TONY DUNASKE

TONY DUNASKE

An Anatomy of Literature

Robert Foulke
Skidmore College

Paul Smith
Trinity College

Harcourt Brace Jovanovich, Inc.

New York   Chicago   San Francisco   Atlanta .

ISBN: 0-15-502710-7

Library of Congress Catalog Card Number: 79-180996

Printed in the United States of America

Cover art by Martha Herman

Credits and Acknowledgments

THE BOBBS-MERRILL COMPANY   For "Now Goth Sonne Under Wode," "Erthe Took of Erthe," "Sodeynly Affrayed," and "Lully, Lullay" from *One Hundred Middle English Lyrics,* edited by Robert D. Stevick, copyright © by the Bobbs-Merrill Company, Inc., reprinted by permission of the publishers.

THE BODLEY HEAD   For "The Lamb," "The Tyger," "Mock on, Mock on, Voltaire, Rousseau," "And Did Those Feet in Ancient Time," "The Sick Rose," and "London" from the Nonesuch Press Edition (1961) of *Poetry and Prose of William Blake,* edited by Sir Geoffrey Keynes.

JONATHAN CAPE LTD   For "Araby," "Ivy Day in the Committee Room," "A Painful Case," and "Grace" from *Dubliners* by James Joyce. Reprinted by permission of the Executors of the James Joyce Estate and Jonathan Cape Ltd.

CLARENDON PRESS   For "Holy Willie's Prayer" from *The Poems and Songs of Robert Burns* (1968), edited by James Kinsley. For "Upon Julia's Clothes," "Delight in Disorder," "To the Virgins, to Make Much of Time," and "Corinna's Going A-Maying" from *Poetical Works of Robert Herrick* (1956), edited by L. C. Martin. For "Lycidas," *Samson Agonistes,* and "On the Morning of Christ's Nativity" from *The Poetical Works of John Milton,* edited by Helen Darbishire. All reprinted by permission of the Clarendon Press, Oxford.

COLLINS-KNOWLTON-WING   For "Saint" from *Collected Poems 1914-1947* by Robert Graves. Copyright © 1947 Robert Graves. For "To Juan at the Winter Solstice" from *Collected Poems* by Robert Graves. Copyright © 1966 by Robert Graves. Both reprinted by permission of Collins-Knowlton-Wing Inc.

J. M. DENT & SONS LTD   For *Heart of Darkness* by Joseph Conrad. Reprinted by permission of J. M. Dent and the Trustees of the Joseph Conrad Estate. For "In My Craft or Sullen Art," "A Winter's Tale," "A Refusal to Mourn the Death, by Fire, of a Child in London," and "A Story" from *Quite Early One Morning.* Reprinted by permission of J. M. Dent and the Literary Executors of the Dylan Thomas Estate.

DOUBLEDAY & COMPANY, INC   For "Little Elegy" copyright © 1960 by X. J. Kennedy, from *Nude Descending A Staircase* by X. J. Kennedy. Originally appeared in *The New Yorker.* Reprinted by permission of Doubleday & Company, Inc.

FABER AND FABER LIMITED   For "Victor Was a Little Baby," "In Memory of W. B. Yeats," and "Law Like Love" from *Collected Shorter Poems* by W. H. Auden. For *Murder in the Cathedral* by T. S. Eliot and *The Waste Land* from *Collected Poems 1909-1962* by T. S. Eliot. For "The Express" and "The Pylons" from *Collected Poems* by Stephen Spender. All reprinted by permission of Faber and Faber Limited.

FARRAR, STRAUS & GIROUX, INC   For "The Lottery" from *The Lottery* by Shirley Jackson. Copyright 1948 by The New Yorker Magazine. Copyright 1949 by Shirley Jackson. For "Skunk Hour" from *Life Studies* by Robert Lowell, copyright © 1958 by Robert Lowell. For "Beyond the Alps" from *For the Union Dead* by Robert Lowell, copyright © 1956 by Robert Lowell. For "The Magic Barrel" from *The Magic Barrel* by Bernard Malamud. Copyright © 1954, 1958 by Bernard Malamud. All reprinted by permission of Farrar, Straus, & Giroux, Inc.

HARCOURT BRACE JOVANOVICH, INC   For "anyone lived in a pretty how town" from *Poems 1923-1954* by E. E. Cummings. Copyright, 1940, by E. E. Cummings, copyright, 1968, by Marion Morehouse Cummings. For *Murder in the Cathedral* by T. S. Eliot, copyright, 1935, by Harcourt, Brace & World, Inc., copyright, 1963, by T. S. Eliot. For *The Waste Land* from *Collected Poems 1909-1962* by T. S. Eliot, copyright, 1936, by Harcourt, Brace & World, Inc.; copyright © 1963, 1964, by T. S. Eliot. For the notes accompanying *The Tragedy of King Lear* and *The Tragedy of Troilus and Cressida* from *Shakespeare: The Complete Works* edited by G. B. Harrison, copyright, 1948, 1952, by Harcourt, Brace & World, Inc. For notes by Charles W. Dunn accompanying "The Wife of Bath's Tale," "The Pardoner's Prologue and Tale," "The Nun's Priest's Tale" and "The Miller's Tale" by Geoffrey Chaucer from *Major British Writers,* Volume I, edited by G. B. Harrison, copyright, 1954, © 1959, by Harcourt, Brace & World, Inc. For "Mother Marie Therese" from *The Mills of the Kavanaughs* by Robert Lowell. Copyright, 1948, by Robert Lowell. For "A Good Man Is Hard to Find" from *A Good Man Is Hard to Find And Other Stories* by Flannery O'Connor. Copyright, 1953, by Flannery O'Connor. For "Advice to a Prophet" from *Advice to A Prophet And Other Poems,* by Richard Wilbur. © 1959 by Richard Wilbur. First printed in *The New Yorker.* All reprinted by permission of Harcourt Brace Jovanovich, Inc.

HARPER & ROW, PUBLISHERS, INCORPORATED   For "The Swimmer" from *The Brigadier and the Golf Widow* by John Cheever. Copyright © 1964 by John Cheever. Reprinted by permission of Harper & Row, Publishers, Inc.

HARVARD UNIVERSITY PRESS   For "Of Bronze—And Blaze" and "I Heard A Fly Buzz—When I Died" by Emily Dickinson from Thomas H. Johnson, Editor, *The Poems of Emily Dickinson,* Cambridge, Mass.: The Belknap Press of Harvard University Press, copyright 1951, 1955, by The President and Fellows of Harvard College. Reprinted by permission of the publishers.

HOLT, RINEHART AND WINSTON, INC   For "Design," "Home Burial," "Dust of Snow," and "The Draft Horse" from *The Poetry of Robert Frost* edited by Edward Connery Lathem. Copyright 1923, 1930, 1939, © 1969 by Holt, Rinehart and Winston, Inc. Copyright 1936, 1951, © 1958, 1962 by Robert Frost. Copyright © 1964, 1967 by Lesley Frost Ballantine. Reprinted by permission of Holt, Rinehart and Winston, Inc.

HOUGHTON MIFFLIN COMPANY   For "Ars Poetica," "Landscape as a Nude," and "Not Marble nor the Gilded Monuments" from *Collected Poems* 1917-1952 by Archibald MacLeish. Copyright, 1952, by Archibald MacLeish. For "The Conversion of the Jews" from *Goodbye Columbus and Five Short Stories* by Philip Roth. Copyright © 1959 by Philip Roth. All reprinted by permission of the publisher, Houghton Mifflin Company.

MARGOT JOHNSON AGENCY   For "A Day on the Big Branch" by Howard Nemerov.

Reprinted by permission of the Estate of the Late Mrs. Frieda Lawrence, William Heinemann Ltd., and Laurence Pollinger Ltd. For "The Basement Room" from *Twenty-One Stories* by Graham Greene. Reprinted by permission of William Heinemann Ltd. and Laurence Pollinger Ltd.

RANDOM HOUSE, INC   For "Law Like Love," "Victor Was A Little Baby," and "In Memory of W. B. Yeats" from *Collected Shorter Poems 1927-1957*, by W. H. Auden. Copyright 1940 and renewed 1968 by W. H. Auden. For "Wash" from *Collected Stories of William Faulkner*. Copyright 1934 and renewed 1962 by William Faulkner. For "Adam and Eve" from *Selected Poems* by Karl Shapiro. Copyright 1951 by Karl Shapiro. For "The Express" and "The Pylons" from *Collected Poems 1928-1953* by Stephen Spender. Copyright 1934 and renewed 1962 by Stephen Spender. For *The Playboy of the Western World* from *The Complete Works of John M. Synge*. Copyright 1907 and renewed 1935 by the Executors of the Estate of John M. Synge. All reprinted by permission of Random House, Inc.

RUSSELL & RUSSELL   For "The Siege," "Oh! For Some Honest Lover's Ghost," and "Constancy" from *The Works of Sir John Suckling in Prose and Verse,* Edited, with an Introduction and Notes, by A. Hamilton Thompson, (1910) New York: Russell & Russell, 1964.

CHARLES SCRIBNER'S SONS   For "The Killers" (Copyright 1927 Charles Scribner's Sons; renewal copyright © 1955) is reprinted with the permission of Charles Scribner's Sons from *Men Without Women* by Ernest Hemingway.

UNIVERSITY OF CHIGAGO PRESS   For the texts of "The Wife of Bath's Tale," "The Pardoner's Prologue and Tale," "The Miller's Tale," and "The Nun's Priest's Tale" from *The Text of the Canterbury Tales* by Geoffrey Chaucer, edited by John Matthews Manley and Edith Rickert. © 1940 by John Matthews Manly. All rights reserved. For *Sir Gawain and the Green Knight* from *The Complete Works of the Gawain Poet*, edited and translated by John Gardner. © 1965 by the University of Chicago. All rights reserved. Both are reprinted by permission of the University of Chicago Press.

THE VIKING PRESS, INC   For "The Basement Room" from *Twenty-One Stories* by Graham Greene. Copyright 1947 by Graham Greene. All rights reserved. For "Araby," "Ivy Day in the Committee Room," "A Painful Case," and "Grace" from *Dubliners* by James Joyce. Copyright © 1967 by The Estate of James Joyce. For "Gloire de Dijon" and "Spring Morning" from *The Complete Poems of D. H. Lawrence,* edited by Vivian de Sola Pinto and F. Warren Roberts. Copyright © 1964, 1971 by Angelo Ravagli and C. M. Weekley. For "The Prussian Officer" from *The Complete Short Stories of D. H. Lawrence,* Vol. I. All rights reserved. For "The Horse Dealer's Daughter" from *The Complete Short Stories of D. H. Lawrence,* Vol. II. Copyright 1922 by Thomas B. Seltzer, Inc., renewed 1950 by Frieda Lawrence. All reprinted by permission of The Viking Press, Inc.

A. P. WATT & SON   For "To Juan at the Winter Solstice" from *Collected Poems* by Robert Graves. Reprinted by permission of A. P. Watt & Son. For "The Wanderings of Oisin," "Sailing to Byzantium," "Nineteen Hundred and Nineteen," "Two Songs from a Play," "Lapis Lazuli," and "Under Ben Bulben" from *The Variorum Edition of the Poems of W. B. Yeats*. Reprinted by permission of Mr. M. B. Yeats, The Macmillan Company of Canada Ltd., and A. P. Watt & Son.

YALE UNIVERSITY PRESS   For *Volpone* by Ben Jonson, edited by Alvin B. Kernan. Copyright © 1962 by Yale University. Reprinted by permission of Yale University Press.

To the memory
of
Frederick Landis Gwynn

Preface

If a student's first impressions last as long as most other people's, there is a reason for this anthology. Many college students begin the formal study of English with a historical survey of literature. From then on, like it or not, many of them are convinced that the first thing to know about a literary work will concern who wrote it, when it was written, and what other writers influenced it or were influenced by it—how, in brief, literature connects with history. These are questions of real value, but it is as pointless to ask them too early as it is irresponsible not to ask them at all. The issue for us, as for anyone interested in a sensible curriculum, is not what questions to ask but when to ask them. And we feel that the questions entertained in historical criticism should not be the first for the English major nor the last for students for whom the introductory course may be their only one in English.

When we set out to devise a new course and this anthology, we wanted to connect and, in a sense, reconcile two major critical activities and the two kinds of courses derived from them. In the later years of secondary school, English courses, whether they are structured around genres or themes, are usually concerned with an intensive reading of the text—the sort of analysis we associate with the varieties of formalist criticism. Any student who has had that sort of course or has learned to think about such elements as plot, character, imagery, and authorial attitude is ready for the selections in this anthology and its critical introductions. The second kind of course the student of English encounters is usually derived from one of the varieties of historical criticism. Whether they are organized by literary periods, movements, or major authors, these courses demand a critical sophistication and range of experience with literature and history that are rather much to expect from the beginning student. Again, we do not mean to dismiss issues of literary history but simply to raise them later in the English curriculum. Furthermore, the study of narrative patterns seems logically prior to the intensive study of literary genres, just as the student's perception of those patterns is likely to precede his perception of the generic features of a literary work. What we needed, then, was a course and an anthology that would lead with some logic from formalist criticism and the courses in textual analysis into historical and generic criticism and courses in literary history or genres. We wanted to widen the students' critical vision to include the individual literary work within the context of the narrative and thematic structures in all of literature, and then to offer them a way of thinking about the interplay of convention and originality, tradition and experiment, upon which an understanding of the historical relevance of literature must finally rest.

For this kind of course we needed a critical theory that was at once comprehensive and practical, one that would order student intuitions about literature and offer a working hypothesis for them to test and revise and then use in their own critical reading and writing. We did not come to Northrop Frye's *Anatomy of Criticism* looking for dogma. Nevertheless, much of what he says seems unarguable—there *are* recurrent patterns in literature like tragedy and comedy, and they *are* well worth our attention. As we selected readings and tested his theory we revised it in a number of ways: at times we simplified it, reducing the number of phases in each narrative pattern from six to three and in some instances redefining them; at other times we refashioned and enlarged certain concepts, like those of mode, displacement, and thematic pattern. However much we have changed or added to Frye's work, we think that most of what he has written is right; or as Huck Finn said of Twain, "He told the truth, mainly."

We have tried to describe, analyze, and illustrate with a wide range of selections the narrative patterns of romance, tragedy, comedy, and irony and their thematic analogues in lyric poetry. In the General Introduction we consider four basic critical concepts: two are primarily descriptive and structural, the concepts of narrative pattern and of thematic pattern; and two are primarily analytic and historical, the concepts of mode and of displacement. In the introductions to each of the narrative sections, we describe the narrative pattern, its recurrent character and setting, and its phases or specific kinds. In the introductions to the thematic sections, we discuss some of the more evident analogies between structural elements in the narrative patterns and organizing principles in lyric poetry.

The selections range from the Anglo-Saxon period to the present, include British and American writers, and represent all the major genres. There are 168 selections by 88 authors: 10 plays; 27 works of fiction; 32 narrative poems, including 12 ballads and dramatic poems; and 99 lyric poems. These are arranged chronologically under the phases in each narrative section and by general themes in the thematic sections. (A table of contents arranged chronologically within genres appears on pages 1111–1115.) We collaborated on all the introductions, but Mr. Foulke was the primary writer of the sections on narrative and thematic patterns in the General Introduction and the introductions to Tragedy and Comedy; Mr. Smith of the sections on mode and displacement in the General Introduction and the introductions to Romance and Irony.

The text may be used in a number of ways. It is large enough (with a few novels) for a year course, but it can be adapted (with a few deletions) to a semester course as well. We think of it as a text in both the prerequisite survey course for English majors and in the general elective course for others. One may follow the sequence of selections through romance, tragedy, comedy, and irony, although recently we have found that the combination of romance and irony in one semester and tragedy and comedy in another works well. In any case, we recommend that the students begin with the selections rather than the critical introductions. The selections are meant to demonstrate that there are narrative and thematic patterns in literature *before* critics talk about them (and after, too, by the way). Whether our sense of them is the right one is less important than the fact that *some* sense can be made of them. So we suggest that students begin with one or two works from each of the narrative sections, enough at least to demonstrate that there are different narrative patterns that recur in literature and for that reason are important—whatever terms we give to them. This might be done by considering some common event or idea that is variously conceptualized in the narrative patterns: the idea of death, for example, in Tennyson's "Passing of Arthur," Crane's "Blue Hotel," Fry's "Phoenix Too Frequent," and Jackson's "Lottery." Once the fact of narrative and thematic patterns and the need for some definition of their elements and relationships have been demonstrated, the students can read our attempts at that definition and the critical uses we make of them in the introductions.

Our debt to Northrop Frye exceeds this book: at an important time for us, as for many of our generation, he reminded us of the ways in which criticism participates in the work of civilization. We are also indebted to Alvin Lee of McMaster University for his commentary on our introductions, to our colleague James Wheatley for his work with the course, and to our students at Trinity College for the encouragement of their hard questions and bright answers.

Robert Foulke
Paul Smith

Contents

TRAGEDY

Thematic Tragedy

Loss and Reconciliation

The Search for Immortality

COMEDY

The Invention of Partial Order

IRONY

The Dismembered World of Experience

The Denial of the Poetic

An
Anatomy of
Literature

General Introduction

At one point in his desperate story, the hero of John Barth's novel *End of the Road* thinks to himself,

> Articulation! There, by Joe, was *my* absolute, if I could be said to have one. At any rate, it is the only thing I can think of about which I ever had, with any frequency at all, the feelings one usually has for one's absolutes. To turn experience into speech— that is, to classify, to categorize, to conceptualize, to grammarize, to syntactify it—is always a betrayal of experience, a falsification of it; but only so betrayed can it be dealt with at all, and only in so dealing with it did I ever feel a man, alive and kicking.

This ambivalent commitment to an absolute, at once serious and ironic, comes close to the attitude represented in this book. Describing the articulation *in* literature, the orders and forms with which writers turn experience into the language of their art, and the articulation *of* literature, the orders and forms in criticism, is what we are about—an absolute if we could be said to have one. This book is concerned with some of the most important forms of literature, on the assumption that literature, like language itself, has a grammar or syntax on which our understanding of it inevitably depends. The simplest child could never learn to speak and the subtlest poet could never write a poem without a knowledge of the grammar of his language. For both, this knowledge may be unconscious but is nonetheless essential. For the reader, the simplest and the most subtle understanding of literature must depend on a similar tacit but necessary knowledge of the grammar of literature. However it happened that there are structures in literature, tragedies and comedies, elegies and songs, each of which is one of a kind, unique and conventional, that fact is in itself enough to call up "the feelings one usually has for one's absolutes."

The articulation of experience in literature is always in some way a betrayal of that experience. Literature is not life. Those who claim that it

1

is and who read it for the slices, gobbets, or mirrored reflections of life miss the point. It is precisely through its falsification of inchoate experience that literature makes its most scrupulous and accurate connection with our lives. There is, however, a way in which the articulation of literary forms in criticism can seriously betray not literature itself—for no literary work ever dies under the critical scalpel—but the possibilities for imaginative reading. This can happen when the concepts of criticism are taken as more real or valuable than the literature they describe or as the final answer to the question that a poem or a novel proposes. Simply to classify or categorize—to say, for example, that John Millington Synge's *Riders to the Sea* is a tragedy and leave it at that—is to betray our experience of that work. To observe that the play is similar to John Milton's *Samson Agonistes* and T. S. Eliot's *Murder in the Cathedral* simply because men die in all three is to miss the intent of this anthology and, worse yet, to trivialize the experience of reading. This does not mean that recognizing the play's tragic pattern is pointless, but only that it is *one* preliminary assumption worth entertaining as a means to the imaginative possession of the play.

At some time in the process of reading *Riders to the Sea* we become aware of the greater importance of its dissimilarities with Milton's and Eliot's dramas. When we try to account for these differences, it may seem as if the concept of tragedy, without which we would never have recognized the three plays as being similar, loses its interest and value as we become more engaged with the single work and its details. This is probably the case for most of us most of the time. But it need not be the case all of the time, at least not for the "ideal reader suffering from an ideal insomnia"—James Joyce's phrase for the critic lurking in all of us. For that reader in his wakeful hours there is a complex interplay between concept and poem, between abstract category (tragedy) and individual play (*this* tragedy). In this ideal situation our early concepts are modified by the evidence of the literary work, and these transformed concepts reveal in turn new dimensions in the work itself. In his essay "Tradition and the Individual Talent," Eliot wrote of a similar mediation between whole and part in literature:

> What happens when a new work of art is created is something that happens simultaneously to all the works of art which preceded it. The existing monuments form an ideal order among themselves, which is modified by the introduction of the new (the really new) work of art among them. The existing order is complete before the new work arrives; for order to persist after the supervention of novelty, the *whole* existing order must be, if ever so slightly, altered; and so the relations, proportions, values of each work of art toward the whole are readjusted; and this is conformity between the old and the new. Whoever has approved this idea of order, of the form of European, of English

literature will not find it preposterous that the past should be altered by the present as much as the present is directed by the past.

We must assume that the same can be said of the relations, proportions, and values of each critical reading in the whole order of criticism. This is especially so if criticism is to be anything more than a private pastime with the defects of its virtues: neither betraying nor falsifying experience because it simply does not deal with it.

In order to entertain Eliot's idea of literature or the idea of criticism it implies, one must imagine that, as he said, "the whole of literature . . . has a simultaneous existence and composes a simultaneous order." We can think of all literature as coeval in space, with its various relationships and proportions expressed in spatial terms of distance and direction. We do this when we say that one novel is "closer" to classical tragedy than another, or that the final scene of a play "points to" the ironic. Some of the basic ideas in this book are "spatial" in this sense: the concepts of narrative and thematic patterns of romance, tragedy, comedy, and irony are meant to describe the features of a work as well as that work's "place" in relation to others within the total order of literature. The concepts of mode and displacement suggest the temporal relationship that a poem or novel or play has to others: they allow us to return the work of literature to its historical scene and to understand it in its original time and place.

Our intention is not to sanctify a system but, as Geoffrey Hartman said of Northrop Frye's work, "to democratize criticism and to demystify the muse." We would not flatten criticism to one simplistic or trivial act in which any critical vote is equal to any other, nor would we deny to literature that mystery and magnificence for which the muse is a classical explanation. Rather, our concern is to make explicit and available the intuitions and concepts that we all share in the experience of literature. In this sense, criticism is democratic and literature is no more or less mysterious than we ourselves. We begin with the fact that for centuries men have thought about literature with terms such as tragedy and comedy. In themselves, these terms and conceptual structures are of little value, but as instruments in the act of criticism they are of great value. For by imagining a work in the context of the simultaneous and total order of literature and discovering through concepts such as comedy and elegy and romantic tragedy its relationships with other works of literature, we come to a more discriminating and coherent sense of its uniqueness. One cannot understand the real differences between Eliot's *Murder in the Cathedral* and George Bernard Shaw's *Saint Joan* without first discounting the similarities called to attention by the concept of romantic tragedy, any more than one can tell T. S. Eliot from G. B. Shaw without first recognizing that both were human beings.

The ideas that articulate literature, then, are like keys for its possession. But possession may not be the best term for what happens between us and a poem or novel or play; it implies too private or even lonely an experience.

It misses our participation in the imaginative vision of all mankind, past and present, as that vision reciprocates with a writer's unique artistic insight. This, as John Barth's character said in another situation, is at least one way to deal with the experience of literature, and in so dealing with it to sense its humanity and ours—to feel a man, alive and kicking.

Narrative Pattern

The Concept of Narrative Pattern

When we read a narrative, we usually find we know more about the characters' lives than they do. A shape or *pattern* emerges from acts or words that may seem ordinary or trivial, and we are likely to perceive this shape sooner and more clearly than any character does. Normally our sense of the whole—of the larger congeries of events in which the character is entangled—comes by implication rather than by direct statement. We are not told how to construe events; rather, we fit them together ourselves, perhaps trying out a number of possible patterns if their meaning is not immediately clear. In most cases we discover some basic pattern rather quickly. We anticipate a tragic hero's destiny before he does, sense the danger in his pride or obsession, and feel the crisis approaching before it happens. We would have some tentative expectations even if literary critics had never written about tragedy because we have to have a pattern in mind to make any sense out of a sequence of events in literature or in our own lives. Random events make us uncomfortable because they resist patterning, as the illusion that the theater of the absurd creates has demonstrated for the past several decades.

Ordinarily literature creates a perspective in which the shape or pattern of events is clearer than in life. The part of everyday experience that includes the irrelevant and disconnected and routine has been left out or transformed. Yet the shape or pattern is never fully drawn *in* the words of the text; much of it lies somewhere between the lines. The narrative pattern is not identical with the observable features of the text but is implicit in them. It is apparent in the unstated connection between what the characters do and say in the context of what has gone before. At certain points a gesture or a bit of ordinary dialogue may take on special significance from its position in the sequence of events, indicating a crisis or a turning point or revealing the hidden meaning in past events. Some parts of the text stand out from their surroundings because they mark important shifts within the narrative pattern, giving the reader a fuller awareness of the total shape of the story. If the reader is alert as he encounters these signals, he will modify his expectations accordingly. On first reading Coleridge's "Rime of the Ancient Mariner," for example, the reader finds in the tale of the voyage itself few clues to its special significance for the Mariner until the end of Part I. The Mariner relates how an albatross appeared suddenly out of the barren wastes of Antarctica, and the ice split and freed the trapped ship. Then the Mariner unaccountably killed the albatross. This gratuitous act of destruction, which might be perfectly normal in another context (an account of a hunting expedition or of starvation at sea), marks a turning point in the narrative pattern: the reader now suspects that the voyage cannot prosper. His awareness has been modified in ways that let him understand why the Mariner will be isolated from the rest of the crew and must suffer some penance for his act. A second turning point is also clearly marked. When the Mariner blesses the water snakes both he and the ship are released, though he alone survives to be haunted by the voyage. The reader is now ready for the return of the opening scene, the wedding festivity—a celebration of life— that frames the Mariner's tale of death. Throughout, the features of the text that signal important stages in the narrative pattern guide the reader's expectations, enabling him to notice the important connections between act and consequence, between pride and suffering and redemption, in Coleridge's poem.

While we are reading, we notice the narrative pattern first as a series of check points on a literary map that we use to discover where we are and predict where we are going. The pattern is a configuration in our awareness confirmed by certain landmarks in the text, giving us orientation and a sense of direction as we move through from beginning to end. How it happens that we have these mental maps available to us as we read is more a question for psychologists than literary critics because such maps are not unique to literary experience. We could not manage our daily lives without recourse to sets of expectations. From the simplest act of inter- preting signs (taking dark clouds to indicate the coming of rain) to slightly more complex inferences (concluding that because both the car and its owner are missing, the owner must have gone on an errand), we constantly depend on past experience to connect observations and make predictions. If we use the wrong set of expectations, we will be mistaken (the clouds may turn out to be smoke from a burning building; the owner of the car may be at the police station because the car was stolen). Sometimes our predictions turn out to be wrong because we have run across something truly new. (Who could have predicted the meaning of a mushroom-shaped cloud before 1945?) Because expectations are analogies, projections of past experience on present events, and because two situations are seldom identical, we often have to adjust our expectations or abandon them. Even when events seem totally incomprehensible, we keep trying out old explanations, or we invent new ones that recombine parts of the old in a new way.

The same processes are at work in literary experience, with a few additional complications. No two narratives are identical—we often value literary works for their freshness or novelty—yet there are always some helpful similarities between the work we are reading and what we have read before. In addition to the expectations we get from our past reading, we usually have another set from direct or indirect knowledge of the kind of experience the story is about—a voyage, a battle, a race, a party, a political campaign, conflicts within a family. Ordinarily these two strands of expectation merge in our imagination to form a network of probabilities.

Consciously or unconsciously, we use this network to fit the pieces of the text together, to maintain a sense of continuity at every stage. We are able to do this more successfully with literature than with the events of our own lives because stories are "made": the writer has absolute power to select, exclude, and arrange details within the limits of his invented world. Because the writer's vision of human experience is not identical with ours —if it were we would be too bored to finish the story—the text continually modifies the very expectations that we use to make sense of it. What happens as we read seems to lie somewhere between the two poles of experiencing the new and recognizing the familiar. We start reading with some minimal notion of pattern gleaned from any number of sources— other stories by the same writer, reviews, information from friends, and so on. Even when we have no initial expectations we quickly construct a tentative pattern to help us connect events and discriminate qualities of character in the opening pages. All sorts of clues are available: the title may suggest an adventure ("The Legende of the Knight of the Red Crosse"); the subtitle may name the pattern ("A Comedy in Three Acts"); the opening may set the ground rules of probability ("Once upon a time . . ."); the setting may suggest what is appropriate (light-hearted court-ship stories seem out of place in jungles and deserts). We use this initial pattern until it begins to fail us, which inevitably happens in a story of any complexity. When it does we modify the pattern, combine it with others, or abandon it for another, and we are likely to continue the process of partial modification as long as we read.

Describing the use of narrative patterns is the best way to understand a controlling shape that is only partly visible in the text. Patterns for physical objects—the blueprint for a house, the mold for a vase, the sketch for a painting—have an exact though limited correspondence with their finished products. Literary patterns are more difficult to isolate because they are intangible, like all mental constructs. An author's prospectus for a story and a critic's paraphrase of a poem are not directly comparable to the finished works for several reasons. In the first place, stories and poems are not "objects" in any important sense, since their physical forms are tangential to their meanings. A great poem may be scrawled on wrapping paper, printed on fine paper, or just memorized without altering its sub-stance. The words of a prospectus and a paraphrase have the same status —they are never wholly observable as blueprints and sketches are. Thus exact correspondence cannot be seen or measured when we are dealing with words. In the second place, verbal constructs do not have any absolute limits within the mind. What we understand as the pattern or shape of a story may be enlarged or changed on subsequent readings as our experience and knowledge accumulate. Moreover, both the writer and the reader draw on their culture for modes of understanding words, and thus different conceptions of the narrative pattern of a work are possible even though the words themselves never change. Thus it is best to define *narrative pattern* as an expected sequence of events; we must understand it as a form that can be filled out in innumerable ways with details of characterization, setting, and style.

Most of the stories that we find permanently satisfying modify a given pattern or combine it with others, but patterns can be discovered easily in the simpler narratives of popular culture—television, movies, magazine fiction. A weekly television comedy may have the following basic pattern, which can be repeated endlessly with minor variations: a rebellious but likeable teenager comes into conflict with a stuffy but equally likeable parent over some rule or habit; everyone becomes exasperated; then a trick or gimmick quickly resolves the difficulty at the end of the show, leaving everybody happy and ready to do it over again a week later. The pattern for a western movie is equally firm but subject to more variation: a stranger (either good or bad) comes into town and the sheriff (either honest or corrupt) tries to run him out; next a crime (bank robbery, rustling) is committed or a distressed heroine appears who needs to be rescued; a gun battle ensues in which the good man wins. In a variation two groups may be opposed (cattlemen and homesteaders, the army and the Indians). After watching five or ten minutes of a situation comedy or a western we can fill in the rest of the pattern—though not the details— partly because we are familiar with these kinds of stories. If we continue watching and meet no surprises or complications, we have encountered a simple formula piece, one in which the story is nearly identical with a single narrative pattern. Even if we had not grown up in a culture loaded with situation comedies and westerns, we would probably recognize such formulas rather quickly as derivatives of more inclusive narrative patterns in literature. The rule that creates the conflict in situation comedy is related to the irrational law that sparks many full-scale comedies and that must be overcome before they can be resolved, and the character with an absurd habit is a staple of drama from Aristophanes to Shaw. There is a close family resemblance between the good cowboys of westerns and the knights of the Round Table in Arthurian romances. We do not need to be aware of such resemblances to make sense of simpler forms, but we depend on them more and more as we try to untangle the complexities of sophis- ticated literature, plays like Tom Stoppard's *Rosencrantz and Guildenstern Are Dead* and novels like William Faulkner's *Absalom, Absalom!* These works modify and combine basic narrative patterns, telling new stories on the basis of older ones that are a part of our cultural inheritance. In such works we are not reading *for* the pattern so much as *with* it. The true uniqueness of literary works lies in what they enable us to discover. They invite us to connect, if we will, a flexible pattern of expectations with the possible meanings of human experience articulated in literature.

How we make such connections between incidents and meanings while we read is not fully understood, but clearly we need no prodigious memory or intelligence. Very early in their lives children can recognize and use narrative patterns; they know that in fairy tales pumpkins can be

The Four Basic Narrative Patterns

transformed into coaches and heroines must not be left permanently in the power of witches or be eaten by wolves. It is not clear where the human capacity for patterning sequences of events comes from, yet we can observe its cultural effects quite simply by looking at the history of literature. Four basic patterns make up the framework of Western literature: *romance*, *tragedy*, *comedy*, and *irony*. All four patterns appear in the literature of ancient Greece—romance in the epic, the idyl, and the prose tale; tragedy and comedy in the drama that developed from religious ritual; and irony in the poetic satire and some forms of comic drama. From their first elaboration in classical literature throughout subsequent literary history, the basic patterns have passed from genre to genre and from age to age without losing their essential shape. This remarkable persistence suggests that they are not identical with literary conventions. Though one pattern may dominate the literature of a particular period, then seem to disappear, as tragedy did in England during the eighteenth and nineteenth centuries, none of the four basic patterns has become extinct.

Narrative patterns persist throughout the literature of various eras and cultures because they are fundamental structures of the human imagination, perennially useful ways of perceiving the world we experience. Repeatedly, human beings invent an idealized world in which all human desires can be realized—a world in which fame, love, and power can be attained simultaneously, in which truth and beauty are indeed compatible. The details of this idealized world vary with the age—they may be derived from nature (Wordsworth), from both nature and art (the gardens in Spenser and Marvell), from a particular culture (Yeats' Byzantium)—but the impulse to imagine a perfect world remains constant. It is also possible to imagine the opposite, a world that frustrates human desires. This world, based on our aversions, is one that we despise and fear but somehow must contemplate. Its dominating images are not gardens and beautiful cities but uninhabitable wildernesses and slums—the jungle, the desert, the ghetto, the industrial wasteland. Both worlds polarize ordinary human experience: the world we desire would give us more power over our environment than we will ever have, while the world we fear seems altogether beyond our control, totally dehumanized. We touch the extremes of these opposed worlds in aesthetic or religious experience, on the one hand, or in cultural facts like Hiroshima and Buchenwald, on the other.

We think of such desired and hated worlds as states of being rather than as processes of becoming. They are the high and low points of human experience and seem to lead nowhere beyond themselves. However, if we let our imaginations play upon less extraordinary experience, we notice that movement and change predominate. No state of being lasts, whether in the general pattern of development from childhood through adolescence to adulthood or in the more specific falling out of events in the life of each individual. Above all we are struck by the fact that individual fates and fortunes change with the passing of time. The word *fate* usually implies a fixed though unknown pattern of change, foreordained and malevolent, whereas *fortune* suggests the unpredictable, an unexpected stroke of good luck. (In ordinary conversation we are more apt to speak of a man's evil fate or good fortune than of his good fate or evil fortune.) It is thus possible to think about what happens to an individual as inevitable or fortuitous, as destiny or luck. If we combine these interpretations of change with the idea of desirable and undesirable worlds, we can generate two movements: an inevitable "downward" plunge from a relatively desirable state in which men are free to do what they wish to an undesirable state in which men seem to have no choice whatsoever; and the reverse, a fortuitous "upward" leap from constraint or bondage to freedom of action. In our imaginations we can then fuse other relationships with these two movements, associating death and a sense of alienation with the downward movement, rebirth and a spirit of social communion with the upward. As the process elaborates within our imaginations, we invent the narrative patterns of tragedy and comedy by working with opposed human possibilities. The following diagram illustrates the structure of such changes:

Desirable and undesirable states of being, though conceived as changeless worlds, can also be pushed into movement. There is something finally unsatisfactory about changeless states. Wallace Stevens senses the lifelessness of an immobile paradise in "Sunday Morning":

> Is there no change of death in paradise?
> Does ripe fruit never fall? Or do the boughs
> Hang always heavy in that perfect sky,
> Unchanging, yet so like our perishing earth,
> With rivers like our own that seek for seas
> They never find, the same receding shores
> That never touch with inarticulate pang?

Put in motion, the desirable and undesirable states become the dream of wish fulfilment and the nightmare, respectively. If we imagine that states of being are scenes for action, we can generate one pattern of movement in which a hero sets out to overcome all obstacles and reaches his desired goal and another in which a victim of circumstances lacks power to accomplish anything he sets out to do. In contrast to the movements of tragedy and comedy, these do not involve as dramatic a change in the protagonist's relation to his world. In his moment of greatest distress, we never doubt that the romantic hero will come through, just as we find it difficult to believe that anything an ironic victim attempts can succeed. The quest in romance is generally progressive, following the hero from his arrival through a sequence of initiatory adventures to a crucial test that he passes and beyond into further successes or a return to a state of being (the wise and good king who rules benignly for the rest of his days). The antiquest in irony is more likely to be regressive, returning the unfortunate protagonist to where he began with nothing accomplished, nothing gained. Like the hero of romance, he is often left in a state of being; the ironic hero is trapped, imprisoned, or perhaps caught in perpetual motion that has no progress or meaning.

Narrative
Patterns
and Literary
Works

The narrative pattern is, then, the implicit form of a sequence of events that guides our expectations as we read; it recurs in narratives very different in subject and style because it is fundamental to any awareness of what stories mean. Since it is not directly observable, we need to be especially careful in determining how it relates to the details of a given text. In the first place, we must remember that words like *shape* and *pattern* can be used in both general and specific senses. The word *oval* can be used to describe a geometric figure, the composition of a painting, or an impression of a human face. What varies in each usage is not the appropriateness of the word—it may fit very well in all of them—but the standard of precision being invoked. To object that a particular human face is not in fact a perfect oval would reveal an inability to abstract and generalize, to know the degree of precision that is wanted or needed. When words suggesting pattern are used to describe processes rather than static shapes, such discriminations are crucial. Characters in novels are said to "rise" in their fictional worlds, and the dramatic shape of plays is often described in terms of "rising" and "falling" action, the parts preceding and follow-ing the climax or turning-point. Or these terms are sometimes used to characterize the general nature of the action; in talking about the pattern of Synge's plays, it is appropriate to speak of the "falling" action of *Riders to the Sea* and the "rising" action of *The Playboy of the Western World*. Such descriptions are highly generalized, not vague. They are useful when they enable us to see the large movements that include and articulate the superstition of old Maurya and the poetic boasting of Christy Mahon.

The "fit" of narrative patterns must be qualified in a second way. As abstractions from a multitude of particulars, they seldom correspond to the shape of an individual literary work unless it is very simple. We have defined a narrative pattern as a set of expectations, a possible way of articulating events that serves the reader much as a rough chart serves an explorer. In this respect a narrative pattern differs from a plot summary because the latter is simply a reduction of fixed events into schematic form. The basic narrative patterns are more like common denominators of specific plots, possible groupings of characters and sequences of events that are capable of variation and transformation. A plot summary of Henry Fielding's *Tom Jones* describes one fixed sequence of events, whereas Fielding's description of the novel as a "comic epic in prose" is open-ended, taking in all the possible developments of narrative pattern suggested by the words *comedy* and *epic*. These words have a wide range of application; they can never be limited to a single instance.

That there is nothing new under the sun is an old cliché that once had a rather precise meaning in Greek physics: matter changes its form but not its substance. The same principle applies to narrative patterns in literature. What is new and original in literature is not the pattern but the details that fill it out and complicate it. It is easy to claim too much for the differences between works by suggesting that shopworn "formula" plots and "flat" characters come from third-rate writers rather than men of genius. But such large claims for the atypical can be refuted rather easily by the work of Shakespeare, who simply renovated earlier versions for most of his plots, and by Charles Dickens, who flattened many of his most effective characters into caricatures. Yet we do not read Shakespeare's plays or Dickens' novels for the patterns they use. At this point we need to qualify the relationship between narrative patterns and individual works of literature in a third way. Just as the pattern of expectations cannot be derived from or limited to a single literary work, so the particulars of the work cannot be reduced to the pattern. Fielding's statement about *Tom Jones* is not the final word but a starting point for critical inquiry. At stake here is the valued "uniqueness" of every literary work, the sense we have that in spite of shared patterns the differences between Fielding's *Tom Jones*, William Thackeray's *Vanity Fair*, Saul Bellow's *Augie March*, and Kingsley Amis' *Lucky Jim* are what count. The full meaning of any story worth our time depends on pattern but can never be reduced to it.

However useful the concepts of narrative patterns may be—and they have served critics for a long time—they are too general to be practicable for very long, especially when we want to talk about an individual work. A discussion of *Macbeth*, for instance, may begin with a fixed definition of tragedy or the version of it we associate with the Elizabethans, but if we stop there we will miss the important ways in which the play challenges conventional ideas of fate or of the moral nature of the tragic hero. So we need more precise definitions of the major variations that have been worked on the patterns of romance, tragedy, comedy, and irony. The history of criticism makes this point: Aristotle's concept of the tragic hero and the tragic pattern—a noble and proud figure who falls from happiness to misery through error rather than vice—suited most of the drama of classical Greece but could not adequately define the tragedies of medieval and Renaissance England, such as *Everyman* and *Antony and Cleopatra*. How could any theory revised to accommodate these plays fit the plays of Samuel Beckett, Harold Pinter, and Edward Albee in our time.

The Phases of Narrative Patterns

Playwrights, either in or out of their plays, are forever posing hard questions for critics who would pin them down with definitions. Can a Christian martyr, like Thomas à Becket in *Murder in the Cathedral*, who deliberately seeks and finds his true being in martyrdom, share the Aristotelian terms we use to describe Aeschylus' Agamemnon? Can Willy Loman's suicide in *Death of a Salesman* have anything to do with Othello's; and is it true, as Linda Loman says of that worn-out man, that "attention, attention must be finally paid to such a person"? If questions like these are of any moment, as they seem to be, they must somehow be partially answered in the theory of narrative patterns.

We can acknowledge some of these questions with the concept of *phase*. A phase of a narrative pattern is a specific type or stage of action that characterizes a major variation on one of the narrative patterns. Since we will consider the phases in more detail in the introductions to the narrative patterns, we need only sketch their general characteristics here.

The Phases of Tragedy and Comedy. The very fact that we hesitate to call *Death of a Salesman* a tragedy and feel rather uncomfortable thinking of *Volpone* as a comedy in the same way that we do of Chaucer's "Miller's Tale" suggests that for each narrative pattern there is a conventional type or norm against which we measure such differences as those in Arthur Miller's play or in Ben Jonson's. For tragedy the norm is familiar in an action like that in Sophocles' *Oedipus*, where a powerful protagonist of noble stature upsets the equilibrium of things, suffers the consequences, accepts responsibility for his acts, and recognizes their transcendent significance. For comedy the norm can be found in a novel like Kingsley Amis' *Lucky Jim*, in which an unobtrusive but honest young man is blocked by a pretentious and mechanical society but finally manages to overcome it through some stroke of fortune and win the woman he loves.

At least two of the most common deviations from these norms in tragedy and comedy are produced by assumptions we would ordinarily expect to find in romance and irony. We can see these variations on the norm in the conception of the hero and the outcome of his actions. The death of Becket is an entry into sainthood, an event familiar in romance, while the death of Willy Loman is an ironically pointless sacrifice. The end of *Volpone* is filled with malice, and the characters suffer the severe punishment we often witness in irony, whereas the romantic playboy of the Western world, Christy Mahon, escapes the unregenerated and boggy world of Irish cottagers. These plots and others like them exemplify specific recurrent types of tragic or comic action. However different from the norms of tragedy or comedy, we are not likely to think of *Murder in the Cathedral* as a comedy or of *Volpone* as a tragedy. These plays suggest, rather, that there are recognizable distinctions between romantic and ironic forms of both tragedy and comedy. That we have terms like *romantic comedy* and *ironic tragedy* in our critical vocabulary may be one final authority for these distinctive phases.

The Phases of Romance and Irony. There are no such conventional terms for the phases of romance and irony, perhaps because their status is somewhat different from that of the phases of tragedy and comedy. That is to say, the phases of romance and irony are less obviously affected by the assumptions of some other pattern, the way that comedy, for example, is modified by irony in ironic comedy. One way to describe the phases of romance and irony begins with the opposition between the worlds of their narrative patterns, the idealized realm of our desires and the unidealized realm of our aversions. This contrast implies that if the most common form of the romance is the heroic quest, then the most common form in irony would be an "antiquest," a pointless series of adventures that ends in failure and ignominy. With the quest and the antiquest as norms for romance and irony, we can think of the variations on these norms more as narratives that emphasize certain events or stages in symbolic actions than as narratives that change the outcome of the action or the conception of the hero, as is the case with the phases of tragedy and comedy. The unusually ritualistic and sequential pattern of the romance quest may account for this apparent structure in the phases of romance as well as in those of irony. In romance, then, the events that introduce and conclude the quest myth define the first and last phases of that narrative pattern. These phases have structures similar to the initiation of the young hero (his ritual birth) and the descent into the underworld of the mature hero (his ritual death). Contrasting versions of these events, a brutalizing and deforming initiation and a meaningless incarceration, may be the demonic rituals that enclose the ironic antiquest and so characterize the first and last phases of irony.

The currency of the terms *tragic irony* and *comic irony* suggests another way of thinking about the principle underlying the phases of irony. Just as the ironic norm parodies or inverts the quest in romance, so the first and last phases of irony parody the patterns of comedy and tragedy. First-phase irony turns the conflict of comedy into a more vicious and satiric confrontation; last-phase irony transforms the scapegoat ritual of tragedy into senseless torture. Whichever structure of irony we finally adopt, it must, like the other concepts of phases, fit our imaginative experience and account for the sense we share of the unity within the diversity of literature.

When we think about literary history, we usually have in mind one of two meanings for the term *history*. We may think of history as a scene or context, the more or less immediate time and place in which a literary work was written. Literature, then, is considered a product of its time, something that was once *in* history. Or we may think of history as a characteristic of literature itself: Yeats' Byzantium poems developed through various manuscript versions, Henry James' fiction progressed through related periods, and the work of the romantic poets in the early nineteenth century influenced that of the Victorians later. In this way literature

Mode

The Concept of Mode

displays the dynamic or evolutionary aspects of a living thing; it is less significant as a product than as a process. Literature, then, *has* a history, or, to reverse our phrase, there is a history *in* literature. Literary history, in the first sense of the term, history as context, directs our attention outward from the work to the world that produced it, and we consider questions such as the influence of Coleridge on Wordsworth or of Elizabethan theatrical conventions on Shakespeare. In the second sense of the term, when we think of the history *in* literature, our attention is directed through periods of time and usually within the limits of some literary form or genre; then we entertain such problems as the development of the pastoral ode or the novel or "nature poetry." To understand the concept of literary modes we need to keep in mind both meanings for the term *history*: first, as the external context of society and events in which a work is written, and second, as the record of the internal development of literature itself.

We will define the term *mode* as a conventional assumption about the nature and limits of a central character's power of action. The definition implies something like an agreement between the author's preliminary ideas and the reader's consequent expectations of a fictional world. When we read a literary work and respond to its mode, we attempt to reconstruct the conditions or terms under which such a concept of action is possible. We become part of that audience contemporary with the writer to the extent that we understand and for the moment assent to his assumptions about what men can do or think they can do. Partly because these assumptions are first principles and partly because they are so deeply embedded in the historical ground on which the work rests, they are like those unspoken beliefs the author can count on his audience knowing and to which he need do no more than allude—perhaps the surest indication of their cultural importance.

Mode as the Hero's Power of Action

By comparing four works from different periods of literary history— *Beowulf, Hamlet, Tom Jones,* and *Death of a Salesman*—we can see broad differences in the assumptions authors make about their central characters. The Anglo-Saxon Beowulf poet found it not only possible but fitting and necessary that his hero should spend a day underwater and that the sword he finds there should melt in a monster's blood, though he might have agreed with Shakespeare and Fielding and Miller that these events are at least improbable. Each of these authors expects us to agree to a different set of implicit terms that establish the boundaries of the possible in the outcome of fictional action. Imagine their characters in a four-way battle: Beowulf with his giant sword, Hamlet with his rapier, Tom Jones with his trusty oaken stick, and Willy Loman with his garden hoe. Their "weapons" are all emblematic. Beowulf's sword gives him supernatural powers, and its golden hilt remains after his death as a sign of a divine victory. Hamlet's rapier, the sign of the ideal courtier, distinguishes him as a cultured and noble figure. Tom Jones' staff links him with the green and hearty countryside whose creative powers and good life he inherits. And Willy Loman's hoe is a useless tool with which he scratches the sterile pavement in a city without earth and trees. The odds would favor Beowulf against all comers, and anyone else against Loman. But imagine Hamlet against Tom Jones. On any "neutral" ground outside the seventeenth-century play or the eighteenth-century novel Hamlet should win. But if Hamlet were to lose, Tom Jones would have to become a more sinister figure than he is and take on the powers of the villain of tragedy. And if Tom Jones were to win, then Hamlet would have to become something of a pretentious fool with the diminished powers of the antagonist of comedy—and even then the worst he would get from Tom would be a good drubbing. If we return Hamlet to his play and Tom Jones to his novel, we notice that both are disinherited young men and that Hamlet never regains his "inheritance," whereas Tom Jones does. Nevertheless, Hamlet is the greater for the events in which he *acts*, while Tom Jones is no greater but simply luckier for the events that *happen* to him. A character's power, then, depends on the sort of act his scene permits. Ultimately characters are unimaginable outside their fictional worlds.

The most obvious fact we notice about these four characters is that they demonstrate a general decline in the power and stature of the hero, from the eighth century to the twentieth. Like most other facts of literary history this one can be badly misconstrued, but it does offer a preliminary sketch of the pattern in the modes. We notice, too, that as the hero descends a scale of being from almost more than human to almost less than human, we can isolate related ideas that define the appropriate social and natural realms in which these characters display their potential for action or lack of it. The definition of a mode, then, should include a description of the central character's power of action, his relationship to society and nature, and the underlying concepts or models that give shape and coherence to his world. In our literature there are at least four identifiable modes.

The Romantic Mode. The central character in the romantic mode, although human, is assumed to have powers beyond those of ordinary men. He may be associated with the divine, display supernatural attributes, or perform miraculous or mysterious deeds. He approaches the conception of man as a god, and thus he transcends and represents a perfection of both his society and the natural world. Other characters and elements in his environment are aligned either for or against him—there is no middle ground—and consequently, as in an allegory, they take on a more abstract or idealized meaning. In the romantic mode the model for society is theocratic in the sense of one governed by a divinely authorized agent. The romantic model for nature implies a similarly transcendent power that gives the world a mysterious coherence and meaning.

The Four Basic Modes

The Formal Mode. The central character is assumed to have a power of action greater than that of most ordinary men but still within the range of the possible. He may demonstrate attributes that make him notably representative of his society and thus seem to exist on a "higher" level of abstraction. Either as a leader or as a representative of his society, he acts or speaks for other men, and thus he affirms man's social status. He shares something of the conception of man as hero, in that the heroic represents the highest or the most significant attributes of man in society. Nature is most often conceived of as formalized in some static hierarchical system and subordinated to or reflecting the social order—thus nature is "socialized." The formal model for society is aristocratic; the model for nature is usually static or mechanistic, exhibiting fixed physical orders and laws.

The Natural Mode. The central character is assumed to have a power of action no greater or less than that of ordinary men—he is, if anything, a little luckier. Like the central character of the formal mode, he acts within the range of the possible, but unlike him, he finds his identity most often in an extra-social condition. His most common role is that of the critic or reformer of conventional society. He represents man as an individual, assuming that this is his natural state and that other conceptions of man primarily as a social being are somehow unnatural. Thus, in contrast to the formal mode, where nature often reflects a social order, in this mode society reflects a natural order—society is "naturalized." Man's ideal is to represent or be an agent of nature rather than to control or order it. Nature is thought of as dynamic rather than static, as a process rather than a fixed order, an organic force rather than a mechanical structure. The natural model for society is democratic, with an emphasis on the free individual, youth, and revolution; the model for nature is organic, with an emphasis on biological process, change, and the generation of new and original forms.

The Ironic Mode. The central character is assumed to have a power of action less than that of ordinary men, one that demonstrates an unusual degree of futility or insignificance in human acts. As in the romantic mode, events seem to move beyond the realm of the possible. Again the central character encounters the mysterious or marvelous, with the important difference that the extraordinary events are not explained by a supernatural order as in the romantic mode but are rendered inexplicable by a sense of chaos and disorder. The central figure of the ironic mode often seems less than human by being physically or psychologically maimed or warped out of the human mold. Victimized by both his society and nature, he approaches the terrifying conception of man as a thing or object. The ordered society of the formal mode is distorted in the ironic mode into a tyrannical world of social automata, and the beneficent organic processes in the natural mode are distorted into ineluctable physical powers that indifferently destroy mankind. The ironic model for society is anarchy, and the ironic model for nature is an "unnatural" chaos, a world poisoned, defoliated, and inhabited only by monstrous and sterile beings.

However simplified a version of complex cultural matters, this description of the modes helps to organize some of our intuitions as readers, without which our experience of literature would be chaotic. It clarifies our impressions that many of the characters of contemporary fiction seem lesser men than those of Renaissance drama, and that the conceptions of nature in the lyrics of the early nineteenth century differ from, but in a sense depend on, those in medieval epics. Finally, the structure implicit in the modes is historical, in the two meanings of the term we have discussed. First, it illustrates that sequence of conceptions of action, society, and nature we find in literary history. Second, it outlines the sequence that we associate with the major periods of European cultural history. Literary works of the Anglo-Saxon and medieval periods most commonly exemplify the romantic mode; those of the Renaissance and early seventeenth century, the formal mode; those of the eighteenth and early nineteenth centuries, the natural mode; and those of the late nineteenth and twentieth centuries, the ironic mode.

Our reasoning so far may seem circular, for it is altogether likely that our image of medieval literature is shaped by our notion of medieval history or that our sense of these ironic times is as much a literary as a historical judgment. However, some more interesting implications of the concept of mode arise when it is related to the concept of narrative pattern. Each mode has a special affinity with one of the narrative patterns. The connections between the romantic mode and romance and between the ironic mode and irony are so apparent that we might well think of the narrative pattern and its related mode as representing functions of each other. The relationships between the formal mode and tragedy and between the natural mode and comedy are less obvious but still visible. The conception of a central figure of greater stature than ordinary men, a hierarchic social structure, and a natural world governed by eternal laws is analogous to the kind of character, setting, and final action we associate with tragedy. Similarly, the concepts of the natural mode are most often associated with the narrative pattern of comedy. It is possible, however, to imagine a combination of either the formal mode and a comic narrative or the natural mode and a tragic narrative: we find the first combination in the Old Comedy of Aristophanes, some of Molière and Shakespeare; the second in a variety of "naturalistic" tragedies, like some of Henrik Ibsen's and Thomas Hardy's, involving ordinary men who stand outside of society and unsuccessfully attempt its reformation. And for this reason we adopt the terms *formal* and *natural* to characterize the two modes that, unlike the romantic and the ironic, can be realized in either the narrative pattern with which they are associated or its opposite.

These literary hybrids, important as they are, do not deny the affinities

The Modes and the Narrative Patterns

among the four modes, the four narrative patterns, and the major eras of literary history. If we surveyed English literature for works in the romantic mode, we would find them most frequently among the epics and narrative poems of the Middle Ages, as we would find works in the formal mode most frequently among the tragic dramas of the Renaissance, those in the natural mode most frequently among the comic novels and dramas of the eighteenth and nineteenth centuries, and those in the ironic mode most frequently among the fiction and drama of the modern period.

When the concepts and attitudes that make up a mode seem to express what the historians call the "mind" of a literary period, the narrative pattern associated with the mode flourishes, as tragedy did when the formal mode seemed to fit the Elizabethan sense of the world. When the mode and narrative pattern are radically contradictory, as are the ironic mode and the romance narrative in our day, the mode seems to inhibit the use of the narrative pattern—at least in serious literature. Critics from Eliot on have lamented the fact that contemporary literature offers no myth for modern man and few works of epic character, another way of saying that the assumptions of the ironic mode deny or at least discourage the panoramic vision of idea and act characteristic of epic and romance. This is not to say, of course, that any one narrative pattern entirely disappears in the presence of an uncongenial mode. Narrative patterns may well be modulated, go underground, or reappear out of critical sight and mind in popular forms, as the romance pattern does in the contemporary comic strip, the film, and the television serial.

The Application of the Concept of Mode

The most effective use we can make of the concept of mode is to think of it first as representing those general historical presuppositions that modify or shape narrative patterns to the tastes of a particular period. Tragedies have been written in every era of English literature; and the deaths of Beowulf and Arthur, Othello and Lear, Willy Loman and Stephen Crane's Swede, share some of the constant elements of that narrative pattern, while their variables represent differing but no less legitimate conceptions of the significance of a man's death. Recognizing these differences should encourage some of the virtues of critical sophistication: a sensitivity to the historical life of literature, an awareness of its potential complexity, and a tolerance for the diverse and the original. In *The Faerie Queene*, for example, when Edmund Spenser invokes his muse to "Lay forth . . . the antique rolls . . . Of Faerie knights," we have evidence to support our impression that we are reading a work that both he and his audience would naturally take to be somewhat archaic in its narrative structure. As a romance narrative it is conventionally associated with the medieval period, and Spenser's deliberate imitation of Middle English linguistic forms recognizes the fact. But the intent of his allegory, the profound concern with the social implications of his moral drama, and the religious and political features of his courtly representatives, are all familiar as assumptions of the formal mode and the Renaissance. As readers we expect one thing from the dominant character of the mode (associated with the poem's historical period) and another from its narrative pattern (associated with an earlier period), and in sorting out these expectations we discover the relationship between Spenser's motive and the form of his epic. Through the concept of mode, then, we can come to an understanding of the complex connection between the history that is external and the history that is internal to literature. The modes fix our attention on the intersection of two lines of critical interest, one outward to the history that surrounds literature and one inward to the history of literature itself. That point of intersection is, of course, the literary work, where we witness the effects of its historical environment and its modal heredity.

We begin with a definition of the modes oriented in cultural or literary history, but our experience argues that as characteristics of the total order of literature the modes may transcend, or in some way be independent of, history. Like the narrative patterns, each mode is available to any author in any historical period. And it is no coincidence that the authors we value most are those whose imaginations could not rest in one mode but ranged over them all. Witness *The Canterbury Tales* and Shakespeare's plays: "The Knight's Tale" and "The Wife of Bath's Tale" work variations on the formal and the romantic, "The Miller's Tale" on the natural, and "The Pardoner's Tale" on the formal and the ironic modes. Shakespeare envisioned Tudor history in the romantic mode with *Henry V*, the legends of ancient Britons in the formal mode with *King Lear*, the various masquerades of love in the natural mode with *Twelfth Night*, and the perfidious affections and diplomacy of the Greeks in the ironic mode with *Troilus and Cressida*. And finally, in those works that speak most eloquently or persuasively of the human condition—*Paradise Lost, Moby Dick, Ulysses*—the ideas of character and action in several modes seem to work in concert. One mode, often the one associated with the work's period of history, may set a dominant tonality, like a key in music. But the conceptual harmony of these works is heard only in an intricate and subtle counterpoint of all the modes. Like music, these works play upon our sense of abstract time itself, and this may be why we think of them as timeless.

The word *theme* seems to be a word for all seasons in literary criticism. Sometimes it is used as a synonym for *subject*, the broad category of human experience that the literary work is somehow "about," or for "thesis," a fragment of truth that the writer is trying to prove by telling a story. Realistic novels appear to be making direct statements about the world that they imitate, yet it is usually a mistake for us to take the author's commentary as the whole truth about the meaning of the narrative. The closing paragraph of Thomas Hardy's *Tess of the d'Urbervilles*, just after Tess has been hanged, begins with "'Justice' was done, and the President

Thematic Pattern

The Concept of Thematic Pattern

of the Immortals, in Aeschylean phrase, had ended his sport with Tess." This ponderous sentence is not an adequate summary of the novel's meaning because it misses too much. At this point Hardy ignores the extent to which Tess *participates* in the tragic action leading to her execution. In other cases the truth or falsity of an authorial statement is irrelevant. The opening sentence of Jane Austen's *Pride and Prejudice* is "It is a truth universally acknowledged, that a single man in possession of a good fortune, must be in want of a wife." This wry assertion reveals the attitude of Mrs. Bennet, a woman with marriageable daughters, but it is not a home truth about the social world or about the novel's meaning. Rather it sets everything in motion, postulating the starting point of the comic action that follows. In works where the narrative interest dominates, whether they are epics, novels, or dramatic monologues, theme is the *total* pattern of meaning that emerges through a continuing action, not a smattering of interpretive paragraphs.

Theme in Narrative Literature   The hero's power to act within the given world of a novel or play defines reasonable expectations about what will happen to him. With an idea of his power, and its limitations, we are able to predict where a sequence of acts may lead and to know when they have been completed. Imagine our dilemma as readers if we lacked these expectations: we would be trying to make sense of a disconnected environment in which literally anything *could* happen. It would be impossible to relate one event to another. We should be as disoriented as the central characters of Tom Stoppard's play *Rosencrantz and Guildenstern Are Dead*—they are unable to tell the time by the sun's position because they do not know where south is.

If the events represented in literary fictions were insulated from each other and random in their occurrence, there could be no sequence, no expectation, and ultimately no meaning. In isolation, events are not self-explanatory; a random series can only express randomness until we find some meaning in it, and we usually do this with concepts like time, causality, or motivation, which allow us to connect one event with another. (Unless this were the case, no series of events could strike us as being disconnected or absurd in the first place.) Working hypotheses guide our awareness as we read, enabling us to sort, fit, and gradually assimilate many actions, ideas, and attitudes to a central structure.

As we follow what a fictional hero does, we begin to sense how his acts will fit together into a completed pattern, something we can grasp statically as an idea. Our dual awareness of narrative and theme depends on the way time and space are related in literary understanding. Whenever we talk about the *structure* of a novel or the *form* of a poem or the dramatic *shape* of a play, we are using spatial metaphors to describe something that can only be apprehended directly in passing moments of time while we read. If we think about the uses of these metaphors, we might conclude that we are trying to freeze literature, to pretend that it exists in space as do paintings and statues and buildings. This habit is more fundamentally an attempt to grasp the actions of literature as complete wholes with beginnings and endings, and to sum up their meaning. By pretending that narratives stand still, we enrich their meaning: the hero's responses as a young man can be set side by side with his mature decisions; we detect foreshadowing in earlier events, ironic gaps between his intentions and their results, recurrent images and motifs that grow in meaning. Talking about the theme of a narrative is a way of holding it in mind and memory; in this sense theme is the residue of vicarious action, what is left over after the experience of reading has stopped.

The Narrative-thematic Scale

We began by assuming that narrative literature—literature primarily concerned with telling a story—makes sense because it is built around some kind of idea or theme. This assumption suggests its converse: literature dealing primarily with ideas or attitudes, that is, thematic literature, contains an implicit "story," a movement that articulates or dramatizes the activity of the writer's mind. This relationship between action and thought in literature can be stated as an axiom: narrative implies theme and theme implies narrative, as long as we understand that the implied structure seldom appears overtly in the text. There are exceptions, of course: the playwright's ideas about his characters and their emotions are sometimes stated explicitly by a surrogate figure in the play, and the "story" of the poet's mental processes may be cued to shifts in scene or date. Where story and idea have nearly equal strength, as they do in some forms of fiction, we are able to see most clearly why neither can do without the other. The political satire of Jonathan Swift's *Gulliver's Travels* and George Orwell's *Animal Farm* reaches us through fantasy. Both tales take shape from the ways in which their ideas are articulated. Thus we understand Gulliver's final hatred of man to be the culmination of the book's argument as well as his disillusioning experiences, and the pigs in *Animal Farm* behave both as pigs will and as some revolutionary groups do after they have gained power.

The conventional genres—drama, fiction, lyric—represent a scale of possibilities in the blending of story and idea, ranging from drama at one end to lyric at the other. In drama, the playwright's *ideas* are usually implicit; in the lyric, the sense of *progression* in the poet's thinking is usually implicit. All literature depends on what we read between the lines, as the cliché has it, far more than philosophy, history, or science. While we are reading we have no immediate grasp of anything but structures of words, yet those words seem to suggest more than they state. Our sense of being in the midst of a tangible scene is the result of imaginative projection; like the director of a play, we look through the words of the text to find ways of making it tangible with costumes, gestures, scenery, lighting, tone of voice, pacing of lines, and so on. Just as no two productions of a play are identical, no two readings of a novel will evoke precisely the same mental imagery. In watching a movie made from a novel we know well, we are often dismayed because we had not *seen* Lord Jim or Heathcliff that way in our own minds. The reader has to work with his own private stock of remembered images, and these he must match as best he can to the verbal structure of a literary narrative. At the narrative end of the scale—in drama, for example—the script provides only the dialogue and sequence of scenes; interpreting their meaning is usually left to the reader. Near the middle of the scale, in fiction, a narrating character is often used to make the connections between act and meaning explicit, although his interpretations are not always reliable or complete. At the thematic end of the scale, in lyrics, the verbal structure is not limited to scenes or commentary on them but may depend on clusters of association in a thinking and feeling mind. At no point can the full meaning of play, novel, or poem be reduced to what is directly stated, and the ways in which implication works vary considerably with the genre.

As we approach the thematic end of the scale, the patterns of development within a work resemble thought more than action. But we should not confuse the process of thought with its product, an idea. Few lyrics stand still; they often ask us to imagine ideas and attitudes moving. It is as if we were looking at the pieces on a chess board in their fixed positions and began to plot all the moves we could make. Nothing has actually changed, but we have imagined a whole series of moves leading to checkmate, the culmination of the game. We often behave in this way while looking at paintings of battles or storms at sea, filling in what we do not actually see —the movements preceding and following the one moment actually there on the canvas. In the fourth stanza of "Ode on a Grecian Urn," Keats responds to the arrested motion of the carved scene by imagining what must have gone before and what must follow:

> What little town by river or sea shore,
> Or mountain-built with peaceful citadel,
> Is emptied of this folk, this pious morn?
> And, little town, thy streets for evermore
> Will silent be; and not a soul to tell
> Why thou art desolate can e'er return.

In "Lapis Lazuli," Yeats enlivens another static scene, this one containing three Chinamen on a mountainside:

> and I
> Delight to imagine them seated there;
> There, on the mountain and the sky,
> On all the tragic scene they stare.
> One asks for mournful melodies;
> Accomplished fingers begin to play.
> Their eyes mid many wrinkles, their eyes,
> Their ancient, glittering eyes, are gay.

In both poems nothing can happen in the external scene being described—
it is carved in stone—but the poet imagines, and we with him, what *might*
happen within limits set by the controlling idea or attitude of the poem.
In this sense many lyrics are "frozen narratives" because they imply action,
using the perspectives of events at rest or of ideas in motion.

Analogy, and all the other metaphoric processes associated with it,
generates the pattern of movement within many lyrics. Often the lyric
poet imitates the motions of his own mind more than that of the external
world; a variety of images can be used as long as some idea joins them. In
John Donne's "A Valediction: Forbidding Mourning," for example, the
lover parting from his beloved justifies their separation with two images
that have no connection in the external world:

> Our two souls therefore, which are one,
>   Though I must go, endure not yet
> A breach, but an expansion,
>   Like gold to airy thinness beat.
>
> If they be two, they are two so
>   As stiff twin compasses are two:
> Thy soul, the fixed foot, makes no show
>   To move, but doth if the other do.

The principle relating the two is analogy. In this case it works because both
images suggest the paradox of a separation that does not sever all connection, a transformation of love depending on physical presence into one
that can grow with absence.

Thus the narrative-thematic scale is a principle of literary relativity.
Thematic pattern is not reducible to a statement of "theme" any more than
narrative pattern is because both are structures of changing relationships
within a work. In thematic works—principally lyrics—this pattern controls
a sequence of ideas or attitudes toward human experience rather than
imitations of experience itself. Ideas are not identical with acts, but they
often fit them appropriately, which is to say that they can share a common
purpose, intention, or meaning. If I wish to express my displeasure at a
meeting, I can phrase my objection in words, get up and stalk out, or do
both. Thus it is possible to connect acts that mean in the process of their
doing with ideas that imply a series of possible enactments. We can suggest
how the analogies between thought and action work in literature schem-
atically:

NARRATIVE ⟷ THEMATIC
Character's power ← (Mode) ⟶ Speaker's role
    of action
Stages of action ⟵ (Movement) → Sequences of attitude and argument
Physical setting ⟵ (Placement) ⟶ Conceptual scene

The hero's *power* of action in a narrative work may be related to the speaker's *role*, his sense of his identity as well as his relationship with his audience and his attitude toward his subject. The *stages* of action in a narrative work may be related to *sequences* of thought and feeling, either the explicit "argument" of the poem or a progression of attitudes in the mind of its speaker, or both. And the physical *setting* may move into the speaker's head as the conceptual scene of the poem, becoming the matrix of imagery that unifies it and creates its mood. Such analogies have the limitations inherent in any set of critical definitions because they separate what is inseparable in literature. Nevertheless they enable us to talk about the meaning of what we read more precisely and intelligibly. Nor are the components of this scheme new: we have simply rearranged traditional terms—character, narrative, setting, and theme—in a way that makes the relationship between act and idea clearer.

Speaker's Role   The first major correlation between narrative and thematic elements in literature is *mode*, the link between a character in a novel or play and the speaking voice in a poem. The question "What did he do?" becomes "What did he say?" Yet there are several obvious complications in this simple conversion of act to speech. Descriptions of acts are often found in lyrics, and dialogue is the central substance of plays and many novels. Such overlapping is perfectly consistent with the notion of a narrative-thematic scale, but it is evident that the ways in which speeches in literature can be acts as well as representations of thoughts will need sorting out. A second complication can be stated simply as a question: Who is speaking in a lyric, the author or someone else? In ordinary usage, our language makes no distinction between the poem and the poet's thought. Unless a poem is quite obviously a dramatic monologue, like Robert Browning's "My Last Duchess" or Tennyson's "Ulysses," we slip into the habit of identifying the speaker of the poem with the person who wrote it.

A direct connection between poet and poem seems natural in the realm of ideas and attitudes, where we are likely to question who said it, when, in what surroundings, and with what intentions. Whenever we listen to another person, we connect what we already know about the man with what he is saying; each kind of information helps us to interpret the other. It is curious that we tend to assume the same rhetorical situation of direct address in reading poems, when it obviously does *not* hold. Ordinarily the speaker of a poem is not addressing us directly, nor is the poet available to us as anything but a name prefixed to the words of the poem. Unless we have biographical information about the poet, we do not see the man in the name, but we generally do imagine a man or woman speaking the words of the poem, and we invent the sort of personality that might match those words. Moreover, when a poet reads his own poems, his physical presence in the room does not alter the rhetorical situation in any essential way; he is not expressing emotions or ideas that represent his mental state at the time of the reading so much as reproducing what he once felt or thought or imagined. The poet has no obligation to be consistent in representing himself from poem to poem; he may give the speaking voice of a poem feelings and attitudes that he has never had or ideas that he disbelieves or abhors.

Let us compare the speaking voices in two poems by Robert Frost about man's relation to nature and consider the kind of personality that each voice implies. In "Dust of Snow" the voice is direct, unassuming, and serious:

> The way a crow
> Shook down on me
> The dust of snow
> From a hemlock tree
>
> Has given my heart
> A change of mood
> And saved some part
> Of a day I had rued.

In "Design" the voice begins in a similarly deliberate tone but soon becomes almost whimsically ironic and consciously "poetic" to avoid the implications of a simple "fact" of nature:

> I found a dimpled spider, fat and white,
> On a white heal-all, holding up a moth
> Like a white piece of rigid satin cloth—
> Assorted characters of death and blight
> Mixed ready to begin the morning right,
> Like the ingredients of a witches' broth—
> A snow-drop spider, a flower like a froth,
> And dead wings carried like a paper kite.

Neither voice is a quintessential, unchanging Robert Frost speaking the truth directly to us. "We" are, rather, a hypothetical audience being addressed by two very different "characters." Each one is a role created by a human being sensitive enough to imagine himself in different relationships with the natural world, one of sympathetic identification, the other of fearful obsession. The poet—the real man behind the name—changes, but the two speakers are fixed ineradicably by the words of the poems.

For such reasons it is more appropriate to think of the speaker than of Robert Frost when we try to comprehend either poem, although this would not be so if we were studying the evolution of Frost's themes or writing his biography. Like the real speaker before a live audience, the hypothetical speaker of a lyric (sometimes called the *persona*) *seems* to make certain assumptions about the effects his words might have on his audience. He may count on evoking responses that he can predict from the age, occupation, status, religion, or politics of his imagined listeners, just as comedians do. But the persona has no basis for such expectations, since his real audience includes anyone who can read the poem, even centuries later; thus he imagines an audience he can depend on and use. This hypothetical audience, unlike the characters in a play or a novel who are directly addressed by other characters, is not really there to respond; it is a construct of the speaker's mind, like a television performer's idea of the live audience he never sees. Some of these imagined listeners are used often enough to become literary conventions—the mistress or friend addressed in Shakespeare's sonnets, the idealized shepherds in Milton's "Lycidas" and Shelley's "Adonais," and the young virgin in Robert Herrick's "Corinna" who is told to make much of time. Others, particularly in dramatic monologues like Browning's "My Last Duchess" and Frost's "Home Burial," are clearly implied by what is said to them. When we "identify" most closely with such poems, we temporarily assume the role of the imagined listener. Thus for a moment we are a part of the society implied by the poem, and the persona is speaking to us. But he is doing so indirectly, just as our responses are imagined rather than spoken. What the poem creates is an imitation of dialogue between speaker and listener, an imaginary conversation that we can enjoy and contemplate all the more because we are never forced to reply to anything that is said.

Sequences of Attitude and Argument   In many lyrics the imagined conversation is so overlaid with elaborate formal conventions (rhyme, meter, stanza pattern) and so dense with clustering images and logical relationships that we may be tempted to treat the poem as if it were a complex static whole, like a painting or a building. To do so is to ignore *movement*, the second major correlation between narrative and thematic elements in literature. Our scheme suggests that stages of action in narratives are transformed into sequences of attitude and argument in lyrics.

To understand how this transformation works, we must answer a basic question: To what extent is the speaking voice of a lyric engaged in acting, *doing* something? Given the notion of the persona as a potential character in a fictional world containing him and us, we can see that the kind of "act" he performs is a verbal act. Then we might expect to find that sequences of words that can be entertained by the mind are correlated with possible sequences of acts in the world. It may be helpful to reconsider a key word that links ideas and acts: the *attitude* of a human being means both a disposition toward another person or object and a pose, a momentary fixation of a body in motion. The connection of the two meanings in language seems natural when we reflect that movement is a constant feature of ordinary human experience. If two persons greeting each other are asked to pose for a photograph, there is an artificial pause in the normal flow of gesture and conversation. In the print, we may find something we would not have noticed—a grimace, an awkward stance—had we been watching a motion, just as we study the form of a skier or diver by looking at individual frames of a film. Similarly, our attitudes toward persons can be made to stand still to reveal their complexity, whereas such dispositions are actually experienced as fluctuating, evolving feelings.

Literature is less interested in naming states of emotion than in representing their rhythms, articulating the changes that make each moment of feeling distinctive and specific. King Lear's soliloquy on the heath during the storm reveals a continually shifting attitude toward his daughters, himself, and nature:

> Rumble thy bellyful! Spit, fire! spout, rain!
> Nor rain, wind, thunder, fire are my daughters;
> I tax not you, you elements, with unkindness.
> I never gave you kingdom, called you children,
> You owe me no subscription. Then let fall
> Your horrible pleasure. Here I stand, your slave,
> A poor, infirm, weak, and despised old man.
> But yet I call you servile ministers
> That have with two pernicious daughters joined
> Your high-engendered battles 'gainst a head
> So old and white as this. Oh, oh! 'Tis foul. . . .
> No, I will be the pattern of all patience,
> I will say nothing.

It is easier to sense the changes in Lear's mood than it is to label them, yet in following the contours of feeling through the passage we may forget the part that ideas play in causing emotion. Feeling and thought sustain each other in a sequence of attitudes: Lear's mood changes because he thinks about ingratitude, servility, and patience, and the intensity of his denunciation depends on the analogy between family and kingdom that his metaphors for the storm establish (tax, subscription, slave, ministers, battles). This interaction of idea and emotion is necessarily dynamic; we are caught up in it because the persona is thinking and feeling simultaneously.

In the lyric, direct experience of Lear's sort may also be put at one remove, transformed into the recaptured life of memory. The process of remembering can have its own drama of shifting attitudes. We can observe the stages of such internal movement in Philip Larkin's "Church Going" by isolating and juxtaposing four fragments:

> Once I am sure there's nothing going on
> I step inside, letting the door thud shut.
>
> .   .   .
>
> Yet stop I did: in fact I often do,
> And always end much at a loss like this,
> Wondering what to look for; . . .
>
> .   .   .

A shape less recognizable each week,
A purpose more obscure. I wonder who
Will be the last, the very last, to seek
This place for what it was: . . .

.   .   .

For, though I've no idea
What this accoutred frowsty barn is worth,
It pleases me to stand in silence here;

A serious house on serious earth it is,
In whose blent air all our compulsions meet,
Are recognized, and robed as destinies.

The speaker starts out as a tourist and ends up talking about "compulsions
. . . robed as destinies"; his musings have obviously gotten him somewhere. The movement from apathy to a far-reaching concern for human
beings has been completed: the persona understands that life has meaning
for men and women because they endow their own acts with symbolic
meaning. This abstract description of his mental trip is a shorthand for a
sequence of attitudes that the persona is trying out, each one tied to its
predecessors in some important way. Thus the peculiar compulsiveness
of the second fragment—in which the persona admits that he continues to
stop at churches for no reason he can explain—depends on the shift from
the self-assured, detached boredom of the first fragment for its force.
Similarly, the third fragment represents a rather crucial abandonment of
his supercilious tone, preparing him for the identification with others that
is signaled by "*our* compulsions" in the last fragment. The persona never
gives up easy flippancy—the church is still a "frowsty barn"—but he has
brought that flippancy into new relations with competing attitudes; it is
now a safeguard against meretricious seriousness, whereas it began as a
barrier to self-discovery.

King Lear's soliloquy and Larkin's poem leave traces of psychological
change within the acts of speaking and remembering that they record.
The words of the passages serve as cues to sequences that end in temporary
resolution, a momentary equilibrium amongst warring impulses. In these
instances words are signs of subtle internal changes, but speech can also
be an overt and conventional act in itself. In many lyrics there is an obvious
argument, an attempt to convince some listener (who may be the persona
himself) of something: many of Shakespeare's sonnets imitate syllogisms,
with the conclusion in the final couplet; Donne's "Valediction: Forbidding Mourning" argues by analogy; Tennyson's "Ulysses" is a series
of rationalizations dismissing the obligations of kingship and justifying
heroic wanderlust; Yeats' "aged man" in "Sailing to Byzantium" concludes two stanzas of argument with the lines "And therefore I have sailed
the seas and come / To the holy city of Byzantium."

In a very important sense, arguments are acts, rituals of the thinking
process. In Dylan Thomas' "A Refusal to Mourn the Death, by Fire, of a

Child in London" speaking *is* acting for the persona. The long first sentence of thirteen lines, which runs into the third stanza, is a very complicated temporal variant of the "if-then" logical form transmuted into "when-then."

> Never until the mankind making
> Bird beast and flower
> Fathering and all humbling darkness
> Tells with silence the last light breaking
> And the still hour
> Is come of the sea tumbling in harness
>
> And I must enter again the round
> Zion of the water bead
> And the synagogue of the ear of corn
> Shall I let pray the shadow of a sound
> Or sow my salt seed
> In the least valley of sackcloth to mourn
>
> The majesty and burning of the child's death.

The sentence has obvious affinities with chronological narration. It is filled with conditions from lines 1 through 9, all of them describing the end of the world and the merging of the individual into the cycles of nature. But the word "never" at the very beginning of the sentence tips us off: we know that the conditions will not be fulfilled *yet* because the word hangs over all of them. In line 10 the "shall" sets us off on a second series, the consequences that would follow the unlikely fulfilment of the preceding conditions. Should this happen, claims the persona, he would then mourn the child's death, but of course he has been engaged in *refusing* to mourn now for thirteen lines. This refusal is an act, just as the remaining lines of the third stanza suggest further refusals to "murder" in words or "blaspheme" by using the literary conventions of the elegy. And all of this argument leads to the final assertion of the poem: "After the first death, there is no other." This is both a reason for refusing to mourn and an act in itself, an affirmation whose truth is inseparable from its *being* affirmed just as the articles of belief in Christian liturgy are both assertions about the world and affirmations of faith for the individual. Repeating a catechism, swearing an oath, saying "I do" in a marriage ceremony, and conducting a poetic argument are all ways in which saying is doing.

Conceptual Scene

Placement provides a third way of correlating narrative and thematic elements in literature. In narratives, the scene at any stage of action is usually a recognizable place in which certain kinds of words and acts are more likely to occur than others; a city street, a living room, a clearing in the forest—each has its own limits of probability. Without much conscious effort, we can imagine the ways in which a meeting between lovers or enemies might be influenced by placement in any one of these settings. We customarily use the word *setting* to refer to scenes that have such clear limits in the visible world; they are familiar places for human beings to act in, and in fiction and drama they are often described in minute detail.

A carefully drawn visible setting may operate as the scene of a lyric, but it seldom *contains* what happens in quite the same way. Frost's "Design," for example, begins with a clearly seen fragment of nature—moth, spider, and flower—but the speaker is less captured by what he sees than excited to ask metaphysical questions; the true scene of the poem has expanded from the minute drama of death on the flower to the workings of the universe. Similarly, Larkin's "Church Going" begins with a concretely realized setting, a typical church that the speaker is visiting, and ends with a conceptual scene that includes all churches and worshipers throughout time. In such instances the scene implied by the poem has broken all the limits that might be expected within the original setting. Thus in Coleridge's "Kubla Khan" the actual contents of the pleasure gardens within "twice five miles of fertile ground / With walls and towers . . . girdled round" are determined by the needs of the speaker's imagination, not by what real gardens may be like. This principle of imaginative rather than mimetic association is one of the themes of Andrew Marvell's "Garden," in which the mind annihilates "all that's made / To a green thought in a green shade."

Images can be associated by the mind in many ways that do not imitate natural groupings of objects in the world. The possibilities of intertwining images in new ways are seemingly endless as long as some rationale of association is implied. The pattern of association, like the ground bass in a fugue, controls the variations in a lyric and gives them coherence. In Shakespeare's Sonnet 64 ("When I have seen by Time's fell hand defaced") for example, the varied images cohere in a common reference to an abstract idea of the transformation of matter, "such interchange of state, / Or state itself confounded to decay." The principle of association may rest in an extended metaphor, as in Donne's "Love's Diet"; the whole poem develops an initial image of "burdenous corpulence." It may be quite particular without being tangible, like an event in history, or it may be a form of thinking itself, like the logic of analogy or the syllogism. Yeats' "Easter 1916" uses a series of allusions to characters and events in the armed revolt of the Irish Republicans as one principle of coherence, and the abstract relation between change and beauty as the other. The third stanza is a remarkable instance of argument by analogy; the idea comes first, equating revolutionary zeal with lack of change:

> Hearts with one purpose alone
> Through summer and winter seem
> Enchanted to a stone
> To trouble the living stream.

The remainder of the stanza builds on other images from nature (horses, birds, clouds, moor-hens) to expand the idea of the "living stream" into a scene, then concludes by restating the idea in terms of the images: "Minute by minute they live: / The stone's in the midst of all." What we observe in such poems is thinking *in* images, a visual and auditory scene that is the result of mental action rather than the setting in which it occurs.

The discovery of recondite connections between phenomena that come together only as the speaker thinks and feels is the principle operating in Emily Dickinson's "Of Bronze—and Blaze."

The images do not set a scene for an action, although one can imagine a narrative work in which they might. For example, the image of the grave, "An Island in dishonored Grass," does not have the same status or function that, say, Ophelia's grave has in *Hamlet*. Rather, the poet uses this image and others to construct a metaphorical discourse on the response to the magnificence of the northern lights. The aurora borealis (imagined as a monarch), the poet (imagined as a flower), her menagerie of splendors, the meteoric show, and the grave with its daisies are conceptual items with which the poet or her persona thinks rather than elements of a world in which she acts. Of course, there are "acts" in the poem—or so they seem. The majesty of the northern lights "infects" the poet's spirit until she "takes" vaster attitudes, "struts" upon her stem, and "disdains" men; and the incomparable celestial show will "entertain" the centuries long after she has died. But these verbs do not describe movements or gestures in a plot, in the ordinary sense, so much as they indicate a sequence of intricately related attitudes or conceptual positions. And there is a "dramatic" movement in the poem from wonder to arrogance to humility; it has some analogy with an ironic narrative, but it is the movement of a mind thinking, not of a character acting. The images establish an imagined cosmos with a hierarchy from the majestically indifferent heavens to the mundane and dishonored grass. Just as a setting with its implied orders of time and space gives a location and meaning to a narrative action, so the implied scene in this poem with its ordered ranks of existence serves the poet's conceptual purposes. The flower images, for example, function primarily as instruments of thought as the poet contemplates the paradoxical effect of the northern lights:

> I take vaster attitudes—
> And strut upon my stem—
> Disdaining Men, and Oxygen,
> For Arrogance of them—

The aurora's grandeur is such that it reduces the poet, demotes her from the human and the animate to the level of the plant, and at the same time it inspires her to rise again to the level of the animate and "strut" upon her stem, disdaining not only men on that higher scale of being but the element oxygen that so intimately connects the lives of men and plants. In the margin of the manuscript for this poem Dickinson considered a possible alternative for the last line that read "Whom none but Beetles—know." Some editors prefer that grimmer version, but whether the poet did is anyone's guess. In the original form, however, the flower image in the last line rounds out the poem's thematic pattern. The imaginative experience of having been diminished to a flower, coming from the earth but strutting with arrogance, raised the thought, almost like a punishment for that pride, of being literally brought back down to earth in death.

These three correlations—between a character's power of action and a speaker's role, between narrative and a sequence of attitude or argument, between the setting in which a character acts and the pattern of imagery with which a poet thinks—suggest that thematic patterns may resemble narrative patterns in a number of other ways. We might expect to find conventions that are as persistent and widespread as the major narrative patterns, but the development of the lyric throughout literary history has been so various that it is hard to isolate patterns with the scope of tragedy or comedy. Some thematic conventions like the elegy and the *carpe diem* poem do persist; others like the epithalamium and the epistle seem limited to particular eras of literary history; still others like the sonnet and the Horatian ode remain consistent only in form. As readers, evidently, we must approach lyrics with far more liberal expectations than we need for narratives. It is nevertheless true that implicit meaning in lyrics depends on the broad sense of convention that enables us to isolate and react to the unexpected. Otherwise we would fail to comprehend Thomas' elegy that paradoxically refuses to mourn or to recognize Matthew Arnold's "Dover Beach" as a despairing philosophical version of the *carpe diem* argument. The freshness and power of lyric poetry often depends on expectations not unlike those we use in understanding the four narrative patterns.

Displacement

The Concept of Displacement

In some ways the concept of displacement is so similar to the concept of mode that it is difficult to keep the two ideas separate. For that matter, it may be better not to make too precise a distinction between them, since they both function in much the same way in our critical thinking: both concepts offer ways of reinvesting literature with its historical context. When we think of a novel or a poem only in terms of its narrative or thematic pattern, we necessarily take it out of its time and place in history. Those patterns are by definition more or less timeless and constant patterns of action and thought; they may be shared by writers as distant from each other in time as Thomas Malory and Saul Bellow, John Donne and Gerard Manley Hopkins. If our critical interest ended rather than began with these common narrative and thematic patterns, then the novels and poems we read would seem anonymous and detached from experience, and we might do without Malory and Hopkins and get along with Bellow and Donne. But literature insists on its personality and history, and even if it did not, the human itch for relevance would name the man behind the poem and fix its time and place. So we draw on the idea of mode to identify the complex culture, and the idea of displacement to characterize the unique mind that makes *Morte Darthur* Malory's, *not* Chaucer's.

We have used the term *mode* to describe four sets of postulates on the character of the hero, his society, and his natural world: romantic, formal, natural, and ironic. They follow a historical sequence; each is associated with a major period of cultural history: the medieval period, the Renaissance, the eighteenth and most of the nineteenth centuries, and the contemporary period. The term *displacement* refers to the writer's adaptation or modification of narrative or thematic patterns to fit some standard of plausibility or morality—what will occur or ought to occur in action or thought. Those pervasive cultural assumptions that constitute a mode obviously can account for the displacement of a pattern; modes, after all, imply standards of plausibility or morality. Yet not all modifications of narrative and thematic patterns are *modal* displacements; in fact, many of the more intricate and profound variations on patterns of structure and thought are *stylistic*, in that they represent the individual writer's characteristic adaptation of literary patterns to his own vision of plausibility or morality—what *he* thinks is possible or right in human action and thought.

Modal and Stylistic Displacement

We must admit that some of the modifications of conventional narrative in the plot of a novel or play and of conventional thematic pattern in the conceptual structure of a lyric poem are impossible or at least difficult to distinguish as either modal or stylistic displacement. There is no sharp line between a writer's social and individual life; so too with his art. However, there are features of Chaucer's work, for instance, that are as medieval as the next man's, and there are features that are his and no one else's in the fourteenth or any other century.

Displacement—particularly what we call stylistic displacement—offers a way into the personality of the writer. The term originated in Freudian psychoanalysis, where it usually refers to those modifications imposed on our instinctual desires or early memories by some censor in our minds. The displaced version at once conceals and reveals the original idea or event. So dreams distort and reform our memories and desires into shapes and meanings that our imagination can accept or momentarily bear but that still allow the analyst to retrieve their original form and import. If the analogy between psychology and literature holds, then displacement in a novel or poem may be read as evidence for the ways in which the writer's imagination has transformed and revised his most profound desires and experiences into forms that meet his or his culture's sense of what is appropriate or significant. Displacement, therefore, is often a feature of style, marking evidence with which we can discover the writer's secret signature.

The danger of the analogy with psychoanalysis lies in the reduction of art to neurosis and literary style to a collection of Freudian slips. The concept of displacement is abused when everything is taken to mean something else or its opposite, there are no pure and simple motives, and Holy Grails are as common as paper cups. But with reasonable tact we can use the concept to discover some of the elusive and private impulses that account for the originality of a literary work and our recognition of its author's characteristic art.

Displacement in Narrative Pattern   In narratives we assume more or less constant patterns of action, character, and setting within which both modal and stylistic displacement function as variables. From the medieval romance *Sir Orfeo* and D. H. Lawrence's story "The Horse Dealer's Daughter," we can abstract a common narrative pattern. A hero descends into a lower region associated with death (in the first a Celtic otherworld, in the second the dead, black water of a pond) from which he rescues a woman with whom he is later reunited in love. Each story is related to the Greek legend of Orpheus and Eurydice but rendered with a more fortunate conclusion. Each shares other significant characteristics: some aura of the occult and mysterious, mature characters, and diametrically opposed forces—the real world and fairyland, the bestial horse dealer's life and that of the more spiritual daughter. These are the features associated with the defining event of last-phase romance, the descent into the underworld, and are sufficient to begin a comparison of the narratives. There are differences between the two stories: some are so large—like those between the two narrative points of view—as to be trivial, although they might be of critical interest on another occasion. Others are factors of mode, like the ease and frequency with which the Orfeo poet introduces the magical and prophetic. Within the romantic mode he can say that "the Queen was taken from their midst by magic." Lawrence must rely on metaphor for the mysterious tone: the doctor watches the woman "as if spell-bound," her memory remains "distinct in his consciousness, like a vision." He must italicize his point—"It *was* portentous, her face. It seemed to mesmerize him"—for Lawrence writes under the constraints of the natural mode.

But there are other differences between the two stories that are neither so large as to make comparison pointless nor so apparently explicable in terms of mode. Dame Heurodis has a rather passive part in the medieval tale; she is simply lost and regained more like an object than a person. Mabel Pervin's role is much less passive; early in the story, during her meeting with the doctor at the graveyard, "a heavy power in her eyes . . . laid hold of his whole being, as if he had drunk some powerful drug. He had been feeling weak and done before. Now the life came back into him, he felt delivered from his own fretted, daily self." In this moment she empowers him, by delivering him from his reticence, with the ability to deliver her later from the "foul earthy" waters of death. And when she revives on the warm hearth, the scene that follows continues this reciprocity between the hero and heroine, unusual for the romance narrative. They are caught in a struggle not so much between themselves as between the symbolic forces figured in the cold, stagnant water and the bright, passionate fire.

The characteristic structure of the romance narrative sets an active subject, the hero, on a quest to rescue the passive object, the heroine. Lawrence's deliberate displacement of this pattern raises questions about the meaning of the narrative and the author's motive. The unilateral emotional arrangement of the typical romance was anathema to Lawrence. For him the ideal, almost mystical, union between a man and a woman should involve no domination of one partner by the other. Rather, he imagined a delicate equilibrium in which the selfhood and power of both were undiminished. In his novel *Women in Love*, he described it as "a pure balance of two single beings:—as the stars balance each other." This much is no critical secret, and the more adequate commentaries on Lawrence mention this criterion for emotional parity in what has been called his "love ethic." One can read of this in biographical studies, yet it seems important to come to this concept through the narrative and thematic features of the story itself, for to do so is to see how the concept is central rather than peripheral to the story and how it contributes to its integrity and coherence. Our primary responsibility is to recognize Lawrence's idea first as a fact of literature. Then, as we see this kind of displacement recur in his other fiction, we can take it as a conscious stylistic choice that is both a critical fact and an original comment on an elemental human experience.

Displacement in Thematic Pattern

Thematic structures in literature are subject to the modifying effects of displacement in ways that are perhaps more subtle and certainly more difficult to recognize. The point was made earlier that a facile identification of the speaker of the poem with the poet usually collides with a contrary identification when we read another of his poems, as it does when we read Frost's "Design" after his "Dust of Snow." The concept of thematic pattern suggests a wide range of authorial attitudes, conceptual structures, and patterns of imagery. Within this array there probably are regularly recurring combinations of attitude, concept, and image. Both this variety and recurrence in thematic structures argue against any immediate or simple identity between the persona and the poet, the poem's meaning and the man's thought, or its imagery and his world. But to leave it at this is to beg a variety of important questions. Why, for instance, do we insist on talking, and legitimately so, about Edgar Allan Poe's conception of death, for example, and mean by the name not some literary abstraction but the man who lived from 1809 to 1849? How is it that, as stylistic critics have noted, readers can identify with no other evidence than the literary work itself a Faulkner story, distinguish it from one by J. D. Salinger, and recognize a parody of it by Peter De Vries. If there is no truth to the statement that style is the man, then literature has only a rather abstract and tangential connection with life. If we go no further into a poem than to meet its persona or are satisfied with attitudes as formalities of literature and little else, then our experience of literature will seem confined. Critical skepticism should use the disparity between the speakers in the two Frost poems to avoid any easy and superficial characterization of the poet. But the two poems still bear Frost's stylistic signature. How we know that—what we respond to as Frost's style—is a difficult question; even to begin to answer it demands some concept like displacement and some procedure for distinguishing significant variations on thematic convention.

The classical elegy offers a recurrent thematic pattern against which we can measure the effects of displacement. This conventional form has provided many lesser poets with a convenient vessel for their lachrymose sentiments, but it has also presented better poets with a challenge to their originality, for it has been an honored tradition since classical times. Milton apparently alludes to that challenge in the opening lines of "Lycidas" when he speaks of plucking the laurel, myrtles, and ivy with "forced fingers rude . . . before the mellowing year." The untimeliness of the act suggests not only the premature death of his friend but his own inexperience with a noble tradition. Most of the conventional elements of the elegy are present in "Lycidas": the invocation of the muse, the recollection of a pastoral life with the dead friend, the sympathetic mourning of nature, the procession of mourners, the floral tribute, and the sequence of attitudes from grief and despair to reconciliation and hope. Walt Whitman's elegy "When Lilacs Last in the Dooryard Bloom'd" is an interesting example of displacement, partly because he thought of himself as an original poet who wrote against tradition and especially its more artificial conventions. In a later invocation to the muse he was more demanding than deferential: "Come Muse migrate from Greece and Ionia / Cross out please those immensely overpaid accounts." And yet his poem on the death of Abraham Lincoln incorporates most of the traditional elements of the classical elegy. The early sections invoke the symbolic lilac, western star, and hermit thrush; the natural world responds to the poet's grief with the great star sinking in the night and the "carol of death" sung by the thrush; the poet follows the president's funeral cortege as it crosses the country; and he moves from inconsolable grief to reconciliation found in "death's outlet song" of the thrush. For all Whitman's disavowal of the elegiac convention, some important part of his meaning depends on the tradition and its displacement in the poem.

We can observe the modification of convention in the version Whitman gives us of the floral tribute, the casting of flowers or wreaths upon the grave as a sign of nature's lament for the dead. Milton's version is an example of the tradition established by Greek and Latin poets from Bion to Virgil:

> return Sicilian Muse,
> And call the vales, and bid them hither cast
> Their bells, and flowerets of a thousand hues.

> Ye valleys low where the mild whispers use,
> Of shades and wanton winds, and gushing brooks,
> On whose fresh lap the swart star sparely looks,
> Throw hither all your quaint enameled eyes,
> That on the green turf suck the honeyed showers,
> And purple all the ground with vernal flowers.
> Bring the rathe primose that forsaken dies,
> The tufted crow-toe, and pale jessamine,
> The white pink, and the pansy freaked with jet,
> The glowing violet,
> The musk-rose, and the well-attired woodbine,
> With cowslips wan that hang the pensive head,
> And every flower that sad embroidery wears:
> Bid amaranthus all his beauty shed,
> And daffadillies fill their cups with tears,
> To strew the laureate hearse where Lycid lies.

In Whitman's poem the floral tribute recurs throughout, and the lilac assumes a more specific meaning as one of its three major symbols. The poet introduces the lilac in the first section of the poem; in the third section he describes the bush, "tall-growing with heart-shaped leaves of rich green," from which he breaks a sprig with its flower. Later he places the sprig on the coffin, not "for one alone" but for "sane and sacred death":

> All over bouquets of roses,
> O death, I cover you with roses and early lilies,
> But mostly and now the lilac that blooms the first,
> Copious I break, I break the sprigs from the bushes,
> With loaded arms I come, pouring for you,
> For you and the coffins all of you O death.

The "mastering odor" of the lilac detains the poet until the moment of reconciliation, achieved after he hears the song of the thrush. Then he passes beyond it: "I leave thee lilac with heart-shaped leaves, / I leave thee there in the dooryard, blooming, returning with spring."

Like any two poems in the same tradition, these contribute to each other's meaning. Whitman's poem shows us how close Milton's is to the original Greek and Latin elegies. In the earlier poem the muse is invoked to arouse the valleys and bid them to gather the flowers for a conventional rite. The flowers are listed not for their simple virtues as flowers but for their human characteristics—"quaint enameled eyes," appropriate attire, pensive manner, and "sad embroidery." The "gathering" of the flowers is a human one; they are brought together to perform as mourners in a kind of floral society. This much is characteristic of the formal mode in which the natural world imitates the social world. The flowers, in obedience to the valleys, take the muse as their leader and spokesman just as the "human" characters—the company of nymphs, Hippotades, Camus, and Saint Peter—respond to the poet's vision.

Whitman finds his inspiration not in the muse but in the "tallying chant" with which his soul echoes the song of the bird. Although some of the attendant natural imagery is animated, it is not so consistently humanized as Milton's. Aside from the implication of its "heart-shaped leaves," the lilac remains a flower; and the obvious personification of the thrush is important not so much as an instance of the poet investing the bird with human poetic talents, as it is of the bird inspiring the poet with a gift for natural song. There may be a whole nation mourning the death of a president (who like Milton's friend Edward King is never mentioned), but Whitman's concern is with his own love and his private loss. The song he learns from the thrush, like the gesture of covering all coffins with flowers, is one for and about "sane and sacred death." Once he unites the thought of this death with the sacred and reconciling knowledge of all death, he can turn his gaze from the darkened star and can leave the lilac behind in the common dooryard, where it will bloom with ever-returning spring.

Both poems begin with the "fact" of tragedy, the death of a representative man; both poems reflect in varying degrees the conventions of the elegy. But Milton's poem ends with the deification of Lycidas as he enters the highest of conventional societies, the "blest kingdoms meek of joy and love." When he becomes

the genius of the shore,
In thy large recompense, and shalt be good
To all that wander in that perilous flood.

Lycidas, like the hero of romance, transcends death, and the poem modulates into the romantic mode. Whitman's poem ends, "With the holders holding my hand hearing the call of the bird, / Comrades mine and I in the midst, and their memory ever to keep, for the dead I loved so well." The idea of death is not so much transcended as it is translated by the comradely gesture of the poet. In a revolutionary act of the imagination, he joins hands with the personified concept of death and literally creates a new society within the natural world. And this poem modulates into the natural mode with an ending analogous to the celebration that concludes comedy.

These two variations on the convention of the floral tribute lead to questions of one kind of historical criticism, to the degree and manner in which Milton was part of seventeenth-century England and Whitman part of nineteenth-century America. To conceive of the poems in this way is to assume, and with some legitimacy, a version of historical determinism —the poems are as they are because of the time and place in which they were written. But when we take the features to be the result of an artistic option the writer has exercised within the limits of any one mode, then we are led to another kind of historical criticism. We ask why Whitman, for example, almost in spite of being part of the nineteenth century in America, is valuable and interesting to us as Whitman.

Not every poet in nineteenth-century America adopted the natural mode, and there are those who did so and did not mind alluding to classical legend or even invoking the muse. In any event Whitman's refusal to invoke the muse in this elegy is individualized by his hearty irreverence for the stately goddess whom he addressed on one occasion as "The dame of dames!" That he chose to tally his song with that of the American hermit thrush rather than with that of the phoenix, the nightingale, or a mechanical golden bird upon a bough is in part a result of the constraints of the natural mode; but it is also in part a result of his own separate and lonely mourning among a nation of mourners and his own separate and lonely vision of death as finally sane and sacred. Casting a sprig of lilac on the coffin may have been suggested by the fact that he saw the president's coffin banked with lilacs in the Capitol Building. And as a fictional act, the gesture may be wholly consonant with the natural mode. But it is more; there is no other elegy in the language in which the tribute, with the symbol of the lilac, takes precisely the shape that it does in this poem. The sprig is broken from a bush in a farmhouse yard, "given" to the coffin as it passes, immediately generalized into a universal gesture covering all the coffins and every death; and the lilac remains at the end of the poem, blooming as a symbol of Whitman's personal faith in the celebrative nature of death.

With the concept of displacement we can begin some tentative account of the general ways in which the narrative and thematic patterns of literature—the more or less permanent abstractions of action and meaning—may be cut to fit the singular shape of an artist's thought and experience in one passing time and one changing place. If the concept of pattern argues for a similarity among a variety of literary works, the concept of displacement argues for the final differences among all of them, and neither idea could be conceived without the other.

Criticism and Literature

Literature is what we talk about, criticism is the way we talk about it. And to take a clear stand on a debated issue, we will say that criticism is the only thing we can teach or learn. Only in a metaphorical sense do we teach literature or learn it. The teacher does not enter the classroom with Shakespeare in his possession and lecture to students who leave with Shakespeare in theirs. What he brings to class and what his students leave with are ways of thinking about Shakespeare, and ultimately all of literature—and that is criticism in our sense of the term. If this is true, then we need to be particularly careful with the way we understand and use critical terms and concepts. They are part of criticism and not of literature; however clear and direct their reference to literature, we do not expect to find critical abstractions themselves embedded in the texture of a poem or novel. The concepts of narrative and theme, for instance, can start us talking intelligibly about act and thought in literature, but the existence of the terms should never leave us with the conviction that act and thought can ever be finally separated in literature any more than in life. Similarly, the major patterns of romance, tragedy, comedy, and irony are not categories into which we place works to dispose of them. The critical act should not stop with identifying *Moby Dick* as romance or tragedy, for we are surely more interested in the ways in which the two patterns help us to embody the intricacies of that novel than in a critical anatomy for its own sake. This can be put simply as a principle of reading: patterns and concepts are entrances into the work's complexity, not exits.

The proper study of narrative and thematic pattern, mode and displacement, becomes clearer when we understand that a literary theory is not the same as a scientific theory. Criticism cannot account for literature in the same way that physics does for relations between mass, motion, and time in the physical world. Nor are we concerned with the possibility of making predictions. More in the manner of historians than of physicists, we want to understand what has already happened, not what happens anytime or might happen tomorrow. We are looking for structures of explanation that will articulate our intuition that the creation of literature is not a random activity, but one that participates in and so reveals the orders and processes of the human imagination.

We do not assume that the set of critical concepts and methods described here make up all of criticism. The body politic of criticism, as we see it now, is at best a loose confederation of states that has had its internecine quarrels, uneasy truces, and some peaceful times.

This political metaphor has its point: the different kinds or activities of criticism—formalist, historical, Freudian, Marxist—are most often distinguishable by the contexts in which they place the literary work. These contexts establish the limits of evidence admissable in the critical argument. Keats' letters, nineteenth-century notions of science and poetry, and the poet's experience as a student of medicine are all relevant evidence to Kenneth Burke and mark out the boundaries for historical criticism of John Keats' "Ode on a Grecian Urn." But little of this evidence is admitted in Cleanth Brooks' *Well Wrought Urn*, an example of formalist criticism. There the structures of attitude and image have priority. So, too, the critic using archetypal criticism imagines the poem within the context of the orders of literature, and finds in both the earlier and later examples of the traditional ode evidence for analysis that a rigid theory of either historical or formalist criticism would deny.

Although no theory we have encountered is all that rigid, distinguishing among the familiar kinds of criticism by their contexts for evidence allows us to entertain a more inclusive concept of criticism and the place in it for archetypal analysis. Any complete and sophisticated reading of a literary work should begin with a close analysis of the text as a discrete structure of syntax, metaphor, and rhetoric. Textual analysis such as this rests on some of the critical assumptions of the formalist critics, and our commentary presupposes that kind of analysis. Archetypal criticism, or the version we have defined here, first places the work in the environment of literary conventions, like the recurrent narrative and thematic patterns, in order to distinguish those elements of plot and character and image that the work shares with other works of literature. With the procedures of mode and displacement, the work is returned to the context assumed by historical criticism, the varied and inimitable experience of one man in one historical time and place. In this way archetypal criticism qualifies the activities in formalist and historical criticism, but more to the point, it offers a way of mediating between these two traditional but often opposed varieties of the critical act.

These are some of the reasons for this book and for its primary, but in no way final, emphasis on criticism. Criticism is too important to civilization to ignore simply because we consider the object it contemplates, literature, more important. Fortunately, we need not and in fact cannot choose between the two: criticism is unimaginable without literature, and literature without criticism is like life without thought. We know that literature gathers in the whole imaginative life of humanity; and the inquiring mind, at once skeptical and desirous of order, insists on knowing how and why we live that life. Criticism will speak to those questions; our purpose here is to ask them.

ROMANCE

Narrative Romance

There is one story and one story only
That will prove worth your telling,
Whether as learned bard or gifted child;
To it all lines or lesser gauds belong
That startle with their shining
Such common stories as they stray into.

Robert Graves, "To Juan at the Winter Solstice"

The one story Robert Graves refers to is the romance, and we may wonder why he makes such a large claim for it. We can agree that elements of the romance narrative recur in a variety of stories in every age and culture. *Beowulf*, in an eighth-century Anglo-Saxon world, and Herman Melville's Ahab, in nineteenth-century America, are both variations of the questing romantic hero. The stories of Edmund Spenser's Redcrosse Knight and James Fenimore Cooper's frontier scout, Leatherstocking, suggest that either hero would have been familiar with the other's romantic forest. But this does not make the romance the only story worth telling; the narrative patterns of tragedy, comedy, and irony are as recurrent and as universal.

However, there may be other grounds on which Graves could rest his claim. Let us consider this typical romance narrative: a young knight, after a series of adventures in which he has proved his valor, encounters a dragon that has laid waste to the land. In a battle that lasts for three days, he finally kills the dragon. He then liberates the kingdom and marries the king's daughter. In later times he becomes the patron saint of the land. Whatever else we might say about this story, most of us would agree, first, that it has something of the supernatural or mysterious about it; second, that it has an old or archaic quality; and finally, that it has a simple, even inevitable, plot. It is a familiar tale whether or not we have read Spenser's more complex version in *The Faerie Queene*. These intuitions about the romance as a narrative that is essentially mysterious or supernatural in character, old in origin, and simple in structure can help us to discover why someone might claim for it a primary status among the narrative patterns.

The mysterious and supernatural character of the romance suggests its resemblance to legend and myth. Spenser called the first book of *The Faerie Queene* "The Legende of the Knight of the Red Crosse." He recognized its similarity to the story of Saint George and the Dragon, which in turn parallels the Greek myth of Perseus' rescue of Andromeda from a sea monster. And, as we saw in the General Introduction, D. H. Lawrence's "Horse Dealer's Daughter" is linked with the Orpheus and Eurydice myth. In romance narratives, as in the myths they often draw on, animals give warnings, dragons threaten, and princes inevitably rescue the beleaguered at the darkest moment. Events and characters come in sets of three, like Gawain's three temptations and the three harpooners in *Moby Dick*. Havelok the Dane's life is threatened during his childhood as are the lives of legendary characters from Oedipus to Snow White. And when the romantic hero dies, he takes on the features of a god or, at least, is memorialized as someone more than human. His final union with the mysterious suggests the romance form's return to the realm of legend and myth, from which, we feel, it has never been too distant.

There are historical reasons for thinking of the romance as a primary form. The romance narrative most often dominates the earliest period in the literary history of a culture. It is the dominant form in Anglo-Saxon and medieval English literature. The same is true in American literary history. From the late eighteenth century when Joel Barlow wrote his ponderous epic about Columbus to the early nineteenth when Cooper wrote his Leatherstocking saga, poets and novelists turned to the romance pattern to fashion heroes and articulate ideals commensurate with the American adventure. Writers in later periods often testify to the archaic quality associated with the romance by setting their narratives in an earlier time when such forms were more frequent. In England Spenser did this with *The Faerie Queene*, as did John Keats with "The Eve of Saint Agnes" and Sir Walter Scott with *Ivanhoe*.

We may think of the romance pattern as simpler than the others because it is so familiar to us in children's literature and in movies, cartoons, comic strips, and television dramas. Much of the popularity of these forms lies in the simplicity of the questions they raise and the inevitability of their answers. Will good triumph over evil? Will the innocent young find protection? Will the skeptical elders be proved wrong? Such questions arise in the suspense we feel over whether the cavalry will arrive in time, whether Dorothy will find the Wizard of Oz, whether Godzilla will be destroyed, and whether the Little Engine That Could can. The romance pattern asks us to entertain these questions as if there were some doubt as to their answers and at the same time assures us that there is none. If we rewrite the conclusion of the story of Snow White so that the young prince visits her glass coffin in the forest, turns away with a shrug, and marries the wicked queen, even a child, however caught up he may be in the story, *knows* it must not end this way, Because of its simplicity, at least in its popular versions, its early place in literary history, and its affinity with legend and myth, we may think of the romance pattern as a primary imaginative form. There is some justice, then, in a poet's saying that to it all lesser things belong "that startle with their shining / Such common stories as they stray into."

One final reason for the primacy of the romance narrative in our thinking is that it provides a variety of assumptions to which the other three narratives respond. The romantic world assumes total human freedom and almost infinite possibilities for significant action. The hero's powers, once learned, are nearly limitless, and his deeds are imbued with a radiant meaning. In romance dreams and desires are realized, suffering is transcended, and human action is attended and ordered by some power whose eternal plan embraces man's most hopeful conception of life. Tragedy may be thought to begin with the assumptions of romance, perhaps an origin for hubris, that overweening pride and insolence we often note in traditional tragic heroes. They seem to have a vision of the romantic world and its possibilities—Oedipus is spiritually blinded by it, Willy Loman glimpses it in the dream-figure of his brother Ben—and the tragic narrative records the fated fall from that ideal. Comedy, on the other hand, reaches toward the world of romance and its postulates concerning human experience. Man's dream of success is affirmed in comedy; often the elder presiding figures—from the various dukes in Shakespeare's comedies to Gore-Urquhart in Kingsley Amis' *Lucky Jim*—enter the final action of the narrative as if they have come from the romantic realm to bestow its traditional rewards, the large inheritance and the lovely maiden. The relationship between irony and romance is different and more complex. Irony twists the assumptions of romance into satire and employs its narrative pattern for parody. Unlike tragedy, irony never replaces those assumptions with affirmations of a higher law; unlike comedy it never imagines a return to the romantic world.

The controlling principle or purpose of romance—its motive—is to realize and to articulate the desirable. Northrop Frye describes romance as the form "nearest . . . to the wish-fulfillment dream. . . . The perennially child-like quality of romance is marked by its extraordinarily persistent nostalgia, its search for some kind of imaginative golden age in time or space." There is a good deal of evidence in the simpler romance narratives to support this definition: Havelok swaggers through the world like a rather burly Horatio Alger hero, and Keats' "Eve of Saint Agnes" is redolent with imagery from other worlds and other times. But we risk implying that the romance narrative is somehow naive or even simple-minded and thus underestimate its potential for intricate modifications by cultural history and by the imaginative resources of the artist.

In some romance narratives, especially those that focus on the initiation of the young hero, it is precisely the attitudes of naiveté and longing for the pure and simple from which the hero is liberated. James Joyce's

The Motive of Narrative Romance

"Araby" may be read this way. Similarly, the poet who wrote *Sir Gawain and the Green Knight* may have been motivated, like Spenser who followed him, to evoke an earlier and somewhat nostalgic vision of the aristocracy of Arthurian times to chasten his audience. But the complexity of Gawain's initiation, the rather dilettantish character of Arthur, and the unfathomable mystery of the Green Knight are not naive or simplistic. So any final definition of the controlling principle of romance only in terms of the simple, the childlike, or the nostalgic misses the point. Perhaps it is better to think of these terms as describing initial assumptions about the nature of experience that the romance pattern first articulates and then revises in the light of its narrative goals. The more intricate and sophisticated romances may so radically modify these assumptions as to seem to verge on the ironic, but for one element: for the writer of romance, man's nostalgia for the past or the innocence of childhood and his yearning for a simple moral world are serious and ultimately necessary aspects of human existence out of which good will come. Irony denies this.

Romantic ideals are originally manifested in the hero's quest with its rewards of the beautiful heroine, great wealth, a position of power, and the attainment of a kind of wisdom, often derived from some arcane source. These prizes, however, point to something more than the satisfaction of specific desires. If we consider any extensive variety of romances, we recognize a common characteristic in their tendency to refine rather than merely to realize human desires. The impulse in romance is to give the desirable rewards—the fair maiden, the hidden treasure, and the ranks of power—a place and a meaning in a higher order and thus to rationalize them as more than mere physical or psychical gratifications.

The narrative pattern of romance, then, reflects more than the human need to give respectability to dreams. Like the abandoned church in Philip Larkin's "Church Going," the romance is a serious place "on serious earth," where "all our compulsions meet, / Are recognized, and robed as destinies." More than simply offering an occasion to sublimate our compulsions, this imaginative form seeks to affirm a destiny that demands that occasion. The outcome of a typical romance seems inevitable; we have an intuition of some mysterious source of order, unity, and immanent meaning. Other narrative patterns may imply a determined shape in events; but whereas they suggest that we contemplate an order within experience, romance asks us to look beyond. Other literary patterns may robe our compulsions as destinies; none but romance so resolutely points, like a church, to the supernal origins of those destinies.

The Characters of Romance

Like the narrative structure, the characters of romance are obedient to a higher order. In spite of the ambiguity of the Green Knight and other shape-shifters in the complex versions of romance, most characters are ranked with good or evil, the divine or the demonic, and openly wear the moral insignia of white or black. It is as if some rules called for Spenser's

Redcrosse Knight to carry a silver shield and for Una to lead a milk-white lamb. When the pattern deviates, the author seems compelled to explain why: Una's stole is black befitting "one that inly mourned" and is thus dissociated from the moral blackness that envelopes Archimago. The dark- and light-haired heroines of Cooper and Hawthorne are later examples of this almost instinctive moral labeling; in their novels no hero ever marries a dark-haired woman, however many sidelong glances he sends her way.

In simple forms of the romance like *Havelok the Dane* the division of characters between the good and the evil is apparent at the outset; in more complex forms like *Sir Gawain and the Green Knight* the relationship of the characters to the forces of good and evil is apt to be ambiguous and to become clear only as the narrative progresses. Like the ordering of the narrative pattern, the characterization implies more than a retreat to the ordered and simple; it suggests once again that man's actions are illuminated by the significance of a cosmic struggle. Human experience and the world it is acted out in become the occasion and the arena for some ultimately profound conflict between divine and demonic forces. In such a struggle it is rare for any thing or person to remain neutral. With its leaning toward the allegorical, romance has little use for characters who have no more fictional purpose than to convince us of the presence of society. Rather, it enlists characters in the service of an ideal through which they may find a more enduring meaning. The romantic hero and the villain, the black magician and the white, exist outside the constraints of the everyday and plausible world. In contemporary fiction, they may move through recognizable scenes and face familiar dilemmas, but they are finally responsible to something beyond the usual demands faced by men and women in realistic situations. Acting more like iconic figures in medieval art, characters in a typical romance, like those of Spenser and Hawthorne, gaze not at one another but outward toward their meaning; they do not participate in a social order but in a conceptual system.

Just as we cannot say that all characters in romance are unambiguous, we cannot ascribe to them the same sort or intensity of ambiguity displayed by characters in irony. In romance the equivocal is more often temporary and usually derives from the hero's inaccurate vision during an early test of his moral insight, as when the Redcrosse Knight fails to recognize the true nature of Duessa. When ambiguity is essential in a character—and the exceptions are of primary significance—it usually appears in the antagonist and in sophisticated versions of the narrative. This may be the first indication of an artist's attempt to weave a moral intricacy into the apparently facile dualism of the romance pattern. In any case, the significant recurrence of ambiguity in the features of the antagonist—the Green Knight's holly branch, a symbol of life and rebirth, contrasts with his battleax, his role as gracious host with his role as terrifying challenger—suggests that ambiguity in romance represents not only the ultimate trial for the hero but the final moral and esthetic problem for the artist of this mode.

**The World
of Romance**
The world in which the characters live, suffer, and triumph responds to
the same desire for order and meaning. It offers an environment amenable
to the mysterious and miraculous. Trees may talk and animals, like men,
align themselves with heroic or villainous forces. The dream-inducing tree
in *Sir Orfeo*, under which Orfeo loses his Queen to the forces of the Celtic
otherworld, the Ancient Mariner's mystic albatross, and the dead pond in
"The Horse Dealer's Daughter" are more than natural elements; they are
agents of supernatural forces attesting to an uncommon significance in
the action. Even abstractions like time and space conform to this moral
ordering. Time is cyclical rather than linear as we usually think of it.
The hero's adventures coincide with the cycle of the seasons: his trials
occur in winter, and his triumph is assured and witnessed by the return
of spring. Quests are set to be accomplished in a year or a year and a
day; and, as in "The Wife of Bath's Tale," it would offend the sense of
decorum we associate with such adventures not only if the knight failed to
achieve his quest by the final day of the limit but also if he achieved it
before that time. This sense of recurrence, of patterned time, orders the
events of the hero's life and links him to the eternal.

The same impulse orders space. The specific scenes in this world—
Dublin, Ireland, or Firetown, Pennsylvania—seem less important for
what they are than for what happens there. That Lawrence's "Horse
Dealer's Daughter" is set in the dark midlands of England is less important
than the sense we share with the doctor, "a slave to the countryside,"
that here, at this moment in the graveyard, it is fitting and necessary that
we have a portentous vision of another world. The setting for romance is
usually some variant of a Spenserian fairyland or the mystical seas of
Coleridge. Distance and dimension are rarely mentioned; localities become habitations of the universal. Places, Arthur's court and Orfeo's
underworld, take on meaning as coordinates of morality and are aligned
with the opposing forces of the narrative: Spenser's hero is detained in
the House of Pride, and he is prepared for his final triumph in the House
of Holiness; the dark pond threatens and the bright hearth restores
Lawrence's characters.

All the major features of romance—narrative, character, setting, and
time and space—reflect the complex impulse to realize and refine human
desires in a quest for a transcendent order. The terms "nostalgia," "wish-
fulfilment," and "compulsion" could be used if they did not imply something childlike or escapist about the romance form. Some of its postulates
may seem simplistic at first; its assurance of the final triumph of good over
evil may seem no more than a pious hope in our ironic age. But the more
intricate and original variations on the romance pattern are neither simple
nor escapist. Writers like the Gawain poet, Shakespeare, Shelley, and
Lawrence do not allow us to avoid the complexity of experience, nor do
they offer us any devious affirmations of our own importance. Rather they
use the romance pattern to show us how men's actions matter in ways our
ordinary conceptions of existence cannot explain. They challenge us

with the thought that, as John Updike once wrote, everything rests "upon an intense radiance we do not see because we see nothing else."

Most of what we know of the romantic mode and everything we have said of the principle governing its narrative argue for some degree of successful completion of the quest or some degree of resolution and reward for the hero. Therefore it seems appropriate to alter slightly Frye's description of the stages of romance. He defines them as "the stage of the perilous journey and the preliminary minor adventures; the crucial struggle, usually some kind of battle in which either the hero or his foe, or both, must die; and the exaltation of the hero." The alternative we propose retains the first stage, the preliminary adventures, and places primary emphasis on the advent and initiation of the hero, his early trials and introduction to the heroic condition. The latter two stages are separated or merged depending on the outcome of the hero's struggle. If the hero overcomes his adversary, as he most often does, and wins the conventional rewards for that struggle, we think of the narrative as typical, as the norm for the romance. But if the hero dies or disappears, as in his descent into the underworld, then the underlying purpose of romance seems to demand the return to life, the exaltation or apotheosis, of the hero. It is this event, the descent and recognition of the hero, that we associate with the last stage of the romance pattern. Had Odysseus never returned from Hades we would be hard pressed to think of the *Odyssey* as a romance; and yet the epic could have incorporated Odysseus' ritual death without a rebirth had his son Telemachus gone on to destroy the suitors and bring order to Ithaca. We would then be able to recognize a version of the hero's return and a variation on the symbolic reincarnation of his heroic virtues. Conceived this way the final fragment of Beowulf's story, his fight with the dragon in which they destroy each other, conforms to the last stage of romance, since it ends not with Beowulf's death but with his exaltation in the building of the memorial barrow and in the mourning of Wiglaf, in whom the older hero's spirit is reborn.

The Phases of Romance

Finally, we should consider the differences between the outcome of the conflict in the usual quest and that in the last phase of romance. In the typical form of the romance the hero is in complete opposition to his antagonist; they struggle and the hero emerges triumphant. Yet often in the more esoteric world of last-phase romance, the antagonist assumes ambiguous characteristics, and the conflict takes on less the quality of a battle than of a redemptive sacrifice. Rather than defeat his antagonist, the hero merges with him. The dragon's reign of terror in the final fragment of *Beowulf* is as just and necessary as is Beowulf's obligation to destroy him; the hero and the dragon mortally wound each other in a contest that unites them in a deathly embrace. Ahab hurls his harpoon as much at his own heart as at Moby Dick's, and the white whale dives with his heroic opponent entangled in the lines and identified with him. Out of the carnage of these encounters arise the new heroes, Wiglaf and Ishmael.

This concept of the romance pattern reflects a symmetry within the total narrative itself. The central quest stands between two mirroring events. Both the advent of the hero and his apotheosis assume a world without him: one into which he is born, the other to which he literally or symbolically returns. Each of the events, his initiation and his return, takes on ritualistic proportions. In the first, the hero faces a test or initiatory rite whose successful completion qualifies him for the climactic quest that is to come; in the second, the hero performs his last ritual act, descends to oppose the forces of darkness, and finally rises. His apotheosis affirms his final heroic status; he transcends the limitations of this world to become a god or godlike in the other.

A cautionary note: no concept of the phases, of course, should be treated as an inflexible prescription or a "hard" fact of literature. Abstract patterns find a variety of individual manifestations and, like all archetypal forms, are subject to the historical influences of displacement. The descent into the underworld, for example, may be as literal as Odysseus' into the regions of the dead or as figurative as Leopold Bloom's journey to a Dublin funeral service in Joyce's *Ulysses*. Furthermore, as in both the *Odyssey* and *Ulysses*, a work will often include more than one of the major phases. *Havelok the Dane* takes its hero from his advent and early trials through his climactic victory and enthronement, though it emphasizes his youthful exploits.

First-Phase Romance: Advent and Initiation

Some kind of initiation or trial marks the first phase of romance. Events take their shape and meaning from a young hero's miraculous or mysterious advent and his early trials. The typical environment for these events is hostile, as was Havelok's, or is cursed with a physical and spiritual sterility that the hero's innocence and creativity seem destined to overcome, as was Arthur's. The hero comes as a redeemer, sometimes unwittingly and with little understanding of his true role. Indeed, part of his initiation involves his education in regard to his heroic destiny. He enters the world of an older and more cynical generation. There may be some figures who counsel him with their occult wisdom—usually older women or men like Merlin who know him for the hero he is to become. But more often the older generation is powerful and corrupt; they set dogs at their gates, or they chatter idly on, as in Joyce's story, while the young hero yearns to be off for Araby. Probably because of his youth the hero is often attuned to the natural world and familiar with the pastoral environment. The beasts and the birds are his allies and affirm his innocence.

The initiation of the hero marks both a departure and an entry; he moves from an innocent world into one beset with obstacles and apparently insurmountable challenges. It signals a rite of passage and functions as an act of both identification and purgation. This symbolic event not only establishes his claim to the heroic role but also marks his loss of unwitting innocence, the characteristic that most clearly identifies him and is most necessary for him to outgrow. The romance usually balances the moral ledger, for to lose innocence is to acquire wisdom, as Gawain is taught in his encounter with the Green Knight. The initiation is, of course, a preliminary rather than a final event. Although the hero of a first-phase romance may perform the same deed as does his older counterpart on a quest, his is clearly seen as a preparatory rather than as a culminating act. The initiation may be the first of the conventional three tests or a singular action intended to qualify the hero for later trials, but in any case it implies or even causes further events. We have the impression, for instance, that Porphyro, the untried hero in "The Eve of Saint Agnes," might ultimately have to conquer rather than deceive his antagonists, while there is little left for the Redcrosse Knight after completing his quest besides a pleasant and allegorical marriage with Una.

Narratives of initiation, however universal, seem to have a particular appeal in times charged with a revolutionary spirit. Rebellion may be part of the experience of any age, but when it is encouraged by political revolution, as it was at the end of the eighteenth century, or by social change, as in the early years of this century, writers find the initiation story most expressive of their times. A "fair seed-time" of the soul like that Wordsworth lived through calls for a youthful hero to test and proclaim his powers. His *Prelude* reads like a thematic commentary on the initiation of a hero, who, unlike his medieval predecessor, proves his powers in the landscape of the imagination rather than on the field of battle. The American romantics, too, saw the outlines of their national experience in this pattern. Again, Cooper's story of Leatherstocking is the most exact example and among the first of a tradition of American narratives that depict the young contender striving for the role of the American hero. Novels of youthful initiation, from *The Adventures of Huckleberry Finn* to *The Catcher in the Rye*, rework this theme. When an age demands more realism, imaginative or verbal acts replace feats of physical power or endurance as the means by which the initiate attains heroic stature.

The Romantic Norm: The Quest

In the romance pattern everything leads to or follows from its primary action, the quest; the hero's advent and initiation mark its prologue, his descent and recognition its epilogue. The most common form of the quest is the journey, often a sequence of three adventures, leading to a climactic struggle between the hero and a dragon or some dark human opponent for the prize of a beautiful maiden, wealth, or power. The journey often describes a movement into the realm of the unknown and back: Odysseus, and Leopold Bloom for that matter, trace paths that circle from the familiar to the mysterious and back to the familiar. We need not explain why the adventures, the temptations, or the battles almost inevitably occur in sequences of three, as in *Beowulf* and Saul Bellow's *Henderson the Rain King*, or in linked sets of three, as in *Sir Gawain and the Green Knight*. It is enough to note that the effect of the three-part sequence contributes to the paradoxical effect of romance: the sense of the inevitable merged with the sense of the mysterious. Even in such "realistic" narratives as

Lawrence's "Horse Dealer's Daughter," Joyce's "Araby," and Updike's "Pigeon Fathers," some feature makes the mystic glance over the tombs, the radiance in the Mangan girl's hair, and the bright pigeon feathers not merely possible but the *only* things possible.

The quest is often initiated and its terms set by an older woman of royal, matriarchal, and, at times, vaguely sibylline features. Like other major characters in romance, she has her darker counterpart—from Morgan le Fay in the Gawain story to the Wicked Witch of the West in *The Wizard of Oz*—who appears near the end of the quest or who presides over its treasure. Older men, practitioners like the women of either white or black magic, assist or thwart the hero in his completion of the quest. Perhaps one of the most interesting characters of romance, sometimes more so than the hero himself, is his companion or helper. His role in early versions is simple: he assists the hero and plays foil to his superior's courage with his timidity or to his bravado with an earthy common sense. He carries armor, bears news, kneels obediently, and is otherwise of little moment except in the hands of a Cervantes.

The evolution of the helper figure in the history of the romance pattern deserves comment. As the romance pattern became more sophisticated, this sometimes simple character tended to assume the features of the hero or to become his reincarnation. *Moby Dick*—which for all its apparatus of tragedy may well be read as a romance—is one culmination of this tradition. It is almost as if the romance writers, becoming restive with the form's "two-party" moral system, trained their imaginative and analytic powers on the quality of evil in the antagonist and found it not all that bad, or at best of some utilitarian value. Then reconsidering the quality of virtue in the protagonist they seem to have found it not all that good, or at worst hell-bent for heaven. In the light of this analysis, the secondary figure gradually assumed a new, more subtle, and often chastened capacity for heroism that his superior lacked. We see something of this capacity in Beowulf's Wiglaf, perhaps even in Arthur's Sir Bedivere; it is developed in Huck Finn's Jim with his simple moral grandeur and in Ahab's Ishmael and Gatsby's Nick Carroway, both of whom serve as witnesses and narrators of quests that fail. The depiction of this character in most important American romances as an Indian or a black—Chingachgook in Cooper, Queequeg in Melville, Jim in Mark Twain, Sam Fathers in Faulkner—is a sign of one rather uneasy cultural accommodation for which the romance pattern has been used.

The goals of the quest may vary from the Holy Grail to a beautiful maiden to a treasure hoard, but, like the protagonists', their functions are remarkably constant. The antagonists in romance—like Milton's Satan—may sometimes command our interest more than the heroes they oppose. Once the antagonist is associated with nature and is freed from the Christian moral system, his ambiguous qualities often make him the most memorable feature of the narrative. Gawain's character can be explained, but the Green Knight remains an enigma, even when he appears in the cultivated figure of Lord Bercilak. The ambiguous white whale in *Moby Dick* is the most familiar example, and from the Green Knight to Old Ben, the bear in Faulkner's story, these "natural" antagonists do not admit to the same sort of moral explanation that poets use for Grendel or the Blatant Beast or even Satan. As the antagonist becomes less purely evil, the protagonist set against him becomes less purely good. Their conflict is no longer a matter of one or the other's victory—who finally wins the contest between Gawain and the Green Knight?—but a mystical confrontation in which neither is defeated. The hero or his surrogate gains a new wisdom drawn from his encounter with the agent of some natural power. In Faulkner's *Bear*, a work that falls near the end of this tradition, the protagonists conceive of the hunt more as a sacrifice than a kill, a curious knowledge they seem to share with their opponent. The antagonists in such works function, sometimes knowingly, much like harsh priests watching over the indoctrination of the heroes, who act as much like acolytes as warriors.

These observations suggest that as the moral system of the romance shifts from the rigid dialectic of the religious quest, and as the antagonist is associated with natural, more neutral forces, the quest takes on the character of a second initiation. The antagonist assumes the role of a neutral or benevolent presiding elder in whose presence the hero, however experienced, becomes childlike. Their meeting is more oblique than head-on, and from it the hero or his surrogate returns spiritually and morally rearmed, bearing mystic tokens of his encounter. To put it another way, this compelling variation on the romance pattern seems to merge elements of both the first and the last phases of the narrative pattern: the initiate of the first phase encounters the mysterious, primeval figure who rules the underworld of the last phase.

The final phase of romance is more ceremonial than eventful. Following the quest, the hero consolidates his position, metes out rewards to the faithful and punishments to his remaining enemies, and awaits the culminating event of his career, the act that will finally reunite him with the divine. Opposition may recur but the conflict is more static than during the quest and seems to represent the last convulsive efforts of the enemy and the final retributive thrusts of the hero. The event that characterizes this phase, the descent to the underworld, infuses nearly every object and act with the aura of the magical and the occult. The mood is ominous, and the mature hero, sensing the presence of other powers, becomes more pensive as a result of his awareness of the divine forces he only distantly perceived in his earlier career. When he acts, he acts alone and often through guile. Sir Orfeo could not storm the battlements of hell, and Odysseus, only incidentally accompanied by his crew, faces the dead heroes of Troy and the seer Tiresias alone, for it is only to him that they will speak. The descent into the underworld is the hero's final act preparatory to his assumption of a divine or semidivine role. He enters the underworld, confronts its rulers, and receives from them knowledge of the

Last-Phase Romance: Descent and Recognition

future and often some prediction of his apotheosis. The descent may be actual, like those of Jesus, Odysseus, and Aeneas; it may be implied in the conventional withdrawal or restorative isolation of the hero; or it may be suggested in a confrontation with forces of darkness and prophecy more symbolic than real.

After receiving the knowledge that insures his future and a prophecy of his apotheosis, the hero returns from the underworld. His return is the second defining feature of last-phase romance and is a form of rebirth. The romantic hero, less than divine, must die; but since he is more than human, his death is not a final or tragic event but a sign of his transcendence. He is set apart in his wisdom; like Oedipus at Colonus, he faces his approaching transformation with philosophic calm, impatient with those lesser figures who cannot comprehend the awesome import of his ascension. The inevitability of the hero's death or descent to the underworld lends final proof of the governance of the supernatural. Again we must note the distinction between romance and tragedy: in romance there is no implication of an order that has been upset and is being reaffirmed, nor is there any sense of retribution or the vindication of a violated law or moral system. The hero's death strikes us as inevitable, as it does in tragedy, but that necessity is never conceived as anything other than benign, a just and fitting transition to another life. The mood may be elegiac, but it derives not from the suffering of the hero but from that of the society that witnesses his passing. Death in the romance narrative, then, is mitigated by the hero's ascension, by his rebirth in the figure of a younger companion, or by the sort of transforming and transcendent wisdom the experience of death has provided. In his final remarks on the death of Arthur, Sir Thomas Malory questions the matter of his hero's immortality:

> Yet some men say in many parts of England that King Arthur is not dead, but had by the will of our Lord Jesu into another place. And men say that he shall come again and he shall win the Holy Cross. Yet I will not say that it shall be so, but rather I will say, Here in this world he changed his life. And many men say that there is written upon his tomb this verse: *Hic iacet Arthurus, rex quondam, rexque futurus.*

Whatever doubts Malory may have over what men have said of the "once and future king," he speaks the final word on the hero of romance: "Here in this world he changed his life."

Narrative and Narration in "Araby"

When elements of the romance pattern survive in modern narratives, they often take on the allusiveness and ambiguity characteristic of contemporary literature. These vestiges of the pattern usually demand a closer reading than we would ordinarily give to, say, a medieval narrative. James Joyce's

"Araby," for example, requires a more analytic response to its metaphors and narrative point of view than does *Havelok the Dane*. Its narrative, characters, and imagery are radically displaced to accommodate our demands for realism. But they still conform to a version of the romantic pattern—at least until the last scene of the story. The boy's expectations, somewhat like ours, draw on romantic conventions. The title, the ancient name for Arabia, calls up "an Eastern enchantment." The narrator imagines himself a young hero set above the rest of the commonplace world and singled out for a quest. The enigmatic last scene, however, raises a question about those expectations: whether they are denied or ultimately realized in some other way.

JAMES JOYCE
1882–1941

Araby

North Richmond Street, being blind, was a quiet street except at the hour when the Christian Brothers' School set the boys free. An uninhabited house of two stories stood at the blind end, detached from its neighbors in a square ground. The other houses of the street, conscious of decent lives within them, gazed at one another with brown imperturbable faces.

The former tenant of our house, a priest, had died in the back drawing-room. Air, musty from having been long enclosed, hung in all the rooms, and the waste room behind the kitchen was littered with old useless papers. Among these I found a few paper-covered books, the pages of which were curled and damp: *The Abbot*, by Walter Scott, *The Devout Communicant* and *The Memoirs of Vidocq*.[1] I liked the last best because its leaves were yellow. The wild garden behind the house contained a central apple-tree and a few straggling bushes under one of which I found the late tenant's rusty bicycle-pump. He had been a very charitable priest; in his will he had left all his money to institutions and the furniture of his house to his sister.

When the short days of winter came dusk fell before we had well eaten our dinners. When we

ARABY. **1. Vidocq:** François Eugène Vidocq (1775–1857), soldier, thief, and later chief of the French detective force.

met in the street the houses had grown somber. The space of sky above us was the color of ever-changing violet and towards it the lamps of the street lifted their feeble lanterns. The cold air stung us and we played till our bodies glowed. Our shouts echoed in the silent street. The career of our play brought us through the dark muddy lanes behind the houses where we ran the gauntlet of the rough tribes from the cottages, to the back doors of the dark dripping gardens where odors arose from the ashpits, to the dark odorous stables where a coachman smoothed and combed the horse or shook music from the buckled harness. When we returned to the street light from the kitchen windows had filled the areas. If my uncle was seen turning the corner we hid in the shadow until we had seen him safely housed. Or if Mangan's sister came out on the doorstep to call her brother in to his tea we watched her from our shadow peer up and down the street. We waited to see whether she would remain or go in and, if she remained, we left our shadow and walked up to Mangan's steps resignedly. She was waiting for us, her figure defined by the light from the half-opened door. Her brother always teased her before he obeyed and I stood by the railings looking at her. Her dress swung as she moved her body and the soft rope of her hair tossed from side to side.

Every morning I lay on the floor in the front parlor watching her door. The blind was pulled down to within an inch of the sash so that I could not be seen. When she came out on the doorstep my heart leaped. I ran to the hall, seized my books and followed her. I kept her brown figure always in my eye and, when we came near the point at which our ways diverged, I quickened my pace and passed her. This happened morning after morning. I had never spoken to her, except for a few casual words, and yet her name was like a summons to all my foolish blood.

Her image accompanied me even in places the most hostile to romance. On Saturday evenings when my aunt went marketing I had to go to carry some of the parcels. We walked through the flaring streets, jostled by drunken men and bargaining women, amid the curses of laborers, the shrill litanies of shopboys who stood on guard by the barrels of pigs' cheeks, the nasal chanting of street-singers, who sang a *come-all-you* about O'Donovan Rossa,[2] or a ballad about the troubles in our native land. These noises converged in a single sensation of life for me: I imagined that I bore my chalice safely through a throng of foes. Her name sprang to my lips at moments in strange prayers and praises which I myself did not understand. My eyes were often full of tears (I could not tell why) and at times a flood from my heart seemed to pour itself out into my bosom. I thought little of the future. I did not know whether I would ever speak to her or not or, if I spoke to her, how I could tell her of my confused adoration. But my body was like a harp and her words and gestures were like fingers running upon the wires.

One evening I went into the back drawing-room in which the priest had died. It was a dark rainy evening and there was no sound in the house. Through one of the broken panes I heard the rain impinge upon the earth, the fine incessant needles of water playing in the sodden beds. Some distant lamp or lighted window gleamed below me. I was thankful that I could see so little. All my senses seemed to desire to veil themselves and, feeling that I was about to slip from them, I pressed the palms of my hands together until they trembled, murmuring: "*O love! O love!*" many times.

At last she spoke to me. When she addressed the first words to me I was so confused that I did not know what to answer. She asked me was I going to *Araby*. I forgot whether I answered yes or no. It would be a splendid bazaar, she said she would love to go.

"And why can't you?" I asked.

While she spoke she turned a silver bracelet round and round her wrist. She could not go, she said, because there would be a retreat that week in her convent.[3] Her brother and two other boys were fighting for their caps and I was alone at the railings. She held one of the spikes, bowing her head towards me. The light from the lamp opposite our door caught the white curve of her neck, lit up her hair that rested there and, falling, lit up the hand upon the railing. It fell over one side of her dress and caught the white border of a petticoat, just visible as she stood at ease.

"It's well for you," she said.

"If I go," I said, "I will bring you something."

What innumerable follies laid waste my waking and sleeping thoughts after that evening! I wished to annihilate the tedious intervening days. I chafed against the work of school. At night in my bedroom and by day in the classroom her image came between me and the page I strove to read. The syllables of the word *Araby* were called to me through the silence in which my soul luxuriated and cast an Eastern enchantment over me. I asked for leave to go to the bazaar on Saturday night. My aunt was surprised and hoped it was not some Freemason affair. I answered few questions in class. I watched my master's face pass from amiability to sternness; he hoped I was not beginning to idle. I could not call my wandering thoughts together. I had hardly any patience with the serious work of life which, now that it stood between me and my desire, seemed to me child's play, ugly monotonous child's play.

On Saturday morning I reminded my uncle that I wished to go to the bazaar in the evening. He was fussing at the hallstand, looking for the hat-brush, and answered me curtly:

"Yes, boy, I know."

As he was in the hall I could not go into the front parlor and lie at the window. I left the house in bad humor and walked slowly towards the school. The air was pitilessly raw and already my heart misgave me.

When I came home to dinner my uncle had not yet been home. Still it was early. I sat staring at the clock for some time and, when its ticking began to irritate me, I left the room. I mounted the staircase and gained the upper part of the house. The high

2. come-all-you . . . Rossa: conventional opening of a street ballad; O'Donovan Rossa (Jeremiah Donovan) was a nineteenth-century Irish nationalist.

3. convent: convent school.

cold empty gloomy rooms liberated me and I went from room to room singing. From the front window I saw my companions playing below in the street. Their cries reached me weakened and indistinct and, leaning my forehead against the cool glass, I looked over at the dark house where she lived. I may have stood there for an hour, seeing nothing but the brown-clad figure cast by my imagination, touched discreetly by the lamplight at the curved neck, at the hand upon the railings and at the border below the dress.

When I came downstairs again I found Mrs. Mercer sitting at the fire. She was an old garrulous woman, a pawnbroker's widow, who collected used stamps for some pious purpose. I had to endure the gossip of the tea-table. The meal was prolonged beyond an hour and still my uncle did not come. Mrs. Mercer stood up to go: she was sorry she couldn't wait any longer, but it was after eight o'clock and she did not like to be out late, as the night air was bad for her. When she had gone I began to walk up and down the room, clenching my fists. My aunt said:

"I'm afraid you may put off your bazaar for this night of our Lord."

At nine o'clock I heard my uncle's latchkey in the halldoor. I heard him talking to himself and heard the hallstand rocking when it had received the weight of his overcoat. I could interpret these signs. When he was midway through his dinner I asked him to give me the money to go to the bazaar. He had forgotten.

"The people are in bed and after their first sleep now," he said.

I did not smile. My aunt said to him energetically:

"Can't you give him the money and let him go? You've kept him late enough as it is."

My uncle said he was very sorry he had forgotten. He said he believed in the old saying: "All work and no play makes Jack a dull boy." He asked me where I was going and, when I had told him a second time he asked me did I know *The Arab's Farewell to his Steed*. When I left the kitchen he was about to recite the opening lines of the piece to my aunt.

I held a florin tightly in my hand as I strode down Buckingham Street towards the station. The sight of the streets thronged with buyers and glaring with gas recalled to me the purpose of my journey. I took my seat in a third-class carriage of a deserted train. After an intolerable delay the train moved out of the station slowly. It crept onward among ruinous houses and over the twinkling river. At Westland Row Station a crowd of people pressed to the carriage doors; but the porters moved them back, saying that it was a special train for the bazaar. I remained alone in the bare carriage. In a few minutes the train drew up beside an improvised wooden platform. I passed out on to the road and saw by the lighted dial of a clock that it was ten minutes to ten. In front of me was a large building which displayed the magical name.

I could not find any sixpenny entrance and, fearing that the bazaar would be closed, I passed in quickly through a turnstile, handing a shilling to a weary-looking man. I found myself in a big hall girdled at half its height by a gallery. Nearly all the stalls were closed and the greater part of the hall was in darkness. I recognized a silence like that which pervades a church after a service. I walked into the center of the bazaar timidly. A few people were gathered about the stalls which were still open. Before a curtain, over which the words *Café Chantant*[4] were written in colored lamps, two men were counting money on a salver. I listened to the fall of the coins.

Remembering with difficulty why I had come I went over to one of the stalls and examined porcelain vases and flowered tea-sets. At the door of the stall a young lady was talking and laughing with two young gentlemen. I remarked their English accents and listened vaguely to their conversation.

"Oh, I never said such a thing!"

"Oh, but you did!"

"Oh, but I didn't!"

"Didn't she say that?"

"Yes. I heard her."

"Oh, there's a . . . fib!"

Observing me the young lady came over and asked me did I wish to buy anything. The tone of her voice was not encouraging; she seemed to have spoken to me out of a sense of duty. I looked humbly at the great jars that stood like Eastern guards at either side of the dark entrance to the stall and murmured:

"No, thank you."

The young lady changed the position of one of the vases and went back to the two young men.

---

4. Café Chantant: café providing musical entertainment.

They began to talk of the same subject. Once or twice the young lady glanced at me over her shoulder.

I lingered before her stall, though I knew my stay was useless, to make my interest in her wares seem the more real. Then I turned away slowly and walked down the middle of the bazaar. I allowed the two pennies to fall against the sixpence in my pocket. I heard a voice call from one end of the gallery that the light was out. The upper part of the hall was now completely dark.

Gazing up into the darkness I saw myself as a creature driven and derided by vanity; and my eyes burned with anguish and anger.

The final scene brings the story to an abrupt and apparently inconclusive ending. Although there are suggestions throughout the narrative that the boy's quest may not be successful—the most immediate of these is the dark and empty hall—his failure is not inevitable and his response to the sales-girl's indifference seems excessive at first. He wasted sixpence in his eagerness to enter the building, most of the stalls were closed, but there is no clear reason why he could not spend his remaining eight pence on a token gift and walk home. Something about the experience, however, makes even that gesture impossible, and we look for an explanation either in the description of the scene or in the dialogue between the "young lady" and the "two young gentlemen." The scene continues the pattern of religious imagery with the "silence like that which pervades a church after a service," and the pattern of romantic imagery with "the great jars that stood like Eastern guards." But the meaning the boy had found earlier in these images is challenged. Two men are "counting money on a salver," an allusion to the New Testament story of the money-changers violating the sanctity of the Temple. And the two men—hardly gentlemen—are there for more than the bazaar; they are Englishmen on a cheap holiday in Dublin and obviously out on the town.

The boy's response is only partly explained by his sense of failure. His reaction is oddly in excess of the event that occasioned it: "Gazing up into the darkness I saw myself as a creature driven and derided by vanity; and my eyes burned with anguish and anger." To put it simply, as his uncle might, the boy missed the bazaar he had been counting on. Yet he sees himself as a "creature"—a contemptuous term that makes him less than heroic, almost less than human. At the same time he imagines some power outside himself that drives and derides him. The abstraction *vanity* is first objectified, for it is his own futility and pride he is speaking of, then personified through association with verbs that take human grammatical subjects, and finally raised to a more than human power, like the allegorical figures of the Seven Deadly Sins who threaten Spenser's Redcrosse Knight. The boy's response, then, is complex: he recognizes the futility of his heroic presumptions—he is no more than a creature—while he persists in a romantic vision of himself persecuted by a powerful adversary from the throng of his foes.

The preceding narrative foreshadows and partially explains the boy's final reaction. It presents two worlds, the realistic neighborhood of Dublin and the romantic realm of the boy's imagination. Although these worlds are opposed, the one is necessary for the other. For any romantic hero, there is an unfriendly or threatening land without which his advent would have little point. It is just as essential to the boy's sense of mission that he move through "places the most hostile to romance." And to the end he seeks out evidence in the real world to confirm and dramatize his heroic encounter.

The narrative begins with the description of the blind or dead-end street, its brown houses, the "waste room" littered with the dead priest's useless papers and books, and the unkempt garden with the single apple tree and rusty bicycle pump—a dead, winter world awaiting a redemptive vision. In the evenings the two children, the narrator and the Mangan boy, watch from the shadows for the two figures who represent the opposed forces in the narrative: the boy's uncle, whom they avoid until he is "safely housed," and Mangan's sister, whom the boy sees "defined by the light" from the doorway. Amidst the commonplace sounds of the street, the boy's silent adoration for the girl grows and is expressed in images of a religious quest: "I imagined that I bore my chalice through a throng of foes." At last the girl speaks to him; she mentions Araby, and with the remark that she is unable to go she elicits from him a promise that he will bring her something. Committed to the quest, he impatiently awaits the day of the bazaar. He feels set apart from his friends, now mere children to him, and sees nothing but the figure of the girl cast by his imagination and outlined by the light that shone at their first conversation. When the time comes to leave, he is detained by his uncle's late return and barely escapes the older man's banal recitation of "The Arab's Farewell to His Steed." Then, recalled to the purpose of his journey by the crowded streets of the ordinary world, the boy travels alone on the "special train for the bazaar." What happens when he enters the hall is, in a sense, another story.

To the moment when the boy first sees the hall with its "magical name," the story includes most of the major elements of the advent and initiation phase of romantic narrative. There is the hostile or sterile environment, the forces of light and darkness clearly opposed, the heroine who sets the quest for the innocent but inspired young hero, the older figures who oppose the quest and detain the hero, and the solitary journey to a magical realm. These elements are displaced to meet modern conventions of probability. In older romances a queen or divine figure sets the quest; here Mangan's sister is touched by the light from a streetlamp, but the effect on the hero would have been no greater had she worn a crown or a halo.

This much similarity between the story and the narrative pattern of romance increases our understanding of the boy's profound sense of failure. What he fails to do at Araby is no more important than what he sees there. He imagines himself on a quest at the command of one he loves with a chaste and nearly religious adoration. At the end of his journey, at the very center of the magical realm, he finds no reward or vindication for his struggle, only the tawdry banter of a mundane sexual encounter and a voice reminding him that "the light was out." In his disappointment he may recognize himself as a creature like any other living thing, no better, incidentally, than the young gentlemen who profane the hall, and this would account for the dramatic image with which he distinguishes himself as one hounded by a furious vanity.

The pattern of romantic initiation defines another ambiguity in the story. In a conventional romance, no matter how bitter the struggle, the hero's initiation signals his advent and prepares him for his most important adventure. But this story ends with its hero gazing tearfully into the darkness. If we restrict our reading to the events in the narrative, the initiation fails and the boy's claim to the heroic is denied rather than proved. As a story of a young boy's first quest, the narrative repudiates the expectations of romance and parodies its initiation. And, as we will see, "Araby" could be read as an ironic narrative, for one of the typical devices of irony is the reversal of a romantic pattern.

There is still the question whether the quest was an utter failure—a question that rests in the story's last sentence. However easily the boy might have imagined himself "a creature driven and derided by vanity," he could not at that time have said so. The best that he can do at any time is to murmur "*O love! O love!*" Earlier he might have heard the girl's name as a summons, but it is as a much older and critical person that he calls it "a summons to all my *foolish* blood." Here, as in the last sentence and elsewhere, there is a mature, somewhat patronizing tone in the narration. For all the passion and disappointment the boy suffers, the story is seen and told from the distance of many years and with a detached point of view. The narrator has lived through the event; his exaggerated despair was not final. Something has been learned. Now the narrator can see, better than he ever could as a boy, where his almost sacramental vision was leading him—not to the bazaar but to the story "Araby." If the final "act" in this narrative is its narration, then the failure to bring something back from the bazaar may have been the necessary test to prove the imagination that would bring "Araby" back from memory.

In March of 1894, when Joyce was twelve and living on North Richmond Street, the bazaar Araby was held in Dublin. The posters proclaimed it a "Grand Oriental Fete" and showed a dashing Arab riding a camel and brandishing a rifle. Joyce may or may not have gone to the bazaar, or if he did, for the least romantic of reasons. But in October of 1905, eleven years later in Trieste, he wrote "Araby" and described it in a letter as one of the stories of his childhood. It reflects both years for it is a confident portrait of the artist as an uncertain child.

First-Phase Romance:
Advent and Initiation

Havelok the Dane

ca. 1300–1325

Translated by John Hampden

Here begins the life of Havelok, one time
King of England and Denmark.

1

Listen to me, all you good folk, wives, maidens
and men! Listen to me, and I will tell you the tale
of Havelok.

He was a very good man. In every gathering he
was the best, and in time of need he was the greatest
champion who ever bestrode a horse, but when he
was little he went naked.

Now you shall hear the story, but first fill me a
cup of your best ale. May Christ keep us all from
hell and grant that we come to him at the last!
Benedicamus domino![1]

Once there was a king who made good laws and
saw that they were obeyed. Young and old loved
him, earl and baron, dreng[2] and thane,[3] knight,
farmer and peasant, widow, maiden, priest and
clerk—everyone loved him for his good deeds. He
loved God, Holy Church and truth with all his
might; he loved all good men and gathered them
around him, and he hated all wrongdoers. Traitors
and informers he brought down, and all the outlaws and thieves that he could find he hanged high
on the gallows; neither wealth nor possessions

could save them. In those days a man could carry
[fifty pounds or more] in red gold on his back, in a
black or white bag, and no one would threaten him
or lay a wicked hand upon him. Chapmen[4] could
travel the length of England with their wares,
buying and selling boldly anywhere they wished, in
good towns, and anyone who wronged them was
brought to poverty and ruin.

Then England was at peace. A king who kept the
country so secure as this deserved high praise
indeed! Christ in Heaven was with him, and he was
the flower of England. There was no lord, from
here to Rome, who was bold enough to bring
hunger or any other evil upon his country. When
he pursued his foes they crept away into corners to
hide, not daring to move, and bowed to his will. He
loved the right above all things, and no one could
bribe him, with silver or gold; he was so careful of
the good of his soul. He protected the fatherless,
and whether it was a cleric or a knight who
wronged them he saw that they had justice. Anyone
who did wrong to a widow, even the most powerful
knight, was soon arrested and put in chains, and
anyone who brought shame or blame upon a
maiden, against her will, had some of his limbs cut
off. In time of need he was the best knight that ever
rode a horse, wielded a weapon or led his people;
he feared no man and was quick as fire to show his
prowess as a warrior. He took his foe's horse or
clothes, or made him spread his hands and cry for
mercy. He was openhanded, not niggardly; he
would give wayfarers the finest roast meat and the
most delicate dishes on his table, to win the favor
of Christ, who bled for us on the cross and guides
and directs all men everywhere.

HAVELOK THE DANE. **1. Benedicamus domino:** May God
bless us. **2. dreng:** king's tenant with military duties. **3.
thane:** man ranking between an ordinary freeman and a
nobleman.

4. Chapmen: peddlers.

This king was called Athelwold. The only child he had to succeed him was a lovely daughter, too young yet to walk or speak properly, so that when dire sickness overtook him and he knew that death was near, he said: "Christ, what shall I do? Where shall I find guidance? I know very well that I have my deserts, but what will happen to my daughter now? I fear for her, not for myself, and it is no wonder, for she cannot speak yet, she cannot walk by herself. If she could ride with a thousand men beside her, if she were old enough to rule England, and look after herself, I should never be uneasy again, even though I were dead!" And he gave a great shudder.

Then he sent writs to every earl and baron from Roxburgh to Dover, bidding them come to their unhappy king who lay night and day in the utmost misery. He was in such pain that he could neither sleep nor eat nor get relief, and no one could cure him; there was nothing for him but death.

All those who received his writs came sorrowfully into his presence, they wrung their hands and wept bitterly, and entreated Christ to cure him of his dreadful sickness. When they had all assembled before the king in the hall at Winchester where he lay, he said to them, "You are always welcome! I am very grateful to you for coming to me now." And when they had all taken their places and had greeted the king, they wept and mourned, but he quietened them and said, "Tears are useless, for I am near death. But I wish you all to pray for my daughter, who will be your lady when I am gone. Who is to take care of her and of England until she comes of age and can govern for herself?"

They answered at once, by Christ and Saint John, that Earl Godrich of Cornwall was a true and loyal man, wise in word and deed, feared and respected by all. "He is the best man to protect her, until she can become queen."

The King was satisfied with this advice. He had a fair cloth brought in and on it were laid the Mass-book, the chalice and the paten,[5] the sacrament-cloth and all the things used in the service of the Mass, and then he made the Earl swear on these to bring the child up properly, until she was twelve years old and able to speak up for herself. Then when she knew how to behave, and could think of marriage, and love anyone who pleased her, Godrich was to marry her to the tallest man alive,

5. **paten:** plate for the Eucharistic bread.

the best, the strongest and most handsome. Thereafter he was to give all England into her charge. All this the King made him swear upon the Book.

When the oath was taken the King gave the maiden into the Earl's keeping, together with all the land he had ever possessed in England, praying the Earl to use her well.

The King could do no more, but earnestly besought God's mercy; he received the sacrament and was shriven many times; many times he had himself sharply scourged, so that blood ran from his tender flesh. He made his will very prudently and carried it out at once in every particular. He did not keep enough to pay for a winding-sheet; everything was so well shared out that nothing was left.

When he had been many times chastised, whipped and shriven, before his tongue fell silent forever he cried out, "Into Thy hands" and called upon Jesus Christ, and then he died in the presence of all his noblemen. There was great sobbing and sighing, wringing of hands and tearing of hair; rich and poor grieved sorely, ladies in the bower and lords in the hall. Then bells were rung, monks and priests sang Mass, and many psalters were read, that God Himself should take the King's soul to heaven, into His Son's presence, to dwell there evermore. Then the King was laid in the earth.

The rich Earl forgot nothing, but soon took possession of all England. He gave the castles to knights whom he could trust, and made all the English swear loyalty to him. He gave to all men what seemed fitting, until the King's daughter was twenty winters old and more.

When he had taken this oath from earls and barons, from friends and foes alike, from knights, servants, bond and free, he appointed new judges to journey through England from Dover to Roxburgh. He set sheriffs, beadles, greaves[6] and officers of the peace with long swords to guard wild woods and paths from evildoers, so that everything was under his control. No baron, knight or peasant dared defy him, he was so rich in men, weapons and goods. In a short time all England feared him as the beast fears the goad.

The King's daughter, whose name was Goldboro, thrived and grew up to be the fairest woman living, wise and full of virtues, and many a tear was shed for her.

6. **sheriffs . . . greaves:** officials responsible for order in counties, church affairs, and towns, respectively.

When Earl Godrich heard how wise, chaste and lovely this maiden was, the rightful heiress of the whole kingdom, then he began to sigh and said, "Shall she be queen over me? Shall she possess all England, me and mine included? A curse on him who lets her! Should I give England to a fool, a servingmaid, because she wants it? A curse on anyone who gives it to her while I live! She has become all too proud, because I have given her too much good food and fine clothing; I've brought her up too softly. It shall not be as she plans. 'Hope often plays tricks on the fool!' I have a son, a fine boy, and all England shall be his. He shall be king, he shall be master, or I'll lose my neck for it!"

When he had planned this treason he thought no more of his oath; he let it go, he didn't give a straw for it. But before food passed his lips, like a wicked traitor Judas, he had her fetched from Winchester to Dover, that stands by our seas, and kept her there like a beggar in wretched clothes. He had the castle guarded so that none of her friends, who might avenge her misery, could come and speak with her.

Now we will leave the tale of Goldboro, who grieves continually as she lies in prison. May Jesus Christ, who brought Lazarus to life, free her with His own hands and grant that she may see that man hanged high on the gallows who brought her to sorrow when she had done no wrong!

2

Let us now go on with our story. It happened at that time that a rich and mighty king ruled in the land of Denmark. His name was Birkabeyn and he had many knights and servants: he was a handsome man and very brave, the best knight who ever led an army, rode a horse, or handled a spear. His wife had borne him three children whom he loved dearly, a son and two daughters, all lovely children. Death, who will spare no man, rich or poor, king or emperor, took him when he most desired to enjoy life, but his days were numbered; neither gold nor silver nor anything he could give would keep him alive.

When he realized this he sent far and wide in haste for priests, both good canons and monks, to direct and advise him, to give him the sacrament and shrive him while he still lived. As soon as his soul was prepared, and he had made his will and

given away all he owned, he gathered his knights about him, for he wanted to know from them who would protect his young children until they could speak for themselves, walk and ride with knights and soldiers beside them. He soon chose a rich man, his friend Godard, whom he thought the truest under the moon, to look after them until his son could don a helmet and lead an army, with a stout spear in his hand, and be made King of Denmark. In perfect trust he laid his hands on Godard and said: "Here I confide to your care my three children, all Denmark and all my possessions, until my son comes of age: but I wish you to swear by the altar, the Mass-gear, the bells that men ring and the Mass-book from which the priest sings, that you will bring up my children well, in a way which will please their kin, until my son is of age; then yield him his right, Denmark and all that goes with it, castles and towns, woods and fields."

Godard started up and swore all that the king bade him, and afterwards he sat with the knights who were there. They all wept sorely for the king, who died soon afterwards. May Jesus Christ, who makes the moon to shine in the dark night, protect his soul from the pains of hell, and grant that it may dwell in heaven with God's Son!

When Birkabeyn was laid in the grave, the Earl soon took the boy Havelok, heir to the kingdom, his sisters Swanborow and Elfred the fair, and imprisoned them in the castle, where none of their kin could come to them. There they often wept bitterly with hunger and cold before they were three winters old. He did not give a straw for his oaths; he neither clothed nor fed them properly, nor put them to sleep in rich beds. Godard was surely the worst traitor, in God's sight, of all who were ever made from clay, except one, the wicked Judas. May he be cursed today by all who can speak!—patriarch, pope, priest, monks and hermits all! And from the holy cross on which God Himself ran with blood, may Christ curse him! May he be cursed by north and south, by all men who can speak, by Christ who made the moon and sun!

When he had gained control over the whole country and people, and all had sworn an oath to him—rich and poor, willing and unwilling—that they would do his will and would not anger him, he made up his mind to do a very cruel and treacherous thing to the children. May the devil from hell take him soon!

When the plan was made, he went to the tower where they were imprisoned, weeping with hunger and cold. The boy, who was bold enough, came to meet him, knelt down and greeted him courteously.

Godard said, "What is wrong with you? Why do you weep and howl?"

"Because we are very hungry," they said, "We have nothing to eat, and in this place we have neither knight nor page to give us drink or meat, even half as much as we could eat. We wish we had never been born. Is there no corn to make bread? We are so hungry, we are nearly dead!"

Godard listened to their complaint, but he did not care a straw for it. He took hold of the maidens both together, as though he were playing with them, sickly and pale with hunger as they were. He cut both their throats, and afterwards cut them to pieces. It was a terrible thing to see the children lying in their blood by the wall. Havelok stood aghast. Well might that innocent lad be afraid, for he saw at his heart a knife that was ready to rob him of his life. But the boy, small as he was, knelt before that Judas, and said,

"My lord, have mercy! My lord, I offer you homage! I will give all Denmark to you, if you let me live. Here I will swear on the Book that I will never bear against you, my lord, shield, spear, or any weapon that may harm you. My lord, have mercy on me! Today I will flee from Denmark and never return. I will swear that Birkabeyn never begot me."

When the devil heard that, he was touched with pity and he lowered the knife that was warm with the innocent children's blood. It was a blessed miracle that he did not kill the boy, and held back through pity. He was very sorry for Havelok, and he could not kill him with his own hands, the foul fiend! but he thought as he stood, staring as though he were mad, "If I let the boy go, he may do me great harm. I shall never be safe; he may watch for a chance to kill me; but if he dies and my children thrive, they may be lords of all Denmark after me. God knows, he shall die. I will have him thrown into the sea, and drowned with an anchor about his neck, so that he cannot float on the waves."

Thereupon he sent for a fisherman who would, he thought, do anything he wanted, and said to him, "Grim, you know you are my thrall; if you will now do exactly as I bid you, tomorrow I will give you your freedom and make you rich—pro-vided that you will take this boy to sea with you tonight, when you see it is moonlight, and throw him in. I will take the sin upon myself."

Grim took the child, and bound him fast with all the ropes he could find, which were of very strong cord.

Then was Havelok in the greatest misery; he never knew such misery before. May Jesus Christ, who makes the lame to walk and the dumb to speak, revenge you, Havelok, on Godard!

When Grim had bound him fast he tied him up in an old cloth, gagged him with a filthy rag so that he could neither speak nor breathe, and put him into a foul black bag, then flung him on his back and carried him home to his cottage. There he handed him over to Dame Leve and said, "Guard this boy as you value my life. I am going to drown him at sea. We shall get our freedom for it, and wealth in plenty. My lord has promised me."

When Dame Leve heard that, she started up and threw the boy down so hard that he cracked his head against a great stone that lay there. Then might Havelok say, "Woe is me that ever I was a king's child!—Woe that neither griffin, eagle, lion nor wolf, she-wolf nor bear nor other dangerous beast carried off Godard!" So the child lay until midnight, when Grim told Leve to get a light.

"Do you care nothing for the oaths I have sworn to my lord? I will not be utterly lost. I will carry the boy down to the sea, as you know I must, and drown him. Get up quickly, go and blow the fire and light a candle."

When she had picked up Grim's clothes she set about blowing the fire, and then she saw a shining light, as bright as day, around the boy. From his mouth there issued a ray like a sunbeam; the room was as bright as though lit by wax candles.

"Jesus Christ!" cried Dame Leve, "What is this light in our cottage? Get up, Grim, and see what it means. What light is this?"

They both rushed to the boy, ungagged him and unbound him quickly, and rolled back his shirt. They soon found a king's birthmark, very bright and fine, on his right shoulder.

"God knows!" cried Grim, "this is our heir, who shall be lord of Denmark. He shall be king, stout and strong; he shall have all Denmark and England in his power; he will make Godard suffer, hang him or flay him or bury him alive; he will have no mercy on him!"

Thus said Grim and wept bitterly. Then he fell at Havelok's feet and cried, "My lord, have mercy on me, and on Leve who stands by me. My lord, we are both your thralls and slaves. My lord, we will feed you well until you can ride a horse, and can bear helm, shield and spear. That foul traitor Godard shall never know of it. No one but you, my lord, shall make me free. I will care for you and keep watch over you."

Then Havelok was glad. He sat up and asked for food, and said, "I am nearly dead with hunger and with the ropes you tied round my hands, and the gag which was thrust so fast into my mouth that it nearly choked me."

"I rejoice that you can eat, God knows!" said Leve, "I will fetch you bread and cheese, butter and milk, pasties[7] and flauns.[8] We will feed you well, my lord, in your great need. It is true, as men say, 'Where God will help, nothing can do harm.' "

As soon as she brought the food, Havelok began to eat heartily and was happy. He could not hide his hunger. He ate a loaf, I guess, and more, for he was famished—he had eaten no food for three days. When he was satisfied, Grim made him a fine bed, undressed him and put him into it, saying, "Sleep, my son, very happily! Sleep soundly and fear nothing. You have been brought from misery to happiness."

As soon as it was daylight, Grim went to the wicked traitor Godard, the steward of Denmark, and said,

"Lord, I have done what you bade me. The boy is drowned in the sea with a good anchor round his neck. He is certainly dead; he will eat bread no more. Now give me my freedom and the rich rewards you promised me."

Godard stood and looked grimly and searchingly at him, and said, "Do you expect to be made an earl? Go home at once, you foul, dirty fellow! Go and be the thrall and slave you have always been! You shall have no other reward. It would not take much for me to send you to the gallows, God help me! You have done a wicked deed. You may stand here too long unless you go at once!"

Grim could not escape quickly enough from that wicked traitor. He thought, "What shall I do? If he finds out that the boy is alive, he will hang us both on the gallows. It is better for us to flee the land, to save all our lives."

Grim soon sold all his corn, his woolly sheep and horned cattle, his horse, swine and bearded goats, the geese and the hens from his yard; he sold everything of any value that he possibly could, and he turned it all into money. He prepared his ship well, tarred it and stopped its seams with pitch, so that neither shoal nor creek would endanger it. He fitted it with an excellent mast, strong cables, good oars and a fine sail—not a nail was missing. When it was ready, he went on board with the young Havelok, and his wife, his three sons and his two fair daughters, and rowed out to the open sea where he might best escape. He was but a mile from land when the wind called Bise[9] came out of the north, and drove them to England, which Havelok was to rule, but not before he had suffered great shame and sorrow and grief. Yet he got all England in the end, as you shall hear if you will listen long enough.

3

Grim came to land in the Humber, in the north of Lindsay. His ship grounded on the sand but he hauled it to the shore, and there he made a little shelter for himself and his family. Then he began to build a small cottage of earth, so that they were well housed, and because Grim owned that place, it was named after him. Everyone calls it Grimsby, and so it shall always be called from now till Doomsday.

Grim was a good fisherman, and a good sailor. He caught many fine fish, with nets and hooks— sturgeon, whale, turbot, salmon, seal and eel. He often did well; he caught cod and porpoise, herring, mackerel, flatfish, plaice and skate. He made good baskets, one for himself and three others for his sons, to carry fish in so that they could sell it on land.

He went to town and village to sell his wares; he never came home empty-handed, but brought bread and something to eat with it in his tunic or cloak, beans and corn in his bag. He never wasted his labor. And when he caught a great lamprey, he went straight to the good town of Lincoln. Often he walked all over the town, until he had sold all his fish at a good price and counted his

---

7. **pasties:** meat pies. 8. **flauns:** cakes containing custard or cheese.

9. **Bise:** (Frencn) dry and cold north wind.

takings. When he came home they were happy, for he often brought wastel-bread[10] and horn-shaped simnel cakes and his bags were full of meal and corn, beef, mutton and pork, besides hemp to make good lines and strong ropes for the nets which he often set in the sea.

So Grim prospered. He fed himself and his household well for twelve winters and more. Havelok knew that Grim worked hard for his food while he stayed at home, and he thought, "I am not a boy now, I can easily eat more than Grim can earn. I eat more than Grim and his five children! This must not go on, God knows! I will go with them and learn to work for my keep. There is nothing to be ashamed of in working; the man who wants to eat and drink well ought to work hard; it is shameful to stay at home. May God reward him who has fed me until now! I will gladly carry a basket, which will do me no harm if it is as heavy as an ox. Tomorrow I will go out."

Next day he got up at dawn, and threw a basket on his back, after he had filled it with fish; he put four basketfuls into one. He did well with it and brought home every silver piece that he got; he didn't keep a farthing. So he went out every day, and learned his trade.

Then there was a great dearth of corn and bread, so that Grim could find no way of feeding his household. He was very anxious about Havelok, who could eat far more than he got, but neither ling nor skate nor any other good fish was to be caught. Grim thought nothing of his children, but cared only for Havelok. He said,

"Havelok, dear son, I think that we must die of hunger, this famine is so bad, and our food has run out. It would be better for you to go away than to stay here. You might go too late. You know the road to Lincoln well, for you have traveled it often. (As for me, I am not worth a sloe.) You will find there many a good man from whom you could earn a living. But woe is me! You are almost naked. I will make you a garment from my sail, so that you can wear it, son, and not take cold."

He took the shears from the hook, and made a cloak from the sail, which Havelok put on. He had neither hose nor shoes, nor any other garment; he went to Lincoln barefoot. When he arrived there he was bewildered, and for two days he went

10. **wastel-bread:** bread made from fine flour.

without food, for he could get no work to do, but on the third day he heard the Earl's cook shouting, "Porters, porters, come here!" A crowd of poor men sprang forward like sparks from a fire, but Havelok knocked down nine or ten of them into the mud, and left them to lie there. All the food which the cook had bought at the bridge[11] Havelok carried up to the castle,[12] and he got a farthing wastel-loaf for himself.

Next day he watched eagerly for the cook, until he saw him on the bridge, with a heap of fish which he had bought for the Earl of Cornwall, shouting, "Porters, porters, come quickly!" Havelok was delighted. He laid out everyone who got in his way, sixteen good lads and more, he knocked them all down in a heap, and bounded up to the cook with his basket and began to pick up the fish. He carried up a whole cartload of cuttlefish, salmon, broad plaice, great lampreys and eels; he never spared himself until he reached the castle. When they had helped him to put down the load from his head, the cook smiled at him and thought him a stalwart man enough. He said, "Will you serve me? I will feed you gladly, for you will earn your keep."

"God knows!" said Havelok, "I will ask for no other payment. If you give me enough to eat, I will fetch fuel and water, blow the fire and make it burn well. I can break and split sticks, and kindle a fire so that it burns brightly. I am very good at cutting firewood and I can skin an eel, wash dishes, and do all you want."

The cook answered, "I want nothing more. Go and sit over there, and I will give you the finest bread, and make broth for you in the pot. Sit down now and eat all you want, and a curse on anyone who begrudges you your food!"

Havelok sat quiet until he had eaten his fill, which he had well earned. When he had had enough, he went to the well to draw water, and filled a great tub there; he asked nobody to help him, but carried it in all by himself to the kitchen. He asked no one to fetch water for him or to bring the food from the bridge. He carried peat and sedge[13] and brought wood from the bridge; everything he used he drew and cut himself. He took no more rest than an animal. He was the meekest of men and always cheerful; he kept his

11. **bridge:** bridge with houses and shops on it. 12. **castle:** Lincoln Castle. 13. **sedge:** marsh grass used for kindling.

sorrows to himself. No boy who wanted a game was too little for him to frolic with, he would do anything for the children who came in his way, and he played with them to their hearts' content. Everyone loved him, the shy and the bold, knights, children, young and old, high and low. Far and wide people talked about him, how big and strong he was, and what a fine man God had made him, except that he was almost naked; for he had nothing to wear but a rough, dirty cloak which wasn't worth a faggot.

The cook took pity on him and brought him some clothes and shoes, all brand new, and when he had put them on he looked the finest man ever born of woman; no king ever looked so kingly as he did then, and when the people had gathered at Lincoln for the games, and all the Earl's men were there, Havelok was head and shoulders taller than any of them. He soon threw anyone he took in his arms, for he was as sturdy and strong as he was tall; no one in England could match him in strength. Yet he was as gentle as he was strong. Even those who wronged him, he would never insult or handle roughly. He was a virgin, for he would no more lie with a woman, in a love-game or in the fields, than he would lie with a witch.

At that time Earl Godrich, who ruled all England, summoned many earls and barons and all the men of England to a parliament at Lincoln. With them came many a champion too, many a brave servingman, all the lesser folk. Nine or ten young men began to play games, and then they all gathered —champions, stout lads, husbandmen with their goads as they came from the plow; there was not a horse-boy, no matter what work he had to do, who did not come to watch the sport. The stout lads, with a tree-trunk at their feet, put a huge stone which was as heavy as an ox. Only a very stalwart man could lift it as high as his knees; there was not a clerk or priest who could lift it to his breast, and anyone who could put it an inch or so farther than another, young or old, was hailed as a champion. As they watched and made a great clamor about the best throw of all, Havelok stood and looked on. He knew nothing about putting, for he had never seen the games before, but his master bade him go and do his best. He was very much afraid, but he laid hold of the stone at once and threw it, the first time more than twelve feet farther than anyone else. The champions who saw the

throw nudged each other and laughed; they would not put the stone again, but said, "We have been here too long!"

This wonderful feat could not be kept secret. Very soon everyone knew how Havelok had cast the stone farther than any of the servingmen, how handsome, tall, brave and strong he was, and how modest. All over England, in the castle, up in the hall, the knights spoke of it, so that Godrich heard it too, and he thought, "By making use of this man I can get all England for myself and for my son after me, which is what I want. King Athelwold made me swear on all the Mass-gear that I would give his daughter to the tallest man alive, the best and strongest and most handsome; he made me swear it on the Book. Where could I find a man as tall and skillful as Havelok, even if I searched as far as India? Havelok is the man for Goldboro."

This was a treacherous plan, for he believed that Havelok was a churl's son, and he did not intend to give a single furrow of England as dowry for Goldboro, although it was all hers and she was a good and lovely woman. In this way, he believed, he would get all England for himself. He was worse than Satan, whom Christ shut up in hell. May he be hanged on a hook!

He sent at once for Goldboro, that fair and gracious lady, and had her brought to Lincoln. He set the bells ringing and made much of her, but he was a traitor all the same. He said that he would give her the finest man alive, but she answered that, by Jesus Christ and Saint John, no man should wed her and bring her to bed unless he were a king or a king's heir, however handsome he might be.

When she took this oath Godrich was angry indeed. "Will you make yourself queen over me?" he cried. "You shall marry not a king but a churl. You shall marry my cook's boy, and a curse on him who gives you any other husband while I live! You shall be wedded and bedded tomorrow, say what you like!"

Goldboro wept, for she was so miserable that she wanted to die; but next morning, as soon as the sun had risen and the matins-bell had rung, that Judas, who was worse than Satan, sent for Havelok and said to him,

"Master, do you want a wife?"

"Not on my life!" answered Havelok. "W should I do with a wife? I could not feed or c her. And where could I take her? I have absolutely nothing: neither house nor cottage, neither stick nor twig, neither bread nor anything to eat with it, no clothing except for an old white cloak. These clothes that I am wearing are the cook's, and I am his servant."

Godrich sprang up and struck him with all his strength. "If you don't take the woman I give you I will hang you, I will put out your eye!"

Havelok was afraid, for he was all alone, so he agreed to everything. Then Godrich sent for Goldboro, the fairest woman under the sun, and said to her—the foul traitor!—

"If you refuse to marry this man I will drive you out of the country or burn you alive!"

She was so terrified that she dared not refuse, and although she hated it she thought that it must be God's will, who makes the corn grow and made her to be born a woman. So Godrich forced them to marry. A great many pennies (which he made Goldboro take) were laid upon the Book, and the Wedding Mass was said by a good priest, the Archbishop of York, who had come to the parliament as if sent by God.

4

When they had been truly wedded, by God's law and in sight of the people, they did not want to stay long, for they saw very well that Godrich hated them, the devil take him! And Havelok was very much afraid that if they remained some shame would be put upon his wife—and he would rather die first—or that some evil would be done to them. So he made up his mind that they must flee to Grim and his three sons, where they might get food and clothing, and they set out as fast as they could for Grimsby. There they found that Grim as dead, but his five children greeted them joy- and loyally. They knelt down, and said,

elcome, dear lord! And welcome to your ! Blessed be the hour in which you were We rejoice to see you alive, and you may ndmen if only you will stay here. We d things: horses, cattle and a ship on nd silver and many other things Grim left us, and he bade us give y with us, and they shall all be ve you and your lady, and our she commands. They shall wash

and wring her clothes, bring water for her hands, and bring you both to bed, for we wish to have her for our lady!"

When they had given them this joyful greeting, they broke sticks and split them, and made the fire blaze up. Neither goose nor hen, duck nor drake was spared, there was food in plenty, with no good dish lacking. Wine and ale were brought in, and they made merry, Havelok and Goldboro leading the wassail many a time.

That night Goldboro lay awake full of sorrow, for she thought she had been betrayed and married below her rank. Then she saw a light in the room, a wonderful light as bright as a blazing fire. She looked about, and found that it shone from the mouth of the man who lay in bed beside her. No wonder that she was afraid! "What can this mean?" she thought. "He will be a nobleman! He will be a nobleman before he dies!" Then she saw a splendid cross of red gold on his shoulder, and the voice of an angel spoke to her:

"Goldboro, do not be sad, for this Havelok who has married you is a king's son and heir. This cross proves it, and it means that he will become King of Denmark and of all England. You shall see this happen and you shall be his queen!"

When she heard that voice from heaven she was so overjoyed that she could not conceal it. She kissed Havelok, who was asleep and had heard nothing of what the angel said, and he awoke and cried,

"Sweetheart, are you asleep? I have just had a wonderful dream. Let me tell you about it. I dreamed I was in Denmark, on one of the highest hills that I ever saw. It was so high that I thought I could see the whole world, and as I sat there I took hold of Denmark, its towns and its strong castles, until my arms grew so long that I embraced the whole country, and when I tried to free my arms everything living in Denmark clung to them, all the strong castles fell on their knees and their keys fell at my feet. Then I had another dream, that I flew over the salt sea to England, and all the people of Denmark, except the bondmen and their wives, went with me. Then I took up the whole of England in my hand and gave it to you, Goldboro. In the name of God, my love, what can this mean?"

"May Jesus Christ, who made the moon, turn all your dreams to joy," said Goldboro. "No king or emperor shall be as strong as you, for you shall wear the crown in England yet, Denmark shall kneel at your feet, and all its castles shall be truly yours. I know as well as if I could see it that all the people of Denmark, father and son, earl and baron, dreng and thane, knights, townsfolk and peasants, shall hail you as king. Every yard of Denmark shall be yours, and within a year you shall be king of it. Do not doubt this, but do as I wish, at once. Let us both go to Denmark without delay. 'Speed and success go together.' I shall never be happy till I see Denmark, because I know it is to be yours. Ask all three of Grim's sons to go with you. I know they won't refuse, for they love you well, and you know how active they are wherever they go. Ask them to get their ship ready quickly and don't delay. 'Delay has often done harm.' "

After listening to her advice Havelok dressed himself, as soon as it was day, and before he did anything else he went to the church and fell on his knees before the Rood,[14] calling on Christ and the Cross.

"Lord," he prayed, "Thou that rulest all things, wind and water, woods and fields, by Thy holy mercy have pity on me now, O Lord! Avenge me on my foe, who slew my sisters with a knife before my very eyes and who would have robbed me of my life, for he bade Grim drown me in the sea. He holds my land most wickedly, for I never did him any harm and he has brought me to misery; he has made me beg my food and live in sorrow and pain. Lord, have mercy upon me and let me cross the sea in safety, although I am so anxious and afraid. Keep me from storms and from drowning, and from destruction for any sin. Bring me safely to the land which Godard rules, which is all of it mine by right,—Jesus Christ, thou knowest that well."

When he had said this prayer and laid his offering on the altar he took his leave of Christ and His sweet mother, and of the Cross before which he lay, and then went weeping on his way.

Grim's sons were getting ready to go fishing, so that Havelok could have a good meal, but he called the eldest brother, Red Robert, then William Wendut and Hugh Raven, all Grim's three sons, and said,

"Now listen to me, lordings, and I will remind you of something about myself which you know already. My father was King of Denmark—all

14. **Rood:** the crucifix.

Denmark was in his hand on the day he died, but then he was given evil counsel, that he should entrust me and my sisters and his kingdom to the care of a villain, a limb of the devil. I saw that foul fiend kill my sisters with his own hands. He slit their throats and cut them to pieces. Then he bade Grim, your father, drown me in the sea, he made your father swear solemnly on the Book to do it and said he would take the sin upon himself. But Grim was wise and clever. He would not damn his soul, he chose instead to break his oath and to save me by fleeing from Denmark. If I had been found there he would have been slain, or bound fast and hanged high on a tree; no bribe could have saved him. So he fled here from Denmark, and looked after me so well that to this very day I have always been fed and cared for. But now that I have come to an age when I can wield a weapon and give great blows with it I shall never rejoice until I see Denmark. I beg you to come with me, and I will make you rich men. Each of you shall have ten castles, with all their lands, boroughs, towns, woods and fields."[15]

5

"I beg your leave," [said Havelok to Earl Ubbe, "to trade in] such goods as I shall buy. I will ask permission of no magistrate but you. I want to travel from town to town, selling my wares."

He took out a gold ring, the stone in which was worth a hundred pounds, and gave it to Ubbe. "He was wise who first gave a bribe," and Havelok was very wise; no merchant ever got such a high price for a ring, as you will hear if you listen to my story.

Once Ubbe had that gold ring he would not have parted with it for anything. He looked closely at Havelok, seeing how well-built he was, broad-shouldered, deep-chested and tall: he looked a very powerful man.

"God!" said Ubbe, "why is he not a knight? He is a man of courage, I swear! He should be wearing helmet, shield and spear, not buying and

15. [Hampden's note] At this point a leaf containing 180 lines has been cut out of the manuscript. Evidently it describes how Havelok and Goldboro, with Grim's three sons, sailed to Denmark and arrived at the castle of the Danish earl named Ubbe, who was a friend of Havelok's father, King Birkabeyn. Havelok begged his permission to live nearby and make a living by trading.

selling. It is a shame that he should have to. God knows, if he would trust me he would give up trade." Nevertheless he said at once, "Havelok, your boon is granted. Come and eat with me to-day, you and your beautiful wife, whom you love as yourself. And have no fear for her, for no one shall put her to shame; I will go surety for that myself."

Havelok heard what he said, but he was afraid for his wife, for he would rather have died than let her come to any harm. Ubbe spurred his horse and rode off, but before he was out of hearing he called, so that his people heard, "See that you both come. I wish it—and command it."

Although he was afraid Havelok did not dare to disobey, and he took his wife with him to the court. Robert the Red went with her, who would have died to save her from insult or injury, and her other escort was Robert's brother, William Wendut, a man of courage in any hour of need.

"Well is it with him who feeds a good man." When they came into the hall Ubbe sprang up to receive them, and so did many a knight and peasant, to look at them and point them out, for Havelok stood up like a hill above everyone there; he was a head taller than any of them. How happy Ubbe was, to see him so handsome and courteous! Ubbe's heart went out to him and his wife, and it seemed to him that there was no one in Denmark whom he could love so much. See the different ways in which God can help a man and his wife!

When it was time to eat, Ubbe had his wife brought in and said to her, in jest, "Dame, you and Havelok shall eat together and Goldboro, who is as beautiful as a flower on a tree, shall eat with me. By Saint John, no woman in Denmark is as lovely!"

When they had sat down and the table was laid and grace had been said, the finest food that any king or emperor could have was set before them: cranes, swans, venison, salmon, lampreys, good sturgeon, spiced wine and good claré,[16] with plenty of white and red wine. In that place even the smallest page would never drink ale. I will not dwell on the food and wine; that is too long a story, it would weary this fair company. But when everything had been served and they had wassailed many times, when they had sat long over their good wine and it was time to go, everyone to his own place, Ubbe thought,

16. claré: spiced wine.

"If I let these four go all alone there will be trouble for this woman, as I hope to keep the use of finger and toe! Someone will kill her lord to get her."

So he sent ten knights and sixty men, at least, with good swords and bows, to the house of the greave, who was named Bernard Brun, with orders that as he valued his life he was to keep Havelok and Goldboro safe until the morning. Bernard was a trusty man and very brave. There was no man in the town who was better on a horse with his helmet on his head and his sword at his side. He welcomed Havelok very warmly and had a very good supper got ready, so that they might feast to their hearts' content, for there was nothing mean about him.

As soon as they had sat down to supper there came a servingman in a loose jacket, with sixty strong men bearing drawn swords and long knives, who shouted,

"Unbar the door, Greave Bernard! Unbar it quickly and let us in, or by Saint Augustine you are a dead man!"

Bernard, that big man, sprang up and donned a coat of mail, he grasped a good ax and rushed to the door like a madman, crying,

"Who are you, out there, making that din? Begone, you dirty thieves, for by the Lord men trust, if I open this door I will kill some of you! And the rest of you I'll put in chains!"

"What's that?" cried a man, "Do you think we're afraid? We shall get through this door, you churl, in spite of you."

He seized a great stone and hurled it with such force that it smashed the door to pieces.

Havelok sprang to the door-bar and pulled it out, rough and heavy as it was, flung open the door and shouted,

"Here I stand! Come on! A curse on him who runs away from you!"

"You shall pay for that!" cried one.

Sword in hand he made at Havelok, and with him came two more. Havelok lifted the door-bar and with a single stroke he slew all three. Their brains lay open to the stars. A fourth he saluted with the bar so well that the man's right eye flew out of its socket, and then Havelok smote him on the crown so that he fell stone-dead. The fifth got such a blow between the shoulders that he spent his heart's blood. The sixth turned to flee, and the bar broke his foul neck in two. When the sixth had been felled the seventh drew his sword and thrust at Havelok's eye, but Havelok let fly with the bar and smote him on the breast; he had no chance to get shriven, for he was dead in less time than it takes to run a mile. Then the rest planned to surround him and beat him so that no leech should be able to heal him with any salve. They drew their swords and rushed at him as dogs rush at a baited bear when they mean to tear it to pieces. They all closed in upon him boldly and fiercely, they smote him with bars and stones, and thrust their swords into his back and sides until he had more than twenty great wounds from head to foot. He was mad with anger. It was a marvel that he kept his feet, for the blood streamed down him, but then he showed them what he could do; he mowed them down with his bar, he cracked the skull of every man he could reach, and in no time he felled twenty of them to the ground. What a din they made! They still attacked him fiercely but they kept their distance now, hurling flints and spears at him. Eager as they were to kill him they no more dared come near than if he were a boar or a lion.

Hugh Raven heard that din, and thought that they were attacking Havelok in order to take his wife. Hugh seized an oar and a long knife and ran like a deer. Then he saw how these mad fellows surrounded his lord and beat him as a smith beats an anvil with a hammer.

"Alas!" cried Hugh, "that ever I was born! That ever I ate bread! That I should see such sorrow! Robert! William! where are you? Arm yourselves with good bars of wood! Not one of these dogs shall escape until our lord is avenged. Come quickly and follow me! I have a good oar in my hand. A curse on him who does not strike hard!"

"Yes, dear brother, yes!" cried Robert. "We can see by the moonlight!"

Robert grasped a staff strong enough to carry an ox, William Wendut seized a bar of wood much thicker than his thigh, Bernard gripped his ax (I swear he was not the last) and they all rushed out as though they were mad. What wounds they gave those rogues! Havelok was well avenged. They broke their ribs, they broke their arms, knees, legs and thighs, they cracked their heads, they beat their backs as soft as their bellies. They made them roar like children in the cradle, like children roaring for their mothers. A curse on anyone who pities them! What were they doing there? They deserved all they got. There were more than sixty of them and not one escaped alive.

6

Next morning there they lay in heaps, like dogs which had been hanged. Some had been thrown into dikes, others had been dragged into ditches by the hair and left there.

The news came quickly to Ubbe that Havelok, with a club, had killed sixty-one servingmen, the best men living.

"God!" cried Ubbe, "What is this? I must go myself to see what has happened, for if I send messengers they may do him harm and I would not have that happen for anything. I love him well, by the King of Heaven!"

He leaped lightly on a horse, and with many a noble knight behind him he rode to Bernard Brun's house in the town, and called to him. Out came Bernard, nearly as naked as he was born and covered with bruises.

"Bernard, what has happened to you?" asked Ubbe. "Who has treated you like this and left you nearly naked?"

"Have mercy on me, my lord," he answered. "Last night, as the moon rose, more than sixty thieves came here to rob me and to kill me and mine. They broke down my door and meant to bind me hand and foot. When the good Havelok saw that, as he lay by the wall, he sprang up and drove them out, though they were as fierce as dogs from a mill. Havelok grasped the door-bar and killed three of them at a blow. He is the best man at need that shall ever ride a horse; God help me, I think he's worth a thousand men! Had it not been for him I should be dead. But it is hard on him, for they gave him three wounds the least of which would bring a horse to the ground. He has a great sword-wound in the side, another very bad one in the arm, and the worst wound ever seen in his thigh, besides more than twenty others. But when he felt the pain of those wounds he fought as no boar ever fought. He smashed the hardest skull and spattered it to pieces. He hunted those thieves as a dog hunts a hare, until every one of them lay still as a stone, and he is not to blame, for if he had not killed them they would have cut him to pieces.

My lord, I have only been roughly handled and the thieves who meant to rob me have paid dearly for it, thank God, but Havelok is very sorely wounded. I think he will soon be a dead man."

"Bernard," said Ubbe, "do you speak the truth?"

"Yes, sire, I do not lie from my teeth. If I speak one untrue word, my lord, hang me high tomorrow."

The townsfolk who stood by, high and low, young and old, swore solemn oaths that Bernard spoke the truth:

"Lord, they would have carried off all his goods and torn him to pieces, but God protected him so that he lost nothing. What knight or man could stand against so many at dead of night? There were seventy of them strong, stalwart men, and their leader was called Griffin Galle. Who could stand against so many except this man from a foreign land who slew them all with a bar of wood? Much joy to him!"

"Bring him quickly," said Ubbe, "so that I can see whether his wounds can be healed, for if he recovers and can walk again I myself will dub him knight for his bravery. And if those foul thieves, the kinsmen of Cain and Eve, were still alive, they should hang by the neck. A curse on anyone who pities them, when they come like this at night to bind burgesses and knights. I have no love for outlaws who bind their victims. I do not care a sloe for them."

Havelok was brought to Ubbe, who grieved over his painful wounds, and feared for his life, but when his wounds were looked at, and a leech declared that he could be cured completely, to speak and walk and ride as well as ever, then Ubbe forgot all his grief and fear and said,

"Come with me, and bring Goldboro your wife, and your three servants. I will keep you safe. I do not want the friends of those you killed to lie in wait for you as you go to and fro. I will lend you a room in a high tower until you can walk again and are cured. There shall be nothing between your room and mine but a good wall of fir-wood, and whether I speak loudly or softly you will be able to hear all I say, and you shall see me whenever you wish. One roof shall cover us at night, so that no man of mine, cleric or knight, shall try to shame your wife, any more than mine, God help me!"

So Havelok went to the tower, taking his wife and his three men, the best men in the world. In the middle of the night Ubbe awoke and saw a great light, as bright as day, in the room where Havelok slept.

"God!" thought Ubbe, "what is this? I had best go myself to see whether they are sitting up wassailing or doing something foolish. If they are, they ought to be thrown into a dike or into the fen. By Christ whom all men believe in, only gluttons or wicked thieves would be up now."

He got up and looked through a crack, without saying a word. They were all lying fast asleep, and the great light was shining out of Havelok's mouth.

"God!" he thought, "what does this mean?" He called together his knights and retainers, more than a hundred of them, and bade them come and look at this marvel. As they came from the hall to Havelok's room a ray of light like a sunbeam shone from his mouth, so that the room was as bright as though a hundred wax-tapers were burning. They were all five sleeping like the dead. Havelok lay on his left side with his lovely bride in his arms and they were naked to the breasts. So handsome a pair never lay together in a bed. The knights thought it a great joke to look at them, and as Havelok lay with his back turned they saw a splendid cross on his right shoulder, brighter than gold against the light, which all of them knew to be the birthmark of a king. It sparkled and shone like a carbuncle; a man could tell one coin from another by its light. Then they looked at him closely, and they knew him at last for the son of their good King Birkabeyn, who had led them so bravely against their foes. "There were never two brothers in all Denmark so much alike as Birkabeyn and this man," they said, "He must be Birkabeyn's heir."

They fell at his feet, weeping for joy, as though he had come back from the grave. They kissed his feet a hundred times, his toes and toenails and the tips of his toes. He awoke and glowered at them, for he thought they meant to kill him or make him prisoner.

"My lord, do not be afraid. I see your thought," said Ubbe. "Dear son, it is well for me that my eyes behold you. I do you homage, my lord. It is right that I should be your liegeman, for you are Birkabeyn's heir. He had many a knight and servant, and so shall you have, young as you are. You shall be King of all Denmark, stronger than any before you. Tomorrow all men in this town shall do you homage, earl, baron, dreng and thane, knight and churl. And I will gladly make you a knight, for you are a brave man."

Then Havelok was very happy and thanked God many times. Next morning, when the darkness of night had gone, Ubbe ordered a man to take horse and call together earls, barons, drengs, thanes, clerics, knights, townsfolk and peasants, on pain of their lives and their wives' and children's lives. No man dared to disobey him; they came at once to see what the magistrate wanted. Then he rose and said,

"Listen to me, all of you, freemen and serfs. I will remind you of something you know well, that all this land was in Birkabeyn's hands on the day he died and that by your advice he put his three children and all his goods into Godard's care. You all heard Godard swear on the Book and the Mass-gear that he would care for them faithfully and well. He was altogether false to his oath. May he suffer for it forever! He killed both the maidens with a knife, and he would have killed the boy too, the knife was at his heart, but God had pity on him and saved him. That foul fiend did not kill the boy himself, he made a fisherman swear to drown him in the raging sea.

"When Grim saw that he was such a fine boy and knew that he was the rightful heir, he fled with him from Denmark to England and took care of him for many a winter, so that he has always been provided for. Look at him now! There is no one in the world to equal him, no one so handsome, so tall and strong, no knight half so brave. Rejoice in him! Come and do homage to your lord. I will be the first to kneel to him."

He fell on his knees and swore to be Havelok's man, for all to see. After him ten servingmen started up and swore to be his men, then every baron in that town, every dreng, thane, knight and peasant; so that, before that day was done there was no one in the whole town who had not paid homage to Havelok.

Then he made them solemnly swear that they would be faithful to him against any man alive, and all of them, rich and poor, willing or not, soon took that oath. Then Ubbe sent writs far and wide to all governors of castles, boroughs and towns, kinsmen or strangers, summoning them to come quickly and hear good news. Not one of them tarried; they came posthaste, on horse or on foot, and within a fortnight there was no knight, constable, or sheriff, born of Adam and Eve, who

had not come before Sir Ubbe, for they feared him as a thief fears the law.

When they had greeted the King and had taken their places, Ubbe said,

"Behold our most dear lord! He is to be King of all this land, he is to rule us all, for he is the son of Birkabeyn, our king that was, who defended us well with his sharp sword and long spear. This is his heir. Fall at his feet, all of you, and swear to be his men."

They all went in fear of Ubbe, so they did what he bade them, and something more: they swore solemnly on the Book that they would stand by Havelok against all his foes, secret or open.

When they had all paid homage and sworn, willingly or not, Ubbe dubbed him knight with the brightest of swords, gave all the people and all the land of Denmark into his care, and nobly made him King. Then the people enjoyed all the greatest pleasures in life: thrusting with sharp spears, fighting with sword and buckler, wrestling, putting the stone, harping and playing on the pipes, playing at backgammon and dice, and reading romances from books; then men could hear gests sung and gleemen striking on the tabor;[17] bulls and bears were baited by fierce hounds, with more and more noise and fury; there was never yet more happiness in the world than there was then in Havelok's kingdom. There were so many gifts of garments that I could not make them seem more than they were; that I can swear in the name of God. There was the best of food and wine, brought from far away, and as plentiful as water in the sea. The feast lasted for forty days; there has never been another so rich. Robert, that stalwart man, William Wendut his brother, and Hugh Raven were there made knights by the King, and then he made all three of them barons, and gave them lands and goods so rich that always, day and night, each of them maintained a retinue of twenty knights.

When at last the feast was over, King Havelok kept with him a thousand well-armed knights, each of them with a good mount, helmet, shield and bright coat of mail, and all the weapons a knight should have. He kept also five thousand good men who were spoiling for a fight. I will not make a long story of it. When all the castles in the country were in his hands, and he had put wardens in

17. **gests . . . tabor:** Notable deeds were celebrated in ballads by minstrels (gleemen) with tabors or small drums.

charge of them, he swore that he would never rest until he was revenged on that Godard of whom I have often told you. Havelok called together half a hundred of his fighting men, and made them swear by Book and Altar that they would never rest, for love or sin, till they had found Godard and brought him bound before their King.

Then they set off as fast as they could to the lands where Godard, that proud man, still went hunting with a great company. Robert was leader of the army, he wore a sword and rode a fine horse which would carry him at a furious gallop, and it was Robert who first spoke to Godard.

"Hey, fellow," he cried, "Listen to me! What are you doing here? You must come to the King at once. He commands you to come, and to remember how you slew his sisters with a knife and gave orders for him to be drowned in the sea. He is full of anger. You are to come to him at once, you foul and wicked traitor, and by Christ who gave His blood for us on the cross, the King will give you your reward!"

At that Godard dealt Robert a heavy blow in the teeth with his fist. Robert drew a long knife and stabbed him through the right arm.—There's no need to be sorry for him!

When Godard's men saw this they would have killed Robert but for his brothers and five more. They slew ten of Godard's best men, and the others fled. Then Godard shouted loudly,

"What are you doing? Will you desert me like this? I have fed you, and will go on feeding you. Help me now. Do not leave me to be killed or for Havelok to do what he likes with me. If you do you put yourselves to shame."

At that his men turned back and killed a knight and a peasant of the King's army, and wounded ten more, but then the whole army rushed upon them, and slew every man of them except Godard himself. Him they flayed later, like a thief that is hanged or a dog that is thrown into a ditch. They bound him now, as tightly as they could, as tightly as the cords would stretch, till he roared like a bull trapped in a hole with dogs baiting him. They bound him so sorely that he cried to them, by God's mercy, not to cut off his hand, but they would not stop. A curse on the man who would! They bound him hand and foot, they beat him like a bear, they threw him on to a scabby mare with his nose at the mare's tail. And so they brought that foul traitor to Havelok, on whom he had brought so much suffering, cold and hunger and wretchedness before the boy was twelve years old, in spite of all the oaths he had sworn. Now he had his reward. "Old sin makes new shame."

When he was brought so shamefully before the King, that foul traitor, the King made Ubbe call together at once all his earls and barons, every dreng and thane, knight and citizen, and ordered them to give the prisoner a fair trial, for the King knew that treacherous fellow again.—How angry God was with him!

They took their places by the wall, rich and poor, high and low, old men and boys. They gave the prisoner a fair trial, and then they said to the King, who sat there still as a stone,

"Our judgment is that he shall be flayed alive, and then dragged to the gallows at this wretched mare's tail, with a strong nail through his feet, and there he shall be hanged in two chains, and there shall be written on the gallows: 'This is the traitor who sought to take the country from the King and who took the lives of both his sisters with a knife.' We have passed sentence. We have no more to say."

When the sentence had been passed and Godard had been shriven by a priest there was nothing for it but that he should lose his life. A man came with a knife and began to flay him from the toes upward, slashing off his skin as though it were a garment. The foul fiend roared loud enough to be heard a mile away, and cried "Mercy, mercy!" but the man would not stop until he had flayed every inch of him, with a knife made of ground steel. Then that scabby raw-boned mare was brought, and Godard was tied at her tail with an old sail-rope and dragged through the north gate, over the plowed fields, to the gallows. There he was hanged by the neck. A curse on anyone who pities him! He was false.

When the devil was dead the King gave all his possessions to Ubbe, with a handsome staff, and said, "Here I give you seizin[18] of all these lands and fees."

7

[So Havelok became a mighty King, and after he had reigned four years and made himself very

18. **seizin:** legal possession.

rich, Goldboro bade him go over into England to conquer her inheritance, from which her uncle had cast her out and so wickedly disinherited her. The King said he would do as she commanded. He got ready his fleet, gathered his hosts, and put to sea when the wind served, taking the Queen with him. Four score and four hundred ships had Havelok, full of men.

He steered and sailed so far that he came to Carleflure. They camped beside the harbor there and sought food in the country round about.][19]

Then Havelok swore that for Grim's sake he would found a priory of black monks[20] to serve Jesus Christ until Doomsday in memory of Grim's kindness to him when he was poor and miserable, and this he founded in the town where Grim was buried, which still bears his name. I will say no more about Grim.

That foul traitor, that filthy churl, Godrich, Earl of Cornwall, heard that Havelok was King of Denmark and had landed in England with a great army to win all the country, and that Goldboro, the lovely lady who was the rightful Queen of England, had arrived at Grimsby. Then Godrich was sad and sorry. "What shall I do?" he thought. "I must have them both killed, God knows. Unless he flees from my land, I will have them hanged—as I hope to keep my right eye! Does he think he can disinherit me?"

Godrich soon called out his army. Every man who could ride a horse, or wear a helmet and a coat of mail and carry a shield and a spear or any other weapon, hand-ax, scythe, halberd, short dagger or good long knife—every man who valued his life and limb must come to Godrich, where he lay at Lincoln, on the seventeenth day of March. All who came would earn his thanks. Anyone who was too proud to come, he swore by Christ and Saint John, should be made a slave, with all his children after him.

None of the Englishmen dared to disobey him, for they feared him as a nag fears the spur, and much more. They came on the day named, well armed and mounted as knights should be. The Earl was very soon ready to march against the Danes, and he said,

"Now listen, all of you. I have not brought you together for sport, and I will tell you why. Invaders have landed at Grimsby and have taken the priory, with all that they can find. They burn churches and bind priests, they strangle monks and nuns. What do you think of this, my friends? If they go on like this for long they may overcome us all—hang us up alive, make us their slaves, or kill us and our wives and children. Now you must do all that I command you, help both me and yourselves, and smite these dogs at once. For I shall never be happy again, or receive the sacrament or be shriven by a priest, until they are driven from the land. Let us go quickly to drive them out and follow me closely, all of you, for in the whole of the army I will be the first man to kill with my drawn sword. A curse on him who does not stand firm by me while his weapons last!"

"Yes, sire, yes!" cried Earl Gunter. "Yes!" cried Reyner, Earl of Chester. So did all who stood there, and they started forward as though mad to fight. They threw on their coats of mail and pulled them straight, and set their helmets high on their heads. They were ready in the time it takes to count a pound; then they sprang on to their horses and rode stealthily on their way until they came near Grimsby.

Havelok had sent to get news of their march. He came to meet them with his whole army, sparing neither knight nor peasant. The first knight whom he met he greeted by striking off his head. No sin could stop him. Robert saw that lovely blow and would not move until he had killed another. William Wendut slew the third, whose left arm went flying with his shield. Neither did Hugh Raven forget to use his sword. He smote an earl who was spurring his horse to a gallop, and cleft the earl's head in two; the keen blade swept down through the shoulder to the heart and the earl fell dead as a stone.

"I have waited too long," cried Ubbe, and taking another knight's spear he rode with it against Godrich. So fiercely and grimly they smote each other that they were both thrown headlong to the ground. Eagerly then they drew their sharp swords and fought like madmen. The sweat ran down them; they rained great blows upon each other. All day long they fought without a pause until the sun

---

19. [Hampden's note] There is a gap in the story here, a column or a page having been omitted by a copyist. The passage in brackets has been taken from *Le Lai d'Havelok*, a twelfth-century Anglo-French version. **20. priory . . . monks:** possibly Grimsby Abbey, with black-robed canons of the Augustinian order.

began to set, and then Godrich gave Ubbe such a wound in the side that it would have been the end of him, and his head would have been cut off, if he had not been saved by God and by Hugh Raven, who dragged him away from Godrich. But before that a thousand knights and more had been killed on both sides. There was such slaughter that blood filled every puddle in that field and flowed down into the hollow.

Then Godrich began to gain upon the Danes and slay them fast. He fell upon them like a lion which spares no beast it meets, so that they gave way before him and he killed everyone, dark or fair, that he could overtake. Neither knight nor man could face his blows. They went down like grass before a sharp scythe. But when Havelok saw them giving way he came galloping up on his horse and shouted.

"Godrich, what is wrong with you that you slay my good knights like this? You are acting wickedly. Remember how Athelwold made you kneel and swear on the Mass-book, the chalice and the paten that when his daughter came of age you would put all England into her hands. Earl Godrich, you know that well. Give up the land to her peacefully now, as is right. Then I will forgive the wrong you have done, and the deaths of my men, because you are so brave a knight of your body."

"That I will never do," answered Earl Godrich, "for I will slay you and hang Goldboro high. I will thrust out your right eye unless you turn and run."

Then he snatched his sword from its sheath, and cleft Havelok's shield in two. Disgraced like that in the sight of all his army, Havelok whipped out his good sword and dealt Godrich such a blow upon the helmet that it felled him to the earth, but he started up at once and smote Havelok on the shoulder. That stroke stripped more rings from Havelok's coat of mail than I can count, and wounded his tender flesh so that his blood ran down to his feet. How ashamed and angry Havelok was then! Fiercely he heaved up his sword and cut off the hand which had wounded him, and what greater shame could he do his foe? Then Havelok took him by the throat like a traitor—a curse on the man who pities him!—and sent him fettered with good steel fetters, to the Queen, bidding her guard him well because he was a knight and must not be beaten or disgraced before knights had judged him.

When the English saw that, they all believed that the beautiful Goldboro was the rightful Queen of England and that the King had wedded her and taken her to bed. With one voice they came to ask mercy of the King. They did homage to him and swore that never again would they take up arms against him, for weal or woe.

The King did not refuse their homage, but first he sent for the Queen, to see if they knew her, so that he could tell whether she ought to be Queen. Six earls set out at once and soon they brought her back who had no equal in courtesy under the moon. When she came all the Englishmen fell upon their knees, and wept bitterly, and cried,

"Lady, by Christ's grace and yours, we have sinned greatly in being disloyal to you, for England should be yours and we should be your men. Not one of us, young or old, but knows that Athelwold was king of all this kingdom and that you are his heiress. This traitor has held it wrongfully. God grant that he may soon hang high!"

"Since you know this to be so," said Havelok, "sit down and pass a fair judgment upon Godrich for what he has done. He has brought himself to grief, and justice spares neither cleric nor knight. Afterwards I will accept your homage, according to the law of the land, and accept your oaths too, if you agree."

They took their places at once, for no one dared to defy Havelok, and their sentence was that Godrich should be lashed to the back of a wretched ass, with his nose to its tail, and that he should be led to Lincoln in this shameful fashion. When he came to the town he should be led through it to a green on the south side—which is still there, I think—and there should be bound to a stake, with a great fire laid about him, and then he should be burned to ashes. And as a warning to other traitors his children should lose their heritage for ever, because of his evildoing.

When this sentence had been given the traitor was soon laid on the ass and taken to that same green and burned to ashes. Then Goldboro was overjoyed. She thanked God many a time that the foul traitor who tried to ruin her had been burned. "Now is the time," she said, "to receive homage from all. Now I am avenged on my foe."

Then Havelok made all the English pay him homage and swear great oaths that they would keep faith with him against any alive. When he had taken sureties as he wished from high and low, he summoned the Earl of Chester, who was a young bachelor, and all his men, and he said,

"Sir Earl, on my life, if you will follow my counsel I will do well by you, for I will give you to wife the finest woman alive, Gunnild of Grimsby, Grim's daughter, by Saint David. It was he who brought me from Denmark to save me from death, and it is certainly owing to his wisdom that I am still alive. Blessed be his soul forever! I advise you to wed her and to treat her courteously, for she is lovely, and generous and most gracious. She stands high in my favor, as I will show you, for I promise you that as long as I live you shall be dear to me because of her, and I wish all these people to hear this."

The Earl would not go against the King; he wedded her that same day. And never came two together in bed, clothed or naked, who lived as they did all their lives. They got five sons who were the best men that could ride a horse in the hour of need.

The good Havelok did not forget Bertram, the Earl's cook, but sent for him too and said,

"Now, my friend, you shall have a rich reward for the kindness that you did me in my great need. For when I had nothing to wear but a cloak, and neither bread nor anything else to eat, you fed me and clothed me well. Now you shall have the earldom of Cornwall as your reward and all the land that Godrich held in town and country, and I wish you to marry Grim's daughter, the beautiful Levive. Provide for her well and treat her courteously, for she is as fair as a flower on a tree. The color in her cheeks is the color of a rose when it first opens to the light and warmth of the sun."

Then he girded Bertram with the sword of the earldom, in the sight of his army, dubbed him knight with his own hand, gave him arms, as was fitting, and soon wed him to this lady who was so sweet in bed. After the wedding the Earl would not linger there but went to take possession of his lands, where he lived a good life with his wife for a hundred winters. They got many children and lived happily always.

When both these maidens were wed, Havelok enriched all his Danes with lands and goods, for he was generous, not mean. Then he marched to London with his army, so that English and Danes, high and low, could see how proudly he wore the crown before his many barons. At this crowning the feast lasted with great joy for forty days or more, after which the Danes began asking the King's leave to depart. He would not grieve them, for he saw that they were eager to go back to Denmark, so he gave them leave and commended them to the care of Saint John. He bade Ubbe govern and guard Denmark so well that no complaint would be made to him.

After they had all gone, Havelok lived joyfully and merrily in England. He and Goldboro ruled there for sixty winters, and there was so much love between these two that all the world spoke of them. They could never be parted; they had no joy in life unless they were together, and they were never angry, for their love was always new; never a word passed between them which could give rise to wrath. They got fifteen sons and daughters, all of whom, by God's will, were kings and queens. "It is well with him who begets a good child."

Now you have heard the tale of Havelok and Goldboro—how they were born and how they were bred, how they met with treachery and evil in their youth, how the traitors sought to rob them of their rights, and how they were well revenged. I have told you everything about them.

So now I beseech all of you who have heard this rhyme to say a Paternoster for him who made the rhyme, and forwent many a night's sleep to make it: that at his life's end Jesus Christ may bring his soul before God the Father.

Amen.

JOHN KEATS
1795–1821

The Eve of Saint Agnes

1

Saint Agnes' Eve°—Ah, bitter chill it was!
The owl, for all his feathers, was a-cold;
The hare limped trembling through the frozen grass,

THE EVE OF SAINT AGNES. **1. Saint . . . Eve:** January 21, anniversary of the martydom of the Roman woman who became the patron saint of virgins.

And silent was the flock in woolly fold:
Numb were the Beadsman's° fingers, while he
    told   5
His rosary, and while his frosted breath,
Like pious incense from a censer old,
Seemed taking flight for heaven, without a death,
Past the sweet Virgin's picture, while his prayer he
    saith.

2

His prayer he saith, this patient, holy man;   10
Then takes his lamp, and riseth from his knees,
And back returneth, meager, barefoot, wan,
Along the chapel aisle by slow degrees:
The sculptured dead, on each side, seem to
    freeze,
Emprisoned in black, purgatorial rails: 15
Knights, ladies, praying in dumb orat'ries,
He passeth by; and his weak spirit fails
To think how they may ache in icy hoods and mails.

3

Northward he turneth through a little door,
And scarce three steps, ere Music's golden
    tongue   20
Flattered to tears this aged man and poor;
But no—already had his deathbell rung;
The joys of all his life were said and sung:
His was harsh penance on Saint Agnes' Eve:
Another way he went, and soon among   25
Rough ashes sat he for his soul's reprieve,
And all night kept awake, for sinners' sake to
    grieve.

4

That ancient Beadsman heard the prelude soft;
And so it chanced, for many a door was wide,
From hurry to and fro. Soon, up aloft,   30
The silver, snarling trumpets 'gan to chide:
The level chambers, ready with their pride,
Were glowing to receive a thousand guests:
The carvèd angels, ever eager-eyed,
Stared, where upon their heads the cornice rests,
With hair blown back, and wings put crosswise on
    their breasts.   36

5. **Beadsman:** person hired to pray (tell beads) for a patron.

5

At length burst in the argent° revelry,
With plume, tiara, and all rich array,
Numerous as shadows haunting faerily
The brain, new stuffed, in youth, with triumphs
    gay   40
Of old romance. These let us wish away,
And turn, sole-thoughted, to one Lady there,
Whose heart had brooded, all that wintry day,
On love, and winged Saint Agnes' saintly care,
As she had heard old dames full many times
    declare.   45

6

They told her how, upon Saint Agnes' Eve,
Young virgins might have visions of delight,
And soft adorings from their loves receive
Upon the honeyed middle of the night,
If ceremonies due they did aright   50
As, supperless to bed they must retire,
And couch supine their beauties, lily white;
Nor look behind, nor sideways, but require
Of Heaven with upward eyes for all that they desire.

['Twas said her future lord would there appear,
Offering as sacrifice—all in the dream—   56
Delicious food even to her lips brought near:
Viands and wine and fruit and sugared cream,
To touch her palate with the fine extreme
Of relish; then soft music heard; and then   60
More pleasures followed in a dizzy stream
Palpable almost; then to wake again
Warm in the virgin morn, no weeping Magdalen.°]

7

Full of this whim was thoughtful Madeline:
The music, yearning like a god in pain,   65
She scarcely heard; her maiden eyes divine,
Fixed on the floor, saw many a sweeping train
Pass by—she needed not at all: in vain
Came many a tiptoe, amorous cavalier,
And back retired; not cooled by high disdain,   70
But she saw not: her heart was otherwhere:
She sighed for Agnes' dreams, the sweetest of the
    year.

37. **argent:** silver. 55–63. **'Twas . . . Magdalen:** This stanza
from a manuscript version of the poem in the de Selincourt
edition (1905) is included here as an explanation of ll. 133 ff.
Magdalen: penitent prostitute.

8

She danced along with vague, regardless eyes,
Anxious her lips, her breathing quick and short:
The hallowed hour was near at hand; she sighs 75
Amid the timbrels,° and the thronged resort
Of whisperers in anger, or in sport;
'Mid looks of love, defiance, hate, and scorn,
Hoodwinked with faery fancy; all amort,°
Save to Saint Agnes and her lambs unshorn,° 80
And all the bliss to be before tomorrow morn.

9

So, purposing each moment to retire,
She lingered still. Meantime, across the moors,
Had come young Porphyro, with heart on fire
For Madeline. Beside the portal doors,   85
Buttressed° from moonlight, stands he, and
    implores
All saints to give him sight of Madeline,
But for one moment in the tedious hours,
That he might gaze and worship all unseen;
Perchance speak, kneel, touch, kiss—in sooth such
    things have been.   90

10

He ventures in: let no buzzed whisper tell;
All eyes be muffled, or a hundred swords
Will storm his heart, love's feverous citadel:
For him, those chambers held barbarian hordes,
Hyena foemen, and hot-blooded lords,   95
Whose very dogs would execrations howl
Against his lineage: not one breast affords
Him any mercy, in that mansion foul,
Save one old beldame, weak in body and in soul.

11

Ah, happy chance! the aged creature came,   100
Shuffling along with ivory-headed wand,
To where he stood, hid from the torch's flame,
Behind a broad hall-pillar, far beyond
The sound of merriment and chorus bland:
He startled her; but soon she knew his face, 105
And grasped his fingers in her palsied hand,

76. timbrels: small tambourines. **79. amort:** deathlike.
80. Saint . . . unshorn: reference to the custom of offering
lambs wool on the altar for nuns to weave into garments;
see ll. 124–26. **86. Buttressed:** hidden by a buttress.

Saying, "Mercy, Porphyro! hie thee from this
    place;
They are all here tonight, the whole bloodthirsty
    race!

12

"Get hence! get hence! there's dwarfish Hilde-
    brand;
He had a fever late, and in the fit   110
He cursèd thee and thine, both house and land;
Then there's that old Lord Maurice, not a whit
More tame for his gray hairs—Alas me! flit!
Flit like a ghost away."—"Ah, Gossip dear,
We're safe enough; here in this armchair sit, 115
And tell me how"—"Good Saints! not here, not
    here;
Follow me, child, or else these stones will be thy
    bier."

13

He followed through a lowly archèd way,
Brushing the cobwebs with his lofty plume,
And as she muttered "Well-a—well-a-day!"   120
He found him in a little moonlight room,
Pale, latticed, chill, and silent as a tomb.
"Now tell me where is Madeline," said he,
"O tell me, Angela, by the holy loom
Which none but secret sisterhood may see,   125
When they Saint Agnes' wool are weaving piously."

14

"Saint Agnes! Ah! it is Saint Agnes' Eve—
Yet men will murder upon holy days:
Thou must hold water in a witch's sieve,
And be liege-lord of all the Elves and Fays, 130
To venture so: it fills me with amaze
To see thee, Porphyro!—Saint Agnes' Eve!
God's help! my lady fair the conjurer plays
This very night: good angels her deceive!
But let me laugh awhile, I've mickle° time to
    grieve."   135

15

Feebly she laugheth in the languid moon,
While Porphyro upon her face doth look,

135. mickle: much.

Like puzzled urchin on an aged crone
Who keepeth closed a wond'rous riddle-book,
As spectacled she sits in chimney nook.   140
But soon his eyes grew brilliant, when she told
His lady's purpose; and he scarce could brook
Tears, at the thought of those enchantments cold,
And Madeline asleep in lap of legends old.

16

Sudden a thought came like a full-blown rose, 145
Flushing his brow, and in his painèd heart
Made purple riot; then doth he propose
A strategem, that makes the beldame start:
"A cruel man and impious thou art:
Sweet lady, let her pray, and sleep, and dream
Alone with her good angels, far apart   151
From wicked men like thee. Go, go!—I deem
Thou canst not surely be the same that thou didst
    seem."

17

"I will not harm her, by all saints I swear,"
Quoth Porphyro: "O may I ne'er find grace   155
When my weak voice shall whisper its last
    prayer,
If one of her soft ringlets I displace,
Or look with ruffian passion in her face;
Good Angela, believe me by these tears,
Or I will, even in a moment's space,   160
Awake, with horrid shout, my foemen's ears,
And beard them, though they be more fanged than
    wolves and bears."

18

"Ah! why wilt thou affright a feeble soul?
A poor, weak, palsy-stricken, churchyard thing,
Whose passing-bell may ere the midnight toll;
Whose prayers for thee, each morn and evening,
Were never missed."—Thus plaining, doth she
    bring   167
A gentler speech from burning Porphyro;
So woeful, and of such deep sorrowing,
That Angela gives promise she will do   170
Whatever he shall wish, betide her weal or woe.

19

Which was, to lead him, in close secrecy,
Even to Madeline's chamber, and there hide
Him in a closet, of such privacy
That he might see her beauty unespied,   175
And win perhaps that night a peerless bride,
While legioned faeries paced the coverlet,
And pale enchantment held her sleepy-eyed.
Never on such a night have lovers met,
Since Merlin paid his Demon all the monstrous
    debt.°   180

20

"It shall be as thou wishest," said the Dame:
"All cates° and dainties shall be stored there
Quickly on this feast-night: by the tambour
    frame°
Her own lute thou wilt see; no time to spare,
For I am slow and feeble, and scarce dare   185
On such a catering trust my dizzy head.
Wait here, my child, with patience; kneel in
    prayer
The while. Ah! thou must needs the lady wed,
Or may I never leave my grave among the dead."

21

So saying, she hobbled off with busy fear.   190
The lover's endless minutes slowly passed;
The dame returned, and whispered in his ear
To follow her; with aged eyes aghast
From fright of dim espial. Safe at last,
Through many a dusky gallery, they gain   195
The maiden's chamber, silken, hushed, and
    chaste;
Where Porphyro took covert, pleased amain.
His poor guide hurried back with agues in her brain.

22

Her faltering hand upon the balustrade,
Old Angela was feeling for the stair,   200

---

180. **Since . . . debt:** allusion to the legend that Merlin,
begotten by a demon, later used his magical powers to
assist Uther in his courtship of Igerna (Ygerne), the
duchess of Cornwall; Uther appeared to her as her husband
and begot Arthur. **182. cates:** delicacies. **183. tambour
frame:** embroidery frame.

When Madeline, Saint Agnes' charmèd maid,
Rose, like a missioned spirit, unaware:
With silver taper's light, and pious care,
She turned, and down the aged gossip led
To a safe level matting. Now prepare,   205
Young Porphyro, for gazing on that bed;
She comes, she comes again, like ringdove frayed°
    and fled.

23

Out went the taper as she hurried in;
Its little smoke, in pallid moonshine, died;
She closed the door, she panted, all akin   210
To spirits of the air, and visions wide:
No uttered syllable, or, woe betide!
But to her heart, her heart was voluble,
Paining with eloquence her balmy side;
As though a tongueless nightingale should swell
Her throat in vain, and die, heart-stifled, in her
    dell.   216

24

A casement high and triple-arched there was,
All garlanded with carven imageries
Of fruits, and flowers, and bunches of knotgrass,
And diamonded with panes of quaint device,   220
Innumerable of stains and splendid dyes,
As are the tiger-moth's deep-damasked wings;
And in the midst, 'mong thousand heraldries,
And twilight saints, and dim emblazonings,
A shielded scutcheon blushed with blood of queens
    and kings.   225

25

Full on this casement shone the wintry moon,
And threw warm gules on Madeline's fair breast,
As down she knelt for heaven's grace and boon;
Rose-bloom fell on her hands, together pressed,
And on her silver cross soft amethyst,   230
And on her hair a glory, like a saint:
She seemed a splendid angel, newly dressed,
Save wings, for heaven:—Porphyro grew faint:
She knelt, so pure a thing, so free from mortal taint.

26

Anon his heart revives: her vespers done,   235
Of all its wreathèd pearls her hair she frees;
Unclasps her warmèd jewels one by one;
Loosens her fragrant bodice; by degrees
Her rich attire creeps rustling to her knees.
Half-hidden, like a mermaid in seaweed,   240
Pensive awhile she dreams awake, and sees,
In fancy, fair Saint Agnes in her bed,
But dares not look behind, or all the charm is fled.

27

Soon, trembling in her soft and chilly nest,
In sort of wakeful swoon, perplexed she lay,   245
Until the poppied warmth of sleep oppressed
Her soothèd limbs, and soul fatigued away;
Flown, like a thought until the morrow-day;
Blissfully havened both from joy and pain;
Clasped like a missal where swart Paynims° pray;
Blinded alike from sunshine and from rain,   251
As though a rose should shut, and be a bud again.

28

Stolen to this paradise, and so entranced,
Porphyro gazed upon her empty dress,
And listened to her breathing, if it chanced   255
To wake into a slumberous tenderness;
Which when he heard, that minute did he bless,
And breathed himself: then from the closet
    crept,
Noiseless as fear in a wide wilderness,
And over the hushed carpet, silent, stepped,   260
And 'tween the curtains peeped, where, lo!—how
    fast she slept.

29

Then by the bedside, where the faded moon
Made a dim, silver twilight, soft he set
A table, and, half anguished, threw thereon
A cloth of woven crimson, gold, and jet:—   265
O for some drowsy Morphean amulet!°
The boisterous, midnight, festive clarion,
The kettledrum, and far-heard clarionet,
Affray his ears, though but in dying tone:—
The hall door shuts again, and all the noise is gone.

207. frayed: frightened.

250. swart Paynims: dark pagans. **266. Morphean amulet:**
opiate; Morpheus was the god of dreams.

30

And still she slept an azure-lidded sleep,   271
In blanchèd linen, smooth, and lavendered,
While he from forth the closet brought a heap
Of candied apple, quince, and plum, and gourd;
With jellies soother than the creamy curd,   275
And lucent syrups, tinct with cinnamon;
Manna and dates, in argosy transferred
From Fez; and spicèd dainties, every one,
From silken Samarkand to cedared Lebanon.

31

These delicates he heaped with glowing hand 280
On golden dishes and in baskets bright
Of wreathèd silver: sumptuous they stand
In the retirèd quiet of the night,
Filling the chilly room with perfume light.—
"And now, my love, my seraph fair, awake!   285
Thou art my heaven, and I thine eremite:
Open thine eyes, for meek Saint Agnes' sake,
Or I shall drowse beside thee, so my soul doth
    ache."

32

Thus whispering, his warm, unnervèd arm
Sank in her pillow. Shaded was her dream   290
By the dusk curtains:—'twas a midnight charm
Impossible to melt as icèd stream:
The lustrous salvers in the moonlight gleam;
Broad golden fringe upon the carpet lies:
It seemed he never, never could redeem   295
From such a steadfast spell his lady's eyes;
So mused awhile, entoiled in woofèd fantasies.°

33

Awakening up, he took her hollow lute,—
Tumultuous,—and, in chords that tenderest be,
He played an ancient ditty, long since mute, 300
In Provence called, "La belle dame sans merci,"°
Close to her ear touching the melody;—
Wherewith disturbed she uttered a soft moan:
He ceased—she panted quick—and suddenly
Her blue affrayèd eyes wide open shone: 305
Upon his knees he sank, pale as smooth-sculptured
    stone.

297. entoiled . . . fantasies: entangled in woven fantasies.
301. "La . . . merci": the beautiful lady without mercy.

34

Her eyes were open, but she still beheld,
Now wide awake, the vision of her sleep:
There was a painful change, that nigh expelled
The blisses of her dream so pure and deep   310
At which fair Madeline began to weep,
And moan forth witless words with many a sigh;
While still her gaze on Porphyro would keep;
Who knelt, with joinèd hands and piteous eye,
Fearing to move or speak, she looked so dream-
    ingly.   315

35

"Ah, Porphyro!" said she, "but even now
Thy voice was at sweet tremble in mine ear,
Made tunable with every sweetest vow;
And those sad eyes were spiritual and clear.
How changed thou art; how pallid, chill, and
    drear!   320
Give me that voice again, my Porphyro,
Those looks immortal, those complainings dear!
Oh, leave me not in this eternal woe,
For if thou diest, my Love, I know not where to
    go."

36

Beyond a mortal man impassioned far   325
At these voluptuous accents, he arose,
Ethereal, flushed, and like a throbbing star
Seen mid the sapphire heaven's deep repose;
Into her dream he melted, as the rose
Blendeth its odor with the violet,—   330
Solution sweet: meantime the frost-wind blows
Like Love's alarum, pattering the sharp sleet
Against the windowpanes; Saint Agnes' moon hath
    set.

37

'Tis dark: quick pattereth the flaw-blown° sleet.
"This is no dream, my bride, my Madeline!"   335
'Tis dark: the icèd gusts still rave and beat.
"No dream, alas! alas! and woe is mine!
Porphyro will leave me here to fade and pine.
Cruel! what traitor could thee hither bring?
I curse not, for my heart is lost in thine,   340

334. flaw-blown: wind-blown.

Though thou forsakest a deceivèd thing;—
A dove forlorn and lost with sick unprunèd wing."

38

"My Madeline! sweet dreamer! lovely bride!
Say, may I be for aye thy vassal blest?
Thy beauty's shield, heart-shaped and vermeil°
    dyed?   345
Ah, silver shrine, here will I take my rest
After so many hours of toil and quest,
A famished pilgrim,—saved by miracle.
Though I have found, I will not rob thy nest
Saving of thy sweet self; if thou think'st well   350
To trust, fair Madeline, to no rude infidel.

39

"Hark! 'tis an elfin-storm from faery land.
Of haggard° seeming, but a boon indeed:
Arise—arise! the morning is at hand;—
The bloated wassailers will never heed: 355
Let us away, my love, with happy speed;
There are no ears to hear, or eyes to see,—
Drowned all in Rhenish° and the sleepy mead:
Awake! arise! my love, and fearless be,
For o'er the southern moors I have a home for
    thee."   360

40

She hurried at his words, beset with fears,
For there were sleeping dragons all around,
At glaring watch, perhaps, with ready spears—
Down the wide stairs a darkling way they found.
In all the house was heard no human sound.   365
A chain-drooped lamp was flickering by each
    door;
The arras, rich with horseman, hawk, and hound,
Fluttered in the besieging wind's uproar;
And the long carpets rose along the gusty floor.

41

They glide, like phantoms, into the wide hall;   370
Like phantoms, to the iron porch they glide;
Where lay the Porter, in uneasy sprawl,
With a huge empty flagon by his side:

345. **vermeil:** vermilion. **353. haggard:** witch-like, wild.
358. Rhenish: Rhine wine.

The wakeful bloodhound rose, and shook his
    hide,
But his sagacious eye an inmate owns: 375
By one, and one, the bolts full easy slide:—
The chains lie silent on the footworn stones;—
The key turns, and the door upon its hinges groans.

42

And they are gone: aye, ages long ago
These lovers fled away into the storm.   380
That night the Baron dreamt of many a woe,
And all his warrior-guests, with shade and form
Of witch, and demon, and large coffin-worm,
Were long be-nightmared. Angela the old
Died palsy-twitched, with meager face deform;
The Beadsman, after thousand aves told,   386
For aye unsought for slept among his ashes cold.

ALFRED, LORD TENNYSON
1809–1892

from Idylls of the King

DEDICATION

These to His Memory—since he held them dear,
Perchance as finding there unconsciously
Some image of himself—I dedicate,°
I dedicate, I consecrate with tears—
These Idylls.

        And indeed he seems to me   5
Scarce other than my king's ideal knight,
"Who reverenced his conscience as his king;
Whose glory was, redressing human wrong;
Who spake no slander, no, nor listened to it;
Who loved one only and who clave to her—"°   10
Her—over all whose realms to their last isle,
Commingled with the gloom of imminent war,°
The shadow of his loss drew like eclipse,

IDYLLS OF THE KING: *Dedication.* **1–4. These . . . dedicate:**
The *Idylls* were dedicated to Prince Albert (1819–61), a
native of Germany, consort of Queen Victoria, and Tennyson's model for King Arthur. **7–10. Who . . . her:** lines
adapted from the concluding *Idyll*, "Guinevere," ll. 464–79.
12. war: In 1861 war was imminent between Great Britain
and the United States.

Darkening the world. We have lost him: he is gone:
We know him now: all narrow jealousies   15
Are silent; and we see him as he moved,
How modest, kindly, all-accomplished, wise,
With what sublime repression of himself,
And in what limits, and how tenderly;
Not swaying to this faction or to that;   20
Not making his high place the lawless perch
Of winged ambitions, nor a vantage-ground
For pleasure; but through all this tract of years
Wearing the white flower of a blameless life,
Before a thousand peering littlenesses,   25
In that fierce light which beats upon a throne,
And blackens every blot: for where is he,
Who dares foreshadow for an only son
A lovelier life, a more unstained, than his?
Or how should England dreaming of *his* sons   30
Hope more for these than some inheritance
Of such a life, a heart, a mind as thine,
Thou noble Father of her Kings to be,
Laborious for her people and her poor—
Voice in the rich dawn of an ampler day—   35
Far-sighted summoner of War and Waste
To fruitful strifes and rivalries of peace—
Sweet nature gilded by the gracious gleam
Of letters, dear to Science, dear to Art,
Dear to thy land and ours, a Prince indeed,   40
Beyond all titles, and a household name,
Hereafter, through all times, Albert the Good.

Break not, O woman's-heart, but still endure;
Break not, for thou art Royal, but endure,
Remembering all the beauty of that star   45
Which shone so close beside thee that ye made
One light together, but has passed and leaves
The Crown a lonely splendor.

                     May all love,
His love, unseen but felt, o'ershadow thee,   50
The love of all thy sons encompass thee,
The love of all thy daughters cherish thee,
The love of all thy people comfort thee,
Till God's love set thee at his side again!

THE COMING OF ARTHUR

Leodogran the king of Cameliard,
Had one fair daughter, and none other child;
And she was fairest of all flesh on earth,
Guinevere, and in her his one delight.

For many a petty king ere Arthur came   5
Ruled in this isle, and ever waging war
Each upon other, wasted all the land;
And still from time to time the heathen host
Swarmed overseas, and harried what was left.
And so there grew great tracts of wilderness,   10
Wherein the beast was ever more and more,
But man was less and less, till Arthur came.
For first Aurelius° lived and fought and died,
And after him King Uther fought and died,
But either failed to make the kingdom one.   15
And after these King Arthur for a space,
And through the puissance of his Table Round,
Drew all their petty princedoms under him,
Their king and head, and made a realm, and
    reigned.

And thus the land of Cameliard was waste,   20
Thick with wet woods, and many a beast therein,
And none or few to scare or chase the beast;
So that wild dog, and wolf and boar and bear
Came night and day, and rooted in the fields,
And wallowed in the gardens of the king.   25
And ever and anon the wolf would steal
The children and devour, but now and then,
Her own brood lost or dead, lent her fierce teat
To human sucklings; and the children, housed
In her foul den, there at their meat would growl,
And mock their foster-mother on four feet,   31
Till, straightened, they grew up to wolflike men,
Worse than the wolves. And King Leodogran
Groaned for the Roman legions here again,
And Caesar's eagle: then his brother king,   35
Urien, assailed him: last a heathen horde,
Reddening the sun with smoke and earth with
    blood,
And on the spike that split the mother's heart
Spitting the child, brake on him, till, amazed,
He knew not whither he should turn for aid.   40

But—for he heard of Arthur newly crowned,
Though not without an uproar made by those
Who cried, "He is not Uther's son"—the king
Sent to him, saying, "Arise, and help us thou!
For here between the man and beast we die."   45

And Arthur yet had done no deed of arms,
But heard the call, and came: and Guinevere
Stood by the castle walls to watch him pass;

The Coming of Arthur. **13. Aurelius:** brother of Uther
and descendant of the last Roman general governing
England.

But since he neither wore on helm or shield
The golden symbol of his kinglihood,   50
But rode a simple knight among his knights,
And many of these in richer arms than he,
She saw him not, or marked not, if she saw,
One among many, though his face was bare.
But Arthur, looking downward as he passed,   55
Felt the light of her eyes into his life
Smite on the sudden, yet rode on, and pitched
His tents beside the forest. Then he drave
The heathen; after, slew the beast, and felled
The forest, letting in the sun, and made   60
Broad pathways for the hunter and the knight
And so returned.

               For while he lingered there,
A doubt that ever smoldered in the hearts
Of those great lords and barons of his realm
Flashed forth and into war: for most of these,   65
Colleaguing with a score of petty kings,
Made head against him, crying, "Who is he
That he should rule us? who hath proven him
King Uther's son? for lo! we look at him,
And find nor face nor bearing, limbs nor voice, 70
Are like to those of Uther whom we knew.
This is the son of Gorloïs, not the king;
This is the son of Anton, not the king."

And Arthur, passing thence to battle, felt
Travail, and throes and agonies of the life,   75
Desiring to be joined with Guinevere;
And thinking as he rode, "Her father said
That there between the man and beast they die.
Shall I not lift her from this land of beasts
Up to my throne, and side by side with me?   80
What happiness to reign a lonely king,
Vexed—O ye stars that shudder over me,
O earth that soundest hollow under me,
Vexed with waste dreams? for saving I be joined
To her that is the fairest under heaven,   85
I seem as nothing in the mighty world,
And cannot will my will, nor work my work
Wholly, nor make myself in mine own realm
Victor and lord. But were I joined with her,
Then might we live together as one life,   90
And reigning with one will in everything
Have power on this dark land to lighten it,
And power on this dead world to make it live."

Thereafter—as he speaks who tells the tale—
When Arthur reached a field-of-battle bright   95

With pitched pavilions of his foe, the world
Was all so clear about him, that he saw
The smallest rock far on the faintest hill,
And even in high day the morning star.
So when the king had set his banner broad,   100
At once from either side, with trumpet-blast,
And shouts, and clarions shrilling unto blood,
The long-lanced battle let their horses run.
And now the barons and the kings prevailed,
And now the king, as here and there that war 105
Went swaying; but the Powers who walk the world
Made lightnings and great thunders over him,
And dazed all eyes, till Arthur by main might,
And mightier of his hands with every blow,
And leading all his knighthood threw the kings
Carádos, Urien, Cradlemont of Wales,   111
Claudius, and Clariance of Northumberland,
The king Brandagoras of Latangor,
With Anguisant of Erin, Morganore,
And Lot of Orkney. Then, before a voice   115
As dreadful as the shout of one who sees
To one who sins, and deems himself alone
And all the world asleep, they swerved and brake
Flying, and Arthur called to stay the brands°
That hacked among the flyers, "Ho! they yield!"
So like a painted battle the war stood   121
Silenced, the living quiet as the dead,
And in the heart of Arthur joy was lord.
He laughed upon his warrior° whom he loved 124
And honored most. "Thou dost not doubt me king,
So well thine arm hath wrought for me today."
"Sir and my liege," he cried, "the fire of God
Descends upon thee in the battlefield:
I know thee for my king!" Whereat the two,
For each had warded either in the fight,   130
Sware on the field of death a deathless love.
And Arthur said, "Man's word is God in man:°
Let chance what will, I trust thee to the death."

Then quickly from the foughten field he sent
Ulfius, and Brastias, and Bedivere,   135
His new-made knights, to King Leodogran,
Saying, "If I in aught have served thee well,
Give me thy daughter Guinevere to wife."

Whom when he heard, Leodogran in heart
Debating—"How should I that am a king,   140
However much he holp me at my need,
Give my one daughter saving to a king,

119. brands: swords. **124. warrior:** Sir Lancelot. **132. Man's . . . man:** Man's word is sacred.

And a king's son?"—lifted his voice, and called
A hoary man, his chamberlain, to whom
He trusted all things, and of him required   145
His counsel: "Knowest thou aught of Arthur's
   birth?"

Then spake the hoary chamberlain and said,
"Sir King, there be but two old men that know:
And each is twice as old as I; and one
Is Merlin, the wise man that ever served   150
King Uther through his magic art; and one
Is Merlin's master (so they call him) Bleys,
Who taught him magic; but the scholar ran
Before the master, and so far, that Bleys
Laid magic by, and sat him down, and wrote   155
All things and whatsoever Merlin did
In one great annal-book, where after-years
Will learn the secret of our Arthur's birth."

To whom the King Leodogran replied,
"O friend, had I been holpen half as well   160
By this King Arthur as by thee today,
Then beast and man had had their share of me:
But summon here before us yet once more
Ulfius, and Brastias, and Bedivere."

Then, when they came before him, the king said, 165
"I have seen the cuckoo chased by lesser fowl,
And reason in the chase: but wherefore now
Do these your lords stir up the heat of war,
Some calling Arthur born of Gorloïs,
Others of Anton? Tell me, ye yourselves,   170
Hold ye this Arthur for King Uther's son?"

And Ulfius and Brastias answered, "Aye."
Then Bedivere, the first of all his knights
Knighted by Arthur at his crowning, spake—
For gold in heart and act and word was he,   175
Whenever slander breathed against the king—

"Sir, there be many rumors on this head:
For there be those who hate him in their hearts,
Call him baseborn, and since his ways are sweet,
And theirs are bestial, hold him less than man: 180
And there be those who deem him more than man,
And dream he dropped from heaven: but my belief
In all this matter—so ye care to learn—
Sir, for ye know that in King Uther's time
The prince and warrior Gorloïs, he that held   185
Tintagil castle by the Cornish sea,
Was wedded with a winsome wife, Ygerne:

And daughters had she borne him,—one whereof,
Lot's wife, the queen of Orkney, Bellicent,
Hath ever like a loyal sister cleaved   190
To Arthur,—but a son she had not borne.
And Uther cast upon her eyes of love:
But she, a stainless wife to Gorloïs,
So loathed the bright dishonor of his love,
That Gorloïs and King Uther went to war: 195
And overthrown was Gorloïs and slain.
Then Uther in his wrath and heat besieged
Ygerne within Tintagil, where her men,
Seeing the mighty swarm about their walls,
Left her and fled, and Uther entered in,   200
And there was none to call to but himself.
So, compassed by the power of the king,
Enforced she was to wed him in her tears,
And with a shameful swiftness: afterward,
Not many moons, King Uther died himself,   205
Moaning and wailing for an heir to rule
After him, lest the realm should go to wrack.
And that same night, the night of the new year,
By reason of the bitterness and grief
That vexed his mother, all before his time   210
Was Arthur born, and all as soon as born
Delivered at a secret postern-gate
To Merlin, to be holden far apart
Until his hour should come; because the lords
Of that fierce day were as the lords of this, 215
Wild beasts, and surely would have torn the child
Piecemeal among them, had they known; for each
But sought to rule for his own self and hand,
And many hated Uther for the sake
Of Gorloïs. Wherefore Merlin took the child,   220
And gave him to Sir Anton, an old knight
And ancient friend of Uther; and his wife
Nursed the young prince, and reared him with her
   own;
And no man knew. And ever since the lords   224
Have foughten like wild beasts among themselves,
So that the realm has gone to wrack: but now,
This year, when Merlin (for his hour had come)
Brought Arthur forth, and set him in the hall,
Proclaiming, 'Here is Uther's heir, your king,'
A hundred voices cried, 'Away with him!   230
No king of ours! a son of Gorloïs he,
Or else the child of Anton, and no king,
Or else baseborn.' Yet Merlin through his craft,
And while the people clamored for a king,
Had Arthur crowned; but after, the great lords
Banded, and so brake out in open war."   236

Then while the king debated with himself
If Arthur were the child of shamefulness,
Or born the son of Gorloïs, after death,
Or Uther's son, and born before his time,   240
Or whether there were truth in anything
Said by these three, there came to Cameliard,
With Gawain and young Modred, her two sons,
Lot's wife, the queen of Orkney, Bellicent;
Whom as he could, not as he would, the king 245
Made feast for, saying, as they sat at meat,

"A doubtful throne is ice on summer seas.
Ye come from Arthur's court. Victor his men
Report him! Yea, but ye—think ye this king—
So many those that hate him, and so strong,   250
So few his knights, however brave they be—
Hath body enow to hold his foemen down?"

"O king," she cried, "and I will tell thee: few,
Few, but all brave, all of one mind with him;
For I was near him when the savage yells   255
Of Uther's peerage died, and Arthur sat
Crowned on the dais, and his warriors cried,
'Be thou the king, and we will work thy will
Who love thee.' Then the king in low deep tones,
And simple words of great authority,   260
Bound them by so strait vows to his own self,
That when they rose, knighted from kneeling, some
Were pale as at the passing of a ghost,
Some flushed, and others dazed, as one who wakes
Half-blinded at the coming of a light.   265

"But when he spake and cheered his Table Round
With large, divine, and comfortable words,
Beyond my tongue to tell thee—I beheld
From eye to eye through all their order flash
A momentary likeness of the king: 270
And ere it left their faces, through the cross
And those around it and the Crucified,
Down from the casement over Arthur, smote
Flame-color, vert° and azure, in three rays,
One falling upon each of three fair queens,   275
Who stood in silence near his throne, the friends
Of Arthur, gazing on him, tall, with bright
Sweet faces, who will help him at his need.

"And there I saw mage Merlin, whose vast wit
And hundred winters are but as the hands   280
Of loyal vassals toiling for their liege.

"And near him stood the Lady of the Lake,
Who knows a subtler magic than his own—

274. vert: green.

Clothed in white samite, mystic, wonderful.
She gave the king his huge cross-hilted sword, 285
Whereby to drive the heathen out: a mist
Of incense curled about her, and her face
Well-nigh was hidden in the minster gloom;
But there was heard among the holy hymns
A voice as of the waters, for she dwells   290
Down in a deep; calm, whatsoever storms
May shake the world, and when the surface rolls,
Hath power to walk the waters like our Lord.

"There likewise I beheld Excalibur
Before him at his crowning borne, the sword   295
That rose from out the bosom of the lake,
And Arthur rowed across and took it—rich
With jewels, elfin Urim, on the hilt,
Bewildering heart and eye—the blade so bright
That men are blinded by it—on one side,   300
Graven in the oldest tongue of all this world,
'Take me,' but turn the blade and ye shall see,
And written in the speech ye speak yourself,
'Cast me away!' And sad was Arthur's face
Taking it, but old Merlin counseled him,   305
'Take thou and strike! the time to cast away
Is yet far-off.' So this great brand the king
Took, and by this will beat his foemen down."

Thereat Leodogran rejoiced, but thought
To sift his doubtings to the last, and asked, 310
Fixing full eyes of question on her face,
"The swallow and the swift are near akin,
But thou art closer to this noble prince,
Being his own dear sister;" and she said,
"Daughter of Gorloïs and Ygerne am I;"   315
"And therefore Arthur's sister?" asked the king.
She answered, "These be secret things," and signed
To those two sons to pass, and let them be.
And Gawain went, and breaking into song
Sprang out, and followed by his flying hair   320
Ran like a colt, and leapt at all he saw:
But Modred laid his ear beside the doors,
And there half-heard; the same that afterward
Struck for the throne, and striking found his doom.

And then the queen made answer, "What know I?
For dark my mother was in eyes and hair,   326
And dark in hair and eyes am I; and dark
Was Gorloïs, yea and dark was Uther too,
Well-nigh to blackness; but this king is fair
Beyond the race of Britons and of men.   330
Moreover, always in my mind I hear

A cry from out the dawning of my life,
A mother weeping, and I hear her say,
'O that ye had some brother, pretty one,   334
To guard thee on the rough ways of the world.' "

"Aye," said the king, "and hear ye such a cry?
But when did Arthur chance upon thee first?"

"O king!" she cried, "and I will tell thee true:
He found me first when yet a little maid:
Beaten had I been for a little fault   340
Whereof I was not guilty; and out I ran
And flung myself down on a bank of heath,
And hated this fair world and all therein,
And wept, and wished that I were dead; and he—
I know not whether of himself he came,   345
Or brought by Merlin, who, they say, can walk
Unseen at pleasure—he was at my side,
And spake sweet words, and comforted my heart,
And dried my tears, being a child with me.
And many a time he came, and evermore   350
As I grew greater grew with me; and sad
At times he seemed, and sad with him was I,
Stern too at times, and then I loved him not,
But sweet again, and then I loved him well.
And now of late I see him less and less,   355
But those first days had golden hours for me,
For then I surely thought he would be king.

"But let me tell thee now another tale:
For Bleys, our Merlin's master, as they say,
Died but of late, and sent his cry to me,   360
To hear him speak before he left his life.
Shrunk like a fairy changeling lay the mage;
And when I entered told me that himself
And Merlin ever served about the king,
Uther, before he died; and on the night   365
When Uther in Tintagil passed away
Moaning and wailing for an heir, the two
Left the still king, and passing forth to breathe,
Then from the castle gateway by the chasm
Descending through the dismal night—a night   370
In which the bounds of heaven and earth were
    lost—
Beheld, so high upon the dreary deeps
It seemed in heaven, a ship, the shape thereof
A dragon winged, and all from stem to stern
Bright with a shining people on the decks,   375
And gone as soon as seen. And then the two
Dropped to the cove, and watched the great sea
    fall,

Wave after wave, each mightier than the last,
Till last, a ninth one, gathering half the deep
And full of voices, slowly rose and plunged   380
Roaring, and all the wave was in a flame:
And down the wave and in the flame was borne
A naked babe, and rode to Merlin's feet,
Who stooped and caught the babe, and cried 'The
    king!
Here is an heir for Uther!' And the fringe   385
Of that great breaker, sweeping up the strand,
Lashed at the wizard as he spake the word,
And all at once all round him rose in fire,
So that the child and he were clothed in fire.
And presently thereafter followed calm,   390
Free sky and stars: 'And this same child,' he said,
'Is he who reigns; nor could I part in peace
Till this were told.' And saying this the seer
Went through the strait and dreadful pass of death,
Not ever to be questioned any more   395
Save on the further side; but when I met
Merlin, and asked him if these things were truth—
The shining dragon and the naked child
Descending in the glory of the seas—
He laughed as is his wont, and answered me   400
In riddling triplets of old time, and said:

" 'Rain, rain, and sun! a rainbow in the sky!
A young man will be wiser by and by;
An old man's wit may wander ere he die.
    Rain, rain, and sun! a rainbow on the lea!   405
And truth is this to me, and that to thee;
And truth or clothed or naked let it be.

Rain, sun, and rain! and the free blossom blows:
Sun, rain, and sun! and where is he who knows?
From the great deep to the great deep he goes.'   410

"So Merlin riddling angered me; but thou
Fear not to give this king thine only child,
Guinevere: so great bards of him will sing
Hereafter; and dark sayings from of old
Ranging and ringing through the minds of men,   415
And echoed by old folk beside their fires
For comfort after their wage-work is done,
Speak of the king; and Merlin in our time
Hath spoken also, not in jest, and sworn
Though men may wound him that he will not die,
But pass, again to come; and then or now   421
Utterly smite the heathen underfoot,
Till these and all men hail him for their king."

She spake and King Leodogran rejoiced,
But musing "Shall I answer yea or nay?" 425
Doubted, and drowsed, nodded and slept, and saw,
Dreaming, a slope of land that ever grew,
Field after field, up to a height, the peak
Haze-hidden, and thereon a phantom king,
Now looming, and now lost; and on the slope 430
The sword rose, the hind fell, the herd was driven,
Fire glimpsed; and all the land from roof and rick,
In drifts of smoke before a rolling wind,
Streamed to the peak, and mingled with the haze
And made it thicker; while the phantom king 435
Sent out at times a voice; and here or there
Stood one who pointed toward the voice, the rest
Slew on and burnt, crying, "No king of ours,
No son of Uther, and no king of ours;"
Till with a wink his dream was changed, the haze
Descended, and the solid earth became 441
As nothing, but the king stood out in heaven,
Crowned. And Leodogran awoke, and sent
Ulfius, and Brastias and Bedivere,
Back to the court of Arthur answering yea. 445

Then Arthur charged his warrior whom he loved
And honored most, Sir Lancelot, to ride forth
And bring the queen;—and watched him from the
   gates:
And Lancelot passed away among the flowers,
(For then was latter April) and returned 450
Among the flowers, in May, with Guinevere.
To whom arrived, by Dubric the high saint,
Chief of the church in Britain, and before
The stateliest of her altar-shrines, the king
That morn was married, while in stainless white,
The fair beginners of a nobler time, 456
And glorying in their vows and him, his knights
Stood round him, and rejoicing in his joy.
Far shone the fields of May through open door,
The sacred altar blossomed white with May, 460
The sun of May descended on their king,
They gazed on all earth's beauty in their queen,
Rolled incense, and there passed along the hymns
A voice as of the waters, while the two
Sware at the shrine of Christ a deathless love: 465
And Arthur said, "Behold, thy doom is mine.
Let chance what will, I love thee to the death!"
To whom the queen replied with drooping eyes,
"King and my lord, I love thee to the death!"
And holy Dubric spread his hands and spake, 470
"Reign ye, and live and love, and make the world

Other, and may thy queen be one with thee,
And all this order of thy Table Round
Fulfill the boundless purpose of their king!"

So Dubric said; but when they left the shrine 475
Great lords from Rome before the portal stood,
In scornful stillness gazing as they passed;
Then while they paced a city all on fire 478
With sun and cloth of gold, the trumpets blew,
And Arthur's knighthood sang before the king:—

"Blow trumpet, for the world is white with May;
Blow trumpet, the long night hath rolled away!
Blow through the living world—'Let the king
   reign.'

"Shall Rome or heathen rule in Arthur's realm?
Flash brand and lance, fall battle-ax upon helm,
Fall battle-ax, and flash brand! Let the king
   reign. 486

"Strike for the king and live! his knights have
   heard
That God hath told the king a secret word.
Fall battle-ax, and flash brand! Let the king reign.

"Blow trumpet! he will lift us from the dust. 490
Blow trumpet! live the strength and die the lust!
Clang battle-ax, and clash brand! Let the king
   reign.

"Strike for the king and die! and if thou diest,
The king is king, and ever wills the highest.
Clang battle-ax, and clash brand! Let the king
   reign. 495

"Blow, for our Sun is mighty in his May!
Blow, for our Sun is mightier day by day!
Clang battle-ax, and clash brand! Let the king
   reign.

"The king will follow Christ, and we the king
In whom high God hath breathed a secret thing.
Fall battle-ax, and flash brand! Let the king
   reign." 501

So sang the knighthood, moving to their hall.
There at the banquet those great lords from Rome,
The slowly-fading mistress of the world,
Strode in, and claimed their tribute as of yore. 505
But Arthur spake, "Behold, for these have sworn
To wage my wars, and worship me their king;
The old order changeth, yielding place to new;
And we that fight for our fair father Christ,

Seeing that ye be grown too weak and old   510
To drive the heathen from your Roman wall,
No tribute will we pay:" so those great lords
Drew back in wrath, and Arthur strove with Rome.

And Arthur and his knighthood for a space
Were all one will, and through that strength the
    king   515
Drew in the petty princedoms under him,
Fought, and in twelve great battles overcame
The heathen hordes, and made a realm and
    reigned.

JOHN UPDIKE
b. 1932

Pigeon Feathers

When they moved to Firetown, things were upset, displaced, rearranged. A red cane-back sofa that had been the chief piece in the living room at Olinger was here banished, too big for the narrow country parlor, to the barn, and shrouded under a tarpaulin. Never again would David lie on its length all afternoon eating raisins and reading mystery novels and science fiction and P. G. Wodehouse. The blue wing chair that had stood for years in the ghostly, immaculate guest bedroom, gazing through the windows curtained with dotted swiss toward the telephone wires and horse-chestnut trees and opposite houses, was here established importantly in front of the smutty little fireplace that supplied, in those first cold April days, their only heat. As a child, David had been afraid of the guest bedroom—it was there that he, lying sick with the measles, had seen a black rod the size of a yardstick jog along at a slight slant beside the edge of the bed and vanish when he screamed—and it was disquieting to have one of the elements of its haunted atmosphere basking by the fire, in the center of the family, growing sooty with use. The books that at home had gathered dust in the case beside the piano were here hastily stacked, all out of order, in the shelves that the carpenters had built along one wall below the deep-silled windows. David, at fourteen, had been more moved than a mover; like the furniture, he had to find a new place, and on the Saturday of the second week he tried to work off some of his disorientation by arranging the books.

It was a collection obscurely depressing to him, mostly books his mother had acquired when she was young: college anthologies of Greek plays and Romantic poetry, Will Durant's *Story of Philosophy*, a soft-leather set of Shakespeare with string bookmarks sewed to the bindings, *Green Mansions* boxed and illustrated with woodcuts, *I, the Tiger*, by Manuel Komroff, novels by names like Galsworthy and Ellen Glasgow and Irvin S. Cobb and Sinclair Lewis and "Elizabeth." The odor of faded taste made him feel the ominous gap between himself and his parents, the insulting gulf of time that existed before he was born. Suddenly he was tempted to dip into this time. From the heaps of books piled around him on the worn old floorboards, he picked up Volume II of a four-volume set of *The Outline of History*, by H. G. Wells. Once David had read *The Time Machine* in an anthology; this gave him a small grip on the author. The book's red binding had faded to orange-pink on the spine. When he lifted the cover, there was a sweetish, atticlike smell, and his mother's maiden name written in unfamiliar handwriting on the flyleaf—an upright, bold, yet careful signature, bearing a faint relation to the quick scrunched backslant that flowed with marvelous consistency across her shopping lists and budget accounts and Christmas cards to college friends from this same, vaguely menacing long ago.

He leafed through, pausing at drawings, done in an old-fashioned stippled style, of bas-reliefs, masks, Romans without pupils in their eyes, articles of ancient costume, fragments of pottery found in unearthed homes. He knew it would be interesting in a magazine, sandwiched between ads and jokes, but in this undiluted form history was somehow sour. The print was determinedly legible, and smug, like a lesson book. As he bent over the pages, yellow at the edges, they seemed rectangles of dusty glass through which he looked down into unreal and irrelevant worlds. He could see things sluggishly move, and an unpleasant fullness came into his throat. His mother and grandmother fussed in the kitchen; the puppy, which they had just acquired, for "protection in the country," was cowering, with a sporadic panicked scrabble of claws, under the dining table that in their old home had been reserved for special days but that here was used for every meal.

Then, before he could halt his eyes, David slipped into Wells's account of Jesus. He had been an obscure political agitator, a kind of hobo, in a minor colony of the Roman Empire. By an accident impossible to reconstruct, he (the small *h* horrified David) survived his own crucifixion and presumably died a few weeks later. A religion was founded on the freakish incident. The credulous imagination of the times retrospectively assigned miracles and supernatural pretensions to Jesus; a myth grew, and then a church, whose theology at most points was in direct contradiction of the simple, rather communistic teachings of the Galilean.

It was as if a stone that for weeks and even years had been gathering weight in the web of David's nerves snapped them and plunged through the page and a hundred layers of paper underneath. These fantastic falsehoods—plainly untrue; churches stood everywhere, the entire nation was founded "under God"—did not at first frighten him; it was the fact that they had been permitted to exist in an actual human brain. This was the initial impact—that at a definite spot in time and space a brain black with the denial of Christ's divinity had been suffered to exist; that the universe had not spit out this ball of tar but allowed it to continue in its blasphemy, to grow old, win honors, wear a hat, write books that, if true, collapsed everything into a jumble of horror. The world outside the deep-silled windows—a rutted lawn, a whitewashed barn, a walnut tree frothy with fresh green—seemed a haven from which he was forever sealed off. Hot washrags seemed pressed against his cheeks.

He read the account again. He tried to supply out of his ignorance objections that would defeat the complacent march of these black words, and found none. Survivals and misunderstandings more far-fetched were reported daily in the papers. But none of them caused churches to be built in every town. He tried to work backwards through the churches, from their brave high fronts through their shabby, ill-attended interiors back into the events at Jerusalem, and felt himself surrounded by shifting gray shadows, centuries of history, where he knew nothing. The thread dissolved in his hands. Had Christ ever come to him, David Kern, and said,

"Here. Feel the wound in My side?" No; but prayers had been answered. What prayers? He had prayed that Rudy Mohn, whom he had purposely tripped so he cracked his head on their radiator, not die, and he had not died. But for all the blood, it was just a cut; Rudy came back the same day, wearing a bandage and repeating the same teasing words. He could never have died. Again, David had prayed for two separate war-effort posters he had sent away for to arrive tomorrow, and though they did not, they did arrive, some days later, together, popping through the clacking letter slot like a rebuke from God's mouth: *I answer your prayers in My way, in My time.* After that, he had made his prayers less definite, less susceptible of being twisted into a scolding. But what a tiny, ridiculous coincidence this was, after all, to throw into battle against H. G. Wells's engines of knowledge! Indeed, it proved the enemy's point: Hope bases vast premises on foolish accidents, and reads a word where in fact only a scribble exists.

His father came home. Though Saturday was a free day for him, he had been working. He taught school in Olinger and spent all his days performing, with a curious air of panic, needless errands. Also, a city boy by birth, he was frightened of the farm and seized any excuse to get away. The farm had been David's mother's birthplace; it had been her idea to buy it back. With an ingenuity and persistence unparalleled in her life, she had gained that end, and moved them all here—her son, her husband, her mother. Granmom, in her prime, had worked these fields alongside her husband, but now she dabbled around the kitchen futilely, her hands waggling with Parkinson's disease. She was always in the way. Strange, out in the country, amid eighty acres, they were crowded together. His father expressed his feelings of discomfort by conducting with Mother an endless argument about organic farming. All through dusk, all through supper, it rattled on.

"Elsie, I *know*, I know from my education, the earth is nothing but chemicals. It's the only damn thing I got out of four years of college, so don't tell me it's not true."

"George, if you'd just walk out on the farm you'd know it's not true. The land has a *soul*."

"Soil, has, no, soul," he said, enunciating stiffly, as if to a very stupid class. To David he said, "You can't argue with a femme. Your mother's a real femme. That's why I married her, and now I'm suffering for it."

"*This* soil has no soul," she said, "because it's been killed with superphosphate. It's been burned bare by Boyer's tenant farmers." Boyer was the rich man they had bought the farm from. "It used to have a soul, didn't it, Mother? When you and Pop farmed it?"

"Ach, yes; I guess." Granmom was trying to bring a forkful of food to her mouth with her less severely afflicted hand. In her anxiety she brought the other hand up from her lap. The crippled fingers, dull red in the orange light of the kerosene lamp in the center of the table, were welded by paralysis into one knobbed hook.

"Only human indi-vidu-als have souls," his father went on, in the same mincing, lifeless voice. "Because the Bible tells us so." Done eating, he crossed his legs and dug into his ear with a match miserably; to get at the thing inside his head he tucked in his chin, and his voice came out low-pitched at David. "When God made your mother, He made a real femme."

"George, don't you read the papers? Don't you know that between the chemical fertilizers and the bug sprays we'll all be dead in ten years? Heart attacks are killing every man in the country over forty-five."

He sighed wearily; the yellow skin of his eyelids wrinkled as he hurt himself with the match. "There's no connection," he stated, spacing his words with pained patience, "between the heart— and chemical fertilizers. It's alcohol that's doing it. Alcohol and milk. There is too much—choles-terol—in the tissues of the American heart. Don't tell me about chemistry, Elsie; I majored in the damn stuff for four years."

"Yes and I majored in Greek and I'm not a penny wiser. Mother, put your waggler a*way!*" The old woman started, and the food dropped from her fork. For some reason, the sight of her bad hand at the table cruelly irritated her daughter. Gran-mom's eyes, worn bits of crazed crystal embedded in watery milk, widened behind her cockeyed spectacles. Circles of silver as fine as thread, they clung to the red notches they had carved over the years into her little white beak. In the orange flicker of the kerosene lamp her dazed misery seemed infernal. David's mother began, without

noise, to cry. His father did not seem to have eyes at all; just jaundiced sockets of wrinkled skin. The steam of food clouded the scene. It was horrible but the horror was particular and familiar, and distracted David from the formless dread that worked, sticky and sore, within him, like a too large wound trying to heal.

He had to go to the bathroom, and took a flashlight down through the wet grass to the out-house. For once, his fear of spiders there felt trivial. He set the flashlight, burning, beside him, and an insect alighted on its lens, a tiny insect, a mosquito or flea, made so fine that the weak light projected its X-ray onto the wall boards; the faint rim of its wings, the blurred strokes, magnified, of its long hinged legs, the dark cone at the heart of its anatomy. The tremor must be its heart beating. Without warning, David was visited by an exact vision of death: a long hole in the ground, no wider than your body, down which you are drawn while the white faces above recede. You try to reach them but your arms are pinned. Shovels pour dirt into your face. There you will be forever, in an upright position, blind and silent, and in time no one will remember you, and you will never be called. As strata of rock shift, your fingers elongate, and your teeth are distended sideways in a great underground grimace indistinguishable from a strip of chalk. And the earth tumbles on, and the sun expires, and unaltering darkness reigns where once there were stars.

Sweat broke out on his back. His mind seemed to rebound off a solidness. Such extinction was not another threat, a graver sort of danger, a kind of pain; it was qualitatively different. It was not even a conception that could be voluntarily pictured; it entered him from outside. His protesting nerves swarmed on its surface like lichen on a meteor. The skin of his chest was soaked with the effort of rejection. At the same time that the fear was dense and internal, it was dense and all around him; a tide of clay had swept up to the stars; space was crushed into a mass. When he stood up, automatic-ally hunching his shoulders to keep his head away from the spider webs, it was with a numb sense of being cramped between two huge volumes of rigidity. That he had even this small freedom to move surprised him. In the narrow shelter of that rank shack, adjusting his pants, he felt—his first spark of comfort—too small to be crushed.

But in the open, as the beam of the flashlight skidded with frightened quickness across the remote surfaces of the barn and the grape arbor and the giant pine that stood by the path to the woods, the terror descended. He raced up through the clinging grass pursued, not by one of the wild animals the woods might hold, or one of the goblins his superstitious grandmother had communicated to his childhood, but by spectres out of science fiction, where gigantic cinder moons fill half the turquoise sky. As David ran, a gray planet rolled inches behind his neck. If he looked back, he would be buried. And in the momentum of his terror, hideous possibilities—the dilation of the sun, the triumph of the insects, the crabs on the shore in *The Time Machine*—wheeled out of the vacuum of make-believe and added their weight to his impending oblivion.

He wrenched the door open; the lamps within the house flared. The wicks burning here and there seemed to mirror one another. His mother was washing the dishes in a little pan of heated pump-water; Granmom flutered near her elbow apprehensive. In the living room—the downstairs of the little square house was two long rooms—his father sat in front of the black fire place restlessly folding and unfolding a newspaper as he sustained his half of the argument. "Nitrogen, phosphorus, potash: these are the three replaceable constituents of the soil. One crop of corn carries away hundreds of pounds of"—he dropped the paper into his lap and ticked them off on three fingers—"nitrogen, phosphorus, potash."

"Boyer didn't grow corn."

"*Any* crop, Elsie. The human animal—"

"You're killing the *earth*worms, George!"

"The human animal, after thousands and *thous*ands of years, learned methods whereby the chemical balance of the soil may be maintained. Don't carry me back to the Dark Ages."

"When we moved to Olinger the ground in the garden was like slate. Just one summer of my cousin's chicken dung and the earthworms came back."

"I'm sure the Dark Ages were a fine place to the poor devils born in them, but I don't want to go there. They give me the creeps." Daddy stared into the cold pit of the fireplace and clung to the rolled newspaper in his lap as if it alone were keeping him from slipping backwards and down, down.

Mother came into the doorway brandishing a fistful of wet forks. "And thanks to your DDT there soon won't be a bee left in the country. When I was a girl here you could eat a peach without washing it."

"It's primitive, Elsie. It's Dark Age stuff."

"Oh what do *you* know about the Dark Ages?"

"I know I don't want to go back to them."

David took from the shelf, where he had placed it this afternoon, the great unabridged Webster's Dictionary that his grandfather had owned. He turned the big thin pages, floppy as cloth, to the entry he wanted, and read

> soul . . . 1. An entity conceived as the essence, substance, animating principle, or actuating cause of life, or of the individual life, esp. of life manifested in psychical activities; the vehicle of individual existence, separate in nature from the body and usually held to be separable in existence.

The definition went on, into Greek and Egyptian conceptions, but David stopped short on the treacherous edge of antiquity. He needed to read no further. The careful overlapping words shingled a temporary shelter for him. "Usually held to be separable in existence"—what could be fairer, more judicious, surer?

His father was saying, "The modern farmer can't go around sweeping up after his cows. The poor devil has thousands and *thou*sands of acres on his hands. Your modern farmer uses a scientifically-arrived-at mixture, like five-ten-five, or six-twelve-six, or *three*-twelve-six, and spreads it on with this wonderful modern machinery which of course we can't afford. Your modern farmer can't *afford* medieval methods."

Mother was quiet in the kitchen; her silence radiated waves of anger.

"No now Elsie; don't play the femme with me. Let's discuss this calmly like two rational twentieth-century people. Your organic farming nuts aren't attacking five-ten-five; they're attacking the chemical fertilizer crooks. The monster firms."

A cup clinked in the kitchen. Mother's anger touched David's face; his cheeks burned guiltily. Just by being in the living room he was associated with his father. She appeared in the doorway with red hands and tears in her eyes, and said to the two of them, "I knew you didn't want to come here but I didn't know you'd torment me like this. You talked Pop into his grave and now you'll kill me.

Go ahead, George, more power to you; at least I'll be buried in good ground." She tried to turn and met an obstacle and screamed, "Mother, stop hanging on my *back*! Why don't you go to *bed*?"

"Let's all go to bed," David's father said, rising from the blue wing chair and slapping his thigh with a newspaper. "This reminds me of death." It was a phrase of his that David had heard so often he never considered its sense.

Upstairs, he seemed to be lifted above his fears. The sheets on his bed were clean. Granmom had ironed them with a pair of flatirons saved from the Olinger attic; she plucked them hot off the stove alternately, with a wooden handle called a goose. It was a wonder, to see how she managed. In the next room, his parents grunted peaceably; they seemed to take their quarrels less seriously than he did. They made comfortable scratching noises as they carried a little lamp back and forth. Their door was open a crack, so he saw the light shift and swing. Surely there would be, in the last five minutes, in the last second, a crack of light, showing the door from the dark room to another, full of light. Thinking of it this vividly frightened him. His own dying, in a specific bed in a specific room, specific walls mottled with wallpaper, the dry whistle of his breathing, the murmuring doctors, the nervous relatives going in and out, but for him no way out but down into the funnel. *Never touch a doorknob again.* A whisper, and his parents' light was blown out. David prayed to be reassured. Though the experiment frightened him, he lifted his hands high into the darkness above his face and begged Christ to touch them. Not hard or long: the faintest, quickest grip would be final for a lifetime. His hands waited in the air, itself a substance, which seemed to move through his fingers; or was it the pressure of his pulse? He returned his hands to beneath the covers uncertain if they had been touched or not. For would not Christ's touch *be* infinitely gentle?

Through all the eddies of its aftermath, David clung to this thought about his revelation of extinction: that there, in the outhouse, he had struck a solidness qualitatively different, a rock of horror firm enough to support any height of construction. All he needed was a little help; a word, a gesture, a nod of certainty, and he would be sealed in, safe. The assurance from the dictionary had melted in

the night. Today was Sunday, a hot fair day. Across a mile of clear air the church bells called, *Celebrate, celebrate.* Only Daddy went. He put on a coat over his rolled-up shirtsleeves and got into the little old black Plymouth parked by the barn and went off, with the same pained hurried grimness of all his actions. His churning wheels, as he shifted too hastily into second, raised plumes of red dust on the dirt road. Mother walked to the far field, to see what bushes needed cutting. David, though he usually preferred to stay in the house, went with her. The puppy followed at a distance, whining as it picked its way through the stubble but floundering off timidly if one of them went back to pick it up and carry it. When they reached the crest of the far field, his mother asked, "David, what's troubling you?"

"Nothing. Why?"

She looked at him sharply. The greening woods crosshatched the space beyond her half-gray hair. Then she showed him her profile, and gestured toward the house, which they had left a half-mile behind them. "See how it sits in the land? They don't know how to build with the land any more. Pop always said the foundations were set with the compass. We must try to get a compass and see. It's supposed to face due south; but south feels a little more *that* way to me." From the side, as she said these things, she seemed handsome and young. The smooth sweep of her hair over her ear seemed white with a purity and calm that made her feel foreign to him. He had never regarded his parents as consolers of his troubles; from the beginning they had seemed to have more troubles than he. Their confusion had flattered him into an illusion of strength; so now on this high clear ridge he jealously guarded the menace all around them, blowing like a breeze on his fingertips, the possibility of all this wide scenery sinking into darkness. The strange fact that though she came to look at the brush she carried no clippers, for she had a fixed prejudice against working on Sundays, was the only consolation he allowed her to offer.

As they walked back, the puppy whimpering after them, the rising dust behind a distant line of trees announced that Daddy was speeding home from church. When they reached the house he was there. He had brought back the Sunday paper and the vehement remark, "Dobson's too intelligent for these farmers. They just sit there with their mouths open and don't hear a thing the poor devil's saying."

"What makes you think farmers are unintelligent? This country was made by farmers. George Washington was a farmer."

"They are, Elsie. They are unintelligent. George Washington's dead. In this day and age only the misfits stay on the farm. The lame, the halt, the blind. The morons with one arm. Human garbage. They remind me of death, sitting there with their mouths open."

"My *father* was a farmer."

"He was a frustrated man, Elsie. He never knew what hit him. The poor devil meant so well, and he never knew which end was up. Your mother'll bear me out. Isn't that right, Mom? Pop never knew what hit him?"

"Ach, I guess not," the old woman quavered, and the ambiguity for the moment silenced both sides.

David hid in the funny papers and sports section until one-thirty. At two, the catechetical class met at the Firetown church. He had transferred from the catechetical class of the Lutheran church in Olinger, a humiliating comedown. In Olinger they met on Wednesday nights, spiffy and spruce, in the atmosphere of a dance. Afterwards, blessed by the brick-faced minister from whose lips the word "Christ" fell like a burning stone, the more daring of them went with their Bibles to a luncheonette and smoked. Here in Firetown, the girls were dull white cows and the boys narrow-faced brown goats in old men's suits, herded on Sunday afternoons into a threadbare church basement that smelled of stale hay. Because his father had taken the car on one of his endless errands to Olinger, David walked, grateful for the open air and the silence. The catechetical class embarrassed him, but today he placed hope in it, as the source of the nod, the gesture, that was all he needed.

Reverend Dobson was a delicate young man with great dark eyes and small white shapely hands that flickered like protesting doves when he preached; he seemed a bit misplaced in the Lutheran ministry. This was his first call. It was a split parish; he served another rural church twelve miles away. His iridescent green Ford, new six months ago, was spattered to the windows with red mud and rattled from bouncing on the rude back roads, where he frequently got lost, to the malicious satisfaction of many. But David's mother liked him, and, more

pertinent to his success, the Haiers, the sleek family of feed merchants and innkeepers and tractor salesmen who dominated the Firetown church, liked him. David liked him, and felt liked in turn; sometimes in class, after some special stupidity, Dobson directed toward him out of those wide black eyes a mild look of disbelief, a look that, though flattering, was also delicately disquieting.

Catechetical instruction consisted of reading aloud from a work booklet answers to problems prepared during the week, problems like, "I am the ———, the ———, and the ———, saith the Lord." Then there was a question period in which no one ever asked any questions. Today's theme was the last third of the Apostles' Creed. When the time came for questions, David blushed and asked, "About the Resurrection of the Body—are we conscious between the time when we die and the Day of Judgment?"

Dobson blinked, and his fine little mouth pursed, suggesting that David was making difficult things more difficult. The faces of the other students went blank, as if an indiscretion had been committed.

"No, I suppose not," Reverend Dobson said.

"Well, where is our soul, then, in this gap?"

The sense grew, in the class, of a naughtiness occurring. Dobson's shy eyes watered, as if he were straining to keep up the formality of attention, and one of the girls, the fattest, simpered toward her twin, who was a little less fat. Their chairs were arranged in a rough circle. The current running around the circle panicked David. Did everybody know something he didn't know?

"I suppose you could say our souls are asleep," Dobson said.

"And then they wake up, and there is the earth like it always is, and all the people who have ever lived? Where will Heaven be?"

Anita Haier giggled. Dobson gazed at David intently, but with an awkward, puzzled flicker of forgiveness, as if there existed a secret between them that David was violating. But David knew of no secret. All he wanted was to hear Dobson repeat the words he said every Sunday morning. This he would not do. As if these words were unworthy of the conversational voice.

"David, you might think of Heaven this way: as the way the goodness Abraham Lincoln did lives after him."

"But is Lincoln conscious of it living on?" He

blushed no longer with embarrassment but in anger; he had walked here in good faith and was being made a fool.

"Is he conscious now? I would have to say no; but I don't think it matters." His voice had a coward's firmness; he was hostile now.

"You don't."

"Not in the eyes of God, no." The unction, the stunning impudence, of this reply sprang tears of outrage in David's eyes. He bowed them to his book, where short words like Duty, Love, Obey, Honor, were stacked in the form of a cross.

"Were there any other questions, David?" Dobson asked with renewed gentleness. The others were rustling, collecting their books.

"No." He made his voice firm, though he could not bring up his eyes.

"Did I answer your question fully enough?"

"Yes."

In the minister's silence the shame that should have been his crept over David: the burden and fever of being a fraud were placed upon *him*, who was innocent, and it seemed, he knew, a confession of this guilt that on the way out he was unable to face Dobson's stirred gaze, though he felt it probing the side of his head.

Anita Haier's father gave him a ride down the highway as far as the dirt road. David said he wanted to walk the rest, and figured that his offer was accepted because Mr. Haier did not want to dirty his bright blue Buick with dust. This was all right; everything was all right, as long as it was clear. His indignation at being betrayed, at seeing Christianity betrayed, had hardened him. The straight dirt road reflected his hardness. Pink stones thrust up through its packed surface. The April sun beat down from the center of the afternoon half of the sky; already it had some of summer's heat. Already the fringes of weeds at the edges of the road were bedraggled with dust. From the reviving grass and scuff of the fields he walked between, insects were sending up a monotonous, automatic chant. In the distance a tiny figure in his father's coat was walking along the edge of the woods. His mother. He wondered what joy she found in such walks; to him the brown stretches of slowly rising and falling land expressed only a huge exhaustion.

Flushed with fresh air and happiness, she returned from her walk earlier than he had expected, and surprised him at his grandfather's Bible. It was a stumpy black book, the boards worn thin where the old man's fingers had held them; the spine hung by one weak hinge of fabric. David had been looking for the passage where Jesus says to the one thief on the cross, "Today shalt thou be with me in paradise." He had never tried reading the Bible for himself before. What was so embarrassing about being caught at it, was that he detested the apparatus of piety. Fusty churches, creaking hymns, ugly Sunday-school teachers and their stupid leaflets—he hated everything about them but the promise they held out, a promise that in the most perverse way, as if the homeliest crone in the kingdom were given the Prince's hand, made every good and real thing, ball games and jokes and pert-breasted girls, possible. He couldn't explain this to his mother. There was no time. Her solicitude was upon him.

"David, what are you doing?"

"Nothing."

"What are you doing at Grandpop's Bible?"

"Trying to read it. This is supposed to be a Christian country, isn't it?"

She sat down on the green sofa, which used to be in the sun parlor at Olinger, under the fancy mirror. A little smile still lingered on her face from the walk. "David, I wish you'd talk to me."

"What about?"

"About whatever it is that's troubling you. Your father and I have both noticed it."

"I asked Reverend Dobson about Heaven and he said it was like Abraham Lincoln's goodness living after him."

He waited for the shock to strike her. "Yes?" she said, expecting more.

"That's all."

"And why didn't you like it?"

"Well; don't you see? It amounts to saying there isn't any Heaven at all."

"I don't see that it amounts to that. What do you want Heaven to be?"

"Well, I don't know. I want it to be *some*thing. I thought he'd tell me what it was. I thought that was his job." He was becoming angry, sensing her surprise at him. She had assumed that Heaven had faded from his head years ago. She had imagined that he had already entered, in the secrecy of silence, the conspiracy that he now knew to be all around him.

"David," she asked gently, "don't you ever want to rest?"

"No. Not forever."

"David, you're so young. When you get older, you'll feel differently."

"Grandpa didn't. Look how tattered this book is."

"I never understood your grandfather."

"Well I don't understand ministers who say it's like Lincoln's goodness going on and on. Suppose you're not Lincoln?"

"I think Reverend Dobson made a mistake. You must try to forgive him."

"It's not a *question* of his making a mistake! It's a question of dying and never moving or seeing or hearing anything ever again."

"But"—in exasperation—"darling, it's so *greedy* of you to want more. When God has given us this wonderful April day, and given us this farm, and you have your whole life ahead of you—"

"You think, then, that there is God?"

"Of course I do"—with deep relief, that smoothed her features into a reposeful oval. He had risen and was standing too near her for his comfort. He was afraid she would reach out and touch him.

"He made everything? You feel that?"

"Yes."

"Then who made Him?"

"Why, Man. Man." The happiness of this answer lit up her face radiantly, until she saw his gesture of disgust. She was so simple, so illogical; such a femme.

"Well that amounts to saying there is none."

Her hand reached for his wrist but he backed away. "David, it's a mystery. A miracle. It's a miracle more beautiful than any Reverend Dobson could have told you about. You don't say houses don't exist because Man made them."

"No. God has to be different."

"But, David, you have the *evidence*. Look out the window at the sun; at the fields."

"Mother, good grief. Don't you see"—he rasped away the roughness in his throat—"if when we die there's nothing, all your sun and fields and what not are all, ah, *horror*? It's just an ocean of horror."

"But David, it's not. It's so clearly not that." And she made an urgent opening gesture with her hands that expressed, with its suggestion of a willingness to receive his helplessness, all her grace, her gentleness, her love of beauty, gathered into a passive intensity that made him intensely hate her. He would not be wooed away from the truth. *I am the Way, the Truth. . . .*

"No," he told her. "Just let me alone."

He found his tennis ball behind the piano and went outside to throw it against the side of the house. There was a patch high up where the brown stucco that had been laid over the sandstone masonry was crumbling away; he kept trying with the tennis ball to chip more pieces off. Superimposed upon his deep ache was a smaller but more immediate worry; that he had hurt his mother. He heard his father's car rattling on the straightaway, and went into the house, to make peace before he arrived. To his relief, she was not giving off the stifling damp heat of her anger, but instead was cool, decisive, maternal. She handed him an old green book, her college text of Plato.

"I want you to read the Parable of the Cave," she said.

"All right," he said, though he knew it would do no good. Some story by a dead Greek just vague enough to please her. "Don't worry about it, Mother."

"I *am* worried. Honestly, David, I'm sure there will be something for us. As you get older, these things seem to matter a great deal less."

"That may be. It's a dismal thought, though."

His father bumped at the door. The locks and jambs stuck here. But before Granmom could totter to the latch and let him in, he had knocked it open. He had been in Olinger dithering with track meet tickets. Although Mother usually kept her talks with David a confidence, a treasure between them, she called instantly, "George, David is worried about death!"

He came to the doorway of the living room, his shirt pocket bristling with pencils, holding in one hand a pint box of melting ice cream and in the other the knife with which he was about to divide it into four sections, their Sunday treat. "Is the kid worried about death? Don't give it a thought, David. I'll be lucky if I live till tomorrow, and I'm not worried. If they'd taken a buckshot gun and shot me in the cradle I'd be better off. The *world*'d be better off. Hell, I think death is a wonderful thing. I look forward to it. Get the garbage out of the way. If I had the man here who invented death, I'd pin a medal on him."

"Hush, George. You'll frighten the child worse than he is."

This was not true; he never frightened David. There was no harm in his father, no harm at all. Indeed, in the man's steep self-disgust the boy felt a kind of ally. A distant ally. He saw his position with a certain strategic coldness. Nowhere in the world of other people would he find the hint, the nod, he needed to begin to build his fortress against death. They none of them believed. He was alone. In that deep hole.

In the months that followed, his position changed little. School was some comfort. All those sexy, perfumed people, wisecracking, chewing gum, all of them doomed to die, and none of them noticing. In their company David felt that they would carry him along into the bright, cheap paradise reserved for them. In any crowd, the fear ebbed a little; he had reasoned that somewhere in the world there must exist a few people who believed what was necessary, and the larger the crowd, the greater the chance that he was near such a soul, within calling distance, if only he was not too ignorant, too ill-equipped, to spot him. The sight of clergymen cheered him; whatever they themselves thought, their collars were still a sign that somewhere, at sometime, someone had recognized that we cannot, *cannot*, submit to death. The sermon topics posted outside churches, the flip, hurried pieties of disc jockeys, the cartoons in magazines showing angels or devils—on such scraps he kept alive the possibility of hope.

For the rest, he tried to drown his hopelessness in clatter and jostle. The pinball machine at the luncheonette was a merciful distraction; as he bent over its buzzing, flashing board of flippers and cushions, the weight and constriction in his chest lightened and loosened. He was grateful for all the time his father wasted in Olinger. Every delay postponed the moment when they must ride together down the dirt road into the heart of the dark farmland, where the only light was the kerosene lamp waiting on the dining-room table, a light that drowned their food in shadow and made it sinister.

He lost his appetite for reading. He was afraid of being ambushed again. In mystery novels people died like dolls being discarded; in science fiction enormities of space and time conspired to crush the humans; and even in P. G. Wodehouse he felt a hollowness, a turning away from reality that was implicitly bitter, and became explicit in the comic figures of futile clergymen. All gaiety seemed minced out on the skin of a void. All quiet hours seemed invitations to dread.

Even on weekends, he and his father contrived to escape the farm; and when, some Saturdays, they did stay home, it was to do something destructive—tear down an old henhouse or set huge brush fires that threatened, while Mother shouted and flapped her arms, to spread to the woods. Whenever his father worked, it was with rapt violence; when he chopped kindling, fragments of the old henhouse boards flew like shrapnel and the ax-head was always within a quarter of an inch of flying off the handle. He was exhilarating to watch, sweating and swearing and sucking bits of saliva back into his lips.

School stopped. His father took the car in the opposite direction, to a highway construction job where he had been hired for the summer as a time-keeper, and David was stranded in the middle of acres of heat and greenery and blowing pollen and the strange, mechanical humming that lay invisibly in the weeds and alfalfa and dry orchard grass.

For his fifteenth birthday his parents gave him, with jokes about him being a hillbilly now, a Remington .22. It was somewhat like a pinball machine to take it out to the old kiln in the woods where they dumped their trash, and set up tin cans on the kiln's sandstone shoulder and shoot them off one by one. He'd take the puppy, who had grown long legs and a rich coat of reddish fur—he was part chow. Copper hated the gun but loved the boy enough to accompany him. When the flat acrid crack rang out, he would race in terrified circles that would tighten and tighten until they brought him, shivering, against David's legs. Depending upon his mood, David would shoot again or drop to his knees and comfort the dog. Giving this comfort to a degree returned comfort to him. The dog's ears, laid flat against his skull in fear, were folded so intricately, so—he groped for the concept —*surely*. Where the dull-studded collar made the fur stand up, each hair showed a root of soft white under the length, black-tipped, of the metal-color that had lent the dog its name. In his agitation Copper panted through nostrils that were elegant slits, like two healed cuts, or like the keyholes of a dainty lock of black, grained wood. His whole whorling, knotted, jointed body was a wealth of such embellishments. And in the smell of the dog's hair David seemed to descend through many finely differentiated layers of earth: mulch, soil, sand, clay, and the glittering mineral base.

But when he returned to the house, and saw the books arranged on the low shelves, fear returned. The four adamant volumes of Wells like four thin bricks, the green Plato that had puzzled him with its queer softness and tangled purity, the dead Galsworthy and "Elizabeth," Grandpa's mammoth dictionary, Grandpa's Bible, the Bible that he himself had received on becoming a member of the Firetown Lutheran Church—at the sight of these, the memory of his fear reawakened and came around him. He had grown stiff and stupid in its embrace. His parents tried to think of ways to entertain him.

"David, I have a job for you to do," his mother said one evening at the table.

"What?"

"If you're going to take that tone perhaps we'd better not talk."

"What tone? I didn't take any tone."

"Your grandmother thinks there are too many pigeons in the barn."

"Why?" David turned to look at his grandmother, but she sat there staring at the burning lamp with her usual expression of bewilderment.

Mother shouted, "Mom, he wants to know why!"

Granmom made a jerky, irritable motion with her bad hand, as if generating the force for utterance, and said, "They foul the furniture."

"That's right," Mother said. "She's afraid for that old Olinger furniture that we'll never use. David, she's been after me for a month about those poor pigeons. She wants you to shoot them."

"I don't want to kill anything especially," David said.

Daddy said, "The kid's like you are, Elsie. He's too good for this world. Kill or be killed, that's my motto."

His mother said loudly, "Mother, he doesn't want to do it."

"Not?" The old lady's eyes distended as if in horror, and her claw descended slowly to her lap.

"Oh, I'll do it, I'll do it tomorrow," David snapped, and a pleasant crisp taste entered his mouth with the decision.

"And I had thought, when Boyer's men made the hay, it would be better if the barn doesn't look like a rookery," his mother added needlessly.

A barn, in day, is a small night. The splinters of light between the dry shingles pierce the high roof like stars, and the rafters and crossbeams and built-in ladders seem, until your eyes adjust, as mysterious as the branches of a haunted forest. David entered silently, the gun in one hand. Copper whined desperately at the door, too frightened to come in with the gun yet unwilling to leave the boy. David stealthily turned, said "Go away," shut the door on the dog, and slipped the bolt across. It was a door within a door; the double door for wagons and tractors was as high and wide as the face of a house.

The smell of old straw scratched his sinuses. The red sofa, half-hidden under its white-splotched tarpaulin, seemed assimilated into this smell, sunk in it, buried. The mouths of empty bins gaped like caves. Rusty oddments of farming—coils of baling wire, some spare tines for a harrow, a handleless shovel—hung on nails driven here and there in the thick wood. He stood stock-still a minute; it took a while to separate the cooing of the pigeons from the rustling in his ears. When he had focused on the cooing, it flooded the vast interior with its throaty, bubbling outpour: there seemed no other sound. They were up behind the beams. What light there was leaked through the shingles and the dirty glass windows at the far end and the small round holes, about as big as basketballs, high on the opposite stone side walls, under the ridge of the roof.

A pigeon appeared in one of these holes, on the side toward the house. It flew in, with a battering of wings, from the outside, and waited there, silhouetted against its pinched bit of sky, preening and cooing in a throbbing, thrilled, tentative way. David tiptoed four steps to the side, rested his gun against the lowest rung of a ladder pegged between two upright beams, and lowered the gunsight into the bird's tiny, jauntily cocked head. The slap of the report seemed to come off the stone wall behind him, and the pigeon did not fall. Neither did it fly. Instead it stuck in the round hole, pirouetting rapidly and nodding its head as if in frantic agreement. David shot the bolt back and forth and had aimed again before the spent cartridge had stopped jingling on the boards by his feet. He eased the tip of the sight a little lower, into the bird's breast, and took care to squeeze the trigger with perfect evenness. The slow contraction of his hand abruptly sprang the bullet; for a half-second there was doubt, and then the pigeon fell like a handful of rags, skimming down the barn wall into the layer of straw that coated the floor of the mow on this side.

Now others shook loose from the rafters, and whirled in the dim air with a great blurred hurtle of feathers and noise. They would go for the hole; he fixed his sight on the little moon of blue, and when a pigeon came to it, shot him as he was walking the ten inches of stone that would have carried him into the open air. This pigeon lay down in that tunnel of stone, unable to fall either one way or the other, although he was alive enough to lift one wing and cloud the light. It would sink back, and he would suddenly lift it again, the feathers flaring. His body blocked that exit. David raced to the other side of the barn's main aisle, where a similar ladder was symmetrically placed, and rested his gun on the same rung. Three birds came together to this hole; he got one, and two got through. The rest resettled in the rafters.

There was a shallow triangular space behind the cross beams supporting the roof. It was here they roosted and hid. But either the space was too small, or they were curious, for now that his eyes were at home in the dusty gloom David could see little dabs of gray popping in and out. The cooing was shriller now; its apprehensive tremolo made the whole volume of air seem liquid. He noticed one little smudge of a head that was especially persistent in peeking out; he marked the place, and fixed his gun on it, and when the head appeared again, had his finger tightened in advance on the trigger. A parcel of fluff slipped off the beam and fell the barn's height onto a canvas covering some Olinger furniture, and where its head had peeked out there was a fresh prick of light in the shingles.

Standing in the center of the floor, fully master now, disdaining to steady the barrel with anything but his arm, he killed two more that way. He felt like a beautiful avenger. Out of the shadowy ragged infinity of the vast barn roof these impudent things dared to thrust their heads, presumed to dirty its starred silence with their filthy timorous life, and he cut them off, tucked them back neatly into the silence. He had the sensation of a creator; these

little smudges and flickers that he was clever to see and even cleverer to hit in the dim recesses of the rafters—out of each of them he was making a full bird. A tiny peek, probe, dab of life, when he hit it, blossomed into a dead enemy, falling with good, final weight.

The imperfection of the second pigeon he had shot, who was still lifting his wing now and then up in the round hole, nagged him. He put a new clip into the stock. Hugging the gun against his body, he climbed the ladder. The barrel sight scratched his ear; he had a sharp, garish vision, like a color slide, of shooting himself and being found tumbled on the barn floor among his prey. He locked his arm around the top rung—a fragile, gnawed rod braced between uprights—and shot into the bird's body from a flat angle. The wing folded, but the impact did not, as he had hoped, push the bird out of the hole. He fired again, and again, and still the little body, lighter than air when alive, was too heavy to budge from its high grave. From up here he could see green trees and a brown corner of the house through the hole. Clammy with the cobwebs that gathered between the rungs, he pumped a full clip of eight bullets into the stubborn shadow, with no success. He climbed down, and was struck by the silence in the barn. The remaining pigeons must have escaped out the other hole. That was all right; he was tired of it.

He stepped with his rifle into the light. His mother was coming to meet him, and it tickled him to see her shy away from the carelessly held gun. "You took a chip out of the house," she said. "What were those last shots about?"

"One of them died up in that little round hole and I was trying to shoot it down."

"Copper's hiding behind the piano and won't come out. I had to leave him."

"Well don't blame me. *I* didn't want to shoot the poor devils."

"Don't smirk. You look like your father. How many did you get?"

"Six."

She went into the barn, and he followed. She listened to the silence. Her hair was scraggly, perhaps from tussling with the dog. "I don't suppose the others will be back," she said wearily. "Indeed, I don't know why I let Mother talk me into it. Their cooing was such a comforting noise." She began to gather up the dead pigeons. Though he didn't want to touch them, David went into the mow and picked up by its tepid, horny, coral-colored feet the first bird he had killed. Its wings unfolded disconcertingly, as if the creature had been held together by threads that now were slit. It did not weigh much. He retrieved the one on the other side of the barn; his mother got the three in the middle and led the way across the road to the little southern slope of land that went down toward the foundations of the vanished tobacco shed. The ground was too steep to plant and mow; wild strawberries grew in the tangled grass. She put her burden down and said, "We'll have to bury them. The dog will go wild."

He put his two down on her three; the slick feathers let the bodies slide liquidly on one another. He asked, "Shall I get you the shovel?"

"Get it for yourself; *you* bury them. They're your kill. And be sure to make the hole deep enough so he won't dig them up." While he went to the tool shed for the shovel, she went into the house. Unlike her, she did not look up, either at the orchard to the right of her or at the meadow on her left, but instead held her head rigidly, tilted a little, as if listening to the ground.

He dug the hole, in a spot where there were no strawberry plants, before he studied the pigeons. He had never seen a bird this close before. The feathers were more wonderful than dog's hair, for each filament was shaped within the shape of the feather, and the feathers in turn were trimmed to fit a pattern that flowed without error across the bird's body. He lost himself in the geometrical tides as the feathers now broadened and stiffened to make an edge for flight, now softened and constricted to cup warmth around the mute flesh. And across the surface of the infinitely adjusted yet somehow effortless mechanics of the feathers played idle designs of color, no two alike, designs executed, it seemed, in a controlled rapture, with a joy that hung level in the air above and behind him. Yet these birds bred in the millions and were exterminated as pests. Into the fragrant open earth he dropped one broadly banded in slate shades of blue, and on top of it another, mottled all over in rhythms of lilac and gray. The next was almost wholly white, but for a salmon glaze at its throat. As he fitted the last two, still pliant, on the top, and stood up, crusty coverings were lifted from him, and with a feminine, slipping sensation along his nerves that seemed to give the air hands, he was robed in this certainty: that the God who had lavished such craft upon these worthless birds would not destroy His whole Creation by refusing to let David live forever.

The Romantic Norm:
The Quest

SIR THOMAS MALORY
1405?–1471?

from Morte Darthur

Translated by A. W. Pollard

SIR GALAHAD

CHAPTER I. *How Sir Galahad fought at a tournament, and how he was known of Sir Gawaine and Sir Ector de Maris.*[1]

. . . The good knight, Galahad, rode so long till he came that night to the Castle of Carboneck; and it befell him thus that he was benighted in an hermitage. So the good man was fain[2] when he saw he was a knight-errant. Tho[3] when they were at rest there came a gentlewoman knocking at the door, and called Galahad, and so the good man came to the door to wit what she would. Then she called the hermit: Sir Ulfin, I am a gentlewoman that would speak with the knight which is with you. Then the good man awaked Galahad, and bade him: Arise, and speak with a gentlewoman that seemeth hath great need of you. Then Galahad went to her and asked her what she would. Galahad, said she, I will that ye arm you, and mount upon your horse and follow me, for I shall show you within these three days the highest adventure that ever any

MORTE DARTHUR: *Sir Galahad.* **1. How . . . Maris:** A brief passage describing Galahad's victory in the tournament is deleted. **2. fain:** glad. **3. Tho:** then.

knight saw. Anon Galahad armed him, and took his horse, and commended him to God, and bade the gentlewoman go, and he would follow thereas she liked.

CHAPTER II. *How Sir Galahad rode with a damosel, and came to the ship whereas Sir Bors and Sir Percivale were in.*

So she rode as fast as her palfrey might bear her, till that she came to the sea, the which was called Collibe. And at the night they came unto a castle in a valley, closed with a running water, and with strong walls and high; and so she entered into the castle with Galahad, and there had he great cheer, for the lady of that castle was the damosel's lady. So when he was unarmed, then said the damosel: Madam, shall we abide here all this day? Nay, said she, but till he hath dined and till he hath slept a little. So he ate and slept a while till that the maid called him, and armed him by torchlight. And when the maid was horsed and he both, the lady took Galahad a fair child and rich; and so they departed from the castle till they came to the seaside; and there they found the ship where Bors and Percivale were in, the which cried on the ship's board: Sir Galahad, ye be welcome, we have abiden you long. And when he heard them he asked them what they were. Sir, said she, leave your horse here, and I shall leave mine; and took their saddles and their bridles with them, and made a cross on them, and so entered into the ship. And the two knights received them both with great joy, and everych knew other; and so the wind arose, and drove them through the sea in a marvellous pace. And within a while it dawned.

Then did Galahad off his helm and his sword, and asked of his fellows from whence came that fair ship. Truly, said they, ye wot as well as we, but of God's grace; and then they told everych to other of all their hard adventures, and of their great temptations. Truly, said Galahad, ye are much bounden to God, for ye have escaped great adventures; and had not the gentlewoman been I had not come here, for as for you I weened never[4] to have found you in these strange countries. Ah Galahad, said Bors, if Launcelot, your father, were here then were we well at ease, for then me-seemed we failed nothing. That may not be, said Galahad, but if it pleased Our Lord.

By then the ship went from the land of Logris, and by adventure it arrived up betwixt two rocks passing great and marvellous; but there they might not land, for there was a swallow[5] of the sea, save there was another ship, and upon it they might go without danger. Go we thither, said the gentle-woman, and there shall we see adventures, for so is Our Lord's will. And when they came thither they found the ship rich enough, but they found neither man nor woman therein. But they found in the end of the ship two fair letters written, which said a dreadful word and a marvellous: Thou man, which shall enter into this ship, beware thou be in stead-fast belief, for I am Faith, and therefore beware how thou enterest, for an[6] thou fail I shall not help thee. Then said the gentlewoman: Percivale, wot[7] ye what I am? Certes, said he, nay, to my witting. Wit ye well, said she, that I am thy sister, which am daughter of King Pellinore, and therefore wit ye well ye are the man in the world that I most love; and if ye be not in perfect belief of Jesu Christ enter not in no manner of wise, for then should ye perish the ship, for he is so perfect he will suffer no sinner in him. When Percivale understood that she was his very sister he was inwardly glad, and said: Fair sister, I shall enter therein, for if I be a mis-creature or an untrue knight there shall I perish.

CHAPTER III. *How Sir Galahad entered into the ship, and of a fair bed therein, with other marvellous things, and of a sword.*

In the meanwhile Galahad blessed him, and entered therein; and then next the gentlewoman,

and then Sir Bors and Sir Percivale. And when they were in, it was so marvellous fair and rich that they marvelled; and in midst of the ship was a fair bed, and Galahad went thereto, and found there a crown of silk. And at the feet was a sword, rich and fair, and it was drawn out of the sheath half a foot and more; and the sword was of divers fashions, and the pommel was of stone, and there was in him all manner of colours that any man might find, and everych of the colours had divers virtues; and the scales[8] of the haft were of two ribs of divers beasts, the one beast was a serpent which was conversant[9] in Calidone, and is called the Serpent of the fiend; and the bone of him is of such a virtue that there is no hand that handleth him shall never be weary nor hurt. And the other beast is a fish which is not right great, and haunteth the flood of Euphrates; and that fish is called Ertanax, and his bones be of such a manner of kind that who that handleth them shall have so much will that he shall never be weary, and he shall not think on joy nor sorrow that he hath had, but only that thing that he beholdeth before him. And as for this sword there shall never man begrip him at the handles but one; but he shall pass all other. In the name of God, said Percivale, I shall assay to handle it. So he set his hand to the sword, but he might not begrip it. By my faith, said he, now have I failed. Bors set his hand thereto and failed.

Then Galahad beheld the sword and saw letters like blood that said: Let see who shall assay to draw me out of my sheath, but if he be more hardier than any other; and who that draweth me, wit ye well that he shall never fail of shame of his body,[10] or to be wounded to the death. By my faith, said Galahad, I would draw this sword out of the sheath, but the offending is so great that I shall not set my hand thereto. Now sirs, said the gentle-woman, wit ye well that the drawing of this sword is warned to all men save all only to you. Also this ship arrived in the realm of Logris; and that time was deadly war between King Labor, which was father unto the maimed king, and King Hurlame, which was a Saracen. But then was he newly christened, so that men held him afterward one of the wittiest men of the world. And so upon a day it

---

8. **scales:** curved or cup-shaped handguards. 9. **conversant:** living. 10. **but . . . body:** unless he is hardier than any other, he who draws me . . . shall never fail to be shamed in his body.

4. **for as . . . never:** for, like you, I would never expect.
5. **swallow:** whirlpool. 6. **an:** if. 7. **wot:** know.

befell that King Labor and King Hurlame had assembled their folk upon the sea where this ship was arrived; and there King Hurlame was discomfit, and his men slain; and he was afeard to be dead, and fled to his ship, and there found this sword and drew it, and came out and found King Labor, the man in the world of all Christendom in whom was then the greatest faith. And when King Hurlame saw King Labor he dressed this sword, and smote him upon the helm so hard that he clave him and his horse to the earth with the first stroke of his sword. And it was in the realm of Logris; and so befell great pestilence and great harm to both realms. For sithen[11] increased neither corn, nor grass, nor well-nigh no fruit, nor in the water was no fish; wherefore men call it the lands of the two marches,[12] the waste land, for that dolorous stroke. And when King Hurlame saw this sword so carving,[13] he turned again to fetch the scabbard, and so came into this ship and entered, and put up the sword in the sheath. And as soon as he had done it he fell down dead afore the bed. Thus was the sword proved, that none ne drew it but he were dead or maimed. So lay he there till a maiden came into the ship and cast him out, for there was no man so hardy of the world to enter into that ship for the defence.

CHAPTER IV. *Of the marvels of the sword and of the scabbard.*

And then beheld they the scabbard, it seemed to be of a serpent's skin, and thereon were letters of gold and silver. And the girdle was but poorly to come to, and not able to sustain such a rich sword. And the letters said: He which shall wield me ought to be more harder than any other, if he bear me as truly as me ought to be borne. For the body of him which I ought to hang by, he shall not be shamed in no place while he is girt with this girdle, nor never none be so hardy to do away this girdle; for it ought not be done away but by the hands of a maid, and that she be a king's daughter and queen's, and she must be a maid all the days of her life, both in will and in deed. And if she break her virginity she shall die the most villainous death that ever died any woman. Sir, said Percivale, turn this sword that we may see what is on the other

side. And it was red as blood, with black letters as any coal, which said: He that shall praise me most, most shall he find me to blame at a great need; and to whom I should be most debonair[14] shall I be most felon,[15] and that shall be at one time.

Fair brother, said she to Percivale, it befell after a forty year after the passion of Jesu Christ that Nacien, the brother-in-law of King Mordrains, was borne into a town more than fourteen days' journey from his country, by the commandment of Our Lord, into an isle, into the parts of the West, that men cleped[16] the Isle of Turnance. So befell it that he found this ship at the entry of a rock, and he found the bed and this sword as we have heard now. Not for then[17] he had not so much hardiness to draw it; and there he dwelled an eight days, and at the ninth day there fell a great wind which departed him out of the isle, and brought him to another isle by a rock, and there he found the greatest giant that ever man might see. Therewith came that horrible giant to slay him; and then he looked about him and might not flee, and he had nothing to defend him with. So he ran to his sword, and when he saw it naked he praised it much, and then he shook it, and therewith he brake it in the midst. Ah, said Nacien, the thing that I most praised ought I now most to blame, and therewith he threw the pieces of his sword over his bed. And after he leapt over the board to fight with the giant, and slew him.

And anon he entered into the ship again, and the wind arose, and drove him through the sea, that by adventure he came to another ship where King Mordrains was, which had been tempted full evil with a fiend in the Port of Perilous Rock. And when that one saw the other they made great joy of other, and either told other of their adventure, and how the sword failed him at his most need. When Mordrains saw the sword he praised it much: But the breaking was not to do but by wickedness of thy selfward, for thou art in some sin. And there he took the sword, and set the pieces together, and they soldered as fair as ever they were to-fore; and there put he the sword in the sheath, and laid it down on the bed. Then heard they a voice that said: Go out of this ship a little while, and enter into the other, for dread ye fall in deadly sin, for and ye be found in deadly sin ye may not escape but perish:

11. **sithen:** since then. 12. **marches:** borders. 13. **carving:** cutting, sharp.

14. **debonair:** gracious, useful. 15. **felon:** harmful. 16. **cleped:** called. 17. **Not for then:** nevertheless.

and so they went into the other ship. And as Nacien went over the board he was smitten with a sword on the right foot, that he fell down noseling[18] to the ship's board; and therewith he said: O God, how am I hurt. And then there came a voice and said: Take thou that for thy forfeit that thou didst in drawing of this sword, therefore thou receivest a wound, for thou were never worthy to handle it, as the writing maketh mention. In the name of God, said Galahad, ye are right wise of these works.

CHAPTER V. *How King Pelles was smitten through both thighs because he drew the sword, and other marvellous histories.*

Sir, said she, there was a king that hight[19] Pelles, the maimed king. And while he might ride he supported much Christendom and Holy Church. So upon a day he hunted in a wood of his which lasted unto the sea; and at the last he lost his hounds and his knights save only one: and there he and his knight went till that they came toward Ireland, and there he found the ship. And when he saw the letters and understood them, yet he entered, for he was right perfect of his life, but his knight had none hardiness to enter; and there found he this sword, and drew it out as much as ye may see. So therewith entered a spear wherewith he was smitten him through both the thighs, and never sith might he be healed, nor nought shall to-fore we come to him. Thus, said she, was not King Pelles, your grandsire, maimed for his hardiness? In the name of God, damosel, said Galahad.

So they went toward the bed to behold all about it, and above the head there hung two swords. Also there were two spindles which were as white as any snow, and other that were as red as blood, and other above green as any emerald: of these three colours were the spindles, and of natural colour within, and without any painting. These spindles, said the damosel, were when sinful Eve came to gather fruit, for which Adam and she were put out of paradise, she took with her the bough on which the apple hung on. Then perceived she that the branch was fair and green, and she remembered her the loss which came from the tree. Then she thought to keep the branch as long as she might. And for she had no coffer to keep it in, she put it in the earth. So by the will of Our Lord the branch grew to a great tree within a little while, and was as white as any snow, branches, boughs, and leaves: that was a token a maiden planted it. But after God came to Adam, and bade him know his wife fleshly as nature required. So lay Adam with his wife under the same tree; and anon the tree which was white was full green as any grass, and all that came out of it; and in the same time that they medled together there was Abel begotten: thus was the tree long of green colour. And so it befell many days after, under the same tree Caym[20] slew Abel, whereof befell great marvel. For anon as Abel had received the death under the green tree, it lost the green colour and became red; an that was in tokening of the blood. And anon all the plants died thereof, but the tree grew and waxed marvellously fair, and it was the fairest tree and the most delectable that any man might behold and see; and so died the plants that grew out of it to-fore that Abel was slain under it. So long dured[21] the tree till that Solomon, King David's son, reigned, and held the land after his father. This Solomon was wise, and knew all the virtues of stones and trees, and so he knew the course of the stars, and many other divers things. This Solomon had an evil wife, wherethrough he weened that there had been no good woman, and so he despised them in his books. So answered a voice him once: Solomon, if heaviness come to a man by a woman, ne reck thou never; for yet shall there come a woman whereof there shall come greater joy to man an hundred times more than this heaviness giveth sorrow; and that woman shall be born of thy lineage. Tho when Solomon heard these words he held himself but a fool, and the truth he perceived by old books. Also the Holy Ghost showed him the coming of the glorious Virgin Mary. Then asked he of the voice, if it should be in the yerde[22] of his lineage. Nay, said the voice, but there shall come a man which shall be a maid, and the last of your blood, and he shall be as good a knight as Duke Josua, thy brother-in-law.

---

18. **noseling**: headlong. 19. **hight**: was called.

20. **Caym**: Cain. 21. **dured**: lasted. 22. **yerde**: branch.

CHAPTER VI. *How Solomon took David's sword by the counsel of his wife, and of other matters marvellous.*

Now have I certified thee of that thou stoodest in doubt. Then was Solomon glad that there should come any such of his lineage; but ever he marvelled and studied who that should be, and what his name might be. His wife perceived that he studied, and thought she would know it at some season; and so she waited her time, and asked of him the cause of his studying, and there he told her altogether how the voice told him. Well, said she, I shall let make a ship of the best wood and most durable that men may find. So Solomon sent for all the carpenters of the land, and the best. And when they had made the ship the lady said to Solomon: Sir, said she, since it is so that this knight ought to pass all knights of chivalry which have been to-fore him and shall come after him, moreover I shall tell you, said she, ye shall go into Our Lord's temple, where is King David's sword, your father, the which is the marvelloust and the sharpest that ever was taken in any knight's hand. Therefore take that, and take off the pommel, and thereto make ye a pommel of precious stones, that it be so subtly made that no man perceive it but that they be all one; and after make there an hilt so marvellously and wonderly that no man may know it; and after make a marvellous sheath. And when ye have made all this I shall let make a girdle thereto, such as shall please me.

All this King Solomon did let make as she devised, both the ship and all the remnant. And when the ship was ready in the sea to sail, the lady let make a great bed and marvellous rich, and set her upon the bed's head, covered with silk, and laid the sword at the feet, and the girdles were of hemp, and therewith the king was angry. Sir, wit ye well, said she, that I have none so high a thing which were worthy to sustain so high a sword, and a maid shall bring other knights thereto, but I wot not when it shall be, nor what time. And there she let make a covering to the ship, of cloth of silk that should never rot for no manner of weather. Yet went that lady and made a carpenter to come to the tree which Abel was slain under. Now, said she, carve me out of this tree as much wood as will make me a spindle. Ah madam, said he, this is the tree the which our first mother planted. Do it, said she,

or else I shall destroy thee. Anon as he began to work there came out drops of blood; and then would he have left, but she would not suffer him, and so he took away as much wood as might make a spindle: and so she made him to take as much of the green tree and of the white tree. And when these three spindles were shapen she made them to be fastened upon the selar[23] of the bed. When Solomon saw this, he said to his wife: Ye have done marvellously, for though all the world were here right now, he could not devise wherefore all this was made, but Our Lord Himself; and thou that hast done it wottest not what it shall betoken. Now let it be, said she, for ye shall hear tidings sooner than ye ween. Now shall ye hear a wonderful tale of King Solomon and his wife.

CHAPTER VII. *A wonderful tale of King Solomon and his wife.*

That night lay Solomon before the ship with little fellowship. And when he was asleep him thought there came from heaven a great company of angels, and alighted into the ship, and took water which was brought by an angel, in a vessel of silver, and sprent[24] all the ship. And after he came to the sword, and drew letters on the hilt. And after went to the ship's board, and wrote there other letters which said: Thou man that wilt enter within me, beware that thou be full within the faith, for I ne am but Faith and Belief. When Solomon espied these letters he was abashed, so that he durst not enter, and so drew him aback; and the ship was anon shoven in the sea, and he went so fast that he lost sight of him within a little while. And then a little voice said: Solomon, the last knight of thy lineage shall rest in this bed. Then went Solomon and awaked his wife, and told her of the adventures of the ship.

Now saith the history that a great while the three fellows beheld the bed and the three spindles. Then they were at certain that they were of natural colours without painting. Then they lift up a cloth which was above the ground, and there found a rich purse by seeming. And Percivale took it, and found therein a writ and so he read it, and devised the manner of the spindles and of the ship, whence it came, and by whom it was made. Now, said

23. **selar:** canopy. 24. **sprent:** sprinkled.

Galahad, where shall we find the gentlewoman that shall make new girdles to the sword? Fair sir, said Percivale's sister, dismay you not, for by the leave of God I shall let make a girdle to the sword, such one as shall long thereto. And then she opened a box, and took out girdles which were seemly wrought with golden threads, and upon that were set full precious stones, and a rich buckle of gold. Lo, lords, said she, here is a girdle that ought to be set about the sword. And wit ye well the greatest part of this girdle was made of my hair, which I loved well while that I was a woman of the world. But as soon as I wist that this adventure was ordained me I clipped off my hair, and made this girdle in the name of God. Ye be well found, said Sir Bors, for certes ye have put us out of great pain, wherein we should have entered ne had your tidings been.

Then went the gentlewoman and set it on the girdle of the sword. Now, said the fellowship, what is the name of the sword, and what shall we call it? Truly, said she, the name of the sword is the Sword with the Strange Girdles; and the sheath, Mover of Blood; for no man that hath blood in him ne shall never see the one part of the sheath which was made of the Tree of Life. Then they said to Galahad: In the name of Jesu Christ, and pray you that ye gird you with this sword which hath been desired so much in the realm of Logris. Now let me begin, said Galahad, to grip this sword for to give you courage; but wit ye well it longeth no more to me than it doth to you. And then he gripped about it with his fingers a great deal; and then she girt him about the middle with the sword. Now reck I not though I die, for now I hold me one of the blessed maidens of the world, which hath made the worthiest knight of the world. Damosel, said Galahad, ye have done so much that I shall be your knight all the days of my life.

Then they went from that ship, and went to the other. And anon the wind drove them into the sea a great pace, but they had no victuals: but it befell that they came on the morn to a castle that men call Carteloise, that was in the marches of Scotland. And when they had passed the port, the gentlewoman said: Lords, here be men arriven that, an they wist that ye were of King Arthur's court, ye should be assailed anon. Damosel, said Galahad, He that cast us out of the rock shall deliver us from them.

CHAPTER VIII. *How Galahad and his fellows came to a castle, and how they were fought withal, and how they slew their adversaries, and other matters.*

So it befell as they spoke thus there came a squire by them, and asked what they were; and they said they were of King Arthur's house. Is that sooth? said he. Now by my head, said he, ye be ill arrayed; and then turned he again unto the cliff fortress. And within a while they heard an horn blow. Then a gentlewoman came to them, and asked them of whence they were; and they told her. Fair lords, said she, for God's love turn again if ye may, for ye be come unto your death. Nay, they said, we will not turn again, for He shall help us in whose service we be entered in. Then as they stood talking there came knights well armed, and bade them yield them or else to die. That yielding, said they, shall be noyous[25] to you. And therewith they let their horses run, and Sir Percivale smote the foremost to the earth, and took his horse, and mounted thereupon, and the same did Galahad. Also Bors served another so, for they had no horses in that country, for they left their horses when they took their ship in other countries. And so when they were horsed then began they to set upon them; and they of the castle fled into the strong fortress, and the three knights after them into the castle, and so alighted on foot, and with their swords slew them down, and gat into the hall.

Then when they beheld the great multitude of people that they had slain, they held themself great sinners. Certes, said Bors, I ween an God had loved them that we should not have had power to have slain them thus. But they have done so much against Our Lord that He would not suffer them to reign no longer. Say ye not so, said Galahad, for if they misdid against God, the vengeance is not ours, but to Him which hath power thereof.

So came there out of a chamber a good man which was a priest, and bare God's body in a cup. And when he saw them which lay dead in the hall he was all abashed; and Galahad did off his helm and kneeled down, and so did his two fellows. Sir, said they, have ye no dread of us, for we be of King Arthur's court. Then asked the good man how they were slain so suddenly, and they told it him. Truly, said the good man, an ye might live as

25. noyous: troublesome.

long as the world might endure, ne might ye have done so great an alms-deed as this. Sir, said Galahad, I repent me much, inasmuch as they were christened. Nay, repent you not, said he, for they were not christened, and I shall tell you how that I wot of this castle. Here was Lord Earl Hernox not but one year, and he had three sons, good knights of arms, and a daughter, the fairest gentlewoman that men knew. So those three knights loved their sister so sore that they brent in love, and so they lay by her, maugre her head.[26] And for she cried to her father they slew her, and took their father and put him in prison, and wounded him nigh to the death, but a cousin of hers rescued him. And then did they great untruth: they slew clerks and priests, and made beat down chapels, that Our Lord's service might not be served nor said. And this same day her father sent to me for to be confessed and houseled;[27] but such shame had never man as I had this day with the three brethren, but the earl bade me suffer, for he said they should not long endure, for three servants of Our Lord should destroy them, and now it is brought to an end. And by this may ye wit that Our Lord is not displeased with your deeds. Certes, said Galahad, an it had not pleased Our Lord, never should we have slain so many men in so little a while.

And then they brought the Earl Hernox out of prison into the midst of the hall, that knew Galahad anon, and yet he saw him never afore but by revelation of Our Lord.

CHAPTER IX. *How the three knights, with Percivale's sister, came unto the same forest, and of an hart*[28] *and four lions, and other things.*

Then began he to weep right tenderly, and said: Long have I abiden your coming, but for God's love hold me in your arms, that my soul may depart out of my body in so good a man's arms as ye be. Gladly, said Galahad. And then one said on high, that all heard: Galahad, well hast thou avenged me on God's enemies. Now behoveth thee to go to the Maimed King as soon as thou mayest, for he shall receive by thee health which he hath abiden so long. And therewith the soul departed from the body, and Galahad made him to be buried as him ought to be.

Right so departed the three knights, and Percivale's sister with them. And so they came into a waste forest, and there they saw afore them a white hart which four lions led. Then they took them to assent for to follow after for to know whither they repaired; and so they rode after a great pace till that they came to a valley, and thereby was an hermitage where a good man dwelled, and the hart and the lions entered also. So when they saw all this they turned to the chapel, and saw the good man in a religious weed and in the armour of Our Lord, for he would sing mass of the Holy Ghost; and so they entered in and heard mass. And at the secrets of the mass they three saw the hart become a man, the which marvelled them, and set him upon the altar in a rich siege;[29] and saw the four lions were changed, the one to the form of a man, the other to the form of a lion, and the third to an eagle, and the fourth was changed unto an ox. Then took they their siege where the hart sat, and went out through a glass window, and there was nothing perished nor broken; and they heard a voice say: In such a manner entered the Son of God in the womb of a maid Mary, whose virginity ne was perished ne hurt. And when they heard these words they fell down to the earth and were astonied; and therewith was a great clearness.

And when they were come to theirself again they went to the good man and prayed him that he would say them truth. What thing have ye seen? said he. And they told him all that they had seen. Ah lords, said he, ye be welcome; now wot I well ye be the good knights the which shall bring the Sangreal[30] to an end; for ye be they unto whom Our Lord shall shew great secrets. And well ought Our Lord be signified to an hart, for the hart when he is old he waxeth young again in his white skin. Right so cometh again Our Lord from death to life, for He lost earthly flesh that was the deadly flesh, which He had taken in the womb of the blessed Virgin Mary; and for that cause appeared Our Lord as a white hart without spot. And the four that were with Him is to understand the four evangelists which set in writing a part of Jesu Christ's deeds that He did sometime when He was among you an earthly man; for wit ye well never erst[31] he might no knight know the truth, for ofttimes or this Our Lord showed Him unto good

26. **maugre her head:** against her will. 27. **houseled:** shriven. 28. **hart:** deer.

29. **siege:** seat. 30. **Sangreal:** Holy Grail. 31. **erst:** before.

men and unto good knights, in likeness of an hart, but I suppose from henceforth ye shall see no more. And then they joyed much, and dwelled there all that day. And upon the morrow when they had heard mass they departed and commended the good man to God: and so they came to a castle and passed by. So there came a knight armed after them and said: Lords, hark what I shall say to you.

CHAPTER X. *How they were desired of a strange custom, the which they would not obey; wherefore they fought and slew many knights.*

This gentlewoman that ye lead with you is a maid? Sir, said she, a maid I am. Then he took her by the bridle and said: By the Holy Cross, ye shall not escape me to-fore ye have yolden[32] the custom of this castle. Let her go, said Percivale, ye be not wise, for a maid in what place she cometh is free. So in the meanwhile there came out a ten or twelve knights armed, out of the castle, and with them came gentlewomen which held a dish of silver. And then they said: This gentlewoman must yield us the custom of this castle. Sir, said a knight, what maid passeth hereby shall give this dish full of blood of her right arm. Blame have ye, said Galahad, that brought up such customs, and so God me save, I ensure you of this gentlewoman ye shall fail while that I live. So God me help, said Percivale, I had liefer[33] be slain. And I also, said Sir Bors. By my troth, said the knight, then shall ye die, for ye may not endure against us though ye were the best knights of the world.

Then let they run each to other, and the three fellows beat the ten knights, and then set their hands to their swords and beat them down and slew them. Then there came out of the castle a three score knights armed. Fair lords, said the three fellows, have mercy on yourself and have not ado with us. Nay, fair lords, said the knights of the castle, we counsel you to withdraw you, for ye be the best knights of the world, and therefore do no more, for ye have done enough. We will let you go with this harm, but we must needs have the custom. Certes, said Galahad, for nought speak ye. Well, said they, will ye die? We be not yet come thereto, said Galahad. Then began they to meddle together, and Galahad, with the strange girdles, drew his sword, and smote on the right hand and on the left

32. **yolden:** complied with. 33. **liefer:** rather.

hand, and slew what that ever abode him, and did such marvels that there was none that saw him but weened he had been none earthly man, but a monster. And his two fellows halp him passing well, and so they held the journey everych in like hard till it was night: then must they needs depart.

So came in a good knight, and said to the three fellows: If ye will come in to-night and take such harbour as here is ye shall be right welcome, and we shall ensure you by the faith of our bodies, and as we be true knights, to leave you in such estate to-morrow as we find you, without any falsehood. And as soon as ye know of the custom we dare say ye will accord therefore. For God's love, said the gentlewoman, go thither and spare not for me. Go we, said Galahad; and so they entered into the chapel. And when they were alighted they made great joy of them. So within a while the three knights asked the custom of the castle and wherefore it was. What it is, said they, we will say you sooth.

CHAPTER XI. *How Sir Percivale's sister bled a dish full of blood for to heal a lady, wherefore she died; and how that the body was put in a ship.*

There is in this castle a gentlewoman which we and this castle is hers, and many other. So it befell many years agone there fell upon her a malady; and when she had lain a great while she fell unto a measle,[34] and of no leech[35] she could have no remedy. But at the last an old man said an she might have a dish full of blood of a maid and a clean virgin in will and in work, and a king's daughter, that blood should be her health, and for to anoint her withal; and for this thing was this custom made. Now, said Percivale's sister, fair knights, I see well that this gentlewoman is but dead. Certes, said Galahad, an ye bleed so much ye may die. Truly, said she, an I die for to heal her I shall get me great worship and soul's health, and worship to my lineage, and better is one harm than twain. And therefore there shall be no more battle, but to-morn I shall yield you your custom of this castle. And then there was great joy more than there was to-fore, for else had there been mortal war upon the morn; notwithstanding she would none other, whether they wold or nold.

34. **measle:** serious illness. 35. **leech:** physician.

That night were the three fellows eased with the best; and on the morn they heard mass, and Sir Percivale's sister bade bring forth the sick lady. So she was, the which was evil at ease. Then said she: Who shall let me blood? So one came forth and let her blood, and she bled so much that the dish was full. Then she lift up her hand and blessed her; and then she said to the lady: Madam, I am come to the death for to make you whole, for God's love pray for me. With that she fell in a swoon. Then Galahad and his two fellows start up to her, and lift her up and staunched her, but she had bled so much that she might not live. Then she said when she was awaked: Fair brother Percivale, I die for the healing of this lady, so I require you that ye bury me not in this country, but as soon as I am dead put me in a boat at the next haven, and let me go to adventure will lead me; and as soon as ye three come to the city of Sarras, there to enchieve the Holy Grail, ye shall find me under a tower arrived, and there bury me in the spiritual place; for I say you so much, there Galahad shall be buried, and ye also, in the same place.

Then Percivale understood these words, and granted it her, weeping. And then said a voice: Lords and fellows, to-morrow at the hour of prime[36] ye three shall depart everych from other, till the adventure bring you to the Maimed King. Then asked she her Saviour; and as soon as she had received it the soul departed from the body. So the same day was the lady healed, when she was anointed withal. Then Sir Percivale made a letter of all that she had holpen them as in strange adventures, and put it in her right hand, and so laid her in a barge, and covered it with black silk; and so the wind arose, and drove the barge from the land, and all knights beheld it till it was out of their sight. Then they drew all to the castle, and so forthwith there fell a sudden tempest and a thunder, lightning, and rain, as all the earth would have broken. So half the castle turned up-so-down. So it passed evensong or the tempest was ceased.

Then they saw afore them a knight armed and wounded hard in the body and in the head, that said: O God, succour me for now it is need. After this knight came another knight and a dwarf, which cried to them afar: Stand, ye may not escape. Then the wounded knight held up his hands to God that he should not die in such tribulation.

36. **prime:** first canonical hour of the day, 9:00 A.M.

Truly, said Galahad, I shall succour him for His sake that he calleth upon. Sir, said Bors, I shall do it, for it is not for you, for he is but one knight. Sir, said he, I grant. So Sir Bors took his horse, and commended him to God, and rode after, to rescue the wounded knight. Now turn we to the two fellows.

CHAPTER XII. *How Galahad and Percivale found in a castle many tombs of maidens that had bled to death.*

Now saith the story that all night Galahad and Percivale were in a chapel in their prayers, for to save Sir Bors. So on the morrow they dressed them in their harness toward the castle, to wit what was fallen of them therein. And when they came there they found neither man nor woman that he ne was dead by the vengeance of Our Lord. With that they heard a voice that said: This vengeance is for blood-shedding of maidens. Also they found at the end of the chapel a churchyard, and therein might they see a three score fair tombs, and that place was so fair and so delectable that it seemed them there had been none tempest, for there lay the bodies of all the good maidens which were martyred for the sick lady's sake. Also they found the names of everych, and of what blood they were come, and all were of kings' blood, and twelve of them were kings' daughters. Then they departed and went into a forest. Now, said Percivale unto Galahad, we must depart, so pray we Our Lord that we may meet together in short time: then they did off their helms and kissed together, and wept at their departing.

THE MIRACLE OF GALAHAD

CHAPTER XVIII.[1] *How Galahad came to King Mordrains, and of other matters and adventures.*

Now, saith the story, Galahad rode many journeys in vain. And at the last he came to the abbey where King Mordrains was, and when he heard that, he thought he would abide to see him. And upon the morn, when he had heard mass, Galahad came

The Miracle of Galahad. **1.** An intervening story, "The Castle of Corbenic," tells of Lancelot's quest for the Holy Grail.

unto King Mordrains, and anon the king saw him, which had lain blind of long time. And then he dressed him against him, and said: Galahad, the servant of Jesu Christ, whose coming I have abiden so long, now embrace me and let me rest on thy breast, so that I may rest between thine arms, for thou art a clean virgin above all knights, as the flower of the lily in whom virginity is signified, and thou art the rose the which is the flower of all good virtues, and in colour of fire. For the fire of the Holy Ghost is taken so in thee that my flesh which was all dead of oldness is become young again. Then Galahad heard his words, then he embraced him and all his body. Then said he: Fair Lord Jesu Christ, now I have my will. Now I require thee, in this point that I am in, thou come and visit me. And anon Our Lord heard his prayer: therewith the soul departed from the body.

And then Galahad put him in the earth as a king ought to be, and so departed and so came into a perilous forest where he found the well the which boileth with great waves, as the tale telleth to-fore. And as soon as Galahad set his hand thereto it ceased, so that it brent no more, and the heat departed. For that it brent it was a sign of lechery, the which was that time much used. But that heat might not abide his pure virginity. And this was taken in the country for a miracle. And so ever after was it called Galahad's well.

Then by adventure he came into the country of Gore, and into the abbey where Launcelot had been to-forehand, and found the tomb of King Bagdemagus, but he was founder thereof, Joseph of Aramathie's[2] son; and the tomb of Simeon where Launcelot had failed. Then he looked into a croft[3] under the minster,[4] and there he saw a tomb which brent full marvellously. Then asked he the brethren what it was. Sir, said they, a marvellous adventure that may not be brought unto none end but by him that passeth of bounty and of knighthood all them of the Round Table. I would, said Galahad, that ye would lead me thereto. Gladly, said they, and so led him till a cave. And he went down upon greses,[5] and came nigh the tomb. And then the flaming failed, and the fire staunched, the which many a day had been

2. **Joseph of Aramathie:** In medieval legend Joseph of Arimathaea obtained the chalice (the Holy Grail) used at the Last Supper, caught Jesus' blood in it at the Crucifixion, and brought it to England. 3. **croft:** crypt. 4. **minster:** monastery. 5. **greses:** steps.

great. Then came there a voice that said: Much are ye beholden to thank Our Lord, the which hath given you a good hour, that ye may draw out the souls of earthly pain, and to put them into the joys of paradise. I am of your kindred, the which hath dwelled in this heat this three hundred winter and four-and-fifty to be purged of the sin that I did against Joseph of Aramathie. Then Galahad took the body in his arms and bare it into the minster. And that night lay Galahad in the abbey; and on the morn he gave him service, and put him in the earth afore the high altar.

CHAPTER XIX. *How Sir Percivale and Sir Bors met with Sir Galahad, and how they came to the castle of Carbonek, and other matters.*

So departed he from thence, and commended the brethren to God; and so he rode five days till that he came to the Maimed King. And ever followed Percivale the five days, asking where he had been; and so one told him how the adventures of Logris were enchieved. So on a day it befell that they came out of a great forest, and there they met at traverse with Sir Bors, the which rode alone. It is none need to tell if they were glad; and them he saluted, and they yielded him honour and good adventure, and everych told other. Then said Bors: It is mo than a year and an half that I ne lay ten times where men dwelled, but in wild forests and in mountains, but God was ever my comfort.

Then rode they a great while till that they came to the castle of Carbonek. And when they were entered within the castle King Pelles knew them; then there was great joy, for they wist well by their coming that they had fulfilled the quest of the Sangreal. Then Eliazar, King Pelles' son, brought to-fore them the broken sword wherewith Joseph was striken through the thigh. Then Bors set his hand thereto, if that he might have soldered it again; but it would not be. Then he took it to Percivale, but he had no more power thereto than he. Now have ye it again, said Percivale to Galahad, for an it be ever enchieved by any bodily man ye must do it. And then he took the pieces and set them together, and they seemed that they had never been broken, and as well as it had been first forged. And when they within espied that the adventure of the sword was enchieved, then they gave the sword to Bors, for it might not be better set; for he was a good knight and a worthy man.

And a little afore even the sword arose great and marvellous, and was full of great heat that many men fell for dread. And anon alighted a voice among them, and said: They that ought not to sit at the table of Jesu Christ arise, for now shall very knights be fed. So they went thence, all save King Pelles and Eliazar, his son, the which were holy men, and a maid which was his niece; and so these three fellows and they three were there, no mo. Anon they saw knights all armed came in at the hall door, and did off their helms and their arms, and said unto Galahad: Sir, we have hied right much for to be with you at this table where the holy meat shall be departed. Then said he: Ye be welcome, but of whence be ye? So three of them said they were of Gaul, and other three said they were of Ireland, and the other three said they were of Denmark. So as they sat thus there came out a bed of tree, of a chamber, the which four gentlewomen brought; and in the bed lay a good man sick, and a crown of gold upon his head; and there in the midst of the place they set him down, and went again their way. Then he lift up his head, and said: Galahad, Knight, ye be welcome, for much have I desired your coming, for in such pain and in such anguish I have been long. But now I trust to God the term is come that my pain shall be allayed, that I shall pass out of this world so as it was promised me long ago. Therewith a voice said: There be two among you that be not in the quest of the Sangreal, and therefore depart ye.

CHAPTER XX. *How Galahad and his fellows were fed of the Holy Sangreal, and how Our Lord appeared to them, and other things.*

Then King Pelles and his son departed. And therewithal beseemed them that there came a man, and four angels from heaven, clothed in likeness of a bishop, and had a cross in his hand; and these four angels bare him up in a chair, and set him down before the table of silver whereupon the Sangreal was; and it seemed that he had in midst of his forehead letters the which said: See ye here Joseph, the first bishop of Christendom, the same which Our Lord succoured in the city of Sarras in the spiritual place. Then the knights marvelled, for that bishop was dead more than three hundred

year to-fore. O knights, said he, marvel not, for I was sometime an earthly man. With that they heard the chamber door open, and there they saw angels; and two bare candles of wax, and the third a towel, and the fourth a spear which bled marvellously, that three drops fell within a box which he held with his other hand. And they set the candles upon the table, and the third the towel upon the vessel, and the fourth the holy spear even upright upon the vessel. And then the bishop made semblaunt[6] as though he would have gone to the sacring[7] of the mass. And then he took an ubblie[8] which was made in likeness of bread. And at the lifting up there came a figure in likeness of a child, and the visage was as red and as bright as any fire, and smote himself into the bread, so that they all saw it that the bread was formed of a fleshly man; and then he put it into the Holy Vessel again, and then he did that longed to a priest to do to a mass. And then he went to Galahad and kissed him, and bade him go and kiss his fellows: and so he did anon. Now, said he, servants of Jesu Christ, ye shall be fed afore this table with sweet meats that never knights tasted. And when he had said, he vanished away. And they set them at the table in great dread, and made their prayers.

Then looked they and saw a man come out of the Holy Vessel, that had all the signs of the passion of Jesu Christ, bleeding all openly, and said: My knights, and my servants, and my true children, which be come out of deadly life into spiritual life, I will now no longer hide me from you, but ye shall see now a part of my secrets and of my hidden things: now hold and receive the high meat which ye have so much desired. Then took he himself the Holy Vessel and came to Galahad; and he kneeled down, and there he received his Saviour, and after him so received all his fellows; and they thought it so sweet that it was marvellous to tell. Then said he to Galahad: Son, wottest thou what I hold betwixt my hands? Nay, said he, but if ye will tell me. This is, said he, the holy dish wherein I ate the lamb on Sheer-Thursday.[9] And now hast thou seen that thou most desired to see, but yet hast thou not seen it so openly as thou shalt see it in the city of Sarras in the spiritual place. Therefore thou must

6. **semblaunt:** appearance. 7. **sacring:** consecration. 8. **ubblie:** wafer. 9. **Sheer-Thursday:** modification of a Scandinavian form for Maundy Thursday, the Thursday before Easter.

go hence and bear with thee this Holy Vessel; for this night it shall depart from the realm of Logris, that it shall never be seen more here. And wottest thou wherefore? For he is not served nor worshipped to his right by them of this land, for they be turned to evil living; therefore I shall disherit them of the honour which I have done them. And therefore go ye three to-morrow unto the sea, where ye shall find your ship ready, and with you take the sword with the strange girdles, and no more with you but Sir Percivale and Sir Bors. Also I will that ye take with you of the blood of this spear for to anoint the Maimed King, both his legs and all his body, and he shall have his health. Sir, said Galahad, why shall not these other fellows go with us? For this cause: for right as I departed my apostles one here and another there, so I will that ye depart; and two of you shall die in my service, but one of you shall come again and tell tidings. Then gave he them his blessing and vanished away.

CHAPTER XXI. *How Galahad anointed with the blood of the spear the Maimed King, and of other adventures.*

And Galahad went anon to the spear which lay upon the table, and touched the blood with his fingers, and came after to the Maimed King and anointed his legs. And therewith he clothed him anon, and start upon his feet out of his bed as an whole man, and thanked Our Lord that He had healed him. And that was not to the worldward, for anon he yielded him to a place of religion of white monks, and was a full holy man. That same night about midnight came a voice among them which said: My sons and not my chief sons, my friends and not my warriors, go ye hence where ye hope best to do and as I bade you. Ah, thanked be Thou, Lord, that Thou wilt vouchsafe to call us, Thy sinners. Now may we well prove that we have not lost our pains. And anon in all haste they took their harness and departed. But the three knights of Gaul, one of them hight Claudine, King Claudas' son, and the other two were great gentlemen. Then prayed Galahad to everych of them, that if they come to King Arthur's court that they should salute my lord, Sir Launcelot, my father, and all the fellowship of the Round Table; and

prayed them if that they came on that part that they should not forget it.

Right so departed Galahad, Percivale and Bors with him; and so they rode three days, and then they came to a rivage,[10] and found the ship whereof the tale speaketh of to-fore. And when they came to the board they found in the midst the table of silver which they had left with the Maimed King, and the Sangreal which was covered with red samite. Then were they glad to have such things in their fellowship; and so they entered and made great reverence thereto; and Galahad fell in his prayer long time to Our Lord, that at what time he asked, that he should pass out of this world. So much he prayed till a voice said to him: Galahad, thou shalt have thy request; and when thou askest the death of thy body thou shalt have it, and then shalt thou find the life of the soul. Percivale heard this, and prayed him, of fellowship that was between them, to tell him wherefore he asked such things. That shall I tell you, said Galahad; the other day when we saw a part of the adventures of the Sangreal I was in such a joy of heart, that I trow never man was that was earthly. And therefore I wot well, when my body is dead my soul shall be in great joy to see the blessed Trinity every day, and the majesty of Our Lord, Jesu Christ.

So long were they in the ship that they said to Galahad: Sir, in this bed ought ye to lie, for so saith the scripture. And so he laid him down and slept a great while; and when he awaked he looked afore him and saw the city of Sarras. And as they would have landed they saw the ship wherein Percivale had put his sister in. Truly, said Percivale, in the name of God, well hath my sister holden us covenant. Then took they out of the ship the table of silver, and he took it to Percivale and to Bors, to go to-fore, and Galahad came behind. And right so they went to the city, and at the gate of the city they saw an old man crooked. Then Galahad called him and bade him help to bear this heavy thing. Truly, said the old man, it is ten year ago that I might not go but with crutches. Care thou not, said Galahad, and arise up and shew thy good will. And so he assayed, and found himself as whole as ever he was. Then ran he to the table, and took one part against Galahad. And anon arose there great noise in the city, that a cripple was made whole by knights marvellous that entered into the city.

10. **rivage:** shore.

Then anon after, the three knights went to the water, and brought up into the palace Percivale's sister, and buried her as richly as a king's daughter ought to be. And when the king of the city, which was cleped Estorause, saw the fellowship, he asked them of whence they were, and what thing it was that they had brought upon the table of silver. And they told him the truth of the Sangreal, and the power which that God had sent there. Then the king was a tyrant, and was come of the line of paynims,[11] and took them and put them in prison in a deep hole.

CHAPTER XXII. *How they were fed with the Sangreal while they were in prison, and how Galahad was made king.*

But as soon as they were there Our Lord sent them the Sangreal, through whose grace they were always fulfilled while that they were in prison. So at the year's end it befell that this King Estorause lay sick, and felt that he should die. Then he sent for the three knights, and they came afore him; and he cried them mercy of that he had done to them, and they forgave it him goodly; and he died anon. When the king was dead all the city was dismayed, and wist not who might be their king. Right so as they were in counsel there came a voice among them, and bade them choose the youngest knight of them three to be their king: For he shall well maintain you and all yours. So they made Galahad king by all the assent of the holy city, and else they would have slain him. And when he was come to behold the land, he let make above the table of silver a chest of gold and of precious stones, that hilled[12] the Holy Vessel. And every day early the three fellows would come afore it, and make their prayers.

Now at the year's end, and the self day after Galahad had borne the crown of gold, he arose up early and his fellows, and came to the palace, and saw to-fore them the Holy Vessel, and a man kneeling on his knees in likeness of a bishop, that had about him a great fellowship of angels, as it had been Jesu Christ himself; and then he arose and began a mass of Our Lady. And when he came to the sacrament of the mass, and had done, anon he called Galahad, and said to him: Come forth the servant of Jesu Christ, and thou shalt see that

thou hast much desired to see. And then he began to tremble right hard when the deadly[13] flesh began to behold the spiritual things. Then he held up his hands toward heaven and said: Lord, I thank thee, for now I see that that hath been my desire many a day. Now, blessed Lord, would I not longer live, if it might please thee, Lord. And therewith the good man took Our Lord's body betwixt his hands, and proffered it to Galahad, and he received it right gladly and meekly. Now wottest thou what I am? said the good man. Nay, said Galahad. I am Joseph of Aramathie, the which Our Lord hath sent here to thee to bear thee fellowship; and wottest thou wherefore that he hath sent me more than any other? For thou hast resembled me in two things; in that thou hast seen the marvels of the Sangreal, in that thou hast been a clean maiden, as I have been and am.

And when he had said these words Galahad went to Percivale and kissed him, and commended him to God; and so he went to Sir Bors and kissed him, and commended him to God, and said: Fair lord, salute me to my lord, Sir Launcelot, my father, and as soon as ye see him, bid him remember of this unstable world. And therewith he kneeled down to-fore the table and made his prayers, and then suddenly his soul departed to Jesu Christ, and a great multitude of angels bare his soul up to heaven, that the two fellows might well behold it. Also the two fellows saw come from heaven an hand, but they saw not the body. And then it came right to the Vessel, and took it and the spear, and so bare it up to heaven. Sithen was there never man so hardy to say that he had seen the Sangreal.

CHAPTER XXIII. *Of the sorrow that Percivale and Bors made when Galahad was dead: and of Percivale how he died, and other matters.*

When Percivale and Bors saw Galahad dead they made as much sorrow as ever did two men. And if they had not been good men they might lightly have fallen in despair. And the people of the country and of the city were right heavy. And then he was buried; and as soon as he was buried Sir Percivale yielded him to an hermitage out of the city, and took a religious clothing. And Bors was alway with him, but never changed he his secular clothing, for that he purposed him to go again into the realm of

---

11. **paynims:** pagans. 12. **hilled:** held.

13. **deadly:** mortal.

Logris. Thus a year and two months lived Sir Percivale in the hermitage a full holy life, and then passed out of this world; and Bors let bury him by his sister and by Galahad in the spiritualities.[14]

When Bors saw that he was in so far countries as in the parts of Babylon he departed from Sarras, and armed him and came to the sea, and entered into a ship; and so it befell him in good adventure he came into the realm of Logris; and he rode so fast till he came to Camelot where the king was. And then was there great joy made of him in the court, for they weened all he had been dead, forasmuch as he had been so long out of the country. And when they had eaten, the king made great clerks to come afore him, that they should chronicle of the high adventures of the good knights. When Bors had told him of the adventures of the Sangreal, such as had befallen him and his three fellows, that was Launcelot, Percivale, Galahad, and himself, there Launcelot told the adventures of the Sangreal that he had seen. All this was made in great books, and put up in almeries[15] at Salisbury. And anon Sir Bors said to Sir Launcelot: Galahad, your own son, saluted you by me, and after you King Arthur and all the court, and so did Sir Percivale, for I buried them with mine own hands in the city of Sarras. Also, Sir Launcelot, Galahad prayed you to remember of this unsiker[16] world as ye behight[17] him when ye were together more than half a year. This is true, said Launcelot; now I trust to God his prayer shall avail me.

The Launcelot took Sir Bors in his arms, and said: Gentle cousin, ye are right welcome to me, and all that ever I may do for you and for yours ye shall find my poor body ready at all times, while the spirit is in it, and that I promise you faithfully, and never to fail. And wit ye well, gentle cousin, Sir Bors, that ye and I will never depart asunder whilst our lives may last. Sir, said he, I will as ye will.

Sir Gawain and the Green Knight

ca. 1375–1400

Translated by John Gardner

PART I

1

After the siege and assault was ended at Troy,
The battlements breached and burnt to brands and ashes,
Antenor,° he who the trammels of treason there wrought,
Was well known for his wrongs—the worst yet on earth.
Aeneas the noble it was and his kingly kinsmen   5
That afterward conquered kingdoms and came to be lords
Of well-nigh all the wealth of the Western Isles;
For royal Romulus to Rome rushed swiftly
And with great splendor established that first of all cities
And named it his own name, as we now know it;   10
And Ticius to Tuskan went and built there his towers;
And Langaberde in Lombardy lifted up houses;
And far over the French flood Felix Brutus°
On the slopes of many broad hills established Britain with joy,
    Where war and wrack and wonder   15
    Have sometimes since held sway,
    And now bliss, now blunder,
    Turned like dark and day.

2

And after Britain was built by that brave baron,
Bold lords were bred there, men who loved battle,   20
And time after time they would turn to the tools of destruction;
More monsters have been met on the moors of that land

---

14. **spiritualities:** consecrated ground. 15. **almeries:** libraries.
16. **unsiker:** uncertain. 17. **behight:** promised.

SIR GAWAIN AND THE GREEN KNIGHT: *Part I.* **3. Antenor:** traitor banished by the Trojans for betraying the slayer of Achilles. **13. Felix Brutus:** grandson of Aeneas and legendary founder of Britain.

Than anywhere else I know of since earliest times.
But of all who built castles there, of Britain's kings,
Arthur was highest in honor, as all men know; 25
And so I intend to recount a tradition of the region,
A strange and surprising thing, as some men hold,
And awesome even among the adventures of
    Arthur.
If you will listen to my lay but a little while
I will tell it all, and at once, as I heard it told in
    town, 30
        Rightly, as it is written,
        A story swift and strong
        With letters locked and linking,
        As scōps° have always sung.

3

King Arthur lay at Camelot over Christmas 35
With many a gentle lord, his gallant-hearted men,
The noble knights of the Round Table, names of
    renown,
With great revels and good, and gladness of heart.
Tournament trumpets rang there time and again,
And knights jarred knights, with jubilant hearts,
    in the joust, 40
And later they came into court to dance caroles;°
For the feast was in full swing for fifteen days
With all the dinners and diversions devised by
    man,
Such explosions of joy, it was beautiful to hear—
Joyful din all day long, and dancing all night; 45
Happiness reigned on high there in halls and in
    chambers
Where lords and ladies delighted themselves as they
    liked.
With all the goodwill in the world they dwelled
    there together,
The most renowned of knights—next to Christ
    himself—
And the loveliest ladies that ever yet lived in the
    land, 50
And their king the comeliest king that had ever
    held court;
For all those excellent people were still in their
    youth on that dais;
        Most highborn under Heaven,
        Their king of all kings best—
        Where but there has there been 55
        A company so blessed?

4

While the New Year was still young—it was newly
    fallen—
The nobles sat two to a serving on the dais,
For the king and all his knights had come down to
    the hall
When the chanting of mass in the chapel had come
    to an end; 60
Joyful cries were cast up by the clergy and others,
Praising Noel anew and naming it often;
And now the great lords rushed about giving out
    handsels,°
Cried out the gifts on high and gave them in
    person;
They debated busily, briskly, about those gifts, 65
And the ladies laughed, delighted, even though
    they lost
(And she who won was not sorry, you may be
    sure);
Thus they all made merry till dinner was made.
Then, when they all had washed, they went to their
    seats,
Arranged by standards of rank, as seemed to them
    right, 70
Queen Guinevere, resplendent, seated in the center,
Placed on the blazing dais, adorned all about
With the finest of silks on all sides, and streaming
    above her
A tapestry-tent out of world-famous Tars and
    Toulouse°
Embroidered and splendidly spangled with spark-
    ling gems 75
That might well prove priceless if anyone wanted
    to buy them some day;
        But the fairest of all to see
        Was the gem° with eyes of gray;
        Fairest of all was she,
        As all our poets say. 80

5

Now Arthur the King would not eat until all were
    served,
So brimming he was with youth and boyish high
    spirits;
He loved all the luster of life, and he little liked

Either to lie in bed late or too long to sit,
So busy his youthful blood, his brain so lively; 85
And also for other reasons he waited there,
  restless:
He had sworn by his sovereignty he would start no
  meal
On the festival of the New Year before he was
  given
Some strange tale about some most mysterious
  thing,
Some Monstrous Marvel that merited belief,   90
Of the Old Ones, or of Arms, or of other adven-
  tures,
Or until some stout lancer had sought of him some
  sure knight
To join with him in the joust and in jeopardy lay
Mortal life against life, each leaving to the other
His fling at the fairer lot, as Fortune might
  fashion.   95
Such was the King's custom when the court came
  together
At each of the fine feasts he held with his freemen
  in the hall;
        Therefore, bold in his manner,
        He stands at his place, tall,
        Waiting, young on the New Year,   100
        Laughing and talking with them all.

6

There at his station the King stood, straight and
  proud,
Taking politely of trifles to all the high table;
The good Sir Gawain was stationed by gray-eyed
  Guinevere,
And Agravain of the Gauntlet on Gawain's
  left,   105
Sure knights both and sons of the King's own
  sister.
Above, at the head of the table, sat Bishop
  Baldwin,
And Ywain, son of Urien, ate with the Bishop.
All these were seated on the dais and served with
  distinction,
And down below many another knight ate at the
  sideboards.   110
Then quickly the first course comes in, with a
  clarion of trumpets
Hung brightly with many a blazing banderole,°

112. **banderole:** banner, streamer.

And now the kettledrums barked, and the brilliant
  pipes
Warbled wildly and richly, awakening echoes
That lifted high every heart by their heavenly
  sound.   115
Then in flooded wonderful cates,° the finest of
  foods,
Mountains of splendid meats, such a marvel of
  dishes
It was hard to find places to place there, in front of
  the people,
The vessels of silver that held all the various stews
  on hand.
        Soon each to suit his wishes   120
        Turned gladly, gay of mind,
        For every two, twelve dishes,
        Cold beer and brilliant wine.

7

But now I will speak no more of their sumptuous
  banquet,
For as every man must know, there was nothing
  missing.   125
Another strain of music now sang through the hall
Encouraging each of the nobles to eat all he might;
And strangely, almost as soon as that sound died
  out
And the first course had been courteously served
  to the court,
There haled through the door of that hall an
  ungodly creature,   130
A man as enormous as any known on earth:
From his wide neck to his rib cage so square and
  so thick,
His loins and his legs so long and so loaded with
  power,
I must hold that man half giant under Heaven—
And yet for all that, a man he must still have
  been,   135
And the handsomest creature that ever yet rode
  horseback;
For his chest and his shoulders were huge as any
  boulder
And yet his waist and his belly were worthily small,
And indeed all his features were princely and
  perfectly formed and clean:

116. **cates:** delicacies.

But astounded, every man there   140
Stared at the stranger's skin,
For though he seemed fine and fair,
His whole great body was green!

A great horse huge and heavy
And hard to keep in hand,
Who bridled and bristled roughly
But knew the knight's command.

8

He came there all in green, both the clothes and
the man,
A coat, tight-fitting and long, fastened to his
sides;   145
On his shoulders a beautiful cloak that was
covered inside
With pelts perfectly pured,° resplendent cloth
Bright with a trimming of blaunner,° and a hood
to match,
Loosened now from his locks and lying on his
shoulders;
Close-fitting, tightly stretched hose of that same
vivid green   150
Clung to his calves; at his ankles hung gleaming
spurs
Of gold on embroidered bangles richly barred;
The guard-leather under his legs, where the large
man rode,
And everything on him, in fact, was entirely
green—
Both the bars of his belt and the beautiful stones
Artfully arranged over all his array   156
Upon settings of silk on himself and the cantle° of
his saddle;
It would be too much to tell half the trimmings and
trifles
Embroidered in brocatelle,° with birds and flies,
Gay weld-glints° of green gleaming gold at the
center,   160
The beautiful bridle with its metal all brightly
enameled,
The stirrups the stranger stood on strained the
same way,
And the saddlebow also, and the mighty steed's
fine skirts
Where they glistered and gleamed and glinted, all
of green stones.
For the charger on which he came was completely
the color of the man—   165

147. **pured:** trimmed to show one color only. 148. **blaunner:**
white fur used to line hoods. 157. **cantle:** rear part of a
saddle. 159. **brocatelle:** heavy fabric like brocade. 160.
weld-glints: beaded work.

9

Splendid that knight errant stood in a splay of
green,   170
And green, too, was the mane of his mighty
destrier;
Fair fanning tresses enveloped the fighting man's
shoulders,
And over his breast hung a beard as big as a bush;
The beard and the huge mane burgeoning forth
from his head
Were clipped off clean in a straight line over his
elbows,   175
And the upper half of each arm was hidden under-
neath
As if covered by a king's chaperon,° closed round
the neck.
The mane of the marvelous horse was much the
same,
Well crisped and combed and carefully pranked
with knots,
Threads of gold interwoven with the glorious
green,   180
Now a thread of hair, now another thread of gold;
The tail of the horse and the forelock were tricked
the same way,
And both were bound up with a band of brilliant
green
Adorned with glittering jewels the length of the
dock,
Then caught up tight with a thong in a crisscross
knot   185
Where many a bell tinkled brightly, all burnished
gold.
So monstrous a mount, so mighty a man in the
saddle
Was never once encountered on all this earth till
then;
His eyes, like lightning, flashed,
And it seemed to many a man,   190
That any man who clashed
With him would not long stand.

177. **chaperon:** hood.

10

But the huge man came unarmed, without helmet
  or hauberk,°
No breastplate or gorget° or iron cleats on his arms;
He brought neither shield nor spearshaft to shove
  or to smite,   195
But instead he held in one hand a bough of the
  holly
That grows most green when all the groves are
  bare
And held in the other an ax, immense and un-
  wieldy,
A pitiless battleblade terrible to tell of.
The head alone was a full ell-yard in length,   200
The branching pike-steel of blinking green and
  gold,
The bit brilliantly burnished, with a broad edge
So carefully ground it could cut like the blade of a
  razor;
The stout shaft which the stern-faced hero gripped
Was wound around with iron to the end of the
  wood   205
And was all engraved in green with graceful
  figures;
And a leather cord lapped around it to lock on the
  head
And, below, lapped round the handle to hold it in
  tight;
And what seemed hundreds of tassels were tacked
  to the cord
On buttons of bright green, brocheed° and em-
  broidered.   210
Thus came the dreadful knight to King Arthur's
  hall
And drove full tilt to the dais, afraid of no man.
He never hailed anyone there but, haughtily staring,
He spoke, and the first words he said were these:
  "Where is
The ruler of this rout? For readily would I   215
Set eyes on that sovereign and say a few words with
  him, man to man."

> He glanced at the company
> And looked them up and down;
> He stood and seemed to study
> Which knight had most renown.   220

193. hauberk: chain-mail tunic. 194. gorget: armor for
the throat. 210. brocheed: brocaded.

11

All the lords sat silent and looked at the stranger
And each duke marveled long what the devil it
  meant
That a hero and horse should have taken such a
  hue,
As growing-green as the grass—and yet greener, it
  seemed;
More brightly glowing than green enamel on
  gold.   225
And every man there stood musing and came more
  near
Wondering what in the world this creature was
  up to,
For many a marvel they'd met with, but nothing
  like this.
They thought it must be magic or illusion,
And for that reason many a lord was too frightened
  to answer;   230
Astounded at the sound of his voice, they sat stone
  still,
And a deathly silence spread throughout the hall
As if they had slipped off to sleep; their sounds
  sank away and died;

> But some (I'm sure) kept still
> From courtesy, not fright;   235
> Since this was Arthur's hall,
> Let him address the knight.

12

King Arthur stared down at the stranger before
  the high dais
And greeted him nobly, for nothing on earth
  frightened him.
And he said to him, "Sir, you are welcome in this
  place;   240
I am the head of this court. They call me Arthur.
Get down from your horse, I beg you, and join us
  for dinner,
And then whatever you seek we will gladly see to."
But the stranger said, "No, so help me God on
  high,
My errand is hardly to sit at my ease in your
  castle!   245
But friend, since your praises are sung so far and
  wide,
Your castle the best ever built, people say, and
  your barons

The stoutest men in steel armor that ever rode
   steeds,
Most mighty and most worthy of all mortal men
And tough devils to toy with in tournament
   games,   250
And since courtesy is in flower in this court, they say,
All these tales, in truth, have drawn me to you at
   this time.
You may be assured by this holly branch I bear
That I come to you in peace, not spoiling for battle.
If I'd wanted to come in finery, fixed up for
   fighting,   255
I have back at home both a helmet and a hauberk,
A shield and a sharp spear that shines like fire,
And other weapons that I know pretty well how to
   use.
But since I don't come here for battle, my clothes
   are mere cloth.   259
Now if you are truly as bold as the people all say,
You will grant me gladly the little game that I ask
   as my right."
      Arthur gave him answer
      And said, "Sir noble knight,
      If it's a duel you're after,
      We'll furnish you your fight."   265

13

"Good heavens, I want no such thing! I assure
   you, Sire,
You've nothing but beardless babes about this
   bench!
If I were hasped in my armor and high on my horse,
You haven't a man that could match me, your
   might is so feeble.
And so all I ask of this court is a Christmas
   game,   270
For the Yule is here, and New Year's, and here sit
   young men;
If any man holds himself, here in this house, so
   hardy,
So bold in his blood—and so brainless in his
   head—
That he dares to stoutly exchange one stroke for
   another,
I shall let him have as my present this lovely
   gisarme,°   275
This ax, as heavy as he'll need, to handle as he
   likes,

275. **gisarme:** two-bladed axlike weapon.

And I will abide the first blow, bare-necked as I sit.
If anyone here has the daring to try what I've
   offered,
Leap to me lightly, lad; lift up this weapon;
I give you the thing forever—you may think it
   your own;   280
And I will stand still for your stroke, steady on the
   floor,
Provided you honor my right, when my inning
   comes, to repay.
      But let the respite be
      A twelvemonth and a day;
      Come now, my boys, let's see   285
      What any here can say."

14

If they were like stone before, they were stiller now,
Every last lord in the hall, both the high and the
   low;
The stranger on his destrier stirred in the saddle
And ferociously his red eyes rolled around;   290
He lowered his grisly eyebrows, glistening green,
And waved his beard and waited for someone to
   rise;
When no one answered, he coughed, as if em-
   barrassed,
And drew himself up straight and spoke again:
"What! Can this be King Arthur's court?" said the
   stranger,   295
"Whose renown runs through many a realm, flung
   far and wide?
What has become of your chivalry and your
   conquest,
Your greatness-of-heart and your grimness and
   grand words?
Behold the radiance and renown of the mighty
   Round Table
Overwhelmed by a word out of one man's
   mouth!   300
You shiver and blanch before a blow's been
   shown!"
And with that he laughed so loud that the lord was
   distressed;
In chagrin, his blood shot up in his face and limbs
   so fair;
      More angry he was then the wind,
      And likewise each man there;   305
      And Arthur, bravest of men,
      Decided now to draw near.

15

And he said, "By heaven, sir, your request is
strange;
But since you have come here for folly, you may as
well find it.
I know no one here who's aghast of your great
words.   310
Give me your gisarme, then, for the love of God,
And gladly I'll grant you the gift you have asked to
be given."
Lightly the King leaped down and clutched it in
his hand;
Then quickly that other lord alighted on his feet.
Arthur lay hold of the ax, he gripped it by the
handle,   315
And he swung it up over him sternly, as if to strike.
The stranger stood before him, in stature higher
By a head or more than any man here in the house;
Sober and thoughtful he stood there and stroked
his beard,
And with patience like a priest's he pulled down
his collar,   320
No more unmanned or dismayed by Arthur's
might
Than he'd be if some baron on the bench had
brought him a glass of wine.
    Then Gawain, at Guinevere's side,
    Made to the king a sign:
    "I beseech you, Sire," he said,   325
    "Let this game be mine."

16

"Now if you, my worthy lord," said Gawain to the
King,
"Would command me to step from the dais and
stand with you there,
That I might without bad manners move down
from my place
(Though I couldn't, of course, if my liege lady
disliked it)   330
I'd be deeply honored to advise you before all the
court;
For I think it unseemly, if I understand the matter,
That challenges such as this churl has chosen to
offer
Be met by Your Majesty—much as it may amuse
you—
When so many bold-hearted barons sit about the
bench: 335

No men under Heaven, I am sure, are more hardy
in will
Or better in body on the fields where battles are
fought;
I myself am the weakest, of course, and in wit the
most feeble;
My life would be least missed, if we let out the
truth.
Only as you are my uncle have I any honor,   340
For excepting your blood, I bear in my body slight
virtue.
And since this affair that's befallen us here is so
foolish,
And since I have asked for it first, let it fall to me.
If I've reasoned incorrectly, let all the court say,
without blame."
    The nobles gather round   345
    And all advise the same:
    "Let the King step down
    And give Sir Gawain the game!"

17

Then King Arthur commanded the knight to rise,
And promptly Gawain leaped up and, approaching
his lord,   350
Kneeled on one knee by the King and caught up
the weapon;
And gently the King released it and lifted up his hand
And gave God's blessing to him, and bid Sir
Gawain
To be hearty both in his heart and in his hand.
"Take care, cousin," said the King, "as you set to
your carving;   355
For in truth, I think, if you tackle the matter rightly
You'll take without much trouble the tap he
returns."
Then Gawain turned to the knight, the gisarme in
his hand.
The Green Knight waited boldly, abashed not a bit.
And then up spoke the knight in green to Sir
Gawain: 360
"My friend, let's go over our terms here before we
go further.
And first, let me ask you, my boy: What is it men
call you?
Now let me hear the truth. Let me know I can
trust you."
"On my faith," said the noble knight, "Sir Gawain
is the name

Of the baron who gives you this blow, befall what
may;   365
And twelve months from now I will take from you
another,
And with any blade you may wish—but from
nobody else alive."
    The Green Knight answered then,
    "I am proud, by Heaven above,
    To get from the famous Sir Gawain   370
    Whatever he may have."

18

"By crimus," the Green Knight said, "Sir Gawain,
I'm glad
To be getting from your own hand the handsel I've
asked.
You've recited without a mistake my whole
agreement—
Quite glibly, in fact, all the terms of my trade with
the King—   375
Except that you still have to promise me, sir, by
your honor
To seek me yourself, alone, wherever you think
You will find me in all the wide world, and win
there such wages
As you pay out today before all these princes on
the dais."
"Where shall I seek you?" said Gawain, "Where is
your castle?   380
By our Lord, sir, I haven't the least idea where you
live;
I know neither your court, Knight, nor your name;
But tell me your name, and tell me truly the way
there,
And I swear I will work all my wits to wend my
way to you,
And that I can swear to you by my certain
troth."   385
"That is enough for the New Year; I need no
more,"
Said the warrior all in green to the worthy Gawain;
"If I tell you truly, after I've taken your tap—
If you lay on too lightly—if quickly I tell you all
Concerning my castle and country and what I am
called,   390
Then you may ask me my path and hold to your
pact.
And if I can bring out no sound, all the better for
you!

You may linger here in your land and look no
further and relax:
    Take up your tool, Sir Gawain,
    And let's see how it smacks."   395
    "Just as you wish, my friend,"
    Said he—and stroked his ax.

19

On the ground, the Green Knight got himself into
position,
His head bent forward a little, the bare flesh
showing,
His long and lovely locks laid over his crown   400
So that any man there might note the naked neck.
Sir Gawain laid hold of the ax and he hefted it high,
His pivot foot thrown forward before him on the
floor,
And then, swiftly, he slashed at the naked neck;
The sharp of the battleblade shattered asunder the
bones   405
And sank through the shining fat and slit it in two,
And the bit of the bright steel buried itself in the
ground.
The fair head fell from the neck to the floor of the
hall
And the people all kicked it away as it came near
their feet.
The blood splashed up from the body and glistened
on the green,   410
But he never faltered or fell for all of that,
But swiftly he started forth upon stout shanks
And rushed to reach out, where the King's retainers
stood,
Caught hold of the lovely head, and lifted it up,
And leaped to his steed and snatched up the reins
of the bridle,   415
Stepped into stirrups of steel and, striding aloft,
He held his head by the hair, high, in his hand;
And the stranger sat there as steadily in his saddle
As a man entirely unharmed, although he was
headless on his steed.
    He turned his trunk about,   420
    That baleful body that bled,
    And many were faint with fright
    When all his say was said.

20

He held his head in his hand up high before him,
Addressing the face to the dearest of all on the
dais;   425

And the eyelids lifted wide, and the eyes looked out,
And the mouth said just this much, as you may
now hear:
"Look that you go, Sir Gawain, as good as your
word,
And seek till you find me, as loyally, my friend,
As you've sworn in this hall to do, in the hearing of
the knights. 430
Come to the Green Chapel, I charge you, and take
A stroke the same as you've given, for well you
deserve
To be readily requited on New Year's morn.
Many men know me, the Knight of the Green
Chapel;
Therefore if you seek to find me, you shall not
fail. 435
Come or be counted a coward, as is fitting."
Then with a rough jerk he turned the reins
And haled away through the hall-door, his head in
his hand,
And fire of the flint flew out from the hooves of
the foal.
To what kingdom he was carried no man there
knew, 440
No more than they knew what country it was he
came from. What then?
　　The King and Gawain there
　　Laugh at the thing and grin;
　　And yet, it was an affair
　　Most marvelous to men. 445

21

Though Arthur the highborn King was amazed in
his heart,
He let no sign of it show but said as if gaily
To the beautiful Guinevere, with courteous
speech:
"Beloved lady, today be dismayed by nothing;
Such things are suitable at the Christmas season—
The playing of interludes, and laughter and
song, 451
Along with the courtly caroles of knights and their
ladies;
Nevertheless, I may now begin my meal,
For I've seen my marvel, that much I must admit."
The King glanced then at Sir Gawain, and gently
he said, 455
"Now, sir, hang up your ax. You've hewn enough."

On the drapes of the throne, above the dais, they
hung it,
Where every man might see for himself the marvel
And tell of the wonder truly by that token.
Then the two of them turned to the table to-
gether, 460
The King and the good Sir Gawain, and quickly
men served them
With double helpings of delicacies, as was right,
All manner of meats, and minstrelsy as well;
In joy they passed that day until darkness came
in the land.
　　And now think well, Sir Gawain, 465
　　Lest you from terror stand
　　Betrayer of the bargain
　　That you have now in hand!

PART II

1

Such was the earnest-pay King Arthur got early,
When the year was young, for his yearning to hear
men boast;
Though words of daring were few when they went
to their seats,
Now they have hard work enough, and their hands
are full.
Sir Gawain was glad to begin those games in the
hall, 5
But if the end should be heavy, it ought not sur-
prise you.
For though men grow merry of mind when there's
much to drink,
A year turns all too soon, and all things change:
The opening and the closing are seldom the same.
And so this Yuletide passed, and so the year
passed, 10
And each season, in order, succeeded the other:
For after Christmas, in came crabbed Lenten
That tries the flesh with fish and foods more plain;
And then the weather of the world contends with
winter:
Cold clutches the earth, the clouds lift up; 15
And then the rain falls, shining, in warm showers,
Falls on the fair plains, and flowers come,
And green are the robes of the ground and all the
groves,
And birds begin to build and sing on the boughs

For joy as summer's softness settles down on the
banks;   20
      The blossoms swell to flowers
      By hedgerows rich as kings;
      And deep in the fair forest,
      Royal music rings.

2

Now comes the season of summer; soft are the
winds;   25
The spirit of Zephyrus whispers to seeds and green
shoots.
Joyful enough is that herb rising up out of earth,
When the dampening dew has dropped from all her
leaves,
To bask in the blissful gaze of the bright sun.   29
But harvest time draws near and soon grows harsh
And warns it to ripen quickly, for winter is coming;
With draft, he drives the dust along before him,
Flying up from the face of the earth to the sky.
Wild winds of the welkin wrestle with the sun,
And leaves tear loose from their limbs and alight
on the ground,   35
And gray is all the grass that was green before;
Then all that rose up proud grows ripe and rots,
And so the year descends into yesterdays,
And winter returns again as the world requires,
we know.
      Comes the Michaelmas moon   40
      And winter's wages flow;
      And now Sir Gawain soon
      Remembers he must go.

3

But yet while the holiday lasts he lingers with
Arthur,
And the King makes a festival of it, for Gawain's
sake,   45
With rich and splendid revels of all the Round
Table—
Courteous knights and the comeliest of ladies—
But all had leaden hearts for love of the hero.
Nevertheless, they hid every hint of sorrow;
Though joyless, they made jokes for the gentle
knight's sake.   50
Then sadly, when dinner was over, he spoke to his
uncle

And talked of the trip he must take, and told him
simply,
"Now, liege lord of my life, I must ask to leave you.
You know of the terms I have taken. I ask no
better.
To worry you with my troubles would waste your
time;   55
I must leave to take my blow tomorrow at the
latest,
And seek the knight in the green as God may
guide me."
The noblest barons in the palace gathered to-
gether,
Ywain, and Eric, and many another man—
Sir Dodinal le Sauvage, the Duke of Clarence, 60
Sir Lancelot, Sir Lionel, Sir Lucan the good,
Sir Bors and also Sir Bedevere, big men both,
And many another noble, with Mador de la Port.
This company of the court came nearer to the
King
To give the knight their counsel, with care in their
hearts;   65
Deep was the secret grief of that great hall
That so worthy a knight as Sir Gawain should go
on that quest,
To suffer one sad stroke and strike no more that
day.
      Sir Gawain feigned good cheer
      And said, "Why should one fly   70
      From fortune dark and drear?
      What can man do but try?"

4

He stayed there all that day and dressed the next
morning.
He asked them, early, for his arms, and all were
brought:
First a carpet of scarlet was spread on the floor   75
And covered with gilt gear that gleamed aloft;
The strong knight stepped up onto it, handled the
steel,
Dressed in a costly doublet wrought at Tars,
On his head a hood made craftily, closed at the top,
Lined and bound within with a brilliant blaunner;
Steel sabots they set on that sure knight's feet,   81
And they lapped his legs in lovely greaves of steel
With kneeplates pinned at the joints and polished
clean
And cinched around his knees with knots of gold;

Cuisses, next, that cunningly enclosed   85
His thick and brawny thighs, they attached with
    thongs;
And then a woven byrnie with bright steel rings,
Set upon costly cloth, encircled the knight,
And beautifully burnished braces about both arms,
And tough, gay elbow cups, and gloves of plate,   90
And all the goodly gear that might give aid on that
    ride:
    Coat-armor of the best,
    His gold spurs pinned with pride,
    A sword the knight might trust
    On a ceinture of silk at his side.   95

5

And when the knight was hasped in his splendid
    harness,
Every last latchet and loop all gleaming gold,
Worthily dressed as he was he went to hear mass,
Made offering, honored his Lord at the high altar.
Then Gawain came to the King and all the
    court,   100
And gently he took his leave of lords and ladies;
They walked with him, kissed him, commended
    him to Christ.
Now Gringolet was ready, girt with a saddle,
Glorious, gleaming with many a golden fringe,
The riveting newly wrought for the coming ride,
The bridle bound about and barred with gold,   106
The proud skirts and the breast-harness splendidly
    tricked,
The crupper and caparison matching the saddle-
    bows;
And all was clamped on red cloth by golden nails
That glittered and glanced like the gleaming beams
    of the sun.   110
Then he caught up the helmet and hastily kissed it,
A helmet heavily stapled and padded within;
It towered high on his head and was hasped in
    back,
With a lightly hanging veil laid over the visor
Embroidered and bound fast with the best of
    gems   115
On a broad silk border, and birds on all the seams—
Brightly painted parrots preening in among
Love knots and turtledoves—so thickly em-
    broidered
The women must have worked on it seven winters
    in the town;

But greater yet the price   120
Of the circlet round his crown:
A rich and rare device
Of diamonds dripping down.

6

Then they showed him his shield, of shining gules,
With the pentangle° upon it, painted in gold;   125
He bore it up by the baldric and hung it on his
    neck,
And that shield was fair to see, and suited him.
And why the sign of the pentangle suited that
    prince
I intend to stop and say, though it slows my tale:
That star is the same that Solomon once set   130
As an emblem of truth by its own just claim and
    title;
For that fair figure is framed upon five points,
And every line overlaps and locks with another,
And everywhere it is endless—thus Englishmen
    call it,
In every dialect, "the endless knot."   135
And therefore it suited this knight and his splendid
    arms,
Five ways ever faithful on five different sides.
Luke purified gold, Sir Gawain was known for his
    goodness,
All dross refined away, adorned with virtues in the
    castle.
    And thus on coat and shield   140
    He bore the New Pentangle;
    A man still undefiled,
    And of all knights most gentle.

7

First, in his five senses they found him faultless;
And next, he was found unfailing in his five
    fingers;   145
And all his faith was fixed on the five wounds
That Christ received on the cross, as the creed tells;
And whenever this man was hard-pressed, in
    murderous battle,
His steady thought, throughout, was this alone:
That he drew all the force he found from the five
    joys°   150

Part II. **125. pentangle:** (pentacle) five-pointed star that
was a legendary symbol of perfection. **150. five joys:** the
Annunciation, Nativity, Resurrection, Ascension, and
Assumption.

That the holy Queen of Heaven had through her
child;
And for this reason the hero had handsomely
painted
On the inside of his shield an image of the Virgin,
So that when he glanced there his courage could
not flag.
And these, I find, were the fifth five of the hero: 155
Franchise° and *Fellowship* before all things,
And *Cleanness* and *Courtesy* that none could
corrupt,
And *Charity*, chief of all virtues. These five things
Were fixed more firmly in him than in all other
men.
Now all these fives, in truth, were firm in him   160
And each was locked with the other that none
might fail,
And fashioned firmly on five unfailing points,
No two on the same side, yet inseparable
Throughout and at every angle, a knot without
end,
Wherever the man who traced it started or
stopped.   165
And so on this shining shield they shaped the knot
Most regally, in gold on a crimson field:
The pentangle of perfection it was to men of lore.
    And now Sir Gawain gay
    Caught up his lance of war;   170
    He gave them all good-day
    And thought: *For evermore!*

8

He struck the steed with his spurs and sprang on
his way
So swiftly that Gringolet's shoes struck fire on the
stone;
And all who saw that sweet knight sighed in their
hearts,   175
And each man there said the same to every other,
Grieving for that knight: "By Christ, it's sad
That you, lad, must be lost, so noble in life!
It would not be easy to find this man's equal on
earth.
It would have been wiser to work more warily;   180
We might one day have made him a mighty duke,
A glowing lord of the people in his land;
Far better that than broken like this into nothing,
Beheaded by an elf for undue pride.

156. Franchise: liberality.

Who ever heard of a king who'd hear the
counsel   185
Of addle-pated knights during Christmas games?"
Many were the warm tears that watered their eyes
When that handsome hero rode from the high hall
that day.
    He paused at no abode
    But swiftly went his way   190
    Down many a devious road,
    As all the old books say.

9

Now through the realm of Logres rides the lord,
Sir Gawain, servant of God. No pleasant game.
Often he sleeps alone at night, and friendless,   195
Where he finds at lunchtime little enough that he
likes.
He had no friend but his horse in the hills and
forests
And no one but God to talk with on the way.
Soon the knight drew near to northern Wales,
And he fared over the fords and past the fore-
lands   200
Over at Holy Head till he came to the hillsides
In the wilderness of Wyral; few lived there
Who loved with a good heart either God or man.
And always he asked of all he met as he passed
Whether they'd ever heard word of a knight of
green,   205
Or knew, in some nearby kingdom, a Green
Chapel.
But all of them shook their heads, saying never yet
Had they heard of any hero with the hue of green.
    He left the roads for the woods
    And rough-grown higher ground,   210
    And many would be his moods
    Before that place was found.

10

A hundred cliffs he climbed in foreign countries,
Far removed from friends, riding as a stranger;
At every hill or river where the hero passed   215
He found—strange to say!—some foe before him,
And a foe so foul and so fell he was forced to fight.
He met so many marvels in those mountains,
A tenth would be too tedious to tell.
Sometimes he takes on dragons, sometimes
wolves,   220

Sometimes wood-satyrs dwelling in the rugged
    rocks;
At times he battles bulls and bears and boars
And giants puffing and snorting down from the
    hilltops;
Had he not been sturdy and doughty, or served
    his God,
He'd doubtless have died or been murdered there
    many times over;   225
For if warring worried him little, the winter was
    worse,
When the cold, clear water showered from the
    clouds
And froze before it could fall to the faded earth;
Nearly slain by sleet, he slept in his irons
Many more nights than he needed in the naked
    rocks   230
Where the cold stream fell down crashing from the
    mountain's crest
And hung, high over his head, in hard icicles.
Thus in peril and pain and terrible plights
The knight roams all through the region till
    Christmas Eve—alone.
        Earnestly that night   235
        He lifted up a moan
        To the Virgin, that she guide
        His way, reveal some home.

11

By a mountain that morning merrily he rides,
And into an old, deep forest, weird and wild,   240
High hills on either hand, and below them a holt
Of huge and hoary oaks, a hundred together;
Hazel and hawthorn were twisted there all into one,
And rough, ragged moss grew rampant all about,
And many small sorrowing birds upon bare twigs
Piteously piped there for pain of the cold.   246
Sir Gawain on Gringolet glided along below them
Through many a quagmire and bog, a man all
    alone
Brooding on his sins, lest he never be brought
To see the service of that Sire who the selfsame
    night   250
Was born of a lady to allay all human griefs;
And therefore, sighing, he said, "I beseech Thee,
    Lord,
And Mary, mildest mother and most dear,
Grant some haven where I may with honor hear
    mass

And also Thy matins tomorrow—meekly I ask
    it—   255
And thereto promptly I pray my Pater and Ave
    and Creed."
        He rode on in prayer
        And wept for each misdeed,
        On four sides signed the air
        And said: "Christ's cross give speed."   260

12

Nor had the hero signed himself but thrice
Before he beheld in that wood a moated dwelling
Above a lawn, on a mound, locked under boughs
Of many a boar-proud bole° that grew by the
    ditches: 264
The comeliest castle that ever a knight had kept,
Ascending like a prayer, and a park all about,
With a sharp-piked palisade, all thickly pinned,
Surrounding many a tree for more than two miles.
The hero stared at that stronghold where it stood
Shimmering and shining through starlit oaks,   270
Then humbly he took off his helmet and nobly gave
    thanks
To Jesus and Saint Julian,° gentle lords both,
Who had guided him courteously and had heard
    his cry.
"I pray, let them grant me lodgings," said the lord,
Then with his gilt heels goaded Gringolet,   275
Who chose, entirely by chance, the chief of the
    gates
And brought the hero in a bound to the end of the
    bridge in haste:
        The bridge was sharply raised,
        The gate bars bolted fast;
        The walls were well arrayed: 280
        They feared no winter's blast.

13

On his great white horse the warrior waited on the
    bank
Of the steep double ditch that drove against the
    wall.
The rock went down in the water wonderfully
    deep,
And above, it hove aloft to a huge height: 285
Of hard-hewn stone it rose to the high tables

264. boar-proud bole: trees proud as boars. **272. Saint
Julian:** patron saint of hospitality.

Built up under the battlements, by the best law,
And above stood splendid watch stations, evenly
    spaced,
With loopholes craftily fashioned and cleanly
    locked.
A better barbican he had never beheld.   290
And then he beheld, beyond, the noble hall:
Towers built on top branched thickly with spires,
Finials floating upward, fearfully tall,
With carved-out capitals, ingeniously wrought;
Chalk-white chimneys his eye caught there in
    plenty   295
Blinking on the high rooftops, all of white.
So many were the painted pinnacles springing up
Among the castle crenels, and they climbed so
    thick,
The castle seemed surely to be cut out of clean
    white paper.
The freehearted knight on his horse thought it fair
    indeed   300
If he might come safely at last to the cloister
    within
To hold up there in that house while the holy days
    lasted, in delight;
        Then there came to his call
        A porter, courtly, polite;
        Taking his place on the wall,   305
        He hailed the errant knight.

14

"Good sir," called Gawain, "would you kindly go
    my errand
To ask the great lord of this castle to take me in?"
"Gladly, by Peter," said the porter; "I'm sure, in
    pure truth,
You'll be welcome, sir, to stay here as long as
    you like."   310
The servingman came back again to him swiftly
And brought a great company with him to greet
    the knight.
They let down the drawbridge, and joyfully they
    rushed out
And kneeled down on their knees on the cold earth
To welcome him in the way that seemed to them
    worthy;   315
They yielded the mighty gate to him, swinging it
    wide,
And he hurried to raise them up, and rode over the
    bridge.

Several men steadied his saddle while he lighted,
Then stabled the dancing steed—men sturdy
    enough!
Knights and squires came down to Sir Gawain
    then   320
To lead the bold knight blissfully to the hall.
When he hefted off his helmet, men hurried to his
    side
To snatch it from his hand, all too eager to serve him,
And they took his sword of steel and his glinting
    shield.
Then nobly the good knight hailed every one of
    those nobles,   325
And many proud lords pressed closer to honor the
    knight;
And still hasped in his armor they led him to the
    hall
Where a fair fire burned fiercely on the hearthrock;
And the lord of the castle himself came down from
    his chamber
To meet with due ceremony the man on the
    floor.   330
He said: "You are welcome to rest here as long as
    you wish;
All I have is yours to use as you will and please."
        "I thank you, sir," said Gawain;
        "May Christ with words so free
        Greet you." The two good men   335
        Embraced in courtesy.

15

Sir Gawain gazed at the lord who so graciously
    met him
And thought it no common knight that kept that
    castle;
An immense man, indeed, mature in years;
A beard broad and bright, and beaver-hued;   340
His stance was proud and staunch, on stalwark
    shanks;
His face flashed like fire; his speech was free:
Surely a man well suited, Sir Gawain saw,
To lead as lord in a land of gallant men.
The lord led him to a chamber and quickly
    commanded   345
Lads delivered to the knight as loyal servants,
And soon there stood at his bidding servants
    a-plenty
Who brought him to a bright room with the finest
    of beds;

Curtains of clearest silk and clear gold hems,
Curious covertures with comely panels,   350
Bright blaunner above, embroidered at the sides,
The draperies running on ropes by red-gold rings,
Tapestries tacked to the walls from Tars and Toulouse,
And under his feet on the floor, fair rugwork to match.
There he was unlocked, with laughing speeches, 355
From his interlinked coat of mail and his colorful robes;
And swiftly the servants sought for him splendid robes
To put on or put aside, picking the best.
As soon as Sir Gawain had chosen, and was dressed   359
In one that perfectly fit him, with flowing skirts,
He looked like Spring itself, as indeed it seemed
To all who gazed at him: a glory of color
Shining and lovely, and not a bare limb showing.
Christ never had made a more handsome knight than he, they thought.

> Wherever on earth he were,   365
> It seemed that Gawain might
> Be prince and without peer
> In fields where bold men fight.

16

A chair before the hearth where charcoal burned
Was readied for Sir Gawain, and suitable covering—   370
Cushions upon counterpanes, both quaintly wrought—
And then a costly mantle was cast on the man,
Of a bright, fine fabric beautifully embroidered
And fairly furred within with the finest of pelts,
All of English ermine, and a hood of the same; 375
And Gawain sat in that settle, handsome and shining,
And soon he had warmed himself, and his spirit quickened.
They built up a table then on gilded trestles
And covered it with a cloth of clean, clear white,
A napkin and a salver and silver spoons;   380
When he wished, Sir Gawain washed and went to his place.
Servingmen served him suitably enough
With stews of many sorts, all artfully seasoned—
Double helpings, as was right—all kinds of fish,
Some kinds baked in bread, some broiled on the coals,   385
Some boiled, still others in stews that were sweet with spice,
And all of the sauces there skillfully made to delight him.
Again and again the good man called it a banquet,
Most courteously, and the courtiers urged him on and said:

> "Now take this penance, lad,   390
> And thou shalt be comforted!"
> And ah, what joy he had
> As the wine got into his head!

17

Then they sought and inquired, in a delicate way,
By putting to him personal, casual questions,   395
That he tell them in courtesy what court he came from;
The knight confessed that he'd come from the court of King Arthur,
The rich and royal king of the Round Table,
And that he who sat in their castle was Gawain himself,
Come there that Christmastime, as chance had fallen.   400
When the lord of the castle learned what lad he had there
He laughed aloud, so pleased was he with his luck,
And all the men around him were overjoyed
And gathered together around Sir Gawain that instant,
For all mortal virtue, both prowess and perfect taste,   405
Were summed up in that name universally praised;
He was honored above all other men on earth.
Softly then each courtier said to his comrade,
"Soon we shall see some ingenious examples of tact,
And faultless, mellifluent figures of fine conversation;   410
What speech can achieve we'll soon find out without asking,
For before us sits the embodiment of good breeding!
God has indeed been gracious unto us
To grant us the gift of so grand a guest as Sir Gawain

At this time when all men take joy at His birth,
   and feast and sing.   415
       The whole art of manners
       No man's more fit to bring;
       It may be, too, his hearers
       Will learn of love-talking."

18

By the time the dinner was done and the knight
   stood up   420
It was late enough; dark night was driving in;
The chaplains made their way toward the chapel
And rang the resounding mass bells, as was right,
For the solemn evensong of Christmastide.
The lord listened and went in, and also the lady, 425
And reverently she walked to her closed pew;
Sir Gawain in gay robes went gliding after.
The lord took him by the sleeve and led him to a
   seat
And looked after him kindly and called him by his
   name,
And called him the welcomest man in all the
   world;   430
And earnestly Gawain thanked him, and they
   embraced
And sat there together soberly through the service.
It pleased the lady then to look at the knight,
And with all her ladies in waiting she left her place;
Fairest of all was she of body and face,   435
Of shape and color and all other qualities—
More lovely than Guinevere, Sir Gawain thought;
He crossed the chancel to cherish her chivalrously.
Another lady led her by the left hand,
A woman much older than she—an ancient, in
   fact—   440
And highly honored by the nobles gathered
   around her.
Hardly similar were those ladies in looks,
The younger ripe with vigor, the other one yellowed,
The one shining radiant, rich red everywhere,
On the other, rough, wrinkled cheeks that hung
   down in rolls,   445
One in sheer kerchiefs and clusters of clear pearls,
Her breast and the flesh of her bright throat
   showing bare,
Purer than snow on the slopes of December hills,
The other one with a gorger covering her neck,
Her black chin hidden in the depths of chalk-white
   veils,   450

Her forehead folded in silk and everywhere
   enveloped,
Ornamented and trellised about with trifles
Until nothing was left in view but that lady's black
   brows,
Her nearsighted eyes, her nose, and her naked lips
(Lips that were sour to see and strangely bleared);
A wonderful lady in this world men might well
   call her—to God.   456
       Her body was short and thick,
       Her buttocks splayed and wide;
       But lovelier was the look
       Of the lady at her side!   460

19

When Gawain's glance met the glance of that
   gracious lady
He left the lord with a bow and lightly stepped to
   them;
He bid good-day to the elder, bowing low,
And he took the more lovely politely in his arms.
He kissed her cheek and most courteously gave her
   greetings;   465
They ask to be better acquainted; he pleads in turn
That they make him their own true servant, if it
   please them.
They take him between them and, talking and
   laughing, lead him
To the chamber, to the hearth, where they call at
   once   469
For spices, which the servants speedily bring them
Together with heart-warming wine whenever they
   ask it.
Again and again the lord of the castle leapt up
To make sure that all were merry on every side;
He took off his hood with a flourish and hung it on
   a spear
And challenged them all to capture it; for who-
   ever   475
Should best please the company, that Christmas,
   should have it;
"—And I shall strive, on my soul, to struggle with
   the best,
With my good friends' help, before I give up my
   clothes."
Thus with laughing words the lord made merry
In order to please Sir Gawain with games that
   night by the fire.   480

Such, as the hours ran,
Was the reign of that good sire;
Then at last Sir Gawain
Rose and prepared to retire.

20

On the morning when every man looks back to that
    time   485
When Christ was born to die to redeem mankind,
Joy wakes for His sake in all the world;
And so it did there that day in due celebration;
Strong men furnished the dais with elegant foods
All day long and again for the great, formal
    dinner;   490
The ancient woman was given the highest seat,
And the lord of the castle, I trust, took his place
    beside her;
Gawain and the lady gay were seated together
At the middle of the feastboard, where the foods
    came first;
And the rest were seated about all the hall as
    seemed best,   495
Each man suitably served in his degree.
There was such meat, such mirth, such marvelous
    joy
That to tell of it all would soon prove tedious
Even if I were to choose only striking details;
Suffice it to say that the knight and that splendid
    lady   500
Found one another's company so amusing,
Through their courtly dalliance and their con-
    fidences,
Their proper and courteous chat—all perfectly
    chaste—
That to play like theirs no other fencing sport
    compares.
        Kettledrums and brasses   505
        Rattled and sang on the stairs;
        Each man minded his business,
        And they two minded theirs.

21

Pleasure filled the palace that day and the next,
And the third day passed, as pleasing as the
    others;   510
Their joy on the day of Saint John° was cheering to
    hear,

511. day . . . John: December 27.

But then fell the close of the feast-time, as all of
    them knew;
The guests would go off again on the gray of the
    morning,
So all that night they stayed wide awake, drank
    wine,
And danced their courtly caroles continuously. 515
At last, when it was late, they took their leave,
Each one to wend his way down his wandering
    road.
Gawain too said good-day, but the lord drew him
    back
And led him to his own chamber, and to the
    chimney,
And there he held him awhile and heartily thanked
    him   520
For the pleasure and the great prestige he'd brought
    by his presence
In honoring the house at that holy season
And ornamenting the castle with his courtliness.
"As long as I live, in truth, I'll be the better
For Gawain's being my guest at God's own
    feast!"   525
"I thank you, sir," said Gawain; "but let me assure
    you,
The honor is all your own. May God defend it.
And I am your servant, my lord, to command as
    you will
In large things and in small, for my debt to you is
    great."
        The lord of the castle said,   530
        "Then stay another night!"
        But Gawain shook his head;
        It lay outside his might.

22

Then most kindly the lord of the castle inquired
What dire and dreadful business drew him out 535
From the court of the king, and at Christmas, to
    ride alone
Before the holiday holly was hauled out of town.
"Indeed, sir," said the knight, "it's just as you've
    guessed;
A high and hasty errand hales me from the hall,
For I am summoned in person to seek out a
    place   540
That I haven't the faintest idea where to turn to
    find;

For all the length and breadth of Logres, Lord help
me,
I must somehow make it there by the morning of
New Year's.
And for that reason, my lord, let me ask you this:
That you tell me truly if ever you've heard any
tale   545
Of a Green Chapel, and where on God's earth it
stands,
Of the knight who keeps that chapel, a man all of
green.
For there was established between us a solemn
agreement
That I look for that man in that place, if my life
should last;
New Year's morning is now no great while off,   550
And by God's son, I'd be gladder to greet that
man
Than any other alive, if God will allow it.
And so, by your leave, I'd better be looking for
him,
For I've barely three days left to be done with this
business,
And by heaven I'd rather fall dead than fail in
this."   555
Then the lord laughed. "I insist that you linger,
now;
For I'll tell you the way to the place when your
time is up.
Worry no more about where you will find the
Green Chapel:
For you shall bask in bed, my boy, at your ease,
While your days pass, and put out on the first of
the year   560
And come to your mark by midmorning to do as
you like out there.
    Stay till New Year's Day,
    Rest and build up your cheer;
    My man will show you the way;
    It's not two miles from here."   565

23

Sir Gawain grew jubilant then. He laughed for joy.
"I thank you now for this above everything else,
For luck is with me at last; I shall be at your will,
To stay or to do whatever may please you most."
The lord threw his arm around him and sat down
beside him,   570

And he asked that the ladies be called, to bring
still more joy;
There was happiness then on all sides as they sat
there together,
And the lord of the castle let out such explosions
of laughter
He seemed half out of his wits, hardly sure who he
was.
Before long he called to the knight, and cried out
loudly,   575
"You've sworn you'll be my servant and do as I
say:
Will you hold to your hasty promise here and
now?"
"Certainly, my lord," said the good Sir Gawain,
"As long as I'm here in your castle, I'm yours to
command."
"You've had a hard trip," said the lord, "and
you've come a long way,   580
And I've kept you cavorting all night; you haven't
caught up
On either your food or your sleep, I know for a fact.
You shall therefore lounge in your bedroom and
lie at your ease
Tomorrow till time for high mass, and then take
your dinner
When you wish, along with my wife, who'll sit
beside you   585
And keep you company till I come back to court.
You stay here;
    And as for me, I'll rise
    At dawn and play the hunter."
    Gawain grants all this
    And bows, as does the other.   590

24

"—And one thing more," said the lord: "we'll
make a pact:
Whatever I win in the woods, I will make it yours,
And anything you may win you'll exchange with
me;
Such is the swap, my sweet. Swear on your word,
Whether the bargain should bring you to better or
worse."   595
"By God," said the gallant knight, "I gladly
accept;
And I'm glad to discover milord has a gambling
heart!"

"Who'll bring us the beverages to bind this
  bargain?"
The lord of the place called out. The people all
  laughed.
They drank and dallied together and dealt in small
  talk,   600
Those splendid lords and ladies, as long as they
  liked,
And then, in the French manner, with many pretty
  words,
They stood and said *bonsoir°* and spoke in whispers,
Kissed with great courtliness and took their leave.
Attended by fleet-footed servants and flaming
  torches,   605
Each of the company came at the last to his bed
  for rest;
            But often before they go
            The lord brings up the jest;
            No man knew better how
            To entertain a guest.   610

PART III

1

Early, before it was daylight, the hunters arose,
The guests who wanted to go, and called to their
  grooms,
Who bustled about and saddled the big white
  horses.
They trimmed their tackle and tied up the saddle-
  bags
And fixed themselves up in their finest attire for
  the hunt,   5
Then leaped to their horses lightly, lifted their reins,
And turned, each man to the hunting trail he
  liked best.
The lord of the land was by no means the last of
  those
Arrayed for riding, his retinue around him;
When he'd heard hunters' mass and had snatched a
  hasty breakfast,   10
He flew with his hunter's bugle to fields of bent
  grasses;
By the time the day's first rays had dawned on the
  hills,
He and his men were all mounted and ready to
  ride.

603. bonsoir: good night.

Kennelmen keen in their craft now coupled the
  hounds,
Caught up the kennel doors, called out loudly to
  the dogs,   15
Blew mightily on their bugles three bare notes,
And the hounds bugled back—bright music in the
  morning—
And those that dashed off too soon were driven to
  place.
A hundred hunters were there, I've heard; all
  hunters of the best.
            The keepers took their posts   20
            And signaled the hounds' release;
            And hard on their bugle blasts,
            A roar rose up in the trees.

2

At the first cry of the quest all the wild creatures
  quaked;
Deer drove down through the dales, half crazy
  with dread,   25
Raced for the ridges, reversed again in a rout,
Driven back by the bellowing shouts of the beaters.
They let the harts with their high-arching antlers
  escape
And also the brave old bucks with their broad-
  palmed horns,
For in close season, the lord of the castle com-
  manded,   30
No man should make so much as a mark on the
  males;
But the hinds were all held in with a "Heigh!" and
  a " 'Ware!"
And the does all driven with a din to the depths of
  the vales.
You could see on all sides the slanting of arrows,
For at every turn in the forest a feather flashed,   35
A broad steel head bit deep into hurtling brown,
And Christ, how they brayed and bled and buckled
  on the bank!—
And always the kennelhounds howling on their
  heels,
And hunters with horns lifted high not a rod
  behind,
Their clear bugles cracking as if all the cliffs had
  exploded;   40
And any deer that escaped the arrow
Was dragged down into its death at the dog
  stations,

Driven there from the high ground, harried to the
water—
So skillful were the men at the lower stations,
So great the greyhounds who got to the deer in a
flash   45
And savagely shook out their life, more swift, I
swear, than sight!
          The lord now leaped like a boy,
          Now riding, now running in delight;
          And thus he drove, in his joy,
          Bright day into dark night.   50

3

Thus plays the lord of the hunt at the edge of the
limewoods,
And good young Gawain lies in his gay bed:
While daylight slides down the walls, he lies
concealed
Under a quaintly made coverture, curtains drawn.
As he lay there half asleep, there slid through his
thought   55
A delicate sound at his door. It was softly drawn
open;
He squirmed his head up stealthily from the bed-
clothes
And caught up a corner of the curtain just a little
And peeked out warily to see what it was.
In slipped the lady of the hall, so lovely to be-
hold,   60
And silently, secretly, drew the door closed behind
her
And bore toward the bed. Sir Gawain blushed.
He lay back craftily, letting on that he slept.
She soundlessly stepped to him, stole up close to
his bed
And lifted the curtain and stealthily crept in   65
And softly seated herself on the bedside, near him,
And stayed there, watching to see the first sign of
his waking.
Sir Gawain lay still for a good long while
Studying in his conscience what this situation
Might lead to or mean. Something most strange,
he was certain.   70
And yet he mused to himself, "It might be more
seemly
To ask and find out in plain words what it is that
she wishes."
And so he awakened and stretched and turned
toward her

And unlocked his eyelids and let on that he was
surprised,
Exclaimed and signed himself to be safer, through
words, with his hand.   75
          Red and white together
          Her pretty cheeks and chin;
          Lightly she leaned nearer,
          With laughing lips, to begin.

4

"Good morning, my good Sir Gawain," the gay
lady said;   80
"You're an unwary sleeper to let one slip in like
this;
I've taken you just like that! You'd better call
'Truce'
Or I'll make your bed your prison, believe you
me!"
Thus the lady laughingly let fly.
"And good morning to you, gay lady," said
Gawain with a grin,   85
"I give myself up to your will, and glad to be
caught!
I surrender my arms at once and sue for kind
treatment—
That being, if I'm not mistaken, my only course."
Thus Gawain replied to the lady and laughed as he
spoke;
"But lovely lady, if you would grant leniency   90
And unlock your prisoner and allow him to rise,
I'd be glad to be free of this bed and be dressed
somewhat better,
And I might enjoy even more exchanging terms."
"No sir! Not on your life!" that sweet one said,
"You'll not budge an inch from your bed. I've a
better idea: 95
I'll lock you up even tighter—inside my two arms.
Then I can chat all I please with the knight I've
caught.
For I see that, sure enough, you're the sweet Sir
Gawain
Whom all this wide world worships, wherever you
ride;
Your honor and handsome bearing are highly
praised   100
By lords and ladies alike, and by all that lives;
And now here you are, I find, and we're all alone:
My lord and most of his men are miles away,
The others still in their beds, and my ladies too,

And the door is closed and locked with a good
    strong bolt.   105
Since here in my house lies the knight whom all the
    world loves,
I'll make good use of my time, while my time may
    last, with chatter.
        You're welcome to my body:
        Do anything whatever.
        Of absolute necessity,   110
        I'm yours, and yours forever!''

5

"Upon my soul!" cried Sir Gawain. "I'm certainly
    honored!—
Though alas, I'm by no means the marvelous man
    you speak of;
I'm wholly unworthy to soar to such splendid
    things
As you've just suggested; I know it myself, I
    assure you.   115
But God knows I'd be glad, if you thought it good,
To contribute to the pleasure of your virtue
By speech or some other low service. I'd think it
    sheer joy!''
"Upon *my* soul, Sir Gawain,'' said the lady,
"If I did not prize the princely glory and
    prowess   120
That please all others, I'd be guilty of puffed-up
    pride!
There are lovely ladies enough, my lord, who
    would liever°
Have you, dear heart, in their clutches, as I have
    here—
To dally with, draw out thy pretty nothings,
Take comfort from, find ease for all their sor-
    rows—   125
Than keep all the gold or great estate they own.
As sure as I love that Lord who rules your life,
I have at hand what every woman hopes for
    through grace.''
        No one could be pleasanter
        Than she so fair of face;   130
        But always Gawain answered her
        In turn, with perfect taste.

6

"Madam,'' said merry Sir Gawain, "may Mary
    defend you,

Part III. **122. liever:** rather.

For truly, I find you freehearted, the noblest of
    women;
No doubt there are men who deserve their renown
    for their deeds,   135
But as for myself, the praise exceeds my merit;
You're so good yourself that you see in me only
    the good.''
"By Mary,'' said the beauty, "I beg to differ.
Were I as worthy as all other women alive
And were all the wealth in the world within my
    grasp   140
And were I to have my choice of the husband I'd
    cherish,
In the light of the lordly virtues that lie here in
    you—
Handsome, courteous, debonair as you are
(Virtues I'd only heard of before, but believed in)—
Then I swear I would care for no sovereign on
    earth but sweet Gawain.''   145
"Alas,'' said the knight, "you have chosen my
    better already.
But I'm proud of the noble price you put upon me,
And I swear myself your servant and you my
    sovereign,
And may I become your true knight, and Christ
    give you joy.''
Thus they chatted of this and that till midmorn-
    ing,   150
And always the lady let on that she loved him most
    dearly,
But Sir Gawain remained, in his graceful way, *en
    garde*.°
Though I were the loveliest lady in the land, she
    thought,
Even so, his mind would be drawn to the dark that
    he need not long await,
        The stroke that must destroy him,   155
        Swift and sure as fate.
        When the lady asked to leave him,
        He did not hesitate.

7

The lady gave him good-day, then laughed and
    looked sly,
And as she stood she surprised him with stern
    words: 160
"May He who speeds our speech pay you well for
    my pleasure;

152. en garde: on guard.

But as for your being the brilliant Sir Gawain—I
  wonder.''
"Why?" asked the knight at once, in some distress,
Afraid that perhaps he had failed at some point in
  his manners.
But the lady blessed him and brought out no charge
  but this: 165
"So good a man as Sir Gawain is granted to be
Could not easily have lingered so long with a lady
Without ever asking a kiss—in courtesy's name—
By means of some delicate hint between dainty
  speeches.''
Sir Gawain answered, "Indeed, it shall be as you
  wish: 170
I shall kiss at your command, since knights must
  obey,
And also for fear of displeasing you. Plead it no
  more.''
With that she came more near him and caught him
  in her arms,
Lovingly leaned toward him and kissed him on the
  lips;
Then courteously they commended each other to
  Christ,   175
And without a word more, the lady went out
  through the door.
Then good Sir Gawain prepared in all haste to get
  up,
Called to his chamberlain, picked out his clothes
  for the day,
And as soon as he had himself dressed, hurried
  down to hear mass
And then to the splendid breakfast the servants
  had set him;   180
All that day till the moon rose, Gawain made
  merry with pleasure

> There never was a knight more bold
> Between two ladies more clever,
> The young one and the old,
> And great was their joy together.   185

8

And still the lord of the land looked after his sport,
The hunt of the barren hinds in the holts and
  heaths.
By the time the sun went down he'd slain such a
  number
Of does and other deer you'd have doubted your
  eyes.

At the end of the hunt, the game was gathered up
  quickly   190
And all the slaughtered deer stacked up in a pile;
The hunters of highest rank stepped up with their
  servants
And selected for themselves the fattest of the slain
And broke them open cleanly, as the code required;
They checked a sample of those that were set
  aside   195
And found on even the leanest two fingers of fat;
They slit the cut still deeper, seized the first
  stomach
And cut it with a sharp knife and scraped the
  white flesh;
Then they struck off the legs and stripped the hide,
Broke the belly open and pulled out the bowels 200
Deftly, lest they loosen the ligature
Of the knot;° they gripped the gullet and dis-
  engaged
The wezand° from the windhole and spilled out the
  guts;
Then with their sharp knives they carved out the
  shoulders
And held them by small holes to preserve the
  sides   205
Intact, then cut the breast and broke it in two.
For the next stage they started again with the gullet,
Opened it neatly, as far as the bright fork,°
Flicked out the shoulder fillets and after that
Clipped away the meat that rimmed the ribs;   210
They cleaned the ridge of the spine, still working
  by rule,
From the center down to the haunch which hung
  below;
And they hefted the haunch up whole and carved
  it away
Reducing it to "numbles"°—a word all too apt,
  I find.

> By the fork of all the thighs   215
> They cut the folds behind;
> At last they split the sides
> Making the back unbind.

9

They cut off, after that, the head and the neck,
And then they swiftly severed the sides from the
  chine,   220

202. **knot:** two pieces of flesh in the neck. 203. **wezand.**
gullet. 208. **fork:** of the throat or windpipe. 214. **numbles:**
entrails.

And they flung the corbies' fee° far up in the trees;
Then finally they thurled each thick side through
By the ribs and hung them on high by the hocks of
    the legs,
And each man there got the meat he had coming to
    him.
From one of the finest of the deer they fed their
    dogs   225
With the lights, the liver, and the leather of the
    paunches
Mingled in with bread that was soaked in blood.
They blew the call of the kill; the kenneldogs
    bayed;
Then the men took their meat and turned toward
    home,
Their bugles striking out many a brilliant note. 230
By the time all daylight was gone, the hunters were
    back
Within the walls of the castle, where Gawain
    awaited their call.
    Joy and the hearthfire leap;
    The lord comes home to the hall;
    When he and Sir Gawain meet   235
    Their cheer lends cheer to all.

10

The lord then commanded the people all called to
    the hall
And summoned the ladies downstairs, and their
    ladies in waiting,
To stand before those now assembled, and he sent
    his men
To haul in the venison and to hold it high;   240
Then gaily, in his game, he called to Sir Gawain
And told him the tally of those tremendous beasts
And showed him the fine meat they'd cut from the
    ribs.
"What do you think of our sport? Have I earned
    your praise?   244
Have I duly proved myself your dutiful servant?"
"You have indeed," said he; "so fine a hunt
I haven't seen in the winter for seven years."
"I give it all to you, Gawain," the man said then,
"For according to our contract, it's yours to claim."
"So it is," said the knight, "and I say the same to
    you: 250
What I have honorably won within your walls
I'll be equally quick to acknowledge wholly yours."

221. corbies' fee: gristle thrown to the birds.

With that he closes his arms round the lord's neck
And gives him the sweetest kiss he can summon up.
"There you have my achievement today. That's
    it.   255
I swear if there were more I'd make it yours."
"Hmmm. Very nice," said the lord, "I thank you
    kindly;
But it might seem better yet if you'd breathe in my
    ear
Whom you won this treasure from by your wits."
"That was not in our contract," said he, "ask no
    more.   260
You've gotten what is yours; more than that you
    must not bid."
    They laughed in their merry manner
    And their talk was clever and good;
    When they turned then to their dinner
    They found no lack of food.   265

11

Later they gathered in the chamber, by the fire-
    place,
Where servants waited on them, bringing in wine;
And after a while, in high spirits, they settled again
On the same contract for tomorrow as they'd made
    today,
That as chance might fall, each would exchange
    with the other   270
Whatever he won that day, when they met at night.
Before all the court they agreed upon the covenant,
And, laughing, saluting once more with wine, they
    sealed it.
At last, late, the lord and the knight took their
    leave,
And every man there made his way in haste to his
    bed.   275
By the time the cock had crowed and cackled but
    thrice
The lord had leaped from his bed, as had all his
    men;
The hunter's mass and breakfast were both behind
    them
And the company dressed for the woods before
    any light showed, for the chase;
    With hunters and with horns   280
    They cross the meadow brush;
    Unleashed, among the thorns,
    The hounds are running in a rush.

12

Soon by the side of a quagmire the hounds hit a
    scent;
The hunting-lord cheered on the hounds that had
    hit it first,   285
Shouted out wild words with a wonderful noise;
And when those hounds heard him shout they
    hurried forward
And fell on the trail in a flash, some forty at once,
And then such a howl and yowl of singing hounds
Rose up that the rocks all around rang out like
    bells;   290
Hunters cheered them on with their horns and
    their voices;
Then, all in a group, they surged together
Between a pool in those woods and a rugged crag,
The dogs in a scrambling heap—at the foot of the
    cliff
By the quagmire's side where rocks had tumbled
    roughly—   295
Rushed to make the find, and the men rushed
    behind them.
They surrounded the knobby rocks and the bog as
    well—
The men—for they knew well enough he was hiding
    there someplace,
The beast whose trail the bellowing bloodhounds
    had caught;   299
They beat the bushes and shouted "Get up! Up!"
And angrily out he came to attack the men—
One of the most amazing swine ever seen,
An ancient loner who'd long ago left the herd,
For he was an old one, and brawny, the biggest of
    them all,
A grim old devil when he grunted, and he grieved
    them plenty,   305
For the first thrust he made threw three to the
    earth
And gave their souls Godspeed as quick as that.
The hunters hollered "Hi-y" on high, and cried out
    "Hey! Hey!"
And lifted their horns to their mouths to recall the
    hounds;
Many were the bugle notes of the men and the
    dogs   310
Who bounded after that boar with boasts and noise
    for the kill;
       Again and again, at bay,
       He rushes the hounds pell-mell

And hurls them high, and they,
They yowp and yowl and yell.   315

13

Up stepped sturdy men to shoot at him,
And their arrows hurtled at him and hit him like
    rain,
But hitting his plated hide, the arrowheads failed
And their barbs would not bite in through the
    bristles of his brow
Though the force of the blow made the smooth
    shafts shatter to bits;   320
Then, insane with anger, he turns on the archers,
Goring them horribly as he hurls himself forward,
And not a few were afraid and fled before him.
But the lord on his light horse lunged in after the
    boar,
Boldly blowing his bugle like a knight in battle;   325
He rallied the hounds and rode through heavy
    thickets
Pursuing the savage swine till the sun went down.
Thus they drove away the day with their hunting;
And meanwhile our handsome hero lies in his bed,
Lies at his ease at home, in all his finery so bright.
       The lady by no means forgot him   331
       Or to bring him what cheer she might;
       Early that day she was at him
       To make his heart more light.

14

The lady came up to the curtain and looked at the
    knight;   335
Sir Gawain welcomed her worthily at once,
And quickly the lady returned his greeting with
    pleasure
And with a loving look she delivered these words:
"Sir, if you're really Sir Gawain, it's surely most
    strange—
A man whose every act is the apex of virtue   340
And yet who has no idea how to act in company;
And if someone teaches you manners they slip
    your mind;
All I taught yesterday you've forgotten already,
Or so it seems to me, by some very sure signs."
"What's that?" said the knight. "I swear, I'm still
    in the dark.   345
If things really stand as you say, I'm sadly at fault."
"I taught you, sir, of kissing," said the lady gay;

"Where favor is conferred, you should quickly
    claim it,
For such is the practice prescribed by the code of
    Courtesy."
"Away with you, my sweet," said the sturdy
    knight,   350
"I didn't dare ask a kiss for fear you'd deny it.
If I asked and you refused I'd be most embar-
    rassed."
"Well mercy!" said the merry wife, "how *could* I
    refuse you?
You're a great strong knight; you could take what
    you wished, if you wanted—
If a woman were so churlish as to refuse you."   355
"True, by God," said Gawain, "your reasoning's
    good;
But where I come from force is not much favored,
Or any gift not given with free good will.
I stand at your commandment, to kiss when you
    wish;
Come, start whenever you like, and stop whenever
    you please."   360
        She bent to him with a smile
        And gently kissed his face;
        And now they talked a while
        Of love, its grief and grace.

15   •

"I should like to know, milord," the lady said
    then,   365
"—If my asking were not to annoy you—what is
    the reason
That one so young and so valiant as you are now,
So courteous and so knightly as you're known to be,
[Has said not one single word of his struggles for
    Love,]°
When in all the romance of Chivalry, what is most
    praised   370
Is the game of love, the ground of all deeds of
    arms?
For to tell of the desperate gambles of trusty
    knights
Is both the title and text of every tale—
How lords have ventured their lives for their ladies'
    love,
Endured for them long and dreary, doleful
    hours,   375

369. Has . . . Love: [Gardner's note] based on the proposed emendation of Sir Israel Gollancz.

And later avenged them valiantly, casting out grief,
And brought by their own joy, joy to all the hall.
It's said, sir, that you're the most splendid knight
    of your time;
You're raved about and honored on every side;
Yet I've sat beside you here on two occasions   380
And I haven't heard from your mouth so much as a
    mumble,
Neither less, nor more, on Courtly Love.
You who are so keen in advice, and so courteous,
Ought to be eager to give a poor young thing some
    guidance
And teach her some trifling details of true love's
    craft.   385
Why? Are you ignorant, really, for all your
    renown?
Or is it perhaps that you think me too stupid to
    learn? For shame!
        I come here alone and sit
        To learn. In heaven's name,
        Come, teach me by your wit   390
        While my lord's away on his game."

16

"In good faith, Madam," said Gawain, "may God
    preserve you!
It's a very great pleasure to me, and game enough,
That one so worthy as you would come to me
And take such pains for so poor a man as to
    play   395
With your knight with looks of any sort. I'm
    charmed!
But to take such travail on myself as to tell *you* of
    love—
To touch on the themes of that text, or tell of
    love's battles,
You who, we both know well, know more of the
    tricks
Of that art by half than a hundred such men
    as I   400
Know now or ever will know in all my life—
That would be manifold folly, my fair one, I swear.
Whatever you ask I will do, to the height of my
    power,
As I'm duty bound, and for ever more I'll be
Your ladyship's humble servant, as God may
    save me."   405
Thus did she tempt the knight and repeatedly test
    him

To win him to wrong (and whatever things worse
   she plotted).
But so fine was his defense that no fault was
   revealed,
Nor was there evil on either side or ought but bliss.
   They laughed and chatted long;   410
   At last she gave him a kiss
   And said she must be gone
   And went her way with this.

17

Then Gawain got himself dressed to go to his mass,
And soon after that their dinner was splendidly
   set,   415
And so the knight spent all that day with the
   ladies;
But the lord again and again lunged over the land
Pursuing his wretched boar that rushed by the cliffs
And broke the backs of the best of the hounds in
   two
Where he stood at bay, until bowmen broke the
   deadlock   420
And forced him, like it or not, to fight in the open;
So fast their arrows flew when the archers as-
   sembled—
Yet sometimes the stoutest there turned tail before
   him—
That at last the boar was so tired he couldn't run
But dragged himself with what haste he could to a
   hole   425
In a mound beside a rock where water ran;
He gets the bank at his back and he scrapes the
   ground
And froth foams at the corners of his ugly mouth
And he whets his huge white tusks. The hunters
   around him
Were tired, by this time, of teasing from a dis-
   tance,   430
But brave as they were they didn't dare draw nearer
   that swine;
   He'd hurt so many before
   That none was much inclined
   To be torn by the tusks of a boar
   So mighty and out of his mind,   435

18

Till up came the lord of the hunt himself, on his
   horse,
And saw him standing at bay, the hunters near by;

He steps from his saddle lightly, leaves his mount,
Draws out his sun-bright sword and boldly strides
   close,
Wades through the water toward where the beast
   lies in wait.   440
But the creature saw him coming, sword in hand,
And his back went up, and so brutal were his snorts
That many there feared for their lord, lest the worst
   befall him,
And then the boar came rushing right straight at
   him
So that baron and boar were both of them hurled
   in a heap   445
In the wildest of the water; but the boar got the
   worst;
For the man had marked him well, and the minute
   he hit,
Coolly set his sword in the slot of his breastbone
And rammed it in to the hilt, so it split the heart.
Squealing, the boar gave way and struggled from
   the water in a fit.   450
   A hundred hounds leaped in
   And murderously bit;
   Men drove him up on the land
   And the dogs there finished it.

19

From many a blazing horn came the blast of the
   kill,   455
And every man there hallooed on high in triumph,
And all the bloodhounds bayed as their masters bid,
Those who were chief huntsmen in that chase.
Then the lord, who was wise in woodcraft,
Began the butchering of the mighty boar.   460
First he hacked off the head and set it on high,
Then roughly opened him up, the length of the
   backbone,
Scooped out the bowels and cooked them on hot
   coals,
And mixed them in with bread to reward his
   hounds;
Next he carved out the flesh in fine broad cuts   465
And drew out the edible inner parts, as is proper,
And he fastened the sides together, still in one piece,
And afterward hung them to swing from a sturdy
   pole.
Now with this same swine they started for home,
And before the lord himself they bore the boar's
   head,   470

The lord who had won him himself in the stream
  by force alone.

    The great lord could not rest
    Until his prize was shown;
    He called, and at once his guest
    Came to claim his own.   475

20

The lord was loud with mirth and merrily laughed
When he saw Sir Gawain, and cheerfully he spoke;
The noble ladies were called and the court brought
  together,
And he showed off the slices of meat and told the
  tale
Of the might and length of the boar, and also the
  meanness,   480
And the fight that beast had fought in the woods
  where he'd fled.
Sir Gawain commended his hunt most generously
And praised it as a proof of remarkable prowess,
For so much meat on a beast, the good man said,
He'd never seen, nor the sides of a swine so
  enormous.   485
When they held up the huge head, our hero praised
  it
And, for the lord's sake, said it half scared him to
  death!
"Now Gawain," said the lord, "this game is yours,
By the covenant we made, as you recall."
"So it is," said Gawain, "and just as surely   490
All I've gained I'll give to you, and at once."
Embracing the lord of the castle, he kisses him
  sweetly,
And after a moment he gives him a second kiss.
"And now we're even," said Gawain, "for this
  evening.
Since first I came, up to now, I'm in no respect in
  your debt."   495
    "Good Saint Giles,"° said the lord,
    "You're the best I ever met!
    Keep on like this, on my word,
    And you'll be a rich man yet!"

21

They raised the tables to the trestles then   500
And covered them with linen cloths. Clear light

496. **Saint Giles:** seventh-century hermit and founder of a
monastery; his symbol was a deer.

Leaped up the length of the walls, where the waxen
  torches
Were set by the servants sweeping through the hall.
There was soon much merriment and amusement
  there
In the comfort of the fire, and a good many
  times   505
At supper and later they launched some noble song,
Old and new caroles and Christmas carols
And every kind of enjoyment a man could name;
And always our handsome knight was beside the
  sweet lady,
And so remarkably warm were her ways with
  him,   510
With her sly and secret glances designed to please,
Our Gawain was downright alarmed, and annoyed
  with himself,
And yet in all courtesy he could hardly be cool to
  her;
He dallied, delighted, and nervously hoped he'd
  escape disgrace.
    They amused themselves in the hall   515
    And, when it suited their taste,
    Went with the lord, at his call,
    To sit by his fireplace.

22

The two men talked there, sipping their wine, and
  spoke
Of playing the same game again on New Year's
  Eve;   520
But the knight asked the lord's permission to leave
  in the morning,
For the twelvemonth-and-a-day was drawing to a
  close;
The lord would not hear of it; he implored him to
  stay
And said, "Now I swear to you on my word as a
  knight,
You'll find your way to the Chapel to finish your
  business,   525
My lad, on New Year's Day, a good deal before
  prime;°
So come now, relax in your bed, catch up on your
  rest,
And I'll go and hunt in the holts and hold to my
  bargain

526. **prime:** first canonical hour of the day, 9:00 A.M.

And later exchange with you all I chase down and
bring in.
For I've tested you twice, my friend, and found you
faithful,   530
But it's always the third strike that counts; so think
of tomorrow;
Eat, drink, and be merry, boy! *Carpe diem!*°
The man who goes hunting for grief, he'll get it in
no time."
It was true enough, Gawain saw, and he said he
would stay.
Bright wine was brought to them, and then to bed
by torches' light.   535
   Sir Gawain lies and sleeps
   Soft and still all night;
   Before it's dawn, up leaps
   That crafty older knight.

23

After mass the lord and his men made breakfast—
A beautiful morning it was!—and he called for his
mount;   541
And every hunter who'd ride to the hounds behind
him
Was dressed and horsed and waiting at the door of
the hall.
The fields were fine to see, all shining with frost,
The sun rising brilliant red on a scaffold of
clouds,   545
Warm and clear, dissolving the clouds from the
welkin.
The hunters uncoupled the hounds by the side of a
holt
And the rocks in the undergrowth rang at the sound
of their horns.
Some few of the dogs fell at once on the scent of
the fox,
A trail that is often a traitoress,° tricky and
sly: 550
A hound cries out his find, the hunters all call to
him,
The other hounds rush to the young hound busily
sniffing,
And they all race off in a rabble, right at last,
That first hound leading the pack. They found the
fox quickly

---

532. **Carpe diem:** Seize the day. 550. **traitoress:** trail of
vixen that crosses that of a male fox to confuse the
hounds.

And when they spied him plain, they sped in
pursuit,   555
Fiercely and angrily shouting with voices of out-
rage.
He twists and turns through many a tangled thicket
And he doubles back or he hides in the hedges to
watch them;
At last by a little ditch he leaped a thorn-hedge
And stole out stealthily down the long slope of a
valley   560
And laughed, believing his wiles had eluded the
hounds;
But before he knew it he'd come to a hunting post
Where suddenly there whirled at him three hounds
at once, all gray!
   He quickly bounded back,
   And his heart leaped high in dismay;   565
   But taking another tack,
   To the woods he raced away.

24

Lord, how sweet it was then to hear those hounds,
When the whole of the pack had met him, all
mingled together!
Such scorn those hounds sang down on that fox's
head   570
It seemed as if all the high cliffs had come smashing
to the ground;
Here he was hallooed when the huntsmen met him,
Yonder saluted with savage snarls,
And over there he was threatened and called a
thief—
And always the hounds on his tail to keep him
a-running.   575
Again and again when he raced for the open they
rushed him
And he ran for the woods once more, old Reddy
the sly;
He led them every which way, the lord and his
men,
Over hill and dale, that devil, until it was midday—
While at home the handsome knight lay asleep in
his bed,   580
In the morning's cold, inside his handsome
curtains.
But for love's sake the lady could not let herself
sleep long
Or forget the purpose so firmly fixed in her heart;
She rose up quickly and hurried to where he lay,

And she wore a splendid gown that went clear to
　the floor　　　　　　585
And luxurious furs of pelts all perfectly pured,
No colors on her head but costly gems
All tressed about her hairnet in clusters of twenty;
Her beautiful face and her throat were revealed
　uncovered,
And her breasts stood all but bare, and her back as
　well.　　　　　　590
She glides through the doorway and closes the
　door behind her,
Throws the wide window open and calls to the
　knight
And warms his heart at once with her glorious
　voice and cheer:
　　　"Lord, man, how can you sleep
　　　When the morning shines so clear?"　　595
　　　Though sunk in gloomy sleep,
　　　He could not help but hear.

25

From the depths of his mournful sleep Sir Gawain
　muttered,
A man who was suffering throngs of sorrowful
　thoughts
Of how Destiny would that day deal him his
　doom　　　　　　600
At the Green Chapel, where he dreamed he was
　facing the giant
Whose blow he must abide without further debate.
But soon our rosy knight had recovered his wits;
He struggled up out of his sleep and responded in
　haste.
The lovely lady came laughing sweetly,　　605
Fell over his fair face and fondly kissed him;
Sir Gawain welcomed her worthily and with
　pleasure;
He found her so glorious, so attractively dressed,
So faultless in every feature, her colors so fine
Welling joy rushed up in his heart at once.　　610
Their sweet and subtle smiles swept them upward
　like wings
And all that passed between them was music and
　bliss and delight.
　　　How sweet was now their state!
　　　Their talk, how loving and light!
　　　But the danger might have been great　　615
　　　Had Mary not watched her knight!

26

For that priceless princess pressed our poor hero
　so hard
And drove him so close to the line that she left him
　no choice
But to take the full pleasure she offered or flatly
　refuse her;
He feared for his name, lest men call him a com-
　mon churl,　　　　　　620
But he feared even more what evil might follow
　his fall
If he dared to betray his just duty as guest to his
　host.
God help me, thought the knight, *I can't let it
　happen!*
With a loving little laugh he parried her lunges,
Those words of undying love she let fall from her
　lips.　　　　　　625
Said the lady then, "It's surely a shameful thing
If you'll lie with a lady like this yet not love her
　at all—
The woman most brokenhearted in all the wide
　world!
Is there someone else?—some lady you love still
　more
To whom you've sworn your faith and so firmly
　fixed　　　　　　630
Your heart that you can't break free? I can't
　believe it!
But tell me if it's so. I beg you—truly—
By all the loves in life, let me know, and hide
　nothing with guile."
　　　The knight said, "By Saint John,"
　　　And smooth was Gawain's smile,
　　　"I've pledged myself to none,　　635
　　　Nor will I for awhile."

27

"Of all the words you might have said," said she,
"That's surely cruelest. But alas, I'm answered.
Kiss me kindly, then, and I'll go from you.　　640
I'll mourn through life as one who loved too
　much."
She bent above him, sighing, and softly kissed
　him:
Then, drawing back once more, she said as she
　stood,
"But my love, since we must part, be kind to me:

Leave me some little remembrance—if only a
   glove—   645
To bring back fond memories sometimes and
   soften my sorrow."
"Truly," said he, "with all my heart I wish
I had here with me the handsomest treasure I own,
For surely you have deserved on so many occasions
A gift more fine than any gift I could give you;   650
But as to my giving some token of trifling value,
It would hardly suit your great honor to have from
   your knight
A glove as a treasured keepsake and gift from
   Gawain;
And I've come here on my errand to countries
   unknown
Without any attendants with treasures in their
   trunks;   655
It sadly grieves me, for love's sake, that it's so,
But every man must do what he must and not
   murmur or pine."
         "Ah no, my prince of all honors,"
         Said she so fair and fine,
         "Though I get nothing of yours,   660
         You shall have something of mine."

28

She held toward him a ring of the yellowest gold
And, standing aloft on the band, a stone like a star
From which flew splendid beams like the light of
   the sun;
And mark you well, it was worth a rich king's
   ransom.   665
But right away he refused it, replying in haste,
"My lady gay, I can hardly take gifts at the
   moment;
Having nothing to give, I'd be wrong to take gifts
   in turn."
She implored him again, still more earnestly, but
   again
He refused it and swore on his knighthood that he
   could take nothing.   670
Grieved that he still would not take it, she told
   him then:
"If taking my ring would be wrong on account of
   its worth,
And being so much in my debt would be bother-
   some to you,
I'll give you merely this sash that's of slighter
   value."

She swiftly unfastened the sash that encircled her
   waist,   675
Tied around her fair tunic, inside her bright
   mantle;
It was made of green silk and was marked of
   gleaming gold
Embroidered along the edges, ingeniously stitched.
This too she held out to the knight, and she
   earnestly begged him
To take it, trifling as it was, to remember her
   by.   680
But again he said no, there was nothing at all he
   could take,
Neither treasure nor token, until such time as the
   Lord
Had granted him some end to his adventure.
"And therefore, I pray you, do not be displeased,
But give up, for I cannot grant it, however fair or
   right.   685
         I know your worth and price,
         And my debt's by no means slight;
         I swear through fire and ice
         To be your humble knight."

29

"Do you lay aside this silk," said the lady then,   690
"Because it seems unworthy—as well it may?
Listen. Little as it is, it seems less in value,
But he who knew what charms are woven within it
Might place a better price on it, perchance.
For the man who goes to battle in this green
   lace,   695
As long as he keeps it looped around him,
No man under Heaven can hurt him, whoever may
   try,
For nothing on earth, however uncanny, can kill
   him."
The knight cast about in distress, and it came to his
   heart
This might be a treasure indeed when the time
   came to take   700
The blow he had bargained to suffer beside the
   Green Chapel.
If the gift meant remaining alive, it might well be
   worth it;
So he listened in silence and suffered the lady to
   speak,
And she pressed the sash upon him and begged
   him to take it,

And Gawain did, and she gave him the gift with great pleasure 705
And begged him, for her sake, to say not a word,
And to keep it hidden from her lord. And he said he would,
That except for themselves, this business would never be known to a man.
  He thanked her earnestly,
  And boldly his heart now ran; 710
  And now a third time she
  Leaned down and kissed her man.

30

And now she takes her leave and leaves him there,
For she knew there was nothing more she could get from the man.
And when she was gone from him, Gawain got up and got dressed, 715
Rose and arrayed himself in his richest robes,
And he laid away the love lace the lady had given
And hid it well, where later he'd find it still waiting;
Then, at once, he went on his way to the chapel
And approached a priest in private and asked him there 720
To purify his life and make plainer for him
What a man had to do to be saved and see Heaven.
He confessed his sins in full, spoke of all his misdeeds,
Both major sins and minor, and asked God's mercy,
And he asked the priest for perfect absolution. 725
The priest assoiled° him and made him as spotless of guilt
As he would if the Day of Doom were to fall the next morning.
And after that Sir Gawain made more merry,
Dancing caroles and joining the hall's entertainments,
Than ever before in his life, until dark, when the owl sang low. 730
  And all who saw him there
  Were pleased, and said: "I vow,
  He was never so debonair
  Since first he came, as now."

31

Now let us leave him there, and may love be with him! 735

726. assoiled: absolved.

For the lord of the hunt is still riding, and all his men.
And behold, he has slain that fox whom he hunted so long!
As he leaped a bramble to get a good look at the villain,
Where he heard the hounds all hurrying Reddy along,
Who should appear but Renard himself from a thicket, 740
And all the rabble in a rush, and right on his heels.
The hunter was quick to spot him, and oh, he was sly!
He waited, half hidden, then whirled out his sword and struck.
The fox darted back—he intended to turn for the trees—
But a hound right behind him shot forward before he could stir, 745
And there, just ahead of the horses' hooves, they hit him,
And they howled, and oh, how they worried that wily one!
The lord came down like lightning and caught up his legs
And snatched him up in a flash from the teeth of the dogs,
And he held him up over his head and hallooed like a fiend 750
And all the hounds there howled at once.
The hunters came galloping up with their horns all blaring,
Sounding the recall on high till they came to the hero;
When the whole of the kingly company had come close
And every last baron that had him a bugle was blowing 755
And all of the others who didn't have horns were hallooing,
Right there was the merriest music a man ever heard,
The hymn that went up for the soul of Renard from horn and throat.
  They grant the hounds their reward
  And fondle their heads and dote; 760
  And then they take Renard
  And part him from his coat.

32

And then they headed for home, for night was near,
And splendidly they sang with their shining horns;
The lord alights at last at his well-loved home,   765
Finds a fire awaiting him there, and his friend,
The good Sir Gawain, so gay tonight in the hall,
Brimming with mirth and love with the merry
  ladies;
He wore a blue robe with skirts that swept the
  flagstones,
His surcoat was softly furred and suited him
  well,   770
And his hood, of the same material, hung on his
  shoulders,
And both were bordered all about with white fur.
In the middle of the floor he met the lord
And greeted him gladly, and graciously said to him:
"I shall for once be first to fulfill the pact   775
We swore to one another and sealed with mine."
Then Gawain embraced the lord and kissed him
  thrice,
The sweetest and solemnest kisses a man could
  bestow.
"By Christ," said the elder knight, "you're quite a
  man
In business, if all your bargains are good as they
  seem."   780
"Yes. Well, no worry there," said Gawain at once,
"Since I've paid in full and promptly all I owe."
"Mary," the other answered him, "mine's not
  worth much,
For I hunted all day long, and all I got
Was this foul-smelling fox—the devil take
  him!—   785
It's hardly decent pay for such precious things
As you've kindly pressed upon me, these kisses so
  sweet and good."
      "Enough now," said Sir Gawain,
      "I thank you, by the rood."°
      Then how the fox was slain   790
      He told them as they stood.

33

With mirth and minstrelsy, and meat at their
  pleasure,
The two made as merry as any man living might—
With the laughter of the ladies and lighthearted
  joking,

789. rood: the Cross.

Both the knight and the hall's noble lord, in their
  happiness—   795
Only a drunk or a madman could make more
  merry.
They laughed, and all the hall laughed with them
  and joked
Until the time came round at last for parting,
When finally they were forced to turn to their beds.
And now my sweet knight says adieu first to the
  lord,   800
Bowing humbly and graciously giving his thanks:
"For the splendid welcome you've given me here
  at your home,
At Christmastime, may the King of Heaven
  reward you.
I'll make myself your servant, if you so desire;
But tomorrow, milord, as you know, I must move
  on;   805
But give me someone to show me the path, as you
  promised,
The road to the Green Chapel, where as God sees
  fit
I must meet on New Year's Day my appointed
  fate."
"In good faith," said the lord, "I'll do so gladly,
All I may ever have promised, I'll pay in full."   810
He assigns a servant to Gawain to show him the
  way
And guide him in through the hills, that he make
  no mistake,
And show him the easiest path through the woods
  to the green one's cell.
      The lord thanks Gawain gravely
      For more than he can tell;   815
      Then to each highborn lady
      Sir Gawain says farewell.

34

With sorrowing heart and with kisses he spoke to
  them both
And urged the two to accept his undying thanks,
And they returned the same again to Gawain,   820
And with heavy sighs of care they commend him
  to Christ.
Then Gawain said good-by to all the hall;
To every man he'd met he gave his thanks
For his service and companionship and the kind-
  ness
With which they'd all attended his every wish; 825

And the servants there were as sorry to see him go
As they'd been if he'd lived with them all their
    lives as their lord.
Then the torchbearers took him upstairs to his
    room
And led him to his bed to lie down and rest.
And did he sleep soundly then? I dare not say! 830
There was much concerning the morning our
    knight might turn in his thought.
        Then let him lie there still:
        He is near to what he's sought;
        If you'll listen for a while,
        I'll tell what morning brought.   835

PART IV

1

Now New Year's Day draws near; the night slides
    past:
Dawn drives out the dark, as the Lord commands;
But the wintry winds of the world awaken outside
And clouds cast down their chilly load on the
    earth;
There's enough of the North Wind's needle to
    trouble the naked;   5
Snow and sleet hurl down to make wild creatures
    cower,
And howling winds come hurtling down from the
    heights
And drive huge drifts to the depth of every dale.
The young man listened well, where he lay in his
    bed,
And although his eyelids were locked, he got little
    sleep;   10
By every cock that crowed he could tell the hour.
He was up and dressed before any faint sign of
    dawn,
For there in his chamber there flickered the light
    of a lamp.
He called to his chamberlain, who cheerfully
    answered,
And he bid him to bring in his byrnie and the
    saddle of his horse;   15
The other was up at once and arranging his clothes,
And he dressed our knight at once in his noble
    attire.
First he put on soft cloth to ward off the cold,
And then all his other equipment, carefully kept:

His chest- and belly-plates, all polished to a
    glow,   20
The rings of his rich byrnie rubbed free of all rust;
And all was as fresh as at first, so that well might he
    thank his men.
        He put on every piece,
        All burnished till they shone,
        Most gay from here to Greece;   25
        And he called for his horse again.

2

When Gawain garbed himself in his handsome
    clothes—
His cloak with its crest of gleaming needlework,
The velvet cloth set off by splendid stones,
Brightly embellished and bound by brilliant
    seams,   30
Beautifully furred within with the finest of pelts—
He by no means left behind that lady's gift,
The last thing on earth it was likely he'd forget!
When he'd lightly belted his sword to his lean hips
He circled the sash around him twice,   35
Winding the girdle around himself with relish,
That green device that seemed only gay decoration
On the proud and royal red of Gawain's robe;
But it wasn't because of its worth he wore that sash,
Or pride of its pendants, polished though they
    were,   40
But in hopes of saving his head when he had to
    endure
Without argument, when the time came for that
    ax to fall.
        Now Gawain, tan and proud,
        Works his way through the hall,
        Nodding and bending to the crowd   45
        And once more thanking them all.

3

And now the great, tall Gringolet was ready,
The war horse carefully stabled while Gawain was
    here,
And how that proud steed pranced in his rage to
    run!
Sir Gawain stepped up beside him, inspecting his
    coat,   50
And said, "Here's a castle that knows how to keep
    its guests;

Good fortune to the man who maintains such
    groomsmen,
And the lady of this place, may love be with her!
May they who see to their guests so splendidly
And welcome them so well be richly re-
    warded—   55
And all of you here—when you come to the
    Kingdom of Heaven!
And if I may stay alive awhile on earth,
May I see some way to repay you at last for such
    kindness!"
He steps in the stirrup and strides aloft;
They show him his shield, and he swings it onto
    his shoulder,   60
Then touches Gringolet once with his gilded heels,
And the charger lunges, lingering no longer to
    dance.
        High on his horse he rides,
        Armed with his spear and lance;
        "This castle be kept by Christ!"   65
        He cried, "May He give it *bonne chance!*"°

4

They dropped the drawbridge down, and the men
    at the gates
Unbarred the blocks, and both halves opened
    wide;
He blessed the company quickly and crossed on
    the planks,
And he praised the porter who knelt by the prince
    of the hall,   70
Praying to God that He grant all good fortune to
    Gawain,
And thus he rode off before dawn with his single
    servant,
The man sent to show him the path to the place
    appointed
Where Sir Gawain was doomed to suffer that
    sorrowful stroke.
They rode by hills where every bough hung
    bare   75
And climbed in the bloom of cliffs where coldspots
    hung—
The dark sky overcast, the low clouds ugly;
Mists moved, wet, on the moor, and the mountain
    walls
Were damp, every mountain a huge man hatted
    and mantled;

Part IV. **66. bonne chance:** good luck.

Brooks boiled up muttering, bursting from banks
    all about them,   80
And shattered, shining, on the stones as they
    showered down.
The way through the wood wound, baffling, out
    and in
Till the hour of sunrise came and the sun rose cold
    and bright.
        They rode on a high hill's crown,
        The snow all around them white;   85
        The servant beside him then
        Reined up and stopped the knight.

5

"Sir," the servant said, "I've brought you this far.
You're pretty near right up on top of that famous
    place
You've asked about and looked for all this
    while;   90
But let me say this, my lord—because I know you,
And because you're a man I love like not many
    alive—
If you'll take my advice in this, you'll be better off.
The place you're pushing to is a perilous place,
And the man who holes up in those rocks is the
    worst in the world,   95
For he's mighty, and he's cruel, and he kills for
    pure joy;
No man between Heaven and Hell is a match for
    that monster,
And his body's bigger than the best four
In Arthur's hall, or Hector, or anyone else.
It's there he plays his game, at the Green
    Chapel,   100
Where no man passes, however proud in battle,
But he cuts him down for sport by the strength of
    his arm;
He's a man without moderation, a stranger to
    mercy,
For chaplain or plowman, whoever goes past that
    chapel—
Monk, mass-priest, mortal of any kind—   105
That green man loves his death as he loves his own
    life.
So I say to you, sir, as sure as you sit in your
    saddle,
Go there and you go to your grave, as the green
    man likes;

Trust me, for if you had twenty more lives, he'd
   take them too.

> How long he's lived, God knows!   110
> —Or who he's cut in two;
> But sir, against his blows
> There's nothing a man can do.

6

"And so, milord, I plead with you, leave him alone!
Go home some other route, by Christ's own
   side—   115
Ride through some far-off country, and Christ be
   with you!
And I'll go back home, I promise you on my honor,
And swear me by God and by all the beloved
   apostles,
By the wounds and by all that's holy—and all other
   oaths—
I'll keep me your secret, sir, and say never a
   word   120
Of your fleeing from any man living that ever I
   heard of."
"I thank you," said Gawain, and grudgingly he
   added:
"Good fortune to you, my friend, for wishing me
   well;
As for your keeping the secret, I'm sure I believe
   you;
But however well you held it in, if I left here   125
Flying in fright from the place, as you feel I should,
I'd prove myself a cowardly knight and past
   pardon.
I'll make my way to the Chapel to meet what I
   must
And have what words I will with the one you tell of.
Whether for better or worse, I'll try my hand on
   this hill.   130

> Cruel as he may be,
> However quick to kill,
> God can find the way
> To save me, if He will."

7

"Mary," the other man said, "since you've as
   much   135
As said you've set your heart on suicide,
And losing your life would please you, who can
   prevent it?

Here's your helmet, then, and here's your spear.
Ride on down this road past the side of that rock
Till it sets you down in the stones on the valley
   floor;   140
Look down the flats to the left a little way
And there, not far away, you'll find the Chapel
And the burly knight that keeps it not far off.
And now good-by, by God's side, noble Gawain.
I wouldn't ride further for all the gold on
   earth—   145
Or walk even one step more in these weird woods."
With that the servingman jerked at his horse's
   reins
And stabbed his horse with his heels with all his
   might
And galloped along the land and left our knight
   alone.

> "By Christ," said Gawain now,   150
> "I'll neither whine nor moan;
> To the will of God I bow
> And make myself His own."

8

He put his spurs to Gringolet, plunged down the
   path,
Shoved through the heavy thicket grown up by the
   woods   155
And rode down the steep slope to the floor of the
   valley;
He looked around him then—a strange, wild place,
And not a sign of a chapel on any side
But only steep, high banks surrounding him,
And great, rough knots of rock and rugged
   crags   160
That scraped the passing clouds, as it seemed to
   him.
He heaved at the heavy reins to hold back his
   horse
And squinted in every direction in search of the
   Chapel,
And still he saw nothing except—and this was
   strange—
A small green hill all alone, a sort of barrow,   165
A low, smooth bulge on the bank of the brimming
   creek
That flowed from the foot of a waterfall,
And the water in the pool was bubbling as if it
   were boiling.

Sir Gawain urged Gringolet on till he came to the
     mound
And lightly dismounted and made the reins
     secure   170
On the great, thick limb of a gnarled and ancient
     tree;
Then he went up to the barrow and walked all
     around it,
Wondering in his wits what on earth it might be.
It had at each end and on either side an entrance,
And patches of grass were growing all over the
     thing,   175
And all the inside was hollow—an old, old cave
Or the cleft of some ancient crag, he couldn't tell
     which it was.
          "Whoo, Lord!" thought the knight,
          "Is *this* the fellow's place?
          Here the Devil might   180
          Recite his midnight mass.

9

"Dear God," thought Gawain, "the place is
     deserted enough!
And it's ugly enough, all overgrown with weeds!
Well might it amuse that marvel of green
To do his devotions here, in his devilish way!   185
In my five senses I fear it's the Fiend himself
Who's brought me to meet him here to murder me.
May fire and fury befall this fiendish Chapel,
As cursed a kirk as I ever yet came across!"
With his helmet on his head and his lance in
     hand   190
He leaped up onto the roof of the rock-walled room
And, high on that hill, he heard, from an echoing
     rock
Beyond the pool, on the hillside, a horrible noise.
Brrrack! It clattered in the cliffs as if to cleave
     them,
A sound like a grindstone grinding on a scythe!   195
Brrrack! It whirred and rattled like water on a mill
     wheel!
Brrrrrack! It rushed and rang till your blood ran
     cold.
And then: "Oh God," thought Gawain, "it grinds,
     I think,
For me—a blade prepared for the blow I must take
     as my right!
          God's will be done! But here!   200
          He may well get his knight,

But still, no use in fear;
I won't fall dead of fright!"

10

And then Sir Gawain roared in a ringing voice,
"Where is the hero who swore he'd be here to
     meet me?   205
Sir Gawain the Good is come to the Green Chapel!
If any man would meet me, make it now,
For it's now or never, I've no wish to dawdle here
     long."
"Stay there!" called someone high above his head,
"I'll pay you promptly all that I promised be-
     fore."   210
But still he went on with that whetting noise a
     while,
Turning again to his grinding before he'd come
     down.
At last, from a hole by a rock he came out into
     sight,
Came plunging out of his den with a terrible
     weapon,
A huge new Danish ax to deliver his blow with, 215
With a vicious swine of a bit bent back to the
     handle,
Filed to a razor's edge and four foot long,
Not one inch less by the length of that gleaming
     lace.
The great Green Knight was garbed as before,
Face, legs, hair, beard, all as before but for
     this: 220
That now he walked the world on his own two legs,
The ax handle striking the stone like a walking-
     stave.
When the knight came down to the water he would
     not wade
But vaulted across on his ax, then with awful strides
Came fiercely over the field filled all around with
     snow.   225
          Sir Gawain met him there
          And bowed—but none too low!
          Said the other, "I see, sweet sir,
          You go where you say you'll go!

11

"Gawain," the Green Knight said, "may God be
     your guard!   230
You're very welcome indeed, sir, here at my place;

You've timed your travel, my friend, as a true man
  should.
You recall the terms of the contract drawn up
  between us:
At this time a year ago you took your chances,
And I'm pledged now, this New Year, to make you
  my payment.   235
And here we are in this valley, all alone,
And no man here to part us, proceed as we may;
Heave off your helmet then, and have here your
  pay;
And debate no more with me than I did then
When you severed my head from my neck with a
  single swipe."   240
"Never fear," said Gawain, "by God who gave
Me life, I'll raise no complaint at the grimness of it;
But take your single stroke, and I'll stand still
And allow you to work as you like and not oppose
  you here."
            He bowed toward the ground   245
            And let his skin show clear;
            However his heart might pound,
            He would not show his fear.

12

Quickly then the man in the green made ready,
Grabbed up his keen-ground ax to strike Sir
  Gawain;   250
With all the might in his body he bore it aloft
And sharply brought it down as if to slay him;
Had he made it fall with the force he first intended
He would have stretched out the strongest man on
  earth.
But Sir Gawain cast a side glance at the ax   255
As it glided down to give him his Kingdom Come,
And his shoulders jerked away from the iron a
  little,
And the Green Knight caught the handle, holding
  it back,
And mocked the prince with many a proud reproof:
"*You* can't be Gawain," he said, "who's thought so
  good,   260
A man who's never been daunted on hill or dale!
For look how you flinch for fear before anything's
  felt!
I never heard tell that Sir Gawain was ever a
  coward!
I never moved a muscle when *you* came down;
In Arthur's hall I never so much as winced.   265

My head fell off at my feet, yet I never flickered;
But you! You tremble at heart before you're
  touched!
I'm bound to be called a better man than you, then,
  my lord."
            Said Gawain, "I shied once:
            No more. You have my word.   270
            But if my head falls to the stones
            It cannot be restored.

13

"But be brisk, man, by your faith, and come to the
  point!
Deal out my doom if you can, and do it at once,
For I'll stand for one good stroke, and I'll start no
  more   275
Until your ax has hit—and that I swear."
"Here goes, then," said the other, and heaves it
  aloft
And stands there waiting, scowling like a madman;
He swings down sharp, then suddenly stops again,
Holds back the ax with his hand before it can
  hurt,   280
And Gawain stands there stirring not even a nerve;
He stood there still as a stone or the stock of a tree
That's wedged in rocky ground by a hundred roots.
O, merrily then he spoke, the man in green:
"Good! You've got your heart back! Now I can
  hit you.   285
May all that glory the good King Arthur gave you
Prove efficacious now—if it ever can—
And save your neck." In rage Sir Gawain shouted,
"*Hit* me, hero! I'm right up to here with your
  threats!
Is it *you* that's the cringing coward after all?" 290
"Whoo!" said the man in green, "he's wrathful,
  too!
No pauses, then; I'll pay up my pledge at once,
  I vow!"
            He takes his stride to strike
            And lifts his lip and brow;
            It's not a thing Gawain can like,   295
            For nothing can save him now!

14

He raises that ax up lightly and flashes it down,
And that blinding bit bites in at the knight's bare
  neck—

But hard as he hammered it down, it hurt him no
more
Than to nick the nape of his neck, so it split the
skin;   300
The sharp blade slit to the flesh through the shiny
hide,
And red blood shot to his shoulders and spattered
the ground.
And when Gawain saw his blood where it blinked
in the snow
He sprang from the man with a leap to the length
of a spear;
He snatched up his helmet swiftly and slapped it
on,   305
Shifted his shield into place with a jerk of his
shoulders,
And snapped his sword out faster than sight; said
boldly—
And, mortal born of his mother that he was,
There was never on earth a man so happy by
half—
"No more strokes, my friend; you've had your
swing!   310
I've stood one swipe of your ax without resistance;
If you offer me any more, I'll repay you at once
With all the force and fire I've got—as you will see.
        I take one stroke, that's all,
        For that was the compact we   315
        Arranged in Arthur's hall;
        But now, no more for me!"

15

The Green Knight remained where he stood,
relaxing on his ax—
Settled the shaft on the rocks and leaned on the
sharp end—
And studied the young man standing there,
shoulders hunched,   320
And considered that staunch and doughty stance
he took,
Undaunted yet, and in his heart he liked it;
And then he said merrily, with a mighty voice—
With a roar like rushing wind he reproved the
knight—
"Here, don't be such an ogre on your ground!   325
Nobody here has behaved with bad manners
toward you
Or done a thing except as the contract said.

I owed you a stroke, and I've struck; consider
yourself
Well paid. And now I release you from all further
duties.
If I'd cared to hustle, it may be, perchance, that I
might   330
Have hit somewhat harder, and then you might
well be cross!
The first time I lifted my ax it was lighthearted
sport,
I merely feinted and made no mark, as was right,
For you kept our pact of the first night with honor
And abided by your word and held yourself true
to me,   335
Giving me all you owed as a good man should.
I feinted a second time, friend, for the morning
You kissed my pretty wife twice and returned me
the kisses;
And so for the first two days, mere feints, nothing
more severe.
        A man who's true to his word,   340
        There's nothing he needs to fear;
        You failed me, though, on the third
        Exchange, so I've tapped you here.

16

"That sash you wear by your scabbard belongs to
me;
My own wife gave it to you, as I ought to know. 345
I know, too, of your kisses and all your words
And my wife's advances, for I myself arranged
them.
It was I who sent her to test you. I'm convinced
You're the finest man that ever walked this earth.
As a pearl is of greater price than dry white
peas,   350
So Gawain indeed stands out above all other
knights.
But you lacked a little, sir; you were less than
loyal;
But since it was not for the sash itself or for lust
But because you loved your life, I blame you less."
Sir Gawain stood in a study a long, long while,   355
So miserable with disgrace that he wept within,
And all the blood of his chest went up to his face
And he shrank away in shame from the man's
gentle words.
The first words Gawain could find to say were
these:

"Cursed be cowardice and coveteousness both, 360
Villainy and vice that destroy all virtue!"
He caught at the knots of the girdle and loosened
    them
And fiercely flung the sash at the Green Knight.
"There, there's my fault! The foul fiend vex it!
Foolish cowardice taught me, from fear of your
    stroke,   365
To bargain, covetous, and abandon my kind,
The selflessness and loyalty suitable in knights;
Here I stand, faulty, and false, much as I've feared
    them,
Both of them, untruth and treachery; may they see
    sorrow and care!
        I can't deny my guilt;   370
        My works shine none too fair!
        Give me your good will
        And henceforth I'll beware."

17

At that, the Green Knight laughed, saying
    graciously,
"Whatever harm I've had, I hold it amended   375
Since now you're confessed so clean, acknowledging
    sins
And bearing the plain penance of my point;
I consider you polished as white and as perfectly
    clean
As if you had never fallen since first you were born.
And I give you, sir, this gold-embroidered girdle,
For the cloth is as green as my gown. Sir Gawain,
    think   381
On this when you go forth among great princes;
Remember our struggle here; recall to your mind
This rich token. Remember the Green Chapel.
And now, come on, let's both go back to my
    castle   385
And finish the New Year's revels with feasting and
    joy, not strife,
        I beg you," said the lord,
        And said, "As for my wife,
        She'll be you friend, no more
        A threat against your life."   390

18

"No, sir," said the knight, and seized his helmet
And quickly removed it, thanking the Green
    Knight,

"I've reveled too well already; but fortune be with
    you;
May He who gives all honors honor you well.
Give my regards to that courteous lady, your
    wife—   395
Both to her and the other, those honorable ladies
Who with such subtlety deceived their knight.
It's no great marvel that a man is made a fool
And through the wiles of woman won to sorrow;
Thus one of them fooled Adam, here on earth,   400
And several of them Solomon, and Samson,
Delilah dealt him his death, and later David
Was blinded by Bathsheba and bitterly suffered.
All these were wrecked by their wiles. What bliss it
    would be
To love them but never believe them—if only one
    could!   405
For all those heroes were once most happy and free
And the greatest thinkers that ever walked this
    side of Heaven.
        Yet these were all defiled
        Through faith in lovely women;
        If I, too, was beguiled,   410
        I think I must be forgiven.

19

"And as for your girdle," said Gawain, "God
    reward you!
I'll take it and gladly, and not for the gleaming gold
Or the weave or the silk or the pendants on its side
Or for wealth or renown or the wonderful orna-
    mentation   415
But instead as a sign of my slip, and I'll look at it
    often
When I move in glory, and humbly I'll remember
The fault and frailty of the foolish flesh,
How tender it is to infection, how easily stained;
And when I am tempted to pride by my prowess in
    arms,   420
A glance at the sash will once more soften my
    heart.
But I'd like to ask one other thing, if it doesn't
    displease you:
Since you are the lord of the land where I've visited
And received such splendid welcome (for which
    may He
Who sits on high upholding the heavens repay
    you),   425
What is your true name? I'll ask nothing else."

"I'll tell you truly, Gawain," the other said,
"I'm known in this land as Bertilak de Hautdesert.°
Through the might of Morgan le Fay, who lives in
    my castle,
Well versed in the occult and cunning in magic   430
(Oh, many the marvelous arts she's learned from
    Merlin,
For she dallied long ago with the love
Of that crafty old scholar, as all your knights are
    aware at home—
        'Morgan the goddess' she's called,
        And it's thus she got her name: 435
        There's none, however bold,
        That Morgan cannot tame—)

20

"—Through Morgan's might I came in this form
    to your hall
To test its pride, to see if the tales were true
Concerning the great nobility of the Round
    Table.   440
She worked this charm on me to rob your wits
In the hope that Queen Guinevere might be shocked
    to her grave
At sight of my game and the ghastly man who
    spoke
With his head held high in his hand before all the
    table.
It's Morgan you met in my castle—the old, old
    woman—   445
Your aunt, as a matter of fact, half-sister to Arthur,
Daughter to the Duchess of Tyntagel, on whom
King Uther got his famous son King Arthur.
But come, I urge you, knight, come visit your aunt;
Make merry in my house, where my servants love
    you,   450
And where I will love you as well, man, I swear,
As I love any lord on earth, for your proven honor."
But Gawain again said no, not by any means,
And so they embraced and kissed and commended
    each other
To the Prince of Paradise, and parted then in the
    cold;   455
        Sir Gawain turned again
        To Camelot and his lord;
        And as for the man of green,
        He went wherever he would.

428. Haut-desert: high hermitage, the Green Chapel in
the mountains.

21

Now Gawain rides through the wild woods of the
    world   460
On Gringolet—a man given back his life
Through grace. Sometimes he slept in houses,
    sometimes
Not. In every vale he fought and conquered,
But of all that I've no intention to tell.
By now the cut in his neck was whole once more 465
And over the scar he wore his shining sash
Bound to his side obliquely, like a baldric,
And tied with a knot on his *left*, below his arm,
As a sign that he had been taken in untruth;
And thus he comes, alive and well, at last   470
To court. What cheer there was when the Round
    Table learned
That good Sir Gawain had come! The King was
    joyful.
He clutched him and kissed him, and Guinevere
    kissed him then,
And many a stalwart knight stepped near to hail
    him,
And they all asked what had happened, and he
    told his story,   475
Recounted his hardships, all his fears and griefs,
The adventure of the Chapel, the green man's
    actions,
The love of the lady, and, last of all, the sash.
He showed them all the scar on his naked neck,
Left by the Green Knight's ax when he was found
    to blame;   480
        He told of his disgrace
        And moaned his fallen name;
        The blood rushed up in his face
        As he showed his badge of shame.

22

"Look, my lord," said Gawain, holding the love
    lace,   485
"Here's the heraldic bend of the brand on my neck,
The sign and symbol of something valued lost,
Of the coveting and cowardice that caught me—
The token that I have been taken once in faith-
    lessness.
I must wear this emblem as long as my life may
    last,   490
For this sign, once attached, is attached for all
    time."

The King and the court all comforted the knight;
And laughing gaily, they graciously agreed
That all the lords and ladies of *La Table Ronde*,
And all in that brotherhood should bear a
    baldric, 495
An oblique heraldic bend of burning green,
And wear that sign forever in honor of Gawain.
Thus was the glory of the Round Table given to
    the sash
And what marked Gawain's shame made Gawain's
    glory
Forever, as all the best books of Romance 500
Record. These things took place in the days of
    King Arthur,
As the ancient Book of the British has borne
    witness,
After bold King Brutus founded Britain,
After the siege and assault was ended at Troy
    at last.
      And many a man has found 505
      Adventures such as this.
      Now He that bore the crown
      Of thorns bring us to bliss! *Amen.*
          HONY SOYT QUI MAL PENCE°

GEOFFREY CHAUCER
1340?–1400

The Wife of Bath's Tale

In th' olde dayes of the Kyng Arthour,
Of which that Britons speken greet honour,
Al was this land fulfild of fairye.°
The elf queene with hir joly compaignye
Daunced ful ofte in many a grene mede.° 5
This was the olde opynyoun,° as I rede;
I speke of many hundred yeres ago.
But now kan no man se none elves mo,°
For now the grete charitee and prayeres
Of lymytours° and othere holy freres, 10

That serchen° every lond and every streem,
As thikke as motes in the sonne beem,
Blessynge halles, chambres, kitchenes, boures,°
Citees, burghes, castels, hye toures,
Thropes,° bernes,° shipnes,° dayeryes— 15
This maketh° that ther been no fairyes.
For, ther-as wont° to walken was an elf,
Ther walketh now the lymytour hymself
In undermeles° and in morwenynges,
And seith his matyns and his holy thynges 20
As he gooth in his lymytacioun.
Wommen may go saufly up and doun
In every bussh or under every tree.
Ther is noon oother incubus° but he,
And he ne wol doon hem but° dishonour. 25
    And so bifel that this Kyng Arthour
Hadde in his hous a lusty bacheler
That on a day cam ridyng fro ryver;°
And happed° that, allone as he was born,
He say° a mayde walkynge hym biforn 30
Of which mayde anoon,° maugree hir hed,°
By verray force he rafte° hir maydenhed;
For which oppressioun was swich° clamour
And swich pursuyte unto the Kyng Arthour
That dampned° was this knyght for to be deed 35
By cours of lawe and sholde han° lost his heed—
Paraventure° swich was the statut tho°—
But° that the queene and othere ladyes mo
So longe preyden° the kyng of° grace
Til he his lyf hym graunted in the place 40
And yaf° hym to the queene, al at hir wille,
To chese° wheither she wolde hym save or spille.°
    The queene thanked the kyng with al hir myght,
And after this thus spak she to the knyght
Whan that she saugh° hir tyme upon a day: 45
"Thow standest yet," quod she, "in swich array°
That of thy lyf yet hastow° no suretee.
I graunte thee lyf if thow kanst tellen me
What thyng is it that wommen moost desiren.

509. Hony . . . pence: "Shame on him who thinks evil (of it)," motto of the Order of the Garter, which was founded about 1350. Its founding has little possible connection with this story.

THE WIFE OF BATH'S TALE. 3. fulfild of fairye: filled with fairy magic. 5. mede: meadow. 6. opynyoun: belief. 8. mo: more. 10. lymytours: friars licensed to beg for a limited time.

11. serchen: search. 13. boures: bedrooms. 15. Thropes: villages. bernes: barns. shipnes: stables. 16. maketh: brings it about. 17. ther-as wont: where accustomed. 19. undermeles: afternoons. 24. incubus: demon believed capable of impregnating women in their sleep. 25. doon . . . but: do them nothing worse than. 28. fro ryver: from hawking. 29. happed: it happened. 30. say: saw. 31. anoon: immediately. maugree . . . hed: despite her resistance. 32. rafte: took away. 33. swich: such. 35. dampned: condemned. 36. sholde han: was to have. 37. Paraventure: perchance. statut tho: law then. 38. But: except. 39. preyden: begged. of: for. 41. yaf: gave. 42. chese: choose. spille: destroy. 45. saugh: saw. 46. array: situation. 47. hastow: you have.

Be war,° and keep thy nekke boon° from iren.°   50
And if thow kanst nat tellen it me anon,
Yet wol I yeve thee leve for to gon
A twelf monthe and a day to seche° and lere°
An answere suffisant in this matere.
And suretee wol I han er that° thow pace,°   55
Thy body for to yelden° in this place."
    Wo° was this knyght, and sorwefully he siketh,°
But what! He may nat doon al as hym liketh.°
And atte laste he chees hym for to wende°
And come agayn right at the yeres ende   60
With swich answere as God wolde hym purveye,°
And taketh his leve and wendeth forth his weye.
    He seketh every hous and every place
Where-as° he hopeth for to fynde grace
To lerne what thyng wommen loven moost,   65
But he ne koude arryven in no coost°
Where-as he myghte° fynde in this matere
Two creatures acordyng in feere.°
    Somme seyden wommen loven best richesse,
Somme seyde honour, somme seyde jolynesse,   70
Somme riche array, somme seyden lust a-bedde,
And ofte tyme to be wydwe° and wedde.°
    Somme seyde that oure herte is moost esed°
When that we been° y-flatered and y-plesed.
    He gooth ful ny° the sothe,° I wol nat lye.   75
A man shal wynne us best with flaterye;
And with attendaunce and with bisynesse°
Been we y-lymed,° bothe moore° and lesse.°
And somme seyn that we loven best
For to be free and do right as us lest,°   80
And that no man repreve° us of oure vice
But seye that we be wise and nothyng nyce.°
For trewely there is noon of us alle,
If any wight° wol clawe us on the galle,°
That we nyl kike for° he seith us sooth.°   85
Assay,° and he shal fynde it that so dooth,
For, be we nevere so vicious withinne,
We wol be holden° wise and clene° of synne.

And somme seyn that greet delit han° we
For to be holden stable and eek secree,°   90
And in o purpos stedefastly to dwelle,
And nat biwreye° thyng that men us telle;
But that tale is nat worth a rake-stele.°
Pardee,° we wommen konne nothyng hele.°
Witnesse on Mida,° wol ye heere the tale.   95
    Ovyde,° amonges othere thynges smale,
Seyde Mida hadde under his longe heres°
Growynge upon his heed two asses eres,°
The whiche vice° he hidde as he best myghte
Ful sotilly° from every mannes sighte   100
That, save his wyf, ther wiste° of it namo.°
He loved hire moost and trusted hire also.
He preyed hire that to no creature
She sholde tellen of his disfigure.
    She swoor hym, "Nay." For al this world to
        wynne,°   105
She nolde° do that vileynye or synne
To make hir housbonde han so foul a name.
She nolde nat telle it for hir owene shame.
But, nathelees,° hir thoughte° that she dyde°
That she so longe sholde a conseil° hyde.   110
Hir thoughte it swal° so soore aboute hir herte,
That nedely° som word hir moste asterte;°
And, sith° she dorste° telle it to no man,
Doun to a marys faste by° she ran.
Til she cam there, hir herte was afyre.   115
And, as a bitore bombleth in the myre,°
She leyde hir mouth unto the water doun.
"Biwrey° me nat, thow water, with thy soun,"°
Quod she. "To thee I telle it and namo.
Myn housbonde hath longe asses erys° two!   120
Now is myn herte al hool.° Now is it oute.
I myghte° no lenger kepe° it, out of doute."
Heere may ye see, thogh we a tyme abyde,
Yet out it moot.° We kan no conseil hyde.
The remenant of the tale if ye wol heere,   125
Redeth Ovyde, and ther ye may it leere.°

---

50. Be war: beware. **boon:** bone. **iren:** iron. **53. seche:** seek **lere:** learn. **55. han er that:** have before. **pace:** go. **56. for to yelden:** to surrender. **57. Wo:** woeful. **siketh:** sighs. **58. liketh:** it pleases. **59. chees . . . wende:** chose to go. **61. purveye:** provide. **64. Where-as:** where. **66. coost:** region. **67. Where-as he myghte:** where he could. **68. acordyng in feere:** agreeing together. **72. wydwe:** widow. **wedde:** wed (again). **73. esed:** satisfied. **74. been:** are. **75. ny:** near. **sothe:** truth. **77. bisynesse:** diligence. **78. y-lymed:** snarled. **moore:** high. **lesse:** low. **80. right . . . lest:** just as we please. **81. repreve:** reprove. **82. nothyng nyce:** in no way foolish. **84. wight:** person. **clawe . . . galle:** scratch us on the sore spot. **85. That . . . for:** that won't kick because. **sooth:** truth. **86. Assay:** try. **88. holden:** considered. **clene:** pure.

89. han: have. **90. eek secree:** also secretive. **92. biwreye:** betray. **93. rake-stele:** rake handle. **94. Pardee:** certainly. **hele:** conceal. **95. Mida:** Midas. **96. Ovyde:** Ovid. **97. heres:** hair. **98. eres:** ears. **99. vice:** defect. **100. sotilly:** skillfully. **101. wiste:** knew. **namo:** no other. **105. wynne:** gain. **106. nolde:** wouldn't. **109. nathelees:** nevertheless. **thoughte:** it seemed to. **dyde:** would die. **110. conseil:** secret. **111. swal:** swelled. **112. nedely:** necessarily. **moste asterte:** escape from. **113. sith:** since. **dorste:** dared. **114. marys . . . by:** marsh nearby. **116. bitore . . . myre:** bittern drones in the swamp. **118. Biwrey:** betray. **soun:** sound. **120. erys:** ears. **121. hool:** whole. **122. myghte:** could. **kepe:** conceal. **124. moot:** must. **126. leere:** learn.

This knyght of which my tale is specially,
Whan that he say° he myghte nat come ther-by,°—
This is to seye, what wommen loven moost—
Withinne his brest ful sorweful was the goost;° 130
But hom he gooth. He myghte nat sojourne.°
The day was come that homward moste he torne;°
And in his wey it happed hym° to ryde,
In al this care, under a forest syde,
Wher-as he say upon a daunce go 135
Of ladyes foure-and-twenty and yet mo,
Toward the whiche daunce he drow° ful yerne°
In hope that som wisdom sholde he lerne.
But certeynly, er° he cam fully there,
Vanysshed was this daunce, he nyste° where. 140
No creature saugh he that bar° lyf,
Save on the grene he say sittynge a wyf.
A fouler wight ther may no man devyse.°
Agayn° the knyght this olde wyf gan ryse°
And seyde, "Sire knyght, heer° forth ne lyth° no
          wey. 145
Tel me what that ye seken, by your fey.°
Paraventure,° it may the bettre be.
Thise olde folk konne muchel° thyng," quod she.
    "My leeve moder,"° quod this knyght, "certeyn
I nam but deed but if that° I kan seyn 150
What thyng it is that wommen moost desire.
Koude ye me wisse,° I wolde wel quyte° youre
          hyre."
    "Plight° me thy trouthe,° here in myn hand,"°
          quod she,
"The nexte thyng that I requere thee,
Thow shalt it do, if it lye in thy myght, 155
And I wol telle it yow er it be nyght."
    "Have here my trouthe," quod the knyght, "I
          graunte."°
    "Thanne," quod she, "I dar me wel avaunte,°
Thy lyf is sauf,° for I wole stonde ther-by,°
Upon my lyf, the queene wol seye as I. 160
Lat see which is the proudeste of hem alle
That wereth on a coverchief° or a calle°

That dar seye 'Nay' of that° I shal thee teche.
Lat us go forth withouten lenger speche."
Tho rowned° she a pistel° in his ere 165
And bad hym to be glad and have no fere.
    Whan they be comen to the court, this knyght
Seyde he hadde holde° his day as he had hight,°
And redy was his answere, as he sayde.
Ful many a noble wyf, and many a mayde, 170
And many a widwe, for that° they ben wise,
The queene hirself sittyng as justise,
Assembled been,° his answere for to here.
And afterward this knyght was bode° appere.
    To every wight comanded was silence, 175
And that the knyght sholde telle in audience
What thyng that worldly wommen loven best.
This knyght ne stood nat stille as dooth a best°
But to his questioun anon answerde
With manly voys that al the court it herde. 180
    "My lige lady, generally," quod he,
"Wommen desiren to have sovereyntee
As wel over hir housbonde as hir love
And for to been in maistrie° hym above.
This is youre mooste° desir, thogh ye me kille. 185
Dooth as yow list.° I am here at youre wille."
    In al the court ne was ther wyf, ne mayde,
Ne wydwe that contraried that° he sayde
But seyden he was worthy han° his lyf.
    And with that word up stirte° that olde wyf 190
Which that the knyght say° sittyng on the grene.
"Mercy," quod she, "my sovereyn lady queene,
Er that youre court departe, do me right.
I taughte this answere unto the knyght,
For which he plighte me his trouthe there, 195
The firste thyng I wolde hym requere,
He wolde it do, if it laye in his myght.
Bifore the court thanne preye I thee, sire knyght,"
Quod she, "that thow me take unto° thy wyf.
For wel thow woost° that I have kept° thy lyf. 200
If I seye fals, sey 'Nay,' upon thy fey."
    This knyght answered, "Allas and weylawey,°
I woot right wel that swich was my biheste.
For Goddes love, as chees° a newe requeste!
Taak al my good,° and lat my body go." 205

---

128. **say:** saw. **come ther-by:** discover it. 130. **goost:**
spirit. 131. **sojourne:** stay. 132. **torne:** turn. 133. **it . . .
hym:** he happened. 137. **drow:** drew. **yerne:** eagerly.
139. **er:** before. 140. **nyste:** knew not. 141. **bar:** bore.
143. **devyse:** imagine. 144. **Agayn:** toward. **gan ryse:**
arose. 145. **heer:** here. **lyth:** lies. 146. **fey:** faith. 147.
Paraventure: perchance. 148. **konne muchel:** know many a.
149. **leeve moder:** dear mother. 150. **nam . . . that:** am but
dead unless. 152. **wisse:** inform. **quyte:** reward. 153. **Plight:**
give. **trouthe:** promise. **in . . . hand:** by a handshake.
157. **graunte:** consent. 158. **dar . . . avaunte:** dare well
boast. 159. **sauf:** safe. **stonde ther-by:** guarantee. 162.
wereth . . . coverchief: has on a kerchief. **calle:** cap.

163. **that:** that which. 165. **Tho rowned:** then whispered.
pistel: lesson. 168. **holde:** kept. **hight:** promised. 171. **for
that:** because. 173. **been:** are. 174. **bode:** ordered to. 178.
best: beast. 184. **maistrie:** mastery. 185. **mooste:** greatest.
186. **list:** it pleases. 188. **contraried that:** contradicted
what. 189. **han:** to have. 190. **stirte:** sprang. 191. **say:**
saw. 199. **unto:** to be. 200. **woost:** know. **kept:** saved.
202. **weylawey:** woe. 204. **as chees:** choose. 205. **good:**
goods.

"Nay, thanne," quod she. "I shrewe° us bothe
 two.
For, thogh that I be foul, old, and poore,
I nolde,° for al the metal ne for oore°
That under erthe is grave° or lith° above,
But if thy wyf I were and eek thy love."   210
  "My love!" quod he. "Nay, my dampnacioun!°
Allas that any of my nacioun°
Sholde evere so foule° disparaged be!"
But al for noght! Th' ende is this that he
Constreyned was, he nedes moste° hir wedde,   215
And taketh his olde wyf, and goth to bedde.

  Now wolden som men seye, paraventure,
That for my necligence I do no cure°
To tellen yow the joye and al th' array
That at the feste was that ilke° day;   220
To which thyng shortly answere I shal.
I seye, ther nas° no joye ne° feste at al!
Ther nas but hevynesse° and muche sorwe,
For pryvely° he wedded hire on morwe,°
And al day after hidde hym° as an owle,   225
So wo was hym,° his wyf looked so foule.

  Greet was the wo the knyght hadde in his thoght
Whan he was with his wyf a-bedde y-broght.
He walweth,° and he turneth to and fro.
His olde wyf lay smylyng evere mo°   230
And seyde, "O deere housbonde, benedicite!°
Fareth° every knyght thus with his wyf as ye?
Is this the lawe of Kyng Arthures hous?
Is every knyght of his thus daungerous?°
I am youre owene love and youre wyf.   235
I am she which that saved hath youre lyf.
And certes yet ne dide I yow nevere unright.
Why fare ye thus with me this firste nyght?
Ye faren° lyk a man hadde° lost his wit.
What is my gilt? For Goddes love, tel it,   240
And it shal ben amended, if I may."°
  "Amended!" quod this knyght. "Allas, nay, nay.
It wol nat ben amended nevere mo.°
Thow art so loothly, and so old also,
And ther-to comen of° so lowe a kynde°   245

That litel wonder is thogh I walwe and wynde.°
So wolde God, myn herte wolde breste!"°
  "Is this," quod she, "the cause of youre unreste?"
  "Ye, certeynly," quod he. "No wonder is."
  "Now sire," quod she, "I koude amende al
 this,   250
If that me liste, er it were dayes thre,
So wel ye myghte bere yow unto me.
  "But, for° ye speken of swich gentilesse
As is descended out of old richesse,°
That therfore sholden ye be gentil men,   255
Swich arrogance is nat worth an hen.
Looke-who-that° is moost vertuous alway,
Pryvee° and apert,° and moost entendeth ay°
To do the gentil dedes that he kan;
Taak hym for the gretteste gentil man.   260
Crist wol,° we clayme of hym oure gentillesse,
Nat of oure eldres for hir° old richesse,
For, thogh they yeve us al hir heritage
For which we clayme to been of heigh parage,°
Yet may° they nat biquethe, for nothyng,   265
To noon of us hir vertuous lyvyng
That made hem gentil men y-called be
And bad° us folwen hem in swich degree.
  "Wel kan the wise poete of Florence
That highte Dant° speken in this sentence.°   270
Lo, in swich maner° rym is Dantes tale:°
'Ful selde° up riseth by his braunches smale
Prowesse° of man, for God of his prowesse
Wol° that of hym we clayme oure gentillesse.'
For of oure eldres may we nothyng clayme   275
But temporel thyng that man may hurte and
 mayme.
  "Eek every wight woot this as wel as I,
If gentillesse were planted naturelly°
Unto° a certeyn lynage doun the lyne,
Pryvee and apert, thanne wolde they nevere fyne° 280
To doon of gentilesse the faire office;   281
They myghte° do no vileynye or vice.
  "Taak fyr, and bere° it in the derkeste hous
Bitwix this and the mount Kaukasous,°

206. shrewe: curse. 208. nolde: wouldn't wish (anything else). oore: ore. 209. grave: buried. lith: lies. 211.
dampnacioun: ruination. 212. nacioun: birth. 213. foule:
foully. 215. nedes moste: needs must. 218. do no cure:
take no care. 220. ilke: same. 222. nas: was. ne: nor. 223.
hevynesse: gloom. 224. pryvely: privately. morwe: the
morrow. 225. hym: himself. 226. wo . . . hym: woeful was
he. 229. walweth: wallows. 230. evere mo: all the while.
231. benedicite!: God bless you! 232. Fareth: behaves.
234. daungerous: reluctant. 239. faren: act. hadde: (who)
had. 241. may: can. 243. nevere mo: ever after. 245. comen
of: descended from. kynde: nature.

246. wynde: twist. 247. breste: burst. 253. for: since. gentilesse: gentility. 254. richesse: wealth. 257. Looke-who-that:
whoever. 258. Pryvee: inwardly. apert: outwardly. entendeth
ay: strives always. 261. wol: desires (that). 262. hir: their.
264. highte Dant: is called Dante. sentence: opinion. 271.
maner: sort of. tale: saying. 272. selde: seldom. 273.
Prowesse: excellence. 274. Wol: wishes. 278. planted
naturelly: implanted by nature. 279. Unto: within. 280.
fyne: cease. 282. myghte: could. If the quality of gentility
could be naturally inherited, the heirs could never be unworthy of their rank. 283. bere: bring. 284. Kaukasous:
Caucasus.

And lat men shette° the dores and go thenne,° 285
Yet wol the fyr as faire lye° and brenne°
As° twenty thousand men myghte it biholde.
His office° naturel ay wol it holde,°
Up° peril of my lyf, til that it dye.
　　"Here may ye se wel how that genterye° 290
Is nat annexed to possessioun,
Sith folk ne doon hir operacioun°
Alwey as dooth the fyr, lo, in his kynde.
For, God it woot, men may wel often fynde
A lordes sone do shame and vileynye. 295
And he that wol han prys of° his gentrye,
For he was born of a gentil hous
And hadde his eldres noble and vertuous,
And nyl° hymselven do no gentil dedis°
Ne folwen his gentil auncestre that deed° is, 300
He nys° nat gentil, be he duc or erl,
For vileyns synful dedes make a cherl.
For gentilesse nys but renomee°
Of thyn auncestres for hir hye bountee,
Which is a straunge° thyng for thy persone. 305
Thy gentilesse cometh fro God allone.
Thanne comth oure verray° gentilesse of grace;
It was nothyng biquethe° us with oure place.
　　"Thenketh how noble, as seith Valerius,°
Was thilke° Tullius Hostillius 310
That out of poverte roos to heigh noblesse.
Redeth Senek,° and redeth eek Boece.°
Ther shul ye seen expres° that no drede° is
That he is gentil that dooth gentil dedis.
And therfore, leve° housbonde, I thus conclude, 315
Al° were it that myne auncestres were rude,
Yet may the hye God, and so hope I,
Graunte me grace to lyven vertuously.
Thanne am I gentil, whan that I bigynne
To lyven vertuously and weyve° synne. 320
　　"And ther-as° ye of poverte me repreve,°
The hye God, on whom that we bileve,

In wilful° poverte chees° to lyve his lyf.
And certes every man, mayden, or wyf
May understonde that Jesus, hevene° Kyng, 325
Ne wolde nat chese° a vicious lyvyng.
Glad° poverte is an honeste thyng, certeyn;
This wol Senek and othere clerkes° seyn.
Who so that halt hym payd of° his poverte,
I holde hym riche, al hadde he nat a sherte. 330
He that coveiteth is a poure wight,
For he wolde han that is nat in his myght;
But he that noght hath ne coveiteth to have
Is riche, althogh ye holde hym but a knave.
　　"Verray poverte, it syngeth properly. 335
Juvenal seith of poverte myrily:°
'The poure man, whan he gooth by the weye,
Biforn° the theves he may synge and pleye.'
Poverte is hateful good and, as I gesse,
A ful greet bryngere out of bisynesse,° 340
A greet amendere eek° of sapience,°
To hym that taketh° it in pacience.
Poverte is this, althogh it seme alenge,°
Possessioun that no wight wol chalenge.
Poverte ful often, whan a man is lowe, 345
Maketh° his God and eek hymself to knowe.
Poverte a spectacle° is, as thynketh° me,
Thurgh which he may his verray freendes se.
And therfore, sire, syn that° I noght yow greve,°
Of my poverte namoore ye me repreve.° 350
　　"Now, sire, of elde° ye repreve me;
And certes, sire, thogh noon auctoritee°
Were in no book, ye gentils of honour
Seyn° that men sholde an old wight doon favour
And clepe° hym fader, for youre gentilesse; 355
And auctours° shal I fynden,° as I gesse.
　　"Now, ther° ye seye that I am foul and old,
Thanne drede yow noght to been a cokewold,°
For filthe and elde, also mote I thee,°
Been grete wardeyns° upon chastitee. 360
But, nathelees,° syn I knowe youre delit,
I shal fulfille youre worldly appetit.

---

285. shette: shut. thenne: thence. 286. lye: blaze. brenne:
burn. 287. As: as if. 288. His office: its function. holde: retain.
289. Up: on. 290. genterye: gentility. 292. ne . . . opera-
cioun: don't behave. 296. han . . . of: have esteem for.
299. nyl: will (not). dedis: deeds. 300. deed: dead. 301. nys:
is (not). 303. renomee: renown. 305. straunge: alien, i.e., the
"high goodness" of your ancestors cannot descend into *your*
character. 307. verray: true. 308. nothyng biquethe: in no
way bequeathed to. 309. Valerius: Valerius Maximus, a
Roman moralist and historian. 310. thilke: that same. 312.
Senek: Seneca, a Roman author. Boece: Boethius, late
fifth-century author of the *Consolation of Philosophy*.
313. expres: expressly. drede: doubt. 315. leve: dear. 316.
Al: even if. 320. weyve: shun. 321. ther-as: whereas.
repreve: reproach.

323. wilful: willing. chees: chose. 325. hevene: heaven's. 326.
chese: choose. 327. Glad: willing. 328. clerkes: scholars.
329. halt . . . of: considers himself rewarded by. 336. myrily:
merrily. 338. Biforn: in front of. 340. bisynesse: care. 341.
amendere eek: improver also. sapience: wisdom. 342. taketh:
receives. 343. alenge: miserable. 346. Maketh: causes (him).
347. spectacle: eyeglass. thynketh: it seems to. 349. syn
that: since. greve: harm. 350. repreve: reproach. 351. elde:
old age. 352. noon auctoritee: no authoritative decision.
354. Seyn: say. 355. clepe: call. 356. auctours: authors.
fynden: find (as authorities). 357. ther: whereas. 358. cokewold: cuckold. 359. also . . . thee: as I may prosper. 360.
wardeyns: guards. 361. nathelees: nevertheless.

"Chees now," quod she, "oon of thise thynges
  tweye:°
To han me foul and old til that I deye,
And be to yow a trewe, humble wyf,   365
And nevere yow displese in al my lyf;
Or elles ye wol han me yong and fair
And take youre aventure° of the repair°
That shal be to youre hous because of me,
Or in som oother place, may wel be.   370
Now chees yourselven wheither that yow liketh."°
  This knyght avyseth hym° and soore siketh,°
But atte laste he seyde in this manere:
"My lady, and my love and wyf so deere,
I putte me in youre wise governaunce.   375
Cheseth° yourself which may be moost plesaunce
And moost honour to yow and me also.
I do no fors the wheither° of the two,
For as yow liketh, it suffiseth me."
  "Thanne have I gete° of yow maistrye," quod
  she,   380
"Syn I may chese and governe as me lest?"°
  "Ye, certes, wyf," quod he. "I holde it best."
  "Kys me," quod she. "We be no lenger wrothe,
For, by my trouthe,° I wol be to yow bothe—
This is to seyn, ye,° bothe fair and good.   385
I pray to God that I mote sterven wood°
But° I to yow be also° good and trewe
As evere was wyf syn that the world was newe.
And but I be to-morn as fair to sene°
As any lady, emperice, or queene   390
That is bitwix the est and eek the west,
Do with my lyf and deth right as yow lest.
Cast up the curtyn. Looke how that it is."
  And whan the knyght sey° verraily al this,
That she so fair was and so yong ther-to,   395
For joye he hente° hire in his armes two.
His herte bathed in a bath of blisse,
A thousand tyme a rewe he gan hir kisse,°
And she obeyed hym in every thyng
That myghte do hym plesance° or likyng.   400
  And thus they lyve unto hir° lyves ende
In parfit joye, and Jesu Crist us sende
Housbondes meke, yonge, and fressh a-bedde,

And grace t' overbyde hem° that we wedde.
And eek I praye Jesu shorte hir lyves   405
That noght wol be governed by hir wyves;
And olde and angry nygardes of dispence,°
God sende hem soone verray pestilence.

EDMUND SPENSER
1552–1599

from The Faerie Queene

from The First Booke of the *Faerie Queene*,
Contayning the Legende of the Knight of the
Red Crosse, or of Holinesse

1

Lo I the man, whose Muse whilome did maske,
As time her taught in lowly Shepheards weeds,°
Am now enforst a far unfitter taske,
For trumpets sterne to chaunge mine Oaten reeds,
And sing of Knights and Ladies gentle deeds;   5
Whose prayses having slept in silence long,
Me, all too meane, the sacred Muse areeds°
To blazon broad emongst her learned throng:
Fierce warres and faithfull loves shall moralize my
  song.

2

Helpe then, O holy Virgin chiefe of nine,°   10
Thy weaker° Novice to performe thy will,
Lay forth out of thine everlasting scryne°
The antique rolles, which there lye hidden still,
Of Faerie knights and fairest Tanaquill,°
Whom that most noble Briton Prince° so long   15

363. tweye: two. 368. aventure: chance. repair: resort. 371.
wheither . . . liketh: whichever pleases you better. 372.
avyseth hym: ponders. siketh: sighs. 376. Cheseth: choose.
378. do . . . wheither: don't care which. 380. gete: gotten.
381. lest: it pleases. 384. trouthe: faith. 385. ye: indeed.
386. mote . . . wood: may die mad. 387. But: unless. also:
as. 389. sene: see. 394. sey: saw. 396. hente: seized. 398.
a rewe . . . kisse: in a row he kissed her. 400. plesance:
pleasure. 401. hir: their.

404. t' overbyde hem: to overrule them. 407. nygardes of
dispence: niggardly spenders.

THE FAERIE QUEENE. 2. Shepheards weeds: conventional
dress of the poet in pastoral poetry; Spenser is alluding to
his earlier verse. 7. areeds: tells. 10. Virgin . . . nine: Clio,
the muse of history. 11. weaker: too weak. 12. scryne:
chest for keeping books or documents. 14. Tanaquill:
Gloriana, representative of Elizabeth I. 15. Briton Prince:
King Arthur.

Sought through the world, and suffered so much
 ill,
That I must rue his undeservèd wrong:
O helpe thou my weake wit, and sharpen my dull
 tong.

3

And thou most dreaded impe° of highest Jove,
Faire Venus sonne, that with thy cruell dart 20
At that good knight so cunningly didst rove,°
That glorious fire it kindled in his hart,
Lay now thy deadly Heben° bow apart,
And with thy mother milde come to mine ayde:
Come both, and with you bring triumphant Mart,°
In loves and gentle jollities arrayd, 26
After his murdrous spoiles and bloudy rage allyd.

4

And with them eke, O Goddesse heavenly bright,
Mirrour of grace and Majestie divine,
Great Lady of the greatest Isle, whose light 30
Like Phoebus lampe throughout the world doth
 shine,
Shed thy faire beames into my feeble eyne,
And raise my thoughts too humble and too vile,
To thinke of that true glorious type of thine,
The argument of mine afflicted stile: 35
The which to heare, vouchsafe, O dearest dred
 a-while.

CANTO I

The Patron of true Holinesse,
 Foule Errour doth defeate:
Hypocrisie him to entrape,
 Doth to his home entreate.

1

A Gentle Knight was pricking on the plaine,
Y cladd in mightie armes and silver shielde,
Wherein old dints of deepe wounds did remaine,
The cruell markes of many a bloudy fielde;
Yet armes till that time did he never wield: 5
His angry steede did chide his foming bitt,
As much disdayning to the curbe to yield:

Full jolly° knight he seemd, and faire did sitt,
As one for knightly giusts and fierce encounters fitt.

2

But on his brest a bloudie Crosse he bore, 10
The deare remembrance of his dying Lord,
For whose sweete sake that glorious badge he wore,
And dead as living ever him adored:
Upon his shield the like was also scored,
For soveraine hope, which in his helpe he had: 15
Right faithfull true he was in deede and word,
But of his cheere° did seeme too solemne sad;
Yet nothing did he dread, but ever was ydrad.°

3

Upon a great adventure he was bond,
That greatest Gloriana to him gave; 20
That greatest Glorious Queene of Faerie lond,
To winne him worship, and her grace to have,
Which of all earthly things he most did crave;
And ever as he rode, his hart did earne°
To prove his puissance in battell brave 25
Upon his foe, and his new force to learne;
Upon his foe, a Dragon horrible and stearne.

4

A lovely Ladie rode him faire beside,
Upon a lowly Asse more white then snow,
Yet she much whiter, but the same did hide 30
Under a vele, that wimpled was full low,
And over all a blacke stole she did throw,
As one that inly mournd: so was she sad,
And heavie sat upon her palfrey slow;
Seemèd in heart some hidden care she had, 35
And by her in a line a milke white lambe she lad.

5

So pure an innocent, as that same lambe,
She was in life and every vertuous lore,
And by descent from Royall lynage came
Of ancient Kings and Queenes, that had of yore 40
Their scepters stretcht from East to Westerne shore,
And all the world in their subjection held;
Till that infernall feend with foule uprore

---

19. impe: child, i.e., Cupid. **21. rove:** shoot. **23. Heben:**
ebony. **25. Mart:** Mars.

Canto I. **8. jolly:** gallant, brave. **17. cheere:** countenance. **18. ydrad:** dreaded. **24. earne:** yearn.

Forwasted all their land, and them expeld:
Whom to avenge, she had this Knight from far
  compeld.   45

6

Behind her farre away a Dwarfe did lag,
That lasie seemed in being ever last,
Or wearièd with bearing of her bag
Of needments at his backe. Thus as they past,
The day with cloudes was suddeine overcast,   50
And angry Jove an hideous storme of raine
Did poure into his Lemans° lap so fast,
That every wight° to shrowd it did constrain,
And this faire couple eke° to shroud themselves
  were fain.

7

Enforst to seeke some covert nigh at hand,   55
A shadie grove not far away they spide,
That promist ayde the tempest to withstand:
Whose loftie trees yclad with sommers pride,
Did spred so broad, that heavens light did hide,
Not perceable with power of any starre: 60
And all within were pathes and alleies wide,
With footing worne, and leading inward farre:
Faire harbour that them seemes; so in they entred
  arre.

8

And foorth they passe, with pleasure forward led,
Joying to heare the birdes sweete harmony,   65
Which therein shrouded from the tempest dred,
Seemd in their song to scorne the cruell sky.
Much can they prayse the trees so straight and hy,
The sayling Pine, the Cedar proud and tall,
The vine-prop Elme, the Poplar never dry,   70
The builder Oake, sole king of forrests all,
The Aspine good for staves, the Cypresse funerall.

9

The Laurell, meed° of mightie Conquerours
And Poets sage, the Firre that weepeth still,
The Willow worne of forlorne Paramours,   75
The Eugh obedient to the benders will,

The Birch for shaftes, the Sallow for the mill,
The Mirrhe sweete bleeding in the bitter wound,°
The warlike Beech, the Ash for nothing ill,
The fruitfull Olive, and the Platane round,   80
The carver Holme, the Maple seeldom inward
  sound.

10

Led with delight, they thus beguile the way,
Untill the blustring storme is overblowne;
When weening° to returne, whence they did stray,
They cannot finde that path, which first was
  showne,   85
But wander too and fro in wayes unknowne,
Furthest from end then, when they neerest weene,
That makes them doubt, their wits be not their
  owne:
So many pathes, so many turnings seene,
That which of them to take, in diverse doubt they
  been.   90

11

At last resolving forward still to fare,
Till that some end they finde or in or out,
That path they take, that beaten seemd most bare,
And like to lead the labyrinth about;
Which when by tract they hunted had throughout,
At length it brought them to a hollow cave,   96
Amid the thickest woods. The Champion stout
Eftsoones dismounted from his courser brave,
And to the Dwarfe a while his needlesse spere° he
  gave.

12

"Be well aware," quoth then that Ladie milde, 100
"Least suddaine mischiefe ye too rash provoke:
The danger hid, the place unknowne and wilde,
Breedes dreadfull doubts: Oft fire is without smoke,
And perill without show: therefore your stroke
Sir knight with-hold, till further triall made." 105
"Ah Ladie," said he, "shame were to revoke
The forward footing for an hidden shade:
Vertue gives her selfe light, through darkenesse for
  to wade."

52. **Lemans:** lover's. 53. **wight:** creature. 54. **eke:** also. 73.
meed: reward.

78. **Mirrhe . . . wound:** The sweet gum of the myrrh was
used in dressing wounds. 84. **weening:** expecting. 99.
needlesse spere: i.e., used only on horseback.

13

"Yea but," quoth she, "the perill of this place
I better wot then you, though now too late   110
To wish you backe returne with foule disgrace,
Yet wisedome warnes, whilest foot is in the gate,
To stay the steppe, ere forcèd to retrate.
This is the wandring wood, this Errours den,
A monster vile, whom God and man does hate: 115
Therefore I read° beware." "Fly fly," quoth then
The fearefull Dwarfe, "this is no place for living
  men."

14

But full of fire and greedy hardiment,
The youthfull knight could not for ought be staide,
But forth unto the darksome hole he went,   120
And lookèd in: his glistring armor made
A litle glooming light, much like a shade,
By which he saw the ugly monster plaine,
Halfe like a serpent horribly displaide,
But th' other halfe did womans shape retaine, 125
Most lothsom, filthie, foule, and full of vile
  disdaine.

15

And as she lay upon the durtie ground,
Her huge long taile her den all overspred,
Yet was in knots and many boughtes° upwound,
Pointed with mortall sting. Of her there bred   130
A thousand yong ones, which she dayly fed,
Sucking upon her poisonous dugs, eachone
Of sundry shapes, yet all ill favorèd:
Soone as that uncouth° light upon them shone,
Into her mouth they crept, and suddain all were
  gone.   135

16

Their dam upstart, out of her den effraide,
And rushèd forth, hurling her hideous taile
About her cursed head, whose folds displaid
Were stretcht now forth at length without entraile.°
She lookt about, and seeing one in mayle   140
Armèd to point, sought backe to turne againe;
For light she hated as the deadly bale,°

116. **read:** advise. 129. **boughtes:** coils. 134. **uncouth:** unfamiliar. 139. **entraile:** twisting. 142. **bale:** evil.

Ay wont in desert darknesse to remaine,
Where plaine none might her see, nor she see any
  plaine.

17

Which when the valiant Elfe° perceived, he lept
As Lyon fierce upon the flying pray,   146
And with his trenchand° blade her boldly kept
From turning backe, and forcèd her to stay:
Therewith enraged she loudly gan to bray,
And turning fierce, her speckled taile advaunst, 150
Threatning her angry sting, him to dismay:
Who nought aghast, his mightie hand enhaunst:
The stroke down from her head unto her shoulder
  glaunst.

18

Much daunted with that dint, her sence was dazd,
Yet kindling rage, her selfe she gathered round, 155
And all attonce her beastly body raizd
With doubled forces high above the ground:
Tho° wrapping up her wrethèd sterne arownd,
Lept fierce upon his shield, and her huge traine
All suddenly about his body wound,   160
That hand or foot to stirre he strove in vaine:
God helpe the man so wrapt in Errours endlesse
  traine.

19

His Lady sad to see his sore constraint,
Cride out, "Now now Sir knight, shew what ye bee,
Add faith unto your force, and be not faint: 165
Strangle her, else she sure will strangle thee."
That when he heard, in great perplexitie,
His gall did grate for griefe and high disdaine,
And knitting all his force got one hand free,   170
Wherewith he grypt her gorge with so great paine,
That soone to loose her wicked bands did her
  constraine.

20

Therewith she spewd out of her filthy maw
A floud of poyson horrible and blacke,

145. **Elfe:** name applied to knight of fairyland. 147. **trenchand:** cutting. 158. **Tho:** then.

Full of great lumpes of flesh and gobbets raw,
Which stunck so vildly, that it forst him slacke 175
His grasping hold, and from her turne him backe:
Her vomit full of bookes and papers was,
With loathly frogs and toades, which eyes did lacke,
And creeping sought way in the weedy gras:
Her filthy parbreake° all the place defilèd has. 180

21

As when old father Nilus gins to swell
With timely pride above the Aegyptian vale,
His fattie waves do fertile slime outwell,
And overflow each plaine and lowly dale:
But when his later spring gins to avale, 185
Huge heapes of mudd he leaves, wherein there
    breed
Ten thousand kindes of creatures, partly male
And partly female of his fruitfull seed;
Such ugly monstrous shapes elsewhere may no
    man reed.°

22

The same so sore annoyèd has the knight, 190
That welnigh chokèd with the deadly stinke,
His forces faile, ne can no longer fight.
Whose corage when the feend perceived to shrinke,
She pourèd forth out of her hellish sinke
Her fruitfull cursed spawne of serpents small, 195
Deformèd monsters, fowle, and blacke as inke,
Which swarming all about his legs did crall,
And him encombred sore, but could not hurt at all.

23

As gentle Shepheard in sweete even-tide,
When ruddy Phoebus gins to welke° in west, 200
High on an hill, his flocke to vewen wide,
Markes which do byte their hasty supper best;
A cloud of combrous gnattes do him molest,
All striving to infixe their feeble stings,
That from their noyance he no where can rest, 205
But with his clownish° hands their tender wings
He brusheth oft, and oft doth mar their murmur-
    ings.

24

Thus ill bestedd, and fearefull more of shame,
Then of the certaine perill he stood in,
Halfe furious unto his foe he came, 210
Resolved in minde all suddenly to win,
Or soone to lose, before he once would lin;°
And strooke at her with more then manly force,
That from her body full of filthie sin
He raft her hatefull head without remorse; 215
A streame of cole black bloud forth gushèd from
    her corse.

25

Her scattred brood, soone as their Parent deare
They saw so rudely falling to the ground,
Groning full deadly, all with troublous feare,
Gathred themselves about her body round, 220
Weening their wonted entrance to have found
At her wide mouth: but being there withstood
They flockèd all about her bleeding wound,
And suckèd up their dying mothers blood,
Making her death their life, and eke her hurt their
    good. 225

26

That detestable sight him much amazde,
To see th' unkindly Impes of heaven accurst,
Devoure their dam; on whom while so he gazd,
Having all satisfide their bloudy thurst,
Their bellies swolne he saw with fulnesse burst, 230
And bowels gushing forth: well worthy end
Of such as drunke her life, the which them nurst;
Now needeth him no lenger labour spend,
His foes have slaine themselves, with whom he
    should contend.

27

His Ladie seeing all, that chaunst, from farre 235
Approcht in hast to greet his victorie,
And said, "Faire knight, borne under happy starre,
Who see your vanquisht foes before you lye:°
Well worthy be you of that Armorie,
Wherein ye have great glory wonne this day, 240
And prooved your strength on a strong enimie,

---

180. parbreake: vomit. **189. reed**: see. **200. welke**: fade. **206. clownish**: rude.

212. lin: stop.

Your first adventure: many such I pray,
And henceforth ever wish, that like succeed it
   may."

28

Then mounted he upon his Steede againe,
And with the Lady backward sought to wend; 245
That path he kept, which beaten was most plaine,
Ne ever would to any by-way bend,
But still did follow one unto the end,
The which at last out of the wood them brought.
So forward on his way (with God to frend)   250
He passèd forth, and new adventure sought;
Long way he travellèd, before he heard of ought.

29

At length they chaunst to meet upon the way
An aged Sire, in long blacke weedes yclad,
His feete all bare, his beard all hoarie gray,   255
And by his belt his booke he hanging had;
Sober he seemde, and very sagely sad,
And to the ground his eyes were lowly bent,
Simple in shew, and voyde of malice bad,
And all the way he prayèd, as he went,   260
And often knockt his brest, as one that did repent.

30

He faire the knight saluted, louting° low,
Who faire him quited, as that courteous was:
And after askèd him, if he did know
Of straunge adventures, which abroad did pas. 265
"Ah my deare Sonne," quoth he, "how should,
   alas,
Silly° old man, that lives in hidden cell,
Bidding his beades all day for his trespas,
Tydings of warre and worldly trouble tell?   269
With holy father sits not with such things to mell.°

31

"But if of daunger which hereby doth dwell,
And homebred evill ye desire to heare,
Of a straunge man I can you tidings tell,
That wasteth all his countrey farre and neare."
"Of such," said he, "I chiefly do inquere,   275

262. **louting**: bowing. 267. **Silly**: innocent. 270. **mell**: meddle.

And shall you well reward to shew the place,
In which that wicked wight his dayes doth weare:
For to all knighthood it is foule disgrace,
That such a cursed creature lives so long a space."

32

"Far hence," quoth he, "in wastfull wildernesse 280
His dwelling is, by which no living wight
May ever passe, but thorough great distresse."
"Now," sayd the Lady, "draweth toward night,
And well I wote, that of your later fight
Ye all forwearied be: for what so strong,   285
But wanting rest will also want of might?
The Sunne that measures heaven all day long,
At night doth baite° his steedes the Ocean waves
   emong.

33

"Then with the Sunne take Sir, your timely rest.
And with new day new worke at once begin: 290
Untroubled night they say gives counsell best."
"Right well Sir knight ye have advisèd bin,"
Quoth then that aged man; "the way to win
Is wisely to advise: now day is spent;
Therefore with me ye may take up your In   295
For this same night." The knight was well content:
So with that godly father to his home they went.

34

A little lowly Hermitage it was,
Downe in a dale, hard by a forests side,
Far from resort of people, that did pas   300
In travell to and froe: a little wyde
There was an holy Chappell edifyde,
Wherein the Hermite dewly wont to say
His holy things each morne and eventyde:
Thereby a Christall streame did gently play,   305
Which from a sacred fountaine wellèd forth alway.

35

Arrivèd there, the little house they fill,
Ne looke for entertainement, where none was:
Rest is their feast, and all things at their will;
The noblest mind the best contentment has.   310
With faire discourse the evening so they pas:

288. **baite**: feed.

For that old man of pleasing wordes had store,
And well could file his tongue as smooth as glas;
He told of Saintes and Popes, and evermore
He strowd an Ave-Mary after and before.   315

36

The drouping Night thus creepeth on them fast,
And the sad humour° loading their eye liddes,
As messenger of Morpheus on them cast
Sweet slombring deaw, the which to sleepe them
    biddes.
Unto their lodgings then his guestes he riddes:° 320
Where when all drownd in deadly sleepe he findes,
He to his study goes, and there amiddes
His Magick bookes and artes of sundry kindes,
He seekes out mighty charmes, to trouble sleepy
    mindes.

37

Then choosing out few wordes most horrible, 325
(Let none them read) thereof did verses frame,
With which and other spelles like terrible,
He bad awake blacke Plutoes griesly Dame,°
And cursèd heaven, and spake reprochfull shame
Of highest God, the Lord of life and light;   330
A bold bad man, that dared to call by name
Great Gorgon,° Prince of darknesse and dead night,
At which Cocytus quakes, and Styx is put to flight.

38

And forth he cald out of deepe darknesse dred
Legions of Sprights, the which like little flyes 335
Fluttring about his ever damnèd hed,
A-waite whereto their service he applyes,
To aide his friends, or fray° his enimies:
Of those he chose out two, the falsest twoo,
And fittest for to forge true-seeming lyes;   340
The one of them he gave a message too,
The other by him selfe staide other worke to doo.

39

He making speedy way through spersèd ayre,
And through the world of waters wide and deepe,

To Morpheus house doth hastily repaire.   345
Amid the bowels of the earth full steepe,
And low, where dawning day doth never peepe,
His dwelling is; there Tethys his wet bed
Doth ever wash, and Cynthia still doth steepe
In silver deaw his ever-drouping hed,   350
Whiles sad Night over him her mantle black doth
    spred.

40

Whose double gates° he findeth lockèd fast,
The one faire framed of burnisht Yvory,
The other all with silver overcast;
And wakefull dogges before them farre do lye, 355
Watching to banish Care their enimy,
Who oft is wont to trouble gentle Sleepe.
By them the Sprite doth passe in quietly,
And unto Morpheus comes, whom drownèd deepe
In drowsie fit he findes: of nothing he takes
    keepe.°   360

41

And more, to lulle him in his slumber soft,
A trickling streame from high rocke tumbling
    downe
And ever-drizling raine upon the loft,
Mixt with a murmuring winde, much like the sowne
Of swarming Bees, did cast him in a swowne: 365
No other noyse, nor peoples troublous cryes,
As still are wont t' annoy the wallèd towne,
Might there be heard: but carelesse Quiet lyes,
Wrapt in eternall silence farre from enemyes.

42

The messenger approching to him spake,   370
But his wast wordes returnd to him in vaine:
So sound he slept, that nought mought him awake.
Then rudely he him thrust, and pusht with paine,
Whereat he gan to stretch: but he againe
Shooke him so hard, that forcèd him to speake. 375
As one then in a dreame, whose dryer braine
Is tost with troubled sights and fancies weake,
He mumbled soft, but would not all his silence
    breake.

---

317. **sad humour:** heavy moisture. 320. **riddes:** leads. 328.
Dame: Proserpine. 332. **Great Gorgon:** Demogorgon.
338. **fray:** frighten.

352. **double gates:** the two legendary gates from which
dreams issue, false dreams from the ivory gate and true
dreams from the gate of horn. 360. **keepe:** notice.

43

The Sprite then gan more boldly him to wake,
And threatned unto him the dreaded name 380
Of Hecate: whereat he gan to quake,
And lifting up his lumpish head, with blame
Halfe angry askèd him, for what he came.
"Hither," quoth he, "me Archimago sent,
He that the stubborne Sprites can wisely tame, 385
He bids thee to him send for his intent
A fit false dreame, that can delude the sleepers
    sent.°

44

The God obayde, and calling forth straight way
A diverse dreame out of his prison darke,
Delivered it to him, and downe did lay 390
His heavie head, devoide of careful carke,°
Whose sences all were straight benumbd and starke.
He backe returning by the Yvorie dore,
Remounted up as light as chearefull Larke,
And on his litle winges the dreame he bore 395
In hast unto his Lord, where he him left afore.

45

Who all this while with charmes and hidden artes,
Had made a Lady of that other Spright,
And framed of liquid ayre her tender partes
So lively, and so like in all mens sight, 400
That weaker sence it could have ravisht quight:
The maker selfe for all his wondrous witt,
Was nigh beguilèd with so goodly sight:
Her all in white he clad, and over it
Cast a blacke stole, most like to seeme for Una°
    fit. 405

46

Now when that ydle dreame was to him brought
Unto that Elfin knight he bad him fly,
Where he slept soundly void of evill thought,
And with false shewes abuse his fantasy,
In sort as he him schoolèd privily: 410
And that new creature borne without her dew,
Full of the makers guile, with usage sly
He taught to imitate that Lady trew,
Whose semblance she did carrie under feignèd
    hew.

387. sent: senses. **391 carke:** sorrow. **405. Una:** Truth.

47

Thus well instructed, to their worke they hast, 415
And comming where the knight in slomber lay,
The one upon his hardy head him plast,
And made him dreame of loves and lustfull play,
That nigh his manly hart did melt away,
Bathèd in wanton blis and wicked joy: 420
Then seemèd him his Lady by him lay,
And to him playnd, how that false wingèd boy,
Her chast hart had subdewd, to learne Dame
    pleasures toy.

48

And she her selfe of beautie soveraigne Queene,
Faire Venus seemde unto his bed to bring 425
Her, whom he waking evermore did weene
To be the chastest flowre, that ay did spring
On earthly braunch, the daughter of a king,
Now a loose Leman to vile service bound:
And eke the Graces seemèd all to sing, 430
Hymen iô Hymen, dauncing all around,
Whilst freshest Flora her with Yvie girlond crownd.

49

In this great passion of unwonted lust,
Or wonted feare of doing ought amis,
He started up, as seeming to mistrust 435
Some secret ill, or hidden foe of his:
Lo there before his face his Lady is,
Under blake stole hyding her bayted hooke,
And as halfe blushing offred him to kis,
With gentle blandishment and lovely looke, 440
Most like that virgin true, which for her knight
    him took.

50

All cleane dismayd to see so uncouth sight,
And halfe enragèd at her shamelesse guise,
He thought have slaine her in his fierce despight:
But hasty heat tempring with sufferance wise, 445
He stayde his hand, and gan himselfe advise
To prove his sense, and tempt her faignèd truth.
Wringing her hands in wemens pitteous wise,
Tho can she weepe, to stirre up gentle ruth,
Both for her noble bloud, and for her tender
    youth. 450

51

And said, "Ah Sir, my liege Lord and my love,
Shall I accuse the hidden cruell fate,
And mightie causes wrought in heaven above,
Or the blind God, that doth me thus amate,°
For hopèd love to winne me certaine hate?   455
Yet thus perforce he bids me do, or die.
Die is my dew: yet rew my wretched state
You, whom my hard avenging destinie
Hath made judge of my life or death indifferently.

52

"Your owne deare sake forst me at first to leave   460
My Fathers kingdome," There she stopt with
    teares;
Her swollen hart her speach seemd to bereave,
And then againe begun, "My weaker yeares
Captived to fortune and frayle worldly feares,
Fly to your faith for succour and sure ayde: 465
Let me not dye in languor and long teares."
"Why Dame," quoth he, "what hath ye thus dis-
    mayd?
What frayes ye, that were wont to comfort me
    affrayd?"

53

"Love of your selfe," she said, "and deare°
    constraint
Lets me not sleepe, but wast the wearie night   470
In secret anguish and unpittied plaint,
Whiles you in carelesse sleepe are drownèd quight."
Her doubtfull words made that redoubted knight
Suspect her truth: yet since no untruth he knew,
Her fawning love with foule disdainefull spight   475
He would not shend,° but said, "Deare dame I rew,
That for my sake unknowne such griefe unto you
    grew.

54

"Assure your selfe, it fell not all to ground;
For all so deare as life is to my hart,
I deeme your love, and hold me to you bound;   480
Ne let vaine feares procure your needlesse smart,
Where cause is none, but to your rest depart."
Not all content, yet seemd she to appease

454. amate: dismay. 469. deare: dire. 476. shend: reject.

Her mournefull plaintes, beguilèd of her art,
And fed with words, that could not chuse but
    please,   485
So slyding softly forth, she turnd as to her ease.

55

Long after lay he musing at her mood,
Much grieved to thinke that gentle Dame so light,
For whose defence he was to shed his blood.
At last dull wearinesse of former fight   490
Having yrockt a sleepe his irkesome spright,
That troublous dreame gan freshly tosse his braine,
With bowres, and beds, and Ladies deare delight:
But when he saw his labour all was vaine,
With that misformèd spright he backe returnd
    againe.   495

CANTO II

The guilefull great Enchanter parts
The Redcrosse Knight from Truth:
Into whose stead faire falshood steps,
And workes him wofull ruth.

1

By this the Northerne wagoner had set
His sevenfold teme behind the stedfast starre,°
That was in Ocean waves yet never wet,
But firme is fixt, and sendeth light from farre
To all, that in the wide deepe wandring arre: 5
And chearefull Chaunticlere with his note shrill
Had warnèd once, that Phoebus fiery carre
In hast was climbing up the Easterne hill,
Full envious that night so long his roome did fill.

2

When those accursed messengers of hell,   10
That feigning dreame, and that faire-forgèd Spright
Came to their wicked maister, and gan tell
Their bootelesse paines, and ill succeeding night:
Who all in rage to see his skilfull might
Deluded so, gan threaten hellish paine   15
And sad Prosèrpines wrath, them to affright.
But when he saw his threatning was but vaine,
He cast about, and searcht his balefull bookes
    againe.

Canto II. **2. By . . . starre:** By this time the Big Dipper
had set behind the polestar.

3

Eftsoones he tooke that miscreated faire,
And that false other Spright, on whom he spred 20
A seeming body of the subtile aire,
Like a young Squire, in loves and lusty-hed
His wanton dayes that ever loosely led,
Without regard of armes and dreaded fight:
Those two he tooke, and in a secret bed, 25
Covered with darknesse and misdeeming night,
Them both together laid, to joy in vaine delight.

4

Forthwith he runnes with feignèd faithfull hast
Unto his guest, who after troublous sights
And dreames, gan now to take more sound
repast, 30
Whom suddenly he wakes with fearefull frights,
As one aghast with feends or damnèd sprights,
And to him cals, "Rise rise unhappy Swaine,
That here wex old in sleepe, whiles wicked wights
Have knit themselves in Venus shamefull chaine; 35
Come see, where your false Lady doth her honour
staine."

5

All in amaze he suddenly up start
With sword in hand, and with the old man went;
Who soone him brought into a secret part,
Where that false couple were fully closely ment° 40
In wanton lust and lewd embracèment:
Which when he saw, he burnt with gealous fire,
The eye of reason was with rage yblent,°
And would have slaine them in his furious ire,
But hardly was restreinèd of that aged sire. 45

6

Returning to his bed in torment great,
And bitter anguish of his guiltie sight,
He could not rest, but did his stout heart eat,
And wast his inward gall with deepe despight,
Yrkesome of life, and too long lingring night. 50
At last faire Hesperus in highest skie
Had spent his lampe, and brought forth dawning
light,
Then up he rose, and clad him hastily;
The Dwarfe him brought his steed: so both away
do fly.

7

Now when the rosy-fingred Morning faire, 55
Weary of aged Tithones saffron bed,
Had spred her purple robe through deawy aire,
And the high hils Titan discoverèd,
The royall virgin shooke off drowsy-hed,
And rising forth out of her baser bowre, 60
Lookt for her knight, who far away was fled,
And for her Dwarfe, that wont to wait each houre;
Then gan she waile and weepe, to see that woefull
stowre.°

8

And after him she rode with so much speede
As her slow beast could make; but all in vaine: 65
For him so far had borne his light-foot steede,
Pricked with wrath and fiery fierce disdaine,
That him to follow was but fruitlesse paine;
Yet she her weary limbes would never rest,
But every hill and dale, each wood and plaine 70
Did search, sore grievèd in her gentle brest,
He so ungently left her, whom she lovèd best.

9

But subtill Archimago, when his guests
He saw divided into double parts,
And Una wandring in woods and forrests, 75
Th' end of his drift, he praisd his divelish arts,
That had such might over true meaning harts;
Yet rests not so, but other meanes doth make,
How he may worke unto her further smarts:
For her he hated as the hissing snake, 80
And in her many troubles did most pleasure take.

10

He then devisde himselfe how to disguise;
For by his mightie science he could take
As many formes and shapes in seeming wise,
As ever Proteus to himselfe could make: 85
Sometime a fowle, sometime a fish in lake,
Now like a foxe, now like a dragon fell,
That of himselfe he oft for feare would quake,
And oft would flie away. O who can tell
The hidden power of herbes, and might of Magicke
spell? 90

40. ment: joined. **43. yblent:** blinded.

63. stowre: affliction.

11

But now seemde best, the person to put on
Of that good knight, his late beguilèd guest:
In mighty armes he was yclad anon,
And silver shield: upon his coward brest
A bloudy crosse, and on his craven crest   95
A bounch of haires discoloured diversly:
Full jolly knight he seemde, and well addrest,
And when he sate upon his course free,
Saint George himself ye would have deemèd him
  to be.

12

But he the knight, whose semblaunt he did beare,
The true Saint George was wandred far away, 101
Still flying from his thoughts and gealous feare;
Will was his guide, and griefe led him astray.
At last him chaunst to meete upon the way
A faithlesse Sarazin all armed to point,   105
In whose great shield was writ with letters gay
Sans foy:° full large of limbe and every joint
He was, and carèd not for God or man a point.

13

He had a faire companion of his way,
A goodly Lady clad in scarlot red,   110
Purfled° with gold and pearle of rich assay,
And like a Persian mitre on her hed
She wore, with crownes and owches° garnishèd,
The which her lavish lovers to her gave;
Her wanton palfrey all was overspred   115
With tinsell trappings, woven like a wave,
Whose bridle rung with golden bels and bosses
  brave.

14

With faire disport and courting dalliaunce
She intertainde her lover all the way:
But when she saw the knight his speare ad-
  vaunce,   120
She soone left off her mirth and wanton play,
And bad her knight addresse him to the fray:
His foe was nigh at hand. He prickt with pride
And hope to winne his Ladies heart that day,

Forth spurrèd fast: adowne his coursers side 125
The red bloud trickling staind the way, as he did
  ride.

15

The knight of the Redcrosse when him he spide,
Spurring so hote with rage dispiteous,
Gan fairely couch his speare, and towards ride:
Soone meete they both, both fell and furious, 130
That daunted with their forces hideous,
Their steeds do stagger, and amazèd stand,
And eke themselves too rudely rigorous,
Astonied with the stroke of their owne hand, 134
Do backe rebut, and each to other yeeldeth land.

16

As when two rams stird with ambitious pride,
Fight for the rule of the rich fleecèd flocke,
Their hornèd fronts so fierce on either side
Do meete, that with the terrour of the shocke
Astonied both, stand sencelesse as a blocke, 140
Forgetfull of the hanging victory:
So stood these twaine, unmovèd as a rocke,
Both staring fierce, and holding idely
The broken reliques of their former cruelty.

17

The Sarazin sore daunted with the buffe   145
Snatcheth his sword, and fiercely to him flies;
Who well it wards, and quyteth cuff with cuff:
Each others equall puissance envies,
And through their iron sides with cruell spies
Does seeke to perce: repining courage yields 150
No foote to foe. The flashing fier flies
As from a forge out of their burning shields,
And streames of purple bloud new dies the verdant
  fields.

18

"Curse on the Crosse," quoth then the Sarazin,
"That keepes thy body from the bitter fit;°   155
Dead long ygoe I wote thou haddest bin,
Had not that charme from thee forwarnèd it:
But yet I warne thee now assurèd sitt,
And hide thy head." Therewith upon his crest

107. **Sans foy:** Without faith. 111. **Purfled:** decorated with a
border. 113. **owches:** gems.

155. **fit:** stroke.

With rigour so outrageous he smitt,   160
That a large share it hewd out of the rest,
And glauncing down his shield, from blame him
   fairely blest.°

19

Who thereat wondrous wroth, the sleeping spark
Of native vertue gan eftsoones revive,
And at his haughtie helmet making mark,   165
So hugely stroke, that it the steele did rive,
And cleft his head. He tumbling downe alive,
With bloudy mouth his mother earth did kis,
Greeting his grave: his grudging ghost did strive
With the fraile flesh; at last it flitted is,   170
Whither the soules do fly of men, that live amis.

20

The Lady when she saw her champion fall,
Like the old ruines of a broken towre,
Staid not to waile his woefull funerall,
But from him fled away with all her powre;   175
Who after her as hastily gan scowre,°
Bidding the Dwarfe with him to bring away
The Sarazins shield, signe of the conqueroure.
Her soone he overtooke, and bad to stay,
For present cause was none of dread her to
   dismay.   180

21

She turning backe with ruefull countenaunce,
Cride, "Mercy mercy Sir vouchsafe to show
On silly Dame, subject to hard mischaunce,
And to your mighty will." Her humblesse low
In so ritch weedes and seeming glorious show, 185
Did much emmove his stout heroicke heart,
And said, "Deare dame, your suddein overthrow
Much rueth me; but now put feare apart,
And tell, both who ye be, and who that tooke your
   part."

22

Melting in teares, then gan she thus lament;   190
"The wretched woman, whom unhappy howre
Hath now made thrall to your commandèment,

Before that angry heavens list to lowre,
And fortune false betraide me to your powre,
Was, (O what now availeth that I was!)   195
Borne the sole daughter of an Emperour,
He that the wide West under his rule has,
And high hath set his throne, where Tiberis doth
   pas.

23

"He in the first flowre of my freshest age,
Betrothèd me unto the onely haire   200
Of a most mighty king, most rich and sage;
Was never Prince so faithfull and so faire,
Was never Prince so meeke and debonaire;
But ere my hopèd day of spousall shone,
My dearest Lord fell from high honours staire, 205
Into the hands of his accursed fone,°
And cruelly was slaine, that shall I ever mone.

24

"His blessed body spoild of lively breath,
Was afterward, I know not how, convaid
And fro me hid: of whose most innocent death
When tidings came to me unhappy maid,   211
O how great sorrow my sad soule assaid.
Then forth I went his woefull corse to find,
And many yeares throughout the world I straid,
A virgin widow, whose deepe wounded mind   215
With love, long time did languish as the striken
   hind.

25

"At last it chauncèd this proud Sarazin
To meete me wandring, who perforce me led
With him away, but yet could never win
The Fort, that Ladies hold in soveraigne dread. 220
There lies he now with foule dishonour dead,
Who whiles he livde, was callèd proud Sans foy,
The eldest of three brethren, all three bred
Of one bad sire, whose youngest is Sans joy,°
And twixt them both was borne the bloudy bold
   Sans loy°   225

---

162. from . . . blest: The cross on the shield served as a blessing that kept him from harm. 176. scowre: pursue.   206. fone: foes. 224. Sans joy: Without joy. 225. Sans loy: Without law.

26

"In this sad plight, friendlesse, unfortunate,
Now miserable I Fidessa° dwell,
Craving of you in pitty of my state,
To do none ill, if please ye not do well."
He in great passion all this while did dwell,   230
More busying his quicke eyes, her face to view,
Then his dull eares, to heare what she did tell;
And said, "Faire Lady hart of flint would rew
The undeservèd woes and sorrowes, which ye shew.

27

"Henceforth in safe assuraunce may ye rest,   235
Having both found a new friend you to aid,
And lost an old foe, that did you molest:
Better new friend then an old foe is said."
With chaunge of cheare the seeming simple maid
Let fall her eyen, as shamefast to the earth,   240
And yeelding soft, in that she nought gain-said,
So forth they rode, he feining seemely merth,
And she coy lookes: so dainty they say maketh
      derth.°

28

Long time they plus together traveilèd,
Till weary of their way, they came at last,   245
Where grew two goodly trees, that faire did spred
Their armes abroad, with gray mosse overcast,
And their greene leaves trembling with every blast,
Made a calme shadow far in compasse round:
The fearefull Shepheard often there aghast   250
Under them never sat, ne wont there sound
His mery oaten pipe, but shund th' unlucky ground.

29

But this good knight soone as he them can spie,
For the coole shade him thither hastly got:
For golden Phoebus now ymounted hie,   255
From fiery wheeles of his faire chariot
Hurlèd his beame so scorching cruell hot,
That living creature mote it not abide;
And his new Lady it endurèd not.
There they alight, in hope themselves to hide   260
From the fierce heat, and rest their weary limbs a
      tide.

227. **Fidessa:** Faith. 243. **so . . . derth:** coyness makes a
dearth of satisfaction.

30

Faire seemely pleasaunce each to other makes,
With goodly purposes there as they sit:
And in his falsèd fancy he her takes
To be the fairest wight, that livèd yit;   265
Which to expresse, he bends his gentle wit,
And thinking of those braunches greene to frame
A girlond for her dainty forehead fit,
He pluckt a bough; out of whose rift there came
Small drops of gory bloud, that trickled downe the
      same.   270

31

Therewith a piteous yelling voyce was heard,
Crying, "O spare with guilty hands to teare
My tender sides in this rough rynd embard,
But fly, ah fly far hence away, for feare
Least to you hap, that happened to me heare,   275
And to this wretched Lady, my deare love,
O too deare love, love bought with death too
      deare."
Astond he stood, and up his haire did hove,
And with that suddein horror could no member
      move.

32

At last whenas the dreadfull passion   280
Was overpast, and manhood well awake,
Yet musing at the straunge occasion,
And doubting much his sence, he thus bespake;
"What voyce of damnèd Ghost from Limbo lake,
Or guilefull spright wandring in empty aire,   285
Both which fraile men do oftentimes mistake,
Sends to my doubtfull eares these speaches rare,
And ruefull plaints, me bidding guiltlesse bloud to
      spare?"

33

Then groning deepe, "Nor damnèd Ghost," quoth
      he,
"Nor guilefull sprite to thee these wordes doth
      speake,   290
But once a man Fradubio,° now a tree,
Wretched man, wretched tree; whose nature weake,
A cruell witch her cursed will to wreake,

291. **Fradubio:** Brother Doubt.

Hath thus transformd, and plast in open plaines,
Where Boreas doth blow full bitter bleake,   295
And scorching Sunne does dry my secret vaines:
For though a tree I seeme, yet cold and heat me
  paines."

34

"Say on Fradubio then, or man, or tree,"
Quoth then the knight, "by whose mischievous arts
Art thou misshapèd thus, as now I see?
He oft finds med'cine, who his griefe imparts;   300
But double griefs afflict concealing harts,
As raging flames who striveth to suppresse."
"The author then," said he, "of all my smarts,
Is one Duessa° a false sorceresse,
That many errant knights hath brought to
  wretchednesse.   305

35

"In prime of youthly yeares, when corage hot
The fire of love and joy of chevalree
First kindled in my brest, it was my lot
To love this gentle Lady, whom ye see,   310
Now not a Lady, but a seeming tree;
With whom as once I rode accompanyde,
Me chauncèd of a knight encountred bee,
That had a like faire Lady by his syde,
Like a faire Lady, but did fowle Duessa hyde.   315

36

"Whose forgèd beauty he did take in hand,°
All other Dames to have exceeded farre;
I in defence of mine did likewise stand,
Mine, that did then shine as the Morning starre:
So both to battell fierce arraungèd arre,   320
In which his harder fortune was to fall
Under my speare: such is the dye° of warre:
His Lady left as a prise martiall,
Did yield her comely person, to be at my call.

37

"So doubly loved of Ladies unlike faire,   325
Th' one seeming such, the other such indeede,
One day in doubt I cast for to compare,

Whether in beauties glorie did exceede;
A Rosy girlond was the victors meede:
Both seemde to win, and both seemde won to
  bee,   330
So hard the discord was to be agreede.
Fraelissa° was as faire, as faire mote bee,
And ever false Duessa seemde as faire as shee.

38

"The wicked witch now seeing all this while
The doubtful ballaunce equally to sway,   335
What not by right, she cast to win by guile,
And by her hellish science raisd streight way
A foggy mist, that overcast the day,
And a dull blast, that breathing on her face,
Dimmèd her former beauties shining ray,   340
And with foule ugly forme did her disgrace:
Then was she faire alone, when none was faire in
  place.

39

"Then cride she out, 'Fye, fye, deformèd wight,
Whose borrowed beautie now appeareth plaine
To have before bewitchèd all mens sight;   345
O leave her soone, or let her soone be slaine.'
Her loathly visage viewing with disdaine,
Eftsoones I thought her such, as she me told,
And would have kild her; but with faignèd paine,
The false witch did my wrathfull hand with-
  hold;   350
So left her, where she now is turnd to treën mould.°

40

"Thens forth I tooke Duessa for my Dame,
And in the witch unweeting joyd long time,
Ne ever wist, but that she was the same,
Till on a day (that day is every Prime,°   355
When Witches wont do penance for their crime)
I chaunst to see her in her proper hew,
Bathing her selfe in origane and thyme:
A filthy foule old woman I did vew,
That ever to have toucht her, I did deadly rew.   360

---

305. Duessa: Fraud. **316. take in hand:** maintain. **322. dye:** chance.

332. Fraelissa: Frailty. **351. treën mould:** form of a tree. **355. Prime:** spring, or the beginning of the year.

41

"Her neather partes misshapen, monstruous,
Were hidd in water, that I could not see,
But they did seeme more foule and hideous,
Then womans shape man would beleeve to bee.
Then forth from her most beastly companie   365
I gan refraine, in minde to slip away,
Soone as appeard safe opportunitie:
For danger great, if not assured decay
I saw before mine eyes, if I were knowne to stray.

42

"The divelish hag by chaunges of my cheare   370
Perceived my thought, and drownd in sleepie night,
With wicked herbes and ointments did besmeare
My bodie all, through charmes and magicke might,
That all my senses were bereavèd quight:
Then brought she me into this desert waste,   375
And by my wretched lovers side me pight,°
Where now enclosd in wooden wals full faste,
Banisht from living wights, our wearie dayes we
    waste."

43

"But how long time," said then the Elfin knight,
"Are you in this misformèd house to dwell?"   380
"We may not chaunge," quoth he, "this evil
    plight,
Till we be bathèd in a living well;
That is the terme prescribèd by the spell."
"O how," said he, "mote I that well out find,
That may restore you to your wonted well?"   385
"Time and suffisèd fates to former kynd
Shall us restore, none else from hence may us
    unbynd."

44

The false Duessa, now Fidessa hight,°
Heard how in vaine Fradubio did lament,
And knew well all was true. But the good
    knight   390
Full of sad feare and ghastly dreriment,
When all this speech the living tree had spent,
The bleeding bough did thrust into the ground,
That from the bloud he might be innocent,

376. pight: placed. 388. hight: called.

And with fresh clay did close the wooden
    wound: 395
Then turning to his Lady, dead with feare her
    found.

45

Her seeming dead he found with feignèd feare,
As all unweeting of that well she knew,
And paynd himselfe with busie care to reare
Her out of carelesse swowne. Her eylids blew   400
And dimnèd sight with pale and deadly hew
At last she up gan lift: with trembling cheare
Her up he tooke, too simple and too trew,
And oft her kist. At length all passèd feare,
He set her on her steede, and forward forth did
    beare.   405

CANTO VII°

*The Redcrosse knight is captive made
By Gyaunt proud opprest,
Prince Arthur meets with Una great-
ly with those newes distrest.*

1

What man so wise, what earthly wit so ware,
As to descry the crafty cunning traine,
By which deceipt doth maske in visour faire,
And cast her colours dyèd deepe in graine,
To seeme like Truth, whose shape she well can
    faine,   5
And fitting geatures to her purpose frame,
The guiltlesse man with guile to entertaine?
Great maistresse of her art was that false Dame,
The false Duessa, clokèd with Fidessaes name.

2

Who when returning from the drery Night,   10
She fownd not in that perilous house of Pryde,
Where she had left, the noble Redcrosse knight,
Her hopèd pray, she would no lenger bide,
But forth she went, to seeke him far and wide.

Canto VII. In the intervening cantos Duessa guides
the Redcrosse Knight to the House of Pride, where Lucifera
presides over the pageant of the Deadly Sins; later the
knight encounters and defeats Sans joy, whose body
Duessa conveys to Hell with the aid of Night.

Ere long she fownd, whereas he wearie sate,   15
To rest him selfe, foreby a fountaine side,
Disarmèd all of yron-coted Plate,
And by his side his steed the grassy forage ate.

3

He feedes upon the cooling shade, and bayes°
His sweatie forehead in the breathing wind,   20
Which through the trembling leaves full gently
    playes
Wherein the cherefull birds of sundry kind
Do chaunt sweet musick, to delight his mind:
The Witch approching gan him fairely greet,
And with reproch of carelesnesse unkind   25
Upbrayd, for leaving her in place unmeet,
With fowle words tempring faire, soure gall with
    hony sweet.

4

Unkindnesse past, they gan of solace treat,
And bathe in pleasaunce of the joyous shade,
Which shielded them against the boyling heat,   30
And with greene boughes decking a gloomy glade,
About the fountaine like a girlond made;
Whose bubbling wave did ever freshly well,
Ne ever would through fervent sommer fade:
The sacred Nymph, which therein wont to dwell, 35
Was out of Dianes favour, as it then befell.

5

The cause was this: one day when Phoebe fayre
With all her band was following the chace,
This Nymph, quite tyred with heat of scorching ayre
Sat downe to rest in middest of the race: 40
The goddesse wroth gan fowly her disgrace,
And bad the waters, which from her did flow,
Be such as she her selfe was then in place.
Thenceforth her waters waxèd dull and slow,
And all that drunke thereof, did faint and feeble
    grow.   45

6

Hereof this gentle knight unweeting was,
And lying downe upon the sandie graile,°
Drunke of the streame, as cleare as cristall glas;

19. **bayes:** bathes. 47. **graile:** gravel.

Eftsoones his manly forces gan to faile,
And mightie strong was turnd to feeble fraile.   50
His chaungèd powres at first them selves not felt,
Till crudled° cold his corage gan assaile,
And chearefull bloud in faintnesse chill did melt,
Which like a fever fit through all his body swelt.

7

Yet goodly court he made still to his Dame,   55
Pourd out in loosnesse on the grassy grownd,
Both carelesse of his health, and of his fame:
Till at the last he heard a dreadfull sownd,
Which through the wood loud bellowing, did
    rebownd,
That all the earth for terrour seemd to shake,   60
And trees did tremble. Th' Elfe therewith astownd,
Upstarted lightly from his looser make,°
And his unready weapons gan in hand to take.

8

But ere he could his armour on him dight,
Or get his shield, his monstrous enimy   65
With sturdie steps came stalking in his sight,
An hideous Geant horrible and hye,
That with his talnesse seemd to threat the skye,
The ground eke gronèd under him for dreed;
His living like saw never living eye,   70
He durst behold: his stature did exceed
The hight of three the tallest sonnes of mortall
    seed.

9

The greatest Earth his uncouth mother was,
And blustring Aeolus his boasted sire,
Who with his breath, which through the world
    doth pas,   75
Her hollow womb did secretly inspire,
And fild her hidden caves with stormie yre,
That she conceived; and trebling the dew time,
In which the wombes of women to expire,
Brought forth this monstrous masse of earthly
    slime,   80
Puft up with emptie wind, and fild with sinfull
    crime.

52. **crudled:** curdled. 62. **make:** companion.

10

So growen great through arrogant delight
Of th' high descent, whereof he was yborne,
And through presumption of his matchlesse might,
All other powres and knighthood he did scorne. 85
Such now he marcheth to this man forlorne,
And left to losse: his stalking steps are stayde
Upon a snaggy Oke, which he had torne
Out of his mothers bowelles, and it made
His mortall mace, wherewith his foemen he dis-
    mayde.   90

11

That when the knight he spide, he gan advance
With huge force and insupportable mayne,
And towardes him with dreadfull fury praunce;
Who haplesse, and eke hopelesse, all in vaine
Did to him pace, sad battaile to darrayne,°   95
Disarmd, disgrast, and inwardly dismayde,
And eke so faint in every joynt and vaine,
Through that fraile fountaine, which him feeble
    made,
That scarsely could he weeld his bootlesse single
    blade.

12

The Geaunt strooke so maynly mercilesse,   100
That could have overthrowne a stony towre,
And were not heavenly grace, that him did blesse,
He had beene pouldred all, as thin as flowre:
But he was wary of that deadly stowre,
And lightly lept from underneath the blow: 105
Yet so exceeding was the villeins powre,
That with the wind it did him overthrow,
And all his sences stound, that still he lay full low.

13

As when that divelish yron Engin wrought
In deepest Hell, and framd by Furies skill,   110
With windy Nitre and quick Sulphur fraught,
And ramd with bullet round, ordaind to kill,
Conceiveth fire, the heavens it doth fill
With thundring noyse, and all the ayre doth choke,
That none can breath, nor see, nor heare at will, 115

95. darrayne: prepare for.

Through smouldry cloud of duskish stincking
    smoke,
That th' onely breath him daunts, who hath escapt
    the stroke.

14

So daunted when the Geaunt saw the knight,
His heavie hand he heavèd up on hye,
And him to dust thought to have battred
    quight,   120
Untill Duessa loud to him gan crye;
O great Orgoglio,° greatest under skye,
O hold thy mortall hand for Ladies sake,
Hold for my sake, and do him not to dye,
But vanquisht thine eternall bondslave make,   125
And me thy worthy meed unto thy Leman take.

15

He hearkned, and did stay from further harmes,
To gayne so goodly guerdon, as she spake:
So willingly she came into his armes,
Who her as willingly to grace did take,   130
And was possessèd of his new found make.
Then up he tooke the slombred sencelesse corse,
And ere he could out of his swowne awake,
Him to his castle brought with hastie forse,
And in a Dongeon deepe him threw without
    remorse.   135

16

From that day forth Duessa was his deare,
And highly honourd in his haughtie eye,
And gave her gold and purple pall to weare,
And triple crowne set on her head full hye,
And her endowd with royall majestye: 140
Then for to make her dreaded more of men,
And peoples harts with awfull terrour tye,
A monstrous beast ybred in filthy fen
He chose, which he had kept long time in darksome
    den.

17

Such one it was, as that renowmèd Snake   145
Which great Alcides in Stremona slew,
Long fostred in the filth of Lerna lake,°

122. Orgoglio: Carnal Pride. **145–47. Snake . . . lake:**
Hercules (Alcides) killed the Hydra, which lived in the
marsh at Lerna.

Whose many heads out budding ever new,
Did breed him endlesse labour to subdew:
But this same Monster much more ugly was;　150
For seven great heads out of his body grew,
An yron brest, and backe of scaly bras,
And all embrewd in bloud, his eyes did shine as
　glas.

18

His tayle was stretchèd out in wondrous length,
That to the house of heavenly gods it raught,　155
And with extorted powre, and borrowed strength,
The ever-burning lamps from thence it brought,
And prowdly threw to ground, as things of nought;
And underneath his filthy feet did tread
The sacred things, and holy heasts° foretaught. 160
Upon this dreadfull Beast with sevenfold head
He set the false Duessa, for more aw and dread.

19

The wofull Dwarfe, which saw his maisters fall,
Whiles he had keeping of his grasing steed,
And valiant knight become a caytive thrall,　165
When all was past, tooke up his forlorne weed,°
His mightie armour, missing most at need;
His silver shield, now idle maisterlesse;
His poynant speare, that many made to bleed,
The ruefull moniments of heavinesse,　170
And with them all departes, to tell his great
　distresse.

20

He had not travaild long, when on the way
He wofull Ladie, wofull Una met,
Fast flying from the Paynims° greedy pray,
Whilst Satyrane° him from pursuit did let:　175
Who when her eyes she on the Dwarfe had set,
And saw the signes, that deadly tydings spake,
She fell to ground for sorrowfull regret,
And lively breath her sad brest did forsake,
Yet might her pitteous hart be seene to pant and
　quake.　180

21

The messenger of so unhappie newes,
Would faine have dyde: dead was his hart within,
Yet outwardly some little comfort shewes:
At last recovering hart, he does begin
To rub her temples, and to chaufe her chin,　185
And every tender part does tosse and turne:
So hardly he the flitted life does win,
Unto her native prison to retourne:
Then gins her grievèd ghost thus to lament and
　mourne.

22

"Ye dreary instruments of dolefull sight,　190
That doe this deadly spectacle behold,
Why do ye lenger feed on loathèd light,
Or liking find to gaze on earthly mould,
Sith cruell fates the carefull threeds unfould,
The which my life and love together tyde?　195
Now let the stony dart of senselesse cold
Perce to my hart, and pas through every side,
And let eternall night so sad sight fro me hide.

23

"O lightsome day, the lampe of highest Jove,
First made by him, mens wandring wayes to
　guyde,　200
When darknesse he in deepest dongeon drove,
Henceforth thy hated face for ever hyde,
And shut up heavens windowes shyning wyde:
For earthly sight can nought but sorrow breed,
And late repentance, which shall long abyde.　205
Mine eyes no more on vanitie shall feed,
But seelèd up with death, shall have their deadly
　meed."

24

Then downe againe she fell unto the ground;
But he her quickly rearèd up againe:
Thrise did she sinke adowne in deadly swownd, 210
And thrise he her revived with busie paine:
At last when life recovered had the raine,
And over-wrestled his strong enemie,
With foltring tong, and trembling every vaine,
"Tell on," quoth she, "the wofull Tragedie,　215
The which these reliques sad present unto mine eie.

160. heasts: commands. 166. forlorne weed: abandoned
garment. 174. Paynims: pagans. 175. Satyrane: child of a
satyr and a mortal who protected Una from Sans loy in
Canto VI.

25

"Tempestuous fortune hath spent all her spight,
And thrilling sorrow throwne his utmost dart;
Thy sad tongue cannot tell more heavy plight,
Then that I feele, and harbour in mine hart: 220
Who hath endured the whole, can beare each part.
If death it be, it is not the first wound,
That launchèd hath my brest with bleeding smart.
Begin, and end the bitter balefull stound;°
If lesse, then that I feare, more favour I have
     found."   225

26

Then gan the Dwarfe the whole discourse declare,
The subtill traines of Archimago old;
The wanton loves of false Fidessa faire,
Bought with the bloud of vanquisht Paynim bold:
The wretched payre transformed to treën
     mould;   230
The house of Pride, and perils round about;
The combat, which he with Sans joy did hould;
The lucklesse conflict with the Gyant stout,
Wherein captived, of life or death he stood in
     doubt.

27

She heard with patience all unto the end,   235
And strove to maister sorrowfull assay,
Which greater grew, the more she did contend,
And almost rent her tender hart in tway;
And love fresh coles unto her fire did lay:
For greater love, the greater is the losse.   240
Was never Ladie lovèd dearer day,
Then she did love the knight of the Redcrosse;
For whose deare sake so many troubles her did
     tosse.

28

At last when fervent sorrow slakèd was,
She up arose, resolving him to find   245
A live or dead: and forward forth doth pas,
All as the Dwarfe the way to her assynd:
And evermore in constant carefull mind
She fed her wound with fresh renewèd bale;
Long tost with stormes, and bet with bitter
     wind,   250

224. stound: disaster.

High over hils, and low adowne the dale,
She wandred many a wood, and measurd many a
     vale.

29

At last she chauncèd by good hap to meet
A goodly knight, faire marching by the way
Together with his Squire, arayèd meet: 255
His glitterand armour shinèd farre away,
Like glauncing light of Phoebus brightest ray;
From top to toe no place appearèd bare,
That deadly dint of steele endanger may:
Athwart his brest a bauldrick brave he ware,   260
That shynd, like twinkling stars, with stons most
     pretious rare.

30

And in the midst thereof one pretious stone
Of wondrous worth, and eke of wondrous mights,
Shapt like a Ladies head, exceeding shone,
Like Hesperus emongst the lesser lights,   265
And strove for to amaze the weaker sights;
Thereby his mortall blade full comely hong
In yvory sheath, ycarved with curious slights;
Whose hilts were burnisht gold, and handle strong
Of mother pearle, and buckled with a golden
     tong.   270

31

His haughtie helmet, horrid all with gold,
Both glorious brightnesse, and great terrour bred;
For all the crest a Dragon did enfold
With greedie pawes, and over all did spred
His golden wings: his dreadfull hideous hed   275
Close couchèd on the bever,° seemed to throw
From flaming mouth bright sparkles fierie red,
That suddeine horror to faint harts did show;
And scaly tayle was stretcht adowne his backe full
     low.

32

Upon the top of all his loftie crest,   280
A bunch of haires discolourd diversly,
With sprincled pearle, and gold full richly drest,
Did shake, and seemed to daunce for jollity,

276. bever: visor.

Like to an Almond tree ymounted hye
On top of greene Selinis all alone,   285
With blossomes brave bedeckèd daintily;
Whose tender locks do tremble every one
At every little breath, that under heaven is blowne.

33

His warlike shield all closely covered was,
Ne might of mortall eye be ever seene;   290
Not made of steele, nor of enduring bras,
Such earthly mettals soone consumèd bene:
But all of Diamond perfect pure and cleene
It framèd was, one massie entire mould,
Hewen out of Adament rocke with engines
keene,   295
That point of speare it never percen could,
Ne dint of direfull sword divide the substance
would.

34

The same to wight he never wont disclose,
But when as monsters huge he would dismay,
Or daunt unequall armies of his foes,   300
Or when the flying heavens he would affray;
For so exceeding shone his glistring ray,
That Phoebus golden face it did attaint,
As when a cloud his beames doth over-lay;
And silver Cynthia wexed pale and faint,   305
As when her face is staynd with magicke arts
constraint.

35

No magicke arts hereof had any might,
Nor bloudie wordes of bold Enchaunters call,
But all that was not such, as seemd in sight,
Before that shield did fade, and suddeine fall: 310
And when him list the raskall routes appall,
Men into stones therewith he could transmew,
And stones to dust, and dust to nought at all;
And when him list the prouder lookes subdew,
He would them gazing blind, or turne to other
hew.   315

36

Ne let it seeme, that credence this exceedes,
For he that made the same, was knowne right well

To have done much more admirable deedes.
It Merlin was, which whylome did excell
All living wightes in might of magicke spell: 320
Both shield, and sword, and armour all he wrought
For this young Prince, when first to armes he fell;
But when he dyde, the Faerie Queene it brought
To Faerie lond, where yet it may be seene, if
sought.

37

A gentle youth, his dearely lovèd Squire   325
His speare of heben wood behind him bare,
Whose harmefull head, thrice heated in the fire,
Had riven many a brest with pikehead square;
A goodly person, and could menage faire
His stubborne steed with curbèd canon bit,°   330
Who under him did trample as the aire,
And chauft, that any on his backe should sit;
The yron rowels into frothy fome he bit.

38

When as this knight nigh to the Ladie drew,
With lovely court he gan her entertaine;   335
But when he heard her answeres loth, he knew
Some secret sorrow did her heart distraine:
Which to allay, and calme her storming paine,
Faire feeling words he wisely gan display,
And for her humour fitting purpose faine,   340
To tempt the cause it selfe for to bewray;°
Wherewith emmoved, these bleeding words she
gan to say.

39

"What worlds delight, or joy of living speach
Can heart, so plunged in sea of sorrowes deepe,
And heapèd with so huge misfortunes, reach? 345
The carefull cold beginneth for to creepe,
And in my heart his yron arrow steepe,
Soone as I thinke upon my bitter bale:
Such helplesse harmes yts better hidden keepe,
Then rip up griefe, where it may not availe,   350
My last left comfort is, my woes to weepe and
waile."

---

330. canon bit: smooth round bit. **341. bewray:** reveal.

40

"Ah Ladie deare," quoth then the gentle knight,
"Well may I weene, your griefe is wondrous great;
For wondrous great griefe groneth in my spright,
Whiles thus I heare you of your sorrowes treat. 355
But wofull Ladie let me you intrete,
For to unfold the anguish of your hart:
Mishaps are maistred by advice discrete,
And counsell mittigates the greatest smart;
Found never helpe, who never would his hurts
    impart."   360

41

"O but," quoth she, "great griefe will not be tould,
And can more easily be thought, then said."
"Right so;" quoth he, "but he, that never would,
Could never: will to might gives greatest aid."
"But griefe," quoth she, "does greater grow dis-
    plaid,   365
If then it find not helpe, and breedes despaire."
"Despaire breedes not," quoth he, "where faith is
    staid."
"No faith so fast," quoth she, "but flesh does
    paire."
"Flesh may empaire," quoth he, "but reason can
    repaire."

42

His goodly reason, and well guided speach   370
So deepe did settle in her gratious thought,
That her perswaded to disclose the breach,
Which love and fortune in her heart had wrought,
And said; "Faire Sir, I hope good hap hath
    brought
You to inquire the secrets of my griefe,   375
Or that your wisedome will direct my thought,
Or that your prowesse can me yield reliefe:
Then heare the storie sad, which I shall tell you
    briefe.

43

"The forlorne Maiden, whom your eyes have seene
The laughing stocke of fortunes mockeries,   380
Am th' only daughter of a King and Queene,
Whose parents deare, whilest equall destinies
Did runne about, and their felicities

The favorable heavens did not envy,
Did spread their rule through all the territories, 385
Which Phison and Euphrates floweth by,
And Gehons° golden waves doe wash continually.

44

"Till that their cruell cursed enemy,
An huge great Dragon horrible in sight,
Bred in the loathly lakes of Tartary,°   390
With murdrous ravine, and devouring might
Their kingdome spoild, and countrey wasted
    quight:
Themselves, for feare into his jawes to fall,
He forst to castle strong to take their flight,
Where fast embard in mightie brasen wall,   395
He has them now foure yeres besiegd to make them
    thrall.

45

"Full many knights adventurous and stout
Have enterprizd that Monster to subdew;
From every coast that heaven walks about,
Have thither come the noble Martiall crew,   400
That famous hard atchievements still pursew,
Yet never any could that girlond win,
But all still shronke, and still he greater grew:
All they for want of faith, or guilt of sin,
The pitteous pray of his fierce crueltie have bin. 405

46

"At last yledd with farre reported praise,
Which flying fame throughout the world had spred,
Of doughtie knights, whom Faery land did raise,
That noble order hight of Maidenhed,
Forthwith to court of Gloriane I sped,   410
Of Gloriane great Queene of glory bright,
Whose kingdomes seat Cleopolis° is red,°
There to obtaine some such redoubted knight,
That Parents deare from tyrants powre deliver
    might.

47

"It was my chance (my chance was faire and
    good)   415
There for to find a fresh unprovèd knight,

386–87. Phison . . . Gehons: names of rivers in Genesis 2:11–14. **390. Tartary:** Tartarus, Hell. **412. Cleopolis:** City of Glory. **red:** called.

Whose manly hands imbrewed in guiltie blood
Had never bene, ne ever by his might
Had throwne to ground the unregarded right:
Yet of his prowesse proofe he since hath made   420
(I witnesse am) in many a cruell fight;
The groning ghosts of many one dismaide
Have felt the bitter dint of his avenging blade.

48

"And ye the forlorne reliques of his powre,
His byting sword, and his devouring speare,   425
Which have endurèd many a dreadfull stowre,
Can speake his prowesse, that did earst you beare,
And well could rule: now he hath left you heare,
To be the record of his ruefull losse,
And of my dolefull disaventurous deare: 430
O heavie record of the good Redcrosse,
Where have you left your Lord, that could so well
    you tosse?

49

"Well hopèd I, and faire beginnings had,
That he my captive langour should redeeme,
Till all unweeting, an Enchaunter bad   435
His sence abusd, and made him to misdeeme
My loyalty, not such as it did seeme;
That rather death desire, then such despight.
Be judge ye heavens, that all things right esteeme,
How I him loved, and love with all my might, 440
So thought I eke of him, and thinke I thought
    aright.

50

"Thenceforth me desolate he quite forsooke,
To wander, where wilde fortune would me lead,
And other bywaies he himselfe betooke,
Where never foot of living wight did tread,   445
That brought not backe the balefull body dead;
In which him chauncèd false Duessa meete,
Mine onely foe, mine onely deadly dread,
Who with her witchcraft and misseeming sweete,
Inveigled him to follow her desires unmeete.   450

51

"At last by subtill sleights she him betraid
Unto his foe, a Gyant huge and tall,

Who him disarmèd, dissolute, dismaid,
Unwares surprisèd, and with mightie mall
The monster mercilesse him made to fall,   455
Whose fall did never foe before behold;
And now in darkesome dungeon, wretched thrall,
Remedilesse, for aie he doth him hold;
This is my cause of griefe, more great, then may be
    told."

52

Ere she had ended all, she gan to faint: 460
But he her comforted and faire bespake,
"Certes, Madame, ye have great cause of plaint,
That stoutest heart, I weene, could cause to quake.
But be of cheare, and comfort to you take:
For till I have acquit your captive knight,   465
Assure your selfe, I will you not forsake."
His chearefull words revived her chearelesse
    spright,
So forth they went, the Dwarfe them guiding ever
    right.

CANTO VIII

Faire virgin to redeeme her deare
*   brings Arthur to the fight:*
Who slayes the Gyant, wounds the beast,
*   and strips Duessa quight.*

1

Ay me, how many perils doe enfold
The righteous man, to make him daily fall?
Were not, that heavenly grace doth him uphold,
And stedfast truth acquite him out of all.
Her love is firme, her care continuall,   5
So oft as he through his owne foolish pride,
Or weaknesse is to sinfull bands made thrall:
Else should this Redcrosse knight in bands have
    dyde,
For whose deliverance she this Prince doth thither
    guide.

2

They sadly traveild thus, untill they came   10
Nigh to a castle builded strong and hie:
Then cryde the Dwarfe, lo yonder is the same,
In which my Lord my liege doth lucklesse lie,

Thrall to that Gyants hatefull tyrannie:
Therefore, deare Sir, your mightie powres assay. 15
The noble knight alighted by and by
From loftie steede, and bad the Ladie stay,
To see what end of fight should him befall that day.

3

So with the Squire, th' admirer of his might,
He marchèd forth towards that castle wall;   20
Whose gates he found fast shut, ne living wight
To ward the same, nor answere commers call.
Then tooke that Squire an horne of bugle small,
Which hong adowne his side in twisted gold,
And tassels gay. Wyde wonders over all   25
Of that same hornes great vertues weren told,
Which had approvèd bene in uses manifold.

4

Was never wight, that heard that shrilling sound,
But trembling feare did feele in every vaine;
Three miles it might be easie heard around,   30
And Ecchoes three answerd it selfe againe:
No false enchauntment, nor deceiptfull traine
Might once abide the terror of that blast,
But presently was voide and wholly vaine:
No gate so strong, no locke so firme and fast,   35
But with that percing noise flew open quite, or
    brast.

5

The same before the Geants gate he blew,
That all the castle quakèd from the ground,
And every dore of freewill open flew.
The Gyant selfe dismaièd with that sownd,   40
Where he with his Duessa dalliance fownd,
In hast came rushing forth from inner bowre,
With staring countenance sterne, as one astownd,
And staggering steps, to weet, what suddein stowre
Had wrought that horror strange, and dared his
    dreaded powre.   45

6

And after him the proud Duessa came,
High mounted on her manyheaded beast,
And every head with fyrie tongue did flame,
And every head was crownèd on his creast,

And bloudie mouthèd with late cruell feast.   50
That when the knight beheld, his mightie shild
Upon his manly arme he soone addrest,
And at him fiercely flew, with courage fild,
And eger greedinesse through every member thrild.

7

Therewith the Gyant buckled him to fight,   55
Inflamed with scornefull wrath and high disdaine,
And lifting up his dreadfull club on hight,
All armed with ragged snubbes and knottie graine,
Him thought at first encounter to have slaine.
But wise and warie was that noble Pere,°   60
And lightly leaping from so monstrous maine,
Did faire avoide the violence him nere;
It booted nought, to thinke, such thunderbolts to
    beare.

8

Ne shame he thought to shunne so hideous might:
The idle stroke, enforcing furious way,   65
Missing the marke of his misaymèd sight
Did fall to ground, and with his heavie sway
So deepely dinted in the driven clay,
That three yardes deepe a furrow up did throw:
The sad earth wounded with so sore assay,   70
Did grone full grievous underneath the blow,
And trembling with strange feare, did like an
    earthquake show.

9

As when almightie Jove in wrathfull mood,
To wreake the guilt of mortall sins is bent,
Hurles forth his thundring dart with deadly food, 75
Enrold in flames, and smouldring dreriment,
Through riven cloudes and molten firmament;
The fierce threeforkèd engin making way,
Both loftie towres and highest trees hath rent,
And all that might his angrie passage stay,   80
And shooting in the earth, casts up a mount of clay.

10

His boystrous club, so buried in the ground,
He could not rearen up againe so light,
But that the knight him at avantage found,

Canto VIII.   **60. Pere:** peer.

And whiles he strove his combred clubbe to
    quight   85
Out of the earth, with blade all burning bright
He smote off his left arme, which like a blocke
Did fall to ground, deprived of native might;
Large streames of bloud out of the trunckèd stocke
Forth gushèd, like fresh water streame from riven
    rocke.   90

11

Dismaièd with so desperate deadly wound,
And eke impatient of unwonted paine,
He loudly brayd with beastly yelling sound,
That all the fields rebellowèd againe;
As great a noyse, as when in Cymbrian plaine 95
An heard of Bulles, whom kindly rage doth sting,
Do for the milkie mothers want complaine,
And fill the fields with troublous bellowing,
The neighbour woods around with hollow murmur
    ring.

12

That when his deare Duessa heard, and saw   100
The evill stownd, that daungerd her estate,
Unto his aide she hastily did draw
Her dreadfull beast, who swolne with bloud of late
Came ramping forth with proud presumpteous
    gate,
And threatned all his heads like flaming brands. 105
But him the Squire made quickly to retrate,
Encountring fierce with single sword in hand,
And twixt him and his Lord did like a bulwarke
    stande.

13

The proud Duessa full of wrathfull spight,
And fierce disdaine, to be affronted so,   110
Enforst her purple beast with all her might
That stop out of the way to overthroe,
Scorning the let° of so unequall foe:
But nathemore would that courageous swayne
To her yeeld passage, gainst his Lord to goe,   115
But with outrageous strokes did him restraine,
And with his bodie bard the way atwixt them
    twaine.

113. let: obstacle.

14

Then tooke the angrie witch her golden cup,
Which still she bore, replete with magick artes;
Death and despeyre did many thereof sup,   120
And secret poyson through their inner parts,
Th' eternall bale of heavie wounded harts;
Which after charmes and some enchauntments said,
She lightly sprinkled on his weaker parts;
Therewith his sturdie courage soone was quayd, 125
And all his senses were with suddeine dread
    dismayd.

15

So downe he fell before the cruell beast,
Who on his necke his bloudie clawes did seize,
That life nigh crusht out of his panting brest:
No powre he had to stirre, nor will to rize.   130
That when the carefull knight gan well arise,
He lightly left the foe, with whom he fought,
And to the beast gan turne his enterprise;
For wondrous anguish in his hart it wrought,
To see his lovèd Squire into such thraldome
    brought.   135

16

And high advancing his bloud-thirstie blade,
Stroke one of those deformèd heads so sore,
That of his puissance proud ensample made;
His monstrous scalpe downe to his teeth it tore,
And that misformèd shape mis-shapèd more: 140
A sea of bloud gusht from the gaping wound,
That her gay garments staynd with filthy gore,
And overflowed all the field around;
That over shoes in bloud he waded on the ground.

17

Thereat he roared for exceeding paine,   145
That to have heard, great horror would have bred,
And scourging th' emptie ayre with his long traine,
Through great impatience of his grievèd hed
His gorgeous ryder from her loftie sted
Would have cast downe, and trod in durtie myre,
Had not the Gyant soone her succourèd;   151
Who all enraged with smart and franticke yre,
Came hurtling in full fierce, and forst the knight
    retyre.

18

The force, which wont in two to be disperst,
In one alone left hand he now unites,   155
Which is through rage more strong then both were
    erst;
With which his hdeous club aloft he dites,
And at his foe with furious rigour smites,
That strongest Oake might seeme to overthrow:
The stroke upon his shield so heavie lites,   160
That to the ground it doubleth him full low:
What mortall wight could ever beare so monstrous
    blow?

19

And in his fall his shield, that covered was,
Did loose his vele by chaunce, and open flew:
The light whereof, that heavens light did pas, 165
Such blazing brightnesse through the aier threw,
That eye mote not the same endure to vew.
Which when the Gyaunt spyde with staring eye,
He downe let fall his arme, and soft withdrew
His weapon huge, that heavèd was on hye   170
For to have slaine the man, that on the ground did
    lye.

20

And eke the fruitfull-headed beast, amazed
At flashing beames of that sunshiny shield,
Became starke blind, and all his senses dazed,
That downe he tumbled on the durtie field,   175
And seemed himselfe as conquerèd to yield.
Whom when his maistresse proud perceived to fall,
Whiles yet his feeble feet for faintnesse reeld,
Unto the Gyant loudly she gan call,
"O helpe Orgoglio, helpe, or else we perish all." 180

21

At her so pitteous cry was much amooved,
Her champion stout, and for to ayde his frend,
Againe his wonted angry weapon prooved:
But all in vaine: for he has read his end
In that bright shield, and all their forces spend 185
Themselves in vaine: for since that glauncing sight,
He hath no powre to hurt, nor to defend;
As where th' Almighties lightning brond does light,
It dimmes the dazèd eyen, and daunts the senses
    quight.

22

Whom when the Prince, to battell new addrest, 190
And threatning high his dreadfull stroke did see,
His sparkling blade about his head he blest,
And smote off quite his right leg by the knee,
That downe he tombled; as an aged tree,
High growing on the top of rocky clift,   195
Whose hartstrings with keene steele nigh hewen be,
The mightie trunck halfe rent, with ragged rift
Doth roll adowne the rocks, and fall with fearefull
    drift.

23

Or as a Castle rearèd high and round,
By subtile engins and malitious slight   200
Is underminèd from the lowest ground,
And her foundation forst, and feebled quight,
At last downe falles, and with her heapèd hight
Her hastie ruine does more heavie make,
And yields it selfe unto the victours might;   205
Such was this Gyaunts fall, that seemd to shake
The stedfast globe of earth, as it for feare did quake.

24

The knight then lightly leaping to the pray,
With mortall steele him smot againe so sore,
That headlesse his unweldy bodie lay,   210
All wallowd in his owne fowle bloudy gore,
Which flowèd from his wounds in wondrous store.
But soone as breath out of his breast did pas,
That huge great body, which the Gyaunt bore,
Was vanisht quite, and of that monstrous mas   215
Was nothing left, but like an emptie bladder was.

25

Whose grievous fall, when false Duessa spide,
Her golden cup she cast unto the ground,
And crownèd mitre rudely threw aside;   219
Such percing griefe her stubborne hart did wound,
That she could not endure that dolefull stound,
But leaving all behind her, fled away:
The light-foot Squire her quickly turnd around,
And by hard meanes enforcing her to stay,
So brought unto his Lord, as his deservèd pray. 225

26

The royall Virgin, which beheld from farre,
In pensive plight, and sad perplexitie,
The whole atchievement of this doubtfull warre,
Came running fast to greet his victorie,
With sober gladnesse, and myld modestie,   230
And with sweet joyous cheare him thus bespake;
"Faire braunch of noblesse, flowre of chevalrie,
That with your worth the world amazèd make,
How shall I quite the paines, ye suffer for my sake?

27

"And you fresh bud of vertue springing fast,   235
Whom these sad eyes saw nigh unto deaths dore,
What hath poore Virgin for such perill past,
Wherewith you to reward? Accept therefore
My simple selfe, and service evermore;
And he that high does sit, and all things see   240
With equall eyes, their merites to restore,
Behold what ye this day have done for mee,
And what I cannot quite, requite with usuree.

28

"But sith the heavens, and your faire handeling
Have made you maister of the field this day,   245
Your fortune maister eke with governing,
And well begun end all so well, I pray,
Ne let that wicked woman scape away;
For she it is, that did my Lord bethrall,
My dearest Lord, and deepe in dongeon lay,   250
Where he his better dayes hath wasted all.
O heare, how piteous he to you for ayd does call."

29

Forthwith he gave in charge unto his Squire,
That scarlot whore to keepen carefully;
Whiles he himselfe with greedie great desire   255
Into the Castle entred forcibly,
Where living creature none he did espye;
Then gan he lowdly through the house to call:
But no man cared to answere to his crye.
There raignd a solemne silence over all,   260
Nor voice was heard, nor wight was seene in bowre
    or hall.

30

At last with creeping crooked pace forth came
An old old man, with beard as white as snow,
That on a staffe his feeble steps did frame,
And guide his wearie gate both too and fro: 265
For his eye sight him failèd long ygo,
And on his arme a bounch of keyes he bore,
The which unusèd rust did overgrow:
Those were the keyes of every inner dore,
But he could not them use, but kept them still in
    store.   270

31

But very uncouth sight was to behold,
How he did fashion his untoward pace,
For as he forward mooved his footing old,
So backward still was turnd his wrincled face,
Unlike to men, who ever as they trace,   275
Both feet and face one way are wont to lead.
This was the auncient keeper of that place,
And foster father of the Gyant dead;
His name Ignaro° did his nature right aread.

32

His reverend haires and holy gravitie   280
The knight much honord, as beseemèd well,
And gently askt, where all the people bee,
Which in that stately building wont to dwell.
Who answered him full soft, he could not tell.   284
Againe he askt, where that same knight was layd,
Whom great Orgoglio with his puissaunce fell
Had made his caytive thrall; againe he sayde,
He could not tell: ne ever other answere made.

33

Then askèd he, which way he in might pas:
He could not tell, againe he answerèd.   290
Thereat the curteous knight displeasèd was,
And said, "Old sire, it seemes thou hast not red
How ill it sits with that same silver hed
In vaine to mocke, or mockt in vaine to bee:
But if thou be, as thou art pourtrahèd   295
With natures pen, in ages grave degree,
Aread in graver wise, what I demaund of thee."

279. **Ignaro:** Ignorance.

34

His answere likewise was, he could not tell.
Whose sencelesse speach, and doted ignorance
When as the noble Prince had markèd well,   300
He ghest his nature by his countenance,
And calmd his wrath with goodly temperance.
Then to him stepping, from his arme did reach
Those keyes, and made himselfe free enterance.
Each dore he opened without any breach;   305
There was no barre to stop, nor foe him to
  empeach.

35

There all within full rich arayd he found,
With royall arras and resplendent gold.
And did with store of every thing abound,
That greatest Princes presence might behold.   310
But all the floore (too filthy to be told)
With bloud of guiltlesse babes, and innocents trew,
Which there were slaine, as sheepe out of the fold,
Defilèd was, that dreadfull was to vew,
And sacred ashes over it was strowèd new.   315

36

And there beside of marble stone was built
An Altare, carved with cunning imagery,
On which true Christians bloud was often spilt,
And holy Martyrs often doen to dye,
With cruell malice and strong tyranny: 320
Whose blessed sprites from underneath the stone
To God for vengeance cryde continually,
And with great griefe were often heard to grone,
That hardest heart would bleede, to heare their
  piteous mone.

37

Through every rowme he sought, and every bowr,
But no where could he find that wofull thrall: 326
At last he came unto an yron doore,
That fast was lockt, but key found not at all
Emongst that bounch, to open it withall;
But in the same a little grate was pight,   330
Through which he sent his voyce, and lowd did call
With all his powre, to weet, if living wight
Were housèd therewithin, whom he enlargen might.

38

Therewith an hollow, dreary, murmuring voyce
These piteous plaints and dolours did resound; 335
"O who is that, which brings me happy choyce
Of death, that here lye dying every stound,
Yet live perforce in balefull darkenesse bound?
For now three Moones have changèd thrice their
  hew,   339
And have beene thrice hid underneath the ground,
Since I the heavens chearefull face did vew:
O welcome thou, that doest of death bring tydings
  trew."

39

Which when that Champion heard, with percing
  point
Of pitty deare his hart was thrillèd sore,
And trembling horrour ran through every joynt, 345
For ruth of gentle knight so fowle forlore:°
Which shaking off, he rent that yron dore,
With furious force, and indignation fell;
Where entred in, his foot could find no flore,
But all a deepe descent, as darke as hell,   350
That breathèd ever forth a filthie banefull smell.

40

But neither darkenesse fowle, nor filthy bands,
Nor noyous smell his purpose could withhold,
(Entire affection hateth nicer hands)
But that with constant zeale, and courage bold, 355
After long paines and labours manifold,
He found the meanes that Prisoner up to reare;
Whose feeble thighes, unhable to uphold
His pinèd corse, him scarse to light could beare,
A ruefull spectacle of death and ghastly drere. 360

41

His sad dull eyes deepe sunck in hollow pits,
Could not endure th' unwonted sunne to view;
His bare thin cheekes for want of better bits,
And empty sides deceivèd of their dew,
Could make a stony hart his hap to rew;   365
His rawbone armes, whose mighty brawnèd bowrs
Were wont to rive steele plates, and helmets hew,
Were cleane consumed, and all his vitall powres
Decayd, and all his flesh shronk up like withered
  flowres.

346. forlore: forlorn.

42

Whom when his Lady saw, to him she ran   370
With hasty joy: to see him made her glad,
And sad to view his visage pale and wan,
Who earst in flowres of freshest youth was clad.
Tho when her well of teares she wasted had,
She said, "Ah dearest Lord, what evill starre 375
On you hath frownd, and pourd his influence bad,
That of your selfe ye thus berobbèd arre,
And this misseeming hew your manly looks doth
   marre?

43

"But welcome now my Lord, in wele or woe,
Whose presence I have lackt too long a day;   380
And fie on Fortune mine avowèd foe,
Whose wrathfull wreakes them selves do now alay.
And for these wrongs shall treble penaunce pay
Of treble good: good growes of evils priefe."°
The chearelesse man, whom sorrow did dismay, 385
Had no delight to treaten of his griefe;
His long endurèd famine needed more reliefe.

44

"Faire Lady," then said that victorious knight,
"The things, that grievous were to do, or beare,
Them to renew, I wote, breeds no delight;   390
Best musicke breeds delight in loathing eare:
But th' onely good, that growes of passèd feare,
Is to be wise, and ware of like agein.
This dayes ensample hath this lesson deare
Deepe written in my heart with yron pen,   395
That blisse may not abide in state of mortall men.

45

"Henceforth sir knight, take to you wonted
   strength,
And maister these mishaps with patient might;
Loe where your foe lyes stretcht in monstrous
   length,
And loe that wicked woman in your sight,   400
The roote of all your care, and wretched plight,
Now in your powre, to let her live, or dye."
"To do her dye," quoth Una, "were despight,°
And shame t' avenge so weake an enimy;   404
But spoile her of her scarlot robe, and let her fly."

384. priefe: experience. 403. despight: spiteful.

46

So as she bad, that witch they disaraid,
And robd of royall robes, and purple pall,
And ornaments that richly were displaid;
Ne sparèd they to strip her naked all.
Then when they had despoild her tire and call,° 410
Such as she was, their eyes might her behold,
That her misshapèd parts did them appall,
A loathly, wrinckled hag, ill favoured, old,
Whose secret filth good manners biddeth not be
   told.

47

Her craftie head was altogether bald,   415
And as in hate of honorable eld,
Was overgrowne with scurfe and filthy scald;
Her teeth out of her rotten gummes were feld,
And her sowre breath abhominably smeld;
Her dried dugs, like bladders lacking wind,   420
Hong downe, and filthy matter from them weld;
Her wrizled skin as rough, as maple rind,
So scabby was, that would have loathd all woman-
   kind.

48

Her neather parts, the shame of all her kind,
My chaster Muse for shame doth blush to write;
But at her rompe she growing had behind   426
A foxes taile, with dong all fowly dight;
And eke her feete most monstrous were in sight;
For one of them was like an Eagles claw,
With griping talaunts armd to greedy fight,   430
The other like a Beares uneven paw:
More ugly shape yet never living creature saw.

49

Which when the knights beheld, amazd they were,
And wondred at so fowle deformèd wight.
"Such then," said Una, "as she seemeth here, 435
Such is the face of falshood, such the sight
Of fowle Duessa, when her borrowed light
Is laid away, and counterfesaunce° knowne."
Thus when they had the witch disrobèd quight,
And all her filthy feature open showne,   440
They let her goe at will, and wander wayes
   unknowne.

410. tire and call: robe and headdress. **438. counterfesaunce:**
counterfeit, deception.

50

She flying fast from heavens hated face,
And from the world that her discovered wide,
Fled to the wastfull wildernesse apace,
From living eyes her open shame to hide,   445
And lurkt in rocks and caves long unespide.
But that faire crew of knights, and Una faire
Did in that castle afterwards abide,
To rest them selves, and weary powres repaire,
Where store they found of all, that dainty was and
    rare.   450

CANTO IX

His loves and lignage Arthur tells:
The knights knit friendly bands:
Sir Trevisan flies from Despayre,
Whom Redcrosse knight withstands.

1

O Goodly golden chaine, wherewith yfere°
The vertues linkèd are in lovely wize:
And noble minds of yore allyèd were,
In brave poursuit of chevalrous emprize,
That none did others safety despize,   5
Nor aid envy to him, in need that stands,
But friendly each did others prayse devise,
How to advaunce with favourable hands,
As this good Prince redeemd the Redcrosse knight
    from bands.

2

Who when their powres, empaird through labour
    long,   10
With dew repast they had recurèd° well,
And that weake captive wight now wexèd strong,
Them list no lenger there at leasure dwell,
But forward fare, as their adventures fell,
But ere they parted, Una faire besought   15
That straunger knight his name and nation tell;
Least so great good, as he for her had wrought,
Should die unknown, and buried be in thanklesse
    thought.

Canto IX. **1. yfere:** together. **11. recurèd:** restored.

3

"Faire virgin," said the Prince, "ye me require
A thing without the compas of my wit: 20
For both the lignage and the certain Sire,
From which I sprong, from me are hidden yit.
For all so soone as life did me admit
Into this world, and shewèd heavens light,
From mothers pap I taken was unfit: 25
And streight delivered to a Faery knight,
To be upbrought in gentle thewes° and martiall
    might.

4

Unto old Timon he me brought bylive,°
Old Timon, who in youthly yeares hath beene
In warlike feates th' expertest man alive,   30
And is the wisest now on earth I weene;
His dwelling is low in a valley greene,
Under the foot of Rauran mossy hore,
From whence the river Dee as silver cleene
His tombling billowes rolls with gentle rore: 35
There all my dayes he traind me up in vertuous lore.

5

"Thither the great Magicien Merlin came,
As was his use, ofttimes to visit me:
For he had charge my discipline to frame,
And Tutours nouriture to oversee.   40
Him oft and oft I askt in privitie,
Of what loines and what lignage I did spring:
Whose aunswere bad me still assurèd bee,
That I was sonne and heire unto a king,
As time in her just terme the truth to light should
    bring."   45

6

"Well worthy impe," said then the Lady gent,
"And Pupill fit for such a Tutours hand.
But what adventure, or what high intent
Hath brought you hither into Faery land,   49
Aread° Prince Arthur, crowne of Martiall band?"
"Full hard it is," quoth he, "to read aright
The course of heavenly cause, or understand
The secret meaning of th' eternall might,
That rules mens wayes, and rules the thoughts of
    living wight.

27. thewes: habits. **28. bylive:** quickly. **50. Aread:** tell.

7

"For whither he through fatall deepe foresight 55
Me hither sent, for cause to me unghest,
Or that fresh bleeding wound, which day and night
Whilome doth rancle in my riven brest,
With forcèd fury following his behest,
Me hither brought by wayes yet never found,   60
You to have helpt I hold my selfe yet blest."
"Ah curteous knight," quoth she, "what secret
    wound
Could ever find, to grieve the gentlest hart on
    ground?"

8

"Deare Dame," quoth he, "you sleeping sparkes
    awake,
Which troubled once, into huge flames will grow, 65
Ne ever will their fervent fury slake
Till living moysture into smoke do flow,
And wasted life do lye in ashes low.
Yet sithens silence lesseneth not my fire,
But told it flames, and hidden it does glow,   70
I will revele, what ye so much desire:
Ah Love, lay downe thy bow, the whiles I may
    respire.

9

"It was in freshest flowre of youthly yeares,
When courage first does creepe in manly chest,
Then first the coale of kindly heat appeares   75
To kindle love in every living brest;
But me had warnd old Timons wise behest,
Those creeping flames by reason to subdew,
Before their rage grew to so great unrest,
As miserable lovers use to rew,   80
Which still wex old in woe, whiles woe still wexeth
    new.

10

"That idle name of love, and lovers life,
As losse of time, and vertues enimy
I ever scornd, and joyd to stirre up strife,
In middest of their mournfull Tragedy,   85
Ay wont to laugh, when them I heard to cry,
And blow the fire, which them to ashes brent:
Their God himselfe, grieved at my libertie,
Shot many a dart at me with fiers intent,
But I them warded all with wary government.   90

11

"But all in vaine: no fort can be so strong,
Ne fleshly brest can armèd be so sound,
But will at last be wonne with battrie long,
Or unawares at disavantage found;
Nothing is sure, that growes on earthly ground: 95
And who most trustes in arme of fleshly might,
And boasts, in beauties chaine not to be bound,
Doth soonest fall in disaventrous fight,
And yeeldes his caytive neck to victours most
    despight.

12

"Ensample make of him your haplesse joy,   100
And of my selfe now mated, as ye see;
Whose prouder vaunt that proud avenging boy
Did soone pluck downe, and curbd my libertie.
For on a day prickt forth with jollitie
Of looser life, and heat of hardiment,   105
Raunging the forest wide on courser free,
The fields, the floods, the heavens with one consent
Did seeme to laugh on me, and favour mine intent.

13

"For-wearied with my sports, I did alight   109
From loftie steed, and downe to sleepe me layd;
The verdant gras my couch did goodly dight,
And pillow was my helmet faire displayd:
Whiles every sence the humour sweet embayd,
And slombring soft my hart did steale away,
Me seemèd, by my side a royall Mayd   115
Her daintie limbes full softly down did lay:
So faire a creature yet saw never sunny day.

14

"Most goodly glee and lovely blandishment
She to me made, and bad me love her deare,
For dearely sure her love was to me bent,   120
As when just time expired should appeare.
But whether dreames delude, or true it were,
Was never hart so ravisht with delight,
Ne living man like words did ever heare,
As she to me delivered all that night;   125
And at her parting said, She Queene of Faeries
    hight.

15

"When I awoke, and found her place devoyd,
And nought but pressèd gras, where she had lyen,
I sorrowed all so much, as earst I joyd,
And washèd all her place with watry eyen.   130
From that day forth I loved that face divine;
From that day forth I cast in carefull mind,
To seeke her out with labour, and long tyne,
And never vow to rest, till her I find,
Nine monethes, I seeke in vaine yet ni'll that vow
   unbind."   135

16

Thus as he spake, his visage wexèd pale,
And chaunge of hew great passion did bewray;
Yet still he strove to cloke his inward bale,
And hide the smoke, that did his fire display,
Till gentle Una thus to him gan say;   140
"O happy Queene of Faeries, that hast found
Mongst many, one that with his prowesse may
Defend thine honour, and thy foes confound:
True Loves are often sown, but seldom grow on
   ground."

17

"Thine, O then," said the gentle Redcrosse knight,
"Next to that Ladies love, shalbe the place,   146
O fairest virgin, full of heavenly light,
Whose wondrous faith, exceeding earthly race,
Was firmest fixt in mine extremest case."
"And you, my Lord, the Patrone of my life,   150
Of that great Queene may well gaine worthy grace:
For onely worthy you through prowes priefe
Yf living man mote worthy be, to be her liefe."°

18

So diversly discoursing of their loves,
The golden Sunne his glistring head gan shew,   155
And sad remembraunce now the Prince amoves,
With fresh desire his voyage to pursew:
Als° Una earnd her traveill to renew.
Then those two knights, fast friendship for to bynd,
And love establish each to other trew,   160
Gave goodly gifts, the signes of gratefull mynd,
And eke as pledges firme, right hands together joynd.

153. liefe: beloved. **158. Als:** so.

19

Prince Arthur gave a boxe of Diamond sure,
Embowd with gold and gorgeous ornament,
Wherein were closd few drops of liquor pure,   165
Of wondrous worth, and vertue excellent,
That any wound could heale incontinent:
Which to requite, the Redcrosse knight him gave
A booke, wherein his Saveours testament
Was writ with golden letters rich and brave;   170
A worke of wondrous grace, and able soules to save.

20

Thus beene they parted, Arthur on his way
To seeke his love, and th' other for to fight
With Unaes foe, that all her realme did pray.
But she now weighing the decayèd plight,   175
And shrunken synewes of her chosen knight,
Would not a while her forward course pursew,
Ne bring him forth in face of dreadfull fight,
Till he recovered had his former hew: 179
For him to be yet weake and wearie well she knew.

21

So as they traveild, lo they gan espy
An armèd knight towards them gallop fast,
That seemèd from some fearèd foe to fly,
Or other griesly thing, that him agast.
Still as he fled, his eye was backward cast,   185
As if his feare still followed him behind;
Als flew his steed, as he his bands had brast,
And with his wingèd heeles did tread the wind,
As he had beene a fole of Pegasus his kind.

22

Nigh as he drew, they might perceive his head   190
To be unarmd, and curld uncombèd heares
Upstaring stiffe, dismayd with uncouth dread;
Nor drop of bloud in all his face appeares
Nor life in limbe: and to increase his feares,
In fowle reproch of knighthoods faire degree,   195
About his neck an hempen rope he weares,
That with his glistring armes does ill agree;
But he of rope or armes has now no memoree.

23

The Redcrosse knight toward him crossèd fast,
To weet, what mister° wight was so dismayd: 200
There him he finds all sencelesse and aghast,
That of him selfe he seemd to be afrayd;
Whom hardly he from flying forward stayd,
Till he these wordes to him deliver might;
"Sir knight, aread who hath ye thus arayd, 205
And eke from whom make ye this hasty flight:
For never knight I saw in such misseeming plight."

24

He answerd nought at all, but adding new
Feare to his first amazment, staring wide
With stony eyes, and hartlesse hollow hew, 210
Astonisht stood, as one that had aspide
Infernall furies, with their chaines untide.
Him yet againe, and yet againe bespake
The gentle knight; who nought to him replide,
But trembling every joynt did inly quake, 215
And foltring tongue at last these words seemd forth
   to shake.

25

"For Gods deare love, Sir knight, do me not stay;
For loe he comes, he comes fast after mee."
Eft° looking backe would faine have runne away;
But he him forst to stay, and tellen free 220
The secret cause of his perplexitie:
Yet nathemore by his bold hartie speach,
Could his bloud-frosen hart emboldned bee,
But through his boldnesse rather feare did reach,
Yet forst, at last he made through silence suddein
   breach. 225

26

"And am I now in safetie sure," quoth he,
"From him, that would have forcèd me to dye?
And is the point of death now turned fro mee,
That I may tell this haplesse history?" 229
"Feare nought," quoth he, "no daunger now is nye."
"Then shall I you recount a ruefull cace,"
Said he, "the which with this unlucky eye
I late beheld, and had not greater grace
Me reft from it, had bene partaker of the place.

27

"I lately chaunst (Would I had never chaunst) 235
With a faire knight to keepen companee,
Sir Terwin hight, that well himselfe advaunst
In all affaires, and was both bold and free,
But not so happie as mote happie bee:
He loved, as was his lot, a Ladie gent, 240
That him againe loved in the least degree:
For she was proud, and of too high intent,
And joyd to see her lover languish and lament.

28

"From whom returning sad and comfortlesse,
As on the way together we did fare, 245
We met that villen (God from him me blesse)
That cursed wight, from whom I scapt whyleare,°
A man of hell, that cals himselfe Despaire:
Who first us greets, and after faire areedes
Of tydings strange, and of adventures rare: 250
So creeping close, as Snake in hidden weedes,
Inquireth of our states, and of our knightly
   deedes.

29

"Which when he knew, and felt our feeble harts
Embost° with bale, and bitter byting griefe,
Which love had launchèd with his deadly darts, 255
With wounding words and termes of foule repriefe,
He pluckt from us all hope of due reliefe,
That earst us held in love of lingring life;
Then hopelesse hartlesse, gan the cunning thiefe
Perswade us die, to stint all further strife: 260
To me he lent this rope, to him a rustie knife.

30

"With which sad instrument of hastie death,
That wofull lover, loathing lenger light,
A wide way made to let forth living breath.
But I more fearefull, or more luckie wight, 265
Dismayd with that deformèd dismal sight,
Fled fast away, halfe dead with dying feare:
Ne yet assured of life by you, Sir knight,
Whose like infirmitie like chaunce may beare:
But God you never let his charmèd speeches
   heare." 270

200. mister: kind of. 219. Eft: again.

247. whyleare: lately.

31

"How may a man," said he, "with idle speach
Be wonne, to spoyle the Castle of his health?"
"I wote," quoth he, "whom triall late did teach,
That like would not for all this worldes wealth:
His subtill tongue, like dropping honny, mealt'h
Into the hart, and searcheth every vaine,   276
That ere one be aware, by secret stealth
His powre is reft, and weaknesse doth remaine.
O never Sir desire to try his guilefull traine."

32

"Certes," said he, "hence shall I never rest,   280
Till I that treachours art have heard and tride;
And you Sir knight, whose name mote I request,
Of grace do me unto his cabin guide."
"I that hight Trevisan," quoth he, "will ride
Against my liking backe, to doe you grace: 285
But not for gold nor glee will I abide
By you, when ye arrive in that same place;
For lever had I die, then see his deadly face."

33

Ere long they come, where that same wicked wight
His dwelling has, low in an hollow cave,   290
Farre underneath a craggie clift ypight,
Darke, dolefull, drearie, like a greedie grave,
That still for carrion carcases doth crave:
On top whereof aye dwelt the ghastly Owle,
Shrieking his balefull note, which ever drave   295
Farre from that haunt all other chearefull fowle;
And all about it wandring ghostes did waile and
   howle.

34

And all about old stockes and stubs of trees,
Whereon nor fruit, nor leafe was ever seene,
Did hang upon the ragged rocky knees;   300
On which had many wretches hangèd beene,
Whose carcases were scattered on the greene,
And throwne about the cliffs. Arrivèd there,
That bare-head knight for dread and dolefull
   teene,°   304
Would faine have fled, ne durst approchen neare,
But th' other forst him stay, and comforted in feare.

304. teene: grief.

35

That darkesome cave they enter, where they find
That cursed man, low sitting on the ground,
Musing full sadly in his sullein mind;
His griesie lockes, long growen, and unbound,   310
Disordred hong about his shoulders round,
And hid his face; through which his hollow eyne
Lookt deadly dull, and starèd as astound;
His raw-bone cheekes through penurie and pine,
Were shronke into his jawes, as he did never
   dine.   315

36

His garment nought but many ragged clouts,
With thornes together pind and patchèd was,
The which his naked sides he wrapt abouts;
And him beside there lay upon the gras
A drearie corse, whose life away did pas,   320
All wallowd in his owne yet luke-warme blood,
That from his wound yet wellèd fresh alas;
In which a rustie knife fast fixèd stood,
And made an open passage for the gushing flood.

37

Which piteous spectacle, approving trew   325
The wofull tale that Trevisan had told,
When as the gentle Redcrosse knight did vew,
With firie zeale he burnt in courage bold,
Him to avenge, before his bloud were cold,
And to the villein said, "Thou damnèd wight,   330
The author of this fact, we here behold,
What justice can but judge against thee right,
With thine owne bloud to price his bloud, here
   shed in sight."

38

"What franticke fit," quoth he, "hath thus dis-
   traught
Thee, foolish man, so rash a doome to give?   335
What justice ever other judgement taught,
But he should die, who merites not to live?
None else to death this man despayring drive,
But his owne guiltie mind deserving death.
Is then unjust to each his due to give?   340
Or let him die, that loatheth living breath?
Or let him die at ease, that liveth here uneath?°

342. uneath: uneasily.

39

"Who travels by the wearie wandring way,
To come unto his wishèd home in haste,
And meetes a flood, that doth his passage stay, 345
Is not great grace to helpe him over past,
Or free his feet, that in the myre sticke fast?
Most envious man, that grieves at neighbours
    good,
And fond, that joyest in the woe thou hast,
Why wilt not let him passe, that long hath stood
Upon the banke, yet wilt thy selfe not passe the
    flood? 351

40

"He there does now enjoy eternall rest
And happie ease, which thou doest want and crave,
And further from it daily wanderest:
What if some litle paine the passage have, 355
That makes fraile flesh to feare the bitter wave?
Is not short paine well borne, that brings long ease,
And layes the soule to sleepe in quiet grave?
Sleepe after toyle, port after stormie seas,
Ease after warre, death after life does greatly
    please." 360

41

The knight much wondred at his suddeine wit,
And said, "The terme of life is limited,
Ne may a man prolong, nor shorten it;
The souldier may not move from watchfull sted,
Nor leave his stand, untill his Captaine bed." 365
"Who life did limit by almightie doome,"
Quoth he, "knowes best the termes establishèd;
And he, that points the Centonell his roome,
Doth license him depart at sound of morning
    droome.

42

"Is not his deed, what ever thing is donne, 370
In heaven and earth? did not he all create
To die againe? all ends that was begonne.
Their times in his eternall booke of fate
Are written sure, and have their certaine date.
Who then can strive with strong necessitie, 375
That holds the world in his still chaunging state,
Or shunne the death ordaynd by destinie?
When houre of death is come, let none aske whence,
    nor why.

43

"The lenger life, I wote the greater sin,
The greater sin, the greater punishment: 380
All those great battels, which thou boasts to win,
Through strife, and bloud-shed, and avengement,
Now praysd, hereafter deare thou shalt repent:
For life must life, and bloud must bloud repay.
Is not enough thy evill life forespent? 385
For he, that once hath missèd the right way,
The further he doth goe, the further he doth stray.

44

"Then do no further goe, no further stray,
But here lie downe, and to thy rest betake,
Th' ill to prevent, that life ensewen may. 390
For what hath life, that may it lovèd make,
And gives not rather cause it to forsake?
Feare, sicknesse, age, losse, labour, sorrow, strife,
Paine, hunger, cold, that makes the hart to quake;
And ever fickle fortune rageth rife, 395
All which, and thousands mo do make a loathsome
    life.

45

"Thou wretched man, of death hast greatest need,
If in true ballance thou wilt weigh thy state:
For never knight, that darèd warlike deede,
More lucklesse disaventures did amate:° 400
Witnesse the dongeon deepe, wherein of late
Thy life shut up, for death so oft did call;
And though good lucke prolongèd hath thy date,
Yet death then, would the like mishaps forestall,
Into the which hereafter thou maiest happen fall.

46

"Why then doest thou, O man of sin, desire 406
To draw thy dayes forth to their last degree?
Is not the measure of thy sinfull hire
High heapèd up with huge iniquitie,
Against the day of wrath, to burden thee? 410
Is not enough, that to this Ladie milde
Thou falsèd hast thy faith with perjurie,
And sold thy selfe to serve Duessa vilde,
With whom in all abuse thou hast thy selfe defilde?

400. amate: appall.

47

"Is not he just, that all this doth behold   415
From highest heaven, and beares an equall eye?
Shall he thy sins up in his knowledge fold,
And guiltie be of thine impietie?
Is not his law, let every sinner die:
Die shall all flesh? what then must needs be
    donne,   420
Is it not better to doe willinglie,
Then linger, till the glasse be all out ronne?
Death is the end of woes: die soone, O faeries
    sonne."

48

The knight was much enmovèd with his speach,
That as a swords point through his hart did
    perse,   425
And in his conscience made a secret breach,
Well knowing true all, that he did reherse,
And to his fresh remembrance did reverse
The ugly vew of his deformèd crimes,
That all his manly powres it did disperse,   430
As he were charmèd with inchaunted rimes,
That oftentimes he quakt, and fainted oftentimes.

49

In which amazement, when the Miscreant
Perceivèd him to waver weake and fraile,
Whiles trembling horror did his conscience dant,
And hellish anguish did his soule assaile,   436
To drive him to despaire, and quite to quaile,
He shewed him painted in a table plaine,
The damnèd ghosts, that doe in torments waile,
And thousand feends that doe them endlesse
    paine   440
With fire and brimstone, which for ever shall
    remaine.

50

The sight whereof so throughly him dismaid,
That nought but death before his eyes he saw,
And ever burning wrath before him laid,
By righteous sentence of th' Almighties law: 445
Then gan the villein him to overcraw,°
And brought unto him swords, ropes, poison, fire,

446. overcraw: exult over.

And all that might him to perdition draw;
And bad him choose, what death he would desire:
For death was due to him, that had provokt Gods
    ire.   450

51

But when as none of them he saw him take,
He to him raught° a dagger sharpe and keene,
And gave it him in hand: his hand did quake,
And tremble like a leafe of Aspin greene,
And troubled bloud through his pale face was
    seene   455
To come, and goe with tydings from the hart,
As it a running messenger had beene.
At last resolved to worke his finall smart,
He lifted up his hand, that backe againe did start.

52

Which when as Una saw, through every vaine   460
The crudled cold ran to her well of life,
As in a swowne: but soone relived againe,
Out of his hand she snatcht the cursed knife,
And threw it to the ground, enragèd rife,
And to him said, "Fie, fie, faint harted knight, 465
What meanest thou by this reprochfull strife?
Is this the battell, which thou vauntst to fight
With that fire-mouthèd Dragon, horrible and
    bright?

53

"Come, come away, fraile, feeble, fleshly wight,
Ne let vaine words bewitch thy manly hart,   470
Ne divelish thoughts dismay thy constant spright.
In heavenly mercies hast thou not a part?
Why shouldst thou then despeire, that chosen art?
Where justice growes, there grows eke greater
    grace,
The which doth quench the brond of hellish
    smart,   475
And that accurst hand-writing doth deface.
Arise, Sir knight arise, and leave this cursed
    place."

54

So up he rose, and thence amounted streight.
Which when the carle° beheld, and saw his guest

452. raught: handed. 479. carle: churl.

Would safe depart, for all his subtill sleight, 480
He chose an halter from among the rest,
And with it hung himselfe, unbid unblest.
But death he could not worke himselfe thereby;
For thousand times he so himselfe had drest,
Yet nathelesse it could not doe him die, 485
Till he should die his last, that is eternally.

CANTO XI°

The knight with that old Dragon fights
two dayes incessantly:
The third him overthrowes, and gayns
most glorious victory.

1

High time now gan it wex for Una faire,
To thinke of those her captive Parents deare,
And their forwasted kingdome to repaire:
Whereto whenas they now approchèd neare,
With hartie words her knight she gan to cheare, 5
And in her modest manner thus bespake;
"Deare knight, as deare, as ever knight was deare,
That all these sorrowes suffer for my sake,
High heaven behold the tedious toyle, ye for me
take.

2

"Now are we come unto my native soyle, 10
And to the place, where all our perils dwell;
Here haunts that feend, and does his dayly spoyle,
Therefore henceforth be at your keeping well,
And ever ready for your foeman fell.
The sparke of noble courage now awake, 15
And strive your excellent selfe to excell;
That shall ye evermore renowmèd make,
Above all knights on earth, that batteill under-
take."

3

And pointing forth, "lo yonder is," said she,
"The brasen towre in which my parents deare 20

Canto XI. In Canto X Una guides the weakened
knight to the House of Holiness, where he is restored by
religious discipline, afforded a vision of the New Jerusalem,
and told that in later times he will become Saint George,
the patron saint of England.

For dread of that huge feend emprisoned be,
Whom I from far see on the walles appeare,
Whose sight my feeble soule doth greatly cheare:
And on the top of all I do espye
The watchman wayting tydings glad to heare, 25
That O my parents might I happily
Unto you bring, to ease you of your misery."

4

With that they heard a roaring hideous sound,
That all the ayre with terrour fillèd wide,
And seemd uneath° to shake the stedfast ground. 30
Eftsoones that dreadful Dragon they espide,
Where stretcht he lay upon the sunny side
Of a great hill, himselfe like a great hill.
But all so soone, as he from far descride
Those glistring armes, that heaven with light did
fill, 35
He roused himselfe full blith, and hastned them
untill.

5

Then bad the knight his Lady yede° aloofe,
And to an hill her selfe with draw aside,
From whence she might behold that battailes
proof
And eke be safe from daunger far descryde: 40
She him obayd, and turned a little wyde.
Now O thou sacred Muse, most learned Dame,
Faire ympe of Phoebus, and his aged bride,°
The Nourse of time, and everlasting fame,
That warlike hands ennoblest with immortall
name; 45

6

O gently come into my feeble brest,
Come gently, but not with that mighty rage,
Wherewith the martiall troupes thou doest infest,
And harts of great Heroës doest enrage,
That nought their kindled courage may aswage, 50
Soone as thy dreadfull trompe begins to sownd;
The God of warre with his fiers equipage
Thou doest awake, sleepe never he so sownd,
And scarèd nations doest with horrour sterne
astownd.

30. **uneath:** almost. 37. **yede:** step. 43. **bride:** Mnemosyne,
memory.

7

Faire Goddesse lay that furious fit aside,   55
Till I of warres and bloudy Mars do sing,
And Britons fields with Sarazin bloud bedyde,
Twixt that great faery Queene and Paynim king,
That with their horrour heaven and earth did ring,
A worke of labour long, and endlesse prayse: 60
But now a while let downe that haughtie string,
And to my tunes thy second tenor rayse,
That I this man of God his godly armes may
     blaze.°

8

By this the dreadfull Beast drew nigh to hand,
Halfe flying, and halfe footing in his hast,   65
That with his largenesse measurèd much land,
And made wide shadow under his huge wast;
As mountaine doth the valley overcast.
Approching nigh, he rearèd high afore
His body monstrous, horrible, and vast,   70
Which to increase his wondrous greatnesse more,
Was swolne with wrath, and poyson, and with
     bloudy gore.

9

And over, all with brasen scales was armd,
Like plated coate of steele, so couchèd neare,
That nought mote perce, ne might his corse be
     harmd   75
With dint of sword, nor push of pointed speare;
Which as an Eagle, seeing pray appeare,
His aery plumes doth rouze, full rudely dight,
So shakèd he, that horrour was to heare,
For as the clashing of an Armour bright,   80
Such noyse his rouzèd scales did send unto the
     knight.

10

His flaggy wings when forth he did display,
Were like two sayles, in which the hollow wynd
Is gathered full, and worketh speedy way: 84
And eke the pennes,° that did his pineons bynd,
Were like mayne-yards, with flying canvas lynd,
With which whenas him list the ayre to beat,
And there by force unwonted passage find,
The cloudes before him fled for terrour great,
And all the heavens stood still amazèd with his
     threat.   90

63. blaze: describe. **85. pennes:** quills.

11

His huge long tayle wound up in hundred foldes,
Does overspred his long bras-scaly backe,
Whose wreathèd boughts when ever he unfoldes,
And thicke entangled knots adown does slacke,
Bespotted as with shields of red and blacke,   95
It sweepeth all the land behind him farre,
And of three furlongs does but litle lacke;
And at the point two stings in-fixèd arre,
Both deadly sharpe, that sharpest steele exceeden
     farre.

12

But stings and sharpest steele did far exceed   100
The sharpnesse of his cruell rending clawes;
Dead was it sure, as sure as death in deed,
What ever thing does touch his ravenous pawes,
Or what within his reach he ever drawes.
But his most hideous head my toung to tell,   105
Does tremble: for his deepe devouring jawes
Wide gapèd, like the griesly mouth of hell,
Through which into his darke abisse all ravin° fell.

13

And that more wondrous was, in either jaw
Three ranckes of yron teeth enraungèd were,   110
In which yet trickling bloud and gobbets raw
Of late devourèd bodies did appeare,
That sight thereof bred cold congealèd feare:
Which to increase, and all atonce to kill,
A cloud of smoothering smoke and sulphur seare
Out of his stinking gorge forth steemèd still,   116
That all the ayre about with smoke and stench did
     fill.

14

His blazing eyes, like two bright shining shields,
Did burne with wrath, and sparkled living fyre;
As two broad Beacons, set in open fields,   120
Send forth their flames farre off to every shyre,
And warning give, that enemies conspyre,
With fire and sword the region to invade;
So flamed his eyne with rage and rancorous yre:
But farre within, as in a hollow glade,   125
Those glaring lampes were set, that made a dread-
     full shade.

108. ravin: prey.

15

So dreadfully he towards him did pas,
Forelifting up aloft his speckled brest,
And often bounding on the brusèd gras,
As for great joyance of his newcome guest.   130
Eftsoones he gan advance his haughtie crest,
As chauffèd° Bore his bristles doth upreare,
And shoke his scales to battell readie drest;
That made the Redcrosse knight nigh quake for
    feare,
As bidding bold defiance to his foeman neare. 135

16

The knight gan fairely couch his steadie speare,
And fiercely ran at him with rigorous might:
The pointed steele arriving rudely theare,
His harder hide would neither perce, nor bight,
But glauncing by forth passed forward right;   140
Yet sore amovèd with so puissant push,
The wrathfull beast about him turnèd light,
And him so rudely passing by, did brush
With his long tayle, that horse and man to ground
    did rush.

17

Both horse and man up lightly rose againe,   145
And fresh encounter towards him addrest:
But th' idle stroke yet backe recoyld in vaine,
And found no place his deadly point to rest.
Exceeding rage enflamed the furious beast,
To be avengèd of so great despight;   150
For never felt his imperceable brest
So wondrous force, from hand of living wight;
Yet had he proved the powre of many a puissant
    knight.

18

Then with his waving wings displayèd wyde,
Himselfe up high he lifted from the ground,   155
And with strong flight did forcibly divide
The yielding aire, which nigh too feeble found
Her flitting partes, and element unsound,
To beare so great a weight: he cutting way
With his broad sayles, about him soarèd round: 160
At last low stouping with unweldie sway,
Snatch up both horse and man, to beare them quite
    away.

132. chauffèd: enraged.

19

Long he them bore above the subject plaine,
So farre as Ewghen° bow a shaft may send,
Till struggling strong did him at last constraine, 165
To let them downe before his flightès end:
As hagard° hauke presuming to contend
With hardie fowle, above his hable° might,
His wearie pounces° all in vaine doth spend,
To trusse the pray too heavie for his flight;   170
Which comming downe to ground, does free it
    selfe by fight.

20

He so disseizèd of his gryping grosse,°
The knight his thrillant° spare againe assayd
In his bras-plated body to embosse,   174
And three mens strength unto the stroke he layd;
Wherewith the stiffe beame quakèd, as affrayd,
And glauncing from his scaly necke, did glyde
Close under his left wing, then broad displayd.
The percing steele there wrought a wound full
    wyde,
That with the uncouth smart the Monster lowdly
    cryde.   180

21

He cryde, as raging seas are wont to rore,
When wintry storme his wrathfull wreck does
    threat,
The rolling billowes beat the ragged shore,
As they the earth would shoulder from her seat,
And greedie gulfe does gape, as he would eat 185
His neighbour element in his revenge:
Then gin the blustring breathren boldly threat,
To move the world from off his stedfast henge,
And boystrous battell make, each other to avenge.

22

The steely head stucke fast still in his flesh,   190
Till with his cruell clawes he snatcht the wood,
And quite a sunder broke. Forth flowèd fresh
A gushing river of blacke goarie blood,
That drownèd all the land, whereon he stood;
The streame thereof would drive a water-mill. 195

164. Ewghen: of yew. 167. hagard: untrained. 168. hable:
powerful. 169. pounces: claws. 172. disseized . . . grosse:
freed from his hard grip. 173. thrillant: piercing.

Trebly augmented was his furious mood
With bitter sense of his deepe rooted ill,
That flames of fire he threw forth from his large
  nosethrill.

23

His hideous tayle then hurlèd he about,
And therewith all enwrapt the nimble thyes   200
Of his froth-fomy steed, whose courage stout
Striving to loose the knot, that fast him tyes,
Himselfe in streighter bandes too rash implyes,
That to the ground he is perforce constraynd
To throw his rider: who can quickly ryse   205
From off the earth, with durty bloud distaynd,
For that reprochfull fall right fowly he disdaynd.

24

And fiercely tooke his trenchand blade in hand,
With which he stroke so furious and so fell,
That nothing seemd the puissance could with-
  stand: 210
Upon his crest the hardned yron fell,
But his more hardned crest was armd so well,
That deeper dint therein it would not make;
Yet so extremely did the buffe him quell,
That from thenceforth he shund the like to take,
But when he saw them come, he did them still
  forsake.   216

25

The knight was wrath to see his stroke beguyld,
And smote againe with more outrageous might;
But backe againe the sparckling steele recoyld,
And left not any marke, where it did light;   220
As if in Adamant rocke it had bene pight.
The beast impatient of his smarting wound,
And of so fierce and forcible despight,
Thought with his wings to stye° above the ground;
But his late wounded wing unserviceable found. 225

26

Then full of griefe and anguish vehement,
He lowdly brayd, that like was never heard,
And from his wide devouring oven sent

224. **stye**: mount.

A flake of fire, that flashing in his beard,
Him all amazd, and almost made affeard: 230
The scorching flame sore swingèd all his face,
And through his armour all his bodie seard,
That he could not endure so cruell cace,
But thought his armes to leave, and helmet to
  unlace.

27

Not that great Champion° of the antique world, 235
Whom famous Poetes verse so much doth vaunt,
And hath for twelve huge labours high extold,
So many furies and sharpe fits did haunt,
When him the poysoned garment did enchaunt
With Centaures bloud, and bloudie verses
  charmed,   240
As did this knight twelve thousand dolours daunt,
Whom fyrie steele now burnt, that earst him armed,
That erst him goodly armed, now most of all him
  harmed.

28

Faint, wearie, sore, emboylèd, grievèd, brent
With heat, toyle, wounds, armes, smart, and inward
  fire   245
That never man such mischiefes did torment;
Death better were, death did he oft desire,
But death will never come, when needes require.
Whom so dismayd when that his foe beheld,
He cast to suffer him no more respire,   250
But gan his sturdie sterne about to weld,
And him so strongly stroke, that to the ground
  him feld.

29

It fortunèd (as faire it then befell)
Behind his backe unweeting, where he stood,
Of auncient time there was a springing well,   255
From which fast trickled forth a silver flood,
Full of great vertues, and for med'cine good.
Whylome, before that cursed Dragon got
That happie land, and all with innocent blood
Defyld those sacred waves, it rightly hot°   260
The well of life, ne yet his vertues had forgot.

235. **Champion**: Hercules. 260. **hot**: was called.

30

For unto life the dead it could restore,
And guilt of sinful crimes cleane wash away,
Those that with sicknesse were infected sore,
It could recure, and aged long decay   265
Renew, as one were borne that very day.
Both Silo this, and Jordan did excell,
And th' English Bath, and eke the german Spau,
Ne can Cephise, nor Hebrus° match this well: 269
Into the same the knight backe overthrowen, fell.

31

Now gan the golden Phoebus for to steepe
His fierie face in billowes of the west,
And his faint steedes watred in Ocean deepe,
Whiles from their journall° labours they did rest,
When that infernall Monster, having kest   275
His wearie foe into that living well,
Can high advance his broad discoloured brest,
Above his wonted pitch, with countenance fell,
And clapt his yron wings, as victor he did dwell.

32

Which when his pensive Ladie saw from farre, 280
Great woe and sorrow did her soule assay,
As weening that the sad end of the warre,
And gan to highest God entirely pray,
That feared chance from her to turne away;
With folded hands and knees full lowly bent 285
All night she watcht, ne once adowne would lay
Her daintie limbs in her sad dreriment,
But praying still did wake, and waking did lament.

33

The morrow next gan early to appeare,
That Titan rose to runne his daily race;   290
But early ere the morrow next gan reare
Out of the sea faire Titans deawy face,
Up rose the gentle virgin from her place,
And looked all about, if she might spy
Her loved knight to move his manly pace: 295
For she had great doubt of his safety,
Since late she saw him fall before his enemy.

267–69. **Silo . . . Hebrus:** references to baptismal or curative waters or rivers in the Bible, England, Europe, and Greece. 274. **journall:** daily.

34

At last she saw, where he upstarted brave
Out of the well, wherein he drenchèd lay;
As Eagle fresh out of the Ocean wave,   300
Where he hath left his plumes all hoary gray,
And deckt himselfe with feathers youthly gay,
Like Eyas° hauke up mounts unto the skies,
His newly budded pineons to assay,
And marveiles at himselfe, still as he flies: 305
So new this new-borne knight to battell new did rise.

35

Whom when the damnèd feend so fresh did spy,
No wonder if he wondred at the sight,
And doubted, whether his late enemy
It were, or other new supplièd knight.   310
He, now to prove his late renewèd might,
High brandishing his bright deaw-burning blade,
Upon his crested scalpe so sore did smite,
That to the scull a yawning wound it made:
That deadly dint his dullèd senses all dismaid. 315

36

I wote not, whether the revenging steele
Were hardnèd with that holy water dew,
Wherein he fell, or sharper edge did feele,
Or his baptizèd hands now greater grew;
Or other secret vertue did ensew;   320
Else never could the force of fleshy arme,
Ne molten mettall in his bloud embrew:°
For till that stownd° could never wight him harme,
But subtilty, nor slight, nor might, nor mighty charme.

37

The cruell wound enragèd him so sore,   325
That loud he yelded for exceeding paine;
As hundred ramping Lyons seemed to rore,
Whom ravenous hunger did thereto constraine:
Then gan he tosse aloft his stretchèd traine,
And therewith scourge that buxome aire so sore,
That to his force to yeelden it was faine;   331
Ne ought his sturdie strokes might stand afore,
That high trees overthrew, and rocks in peeces tore.

303. **Eyas:** young. 322. **embrew:** plunge. 323. **stownd:** moment.

38

The same advauncing high above his head,
With sharpe intended sting so rude him smot,   335
That to the earth him drove, as stricken dead,
Ne living wight would have him life behot:°
The mortall sting his angry needle shot
Quite through his shield, and in his shoulder seasd,
Where fast it stucke, ne would there out be got: 340
The griefe thereof him wondrous sore diseasd,
Ne might his ranckling paine with patience be
    appeasd.

39

But yet more mindfull of his honour deare,
Then of the grievous smart, which him did wring,
From loathèd soile he gan him lightly reare,   345
And strove to loose the farre infixèd sting:
Which when in vaine he tryde with struggeling,
Inflamed with wrath, his raging blade he heft,
And strooke so strongly, that the knotty string
Of his huge taile he quite a sunder cleft,   350
Five joynts thereof he hewd, and but the stump him
    left.

40

Hart cannot thinke, what outrage, and what cryes,
With foule enfouldred° smoake and flashing fire,
The hell-bred beast threw forth unto the skyes,
That all was coverèd with darknesse dire: 355
Then fraught with rancour, and engorgèd ire,
He cast at once him to avenge for all,
And gathering up himselfe out of the mire,
With his uneven wings did fiercely fall
Upon his sunne-bright shield, and gript it fast
    withall.   360

41

Much was the man encombred with his hold,
In feare to lose his weapon in his paw,
Ne wist yet, how his talants to unfold;
Nor harder was from Cerberus greedie jaw
To plucke a bone, then from his cruell claw   365
To reave by strength the gripèd gage away:
Thrise he assayd it from his foot to draw,

And thrise in vaine to draw it did assay,
It booted nought to thinke, to robbe him of his
    pray.

42

Tho when he saw no power might prevaile,   370
His trustie sword he cald to his last aid,
Wherewith he fiercely did his foe assaile,
And double blowes about him stoutly laid,
That glauncing fire out of the yron plaid;
As sparckles from the Andvile use to fly,   375
When heavie hammers on the wedge are swaid;°
Therewith at last he forst him to unty
One of his grasping feete, him to defend thereby.

43

The other foot, fast fixèd on his shield,
Whenas no strength, nor stroks mote him con-
    straine   380
To loose, ne yet the warlike pledge to yield,
He smot thereat with all his might and maine,
That nought so wondrous puissance might sustaine;
Upon the joynt the lucky steele did light,
And made such way, that hewd it quite in
    twaine;   385
The paw yet missèd not his minisht might,
But hong still on the shield, as it at first was pight.

44

For griefe thereof, and divelish despight,
From his infernall fournace forth he threw
Huge flames, that dimmèd all the heavens light, 390
Enrold in duskish smoke and brimstone blew;
As burning Aetna from his boyling stew
Doth belch out flames, and rockes in peeces broke,
And ragged ribs of mountaines molten new,
Enwrapt in coleblacke clouds and filthy smoke, 395
That all the land with stench, and heaven with
    horror choke.

45

The heate whereof, and harmefull pestilence
So sore him noyd, that forst him to retire
A little backward for his best defence,
To save his bodie from the scorching fire,   400

337. life behot: held out hope of life. 353. enfouldred:
like a thundercloud.

376. swaid: struck.

Which he from hellish entrailes did expire.
It chaunst (eternall God that chaunce did guide)
As he recoylèd backward, in the mire
His nigh forwearied feeble feet did slide,
And downe he fell, with dread of shame sore
   terrifide.   405

46

There grew a goodly tree him faire beside,
Loaden with fruit and apples rosie red,
As they in pure vermilion had beene dide,
Whereof great vertues over all were red:°
For happie life to all, which thereon fed,   410
And life eke everlasting did befall:
Great God it planted in that blessed sted
With his almightie hand, and did it call
The tree of life, the crime of our first fathers fall.

47

In all the world like was not to be found,   415
Save in that soile, where all good things did grow,
And freely sprong out of the fruitfull ground,
As incorrupted Nature did them sow,
Till that dread Dragon all did overthrow.
Another like faire tree eke grew thereby,   420
Whereof who so did eat, eftsoones did know
Both good and ill: O mornefull memory:
That tree through one mans fault hath doen us all
   to dy.

48

From that first tree forth flowd, as from a well,
A trickling streame of Balme, most soveraine   425
And daintie deare, which on the ground still fell,
And overflowèd all the fertill plaine,
As it had deawèd bene with timely raine:
Life and long health that gratious ointment gave,
And deadly woundes could heale, and reare againe
The senselesse corse appointed for the grave.   431
Into the same he fell: which did from death him
   save.

49

For nigh thereto the ever damnèd beast
Durst not approach, for he was deadly made,

409. red: declared.

And all that life preservèd, did detest: 435
Yet he it oft adventured to invade.
By this the drouping day-light gan to fade,
And yeeld his roome to sad succeeding night,
Who with her sable mantle gan to shade
The face of earth, and wayes of living wight,   440
And high her burning torch set up in heaven bright.

50

When gentle Una saw the second fall
Of her deare knight, who wearie of long fight,
And faint through losse of bloud, moved not at all,
But lay as in a dreame of deepe delight,   445
Besmeard with pretious Balme, whose vertuous
   might
Did heale his wounds, and scorching heat alay,
Againe she stricken was with sore affright,
And for his safetie gan devoutly pray;
And watch the noyous° night, and wait for joyous
   day.   450

51

The joyous day gan early to appeare,
And faire Aurora from the deawy bed
Of aged Tithone gan her selfe to reare,
With rosie cheekes, for shame as blushing red;
Her golden lockes for haste were loosely shed   455
About her eares, when Una her did marke
Clymbe to her charet, all with flowers spred,
From heaven high to chase the chearelesse darke;
With merry note her loud salutes the mounting
   larke.

52

Then freshly up arose the doughtie knight,   460
All healèd of his hurts and woundès wide,
And did himselfe to battell readie dight;
Whose early foe awaiting him beside
To have devourd, so soone as day he spyde,
When now he saw himselfe so freshly reare,   465
As if late fight had nought him damnifyde,
He woxe dismayd, and gan his fate to feare;
Nathlesse with wonted rage he him advauncèd
   neare.

450. noyous: afflicting.

53

And in his first encounter, gaping wide,
He thought attonce him to have swallowed
   quight,   470
And rusht upon him with outragious pride;
Who him r'encountring fierce, as hauke in flight,
Perforce rebutted backe. The weapon bright
Taking advantage of his open jaw,   474
Ran through his mouth with so importune might,
That deepe emperst his darksome hollow maw,
And back retyrd, his life bloud forth with all did
   draw.

54

So downe he fell, and forth his life did breath,
That vanisht into smoke and cloudès swift;
So downe he fell, that th' earth him underneath 480
Did grone, as feeble so great load to lift;
So downe he fell, as an huge rockie clift,
Whose false foundation waves have washt away,
With dreadfull poyse° is from the mayneland rift,
And rolling downe, great Neptune doth dis-
   may;   485
So downe he fell, and like an heapèd mountaine lay.

55

The knight himselfe even trembled at his fall,
So huge and horrible a masse it seemed;
And his deare Ladie, that beheld it all,
Durst not approch for dread, which she mis-
   deemed,   490
But yet at last, when as the direfull feend
She saw not stirre, off-shaking vaine affright,
She nigher drew, and saw that joyous end:
Then God she praysd, and thankt her faithfull
   knight,
That had atchieved so great a conquest by his
   might.   495

CANTO XII

Faire Una to the Redcrosse knight
betrouthèd is with joy:
Though false Duessa it to barre
her false sleights doe imploy.

484. **poyse:** force.

1

Behold I see the haven nigh at hand,
To which I meane my wearie course to bend;
Vere the maine shete,° and beare up with the land,
The which afore is fairely to be kend,°
And seemeth safe from stormes, that may offend; 5
There this faire virgin wearie of her way
Must landed be, now at her journeyes end:
There eke my feeble barke a while may stay,
Till merry wind and weather call her thence away.

2

Scarsely had Phoebus in the glooming East   10
Yet harnessèd his firie-footed teeme,
Ne reard above the earth his flaming creast,
When the last deadly smoke aloft did steeme,
That signe of last outbreathèd life did seeme,
Unto the watchman on the castle wall;   15
Who thereby dead that balefull Beast did deeme,
And to his Lord and Ladie lowd gan call,
To tell, how he had seene the Dragons fatall fall.

3

Uprose with hastie joy, and feeble speed
That aged Sire, the Lord of all that land,   20
And lookèd forth, to weet, if true indeede
Those tydings were, as he did understand,
Which whenas true by tryall he out fond,
He bad to open wyde his brazen gate,   24
Which long time had bene shut, and out of hond
Proclaymèd joy and peace through all his state;
For dead now was their foe, which them forrayèd
   late.

4

Then gan triumphant Trompets sound on hie,
That sent to heaven the ecchoèd report
Of their new joy, and happie victorie   30
Gainst him, that had them long opprest with tort°
And fast imprisonèd in siegèd fort.
Then all the people, as in solemne feast,
To him assembled with one full consort,
Rejoycing at the fall of that great beast,   35
From whose eternall bondage now they were
   release.

Canto XII. **3. Vere . . . shete:** readjust the mainsail line
to change course. **4. kend:** recognized. **31. tort:** wrong.

5

Forth came that auncient Lord and aged Queene,
Arayd in antique robes downe to the ground,
And sad habiliments right well beseene;
A noble crew about them waited round   40
Of sage and sober Peres, all gravely gownd;
Whom farre before did march a goodly band
Of tall young men, all hable armes to sownd,°
But now they laurell braunches bore in hand;   44
Glad signe of victorie and peace in all their land.

6

Unto that doughtie Conquerour they came,
And him before themselves prostrating low,
Their Lord and Patrone loud did him proclame,
And at his feet their laurell boughes did throw.
Soone after them all dauncing on a row   50
The comely virgins came, with girlands dight,
As fresh as flowres in medow greene do grow,
When morning deaw upon their leaves doth light:
And in their hands sweet Timbrels° all upheld on
    hight.

7

And them before, the fry of children young   55
Their wanton sports and childish mirth did play,
And to the Maydens sounding tymbrels sung
In well attunèd notes, a joyous lay,
And made delightfull musicke all the way,
Untill they came, where that faire virgin stood; 60
As faire Diana in fresh sommers day
Beholds her Nymphes, enraunged in shadie wood,
Some wrestle, some do run, some bathe in christall
    flood.

8

So she beheld those maydens meriment
With chearefull vew; who when to her they came,
Themselves to ground with gratious humblesse
    bent,   66
And her adored by honorable name,
Lifting to heaven her everlasting fame:
Then on her head they set a girland greene,
And crownèd her twixt earnest and twixt game; 70

Who in her selfe-resemblance well beseene,
Did seeme such, as she was, a goodly maiden
    Queene.

9

And after, all the raskall° many ran,
Heapèd together in rude rablement,
To see the face of that victorious man: 75
Whom all admirèd, as from heaven sent,
And gazd upon with gaping wonderment.
But when they came, where that dead Dragon lay,
Stretcht on the ground in monstrous large extent,
The sight with idle feare did them dismay,   80
Ne durst approch him nigh, to touch, or once assay.

10

Some feard, and fled; some feard and well it faynd;
One that would wiser seeme, then all the rest,
Warnd him not touch, for yet perhaps remaynd
Some lingring life within his hollow brest,   85
Or in his wombe might lurke some hidden nest
Of many Dragonets, his fruitfull seed;
Another said, that in his eyes did rest
Yet sparckling fire, and bad thereof take heed;
Another said, he saw him move his eyes indeed. 90

11

One mother, when as her foolehardie chyld
Did come too neare, and with his talants play,
Halfe dead through feare, her litle babe revyld,
And to her gossips gan in counsell say;
"How can I tell, but that his talants may   95
Yet scratch my sonne, or rend his tender hand?"
So diversly themselves in vaine they fray;
Whiles some more bold, to measure him nigh
    stand,
To prove how many acres he did spread of land.

12

Thus flockèd all the folke him round about,   100
The whiles that hoarie king, with all his traine,
Being arrivèd, where that champion stout
After his foes defeasance did remaine,
Him goodly greetes, and faire does entertaine,

---

43. sownd: wield. **54. Timbrels:** tambourines.

73. raskall: base, worthless.

With princely gifts of yvorie and gold,   105
And thousand thankes him yeelds for all his paine.
Then when his daughter deare he does behold,
Her dearely doth imbrace, and kisseth manifold.

13

And after to his Pallace he them brings,
With shaumes,° and trompets, and with Clarions
     sweet;   110
And all the way the joyous people sings,
And with their garments strowes the pavèd street:
Whence mounting up, they find purveyance meet
Of all, that royall Princes court became,
And all the floore was underneath their feet   115
Bespred with costly scarlot of great name,
On which they lowly sit, and fitting purpose frame.

14

What needs me tell their feast and goodly guize,
In which was nothing riotous nor vaine?
What needs of daintie dishes to devize,   120
Of comely services, or courtly trayne?
My narrow leaves cannot in them containe
The large discourse of royall Princes state.
Yet was their manner then but bare and plaine:
For th' antique world excesse and pride did
     hate;   125
Such proud luxurious pompe is swollen up but late.

15

Then when with meates and drinkes of every kinde
Their fervent appetites they quenchèd had,
That auncient Lord gan fit occasion finde,
Of straunge adventures, and of perils sad,   130
Which in his travell him befallen had,
For to demaund of his renowmèd guest:
Who then with utt'rance grave, and count'nance
     sad,
From point to point, as is before exprest,   134
Discourst his voyage long, according his request.

16

Great pleasure mixt with pitifull regard,
That godly King and Queene did passionate,
Whiles they his pittifull adventures heard,

That oft they did lament his lucklesse state,
And often blame the too importune fate,   140
That heapd on him so many wrathfull wreakes:
For never gentle knight, as he of late,
So tossèd was in fortunes cruell freakes;
And all the while salt teares bedeawd the hearers
     cheaks.

17

Then said that royall Pere in sober wise;   145
"Deare Sonne, great beene the evils, which ye bore
From first to last in your late enterprise,
That I note,° whether prayse, or pitty more:
For never living man, I weene, so sore
In sea of deadly daungers was distrest;   150
But since now safe ye seisèd have the shore,
And well arrivèd are, (high God be blest)
Let us devize of ease and everlasting rest."

18

"Ah dearest Lord," said then that doughty knight,
"Of ease or rest I may not yet devize;   155
For by the faith, which I to armes have plight,
I bounden am streight after this emprize,
As that your daughter can ye well advize,
Backe to returne to that great Faerie Queene,
And her to serve six yeares in warlike wize,   160
Gainst that proud Paynim king, that workes her
     teene:°
Therefore I ought crave pardon, till I there have
     beene."

19

"Unhappie falles that hard necessitie,"
Quoth he, "the troubler of my happie peace,
And vowèd foe of my felicitie;   165
Ne I against the same can justly preace:°
But since that band ye cannot now release,
Nor doen undo; (for vowes may not be vaine)
Soone as the terme of those six yeares shall cease,
Ye then shall hither backe returne againe,   170
The marriage to accomplish vowd betwixt you
     twaine.

---

110. **shaumes:** ancient instruments similar to the oboe.   148. **note:** know not. 161. **teene:** injury. 166. **preace:** press.

20

"Which for my part I covet to performe,
In sort as through the world I did proclame,
That who so kild that monster most deforme,
And him in hardy battaile overcame,   175
Should have mine onely daughter to his Dame,
And of my kingdome heire apparaunt bee:
Therefore since now to thee perteines the same,
By dew desert of noble chevalree,   179
Both daughter and eke kingdome, lo I yield to thee."

21

Then forth he callèd that his daughter faire,
The fairest Un' his onely daughter deare,
His onely daughter, and his onely heyre;
Who forth proceeding with sad sober cheare,
As bright as doth the morning starre appeare   185
Out of the East, with flaming lockes bedight,
To tell that dawning day is drawing neare,
And to the world does bring long wishèd light;
So faire and fresh that Lady shewd her selfe in
    sight.

22

So faire and fresh, as freshest flowre in May;   190
For she had layd her mournefull stole aside,
And widow-like sad wimple throwne away,
Wherewith her heavenly beautie she did hide,
Whiles on her wearie journey she did ride;
And on her now a garment she did weare,   195
All lilly white, withoutten spot, or pride,
That seemd like silke and silver woven neare,
But neither silke nor silver therein did appeare.

23

The blazing brightnesse of her beauties beame,
And glorious light of her sunshyny face   200
To tell, were as to strive against the streame.
My ragged rimes are all too rude and bace,
Her heavenly lineaments for to enchace.
Ne wonder; for her owne deare lovèd knight,
All were she dayly with himselfe in place,   205
Did wonder much at her celestiall sight:
Oft had he seene her faire, but never so faire dight.

24

So fairely dight, when she in presence came,
She to her Sire made humble reverence,
And bowèd low, that her right well became,   210
And added grace unto her excellence:
Who with great wisedome, and grave eloquence
Thus gan to say. But eare he thus had said,
With flying speede, and seeming great pretence,
Came running in, much like a man dismaid,   215
A Messenger with letters, which his message said.

25

All in the open hall amazèd stood,
At suddeinnesse of that unwarie sight,
And wondred at his breathlesse hastie mood.
But he for nought would stay his passage right, 220
Till fast before the king he did alight;
Where falling flat, great humblesse he did make,
And kist the ground, whereon his foot was pight;
Then to his hands that writ he did betake,   224
Which he disclosing, red thus, as the paper spake.

26

"To thee, most mighty king of Eden faire,
Her greeting sends in these sad lines addrest,
The wofull daughter, and forsaken heire
Of that great Emperour of all the West;
And bids thee be advizèd for the best,   230
Ere thou thy daughter linck in holy band
Of wedlocke to that new unknowen guest:
For he already plighted his right hand
Unto another love, and to another land.

27

"To me sad mayd, or rather widow sad,   235
He was affiauncèd long time before,
And sacred pledges he both gave, and had,
False erraunt knight, infamous, and forswore:
Witnesse the burning Altars, which he swore,
And guiltie heavens of° his bold perjury,   240
Which though he hath polluted oft of yore,
Yet I to them for judgement just do fly,
And them conjure t' avenge this shamefull injury.

240. guiltie . . . of: heavens corrupted by.

28

"Therefore since mine he is, or free or bond,
Or false or trew, or living or else dead,   245
Withhold, O soveraine Prince, your hasty hond
From knitting league with him, I you aread;
Ne weene my right with strength adowne to tread,
Through weakenesse of my widowhed, or woe:
For truth is strong, her rightfull cause to plead, 250
And shall find friends, if need requireth soe.
So bids thee well to fare, Thy neither friend, nor
     foe, Fidessa."

29

When he these bitter byting words had red,
The tydings straunge did him abashèd make,
That still he sate long time astonishèd   255
As in great muse, ne word to creature spake.
At last his solemne silence thus he brake,
With doubtfull eyes fast fixèd on his guest;
"Redoubted knight, that for mine onely sake
Thy life and honour late adventurest,   260
Let nought be hid from me, that ought to be
     exprest.

30

"What meane these bloudy vowes, and idle threats
Throwne out from womanish impatient mind?
What heavens? what altars? what enragèd heates
Here heapèd up with termes of love unkind,   265
My conscience cleare with guilty bands would
     bind?
High God be witnesse, that I guiltlesse ame.
But if your selfe, Sir knight, ye faultie find,
Or wrappèd be in loves of former Dame,   269
With crime do not it cover, but disclose the same."

31

To whom the Redcrosse knight this answere sent,
"My Lord, my King, be nought hereat dismayd,
Till well ye wote by grave intendiment,
What woman, and wherefore doth me upbrayd
With breach of love, and loyalty betrayd.   275
It was in my mishaps, as hitherward
I lately traveild, that unwares I strayd
Out of my way, through perils straunge and hard;
That day should faile me, ere I had them all
     declard.

32

"There did I find, or rather I was found   280
Of this false woman, that Fidessa hight,
Fidessa hight the falsest Dame on ground,
Most false Duessa, royall richly dight,
That easie was t' invegle weaker sight:
Who by her wicked arts, and wylie skill,   285
Too false and strong for earthly skill or might,
Unwares me wrought unto her wicked will,
And to my foe betrayd, when least I fearèd ill."

33

Then steppèd forth the goodly royall Mayd,
And on the ground her selfe prostrating low,   290
With sober countenaunce thus to him sayd;
"O pardon me, my soveraigne Lord, to show
The secret treasons, which of late I know
To have bene wroght by that false sorceresse.
She onely she it is, that earst did throw   295
This gentle knight into so great distresse,
That death him did awaite in dayly wretchednesse.

34

"And now it seemes, that she subornèd hath
This craftie messenger with letters vaine,
To worke new woe and improvided scath,°   300
By breaking of the band betwixt us twaine;
Wherein she usèd hath the practicke paine
Of this false footman, clokt with simplenesse,
Whom if ye please for to discover plaine,
Ye shall him Archimago find, I ghesse,   305
The falsest man alive; who tries shall find no lesse."

35

The king was greatly movèd at her speach,
And all with suddein indignation fraight,°
Bad on that Messenger rude hands to reach.
Eftsoones the Gard, which on his state did wait, 310
Attacht that faitor° false, and bound him strait:
Who seeming sorely chauffèd at his band,
As chainèd Beare, whom cruell dogs do bait,
With idle force did faine them to withstand,
And often semblaunce made to scape out of their
     hand.   315

300. improvided scath: unexpected harm. **308. fraight:**
fraught. **311. faitor:** impostor.

36

But they him layd full low in dungeon deepe,
And bound him hand and foote with yron chaines,
And with continuall watch did warely keepe;
Who then would thinke, that by his subtile trains
He could escape fowle death or deadly paines? 320
Thus when that Princes wrath was pacifide,
He gan renew the late forbidden banes,°
And to the knight his daughter deare he tyde,
With sacred rites and vowes for ever to abyde.

37

His owne two hands the holy knots did knit, 325
That none but death for ever can devide;
His owne two hands, for such a turne most fit,
The housling° fire did kindle and provide,
And holy water thereon sprinckled wide;
At which the bushy Teade° a groome did light, 330
And sacred lampe in secret chamber hide,
Where it should not be quenchèd day nor night,
For feare of evill fates, but burnen ever bright.

38

Then gan they sprinckle all the posts with wine,
And made great feast to solemnize that day; 335
They all perfumde with frankencense divine,
And precious odours fetcht from far away,
That all the house did sweat with great aray:
And all the while sweete Musicke did apply
Her curious skill, the warbling notes to play, 340
To drive away the dull Melancholy;
The whiles one sung a song of love and jollity.

39

During the which there was an heavenly noise
Heard sound through all the Pallace pleasantly,
Like as it had bene many an Angels voice, 345
Singing before th' eternall majesty,
In their trinall triplicities° on hye;
Yet wist no creature, whence that heavenly sweet
Proceeded, yet eachone felt secretly
Himselfe thereby reft of his sences meet, 350
And ravishèd with rare impression in his sprite.

40

Great joy was made that day of young and old,
And solemne feast proclaimd throughout the land,
That their exceeding merth may not be told:
Suffice it heare by signes to understand 355
The usual joyes at knitting of loves band.
Thrise happy man the knight himselfe did hold,
Possessèd of his Ladies hart and hand,
And ever, when his eye did her behold, 359
His heart did seeme to melt in pleasures manifold.

41

Her joyous presence and sweet company
In full content he there did long enjoy,
Ne wicked envie, ne vile gealosy
His deare delights were able to annoy:
Yet swimming in that sea of blisfull joy, 365
He nought forgot, how he whilome had sworne,
In case he could that monstrous beast destroy,
Unto his Farie Queene backe to returne:
The which he shortly did, and Una left to mourne.

42

Now strike your sailes ye jolly Mariners, 370
For we be come unto a quiet rode,
Where we must land some of our passengers,
And light this wearie vessell of her lode.
Here she a while may make her safe abode,
Till she repairèd have her tackles spent, 375
And wants supplide. And then againe abroad
On the long voyage whereto she is bent:
Well may she speede and fairely finish her intent.

322. **banes:** banns. 328. **housling:** sacramental. 330. **Teade:**
marriage torch. 347. **trinall triplicities:** threefold trinity,
i.e., the nine ranks of angels.

PERCY BYSSHE SHELLEY
1792–1822

Prometheus Unbound

A LYRICAL DRAMA IN FOUR ACTS

DRAMATIS PERSONAE

PROMETHEUS
DEMOGORGON
JUPITER
THE EARTH
OCEAN
APOLLO
THE PHANTASM OF JUPITER
THE SPIRIT OF THE EARTH
THE SPIRIT OF THE MOON
SPIRITS OF THE HOURS
SPIRITS. ECHOES. FAUNS. FURIES
MERCURY
HERCULES
ASIA ⎫
PANTHEA ⎬ *Oceanides*
IONE ⎭

ACT I

SCENE—*A Ravine of Icy Rocks in the Indian Caucasus.* PROMETHEUS *is discovered bound to the Precipice.* PANTHEA *and* IONE *are seated at his feet. Time, night. During the Scene, morning slowly breaks.*

PROMETHEUS   Monarch of Gods and Daemons, and all Spirits
But One,° who throng those bright and rolling worlds
Which Thou and I alone of living things
Behold with sleepless eyes! regard this Earth   4
Made multitudinous with thy slaves, whom thou
Requitest for knee-worship, prayer, and praise,
And toil, and hecatombs of broken hearts,
With fear and self-contempt and barren hope.
Whilst me, who am thy foe, eyeless in hate,   9

Hast thou made reign and triumph, to thy scorn,
O'er mine own misery and thy vain revenge.
Three thousand years of sleep-unsheltered hours,
And moments aye divided by keen pangs
Till they seemed years, torture and solitude,
Scorn and despair,—these are mine empire:—   15
More glorious far than that which thou surveyest
From thine unenvied throne, O Mighty God!
Almighty, had I deigned to share the shame
Of thine ill tyranny, and hung not here   19
Nailed to this wall of eagle-baffling mountain,
Black, wintry, dead, unmeasured; without herb,
Insect, or beast, or shape or sound of life.
Ah me! alas, pain, pain ever, for ever!

No change, no pause, no hope! Yet I endure.
I ask the Earth, have not the mountains felt?   25
I ask yon Heaven, the all-beholding Sun,
Hast it not seen? The Sea, in storm or calm,
Heaven's ever-changing Shadow, spread below,
Have its deaf waves not heard my agony?
Ah me! alas, pain, pain ever, for ever!   30

The crawling glaciers pierce me with the spears
Of their moon-freezing crystals, the bright chains
Eat with their burning cold into my bones.
Heaven's wingèd hound,° polluting from thy lips
His beak in poison not his own, tears up   35
My heart; and shapeless sights come wandering by,
The ghastly people of the realm of dream,
Mocking me: and the Earthquake-fiends are charged
To wrench the rivets from my quivering wounds
When the rocks split and close again behind: 40
While from their loud abysses howling throng
The genii of the storm, urging the rage
Of whirlwind, and afflict me with keen hail.
And yet to me welcome is day and night,
Whether one breaks the hoar frost of the morn,
Or starry, dim, and slow, the other climbs   46
The leaden-colored east; for then they lead
The wingless, crawling hours, one among whom
—As some dark Priest hales the reluctant victim—
Shall drag thee, cruel King, to kiss the blood   50
From these pale feet, which then might trample thee

PROMETHEUS UNBOUND: *Act I.* **2.** One: Prometheus.

34. Heaven's . . . hound: vulture.

If they disdained not such a prostrate slave.
Disdain! Ah no! I pity thee. What ruin
Will hunt thee undefended through wide
    Heaven!
How will thy soul, cloven to its depth with
    terror,   55
Gape like a hell within! I speak in grief,
Not exultation, for I hate no more,
As then ere misery made me wise. The curse
Once breathed on thee I would recall. Ye
    Mountains,   59
Whose many-voicèd Echoes, through the mist
Of cataracts, flung the thunder of that spell!
Ye icy Springs, stagnant with wrinkling frost,
Which vibrated to hear me, and then crept
Shuddering through India! Thou serenest Air,
Through which the Sun walks burning without
    beams!   65
And ye swift Whirlwinds, who on poisèd wings
Hung mute and moveless o'er yon hushed abyss,
As thunder, louder than your own, made rock
The orbèd world! If then my words had power,
Though I am changed so that aught evil wish
Is dead within; although no memory be   71
Of what is hate, let them not lose it now!
What was that curse? for ye all heard me
    speak.

FIRST VOICE (*from the Mountains*)

Thrice three hundred thousand years
    O'er the Earthquake's couch we stood: 75
Oft, as men convulsed with fears,
    We trembled in our multitude.

SECOND VOICE (*from the Springs*)

Thunderbolts had parched our water,
    We had been stained with bitter blood,
And had run mute, 'mid shrieks of slaughter,   80
    Thro' a city and a solitude.

THIRD VOICE (*from the Air*)

I had clothed, since Earth uprose,
    Its wastes in colors not their own,
And oft had my serene repose
    Been cloven by many a rending groan.   85

FOURTH VOICE (*from the Whirlwinds*)

We had soared beneath these mountains
    Unresting ages; nor had thunder,

Nor yon volcano's flaming fountains,
    Nor any power above or under
Ever made us mute with wonder.   90

FIRST VOICE

But never bowed our snowy crest
As at the voice of thine unrest.

SECOND VOICE

Never such a sound before
To the Indian waves we bore.
A pilot asleep on the howling sea   95
Leaped up from the deck in agony,
And heard, and cried, "Ah, woe is me!"
And died as mad as the wild waves be.

THIRD VOICE

By such dread words from Earth to Heaven
My still realm was never riven: 100
When its wound was closed, there stood
Darkness o'er the day like blood.

FOURTH VOICE

And we shrank back: for dreams of ruin
To frozen caves our flight pursuing
Made us keep silence—thus—and thus—   105
Though silence is as hell to us.

THE EARTH   The tongueless Caverns of the craggy
    hills
    Cried, "Misery!" then; the hollow Heaven re-
        plied,
    "Misery!" And the Ocean's purple waves,   109
    Climbing the land, howled to the lashing winds,
    And the pale nations heard it, "Misery!"
PROMETHEUS   I heard a sound of voices: not the
    voice
    Which I gave forth. Mother, thy sons and thou
    Scorn him, without whose all-enduring will
    Beneath the fierce omnipotence of Jove,   115
    Both they and thou had vanished, like thin mist
    Unrolled on the morning wind. Know ye not me,
    The Titan? He who made his agony
    The barrier to your else all-conquering foe?
    Oh, rock-embosomed lawns, and snow-fed
        streams,   120
    Now seen athwart frore° vapors, deep below,

121. frore: frosty.

Through whose o'ershadowing woods I wan-
dered once
With Asia, drinking life from her loved eyes;
Why scorns the spirit which informs ye, now 124
To commune with me? me alone, who checked,
As one who checks a fiend-drawn charioteer,
The falsehood and the force of him who reigns
Supreme, and with the groans of pining slaves
Fills your dim glens and liquid wildernesses:
Why answer ye not, still? Brethren!
THE EARTH   They dare not.
PROMETHEUS   Who dares? for I would hear that
  curse again.   131
  Ha, what an awful whisper rises up!
  'Tis scarce like sound: it tingles through the
  frame
  As lightning tingles, hovering ere it strike.
  Speak, Spirit! from thine inorganic voice   135
  I only know that thou art moving near
  And love. How cursed I him?
THE EARTH   How canst thou hear
  Who knowest not the language of the dead?
PROMETHEUS   Thou are a living spirit; speak as
  they.
THE EARTH   I dare not speak like life, lest Heaven's
  fell King   140
  Should hear, and link me to some wheel of pain
  More torturing than the one whereon I roll.
  Subtle thou art and good, and though the Gods
  Hear not this voice, yet thou art more than God,
  Being wise and kind: earnestly hearken now. 145
PROMETHEUS   Obscurely through my brain, like
  shadows dim,
  Sweep awful thoughts, rapid and thick. I feel
  Faint, like one mingled in entwining love;
  Yet 'tis not pleasure.
THE EARTH   No, thou canst not hear:
  Thou art immortal, and this tongue is known 150
  Only to those who die.
PROMETHEUS   And what art thou,
  O, melancholy Voice?
THE EARTH   I am the Earth,
  Thy mother; she within whose stony veins,
  To the last fiber of the loftiest tree   154
  Whose thin leaves trembled in the frozen air,
  Joy ran, as blood within a living frame,
  When thou didst from her bosom, like a cloud
  Of glory, arise, a spirit of keen joy!
  And at thy voice her pining sons uplifted   159
  Their prostrate brows from the polluting dust,

And our almighty Tyrant with fierce dread
Grew pale, until his thunder chained thee here.
Then, see those million worlds which burn and
  roll
Around us: their inhabitants beheld
My spherèd light wane in wide Heaven; the sea
Was lifted by strange tempest, and new fire 166
From earthquake-rifted mountains of bright
  snow
Shook its portentous hair beneath Heaven's
  frown;
Lightning and Inundation vexed the plains; 169
Blue thistles bloomed in cities; foodless toads
Within voluptuous chambers panting crawled:
When Plague had fallen on man, and beast, and
  worm,
And Famine; and black blight on herb and tree;
And in the corn, and vines, and meadow-grass,
Teemed ineradicable poisonous weeds   175
Draining their growth, for my wan breast was
  dry
With grief; and the thin air, my breath, was
  stained
With the contagion of a mother's hate
Breathed on her child's destroyer; ay, I heard
Thy curse, the which, if thou rememberest not,
Yet my innumerable seas and streams,   181
Mountains, and caves, and winds, and yon
  wide air,
And the inarticulate people of the dead,
Preserve, a treasured spell. We meditate
In secret joy and hope those dreadful words, 185
But dare not speak them.
PROMETHEUS   Venerable mother!
  All else who live and suffer take from thee
  Some comfort; flowers, and fruits, and happy
  sounds,
  And love, though fleeting; these may not be
  mine.
  But mine own words, I pray, deny me not.   190
THE EARTH   They shall be told. Ere Babylon was
  dust,
  The Magus Zoroaster, my dead child,
  Met his own image walking in the garden.
  The apparition, sole of men, he saw.
  For know there are two worlds of life and
  death: 195
  One that which thou beholdest; but the other
  Is underneath the grave, where do inhabit
  The shadows of all forms that think and live

Till death unite them and they part no more;
Dreams and the light imaginings of men,   200
And all that faith creates or love desires,
Terrible,   strange,   sublime   and   beauteous
   shapes.°
There   thou   art,   and   dost   hang,   a   writhing
   shade,
'Mid whirlwind-peopled mountains; all the gods
Are   there,   and   all   the   powers   of   nameless
   worlds,   205
Vast,   sceptered   phantoms;   heroes,   men,   and
   beasts;
And Demogorgon, a tremendous gloom;
And he, the supreme Tyrant, on his throne
Of burning gold. Son, one of these shall utter
The curse which all remember. Call at will   210
Thine own ghost, or the ghost of Jupiter,
Hades or Typhon, or what mightier Gods
From all-prolific Evil, since thy ruin
Have   sprung,   and   trampled   on   my   prostrate
   sons.
Ask, and they must reply: so the revenge   215
Of   the   Supreme   may   sweep   through   vacant
   shades,
As rainy wind through the abandoned gate
Of a fallen palace.
PROMETHEUS   Mother, let not aught
Of that which may be evil, pass again
My lips, or those of aught resembling me.   220
Phantasm of Jupiter, arise, appear!

IONE

My wings are folded o'er mine ears:
   My wings are crossèd o'er mine eyes:
Yet through their silver shade appears,
   And through their lulling plumes arise,   225
A Shape, a throng of sounds;
   May it be no ill to thee
O thou of many wounds!
Near whom, for our sweet sister's sake,
Ever thus we watch and wake.   230

PANTHEA

The sound is of whirlwind underground,
   Earthquake, and fire, and mountains cloven;

The shape is awful like the sound,
   Clothed in dark purple, star-inwoven.
A scepter of pale gold   235
   To stay steps proud, o'er the slow cloud
His veinèd hand doth hold.
Cruel he looks, but calm and strong,
Like one who does, not suffers wrong.

PHANTASM OF JUPITER   Why   have   the   secret
   powers of this strange world   240
Driven me, a frail and empty phantom, hither
On direst storms? What unaccustomed sounds
Are hovering on my lips, unlike the voice
With which our pallid race hold ghastly talk
In   darkness?   And,   proud   sufferer,   who   are
   thou?   245
PROMETHEUS   Tremendous   Image,   as   thou   art
   must be
He whom thou shadowest forth. I am his foe,
The Titan. Speak the words which I would hear,
Although no thought inform thine empty voice.
THE EARTH   Listen!   And   though   your   echoes
   must be mute,   250
Gray   mountains,   and   old   woods,   and   haunted
   springs,
Prophetic caves, and isle-surrounding streams,
Rejoice to hear what yet ye cannot speak.
PHANTASM   A spirit seizes me and speaks within:
   It tears me as fire tears a thundercloud.   255
PANTHEA   See, how he lifts his mighty looks,
   the Heaven
Darkens above.
IONE   He speaks! O shelter me!
PROMETHEUS   I see the curse on gestures proud
   and cold,
And looks of firm defiance, and calm hate,
And such despair as mocks itself with smiles,   260
Written as on a scroll: yet speak: Oh, speak!

PHANTASM°

Fiend, I defy thee! with a calm, fixed mind,
   All that thou canst inflict I bid thee do;
Foul Tyrant both of Gods and Humankind,
   One only being shalt thou not subdue.   265
Rain then thy plagues upon me here,
Ghastly disease, and frenzying fear;
And let alternate frost and fire
Eat into me, and be thine ire   269

192–202. Zoroaster . . . shapes: reference to the Persian
religious leader (fl. 1000 B.C.) or a later wizard; the doctrine
of corresponding worlds of reality and phantasms is
common in Platonic thought and in later folklore.

262. The phantasm repeats Prometheus' curse on Jupiter.

Lightning, and cutting hail, and legioned forms
Of furies, driving by upon the wounding storms.

Ay, do thy worst. Thou art omnipotent.
  O'er all things but thyself I gave thee power,
And my own will. Be thy swift mischiefs sent
  To blast mankind, from yon ethereal tower.
Let thy malignant spirit move   276
In darkness over those I love:
On me and mine I imprecate
The utmost torture of thy hate;
And thus devote to sleepless agony,   280
This undeclining head while thou must reign on
  high.

But thou, who art the God and Lord: O, thou,
  Who fillest with thy soul this world of woe,
To whom all things of Earth and Heaven do
  bow
  In fear and worship: all-prevailing foe!   285
I curse thee! let a sufferer's curse
Clasp thee, his torturer, like remorse;
Till thine Infinity shall be
A robe of envenomed agony;
And thine Omnipotence a crown of pain,   290
To cling like burning gold round thy dissolving
  brain.

Heap on the soul, by virtue of this Curse,
  Ill deeds, then be thou damned, beholding
  good;
Both infinite as is the universe,
  And thou, and thy self-torturing solitude.   295
An awful image of calm power
Though now thou sittest, let the hour
Come, when thou must appear to be
That which thou art internally;
And after many a false and fruitless crime   300
Scorn track thy lagging fall through boundless
  space and time

PROMETHEUS   Were these my words, O Parent?
THE EARTH   They were thine.
PROMETHEUS   It doth repent me: words are quick
  and vain;
  Grief for a while is blind, and so was mine.
I wish not living thing to suffer pain.   305

THE EARTH

Misery, Oh misery to me,
That Jove at length should vanquish thee.

Wail, howl aloud, Land and Sea,
  The Earth's rent heart shall answer ye.
Howl, Spirits of the living and the dead,   310
Your refuge, your defense lies fallen and
  vanquishèd.

FIRST ECHO

Lies fallen and vanquishèd!

SECOND ECHO
                        Fallen and vanquishèd!

IONE

Fear not: 'tis but some passing spasm,
  The Titan is unvanquished still.
But see, where through the azure chasm   315
  Of yon forked and snowy hill
Trampling the slant winds on high
  With golden-sandled feet, that glow
Under plumes of purple dye,
Like rose-ensanguined ivory,   320
    A Shape comes now,
  Stretching on high from his right hand
A serpent-cinctured wand.

PANTHEA   'Tis Jove's world-wandering herald,
  Mercury.

IONE

And who are those with hydra tresses   325
  And iron wings that climb the wind,
Whom the frowning God represses
  Like vapors steaming up behind,
Clanging loud, and endless crowd—

PANTHEA

These are Jove's tempest-walking hounds   330
Whom he gluts with groans and blood,
When charioted on sulfurous cloud
  He bursts Heaven's bounds.

IONE

Are they now led, from the thin dead
On new pangs to be fed?   335

PANTHEA

The Titan looks as ever, firm, not proud.

FIRST FURY   Ha! I scent life!

SECOND FURY   Let me but look into his eyes!

THIRD FURY   The hope of torturing him smells
  like a heap
Of corpses to a death-bird after battle.   340

FIRST FURY   Darest thou delay, O Herald! take
  cheer, Hounds
Of Hell: what if the Son of Maia° soon
Should make us food and sport—who can
  please long   343
The Omnipotent?

MERCURY   Back to your towers of iron,
And gnash, beside the streams of fire and wail,
Your foodless teeth. Geryon, arise! and Gorgon,
Chimaera, and thou Sphinx, subtlest of fiends
Who ministered to Thebes Heaven's poisoned
  wine,°
Unnatural love, and more unnatural hate: 349
These shall perform your task.

FIRST FURY   Oh, mercy! mercy!
We die with our desire: drive us not back!

MERCURY   Crouch then in silence.

                        Awful Sufferer!
To thee unwilling, most unwillingly
I come, by the great Father's will driven down,
To execute a doom of new revenge.   355
Alas! I pity thee, and hate myself
That I can do no more: aye from the sight
Returning, for a season, Heaven seems Hell,
So thy worn form pursues me night and day, 359
Smiling reproach. Wise art thou, firm and good,
But vainly wouldst stand forth alone in strife
Against the Omnipotent; as yon clear lamps
That measure and divide the weary years
From which there is no refuge, long have taught
And long must teach. Even now thy Torturer
  arms   365
With the strange might of unimagined pains
The powers who scheme slow agonies in Hell,
And my commission is to lead them here,
Or what more subtle, foul, or savage fiends 369
People the abyss, and leave them to their task.
Be it not so! there is a secret known
To thee, and to none else of living things,
Which may transfer the scepter of wide Heaven,
The fear of which perplexes the Supreme: 374

Clothe it in words, and bid it clasp his throne
In intercession; bend thy soul in prayer,
And like a suppliant in some gorgeous fane,°
Let the will kneel within thy haughty heart:
For benefits and meek submission tame
The fiercest and the mightiest.

PROMETHEUS   Evil minds   380
Change good to their own nature. I gave all
He has; and in return he chains me here
Years, ages, night and day: whether the Sun
Split my parched skin, or in the moony night 384
The crystal-wingèd snow cling round my hair:
Whilst my belovèd race is trampled down
By his thought-executing ministers.
Such is the tyrant's recompense: 'tis just:
He who is evil can receive no good;
And for a world bestowed, or a friend lost, 390
He can feel hate, fear, shame; not gratitude:
He but requites me for his own misdeed.
Kindness to such is keen reproach, which breaks
With bitter stings the light sleep of Revenge.
Submission, thou dost know I cannot try: 395
For what submission but that fatal word,
The death-seal of mankind's captivity,
Like the Sicilian's hair-suspended sword,°
Which trembles o'er his crown, would he accept,
Or could I yield? Which yet I will not yield. 400
Let others flatter Crime, where it sits throned
In brief Omnipotence: secure are they:
For Justice, when triumphant, will weep down
Pity, not punishment, on her own wrongs,
Too much avenged by those who err. I wait, 405
Enduring thus, the retributive hour
Which since we spake is even nearer now.
But hark, the hellhounds clamor: fear delay:
Behold! Heaven lowers under thy Father's frown.

MERCURY   Oh, that we might be spared: I to inflict
And thou to suffer! Once more answer me: 411
Thou knowest not the period of Jove's power?

PROMETHEUS   I know but this, that it must come.

MERCURY   Alas!
Thou canst not count thy years to come of pain?

PROMETHEUS   They last while Jove must reign: no
  more, nor less   415
Do I desire or fear.

MERCURY   Yet pause, and plunge
Into Eternity, where recorded time,
Even all that we imagine, age on age,

---

342. Son of Maia: Mercury. 346–48. Geryon . . . wine:
Geryon, Gorgon, Chimera, and the Sphinx were monsters
in Greek legend; the poisoned wine is a figurative reference
to the events following the riddle the Sphinx asked of
Oedipus.

377. fane: temple. 398. sword: sword suspended by a thread
over the head of Damocles.

Seems but a point, and the reluctant mind
Flags wearily in its unending flight,   420
Till it sink, dizzy, blind, lost, shelterless;
Perchance it has not numbered the slow years
Which thou must spend in torture, unreprieved?

PROMETHEUS   Perchance no thought can count them, yet they pass.

MERCURY   If thou might'st dwell among the Gods the while   425
Lapped in voluptuous joy?

PROMETHEUS   I would not quit
This bleak ravine, these unrepentant pains.

MERCURY   Alas! I wonder at, yet pity thee.

PROMETHEUS   Pity the self-despising slaves of Heaven,   429
Not me, within whose mind sits peace serene,
As light in the sun, throned: how vain is talk!
Call up the fiends.

IONE   O, sister, look! White fire
Has cloven to the roots yon huge snowloaded cedar;
How fearfully God's thunder howls behind!

MERCURY   I must obey his words and thine: alas!
Most heavily remorse hangs at my heart!   436

PANTHEA   See where the child of Heaven, with wingèd feet,
Runs down the slanted sunlight of the dawn. 438

IONE   Dear sister, close thy plumes over thine eyes
Lest thou behold and die: they come: they come
Blackening the birth of day with countless wings,
And hollow underneath like death.

FIRST FURY   Prometheus!

SECOND FURY   Immortal Titan!

THIRD FURY   Champion of Heaven's slaves!

PROMETHEUS   He whom some dreadful voice invokes is here,   444
Prometheus, the chained Titan. Horrible forms,
What and who are ye? Never yet there came
Phantasms so foul through monster-teeming Hell
From the all-miscreative brain of Jove;
Whilst I behold such excrable shapes,
Methinks I grow like what I contemplate,   450
And laugh and stare in loathsome sympathy.

FIRST FURY   We are the ministers of pain, and fear,
And disappointment, and mistrust, and hate,
And clinging crime; and as lean dogs pursue
Through wood and lake some struck and sobbing fawn,   455
We track all things that weep, and bleed, and live,
When the great King betrays them to our will.

PROMETHEUS   Oh! many fearful natures in one name,
I know ye; and these lakes and echoes know
The darkness and the clangor of your wings. 460
But why more hideous than your loathèd selves
Gather ye up in legions from the deep?

SECOND FURY   We knew not that: Sisters, rejoice, rejoice!

PROMETHEUS   Can aught exult in its deformity?

SECOND FURY   The beauty of delight makes lovers glad,   465
Gazing on one another: so are we.
As from the rose which the pale priestess kneels
To gather for her festal crown of flowers
The aëreal crimson falls, flushing her cheek,
So from our victim's destined agony   470
The shape which is our form invests us round,
Else we are shapeless as our mother Night.

PROMETHEUS   I laugh your power, and his who sent you here,
To lowest scorn. Pour forth the cup of pain.

FIRST FURY   Thou thinkest we will rend thee bone from bone,   475
And nerve from nerve, working like fire within?

PROMETHEUS   Pain is my element, as hate is thine;
Ye rend me now: I care not.

SECOND FURY   Dost imagine
We will but laugh into thy lidless eyes?

PROMETHEUS   I weigh not what ye do, but what ye suffer,   480
Being evil. Cruel was the power which called
You, or aught else so wretched, into light.

THIRD FURY   Thou think'st we will live through thee, one by one,
Like animal life, and though we can obscure not
The soul which burns within, that we will dwell
Beside it, like a vain loud multitude   486
Vexing the self-content of wisest men:
That we will be dread thought beneath thy brain,
And foul desire round thine astonished heart,
And blood within thy labyrinthine veins   490
Crawling like agony?

PROMETHEUS   Why, ye are thus now;
Yet am I king over myself, and rule
The torturing and conflicting throngs within,
As Joy rules you when Hell grows mutinous.

CHORUS OF FURIES

From the ends of the earth, from the ends of the earth,   495

Where the night has its grave and the morning
    its birth,
        Come, come, come!
Oh, ye who shake hills with the scream of your
    mirth,
When cities sink howling in ruin; and ye
Who with wingless footsteps trample the sea,   500
And close upon Shipwreck and Famine's track,
Sit chattering with joy on the foodless wreck;
        Come, come, come!
Leave the bed, low, cold, and red,
Strewed beneath a nation dead;   505
Leave the hatred, as in ashes
    Fire is left for future burning:
It will burst in bloodier flashes
    When ye stir it, soon returning:
Leave the self-contempt implanted   510
In young spirits, sense-enchanted,
    Misery's yet unkindled fuel:
Leave Hell's secrets half unchanted,
    To the maniac dreamer; cruel
More than ye can be with hate   515
    Is he with fear.
        Come, come, come!
We are steaming up from Hell's wide gate
And we burthen the blast of the atmosphere,
But vainly we toil till ye come here.   520

IONE   Sister, I hear the thunder of new wings.
PANTHEA   These solid mountains quiver with the
    sound
    Even as the tremulous air: their shadows make
    The space within my plumes more black than
    night.

FIRST FURY

Your call was as a wingèd car   525
Driven on whirlwinds fast and far;
It rapt us from red gulfs of war.

SECOND FURY

From wide cities, famine-wasted;

THIRD FURY

Groans half heard, and blood untasted;

FOURTH FURY

Kingly conclaves stern and cold,   530
Where blood with gold is brought and sold;

FIFTH FURY

From the furnace, white and hot,
In which—

A FURY

    Speak not: whisper not:
I know all that ye would tell,
But to speak might break the spell   535
    Which must bend the Invincible,
        The stern of thought;
He yet defies the deepest power of Hell.

A FURY

Tear the veil!

ANOTHER FURY

    It is torn.

CHORUS

           The pale stars of the morn
Shine on a misery, dire to be borne.   540
Dost thou faint, mighty Titan? We laugh thee to
    scorn.
Dost thou boast the clear knowledge thou
    waken'dst for man?
Then was kindled within him a thirst which
    outran
Those perishing waters; a thirst of fierce fever,
Hope, love, doubt, desire, which consume him
    for ever.   545
One° came forth of gentle worth
Smiling on the sanguine earth;
His words outlived him, like swift poison
    Withering up truth, peace, and pity.
Look! where round the wide horizon   550
    Many a million-peopled city
Vomits smoke in the bright air.
Hark that outcry of despair!
'Tis his mild and gentle ghost
    Wailing for the faith he kindled: 555
Look again, the flames almost
    To a glowworm's lamp have dwindled:
The survivors round the embers
    Gather in dread.
        Joy, joy, joy!   560
Past ages crowd on thee, but each one remembers,
And the future is dark, and the present is spread
Like a pillow of thorns for thy slumberless head.
546. One: Jesus.

SEMICHORUS I

Drops of bloody agony flow
From his white and quivering brow.   565
Grant a little respite now:
See a disenchanted nation
Springs like day from desolation;
To Truth its state is dedicate,
And Freedom leads it forth, her mate;   570
A legioned band of linkèd brothers
Whom Love calls children—

SEMICHORUS II

'Tis another's:
See how kindred murder kin:
'Tis the vintage-time for death and sin:
Blood, like new wine, bubbles within: 575
Till Despair smothers
The struggling world, which slaves and tyrants win.
[*All the* FURIES *vanish, except one.*]

IONE   Hark, sister! what a low yet dreadful groan
Quite unsuppressed is tearing up the heart
Of the good Titan, as storms tear the deep,   580
And beasts hear the sea moan in inland caves.
Darest thou observe how the fiends torture him?
PANTHEA   Alas! I looked forth twice, but will no
more.
IONE   What didst thou see?
PANTHEA   A woful sight: a youth
With patient looks nailed to a crucifix.   585
IONE   What next?
PANTHEA   The heaven around, the earth below
Was peopled with thick shapes of human death,
All horrible, and wrought by human hands,
And some appeared the work of human hearts.
For men were slowly killed by frowns and
smiles: 590
And other sights too foul to speak and live
Were wandering by. Let us not tempt worse fear
By looking forth: those groans are grief enough.
FURY   Behold an emblem: those who do endure
Deep wrongs for man, and scorn, and chains,
but heap   595
Thousandfold torment on themselves and him.
PROMETHEUS   Remit the anguish of that lighted
stare;
Close those wan lips; let that thorn-wounded brow
Stream not with blood; it mingles with thy tears!
Fix, fix those tortured orbs in peace and death,
So thy sick throes shake not that crucifix,   601

So those pale fingers play not with thy gore.
O, horrible! Thy name I will not speak,
It hath become a curse. I see, I see
The wise, the mild, the lofty, and the just,   605
Whom thy slaves hate for being like to thee,
Some hunted by foul lies from their heart's home,
An early-chosen, late-lamented home;
As hooded ounces cling to the driven hind;°
Some linked to corpses in unwholesome cells: 610
Some—hear I not the multitude laugh loud?—
Impaled in lingering fire: and mighty realms
Float by my feet, like sea-uprooted isles,
Whose sons are kneaded down in common blood
By the red light of their own burning homes.   615
FURY   Blood thou canst see, and fire; and canst
hear groans;
Worse things, unheard, unseen, remain behind.
PROMETHEUS   Worse?
FURY   In each human heart terror survives
The ravin° it has gorged: the loftiest fear   619
All that they would disdain to think were true:
Hypocrisy and custom make their minds
The fanes of many a worship, now outworn.
They dare not devise good for man's estate,
And yet they know not that they do not dare.   624
The good want power, but to weep barren tears.
The powerful goodness want: worse need for
them.
The wise want love; and those who love want
wisdom;
And all best things are thus confused to ill.
Many are strong and rich, and would be just,
But live among their suffering fellow-men   630
As if none felt: they know not what they do.
PROMETHEUS   Thy words are like a cloud of
wingèd snakes;
And yet I pity those they torture not.
FURY   Thou pitiest them? I speak no more!
[*Vanishes.*]
PROMETHEUS   Ah woe!
Ah woe! Alas! pain, pain ever, for ever!   635
I close my tearless eyes, but see more clear
Thy works within my woe-illumèd mind,
Thou subtle tyrant! Peace is in the grave.
The grave hides all things beautiful and good:
I am a God and cannot find it there,   640
Nor would I seek it: for, though dread revenge,

609. **hooded . . . hind:** ounces or wildcats blindfolded for
hunting deer; the hind is a female red deer. **619. ravin:**
prey.

This is defeat, fierce king, not victory.
The sights with which thou torturest gird my soul
With new endurance, till the hour arrives 644
When they shall be no types of things which are.
PANTHEA Alas! what sawest thou more?
PROMETHEUS There are two woes:
To speak, and to behold; thou spare me one.
Names are there, Nature's sacred watchwords,
they
Were borne aloft in bright emblazonry; 649
The nations thronged around, and cried aloud,
As with one voice, Truth, liberty, and love!
Suddenly fierce confusion fell from heaven
Among them: there was strife, deceit, and fear:
Tyrants rushed in, and did divide the spoil.°
This was the shadow of the truth I saw. 655
THE EARTH I felt thy torture, son; with such
mixed joy
As pain and virtue give. To cheer thy state
I bid ascend those subtle and fair spirits,
Whose homes are the dim caves of human
thought,
And who inhabit, as birds wing the wind, 660
Its world-surrounding aether: they behold
Beyond that twilight realm, as in a glass,
The future: may they speak comfort to thee!
PANTHEA Look, sister, where a troop of spirits
gather,
Like flocks of clouds in spring's delightful
weather, 665
Thronging in the blue air!
IONE And see! more come,
Like fountain-vapors when the winds are dumb,
That climb up the ravine in scattered lines.
And, hark! is it the music of the pines?
Is it the lake? Is it the waterfall? 670
PANTHEA 'Tis something sadder, sweeter far
than all.

CHORUS OF SPIRITS

From unremembered ages we
Gentle guides and guardians be
Of heaven-oppressed mortality;
And we breathe, and sicken not, 675
The atmosphere of human thought:
Be it dim, and dank, and gray,
Like a storm-extinguished day,

Traveled o'er by dying gleams;
Be it bright as all between 680
Cloudless skies and windless streams,
Silent, liquid, and serene;
As the birds within the wind,
As the fish within the wave,
As the thoughts of man's own mind 685
Float through all above the grave;
We make there our liquid lair,
Voyaging cloudlike and unpent
Through the boundless element:
Thence we bear the prophecy 690
Which begins and ends in thee!

IONE More yet come, one by one: the air around
them
Looks radiant as the air around a star.

FIRST SPIRIT

On a battle-trumpet's blast
I fled hither, fast, fast, fast, 695
'Mid the darkness upward cast.
From the dust of creeds outworn,
From the tyrant's banner torn,
Gathering 'round me, onward borne,
There was mingled many a cry— 700
Freedom! Hope! Death! Victory!
Till they faded through the sky;
And one sound, above, around,
One sound beneath, around, above,
Was moving; 'twas the soul of Love; 705
'Twas the hope, the prophecy,
Which begins and ends in thee.

SECOND SPIRIT

A rainbow's arch stood on the sea,
Which rocked beneath, immovably;
And the triumphant storm did flee, 710
Like a conqueror, swift and proud,
Between, with many a captive cloud,
A shapeless, dark and rapid crowd,
Each by lightning riven in half:
I heard the thunder hoarsely laugh: 715
Mighty fleets were strewn like chaff
And spread beneath a hell of death
O'er the white waters. I alit
On a great ship lightning-split,
And speeded hither on the sigh 720
Of one who gave an enemy,
His plank, then plunged aside to die.

648–54. Names . . . spoil: reference to the French
Revolution.

THIRD SPIRIT

I sate beside a sage's bed,
And the lamp was burning red
Near the book where he had fed,   725
When a Dream with plumes of flame,
To his pillow hovering came,
And I knew it was the same
Which had kindled long ago
Pity, eloquence, and woe;   730
And the world awhile below
Wore the shade, its luster made.
It has borne me here as fleet
As Desire's lightning feet:
I must ride it back ere morrow,   735
Or the sage will wake in sorrow.

FOURTH SPIRIT

On a poet's lips I slept
Dreaming like a love-adept
In the sound his breathing kept;
Nor seeks nor finds he mortal blisses,   740
But feeds on the aëreal kisses
Of shapes that haunt thought's wildernesses.
He will watch from dawn to gloom
The lake-reflected sun illume
The yellow bees in the ivy-bloom,   745
Nor heed nor see, what things they be;
But from these create he can
Forms more real than living man,
Nurslings of immortality!
One of these awakened me,   750
And I sped to succour thee.

IONE

Behold'st thou not two shapes from the east and
        west
Come, as two doves to one belovèd nest,
Twin nurslings of the all-sustaining air   754
On swift still wings glide down the atmosphere?
And, hark! their sweet, sad voices! 'tis despair
Mingled with love and then dissolved in sound.

PANTHEA   Canst thou speak, sister? all my words
    are drowned.
IONE   Their beauty gives me voice. See how they
    float
        On their sustaining wings of skiey grain,   760
        Orange and azure deepening into gold:
        Their soft smiles light the air like a star's fire.

CHORUS OF SPIRITS

Hast thou beheld the form of Love?

FIFTH SPIRIT

                    As over wide dominions
    I sped, like some swift cloud that wings the
        wide air's wildernesses,
That planet-crested shape swept by on lightning-
        braided pinions,   765
    Scattering the liquid joy of life from his
        ambrosial tresses:
His footsteps paved the world with light; but as
        I passed 'twas fading,
    And hollow Ruin yawned behind: great sages
        bound in madness,
And headless patriots, and pale youths who
        perished, unupbraiding,
    Gleamed in the night. I wandered o'er, till
        thou, O King of sadness,   770
    Turned by thy smile the worst I saw to
        recollected gladness.

SIXTH SPIRIT

Ah, sister! Desolation is a delicate thing:
    It walks not on the earth, it floats not on the
        air,
But treads with lulling footsteps, and fans with
        silent wing
    The tender hopes which in their hearts the best
        and gentlest bear;   775
Who, soothed to false repose by the fanning
        plumes above
    And the music-stirring motion of its soft and
        busy feet,
Dream visions of aëreal joy, and call the monster,
        Love,
    And wake, and find the shadow Pain, as he
        whom now we greet.

CHORUS

Though Ruin now Love's shadow be,   780
Following him, destroyingly,
    On Death's white and wingèd steed,
Which the fleetest cannot flee,
    Trampling down both flower and weed,
Man and beast, and foul and fair,   785
Like a tempest through the air;
Thou shalt quell this horseman grim,
Woundless though in heart or limb.

PROMETHEUS Spirits! how know ye this shall be?

CHORUS

In the atmosphere we breathe,   790
As buds grow red when the snowstorms flee,
  From Spring gathering up beneath,
  Whose mild winds shake the elder brake,
  And the wandering herdsmen know
That the white-thorn soon will blow: 795
    Wisdom, Justice, Love, and Peace,
    When they struggle to increase,
      Are to us as soft winds be
      To shepherd boys, the prophecy
      Which begins and ends in thee.   800

IONE Where are the Spirits fled?
PANTHEA   Only a sense
  Remains of them, like the omnipotence
  Of music, when the inspired voice and lute
  Languish, ere yet the responses are mute,   804
  Which through the deep and labyrinthine soul,
  Like echoes through long caverns, wind and
    roll.
PROMETHEUS How fair these airborn shapes!
  and yet I feel
  Most vain all hope but love; and thou art far,
  Asia! who, when my being overflowed,
  Wert like a golden chalice to bright wine   810
  Which else had sunk into the thirsty dust.
  All things are still: alas! how heavily
  This quiet morning weighs upon my heart;
  Though I should dream I could even sleep with
    grief
  If slumber were denied not. I would fain   815
  Be what it is my destiny to be,
  The savior and the strength of suffering man,
  Or sink into the original gulf of things:
  There is no agony, and no solace left;   819
  Earth can console, Heaven can torment no more.
PANTHEA Hast thou forgotten one who watches
    thee
  The cold dark night, and never sleeps but when
  The shadow of thy spirit falls on her?
PROMETHEUS I said all hope was vain but love:
  thou lovest.
PANTHEA Deeply in truth; but the eastern star
  looks white,   825
  And Asia waits in that far Indian vale,
  The scene of her sad exile; rugged once
  And desolate and frozen, like this ravine;

But now invested with fair flowers and herbs,
And haunted by sweet airs and sounds, which
  flow   830
Among the woods and waters, from the aether
Of her transforming presence, which would fade
If it were mingled not with thine. Farewell!

END OF THE FIRST ACT

ACT II

SCENE I—*Morning. A lovely Vale in the Indian
Caucasus.* ASIA *alone.*

ASIA From all the blasts of heaven thou hast
    descended:
  Yes, like a spirit, like a thought, which makes
  Unwonted tears throng to the horny eyes,
  And beatings haunt the desolated heart,
  Which should have learnt repose: thou hast
    descended   5
  Cradled in tempests; thou dost wake, O Spring!
  O child of many winds! As suddenly
  Thou comest as the memory of a dream,
  Which now is sad because it hath been sweet;
  Like genius, or like joy which riseth up   10
  As from the earth, clothing with golden clouds
  The desert of our life.
  This is the season, this the day, the hour;
  At sunrise thou shouldst come, sweet sister mine,
  Too long desired, too long delaying, come!   15
  How like death-worms the wingless moments
    crawl!
  The point of one white star is quivering still
  Deep in the orange light of widening morn
  Beyond the purple mountains: through a chasm
  Of wind-divided mist the darker lake   20
  Reflects it: now it wanes: it gleams again
  As the waves fade, and as the burning threads
  Of woven cloud unravel in pale air:
  'Tis lost! and through yon peaks of cloudlike
    snow
  The roseate sunlight quivers: hear I not   25
  The Aeolian music of her sea-green plumes
  Winnowing the crimson dawn?
                          [PANTHEA *enters.*]
                          I feel, I see
  Those eyes which burn through smiles that fade
    in tears,
  Like stars half quenched in mists of silver dew.

Belovèd and most beautiful, who wearest   30
The shadow of that soul by which I live,
How late thou art! the spherèd sun had climbed
The sea; my heart was sick with hope, before
The printless air felt thy belated plumes.
PANTHEA   Pardon, great Sister! but my wings
    were faint   35
With the delight of a remembered dream,
As are the noontide plumes of summer winds
Satiate with sweet flowers. I was wont to sleep
Peacefully, and awake refreshed and calm
Before the sacred Titan's fall, and thy   40
Unhappy love, had made, through use and pity,
Both love and woe familiar to my heart
As they had grown to thine: erewhile I slept
Under the glaucous° caverns of old Ocean
Within dim bowers of green and purple moss, 45
Our young Ione's soft and milky arms
Locked then, as now, behind my dark, moist hair,
While my shut eyes and cheek were pressed
    within
The folded depth of her life-breathing bosom:
But not as now, since I am made the wind   50
Which fails beneath the music that I bear
Of thy most wordless converse; since dissolved
Into the sense with which love talks, my rest
Was troubled and yet sweet; my waking hours
Too full of care and pain.
ASIA   Lift up thine eyes,   55
And let me read thy dream.
PANTHEA   As I have said
With our sea-sister at his feet I slept.
The mountain mists, condensing at our voice
Under the moon, had spread their snowy flakes,
From the keen ice shielding our linkèd sleep. 60
Then two dreams came. One, I remember not.
But in the other his pale wound-worn limbs
Fell from Prometheus, and the azure night
Grew radiant with the glory of that form   64
Which lives unchanged within, and his voice fell
Like music which makes giddy the dim brain,
Faint with intoxication of keen joy:
"Sister of her whose footsteps pave the world
With loveliness—more fair than aught but her,
Whose shadow thou art—lift thine eyes on me."
I lifted them: the overpowering light   71
Of that immortal shape was shadowed o'er
By love; which, from his soft and flowing limbs,
And passion-parted lips, and keen, faint eyes, 74

Act II, scene i.   **44. glaucous:** sea-green.

Steamed forth like vaporous fire; an atmosphere
Which wrapped me in its all-dissolving power,
As the warm aether of the morning sun
Wraps ere it drinks some cloud of wandering dew.
I saw not, heard not, moved not, only felt   79
His presence flow and mingle through my blood
Till it became his life, and his grew mine,
And I was thus absorbed, until it passed,
And like the vapors when the sun sinks down,
Gathering again in drops upon the pines,
And tremulous as they, in the deep night   85
My being was condensed; and as the rays
Of thought were slowly gathered, I could hear
His voice, whose accents lingered ere they died
Like footsteps of weak melody: thy name
Among the many sounds alone I heard   90
Of what might be articulate; though still
I listened through the night when sound was none.
Ione wakened then, and said to me:
"Canst thou divine what troubles me tonight?
I always knew what I desired before,   95
Nor ever found delight to wish in vain.
But now I cannot tell thee what I seek;
I know not; something sweet, since it is sweet
Even to desire; it is thy sport, false sister;
Thou hast discovered some enchantment old, 100
Whose spells have stolen my spirit as I slept
And mingled it with thine: for when just now
We kissed, I felt within thy parted lips
The sweet air that sustained me, and the warmth
Of the lifeblood, for loss of which I faint,   105
Quivered between our intertwining arms."
I answered not, for the Eastern star grew pale,
But fled to thee.
ASIA   Thou speakest, but thy words
Are as the air: I feel them not: Oh, lift
Thine eyes, that I may read his written soul! 110
PANTHEA   I lift them though they droop beneath
    the load
Of that they would express: what canst thou see
But thine own fairest shadow imaged there?
ASIA   Thine eyes are like the deep, blue, boundless
    heaven
Contracted to two circles underneath   115
Their long, fine lashes; dark, far, measureless,
Orb within orb, and line through line inwoven.
PANTHEA   Why lookest thou as if a spirit passed?
ASIA   There is a change: beyond their inmost depth
I see a shade, a shape: 'tis He, arrayed   120
In the soft light of his own smiles, which spread

Like radiance from the cloud-surrounded moon.
Prometheus, it is thine! depart not yet!
Say not those smiles that we shall meet again
Within that bright pavilion which their beams 125
Shall build o'er the waste world? The dream is
    told.
What shape is that between us? Its rude hair
Roughens the wind that lifts it, its regard
Is wild and quick, yet 'tis a thing of air,
For through its grey robe gleams the golden dew
Whose stars the noon has quenched not.   131
DREAM   Follow! Follow!
PANTHEA   It is mine other dream.
ASIA   It disappears.
PANTHEA   It passes now into my mind. Methought
As we sate here, the flower-infolding buds
Burst on yon lightning-blasted almond-tree, 135
When swift from the white Scythian wilderness
A wind swept forth wrinkling the Earth with
    frost:
I looked, and all the blossoms were blown down;
But on each leaf was stamped, as the blue bells
Of Hyacinth tell Apollo's written grief,°   140
O, FOLLOW, FOLLOW!
ASIA   As you speak, your words
Fill, pause by pause, my own forgotten sleep
With shapes. Methought among these lawns
    together
We wandered, underneath the young gray dawn,
And multitudes of dense white fleecy clouds 145
Were wandering in thick flocks along the
    mountains
Shepherded by the slow, unwilling wind;
And the white dew on the new-bladed grass,
Just piercing the dark earth, hung silently;
And there was more which I remember not 150
But on the shadows of the morning clouds,
Athwart the purple mountain slope, was written
FOLLOW, O, FOLLOW! as they vanished by;
And on each herb, from which Heaven's dew
    had fallen,
The like was stamped, as with withering fire; 155
A wind arose among the pines; it shook
The clinging music from their boughs, and then
Low, sweet, faint sounds, like the farewell of
    ghosts,

139–40. as . . . grief: Hyacinthus, beloved of Apollo and
Zephyr, was accidentally killed by Apollo with a discus
blown by Zephyr; from his blood sprang the flower
marked by the letters *AI AI* (Alas!).

Were heard: O, FOLLOW, FOLLOW, FOLLOW ME!
And then I said: "Panthea, look on me."   160
But in the depth of those belovèd eyes
Still I saw, FOLLOW, FOLLOW!
ECHO   Follow, follow!
PANTHEA   The crags, this clear spring morning,
    mock our voices
As they were spirit-tongued.
ASIA   It is some being
Around the crags. What fine clear sounds! O,
    list!   165

ECHOES (*unseen*)

Echoes we: listen!
    We cannot stay:
As dew-stars glisten
    Then fade away—
        Child of Ocean!   170

ASIA   Hark! Spirits speak. The liquid responses
Of their aëreal tongues yet sound.

PANTHEA   I hear.

ECHOES

O, follow, follow,
    As our voice recedeth
Through the caverns hollow,   175
    Where the forest spreadeth;

(*More distant*)

    O, follow, follow!
Through the caverns hollow,
As the song floats thou pursue,
Where the wild bee never flew,   180
Through the noontide darkness deep,
By the odor-breathing sleep
Of faint night flowers, and the waves
At the fountain-lighted caves
While our music, wild and sweet,   185
Mocks thy gently falling feet,
        Child of Ocean!

ASIA   Shall we pursue the sound? It grows more
    faint
    And distant.
PANTHEA   List! the strain floats nearer now.

ECHOES

In the world unknown   190
    Sleeps a voice unspoken;
By thy step alone
    Can its rest be broken;
        Child of Ocean!   194

ASIA   How the notes sink upon the ebbing wind!

ECHOES

O, follow, follow!
    Through the caverns hollow,
As the song floats thou pursue,
By the woodland noontide dew;
By the forest, lakes, and fountains,   200
Through the many-folded mountains;
To the rents, and gulfs, and chasms,
Where the Earth reposed from spasms,
On the day when He° and thou
Parted, to commingle now: 205
        Child of Ocean!

ASIA   Come, sweet Panthea, link thy hand in mine,
        And follow, ere the voices fade away.

SCENE II—*A Forest, intermingled with Rocks
and Caverns.* ASIA *and* PANTHEA *pass into it.
Two young Fauns are sitting on a Rock listening.*

SEMICHORUS I OF SPIRITS

The path through which that lovely twain
    Have passed, by cedar, pine, and yew,
    And each dark tree that ever grew,
    Is curtained out from Heaven's wide blue;
Nor sun, nor moon, nor wind, nor rain,   5
    Can pierce its interwoven bowers,
    Nor aught, save where some cloud of dew,
Drifted along the earth-creeping breeze,
Between the trunks of the hoar trees,
    Hangs each a pearl in the pale flowers   10
    Of the green laurel, blown anew;
And bends, and then fades silently,
One frail and fair anemone:
Or when some star of many a one
That climbs and wanders through steep night,   15
Has found the cleft through which alone

204. He: Prometheus.

Beams fall from high those depths upon
Ere it is borne away, away,
By the swift Heavens that cannot stay,
It scatters drops of golden light,   20
Like lines of rain that ne'er unite:
And the gloom divine is all around,
And underneath is the mossy ground.

SEMICHORUS II

There the voluptuous nightingales,
    Are awake through all the broad noon-day. 25
When one with bliss or sadness fails,
    And through the windless ivy-boughs,
    Sick with sweet love, droops dying away
On its mate's music-panting bosom;
Another from the swinging blossom,   30
    Watching to catch the languid close
    Of the last strain, then lifts on high
    The wings of the weak melody,
'Till some new strain of feeling bear
    The song, and all the woods are mute;   35
When there is heard through the dim air
The rush of wings, and rising there
    Like many a lake-surrounded flute,
Sounds overflow the listener's brain
So sweet, that joy is almost pain.   40

SEMICHORUS I

There those enchanted eddies play
    Of echoes, music-tongued, which draw,
    By Demogorgon's mighty law,
    With melting rapture, or sweet awe,
All spirits on that secret way;   45
    As inland boats are driven to Ocean
Down streams made strong with mountain-thaw:
    And first there comes a gentle sound
    To those in talk or slumber bound,
    And wakes the destined soft emotion,—   50
Attracts, impels them; those who saw
    Say from the breathing earth behind
    There steams a plume-uplifting wind
Which drives them on their path, while they
    Believe their own swift wings and feet   55
The sweet desires within obey:
And so they float upon their way,
Until, still sweet, but loud and strong
The storm of sound is driven along,
    Sucked up and hurrying: as they fleet   60
    Behind, its gathering billows meet

And to the fatal mountain° bear
Like clouds amid the yielding air.

FIRST FAUN Canst thou imagine where those
    spirits live   64
    Which make such delicate music in the woods?
    We haunt within the least frequented caves
    And closest coverts, and we know these wilds,
    Yet never meet them, though we hear them oft:
    Where may they hide themselves?
SECOND FAUN   'Tis hard to tell:
    I have heard those more skilled in spirits say, 70
    The bubbles, which the enchantment of the sun
    Sucks from the pale faint water-flowers that pave
    The oozy bottom of clear lakes and pools,
    Are the pavilions where such dwell and float
    Under the green and golden atmosphere   75
    Which noontide kindles through the woven leaves;
    And when these burst, and the thin fiery air,
    The which they breathed within those lucent
      domes,
    Ascends to flow like meteors through the night,
    They ride on them, and rein their headlong speed,
    And bow their burning crests, and glide in fire
    Under the waters of the earth again.   82
FIRST FAUN If such live thus, have others other
    lives,
    Under pink blossoms or within the bells
    Of meadow flowers, or folded violets deep,   85
    Or on their dying odors, when they die,
    Or in the sunlight of the spherèd dew?
SECOND FAUN Ay, many more which we may
    well divine.
    But, should we stay to speak, noontide would
    come,
    And thwart Silenus° find his goats undrawn, 90
    And grudge to sing those wise and lovely songs
    Of Fate, and Chance, and God, and Chaos old,
    And Love, and the chained Titan's woful doom,
    And how he shall be loosed, and make the earth
    One brotherhood: delightful strains which cheer
    Our solitary twilights, and which charm   96
    To silence the unenvying nightingales.

SCENE III—*A Pinnacle of Rock among Mountains.* ASIA *and* PANTHEA

Scene ii. **62. fatal mountain:** i.e., fateful mountain because of Demogorgon's presence. **90. thwart Silenus:** perverse or bad-tempered Silenus, a woodland deity (satyr).

PANTHEA Hither the sound has borne us—to the
    realm
    Of Demogorgon, and the mighty portal,
    Like a volcano's meteor-breathing chasm,
    Whence the oracular vapor is hurled up
    Which lonely men drink wandering in their
      youth,   5
    And call truth, virtue, love, genius, or joy,
    That maddening wine of life, whose dregs they
      drain
    To deep intoxication; and uplift,
    Like Maenads° who cry loud, Evoe! Evoe!
    The voice which is contagion to the world.   10
ASIA Fit throne for such a Power! Magnificent!
    How glorious art thou, Earth! And if thou be
    The shadow of some spirit lovelier still,
    Though evil stain its work, and it should be
    Like its creation, weak yet beautiful,   15
    I could fall down and worship that and thee.
    Even now my heart adoreth: Wonderful!
    Look, sister, ere the vapor dim thy brain:
    Beneath is a wide plain of billowy mist,
    As a lake, paving in the morning sky,   20
    With azure waves which burst in silver light,
    Some Indian vale. Behold it, rolling on
    Under the curdling winds, and islanding
    The peak whereon we stand, midway, around,
    Encinctured by the dark and blooming forests, 25
    Dim twilight-lawns, and stream-illumèd caves,
    And wind-enchanted shapes of wandering mist;
    And far on high the keen sky-cleaving mountains
    From icy spires of sunlike radiance fling
    The dawn, as lifted Ocean's dazzling spray,   30
    From some Atlantic islet scattered up,
    Spangles the wind with lamplike water-drops.
    The vale is girdled with their walls, a howl
    Of cataracts from their thaw-cloven ravines,
    Satiates the listening wind, continuous, vast, 35
    Awful as silence. Hark! the rushing snow!
    The sun-awakened avalanche! whose mass,
    Thrice sifted by the storm, had gathered there
    Flake after flake, in heaven-defying minds
    As thought by thought is piled, till some great
      truth   40
    Is loosened, and the nations echo round,
    Shaken to their roots, as do the mountains now.
PANTHEA Look how the gusty sea of mist is
    breaking

Scene iii. **9. Maenads:** frenzied female worshipers of Bacchus.

In crimson foam, even at our feet! it rises
As Ocean at the enchantment of the moon   45
Round foodless men wrecked on some oozy
        isle.
ASIA   The fragments of the cloud are scattered up;
The wind that lifts them disentwines my hair;
Its billows now sweep o'er mine eyes; my brain
Grows dizzy; see'st thou shapes within the mist?
PANTHEA   A countenance with beckoning smiles:
        there burns   51
An azure fire within its golden locks!
Another and another: hark! they speak!

SONG OF SPIRITS

To the deep, to the deep,
                    Down, down!   55
Through the shade of sleep,
Through the cloudy strife
Of Death and of Life;
Through the veil and the bar
Of things which seem and are   60
Even to the steps of the remotest throne,
                    Down, down!

While the sound whirls around,
                    Down, down!
As the fawn draws the hound,   65
As the lightning the vapor,
As a weak moth the taper;
Death, despair; love, sorrow;
Time both; today, tomorrow;
As steel obeys the spirit of the stone,   70
                    Down, down!

Through the gray, void abysm,
                    Down, down!
Where the air is no prism,
And the moon and stars are not,   75
And the cavern-crags wear not
The radiance of Heaven,
Nor the gloom to Earth given,
Where there is One pervading, One alone,
                    Down, down!   80

In the depth of the deep,
                    Down, down!
Like veiled lightning asleep,
Like the spark nursed in embers,
The last look Love remembers,   85
Like a diamond, which shines
On the dark wealth of mines,

A spell is treasured but for thee alone.
                    Down, down!

We have bound thee, we guide thee;   90
                    Down, down!
With the bright form beside thee;
Resist not the weakness,
Such strength is in meekness
That the Eternal, the Immortal,   95
Must unloose through life's portal,
The snakelike Doom coiled underneath his throne
                    By that alone.

SCENE IV—*The Cave of* DEMOGORGON. ASIA *and*
PANTHEA

PANTHEA   What veilèd form sits on that ebon
        throne?
ASIA   The veil has fallen.
PANTHEA   I see a mighty darkness
Filling the seat of power, and rays of gloom
Dart round, as light from the meridian sun.
—Ungazed upon and shapeless; neither limb, 5
Nor form, nor outline; yet we feel it is
A living Spirit.
DEMOGORGON   Ask what thou wouldst know.
ASIA   What canst thou tell?
DEMOGORGON   All things thou dar'st demand.
ASIA   Who made the living world?
DEMOGORGON   God.
ASIA   Who made all
That it contains? thought, passion, reason, will,
Imagination?
DEMOGORGON   God: Almighty God.   11
ASIA   Who made that sense which, when the
        winds of Spring
In rarest visitation, or the voice
Of one belovèd heard in youth alone,   14
Fills the faint eyes with falling tears which dim
The radiant looks of unbewailing flowers,
And leaves this peopled earth a solitude
When it returns no more?
DEMOGORGON   Merciful God.
ASIA   And who made terror, madness, crime,
        remorse,
Which from the links of the great chain of
        things,   20
To every thought within the mind of man
Sway and drag heavily, and each one reels
Under the load towards the pit of death:
Abandoned hope, and love that turns to hate;

And self-contempt, bitterer to drink than blood;
Pain, whose unheeded and familiar speech   26
Is howling, and keen shrieks, day after day;
And Hell, or the sharp fear of Hell?
DEMOGORGON   He reigns.
ASIA Utter his name: a world pining in pain 29
Asks but his name: curses shall drag him down.
DEMOGORGON He reigns.
ASIA   I feel, I know it: who?
DEMOGORGON   He reigns.
ASIA Who reigns? There was the Heaven and
        Earth at first,
    And Light and Love; then Saturn, from whose
        throne
    Time fell, an envious shadow: such the state
    Of the earth's primal spirits beneath his sway, 35
    As the calm joy of flowers and living leaves
    Before the wind or sun has withered them
    And semivital worms! but he refused
    The birthright of their being, knowledge, power,
    The skill which wields the elements, the thought
    Which pierces this dim universe like light,   41
    Self-empire, and the majesty of love;
    For thirst of which they fainted. Then Prome-
        theus
    Gave wisdom, which is strength, to Jupiter,
    And with this law alone, "Let man be free," 45
    Clothed him with the dominion of wide Heaven.
    To know nor faith, nor love, nor law; to be
    Omnipotent but friendless is to reign;
    And Jove now reigned; for on the race of man
    First famine, and then toil, and then disease, 50
    Strife, wounds, and ghastly death unseen before,
    Fell; and the unseasonable seasons drove
    With alternating shafts of frost and fire,
    Their shelterless, pale tribes to mountain caves:
    And in their desert hearts fierce wants he sent, 55
    And mad disquietudes, and shadows idle
    Of unreal good, which levied mutual war,
    So ruining the lair wherein they raged.
    Prometheus saw, and waked the legioned hopes
    Which sleep within folded Elysian flowers,   60
    Nepenthe, Moly, Amaranth,° fadeless blooms,
    That they might hide with thin and rainbow
        wings
    The shape of Death; and Love he sent to bind
    The disunited tendrils of that vine

Which bears the wine of life, the human heart; 65
And he tamed fire which, like some beast of prey,
Most terrible, but lovely, played beneath
The frown of man; and tortured to his will
Iron and gold, the slaves and signs of power,
And gems and poisons, and all subtlest forms 70
Hidden beneath the mountains and the waves.
He gave man speech, and speech created thought,
Which is the measure of the universe;
And Science struck the thrones of earth and
    heaven,
Which shook, but fell not; and the harmonious
    mind   75
Poured itself forth in all-prophetic song;
And music lifted up the listening spirit
Until it walked, exempt from mortal care,
Godlike, o'er the clear billows of sweet sound;
And human hands first mimicked and then
    mocked,   80
With molded limbs more lovely than its own,
The human form, till marble grew divine;
And mothers, gazing, drank the love men see
Reflected in their race, behold, and perish.°
He told the hidden power of herbs and springs, 85
And Disease drank and slept. Death grew like
    sleep.
He taught the implicated orbits woven
Of the wide-wandering stars; and how the sun
Changes his lair, and by what secret spell
The pale moon is transformed, when her broad
    eye   90
Gazes not on the interlunar sea:
He taught to rule, as life directs the limbs,
The tempest-wingèd chariots of the Ocean,
And the Celt knew the Indian. Cities then
Were built, and through their snowlike columns
    flowed   95
The warm winds, and the azure aether shone,
And the blue sea and shadowy hills were seen.
Such, the alleviations of his state,
Prometheus gave to man, for which he hangs
Withering in destined pain: but who rains down
Evil, the immedicable plague, which, while 101
Man looks on his creation like a God
And sees that it is glorious, drives him on,
The wreck of his own will, the scorn of earth,
The outcast, the abandoned, the alone?   105

Scene iv. **61. Nepenthe . . . Amaranth:** The first two are legendary drugs; the third, a never-fading flower (Amaranthus).

82–84. till . . . perish: reference to the belief that pregnant women, gazing at a beautiful statue, bear children like them, while men behold the statues and perish for love.

Not Jove: while yet his frown shook Heaven,
   ay, when
His adversary from adamantine chains
Cursed him, he trembled like a slave. Declare
Who is his master? Is he too a slave?
DEMOGORGON   All spirits are enslaved which
   serve things evil: 110
Thou knowest if Jupiter be such or no.
ASIA   Whom called'st thou God?
DEMOGORGON   I spoke but as ye speak,
   For Jove is the supreme of living things.
ASIA   Who is the master of the slave?
DEMOGORGON   If the abysm
   Could vomit forth its secrets. . . . But a voice 115
   Is wanting, the deep truth is imageless;
   For what would it avail to bid thee gaze
   On the revolving world? What to bid speak
   Fate, Time, Occasion, Chance, and Change?
   To these
   All things are subject but eternal Love.   120
ASIA   So much I asked before, and my heart gave
   The response thou hast given; and of such truths
   Each of itself must be the oracle.
   One more demand; and do thou answer me
   As mine own soul would answer, did it know 125
   That which I ask. Prometheus shall arise
   Henceforth the sun of this rejoicing world:
   When shall the destined hour arrive?
DEMOGORGON   Behold!
ASIA   The rocks are cloven, and through the
   purple night
   I see cars drawn by rainbow-wingèd steeds 130
   Which trample the dim winds: in each there stands
   A wild-eyed charioteer urging their flight.
   Some look behind, as fiends pursued them there,
   And yet I see no shapes but the keen stars: 134
   Others, with burning eyes, lean forth, and drink
   With eager lips the wind of their own speed,
   As if the thing they loved fled on before,
   And now, even now, they clasped it. Their
   bright locks
   Stream like a comet's flashing hair: they all
   Sweep onward.
DEMOGORGON   These are the immortal Hours, 140
   Of whom thou didst demand. One waits for thee.
ASIA   A spirit with a dreadful countenance
   Checks its dark chariot by the craggy gulf.
   Unlike thy brethren, ghastly charioteer,
   Who are thou? Whither wouldst thou bear me?
   Speak!   145

SPIRIT   I am the shadow of a destiny
   More dread than is my aspect: ere yon planet
   Has set, the darkness which ascends with me
   Shall wrap in lasting night heaven's kingless
   throne.
ASIA   What meanest thou?
PANTHEA   That terrible shadow floats 150
   Up from its throne, as may the lurid smoke
   Of earthquake-ruined cities o'er the sea.
   Lo! it ascends the car; the coursers fly
   Terrified: watch its path among the stars   154
   Blackening the night!
ASIA   Thus I am answered: strange!
PANTHEA   See, near the verge, another chariot
   stays;
   An ivory shell inlaid with crimson fire,
   Which comes and goes within its sculptured rim
   Of delicate strange tracery; the young spirit 159
   That guides it has the dovelike eyes of hope;
   How its soft smiles attract the soul! as light
   Lures wingèd insects through the lampless air.

SPIRIT

My coursers are fed with the lightning,
   They drink of the whirlwind's stream,
And when the red morning is bright'ning   165
   They bathe in the fresh sunbeam;
   They have strength for their swiftness I deem,
Then ascend with me, daughter of Ocean.

I desire: and their speed makes night kindle;
   I fear: they outstrip the Typhoon;   170
Ere the cloud piled on Atlas can dwindle
   We encircle the earth and the moon:
   We shall rest from long labors at noon:
Then ascend with me, daughter of Ocean.

SCENE V—*The Car pauses within a Cloud on the
top of a snowy Mountain.* ASIA, PANTHEA, *and
the* SPIRIT OF THE HOUR.

SPIRIT

On the brink of the night and the morning
   My coursers are wont to respire;
But the Earth has just whispered a warning
   That their flight must be swifter than fire:
   They shall drink the hot speed of desire!   5

ASIA   Thou breathest on their nostrils, but my
   breath
   Would give them swifter speed.

SPIRIT   Alas! it could not.

PANTHEA Oh Spirit! pause, and tell whence is
    the light
Which fills this cloud? the sun is yet unrisen.

SPIRIT The sun will rise not until noon. Apollo 10
    Is held in heaven by wonder; and the light
    Which fills this vapor, as the aëreal hue
    Of fountain-gazing roses fills the water,
    Flowers from thy mighty sister.

PANTHEA   Yes, I feel— 14

ASIA What is it with thee, sister? Thou art pale.

PANTHEA How thou art changed! I dare not look
    on thee;
    I feel but see thee not. I scarce endure
    The radiance of thy beauty. Some good change
    Is working in the elements, which suffer
    Thy presence thus unveiled. The Nereids° tell 20
    That on the day when the clear hyaline°
    Was cloven at thine uprise, and thou didst stand
    Within a veinèd shell, which floated on
    Over the calm floor of the crystal sea,
    Among the Aegean isles, and by the shores 25
    Which bear thy name; love, like the atmosphere
    Of the sun's fire filling the living world,
    Burst from thee, and illumined earth and
    heaven
    And the deep ocean and the sunless caves
    And all that dwells within them; till grief cast
    Eclipse upon the soul from which it came: 31
    Such art thou now; nor is it I alone,
    Thy sister, thy companion, thine own chosen one,
    But the whole world which seeks thy sympathy.
    Hearest thou not sounds i' the air which speak
    the love   35
    Of all articulate beings? Feelest thou not
    The inanimate winds enamored of thee? List!
                        [*Music.*]

ASIA Thy words are sweeter than aught else but his
    Whose echoes they are: yet all love is sweet,
    Given or returned. Common as light is love, 40
    And its familiar voice wearies not ever.
    Like the wide heaven, the all-sustaining air,
    It makes the reptile equal to the God:
    They who inspire it most are fortunate,
    As I am now; but those who feel it most   45
    Are happier still, after long sufferings,
    As I shall soon become.

PANTHEA   List! Spirits speak.

Scene v. **20. Nereids:** sea nymphs. **21. hyaline:** glassy
stone.

VOICE IN THE AIR, SINGING

Life of Life! thy lips enkindle
    With their love the breath between them;
And thy smiles before they dwindle   50
    Make the cold air fire; then screen them
In those looks, where whoso gazes
Faints, entangled in their mazes.

Child of Light! thy limbs are burning
    Through the vest which seems to hide them; 55
As the radiant lines of morning
    Through the clouds ere they divide them;
And this atmosphere divinest
Shrouds thee wheresoe'er thou shinest.

Fair are others; none beholds thee,   60
    But thy voice sounds low and tender
Like the fairest, for it folds thee
    From the sight, that liquid splendor,
And all feel, yet see thee never,
As I feel now, lost for ever!   65

Lamp of Earth! where'er thou movest
    Its dim shapes are clad with brightness,
And the souls of whom thou lovest
    Walk upon the winds with lightness,
Till they fail, as I am failing,   70
Dizzy, lost, yet unbewailing!

ASIA

My soul is an enchanted boat,
    Which, like a sleeping swan, doth float
Upon the silver waves of thy sweet singing;
    And thine doth like an angel sit   75
    Beside a helm conducting it,
Whilst all the winds with melody are ringing.
    It seems to float ever, for ever,
    Upon that many-winding river,
    Between mountains, woods, abysses,   80
    A paradise of wildernesses!
Till, like one in slumber bound,
Borne to the ocean, I float down, around,
Into a sea profound, of ever-spreading sound:

    Meanwhile thy spirit lifts its pinions   85
    In music's most serene dominions;
Catching the winds that fan that happy heaven.
    And we sail on, away, afar,
    Without a course, without a star,
But, by the instinct of sweet music driven; 90
    Till through Elysian garden islets

By thee, most beautiful of pilots,
Where never mortal pinnace glided,
The boat of my desire is guided:
Realms where the air we breathe is love,   95
Which in the winds and on the waves doth move,
Harmonizing this earth with what we feel above.

We have passed Age's icy caves,
And Manhood's dark and tossing waves,
And Youth's smooth ocean, smiling to betray: 100
Beyond the glassy gulfs we flee
Of shadow-peopled Infancy,
Through Death and Birth, to a diviner day;
A paradise of vaulted bowers,
Lit by downward-gazing flowers,   105
And watery paths that wind between
Wildernesses calm and green,
Peopled by shapes too bright to see,
And rest, having beheld; somewhat like thee; 109
Which walk upon the sea, and chant melodiously!

END OF THE SECOND ACT

ACT III

SCENE I—*Heaven.* JUPITER *on his Throne;*
THETIS *and the other Deities assembled.*

JUPITER   Ye congregated powers of heaven, who
    share
The glory and the strength of him ye serve,
Rejoice! henceforth I am omnipotent,
All else had been subdued to me; alone
The soul of man, like unextinguished fire,   5
Yet burns towards heaven with fierce reproach,
    and doubt,
And lamentation, and reluctant prayer,
Hurling up insurrection, which might make
Our antique empire insecure, though built
On eldest faith, and hell's coeval, fear;   10
And though my curses through the pendulous air,
Like snow on herbless peaks, fall flake by flake,
And cling to it; though under my wrath's night
It climbs the crags of life, step after step,   14
Which wound it, as ice wounds unsandaled feet,
It yet remains supreme o'er misery,
Aspiring, unrepressed, yet soon to fall:
Even now have I begotten a strange wonder,
That fatal child, the terror of the earth,
Who waits but till the destined hour arrive,   20

Bearing from Demogorgon's vacant throne
The dreadful might of ever-living limbs
Which clothed that awful spirit unbeheld,
To redescend, and trample out the spark.
Pour forth heaven's wine, Idaean Ganymede,° 25
And let it fill the Daedal° cups like fire,
And from the flower-inwoven soil divine
Ye all-triumphant harmonies arise,
As dew from earth under the twilight stars: 29
Drink! be the nectar circling through your veins
The soul of joy, ye ever-living Gods,
Till exultation burst in one wide voice
Like music from Elysian winds.
                              And thou
Ascend beside me, veilèd in the light
Of the desire which makes thee one with me, 35
Thetis,° bright image of eternity!
When thou didst cry, "Insufferable might!
God! Spare me! I sustain not the quick flames,
The penetrating presence; all my being,
Like him whom the Numidian seps° did thaw 40
Into a dew with poison, is dissolved,
Sinking through its foundations": even then
Two mighty spirits, mingling, made a third
Mightier than either, which, unbodied now,
Between us floats, felt, although unbeheld,   45
Waiting the incarnation, which ascends,
(Hear ye the thunder of the fiery wheels
Griding° the winds?) from Demogorgon's
    throne.
Victory! victory! Feel'st thou not, O world,
The earthquake of his chariot thundering up 50
Olympus?
              [*The Car of the* HOUR *arrives.* DEMO-
              GORGON *descends, and moves towards
              the Throne of* JUPITER.]
              Awful shape, what are thou? Speak!
DEMOGORGON   Eternity. Demand no direr name.
Descend, and follow me down the abyss.
I am thy child, as thou wert Saturn's child: 54
Mightier than thee: and we must dwell together
Henceforth in darkness. Lift thy lightnings not.
The tyranny of heaven none may retain,
Or reassume, or hold, succeeding thee:

Act III, scene i.   **25. Idaean Ganymede:** the gods' cup-
bearer from Mount Ida. **26. Daedal:** skillfully wrought, as
by the ancient artificer Daedalus. **36. Thetis:** sea nymph by
whom Jupiter incorrectly imagines he will produce a child
to overcome Demogorgon. **40. Numidian seps:** snake whose
bite was thought to produce putrefaction. **48. Griding:**
cutting.

Yet if thou wilt, as 'tis the destiny
Of trodden worms to writhe till they are dead, 60
Put forth thy might.
JUPITER   Detested prodigy!
Even thus beneath the deep Titanian prisons
I trample thee! thou lingerest?
                                        Mercy! mercy!
No pity, no release, no respite! Oh,   64
That thou wouldst make mine enemy my judge,
Even where he hangs, seared by my long
    revenge,
On Caucasus! he would not doom me thus.
Gentle, and just, and dreadless, is he not
The monarch of the world? What then art
    thou?
No refuge! no appeal!
                        Sink with me then,   70
We two will sink on the wide waves of ruin,
Even as a vulture and a snake outspent
Drop, twisted in inextricable fight,
Into a shoreless sea. Let hell unlock
Its mounded oceans of tempestuous fire,   75
And whelm on them into the bottomless void
This desolated world, and thee, and me,
The conqueror and the conquered, and the
    wreck
Of that for which they combated.
                                        Ai! Ai!
The elements obey me not. I sink   80
Dizzily down, ever, for ever, down.
And, like a cloud, mine enemy above
Darkens my fall with victory! Ai! Ai!

SCENE II—*The Mouth of a great River in the
Island Atlantis.* OCEAN *is discovered reclining
near the Shore;* APOLLO *stands beside him.*

OCEAN He fell, thou sayest, beneath his con-
    queror's frown?
APOLLO Ay, when the strife was ended which
    made dim
The orb I rule, and shook the solid stars,
The terrors of his eye illumined heaven
With sanguine light, through the thick ragged
    skirts   5
Of the victorious darkness, as he fell:
Like the last glare of day's red agony,
Which, from a rent among the fiery clouds,
Burns far along the tempest-wrinkled deep.   9

OCEAN He sunk to the abyss? To the dark void?
APOLLO An eagle so caught in some bursting cloud
On Caucasus, his thunder-baffled wings
Entangled in the whirlwind, and his eyes
Which gazed on the undazzling sun, now blinded
By the white lightning, while the ponderous hail
Beats on his struggling form, which sinks at
    length   16
Prone, and the aëreal ice clings over it.
OCEAN Henceforth the fields of heaven-reflecting
    sea
Which are my realm, will heave, unstained
    with blood,
Beneath the uplifting winds, like plains of corn 20
Swayed by the summer air; my streams will flow
Round many-peopled continents, and round
Fortunate isles; and from their glassy thrones
Blue Proteus and his humid nymphs shall mark
The shadow of fair ships, as mortals see   25
The floating bark of the light-laden moon
With the white star, its sightless pilot's crest,
Borne down the rapid sunset's ebbing sea;
Tracking their path no more by blood and
    groans,
And desolation, and the mingled voice   30
Of slavery and command; but by the light
Of wave-reflected flowers, and floating odors,
And music soft, and mild, free, gentle voices,
And sweetest music, such as spirits love.
APOLLO And I shall gaze not on the deeds which
    make   35
My mind obscure with sorrow, as eclipse
Darkens the sphere I guide; but list, I hear
The small, clear, silver lute of the young Spirit
That sits i' the morning star.
OCEAN   Thou must away;
Thy steeds will pause at even, till when farewell:
The loud deep calls me home even now to feed it
With azure calm out of the emerald urns   42
Which stand for ever full beside my throne.
Behold the Nereids under the green sea,
Their wavering limbs borne on the windlike
    stream,   45
Their white arms lifted o'er their streaming hair
With garlands pied and starry sea-flower crowns,
Hastening to grace their mighty sister's joy.
                    [*A sound of waves is heard.*]
It is the unpastured sea hungering for calm. 49
Peace, monster; I come now. Farewell.
APOLLO   Farewell.

SCENE III—*Caucasus.* PROMETHEUS, HERCULES,
IONE, *the* EARTH, SPIRITS, ASIA, *and* PANTHEA,
borne in the Car with the SPIRIT OF THE HOUR.
HERCULES *unbinds* PROMETHEUS, *who descends.*

HERCULES   Most glorious among Spirits, thus
    doth strength
To wisdom, courage, and long-suffering love,
And thee, who art the form they animate,
Minister like a slave.
PROMETHEUS   Thy gentle words
Are sweeter even than freedom long desired   5
And long delayed.
            Asia, thou light of life,
Shadow of beauty unbeheld: and ye,
Fair sister nymphs, who made long years of pain
Sweet to remember, through your love and care:
Henceforth we will not part. There is a cave,   10
All overgrown with trailing odorous plants,
Which curtain out the day with leaves and
    flowers,
And paved with veinèd emerald, and a fountain
Leaps in the midst with an awakening sound. 14
From its curved roof the mountain's frozen tears
Like snow, or silver, or long diamond spires,
Hang downward, raining forth a doubtful light:
And there is heard the ever-moving air,
Whispering without from tree to tree, and birds,
And bees; and all round are mossy seats,   20
And the rough walls are clothed with long soft
    grass;
A simple dwelling, which shall be our own;
Where we will sit and talk of time and change,
As the world ebbs and flows, ourselves un-
    changed.
What can hide man from mutability?   25
And if ye sigh, then I will smile; and thou,
Ione, shalt chant fragments of sea-music,
Until I weep, when ye shall smile away
The tears she brought, which yet were sweet
    to shed.
We will entangle buds and flowers and beams   30
Which twinkle on the fountain's brim, and make
Strange combinations out of common things,
Like human babes in their breif innocence;
And we will search, with looks and words of
    love,
For hidden thoughts, each lovelier than the last,
Our unexhausted spirits; and like lutes   36
Touched by the skill of the enamored wind,

Weave harmonies divine, yet ever new,
From difference sweet where discord cannot be;
And hither come, sped on the charmèd winds,   40
Which meet from all the points of heaven, as
    bees
From every flower aëreal Enna° feeds,
At their known island-homes in Himera,°
The echoes of the human world, which tell
Of the low voice of love, almost unheard,   45
And dove-eyed pity's murmured pain, and
    music,
Itself the echo of the heart, and all
That tempers or improves man's life, now free;
And lovely apparitions,—dim at first,
Then radiant, as the mind, arising bright   50
From the embrace of beauty (whence the forms
Of which these are the phantoms) casts on them
The gathered rays which are reality—
Shall visit us, the progeny immortal
Of Painting, Sculpture, and rapt Poesy,   55
And arts, though unimagined, yet to be.
The wandering voices and the shadows these
Of all that man becomes, the mediators
Of that best worship, love, by him and us
Given and returned; swift shapes and sounds,
    which grow   60
More fair and soft as man grows wise and kind,
And, veil by veil, evil and error fall:
Such virtue has the cave and place around.
            [*Turning to the* SPIRIT OF THE HOUR.]
For thee, fair Spirit, one toil remains. Ione,
Give her that curvèd shell, which Proteus old 65
Made Asia's nuptial boon, breathing within it
A voice to be accomplished, and which thou
Didst hide in grass under the hollow rock.
IONE   Thou most desired Hour, more loved and
    lovely
Than all thy sisters, this is the mystic shell;   70
See the pale azure fading into silver
Lining it with a soft yet glowing light:
Looks it not like lulled music sleeping there?
SPIRIT   It seem in truth the fairest shell of Ocean:
Its sounds must be at once both sweet and
    strange.   75
PROMETHEUS   Go, borne over the cities of mankind
On whirlwind-footed coursers: once again
Outspeed the sun around the orbèd world;
And as thy chariot cleaves the kindling air,

Scene iii.   **42. Enna:** valley in Sicily. **43. Himera:** ancient
town in Sicily.

Thou breathe into the many-folded shell,   80
Loosening its mighty music; it shall be
As thunder mingled with clear echoes: then
Return; and thou shalt dwell beside our cave.
And thou, O, Mother Earth!—

THE EARTH   I hear, I feel;
Thy lips are on me, and their touch runs down
Even to the adamantine central gloom   86
Along these marble nerves; 'tis life, 'tis joy,
And through my withered, old, and icy frame
The warmth of an immortal youth shoots down
Circling. Henceforth the many children fair   90
Folded in my sustaining arms; all plants,
And creeping forms, and insects rainbow-
          winged,
And birds, and beasts, and fish, and human
          shapes,
Which drew disease and pain from my wan
          bosom,
Draining the poison of despair, shall take   95
And interchange sweet nutriment; to me
Shall they become like sister-antelopes
By one fair dam, snow-white and swift as wind,
Nursed among lilies near a brimming stream.
The dew-mists of my sunless sleep shall float   100
Under the stars like balm: night-folded flowers
Shall suck unwithering hues in their repose:
And men and beasts in happy dreams shall
          gather
Strength for the coming day, and all its joy:
And death shall be the last embrace of her   105
Who takes the life she gave, even as a mother
Folding her child, says, "Leave me not again."

ASIA   Oh, mother! wherefore speak the name of
          death?
Cease they to love, and move, and breathe, and
          speak,
Who die?

THE EARTH   It would avail not to reply;   110
Thou art immortal, and this tongue is known
But to the uncommunicating dead.
Death is the veil which those who live call life:
They sleep, and it is lifted: and meanwhile
In mild variety the seasons mild   115
With rainbow-skirted showers, and odorous
          winds,
And long blue meteors cleansing the dull night,
And the life-kindling shafts of the keen sun's
All-piercing bow, and the dew-mingled rain   119
Of the calm moonbeams, a soft influence mild,

Shall clothe the forests and the fields, ay, even
The crag-built deserts of the barren deep,
With ever-living leaves, and fruits, and flowers.
And thou! There is a cavern where my spirit
Was panted forth in anguish whilst thy pain   125
Made my heart mad, and those who did inhale it
Became mad too, and built a temple there,
And spoke, and were oracular, and lured
The erring nations round to mutual war.   129
And faithless faith, such as Jove kept with thee;
Which breath now rises, as amongst tall weeds
A violet's exhalation, and it fills
With a serener light and crimson air
Intense, yet soft, the rocks and woods around;
It feeds the quick growth of the serpent vine,   135
And the dark linkèd ivy tangling wild,
And budding, blown, or odor-faded blooms
Which star the winds with points of colored light,
As they rain through them, and bright golden
          globes   139
Of fruit, suspended in their own green heaven,
And through their veinèd leaves and amber stems
The flowers whose purple and translucid bowls
Stand ever mantling with aëreal dew,
The drink of spirits: and it circles round,   144
Like the soft waving wings of noonday dreams,
Inspiring calm and happy thoughts, like mine,
And thou art thus restored. This cave is thine.
Arise! Appear!

          [A SPIRIT *rises in the likeness of a*
                    winged child.]
                    This is my torch-bearer;
Who let his lamp out in old time gazing
On eyes from which he kindled it anew   150
With love, which is as fire, sweet daughter mine,
For such is that within thine own. Run, way-
          ward,
And guide this company beyond the peak
Of Bacchic Nysa,° Maenad-haunted mountain,
And beyond Indus and its tribute rivers,   155
Trampling the torrent streams and glassy lakes
With feet unwet, unwearied, undelaying,
And up the green ravine, across the vale,
Beside the windless and crystalline pool,
Where ever lies, on unerasing waves,   160
The image of a temple, built above,
Distinct with column, arch, and architrave,
And palmlike capital, and over-wrought,
And populous with most living imagery,

154. Nysa: mountain home of Bacchus.

Praxitelean shapes, whose marble smiles   165
Fill the hushed air with everlasting love.
It is deserted now, but once it bore
Thy name, Prometheus; there the emulous youths
Bore to thy honor through the divine gloom
The lamp which was thine emblem; even as those
Who bear the untransmitted torch of hope   171
Into the grave, across the night of life,
As thou hast borne it most triumphantly
To this far goal of Time. Depart, farewell.
Beside that temple is the destined cave.   175

SCENE IV—*A Forest. In the Background a Cave.*
PROMETHEUS, ASIA, PANTHEA, IONE, *and the*
SPIRIT OF THE EARTH.

IONE   Sister, it is not earthly: how it glides
Under the leaves! how on its head there burns
A light, like a green star, whose emerald beams
Are twined with its fair hair! how, as it moves,
The splendor drops in flakes upon the grass!   5
Knowest thou it?
PANTHEA   It is the delicate spirit
That guides the earth through heaven. From afar
The populous constellations call that light
The loveliest of the planets; and sometimes
It floats along the spray of the salt sea,   10
Or makes it chariot of a foggy cloud,
Or walks through fields or cities while men sleep,
Or o'er the mountain tops, or down the rivers,
Or through the green waste wilderness, as now,
Wondering at all it sees. Before Jove reigned   15
It loved our sister Asia, and it came
Each leisure hour to drink the liquid light
Out of her eyes, for which it said it thirsted
As one bit by a dipsas,° and with her
It made its childish confidence, and told her   20
All it had known or seen, for it saw much,
Yet idly reasoned what it saw; and called her—
For whence it sprung it knew not, nor do I—
Mother, dear mother.
THE SPIRIT OF THE EARTH   (*running to Asia*)
                Mother, dearest mother;
May I then talk with thee as I was wont?   25
May I then hide my eyes in thy soft arms,
After thy looks have made them tired of joy?

Scene iv. **19. dipsas:** legendary snake whose bite was
said to cause intense thirst.

May I then play beside thee the long noons,
When work is none in the bright silent air?
ASIA   I love thee, gentlest being, and henceforth   30
Can cherish thee unenvied: speak, I pray:
Thy simple talk once solaced, now delights.
SPIRIT OF THE EARTH   Mother, I am grown wiser, though a child
Cannot be wise like thee, within this day;
And happier too; happier and wiser both.   35
Thou knowest that toads, and snakes, and loathly worms,
And venomous and malicious beasts, and boughs
That bore ill berries in the woods, were ever
An hindrance to my walks o'er the green world:
And that, among the haunts of humankind,   40
Hard-featured men, or with proud, angry looks,
Or cold, staid gait, or false and hollow smiles,
Or the dull sneer of self-loved ignorance,
Or other such foul masks, with which ill thoughts
Hide that fair being whom we spirits call man;   45
And women too, ugliest of all things evil,
(Though fair, even in a world where thou art fair,
When good and kind, free and sincere like thee),
When false or frowning made me sick at heart
To pass them, though they slept, and I unseen.   50
Well, my path lately lay through a great city
Into the woody hills surrounding it:
A sentinel was sleeping at the gate:
When there was heard a sound, so loud, it shook
The towers amid the moonlight, yet more sweet
Than any voice but thine, sweetest of all;   56
A long, long sound, as it would never end:
And all the inhabitants leaped suddenly
Out of their rest, and gathered in the streets,
Looking in wonder up to Heaven, while yet   60
The music pealed along. I hid myself
Within a fountain in the public square,
Where I lay like the reflex of the moon
Seen in a wave under green leaves; and soon
Those ugly human shapes and visages   65
Of which I spoke as having wrought me pain,
Passed floating through the air, and fading still
Into the winds that scattered them; and those
From whom they passed seemed mild and lovely forms
After some foul disguise had fallen, and all   70
Were somewhat changed, and after brief surprise
And greetings of delighted wonder, all

Went to their sleep again: and when the dawn
Came, wouldst thou think that toads, and
  snakes, and efts,
Could e'er be beautiful? yet so they were,   75
And that with little change of shape or hue:
All things had put their evil nature off:
I cannot tell my joy, when o'er a lake
Upon a drooping bough with nightshade
  twined,
I saw two azure halcyons clinging downward 80
And thinning one bright bunch of amber
  berries,
With quick long beaks, and in the deep there lay
Those lovely forms imaged as in a sky;
So, with my thoughts full of these happy
  changes,
We meet again, the happiest change of all.   85
ASIA   And never will we part, till thy chaste sister
  Who guides the frozen and inconstant moon
  Will look on thy more warm and equal light
  Till her heart thaw like flakes of April snow
  And love thee.
SPIRIT OF THE EARTH   What; as Asia loves
  Prometheus?   90
ASIA   Peace, wanton, thou art yet not old enough.
  Think ye by gazing on each other's eyes
  To multiply your lovely selves, and fill
  With sphered fires the interlunar air?
SPIRIT OF THE EARTH   Nay, mother, while my
  sister trims her lamp   95
  'Tis hard I should go darkling.
ASIA   Listen; look!
      [*The* SPIRIT OF THE HOUR *enters.*]
PROMETHEUS   We feel what thou hast heard and
  seen: yet speak.
SPIRIT OF THE HOUR   Soon as the sound had
  ceased whose thunder filled
The abysses of the sky and the wide earth,
There was a change: the impalpable thin air 100
And the all-circling sunlight were transformed,
As if the sense of love dissolved in them
Had folded itself round the sphered world.
My vision then grew clear, and I could see
Into the mysteries of the universe: 105
Dizzy as with delight I floated down,
Winnowing the lightsome air with languid
  plumes,
My coursers sought their birthplace in the sun,
Where they henceforth will live exempt from toil,
Pasturing flowers of vegetable fire;   110

And where my moonlike car will stand within
A temple, gazed upon by Phidian forms
Of thee, and Asia, and the Earth, and me,
And you fair nymphs looking the love we feel,—
In memory of the tidings it has born,—   115
Beneath a dome fretted with graven flowers,
Poised on twelve columns of resplendent stone,
And open to the bright and liquid sky.
Yoked to it by an amphisbaenic snake°   119
The likeness of those wingèd steeds will mock
The flight from which they find repose. Alas,
Whither has wandered now my partial tongue
When all remains untold which ye would hear?
As I have said, I floated to the earth:
It was, as it is still, the pain of bliss   125
To move, to breathe, to be; I wandering went
Among the haunts and dwellings of mankind,
And first was disappointed not to see
Such mighty change as I had felt within
Expressed in outward things; but soon I
  looked,   130
And behold, thrones were kingless, and men
  walked
One with the other even as spirits do,
None fawned, none trampled; hate, disdain, or
  fear,
Self-love or self-contempt, on human brows
No more inscribed, as o'er the gate of hell, 135
"All hope abandon ye who enter here";
None frowned, none trembled, none with
  eager fear
Gazed on another's eye of cold command,
Until the subject of a tyrant's will
Became, worse fate, the abject° of his own, 140
Which spurred him, like an outspent horse, to
  death.
None wrought his lips in truth-entangling lines
Which smiled the lie his tongue disdained to
  speak;
None, with firm sneer, trod out in his own heart
The sparks of love and hope till these re-
  mained   145
Those bitter ashes, a soul self-consumed,
And the wretch crept a vampire among men,
Infecting all with his own hideous ill;
None talked that common, false, cold, hollow
  talk
Which makes the heart deny the *yes* it breathes,

119. amphisbaenic snake: legendary snake with a head
at each end. **140. abject:** slave.

Yet question that unmeant hypocrisy   151
With such a self-mistrust as has no name.
And women, too, frank, beautiful, and kind
As the free heaven which rains fresh light and
    dew
On the wide earth, past; gentle radiant forms, 155
From custom's evil taint exempt and pure;
Speaking the wisdom once they could not think,
Looking emotions once they feared to feel,
And changed to all which once they dared
    not be,
Yet being now, made earth like heaven; nor pride,
Nor jealousy, nor envy, nor ill shame,   161
The bitterest of those drops of treasured gall,
Spoilt the sweet taste of the nepenthe, love.
Thrones, altars, judgment-seats, and prisons;
    wherein,   164
And beside which, by wretched men were borne
Scepters, tiaras, swords, and chains, and tomes
Of reasoned wrong, glozed on by ignorance,
Were like those monstrous and barbaric shapes,
The ghosts of a no-more-remembered fame,
Which, from their unworn obelisks, look forth
In triumph o'er the palaces and tombs   171
Of those who were their conquerors: mould-
    ering round,
These imaged to the pride of kings and priests
A dark yet mighty faith, a power as wide
As is the world it wasted, and are now   175
But an astonishment; even so the tools
And emblems of its last captivity,
Amid the dwellings of the peopled earth,
Stand, not o'erthrown, but unregarded now.
And those foul shapes, abhorred by god and
    man,—   180
Which, under many a name and many a form
Strange, savage, ghastly, dark and execrable,
Were Jupiter, the tyrant of the world;
And which the nations, panic-stricken, served
With blood, and hearts broken by long hope,
    and love   185
Dragged to his altars soiled and garlandless,
And slain amid men's unreclaiming tears,
Flattering the thing they feared, which fear was
    hate,—
Frown, moldering fast, o'er their abandoned
    shrines:
The painted veil, by those who were, called life,
Which mimicked, as with colors idly spread, 191
All men believed or hoped, is torn aside;

The loathsome mask has fallen, the man re-
    mains
Scepterless, free, uncircumscribed, but man
Equal, unclassed, tribeless, and nationless,   195
Exempt from awe, worship, degree, the king
Over himself; just, gentle, wise: but man
Passionless?—no, yet free from guilt or pain,
Which were, for his will made or suffered them,
Nor yet exempt, though ruling them like slaves,
From chance, and death, and mutability,   201
The clogs of that which else might oversoar
The loftiest star of unascended heaven,
Pinnacled dim in the intense inane.

END OF THE THIRD ACT

ACT IV

SCENE—*A Part of the Forest near the Cave of*
PROMETHEUS. PANTHEA *and* IONE *are sleeping:*
they awaken gradually during the first song.

VOICE OF UNSEEN SPIRITS

The pale stars are gone!
For the sun, their swift shepherd,
To their folds them compelling,
In the depths of the dawn,
Hastes, in meteor-eclipsing array, and they flee   5
    Beyond his blue dwelling,
    As fawns flee the leopard.
        But where are ye?

A TRAIN OF DARK FORMS AND SHADOWS PASSES
BY CONFUSEDLY, SINGING.

Here, oh, here:
    We bear the bier   10
Of the Father of many a canceled year!
    Specters we
    Of the dead Hours be,
We bear Time to his tomb in eternity.

    Strew, oh, strew   15
    Hair, not yew!
Wet the dusty pall with tears, not dew!
    Be the faded flowers
    Of Death's bare bowers
Spread on the corpse of the King of Hours!   20

Haste, oh, haste!
As shades are chased,
Trembling, by day, from heaven's blue waste.
We melt away,
Like dissolving spray,   25
From the children of a diviner day,
With the lullaby
Of winds that die
On the bosom of their own harmony!

IONE

What dark forms were they?   30

PANTHEA

The past Hours weak and gray,
With the spoil which their toil
Raked together
From the conquest but One could foil.

IONE

Have they passed?

PANTHEA

They have passed;   35
They outspeeded the blast,
While 'tis said, they are fled:

IONE

Whither, oh, whither?

PANTHEA

To the dark, to the past, to the dead.

VOICE OF UNSEEN SPIRITS

Bright clouds float in heaven,   40
Dew-stars gleam on earth,
Waves assemble on ocean,
They are gathered and driven
By the storm of delight, by the panic of glee!
They shake with emotion,   45
They dance in their mirth.
But where are ye?

The pine boughs are singing
Old songs with new gladness,
The billows and fountains   50
Fresh music are flinging,

Like the notes of a spirit from land and from
    sea;
The storms mock the mountains
With the thunder of gladness.
But where are ye?   55

IONE   What charioteers are these?
PANTHEA   Where are their chariots?

SEMICHORUS OF HOURS

The voice of the Spirits of Air and of Earth
    Have drawn back the figured curtain of sleep
Which covered our being and darkened our birth
    In the deep.

A VOICE

In the deep?

SEMICHORUS II

Oh, below the deep. 60

SEMICHORUS I

An hundred ages we had been kept
    Cradled in visions of hate and care,
And each one who waked as his brother slept,
    Found the truth—

SEMICHORUS II

Worse than his visions were!

SEMICHORUS I

We have heard the lute of Hope in sleep;   65
    We have known the voice of Love in dreams;
We have felt the wand of Power, and leap—

SEMICHORUS II

As the billows leap in the morning beams!

CHORUS

Weave the dance on the floor of the breeze,
    Pierce with song heaven's silent light,   70
Enchant the day that too swiftly flees,
    To check its flight ere the cave of Night.

Once the hungry Hours were hounds
    Which chased the day like a bleeding deer,   74
And it limped and stumbled with many wounds
    Through the nightly dells of the desert year.

But now, oh weave the mystic measure
   Of music, and dance, and shapes of light,
Let the Hours, and the spirits of might and
   pleasure,
   Like the clouds and sunbeams, unite.

A VOICE

               Unite! 80
PANTHEA See, where the Spirits of the human
   mind
   Wrapped in sweet sounds, as in bright veils,
   approach.

CHORUS OF SPIRITS

   We join the throng
   Of the dance and the song,
By the whirlwind of gladness borne along,   85
   As the flying-fish leap
   From the Indian deep,
And mix with the sea-birds, half asleep.

CHORUS OF HOURS

Whence come ye, so wild and so fleet,
For sandals of lightning are on your feet,   90
And your wings are soft and swift as thought,
And your eyes are as love which is veilèd not?

CHORUS OF SPIRITS

   We come from the mind
   Of human kind   94
Which was late so dusk, and obscene, and blind,
   Now 'tis an ocean
   Of clear emotion,
A heaven of serene and mighty motion.

   From that deep abyss
   Of wonder and bliss,   100
Whose caverns are crystal palaces;
   From those skiey towers
   Where Thought's crowned powers
Sit watching your dance, ye happy Hours!
   From the dim recesses   105
   Of woven caresses,
Where lovers catch ye by your loose tresses;
   From the azure isles,
   Where sweet Wisdom smiles,
Delaying your ships with her siren wiles.   110

   From the temples high
   Of Man's ear and eye,

Roofed over Sculpture and Poesy;
   From the murmurings
   Of the unsealed springs   115
Where Science bedews her Daedal wings.

   Years after years,
   Through blood, and tears,
And a thick hell of hatreds, and hopes, and fears;
   We waded and flew,   120
   And the islets were few
Where the bud-blighted flowers of happiness grew.

   Our feet now, every palm,
   Are sandaled with calm,
And the dew of our wings is a rain of balm;   125
   And, beyond our eyes,
   The human love lies
Which makes all it gazes on Paradise.

CHORUS OF SPIRITS AND HOURS

   Then weave the web of the mystic measure;
From the depths of the sky and the ends of the
   earth,   130
Come, swift Spirits of might and of pleasure,
Fill the dance and the music of mirth,
   As the waves of a thousand streams rush by
   To an ocean of splendor and harmony!

CHORUS OF SPIRITS

   Our spoil is won,   135
   Our task is done,
We are free to dive, or soar, or run;
   Beyond and around,
   Or within the bound
Which clips the world with darkness round.   140

   We'll pass the eyes
   Of the starry skies
Into the hoar deep to colonize:
   Death, Chaos, and Night,
   From the sound of our flight,   145
Shall flee, like mist from a tempest's might.

   And Earth, Air, and Light,
   And the Spirit of Might,
Which drives round the stars in their fiery flight;
   And love, Thought, and Breath,   150
   The powers that quell Death,
Wherever we soar shall assemble beneath.

   And our singing shall build
   In the void's loose field

A world for the Spirit of Wisdom to wield;   155
   We will take our plan
   From the new world of man,
And our work shall be called the Promethean.

CHORUS OF HOURS

Break the dance, and scatter the song;
   Let some depart, and some remain.   160

SEMICHORUS I

We, beyond heaven, are driven along:

SEMICHORUS II

Us the enchantments of earth retain:

SEMICHORUS I

Ceaseless, and rapid, and fierce, and free,
With the Spirits which build a new earth and sea,
And a heaven where yet heaven could never be; 165

SEMICHORUS II

Solemn, and slow, and serene, and bright,
Leading the Day and outspeeding the Night,
With the powers of a world of perfect light;

SEMICHORUS I

We whirl, singing loud, round the gathering sphere,
Till the trees, and the beasts, and the clouds appear
From its chaos made calm by love, not fear.   171

SEMICHORUS II

We encircle the ocean and mountains of earth,
And the happy forms of its death and birth
Change to the music of our sweet mirth.

CHORUS OF HOURS AND SPIRITS

Break the dance, and scatter the song,   175
   Let some depart, and some remain,
Wherever we fly we lead along
In leashes, like starbeams, soft yet strong,
   The clouds that are heavy with love's sweet rain.

PANTHEA Ha! they are gone!
IONE   Yet feel you no delight 180
  From the past sweetness?
PANTHEA   As the bare green hill

When some soft cloud vanishes into rain,
  Laughs with a thousand drops of sunny water
  To the unpavilioned sky!
IONE   Even whilst we speak
  New notes arise. What is that awful sound? 185
PANTHEA 'Tis the deep music of the rolling world
  Kindling within the strings of the waved air
  Aeolian modulations.
IONE   Listen too,
  How every pause is filled with under-notes,
  Clear, silver, icy, keen, awakening tones,   190
  Which pierce the sense, and live within the soul,
  As the sharp stars pierce winter's crystal air
  And gaze upon themselves within the sea.
PANTHEA But see where through two openings in
    the forest
  Which hanging branches overcanopy,   195
  And where two runnels of a rivulet,
  Between the close moss violet-inwoven,
  Have made their path of melody, like sisters
  Who part with sighs that they may meet in smiles,
  Turning their dear disunion to an isle   200
  Of lovely grief, a wood of sweet sad thoughts;
  Two visions of strange radiance float upon
  The oceanlike enchantment of strong sound,
  Which flows intenser, keener, deeper yet   204
  Under the ground and through the windless air.
IONE   I see a chariot like that thinnest boat,
  In which the Mother of the Months is borne
  By ebbing light into her western cave,
  When she upsprings from interlunar dreams;
  O'er which is curved an orblike canopy   210
  Of gentle darkness, and the hills and woods,
  Distinctly seen through that dusk aery veil,
  Regard like shapes in an enchanter's glass;
  Its wheels are solid clouds, azure and gold,
  Such as the genii of the thunderstorm   215
  Pile on the floor of the illuminated sea
  When the sun rushes under it; they roll
  And move and grow as with an inward wind;
  Within it sits a wingèd infant, white
  Its countenance, like the whiteness of bright
    snow,   220
  Its plumes are as feathers of sunny frost,
  Its limbs gleam white, through the wind-
    flowing folds
  Of its white robe, woof of ethereal pearl.
  Its hair is white, the brightness of white light
  Scattered in strings; yet its two eyes are
    heavens   225

Of liquid darkness, which the Deity
Within seems pouring, as a storm is poured
From jaggèd clouds, out of their arrowy lashes,
Tempering the cold and radiant air around,
With fire that is not brightness; in its hand   230
It sways a quivering moonbeam, from whose
    point
A guiding power directs the chariot's prow
Over its wheelèd clouds, which as they roll
Over the grass, and flowers, and waves, wake
    sounds,
Sweet as a singing rain of silver dew.   235
PANTHEA   And from the other opening in the wood
Rushes, with loud and whirlwind harmony,
A sphere, which is as many thousand spheres,
Solid as crystal, yet through all its mass   239
Flow, as through empty space, music and light:
Ten thousand orbs involving and involved,
Purple and azure, white, and green, and golden,
Sphere within sphere; and every space between
Peopled with unimaginable shapes,   244
Such as ghosts dream dwell in the lampless deep,
Yet each inter-transpicuous, and they whirl
Over each other with a thousand motions,
Upon a thousand sightless axles spinning,
And with the force of self-destroying swiftness,
Intensely, slowly, solemnly roll on,   250
Kindling with mingled sounds, and many tones,
Intelligible words and music wild.
With mighty whirl the multitudinous orb
Grinds the bright brook into an azure mist
Of elemental subtlety, like light;   255
And the wild odor of the forest flowers,
The music of the living grass and air,
The emerald light of leaf-entangled beams
Round its intense yet self-conflicting speed,
Seem kneaded into one aëreal mass   260
Which drowns the sense. Within the orb itself,
Pillowed upon its alabaster arms,
Like to a child o'erwearied with sweet toil,
On its own folded wings, and wavy hair,
The Spirit of the Earth is laid asleep,   265
And you can see its little lips are moving,
Amid the changing light of their own smiles,
Like one who talks of what he loves in dream.
IONE   'Tis only mocking the orb's harmony.
PANTHEA   And from a star upon its forehead,
    shoot,   270
Like swords of azure fire, or golden spears
With tyrant-quelling myrtle overtwined,

Embleming heaven and earth united now,
Vast beams like spokes of some invisible wheel
Which whirl as the orb whirls, swifter than
    thought,   275
Filling the abyss with sunlike lightenings,
And perpendicular now, and now transverse,
Pierce the dark soil, and as they pierce and pass,
Make bare the secrets of the earth's deep heart;
Infinite mines of adamant and gold,   280
Valueless stones, and unimagined gems,
And caverns on crystalline columns poised
With vegetable silver overspread;
Wells of unfathomed fire, and water springs
Whence the great sea, even as a child is fed, 285
Whose vapors clothe earth's monarch mountain-
    tops
With kingly, ermine snow. The beams flash on
And make appear the melancholy ruins
Of canceled cycles; anchors, beaks of ships;
Planks turned to marble; quivers, helms, and
    spears,   290
And gorgon-headed targes,° and the wheels
Of scythèd chariots, and the emblazonry
Of trophies, standards, and armorial beasts,
Round which death laughed, sepulchered em-
    blems
Of dead destruction, ruin within ruin!   295
The wrecks beside of many a city vast,
Whose population which the earth grew over
Was mortal, but not human; see, they lie,
Their monstrous works, and uncouth skeletons,
Their statues, homes and fanes; prodigious
    shapes   300
Huddled in gray annihilation, split,
Jammed in the hard, black deep; and over these,
The anatomies of unknown wingèd things,
And fishes which were isles of living scale,
And serpents, bony chains, twisted around 305
The iron crags, or within heaps of dust
To which the tortuous strength of their last pangs
Had crushed the iron crags; and over these
The jagged alligator, and the might
Of earth-convulsing behemoth, which once 310
Were monarch beasts, and on the slimy shores,
And weed-overgrown continents of earth,
Increased and multiplied like summer worms
On an abandoned corpse, till the blue globe 314
Wrapped deluge round it like a cloak, and they

Act IV.   291. gorgon-headed targes: shields with the
Gorgon-like power to turn a man to stone.

Yelled, gasped, and were abolished; or some God
Whose throne was in a comet, passed, and cried,
"Be not!" And like my words they were no
    more.

THE EARTH

The joy, the triumph, the delight, the madness!
The boundless, overflowing, bursting gladness,
The vaporous exultation not to be confined!
    Ha! ha! the animation of delight   322
    Which wraps me, like an atmosphere of light,
And bears me as a cloud is borne by its own
    wind.

THE MOON

    Brother mine, calm wanderer,   325
    Happy globe of land and air,
Some Spirit is darted like a beam from thee,
    Which penetrates my frozen frame,
    And passes with the warmth of flame,
With love, and odor, and deep melody   330
    Through me, through me!

THE EARTH

Ha! ha! the caverns of my hollow mountains,
    My cloven fire-crags, sound-exulting fountains
Laugh with a vast and inextinguishable laughter.
    The oceans, and the deserts, and the abysses, 335
    And the deep air's unmeasured wildernesses,
Answer from all their clouds and billows, echoing
    after.

    They cry aloud as I do. Sceptered curse,
    Who all our green and azure universe
Threatenedst to muffle round with black destruc-
    tion, sending   340
    A solid cloud to rain hot thunderstones,
    And splinter and knead down my children's
        bones,
All I bring forth, to one void mass battering and
    blending,—

    Until each craglike tower, and storied column,
    Palace, and obelisk, and temple solemn,   345
My imperial mountains crowned with cloud, and
    snow, and fire;
    My sealike forests, every blade and blossom
    Which finds a grave or cradle in my bosom,
Were stamped by thy strong hate into a lifeless
    mire:

How art thou sunk, withdrawn, covered, drunk
    up   350
By thirsty nothing, as the brackish cup
Drained by a desert-troop, a little drop for all;
    And from beneath, around, within, above,
    Filling the void annihilation, love
Burst in like light on caves cloven by the thunder-
    ball.   355

THE MOON

    The snow upon my lifeless mountains
    Is loosened into living fountains,
My solid oceans flow, and sing, and shine:
    A spirit from my heart bursts forth,
    It clothes with unexpected birth   360
My cold bare bosom: Oh! it must be thine
    On mine, on mine!

    Gazing on thee I feel, I know
    Green stalks burst forth, and bright flowers
        grow,
And living shapes upon my bosom move: 365
    Music is in the sea and air,
    Wingèd clouds soar here and there,
Dark with the rain new buds are dreaming of:
    'Tis, love, all love!

THE EARTH

    It interpenetrates my granite mass,   370
    Through tangled roots and trodden clay doth
        pass
Into the utmost leaves and delicatest flowers;
    Upon the winds, among the clouds 'tis spread,
    It wakes a life in the forgotten dead,
They breathe a spirit up from their obscurest
    bowers.   375

    And like a storm bursting its cloudy prison
    With thunder, and with whirlwind, has arisen
Out of the lampless caves of unimagined being:
    With earthquake shock and swiftness making
        shiver   379
    Thought's stagnant chaos, unremoved for ever,
Till hate, and fear, and pain, light-vanquished
    shadows, fleeing,

    Leave Man, who was a many-sided mirror,
    Which could distort to many a shape of error,
This true fair world of things, a sea reflecting love;
    Which over all his kind, as the sun's heaven 385

Gliding o'er ocean, smooth, serene, and even,
Darting from starry depths radiance and life, doth
    move:

Leave Man, even as a leprous child is left,
Who follows a sick beast to some warm cleft
Of rocks, through which the might of healing
    springs is poured;   390
Then when it wanders home with rosy smile,
Unconscious, and its mother fears awhile
It is a spirit, then, weeps on her child restored.

Man, oh, not men! a chain of linkèd thought,
Of love and might to be divided not,   395
Compelling the elements with adamantine stress;
As the sun rules, even with a tyrant's gaze,
The unquiet republic of the maze
Of planets, struggling fierce towards heaven's free
    wilderness.

Man, one harmonious soul of many a soul,   400
Whose nature is its own divine control,
Where all things flow to all, as rivers to the sea;
Familiar acts are beautiful through love;
Labor, and pain, and grief, in life's green grove
Sport like tame beasts, none knew how gentle
    they could be!   405

His will, with all mean passions, bad delights,
And selfish cares, its trembling satellites,
A spirit ill to guide, but mighty to obey,
Is as a tempest-wingèd ship, whose helm
Love rules, through waves which dare not
    overwhelm,   410
Forcing life's wildest shores to own its sovereign
    sway.

All things confess his strength. Through the
    cold mass
Of marble and of color his dreams pass;
Bright threads whence mothers weave the robes
    their children wear;
Language is a perpetual Orphic song,   415
Which rules with Daedal harmony a throng
Of thoughts and forms, which else senseless and
    shapeless were.

The lightning is his slave; heavén's utmost deep
Gives up her stars, and like a flock of sheep
They pass before his eye, are numbered, and
    roll on!   420
The tempest is his steed, he strides the air;

And the abyss shouts from her depth laid bare,
Heaven, hast thou secrets? Man unveils me;
    I have none.

THE MOON

The shadow of white death has passed
From my path in heaven at last,   425
A clinging shroud of solid frost and sleep;
And through my newly-woven bowers,
Wander happy paramours,
Less mighty, but as mild as those who keep
    Thy vales more deep.   430

THE EARTH

As the dissolving warmth of dawn may fold
A half unfrozen dew-globe, green, and gold,
And crystalline, till it becomes a wingèd mist,
And wanders up the vault of the blue day,
Outlives the noon, and on the sun's last ray 435
Hangs o'er the sea, a fleece of fire and amethyst.

THE MOON

Thou art folded, thou art lying
In the light which is undying
Of thine own joy, and heaven's smile divine;
All suns and constellations shower   440
On thee a light, a life, a power
Which doth array thy sphere; thou pourest thine
    On mine, on mine!

THE EARTH

I spin beneath my pyramid of night,
Which points into the heavens dreaming
    delight,   445
Murmuring victorious joy in my enchanted sleep;
As a youth lulled in love-dreams faintly sighing,
Under the shadow of his beauty lying,
Which round his rest a watch of light and warmth
    doth keep.

THE MOON

As in the soft and sweet eclipse,   450
When soul meets soul on lovers' lips,
High hearts are calm, and brightest eyes are dull;
So when thy shadow falls on me,
Then am I mute and still, by thee
Covered; of thy love, Orb most beautiful,   455
    Full, oh, too full!

Thou art speeding round the sun
Brightest world of many a one;
Green and azure sphere which shinest
With a light which is divinest   460
Among all the lamps of Heaven
To whom life and light is given;
I, thy crystal paramour
Borne beside thee by a power
Like the polar Paradise,   465
Magnet-like of lovers' eyes;
I, a most enamored maiden
Whose weak brain is overladen
With the pleasure of her love,
Maniac-like around thee move   470
Gazing, an insatiate bride,
On thy form from every side
Like a Maenad, round the cup
Which Agave° lifted up
In the weird Cadmaean forest.   475
Brother, wheresoe'er thou soarest
I must hurry, whirl and follow
Through the heavens wide and hollow,
Sheltered by the warm embrace
Of thy soul from hungry space,   480
Drinking from thy sense and sight
Beauty, majesty, and might,
As a lover or a chameleon
Grows like what it looks upon,

As a violet's gentle eye   485
Gazes on the azure sky
Until its hue grows like what it beholds,
As a gray and watery mist
Glows like solid amethyst
Athwart the western mountain it enfolds,   490
When the sunset sleeps
Upon its snow—

THE EARTH

And the weak day weeps
That it should be so.
Oh, gentle Moon, the voice of thy delight   495
Falls on me like thy clear and tender light
Soothing the seaman, borne the summer night,
Through isles for ever calm;
Oh, gentle Moon, thy crystal accents pierce
The caverns of my pride's deep universe,   500

474. Agave: Agave, the daughter of Cadmus, unwittingly killed her son when he tried to prevent a Dionysian festival.

Charming the tiger joy, whose tramplings fierce
Made wounds which need thy balm.

PANTHEA   I rise as from a bath of sparkling water,
    A bath of azure light, among dark rocks,   504
    Out of the stream of sound.
IONE   Ah me! sweet sister,
    The stream of sound has ebbed away from us,
    And you pretend to rise out of its wave,
    Because your words fall like the clear, soft dew
    Shaken from a bathing wood-nymph's limbs and
    hair.
PANTHEA   Peace! peace! A mighty Power, which
    is as darkness,   510
    Is rising out of Earth, and from the sky
    Is showered like night, and from within the air
    Bursts, like eclipse which had been gathered up
    Into the pores of sunlight: the bright visions,
    Wherein the singing spirits rode and shone,   515
    Gleam like pale meteors through a watery night.
IONE   There is a sense of words upon mine ear.
PANTHEA   An universal sound like words:
    Oh, list!

DEMOGORGON

Thou, Earth, calm empire of a happy soul,
    Sphere of divinest shapes and harmonies,   520
Beautiful orb! gathering as thou dost roll
    The love which paves thy path along the skies:

THE EARTH

I hear: I am as a drop of dew that dies.

DEMOGORGON

Thou, Moon, which gazest on the nightly Earth
    With wonder, as it gazes upon thee;   525
Whilst each to men, and beasts, and the swift birth
    Of birds, is beauty, love, calm, harmony:

THE MOON

I hear: I am a leaf shaken by thee!

DEMOGORGON

Ye Kings of suns and stars, Daemons and Gods,
    Aethereal Dominations, who possess   530
Elysian, windless, fortunate abodes
    Beyond Heaven's constellated wilderness:

A VOICE FROM ABOVE

Our great Republic hears, we are blest, and bless.

DEMOGORGON

Ye happy Dead, whom beams of brightest verse
    Are clouds to hide, not colors to portray,   535
Whether your nature is that universe
    Which once ye saw and suffered—

A VOICE FROM BENEATH

                                Or as they
Whom we have left, we change and pass away.

DEMOGORGON

Ye elemental Genii, who have homes
    From man's high mind even to the central
    stone   540
Of sullen lead; from heaven's star-fretted domes
To the dull weed some sea-worm battens on:

A CONFUSED VOICE

We hear: thy words waken Oblivion.

DEMOGORGON

Spirits, whose homes are flesh: ye beasts and
    birds,
    Ye worms, and fish; ye living leaves and
    buds;   545
Lightning and wind; and ye untameable herds,
    Meteors and mists, which throng air's soli-
    tudes:—

A VOICE

Thy voice to us is wind among still woods.

DEMOGORGON

Man, who wert once a despot and a slave;
    A dupe and a deceiver; a decay;   550
A traveler from the cradle to the grave
    Through the dim night of this immortal day:

ALL

Speak: thy strong words may never pass away.

DEMOGORGON

This is the day, which down the void abysm
At the Earth-born's° spell yawns for Heaven's
    depotism,   555
    And Conquest is dragged captive through the
    deep:
Love, from its awful throne of patient power
In the wise heart, from the last giddy hour
    Of dread endurance, from the slippery, steep,
And narrow verge of craglike agony, springs   560
And folds over the world its healing wings.

Gentleness, Virtue, Wisdom, and Endurance,
These are the seals of that most firm assurance
    Which bars the pit over Destruction's strength;
And if, with infirm hand, Eternity,   565
Mother of many acts and hours, should free
    The serpent that would clasp her with its length;
These are the spells by which to reassume
An empire o'er the disentangled doom.

To suffer woes which Hope thinks infinite;   570
To forgive wrongs darker than death or night;
    To defy Power, which seems omnipotent;
To love, and bear; to hope till Hope creates
From its own wreck the thing it contemplates;
    Neither to change, nor falter, nor repent;   575
This, like thy glory, Titan, is to be
Good, great and joyous, beautiful and free;
This is alone Life, Joy, Empire, and Victory.

WILLIAM BUTLER YEATS
1865–1939

The Wanderings of Oisin°

BOOK I

SAINT PATRICK   You who are bent, and bald, and
    blind,
    With a heavy heart and a wandering mind,
    Have known three centuries, poets sing,
    Of dalliance with a demon thing.

555. Earth-born: Prometheus.

THE WANDERINGS OF OISIN. The poem is based on several
ancient and medieval versions of a dialogue between Saint
Patrick, apostle and patron saint of Ireland, and Oisin
(pronounced *Ushéen*), a great poet and warrior of the
Fianna, a military order in Irish legend.

OISIN   Sad to remember, sick with years,   5
   The swift innumerable spears,
   The horsemen with their floating hair,
   And bowls of barley, honey, and wine,
   Those merry couples dancing in tune,
   And the white body that lay by mine;   10
   But the tale, though words be lighter than air,
   Must live to be old like the wandering moon.

   Caoilte, and Conan, and Finn° were there,
   When we followed a deer with our baying
      hounds,
   With Bran, Sceolan, and Lomair,°   15
   And passing the Firbolgs° burial-mounds,
   Came to the cairn-heaped grassy hill
   Where passionate Maeve° is stony-still;
   And found on the dove-gray edge of the sea
   A pearl-pale, highborn lady, who rode   20
   On a horse with bridle of findrinny;°
   And like a sunset were her lips,
   A stormy sunset on doomed ships;
   A citron color gloomed in her hair,
   But down to her feet white vesture flowed,   25
   And with the glimmering crimson glowed
   Of many a figured embroidery;
   And it was bound with a pearl-pale shell
   That wavered like the summer streams,
   As her soft bosom rose and fell.   30
SAINT PATRICK   You are still wrecked among
   heathen dreams.
OISIN   "Why do you wind no horn?" she said.
   "And every hero droop his head?
   The hornless deer is not more sad
   That many a peaceful moment had,   35
   More sleek than any granary mouse,
   In his own leafy forest house
   Among the waving fields of fern:
   The hunting of heroes should be glad."

   "O pleasant woman," answered Finn,   40
   "We think on Oscar's° penciled urn,
   And on the heroes lying slain
   On Gabhra's° raven-covered plain;

   But where are your noble kith and kin,
   And from what country do you ride?"   45

   "My father and my mother are
   Aengus° and Edain,° my own name
   Niamh,° and my country far
   Beyond the tumbling of this tide."

   "What dream came with you that you came   50
   Through bitter tide on foam-wet feet?
   Did your companion wander away
   From where the birds of Aengus wing?"

   Thereon did she look haughty and sweet:
   "I have not yet, war-weary king,   55
   Been spoken of with any man;
   Yet now I choose, for these four feet
   Ran through the foam and ran to this
   That I might have your son to kiss."

   "Were there no better than my son   60
   That you through all that foam should run?"

   "I loved no man, though kings besought
   Until the Danaan° poets brought
   Rhyme that rhymed upon Oisin's name,
   And now I am dizzy with the thought   65
   Of all that wisdom and the fame
   Of battles broken by his hands,
   Of stories builded by his words
   That are like colored Asian birds
   At evening in their rainless lands."   70

   O Patrick, by your brazen bell,
   There was no limb of mine but fell
   Into a desperate gulf of love!
   "You only will I wed," I cried,
   "And I will make a thousand songs,   75
   And set your name all names above,
   And captives bound with leathern thongs
   Shall kneel and praise you, one by one,
   At evening in my western dun."°

   "O Oisin, mount by me and ride   80
   To shores by the wash of the tremulous tide,
   Where men have heaped no burial-mounds,
   And the days pass by like a wayward tune,

Book I.   **13. Caoilte . . . Finn:** Caoilte was Oisin's companion and Finn's favorite among his warriors; Conan, a foul and garrulous braggart (see Book III, l. 116); Finn, chief of the Fianna and Oisin's father. **15. Bran . . . Lomair:** favorite hunting dogs. **16. Firbolgs:** legendary race of prehistoric invaders of Ireland. **18. Maeve:** in folk tradition the queen of the fairies. **21. findrinny:** variety of white bronze. **41. Oscar:** Oisin's son. **43. Gabhra:** scene of the final battle in which the Fianna were nearly destroyed.

47. Aengus: god of youth, beauty, and poetry who ruled over the country of the young. **Edain:** legendary queen who was lured away to live among the fairies. **48. Niamh:** brightness and beauty. **63. Danaan:** Tuatha De Danaan (Race of the Gods of Dana); Dana was the mother of all Irish gods. They defeated the Firbolgs and were later defeated by the Milesians and became the Side, or fairy-folk. **79. dun:** ancient hill fortress.

Where broken faith has never been known,
And the blushes of first love never have flown; 85
And there I will give you a hundred hounds;
No mightier creatures bay at the moon;
And a hundred robes of murmuring silk,
And a hundred calves and a hundred sheep
Whose long wool whiter than sea-froth flows 90
And a hundred spears and a hundred bows,
And oil and wine and honey and milk,
And always never-anxious sleep;
While a hundred youths, mighty of limb,
But knowing nor tumult nor hate nor strife, 95
And a hundred ladies, merry as birds,
Who when they dance to a fitful measure
Have a speed like the speed of the salmon herds,
Shall follow your horn and obey your whim,
And you shall know the Danaan leisure; 100
And Niamh be with you for a wife."
Then she sighed gently, "It grows late.
Music and love and sleep await,
Where I would be when the white moon climbs,
The red sun falls and the world grows dim." 105

And then I mounted and she bound me
With her triumphing arms around me,
And whispering to herself enwound me;
But when the horse had felt my weight,
He shook himself and neighed three times: 110
Caoilte, Conan, and Finn came near,
And wept, and raised their lamenting hands,
And bid me stay, with many a tear;
But we rode out from the human lands.

In what far kingdom do you go, 115
Ah, Fenians, with the shield and bow?
Or are you phantoms white as snow,
Whose lips had life's most prosperous glow?
O you, with whom in sloping valleys,
Or down the dewy forest alleys, 120
I chased at morn the flying deer,
With whom I hurled the hurrying spear,
And heard the foemen's bucklers rattle,
And broke the heaving ranks of battle!
And Bran, Sceolan, and Lomair, 125
Where are you with your long rough hair?
You go not where the red deer feeds,
Nor tear the foemen from their steeds.

SAINT PATRICK Boast not, nor mourn with
    drooping head
Companions long accurst and dead, 130
And hounds for centuries dust and air.

OISIN   We galloped over the glossy sea:
I know not if days passed or hours,
And Niamh sang continually
Danaan songs, and their dewy showers 135
Of pensive laughter, unhuman sound,
Lulled weariness, and softly round
My human sorrow her white arms wound.
We galloped; now a hornless deer
Passed by us, chased by a phantom hound 140
All pearly white, save one red ear;
And now a lady rode like the wind
With an apple of gold in her tossing hand;
And a beautiful young man followed behind
With quenchless gaze and fluttering hair. 145

"Were these two born in the Danaan land
Or have they breathed the mortal air?"

"Vex them no longer," Niamh said,
And sighing bowed her gentle head,
And sighing laid the pearly tip 150
Of one long finger on my lip.

But now the moon like a white rose shone
In the pale west, and the sun's rim sank,
And clouds arrayed their rank on rank
About his fading crimson ball: 155
The floor of Almhuin's° hosting hall
Was not more level than the sea,
As, full of loving fantasy,
And with low murmurs, we rode on,
Where many a trumpet-twisted shell 160
That in immortal silence sleeps
Dreaming of her own melting hues,
Her golds, her ambers, and her blues,
Pierced with soft light the shallowing deeps
But now a wandering land breeze came 165
And a far sound of feathery quires;°
It seemed to blow from the dying flame,
They seemed to sing in the smoldering fires.
The horse towards the music raced,
Neighing along the lifeless waste; 170
Like sooty fingers, many a tree
Rose ever out of the warm sea;
And they were trembling ceaselessly,
As though they all were beating time,
Upon the center of the sun, 175
To that low laughing woodland rhyme.
And, now our wandering hours were done,
We cantered to the shore, and knew

156. **Almhuin's:** Finn's. 166. **quires:** choirs.

The reason of the trembling trees:
Round every branch the songbirds flew,   180
Or clung thereon like swarming bees;
While round the shore a million stood
Like drops of frozen rainbow light,
And pondered in a soft vain mood
Upon their shadows in the tide,   185
And told the purple deeps their pride,
And murmured snatches of delight;
And on the shores were many boats
With bending sterns and bending bows,
And carven figures on their prows   190
Of bitterns, and fish-eating stoats,
And swans with their exultant throats:
And where the wood and waters meet
We tied the horse in a leafy clump,
And Niamh blew three merry notes   195
Out of a little silver trump;
And then an answering whispering flew
Over the bare and woody land,
A whisper of impetuous feet,
And ever nearer, nearer grew;   200
And from the woods rushed out a band
Of men and ladies, hand in hand,
And singing, singing all together;
Their brows were white as fragrant milk,
Their cloaks made out of yellow silk,   205
And trimmed with many a crimson feather;
And when they saw the cloak I wore
Was dim with mire of a mortal shore,
They fingered it and gazed on me
And laughed like murmurs of the sea;   210
But Niamh with a swift distress
Bid them away and hold their peace;
And when they heard her voice they ran
And knelt there, every girl and man,
And kissed, as they would never cease,   215
Her pearl-pale hand and the hem of her dress.
She bade them bring us to the hall
Where Aengus dreams, from sun to sun,
A Druid dream of the end of days
When the stars are to wane and the world be
    done.   220

They led us by long and shadowy ways
Where drops of dew in myriads fall,
And tangled creepers every hour
Blossom in some new crimson flower,
And once a sudden laughter sprang   225
From all their lips, and once they sang

Together, while the dark woods rang,
And made in all their distant parts,
With boom of bees in honey-marts,
A rumor of delighted hearts.   230
And once a lady by my side
Gave me a harp, and bid me sing,
And touch the laughing silver string;
But when I sang of human joy
A sorrow wrapped each merry face,   235
And, Patrick! by your beard, they wept,
Until one came, a tearful boy;
"A sadder creature never stept
Than this strange human bard," he cried;
And caught the silver harp away,   240
And, weeping over the white strings, hurled
It down in a leaf-hid, hollow place
That kept dim waters from the sky;
And each one said, with a long, long sigh,
"O saddest harp in all the world,   245
Sleep there till the moon and the stars die!"

And now, still sad, we came to where
A beautiful young man dreamed within
A house of wattles, clay, and skin;
One hand upheld his beardless chin,   250
And one a scepter flashing out
Wild flames of red and gold and blue,
Like to a merry wandering rout
Of dancers leaping in the air;
And men and ladies knelt them there   255
And showed their eyes with teardrops dim,
And with low murmers prayed to him,
And kissed the scepter with red lips,
And touched it with their finger-tips.

He held that flashing scepter up.   260
"Joy drowns the twilight in the dew,
And fills with stars night's purple cup,
And wakes the sluggard seeds of corn,
And stirs the young kid's budding horn,
And makes the infant ferns unwrap,   265
And for the peewit paints his cap,
And rolls along the unwieldy sun,
And makes the little planets run:
And if joy were not on the earth,
There were an end of change and birth,   270
And Earth and Heaven and Hell would die,
And in some gloomy barrow lie
Folded like a frozen fly;
Then mock at Death and Time with glances
And wavering arms and wandering dances.   275

"Men's hearts of old were drops of flame
That from the saffron morning came,
Or drops of silver joy that fell
Out of the moon's pale twisted shell;
But now hearts cry that hearts are slaves,   280
And toss and turn in narrow caves;
But here there is nor law nor rule,
Nor have hands held a weary tool;
And here there is nor Change nor Death,
But only kind and merry breath,   285
For joy is God and God is joy."
With one long glance for girl and boy
And the pale blossom of the moon,
He fell into a Druid swoon.

And in a wild and sudden dance   290
We mocked at Time and Fate and Chance
And swept out of the wattled hall
And came to where the dewdrops fall
Among the foamdrops of the sea,
And there we hushed the revelry;   295
And, gathering on our brows a frown,
Bent all our swaying bodies down,
And to the waves that glimmer by
That sloping green De Danaan sod
Sang, "God is joy and joy is God,   300
And things that have grown sad are wicked,
And things that fear the dawn of the morrow
Or the gray wandering osprey Sorrow."

We danced to where in the winding thicket
The damask roses, bloom on bloom,   305
Like crimson meteors hang in the gloom,
And bending over them softly said,
Bending over them in the dance,
With a swift and friendly glance
From dewy eyes: "Upon the dead   310
Fall the leaves of other roses,
On the dead dim earth encloses:
But never, never on our graves,
Heaped beside the glimmering waves,
Shall fall the leaves of damask roses.   315
For neither Death nor Change comes near us,
And all listless hours fear us,
And we fear no dawning morrow,
Nor the gray wandering osprey Sorrow."   319

The dance wound through the windless woods;
The ever-summered solitudes;
Until the tossing arms grew still
Upon the woody central hill;

And, gathered in a panting band,
We flung on high each waving hand,   325
And sang unto the starry broods.
In our raised eyes there flashed a glow
Of milky brightness to and fro
As thus our song arose: "You stars,
Across your wandering ruby cars   330
Shake the loose reins: you slaves of God,
He rules you with an iron rod,
He holds you with an iron bond,
Each one woven to the other,
Each one woven to his brother   335
Like bubbles in a frozen pond;
But we in a lonely land abide
Unchainable as the dim tide,
With hearts that know nor law nor rule,
And hands that hold no wearisome tool,   340
Folded in love that fears no morrow,
Nor the gray wandering osprey Sorrow."

O Patrick! for a hundred years
I chased upon that woody shore
The deer, the badger, and the boar.   345
O Patrick! for a hundred years
At evening on the glimmering sands,
Beside the piled-up hunting spears,
These now outworn and withered hands
Wrestled among the island bands.   350
O Patrick! for a hundred years
We went a-fishing in long boats
With bending sterns and bending bows,
And carven figures on their prows
Of bitterns and fish-eating stoats.   355
O Patrick! for a hundred years
The gentle Niamh was my wife;
But now two things devour my life;
The things that most of all I hate:
Fasting and prayers.

SAINT PATRICK   Tell on.
OISIN   Yes, yes,   360
For these were ancient Oisin's fate
Loosed long ago from Heaven's gate,
For his last days to lie in wait.
When one day by the tide I stood,
I found in that forgetfulness   365
Of dreamy foam a staff of wood
From some dead warrior's broken lance:
I turned it in my hands; the stains
Of war were on it, and I wept,
Remembering how the Fenians stept   370

Along the blood-bedabbled plains,
Equal to good or grievous chance:
Thereon young Niamh softly came
And caught my hands, but spake no word
Save only many times my name,   375
In murmurs, like a frighted bird.
We passed by woods, and lawns of clover,
And found the horse and bridled him,
For we knew well the old was over.
I heard one say, "His eyes grow dim   380
With all the ancient sorrow of men";
And wrapped in dreams rode out again
With hoofs of the pale findrinny
Over the glimmering purple sea.
Under the golden evening light,   385
The Immortals moved among the fountains
By rivers and the woods' old night;
Some danced like shadows on the mountains,
Some wandered ever hand in hand;
Or sat in dreams on the pale strand,   390
Each forehead like an obscure star
Bent down above each hookèd knee,
And sang, and with a dreamy gaze
Watched where the sun in a saffron blaze
Was slumbering half in the sea-ways;   395
And, as they sang, the painted birds
Kept time with their bright wings and feet;
Like drops of honey came their words,
But fainter than a young lamb's bleat.

"An old man stirs the fire to a blaze,   400
In the house of a child, of a friend, of a brother.
He has over-lingered his welcome; the days,
Grown desolate, whisper and sigh to each other;
He hears the storm in the chimney above, 404
And bends to the fire and shakes with the cold,
While his heart still dreams of battle and love,
And the cry of the hounds on the hills of old.

"But we are apart in the grassy places,
Where care cannot trouble the least of our days,
Or the softness of youth be gone from our faces,
Or love's first tenderness die in our gaze. 411
The hare grows old as she plays in the sun
And gazes around her with eyes of brightness;
Before the swift things that she dreamed of were
    done
She limps along in an aged whiteness;   415
A storm of birds in the Asian trees
Like tulips in the air a-winging,
And the gentle waves of the summer seas,

That raise their heads and wander singing,
Must murmur at last, 'Unjust, unjust';   420
And 'My speed is a weariness,' falters the mouse,
And the kingfisher turns to a ball of dust,
And the roof falls in of his tunnelled house.
But the love-dew dims our eyes till the day 424
When God shall come from the sea with a sigh
And bid the stars drop down from the sky,
And the moon like a pale rose wither away."

BOOK II

Now, man of croziers, shadows called our
    names
And then away, away, like whirling flames;
And now fled by, mist-covered, without sound,
The youth and lady and the deer and hound; 4
"Gaze no more on the phantoms," Niamh said,
And kissed my eyes, and, swaying her bright
    head
And her bright body, sang of faery and man
Before God was or my old line began;
Wars shadowy, vast, exultant; faeries of old 10
Who wedded men with rings of Druid gold;
And how those lovers never turn their eyes
Upon the life that fades and flickers and dies,
Yet love and kiss on dim shores far away
Rolled round with music of the sighing spray:
Yet sang no more as when, like a brown bee 15
That has drunk full, she crossed the misty sea
With me in her white arms a hundred years
Before this day; for now the fall of tears
Troubled her song.
                    I do not know if days
Or hours passed by, yet hold the morning rays 20
Shone many times among the glimmering
    flowers
Woven into her hair, before dark towers
Rose in the darkness, and the white surf gleamed
About them; and the horse of Faery screamed 24
And shivered, knowing the Isle of Many Fears,
Nor ceased until white Niamh stroked his ears
And named him by sweet names.
                                A foaming tide
Whitened afar with surge, fan-formed and wide,
Burst from a great door marred by many a blow
From mace and sword and poleax, long ago   30
When gods and giants warred. We rode between
The seaweed-covered pillars; and the green
And surging phosphorus alone gave light

On our dark pathway, till a countless flight   34
Of moonlit steps glimmered; and left and right
Dark statues glimmered over the pale tide
Upon dark thrones. Between the lids of one
The imaged meteors had flashed and run
And had disported in the stilly jet,°
And the fixed stars had dawned and shone and
    set,   40
Since God made Time and Death and Sleep: the
    other
Stretched his long arm to where, a misty smother,
The stream churned, churned, and churned—his
    lips apart,
As though he told his never-slumbering heart
Of every foamdrop on its misty way.   45
Tying the horse to his vast foot that lay
Half in the unvesseled sea, we climbed the stair
And climbed so long, I thought the last steps
    were
Hung from the morning star; when these mild
    words
Fanned the delighted air like wings of birds: 50
"My brothers spring out of their beds at morn,
A-murmur like young partridge: with loud horn
They chase the noontide deer;
And when the dew-drowned stars hang in the air
Look to long fishing-lines, or point and pare   55
An ashen hunting spear.
O sigh, O fluttering sigh, be kind to me;
Flutter along the froth lips of the sea,
And shores the froth lips wet:
And stay a little while, and bid them weep: 60
Ah, touch their blue-veined eyelids if they sleep,
And shake their coverlet.
When you have told how I weep endlessly,
Flutter along the froth lips of the sea
And home to me again,   65
And in the shadow of my hair lie hid,
And tell me that you found a man unbid,
The saddest of all men."

A lady with soft eyes like funeral tapers,
And face that seemed wrought out of moonlit
    vapors,   70
And a sad mouth, that fear made tremulous
As any ruddy moth, looked down on us;
And she with a wave-rusted chain was tied
To two old eagles, full of ancient pride,
That with dim eyeballs stood on either side.   75

Book II. **39. stilly jet:** still, jet black of the statue's eyes.

Few feathers were on their disheveled wings,
For their dim minds were with the ancient things

"I bring deliverance," pearl-pale Niamh said.

"Neither the living, nor the unlaboring dead,
Nor the high gods who never lived, may fight   80
My enemy and hope; demons for fright
Jabber and scream about him in the night;
For he is strong and crafty as the seas
That sprang under the Seven Hazel Trees,°
And I must needs endure and hate and weep,   85
Until the gods and demons drop asleep,
Hearing Aed° touch the mournful strings of
    gold."

"Is he so dreadful?"
                    "Be nor over-bold,
But fly while still you may."
                            And thereon I:
"This demon shall be battered till he die,   90
And his loose bulk be thrown in the loud tide."

"Flee from him," pearl-pale Niamh weeping
    cried,
"For all men flee the demons"; but moved not
My angry king-remembering soul one jot.
There was no mightier soul of Heber's° line;   95
Now it is old and mouse-like. For a sign
I burst the chain: still earless, nerveless, blind,
Wrapped in the things of the unhuman mind,
In some dim memory or ancient mood,
Still earless, nerveless, blind, the eagles stood.   100

And then we climbed the stair to a high door;
A hundred horsemen on the basalt floor
Beneath had paced content: we held our way
And stood within: clothed in a misty ray
I saw a foam-white seagull drift and float   105
Under the roof, and with a straining throat
Shouted, and hailed him: he hung there a star,
For no man's cry shall ever mount so far;
Not even your God could have thrown down
    that hall;   109
Stabling His unloosed lightnings in their stall,
He had sat down and sighed with cumbered
    heart,
As though His hour were come.

84. Seven . . . Trees: According to Yeats, the trees guarded a sacred well, and when a woman stole their fruit, seven rivers sprang from the well, swept her away, and became the seven seas of the world. **87. Aed:** god of death; all who hear him playing his harp die. **95. Heber:** early ancestor of the Irish and ruler of southern Ireland.

We sought the part
That was most distant from the door; green slime
Made the way slippery, and time on time
Showed prints of sea-born scales, while down
    through it   115
The captive's journeys to and fro were writ
Like a small river, and where feet touched came
A momentary gleam of phosphorus flame.
Under the deepest shadows of the hall
That woman found a ring hung on the wall, 120
And in the ring a torch, and with its flare
Making a world about her in the air,
Passed under the dim doorway, out of sight,
And came again, holding a second light
Burning between her fingers, and in mine   125
Laid it and sighed: I held a sword whose shine
No centuries could dim, and a word ran
Thereon in Ogham° letters, "Manannan";
That sea-god's name, who in a deep content 129
Sprang dripping, and, with captive demons sent
Out of the sevenfold seas, built the dark hall
Rooted in foam and clouds, and cried to all
The mightier masters of a mightier race;
And at his cry there came no milk-pale face 134
Under a crown of thorns and dark with blood,
But only exultant faces.
                Niamh stood
With bowed head, trembling when the white
    blade shone,
But she whose hours of tenderness were gone
Had neither hope nor fear. I bade them hide
Under the shadows till the tumults died   140
Of the loud-crashing and earth-shaking fight,
Lest they should look upon some dreadful sight;
And thrust the torch between the slimy flags.
A dome made out of endless carven jags,   144
Where shadowy face flowed into shadowy face,
Looked down on me; and in the selfsame place
I waited hour by hour, and the high dome,
Windowless, pillarless, multitudinous home
Of faces, waited; and the leisured gaze
Was loaded with the memory of days   150
Buried and mighty. When through the great door
The dawn came in, and glimmered on the floor
With a pale light, I journeyed round the hall
And found a door deep sunken in the wall,
The least of doors; beyond on a dim plain   155
A little runnel made a bubbling strain,
And on the runnel's stony and bare edge

128. **Ogham:** alphabetic engraving adapted from Latin.

A dusky demon dry as a withered sedge
Swayed, crooning to himself an unknown
    tongue:
In a sad revelry he sang and swung   160
Bacchant° and mournful, passing to and fro
His hand along the runnel's side, as though
The flowers still grew there: far on the sea's waste
Shaking and waving, vapor vapor chased,   164
While high frail cloudlets, fed with a green light,
Like drifts of leaves, immovable and bright,
Hung in the passionate dawn. He slowly turned:
A demon's leisure: eyes, first white, now burned
Like wings of kingfishers; and he arose   169
Barking. We trampled up and down with blows
Of sword and brazen battle-ax, while day
Gave to high noon and noon to night gave way;
And when he knew the sword of Manannan
Amid the shades of night, he changed and ran
Through many shapes; I lunged at the smooth
    throat   175
Of a great eel; it changed, and I but smote
A fir-tree roaring in its leafless top;
And thereupon I drew the livid chop
Of a drowned dripping body to my breast;
Horror from horror grew; but when the west   180
Had surged up in a plumy fire, I drave
Through heart and spine; and cast him in the
    wave
Lest Niamh shudder.
                Full of hope and dread
Those two came carrying wine and meat and
    bread,
And healed my wounds with unguents out of
    flowers   185
That feed white moths by some De Danaan
    shrine;
Then in that hall, lit by the dim sea-shine,
We lay on skins of otters, and drank wine,
Brewed by the sea-gods, from huge cups that lay
Upon the lips of sea-gods in their day;   190
And then on heaped-up skins of otters slept.
And when the sun once more in saffron stept,
Rolling his flagrant wheel out of the deep,
We sang the loves and angers without sleep,
And all the exultant labors of the strong.   195
But now the lying clerics murder song
With barren words and flatteries of the weak.
In what land do the powerless turn the beak

161. **Bacchant:** riotous.

Of ravening Sorrow, or the hand of Wrath?
For all your croziers, they have left the path 200
And wander in the storms and clinging snows,
Hopeless forever: ancient Oisin knows,
For he is weak and poor and blind, and lies
On the anvil of the world.

SAINT PATRICK   Be still: the skies
Are choked with thunder, lightning, and fierce
    wind,   205
For God has heard, and speaks His angry mind;
Go cast your body on the stones and pray,
For He has wrought midnight and dawn and day.

OISIN Saint, do you weep? I hear amid the thunder
The Fenian horses; armor torn asunder;   210
Laughter and cries. The armies clash and shock,
And now the daylight-darkening ravens flock.
Cease, cease, O mournful, laughing Fenian horn!

We feasted for three days. On the fourth morn
I found, dropping sea-foam on the wide stair, 215
And hung with slime, and whispering in his hair,
That demon dull and unsubduable;
And once more to a day-long battle fell,
And at the sundown threw him in the surge,
To lie until the fourth morn saw emerge   220
His new-healed shape; and for a hundred years
So warred, so feasted, with nor dreams nor fears,
Nor languor nor fatigue: an endless feast,
An endless war.

            The hundred years had ceased;
I stood upon the stair: the surges bore   225
A beech-bough to me, and my heart grew sore,
Remembering how I had stood by white-haired
    Finn
Under a beech at Almhuin and heard the thin
Outcry of bats.

            And then young Niamh came
Holding that horse, and sadly called my name;
I mounted, and we passed over the lone   231
And drifting grayness, while this monotone,
Surly and distant, mixed inseparably
Into the clangor of the wind and sea.

"I hear my soul drop down into decay,   235
And Manannan's dark tower, stone after stone,
Gather sea-slime and fall the seaward way,
And the moon goad the waters night and day,
That all be overthrown.

"But till the moon has taken all, I wage   240
War on the mightiest men under the skies,

And they have fallen or fled, age after age.
Light is man's love, and lighter is man's rage;
His purpose drifts and dies."   244

And then lost Niamh murmured, "Love, we go
To the Island of Forgetfulness, for lo!
The Islands of Dancing and of Victories
Are empty of all power."

                    "And which of these
Is the Island of Content?"

                    "None know," she said;
And on my bosom laid her weeping head.   250

BOOK III

Fled foam underneath us, and round us, a
    wandering and milky smoke,
High as the saddle-girth, covering away from our
    glances the tide;
And those that fled, and that followed, from the
    foam-pale distance broke;
The immortal desire of Immortals we saw in
    their faces, and sighed.

I mused on the chase with the Fenians, and Bran,
    Sceolan, Lomair,   5
And never a song sang Niamh, and over my
    finger-tips
Came now the sliding of tears and sweeping of
    mist-cold hair,
And now the warmth of sighs, and after the
    quiver of lips.

Were we days long or hours long in riding, when,
    rolled in a grisly peace,
An isle lay level before us, with dripping hazel
    and oak?   10
And we stood on a sea's edge we saw not; for
    whiter than new-washed fleece
Fled foam underneath us, and round us, a
    wandering and milky smoke.

And we rode on the plains of the sea's edge; the
    sea's edge barren and gray,
Gray sand on the green of the grasses and over
    the dripping trees,
Dripping and doubling landward, as though they
    would hasten away,   15
Like an army of old men longing for rest from
    the moan of the seas.

But the trees grew taller and closer, immense in
    their wrinkling bark;
Dropping; a murmurous dropping; old silence
    and that one sound;
For no live creatures lived there, no weasels
    moved in the dark;
Long sighs arose in our spirits, beneath us
    bubbled the ground.   20
And the ears of the horse went sinking away in
    the hollow night,
For, as drift from a sailor slow drowning the
    gleams of the world and the sun,
Ceased on our hands and our faces, on hazel and
    oak leaf, the light,
And the stars were blotted above us, and the
    whole of the world was one.

Till the horse gave a whinny; for, cumbrous with
    stems of the hazel and oak,   25
A valley flowed down from his hoofs, and there
    in the long grass lay,
Under the starlight and shadow, a monstrous
    slumbering folk,
Their naked and gleaming bodies poured out
    and heaped in the way.
And by them were arrow and war-ax, arrow and
    shield and blade;
And dew-blanched horns, in whose hollow a
    child of three years old   30
Could sleep on a couch of rushes, and all in-
    wrought and inlaid,
And more comely than man can make them with
    bronze and silver and gold.

And each of the huge white creatures was huger
    than fourscore men;
The tops of their ears were feathered, their hands
    were the claws of birds,
And, shaking the plumes of the grasses and the
    leaves of the mural° glen,   35
The breathing came from those bodies, long
    warless, grown whiter than curds.

The wood was so spacious above them, that He
    who has stars for His flocks
Could fondle the leaves with His fingers, nor go
    from His dew-cumbered skies;
So long were they sleeping, the owls had builded
    their nests in their locks,

Book III.   **35. mural:** walled.

Filling the fibrous dimness with long generations
    of eyes.   40

And over the limbs and the valley the slow owls
    wandered and came,
Now in a place of star-fire, and now in a shadow-
    place wide;
And the chief of the huge white creatures, his
    knees in the soft star-flame,
Lay loose in a place of shadow: we drew the
    reins by his side.

Golden the nails of his bird-claws, flung loosely
    along the dim ground;   45
In one was a branch° soft-shining with bells more
    many than sighs
In midst of an old man's bosom; owls ruffling
    and pacing around
Sidled their bodies against him, filling the shade
    with their eyes.

And my gaze was thronged with the sleepers; no,
    not since the world began,
In realms where the handsome were many, nor
    in glamors by demons flung,   50
Have faces alive with such beauty been known to
    the salt eye of man,
Yet weary with passions that faded when the
    sevenfold seas were young.

And I gazed on the bell-branch, sleep's forebear,
    far sung by the Sennachies.°
I saw how those slumberers, grown weary, there
    camping in grasses deep,
Of wars with the wide world and pacing the
    shores of the wandering seas,   55
Laid hands on the bell-branch and swayed it,
    and fed of unhuman sleep.

Snatching the horn of Niamh, I blew a long
    lingering note.
Came sound from those monstrous sleepers, a
    sound like the stirring of flies.
He, shaking the fold of his lips, and heaving the
    pillar of his throat,
Watched me with mournful wonder out of the
    wells of his eyes.   60

I cried, "Come out of the shadow, king of the
    nails of gold!

46. branch: legendary bell-branch that casts men into a
deep sleep when it is waved. **53. Sennachies:** tellers of
legendary romances.

And tell of your goodly household and the
goodly works of your hands,
That we may muse in the starlight and talk of
the battles of old;
Your questioner, Oisin, is worthy, he comes
from the Fenian lands.''

Half open his eyes were, and held me, dull with
the smoke of their dreams;   65
His lips moved slowly in answer, no answer out
of them came;
Then he swayed in his fingers the bell-branch,
slow dropping a sound in faint streams
Softer than snowflakes in April and piercing the
marrow like flame.

Wrapt in the wave of that music, with weariness
more than of earth,
The moil of my centuries filled me; and gone like
a sea-covered stone   70
Were the memories of the whole of my sorrow
and the memories of the whole of my mirth,
And a softness came from the starlight and filled
me full to the bone.

In the roots of the grasses, the sorrels, I laid my
body as low;
And the pearl-pale Niamh lay by me, her brow
on the midst of my breast;
And the horse was gone in the distance, and years
after years 'gan flow;   75
Square leaves of the ivy moved over us, binding
us down to our rest.

And, man of the many white croziers, a century
there I forgot
How the fetlocks drip blood in the battle, when
the fallen on fallen lie rolled;
How the falconer follows the falcon in the weeds
of the heron's plot,
And the name of the demon whose hammer made
Conchubar's° sword-blade of old.   80

And, man of the many white croziers, a century
there I forgot
That the spear-shaft is made out of ashwood, the
shield out of osier and hide;
How the hammers spring on the anvil, on the
spearhead's burning spot;
How the slow, blue-eyed oxen of Finn low sadly
at evening tide.

80. **Conchubar:** king of the Red Branch heroes.

But in dreams, mild man of the croziers, driving
the dust with their throngs,   85
Moved round me, of seamen or landsmen, all
who are winter tales;
Came by me the kings of the Red Branch, with
roaring of laughter and songs,
Or moved as they moved once, love-making or
piercing the tempest with sails.

Came Blanid, Mac Nessa, tall Fergus° who
feastward of old time slunk,
Cook Barach, the traitor; and warward, the
spittle on his beard never dry,   90
Dark Balor,° as old as a forest, car-borne, his
mighty head sunk
Helpless, men lifting the lids of his weary and
death-making eye.

And by me, in soft red raiment, the Fenians
moved in loud streams,
And Grania,° walking and smiling, sewed with
her needle of bone.
So lived I and lived not, so wrought I and
wrought not, with creatures of dreams,   95
In a long iron sleep, as a fish in the water goes
dumb as a stone.

At times our slumber was lightened. When the
sun was on silver or gold;
When brushed with the wings of the owls, in the
dimness they love going by;
When a glowworm was green on a grass-leaf,
lured from his lair in the mold;
Half wakening, we lifted our eyelids, and gazed
on the grass with a sigh.   100

So watched I when, man of the croziers, at the
heel of a century fell,
Weak, in the midst of the meadow, from his
miles in the midst of the air,
A starling like them that forgathered 'neath a
moon waking white as a shell
When the Fenians made foray at morning with
Bran, Sceolan, Lomair.

89. **Blanid . . . Fergus:** Blanid was a legendary heroine
and a king's wife who loved Cuchulain; Mac Nessa,
Conchubar Mac Nessa, i.e., the son of Nessa; Fergus, the
king and poet of the Red Branch who was enticed to a feast
by Barach (see l. 90) so that the sons of Usna could be
killed in his absence. **91. Balor:** leader of the hosts of darkness. **94. Grania:** beautiful woman beloved by the aged
Finn.

I awoke: the strange horse without summons out
  of the distance ran,   105
Thrusting his nose to my shoulder; he knew in
  his bosom deep
That once more moved in my bosom the ancient
  sadness of man,
And that I would leave the Immortals, their
  dimness, their dews dropping sleep.

O, had you seen beautiful Niamh grow white as
  the waters are white,
Lord of the croziers, you even had lifted your
  hands and wept: 110
But, the bird in my fingers, I mounted, remembering alone that delight
Of twilight and slumber were gone, and that hoofs
  impatiently stept.

I cried, "O Niamh! O white one! if only a
  twelve-houred day,
I must gaze on the beard of Finn, and move
  where the old men and young
In the Fenians' dwellings of wattle lean on the
  chessboards and play,   115
Ah, sweet to me now were even bald Conan's
  slanderous tongue!

"Like me were some galley forsaken far off in
  Meridian isle,
Remembering its long-oared companions, sails
  turning to threadbare rags;
No more to crawl on the seas with long oars mile
  after mile,
But to be amid shooting of flies and flowering of
  rushes and flags."   120

Their motionless eyeballs of spirits grown mild
  with mysterious thought,
Watched her those seamless faces from the
  valley's glimmering girth;
As she murmured, "O wandering Oisin, the
  strength of the bell-branch is naught,
For there moves alive in your fingers the
  fluttering sadness of earth.

"Then go through the lands in the saddle and see
  what the mortals do,   125
And softly come to your Niamh over the tops of
  the tide;
But weep for your Niamh, O Oisin, weep; for if
  only your shoe
Brush lightly as haymouse earth's pebbles, you
  will come no more to my side.

"O flaming lion of the world, O when will you
  turn to your rest?"
I saw from a distant saddle; from the earth she
  made her moan: 130
"I would die like a small withered leaf in the
  autumn, for breast unto breast
We shall mingle no more, nor our gazes empty
  their sweetness lone

"In the isles of the farthest seas where only the
  spirits come.
Were the winds less soft than the breath of a
  pigeon who sleeps on her nest,
Nor lost in the star-fires and odors the sound of
  the sea's vague drum?   135
O flaming lion of the world, O when will you
  turn to your rest?"

The wailing grew distant; I rode by the woods of
  the wrinkling bark,
Where ever is murmurous dropping, old silence
  and that one sound;
For no live creatures live there, no weasels move
  in the dark;
In a reverie forgetful of all things, over the
  bubbling ground.   140

And I rode by the plains of the sea's edge, where
  all is barren and gray,
Gray sand on the green of the grasses and over
  the dripping trees,
Dripping and doubling landward, as though they
  would hasten away,
Like an army of old men longing for rest from
  the moan of the seas.

And the winds made the sands on the sea's edge
  turning and turning go,   145
As my mind made the names of the Fenians. Far
  from the hazel and oak,
I rode away on the surges, where, high as the
  saddle-bow,
Fled foam underneath me, and round me, a
  wandering and milky smoke.

Long fled the foam-flakes around me, the winds
  fled out of the vast,
Snatching the bird in secret; nor knew I,
  embosomed apart,   150
When they froze the cloth on my body like
  armor riveted fast,
For Remembrance, lifted her leanness, keened in
  the gates of my heart.

Till, fattening the winds of the morning, an odor
of new-mown hay
Came, and my forehead fell low, and my tears
like berries fell down;
Later a sound came, half lost in the sound of a
shore far away,   155
From the great grass-barnacle calling, and later
the shore-weeds brown.

If I were as I once was, the strong hoofs crushing
the sand and the shells,
Coming out of the sea as the dawn comes, a
chaunt of love on my lips,
Not coughing, my head on my knees, and
praying, and wroth with the bells,
I would leave no saint's head on his body from
Rachlin to Bera of ships.   160

Making way from the kindling surges, I rode on a
bridle-path
Much wondering to see upon all hands, of wattles
and woodwork made,
Your bell-mounted churches, and guardless the
sacred cairn and the rath,°
And a small and a feeble populace stooping with
mattock and spade,

Or weeding or ploughing with faces a-shining
with much-toil wet;   165
While in this place and that place, with bodies
unglorious, their chieftains stood,
Awaiting in patience the straw-death,° croziered
one, caught in your net:
Went the laughter of scorn from my mouth like
the roaring of wind in a wood.

And before I went by them so huge and so
speedy with eyes so bright,
Came after the hard gaze of youth, or an old man
lifted his head: 170
And I rode and I rode, and I cried out, "The
Fenians hunt wolves in the night,
So sleep thee by daytime." A voice cried. "The
Fenians a long time are dead."

A whitebeard stood hushed on the pathway, the
flesh of his face as dried grass,
And in folds round his eyes and his mouth, he
sad as a child without milk;

And the dreams of the islands were gone, and I
knew how men sorrow and pass,   175
And their hound, and their horse, and their love,
and their eyes that glimmer like silk.

And wrapping my face in my hair, I murmured,
"In old age they ceased";
And my tears were larger than berries, and I
murmured, "Where white clouds lie spread
On Crevroe or broad Knockfefin, with many of
old they feast
On the floors of the gods." He cried, "No, the
gods a long time are dead."   180

And lonely and longing for Niamh, I shivered
and turned me about,
The heart in me longing to leap like a grasshopper into her heart;
I turned and rode to the westward, and followed
the sea's old shout
Till I saw where Maeve lies sleeping till starlight
and midnight part.

And there at the foot of the mountain, two
carried a sack full of sand,   185
They bore it with staggering and sweating, but
fell with their burden at length.
Leaning down from the gem-studded saddle, I
flung it five yards with my hand,
With a sob for men waxing so weakly, a sob for
the Fenians' old strength.

The rest you have heard of, O croziered man;
how, when divided the girth,
I fell on the path, and the horse went away like a
summer fly;   190
And my years three hundred fell on me, and I
rose, and walked on the earth,
A creeping old man, full of sleep, with the spittle
on his beard never dry.

How the men of the sand-sack showed me a
church with its belfry in air;
Sorry place, where for swing of the war-ax in my
dim eyes that crozier gleams;
What place have Caoilte and Conan, and Bran,
Sceolan, Lomair?   195
Speak, you too are old with your memories, an
old man surrounded with dreams.

SAINT PATRICK Where the flesh of the footsole
clingeth on the burning stones is their place;
Where the demons whip them with wires on the
burning stones of wide Hell,

---

163. rath: fortified enclosure that served as a residence for
a tribal chief. 167. straw-death: natural death.

Watching the blessèd ones move far off, and the
    smile on God's face.
Between them a gateway of brass, and the howl
    of the angels who fell.   200
OISIN Put the staff in my hands; for I go to the
    Fenians, O cleric, to chaunt
The war-songs that roused them of old; they will
    rise, making clouds with their breath,
Innumerable, singing, exultant; the clay under-
    neath them shall pant,
And demons be broken in pieces, and trampled
    beneath them in death.

And demons afraid in their darkness; deep
    horror of eyes and of wings,   205
Afraid, their ears on the earth laid, shall listen
    and rise up and weep;
Hearing the shaking of shields and the quiver of
    stretched bowstrings,
Hearing Hell loud with a murmur, as shouting
    and mocking we sweep.

We will tear out the flaming stones, and batter
    the gateway of brass
And enter, and none sayeth "No" when there
    enters the strongly armed guest;   210
Make clean as a broom cleans, and march on as
    oxen move over young grass;
Then feast, making converse of wars, and of old
    wounds, and turn to our rest.

SAINT PATRICK On the flaming stones, without
    refuge, the limbs of the Fenians are tost;
None war on the masters of Hell, who could
    break up the world in their rage;
But kneel and wear out the flags and pray for
    your soul that is lost   215
Through the demon love of its youth and its
    godless and passionate age.

OISIN Ah me! to be shaken with coughing and
    broken with old age and pain,
Without laughter, a show unto children, alone
    with remembrance and fear;
All emptied of purple hours as a beggar's cloak
    in the rain,
As a haycock out on the flood, or a wolf sucked
    under a weir.   220

It were sad to gaze on the blessèd and no man I
    loved of old there;
I throw down the chain of small stones!° when
    life in my body has ceased,

222. chain . . . stones: rosary.

I will go to Caoilte, and Conan, and Bran,
    Sceolan, Lomair,
And dwell in the house of the Fenians, be they in
    flames or at feast.

Hind Horn°
ca. 1300–1400

In Scotland there was a baby born,
    Lill lal, etc.°
And his name it was called young Hind Horn.°
    With a fal lal, etc.

He sent a letter to our king   5
That he was in love with his daughter Jean.

He's gi'en to her a silver wand,
With seven living lavrocks° sitting thereon.

She's gi'en to him a diamond ring,
With seven bright diamonds set therein.   10

"When this ring grows pale and wan,
You may know by it my love is gane."

One day° as he looked his ring upon,
He saw the diamonds pale and wan.

He left the sea and came to land,   15
And the first that he met was an old beggar man.

"What news, what news?" said young Hind Horn;
"No news, no news," said the old beggar man.

"No news," said the beggar, "no news at a',
But there is a wedding in the king's ha'.   20

"But there is a wedding in the king's ha',
That has halden° these forty days and twa."

"Will ye lend me your begging coat?
And I'll lend you my scarlet cloak.

HIND HORN. "Hind Horn" and the two ballads that follow,
"Kemp Owyne" and "Thomas Rymer" were probably
composed during the fourteenth or fifteenth century; they
were not collected and printed however until several
centuries later. The texts are based on versions in F. J.
Child, *The English and Scottish Popular Ballads* (1882),
Volume I, numbers 17, 34, and 37. **2. etc.**: refrain to be
repeated in each stanza. **3. Hind Horn:** Young Horn.
8. lavrocks: larks. **13. One day:** Another version of the
ballad describes the exile implied here: "Seven long years
he served the king, / An it's a' for the sake of his daughter
Jean. / The king an angry man was he; / He send young
Hyn Horn to the sea." **22. halden:** been held.

"Will you lend me your beggar's rung?°   25
And I'll gi'e you my steed to ride upon.

"Will you lend me your wig o' hair,
To cover mine, because it is fair?"

The old beggar man was bound for the mill,
But young Hind Horn for the king's hall.   30

The old beggar man was bound for to ride,
But young Hind Horn was bound for the bride.

When he came to the king's gate,
He sought a drink for Hind Horn's sake.

The bride came down with a glass of wine,   35
When he drank out the glass, and dropped in the
    ring.

"O got ye this by sea or land?
Or got ye it off a dead man's hand?"

"I got not it by sea, I got it by land,
And I got it, madam, out of your hand."   40

"O I'll cast off my gowns of brown,
And beg wi' you frae town to town.

"O I'll cast off my gowns of red,
And I'll beg wi' you to win my bread."

"Ye needna cast off your gowns of brown,   45
For I'll make you lady o' many a town.

"Ye needna cast off your gowns of red,
It's only a sham, the begging o' my bread."

The bridegroom he had wedded the bride,
But young Hind Horn he took her to bed.   50

Kemp Owyne°
ca. 1300–1400

Her mother died when she was young,
    Which gave her cause to make great moan;
Her father married the warst woman
    That ever lived in Christendom.

She served her with foot and hand,   5
    In every thing that she could dee,
Till once, in an unlucky time,
    She threw her in ower Craigy's sea.°

Says, "Lie you there, dove Isabel,
    And all my sorrows lie with thee;   10
Till Kemp Owyne come ower the sea,
    And borrow you with kisses three,
Let all the warld do what they will,
    Oh borrowed shall you never be!"

Her breath grew strang, her hair grew lang,   15
    And twisted thrice about the tree,
And all the people, far and near,
    Thought that a savage beast was she.

These news did come to Kemp Owyne,
    Where he lived, far beyond the sea;   20
He hasted him to Craigy's sea,
    And on the savage beast looked he.

Her breath was strang, her hair was lang,
    And twisted was about the tree,
And with a swing she came about: 25
    "Come to Craigy's sea, and kiss with me.

"Here is a royal belt," she cried,
    "That I have found in the green sea;
And while your body it is on,
    Drawn shall your blood never be;   30
But if you touch me, tail or fin,
    I vow my belt your death shall be."

He stepped in, gave her a kiss,
    The royal belt he brought him wi';
Her breath was strang, her hair was lang,   35
    And twisted twice about the tree,
And with a swing she came about:
    "Come to Craigy's sea, and kiss with me.°

"Here is a royal ring," she said,
    "That I have found in the green sea;   40
And while your finger it is on,
    Drawn shall your blood never be;
But if you touch me, tail or fin,
    I swear my ring your death shall be."

He stepped in, gave her a kiss,   45
    The royal ring he brought him wi';
Her breath was strang, her hair was lang,
    And twisted ance about the tree,

---

25. rung: staff.

KEMP OWYNE. Champion Owain, one of King Arthur's knights. **8. ower . . . sea:** over Craigy's sea; a variant of this line is "craig (crag) of the sea."

29–38. And . . . me: The apparent contradiction between the belt (and later the ring and sword) as a protection in one instance and a threat in another is explained by the Icelandic saga that is one source for the ballad. In the saga the condition is set that if the hero hesitates to kiss the monster (here, "if you touch me, tail or fin"), he will be killed by the object that would otherwise protect him.

And with a swing she came about:
   "Come to Craigy's sea, and kiss with me.   50

"Here is a royal brand,"° she said,
   "That I have found in the green sea;
And while your body it is on,
   Drawn shall your blood never be;
But if you touch me, tail or fin,   55
   I swear my brand your death shall be."

He stepped in, gave her a kiss,
   The royal brand he brought him wi';
Her breath was sweet, her hair grew short,
   And twisted nane about the tree,   60
And smilingly she came about,
   As fair a woman as fair could be.

Thomas Rymer°

ca. 1300–1400

True Thomas lay on Huntly bank;°
   A ferly° he spied wi' his ee;
And there he saw a lady bright
   Come riding down by the Eildon Tree.

Her shirt was o' the grass-green silk,   5
   Her mantle o' the velvet fine;
At ilka tett° of her horse's mane
   Hung fifty sil'er bells and nine.

True Thomas, he pulled off his cap
   And louted° low down to his knee: 10
"All hail, thou mighty Queen of Heaven!
   For thy peer on earth I never did see."

"O no, O no, Thomas," she said,
   "That name does not belang to me;
I am but the Queen of fair Elfland,   15
   That am hither come to visit thee.

"Harp and carp,° Thomas," she said,
   "Harp and carp along wi' me,
And if ye dare to kiss my lips,
   Sure of your body I will be."   20

51. brand: sword.

THOMAS RYMER. A prophet ("True Thomas") and poet ("rhymer") reputed to have lived in Scotland in the thirteenth or fourteenth century; the ballad, however, is based on an earlier romance narrative, which it uses to record Thomas' achievement of prophetic powers. **1. Huntly bank:** Huntly bank and the stone marking the Eildon Tree are in southern Scotland. **2. ferly:** marvel. **7. ilka tett:** each lock of hair. **10. louted:** bowed. **17. harp and carp:** sing and chant tales.

"Betide me weal, betide me woe,
   That weird° shall never daunten me."
Sine° he has kissed her rosy lips,
   All underneath the Eildon Tree.

"Now, ye maun go wi' me," she said,   25
   "True Thomas, ye maun go wi' me;
And ye maun serve me seven years
   Through weal or woe, as may chance to be."

She mounted on her milk-white steed;
   She's ta'en True Thomas up behind;   30
And aye whene'er her bridle rung,
   The steed flew swifter than the wind.

O they rade on, and farther on;
   The steed gaed swifter than the wind,
Until they reached a desert wide,   35
   And living land was left behind.

"Light down, light down, now, True Thomas,
   And lean your head upon my knee;
Abide and rest a little space,
   And I will show you ferlies three.   40

"O see ye not yon narrow road,
   So thick beset with thorns and briers?
That is the path of righteousness,
   Though after it but few inquires.

"And see not ye that braid braid road,   45
   That lies across that lily leven?°
That is the path of wickedness,
   Though some call it the road to heaven.

"And see not ye that bonny road,
   That winds about the ferny brae?°   50
That is the road to fair Elfland,
   Where thou and I this night maun gae.

"But, Thomas, ye maun hold your tongue,
   Whatever ye may hear or see;
For, if you speak word in Elfenland,   55
   Ye'll ne'er get back to your ain country."

O they rade on and farther on,
   And they waded through rivers aboon the knee,
And they saw neither sun nor moon,
   But they heard the roaring of the sea.   60

It was mirk° mirk night, and there was nae stern-
    light,°
   And they waded through red blude to the knee;

22. weird: fate. **23. sine:** then. **46. leven:** glade or lawn. **50. ferny brae:** fern-covered hillside. **61. mirk:** dark. **stern-light:** starlight.

For a' the blude that's shed on earth
　　Rins through the springs o' that country.

Sine they came on to a garden green,　　65
　　And she pulled an apple frae a tree:
"Take this for thy wages, True Thomas,
　　It will give the tongue that can never lie."

"My tongue is mine ain," True Thomas said;
　　"A gudely gift ye wad gi'e to me!　　70
I neither dought° to buy nor sell,
　　At fair or tryst where I may be.

71. dought: feared.

"I dought neither speak to prince or peer,
　　Nor ask of grace frae fair lady."
"Now hold thy peace," the lady said,　　75
　　"For as I say, so must it be."

He has gotten a coat of the even cloth,
　　And a pair of shoes of velvet green;
And till seven years were gane and past,
　　True Thomas on earth was never seen.　　80

Last-Phase Romance:
Descent and Recognition

Sir Orfeo

ca. 1300–1325

Translated by John Hampden

The lays which minstrels sing to their harps are full of good things. Some of them sing of happiness and some of sorrow, some of joy and mirth, others of treachery and guile, jests or ribaldry, and some of fairyland. But above all they sing of love.

These lays were first sung in Brittany, for when Bretons heard of daring deeds or great events they took up their harps gaily and made new songs. I do not know them all, but if you will listen, my lords, I will sing you the lay of Sir Orfeo.

Orfeo was a king, a very noble English lord, bold and valiant, generous and courteous too. His father was descended from King Pluto[1] and his mother from King Juno,[2] who were once believed to be gods because of the things which they did.

Orfeo took more pleasure in harping than in anything else, and always did honor to a good minstrel. He loved to play the harp himself; he gave his keen mind to it and learned to play so well that there was not a better harper in the world. Any man who heard Orfeo play would think himself in paradise, there was such melody in that harping.

This King lived in Thrace,[3] a city with noble defenses, which was no doubt the city now called Winchester. He had a good Queen, Dame Heurodis, the most beautiful lady alive, who was full of love and goodness. No man can say how beautiful she was.

Now early in the month of May, when the days are warm and happy, wintry showers are over, and every field is full of flowers and every branch is glorious with blossom, this Queen, Dame Heurodis, with two noble maidens, went one morning to enjoy herself beside an orchard, to look at the flowers and listen to the birds singing.

They all three sat down under a fair orchard-tree, and very soon the Queen fell asleep on the green grass. The maidens dared not wake her; they let her lie and take her rest, so she slept unto the afternoon. But when she awoke she cried and screamed, she tore at her hands and her feet, she clawed her face until it streamed with blood, and tore her rich dress to shreds; she was out of her mind. The two maidens dared not stay with her. They ran to the palace and bade the knights and squires to come and restrain her. The knights and ladies, sixty maidens and more, ran to the Queen in the orchard, and they took her up in their arms and carried her to her bed. They held her fast, but still she screamed and struggled to break free.

When Orfeo heard this news he was more miserable than ever in his life before. He came with ten knights to the Queen's chamber, and looked at her, and then, full of pity, he said,

"My dear life, what ails you, who have always been so quiet and now cry out so shrilly? Your lovely white body is torn by your nails. Your beautiful face, which was full of color, is as pale as if you were dead. Your little fingers are blood-stained and white. Your lovely eyes are like the

SIR ORFEO. **1. Pluto:** Greek god of the underworld. **2. Juno:** Roman goddess (not a king) and consort of Jupiter. **3. Thrace:** part of Greece, taken by the poet to be the ancient name for Winchester, which was the capital of medieval England.

eyes of a man glaring at his foe. Oh, my lady, I beg you, cease this pitiful crying and tell me what ails you, and how it came about, and what can be done to help you now."

Then she lay still at last and began to weep bitterly, and she said to the King,

"Alas, my lord, Sir Orfeo, since we first came together there has never once been any discord between us; I have always loved you as my life, and so have you loved me. But now we must part. You must do the best you can, for I must leave you."

"Alas!" he said, "Where are you going, and to whom? Wherever you go I will go with you, and wherever I go you shall come with me."

"No, no, sir! That cannot be. I will tell you everything. As I lay asleep beside the orchard at noon there came to me two fair knights, armed point-device,[4] who bade me come in haste to speak with their King. I answered boldly that I dared not and would not go. They galloped away as fast as they could, and then their King appeared, with a hundred knights and more, and a hundred damsels, all mounted on snow-white steeds and wearing clothes as white as milk. Never before have I seen such noble beings. The King wore a crown which was not made of silver or red gold; it was a precious stone which shone like the sun. He seized me and compelled me, against my will, to ride beside him on a palfrey to his palace. It was furnished nobly in every way, and he showed me castles and towers, rivers, forests, parks full of flowers, and all his splendid horses. Then he brought me back to our orchard, and he said, 'See to it, lady, that to-morrow you are here under this orchard-tree, for then you are to go with us and live with us for ever. If you resist you will be found and brought to me, no matter where you are, and even if we have to tear you limb from limb we shall carry you off.'"

When King Orfeo heard this he cried, "Alas, alas, I would rather lose my life than lose the Queen, my wife, like this." He asked counsel from them all but no one could help him.

At noon next day Orfeo seized his weapons and with fully a thousand knights, all of them strongly armed, he escorted the queen to the orchard-tree. There, drawn up in ranks around her, they swore that they would hold their ground and die to the last man before the Queen should be taken away.

And yet the Queen was taken from their midst by magic, and no one knew what had become of her.

Then there was crying, weeping and grief. The King went to his chamber, and there he lay swooning and lamenting on the stone floor until he was near to death, but nothing was of any use.

He called for his barons, earls and famous lords and when they had all gathered he said,

"My lords, here before you all I appoint my high steward to be regent of my kingdom. He shall stand in my place, to guard my lands everywhere. For now that I have lost my Queen, the fairest lady that was ever born, I will never look upon a woman again; I shall go into the wilderness, to live with wild beasts in the gray woods. When you know that I am dead, then call a parliament and choose a new king. Now do the best that you can with all my affairs."

Then there was weeping and a great outcry in the hall. Hardly anyone, young or old, could speak a word; they all kneeled down and begged him not to leave them. "Say no more!" he said, "It shall be so."

He forsook his kingdom. He put on a pilgrim's mantle, without kirtle or hood, he took nothing but his harp, and he went barefoot out of the gate. He allowed no one to go with him.

What weeping and grief there was, when he who had been a crowned king left them in that humble dress! Through wood and heath he went out into the wilderness, and there was nothing but hardship in the life he lived. He who had worn vair[5] and gray fur, and had fine purple linen on his bed, now lay on the hard ground, covering himself with leaves and grass. He who had owned castles and towers, rivers, forests and flowering parklands, had now to make his bed of moss, even in frost and snow. He who had had noble knights and ladies kneeling before him now saw only snakes gliding by. He who had had plenty of food and drink, and every delicacy, had now to dig and grub in the earth all day before he found his fill of roots. In summer he lived on wild fruit and berries that were poor food indeed: in winter he could find nothing but roots, grasses and the bark of trees. His whole body was scarred and wasted away by hardship. Lord, who can tell how this King suffered for ten years or more? His rough, black

4. point-device: completely and correctly.

5. vair: fur made of alternate pieces of the gray back and white belly of the squirrel.

beard grew down to his waist. His harp, his only joy, he hid in a hollow tree, but when the weather was clear and bright he took it out and played on it to his heart's content. The music sounded through the wood until all the wild beasts drew near in delight and all the birds perched on the briars around him to listen to his harping, the melody was so sweet. But when he stopped no creature would stay with him.

Often in the heat of noon Orfeo saw the King of Fairyland and all his company come to hunt, with thin cries, with blowing of horns and baying of hounds, but they caught nothing and Orfeo never knew what became of them. At other times a great host would sweep by him, a thousand knights armed point-device, looking fierce and proud, with their swords drawn and their banners unfurled, but he never knew where they went. Sometimes he saw knights and ladies in elegant attire, dancing with light and skillful steps while tabors and trumpets went beside them, and all manner of minstrelsy.

Then one day sixty ladies came riding by as gay and graceful as birds on a leafy spray, and not one man with them. They rode hawking by a river, for they all carried falcons on their hands. There were plenty of game-birds—mallards, herons and cormorants. The waterfowl rose, the falcons descried them and every one brought down his prey. When Orfeo saw that he laughed. "On my word," he said, "that is good sport! I will go to them in God's name, for I was once well used to seeing such things." As he drew near he saw that one of the ladies was his own Queen, Dame Heurodis. Longingly they gazed at each other, but neither spoke a word. When she saw him in that plight, who had been so rich and noble, the tears fell from her eyes, but the other ladies forced her to ride away.

"Alas," he cried, "why does not death take me now? I have lived too long when I dare not speak a word to my wife and she dare not speak to me. But come what may I will ride after these ladies. I do not care whether I live or die." At that he put on his pilgrim's mantle, and hung his harp upon his back, and went eagerly on his way. He stopped for nothing. When the ladies rode into a rock he followed them at once.

Three miles or more he traveled through the rock until he came into a fair country, bright as a summer's day, and green and flat; there was not a hill or valley to be seen. In the midst of it stood a magnificent royal castle. Its outer wall shone like crystal, a hundred battlemented towers surrounded it, and the buttresses which rose from its moat were bright with red gold. The vaulting was adorned with carvings of every kind of animal in the world, the wide halls within were all of precious stones, and the meanest pillar was made of burnished gold. In that country it was always light, for at night the rich stones shone as brightly as the sun at noon. No man can imagine how splendid the castle was. Orfeo thought that it was the glorious court of Paradise.

The ladies entered this castle, and he wished to follow them, so when he reached the gate he knocked. The porter asked him what he wanted.

"On my word," said Sir Orfeo, "I am a minstrel, as you see. I will entertain your Lord with my music, if he be willing to listen."

The porter opened the gate at once and let him into the castle, and Orfeo began to look about him. He saw in the courtyard many folk who are believed to be dead, but have not died. Some stood there without their heads, some had no arms, or were wounded through the body, and some were madmen, lying in bonds. Others were fully armed and mounted on horseback. Some had been strangled as they were eating, or drowned in water, or burned with fire. Women lay there in childbed, dead or raving. Others slept as though they were taking a noonday rest. All were just as they had been when the fairies took them out of this world. And there Sir Orfeo saw his wife, Dame Heurodis, who was as dear to him as his own life, sleeping under an orchard-tree; he knew her by her clothes.

When he had seen all these marvels he went into the King's hall. There stood a glorious throne, under a canopy, and the King and Queen were seated there, wearing crowns and robes which shone so brightly that he could hardly bear to look at them. He knelt before the throne and said,

"My lord, if you will you shall hear my minstrelsy."

"Who are you?" asked the King. "Neither I nor anyone about me sent for you. Since I began to reign here I have never seen any other man foolhardy enough to journey hither unless he was sent for."

"My lord," said Sir Orfeo, "I am only a poor minstrel, and, sir, it is the custom among us to visit many a lord's house. Even if we are not welcome we must offer to make music."

Sitting down before the King he took his merry-sounding harp and tuned it skillfully, and then he struck from it notes so blissful that all who were in the palace came to hear him and lay down at his feet, they thought his melody so sweet. The King sat very still, for both he and his noble Queen took great joy in Orfeo's harping.

When it came to an end the King said to him.

"Minstrel, your playing pleases me greatly. Ask of me whatever you wish and I will give it to you."

"Sir," answered Orfeo, "I beseech you to give me the lady with the beautiful face who is sleeping under the orchard-tree."

"No," said the King, "That is impossible. What an ill-matched pair you would be! You are so gaunt, black and unkempt, while she is lovely, without a blemish. It would be a horrible thing to see her in your company."

"Oh sir," he cried, "noble King, it would be more horrible still to hear a lie from your lips. You said that I should have anything I asked. You must keep your word."

The King answered, "Since it must be so, take her by the hand and go. I wish you joy of her."

Then Sir Orfeo knelt and thanked him exceedingly. He took his wife by the hand and went quickly from that country, returning by the way he had come.

He traveled on until he came to Winchester, his own city, but he dared not go beyond the town's end, for fear of being known, so he found a poor lodging there, with a beggar, for himself and his wife, as though he were a minstrel of low degree; and he asked what was the news of that country, and who was the ruler of it. The poor beggar told him everything: how the Queen had been stolen away by the fairies ten years ago, how the King had gone into exile, no man knew where; and how the steward ruled the land. And many other things the beggar told him.

The next day, towards noon, he borrowed the beggar's clothes, hung his harp on his back and, bidding his wife stay in the cottage, he went into the city, so that he could be seen. Earls and bold barons, burgesses and ladies, looked at him and said, "What a man! His hair is so long and his beard reaches to his knees! And he is as withered as a dead tree!"

Walking along the street he met his steward and called to him loudly, "Sir Steward, take pity on me! I am a harper from heathen lands. Help me in my need!"

The steward answered, "Come with me. You shall share what I have. Every good harper is welcome to me, for the love of my lord Sir Orfeo."

In the castle the steward sat at table, with many lords beside him, while trumpeters and tabor-players, harpers and fiddlers made great music. Sir Orfeo sat quiet in the hall and listened. When they were all silent he took his harp and tuned it loudly, and then he played there the most joyful melody that ever man heard. They were all enchanted by his harping.

The Steward knew the harp at once. "Minstrel!" he said, "as you hope to thrive, where and how did you get that harp? I pray you, tell me at once."

"My lord," he answered, "I was traveling through a wilderness in a strange country when I found, in a dale, a man who had been torn to pieces by lions and wolves, and beside his body I found this harp. It was a full ten years ago."

"Oh," cried the Steward, "alas! That was my lord Sir Orfeo! Unhappy wretch that I am, what shall I do now that I have lost so good a lord? Alas, that I was ever born! that so hard a lot was ordained for him and he was marked out for so vile a death!"

He fell swooning to the ground, but his baron lifted him up and told him that in the course of nature there is no remedy for death.

Then King Orfeo was certain that his steward was a true man, who loved his King as he ought to do, so Orfeo stood up and cried,

"Now, steward, listen to this! If I were King Orfeo, and had long suffered greatly in the wilderness, and had won my Queen back from the realm of the fairies and had come here in this humble disguise to test you, and had found you true, you should never regret it. In any case you should certainly be king after me. But if you had been glad to hear that I was dead you would have been quickly dismissed from your office."

Then all those gathered there saw that it was King Orfeo, and the Steward knew him well. He overturned the table and threw himself at the King's feet. All the lords did the same, and they all cried,

"You are our lord, sire, and our king!"

They were overjoyed to see him alive; they took him at once to a chamber, bathed him and shaved his beard, and robed him like a king, for all to see. Then they brought the Queen into the town in a great procession, with all manner of minstrelsy. Lord, there was great music-making! They wept for joy to see the King and Queen return unharmed.

Now King Orfeo was crowned afresh, with his Queen Heurodis. They lived for many years, and then the Steward was made king.

Afterwards minstrels in Brittany heard this marvelous tale, and made it into a pleasant lay to which they gave the King's name, Sir Orfeo. Good is the lay, and sweet its melody.

Thus Sir Orfeo came out of his sorrow. God grant us all to fare as well.

SAMUEL TAYLOR COLERIDGE
1772–1834

The Rime
of the Ancient Mariner

IN SEVEN PARTS

PART I

An ancient Mariner meeteth three Gallants bidden to a wedding-feast, and detaineth one.

It is an ancient Mariner,
And he stoppeth one of three.
"By thy long gray beard and glittering eye,
Now wherefore stopp'st thou me?

The Bridegroom's doors are opened wide,   5
And I am next of kin;
The guests are met, the feast is set:
May'st hear the merry din."

He holds him with his skinny hand,
"There was a ship," quoth he.   10
"Hold off! unhand me, graybeard loon!"
Eftsoons° his hand dropped he.

The Wedding-Guest is spellbound by the eye of the old seafaring man, and constrained to hear his tale.

He holds him with his glittering eye—
The Wedding-Guest stood still,   14
And listens like a three years' child:
The Mariner hath his will.

The Wedding-Guest sat on a stone:
He cannot choose but hear;
And thus spake on that ancient man,
The bright-eyed Mariner.   20

The Mariner tells how the ship sailed southward with a good wind and fair weather, till it reached the Line.

"The ship was cheered, the harbor cleared,
Merrily did we drop
Below the kirk, below the hill,
Below the lighthouse top.

The Sun came up upon the left,   25
Out of the sea came he!
And he shone bright, and on the right
Went down into the sea.

Higher and higher every day,
Till over the mast at noon—"°   30
The Wedding-Guest here beat his breast,
For he heard the loud bassoon.

The Wedding-Guest heareth the bridal music; but the Mariner continueth his tale.

The bride hath paced into the hall,
Red as a rose is she;   34
Nodding their heads before her goes
The merry minstrelsy.

The Wedding-Guest he beat his breast,
Yet he cannot choose but hear;
And thus spake on that ancient man,
The bright-eyed Mariner.   40

The ship driven by a storm toward the South Pole.

"And now the STORM-BLAST came, and he
Was tyrannous and strong:
He struck with his o'ertaking wings
And chased us south along.

With sloping masts and dipping prow,   45
As who pursued with yell and blow
Still treads the shadow of his foe,
And forward bends his head,
The ship drove fast, loud roared the blast,
And southward aye we fled.   50

THE RIME OF THE ANCIENT MARINER. **12. Eftsoons:** soon.

30. noon: The ship had reached the equator (the "Line").

And now there came both mist and
    snow,
And it grew wondrous cold:
And ice, mast-high, came floating by,
As green as emerald.

*The land of
ice, and of
fearful sounds
where no
living thing
was to be
seen.*

And through the drifts the snowy
    clifts   55
Did send a dismal sheen:
Nor shapes of men nor beasts we
    ken—
The ice was all between.

The ice was here, the ice was there,
The ice was all around: 60
It cracked and growled, and roared
    and howled,
Like noises in a swound!°

*Till a great
sea-bird
called the
Albatross,
came through
the snow-fog,
and was
received with
great joy and
hospitality.*

At length did cross an Albatross,
Through the fog it came;
As if it had been a Christian soul,   65
We hailed it in God's name.

It ate the food it ne'er had eat,
And round and round it flew.
The ice did split with a thunder-fit;
The helmsman steered us through! 70

*And lo! the
Albatross
proveth a bird
of good omen,
and followeth
the ship as it
returned
northward
through fog
and floating
ice.*

And a good south wind sprung up
    behind;
The Albatross did follow,
And every day, for food or play,
Came to the mariners' hollo!

In mist or cloud, on mast or
    shroud,   75
It perched for vespers nine;
Whiles all the night, through fog-
    smoke white,
Glimmered the white Moon-shine."

*The ancient
Mariner
inhospitably
killeth the
pious bird of
good omen.*

"God save thee, ancient Mariner!
From the fiends, that plague thee
    thus!—   80
Why look'st thou so?"—With my
    crossbow
I shot the ALBATROSS.

PART II

The Sun now rose upon the right:°
Out of the sea came he,
Still hid in mist, and on the left   85
Went down into the sea.

And the good south wind still blew
    behind,
But no sweet bird did follow,
Nor any day for food or play
Came to the mariners' hollo!   90

*His shipmates
cry out against
the ancient
Mariner, for
killing the
bird of good
luck.*

And I had done a hellish thing,
And it would work 'em woe:
For all averred, I had killed the bird
That made the breeze to blow.
Ah wretch! said they, the bird to
    slay,   95
That made the breeze to blow!

*But when the
fog cleared
off, they
justify the
same, and
thus make
themselves
accomplices
in the crime.*

Nor dim nor red, like God's own
    head,
The glorious Sun uprist:
Then all averred, I had killed the bird
That brought the fog and mist.   100
'Twas right, said they, such birds to
    slay,
That bring the fog and mist.

*The fair
breeze con-
tinues; the
ship enters the
Pacific Ocean,
and sails
northward,
even till it
reaches the
Line.*

The fair breeze blew, the white foam
    flew,
The furrow followed free;
We were the first that ever burst 105
Into that silent sea.

*The ship hath
been suddenly
becalmed.*

Down dropped the breeze, the sails
    dropped down,
'Twas sad as sad could be;
And we did speak only to break
The silence of the sea!   110

All in a hot and copper sky,
The bloody Sun, at noon,
Right up above the mast did stand,
No bigger than the Moon.

Day after day, day after day,   115
We stuck, nor breath nor motion;
As idle as a painted ship
Upon a painted ocean.

---

62. swound: swoon.

83. Sun . . . right: The ship has rounded Cape Horn and is
heading north.

And the Albatross begins to be avenged.

Water, water, everywhere,
And all the boards did shrink;   120
Water, water, everywhere,
Nor any drop to drink.

A Spirit had followed them; one of the invisible inhabitants of this planet, neither departed souls nor angels; concerning whom the learned Jew, Josephus, and the Platonic Constantinopolitan, Michael Psellus, may be consulted. They are very numerous, and there is no climate or element without one or more.

The very deep did rot; O Christ!
That ever this should be!   124
Yea, slimy things did crawl with legs
Upon the slimy sea.

About, about in reel and rout
The death-fires° danced at night;
The water, like a witch's oils,
Burnt green, and blue and white.   130

And some in dreams assurèd were
Of the Spirit that plagued us so;
Nine fathom deep he had followed us
From the land of mist and snow.

The shipmates, in their sore distress, would fain throw the whole guilt on the ancient Mariner: in sign whereof they hang the dead sea-bird round his neck.

And every tongue, through utter drought,   135
Was withered at the root;
We could not speak, no more than if
We had been choked with soot.

Ah! well a-day! what evil looks
Had I from old and young!   140
Instead of the cross, the Albatross
About my neck was hung.

PART III

There passed a weary time. Each throat
Was parched, and glazed each eye.
A weary time! a weary time!   145
How glazed each weary eye,
When looking westward, I beheld
A something in the sky.

The ancient Mariner beholdeth a sign in the element afar off.

At first it seemed a little speck,
And then it seemed a mist;   150
It moved and moved, and took at last
A certain shape, I wist.°

A speck, a mist, a shape, I wist!
And still it neared and neared:

As if it dodged a water-sprite,   155
It plunged and tacked and veered.

At its nearer approach, it seemeth him to be a ship; and at a dear ransom he freeth his speech from the bonds of thirst.

With throats unslaked, with black lips baked,
We could nor laugh nor wail;
Through utter drought all dumb we stood!
I bit my arm, I sucked the blood,   160
And cried, A sail! a sail!

A flash of joy;

With throats unslaked, with black lips baked,
Agape they heard me call:
Gramercy! they for joy did grin,   164
And all at once their breath drew in,
As° they were drinking all.

And horror follows. For can it be a ship that comes onward without wind or tide?

See! see! (I cried) she tacks no more!
Hither to work us weal;
Without a breeze, without a tide,
She steadies with upright keel!   170

The western wave was all aflame.
The day was well nigh done!
Almost upon the western wave
Rested the broad bright Sun;
When that strange shape drove suddenly   175
Betwixt us and the Sun.

It seemeth him but the skeleton of a ship.

And straight the Sun was flecked with bars,
(Heaven's Mother send us grace!)
As if through a dungeon-grate he peered
With broad and burning face.   180

And its ribs are seen as bars on the face of the setting Sun.

Alas! (thought I, and my heart beat loud)
How fast she nears and nears!
Are those *her* sails that glance in the Sun,
Like restless gossameres?°

The Specter-Woman and her Death-mate, and no other on board the skeleton ship.

Are those *her* ribs through which the Sun   185
Did peer, as through a grate?
And is that Woman all her crew?
Is that a DEATH? and are there two?
Is DEATH that woman's mate?

128. **death-fires:** Saint Elmo's fire, atmospheric electricity in the rigging, taken by sailors as a bad omen. 152. **wist:** knew.

166. **as:** as if. 184. **gossameres:** cobwebs.

Like vessel, like crew! Death and Life-in-Death have diced for the ship's crew, and she (the latter) winneth the ancient Mariner.

Her lips were red, *her* looks were free,   190
Her locks were yellow as gold:
Her skin was as white as leprosy,
The Nightmare LIFE-IN-DEATH was she,
Who thicks man's blood with cold.

The naked hulk alongside came, 195
And the twain were casting dice;
"The game is done! I've won! I've won!"
Quoth she, and whistles thrice.

No twilight within the courts of the Sun.

The Sun's rim dips; the stars rush out:
At one stride comes the dark;   200
With far-heard whisper, o'er the sea,
Off shot the specter-bark.

At the rising, of the Moon,

We listened and looked sideways up!
Fear at my heart, as at a cup,
My lifeblood seemed to sip!   205
The stars were dim, and thick the night,
The steersman's face by his lamp gleamed white;
From the sails the dew did drip—
Till clomb° above the eastern bar
The hornèd Moon, with one bright star   210
Within the nether tip.

One after another,

One after one, by the star-dogged Moon,
Too quick for groan or sigh,
Each turned his face with a ghastly pang,
And cursed me with his eye.   215

His shipmates drop down dead.

Four times fifty living men,
(And I heard nor sigh nor groan)
With heavy thump, a lifeless lump,
They dropped down one by one. 219

But Life-in-Death begins her work on the ancient Mariner.

The souls did from their bodies fly,—
They fled to bliss or woe!
And every soul, it passed me by,
Like the whizz of my crossbow!

PART IV

The Wedding-Guest feareth that a Spirit is talking to him;

"I fear thee, ancient Mariner!
I fear thy skinny hand!   225
And thou art long, and lank, and brown,
As is the ribbed sea-sand.

I fear thee and thy glittering eye,
And thy skinny hand, so brown."—

But the ancient Mariner assureth him of his bodily life, and proceedeth to relate his horrible penance.

Fear not, fear not, thou Wedding-Guest!   230
This body dropped not down.

Alone, alone, all, all alone,
Alone on a wide wide sea!
And never a saint took pity on
My soul in agony.   235

He despiseth the creatures of the calm,

The many men, so beautiful!
And they all dead did lie:
And a thousand thousand slimy things
Lived on; and so did I.

And envieth that *they* should live, and so many lie dead.

I looked upon the rotting sea,   240
And drew my eyes away;
I looked upon the rotting deck,
And there the dead men lay.

I looked to heaven, and tried to pray;
But or° ever a prayer had gushed. 245
A wicked whisper came, and made
My heart as dry as dust.

I closed my lids, and kept them close,
And the balls like pulses beat;
For the sky and the sea, and the sea and the sky   250
Lay like a load on my weary eye,
And the dead were at my feet.

But the curse liveth for him in the eye of the dead men.

The cold sweat melted from their limbs,
Nor rot nor reek did they:
The look with which they looked on me   255
Had never passed away.

An orphan's curse would drag to hell
A spirit from on high;
But oh! more horrible than that
Is the curse in a dead man's eye! 260
Seven days, seven nights, I saw that curse,

---

209. clomb: climbed.   **245. or:** before.

In his lone-
liness and
fixedness he
yearneth to-
wards the
journeying
Moon, and
the stars that
still sojourn,
yet still move
onward; and
everywhere
the blue sky
belongs to

And yet I could not die.
The moving Moon went up the sky,
And nowhere did abide:
Softly she was going up,   265
And a star or two beside—
Her beams bemocked the sultry main,
Like April hoar-frost spread;
But where the ship's huge shadow lay,
The charmèd water burnt alway   270
A still and awful red.

them, and is their appointed rest, and their native country
and their own natural homes, which they enter unan-
nounced, as lords that are certainly expected and yet there
is a silent joy at their arrival.

By the light of
the Moon he
beholdeth
God's crea-
tures of the
great calm.

Beyond the shadow of the ship,
I watched the water-snakes:
They moved in tracks of shining
     white,
And when they reared, the elfish
     light   275
Fell off in hoary flakes.

Within the shadow of the ship
I watched their rich attire:
Blue, glossy green, and velvet black,
They coiled and swam; and every
     track   280
Was a flash of golden fire.

Their beauty
and their
happiness.

O happy living things! no tongue
Their beauty might declare:
A spring of love gushed from my
     heart,

He blesseth
them in his
heart.

And I blessed them unaware: 285
Sure my kind saint took pity on me,
And I blessed them unaware.

The spell be-
gins to break.

The selfsame moment I could pray;
And from my neck so free
The Albatross fell off, and sank 290
Like lead into the sea.

PART V

O sleep! it is a gentle thing,
Beloved from pole to pole!
To Mary Queen the praise be given!
She sent the gentle sleep from
     Heaven,   295
That slid into my soul.

By grace of
the holy
Mother, the
ancient
Mariner is re-
freshed with
rain.

The silly° buckets on the deck,
That had so long remained,
I dreamt that they were filled with
     dew;
And when I awoke, it rained.   300

My lips were wet, my throat was cold,
My garments all were dank;
Sure I had drunken in my dreams,
And still my body drank.

I moved, and could not feel my
     limbs: 305
I was so light—almost
I thought that I had died in sleep,
And was a blessed ghost.

He heareth
sounds and
seeth strange
sights and
commotions
in the sky and
the element.

And soon I heard a roaring wind:
It did not come anear;   310
But with its sound it shook the sails,
That were so thin and sere.

The upper air burst into life!
And a hundred fire-flags° sheen,
To and fro they were hurried
     about!   315
And to and fro, and in and out,
The wan stars danced between.

And the coming wind did roar more
     loud,
And the sails did sigh like sedge;°
And the rain poured down from one
     black cloud;   320
The Moon was at its edge.

The thick black cloud was cleft, and
     still
The Moon was at its side:
Like waters shot from some high
     crag,   324
The lightning fell with never a jag,
A river steep and wide.

The bodies of
the ship's crew
are inspired
and the ship
moves on;

The loud wind never reached the
     ship,
Yet now the ship moved on!
Beneath the lightning and the Moon
The dead men gave a groan.   330

297. silly: useless. **314. fire-flags:** aurora australis or the
southern lights. **319. sedge:** rushlike plant.

They groaned, they stirred, they all
    uprose,
Nor spake, nor moved their eyes;
It had been strange, even in a dream,
To have seen those dead men rise.

The helmsman steered, the ship
    moved on;   335
Yet never a breeze up-blew;
The mariners all 'gan work the ropes,
Where they were wont to do;
They raised their limbs like lifeless
    tools—
We were a ghastly crew.   340

The body of my brother's son
Stood by me, knee to knee:
The body and I pulled at one rope,
But he said nought to me.

But not by the souls of the men, nor by daemons of earth, or middle air, but by a blessed troop of angelic spirits, sent down by the invocation of the guardian saint.

"I fear thee, ancient Mariner!"   345
Be calm, thou Wedding-Guest!
'Twas not those souls that fled in
    pain,
Which to their corses° came again,
But a troop of spirits blest:

For when it dawned—they dropped
    their arms,   350
And clustered round the mast;
Sweet sounds rose slowly through
    their mouths,
And from their bodies passed.

Around, around, flew each sweet
    sound,
Then darted to the Sun;   355
Slowly the sounds came back again,
Now mixed, now one by one.

Sometimes a-dropping from the sky
I heard the skylark sing;
Sometimes all little birds that are,   360
How they seemed to fill the sea and
    air
With their sweet jargoning!

And now 'twas like all instruments,
Now like a lonely flute;
And now it is an angel's song,   365
That makes the heavens be mute.

348. corses: corpses.

It ceased; yet still the sails made on
A pleasant noise till noon,
A noise like of a hidden brook
In the leafy month of June,   370
That to the sleeping woods all night
Singeth a quiet tune.

Till noon we quietly sailed on,
Yet never a breeze did breathe: 374
Slowly and smoothly went the ship,
Moved onward from beneath.

The lonesome Spirit from the South Pole carries on the ship as far as the Line, in obedience to the angelic troop, but still requireth vengeance.

Under the keel nine fathom deep,
From the land of mist and snow,
The spirit slid: and it was he
That made the ship to go.   380
The sails at noon left off their tune,
And the ship stood still also.

The Sun, right up above the mast,
Had fixed her to the ocean:
But in a minute she 'gan stir,   385
With a short uneasy motion—
Backwards and forwards half her
    length
With a short uneasy motion.

Then like a pawing horse let go,
She made a sudden bound: 390
It flung the blood into my head,
And I fell down in a swound.

The Polar Spirit's fellow-daemons, the invisible inhabitants of the element, take part in his wrong; and two of them relate, one to the other, that penance long and heavy for the ancient Mariner hath been accorded to the Polar Spirit, who returneth southward.

How long in that same fit I lay,
I have not to declare;
But ere my living life returned,   395
I heard and in my soul discerned
Two voices in the air.

"Is it he?" quoth one, "Is this the
    man?
By him who died on cross,   399
With his cruel bow he laid full low
The harmless Albatross.

The spirit who bideth by himself
In the land of mist and snow,
He loved the bird that loved the man
Who shot him with his bow."   405

The other was a softer voice,
As soft as honeydew:
Quoth he, "The man hath penance
    done,
And penance more will do."   409

PART VI

FIRST VOICE

"But tell me, tell me! speak again,
Thy soft response renewing—
What makes that ship drive on so
  fast?
What is the ocean doing?"

SECOND VOICE

"Still as a slave before his lord,
The ocean hath no blast;   415
His great bright eye most silently
Up to the Moon is cast—

If he may know which way to go;
For she guides him smooth or grim.
See, brother, see! how graciously 420
She looketh down on him."

FIRST VOICE

The Mariner hath been cast into a trance; for the angelic power causeth the vessel to drive northward faster than human life could endure.

"But why drives on that ship so fast,
Without or wave or wind?"

SECOND VOICE

"The air is cut away before,
And closes from behind.   425

Fly, brother, fly! more high, more
  high!
Or we shall be belated:

For slow and slow that ship will go,
When the Mariner's trance is
  abated."

The supernatural motion is retarded; the Mariner awakes, and his penance begins anew.

I woke, and we were sailing on   430
As in a gentle weather:
'Twas night, calm night, the moon
  was high;
The dead men stood together.

All stood together on the deck,
For a charnel-dungeon fitter: 435
All fixed on me their stony eyes,
That in the Moon did glitter.

The pang, the curse, with which they
  died,
Had never passed away:

The curse is finally expiated.

I could not draw my eyes from
  theirs,   440
Nor turn them up to pray.

And now this spell was snapped:
  once more
I viewed the ocean green,
And looked far forth, yet little saw
Of what had else been seen—   445

Like one, that on a lonesome road
Doth walk in fear and dread,
And having once turned round walks
  on,
And turns no more his head;   449
Because he knows, a frightful fiend
Doth close behind him tread.

But soon there breathed a wind on
  me,
Nor sound nor motion made:
Its path was not upon the sea,
In ripple or in shade.   455

It raised my hair, it fanned my cheek
Like a meadow-gale of spring—
It mingled strangely with my fears,
Yet it felt like a welcoming.

Swiftly, swiftly flew the ship,   460
Yet she sailed softly too:
Sweetly, sweetly blew the breeze—
On me alone it blew.

And the ancient Mariner beholdeth his native country.

Oh! dream of joy! is this indeed
The lighthouse top I see?   465
Is this the hill? is this the kirk?
Is this mine own countree?

We drifted o'er the harbor-bar,
And I with sobs did pray—
O let me be awake, my God!   470
Or let me sleep alway.

The harbor-bay was clear as glass,
So smoothly it was strewn!
And on the bay the moonlight lay,
And the shadow of the Moon.   475

The rock shone bright, the kirk no
  less,
That stands above the rock:
The moonlight steeped in silentness
The steady weathercock.

And the bay was white with silent
    light,   480
Till rising from the same,

The angelic
spirits leave
the dead
bodies,
Full many shapes, that shadows were,
In crimson colors came.

A little distance from the prow

And appear in
their own
forms of light.
Those crimson shadows were: 485
I turned my eyes upon the deck—
Oh, Christ! what saw I there!

Each corse lay flat, lifeless and flat,
And, by the holy rood!°
A man all light, a seraph-man,   490
On every corse there stood.

This seraph-band, each waved his
    hand:
It was a heavenly sight!
They stood as signals to the land,
Each one a lovely light;   495

This seraph-band, each waved his
    hand,
No voice did they impart—
No voice; but oh! the silence sank
Like music on my heart.

But soon I heard the dash of oars, 500
I heard the Pilot's cheer;
My head was turned perforce away
And I saw a boat appear.

The Pilot and the Pilot's boy,
I heard them coming fast: 505
Dear Lord in Heaven! it was a joy
The dead men could not blast.

I saw a third—I heard his voice:
It is the Hermit good!
He singeth loud his godly hymns 510
That he makes in the wood.
He'll shrieve my soul, he'll wash away
The Albatross's blood.

PART VII

The Hermit of
the Wood,
This Hermit good lives in that wood
Which slopes down to the sea.   515
How loudly his sweet voice he rears!
He loves to talk with marineres
That come from a far countree.

He kneels at morn, and noon, and
    eve—
He hath a cushion plump: 520
It is the moss that wholly hides
The rotted old oak-stump.

The skiff-boat neared: I heard them
    talk,
"Why, this is strange, I trow!°
Where are those lights so many and
    fair,   525
That signal made but now?"

Approacheth
the ship with
wonder.
"Strange, by my faith!" the Hermit
    said—
"And they answered not our cheer!
The planks looked warped! and see
    those sails,
How thin they are and sere!   530
I never saw aught like to them,
Unless perchance it were

Brown skeletons of leaves that lag
My forest-brook along;
When the ivy-tod° is heavy with
    snow,   535
And the owlet whoops to the wolf
    below,

That eats the she-wolf's young."
"Dear Lord! it hath a fiendish look—
(The Pilot made reply)
I am a-feared"—"Push on, push
    on!"   540
Said the Hermit cheerily.

The boat came closer to the ship,
But I nor spake nor stirred;
The boat came close beneath the ship,
And straight a sound was heard.   545

The ship
suddenly
sinketh.
Under the water it rumbled on,
Still louder and more dread:
It reached the ship, it split the bay;
The ship went down like lead.

The ancient
Mariner is
saved in the
Pilot's boat.
Stunned by that loud and dreadful
    sound,   550
Which sky and ocean smote,
Like one that hath been seven days
    drowned
My body lay afloat;

---

489. rood: Cross.

524. trow: think. **535. ivy-tod:** ivy bush.

But swift as dreams, myself I found
Within the Pilot's boat.   555

Upon the whirl, where sank the ship,
The boat spun round and round;
And all was still, save that the hill
Was telling of the sound.

I moved my lips—the Pilot shrieked
And fell down in a fit;   561
The holy Hermit raised his eyes,
And prayed where he did sit.

I took the oars: the Pilot's boy,
Who now doth crazy go,   565
Laughed loud and long, and all the
    while
His eyes went to and fro.
"Ha! ha!" quoth he, "full plain I see,
The Devil knows how to row."

And now, all in my own countree, 570
I stood on the firm land!
The Hermit stepped forth from the
    boat,
And scarcely he could stand.

The ancient Mariner earnestly entreateth the Hermit to shrieve him; and the penance of life falls on him.
"O shrieve me, shrieve me, holy
    man!"
The Hermit crossed his brow.   575
"Say quick," quoth he, "I bid thee
    say—
What manner of man art thou?"

Forthwith this frame of mine was
    wrenched
With a woeful agony,   579
Which forced me to begin my tale;
And then it left me free.

And ever and anon throughout his future life an agony constraineth him to travel from land to land;
Since then, at an uncertain hour,
That agony returns:
And till my ghastly tale is told,
This heart within me burns.   585

I pass, like night, from land to land;
I have strange power of speech;
That moment that his face I see,
I know the man that must hear me:
To him my tale I teach.   590

What loud uproar bursts from that
    door!
The wedding-guests are there:

But in the garden-bower the bride
And bride-maids singing are:
And hark the little vesper bell,   595
Which biddeth me to prayer!

O Wedding-Guest! this soul hath
    been
Alone on a wide wide sea:
So lonely 'twas, that God himself
Scarce seemèd there to be.   600

O sweeter than the marriage-feast,
'Tis sweeter far to me,
To walk together to the kirk
With a goodly company!—

To walk together to the kirk,   605
And all together pray,
While each to his great Father bends,
Old men, and babes, and loving
    friends
And youths and maidens gay!

And to teach, by his own example, love and reverence to all things that God made and loveth.
Farewell, farewell! but this I tell   610
To thee, thou Wedding-Guest!
He prayeth well, who loveth well
Both man and bird and beast.

He prayeth best, who loveth best
All things both great and small;   615
For the dear God who loveth us,
He made and loveth all.

The Mariner, whose eye is bright,
Whose beard with age is hoar,
Is gone: and now the Wedding-
    Guest   620
Turned from the bridegroom's door.

He went like one that hath been
    stunned,
And is of sense forlorn:
A sadder and a wiser man,
He rose the morrow morn.   625

ALFRED, LORD TENNYSON
1809–1892

from Idylls of the King

THE PASSING OF ARTHUR

That story which the bold Sir Bedivere,
First made and latest left of all the knights,
Told, when the man was no more than a voice
In the white winter of his age, to those
With whom he dwelt, new faces, other minds.   5

For on their march to westward, Bedivere,
Who slowly paced among the slumbering host,
Heard in his tent the moanings of the king:

"I found Him in the shining of the stars,
I marked Him in the flowering of His fields,   10
But in His ways with men I find Him not.
I waged His wars, and now I pass and die.
O me! for why is all around us here
As if some lesser god had made the world,
But had not force to shape it as he would,   15
Till the High God behold it from beyond,
And enter it, and make it beautiful?
Or else as if the world were wholly fair,
But that these eyes of men are dense and dim,
And have not power to see it as it is: 20
Perchance, because we see not to the close;—
For I, being simple, thought to work His will,
And have but stricken with the sword in vain;
And all whereon I leaned in wife and friend°
Is traitor to my peace, and all my realm   25
Reels back into the beast, and is no more.
My God, thou hast forgotten me in my death:
Nay—God my Christ—I pass but shall not die."

Then, ere that last weird battle in the west,
There came on Arthur sleeping, Gawain killed   30
In Lancelot's war, the ghost of Gawain blown
Along a wandering wind, and past his ear
Went shrilling, "Hollow, hollow all delight!
Hail, King! tomorrow thou shalt pass away.
Farewell! there is an isle of rest for thee.   35

And I am blown along a wandering wind,
And hollow, hollow, hollow all delight."
And fainter onward, like wild birds that change
Their season in the night and wail their way
From cloud to cloud, down the long wind the
    dream   40
Shrilled; but in going mingled with dim cries
Far in the moonlight haze among the hills,
As of some lonely city sacked by night,
When all is lost, and wife and child with wail
Pass to new lords; and Arthur woke and called,   45
"Who spake? A dream. O light upon the wind,
Thine, Gawain, was the voice—are these dim cries
Thine? or doth all that haunts the waste and wild
Mourn, knowing it will go along with me?"

This heard the bold Sir Bedivere and spake: 50
"O me, my king, let pass whatever will,
Elves, and the harmless glamor° of the field;
But in their stead thy name and glory cling
To all high places like a golden cloud
Forever: but as yet thou shalt not pass.   55
Light was Gawain in life, and light in death
Is Gawain, for the ghost is as the man;
And care not thou for dreams from him, but rise—
I hear the steps of Modred in the west,
And with him many of thy people, and knights   60
Once thine, whom thou hast loved, but grosser
    grown
Than heathen, spitting at their vows and thee.
Right well in heart they know thee for the king.
Arise, go forth and conquer as of old."

Then spake King Arthur to Sir Bedivere: 65
"Far other is this battle in the west
Whereto we move, than when we strove in youth,
And brake the petty kings, and fought with Rome,
Or thrust the heathen from the Roman wall,
And shook him through the north. Ill doom is
    mine   70
To war against my people and my knights.
The king who fights his people fights himself.
And they my knights, who loved me once, the
    stroke
That strikes them dead is as my death to me.
Yet let us hence, and find or feel a way   75
Through this blind haze, which ever since I saw
One lying in the dust at Almesbury,°

Hath folded in the passes of the world."

Then rose the king and moved his host by night,
And ever pushed Sir Modred, league by league,   80
Back to the sunset bound of Lyonesse—°
A land of old upheaven from the abyss
By fire, to sink into the abyss again;
Where fragments of forgotten peoples dwelt,
And the long mountains ended in a coast   85
Of ever-shifting sand, and far away
The phantom circle of a moaning sea.
There the pursuer could pursue no more,
And he that fled no further fly the king;
And there, that day when the great light of heaven
Burned at his lowest in the rolling year,°   91
On the waste sand by the waste sea they closed.
Nor ever yet had Arthur fought a fight
Like this last, dim, weird battle of the west.
A death-white mist slept over sand and sea: 95
Whereof the chill, to him, who breathed it, drew
Down with his blood, till all his heart was cold
With formless fear; and ev'n on Arthur fell
Confusion, since he saw not whom he fought.
For friend and foe were shadows in the mist,   100
And friend slew friend not knowing whom he slew;
And some had visions out of golden youth,
And some beheld the faces of old ghosts
Look in upon the battle; and in the mist
Was many a noble deed, many a base,   105
And chance and craft and strength in single fights,
And ever and anon with host to host
Shocks, and the splintering spear, the hard mail
   hewn,
Shield-breakings, and the clash of brands, the crash
Of battle-axes on shattered helms, and shrieks 110
After the Christ, of those who falling down
Looked up for heaven, and only saw the mist;
And shouts of heathen and the traitor knights,
Oaths, insult, filth, and monstrous blasphemies,
Sweat, writhings, anguish, laboring of the lungs 115
In that close mist, and cryings for the light,
Moans of the dying, and voices of the dead.

Last, as by some one deathbed after wail
Of suffering, silence follows, or through death
Or deathlike swoon, thus over all that shore,   120
Save for some whisper of the seething seas,
A dead hush fell; but when the dolorous day
Grew drearier toward twilight falling, came

A bitter wind, clear from the north, and blew
The mist aside, and with that wind the tide   125
Rose, and the pale king glanced across the field
Of battle: but no man was moving there;
Nor any cry of Christian heard thereon,
Nor yet of heathen; only the wan wave
Brake in among dead faces, to and fro   130
Swaying the helpless hands, and up and down
Tumbling the hollow helmets of the fallen,
And shivered brands° that once had fought with
   Rome,
And rolling far along the gloomy shores
The voice of days of old and days to be.   135

Then spake King Arthur to Sir Bedivere,
And whiter than the mist that all day long
Had held the field of battle was the king:

"Hearest thou this great voice that shakes the
   world,   139
And wastes the narrow realm whereon we move,
And beats upon the faces of the dead,
My dead, as though they had not died for me?—
O Bedivere, for on my heart hath fall'n
Confusion, till I know not what I am,
Nor whence I am, nor whether I be king.   145
Behold, I seem but king among the dead."

Then spake the bold Sir Bedivere: "My king,
King everywhere! and so the dead have kings,
There also will I worship thee as king.
Yet still thy life is whole, and still I live   150
Who love thee; but who hates thee, he that
   brought
The heathen back among us, yonder stands,
Modred, unharmed, the traitor of thine house."

Then spake the king: "My house hath been my
   doom.
But call not thou this traitor of my house   155
Who hath but dwelt beneath one roof with me.
My house are rather they who sware my vows,
Yea, even while they brake them, owned me king.
And well for thee, saying in my dark hour,
When all the purport of my throne hath failed, 160
That quick or dead thou holdest me for king.
King am I, whatsoever be their cry;
And one last act of kinghood shalt thou see
Yet, ere I pass." And uttering this the king
Made at the man: then Modred smote his liege 165

81. **Lyonesse:** region between Land's End and Scilly, including Cornwall. 91. **Burned . . . year:** winter solstice.

133. **brands:** swords.

Hard on that helm which many a heathen sword
Had beaten thin; while Arthur at one blow,
Striking the last stroke with Excalibur,
Slew him, and all but slain himself, he fell.

So all day long the noise of battle rolled   170
Among the mountains by the winter sea;
Until King Arthur's Table, man by man,
Had fall'n in Lyonesse about their lord,
King Arthur. Then, because his wound was deep,
The bold Sir Bedivere uplifted him,   175
And bore him to a chapel nigh the field,
A broken chancel with a broken cross,
That stood on a dark strait of barren land:
On one side lay the ocean, and on one
Lay a great water, and the moon was full.   180

Then spake King Arthur to Sir Bedivere:
"The sequel of today unsolders all
The goodliest of fellowship of famous knights
Whereof this world holds record. Such a sleep
They sleep—the men I loved. I think that we   185
Shall never more, at any future time,
Delight our souls with talk of knightly deeds,
Walking about the gardens and the halls
Of Camelot, as in the days that were.
I perish by this people which I made,—   190
Though Merlin sware° that I should come again
To rule once more; but, let what will be, be,
I am so deeply smitten through the helm
That without help I cannot last till morn.
Thou therefore take my brand Excalibur,   195
Which was my pride: for thou rememberest how
In those old days, one summer noon, an arm
Rose up from out the bosom of the lake,
Clothed in white samite, mystic, wonderful,
Holding the sword—and how I rowed across   200
And took it, and have worn it, like a king;
And, wheresoever I am sung or told
In aftertime, this also shall be known:
But now delay not: take Excalibur,
And fling him far into the middle mere: 205
Watch what thou seest, and lightly bring me
   word."

To him replied the bold Sir Bedivere:
"It is not meet, Sir King, to leave thee thus,
Aidless, alone, and smitten through the helm—
A little thing may harm a wounded man;   210

191. Merlin sware: See his prophecy in "The Coming of
Arthur," l. 421.

Yet I thy hest will all perform at full,
Watch what I see, and lightly bring thee word."

So saying, from the ruined shrine he stepped,
And in the moon athwart the place of tombs,
Where lay the mighty bones of ancient men,   215
Old knights, and over them the sea-wind sang
Shrill, chill, with flakes of foam. He, stepping down
By zigzag paths, and juts of pointed rock,
Came on the shining levels of the lake.

There drew he forth the brand° Excalibur,   220
And o'er him, drawing it, the winter moon,
Brightening the skirts of a long cloud, ran forth
And sparkled keen with frost against the hilt:
For all the haft twinkled with diamond sparks,
Myriads of topaz-lights, and jacinth-work   225
Of subtlest jewelery. He gazed so long
That both his eyes were dazzled as he stood,
This way and that dividing the swift mind,
In act to throw: but at the last it seemed
Better to leave Excalibur concealed   230
There in the many-knotted waterflags,
That whistled stiff and dry about the marge.
So strode he back slow to the wounded king.

Then spake King Arthur to Sir Bedivere: 234
"Hast thou performed my mission which I gave?
What is it thou hast seen? or what hast heard?"

And answer made the bold Sir Bedivere:
"I heard the ripple washing in the reeds,
And the wild water lapping on the crag."

To whom replied King Arthur, faint and pale: 240
"Thou hast betrayed thy nature and thy name,
Not rendering true answer, as beseemed
Thy fealty, nor like a noble knight:
For surer sign had followed, either hand,
Or voice, or else a motion of the mere.   245
This is a shameful thing for men to lie.
Yet now, I charge thee, quickly go again,
As thou art lief and dear, and do the thing
I bade thee, watch, and lightly bring me word."

Then went Sir Bedivere the second time   250
Across the ridge, and paced beside the mere,
Counting the dewy pebbles, fixed in thought;
But when he saw the wonder of the hilt,
How curiously and strangely chased, he smote
His palms together, and he cried aloud: 255

"And if indeed I cast the brand away,
Surely a precious thing, one worthy note,

Should thus be lost forever from the earth,
Which might have pleased the eyes of many men.
What good should follow this, if this were done?
What harm, undone? Deep harm to disobey,   261
Seeing obedience is the bond of rule.
Were it well to obey then, if a king demand
An act unprofitable, against himself?
The king is sick, and knows not what he does.   265
What record, or what relic of my lord
Should be to aftertime, but empty breath
And rumours of a doubt? But were this kept,
Stored in some treasure-house of mighty kings,
Some one might show it at a joust of arms,   270
Saying, 'King Arthur's sword, Excalibur,
Wrought by the lonely maiden of the lake.
Nine years she wrought it, sitting in the deeps
Upon the hidden bases of the hills.'
So might some old man speak in the aftertime 275
To all the people, winning reverence.
But now much honor and much fame were lost."

So spake he, clouded with his own conceit,
And hid Excalibur the second time,
And so strode back slow to the wounded king. 280

Then spoke King Arthur, breathing heavily:
"What is it thou hast seen? or what hast heard?"

And answer made the bold Sir Bedivere:
"I heard the water lapping on the crag,
And the long ripple washing in the reeds."   285

To whom replied King Arthur, much in wrath:
"Ah, miserable and unkind, untrue,
Unknightly, traitor-hearted! Woe is me!
Authority forgets a dying king,
Laid widowed of the power in his eye   290
That bowed the will. I see thee what thou art,
For thou, the latest-left of all my knights,
In whom should meet the offices of all,
Thou wouldst betray me for the precious hilt;
Either from lust of gold, or like a girl   295
Valuing the giddy pleasure of the eyes.
Yet, for a man may fail in duty twice,
And the third time may prosper, get thee hence:
But, if thou spare to fling Excalibur,
I will arise and slay thee with my hands."   300

Then quickly rose Sir Bedivere, and ran,
And, leaping down the ridges lightly, plunged
Among the bulrush beds, and clutched the sword
And strongly wheeled and threw it. The great brand

Made lightnings in the splendor of the moon, 305
And flashing round and round, and whirled in an
   arch,
Shot like a streamer of the northern morn,°
Seen where the moving isles of winter shock
By night, with noises of the northern sea.
So flashed and fell the brand Excalibur: 310
But ere he dipped the surface, rose an arm
Clothed in white samite, mystic, wonderful,
And caught him by the hilt, and brandished him
Three times, and drew him under in the mere.
And lightly went the other to the king.   315

Then spoke King Arthur, drawing thicker breath:
"Now see I by thine eyes that this is done.
Speak out: what is it thou hast heard, or seen?"

And answer made the bold Sir Bedivere:
"Sir King, I closed mine eyelids, lest the gems 320
Should blind my purpose, for I never saw,
Nor shall see, here or elsewhere, till I die,
Not though I live three lives of mortal men,
So great a miracle as yonder hilt.   324
Then with both hands I flung him, wheeling him;
But when I looked again, behold an arm,
Clothed in white samite, mystic, wonderful,
That caught him by the hilt, and brandished him
Three times, and drew him under in the mere."

And answer made King Arthur, breathing hard: 330
"My end draws nigh; 'tis time that I were gone.
Make broad thy shoulders to receive my weight,
And bear me to the margin; yet I fear
My wound hath taken cold, and I shall die."

So saying, from the pavement° he half rose,   335
Slowly, with pain, reclining on his arm,
And looking wistfully with wide blue eyes
As in a picture. Him Sir Bedivere
Remorsefully regarded through his tears,   339
And would have spoken, but he found not words;
Then took with care, and kneeling on one knee,
O'er both his shoulders drew the languid hands,
And rising bore him through the place of tombs.

But, as he walked, King Arthur panted hard,
Like one that feels a nightmare on his bed   345
When all the house is mute. So sighed the king,
Muttering and murmuring at his ear, "Quick,
   quick!

307. streamer . . . morn: aurora borealis. 335. pavement:
stone floor of the chapel.

I fear it is too late, and I shall die."
But the other swiftly strode from ridge to ridge,
Clothed with his breath, and looking, as he walked
Larger than human on the frozen hills.   351
He heard the deep behind him, and a cry
Before. His own thought drove him like a goad.
Dry clashed his harness in the icy caves
And barren chasms, and all to left and right   355
The bare black cliff clanged round him, as he
    based
His feet on juts of slippery crag that rang
Sharp-smitten with the dint of armèd heels—
And on a sudden, lo! the level lake,
And the long glories of the winter moon.   360

Then saw they how there hove a dusky barge,
Dark as a funeral scarf from stem to stern,
Beneath them; and descending they were ware
That all the decks were dense with stately forms,
Black-stoled, black-hooded, like a dream—by
    these   365
Three queens° with crowns of gold: and from them
    rose
A cry that shivered to the tingling stars,
And, as it were one voice, an agony
Of lamentation, like a wind that shrills
All night in a waste land, where no one comes, 370
Or hath come, since the making of the world.

Then murmured Arthur, "Place me in the barge."
So to the barge they came. There those three
    queens
Put forth their hands, and took the king, and wept.
But she, that rose the tallest of them all   375
And fairest, laid his head upon her lap,
And loosed the shattered casque and chafed his
    hands,
And called him by his name, complaining loud,
And dropping bitter tears against a brow
Striped with dark blood: for all his face was
    white   380
And colorless, and like the withered moon
Smote by the fresh beam of the springing east;
And all his greaves and cuisses° dashed with drops
Of onset;° and the light and lustrous curls—
That made his forehead like a rising sun   385
High from the dais-throne—were parched with
    dust;

366. **Three queens:** See "The Coming of Arthur," ll.
275 ff. **383. greaves and cuisses:** leg armor. **384. onset:**
onslaught, blood.

Or, clotted into points and hanging loose,
Mixed with the knightly growth that fringed his
    lips.
So like a shattered column lay the king;
Not like that Arthur who, with lance in rest,   390
From spur to plume a star of tournament,
Shot through the lists at Camelot, and charged
Before the eyes of ladies and of kings.

Then loudly cried the bold Sir Bedivere:
"Ah! my Lord Arthur, whither shall I go?   395
Where shall I hide my forehead and my eyes?
For now I see the true old times are dead
When every morning brought a noble chance,
And every chance brought out a noble knight.
Such times have been not since the light that led 400
The holy Elders° with the gift of myrrh.
But now the whole Round Table is dissolved
Which was an image of the mighty world,
And I, the last, go forth companionless,
And the days darken round me, and the years, 405
Among new men, strange faces, other minds."

And slowly answered Arthur from the barge
"The old order changeth, yielding place to new,
And God fulfills himself in many ways,   409
Lest one good custom should corrupt the world.
Comfort thyself: what comfort is in me?
I have lived my life, and that which I have done
May He within himself make pure! but thou,
If thou shouldst never see my face again,
Pray for my soul. More things are wrought by
    prayer   415
Than this world dreams of. Wherefore, let thy voice
Rise like a fountain for me night and day.
For what are men better than sheep or goats
That nourish a blind life within the brain,
If, knowing God, they lift not hands of prayer 420
Both for themselves and those who call them
    friend?
For so the whole round earth is every way
Bound by gold chains about the feet of God.
But now farewell. I am going a long way
With these thou seest—if indeed I go   425
(For all my mind is clouded with a doubt)—
To the island-valley of Avilion;°
Where falls not hail, or rain, or any snow,
Nor ever wind blows loudly; but it lies   429
Deep-meadowed, happy, fair with orchard lawns

401. Elders: Magi. **427. Avilion:** happy island of the blessed
in Celtic mythology.

And bowery hollows crowned with summer sea,
Where I will heal me of my grievous wound."

So said he, and the barge with oar and sail
Moved from the brink, like some full-breasted swan
That, fluting a wild carol ere her death,   435
Ruffles her pure cold plume, and takes the flood
With swarthy webs. Long stood Sir Bedivere
Revolving many memories, till the hull
Looked one black dot against the verge of dawn,
And on the mere the wailing died away.   440

But when the moan had passed for evermore,
The stillness of the dead world's winter dawn
Amazed him, and he groaned, "The king is gone."
And therewithal came on him the weird rhyme,
"From the great deep to the great deep he goes."°

Whereat he slowly turned and slowly clomb   446
The last hard footstep of that iron crag;
Thence marked the black hull moving yet and
    cried,
"He passes to be king among the dead,
And after healing of his grievous wound   450
He comes again; but—if he come no more—
O me, be yon dark queens in yon black boat,
Who shrieked and wailed, the three whereat we
    gazed
On that high day, when, clothed with living light,
They stood before his throne in silence, friends 455
Of Arthur who should help him at his need?"

Then from the dawn it seemed there came, but
    faint
As from beyond the limit of the world,
Like the last echo born of a great cry,
Sounds, as if some fair city were one voice   460
Around a king returning from his wars.

Thereat once more he moved about, and clomb
Ev'n to the highest he could climb, and saw,
Straining his eyes beneath an arch of hand,
Or thought he saw, the speck that bare the king 465
Down that long water opening on the deep
Somewhere far off, pass on and on, and go
From less to less and vanish into light.
And the new sun rose bringing the new year.

---

445. From . . . goes: See "The Coming of Arthur,"
l. 410.

D. H. LAWRENCE
1885–1930

The Horse Dealer's Daughter

"Well, Mabel, and what are you going to do with yourself?" asked Joe, with foolish flippancy. He felt quite safe himself. Without listening for an answer, he turned aside, worked a grain of tobacco to the tip of his tongue, and spat it out. He did not care about anything, since he felt safe himself.

The three brothers and the sister sat round the desolate breakfast table, attempting some sort of desultory consultation. The morning's post had given the final tap to the family fortune, and all was over. The dreary dining-room itself, with its heavy mahogany furniture, looked as if it were waiting to be done away with.

But the consultation amounted to nothing. There was a strange air of ineffectuality about the three men, as they sprawled at table, smoking and reflecting vaguely on their own condition. The girl was alone, a rather short, sullen-looking young woman of twenty-seven. She did not share the same life as her brothers. She would have been good-looking, save for the impassive fixity of her face, "bull-dog," as her brothers called it.

There was a confused trampling of horses' feet outside. The three men all sprawled round in their chairs to watch. Beyond the dark holly-bushes that separated the strip of lawn from the highroad, they could see a cavalcade of shire horses swinging out of their own yard, being taken for exercise. This was the last time. These were the last horses that would go through their hands. The young men watched with critical, callous look. They were all frightened at the collapse of their lives, and the sense of disaster in which they were involved left them no inner freedom.

Yet they were three fine, well-set fellows enough. Joe, the eldest, was a man of thirty-three, broad and handsome in a hot, flushed way. His face was red, he twisted his black mustache over a thick finger, his eyes were shallow and restless. He had a sensual way of uncovering his teeth when he laughed, and his bearing was stupid. Now he watched the horses with a glazed look of helplessness in his eyes, a certain stupor of downfall.

The great draft-horses swung past. They were tied head to tail, four of them, and they heaved along to where a lane branched off from the highroad, planting their great hoofs floutingly in the fine black mud, swinging their great rounded haunches sumptuously, and trotting a few sudden steps as they were led into the lane, round the corner. Every movement showed a massive, slumbrous strength, and a stupidity which held them in subjection. The groom at the head looked back, jerking the leading rope. And the cavalcade moved out of sight up the lane, the tail of the last horse, bobbed up tight and stiff, held out taut from the swinging great haunches as they rocked behind the hedges in a motionlike sleep.

Joe watched with glazed hopeless eyes. The horses were almost like his own body to him. He felt he was done for now. Luckily he was engaged to a woman as old as himself, and therefore her father, who was steward of a neighbouring estate, would provide him with a job. He would marry and go into harness. His life was over, he would be a subject animal now.

He turned uneasily aside, the retreating steps of the horses echoing in his ears. Then, with foolish restlessness, he reached for the scraps of bacon-rind from the plates, and making a faint whistling sound, flung them to the terrier that lay against the fender. He watched the dog swallow them, and waited till the creature looked into his eyes. Then a faint grin came on his face, and in a high, foolish voice he said:

"You won't get much more bacon, shall you, you little bitch?"

The dog faintly and dismally wagged its tail, then lowered its haunches, circled round, and lay down again.

There was another helpless silence at the table. Joe sprawled uneasily in his seat, not willing to go till the family conclave was dissolved. Fred Henry, the second brother, was erect, clean-limbed, alert. He had watched the passing of the horses with more sang-froid. If he was an animal, like Joe, he was an animal which controls, not one which is controlled. He was master of any horse, and he carried himself with a well-tempered air of mastery. But he was not master of the situations of life. He pushed his coarse brown mustache upwards, off his lip, and glanced irritably at his sister, who sat impassive and inscrutable.

"You'll go and stop with Lucy for a bit, shan't you?" he asked. The girl did not answer.

"I don't see what else you can do," persisted Fred Henry.

"Go as a skivvy,"[1] Joe interpolated laconically. The girl did not move a muscle.

"If I was her, I should go in for training for a nurse," said Malcolm, the youngest of them all. He was the baby of the family, a young man of twenty-two, with a fresh, jaunty *museau*.[2]

But Mabel did not take any notice of him. They had talked at her and round her for so many years, that she hardly heard them at all.

The marble clock on the mantelpiece softly chimed the half-hour, the dog rose uneasily from the hearthrug and looked at the party at the breakfast table. But still they sat on in ineffectual conclave.

"Oh, all right," said Joe suddenly, apropos of nothing. "I'll get a move on."

He pushed back his chair, straddled his knees with a downward jerk, to get them free, in horsey fashion, and went to the fire. Still he did not go out of the room; he was curious to know what the others would do or say. He began to charge his pipe, looking down at the dog and saying, in a high, affected voice:

"Going wi' me? Going wi' me are ter? Tha'rt goin' further than tha counts on just now, dost hear?"

The dog faintly wagged its tail, the man stuck out his jaw and covered his pipe with his hands, and puffed intently, losing himself in the tobacco, looking down all the while at the dog with an absent brown eye. The dog looked up at him in mournful distrust. Joe stood with his knees stuck out, in real horsey fashion.

"Have you had a letter from Lucy?" Fred Henry asked of his sister.

"Last week," came the neutral reply.

"And what does she say?"

There was no answer.

"Does she *ask* you to go and stop there?" persisted Fred Henry.

"She says I can if I like."

"Well, then, you'd better. Tell her you'll come on Monday."

This was received in silence.

THE HORSE DEALER'S DAUGHTER.   **1. skivvy:** female servant.
2. museau: face.

"That's what you'll do then, is it?" said Fred Henry, in some exasperation.

But she made no answer. There was a silence of futility and irritation in the room. Malcolm grinned fatuously.

"You'll have to make up your mind between now and next Wednesday," said Joe loudly, "or else find yourself lodgings on the curbstone."

The face of the young woman darkened, but she sat on immutable.

"Here's Jack Fergusson!" exclaimed Malcolm, who was looking aimlessly out of the window.

"Where?" exclaimed Joe, loudly.

"Just gone past."

"Coming in?"

Malcolm craned his neck to see the gate.

"Yes," he said.

There was a silence. Mabel sat on like one condemned, at the head of the table. Then a whistle was heard from the kitchen. The dog got up and barked sharply. Joe opened the door and shouted:

"Come on."

After a moment a young man entered. He was muffled up in overcoat and a purple woollen scarf, and his tweed cap, which he did not remove, was pulled down on his head. He was of medium height, his face was rather long and pale, his eyes looked tired.

"Hello, Jack! Well, Jack!" exclaimed Malcolm and Joe. Fred Henry merely said, "Jack."

"What's doing?" asked the newcomer, evidently addressing Fred Henry.

"Same. We've got to be out by Wednesday. Got a cold?"

"I have—got it bad, too."

"Why don't you stop in?"

"*Me* stop in? When I can't stand on my legs, perhaps I shall have a chance." The young man spoke huskily. He had a slight Scotch accent.

"It's a knockout, isn't it," said Joe, boisterously, "if a doctor goes round croaking with a cold. Looks bad for the patients, doesn't it?"

The young doctor looked at him slowly.

"Anything the matter with *you*, then?" he asked sarcastically.

"Not as I know of. Damn your eyes, I hope not. Why?"

"I thought you were very concerned about the patients, wondered if you might be one yourself."

"Damn it, no, I've never been patient to no flaming doctor, and hope I never shall be," returned Joe.

At this point Mabel rose from the table, and they all seemed to become aware of her existence. She began putting the dishes together. The young doctor looked at her, but did not address her. He had not greeted her. She went out of the room with the tray, her face impassive and unchanged.

"When are you off then, all of you?" asked the doctor.

"I'm catching the eleven-forty," replied Malcolm. "Are you goin' down wi' th' trap, Joe?"

"Yes, I've told you I'm going down wi' th' trap, haven't I?"

"We'd better be getting her in then. So long, Jack, if I don't see you before I go," said Malcolm, shaking hands.

He went out, followed by Joe, who seemed to have his tail between his legs.

"Well, this is the devil's own," exclaimed the doctor, when he was left alone with Fred Henry. "Going before Wednesday, are you?"

"That's the orders," replied the other.

"Where, to Northampton?"

"That's it."

"The devil!" exclaimed Fergusson, with quiet chagrin.

And there was silence between the two.

"All settled up, are you?" asked Fergusson.

"About."

There was another pause.

"Well, I shall miss yer, Freddy, boy," said the young doctor.

"And I shall miss thee, Jack," returned the other.

"Miss you like hell," mused the doctor.

Fred Henry turned aside. There was nothing to say. Mabel came in again, to finish clearing the table.

"What are *you* going to do, then, Miss Pervin?" asked Fergusson. "Going to your sister's, are you?"

Mabel looked at him with her steady, dangerous eyes, that always made him uncomfortable, unsettling his superficial ease.

"No," she said.

"Well, what in the name of fortune *are* you going to do? Say what you mean to do," cried Fred Henry, with futile intensity.

But she only averted her head, and continued

her work. She folded the white tablecloth, and put on the chenille cloth.

"The sulkiest bitch that ever trod!" muttered her brother.

But she finished her task with perfectly impassive face, the young doctor watching her interestedly all the while. Then she went out.

Fred Henry stared after her, clenching his lips, his blue eyes fixing in sharp antagonism, as he made a grimace of sour exasperation.

"You could bray her into bits, and that's all you'd get out of her," he said in a small, narrowed tone.

The doctor smiled faintly.

"What's she *going* to do, then?" he asked.

"Strike me if *I* know!" returned the other.

There was a pause. Then the doctor stirred.

"I'll be seeing you tonight, shall I?" he said to his friend.

"Aye—where's it to be? Are we going over to Jessdale?"

"I don't know. I've got such a cold on me. I'll come round to the Moon and Stars, anyway."

"Let Lizzie and May miss their night for once, eh?"

"That's it—if I feel as I do now."

"All's one—"

The two young men went through the passage and down to the back door together. The house was large, but it was servantless now, and desolate. At the back was a small bricked house-yard, and beyond that a big square, graveled fine and red, and having stables on two sides. Sloping, dank, winter-dark fields stretched away on the open sides.

But the stables were empty. Joseph Pervin, the father of the family, had been a man of no education, who had become a fairly large horse dealer. The stables had been full of horses, there was a great turmoil and come-and-go of horses and of dealers and grooms. Then the kitchen was full of servants. But of late things had declined. The old man had married a second time, to retrieve his fortunes. Now he was dead and everything was gone to the dogs, there was nothing but debt and threatening.

For months, Mabel had been servantless in the big house, keeping the home together in penury for her ineffectual brothers. She had kept house for ten years. But previously it was with unstinted means. Then, however brutal and coarse everything

was, the sense of money had kept her proud, confident. The men might be foul-mouthed, the women in the kitchen might have bad reputations, her brothers might have illegitimate children. But so long as there was money, the girl felt herself established, and brutally proud, reserved.

No company came to the house, save dealers and coarse men. Mabel had no associates of her own sex, after her sister went away. But she did not mind. She went regularly to church, she attended to her father. And she lived in the memory of her mother, who had died when she was fourteen, and whom she had loved. She had loved her father, too, in a different way, depending upon him, and feeling secure in him, until at the age of fifty-four he married again. And then she had set hard against him. Now he had died and left them all hopelessly in debt.

She had suffered badly during the period of poverty. Nothing, however, could shake the curious sullen, animal pride that dominated each member of the family. Now, for Mabel, the end had come. Still she would not cast about her. She would follow her own way just the same. She would always hold the keys of her own situation. Mindless and persistent, she endured from day to day. Why should she think? Why should she answer anybody? It was enough that this was the end, and there was no way out. She need not pass any more darkly along the main street of the small town, avoiding every eye. She need not demean herself any more, going into the shops and buying the cheapest food. This was at an end. She thought of nobody, not even of herself. Mindless and persistent, she seemed in a sort of ecstasy to be coming near to her fulfilment, her own glorification, approaching her dead mother, who was glorified.

In the afternoon she took a little bag, with shears and sponge and a small scrubbing brush, and went out. It was a gray, wintry day, with saddened, dark green fields and an atmosphere blackened by the smoke of foundries not far off. She went quickly, darkly along the causeway, heeding nobody, through the town to the churchyard.

There she always felt secure, as if no one could see her, although as a matter of fact she was exposed to the stare of everyone who passed along under the churchyard wall. Nevertheless, once under the shadow of the great looming church, among the graves, she felt immune from the world, reserved within the thick churchyard wall as in another country.

Carefully she clipped the grass from the grave, and arranged the pinky white, small chrysanthemums in the tin cross. When this was done, she took an empty jar from a neighboring grave, brought water, and carefully, most scrupulously sponged the marble headstone and the coping-stone.

It gave her sincere satisfaction to do this. She felt in immediate contact with the world of her mother. She took minute pains, went through the park in a state bordering on pure happiness, as if in performing this task she came into a subtle, intimate connection with her mother. For the life she followed her in the world was far less real than the world of death she inherited from her mother.

The doctor's house was just by the church. Fergusson, being a mere hired assistant, was slave to the countryside. As he hurried now to attend to the outpatients in the surgery, glancing across the graveyard with his quick eye, he saw the girl at her task at the grave. She seemed so intent and remote, it was like looking into another world. Some mystical element was touched in him. He slowed down as he walked, watching her as if spellbound.

She lifted her eyes, feeling him looking. Their eyes met. And each looked away again at once, each feeling, in some way, found out by the other. He lifted his cap and passed on down the road. There remained distinct in his consciousness, like a vision, the memory of her face, lifted from the tombstone in the churchyard, and looking at him with slow, large, portentous eyes. It *was* portentous, her face. It seemed to mesmerize him. There was a heavy power in her eyes which laid hold of his whole being, as if he had drunk some powerful drug. He had been feeling weak and done before. Now the life came back into him, he felt delivered from his own fretted, daily self.

He finished his duties at the surgery as quickly as might be, hastily filling up the bottles of the waiting people with cheap drugs. Then, in perpetual haste, he set off again to visit several cases in another part of his round, before teatime. At all times he preferred to walk if he could, but particularly when he was not well. He fancied the motion restored him.

The afternoon was falling. It was gray, deadened, and wintry, with a slow, moist, heavy coldness sinking in and deadening all the faculties. But why should he think or notice? He hastily climbed the hill and turned across the dark green fields, following the black cinder-track. In the distance, across a shallow dip in the country, the small town was clustered like smoldering ash, a tower, a spire, a heap of low, raw, extinct houses. And on the nearest fringe of the town, sloping into the dip, was Oldmeadow, the Pervins' house. He could see the stables and the outbuildings distinctly, as they lay towards him on the slope. Well, he would not go there many more times! Another resource would be lost to him, another place gone: the only company he cared for in the alien, ugly little town he was losing. Nothing but work, drudgery, constant hastening from dwelling to dwelling among the colliers and the iron-workers. It wore him out, but at the same time he had a craving for it. It was a stimulant to him to be in the homes of the working people, moving as it were through the innermost body of their life. His nerves were excited and gratified. He could come so near, into the very lives of the rough, inarticulate, powerfully emotional men and women. He grumbled, he said he hated the hellish hole. But as a matter of fact it excited him, the contact with the rough, strongly-feeling people was a stimulant applied direct to his nerves.

Below Oldmeadow, in the green, shallow, soddened hollow of fields, lay a square, deep pond. Roving across the landscape, the doctor's quick eye detected a figure in black passing through the gate of the field, down towards the pond. He looked again. It would be Mabel Pervin. His mind suddenly became alive and attentive.

Why was she going down there? He pulled up on the path on the slope above, and stood staring. He could just make sure of the small black figure moving in the hollow of the failing day. He seemed to see her in the midst of such obscurity, that he was like a clairvoyant, seeing rather with the mind's eye than with ordinary sight. Yet he could see her positively enough, whilst he kept his eye attentive. He felt, if he looked away from her, in the thick, ugly falling dusk, he would lose her altogether.

He followed her minutely as she moved, direct and intent, like something transmitted rather than stirring in voluntary activity, straight down the field towards the pond. There she stood on the bank for a moment. She never raised her head. Then she waded slowly into the water.

He stood motionless as the small black figure walked slowly and deliberately towards the center of the pond, very slowly, gradually moving deeper into the motionless water, and still moving forward as the water got up to her breast. Then he could see her no more in the dusk of the dead afternoon.

"There!" he exclaimed. "Would you believe it?"

And he hastened straight down, running over the wet, soddened fields, pushing through the hedges, down into the depression of callous wintry obscurity. It took him several minutes to come to the pond. He stood on the bank, breathing heavily. He could see nothing. His eyes seemed to penetrate the dead water. Yes, perhaps that was the dark shadow of her black clothing beneath the surface of the water.

He slowly ventured into the pond. The bottom was deep, soft clay, he sank in, and the water clasped dead cold round his legs. As he stirred he could smell the cold, rotten clay that fouled up into the water. It was objectionable in his lungs. Still, repelled and yet not heeding, he moved deeper into the pond. The cold water rose over his thighs, over his loins, upon his abdomen. The lower part of his body was all sunk in the hideous cold element. And the bottom was so deeply soft and uncertain, he was afraid of pitching with his mouth underneath. He could not swim, and was afraid.

He crouched a little, spreading his hands under the water and moving them round, trying to feel for her. The dead cold pond swayed upon his chest. He moved again, a little deeper, and again, with his hands underneath, he felt all around under the water. And he touched her clothing. But it evaded his fingers. He made a desperate effort to grasp it.

And so doing he lost his balance and went under, horribly, suffocating in the foul earthy water, struggling madly for a few moments. At last, after what seemed an eternity, he got his footing, rose again into the air and looked around. He gasped, and knew he was in the world. Then he looked at the water. She had risen near him. He grasped her clothing, and drawing her nearer, turned to take his way to land again.

He went very slowly, carefully, absorbed in the slow progress. He rose higher, climbing out of the

pond. The water was now only about his legs; he was thankful, full of relief to be out of the clutches of the pond. He lifted her and staggered on to the bank, out of the horror of wet, gray clay.

He laid her down on the bank. She was quite unconscious and running with water. He made the water come from her mouth, he worked to restore her. He did not have to work very long before he could feel the breathing begin again in her; she was breathing naturally. He worked a little longer. He could feel her live beneath his hands; she was coming back. He wiped her face, wrapped her in his overcoat, looked round into the dim, dark gray world, then lifted her and staggered down the bank and across the fields.

It seemed an unthinkably long way, and his burden so heavy he felt he would never get to the house. But at last he was in the stable-yard, and then in the house-yard. He opened the door and went into the house. In the kitchen he laid her down on the hearthrug, and called. The house was empty. But the fire was burning in the grate.

Then again he kneeled to attend to her. She was breathing regularly, her eyes were wide open and as if conscious, but there seemed something missing in her look. She was conscious in herself, but unconscious of her surroundings.

He ran upstairs, took blankets from a bed, and put them before the fire to warm. Then he removed her saturated, earthy-smelling clothing, rubbed her dry with a towel, and wrapped her naked in the blankets. Then he went into the dining-room, to look for spirits. There was a little whisky. He drank a gulp himself, and put some into her mouth.

The effect was instantaneous. She looked full into his face, as if she had been seeing him for some time, and yet had only just become conscious of him.

"Dr. Fergusson?" she said.

"What?" he answered.

He was divesting himself of his coat, intending to find some dry clothing upstairs. He could not bear the smell of the dead, clayey water, and he was mortally afraid for his own health.

"What did I do?" she asked.

"Walked into the pond," he replied. He had begun to shudder like one sick, and could hardly attend to her. Her eyes remained full on him, he seemed to be going dark in his mind, looking back at her helplessly. The shuddering became quieter in

THE HORSE DEALER'S DAUGHTER

him, his life came back in him, dark and un-knowing, but strong again.

"Was I out of my mind?" she asked, while her eyes were fixed on him all the time.

"Maybe, for the moment," he replied. He felt quiet, because his strength had come back. The strange fretful strain had left him.

"Am I out of my mind now?" she asked.

"Are you?" he reflected a moment. "No," he answered truthfully, "I don't see that you are." He turned his face aside. He was afraid now, because he felt dazed, and felt dimly that her power was stronger than his, in this issue. And she continued to look at him fixedly all the time. "Can you tell me where I shall find some dry things to put on?" he asked.

"Did you dive into the pond for me?" she asked.

"No," he answered. "I walked in. But I went in overhead as well."

There was silence for a moment. He hesitated. He very much wanted to go upstairs to get into dry clothing. But there was another desire in him. And she seemed to hold him. His will seemed to have gone to sleep, and left him, standing there slack before her. But he felt warm inside himself. He did not shudder at all, though his clothes were sodden on him.

"Why did you?" she asked.

"Because I didn't want you to do such a foolish thing," he said.

"It wasn't foolish," she said, still gazing at him as she lay on the floor, with a sofa cushion under her head. "It was the right thing to do. I knew best, then."

"I'll go and shift these wet things," he said. But still he had not the power to move out of her presence, until she sent him. It was as if she had the life of his body in her hands, and he could not extricate himself. Or perhaps he did not want to.

Suddenly she sat up. Then she became aware of her own immediate condition. She felt the blankets about her, she knew her own limbs. For a moment it seemed as if her reason were going. She looked round, with wild eye, as if seeking something. He stood still with fear. She saw her clothing lying scattered.

"Who undressed me?" she asked, her eyes resting full and inevitable on his face.

"I did," he replied, "to bring you round."

For some moments she sat and gazed at him awfully, her lips parted.

"Do you love me, then?" she asked.

He only stood and stared at her, fascinated. His soul seemed to melt.

She shuffled forward on her knees, and put her arms round him, round his legs, as he stood there, pressing her breasts against his knees and thighs, clutching him with strange, convulsive certainty, pressing his thighs against her, drawing him to her face, her throat, as she looked up at him with flaring, humble eyes of transfiguration, triumphant in first possession.

"You love me," she murmured, in strange transport, yearning and triumphant and confident. "You love me. I know you love me, I know."

And she was passionately kissing his knees, through the wet clothing, passionately and in-discriminately kissing his knees, his legs, as if unaware of everything.

He looked down at the tangled wet hair, the wild, bare, animal shoulders. He was amazed, bewildered, and afraid. He had never thought of loving her. He had never wanted to love her. When he rescued her and restored her, he was a doctor, and she was a patient. He had had no single personal thought of her. Nay, this introduction of the personal element was very distasteful to him, a violation of his professional honor. It was horrible to have her there embracing his knees. It was horrible. He revolted from it, violently. And yet—and yet—he had not the power to break away.

She looked at him again, with the same supplica-tion of powerful love, and that same transcendent, frightening light of triumph. In view of the delicate flame which seemed to come from her face like a light, he was powerless. And yet he had never intended to love her. He had never intended. And something stubborn in him could not give way.

"You love me," she repeated, in a murmur of deep, rhapsodic assurance. "You love me."

Her hands were drawing him, drawing him down to her. He was afraid, even a little horrified. For he had, really, no intention of loving her. Yet her hands were drawing him towards her. He put out his hand quickly to steady himself, and grasped her bare shoulder. A flame seemed to burn the hand that grasped her soft shoulder. He had no intention of loving her: his whole will was against his yield-ing. It was horrible. And yet wonderful was the touch of her shoulders, beautiful the shining of her face. Was she perhaps mad? He had a horror of yielding to her. Yet something in him ached also.

He had been staring away at the door, away from her. But his hand remained on her shoulder. She had gone suddenly very still. He looked down at her. Her eyes were now wide with fear, with doubt, the light was dying from her face, a shadow of terrible grayness was returning. He could not bear the touch of her eyes' question upon him, and the look of death behind the question.

With an inward groan he gave way, and let his heart yield towards her. A sudden gentle smile came on his face. And her eyes, which never left his face, slowly, slowly filled with tears. He watched the strange water rise in her eyes, like some slow fountain coming up. And his heart seemed to burn and melt away in his breast.

He could not bear to look at her any more. He dropped on his knees and caught her head with his arms and pressed her face against his throat. She was very still. His heart, which seemed to have broken, was burning with a kind of agony in his breast. And he felt her slow, hot tears wetting his throat. But he could not move.

He felt the hot tears wet his neck and the hollows of his neck, and he remained motionless, suspended through one of man's eternities. Only now it had become indispensable to him to have her face pressed close to him; he could never let her go again. He could never let her head go away from the close clutch of his arm. He wanted to remain like that forever, with his heart hurting him in a pain that was also life to him. Without knowing, he was looking down on her damp, soft brown hair.

Then, as it were suddenly, he smelt the horrid stagnant smell of that water. And at the same moment she drew away from him and looked at him. Her eyes were wistful and unfathomable. He was afraid of them, and he fell to kissing her, not knowing what he was doing. He wanted her eyes not to have that terrible, wistful, unfathomable look.

When she turned her face to him again, a faint delicate flush was glowing, and there was again dawning that terrible shining of joy in her eyes, which really terrified him, and yet which he now wanted to see, because he feared the look of doubt still more.

"You love me?" she said, rather faltering.

"Yes." The word cost him a painful effort. Not because it wasn't true. But because it was too newly true, the *saying* seemed to tear open again his newly torn heart. And he hardly wanted it to be true, even now.

She lifted her face to him, and he bent forward and kissed her on the mouth, gently, with the one kiss that is an eternal pledge. And as he kissed her his heart strained again in his breast. He never intended to love her. But now it was over. He had crossed over the gulf to her, and all that he had left behind had shriveled and become void.

After the kiss, her eyes again slowly filled with tears. She sat still, away from him, with her face drooped aside, and her hands folded in her lap. The tears fell very slowly. There was complete silence. He too sat there motionless and silent on the hearthrug. The strange pain of his heart that was broken seemed to consume him. That he should love her? That this was love! That he should be ripped open in this way! Him, a doctor! How they would all jeer if they knew! It was agony to him to think they might know.

In the curious naked pain of the thought he looked again to her. She was sitting there drooped into a muse. He saw a tear fall, and his heart flared hot. He saw for the first time that one of her shoulders was quite uncovered, one arm bare, he could see one of her small breasts; dimly, because it had become almost dark in the room.

"Why are you crying?" he asked, in an altered voice.

She looked up at him, and behind her tears the consciousness of her situation for the first time brought a dark look of shame to her eyes.

"I'm not crying, really," she said, watching him half frightened.

He reached his hand, and softly closed it on her bare arm.

"I love you! I love you!" he said in a soft, low vibrating voice, unlike himself.

She shrank, and dropped her head. The soft, penetrating grip of his hand on her arm distressed her. She looked up at him.

"I want to go," she said. "I want to go and get you some dry things."

"Why?" he said. "I'm all right."

"But I want to go," she said. "And I want you to change your things."

He released her arm, and she wrapped herself in the blanket, looking at him rather frightened. And still she did not rise.

"Kiss me," she said wistfully.

He kissed her, but briefly, half in anger.

Then, after a second, she rose nervously, all mixed up in the blanket. He watched her in her confusion, as she tried to extricate herself and wrap herself up so that she could walk. He watched her relentlessly, as she knew. And as she went, the blanket trailing, and as he saw a glimpse of her feet and her white leg, he tried to remember her as she was when he had wrapped her in the blanket. But then he didn't want to remember, because she had been nothing to him then, and his nature revolted from remembering her as she was when she was nothing to him.

A tumbling, muffled noise from within the dark house startled him. Then he heard her voice:— "There are clothes." He rose and went to the foot of the stairs, and gathered up the garments she had thrown down. Then he came back to the fire, to rub himself down and dress. He grinned at his own appearance when he had finished.

The fire was sinking, so he put on coal. The house was now quite dark, save for the light of a street-lamp that shone in faintly from beyond the holly-trees. He lit the gas with matches he found on the mantelpiece. Then he emptied the pockets of his own clothes, and threw all his wet things in a heap into the scullery. After which he gathered up her sodden clothes, gently, and put them in a separate heap on the copper-top in the scullery.

It was six o'clock on the clock. His own watch had stopped. He ought to go back to the surgery. He waited, and still she did not come down. So he went to the foot of the stairs and called:

"I shall have to go."

Almost immediately he heard her coming down. She had on her best dress of black voile, and her hair was tidy, but still damp. She looked at him— and in spite of herself, smiled.

"I don't like you in those clothes," she said.

"Do I look a sight?" he answered.

They were shy of one another.

"I'll make you some tea," she said.

"No, I must go."

"Must you?" And she looked at him again with the wide, strained, doubtful eyes. And again, from the pain of his breast, he knew how he loved her. He went and bent to kiss her, gently, passionately, with his heart's painful kiss.

"And my hair smells so horrible," she murmured in distraction. "And I'm so awful, I'm so awful! Oh, no, I'm too awful." And she broke into bitter, heartbroken sobbing. "You can't want to love me, I'm horrible."

"Don't be silly, don't be silly," he said, trying to comfort her, kissing her, holding her in his arms. "I want you, I want to marry you, we're going to be married, quickly, quickly—tomorrow if I can."

But she only sobbed terribly, and cried:

"I feel awful. I feel awful. I feel I'm horrible to you."

"No, I want you, I want you," was all he answered, blindly, with that terrible intonation which frightened her almost more than her horror lest he should *not* want her.

DYLAN THOMAS
1914–1953

A Winter's Tale

It is a winter's tale
That the snow blind twilight ferries over the lakes
And floating fields from the farm in the cup of the
    vales,
Gliding windless through the hand folded flakes,
The pale breath of cattle at the stealthy sail,°   5

    And the stars falling cold,
And the smell of hay in the snow, and the far owl
Warning among the folds, and the frozen hold°
Flocked with the sheep white smoke of the farm
    house cowl
In the river wended vales where the tale was told. 10

    Once when the world turned old
On a star of faith pure as the drifting bread,°

A WINTER'S TALE. **5. The pale . . . sail:** The cattle breathe on and move the twilight's sail. **8. hold:** pen, enclosure. **11–12. Once . . . bread:** The action of the poem takes place in an earlier time, before "the rite is shorn" (l. 116), when the world of nature, particularly the snow, is conceived of as sacramental (see ll. 28 ff.).

As the food and flames of the snow, a man unrolled
The scrolls of fire that burned in his heart and head,
Torn and alone in a farm house in a fold   15

        Of fields. And burning then
In his firelit island ringed by the winged snow
And the dung hills white as wool and the hen
Roosts sleeping chill till the flame of the cock crow
Combs through the mantled yards and the morning
        men   20

        Stumble out with their spades,
The cattle stirring, the mousing cat stepping shy,
The puffed birds hopping and hunting, the milk-
        maids
Gentle in their clogs over the fallen sky,
And all the woken farm at its white trades,   25

        He knelt, he wept, he prayed,
By the spit and the black pot in the log bright light
And the cup and the cut bread in the dancing shade,
In the muffled house, in the quick of night,°
At the point of love, forsaken and afraid.   30

        He knelt on the cold stones,
He wept from the crest of grief, he prayed to the
        veiled sky
May his hunger go howling on bare white bones
Past the statues of the stables and the sky roofed
        sties
And the duck pond glass and the blinding byres°
        alone   35

        Into the home of prayers
And fires where he should prowl down the cloud
Of his snow blind love and rush in the white lairs.°
His naked need struck him howling and bowed 39
Though no sound flowed down the hand folded air

        But only the wind strung
Hunger of birds in the fields of the bread of water,
        tossed
In high corn and the harvest melting on their
        tongues.
And his nameless need bound him burning and lost
When cold as snow he should run the wended
        vales among°   45

The rivers mouthed in night,
And drown in the drifts of his need, and lie curled
        caught
In the always desiring center of the white
Inhuman cradle and the bride bed forever sought
By the believer lost and the hurled outcast of light.

        Deliver him, he cried,   51
By losing him all in love, and cast his need
Alone and naked in the engulfing bride,
Never to flourish in the fields of the white seed
Or flower under the time dying flesh astride.   55

        Listen. The minstrels sing
In the departed villages. The nightingale,
Dust in the buried wood, flies on the grains of her
        wings
And spells on the winds of the dead his winter's
        tale.
The voice of the dust of water from the withered
        spring   60

        Is telling. The wizened
Stream with bells and baying water bounds. The
        dew rings
On the gristed° leaves and the long gone glistening
Parish of snow. The carved mouths in the rock are
        wind swept strings.
Time sings through the intricately dead snow
        drop. Listen.   65

        It was a hand or sound
In the long ago land that glided the dark door°
        wide
And there outside on the bread of the ground
A she bird rose and rayed like a burning bride.
A she bird dawned, and her breast with snow and
        scarlet downed.   70

        Look. And the dancers move
On the departed, snow bushed green, wanton in
        moon light
As a dust of pigeons. Exulting, the grave hooved
Horses, centaur dead, turn and tread the drenched
        white
Paddocks in the farms of birds. The dead oak
        walks for love.   75

---

29. quick of night: quick in the sense of alive (cf. in the dead of night). **33–38. May . . . lairs:** May his hunger go howling . . . and be answered by heaven. **35. byres:** cowsheds. **44–45. And his . . . among:** His need restrained him at a time when he should have actively sought his vision.

56–65. Listen . . . Listen: The narrative is interrupted just before and after (ll. 71–80) the mystical she bird rises; the first passage describes the other tellers of the tale, the second the rebirth of all that was once dead. **63. gristed:** ground up. **67. dark door:** door of perception and later the door of death.

The carved limbs in the rock
Leap, as to trumpets. Calligraphy of the old
Leaves is dancing. Lines of age on the stones
    weave in a flock.
And the harp shaped voice of the water's dust
    plucks in a fold
Of fields. For love, the long ago she bird rises.
    Look.   80

    And the wild wings were raised
Above her folded head, and the soft feathered
    voice
Was flying through the house as though the she
    bird praised
And all the elements of the slow fall rejoiced
That a man knelt alone in the cup of vales,   85

    In the mantle and calm,
By the spit and the black pot in the log bright light.
And the sky of birds in the plumed voice charmed
Him up and he ran like a wind after the kindling
    flight
Past the blind barns and byres of the windless
    farm.   90

    In the poles of the year°
When black birds died like priests in the cloaked
    hedge row
And over the cloth of counties the far hills rode
    near,
Under the one leaved trees ran a scarecrow of snow
And fast through the drifts of the thickets antlered
    like deer,   95

    Rags and prayers down the knee-
Deep hillocks and loud on the numbered lakes,
All night lost and long wading in the wake of
    the she
Bird through the times and lands and tribes of the
    slow flakes.
Listen and look where she sails the goose plucked
    sea,   100

    The sky, the bird, the bride,
The cloud, the need, the planted stars, the joy
    beyond
The fields of seed and the time dying flesh astride,
The heavens, the heaven, the grave, the burning
    font,
In the far ago land the door of his death glided
    wide,   105

And the bird descended.
On a bread white hill over the cupped farm
And the lakes and floating fields and the river
    wended
Vales where he prayed to come to the last harm
And the home of prayers and fires, the tale
    ended.   110

    The dancing perishes
On the white, no longer growing green, and,
    minstrel dead,
The singing breaks in the snow shoed villages of
    wishes
That once cut the figures of birds on the deep
    bread
And over the glazed lakes skated the shapes of
    fishes   115

    Flying. The rite is shorn
Of nightingale and centaur dead horse. The
    springs wither
Back. Lines of age sleep on the stones till trumpet-
    ing dawn.°
Exultation lies down. Time buries the spring
    weather
That belled and bounded with the fossil and the
    dew reborn.   120

    For the bird lay bedded
In a choir of wings, as though she slept or died,
And the wings glided wide and he was hymned
    and wedded,
And through the thighs of the engulfing bride,
The woman breasted and the heaven headed   125

    Bird, he was brought low,
Burning in the bride bed of love, in the whirl-
Pool at the wanting center, in the folds
Of Paradise, in the spun bud of the world.
And she rose with him flowering in her melting
    snow.   130

---

91. poles . . . year: arctic and antarctic winter united.

118. trumpeting dawn: the Resurrection.

Thematic Romance

Lyric poems in the romantic mode work a variety of "translations" on the characters, actions, and motives of narrative romance. The events in the narrative are transformed into analogous attitudes or states of mind. As action becomes thought, patterns in what the narrative hero does find parallels in what the thematic poet or, more properly, the speaker in the poem thinks or imagines. There are other more specific analogies between components of narrative and thematic romance. Attributes of the persona's role in the poem correspond to those of the narrative hero; the audience imagined by the speaker resembles the society surrounding the hero in the narrative, particularly when his superior powers are revealed; and finally, thematic romance, as if freed from the exigencies of narration, openly pays homage to the divine order implicit in romance narratives.

In the tradition of religious or visionary verse, a number of poems are close analogs of narratives of advent and initiation. The closest thematic parallel to those narratives is found, of course, in poems that are nearly narrative in form and that celebrate the advent of Jesus or the early career of a saint—Milton's ode "On the Morning of Christ's Nativity" and Richard Crashaw's "Hymn to Saint Teresa," are two examples. Perhaps a more interesting similarity to the narrative pattern is the depiction of Jesus or the saint with the features and armor of the romantic hero. In "A Dream of the Rood" Jesus is described as "the young Warrior, God, the All-Wielder," an almost natural reflex for an Anglo-Saxon poet. Later in Hopkins' sonnet "The Windhover" a similar conception of a heroic Jesus is derived from the tradition of the militant Christ and embodied in romantic images of the "kingdom of daylight's dauphin" and "my chevalier." In Crashaw's "Hymn to Saint Teresa" the imagery of knighthood and a pattern of events much like a quest contrasts with the innocence of Teresa and her vision of love. Walt Whitman's "Passage to India" indicates that the romantic lyricist may employ this heroic convention with a secular subject. In a gesture typical of the nineteenth-century visionary poet, Whitman imagines the quest for the New World,

The Vision of the Heroic

and with incantatory lines of prophetic daring, he finds his hero in a poet not unlike himself. In its thematic form, the advent and initiation is as often experienced as it is witnessed by the poet: the Anglo-Saxon poet's initiation is presided over by the cross and vicariously performed in the narrative of the Crucifixion, and Hopkins' oracular insight comes like the gift of tongues from the windhover.

Visions like these confer on the romantic poet a status similar to that of the romantic hero, midway between the human and the divine. Like the hero's initiation, the romantic poet's vision becomes an event that at once strips him of his innocence and sets him apart, as "the dearest of dreams" does the Dream of the Rood poet "when mortal men / Were sunk in slumber." Moreover, the vision makes manifest the tone of the romantic mode, for all things are now invested with the aura of the sacramental. Tradition, history, and the common wisdom of the world are infused with the light of revelation. The poet's stance is similarly determined by the vision that commands his expression. It is as if he is startled or enchanted into prophetic speech. Yet the very fact that it is a vision will not allow him to sully the experience with further argument or proof. Any extensive comment to his audience would turn his eyes from the mystery and might suggest that his vision is something less than self-evident. Coleridge's account of the writing of "Kubla Khan" is almost too appropriate to be true. He tells us that in an opium dream he imagined himself writing a poem of two to three hundred lines. When he awoke he hurriedly wrote down the lines we now know, but then was interrupted by a man on business from the village of Porlock. When he returned to his poem the vision was gone; and perhaps fortunately so, for much of its authority as a vision lies in its fragmentary and oracular form. One suspects that if there had not been a man from Porlock, Coleridge would have had to invent him.

The Ideal World of the Imagination

For the lyric poet the counterpart of the quest is the metaphysical journey, the search for an ideal world like that of Kubla Khan's "stately pleasure-dome" or the gold mosaics of Byzantium. This pattern is similar to that in the lyrics of thematic comedy that seek resolution in an imaginative order. However, the romantic poet depends more on some supernal power, and his quest is for some version of the celestial city or court, like the ruling courts of narrative romance, presided over by "lords and ladies of Byzantium" or some figure like Kubla Khan. The poet of thematic comedy is content with the natural world and is more democratic; Tennyson, on the other hand, takes up Ulysses' story *after* his worldly adventures and sets him on a journey to the west seeking "knowledge like a sinking star." The world of Ithaca, where lesser men like Telemachus may do their work, will not accommodate the motives of the romance lyric. For Marvell the real world is one of human vanity and unending labor; for Yeats, it is a teeming and transient world that troubles his mature vision with the natural rounds of "whatever is begotten, born, and dies." And even for Wordsworth, "the common light of day" compels the poet to seek an older man's philosophic resolve and to affirm intimations of immortality.

In most of these lyrics there is a pattern of thematic movement between two realms, from the world of the real, the living, and the natural to the world of the ideal, the eternal, and the supernatural, a progress from all that we can see to all that we can imagine. Thus the role of the seer is merged with the role of the wanderer; the poet seeks and affirms new states of consciousness, questions and rejects the conventional and the normal. In this sense Allen Ginsberg and Lawrence Ferlinghetti are, perhaps to their dismay, traditional poets. The romantic poet encounters his adversary in those conditions of life that will not accommodate his vision, in the present world that has fallen from the imagined world of innocence, or in a society that will not venture toward his vision of the future. Like the characters in narrative romance, his audience is either for him or against him, a slumbering generation or a saving remnant. Yet he remains detached. Though nothing is more important than his vision, his very engagement in that vision and his dependence on the mysterious source of his inspiration prevent him from joining his audience. Nor can he speak explicitly, like the poet of thematic tragedy, as an advocate either for his audience or for the supernatural powers he serves. His voice has the singular finality of a prophet's, for his role is to convey, not to explain, the mystery. Out of his sense of conviction rise the accents of impatience heard in the voices of Tennyson's Ulysses and Yeats' voyager to Byzantium.

The Oracular Role

Just as the events in narrative romance culminate in the hero's confrontation with the otherworld, so the ideas and attitudes of thematic romance culminate in the tradition of oracular poetry, those lyrics in which the poet is absorbed in some enigmatic event or force and is moved to speak as a mystic or seer. With a few exceptions, such as Shelley's "Ode to the West Wind" and the first of Yeats' "Two Songs from a Play," the speaker is lost in the enigma he confronts. His tone takes on the accents of fearsome awe rather than delighted wonder. The mood of the prophecy, though still ordering the world with transcendent powers, assumes a darker, more elegiac character than that of the vision poems considered earlier. The poet, like the hero of narrative romance, senses his isolation and shows little awareness of an audience.

Just as the romantic death differs from the tragic in the narrative patterns, the theme of loss and reconciliation characteristic of the elegy is conceived differently in thematic romance. The initial despair and anguish typical of the elegy is lessened by the awesome confidence in the miraculous. George Herbert's Easter poems are infused with a serenity that is more a prior axiom than a conclusion to be worked toward as it is in the classical elegy. Poems that witness scenes of death and imminent rebirth are marked by the almost monumental stillness of the final events in the romance narrative. The medieval lyrics "Now goth sonne under wode" and "Lully, lullay" and Yeats' "Two Songs from a Play" are like painted tableaux or stone carvings; gestures, when they occur, are iconic and ritualistic. Shelley's ode is only an apparent exception, for even there the turbulence he invokes is contained and controlled within the long apostrophes and imperative sentences.

As romantic poems confront the mysterious they became more imbued with paradoxical and enigmatic qualities. Blake's lamb and tiger merge in the one deity, winter breeds spring, the "staring virgin" is both Aphrodite and the Virgin Mary, and "Erthe" shifts its meaning in every phrase. Oracular, prophetic, incantatory, the haunting medieval lyric "Erthe took of Erthe" reads at once like a mystic charm to summon dark fields to life again and like the story in little of man's fall and redemption. It would serve as an epitaph for the tombs of all the heroes of romance.

Thematic Parallels to Narrative Romance in "The Garden"

Andrew Marvell's "Garden" offers the chance to trace the poet's use of the concepts of thematic romance. With the intellectual habits of a seventeenth-century metaphysical poet, he trained his analytic talents on some of the literary themes, like those of the pastoral tradition, that are closely associated with the romantic mode. Versions of the contemplative pastoral life and the refined passions of romance appear in "The Garden." Although these themes are expressed with a wit and humorous logic unusual in thematic romance, Marvell still displays some of the distinctive attitudes and strategies of the romantic lyricist.

ANDREW MARVELL
1621–1678

The Garden

How vainly men themselves amaze
To win the palm, the oak, or bays;°
And their incessant labors see
Crowned from some single herb or tree,
Whose short and narrow-vergèd shade   5
Does prudently their toils upbraid;
While all flowers and all trees do close
To weave the garlands of repose!

THE GARDEN. **2. palm . . . bays:** Crowns were woven of these leaves for winners of athletic, military, and poetic contests, respectively.

Fair Quiet, have I found thee here,
And Innocence, thy sister dear?   10
Mistaken long, I sought you then
In busy companies of men.
Your sacred plants, if here below,
Only among the plants will grow;
Society is all but rude,   15
To° this delicious solitude.

No white nor red was ever seen
So amorous as this lovely green.
Fond° lovers, cruel as their flame,
Cut in these trees their mistress' name.   20
Little, alas, they know or heed,
How far these beauties hers exceed!
Fair trees! wheresoe'er your barks I wound,
No name shall but your own be found.

16. To: compared to. **19. Fond:** foolish.

When we have run our passion's heat, 25
Love hither makes his best retreat.
The gods, that mortal beauty chase,
Still in a tree did end their race:
Apollo hunted Daphne so,
Only that she might laurel grow; 30
And Pan did after Syrinx speed,
Not as a nymph, but for a reed.°

What wondrous life is this I lead!
Ripe apples drop about my head;
The luscious clusters of the vine 35
Upon my mouth do crush their wine;
The nectarine and curious° peach
Into my hands themselves do reach;
Stumbling on melons, as I pass,
Insnared with flowers, I fall on grass. 40

Meanwhile the mind, from pleasure less,
Withdraws into its happiness:
The mind, that ocean where each kind
Does straight its own resemblance find;°
Yet it creates, transcending these, 45
Far other worlds, and other seas,
Annihilating all that's made
To a green thought in a green shade.

Here at the fountain's sliding foot,
Or at some fruit-tree's mossy root, 50
Casting the body's vest° aside,
My soul into the boughs does glide:
There like a bird it sits and sings,
Then whets° and combs its silver wings,
And, till prepared for longer flight, 55
Waves in its plumes the various light.

Such was the happy garden-state,
While man there walked without a mate:
After a place so pure, and sweet,
What other help could yet be meet! 60
But 'twas beyond a mortal's share
To wander solitary there:
Two paradises 'twere in one,
To live in Paradise alone.

How well the skillful gardener drew 65
Of flowers and herbs this dial° new!
Where, from above, the milder sun
Does through a fragrant zodiac run;
And, as it works, th' industrious bee
Computes its time as well as we! 70
How could such sweet and wholesome hours
Be reckoned but with herbs and flowers?

29–32. Apollo . . . reed: In myth Daphne was turned into a laurel to escape Apollo, and Syrinx into a reed to escape Pan. 37. curious: exquisite. 43–44. The . . . find: reference to the notion that all creatures on earth have their counterparts in the sea.

51. vest: garment. 54. whets: preens. 66. dial: probably a formal garden arranged as a clock, or flowers measuring time in their growth and decline.

The poem begins with a departure, a farewell contrast between that rude society where "men themselves amaze / To win the palm, the oak, or bays" and the garden where "all flowers and all trees do close / To weave the garlands of repose!" The objects of the quest are the personified figures of Fair Quiet and Innocence, for whom the speaker has searched so long. Personification is, as we have noted, a frequent device in romance though not unique to the mode. The second to the fifth stanzas, once the speaker has left the "busy companies of men," relate his contemplative love for the beauties of nature (in the third stanza) to the love of the gods Apollo and Pan for two beautiful mortals who were transformed into plants. Each kind of love involves a specific kind of metamorphosis: the speaker, shunning the world of fond lovers, sublimates his love in a transcendent passion for the garden, while the gods, seeking love on a plane lower than the divine, find their love transformed in a "descendent" passion for the laurel and reed. Thus both human and divine passions meet in the natural world, with the divine descent lending poetic justification to the ascent of human love. This reading is supported by the poetic logic of the fifth stanza, the conclusion of the first half of the poem. The stanza, by itself, celebrates in luxuriant imagery the wondrous life of the speaker in a receptive natural world. But in the context of the poetic argument on human, "natural," and divine passion, the stanza does something more. With its overtly sensual metaphors, it transforms the kiss and the caress in a fruitful sublimation of the human gestures of love. We may set our own limits on this reading, but Marvell's wit invites us to be liberal.

The celebrated sixth stanza, with its suggestive culmination in "a green thought in a green shade," is the logical center of the poem. It presents an analogy between the sea and the mind that contains images of all things in this world and possesses as well the power to imagine other worlds. In the next stanza the poet's soul, as if in response to the movement of his mind, transcends time and space, gliding from his body like a silver bird, in an act that foreshadows its future ascent to heaven. And in the eighth stanza, the mind again escapes the temporal and spatial to look backward to the Edenic state now mentally recreated and purified with solitude.

With his imaginative quest ended, the poet unites the realms of the natural and the divine in the image of the floral zodiac: here the flowers of this world are patterned after the stars in a higher one. The poem, like the final image of the garden, epitomizes the romantic mode. However much the romantic imagination withdraws into its own happiness, it contains resemblances for everything in our experience, while it creates "far other worlds, and other seas." The symbol of the garden joins the world our mind reflects and the world it creates. Like the romantic mode, the dial of flowers orders space and records time as it recreates the figures in the constellations that are said to govern the lives of men.

The Vision of the Heroic

A Dream of the Rood

ca. 750–800

Translated by Charles W. Kennedy

Lo! I will tell   the dearest of dreams
That I dreamed in the midnight   when mortal men
Were sunk in slumber.   Meseemed I saw
A wondrous Tree   towering in air,
Most shining of crosses   compassed with light.
Brightly that beacon   was gilded with gold;   6
Jewels adorned it   fair at the foot,
Five on the shoulder-beam,°   blazing in splendor.
Through all creation   the angels of God
Beheld it shining—   no cross of shame!   10
Holy spirits   gazed on its gleaming,
Men upon earth   and all this great creation.
  Wondrous that Tree,   that Token of triumph,
And I a transgressor   soiled with my sins!
I gazed on the Rood   arrayed in glory,   15
Shining in beauty   and gilded with gold,
The Cross of the Savior   beset with gems.
But through the gold-work   outgleamed a token
Of the ancient evil   of sinful men
Where the Rood on its right side   once sweat blood.   20
Saddened and rueful,   smitten with terror
At the wondrous Vision,   I saw the Cross
Swiftly varying   vesture and hue,
Now wet and stained   with the Blood outwelling,

Now fairly jeweled   with gold and gems.   25
  Then, as I lay there,   long I gazed
In rue and sadness   on my Savior's Tree,
Till I heard in dream   how the Cross addressed me,
Of all woods worthiest,   speaking these words:
  "Long years ago   (well yet I remember)   30
They hewed me down   on the edge of the holt,
Severed my trunk;   strong foemen took me,
For a spectacle wrought me,   a gallows for rogues.
High on their shoulders   they bore me to hilltop,
Fastened me firmly,   an army of foes!   35
  "Then I saw the King   of all mankind
In brave mood hasting   to mount upon me.
Refuse I dared not,   nor bow nor break,
Though I felt earth's confines   shudder in fear;
All foes I might fell,   yet still I stood fast.   40
  "Then the young Warrior,   God, the All-Wielder,
Put off His raiment,   steadfast and strong;
With lordly mood   in the sight of many
He mounted the Cross   to redeem mankind.
When the Hero clasped me   I trembled in terror,   45
But I dared not bow me   nor bend to earth;
I must needs stand fast.   Upraised as the Rood
I held the High King,   the Lord of heaven.
I dared not bow!   With black nails driven
Those sinners pierced me;   the prints are clear,
The open wounds.   I dared injure none.   51
They mocked us both.   I was wet with blood
From the Hero's side   when He sent forth His spirit.
  "Many a bale°   I bore on that hillside

A DREAM OF THE ROOD.   **8. shoulder-beam:** crosspiece.   **54. bale:** sorrow.

Seeing the Lord   in agony outstretched.   55
Black darkness covered   with clouds God's
  body,
That radiant splendor.   Shadow went forth
Wan under heaven;   all creation wept
Bewailing the King's death.   Christ was on the
  Cross.
  "Then many came quickly,   faring from far,
Hurrying to the Prince.   I beheld it all.   61
Sorely smitten with sorrow   in meekness I
  bowed
To the hands of men.   From His heavy and
  bitter pain
They lifted Almighty God.   Those warriors left
  me
Standing bespattered with blood,   I was wound-
  ed with spears.   65
Limb-weary they laid Him down;   they stood at
  His head,
Looked on the Lord of heaven   as He lay there
  at rest
From His bitter ordeal all forspent.°   In sight of
  His slayers
They made Him a sepulcher   carved from the
  shining stone;
Therein laid the Lord of triumph.   At evening
  tide   70
Sadly they sang their dirges   and wearily turned
  away
From their lordly Prince;   there He lay all still
  and alone.
  "There at our station   a long time we stood
Sorrowfully weeping   after the wailing of men
Had died away.   The corpse grew cold,   75
The fair life-dwelling.   Down to earth
Men hacked and felled us,   a grievous fate!
They dug a pit   and buried us deep.
But there God's friends   and followers found me
And graced me with treasure   of silver and gold.
  "Now may you learn,   O man beloved,   81
The bitter sorrows   that I have borne,
The work of caitiffs.°   But the time is come
That men upon earth   and through all creation
Show me honor   and bow to this sign.   85
On me a while   God's Son once suffered;
Now I tower under heaven   in glory attired
With healing for all   that hold me in awe.
Of old I was once   the most woeful of tortures,
Most hateful to all men,   till I opened for them

68. forspent: exhausted. 83. caitiffs: scoundrels.

The true Way of life.   Lo! the Lord of glory, 91
The Warden of heaven,   above all wood
Has glorified me   as Almighty God
Has honored His Mother,   even Mary herself,
Over all womankind   in the eyes of men.   95
  "Now I give you bidding,   O man beloved,
Reveal this Vision   to the sons of men,
And clearly tell   of the Tree of glory
Whereon God suffered   for man's many sins
And the evil that Adam   once wrought of old.
  "Death He suffered,   but our Savior rose 101
By virtue of His great might   as a help to men.
He ascended to heaven.   But hither again
He shall come unto earth   to seek mankind,
The Lord Himself   on the Day of Doom,   105
Almighty God   with His angel hosts.
And then will He judge,   Who has power of
  judgment,
To each man according   as here on earth
In this fleeting life   he shall win reward.
  "Nor there may any   be free from fear   110
Hearing the words   which the Wielder shall
  utter.
He shall ask before many: Where is the man
Who would taste bitter death   as He did on the
  Tree?
And all shall be fearful   and few shall know
What to say unto Christ.   But none at His
  Coming   115
Shall need to fear   if he bears in his breast
This best of symbols;   and every soul
From the ways of earth   through the Cross shall
  come
To heavenly glory,   who would dwell with God."
  Then with ardent spirit   and earnest zeal,   120
Companionless, lonely,   I prayed to the Cross.
My soul was fain of° death.   I had endured
Many an hour of longing.   It is my life's hope
That I may turn   to this Token of triumph,
I above all men,   and revere it well.   125
  This is my heart's desire,   and all my hope
Waits on the Cross.   In this world now
I have few powerful friends;   they have fared
  hence
Away from these earthly gauds   seeking the
  King of glory,
Dwelling now with the High Father   in heaven
  above,   130
Abiding in rapture.   Each day I dream

122. fain of: pleased with.

Of the hour when the Cross of my Lord,   where-
of here on earth
I once had vision,   from this fleeting life may
fetch me
And bring me where is great gladness   and
heavenly bliss,
Where the people of God   are planted and
stablished for ever   135
In joy everlasting.   There may it lodge me
Where I may abide in glory   knowing bliss with
the saints.
    May the Lord be gracious   who on earth of
old
Once suffered on the Cross   for the sins of men.
He redeemed us, endowed us with life   and a
heavenly home.   140
Therein was hope renewed   with blessing and
bliss
For those who endured the burning.   In that
great deed
God's Son was triumphant,   possessing power
and strength!
Almighty, Sole-Ruling   He came to the king-
dom of God
Bringing a host of souls   to angelic bliss,   145
To join the saints   who abode in the splendor of
glory,
When the Lord, Almighty God,   came again to
His throne.

RICHARD CRASHAW
1612?–1649

A Hymn to the Name and Honor
of the Admirable Saint Teresa°

*Foundress of the reformation of the Discalced
Carmelites, both men and women. A woman for
angelical height of speculation, for masculine
courage of performance, more than a woman,
who yet a child outran maturity, and durst plot
a martyrdom.*

Love, thou art absolute sole lord
Of life and death. To prove the word,

A HYMN TO SAINT TERESA. Theresa of Avila (1515–82) was
a Spanish nun who founded the reformed order of the
Discalced (barefooted) Carmelites.

We'll now appeal to none of all
Those thy old soldiers, great and tall,
Ripe men of martyrdom, that could reach down 5
With strong arms their triumphant crown,
Such as could with lusty breath
Speak loud into the face of death
Their great Lord's glorious name; to none
Of those whose spacious bosoms spread a throne 10
For love at large to fill; spare blood and sweat,
And see him take a private seat,
Making his mansion in the mild
And milky soul of a soft child.
    Scarce has she learned to lisp the name   15
Of martyr, yet she thinks it shame
Life should so long play with that breath
Which spent can buy so brave a death.
She never undertook to know
What death with love should have to do;   20
Nor has she e'er yet understood
Why to show love she should shed blood;
Yet though she cannot tell you why,
She can love and she can die.
    Scarce has she blood enough to make   25
A guilty sword blush for her sake;
Yet has she a heart dares hope to prove
How much less strong is death than love.
    Be love but there, let poor six years
Be posed with the maturest fears   30
Man trembles at, you straight shall find
Love knows no nonage, nor the mind.
'Tis love, not years or limbs that can
Make the martyr or the man.
    Love touched her heart, and lo it beats   35
High, and burns with such brave heats,
Such thirsts to die, as dares drink up
A thousand cold deaths in one cup.
Good reason, for she breathes all fire;
Her weak breast heaves with strong desire   40
Of what she may with fruitless wishes
Seek for amongst her mother's kisses.
    Since 'tis not to be had at home,
She'll travel to a martyrdom.
No home for hers confesses she   45
But where she may a martyr be.
    She'll to the Moors,° and trade with them
For this unvalued diadem.°

47. **Moors:** As children, she and her brother, inspired by
the lives of the saints, tried unsuccessfully to go to the
land of the Moors and die for their faith. **48. unvalued
diadem:** martyrdom not valued by the Moslem Moors
but invaluable to her.

She'll offer them her dearest breath,
With Christ's name in 't, in change for death.   50
She'll bargain with them, and will give
Them God, teach them how to live
In him; or if they this deny,
For him she'll teach them how to die.
So shall she leave amongst them sown   55
Her Lord's blood, or at least her own.
   Farewell then, all the world, adieu!
Teresa is no more for you.
Farewell, all pleasures, sports, and joys,
Never till now esteemèd toys,   60
Farewell, whatever dear may be,
Mother's arms or father's knee;
Farewell house and farewell home,
She's for the Moors and martyrdom!
   Sweet, not so fast! lo, thy fair spouse°   65
Whom thou seek'st with so swift vows
Calls thee back, and bids thee come
T' embrace a milder martyrdom.
   Blest powers forbid thy tender life
Should bleed upon a barbarous knife;   70
Or some base hand have power to rase°
Thy breast's chaste cabinet and uncase
A soul kept there so sweet; oh no,
Wise heav'n will never have it so:
Thou art love's victim, and must die   75
A death more mystical and high;
Into love's arms thou shalt let fall
A still surviving funeral.°
His is the dart must make the death
Whose stroke shall taste thy hallowed breath;   80
A dart thrice dipped in that rich flame°
Which writes thy spouse's radiant name
Upon the roof of heav'n, where aye
It shines, and with a sovereign ray
Beats bright upon the burning faces   85
Of souls, which in that name's sweet graces
Find everlasting smiles. So rare,
So spiritual, pure, and fair
Must be th' immortal instrument
Upon whose choice point shall be sent   90
A life so loved; and that there be
Fit executioners for thee,
The fair'st and firstborn sons of fire,
Blest seraphim, shall leave their choir

And turn love's soldiers, upon thee   95
To exercise their archery.
   Oh, how oft shalt thou complain
Of a sweet and subtle pain,
Of intolerable joys,
Of a death in which who dies   100
Loves his death, and dies again,
And would forever so be slain,
And lives and dies, and knows not why
To live, but that he thus may never leave to die.
   How kindly will thy gentle heart   105
Kiss the sweetly killing dart!
And close in his embraces keep
Those delicious wounds, that weep
Balsam to heal themselves with. Thus
When these thy deaths, so numerous,   110
Shall all at last die into one,
And melt thy soul's sweet mansïon
Like a soft lump of incense, hasted
By too hot a fire, and wasted
Into perfuming clouds, so fast   115
Shalt thou exhale to heav'n at last
In a resolving sigh; and then,
Oh, what? Ask not the tongues of men;
Angels cannot tell; suffice,
Thyself shall feel thine own full joys   120
And hold them fast forever. There
So soon as thou shalt first appear,
The moon of maiden stars, thy white
Mistress, attended by such bright
Souls as thy shining self, shall come   125
And in her first ranks make thee room;
Where 'mongst her snowy family
Immortal welcomes wait for thee.
   Oh, what delight when revealèd life shall stand
And teach thy lips heav'n with his hand,   130
On which thou now mayst to thy wishes
Heap up thy consecrated kisses.
What joys shall seize thy soul when she,
Bending her blessed eyes on thee,
Those second smiles of heaven, shall dart   135
Her mild rays through thy melting heart!
   Angels, thy old friends, there shall greet thee,
Glad at their own home now to meet thee.
   All thy good works which went before
And waited for thee at the door   140
Shall own thee there, and all in one
Weave a constellatïon
Of crowns, with which the King, thy spouse,
Shall build up thy triumphant brows.

65. spouse: Jesus. **71. rase:** cut, slash. **78. still . . . funeral:** still body still surviving its own funeral. **79–81. His . . . flame:** In a vision an angel thrust a golden dart tipped with fire into her heart and left her inflamed with the love of God.

All thy old woes shall now smile on thee,   145
And thy pains sit bright upon thee;
All thy sorrows here shall shine,
All thy sufferings be divine;
Tears shall take comfort and turn gems,
And wrongs repent to diadems.   150
Even thy deaths shall live, and new
Dress the soul that erst they slew;
Thy wounds shall blush to such bright scars
As keep account of the Lamb's wars.
 Those rare works where thou shalt leave writ   155
Love's noble history, with wit
Taught thee by none but him, while here
They feed our souls, shall clothe thine there.
Each heav'nly word by whose hid flame
Our hard hearts shall strike fire, the same   160
Shall flourish on thy brows, and be
Both fire to us and flame to thee,
Whose light shall live bright in thy face
By glory, in our hearts by grace.
 Thou shalt look round about and see   165
Thousands of crownèd souls throng to be
Themselves thy crown; sons of thy vows,
The virgin-births with which thy sovereign spouse
Made fruitful thy fair soul, go now
And with them all about thee, bow   170
To him. "Put on," he'll say, "put on,
My rosy love, that thy rich zone
Sparkling with the sacred flames
Of thousand souls whose happy names
Heav'n keeps upon thy score. Thy bright   175
Life brought them first to kiss the light
That kindled them to stars." And so
Thou with the Lamb, thy Lord, shalt go,
And wheresoe'er he sets his white
Steps, walk with him those ways of light   180
Which who in death would live to see
Must learn in life to die like thee.

JOHN MILTON
1608–1674

On the Morning
of Christ's Nativity

1

This is the month, and this the happy morn,
Wherein the Son of Heaven's eternal King,
Of wedded maid and virgin mother born,
Our great redemption from above did bring;
For so the holy sages° once did sing,   5
 That he our deadly forfeit° should release,
And with his Father work us a perpetual peace.

2

That glorious form, that light unsufferable,
And that far-beaming blaze of majesty,
Wherewith he wont° at Heaven's high council-
  table   10
To sit the midst of Trinal Unity,°
He laid aside, and, here with us to be,
 Forsook the courts of everlasting day,
And chose with us a darksome house of mortal clay.

3

Say, Heavenly Muse,° shall not thy sacred vein   15
Afford a present to the Infant God,
Hast thou no verse, no hymn, or solemn strain,
To welcome him to this his new abode,
Now while the heaven, by the Sun's team untrod,
 Hath took no print of the approaching light,   20
And all the spangled host keep watch in squadrons
  bright?

4

See how from far upon the eastern road
The star-led wizards° haste with odors sweet:

ON THE MORNING OF CHRIST'S NATIVITY. **5. holy sages:**
prophets of the Old Testament. **6. deadly forfeit:** original
sin. **10. wont:** was wont. **11. midst . . . Unity:** between God
the Father and the Holy Ghost. **15. Heavenly Muse:**
Urania, muse of sacred poetry. **23. wizards:** the three wise
men.

O run, prevent° them with thy humble ode,
And lay it lowly at his blessèd feet;   25
Have thou the honor first thy Lord to greet,
   And join thy voice unto the angel quire,
From out his secret altar touched with hallowed
    fire.

THE HYMN

1

It was the winter wild,
While the Heaven-born child   30
   All meanly wrapped in the rude manger lies;
Nature, in awe to him,
Had doffed her gaudy trim,
   With her great Master so to sympathize:
It was no season then for her   35
To wanton with the Sun, her lusty paramour.

2

Only with speeches fair
She woos the gentle air
   To hide her guilty front with innocent snow,
And on her naked shame,   40
Pollute° with sinful blame,
   The saintly veil of maiden white to throw;
Confounded, that her Maker's eyes
Should look so near upon her foul deformities.

3

But he, her fears to cease,°   45
Sent down the meek-eyed Peace:
   She, crowned with olive green, came softly sliding
Down through the turning sphere,
His ready harbinger,
   With turtle° wing the amorous clouds dividing 50
And, waving wide her myrtle wand,
She strikes a universal peace through sea and land.

4

No war, or battle's sound,
Was heard the world around:

The idle spear and shield were high uphung;   55
The hookèd chariot stood,
Unstained with hostile blood;
   The trumpet spake not to the armed throng;
And kings sat still with awful eye,
As if they surely knew their sovran Lord was by. 60

5

But peaceful was the night
Wherein the Prince of Light
   His reign of peace upon the earth began:
The winds, with wonder whist,°
Smoothly the waters kissed,   65
   Whispering new joys to the mild ocëan,
Who now hath quite forgot to rave,
While birds of calm sit brooding on the charmèd
    wave.°

6

The stars, with deep amaze,
Stand fixed in steadfast gaze,   70
   Bending one way their precious influence,
And will not take their flight,
For all the morning light,
   Or Lucifer° that often warned them thence;
But in their glimmering orbs did glow,   75
Until their Lord himself bespake, and bid them go.

7

And, though the shady gloom
Had given day her room,
   The sun himself withheld his wonted speed,
And hid his head for shame,   80
As his inferior flame
   The new-enlightened world no more should
    need;
He saw a greater Sun appear
Than his bright throne or burning axletree could
    bear.

8

The shepherds on the lawn,°   85
Or ere the point of dawn,

---

24. **prevent:** come before. 41. **pollute:** polluted. 45. **cease:** allay. 50. **turtle:** turtledove, symbol of peace and love.

56. **hooked chariot:** armed with hooks at the hub of each wheel. 64. **whist:** hushed. 68. **While . . . wave:** reference to the belief that the seas become calm in December when the halcyons nest on the surface. 74. **Lucifer:** the morning star or the sun. 85. **lawn:** grassland or pasture.

Sat simply chatting in a rustic row;
Full little thought they than°
That the mighty Pan°
    Was kindly come to live with them below;   90
Perhaps their loves, or else their sheep,
Was all that did their silly° thoughts so busy keep.

9

When such music sweet
Their hearts and ears did greet
    As never was by mortal finger strook,   95
Divinely-warbled voice
Answering the stringèd noise,
    As all their souls in blissful rapture took:
The air, such pleasure loath to lose,
With thousand echoes still prolongs each heavenly
    close.°   100

10

Nature, that heard such sound
Beneath the hollow round
    Of Cynthia's seat, the airy region thrilling,
Now was almost won
To think her part was done,   105
    And that her reign had here its last fulfilling;
She knew such harmony alone
Could hold all Heaven and Earth in happier union.°

11

At last surrounds their sight
A globe of circular light,   110
    That with long beams the shamefaced night
    arrayed;
The helmèd cherubim
And sworded seraphim
    Are seen in glittering ranks with wings displayed,
Harping in loud and solemn quire,   115
With unexpressive° notes, to Heaven's newborn
    Heir.

12

Such music (as 'tis said)
Before was never made,
    But when of old the sons of morning° sung,
While the Creator great   120
His constellations set,
    And the well-balanced world on hinges hung,
And cast the dark foundations deep,
And bid the weltering waves their oozy channel
    keep.

13

Ring out, ye crystal spheres!   125
Once bless our human ears,°
    (If ye have power to touch our senses so),
And let your silver chime
Move in melodious time;
    And let the bass of heaven's deep organ blow; 130
And with your ninefold harmony
Make up full consort to th' angelic symphony.

14

For, if such holy song
Enwrap our fancy long,
    Time will run back and fetch the age of gold; 135
And speckled Vanity
Will sicken soon and die,
    And leprous Sin will melt from earthly mold;
And Hell itself will pass away,
And leave her dolorous mansions to the peering
    day.   140

15

Yea, Truth and Justice then
Will down return to men,
    Orbed in a rainbow; and, like glories wearing,
Mercy will sit between,
Throned in celestial sheen,   145
    With radiant feet the tissued clouds down
    steering;
And Heaven, as at some festival,
Will open wide the gates of her high palace-hall.

---

88. than: then. **89. Pan:** Greek god, guardian of flocks, associated with Christ as shepherd. **92. silly:** simple or innocent. **100. close:** cadence. **101–08. Nature . . . union:** Nature, hearing the angelic song, fears that it may replace the music of the spheres as a force binding and unifying the cosmos (see stanza 13, where the two harmonies are asked to join in concert). **116. unexpressive:** inexpressible.

119. sons of morning: morning stars (see Job 38:6–7). **126. Once . . . ears:** reference to the belief that the divine harmony has not been heard since the Fall.

16

But wisest Fate says no,
This must not yet be so;   150
  The Babe lies yet in smiling infancy
That on the bitter cross
Must redeem our loss,
  So both himself and us to glorify:
Yet first, to those ychained in sleep,   155
The wakeful trump of doom must thunder through
    the deep,

17

With such a horrid clang
As on Mount Sinai rang
  While the red fire and smoldering clouds
    outbrake:°
The agèd Earth, aghast   160
With terror of that blast,
  Shall from the surface to the center shake,
When, at the world's last session,
The dreadful Judge in middle air shall spread his
    throne.

18

And then at last our bliss   165
Full and perfect is,
  But now begins; for from this happy day
The old Dragon° under ground,
  In straiter limits bound,
  Not half so far casts his usurpèd sway,   170
And, wroth to see his kingdom fail,
Swinges the scaly horror of his folded tail.

19

The Oracles are dumb,
No voice or hideous hum
  Runs through the archèd roof in words de-
    ceiving.   175
Apollo from his shrine
Can no more divine,
  With hollow shriek the steep of Delphos° leaving.
No nightly trance, or breathèd spell,
Inspires the pale-eyed priest from the prophetic
    cell.   180

158–59. As . . . outbrake: reference to Moses receiving the Ten Commandments (see Exodus 19:16). 168. Dragon: Satan. 178. Delphos: Apollo's oracle at Delphi.

20

The lonely mountains o'er,
And the resounding shore,
  A voice of weeping heard and loud lament;
From hunted spring, and dale
Edged with poplar pale,   185
  The parting Genius° is with sighing sent;
With flower-inwoven tresses torn
The nymphs in twilight shade of tangled thickets
    mourn.

21

In consecrated earth,
And on the holy hearth,   190
  The Lars and Lemures° moan with midnight
    plaint;
In urns, and altars round,
A drear and dying sound
  Affrights the flamens° at their service quaint;
And the chill marble seems to sweat,   195
While each peculiar power forgoes his wonted seat.

22

Peor and Baälim°
Forsake their temples dim,
  With that twice-battered god° of Palestine;
And moonèd Ashtaroth,°   200
Heaven's queen and mother both,
  Now sits not girt with tapers' holy shine:
The Libyc Hammon° shrinks his horn;
In vain the Tyrian maids their wounded Thammuz
    mourn.°

23

And sullen Moloch,° fled,   205
Hath left in shadows dread

186. Genius: god of a locality. 191. Lars and Lemures: Roman gods of cities, houses, or families; spirits of the dead. 194. flamens: Roman priests. 197. Peor and Baälim: Baal, the chief Canaanite god worshiped at Mount Peor, and (Baälim) minor Canaanite deities. 199. twice-battered god: Dagon, god of the Philistines, whose image was miraculously destroyed twice (see I Samuel 5:4). 200. Ashtaroth: Astarte, fertility goddess identified with the moon. 203. Libyc Hammon: Egyptian god, Ammon, represented as a ram with great horns; his shrine was in Libya. 204. Tyrian . . . mourn: Phoenician women mourned the death of Thammuz (Adonis), who was killed by a boar. 205. Moloch: god of the Ammonites, to whom children were sacrificed.

His burning idol all of blackest hue;
In vain with cymbals' ring
They call the grisly king,
    In dismal dance about the furnace blue;   210
The brutish gods of Nile as fast,
Isis, and Orus, and the dog Anabis,° haste.

24

Nor° is Osiris seen
In Memphian grove or green,
    Trampling the unshowered grass with lowings
        loud;   215
Nor can he be at rest
Within his sacred chest;
    Nought but profoundest Hell can be his shroud;
In vain, with timbreled° anthems dark,   219
The sable-stolèd sorcerers bear his worshiped ark.

25

He feels from Juda's land
The dreaded Infant's hand;
    The rays of Bethlehem blind his dusky eyn;
Nor all the gods beside
Longer dare abide,   225
    Not Typhon° huge ending in snaky twine:
Our Babe, to show his Godhead true,
Can in his swaddling bands control the damnèd
    crew.°

26

So, when the sun in bed,
Curtained with cloudy red,   230
    Pillows his chin upon an orient wave,
The flocking shadows pale
Troop to the infernal jail,
    Each fettered ghost slips to his several° grave,
And the yellow-skirted fays   235
Fly after the night-steeds, leaving their moon-loved
    maze.°

212. **Isis . . . Anubis:** Egyptian gods portrayed with the head of a cow, a hawk, and a jackal, respectively. 213–20. **Nor . . . ark:** The Egyptian god Osiris was portrayed as a bull, had his shrine at Memphis, and was worshiped by priests carrying his image in a small chest. 219. **timbreled:** accompanied by timbrels, tambourines. 226. **Typhon:** monster, half-man and half-snake, killed by Hercules. 227–28. **Our . . . crew:** Hercules, here associated with Christ, killed two snakes as an infant. 234. **several:** separate. 236. **maze:** forest where Diana loved to hunt.

27

But see! the Virgin blest
Hath laid her Babe to rest.
    Time is our tedious song should here have
        ending:
Heaven's youngest-teemèd star°   240
Hath fixed her polished car,
    Her sleeping Lord with handmaid lamp at-
        tending;
And all about the courtly stable
Bright-harnessed angels sit in order serviceable.

WALT WHITMAN
1819–1892

Passage to India

1

Singing my days,
Singing the great achievements of the present,
Singing the strong light works of engineers,
Our modern wonders, (the antique ponderous
    Seven outvied,)
In the Old World the east the Suez canal,   5
The New by its mighty railroad spann'd,
The seas inlaid with eloquent gentle wires;°
Yet first to sound, and ever sound, the cry with
    thee O soul,
The Past! the Past! the Past!

The Past—the dark unfathom'd retrospect!   10
The teeming gulf—the sleepers and the shadows!
The past—the infinite greatness of the past!
For what is the present after all but a growth out
    of the past?
(As a projectile form'd, impell'd, passing a certain
    line, still keeps on,
So the present, utterly form'd, impell'd by the
    past.)   15

240. **youngest-teemed star:** newest-born star, the star of Bethlehem.

PASSAGE TO INDIA. 5–7. **In . . . wires:** references to the Suez Canal and the transcontinental railroad, completed in 1869, and to the laying of the Atlantic cable in 1866.

2

Passage O soul to India!
Eclaircise° the myths Asiatic, the primitive fables.

Not you alone proud truths of the world,
Nor you alone ye facts of modern science,
But myths and fables of eld, Asia's, Africa's
    fables,   20
The far-darting beams of the spirit, the unloos'd
    dreams,
The deep diving bibles and legends,
The daring plots of the poets, the elder religions;
O you temples fairer than lilies pour'd over by the
    rising sun!
O you fables spurning the known, eluding the hold
    of the known, mounting to heaven!   25
You lofty and dazzling towers, pinnacled, red as
    roses, burnish'd with gold!
Towers of fables immortal fashion'd from mortal
    dreams!
You too I welcome and fully the same as the rest!
You too with joy I sing.

Passage to India!   30
Lo, soul, seest thou not God's purpose from the
    first?
The earth to be spann'd, connected by network,
The races, neighbors, to marry and be given in
    marriage,
The oceans to be cross'd, the distant brought near,
The lands to be welded together.   35

A worship new I sing,
You captains, voyagers, explorers, yours,
You engineers, you architects, machinists, yours,
You, not for trade or transportation only,
But in God's name, and for thy sake O soul.   40

3

Passage to India!
Lo soul for thee of tableaus twain.
I see in one the Suez canal initiated, open'd.
I see the procession of steamships, the Empress
    Eugenie's leading the van,
I mark from on deck the strange landscape, the
    pure sky, the level sand in the distance,   45
I pass swiftly the picturesque groups, the workmen
    gather'd,
The gigantic dredging machines.

17. **Eclaircise:** clarify.

In one again, different, (yet thine, all thine, O soul,
    the same,)
I see over my own continent the Pacific railroad
    surmounting every barrier,
I see continual trains of cars winding along the
    Platte carrying freight and passengers,   50
I hear the locomotives rushing and roaring, and
    the shrill steam-whistle,
I hear the echoes reverberate through the grandest
    scenery in the world,
I cross the Laramie plains, I note the rocks in
    grotesque shapes, the buttes,
I see the plentiful larkspur and wild onions, the
    barren, colorless, sage-deserts,
I see in glimpses afar or towering immediately above
    me the great mountains, I see the Wind river and
    the Wahsatch mountains,   55
I see the Monument mountain and the Eagle's
    Nest, I pass the Promontory, I ascend the
    Nevadas,
I scan the noble Elk mountain and wind around its
    base,
I see the Humboldt range, I thread the valley and
    cross the river,
I see the clear waters of lake Tahoe, I see forests of
    majestic pines,
Or crossing the great desert, the alkaline plains, I
    behold enchanting mirages of waters and
    meadows,   60
Marking through these and after all, in duplicate
    slender lines,
Bridging the three or four thousand miles of land
    travel,
Tying the Eastern to the Western sea,
The road between Europe and Asia.

(Ah Genoese° thy dream! thy dream!   65
Centuries after thou art laid in thy grave,
The shore thou foundest verifies thy dream.)

4

Passage to India!
Struggles of many a captain, tales of many a sailor
    dead,   69
Over my mood stealing and spreading they come,
Like clouds and cloudlets in the unreach'd sky.

Along all history, down the slopes,
As the rivulet running, sinking now, and now again
    to the surface rising,

65. **Genoese:** Columbus.

A ceaseless thought, a varied train—lo, soul, to
   thee, thy sight, they rise,
The plans, the voyages again, the expeditions;   75
Again Vasco da Gama sails forth,
Again the knowledge gain'd, the mariner's compass,
Lands found and nations born, thou born America,
For purpose vast, man's long probation fill'd,   79
Thou rondure of the world at last accomplish'd.

5

O vast Rondure, swimming in space,
Cover'd all over with visible power and beauty,
Alternate light and day and the teeming spiritual
   darkness,
Unspeakable high processions of sun and moon
   and countless stars above,
Below, the manifold grass and waters, animals,
   mountains, trees,   85
With inscrutable purpose, some hidden prophetic
   intention,
Now first it seems my thought begins to span thee.

Down from the gardens of Asia descending
   radiating,
Adam and Eve appear, then their myriad progeny
   after them,
Wandering, yearning, curious, with restless explorations,   90
With questionings, baffled, formless, feverish, with
   never-happy hearts,
With that sad incessant refrain, *Wherefore unsatisfied
   soul?* and *Whither O mocking life?*

Ah who shall soothe these feverish children?
Who justify these restless explorations?
Who speak the secret of impassive earth?   95
Who bind it to us? what is this separate Nature so
   unnatural?
What is this earth to our affections? (unloving
   earth, without a throb to answer ours,
Cold earth, the place of graves.)

Yet soul be sure the first intent remains, and shall
   be carried out,
Perhaps even now the time has arrived.   100

After the seas are all cross'd, (as they seem already
   cross'd,)
After the great captains and engineers have
   accomplish'd their work,

After the noble inventors, after the scientists, the
   chemist, the geologist, ethnologist,
Finally shall come the poet worthy of that name,
The true son of God shall come singing his
   songs.   105

Then not your deeds only O voyagers, O scientists
   and inventors, shall be justified,
All these hearts as of fretted children shall be
   sooth'd,
All affection shall be fully responded to, the secret
   shall be told,
All these separations and gaps shall be taken up
   and hook'd and link'd together,
The whole earth, this cold, impassive, voiceless
   earth, shall be completely justified,   110
Trinitas divine shall be gloriously accomplish'd
   and compacted by the true son of God, the poet,
(He shall indeed pass the straits and conquer the
   mountains,
He shall double the cape of Good Hope to some
   purpose,)
Nature and Man shall be disjoin'd and diffused no
   more,
The true son of God shall absolutely fuse them.   115

6

Year at whose wide-flung door I sing!
Year of the purpose accomplish'd!
Year of the marriage of continents, climates and
   oceans!
(No mere doge of Venice now wedding the
   Adriatic,°)
I see O year in you the vast terraqueous globe given
   and giving all,   120
Europe to Asia, Africa join'd, and they to the New
   World,
The lands, geographies, dancing before you,
   holding a festival garland,
As brides and bridegrooms hand in hand.

Passage to India!
Cooling airs from Caucasus, far, soothing cradle
   of man,   125
The river Euphrates flowing, the past lit up again.

Lo soul, the retrospect brought forward,
The old, most populous, wealthiest of earth's
   lands,

119. doge . . . Adriatic: chief magistrate of Venice who
annually performed a ritual wedding of the city with the sea.

The streams of the Indus and the Ganges and their
    many affluents,
(I my shores of America walking today behold,
    resuming all,)   130
The tale of Alexander on his warlike marches
    suddenly dying,
On one side China and on the other Persia and
    Arabia,
To the south the great seas and the bay of Bengal,
The flowing literatures, tremendous epics, religions,
    castes,
Old occult Brahma interminably far back, the
    tender and junior Buddha,   135
Central and southern empires and all their be-
    longings, possessors,
The wars of Tamerlane,° the reign of Aurungzebe,°
The traders, rulers, explorers, Moslems, Venetians,
    Byzantium, the Arabs, Portuguese,
The first traveler famous yet, Marco Polo, Batouta,°
    the Moor,
Doubts to be solv'd, the map incognita, blanks to
    be fill'd,   140
The foot of man unstay'd, the hands never at rest,
Thyself O soul that will not brook a challenge.

The medieval navigators rise before me,
The world of 1492, with its awaken'd enterprise,
Something swelling in humanity now like the sap
    of the earth in spring,   145
The sunset splendor of chivalry declining.

And who art thou sad shade?
Gigantic, visionary, thyself a visionary,
With majestic limbs and pious beaming eyes,
Spreading around with every look of thine a
    golden world,   150
Enhuing it with gorgeous hues.

As the chief histrion,°
Down to the footlights walks in some great scena,
Dominating the rest I see the Admiral° himself,
(History's type of courage, action, faith,)   155
Behold him sail from Palos° leading his little fleet,
His voyage behold, his return, his great fame,
His misfortunes, calumniators, behold him a
    prisoner, chain'd,
Behold his dejection, poverty, death.

(Curious in time I stand, noting the efforts of
    heroes,   160
Is the deferment long? bitter the slander, poverty,
    death?
Lies the seed unreck'd for centuries in the ground?
    lo, to God's due occasion,
Uprising in the night, it sprouts, blooms,
And fills the earth with use and beauty.)

7

Passage indeed O soul to primal thought,   165
Not lands and seas alone, thy own clear freshness,
The young maturity of brood and bloom,
To realms of budding bibles.

O soul, repressless, I with thee and thou with me,
Thy circumnavigation of the world begin,   170
Of man, the voyage of his mind's return,
To reason's early paradise,
Back, back to wisdom's birth, to innocent in-
    tuitions,
Again with fair creation.

8

O we can wait no longer,   175
We too take ship O soul,
Joyous we too launch out on trackless seas,
Fearless for unknown shores on waves of ecstasy
    to sail,
Amid the wafting winds, (thou pressing me to thee,
    I thee to me, O soul,)
Caroling free, singing our song of God,   180
Chanting our chant of pleasant exploration.

With laugh and many a kiss,
(Let others deprecate, let others weep for sin,
    remorse, humiliation,)
O soul thou pleasest me, I thee.

Ah more than any priest O soul we too believe in
    God,   185
But with the mystery of God we dare not dally.

O soul thou pleasest me, I thee,
Sailing these seas or on the hills, or waking in the
    night,
Thoughts, silent thoughts, of Time and Space and
    Death, like waters flowing,
Bear me indeed as through the regions infinite,   190
Whose air I breathe, whose ripples hear, lave me all
    over,

137. Tamerlane: Oriental conqueror of the lands from the
Persian Gulf to the Ganges in India. **Aurungzebe:** seventeenth-century Mogul emperor of Hindustan. **139. Batouta:**
fourteenth-century traveler in Africa and Asia. **152.
histrion:** actor. **154. Admiral:** Columbus. **156. Palos:**
Spanish port from which Columbus sailed.

Bathe me O God in thee, mounting to thee,
I and my soul to range in range of thee.

O Thou transcendent,
Nameless, the fiber and the breath,   195
Light of the light, shedding forth universes, thou
 center of them,
Thou mightier center of the true, the good, the
 loving,
Thou moral, spiritual fountain—affection's source
 —thou reservoir,
(O pensive soul of me—O thirst unsatisfied—
 waitest not there?
Waitest not haply for us somewhere there the
 Comrade perfect?)   200
Thou pulse—thou motive of the stars, suns, systems,
That, circling, move in order, safe, harmonious,
Athwart the shapeless vastnesses of space,
How should I think, how breathe a single breath,
 how speak, if out of myself,
I could not launch, to those, superior universes? 205

Swiftly I shrivel at the thought of God,
At Nature and its wonders, Time and Space and
 Death,
But that I, turning, call to thee O soul, thou actual
 Me,
And lo, thou gently masterest the orbs,
Thou matest Time, smilest content at Death,   210
And fillest, swellest full the vastnesses of Space.

Greater than stars or suns,
Bounding O soul thou journeyest forth;
What love than thine and ours could wider
 amplify?
What aspirations, wishes, outvie thine and ours O
 soul?   215
What dreams of the ideal? what plans of purity,
 perfection, strength,
What cheerful willingness for others' sake to give
 up all?
For others' sake to suffer all?

Reckoning ahead O soul, when thou, the time
 achiev'd,
The seas all cross'd, weather'd the capes, the
 voyage done,   220
Surrounded, copest, frontest God, yieldest, the
 aim attain'd,
As fill'd with friendship, love complete, the Elder
 Brother found,
The Younger melts in fondness in his arms.

9

Passage to more than India!
Are thy wings plumed indeed for such far
 flights?   225
O soul, voyagest thou indeed on voyages like those?
Disportest thou on waters such as those?
Soundest below the Sanskrit and the Vedas?°
Then have thy bent unleash'd.

Passage to you, your shores, ye aged fierce
 enigmas!   230
Passage to you, to mastership of you, ye strangling
 problems!
You, strew'd with the wrecks of skeletons, that,
 living, never reach'd you.

Passage to more than India!
A secret of the earth and sky!
Of you O waters of the sea! O winding creeks and
 rivers!   235
Of you O woods and fields! of you strong moun-
 tains of my land!
Of you O prairies! of you gray rocks!
O morning red! O clouds! O rain and snows!
O day and night, passage to you!

O sun and moon and all you stars! Sirius and
 Jupiter!   240
Passage to you!

Passage, immediate passage! the blood burns in
 my veins!
Away O Soul! hoist instantly the anchor!
Cut the hawsers—haul out—shake out every sail!
Have we not stood here like trees in the ground
 long enough?   245
Have we not grovel'd here long enough, eating and
 drinking like mere brutes?
Have we not darken'd and dazed ourselves with
 books long enough?

Sail forth—steer for the deep waters only
Reckless O soul, exploring, I with thee, and thou
 with me,
For we are bound where mariner has not yet dared
 to go,   250
And we will risk the ship, ourselves and all.

O my brave soul!
O farther farther sail!

228. Vedas: sacred writings of Hinduism.

O daring joy, but safe! are they not all the seas of
   God?
O farther, farther, farther sail!   255

GERARD MANLEY HOPKINS
1844–1889

The Blessed Virgin
Compared to the Air We Breathe

Wild air, world-mothering air,
Nestling me everywhere,
That each eyelash or hair
Girdles; goes home betwixt
The fleeciest, frailest-flixed°   5
Snowflake, that's fairly mixed
With, riddles, and is rife
In every least thing's life;
This needful, never spent,
And nursing element;   10
My more than meat and drink,
My meal at every wink;
This air, which, by life's law,
My lung must draw and draw
Now but to breathe its praise,   15
Minds me in many ways
Of her who not only
Gave God's infinity
Dwindled to infancy
Welcome in womb and breast,   20
Birth, milk, and all the rest
But mothers each new grace
That does now reach our race—
Mary Immaculate,
Merely a woman, yet   25
Whose presence, power is
Great as no goddess's
Was deemèd, dreamèd; who
This one work has to do—
Let all God's glory through,   30
God's glory which would go
Through her and from her flow
Off, and no way but so.

THE BLESSED VIRGIN COMPARED TO THE AIR WE BREATHE.
5. frailest-flixed: softest-furred (flix: down or fur).

I say that we are wound
With mercy round and round   35
As if with air: the same
Is Mary, more by name.
She, wild web, wondrous robe,
Mantles the guilty globe,
Since God has let dispense   40
Her prayers his providence:
Nay, more than almoner,
The sweet alms' self is her
And men are meant to share
Her life as life does air.   45
  If I have understood,
She holds high motherhood
Towards all our ghostly good
And plays in grace her part
About man's beating heart,   50
Laying, like air's fine flood,
The deathdance in his blood;
Yet no part but what will
Be Christ our Savior still.
Of her flesh he took flesh: 55
He does take fresh and fresh,
Though much the mystery how,
Not flesh but spirit now
And makes, O marvelous!
New Nazareths in us,   60
Where she shall yet conceive
Him, morning, noon, and eve;
New Bethlems, and he born
There, evening, noon, and morn—
Bethlem or Nazareth,   65
Men here may draw like breath
More Christ and baffle death;
Who, born so, comes to be
New self and nobler me
In each one and each one   70
More makes, when all is done,
Both God's and Mary's Son.
  Again, look overhead
How air is azurèd;
O how! nay do but stand   75
Where you can lift your hand
Skywards: rich, rich it laps
Round the four fingergaps.
Yet such a sapphire-shot,
Charged, steepèd sky will not   80
Stain light. Yea, mark you this:
It does no prejudice.
The glass-blue days are those

When every color glows,
Each shape and shadow shows.   85
Blue be it: this blue heaven
The seven or seven times seven
Hued sunbeam will transmit
Perfect, not alter it.
Or if there does some soft,   90
On things aloof, aloft,
Bloom breathe, that one breath more
Earth is the fairer for.
Whereas did air not make
This bath of blue and slake   95
His fire, the sun would shake,
A blear and blinding ball
With blackness bound, and all
The thick stars round him roll
Flashing like flecks of coal,   100
Quartz-fret,° or sparks of salt,
In grimy vasty vault.
    So God was god of old:
A mother came to mold
Those limbs like ours which are   105
What must make our daystar
Much dearer to mankind;
Whose glory bare would blind
Or less would win man's mind.
Through her we may see him   110
Made sweeter, not made dim,
And her hand leaves his light
Sifted to suit our sight.
    Be thou then, O thou dear
Mother, my atmosphere;   115
My happier world, wherein
To wend and meet no sin;
Above me, round me lie
Fronting my froward° eye
With sweet and scarless sky;   120
Stir in my ears, speak there
Of God's love, O live air,
Of patience, penance, prayer:

101. quartz-fret: lines or marks on quartz. **119. froward:**
stubbornly contrary and disobedient.

World-mothering air, air wild,
Wound with thee, in thee isled,   125
Fold home, fast fold thy child.

The Windhover°

TO CHRIST OUR LORD

I caught this morning morning's minion, king-
    dom of daylight's dauphin, dapple-dawn-
    drawn Falcon, in his riding
Of the rolling level underneath him steady air,
    and striding
High there, how he rung° upon the rein of a
    wimpling wing
In his ecstasy! then off, off forth on swing,   5
    As a skate's heel sweeps smooth on a bow-bend:
    the hurl and gliding
    Rebuffed the big wind. My heart in hiding
Stirred for a bird,—the achieve of, the mastery of
    the thing!

Brute beauty and valor and act, oh, air, pride,
    plume, here
    Buckle!° AND the fire that breaks from thee then,
    a billion   10
Times told lovelier, more dangerous, O my
    chevalier!°

    No wonder of it: shéer plód makes plow down
    sillion
Shine,° and blue-bleak embers, ah my dear,
    Fall, gall themselves, and gash° gold-vermilion.

THE WINDHOVER. The windhover is a small hovering
hawk. **4. rung:** rose in a spiral. **10. Buckle:** to break or
crumple; to fasten or enclose; to grapple or engage. **11.
chevalier:** knight; both the falcon and Christ. **12–13.
sheer . . . Shine:** Sheer plod (plowshare?) and plodding
make the plowshare in the sillion (furrow) and the furrow
itself shine. **14. Fall . . . gash:** allusion to the wounds and
suffering of Christ.

The Ideal World
of the Imagination

The Phoenix

ca. 750–800

Translated by Charles W. Kennedy

Lo! I have learned   of the loveliest of lands
Far to the eastward,   famous among men.
But few ever fare   to that far-off realm
Set apart from the sinful   by the power of God.
Beauteous that country   and blessed with joys,
With the fairest odors   of all the earth;   6
Goodly the island,   gracious the Maker,
Matchless and mighty,   who stablished the world.
There ever stand open   the portals of heaven
With songs of rapture   for blessed souls.   10
   The plain is winsome,   the woods are green,
Widespread under heaven.   No rain or snow,
Or breath of frost   or blast of fire,
Or freezing hail   or fall of rime,
Or blaze of sun   or bitter-long cold,   15
Or scorching summer   or winter storm
Work harm a whit,   but the plain endures
Sound and unscathed.   The lovely land
Is rich with blossoms.   No mountains rise,
No lofty hills,   as here with us;   20
No high rock-cliffs,   no dales or hollows,
No mountain gorges,   no caves or crags,
Naught rough or rugged,   but the pleasant plain
Basks under heaven   laden with bloom.
   Twelve cubits higher   is that lovely land,   25
As learned writers   in their books relate,
Than any of these hills   that here in splendor
Tower on high   under heavenly stars.
Serene that country   sunny groves gleaming;

Winsome the woodlands;   fruits never fail   30
Or shining blossoms.   As God gave bidding
The groves stand for ever   growing and green.
Winter and summer   the woods alike
Are hung with blossoms;   under heaven no leaf
Withers, no fire   shall waste the plain   35
To the end of the world.   As the waters of old,
The sea-floods, covered   the compass of earth
And the pleasant plain   stood all uninjured,
By the grace of God   unhurt and unharmed,
So shall it flourish   till the fire of Judgment   40
When graves shall open,   the dwellings of death.
   Naught hostile lodges   in all that land,
No pain or weeping   or sign of sorrow,
No age or anguish   or narrow death;
No ending of life   or coming of evil,   45
No feud or vengeance   or fret of care;
No lack of wealth   or pressure of want,
No sorrow or sleeping   or sore disease.
No winter storm   or change of weather
Fierce under heaven,   or bitter frost   50
With wintry icicles   smites any man there.
No hail or hoarfrost   descends to earth,
No windy cloud;   no water falls
Driven by storm.   But running streams
And welling waters   wondrously spring   55
Overflowing earth   from fountains fair.
   From the midst of the wood   a winsome water
Each month breaks out   from the turf of earth,
Cold as the sea-stream,   coursing sweetly
Through all the grove.   By the bidding of God
The flood streams forth   through the glorious land   61
Twelve times yearly.   The trees are hung
With beauteous increase,   flowering buds;
Holy under heaven   the woodland treasures

Wane not nor wither;   no failing bloom,   65
No fruits of the wildwood,   fall to earth;
But in every season   on all the trees
The boughs bear their burden   of fruit anew.
Green are the groves   in the grassy meadow,
Gaily garnished   by the might of God.   70
No branch is broken,   and fragrance fair
Fills all the land.   Nor ever comes change
Till the Ruler Whose wisdom   wrought its
     beginning
His ancient Creation   shall bring to its end.
     In that woodland dwelleth,   most wondrous
          fair
                                             75
And strong of wing,   a fowl called Phoenix;
There dauntless-hearted   he has his home,
His lonely lodging.   In that lovely land
Death shall never   do him a hurt,
Or work him harm   while the world standeth. 80
     Each day he observes   the sun's bright
          journey
Greeting God's candle,   the gleaming gem,
Eagerly watching   till over the ocean
The fairest of orbs   shines forth from the East,
God's bright token   glowing in splendor,   85
The ancient handwork   of the Father of all.
The stars are hid   in the western wave,
Dimmed at dawn,   and the dusky night
Steals darkly away;   then, strong of wing
And proud of pinion,   the bird looks out   90
Over the ocean   under the sky,
Eagerly waiting   when up from the East
Heaven's gleam comes gliding   over the wide
     water.
     Then the fair bird,   changeless in beauty,
Frequents   at   the   fountain   the   welling
     streams;
                                             95
Twelve times the blessed one   bathes in the
     burn°
Ere the bright beacon comes,   the candle of
     heaven;
And even as often   at every bath
Tastes the pleasant water   of brimcold° wells.
     Thereafter the proud one   after his water-
          play
                                             100
Takes his flight   to a lofty tree
Whence most easily   o'er the eastern ways
He beholds the course   of the heavenly taper
Brightly shining   over the tossing sea,   104

THE PHOENIX. **96. burn:** stream. **99. brimcold:** as cold as
the ocean.

A blaze of light.   The land is made beautiful,
The world made fair,   when the famous gem
O'er the ocean-stretches   illumines the earth
All the world over,   noblest of orbs.
     When the sun climbs high   over the salt
          streams
The gray bird wings   from his woodland tree 110
And, swift of pinion,   soars to the sky
Singing and caroling   to meet the sun.
Then is the bearing   of the bird so fair,
Its heart so gladsome   and so graced with joy,
It trills its song   in clear-voiced strain,   115
More wondrous music   than ever child of man
Heard under heaven   since the High-King,
Author of glory,   created the world,
The earth and the heavens.   The music of its
     hymn
Is sweeter than all song-craft,   more winsome
     and fair
                                             120
Than any harmony.   Neither trumpet nor horn,
Nor melody of harp   is like to that lay,
Nor voice of man,   nor strain of organ music,
Nor swan's singing feathers,   nor any pleasant
     sound
That God gave for joy to men   in this mournful
     world.
                                             125
     So he hymns and carols   with joyous heart
Until the sun   in the southern sky
Sinks to its setting.   Then in silence he listens;
Thrice the wise-hearted   lifts his head,
Thrice shakes his feathers   strong in flight,   130
Then broods in silence.   Twelve times the bird
Notes the hours   of night and day.
     So is it ordained   for the forest dweller
To live in that land   having joy of life,
Well-being and bliss   and all the world's
     beauty,
                                             135
Till the warden of the wood   of this life's
     winters
Has numbered a thousand.   Aged and old
The gray-plumed is weary   and weighted with
     years.
     Then the fairest of fowls   flies from the
          greenwood,
The blossoming earth,   seeks a boundless realm,
A land and lodging   where no man dwells; 141
And there exalted   over all the host
Has dominion and rule   of the race of birds,
With them in the waste   resides for a season.
Swift of pinion   and strong in flight   145

He wings to the westward,   heavy with years.
Around the royal one   throng the birds,
Servants and thanes°   of a peerless prince.
And so he seeks out   the Syrian land   149
With a lordly following.   There the pure fowl
Suddenly leaves them,   lodging in shadow
In a woodland covert,   a secret spot
Sequestered and hidden   from the hosts of men.
    There he takes lodging   in a lofty tree
Fast by its roots   in the forest-wood   155
Under heaven's roof.   The race of men
Call the tree Phoenix   from the name of the
    fowl.
Unto that tree,   as I have heard tell,
The Great King has granted,   the Lord of
    mankind,
That it alone   of all tall trees   160
Is the brightest blooming   in all the earth.
Nor may aught of evil   work it a harm;
For ever shielded,   for ever unscathed,
It stands to the end   while the world standeth.
    When the wind lies at rest   and weather is
    fair,   165
And heaven's bright gem   shines holy on high,
When clouds are dispersed   and seas are
    tranquil
And every storm   is stilled under heaven,
When the weather-candle   shines warm from
    the south
Lighting earth's legions,   then in the boughs 170
He begins to form   and fashion a nest.
His sage heart stirs   with a great desire
Swiftly to alter   old age to youth,
To renew his life.   From near and far
He gleans and gathers   to his lodging-place 175
Pleasant plants   and fruits of the forest,
All sweetest spices   and fragrant herbs
Which the King of glory,   Lord of beginnings,
Created on earth   for a blessing to men,
The sweetest under heaven.   So he assembles 180
In the boughs of the tree   his shining treasures.
There in that wasteland   the wild bird
In the tall tree's top   timbers his house
Pleasant and lovely.   And there he lodges
In that lofty chamber;   in the leafy shade   185
Besets his feathered body   on every side
With the sweetest odors   and blossoms of earth.
    When the gem of the sky   in the summer season,

The burning sun,   shines over the shades
Scanning the world,   the Phoenix sits   190
Fain of departure,°   fulfilling his fate.
His house is kindled   by heat of the sun;
The herbs grow hot,   the pleasant hall steams
With sweetest odors;   in the surging flame,
In the fire-grip, burns   the bird with his nest. 195
The pyre is kindled,   the fire enfolds
The home of the heartsick.   The yellow flame
Fiercely rages;   the Phoenix burns,
Full of years,   as the fire consumes
The fleeting body.   The spirit fades,   200
The soul of the fated.   The bale-fire seizes
Both bone and flesh.
                    But his life is reborn
After a season,   when the ashes begin
After the fire-surge   fusing together   204
Compressed to a ball.   The brightest of nests,
The house of the stout-heart,   by force of the
    flame
Is clean consumed;   the corpse grows chill;
The bone-frame is broken;   the burning sub-
    sides.
From the flame of the fire   is found thereafter
In the ash of the pyre   an apple's likeness, 210
Of which grows a worm   most wondrous fair,
As it were a creature   come from an egg,
Shining from the shell.   In the shadow it grows
Fashioned first   as an eagle's young,
A comely fledgling;   then flourishing fair   215
Is like in form   to a full-grown eagle
Adorned with feathers   as he was at first,
Brightly gleaming.
                    Then is beauty reborn,
Sundered from sin,   once more made new;
Even in such fashion   as men, for food,   220
Bring home in harvest   at reaping time
Pleasant fare,   the fruits of earth,
Ere coming of winter   lest rainstorms waste;
Find joy and strength   in their garnered store
When frost and snow   with furious might   225
Cover earth over   with winter weeds:
From these grains again   grow riches for men
Through the sprouting kernels,   first sowed pure
    seed;
Then the warm sun in Springtime,   symbol of
    life,   229
Wakes the world's wealth   and new crops rise,

148. thanes: persons ranking above freemen and below
noblemen.

191. Fain of departure: either declining to leave the nest or
willing to die.

Each after its kind,   the treasures of earth.
    Even so the Phoenix   after long life
Grows young and fashioned   with flesh anew.
He eats no food,   no fare of earth,
But only a drop   of honeydew   235
Which falls in the midnight;   thereby the Phoenix
Comforts his life   till he comes again
To his own habitation,   his ancient seat.
    Beset with his sweet herbs,   proud of plumage,
The bird is reborn,   his life made young,   240
Youthful and gifted   with every grace.
Then from the ground   he gathers together
The nimble body   that the bale-fire broke;
With skill assembles   the ashy remnants,
The crumbling bones   left after the blaze;   245
Brings together there   bone and ashes
And covers over   with savory herbs
The spoil of the death-fire,   fairly adorned.
    Then he takes his departure,   turns to his home,
Grasps in his talons,   clasps in his claws,   250
What the fire has left;   joyously flying
To his native dwelling,   his sun-bright seat,
His happy homeland.   All is renewed,
Life and feathered body   as it was at first
What time God placed him   in that pleasant plain.   255
He brings there the bones   which the fiery surges
Swallowed in flame   on the funeral pyre,
The ashes as well;   and all together
Buries the leavings,   ashes and bone,
In his island home.   For him is renewed   260
The sign of the sun   when the light of heaven,
Brightest of orbs,   most joyous of jewels,
Over the ocean   shines from the East.
    Fair-breasted that fowl   and comely of hue
With varied colors;   the head behind   265
Is emerald burnished   and blended with scarlet.
The tail plumes are colored   some crimson, some brown,
And cunningly speckled   with shining spots.
White of hue   are the backs of the wings,
The neck all green   beneath and above.   270
The strong neb° gleams   like glass or gem;
Without and within   the beak is fair.
The eye is stark,   most like to stone
Or shining jewel   skillfully wrought
In a golden setting   by cunning smiths.   275

271. neb: beak.

All round the neck   like the ring of the sun
Is a shining circlet   fashioned of feathers.
Wondrously bright   and shining the belly,
Brilliant and comely;   over the back
Splendidly fashioned   the shield is spread.   280
The fair bird's shanks,   its yellow feet
Are patterned with scales.   'Tis a peerless fowl
Most like in appearance   to a peacock proud,
As the writings say;   neither sluggish or slow,
Torpid or slothful,   as some birds are   285
Heavily winging   their way in the sky;
But swift and lively   and very light,
Fair and goodly   and marked with glory.
Eternal the God   who grants him that grace!
    Then from that country   the Phoenix flies   290
To seek his homeland,   his ancient seat.
He wings his way   observed of men
Assembled together   from south and north,
From East and west,   in hurrying hosts.
A great folk gathers   from far and near   295
To behold God's grace   in the beauteous bird
For whom at Creation   the Lord of all
Ordained and stablished   a special nature,
A fairer perfection   beyond all fowl.
Men on earth   all marvel in wonder   300
At the fair fowl's beauty   inscribing in books
And skillfully carving   on marble stone
When the day and the hour   shall exhibit to men
The gleaming beauty   of the flying bird.
    Then all about him   the race of birds   305
In flocks assemble   on every side,
Winging from far ways,   singing his praises,
Hymning their hero   in fervent strains;
Around the Phoenix   in circling flight
They attend the holy one   high in air,   310
Thronging in multitudes.   Men look up,
Marvel to see   that happy host
Worship the wild bird,   flock after flock,
Keenly acclaiming   and praising as King
Their beloved lord;   joyously leading   315
Their liege to his home;   till at last alone
He swiftly soars   where that blissful band
May not follow after   when the best of birds
From the turf of earth   returns to his homeland.
    So the blessed bird   after his death-bale   320
Enters once more   his ancient abode,
His fatherland fair.   Leaving their leader
The birds sad-hearted   return to their home,
Their prince to his palace.   God only knows,
The Almighty King,   what his breed may be,   325

Or male or female;   and no man knows,
But only the Maker,   the ancient edict
And wondrous causes   of that fowl's kind.
    There blessed abiding   the bird has bliss 329
In the welling streams   and the woodland grove
Till a thousand winters   have waxed and waned,
And again life ends   as the bale-fire burns,
The ravaging flames;   yet he rises again,
Strangely, wondrously   wakened to life.
Therefore drooping   he dreads not death,   335
Dire death-pangs,   but ever he knows
After the fire's force   life refashioned,
Breath after burning,   and straight transformed
Out of the ashes,   once more restored
Unto bird's form   his youth is reborn   340
Under sheltering skies.   He is himself
Both his own son   and his own dear father;
Ever the heir   of his former remains.
The Almighty Maker   of all mankind   344
Has granted him wondrously   once more to be
What before he was,   with feathers appareled
Though fire clasp him   close in its grip.
    So each blessed soul   through somber death
After his life-days   of sore distress
Gains life everlasting,   knowing God's grace 350
In bliss never-ending;   and ever thereafter
Resides in glory   as reward for his works.
The traits of this bird   clearly betoken
Christ's chosen thanes,   how on earth they thrill
By the Father's grace   with a gleaming joy 355
In this perilous time,   and attain thereafter
Bliss on high   in the heavenly home.

WILLIAM WORDSWORTH
1770–1850

Ode: Intimations of Immortality from Recollections of Early Childhood

The Child is father of the Man;
And I could wish my days to be
Bound each to each by natural piety.°

1

There was a time when meadow, grove, and stream,
The earth, and every common sight,
        To me did seem
        Appareled in celestial light,
The glory and the freshness of a dream.   5
It is not now as it hath been of yore;—
        Turn wheresoe'er I may,
            By night or day,
The things which I have seen I now can see no more.

2

        The Rainbow comes and goes,   10
        And lovely is the Rose,
        The Moon doth with delight
Look round her when the heavens are bare;
        Waters on a starry night
        Are beautiful and fair;   15
    The sunshine is a glorious birth;
    But yet I know, where'er I go,
That there hath passed away a glory from the
        earth.

3

Now, while the birds thus sing a joyous song,
    And while the young lambs bound   20
        As to the tabor's° sound,
To me alone there came a thought of grief:
A timely utterance gave that thought relief,
        And I again am strong: 24

ODE: INTIMATIONS OF IMMORTALITY. **The Child . . . piety:**
conclusion of Wordsworth's poem "My Heart Leaps Up."
21. tabor: drum.

The cararacts blow their trumpets from the steep;
No more shall grief of mine the season wrong;
I hear the Echoes through the mountains throng,
The Winds come to me from the fields of sleep,
     And all the earth is gay;
        Land and sea   30
     Give themselves up to jollity,
      And with the heart of May
     Doth every Beast keep holiday;—
       Thou Child of Joy,
Shout round me, let me hear thy shouts, thou happy
        Shepherd-boy!   35

4

Ye blessed Creatures, I have heard the call
   Ye to each other make; I see
The heavens laugh with you in your jubilee;
   My heart is at your festival,
    My head hath its coronal,   40
The fullness of your bliss, I feel—I feel it all,
   Oh evil day! if I were sullen
   While Earth herself is adorning,
    This sweet May-morning,
   And the Children are culling   45
    On every side,
  In a thousand valleys far and wide,
  Fresh flowers; while the sun shines warm,
And the Babe leaps up on his Mother's arm:—
   I hear, I hear, with joy I hear!   50
  —But there's a Tree, of many, one,
A single Field which I have looked upon,
Both of them speak of something that is gone:
   The Pansy at my feet
   Doth the same tale repeat: 55
Whither is fled the visionary gleam?
Where is it now, the glory and the dream?

5

Our birth is but a sleep and a forgetting:
The Soul that rises with us, our life's Star,
   Hath had elsewhere its setting,   60
    And cometh from afar:
   Not in entire forgetfulness,
   And not in utter nakedness,
But trailing clouds of glory do we come
   From God, who is our home: 65
Heaven lies about us in our infancy!
Shades of the prison-house begin to close

   Upon the growing Boy,
    But He
Beholds the light, and whence it flows,   70
   He sees it in his joy;
The Youth, who daily farther from the east
   Must travel, still is Nature's Priest,
   And by the vision splendid
   Is on his way attended;   75
At length the Man perceives it die away,
And fade into the light of common day.

6

Earth fills her lap with pleasures of her own;
Yearnings she hath in her own natural kind,
And, even with something of a Mother's mind, 80
   And no unworthy aim,
   The homely Nurse doth all she can
To make her Foster-child, her Inmate Man,
   Forget the glories he hath known,
And that imperial palace whence he came.   85

7

Behold the Child among his newborn blisses,
A six years' Darling of a pigmy size!
See, where 'mid work of his own hand he lies,
Fretted by sallies of his mother's kisses,
With light upon him from his father's eyes!   90
See, at his feet, some little plan or chart,
Some fragment from his dream of human life,
Shaped by himself with newly-learned art;
   A wedding or a festival,
   A mourning or a funeral;   95
    And this hath now his heart,
   And unto this he frames his song:
    Then will he fit his tongue
To dialogues of business, love, or strife;
   But it will not be long   100
   Ere this be thrown aside,
   And with new joy and pride
The little Actor cons° another part;
Filling from time to time his "humorous stage"°
With all the Persons, down to palsied Age,   105
That Life brings with her in her equipage;
   As if his whole vocation
   Were endless imitation.

103. cons: learns. 104. "humorous stage": phrase from
Samuel Daniel (1562–1619), Britain's poet laureate between
Spenser and Jonson; it means the various parts in a play.

8

Thou, whose exterior semblance doth belie
   Thy Soul's immensity;   110
Thou best Philosopher, who yet dost keep
Thy heritage, thou Eye among the blind,
That, deaf and silent, read'st the eternal deep,
Haunted for ever by the eternal mind,—
     Mighty Prophet! Seer blest!   115
     On whom those truths do rest,
Which we are toiling all our lives to find,
In darkness lost, the darkness of the grave;
Thou, over whom thy Immortality
Broods like the Day, a Master o'er a Slave,   120
A Presence which is not to be put by;
Thou little Child, yet glorious in the might
Of heaven-born freedom on thy being's height,
Why with such earnest pains dost thou provoke
The years to bring the inevitable yoke,   125
Thus blindly with thy blessedness at strife?
Full soon thy Soul shall have her earthly freight,
And custom lie upon thee with a weight,
Heavy as frost, and deep almost as life!

9

   O joy! that in our embers   130
   Is something that doth live,
   That nature yet remembers
   What was so fugitive!
The thought of our past years in me doth breed
Perpetual benediction: not indeed   135
For that which is most worthy to be blest;
Delight and liberty, the simple creed
Of Childhood, whether busy or at rest,
With new-fledged hope still fluttering in his
     breast:—
     Not for these I raise   140
     The song of thanks and praise;
   But for those obstinate questionings
   Of sense and outward things,
   Fallings from us, vanishings;
   Blank misgivings of a Creature   145
Moving about in worlds not realized,
High instincts before which our mortal Nature
Did tremble like a guilty Thing surprised:
     But for those first affections,
     Those shadowy recollections,   150
   Which, be they what they may,
Are yet the fountain light of all our day,
Are yet a master light of all our seeing;

Uphold us, cherish, and have power to make
Our noisy years seem moments in the being   155
Of the eternal Silence: truths that wake,
   To perish never;
Which neither listlessness, nor mad endeavor,
   Nor Man nor Boy,
Nor all that is at enmity with joy,   160
Can utterly abolish or destroy!
     Hence in a season of calm weather
     Though inland far we be,
Our Souls have sight of that immortal sea
     Which brought us hither,   165
   Can in a moment travel thither,
And see the Children sport upon the shore,
And hear the mighty waters rolling evermore.

10

Then sing, ye Birds, sing, sing a joyous song!
     And let the young Lambs bound   170
     As to the tabor's sound!
We in thought will join your throng,
     Ye that pipe and ye that play,
     Ye that through your hearts today
     Feel the gladness of the May!   175
What though the radiance which was once so
  bright
Be now for ever taken from my sight,
     Though nothing can bring back the hour
Of splendor in the grass, of glory in the flower;
     We will grieve not, rather find   180
     Strength in what remains behind;
     In the primal sympathy
     Which having been must ever be;
     In the soothing thoughts that spring
     Out of human suffering;   185
     In the faith that looks through death,
In years that bring the philosophic mind.

11

And O, ye Fountains, Meadows, Hills, and Groves,
Forebode not any severing of our loves!
Yet in my heart of hearts I feel your might;   190
I only have relinquished one delight
To live beneath your more habitual sway.
I love the Brooks which down their channels fret,
Even more than when I tripped lightly as they;
The innocent brightness of a newborn Day   195
     Is lovely yet;

The Clouds that gather round the setting sun
Do take a sober coloring from an eye
That hath kept watch o'er man's mortality;   199
Another race hath been, and other palms are won.
Thanks to the human heart by which we live,
Thanks to its tenderness, its joys, and fears,
To me the meanest flower that blows° can give
Thoughts that do often lie too deep for tears.

SAMUEL TAYLOR COLERIDGE
1772–1834

Kubla Khan

In Xanadu° did Kubla Khan
A stately pleasure-dome decree:
Where Alph,° the sacred river, ran
Through caverns measureless to man
   Down to a sunless sea.   5
So twice five miles of fertile ground
With walls and towers were girdled round:
And here were gardens bright with sinuous rills
Where blossomed many an incense-bearing tree;
And here were forests ancient as the hills,   10
Enfolding sunny spots of greenery.

But oh! that deep romantic chasm which slanted
Down the green hill athwart a cedarn cover!
A savage place! as holy and enchanted
As e'er beneath a waning moon was haunted   15
By woman wailing for her demon-lover!
And from this chasm, with ceaseless turmoil
   seething,
As if this earth in fast thick pants were breathing,
A mighty fountain momently was forced:
Amid whose swift half-intermitted burst   20
Huge fragments vaulted like rebounding hail,
Or chaffy grain beneath the thresher's flail:
And 'mid these dancing rocks at once and ever
It flung up momently the sacred river.
Five miles meandering with a mazy motion   25
Through wood and dale the sacred river ran,

Then reached the caverns measureless to man,
And sank in tumult to a lifeless ocean;
And 'mid this tumult Kubla heard from far
Ancestral voices prophesying war!   30
   The shadow of the dome of pleasure
   Floated midway on the waves;
   Where was heard the mingled measure
   From the fountain and the caves.
It was a miracle of rare device,°   35
A sunny pleasure-dome with caves of ice!

   A damsel with a dulcimer
   In a vision once I saw:
   It was an Abyssinian maid,
   And on her dulcimer she played,   40
   Singing of Mount Abora.
   Could I revive within me
   Her symphony° and song,
   To such a deep delight 'twould win me,
That with music loud and long,   45
I would build that dome in air,
That sunny dome! those caves of ice!
And all who heard should see them there,
And all should cry, Beware! Beware!
His flashing eyes, his floating hair!   50
Weave a circle round him thrice,
And close your eyes with holy dread,
For he on honeydew hath fed,
And drunk the milk of Paradise.

ALFRED, LORD TENNYSON
1809–1892

Ulysses

It little profits that an idle king,
By this still hearth, among these barren crags,
Matched with an aged wife, I mete and dole
Unequal laws unto a savage race,
That hoard, and sleep, and feed, and know not
   me.   5
I cannot rest from travel; I will drink
Life to the lees. All times I have enjoyed
Greatly, have suffered greatly, both with those
That loved me, and alone; on shore, and when

203. **blows:** blooms.

KUBLA KHAN. **1. Xanadu:** Xamdu or Shantu, the summer capital of Kublai Khan, thirteenth-century Mongolian emperor of China. **3. Alph:** Cf. Alpheus, the mythological Greek river that ran underground and rose in a fountain.

35. **device:** invention. **43. symphony:** harmony.

Through scudding drifts the rainy Hyades°   10
Vexed the dim sea. I am become a name;
For always roaming with a hungry heart
Much have I seen and known,—cities of men
And manners, climates, councils, governments,
Myself not least, but honored of them all,—   15
And drunk delight of battle with my peers,
Far on the ringing plains of windy Troy.
I am a part of all that I have met;
Yet all experience is an arch wherethrough
Gleams that untraveled world, whose margin fades
Forever and forever when I move.   21
How dull it is to pause, to make an end,
To rust unburnished, not to shine in use!
As though to breathe were life! Life piled on life
Were all too little, and of one to me   25
Little remains; but every hour is saved
From that eternal silence, something more,
A bringer of new things; and vile it were
For some three suns° to store and hoard myself,
And this gray spirit yearning in desire   30
To follow knowledge, like a sinking star,
Beyond the utmost bound of human thought.

    This is my son, mine own Telemachus,
To whom I leave the scepter and the isle,—
Well-loved of me, discerning to fulfill   35
This labor, by slow prudence to make mild
A rugged people, and through soft degrees
Subdue them to the useful and the good.
Most blameless is he, centered in the sphere
Of common duties, decent not to fail   40
In offices of tenderness, and pay
Meet adoration to my household gods,
When I am gone. He works his work, I mine.

    There lies the port; the vessel puffs her sail;
There gloom the dark, broad seas. My mariners,   45
Souls that have toiled, and wrought, and thought
    with me,—
That ever with a frolic welcome took
The thunder and the sunshine, and opposed
Free hearts, free foreheads—you and I are old;
Old age hath yet his honor and his toil.   50
Death closes all; but something ere the end,
Some work of noble note, may yet be done,
Not unbecoming men that strove with gods.
The lights begin to twinkle from the rocks;
The long day wanes; the slow moon climbs; the
    deep   55

Moans round with many voices. Come, my friends,
'Tis not too late to seek a newer world.
Push off, and sitting well in order smite
The sounding furrows; for my purpose holds
To sail beyond the sunset, and the baths   60
Of all the western stars, until I die.
It may be that the gulfs will wash us down;
It may be we shall touch the Happy Isles,
And see the great Achilles, whom we knew.
Though much is taken, much abides; and though   65
We are not now that strength which in old days
Moved earth and heaven, that which we are, we
    are,—
One equal temper of heroic hearts,
Made weak by time and fate, but strong in will
To strive, to seek, to find, and not to yield.   70

WILLIAM BUTLER YEATS
1865–1939

Sailing to Byzantium

1

That is no country for old men. The young
In one another's arms, birds in the trees
—Those dying generations—at their song,
The salmon-falls, the mackerel-crowded seas,
Fish, flesh, or fowl, commend all summer long   5
Whatever is begotten, born, and dies.
Caught in that sensual music all neglect
Monuments of unaging intellect.

2

An aged man is but a paltry thing,
A tattered coat upon a stick, unless   10
Soul clap its hands and sing, and louder sing
For every tatter in its mortal dress,
Nor is there singing school but studying
Monuments of its own magnificence;
And therefore I have sailed the seas and come   15
To the holy city of Byzantium.°

SAILING TO BYZANTIUM. **16. Byzantium:** ancient Istanbul;
here symbolic of a culture noted for impersonal, abstract,
and timeless art.

ULYSSES.   **10. Hyades:** cluster of stars that when rising with
the sun was thought to indicate rain. **29. suns:** years.

3

O sages standing in God's holy fire
As in the gold mosaic of a wall,
Come from the holy fire, perne in a gyre,°
And be the singing-masters of my soul. 20
Consume my heart away; sick with desire
And fastened to a dying animal
It knows not what it is; and gather me
Into the artifice of eternity.

19. **perne . . . gyre:** turn and descend in a spiral motion.

4

Once out of nature I shall never take 25
My bodily form from any natural thing,
But such a form as Grecian goldsmiths make
Of hammered gold and gold enameling
To keep a drowsy Emperor awake;
Or set upon a golden bough to sing 30
To lords and ladies of Byzantium
Of what is past, or passing, or to come.

The Oracular Role

Now Goth Sonne Under Wode
ca. 1240

Now goth sonne under wode,°—
Me reweth,° Marie, thy faire rode.°
Now goth sonne under tree,—
Me reweth, Marie, thy sone and thee.

Erthe Took of Erthe
ca. 1320

Erthe° took of erthe, erthe wyth wogh;°
Erthe other erthe to the erthe drough;°
Erthe leyde erthe in erthen through:°
Than hadde erthe of erthe erthe ynough.

Sodeynly Affrayed
ca. 1450

Sodeynly affrayed, half wakyng, half slepyng,
And greetly dismayde, a womman sat wepyng.

Wyth favour in hir face fer passyng my resoun,
And of hir sore wepyng this was the enchesoun:°

Hir sone in hir lappe lay, she seyde, slayn by
   tresoun.   5
If wepyng myghte ripe ben, it semed than in sesoun.
  "Jhesu!" so she sobbed,
  So hir sone was bobbed°
  And of his lyf robbed;
Seying thise wordes, as I seye thee: 10
"Who can not wepe, come lerne at me."

I seyde I coude not wepe, I was so hard-herted.
She answerde me wyth wordes shortely that
   smerted:
"Lo, nature shal meve° thee, thou most be con-
   verted.
Thyn owene fader this nyght is deed," lo, thus she
   thwarted,°   15
  "So my sone is bobbed
  And of his lyf robbed."
  For sothe° than I sobbed,
Verifying the wordes she seyde to me:
Who can not wepe may lerne at thee.   20

"Now breek, herte, I thee preye! This cors° lieth so
   rewely,°
So beten, so wounded, entreted° so Jewely,°
What wight° may me biholde and wepe not? Non,
   trewely,
To see my dede dere sone lie bledyng, lo, this
   newely."
  Ay stille she sobbed   25
  So hir sone was bobbed
  And of his lyf robbed,
Newyng the wordes, as I seye thee:
"Who can not wepe, come lerne at me."

NOW GOTH SONNE UNDER WODE. **1. wode:** forest. **2. Me reweth:** I have pity for. **rode:** face; but note the similarity to the word *rood*, or cross.

ERTHE TOOK OF ERTHE. **1. Erthe:** Consider the various meanings of the word *earth:* the physical earth, a creative or natural force, man, as in Genesis, and so on. **wogh:** wrong or harm. **2. drough:** drew, added. **3. through:** coffin or grave.

SODEYNLY AFFRAYED. **4. enchesoun:** occasion, reason.

8. bobbed: hurt and ridiculed. **14. meve:** move. **15. thwarted:** retorted. **18. For sothe:** in truth, truly. **21. cors:** body. **rewely:** ruefully. **22. entreted:** dealt with. **Jewely:** like a Jew. **23. wight:** person.

On me she caste hir eye, seyde, "See, man, thy
   brother!"   30
She kiste him and seyde, "Swete, am I not thy
   moder?"
In swownyng she fil ther, it wolde be non other.
I not° which more deedly, that oon or that other.
   Yet she revived and sobbed
   So hir sone was bobbed   35
   And of his lyf robbed.
"Who can not wepe"—this was the laye°—
And wyth that word she vanisht awey.

Lully, Lullay

ca. 1500

Lully, lullay, lully, lullay,
The faucon° hath born my make° awey.

He bar him up, he bar him down,
He bar him into an orchard broun.

In that orchard ther was an halle   5
That was hanged wyth purpre and palle.°

And in that halle ther was a bed,
It was hanged wyth gold so red.

And in that bed ther lieth a knight,
His woundes bledyng day and nyght.   10

By that beddes side ther kneleth a may,°
And she wepeth bothe nyght and day.

And by that beddes side ther stondeth a ston,
Corpus Cristi° writen ther-on.

GEORGE HERBERT
1593–1633

Easter

Rise, heart, thy Lord is risen, sing his praise
            Without delays,
Who takes thee by the hand, that thou likewise
            With him mayst rise;

33. not: know not. 37. laye: strain, the meaning.

LULLY, LULLAY. 2. faucon: falcon. make: mate. 6. purpre
and palle: rich and fine purple cloth. 11. may: maid. 14.
Corpus Cristi: body of Christ.

That, as his death calcinèd thee to dust,   5
His life may make thee gold, and much more, just.

Awake, my lute, and struggle for thy part
            With all thy art;
The cross taught all wood to resound his name,
            Who bore the same;   10
His stretchèd sinews taught all strings, what key
Is best to celebrate this most high day.

Consort both heart and lute, and twist a song
            Pleasant and long;
Or, since all music is but three parts vied°   15
            And multiplied,

O let thy blessed Spirit bear a part,
And make up our defects with his sweet art.

I got me flowers to straw° thy way;
I got me boughs off many a tree: 20
But thou wast up by break of day,
And brought'st thy sweets along with thee.

The sun arising in the east,
Though he give light, and the east perfume,
If they should offer to contest   25
With thy arising, they presume.

Can there be any day but this,
Though many suns to shine endeavor?
We count three hundred, but we miss:
There is but one, and that one ever.   30

Easter Wings

Lord, who createdst man in wealth and store,
   Though foolishly he lost the same,
      Decaying more and more,
         Till he became
            Most poor: 5
            With thee
         O let me rise
      As larks, harmoniously,
   And sing this day thy victories:
Then shall the fall further the flight in me.° 10

EASTER. 15. three . . . vied: the heart, lute, and spirit vie
(combine) to complete the musical chord. 19. straw: strew.

EASTER WINGS. 10. the fall . . . me: reference to the
concept of the fortunate fall; Adam's fall provided the
occasion for Christ's redemption of man.

My tender age in sorrow did begin:
And still with sicknesses and shame
Thou didst so punish sin,
That I became
Most thin.   15
With thee
Let me combine,
And feel this day thy victory:
For, if I imp° my wing on thine,
Affliction shall advance the flight in me. 20

WILLIAM BLAKE
1757–1827

The Lamb

Little Lamb, who made thee?
Dost thou know who made thee?
Gave thee life, & bid thee feed
By the stream & o'er the mead;
Gave thee clothing of delight,   5
Softest clothing, wooly, bright;
Gave thee such a tender voice,
Making all the vales rejoice?
  Little Lamb, who made thee?
  Dost thou know who made thee?   10

  Little Lamb, I'll tell thee,
  Little Lamb, I'll tell thee:
He is callèd by thy name,
For he calls himself a Lamb.
He is meek, & he is mild;   15
He became a little child.
I a child, & thou a lamb,
We are callèd by his name.
  Little Lamb, God bless thee!
  Little Lamb, God bless thee!   20

The Tyger

Tyger! Tyger! burning bright
In the forests of the night,
What immortal hand or eye
Could frame thy fearful symmetry?

19. imp: in falconry, to repair a damaged wing by insert-
ing feathers from another bird.

In what distant deeps or skies   5
Burnt the fire of thine eyes?
On what wings dare he aspire?
What the hand dare seize the fire?

And what shoulder, & what art,
Could twist the sinews of thy heart?   10
And when thy heart began to beat,
What dread hand? & what dread feet?

What the hammer? what the chain?
In what furnace was thy brain?
What the anvil? what dread grasp   15
Dare its deadly terrors clasp?

When the stars threw down their spears,
And water'd heaven with their tears,
Did he smile his work to see?
Did he who made the Lamb make thee?   20

Tyger! Tyger! burning bright
In the forests of the night,
What immortal hand or eye
Dare frame thy fearful symmetry?

Mock on, Mock on, Voltaire, Rousseau

Mock on, Mock on, Voltaire, Rousseau:°
Mock on, Mock on: 'tis all in vain.
You throw the sand against the wind,
And the wind blows it back again.

And every sand becomes a Gem   5
Reflected in the beams divine;
Blown back they blind the mocking Eye,
But still in Israel's paths they shine.

The Atoms of Democritus
And Newton's Particles of light°   10
Are sands upon the Red sea shore,
Where Israel's tents do shine so bright.

MOCK ON, MOCK ON, VOLTAIRE, ROUSSEAU. **1. Voltaire,
Rousseau:** eighteenth-century leaders of the French Enlightenment, whose criticism of the established order is
described here as pointless. **9–10. Atoms . . . light:** philosophical reductions of nature to inanimate matter or
physical laws by the Greek philosopher Democritus
(fifth century B.C.) and by Sir Isaac Newton (1642–1727).

And Did Those Feet in Ancient Time

And did those feet in ancient time
Walk upon England's mountains green?°
And was the holy Lamb of God
On England's pleasant pastures seen?

And did the Countenance Divine   5
Shine forth upon our clouded hills?
And was Jerusalem builded here
Among these dark Satanic Mills?

Bring me my Bow of burning gold:
Bring me my Arrows of desire: 10
Bring me my Spear: O clouds unfold!
Bring me my Chariot of fire!

I will not cease from Mental Fight,
Nor shall my Sword sleep in my hand
Till we have built Jerusalem°   15
In England's green & pleasant Land.

PERCY BYSSHE SHELLEY
1792–1822

Ode to the West Wind

1

O wild West Wind, thou breath of Autumn's being,
Thou, from whose unseen presence the leaves dead
Are driven, like ghosts from an enchanter fleeing,

Yellow, and black, and pale, and hectic red,
Pestilence-stricken multitudes: O thou,   5
Who chariotest to their dark wintry bed

The wingèd seeds, where they lie cold and low,
Each like a corpse within its grave, until
Thine azure sister of the Spring shall blow.

Her clarion o'er the dreaming earth, and fill   10
(Driving sweet buds like flocks to feed in air)
With living hues and odors plain and hill:

AND DID THOSE FEET IN ANCIENT TIME. **1–2. And . . .
green:** reference to the notion that the Celtic Druids were
the Old Testament patriarchs. **15. Jerusalem:** New Jerusalem (see Revelation 21).

Wild Spirit, which are moving everywhere;
Destroyer and preserver; hear, oh hear!

2

Thou on whose stream, mid the steep sky's
    commotion,   15
Loose clouds like earth's decaying leaves are shed,
Shook from the tangled boughs of Heaven and
    Ocean,

Angels of rain and lightning: there are spread
On the blue surface of thine aëry surge,
Like the bright hair uplifted from the head   20

Of some fierce Maenad,° even from the dim verge
Of the horizon to the zenith's height,
The locks of the approaching storm. Thou dirge

Of the dying year, to which this closing night
Will be the dome of a vast sepulcher,   25
Vaulted with all thy congregated might

Of vapors, from whose solid atmosphere
Black rain, and fire, and hail will burst: oh, hear!

3

Thou who didst waken from his summer dreams
The blue Mediterranean, where he lay,   30
Lulled by the coil of his crystalline streams,

Beside a pumice isle in Baiae's bay.°
And saw in sleep old palaces and towers
Quivering within the wave's intenser day,

All overgrown with azure moss and flowers   35
So sweet, the sense faints picturing them! Thou
For whose path the Atlantic's level powers

Cleave themselves into chasms, while far below
The sea-blooms and the oozy woods which wear
The sapless foliage of the ocean, know   40

Thy voice, and suddenly grow gray with fear,
And tremble and despoil themselves: oh, hear!

4

If I were a dead leaf thou mightest bear;
If I were a swift cloud to fly with thee;
A wave to pant beneath thy power, and share   45

ODE TO THE WEST WIND. **21. Maenad:** frenzied female
worshiper of Dionysus. **32. pumice . . . bay:** volcanic
island near Naples.

The impulse of thy strength, only less free
Than thou, O uncontrollable! If even
I were as in my boyhood, and could be

The comrade of thy wanderings over Heaven,
As then, when to outstrip thy skiey speed   50
Scarce seemed a vision; I would ne'er have striven

As thus with thee in prayer in my sore need.
Oh, lift me as a wave, a leaf, a cloud!
I fall upon the thorns of life! I bleed!

A heavy weight of hours has chained and bowed   55
One too like thee: tameless, and swift, and proud.

5

Make me thy lyre, even as the forest is:
What if my leaves are falling like its own!
The tumult of thy mighty harmonies

Will take from both a deep, autumnal tone,   60
Sweet though in sadness. Be thou, Spirit fierce,
My spirit! Be thou me, impetuous one!

Drive my dead thoughts over the universe
Like withered leaves to quicken a new birth!
And, by the incantation of this verse,   65

Scatter, as from an unextinguished hearth
Ashes and sparks, my words among mankind!
Be through my lips to unawakened earth

The trumpet of a prophecy! O Wind,
If Winter comes, can Spring be far behind?   70

WILLIAM BUTLER YEATS
1865–1939

Two Songs from a Play°

1

I saw a staring virgin° stand
Where holy Dionysus died,
And tear the heart out of his side,
And lay the heart upon her hand
And bear that beating heart away;   5
And then did all the Muses sing
Of Magnus Annus° at the spring,
As though God's death were but a play.

Another Troy must rise and set,
Another lineage feed the crow,   10
Another Argo's painted prow
Drive to a flashier bauble yet.°
The Roman Empire stood appalled:
It dropped the reigns of peace and war
When that fierce virgin and her Star   15
Out of the fabulous darkness called.

2

In pity for man's darkening thought
He walked that room and issued thence
In Galilean turbulence;°
The Babylonian starlight° brought   20
A fabulous, formless darkness in;
Odor of blood when Christ was slain
Made all Platonic tolerance vain
And vain all Doric discipline.

Everything that man esteems   25
Endures a moment or a day.
Love's pleasure drives his love away,
The painter's brush consumes his dreams;
The herald's cry, the soldier's tread
Exhaust his glory and his might: 30
Whatever flames upon the night
Man's own resinous heart has fed.

TWO SONGS FROM A PLAY. The prologue and epilogue to
The Resurrection, in which the Resurrection of Christ
occurs during the ritual celebration of the death and resurrection of Dionysus. **1. virgin:** Athena, the Virgin Mary, and
the constellation Virgo, who holds the star Spica in her
hand (see l. 15). When Dionysus was dismembered by the
Titans, Athena rescued his heart and insured his resurrection.

7. Magnus Annus: (Great Year) the year that marks the
rise and fall of civilizations, here the fall of the Greek and
the rise of the Christian. **9–12. Another . . . yet:** allusion to
Virgil's *Eclogue* IV, 31–36. **17–19. In . . . turbulence:**
reference to the conclusion of the play, in which Christ
leaves the room where his Resurrection has been witnessed
and, in Yeats' thought, introduces the dominant emotion
of the new era, pity. **20. Babylonian starlight:** both the
Star of Bethlehem and a recurrence of the starlight that
ushered in the civilization that preceded the Greek, the
Babylonian.

TRAGEDY

Narrative Tragedy

Evil seems deep-rooted in a world where men often bring destruction on themselves unwittingly before they have realized their potential or suffer retribution that is out of keeping with their offenses. For more than two thousand years philosophers and historians have been preoccupied with finding meaning in this vision of life. The Christian doctrine of original sin and the Greek concept of fate are two attempts to account for the persistence of human suffering. Tragedy is not only an idea or sense of life but a literary form, a pattern of action that keeps recurring in the literature of different times and places and has included such central figures in the imaginative life of Western civilization as Oedipus and Hamlet. When Oedipus tries to evade the prophecy that he will kill his father and marry his mother, his efforts only serve to fulfill it. Both of Hamlet's choices—avenging his murdered father and refusing to do so—would implicate him in evil and cut off his future. Tragedy tries to understand the mysterious workings of a world that repeatedly frustrate human wishes and crush human capacities. It appeals to our desire for some order that can explain the evident contradictions of human existence.

The sense in which tragedy is a literary concept, a way of describing the structure that keeps recurring in the novels and poems and plays we read, is the most important one for our purposes as students of literature, but it is not the only relevant one. Buried within the literary structure is something that historians and philosophers can abstract as the idea of tragedy. It has been particularly useful to biographers in reconstructing the lives of such figures as Julius Caesar, Thomas à Becket, Joan of Arc, Mary Queen of Scots, Napoleon, Abraham Lincoln, and John and Robert Kennedy; it has also served as the principle for explaining whole epochs, such as the French Revolution and the Second World War. As an idea, tragedy is central to the philosophical tradition stretching from Hegel through Nietzsche to Karl Jaspers. What history and philosophy describe, literature vividly *presents* to the imagination, so we should not be surprised at the connection between the idea of tragedy as a way of explaining events and the literary structure as a way of ordering events.

The closely linked thought and action of tragedy seem to represent and evoke strong emotions that are often valued for their own sake. One of the nonliterary uses of the word *tragedy* is instructive. When we are strongly moved by someone else's misfortune or by some natural or man-made catastrophe, we are likely to say that the event is "tragic." Though this usage is often so loose as to be nearly meaningless, it can dignify the person or suggest that the event is not simply a random phenomenon without human significance. Only the most careless speaker would say that a dog's death is "tragic" or that an assassination is merely "sad," though many other qualifying words might be appropriate in either case. Even in casual speech we are likely to reserve the word *tragic* for those situations in which we feel attracted to another human being but are simultaneously repelled by what happens to him.

Relating this state of mixed feelings to literary tragedy is not so easy as it may seem. The temptation, of course, is to reduce the complex experience of watching tragic drama to feelings produced within the audience. Aristotle's notion of tragic *catharsis* has sometimes been interpreted as an emotional state within the spectator, a combination of pity (sympathy for one who experiences undeserved misfortune) and fear (unwilling identi-fication with the hero in his disaster). There are obvious difficulties in this way of thinking about literary tragedy that are not so apparent in the everyday use of the word. *Pity* and *fear*, like most words referring to human emotions, are too broadly inclusive and vague to tell us much about the feelings they refer to, and there is very little reason to believe that any abstract label can describe psychological conditions adequately. Connecting the feelings we may have as we watch a play or read a novel with the permanent qualities of that literary work is even more difficult. As individuals, we may be moved by Lear, Billy Budd, or Willy Loman yet not respond to Coriolanus, Macbeth, or Clyde Griffiths; perhaps the young identify with Hamlet more readily than do the old. It may be the case that empathy—identifying with a character and vicariously experi-encing his feelings—can never be counted on as an inevitable or constant effect of literary tragedy.

Yet we know that the complex impulses referred to by words like *pity* and *fear* are somehow built into the literary structure itself. Though the spectator or reader need not feel these emotions, he does come to under-stand them as he sees them being acted out in the lives of the characters. Sometimes the literary structure includes an imitation of our response to the fortunes of the hero through the words of a commentator or a hypo-thetical audience. The narrator in many of Bertolt Brecht's plays performs this function, as does the chorus in Greek tragedy, and in later plays like John Milton's *Samson Agonistes* and T. S. Eliot's *Murder in the Cathedral*. In these two, the chorus displays a whole range of feelings toward a hero who is both admired and hated for disrupting the normal world. Whether implicit or expressed, such emotions are a permanent dimension of tragic structure, independent of the spectator's temperament and circumstances. We are far more likely to agree about Hamlet's feelings in Act II, which never change, than we are about our feelings at three separate performances of the play. Our understanding of Hamlet's feelings depends on what happens to him and on the kind of world he lives in more than our own emotional states. For example, Hamlet's problem would disappear if the duty of revenge were eliminated as a principle of his world. This conventional duty sets up the ambivalence between his need to act and his doubt of the significance of all action, yet it is not part of *our* moral code. We may not feel his needs pressing upon us, but we do understand them. Unlike the misfortunes and catastrophes of our everyday lives, literary tragedy does not necessarily produce strong feelings, but it does demand awareness. We must have a full conception of the world in which the action occurs, and we must try to understand why certain acts in that world inevitably bring disaster to the hero.

The Idea of Tragedy

Our sense that the world *should* not contain evil generates the idea of tragedy. The mystery at the heart of human experience is the inexplicable presence of both good and evil in the world. An awareness of life-enhancing forces—like the simple vitality that allows us to enjoy our senses—is coupled with the sure knowledge that lives not yet fulfilled will be destroyed or mutilated. Human beings keep getting caught up in acts with consequences beyond their control and against their desires, and their personal fates or destinies cannot be fully understood in moral terms. The tragic hero is not simply a grand criminal who gets his just deserts in the final catastrophe. He usually appears to be both good and evil, which makes his destruction both undeserved *and* just at the same time. If the tragic hero moves within a moral order, it is one whose operations are not clearly linked to his good and bad impulses. It is sometimes claimed that the paradox will disappear if we think of tragedy as a battle between incompatible values, but it is hard to regard the violence of much tragic action—murder, rape, suicide, war—as an instrument of benevolence. Even when there are accepted moral or legal sanctions supporting both sides of a human conflict, we may doubt whether the struggle offers a choice between essentially good actions. Can we say that Hamlet's obligations to avenge his father and to honor his mother are morally equivalent, or that Antigone's right to her brother's body and Creon's refusal to honor that right in the name of authority are directly comparable? The systems of moral order we use—elaborate taboo structures in primitive societies, gradations of crime in legal codes, imperatives like the Ten Commandments, even the radical altruism of the Sermon on the Mount—do not explain everything we need to understand. What happens in the world does not seem to be aligned with what human beings value. As Max Scheler puts it, "the simple fact that the sun shines on the good and bad alike makes tragedy possible." And necessary, we might add.

The idea of tragedy comes from our attempt to relate human values to a seemingly hostile universe without abandoning those values. Moral principles as we usually understand them do not have the power or scope to explain tragic action. Our sense of justice, for example, derived as it is from the context of everyday social relationships, does not tell us why an already enlightened Lear must suffer through the death of his daughter Cordelia. A senile old king would not be punished that much for folly and presumption under any humane code of justice. The conflict of tragedy usually transcends moral principles because it sets human desires and human conceptions of order against the workings of an inhospitable world. Northrop Frye observes that "the hero's act has thrown a switch in a larger machine than his own life, or even his own society." Men cannot avoid responsibility for being born, for the defects in their own characters that they did not wholly create, for the unwanted and unforeseen consequences of seemingly innocent acts. Disasters come upon them because every act is part of a process occurring *in* time. Human decisions are inherently flawed: they are made within the context suggested by past experience, whereas the effects of any choice occur in a future never wholly identical with that past. Thus, Lear fractures political order through his scheme for maintaining it, and his rejection of Cordelia in the opening scene is fulfilled by her death long after he has learned to value her properly. In Arthur Miller's *Death of a Salesman*, Willy Loman assures his own subsequent failure when he lives by illusions about the magnificent "success" of his brother Ben. Once started, a sequence of cause and effect in time cannot be stopped, reversed, or even understood until it is too late.

Awareness of the tragic has usually depended on such a linear conception of time and causality. We attach importance to this pattern of events because it is typical rather than unique; the pattern repeats itself endlessly in human history and art. Our awareness of the tragic, then, must also involve the idea of recurrence. The fatal chain of cause and effect that moves toward completion in individual lives is continually being reenacted. One obvious model for the tragic sequence is the natural cycle of human life. Men are born, gain strength and knowledge as they grow, reach their full powers in maturity, decay into senility, and die. But tragedy usually deals with an interruption of the cycle, a sudden cutting off of power in the mature or a waste of promise in the young. It foreshortens the cycle by concentrating the energy of a lifetime into a few acts rather than measuring it out over a span of years. When released, such compacted energy is dangerous because it has more than human force. We are not surprised when innocents like Ophelia and Cordelia are swept away in the general carnage of *Hamlet* and *King Lear* because the destruction latent in most human action has been magnified many times and cannot be contained. The political and moral order that is partly restored in the last scene of each play is meaningful because it replaces a chaos of unbridled energy. Again and again, men must rediscover the limits of human power by acting rashly and suffering consequences that they could not foresee. In this important sense the tragic hero's "fate" or "destiny" is what he does rather than what is done to him.

Savage acts have no human meaning in themselves and thus are not enough to create tragedy. The value of foreshortened time and heightened energy, whether they occur in life or in art, lies in the enlightenment they give us. Events ordinarily separated by years are jammed together, preventing the diffusion of relevance that interruptions and lapses of memory usually produce. Of course, compression is one of the sources of power in all literature, and particularly in drama, but it is especially necessary in tragedy. Events must crowd and push, conveying the sense of energy and the illusion of power that men feel as they assert themselves. An Othello who trusted Iago for years before becoming jealous would be more pathetic than tragic. If the containing shape of a life is to be seen at all, it must be seen all at once in sharp outline with no distractions, no relief. In this respect the moment of understanding or recognition in tragedy is quite similar to religious epiphany, the suddenly glimpsed manifestation of the divine in human form.

The recognition that comes to tragic heroes depends on the idea of death, not death itself. A man has the chance to reflect on the shape of his whole life only just before a certain death, the one moment at which everything can be known. But the hero has no use for the knowledge he gains at the point of death; we who are still living do. Few of us wish to gain tragic knowledge through experience, whereas we might like to participate in the festival at the end of comedy, and we sometimes do wish we were the hero of romance. We want to come by our tragic knowledge vicariously, and we want to use it as a bulwark against the images of disorder that flood our minds. Thus tragic action performs the function of a ritual for the living. It makes sense of events that are otherwise meaningless and fearful. Life must end in death for each individual man, but energy and potency continue in the human community.

No matter how much the career of the tragic hero may horrify us, his death has meaning because it resembles sacrifice. In myths of dying and reviving gods like Adonis and Osiris, in Old Testament stories about Abraham and Samson, and in the Crucifixion, individual death is associated with communal rejuvenation. Figures of innocence, beauty, fidelity, and strength die, but their qualities are symbolically transferred to the living or reabsorbed within nature; death becomes a means of partial rejuvenation because it brings together the remnants of society. In this sense, the final scene of tragic plays resembles the rite of communion. Although the religious meaning of sacrifice is muted in literary tragedy, the hero's death does affect his society. In *Samson Agonistes* and *Murder in the Cathedral* the heroes are martyrs, men in league with God against a sinful world, and their acts are a means of restoring that world to its divine purposes. More often the hero's death represents a political sacrifice that destroys usurped power and restores health to the state. Both *Hamlet* and *King Lear* include this kind of political renewal, and it is the substance of Miller's *Crucible*. Sometimes the protagonists, usually women or youths, are too innocent to survive in the totally corrupt society around them:

Romeo and Juliet are sacrificed to an implacable feud in Verona; young Morgan Moreen, the hero of Henry James' "Pupil," to the crassness of his parents. Thus, the way in which tragedy assigns meaning to death depends largely on the kind of world surrounding the hero.

The Tragic Scene   The scene in tragedy establishes the scope of human power, norms of conduct, and the connections between cause and effect that determine the outcome of the action. Such assumptions about the workings of nature and human society are conditions of understanding for the reader whether or not they reflect scientific and historical truths. These underlying conventions of the tragic world are usually associated with "fate" or "destiny" or "necessity." The tragic scene is a closed system that limits freedom of action; it confines human energy and prevents any escape from the irreversible processes of linear time. Nothing can be done over again within the tragic scene because a choice once made sets some social or cosmic machinery going.

The given world of any tragedy must convince us that a logic of necessity operates, that whatever does happen must happen in that world. Its specific postulates may vary—the will of the gods, the eye-for-an-eye code of revenge, the gnawing demands of an obsession—but they have the clarity of axioms and the force of natural law. In Macbeth's case, some of these postulates are his own ambition, his belief in prophecy, his wife's urging, the opportunity provided by Duncan's visit, and the unsteadiness of government based on personal loyalty. Accidental events—for example, Hamlet's encounter with the pirate ship, which prevents his being murdered in England and brings about his return to Denmark—never seem to be an essential part of the tragic scene. An accidental event may serve as the occasion for a decisive act, or it may intensify the emotion leading to a character's choice, but it is not crucial. It has no more than a triggering function. The violence of tragic action can be detonated by an insignificant object like Desdemona's handkerchief or by an unlucky coincidence as simple as the letters that go astray in *Romeo and Juliet* and in Thomas Hardy's *Tess of the D'Urbervilles*. The pent-up energy of the tragic scene is often released by a trivial act that is no fundamental cause of the catastrophe, just as a chance remark can destroy a friendship or an assassination start a war. Thus the world enclosing tragic action is precarious but not haphazard. In it, false steps precipitate the "fall" and missed chances bring remorse because there is no proportion between acts and consequences. The destructive forces unleashed by the hero are regular enough in their working, even though he cannot foresee them. They are the electric potential of the tragic scene discharged.

As we might expect, the destructive forces take many forms. They appear as nature in John Millington Synge's *Riders to the Sea*, in which an indifferent, remorseless sea claims all Maurya's sons, yet no one knows how or when. They can also be an internal psychological obsession, as they are in James Joyce's "Painful Case": Mr. Duffy is totally imprisoned by the sexual inhibitions that destroy his relationship with Mrs. Sinico. More frequently, discord between a character's moral principles or fixations and the conditions of external scene produces tragic action. Thus characters sometimes help in provoking their own murders, as the Swede does in Stephen Crane's "Blue Hotel" when he forces hostile roles on the men of a little Nebraska town, or as Sutpen does in William Faulkner's "Wash" by treating Milly Jones as if she were a foaling mare, someone to be paid attention to only if she gives birth to his son. Similarly, in D. H. Lawrence's "Prussian Officer" the Captain's sadism is part of the given scene, and the other part is furnished by the code of military discipline and the mere presence of the young orderly. The cosmic order of God's will on earth is the larger scene of *Samson Agonistes* and also of *Murder in the Cathedral*, where it is set in opposition to Becket's desire for sainthood and the political order of Henry II. And all these elements—natural, psychological, political, cosmic—are interlocking forces at work against King Lear.

The Hero and His Society

The Hero

Within the tragic scene, the central figure has an extraordinary importance. Lear and Samson have a hand in creating the world that constrains them; acts like dividing the kingdom and confiding in Delilah are voluntary. For this reason it seems irrelevant to debate whether or not the hero has an opportunity to evade catastrophe. Some of the acts leading up to the hero's fall are unmistakably willed. Oedipus actively seeks the murderer of Laius; Jesus goes to the Garden of Gethsemane knowing that he will be betrayed; Captain Ahab vows revenge on a brute, the white whale that gradually comes to represent all the forces set against man in the world. What becomes the hero's nemesis originates in part from his own will and is transferred to the external scene. Adam's fall reminds us that human choice and self-assertion are at the core of the tragic situation. This "use of freedom to lose freedom," in Frye's phrase, is not a mystical paradox if we are willing to grant that for the most part men act with only fleeting glimpses of the consequences to follow. The tragic hero is overwhelmed by those consequences.

Like all men, the tragic hero is the victim of his decisions, but he is more than an ordinary man. He represents human potency and therefore is often remarkable in strength, skill, wisdom, or persistence. According to Frye, "tragic heroes are so much the highest points in their human landscape that they seem the inevitable conductors of the power about them, great trees more likely to be struck by lightning than a clump of grass." It is important that we not misconstrue this remark. It applies to the Willy Lomans of tragedy as well as the King Lears because it describes the *function* of the hero within a given scene rather than his degree of absolute power. Belief in Great Men, a characteristic of the formal mode, is not a necessary condition of tragedy. However limited or expansive the view of human nature may be in a culture, its dominant traits can be concentrated and exaggerated in one representative man and thereby gain tragic potentiality.

In the process of such heightening, the tragic hero's interests are narrowed and intensified, giving us the ambition of Lady Macbeth and the jealousy of Othello purified of irrelevancy. But this does not imply that the action must be grandiose in the manner of Satan rebelling against God or Samson destroying a nation of Philistines. We see the same willful narrowing of possibilities in Faulkner's "Wash," in which Sutpen follows the principles of his inhuman "design" single-mindedly, and in James' "Pupil," in which young Morgan Moreen struggles against the overwhelming corruption of his parents. The hero's talents are wasted. Human possibilities of some kind are concentrated in him, so his failure brings us a pained awareness of the gap between promise and accomplishment. Young men like Hamlet are immobilized by doubt; men in their prime like Mark Antony are torn between two courses of action; old men like Lear, with rich lives behind them, must watch the worlds they have built dissolve before their eyes. We have a sense of communion with the tragic hero because he suffers for us.

The hero's role as a representative man, his unusual prowess, his pride, and his vulnerability may come out in a number of ways as the action develops, but they often appear through an obsession. The tremendous concentration of energy and purpose that gives heroes their power may also throw them off balance; they seem to lack the sense of proportion that comes from ordinary living. The same impulse for perfection that makes tragic heroes extraordinary often leads them to embrace the logic of their designs absolutely. Our attitude toward such men reveals an important difference between historical and fictional characters. We are appalled by the self-sufficiency of a Caesar, a Napoleon, or a Hitler, yet we are awed by the same single-mindedness in Oedipus, Othello, Ahab. We grant the latter their world of self-created horrors when aesthetic distance intervenes. The union of greatness and obsession, of accomplishment and intolerance, makes the tragic hero particularly susceptible to delusion. He is often too sure that his vision is clear, that his power is sufficient, that his purpose is benign.

Nemesis   Undermining such illusions is the function of many characters set against the hero in tragedy. They often seem to epitomize all the evil in human nature—the traitor Iago in *Othello*, the bastard Edmund in *King Lear*, the misanthropic Claggart who hates without cause in Herman Melville's *Billy Budd*, the satanic Misfit with his sinister self-confidence in Flannery O'Connor's "A Good Man Is Hard to Find." Ordinary human motives cannot account for what such villains do: their pure evil resembles that of black magicians and malign spirits in romance. Within the narrative pattern, they are the agents of retribution who stand ready to thwart the exorbitant designs of the hero.

Sometimes ultimate control over the action is vested in a superhuman figure like the ghost of Hamlet's father or Jehovah in *Samson Agonistes*. The same function can be performed indirectly by the words of a prophet like Tiresias or Cassandra in Greek tragedy, the instructions of the mysterious old man in Chaucer's "Pardoner's Tale," or the superstitious visions of an ordinary woman like Maurya in *Riders to the Sea*. The blood feud between families that starts the action of most revenge tragedies is another indirect nemesis. There is no point in distinctions between characters and impersonal forces. The characters of nemesis are often both less and more than fully human, lacking the capacity for pity and remorse yet wielding power that is unquestioned within the tragic scene. They cannot be banished or converted like the characters who oppose the hero and heroine in comedy.

Victims

The hero and his nemesis represent the two necessary character functions of the tragic pattern. A third major function is complementing and reinforcing the hero's fall to symbolize its universality. Whether the hero is an aged king like Lear, a usurping rebel like Macbeth, or an immobilized avenger like Hamlet, his agonies spread throughout the realm. Tragedies are full of victims and scapegoats, characters who get pulled down accidentally and who bear little or no responsibility for their own destruction. The drowning of Ophelia in *Hamlet* and the hanging of Cordelia in *King Lear* deepen the sense of wasted beauty and innocence. Murdered children in *Macbeth*, *Richard II*, Hardy's *Jude the Obscure*, Faulkner's "Wash," and O'Connor's "A Good Man Is Hard to Find" become emblems of waste through their peripheral connection with tragic events. Tragedy subverts the stability and permanence of human society through wanton carnage.

Spokesmen for Common Sense

Some characters speak for the sane world that the hero's presumption has upset. They serve a fourth function, opposing the havoc of tragic action and suggesting the continuity of society. They are usually mature men with blunt advice, unaffected, candid, and honest. Comrades-in-arms like Horatio in *Hamlet*, Kent in *King Lear*, and Enobarbus in *Antony and Cleopatra* try to talk common sense to their errant heroes and are sometimes punished for their interference; Starbuck has the same relation to Ahab in *Moby Dick*. Groups like the priests and the chorus of women in *Murder in the Cathedral* and the chorus of Danites in *Samson Agonistes* often display the same kind of homespun wisdom with an equal lack of persuasiveness. The very fact that the chorus is composed of many people symbolizes the degree to which the tragic hero has isolated himself from common humanity. The chorus also contains the germ of comic action because it survives the catastrophe and welcomes the return of ordinary routine, with its promise for the future.

**Stages
of Action**
The action of tragedy is one development of the combat myth at the heart of all drama. The four character functions just described are naturally polarized: hero against nemesis, sacrificial victims against spokesmen for common sense in a normal world. In its simplest form, the conflict that makes literary narratives move is a matter of choosing sides. Characters align themselves with or against the hero on the basis of personal loyalties. It is easy to see how this principle works in overtly political tragedies like *Macbeth* or *Coriolanus*. It also organizes the metaphysical battle between God and Satan in *Paradise Lost* and the implied test of power between Jehovah and Baal in *Samson Agonistes*.

The persistence of triangular relationships in literature is testimony to the power of the combat myth; the father must choose between sons, the son between mother and lover, the husband between wife and mistress. Splitting the family unit into warring parts creates the necessity of exclusive choice; we see this principle at work in the Old Testament story of Absalom, in Aeschylus' Agamemnon trilogy, in *Hamlet* and *King Lear,* in Eugene O'Neill's *Desire Under the Elms,* in Tennessee Williams' *Streetcar Named Desire*. But all forms of the combat myth are not tragic. We can observe simplified variants of it in the play of children: comedy is something like a tug-of-war in which everyone takes part, and it is resolved when the winning side pulls the losers along too; in tragedy the subsidiary characters are watching someone else play king-of-the-hill, a far more dangerous game because no one can stay up there forever. Tragic action isolates the hero from the society he represents, giving him the double role of leader and sacrificial victim. Although it is impossible to describe this loss of social cohesion in a way that fits in all tragedies, five stages are sometimes discernible.

Encroachment
The first stage of action may be called the *encroachment*. In this stage, the hero takes on more than he should and makes a mistake that ultimately causes his own "fall" (the metaphor ordinarily used to describe the whole curve of tragic action). He goes beyond the bounds of his power or peculiar talent, and in his refusal to recognize these bounds he exhibits both the grandeur and the folly of human assertiveness. Aristotle and his commentators used the concepts of *hubris* (pride) and *hamartia* (error or flaw) to explain this stage of action. It is probably a mistake to interpret either concept psychologically. To say that the hero might or should have been more humble and less fallible is irrelevant. Pride and error are conditions of tragic narrative; nothing would happen without them.

Those with a special interest in the ethical motives of tragedy are likely to speak of the "sin" of pride, but the act that sets the machinery going is not always morally blameworthy. It is often an act blindly done, demonstrating the hero's faith in his power to regulate the world or his insensitivity to others. (The physical blindness of Oedipus and Samson is obviously symbolic.) When Lear demands that an overt expression of love by his three daughters be part of his abdication ceremony, he misunderstands both the nature of love and his daughters' motives. Similarly, the well-meaning husband in Robert Frost's "Home Burial" unintentionally alienates his wife by digging a needed grave for their dead child, and the unpleasant family in O'Connor's "A Good Man Is Hard to Find" goes sightseeing quite innocently on the road that leads to their slaughter. Even in such cases as these some *act* is committed, consciously or unconsciously, that is an encroachment in terms of norms of human conduct within a given world. And here literature is not so far from life as we might like to think. People do, like the wife in "Home Burial," fall prey to mistakes and fixations in moments of great stress, and they do, like the family in "A Good Man Is Hard to Find," wander into unlucky confrontations with evil. To be alive is to take up space in the world and run the risk of conflict with whatever laws govern it. When we trespass unknowingly we are still asserting our existence, although not so obviously as the Oedipus or Lear who lays claim to great power in the world.

The second stage of both comic and tragic action may be called the *complication*. In both patterns it includes the events that build up and align opposing forces. For our purposes at the moment, the difference between comic and tragic action is more important than the similarity. Although the rift between opponents widens in both actions, the network of cause and effect disintegrates in comedy but expands its scope in tragedy. Frye states the difference succinctly: "Just as comedy often sets up an arbitrary law and then organizes the action to break or evade it, so tragedy presents the reverse theme of narrowing a comparatively free life into a process of causation." The conflict of comedy can sometimes be resolved by one event or discovery that allows the hero and heroine to marry or the sanity of society to return, whereas in tragedy the causes of disruption grow enormously. This difference may explain why *Romeo and Juliet* (not far removed from the pattern of comedy) needs an ancient and implacable feud between Montagues and Capulets, fatal duels, and a large dose of human bumbling to establish a tragic context for "star-crossed lovers." It may also help to explain why disguises and deceptions—often the major devices of comic plot—are not important in tragedy. The whole structure of *Twelfth Night* depends on Viola's disguise, but Edgar playing "Poor Tom" before Lear and Gloucester cannot change their destinies by unmasking himself. Edgar, Lear, Gloucester, Albany, Kent, Cordelia, France, Goneril, Regan, and Edmund are all enmeshed in a network of causation that no one of them can control. Up to the point of crisis in tragedy, forces accumulate until they threaten to crack the order of society.

Complication

The moment of crisis itself, *reversal*, is the third important stage of tragic action. Again, the comparison between comedy and tragedy is instructive. In comedy, the reversal is often as simple as discovering that the humble hero has royal blood in his veins and is therefore eligible to marry the rich and beautiful daughter of an aristocratic family. In tragedy,

Reversal

it is the point at which it becomes clear that the hero's expectations are mistaken, that his fate will be the reverse of what he had hoped. In contrast to comedy, the reversal does not trigger the dénouement immediately; it is more often an act that leads to rather incomplete and mysterious discoveries, and it sometimes produces effects directly contrary to the hero's expectations. Since Aristotle, such effects have been called "tragic irony" and assigned a pivotal role in the development of the action. The classic instance, of course, is Oedipus, who *seeks* the knowledge that proves him guilty of murdering his father and marrying his mother; when the facts are discovered, he has accomplished his objective and destroyed himself in doing so. In such reversals the cure for evil or the means of achieving prosperity turns out to be the hero's nemesis. As spectators we are detached enough from the hero to see what he cannot yet know; he may have premonitions of disaster, but we apprehend design, although we do not always see it clearly or entirely at this stage of the action.

The reversal is sometimes thought of as the hero's apogee on the wheel of fortune, the high point of his power before the downward swing toward catastrophe. This figure is misleading if we try to apply it too literally. We can locate in the text the point at which Samson makes the crucial decision leading to his death (when he gives in to demands that he display his strength before the assembled Philistines), but that death is also his final achievement. Again, in "The Pardoner's Tale," the three revelers seem to reach a turning point when they consciously plot to kill each other, but this ironic reversal is already implicit in their initial quest to seek out death. Similarly, the fact of Lear's having divided the kingdom in the first scene makes his fate irreversible, although the implications of that decision are not clear to him until he is cast out upon the heath during the storm. In *Murder in the Cathedral*, Becket wills his reversal by returning from France; that decision has been made when the play begins. These examples suggest that the reversal is less a sudden turn of the wheel of fortune, as it often is in comedy, than a manifest working out of what has been latent in the tragic scene from the beginning. The hero starts to feel and understand the consequences of his former acts, and he may dimly foresee where they will lead him.

Catastrophe   The fourth stage of tragic action is a *catastrophe*. It may be a moment of passionate action—Samson destroying the Philistines, Jones cutting down Sutpen in Faulkner's "Wash," the orderly throttling the Captain in Lawrence's "Prussian Officer"—but it may also be almost completely passive, as it is in James's "Pupil," Graham Greene's "Basement Room," and Joyce's "Painful Case." The catastrophe has at least two functions in the working out of tragic action: to expose the limits of the hero's power and to dramatize the waste of his life. Whatever the context established by the tragic scene, its laws prove too much for the power of the hero; he is destroyed and so is much of his world. In the last act of many tragic plays, the stage is littered with dead bodies to remind us that the forces unleashed are not easily contained, and there are often elaborate subplots like that of Gloucester and his sons in *King Lear* to reinforce the impression of a world inundated with evil. Further, we are not allowed to forget how much has been destroyed since the hero's extraordinary promise represents our own aspirations for power and accomplishment.

The final stage of tragic action is full *recognition* of the larger pattern, by the audience alone or by the hero as well. This completes the movement toward knowledge begun in the reversal, and it may occur simultaneously with that third stage. Oedipus knows all that he needs to know when the shepherd confirms his identity as the son of Laius and Jocasta, but Lear has to wait for Cordelia's death before he gains full recognition. The hero himself usually reaches this stage *only* when he sees his life as complete, when he can stand outside of his own existence and discern its shape. Because the heroes of Aeschylus, Sophocles, and Shakespeare are detached from themselves in this sense at the end of the action, some critics have observed that tragic heroes must be capable of self-awareness. The demand seems excessive. Many tragic figures are too innocent (Joan of Arc, Billy Budd) or too helpless (Philip in Greene's "Basement Room," Hardy's Tess) or too impassioned (Coriolanus, Hedda Gabler) or too deluded (Emma Bovary, Willy Loman) for meaningful self-examination. Even in the case of heroes who are agonizingly reflective, like Hamlet and Raskolnikov, their position *in* the action makes them less fit to see the whole of it. They see the connections between intentions and deeds only momentarily and incompletely. As readers, we are not limited to a single perspective. Thus it is more useful for us to think of recognition as the total implication of tragic action rather than limiting it to the hero's perception. Karl Jaspers has claimed that even this kind of tragic knowledge is faulty because it deludes men into thinking they can transcend "the terrifying abysses of reality." Yet an awareness of order is the residue of tragic action. Tragedy has grandeur and dignity because art lends such qualities to repugnant events without eliminating their horror. And recognition, as the final stage of tragic action, is peculiarly important because it links what can be imagined with what has been done, containing, for a moment, both the vision of romance and the experience of irony.

Recognition

It is quite clear that not all the stories we consider tragic have five stages of action or four character functions. Some include no explicit act of encroachment because they assume general knowledge of the history or myth of a culture. An American tragedy built around Abraham Lincoln or John Kennedy could begin on the day of assassination. The bulk of Oedipus' history comes to us through fragmentary allusions by the chorus, and in the dramatic action proper the stages of reversal and recognition coalesce in one moment preceding the catastrophe. *Murder in the Cathedral* and *Samson Agonistes* begin in the middle of tragic action; the earlier

The Phases of Tragedy

stages are narrated by the chorus and by characters who retell the missing history of the hero. Other stories like Greene's "Basement Room" and Joyce's "Painful Case" carry the hero beyond a psychological catastrophe (and beyond the time span of the story proper) by implying the sterility of his future life. There are no subsidiary victims or blunt advisers in Lawtence's "Prussian Officer," no dominating "hero" in Chaucer's "Pardoner's Tale," and only hints of what the whole action might be in Robert Browning's "My Last Duchess" and Robert Lowell's "Mother Marie Therese." Such anomalies suggest the need for some means of recognizing transformations and condensations of the basic pattern. The full action has a logic of its own, with stark contrasts between the hero's power at the beginning and his impotence at the end, between his initial ignorance and his self-knowledge gained through suffering, between those supporting characters who are sucked down in his disaster and those survivors who escape the current of tragic action. When stages are missing or when the cast of characters is incomplete, the normal equilibrium is destroyed, and the meaning of the action changes.

The Tragic Norm: Conflict with Cosmic Law

The tragic norm is essentially the full action described in preceding sections: the hero aspires to more power than the scene will allow, unwittingly contributes to his own catastrophe by acting, and comes to recognize the limits of human will in an alien universe. One central example of this phase is *King Lear*. Lear acts as if he has the divine right to rule family, kingdom, and nature itself. The storm scene, the defeat of France's army, and the execution of Cordelia destroy his illusions of power. He moves down the social hierarchy as the play progresses—king, dependent, outcast—until he is indeed reduced to a "poor, bare, forked animal." *Samson Agonistes*, though still close to the norm, is more romantic because the hero's catastrophe is simultaneously his triumph through God's will. Since tragedy begins with the hero's impulse to grasp more than human power and ends in his bondage or mutilation, its mutations shift either toward pure romance or total irony.

The Romantic Phase: Escape from Bondage

In the romantic phase of tragedy, the hero's innocence or dignity receives more emphasis, but he usually lacks the strength to enforce his will because he is subject to some greater power. Karl Shapiro's "Adam and Eve," in capsule form, uses the archetype of subjection to God that is the center of a full-blown epic in *Paradise Lost*. Other forms of romantic tragedy are not overtly or wholly dependent on a divine scene. In one variant, young and naive heroes like Morgan Moreen in James's "Pupil" and the orderly in Lawrence's "Prussian Officer" are paralyzed by their initiation into code-ruled adult societies; in another, mature men like Becket in *Murder in the Cathedral* balance the demands of this world against their vision of God's will. In both cases death is an *escape* for the hero. The catastrophe is comparable to the final victory of romance because the hero does not lose his innocence or dignity. A passion for the sanctity of human personality is often the central motive in the romantic phase of tragedy. Through death the hero escapes the full force of experience, the debilitation of a fall.

In ironic tragedy the hero is an ordinary man, somehow trapped and forced into a contest he never sought. The action depends rather heavily on accident in an inexplicable world where time and human impulse are out of joint. The forces isolating the hero from the community are at their strongest in this phase. The hero loses his bearings; after the conflict he no longer knows who he is. The supports for his normal identity have disappeared. *The Ironic Phase: Defeat and Humiliation*

We tend to look down on the hero of this phase, since he often has less power than we do. Yet his plight is still tragic because he is inadequately armed for the encounters he must face. Bailey and his family do not have a chance against the diabolic Misfit in "A Good Man Is Hard to Find." Again, in "The Basement Room," young Philip sees the demonic in the familiar face of a housekeeper, Mrs. Baines; her face appears in his nightmares and prompts a betrayal that empties his own life of vitality and creativity. Ordinary men fighting everyday battles give us ironic versions of tragic action—versions in which there is still a real contest between power and law although the events may be commonplace rather than heroic. Ironic tragedy requires a vision of man precariously balancing his own capacity against the laws of his environment.

What seems to be lacking in the hero of ironic tragedy is any disposition to act. In "A Painful Case" Mr. Duffy's life was "an adventureless tale" until circumstances thrust Mrs. Sinico in his way. As a man who "lived his spiritual life without any communion with others," he misjudges her character and desires in a painfully obvious way: he thinks he is talking to "a temperament of great sensibility" about the "soul's incurable loneliness" until Mrs. Sinico touches him. The truth of Mr. Duffy's words ("we cannot give ourselves . . . we are our own") is confirmed by his failure to respond to Mrs. Sinico's appeal for "communion" in all senses of that word, physical as well as spiritual. The consequences of his rejection do not become apparent until four years later when Mrs. Sinico's suicide is reported in the newspaper. Mr. Duffy's unwillingness to respond destroys her life and leads him to a full recognition through stages of disgust and guilt leading to a final sense of his earlier self-betrayal. He sees the completed shape of his own life: "No one wanted him; he was outcast from life's feast." Mr. Duffy is left with nothing more to learn, no more life to live. The pattern is complete. Although he is an ordinary man, a captive of his own inhibitions, Mr. Duffy is nevertheless tragic rather than ironic because he has matched himself against a world not entirely of his own making and has lost.

The humdrum but secure world that such characters understand has been pulled out from under them, yet it has not been replaced by chaos. What saves these stories from total irony is our feeling that the hero might have been able to stand the test had he fully used such human capacities as foresight and strength of will. He has stumbled on some truth about nature or society or human character that other men do cope with successfully at least part of the time. He has been living in culpable ignorance, by illusions that ordinary human experience will not sustain. There is no reason for Maurya, the old woman in *Riders to the Sea*, to believe that the sea will not take the whole of her family nor for the three revelers in "The Pardoner's Tale" to think that they will not betray each other. When the young or the weak discover such truths through debilitating experience, they relive in miniature the Herculean quests and failures of kings and heroes. Even in its ironic phase, the tragic pattern affirms law. Weak and culpable characters reveal unpleasant truths about a world whose order is at least partly comprehensible.

Tragedy in the Natural Mode: "The Blue Hotel"

The possibility of tragic action cast in the natural mode—with a hero whose power is no greater than that of ordinary men—has been seriously questioned. Some critics follow Joseph Wood Krutch in claiming that tragedy requires a belief in great men and that it flourishes only in cultures dominated by generals, statesmen, or kings. It is easy to find a rationale for this view: if the hero is an ordinary man of no special eminence or talent, his actions may seem insignificant. But we still want to account for his suffering, and in doing so we may be led to apply what Frye calls "reductive formulas" to his case, either by making him a victim of fate or by finding him morally blameworthy. In the first instance the hero's acts are seen to be totally determined by some powerful external force; he is a victim because the odds are stacked against him. In the second, the hero is seen as committing crimes or sins rather than making mistakes; he is fully responsible for his own destruction and is not worth saving. Becket, Lear, and Samson do not tempt us into using these reductive formulas, but the less impressive heroes of Lawrence's "Prussian Officer," Greene's "Basement Room," and Crane's "Blue Hotel" may. Yet these stories are essentially tragic; the young Swede of "The Blue Hotel," a tailor from New York, is King Lear in miniature, a man who destroys himself through his own willed acts. He is not a passive victim of circumstances.

STEPHEN CRANE
1871–1900

The Blue Hotel

1

The Palace Hotel at Fort Romper was painted a light blue, a shade that is on the legs of a kind of heron, causing the bird to declare its position against any background. The Palace Hotel, then, was always screaming and howling in a way that made the dazzling winter landscape of Nebraska seem only a gray swampish hush. It stood alone on the prairie, and when the snow was falling the town two hundred yards away was not visible. But when the traveler alighted at the railway station he was obliged to pass the Palace Hotel before he could come upon the company of low clapboard houses which composed Fort Romper, and it was not to be thought that any traveler could pass the Palace Hotel without looking at it. Pat Scully, the proprietor, had proved himself a master of strategy when he chose his paints. It is true that on clear days, when the great transcontinental expresses, long lines of swaying Pullmans, swept through Fort Romper, passengers were overcome at the sight, and the cult that knows the brown-reds and the subdivisions of the dark greens of the East expressed shame, pity, horror, in a laugh. But to the citizens of this prairie town and to the people who would naturally stop there, Pat Scully had performed a feat. With this opulence and splendor, these creeds, classes, egotisms, that streamed through Romper on the rails day after day, they had no color in common.

As if the displayed delights of such a blue hotel were not sufficiently enticing, it was Scully's habit to go every morning and evening to meet the leisurely trains that stopped at Romper and work his seductions upon any man that he might see wavering, gripsack in hand.

One morning, when a snow-crusted engine dragged its long string of freight cars and its one passenger coach to the station, Scully performed the marvel of catching three men. One was a shaky and quick-eyed Swede, with a great shining cheap valise; one was a tall bronzed cowboy, who was on his way to a ranch near the Dakota line; one was a little silent man from the East, who didn't look it, and didn't announce it. Scully practically made them prisoners. He was so nimble and merry and kindly that each probably felt it would be the height of brutality to try to escape. They trudged off over the creaking board sidewalks in the wake of the eager little Irishman. He wore a heavy fur cap squeezed tightly down on his head. It caused his two red ears to stick out stiffly, as if they were made of tin.

At last, Scully, elaborately, with boisterous hospitality, conducted them through the portals of the blue hotel. The room which they entered was small. It seemed to be merely a proper temple for an enormous stove, which, in the center, was humming with godlike violence. At various points on its surface the iron had become luminous and glowed yellow from the heat. Beside the stove Scully's son Johnnie was playing High-Five with an old farmer who had whiskers both gray and sandy. They were quarreling. Frequently the old farmer turned his face toward a box of sawdust—colored brown from tobacco juice—that was behind the stove, and spat with an air of great impatience and irritation. With a loud flourish of words Scully destroyed the game of cards, and bustled his son upstairs with part of the baggage of the new guests. He himself conducted them to three basins of the coldest water in the world. The cowboy and the Easterner burnished themselves fiery red with this water, until it seemed to be some kind of metal-polish. The Swede, however, merely dipped his fingers gingerly and with trepidation. It was notable that throughout this series of small ceremonies the three travelers were made to feel that Scully was very benevolent. He was conferring great favors upon them. He handed the towel from one to another with an air of philanthropic impulse.

Afterward they went to the first room, and, sitting about the stove, listened to Scully's officious clamor at his daughters, who were preparing the midday meal. They reflected in the silence of experienced men who tread carefully amid new people. Nevertheless, the old farmer, stationary, invincible in his chair near the warmest part of the stove, turned his face from the sawdust-box frequently and addressed a glowing commonplace to the strangers. Usually he was answered in short but adequate sentences by either the cowboy or the Easterner. The Swede said nothing. He seemed to be occupied in making furtive estimates of each man in the room. One might have thought that he had the sense of silly suspicion which comes to guilt. He resembled a badly frightened man.

Later, at dinner, he spoke a little, addressing his conversation entirely to Scully. He volunteered that he had come from New York, where for ten years he had worked as a tailor. These facts seemed to strike Scully as fascinating, and afterward he volunteered that he had lived at Romper for fourteen years. The Swede asked about the crops and the price of labor. He seemed barely to listen to Scully's extended replies. His eyes continued to rove from man to man.

Finally, with a laugh and a wink, he said that some of these Western communities were very dangerous; and after his statement he straightened his legs under the table, tilted his head, and laughed again, loudly. It was plain that the demonstration had no meaning to the others. They looked at him wondering and in silence.

2

As the men trooped heavily back into the front room, the two little windows presented views of a turmoiling sea of snow. The huge arms of the wind were making attempts—mighty, circular, futile—to embrace the flakes as they sped. A gatepost like a still man with a blanched face stood aghast amid this profligate fury. In a hearty voice Scully announced the presence of a blizzard. The guests of the blue hotel, lighting their pipes, assented with grunts of lazy masculine contentment. No island of the sea could be exempt in the degree of this little room with its humming stove. Johnnie, son of Scully, in a tone which defined his opinion of his ability as a cardplayer, challenged the old farmer of both gray and sandy whiskers to a game of High-Five. The farmer agreed with a contemptuous and bitter scoff. They sat close to the stove, and squared their knees under a wide board. The cowboy and the Easterner watched the game with interest. The Swede remained near the window, aloof, but with a countenance that showed signs of an inexplicable excitement.

The play of Johnnie and the graybeard was suddenly ended by another quarrel. The old man arose while casting a look of heated scorn at his adversary. He slowly buttoned his coat, and then stalked with fabulous dignity from the room. In the discreet silence of all the other men the Swede laughed. His laughter rang somehow childish. Men by this time had begun to look at him askance, as if they wished to inquire what ailed him.

A new game was formed jocosely. The cowboy volunteered to become the partner of Johnnie, and they all then turned to ask the Swede to throw in his lot with the little Easterner. He asked some questions about the game, and, learning that it wore many names, and that he had played it when it was under an alias, he accepted the invitation. He strode toward the men nervously, as if he expected to be assaulted. Finally, seated, he gazed from face to face and laughed shrilly. This laugh was so strange that the Easterner looked up quickly, the cowboy sat intent and with his mouth open, and Johnnie paused, holding the cards with still fingers.

Afterward there was a short silence. Then Johnnie said, "Well let's get at it. Come on now!" They pulled their chairs forward until their knees were bunched under the board. They began to play, and their interest in the game caused the others to forget the manner of the Swede.

The cowboy was a board-whacker. Each time that he held superior cards he whanged them, one by one, with exceeding force, down upon the improvised table, and took the tricks with a glowing air of prowess and pride that sent thrills of indignation into the hearts of his opponents. A game with a board-whacker in it is sure to become intense. The countenances of the Easterner and the Swede were miserable whenever the cowboy thundered down his aces and kings, while Johnnie, his eyes gleaming with joy, chuckled and chuckled.

Because of the absorbing play none considered the strange ways of the Swede. They paid strict heed to the game. Finally, during a lull caused by a new deal, the Swede suddenly addressed Johnnie: "I suppose there have been a good many men killed in this room." The jaws of the others dropped and they looked at him.

"What in hell are you talking about?" said Johnnie.

The Swede laughed again his blatant laugh, full of a kind of false courage and defiance. "Oh, you know what I mean all right," he answered.

"I'm a liar if I do!" Johnnie protested. The card was halted, and the men stared at the Swede. Johnnie evidently felt that as the son of the proprietor he should make a direct inquiry. "Now, what might you be drivin' at, mister?" he asked. The Swede winked at him. It was a wink full of cunning. His fingers shook on the edge of the board. "Oh, maybe you think I have been to no-wheres. Maybe you think I'm a tenderfoot?"

"I don't know nothin' about you," answered Johnnie, "and I don't give a damn where you've been. All I got to say is that I don't know what you're driving at. There hain't never been nobody killed in this room."

The cowboy, who had been steadily gazing at the Swede, then spoke: "What's wrong with you, mister?"

Apparently it seemed to the Swede that he was formidably menaced. He shivered and turned white near the corners of his mouth. He sent an appealing glance in the direction of the little Easterner. During these moments he did not forget to wear his air of advanced pot-valor. "They say they don't know what I mean," he remarked mockingly to the Easterner.

The latter answered after prolonged and cautious reflection. "I don't understand you," he said, impassively.

The Swede made a movement then which announced that he thought he had encountered treachery from the only quarter where he had expected sympathy, if not help. "Oh, I see you are all against me. I see—"

The cowboy was in a state of deep stupefaction. "Say," he cried, as he tumbled the deck violently down upon the board, "say, what are you gittin' at, hey?"

The Swede sprang up with the celerity of a man escaping from a snake on the floor. "I don't want to fight!" he shouted. "I don't want to fight!"

The cowboy stretched his long legs indolently and deliberately. His hands were in his pockets. He spat into the sawdust-box. "Well, who the hell thought you did?" he inquired.

The Swede backed rapidly toward a corner of the room. His hands were out protectingly in front of his chest, but he was making an obvious struggle to control his fright. "Gentlemen," he quavered, "I suppose I am going to be killed before I can leave this house! I suppose I am going to be killed before

I can leave this house!" In his eyes was the dying-swan look. Through the windows could be seen the snow turning blue in the shadow of dusk. The wind tore at the house, and some loose things beat regularly against the clapboards like a spirit tapping.

A door opened, and Scully himself entered. He paused in surprise as he noted the tragic attitude of the Swede. Then he said, "What's the matter here?"

The Swede answered him swiftly and eagerly: "These men are going to kill me."

"Kill you!" ejaculated Scully. "Kill you! What are you talkin'?"

The Swede made the gesture of a martyr.

Scully wheeled sternly upon his son. "What is this, Johnnie?"

The lad had grown sullen. "Damned if I know," he answered. "I can't make no sense to it." He began to shuffle the cards, fluttering them together with an angry snap. "He says a good many men have been killed in this room, or something like that. And he says he's goin' to be killed here too. I don't know what ails him. He's crazy, I shouldn't wonder."

Scully then looked for explanation to the cowboy, but the cowboy simply shrugged his shoulders.

"Kill you?" said Scully again to the Swede. "Kill you? Man, you're off your nut."

"Oh, I know," burst out the Swede. "I know what will happen. Yes, I'm crazy—yes. Yes, of course, I'm crazy—yes. But I know one thing—" There was a sort of sweat of misery and terror upon his face. "I know I won't get out of here alive."

The cowboy drew a deep breath, as if his mind was passing into the last stages of dissolution. "Well, I'm doggoned," he whispered to himself.

Scully wheeled suddenly and faced his son. "You've been troublin' this man!"

Johnnie's voice was loud with its burden of grievance. "Why, good Gawd, I ain't done nothin' to 'im."

The Swede broke in. "Gentlemen, do not disturb yourselves. I will leave this house. I will go away, because"—he accused them dramatically with his glance—"because I do not want to be killed."

Scully was furious with his son. "Will you tell me what is the matter, you young divil? What's the matter, anyhow? Speak out!"

"Blame it!" cried Johnnie in despair, "don't I tell you I don't know? He—he says we want to kill him, and that's all I know. I can't tell what ails him."

The Swede continued to repeat: "Never mind, Mr. Scully; never mind. I will leave this house. I will go away, because I do not wish to be killed. Yes, of course, I am crazy—yes. But I know one thing! I will go away. I will leave this house. Never mind, Mr. Scully; never mind. I will go away."

"You will not go 'way," said Scully. "You will not go 'way until I hear the reason of this business. If anybody has troubled you I will take care of him. This is my house. You are under my roof, and I will not allow any peaceable man to be troubled here." He cast a terrible eye upon Johnnie, the cowboy, and the Easterner.

"Never mind, Mr. Scully; never mind. I will go away. I do not wish to be killed." The Swede moved toward the door which opened upon the stairs. It was evidently his intention to go at once for his baggage.

"No, no," shouted Scully peremptorily; but the white-faced man slid by him and disappeared. "Now," said Scully severely, "what does this mane?"

Johnnie and the cowboy cried together: "Why, we didn't do nothin' to 'im!"

Scully's eyes were cold. "No," he said, "you didn't?"

Johnnie swore a deep oath. "Why, this is the wildest loon I ever see. We didn't do nothin' at all. We were jest sittin' here playin' cards, and he—"

The father suddenly spoke to the Easterner. "Mr. Blanc," he asked, "what has these boys been doin'?"

The Easterner reflected again. "I didn't see anything wrong at all," he said at last, slowly.

Scully began to howl. "But what does it mane?" He stared ferociously at his son. "I have a mind to lather you for this, me boy."

Johnnie was frantic. "Well, what have I done?" he bawled at his father.

3

"I think you are tongue-tied," said Scully finally to his son, the cowboy, and the Easterner; and at the end of this scornful sentence he left the room.

Upstairs the Swede was swiftly fastening the straps of his great valise. Once his back happened to be half turned toward the door, and, hearing a noise there, he wheeled and sprang up, uttering a loud cry. Scully's wrinkled visage showed grimly in the light of the small lamp he carried. This yellow effulgence, streaming upward, colored only his prominent features, and left his eyes, for instance, in mysterious shadow. He resembled a murderer.

"Man! man!" he exclaimed, "have you gone daffy?"

"Oh, no! Oh, no!" rejoined the other. "There are people in this world who know pretty nearly as much as you do—understand?"

For a moment they stood gazing at each other. Upon the Swede's deathly pale cheeks were two spots brightly crimson and sharply edged, as if they had been carefully painted. Scully placed the light on the table and sat himself on the edge of the bed. He spoke ruminatively. "By cracky, I never heard of such a thing in my life. It's a complete muddle. I can't, for the soul of me, think how you ever got this idea into your head." Presently he lifted his eyes and asked: "And did you sure think they were going to kill you?"

The Swede scanned the old man as if he wished to see into his mind. "I did," he said at last. He obviously suspected that this answer might precipitate an outbreak. As he pulled on a strap his whole arm shook, the elbow wavering like a bit of paper.

Scully banged his hand impressively on the foot-board of the bed. "Why, man, we're goin' to have a line of ilictric streetcars in this town next spring."

"'A line of electric streetcars,'" repeated the Swede, stupidly.

"And," said Scully, "there's a new railroad goin' to be built down from Broken Arm to here. Not to mintion the four churches and the smashin' big brick schoolhouse. Then there's the big factory, too. Why, in two years Romper'll be a met-tro-pol-is."

Having finished the preparation of his baggage, the Swede straightened himself. "Mr. Scully," he said, with sudden hardihood, "how much do I owe you?"

"You don't owe me anythin'," said the old man, angrily.

"Yes, I do," retorted the Swede. He took seventy-five cents from his pocket and tendered it to Scully; but the latter snapped his fingers in disdainful refusal. However, it happened that they both stood gazing in a strange fashion at three silver pieces on the Swede's open palm.

"I'll not take your money," said Scully at last. "Not after what's been goin' on here." Then a plan seemed to strike him. "Here," he cried, picking up his lamp and moving toward the door. "Here! Come with me a minute."

"No," said the Swede, in overwhelming alarm.

"Yes," urged the old man. "Come on! I want you to come and see a picter—just across the hall—in my room."

The Swede must have concluded that his hour was come. His jaw dropped and his teeth showed like a dead man's. He ultimately followed Scully across the corridor, but he had the step of one hung in chains.

Scully flashed the light high on the wall of his own chamber. There was revealed a ridiculous photograph of a little girl. She was leaning against a balustrade of gorgeous decoration, and the formidable bang to her hair was prominent. The figure was as graceful as an upright sled-stake, and, withal, it was of the hue of lead. "There," said Scully, tenderly, "that's the picter of my little girl that died. Her name was Carrie. She had the purtiest hair you ever saw! I was that fond of her, she—"

Turning then, he saw that the Swede was not contemplating the picture at all, but, instead, was keeping keen watch on the gloom in the rear.

"Look, man!" cried Scully, heartily. "That's the picter of my little gal that died. Her name was Carrie. And then here's the picter of my oldest boy, Michael. He's a lawyer in Lincoln, an' doin' well. I gave that boy a grand eddication, and I'm glad for it now. He's a fine boy. Look at 'im now. Ain't he bold as blazes, him there in Lincoln, an honored an' respicted gintleman! An honored and respicted gintleman," concluded Scully with a flourish. And, so saying, he smote the Swede jovially on the back.

The Swede faintly smiled.

"Now," said the old man, "there's only one more thing." He dropped suddenly to the floor and thrust his head beneath the bed. The Swede could hear his muffled voice. "I'd keep it under me piller if it wasn't for that boy Johnnie. Then there's the old woman—Where is it now? I never put it twice in the same place. Ah, now come out with you!"

Presently he backed clumsily from under the bed, dragging with him an old coat rolled into a bundle.

"I've fetched him," he muttered. Kneeling on the floor, he unrolled the coat and extracted from its heart a large yellow-brown whisky-bottle.

His first maneuver was to hold the bottle up to the light. Reassured, apparently, that nobody had been tampering with it, he thrust it with a generous movement toward the Swede.

The weak-kneed Swede was about to eagerly clutch this element of strength, but he suddenly jerked his hand away and cast a look of horror upon Scully.

"Drink," said the old man affectionately. He had risen to his feet, and now stood facing the Swede.

There was a silence. Then again Scully said: "Drink!"

The Swede laughed wildly. He grabbed the bottle, put it to his mouth; and as his lips curled absurdly around the opening and his throat worked, he kept his glance, burning with hatred, upon the old man's face.

4

After the departure of Scully the three men, with the card-board still upon their knees, preserved for a long time an astounded silence. Then Johnnie said: "That's the dod-dangedest Swede I ever see."

"He ain't no Swede," said the cowboy, scornfully.

"Well, what is he then?" cried Johnnie. "What is he then?"

"It's my opinion," replied the cowboy deliberately, "he's some kind of a Dutchman." It was a venerable custom of the country to entitle as Swedes all light-haired men who spoke with a heavy tongue. In consequence the idea of the cowboy was not without its daring. "Yes, sir," he repeated. "It's my opinion this feller is some kind of a Dutchman."

"Well, he says he's a Swede, anyhow," muttered Johnnie, sulkily. He turned to the Easterner: "What do you think, Mr. Blanc?"

"Oh, I don't know," replied the Easterner.

"Well, what do you think makes him act that way?" asked the cowboy.

"Why, he's frightened." The Easterner knocked his pipe against a rim of the stove. "He's clear frightened out of his boots."

"What at?" cried Johnnie and the cowboy together.

The Easterner reflected over his answer.

"What at?" cried the others again.

"Oh, I don't know, but it seems to me this man has been reading dime novels, and he thinks he's right out in the middle of it—the shootin' and stabbin' and all."

"But," said the cowboy, deeply scandalized, "this ain't Wyoming, ner none of them places. This is Nebrasker."

"Yes," added Johnnie. "an' why don't he wait till he gits *out West*?"

The traveled Easterner laughed. "It isn't different there even—not in these days. But he thinks he's right in the middle of hell."

Johnnie and the cowboy mused long.

"It's awful funny," remarked Johnnie at last.

"Yes," said the cowboy. "This is a queer game. I hope we don't git snowed in, because then we'd have to stand this here man bein' around with us all the time. That wouldn't be no good."

"I wish pop would throw him out," said Johnnie.

Presently they heard a loud stamping on the stairs, accompanied by ringing jokes in the voice of old Scully, and laughter, evidently from the Swede. The men around the stove stared vacantly at each other. "Gosh!" said the cowboy. The door flew open, and old Scully, flushed and anecdotal, came into the room. He was jabbering at the Swede, who followed him, laughing bravely. It was the entry of two roisterers from a banquet hall.

"Come now," said Scully sharply to the three seated men, "move up and give us a chance at the stove." The cowboy and the Easterner obediently sidled their chairs to make room for the newcomers. Johnnie, however, simply arranged himself in a more indolent attitude, and then remained motionless.

"Come! Git over, there," said Scully.

"Plenty of room on the other side of the stove," said Johnnie.

"Do you think we want to sit in the draft?" roared the father.

But the Swede here interposed with a grandeur of confidence. "No, no. Let the boy sit where he likes," he cried in a bullying voice to the father.

"All right! All right!" said Scully, deferentially. The cowboy and the Easterner exchanged glances of wonder.

The five chairs were formed in a crescent about one side of the stove. The Swede began to talk; he talked arrogantly, profanely, angrily. Johnnie, the cowboy, and the Easterner maintained a morose silence, while old Scully appeared to be receptive and eager, breaking in constantly with sympathetic ejaculations.

Finally the Swede announced that he was thirsty. He moved in his chair, and said that he would go for a drink of water.

"I'll git it for you," cried Scully at once.

"No," said the Swede, contemptuously. "I'll get it for myself." He arose and stalked with the air of an owner off into the executive parts of the hotel.

As soon as the Swede was out of hearing Scully sprang to his feet and whispered intensely to the others: "Upstairs he thought I was tryin' to poison 'im."

"Say," said Johnnie, "this makes me sick. Why don't you throw 'im out in the snow?"

"Why, he's all right now," declared Scully. "It was only that he was from the East, and he thought this was a tough place. That's all. He's all right now."

The cowboy looked with admiration upon the Easterner. "You were straight," he said. "You were on to that there Dutchman."

"Well," said Johnnie to his father, "he may be all right now, but I don't see it. Other time he was scared, but now he's too fresh."

Scully's speech was always a combination of Irish brogue and idiom, Western twang and idiom, and scraps of curiously formal diction taken from the storybooks and newspapers. He now hurled a strange mass of language at the head of his son. "What do I keep? What do I keep? What do I keep?" he demanded, in a voice of thunder. He slapped his knee impressively, to indicate that he himself was going to make reply, and that all should heed. "I keep a hotel," he shouted. "A hotel, do you mind? A guest under my roof has sacred privileges. He is to be intimidated by none. Not one word shall he hear that would prijudice him in favor of goin' away. I'll not have it. There's no place in this here town where they can say they iver took in a guest of mine because he was afraid to stay here." He wheeled suddenly upon the cowboy and the Easterner. "Am I right?"

"Yes, Mr. Scully," said the cowboy, "I think you're right."

Yes, Mr. Scully," said the Easterner, "I think you're right."

5

At six-o'clock supper, the Swede fizzed like a fire-wheel. He sometimes seemed on the point of bursting into riotous song, and in all his madness he was encouraged by old Scully. The Easterner was encased in reserve; the cowboy sat in wide-mouthed amazement, forgetting to eat, while Johnnie wrathily demolished great plates of food. The daughters of the house, when they were obliged to replenish the biscuits, approached as warily as Indians, and, having succeeded in their purpose, fled with ill-concealed trepidation. The Swede domineered the whole feast, and he gave it the appearance of a cruel bacchanal. He seemed to have grown suddenly taller; he gazed, brutally disdainful, into every face. His voice rang through the room. Once when he jabbed out harpoon-fashion with his fork to pinion a biscuit, the weapon nearly impaled the hand of the Easterner, which had been stretched quietly out for the same biscuit.

After supper, as the men filed toward the other room, the Swede smote Scully ruthlessly on the shoulder. "Well, old boy, that was a good square meal." Johnnie looked hopefully at his father; he knew that shoulder was tender from an old fall; and, indeed, it appeared for a moment as if Scully was going to flame out over the matter, but in the end he smiled a sickly smile and remained silent. The others understood from his manner that he was admitting his responsibility for the Swede's new viewpoint.

Johnnie, however, addressed his parent in an aside. "Why don't you license somebody to kick you downstairs?" Scully scowled darkly by way of reply.

When they were gathered about the stove, the Swede insisted on another game of High-Five. Scully gently deprecated the plan at first, but the Swede turned a wolfish glare upon him. The old man subsided, and the Swede canvassed the others. In his tone there was always a great threat. The cowboy and the Easterner both remarked indifferently that they would play. Scully said that he would presently have to go to meet the 6:58 train, and so the Swede turned menacingly upon Johnnie. For a moment their glances crossed like blades, and then Johnnie smiled and said, "Yes, I'll play."

They formed a square, with the little board on their knees. The Easterner and the Swede were again partners. As the play went on, it was noticeable that the cowboy was not board-whacking as usual. Meanwhile, Scully, near the lamp, had put on his spectacles and, with an appearance curiously like an old priest, was reading a newspaper. In time he went out to meet the 6:58 train, and, despite his precautions, a gust of polar wind whirled into the room as he opened the door. Besides scattering the cards, it chilled the players to the marrow. The Swede cursed frightfully. When Scully returned, his entrance disturbed a cozy and friendly scene. The Swede again cursed. But presently they were once more intent, their heads bent forward and their hands moving swiftly. The Swede had adopted the fashion of board-whacking.

Scully took up his paper and for a long time remained immersed in matters which were extra-ordinarily remote from him. The lamp burned badly, and once he stopped to adjust the wick. The newspaper, as he turned from page to page, rustled with a slow and comfortable sound. Then suddenly he heard three terrible words: "You are cheatin'!"

Such scenes often prove that there can be little of dramatic import in environment. Any room can present a tragic front; any room can be comic. This little den was now hideous as a torture-chamber. The new faces of the men themselves had changed it upon the instant. The Swede held a huge fist in front of Johnnie's face, while the latter looked steadily over it into the blazing orbs of his accuser. The Easterner had grown pallid; the cowboy's jaw had dropped in that expression of bovine amazement which was one of his important mannerisms. After the three words, the first sound in the room was made by Scully's paper as it floated forgotten to his feet. His spectacles had also fallen from his nose, but by a clutch he had saved them in air. His hand, grasping the spectacles, now remained poised awkwardly and near his shoulder. He stared at the cardplayers.

Probably the silence was while a second elapsed. Then, if the floor had been suddenly twitched out from under the men they could not have moved quicker. The five had projected themselves headlong toward a common point. It happened that Johnnie, in rising to hurl himself upon the Swede, had stumbled slightly because of his curiously instinctive care for the cards and the board. The loss of the moment allowed time for the arrival of Scully, and also allowed the cowboy time to give the Swede a great push which sent him staggering back. The men found tongue together, and hoarse shouts of rage, appeal, or fear burst from every throat. The cowboy pushed and jostled feverishly at the Swede, and the Easterner and Scully clung wildly to Johnnie; but through the smoky air, above the swaying bodies of the peace-compellers, the eyes of the two warriors ever sought each other in glances of challenge that were at once hot and steely.

Of course the board had been overturned, and now the whole company of cards was scattered over the floor, where the boots of the men trampled the fat and painted kings and queens as they gazed with their silly eyes at the war that was waging above them.

Scully's voice was dominating the yells. "Stop now! Stop, I say! Stop, now——"

Johnnie, as he struggled to burst through the rank formed by Scully and the Easterner, was crying, "Well, he says I cheated! He says I cheated! I won't allow no man to say I cheated! If he says I cheated, he's a —— ——!"

The cowboy was telling the Swede, "Quit, now! Quit, d'ye hear——"

The screams of the Swede never ceased: "He did cheat! I saw him! I saw him——"

As for the Easterner, he was importuning in a voice that was not heeded: "Wait a moment, can't you? Oh, wait a moment. What's the good of a fight over a game of cards? Wait a moment——"

In this tumult no complete sentences were clear. "Cheat"—"Quit"—"He says"—these fragments pierced the uproar and rang out sharply. It was remarkable that, whereas Scully undoubtedly made the most noise, he was the least heard of any of the riotous band.

Then suddenly there was a great cessation. It was as if each man had paused for breath; and although the room was still lighted with the anger of men, it could be seen that there was no danger of immediate conflict, and at once Johnnie, shouldering his way forward, almost succeeded in confronting the Swede. "What did you say I cheated for? What did you say I cheated for? I don't cheat, and I won't let no man say I do!"

The Swede said, "I saw you! I saw you!"

"Well," cried Johnnie, "I'll fight any man what says I cheat!"

"No, you won't," said the cowboy, "Not here."

"Ah, be still, can't you?" said Scully, coming between them.

The quiet was sufficient to allow the Easterner's voice to be heard. He was repeating, "Oh, wait a moment, can't you? What's the good of a fight over a game of cards? Wait a moment!"

Johnnie, his red face appearing above his father's shoulder, hailed the Swede again. "Did you say I cheated?"

The Swede showed his teeth. "Yes."

"Then," said Johnnie, "we must fight."

"Yes, fight," roared the Swede. He was like a demoniac. "Yes, fight! I'll show you what kind of a man I am! I'll show you who you want to fight! Maybe you think I can't fight! Maybe you think I can't! I'll show you, you skin, you cardsharp! Yes, you cheated! You cheated! You cheated!"

"Well, let's go at it, then, mister," said Johnnie, coolly.

The cowboy's brow was beaded with sweat from his efforts in intercepting all sorts of raids. He turned in despair to Scully. "What are you goin' to do now?"

A change had come over the Celtic visage of the old man. He now seemed all eagerness; his eyes glowed.

"We'll let them fight," he answered, stalwartly. "I can't put up with it any longer. I've stood this damned Swede till I'm sick. We'll let them fight."

6

The men prepared to go out of doors. The Easterner was so nervous that he had great difficulty in getting his arms into the sleeves of his new leather coat. As the cowboy drew his fur cap down over his ears his hands trembled. In fact, Johnnie and old Scully were the only ones who displayed no agitation. These preliminaries were conducted without words.

Scully threw open the door. "Well, come on," he said. Instantly a terrific wind caused the flame of the lamp to struggle at its wick, while a puff of black smoke sprang from the chimney-top. The stove was in mid-current of the blast, and its voice swelled to equal the roar of the storm. Some of the scarred and bedabbled cards were caught up from the floor and dashed helplessly against the farther wall. The men lowered their heads and plunged into the tempest as into a sea.

No snow was falling, but great whirls and clouds of flakes, swept up from the ground by the frantic winds, were streaming southward with the speed of bullets. The covered land was blue with the sheen of an unearthly satin, and there was no other hue save where, at the low, black railway station—which seemed incredibly distant—one light gleamed like a tiny jewel. As the men floundered into a thigh-deep drift, it was known that the Swede was bawling out something. Scully went to him, put a hand on his shoulder, and projected an ear. "What's that you say?" he shouted.

"I say," bawled the Swede again, "I won't stand much show against this gang. I know you'll all pitch on me."

Scully smote him reproachfully on the arm. "Tut, man!" he yelled. The wind tore the words from Scully's lips and scattered them far alee.

"You are all a gang of—" boomed the Swede, but the storm also seized the remainder of this sentence.

Immediately turning their backs upon the wind, the men had swung around a corner to the sheltered side of the hotel. It was the function of the little house to preserve here, amid this great devastation of snow, an irregular V-shape of heavily encrusted grass, which crackled beneath the feet. One could imagine the great drifts piled against the windward side. When the party reached the comparative peace of this spot it was found that the Swede was still bellowing.

"Oh, I know what kind of a thing this is! I know you'll all pitch on me. I can't lick you all!"

Scully turned upon him panther-fashion. "You'll not have to whip all of us. You'll have to whip my son Johnnie. An' the man what troubles you durin' that time will have me to dale with."

The arrangements were swiftly made. The two men faced each other, obedient to the harsh commands of Scully, whose face, in the subtly luminous gloom, could be seen set in the austere impersonal lines that are pictured on the countenances of the Roman veterans. The Easterner's teeth were chattering, and he was hopping up and down like a mechanical toy. The cowboy stood rocklike.

The contestants had not stripped off any clothing. Each was in his ordinary attire. Their fists were up, and they eyed each other in a calm that had the elements of leonine cruelty in it.

During this pause, the Easterner's mind, like a film, took lasting impressions of three men—the iron-nerved master of the ceremony; the Swede, pale, motionless, terrible; and Johnnie, serene yet ferocious, brutish yet heroic. The entire prelude had in it a tragedy greater than the tragedy of action, and this aspect was accentuated by the long, mellow cry of the blizzard, as it sped the tumbling and wailing flakes into the black abyss of the south.

"Now!" said Scully.

The two combatants leaped forward and crashed together like bullocks. There was heard the cushioned sound of blows, and of a curse squeezing out from between the tight teeth of one.

As for the spectators, the Easterner's pent-up breath exploded from him with a pop of relief, absolute relief from the tension of the preliminaries. The cowboy bounded into the air with a yowl. Scully was immovable as from supreme amazement and fear at the fury of the fight which he himself had permitted and arranged.

For a time the encounter in the darkness was such a perplexity of flying arms that it presented no more detail than would a swiftly revolving wheel. Occasionally a face, as if illumined by a flash of light, would shine out, ghastly and marked with pink spots. A moment later, the men might have been known as shadows, if it were not for the involuntary utterance of oaths that came from them in whispers.

Suddenly a holocaust of warlike desire caught the cowboy, and he bolted forward with the speed of a broncho. "Go it, Johnnie! go it! Kill him! Kill him!"

Scully confronted him. "Kape back," he said; and by his glance the cowboy could tell that this man was Johnnie's father.

To the Easterner there was a monotony of unchangeable fighting that was an abomination. This confused mingling was eternal to his sense, which was concentrated in a longing for the end, the priceless end. Once the fighters lurched near him, and as he scrambled hastily backward he heard them breathe like men on the rack.

"Kill him, Johnnie! Kill him! Kill him! Kill him!" The cowboy's face was contorted like one of those agony masks in museums.

"Keep still," said Scully, icily.

Then there was a sudden loud grunt, incomplete, cut short, and Johnnie's body swung away from the Swede and fell with sickening heaviness to the grass. The cowboy was barely in time to prevent the mad Swede from flinging himself upon his prone adversary. "No, you don't," said the cowboy, interposing an arm. "Wait a second."

Scully was at his son's side. "Johnnie! Johnnie, me boy!" His voice had a quality of melancholy tenderness. "Johnnie! Can you go on with it?" He looked anxiously down into the bloody, pulpy face of his son.

There was a moment of silence, and then Johnnie answered in his ordinary voice, "Yes, I—it—yes."

Assisted by his father he struggled to his feet. "Wait a bit now till you git your wind," said the old man.

A few paces away the cowboy was lecturing the Swede. "No, you don't! Wait a second!"

The Easterner was plucking at Scully's sleeve. "Oh, this is enough," he pleaded. "This is enough! Let it go as it stands. This is enough!"

"Bill," said Scully, "git out of the road." The cowboy stepped aside. "Now." The combatants were actuated by a new caution as they advanced toward collision. They glared at each other, and then the Swede aimed a lightning blow that carried with it his entire weight. Johnnie was evidently half stupid from weakness, but he miraculously dodged, and his fist sent the overbalanced Swede sprawling.

The cowboy, Scully, and the Easterner burst into a cheer that was like a chorus of triumphant soldiery, but before its conclusion the Swede had scuffled agilely to his feet and come in berserk abandon at his foe. There was another perplexity of flying arms, and Johnnie's body again swung away and fell, even as a bundle might fall from a roof. The Swede instantly staggered to a little wind-waved tree and leaned upon it, breathing like an engine, while his savage and flame-lit eyes roamed from face to face as the men bent over Johnnie. There was a splendor of isolation in his situation at this time which the Easterner felt once when, lifting his eyes from the man on the ground, he beheld that mysterious and lonely figure, waiting.

"Are you any good yet, Johnnie?" asked Scully in a broken voice.

The son gasped and opened his eyes languidly. After a moment he answered, "No—I ain't—any good—any—more." Then, from shame and bodily ill, he began to weep, the tears furrowing down through the bloodstains on his face. "He was too—too—too heavy for me."

Scully straightened and addressed the waiting figure. "Stranger," he said, evenly, "it's all up with our side." Then his voice changed into that vibrant huskiness which is commonly the tone of the most simple and deadly announcements. "Johnnie is whipped."

Without replying, the victor moved off on the route to the front door of the hotel.

The cowboy was formulating new and unspellable blasphemies. The Easterner was startled to find that they were out in a wind that seemed to come direct from the shadowed arctic floes. He heard again the wail of the snow as it was flung to its grave in the south. He knew now that all this time the cold had been sinking into him deeper and deeper, and he wondered that he had not perished. He felt indifferent to the condition of the vanquished man.

"Johnnie, can you walk?" asked Scully.

"Did I hurt—hurt him any?" asked the son.

"Can you walk, boy? Can you walk?"

Johnnie's voice was suddenly strong. There was a robust impatience in it. "I asked you whether I hurt him any!"

"Yes, yes, Johnnie," answered the cowboy, consolingly; "he's hurt a good deal."

They raised him from the ground, and as soon as he was on his feet he went tottering off, rebuffing all attempts at assistance. When the party rounded the corner they were fairly blinded by the pelting of the snow. It burned their faces like fire. The cowboy carried Johnnie through the drift to the door. As they entered, some cards again rose from the floor and beat against the wall.

The Easterner rushed to the stove. He was so profoundly chilled that he almost dared to embrace the glowing iron. The Swede was not in the room. Johnnie sank into a chair and, folding his arms on his knees, buried his face in them. Scully, warming one foot and then the other at a rim of the stove, muttered to himself with Celtic mournfulness. The cowboy had removed his fur cap, and with a dazed and rueful air he was running one hand through his tousled locks. From overhead they could hear the creaking of boards, as the Swede tramped here and there in his room.

The sad quiet was broken by the sudden flinging open of a door that led toward the kitchen. It was instantly followed by an inrush of women. They precipitated themselves upon Johnnie amid a chorus of lamentation. Before they carried their prey off to the kitchen, there to be bathed and harangued with that mixture of sympathy and abuse which is a feat of their sex, the mother straightened herself and fixed old Scully with an eye of stern reproach. "Shame be upon you, Patrick Scully!" she cried. "Your own son, too. Shame be upon you!"

"There, now! Be quiet, now!" said the old man, weakly.

"Shame be upon you, Patrick Scully!" The girls, rallying to this slogan, sniffed disdainfully in the direction of those trembling accomplices, the cowboy and the Easterner. Presently they bore Johnnie away, and left the three men to dismal reflection.

7

"I'd like to fight this here Dutchman myself," said the cowboy, breaking a long silence.

Scully wagged his head sadly. "No, that wouldn't do. It wouldn't be right. It wouldn't be right."

"Well, why wouldn't it?" argued the cowboy. "I don't see no harm in it."

"No," answered Scully, with mournful heroism. "It wouldn't be right. It was Johnnie's fight, and now we mustn't whip the man just because he whipped Johnnie."

"Yes, that's true enough," said the cowboy; "but—he better not get fresh with me, because I couldn't stand no more of it."

"You'll not say a word to him," commanded Scully, and even then they heard the tread of the Swede on the stairs. His entrance was made theatric. He swept the door back with a bang and swaggered to the middle of the room. No one looked at him. "Well," he cried, insolently, at Scully, "I s'pose you'll tell me now how much I owe you?"

The old man remained stolid. "You don't owe me nothin'."

"Huh!" said the Swede, "huh! Don't owe 'im nothin'."

The cowboy addressed the Swede. "Stranger, I don't see how you come to be so gay around here."

Old Scully was instantly alert. "Stop!" he shouted, holding his hand forth, fingers upward. "Bill, you shut up!"

The cowboy spat carelessly into the sawdust-box. "I didn't say a word, did I?" he asked.

"Mr. Scully," called the Swede, "how much do I owe you?" It was seen that he was attired for departure, and that he had his valise in his hand.

"You don't owe me nothin'," repeated Scully in the same imperturbable way.

"Huh!" said the Swede. "I guess you're right. I guess if it was any way at all, you'd owe me somethin'. That's what I guess." He turned to the cowboy. "'Kill him! Kill him! Kill him!'" he mimicked, and then guffawed victoriously. "'Kill him!'" He was convulsed with ironical humor.

But he might have been jeering the dead. The three men were immovable and silent, staring with glassy eyes at the stove.

The Swede opened the door and passed into the storm, giving one derisive glance backward at the still group.

As soon as the door was closed, Scully and the cowboy leaped to their feet and began to curse. They trampled to and fro, waving their arms and smashing into the air with their fists. "Oh, but that was a hard minute!" wailed Scully. "That was a hard minute! Him there leerin' and scoffin'! One bang at his nose was worth forty dollars to me that minute! How did you stand it, Bill?"

"How did I stand it?" cried the cowboy in a quivering voice. "How did I stand it? Oh!"

The old man burst into sudden brogue. "I'd loike to take that Swade," he wailed, "and hould 'im down on a shtone flure and bate 'im to a jelly wid a shtick!"

The cowboy groaned in sympathy. "I'd like to git him by the neck and ha-ammer him"—he brought his hand down on a chair with a noise like a pistol-shot—"hammer that there Dutchman until he couldn't tell himself from a dead coyote!"

"I'd bate 'im until he—"

"I'd show *him* some things—"

And then together they raised a yearning, fanatic cry—"Oh-o-oh! if we only could—"

"Yes!"

"Yes!"

"And then I'd—"

"O-o-oh!"

8

The Swede, tightly gripping his valise, tacked across the face of the storm as if he carried sails. He was following a line of little naked, gasping trees which, he knew, must mark the way of the road. His face, fresh from the pounding of Johnnie's fists, felt more pleasure than pain in the wind and the driving snow. A number of square shapes loomed upon him finally, and he knew them as the houses of the main body of the town. He found a street and made travel along it, leaning heavily upon the wind whenever, at a corner, a terrific blast caught him.

He might have been in a deserted village. We picture the world as thick with conquering and elate humanity, but here, with the bugles of the tempest pealing, it was hard to imagine a peopled earth. One viewed the existence of man then as a marvel, and conceded a glamor of wonder to these lice which were caused to cling to a whirling, fire-smitten, ice-locked, disease-stricken, space-lost bulb. The conceit of man was explained by this storm to be the very engine of life. One was a coxcomb not to die in it. However, the Swede found a saloon.

In front of it an indomitable red light was burning, and the snowflakes were made blood-color as they flew through the circumscribed territory of the lamp's shining. The Swede pushed open the door of the saloon and entered. A sanded expanse was before him, and at the end of it four men sat about a table drinking. Down one side of the room extended a radiant bar, and its guardian was leaning upon his elbows listening to the talk of the men at the table. The Swede dropped his valise upon the floor and, smiling fraternally upon the barkeeper, said, "Gimme some whisky, will you?" The man placed a bottle, a whisky-glass, and a glass of ice-thick water upon the bar. The Swede poured himself an abnormal portion of whisky and drank it in three gulps. "Pretty bad night," remarked the bartender, indifferently. He was making the pretension of blindness which is usually a distinction of his class; but it could have been seen that he was furtively studying the half-erased blood-stains on the face of the Swede. "Bad night," he said again.

"Oh, it's good enough for me," replied the Swede, hardily, as he poured himself some more

whisky. The barkeeper took his coin and maneuvered it through its reception by the highly nickeled cash-machine. A bell rang; a card labeled "20 cts." had appeared.

"No," continued the Swede, "this isn't too bad weather. It's good enough for me."

"So?" murmured the barkeeper, languidly.

The copious drams made the Swede's eyes swim, and he breathed a trifle heavier. "Yes, I like this weather. I like it. It suits me." It was apparently his design to impart a deep significance to these words.

"So?" murmured the bartender again. He turned to gaze dreamily at the scroll-like birds and birdlike scrolls which had been drawn with soap upon the mirrors in back of the bar.

"Well, I guess I'll take another drink," said the Swede, presently. "Have something?"

"No, thanks; I'm not drinkin'," answered the bartender. Afterward he asked, "How did you hurt your face?"

The Swede immediately began to boast loudly. "Why, in a fight. I thumped the soul out of a man down here at Scully's hotel."

The interest of the four men at the table was at last aroused.

"Who was it?" said one.

"Johnnie Scully," blustered the Swede. "Son of the man what runs it. He will be pretty near dead for some weeks, I can tell you. I made a nice thing of him, I did. He couldn't get up. They carried him in the house. Have a drink?"

Instantly the men in some subtle way encased themselves in reserve. "No, thanks," said one. The group was of curious formation. Two were prominent local business men; one was the district attorney; and one was a professional gambler of the kind known as "square." But a scrutiny of the group would not have enabled an observer to pick the gambler from the men of more reputable pursuits. He was, in fact, a man so delicate in manner, when among people of fair class, and so judicious in his choice of victims, that in the strictly masculine part of the town's life he had come to be explicitly trusted and admired. People called him a thoroughbred. The fear and contempt with which his craft was regarded were undoubtedly the reason why his quiet dignity shone conspicuous above the quiet dignity of men who might be merely hatters, billiard-markers, or grocery clerks. Beyond an occasional unwary traveler who came by rail, this gambler was supposed to prey solely upon reckless and senile farmers, who, when flush with good crops, drove into town in all the pride and confidence of an absolutely invulnerable stupidity. Hearing at times in circuitous fashion of the despoilment of such a farmer, the important men of Romper invariably laughed in contempt of the victim, and if they thought of the wolf at all, it was with a kind of pride at the knowledge that he would never dare think of attacking their wisdom and courage. Besides, it was popular that this gambler had a real wife and two real children in a neat cottage in a suburb, where he led an exemplary home life; and when anyone even suggested a discrepancy in his character, the crowd immediately vociferated descriptions of this virtuous family circle. Then men who led exemplary home lives, and men who did not lead exemplary home lives, all subsided in a bunch, remarking that there was nothing more to be said.

However, when a restriction was placed upon him—as, for instance, when a strong clique of members of the new Pollywog Club refused to permit him, even as a spectator, to appear in the rooms of the organization—the candor and gentleness with which he accepted the judgment disarmed many of his foes and made his friends more desperately partisan. He invariably distinguished between himself and a respectable Romper man so quickly and frankly that his manner actually appeared to be a continual broadcast compliment.

And one must not forget to declare the fundamental fact of his entire position in Romper. It is irrefutable that in all affairs outside his business, in all matters that occur eternally and commonly between man and man, this thieving cardplayer was so generous, so just, so moral, that, in a contest, he could have put to flight the consciences of nine tenths of the citizens of Romper.

And so it happened that he was seated in this saloon with the two prominent local merchants and the district attorney.

The Swede continued to drink raw whisky, meanwhile babbling at the barkeeper and trying to induce him to indulge in potations. "Come on. Have a drink. Come on. What—no? Well, have a little one, then. By gawd, I've whipped a man tonight, and I want to celebrate. I whipped him good,

too. Gentlemen," the Swede cried to the men at the table, "have a drink?"

"Ssh!" said the barkeeper.

The group at the table, although furtively attentive, had been pretending to be deep in talk, but now a man lifted his eyes toward the Swede and said, shortly, "Thanks. We don't want any more."

At this reply the Swede ruffled out his chest like a rooster. "Well," he exploded, "it seems I can't get anybody to drink with me in this town. Seems so, don't it? Well!"

"Ssh!" said the barkeeper.

"Say," snarled the Swede, "don't you try to shut me up. I won't have it. I'm a gentleman, and I want people to drink with me. And I want 'em to drink with me now. *Now*—do you understand?" He rapped the bar with his knuckles.

Years of experience had calloused the bartender. He merely grew sulky. "I hear you," he answered.

"Well," cried the Swede, "listen hard then. See those men over there? Well, they're going to drink with me, and don't you forget it. Now you watch."

"Hi!" yelled the barkeeper, "this won't do!"

"Why won't it?" demanded the Swede. He stalked over to the table, and by chance laid his hand upon the shoulder of the gambler. "How about this?" he asked wrathfully. "I asked you to drink with me."

The gambler simply twisted his head and spoke over his shoulder. "My friend, I don't know you."

"Oh, hell!" answered the Swede, "come and have a drink."

"Now, my boy," advised the gambler, kindly, "take your hand off my shoulder and go 'way and mind your own business." He was a little, slim man, and it seemed strange to hear him use this tone of heroic patronage to the burly Swede. The other men at the table said nothing.

"What! You won't drink with me, you little dude? I'll make you, then! I'll make you!" The Swede had grasped the gambler frenziedly at the throat, and was dragging him from his chair. The other men sprang up. The barkeeper dashed around the corner of his bar. There was a great tumult, and then was seen a long blade in the hand of the gambler. It shot forward, and a human body, this citadel of virtue, wisdom, power, was pierced as easily as if it had been a melon. The Swede fell with a cry of supreme astonishment.

The prominent merchants and the district attorney must have at once tumbled out of the place backward. The bartender found himself hanging limply to the arm of a chair and gazing into the eyes of a murderer.

"Henry," said the latter, as he wiped his knife on one of the towels that hung beneath the bar rail, "you tell 'em where to find me. I'll be home, waiting for 'em." Then he vanished. A moment afterward the barkeeper was in the street dinning through the storm for help and, moreover, companionship.

The corpse of the Swede, alone in the saloon, had its eyes fixed upon a dreadful legend that dwelt atop of the cash-machine: "This registers the amount of your purchase."

9

Months later, the cowboy was frying pork over the stove of a little ranch near the Dakota line, when there was a quick thud of hoofs outside, and presently the Easterner entered with the letters and the papers.

"Well," said the Easterner at once, "the chap that killed the Swede has got three years. Wasn't much, was it?"

"He has? Three years?" The cowboy poised his pan of pork, while he ruminated upon the news. "Three years. That ain't much."

"No. It was a light sentence," replied the Easterner as he unbuckled his spurs. "Seems there was a good deal of sympathy for him in Romper."

"If the bartender had been any good," observed the cowboy, thoughtfully, "he would have gone in and cracked that there Dutchman on the head with a bottle in the beginnin' of it and stopped all this here murderin'."

"Yes, a thousand things might have happened," said the Easterner, tartly.

The cowboy returned his pan of pork to the fire, but his philosophy continued. "It's funny, ain't it? If he hadn't said Johnnie was cheatin' he'd be alive this minute. He was an awful fool. Game played for fun, too. Not for money. I believe he was crazy."

"I feel sorry for that gambler," said the Easterner.

"Oh, so do I," said the cowboy. "He don't deserve none of it for killin' who he did."

"The Swede might not have been killed if everything had been square."

"Might not have been killed?" exclaimed the cowboy. "Everythin' square? Why, when he said that Johnnie was cheatin' and acted like such a jackass? And then in the saloon he fairly walked up to git hurt?" With these arguments the cowboy browbeat the Easterner and reduced him to rage.

"You're a fool!" cried the Easterner, viciously. "You're a bigger jackass than the Swede by a million majority. Now let me tell you one thing. Let me tell you something. Listen! Johnnie *was* cheating!"

" 'Johnnie,' " said the cowboy, blankly. There was a minute of silence, and then he said, robustly, "Why, no. The game was only for fun."

"Fun or not," said the Easterner, "Johnnie was cheating. I saw him. I know it. I saw him. And I refused to stand up and be a man. I let the Swede fight it out alone. And you—you were simply puffing around the place and wanting to fight. And then old Scully himself! We are all in it! This poor gambler isn't even a noun. He is kind of an adverb. Every sin is the result of a collaboration. We, five of us, have collaborated in the murder of this Swede. Usually there are from a dozen to forty women really involved in every murder, but in this case it seems to be only five men—you, I, Johnnie, old Scully; and that fool of an unfortunate gambler came merely as a culmination, the apex of a human movement, and gets all the punishment."

The cowboy, injured and rebellious, cried out blindly into this fog of mysterious theory: "Well, I didn't do anythin', did I?"

Stephen Crane was fully aware of his young greenhorn's insignificance, but he called attention to it in ways that made the Swede represent all of us. The whole human action is set in the midst of a blizzard. An unnamed narrator (probably to be identified with the Easterner) makes the point of this scene explicit:

We picture the world as thick with conquering and elate humanity, but here, with the bugles of the tempest pealing, it was hard to imagine a peopled earth. One viewed the existence of man then as a marvel, and conceded a glamor of wonder to these lice which were caused to cling to a whirling, fire-smitten, ice-locked, disease-stricken, space-lost bulb. The conceit of man was explained by this storm to be the very engine of life. One was a coxcomb not to die in it.

The passage manipulates perspective by calling attention to the insignificance of *all* men, no matter what their rank or position, thus deemphasizing the Swede's relative unimportance in human society. When we look through the wrong end of a telescope the world we see becomes smaller without changing its proportions. The Swede is important in the small human world of the Blue Hotel, where his arrival is a matter of note and where his conduct becomes a matter of speculation until he makes that world convulse with rage and catapults it out into the storm. The imagery continually reminds us that any human habitation can become a self-contained universe. The small parlor in which most of the action occurs is a complete world, "a proper temple for an enormous stove, which, in the center, was humming with godlike violence." That same room presents "a tragic front" and becomes as "hideous as a torture chamber" when the symbolic violence of the stove erupts into a human brawl over the card game: "the whole company of cards was scattered over the floor, where the boots of the men trampled the fat and painted kings and queens as they gazed with their silly eyes at the war that was waging above them." Yet when the door is opened to the blizzard outside, all the human violence within is absorbed by the storm: "The stove was in mid-current of the blast, and its voice swelled to equal the roar of the storm. Some of the scarred and bedabbled cards were caught up from the floor and dashed helplessly against the farther wall. The men lowered their heads and plunged into the tempest as into a sea." Images of the stove, the cards, and the blizzard give us the sense of proportion we need. Within the walls of the Blue Hotel in Fort Romper, Nebraska, the Swede's story is just as important as the silly kings and queens and wars symbolized by the cards trampled underfoot might be in a wider scene.

The world of Fort Romper can contain tragic action because it is not chaotic. It has the laws and customs of a civilization; one can have expectations, lay plans, and predict human responses to some extent. All the characters except the Swede have adjusted their behavior to their sense of world order, but he is totally governed by an illusion garnered from dime novels. He believes that the west is wild and demonic according to the Easterner: "he thinks he's right in the middle of hell." Thinking can and does make it so in this story—to a degree. If there were no sources of disorder in Fort Romper—no potential violence underneath the veneer of four churches, a brick schoolhouse, and electric streetcars—the Swede would not have been killed. This violence waiting beneath a placid surface emerges three times in the cowboy's shouts during the fight ("Kill him! Kill him! Kill him!"), in the fanatic desire to maim shared by Scully and the cowboy after the fight, and in the swift knife thrust of the gambler. Yet nothing would have happened without the Swede's illusion. His show of false wisdom ("I suppose there have been a good many men killed in this room") meets with astonishment and disbelief from the other men, although it starts the chain of events that proves it nearly true. The Swede imposes his illusion on everyone else in the Blue Hotel relentlessly. His first supposition about men being killed is quickly followed by a second ("I suppose I am going to be killed before I can leave this house!") and is transformed into a third ("These men are going to kill me"). Such quick assumptions are a sign of the Swede's fear, and they are also his act of encroachment. He does not let the other men control their own attitudes toward him but insists on believing that they do in fact play the roles he imagines. As long as these imposed roles do not upset the order they know, the men can put up with their exasperation. The Swede has been deluding himself that he is powerless against a roomful of enemies. After Scully forces the whisky on him, the relationship is inverted in a dangerous way: he now believes he is all powerful and begins to impose his will directly on the other men. Johnnie accurately senses this change when he tells his father, "he may be all right now, but I don't see it. Other time he was scared, but now he's too fresh."

While he remains in the Blue Hotel, the Swede can live by this new illusion because he has Scully's protection. The hotelkeeper is very much in charge of what happens in his domain from the moment his guests enter it. The imagery suggests that his role is both priestly and regal, for he officiates at a "series of small ceremonies"—a kind of baptism in the washroom for his guests—"conferring great favors upon them." Later he tries to reassure the Swede that Nebraska is not the wild west, forces drink on him in a gesture of communion, refuses to let him leave the Blue Hotel ("a guest under my roof has sacred privileges"), serves like a "Roman Veteran" as "the iron-nerved master of the ceremony" at the fight, and preserves fairness to the Swede after his own son has been defeated by him. Under his aegis there is a chivalric overtone to everything that occurs, with Scully assuming the role of the benevolent lord who fully appreciates the medieval meaning of hospitality: "This is my house. You are under my roof, and I will not allow any peaceable man to be troubled here." He and the Swede return from the second floor like "two roisterers from a banquet hall"; he refuses to accept any money from the Swede and repudiates him only after he has left the Blue Hotel. While such codes are enforced, the Swede is not harmed; but when he assumes that they hold in the saloon as well, he is rewarded with the "supreme astonishment" of being knifed. The barkeeper is no substitute for Scully, and the respectable gentlemen (two merchants and the district attorney) who are playing with the equally respectable gambler subscribe to no code of honor. The Swede has little time to discover anything, but the reader is given a "dreadful legend" on the cash register to reflect on: "This registers the amount of your purchase."

Had the story ended here, we might overlook many earlier allusions to communal responsibility for the Swede's death. The final part, like the interview with the "Intended" appended to Joseph Conrad's *Heart of Darkness*, destroys any neat balance between what happens and what the hero deserves. The Easterner's statement—"We, five of us, have collaborated in the murder of this Swede"—makes sense only in the context of a tragic world. Johnnie *had* cheated; the Easterner saw the cheating and kept silent. The cowboy and Scully had gloated over images of dismembering the Swede. Scully's benevolence itself led to the Swede's death; he forced the Swede to drink and thus assumed responsibility for his transformation, and he refused to let him leave the Blue Hotel; upstairs with the Swede "he resembled a murderer," and in a sense he was. Oedipus did not intend to kill his father any more or less than Scully intended harm to the Swede, but both are responsible because they acted. We are brought back to the central principle of the tragic world: men cannot know or control all the consequences of their acts, but they must accept responsibility for everything they do. Ultimately, every tragic catastrophe is ritualistic and communal. Thus we can accept the verdict of the Easterner: "We are all in it! . . . Every sin is the result of a collaboration." The Swede himself cannot be reduced to a dupe of fate or a man who deserves what he gets. Both principles operate in somewhat mysterious ways within any tragic scene, even an ordinary little Nebraska town with an uncommon hotel.

The Tragic Norm:
Conflict with Cosmic Law

WILLIAM SHAKESPEARE
1564–1616

King Lear

DRAMATIS PERSONAE

LEAR, *king of Britain*
KING OF FRANCE
DUKE OF BURGUNDY
DUKE OF CORNWALL
DUKE OF ALBANY
EARL OF KENT
EARL OF GLOUCESTER
EDGAR, *son to Gloucester*
EDMUND, *bastard son to Gloucester*
CURAN, *a courtier*
OLD MAN, *tenant to Gloucester*
DOCTOR
FOOL
OSWALD, *steward to Goneril*
A CAPTAIN *employed by Edmund*
GENTLEMAN *attendant on Cordelia*
HERALD
SERVANTS *to Cornwall*
GONERIL ⎫
REGAN ⎬ *daughters to Lear*
CORDELIA ⎭
KNIGHTS *of Lear's train,* CAPTAINS, MESSENGERS, SOLDIERS, *and* ATTENDANTS

SCENE—*Britain.*

ACT I

SCENE I.° KING LEAR's *palace.*

[*Enter* KENT, GLOUCESTER, *and* EDMUND.]

KENT I thought the king had more affected° the duke of Albany than Cornwall.

GLOUCESTER It did always seem so to us. But now, in the division of the kingdom, it appears not which of the dukes he values most, for equalities are so weighed that curiosity in neither can make choice of either's moiety.°   7

KENT Is not this your son, my lord?

GLOUCESTER His breeding, sir, hath been at my charge. I have so often blushed to acknowledge him that now I am brazed° to it.   11

KENT I cannot conceive° you.

GLOUCESTER Sir, this young fellow's mother could. Whereupon she grew round-wombed, and had indeed, sir, a son for her cradle ere she had a husband for her bed. Do you smell a fault? 16

KENT I cannot wish the fault undone, the issue° of it being so proper.°

GLOUCESTER But I have, sir, a son by order of law, some year elder than this, who yet is no dearer in my account. Though this knave came something saucily into the world before he was sent for, yet was his mother fair, there was

---

KING LEAR: *Act I, scene i.* As the opening words of this scene show, Lear has already decided on the division of the kingdom. There remains only the public and ceremonious announcement of his abdication. **1. more affected:** had more affection for. **5–7. equalities . . . moiety:** for their shares are so equal that a close examination (*curiosity*) cannot decide which share (*moiety*) is to be preferred. **11. brazed:** become brazen; lit., brass-plated. **12. conceive:** understand. **17. issue:** result; i.e., child. **18. proper:** handsome.

363

good sport at his making, and the whoreson° must be acknowledged. Do you know this noble gentleman, Edmund?   26

EDMUND   No, my lord.

GLOUCESTER   My lord of Kent. Remember him hereafter as my honorable friend.

EDMUND   My services to your lordship.   30

KENT   I must love you, and sue to know you better.

EDMUND   Sir, I shall study deserving.°

GLOUCESTER   He hath been out nine years, and away he shall again. The king is coming.   35

[*Sennet.*° *Enter one bearing a coronet,*° KING LEAR, CORNWALL, ALBANY, GONERIL, REGAN, CORDELIA, *and* ATTENDANTS.]

LEAR   Attend° the lords of France and Burgundy, Gloucester.

GLOUCESTER   I shall, my liege.

[*Exeunt* GLOUCESTER *and* EDMUND.]

LEAR   Meantime we shall express our darker purpose.°

Give me the map there. Know that we have divided
In three our kingdom. And 'tis our fast intent 40
To shake all cares and business from our age,
Conferring them on younger strengths while we
Unburdened crawl toward death. Our son° of Cornwall,
And you, our no less loving son of Albany,
We have this hour a constant will° to publish 45
Our daughters' several° dowers, that future strife
May be prevented° now. The princes, France and Burgundy,
Great rivals in our youngest daughter's love,
Long in our court have made their amorous sojourn,
And here are to be answered. Tell me, my daughters,   50
Since now we will divest us both of rule,
Interest of territory, cares of state,
Which of you shall we say doth love us most?
That we our largest bounty may extend

Where nature doth with merit challenge.° Goneril,
Our eldest-born, speak first.   56

GONERIL   Sir, I love you more than words can wield° the matter,
Dearer than eyesight, space, and liberty,
Beyond what can be valued, rich or rare,
No less than life, with grace, health, beauty, honor,   60
As much as child e'er loved or father found—
A love that makes breath poor and speech unable—
Beyond all manner of so much° I love you.

CORDELIA   [*Aside*] What shall Cordelia do? Love, and be silent.

LEAR   Of all these bounds, even from this line to this,   65
With shadowy forests and with champaigns riched,°
With plenteous rivers and wide-skirted meads,°
We make thee lady. To thine and Albany's issue
Be this perpetual. What says our second daughter,
Our dearest Regan, wife to Cornwall? Speak. 70

REGAN   I am made of that self metal° as my sister,
And prize me at her worth.° In my true heart
I find she names my very deed of love,
Only she comes too short. That I profess
Myself an enemy to all other joys   75
Which the most precious square° of sense possesses,°
And find I am alone felicitate°
In your dear highness' love.

CORDELIA   [*Aside*] Then poor Cordelia!
And yet not so, since I am sure my love's
More ponderous than my tongue.°   80

LEAR   To thee and thine hereditary ever
Remain this ample third of our fair kingdom,
No less in space, validity° and pleasure
Than that conferred on Goneril. Now, our joy,
Although the last, not least, to whose young love
The vines of France and milk of Burgundy   86
Strive to be interested,° what can you say to draw

---

55. **Where . . . challenge:** where natural affection and desert have an equal claim on our bounty. **57. wield:** declare. **63. Beyond . . . much:** i.e., beyond all these things. **66. champaigns riched:** enriched with fertile fields. **67. wide-skirted meads:** extensive pasture lands. **71. self metal:** same material. **72. prize . . . worth:** value me at the same price. **76. most . . . possesses:** feeling in the highest degree possesses. **square:** the carpenter's rule; i.e., measurement. **77. felicitate:** made happy. **79–80. love's . . . tongue:** love is heavier than my words. **83. validity:** value. **87. interested:** have a share in.

---

24. **whoreson:** rogue; lit., son of a whore. **33. I . . . deserving:** I shall do my best to deserve your favor. **35 s.d., Sennet:** trumpet call used to announce the approach of a procession. **coronet:** a small crown worn by those of lesser rank than king. **36. Attend:** wait on. **38. we . . . purpose:** we will explain what we have hitherto kept dark. Lear, speaking officially as king, uses the royal "we." **43. son:** son-in-law. **45. constant will:** firm intention. **46. several:** separate. **47. prevented:** forestalled.

A third more opulent than your sisters? Speak.

CORDELIA Nothing, my lord.

LEAR Nothing! 90

CORDELIA Nothing.

LEAR Nothing will come of nothing.° Speak again.

CORDELIA Unhappy that I am, I cannot heave
My heart into my mouth. I love your majesty
According to my bond,° nor more nor less. 95

LEAR How, how, Cordelia! Mend your speech a little,
Lest it may mar your fortunes.

CORDELIA   Good my lord,
You have begot me, bred me, loved me. I
Return those duties back as are right fit,
Obey you, love you, and most honor you. 100
Why have my sisters husbands if they say
They love you all? Haply,° when I shall wed,
That lord whose hand must take my plight° shall carry
Half my love with him, half my care and duty.
Sure, I shall never marry like my sisters, 105
To love my father all.

LEAR But goes thy heart with this?

CORDELIA   Aye, good my lord.

LEAR So young, and so untender?

CORDELIA So young, my lord, and true.

LEAR Let it be so. Thy truth then be thy dower.
For, by the sacred radiance of the sun, 111
The mysteries of Hecate,° and the night,
By all the operation of the orbs°
From whom we do exist and cease to be,
Here I disclaim° all my paternal care, 115
Propinquity,° and property of blood,°
And as a stranger to my heart and me
Hold thee from this forever. The barbarous Scythian,°
Or he that makes his generation messes
To gorge his appetite° shall to my bosom 120
Be as well neighbored, pitied, and relieved°
As thou my sometime daughter.

KENT   Good my liege——

LEAR Peace, Kent!
Come not between the dragon° and his wrath.
I loved her most, and thought to set my rest° 125
On her kind nursery.° Hence, and avoid° my sight!
So be my grave my peace, as here I give
Her father's heart from her! Call France. Who stirs?
Call Burgundy. Cornwall and Albany, 129
With my two daughter's dowers digest° this third.
Let pride, which she calls plainness,° marry her.
I do invest you jointly with my power,
Preeminence,° and all the large effects
That troop with majesty.° Ourself, by monthly course,°
With reservation of a hundred knights 135
By you to be sustained, shall our abode
Make with you by due turns. Only we still retain
The name and all the additions° to a king.
The sway, revenue, execution of the rest,
Beloved Sons, be yours, which to confirm, 140
This coronet° part betwixt you.

KENT   Royal Lear,
Whom I have ever honored as my king,
Loved as my father, as my master followed,
As my great patron thought on in my prayers——

LEAR The bow is bent and drawn, make from the shaft.° 145

KENT Let it fall rather, though the fork° invade
The region of my heart. Be Kent unmannerly
When Lear is mad. What wouldst thou do, old man?°
Think'st thou that duty shall have dread to speak
When power to flattery bows? To plainness honor's bound 150
When majesty stoops to folly.° Reverse thy doom°

92. Nothing . . . nothing: the old maxim *Ex nihilo nihil fit.* 95. bond: i.e., the tie of natural affection and duty which binds daughter to father. 102. Haply: it may happen. 103. plight: promise made at betrothal. 112. Hecate: goddess of witchcraft. 113. orbs: stars. 115. disclaim: renounce. 116. Propinquity: relationship. property of blood: claim which you have as being of my blood. 118. Scythian: inhabitant of South Russia, regarded as the worst kind of savage. 119–20. Or . . . appetite: or he that feeds gluttonously on his own children. 121. relieved: helped in distress.

124. dragon: the dragon of Britain was Lear's heraldic device and also a symbol of his ferocity. 125. set . . . my rest: lit., to risk all—a term in the card game called primero. Lear uses it with the double meaning of "find rest." 126. nursery: care. avoid: depart from. 130. digest: absorb. 131. plainness: honest plain speech. 133. Preeminence: authority. 133–34. large . . . majesty: the outward show of power that goes with rule. 134. course: turn. 138. additions: titles of honor. 141. coronet: i.e., the coronet which was to have been the symbol of Cordelia's kingdom. 145. shaft: arrow. 146. fork: point of a forked arrow. 148. old man: Kent, who is as quick-tempered as Lear, has lost control of his tongue. The phrase to a still ruling king is grossly insulting. 149–51. Think'st . . . folly: This is one of many passages in *Lear* where the abstract is strikingly and effectively used for the person. It means: "Do you think that a man who keeps his sense of duty will be afraid to speak when he sees a king yielding to his flatterers? An honorable man is forced to speak plainly when a king becomes a fool." 151. doom: sentence.

And in thy best consideration check
This hideous rashness. Answer my life my
    judgment,
Thy youngest daughter does not love thee least,
Nor are those empty-hearted whose low sound
Reverbs° no hollowness.   156
LEAR   Kent, on thy life, no more.
KENT   My life I never held but as a pawn°
To wage against thy enemies, nor fear to lose it,
Thy safety being the motive.
LEAR   Out of my sight!
KENT   See better, Lear, and let me still remain   160
The true blank° of thine eye.
LEAR   Now, by Apollo——
KENT   Now, by Apollo, king.
Thou swear'st thy gods in vain.
LEAR   O vassal!° Miscreant!°
                        [Laying his hand on his sword.]
ALBANY and CORDELIA   Dear sir, forbear.
KENT   Do.   165
Kill thy physician, and the fee bestow
Upon the foul disease. Revoke thy doom,
Or whilst I can vent clamor° from my throat
I'll tell thee thou dost evil.
LEAR   Hear me, recreant!°
On thy allegiance,° hear me!   170
Since thou hast sought to make us break our
    vow,
Which we durst never yet, and with strained°
    pride
To come between our sentence and our power°—
Which nor our nature nor our place can bear,
Our potency made good°—take thy reward.   175
Five days we do allot thee, for provision°
To shield thee from diseases of the world,
And on the sixth to turn thy hated back
Upon our kingdom. If on the tenth day following
Thy banished trunk° be found in our dominions,
The moment is thy death. Away! By Jupiter,   181
This shall not be revoked.

KENT   Fare° thee well, king. Sith° thus thou wilt
    appear,
Freedom lives hence, and banishment is here.
[To CORDELIA] The gods to their dear shelter take
    thee, maid,   185
That justly think'st and hast most rightly said!
[To REGAN and GONERIL] And your large° speeches
    may your deeds approve,°
That good effects° may spring from words of
    love.
Thus Kent, O princes, bids you all adieu.
He'll shape his old course in a country new.   190
                                                [Exit.]
[Flourish.° Reenter GLOUCESTER, with FRANCE,
        BURGUNDY, and ATTENDANTS.]
GLOUCESTER   Here's France and Burgundy, my
    noble lord.
LEAR   My lord of Burgundy,
We first address toward you, who with this king
Hath rivaled for our daughter. What, in the least,
Will you require° in present° dower with her,   195
Or cease your quest of love?
BURGUNDY   Most royal majesty,
I crave no more than what your highness offered,
Nor will you tender° less.
LEAR   Right noble Burgundy,
When she was dear° to us, we did hold her so,
But now her price is fall'n. Sir, there she stands.
If aught within that little seeming substance,°   201
Or all of it, with our displeasure pieced°
And nothing more, may fitly like° your grace,
She's there, and she is yours.
BURGUNDY   I know no answer.
LEAR   Will you, with those infirmities she owes,°
Unfriended, new-adopted to our hate,   206
Dowered with our curse and strangered with our
    oath,°
Take her, or leave her?
BURGUNDY   Pardon me, royal sir,

---

156. **Reverbs:** reechoes. **157. pawn:** a pledge to be
sacrificed. **161. blank:** aim; i.e., something which you
look at. The blank is the center of the target. **163.
vassal:** wretch. **Miscreant:** lit., misbeliever. **168. vent
clamor:** utter a cry. **169. recreant:** traitor. **170. On . . .
allegiance:** The most solemn form of command that can be
laid upon a subject, for to disobey it is to commit high
treason. **172. strained:** excessive. **173. To . . . power:** to
interpose yourself between my decree and my royal will;
i.e., to make me revoke an order. **175. Our . . . good:** my
power being now asserted. **176. for provision:** for making
your preparations. **180. trunk:** body.

183–90. **Fare . . . new:** The rhyme in this passage and
elsewhere in the play is used for the particular purpose
of stiffening the speech and giving it a special prophetic
or moral significance; cf. III.vi.109–20. **183. Sith:** since.
187. large: fine-sounding. **approve:** i.e., be shown in
deeds. **188. effects:** results. **190. s.d., Flourish:** trumpet
fanfare. **195. require:** request. **present:** immediate. **198.
tender:** offer. **199. dear:** in the double sense of "beloved" and "valuable." **201. little . . . substance:** creature
that seems so small. Part of Lear's anger with Cordelia is
that so small a body seems to hold so proud a heart. **202.
pieced:** added to it. **203. fitly like:** suitably please. **205. owes:**
possesses. **207. strangered . . . oath:** made a stranger to me
by my oath.

Election makes not up on such conditions.°

LEAR   Then leave her, sir. For, by the power that
    made me,   210
I tell you all her wealth. [*To* FRANCE] For you,
    great king,
I would not from your love make such a stray °
To match you where I hate. Therefore beseech
    you
To avert your liking° a more worthier way
Than on a wretch whom Nature is ashamed 215
Almost to acknowledge hers.

FRANCE   This is most strange,
That she that even but now was your best object,
The argument° of your praise, balm of your age,
Most best, most dearest, should in this trice of
    time
Commit a thing so monstrous, to dismantle° 220
So many folds of favor. Sure, her offense
Must be of such unnatural degree
That monsters it,° or your forevouched° affection
Fall'n into taint.° Which to believe of her
Must be a faith that reason without miracle 225
Could never plant in me.°

CORDELIA   I yet beseech your majesty—
If for I want that glib and oily art,
To speak and purpose not,° since what I well
    intend
I'll do't before I speak—that you make known
It is no vicious blot,° murder, or foulness,   230
No unchaste action or dishonored step,
That hath deprived me of your grace and favor,
But even for want of that for which I am richer,
A still-soliciting° eye, and such a tongue
As I am glad I have not, though not to have it 235
Hath lost me in° your liking.

LEAR   Better thou
Hadst not been born than not to have pleased me
    better.

FRANCE   Is it but this? A tardiness in nature°
Which often leaves the history unspoke

That it intends to do? My lord of Burgundy, 240
What say you to the lady? Love's not love
When it is mingled with regards that stand
Aloof from the entire point.° Will you have her?
She is herself a dowry.

BURGUNDY   Royal Lear,
Give but that portion which yourself proposed,
And here I take Cordelia by the hand,   246
Duchess of Burgundy.

LEAR   Nothing. I have sworn, I am firm.

BURGUNDY   I am sorry then you have so lost a
    father
That you must lose a husband.   250

CORDELIA   Peace be with Burgundy!
Since that respects of fortune° are his love,
I shall not be his wife.

FRANCE   Fairest Cordelia, that art most rich
    being poor,
Most choice forsaken, and most loved despised,
Thee and thy virtues here I seize upon,   255
Be it lawful I take up what's cast away.
Gods, gods! 'Tis strange that from their cold'st
    neglect
My love should kindle to inflamed respect.°
Thy dowerless daughter, king, thrown to my
    chance,
Is queen of us, of ours, and our fair France.   260
Not all the dukes of waterish° Burgundy
Can buy this unprized precious maid of me.
Bid them farewell, Cordelia, though unkind.
Thou losest here, a better where to find.

LEAR   Thou hast her, France. Let her be thine, for
    we   265
Have no such daughter, nor shall ever see
That face of hers again. Therefore be gone
Without our grace, our love, our benison.°
Come, noble Burgundy. [*Flourish. Exeunt all but*
    FRANCE, GONERIL, REGAN, *and* CORDELIA.]

FRANCE   Bid farewell to your sisters.   270

CORDELIA   The jewels of our father,° with washed°
    eyes
Cordelia leaves you. I know you what you are,
And, like a sister, am most loath to call

---

209. **Election . . . conditions:** i.e., one does not choose one's wife on such conditions. 212. **from . . . stray:** remove myself so far from showing love to you. 214. **avert . . . liking:** turn your affection. 218. **argument:** topic. 220. **dismantle:** lit., take off (as a cloak). 223. **monsters it:** makes it a monster. **forevouched:** previously declared. 224. **Fall'n . . . taint:** become bad. 224–26. **Which . . . me:** that is so contrary to reason that only a miracle could make me believe it. 228. **and . . . not:** and not mean it. 230. **vicious blot:** vicious act which blots my honor. 234. **still-soliciting:** always begging favors. 236. **lost me in:** deprived me of. 238. **tardiness in nature:** natural slowness.

242–43. **When . . . point:** when it is mixed with other motives (the amount of the dowry) which have nothing to do with the thing itself (love). 251. **respects of fortune:** considerations of my dowry. 258. **inflamed respect:** warmer affection. 261. **waterish:** with the double meaning of "with many rivers" and "feeble." 268. **benison:** blessing. 271. **The . . . father:** i.e., creatures whom my father values so highly. **washed:** weeping, but also made clearsighted by tears.

Your faults as they are named. Use well our
father.
To your professèd° bosoms I commit him.   275
But yet, alas, stood I within his grace,°
I would prefer° him to a better place.
So farewell to you both.
REGAN   Prescribe not us our duties.
GONERIL   Let your study
Be to content your lord, who hath received you
At Fortune's alms.° You have obedience
scanted,°   281
And well are worth the want that you have
wanted.°
CORDELIA   Time shall unfold what plaited° cunning
hides.
Who cover faults, at last shame them derides.
Well may you prosper!   285
FRANCE   Come, my fair Cordelia.
        [Exeunt FRANCE and CORDELIA.]
GONERIL   Sister,° it is not a little I have to say of
what most nearly appertains to us both. I think
our father will hence tonight.
REGAN   That's most certain, and with you, next
month with us.   290
GONERIL   You see how full of changes his age is,
the observation we have made of it hath not
been little. He always loved our sister most, and
with what poor judgment he hath now cast her
off appears too grossly.   295
REGAN   'Tis the infirmity of his age. Yet he hath
ever but slenderly known himself.   297
GONERIL   The best and soundest of his time hath
been but rash. Then must we look to receive
from his age not alone the imperfections of
long-ingrafted condition,° but therewithal the
unruly waywardness that infirm and choleric
years bring with them.   303
REGAN   Such unconstant starts° are we like to
have from him as this of Kent's banishment.
GONERIL   There is further compliment° of leave-
taking between France and him. Pray you, let's

hit° together. If our father carry authority with
such dispositions° as he bears, this last surrender
of his will but offend us.   310
REGAN   We shall further think on 't.
GONERIL   We must do something, and i' the heat.°
                                          [Exeunt.]

SCENE II. The EARL OF GLOUCESTER's castle.

        [Enter EDMUND, with a letter.]
EDMUND   Thou, Nature,° art my goddess, to thy
law
My services are bound. Wherefore should I
Stand in the plague of custom, and permit
The curiosity of nations to deprive me,
For that I am some twelve or fourteen moon-
shines   5
Lag of a brother?° Why bastard? Wherefore
base?
When my dimensions are as well compact,°
My mind as generous° and my shape as true,
As honest madam's issue? Why brand they us
With base? With baseness? Bastardy? Base,
base?   10
Who in the lusty stealth of nature take
More composition and fierce quality°
Than doth, within a dull, stale, tired bed,
Go to the creating a whole tribe of fops°
Got° 'tween asleep and wake? Well then,   15
Legitimate Edgar, I must have your land.
Our father's love is to the bastard Edmund
As to the legitimate—fine word, "legitimate"!
Well, my legitimate, if this letter speed°
And my invention° thrive, Edmund the base   20
Shall top the legitimate. I grow, I prosper.
Now, gods, stand up for bastards!
                    [Enter GLOUCESTER.]
GLOUCESTER   Kent banished thus! And France in
choler parted!

275. professed: which profess such love. 276. within . . .
grace: in his favor. 277. prefer: promote. 281. At . . . alms:
as an act of charity from Fortune. scanted: neglected. 282.
And . . . wanted: and well deserve the same lack of love
which you have shown. 283. plaited: pleated, enfolded. Cf.
ll. 220–21. 286–312. Sister . . . heat: The abrupt change
from rhyme to prose marks the change from the emotion
of the previous episodes to the cynical frankness of the
two sisters. 301. long-ingrafted condition: temper which
has long been part of his nature. 304. unconstant starts:
sudden outbursts. 306. compliment: formality.

308. hit: agree. 309. dispositions: frame of mind. 312. i'
the heat: while the iron is hot.
    Scene ii. 1. Thou, Nature: Edmund, the "natural" son
of his father, appeals to Nature, whose doctrine is every
man ruthlessly for himself. 2–6. Wherefore . . . brother:
Why should I allow myself to be plagued by custom and
nice distinctions (curiosity) which deprive me of my natural
rights, because I am a year younger (lag: lagging behind)
than my legitimate brother? 7. compact: put together,
framed. 8. generous: noble. 12. More . . . quality: more fiber
and ferocity. 14. fops: fools. 15. Got: begotten. 19. speed:
prosper. 20. invention: plan.

And the king gone tonight! Subscribed° his
power!
Confined to exhibition!° All this done   25
Upon the gad!° Edmund, how now! What
news?

EDMUND   So please your lordship, none.

[*Putting up the letter.*]

GLOUCESTER   Why so earnestly seek you to put up
that letter?

EDMUND   I know no news, my lord.

GLOUCESTER   What paper were you reading?   30

EDMUND   Nothing, my lord.°

GLOUCESTER   No? What needed then that terrible
dispatch° of it into your pocket? The quality of
nothing hath not such need to hide itself. Let's
see. Come, if it be nothing, I shall not need
spectacles.   36

EDMUND   I beseech you, sir, pardon me. It is a
letter from my brother that I have not all
o'erread, and for so much as I have perused, I
find it not fit for your o'erlooking.°   40

GLOUCESTER   Give me the letter, sir.

EDMUND   I shall offend, either to detain or give it.
The contents, as in part I understand them, are
to blame.

GLOUCESTER   Let's see, let's see.   45

EDMUND   I hope, for my brother's justification, he
wrote this but as an essay° or taste of my virtue.

GLOUCESTER   [*Reads*] "This policy and reverence
of age° makes the world bitter to the best of our
times,° keeps our fortunes from us till our
oldness cannot relish them. I begin to find an
idle and fond° bondage in the oppression of aged
tyranny, who sways not as it hath power, but as
it is suffered.° Come to me, that of this I may
speak more. If our father would sleep till I
waked him, you should enjoy half his revenue
forever, and live the beloved of your brother, 57
                                        EDGAR."

Hum! Conspiracy!—"Sleep till I waked him, you
should enjoy half his revenue!"—My son Edgar!
Had he a hand to write this? A heart and brain to

breed it in? When came this to you? Who
brought it?   63

EDMUND   It was not brought me, my lord, there's
the cunning of it. I found it thrown in at the
casement° of my closet.°

GLOUCESTER   You know the character° to be your
brother's?   68

EDMUND   If the matter were good, my lord, I durst
swear it were his, but in respect of that, I would
fain think it were not.   71

GLOUCESTER   It is his.

EDMUND   It is his hand, my lord, but I hope his
heart is not in the contents.

GLOUCESTER   Hath he never heretofore sounded
you in this business?   76

EDMUND   Never, my lord. But I have heard him oft
maintain it to be fit that, sons at perfect age and
fathers declining, the father should be as ward
to the son, and the son manage his revenue.   80

GLOUCESTER   Oh, villain, villain! His very opinion
in the letter! Abhorred villain! Unnatural,
detested, brutish villain! Worse than brutish!
Go, sirrah, seek him——aye, apprehend him.
Abominable villain! Where is he?   85

EDMUND   I do not well know, my lord. If it shall
please you to suspend your indignation against
my brother till you can derive from him better
testimony of his intent, you should run a certain
course.° Where, if you violently proceed against
him, mistaking his purpose, it would make a
great gap° in your own honor and shake in
pieces the heart of his obedience.° I dare pawn
down my life for him that he hath wrote this to
feel° my affection to your honor and to no
further pretense of danger.   96

GLOUCESTER   Think you so?

EDMUND   If your honor judge it meet, I will place
you where you shall hear us confer of this,
and by an auricular assurance° have your satisfaction, and that without any further delay
than this very evening.   102

GLOUCESTER   He cannot be such a monster—

EDMUND   Nor is not, sure.

GLOUCESTER   ——to his father, that so tenderly
and entirely loves him. Heaven and earth!

---

24. **Subscribed:** signed away. 25. **Confined to exhibition:**
reduced to a pension. 26. **gad:** prick of a goad; i.e., the
spur of the moment. 31. **Nothing, my lord:** Gloucester's
tragedy also begins with the word "nothing." See I.i.89.
32–33. **terrible dispatch:** i.e., hasty thrusting. 40. **o'erlooking:** reading. 47. **essay:** trial. 48–49. **policy . . . age:**
this custom of respecting old men. 49–50. **best . . . times:**
i.e., when we are still young. 52. **fond:** foolish. 54.
suffered: allowed.

66. **casement:** window. **closet:** room. 67. **character:** handwriting. 89–90. **certain course:** i.e., know where you are
going. 92. **gap:** hole. 92–93. **shake . . . obedience:** cause
him no longer to obey you loyally. 95. **feel:** test. 100.
auricular assurance: proof heard with your own ears.

Edmund, seek him out, wind me into him,° I pray you. Frame the business after your own wisdom. I would unstate myself, to be in a due resolution.°   110

EDMUND   I will seek him, sir, presently,° convey° the business as I shall find means, and acquaint you withal.   113

GLOUCESTER   These late eclipses in the sun and moon portend no good to us. Though the wisdom of nature° can reason° it thus and thus, yet nature finds itself scourged by the sequent° effects. Love cools, friendship falls off, brothers divide. In cities, mutinies; in countries, discord; in palaces, treason; and the bond cracked 'twixt son and father. This villain of mine comes under the prediction, there's son against father. The king falls from bias of nature,° there's father against child. We have seen the best of our time. Machinations, hollowness, treachery, and all ruinous disorders follow us disquietly to our graves. Find out this villain Edmund, it shall lose thee nothing. Do it carefully. And the noble and true-hearted Kent banished! His offense, honesty! 'Tis strange. [Exit]   130

EDMUND   This is the excellent foppery° of the world, that when we are sick in fortune—often the surfeit° of our own behavior—we make guilty of our disasters the sun, the moon, and the stars, as if we were villains by necessity, fools by heavenly compulsion; knaves, thieves and treachers by spherical predominance;° drunkards, liars, and adulterers by an enforced obedience of planetary influence;° and all that we are evil in, by a divine thrusting on—an admirable evasion of whoremaster° man, to lay his goatish disposition to the charge of a star!° My father compounded with my mother under the dragon's

tail, and my nativity° was under Ursa Major,° so that it follows I am rough and lecherous. Tut, I should have been that I am had the maidenliest star in the firmament twinkled on my bastardizing. Edgar——[Enter EDGAR.] And pat he comes like the catastrophe° of the old comedy. My cue is villainous melancholy, with a sigh like Tom o' Bedlam.° Oh, these eclipses do portend these divisions! Fa, sol, la, mi.°   153

EDGAR   How now, Brother Edmund! What serious contemplation are you in?

EDMUND   I am thinking, brother, of a prediction I read this other day, what should follow these eclipses.   158

EDGAR   Do you busy yourself about that?

EDMUND   I promise you the effects he writes of succeed° unhappily, as of unnaturalness between the child and the parent; death, dearth, dissolutions of ancient amities;° divisions in state, menaces and maledictions against king and nobles; needless diffidences,° banishment of friends, dissipation of cohorts,° nuptial breaches, and I know not what.   167

EDGAR   How long have you been a sectary astronomical?°

EDMUND   Come, come, when saw you my father last?   171

EDGAR   Why, the night gone by.

EDMUND   Spake you with him?

EDGAR   Aye, two hours together.

EDMUND   Parted you in good terms? Found you no displeasure in him by word or countenance?

EDGAR   None at all.   177

EDMUND   Bethink yourself wherein you may have offended him. And at my entreaty forbear his presence till some little time hath qualified° the heat of his displeasure, which at this instant so rageth in him that with the mischief of your person it would scarcely allay.°   183

107. wind . . . him: worm your way into his confidence for me. 109–10. I . . . resolution: I would lose my earldom to learn the truth. This is one of many touches of bitter irony in this tragedy, for it is not until he has "unstated himself" that Gloucester does indeed learn the truth about his two sons. 111. presently: at once. convey: manage. 116. wisdom of nature: i.e., a rational explanation. reason: explain. 117. sequent: subsequent. 123. bias of nature: natural inclination. 131. foppery: folly. 133. surfeit: lit., eating to excess and its results. 137. treachers . . . predominance: traitors because the stars so decreed when we were born. 138–39. enforced . . . influence: because we were forced to be so in obeying the influence of the stars. 141. whoremaster: lecherous. 142. to . . . star: to say that some star caused him to have the morals of a goat.

144. nativity: moment of birth. Ursa Major: the Great Bear. 149. catastrophe: the final episode. 150–51. My . . . Bedlam: I must now pretend to be a melancholic and sigh like a lunatic beggar. Tom o' Bedlam was a lunatic discharged from Bedlam (Bethlehem Hospital for lunatics). See II.iii.14. 152–53. Fa . . . mi: Edmund hums to himself. 161. succeed: follow. 163. amities: friendships. 165. diffidences: distrusts. 166. dissipation of cohorts: breaking-up of established friendships (lit., of troops of soldiers). 168–89. sectary astronomical: a follower of the sect of astrologers. 180. qualified: lessened. 182–83. with . . . allay: it would scarcely be lessened even if he did you some bodily injury.

EDGAR   Some villain hath done me wrong.

EDMUND   That's my fear. I pray you have a continent forbearance° till the speed of his rage goes slower, and, as I say, retire with me to my lodging, from whence I will fitly bring you to hear my lord speak. Pray ye, go, there's my key. If you do stir abroad, go armed. 190

EDGAR   Armed, brother!

EDMUND   Brother, I advise you to the best—go armed. I am no honest man if there be any good meaning toward you. I have told you what I have seen and heard, but faintly, nothing like the image and horror of it. Pray you, away. 196

EDGAR   Shall I hear from you anon?

EDMUND   I do serve you in this business.

[Exit EDGAR.]

A credulous father, and a brother noble,
Whose nature is so far from doing harms   200
That he suspects none, on whose foolish honesty
My practices° ride easy. I see the business.
Let me, if not by birth, have lands by wit.
All with me's meet° that I can fashion fit.° [Exit]

SCENE III. *The* DUKE OF ALBANY'*s palace.*

[*Enter* GONERIL *and* OSWALD, *her steward.*]

GONERIL   Did my father strike my gentleman for chiding of his fool?°

OSWALD   Yes, madam.

GONERIL   By day and night he wrongs me. Every hour
He flashes into one gross crime or other
That sets us all at odds. I'll not endure it.   5
His knights grow riotous, and himself upbraids us
On every trifle. When he returns from hunting,
I will not speak with him. Say I am sick.
If you come slack of former services,°
You shall do well, the fault of it I'll answer.   10

OSWALD   He's coming, madam, I hear him.

[*Horns within.*]

GONERIL   Put on what weary negligence you please,
You and your fellows, I'd have it come to question.°

If he distaste it, let him to our sister,
Whose mind and mine, I know, in that are one,   15
Not to be overruled. Idle old man,
That still would manage those authorities
That he hath given away! Now, by my life,
Old fools are babes again, and must be used
With checks as flatteries when they are seen abused.°   20
Remember what I tell you.

OSWALD   Very well, madam.

GONERIL   And let his knights have colder looks among you.
What grows of it, no matter, advise your fellows so.
I would breed from hence occasions,° and I shall,
That I may speak. I'll write straight to my sister   25
To hold my very course. Prepare for dinner.

[*Exeunt.*]

SCENE IV. *A hall in the same.*

[*Enter* KENT, *disguised.*]

KENT   If but as well I other accents borrow
That can my speech defuse,° my good intent
May carry through itself to that full issue
For which I razed° my likeness. Now, banished Kent,
If thou canst serve where thou dost stand condemned,   5
So may it come, thy master whom thou lovest
Shall find thee full of labors.

[*Horns within.° Enter* LEAR, KNIGHTS, *and* ATTENDANTS.]

LEAR   Let me not stay at jot for dinner. Go get it ready. [*Exit an* ATTENDANT.] How now! What art thou?   10

KENT   A man, sir.

LEAR   What dost thou profess?° What wouldst thou with us?

KENT   I do profess to be no less than I seem—to serve him truly that will put me in trust, to love him that is honest, to converse with him that

---

186. continent forbearance: self-control which will keep you from any rash action. 202. practices: plots. 204. meet: suitable. fashion fit: make fit my purposes.
   Scene iii. 1. fool: professional jester. 9. come . . . services: do not wait on him as efficiently as you used to. 13. to question: or in modern slang, to a showdown.

19–20. Old . . . abused: old men must be treated like babies, and scolded, not flattered, when they are naughty. 24. breed . . . occasions: find excuses for taking action. *Scene iv.* 2. defuse: make indistinct, disguise. 4. razed: lit., shaved off, disguised. 7. s.d., within: off stage. 12. What . . . profess: what is your profession?

is wise and says little, to fear judgment,° to fight when I cannot choose, and to eat no fish.°

LEAR   What art thou?   19

KENT   A very honest-hearted fellow, and as poor as the king.

LEAR   If thou be as poor for a subject as he is for a king, thou art poor enough. What wouldst thou?

KENT   Service.   25

LEAR   Who wouldst thou serve?

KENT   You.

LEAR   Dost thou know me, fellow?

KENT   No, sir, but you have that in your countenance° which I would fain call master.   30

LEAR   What's that?

KENT   Authority.

LEAR   What services canst thou do?

KENT   I can keep honest counsel, ride, run, mar a curious tale in telling it,° and deliver a plain message bluntly. That which ordinary men are fit for, I am qualified in, and the best of me is diligence.   38

LEAR   How old art thou?

KENT   Not so young, sir, to love a woman for singing, nor so old to dote on her for anything. I have years on my back forty-eight.   42

LEAR   Follow me, thou shalt serve me. If I like thee no worse after dinner, I will not part from thee yet. Dinner, ho, dinner! Where's my knave? My fool? Go you, and call my fool hither. [*Exit an* ATTENDANT. *Enter* OSWALD.] You, you, sirrah, where's my daughter?   48

OSWALD   So please you——   [*Exit.*]

LEAR   What says the fellow there? Call the clotpoll° back. [*Exit a* KNIGHT.] Where's my fool, ho? I think the world's asleep. [*Reenter* KNIGHT.] How now! Where's that mongrel?   53

KNIGHT   He says, my lord, your daughter is not well.

LEAR   Why came not the slave back to me when I called him?   57

KNIGHT   Sir, he answered me, in the roundest° manner, he would not.

LEAR   He would not!   60

KNIGHT   My lord, I know not what the matter is, but, to my judgment, your highness is not entertained° with that ceremonious affection° as you were wont. There's a great abatement of kindness appears as well in the general dependents° as in the duke himself also and your daughter.   66

LEAR   Ha! Sayest thou so?

KNIGHT   I beseech you pardon me, my lord, if I be mistaken, for my duty cannot be silent when I think your highness wronged.   70

LEAR   Thou but rememberest° me of mine own conception. I have perceived a most faint neglect° of late, which I have rather blamed as mine own jealous curiosity° than as a very pretense° and purpose of unkindness. I will look further into 't. But where's my fool? I have not seen him this two days.   77

KNIGHT   Since my young lady's going into France, sir, the fool hath much pined away.

LEAR   No more of that, I have noted it well. Go you, and tell my daughter I would speak with her. [*Exit an* ATTENDANT.] Go you, call hither my fool. [*Exit an* ATTENDANT. *Reenter* OSWALD.] Oh, you sir, you, come you hither, sir. Who am I, sir?   85

OSWALD   My lady's father.

LEAR   My lady's father! My lord's knave. You whoreson dog! You slave! You cur!

OSWALD   I am none of these, my lord, I beseech your pardon.   90

LEAR   Do you bandy° looks with me, you rascal?
                                        [*Striking him.*]

OSWALD   I'll not be struck, my lord.

KENT   Nor tripped neither, you base football player.   [*Tripping up his heels.*]

LEAR   I thank thee, fellow. Thou servest me, and I'll love thee.   96

KENT   Come, sir, arise, away! I'll teach you differences.° Away, away! If you will measure your lubber's length again, tarry. But away! Go to, have you wisdom? So.   [*Pushes* OSWALD *out.*]

---

17. judgment: the Day of Judgment; i.e., I have a conscience. 18. eat no fish: I don't observe fast days, and am therefore no Catholic. 29–30. countenance: bearing. 34–35. mar . . . it: I'm not one to delight in overelaborate (*curious*) phrases when telling my tale; i.e., he will have none of the fantastic talk of the typical courtier. Kent himself mimics this fashion later (II.ii.113–16). 50–51. clotpoll: clodpole, blockhead. 58. roundest: plainest.

62–63. entertained: treated. 63. ceremonious affection: affection which shows itself in ceremony. Manners even between children and parents were very formal. Neglect of courtesies to the ex-king shows deliberate disrespect. 65. dependents: servants of the house. 71. rememberest: remind. 72. faint neglect: i.e., the "weary negligence" commanded by Goneril (I.iii.12). 74. jealous curiosity: excessive suspicion. pretense: deliberate intention. 91. bandy: lit., hit the ball to and fro as in tennis. 97–98. differences: of rank.

LEAR Now, my friendly knave, I thank thee.
There's earnest° of thy service.   102

[*Giving* KENT *money*.]

[*Enter* FOOL.]

FOOL Let me hire him too. Here's my coxcomb.°

[*Offering* KENT *his cap*.]

LEAR How now, my pretty knave! How dost
thou?   105

FOOL Sirrah, you were best take my coxcomb.

KENT Why, fool?

FOOL Why, for taking one's part that's out of
favor. Nay, an thou canst not smile as the wind
sits,° thou'lt catch cold shortly. There, take my
coxcomb. Why, this fellow hath banished two
on 's daughters, and done the third a blessing
against his will. If thou follow him, thou must
needs wear my coxcomb. How now, nuncle!°
Would I had two coxcombs and two daughters!

LEAR Why, my boy?   116

FOOL If I gave them all my living, I'd keep my
coxcombs myself. There's mine, beg another of
thy daughters.

LEAR Take heed, sirrah, the whip.°   120

FOOL Truth's a dog must to kennel. He must be
whipped out, when Lady the brach° may stand
by the fire and stink.

LEAR A pestilent gall to me!°

FOOL Sirrah, I'll teach thee a speech.   125

LEAR Do.

FOOL Mark it, nuncle:
"Have more than thou showest,
    Speak less than thou knowest,
    Lend less than thou owest,°   130
    Ride more than thou goest,°
    Learn more than thou trowest,°
    Set less than thou throwest.°
Leave thy drink and thy whore
And keep in-a-door,   135

And thou shalt have more
    Than two tens to a score."°

KENT This is nothing, fool.

FOOL Then 'tis like the breath of an unfeed lawyer. You gave me nothing for 't. Can you make
no use of nothing, nuncle?   141

LEAR Why, no, boy, nothing can be made out
of nothing.°

FOOL [*To* KENT] Prithee tell him so much the
rent of his land comes to. He will not believe a
fool.   146

LEAR A bitter fool!

FOOL Dost thou know the difference, my boy, between a bitter fool and a sweet fool?

LEAR No, lad, teach me.   150

FOOL "That lord that counseled thee
    To give away thy land,
    Come place him here by me,
    Do thou for him stand.
The sweet and bitter fool   155
    Will presently appear—
    The one in motley° here,
    The other found out there."

LEAR Dost thou call me fool, boy?

FOOL All thy other titles thou hast given away.
That thou wast born with.   161

KENT This is not altogether fool, my lord.

FOOL No, faith, lords and great men will not let
me.° If I had a monopoly° out, they would have
part on 't. And ladies too, they will not let me
have all the fool to myself, they'll be snatching.
Give me an egg, nuncle, and I'll give thee two
crowns.   168

LEAR What two crowns shall they be?

FOOL Why, after I have cut the egg in the middle
and eat up the meat, the two crowns of the egg.
When thou clovest thy crown i' the middle
and gavest away both parts, thou borest thine
ass on thy back o'er the dirt.° Thou hadst little
wit in thy bald crown when thou gavest thy
golden one away. If I speak like myself° in this,
let him be whipped that first finds it so.   177

---

102. **earnest:** money given on account of services to be rendered. Lear thus formally engages Kent as his servant. 103. **coxcomb:** the cap shaped like a cock's comb (crest) worn by the professional fool. 109–10. **an . . . sits:** i.e., if you can't curry favor with those in power. 114. **nuncle:** uncle. 120. **the whip:** The fool's profession was precarious, and in real life too smart a joke brought its painful reward. In March 1605 Stone, a professional fool, was whipped for commenting on the diplomatic mission about to sail for Spain that "there went sixty fools into Spain, besides my lord admiral and his two sons." 122. **Lady . . . brach:** Lady the pet bitch. 124. **A . . . me:** this pestilent fool rubs me on a sore spot. 130. **owest:** possess. 131. **goest:** walk. 132. **trowest:** know. 133. **Set . . . throwest:** don't bet a larger stake than you can afford to lose.

136–37. **And . . . score:** and then your money will increase. 142–43. **nothing . . . nothing:** Lear unconsciously repeats himself. See I.i.92. 157. **motley:** the particolored uniform worn by a fool. 163–64. **will . . . me:** i.e., keep all my folly to myself. 164. **monopoly:** a royal patent giving the holders the sole right to deal in some commodity. The granting of such monopolies to courtiers was one of the crying scandals of the time. 173–74. **thine . . . dirt:** an old tale of the typical simple-minded countryman. 176. **like myself:** i.e., like a fool.

[*Singing*]

"Fools had ne'er less wit in a year,
    For wise men are grown foppish,
    And know not how their wits to wear,
        Their manners are so apish."°   181

LEAR   When were you wont to be so full of songs, sirrah?

FOOL   I have used it, nuncle, ever since thou madest thy daughters thy mother. For when thou gavest them the rod and puttest down thine own breeches, [*Singing*]   187

"Then they for sudden joy did weep,
    And I for sorrow sung,
    That such a king should play bopeep, 190
    And go the fools among."

Prithee, nuncle, keep a schoolmaster that can teach thy fool to lie. I would fain learn to lie.

LEAR   An° you lie, sirrah, we'll have you whipped.

FOOL   I marvel what kin thou and thy daughters are. They'll have me whipped for speaking true, thou'lt have me whipped for lying, and sometimes I am whipped for holding my peace. I had rather be any kind o' thing than a fool. And yet I would not be thee, nuncle. Thou has pared thy wit o' both sides and left nothing i' the middle. Here comes one o' the parings.   202

[*Enter* GONERIL.]

LEAR   How now, daughter! What makes that frontlet° on? Methinks you are too much of late i' the frown.   205

FOOL   Thou was pretty fellow when thou hadst no need to care for her frowning. Now thou art an O without a figure.° I am better than thou art now. I am a fool, thou art nothing. [*To* GONERIL] Yes, forsooth, I will hold my tongue, so your face bids me, though you say nothing.

"Mum, mum.   212
    He that keeps nor crust nor crumb,°
    Weary of all, shall want some."

[*Pointing to* LEAR] That's a shealed peascod.° 215

GONERIL   Not only, sir, this your all-licensed° fool,
But other of your insolent retinue
Do hourly carp° and quarrel, breaking forth
In rank and not to be endurèd riots. Sir,

I had thought, by making this well known unto you,   220
To have found a safe redress, but now grow fearful
By what yourself too late have spoke and done
That you protect this course and put it on°
By your allowance.° Which if you should, the fault
Would not 'scape censure, nor the redresses sleep,
Which, in the tender of a wholesome weal,   226
Might in their working do you that offense
Which else were shame, that then necessity
Will call discreet proceeding.°

FOOL   For, you know, nuncle,   230

"The hedge sparrow fed the cuckoo so long
That it had it head bit off by it young."

So out went the candle, and we were left darkling.°

LEAR   Are you our daughter?

GONERIL   Come, sir,   235
I would you would make use of that good wisdom
Whereof I know you are fraught,° and put away
These dispositions° that of late transform you
From what you rightly are.

FOOL   May not an ass know when the cart draws the horse? Whoop, Jug! I love thee.°   241

LEAR   Doth any here know me? This is not Lear. Doth Lear walk thus? Speak thus? Where are his eyes?
Either his notion° weakens, his discernings
Are lethargied°——Ha! Waking? 'Tis not so.
Who is it that can tell me who I am?   246

FOOL   Lear's shadow.

LEAR   I would learn that, for, by the marks of sovereignty,° knowledge, and reason, I should be false persuaded I had daughters.   250

FOOL   Which they will make an obedient father.

LEAR   Your name, fair gentlewoman?

GONERIL   This admiration,° sir, is much o' the savor
Of° other your new pranks. I do beseech you

178–81. Fools . . . apish: there's no job left for fools nowadays, because the wise men are so like them. **apish:** like apes, who always imitate. **194. An:** if. **204. frontlet:** frown; lit., a band worn on the forehead. **208. an . . . figure:** a cipher. **213. crumb:** inside of the loaf. **215. shealed peascod:** a shelled peapod. **216. all-licensed:** allowed to take all liberties. **218. carp:** find fault.

223. put it on: encourage it. **224. allowance:** approval. **226–29. Which . . . proceeding:** if you continue to be a nuisance I shall be forced to keep my state peaceful by taking measures which will annoy you and would at other times be shameful toward a father, but would be justified as mere discretion. **233. darkling:** in the dark. **237. fraught:** stored, endowed. **238. dispositions:** moods. **241. Whoop . . . thee:** one of the meaningless cries made by the fool to distract attention. **244. notion:** understanding. **245. lethargied:** paralyzed. **248–49. marks of sovereignty:** the outward signs which show that I am king. **253. admiration:** pretended astonishment. **253–54. much . . . Of:** tastes much the same as.

To understand my purposes aright.   255
As you are old and reverend, you should be
  wise.
Here do you keep a hundred knights and squires,
Men so disordered,° so deboshed° and bold,
That this our court, infected with their manners,
Shows like a riotous inn. Epicurism° and lust
Make it more like a tavern or a brothel   261
Than a graced° palace. The shame itself doth
  speak
For instant remedy. Be then desired
By her that else will take the thing she begs
A little to disquantity your train,°   265
And the remainder that shall still depend,°
To be such men as may besort° your age,
Which know themselves and you.
LEAR   Darkness and devils!
Saddle my horses, call my train together.
Degenerate bastard! I'll not trouble thee.   270
Yet have I left a daughter.
GONERIL You strike my people, and your dis-
  ordered rabble
Make servants of their betters.
                    [Enter ALBANY.]
LEAR Woe, that too late repents.—[To ALBANY]
  Oh, sir, are you come?
Is it your will? Speak, sir. Prepare my horses. 275
Ingratitude, thou marble-hearted fiend,
More hideous when thou show'st thee in a child
Than the sea monster!
ALBANY   Pray, sir, be patient.
LEAR [To GONERIL] Detested kite!° Thou liest.
My train are men of choice and rarest parts,°
That all particulars of duty know,   281
And in the most exact regard support
The worships of their name.° O most small fault,
How ugly didst thou in Cordelia show!
That, like an engine, wrenched my frame of
  nature   285
From the fixed place,° drew from my heart all
  love
And added to the gall.° O Lear, Lear, Lear!

258. **disordered:** disorderly. **deboshed:** debauched. 260. **Epi-curism:** self-indulgence, riotous living. 262. **graced:** gracious. 265. **disquantity . . . train:** diminish the number of your followers. 266. **depend:** be your dependents. 267. **besort:** be suitable for. 279. **kite:** the lowest of the birds of prey, an eater of offal. 280. **parts:** accomplishments. 282–83. **in . . . name:** and in every minute detail uphold their honorable names. 285–86. **like . . . place:** like a little instrument (e.g., a lever) dislodged my firm nature. 287. **gall:** bitterness.

Beat at this gate, that let thy folly in
                    [Striking his head]
And thy dear judgment out!° Go, go, my people.
ALBANY My lord, I am guiltless, as I am ignorant
Of what hath moved you.
LEAR   It may be so, my lord.
Hear, Nature, hear,° dear goddess, hear!   292
Suspend thy purpose if thou didst intend
To make this creature fruitful.
Into her womb convey sterility.   295
Dry up in her the organs of increase,°
And from her derogate° body never spring
A babe to honor her! If she must teem,°
Create her child of spleen,° that it may live
And be a thwart disnatured° torment to her. 300
Let it stamp wrinkles in her brow of youth,
With cadent° tears fret° channels in her cheeks,
Turn all her mother's pains and benefits
To laughter and contempt, that she may feel
How sharper than a serpent's tooth it is   305
To have a thankless child! Away, away! [Exit.]
ALBANY Now, gods that we adore, whereof comes
  this?
GONERIL Never afflict yourself to know the cause,
But let his disposition have that scope
That dotage gives it.   310
                    [Reenter LEAR.]
LEAR What, fifty of my followers at a clap!°
Within a fortnight!°
ALBANY   What's the matter, sir?
LEAR I'll tell thee. [To GONERIL] Life and death!
  I am ashamed
That thou hast power to shake my manhood° thus,
That these hot tears, which break from me
  perforce,   315
Should make thee worth them. Blasts and fogs
  upon thee!
The untented woundings° of a father's curse

288–89. **Beat . . . out:** the first signs of madness in Lear. 292. **Hear . . . hear:** In making this terrible curse, Lear also calls on Nature, but as goddess of natural affection. Cf. I.ii.1–22. 296. **increase:** childbearing. 297. **derogate:** debased. 298. **teem:** conceive. 299. **spleen:** malice. 300. **thwart disnatured:** perverse and unnatural. 302. **cadent:** falling. **fret:** wear away. 311. **at a clap:** at one blow. 311–12. **What . . . fortnight:** As Lear goes out he learns that Goneril has herself already begun to take steps "a little to disquantity his train" by ordering that fifty of them shall depart within a fortnight. To a man who regards his own dignity so highly, this fresh blow is devastating. 314. **shake my manhood:** i.e., with sobs. 317. **untented woundings:** raw wounds. A tent was a small roll of lint used to clean out a wound before it was bound up.

Pierce every sense about thee! Old fond° eyes,
Beweep this cause again, I'll pluck ye out
And cast you with the waters that you lose   320
To temper° clay. Yea, is it come to this?
Let it be so. Yet have I left a daughter
Who I am sure is kind and comfortable.°
When she shall hear this of thee, with her nails
She'll flay thy wolvish visage. Thou shalt find
That I'll resume the shape which thou dost think
I have cast off forever. Thou shalt, I warrant thee.
             [*Exeunt* LEAR, KENT, *and* ATTENDANTS.]
GONERIL   Do you mark that, my lord?   328
ALBANY   I° cannot be so partial, Goneril,
To the great love I bear you——   330
GONERIL   Pray you, content. What, Oswald, ho!
[*To the* FOOL] You, sir, more knave than fool,
after your master.
FOOL   Nuncle Lear, Nuncle Lear, tarry, take the
fool with thee.°
             "A fox, when one has caught her,   335
             And such a daughter,
             Should sure to the slaughter,
             If my cap would buy a halter.
             So the fool follows after."   [*Exit.*]
GONERIL   This man hath had good counsel. A
hundred knights!   340
'Tis politic° and safe to let him keep
At point° a hundred knights. Yes, that on every
dream,
Each buzz° each fancy, each complaint, dislike,
He may enguard his dotage with their powers
And hold our lives in mercy. Oswald, I say!   345
ALBANY   Well, you may fear too far.
GONERIL   Safer than trust too far.
Let me still take away the harms I fear,
Not fear still to be taken.° I know his heart.
What he hath uttered I have writ my sister.
If she sustain him and his hundred knights   350
When I have showed the unfitness——
             [*Reenter* OSWALD.] How now, Oswald!
What, have you writ that letter to my sister?
OSWALD   Yes, madam.
GONERIL   Take you some company, and away to
horse.

Inform her full of my particular fear,   355
And thereto add such reasons of your own
As may compact it more.° Get you gone,
And hasten your return. [*Exit* OSWALD.] No, no,
my lord,
This milky gentleness and course° of yours
Though I condemn not, yet, under pardon,   360
You are much more attasked° for want of
wisdom
Than praised for harmful mildness.°
ALBANY   How far your eyes may pierce I cannot
tell.
Striving to better, oft we mar what's well.
GONERIL   Nay, then——   365
ALBANY   Well, well, the event.°   [*Exeunt.*]

SCENE V. *Court before the same.*

[*Enter* LEAR, KENT, *and* FOOL.]
LEAR   Go you before to Gloucester with these letters. Acquaint my daughter no further with anything you know than comes from her demand out
of the letter. If your diligence be not speedy, I
shall be there afore you.   5
KENT   I will not sleep my, lord, till I have delivered
your letter.   [*Exit.*]
FOOL   If a man's brains were in 's heels, were 't
not in danger of kibes?°
LEAR   Aye, boy.   10
FOOL   Then I prithee be merry. Thy wit shall ne'er
go slipshod.°
LEAR   Ha, ha, ha!
FOOL   Shalt see thy other daughter will use thee
kindly,° for though she's as like this as a crab's°
like an apple, yet I can tell what I can tell.   16
LEAR   Why, what canst thou tell, my boy?
FOOL   She will taste as like this as a crab does to
a crab. Thou canst tell why one's nose stands i'
the middle on 's face?   20
LEAR   No.
FOOL   Why, to keep one's eyes of either side 's
nose, that what a man cannot smell out he may
spy into.

---

318. fond: foolish. **321. temper:** mix. **323. comfortable:** full
of comfort. **329–30. I . . . you:** i.e., although my love
makes me partial to you, yet I must protest. **333–34. take
. . . thee:** i.e., take your fool and your own folly. **341.
politic:** good policy. **342. At point:** fully armed. **343. buzz:**
rumor. **347–48. Let . . . taken:** let me always remove what
I fear will harm me rather than live in perpetual fear.

357. compact it more: make my argument more convincing.
359. milky . . . course: this milksop behavior. **361. attasked:**
blamed. **362. harmful mildness:** a mildness which may prove
harmful. **366. the event:** i.e., we must see what will happen.
   Scene v.   **9. kibes:** chilblains. **11–12. Thy . . . slipshod:**
i.e., you don't need slippers, for you have no brains to be
protected from chilblains. **15. kindly:** after her kind; i.e.,
nature. **crab:** crab apple.

LEAR I did her wrong——   25

FOOL Canst tell how an oyster makes his shell?

LEAR No.

FOOL Nor I neither, but I can tell why a snail has a house.

LEAR Why?   30

FOOL Why, to put 's head in, not to give it away to his daughters and leave his horns without a case.

LEAR. I will forget my nature.—So kind a father! —Be my horses ready?   35

FOOL Thy asses are gone about 'em. The reason why the seven stars are no more than seven is a pretty reason.

LEAR Because they are not eight?

FOOL Yes, indeed. Thou wouldst make a good fool.   41

LEAR To take 't again perforce!° Monster ingratitude!

FOOL If thou wert my fool, nuncle, I'd have thee beaten for being old before thy time.   45

LEAR How's that?

FOOL Thou shouldst not have been old till thou hadst been wise.

LEAR Oh, let me not be mad, not mad, sweet Heaven!   50
Keep me in temper.° I would not be mad!

[Enter GENTLEMAN.] How now! Are the horses ready?

GENTLEMAN Ready, my lord.

LEAR Come, boy.

FOOL She that's a maid now and laughs at my departure   55
Shall not be maid long, unless things be cut shorter.

[Exeunt.]

ACT II

SCENE I. The EARL OF GLOUCESTER's castle.

[Enter EDMUND and CURAN, meeting.]

EDMUND Save thee,° Curan.

CURAN And you, sir. I have been with your father, and given him notice that the duke of Cornwall and Regan his duchess will be here with him this night.   5

EDMUND How comes that?

CURAN Nay, I know not. You have heard of the news abroad—I mean the whispered ones, for they are yet but ear-kissing° arguments?

EDMUND Not I. Pray you what are they?   10

CURAN Have you heard of no likely wars toward 'twixt the dukes of Cornwall and Albany?

EDMUND Not a word.

CURAN You may do, then, in time. Fare you well, sir.   [Exit.]

EDMUND The duke be here tonight? The better! Best!   16
This weaves itself perforce into my business.
My father hath set guard to take my brother,
And I have one thing, of a queasy question,°
Which I must act. Briefness and fortune, work!
Brother, a word, descend.° Brother, I say!   21
[Enter EDGAR.] My father watches. O sir, fly this place.
Intelligence° is given where you are hid.
You have now the good advantage of the night.
Have you not spoken 'gainst the duke of Cornwall?   25
He's coming hither, now, i' the night, i' the haste,
And Regan with him. Have you nothing said
Upon his party 'gainst the duke of Albany?
Advise yourself.

EDGAR   I am sure on 't, not a word.

EDMUND I hear my father coming. Pardon me, 30
In cunning° I must draw my sword upon you.
Draw. Seem to defend yourself. Now quit you well.°
Yield. Come before my father. Light, ho, here!
Fly, brother. Torches, torches! So farewell.
[Exit EDGAR.]
Some blood drawn on me would beget opinion°
[Wounds his arm]
Of my more fierce endeavor. I have seen drunkards   36
Do more than this in sport. Father, father!
Stop, stop! No help?
[Enter GLOUCESTER and SERVANTS with torches.]

---

42. To . . . perforce: I will take back my kingdom by force.
51. temper: sanity.
Act II, scene i. 1. Save thee: God save thee.

9. ear-kissing: whispered close in the ear. 19. queasy question: which needs delicate handling; queasy means on the point of vomiting. 21. descend: i.e., from the chamber where he has been hiding. 23. Intelligence: information. 31. In cunning: as a pretense. 32. quit . . . well: defend yourself well. Here they clash their swords together. 35. beget opinion: give the impression.

GLOUCESTER   Now, Edmund, where's the villain?

EDMUND   Here stood he in the dark, his sharp
   sword out,   40
   Mumbling° of wicked charms, conjuring the
   moon°
   To stand 's auspicious° mistress.

GLOUCESTER   But where is he?

EDMUND   Look, sir, I bleed.

GLOUCESTER   Where is the villain, Edmund?

EDMUND   Fled this way, sir. When by no means he
   could——

GLOUCESTER   Pursue him, ho!—Go after.   45
               [Exeunt some SERVANTS.]
               "By no means" what?

EDMUND   Persuade me to the murder of your
   lordship,
   But that I told him the revenging gods
   'Gainst parricides did all their thunders bend,
   Spoke with how manifold and strong a bond
   The child was bound to the father. Sir, in fine,°
   Seeing how loathly opposite I stood°   51
   To his unnatural purpose, in fell° motion
   With his preparèd° sword he charges home
   My unprovided° body, lanced mine arm.
   But when he saw my best alarumed spirits°   55
   Bold in the quarrel's right, roused to the en-
   counter,
   Or whether gasted° by the noise I made,
   Full suddenly he fled.

GLOUCESTER   Let him fly far.
   Not in this land shall he remain uncaught,
   And found—dispatch.° The noble duke my
   master,   60
   My worthy arch and patron,° comes tonight.
   By his authority I will proclaim it,
   That he which finds him shall deserve our thanks,
   Bringing the murderous caitiff° to the stake.°
   He that conceals him, death.   65

EDMUND   When I dissuaded him from his intent
   And found him pight° to do it, with curst° speech
   I threatened to discover him. He replied,

"Thou unpossessing bastard! Dost thou think,
If I would stand against thee, could the reposal 70
Of any trust, virtue, or worth in thee
Make thy words faithed?° No. What I should
   deny—
As this I would, aye, though thou didst produce
My very character°—I'd turn it all°
To thy suggestion,° plot, and damnèd practice.°
And thou must make° a dullard of the world 76
If they not thought the profits of my death
Were very pregnant and potential spurs°
To make thee seek it."

GLOUCESTER   Strong and fastened° villain!
Would he deny his letter? I never got° him.   80
              [Tucket° within.]
Hark, the duke's trumpets! I know not why he
   comes.
All ports I'll bar,° the villain shall not 'scape,
The duke must grant me that. Besides, his
   picture
I will send far and near, that all the kingdom
May have due note of him, and of my land,   85
Loyal and natural° boy, I'll work the means
To make thee capable.°

[Enter CORNWALL, REGAN, and ATTENDANTS.]

CORNWALL   How now, my noble friend! Since I
   came hither,
   Which I can call but now, I have heard strange
   news.

REGAN   If it be true, all vengeance comes too
   short   90
   Which can pursue the offender. How dost, my
   lord?

GLOUCESTER   Oh, madam, my old heart is cracked,
   is cracked!

REGAN   What, did my father's godson seek your
   life?
   He whom my father named? Your Edgar?

GLOUCESTER   Oh, lady, lady, shame would have it
   hid!   95

41–42. **Mumbling . . . mistress:** This is the kind of story
which would especially appeal to Gloucester. Cf. I.ii.114.
41. **conjuring . . . moon:** calling on Hecate, goddess of witchcraft. 42. **auspicious:** favorable. 50. **in fine:** in short. 51. **how
. . . stood:** with what loathing I opposed. 52. **fell:** fearful.
53. **prepared:** drawn. 54. **unprovided:** unguarded. 55. **my
. . . spirits:** my stoutest spirits called out by the alarm.
57. **gasted:** terrified. 60. **And . . . dispatch:** and when he's
found, kill him. 61. **arch . . . patron:** chief support and
protector. 64. **caitiff:** wretch; lit., captive. **to . . . stake:** i.e.,
place of execution. 67. **pight:** determined. **curst:** bitter.

72. **faithed:** believed. 74. **character:** handwriting. Cf. I.ii.67.
turn it all: make it appear to be. 75. **suggestion:** idea.
practice: plot. 76–79. **make . . . it:** you would have to make
people dull indeed before they would disbelieve that your
chief motive was to benefit by my death. 78. **pregnant . . .
spurs:** obvious and powerful encouragements. 79. **fastened:**
confirmed. 80. **got:** begot. s.d., **Tucket:** trumpet call. 82.
ports . . . bar: I'll have the seaports watched to prevent
his escape. 86. **natural:** i.e., one who has the proper feelings
of son to father. Gloucester does not as yet realize what
"nature" means to Edmund. See I.ii.1. 87. **capable:** i.e.,
legitimate; lit., capable of succeeding as my heir.

REGAN　Was he not companion with the riotous knights
That tend upon my father?

GLOUCESTER　I know not, madam. 'Tis too bad, too bad.

EDMUND　Yes, madam, he was of that consort.°

REGAN　No marvel then, though he were ill affected.°　　100
'Tis they have put him on° the old man's death,
To have the waste and spoil of his revènues.
I have this present evening from my sister
Been well informed of them, and with such cautions
That if they come to sojourn at my house,　105
I'll not be there.

CORNWALL　　Nor I, assure thee, Regan.
Edmund, I hear that you have shown your father
A childlike office.°

EDMUND　　'Twas my duty, sir.

GLOUCESTER　He did bewray° his practice, and received　　109
This hurt you see, striving to apprehend him.

CORNWALL　Is he pursued?

GLOUCESTER　　Aye, my good lord.

CORNWALL　If he be taken, he shall never more
Be feared of doing° harm. Make your own purpose,
How in my strength you please.° For you, Edmund,
Whose virtue and obedience doth this instant
So much commend itself, you shall be ours.　116
Natures of such deep trust we shall much need.
You we first seize on.

EDMUND　　I shall serve you, sir,
Truly, however else.

GLOUCESTER　　For him I thank your grace.

CORNWALL　You know not why we came to visit you——　　120

REGAN　Thus out of season, threading dark-eyed night.°
Occasions, noble Gloucester, of some poise,°
Wherein we must have use of your advice.
Our father he hath writ, so hath our sister,

Of differences, which I least thought it fit　125
To answer from° our home. The several messengers
From hence attend dispatch.° Our good old friend,
Lay comforts to your bosom, and bestow
Your needful counsel to our business,
Which craves the instant use.°　　130

GLOUCESTER　　I serve you, madam.
Your graces are right welcome.

[Flourish. Exeunt.]

SCENE II. *Before* GLOUCESTER'*s castle.*

[Enter KENT *and* OSWALD, *severally.°]*

OSWALD　Good dawning to thee, friend. Art of this house?

KENT　Aye.

OSWALD　Where may we set our horses?

KENT　I' the mire.　　5

OSWALD　Prithee, if thou lovest me, tell me.

KENT　I love thee not.

OSWALD　Why, then I care not for thee.

KENT　If I had thee in Lipsbury pinfold,° I would make thee care for me.　　10

OSWALD　Why dost thou use me thus? I know thee not.

KENT　Fellow, I know thee.

OSWALD　What dost thou know me for?　　14

KENT　A° knave, a rascal, an eater of broken meats; a base, proud, shallow, beggarly, three-suited, hundred-pound, filthy, worsted-stocking knave; a lily-livered, action-taking knave; a whoreson, glassgazing, superserviceable, finical

---

99. **consort:** party. 100. **though . . . affected:** if he had traitorous thoughts. 101. **put . . . on:** persuaded him to cause. 108. **childlike office:** filial service. 109. **bewray:** reveal. 113. **of doing:** because he might do. 113–14. **Make . . . please:** use my authority for any action you care to take. 121. **threading . . . night:** making our way through the darkness.

122. **poise:** weight. 126. **from:** away from. 127. **attend dispatch:** are waiting to be sent back. 130. **craves . . . use:** requires immediate action.
Scene ii. **s.d., severally:** by different entrances. 9. **Lipsbury pinfold:** This phrase has not been convincingly explained. A pinfold is a village pound, a small enclosure in which strayed beasts are kept until reclaimed by their owners; a pinfold was a good place for a fight whence neither side could escape. 15–26. **A . . . addition:** Kent here sums up the characteristics of the more unpleasant kind of gentleman servingman of whom Oswald is a fair specimen. **broken meats:** remains of food sent down from the high table. **three-suited:** allowed three suits a year. **hundred-pound:** i.e., the extent of his wealth. **worsted-stocking:** no gentleman, or he would have worn silk. **lily-livered:** cowardly. **action-taking knave:** one who goes to law instead of risking a fight. **glass-gazing:** always looking at himself in a mirror. **superserviceable:** too eager to do what his master wishes. **finical:** finicky.

rogue, one-trunkinheriting slave; one that wouldst be a bawd in way of good service, and art nothing but the composition of a knave, beggar, coward, pander, and the son and heir of a mongrel bitch—one whom I will beat into clamorous whining if thou deniest the least syllable of thy addition.   26

OSWALD   Why, what a monstrous fellow art thou, thus to rail on one that is neither known of thee nor knows thee!   29

KENT   What a brazen-faced varlet art thou, to deny thou knowest me! Is it two days ago since I tripped up thy heels and beat thee before the king? Draw, you rogue. For though it be night, yet the moon shines. I'll make a sop o' the moonshine° of you.° Draw, you whoreson cullionly° barbermonger,° draw.   36

[*Drawing his sword.*]

OSWALD   Away! I have nothing to do with thee.

KENT   Draw, you rascal. You come with letters against the king, and take vanity the puppet's part° against the royalty of her father. Draw, you rogue, or I'll so carbonado° your shanks. Draw, you rascal, come your ways.   42

OSWALD   Help, ho! Murder! Help!

KENT   Strike, you slave. Stand, rogue, stand, you neat slave, strike.   [*Beating him.*]

OSWALD   Help, ho! Murder! Murder!   46

[*Enter* EDMUND, *with his rapier drawn,* CORNWALL, REGAN, GLOUCESTER, *and* SERVANTS.]

EDMUND   How now! What's the matter?

[*Parting them.*]

KENT   With you, goodman boy,° an you please. Come, I'll flesh you,° come on, young master.

GLOUCESTER   Weapons! Arms! What's the matter here?   51

CORNWALL   Keep peace, upon your lives. He dies that strikes again. What is the matter?

REGAN   The messengers from our sister and the king.   55

CORNWALL   What is your difference?° Speak.

OSWALD   I am scarce in breath, my lord.

KENT   No marvel, you have so bestirred your valor. You cowardly rascal, Nature disclaims in thee. A tailor made thee.°   60

CORNWALL   Thou art a strange fellow—a tailor make a man?

KENT   Aye, a tailor, sir. A stonecutter or a painter could not have made him so ill, though he had been but two hours at the trade.   65

CORNWALL   Speak yet, how grew your quarrel?

OSWALD   This ancient ruffian, sir, whose life I have spared at suit of his gray beard——

KENT   Thou whoreson zed! Thou unnecessary letter!° My lord, if you will give me leave, I will tread this unbolted° villain into mortar, and daub the wall of a jakes° with him. Spare my gray beard, you wagtail?°   73

CORNWALL   Peace, sirrah! You beastly knave, know you no reverence?° 75

KENT   Yes, sir, but anger hath a privilege.°

CORNWALL   Why art thou angry?

KENT   That such a slave as this should wear a sword,
Who wears no honesty. Such smiling rogues as these,
Like rats, oft bite the holy cords a-twain   80
Which are too intrinse to unloose;° smooth° every passion
That in the natures of their lords rebel;
Bring oil to fire, snow to their colder moods;
Renege, affirm,° and turn their halcyon° beaks
With every gale and vary of their masters,   85

---

one-trunkinheriting: whose whole inheritance from his father will go into one trunk. bawd . . . service: ready to serve his master's lusts if it will please him. composition: mixture. pander: pimp. addition: lit., title of honor added to a man's name. 34–35. sop . . . you: Not satisfactorily explained, but obviously something unpleasant; probably Kent means no more than "I'll make a wet mess of you." 36. cullionly: base. barber-monger: a man always in the barber's shop. Elizabethan gentlemen frequented the beauty parlor as much as our modern ladies do. 39–40. vanity . . . part: Vanity appeared as an evil character in the old morality plays of the early sixteenth century, which still survived in a degenerate form in puppet shows exhibited at fairs. 41. carbonado: lit., a steak slashed for cooking, so "slice." 48. goodman boy: my young man. Edmund is still a young man, but it was an insult to call him boy. 49. flesh you: give you your first fight.

56. difference: disagreement. 59–60. Nature . . . thee: Nature refuses to own you, you are nothing but clothes —from the English proverb "The tailor makes the man." 69–70. zed . . . letter: because z does not exist in Latin and is not necessary in the English alphabet, since s can usually take its place. 71. unbolted: unsifted, coarse. 72. jakes: privy. 73. wagtail: a small bird which wags its tail up and down as it struts. 75. know . . . reverence: i.e., do you have the impertinence to raise your voice in the presence of your betters? 76. anger . . . privilege: something must be allowed to a man who has lost temper. 80–81. bite . . . unloose: i.e., cause the bonds of holy matrimony to be broken by serving the lusts of their employers. 81. smooth: help to gratify. 84. Renege, affirm: deny or agree; i.e., a perfect "yes man." halcyon: kingfisher. A kingfisher hung up by the neck was supposed to turn its bill into the prevailing wind.

Knowing naught, like dogs, but following.
A plague upon your epileptic visage!
Smile you my speeches, as I were a fool?
Goose,° if I had you upon Sarum° plain,
I'd drive ye cackling home to Camelot.°   90
CORNWALL   What, art thou mad, old fellow?
GLOUCESTER   How fell you out? Say that.
KENT   No contraries hold more antipathy
Than I and such a knave.
CORNWALL   Why dost thou call him knave? What
is his fault?   95
KENT   His countenance likes me not.°
CORNWALL   No more perchance does mine, nor
his, nor hers.
KENT   Sir, 'tis my occupation to be plain.
I have seen better faces in my time
Than stands on any shoulder that I see   100
Before me at this instant.
CORNWALL   This is some fellow
Who, having been praised for bluntness, doth
affect
A saucy roughness,° and constrains the garb
Quite from his nature.° He cannot flatter, he—
An honest mind and plain—he must speak
truth!   105
An they will take it, so. If not, he's plain.
These kind of knaves I know, which in this
plainness
Harbor more craft and more corrupter ends
Than twenty silly ducking observants
That stretch their duties nicely.°   110
KENT   Sir,° in good faith, in sincere verity,
Under the allowance of your great aspéct,
Whose influence, like the wreath of radiant fire
On flickering Phoebus'° front——   114
CORNWALL   What mean'st by this?
KENT   To go out of my dialect, which you discom-
mend so much. I know, sir, I am no flatterer. He
that beguiled you in a plain accent was a plain

knave, which, for my part, I will not be, though I
should win your displeasure to entreat me to 't.°
CORNWALL   What was the offense you gave him?
OSWALD   I never gave him any.   121
It pleased the king his master very late
To strike at me, upon his misconstruction,°
When he, conjunct,° and flattering his dis-
pleasure,
Tripped me behind; being down, insulted, railed,
And put upon him such a deal of man   126
That worthied him,° got praises of the king
For him attempting° who was self-subdued,°
And in the fleshment° of this dread exploit
Drew on me here again.   130
KENT   None of these rogues and cowards
But Ajax is their fool.°
CORNWALL   Fetch forth the stocks!
You stubborn° ancient knave, you reverend°
braggart,
We'll teach you——
KENT   Sir, I am too old to learn.
Call not your stocks for me. I serve the king,
On whose employment I was sent to you.   135
You shall do small respect, show too bold
malice
Against the grace and person of my master,
Stocking his messenger.°
CORNWALL   Fetch forth the stocks! As I have life
and honor,
There shall he sit till noon.   140
REGAN   Till noon! Till night, my lord, and all
night too.
KENT   Why, madam, if I were your father's dog,
You should not use me so.
REGAN   Sir, being his knave, I will.

123. upon . . . misconstruction: because he deliberately misinterpreted my words. 124. conjunct: i.e., joining with the king. 127. worthied him: got him favor. 128. attempting: attacking. self-subdued: made no resistance. 129. fleshment: excitement. 130–31. None . . . fool: This cryptic but devastating remark rouses Cornwall to fury, for he realizes from Kent's insolent tone, manner, and gesture that by "Ajax" he is himself intended. Ajax was the ridiculous braggart of the Greek army whom Shakespeare had already dramatized in *Troilus and Cressida*. The name Ajax had further unsavory significances for the original audience, for "Ajax" was a common synonym for a jakes— a very evil-smelling place. Kent thus implies "All these knaves and cowards are fooling this stinking braggart." 132. stubborn: rude. reverend: old. 136–38. You . . . messenger: As the king's representative, Kent is entitled to respectful treatment; to put him in the stocks is to offer an intolerable insult to the king. See ll. 146–53 below and II.iv.22–24.

89–90. Goose . . . Camelot: These lines cannot be explained. Sarum: Salisbury Plain, in the south of England. Camelot: the home of King Arthur and the knights of his Round Table. 96. His . . . not: I don't like his face. 103. saucy roughness: impudent rudeness. 103–04. constrains . . . nature: affects a manner which is quite unnatural. 109–10. silly . . . nicely: silly servants who are always bowing to their masters as they strain to carry out their orders. 111–14. Sir . . . front: Kent now changes his tone from the honest blunt man to the affected courtier. See I.iv.34. Phoebus: the sun god. 116–19. He . . . to 't: the man who posed as blunt and honest and deceived you was simply a knave. I shall never be a knave, even if you ask me and are angry because I refuse.

CORNWALL   This is a fellow of the selfsame color
Our sister speaks of. Come, bring away° the
stocks!   [*Stocks brought out.*]
GLOUCESTER   Let me beseech your grace not to do
so.   146
His fault is much, and the good king his master
Will check° him for 't. Your purposed low
correction°
Is such as basest and contemnèd'st° wretches
For pilferings and most common trespasses   150
Are punished with. The king must take it ill
That he, so slightly valued in his messenger,
Should have him thus restrained.
CORNWALL   I'll answer that.
REGAN   My sister may receive it much more
worse
To have her gentleman abused, assaulted,   155
For following her affairs. Put in his legs.
                          [KENT *is put in the stocks.*]
Come, my good lord, away.
                [*Exeunt all but* GLOUCESTER *and* KENT.]
GLOUCESTER   I am sorry for thee, friend. 'Tis the
duke's pleasure,
Whose disposition all the world well knows
Will not be rubbed° nor stopped. I'll entreat for
thee.   160
KENT   Pray do not, sir. I have watched and
traveled hard,
Some time I shall sleep out, the rest I'll whistle.
A good man's fortune may grow out at heels.°
Give you good morrow!°
GLOUCESTER   The duke's to blame in this, 'twill
be illtaken.   [*Exit.*]
KENT   Good king, that must approve the common
saw,°   166
Thou out of Heaven's benediction comest
To the warm sun!°
Approach, thou beacon to this underglobe,°
That by the comfortable beams I may   170
Peruse this letter! Nothing almost sees miracles
But misery.° I know 'tis from Cordelia,

Who hath most fortunately been informed
Of my obscurèd course,° and shall find time
From this enormous state,° seeking to give   175
Losses their remedies. All weary and o'erwatched,
Take vantage, heavy eyes, not to behold
This shameful lodging.
Fortune, good night. Smile once more, turn thy
wheel!   [*Sleeps.*]

SCENE III. *A wood.*

[*Enter* EDGAR.]
EDGAR   I heard myself proclaimed,°
And by the happy° hollow of a tree
Escaped the hunt. No port is free, no place,
That guard and most unusual vigilance
Does not attend my taking.° Whiles I may
'scape   5
I will preserve myself, and am bethought°
To take the basest and most poorest shape
That ever penury in contempt of man
Brought near to beast.° My face I'll grime with
filth,
Blanket° my loins, elf° all my hair in knots,   10
And with presented nakedness° outface
The winds and persecutions of the sky.
The country gives me proof and precedent°
Of Bedlam beggars,° who with roaring voices   14
Strike in their numbed and mortified° bare arms
Pins, wooden pricks, nails, sprigs of rosemary,
And with this horrible object, from low° farms,
Poor pelting° villages, sheepcotes and mills,
Sometime with lunatic bans,° sometime with
prayers,
Enforce their charity. Poor Turlygod! Poor
Tom!°   20
That's something yet. Edgar I nothing am.° [*Exit.*]

---

145. **bring away:** fetch out. 148. **check:** rebuke, punish.
purposed . . . correction: the degrading punishment which
you propose. 149. **contemnèd'st:** most despised. 160.
rubbed: turned aside, a metaphor from the game of bowls.
163. **A . . . heels:** even a good man may suffer a shabby
fate. 164. **Give . . . morrow:** a good morning to you. 166.
approve . . . saw: stress the truth of the common proverb.
167–68. **Thou . . . sun:** you are coming out of the shade
into the heat. 169. **beacon . . . underglobe:** the rising sun.
171–72. **Nothing . . . misery:** only those who are wretched
appreciate miracles.

174. **obscurèd course:** i.e., my actions in disguise. 175. **this
. . . state:** these wicked times.
Scene iii. 1. **proclaimed:** See II.i.82–85. 2. **happy:** lucky.
5. **attend my taking:** watch to take me. 6. **am bethought:** have
decided. 8–9. **penury . . . beast:** poverty, to show that man
is a contemptible creature, reduced to the level of a beast.
10. **Blanket:** cover with only a blanket. **elf:** mat. Matted
hair was believed to be caused by elves. 11. **with . . . nakedness:** bold in my nakedness. 13. **proof . . . precedent:**
examples. 14. **Bedlam beggars:** lunatics discharged from
Bedlam (or Bethlehem) Hospital, the London madhouse.
These sturdy beggars were the terror of the countryside. See
I.ii.151. 15. **mortified:** numbed. 17. **low:** humble. 18. **pelting:**
paltry. 19. **bans:** curses. 20. **Poor . . . Tom:** Edgar rehearses
the names which a bedlam calls himself. 21. **That's . . . am:**
there's still a chance for me; as Edgar I am a dead man.

SCENE IV. *Before* GLOUCESTER's *castle.* KENT *in the stocks.*

[*Enter* LEAR, FOOL, *and* GENTLEMAN.]

LEAR 'Tis strange that they should so depart from home
And not send back my messenger.

GENTLEMAN   As I learned,
The night before there was no purpose° in them
Of this remove.

KENT   Hail to thee, noble master!

LEAR Ha!   5
Makest thou this shame thy pastime?°

KENT   No, my lord.

FOOL Ha, ha! He wears cruel° garters. Horses are tied by the heads, dogs and bears by the neck, monkeys by the loins, and men by the legs. When a man's overlusty at legs,° then he wears wooden netherstocks.°   11

LEAR What's he that hath so much thy place mistook
To set thee here?

KENT   It is both he and she,
Your son and daughter.

LEAR No.   15

KENT Yes.

LEAR No, I say.

KENT I say yea.

LEAR No, no, they would not.

LENT Yes, they have.   20

LEAR By Jupiter, I swear no.

KENT By Juno, I swear aye.

LEAR   They durst not do 't,
They could not, would not do 't. 'Tis worse than murder
To do upon respect° such violent outrage.
Resolve° me with all modest haste which way 25
Thou mightest deserve, or they impose, this usage,
Coming from us.°

KENT   My lord, when at their home
I did commend your highness' letters to them,
Ere I was risen from the place that showed

My duty kneeling, came there a reeking post,° 30
Stewed in his haste, half-breathless, panting forth
From Goneril his mistress salutations,
Delivered letters, spite of intermission,°
Which presently° they read. On whose contents
They summoned up their meiny,° straight took horse,   35
Commanded me to follow and attend
The leisure of their answer, gave me cold looks.
And meeting here the other messenger,
Whose welcome, I perceived, had poisoned mine—
Being the very fellow that of late   40
Displayed so saucily° against your highness—
Having more man than wit about me, drew.
He raised the house with loud and coward cries.
Your son and daughter found this trespass worth°
The shame which here it suffers.   45

FOOL Winter's not gone yet° if the wild geese fly that way.

        "Fathers that wear rags
            Do make their children blind,
        But fathers that bear bags°   50
            Shall see their children kind.
        Fortune, that arrant whore,
            Ne'er turns the key° to the poor."

But for all this, thou shalt have as many dolors°
for thy daughters as thou canst tell° in a year.

LEAR Oh,° how this mother swells up toward my heart!   56
Hysterica passio, down, thou climbing sorrow,
Thy element's° below! Where is this daughter?

KENT With the earl, sir, here within.

LEAR Follow me not, stay here.   [*Exit.*]

GENTLEMAN Made you no more offense but what you speak of?   62

KENT None.

---

30. **reeking post:** sweating messenger. 33. **spite of intermission:** in spite of the delay in reading my letter (which should have come first). 34. **presently:** immediately. 35. **meiny:** followers. 41. **Displayed so saucily:** behaved so insolently. 44. **worth:** deserving. 46. **Winter's . . . yet:** there's more trouble to come. 50. **bear bags:** have money. 53. **turns . . . key:** opens the door. 54. **dolors:** with a pun on "dollars." 55. **tell:** count. 56–58. **Oh . . . below:** The *mother*, called also *hysterica passio*, was an overwhelming feeling of physical distress and suffocation. Lear's mental suffering is now beginning to cause a physical breakdown. This sensation, and the violent throbbing of his heart until finally it ceases, can be traced in Lear's speeches, See ll. 122, 138, 201–02; III.iv.14. 58. **element:** natural place.

Scene iv. 3. **purpose:** intention. 6. **Makest . . . pastime:** are you sitting there for amusement? 7. **cruel:** with a pun on "crewel"—worsted. 10. **overlusty at legs:** i.e., a vagabond. 11. **netherstocks:** stockings. 24. **upon respect:** the respect due to me, their king and father. 25. **Resolve:** inform. 27. **Coming . . . us:** Lear uses the royal "we"—"from us, the king."

How chance the king comes with so small a
train?

FOOL   An thou hadst been set i' the stocks for that
question, thou hadst well deserved it.   66

KENT   Why, fool?

FOOL   We'll° set thee to school to an ant, to teach
thee there's no laboring i' the winter. All that
follow their noses° are led by their eyes but blind
men, and there's not a nose among twenty but
can smell him that's stinking. Let go thy hold
when a great wheel runs down a hill, lest it break
thy neck with following it, but the great one that
goes up the hill, let him draw thee after. When a
wise man gives thee better counsel, give me mine
again. I would have none but knaves follow it,
since a fool gives it.   78

"That sir which serves and seeks for gain,
    And follows but for form,°   80
Will pack° when it begins to rain,
    And leave thee in the storm.

"But I will tarry, the fool will stay,
    And let the wise man fly.
The knave turns fool that runs away,   85
    The fool no knave, perdy."°

KENT   Where learned you this, fool?

FOOL   Not i' the stocks, fool.

[*Reenter* LEAR, *with* GLOUCESTER.]

LEAR   Deny to speak with me? They are sick?
They are weary?

They have traveled all the night? Mere fetches,°
The images° of revolt and flying off.   91
Fetch me a better answer.

GLOUCESTER   My dear lord,
You know the fiery quality° of the duke,
How unremovable and fixed he is
In his own course.   95

LEAR   Vengeance! Plague! Death! Confusion!
Fiery? What quality? Why, Gloucester,
Gloucester,
I'd speak with the duke of Cornwall and his wife.

GLOUCESTER   Well, my good lord, I have informed
them so.

LEAR   Informed them! Dost thou understand me,
man?   100

GLOUCESTER   Aye, my good lord.

LEAR   The king would speak with Cornwall, the
dear father
Would with his daughter speak, commands her
service.
Are they informed of this? My breath and blood!
"Fiery"? "The fiery duke"? Tell the hot duke
that——   105
No, but not yet. Maybe he is not well.
Infirmity doth still neglect all office
Whereto our health is bound.° We are not
ourselves
When nature being oppressed commands the
mind
To suffer with the body. I'll forbear,   110
And am fall'n out with my more headier will,°
To take the indisposed and sickly fit
For the sound man. [*Looking on* KENT] Death on
my state! Wherefore
Should he sit here? This act persuades me
That this remotion° of the duke and her   115
Is practice° only. Give me my servant forth.°
Go tell the duke and 's wife I'd speak with them,
Now, presently. Bid them come forth and hear
me,
Or at their chamber door I'll beat the drum
Till it cry sleep to death.°   120

GLOUCESTER   I would have all well betwixt you.
[*Exit.*]

LEAR   Oh, me, my heart, my rising heart! But
down!°

FOOL   Cry to it, nuncle, as the cockney° did to
the eels when she put 'em i' the paste alive. She
knapped° 'em o' the coxcombs with a stick, and
cried "Down, wantons, down!" 'Twas her
brother that, in pure kindness to his horse,
buttered his hay.   128

[*Reenter* GLOUCESTER, *with* CORNWALL, REGAN, *and*
SERVANTS.]

LEAR   Good morrow to you both.

CORNWALL   Hail to your grace!   130
[KENT *is set at liberty.*]

REGAN   I am glad to see your highness.

LEAR   Regan, I think you are, I know what reason
I have to think so. If thou shouldst not be glad,

68–78. We'll . . . it: The fool is so much amused at Kent's
discomfiture that he strings off a series of wise sayings to
show his own clearer understanding of Lear's state. 70.
follow . . . noses: go straight ahead. 80. but . . . form:
merely for show. 81. pack: clear out. 86. perdy: by God.
90. fetches: excuses. 91. images: exact likenesses. 93. quality:
nature.

107–08. Infirmity . . . bound: when a man is sick, he
neglects his proper duty. 111. am . . . will: regret my
hastiness. 115. remotion: removal. 116. practice: pretense.
Give . . . forth: release my servant at once. 120. cry . . .
death: kill sleep by its noise. 122. Oh . . . down: See ll.
56–58. 123. cockney: Londoner. 125. knapped: cracked.

I would divorce me from thy mother's tomb,
Sepúlchring an adultress.° [*To* KENT] Oh, are you
  free? 135
Some other time for that. Beloved Regan,
Thy sister's naught.° O Regan, she hath tied
Sharp-toothed unkindness, like a vulture, here.
                  [*Points to his heart.*]
I can scarce speak to thee, thou'lt not believe
With how depraved a quality——O Regan! 140
REGAN   I pray you, sir, take patience. I have hope
  You less know how to value her desert
  Than she to scant her duty.
LEAR   Say, how is that?
REGAN   I cannot think my sister in the least
  Would fail her obligation. If, sir, perchance 145
  She have restrained the riots of your followers,
  'Tis on such ground and to such wholesome end
  As clears her from all blame.
LEAR   My curses on her!
REGAN   Oh, sir, you are old,
  Nature in you stands on the very verge 150
  Of her confine.° You should be ruled and led
  By some discretion that discerns your state
  Better than you yourself. Therefore I pray you
  That to our sister you do make return.
  Say you have wronged her, sir. 155
LEAR   Ask her forgiveness?
Do you but mark how this becomes the house°—
[*Kneeling.*] "Dear daughter, I confess that I am
  old,
Age is unnecessary. On my knees I beg
That you'll vouchsafe me raiment, bed, and
  food."
REGAN   Good sir, no more, these are unsightly
  tricks. 160
  Return you to my sister.
LEAR   [*Rising*]   Never, Regan.
She hath abated me of half my train,
Looked black upon me, struck me with her
  tongue,
Most serpentlike, upon the very heart.
All the stored vengeances of Heaven fall 165
On her ingrateful top!° Strike her young
  bones,
You taking airs, with lameness.
CORNWALL   Fie, sir, fie!

LEAR   You nimble lightnings, dart your blinding
  flames
Into her scornful eyes. Infect her beauty,
You fen-sucked fogs,° drawn by the powerful
  sun 170
To fall° and blast her pride.
REGAN   Oh, the blest gods! So will you wish on me
  When the rash mood is on.
LEAR   No, Regan, thou shalt never have my
  curse.
Thy tender-hefted° nature shall not give 175
Thee o'er to harshness. Her eyes are fierce, but
  thine
Do comfort and not burn. 'Tis not in thee
To grudge my pleasures, to cut off my train,
To bandy hasty words, to scant my sizes,°
And in conclusion to oppose the bolt° 180
Against my coming in. Thou better know'st
The offices of nature, bond of childhood,
Effects of courtesy, dues of gratitude.
Thy half o' the kingdom hast thou not forgot,
Wherein I thee endowed. 185
REGAN   Good sir, to the purpose.°
LEAR   Who put my man i' the stocks?
                [*Tucket within.*]
CORNWALL   What trumpet's that?
REGAN   I know 't, my sister's. This approves° her
  letter,
That she would soon be here.
      [*Enter* OSWALD.]   Is your lady come?
LEAR   This is a slave whose easy-borrowed pride
Dwells in the fickle grace of her he follows.° 190
Out, varlet,° from my sight!
CORNWALL   What means your grace?
LEAR   Who stocked my servant? Regan, I have
  good hope
Thou didst not know on 't. Who comes here?
[*Enter* GONERIL.]   O Heavens,
If you do love old men, if your sweet sway
Allow° obedience, if yourselves are old, 195
Make it your cause. Send down, and take my
  part!
[*To* GONERIL] Art not ashamed to look upon this
  beard?

134–35. **divorce . . . adultress:** i.e., I would suspect that your dead mother had been false to me. 137. **naught:** wicked. 151. **confine:** boundary, edge. 156. **becomes . . . house:** i.e., suits my dignity. 166. **top:** head.

170. **fen-sucked fogs:** Cf. I.iv.316. 171. **fall:** fall upon. 175. **tender-hefted:** gently framed. 179. **scant my sizes:** reduce my allowances. 180. **oppose . . . bolt:** bar the door. 185. **Good . . . purpose:** and in good time to; or, please talk sense. 187. **approves:** confirms. 189–90. **whose . . . follows:** who soon puts on airs because his fickle mistress favors him. 191. **varlet:** knave. 195. **Allow:** approve of.

O Regan, wilt thou take her by the hand?

GONERIL   Why not by the hand, sir? How have I
offended?

All's not offense that indiscretion finds   200
And dotage terms so.°

LEAR   O sides, you are too tough,
Will you yet hold?° How came my man i' the
stocks?

CORNWALL   I set him there, sir. But his own
disorders
Deserved much less advancement.°

LEAR   You! Did you?

REGAN   I pray you, father, being weak, seem so.°
If till the expiration of your month   206
You will return and sojourn with my sister,
Dismissing half your train, come then to me.
I am now from home and out of that provision
Which shall be needful for your entertainment.°

LEAR   Return to her, and fifty men dismissed? 211
No, rather I abjure° all roofs, and choose
To wage against the enmity o' the air,
To be a comrade with the wolf and owl—
Necessity's sharp pinch! Return with her?   215
Why, the hot-blooded France, that dowerless
took
Our youngest-born—I could as well be brought
To knee his throne and, squirelike,° pension beg
To keep base life afoot. Return with her?
Persuade me rather to be slave and sumpter° 220
To this detested groom.   [*Pointing at* OSWALD.]

GONERIL   At your choice, sir.

LEAR   I prithee, daughter, do not make me mad.
I will not trouble thee, my child. Farewell.
We'll no more meet, no more see one another.
But yet thou art my flesh, my blood, my daughter,
Or rather a disease that's in my flesh   226
Which I must needs call mine. Thou art a boil,
A plague sore, an embossed carbuncle,°
In my corrupted blood. But I'll not chide thee.
Let shame come when it will, I do not call it. 230
I do not bid the thunderbearer° shoot,
Nor tell tales of thee to high-judging Jove.
Mend when thou canst, be better at thy leisure.
I can be patient, I can stay with Regan,

I and my hundred knights.

REGAN   Not altogether so. 235
I looked not for you yet, nor am provided
For your fit welcome. Give ear, sir, to my sister,
For those that mingle reason with your passion
Must be content to think you old,° and so——
But she knows what she does.   240

LEAR   Is this well spoken?

REGAN   I dare avouch° it, sir. What, fifty followers?
Is it not well? What should you need of more?
Yea, or so many, sith° that both charge and
danger°
Speak 'gainst so great a number? How in one
house
Should many people under two commands 245
Hold amity? 'Tis hard, almost impossible.

GONERIL   Why might not you, my lord, receive
attendance
From those that she calls servants or from mine?

REGAN   Why not, my lord? If then they chanced
to slack° you,
We could control them. If you will come to me,
For now I spy a danger, I entreat you   251
To bring but five and twenty. To no more
Will I give place or notice.

LEAR   I gave you all——

REGAN   And in good time you gave it.

LEAR   Made you my guardians, my depositaries,°
But kept a reservation° to be followed   256
With such a number. What, must I come to you
With five and twenty, Regan? Said you so?

REGAN   And speak 't again, my lord, no more
with me.

LEAR   Those wicked creatures yet do look well-
favored,°   260
When others are more wicked. Not being the
worst
Stands in some rank of praise.° [*To* GONERIL]
I'll go with thee.
Thy fifty yet doth double five and twenty,
And thou art twice her love.

GONERIL   Hear me, my lord.
What need you five and twenty, ten, or five, 265

200–01. that . . . so: because a silly old man says so. See
I.i.149–51,n. **201–02. O . . . hold:** See II.iv.56–58,n, above.
204. advancement: promotion. **205. seem so:** i.e., behave
suitably. **210. entertainment:** maintenance. **212. abjure:**
refuse with an oath. **218. squirelike:** like a servant. **220.
sumpter:** pack horse, beast of burden. **228. embossed carbuncle:** swollen boil. **231. thunderbearer:** Jupiter.

238–39. those . . . old: those who consider your passion
with reason realize that you are old—and should be wise.
241. avouch: guarantee. **243. sith:** since. **charge . . .
danger:** expense and risk of maintaining. **249. slack:** neglect.
255. depositaries: trustees. **256. reservation:** condition. See
I.i.134–41. **260. well-favored:** handsome. **261–62. Not . . .
praise:** i.e., since Goneril is not so bad as Regan, that is one
thing in her favor.

To follow in a house where twice so many
Have a command to tend you?
REGAN   What need one?
LEAR Oh,° reason not the need. Our basest
  beggars
Are in the poorest thing superfluous.°
Allow not nature more than nature needs,   270
Man's life's as cheap as beast's. Thou art a
  lady.
If only to go warm were gorgeous,
Why, nature needs not what thou gorgeous
  wear'st,
Which scarcely keeps thee warm. But for true
  need——
You Heavens, give me that patience, patience I
  need!   275
You see me here, you gods, a poor old man,
As full of grief as age, wretched in both.
If it be you that stirs these daughters' hearts
Against their father, fool me not so much
To bear it tamely.° Touch me with noble anger,
And let not women's weapons, water drops,   281
Stain my man's cheeks! No, you unnatural
  hags,
I will have such revenges on you both
That all the world shall——I will do such
  things——
What they are, yet I know not, but they shall be
The terrors of the earth. You think I'll weep.
No, I'll not weep.   287
I have full cause of° weeping, but this heart
Shall break into a hundred thousand flaws°
Or ere I'll weep. O fool, I shall go mad!   290
  [Exeunt LEAR, GLOUCESTER, KENT, and FOOL.]
CORNWALL Let us withdraw, 'twill be a storm.
                          [Storm and tempest.]
REGAN This house is little. The old man and his
  people
Cannot be well bestowed.
GONERIL 'Tis his own blame. Hath put himself
  from rest,
And must needs taste his folly.   295
REGAN For his particular,° I'll receive him gladly,
But not one follower.

GONERIL   So am I purposed.
Where is my lord of Gloucester?
CORNWALL Followed the old man forth. He is
  returned.
           [Reenter GLOUCESTER]
GLOUCESTER The king is in high rage.
CORNWALL   Whither is he going?
GLOUCESTER He calls to horse, but will I know
  not whither.   301
CORNWALL 'Tis best to give him way, he leads
  himself.
GONERIL My lord, entreat him by no means to
  stay.
GLOUCESTER Alack, the night comes on, and the
  bleak winds
Do sorely ruffle. For many miles about   305
There's scarce a bush.
REGAN   Oh, sir, to willful men
The injuries that they themselves procure
Must be their schoolmasters. Shut up your
  doors.
He is attended with a desperate train,
And what they may incense° him to, being apt°
To have his ear abused,° wisdom bids fear.   311
CORNWALL Shut up your doors, my lord, 'tis a
  wild night.
My Regan counsels well. Come out o' the
  storm.   [Exeunt.]

           ACT III

       SCENE I. A heath.

  [Storm still.° Enter KENT and a GENTLEMAN,
                meeting.]
KENT Who's there, besides foul weather?
GENTLEMAN One minded like the weather, most
  unquietly.
KENT I know you. Where's the king?
GENTLEMAN Contending with the fretful elements.
Bids the wind blow the earth into the sea,   5
Or swell the curlèd waters 'bove the main,°
That things might change or cease; tears his white
  hair,

268–75. Oh . . . need: the needs of a beggar are very
different from the needs of a king—but above all Lear
needs not dignity but patience. 268–69. Our . . . superfluous: even the few possessions of a beggar are not
absolutely necessary. 279–80. fool . . . tamely: do not
degrade me so much that I just tamely endure it. 288. of:
for. 289. flaws: broken pieces. 296. his particular: himself
personally.

310. incense: incite. apt: ready. 311. abused: deceived.
  Act III, scene i. s.d., still: continuing. 6. main: mainland.

Which the impetuous blasts, with eyeless° rage,
Catch in their fury, and make nothing of;
Strives in his little world of man° to outscorn 10
The to-and-fro-conflicting wind and rain.
This night, wherein the cub-drawn bear° would couch,°
The lion and the belly-pinchèd° wolf
Keep their fur dry, unbonneted° he runs,
And bids what will take all.   15

KENT   But who is with him?

GENTLEMAN   None but the fool, who labors to outjest
His heart-struck injuries.

KENT   Sir, I do know you,
And dare, upon the warrant of my note,°
Commend a dear° thing to you. There is division,
Although as yet the face of it be covered   20
With mutual cunning, 'twixt Albany and Cornwall,
Who have—as who have not that their great stars
Throned and let high?°—servants, who seem no less,
Which are to France the spies and speculations°
Intelligent of our state°—what hath been seen, 25
Either in snuffs and packings° of the dukes,
Or the hard rein which both of them have borne
Against the old kind king, or something deeper,
Whereof perchance these are but furnishings°——
But true it is, from France there comes a power°   30
Into this scattered kingdom, who already,
Wise in our negligence, have secret feet
In some of our best ports and are at point°
To show their open banner. Now to you.
If on my credit° you dare build so far   35
To make your speed to Dover, you shall find
Some that will thank you, making just report

Of how unnatural and bemadding sorrow
The king hath cause to plain.°
I am a gentleman of blood° and breeding,   40
And from some knowledge and assurance° offer
This office° to you.

GENTLEMAN   I will talk further with you.

KENT   No, do not.
For confirmation that I am much more
Than my outwall,° open this purse and take   45
What it contains. If you shall see Cordelia—
As fear not but you shall—show her this ring,
And she will tell you who your fellow° is
That yet you do not know. Fie on this storm!
I will go seek the king.

GENTLEMAN   Give me your hand.   50
Have you no more to say?

KENT   Few words, but, to effect, more than all yet—
That when we have found the king—in which your pain°
That way, I'll this—he that first lights on him 54
Holloa the other.   [Exeunt severally.]

SCENE II. *Another part of the heath.*
Storm still.

[*Enter* LEAR *and* FOOL.]

LEAR   Blow, winds, and crack your cheeks! Rage! Blow!
You cataracts and hurricanoes,° spout
Till you have drenched our steeples, drowned the cocks!°
You sulfurous and thought-executing° fires,
Vaunt-couriers° to oak-cleaving thunderbolts, 5
Singe my white head! And thou, all-shaking thunder,
Smite, flat the thick rotundity o' the world!
Crack nature's molds,° all germens° spill at once
That make ingrateful man!   9

FOOL   O nuncle, court holy water° in a dry house is better than this rainwater out o' door.

---

8. eyeless: blind. 10. little . . . man: It was a common Elizabethan idea, sometimes elaborately worked out, that individual man was a little world (microcosm) and reproduced in himself the universe (macrocosm). 12. cubdrawn bear: she-bear sucked dry, and therefore hungry. couch: take shelter. 13. belly-pinched: ravenous. 14. unbonneted: without a hat. 18. upon . . . note: guaranteed by my observation of you. 19. dear: precious. 22–23. that . . . high: whom Fate has set in a great position. 24. speculations: informers. 25. Intelligent . . . state: report on the state of our affairs. 26. snuffs . . . packings: resentment and plotting against each other. 29. furnishings: excuses. The sentence is not finished. 30. power: army. 33. at point: on the point of, about to. 35. credit: trustworthiness.

39. plain: complain. 40. blood: noble family. 41. knowledge . . . assurance: sure knowledge. 42. office: undertaking. 45. outwall: outside. 48. fellow: companion. 53. pain: labor.
Scene ii. 2. hurricanoes: waterspouts. 3. cocks: weathercocks on top of the steeples. 4. thought-executing: killing as quick as thought. 5. Vaunt-couriers: forerunners. 8. nature's molds: the molds in which men are made. germens: seeds of life. 10. court . . . water: flattery of great ones.

Good nuncle, in and ask thy daughters' blessing.
Here's a night pities neither wise man nor fool.
LEAR   Rumble thy bellyful! Spit, fire! Spout, rain!
Nor rain, wind, thunder, fire, are my daughters. 15
I tax° not you, you elements, with unkindness.
I never gave you kingdom, called you children,
You owe me no subscription.° Then let fall
Your horrible pleasure. Here I stand, your slave,
A poor, infirm, weak, and despised old man. 20
But yet I call you servile ministers°
That have with two pernicious daughters joined
Your high-engendered battles° 'gainst a head
So old and white as this. Oh, oh! 'Tis foul!
FOOL   He that has a house to put 's head in has a
good headpiece.   26
     "The° codpiece° that will house
         Before the head has any,
     The head and he shall louse
         So beggars marry many.   30
     The man that makes his toe
         What he his heart should make
     Shall of a corn cry woe,
         And turn his sleep to wake."
For there was never yet fair woman but she
made mouths in a glass.°   36
LEAR   No, I will be the pattern of all patience,
I will say nothing.
                    [*Enter* KENT.]
KENT   Who's there?
FOOL   Marry,° here's grace and a codpiece—
that's a wise man and a fool.   41
KENT   Alas, sir, are you here? Things that love
night
Love not such nights as these. The wrathful skies
Gallow° the very wanderers of the dark
And make them keep their caves. Since I was
man,   45
Such sheets of fire, such bursts of horrid thunder,
Such groans of roaring wind and rain, I never

Remember to have heard. Man's nature cannot carry°
The affliction nor the fear.
LEAR   Let the great gods, 49
That keep this dreadful pother° o'er our heads,
Find out their enemies now. Tremble, thou wretch,
That has within thee undivulgèd crimes
Unwhipped of justice. Hide thee, thou bloody hand,
Thou perjured, and thou simular man of virtue°
That art incestuous. Caitiff, to pieces shake, 55
That under covert and convenient seeming°
Has practiced on man's life. Close pent-up guilts,
Rive your concealing continents° and cry
These dreadful summoners grace.° I am a man
More sinned against than sinning.   60
KENT   Alack, bareheaded!
Gracious my lord, hard by here is a hovel.
Some friendship will it lend you 'gainst the tempest.
Repose you there while I to this hard house—
More harder than the stones whereof 'tis raised,
Which even but now, demanding after you, 65
Denied me to come in—return, and force
Their scanted courtesy.
LEAR   My wits begin to turn.
Come on, my boy. How dost, my boy? Art cold?
I am cold myself. Where is this straw, my fellow?
The art of our necessities is strange,   70
That can make vile things precious.° Come, your hovel.
Poor fool and knave, I have one part in my heart
That's sorry yet for thee.
FOOL   [*Singing*]
     "He° that has and a little tiny wit—
         With hey, ho, the wind and the rain—   75

16. **tax:** accuse. 18. **subscription:** submission. 21. **servile ministers:** servants who slavishly obey your masters. 23. **high-engendered battles:** armies begotten on high. 27–34. **The . . . wake:** the man who goes wenching before he has a roof over his head will become a lousy beggar. The man who is kinder to his toe than to his heart will be kept awake by his corns—i.e., Lear has been kinder to his feet (his daughters) than to his heart (himself). The Fool's remarks, especially when cryptic and indecent, are not easy to paraphrase. 27. **codpiece:** lit., the opening in the hose. 36. **made . . . glass:** made faces in a mirror. 40. **Marry:** Mary, by the Virgin. 44. **Gallow:** terrify.

48. **carry:** endure. 50. **pother:** turmoil. 54. **simular . . . virtue:** a man who pretends to be virtuous. 56. **under . . . seeming:** under a false appearance of propriety. 58. **Rive . . . continents:** split open that which covers and conceals you. 58–59. **cry . . . grace:** ask for mercy from these dreadful summoners. The summoner was the officer of the ecclesiastical court who summoned a man to appear to answer a charge of immorality. 70–71. **art . . . precious:** our needs are like the art of the alchemist (who was forever experimenting to try to transmute base metal into gold). 74–77. **He . . . day:** another stanza of the song which the Fool in *Twelfth Night* sings at the end of the play.

Must make content with his fortunes fit,°
For the rain it raineth every day."
LEAR   True, my good boy. Come, bring us to this
hovel.   [*Exeunt* LEAR *and* KENT.]
FOOL   This is a brave night to cool a courtesan.
I'll speak a prophecy° ere I go: 80
"When priests are more in word than matter,
When brewers mar their malt with water,
When nobles are their tailors' tutors,°
No heretics burned, but wenches' suitors,
When every case in law is right,   85
No squire in debt, nor no poor knight,
When slanders do not live in tongues,
Nor cutpurses come not to throngs,
When usurers tell their gold i' the field,
And bawds and whores do churches build—
Then shall the realm of Albion°   91
Come to great confusion.
Then comes the time, who lives to see 't,
That going shall be used with feet."°   94
This prophecy Merlin shall make, for I live
before his time.°   [*Exit.*]

SCENE III. GLOUCESTER'*s castle.*

[*Enter* GLOUCESTER *and* EDMUND.]

GLOUCESTER   Alack, alack, Edmund, I like not this
unnatural dealing. When I desired their leave
that I might pity him,° they took from me the use
of mine own house, charged me, on pain of their
perpetual displeasure, neither to speak of him,
entreat for him, nor any way sustain° him.   6
EDMUND   Most savage and unnatural!
GLOUCESTER   Go to, say you nothing. There's a
division betwixt the dukes, and a worse matter
than that. I have received a letter this night, 'tis
dangerous to be spoken.—I have locked the
letter in my closet. These injuries the king now

bears will be revenged home.° There is part of a
power already footed.° We must incline to the
king. I will seek him and privily° relieve him. Go
you, and maintain talk with the duke, that my
charity be not of him perceived. If he ask for
me, I am ill and gone to bed. Though I die for
it, as no less is threatened me, the king my old
master must be relieved. There is some strange
thing toward, Edmund. Pray you be careful.   21
[*Exit.*]
EDMUND   This courtesy, forbid thee,° shall the
duke
Instantly know, and of that letter too.
This seems a fair deserving,° and must draw me
That which my father loses, no less than all.   25
The younger rises when the old doth fall.   [*Exit.*]

SCENE IV. *The heath. Before a hovel.*

[*Enter* LEAR, KENT, *and* FOOL.]

KENT   Here is the place, my lord. Good my lord,
enter.
The tyranny° of the open night's too rough
For nature to endure.   [*Storm still.*]
LEAR   Let me alone.
KENT   Good my lord, enter here.
LEAR   Wilt break my heart?
KENT   I had rather break mine own. Good my
lord, enter.   5
LEAR   Thou think'st 'tis much that this conten-
tious° storm
Invades us to the skin. So 'tis to thee,
But where the greater malady is fixed°
The lesser is scarce felt. Thou'dst shun a bear,
But if thy flight lay toward the raging sea   10
Thou'dst meet the bear i' the mouth. When the
mind's free°
The body's delicate. The tempest in my mind
Doth from my senses take all feeling else
Save what beats there.° Filial ingratitude!
Is it not as this mouth should tear this hand   15
For lifting food to 't? But I will punish home.

76. Must . . . fit: i.e., must be content with a fortune
as slim as his wit. 80–94. prophecy . . . feet: The fool
gives a list of common events, pretending that they
are never likely to happen. The prophecy is a parody of
riddling prophecies popular at this time which were
attributed to Merlin, the old magician of King Arthur's
court. 83. nobles . . . tutors: Young noblemen and gallants
were very particular about the fashion and cut of their
clothes. 91. Albion: England. 94. going . . . feet: feet will be
used for walking. 95. This . . . time: A piece of mock
pedantry, for—according to Holinshed's *Chronicles*—
King Lear died some generations before King Arthur.
Scene iii. 3. him: Lear. 6. sustain: relieve.

13. home: to the utmost. 14. footed: landed. 15. privily:
secretly. 22. forbid thee: forbidden to thee. 24. This . . .
deserving: i.e., by betraying my father, I shall deserve
much of (be rewarded by) the duke.
Scene iv. 2. tyranny: cruelty. 6. contentious: striving
against us. 8. the . . . fixed: i.e., in the mind. 11. free: i.e.,
from cares. 14. what . . . there: i.e., the mental anguish
which is increased by the thumping of Lear's overtaxed
heart.

No, I will weep no more. In such a night
To shut me out! Pour on, I will endure.
In such a night as this! O Regan, Goneril!
Your old kind father, whose frank heart gave
    all——   20
Oh, that way madness lies, let me shun that,
No more of that.
KENT   Good my lord, enter here.
LEAR   Prithee, go in thyself, seek thine own ease.
This tempest will not give me leave to ponder
On things would hurt me more. But I'll go in. 25
[*To the* FOOL] In, boy, go first. You houseless
    poverty°——
Nay, get thee in. I'll pray, and then I'll sleep.
                           [FOOL *goes in.*]
Poor naked wretches, wheresoe'er you are,
That bide° the pelting of this pitiless storm,
How shall your houseless heads and unfed sides,
Your looped and windowed° raggedness, defend
    you   31
From seasons such as these? Oh, I have ta'en
Too little care of this! Take physic, pomp.°
Expose thyself to feel what wretches feel,
That thou mayst shake the superflux° to them 35
And show the Heavens more just.
EDGAR [*Within*] Fathom and half, fathom and
half! Poor Tom!
              [*The* FOOL *runs out from the hovel.*]
FOOL   Come not in here, nuncle, here's a spirit.
Help me, help me!   40
KENT   Give me thy hand. Who's there?
FOOL   A spirit, a spirit. He says his name's Poor
Tom.
KENT   What art thou that dost grumble there i'
the straw?
Come forth.   45
      [*Enter* EDGAR *disguised as a madman.*]
EDGAR   Away! The foul fiend follows me!
    "Though the sharp hawthorn blows the cold
    wind."
Hum! Go to thy cold bed and warm thee.
LEAR   Hast thou given all to thy two daughters?
And are thou come to this?°   50
EDGAR   Who gives anything to Poor Tom? Whom

the foul fiend hath led through fire and through
flame, through ford and whirlpool, o'er bog and
quagmire, that hath laid knives under his pillow
and halters in his pew,° set ratsbane° by his
porridge, made him proud of heart to ride on a
bay trotting horse over four-inched° bridges, to
course° his own shadow for a traitor. Bless thy
five wits!° Tom's a-cold Oh, do de, do de, do de.
Bless thee from whirlwinds, star-blasting,° and
taking!° Do Poor Tom some charity, whom the
foul fiend vexes. There could I have him now,
and there, and there again, and there.°   63
                         [*Storm still.*]
LEAR   What, have his daughters brought him to
this pass?
Couldst thou save nothing? Didst thou give
them all?   65
FOOL   Nay, he reserved a blanket,° else we had
been all shamed.
LEAR   Now, all the plagues that in the pendulous°
air
Hang fated o'er men's faults light on thy
daughters!
KENT   He hath no daughters, sir.   70
LEAR   Death, traitor! Nothing could have sub-
dued nature
To such a lowness but his unkind daughters.
Is it the fashion that discarded fathers
Should have thus little mercy on their flesh!
Judicious punishment! 'Twas this flesh begot 75
Those pelican° daughters.
EDGAR   "Pillicock sat on Pillicock Hill.
    Halloo, halloo, loo, loo!"°
FOOL   This cold night will turn us all to fools and
madmen.   80
EDGAR   Take heed o' the foul fiend. Obey thy par-
ents, keep thy word justly, swear not, commit not
with man's sworn spouse, set not thy sweet
heart on proud array. Tom's a-cold.
LEAR   What hast thou been?   85

---

26. **houseless poverty:** poor homeless people. 29. **bide:**
endure. 31. **looped . . . windowed:** full of holes and gaps.
33. **Take . . . pomp:** i.e., cure yourselves, you great men.
35. **superflux:** superfluity, what you do not need. 49–50.
Hast . . . this: At the sight of the supposed lunatic Lear goes
quite mad. Such utter destitution, he says, can only have
been caused by daughters as unkind as his own.

55. **pew:** seat. **ratsbane:** rat poison. 57. **four-inched:** i.e.,
narrow. 58. **course:** hunt after. 58. **five wits:** i.e., common
wit, imagination, fantasy, estimation, and memory. 60.
star-blasting: evil caused by a planet. 61. **taking:** malignant
influence of fairies. 62–63. **There . . . there:** Poor Tom
is chasing his own vermin. 66. **blanket:** i.e., his only covering. See II.iii.10. 68. **pendulous:** overhanging. 76. **pelican:**
The pelican was the pattern of devoted motherhood
because it fed its young on its own blood; but when the
young grew strong, they turned on their parents. 77–78.
Pillocock . . . loo: an old rhyme.

EDGAR   A servingman,° proud in heart and mind,
that curled my hair, wore gloves in my cap,
served the lust of my mistress's heart and did
the act of darkness with her, swore as many
oaths as I spake words and broke them in the
sweet face of Heaven. One that slept in the contriving of lust and waked to do it. Wine loved I
deeply, dice dearly, and in woman outpara-
moured° the Turk.° False of heart, light of ear,
bloody of hand, hog in sloth, fox in stealth, wolf
in greediness, dog in madness, lion in prey. Let
not the creaking of shoes nor the rustling of
silks betray thy poor heart to woman. Keep thy
foot out of brothels, thy hand out of plackets,°
thy pen from lenders' books,° and defy the foul
fiend.   101
"Still through the hawthorn blows the cold wind.
   Says suum, mun, ha, no, nonny.
   Dolphin my boy, my boy, sessa! Let him trot
   by."   [Storm still.]   104

LEAR   Why, thou wert better in thy grave than to
answer with thy uncovered body this extremity
of the skies. Is man no more than this! Consider
him well. Thou° owest the worm no silk, the
beast no hide, the sheep no wool, the cat no perfume.° Ha! Here's three on 's are sophisticated.
Thou art the thing itself. Unaccommodated man
is no more but such a poor, bare, forked animal
as thou art. Off, off, you lendings!° Come, un-
button here.   [Tearing off clothes.]   114

FOOL   Prithee, nuncle, be contented, 'tis a naughty
night to swim in. Now a little fire in a wild field
were like an old lecher's heart, a small spark, all
the rest on 's body cold. Look, here comes a
walking fire.   119
   [Enter GLOUCESTER, with a torch.]

EDGAR   This is the foul fiend Flibbertigibbet. He
begins at curfew° and walks till the first cock, he
gives the web and the pin,° squints the eye and
makes the harelip, mildews the white wheat and
hurts the poor creature of earth.
   "Saint° Withold footed thrice the 'old.°   125
      He met the nightmare° and her ninefold.°
         Bid her alight,
         And her troth plight,
      And aroint thee, witch, aroint° thee!"

KENT   How fares your grace?   130

LEAR   What's he?

KENT   Who's there? What is 't you seek?

GLOUCESTER   What are you there? Your names?

EDGAR   Poor Tom, that eats the swimming frog,
the toad, the tadpole, the wall newt, and the
water; that in the fury of his heart, when the foul
fiend rages, eats cow dung for sallets;° swallows
the old rat and the ditch dog;° drinks the green
mantle of the standing pool; who is whipped
from tithing to tithing,° and stock-punished, and
imprisoned; who hath had three suits° to his
back, six shirts to his body, horse to ride, and
weapon to wear.   142
   "But mice and rats and such small deer
   Have been Tom's food for seven long year."
Beware my follower. Peace, Smulkin,° peace,
thou fiend!   145

GLOUCESTER   What, hath your grace no better
company?

EDGAR   The Prince of Darkness is a gentleman.
Modo he's called, and Mahu.

GLOUCESTER   Our flesh and blood is grown so vile,
my lord,   150
That it doth hate what gets° it.

EDGAR   Poor Tom's a-cold.

GLOUCESTER   Go in with me. My duty cannot
suffer
To obey in all your daughters' hard commands.
Though their injunction be to bar my doors   155
And let this tyrannous night take hold upon you,
Yet have I ventured to come seek you out
And bring you where both fire and food is ready.

86–96. A servingman . . . prey: This is another description
of the gentleman servingman. See II.ii.15–26. **93–94. out-
paramoured:** had more mistresses than. **94. the Turk:** the
Turkish emperor. **99. plackets:** openings in a petticoat.
100. pen . . . books: The debtor often acknowledged the
debt by signing in the lender's account book. **108–14. Thou
. . . here:** There is usually an underlying sense in Lear's
ravings. The bedlam, he says, has not borrowed silk from
the silkworm, or furs from the beast, or wool from the
sheep to cover himself. Kent, the Fool, and he himself are
therefore *sophisticated*—adulterated, wearing coverings not
their own. Natural man, *unaccommodated* (i.e., not provided with such conveniences), is just a naked animal. Lear
will therefore strip himself naked and cease to be artificial.
109–10. cat . . . perfume: a perfume taken from the civet
cat, which has glands that function in the same manner as
the skunk's. **113. lendings:** things borrowed.

121. curfew: sounded at 9:00 P.M. **122. web . . . pin:** eye
diseases, cataract. **125–29. Saint . . . thee:** a charm to
keep horses from suffering from nightmare. **125. 'old:** wold,
uncultivated downland. **126. nightmare:** nightmare was
believed to be caused by a fiend. **ninefold:** nine young. **129.
aroint:** be gone. **137. sallets:** salads. **138. ditch dog:** dog
drowned in a ditch. **140. tithing:** district, parish. **141. three
suits:** See II.ii.16. **145–49. Smulkin . . . Mahu:** familiar
spirits. **151. gets:** begets.

LEAR   First let me talk with this philosopher.
   What is the cause of thunder?°   160

KENT   Good my lord, take his offer, go into the
   house.

LEAR   I'll take a word with this same learned
   Theban.°
   What is your study?°

EDGAR   How to prevent the fiend and to kill vermin.

LEAR   Let me ask you one word in private.   165

KENT   Impórtune him once more to go, my lord.
   His wits begin to unsettle.

GLOUCESTER   Canst thou blame him? [*Storm still.*]
   His daughters seek his death. Ah, that good
   Kent!
   He said it would be thus, poor banished man!
   Thou say'st the king grows mad. I'll tell thee,
   friend,   171
   I am almost mad myself. I had a son,
   Now outlawed from my blood. He sought my
   life
   But lately, very late. I loved him, friend,
   No father his son dearer. Truth to tell thee, 175
   The grief hath crazed my wits. What a night's
   this!
   I do beseech your grace——

LEAR   Oh, cry you mercy, sir.
   Noble philosopher, your company.

EDGAR   Tom's a-cold.

GLOUCESTER   In, fellow, there, into the hovel.
   Keep thee warm.   180

LEAR   Come, let's in all.

KENT   This way, my lord.

LEAR   With him,
   I will keep still with my philosopher.

KENT   Good my lord, soothe him, let him take the
   fellow.

GLOUCESTER   Take him you on.

KENT   Sirrah, come on, go along with us.   185

LEAR   Come, good Athenian.°

GLOUCESTER   No words, no words. Hush.

EDGAR   "Child° Rowland to the dark tower came.
   His word was still 'Fie, foh, and fum,
   I smell the blood of a British man'."   190
                                   [*Exeunt.*]

---

160. **cause of thunder:** This was much disputed by philosophers of the time. 162. **Theban:** i.e., Greek philosopher. 163. **study:** particular interest, or in modern academic jargon, "special field." 186. **Athenian:** like "Theban," l. 162. 188–90. **Child . . . man:** jumbled snatches of old ballads. *Child* in old ballads is used of young warriors who have not yet been knighted.

SCENE V. GLOUCESTER'*s castle.*

[*Enter* CORNWALL *and* EDMUND.]

CORNWALL   I will have my revenge ere I depart
   his house.

EDMUND   How, my lord, I may be censured,° that
   nature° thus gives way to loyalty, something
   fears me to think of.   5

CORNWALL   I now perceive it was not altogether
   your brother's evil disposition made him seek his
   death, but a provoking merit, set a-work by a
   reprovable badness in himself.°   9

EDMUND   How malicious is my fortune, that I
   must repent to be just!° This is the letter he
   spoke of, which approves° him an intelligent
   party° to the advantages of France. Oh heavens,
   that this treason were not, or not I the detector!

CORNWALL   Go with me to the duchess.   15

EDMUND   If the matter of this paper be certain,
   you have mighty business in hand.

CORNWALL   True or false, it hath made thee earl of
   Gloucester. Seek out where thy father is, that he
   may be ready for our apprehension.°   20

EDMUND   [*Aside*] If I find him comforting the king,
   it will stuff his suspicion more fully.—I will persever° in my course of loyalty, though the
   conflict be sore between that and my blood. 24

CORNWALL   I will lay trust upon thee, and thou
   shalt find a dearer father in my love. [*Exeunt.*]

SCENE VI.° *A chamber in a farmhouse
adjoining the castle.*

[*Enter* GLOUCESTER, LEAR, KENT, FOOL, *and* EDGAR.]

GLOUCESTER   Here is better than the open air, take
   it thankfully. I will piece out the comfort with
   what addition I can. I will not be long from you.

KENT   All the power of his wits has given way to
   his impatience.° The gods reward your kindness!   [*Exit* GLOUCESTER.]   6

Scene v. 3. **censured:** judged. 4. **nature:** i.e., natural affection toward my father yielding to loyalty to my duke. For Edmund's real sentiments on nature see I.ii.1–2. 8–9. **but . . . himself:** i.e., but a good quality in Edgar that provoked him to commit murder because of the reprehensible badness in Gloucester. 11. **repent . . . just:** be sorry because I have acted rightly (in betraying my father). 12. **approves:** proves. 12–13. **intelligent party:** spy, one with secret information. 20. **apprehension:** arrest. 22–23. **persever:** persevere.
Scene vi. In this scene Lear is completely mad, the Fool is half-witted, and Edgar is pretending to be a lunatic. 5. **impatience:** suffering.

EDGAR   Frateretto° calls me, and tells me Nero° is
an angler in the lake of darkness. Pray, innocent,°
and beware the foul fiend.   9

FOOL   Prithee, nuncle, tell me whether a madman
be a gentleman or a yeoman.°

LEAR   A king, a king!

FOOL   No, he's a yeoman that has a gentleman to
his son, for he's a mad yeoman that sees his son
a gentleman before him.°   15

LEAR   To have a thousand with red burning spits°
Come hissing in upon 'em——

EDGAR   The foul fiend bites my back.

FOOL   He's mad that trusts in the tameness of a
wolf, a horse's health, a boy's love, or a
whore's oath.   21

LEAR   It shall be done, I will arraign them straight.°
[To EDGAR] Come, sit thou here, most learned
justicer.°
[To the FOOL] Thou, sapient° sir, sit here. Now,
you she-foxes!

EDGAR   Look where he stands and glares! Wantest
thou eyes at trial,° madam?   26
    "Come o'er the bourn, Bessy, to me."

FOOL   "Her boat hath a leak,
    And she must not speak
    Why she dares not come over to thee." 30

EDGAR   The foul fiend haunts poor Tom in the
voice of a nightingale. Hopdance° cries in Tom's
belly for two white herring. Croak not,° black
angel, I have no food for thee.

KENT   How do you, sir? Stand you not so
amazed.°   35
Will you lie down and rest upon the cushions?

LEAR   I'll see their trial first. Bring in the evidence.
    [To EDGAR] Thou robèd man of justice,° take thy
    place.
    [To the FOOL] And thou, his yokefellow of
    equity,°
Bench° by his side. [To KENT] You are o' the
commission,°   40
Sit you too.

EDGAR   Let us deal justly.
    "Sleepest or wakest thou, jolly shepherd?
        Thy sheep be in the corn,
    And for one blast of thy minikin° mouth, 45
        Thy sheep shall take no harm."
Purr! The cat is gray.

LEAR   Arraign her first. 'Tis Goneril. I here take
my oath before this honorable assembly, she
kicked the poor king her father.   50

FOOL   Come hither, mistress. Is your name
Goneril?

LEAR   She cannot deny it.

FOOL   Cry you mercy,° I took you for a joint
stool.°   55

LEAR   And here's another, whose warped° looks
proclaim
What store° her heart is made on. Stop her there!
Arms, arms, sword, fire! Corruption° in the
place!
False justicer, why hast thou let her 'scape?

EDGAR   Bless thy five wits!   60

KENT   Oh, pity! Sir, where is the patience now,
That you so oft have boasted to retain?

EDGAR   [Aside] My tears begin to take his part so
much
They'll mar my counterfeiting.°

LEAR   The little dogs and all,   65
Tray, Blanch, and Sweetheart, see, they bark at
me.

EDGAR   Tom will throw his head at them. Avaunt,
you curs!
    Be thy mouth or black or white,
    Tooth that poisons if it bite,   70
    Mastiff, greyhound, mongrel grim,

7. Frateretto: a fiend's name. **Nero:** the debauched
Roman emperor who fiddled while Rome burned. **8.
innocent:** fool. **10–11. whether . . . yeoman:** The fool is
much interested in the social status of a madman and
proceeds to discuss the problem. **yeoman:** farmer, a notor-
iously wealthy class at this time. **13–15. No . . . him:** Many
yeomen farmers who had become wealthy by profiteering
from the wars and dearths sent their sons to London to
become gentlemen, as fifty years ago Chicago meat packers
sent their sons to Harvard and their daughters to England,
to be presented at court. This social change was much
commented on, and is illustrated in Jonson's comedy *Every
Man out of His Humour.* **16. spits:** thin iron rods thrust
through meat on which the meat was turned before the fire
in roasting; very useful weapons in emergency. **22. straight:**
straightway. **23. justicer:** judge. **24. sapient:** wise. **25–26.
Wantest . . . trial:** can you not see who is at your trial (i.e.,
this fiend)? But Edgar is deliberately talking madly. **32.
Hopdance:** a fiend's name. Cf. l. 7 above. **33. Croak not:**
don't rumble in my empty belly. The correct Elizabethan
word for this embarrassing manifestation is "wamble."
35. amazed: astonished—a strong word.

38. robed . . . justice: another glance at Edgar's blanket. **39.
yokefellow of equity:** partner in the law. **40. Bench:** sit on
the judge's bench. **commission:** Persons of high rank or
those accused of extraordinary crimes were not tried before
the ordinary courts, but by a commission specially appointed. **45. minikin:** dainty. **54. Cry . . . mercy:** I beg your
pardon. **54–55. joint stool:** wooden stool of joiner's work. **56.
warped:** malignant. **57. store:** material. **58. Corruption:**
bribery. **63–64. My . . . counterfeiting:** i.e., I am so sorry
for the king that I can hardly keep up this pretense.

Hound or spaniel, brach° or lym,°
Or bobtail tike or trundletail,°
Tom will make them weep and wail.
For, with throwing thus my head,   75
Dogs leap the hatch, and all are fled.
Do de, de, de. Sessa! Come, march to wakes°
and fairs and market towns. Poor Tom, thy
horn° is dry.   79

LEAR   Then let them anatomize° Regan, see what
breeds about her heart. Is there any cause in
nature that makes these hard hearts? [*To* EDGAR]
You, sir, I entertain° for one of my hundred, only
I do not like the fashion of your garments. You
will say they are Persian attire,° but let them be
changed.   86

KENT   Now, good my lord, lie here and rest
awhile.

LEAR   Make no noise, make no noise. Draw the
curtains. So, so, so.° We'll go to supper i' the
morning. So, so, so.   91

FOOL   And I'll go to bed at noon.°

[*Reenter* GLOUCESTER.]

GLOUCESTER   Come hither, friend. Where is the
king my master?

KENT   Here, sir, but trouble him not. His wits are
gone.

GLOUCESTER   Good friend, I prithee take him in
thy arms.   95
I have o'erheard a plot of death upon him.
There is a litter° ready, lay him in 't,
And drive toward Dover, friend, where thou
shalt meet
Both welcome and protection. Take up thy
master.
If thou shouldst dally° half an hour, his life, 100
With thine and all that offer to defend him,
Stand in assuréd loss. Take up, take up,
And follow me, that will to some provision
Give thee quick conduct.

KENT   Oppressèd nature sleeps.

This rest might yet have balmed° thy broken
sinews,   105
Which, if convenience will not allow,
Stand in hard cure.° [*To the* FOOL] Come, help to
bear thy master.
Thou must not stay behind.

GLOUCESTER   Come, come, away.

[*Exeunt all but* EDGAR.]

EDGAR   When we our betters see bearing our woes,
We scarcely think our miseries our foes.   110
Who alone suffers suffers most i' the mind,
Leaving free things and happy shows behind.
But then the mind much sufferance doth o'erskip
When grief hath mates, and bearing fellowship.°
How light and portable my pain seems now 115
When that which makes me bend makes the king
bow,
He childed as I fathered! Tom, away!
Mark the high noises,° and thyself° bewray
When false opinion, whose wrong thought defiles
thee,
In the just proof repeals° and reconciles thee. 120
What will hap more tonight, safe 'scape the
king!
Lurk,° lurk.   [*Exit.*]

SCENE VII. GLOUCESTER'*s castle.*

[*Enter* CORNWALL, REGAN, GONERIL, EDMUND, *and*
SERVANTS.]

CORNWALL   Post speedily to my lord your husband.° Show him this letter. The army of France
is landed. Seek out the traitor Gloucester.

[*Exeunt some of the* SERVANTS.]

REGAN   Hang him instantly.

GONERIL   Pluck out his eyes.   5

CORNWALL   Leave him to my displeasure. Edmund,
keep you our sister company. The revenges we
are bound to take upon your traitorous father

---

72. brach: bitch. **lym:** bloodhound. **73. trundletail:** curly tail.
77. wakes: merrymakings. **79. horn:** a horn bottle carried by
beggars in which they stored the drink given by the charitable. **80. anatomize:** dissect. **83. entertain:** engage. **85.
Persian attire:** i.e., of a magnificent and foreign fashion. **90.
So . . . so:** In dialogue "so, so" usually indicates action.
Here Lear imagines the bed curtains are being drawn. **92.
And . . . noon:** i.e., if it's suppertime in the morning, it will
be bedtime at noon. The fool disappears after this scene.
97. litter: a form of bed or stretcher enclosed by curtains
used for carrying the sick or the wealthy. **100. dally:**
hesitate.

105. balmed: soothed. **107. Stand . . . cure:** will hardly be
cured. **109–14. When . . . fellowship:** when we see better men
than ourselves suffering as we do, our sufferings seem slight.
The man who suffers endures most in his mind because he
contrasts his present misery with his happy past; but when
he has companions in misery (*bearing fellowship*), his mind
suffers less. **118. high noises:** i.e., the "hue and cry" of the
pursuers. **118–20. thyself . . . thee:** do not reveal yourself
until the belief in your guilt is proved wrong and you are
called back. **120. repeals:** calls back from banishment.
122. Lurk: lie hid.
Scene vii. **1–2. Post . . . husband:** These words are
addressed to Goneril. **Post:** ride fast.

are not fit for your beholding. Advise the duke,
where you are going, to a most festinate°
preparation. We are bound to the like. Our
posts° shall be swift and intelligent° betwixt us.
Farewell, dear sister. Farewell, my lord of
Gloucester.°   14
[*Enter* OSWALD.] How now! Where's the king?

OSWALD My lord of Gloucester° hath conveyed
him hence.
Some five or six and thirty of his knights,
Hot questrists° after him, met him at gate,
Who, with some other of the lords dependents,°
Are gone with him toward Dover, where they
boast   20
To have well-armèd friends.

CORNWALL   Get horses for your mistress.

GONERIL Farewell, sweet lord, and sister.

CORNWALL Edmund, farewell.
        [*Exeunt* GONERIL, EDMUND, *and* OSWALD.]
                Go seek the traitor Gloucester.
Pinion him like a thief, bring him before us.
                        [*Exeunt other* SERVANTS.]
Though well we may not pass° upon his life   25
Without the form of justice, yet our power
Shall do a courtesy to our wrath,° which men
May blame but not control. Who's there? The
traitor?
[*Enter* GLOUCESTER, *brought in by two or three.*]

REGAN Ungrateful fox! 'Tis he.

CORNWALL Bind fast his corky° arms.   30

GLOUCESTER What mean your graces? Good my
friends, consider
You are my guests. Do me no foul play,
friends.

CORNWALL Bind him, I say. [SERVANTS *bind him.*]

REGAN   Hard, hard. O filthy traitor!

GLOUCESTER Unmerciful lady as you are, I'm none.

CORNWALL To this chair bind him. Villain, thou
shalt find——   [REGAN *plucks his beard.*]

GLOUCESTER By the kind gods, 'tis most ignobly
done   36
To pluck me by the beard.°

REGAN So white, and such a traitor!

GLOUCESTER   Naughty lady,
These hairs which thou dost ravish° from my
chin   39
Will quicken° and accuse thee. I am your host.
With robbers' hands my hospitable favors°
You should not ruffle thus. What will you do?

CORNWALL Come, sir, what letters had you late
from France?

REGAN Be simple answerer, for we know the
truth.

CORNWALL And what confederacy° have you with
the traitors   45
Late footed in the kingdom?

REGAN To whose hands have you sent the lunatic
king?
Speak.

GLOUCESTER I have a letter guessingly set down,
Which came from one that's of a neutral heart,
And not from one opposed.   51

CORNWALL   Cunning.

REGAN   And false

CORNWALL Where hast thou sent the king?

GLOUCESTER   To Dover.

REGAN Wherefore to Dover? Wast thou not
charged at peril°——

CORNWALL Wherefore to Dover? Let him first
answer that.

GLOUCESTER I am tied to the stake, and I must
stand the course.°   55

REGAN Wherefore to Dover, sir?

GLOUCESTER Because I would not see thy cruel
nails
Pluck out his poor old eyes, nor thy fierce sister
In his anointed° flesh stick boarish fangs.
The sea, with such a storm as his bare head   60
In hell-black night endured, would have buoyed
up,°
And quenched the stellèd fires.°
Yet, poor old heart, he holp° the heavens to
rain.
If wolves had at thy gate howled that stern time,
Thou shouldst have said, "Good porter, turn the
key,"°   65

---

10. festinate: hasty. **12. posts:** messengers. **intelligent:**
full of information. **13–14. lord of Gloucester:** i.e., Edmund,
who has been promoted for his treachery. **16. lord of
Gloucester:** i.e., the old earl. **18. questrists:** seekers. **19.
lords dependents:** lords of his party. **25. pass:** pass judgment
on. **26–27. yet . . . wrath:** yet because we are all-powerful
we will give way to our wrath. **30. corky:** dry and withered.
37. pluck . . . beard: the greatest indignity that could be
offered.

39. ravish: seize. **40. quicken:** come to life. **41. hospitable
favors:** the face of your host. **45. confederacy:** alliance,
understanding. **53. at peril:** under penalty. **55. I . . . course:**
like a bear in the bear pit I must endure the onslaught. **59.
anointed:** i.e., anointed as a king, and therefore holy. **61.
buoyed up:** swelled up. **62. stelled fires:** the light of the
stars. **63. holp:** helped. **65. turn . . . key:** open the gate.

All cruels else subscribed.° But I shall see

The wingèd vengeance overtake such children.

CORNWALL   See 't shalt thou never. Fellows, hold
the chair.

Upon these eys of thine I'll set my foot.

GLOUCESTER   He that will think to live till he be
old,   70

Give me some help! Oh, cruel! Oh, you gods!

[GLOUCESTER's eye is put out.]

REGAN   One side will mock another, the other too.

CORNWALL   If you see vengeance——

FIRST SERVANT   Hold your hand, my lord.

I have served you ever since I was a child,

But better service have I never done you   75

Than now to bid you hold.

REGAN   How now, you dog!

FIRST SERVANT   If you did wear a beard upon your
chin,

I'd shake it on this quarrel. What do you
mean?

CORNWALL   My villain!

[They draw and fight. CORNWALL is wounded.]

FIRST SERVANT   Nay, then, come on, and take the
chance of anger.   80

REGAN   Give me thy sword. A peasant stand up
thus!

[Takes a sword and runs at him behind.]

FIRST SERVANT   Oh, I am slain! My lord, you have
one eye left

To see some mischief on him. Oh!   [Dies.]

CORNWALL   Lest it see more, prevent it. Out, vile
jelly!

Where is thy luster now?   85

[Puts out GLOUCESTER's other eye.]

GLOUCESTER   All dark and comfortless. Where's
my son Edmund?

Edmund, enkindle all the sparks° of nature,

To quit° this horrid act.

REGAN   Out, treacherous villain!

Thou call'st on him that hates thee. It was he

That made the overture° of thy treasons to us,   90

Who is too good to pity thee.

GLOUCESTER   Oh, my follies! Then Edgar was
abused.

Kind gods, forgive me that, and prosper him!

REGAN   Go thrust him out at gates, and let him
smell

His way to Dover.   [Exit one with GLOUCESTER.]

How is 't, my lord? How look you?

CORNWALL   I have received a hurt. Follow me,
lady.   96

Turn out that eyeless villain. Throw this slave

Upon the dunghill. Regan, I bleed apace.°

Untimely comes this hurt. Give me your arm.

[Exit CORNWALL, led by REGAN.]

SECOND SERVANT   I'll never care what wickedness
I do   100

If this man come to good.

THIRD SERVANT   If she live long,

And in the end meet the old course of death,°

Women will all turn monsters.

SECOND SERVANT   Let's follow the old earl, and
get the bedlam°

To lead him where he would. His roguish mad-
ness   105

Allows itself to anything.

THIRD SERVANT   Go thou. I'll fetch some flax and
whites of eggs.

To apply to his bleeding face. Now, Heaven help
him!   [Exeunt severally.]

ACT IV

SCENE I. The heath.

[Enter EDGAR.]

EDGAR   Yet better thus, and known to be contemned,°

Than still° contemned and flattered. To° be
worst,

The lowest and most dejected thing of fortune,

Stands still in esperance, lives not in fear.

The lamentable change is from the best,   5

The worst returns to laughter. Welcome then,

Thou unsubstantial air that I embrace!

The wretch that thou has blown unto the worst

---

98. apace: quickly, profusely. 102. old . . . death: natural
death in old age. 104. bedlam: i.e., Poor Tom. See I.ii.151;
II.iii.14.

Act IV, scene i.   1. contemned: despised; i.e., as a beggar.
2. still: always. 2–12. To . . . age: when a man has reached
the lowest state of misfortune, he has hope (esperance) for
the better, and no fear for the worse. The change to be
lamented is when the best things turn to bad; the worst can
only change to joy. After this poor consolation that nothing
worse can happen to him, Edgar sees his blinded father and
continues (l. 10): One would not trouble to live to old age
except to spite the world.

66. All . . . subscribed: all other cruel things were on his
side. 87. enkindle . . . sparks: i.e., blow into flame your
natural love. 88. quit: require. 90. overture: revelation.

Owes nothing to thy blasts.—But who comes
here?

[*Enter* GLOUCESTER, *led by an* OLD MAN.]

My father, poorly led?° World, world, O world!
But that thy strange mutations make us hate
thee,   11
Life would not yield to age.

OLD MAN   Oh, my good lord, I have been your
tenant, and your father's tenant, these four-
score years.   15

GLOUCESTER   Away, get thee away. Good friend,
be gone.
Thy comforts can do me no good at all,
Thee they may hurt.

OLD MAN   Alack, sir, you cannot see your way.

GLOUCESTER   I have no way and therefore want no
eyes.   20
I stumbled when I saw. Full oft 'tis seen,
Our means secure us, and our mere defects
Prove our commodities.° Ah, dear son Edgar,
The food° of thy abusèd father's wrath,
Might I but live to see thee in my touch,   25
I'd say I had eyes again!

OLD MAN   How now! Who's there?

EDGAR   [*Aside*] Oh gods! Who is 't can say "I am
at the worst"?
I am worse than e'er I was.

OLD MAN   'Tis poor mad Tom.

EDGAR   [*Aside*] And worse I may be yet. The worst
is not
So long as we can say "This is the worst."°   30

OLD MAN   Fellow, where goest?

GLOUCESTER   Is it a beggarman?

OLD MAN   Madman and beggar too.

GLOUCESTER   He has some reason, else he could
not beg.
I' the last night's storm I such a fellow saw,
Which made me think a man a worm. My son
Came then into my mind, and yet my mind   36
Was then scarce friends with him. I have heard
more since.
As flies to wanton boys are we to the gods,
They kill us for their sport.

EDGAR   [*Aside*] How should this be?
Bad is the trade that must play fool to sorrow,

Angering itself and others.° Bless thee, master! 41

GLOUCESTER   Is that the naked fellow?

OLD MAN   Aye, my lord.

GLOUCESTER   Then, prithee get thee gone. If for
my sake
Thou wilt o'ertake us hence a mile or twain
I' the way toward Dover, do it for ancient love,
And bring some covering for this naked soul, 46
Who I'll entreat to lead me.

OLD MAN   Alack, sir, he is mad.

GLOUCESTER   'Tis the times' plague° when madmen
lead the blind.
Do as I bid thee, or rather do thy pleasure.
Above the rest, be gone.   50

OLD MAN   I'll bring him the best 'parel° that I have,
Come on 't what will.   [*Exit.*]

GLOUCESTER   Sirrah, naked fellow——

EDGAR   Poor Tom's a-cold [*Aside*] I cannot daub°
it further.

GLOUCESTER   Come hither, fellow.   55

EDGAR   [*Aside*] And yet I must.—Bless thy sweet
eyes, they bleed.

GLOUCESTER   Know'st thou the way to Dover?

EDGAR   Both stile and gate, horseway and footpath. Poor Tom hath been scared out of his good
wits. Bless thee, good man's son, from the foul
fiend! Five fiends have been in Poor Tom at
once—of last, as Obidicut; Hobbididence, prince
of dumbness; Mahu, of stealing; Modo, of
murder; Flibbertigibbet,° of mopping and
mowing,° who since possesses chambermaids and
waiting-women. So, bless thee, master!   66

GLOUCESTER   Here, take this purse, thou whom the
Heavens' plagues
Have humbled to all strokes.° That I am wretched
Makes thee the happier. Heavens, deal so still!
Let the superfluous and lust-dieted man,   70
That slaves your ordinance, that will not see
Because he doth not feel, feel your power quickly.°

40–41. Bad . . . others: this business of pretending to
be mad and fooling a man in such distress as Gloucester
is now hateful. **48. times' plague:** a sign of these diseased
times. **51. 'parel:** apparel. **54. daub:** plaster it over, pretend. **62–64: Obidicut . . . Flibbertigibbet:** names of fiends.
Cf. III.vi.7, 32. **64–65. mopping . . . mowing:** making
faces and grimaces. **68. humbled . . . strokes:** made so
humble that you can endure anything. **69–72. Heavens . . .
quickly:** you gods, deal with others as you have dealt with
me; let the man who has too much and pampers his own
lusts, who regards your commands as contemptuously as
he regards his slaves, that will not understand until he is
hurt, feel your power quickly. This passage echoes Lear's
words (III.iv.33–36).

10. poorly led: led by one poor old man—and not accompanied by the usual party of servants. **22–23.
Our . . . commodities:** when we are well off we grow
careless, and then our misfortunes prove blessings. **24. food:**
object. **29–30. The . . . worst:** so long as a man is alive, he
may yet reach a lower depth of misery.

So distribution should undo excess°
And each man have enough. Dost thou know
Dover?
EDGAR Aye, master.   75
GLOUCESTER There is a cliff whose high and
bending° head
Looks fearfully in the confinèd deep.
Bring me but to the very brim of it,
And I'll repair the misery thou dost bear
With something rich about me. From that place
I shall no leading need.
EDGAR   Give me thy arm.   81
Poor Tom shall lead thee.   [Exeunt.]

SCENE II. *Before the* DUKE OF ALBANY'*s palace.*

[*Enter* GONERIL *and* EDMUND.]

GONERIL Welcome, my lord. I marvel our mild
husband
Not met us on the way.
          [*Enter* OSWALD.] Now, where's your master?
OSWALD Madam, within, but never man so
changed.
I told him of the army that was landed.
He smiled at it. I told him you were coming. 5
His answer was "The worse." Of Gloucester's
treachery
And of the loyal service of his son
When I informed him, then he called me sot
And told me I had turned the wrong side out.
What most he should dislike seems pleasant to
him,   10
What like, offensive.
GONERIL [*To* EDMUND] Then shall you go no
further.
It is the cowish° terror of his spirit,
That dares not undertake.° He'll not feel
wrongs
Which tie° him to an answer. Our wishes on the
way
May prove effects.° Back, Edmund, to my
brother.   15
Hasten his musters° and conduct his powers.°

I° must change arms at home and give the distaff°
Into my husband's hands. This trusty servant
Shall pass between us. Ere long you are like to
hear,
If you dare venture in your own behalf,   20
A mistress's° command. Wear this. Spare speech.
                              [*Giving a favor.*]
Decline your head. This kiss, if it durst speak,
Would stretch thy spirits up into the air.
Conceive,° and fare thee well.
EDMUND Yours in the ranks of death.   25
GONERIL   My most dear Gloucester!
                              [*Exit* EDMUND.]
Oh, the difference of man and man!
To thee a woman's services are due,
My fool° usurps my body.
OSWALD   Madam, here comes my lord.
                              [*Exit.*]
          [*Enter* ALBANY.]
GONERIL I have been worth the whistle.°
ALBANY   O Goneril!
You are not worth the dust which the rude
wind   30
Blows in your face. I fear your disposition.
That° nature which contemns its origin
Cannot be bordered certain in itself.
She that herself will sliver° and disbranch
From her material sap,° perforce must wither 35
And come to deadly use.
GONERIL No more, the text is foolish.°
ALBANY Wisdom and goodness to the vile seem
vile.
Filths savor but themselves.° What have you
done?
Tigers, not daughters, what have you per-
formed?   40

17–18. I . . . hands: I must become the soldier and leave
my husband to do the spinning. 17. distaff: stick used in
spinning, essentially the work of the housewife. 21. mistress's: in the double sense of lady and lover. Edmund,
having disposed of his brother and father, now looks
higher; he will through Goneril become possessed of her
half of the kingdom of Lear. 24. Conceive: use your imagination. 28. My fool: i.e., my husband is no more than a fool
to me. 29. worth . . . whistle: There is a proverb " 'Tis a
poor dog that is not worth the whistle." Goneril means:
I was once worth being regarded as your dog. 32–36. That
. . . use: that creature which despises its father (origin)
cannot be kept within bounds; she that cuts herself off
from her family tree will perish and like a dead branch come
to the burning. 34. sliver: slice off. 35. material sap: that sap
which is part of herself. 37. text is foolish: i.e., this is a silly
sermon. 39. Filths . . . themselves: the filthy like the taste
only of filth.

73. So . . . excess: then the man with too much would
distribute his excessive wealth. 76. bending: overhanging.
   Scene ii. 12. cowish: cowardly. 13. undertake: show
initiative, venture. 14. tie: force. 14–15. Our . . . effects:
our hopes (of love) as we rode together may be fulfilled. 16.
musters: troops which have been collected. powers: forces.

A father, and a gracious aged man
Whose reverence even the head-lugged bear°
   would lick,
Most barbarous, most degenerate, have you
   madded!
Could my good brother° suffer you to do it?
A man, a prince, by him so benefited!   45
If that the Heavens do not their visible spirits°
Send quickly down to tame these vile offenses,
It will come.
Humanity must perforce prey on itself,
Like monsters of the deep.°   50
GONERIL   Milk-livered° man!
That bear'st a cheek for blows, a head for
   wrongs,
Who hast not in thy brows an eye discerning
Thine honor from thy suffering;° that not
   know'st
Fools do those villains pity who are punished
Ere they have done their mischief.° Where's thy
   drum?   55
France spreads his banners in our noiseless land,
With plumèd helm thy state begins to threat,
Whiles thou, a moral° fool, sit'st still and criest
"Alack, why does he so?"
ALBANY   See thy self, devil!
Proper deformity° seems not in the fiend   60
So horrid as in woman.
GONERIL   O vain fool!
ALBANY Thou changèd and self-covered° thing,
   for shame,
Bemonster not thy feature.° Were 't my fitness
To let these hands obey my blood,°
They are apt enough to dislocate and tear   65
They flesh and bones. Howe'er° thou art a fiend,
A woman's shape doth shield thee.
GONERIL Marry, your manhood!° Mew!°

42. head-lugged bear: a bear with its head torn by the
hounds. 44. good brother: Cornwall. 46. visible spirits:
avenging spirits in visible form. 49–50. Humanity . . . deep:
A thought more than once expressed by Shakespeare—that
when natural law is broken, men will degenerate into beasts
and prey on each other. 50. Milk-livered: cowardly; the
liver was regarded as the seat of courage. 52–53. Who . . .
suffering: who cannot see when the insults which you endure are dishonorable to you. 54–55. Fools . . . mischief:
only a fool pities a villain when he is punished to prevent his
committing a crime. 58. moral: moralizing. 60. Proper
deformity: deformity natural to a fiend. 62. self-covered:
hiding your true self (i.e., devil) under the guise of a woman.
63. Bemonster . . . feature: do not change your shape into
a fiend. 64. blood: anger. 66. Howe'er: although. 68. Marry
. . . manhood: you're a fine specimen of a man! Mew: a
catcall.

[*Enter a* MESSENGER.]
ALBANY What news?
MESSENGER O my good lord, the duke of Corn-
   wall's dead,   70
Slain, by his servant, going to put out
The other eye of Gloucester.
ALBANY   Gloucester's eyes!
MESSENGER A servant that he bred, thrilled with
   remorse,°
Opposed against the act, bending his sword
To his great master, who thereat enraged   75
Flew on him and amongst them felled him
   dead,
But not without that harmful stroke which since
Hath plucked him after.
ALBANY   This shows you are above,
You justicers, that these our nether crimes°
So speedily can venge. But, oh, poor Gloucester!
Lost he his other eye?
MESSENGER   Both, both, my lord.   81
This letter, madam, craves a speedy answer.
'Tis from your sister.
GONERIL   [*Aside*] One way I like this well,
But being widow, and my Gloucester° with her,
May all the building in my fancy pluck°   85
Upon my hateful life. Another way,
The news is not so tart.—I'll read, and answer.
                                        [*Exit.*]
ALBANY Where was his son when they did take
   his eyes?
MESSENGER Come with my lady hither.
ALBANY   He is not here.
MESSENGER No, my good lord, I met him back
   again.°   90
ALBANY Knows he the wickedness?
MESSENGER Aye, my good lord, 'twas he informed
   against him,
And quit the house on purpose, that their
   punishment
Might have the freer course.
ALBANY   Gloucester, I live
To thank thee for the love thou show'dst the
   king,   95
And to revenge thine eyes. Come hither, friend.
Tell me what more thou know'st.   [*Exeunt.*]

73. thrilled . . . remorse: trembling with pity. 79. nether
crimes: crimes committed on earth below. 84. my Gloucester: i.e., Edmund. 85. May . . . pluck: may pull down
my castle in the air (i.e., her desire to marry Edmund). 90.
met . . . again: met him as he was on his way back.

SCENE III. *The French camp near Dover.*

[*Enter* KENT *and a* GENTLEMAN.]

KENT Why the king of France is so suddenly gone
back know you the reason?

GENTLEMAN Something he left imperfect in the
state which since his coming-forth is thought of,
which imports to the kingdom so much fear and
danger that his personal return was most
required and necessary.   7

KENT Who hath he left behind him general?

GENTLEMAN The marshal of France, Monsieur
La Far.   10

KENT Did your letters pierce the queen to any
demonstration of grief?

GENTLEMAN Aye, sir. She took them, read them
in my presence,
And now and then an ample tear trilled down
Her delicate cheek. It seemed she was a queen
Over her passion,° who most rebel-like   16
Sought to be king o'er her.

KENT   Oh, then it moved her.

GENTLEMAN Not to a rage. Patience and Sorrow
strove
Who should express her goodliest.° You have
seen   19
Sunshine and rain at once. Her smiles and tears
Were like a better way.° Those happy smilets°
That played on her ripe lip seemed not to know
What guests were in her eyes, which parted
thence
As pearls from diamonds dropped. In brief,
Sorrow would be a rarity most beloved   25
If all could so become it.°

KENT   Made she no verbal question?

GENTLEMAN Faith, once or twice she heaved the
name of "Father"
Pantingly forth, as if it pressed her heart,
Cried "Sisters! Sisters! Shame of ladies! Sisters!
Kent! Father! Sisters! What, i' the storm? i' the
night?   30
Let pity not be believed!" There she shook
The holy water from her heavenly eyes,
And clamor-moistened.° Then away she started

To deal with grief alone.

KENT   It is the stars,
The stars above us, govern our conditions,   35
Else one self° mate and mate could not beget
Such different issues.° You spoke not with her
since?

GENTLEMAN No.

KENT Was this before the king returned?

GENTLEMAN   No, since.

KENT Well, sir, the poor distressèd Lear's i' the
town,   40
Who sometime in his better tune remembers
What we are come about, and by no means
Will yield to see his daughter.

GENTLEMAN   Why, good sir?

KENT A sovereign° shame so elbows° him. His
own unkindness
That stripped her from his benediction, turned
her   45
To foreign casualties,° gave her dear rights
To his doghearted daughters. These things sting
His mind so venomously that burning shame
Detains him from Cordelia.

GENTLEMAN   Alack, poor gentleman!

KENT Of Albany's and Cornwall's powers you
heard not?   50

GENTLEMAN 'Tis so, they are afoot.

KENT Well, sir, I'll bring you to our master Lear,
And leave you to attend him. Some dear cause°
Will in concealment wrap me up awhile.
When I am known aright, you shall not grieve
Lending° me this acquaintance. I pray you, go 56
Along with me.   [*Exeunt.*]

SCENE IV. *The same. A tent.*

[*Enter, with drum and colors,*° CORDELIA, DOCTOR,
and SOLDIERS.]

CORDELIA Alack, 'tis he. Why, he was met even
now
As mad as the vexed sea, singing aloud,
Crowned with rank fumiter and furrow weeds,
With burdocks, hemlock, nettles, cuckoo flowers,
Darnel,° and all the idle weeds that grow   5

Scene iii. **16. passion:** emotion. **19. express her good-liest:** make her seem more beautiful. **21. like . . . way:** even more lovely. **smilets:** little smiles. **25–26. Sorrow . . . it:** if everyone looked so beautiful in sorrow, it would be a quality much sought after. **33. clamor-moistened:** wet her cries of grief with tears.

36. self: same. **37. issues:** children. **44. sovereign:** over-powering. **elbows:** plucks him by the elbow, reminding him of the past. **46. casualties:** chances, accidents. **53. dear cause:** important reason. **56. Lending:** bestowing on.
Scene iv. **s.d., drum . . . colors:** a drummer and a soldier carrying a flag. **3–5. fumiter . . . Darnel:** These are all English wild flowers and weeds.

In our sustaining° corn. A century° send forth.
Search every acre in the high-grown° field,
And bring him to our eye. [*Exit an* OFFICER.]
     What can man's wisdom
In the restoring his bereavèd sense?
He that helps him take all my outward worth.° 10
DOCTOR   There is means, madam.
     Our foster nurse° of nature is repose,
The which he lacks. That to provoke in him
Are many simples operative,° whose power
Will close the eye of anguish.
CORDELIA   All blest secrets, 15
All you unpublished virtues° of the earth,
Spring with my tears! Be aidant and remediate°
In the good man's distress! Seek, seek for him,
Lest his ungoverned rage dissolve the life
That wants the means to lead it.°
          [*Enter a* MESSENGER.]
MESSENGER   News, madam.
     The British powers are marching hitherward. 21
CORDELIA   'Tis known before, our preparation
     stands
In expectation of them.° O dear father,
It is thy business that I go about,
Therefore great France   25
My mourning and important° tears hath pitied.
No blown° ambition doth our arms incite,
But love, dear love, and our aged father's
     right.
Soon may I hear and see him!   [*Exeunt.*]

SCENE V. GLOUCESTER'*s castle.*

          [*Enter* REGAN *and* OSWALD.]
REGAN   But are my brother's powers set forth?
OSWALD   Aye, madam.
REGAN   Himself in person there?
OSWALD   Madam, with much ado.
     Your sister is the better soldier.
REGAN   Lord Edmund spake not with your lord
     at home?

OSWALD   No, madam.   5
REGAN   What might import my sister's letter to
     him?
OSWALD   I know not, lady.
REGAN   Faith, he is posted° hence on serious
     matter.
     It was great ignorance, Gloucester's eyes being
          out,
To let him live. Where he arrives he moves   10
All hearts against us. Edmund, I think, is gone,
In pity of his misery, to dispatch
His nighted° life, moreover to descry
The strength o' the enemy.
OSWALD   I must needs after him, madam, with my
     letter.   15
REGAN   Our troops set forth tomorrow. Stay with
     us,
The ways are dangerous.
OSWALD   I may not, madam.
     My lady charged my duty° in this business.
REGAN   Why should she write to Edmund?
     Might not you
Transport her purposes by word? Belike,   20
Something—I know not what——I'll love thee
     much,
Let me unseal the letter.
OSWALD   Madam, I had rather——
REGAN   I know your lady does not love her
     husband,
I am sure of that. And at her late being here
She gave strange oeillades° and most speaking
     looks   25
To noble Edmund. I know you are of her
     bosom.°
OSWALD   I, madam?
REGAN   I speak in understanding. You are, I
     know 't.
Therefore I do advise you, take this note.°
My lord is dead, Edmund and I have talked, 30
And more convenient is he for my hand
Than for your lady's. You may gather more.
If you do find him, pray you give him this,
And when your mistress hears thus much
     from you,
I pray desire her call her wisdom to her.   35
So, fare you well.

---

6. **sustaining:** which maintains life. **century:** company of a hundred soldiers. 7. **high-grown:** The season is therefore late summer. 10. **outward worth:** visible wealth. 12. **foster nurse:** the nurse who feeds. 14. **simples operative:** efficacious herbs. 16. **unpublished virtues:** secret remedies. 17. **aidant . . . remediate:** helpful and remedial. 20. **wants . . . it:** that has no sense to guide it. 22–23. **our . . . them:** our army is ready to meet them. 26. **important:** importunate, pleading. 27. **blown:** puffed up.

Scene v. 8. **is posted:** has ridden fast. 13. **nighted:** blinded. 18. **charged my duty:** entrusted it to me as a solemn duty. 25. **oeillades:** loving looks. 26. **of . . . bosom:** in her confidence. 29. **take . . . note:** observe this.

If you do chance to hear of that blind traitor,
Preferment° falls on him that cuts him off.

OSWALD   Would I could meet him, madam! I should show
What party I do follow.   40

REGAN   Fare thee well. [*Exeunt.*]

SCENE VI. *Fields near Dover.*

[*Enter* GLOUCESTER, *and* EDGAR *dressed like a peasant.*]

GLOUCESTER   When shall we come to the top of
that same hill?

EDGAR   You do climb up it now. Look how we
labor.

GLOUCESTER   Methinks the ground is even.

EDGAR   Horrible steep.
Hark, do you hear the sea?

GLOUCESTER   No, truly.

EDGAR   Why then your other senses grow im-
perfect   5
By your eyes' anguish.

GLOUCESTER   So may it be, indeed.
Methinks thy voice is altered, and thou speak'st
In better phrase and matter than thou didst.

EDGAR   You're much deceived. In nothing am I
changed
But in my garments.   10

GLOUCESTER   Methinks you're better-spoken.

EDGAR   Come on, sir, here's the place. Stand
still. How° fearful
And dizzy 'tis to cast one's eyes so low!
The crows and choughs° that wing the midway
air
Show scarce so gross as beetles. Halfway down
Hangs one that gathers samphire,° dreadful trade!
Methinks he seems no bigger than his head.   16
The fishermen that walk upon the beach
Appear like mice, and yond tall anchoring
bark°
Diminished to her cock°—her cock, a buoy
Almost too small for sight. The murmuring surge
That on the unnumbered idle pebbles chafes   21

Cannot be heard so high. I'll look no more,
Lest my brain turn and the deficient sight
Topple down headlong.°

GLOUCESTER   Set me where you stand.

EDGAR   Give me your hand. You are now within
a foot   25
Of the extreme verge. For all beneath the moon
Would I not leap upright.

GLOUCESTER   Let go my hand.
Here, friend, 's another purse, in it a jewel
Well worth a poor man's taking. Fairies and
gods°
Prosper it with thee! Go thou further off.   30
Bid me farewell, and let me hear thee going.

EDGAR   Now fare you well, good sir.

GLOUCESTER   With all my heart.

EDGAR   Why I do trifle thus with his despair
Is done to cure it.°

GLOUCESTER   [*Kneeling*] O you mighty gods!
This world I do renounce, and in your sights   35
Shake patiently my great affliction off.
If° I could bear it longer and not fall
To quarrel with your great opposeless wills,
My snuff° and loathèd part of nature should
Burn itself out. If Edgar live, oh, bless him!   40
Now, fellow, fare thee well. [*He falls forward.°*]

EDGAR   Gone, sir. Farewell.
And yet I know not how conceit° may rob
The treasury of life when life itself
Yields to the theft.° Had he been where he
thought,
By this had thought been past. Alive or dead? 45
Ho, you sir! Friend! Hear you, sir! Speak!
Thus might he pass° indeed. Yet he revives.
What are you, sir?

---

38. **Preferment:** promotion.
Scene vi. **11–24. How . . . headlong:** This vivid description of the cliffs at Dover seems to have been written
from direct observation. **13. choughs:** jackdaws. **15.
samphire:** a strongly perfumed plant which grows on the
chalk cliffs of Dover. **18. bark:** ship. **19. cock:** cockboat,
the small ship's boat, usually towed behind.

23–24. **deficient . . . headlong:** my sight failing, cause me
to topple headlong. **29. Fairies . . . gods:** As this tale is
pre-Christian, it is natural for the characters to call on the
gods of the "elder world." **33–34. Why . . . it:** Edgar's
purpose is to persuade his blinded father to go on living by
the thought that he has been miraculously preserved after
falling from a great height. When Gloucester begins to
recover from the shock, Edgar has dropped his pretense
of being a bedlam and speaks in a natural (but still
disguised) voice. **37–40. If . . . out:** if I could endure
my misery longer without quarreling with the wish of
Heaven, I would wait for the rest of my hateful life to
burn itself out. **39. snuff:** lit., smoking end of a burnt out
candle. **41. s.d., falls forward.** To be effective this episode
needs an actor who is not afraid of hurting himself, for unless Gloucester's fall is heavy it is quite unconvincing.
After his fall, he lies stunned for a few moments. **42. conceit:** imagination. **44. Yields . . . theft:** i.e., is willing to
die. **47. pass:** pass away, die.

GLOUCESTER   Away, and let me die.

EDGAR   Hadst thou been aught but gossamer,°
feathers, air,
So many fathom down precipitating,   50
Thou'dst shivered like an egg. But thou dost
breathe,
Hast heavy substance, bleed'st not, speak'st, art
sound.
Ten masts at each° make not the altitude
Which thou hast perpendicularly fell.
Thy life's a miracle. Speak yet again.   55

GLOUCESTER   But have I fall'n, or no?

EDGAR   From the dread summit of this chalky
bourn.°
Look up a-height, the shrill-gorged° lark so far
Cannot be seen or heard. Do but look up.

GLOUCESTER   Alack, I have no eyes.   60
Is wretchedness deprived that benefit,
To end itself by death? 'Twas yet some comfort
When misery could beguile° the tyrant's rage
And frustrate his proud will.

EDGAR   Give me your arm.
Up so. How is 't? Feel you your legs? You
stand.   65

GLOUCESTER   Too well, too well.

EDGAR   This is above all strangeness.
Upon the crown o' the cliff, what thing was that
Which parted from you?

GLOUCESTER   A poor unfortunate beggar.

EDGAR   As I stood here below, methought his eyes
Were two full moons, he had a thousand noses,
Horns whelked° and waved like the enridgèd°
sea.   71
It was some fiend, therefore, thou happy father,
Think that the clearest° gods, who make them
honors
Of men's impossibilities,° have preserved thee.

GLOUCESTER   I do remember now. Henceforth I'll
bear   75
Affliction till it do cry out itself
"Enough, enough," and die. That thing you
speak of,

I took it for a man. Often 'twould say
"The fiend, the fiend." He led me to that place.

EDGAR   Bear free° and patient thoughts. But who
comes here?   80
[Enter LEAR, fantastically dressed with wild
flowers.]
The safer sense will n'er accommodate
His master thus.°

LEAR   No,° they cannot touch me for coining, I
am the king himself.

EDGAR   O thou side-piercing sight!   85

LEAR   Nature's above art in that respect. There's
your press money. That fellow handles his bow
like a crowkeeper,° draw me a clothier's yard.°
Look, look, a mouse! Peace, peace, this piece of
toasted cheese will do 't. There's my gauntlet,°
I'll prove it on a° giant. Bring up the brown bills.°
Oh, wellflown, bird! I' the clout,° i' the clout.
Hewgh!° Give the word.°   93

EDGAR   Sweet marjoram.°

LEAR   Pass.   95

GLOUCESTER   I know that voice.

LEAR   Ha! Goneril, with a white beard! They
flattered me like a dog, and told me I had white
hairs in my beard ere the black ones were there.
To say "aye" and "no" to everything that I said!
"Aye" and "no" too was no good divinity.°
When the rain came to wet me once and the wind
to make me chatter, when the thunder would not
peace at my bidding, there I found 'em, there I
smelt 'em out. Go to, they are not men o' their
words. They told me I was everything. 'Tis a lie,
I am not agueproof.   107

49. gossamer: the parachutelike web made by a species of
small spider by which it floats through the air. 53. Ten . . .
each: ten masts, one on top of the other. 57. bourn:
boundary. 58. shrill-gorged: shrill-throated. The lark is
a small brown bird which flies to a great height and there
remains fluttering and singing a shrill but beautiful song.
63. beguile: cheat (by death). 71. whelked: with spiral twists.
enridged: wavy. 73. clearest: most glorious. 73–74. who . . .
impossibilities: who cause themselves to be honored by performing miracles impossible to men.

80. free: innocent. 81–82. The . . . thus: a man in his right
senses would never adorn himself thus. Edgar with unconscious irony repeats Lear's "accommodated." See
III.iv.111. 83–93. No . . . word: Lear's madness has a
sort of logical coherence. He begins by saying that he
cannot be charged with coining, because it was his right as
king to issue the coin, a natural right. From coin his mind
goes to the use of coin as *press money* for soldiers (money
given to a conscripted recruit as token that he has been
engaged), thence to the recruits at archery practice. Then
his mind is distracted by a mouse, but comes back to his
quarrel with his sons-in-law. He will throw down his
gauntlet as a challenge to single combat against any odds.
He comes back to the archery range, and a good shot right in
the bull's-eye. 88. crowkeeper: a man hired to scare away
crows from the crop. clothier's yard: The expert archer
drew his arrow back a full yard to the ear. 90. gauntlet:
glove, token of challenge. 91. prove . . . a: i.e., fight even
a. brown bills: i.e., the infantry. brown: varnished to keep
from rusting. 92. clout: the canvas target. 93. Hewgh: imitation of the whizz of the arrow. word: password. 94. marjoram:
a savory herb. 101. no . . . divinity: i.e., false doctrine.

GLOUCESTER   The trick° of that voice I do well
  remember.

Is 't not the king?

LEAR   Aye, every inch a king.
  When I do stare, see how the subject quakes. 110
  I pardon that man's life. What was thy cause?
  Adultery?
  Thou shalt not die. Die for adultery! No.
  The wren goes to 't, and the small gilded fly
  Does lecher in my sight.   115
  Let copulation thrive, for Gloucester's bastard
    son
  Was kinder to his father than my daughters
  Got 'tween the lawful sheets.
  To 't, luxury,° pell-mell! For I lack soldiers.
  Behold yond simpering dame,   120
  Whose face between her forks° presages snow,
  That minces virtue° and does shake the head
  To hear of pleasure's name.
  The fitchew,° nor the soilèd° horse, goes to 't
  With a more riotous appetite.   125
  Down from the waist they are Centaurs,°
  Though women all above.
  But to° the girdle do the gods inherit,
  Beneath is all the fiends'.
  There's hell, there's darkness, there's the
    sulfurous pit,   130
  Burning, scalding, stench, consumption, fie,
    fie, fie!
  Pah, pah! Give me an ounce of civet,° good
  apothecary,   to   sweeten   my   imagination.
  There's money for thee.

GLOUCESTER   Oh, let me kiss that hand!   135

LEAR   Let me wipe it first, it smells of mortality.

GLOUCESTER   O ruined piece of nature! This great
  world
  Shall so wear out to naught.° Dost thou know
  me?

LEAR   I remember thine eyes well enough. Dost
  thou squiny° at me? No, do thy worst, blind
  Cupid,° I'll not love. Read thou this challenge,
  mark but the penning on 't.   142

GLOUCESTER   Were all the letters suns, I could not
  see one.

EDGAR   I would not take this from report. It is,
  And my heart breaks at it.   145

LEAR   Read.

GLOUCESTER   What, with the case of eyes?

LEAR   Oh ho, are you there with me?° No eyes in
  your head, nor no money in your purse? Your
  eyes are in a heavy case, your purse in a light.
  Yet you see how this world goes.   151

GLOUCESTER   I see it feelingly.

LEAR   What, art mad? A man may see how this
  world goes with no eyes. Look with thine ears.
  See how yond Justice rails upon yond simple
  thief. Hark, in thine ear. Change places and,
  handy-dandy,° which is the Justice, which is the
  thief? Thou hast seen a farmer's dog bark at a
  beggar?

GLOUCESTER   Aye, sir.   160

LEAR   And the creature run from the cur? There
  thou   mightst   behold   the   great   image   of
  authority.°
  A dog's obeyed in office.
  Thou rascal beadle,° hold thy bloody hand!   165
  Why dost thou lash that whore? Strip thine
    own back.
  Thou hotly lust'st to use her in that kind°
  For which thou whip'st her. The usurer hangs
    the cozener.°
  Through tattered clothes small vices do appear,
  Robes and furred gowns hide all. Plate sin with
    gold   170
  And the strong lance of justice hurtless breaks.
  Arm it in rags, a pigmy's straw does pierce it.
  None does offend, none, I say, none, I'll able°
    'em.
  Take that of me, my friend, who have the
    power
  To seal the accuser's lips. Get thee glass eyes°
  And, like a scurvy° politician, seem   176
  To see the things thou dost not.
  Now, now, now, now. Pull off my boots.
  Harder, harder. So.

---

108. trick: peculiar note. 119. luxury: lust. 121. forks: legs.
122. minces virtue: walks with a great air of virtue. 124. fitchew: polecat, a creature demonstratively oversexed. soilèd:
fed on spring grass. 126. Centaurs: creatures half man and
half stallion. 128. But to: only down to. 132. civet:
perfume. See III.iv. 109–10,n. 137–38. O . . . naught: O
ruined masterpiece of nature, the universe likewise will
come to nothing. 140. squiny: look sideways, like a prostitute. 140–41. blind Cupid: the usual sign hung over a
brothel.

148. are . . . me: do you agree with me? 157. handy-dandy:
the nursery game of "Handy-pandy, sugar candy, which
hand will you have?" 162–63. image of authority: figure
showing the true meaning of authority. 165. beadle: parish
officer. 167. kind: manner. 168. usurer . . . cozener: the
swindler hangs the crook. 173. able: give power to. 174.
glass eyes: spectacles. 176. scurvy: lit., with skin disease,
"lousy."

EDGAR   Oh, matter and impertinency° mixed!
   Reason in madness!   180
LEAR   If thou wilt weep my fortunes, take my
   eyes.
   I know thee well enough. Thy name is Gloucester.
   Thou must be patient, we came crying hither.
   Thou know'st the first time that we smell the air,
   We wawl and cry. I will preach to thee. Mark. 185
GLOUCESTER   Alack, alack the day!
LEAR   When we are born, we cry that we are come
   To this great stage of fools. This 's a good
   block.°
   It were a delicate stratagem to shoe   189
   A troop of horse with felt. I'll put 't in proof,°
   And when I have stol'n upon these sons-in-law,
   Then, kill, kill, kill, kill, kill, kill!
          [Enter a GENTLEMAN, with ATTENDANTS.]
GENTLEMAN   Oh, here he is. Lay hand upon him.
   Sir,
   Your most dear daughter——
LEAR   No rescue? What, a prisoner? I am even
   The natural fool of Fortune.° Use me well, 196
   You shall have ransom.° Let me have a surgeon,
   I am cut to the brains.
GENTLEMAN   You shall have anything.
LEAR   No seconds?° All myself?
   Why, this would make a man a man of salt,° 200
   To use his eyes for garden waterpots,
   Aye, and laying autumn's dust.
GENTLEMAN   Good sir——
LEAR   I will die bravely, like a smug bridegroom.°
   What!
   I will be jovial. Come, come, I am a king, 205
   My masters, know you that.
GENTLEMAN   You are a royal one, and we obey
   you.
LEAR   Then there's life in 't. Nay, an you get it,
   you shall get it by running. Sa, sa, sa, sa.°
          [Exit running. ATTENDANTS follow.]
GENTLEMAN   A sight most pitiful in the meanest
   wretch,   210

Past speaking of in a king! Thou hast one
   daughter
Who redeems nature from the general curse
Which twain have brought her to.
EDGAR   Hail, gentle sir.
GENTLEMAN   Sir, speed you. What's your will?
EDGAR   Do you hear aught, sir, of a battle
   toward?°   215
GENTLEMAN   Most sure and vulgar.° Everyone
   hears that
Which can distinguish sound.
EDGAR   But, by your favor,
   How near's the other army?
GENTLEMAN   Near and on speedy foot, the main
   descry
   Stands on the hourly thought.°   220
EDGAR   I thank you, sir. That's all.
GENTLEMAN   Though that the queen on special
   cause is here,
   Her army is moved on.
EDGAR   I thank you, sir. [Exit GENTLEMAN.]
GLOUCESTER   You ever-gentle gods, take my breath
   from me.
   Let not my worser spirit tempt me again
   To die before you please!   225
EDGAR   Well pray you, father.
GLOUCESTER   Now, good sir, what are you?
EDGAR   A most poor man, made tame to fortune's
   blows,
   Who, by the art° of known and feeling sorrows,
   Am pregnant to° good pity. Give me your hand.
   I'll lead you to some biding.°
GLOUCESTER   Hearty thanks. 230
   The bounty and the benison° of Heaven
   To boot, and boot!°
          [Enter OSWALD.]
OSWALD   A proclaimed° prize! Most happy!
   That eyeless head of thine was first framed
   flesh
   To raise my fortunes. Thou old unhappy
   traitor,
   Briefly thyself remember.° The sword is out 235
   That must destroy thee.

179. matter . . . impertinency: sense and nonsense. 188.
block: hat; lit., the block on which a felt hat is molded.
From hat Lear's mind turns to *felt*. 190. put . . . proof: try
it out. 196. natural . . . Fortune: born to be fooled by
Fortune. 197. ransom: Prisoners of good family could buy
their freedom from their captors. 198. No seconds: no one
to help me. 200. man of salt: because tears are salt. 204.
like . . . bridegroom: It was said of Lord Grey of Wilton,
who was led out as if to be executed on December 9, 1603,
that he "had such gaiety and cheer in his countenance that
he seemed a dapper young bridegroom." 209. Sa . . . sa:
a cry used sometimes in sudden action.

215. toward: at hand. 216. vulgar: common, in everyone's
mouth. 219–20. the . . . thought: the main body is
expected to come into sight at any time now. 228.
art: long experience. 229. pregnant to: able to conceive.
230. biding: resting-place. 231. benison: blessing. 232. To
. . . boot: in the highest degree. proclaimed: Cf. IV.v.37–8.
235. thyself remember: prepare for death—by confessing
your sins.

GLOUCESTER   Now let thy friendly hand
Put strength enough to 't. [EDGAR *interposes*.]
OSWALD   Wherefore, bold peasant,
Darest thou support a published° traitor?
Hence,
Lest that the infection of his fortune take
Like hold on thee! Let go his arm.   240
EDGAR   Chill° not let go, zir, without vurther
'casion.°
OSWALD   Let go, slave, or thou diest!
EDGAR   Good gentleman, go your gait,° and let
poor volk pass. An chud° ha' been zwaggered
out of my life, 'twould not ha' been zo long as
'tis by a vortnight. Nay, come not near th' old
man, keep out, che vor ye,° or I'se try whether
your costard° or my ballow° be the harder.
Chill be plain with you.   250
OSWALD   Out, dunghill!   [*They fight.*]
EDGAR   Chill pick your teeth, zir. Come, no
matter vor your foins.°   [OSWALD *falls.*]
OSWALD   Slave, thou hast slain me. Villain, take
my purse.
If ever thou wilt thrive, bury my body,   255
And give the letters which thou find'st about me
To Edmund earl of Gloucester. Seek him out
Upon the British party. Oh, untimely death!
Death!   [*Dies.*]
EDGAR   I know thee well—a serviceable° villain,
As duteous to the vices of thy mistress   261
As badness would desire.
GLOUCESTER   What, is he dead?
EDGAR   Sit you down, father, rest you.
Let's see these pockets. The letters that he speaks
of
May be my friends. He's dead. I am only sorry
He had no other deathsman. Let us see.   266
Leave, gentle wax,° and, manners, blame us
not.
To know our enemies' minds, we'd rip their
hearts,
Their papers is more lawful. [*Reads*]   269
"Let our reciprocal vows be remembered. You
have many opportunities to cut him off. If your
will want not,° time and place will be fruitfully

offered. There is nothing done if he return the
conqueror. Then am I the prisoner, and his
bed my jail, from the loathed warmth whereof
deliver me, and supply the place for your labor.
"Your—wife, so I would say—affectionate
servant,   GONERIL."
Oh, undistinguished space° of woman's will!
A plot upon her virtuous husband's life,   280
And the exchange my brother! Here, in the
sands,
Thee I'll rake up,° the post unsanctified°
Of murderous lechers, and in the mature time
With this ungracious paper strike the sight
Of the death-practiced° duke. For him 'tis well
That of thy death and business I can tell.   286
GLOUCESTER   The king is mad. How° stiff° is my
vile sense,°
That I stand up, and have ingenious° feeling
Of my huge sorrows! Better I were distract.°
So should my thoughts be severed from my
griefs,   290
And woes by wrong imaginations lose
The knowledge of themselves.   [*Drum afar off.*]
EDGAR   Give me your hand.
Far off methinks I hear the beaten drum.
Come, father, I'll bestow you with a friend.
[*Exeunt.*]

SCENE VII. *A tent in the French camp.* LEAR *on a
bed asleep, soft music playing,* GENTLEMAN, *and
others attending.*

[*Enter* CORDELIA, KENT, *and* DOCTOR.]
CORDELIA   O thou good Kent, how shall I live
and work,
To match thy goodness? My life will be too
short,
And every measure fail me.
KENT   To be acknowledged, madam, is o'erpaid.
All my reports go with the modest truth,   5
Nor more nor clipped, but so.°
CORDELIA   Be better suited.°

238. **published:** publicly proclaimed. **241–50. Chill . . . you:**
Edgar speaks stage rustic dialect. **241. Chill:** I'll. **241–42**
vurther 'casion: further occasion, reason. **244. go . . . gait:**
go your own way. **245. chud:** should. **248. che . . . ye:** I
warn yer. **249. costard:** head; lit., apple. **ballow:** cudgel.
253. foins: thrusts. **260. serviceable:** diligent. **267. Leave . . .**
wax: Here he breaks the seal. **272. will . . . not:** desire is
not lacking. *Will* means both willingness and lust.

279. **undistinguished space:** limitless, extending beyond
the range of sight. **282. rake up:** hide in the dust. **post**
unsanctified: unholy messenger. **285. death-practiced:**
whose death is plotted. **287–89. How . . . sorrows:** i.e., if
only I could go mad and forget my sorrows. **287. stiff:**
strong. **sense:** sanity. **288. ingenious:** sensitive. **289. distract:**
mad.
Scene vii. **6. Nor . . . so:** neither exaggerated nor cur-
tailed, but exact. **suited:** garbed.

These weeds° are memories of those worser
hours.
I prithee put them off.

KENT   Pardon me, dear madam,
Yet to be known shortens my made intent.°
My boon° I make it that you know me not   10
Till time and I think meet.

CORDELIA   Then be 't so, my good lord. [*To the*
DOCTOR] How does the king?

DOCTOR   Madam, sleeps still.

CORDELIA   O you kind gods,
Cure this great breach in his abusèd nature!   15
The untuned and jarring senses, oh, wind up°
Of this child-changèd° father!

DOCTOR   So please your Majesty
That we may wake the king. He hath slept long.

CORDELIA   Be governed by your knowledge, and
proceed
I' the sway° of your own will. Is he arrayed?   20

GENTLEMAN   Aye, madam. In the heaviness of his
sleep
We put fresh garments on him.

DOCTOR   Be by, good madam, when we do awake
him.
I doubt not of his temperance.°

CORDELIA   Very well.

DOCTOR   Please you, draw near. Louder the music
there!   25

CORDELIA   O my dear father! Restoration hang
Thy medicine on my lips, and let this kiss
Repair those violent harms that my two sisters
Have in thy reverence made!

KENT   Kind and dear princess!

CORDELIA   Had you not been their father, these
white flakes   30
Had challenged pity of them. Was this a face
To be opposed against the warring winds?
To stand against the deep dread-bolted thunder?
In the most terrible and nimble stroke
Of quick, cross lightning?° To watch—poor
perdu!°—   35
With this thin helm? Mine enemy's dog,
Though he had bit me, should have stood that
night

Against my fire, and was thou fain, poor father,
To hovel thee with swine and rogues forlorn
In short and musty straw? Alack, alack!   40
'Tis wonder that thy life and wits at once
Had not concluded all. He wakes. Speak to him.

DOCTOR   Madam, do you, 'tis fittest.

CORDELIA   How does my royal lord? How fares
your majesty?

LEAR   You do me wrong to take me out o' the
grave.   45
Thou art a soul in bliss,° but I am bound
Upon a wheel of fire that mine own tears
Do scald like molten lead.

CORDELIA   Sir, do you know me?

LEAR   You are a spirit, I know. When did you
die?

CORDELIA   Still, still far wide!   50

DOCTOR   He's scarce awake. Let him alone awhile.

LEAR   Where have I been? Where am I? Fair
daylight?
I am mightily abused. I should e'en die with
pity
To see another thus. I know not what to say.
I will not swear these are my hands. Let's see,   55
I feel this pin prick. Would I were assured
Of my condition!

CORDELIA   Oh, look upon me, sir,
And hold your hands in benediction o'er me.
No, sir, you must not kneel.

LEAR   Pray do not mock me.
I am a very foolish fond old man,   60
Fourscore and upward, not an hour more nor
less,
And, to deal plainly,
I fear I am not in my perfect mind.
Methinks I should know you and know this man,
Yet I am doubtful, for I am mainly ignorant   65
What place this is, and all the skill I have
Remembers not these garments, nor I know not
Where I did lodge last night. Do not laugh at me,
For, as I am a man, I think this lady
To be my child Cordelia.

CORDELIA   And so I am, I am.   70

LEAR   Be your tears wet? Yes, faith. I pray weep
not.
If you have poison for me, I will drink it.
I know you do not love me, for your sisters
Have, as I do remember, done me wrong.
You have some cause, they have not.   75

7. **weeds**: garments; i.e., his livery as Lear's servant. **9. Yet
. . . intent**: my plan will be frustrated if I am revealed now.
10. boon: request for a favor. **16. wind up**: i.e., as the
loose string of a musical instrument is tightened. **17.
child-changed**: transformed by the treatment of his children. **20. sway**: direction. **24. temperance**: sanity. **35. cross
lightning**: forked lightning. **perdu**: sentry in an exposed
position.

46. bliss: Heaven.

CORDELIA   No cause, no cause.

LEAR   Am I in France?

KENT   In your own kingdom, sir.

LEAR   Do not abuse me.

DOCTOR   Be comforted, good madam. The great
   rage,
You see, is killed in him. And yet it is danger
To make him even o'er° the time he has lost.   80
Desire him to go in, trouble him no more
Till further settling.

CORDELIA   Will 't please your highness walk?

LEAR   You must bear with me.
Pray you now, forget and forgive. I am old and
   foolish.
             [*Exeunt all but* KENT *and* GENTLEMAN.]

GENTLEMAN   Holds it true, sir, that the duke of
Cornwall was so slain?   86

KENT   Most certain, sir.

GENTLEMAN   Who is conductor of his people?

KENT   As 'tis said, the bastard son of Gloucester.

GENTLEMAN   They say Edgar, his banished son, is
with the earl of Kent in Germany.   91

KENT   Report is changeable.° 'Tis time to look
about. The powers of the kingdom approach
apace.

GENTLEMAN   The arbiterment° is like to be bloody.
Fare you well, sir.   [*Exit.*]

KENT   My point and period° will be throughly°
wrought,   97
Or well or ill, as this day's battle's fought. [*Exit.*]

ACT V

SCENE I. *The British camp near Dover.*

[*Enter, with drum and colors,* EDMUND, REGAN,
GENTLEMEN, *and* SOLDIERS.]

EDMUND   Know° of the duke if his last purpose
hold,
Or whether since he is advised by aught
To change the course. He's full of alteration
And self-reproving. Bring his constant° pleasure.
                [*To a* GENTLEMAN, *who goes out.*]

REGAN   Our sister's man is certainly miscarried.   5

EDMUND   'Tis to be doubted,° madam.

REGAN   Now, sweet lord,
You know the goodness I intend upon you.
Tell me, but truly, but then speak the truth,
Do you not love my sister?

EDMUND   In honored love.

REGAN   But have you never found my brother's
way   10
To the forfended° place?

EDMUND   That thought abuses° you.

REGAN   I am doubtful that you have been conjunct
And bosomed with her, as far as we call hers.°

EDMUND   No, by mine honor, madam.

REGAN   I never shall endure her. Dear my lord,   15
Be not familiar with her.

EDMUND   Fear me not.—
She and the duke her husband!
[*Enter, with drum and colors,* ALBANY, GONERIL, *and*
                  SOLDIERS.]

GONERIL   [*Aside*] I had rather lose the battle than
   that sister
Should loosen him and me.

ALBANY   Our very loving sister, well bemet.   20
Sir, this I hear: The king is come to his daughter,
With others whom the rigor of our state°
Forced to cry out.° Where I could not be honest,
I never yet was valiant. For this business,
It toucheth us, as France invades our land,   25
Not bolds the king, with others, whom I fear
Most just and heavy causes make oppose.°

EDMUND   Sir, you speak nobly.

REGAN   Why is this reasoned?°

GONERIL   Combine together 'gainst the enemy,
For these domestic and particular broils   30
Are not the question here.

ALBANY   Let's then determine
With the ancient of war° on our proceedings.

EDMUND   I shall attend you presently at your tent.

REGAN   Sister, you'll go with us?

GONERIL   No.   35

REGAN   'Tis most convenient. Pray you go with us.

---

80. even o'er: go over. **92. Report . . . changeable:** rumors are not reliable. **94. arbiterment:** decision. **97. point . . . period:** lit., full stop; the end of my chapter. **throughly:** thoroughly.
Act V, scene i. **1. Know:** learn. **4. constant:** firm; i.e., final decision.

6. doubted: feared. **11. forfended:** forbidden. **abuses:** wrongs; i.e., you should not have such a thought. **12–13. I . . . hers:** I am afraid that you have been united in intimacy with her in every way. **22. rigor . . . state:** our harsh government. **23. cry out:** protest. **24–27. For . . . oppose:** this business concerns us particularly, not because France is encouraging Lear and others who rightly oppose us, but because he is invading our country. **28. reasoned:** argued. **32. ancient of war:** experienced commanders.

GONERIL [*Aside*] Oh ho, I know the riddle.°—I
    will go.
[*As they are going out, enter* EDGAR *disguised.*]
EDGAR   If e'er your grace had speech with man so
    poor,
    Hear me one word.
ALBANY   I'll overtake you. Speak.
            [*Exeunt all but* ALBANY *and* EDGAR.]
EDGAR   Before you fight the battle, ope this letter.
    If you have victory, let the trumpet sound   41
    For him that brought it. Wretched though I seem,
    I can produce a champion that will prove
    What is avouchèd° there. If you miscarry,
    Your business of the world hath so an end,   45
    And machination ceases. Fortune love you!
ALBANY   Stay till I have read the letter.
EDGAR   I was forbid it.
    When time shall serve, let but the herald cry
    And I'll appear again.   49
ALBANY   Why, fare thee well. I will o'erlook° thy
    paper.   [*Exit* EDGAR.]
            [*Reenter* EDMUND.]
EDMUND   The enemy's in view. Draw up your
    powers.
    Here is the guess° of their true strength and
    forces
    By diligent discovery, but your haste
    Is now urged on you.
ALBANY   We will greet the time.° [*Exit.*]
EDMUND   To° both these sisters have I sworn my
    love,   55
    Each jealous of the other, as the stung
    Are of the adder. Which of them shall I take?
    Both? One? Or neither? Neither can be enjoyed
    If both remain alive. To take the widow
    Exasperates, makes mad her sister Goneril,   60
    And hardly shall I carry out my side,°
    Her husband being alive. Now then we'll use
    His countenance° for the battle, which being
    done,
    Let her who would be rid of him devise
    His speedy taking-off. As for the mercy   65

Which he intends to Lear and to Cordelia,
The battle done, and they within our power,
Shall never see his pardon, for my state
Stands on me to defend, not to debate.° [*Exit.*]

SCENE II. *A field between the two camps.*

[*Alarum within. Enter, with drum and colors,* LEAR,
CORDELIA, *and* SOLDIERS, *over the stage; and exeunt.
Enter* EDGAR *and* GLOUCESTER.]
EDGAR   Here, father, take the shadow of this tree
    For your good host. Pray that the right may
    thrive.
    If ever I return to you again,
    I'll bring you comfort.   4
GLOUCESTER   Grace go with you, sir! [*Exit* EDGAR.]
        [*Alarum and retreat within. Reenter* EDGAR.]
EDGAR   Away, old man. Give me thy hand, away!
    King Lear hath lost, he and his daughter ta'en.°
    Give me thy hand, come on.
GLOUCESTER   No farther, sir. A man may rot
    even here.
EDGAR   What, in ill thoughts again? Men must
    endure   9
    Their going hence, even as their coming hither.
    Ripeness° is all. Come on.
GLOUCESTER   And that's true too. [*Exeunt.*]

SCENE III. *The British camp near Dover.*

[*Enter, in conquest, with drum and colors,* EDMUND,
LEAR *and* CORDELIA, *as prisoners,* CAPTAIN, SOLDIERS,
etc.]
EDMUND   Some officers take them away. Good
    guard,
    Until their greater pleasures° first be known
    That are to censure them.
CORDELIA   We are not the first
    Who with best meaning have incurred the worst.
    For thee, oppressèd king, am I cast down.   5
    Myself could else outfrown false fortune's
    frown.°
    Shall we not see these daughters and these
    sisters?

---

37. Oh . . . riddle: i.e., you are afraid to leave me alone with
Edmund. 44. avouched: declared. 50. o'erlook: read. 52.
guess: estimate. 54. greet . . . time: i.e., go to meet our
enemy. 55–69. To . . . debate: Edmund has now reached
the crisis in his fortunes. Both sisters are in love with him,
he can have either. Or he can aim higher and, with Lear
and Cordelia out of the way, achieve the whole kingdom
for himself. 61. my side: i.e., of the bargain. 63. countenance: authority.

68–69. for . . . debate: my fortune is now in such a state
that I must act, not argue.
    Scene ii. 6. ta'en: taken. 11. Ripeness: perfect readiness.
    Scene iii. 2. their . . . pleasures: the will of my superiors.
3–6. We . . . frown: See I.i.183–90,n.

LEAR No, no, no, no! Come, let's away to prison.
We two alone will sing like birds i' the cage.
When thou dost ask me blessing, I'll kneel
down 10
And ask of thee forgiveness. So we'll live,
And pray, and sing, and tell old tales, and laugh
At gilded butterflies,° and hear poor rogues
Talk of court news. And we'll talk with them too,
Who loses and who wins, who's in, who's out,
And take upon 's the mystery of things° 16
As if we were God's spies. And we'll wear out,
In a walled prison, packs and sects of great ones
That ebb and flow by the moon.°
EDMUND Take them away.
LEAR Upon such sacrifices, my Cordelia, 20
The gods themselves throw incense. Have I
caught thee?
He that parts us shall bring a brand° from
Heaven,
And fire us° hence like foxes. Wipe thine eyes.
The goodyears° shall devour them, flesh and fell,°
Ere they shall make us weep. We'll see 'em starve
first. 25
Come. [*Exeunt* LEAR *and* CORDELIA, *guarded.*]
EDMUND Come hither, captain, hark.
Take thou this note. Go follow them to prison.
One step I have advanced thee. If thou dost
As this instructs thee, thou dost make thy way
To noble fortunes. Know thou this, that men 30
Are as the time is.° To be tender-minded
Does not become a sword.° Thy great em-
ployment
Will not bear question.° Either say thou'lt do 't,
Or thrive by other means.
CAPTAIN I'll do 't, my lord.
EDMUND About it, and write happy° when thou
hast done. 35
Mark, I say, instantly, and carry it so
As I have set it down.
CAPTAIN I cannot draw a cart, nor eat dried oats.
If it be man's work, I'll do 't. [*Exit.*]

[*Flourish. Enter* ALBANY, GONERIL, REGAN, *another*
CAPTAIN, *and* SOLDIERS.]
ALBANY Sir, you have shown today your valiant
strain,° 40
And fortune led you well. You have the captives
That were the opposites° of this day's strife.
We do require them of you, so to use them
As we shall find their merits and our safety
May equally determine.
EDMUND Sir, I thought it fit 45
To send the old and miserable king
To some retention and appointed guard,°
Whose age has charms in it, whose title more,
To pluck the common bosom° on his side
And turn our impressed lances° in our eyes 50
Which do command them. With him I sent the
queen,
My reason all the same, and they are ready
Tomorrow or at further space to appear
Where you shall hold your session.° At this
time
We sweat and bleed. The friend hath lost his
friend, 55
And the best quarrels, in the heat, are cursed
By those that feel their sharpness.°
The question of Cordelia and her father
Requires a fitter place.
ALBANY Sir, by your patience,
I hold you but a subject° of this war, 60
Not as a brother.
REGAN That's as we list to grace him.
Methinks our pleasure might have been de-
manded
Ere you had spoke so far. He led our powers,
Bore the commission of my place and person,°
The which immediacy may well stand up 65
And call itself your brother.°
GONERIL Not so hot.
In his own grace he doth exalt himself
More than in your addition.°

---

13. **gilded butterflies:** i.e., court folk. 16. **take . . . things:**
pretend to understand deep secrets. 18–19. **packs . . .
moon:** parties at court whose fortunes change monthly. 22.
a brand: fire. 23. **fire us:** drive us out by fire. 24. **goodyears:**
The phrase "what the goodyear" meant "what the deuce";
hence "goodyear" means something vaguely evil. Lear is
talking baby talk—"The bogeymen shall have them." **fell:**
skin. 30–31. **men . . . is:** i.e., in brutal times men must be
brutes. 32. **sword:** soldier. 32–33. **Thy . . . question:** the
duty now laid on you is too important and brutal to be
argued about. 35. **happy:** fortunate.

40. **strain:** blood, courage. 42. **opposites:** opponents. 47.
retention . . . guard: where he can be kept and properly
guarded. 49. **common bosom:** the sympathies of our soldiers.
50. **impressed lances:** the soldiers we have conscripted. 54.
session: trial. 56–57. **And . . . sharpness:** i.e., with the battle
hardly over we are in no condition to judge this matter
calmly. 60. **subject:** i.e., not one who gives orders. 64. **commission . . . person:** commission appointing him commander as my deputy. 65–66. **The . . . brother:** since he is
my general, he is fit to be considered your equal. 68. **your
addition:** the title which you have given him. See I.i.138.

REGAN   In my rights,
By me invested, he compeers° the best.

GONERIL That were the most, if he should
husband you.   70

REGAN Jesters do oft prove prophets.

GONERIL   Holloa, holloa!
That eye that told you so looked but a-squint.

REGAN Lady, I am not well, else I should answer
From a full-flowing stomach.° General,
Take thou my soldiers, prisoners, patrimony, 75
Dispose of them, of me, the walls are thine.°
Witness the world that I create thee here
My lord and master.

GONERIL   Mean you to enjoy him?

ALBANY The let-alone° lies not in your goodwill.

EDMUND Nor in thine, lord.   80

ALBANY   Half-blooded fellow, yes.

REGAN [To EDMUND] Let the drum strike, and
prove my title thine.

ALBANY Stay yet, hear reason. Edmund, I arrest
thee
On capital treason,° and in thine attaint°
This gilded serpent. [Pointing to GONERIL.] For
your claim, fair sister,
I bar it in the interest of my wife.   85
'Tis she is subcontracted° to this lord,
And I, her husband, contradict your bans.°
If you will marry, make your loves to me.
My lady is bespoke.°

GONERIL   An interlude!°

ALBANY Thou art armed, Gloucester. Let the
trumpet sound.   90
If none appear to prove upon thy person
Thy heinous,° manifest, and many treasons,
There is my pledge. [Throwing down a glove.] I'll
prove it on thy heart
Ere I taste bread, thou art in nothing less
Than I have here proclaimed thee.

REGAN   Sick, oh, sick! 95

GONERIL [Aside] If not, I'll ne'er trust medicine.°

EDMUND [Throwing down a glove] There's my exchange. What in the world he is

That names me traitor, villainlike he lies.°
Call by thy trumpet. He that dares approach,
On him, on you—who not?—I will maintain 100
My truth and honor firmly.

ALBANY A herald, ho!

EDMUND   A herald, ho, a herald!

ALBANY Trust to thy single° virtue, for thy
soldiers,
All levied in my name, have in my name
Took their discharge.   105

REGAN   My sickness grows upon me.

ALBANY She is not well. Convey her to my tent.
                          [Exit REGAN, led.]
[Enter a HERALD.] Come hither, herald.—Let the
trumpet sound.—
And read out this.   108

CAPTAIN Sound trumpet!   [A trumpet sounds.]

HERALD [Reads] "If any man of quality or degree°
within the lists° of the army will maintain upon
Edmund, supposed earl of Gloucester, that he is
a manifold traitor, let him appear by the third
sound of the trumpet. He is bold in his defense."

EDMUND Sound!   [First trumpet.]

HERALD Again!   [Second trumpet.]
Again!   [Third trumpet.]
                   [Trumpet answers within.]
[Enter EDGAR at the third sound, armed, with a
trumpet before him.]

ALBANY Ask him his purposes, why he appears
Upon this call o' the trumpet.°   119

HERALD   What are you?
Your name, your quality? And why you answer
This present summons?

EDGAR   Know my name is lost,
By treason's tooth bare-gnawn and canker-bit.°
Yet am I noble as the adversary
I come to cope.°

ALBANY   Which is that adversary?

EDGAR What's he that speaks for Edmund, earl of
Gloucester?   125

EDMUND Himself. What say'st thou to him?

EDGAR   Draw thy sword,
That if my speech offend a noble heart,

---

69. **compeers:** equals. 74. **full-flowing stomach:** in full wrath.
76. **walls . . . thine:** i.e., you have won the outer defenses.
79. **let-alone:** power to prevent. 83. **capital treason:** treason
deserving death. **and . . . attaint:** and accused with you
(*attaint:* impeachment). 86. **subcontracted:** already betrothed.
87. **bans:** notice of intention to marry, read out in church
for three Sundays previous to the marriage. 89. **bespoke:**
already reserved. **An interlude:** i.e., this is mere play-
acting. 92. **heinous:** odious. 96. **medicine:** poison.

98. **villainlike . . . lies:** he lies like a villain. This is the lie
direct, which was a direct challenge to mortal combat.
103. **single:** solitary, unaided. 110. **quality or degree:** rank
or high position. 111. **lists:** roll call, roster. 118–19. **Ask
. . . trumpet:** The combat follows the normal procedure of
chivalry. Edgar is wearing full armor, his face concealed by
his closed helmet. 122. **canker-bit:** corrupted by maggots.
124. **cope:** meet, encounter.

Thy arm may do thee justice. Here is mine.
Behold, it is the privilege of mine honors,
My oath, and my profession.° I protest,   130
Mauger° thy strength, youth, place, and emi-
nence,
Despite thy victor sword and fire-new° fortune,
Thy valor and thy heart, thou art a traitor,
False to thy gods, thy brother, and thy father,
Conspirant° 'gainst this high illustrious prince,
And from the extremest upward of thy head 136
To the descent and dust below thy foot
A most toad-spotted° traitor. Say thou "No,"
This sword, this arm, and my best spirits are
bent
To prove upon thy heart, whereto I speak, 140
Thou liest.
EDMUND   In wisdom I should ask thy name,
But since thy outside looks so fair and warlike
And that thy tongue some say of breeding°
breathes,
What safe and nicely° I might well delay
By rule of knighthood I disdain and spurn. 145
Back do I toss these treasons to thy head,
With the hell-hated lie o'erwhelm thy heart,
Which for they yet glance by and scarcely bruise,
This sword of mine shall give them instant way
Where they shall rest forever. Trumpets, speak!
          [Alarums. They fight. EDMUND falls.]
ALBANY Save him, save him!   151
GONERIL   This is practice,° Gloucester.
By the law of arms thou wast not bound to
answer
An unknown opposite. Thou art not vanquished,
But cozened° and beguiled.
ALBANY   Shut your mouth, dame,
Or with this paper° shall I stop it. Hold, sir, 155
Thou worse than any name, read thine own evil.
No tearing, lady. I perceive you know it.
GONERIL Say if I do, the laws are mine, not thine.
Who can arraign me for 't?
ALBANY   Most monstrous!
Know'st thou this paper?   160
GONERIL   Ask me not what I know. [Exit.]

ALBANY Go after her. She's desperate, govern°
her.
EDMUND What you have charged me with, that
have I done,
And more, much more. The time will bring it out.
'Tis past, and so am I. But what art thou
That hast this fortune on me? If thou 'rt noble,
I do forgive thee.
EDGAR   Let's exchange charity.   166
I am no less in blood than thou art, Edmund.
If more, the more thou hast wronged me.
My name is Edgar, and thy father's son.
The gods are just, and of our pleasant vices 170
Make instruments to plague us.°
The dark and vicious place where thee he got°
Cost him his eyes.
EDMUND   Thou hast spoken right, 'tis true.
The wheel is come full circle,° I am here.   174
ALBANY Methought thy very gait did prophesy
A royal nobleness. I must embrace thee.
Let sorrow split my heart if ever I
Did hate thee or thy father!
EDGAR   Worthy prince, I know 't.
ALBANY Where have you hid yourself?
How have you known the miseries of your
father?   180
EDGAR By nursing them, my lord. List a brief tale,
And when 'tis told, oh, that my heart would
burst!
The bloody proclamation to escape°
That followed me so near—Oh, our lives'
sweetness!
That we the pain of death would hourly die 185
Rather than die at once!°—taught me to shift
Into a madman's rags, to assume a semblance
That very dogs disdained. And in this habit
Met I my father with his bleeding rings,   189
Their precious stones new-lost, became his guide,
Led him, begged for him, saved him from despair,
Never—oh, fault—revealed myself unto him
Until some half-hour past, when I was armed.
Not sure, though hoping, of this good success,
I asked his blessing, and from first to last   195

---

130. **profession:** i.e., as a knight. 131. **Mauger:** in spite of. 132. **fire-new:** brand-new—like a new coin. 135. **Conspirant:** conspiring. 138. **toad-spotted:** i.e., venomous as a toad. 143. **say of breeding:** accent of a gentleman. 144. **nicely:** i.e., if I stood on niceties of procedure. 151. **practice:** treachery. 154. **cozened:** cheated. 155. **this paper:** her love letter to Edmund, which Edgar had taken from Oswald's corpse. See IV.vi. 270–78.

161. **govern:** control. **170–71. of . . . us:** This is the answer to Gloucester's lighthearted words at the opening of the play—"Do you smell a fault?" (I.i.16). 172. **got:** begot. 174. **The . . . circle:** i.e., I end as I began—an outcast of fortune. 183. **The . . . escape:** in order to escape after the proclamation for my arrest. See II.iii.1. **184–86. Oh . . . once:** life is so sweet to us that we will endure the pains of death hourly if only we can live.

Told him my pilgrimage. But his flawed heart—
Alack, too weak the conflict to support!—
'Twixt two extremes of passion, joy and grief,
Burst smilingly,°

EDMUND   This speech of yours hath moved me,
And shall perchance do good. But speak you on.
You look as you had something more to say. 201

ALBANY   If there be more, more woeful, hold it in,
For I am almost ready to dissolve,
Hearing of this.

EDGAR   This would have seemed a period°
To such as love not sorrow, but another,   205
To amplify too much, would make much more,
And top extremity.°
Whilst I was big in clamor,° came there in a man
Who, having seen me in my worst estate,   209
Shunned my abhorred society. But then, finding
Who 'twas that so endured, with his strong arms
He fastened on my neck, and bellowed out
As he'd burst heaven, threw him on my father,
Told the most piteous tale of Lear and him
That ever ear received. Which in recounting 215
His grief grew puissant,° and the strings of life°
Began to crack. Twice then the trumpets sounded,
And there I left him tranced.°

ALBANY   But who was this?

EDGAR   Kent, sir, the banished Kent, who in
disguise
Followed his enemy king,° and did him service
Improper for a slave.   221

[Enter a GENTLEMAN, with a bloody knife.]

GENTLEMAN   Help, help, oh, help!

EDGAR   What kind of help?

ALBANY   Speak, man.

EDGAR   What means this bloody knife?

GENTLEMAN   'Tis hot, it smokes.
It came even from the heart of—oh, she's dead!

ALBANY   Who dead? Speak, man.   225

GENTLEMAN   Your lady, sir, your lady. And her
sister
By her is poisoned. She hath confessed it.

EDMUND   I was contracted° to them both. All three
Now marry in an instant.

196–99. But . . . smilingly: In the performance the significance of Edgar's speech can easily be missed. Gloucester has died from excessive emotion (passion), and Kent is near his end. 204. period: end. 207. top extremity: exceed the extreme limit of what could be endured. 208. clamor: grief. 216. puissant: powerful, overwhelming. strings of life: heartstrings. 218. tranced: in a faint. 220. enemy king: the king who had declared him an enemy. 228. contracted: betrothed.

EDGAR   Here comes Kent. 229

ALBANY   Produce the bodies, be they alive or
dead.   [Exit GENTLEMAN.]
This judgment of the Heavens, that makes us
tremble,
Touches us not with pity.
                    [Enter KENT.] Oh, is this he?
The time will not allow the compliment
Which very manners urges.

KENT   I am come
To bid my king and master aye good night. 235
Is he not here?

ALBANY   Great thing of us forgot!
Speak, Edmund, where's the king? And where's
Cordelia?
See's thou this object, Kent?

[The bodies of GONERIL and REGAN are brought in.]

KENT   Alack, why thus?

EDMUND   Yet Edmund was beloved.°
The one the other poisoned for my sake,   240
And after slew herself.

ALBANY   Even so. Cover their faces.

EDMUND   I pant for life. Some good I mean to do,
Despite of mine own nature. Quickly send—
Be brief in it—to the castle, for my writ   245
Is on the life of Lear and on Cordelia.
Nay, send in time.

ALBANY   Run, run, oh, run!

EDGAR   To who, my lord? Who hath the office?
Send
Thy token of reprieve.°

EDMUND   Well thought on. Take my sword.   250
Give it the captain.

ALBANY   Haste thee, for thy life. [Exit EDGAR.]

EDMUND   He hath commission from thy wife and me
To hang Cordelia in the prison and
To lay the blame upon her own despair,
That she fordid° herself.   255

ALBANY   The gods defend her! Bear him hence
awhile.   [EDMUND is borne off.]

[Reenter LEAR, with CORDELIA dead in his arms,
EDGAR, CAPTAIN, and others following.]

LEAR   Howl, howl, howl, howl! Oh, you are men
of stones.
Had I your tongues and eyes, I'd use them so
That heaven's vault should crack. She's gone
forever!

239. Yet . . . beloved: The bastard's last grim triumph—two women died for his love. 249. token of reprieve: sign that they are reprieved. 255. fordid: destroyed.

I know when one is dead and when one lives. 260
  She's dead as earth. Lend me a looking-glass.
  If that her breath will mist or stain the stone,°
  Why, then she lives.
KENT   Is this the promised end?°
EDGAR Or image of that horror?
ALBANY   Fall and cease.°
LEAR This feather stirs, she lives. If it be so, 265
  It is a chance which does redeem all sorrows
  That ever I have felt.
KENT   [*Kneeling*] Oh, my good master!
LEAR Prithee, away.
EDGAR   'Tis noble Kent, your friend.
LEAR A plague upon you, murderers, traitors all!
  I might have saved her. Now she's gone forever!
  Cordelia, Cordelia! Stay a little. Ha! 271
  What is 't thou say'st? Her voice was ever soft,
  Gentle and low, an excellent thing in woman.
  I killed the slave that was a-hanging thee.
CAPTAIN 'Tis true, my lords, he did. 275
LEAR   Did I not, fellow?
  I have seen the day with my good biting falchion°
  I would have made them skip. I am old now,
  And these same crosses° spoil me. Who are you?
  Mine eyes are not o' the best, I'll tell you
    straight.
KENT If fortune brag of two she loved and
    hated, 280
  One of them we behold.
LEAR This is a dull sight. Are you not Kent?
KENT   The same,
  Your servant Kent. Where is your servant Caius?
LEAR He's a good fellow, I can tell you that.
  He'll strike, and quickly too. He's dead and
    rotten. 285
KENT No, my good lord, I am the very man°—
LEAR I'll see that straight.
KENT That from your first of difference° and decay
  Have followed your sad steps.
LEAR   You are welcome hither.
KENT Nor no man else. All's cheerless, dark, and
    deadly. 290
  Your eldest daughters have fordone themselves,
  And desperately are dead.
LEAR   Aye, so I think.

ALBANY He knows not what he says, and vain is it
  That we present us to him.
EDGAR   Very bootless.°
             [*Enter a* CAPTAIN.]
CAPTAIN Edmund is dead, my lord. 295
ALBANY   That's but a trifle here.
  You lords and noble friends, know our intent.
  What comfort to this great decay° may come
  Shall be applied. For us, we will resign,
  During the life of this old majesty,
  To him our absolute power. 300
      [*To* EDGAR *and* KENT] You, to your rights,
  With boot,° and such addition as your honors
  Have more than merited. All friends shall taste
  The wages of their virtue, and all foes
  The cup of their deservings. Oh, see, see!°
LEAR And my poor fool° is hanged! No, no, no life!
  Why should a dog, a horse, a rat, have life 306
  And thou no breath at all? Thou'lt come no more,
  Never, never, never, never, never!
  Pray you, undo this button.° Thank you sir. 309
  Do you see this? Look on her, look, her lips,
  Look there, look there!   [*Dies.*]
EDGAR   He faints. My lord, my lord!
KENT Break, heart, I prithee break!
EDGAR   Look up, my lord.
KENT Vex not his ghost. Oh, let him pass! He
    hates him
  That would upon the rack of this tough world
  Stretch him out longer.
EDGAR   He is gone indeed. 315
KENT The wonder is he hath endured so long.
  He but usurped his life.
ALBANY Bear them from hence. Our present
    business
  Is general woe. [*To* KENT *and* EDGAR] Friends of
    my soul, you twain
  Rule in this realm and the gored state sustain.
KENT I have a journey, sir, shortly to go. 321
  My master calls me,° I must not say no.
ALBANY The weight of this sad time we must obey,
  Speak what we feel, not what we ought to say.
  The oldest hath borne most. We that are young
  Shall never see so much, nor live so long. 326
         [*Exeunt, with a dead march.*]

---

262. stone: glass. **263. the . . . end:** i.e., Doomsday. **264. Fall . . . cease:** i.e., let Doomsday come and the world end. **276. falchion:** curved sword. **278. crosses:** troubles. **283–86. Your . . . man:** This is the first and only mention of a Caius, which was apparently the name assumed by Kent in his disguise. **288. difference:** changed state.

294. bootless: useless. **297. decay:** i.e., Lear. **301. boot:** advantage. **304. Oh . . . see:** There is a sudden change in Lear. **305. fool:** Cordelia; *fool* is often used as a term of affection. **309. Pray . . . button:** For the last time Lear is oppressed by the violent beating of his heart before it is stilled forever. **322. calls me:** i.e., to follow him into the darkness.

JOHN MILTON
1608–1674

Samson Agonistes°

THE ARGUMENT

Samson, made captive, blind, and now in the prison at Gaza,[1] there to labor as in a common workhouse, on a festival day, in the general cessation from labor, comes forth into the open air, to a place nigh, somewhat retired, there to sit a while and bemoan his condition. Where he happens at length to be visited by certain friends and equals of his tribe, which make the chorus, who seek to comfort him what they can; then by his old father, Manoa, who endeavors the like, and withal tells him his purpose to procure his liberty by ransom; lastly, that this feast was proclaimed by the Philistines[2] as a day of thanksgiving for their deliverance from the hands of Samson—which yet more troubles him. Manoa then departs to prosecute his endeavor with the Philistian lords for Samson's redemption: who, in the meanwhile, is visited by other persons, and, lastly, by a public officer to require his coming to the feast before the lords and people, to play or show his strength in their presence. He at first refuses, dismissing the public officer with absolute denial to come; at length, persuaded inwardly that this was from God, he yields to go along with him, who came now the second time with great threatenings to fetch him. The chorus yet remaining on the place, Manoa returns full of joyful hope to procure ere long his son's deliverance; in the midst of which discourse an Hebrew comes in haste, confusedly at first, and afterwards more distinctly, relating the catastrophe—what Samson had done to the Philistines, and by accident to himself; wherewith the tragedy ends.

THE PERSONS

SAMSON

MANOA, *the father of Samson*

DALILA, *his wife*

HARAPHA *of Gath*

PUBLIC OFFICER

MESSENGER

CHORUS OF DANITES[3]

THE SCENE—*Before the Prison in Gaza.*

SAMSON A little onward lend thy guiding hand
　　To these dark steps, a little further on;
　　For yonder bank hath choice of sun or shade.
　　There I am wont to sit, when any chance
　　Relieves me from my task of servile toil,　　5
　　Daily in the common prison else enjoined me,
　　Where I, as prisoner chained, scarce freely draw
　　The air, imprisoned also, close and damp,
　　Unwholesome draft. But here I feel amends—
　　The breath of Heaven fresh blowing, pure and
　　　　sweet,　　10
　　With day-spring° born; here leave me to respire.
　　This day a solemn feast the people hold
　　To Dagon their sea-idol, and forbid
　　Laborious works. Unwillingly this rest
　　Their superstition yields me; hence, with leave 15
　　Retiring from the popular noise, I seek
　　This unfrequented place to find some ease—
　　Ease to the body some, none to the mind
　　From restless thoughts, that, like a deadly swarm
　　Of hornets armed, no sooner found alone,　　20
　　But rush upon me thronging, and present
　　Times past, what once I was, and what am now.
　　O, wherefore was my birth from Heaven
　　　　foretold
　　Twice by an angel, who at last, in sight
　　Of both my parents, all in flames ascended　　25
　　From off the altar where an offering burned,
　　As in a fiery column charioting
　　His godlike presence, and from some great act
　　Or benefit revealed to Abraham's race?
　　Why was my breeding ordered and prescribed 30
　　As of a person separate to God,°
　　Designed for great exploits, if I must die
　　Betrayed, captived, and both my eyes put out,
　　Made of my enemies the scorn and gaze,
　　To grind in brazen fetters under task　　35
　　With this Heaven-gifted strength? O glorious
　　　　strength,
　　Put to the labor of a beast, debased

SAMSON AGONISTES. See Judges 13–16 for the source of the narrative. **1. Gaza:** important Philistine city. **2. Philistines:** enemies of the Israelites.

3. Danites: members of Samson's tribe. **11. day-spring:** daybreak. **31. separate to God:** as a Nazarite, one dedicated to God.

Lower than bondslave! Promise was that I
Should Israel from Philistian yoke deliver!
Ask for this great deliverer now, and find him 40
Eyeless in Gaza, at the mill with slaves,
Himself in bonds under Philistian yoke;
Yet stay, let me not rashly call in doubt
Divine prediction. What if all foretold
Had been fulfilled but through mine own
    default? 45
Whom have I to complain of but myself?
Who this high gift of strength committed to me,
In what part lodged, how easily bereft me,
Under the seal of silence could not keep,
But weakly to a woman must reveal it, 50
O'ercome with importunity and tears.
O impotence of mind in body strong!
But what is strength without a double share
Of wisdom? Vast, unwieldy, burdensome,
Proudly secure, yet liable to fall 55
By weakest subtleties; not made to rule,
But to subserve where wisdom bears command.
God, when he gave me strength, to show withal
How slight the gift was, hung it in my hair.
But peace! I must not quarrel with the will 60
Of highest dispensation, which herein
Haply had ends above my reach to know.
Suffices that to me strength is my bane,
And proves the source of all my miseries;
So many, and so huge, that each apart 65
Would ask a life to wail. But, chief of all,
O loss of sight, of thee I most complain!
Blind among enemies! O worse than chains,
Dungeon, or beggary, or decrepit age!
Light, the prime work of God, to me is extinct, 70
And all her various objects of delight
Annulled, which might in part my grief have
    eased.
Inferior to the vilest now become
Of man or worm, the vilest here excel me:
They creep, yet see; I, dark in light, exposed 75
To daily fraud, contempt, abuse, and wrong,
Within doors, or without, still° as a fool,
In power of others, never in my own;
Scarce half I seem to live, dead more than half.
O dark, dark, dark, amid the blaze of noon, 80
Irrecoverably dark, total eclipse
Without all hope of day!
O first-created beam, and thou great Word,°

"Let there be light, and light was over all,"°
Why am I thus bereaved thy prime decree?° 85
The Sun to me is dark
And silent as the Moon,
When she deserts the night,
Hid in her vacant interlunar cave.°
Since light so necessary is to life, 90
And almost life itself, if it be true
That light is in the soul,
She all in every part, why was the sight
To such a tender ball as the eye confined,
So obvious and so easy to be quenched, 95
And not, as feeling, through all parts diffused,
That she might look at will through every pore?
Then had I not been thus exiled from light,
As in the land of darkness, yet in light,
To live a life half dead, a living death, 100
And buried; but, O yet more miserable!
Myself my sepulcher, a moving grave;
Buried, yet not exempt,
By privilege of death and burial,
From worst of other evils, pains, and wrongs; 105
But made hereby obnoxious° more
To all the miseries of life,
Life in captivity
Among inhuman foes.
But who are these? for with joint pace I hear 110
The tread of many feet steering this way;
Perhaps my enemies, who come to stare
At my affliction, and perhaps to insult;
Their daily practice to afflict me more.
CHORUS This, this is he; softly a while; 115
    Let us not break in upon him.
    O change beyond report, thought, or belief!
    See how he lies at random, carelessly diffused,°
    With languished head unpropped,
    As one past hope, abandoned, 120
    And by himself given over,
    In slavish habit,° ill-fitted weeds°
    O'er-worn and soiled.
    Or do my eyes misrepresent? Can this be he,
    That heroic, that renowned, 125
    Irresistible Samson? whom, unarmed,
    No strength of man, or fiercest wild beast, could
        withstand;
    Who tore the lion as the lion tears the kid;

---

77. **still:** always. **83. Word:** See John 1:1.

84. **Let . . . all:** Cf. Genesis 1:3. **85. prime decree:** light (God's first decree). **88–89. When . . . cave:** at new moon. **106. obnoxious:** exposed. **118. diffused:** sprawled. **122. habit:** dress. **weeds:** clothes.

Ran on embattled armies clad in iron,
And, weaponless himself,   130
Made arms ridiculous, useless the forgery°
Of brazen shield and spear, the hammered
     cuirass,
Chalybean-tempered° steel, and frock of mail
Adamantean proof:°
But safest he who stood aloof,   135
When insupportably° his foot advanced,
In scorn of their proud arms and warlike tools,
Spurned them to death by troops. The bold
     Ascalonite°
Fled from his lion ramp; old warriors turned
Their plated backs under his heel,   140
Or groveling soiled their crested helmets in the
     dust.
Then with what trivial weapon came to hand,
The jaw of a dead ass, his sword of bone,
A thousand foreskins fell, the flower of Palestine,
In Ramath-lechi,° famous to this day: 145
Then by main force pulled up, and on his
     shoulders bore,
The gates of Azza,° post and massy bar,
Up to the hill by Hebron, seat of giants old,
No journey of a sabbath-day, and loaded so;
Like whom the Gentiles feign to bear up
     Heaven.°   150
Which shall I first bewail,
Thy bondage or lost sight,
Prison within prison
Inseparably dark?
Thou art become (O worst imprisonment!)   155
The dungeon of thyself; thy soul
(Which men enjoying sight oft without cause
     complain)
Imprisoned now indeed,
In real darkness of the body dwells,
Shut up from outward light   160
To incorporate with gloomy night;
For inward light, alas!
Puts forth no visual beam.
O mirror of our fickle state,
Since man on earth, unparalleled,   165

The rarer thy example stands,
By how much from the top of wondrous glory,
Strongest of mortal men,
To lowest pitch of abject fortune thou are fallen.
For him I reckon not in high estate   170
Whom long descent of birth,
Or the sphere of fortune,° raises;
But thee, whose strength, while virtue was her
     mate,
Might have subdued the earth,
Universally crowned with highest praises.   175

SAMSON   I hear the sound of words; their sense the
     air
Dissolves unjointed ere it reach my ear.

CHORUS   He speaks: let us draw nigh. Matchless in
     might,
The glory late of Israel, now the grief!
We come, thy friends and neighbors not un-
     known,   180
From Eshtaol and Zora's° fruitful vale,
To visit or bewail thee; or, if better,
Counsel or consolation we may bring,
Salve to thy sores: apt words have power to
     swage°
The tumors of a troubled mind,   185
And are as balm to festered wounds.

SAMSON   Your coming, friends, revives me; for I
     learn
Now of my own experience, not by talk,
How counterfeit a coin they are who "friends"
Bear in their superscription (of the most   190
I would be understood). In prosperous days
They swarm, but in adverse withdraw their head,
Not to be found, though sought. Ye see, O
     friends,
How many evils have enclosed me round;
Yet that which was the worst now least afflicts
     me,   195
Blindness; for, had I sight, confused with shame,
How could I once look up, or heave° the head,
Who, like a foolish pilot, have shipwracked
My vessel trusted to me from above,
Gloriously rigged, and for a word, a tear,   200
Fool! have divulged the secret gift of God
To a deceitful woman? Tell me, friends,
Am I not sung and proverbed for a fool
In every street? Do they not say, "How well

131. forgery: forging. 133. Chalybean-tempered: tempered
by a people in Asia Minor who were famous as metalsmiths.
134. Adamantean proof: harder than the legendary mineral
adamant. 136. insupportably: irresistibly. 138. Ascalonite:
citizen of Askalon, a Philistine city raided by Samson. 145.
Ramath-lechi: the place where Samson killed a thousand of
his enemies with the jawbone of an ass (see Judges 15:17).
147. Azza: Gaza. 150. Like . . . Heaven: Atlas.

172. sphere of fortune: wheel of fortune. 181. Eshtaol and
Zora: towns of the Danites. 184. swage: assuage. 197.
heave: lift up.

Are come upon him his deserts"? Yet why? 205
Immeasurable strength they might behold
In me; of wisdom nothing more than mean.
This with the other should at least have paired;
These two, proportioned ill, drove me transverse.°
CHORUS Tax not divine disposal. Wisest men 210
Have erred, and by bad women been deceived;
And shall again, pretend they ne'er so wise.
Deject not, then, so overmuch thyself,
Who hast of sorrow thy full load besides.
Yet, truth to say, I oft have heard men wonder 215
Why thou should'st wed Philistian women
        rather
Than of thine own tribe fairer, or as fair,
At least of thy own nation, and as noble.
SAMSON   The first I saw at Timna,° and she pleased
Me, not my parents, that I sought to wed   220
The daughter of an infidel. They knew not
That what I motioned was of God; I knew
From intimate° impulse, and therefore urged
The marriage on, that, by occasion hence,
I might begin Israel's deliverance,   225
The work to which I was divinely called;
She proving false, the next I took to wife
(O that I never had! fond wish too late)
Was in the vale of Sorec, Dalila,
That specious monster, my accomplished
        snare.   230
I thought it lawful° from my former act,
And the same end, still watching to oppress
Israel's oppressors. Of what now I suffer
She was not the prime cause, but I myself,
Who, vanquished with a peal of words, (O
        weakness!)   235
Gave up my fort of silence to a woman.
CHORUS   In seeking just occasion to provoke
The Philistine, thy country's enemy,
Thou never wast remiss, I bear thee witness:
Yet Israel still serves° with all his sons.   240
SAMSON   That fault I take not on me, but transfer
On Israel's governors and heads of tribes,
Who, seeing those great acts which God had
        done
Singly by me against their conquerors,
Acknowledged not, or not at all considered,° 245

Deliverance offered. I, on the other side,
Used no ambition to commend my deeds;
The deeds themselves, though mute, spoke loud
        the doer.°
But they persisted deaf, and would not seem
To count them things worth notice, till at
        length   250
Their lords, the Philistines, with gathered
        powers,
Entered Judea, seeking me, who then
Safe to the rock of Etham was retired;
Not flying, but forecasting in what place
To set upon them, what advantaged best.   255
Meanwhile the men of Judah, to prevent
The harass of their land, beset me round;
I willingly on some conditions came
Into their hands, and they as gladly yield me
To the uncircumcised a welcome prey,   260
Bound with two cords. But cords to me were
        threads
Touched with the flame: on their whole host I
        flew
Unarmed, and with a trivial weapon felled
Their choicest youth;° they only lived who fled.
Had Judah that day joined, or one whole
        tribe,   265
They had by this possessed the towers of Gath,°
And lorded over them whom now they serve.
But what more oft, in nations grown corrupt,
And by their vices brought to servitude,
Than to love bondage more than liberty,   270
Bondage with ease than strenuous liberty;
And to despise, or envy, or suspect,
Whom God hath of his special favor raised
As their deliverer? If he aught begin,
How frequent to desert him, and at last   275
To heap ingratitude on worthiest deeds!
CHORUS   Thy words to my remembrance bring
How Succoth and the fort of Penuel
Their great deliverer contemned,
The matchless Gideon, in pursuit   280
Of Madian, and her vanquished kings:°
And how ingrateful Ephraim
Had dealt with Jephtha, who by argument,

---

209. transverse: astray. **219. Timna:** Philistine city. **223. intimate:** inward. **231. lawful:** by the precedent of his former marriage and because of the political objective. **240. serves:** is in subjection to the Philistines. **245. considered:** valued.

248. doer: God, acting through Samson's strength. **262–64. Bound . . . youth:** Cf. ll. 142–45. **266. Gath:** one of the five principal Philistine cities, here used as a synecdoche for the whole country. **278–81. How . . . kings:** When Gideon pursued the kings of Madian, men from the cities of Succoth and Penuel refused to help him (see Judges 8:4–9).

Not worse than by his shield and spear,
Defended Israel from the Ammonite,   285
Had not his prowess quelled their pride
In that sore battle when so many died
Without reprieve, adjudged to death
For want of well pronouncing *Shibboleth.*°
SAMSON   Of such examples add me to the roll. 290
Me easily indeed mine may neglect,
But God's proposed deliverance not so.
CHORUS   Just are the ways of God,
And justifiable to men,
Unless there be who think not God at all.   295
If any be, they walk obscure;
For of such doctrine never was there school,
But the heart of the fool,°
And no man therein doctor° but himself.
Yet more there be who doubt his ways not just, 300
As to his own edicts found contradicting,
Then give the reins to wandering thought,
Regardless of his glory's diminution,
Till, by their own perplexities involved,
They ravel° more, still less resolved,   305
But never find self-satisfying solution.
     As if they would confine the Interminable,°
And tie him to his own prescript,
Who made our laws to bind us, not himself,
And hath full right to exempt   310
Whomso it pleases him by choice
From national obstriction° without taint
Of sin, or legal debt;
For with his own laws he can best dispense.
     He   would   not   else,   who   never   wanted
          means,   315
Nor in respect of the enemy just cause,
To set his people free,
Have prompted this heroic Nazarite,
Against his vow of strictest purity,°
To seek in marriage that fallacious bride,   320
Unclean,° unchaste.
     Down, Reason, then; at least, vain reasonings
          down;

Though Reason here aver
That moral verdict quits her of unclean:
Unchaste was subsequent; her stain, not his. 325
     But see! here comes thy reverend sire,
With careful° step, locks white as down,
Old Manoa: advise°
Forthwith how thou ought'st to receive him.
SAMSON   Ay me, another inward grief, awaked 330
With mention of that name, renews the assault,
MANOA   Brethren and men of Dan, for such ye
     seem
Though in this uncouth° place; if old respect,
As I suppose, towards your once gloried friend,
My son, now captive, hither hath informed 335
Your younger feet, while mine, cast back with
     age,
Came lagging after, say if he be here.
CHORUS   As signal° now in low dejected state
As erst in highest, behold him where he lies.
MANOA   O miserable change! Is this the man, 340
That invincible Samson, far renowned,
The dread of Israel's foes, who with a strength
Equivalent to angels' walked their streets,
None offering fight; who, single combatant,
Dueled their armies ranked in proud array, 345
Himself an army, now unequal match
To save himself against a coward armed
At one spear's length? O ever-failing trust
In mortal strength! and, oh, what not in man
Deceivable and vain? Nay, what thing good 350
Prayed for, but often proves our woe, our bane?
I prayed for children, and thought barrenness
In wedlock a reproach; I gained a son,
And such a son as° all men hailed me happy:
Who would be now a father in my stead?   355
O, wherefore did God grant me my request,
And as a blessing with such pomp adorned?
Why are his gifts desirable, to tempt
Our earnest prayers, then, given with solemn
     hand
As graces, draw a scorpion's tail behind?   360
For this did the angel twice descend? for this
Ordained thy nurture holy, as of a plant
Select and sacred? glorious for a while,
The miracle of men; then in an hour
Ensnared, assaulted, overcome, led bound,   365
Thy foes' derision, captive, poor, and blind,

282–89. And . . . Shibboleth: In Jephthah's quarrels with
the Gileadite Hebrews, who refused to support him against
the Ammonites, pronunciation of the word *Shibboleth* was
used to distinguish friend from enemy (see Judges 12:1–6).
296–98. If . . . fool: Cf. Psalms 14:1: "The fool hath said
in his heart, There is no God." **299. doctor:** teacher. **305.
ravel:** confuse themselves. **307. Interminable:** infinite (i.e.,
God). **312. national obstriction:** prohibition in Mosaic law
against marriage with Gentiles. **319. strictest purity:** not
celibacy but exact obedience of the Law. **321. unclean:**
technically, because Dalila was a Gentile.

327. careful: full of care. **328. advise:** consider. **332.
men of Dan:** tribe of Samson and Manoa. **333. uncouth:**
unknown. **338. signal:** striking. **354. as:** that.

Into a dungeon thrust, to work with slaves?
Alas! methinks whom God hath chosen once
To worthiest deeds, if he through frailty err,
He should not so o'erwhelm, and as a thrall 370
Subject him to so foul indignities,
Be it but for honor's sake of former deeds.

SAMSON   Appoint not heavenly disposition, father.
Nothing of all these evils hath befallen me
But justly; I myself have brought them on, 375
Sole author I, sole cause. If aught seem vile,
As vile hath been my folly, who have profaned
The mystery of God, given me under pledge
Of vow, and have betrayed it to a woman,
A Canaanite,° my faithless enemy.   380
This well I knew, nor was at all surprised,
But warned by oft experience. Did not she
Of Timna first betray me, and reveal
The secret wrested from me in her highth
Of nuptial love professed, carrying it straight 385
To them who had corrupted her, my spies
And rivals?° In this other was there found
More faith, who, also in her prime of love,
Spousal embraces, vitiated with gold,
Though offered only, by the scent° conceived 390
Her spurious firstborn, treason against me?
Thrice she assayed, with flattering prayers and
      sighs,
And amorous reproaches, to win from me
My capital secret,° in what part my strength
Lay stored, in what part summed, that she might
      know: 395
Thrice I deluded her, and turned to sport
Her importunity, each time perceiving
How openly and with what impudence
She purposed to betray me, and (which was
      worse
Than undissembled hate) with what contempt 400
She sought to make me traitor to myself.
Yet, the fourth time, when mustering all her
      wiles,
With blandished parleys, feminine assaults,
Tongue-batteries, she surceased not day nor
      night
To storm me, overwatched° and wearied out, 405
At times when men seek most repose and rest,
I yielded, and unlocked her all my heart,

Who, with a grain of manhood well resolved,
Might easily have shook off all her snares:
But foul effeminacy held me yoked   410
Her bondslave; O indignity, O blot
To honor and religion! servile mind
Rewarded well with servile punishment!
The base degree to which I now am fallen,
These rags, this grinding, is not yet so base 415
As was my former servitude, ignoble,
Unmanly, ignominious, infamous,
True slavery, and that blindness worse than this,
That saw not how degenerately I served.

MANOA   I cannot praise thy marriage-choices,
      son,   420
Rather approved them not; but thou didst plead
Divine impulsion prompting how thou might'st
Find some occasion to infest° our foes.
I state° not that; this I am sure; our foes
Found soon occasion thereby to make thee 425
Their captive, and their triumph; thou the
      sooner
Temptation found'st, or over-potent charms,
To violate the sacred trust of silence
Deposited within thee; which to have kept
Tacit was in thy power; true; and thou bear'st 430
Enough, and more, the burden of that fault;
Bitterly hast thou paid, and still art paying,
That rigid score. A worse thing yet remains:
This day the Philistines a popular feast
Here celebrate in Gaza, and proclaim   435
Great pomp, and sacrifice, and praises loud,
To Dagon, as their god who hath delivered
Thee, Samson, bound and blind, into their
      hands,
Them out of thine, who slew'st them many a slain.
So Dagon shall be magnified, and God,   440
Besides whom is no god, compared with idols,
Disglorified, blasphemed, and had in scorn
By the idolatrous rout amidst their wine;
Which to have come to pass by means of thee,
Samson, of all thy sufferings think the
      heaviest,   445
Of all reproach the most with shame that ever
Could have befallen thee and thy father's house.

SAMSON   Father, I do acknowledge and confess
That I this honor, I this pomp, have brought
To Dagon, and advanced his praises high   450
Among the heathen round; to God have
      brought

---

380. Canaanite: Philistine living in Canaan. **383–87. Of
. . . rivals:** For the story of this betrayal, a parallel to
Dalila's, see Judges 14:11–18. **390. scent:** of gold. **394.
capital secret:** important secret kept in the head. **405. over-
watched:** tired from being kept awake.

423. infest: annoy. **424. state:** make a statement about.

Dishonor, obloquy, and oped the mouths
Of idolists and atheists; have brought scandal
To Israel, diffidence° of God, and doubt
In feeble hearts, propense° enough before   455
To waver, or fall off and join with idols:
Which is my chief affliction, shame and sorrow,
The anguish of my soul, that suffers not
Mine eye to harbor sleep, or thoughts to rest.
This only hope relieves me, that the strife   460
With me hath end; all the contest is now
'Twixt God and Dagon; Dagon hath presumed,
Me overthrown,° to enter lists with God,
His deity comparing and preferring
Before the God of Abraham. He, be sure,   465
Will not connive,° or linger, thus provoked,
But will arise, and his great name assert.
Dagon must stoop, and shall ere long receive
Such a discomfit° as shall quite despoil him
Of all these boasted trophies won on me,   470
And with confusion blank° his worshipers.

MANOA With cause this hope relieves thee; and
    these words
I as a prophecy receive: for God,
Nothing more certain will not long defer
To vindicate the glory of his name   475
Against all competition, nor will long
Endure it doubtful whether God be Lord
Or Dagon. But for thee what shall be done?
Thou must not in the meanwhile, here forgot,
Lie in this miserable loathsome plight   480
Neglected. I already have made way
To some Philistian lords, with whom to treat
About thy ransom: well they may by this
Have satisfied their utmost of revenge,
By pains and slaveries, worse than death,
    inflicted   485
On thee, who now no more canst do them harm.

SAMSON Spare that proposal, father, spare the
    trouble
Of that solicitation; let me here,
As I deserve, pay on my punishment,
And expiate, if possible, my crime,   490
Shameful garrulity. To have revealed
Secrets of men, the secrets of a friend,
How heinous had the fact° been, how deserving
Contempt and scorn of all, to be excluded
All friendship, and avoided as a blab,   495

The mark of fool set on his front! But I
God's counsel have not kept, his holy secret
Presumptuously have published, impiously,
Weakly at least and shamefully: A sin
That Gentiles in their parables condemn   500
To their abyss and horrid pains confined.°

MANOA Be penitent, and for thy fault contrite;
But act not in thy own affliction, son;
Repent the sin; but, if the punishment
Thou canst avoid, self-preservation bids;   505
Or the execution leave to high disposal,
And let another hand, not thine, exact
Thy penal forfeit from thyself; perhaps
God will relent, and quit thee all his debt;
Who evermore approves and more accepts   510
(Best pleased with humble and filial submission)
Him who, imploring mercy, sues for life,
Than who, self-rigorous, chooses death as due;
Which argues over-just, and self-displeased
For self-offense more than for God offended.° 515
Reject not, then, what offered means° who
    knows
But God hath set before us to return thee
Home to thy country and his sacred house,
Where thou may'st bring thy offerings, to avert
His further ire, with prayers and vows
    renewed.   520

SAMSON His pardon I implore; but, as for life,
To what end should I seek it? When in strength
All mortals I excelled, and great in hopes,
With youthful courage, and magnanimous
    thoughts
Of birth from Heaven foretold and high
    exploits,   525
Full of divine instinct, after some proof
Of acts indeed heroic, far beyond
The sons of Anak,° famous now and blazed,
Fearless of danger, like a petty god
I walked about, admired of all, and dreaded 530
On hostile ground, none daring my affront.°
Then, swollen with pride, into the snare I fell
Of fair fallacious looks, venereal trains,°
Softened with pleasure and voluptuous life,
At length to lay my head and hallowed pledge 535

---

454. **diffidence:** distrust. 455. **propense:** inclined. 463. **Me overthrown:** having overthrown me. 466. **connive:** ignore. 469. **discomfit:** defeat. 471. **blank:** confound. 493. **fact:** deed.

499–501. **A . . . confined:** Tantalus suffered in Hades for failing to keep the gods' secrets. 514–15. **Which . . . offended:** motivated by excessive pride rather than by submission to the will of God. 516. **offered means:** the means available, which may represent God's providence. 528. **sons of Anak:** giants (see Numbers 13:33). 531. **my affront:** to confront me. 533. **venereal trains:** sexual passion.

Of all my strength in the lascivious lap
Of a deceitful concubine, who shore me,°
Like a tame wether, all my precious fleece,
Then turned me out ridiculous, despoiled,
Shaven, and disarmed among my enemies.   540
CHORUS   Desire of wine and all delicious drinks,
Which many a famous warrior overturns,
Thou could'st repress; nor did the dancing ruby,
Sparkling out-poured, the flavor, or the smell,
Or taste that cheers the heart of gods and
    men,   545
Allure thee from the cool crystálline stream.
SAMSON   Wherever fountain or fresh current
    flowed
Against the eastern ray, translucent, pure
With touch ethereal of Heaven's fiery rod,°
I drank, from the clear milky juice allaying 550
Thirst, and refreshed; nor envied them the grape
Whose heads that turbulent liquor fills with
    fumes.
CHORUS   O madness, to think use of strongest
    wines
And strongest drinks our chief support of
    health,
When God with these forbidden made choice to
    rear   555
His mighty champion, strong above compare,
Whose drink was only from the liquid brook.
SAMSON   But what availed this temperance, not
    complete
Against another object more enticing?
What boots it° at one gate to make defense, 560
And at another to let in the foe,
Effeminately vanquished? by which means,
Now blind, disheartened, shamed, dishonored,
    quelled,
To what can I be useful? wherein serve
My nation, and the work from Heaven im-
    posed,   565
But to sit idle on the household hearth,
A burdenous drone; to visitants a gaze,
Or pitied object; these redundant° locks,
Robustious to no purpose, clustering down,
Vain monument of strength; till length of
    years   570
And sedentary numbness craze my limbs
To a contemptible old age obscure.
Here rather let me drudge, and earn my bread,

Till vermin, or the draff° of servile food,
Consume me, and oft-invocated death   575
Hasten the welcome end of all my pains.
MANOA   Wilt thou then serve the Philistines with
    that gift
Which was expressly given thee to annoy them?
Better at home lie bed-rid, not only idle,
Inglorious, unemployed, with age out-worn. 580
But God who caused a fountain at thy prayer
From the dry ground to spring, thy thirst to
    allay
After the brunt of battle, can as easy
Cause light again within thy eyes to spring,
Wherewith to serve him better than thou
    hast.   585
And I persuade me so; why else this strength
Miraculous yet remaining in those locks?
His might continues in thee not for naught,
Nor shall his wondrous gifts be frustrate thus.
SAMSON   All otherwise to me my thoughts por-
    tend,   590
That these dark orbs no more shall treat with
    light,
Nor the other light of life continue long,
But yield to double darkness° nigh at hand:
So much I feel my genial spirits droop,
My hopes all flat, nature within me seems 595
In all her functions weary of herself;
My race of glory run, and race of shame,
And I shall shortly be with them that rest.
MANOA   Believe not these suggestions, which
    proceed
From anguish of the mind, and humors black 600
That mingle with thy fancy. I, however,
Must not omit a father's timely care
To prosecute the means of thy deliverance
By ransom or how else: meanwhile be calm,
And healing words from these thy friends
    admit.   605
SAMSON   Oh, that torment should not be confined
To the body's wounds and sores,
With maladies innumerable
In heart, head, breast, and reins,°
But must secret passage find   610
To the inmost mind,
There exercise all his fierce accidents,°
And on her purest spirits prey,
As on entrails, joints, and limbs,

---

537. me: from me. **549. rod:** the sun. **560. What . . . it:**
what good is it. **568. redundant:** flowing.

574. draff: offal. **593. double darkness:** blindness and death.
609. reins: kidneys. **612. accidents:** symptoms.

With answerable° pains, but more intense,   615
Though void of corporal sense.
    My griefs not only pain me
As a lingering disease,
But, finding no redress, ferment and rage;
Nor less than wounds immedicable°   620
Rankle, and fester, and gangrene,
To black mortification.°
Thoughts, my tormentors, armed with deadly
    stings,
Mangle my apprehensive° tenderest parts,
Exasperate, exulcerate, and raise   625
Dire inflammation, which no cooling herb
Or med'cinal liquor can assuage,
Nor breath of vernal air from snowy Alp.
Sleep hath forsook and given me o'er
To death's benumbing opium as my only cure.
Thence faintings, swoonings of despair,   631
And sense of Heaven's desertion.
    I was His nursling once and choice delight,
His destined from the womb,
Promised by heavenly message twice descending.
Under his special eye   636
Abstemious I grew up and thrived amain;
He led me on to mightiest deeds,
Above the nerve of mortal arm,
Against the uncircumcised, our enemies: 640
But now hath cast me off as never known,
And to those cruel enemies,
Whom I by his appointment had provoked,
Left me all helpless, with the irreparable loss
Of sight, reserved alive to be repeated°   645
The subject of their cruelty or scorn.
Nor am I in the list of them that hope;
Hopeless are all my evils, all remediless;
This one prayer yet remains, might I be heard,
No long petition, speedy death,   650
The close of all my miseries and the balm.
CHORUS   Many are the sayings of the wise,
In ancient and in modern books enrolled,
Extolling patience as the truest fortitude,
And to the bearing well of all calamities,   655
All chances incident to man's frail life,
Consolatories writ
With studied argument, and much persuasion
    sought,

Lenient of° grief and anxious thought;
But with the afflicted in his pangs their sound   660
Little prevails, or rather seems a tune
Harsh, and of dissonant mood from his com-
    plaint,
Unless he feel within
Some source of consolation from above,
Secret refreshings that repair his strength   665
And fainting spirits uphold.
    God of our fathers! what is man!
That thou towards him with hand so various,
Or might I say contrarious,
Temper'st thy providence through his short
    course,   670
Not evenly, as thou rul'st
The angelic orders, and inferior creatures mute,
Irrational and brute?°
Nor do I name of men the common rout,
That, wandering loose about,   675
Grow up and perish as the summer fly,
Heads without name, no more remembered,
But such as thou hast solemnly elected,
With gifts and graces eminently adorned,
To some great work, thy glory,   680
And people's safety, which in part they effect:
Yet toward these, thus dignified, thou oft,
Amidst their highth of noon,
Changest thy countenance and thy hand, with
    no regard
Of highest favors past   685
From thee on them, or them to thee of service.
    Nor only dost degrade them, or remit
To life obscured, which were a fair dismission,
But throw'st them lower than thou didst exalt
    them high,
Unseemly falls in human eye,   690
Too grievous for the trespass or omission,
Oft leav'st them to the hostile sword
Of heathen and profane, their carcasses
To dogs and fowls a prey, or else captived,
Or to the unjust tribunals, under change of
    times,   695
And condemnation of the ungrateful multitude.
If these they scape, perhaps in poverty
With sickness and disease thou bow'st them
    down,
Painful diseases and deformed,

---

615. answerable: corresponding. 620. immedicable: un-
treatable. 621–22. gangrene . . . mortification: require
amputation. 624. apprehensive: sensitive. 645. repeated:
made repeatedly.

659. Lenient of: allaying. 667–73. What . . . brute: Cf.
Psalm 8:4: "What is man that thou art mindful of him?"

In crude° old age;   700
Though not disordinate, yet causeless suffering
The punishment of dissolute days:° in fine,
Just or unjust alike seem miserable,
For oft alike, both come to evil end.
    So deal not with this once thy glorious
        champion,   705
The image of thy strength, and mighty minister.
What do I beg? how hast thou dealt already?
Behold him in this state calamitous, and turn
His labors, for thou canst, to peaceful end.
    But who is this? what thing of sea or land? 710
Female of sex it seems,
That, so bedecked, ornate, and gay,
Comes this way sailing,
Like a stately ship
Of Tarsus, bound for the isles   715
Of Javan or Gadire,°
With all her bravery° on, and tackle trim,
Sails filled, and streamers waving,
Courted by all the winds that hold them play,°
An amber° scent of odorous perfume   720
Her harbinger, a damsel train behind;
Some rich Philistian matron she may seem,
And now, at nearer view, no other certain
Than Dalila thy wife.
SAMSON My wife! my traitress! let her not come
    near me.   725
CHORUS Yet on she moves, now stands and eyes
    thee fixed,
    About to have spoke, but now, with head
      declined,
    Like a fair flower surcharged with dew, she weeps,
    And words addressed seem into tears dissolved,
    Wetting the borders of her silken veil;   730
    But now again she makes address° to speak.
DALILA With doubtful feet and wavering resolu-
    tion
I came, still dreading thy displeasure, Samson,
Which to have merited, without excuse,
I cannot but acknowledge; yet, if tears   735
May expiate (though the fact more evil drew
In the perverse event than I foresaw)
My penance hath not slackened, though my
    pardon°

No way assured. But conjugal affection,
Prevailing over fear and timorous doubt,   740
Hath led me on, desirous to behold
Once more thy face, and know of thy estate,°
If aught in my ability may serve
To lighten what thou suffer'st, and appease
Thy mind with what amends is in my power, 745
Though late, yet in some part to recompense
My rash but more unfortunate misdeed.
SAMSON Out, out, hyena! These are thy wonted
    arts,
And arts of every woman false like thee,
To break all faith, all vows, deceive, betray, 750
Then, as repentant, to submit, beseech,
And reconcilement move° with feigned remorse,
Confess, and promise wonders in her change,
Not truly penitent, but chief to try
Her husband, how far urged his patience
    bears,   755
His virtue or weakness which way to assail:
Then, with more cautious and instructed skill,
Again transgresses, and again submits;
That wisest and best men, full oft beguiled,
With goodness principled° not to reject   760
The penitent, but ever to forgive,
Are drawn to wear out miserable days,
Entangled with a poisonous bosom-snake,
If not by quick destruction soon cut off,
As I by thee, to ages an example.   765
DALILA Yet hear me, Samson; not that I endeavor
To lessen or extenuate my offense,
But that, on the other side, if it be weighed
By itself, with aggravations not surcharged,
Or else with just allowance counterpoised,   770
I may, if possible, thy pardon find
The easier towards me, or thy hatred less.
First granting, as I do, it was a weakness
In me, but incident to all our sex,
Curiosity, inquisitive, importúne   775
Of secrets, then with like infirmity
To publish them, both common female faults:
Was it not weakness also to make known
For importunity, that is for naught,
Wherein consisted all thy strength and safety?
To what I did thou show'dst me first the way.
But I to enemies revealed, and should not.   782
Nor should'st thou have trusted that to woman's
    frailty:

700. crude: premature. **701–02. Though . . . days:** physically punished as if they had been intemperate. **715–16. the
. . . Gadire:** the Greek isles or Cadiz. **717. bravery:** finery.
719. hold them play: play with them. **720. amber:** ambergris,
used in perfumes. **731. address:** preparation. **738. pardon:**
pardon is.

742. estate: condition. **752. move:** urge. **760. principled:**
acting on principle.

Ere I to thee, thou to thyself wast cruel.
Let weakness, then, with weakness come to
    parle,°   785
So near related, or the same of kind,
Thine forgive mine, the men may censure thine
The gentler, if severely thou exact not
More strength from me than in thyself was
    found.
And what if love, which thou interpret'st
    hate,   790
The jealousy of love, powerful of sway
In human hearts, nor less in mine towards thee,
Caused what I did? I saw thee mutable
Of fancy, feared lest one day thou would'st
    leave me
As her at Timna, sought by all means, there-
    fore,   795
How to endear, and hold thee to me firmest:
No better way I saw than by importuning
To learn thy secrets, get into my power
Thy key of strength and safety: thou wilt say,
"Why, then, revealed?" I was assured by those
Who tempted me that nothing was designed 801
Against thee but safe custody and hold:°
That made for me,° I knew that liberty
Would draw thee forth to perilous enterprises,
While I at home sat full of cares and fears,   805
Wailing thy absence in my widowed bed;
Here I should still enjoy thee, day and night,
Mine and love's prisoner, not the Philistines',
Whole to myself, unhazarded abroad,
Fearless at home of partners in my love.   810
These reasons in Love's law have passed for
    good,
Though fond° and reasonless to some perhaps;
And love hath oft, well meaning, wrought much
    woe,
Yet always pity or pardon hath obtained.
Be not unlike all others, not austere   815
As thou art strong, inflexible as steel.
If thou in strength all mortals dost exceed,
In uncompassionate anger do not so.
SAMSON   How cunningly the sorceress displays
    Her own transgressions, to upbraid me mine! 820
    That malice, not repentance, brought thee hither
    By this appears: I gave, thou say'st, the example,

I led the way; bitter reproach, but true,
I to myself was false ere thou to me,
Such pardon, therefore, as I give my folly   825
Take to thy wicked deed: which when thou seest
Impartial, self-severe, inexorable,
Thou wilt renounce thy seeking, and much
    rather
Confess it feigned. Weakness is thy excuse,
And I believe it, weakness to resist   830
Philistian gold: if weakness may excuse,
What murtherer, what traitor, parricide,
Incestuous, sacrilegious, but may plead it?
All wickedness is weakness: that plea therefore
With God or man will gain thee no remission. 835
But love constrained thee;° call it furious rage
To satisfy thy lust: Love seeks to have love;
My love how could'st thou hope, who took'st the
    way
To raise in me inexpiable hate,
Knowing,° as needs I must, by thee betrayed? 840
In vain thou striv'st to cover shame with shame,
Or by evasions thy crime uncover'st more.
DALILA   Since thou determin'st weakness for no
    plea
    In man or woman, though to thy own con-
     demning,
    Hear what assaults I had, what snares besides, 845
    What sieges girt me round, ere I consented;
    Which might have awed the best-resolved of
     men,
    The constantest, to have yielded without
     blame.
    It was not gold, as to my charge thou lay'st,
    That wrought with° me: thou know'st the
     magistrates   850
    And princes of my country came in person,
    Solicited, commanded, threatened, urged,
    Adjured by all the bonds of civil duty
    And of religion, pressed° how just it was,
    How honorable, how glorious, to entrap   855
    A common enemy, who had destroyed
    Such numbers of our nation: and the priest
    Was not behind, but ever at my ear,
    Preaching how meritorious with the gods
    It would be to ensnare an irreligious   860
    Dishonorer of Dagon: what had I
    To oppose against such powerful arguments?

---

785. parle: parley. 800–02. I . . . hold: not true according
to the Biblical account (see Judges 16:5); Dalila is aware
that the Philistines intend to overpower Samson and make
him a captive. 803. made for me: was in my interest. 812.
fond: foolish.

836. But . . . thee: Samson turns to Dalila's second argument (ll. 790–814). 840. Knowing: knowing myself. 850.
wrought with: influenced. 854. pressed: urged.

Only my love of thee held long debate,
And combated in silence all these reasons
With hard contest. At length, that grounded
   maxim, 865
So rife° and celebrated in the mouths
Of wisest men, that to the public good
Private respects° must yield, with grave authority
Took full possession of me, and prevailed;
Virtue, as I thought, truth, duty, so enjoin-
   ing. 870
SAMSON I thought where all thy circling wiles
   would end;
In feigned religion, smooth hypocrisy.
But had thy love, still odiously pretended,
Been, as it ought, sincere, it would have taught
   thee
Far other reasonings, brought forth other
   deeds. 875
I before all the daughters of my tribe
And of my nation chose thee from among
My enemies, loved thee, as too well thou
   knew'st,
Too well, unbosomed all my secrets to thee,
Not out of levity, but overpowered 880
By thy request, who could deny thee nothing;
Yet now am judged an enemy. Why then
Didst thou at first receive me for thy husband,
Then, as since then, thy country's foe professed?
Being once a wife, for me thou wast to leave 885
Parents and country; nor was I their subject,
Nor under their protection, but my own,
Thou mine, not theirs: if aught against my life
Thy country sought of thee, it sought unjustly,
Against the law of nature, law of nations, 890
No more thy country, but an impious crew
Of men conspiring to uphold their state
By worse than hostile deeds, violating the ends
For which our country is a name so dear;
Not therefore to be obeyed. But zeal moved
   thee;° 895
To please thy gods thou didst it! gods unable
To acquit themselves and prosecute their foes
But by ungodly deeds, the contradiction
Of their own deity, gods cannot be:
Less therefore to be pleased, obeyed, or
   feared. 900
These false pretexts and varnished colors failing,
Bare in thy guilt, how foul must thou appear!

866. **rife:** prevalent. 868. **respects:** interests. 895. **But . . . thee:** reference to Dalila's third argument (ll. 857–61).

DALILA In argument with men a woman ever
   Goes by° the worse, whatever be her cause.
SAMSON For want of words, no doubt, or lack of
   breath! 905
   Witness when I was worried with thy peals.
DALILA I was a fool, too rash, and quite mistaken
   In what I thought would have succeeded best.
   Let me obtain forgiveness of thee, Samson,
   Afford me place to show what recompense 910
   Towards thee I intend for what I have misdone,
   Misguided; only what remains past cure
   Bear not too sensibly,° nor still insist
   To afflict thyself in vain: though sight be lost,
   Life yet hath many solaces, enjoyed 915
   Where other senses want° not their delights
   At home, in leisure and domestic ease,
   Exempt from many a care and chance to which
   Eyesight exposes, daily, men abroad.
   I to the lords will intercede, not doubting 920
   Their favorable ear, that I may fetch thee
   From forth this loathsome prison-house, to abide
   With me, where my redoubled love and care
   With nursing diligence, to me glad office,°
   May ever tend about thee to old age, 925
   With all things grateful cheered, and so supplied
   That what by me thou hast lost thou least shalt
   miss.
SAMSON No, no, of my condition take no care;
   It fits not; thou and I long since are twain;
   Nor think me so unwary or accursed 930
   To bring my feet again into the snare
   Where once I have been caught; I know thy
   trains,°
   Though dearly to my cost, thy gins, and toils;°
   Thy fair enchanted cup, and warbling charms,°
   No more on me have power, their force is
   nulled, 935
   So much of adder's wisdom° I have learned,
   To fence my ear against thy sorceries.
   If in my flower of youth and strength, when all
   men
   Loved, honored, feared me, thou alone could
   hate me,
   Thy husband, slight me, sell me, and forgo
   me; 940

904. **Goes by:** gets. 913. **sensibly:** acutely. 916. **want:** lack. 924. **office:** task. 932. **trains:** lures (used to lead animals into traps). 933. **gins and toils:** snares and nets. 934. **Thy . . . charms:** allusion to Circe, an enchantress in the *Odyssey* who turns men into swine. 936. **adder's wisdom:** deafness (a popular superstition).

How would'st thou use me now, blind, and
   thereby
Deceivable, in most things as a child
Helpless, thence easily contemned and scored,
And last neglected? How would'st thou insult,
When I must live uxorious to thy will   945
In perfect thralldom, how again betray me,
Bearing my words and doings to the lords
To gloss° upon, and, censuring, frown or smile?
This jail I count the house of liberty
To thine, whose doors my feet shall never
   enter.   950
DALILA Let me approach at least, and touch thy
   hand.
SAMSON Not for thy life, lest fierce remembrance
   wake
My sudden rage to tear thee joint by joint.
At distance I forgive thee, go with that;
Bewail thy falsehood, and the pious works   955
It hath brought forth to make thee memorable
Among illustrious women, faithful wives:
Cherish thy hastened widowhood with the gold
Of matrimonial treason: so farewell.
DALILA I see thou art implacable, more deaf   960
To prayers than winds and seas, yet winds to seas
Are reconciled at length, and sea to shore:
Thy anger, unappeasable, still rages,
Eternal tempest never to be calmed.
Why do I humble thus myself, and, suing   965
For peace, reap nothing but repulse and hate?
Bid go with evil omen, and the brand
Of infamy upon my name denounced?
To mix with thy concernments° I desist
Henceforth, nor too much disapprove my
   own.   970
Fame, if not double-faced, is double-mouthed,
And with contrary blast proclaims most deeds;
On both his wings, one black, the other white,
Bears greatest names in his wild aery flight.
My name, perhaps, among the circumcised   975
In Dan, in Judah, and the bordering tribes,
To all posterity may stand defamed,
With malediction mentioned, and the blot
Of falsehood most unconjugal traduced.
But in my country, where I most desire,   980
In Ecron, Gaza, Asdod, and in Gath,°
I shall be named among the famousest
Of women, sung at solemn festivals,

Living and dead recorded, who, to save
Her country from a fierce destroyer, chose   985
Above the faith of wedlock bands, my tomb
With odors visited and annual flowers;
Not less renowned than in Mount Ephraim
Jael,° who, with inhospitable guile,
Smote Sisera sleeping, through the temples
   nailed.   990
Nor shall I count it heinous to enjoy
The public marks of honor and reward
Conferred upon me for the piety°
Which to my country I was judged to have
   shown.
At this whoever envies or repines,   995
I leave him to his lot, and like my own.
CHORUS She's gone—a manifest serpent by her
   sting
Discovered in the end, till now concealed.
SAMSON So let her go. God sent her to debase me,
And aggravate my folly, who committed   1000
To such a viper his most sacred trust
Of secrecy, my safety, and my life.
CHORUS Yet beauty, though injurious, hath
   strange power,
After offense returning, to regain
Love once possessed, nor can be easily   1005
Repulsed, without much inward passion felt,
And secret sting of amorous remorse.
SAMSON Love-quarrels oft in pleasing concord
   end,
Not wedlock-treachery endangering life.
CHORUS It is not virtue, wisdom, valor, wit,   1010
Strength, comeliness of shape, or amplest merit,
That woman's love can win, or long inherit;°
But what it is, hard is to say,
Harder to hit,
(Which way soever men refer it)   1015
Much like thy riddle, Samson, in one day
Or seven, though one should musing sit;
   If any of these,° or all, the Timnian bride
Had not so soon preferred
Thy paranymph,° worthless to thee com-
   pared,   1020
Successor in thy bed,
Nor both° so loosely disallied

---

948. **gloss:** comment. 969. **concernments:** affairs. 981.
Ecron . . . Gath: principal cities of Palestine.

989. **Jael:** Jael's murder of Sisera was also a political betrayal of trust (see Judges 4–5). 993. **piety:** devotion. 1012.
inherit: keep. 1018. **these:** the qualities listed in ll. 1010–11.
1020. **paranymph:** groomsman to whom the woman of
Timna was given during Samson's absence. 1022. **both:**
the woman of Timna and Dalila.

Their nuptials, nor this last so treacherously
Had shorn the fatal harvest of thy head.
Is it for that such outward ornament 1025
Was lavished on their sex, that inward gifts
Were left for haste unfinished, judgment scant,
Capacity not raised to apprehend
Or value what is best
In choice, but oftest to affect° the wrong? 1030
Or was too much of self-love mixed,
Of constancy nor root infixed,
That either they love nothing, or not long?
    Whate'er it be, to wisest men and best,
Seeming at first all heavenly under virgin
    veil, 1035
Soft, modest, meek, demure,
Once joined, the contrary she proves, a thorn
Intestine,° far within defensive arms
A cleaving mischief, in his way to virtue
Adverse and turbulent, or by her charms 1040
Draws him awry, enslaved
With dotage, and his sense depraved
To folly and shameful deeds, which ruin ends.
What pilot so expert but needs must wreck
Embarked with such a steers-mate at the
    helm? 1045
    Favoured of Heaven who finds
One virtuous, rarely found,
That in domestic good combines:
Happy that house! his way to peace is smooth:
But virtue which breaks through all opposi-
    tion, 1050
And all temptation can remove,
Most shines and most is acceptable above.
    Therefore God's universal law°
Gave to the man despotic power
Over his female in due awe, 1055
Nor from that right to part an hour,
Smile she or lour:
So shall he least confusion draw
On his whole life, not swayed
By female usurpation, nor dismayed. 1060
    But had we best retire? I see a storm.
SAMSON Fair days have oft contracted° wind and
    rain.
CHORUS But this another kind of tempest brings.

SAMSON Be less abstruse, my riddling° days are
    past.
CHORUS Look now for no enchanting voice, nor
    fear 1065
The bait of honeyed words; a rougher tongue
Draws hitherward, I know him by his stride,
The giant Harapha° of Gath, his look
Haughty, as is his pile° high-built and proud.
Comes he in peace? What wind hath blown him
    hither 1070
I less conjecture than when first I saw
The sumptuous Dalila floating this way:
His habit carries peace, his brow defiance.
SAMSON Or peace or not, alike to me he comes.
CHORUS His fraught° we soon shall know, he
    now arrives. 1075
HARAPHA I come not, Samson, to condole thy
    chance,
As these° perhaps, yet wish it had not been,
Though for no friendly intent. I am of Gath;
Men call me Harapha, of stock renowned
As Og, or Anak, and the Emins° old 1080
That Kiriathaim held: Thou know'st me now
If thou at all art known. Much I have heard
Of thy prodigious might and feats performed,
Incredible to me, in this displeased,
That I was never present on the place 1085
Of those encounters, where we might have tried
Each other's force in camp or listed field;°
And now am come to see of whom such noise°
Hath walked about, and each limb to survey,
If thy appearance answer loud report. 1090
SAMSON The way to know were not to see but
    taste.
HARAPHA Dost thou already single° me? I
    thought
Gyves° and the mill had tamed thee. O that
    fortune
Had brought me to the field where thou art
    famed
To have wrought such wonders with an ass's
    jaw; 1095
I should have forced thee soon wish other arms,
Or left thy carcass where the ass lay thrown:

1025. for that: because. 1030. affect: desire. 1038. Intestine:
domestic. 1048. combines: i.e., unites with her husband.
1053. God's . . . law: See I Timothy 2:12. 1062. contracted: drawn together.

1064. riddling: at Timna; see Judges 14:11–18 for the story
of Samson's use of riddles. 1068. Harapha: (Hebrew)
giant. 1069. pile: frame. 1075. fraught: business. 1077.
these: the chorus. 1080. Og . . . Emins: giants; the Emins
were defeated at Kiriathaim (l. 1081.) 1087. in . . . field:
in battle or tournament. 1088. noise: fame. 1092. single:
challenge. 1093. Gyves: fetters.

So had the glory of prowess been recovered
To Palestine, won by a Philistine
From the unforeskinned race, of whom thou
    bear'st   1100
The highest name for valiant acts; that honor,
Certain to have won by mortal duel from thee,
I lose, prevented by thy eyes put out.
SAMSON   Boast not of what thou would'st have
    done, but do
What then thou would'st, thou seest it in thy
    hand.°   1105
HARAPHA   To combat with a blind man I disdain,
And thou has need much washing to be touched.
SAMSON   Such usage as your honorable lords
Afford me, assassinated° and betrayed,
Who durst not with their whole united powers
In fight withstand me single and unarmed,   1111
Nor in the house with chamber ambushes
Close-banded durst attack me, no, not sleeping,
Till they had hired a woman with their gold,
Breaking her marriage faith, to circumvent
    me.   1115
Therefore without feigned shifts° let be assigned
Some narrow place enclosed, where sight may
    give thee,
Or rather flight, no great advantage on me;
Then put on all thy gorgeous arms, thy helmet
And brigandine° of brass, thy broad haber-
    geon,°   1120
Vant-brace and greaves and gauntlet,° add thy
    spear,
A weaver's beam,° and seven-times-folded°
    shield,
I only with an oaken staff will meet thee,
And raise such outcries on thy clattered iron,
Which long shall not withhold me from thy
    head,   1125
That in a little time, while breath remains thee,
Thou oft shalt wish thyself at Gath to boast
Again in safety what thou would'st have done
To Samson, but shalt never see Gath more.
HARAPHA   Thou durst not thus disparage glorious
    arms   1130
Which greatest heroes have in battle worn,

Their ornament and safety, had not spells
And black enchantments, some magician's art,
Armed thee or charmed thee strong, which thou
    from Heaven
Feign'dst at thy birth was given thee in thy
    hair,   1135
Where strength can least abide, though all thy
    hairs
Were bristles ranged like those that ridge the
    back
Of chafed wild boars or ruffled porcupines.
SAMSON   I know no spells, use no forbidden arts;
My trust is in the Living God who gave me   1140
At my nativity this strength, diffused
No less through all my sinews, joints and bones,
Than thine, while I preserved these locks
    unshorn,
The pledge of my unviolated vow.
For proof hereof, if Dagon be thy god,   1145
Go to his temple, invocate his aid
With solemnest devotion, spread before him
How highly it concerns his glory now
To frustrate and dissolve these magic spells,
Which I to be the power of Israel's God   1150
Avow, and challenge Dagon to the test,
Offering to combat thee his champion bold,
With the utmost of his godhead seconded:
Then thou shalt see, or rather to thy sorrow
Soon feel, whose God is strongest, thine or
    mine.   1155
HARAPHA   Presume not on thy God, whate'er he be,
Thee he regards not, owns not, hath cut off
Quite from his people, and delivered up
Into thy enemies' hand, permitted them
To put out both thine eyes, and fettered send
    thee   1160
Into the common prison, there to grind
Among the slaves and asses, thy comrades,
As good for nothing else, no better service
With those thy boisterous° locks, no worthy
    match
For valor to assail, nor by the sword   1165
Of noble warrior, so to stain his honor,
But by the barber's razor best subdued.
SAMSON   All these indignities,° for such they are
From thine,° these evils I deserve and more,
Acknowledge them from God inflicted on
    me   1170

1105. in thy hand: in thy power. **1109. assassinated:** attacked.
1116. feigned shifts: treacheries. **1120. brigandine:** body
armor (metal plates sewn to cloth). **habergeon:** tunic of mail.
1121. Vant-brace . . . gauntlet: armor protecting the
forearm, lower leg, and hand, respectively. **1122. weaver's
beam:** as thick as the main cylinder of a loom. **seven-times-
folded:** seven-layered.

1164. boisterous: thick. **1168. indignities:** taunts. **1169.
thine:** Harapha's nation.

Justly, yet despair not of his final pardon
Whose ear is ever open; and his eye
Gracious to readmit the suppliant;
In confidence whereof I once again
Defy thee to the trial of mortal fight,   1175
By combat to decide whose god is God,
Thine, or whom I with Israel's sons adore.

HARAPHA   Fair honor that thou dost thy God, in
trusting
He will accept thee to defend his cause,
A murtherer, a revolter, and a robber.   1180

SAMSON   Tongue-doughty giant, how dost thou
prove me these?

HARAPHA   Is not thy nation subject to our lords?
Their magistrates confessed it when they took
thee
As a league-breaker° and delivered bound
Into our hands: for hadst thou not com-
mitted   1185
Notorious murder on those thirty men
At Ascalon, who never did thee harm,
Then like a robber stripp'dst them of their
robes?
The Philistines, when thou hadst broke the
league,
Went up with armèd powers thee only seeking,
To others did no violence nor spoil.   1191

SAMSON   Among the daughters of the Philistines
I chose a wife, which argued me no foe;
And in your city held my nuptial feast:
But your ill-meaning politician lords,   1195
Under pretense of the bridal friends and guests,
Appointed to await me thirty spies,
Who, threatening cruel death, constrained the
bride
To wring from me and tell to them my secret,
That solved the riddle which I had proposed. 1200
When I perceived all set on enmity,
As on my enemies, wherever chanced,
I used hostility, and took their spoil
To pay my underminers in their coin.
My nation was subjected to your lords!   1205
It was the force of conquest; force with force
Is well ejected when the conquered can.
But I a private person, whom my country
As a league-breaker gave up bound, presumed
Single rebellion and did hostile acts!   1210
I was no private but a person raised

With strength sufficient and command from
Heaven
To free my country; if their servile minds
Me their deliverer sent would not receive,
But to their masters gave me up for nought, 1215
The unworthier they; whence to this day they
serve.
I was to do my part from Heaven assigned,
And had performed it if my known offense
Had not disabled me, not all your force:
These shifts° refuted, answer thy appellant,° 1220
Though by his blindness maimed for high
attempts,°
Who now defies thee thrice to single fight,
As a petty enterprise of small enforce.

HARAPHA   With thee a man condemned, a slave
enrolled,
Due by the law to capital punishment?   1225
To fight with thee no man of arms will deign.

SAMSON   Cam'st thou for this, vain boaster, to
survey me,
To descant° on my strength, and give thy
verdict?
Come nearer, part not hence so slight informed;
But take good heed my hand survey not thee. 1230

HARAPHA   O Baal-zebub!° can my ears unused°
Hear these dishonors, and not render death?

SAMSON   No man withholds thee, nothing from
thy hand
Fear I incurable; bring up thy van,°
My heels are fettered, but my fist is free.   1235

HARAPHA   This insolence other kind of answer
fits.

SAMSON   Go baffled coward, lest I run upon thee,
Though in these chains, bulk without spirit
vast,
And with one buffet lay thy structure low,
Or swing thee in the air, then dash thee down 1240
To the hazard of thy brains and shattered sides.

HARAPHA   By Astaroth, ere long thou shalt
lament
These braveries° in irons loaden on thee.

CHORUS   His giantship is gone somewhat crestfallen,

1184. league-breaker: Cf. ll. 253–64.

1220. shifts: excuses. appellant: challenger. 1221. high
attempts: great deeds. 1228. descant: make unfavorable
comments. 1231. Baal-zebub: Beelzebub or Baal, the sun
god of the Philistines. unused: unaccustomed to such
insults. 1234. bring . . . van: begin fighting. 1243. braveries:
boasts.

Stalking with less unconscionable° strides,   1245
And lower looks, but in a sultry chafe.

SAMSON   I dread him not, nor all his giant-brood,
Though fame divulge him father of five sons
All of gigantic size, Goliah° chief.

CHORUS   He will° directly to the lords, I fear,   1250
And with malicious counsel stir them up
Some way or other yet further to afflict thee.

SAMSON   He must allege some cause, and offered
    fight
Will not dare mention, lest a question rise
Whether he durst accept the offer or not,   1255
And that he durst not plain enough appeared.
Much more affliction than already felt
They cannot well impose, nor I sustain;
If they intend advantage of my labors,
The work of many hands, which earns my
    keeping   1260
With no small profit daily to my owners.
But come what will, my deadliest foe will prove
My speediest friend, by death to rid me hence,
The worst that he can give to me the best.
Yet so it may fall out, because their end   1265
Is hate, not help to me, it may with mine
Draw their own ruin who attempt the deed.

CHORUS   O how comely it is and how reviving
To the spirits of just men long oppressed!
When God into the hands of their deliverer   1270
Puts invincible might
To quell the mighty of the earth, the oppressor,
The brute and boisterous force of violent men
Hardy and industrious to support
Tyrannic power, but raging to pursue   1275
The righteous and all such as honor truth;
He° all their ammunition
And feats of war defeats,
With plain heroic magnitude of mind
And celestial vigor armed,   1280
Their armories and magazines contemns,
Renders them useless, while
With wingèd expedition
Swift as the lightning glance he executes
His errand on the wicked, who, surprised   1285
Lose their defense, distracted and amazed.
    But patience is more oft the exercise
Of saints, the trial of their fortitude,

Making them each his own deliverer,
And victor over all   1290
That tyranny or fortune can inflict.
Either of these is in thy lot,
Samson, with might endued
Above the sons of men; but sight bereaved
May chance to number thee with those   1295
Whom patience finally must crown.
    This idol's day hath been to thee no day of
        rest,
Laboring thy mind
More than the working day thy hands.
And yet perhaps more trouble is behind,   1300
For I descry this way
Some other tending, in his hand
A scepter or quaint° staff he bears,
Comes on amain, speed in his look.
By his habit I discern him now   1305
A public officer, and now at hand.
His message will be short and voluble.°

OFFICER   Hebrews, the prisoner Samson here I
    seek.

CHORUS   His manacles remark° him, there he sits.

OFFICER   Samson, to thee our lords thus bid me
    say;   1310
This day to Dagon is a solemn feast,
With sacrifices, triumph,° pomp, and games;
Thy strength they know surpassing human rate,
And now some public proof thereof require   1314
To honor this great feast, and great assembly;
Rise, therefore with all speed and come
    along,
Where I will see thee heartened and fresh clad,
To appear as fits before the illustrious lords.

SAMSON   Thou know'st I am an Hebrew, therefore
    tell them,
Our law forbids at their religious rites   1320
My presence; for the cause I cannot come.

OFFICER   This answer, be assured, will not content
    them.

SAMSON   Have they not sword-players, and every
    sort
Of gymnic artists, wrestlers, riders, runners,
Jugglers and dancers, antics,° mummers,°
    mimics,   1325
But they must pick me out with shackles tired,
And overlabored at their public mill,

1245. unconscionable: absurdly arrogant. 1249. Goliah:
Goliath, fifth son of the giant brood defeated by David
(see II Samuel 21). 1250. will: will go. 1277. He: the
deliverer.

1303. quaint: cunningly made or decorated. 1307. voluble:
pointed. 1309. remark: identify. 1312. triumph: public
festivity. 1325. antics: clowns. mummers: pantomimists.

To make them sport with blind activity?
Do they not seek occasion of new quarrels
On my refusal, to distress me more,   1330
Or make a game of my calamities?
Return the way thou cam'st, I will not come.

OFFICER   Regard° thyself, this will offend them
highly.

SAMSON   Myself? my conscience and internal
peace.
Can they think me so broken, so debased   1335
With corporal servitude, that my mind ever
Will condescend to such absurd commands?
Although their drudge, to be their fool or jester,
And in my midst of sorrow and heart-grief,
To show them feats, and play before their
god,   1340
The worst of all indignities, yet on me
Joined° with extreme contempt? I will not come.

OFFICER   My message was imposed on me with
speed,
Brooks° no delay: is this thy resolution?

SAMSON   So take it with what speed thy message
needs.   1345

OFFICER   I am sorry what this stoutness° will
produce.

SAMSON   Perhaps thou shalt have cause to sorrow
indeed.

CHORUS   Consider, Samson; matters now are
strained
Up to the highth, whether to hold or break;
He's gone, and who knows how he may
report   1350
Thy words by adding fuel to the flame?
Expect another message more imperious,
More lordly thundering than thou well wilt
bear.

SAMSON   Shall I abuse this consecrated gift
Of strength, again returning with my hair   1355
After my great transgression, so requite
Favor° renewed, and add a greater sin
By prostituting holy things to idols;
A Nazarite in place abominable
Vaunting° my strength in honor to their
Dagon?   1360
Besides, how vile, contemptible, ridiculous,
What act more execrably unclean, profane?

CHORUS   Yet with this strength thou serv'st the
Philistines,
Idolatrous, uncircumcised, unclean.°

SAMSON   Not in their idol-worship, but by labor
Honest and lawful to deserve my food   1366
Of those who have me in their civil power.

CHORUS   Where the heart joins not, outward acts
defile not.

SAMSON   Where outward force constrains, the
sentence° holds: 1369
But who constrains me to the temple of Dagon,
Not dragging? The Philistian lords command.
Commands are no constraints. If I obey them,
I do it freely; venturing to displease
God for the fear of man, and man prefer,
Set God behind: which in his jealousy   1375
Shall never, unrepented, find forgiveness.
Yet that he may dispense° with me or thee
Present in temples at idolatrous rites
For some important cause, thou need'st not
doubt.

CHORUS   How thou wilt here come off surmounts
my reach.   1380

SAMSON   Be of good courage, I begin to feel
Some rousing motions in me which dispose
To something extraordinary my thoughts.
I with this messenger will go along,
Nothing to do, be sure, that may dishonor   1385
Our Law, or stain my vow of Nazarite.
If there be aught of presage° in the mind,
This day will be remarkable in my life
By some great act, or of my days the last.

CHORUS   In time thou hast resolved, the man
returns.   1390

OFFICER   Samson, this second message from our
lords
To thee I am bid say. Art thou our slave,
Our captive, at the public mill our drudge,
And dar'st thou at our sending and command
Dispute thy coming? come without delay;   1395
Or we shall find such engines° to assail
And hamper thee, as thou shalt come of force,
Though thou wert firmlier fastened than a rock.

SAMSON   I could be well content to try their art,
Which to no few of them would prove perni-
cious.   1400

1333. Regard: watch out for. 1342. Joined: enjoined, imposed. 1344. Brooks: permits. 1346. stoutness: pride,
arrogance. 1357. Favor: God's favor. 1360. Vaunting:
exhibiting.

1364. unclean: in the Jewish legal sense, by association
with Gentiles. 1369. sentence: maxim of the preceding line.
1377. dispense: allow a dispensation permitting a forbidden act. 1387. presage: presentiment, foreknowledge.
1396. engines: i.e., engines of torture.

Yet, knowing their advantages too many,
Because° they shall not trail me through their
   streets
Like a wild beast, I am content to go.
Masters' commands come with a power resistless
To such as owe them absolute subjection;   1405
And for a life who will not change his purpose?
(So mutable are all the ways of men)
Yet this be sure, in nothing to comply
Scandalous of forbidden in our Law.

OFFICER   I praise thy resolution, doff these
   links: 1410
By this compliance thou wilt win the lords
To favor, and perhaps to set thee free.

SAMSON   Brethren farewell. Your company along
I will not wish, lest it perhaps offend them
To see me girt with friends; and how the sight
Of me as of a common enemy,   1416
So dreaded once, may now exasperate them
I know not. Lords are lordliest in their wine;
And the well-feasted priest then soonest fired
With zeal, if aught° religion seem concerned:
No less the people, on their holy-days   1421
Impetuous, insolent, unquenchable.
Happen what may, of me expect to hear
Nothing dishonorable, impure, unworthy
Our God, our Law, my nation, or myself;   1425
The last of me or no I cannot warrant.°

CHORUS   Go, and the Holy One
Of Israel be thy guide
To what may serve his glory best, and spread
   his name
Great among the heathen round: 1430
Send° thee the angel of thy birth, to stand
Fast by thy side, who from thy father's field
Rode up in flames after his message told
Of thy conception, and be now a shield
Of fire; that spirit that first rushed on thee   1435
In the camp of Dan
Be efficacious in thee now at need.
For never was from Heaven imparted
Measure of strength so great to mortal seed,
As in thy wondrous actions hath been seen.   1440
But wherefore comes old Manoa in such haste
With youthful steps? Much livelier than erewhile
He seems: supposing here to find his son,

Or of him bringing to us some glad news?

MANOA   Peace with you, brethren; my inducement
   hither   1445
Was not at present here to find my son,
By order of the lords new parted hence
To come and play before them at their feast.
I heard all as I came, the city rings
And numbers thither flock; I had no will,°   1450
Lest I should see him forced to things unseemly.
But that which moved my coming now, was
   chiefly
To give ye part with me° what hope I have
With good success to work his liberty.

CHORUS   That hope would much rejoice us to
   partake   1455
With thee; say, reverend sire, we thirst to hear.

MANOA   I have attempted° one by one the lords
Either at home, or through the high street
   passing,
With supplication prone and father's tears
To accept of ransom for my son their
   prisoner;   1460
Some much averse I found and wondrous harsh,
Contemptuous, proud, set on revenge and spite;
That part most reverenced Dagon and his
   priests;
Others more moderate seeming, but their aim
Private reward, for which both God and state
They easily would set to sale; a third   1466
More generous far and civil, who confessed
They had enough revenged, having reduced
Their foe to misery beneath their fears,°
The rest was magnanimity to remit,   1470
If some convenient ransom were proposed.
What noise or shout was that? it tore the sky.

CHORUS   Doubtless the people shouting to behold
Their once great dread, captive, and blind
   before them,
Or at some proof of strength before them
   shown.   1475

MANOA   His ransom, if my whole inheritance
May compass it, shall willingly be paid
And numbered down: much rather I shall
   choose
To live the poorest in my tribe, than richest,
And he in that calamitous prison left.   1480

1402. **Because:** in order that. **1420. aught:** in any way.
1426. The . . . warrant: Samson is not sure whether this is
the last time his friends will see him. **1431. Send:** may he
send.

1450. **will:** alternative. **1453. give . . . me:** share with you.
1457. attempted: approached, appealed to. **1468–69.**
having . . . fears: having no longer any reason to fear a
weak and blind Samson.

No, I am fixed not to part hence without him.
For his redemption all my patrimony,
If need be, I am ready to forgo
And quit: not wanting° him, I shall want
    nothing.
CHORUS Fathers are wont to lay up for their
    sons,   1485
    Thou for thy son art bent to lay out all;
    Sons wont° to nurse their parents in old age,
    Thou in old age car'st how to nurse thy son,
    Made older than thy age through eyesight lost.
MANOA It shall be my delight to tend his eyes, 1490
    And view him sitting in the house, ennobled
    With all those high exploits by him achieved,
    And on his shoulders waving down those locks,
    That of a nation armed the strength contained:
    And I persuade me God had not° permitted 1495
    His strength again to grow up with his hair
    Garrisoned round about him like a camp
    Of faithful soldiery, were not his purpose
    To use him further yet in some great service,
    Not to sit idle with so great a gift   1500
    Useless, and thence ridiculous about him.
    And since his strength with eyesight was not lost,
    God will restore him eyesight to° his strength.
CHORUS Thy hopes are not ill founded nor
    seem vain
    Of his delivery, and thy joy thereon   1505
    Conceived, agreeable to a father's love;
    In both which we, as next,° participate.
MANOA I know your friendly minds and . . . O,
    what noise!
    Mercy of Heaven what hideous noise was that!
    Horribly loud unlike the former shout.   1510
CHORUS Noise call you it or universal groan
    As if the whole inhabitation perished?
    Blood, death, and deathful deeds are in that
    noise,
    Ruin,° destruction at the utmost point.
MANOA Of ruin indeed methought I heard the
    noise,   1515
    Oh it continues, they have slain my son.
CHORUS Thy son is rather slaying them, that
    outcry
    From slaughter of one foe could not ascend.
MANOA Some dismal accident it needs must be;
    What shall we do, stay here or run and see? 1520

CHORUS Best keep together here, lest running
    thither
    We unawares run into danger's mouth.
    This evil on the Philistines is fallen,
    From whom could else a general cry be heard?
    The sufferers then will scarce molest us here, 1525
    From other hands we need not much to fear.
    What if his eyesight (for to Israel's God
    Nothing is hard) by miracle restored,
    He now be dealing dole° among his foes,
    And over heaps of slaughtered walk his way?
MANOA That were a joy presumptuous to be
    thought.   1531
CHORUS Yet God hath wrought things as in-
    credible
    For his people of old; what hinders now?
MANOA He can I know, but doubt to think he will;
    Yet hope would fain subscribe, and tempts
    belief.   1535
    A little stay will bring some notice hither.
CHORUS Of good or bad so great, of bad the
    sooner;
    For evil news rides post, while good news baits.°
    And to our wish I see one hither speeding,
    An Hebrew, as I guess, and of our tribe.   1540
MESSENGER O whither shall I run, or which way fly
    The sight of this so horrid spectacle
    Which erst° my eyes beheld and yet behold?
    For dire imagination still pursues me.
    But providence or instinct of nature seems, 1545
    Or reason though disturbed, and scarce con-
    sulted
    To have guided me aright, I know not how,
    To thee first reverend Manoa, and to these
    My countrymen, whom here I knew remaining,
    As at some distance from the place of horror,
    So in the sad event too much concerned.   1551
MANOA The accident was loud, and here before
    thee
    With rueful cry, yet what it was we hear not;
    No preface needs, thou seest we long to know.
MESSENGER It would burst forth, but I recover°
    breath   1555
    And sense distract,° to know well what I utter.
MANOA Tell us the sum, the circumstance defer.
MESSENGER Gaza yet stands, but all her sons are
    fallen,

1484. wanting: lacking. 1487. wont: are wont. 1495. had
not: would not have. 1503. to: in addition to. 1507. next:
next of kin. 1514. ruin: downfall, collapse.

1529. dole: grief, pain. 1538. baits: travels slowly. 1543.
erst: just now. 1555. recover: must recover. 1556. distract:
distracted.

All in a moment overwhelmed and fallen.

MANOA   Sad, but thou know'st to Israelites not
    saddest   1560
The desolation of a hostile city.

MESSENGER   Feed on the first, there may in grief be
    surfeit.

MANOA   Relate by whom.

MESSENGER   By Samson.

MANOA   That still lessens
The sorrow, and converts it nigh to joy.

MESSENGER   Ah Manoa I refrain too suddenly
To utter what will come at last too soon;   1566
Lest evil tidings with too rude irruption
Hitting thy aged ear should pierce too deep.

MANOA   Suspense in news is torture, speak them
    out.

MESSENGER   Then take the worst in brief, Samson
    is dead.   1570

MANOA   The worst indeed! O all my hope's
    defeated
To free him hence! but Death, who sets all free,
Hath paid his ransom now and full discharge.
What windy° joy this day had I conceived
Hopeful of his delivery, which now proves   1575
Abortive as the firstborn bloom of spring
Nipped with the lagging rear of winter's frost.
Yet ere I give the reins to grief, say first,
How died he? Death to life is crown or shame.
All by him fell thou say'st, by whom fell he? 1580
What glorious hand gave Samson his death's
    wound?

MESSENGER   Unwounded of his enemies he fell.

MANOA   Wearied with slaughter then or how?
    explain.

MESSENGER   By his own hands.

MANOA   Self-violence? What cause
Brought him so soon at variance with himself
Among his foes?

MESSENGER   Inevitable cause   1586
At once both to destroy and be destroyed;
The edifice where all were met to see him
Upon their heads and on his own he pulled.

MANOA   O lastly overstrong against thyself!   1590
A dreadful way took'st thou to thy revenge.
More than enough we know; but while things yet
Are in confusion, give us if thou canst,
Eyewitness of what first or last was done,
Relation more particular and distinct.   1595

MESSENGER   Occasions° drew me early to this city,

1574. windy: vain. 1596. Occasions: affairs, business.

And as the gates I entered with sunrise,
The morning trumpets festival proclaimed
Through each high street: little I had dispatched°
When all abroad was rumored that this day 1600
Samson should be brought forth to show the
    people
Proof of his mighty strength in feats and games;
I sorrowed at his captive state, but minded
Not to be absent at that spectacle.
The building was a spacious theater   1605
Half round on two main pillars vaulted high,
With seats where all the lords and each degree
Of sort,° might sit in order to behold;
The other side was open, where the throng
On banks° and scaffolds under sky might stand;
I among these aloof obscurely stood.   1611
The feast and noon grew high, and sacrifice
Had filled their hearts with mirth, high cheer, and
    wine,
When to their sports they turned. Immediately
Was Samson as a public servant brought,   1615
In their state livery clad; before him pipes
And timbrels, on each side went armèd guards,
Both horse and foot before him and behind,
Archers and slingers, cataphracts° and spears.°
At sight of him the people with a shout   1620
Rifted the air, clamoring their god with praise,
Who had made their dreadful enemy their thrall.
He patient but undaunted where they led him,
Came to the place, and what was set before him
Which without help of eye, might be assayed, 1625
To heave, pull, draw, or break, he still performed
All with incredible, stupendious force,
None daring to appear antagonist.
At length for intermission sake they led him
Between the pillars; he his guide requested 1630
(For so from such as nearer stood we heard)
As overtired to let him lean a while
With both his arms on those two massy pillars
That to the archèd roof gave main support.
He° unsuspicious led him; which when Samson
Felt in his arms, with head a while inclined, 1636
And eyes fast fixed he stood, as one who prayed,
Or some great matter in his mind revolved.
At last, with head erect, thus cried aloud,
  "Hitherto, lords, what your commands imposed

1599. dispatched: accomplished. 1607–08. each . . . sort:
the upper social classes. 1610. banks: benches. 1619.
cataphracts: heavily armored soldiers and horses. spears:
spearmen. 1635. He: the guide.

I have performed, as reason was, obeying,   1641
Not without wonder or delight beheld.
Now of my own accord such other trial
I mean to show you of my strength, yet greater;
As with amaze° shall strike all who behold." 1645
This uttered, straining all his nerves he bowed;
As with the force of winds and waters pent,
When mountains tremble, those two massy
    pillars
With horrible convulsion to and fro,
He tugged, he shook, till down they came and
    drew   1650
The whole roof after them, with burst of thunder
Upon the heads of all who sat beneath,
Lords, ladies, captains, counselors, or priests,
Their choice nobility and flower, not only
Of this but each Philistian city round   1655
Met from all parts to solemnize this feast.
Samson with these immixed, inevitably
Pulled down the same destruction on himself;
The vulgar° only scaped who stood without.
CHORUS   O dearly bought revenge, yet glorious!
Living or dying thou has fulfilled   1661
The work for which thou wast foretold
To Israel, and now liest victorious
Among the slain self-killed
Not willingly, but tangled in the fold   1665
Of dire necessity,° whose law in death conjoined
Thee with thy slaughtered foes in number more
Than all thy life had slain before.
SEMICHORUS   While their hearts were jocund and
    sublime,°
Drunk with idolatry, drunk with wine   1670
And fat regorged° of bulls and goats,
Chaunting their idol, and preferring
Before our living Dread who dwells
In Silo° his bright sanctuary:
Among them he° a spirit of frenzy sent, 1675
Who hurt their minds,
And urged them on with mad desire
To call in haste for their destroyer;
They only set on sport and play
Unweetingly importuned   1680
Their own destruction to come speedy upon
    them.

So fond are mortal men
Fallen into wrath divine,°
As their own ruin on themselves to invite,
Insensate left, or to sense reprobate,°   1685
And with blindness internal struck.
SEMICHORUS   But he, though blind of sight,
Despised and thought extinguished quite,
With inward eyes illuminated
His fiery virtue roused   1690
From under ashes into sudden flame,
And as an evening dragon came,
Assailant on the perchèd roosts,
And nests in order ranged
Of tame villatic° fowl; but as an eagle   1695
His cloudless thunder bolted on their heads.
So Virtue given° for lost,
Depressed, and overthrown, as seemed,
Like that self-begotten bird°
In the Arabian woods embossed,°   1700
That no second knows nor third,
And lay erewhile a holocaust,
From out her ashy womb now teemed
Revives, reflourishes, then vigorous most
When most unactive deemed,   1705
And though her body die, her fame survives,
A secular bird,° ages of lives.
MANOA   Come, come, no time for lamentation
    now,
Nor much more cause: Samson hath quit
    himself
Like Samson, and heroicly hath finished   1710
A life heroic, on his enemies
Fully revenged, hath left them years of mourning,
And lamentation to the sons of Caphtor°
Through all Philistian bounds. To Israel
Honor hath left, and freedom, let but them 1715
Find courage to lay hold on this occasion;
To himself and father's house eternal fame;
And, which is best and happiest yet, all this
With God not parted from him, as was feared,
But favoring and assisting to the end.   1720
Nothing is here for tears, nothing to wail

1645. amaze: confusion. 1659. vulgar: throng, general populace. 1665–66. Not . . . necessity: Samson's death was not a suicide because it was inseparable from the deaths of his enemies. 1669. sublime: uplifted. 1671. regorged: belched up. 1674. Silo: tabernacle at Shiloh (see Joshua 18:1). 1675. he: God.

1683. Fallen . . . divine: urged to madness for their own destruction by gods (cf. ll. 1675–79). 1685. Insensate . . . reprobate: both senseless (foolish) and sensual. 1695. villatic: barnyard. 1697. given: given up. 1699. self-begotten bird: The phoenix, reborn by rising from its own ashes, is metaphorically identified with the fame of Samson's virtue in the following lines. 1700. embossed: hidden, sheltered. 1707. secular bird: i.e., fame as a kind of human rather than divine immortality. 1713. sons of Caphtor: Philistines.

Or knock the breast, no weakness, no contempt,
Dispraise, or blame, nothing but well and fair,
And what may quiet us in a death so noble.
Let us go find the body where it lies   1725
Soaked in his enemies' blood, and from the
    stream
With lavers° pure and cleansing herbs wash off
The clotted gore. I with what speed° the while
(Gaza is not in plight to say us nay)
Will send for all my kindred, all my friends 1730
To fetch him hence and solemnly attend
With silent obsequy and funeral train
Home to his father's house: there will I build
    him
A monument, and plant it round with shade
Of laurel° ever green, and branching palm,° 1735
With all his trophies° hung, and acts enrolled
In copious legend, or sweet lyric song.
Thither shall all the valiant youth resort,
And from his memory inflame their breasts
To matchless valor and adventures high: 1740
The virgins also shall on feastful days
Visit his tomb with flowers, only bewailing
His lot unfortunate in nuptial choice,
From whence captivity and loss of eyes.
CHORUS   All is best, though we oft doubt   1745
What the unsearchable dispose°
Of highest wisdom brings about,
And ever best found in the close.°
Oft he° seems to hide his face,
But unexpectedly returns   1750
And to his faithful champion hath in place°
Bore witness gloriously; whence Gaza mourns,
And all that band them to resist
His uncontrollable intent;
His servants he, with new acquist°   1755
Of true experience from this great event
With peace and consolation hath dismissed,
And calm of mind, all passion spent.

1727. lavers: basins. 1728. what speed: what speed I can.
1735. laurel, palm: symbols of victory. 1736. trophies:
spoils from his enemies. 1746. dispose: dispensation. 1748.
close: conclusion. 1749. he: God. 1751. in place: on this
spot. 1755. acquist: increase, acquisition.

WILLIAM FAULKNER
1897–1962

Wash

Sutpen stood above the pallet bed on which the mother and child lay. Between the shrunken planking of the wall the early sunlight fell in long pencil strokes, breaking upon his straddled legs and upon the riding whip in his hand, and lay across the still shape of the mother, who lay looking up at him from still, inscrutable, sullen eyes, the child at her side wrapped in a piece of dingy though clean cloth. Behind them an old Negro woman squatted beside the rough hearth where a meager fire smoldered.

"Well, Milly," Sutpen said, "too bad you're not a mare. Then I could give you a decent stall in the stable."

Still the girl on the pallet did not move. She merely continued to look up at him without expression, with a young, sullen, inscrutable face still pale from recent travail. Sutpen moved, bringing into the splintered pencils of sunlight the face of a man of sixty. He said quietly to the squatting Negress, "Griselda foaled this morning."

"Horse or mare?" the Negress said.

"A horse. A damned fine colt. . . . What's this?" He indicated the pallet with the hand which held the whip.

"That un's a mare, I reckon."

"Hah," Sutpen said. "A damned fine colt. Going to be the spit and image of old Rob Roy when I rode him North in '61. Do you remember?"

"Yes, Marster."

"Hah." He glanced back towards the pallet. None could have said if the girl still watched him or not. Again his whip hand indicated the pallet. "Do whatever they need with whatever we've got to do it with." He went out, passing out the crazy doorway and stepping down into the rank weeds (there yet leaned rusting against the corner of the porch the scythe which Wash had borrowed from him three months ago to cut them with) where his horse waited, where Wash stood holding the reins.

When Colonel Sutpen rode away to fight the Yankees, Wash did not go. "I'm looking after the Kernel's place and niggers," he would tell all who asked him and some who had not asked—a gaunt, malaria-ridden man with pale, questioning eyes, who looked about thirty-five, though it was known that he had not only a daughter but an eight-year-old granddaughter as well. This was a lie, as most of them—the few remaining men between eighteen and fifty—to whom he told it, knew, though there were some who believed that he himself really believed it, though even these believed that he had better sense than to put it to the test with Mrs. Sutpen or the Sutpen slaves. Knew better or was just too lazy and shiftless to try it, they said, knowing that his sole connection with the Sutpen plantation lay in the fact that for years now Colonel Sutpen had allowed him to squat in a crazy shack on a slough in the river bottom on the Sutpen place, which Sutpen had built for a fishing lodge in his bachelor days and which had since fallen in dilapidation from disuse, so that now it looked like an aged or sick wild beast crawled terrifically there to drink in the act of dying.

The Sutpen slaves themselves heard of his statement. They laughed. It was not the first time they had laughed at him, calling him white trash behind his back. They began to ask him themselves, in groups, meeting him in the faint road which led up from the slough and the old fish camp, "Why ain't you at de war, white man?"

Pausing, he would look about the ring of black faces and white eyes and teeth behind which derision lurked. "Because I got a daughter and family to keep," he said. "Git out of my road, niggers."

"Niggers?" they repeated; "niggers?" laughing now. "Who him calling us niggers?"

"Yes," he said. "I ain't got no niggers to look after my folks if I was gone."

"Nor nothing else but dat shack down yon dat Cunnel wouldn't *let* none of us live in."

Now he cursed them; sometimes he rushed at them, snatching up a stick from the ground while they scattered before him, yet seeming to surround him still with that black laughing, derisive, evasive, inescapable, leaving him panting and impotent and raging. Once it happened in the very back yard of the big house itself. This was after bitter news had come down from the Tennessee mountains and from Vicksburg, and Sherman had passed through the plantation, and most of the Negroes had followed him. Almost everything else had gone with the Federal troops, and Mrs. Sutpen had sent word to Wash that he could have the scuppernongs[1] ripening in the arbor in the back yard. This time it was a house servant, one of the few Negroes who remained; this time the Negress had to retreat up the kitchen steps, where she turned. "Stop right dar, white man. Stop right whar you is. You ain't never crossed dese steps whilst Cunnel here, and you ain't ghy' do hit now."

This was true. But there was this of a kind of pride: he had never tried to enter the big house, even though he believed that if he had, Sutpen would have received him, permitted him. "But I ain't going to give no black nigger the chance to tell me I can't go nowhere," he said to himself. "I ain't even going to give Kernel the chance to have to cuss a nigger on my account." This, though he and Sutpen had spent more than one afternoon together on those rare Sundays when there would be no company in the house. Perhaps his mind knew that it was because Sutpen had nothing else to do, being a man who could not bear his own company. Yet the fact remained that the two of them would spend whole afternoons in the scuppernong arbor, Sutpen in the hammock and Wash squatting against a post, a pail of cistern water between them, taking drink for drink from the same demijohn. Meanwhile on weekdays he would see the fine figure of the man—they were the same age almost to a day, though neither of them (perhaps because Wash had a grandchild while Sutpen's son was a youth in school) ever thought of himself as being so—on the fine figure of the black stallion, galloping about the plantation. For the moment his heart would be quiet and proud. It would seem to him that that world in which Negroes, whom the Bible told him had been created and cursed by God to be brute and vassal to all men of white skin, were better found and housed and even clothed than he and his; that world in which he sensed always about him mocking echoes of black laughter was but a dream and an illusion, and that the actual world was this one across which his own lonely apotheosis seemed to gallop on the black thoroughbred, thinking how the Book said also that all men were created in the image of God and hence all men made the same image in God's eyes at least; so that he could say, as though speaking of himself,

WASH.   **1. scuppernongs:** grapes.

"A fine proud man. If God Himself was to come down and ride the natural earth, that's what He would aim to look like."

Sutpen returned in 1865, on the black stallion. He seemed to have aged ten years. His son had vanished the same winter in which his wife had died. He returned with his citation for gallantry from the hand of General Lee to a ruined plantation, where for a year now his daughter had subsisted partially on the meager bounty of the man to whom fifteen years ago he had granted permission to live in that tumbledown fishing camp whose very existence he had at the time forgotten. Wash was there to meet him, unchanged: still gaunt, still ageless, with his pale, questioning gaze, his air diffident, a little servile, a little familiar. "Well, Kernel," Wash said, "they kilt us but they ain't whupped us yit, air they?"

That was the tenor of their conversation for the next five years. It was inferior whisky which they drank now together from a stoneware jug, and it was not in the scuppernong arbor. It was in the rear of the little store which Sutpen managed to set up on the highroad: a frame shelved room where, with Wash for clerk and porter, he dispensed kerosene and staple foodstuffs and stale gaudy candy and cheap beads and ribbons to Negroes or poor whites of Wash's own kind, who came afoot or on gaunt mules to haggle tediously for dimes and quarters with a man who at one time could gallop (the black stallion was still alive; the stable in which his jealous get lived was in better repair than the house where the master himself lived) for ten miles across his own fertile land and who had led troops gallantly in battle; until Sutpen in fury would empty the store, close and lock the doors from the inside. Then he and Wash would repair to the rear and the jug. But the talk would not be quiet now, as when Sutpen lay in the hammock, delivering an arrogant monologue while Wash squatted guffawing against his post. They both sat now, though Sutpen had the single chair while Wash used whatever box or keg was handy, and even this for just a little while, because soon Sutpen would reach that stage of impotent and furious undefeat in which he would rise, swaying and plunging, and declare again that he would take his pistol and the black stallion and ride single-handed into Washington and kill Lincoln, dead now, and Sherman, now a private citizen. "Kill them!" he would shout. "Shoot them down like the dogs they are—"

"Sho, Kernel; sho, Kernel," Wash would say, catching Sutpen as he fell. Then he would commandeer the first passing wagon or, lacking that, he would walk the mile to the nearest neighbor and borrow one and return and carry Sutpen home. He entered the house now. He had been doing so for a long time, taking Sutpen home in whatever borrowed wagon might be, talking him into locomotion with cajoling murmurs as though he were a horse, a stallion himself. The daughter would meet them and hold open the door without a word. He would carry his burden through the once white formal entrance, surmounted by a fanlight imported piece by piece from Europe and with a board now nailed over a missing pane, across a velvet carpet from which all nap was now gone, and up a formal stairs, now but a fading ghost of bare boards between two strips of fading paint, and into the bedroom. It would be dusk by now, and he would let his burden sprawl onto the bed and undress it and then he would sit quietly in a chair beside. After a time the daughter would come to the door. "We're all right now," he would tell her. "Don't you worry none, Miss Judith."

Then it would become dark, and after a while he would lie down on the floor beside the bed, though not to sleep, because after a time—sometimes before midnight—the man on the bed would stir and groan and then speak. "Wash?"

"Hyer I am, Kernel. You go back to sleep. We ain't whupped yit, air we? Me and you kin do hit."

Even then he had already seen the ribbon about his granddaughter's waist. She was now fifteen, already mature, after the early way of her kind. He knew where the ribbon came from; he had been seeing it and its kind daily for three years, even if she had lied about where she got it, which she did not, at once bold, sullen, and fearful.

"Sho now," he said. "Ef Kernel wants to give hit to you, I hope you minded to thank him."

His heart was quiet, even when he saw the dress, watching her secret, defiant, frightened face when she told him that Miss Judith, the daughter, had helped her to make it. But he was quite grave when he approached Sutpen after they closed the store that afternoon, following the other to the rear.

"Get the jug," Sutpen directed.

"Wait," Wash said. "Not yit for a minute."

Neither did Sutpen deny the dress. "What about it?" he said.

But Wash met his arrogant stare; he spoke quietly. "I've knowed you for going on twenty years. I ain't never yit denied to do what you told me to do. And I'm a man nigh sixty. And she ain't nothing but a fifteen-year-old gal."

"Meaning that I'd harm a girl? I, a man as old as you are?"

"If you was ara other man, I'd say you was as old as me. And old or no old, I wouldn't let her keep that dress nor nothing else that come from your hand. But you are different."

"How different?" But Wash merely looked at him with his pale, questioning, sober eyes. "So that's why you are afraid of me?"

Now Wash's gaze no longer questioned. It was tranquil, serene. "I ain't afraid. Because you air brave. It ain't that you were a brave man at one minute or day of your life and got a paper to show hit from General Lee. But you air brave, the same as you air alive and breathing. That's where hit's different. Hit don't need no ticket from nobody to tell me that. And I know that whatever you handle or tech, whether hit's a regiment of men or a ignorant gal or just a hound dog, that you will make hit right."

Now it was Sutpen who looked away, turning suddenly, brusquely. "Get the jug," he said sharply.

"Sho, Kernel," Wash said.

So on that Sunday dawn two years later, having watched the Negro midwife, whom he had walked three miles to fetch, enter the crazy door beyond which his granddaughter lay wailing, his heart was still quiet though concerned. He knew what they had been saying—the Negroes in cabins about the land, the white men who loafed all day long about the store, watching quietly the three of them: Sutpen, himself, his granddaughter with her air of brazen and shrinking defiance as her condition became daily more and more obvious, like three actors that came and went upon a stage. "I know what they say to one another," he thought. "I can almost hyear them: *Wash Jones has fixed old Sutpen at last. Hit taken him twenty years, but he has done hit at last.*"

It would be dawn after a while, though not yet.

From the house, where the lamp shone dim beyond the warped door frame, his granddaughter's voice came steadily as though run by a clock, while thinking went slowly and terrifically, fumbling, involved somehow with a sound of galloping hooves, until there broke suddenly free in mid-gallop the fine proud figure of the man on the fine proud stallion, galloping; and then that at which thinking fumbled, broke free too and quite clear, not in justification nor even explanation, but as the apotheosis, lonely, explicable, beyond all fouling by human touch: "He is bigger than all them Yankees that kilt his son and his wife and taken his niggers and ruined his land, bigger than this hyer durn country that he fit for and that has denied him into keeping a little country store; bigger than the denial which hit helt to his lips like the bitter cup in the Book. And how could I have lived this nigh to him for twenty years without being teched and changed by him? Maybe I ain't as big as him and maybe I ain't done none of the galloping. But at least I done been drug along. Me and him kin do hit, if so be he will show me what he aims for me to do."

Then it was dawn. Suddenly he could see the house, and the old Negress in the door looking at him. Then he realized that his granddaughter's voice had ceased. "It's a girl," the Negress said. "You can go tell him if you want to." She re-entered the house.

"A girl," he repeated; "a girl"; in astonishment, hearing the galloping hooves, seeing the proud galloping figure emerge again. He seemed to watch it pass, galloping through avatars which marked the accumulation of years, time, to the climax where it galloped beneath a brandished saber and a shot-torn flag rushing down a sky in color like thunderous sulfur, thinking for the first time in his life that perhaps Sutpen was an old man like himself. "Gittin a gal," he thought in that astonishment; then he thought with the pleased surprise of a child: "Yes, sir. Be dawg if I ain't lived to be a great-grandpaw after all."

He entered the house. He moved clumsily, on tiptoe, as if he no longer lived there, as if the infant which had just drawn breath and cried in light had dispossessed him, be it of his own blood too though it might. But even above the pallet he could see little save the blur of his granddaughter's exhausted face. Then the Negress squatting at the hearth spoke, "You better gawn tell him if you going to. Hit's daylight now."

But this was not necessary. He had no more than turned the corner of the porch where the scythe leaned which he had borrowed three months ago to clear away the weeds through which he walked, when Sutpen himself rode up on the old stallion. He did not wonder how Sutpen had got the word. He took it for granted that this was what had brought the other out at this hour on Sunday morning, and he stood while the other dismounted, and he took the reins from Sutpen's hand, an expression on his gaunt face almost imbecile with a kind of weary triumph, saying, "Hit's a gal, Kernel. I be dawg if you ain't as old as I am—" until Sutpen passed him and entered the house. He stood there with the reins in his hand and heard Sutpen cross the floor to the pallet. He heard what Sutpen said, and something seemed to stop dead in him before going on.

The sun was now up, the swift sun of Mississippi latitudes, and it seemed to him that he stood beneath a strange sky, in a strange scene, familiar only as things are familiar in dream, like the dreams of falling to one who has never climbed. "I kain't have heard what I thought I heard," he thought quietly. "I know I kain't." Yet the voice, the familiar voice which had said the words was still speaking, talking now to the old Negress about a colt foaled that morning. "That's why he was up so early," he thought. "That was hit. Hit ain't me and mine. Hit ain't even hisn that got him outen bed."

Sutpen emerged. He descended into the weeds, moving with that heavy deliberation which would have been haste when he was younger. He had not yet looked full at Wash. He said, "Dicey will stay and tend to her. You better—" Then he seemed to see Wash facing him and paused. "What?" he said.

"You said—" To his own ears Wash's voice sounded flat and ducklike, like a deaf man's. "You said if she was a mare, you could give her a good stall in the stable."

"Well?" Sutpen said. His eyes widened and narrowed, almost like a man's fists flexing and shutting, as Wash began to advance towards him, stooping a little. Very astonishment kept Sutpen still for the moment, watching that man whom in twenty years he had no more known to make any

motion save at command than he had the horse which he rode. Again his eyes narrowed and widened; without moving he seemed to rear suddenly upright. "Stand back," he said suddenly and sharply. "Don't you touch me."

"I'm going to tech you, Kernel," Wash said in that flat, quiet, almost soft voice, advancing.

Sutpen raised the hand which held the riding whip; the old Negress peered around the crazy door with her black gargoyle face of worn gnome. "Stand back, Wash," Sutpen said. Then he struck. The old Negress leaped down into the weeds with the agility of a goat and fled. Sutpen slashed Wash again across the face with the whip, striking him to his knees. When Wash rose and advanced once more he held in his hands the scythe which he had borrowed from Sutpen three months ago and which Sutpen would never need again.

When he reentered the house his granddaughter stirred on the pallet bed and called his name fretfully. "What was that?" she said.

"What was what, honey?"

"That ere racket out there."

"'Twarn't nothing," he said gently. He knelt and touched her hot forehead clumsily. "Do you want ara thing?"

"I want a sup of water," she said querulously. "I been laying here wanting a sup of water a long time, but don't nobody care enough to pay me no mind."

"Sho now," he said soothingly. He rose stiffly and fetched the dipper of water and raised her head to drink and laid her back and watched her turn to the child with an absolutely stonelike face. But a moment later he saw that she was crying quietly. "Now, now," he said, "I wouldn't do that. Old Dicey says hit's a right fine gal. Hit's all right now. Hit's all over now. Hit ain't no need to cry now."

But she continued to cry quietly, almost sullenly, and he rose again and stood uncomfortably above the pallet for a time, thinking as he had thought when his own wife lay so and then his daughter in turn: "Women. Hit's a mystry to me. They seem to want em, and yit when they git em they cry about hit. Hit's a mystry to me. To ara man." Then he moved away and drew a chair up to the window and sat down.

Through all that long, bright, sunny forenoon he sat at the window, waiting. Now and then he rose and tiptoed to the pallet. But his grand-daughter slept now, her face sullen and calm and weary, the child in the crook of her arm. Then he returned to the chair and sat again, waiting, wonder-ing why it took them so long, until he remembered that it was Sunday. He was sitting there at mid-afternoon when a half-grown white boy came around the corner of the house upon the body and gave a choked cry and looked up and glared for a mesmerized instant at Wash in the window before he turned and fled. Then Wash rose and tiptoed again to the pallet.

The granddaughter was awake now, wakened perhaps by the boy's cry without hearing it. "Milly," he said, "air you hungry?" She didn't answer, turning her face away. He built up the fire on the hearth and cooked the food which he had brought home the day before: fatback it was, and cold corn pone; he poured water into the stale coffee pot and heated it. But she would not eat when he carried the plate to her, so he ate him-self, quietly, alone, and left the dishes as they were and returned to the window.

Now he seemed to sense, feel, the men who would be gathering with horses and guns and dogs—the curious, and the vengeful: men of Sutpen's own kind, who had made the company about Sutpen's table in the time when Wash himself had yet to approach nearer to the house than the scuppernong arbor—men who had also shown the lesser ones how to fight in battle, who maybe also had signed papers from the generals saying that they were among the first of the brave; who had also galloped in the old days arrogant and proud on the fine horses across the fine plantations —symbols also of admiration and hope; instru-ments too of despair and grief.

That was who they would expect him to run from. It seemed to him that he had no more to run from than he had to run to. If he ran, he would merely be fleeing one set of bragging and evil shadows for another just like them, since they were all of a kind throughout all the earth which he knew, and he was old, too old to flee far even if he were to flee. He could never escape them, no matter how much or how far he ran: a man going on sixty could not run that far. Not far enough to escape beyond the boundaries of earth where such men lived, set the order and the rule of living. It seemed to him that he now saw for the

first time, after five years, how it was that Yankees or any other living armies had managed to whip them: the gallant, the proud, the brave; the acknowledged and chosen best among them all to carry courage and honor and pride. Maybe if he had gone to the war with them he would have discovered them sooner. But if he had discovered them sooner, what would he have done with his life since? How could he have borne to remember for five years what his life had been before?

Now it was getting toward sunset. The child had been crying; when he went to the pallet he saw his granddaughter nursing it, her face still bemused, sullen, inscrutable. "Air you hungry yit?" he said.

"I don't want nothing."

"You ought to eat."

This time she did not answer at all, looking down at the child. He returned to his chair and found that the sun had set. "Hit kain't be much longer," he thought. He could feel them quite near now, the curious and the vengeful. He could even seem to hear what they were saying about him, the undercurrent of believing beyond the immediate fury: *Old Wash Jones he come a tumble at last. He thought he had Sutpen, but Sutpen fooled him. He thought he had Kernel where he would have to marry the gal or pay up. And Kernel refused.* "But I never expected that, Kernel!" he cried aloud, catching himself at the sound of his own voice, glancing quickly back to find his granddaughter watching him.

"Who you talking to now?" she said.

"Hit ain't nothing. I was just thinking and talked out before I knowed hit."

Her face was becoming indistinct again, again a sullen blur in the twilight. "I reckon so. I reckon you'll have to holler louder than that before he'll hear you, up yonder at that house. And I reckon you'll need to do more than holler before you get him down here too."

"Sho now," he said. "Don't you worry none." But already thinking was going smoothly on: "You know I never. You know how I ain't never expected or asked nothing from ara living man but what I expected from you. And I never asked that. I didn't think hit would need. I said, *I don't need to. What need has a fellow like Wash Jones to question or doubt the man that General Lee himself says in a handwrote ticket that he was brave?* Brave," he thought. "Better if nara one of them had never rid back home in '65''; thinking *Better if his kind and mine too had never drawn the breath of life on this earth. Better that all who remain of us be blasted from the face of earth than that another Wash Jones should see his whole life shredded from him and shrivel away like a dried shuck thrown onto the fire.*

He ceased, became still. He heard the horses, suddenly and plainly; presently he saw the lantern and the movement of men, the glint of gun barrels, in its moving light. Yet he did not stir. It was quite dark now, and he listened to the voices and the sounds of underbrush as they surrounded the house. The lantern itself came on; its light fell upon the quiet body in the weeds and stopped, the horses tall and shadowy. A man descended and stooped in the lantern light, above the body. He held a pistol; he rose and faced the house. "Jones," he said.

"I'm here," Wash said quietly from the window. "That you, Major?"

"Come out."

"Sho," he said quietly. "I just want to see to my granddaughter."

"We'll see to her. Come on out."

"Sho, Major. Just a minute."

"Show a light. Light your lamp."

"Sho. In just a minute." They could hear his voice retreat into the house, though they could not see him as he went swiftly to the crack in the chimney where he kept the butcher knife: the one thing in his slovenly life and house in which he took pride, since it was razor sharp. He approached the pallet, his granddaughter's voice:

"Who is it? Light the lamp, grandpaw."

"Hit won't need no light, honey. Hit won't take but a minute," he said, kneeling, fumbling toward her voice, whispering now. "Where air you?"

"Right here," she said fretfully. "Where would I be? What is. . . ." His hand touched her face. "What is. . . . Grandpaw! Grand. . . ."

"Jones!" the sheriff said. "Come out of there!"

"In just a minute, Major," he said. Now he rose and moved swiftly. He knew where in the dark the can of kerosene was, just as he knew that it was full, since it was not two days ago that he had filled it at the store and held it there until he got a ride home with it, since the five gallons were heavy. There were still coals on the hearth; besides the crazy building itself was like tinder: the coals, the

hearth, the walls exploding in a single blue glare. Against it the waiting men saw him in a wild instant springing toward them with the lifted scythe before the horses reared and whirled. They checked the horses and turned them back toward the glare, yet still in wild relief against it the gaunt figure ran toward them with the lifted scythe.

"Jones!" the sheriff shouted. "Stop! Stop, or I'll shoot. Jones! *Jones!*" Yet still the gaunt, furious figure came on against the glare and roar of the flames. With the scythe lifted, it bore down upon them, upon the wild glaring eyes of the horses and the swinging glints of gun barrels, without any cry, any sound.

ROBERT BROWNING
1812–1889

My Last Duchess

FERRARA°

That's my last Duchess painted on the wall,
Looking as if she were alive. I call
That piece a wonder, now: Frà Pandolf's° hands
Worked busily a day, and there she stands.
Will 't please you sit and look at her? I said   5
"Frà Pandolf" by design, for never read
Strangers like you that pictured countenance,
The depth and passion of its earnest glance,
But to myself they turned (since none puts by
The curtain I have drawn for you, but I)   10
And seemed as they would ask me, if they durst,
How such a glance came there; so, not the first
Are you to turn and ask thus. Sir, 'twas not
Her husband's presence only, called that spot
Of joy into the Duchess' cheek: perhaps   15
Frà Pandolf chanced to say "Her mantle laps
Over my lady's wrist too much," or "Paint
Must never hope to reproduce the faint
Half-flush that dies along her throat": such stuff
Was courtesy, she thought, and cause enough   20
For calling up that spot of joy. She had

MY LAST DUCHESS. **Ferrara:** Italian city prominent in the Renaissance. **3. Fra Pandolf:** imaginary painter.

A heart—how shall I say?—too soon made glad,
Too easily impressed; she liked whate'er
She looked on, and her looks went everywhere.
Sir, 'twas all one! My favor° at her breast,   25
The dropping of the daylight in the West,
The bough of cherries some officious fool
Broke in the orchard for her, the white mule
She rode with round the terrace—all and each
Would draw from her alike the approving
   speech,   30
Or blush, at least. She thanked men,—good! but
   thanked
Somehow—I know not how—as if she ranked
My gift of a nine-hundred-years-old name
With anybody's gift. Who 'd stoop to blame
This sort of trifling? Even had you skill   35
In speech—(which I have not)—to make your will
Quite clear to such an one, and say, "Just this
Or that in you disgusts me; here you miss,
Or there exceed the mark"—and if she let
Herself be lessoned so, nor plainly set   40
Her wits to yours, forsooth, and made excuse,
—E'en then would be some stooping; and I choose
Never to stoop. Oh, sir, she smiled, no doubt,
Whene'er I passed her; but who passed without
Much the same smile? This grew; I gave com-
   mands;   45
Then all smiles stopped together. There she stands
As if alive.° Will 't please you rise? We'll meet
The company below, then. I repeat,
The Count your master's known munificence
Is ample warrant that no just pretense°   50
Of mine for dowry will be disallowed;
Though his fair daughter's self, as I avowed
At starting, is my object. Nay, we 'll go
Together down, sir. Notice Neptune, though,
Taming a sea-horse, thought a rarity,   55
Which Claus of Innsbruck° cast in bronze for me!

25. favor: ornament. **45–47. I . . . alive:** When questioned about these lines by Professor Hiram Corson of Cornell, Browning suggested that the duke may have had the duchess executed or put in a convent. **50. pretense:** claim. **56. Claus of Innsbruck:** imaginary sculptor.

ROBERT FROST
1875–1963

Home Burial

He saw her from the bottom of the stairs
Before she saw him. She was starting down,
Looking back over her shoulder at some fear.
She took a doubtful step and then undid it
To raise herself and look again. He spoke   5
Advancing toward her: "What is it you see
From up there always—for I want to know."
She turned and sank upon her skirts at that,
And her face changed from terrified to dull.
He said to gain time: "What is it you see,"   10
Mounting until she cowered under him.
"I will find out now—you must tell me, dear."
She, in her place, refused him any help
With the least stiffening of her neck and silence.
She let him look, sure that he wouldn't see,   15
Blind creature; and a while he didn't see.
But at last he murmured, "Oh," and again, "Oh."

"What is it—what?" she said.

                     "Just that I see."

"You don't," she challenged. "Tell me what it is."

"The wonder is I didn't see at once.   20
I never noticed it from here before.
I must be wonted to it—that's the reason.
The little graveyard where my people are!
So small the window frames the whole of it.
Not so much larger than a bedroom, is it?   25
There are three stones of slate and one of marble,
Broad-shouldered little slabs there in the sunlight
On the sidehill. We haven't to mind *those*.
But I understand: it is not the stones,
But the child's mound—"

           "Don't, don't, don't, don't," she cried.

She withdrew shrinking from beneath his arm   31
That rested on the banister, and slid downstairs;
And turned on him with such a daunting look,
He said twice over before he knew himself:
"Can't a man speak of his own child he's lost?" 35

"Not you! Oh, where's my hat? Oh, I don't need it!
I must get out of here. I must get air.
I don't know rightly whether any man can."

"Amy! Don't go to someone else this time.
Listen to me. I won't come down the stairs."   40
He sat and fixed his chin between his fists.
"There's something I should like to ask you, dear."

"You don't know how to ask it."

                        "Help me, then."

Her fingers moved the latch for all reply.

"My words are nearly always an offense.   45
I don't know how to speak of anything
So as to please you. But I might be taught,
I should suppose. I can't say I see how.
A man must partly give up being a man
With womenfolk. We could have some arrange-
    ment   50
By which I'd bind myself to keep hands off
Anything special you're a-mind to name.
Though I don't like such things 'twixt those that
    love.
Two that don't love can't live together without
    them.
But two that do can't live together with them."   55
She moved the latch a little. "Don't—don't go.
Don't carry it to someone else this time.
Tell me about it if it's something human.
Let me into your grief. I'm not so much
Unlike other folks as your standing there   60
Apart would make me out. Give me my chance.
I do think, though, you overdo it a little.
What was it brought you up to think it the thing
To take your mother-loss of a first child
So inconsolably—in the face of love.   65
You'd think his memory might be satisfied—"
"There you go sneering now!"

                        "I'm not, I'm not!
You make me angry. I'll come down to you.
God, what a woman! And it's come to this,   69
A man can't speak of his own child that's dead."

"You can't because you don't know how to speak
If you had any feelings, you that dug
With your own hand—how could you?—his little
    grave;
I saw you from that very window there,
Making the gravel leap and leap in air,   75
Leap up, like that, like that, and land so lightly
And roll back down the mound beside the hole.
I thought, Who is that man? I didn't know you.

And I crept down the stairs and up the stairs
To look again, and still your spade kept lifting.   80
Then you came in. I heard your rumbling voice
Out in the kitchen, and I don't know why,
But I went near to see with my own eyes.
You could sit there with the stains on your shoes
Of the fresh earth from your own baby's grave   85
And talk about your everyday concerns.
You had stood the spade up against the wall
Outside there in the entry, for I saw it."

"I shall laugh the worst laugh I ever laughed.
I'm cursed. God, if I don't believe I'm cursed."   90

"I can repeat the very words you were saying.
'Three foggy mornings and one rainy day
Will rot the best birch fence a man can build.'
Think of it, talk like that at such a time!
What had how long it takes a birch to rot   95
To do with what was in the darkened parlor.
You *couldn't* care! The nearest friends can go
With anyone to death, comes so far short
They might as well not try to go at all.
No, from the time when one is sick to death,   100
One is alone, and he dies more alone.
Friends make pretense of following to the grave,
But before one is in it, their minds are turned
And making the best of their way back to life
And living people, and things they understand.   105
But the world's evil. I won't have grief so
If I can change it. Oh, I won't, I won't!"

"There, you have said it all and you feel better.
You won't go now, you're crying. Close the door.
The heart's gone out of it: why keep it up.   110
Amy! There's someone coming down the road!"

"*You*—oh, you think the talk is all. I must go—
Somewhere out of this house. How can I make
    you—"

"If—you—do!" She was opening the door wider.
"Where do you mean to go? First tell me that.   115
I'll follow and bring you back by force. I *will!*—"

ROBERT LOWELL
b. 1917

Mother Marie Therese

Drowned in 1912
The speaker is a Canadian nun stationed
in New Brunswick

Old sisters at our Maris Stella House
Remember how the Mother's strangled grouse
And snowshoe rabbits matched the royal glint
Of Pio Nono's° vestments in the print
That used to face us, while our aching ring   5
Of stationary rockers saw her bring
Our cake. Often, when sunset hurt the rocks
Off Carthage, and surprised us knitting socks
For victims of the Franco-Prussian War,
Our scandal'd set her frowning at the floor;   10
And vespers struck like lightning through the
    gloom
And oaken ennui of her sitting room.
It strikes us now, but cannot reinspire;
False, false and false, I mutter to my fire.
The good old times, ah yes! But good, that all's   15
Forgotten like our Province's cabals;
And Jesus, smiling earthward, finds it good;
For we were friends of Cato,° not of God.
This sixtieth Christmas, I'm content to pray
For what life's shrinkage leaves from day to day;   20
And it's a sorrow to recall our young
Raptures for Mother, when her trophies hung,
Fresh in their blood and color, to convince
Even Probationers that Heaven's Prince,
Befriending, whispered: "Is it then so hard?   25
Tarry a little while, O disregard
Time's wings and armor, when it flutters down
Papal tiaras and the Bourbon crown;
For quickly, priest and prince will stand, their
    shields
Before each other's faces, in the fields,   30
Where, as I promised, virtue will compel

Michael and all his angels to repel
Satan's advances, till his forces lie
Beside the Lamb in blissful fealty."
Our Indian summer! Then, our skies could lift,   35
God willing; but an Indian brought the gift.°
"A sword," said Father Turbot, "not a saint";
Yet He who made the Virgin without taint,
Chastised our Mother to the Rule's restraint.
Was it not fated that the sweat of Christ   40
Would wash the worldly serpent? Christ enticed
Her heart that fluttered, while she whipped her
    hounds
Into the quicksands of her manor grounds
A lordly child, her habit fleur-de-lys'd
There she dismounted, sick; with little heed,   45
Surrendered. Like Proserpina,° who fell
Six months a year from earth to flower in hell;
She half-renounced by Candle, Book and Bell
Her flowers and fowling pieces for the Church.
She never spared the child and spoiled the birch;   50
And how she'd chide her novices, and pluck
Them by the ears for gabbling in Canuck,
While she was reading Rabelais from her chaise,
Or parroting the *Action Française.*°
Her letter from the soi-disant° French King,   55
And the less treasured golden wedding ring
Of her shy Bridegroom, yellow; and the regal
Damascus shotguns, pegged upon her eagle
Emblems from Hohenzollern standards, rust.
Our world is passing; even she, whose trust   60
Was in its princes, fed the gluttonous gulls,
That whiten our Atlantic, when like skulls
They drift for sewage with the emerald tide.
Perpetual novenas cannot tide
Us past that drowning. After Mother died,   65
"An émigrée in this world and the next,"
Said Father Turbot, playing with his text.
Where is he? Surely, he is one of those,
Whom Christ and Satan spew! But no one knows
What's happened to that porpoise-bellied priest.   70
He lodged with us on Louis Neuvième's Feast,
And celebrated her memorial mass.
His bald spot tapestried by colored glass,
Our angels, Prussian blue and flaking red,
He squeaked and stuttered: "N-n-nothing is so
    d-dead   75

MOTHER MARIE THERESE. **4. Pio Nono:** Pope Pius IX
(1846–78). **18. Cato:** Roman ambassador to Carthage (l. 8)
in the second century B.C. The prosperity of the ancient
North African city, Rome's rival, led Cato to advocate
war against Carthage. The Third Punic War broke out in
149 B.C., and the city was totally destroyed.

36. an . . . gift: Cf. Indian giver. **46. Proserpina:** daughter
of Jupiter and Ceres, goddess of fertility. She was abducted
by Pluto and compelled to spend six months each year as
his wife in the underworld. **54. Action Française:** French
royalist journal. **55. soi-disant:** pretender.

as a dead s-s-sister." Off Saint Denis' Head,
Our Mother, drowned on an excursion, sleeps.
Her billy goat, or its descendant, keeps
Watch on a headland, and I hear it bawl
into this sixty-knot Atlantic squall,   80
"Mamamma's Baby," past Queen Mary's Neck,
The ledge at Carthage—almost to Quebec,
Where Monsieur de Montcalm,° on Abraham's
Bosom, asleep, perceives our world that shams
His New World, lost—however it atones   85
For Wolfe, the Englishman, and Huron bones
And priests'. O Mother, here our snuffling crones
and cretins feared you, but I owe you flowers:
The dead, the sea's dead, has her sorrows, hours
on end to lie tossing to the east, cold,   90
Without bedfellows, washed and bored and old,
Bilged by her thoughts, and worked on by the
     worms,
Until her fossil convent come to terms
With the Atlantic. Mother, there is room
Beyond our harbor. Past its wooden Boom   95
Now weak and waterlogged, that Frontenac°
Once diagrammed, she welters on her back.
The bell-buoy, whom she called the Cardinal,
Dances upon her. If she hears at all,

She only hears it tolling to this shore,   100
Where our frost-bitten sisters know the roar
Of water, inching, always on the move
For virgins, when they wish the times were love,
And their hysterical hosannas rouse
The loveless harems of the buck ruffed grouse, 105
Who drums, untroubled now, beside the sea—
As if he found our stern virginity
Contra naturam. We are ruinous;
God's Providence through time has mastered us:
Now all the bells are tongueless, now we freeze, 110
A later Advent, pruner of warped trees,
Whistles about our nunnery slabs, and yells,
And water oozes from us into wells;
A new year swells and stirs. Our narrow Bay
Freezes itself and us. We cannot say   115
Christ even sees us, when the ice floes toss
His statue, made by Hurons, on the cross,
That Father Turbot sank on Mother's mound—
A whirligig! Mother, we must give ground,
Little by little; but it does no good.   120
Tonight, while I am piling on more driftwood,
And stooping with the poker, you are here,
Telling your beads; and breathing in my ear,
You watch your orphan swording at her fears.
I feel you twitch my shoulder. No one hears   125
Us mock the sisters, as we used to, years
And years behind us, when we heard the spheres
Whirring *venite*; and we held our ears.
My mother's hollow sockets fill with tears.

83. Monsieur de Montcalm: French general defeated by the British general Wolfe on the Plains of Abraham, Quebec, in 1759 in the decisive battle between the French and the British for possession of Canada. **96. Frontenac:** French governor of Canada in the last quarter of the seventeenth century.

The Romantic Phase:
Escape from Bondage

HENRY JAMES
1843–1916

The Pupil

1

The poor young man hesitated and procrastinated: it cost him such an effort to broach the subject of terms, to speak of money to a person who spoke only of feelings and, as it were, of the aristocracy. Yet he was unwilling to take leave, treating his engagement as settled, without some more conventional glance in that direction than he could find an opening for in the manner of the large, affable lady who sat there drawing a pair of soiled *gants de Suède*[1] through a fat, jeweled hand and, at once pressing and gliding, repeated over and over everything but the thing he would have liked to hear. He would have liked to hear the figure of his salary; but just as he was nervously about to sound that note the little boy came back—the little boy Mrs. Moreen had sent out of the room to fetch her fan. He came back without the fan, only with the casual observation that he couldn't find it. As he dropped this cynical confession he looked straight and hard at the candidate for the honor of taking his education in hand. This personage reflected, somewhat grimly, that the first thing he should have to teach his little charge would be to appear to address himself to his mother when he spoke to her—especially not to make her such an improper answer as that.

THE PUPIL. **1. gants de Suède:** suede gloves.

When Mrs. Moreen bethought herself of this pretext for getting rid of their companion, Pemberton supposed it was precisely to approach the delicate subject of his remuneration. But it had been only to say some things about her son which it was better that a boy of eleven shouldn't catch. They were extravagantly to his advantage, save when she lowered her voice to sigh, tapping her left side familiarly: "And all overclouded by *this*, you know—all at the mercy of a weakness—!" Pemberton gathered that the weakness was in the region of the heart. He had known the poor child was not robust: this was the basis on which he had been invited to treat, through an English lady, an Oxford acquaintance, then at Nice, who happened to know both his needs and those of the amiable American family looking out for something really superior in the way of a resident tutor.

The young man's impression of his prospective pupil, who had first come into the room, as if to see for himself, as soon as Pemberton was admitted, was not quite the soft solicitation the visitor had taken for granted. Morgan Moreen was, somehow, sickly without being delicate, and that he looked intelligent (it is true Pemberton wouldn't have enjoyed his being stupid), only added to the suggestion that, as with his big mouth and big ears he really couldn't be called pretty, he might be unpleasant. Pemberton was modest—he was even timid; and the chance that his small scholar might prove cleverer than himself had quite figured, to his nervousness, among the dangers of an untried experiment. He reflected, however, that these were risks one had to run when one accepted a position, as it was called, in a private family; when as yet one's University honors had, pecuniarily speaking,

449

remained barren. At any rate, when Mrs. Moreen got up as if to intimate that, since it was understood he would enter upon his duties within the week she would let him off now, he succeeded, in spite of the presence of the child, in squeezing out a phrase about the rate of payment. It was not the fault of the conscious smile which seemed a reference to the lady's expensive identity, if the allusion did not sound rather vulgar. This was exactly because she became still more gracious to reply: "Oh! I can assure you that all that will be quite regular."

Pemberton only wondered, while he took up his hat, what "all that" was to amount to—people had such different ideas. Mrs. Moreen's words, however, seemed to commit the family to a pledge definite enough to elicit from the child a strange little comment, in the shape of the mocking, foreign ejaculation, "Oh, là-là!"

Pemberton, in some confusion, glanced at him as he walked slowly to the window with his back turned, his hands in his pockets and the air in his elderly shoulders of a boy who didn't play. The young man wondered if he could teach him to play, though his mother had said it would never do and that this was why school was impossible. Mrs. Moreen exhibited no discomfiture; she only continued blandly: "Mr. Moreen will be delighted to meet your wishes. As I told you, he has been called to London for a week. As soon as he comes back you shall have it out with him."

This was so frank and friendly that the young man could only reply, laughing as his hostess laughed: "Oh! I don't imagine we shall have much of a battle."

"They'll give you anything you like," the boy remarked unexpectedly, returning from the window. "We don't mind what anything costs—we live awfully well."

"My darling, you're too quaint!" his mother exclaimed, putting out to caress him a practiced but ineffectual hand. He slipped out of it, but looked with intelligent, innocent eyes at Pemberton, who had already had time to notice that from one moment to the other his small satiric face seemed to change its time of life. At this moment it was infantine; yet it appeared also to be under the influence of curious intuitions and knowledges. Pemberton rather disliked precocity, and he was disappointed to find gleams of it in a disciple not yet in his teens. Nevertheless he divined on the

spot that Morgan wouldn't prove a bore. He would prove on the contrary a kind of excitement. This idea held the young man, in spite of a certain repulsion.

"You pompous little person! We're not extravagant!" Mrs. Moreen gayly protested, making another unsuccessful attempt to draw the boy to her side. "You must know what to expect," she went on to Pemberton.

"The less you expect the better!" her companion interposed. "But we *are* people of fashion."

"Only so far as *you* make us so!" Mrs. Moreen mocked, tenderly. "Well, then, on Friday—don't tell me you're superstitious—and mind you don't fail us. Then you'll see us all. I'm so sorry the girls are out. I guess you'll like the girls. And, you know, I've another son, quite different from this one."

"He tries to imitate me," said Morgan to Pemberton.

"He tries? Why, he's twenty years old!" cried Mrs. Moreen.

"You're very witty," Pemberton remarked to the child—a proposition that his mother echoed with enthusiasm, declaring that Morgan's sallies were the delight of the house. The boy paid no heed to this; he only inquired abruptly of the visitor, who was surprised afterwards that he hadn't struck him as offensively forward: "Do you *want* very much to come?"

"Can you doubt it, after such a description of what I shall hear?" Pemberton replied. Yet he didn't want to come at all; he was coming because he had to go somewhere, thanks to the collapse of his fortune at the end of a year abroad, spent on the system of putting his tiny patrimony into a single full wave of experience. He had had his full wave, but he couldn't pay his hotel bill. Moreover, he had caught in the boy's eyes the glimpse of a far-off appeal.

"Well, I'll do the best I can for you," said Morgan; with which he turned away again. He passed out of one of the long windows; Pemberton saw him go and lean on the parapet of the terrace. He remained there while the young man took leave of his mother, who, on Pemberton's looking as if he expected a farewell from him, interposed with: "Leave him, leave him; he's so strange!" Pemberton suspected she was afraid of something he might say. "He's a genius—you'll love him," she added. "He's much the most interesting person in the family." And before he could invent some civility to oppose to this, she wound up with: "But we're all good, you know!"

"He's a genius—you'll love him!" were words that recurred to Pemberton before the Friday, suggesting, among other things that geniuses were not invariably lovable. However, it was all the better if there was an element that would make tutoring absorbing: he had perhaps taken too much for granted that it would be dreary. As he left the villa after his interview, he looked up at the balcony and saw the child leaning over it. "We shall have great larks!" he called up.

Morgan hesitated a moment; then he answered, laughing: "By the time you come back I shall have thought of something witty!"

This made Pemberton say to himself: "After all he's rather nice."

2

On the Friday he saw them all, as Mrs. Moreen had promised, for her husband had come back and the girls and the other son were at home. Mr. Moreen had a white mustache, a confiding manner and, in his buttonhole, the ribbon of a foreign order—bestowed, as Pemberton eventually learned, for services. For what services he never clearly ascertained: this was a point—one of a large number—that Mr. Moreen's manner never confided. What it emphatically did confide was that he was a man of the world. Ulick, the firstborn, was in visible training for the same profession—under the disadvantage as yet, however, of a buttonhole only feebly floral and a mustache with no pretensions to type. The girls had hair and figures and manners and small fat feet, but had never been out alone. As for Mrs. Moreen, Pemberton saw on a nearer view that her elegance was intermittent and her parts didn't always match. Her husband, as she had promised, met with enthusiasm Pemberton's ideas in regard to a salary. The young man had endeavored to make them modest, and Mr. Moreen confided to him that *he* found them positively meager. He further assured him that he aspired to be intimate with his children, to be their best friend, and that he was always looking out for them. That was what he went off for, to London and other places—to look out; and this vigilance

was the theory of life, as well as the real occupation, of the whole family. They all looked out, for they were very frank on the subject of its being necessary. They desired it to be understood that they were earnest people, and also that their fortune, though quite adequate for earnest people, required the most careful administration. Mr. Moreen, as the parent bird, sought sustenance for the nest. Ulick found sustenance mainly at the club, where Pemberton guessed that it was usually served on green cloth. The girls used to do up their hair and their frocks themselves, and our young man felt appealed to to be glad, in regard to Morgan's education, that, though it must naturally be of the best, it didn't cost too much. After a little he *was* glad, forgetting at times his own needs in the interest inspired by the child's nature and education and the pleasure of making easy terms for him.

During the first weeks of their acquaintance Morgan had been as puzzling as a page in an unknown language—altogether different from the obvious little Anglo-Saxons who had misrepresented childhood to Pemberton. Indeed the whole mystic volume in which the boy had been bound demanded some practice in translation. Today, after a considerable interval, there is something phantasmagoric, like a prismatic reflection or a serial novel, in Pemberton's memory of the queerness of the Moreens. If it were not for a few tangible tokens—a lock of Morgan's hair, cut by his own hand, and the half-dozen letters he got from him when they were separated—the whole episode and the figures peopling it would seem too inconsequent for anything but dreamland. The queerest thing about them was their success (as it appeared to him for a while at the time), for he had never seen a family so brilliantly equipped for failure. Wasn't it success to have kept him so hatefully long? Wasn't it success to have drawn him in that first morning at *déjeuner*,[2] the Friday he came—it was enough to *make* one superstitious —so that he utterly committed himself, and this not by calculation or a *mot d'ordre*,[3] but by a happy instinct which made them, like a band of gypsies, work so neatly together? They amused him as much as if they had really been a band of gypsies. He was still young and had not seen much of the world—his English years had been intensely

2. dejeuner: late breakfast or lunch. 3. mot d'ordre: password.

usual; therefore the reversed conventions of the Moreens (for they had their standards), struck him as topsyturvy. He had encountered nothing like them at Oxford; still less had any such note been struck to his younger American ear during the four years at Yale in which he had richly supposed himself to be reacting against Puritanism. The reaction of the Moreens, at any rate, went ever so much further. He had thought himself very clever that first day in hitting them all off in his mind with the term "cosmopolite." Later, it seemed feeble and colorless enough—confessedly, helplessly provisional.

However, when he first applied it to them he had a degree of joy—for an instructor he was still empirical—as if from the apprehension that to live with them would really be to see life. Their sociable strangeness was an intimation of that— their chatter of tongues, their gaiety and good humor, their infinite dawdling (they were always getting themselves up, but it took forever, and Pemberton had once found Mr. Moreen shaving in the drawing-room), their French, their Italian and, in the spiced fluency, their cold, tough slices of American. They lived on macaroni and coffee (they had these articles prepared in perfection); but they knew recipes for a hundred other dishes. They overflowed with music and song, were always humming and catching each other up, and had a kind of professional acquaintance with continental cities. They talked of "good places" as if they had been strolling players. They had at Nice a villa, a carriage, a piano and a banjo, and they went to official parties. They were a perfect calendar of the "days" of their friends, which Pemberton knew them, when they were indisposed, to get out of bed to go to, and which made the week larger than life when Mrs. Moreen talked of them with Paula and Amy. Their romantic initiations gave their new inmate at first an almost dazzling sense of culture. Mrs. Moreen had translated something, at some former period—an author whom it made Pemberton feel *borné*[4] never to have heard of. They could imitate Venetian and sing Neapolitan, and when they wanted to say something very particular they communicated with each other in an ingenious dialect of their own—a sort of spoken cipher, which Pemberton at first took for Volapuk,[5] but

which he learned to understand as he would not have understood Volapuk.

"It's the family language—Ultramoreen," Morgan explained to him drolly enough; but the boy rarely condescended to use it himself, though he attempted colloquial Latin as if he had been a little prelate.

Among all the "days" with which Mrs. Moreen's memory was taxed she managed to squeeze in one of her own, which her friends sometimes forgot. But the house derived a frequented air from the number of fine people who were freely named there and from several mysterious men with foreign titles and English clothes whom Morgan called the princes and who, on sofas with the girls, talked French very loud, as if to show they were saying nothing improper. Pemberton wondered how the princes could ever propose in that tone and so publicly: he took for granted cynically that this was what was desired of them. Then he acknowledged that even for the chance of such an advantage Mrs. Moreen would never allow Paula and Amy to receive alone. These young ladies were not at all timid, but it was just the safeguards that made them so graceful. It was a houseful of Bohemians who wanted tremendously to be Philistines.

In one respect, however, certainly, they achieved no rigor—they were wonderfully amiable and ecstatic about Morgan. It was a genuine tenderness, an artless admiration, equally strong in each. They even praised his beauty, which was small, and were rather afraid of him, as if they recognised that he was of a finer clay. They called him a little angel and a little prodigy and pitied his want of health effusively. Pemberton feared at first that their extravagance would make him hate the boy, but before this happened he had become extravagant himself. Later, when he had grown rather to hate the others, it was a bribe to patience for him that they were at any rate nice about Morgan, going on tiptoe if they fancied he was showing symptoms, and even giving up somebody's "day" to procure him a pleasure. But mixed with this was the oddest wish to make him independent, as if they felt that they were not good enough for him. They passed him over to Pemberton very much as if they wished to force a constructive adoption on the obliging bachelor and shirk altogether a responsibility. They were delighted when they perceived

---

4. **borné:** inexperienced. 5. **Volapuk:** an invented universal language.

that Morgan liked his preceptor, and could think of no higher praise for the young man. It was strange how they contrived to reconcile the appearance, and indeed the essential fact, of adoring the child with their eagerness to wash their hands of him. Did they want to get rid of him before he should find them out? Pemberton was finding them out month by month. At any rate, the boy's relations turned their backs with exaggerated delicacy, as if to escape the charge of interfering. Seeing in time how little he had in common with them (it was by *them* he first observed it —they proclaimed it with complete humility), his preceptor was moved to speculate on the mysteries of transmission, the far jumps of heredity. Where his detachment from most of the things they represented had come from was more than an observer could say—it certainly had burrowed under two or three generations.

As for Pemberton's own estimate of his pupil, it was a good while before he got the point of view, so little had he been prepared for it by the smug young barbarians to whom the tradition of tutorship, as hitherto revealed to him, had been adjusted. Morgan was scrappy and surprising, deficient in many properties supposed common to the *genus* and abounding in others that were the portion only of the supernaturally clever. One day Pemberton made a great stride: it cleared up the question to perceive that Morgan *was* supernaturally clever and that, though the formula was temporarily meager, this would be the only assumption on which one could successfully deal with him. He had the general quality of a child for whom life had not been simplified by school, a kind of homebred sensibility which might have been bad for himself but was charming for others, and a whole range of refinement and perception—little musical vibrations as taking as picked-up airs— begotten by wandering about Europe at the tail of his migratory tribe. This might not have been an education to recommend in advance, but its results with Morgan were as palpable as a fine texture. At the same time he had in his composition a sharp spice of stoicism, doubtless the fruit of having had to begin early to bear pain, which produced the impression of pluck and made it of less consequence that he might have been thought at school rather a polyglot little beast. Pemberton indeed quickly found himself rejoicing that school

was out of the question: in any million of boys it was probably good for all but one, and Morgan was that millionth. It would have made him comparative and superior—it might have made him priggish. Pemberton would try to be school himself—a bigger seminary than five hundred grazing donkeys; so that, winning no prizes, the boy would remain unconscious and irresponsible and amusing —amusing, because, though life was already intense in his childish nature, freshness still made there a strong draft for jokes. It turned out that even in the still air of Morgan's various disabilities jokes flourished greatly. He was a pale, lean, acute, undeveloped little cosmopolite, who liked intellectual gymnastics and who, also, as regards the behavior of mankind, had noticed more things than you might suppose, but who nevertheless had his proper playroom of superstitions, where he smashed a dozen toys a day.

3

At Nice once, towards evening, as the pair sat resting in the open air after a walk, looking over the sea at the pink western lights, Morgan said suddenly to his companion: "Do you like it—you know, being with us all in this intimate way?"

"My dear fellow, why should I stay if I didn't?"

"How do I know you will stay? I'm almost sure you won't, very long."

"I hope you don't mean to dismiss me," said Pemberton.

Morgan considered a moment, looking at the sunset. "I think if I did right I ought to."

"Well, I know I'm supposed to instruct you in virtue; but in that case don't do right."

"You're very young—fortunately," Morgan went on, turning to him again.

"Oh yes, compared with you!"

"Therefore, it won't matter so much if you do lose a lot of time."

"That's the way to look at it," said Pemberton accommodatingly.

They were silent a minute; after which the boy asked: "Do you like my father and mother very much?"

"Dear me, yes. They're charming people."

Morgan received this with another silence; then, unexpectedly, familiarly, but at the same time affectionately, he remarked: "You're a jolly old humbug!"

For a particular reason the words made Pemberton change color. The boy noticed in an instant that he had turned red, whereupon he turned red himself and the pupil and the master exchanged a longish glance in which there was a consciousness of many more things than are usually touched upon, even tacitly, in such a relation. It produced for Pemberton an embarrassment; it raised, in a shadowy form, a question (this was the first glimpse of it), which was destined to play a singular and, as he imagined, owing to the altogether peculiar conditions, an unprecedented part in his intercourse with his little companion. Later, when he found himself talking with this small boy in a way in which few small boys could ever have been talked with, he thought of that clumsy moment on the bench at Nice as the dawn of an understanding that had broadened. What had added to the clumsiness then was that he thought it his duty to declare to Morgan that he might abuse him (Pemberton) as much as he liked, but must never abuse his parents. To this Morgan had the easy reply that he hadn't dreamed of abusing them; which appeared to be true: it put Pemberton in the wrong.

"Then why am I a humbug for saying *I* think them charming?" the young man asked, conscious of a certain rashness.

"Well—they're not *your* parents."

"They love you better than anything in the world—never forget that," said Pemberton.

"Is that why you like them so much?"

"They're very kind to me," Pemberton replied, evasively.

"You *are* a humbug!" laughed Morgan, passing an arm into his tutor's. He leaned against him, looking off at the sea again and swinging his long, thin legs.

"Don't kick my shins," said Pemberton, while he reflected: "Hang it, I can't complain of them to the child!"

"There's another reason, too," Morgan went on, keeping his legs still.

"Another reason for what?"

"Besides their not being your parents."

"I don't understand you," said Pemberton.

"Well, you will before long. All right!"

Pemberton did understand, fully, before long;

but he made a fight even with himself before he confessed it. He thought it the oddest thing to have a struggle with the child about. He wondered he didn't detest the child for launching him in such a struggle. But by the time it began the resource of detesting the child was closed to him. Morgan was a special case, but to know him was to accept him on his own odd terms. Pemberton had spent his aversion to special cases before arriving at knowledge. When at last he did arrive he felt that he was in an extreme predicament. Against every interest he had attached himself. They would have to meet things together. Before they went home that evening, at Nice, the boy had said, clinging to his arm:

"Well, at any rate you'll hang on to the last."

"To the last?"

"Till you're fairly beaten."

"*You* ought to be fairly beaten!" cried the young man, drawing him closer.

4

A year after Pemberton had come to live with them Mr. and Mrs. Moreen suddenly gave up the villa at Nice. Pemberton had got used to suddenness, having seen it practiced on a considerable scale during two jerky little tours—one in Switzerland the first summer, and the other late in the winter, when they all ran down to Florence and then, at the end of ten days, liking it much less than they had intended, straggled back in mysterious depression. They had returned to Nice "forever," as they said; but this didn't prevent them from squeezing, one rainy, muggy May night, into a second-class railway-carriage—you could never tell by which class they would travel—where Pemberton helped them to stow away a wonderful collection of bundles and bags. The explanation of this maneuver was that they had determined to spend the summer "in some bracing place"; but in Paris they dropped into a small furnished apartment—a fourth floor in a third-rate avenue, where there was a smell on the staircase and the *portier*[6] was hateful—and passed the next four months in blank indigence.

The better part of this baffled sojourn was for the preceptor and his pupil, who, visiting the Invalides and Notre Dame, the Conciergerie and all

6. **portier:** porter.

the museums, took a hundred remunerative rambles. They learned to know their Paris, which was useful, for they came back another year for a longer stay, the general character of which in Pemberton's memory today mixes pitiably and confusedly with that of the first. He sees Morgan's shabby knickerbockers—the everlasting pair that didn't match his blouse and that as he grew longer could only grow faded. He remembers the particular holes in his three or four pair of colored stockings.

Morgan was dear to his mother, but he never was better dressed than was absolutely necessary—partly, no doubt, by his own fault, for he was as indifferent to his appearance as a German philosopher. "My dear fellow, you *are* coming to pieces," Pemberton would say to him in skeptical remonstrance; to which the child would reply, looking at him serenely up and down: "My dear fellow, so are you! I don't want to cast you in the shade." Pemberton could have no rejoinder for this—the assertion so closely represented the fact. If however the deficiencies of his own wardrobe were a chapter by themselves he didn't like his little charge to look too poor. Later he used to say: "Well, if we are poor, why, after all, shouldn't we look it?" and he consoled himself with thinking there was something rather elderly and gentlemanly in Morgan's seediness—it differed from the untidiness of the urchin who plays and spoils his things. He could trace perfectly the degrees by which, in proportion as her little son confined himself to his tutor for society, Mrs. Moreen shrewdly forbore to renew his garments. She did nothing that didn't show, neglected him because he escaped notice, and then, as he illustrated this clever policy, discouraged at home his public appearances. Her position was logical enough—those members of her family who did show had to be showy.

During this period and several others Pemberton was quite aware of how he and his comrade might strike people; wandering languidly through the Jardin des Plantes as if they had nowhere to go, sitting, on the winter days, in the galleries of the Louvre, so splendidly ironical to the homeless, as if for the advantage of the *calorifère*.[7] They joked about it sometimes: it was the sort of joke that was perfectly within the boy's compass. They

7. calorifère: central heating.

figured themselves as part of the vast, vague, hand-to-mouth multitude of the enormous city and pretended they were proud of their position in it—it showed them such a lot of life and made them conscious of a sort of democratic brotherhood. If Pemberton could not feel a sympathy in destitution with his small companion (for after all, Morgan's fond parents would never have let him really suffer), the boy would at least feel it with him, so it came to the same thing. He used sometimes to wonder what people would think they were—fancy they were looked askance at, as if it might be a suspected case of kidnapping. Morgan wouldn't be taken for a young patrician with a preceptor—he wasn't smart enough; though he might pass for his companion's sickly little brother. Now and then he had a five-franc piece, and except once, when they bought a couple of lovely neckties, one of which he made Pemberton accept, they laid it out scientifically in old books. It was a great day, always spent on the quays, rummaging among the dusty boxes that garnish the parapets. These were occasions that helped them to live, for their books ran low very soon after the beginning of their acquaintance. Pemberton had a good many in England, but he was obliged to write to a friend and ask him kindly to get some fellow to give him something for them.

If the bracing climate was untasted that summer the young man had an idea that at the moment they were about to make a push the cup had been dashed from their lips by a movement of his own. It had been his first blow-out, as he called it, with his patrons; his first successful attempt (though there was little other success about it), to bring them to a consideration of his impossible position. As the ostensible eve of a costly journey the moment struck him as a good one to put in a signal protest—to present an ultimatum. Ridiculous as it sounded he had never yet been able to compass an uninterrupted private interview with the elder pair or with either of them singly. They were always flanked by their elder children, and poor Pemberton usually had his own little charge at his side. He was conscious of its being a house in which the surface of one's delicacy got rather smudged; nevertheless he had kept the bloom of his scruple against announcing to Mr. and Mrs. Moreen with publicity that he couldn't go on longer without a little money. He was still simple enough to suppose Ulick and Paula and Amy might not know that since his arrival he had only had a hundred and forty francs; and he was magnanimous enough to wish not to compromise their parents in their eyes. Mr. Moreen now listened to him, as he listened to every one and to everything, like a man of the world, and seemed to appeal to him—though not of course too grossly—to try and be a little more of one himself. Pemberton recognized the importance of the character from the advantage it gave Mr. Moreen. He was not even confused, whereas poor Pemberton was more so than there was any reason for. Neither was he surprised—at least any more than a gentleman had to be who freely confessed himelf a little shocked, though not, strictly, at Pemberton.

"We must go into this, mustn't we, dear?" he said to his wife. He assured his young friend that the matter should have his very best attention; and he melted into space as elusively as if, at the door, he were taking an inevitable but deprecatory precedence. When, the next moment, Pemberton found himself alone with Mrs. Moreen it was to hear her say: "I see, I see," stroking the roundness of her chin and looking as if she were only hesitating between a dozen easy remedies. If they didn't make their push Mr. Moreen could at least disappear for several days. During his absence his wife took up the subject again spontaneously, but her contribution to it was merely that she had thought all the while they were getting on so beautifully. Pemberton's reply to this revelation was that unless they immediately handed him a substantial sum he would leave them forever. He knew she would wonder how he would get away, and for a moment expected her to inquire. She didn't, for which he was almost grateful to her, so little was he in a position to tell.

"You won't, you know you won't—you're too interested," she said. "You *are* interested, you know you are, you dear, kind man!" She laughed, with almost condemnatory archness, as if it were a reproach (but she wouldn't insist), while she flirted a soiled pocket-handkerchief at him.

Pemberton's mind was fully made up to quit the house the following week. This would give him time to get an answer to a letter he had despatched to England. If he did nothing of the sort—that is, if he stayed another year and then went away only for three months—it was not merely because before the answer to his letter came (most unsatisfactory when it did arrive), Mr. Moreen generously presented him—again with all the precautions of a man of the world—three hundred francs. He was exasperated to find that Mrs. Moreen was right, that he couldn't bear to leave the child. This stood out clearer for the very reason that, the night of his desperate appeal to his patrons, he had seen fully for the first time where he was. Wasn't it another proof of the success with which those patrons practiced their arts that they had managed to avert for so long the illuminating flash? It descended upon Pemberton with a luridness which perhaps would have struck a spectator as comically excessive, after he had returned to his little servile room, which looked into a close court where a bare, dirty opposite wall took, with the sound of shrill clatter, the reflection of lighted back-windows. He had simply given himself away to a band of adventurers. The idea, the word itself, had a sort of romantic horror for him—he had always lived on such safe lines. Later it assumed a more interesting, almost a soothing, sense: it pointed a moral, and Pemberton could enjoy a moral. The Moreens were adventurers not merely because they didn't pay their debts, because they lived on society, but because their whole view of life, dim and confused and instinctive, like that of clever colorblind animals, was speculative and rapacious and mean. Oh! they were "respectable," and that only made them more *immondes.*[8] The young man's analysis of them put it at last very simply—they were adventurers because they were abject snobs. That was the completest account of them—it was the law of their being. Even when this truth became vivid to their ingenious inmate he remained unconscious of how much his mind had been prepared for it by the extraordinary little boy who had now become such a complication in his life. Much less could he then calculate on the information he was still to owe to the extraordinary little boy.

5

But it was during the ensuing time that the real problem came up—the problem of how far it was excusable to discuss the turpitude of parents with a child of twelve, of thirteen, of fourteen. Absolutely inexcusable and quite impossible it of course

8. immondes: unclean.

at first appeared; and indeed the question didn't press for a while after Pemberton had received his three hundred francs. They produced a sort of lull, a relief from the sharpest pressure. Pemberton frugally amended his wardrobe and even had a few francs in his pocket. He thought the Moreens looked at him as if he were almost too smart, as if they ought to take care not to spoil him. If Mr. Moreen hadn't been such a man of the world he would perhaps have said something to him about his neckties. But Mr. Moreen was always enough a man of the world to let things pass—he had certainly shown that. It was singular how Pemberton guessed that Morgan, though saying nothing about it, knew something had happened. But three hundred francs, especially when one owed money, couldn't last forever; and when they were gone— the boy knew when they were gone—Morgan did say something. The party had returned to Nice at the beginning of the winter, but not to the charming villa. They went to an hotel, where they stayed three months, and then they went to another hotel, explaining that they had left the first because they had waited and waited and couldn't get the rooms they wanted. These apartments, the rooms they wanted, were generally very splendid; but fortunately they never *could* get them—fortunately, I mean, for Pemberton, who reflected always that if they had got them there would have been still less for educational expenses. What Morgan said at last was said suddenly, irrelevantly, when the moment came, in the middle of a lesson, and consisted of the apparently unfeeling words: "You ought to *filer*,[9] you know—you really ought."

Pemberton stared. He had learnt enough French slang from Morgan to know that to *filer* meant to go away. "Ah, my dear fellow, don't turn me off!"

Morgan pulled a Greek lexicon towards him (he used a Greek-German), to look out a word, instead of asking it of Pemberton. "You can't go on like this, you know."

"Like what, my boy?"

"You know they don't pay you up," said Morgan, blushing and turning his leaves.

"Don't pay me?" Pemberton stared again and feigned amazement. "What on earth put that into your head?"

9. **filer:** sneak off.

"It has been there a long time," the boy replied, continuing his search.

Pemberton was silent, then he went on: "I say, what are you hunting for? They pay me beautifully."

"I'm hunting for the Greek for transparent fiction," Morgan dropped.

"Find that rather for gross impertinence, and disabuse your mind. What do I want of money?"

"Oh, that's another question!"

Pemberton hesitated—he was drawn in different ways. The severely correct thing would have been to tell the boy that such a matter was none of his business and bid him go on with his lines. But they were really too intimate for that; it was not the way he was in the habit of treating him; there had been no reason it should be. On the other hand Morgan had quite lighted on the truth—he really shouldn't be able to keep it up much longer; therefore why not let him know one's real motive for forsaking him? At the same time it wasn't decent to abuse to one's pupil the family of one's pupil; it was better to misrepresent than to do that. So in reply to Morgan's last exclamation he just declared, to dismiss the subject, that he had received several payments.

"I say—I say!" the boy ejaculated, laughing.

"That's all right," Pemberton insisted. "Give me your written rendering."

Morgan pushed a copybook across the table, and his companion began to read the page, but with something running in his head that made it no sense. Looking up after a minute or two he found the child's eyes fixed on him, and he saw something strange in them. Then Morgan said: "I'm not afraid of the reality."

"I haven't yet seen the thing that you *are* afraid of—I'll do you that justice!"

This came out with a jump (it was perfectly true), and evidently gave Morgan a pleasure. "I've thought of it a long time," he presently resumed.

"Well, don't think of it any more."

The child appeared to comply, and they had a comfortable and even an amusing hour. They had a theory that they were very thorough, and yet they seemed always to be in the amusing part of lessons, the intervals between the tunnels, where there were waysides and views. Yet the morning was brought to a violent end by Morgan's suddenly leaning his arms on the table, burying his head in them and bursting into tears. Pemberton would have been startled at any rate; but he was doubly startled because, as it then occurred to him, it was the first time he had ever seen the boy cry. It was rather awful.

The next day, after much thought, he took a decision and, believing it to be just, immediately acted upon it. He cornered Mr. and Mrs. Moreen again and informed them that if, on the spot, they didn't pay him all they owed him, he would not only leave their house, but would tell Morgan exactly what had brought him to it.

"Oh, you *haven't* told him?" cried Mrs. Moreen, with a pacifying hand on her well-dressed bosom.

"Without warning you? For what do you take me?"

Mr. and Mrs. Moreen looked at each other, and Pemberton could see both that they were relieved and that there was a certain alarm in their relief. "My dear fellow," Mr. Moreen demanded, "what use *can* you have, leading the quiet life we all do, for such a lot of money?"—an inquiry to which Pemberton made no answer, occupied as he was in perceiving that what passed in the mind of his patrons was something like: "Oh, then, if we've felt that the child, dear little angel, has judged us and how he regards us, and we haven't been betrayed, he must have guessed—and, in short, it's *general!*" an idea that rather stirred up Mr. and Mrs. Moreen, as Pemberton had desired that it should. At the same time, if he had thought that his threat would do something towards bringing them round, he was disappointed to find they had taken for granted (how little they appreciated his delicacy!) that he had already given them away to his pupil. There was mystic uneasiness in their parental breasts, and that was the way they had accounted for it. Nonetheless his threat did touch them; for if they had escaped it was only to meet a new danger. Mr. Moreen appealed to Pemberton, as usual, as a man of the world; but his wife had recourse, for the first time since the arrival of their inmate, to a fine *hauteur*, reminding him that a devoted mother, with her child, had arts that protected her against gross misrepresentation.

"I should misrepresent you grossly if I accused you of common honesty!" the young man replied; but as he closed the door behind him sharply, thinking he had not done himself much good, while Mr. Moreen lighted another cigarette, he heard Mrs. Moreen shout after him, more touchingly:

"Oh, you do, you *do*, put the knife to one's throat!"

The next morning, very early, she came to his room. He recognized her knock, but he had no hope that she brought him money; as to which he was wrong, for she had fifty francs in her hand. She squeezed forward in her dressing-gown, and he received her in his own, between his bathtub and his bed. He had been tolerably schooled by this time to the "foreign ways" of his hosts. Mrs. Moreen was zealous, and when she was zealous she didn't care what she did; so she now sat down on his bed, his clothes being on the chairs, and, in her preoccupation, forgot, as she glanced round, to be ashamed of giving him such a nasty room. What Mrs. Moreen was zealous about on this occasion was to persuade him that in the first place she was very good-natured to bring him fifty francs, and, in the second, if he would only see it, he was really too absurd to expect to be *paid*. Wasn't he paid enough, without perpetual money —wasn't he paid by the comfortable, luxurious home that he enjoyed with them all, without a care, an anxiety, a solitary want? Wasn't he sure of his position, and wasn't that everything to a young man like him, quite unknown, with singularly little to show, the ground of whose exorbitant pretensions it was not easy to discover? Wasn't he paid, above all, by the delightful relation he had established with Morgan—quite ideal, as from master to pupil—and by the simple privilege of knowing and living with so amazingly gifted a child, than whom really—she meant literally what she said—there was no better company in Europe? Mrs. Moreen herself took to appealing to him as a man of the world; she said "Voyons, mon cher," and "My dear sir, look here now"; and urged him to be reasonable, putting it before him that it was really a chance for him. She spoke as if, according as he *should* be reasonable, he would prove himself worthy to be her son's tutor and of the extraordinary confidence they had placed in him.

After all, Pemberton reflected, it was only a difference of theory, and the theory didn't matter much. They had hitherto gone on that of remunerated, as now they would go on that of gratuitous, service; but why should they have so many words about it? Mrs. Moreen, however, continued to be convincing; sitting there with her fifty francs she talked and repeated, as women repeat, and bored and irritated him, while he leaned against the wall with his hands in the pockets of his wrapper, drawing it together round his legs and looking over the head of his visitor at the gray negations of his window. She wound up with saying: "You see I bring you a definite proposal."

"A definite proposal?"

"To make our relations regular, as it were—to put them on a comfortable footing."

"I see—it's a system," said Pemberton, "A kind of blackmail."

Mrs. Moreen bounded up, which was what the young man wanted.

"What do you mean by that?"

"You practice on one's fears—one's fears about the child if one should go away."

"And, pray, what would happen to him in that event?" demanded Mrs. Moreen, with majesty.

"Why, he'd be alone with *you*."

"And pray, with whom *should* a child be but with those whom he loves most?"

"If you think that, why don't you dismiss me?"

"Do you pretend that he loves you more than he loves *us*?" cried Mrs. Moreen.

"I think he ought to. I make sacrifices for him. Though I've heard of those *you* make, I don't see them."

Mrs. Moreen stared a moment; then, with emotion, she grasped Pemberton's hand. "*Will you* make it—the sacrifice?"

Pemberton burst out laughing. "I'll see—I'll do what I can—I'll stay a little longer. Your calculation is just—I *do* hate intensely to give him up; I'm fond of him and he interests me deeply, in spite of the inconvenience I suffer. You know my situation perfectly; I haven't a penny in the world, and, occupied as I am with Morgan, I'm unable to earn money."

Mrs. Moreen tapped her undressed arm with her folded bank-note. "Can't you write articles? Can't you translate, as *I* do?"

"I don't know about translating; it's wretchedly paid."

"I am glad to earn what I can," said Mrs. Moreen virtuously, with her head high.

"You ought to tell me who you do it for." Pemberton paused a moment, and she said nothing; so

he added: "I've tried to turn off some little sketches, but the magazines won't have them—they're declined with thanks."

"You see then you're not such a phoenix—to have such pretensions," smiled his interlocutress.

"I haven't time to do things properly," Pemberton went on. Then as it came over him that he was almost abjectly good-natured to give these explanations he added: "If I stay on longer it must be on one condition—that Morgan shall know distinctly on what footing I am."

Mrs. Moreen hesitated. "Surely you don't want to show off to a child?"

"To show *you* off, do you mean?"

Again Mrs. Moreen hesitated, but this time it was to produce a still finer flower. "And *you* talk of blackmail!"

"You can easily prevent it," said Pemberton.

"And *you* talk of practicing on fears," Mrs. Moreen continued.

"Yes, there's no doubt I'm a great scoundrel."

His visitor looked at him a moment—it was evident that she was sorely bothered. Then she thrust out her money at him. "Mr. Moreen desired me to give you this on account."

"I'm much obliged to Mr. Moreen; but we have no account."

"You won't take it?"

"That leaves me more free," said Pemberton.

"To poison my darling's mind?" groaned Mrs. Moreen.

"Oh, your darling's mind!" laughed the young man.

She fixed him a moment, and he thought she was going to break out tormentedly, pleadingly: "For God's sake, tell me what *is* in it!" But she checked this impulse—another was stronger. She pocketed the money—the crudity of the alternative was comical—and swept out of the room with the desperate concession: "You may tell him any horror you like!"

6

A couple of days after this, during which Pemberton had delayed to profit by Mrs. Moreen's permission to tell her son any horror, the two had been for a quarter of an hour walking together in silence when the boy became sociable again with the remark: "I'll tell you how I know it; I know it through Zénobie."

"Zénobie? Who in the world is *she?*"

"A nurse I used to have—ever so many years ago. A charming woman. I liked her awfully, and she liked me."

"There's no accounting for tastes. What is it you know through her?"

"Why, what their idea is. She went away because they didn't pay her. She did like me awfully, and she stayed two years. She told me all about it—that at last she could never get her wages. As soon as they saw how much she liked me they stopped giving her anything. They thought she'd stay for nothing, out of devotion. And she did stay ever so long—as long as she could. She was only a poor girl. She used to send money to her mother. At last she couldn't afford it any longer, and she went away in a fearful rage one night—I mean of course in a rage against *them.* She cried over me tremendously, she hugged me nearly to death. She told me all about it," Morgan repeated. "She told me it was their idea. So I guessed, ever so long ago, that they have had the same idea with you."

"Zénobie was very shrewd," said Pemberton. "And she made you so."

"Oh, that wasn't Zénobie; that was nature. And experience!" Morgan laughed.

"Well, Zénobie was a part of your experience."

"Certainly I was a part of hers, poor dear!" the boy exclaimed. "And I'm a part of yours."

"A very important part. But I don't see how you know that I've been treated like Zénobie."

"Do you take me for an idiot?" Morgan asked. "Haven't I been conscious of what we've been through together?"

"What we've been through?"

"Our privations—our dark days."

"Oh, our days have been bright enough."

Morgan went on in silence for a moment. Then he said: "My dear fellow, you're a hero!"

"Well, you're another!" Pemberton retorted.

"No, I'm not; but I'm not a baby. I won't stand it any longer. You must get some occupation that pays. I'm ashamed, I'm ashamed!" quavered the boy in a little passionate voice that was very touching to Pemberton.

"We ought to go off and live somewhere together," said the young man.

"I'll go like a shot if you'll take me."

"I'd get some work that would keep us both afloat," Pemberton continued.

"So would I. Why shouldn't *I* work? I ain't such a *crétin!*"[10]

"The difficulty is that your parents wouldn't hear of it," said Pemberton. "They would never part with you; they worship the ground you tread on. Don't you see the proof of it? They don't dislike me; they wish me no harm; they're very amiable people; but they're perfectly ready to treat me badly for your sake."

The silence in which Morgan received this graceful sophistry struck Pemberton somehow as expressive. After a moment Morgan repeated: "You *are* a hero!" Then he added: "They leave me with you altogether. You've all the responsibility. They put me off on you from morning till night. Why, then, should they object to my taking up with you completely? I'd help you."

"They're not particularly keen about my being helped, and they delight in thinking of you as *theirs.* They're tremendously proud of you."

"I'm not proud of them. But you know *that,*" Morgan returned.

"Except for the little matter we speak of they're charming people," said Pemberton, not taking up the imputation of lucidity, but wondering greatly at the child's own, and especially at this fresh reminder of something he had been conscious of from the first—the strangest thing in the boy's large little composition, a temper, a sensibility, even a sort of ideal, which made him privately resent the general quality of his kinsfolk. Morgan had in secret a small loftiness which begot an element of reflection, a domestic scorn not imperceptible to his companion (though they never had any talk about it), and absolutely anomalous in a juvenile nature, especially when one noted that it had not made this nature "old-fashioned," as the word is of children—quaint or wizened or offensive. It was as if he had been a little gentleman and had paid the penalty by discovering that he was the only such person in the family. This comparison didn't make him vain; but it could make him melancholy and a trifle austere. When Pemberton guessed at these young dimnesses he saw him serious and gallant, and was partly drawn on and partly checked, as if with a scruple, by the charm of

10. **cretin:** dunce.

attempting to sound the little cool shallows which were quickly growing deeper. When he tried to figure to himself the morning twilight of childhood, so as to deal with it safely, he perceived that it was never fixed, never arrested, that ignorance, at the instant one touched it, was already flushing faintly into knowledge, that there was nothing that at a given moment you could say a clever child didn't know. It seemed to him that *he* both knew too much to imagine Morgan's simplicity and too little to disembroil his tangle.

The boy paid no heed to his last remark; he only went on: "I should have spoken to them about their idea, as I call it, long ago, if I hadn't been sure what they would say."

"And what would they say?"

"Just what they said about what poor Zénobie told me—that it was a horrid, dreadful story, that they had paid her every penny they owed her."

"Well, perhaps they had," said Pemberton.

"Perhaps they've paid you!"

"Let us pretend they have, and *n'en parlons plus.*"[11]

"They accused her of lying and cheating," Morgan insisted perversely. "That's why I don't want to speak to them."

"Lest they should accuse me, too?"

To this Morgan made no answer, and his companion, looking down at him (the boy turned his eyes, which had filled, away), saw that he couldn't have trusted himself to utter.

"You're right. Don't squeeze them," Pemberton pursued. "Except for that, they *are* charming people."

"Except for *their* lying and *their* cheating?"

"I say—I say!" cried Pemberton, imitating a little tone of the lad's which was itself an imitation.

"We must be frank, at the last; we *must* come to an understanding," said Morgan, with the importance of the small boy who lets himself think he is arranging great affairs—almost playing at shipwreck or at Indians. "I know all about everything," he added.

"I daresay your father has his reasons," Pemberton observed, too vaguely, as he was aware.

"For lying and cheating?"

"For saving and managing and turning his

means to the best account. He has plenty to do with his money. You're an expensive family."

"Yes, I'm very expensive," Morgan rejoined, in a manner which made his preceptor burst out laughing.

"He's saving for *you*," said Pemberton. "They think of you in everything they do."

"He might save a little——" The boy paused. Pemberton waited to hear what. Then Morgan brought out oddly: "A little reputation."

"Oh, there's plenty of that. That's all right!"

"Enough of it for the people they know, no doubt. The people they know are awful."

"Do you mean the princes? We mustn't abuse the princes."

"Why not? They haven't married Paula—they haven't married Amy. They only clean out Ulick."

"You *do* know everything!" Pemberton exclaimed.

"No, I don't, after all. I don't know what they live on, or how they live, or *why* they live! What have they got and how did they get it? Are they rich, are they poor, or have they a *modeste aisance?*[12] Why are they always chiveying about—living one year like ambassadors and the next like paupers? Who are they, anyway, and what are they? I've thought of all that—I've thought of a lot of things. They're so beastly worldly. That's what I hate most—oh, I've *seen* it! All they care about is to make an appearance and to pass for something or other. What do they want to pass for? What *do* they, Mr. Pemberton?"

"You pause for a reply," said Pemberton, treating the inquiry as a joke, yet wondering too, and greatly struck with the boy's intense, if imperfect, vision. "I haven't the least idea."

"And what good does it do? Haven't I seen the way people treat them—the 'nice' people, the ones they want to know? They'll take anything from them—they'll lie down and be trampled on. The nice ones hate that—they just sicken them. You're the only really nice person we know."

"Are you sure? They don't lie down for me!"

"Well, you shan't lie down for them. You've got to go—that's what you've got to do," said Morgan.

"And what will become of you?"

"Oh, I'm growing up. I shall get off before long. I'll see you later."

11. **n'en . . . plus:** let us talk of it no more.

12. **modeste aisance:** comfortable income.

"You had better let me finish you," Pemberton urged, lending himself to the child's extraordinarily competent attitude.

Morgan stopped in their walk, looking up at him. He had to look up much less than a couple of years before—he had grown, in his loose leanness, so long and high. "Finish me?" he echoed.

"There are such a lot of jolly things we can do together yet. I want to turn you out—I want you to do me credit."

Morgan continued to look at him. "To give you credit—do you mean?"

"My dear fellow, you're too clever to live."

"That's just what I'm afraid you think. No, no; it isn't fair—I can't endure it. We'll part next week. The sooner it's over the sooner to sleep."

"If I hear of anything—any other chance, I promise to go," said Pemberton.

Morgan consented to consider this. "But you'll be honest," he demanded; "you won't pretend you haven't heard?"

"I'm much more likely to pretend I have."

"But what can you hear of, this way, stuck in a hole with us? You ought to be on the spot, to go to England—you ought to go to America."

"One would think you were *my* tutor!" said Pemberton.

Morgan walked on, and after a moment he began again: "Well, now that you know that I know and that we look at the facts and keep nothing back—it's much more comfortable, isn't it?"

"My dear boy, it's so amusing, so interesting, that it surely will be quite impossible for me to forego such hours as these."

This made Morgan stop once more. "You *do* keep something back. Oh, you're not straight—*I* am!"

"Why am I not straight?"

"Oh, you've got your idea!"

"My idea?"

"Why, that I probably sha'n't live, and that you can stick it out till I'm removed."

"You *are* too clever to live!" Pemberton repeated.

"I call it a mean idea," Morgan pursued. "But I shall punish you by the way I hang on."

"Look out or I'll poison you!" Pemberton laughed.

"I'm stronger and better every year. Haven't you noticed that there hasn't been a doctor near me since you came?"

"I'm your doctor," said the young man, taking his arm and drawing him on again.

Morgan proceeded, and after a few steps he gave a sigh of mingled weariness and relief. "Ah, now that we look at the facts, it's all right!"

7

They looked at the facts a good deal after this; and one of the first consequences of their doing so was that Pemberton stuck it out, as it were, for the purpose. Morgan made the facts so vivid and so droll, and at the same time so bald and so ugly, that there was fascination in talking them over with him, just as there would have been heartlessness in leaving him alone with them. Now that they had such a number of perceptions in common it was useless for the pair to pretend that they didn't judge such people; but the very judgment, and the exchange of perceptions, created another tie. Morgan had never been so interesting as now that he himself was made plainer by the sidelight of these confidences. What came out in it most was the soreness of his characteristic pride. He had plenty of that, Pemberton felt—so much that it was perhaps well it should have had to take some early bruises. He would have liked his people to be gallant, and he had waked up too soon to the sense that they were perpetually swallowing humble-pie. His mother would consume any amount, and his father would consume even more than his mother. He had a theory that Ulick had wriggled out of an "affair" at Nice: there had once been a flurry at home, a regular panic, after which they all went to bed and took medicine, not to be accounted for on any other supposition. Morgan had a romantic imagination, fed by poetry and history, and he would have liked those who "bore his name" (as he used to say to Pemberton with the humor that made his sensitiveness manly), to have a proper spirit. But their one idea was to get in with people who didn't want them and to take snubs as if they were honorable scars. Why people didn't want them more he didn't know—that was people's own affair; after all they were not superficially repulsive—they were a hundred times cleverer than most of the dreary grandees, the "poor swells" they rushed about Europe to catch up with. "After all, they *are* amusing—they are!" Morgan used to say, with the wisdom of the ages. To which Pemberton always replied: "Amusing—the great Moreen troupe? Why, they're altogether delightful; and if it were not for the hitch that you and I (feeble performers!) make in the *ensemble*, they would carry everything before them."

What the boy couldn't get over was that this particular blight seemed, in a tradition of self-respect, so undeserved and so arbitrary. No doubt people had a right to take the line they liked; but why should *his* people have liked the line of pushing and toadying and lying and cheating? What had their forefathers—all decent folk, so far as he knew—done to them, or what had *he* done to them? Who had poisoned their blood with the fifth-rate social ideal, the fixed idea of making smart acquaintances and getting into the *monde chic*,[13] especially when it was foredoomed to failure and exposure? They showed so what they were after; that was what made the people they wanted not want *them*. And never a movement of dignity, never a throb of shame at looking each other in the face, never any independence or resentment or disgust. If his father or his brother would only knock someone down once or twice a year! Clever as they were they never guessed how they appeared. They were good-natured, yes—as good-natured as Jews at the doors of clothing-shops! But was that the model one wanted one's family to follow? Morgan had dim memories of an old grandfather, the maternal, in New York, whom he had been taken across the ocean to see, at the age of five: a gentleman with a high neckcloth and a good deal of pronunciation, who wore a dress-coat in the morning, which made one wonder what he wore in the evening, and had, or was supposed to have, "property" and something to do with the Bible Society. It couldn't have been but that *he* was a good type. Pemberton himself remembered Mrs. Clancy, a widowed sister of Mr. Moreen's, who was as irritating as a moral tale and had paid a fortnight's visit to the family at Nice shortly after he came to live with them. She was "pure and refined," as Amy said, over the banjo, and had the air of not knowing what they meant and of keeping something back. Pemberton judged that what she kept back was an approval of many of their ways; therefore it was to be supposed that she too was of a good type, and that Mr. and Mrs. Moreen

and Ulick and Paula and Amy might easily have been better if they would.

But that they wouldn't was more and more perceptible from day to day. They continued to "chivey," as Morgan called it, and in due time became aware of a variety of reasons for proceeding to Venice. They mentioned a great many of them—they were always strikingly frank, and had the brightest friendly chatter, at the late foreign breakfast in especial, before the ladies had made up their faces, when they leaned their arms on the table, had something to follow the *demitasse*, and, in the heat of familiar discussion as to what they "really ought" to do, fell inevitably into the languages in which they could *tutoyer*.[14] Even Pemberton liked them, then; he could endure even Ulick when he heard him give his little flat voice for the "sweet sea-city." That was what made him have a sneaking kindness for them—that they were so out of the workaday world and kept him so out of it. The summer had waned when, with cries of ecstasy, they all passed out on the balcony that overhung the Grand Canal; the sunsets were splendid—the Dorringtons had arrived. The Dorringtons were the only reason they had not talked of at breakfast; but the reasons that they didn't talk of at breakfast always came out in the end. The Dorringtons, on the other hand, came out very little; or else, when they did, they stayed—as was natural—for hours, during which periods Mrs. Moreen and the girls sometimes called at their hotel (to see if they had returned) as many as three times running. The gondola was for the ladies; for in Venice too there were "days," which Mrs. Moreen knew in their order an hour after she arrived. She immediately took one herself, to which the Dorringtons never came, though on a certain occasion when Pemberton and his pupil were together at St. Mark's—where, taking the best walks they had ever had and haunting a hundred churches, they spent a great deal of time—they saw the old lord turn up with Mr. Moreen and Ulick, who showed him the dim basilica as if it belonged to them. Pemberton noted how much less, among its curiosities, Lord Dorrington carried himself as a man of the world; wondering too whether, for such services, his companions took a fee from him. The autumn, at any rate, waned, the

13. **monde chic:** fashionable society.

14. **tutoyer:** use the second-person singular, reserved for conversation with intimates.

Dorringtons departed, and Lord Verschoyle, the eldest son, had proposed neither for Amy nor for Paula.

One sad November day, while the wind roared round the old palace and the rain lashed the lagoon, Pemberton, for exercise and even somewhat for warmth (the Moreens were horribly frugal about fires—it was a cause of suffering to their inmate), walked up and down the big bare *sala*[15] with his pupil. The scagliola floor was cold, the high battered casements shook in the storm, and the stately decay of the place was unrelieved by a particle of furniture. Pemberton's spirits were low, and it came over him that the fortune of the Moreens was now even lower. A blast of desolation, a prophecy of disaster and disgrace, seemed to draw through the comfortless hall. Mr. Moreen and Ulick were in the Piazza, looking out for something, strolling drearily, in mackintoshes, under the arcades; but still, in spite of mackintoshes, unmistakable men of the world. Paula and Amy were in bed—it might have been thought they were staying there to keep warm. Pemberton looked askance at the boy at his side, to see to what extent he was conscious of these portents. But Morgan, luckily for him, was now mainly conscious of growing taller and stronger and indeed of being in his fifteenth year. This fact was intensely interesting to him—it was the basis of a private theory (which, however, he had imparted to his tutor) that in a little while he should stand on his own feet. He considered that the situation would change—that, in short, he should be "finished," grown up, producible in the world of affairs and ready to prove himself of sterling ability. Sharply as he was capable, at times, of questioning his circumstances, there were happy hours when he was as superficial as a child; the proof of which was his fundamental assumption that he should presently go to Oxford, to Pemberton's college, and, aided and abetted by Pemberton, do the most wonderful things. It vexed Pemberton to see how little, in such a project, he took account of ways and means: on other matters he was so skeptical about them. Pemberton tried to imagine the Moreens at Oxford, and fortunately failed; yet unless they were to remove there as a family there would be no *modus vivendi* for Morgan. How could he live without an allowance, and where was the

15. **sala:** hall or drawing room.

allowance to come from? He (Pemberton) might live on Morgan; but how could Morgan live on him? What was to become of him anyhow? Somehow, the fact that he was a big boy now, with better prospects of health, made the question of his future more difficult. So long as he was frail the consideration that he inspired seemed enough of an answer to it. But at the bottom of Pemberton's heart was the recognition of his probably being strong enough to live and not strong enough to thrive. He himself, at any rate, was in a period of natural, boyish rosiness about all this, so that the beating of the tempest seemed to him only the voice of life and the challenge of fate. He had on his shabby little overcoat, with the collar up, but he was enjoying his walk.

It was interrupted at last by the appearance of his mother at the end of the *sala*. She beckoned to Morgan to come to her, and while Pemberton saw him, complacent, pass down the long vista, over the damp false marble, he wondered what was in the air. Mrs. Moreen said a word to the boy and made him go into the room she had quitted. Then, having closed the door after him, she directed her steps swiftly to Pemberton. There *was* something in the air, but his wildest flight of fancy wouldn't have suggested what it proved to be. She signified that she had made a pretext to get Morgan out of the way, and then she inquired—without hesitation—if the young man could lend her sixty francs. While, before bursting into a laugh, he stared at her with surprise, she declared that she was awfully pressed for the money; she was desperate for it—it would save her life.

"Dear lady, *c'est trop fort!*"[16] Pemberton laughed. "Where in the world do you suppose I should get sixty francs, *du train dont vous allez?*"[17]

"I thought you worked—wrote things; don't they pay you?"

"Not a penny."

"Are you such a fool as to work for nothing?"

"You ought surely to know that."

Mrs. Moreen stared an instant, then she colored a little. Pemberton saw she had quite forgotten the terms—if "terms" they could be called—that he had ended by accepting from herself; they had burdened her memory as little as her conscience. "Oh, yes, I see what you mean—you have been

16. **c'est trop fort:** this is going too far. 17. **du . . . allez:** considering the way you are behaving.

very nice about that; but why go back to it so often?" She had been perfectly urbane with him ever since the rough scene of explanation in his room, the morning he made her accept *his* "terms" —the necessity of his making his case known to Morgan. She had felt no resentment, after seeing that there was no danger of Morgan's taking the matter up with her. Indeed, attributing this immunity to the good taste of his influence with the boy, she had once said to Pemberton: "My dear fellow; it's an immense comfort you're a gentleman." She repeated this, in substance, now. "Of course you're a gentleman—that's a bother the less!" Pemberton reminded her that he had not "gone back" to anything; and she also repeated her prayer that, somewhere and somehow, he would find her sixty francs. He took the liberty of declaring that if he could find them it wouldn't be to lend them to *her*—as to which he consciously did himself injustice, knowing that if he had them he would certainly place them in her hand. He accused himself, at bottom and with some truth, of a fantastic, demoralized sympathy with her. If misery made strange bedfellows it also made strange sentiments. It was moreover a part of the demoralization and of the general bad effect of living with such people that one had to make rough retorts, quite out of the tradition of good manners. "Morgan, Morgan, to what pass have I come for you?" he privately exclaimed, while Mrs. Moreen floated voluminously down the *sala* again, to liberate the boy; groaning, as she went, that everything was too odious.

Before the boy was liberated there came a thump at the door communicating with the staircase, followed by the apparition of a dripping youth who poked in his head. Pemberton recognized him as the bearer of a telegram and recognized the telegram as addressed to himself. Morgan came back as, after glancing at the signature (that of a friend in London), he was reading the words: "Found jolly job for you—engagement to coach opulent youth on own terms. Come immediately." The answer, happily, was paid, and the messenger waited. Morgan, who had drawn near, waited too, and looked hard at Pemberton; and Pemberton, after a moment, having met his look, handed him the telegram. It was really by wise looks (they knew each other so well), that, while the telegraph-boy, in his waterproof cape, made a great puddle on the floor, the thing was settled between them. Pemberton wrote the answer with a pencil against the frescoed wall, and the messenger departed. When he had gone Pemberton said to Morgan:

"I'll make a tremendous charge; I'll earn a lot of money in a short time, and we'll live on it."

"Well, I hope the opulent youth will be stupid —he probably will—" Morgan parenthesized, "and keep you a long time."

"Of course, the longer he keeps me the more we shall have for our old age."

"But suppose *they* don't pay you!" Morgan awfully suggested.

"Oh, there are not two such—!" Pemberton paused, he was on the point of using an invidious term. Instead of this he said "two such chances."

Morgan flushed—the tears came to his eyes. "*Dites toujours*,[18] two such rascally crews!" Then, in a different tone, he added: "Happy opulent youth!"

"Not if he's stupid!"

"Oh, they're happier then. But you can't have everything, can you?" the boy smiled.

Pemberton held him, his hands on his shoulders. "What will become of *you*, what will you do?" He thought of Mrs. Moreen, desperate for sixty francs.

"I shall turn into a man." And then, as if he recognized all the bearings of Pemberton's allusion: "I shall get on with them better when you're not here."

"Ah, don't say that—it sounds as if I set you against them!"

"You do—the sight of you. It's all right; you know what I mean. I shall be beautiful. I'll take their affairs in hand; I'll marry my sisters."

"You'll marry yourself!" joked Pemberton; as high, rather tense pleasantry would evidently be the right, or the safest, tone for their separation.

It was, however, not purely in this strain that Morgan suddenly asked: "But I say—how will you get to your jolly job? You'll have to telegraph to the opulent youth for money to come on."

Pemberton bethought himself. "They won't like that, will they?"

"Oh, look out for them!"

Then Pemberton brought out his remedy. "I'll go to the American Consul; I'll borrow some

18. **Dites toujours:** speak frankly.

money of him—just for the few days, on the strength of the telegram."

Morgan was hilarious. "Show him the telegram —then stay and keep the money!"

Pemberton entered into the joke enough to reply that, for Morgan, he was really capable of that; but the boy, growing more serious, and to prove that he hadn't meant what he said, not only hurried him off to the Consulate (since he was to start that evening, as he had wired to his friend), but insisted on going with him. They splashed through the tortuous perforations and over the hump-backed bridges, and they passed through the Piazza, where they saw Mr. Moreen and Ulick go into a jeweler's shop. The Consul proved accommodating (Pemberton said it wasn't the letter, but Morgan's grand air), and on their way back they went into St. Mark's for a hushed ten minutes. Later they took up and kept up the fun of it to the very end; and it seemed to Pemberton a part of that fun that Mrs. Moreen, who was very angry when he had announced to her his intention, should charge him, grotesquely and vulgarly, and in reference to the loan she had vainly endeavored to effect, with bolting lest they should "get something out" of him. On the other hand he had to do Mr. Moreen and Ulick the justice to recognize that when, on coming in, *they* heard the cruel news, they took it like perfect men of the world.

8

When Pemberton got at work with the opulent youth, who was to be taken in hand for Balliol, he found himself unable to say whether he was really an idiot or it was only, on his own part, the long association with an intensely living little mind that made him seem so. From Morgan he heard half-a-dozen times: the boy wrote charming young letters, a patchwork of tongues, with indulgent postscripts in the family Volapuk and, in little squares and rounds and crannies of the text, the drollest illustrations—letters that he was divided between the impulse to show his present disciple, as a kind of wasted incentive, and the sense of something in them that was profanable by pub-licity. The opulent youth went up, in due course, and failed to pass; but it seemed to add to the pre-sumption that brilliancy was not expected of him all at once that his parents, condoning the lapse,

which they good-naturedly treated as little as possible as if it were Pemberton's, should have sounded the rally again, begged the young coach to keep his pupil in hand another year.

The young coach was now in a position to lend Mrs. Moreen sixty francs, and he sent her a post-office order for the amount. In return for this favor he received a frantic, scribbled line from her: "Implore you to come back instantly—Morgan dreadfully ill." They were on the rebound, once more in Paris—often as Pemberton had seen them depressed he had never seen them crushed—and communication was therefore rapid. He wrote to the boy to ascertain the state of his health, but he received no answer to his letter. Accordingly he took an abrupt leave of the opulent youth and, crossing the Channel, alighted at the small hotel, in the quarter of the Champs Elysées, of which Mrs. Moreen had given him the address. A deep if dumb dissatisfaction with this lady and her com-panions bore him company: they couldn't be vulgarly honest, but they could live at hotels, in velvety *entresols*,[19] amid a smell of burnt pastilles, in the most expensive city in Europe. When he had left them, in Venice, it was with an irrepressible suspicion that something was going to happen; but the only thing that had happened was that they succeeded in getting away. "How is he? where is he?" he asked of Mrs. Moreen; but before she could speak, these questions were answered by the pressure round his neck of a pair of arms, in shrunken sleeves, which were perfectly capable of an effusive young foreign squeeze.

"Dreadfully ill—I don't see it!" the young man cried. And then, to Morgan: "Why on earth didn't you relieve me? Why didn't you answer my letter?"

Mrs. Moreen declared that when she wrote he was very bad, and Pemberton learned at the same time from the boy that he had answered every letter he had received. This led to the demonstra-tion that Pemberton's note had been intercepted. Mrs. Moreen was prepared to see the fact exposed, as Pemberton perceived, the moment he faced her, that she was prepared for a good many other things. She was prepared above all to maintain that she had acted from a sense of duty, that she was enchanted she had got him over, whatever they might say; and that it was useless of him to pretend that he didn't *know*, in all his bones, that

19. **entresols:** mezzanines.

his place at such a time was with Morgan. He had taken the boy away from them, and now he had no right to abandon him. He had created for himself the gravest responsibilities; he must at least abide by what he had done.

"Taken him away from you?" Pemberton exclaimed indignantly.

"Do it—do it, for pity's sake; that's just what I want. I can't stand *this*—and such scenes. They're treacherous!" These words broke from Morgan, who had intermitted his embrace, in a key which made Pemberton turn quickly to him, to see that he had suddenly seated himself, was breathing with evident difficulty and was very pale.

"*Now* do you say he's not ill—my precious pet?" shouted his mother, dropping on her knees before him with clasped hands, but touching him no more than if he had been a gilded idol. "It will pass—it's only for an instant; but don't say such dreadful things!"

"I'm all right—all right," Morgan panted to Pemberton, whom he sat looking up at with a strange smile, his hands resting on either side on the sofa.

"Now do you pretend I've been treacherous— that I've deceived?" Mrs. Moreen flashed at Pemberton as she got up.

"It isn't *he* says it, it's I!" the boy returned, apparently easier, but sinking back against the wall; while Pemberton, who had sat down beside him, taking his hand, bent over him.

"Darling child, one does what one can; there are so many things to consider," urged Mrs. Moreen. "It's his *place*—his only place. You see *you* think it is now."

"Take me away—take me away," Morgan went on, smiling to Pemberton from his white face.

"Where shall I take you, and how—oh, *how*, my boy?" the young man stammered, thinking of the rude way in which his friends in London held that, for his convenience, and without a pledge of instantaneous return, he had thrown them over; of the just resentment with which they would already have called in a successor, and of the little help as regarded finding fresh employment that resided for him in the flatness of his having failed to pass his pupil.

"Oh, we'll settle that. You used to talk about it," said Morgan. "If we can only go, all the rest's a detail."

"Talk about it as much as you like, but don't think you can attempt it. Mr. Moreen would never consent—it would be so precarious," Pemberton's hostess explained to him. Then to Morgan she explained: "It would destroy our peace, it would break our hearts. Now that he's back it will be all the same again. You'll have your life, your work and your freedom, and we'll all be happy as we used to be. You'll bloom and grow perfectly well, and we won't have any more silly experiments, will we? They're too absurd. It's Mr. Pemberton's place—everyone in his place. You in yours, your papa in his, me in mine—*n'est-ce pas, chéri?*[20] We'll all forget how foolish we've been, and we'll have lovely times."

She continued to talk and to surge vaguely about the little draped, stuffy *salon*, while Pemberton sat with the boy, whose color gradually came back; and she mixed up her reasons, dropping that there were going to be changes, that the other children might scatter (who knew?—Paula had her ideas), and that then it might be fancied how much the poor old parent-birds would want the little nestling. Morgan looked at Pemberton, who wouldn't let him move; and Pemberton knew exactly how he felt at hearing himself called a little nestling. He admitted that he had had one or two bad days, but he protested afresh against the iniquity of his mother's having made them the ground of an appeal to poor Pemberton. Poor Pemberton could laugh now, apart from the comicality of Mrs. Moreen's producing so much philosophy for her defense (she seemed to shake it out of her agitated petticoats, which knocked over the light gilt chairs), so little did the sick boy strike him as qualified to repudiate any advantage.

He himself was in for it, at any rate. He should have Morgan on his hands again indefinitely; though indeed he saw the lad had a private theory to produce which would be intended to smooth this down. He was obliged to him for it in advance; but the suggested amendment didn't keep his heart from sinking a little, any more than it prevented him from accepting the prospect on the spot, with some confidence moreover that he would do so even better if he could have a little supper. Mrs. Moreen threw out more hints about the changes that were to be looked for, but she was

20. n'est-ce pas, cheri: isn't it so, dear?

such a mixture of smiles and shudders (she confessed she was very nervous), that he couldn't tell whether she were in high feather or only in hysterics. If the family were really at last going to pieces why shouldn't she recognize the necessity of pitching Morgan into some sort of lifeboat? This presumption was fostered by the fact that they were established in luxurious quarters in the capital of pleasure; that was exactly where they naturally *would* be established in view of going to pieces. Moreover didn't she mention that Mr. Moreen and the others were enjoying themselves at the opera with Mr. Granger, and wasn't *that* also precisely where one would look for them on the eve of a smash? Pemberton gathered that Mr. Granger was a rich, vacant American—a big bill with a flourishy heading and no items; so that one of Paula's "ideas" was probably that this time she had really done it, which was indeed an unprecedented blow to the general cohesion. And if the cohesion was to terminate what was to become of poor Pemberton? He felt quite enough bound up with them to figure, to his alarm, as a floating spar in case of a wreck.

It was Morgan who eventually asked if no supper had been ordered for him; sitting with him below, later, at the dim, delayed meal, in the presence of a great deal of corded green plush, a plate of ornamental biscuit and a languor marked on the part of the waiter. Mrs. Moreen had explained that they had been obliged to secure a room for the visitor out of the house; and Morgan's consolation (he offered it while Pemberton reflected on the nastiness of lukewarm sauces), proved to be, largely, that this circumstance would facilitate their escape. He talked of their escape (recurring to it often afterwards), as if they were making up a "boy's book" together. But he likewise expressed his sense that there was something in the air, that the Moreens couldn't keep it up much longer. In point of fact, as Pemberton was to see, they kept it up for five or six months. All the while, however, Morgan's contention was designed to cheer him. Mr. Moreen and Ulick, whom he had met the day after his return, accepted that return like perfect men of the world. If Paula and Amy treated it even with less formality an allowance was to be made for them, inasmuch as Mr. Granger had not come to the opera after all. He had only placed his box at their service, with a bouquet for each of the party; there was even one apiece, embittering the thought of his profusion, for Mr. Moreen and Ulick. "They're all like that," was Morgan's comment; "at the very last, just when we think we've got them fast, we're chucked!"

Morgan's comments, in these days, were more and more free; they even included a large recognition of the extraordinary tenderness with which he had been treated while Pemberton was away. Oh, yes, they couldn't do enough to be nice to him, to show him they had him on their mind and make up for his loss. That was just what made the whole thing so sad, and him so glad, after all, of Pemberton's return—he had to keep thinking of their affection less, had less sense of obligation. Pemberton laughed out at this last reason, and Morgan blushed and said: "You know what I mean." Pemberton knew perfectly what he meant; but there were a good many things it didn't make any clearer. This episode of his second sojourn in Paris stretched itself out wearily, with their resumed readings and wanderings and maunderings, their potterings on the quays, their hauntings of the museums, their occasional lingerings in the Palais Royal, when the first sharp weather came on and there was a comfort in warm emanations, before Chevet's wonderful succulent window. Morgan wanted to hear a great deal about the opulent youth—he took an immense interest in him. Some of the details of his opulence—Pemberton could spare him none of them—evidently intensified the boy's appreciation of all his friend had given up to come back to him; but in addition to the greater reciprocity established by such a renunciation he had always his little brooding theory, in which there was a frivolous gaiety too, that their long probation was drawing to a close. Morgan's conviction that the Moreens couldn't go on much longer kept pace with the unexpended impetus with which, from month to month, they did go on. Three weeks after Pemberton had rejoined them they went on to another hotel, a dingier one than the first; but Morgan rejoiced that his tutor had at least still not sacrificed the advantage of a room outside. He clung to the romantic utility of this when the day, or rather the night, should arrive for their escape.

For the first time, in this complicated connection, Pemberton felt sore and exasperated. It was, as he had said to Mrs. Moreen in Venice, *trop fort*

—everything was *trop fort*. He could neither really throw off his blighting burden nor find in it the benefit of a pacified conscience or of a rewarded affection. He had spent all the money that he had earned in England, and he felt that his youth was going and that he was getting nothing back for it. It was all very well for Morgan to seem to consider that he would make up to him for all inconveniences by settling himself upon him permanently—there was an irritating flaw in such a view. He saw what the boy had in his mind; the conception that as his friend had had the generosity to come back to him he must show his gratitude by giving him his life. But the poor friend didn't desire the gift—what could he do with Morgan's life? Of course at the same time that Pemberton was irritated he remembered the reason, which was very honorable to Morgan and which consisted simply of the fact that he was perpetually making one forget that he was after all only a child. If one dealt with him on a different basis one's misadventures were one's own fault. So Pemberton waited in a queer confusion of yearning and alarm for the catastrophe which was held to hang over the house of Moreen, of which he certainly at moments felt the symptoms brush his cheek and as to which he wondered much in what form it would come.

Perhaps it would take the form of dispersal—a frightened *sauve qui peut*,[21] a scuttling into selfish corners. Certainly they were less elastic than of yore; they were evidently looking for something they didn't find. The Dorringtons hadn't reappeared, the princes had scattered; wasn't that the beginning of the end? Mrs. Moreen had lost her reckoning of the famous "days"; her social calendar was blurred—it had turned its face to the wall. Pemberton suspected that the great, the cruel, discomfiture had been the extraordinary behavior of Mr. Granger, who seemed not to know what he wanted, or, what was much worse, what *they* wanted. He kept sending flowers, as if to bestrew the path of his retreat, which was never the path of return. Flowers were all very well, but —Pemberton could complete the proposition. It was now positively conspicuous that in the long run the Moreens were a failure; so that the young man was almost grateful the run had not been short. Mr. Moreen, indeed, was still occasionally

21. **sauve qui peut:** every man for himself.

able to get away on business, and, what was more surprising, he was also able to get back. Ulick had no club, but you could not have discovered it from his appearance, which was as much as ever that of a person looking at life from the window of such an institution; therefore Pemberton was doubly astonished at an answer he once heard him make to his mother, in the desperate tone of a man familiar with the worst privations. Her question Pemberton had not quite caught; it appeared to be an appeal for a suggestion as to whom they could get to take Amy. "Let the devil take her!" Ulick snapped; so that Pemberton could see that not only they had lost their amiability, but had ceased to believe in themselves. He could also see that if Mrs. Moreen was trying to get people to take her children she might be regarded as closing the hatches for the storm. But Morgan would be the last she would part with.

One winter afternoon—it was a Sunday—he and the boy walked far together in the Bois de Boulogne. The evening was so splendid, the cold lemon-colored sunset so clear, the stream of carriages and pedestrians so amusing and the fascination of Paris so great, that they stayed out later than usual and became aware that they would have to hurry home to arrive in time for dinner. They hurried accordingly, arm-in-arm, good-humored and hungry, agreeing that there was nothing like Paris after all and that after all, too, that had come and gone they were not yet sated with innocent pleasures. When they reached the hotel they found that, though scandalously late, they were in time for all the dinner they were likely to sit down to. Confusion reigned in the apartments of the Moreens (very shabby ones this time, but the best in the house), and before the interrupted service of the table (with objects displaced almost as if there had been a scuffle, and a great wine stain from an overturned bottle), Pemberton could not blink the fact that there had been a scene of proprietary mutiny. The storm had come —they were all seeking refuge. The hatches were down—Paula and Amy were invisible (they had never tried the most casual art upon Pemberton, but he felt that they had enough of an eye to him not to wish to meet him as young ladies whose frocks had been confiscated), and Ulick appeared to have jumped overboard. In a word, the host and his staff had ceased to "go on" at the pace of their guests, and the air of embarrassed detention, thanks to a pile of gaping trunks in the passage, was strangely commingled with the air of indignant withdrawal.

When Morgan took in all this—and he took it in very quickly—he blushed to the roots of his hair. He had walked, from his infancy, among difficulties and dangers, but he had never seen a public exposure. Pemberton noticed, in a second glance at him, that the tears had rushed into his eyes and that they were tears of bitter shame. He wondered for an instant, for the boy's sake, whether he might successfully pretend not to understand. Not successfully, he felt, as Mr. and Mrs. Moreen, dinnerless by their extinguished hearth, rose before him in their little dishonored *salon*, considering apparently with much intensity what lively capital would be next on their list. They were not prostrate, but they were very pale, and Mrs. Moreen had evidently been crying. Pemberton quickly learned however that her grief was not for the loss of her dinner, much as she usually enjoyed it, but on account of a necessity much more tragic. She lost no time in laying this necessity bare, in telling him how the change had come, the bolt had fallen, and how they would all have to turn themselves about. Therefore cruel as it was to them to part with their darling she must look to him to carry a little further the influence he had so fortunately acquired with the boy—to induce his young charge to follow him into some modest retreat. They depended upon him, in a word, to take their delightful child temporarily under his protection—it would leave Mr. Moreen and herself so much more free to give the proper attention (too little, alas! had been given), to the readjustment of their affairs.

"We trust you—we feel that we can," said Mrs. Moreen, slowly rubbing her plump white hands and looking, with compunction, hard at Morgan, whose chin, not to take liberties, her husband stroked with a tentative paternal forefinger.

"Oh, yes; we feel that we can. We trust Mr. Pemberton fully, Morgan," Mr. Moreen conceded.

Pemberton wondered again if he might pretend not to understand; but the idea was painfully complicated by the immediate perception that Morgan had understood.

"Do you mean that he may take me to live with him—forever and ever?" cried the boy. "Away, away, anywhere he likes?"

"Forever and ever? *Comme vous-y-allez!*"[22] Mr. Moreen laughed indulgently. "For as long as Mr. Pemberton may be so good."

"We've struggled, we've suffered," his wife went on; "but you've made him so your own that we've already been through the worst of the sacrifice."

Morgan had turned away from his father—he stood looking at Pemberton with a light in his face. His blush had died out, but something had come that was brighter and more vivid. He had a moment of boyish joy, scarcely mitigated by the reflection that, with this unexpected consecration of his hope—too sudden and too violent; the thing was a good deal less like a boy's book—the "escape" was left on their hands. The boyish joy was there for an instant, and Pemberton was almost frightened at the revelation of gratitude and affection that shone through his humiliation. When Morgan stammered "My dear fellow, what do you say to *that?*" he felt that he should say something enthusiastic. But he was still more frightened at something else that immediately followed and that made the lad sit down quickly on the nearest chair. He had turned very white and had raised his hand to his left side. They were all three looking at him, but Mrs. Moreen was the first to bound forward. "Ah, his darling little heart!" she broke out; and this time, on her knees before him and without respect for the idol, she caught him ardently in her arms. "You walked him too far, you hurried him too fast!" she tossed over her shoulder at Pemberton. The boy made no protest, and the next instant his mother, still holding him, sprang up with her face convulsed and with the terrified cry "Help, help! he's going, he's gone!" Pemberton saw, with equal horror, by Morgan's own stricken face, that he *was* gone. He pulled him half out of his mother's hands, and for a moment, while they held him together, they looked, in their dismay, into each other's eyes. "He couldn't stand it, with his infirmity," said Pemberton—"the shock, the whole scene, the violent emotion."

"But I thought he *wanted* to go to you!" wailed Mrs. Moreen.

22. **Comme vous-y-allez:** how you do go on!

"I *told* you he didn't, my dear," argued Mr. Moreen. He was trembling all over, and he was, in his way, as deeply affected as his wife. But, after the first, he took his bereavement like a man of the world.

D. H. LAWRENCE
1885–1930

The Prussian Officer

1

They had marched more than thirty kilometers since dawn, along the white, hot road where occasional thickets of trees threw a moment of shade, then out into the glare again. On either hand, the valley, wide and shallow, glittered with heat; dark green patches of rye, pale young corn, fallow and meadow and black pine woods spread in a dull, hot diagram under a glistening sky. But right in front the mountains ranged across, pale blue and very still, snow gleaming gently out of the deep atmosphere. And towards the mountains, on and on, the regiment marched between the rye fields and the meadows, between the scraggy fruit trees set regularly on either side the high road. The burnished, dark green rye threw off a suffocating heat, the mountains drew gradually nearer and more distinct. While the feet of the soldiers grew hotter, sweat ran through their hair under their helmets, and their knapsacks could burn no more in contact with their shoulders, but seemed instead to give off a cold, prickly sensation.

He walked on and on in silence, staring at the mountains ahead, that rose sheer out of the land, and stood fold behind fold, half earth, half heaven, the heaven, the barrier with slits of soft snow, in the pale, bluish peaks.

He could now walk almost without pain. At the start, he had determined not to limp. It had made him sick to take the first steps, and during the first mile or so, he had compressed his breath, and the cold drops of sweat had stood on his forehead. But he had walked it off. What were they after all but bruises! He had looked at them, as he was

getting up: deep bruises on the backs of his thighs. And since he had made his first step in the morning, he had been conscious of them, till now he had a tight hot place in his chest, with suppressing the pain, and holding himself in. There seemed no air when he breathed. But he walked almost lightly.

The Captain's hand had trembled at taking his coffee at dawn: his orderly saw it again. And he saw the fine figure of the Captain wheeling on horseback at the farmhouse ahead, a handsome figure in pale blue uniform with facings of scarlet, and the metal gleaming on the black helmet and the sword-scabbard, and dark streaks of sweat coming on the silky bay horse. The orderly felt he was connected with that figure moving so suddenly on horseback: he followed it like a shadow, mute and inevitable and damned by it. And the officer was always aware of the tramp of the company behind, the march of his orderly among the men.

The Captain was a tall man of about forty, gray at the temples. He had a handsome, finely knit figure, and was one of the best horsemen in the West. His orderly, having to rub him down, admired the amazing riding muscles of his loins.

For the rest, the orderly scarcely noticed the officer any more than he noticed himself. It was rarely he saw his master's face: he did not look at it. The Captain had reddish-brown, stiff hair, that he wore short upon his skull. His mustache was also cut short and bristly over a full, brutal mouth. His face was rather rugged, the cheeks thin. Perhaps the man was the more handsome for the deep lines of his face, the irritable tension of his brow, which gave him the look of a man who fights with life. His fair eyebrows stood bushy over light blue eyes that were always flashing with cold fire.

He was a Prussian aristocrat, haughty and overbearing. But his mother had been a Polish countess. Having made too many gambling debts when he was young, he had ruined his prospects in the army, and remained an infantry captain. He had never married: his position did not allow of it, and no woman had ever moved him to it. His time he spent riding—occasionally he rode one of his own horses at the races—and at the officers' club. Now and then he took himself a mistress. But after such an event, he returned to duty with his brow still more tense, his eyes still more hostile and irritable. With the men, however, he was merely impersonal, though a devil when roused; so that, on the whole, they feared him, but had no great aversion from him. They accepted him as the inevitable.

To his orderly he was at first cold and just and indifferent: he did not fuss over trifles. So that his servant knew practically nothing about him, except just what orders he would give, and how he wanted them obeyed. That was quite simple. Then the change gradually came.

The orderly was a youth of about twenty-two, of medium height, and well built. He had strong, heavy limbs, was swarthy, with a soft, black, young mustache. There was something altogether warm and young about him. He had firmly marked eyebrows over dark, expressionless eyes, that seemed never to have thought, only to have received life direct through his senses and acted straight from instinct.

Gradually the officer had become aware of his servant's young, vigorous, unconscious presence about him. He could not get away from the sense of the youth's person, while he was in attendance. It was like a warm flame upon the older man's tense, rigid body, that had become almost unliving, fixed. There was something so free and self-contained about him, and something in the young fellow's movement, that made the officer aware of him. And this irritated the Prussian. He did not choose to be touched into life by his servant. He might easily have changed his man, but he did not. He now very rarely looked direct at his orderly, but kept his face averted, as if to avoid seeing him. And yet as the young soldier moved unthinking about the apartment, the elder watched him, and would notice the movement of his strong young shoulders under the blue cloth, the bend of his neck. And it irritated him. To see the soldier's young, brown, shapely peasant's hand grasp the loaf or the wine-bottle sent a flash of hate or of anger through the elder man's blood. It was not that the youth was clumsy: it was rather the blind, instinctive sureness of movement of an unhampered young animal that irritated the officer to such a degree.

Once, when a bottle of wine had gone over, and the red gushed out on to the tablecloth, the officer had started up with an oath, and his eyes, bluey like fire, had held those of the confused youth for a moment. It was a shock for the young soldier. He felt something sink deeper, deeper into his soul, where nothing had ever gone before. It left him rather blank and wondering. Some of his natural completeness in himself was gone, a little uneasiness took its place. And from that time an undiscovered feeling had held between the two men.

Henceforward the orderly was afraid of really meeting his master. His subconsciousness remembered those steely blue eyes and the harsh brows, and did not intend to meet them again. So he always stared past his master, and avoided him. Also, in a little anxiety, he waited for the three months to have gone, when his time would be up. He began to feel a constraint in the Captain's presence, and the soldier even more than the officer wanted to be left alone, in his neutrality as servant.

He had served the Captain for more than a year, and knew his duty. This he performed easily, as if it were natural to him. The officer and his commands he took for granted, as he took the sun and the rain, and he served as a matter of course. It did not implicate him personally.

But now if he were going to be forced into a personal interchange with his master he would be like a wild thing caught; he felt he must get away.

But the influence of the young soldier's being had penetrated through the officer's stiffened discipline, and perturbed the man in him. He, however, was a gentleman, with long, fine hands and cultivated movements, and was not going to allow such a thing as the stirring of his innate self. He was a man of passionate temper, who had always kept himself suppressed. Occasionally there had been a duel, an outburst before the soldiers. He knew himself to be always on the point of breaking out. But he kept himself hard to the idea of the Service. Whereas the young soldier seemed to live out his warm, full nature, to give it off in his very movements, which had a certain zest, such as wild animals have in free movement. And this irritated the officer more and more.

In spite of himself, the Captain could not regain his neutrality of feeling towards his orderly. Nor could he leave the man alone. In spite of himself, he watched him, gave him sharp orders, tried to take up as much of his time as possible. Sometimes he flew into a rage with the young soldier, and bullied him. Then the orderly shut himself off, as it were out of earshot, and waited, with sullen, flushed face, for the end of the noise. The words never pierced to his intelligence. He made himself, protectively, impervious to the feelings of his master.

He had a scar on his left thumb, a deep seam going across the knuckle. The officer had long suffered from it, and wanted to do something to it. Still it was there, ugly and brutal on the young, brown hand. At last the Captain's reserve gave way. One day, as the orderly was smoothing out the tablecloth, the officer pinned down his thumb with a pencil, asking:

"How did you come by that?"

The young man winced and drew back at attention.

"A wood ax, Herr Hauptmann," he answered.

The officer waited for further explanation. None came. The orderly went about his duties. The elder man was sullenly angry. His servant avoided him. And the next day he had to use all his will power to avoid seeing the scarred thumb. He wanted to get hold of it and—A hot flame ran in his blood.

He knew his servant would soon be free, and would be glad. As yet, the soldier had held himself off from the elder man. The Captain grew madly irritable. He could not rest when the soldier was away, and when he was present, he glared at him with tormented eyes. He hated those fine, black brows over the unmeaning, dark eyes, he was infuriated by the free movement of the handsome limbs, which no military discipline could make stiff. And he became harsh and cruelly bullying, using contempt and satire. The young soldier only grew more mute and expressionless.

"What cattle were you bred by, that you can't keep straight eyes? Look me in the eyes when I speak to you."

And the soldier turned his dark eyes to the other's face, but there was no sight in them: he stared with the slightest possible cast, holding back his sight, perceiving the blue of his master's eyes, but receiving no look from them. And the elder man went pale, and his reddish eyebrows twitched. He gave his order, barrenly.

Once he flung a heavy military glove into the young soldier's face. Then he had the satisfaction of seeing the black eyes flare up into his own, like a blaze when straw is thrown on a fire. And he had laughed with a little tremor and a sneer.

But there were only two months more. The youth instinctively tried to keep himself intact: he tried to serve the officer as if the latter were an abstract authority and not a man. All his instinct was to avoid personal contact, even definite hate. But in spite of himself the hate grew, responsive to the officer's passion. However, he put it in the background. When he had left the Army he could dare acknowledge it. By nature he was active, and had many friends. He thought what amazing good fellows they were. But, without knowing it, he was alone. Now this solitariness was intensified. It would carry him through his term. But the officer seemed to be going irritably insane, and the youth was deeply frightened.

The soldier had a sweetheart, a girl from the mountains, independent and primitive. The two walked together, rather silently. He went with her, not to talk, but to have his arm round her, and for the physical contact. This eased him, made it easier for him to ignore the Captain; for he could rest with her held fast against his chest. And she, in some unspoken fashion, was there for him. They loved each other.

The Captain perceived it, and was mad with irritation. He kept the young man engaged all the evenings long, and took pleasure in the dark look that came on his face. Occasionally, the eyes of the two men met, those of the younger sullen and dark, doggedly unalterable, those of the elder sneering with restless contempt.

The officer tried hard not to admit the passion that had got hold of him. He would not know that his feeling for his orderly was anything but that of a man incensed by his stupid, perverse servant. So, keeping quite justified and conventional in his consciousness, he let the other thing run on. His nerves, however, were suffering. At last he slung the end of a belt in his servant's face. When he saw the youth start back, the pain-tears in his eyes and the blood on his mouth, he had felt at once a thrill of deep pleasure and of shame.

But this, he acknowledged to himself, was a thing he had never done before. The fellow was too exasperating. His own nerves must be going to pieces. He went away for some days with a woman.

It was a mockery of pleasure. He simply did not want the woman. But he stayed on for his time. At the end of it, he came back in an agony of irritation, torment, and misery. He rode all the evening, then came straight in to supper. His orderly was out. The officer sat with his long, fine hands lying on the table, perfectly still, and all his blood seemed to be corroding.

At last his servant entered. He watched the strong, easy young figure, the fine eyebrows, the thick black hair. In a week's time the youth had got back his old well-being. The hands of the officer twitched and seemed to be full of mad flame. The young man stood at attention, unmoving, shut off.

The meal went in silence. But the orderly seemed eager. He made a clatter with the dishes.

"Are you in a hurry?" asked the officer, watching the intent, warm face of his servant. The other did not reply.

"Will you answer my question?" said the Captain.

"Yes, sir," replied the orderly, standing with his pile of deep Army plates. The Captain waited, looked at him, then asked again:

"Are you in a hurry?"

"Yes, sir," came the answer, that sent a flash through the listener.

"For what?"

"I was going out, sir."

"I want you this evening."

There was a moment's hesitation. The officer had a curious stiffness of countenance.

"Yes, sir," replied the servant, in his throat.

"I want you tomorrow evening also—in fact, you may consider your evenings occupied, unless I give you leave."

The mouth with the young mustache set close.

"Yes, sir," answered the orderly, loosening his lips for a moment.

He again turned to the door.

"And why have you a piece of pencil in your ear?"

The orderly hesitated, then continued on his way without answering. He set the plates in a pile outside the door, took the stump of pencil from his ear, and put it in his pocket. He had been copying a verse for his sweetheart's birthday card. He returned to finish clearing the table. The officer's eyes were dancing, he had a little, eager smile.

"Why have you a piece of pencil in your ear?" he asked.

The orderly took his hands full of dishes. His master was standing near the great green stove, a little smile on his face, his chin thrust forward. When the young soldier saw him his heart suddenly ran hot. He felt blind. Instead of answering, he

turned dazedly to the door. As he was crouching to set down the dishes, he was pitched forward by a kick from behind. The pots went in a stream down the stairs, he clung to the pillar of the banisters. And as he was rising he was kicked heavily again, and again, so that he clung sickly to the post for some moments. His master had gone swiftly into the room and closed the door. The maid-servant downstairs looked up the staircase and made a mocking face at the crockery disaster.

The officer's heart was plunging. He poured himself a glass of wine, part of which he spilled on the floor, and gulped the remainder, leaning against the cool, green stove. He heard his man collecting the dishes from the stairs. Pale, as if intoxicated, he waited. The servant entered again. The Captain's heart gave a pang, as of pleasure, seeing the young fellow bewildered and uncertain on his feet, with pain.

"Schöner!" he said.

The soldier was a little slower in coming to attention.

"Yes, sir!"

The youth stood before him, with pathetic young mustache, and fine eyebrows very distinct on his forehead of dark marble.

"I asked you a question."

"Yes, sir."

The officer's tone bit like acid.

"Why had you a pencil in your ear?"

Again the servant's heart ran hot, and he could not breathe. With dark, strained eyes, he looked at the officer, as if fascinated. And he stood there sturdily planted, unconscious. The withering smile came into the Captain's eyes, and he lifted his foot.

"I—I forgot it—sir," panted the soldier, his dark eyes fixed on the other man's dancing blue ones.

"What was it doing there?"

He saw the young man's breast heaving as he made an effort for words.

"I had been writing."

"Writing what?"

Again the soldier looked him up and down. The officer could hear him panting. The smile came into the blue eyes. The soldier worked his dry throat, but could not speak. Suddenly the smile lit like a flame on the officer's face, and a kick came heavily against the orderly's thigh. The youth moved a pace sideways. His face went dead, with two black staring eyes.

"Well?" said the officer.

The orderly's mouth had gone dry, and his tongue rubbed in it as on dry brown-paper. He worked his throat. The officer raised his foot. The servant went stiff.

"Some poetry, sir," came the crackling, unrecognizable sound of his voice.

"Poetry, what poetry?" asked the Captain with a sickly smile.

Again there was the working in the throat. The Captain's heart had suddenly gone down heavily, and he stood sick and tired.

"For my girl, sir," he heard the dry, inhuman sound.

"Oh!" he said, turning away. "Clear the table."

"Click!" went the soldier's throat; then again, "click!" and then the half-articulate:

"Yes, sir."

The young soldier was gone, looking old, and walking heavily.

The officer, left alone, held himself rigid, to prevent himself from thinking. His instinct warned him that he must not think. Deep inside him was the intense gratification of his passion, still working powerfully. Then there was a counteraction, a horrible breaking down of something inside him, a whole agony of reaction. He stood there for an hour motionless, a chaos of sensations, but rigid with a will to keep blank his consciousness, to prevent his mind grasping. And he held himself so until the worst of the stress had passed, when he began to drink, drank himself to an intoxication, till he slept obliterated. When he woke in the morning he was shaken to the base of his nature. But he had fought off the realization of what he had done. He had prevented his mind from taking it in, had suppressed it along with his instincts, and the conscious man had nothing to do with it. He felt only as after a bout of intoxication, weak, but the affair itself all dim and not to be recovered. Of the drunkenness of his passion he successfully refused remembrance. And when his orderly appeared with coffee, the officer assumed the same self he had had the morning before. He refused the event of the past night—denied it had ever been—and was successful in his denial. He had not done any such thing—not he himself. Whatever there might be lay at the door of a stupid, insubordinate servant.

The orderly had gone about in a stupor all the evening. He drank some beer because he was parched, but not much, the alcohol made his feeling come back, and he could not bear it. He was dulled, as if nine-tenths of the ordinary man in him were inert. He crawled about disfigured. Still, when he thought of the kicks, he went sick, and when he thought of the threat of more kicking, in the room afterwards, his heart went hot and faint, and he panted, remembered the one that had come. He had been forced to say, "For my girl." He was much too done even to want to cry. His mouth hung slightly open, like an idiot's. He felt vacant, and wasted. So, he wandered at his work, painfully, and very slowly and clumsily, fumbling blindly with the brushes, and finding it difficult, when he sat down, to summon the energy to move again. His limbs, his jaw, were slack and nerveless. But he was very tired. He got to bed at last, and slept inert, relaxed, in a sleep that was rather stupor than slumber, a dead night of stupefaction shot through with gleams of anguish.

In the morning were the maneuvers. But he woke even before the bugle sounded. The painful ache in his chest, the dryness of his throat, the awful steady feeling of misery made his eyes come awake and dreary at once. He knew, without thinking, what had happened. And he knew that the day had come again, when he must go on with his round. The last bit of darkness was being pushed out of the room. He would have to move his inert body and go on. He was so young, and had known so little trouble, that he was bewildered. He only wished it would stay night, so that he could lie still, covered up by the darkness. And yet nothing would prevent the day from coming, nothing would save him from having to get up and saddle the Captain's horse, and make the Captain's coffee. It was there, inevitable. And then, he thought, it was impossible. Yet they would not leave him free. He must go and take the coffee to the Captain. He was too stunned to understand it. He only knew it was inevitable—inevitable, however long he lay inert.

At last, after heaving at himself, for he seemed to be a mass of inertia, he got up. But he had to force every one of his movements from behind, with his will. He felt lost, and dazed, and helpless. Then he clutched hold of the bed, the pain was so keen. And looking at his thighs, he saw the darker bruises on his swarthy flesh and he knew that, if he pressed one of his fingers on one of the bruises, he should faint. But he did not want to faint—he did not want anybody to know. No one should ever know. It was between him and the Captain. There were only the two people in the world now—himself and the Captain.

Slowly, economically, he got dressed and forced himself to walk. Everything was obscure, except just what he had his hands on. But he managed to get through his work. The very pain revived his dull senses. The worst remained yet. He took the tray and went up to the Captain's room. The officer, pale and heavy, sat at the table. The orderly, as he saluted, felt himself put out of existence. He stood still for a moment submitting to his own nullification—then he gathered himself, seemed to regain himself, and then the Captain began to grow vague, unreal, and the younger soldier's heart beat up. He clung to this situation—that the Captain did not exist—so that he himself might live. But when he saw his officer's hand tremble as he took the coffee, he felt everything falling shattered. And he went away, feeling as if he himself were coming to pieces, disintegrated. And when the Captain was there on horseback, giving orders, while he himself stood, with rifle and knapsack, sick with pain, he felt as if he must shut his eyes—as if he must shut his eyes on everything. It was only the long agony of marching with a parched throat that filled him with one single, sleep-heavy intention: to save himself.

2

He was getting used even to his parched throat. That the snowy peaks were radiant among the sky, that the whity-green glacier-river twisted through its pale shoals, in the valley below, seemed almost supernatural. But he was going mad with fever and thirst. He plodded on uncomplaining. He did not want to speak, not to anybody. There were two gulls, like flakes of water and snow, over the river. The scene of green rye soaked in sunshine came like a sickness. And the march continued, monotonously, almost like a bad sleep.

At the next farmhouse, which stood low and broad near the high road, tubs of water had been put out. The soldiers clustered round to drink. They took off their helmets, and the steam mounted from their wet hair. The Captain sat on horseback, watching. He needed to see his orderly. His helmet threw a dark shadow over his light, fierce eyes, but his mustache and mouth and chin were distinct in the sunshine. The orderly must move under the presence of the figure of the horseman. It was not that he was afraid, or cowed. It was as if he were disemboweled, made empty, like an empty shell. He felt himself as nothing, a shadow creeping under the sunshine. And, thirsty as he was, he could scarcely drink, feeling the Captain near him. He would not take off his helmet to wipe his wet hair. He wanted to stay in shadow, not to be forced into consciousness. Starting, he saw the light heel of the officer prick the belly of the horse; the Captain cantered away, and he himself could relapse into vacancy.

Nothing, however, could give him back his living place in the hot, bright morning. He felt like a gap among it all. Whereas the Captain was prouder, overriding. A hot flash went through the young servant's body. The Captain was firmer and prouder with life, he himself was empty as a shadow. Again the flash went through him, dazing him out. But his heart ran a little firmer.

The company turned up the hill, to make a loop for the return. Below, from among the trees, the farm-bell clanged. He saw the laborers, mowing barefoot at the thick grass, leave off their work and go downhill, their scythes hanging over their shoulders, like long, bright claws curving down behind them. They seemed like dream-people, as if they had no relation to himself. He felt as in a blackish dream: as if all the other things were there and had form, but he himself was only a consciousness, a gap that could think and perceive.

The soldiers were tramping silently up the glaring hillside. Gradually his head began to revolve, slowly, rhythmically, Sometimes it was dark before his eyes, as if he saw this world through a smoked glass, frail shadows and unreal. It gave him a pain in his head to walk.

The air was too scented, it gave no breath. All the lush green-stuff seemed to be issuing its sap, till the air was deathly, sickly with the smell of greenness. There was the perfume of clover, like pure honey and bees. Then there grew a faint acrid tang—they were near the beeches; and then a queer clattering noise, and a suffocating, hideous smell; they were passing a flock of sheep, a shepherd in a black smock, holding his crook. Why should the sheep huddle together under this fierce sun? He felt that the shepherd would not see him, though he could see the shepherd.

At last there was the halt. They stacked rifles in a conical stack, put down their kit in a scattered circle around it, and dispersed a little, sitting on a small knoll high on the hillside. The chatter began. The soldiers were steaming with heat, but were lively. He sat still, seeing the blue mountains rising upon the land, twenty kilometers away. There was a blue fold in the ranges, then out of that, at the foot, the broad, pale bed of the river, stretches of whity-green water between pinkish-gray shoals among the dark pine woods. There it was, spread out a long way off. And it seemed to come downhill, the river. There was a raft being steered, a mile away. It was a strange country. Nearer, a red-roofed, broad farm with white base and square dots of windows crouched beside the wall of beech foliage on the wood's edge. There were long strips of rye and clover and pale green corn. And just at his feet, below the knoll, was a darkish bog, where globe flowers stood breathless still on their slim stalks. And some of the pale gold bubbles were burst, and a broken fragment hung in the air. He thought he was going to sleep.

Suddenly something moved in the colored mirage before his eyes. The Captain, a small, light-blue and scarlet figure, was trotting evenly between the strips of corn, along the level brow of the hill. And the man making flag-signals was coming on. Proud and sure moved the horseman's figure, the quick, bright thing, in which was concentrated all the light of this morning, which for the rest lay a fragile, shining shadow. Submissive, apathetic, the young soldier sat and stared. But as the horse slowed to a walk, coming up the last steep path, the great flash flared over the body and soul of the orderly. He sat waiting. The back of his head felt as if it were weighted with a heavy piece of fire. He did not want to eat. His hands trembled slightly as he moved them. Meanwhile the officer on horseback was approaching slowly and proudly. The tension grew in the orderly's soul. Then again, seeing the Captain ease himself on the saddle, the flash blazed through him.

The Captain looked at the patch of light blue and scarlet, and dark heads, scattered closely on the hillside. It pleased him. The command pleased him. And he was feeling proud. His orderly was among them in common subjection. The officer rose a little on his stirrups to look. The young soldier sat with averted, dumb face. The Captain relaxed on his seat. His slim-legged, beautiful horse, brown as a beech nut, walked proudly uphill. The Captain passed into the zone of the company's atmosphere: a hot smell of men, sweat, of leather. He knew it very well. After a word with the lieutenant, he went a few paces higher, and sat there, a dominant figure, his sweat-marked horse swishing its tail, while he looked down on his men, on his orderly, a nonentity among the crowd.

The young soldier's heart was like fire in his chest, and he breathed with difficulty. The officer, looking downhill, saw three of the young soldiers, two pails of water between them, staggering across a sunny green field. A table had been set up under a tree, and there the slim lieutenant stood, importantly busy. Then the Captain summoned himself to an act of courage. He called his orderly.

The flame leapt into the young soldier's throat as he heard the command, and he rose blindly, stifled. He saluted, standing below the officer. He did not look up. But there was the flicker in the Captain's voice.

"Go to the inn and fetch me . . ." the officer gave his commands. "Quick!" he added.

At the last word, the heart of the servant leapt with a flash, and he felt the strength come over his body. But he turned in mechanical obedience, and set off at a heavy run downhill, looking almost like a bear, his trousers bagging over his military boots. And the officer watched this blind, plunging run all the way.

But it was only the outside of the orderly's body that was obeying so humbly and mechanically. Inside had gradually accumulated a core into which all the energy of that young life was compact and concentrated. He executed his commission, and plodded quickly back uphill. There was a pain in his head, as he walked, that made him twist his features unknowingly. But hard there in the center of his chest was himself, himself, firm, and not to be plucked to pieces.

The Captain had gone up into the wood. The orderly plodded through the hot, powerfully smelling zone of the company's atmosphere. He had a curious mass of energy inside him now. The

Captain was less real than himself. He approached the green entrance to the wood. There, in the half-shade, he saw the horse standing, the sunshine and the flickering shadow of leaves dancing over his brown body. There was a clearing where timber had lately been felled. Here, in the gold-green shade beside the brilliant cup of sunshine, stood two figures, blue and pink, the bits of pink showing out plainly. The Captain was talking to his lieutenant.

The orderly stood on the edge of the bright clearing, where great trunks of trees, stripped and glistening, lay stretched like naked, brown-skinned bodies. Chips of wood littered the trampled floor, like splashed light, and the bases of the felled trees stood here and there, with their raw, level tops. Beyond was the brilliant, sunlit green of a beech.

"Then I will ride forward," the orderly heard his Captain say. The lieutenant saluted and strode away. He himself went forward. A hot flash passed through his belly, as he tramped towards his officer.

The Captain watched the rather heavy figure of the young soldier stumble forward, and his veins, too, ran hot. This was to be man to man between them. He yielded before the solid, stumbling figure with bent head. The orderly stooped and put the food on a level-sawn tree-base. The Captain watched the glistening, sun-inflamed, naked hands. He wanted to speak to the young soldier, but could not. The servant propped a bottle against his thigh, pressed open the cork, and poured out the beer into the mug. He kept his head bent. The Captain accepted the mug.

"Hot!" he said, as if amiably.

The flame sprang out of the orderly's heart, nearly suffocating him.

"Yes, sir," he replied, between shut teeth.

And he heard the sound of the Captain's drinking and he clenched his fists, such a strong torment came into his wrists. Then came the faint clang of the closing of the pot-lid. He looked up. The Captain was watching him. He glanced swiftly away. Then he saw the officer stoop and take a piece of bread from the tree-base. Again the flash of flame went through the young soldier, seeing the stiff body stoop beneath him, and his hands jerked. He looked away. He could feel the officer was nervous. The bread fell as it was being broken. The officer ate the other piece. The two men stood tense and still, the master laboriously chewing his bread, the servant staring with averted face, his fist clenched.

Then the young soldier started. The officer had pressed open the lid of the mug again. The orderly watched the lid of the mug, and the white hand that clenched the handle, as if he were fascinated. It was raised. The youth followed it with his eyes. And then he saw the thin, strong throat of the elder man moving up and down as he drank, the strong jaw working. And the instinct which had been jerking at the young man's wrist suddenly jerked free. He jumped, feeling as if it were rent in two by a strong flame.

The spur of the officer caught in a tree-root, he went down backwards with a crash, the middle of his back thudding sickeningly against a sharp-edged tree-base, the pot flying away. And in a second the orderly, with serious, earnest young face, and underlip between his teeth, had got his knee in the officer's chest and was pressing the chin backward over the farther edge of the tree-stump, pressing, with all his heart behind in a passion of relief, the tension of his wrists exquisite with relief. And with the base of his palms he shoved at the chin, with all his might. And it was pleasant, too, to have that chin, that hard jaw already slightly rough with beard, in his hands. He did not relax one hair's breadth, but, all the force of all his blood exulting in his thrust, he shoved back the head of the other man, till there was a little "cluck" and a crunching sensation. Then he felt as if his head went to vapor. Heavy convulsions shook the body of the officer, frightening and horrifying the young soldier. Yet it pleased him, too, to repress them. It pleased him to keep his hands pressing back the chin, to feel the chest of the other man yield in expiration to the weight of his strong, young knees, to feel the hard twitchings of the prostrate body jerking his own whole frame, which was pressed down on it.

But it went still. He could look into the nostrils of the other man, the eyes he could scarcely see. How curiously the mouth was pushed out, ex-aggerating the full lips, and the mustache bristling up from them. Then, with a start, he noticed the nostrils gradually filled with blood. The red brimmed, hesitated, ran over, and went in a thin trickle down the face to the eyes.

It shocked and distressed him. Slowly, he got

up. The body twitched and sprawled there, inert. He stood and looked at it in silence. It was a pity *it* was broken. It represented more than the thing which had kicked and bullied him. He was afraid to look at the eyes. They were hideous now, only the whites showing, and the blood running to them. The face of the orderly was drawn with horror at the sight. Well, it was so. In his heart he was satisfied. He had hated the face of the Captain. It was extinguished now. There was a heavy relief in the orderly's soul. That was as it should be. But he could not bear to see the long, military body lying broken over the tree-base, the fine fingers crisped. He wanted to hide it away.

Quickly, busily, he gathered it up and pushed it under the felled tree-trunks, which rested their beautiful, smooth length either end on logs. The face was horrible with blood. He covered it with the helmet. Then he pushed the limbs straight and decent, and brushed the dead leaves off the fine cloth of the uniform. So, it lay quite still in the shadow under there. A little strip of sunshine ran along the breast, from a chink between the logs. The orderly sat by it for a few moments. Here his own life also ended.

Then, through his daze, he heard the lieutenant, in a loud voice, explaining to the men outside the wood, that they were to suppose the bridge on the river below was held by the enemy. Now they were to march to the attack in such and such a manner. The lieutenant had no gift of expression. The orderly, listening from habit, got muddled. And when the lieutenant began it all again he ceased to hear.

He knew he must go. He stood up. It surprised him that the leaves were glittering in the sun, and the chips of wood reflecting white from the ground. For him a change had come over the world. But for the rest it had not—all seemed the same. Only he had left it. And he could not go back. It was his duty to return with the beer-pot and the bottle. He could not. He had left all that. The lieutenant was still hoarsely explaining. He must go, or they would overtake him. And he could not bear contact with any one now.

He drew his fingers over his eyes, trying to find out where he was. Then he turned away. He saw the horse standing in the path. He went up to it and mounted. It hurt him to sit in the saddle. The pain of keeping his seat occupied him as they cantered through the wood. He would not have minded anything, but he could not get away from the sense of being divided from the others. The path led out of the trees. On the edge of the wood he pulled up and stood watching. There in the spacious sunshine of the valley soldiers were moving in a little swarm. Every now and then, a man harrowing on a strip of fallow shouted to his oxen, at the turn. The village and the white-towered church was small in the sunshine. And he no longer belonged to it—he sat there, beyond, like a man outside in the dark. He had gone out from everyday life into the unknown, and he could not, he even did not want to go back.

Turning from the sun-blazing valley, he rode deep into the wood. Tree-trunks, like people standing gray and still, took no notice as he went. A doe, herself a moving bit of sunshine and shadow, went running through the flecked shade. There were bright green rents in the foliage. Then it was all pine wood, dark and cool. And he was sick with pain, he had an intolerable great pulse in his head, and he was sick. He had never been ill in his life. He felt lost, quite dazed with all this.

Trying to get down from the horse, he fell, astonished at the pain and his lack of balance. The horse shifted uneasily. He jerked its bridle and sent it cantering jerkily away. It was his last connection with the rest of things.

But he only wanted to lie down and not be disturbed. Stumbling through the trees, he came on a quiet place where beeches and pine trees grew on a slope. Immediately he had lain down and closed his eyes, his consciousness went racing on without him. A big pulse of sickness beat in him as if it throbbed through the whole earth. He was burning with dry heat. But he was too busy, too tearingly active in the incoherent race of delirium to observe.

3

He came to with a start. His mouth was dry and hard, his heart beat heavily, but he had not the energy to get up. His heart beat heavily. Where was he?—the barracks—at home? There was something knocking. And, making an effort, he looked round—trees, and litter of greenery, and reddish, bright, still pieces of sunshine on the floor. He did not believe he was himself, he did not believe what he saw. Something was knocking. He made a struggle towards consciousness, but relapsed. Then he struggled again. And gradually his surroundings fell into relationship with himself. He knew, and a great pang of fear went through his heart. Somebody was knocking. He could see the heavy, black rags of a fir tree overhead. Then everything went black. Yet he did not believe he had closed his eyes. He had not. Out of the blackness sight slowly emerged again. And some-one was knocking. Quickly, he saw the blood-disfigured face of his Captain, which he hated. And he held himself still with horror. Yet, deep inside him, he knew that it was so, the Captain should be dead. But the physical delirium got hold of him. Someone was knocking. He lay perfectly still, as if dead with fear. And he went unconscious.

When he opened his eyes again, he started, seeing something creeping swiftly up a tree-trunk. It was a little bird. And the bird was whistling overhead. Tap-tap-tap—it was the small, quick bird rapping the tree-trunk with its beak, as if its head were a little round hammer. He watched it curiously. It shifted sharply, in its creeping fashion. Then, like a mouse, it slid down the bare trunk. Its swift creeping sent a flash of revulsion through him. He raised his head. It felt a great weight. Then, the little bird ran out of the shadow across a still patch of sunshine, its little head bobbing swiftly, its white legs twinkling brightly for a moment. How neat it was in its build, so compact, with pieces of white on its wings. There were several of them. They were so pretty—but they crept like swift, erratic mice, running here and there among the beechmast.

He lay down again exhausted, and his con-sciousness lapsed. He had a horror of the little creeping birds. All his blood seemed to be darting and creeping in his head. And yet he could not move.

He came to with a further ache of exhaustion. There was the pain in his head, and the horrible sickness, and his inability to move. He had never been ill in his life. He did not know where he was or what he was. Probably he had got sunstroke. Or what else?—he had silenced the Captain forever—some time ago—oh, a long time ago. There had been blood on his face, and his eyes had turned upwards. It was all right, somehow. It was peace. But now he had got beyond himself.

He had never been here before. Was it life, or not life? He was by himself. They were in a big, bright place, those others, and he was outside. The town, all the country, a big bright place of light: and he was outside, here, in the darkened open beyond, where each thing existed alone. But they would all have to come out there sometime, those others. Little, and left behind him, they all were. There had been father and mother and sweetheart. What did they all matter? This was the open land.

He sat up. Something scuffled. It was a little, brown squirrel running in lovely, undulating bounds over the floor, its red tail completing the undulation of its body—and then, as it sat up, furling and unfurling. He watched it, pleased. It ran on again, friskily, enjoying itself. It flew wildly at another squirrel, and they were chasing each other, and making little scolding, chattering noises. The soldier wanted to speak to them. But only a hoarse sound came out of his throat. The squirrels burst away—they flew up the trees. And then he saw the one peeping round at him, halfway up a tree-trunk. A start of fear went through him, though, insofar as he was conscious, he was amused. It still stayed, its little, keen face staring at him halfway up the tree-trunk, its little ears pricked up, its clawy little hands clinging to the bark, its white breast reared. He started from it in panic.

Struggling to his feet, he lurched away. He went on walking, walking, looking for something—for a drink. His brain felt hot and inflamed for want of water. He stumbled on. Then he did not know anything. He went unconscious as he walked. Yet he stumbled on, his mouth open.

When, to his dumb wonder, he opened his eyes on the world again, he no longer tried to remember what it was. There was thick, golden light behind golden-green glitterings, and tall gray-purple shafts, and darknesses farther off, surrounding him, growing deeper. He was conscious of a sense of arrival. He was amid the reality, on the real, dark bottom. But there was the thirst burning in his brain. He felt lighter, not so heavy. He supposed it was newness. The air was muttering with thunder. He thought he was walking wonderfully swiftly and was coming straight to relief—or was it to water?

Suddenly he stood still with fear. There was a tremendous flare of gold, immense—just a few dark trunks like bars between him and it. All the young level wheat was burnished gold glaring on its silky green. A woman, full-skirted, a black cloth on her head for headdress, was passing like a block of shadow through the glistening, green corn, into the full glare. There was a farm, too, pale blue in shadow, and the timber black. And there was a church spire, nearly fused away in the gold. The woman moved on, away from him. He had no language with which to speak to her. She was the bright, solid unreality. She would make a noise of words that would confuse him, and her eyes would look at him without seeing him. She was crossing there to the other side. He stood against a tree.

When at last he turned, looking down the long, bare grove whose flat bed was already filling dark, he saw the mountains in a wonderlight, not far away, and radiant. Behind the soft, gray ridge of the nearest range the further mountains stood golden and pale gray, the snow all radiant like pure, soft gold. So still, gleaming in the sky, fashioned pure out of the ore of the sky, they shone in their silence. He stood and looked at them, his face illuminated. And like the golden, lustrous gleaming of the snow he felt his own thirst bright in him. He stood and gazed, leaning against a tree. And then everything slid away into space.

During the night the lightning fluttered perpetually, making the whole sky white. He must have walked again. The world hung livid round him for moments, fields a level sheen of gray-green light, trees in dark bulk, and the range of clouds black across a white sky. Then the darkness fell like a shutter, and the night was whole. A faint flutter of a half-revealed world, that could not quite leap out of the darkness!—Then there again stood a sweep of pallor for the land, dark shapes looming, a range of clouds hanging overhead. The world was a ghostly shadow, thrown for a moment upon the pure darkness, which returned ever whole and complete.

And the mere delirium of sickness and fever went on inside him—his brain opening and shutting like the night—then sometimes convulsions of terror from something with great eyes that stared round a tree—then the long agony of the march, and the sun decomposing his blood—then the pang of hate for the Captain, followed by a pang of tenderness and ease. But everything was distorted, born of an ache and resolving into an ache.

In the morning he came definitely awake. Then his brain flamed with the sole horror of thirstiness! The sun was on his face, the dew was steaming from his wet clothes. Like one possessed, he got up. There, straight in front of him, blue and cool and tender, the mountains ranged across the pale edge of the morning sky. He wanted them—he wanted them alone—he wanted to leave himself and be identified with them. They did not move, they were still and soft, with white, gentle markings of snow. He stood still, mad with suffering, his hands crisping and clutching. Then he was twisting in a paroxysm on the grass.

He lay still, in a kind of dream of anguish. His thirst seemed to have separated itself from him, and to stand apart, a single demand. Then the pain he felt was another single self. Then there was the clog of his body, another separate thing. He was divided among all kinds of separate beings. There was some strange, agonized connection between them, but they were drawing further apart. Then they would all split. The sun, drilling down on him, was drilling through the bond. Then they would all fall, fall through the everlasting lapse of space. Then again, his consciousness reasserted itself. He roused on to his elbow and stared at the gleaming mountains. There they ranked, all still and wonderful between earth and heaven. He stared till his eyes went black, and the mountains, as they stood in their beauty, so clean and cool, seemed to have it, that which was lost in him.

4

When the soldiers found him, three hours later, he was lying with his face over his arm, his black hair giving off heat under the sun. But he was still alive. Seeing the open, black mouth[1] the young soldiers dropped him in horror.

He died in the hospital at night, without having seen again.

The doctors saw the bruises on his legs, behind, and were silent.

The bodies of the two men lay together, side by side, in the mortuary, the one white and slender, but laid rigidly at rest, the other looking as if every moment it must rouse into life again, so young and unused, from a slumber.

THE PRUSSIAN OFFICER. **1. black mouth:** a symptom of bubonic plague.

T. S. ELIOT
1888–1965

Murder in the Cathedral

THOMAS BECKET, *Archbishop of Canterbury*
THREE PRIESTS *of Canterbury Cathedral*
FOUR TEMPTERS
FOUR KNIGHTS
MESSENGER
ATTENDANTS
CHORUS OF WOMEN OF CANTERBURY

PART I

The scene is the Archbishop's Hall, on December 2nd, 1170.

CHORUS   Here let us stand, close by the cathedral.
   Here let us wait.
   Are we drawn by danger? Is it the knowledge of
   safety, that draws our feet
   Towards the cathedral? What danger can be
   For us, the poor, the poor women of Canterbury?
   What tribulation
   With which we are not already familiar? There is
   no danger   5
   For us, and there is no safety in the cathedral.
   Some presage of an act
   Which our eyes are compelled to witness, has
   forced our feet
   Towards the cathedral. We are forced to bear
   witness.

   Since golden October declined into sombre
   November
   And the apples were gathered and stored, and
   the land became brown sharp points of death
   in a waste of water and mud,   10
   The New Year waits, breathes, waits, whispers
   in darkness.
   While the labourer kicks off a muddy boot and
   stretches his hand to the fire,
   The New Year waits, destiny waits for the
   coming.
   Who has stretched out his hand to the fire and
   remembered the Saints at All Hallows,
   Remembered the martyrs and saints who wait?
   And who shall   15

Stretch out his hand to the fire, and deny his
   master?° Who shall be warm
By the fire, and deny his master?

Seven years° and the summer is over,
Seven years since the Archbishop left us,
He who was always kind to his people.   20
But it would not be well if he should return.
King rules or barons rule;
We have suffered various oppression,
But mostly we are left to our own devices,
And we are content if we are left alone.   25
We try to keep our households in order;
The merchant, shy and cautious, tries to compile
   a little fortune,
And the labourer bends to his piece of earth,
   earth-colour, his own colour,
Preferring to pass unobserved.
Now I fear disturbance of the quiet seasons: 30
Winter shall come bringing death from the sea,
Ruinous spring shall beat at our doors,
Root and shoot shall eat our eyes and our ears,
Disastrous summer burn up the beds of our
   streams
And the poor shall wait for another decaying
   October.   35
Why should the summer bring consolation
For autumn fires and winter fogs?
What shall we do in the heat of summer
But wait in barren orchards for another October?
Some malady is coming upon us. We wait, we
   wait,   40
And the saints and martyrs wait, for those who
   shall be martyrs and saints.
Destiny waits in the hand of God, shaping the
   still unshapen:
I have seen these things in a shaft of sunlight.
Destiny waits in the hand of God, not in the
   hands of statesmen
Who do, some well, some ill, planning and
   guessing,   45
Having their aims which turn in their hands in
   the pattern of time.
Come, happy December, who shall observe you,
   who shall preserve you?
Shall the Son of Man be born again in the litter
   of scorn?

MURDER IN THE CATHEDRAL: *Part I.* **16. Stretch . . .
master:** as Saint Peter denied Jesus (see Mark 14:66–68).
18. Seven years: Becket's exile in France (1164–70).

For us, the poor, there is no action,
But only to wait and to witness.   50
[*Enter* PRIESTS.]
FIRST PRIEST   Seven years and the summer is over.
Seven years since the Archbishop left us.
SECOND PRIEST   What does the Archbishop do,
and our Sovereign Lord the Pope
With the stubborn King° and the French King
In ceaseless intrigue, combinations,   55
In conference, meetings accepted, meetings
refused,
Meetings unended or endless
At one place or another in France?
THIRD PRIEST   I see nothing quite conclusive in
the art of temporal government,
But violence, duplicity and frequent malversation.
King rules or barons rule: 61
The strong man strongly and the weak man by
caprice.
They have but one law, to seize the power and
keep it,
And the steadfast can manipulate the greed and
lust of others,
The feeble is devoured by his own.   65
FIRST PRIEST   Shall these things not end
Until the poor at the gate
Have forgotten their friend, their Father in
God, have forgotten
That they had a friend?
[*Enter* MESSENGER.]
MESSENGER   Servants of God, and watchers of the
temple,   70
I am here to inform you, without circumlocu-
tion:
The Archbishop is in England, and is close
outside the city.
I was sent before in haste
To give you notice of his coming, as much as
was possible,
That you may prepare to meet him.   75
FIRST PRIEST   What, is the exile ended, is our
Lord Archbishop
Reunited with the King? What reconciliation
Of two proud men?
THIRD PRIEST   What peace can be found
To grow between the hammer and the anvil?
SECOND PRIEST   Tell us,
Are the old disputes at an end, is the wall of
pride cast down   80

54. stubborn King: Henry II.

That divided them? Is it peace or war?
FIRST PRIEST   Does he come
In full assurance, or only secure
In the power of Rome, the spiritual rule,
The assurance of right, and the love of the
people?
MESSENGER   You are right to express a certain
incredulity.   85
He comes in pride and sorrow, affirming all his
claims,
Assured, beyond doubt, of the devotion of the
people,
Who receive him with scenes of frenzied en-
thusiasm,
Lining the road and throwing down their capes,
Strewing the way with leaves and late flowers of
the season.   90
The streets of the city will be packed to suffoca-
tion,
And I think that his horse will be deprived of its
tail,
A single hair of which becomes a precious relic.
He is at one with the Pope, and with the King of
France,
Who indeed would have liked to detain him in
his kingdom: 95
But as for our King, that is another matter.
FIRST PRIEST   But again, is it war or peace?
MESSENGER   Peace, but not the kiss of peace.°
A patched up affair, if you ask my opinion.
And if you ask me, I think the Lord Archbishop
Is not the man to cherish any illusions,   100
Or yet to diminish the least of his pretensions.
If you ask my opinion, I think that this peace
Is nothing like an end, or like a beginning.
It is common knowledge that when the Arch-
bishop
Parted from the King, he said to the King,   105
My Lord, he said, I leave you as a man
Whom in this life I shall not see again.
I have this, I assure you, on the highest authority;
There are several opinions as to what he meant,
But no one considers it a happy prognostic.
[*Exit.*]
FIRST PRIEST   I fear for the Archbishop, I fear for
the Church,   111
I know that the pride bred of sudden prosperity
Was but confirmed by bitter adversity.

97. kiss of peace: public demonstration of intention, which
King Henry refused Becket.

I saw him as Chancellor,° flattered by the King,
Liked or feared by courtiers, in their overbearing
    fashion,   115
Despised and despising, always isolated,
Never one among them, always insecure;
His pride always feeding upon his own virtues,
Pride drawing sustenance from impartiality,
Pride drawing sustenance from generosity,   120
Loathing power given by temporal devolution,°
Wishing subjection to God alone.
Had the King been greater, or had he been
    weaker
Things had perhaps been different for Thomas.

SECOND PRIEST   Yet our lord is returned. Our lord
    has come back to his own again.   125
We have had enough of waiting, from December
    to dismal December.
The Archbishop shall be at our head, dispelling
    dismay and doubt.
He will tell us what we are to do, he will give us
    our orders, instruct us.
Our Lord is at one with the Pope, and also the
    King of France.
We can lean on a rock, we can feel a firm foot-
    hold   130
Against the perpetual wash of tides of balance of
    forces of barons and landholders.
The rock of God is beneath our feet. Let us meet
    the Archbishop with cordial thanksgiving:
Our lord, our Archbishop returns. And when the
    Archbishop returns
Our doubts are dispelled. Let us therefore rejoice,
I say rejoice, and show a glad face for his
    welcome.   135
I am the Archbishop's man. Let us give the
    Archbishop welcome!

THIRD PRIEST   For good or ill, let the wheel turn.
The wheel has been still, these seven years, and
    no good.
For ill or good, let the wheel turn.
For who knows the end of good or evil?   140
Until the grinders cease
And the door shall be shut in the street,
And all the daughters of music shall be brought
    low.°

114. Chancellor: Before he became archbishop of Canterbury, Becket was King Henry's chancellor (1155–62). 121.
temporal devolution: secular authority. 141–43. Until . . .
low: reference to the end of the world (see Ecclesiastes
12:3–4).

CHORUS   Here is no continuing city, here is no
    abiding stay.
Ill the wind, ill the time, uncertain the profit,
    certain the danger.   145
O late late late, late is the time, late too late,
    and rotten the year;
Evil the wind, and bitter the sea, and grey the
    sky, grey grey grey.
O Thomas, return, Archbishop; return, return to
    France.
Return. Quickly. Quietly. Leave us to perish in
    quiet.
You come with applause, you come with rejoic-
    ing, but you come bringing death into Canter-
    bury: 150
A doom on the house, a doom on yourself, a
    doom on the world.

We do not wish anything to happen.
Seven years we have lived quietly,
Succeeded in avoiding notice,
Living and partly living.   155
There have been oppression and luxury,
There have been poverty and licence,
There has been minor injustice.
Yet we have gone on living,
Living and partly living.   160
Sometimes the corn has failed us,
Sometimes the harvest is good,
One year is a year of rain,
Another a year of dryness,
One year the apples are abundant,   165
Another year the plums are lacking.
Yet we have gone on living,
Living and partly living.
We have kept the feasts, heard the masses,
We have brewed beer and cyder,   170
Gathered wood against the winter,
Talked at the corner of the fire,
Talked at the corners of streets,
Talked not always in whispers,
Living and partly living.   175
We have seen births, deaths and marriages,
We have had various scandals,
We have been afflicted with taxes,
We have had laughter and gossip,
Several girls have disappeared   180
Unaccountably, and some not able to.
We have all had our private terrors,
Our particular shadows, our secret fears.

But now a great fear is upon us, a fear not of
    one but of many,
A fear like birth and death, when we see birth
    and death alone   185
In a void apart. We
Are afraid in a fear which we cannot know,
    which we cannot face, which none under-
    stands,
And our hearts are torn from us, our brains un-
    skinned like the layers of an onion, our selves
    are lost lost
In a final fear which none understands. O Thomas
    Archbishop,
O Thomas our Lord, leave us and leave us be, in
    our humble and tarnished frame of existence,
    leave us; do not ask us   190
To stand to the doom on the house, the doom on
    the Archbishop, the doom on the world.
Archbishop, secure and assured of your fate,
    unaffrayed° among the shades, do you realise
    what you ask, do you realise what it means
To the small folk drawn into the pattern of fate,
    the small folk who live among small things,
The strain on the brain of the small folk who
    stand to the doom of the house, the doom of
    their lord, the doom of the world?
O Thomas, Archbishop, leave us, leave us, leave
    sullen Dover, and set sail for France. Thomas
    our Archbishop still our Archbishop even in
    France. Thomas Archbishop, set the white sail
    between the grey sky and the bitter sea, leave
    us, leave us for France.   195
SECOND PRIEST What a way to talk at such a
    juncture!
You are foolish, immodest and babbling women.
Do you not know that the good Archbishop
Is likely to arrive at any moment?
The crowds in the streets will be cheering and
    cheering,   200
You go on croaking like frogs in the treetops:
But frogs at least can be cooked and eaten.
Whatever you are afraid, of, in your craven
    apprehension,
Let me ask you at the least to put on pleasant
    faces,
And give a hearty welcome to our good Arch-
    bishop.   205
        [*Enter* THOMAS.]

192. **unaffrayed:** not startled or frightened.

THOMAS Peace. And let them be, in their exalta-
    tion.
They speak better than they know, and beyond
    your understanding.
They know and do not know, what it is to act or
    suffer.
They know and do not know, that action is
    suffering
And suffering is action. Neither does the agent
    suffer   210
Nor the patient act. But both are fixed
In an eternal action, an eternal patience
To which all must consent that it may be willed
And which all must suffer that they may will it,
That the pattern may subsist, for the pattern is
    the action   215
And the suffering, that the wheel may turn and
    still
Be forever still.
SECOND PRIEST O my Lord, forgive me, I did not
    see you coming,
Engrossed by the chatter of these foolish women.
Forgive us, my Lord, you would have had a
    better welcome   220
If we had been sooner prepared for the event.
But your Lordship knows that seven years of
    waiting,
Seven years of prayer, seven years of emptiness,
Have better prepared our hearts for your
    coming   224
Than seven days could make ready Canterbury.
However, I will have fires laid in all your rooms
To take the chill off our English December,
Your Lordship now being used to a better
    climate.
Your Lordship will find your rooms in order as
    you left them.
THOMAS And will try to leave them in order as I
    find them.   230
I am more than grateful for all your kind
    attentions.
These are small matters. Little rest in Canterbury
With eager enemies restless about us.
Rebellious bishops, York, London, Salisbury,
Would have intercepted our letters,   235
Filled the coast with spies and sent to meet me
Some who hold me in bitterest hate.
By God's grace aware of their prevision
I sent my letters on another day,
Had fair crossing, found at Sandwich   240

Broc, Warenne, and the Sheriff of Kent,
Those who had sworn to have my head from me.
Only John, the Dean of Salisbury,
Fearing for the King's name, warning against treason,
Made them hold their hands. So for the time 245
We are unmolested.

FIRST PRIEST   But do they follow after?

THOMAS   For a little time the hungry hawk
Will only soar and hover, circling lower,
Waiting excuse, pretence, opportunity.
End will be simple, sudden, God-given.   250
Meanwhile the substance of our first act
Will be shadows, and the strife with shadows.
Heavier the interval than the consummation.
All things prepare the event. Watch.

[*Enter* FIRST TEMPTER.]

FIRST TEMPTER   You see, my Lord, I do not wait
upon ceremony: 255
Here I have come, forgetting all acrimony,
Hoping that your present gravity
Will find excuse for my humble levity
Remembering all the good time past.
Your Lordship won't despise an old friend out
of favour?   260
Old Tom, gay Tom, Becket of London,
Your Lordship won't forget that evening on the
river
When the King, and you and I were all friends
together?
Friendship should be more than biting Time can
sever.
What, my Lord, now that you recover   265
Favour with the King, shall we say that summer's
over
Or that the good time cannot last?
Fluting in the meadows, viols in the hall,
Laughter and apple-blossom floating on the
water,
Singing at nightfall, whispering in chambers, 270
Fires devouring the winter season,
Eating up the darkness, with wit and wine and
wisdom!
Now that the King and you are in amity,
Clergy and laity may return to gaiety,
Mirth and sportfulness need not walk warily. 275

THOMAS   You talk of seasons that are past. I remember
Not worth forgetting.

TEMPTER   And of the new season.

Spring has come in winter. Snow in the branches
Shall float as sweet as blossoms. Ice along the
ditches
Mirror the sunlight. Love in the orchard   280
Send the sap shooting. Mirth matches melan-
choly.

THOMAS   We do not know very much of the future
Except that from generation to generation
The same things happen again and again.
Men learn little from others' experience.   285
But in the life of one man, never
The same time returns. Sever
The cord, shed the scale. Only
The fool, fixed in his folly, may think
He can turn the wheel on which he turns.   290

TEMPTER   My Lord, a nod is as good as a wink.
A man will often love what he spurns.
For the good times past, that are come again
I am your man.

THOMAS   Not in this train.
Look to your behaviour. You were safer   295
Think of penitence and follow your master.

TEMPTER   Not at this gait!
If you go so fast, others may go faster.
Your Lordship is too proud!
The safest beast is not the one that roars most
loud,   300
This was not the way of the King our master!
You were not used to be so hard upon sinners
When they were your friends. Be easy, man!
The easy man lives to eat the best dinners.
Take a friend's advice. Leave well alone,   305
Or your goose may be cooked and eaten to the
bone.

THOMAS   You come twenty years too late.

TEMPTER   Then I leave you to your fate.
I leave you to the pleasures of your higher vices,
Which will have to be paid for at higher prices.
Farewell, my Lord, I do not wait upon ceremony,
I leave as I came, forgetting all acrimony,   312
Hoping that your present gravity
Will find excuse for my humble levity.
If you will remember me, my Lord, at your
prayers,   315
I'll remember you at kissing-time below the
stairs.

THOMAS   Leave-well-alone, the springtime fancy,
So one thought goes whistling down the wind.
The impossible is still temptation.
The impossible, the undesirable,   320

Voices under sleep, waking a dead world,
So that the mind may not be whole in the
    present.
      [*Enter* SECOND TEMPTER.]
SECOND TEMPTER   Your Lordship has forgotten
    me, perhaps. I will remind you.
We met at Clarendon, at Northampton,
And last at Montmirail, in Maine.° Now that I
    have recalled them,   325
Let us but set these not too pleasant memories
In balance against other, earlier
And weightier ones: those of the Chancellorship.
See how the late ones rise! You, master of
    policy
Whom all acknowledged, should guide the state
    again.   330
THOMAS   Your meaning?
TEMPTER   The Chancellorship that you resigned
When you were made Archbishop—that was a
    mistake
On your part—still may be regained. Think, my
    Lord,
Power obtained grows to glory,
Life lasting, a permanent possession,   335
A templed tomb, monument of marble.
Rule over men reckon no madness.
THOMAS   To the man of God what gladness?
TEMPTER   Sadness
Only to those giving love to God alone.
Shall he who held the solid substance   340
Wander waking with deceitful shadows?
Power is present. Holiness hereafter.
THOMAS   Who then?
TEMPTER   The Chancellor. King and Chancellor.
King commands. Chancellor richly rules.
This is a sentence° not taught in the schools. 345
To set down the great, protect the poor,
Beneath the throne of God can man do more?
Disarm the ruffian, strengthen the laws,
Rule for the good of the better cause,
Dispensing justice make all even,   350
Is thrive on earth, and perhaps in heaven.
THOMAS   What means?
TEMPTER   Real Power
Is purchased at price of a certain submission.
Your spiritual power is earthly perdition.
Power is present, for him who will wield.   355

324–25. **Clarendon . . . Maine:** places where Becket met
with King Henry in attempts to settle their dispute by
compromise. 345. **sentence:** aphorism.

THOMAS   Who shall have it?
TEMPTER   He who will come.
THOMAS   What shall be the month?
TEMPTER   The last from the first.
THOMAS   What shall we give for it?
TEMPTER   Pretence of priestly power.
THOMAS   Why should we give it?
TEMPTER   For the power and the glory.
THOMAS   No!   360
TEMPTER   Yes! Or bravery will be broken,
Cabined in Canterbury, realmless ruler,
Self-bound servant of a powerless Pope,
The old stag, circled with hounds.
THOMAS   No!   365
TEMPTER   Yes! men must manoeuvre. Monarchs
    also,
Waging war abroad, need fast friends at home.
Private policy is public profit;
Dignity still shall be dressed with decorum.
THOMAS   You forget the bishops   370
Whom I have laid under excommunication.
TEMPTER   Hungry hatred
Will not strive against intelligent self-interest.
THOMAS   You forget the barons. Who will not
    forget
Constant curbing for pretty privilege.   375
TEMPTER   Against the barons.
Is King's cause, churl's cause, Chancellor's cause.
THOMAS   No! shall I, who keep the keys
Of heaven and hell, supreme alone in England,
Who bind and loose, with power from the Pope,
Descend to desire a punier power?   381
Delegate to deal the doom of damnation,
To condemn kings, not serve among their
    servants,
Is my open office. No! Go.
TEMPTER   Then I leave you to your fate.   385
Your sin soars sunward, covering kings' falcons.
THOMAS   Temporal power, to build a good world,
To keep order, as the world knows order.
Those who put their faith in worldly order
Not controlled by the order of God,   390
In confident ignorance, but arrest disorder,
Make it fast, breed fatal disease,
Degrade what they exalt. Power with the King—
I *was* the King, his arm, his better reason.
But what was once exaltation   395
Would now be only mean descent.
      [*Enter* THIRD TEMPTER.]
THIRD TEMPTER   I am an unexpected visitor.

THOMAS   I expected you.

TEMPTER   But not in this guise, or for my present
    purpose.

THOMAS   No purpose brings surprise.

TEMPTER   Well, my Lord,
    I am no trifler, and no politician.   400
    To idle or intrigue at court
    I have no skill. I am no courtier.
    I know a horse, a dog, a wench;
    I know how to hold my estates in order,
    A country-keeping lord who minds his own
      business.   405
    It is we country lords who know the country
    And we who know what the country needs.
    It is our country. We care for the country.
    We are the backbone of the nation.
    We, not the plotting parasites   410
    About the King. Excuse my bluntness:
    I am a rough straightforward Englishman.

THOMAS   Proceed straight forward.

TEMPTER   Purpose is plain.
    Endurance of friendship does not depend
    Upon ourselves, but upon circumstance.   415
    But circumstance is not undetermined.
    Unreal friendship may turn to real
    But real friendship, once ended, cannot be
      mended.
    Sooner shall enmity turn to alliance.
    The enmity that never knew friendship   420
    Can sooner know accord.

THOMAS   For a countryman
    You wrap your meaning in as dark generality
    As any courtier.

TEMPTER   This is the simple fact!
    You have no hope of reconciliation
    With Henry the King. You look only   425
    To blind assertion in isolation.
    That is a mistake.

THOMAS   O Henry, O my King!

TEMPTER   Other friends
    May be found in the present situation.
    King in England is not all-powerful;
    King is in France, squabbling in Anjou;   430
    Round him waiting hungry sons.
    We are for England. We are in England.
    You and I, my Lord, are Normans.
    England is a land for Norman
    Sovereignty. Let the Angevin°   435

---

435. Angevin: Henry II was hereditary ruler of Anjou and
other French territories.

Destroy himself, fighting in Anjou.
He does not understand us, the English barons.
We are the people.

THOMAS   To what does this lead?

TEMPTER   To a happy coalition
    Of intelligent interests.

THOMAS   But what have you—   440
    If you do speak for barons—

TEMPTER   For a powerful party
    Which has turned its eyes in your direction—
    To gain from you, your Lordship asks.
    For us, Church favour would be an advantage,
    Blessing of Pope powerful protection   445
    In the fight for liberty. You, my Lord,
    In being with us, would fight a good stroke
    At once, for England and for Rome,
    Ending the tyrannous jurisdiction
    Of king's court over bishop's court,   450
    Of king's court over baron's court.

THOMAS   Which I helped to found.

TEMPTER   Which you helped to found.
    But time past is time forgotten.
    We expect the rise of a new constellation.

THOMAS   And if the Archbishop cannot trust the
    King,   455
    How can he trust those who work for King's
      undoing?

TEMPTER   Kings will allow no power but their own;
    Church and people have good cause against the
      throne.

THOMAS   If the Archbishop cannot trust the Throne,
    He has good cause to trust none but God alone.
    I ruled once as Chancellor   461
    And men like you were glad to wait at my door.
    Not only in the court, but in the field
    And in the tilt-yard I made many yield.
    Shall I who ruled like an eagle over doves   465
    Now take the shape of a wolf among wolves?
    Pursue your treacheries as you have done before:
    No one shall say that I betrayed a king.

TEMPTER   Then, my Lord, I shall not wait at your
    door;
    And I well hope, before another spring   470
    The King will show his regard for your loyalty.

THOMAS   To make, then break, this thought has
    come before,
    The desperate exercise of failing power.
    Samson in Gaza° did no more.

---

474. Samson in Gaza: the subject of Milton's *Samson
Agonistes* (see Judges 16:21–30).

But if I break, I must break myself alone. 475
[*Enter* FOURTH TEMPTER.]
FOURTH TEMPTER   Well done, Thomas, your will
is hard to bend.
And with me beside you, you shall not lack a
friend.
THOMAS   Who are you? I expected
Three visitors, not four.
TEMPTER   Do not be surprised to receive one more.
Had I been expected, I had been here before. 481
I always precede expectation.
THOMAS   Who are you?
TEMPTER   As you do not know me, I do not need a
name,
And, as you know me, that is why I come.
You know me, but have never seen my face. 485
To meet before was never time or place.
THOMAS   Say what you come to say.
TEMPTER   It shall be said at last.
Hooks have been baited with morsels of the past.
Wantonness is weakness. As for the King,
His hardened hatred shall have no end. 490
You know truly, the King will never trust
Twice, the man who has been his friend.
Borrow use cautiously, employ
Your services as long as you have to lend.
You would wait for trap to snap 495
Having served your turn, broken and crushed.
As for barons, envy of lesser men
Is still more stubborn than king's anger.
Kings have public policy, barons private profit,
Jealousy raging possession of the fiend. 500
Barons are employable against each other;
Greater enemies must kings destroy.
THOMAS   What is your counsel?
TEMPTER   Fare forward to the end.
All other ways are closed to you
Except the way already chosen. 505
But what is pleasure, kingly rule,
Or rule of men beneath a king,
With craft in corners, stealthy stratagem,
To general grasp of spiritual power?
Man oppressed by sin, since Adam fell— 510
You hold the keys of heaven and hell.
Power to bind and loose: bind, Thomas, bind,
King and bishop under your heel.
King, emperor, bishop, baron, king:
Uncertain mastery of melting armies, 515
War, plague, and revolution,
New conspiracies, broken pacts;

To be master or servant within an hour,
This is the course of temporal power.
The Old King° shall know it, when at last
breath, 520
No sons, no empire, he bites broken teeth.
You hold the skein: wind, Thomas, wind
The thread of eternal life and death.
You hold this power, hold it.
THOMAS   Supreme, in this land?
TEMPTER   Supreme, but for one.° 525
THOMAS   That I do not understand.
TEMPTER   It is not for me to tell you how this may
be so;
I am only here, Thomas, to tell you what you
know.
THOMAS   How long shall this be?
TEMPTER   Save what you know already, ask
nothing of me.
But think, Thomas, think of glory after death.
When king is dead, there's another king, 531
And one more king is another reign.
King is forgotten, when another shall come:
Saint and Martyr rule from the tomb.
Think, Thomas, think of enemies dismayed, 535
Creeping in penance, frightened of a shade;
Think of pilgrims, standing in line
Before the glittering jewelled shrine,
From generation to generation
Bending the knee in supplication. 540
Think of the miracles, by God's grace,
And think of your enemies, in another place.
THOMAS   I have thought of these things.
TEMPTER   That is why I tell you.
Your thoughts have more power than kings to
compel you.
You have also thought, sometimes at your
prayers, 545
Sometimes hesitating at the angles of stairs,
And between sleep and waking, early in the
morning,
When the bird cries, have thought of further
scorning.
That nothing lasts, but the wheel turns,
The next is rifled, and the bird mourns; 550
That the shrine shall be pillaged, and the gold
spent,
The jewels gone for light ladies' ornament,
The sanctuary broken, and its stores

520. Old King: Henry's son had been crowned in advance by
the rebellious bishops in 1170. **525. one:** Satan.

Swept into the laps of parasites and whores.

When miracles cease, and the faithful desert
  you.   555

And men shall only do their best to forget you.

And later is worse, when men will not hate you

Enough to defame or to execrate you,

But pondering the qualities that you lacked

Will only try to find the historical fact.   560

When men shall declare that there was no
  mystery

About this man who played a certain part in
  history.

THOMAS   But what is there to do? What is left to
  be done?

Is there no enduring crown to be won?

TEMPTER   Yes, Thomas, yes; you have thought of
  that too.   565

What can compare with glory of Saints

Dwelling forever in presence of God?

What earthly glory, of king or emperor,

What earthly pride, that is not poverty

Compared with richness of heavenly grandeur?

Seek the way of martyrdom, make yourself the
  lowest   571

On earth, to be high in heaven.

And see far off below you, where the gulf is
  fixed,

Your persecutors, in timeless torment,

Parched passion, beyond expiation.

THOMAS   No!   575

Who are you, tempting with my own desires?

Others have come, temporal tempters,

With pleasure and power at palpable price.

What do you offer? What do you ask?

TEMPTER   I offer what you desire. I ask   580

What you have to give. Is it too much

For such a vision of eternal grandeur?

THOMAS   Others offered real goods, worthless

But real. You only offer

Dreams to damnation.

TEMPTER   You have often dreamt them. 585

THOMAS   Is there no way, in my soul's sickness,

Does not lead to damnation in pride?

I well know that these temptations

Mean present vanity and future torment.

Can sinful pride be driven out   590

Only by more sinful? Can I neither act nor suffer

Without perdition?

TEMPTER   You know and do not know, what it is
  to act or suffer.

You know and do not know, that action is
  suffering,

And suffering action. Neither does the agent suffer

Nor the patient act. But both are fixed   596

In an eternal action, an eternal patience

To which all must consent that it may be willed

And which all must suffer that they may will it,

That the pattern may subsist, that the wheel
  may turn and still   600

Be forever still.

CHORUS   There is no rest in the house. There is no
  rest in the street.

I hear restless movement of feet. And the air is
  heavy and thick.

Thick and heavy the sky. And the earth presses
  up against our feet.

What is the sickly smell, the vapour? The dark
  green light from a cloud on a withered tree?
  The earth is heaving to parturition of issue of
  hell. What is the sticky dew that forms on the
  back of my hand?   605

THE FOUR TEMPTERS   Man's life is a cheat and a
  disappointment;

All things are unreal,

Unreal or disappointing:

The Catherine wheel,° the pantomime cat,

The prizes given at the children's party,   610

The prize awarded for the English Essay,

The scholar's degree, the statesman's decoration.

All things become less real, man passes

From unreality to unreality.

This man is obstinate, blind, intent   615

On self-destruction.

Passing from deception to deception,

From grandeur to grandeur to final illusion,

Lost in the wonder of his own greatness,

The enemy of society, enemy of himself.   620

THE THREE PRIESTS   O Thomas my Lord do not
  fight the intractable tide,

Do not sail the irresistible wind; in the storm,

Should we not wait for the sea to subside, in
  the night

Abide the coming of day, when the traveller may
  find his way,

The sailor lay course by the sun?   625

[CHORUS, PRIESTS and TEMPTERS alternately.]

CHORUS   Is it the owl that calls, or a signal between
  the trees?

609. Catherine wheel: pinwheel, but also the spiked wheel
used to torture Saint Catherine.

PRIESTS   Is the window-bar made fast, is the door
    under lock and bolt?
TEMPTERS   Is it rain that taps at the window, is it
    wind that pokes at the door?
CHORUS   Does the torch flame in the hall, the
    candle in the room?
PRIESTS   Does the watchman walk by the wall? 630
TEMPTERS   Does the mastiff prowl by the gate?
CHORUS   Death has a hundred hands and walks
    by a thousand ways.
PRIESTS   He may come in the sight of all, he may
    pass unseen unheard.
TEMPTERS   Come whispering through the ear, or a
    sudden shock on the skull.
CHORUS   A man may walk with a lamp at night,
    and yet be drowned in a ditch.   635
PRIESTS   A man may climb the stair in the day, and
    slip on a broken step.
TEMPTERS   A man may sit at meat, and feel the
    cold in his groin.
CHORUS   We have not been happy, my Lord, we
    have not been too happy.
    We are not ignorant women, we know what we
      must expect and not expect.
    We know of oppression and torture,   640
    We know of extortion and violence,
    Destitution, disease,
    The old without fire in winter,
    The child without milk in summer,
    Our labour taken away from us,   645
    Our sins made heavier upon us.
    We have seen the young man mutilated,
    The torn girl trembling by the mill-stream.
    And meanwhile we have gone on living,
    Living and partly living,   650
    Picking together the pieces,
    Gathering faggots at nightfall,
    Building a partial shelter,
    For sleeping, and eating and drinking and
      laughter.

    God gave us always some reason, some hope;
      but now a new terror has soiled us, which none
      can avert, none can avoid, flowing under our
      feet and over the sky;   655
    Under doors and down chimneys, flowing in at
      the ear and the mouth and the eye.
    God is leaving us, God is leaving us, more pang,
      more pain than birth or death.
    Sweet and cloying through the dark air

Falls the stifling scent of despair;
The forms take shape in the dark air: 660
Puss-purr of leopard, footfall of padding bear,
Palm-pat of nodding ape, square hyaena waiting
For laughter, laughter, laughter. The Lords of
    Hell are here.
They curl round you, lie at your feet, swing and
    wing through the dark air.
O Thomas Archbishop, save us, save us, save
    yourself that we may be saved;   665
Destroy yourself and we are destroyed.
THOMAS   Now is my way clear, now is the meaning
    plain:
Temptation shall not come in this kind again.
The last temptation is the greatest treason:
To do the right deed for the wrong reason.   670
The natural vigour in the venial sin
Is the way in which our lives begin.
Thirty years ago, I searched all the ways
That lead to pleasure, advancement and praise.
Delight in sense, in learning and in thought, 675
Music and philosophy, curiosity,
The purple bullfinch in the lilac tree,
The tilt-yard skill, the strategy of chess,
Love in the garden, singing to the instrument,
Were all things equally desirable.   680
Ambition comes when early force is spent
And when we find no longer all things possible.
Ambition comes behind and unobservable.
Sin grows with doing good. When I imposed the
    King's law
In England, and waged war with him against
    Toulouse,   685
I beat the barons at their own game. I
Could then despise the men who thought me most
    contemptible,
The raw nobility, whose manners matched their
    fingernails.
While I ate out of the King's dish
To become servant of God was never my wish.
Servant of God has chance of greater sin   691
And sorrow, than the man who serves a king.
For those who serve the greater cause may make
    the cause serve them,
Still doing right: and striving with political men
May make that cause political, not by what they
    do   695
But by what they are. I know
What yet remains to show you of my history
Will seem to most of you at best futility,

Senseless self-slaughter of a lunatic,
Arrogant passion of a fanatic.   700
I know that history at all times draws
The strangest consequence from remotest cause.
But for every evil, every sacrilege,
Crime, wrong, oppression and the axe's edge,
Indifference, exploitation, you, and you,   705
And you, must all be punished. So must you.
I shall no longer act or suffer, to the sword's end.
Now my good Angel, whom God appoints
To be my guardian hover over the swords'
    points.

INTERLUDE

THE ARCHBISHOP *preaches in the Cathedral on Christmas Morning, 1170.*

"Glory to God in the highest, and on earth peace to men of good will." *The fourteenth verse of the second chapter of the Gospel according to Saint Luke.* In the Name of the Father, and of the Son, and of the Holy Ghost. Amen.   5

Dear children of God, my sermon this Christmas morning will be a very short one. I wish only that you should meditate in your hearts the deep meaning and mystery of our masses of Christmas Day. For whenever Mass is said, we re-enact the Passion and Death of Our Lord; and on this Christmas Day we do this in celebration of His Birth. So that at the same moment we rejoice in His coming for the salvation of men, and offer again to God His Body and Blood in sacrifice, oblation and satisfaction for the sins of the whole world. It was in this same night that has just passed, that a multitude of the heavenly host appeared before the shepherds at Bethlehem, saying "Glory to God in the highest, and on earth peace to men of good will"; at this same time of all the year that we celebrate at once the Birth of Our Lord and His Passion and Death upon the Cross. Beloved, as the World sees, this is to behave in a strange fashion. For who in the World will both mourn and rejoice at once and for the same reason? For either joy will be overborne by mourning, or mourning will be cast out by joy; so it is only in these our Christian mysteries that we can rejoice and mourn at once for the same reason. Now think for a moment about the meaning of this word "peace." Does it seem strange to you that the

angels should have announced Peace, when ceaselessly the world has been stricken with War and the fear of War? Does it seem to you that the angelic voices were mistaken, and that the promise was a disappointment and a cheat?   37

Reflect now, how Our Lord Himself spoke of Peace. He said to His disciples, "My peace I leave with you, my peace I give unto you." Did He mean peace as we think of it: the kingdom of England at peace with its neighbours, the barons at peace with the King, the householder counting over his peaceful gains, the swept hearth, his best wine for a friend at the table, his wife singing to the children? Those men His disciples knew no such things: they went forth to journey afar, to suffer by land and sea, to know torture, imprisonment, disappointment, to suffer death by martyrdom. What then did He mean? If you ask that, remember then that He said also, "Not as the world gives, give I unto you." So then, He gave to His disciples peace, but not peace as the world gives.   54

Consider also one thing of which you have probably never thought. Not only do we at the feast of Christmas celebrate at once Our Lord's Birth and His Death: but on the next day we celebrate the martyrdom of His first martyr, the blessed Stephen. Is it an accident, do you think, that the day of the first martyr follows immediately the day of the Birth of Christ? By no means. Just as we rejoice and mourn at once, in the Birth and in the Passion of Our Lord; so also, in a smaller figure, we both rejoice and mourn in the death of martyrs. We mourn, for the sins of the world that has martyred them; we rejoice, that another soul is numbered among the Saints in Heaven, for the glory of God and for the salvation of men.   69

Beloved, we do not think of a martyr simply as a good Christian who has been killed because he is a Christian: for that would be solely to mourn. We do not think of him simply as a good Christian who has been elevated to the company of the Saints: for that would be simply to rejoice: and neither our mourning nor our rejoicing is as the world's is. A Christian martyrdom is never an accident, for Saints are not made by accident. Still less is a Christian martyrdom the effect of a man's will to become a Saint, as a man by willing and contriving may become a ruler of men. A martyrdom is always the design of God, for His love of men, to warn them and to lead them, to bring them back to His ways. It is never the design of man; for the true martyr is he who has become the instrument of God, who has lost his will in the will of God, and who no longer desires anything for himself, not even the glory of being a martyr. So thus as on earth the Church mourns and rejoices at once, in a fashion that the world cannot understand; so in Heaven the Saints are most high, having made themselves most low, and are seen, not as we see them, but in the light of the Godhead from which they draw their being. 95

I have spoken to you to-day, dear children of God, of the martyrs of the past, asking you to remember especially our martyr of Canterbury, the blessed Archbishop Elphege; because it is fitting, on Christ's birth day, to remember what is that Peace which He brought; and because, dear children, I do not think I shall ever preach to you again; and because it is possible that in a short time you may have yet another martyr, and that one perhaps not the last. I would have you keep in your hearts these words that I say, and think of them at another time. In the Name of the Father, and of the Son, and of the Holy Ghost. Amen. 109

PART II

The first scene is in the Archbishop's Hall, the second scene is in the Cathedral, on December 29th, 1170.

CHORUS Does the bird sing in the South?
Only the sea-bird cries, driven inland by the storm.
What sign of the spring of the year?
Only the death of the old: not a stir, not a shoot, not a breath.
Do the days begin to lengthen? 5
Longer and darker the day, shorter and colder the night.
Still and stifling the air: but a wind is stored up in the East.
The starved crow sits in the field, attentive; and in the wood
The owl rehearses the hollow note of death.
What signs of a bitter spring? 10
The wind stored up in the East.

What, at the time of the birth of Our Lord, at Christmastide,
Is there not peace upon earth, goodwill among men?
The peace of this world is always uncertain, unless men keep the peace of God.
And war among men defiles this world, but death in the Lord renews it, 15
And the world must be cleaned in the winter, or we shall have only
A sour spring, a parched summer, an empty harvest.
Between Christmas and Easter what work shall be done?
The ploughman shall go out in March and turn the same earth
He has turned before, the bird shall sing the same song. 20
When the leaf is out on the tree, when the elder and may
Burst over the stream, and the air is clear and high,
And voices trill at windows, and children tumble in front of the door,
What work shall have been done, what wrong
Shall the bird's song cover, the green tree cover, what wrong 25
Shall the fresh earth cover? We wait, and the time is short
But waiting is long.

[*Enter the* FIRST PRIEST *with a banner of St. Stephen borne before him. The lines sung are in italics.*]

FIRST PRIEST Since Christmas a day: and the day of St. Stephen, First Martyr.
Princes moreover did sit, and did witness falsely against me.
A day that was always most dear to the Archbishop Thomas. 30
And he kneeled down and cried with a loud voice: Lord, lay not this sin to their charge.
Princes moreover did sit.

[*Introit of St. Stephen is heard.*]

[*Enter the* SECOND PRIEST, *with a banner of St. John the Apostle borne before him.*]

SECOND PRIEST Since St. Stephen a day: and the day of St. John the Apostle.
In the midst of the congregation he opened his mouth. 35
That which was from the beginning, which we have heard,

Which we have seen with our eyes, and our
hands have handled

Of the word of life; that which we have seen and
heard

Declare we unto you.

In the midst of the congregation.   40

[*Introt of St. John is heard.*]

[*Enter the* THIRD PRIEST, *with a banner of the Holy
Innocents borne before him.*]

THIRD PRIEST   Since St. John the Apostle a day:
and the day of the Holy Innocents.

Out of the mouth of very babes, O God.

As the voice of many waters, of thunder, of
harps,

They sung as it were a new song.

The blood of thy saints have they shed like
water,   45

And there was no man to bury them. Avenge, O
Lord,

The blood of thy saints. In Rama, a voice heard,
weeping.

Out of the mouth of very babes, O God!

[*The* PRIESTS *stand together with the banners behind
them.*]

FIRST PRIEST   Since the Holy Innocents a day: the
fourth day from Christmas.

THE THREE PRIESTS   *Rejoice we all, keeping holy
day.*   50

FIRST PRIEST   As for the people, so also for himself, he offereth for sins.

He lays down his life for the sheep.

THE THREE PRIESTS   *Rejoice we all, keeping holy day.*

FIRST PRIEST   To-day?

SECOND PRIEST   To-day, what is to-day? For the
day is half gone.

FIRST PRIEST   To-day, what is to-day? But another
day, the dusk of the year.   55

SECOND PRIEST   To-day, what is to-day? Another
night, and another dawn.

THIRD PRIEST   What day is the day that we know
that we hope for or fear for?

Every day is the day we should fear from or hope
from. One moment

Weighs like another. Only in retrospection,
selection,

We say, that was the day. The critical moment

That is always now, and here. Even now, in
sordid particulars   61

The eternal design may appear.

[*Enter the* FOUR KNIGHTS. *The banners disappear.*]

FIRST KNIGHT   Servants of the king.

FIRST PRIEST   And known to us.

You are welcome. Have you ridden far?

FIRST KNIGHT   Not far to-day, but matters urgent

Have brought us from France. We rode hard,   66

Took ship yesterday, landed last night,

Having business with the Archbishop.

SECOND KNIGHT   Urgent business.

THIRD KNIGHT   From the King.

SECOND KNIGHT   By the King's order.

FIRST KNIGHT   Our men are outside.

FIRST PRIEST   You know the Archbishop's hospitality.   71

We are about to go to dinner.

The good Archbishop would be vexed

If we did not offer you entertainment

Before your business. Please dine with us.   75

Your men shall be looked after also.

Dinner before business. Do you like roast pork?

FIRST KNIGHT   Business before dinner. We will
roast your pork

First, and dine upon it after.

SECOND KNIGHT   We must see the Archbishop.

THIRD KNIGHT   Go, tell the Archbishop

We have no need of his hospitality.   81

We will find our own dinner.

FIRST PRIEST   [*To* ATTENDANT]

Go, tell His Lordship.

FOURTH KNIGHT   How much longer will you
keep us waiting?

[*Enter* THOMAS.]

THOMAS   [*To* PRIESTS] However certain our expectation

The moment foreseen may be unexpected   85

When it arrives. It comes when we are

Engrossed with matters of other urgency.

On my table you will find

The papers in order, and the documents signed.

[*To* KNIGHTS] You are welcome, whatever your
business may be.   90

You say, from the King?

FIRST KNIGHT   Most surely from the King.

We must speak with you alone.

THOMAS   [*To* PRIESTS] Leave us then alone.

Now what is the matter?

FIRST KNIGHT   This is the matter.

THE THREE KNIGHTS   You are the Archbishop in
revolt against the King; in rebellion to the
King and the law of the land;

You are the Archbishop who was made by the

King; whom he set in your place to carry out
  his command.   95
You are his servant, his tool, and his jack,°
You wore his favours on your back,
You had your honours all from his hand; from
  him you had the power, the seal and the ring.
This is the man who was the tradesman's son;
  the backstairs brat who was born in Cheap-
  side;
This is the creature that crawled upon the King;
  swollen with blood and swollen with pride. 100
Creeping out of the London dirt,
Crawling up like a louse on your shirt,
The man who cheated, swindled, lied; broke his
  oath and betrayed his King.

THOMAS   This is not true.
  Both before and after I received the ring   105
  I have been a loyal subject to the King.
  Saving my order, I am at his command,
  As his most faithful vassal in the land.

FIRST KNIGHT   Saving your order! let your order
  save you—
  As I do not think it is like to do.   110
  Saving your ambition is what you mean,
  Saving your pride, envy and spleen.

SECOND KNIGHT   Saving your insolence and greed.
  Won't you ask us to pray to God for you, in
  your need?

THIRD KNIGHT   Yes, we'll pray for you!

FIRST KNIGHT   Yes, we'll pray for you!   115

THE THREE KNIGHTS   Yes, we'll pray that God
  may help you!

THOMAS   But, gentlemen, your business
  Which you said so urgent, is it only
  Scolding and blaspheming?

FIRST KNIGHT   That was only
  Our indignation, as loyal subjects.   120

THOMAS   Loyal? To whom?

FIRST KNIGHT   To the King!

SECOND KNIGHT   The King!

THIRD KNIGHT   The King!

THE THREE KNIGHTS   God bless him!

THOMAS   Then let your new coat of loyalty be worn
  Carefully, so it get not soiled or torn.
  Have you something to say?

FIRST KNIGHT   By the King's command   125
  Shall we say it now?

SECOND KNIGHT   Without delay,

Before the old fox is off and away.

THOMAS   What you have to say
  By the King's command—if it be the King's
  command—
  Should be said in public. If you make charges,
  Then in public I will refute them.

FIRST KNIGHT   No! here and now!   130
[*They make to attack him, but the* PRIESTS *and*
ATTENDANTS *return and quietly interpose themselves.*]

THOMAS   Now and here!

FIRST KNIGHT   Of your earlier misdeeds I shall
  make no mention.
  They are too well known. But after dissension
  Had ended, in France, and you were endued
  With your former privilege, how did you show
  your gratitude?   135
  You had fled from England, not exiled
  Or threatened, mind you; but in the hope
  Of stirring up trouble in the French dominions.
  You sowed strife abroad, you reviled
  The King to the King of France, to the Pope, 140
  Raising up against him false opinions.

SECOND KNIGHT   Yet the King, out of his charity,
  And urged by your friends, offered clemency,
  Made a pact of peace, and all dispute ended
  Sent you back to your See as you demanded. 145

THIRD KNIGHT   And burying the memory of your
  transgressions
  Restored your honours and your possessions.
  All was granted for which you sued:
  Yet how, I repeat, did you show your gratitude?

FIRST KNIGHT   Suspending those who had crowned
  the young prince,   150
  Denying the legality of his coronation.

SECOND KNIGHT   Binding with the chains of
  anathema.

THIRD KNIGHT   Using every means in your power
  to evince°
  The King's faithful servants, every one who
  transacts
  His business in his absence, the business of the
  nation.   155

FIRST KNIGHT   These are the facts.
  Say therefore if you will be content
  To answer in the King's presence. Therefore
  were we sent.

THOMAS   Never was it my wish
  To uncrown the King's son, or to diminish 160
  His honour and power. Why should he wish

Part II. **96. jack:** man, i.e., bound as a follower of
King Henry.

153. evince: overcome.

To deprive my people of me and keep me from
my own
And bid me sit in Canterbury, alone?
I would wish him three crowns rather than one,
And as for the bishops, it is not my yoke   165
That is laid upon them, or mine to revoke.
Let them go to the Pope. It was he who con-
demned them.

FIRST KNIGHT   Through you they were suspended.
SECOND KNIGHT   By you be this amended.
THIRD KNIGHT   Absolve them.
FIRST KNIGHT   Absolve them.
THOMAS   I do not deny
That this was done through me. But it is not I   170
Who can loose whom the Pope has bound.
Let them go to him, upon whom redounds
Their contempt towards me, their contempt
towards the Church shown.

FIRST KNIGHT   Be that as it may, here is the
King's command:
That you and your servants depart from this
land.   175

THOMAS   If that *is* the King's command, I will be
bold
To say: seven years were my people without
My presence; seven years of misery and pain.
Seven years a mendicant on foreign charity
I lingered abroad: seven years is no brevity.   180
I shall not get those seven years back again.
Never again, you must make no doubt,
Shall the sea run between the shepherd and his
fold.

FIRST KNIGHT   The King's justice, the King's
majesty,
You insult with gross indignity,   185
Insolent madman, whom nothing deters.
From attainting his servants and ministers.

THOMAS   It is not I who insult the King,
And there is higher than I or the King
It is not I, Becket from Cheapside,   190
It is not against me, Becket, that you strive.
It is not Becket who pronounces doom,
But the Law of Christ's Church, the judgement of
Rome.

FIRST KNIGHT   Priest, you have spoken in peril
of your life.
SECOND KNIGHT   Priest, you have spoken in danger of the knife.   195
THIRD KNIGHT   Priest, you have spoken treachery
and treason.

THE THREE KNIGHTS   Priest! traitor, confirmed in
malfeasance.
THOMAS   I submit my cause to the judgement of
Rome.
But if you kill me, I shall rise from my tomb
To submit my cause before God's throne.   200
                                         [*Exit.*]

FOURTH KNIGHT   Priest! monk! and servant! take,
hold, detain,
Restrain this man, in the King's name.
FIRST KNIGHT   Or answer with your bodies.
SECOND KNIGHT   Enough of words.
THE FOUR KNIGHTS   We come for the King's
justice, we come with swords.   [*Exeunt.*]

CHORUS   I have smelt them, the death-bringers,
senses are quickened   205
By subtile forebodings; I have heard
Fluting in the night-time, fluting and owls, have
seen at noon
Scaly wings slanting over, huge and ridiculous.
I have tasted
The savour of putrid flesh in the spoon. I have
felt
The heaving of earth at nightfall, restless,
absurd. I have heard   210
Laughter in the noises of beasts that make
strange noises: jackal, jackass, jackdaw; the
scurrying noise of mouse and jerboa; the
laugh of the loon, the lunatic bird. I have seen
Grey necks twisting, rat tails twining, in the
thick light of dawn. I have eaten
Smooth creatures still living, with the strong salt
taste of living things under sea; I have tasted
The living lobster, the crab, the oyster, the whelk
and the prawn; and they live and spawn in
my bowels, and my bowels dissolve in the light
of dawn. I have smelt
Death in the rose, death in the hollyhock, sweet
pea, hyacinth, primrose and cowslip. I have
seen   215
Trunk and horn, tusk and hoof, in odd places;
I have lain on the floor of the sea and breathed
with the breathing of the sea-anemone, swallowed with ingurgitation of the sponge. I
have lain in the soil and criticised the worm.
In the air
Flirted with the passage of the kite, I have
plunged with the kite and cowered with the
wren. I have felt
The horn of the beetle, the scale of the viper, the

mobile hard insensitive skin of the elephant,
the evasive flank of the fish. I have smelt
Corruption in the dish, incense in the latrine, the
sewer in the incense, the smell of sweet soap
in the woodpath, a hellish sweet scent in the
woodpath, while the ground heaved. I have
seen   220
Rings of light coiling downwards, descending
To the horror of the ape. Have I not known, not
known
What was coming to be? It was here, in the
kitchen, in the passage,
In the mews in the barn in the byre in the
market-place
In our veins our bowels our skulls as well   225
As well as in the plottings of potentates
As well as in the consultations of powers.
What is woven on the loom of fate
What is woven in the councils of princes
Is woven also in our veins, our brains,   230
Is woven like a pattern of living worms
In the guts of the women of Canterbury.

I have smelt them, the death-bringers; now is
too late
For action, too soon for contrition.
Nothing is possible but the shamed swoon   235
Of those consenting to the last humiliation.
I have consented, Lord Archbishop, have
consented.
Am torn away, subdued, violated,
United to the spiritual flesh of nature,
Mastered by the animal powers of spirit,   240
Dominated by the lust of self-demolition,
By the final utter uttermost death of spirit,
By the final ecstasy of waste and shame,
O Lord Archbishop, O Thomas Archbishop, for-
give us, forgive us, pray for us that we may
pray for you, out of our shame.
                [*Enter* THOMAS.]
THOMAS   Peace, and be at peace with your thoughts
and visions.   245
These things had to come to you and you to
accept them.
This is your share of the eternal burden,
The perpetual glory. This is one moment,
But know that another
Shall pierce you with a sudden painful joy   250
When the figure of God's purpose is made
complete.

You shall forget these things, toiling in the
household,
You shall remember them, droning by the fire,
When age and forgetfulness sweeten memory
Only like a dream that has often been told   255
And often been changed in the telling. They will
seem unreal.
Human kind cannot bear very much reality.
                [*Enter* PRIESTS.]
PRIESTS   [*Severally*] My Lord, you must not stop
here. To the minster.
Through the cloister. No time to waste. They are
coming back, armed. To the altar, to the altar.
THOMAS   All my life they have been coming, these
feet. All my life   260
I have waited. Death will come only when I am
worthy,
And if I am worthy, there is no danger.
I have therefore only to make perfect my will.
PRIESTS   My Lord, they are coming. They will
break through presently.
You will be killed. Come to the altar.   265
Make haste, my Lord. Don't stop here talking.
It is not right.
What shall become of us, my Lord, if you are
killed; what shall become of us?
THOMAS   Peace! be quiet! remember where you
are, and what is happening;
No life here is sought for but mine,
And I am not in danger: only near to death. 270
PRIESTS   My Lord, to vespers! You must not be
absent from vespers. You must not be absent
from the divine office. To vespers. Into the
cathedral!
THOMAS   Go to vespers, remember me at your
prayers.
They shall find the shepherd here; the flock shall
be spared.
I have had a tremour of bliss, a wink of heaven,
a whisper,
And I would no longer be denied; all things 275
Proceed to a joyful consummation.
PRIESTS   Seize him! force him! drag him!
THOMAS   Keep your hands off!
PRIESTS   To vespers! Hurry.
[*They drag him off. While the* CHORUS *speak, the
scene is changed to the cathedral.*]
CHORUS   [*While a* Dies Irae° *is sung in Latin by a
choir in the distance.*]

280. s.d. Dies Irae: Day of Judgment, a medieval hymn

Numb the hand and dry the eyelid,   280
Still the horror, but more horror
Than when tearing in the belly.

Still the horror, but more horror
Than when twisting in the fingers,
Than when splitting in the skull.   285

More than footfall in the passage,
More than shadow in the doorway,
More than fury in the hall.

The agents of hell disappear, the human, they
    shrink and dissolve
Into dust on the wind, forgotten, unmemorable;
    only is here   290
The white flat face of Death, God's silent servant,
And behind the face of Death the Judgement
And behind the Judgement the Void, more horrid
    than active shapes of hell;
Emptiness, absence, separation from God;
The horror of the effortless journey, to the empty
    land   295
Which is no land, only emptiness, absence, the
    Void.
Where those who were men can no longer turn
    the mind.
To distraction, delusion, escape into dream,
    pretence,
Where the soul is no longer deceived, for there
    are no objects, no tones,
No colours, no forms to distract, to divert the
    soul   300
From seeing itself, foully united forever, nothing
    with nothing,
Not what we call death, but what beyond death
    is not death,
We fear, we fear. Who shall then plead for me,
Who intercede for me, in my most need?

Dead upon the tree, my Saviour,   305
Let not be in vain Thy labour;
Help me, Lord, in my last fear.

Dust I am, to dust am bending,
From the final doom impending
Help me, Lord, for death is near.   310
    [*In the Cathedral.* THOMAS *and* PRIESTS.]
PRIESTS   Bar the door. Bar the door.
    The door is barred.
    We are safe. We are safe.
    They dare not break in.

They cannot break in. They have not the force.
    We are safe. We are safe.   316
THOMAS   Unbar the doors! throw open the doors!
    I will not have the house of prayer, the church of
        Christ,
    The sanctuary, turned into a fortress.
    The Church shall protect her own, in her own
        way, not   320
    As oak and stone; stone and oak decay,
    Give no stay, but the Church shall endure.
    The church shall be open, even to our enemies.
        Open the door!
PRIEST   My Lord! these are not men, these come
    not as men come, but
    Like maddened beasts. They come not like men,
        who   325
    Respect the sanctuary, who kneel to the Body
        of Christ,
    But like beasts. You would bar the door
    Against the lion, the leopard, the wolf or the
        boar,
    Why not more
    Against beasts with the souls of damned men,
        against men   330
    Who would damn themselves to beasts. My
        Lord! My Lord!
THOMAS   You think me reckless, desperate and
    mad.
    You argue by results, as this world does,
    To settle if an act be good or bad.
    You defer to the fact. For every life and every
        act   335
    Consequence of good and evil can be shown.
    And as in time results of many deeds are blended
    So good and evil in the end become confounded.
    It is not in time that my death shall be known;
    It is out of time that my decision is taken   340
    If you call that decision
    To which my whole being gives entire consent.
    I give my life
    To the Law of God above the Law of Man.
    Unbar the door! unbar the door!   345
    We are not here to triumph by fighting, by
        stratagem, or by resistance,
    Not to fight with beasts as men. We have fought
        the beast
    And have conquered. We have only to conquer
    Now, by suffering. This is the easier victory.
    Now is the triumph of the Cross, now   350
    Open the door! I command it. OPEN THE DOOR!

[*The door is opened. The* KNIGHTS *enter, slightly tipsy.*]

PRIESTS This way, my Lord! Quick. Up the stair. To the roof. To the crypt. Quick. Come. Force him.

KNIGHTS Where is Becket, the traitor to the King?
Where is Becket, the meddling priest?
Come down Daniel to the lions' den,   355
Come down Daniel for the mark of the beast.

Are you washed in the blood of the Lamb?
Are you marked with the mark of the beast?
Come down Daniel to the lions' den,
Come down Daniel and join in the feast.   360

Where is Becket the Cheapside brat?
Where is Becket the faithless priest?
Come down Daniel to the lions' den,
Come down Daniel and join in the feast.

THOMAS It is the just man who   365
Like a bold lion, should be without fear.
I am here.
No traitor to the King. I am a priest,
A Christian, saved by the blood of Christ,
Ready to suffer with my blood.   370
This is the sign of the Church always,
The sign of blood. Blood for blood.
His blood given to buy my life,
My blood given to pay for His death,
My death for His death.   375

FIRST KNIGHT Absolve all those you have excommunicated.

SECOND KNIGHT Resign the powers you have arrogated.

THIRD KNIGHT Restore to the King the money you appropriated.

FIRST KNIGHT Renew the obedience you have violated.

THOMAS For my Lord I am now ready to die, 380
That His Church may have peace and liberty.
Do with me as you will, to your hurt and shame;
But none of my people, in God's name,
Whether layman or clerk, shall you touch.
This I forbid.   385

KNIGHT Traitor! traitor! traitor!

THOMAS You, Reginald,° three times traitor you:
Traitor to me as my temporal vassal,
Traitor to me as your spiritual lord,

387. Reginald: Reginald Fitz Urse had received benefits from Becket.

Traitor to God in desecrating His Church.   390

FIRST KNIGHT No faith do I owe to a renegade,
And what I owe shall now be paid.

THOMAS Now to Almighty God, to the Blessed Mary ever Virgin, to the blessed John the Baptist, the holy apostles Peter and Paul, to the blessed martyr Denys, and to all the Saints, I commend my cause and that of the Church.

[*While the* KNIGHTS *kill him, we hear the* CHORUS.]

CHORUS Clear the air! clean the sky! wash the wind! take stone from stone and wash them.
The land is foul, the water is foul, our beasts and ourselves defiled with blood.
A rain of blood has blinded my eyes. Where is England? Where is Kent? Where is Canterbury?   400
O far far far far in the past; and I wander in a land of barren boughs: if I break them, they bleed; I wander in a land of dry stones: if I touch them they bleed.
How how can I ever return, to the soft quiet seasons?
Night stay with us, stop sun, hold season, let the day not come, let the spring not come.
Can I look again at the day and its common things, and see them all smeared with blood through a curtain of falling blood?
We did not wish anything to happen.   405
We understood the private catastrophe,
The personal loss, the general misery,
Living and partly living;
The terror by night that ends in daily action,
The terror by day that ends in sleep;   410
But the talk in the market-place, the hand on the broom,
The night-time heaping of the ashes,
The fuel laid on the fire at daybreak,
These acts marked a limit to our suffering.
Every horror had its definition,   415
Every sorrow had a kind of end:
In life there is not time to grieve long.
But this, this is out of life, this is out of time,
An instant eternity of evil and wrong.
We are soiled by a filth that we cannot clean, united to supernatural vermin,   420
It is not we alone, it is not the house, it is not the city that is defiled,
But the world that is wholly foul.
Clear the air! clean the sky! wash the wind! take the stone from the stone, take the skin from

the arm, take the muscle from the bone, and wash them. Wash the stone, wash the bone, wash the brain, wash the soul, wash them wash them!   423

[*The* KNIGHTS, *having completed the murder, advance to the front of the stage and address the audience.*]

FIRST KNIGHT We beg you to give us your attention for a few moments. We know that you may be disposed to judge unfavourably of our action. You are Englishmen, and therefore you believe in fair play: and when you see one man being set upon by four, then your sympathies are all with the under dog. I respect such feelings, I share them. Nevertheless, I appeal to your sense of honour. You are Englishmen, and therefore will not judge anybody without hearing both sides of the case. That is in accordance with our long-established principle of Trial by Jury. I am not myself qualified to put our case to you. I am a man of action and not of words. For that reason I shall do no more than introduce the other speakers, who, with their various abilities, and different points of view, will be able to lay before you the merits of this extremely complex problem. I shall call upon our eldest member to speak first, my neighbour in the country: Baron William de Traci.   444

THIRD KNIGHT I am afraid I am not anything like such an experienced speaker as my old friend Reginald Fitz Urse would lead you to believe. But there is one thing I should like to say, and I might as well say it at once. It is this: in what we have done, and whatever you may think of it, we have been perfectly disinterested. [*The other* KNIGHTS: "Hear! hear!"] *We* are not getting anything out of this. We have much more to lose than to gain. We are four plain Englishmen who put our country first. I dare say that we didn't make a very good impression when we came in just now. The fact is that we knew we had taken on a pretty stiff job; I'll only speak for myself, but I had drunk a good deal—I am not a drinking man ordinarily—to brace myself up for it. When you come to the point, it does go against the grain to kill an Archbishop, especially when you have been brought up in good Church traditions. So if we seemed a bit rowdy, you will understand why it was; and for my part I am awfully sorry about it. We realised this was

our duty, but all the same we had to work ourselves up to it. And, as I said, *we* are not getting a penny out of this. We know perfectly well how things will turn out. King Henry—God bless him—will have to say, for reasons of state, that he never meant this to happen; and there is going to be an awful row; and at the best we shall have to spend the rest of our lives abroad. And even when reasonable people come to see that the Archbishop *had* to be put out of the way —and personally I had a tremendous admiration for him—you must have noticed what a good show he put up at the end—they won't give *us* any glory. No, we have done for ourselves, there's no mistake about that. So, as I said at the beginning, please give us at least the credit for being completely disinterested in this business. I think that is about all I have to say.   484

FIRST KNIGHT I think we will all agree that William de Traci has spoken well and has made a very important point. The gist of his argument is this: that we have been completely disinterested. But our act itself needs more justification than that; and you must hear our other speakers. I shall next call upon Hugh de Morville, who has made a special study of statecraft and constitutional law. Sir Hugh de Morville.   493

SECOND KNIGHT I should like first to recur to a point that was very well put by our leader, Reginald Fitz Urse: that you are Englishmen, and therefore your sympathies are always with the under dog. It is the English spirit of fair play. Now the worthy Archbishop, whose good qualities I very much admired, has throughout been presented as the under dog. But is this really the case? I am going to appeal not to your emotions but to your reason. You are hard-headed sensible people, as I can see, and not to be taken in by emotional clap-trap. I therefore ask you to consider soberly: what were the Archbishop's aims? And what are King Henry's aims? In the answer to these questions lies the key to the problem.   509

The King's aim has been perfectly consistent. During the reign of the late Queen Matilda and the irruption of the unhappy usurper Stephen, the kingdom was very much divided. Our King saw that the one thing needful was to restore order: to curb the excessive powers of local government, which were usually exercised for selfish and often for seditious ends, and to reform the legal system. He therefore intended that Becket, who had proved himself an extremely able administrator—no one denies that—should unite the offices of Chancellor and Archbishop. Had Becket concurred with the King's wishes, we should have had an almost ideal State: a union of spiritual and temporal administration, under the central government. I knew Becket well, in various official relations; and I may say that I have never known a man so well qualified for the highest rank of the Civil Service. And what happened? The moment that Becket, at the King's instance, had been made Archbishop, he resigned the office of Chancellor, he became more priestly than the priests, he ostentatiously and offensively adopted an ascetic manner of life, he affirmed immediately that there was a higher order than that which our King, and he as the King's servant, had for so many years striven to establish; and that—God knows why—the two orders were incompatible.   538

You will agree with me that such interference by an Archbishop offends the instincts of a people like ours. So far, I know that I have your approval: I read it in your faces. It is only with the measures we have had to adopt, in order to set matters to rights, that you take issue. No one regrets the necessity for violence more than we do. Unhappily, there are times when violence is the only way in which social justice can be secured. At another time, you would condemn an Archbishop by vote of Parliament and execute him formally as a traitor, and no one would have to bear the burden of being called murderer. And at a later time still, even such temperate measures as these would become unnecessary. But, if you have now arrived at a just subordination of the pretensions of the Church to the welfare of the State, remember that it is we who took the first step. We have been instrumental in bringing about the state of affairs that you approve. We have served your interests; we merit your applause; and if there is any guilt whatever in the matter, you must share it with us.   562

FIRST KNIGHT Morville has given us a great deal to think about. It seems to me that he has said almost the last word, for those who have been able to follow his very subtle reasoning. We have,

however, one more speaker, who has I think another point of view to express. If there are any who are still unconvinced, I think that Richard Brito, coming as he does of a family distinguished for its loyalty to the Church, will be able to convince them. Richard Brito.   572

FOURTH KNIGHT The speakers who have preceded me, to say nothing of our leader, Reginald Fitz Urse, have all spoken very much to the point. I have nothing to add along their particular lines of argument. What I have to say may be put in the form of a question: *Who killed the Archbishop?* As you have been eye-witnesses of this lamentable scene, you may feel some surprise at my putting it in this way. But consider the course of events. I am obliged, very briefly, to go over the ground traversed by the last speaker. While the late Archbishop was Chancellor, no one, under the King, did more to weld the country together, to give it the unity, the stability, order, tranquillity, and justice that it so badly needed. From the moment he became Archbishop, he completely reversed his policy; he showed himself to be utterly indifferent to the fate of the country, to be, in fact, a monster of egotism. This egotism grew upon him, until it became at last an undoubted mania. I have unimpeachable evidence to the effect that before he left France he clearly prophesied, in the presence of numerous witnesses, that he had not long to live, and that he would be killed in England. He used every means of provocation; from his conduct, step by step, there can be no inference except that he had determined upon a death by martyrdom. Even at the last, he could have given us reason: you have seen how he evaded our questions. And when he had deliberately exasperated us beyond human endurance, he could still have easily escaped; he could have kept himself from us long enough to allow our righteous anger to cool. That was just what he did not wish to happen; he insisted, while we were still inflamed with wrath, that the doors should be opened. Need I say more? I think, with these facts before you, you will unhesitatingly render a verdict of Suicide while of Unsound Mind. It is the only charitable verdict you can give, upon one who was, after all, a great man.   615

FIRST KNIGHT Thank you, Brito, I think that

there is no more to be said; and I suggest that you now disperse quietly to your homes. Please be careful not to loiter in groups at street corners, and do nothing that might provoke any public outbreak.   [*Exeunt* KNIGHTS.]   621

FIRST PRIEST   O father, father, gone from us, lost to us,
How shall we find you, from what far place
Do you look down on us? You now in Heaven,
Who shall now guide us, protect us, direct us?   625
After what journey through what further dread
Shall we recover your presence? When inherit
Your strength? The Church lies bereft,
Alone, desecrated, desolated, and the heathen shall build on the ruins,
Their world without God. I see it. I see it.   630

THIRD PRIEST   No. For the Church is stronger for this action,
Triumphant in adversity. It is fortified
By persecution: supreme, so long as men will die for it.
Go, weak sad men, lost erring souls, homeless in earth or heaven.
Go where the sunset reddens the last grey rock
Of Brittany, or the Gates of Hercules.   636
Go venture shipwreck on the sullen coasts
Where blackamoors make captive Christian men;
Go to the northern seas confined with ice
Where the dead breath makes numb the hand, makes dull the brain;   640
Find an oasis in the desert sun,
Go seek alliance with the heathen Saracen,
To share his filthy rites, and try to snatch
Forgetfulness in his libidinous courts,
Oblivion in the fountain by the date-tree;   645
Or sit and bite your nails in Aquitaine.
In the small circle of pain within the skull
You still shall tramp and tread one endless round
Of thought, to justify your action to yourselves,
Weaving a fiction which unravels as you weave,
Pacing forever in the hell of make-believe   651
Which never is belief: this is your fate on earth
And we must think no further of you.

FIRST PRIEST   O my lord
The glory of whose new state is hidden from us,
Pray for us of your charity.   655

SECOND PRIEST   Now in the sight of God
Conjoined with all the saints and martyrs gone before you,
Remember us.

THIRD PRIEST   Let our thanks ascend
To God, who has given us another Saint in Canterbury.

CHORUS   [*While a* Te Deum *is sung in Latin by a choir in the distance.*]
We praise Thee, O God, for Thy glory displayed in all the creatures of the earth,
In the snow, in the rain, in the wind, in the storm; in all of Thy creatures, both the hunters and the hunted.   660
For all things exist only as seen by Thee, only as known by Thee, all things exist
Only in Thy light, and Thy glory is declared even in that which denies Thee; the darkness declares the glory of light.
Those who deny Thee could not deny, if Thou didst not exist; and their denial is never complete, for if it were so, they would not exist.
They affirm Thee in living; all things affirm Thee in living; the bird in the air, both the hawk and the finch; the beast on the earth, both the wolf and the lamb; the worm in the soil and the worm in the belly.
Therefore man, whom Thou hast made to be conscious of Thee, must consciously praise Thee, in thought and in word and in deed.   665
Even with the hand to the broom, the back bent in laying the fire, the knee bent in cleaning the hearth, we, the scrubbers and sweepers of Canterbury,
The back bent under toil, the knee bent under sin, the hands to the face under fear, the head bent under grief,
Even in us the voices of seasons, the snuffle of winter, the song of spring, the drone of summer, the voices of beasts and of birds, praise Thee.
We thank Thee for Thy mercies of blood, for Thy redemption by blood. For the blood of Thy martyrs and saints
Shall enrich the earth, shall create the holy places.   670
For wherever a saint has dwelt, wherever a martyr has given his blood for the blood of Christ,
There is holy ground, and the sanctity shall not depart from it

Though armies trample over it, though sight-
   seers come with guide-books looking over it;
From where the western seas gnaw at the coast
   of Iona,
To the death in the desert, the prayer in forgotten places by the broken imperial column,
From such ground springs that which forever
   renews the earth   676
Though it is forever denied. Therefore, O God,
   we thank Thee
Who hast given such blessing to Canterbury.
Forgive us, O Lord, we acknowledge ourselves as
   type of the common man,
Of the men and women who shut the door and
   sit by the fire;   680
Who fear the blessing of God, the loneliness of
   the night of God, the surrender required, the
   deprivation inflicted;
Who fear the injustice of men less than the
   justice of God;
Who fear the hand at the window, the fire in the
   thatch, the fist in the tavern, the push into the
   canal,
Less than we fear the love of God.
We acknowledge our trespass, our weakness, our
   fault; we acknowledge   685
That the sin of the world is upon our heads; that
   the blood of the martyrs and the agony of the
   saints
Is upon our heads.
Lord, have mercy upon us.
Christ, have mercy upon us.
Lord, have mercy upon us.   690
Blessed Thomas, pray for us.

KARL SHAPIRO
b. 1913

Adam and Eve

1 THE SICKNESS OF ADAM

In the beginning, at every step, he turned
As if by instinct to the East to praise
The nature of things. Now every path was learned
He lost the lifted, almost flowerlike gaze

Of a temple dancer. He began to walk   5
Slowly, like one accustomed to be alone.
He found himself lost in the field of talk;
Thinking became a garden of its own.

In it were new things: words he had never said,
Beasts he had never seen and knew were not   10
In the true garden, terrors, and tears shed
Under a tree by him, for some new thought.

And the first anger. Once he flung a staff
At softly coupling sheep and struck the ram.
It broke away. And God heard Adam laugh   15
And for his laughter made the creature lame.

And wanderlust. He stood upon the Wall
To search the unfinished countries lying wide
And waste, where not a living thing could crawl,
And yet he would descend, as if to hide.   20

His thought drew down the guardian at the gate,
To whom man said, "What danger am I in?"
And the angel, hurt in spirit, seemed to hate
The wingless thing that worried after sin,

For it said nothing but marvelously unfurled   25
Its wings and arched them shimmering overhead,
Which must have been the signal from the world
That the first season of our life was dead.

Adam fell down with labor in his bones,
And God approached him in the cool of day   30
And said, "This sickness in your skeleton
Is longing. I will remove it from your clay."

He said also, "I made you strike the sheep."
It began to rain and God sat down beside
The sinking man. When he was fast asleep   35
He wet his right hand deep in Adam's side

And drew the graceful rib out of his breast.
Far off, the latent streams began to flow
And birds flew out of Paradise to nest
On earth. Sadly the angel watched them go.   40

2 THE RECOGNITION OF EVE

Whatever it was she had so fiercely fought
Had fled back to the sky, but still she lay
With arms outspread, awaiting its assault,
Staring up through the branches of the tree,
The fig tree. Then she drew a shuddering breath 45
And turned her head instinctively his way.
She had fought birth as dying men fight death.

Her sigh awakened him. He turned and saw
A body swollen, as though formed of fruits,
White as the flesh of fishes, soft and raw.   50
He hoped she was another of the brutes
So he crawled over and looked into her eyes,
The human wells that pool all absolutes.
It was like looking into double skies.

And when she spoke the first word (it was *thou*) 55
He was terror-stricken, but she raised her hand
And touched his wound where it was fading now,
For he must feel the place to understand.
Then he recalled the longing that had torn
His side, and while he watched it whitely mend, 60
He felt it stab him suddenly like a thorn.

He thought the woman had hurt him. Was it she
Or the same sickness seeking to return;
Or was there any difference, the pain set free
And she who seized him now as hard as iron?   65
Her fingers bit his body. She looked old
And involuted, like the newly-born.
He let her hurt him till she loosed her hold.

Then she forgot him and she wearily stood
And went in search of water through the grove. 70
Adam could see her wandering through the wood,
Studying her footsteps as her body wove
In light and out of light. She found a pool
And there he followed shyly to observe.
She was already turning beautiful.   75

3 THE KISS

The first kiss was with stumbling fingertips.
Their bodies grazed each other as if by chance
And touched and untouched in a kind of dance.
Second, they found out touching with their lips.

Some obscure angel, pausing on his course,   80
Shed such a brightness on the face of Eve
That Adam in grief was ready to believe
He had lost her love. The third kiss was by force.

Their lips formed foreign, unimagined oaths
When speaking of the Tree of Guilt. So wide   85
Their mouths, they drank each other from inside.
A gland of honey burst within their throats.

But something rustling hideously overhead,
They jumped up from the fourth caress and hid.

4 THE TREE OF GUILT

Why, on her way to the oracle of Love,   90
Did she not even glance up at the Tree
Of Life, that giant with the whitish cast
And glinting leaves and berries of dull gray,
As though covered with mold? But who would taste
The medicine of immortality,   95
And who would "be as God"? And in what way?

So she came breathless to the lowlier one
And like a priestess of the cult she knelt,
Holding her breasts in token for a sign,
And prayed the spirit of the burdened bough   100
That the great power of the tree be seen
And lift itself out of the Tree of Guilt
Where it had hidden in the leaves till now.

Or did she know already? Had the peacock
Rattling its quills, glancing its thousand eyes 105
At her, the iridescence of the dove,
Stench of the he-goat, everything that joins
Told her the mystery? It was not enough,
So from the tree the snake began to rise
And dropt its head and pointed at her loins.   110

She fell and hid her face and still she saw
The spirit of the tree emerge and slip
Into the open sky until it stood
Straight as a standing-stone and spilled its seed.
And all the seed were serpents of the good.   115
Again he seized the snake and from its lip
It spat the venomous evil of the deed.

And it was over. But the woman lay
Stricken with what she knew, ripe in her thought
Like a fresh apple fallen from the limb   120
And rotten, like a fruit that lies too long.
This way she rose, ripe-rotten in her prime
And spurned the cold thing coiled against her foot
And called her husband, in a kind of song.

5 THE CONFESSION

As on the first day her first word was *thou*. 125
He waited while she said, "Thou art the tree."
And while she said, almost accusingly,
Looking at nothing, "Thou art the fruit I took."
She seemed smaller by inches as she spoke,
And Adam wondering touched her hair and shook, 130
Half understanding. He answered softly, "How?"

And for the third time, in the third way, Eve:
"The tree that rises from the middle part
Of the garden." And almost tenderly, "Thou art
The garden. We." Then she was overcome,   135
And Adam coldly, lest he should succumb
To pity, standing at the edge of doom,
Comforted her like one about to leave.

She sensed departure and she stood aside
Smiling and bitter. But he asked again,   140
"How did you eat? With what thing did you sin?"
And Eve with body slackened and uncouth,
"Under the tree I took the fruit of truth
From an angel. I ate it with my other mouth."
And saying so, she did not know she lied.   145

It was the man who suddenly released
From doubt, wept in the woman's heavy arms,
Those double serpents, subtly winding forms
That climb and drop about the manly boughs;
And dry with weeping, fiery and aroused,   150
Fell on her face to slake his terrible thirst
And bore her body earthward like a beast.

6 SHAME

The hard blood falls back in the manly fount,
The soft door closes under Venus' mount,
The ovoid moon moves to the Garden's side   155
And dawn comes, but the lovers have not died.
They have not died but they have fallen apart
In sleep, like equal halves of the same heart.

How to teach shame? How to teach nakedness
To the already naked? How to express   160
Nudity? How to open innocent eyes
And separate the innocent from the wise?
And how to reestablish the guilty tree
In infinite gardens of humanity?

By marring the image, by the black device   165
Of the goat-god, by the clown of Paradise,
By fruits of cloth and by the navel's bud,
By itching tendrils and by strings of blood,
By ugliness, by the shadow of our fear,
By ridicule, by the fig-leaf patch of hair.   170

Whiter than tombs, whiter than whitest clay,
Exposed beneath the whitening eye of day,
They awoke and saw the covering that reveals.
They thought they were changing into animals.
Like animals they bellowed terrible cries   175
And clutched each other, hiding each other's eyes.

7 EXILE

The one who gave the warning with his wings,
Still doubting them, held out the sword of flame
Against the Tree of Whiteness as they came
Angrily, slowly by, like exiled kings,   180

And watched them at the broken-open gate
Stare in the distance long and overlong,
And then, like peasants, pitiful and strong,
Take the first step toward earth and hesitate.

For Adam raised his head and called aloud,   185
"My Father, who has made the garden pall,
Giving me all things and then taking all,
Who with your opposite nature has endowed

Woman, give us your hand for our descent.
Needing us greatly, even in our disgrace,   190
Guide us, for gladly do we leave this place
For our own land and wished-for banishment."

But woman prayed, "Guide us to Paradise."
Around them slunk the uneasy animals,
Strangely excited, uttering coughs and growls, 195
And bounded down into the wild abyss.

And overhead the last migrating birds,
Then empty sky. And when the two had gone
A slow half-dozen steps across the stone,
The angel came and stood among the shards   200

And called them, as though joyously, by name.
They turned in dark amazement and beheld
Eden ablaze with fires of red and gold,
The garden dressed for dying in cold flame,

And it was autumn, and the present world.   205

The Ironic Phase:
Defeat and Humiliation

GEOFFREY CHAUCER
1340?–1400

The Pardoner's Prologue

"Lordynges," quod° he, "in chirches whan I
    preche,
I peyne me° to han an hauteyn° speche
And rynge it out as round as gooth a belle,
For I kan° al by rote that I telle.
My theme is alwey oon,° and ever was—   5
Radix malorum est cupiditas.°
   "First I pronounce whennes that° I come,
And thanne my bulles° shewe I alle and some.°
Oure lige lordes° seel on my patente,
That shewe I first, my body to warante,°   10
That no man be so bold, ne° preest ne° clerk,
Me to destourbe of Cristes holy werk.
And after that thanne telle I forth my tales.
Bulles of popes and of cardynales,
Of patriarkes and bisshopes I shewe,   15
And in Latyn I speke a wordes fewe
To saffron with my predicacioun,°
And for to stire hem to devocioun.
Thanne shewe I forth my longe cristal stones°
Y-crammed ful of cloutes° and of bones;   20

Relikes been° they, as wenen° they echon.°
Thanne have I in latoun° a shulder-bon
Which that was of an holy Jewes sheep.°
'Goode men,' I seye, 'tak of my wordes keep.°
If that this boon be wasshe° in any welle,   25
If cow, or calfe, or sheep, or oxe swelle,
That any worm hath ete or worm y-stonge,°
Taak water of that welle, and wassh his° tonge,
And it is hool anoon.° And further moor,
Of pokkes,° and of scabbe, and every soor   30
Shal every sheep be hool that of this welle
Drynketh a draughte. Taak kepe, eek, what° I telle:
If that the goode man that the bestes oweth°
Wol every wyke,° er that the cok hym croweth,°
Fastynge, drynken of this welle a draughte,   35
As thilke° holy Jew oure eldres taughte,
Hise bestes and his stoor° shal multiplie.
   " 'And, sire, also it heeleth jalousie,
For thogh a man be falle in jalous rage,
Lat maken° with this water his potage,   40
And nevere shal he moore his wyfe mystriste,°
Thogh he the soothe° of hir defaute wiste,°
Al° hadde she taken preestes two or thre.
   " 'Heere is a miteyn,° eek,° that ye may se.

21. **been:** are. **wenen:** believe. **echon:** each one. **22. in latoun:** (set) in copper alloy. **23. Which . . . sheep:** which was taken from the sheep of a holy Jew (that is, some Old Testament hero). The ancient practice of divination by the shape of a shoulder bone survived among the credulous in the Middle Ages. **24. keep:** heed. **25. wasshe:** washed. **27. That . . . y-stonge:** which has eaten any worm (i.e., injurious serpent), or which any worm has stung. **28. his:** its. **29. hool anoon:** cured at once. **30. pokkes:** pocks. **32. kepe . . . what:** heed, also, of what. **33. oweth:** owns. **34. wyke:** week. **er . . . croweth:** before the cock crows. **36. thilke:** that same. **37. stoor:** stock. **40. Lat maken:** have made. **41. mystriste:** mistrust. **42. soothe:** truth. **defaute wiste:** fault should know. **43. Al:** even if. **44. miteyn:** mitten. **eek:** also.

THE PARDONER'S PROLOGUE. **1. quod:** said. **2. peyne me:** take pains. **hauteyn:** dominating. **4. kan:** know. **5. alwey oon:** always one. **6. Radix . . . cupiditas:** The root of evils is avarice. **7. whennes that:** whence. **8. bulles:** grants issued by the pope. **alle . . . some:** one and all. **9. lige lordes:** liege lord's (bishop's). **10. my . . . warante:** to safeguard my person. **11. ne . . . ne:** neither . . . nor. **17. saffron . . . predicacioun:** flavor my preaching with. **19. cristal stones:** glass cases (reliquaries). **20. cloutes:** rags.

He that his hand wol putte in this mitayn, 45
He shal have multiplyyng of his grayn
Whan he hath sowen, be it whete or otes,
So that° he offre pens or ellis grotes.°
 " 'Goode men and wommen, o° thyng warne I
  yow,
If any wight° be in this chirche now 50
That hath doon synne horrible, that he
Dar° nat for shame of it y-shryven° be,
Or any womman, be she yong or old,
That hath y-maked hir housbond cokewold,°
Swich° folk shal have no power, ne no grace, 55
To offren to my relikes in this place.
And whoso° fyndeth hym° out of swich blame,
They wol come up and offre, a° Goddes name,
And I assoille° hym by the auctoritee°
Which that by bulle y-graunted was to me.' 60
 "By this gaude° have I wonne yeer by yeer
An hundred mark° sith° I was pardoner.
I stonde° lyk a clerk° in my pulpet;
And whan the lewed° peple is doun y-set,
I preche so as ye han° herd bifore, 65
And telle an hundred false japes° more.
Thanne peyne I me° to strecche forth the nekke,
And est and west upon the peple I bekke,°
As dooth a dowve° sittyng on a berne.°
Myne handes and my tonge goon° so yerne° 70
That it is joye to se my bisynesse.°
Of avarice and of swich cursednesse
Is al my prechyng, for to make hem free
To yeven hir° pens, and namely° unto me.
For myn entente is nat but for to wynne,° 75
And nothyng° for correccioun of synne.
I rekke° nevere, whan that° they been beryed,°
Thogh that hir soules goon a-blakeberyed.°
For certes° many a predicacioun°
Comth ofte tyme of yvel entencioun, 80

Som for plesance° of folk and flaterye,
To been avanced by ypocrisye,
And some for veyne glorie, and som for hate.
For whan I dar noon oother weyes debate,°
Thanne wol I stynge hym with my tonge smerte° 85
In prechyng, so that he shal nat asterte°
To been defamed falsly, if that he
Hath trespased to° my bretheren or to me.
For thogh I telle noght his propre name,
Men shal wel knowe that it is the same 90
By signes and by othere circumstances.
Thus quyte° I folk that doon° us displesances;
Thus spitte I out my venym under hewe°
Of holynesse, to seme holy and trewe.
 "But shortly myn entente I wol devyse:° 95
I preche of no thyng but for coveityse.°
Therfore my theme is yet, and evere was,
Radix malorum est cupiditas.
Thus kan I preche agayn° that same vice
Which that I use, and that is avarice. 100
But though myself be gilty in that synne,
Yet kan I maken oother folk to twynne°
From avarice, and soore° to repente.
But that is nat my principal entente.
I preche no thyng but for coveitise. 105
Of this matere it oghte ynow° suffise.
 "Thanne telle I hem ensamples° many oon°
Of olde stories longe tyme agoon,°
For lewed peple loven tales olde.
Swiche thynges kan they wel reporte° and holde.°
What! Trowe° ye that, whiles I may preche, 111
And wynne gold and silver for° I teche,
That I wol lyve in poverte wilfully?°
Nay, nay! I thoghte it nevere, trewely.
For I wol preche and begge in sondry landes; 115
I wol nat do no labour with myne handes,
Ne make baskettes and lyve ther-by,
Bycause I wol nat beggen ydelly.°
I wol noon of the apostles countrefete.°
I wol have moneye, wolle,° chese, and whete, 120
Al° were it yeven° of the pouereste° page,

48. So that: provided that. **ellis grotes:** else groats (four-pennies). **49. o:** one. **50. wight:** person. **52. Dar:** dare. **y-shryven:** confessed and absolved. **54. cokewold:** cuckold. **55. Swich:** such. **57. whoso:** whoever. **hym:** himself. **58. a:** in. **59. assoille:** absolve. **auctoritee:** authority. **61. gaude:** trick. **62. mark:** marks (13*s.* 4*d.*). **sith:** since. **63. stonde:** stand. **clerk:** ecclesiastical scholar. **64. lewed:** ignorant. **65. han:** have. **66. japes:** frauds. **67. peyne I me:** I take pains. **68. bekke:** nod. **69. dowve:** dove. **berne:** barn. **70. goon:** go. **yerne:** eagerly. **71. bisynesse:** industriousness. **74. yeven hir:** give their. **namely:** particularly. **75. but . . . wynne:** only to gain. **76. nothyng:** in no way. **77. rekke:** care. **whan that:** when. **been beryed:** are buried. **78. Thogh . . . a-blakeberyed:** though their souls go blackberrying (that is, go wandering without direction). **79. certes:** certainly. **predicacioun:** sermon.

81. plesance: the satisfying. **84. weyes debate:** way contend. **85. smerte:** sharp. **86. asterte:** avoid. **88. trespased to:** wronged. **92. quyte:** repay. **doon:** cause. **93. hewe:** pretext. **95. devyse:** explain. **96. coveityse:** covetousness. **99. agayn:** against. **102. twynne:** depart. **103. soore:** sorely. **106. ynow:** enough. **107. ensamples:** (illustrative) examples. **oon:** a one. **108. agoon:** past. **110. report:** repeat. **holde:** remember. **111. Trowe:** believe. **112. for:** because. **113. wilfully:** willingly. **118. ydelly:** in vain. **119. countrefete:** imitate. **120. wolle:** wool. **121. Al:** though. **yeven:** given. **pouereste:** poorest.

Or of the poureste widwe° in a village,
Al sholde hir children sterve° for famyne.
Nay, I wol drynke licour of the vyne
And have a joly wenche in every toun.   125
    "But herkneth, lordynges, in conclusioun.
Youre likyng is that I shal telle a tale.
Now have I dronke a draghte of corny° ale,
By God, I hope I shal yow telle a thyng
That shal by resoun been at youre likyng.   130
For, thogh myself be a ful vicious man,
A moral tale yet I yow telle kan,
Which I am wont° to preche for to wynne.°
Now, holde youre pees.° My tale I wol bigynne.''

The Pardoner's Tale

In Flaundres whilom° was a compaignye
Of yonge folk that haunteden° folye,
As° riot, hasard,° stewes,° and tavernes
Where-as° with harpes, lutes, and gyternes°
They daunce and pleyen at dees° bothe day and
    nyght,   5
And ete also and drynke over hir myght,°
Thurgh which they doon the devel sacrifise
Withinne that develes temple in cursed wise
By superfluytee abhomynable.
Hir othes been° so grete and so dampnable   10
That it is grisly for to heere hem swere;
Oure blissed Lordes body they to-tere;°
Hem thoughte° that Jewes rente hym noght
    ynough!
And ech° of hem at otheres synne lough.°
And right anon thanne comen tombesteres,°   15
Fetys° and smale,° and yonge frutesteres,°
Syngeres with harpes, baudes° wafereres,°
Whiche been the verray develes officeres,
To kyndle and blowe the fyr of lecherye,
That is annexed unto glotonye.   20

The Holy Writ take I to my witnesse
That luxurie° is in wyn and dronkenesse.
    Lo how that dronken Loth° unkyndely°
Lay by his doghtres two unwityngly.°
So dronke he was, he nyste° what he wroghte.° 25
Herodes,° whoso° wel the stories soghte,
Whan he of wyn was replet° at his feste,
Right at his owene table he yaf° his heste°
To sleen° the Baptist John ful giltelees.
Senec° seith a good word, doutelees.   30
He seith he kan no difference fynde
Bitwix a man that is out of his mynde
And a man which that is dronkelewe,°
But° that woodnesse y-fallen° in a shrewe
Persevereth lenger than dooth dronkenesse.   35
    O glotonye, ful of cursednesse,
O cause first of oure confusioun!°
O original of oure dampnacioun,
Til Crist hadde boght us with his blood agayn!°
Lo how deere,° shortly for to sayn,°   40
Aboght° was thilke° cursed vileynye.
Corrupt was al this world for glotonye.
    Adam oure fader, and his wyf also,
Fro° Paradys to labour and to wo
Were dryven for that vice, it is no drede.°   45
For whil that Adam fasted, as I rede,
He was in Paradys; and whan that he
Eet of the fruyt defended° on the tree,
Anon° he was out cast to wo and peyne.
O glotonye, on thee wel oghte us pleyne.°   50
O, wiste° a man how manye maladies
Folwen of° excesse and of glotonyes,
He wolde been the moore mesurable°
Of his diete, sittyng at his table.
Allas, the shorte throte, the tendre mouth,   55
Maketh that, est and west and north and south,
In erthe, in eyr, in water, men to swynke°
To gete a gloton deyntee mete and drynke.
Of this matere, O Paul, wel kanstow° trete.
"Mete unto wombe,° and wombe eek° unto mete,   60

---

122. widwe: widow. 123. sterve: perish. 128. corny: tasting
strongly of malt. 133. wont: accustomed. wynne: gain.
134. pees: peace.
THE PARDONER'S TALE. 1. Flaundres whilom: Flanders once.
2. haunteden: practiced. 3. As: such as. hasard: dicing.
stewes: brothels. 4. Where-as: where. gyternes: gitterns, a
type of guitar. 5. dees: dice. 6. over . . . myght: beyond
their capacity. 10. Hir . . . been: their oaths are. 12. to-
tere: tear apart, i.e., when they swear by parts of Christ's
body. 13. Hem thoughte: It seemed to them. 14. ech: each.
lough: laughed. 15. tombesteres: dancing girls. 16. Fetys:
trim. smale: slender. frutesteres: fruit sellers. 17. baudes:
bawds. wafereres: confectioners.

22. luxurie: excess. 23. Loth: Lot (Gen. 19:33, 35). unkyndely:
unnaturally. 24. unwityngly: unknowingly. 25. nyste: didn't
know. wroghte: was doing. 26. Herodes: Herod (Matt. 14).
whoso: as one would know who. 27. replet: overfilled. 28.
yaf: gave. heste: order. 29. sleen: slay. 30. Senec: Seneca.
33. dronkelewe: drunken. 34. But: except. woodnesse
y-fallen: madness occurring. 37. confusioun: ruin. 39. boght
agayn: redeemed. 40. deere: dearly. sayn: say. 41. Aboght:
paid for. thilke: that same. 44. Fro: from. 45. drede:
doubt. 48. defended: forbidden. 49. Anon: at once. 50.
oghte us pleyne: should we complain. 51. wiste: knew. 52.
Folwen of: follow. 53. mesurable: moderate. 57. swynke:
toil. 59. kanstow: can you. 60. wombe: belly. eek: also.

Shal God destroyen bothe," as Paulus seith.　61
Alas, a foul thyng is it, by my feith,
To seye this word, and fouler is the dede,
Whan man so drynketh of the white and rede°
That of his throte he maketh his pryvee°　65
Thurgh thilke cursed superfluitee.
　The apostle° wepyng seith ful pitously,
"There walken manye of whiche yow toold have I,—
I seye it now wepyng with pitous voys—
They been enemys of Cristes croys,　70
Of whiche° the ende is deth; wombe is hir° God."
O wombe, O bely, O stynkyng cod,°
Fulfilled of donge and of corrupcioun,
At either ende of thee foul is the soun!°
How greet labour and cost is thee to fynde!°　75
Thise cokes,° how they stampe, and streyne, and
　　grynde,
And turnen substaunce into accident,°
To fulfillen° al thy likerous talent.°
Out of the harde bones knokke they
The mary,° for they caste noght awey　80
That may go thurgh the golet° softe and soote.°
Of spicerie of leef, and bark, and roote
Shal been his sauce y-maked, by delit°
To make hym yet a newer appetit.
But, certes,° he that haunteth swiche delices°　85
Is deed whil that° he lyveth in tho° vices.
　A lecherous thyng is wyn, and dronkenesse
Is ful of stryvyng° and of wrecchednesse.
O dronke man, disfigured is thy face,
Sour is thy breeth, foul artow° to embrace,　90
And thurgh thy dronke nose semeth the soun
As thogh thou seydest ay,° "Sampsoun, Samp-
　soun."
And yet, God woot,° Sampsoun° drank nevere no
　wyn.
Thou fallest as it were a stiked swyn,°
Thy tonge is lost, and al thyn honeste cure.°　95

For dronkenesse is verray sepulture°
Of mannes wit° and his discrecioun.
In whom that drynke hath dominacioun,
He kan no conseil kepe, it is no drede.
Now kepe yow fro the white and fro the rede,　100
And namely° fro the white wyn of Lepe°
That is to selle in Fisshstrete° or in Chepe.°
This wyn of Spaigne crepeth subtilly
In othere wynes growynge faste by,°
Of which ther riseth swich fumositee°　105
That, whan a man hath dronken draghtes thre,
And weneth° that he be at hoom in Chepe,
He is in Spaigne right at the toune of Lepe,
Nat at the Rochel° ne at Burdeux° toun.　109
And thanne wol he seyn, "Sampsoun, Sampsoun."
　But herkneth, lordynges, o° word, I yow preye,
That alle the sovereyn actes, dar I seye,
Of victories in the Olde Testament,
Thurgh verray God, that is omnipotent,
Were doon in abstinence and in prayere.　115
Looketh° the Bible, and ther ye may it leere.°
　Looke, Attila,° the grete conquerour,
Deyde in his sleep with shame and dishonour,
Bledyng at his nose in dronkenesse.
A capitayn sholde lyve in sobrenesse.　120
And over al this, avyseth yow° right wel
What was comaunded unto Lamwel°—
Nat Samuel but Lamwel, seye I.
Redeth the Bible, and fynd it expresly
Of wyn-yevyng° to hem that han justise.　125
Namoore of this, for it may wel suffise.
　And now that I have spoken of glotonye,
Now wol I yow defenden hasardrye.°
Hasard is verray moder of lesynges,°
And of deceite, and cursed forswerynges,°　130
Blaspheme° of Crist, manslaughtre, and wast° also
Of catel° and of tyme; and forther mo

---

64. rede: red (wine). **65. pryvee:** privy. **67. apostle:** Paul. **71. whiche:** whom. **hir:** their. **72. cod:** paunch. **74. soun:** sound. **75. fynde:** provide for. **76. cokes:** cooks. **77. turnen . . . accident:** turn substance into accident—a facetious allusion to the philosophical theory that "substance" only becomes apparent when it takes on the "accidents" of some particular shape, size, color, etc. **78. fulfillen:** satisfy. **likerous talent:** unrestrained appetite. **80. mary:** marrow. **81. golet:** gullet. **soote:** sweet. **83. delit:** delight. **85. certes:** certainly. **haunteth . . . delices:** pursues such delights. **86. deed . . . that:** dead while. **tho:** those. **88. stryvyng:** strife. **90. artow:** are you. **92. ay:** always. **93. woot:** knows. **Sampsoun:** Samson, who was bound by his vow as a Nazarite never to drink wine. **94. as . . . swyn:** like a stuck pig. **95. honeste cure:** care for honor.

96. verray sepulture: the very burial. **97. wit:** understanding. **101. namely:** particularly. **Lepe:** in Spain. **102. Fisshstrete:** Fish Street (London). **Chepe:** Cheapside. **104. faste by:** near by, that is, the more expensive vintages of France, which were evidently adulterated in England with coarser Spanish wines. **105. swich fumositee:** such spirituous vapors. **107. weneth:** believes. **109. the Rochel:** La Rochelle. **Burdeux:** Bordeaux (in France). **111. o:** one. **116. Looketh:** look at. **leere:** learn. **117. Attila:** the invader of Rome, who, according to tradition, died of drunkenness on his wedding night. **121. avyseth yow:** consider. **122. Lamwel:** Lemuel, an otherwise unknown king enjoined in Prov. 31:4–7 to avoid wine. **125. wyn-yevyng:** wine-giving. **128. defenden hasardrye:** forbid dicing. **129. verray . . . lesynges:** the very mother of falsehood. **130. forswerynges:** perjuries. **131. Blaspheme:** blasphemy. **wast:** waste. **132. catel:** substance.

It is repreve° and contrarie of honour
For to ben holde° a commune hasardour.
And evere the hyer he is of estaat,   135
The moore is he holden desolat.
If that a prynce useth hasardrye,
In alle governaunce and policye
He is, as by° commune opynyoun,
Y-holde the lasse in reputacioun.   140
   Stilbon, that was a wys embassadour,
Was sent to Corynthe in ful gret honour
Fro Lacedomye° to make hire alliaunce;
And whan he cam, hym happed° par chaunce
That alle the gretteste that were of that lond   145
Pleiynge atte hasard he hem fond.°
For which, as soone as it myghte be,
He stal° hym hoom agayn to his contree,
And seyde, "Ther wol I nat lese° my name,
N' I wol nat° take on me so greet defame   150
Yow for to allie unto none hasardours.
Sendeth othere wise embassadours,
For, by my trouthe, me were levere° dye
Than I yow sholde to hasardours allye.
For ye that been so glorious in honours   155
Shal nat allye yow with hasardours
As by my wyl ne as by my tretee."°
This wise philosophre thus seyde he.
   Looke eek that to the kyng Demetrius
The kyng of Parthes,° as the book seith us,   160
Sente hym a paire of dees° of gold in scorn,
For° he hadde used hasard their-biforn;°
For which he heeld his glorie or his renoun
At no value or reputacioun.
Lordes may fynden oother manere° pley   165
Honeste ynow° to dryve the day awey.
   Now wol I speke of oothes false and grete
A word or two, as olde bokes trete.
Greet sweryng is a thyng abhomynable,
And fals sweryng is yet moore reprevable.°   170
The heighe God forbad sweryng at al.
Witnesse on Mathew; but in special
Of sweryng seith the holy Jeremye,°
"Thow shalt swere sooth° thyne othes and nat lye,

And swere in doom° and eek in rightwisnesse."°
But ydel° sweryng is a cursednesse.   176
Bihoold and se that, in the firste table
Of heighe Goddes Hestes° honurable,
How that the Seconde Heste of hym is this:
"Take nat my name in ydel° or amys."   180
Lo, rather he forbedeth swich sweryng
Than homycide or many a cursed thyng.
I seye that, as by ordre,° thus it standeth;
This knowen, that hise Hestes understandeth,
How that the Seconde Heste of God is that.   185
And forther over, I wol thee telle al plat°
That vengeance shal nat parten° from his hous
That of hise othes is to° outrageous.
"By Goddes precious herte," and "By his nayles,"
And "By the blood of Crist that is in Hayles,°   190
Sevene is my chaunce, and thyn is cynk° and
   treye,"°
"By Goddes armes, if thow falsly pleye,
This daggere shal thurgh out thyn herte go,"—
This fruyt cometh of the bicched bones° two,
Forsweryng, ire, falsnesse, homycide.   195
Now, for the love of Crist, that for us dyde,
Lete° youre othes, bothe grete and smale.
But, sires, now wol I telle forth my tale.
   Thise riotoures° thre of whiche I telle,
Longe erst er pryme rong° of any belle,   200
Were set hem° in a taverne to drynke;
And, as they sat, they herde a belle clynke°
Biforn a cors° was caried to his grave.
That oon° of hem gan callen to his knave:°
"Go bet,"° quod° he, "and axe redily   205
What cors is this that passeth heer forby.
And looke that thow reporte his name wel."
   "Sir," quod this boy, "it nedeth° never a del.°
It was me told er ye cam here two houres.
He was, pardee,° an old felawe° of youres,   210
And sodeynly he was y-slayn to-nyght,°
Fordronke,° as he sat on his bench upright.

---

133. **repreve**: reproach. 134. **For . . . holde**: to be considered.
139. **as by**: by. 143. **Lacedomye**: Lacedaemon (Sparta).
144. **hym happed**: it happened to him. 146. **fond**: found.
148. **stal**: stole. 149. **lese**: lose. 150. **N' . . . nat**: nor will I.
153. **me . . . levere**: I would rather. 157. **tretee**: agreement.
160. **Parthes**: Parthia. 161. **dees**: dice. 162. **For**: because.
ther-biforn: previously. 165. **manere**: sort of. 166. **ynow**:
enough. 170. **reprevable**: reprovable. 173. **Jeremye**: Jeremiah. 174. **sooth**: truthfully.

175. **doom**: judgment. **rightwisnesse**: righteousness. 176.
ydel: vain. 178. **Hestes**: (Ten) Commandments. 180.
in ydel: in vain. 183. **as by ordre**: in order. 186. **plat**:
plainly. 187. **parten**: depart. 188. **to**: too. 190. **in Hayles**:
(preserved) at Hayles, Gloucestershire. 191. **cynk**: five.
treye: three. 194. **bicched bones**: cursed dice. 197. **Lete**:
restrain. 199. **riotoures**: profligates. 200. **erst . . . rong**:
before prime (9:00 A.M.) rang. 201. **set hem**: seated. 202.
clynke: clang. 203. **cors**: corpse (which). 204. **That oon**:
one. **knave**: boy. 205. **Go bet**: go faster, i.e., hurry. **quod**:
said. **axe**: ask. 208. **nedeth**: is necessary. **a del**: one bit.
210. **pardee**: certainly. **felawe**: companion. 211. **to-nyght**:
last night. 212. **Fordronke**: very drunk.

Ther cam a pryvee° theef, men clepeth° Deeth,
That in this contree al the peple sleeth,°
And with his spere he smoot his herte a-two,°   215
And wente his wey withouten wordes mo.
He hath a thousand slayn, this pestilence.
And, maister, er ye come in his presence,
Me thynketh that it were necessarie
For to be war of swich an adversarie.   220
Beth° redy for to meete hym evere moore.°
Thus taughte me my dame.° I sey namoore."

    "By seinte Marie," seyde this taverner,°
"The child seith sooth, for he hath slayn this yer,
Henne over a myle,° withinne a greet village,   225
Bothe man and womman, child, and hyne,° and page.
I trowe° his habitacioun be there.
To been avysed° greet wisdom it were,
Er that he dide a man a dishonour."

    "Ye,° Goddes armes!" quod this riotour.   230
"Is it swich peril with hym for to meete?
I shal hym seke by wey and eek by strete,
I make avow to Goddes digne° bones.
Herkneth, felawes. We thre been al ones.°
Lat ech of us holde up his hand til° oother,   235
And ech of us bicome otheres brother,°
And we wol sleen this false traytour Deeth.
He shal be slayn, he that so manye sleeth,
By Goddess dignytee, er it be nyght."

    Togidres° han thise thre hir trouthes plight°   240
To lyve and dyen ech of hem for oother,
As thogh he were his owene y-bore° brother.
And up they stirte,° al dronken in this rage,
And forth they goon towardes that village
Of which the taverner hadde spoke biforn.   245
And many a grisly ooth thanne han they sworn,
And Cristes blessed body they to-rente.°
Deeth shal be deed, if that they may hym hente!°

    Whan they han goon nat fully half a myle,
Right° as they wolde han treden° over a stile,   250
An old man and a poure° with hem mette.
This olde man ful mekely hem grette°
And seyde thus, "Now, lordes, God yow se."°

The proudeste of thise riotoures thre
Answerde agayn,° "What, carl!° With sory grace!°
Why artow° al forwrapped° save thy face?   256
Why lyvestow° so longe in so greet age?"

    This olde man gan looke° in his visage
And seyde thus: "For I ne kan nat fynde
A man, thogh that I walked into Inde,°   260
Neither in citee ne in no village,
That wolde chaunge his youthe for myn age.
And, therefore, moot I han° myn age stille,
As longe tyme as it is Goddes wille.

    "Ne Deeth, allas, ne wol nat han my lyf.   265
Thus walke I lyk a restelees caytyf,°
And on the ground, which is my modres° gate,
I knokke with my staf bothe erly and late,
And seye, 'Leeve° moder, leet me in.
Lo, how I vanysshe, flessh, and blood, and skyn.   270
Allas, whan shul my bones been at reste?
Moder, with yow wolde I chaunge my cheste,°
That in my chambre longe tyme hath be,°
Ye, for an heyre clowt° to wrappe me!'
But yet to me she wol nat do that grace,   275
For which full pale and welked° is my face.

    "But, sires, to yow it is no curteisye
To speken to an old man vileynye
But° he trespase in word or elles° in dede.
In Holy Writ ye may yourself wel rede,   280
'Agayns° an old man, hoor° upon his heed,
Ye sholde arise.' Wherefore I yeve° yow reed:°
Ne dooth° unto an old man noon harm now,
Namoore than that ye wolde men dide to yow
In age, if that ye so longe abyde.   285
And God be with yow, wher° ye go° or ryde.
I moot° go thider as° I have to go."

    "Nay, olde cherl. By God, thow shalt nat so,"
Seyde this oother hasardour° anon.
"Thow partest° nat so lightly,° by seint John.   290
Thow spak right now of thilke° traytour Deeth,
That in this contree alle oure freendes sleeth.
Have here my trouthe,° as thow art his espye,°
Telle where he is, or thow shalt it abye,°

213. **pryvee:** secretive. **men clepeth:** (whom) they call. 214. **sleeth:** slays. 215. **a-two:** in two. 221. **Beth:** be. **evere moore:** always. 222. **dame:** mother. 223. **taverner:** innkeeper. 225. **Henne . . . myle:** within a mile hence. 226. **hyne:** servant. 227. **trowe:** believe. 228. **been avysed:** be prepared. 230. **Ye:** yes. 233. **digne:** worthy. 234. **ones:** one. 235. **til:** to. 236. **otheres brother:** the other's sworn brother. 240. **Togidres:** together. **hir . . . plight:** pledged their faith. 242. **y-bore:** born. 243. **stirte:** sprang. 247. **to-rente:** tore to pieces. 248. **hente:** catch. 250. **Right:** just. **han treden:** have stepped. 251. **poure:** poor. 252. **grette:** greeted. 253. **se:** save.

255. **agayn:** back. **carl:** churl. **With . . . grace:** curse you. 256. **artow:** are you. **forwrapped:** wrapped up. 257. **lyvestow:** live you. 258. **gan looke:** looked. 260. **Inde:** India. 263. **moot I han:** must I have. 266. **caytyf:** wretch. 267. **modres:** mother's. 269. **Leeve:** dear. 272. **cheste:** clothes chest. 273. **be:** been. 274. **heyre clowt:** hair rag. 276. **welked:** withered. 279. **But:** unless. **elles:** else. 281. **Agayns:** before. **hoor:** hoar. 282. **yeve:** give. **reed:** advice. 283. **Ne dooth:** don't do. 286. **wher:** whether. **go:** walk. 287. **moot:** must. **as:** where. 289. **hasardour:** gambler. 290. **partest:** depart. **lightly:** easily. 291. **thilke:** that same. 293. **trouthe:** oath. **espye:** spy. 294. **abye:** pay for.

By God and by the holy sacrament!   295
For soothly thow art oon of his assent°
To sleen us yonge folk, thow false theef!"
    "Now, sires," quod he, "if that yow be so leef°
To fynde Deeth, turn up this croked wey.
For in that grove I lafte° hym, by my fey,°   300
Under a tree, and ther he wol abyde.
Nat for youre boost he wol hym° nothyng hyde.
Se yet that ook?° Right ther ye shal hym fynde.
God save yow, that boghte agayn° mankynde,
And yow amende." Thus seyde this olde man. 305
And everich° of thise riotoures ran
Til they came to that tree, and ther they founde
Of floryns° fyne of gold y-coyned rounde
Wel ny an eighte° busshels, as hem thoughte.°
No lenger thanne after Deeth thy soughte;   310
But ech of hem so glad was of the sighte,
For that the floryns been so faire and brighte,
That doun they sette hem° by this precious hoord.
The worste of hem he spak the firste word.
    "Brethren," quod he, "taak kepe° what I seye.
My wit° is greet, thogh that I bourde° and pleye.
This tresor hath fortune unto us yeven,°   317
In myrthe and jolitee oure lyf to lyven.
And lightly as it cometh, so wol we spende.
By Goddes precious dignytee, who wende°   320
Today that we sholde han so fair a grace?
But, myghte this gold be caried fro this place
Hoom to myn hous, or ellis unto youres—
For wel ye woot° that al this gold is oures—
Thanne were we in heigh felicitee.   325
But, trewely, by daye it may nat be.
Men wolde seyn° that we were theves stronge°
And for oure owene tresor doon us honge.°
This tresor moste y-caried be by nyghte
As wisly° and as slyly as it myghte.   330
Wherfore I rede° that cut° among us alle
Be drawe, and lat se° wher the cut wol falle.
And he that hath the cut, with herte blithe
Shal renne° to the toune, and that ful swithe,°
And brynge us breed and wyn ful pryvely.   335

And two of us shul kepen subtilly°
This tresor wel; and if he wol nat tarie,
Whan it is nyght, we wol this tresor carie
By oon assent wher-as us thynketh° best."
    That oon° of hem the cut broghte in his fest,° 340
And bad hem drawe and looke wher it wol falle,
And it fil on the youngeste of hem alle,
And forth toward the toun he wente anon.
And also° soone as that he was agon,°
That oon of hem spak thus unto that oother: 345
"Thow knowest wel, thow art my sworn brother.
Thy profit wol I telle thee anon.
Thow woost° wel that oure felawe is agon,
And heere is gold, and that ful greet plentee,
That shall departed° been among us thre.   350
But, nathelees,° if I kan shape it so
That it departed were among us two,
Hadde I nat doon a freendes torn° to thee?"
    That oother answerde, "I noot° how that may be.
He woot that the gold is with us tweye.°   355
What shal we doon? What shall we to hym seye?"
    "Shal it be conseil?"° seyde the firste shrewe.°
"And I shal tellen in a wordes fewe
What we shul doon, and brynge it wel aboute."
    "I graunte," quod that oother, "out of doute, 360
That, by my trouthe, I wol thee nat biwreye."°
    "Now," quod the firste, "thow woost wel we be
          tweye,
And two of us shul strenger be than oon.
Looke, whan that he is set, that right anoon
Arys as though thow woldest with hym pleye, 365
And I shall ryve° hym thurgh the sydes tweye,
Whil that thow strogelest with him as in game.
And with thy daggere looke thow do the same,
And thanne shal al this gold departed be,
My deere freend, bitwixe me and thee.   370
Thanne may we bothe oure lustes al fulfille,
And pleye at dees° right at oure owene wille."
And thus acorded been thise shrewes tweye
To sleen° the thridde, as ye han herd me seye.
    This youngeste, which that wente to the toun, 375
Ful ofte in herte he rolleth up and doun
The beautee of thise floryns newe and brighte.
"O Lord," quod he, "if so were that I myghte

296. of . . . assent: in agreement with him. 298. leef: eager.
300. lafte: left. fey: faith. 302. hym: himself. 303. ook: oak.
304. boghte agayn: redeemed. 306. everich: each. 308.
floryns: florins (coins). 309. Wel . . . eighte: very nearly
eight. hem thoughte: it seemed to them. 313. hem: themselves. 315. kepe: heed to. 316. wit: understanding. bourde:
jest. 317. yeven: given. 320. wende: would have believed
324. woot: know. 327. seyn: say. stronge: violent. 328. doon
us honge: have us hanged. 330. wisly: cautiously. 331. rede:
advise. cut: cuts. 332. lat se: let see. 334. renne: run.
swithe: quickly.

336. kepen subtilly: guard craftily. 339. wher-as us thynketh:
where it seems to us. 340. That oon: the one. fest: fist.
344. also: as. agon: gone. 348. woost: know. 350. departed:
divided. 351. nathelees: nevertheless. 353. torn: turn. 354.
noot: don't know. 355. tweye: two. 357. conseil: secret.
shrewe: wretch. 361. biwreye: betray. 366. ryve: stab. 372.
dees: dice. 374. sleen: slay.

Have al this tresor to myself allone,
There is no man that lyveth under the trone 380
Of God that sholde lyve so myrie as I!''
And atte laste the feend,° oure enemy,
Putte in his thoght that he sholde poyson beye,°
With which he myghte sleen his felawes tweye,
For-why° the feend foond° hym in swich lyvynge
That he hadde leve° hym to sorwe brynge. 386
For this was outrely° his full entente,
To sleen hem bothe and nevere to repente.
And forth he goth—no lenger wholde he tarie—
Into the toun unto a pothecarie,° 390
And preyed hym that he hym wolde selle
Som poysoun that he myghte his rattes quelle,°
And eek ther was a polcat° in his hawe,°
That, as he seyde, his capouns° hadde y-slawe,°
And fayn° he wolde wreke hym,° if he myghte, 395
On vermyn that destroyed° hym by nyghte.

The pothecarie answerde, "And thow shalt have
A thyng that, also° God my soule save,
In al this world ther is no creature
That ete° or dronke hath of this confiture° 400
Nat but the montaunce° of a corn° of whete,
That he ne shal his lyf anoon forlete.°
Ye,° sterve° he shal, and that in lasse while
Than thow wolt goon a paas° nat but a myle,
The poysoun is so strong and violent." 405

This cursed man hath in his hond y-hent°
This poysoun in a box, and sith° he ran
Into the nexte strete unto a man
And borwed of hym large botels thre,
And in the two his poyson poured he. 410
The thridde he kepte clene for his drynke,
For al the nyght he shoop hym for to swynke°
In cariyng of the gold out of that place.
And whan this riotour—with sory grace!°—
Hadde filled with wyn hise grete botels thre, 415
To hise felawes agayn repaireth he.

What nedeth it to sermone of it moore?
For right as they hadde cast° his deeth bifore,
Right so they han hym slayn, and that anon. 419
And whan that this was doon, thus spak that oon:
"Now lat us sitte, and drynke, and make us merye,
And afterward we wol his body berye."
And with that word it happed hym par cas°
To take the botel ther° the poysoun was,
And drank, and yaf° his felawe drynke also, 425
For which anon they storven° bothe two.

But, certes,° I suppose that Avycen
Wroot nevere in no canon ne in no fen°
Mo wonder signes° of empoysonyng 429
Than hadde thise wrecches two er hir° endyng.
Thus ended been thise homicides two,
And eek the false empoysonere also.

O cursed synne of alle cursednesse!
O traytours homicide! O wikkednesse!
O glotonye, luxurie,° and hasardrye! 435
Thou blasphemour of Crist with vileynye
And othes grete of usage° and of pryde!°
Allas, mankynde, how may it bityde
That to thy Creatour, which that thee wroghte°
And with his precious herte-blood thee boghte, 440
Thow art so fals and so unkynde,° allas?
Now, goode men, God foryeve° yow youre trespas,
And ware yow fro° the synne of avarice.
Myn holy pardoun may yow alle warice,°
So° that ye offre nobles° or sterlynges,° 445
Or elles silver broches, spones, rynges.
Boweth youre heed under this holy bulle!
Cometh up, ye wyves! Offreth of youre wolle!°
Youre name I entre here in my rolle anon;
Into the blisse of hevene shul ye gon. 450
I yow assoille,° by myn heigh power,
Yow that wol offre, as clene and eek as cler
As ye were born.—And lo, sires, thus I preche.
And Jesu Crist, that is oure soules leche,°
So graunte yow his pardoun to receyve, 455
For that is best. I wol yow nat deceyve.

---

382. feend: Devil. **383. beye:** buy. **385. For-why:** because. **foond:** found. **386. leve:** permission (from God). **387. outrely:** entirely. **390. pothecarie:** apothecary. **392. quelle:** kill. **393. polcat:** fitchet (member of the weasel family). **hawe:** hedge. **394. capouns:** capons. **y-slawe:** killed. **395. fayn:** gladly. **wreke hym:** avenge himself. **396. destroyed:** annoyed. **398. also:** as. **400. ete:** eaten. **confiture:** preparation. **401. montaunce:** quantity. **corn:** grain. **402. forlete:** lose. **403. Ye:** yes. **sterve:** die. **404. goon a paas:** walk at footpace. **406. y-hent:** taken. **407. sith:** then. **412. shoop . . . swynke:** intended to work. **414. with . . . grace:** curse him. **418. cast:** planned.

423. it . . . cas: he happened by chance. **424. ther:** where. **425. yaf:** gave. **426. storven:** died. **427. certes:** certainly. **428. fen:** Avicenna's Arabic treatise on medicine was divided into fens (sections), containing the canons (rules) of procedure appropriate to various illnesses, including poisoning. **429. Mo . . . signes:** more wonderful symptoms. **430. er hir:** before their. **435. luxurie:** lechery. **437. usage:** habit. **pryde:** ostentation. **439. wroghte:** made. **441. unkynde:** unnatural. **442. foryeve:** forgive. **443. ware . . . fro:** beware of. **444. warice:** cure. **445. So:** providing. **nobles:** nobles (6s. 8d.). **sterlynges:** silver pennies. **448. wolle:** wool. **451. assoille:** absolve. **454. leche:** leech (physician).

THE EPILOGUE

"But, sires, o° word forgat I in my tale.
I have relikes and pardon in my male°
As faire as any man in Engelond,
Whiche were me yeven by the Popes hond.   460
If any of yow wol, of° devocioun,
Offren and han myn absolucioun,
Com forth anon, and kneleth here adoun,
And mekely receyveth my pardoun;
Or ellis taketh pardoun, as ye wende,°   465
Al newe and fressh at every myles ende,
So that ye offren, alwey newe and newe,°
Nobles or pens whiche that been goode and trewe.
It is an honour to everich° that is heer
That ye mowe° have a suffisant° pardoner   470
T' assoille yow, in contree as ye ryde,
For aventures° whiche that may bityde.
Peraventure ther may falle oon or two
Doun of° his hors, and breke his nekke atwo.
Looke which° a seuretee° is it to yow alle   475
That I am in youre felaweship y-falle,°
That may assoille yow, bothe moore° and lasse,°
Whan that the soule shal fro the body passe.
I rede° that oure Hoost shal bigynne,
For he is moost envoluped° in synne.   480
Com forth, sire Hoost, and offre first anon,
And thow shalt kisse the relikes everychon,°
Ye, for a grote.° Unbokele anon thy purs."
    "Nay, nay!" quod he. "Thanne have I Cristes curs!
Lat be!" quod he. "It shal nat be, so thee'ch.°   485
Thow woldest make me kisse thyn olde breech,
And swere it were a relyk of a seint,
Thogh it were with thy fundement depeynt.°
But, by the croys which that Seint Eleyne fond,°
I wolde I hadde thy coylons° in myn hond   490
In stede of relikes or of seintuarie.°
Lat kutte hem of!° I wol thee helpe hem carie.

---

457. o: one. 458. male: wallet. 461. of: out of. 465.
wende: travel. 467. newe . . . newe: again and again.
469. everich: each one. 470. mowe: can. suffisant: adequate.
472. aventures: incidents. 474. of: off. 475. which: what.
seuretee: security. 476. y-falle: fallen. 477. moore: high.
lasse: low. 479. rede: advise. 480. envoluped: enveloped.
482. everychon: each one. 483. grote: groat (4d.). 485.
thee'ch: may I prosper. 488. depeynt: discolored. 489.
which . . . fond: which St. Helena found. Helena, the
Emperor Constantine's mother, who was believed to have
rediscovered the true Cross, was especially revered in
England, since legend claimed her to be of British origin.
490. coylons: testicles. 491. seintuarie: holy objects. 492.
Lat . . . of: have them cut off.

They shul be shryned—in an hogges toord!"°
This Pardoner answerde nat a word;
So wrooth he was, no word ne wolde he seye.   495
    "Now," quod oure Hoost, "I wol no lenger pleye
With thee, ne with noon oother angry man."
But right anon the worthy Knyght bigan,
Whan that he saugh that al the peple lough,
"Namoore of this, for it is right ynough.   500
Sire Pardoner, be glad and murye° of cheere.
And ye, sire Hoost, that been to me so deere,
I pray yow that ye kisse the Pardoner.
And, Pardoner, I pray thee, drawe thee neer.
And, as we diden, lat us laughe and pleye."   505
Anon they kiste, and ryden° forth hir weye.

JOHN MILLINGTON SYNGE
1871–1909

Riders to the Sea

CHARACTERS

MAURYA, *an old woman*
BARTLEY, *her son*
CATHLEEN, *her daughter*
NORA, *a younger daughter*
MEN *and* WOMEN

SCENE—*An island off the west of Ireland. Cottage kitchen, with nets, oilskins, spinning-wheel, some new boards standing by the wall, etc.* CATHLEEN, *a girl of about twenty, finishes kneading cake, and puts it down in the pot-oven by the fire; then wipes her hands, and begins to spin at the wheel.* NORA, *a young girl, puts her head in at the door.*

NORA [*In a low voice*] Where is she?

CATHLEEN She's lying down, God help her, and maybe sleeping, if she's able.

[NORA *comes in softly, and takes a bundle from under her shawl.*]

CATHLEEN [*Spinning the wheel rapidly*] What is it you have?

---

493. toord: turd. 501. murye: merry. 506. ryden: rode.

NORA The young priest is after bringing them. It's a shirt and a plain stocking were got off a drowned man in Donegal.

[CATHLEEN *stops her wheel with a sudden movement, and leans out to listen.*]

NORA We're to find out if it's Michael's they are, some time herself will be down looking by the sea.

CATHLEEN How would they be Michael's, Nora? How would he go the length of that way to the far north?

NORA The young priest says he's known the like of it. "If it's Michael's they are," says he, "you can tell herself he's got a clean burial by the grace of God, and if they're not his, let no one say a word about them, for she'll be getting her death," says he, "with crying and lamenting."

[*The door which* NORA *half closed is blown open by a gust of wind.*]

CATHLEEN [*Looking out anxiously*] Did you ask him would he stop Bartley going this day with the horses to the Galway fair?

NORA "I won't stop him," says he, "but let you not be afraid. Herself does be saying prayers half through the night, and the Almighty God won't leave her destitute, "says he, "with no son living."

CATHLEEN Is the sea bad by the white rocks, Nora?

NORA Middling bad, God help us. There's a great roaring in the west, and it's worse it'll be getting when the tide's turned to the wind. [*She goes over to the table with the bundle.*] Shall I open it now?

CATHLEEN Maybe she'd wake up on us, and come in before we'd done. [*Coming to the table.*] It's a long time we'll be, and the two of us crying.

NORA [*Goes to the inner door and listens*] She's moving about on the bed. She'll be coming in a minute.

CATHLEEN Give me the ladder, and I'll put them up in the turf-loft, the way she won't know of them at all, and maybe when the tide turns she'll be going down to see would he be floating from the east.

[*They put the ladder against the gable of the chimney;* CATHLEEN *goes up a few steps and hides the bundle in the turf-loft.* MAURYA *comes from the inner room.*]

MAURYA [*Looking up at* CATHLEEN *and speaking querulously*] Isn't it turf enough you have for this day and evening?

CATHLEEN There's a cake baking at the fire for a short space [*throwing down the turf*] and Bartley will want it when the tide turns if he goes to Connemara.

[NORA *picks up the turf and puts it round the pot-oven.*]

MAURYA [*Sitting down on a stool at the fire*] He won't go this day with the wind rising from the south and west. He won't go this day, for the young priest will stop him surely.

NORA He'll not stop him, mother, and I heard Eamon Simon and Stephen Pheety and Colum Shawn saying he would go.

MAURYA Where is he itself?

NORA He went down to see would there be another boat sailing in the week, and I'm thinking it won't be long till he's here now, for the tide's turning at the green head, and the hooker's[1] tacking from the east.

CATHLEEN I hear someone passing the big stones.

NORA [*Looking out*] He's coming now, and he in a hurry.

BARTLEY [*Comes in and looks round the room; speaking sadly and quietly*] Where is the bit of new rope, Cathleen, which was bought in Connemara?

CATHLEEN [*Coming down*] Give it to him, Nora; it's on a nail by the white boards. I hung it up this morning, for the pig with the black feet was eating it.

NORA [*Giving him a rope*] Is that it, Bartley?

MAURYA You'd do right to leave that rope, Bartley, hanging by the boards. [BARTLEY *takes the rope.*] It will be wanting in this place, I'm telling you, if Michael is washed up tomorrow morning, or the next morning, or any morning in the week, for it's a deep grave we'll make him by the grace of God.

BARTLEY [*Beginning to work with the rope*] I've no halter the way I can ride down on the mare, and I must go now quickly. This is the one boat going for two weeks or beyond it, and the fair will be a good fair for horses I heard them saying below.

MAURYA It's a hard thing they'll be saying below if the body is washed up and there's no

RIDERS TO THE SEA. **1. hooker:** sailing vessel.

man in it to make the coffin, and I after giving a big price for the finest white boards you'd find in Connemara.

[*She looks round at the boards.*]

BARTLEY How would it be washed up, and we after looking each day for nine days, and a strong wind blowing a while back from the west and south?

MAURYA If it wasn't found itself, that wind is raising the sea, and there was a star up against the moon, and it rising in the night. If it was a hundred horses, or a thousand horses you had itself, what is the price of a thousand horses against a son where there is one son only?

BARTLEY [*Working at the halter, to* CATHLEEN] Let you go down each day, and see the sheep aren't jumping in on the rye, and if the jobber comes you can sell the pig with the black feet if there is a good price going.

MAURYA How would the like of her get a good price for a pig?

BARTLEY [*To* CATHLEEN] If the west wind holds with the last bit of the moon let you and Nora get up weed enough for another cock for the kelp. It's hard set we'll be from this day with no one in it but one man to work.

MAURYA It's hard set we'll be surely the day you're drownd'd with the rest. What way will I live and the girls with me, and I an old woman looking for the grave?

[BARTLEY *lays down the halter, takes off his old coat, and puts on a newer one of the same flannel.*]

BARTLEY [*To* NORA] Is she coming to the pier?

NORA [*Looking out*] She's passing the green head and letting fall her sails.

BARTLEY [*Getting his purse and tobacco*] I'll have half an hour to go down, and you'll see me coming again in two days, or in three days, or maybe in four days if the wind is bad.

MAURYA [*Turning round to the fire, and putting her shawl over her head*] Isn't it a hard and cruel man won't hear a word from an old woman, and she holding him from the sea?

CATHLEEN It's the life of a young man to be going on the sea, and who would listen to an old woman with one thing and she saying it over?

BARTLEY [*Taking the halter*] I must go now quickly. I'll ride down on the red mare, and the gray pony'll run behind me. . . . The blessing of God on you. [*He goes out.*]

MAURYA [*Crying out as he is in the door*] He's gone now, God spare us, and we'll not see him again. He's gone now, and when the black night is falling I'll have no son left me in the world.

CATHLEEN Why wouldn't you give him your blessing and he looking round in the door? Isn't it sorrow enough is on every one in this house without your sending him out with an unlucky word behind him, and a hard word in his ear?

[MAURYA *takes up the tongs and begins raking the fire aimlessly without looking round.*]

NORA [*Turning toward her*] You're taking away the turf from the cake.

CATHLEEN [*Crying out*] The Son of God forgive us, Nora, we're after forgetting his bit of bread.

[*She comes over to the fire.*]

NORA And it's destroyed he'll be going till dark night, and he after eating nothing since the sun went up.

CATHLEEN [*Turning the cake out of the oven*] It's destroyed he'll be, surely. There's no sense left on any person in a house where an old woman will be talking forever.

[MAURYA *sways herself on her stool.*]

CATHLEEN [*Cutting off some of the bread and rolling it in a cloth; to* MAURYA] Let you go down now to the spring well and give him this and he passing. You'll see him then and the dark word will be broken, and you can say "God speed you," the way he'll be easy in his mind.

MAURYA [*Taking the bread*] Will I be in it as soon as himself?

CATHLEEN If you go now quickly.

MAURYA [*Standing up unsteadily*] It's hard set I am to walk.

CATHLEEN [*Looking at her anxiously*] Give her the stick, Nora, or maybe she'll slip on the big stones.

NORA What stick?

CATHLEEN The stick Michael brought from Connemara.

MAURYA [*Taking a stick* NORA *gives her*] In the big world the old people do be leaving things after them for their sons and children, but in this place it is the young men do be leaving things behind for them that do be old.

[*She goes out slowly.* NORA *goes over to the ladder.*]

CATHLEEN Wait, Nora, maybe she'd turn back quickly. She's that sorry, God help her, you wouldn't know the thing she'd do.

NORA Is she gone round by the bush?

CATHLEEN [*Looking out*] She's gone now. Throw it down quickly, for the Lord knows when she'll be out of it again.

NORA [*Getting the bundle from the loft*] The young priest said he'd be passing tomorrow, and we might go down and speak to him below if it's Michael's they are surely.

CATHLEEN [*Taking the bundle*] Did he say what way they were found?

NORA [*Coming down*] "There were two men," says he, "and they rowing round with poteen before the cocks crowed, and the oar of one of them caught the body, and they passing the black cliffs of the north."

CATHLEEN [*Trying to open the bundle*] Give me a knife, Nora, the string's perished with the salt water, and there's a black knot on it you wouldn't loosen in a week.

NORA [*Giving her a knife*] I've heard tell it was a long way to Donegal.

CATHLEEN [*Cutting the string*] It is surely. There was a man in here a while ago—the man sold us that knife—and he said if you set off walking from the rocks beyond, it would be seven days you'd be in Donegal.

NORA And what time would a man take, and he floating?

[CATHLEEN *opens the bundle and takes out a bit of a stocking. They look at them eagerly.*]

CATHLEEN [*In a low voice*] The Lord spare us, Nora! isn't it a queer hard thing to say if it's his they are surely?

NORA I'll get his shirt off the hook the way we can put the one flannel on the other. [*She looks through some clothes hanging in the corner.*] It's not with them, Cathleen, and where will it be?

CATHLEEN I'm thinking Bartley put it on him in the morning, for his own shirt was heavy with the salt in it. [*Pointing to the corner.*] There's a bit of a sleeve was of the same stuff. Give me that and it will do.

[NORA *brings it to her and they compare the flannel.*]

CATHLEEN It's the same stuff, Nora; but if it is itself aren't there great rolls of it in the shops of Galway, and isn't it many another man may have a shirt of it as well as Michael himself?

NORA [*Who has taken up the stocking and counted the stitches, crying out*] It's Michael, Cathleen, it's Michael; God spare his soul, and what will herself say when she hears this story, and Bartley on the sea?

CATHLEEN [*Taking the stocking*] It's a plain stocking.

NORA It's the second one of the third pair I knitted, and I put up threescore stitches, and I dropped four of them.

CATHLEEN [*Counts the stitches*] It's that number is in it. [*Crying out.*] Ah, Nora, isn't it a bitter thing to think of him floating that way to the far north, and no one to keen him but the black hags that do be flying on the sea?

NORA [*Swinging herself round, and throwing out her arms on the clothes*] And isn't it a pitiful thing when there is nothing left of a man who was a great rower and fisher, but a bit of an old shirt and a plain stocking?

CATHLEEN [*After an instant*] Tell me is herself coming, Nora? I hear a little sound on the path.

NORA [*Looking out*] She is, Cathleen. She's coming up to the door.

CATHLEEN Put these things away before she'll come in. Maybe it's easier she'll be after giving her blessing to Bartley, and we won't let on we've heard anything the time he's on the sea.

NORA [*Helping* CATHLEEN *to close the bundle*] We'll put them here in the corner.

[*They put them into a hole in the chimney corner.* CATHLEEN *goes back to the spinning-wheel.*]

NORA Will she see it was crying I was?

CATHLEEN Keep your back to the door the way the light'll not be on you.

[NORA *sits down at the chimney corner, with her back to the door.* MAURYA *comes in very slowly, without looking at the girls, and goes over to her stool at the other side of the fire. The cloth with the bread is still in her hand. The girls look at each other, and* NORA *points to the bundle of bread.*]

CATHLEEN [*After spinning for a moment*] You didn't give him his bit of bread?

[MAURYA *begins to keen softly, without turning round.*]

CATHLEEN Did you see him riding down?

[MAURYA *goes on keening.*]

CATHLEEN [*A little impatiently*] God forgive you; isn't it a better thing to raise your voice and tell what you seen, than to be making lamentation for a thing that's done? Did you see Bartley, I'm saying to you.

MAURYA [*With a weak voice*] My heart's broken from this day.

CATHLEEN [*As before*] Did you see Bartley?

MAURYA I seen the fearfulest thing.

CATHLEEN [*Leaves her wheel and looks out*] God forgive you; he's riding the mare now over the green head, and the gray pony behind him.

MAURYA [*Starts, so that her shawl falls back from her head and shows her white tossed hair; with a frightened voice*] The gray pony behind him. . . .

CATHLEEN [*Coming to the fire*] What is it ails you at all?

MAURYA [*Speaking very slowly*] I've seen the fearfulest thing any person has seen, since the day Bride Dara seen the dead man with a child in his arms.

CATHLEEN AND NORA Uah.

[*They crouch down in front of the old woman at the fire.*]

NORA Tell us what it is you seen.

MAURYA I went down to the spring well, and I stood there saying a prayer to myself. Then Bartley came along, and he riding on the red mare with the gray pony behind him. [*She puts up her hands, as if to hide something from her eyes.*] The Son of God spare us, Nora!

CATHLEEN What is it you seen?

MAURYA I seen Michael himself.

CATHLEEN [*Speaking softly*] You did not, mother; it wasn't Michael you seen, for his body is after being found in the far north, and he's got a clean burial, by the grace of God.

MAURYA [*A little defiantly*] I'm after seeing him this day, and he riding and galloping. Bartley came first on the red mare; and I tried to say, "God speed you," but something choked the words in my throat. He went by quickly; and "the blessing of God on you," says he, and I could say nothing. I looked up then, and I crying, at the gray pony, and there was Michael upon it—with fine clothes on him, and new shoes on his feet.

CATHLEEN [*Begins to keen*] It's destroyed we are from this day. It's destroyed, surely.

NORA Didn't the young priest say the Almighty God wouldn't leave her destitute with no son living?

MAURYA [*In a low voice, but clearly*] It's little the like of him knows of the sea. . . . Bartley will be lost now, and let you call in Eamon and make me a good coffin out of the white boards, for I won't live after them. I've had a husband, and a husband's father, and six sons in this house—six fine men, though it was a hard birth I had with every one of them and they coming to the world—and some of them were found and some of them were not found, but they're gone now the lot of them. . . . There were Stephen, and Shawn, were lost in the great wind, and found after in the Bay of Gregory of the Golden Mouth, and carried up the two of them on the one plank, and in by that door.

[*She pauses for a moment; the girls start as if they heard something through the door that is half open behind them.*]

NORA [*In a whisper*] Did you hear that, Cathleen? Did you hear a noise in the northeast?

CATHLEEN [*In a whisper*] There's someone after crying out by the seashore.

MAURYA [*Continues without hearing anything*] There was Sheamus and his father, and his own father again, were lost in a dark night, and not a stick or sign was seen of them when the sun went up. There was Patch after was drowned out of a curagh that turned over. I was sitting here with Bartley, and he a baby, lying on my two knees, and I seen two women, and three women, and four women coming in, and they crossing themselves, and not saying a word. I looked out then, and there were men coming after them, and they holding a thing in the half of a red sail, and water dripping out of it—it was a dry day, Nora—and leaving a track to the door.

[*She pauses again with her hand stretched out toward the door. It opens softly and old women begin to come in, crossing themselves on the threshold, and kneeling down in front of the stage with red petticoats over their heads.*]

MAURYA [*Half in a dream, to* CATHLEEN] Is it Patch, or Michael, or what is it at all?

CATHLEEN Michael is after being found in the far north, and when he is found there how could he be here in this place?

MAURYA There does be a power of young men floating round in the sea, and what way would they know if it was Michael they had, or another man like him, for when a man is nine days in the sea, and the wind blowing, it's hard set his own mother would be to say what man was it.

CATHLEEN   It's Michael, God spare him, for they're after sending us a bit of his clothes from the far north.

[*She reaches out and hands* MAURYA *the clothes that belonged to* MICHAEL. MAURYA *stands up slowly, and takes them in her hands.* NORA *looks out.*]

NORA   They're carrying a thing among them and there's water dripping out of it and leaving a track by the big stones.

CATHLEEN   [*In a whisper to the women who have come in*]   Is it Bartley it is?

ONE OF THE WOMEN   It is, surely, God rest his soul.

[*Two younger women come in and pull out the table. Then men carry in the body of* BARTLEY, *laid on a plank, with a bit of a sail over it, and lay it on the table.*]

CATHLEEN   [*To the women, as they are doing so*]   What way was he drowned?

ONE OF THE WOMEN   The gray pony knocked him into the sea, and he was washed out where there is a great surf on the white rocks.

[MAURYA *has gone over and knelt down at the head of the table. The women are keening softly and swaying themselves with a slow movement.* CATHLEEN *and* NORA *kneel at the other end of the table. The men kneel near the door.*]

MAURYA   [*Raising her head and speaking as if she did not see the people around her*]   They're all gone now, and there isn't anything more the sea can do to me. . . . I'll have no call now to be up crying and praying when the wind breaks from the south, and you can hear the surf is in the east, and the surf is in the west, making a great stir with the two noises, and they hitting one on the other. I'll have no call now to be going down and getting holy water in the dark nights after Samhain,[2] and I won't care what way the sea is when the other women will be keening. [*To* NORA.]   Give me the holy water, Nora; there's a small sup still on the dresser.

MAURYA   [*Drops* MICHAEL'S *clothes across* BARTLEY'S *feet, and sprinkles the holy water over him*]   It isn't that I haven't prayed for you, Bartley, to the Almighty God. It isn't that I haven't said prayers in the dark night till you wouldn't know what I'd be saying; but it's a great rest I'll have now, and it's time surely. It's a great rest I'll have now, and great sleeping in the long nights

2. **Samhain:** feast of All Saints, November 1.

after Samhain, if it's only a bit of wet flour we do have to eat, and maybe a fish that would be stinking.

[*She kneels down again, crossing herself, and saying prayers under her breath.*]

CATHLEEN   [*To an old man*]   Maybe yourself and Eamon would make a coffin when the sun rises. We have fine white boards herself bought, God help her, thinking Michael would be found, and I have a new cake you can eat while you'll be working.

THE OLD MAN   [*Looking at the boards*]   Are there nails with them?

CATHLEEN   There are not, Colum; we didn't think of the nails.

ANOTHER MAN   It's a great wonder she wouldn't think of the nails, and all the coffins she's seen made already.

CATHLEEN   It's getting old she is, and broken.

[MAURYA *stands up again very slowly and spreads out the pieces of* MICHAEL'S *clothes beside the body, sprinkling them with the last of the holy water.*]

NORA   [*In a whisper to* CATHLEEN]   She's quiet now and easy; but the day Michael was drowned you could hear her crying out from this to the spring well. It's fonder she was of Michael, and would any one have thought that?

CATHLEEN   [*Slowly and clearly*]   An old woman will be soon tired with anything she will do, and isn't it nine days herself is after crying and keening, and making great sorrow in the house?

MAURYA   [*Puts the empty cup, mouth downwards, on the table, and lays her hands together on* BARTLEY'S *feet*]   They're all together this time, and the end is come. May the Almighty God have mercy on Bartley's soul, and on Michael's soul, and on the souls of Sheamus and Patch, and Stephen and Shawn; [*bending her head*] and may he have mercy on my soul, Nora, and on the soul of every one is left living in the world.

[*She pauses, and the keen rises a little more loudly from the women, then sinks away.*]

MAURYA   [*Continuing*]   Michael has a clean burial in the far north, by the grace of the Almighty God. Bartley will have a fine coffin out of the white boards, and a deep grave surely. What more can we want than that? No man at all can be living forever, and we must be satisfied.

[*She kneels down again and the curtain falls slowly.*]

JAMES JOYCE
1882–1941

A Painful Case

Mr. James Duffy lived in Chapelizod because he wished to live as far as possible from the city of which he was a citizen and because he found all the other suburbs of Dublin mean, modern and pretentious. He lived in an old somber house and from his windows he could look into the disused distillery or upwards along the shallow river on which Dublin is built. The lofty walls of his uncarpeted room were free from pictures. He had himself bought every article of furniture in the room: a black iron bedstead, an iron washstand, four cane chairs, a clothes-rack, a coal-scuttle, a fender and irons and a square table on which lay a double desk. A bookcase had been made in an alcove by means of shelves of white wood. The bed was clothed with white bedclothes and a black and scarlet rug covered the foot. A little hand-mirror hung above the washstand and during the day a white-shaded lamp stood as the sole ornament of the mantelpiece. The books on the white wooden shelves were arranged from below upwards according to bulk. A complete Wordsworth stood at one end of the lowest shelf and a copy of the *Maynooth Catechism*, sewn into the cloth cover of a notebook, stood at one end of the top shelf. Writing materials were always on the desk. In the desk lay a manuscript translation of Hauptmann's *Michael Kramer*, the stage directions of which were written in purple ink, and a little sheaf of papers held together by a brass pin. In these sheets a sentence was inscribed from time to time and, in an ironical moment, the headline of an advertisement for *Bile Beans* had been pasted on to the first sheet. On lifting the lid of the desk a faint fragrance escaped—the fragrance of new cedarwood pencils or of a bottle of gum or of an overripe apple which might have been left there and forgotten.

Mr. Duffy abhorred anything which betokened physical or mental disorder. A medieval doctor would have called him saturnine. His face, which carried the entire tale of his years, was of the brown tint of Dublin streets. On his long and rather large head grew dry black hair and a tawny mustache did not quite cover an unamiable mouth. His cheekbones also gave his face a harsh character; but there was no harshness in the eyes which, looking at the world from under their tawny eyebrows, gave the impression of a man ever alert to greet a redeeming instinct in others but often disappointed. He lived at a little distance from his body, regarding his own acts with doubtful side-glances. He had an odd autobiographical habit which led him to compose in his mind from time to time a short sentence about himself containing a subject in the third person and a predicate in the past tense. He never gave alms to beggars and walked firmly, carrying a stout hazel.

He had been for many years cashier of a private bank in Baggot Street. Every morning he came in from Chapelizod by tram. At midday he went to Dan Burke's and took his lunch—a bottle of lager beer and a small trayful of arrowroot biscuits. At four o'clock he was set free. He dined in an eating-house in George's Street where he felt himself safe from the society of Dublin's gilded youth and where there was a certain plain honesty in the bill of fare. His evenings were spent either before his landlady's piano or roaming about the outskirts of the city. His liking for Mozart's music brought him sometimes to an opera or a concert: these were the only dissipations of his life.

He had neither companions nor friends, church nor creed. He lived his spiritual life without any communion with others, visiting his relatives at Christmas and escorting them to the cemetery when they died. He performed these two social duties for old dignity's sake but conceded nothing further to the conventions which regulate the civic life. He allowed himself to think that in certain circumstances he would rob his bank but, as these circumstances never arose, his life rolled out evenly—an adventureless tale.

One evening he found himself sitting beside two ladies in the Rotunda. The house, thinly peopled and silent, gave distressing prophecy of failure. The lady who sat next him looked round at the deserted house once or twice and then said:

"What a pity there is such a poor house to-night! It's so hard on people to have to sing to empty benches."

He took the remark as an invitation to talk. He

was surprised that she seemed so little awkward. While they talked he tried to fix her permanently in his memory. When he learned that the young girl beside her was her daughter he judged her to be a year or so younger than himself. Her face, which must have been handsome, had remained intelligent. It was an oval face with strongly marked features. The eyes were very dark blue and steady. Their gaze began with a defiant note but was confused by what seemed a deliberate swoon of the pupil into the iris, revealing for an instant a temperament of great sensibility. The pupil reasserted itself quickly, this half-disclosed nature fell again under the reign of prudence, and her astrakhan jacket, molding a bosom of a certain fullness, struck the note of defiance more definitely.

He met her again a few weeks afterwards at a concert in Earlsfort Terrace and seized the moments when her daughter's attention was diverted to become intimate. She alluded once or twice to her husband but her tone was not such as to make the allusion a warning. Her name was Mrs. Sinico. Her husband's great-great-grandfather had come from Leghorn. Her husband was captain of a mercantile boat plying between Dublin and Holland; and they had one child.

Meeting her a third time by accident he found courage to make an appointment. She came. This was the first of many meetings; they met always in the evening and chose the most quiet quarters for their walks together. Mr. Duffy, however, had a distaste for underhand ways and, finding that they were compelled to meet stealthily, he forced her to ask him to her house. Captain Sinico encouraged his visits, thinking that his daughter's hand was in question. He had dismissed his wife so sincerely from his gallery of pleasures that he did not suspect that anyone else would take an interest in her. As the husband was often away and the daughter out giving music lessons Mr. Duffy had many opportunities of enjoying the lady's society. Neither he nor she had had any such adventure before and neither was conscious of any incongruity. Little by little he entangled his thoughts with hers. He lent her books, provided her with ideas, shared his intellectual life with her. She listened to all.

Sometimes in return for his theories she gave out some fact of her own life. With almost maternal solicitude she urged him to let his nature open to

the full: she became his confessor. He told her that for some time he had assisted at the meetings of an Irish Socialist Party where he had felt himself a unique figure amidst a score of sober workmen in a garret lit by an inefficient oil-lamp. When the party had divided into three sections, each under its own leader and in its own garret, he had discontinued his attendances. The workmen's discussions, he said, were too timorous; the interest they took in the question of wages was inordinate. He felt that they were hard-featured realists and that they resented an exactitude which was the produce of a leisure not within their reach. No social revolution, he told her, would be likely to strike Dublin for some centuries.

She asked him why did he not write out his thoughts. For what, he asked her, with careful scorn. To compete with phrasemongers, incapable of thinking consecutively for sixty seconds? To submit himself to the criticisms of an obtuse middle class which entrusted its morality to policemen and its fine arts to impresarios?

He went often to her little cottage outside Dublin; often they spent their evenings alone. Little by little, as their thoughts entangled, they spoke of subjects less remote. Her companionship was like a warm soil about an exotic. Many times she allowed the dark to fall upon them, refraining from lighting the lamp. The dark discreet room, their isolation, the music that still vibrated in their ears united them. This union exalted him, wore away the rough edges of his character, emotionalized his mental life. Sometimes he caught himself listening to the sound of his own voice. He thought that in her eyes he would ascend to an angelical stature; and, as he attached the fervent nature of his companion more and more closely to him, he heard the strange impersonal voice which he recognized as his own, insisting on the soul's incurable loneliness. We cannot give ourselves, it said: we are our own. The end of these discourses was that one night during which she had shown every sign of unusual excitement, Mrs. Sinico caught up his hand passionately and pressed it to her cheek.

Mr. Duffy was very much surprised. Her interpretation of his words disillusioned him. He did not visit her for a week, then he wrote to her asking her to meet him. As he did not wish their last interview to be troubled by the influence of their ruined confessional they met in a little cakeshop near the Parkgate. It was cold autumn weather but in spite of the cold they wandered up and down the roads of the park for nearly three hours. They agreed to break off their intercourse: every bond, he said, is a bond to sorrow. When they came out of the park they walked in silence towards the tram; but here she began to tremble so violently that, fearing another collapse on her part, he bade her good-by quickly and left her. A few days later he received a parcel containing his books and music.

Four years passed. Mr. Duffy returned to his even way of life. His room still bore witness of the orderliness of his mind. Some new pieces of music encumbered the music-stand in the lower room and on his shelves stood two volumes by Nietzsche: *Thus Spake Zarathustra* and *The Gay Science*. He wrote seldom in the sheaf of papers which lay in his desk. One of his sentences, written two months after his last interview with Mrs. Sinico, read: Love between man and man is impossible because there must not be sexual intercourse and friendship between man and woman is impossible because there must be sexual intercourse. He kept away from concerts lest he should meet her. His father died; the junior partner of the bank retired. And still every morning he went into the city by tram and every evening walked home from the city after having dined moderately in George's Street and read the evening paper for dessert.

One evening as he was about to put a morsel of corned beef and cabbage into his mouth his hand stopped. His eyes fixed themselves on a paragraph in the evening paper which he had propped against the water-carafe. He replaced the morsel of food on his plate and read the paragraph attentively. Then he drank a glass of water, pushed his plate to one side, doubled the paper down before him between his elbows and read the paragraph over and over again. The cabbage began to deposit a cold white grease on his plate. The girl came over to him to ask was his dinner not properly cooked. He said it was very good and ate a few mouthfuls of it with difficulty. Then he paid his bill and went out.

He walked along quickly through the November twilight, his stout hazel stick striking the ground regularly, the fringe of the buff *Mail* peeping out of a side-pocket of his tight reefer overcoat. On the lonely road which leads from the Parkgate to Chapelizod he slackened his pace. His stick struck the ground less emphatically and his breath, issuing irregularly, almost with a sighing sound, condensed in the wintry air. When he reached his house he went up at once to his bedroom and, taking the paper from his pocket, read the paragraph again by the failing light of the window. He read it not aloud, but moving his lips as a priest does when he reads the prayers *Secreto*. This was the paragraph:

DEATH OF A LADY AT SYDNEY PARADE

A Painful Case

Today at the City of Dublin Hospital the deputy coroner (in the absence of Mr. Leverett) held an inquest on the body of Mrs. Emily Sinico, aged forty-three years, who was killed at Sydney Parade Station yesterday evening. The evidence showed that the deceased lady, while attempting to cross the line, was knocked down by the engine of the ten o'clock slow train from Kingstown, thereby sustaining injuries of the head and right side which led to her death.

James Lennon, driver of the engine, stated that he had been in the employment of the railway company for fifteen years. On hearing the guard's whistle he set the train in motion and a second or two afterwards brought it to rest in response to loud cries. The train was going slowly.

P. Dunne, railway porter, stated that as the train was about to start he observed a woman attempting to cross the lines. He ran towards her and shouted, but, before he could reach her, she was caught by the buffer of the engine and fell to the ground.

A juror. "You saw the lady fall?"

Witness. "Yes."

Police Sergeant Croly deposed that when he arrived he found the deceased lying on the platform apparently dead. He had the body taken to the waiting-room pending the arrival of the ambulance.

Constable 57 corroborated.

Dr. Halpin, assistant house surgeon of the City of Dublin Hospital, stated that the deceased had two lower ribs fractured and had sustained severe contusions of the right shoulder. The right side of the head had been injured in the fall. The injuries were not sufficient to have caused death in a normal person. Death, in his opinion, had been probably due to shock and sudden failure of the heart's action.

Mr. H. B. Patterson Finlay, on behalf of the railway company, expressed his deep regret at the accident. The company had always taken every precaution to prevent people crossing the lines except by the bridges, both by placing notices in every station and by the use of patent spring gates at level crossings. The deceased had been in the habit of crossing the lines late at night from platform to platform and, in view of certain other circumstances of the case, he did not think the railway officials were to blame.

Captain Sinico, of Leoville, Sydney Parade, husband of the deceased, also gave evidence. He stated that the deceased was his wife. He was not in Dublin at the time of the accident as he had arrived only that morning from Rotterdam. They had been married for twenty-two years and had lived happily until about two years ago when his wife began to be rather intemperate in her habits.

Miss Mary Sinico said that of late her mother had been in the habit of going out at night to buy spirits. She, witness, had often tried to reason with her mother and had induced her to join a league. She was not at home until an hour after the accident. The jury returned a verdict in accordance with the medical evidence and exonerated Lennon from all blame.

The deputy coroner said it was a most painful case, and expressed great sympathy with Captain Sinico and his daughter. He urged on the railway company to take strong measures to prevent the possibility of similar accidents in the future. No blame attached to anyone.

Mr. Duffy raised his eyes from the paper and gazed out of his window on the cheerless evening landscape. The river lay quiet beside the empty distillery and from time to time a light appeared in some house on the Lucan road. What an end! The whole narrative of her death revolted him and it revolted him to think that he had ever spoken to her of what he held sacred. The threadbare phrases, the inane expressions of sympathy, the cautious words of a reporter won over to conceal the details of a commonplace vulgar death attacked his stomach. Not merely had she degraded herself; she had degraded him. He saw the squalid tract of her vice, miserable and malodorous. His

soul's companion! He thought of the hobbling wretches whom he had seen carrying cans and bottles to be filled by the barman. Just God, what an end! Evidently she had been unfit to live, without any strength of purpose, an easy prey to habits, one of the wrecks on which civilization has been reared. But that she could have sunk so low! Was it possible he had deceived himself so utterly about her? He remembered her outburst of that night and interpreted it in a harsher sense than he had ever done. He had no difficulty now in approving of the course he had taken.

As the light failed and his memory began to wander he thought her hand touched his. The shock which had first attacked his stomach was now attacking his nerves. He put on his overcoat and hat quickly and went out. The cold air met him on the threshold; it crept into the sleeves of his coat. When he came to the public-house at Chapelizod Bridge he went in and ordered a hot punch.

The proprietor served him obsequiously but did not venture to talk. There were five or six working-men in the shop discussing the value of a gentleman's estate in County Kildare. They drank at intervals from their huge pint tumblers and smoked, spitting often on the floor and sometimes dragging the sawdust over their spits with their heavy boots. Mr. Duffy sat on his stool and gazed at them, without seeing or hearing them. After a while they went out and he called for another punch. He sat a long time over it. The shop was very quiet. The proprietor sprawled on the counter reading the *Herald* and yawning. Now and again a tram was heard swishing along the lonely road outside.

As he sat there, living over his life with her and evoking alternately the two images in which he now conceived her, he realized that she was dead, that she had ceased to exist, that she had become a memory. He began to feel ill at ease. He asked himself what else could he have done. He could not have carried on a comedy of deception with her; he could not have lived with her openly. He had done what seemed to him best. How was he to blame? Now that she was gone he understood how lonely her life must have been, sitting night after night alone in that room. His life would be lonely too until he, too, died, ceased to exist, became a memory—if anyone remembered him.

It was after nine o'clock when he left the shop. The night was cold and gloomy. He entered the park by the first gate and walked along under the gaunt trees. He walked through the bleak alleys where they had walked four years before. She seemed to be near him in the darkness. At moments he seemed to feel her voice touch his ear, her hand touch his. He stood still to listen. Why had he withheld life from her? Why had he sentenced her to death? He felt his moral nature falling to pieces.

When he gained the crest of the Magazine Hill he halted and looked along the river towards Dublin, the lights of which burned redly and hospitably in the cold night. He looked down the slope and, at the base, in the shadow of the wall of the park, he saw some human figures lying. Those venal and furtive loves filled him with despair. He gnawed the rectitude of his life; he felt that he had been outcast from life's feast. One human being had seemed to love him and he had denied her life and happiness: he had sentenced her to ignominy, a death of shame. He knew that the prostrate creatures down by the wall were watching him and wished him gone. No one wanted him; he was outcast from life's feast. He turned his eyes to the gray gleaming river, winding along towards Dublin. Beyond the river he saw a goods train winding out of Kingsbridge Station, like a worm with a fiery head winding through the darkness, obstinately and laboriously. It passed slowly out of sight; but still he heard in his ears the laborious drone of the engine reiterating the syllables of her name.

He turned back the way he had come, the rhythm of the engine pounding in his ears. He began to doubt the reality of what memory told him. He halted under a tree and allowed the rhythm to die away. He could not feel her near him in the darkness nor her voice touch his ear. He waited for some minutes listening. He could hear nothing: the night was perfectly silent. He listened again: perfectly silent. He felt that he was alone.

GRAHAM GREENE
b. 1904

The Basement Room

1

When the front door had shut them out and the butler Baines had turned back into the dark heavy hall, Philip began to live. He stood in front of the nursery door, listening until he heard the engine of the taxi die out along the street. His parents were gone for a fortnight's holiday; he was "between nurses," one dismissed and the other not arrived; he was alone in the great Belgravia house with Baines and Mrs. Baines.

He could go anywhere, even through the green baize door to the pantry or down the stairs to the basement living-room. He felt a stranger in his home because he could go into any room and all the rooms were empty.

You could only guess who had once occupied them: the rack of pipes in the smoking-room beside the elephant tusks, the carved wood tobacco jar; in the bedroom the pink hangings and pale perfumes and the three-quarter finished jars of cream which Mrs. Baines had not yet cleared away; the high glaze on the never-opened piano in the drawing-room, the china clock, the silly little tables and the silver: but here Mrs. Baines was already busy, pulling down the curtains, covering the chairs in dust-sheets.

"Be off out of here, Master Philip," and she looked at him with her hateful peevish eyes, while she moved round, getting everything in order, meticulous and loveless and doing her duty.

Philip Lane went downstairs and pushed at the baize door; he looked into the pantry, but Baines was not there, then he set foot for the first time on the stairs to the basement. Again he had the sense: this is life. All his seven nursery years vibrated with the strange, the new experience. His crowded busy brain was like a city which feels the earth tremble at a distant earthquake shock. He was apprehensive, but he was happier than he had ever been. Everything was more important than before.

Baines was reading a newspaper in his shirt-sleeves. He said: "Come in, Phil, and make yourself at home. Wait a moment and I'll do the honors," and going to a white cleaned cupboard he brought out a bottle of ginger-beer and half a Dundee cake. "Half-past eleven in the morning," Baines said. "It's opening time, my boy," and he cut the cake and poured out the ginger-beer. He was more genial than Philip had ever known him, more at his ease, a man in his own home.

"Shall I call Mrs. Baines?" Philip asked, and he was glad when Baines said no. She was busy. She liked to be busy, so why interfere with her pleasure?

"A spot of drink at half-past eleven," Baines said, pouring himself out a glass of ginger-beer, "gives an appetite for chop and does no man any harm."

"A chop?" Philip asked.

"Old Coasters," Baines said, "call all food chop."

"But it's not a chop?"

"Well, it might be, you know, cooked with palm oil. And then some paw-paw to follow."

Philip looked out of the basement window at the dry stone yard, the ash-can and the legs going up and down beyond the railings.

"Was it hot there?"

"Ah, you never felt such heat. Not a nice heat, mind, like you get in the park on a day like this. Wet," Baines said, "corruption." He cut himself a slice of cake. "Smelling of rot," Baines said, rolling his eyes round the small basement room from clean cupboard to clean cupboard, the sense of bareness, of nowhere to hide a man's secrets. With an air of regret for something lost he took a long draft of ginger-beer.

"Why did father live out there?"

"It was his job," Baines said, "same as this is mine now. And it was mine then too. It was a man's job. You wouldn't believe it now, but I've had forty niggers under me, doing what I told them to."

"Why did you leave?"

"I married Mrs. Baines."

Philip took the slice of Dundee cake in his hand and munched it round the room. He felt very old, independent and judicial; he was aware that Baines was talking to him as man to man. He never called him Master Philip as Mrs. Baines did, who was servile when she was not authoritative.

Baines had seen the world; he had seen beyond the railings, beyond the tired legs of typists, the Pimlico parade to and from Victoria.[1] He sat there over his ginger pop with the resigned dignity of an exile; Baines didn't complain; he had chosen his fate; and if his fate was Mrs. Baines he had only himself to blame.

But today, because the house was almost empty and Mrs. Baines was upstairs and there was nothing to do, he allowed himself a little acidity.

"I'd go back tomorrow if I had the chance."

"Did you ever shoot a nigger?"

"I never had any call to shoot," Baines said. "Of course I carried a gun. But you didn't need to treat them bad. That just made them stupid. Why," Baines said, bowing his thin gray hair with embarrassment over the ginger pop, "I loved some of those damned niggers. I couldn't help loving them. There they'd be laughing, holding hands; they liked to touch each other; it made them feel fine to know the other fellow was round.

"It didn't mean anything we could understand; two of them would go about all day without loosing hold, grown men; but it wasn't love; it didn't mean anything we could understand."

"Eating between meals," Mrs. Baines said. "What would your mother say, Master Philip?"

She came down the steep stairs to the basement, her hands full of pots of cream and salve, tubes of grease and paste. "You oughtn't to encourage him, Baines," she said, sitting down in a wicker armchair and screwing up her small ill-humored eyes at the Coty lipstick, Pond's cream, the Leichner rouge and Cyclax powder and Elizabeth Arden astringent.

She threw them one by one into the wastepaper basket. She saved only the cold cream. "Telling the boy stories," she said. "Go along to the nursery, Master Philip, while I get lunch."

Philip climbed the stairs to the baize door. He heard Mrs. Baines's voice like the voice in a nightmare when the small Price light has guttered in the saucer and the curtains move; it was sharp and shrill and full of malice, louder than people ought to speak, exposed.

"Sick to death of your ways, Baines, spoiling the boy. Time you did some work about the house," but he couldn't hear what Baines said in reply. He pushed open the baize door, came up like a small

THE BASEMENT ROOM. **1. Pimlico . . . Victoria:** the section near Victoria Station in southwest London.

earth animal in his gray flannel shorts into a wash of sunlight on a parquet floor, the gleam of mirrors dusted and polished and beautified by Mrs. Baines.

Something broke downstairs, and Philip sadly mounted the stairs to the nursery. He pitied Baines; it occurred to him how happily they could live together in the empty house if Mrs. Baines were called away. He didn't want to play with his Meccano sets; he wouldn't take out his train or his soldiers; he sat at the table with his chin on his hands: this is life; and suddenly he felt responsible for Baines, as if he were the master of the house and Baines an aging servant who deserved to be cared for. There was not much one could do; he decided at least to be good.

He was not surprised when Mrs. Baines was agreeable at lunch; he was used to her changes. Now it was "another helping of meat, Master Philip," or "Master Philip, a little more of this nice pudding." It was a pudding he liked, queen's pudding with a perfect meringue, but he wouldn't eat a second helping lest she might count that a victory. She was the kind of woman who thought that any injustice could be counterbalanced by something good to eat.

She was sour, but she liked making sweet things; one never had to complain of a lack of jam or plums; she ate well herself and added soft sugar to the meringue and the strawberry jam. The half light through the basement window set the motes moving above her pale hair like dust as she sifted the sugar, and Baines crouched over his plate saying nothing.

Again Philip felt responsibility. Baines had looked forward to this, and Baines was disappointed: everything was being spoilt. The sensation of disappointment was one which Philip could share; knowing nothing of love or jealousy or passion he could understand better than anyone this grief, something hoped for not happening, something promised not fulfilled, something exciting turning dull. "Baines," he said, "will you take me for a walk this afternoon?"

"No," Mrs. Baines said, "no. That he won't. Not with all the silver to clean."

"There's a fortnight to do it in," Baines said.

"Work first, pleasure afterwards." Mrs. Baines helped herself to some more meringue.

Baines suddenly put down his spoon and fork and pushed his plate away. "Blast," he said.

"Temper," Mrs. Baines said softly, "temper. Don't you go breaking any more things, Baines, and I won't have you swearing in front of the boy. Master Philip, if you've finished you can get down." She skinned the rest of the meringue off the pudding.

"I want to go for a walk," Philip said.

"You'll go and have a rest."

"I will go for a walk."

"Master Philip," Mrs. Baines said. She got up from the table leaving her meringue unfinished, and came towards him, thin, menacing, dusty in the basement room. "Master Philip, you do as you're told." She took him by the arm and squeezed it gently; she watched him with a joyless passionate glitter and above her head the feet of the typists trudged back to the Victoria offices after the lunch interval.

"Why shouldn't I go for a walk?" But he weakened; he was scared and ashamed of being scared. This was life; a strange passion he couldn't understand moving in the basement room. He saw a small pile of broken glass swept into a corner by the wastepaper basket. He looked to Baines for help and only intercepted hate; the sad hopeless hate of something behind bars.

"Why shouldn't I?" he repeated.

"Master Philip," Mrs. Baines said, "you've got to do as you're told. You mustn't think just because your father's away there's nobody here to——"

"You wouldn't dare," Philip cried, and was startled by Baines's low interjection:

"There's nothing she wouldn't dare."

"I hate you," Philip said to Mrs. Baines. He pulled away from her and ran to the door, but she was there before him; she was old, but she was quick.

"Master Philip," she said, "you'll say you're sorry." She stood in front of the door quivering with excitement. "What would your father do if he heard you say that?"

She put a hand out to seize him, dry and white with constant soda, the nails cut to the quick, but he backed away and put the table between them, and suddenly to his surprise she smiled; she became again as servile as she had been arrogant. "Get along with you, Master Philip," she said with glee, "I see I'm going to have my hands full till your father and mother come back."

She left the door unguarded and when he passed her she slapped him playfully. "I've got too much to do today to trouble about you. I haven't covered half the chairs," and suddenly even the upper part of the house became unbearable to him as he thought of Mrs. Baines moving round shrouding the sofas, laying out the dust-sheets.

So he wouldn't go upstairs to get his cap but walked straight out across the shining hall into the street, and again, as he looked this way and looked that way, it was life he was in the middle of.

2

It was the pink sugar cakes in the window on a paper doily, the ham, the slab of mauve sausage, the wasps driving like small torpedoes across the pane that caught Philip's attention. His feet were tired by pavements; he had been afraid to cross the road, had simply walked first in one direction, then in the other. He was nearly home now; the square was at the end of the street; this was a shabby outpost of Pimlico, and he smudged the pane with his nose looking for sweets, and saw between the cakes and ham a different Baines. He hardly recognized the bulbous eyes, the bald forehead. It was a happy, bold and buccaneering Baines, even though it was, when you looked closer, a desperate Baines.

Philip had never seen the girl. He remembered Baines had a niece and he thought that this might be her. She was thin and drawn, and she wore a white mackintosh; she meant nothing to Philip; she belonged to a world about which he knew nothing at all. He couldn't make up stories about her, as he could make them up about withered Sir Hubert Reed, the Permanent Secretary, about Mrs. Wince-Dudley who came up once a year from Penstanley in Suffolk with a green umbrella and an enormous black handbag, as he could make them up about the upper servants in all the houses where he went to tea and games. She just didn't belong; he thought of mermaids and Undine; but she didn't belong there either, nor to the adventures of Emil, nor to the Bastables. She sat there looking at an iced pink cake in the detachment and mystery of the completely disinherited, looking at the half-used pots of powder which Baines had set out on the marble-topped table between them.

Baines was urging, hoping, entreating, commanding, and the girl looked at the tea and the china pots and cried. Baines passed his handkerchief across the table, but she wouldn't wipe her eyes; she screwed it in her palm and let the tears run down, wouldn't do anything, wouldn't speak, would only put up a silent despairing resistance to what she dreaded and wanted and refused to listen to at any price. The two brains battled over the teacups loving each other, and there came to Philip outside, beyond the ham and wasps and dusty Pimlico pane, a confused indication of the struggle.

He was inquisitive and he didn't understand and he wanted to know. He went and stood in the doorway to see better, he was less sheltered than he had ever been; other people's lives for the first time touched and pressed and molded. He would never escape that scene. In a week he had forgotten it, but it conditioned his career, the long austerity of his life; when he was dying he said: "Who is she?"

Baines had won; he was cocky and the girl was happy. She wiped her face, she opened a pot of powder, and their fingers touched across the table. It occurred to Philip that it would be amusing to imitate Mrs. Baines's voice and call "Baines" to him from the door.

It shriveled them; you couldn't describe it in any other way; it made them smaller, they weren't happy any more and they weren't bold. Baines was the first to recover and trace the voice, but that didn't make things as they were. The sawdust was spilled out of the afternoon; nothing you did could mend it, and Philip was scared. "I didn't mean . . ." He wanted to say that he loved Baines, that he had only wanted to laugh at Mrs. Baines. But he had discovered that you couldn't laugh at Mrs. Baines. She wasn't Sir Hubert Reed, who used steel nibs and carried a pen-wiper in his pocket; she wasn't Mrs. Wince-Dudley; she was darkness when the night-light went out in a draft; she was the frozen blocks of earth he had seen one winter in a graveyard when someone said, "They need an electric drill"; she was the flowers gone bad and smelling in the little closet room at Penstanley. There was nothing to laugh about. You had to endure her when she was there and forget about her quickly when she was away, suppress the thought of her, ram it down deep.

Baines said: "It's only Phil," beckoned him in

and gave him the pink iced cake the girl hadn't eaten, but the afternoon was broken, the cake was like dry bread in the throat. The girl left them at once; she even forgot to take the powder; like a small blunt icicle in her white mackintosh she stood in the doorway with her back to them, then melted into the afternoon.

"Who is she?" Philip asked. "Is she your niece?"

"Oh, yes," Baines said, "that's who she is; she's my niece," and poured the last drops of water on to the coarse black leaves in the teapot.

"May as well have another cup," Baines said.

"The cup that cheers," he said hopelessly, watching the bitter black fluid drain out of the spout.

"Have a glass of ginger pop, Phil?"

"I'm sorry. I'm sorry, Baines."

"It's not your fault, Phil. Why, I could believe it wasn't you at all, but her. She creeps in everywhere." He fished two leaves out of his cup and laid them on the back of his hand, a thin soft flake and a hard stalk. He beat them with his hand: "Today," and the stalk detached itself, "tomorrow, Wednesday, Thursday, Friday, Saturday, Sunday," but the flake wouldn't come, stayed where it was, drying under his blows, with a resistance you wouldn't believe it to possess. "The tough one wins," Baines said.

He got up and paid the bill and out they went into the street. Baines said, "I don't ask you to say what isn't true. But you needn't mention to Mrs. Baines you met us here."

"Of course not," Philip said, and catching something of Sir Hubert Reed's manner, "I understand, Baines." But he didn't understand a thing; he was caught up in other people's darkness.

"It was stupid," Baines said. "So near home, but I hadn't time to think, you see. I'd got to see her."

"Of course, Baines."

"I haven't time to spare," Baines said. "I'm not young. I've got to see that she's all right."

"Of course you have, Baines."

"Mrs. Baines will get it out of you if she can."

"You can trust me, Baines," Philip said in a dry important Reed voice; and then, "Look out. She's at the window watching." And there indeed she was, looking up at them, between the lace curtains, from the basement room, speculating. "Need we go in, Baines?" Philip asked, cold

lying heavy on his stomach like too much pudding; he clutched Baines's arm.

"Careful," Baines said softly, "careful."

"But need we go in, Baines? It's early. Take me for a walk in the park."

"Better not."

"But I'm frightened, Baines."

"You haven't any cause," Baines said. "Nothing's going to hurt you. You just run along upstairs to the nursery. I'll go down by the area and talk to Mrs. Baines." But even he stood hesitating at the top of the stone steps pretending not to see her, where she watched between the curtains. "In at the front door, Phil, and up the stairs."

Philip didn't linger in the hall; he ran, slithering on the parquet Mrs. Baines had polished, to the stairs. Through the drawing-room doorway on the first floor he saw the draped chairs; even the china clock on the mantel was covered like a canary's cage; as he passed it, it chimed the hour, muffled and secret under the duster. On the nursery table he found his supper laid out: a glass of milk and a piece of bread and butter, a sweet biscuit, and a little cold queen's pudding without the meringue. He had no appetite; he strained his ears for Mrs. Baines's coming, for the sound of voices, but the basement held its secrets; the green baize door shut off that world. He drank the milk and ate the biscuit, but he didn't touch the rest, and presently he could hear the soft precise footfalls of Mrs. Baines on the stairs: she was a good servant, she walked softly; she was a determined woman, she walked precisely.

But she wasn't angry when she came in; she was ingratiating as she opened the night nursery door— "Did you have a good walk, Master Philip?"— pulled down the blinds, laid out his pajamas, came back to clear his supper. "I'm glad Baines found you. Your mother wouldn't have liked your being out alone." She examined the tray. "Not much appetite, have you, Master Philip? Why don't you try a little of this nice pudding? I'll bring you up some more jam for it."

"No, no, thank you, Mrs. Baines," Philip said.

"You ought to eat more," Mrs. Baines said. She sniffed round the room like a dog. "You didn't take any pots out of the wastepaper basket in the kitchen, did you, Master Philip?"

"No," Philip said.

"Of course you wouldn't. I just wanted to make sure." She patted his shoulder and her fingers flashed to his lapel; she picked off a tiny crumb of pink sugar. "Oh, Master Philip," she said, "that's why you haven't any appetite. You've been buying sweet cakes. That's not what your pocket money's for."

"But I didn't," Philip said. "I didn't."

She tasted the sugar with the tip of her tongue.

"Don't tell lies to me, Master Philip. I won't stand for it any more than your father would."

"I didn't, I didn't," Philip said. "They gave it me. I mean Baines," but she had pounced on the word *they*. She had got what she wanted; there was no doubt about that, even when you didn't know what it was she wanted. Philip was angry and miserable and disappointed because he hadn't kept Baines's secret. Baines oughtn't to have trusted him; grown-up people should keep their own secrets, and yet here was Mrs. Baines immediately entrusting him with another.

"Let me tickle your palm and see if you can keep a secret." But he put his hand behind him; he wouldn't be touched. "It's a secret between us, Master Philip, that I know all about them. I suppose she was having tea with him," she speculated.

"Why shouldn't she?" he said, the responsibility for Baines weighing on his spirit, the idea that he had got to keep her secret when he hadn't kept Baines's making him miserable with the unfairness of life. "She was nice."

"She was nice, was she?" Mrs. Baines said in a bitter voice he wasn't used to.

"And she's his niece."

"So that's what he said," Mrs. Baines struck softly back at him like the clock under the duster. She tried to be jocular. "The old scoundrel. Don't you tell him I know, Master Philip." She stood very still between the table and the door, thinking very hard, planning something. "Promise you won't tell. I'll give you that Meccano set, Master Philip. . . ."

He turned his back on her; he wouldn't promise, but he wouldn't tell. He would have nothing to do with their secrets, the responsibilities they were determined to lay on him. He was only anxious to forget. He had received already a larger dose of life than he had bargained for, and he was scared. "A 2A Meccano set, Master Philip." He never

opened his Meccano set again, never built anything, never created anything, died, the old dilettante, sixty years later with nothing to show rather than preserve the memory of Mrs. Baines's malicious voice saying good night, her soft determined footfalls on the stairs to the basement, going down, going down.

3

The sun poured in between the curtains and Baines was beating a tattoo on the water-can. "Glory, glory," Baines said. He sat down on the end of the bed and said, "I beg to announce that Mrs. Baines has been called away. Her mother's dying. She won't be back till tomorrow."

"Why did you wake me up so early?" Philip said. He watched Baines with uneasiness; he wasn't going to be drawn in; he'd learnt his lesson. It wasn't right for a man of Baines's age to be so merry. It made a grown person human in the same way that you were human. For if a grown-up could behave so childishly, you were liable too to find yourself in their world. It was enough that it came at you in dreams: the witch at the corner, the man with a knife. So "It's very early," he complained, even though he loved Baines, even though he couldn't help being glad that Baines was happy. He was divided by the fear and the attraction of life.

"I want to make this a long day," Baines said. "This is the best time." He pulled the curtains back. "It's a bit misty. The cat's been out all night. There she is, sniffing round the area. They haven't taken in any milk at 59. Emma's shaking out the mats at 63." He said: "This was what I used to think about on the Coast: somebody shaking mats and the cat coming home. I can see it today," Baines said, "just as if I was still in Africa. Most days you don't notice what you've got. It's a good life if you don't weaken." He put a penny on the washstand. "When you've dressed, Phil, run and get a *Mail* from the barrow at the corner. I'll be cooking the sausages."

"Sausages?"

"Sausages," Baines said. "We're going to celebrate today. A fair bust." He celebrated at breakfast, restless, cracking jokes, unaccountably merry and nervous. It was going to be a long long day, he kept on coming back to that: for years he had waited for a long day, he had sweated in the damp

Coast heat, changed shirts, gone down with fever, lain between the blankets and sweated, all in the hope of this long day, that cat sniffing round the area, a bit of mist, the mats beaten at 63. He propped the *Mail* in front of the coffeepot and read pieces aloud. He said, "Cora Down's been married for the fourth time." He was amused, but it wasn't his idea of a long day. His long day was the park, watching the riders in the row, seeing Sir Arthur Stillwater pass beyond the rails ("He dined with us once in Bo; up from Freetown; he was governor there"), lunch at the Corner House for Philip's sake (he'd have preferred himself a glass of stout and some oysters at the York bar), the zoo, the long bus ride home in the last summer light: the leaves in the Green Park were beginning to turn and the motors nuzzled out of Berkeley Street with the low sun gently glowing on their windscreens. Baines envied no one, not Cora Down, or Sir Arthur Stillwater, or Lord Sandale, who came out on to the steps of the Army and Navy and then went back again because he hadn't got anything to do and might as well look at another paper. "I said don't let me see you touch that black again." Baines had led a man's life; everyone on top of the bus pricked their ears when he told Philip all about it.

"Would you have shot him?" Philip asked, and Baines put his head back and tilted his dark respectable man-servant's hat to a better angle as the bus swerved round the artillery memorial.

"I wouldn't have thought twice about it. I'd have shot to kill," he boasted, and the bowed figure went by, the steel helmet, the heavy cloak, the down-turned rifle and the folded hands.

"Have you got the revolver?"

"Of course I've got it," Baines said. "Don't I need it with all the burglaries there've been?" This was the Baines whom Philip loved: not Baines singing and carefree, but Baines responsible, Baines behind barriers, living his man's life.

All the buses streamed out from Victoria like a convoy of aeroplanes to bring Baines home with honor. "Forty blacks under me," and there waiting near the area steps was the proper conventional reward, love at lighting-up time.

"It's your niece," Philip said, recognizing the white mackintosh, but not the happy sleepy face. She frightened him like an unlucky number; he nearly told Baines what Mrs. Baines had said;

but he didn't want to bother, he wanted to leave things alone.

"Why, so it is," Baines said. "I shouldn't wonder if she was going to have a bite of supper with us." But he said they'd play a game, pretend they didn't know her, slip down the area steps, "and here," Baines said, "we are," lay the table, put out the cold sausages, a bottle of beer, a bottle of ginger pop, a flagon of harvest burgundy. "Everyone his own drink," Baines said. "Run upstairs, Phil, and see if there's been a post."

Philip didn't like the empty house at dusk before the lights went on. He hurried. He wanted to be back with Baines. The hall lay there in quiet and shadow prepared to show him something he didn't want to see. Some letters rustled down, and someone knocked. "Open in the name of the Republic." The tumbrils rolled, the head bobbed in the bloody basket. Knock, knock, and the postman's footsteps going away. Philip gathered the letters. The slit in the door was like the grating in a jeweler's window. He remembered the policeman he had seen peer through. He had said to his nurse, "What's he doing?" and when she said, "He's seeing if everything's all right," his brain immediately filled with images of all that might be wrong. He ran to the baize door and the stairs. The girl was already there and Baines was kissing her. She leant breathless against the dresser. "This is Emmy, Phil."

"There's a letter for you, Baines."

"Emmy," Baines said, "it's from her." But he wouldn't open it. "You bet she's coming back."

"We'll have supper, anyway," Emmy said. "She can't harm that."

"You don't know her," Baines said. "Nothing's safe. Damn it," he said, "I was a man once," and he opened the letter.

"Can I start?" Philip asked, but Baines didn't hear; he presented in his stillness and attention an example of the importance grown-up people attached to the written word: you had to write your thanks, not wait and speak them, as if letters couldn't lie. But Philip knew better than that, sprawling his thanks across a page to Aunt Alice who had given him a doll he was too old for. Letters could lie all right, but they made the lie permanent: they lay as evidence against you; they made you meaner than the spoken word.

"She's not coming back till tomorrow night,"

Baines said. He opened the bottles, he pulled up the chairs, he kissed Emmy again against the dresser.

"You oughtn't to," Emmy said, "with the boy here."

"He's got to learn," Baines said, "like the rest of us," and he helped Philip to three sausages. He only took one himself; he said he wasn't hungry; but when Emmy said she wasn't hungry either he stood over her and made her eat. He was timid and rough with her; he made her drink the harvest burgundy because he said she needed building up; he wouldn't take no for an answer, but when he touched her his hands were light and clumsy too, as if he was afraid to damage something delicate and didn't know how to handle anything so light.

"This is better than milk and biscuits, eh?"

"Yes," Philip said, but he was scared, scared for Baines as much as for himself. He couldn't help wondering at every bite, at every draft of the ginger pop, what Mrs. Baines would say if she ever learnt of this meal; he couldn't imagine it, there was a depth of bitterness and rage in Mrs. Baines you couldn't sound. He said, "She won't be coming back tonight?" but you could tell by the way they immediately understood him that she wasn't really away at all; she was there in the basement with them, driving them to longer drinks and louder talk, biding her time for the right cutting word. Baines wasn't really happy; he was only watching happiness from close to instead of from far away.

"No," he said, "she'll not be back till late tomorrow." He couldn't keep his eyes off happiness; he'd played around as much as other men, he kept on reverting to the Coast as if to excuse himself for his innocence; he wouldn't have been so innocent if he'd lived his life in London, so innocent when it came to tenderness. "If it was you Emmy," he said, looking at the white dresser, the scrubbed chairs, "this'd be like a home." Already the room was not quite so harsh; there was a little dust in corners, the silver needed a final polish, the morning's paper lay untidily on a chair. "You'd better go to bed, Phil; it's been a long day."

They didn't leave him to find his own way up through the dark shrouded house; they went with him, turning on lights, touching each other's fingers on the switches; floor after floor they drove the night back; they spoke softly among the covered chairs; they watched him undress, they didn't make him wash or clean his teeth, they saw him into bed and lit his night-light and left his door ajar. He could hear their voices on the stairs, friendly like the guests he heard at dinner-parties when they moved down to the hall, saying good night. They belonged; wherever they were they made a home. He heard a door open and a clock strike, he heard their voices for a long while, so that he felt they were not far away and he was safe. The voices didn't dwindle, they simply went out, and he could be sure that they were still somewhere not far from him, silent together in one of the many empty rooms, growing sleepy together as he grew sleepy after the long day.

He just had time to sigh faintly with satisfaction, because this too perhaps had been life, before he slept and the inevitable terrors of sleep came round him: a man with a tricolor hat beat at the door on His Majesty's service, a bleeding head lay on the kitchen table in a basket, and the Siberian wolves crept closer. He was bound hand and foot and couldn't move; they leapt round him breathing heavily; he opened his eyes and Mrs. Baines was there, her gray untidy hair in threads over his face, her black hat askew. A loose hairpin fell on the pillow and one musty thread brushed his mouth. "Where are they?" she whispered. "Where are they?"

4

Philip watched her in terror. Mrs. Baines was out of breath as if she had been searching all the empty rooms, looking under loose covers.

With her untidy gray hair and her black dress buttoned to her throat, her gloves of black cotton, she was so like the witches of his dreams that he didn't dare to speak. There was a stale smell in her breath.

"She's here," Mrs. Baines said; "you can't deny she's here." Her face was simultaneously marked with cruelty and misery; she wanted to "do things" to people, but she suffered all the time. It would have done her good to scream, but she daren't do that: it would warn them. She came ingratiatingly back to the bed where Philip lay rigid on his back and whispered, "I haven't forgotten the Meccano set. You shall have it tomorrow, Master Philip. We've got secrets together, haven't we? Just tell me where they are."

He couldn't speak. Fear held him as firmly as any nightmare. She said, "Tell Mrs. Baines, Master Philip. You love your Mrs. Baines, don't you?" That was too much; he couldn't speak, but he could move his mouth in terrified denial, wince away from her dusty image.

She whispered, coming closer to him, "Such deceit. I'll tell your father. I'll settle with you myself when I've found them. You'll smart; I'll see you smart." Then immediately she was still, listening. A board had creaked on the floor below, and a moment later, while she stooped listening above his bed, there came the whispers of two people who were happy and sleepy together after a long day. The night-light stood beside the mirror and Mrs. Baines could see bitterly there her own reflection, misery and cruelty wavering in the glass, age and dust and nothing to hope for. She sobbed without tears, a dry, breathless sound; but her cruelty was a kind of pride which kept her going; it was her best quality, she would have been merely pitiable without it. She went out of the door on tiptoe, feeling her way across the landing, going so softly down the stairs that no one behind a shut door could hear her. Then there was complete silence again; Philip could move; he raised his knees; he sat up in bed; he wanted to die. It wasn't fair, the walls were down again between his world and theirs; but this time it was something worse than merriment that the grown people made him share; a passion moved in the house he recognized but could not understand.

It wasn't fair, but he owed Baines everything: the zoo, the ginger pop, the bus ride home. Even the supper called on his loyalty. But he was frightened; he was touching something he touched in dreams: the bleeding head, the wolves, the knock, knock, knock. Life fell on him with savagery: you couldn't blame him if he never faced it again in sixty years. He got out of bed, carefully from habit put on his bedroom slippers, and tiptoed to the door: it wasn't quite dark on the landing below because the curtain had been taken down for the cleaners and the light from the street came in through the tall windows. Mrs. Baines had her hand on the glass doorknob; she was very carefully turning it; he screamed: "Baines, Baines."

Mrs. Baines turned and saw him cowering in his pajamas by the banisters; he was helpless, more helpless even than Baines, and cruelty grew at the sight of him and drove her up the stairs. The nightmare was on him again and he couldn't move; he hadn't any more courage left forever; he'd spent it all, had been allowed no time to let it grow, no years of gradual hardening; he couldn't even scream.

But the first cry had brought Baines out of the best spare bedroom and he moved quicker than Mrs. Baines. She hadn't reached the top of the stairs before he'd caught her round the waist. She drove her black cotton gloves at his face and he bit her hand. He hadn't time to think, he fought her savagely like a stranger, but she fought back with knowledgeable hate. She was going to teach them all and it didn't really matter whom she began with; they had all deceived her; but the old image in the glass was by her side, telling her she must be dignified, she wasn't young enough to yield her dignity; she could beat his face, but she mustn't bite; she could push, but she mustn't kick.

Age and dust and nothing to hope for were her handicaps. She went over the banisters in a flurry of black clothes and fell into the hall; she lay before the front door like a sack of coals which should have gone down the area into the basement. Philip saw; Emmy saw; she sat down suddenly in the doorway of the best spare bedroom with her eyes open as if she were too tired to stand any longer. Baines went slowly down into the hall.

It wasn't hard for Philip to escape; they'd forgotten him completely; he went down the back, the servants' stairs because Mrs. Baines was in the hall; he didn't understand what she was doing lying there; like the startling pictures in a book no one had read to him, the things he didn't understand terrified him. The whole house had been turned over to the grown-up world; he wasn't safe in the night nursery; their passions had flooded it. The only thing he could do was to get away, by the back stair, and up through the area, and never come back. You didn't think of the cold, of the need of food and sleep; for an hour it would seem quite possible to escape from people forever.

He was wearing pajamas and bedroom slippers when he came up into the square, but there was no one to see him. It was that hour of the evening in a residential district when everyone is at the theatre or at home. He climbed over the iron railings into the little garden: the plane-trees spread their large pale palms between him and the sky. It might have been an illimitable forest into which he had escaped. He crouched behind a trunk and the wolves retreated; it seemed to him between the little iron seat and the tree-trunk that no one would ever find him again. A kind of embittered happiness and self-pity made him cry; he was lost; there wouldn't be any more secrets to keep; he surrendered responsibility once and for all. Let grown-up people keep to their world and he would keep to his, safe in the small garden between the plane-trees. "In the lost childhood of Judas Christ was betrayed"; you could almost see the small unformed face hardening into the deep dilettante selfishness of age.

Presently the door of 48 opened and Baines looked this way and that; then he signaled with his hand and Emmy came; it was as if they were only just in time for a train, they hadn't a chance of saying good-by; she went quickly by like a face at a window swept past the platform, pale and unhappy and not wanting to go. Baines went in again and shut the door; the light was lit in the basement, and a policeman walked round the square, looking into the areas. You could tell how many families were at home by the lights behind the first-floor curtains.

Philip explored the garden: it didn't take long: a twenty-yard square of bushes and plane-trees, two iron seats and a gravel path, a padlocked gate at either end, a scuffle of old leaves. But he couldn't stay: something stirred in the bushes and two illuminated eyes peered out at him like a Siberian wolf and he thought how terrible it would be if Mrs. Baines found him there. He'd have no time to climb the railings; she'd seize him from behind.

He left the square at the unfashionable end and was immediately among the fish-and-chip shops, the little stationers selling Bagatelle, among the accommodation addresses and the dingy hotels with open doors. There were few people about because the pubs were open, but a blowsy woman carrying a parcel called out to him across the street and the commissionaire outside a cinema would have stopped him if he hadn't crossed the road. He went deeper: you could go farther and lose yourself more completely here than among the plane-trees. On the fringe of the square he was in danger of being stopped and taken back: it was obvious where he belonged: but as he went deeper he lost the marks of his origin. It was a warm night: any child in those free-living parts might be expected to play truant from bed. He found a kind of camaraderie even among grown-up people; he might have been a neighbor's child as he went quickly by, but they weren't going to tell on him, they'd been young once themselves. He picked up a protective coating of dust from the pavements, of smuts from the trains which passed along the backs in a spray of fire. Once he was caught in a knot of children running away from something or somebody, laughing as they ran; he was whirled with them round a turning and abandoned, with sticky fruit-drop in his hand.

He couldn't have been more lost; but he hadn't the stamina to keep on. At first he feared that someone would stop him; after an hour he hoped that someone would. He couldn't find his way back, and in any case he was afraid of arriving home alone; he was afraid of Mrs. Baines, more afraid than he had ever been. Baines was his friend, but something had happened which gave Mrs. Baines all the power. He began to loiter on purpose to be noticed, but no one noticed him. Families were having a last breather on the doorsteps, the refuse bins had been put out and bits of cabbage stalks soiled his slippers. The air was full of voices, but he was cut off; these people were strangers and would always now be strangers; they were marked by Mrs. Baines and he shied away from them into a deep class-consciousness. He had been afraid of policemen, but now he wanted one to take him home; even Mrs. Baines could do nothing against a policeman. He sidled past a constable who was directing traffic, but he was too busy to pay him any attention. Philip sat down against a wall and cried.

It hadn't occurred to him that that was the easiest way, that all you had to do was to surrender, to show you were beaten and accept kindness. . . . It was lavished on him at once by two women and a pawnbroker. Another policeman appeared, a young man with a sharp incredulous face. He looked as if he noted everything he saw in pocketbooks and drew conclusions. A woman offered to see Philip home, but he didn't trust her: she wasn't a match for Mrs. Baines immobile in the hall. He wouldn't give his address; he said he was afraid to go home. He had his way; he got his protection. "I'll take him to the station," the policeman said, and holding him awkwardly by the hand (he wasn't married; he had his career to make) he led him round the corner, up the stone stairs into the little bare overheated room where Justice waited.

5

Justice waited behind a wooden counter on a high stool; it wore a heavy mustache; it was kindly and had six children ("three of them nippers like yourself"); it wasn't really interested in Philip, but it pretended to be, it wrote the address down and sent a constable to fetch a glass of milk. But the young constable was interested; he had a nose for things.

"Your home's on the telephone, I suppose," Justice said. "We'll ring them up and say you are safe. They'll fetch you very soon. What's your name, sonny?"

"Philip."

"Your other name."

"I haven't got another name." He didn't want to be fetched; he wanted to be taken home by someone who would impress even Mrs. Baines. The constable watched him, watched the way he drank the milk, watched him when he winced away from questions.

"What made you run away? Playing truant, eh?"

"I don't know."

"You oughtn't to do it, young fellow. Think how anxious your father and mother will be."

"They are away."

"Well, your nurse."

"I haven't got one."

"Who looks after you, then?" That question went home. Philip saw Mrs. Baines coming up the stairs at him, the heap of black cotton in the hall. He began to cry.

"Now, now, now," the sergeant said. He didn't know what to do; he wished his wife were with him; even a policewoman might have been useful.

"Don't you think it's funny," the constable said, "that there hasn't been an inquiry?"

"They think he's tucked up in bed."

"You are scared, aren't you?" the constable said. "What scared you?"

"I don't know."

"Somebody hurt you?"

"No."

"He's had bad dreams," the sergeant said. "Thought the house was on fire, I expect. I've

brought up six of them. Rose is due back. She'll take him home."

"I want to go home with you," Philip said; he tried to smile at the constable, but the deceit was immature and unsuccessful.

"I'd better go," the constable said. "There may be something wrong."

"Nonsense," the sergeant said. "It's a woman's job. Tact is what you need. Here's Rose. Pull up your stockings, Rose. You're a disgrace to the force. I've got a job of work for you." Rose shambled in: black cotton stockings drooping over her boots, a gawky Girl Guide manner, a hoarse hostile voice. "More tarts, I suppose."

"No, you've got to see this young man home." She looked at him owlishly.

"I won't go with her," Philip said. He began to cry again. "I don't like her."

"More of that womanly charm, Rose," the sergeant said. The telephone range on his desk. He lifted the receiver. "What? What's that?" he said. "Number 48? You've got a doctor?" He put his hand over the telephone mouth. "No wonder this nipper wasn't reported," he said. "They've been too busy. An accident. Woman slipped on the stairs."

"Serious?" the constable asked. The sergeant mouthed at him; you didn't mention the word death before a child (didn't he know? he had six of them), you made noises in the throat, you grimaced, a complicated shorthand for a word of only five letters anyway.

"You'd better go, after all," he said, "and make a report. The doctor's there."

Rose shambled from the stove; pink apply-dapply cheeks, loose stockings. She stuck her hands behind her. Her large morguelike mouth was full of blackened teeth. "You told me to take him and now just because something interesting . . . I don't expect justice from a man . . ."

"Who's at the house?" the constable asked.

"The butler."

"You don't think," the constable said, "he saw . . ."

"Trust me," the sergeant said. "I've brought up six. I know 'em through and through. You can't teach me anything about children."

"He seemed scared about something."

"Dreams," the sergeant said.

"What name?"

"Baines."

"This Mr. Baines," the constable said to Philip, "you like him, eh? He's good to you?" They were trying to get something out of him; he was suspicious of the whole roomful of them; he said "yes" without conviction because he was afraid at any moment of more responsibilities, more secrets.

"And Mrs. Baines?"

"Yes."

They consulted together by the desk: Rose was hoarsely aggrieved; she was like a female impersonator, she bore her womanhood with an unnatural emphasis even while she scorned it in her creased stockings and her weather-exposed face. The charcoal shifted in the stove; the room was overheated in the mild late summer evening. A notice on the wall described a body found in the Thames, or rather the body's clothes: wool vest, wool pants, wool shirt with blue stripes, size ten boots, blue serge suit worn at the elbows, fifteen and a half celluloid collar. They couldn't find anything to say about the body, except its measurements, it was just an ordinary body.

"Come along," the constable said. He was interested, he was glad to be going, but he couldn't help being embarrassed by his company, a small boy in pajamas. His nose smelt something, he didn't know what, but he smarted at the sight of the amusement they caused: the pubs had closed and the streets were full again of men making as long a day of it as they could. He hurried through the less frequented streets, chose the darker pavements, wouldn't loiter, and Philip wanted more and more to loiter, pulling at his hand, dragging with his feet. He dreaded the sight of Mrs. Baines waiting in the hall: he knew now that she was dead. The sergeant's mouthings had conveyed that; but she wasn't buried, she wasn't out of sight; he was going to see a dead person in the hall when the door opened.

The light was on in the basement, and to his relief the constable made for the area steps. Perhaps he wouldn't have to see Mrs. Baines at all. The constable knocked on the door because it was too dark to see the bell, and Baines answered. He stood there in the doorway of the neat bright basement room and you could see the sad complacent plausible sentence he had prepared wither at the sight of Philip; he hadn't expected Philip to return like that in the policeman's company. He

had to begin thinking all over again; he wasn't a deceptive man; if it hadn't been for Emmy he would have been quite ready to let the truth lead him where it would.

"Mr. Baines?" the constable asked.

He nodded; he hadn't found the right words; he was daunted by the shrewd knowing face, the sudden appearance of Philip there.

"This little boy from here?"

"Yes," Baines said. Philip could tell that there was a message he was trying to convey, but he shut his mind to it. He loved Baines, but Baines had involved him in secrets, in fears he didn't understand. The glowing morning thought "This is life" had become under Baines's tuition the repugnant memory, "That was life": the musty hair across the mouth, the breathless cruel tortured inquiry "Where are they," the heap of black cotton tipped into the hall. That was what happened when you loved: you got involved; and Philip extricated himself from life, from love, from Baines with a merciless egotism.

There had been things between them, but he laid them low, as a retreating army cuts the wires, destroys the bridges. In the abandoned country you may leave much that is dear—a morning in the park, an ice at a corner house, sausages for supper —but more is concerned in the retreat than temporary losses. There are old people who, as the tractors wheel away, implore to be taken, but you can't risk the rearguard for their sake: a whole prolonged retreat from life, from care, from human relationships is involved.

"The doctor's here," Baines said. He nodded at the door, moistened his mouth, kept his eyes on Philip, begging for something like a dog you can't understand. "There's nothing to be done. She slipped on these stone basement stairs. I was in here. I heard her fall." He wouldn't look at the notebook, at the constable's tiny spidery writing which got a terrible lot on one page.

"Did the boy see anything?"

"He can't have done. I thought he was in bed. Hadn't he better go up? It's a shocking thing. O," Baines said, losing control, "it's a shocking thing for a child."

"She's through there?" the constable asked.

"I haven't moved her an inch," Baines said.

"He'd better then——"

"Go up the area and through the hall," Baines

said and again he begged dumbly like a dog: one more secret, keep this secret, do this for old Baines, he won't ask another.

"Come along," the constable said. "I'll see you up to bed. You're a gentleman; you must come in the proper way through the front door like the master should. Or will you go along with him, Mr. Baines, while I see the doctor?"

"Yes," Baines said, "I'll go." He came across the room to Philip, begging, begging, all the way with his soft old stupid expression: this is Baines, the old Coaster; what about a palm-oil chop, eh?; a man's life; forty niggers; never used a gun; I tell you I couldn't help loving them: it wasn't what we call love, nothing we could understand. The messages flickered out from the last posts at the border, imploring, beseeching, reminding: this is your old friend Baines; what about an eleven's; a glass of ginger pop won't do you any harm; sausages; a long day. But the wires were cut, the messages just faded out into the enormous vacancy of the neat scrubbed room in which there had never been a place where a man could hide his secrets.

"Come along, Phil, it's bedtime. We'll just go up the steps . . ." Tap, tap, tap, at the telegraph; you may get through, you can't tell, somebody may mend the right wire. "And in at the front door."

"No," Philip said, "no. I won't go. You can't make me go. I'll fight. I won't see her."

The constable turned on them quickly. "What's that? Why won't you go?"

"She's in the hall," Philip said. "I know she's in the hall. And she's dead. I won't see her."

"You moved her then?" the constable said to Baines. "All the way down here? You've been lying, eh? That means you had to tidy up. . . . Were you alone?"

"Emmy," Philip said, "Emmy." He wasn't going to keep any more secrets: he was going to finish once and for all with everything, with Baines and Mrs. Baines and the grown-up life beyond him; it wasn't his business and never, never again, he decided, would he share their confidences and companionship. "It was all Emmy's fault," he protested with a quaver which reminded Baines that after all he was only a child; it had been hopeless to expect help there; he was a child; he didn't understand what it all meant; he couldn't read this shorthand of terror; he'd had a long day and he was tired out. You could see him dropping asleep where he stood against the dresser, dropping back into the comfortable nursery peace. You couldn't blame him. When he woke in the morning, he'd hardly remember a thing.

"Out with it," the constable said, addressing Baines with professional ferocity, "who is she?" just as the old man sixty years later startled his secretary, his only watcher, asking, "Who is she? Who is she?" dropping lower and lower into death, passing on the way perhaps the image of Baines: Baines hopeless, Baines letting his head drop, Baines "coming clean."

FLANNERY O'CONNOR
1925–1964

A Good Man Is Hard to Find

The grandmother didn't want to go to Florida. She wanted to visit some of her connections in east Tennessee and she was seizing at every chance to change Bailey's mind. Bailey was the son she lived with, her only boy. He was sitting on the edge of his chair at the table, bent over the orange sports section of the *Journal*. "Now look here, Bailey," she said, "see here, read this," and she stood with one hand on her thin hip and the other rattling the newspaper at his bald head. "Here this fellow that calls himself The Misfit is aloose from the federal pen and headed toward Florida and you read what it says he did to these people. Just you read it. I wouldn't take my children in any direction with a criminal like that aloose in it. I couldn't answer to my conscience if I did."

Bailey didn't look up from his reading so she wheeled around then and faced the children's mother, a young woman in slacks, whose face was as broad and innocent as a cabbage and was tied around with a green headkerchief that had two points on the top like rabbit's ears. She was sitting on the sofa, feeding the baby his apricots out of a jar. "The children have been to Florida before," the old lady said. "You all ought to take them somewhere else for a change so they would see different parts of the world and be broad. They never have been to east Tennessee.''

The children's mother didn't seem to hear her but the eight-year-old boy, John Wesley, a stocky child with glasses, said, "If you don't want to go to Florida, why dontcha stay at home?" He and the little girl, June Star, were reading the funny papers on the floor.

"She wouldn't stay at home to be queen for a day," June Star said without raising her yellow head.

"Yes, and what would you do if this fellow, The Misfit, caught you?" the grandmother asked.

"I'd smack his face," John Wesley said.

"She wouldn't stay at home for a million bucks," June Star said. "Afraid she'd miss something. She has to go everywhere we go."

"All right, miss," the grandmother said. "Just remember that the next time you want me to curl your hair."

June Star said her hair was naturally curly.

The next morning the grandmother was the first one in the car, ready to go. She had her big black valise that looked like the head of a hippopotamus in one corner, and underneath it she was hiding a basket with Pitty Sing, the cat, in it. She didn't intend for the cat to be left alone in the house for three days because he would miss her too much and she was afraid he might brush against one of the gas burners and accidentally asphyxiate himself. Her son, Bailey, didn't like to arrive at a motel with a cat.

She sat in the middle of the back seat with John Wesley and June Star on either side of her. Bailey and the children's mother and the baby sat in front and they left Atlanta at eight forty-five with the mileage on the car at 55890. The grandmother wrote this down because she thought it would be interesting to say how many miles they had been when they got back. It took them twenty minutes to reach the outskirts of the city.

The old lady settled herself comfortably, removing her white cotton gloves and putting them up with her purse on the shelf in front of the back window. The children's mother still had on slacks and still had her head tied up in a green kerchief, but the grandmother had on a navy blue straw sailor hat with a bunch of white violets on the brim and a navy blue dress with a small white dot in the print. Her collars and cuffs were white organdy trimmed with lace and at her neckline she had pinned a purple spray of cloth violets containing a sachet. In case of an accident, anyone seeing her dead on the highway would know at once that she was a lady.

She said she thought it was going to be a good day for driving, neither too hot nor too cold, and she cautioned Bailey that the speed limit was fifty-five miles an hour and that the patrolmen hid themselves behind billboards and small clumps of trees and sped out after you before you had a chance to slow down. She pointed out interesting details of the scenery: Stone Mountain; the blue granite that in some places came up to both sides of the highway; the brilliant red clay banks slightly streaked with purple; and the various crops that made rows of green lacework on the ground. The trees were full of silver-white sunlight and the meanest of them sparkled. The children were reading comic magazines and their mother had gone back to sleep.

"Let's go through Georgia fast so we won't have to look at it much," John Wesley said.

"If I were a little boy," said the grandmother, "I wouldn't talk about my native state that way. Tennessee has the mountains and Georgia has the hills."

"Tennessee is just a hillbilly dumping ground," John Wesley said, "and Georgia is a lousy state too."

"You said it," June Star said.

"In my time," said the grandmother, folding her thin veined fingers, "children were more respectful of their native states and their parents and everything else. People did right then. Oh look at the cute little pickaninny!" she said and pointed to a Negro child standing in the door of a shack. "Wouldn't that make a picture, now?" she asked and they all turned and looked at the little Negro out of the back window. He waved.

"He didn't have any britches on," June Star said.

"He probably didn't have any," the grandmother explained. "Little niggers in the country don't have things like we do. If I could paint, I'd paint that picture," she said.

The children exchanged comic books.

The grandmother offered to hold the baby and the children's mother passed him over the front seat to her. She set him on her knee and bounced him and told him about the things they were passing. She rolled her eyes and screwed up her mouth and stuck her leathery thin face into his smooth bland one. Occasionally he gave her a faraway smile. They passed a large cotton field with five or six graves fenced in the middle of it, like a small island. "Look at the graveyard!" the grandmother said, pointing it out. "That was the old family burying ground. That belonged to the plantation."

"Where's the plantation?" John Wesley asked.

"Gone with the Wind," said the grandmother. "Ha. Ha."

When the children finished all the comic books they had brought, they opened the lunch and ate it. The grandmother ate a peanut butter sandwich and an olive and would not let the children throw the box and the paper napkins out the window. When there was nothing else to do they played a game by choosing a cloud and making the other two guess what shape it suggested. John Wesley took one the shape of a cow and June Star guessed a cow and John Wesley said, no, an automobile, and June Star said he didn't play fair, and they began to slap each other over the grandmother.

The grandmother said she would tell them a story if they would keep quiet. When she told a story, she rolled her eyes and waved her head and was very dramatic. She said once when she was a maiden lady she had been courted by a Mr. Edgar Atkins Teagarden from Jasper, Georgia. She said he was a very good-looking man and a gentleman and that he brought her a watermelon every Saturday afternoon with his initials cut in it, E. A. T. Well, one Saturday, she said, Mr. Teagarden brought the watermelon and there was nobody at home and he left it on the front porch and returned in his buggy to Jasper, but she never got the watermelon, she said, because a nigger boy ate it when he saw the initials, E. A. T.! This story tickled John Wesley's funny bone and he giggled and giggled but June Star didn't think it was any good. She said she wouldn't marry a man that just brought her a watermelon on Saturday. The grandmother said she would have done well to marry Mr. Teagarden because he was a gentleman and had bought Coca-Cola stock when it first came out and that he had died only a few years ago, a very wealthy man.

They stopped at The Tower for barbecued sandwiches. The Tower was a part stucco and part wood filling station and dance hall set in a clearing outside of Timothy. A fat man named Red Sammy Butts ran it and there were signs stuck here and there on the building and for miles up and down the highway saying, TRY RED SAMMY'S FAMOUS BARBECUE. NONE LIKE FAMOUS RED SAMMY'S! RED SAM! THE FAT BOY WITH THE HAPPY LAUGH. A VETERAN! RED SAMMY'S YOUR MAN!

Red Sammy was lying on the bare ground outside The Tower with his head under a truck while a gray monkey about a foot high, chained to a small chinaberry tree, chattered nearby. The monkey sprang back into the tree and got on the highest limb as soon as he saw the children jump out of the car and run toward him.

Inside, The Tower was a long dark room with a counter at one end and tables at the other and dancing space in the middle. They all sat down at a board table next to the nickelodeon and Red Sam's wife, a tall burnt-brown woman with hair and eyes lighter than her skin, came and took their order. The children's mother put a dime in the machine and played "The Tennessee Waltz," and the grandmother said that tune always made her want to dance. She asked Bailey if he would like to dance but he only glared at her. He didn't have a naturally sunny disposition like she did and trips made him nervous. The grandmother's brown eyes were very bright. She swayed her head from side to side and pretended she was dancing in her chair. June Star said play something she could tap to so the children's mother put in another dime and played a fast number and June Star stepped out onto the dance floor and did her tap routine.

"Ain't she cute?" Red Sam's wife said, leaning over the counter. "Would you like to come be my little girl?"

"No I certainly wouldn't," June Star said. "I wouldn't live in a broken-down place like this for a million bucks!" and she ran back to the table.

"Ain't she cute?" the woman repeated, stretching her mouth politely.

"Aren't you ashamed?" hissed the grandmother.

Red Same came in and told his wife to quit lounging on the counter and hurry up with these people's order. His khaki trousers reached just to his hip bones and his stomach hung over them like a sack of meal swaying under his shirt. He came over and sat down at a table nearby and let out a combination sigh and yodel. "You can't win," he said. "You can't win," and he wiped his sweating red face off with a gray handkerchief. "These days you don't know who to trust," he said. "Ain't that the truth?"

"People are certainly not nice like they used to be," said the grandmother.

"Two fellers come in here last week," Red Sammy said, "driving a Chrysler. It was a old beat-up car but it was a good one and these boys looked all right to me. Said they worked at the mill and you know I let them fellers charge the gas they bought? Now why did I do that?"

"Because you're a good man!" the grandmother said at once.

"Yes'm, I suppose so," Red Sam said as if he were struck with this answer.

His wife brought the orders, carrying the five plates all at once without a tray, two in each hand and one balanced on her arm. "It isn't a soul in this green world of God's that you can trust," she said. "And I don't count nobody out of that, not nobody," she repeated, looking at Red Sammy.

"Did you read about that criminal, The Misfit, that's escaped?" asked the grandmother.

"I wouldn't be a bit surprised if he didn't attack this place right here," said the woman. "If he hears about it being here, I wouldn't be none surprised to see him. If he hears it's two cent in the cash register, I wouldn't be at all surprised if he. . . ."

"That'll do," Red Sam said. "Go bring these people their Co'-Colas," and the woman went off to get the rest of the order.

"A good man is hard to find," Red Sammy said. "Everything is getting terrible. I remember the day you could go off and leave your screen door unlatched. Not no more."

He and the grandmother discussed better times. The old lady said that in her opinion Europe was entirely to blame for the way things were now. She said the way Europe acted you would think we were made of money and Red Sam said it was no use talking about it, she was exactly right. The children ran outside into the white sunlight and looked at the monkey in the lacy chinaberry tree. He was busy catching fleas on himself and biting each one carefully between his teeth as if it were a delicacy.

They drove off again into the hot afternoon. The grandmother took cat naps and woke up every few minutes with her own snoring. Outside of Toombsboro she woke up and recalled an old plantation that she had visited in this neighborhood once when she was a young lady. She said the house had six white columns across the front and that there was an avenue of oaks leading up to it and two little wooden trellis arbors on either side in front where you sat down with your suitor after a stroll in the garden. She recalled exactly which road to turn off to get to it. She knew that Bailey would not be willing to lose any time looking at an old house, but the more she talked about it, the more she wanted to see it once again and find out if the little twin arbors were still standing. "There was a secret panel in this house," she said craftily, not telling the truth but wishing that she were, "and the story went that all the family silver was hidden in it when Sherman came through but it was never found. . . ."

"Hey!" John Wesley said. "Let's go see it! We'll find it! We'll poke all the woodwork and find it! Who lives there? Where do you turn off at? Hey Pop, can't we turn off there?"

"We never have seen a house with a secret panel!" June Star shrieked. "Let's go to the house with the secret panel! Hey Pop, can't we go see the house with the secret panel!"

"It's not far from here, I know," the grandmother said. "It wouldn't take over twenty minutes."

Bailey was looking straight ahead. His jaw was as rigid as a horseshoe. "No," he said.

The children began to yell and scream that they wanted to see the house with the secret panel. John Wesley kicked the back of the front seat and June Star hung over her mother's shoulder and whined desperately into her ear that they never had any fun even on their vacation, that they could never do what THEY wanted to do. The baby began to scream and John Wesley kicked the back of the seat so hard that his father could feel the blows in his kidney.

"All right!" he shouted and drew the car to a stop at the side of the road. "Will you all shut up? Will you all just shut up for one second? If you don't shut up, we won't go anywhere."

"It would be very educational for them," the grandmother murmured.

"All right," Bailey said, "but get this: this is the only time we're going to stop for anything like this. This is the one and only time."

"The dirt road that you have to turn down is about a mile back," the grandmother directed. "I marked it when we passed."

"A dirt road," Bailey groaned.

After they had turned around and were headed toward the dirt road, the grandmother recalled other points about the house, the beautiful glass over the front doorway and the candle-lamp in the hall. John Wesley said that the secret panel was probably in the fireplace.

"You can't go inside this house," Bailey said. "You don't know who lives there."

"While you all talk to the people in front, I'll run around behind and get in a window," John Wesley suggested.

"We'll all stay in the car," his mother said.

They turned onto the dirt road and the car raced roughly along in a swirl of pink dust. The grandmother recalled the times when there were no paved roads and thirty miles was a day's journey. The dirt road was hilly and there were sudden washes in it and sharp curves on dangerous embankments. All at once they would be on a hill, looking down over the blue tops of trees for miles around, then the next minute, they would be in a red depression with the dust-coated trees looking down on them.

"This place had better turn up in a minute," Bailey said, "or I'm going to turn around."

The road looked as if no one had traveled on it in months.

"It's not much farther," the grandmother said and just as she said it, a horrible thought came to her. The thought was so embarrassing that she turned red in the face and her eyes dilated and her feet jumped up, upsetting her valise in the corner. The instant the valise moved, the newspaper top she had over the basket under it rose with a snarl and Pitty Sing, the cat, sprang onto Bailey's shoulder.

The children were thrown to the floor and their mother, clutching the baby, was thrown out the door onto the ground; the old lady was thrown into the front seat. The car turned over once and landed right-side-up in a gulch off the side of the road. Bailey remained in the driver's seat with the cat—gray-striped with a broad white face and an orange nose—clinging to his neck like a caterpillar.

As soon as the children saw they could move their arms and legs, they scrambled out of the car, shouting, "We've had an ACCIDENT!" The grandmother was curled up under the dashboard, hoping she was injured so that Bailey's wrath would not come down on her all at once. The horrible thought she had had before the accident was that the house she had remembered so vividly was not in Georgia but in Tennessee.

Bailey removed the cat from his neck with both hands and flung it out the window against the side of a pine tree. Then he got out of the car and started looking for the children's mother. She was sitting against the side of the red gutted ditch, holding the screaming baby, but she only had a cut down her face and a broken shoulder. "We've had an ACCIDENT!" the children screamed in a frenzy of delight.

"But nobody's killed," June Star said with disappointment as the grandmother limped out of the car, her hat still pinned to her head but the broken front brim standing up at a jaunty angle and the violet spray hanging off the side. They all sat down in the ditch, except the children, to recover from the shock. They were all shaking.

"Maybe a car will come along," said the children's mother hoarsely.

"I believe I have an injured organ," said the grandmother, pressing her side, but no one answered her. Bailey's teeth were clattering. He had on a yellow sport shirt with bright blue parrots designed on it and his face was as yellow as the shirt. The grandmother decided that she would not mention that the house was in Tennessee.

The road was about ten feet above and they could see only the tops of the trees on the other side of it. Behind the ditch they were sitting in there were more woods, tall and dark and deep. In a few minutes they saw a car some distance away on top of a hill, coming slowly as if the occupants were watching them. The grandmother stood up and waved both arms dramatically to attract their attention. The car continued to come on slowly, disappeared around a bend and appeared again, moving even slower, on top of the hill they had gone over. It was a big black battered hearselike automobile. There were three men in it.

It came to a stop just over them and for some minutes, the driver looked down with a steady expressionless gaze to where they were sitting, and didn't speak. Then he turned his head and muttered something to the other two and they got out. One was a fat boy in black trousers and a red sweat shirt with a silver stallion embossed on the front of it. He moved around on the right side of them and stood staring, his mouth partly open in a kind of loose grin. The other had on khaki pants and a blue striped coat and a gray hat pulled down very low, hiding most of his face. He came around slowly on the left side. Neither spoke.

The driver got out of the car and stood by the side of it, looking down at them. He was an older man than the other two. His hair was just beginning to gray and he wore silver-rimmed spectacles that gave him a scholarly look. He had a long creased face and didn't have on any shirt or undershirt. He had on blue jeans that were too tight for him and was holding a black hat and a gun. The two boys also had guns. "We've had an ACCIDENT!" the children screamed.

The grandmother had the peculiar feeling that the bespectacled man was someone she knew. His face was as familiar to her as if she had known him all her life but she could not recall who he was. He moved away from the car and began to come down the embankment, placing his feet carefully so that he wouldn't slip. He had on tan and white shoes and no socks, and his ankles were red and thin. "Good afternoon," he said. "I see you all had you a little spill."

"We turned over twice!" said the grandmother.

"Oncet," he corrected. "We seen it happen. Try their car and see will it run, Hiram," he said quietly to the boy with the gray hat.

"What you got that gun for?" John Wesley asked. "Whatcha gonna do with that gun?"

"Lady," the man said to the children's mother, "would you mind calling them children to sit down by you? Children make me nervous. I want all you to sit down right together there where you're at."

"What are you telling US what to do for?" June Star asked.

Behind them the line of woods gaped like a dark open mouth. "Come here," said their mother.

"Look here now," Bailey began suddenly, "we're in a predicament! We're in . . ."

The grandmother shrieked. She scrambled to her feet and stood staring. "You're The Misfit!" she said. "I recognized you at once!"

"Yes'm," the man said, smiling slightly as if he were pleased in spite of himself to be known, "but it would have been better for all of you, lady, if you hadn't of reckernized me."

Bailey turned his head sharply and said something to his mother that shocked even the children. The old lady began to cry and The Misfit reddened.

"Lady," he said, "don't you get upset. Sometimes a man says things he don't mean. I don't reckon he meant to talk to you thataway."

"You wouldn't shoot a lady, would you?" the grandmother said and removed the clean handkerchief from her cuff and began to slap at her eyes with it.

The Misfit pointed the toe of his shoe into the ground and made a little hole and then covered it up again. "I would hate to have to," he said.

"Listen," the grandmother almost screamed, "I know you're a good man. You don't look a bit like you have common blood. I know you must come from nice people!"

"Yes mam," he said, "finest people in the world." When he smiled he showed a row of strong white teeth. "God never made a finer woman than my mother and my daddy's heart was pure gold," he said. The boy with the red sweat shirt had come around behind them and was standing with his gun at his hip. The Misfit squatted down on the ground. "Watch them children, Bobby Lee," he said. "You know they make me nervous." He looked at the six of them huddled together in front of him and he seemed to be embarrassed as if he couldn't think of anything to say. "Ain't a cloud in the sky," he remarked, looking up at it. "Don't see no sun but don't see no cloud neither."

"Yes, it's a beautiful day," said the grandmother. "Listen," she said, "you shouldn't call yourself The Misfit because I know you're a good man at heart. I can just look at you and tell."

"Hush!" Bailey yelled. "Hush! Everybody shut up and let me handle this!" He was squatting in the position of a runner about to sprint forward but he didn't move.

"I pre-chate that, lady," The Misfit said and drew a little circle in the ground with the butt of his gun.

"It'll take a half a hour to fix this here car," Hiram called, looking over the raised hood of it.

"Well, first you and Bobby Lee get him and that little boy to step over yonder with you," The Misfit said, pointing to Bailey and John Wesley. "The boys want to ask you something," he said to Bailey. "Would you mind stepping back in them woods there with them?"

"Listen," Bailey began, "we're in a terrible predicament! Nobody realizes what this is," and his voice cracked. His eyes were as blue and intense as the parrots on his shirt and he remained perfectly still.

The grandmother reached up to adjust her hat brim as if she were going to the woods with him but it came off in her hand. She stood staring at it and after a second she let it fall on the ground. Hiram pulled Bailey up by the arm as if he were assisting an old man. John Wesley caught hold of his father's hand and Bobby Lee followed. They went off toward the woods and just as they reached the dark edge, Bailey turned and supported himself against a gray naked pine trunk, he shouted, "I'll be back in a minute, Mamma, wait on me!"

"Come back this instant!" his mother shrilled but they all disappeared into the woods.

"Bailey Boy!" the grandmother called in a tragic voice but she found she was looking at The Misfit squatting on the ground in front of her. "I just know you're a good man," she said desperately. "You're not a bit common!"

"Nome, I ain't a good man," The Misfit said after a second as if he had considered her statement carefully, "but I ain't the worst in the world neither. My daddy said I was a different breed of dog from my brothers and sisters. 'You know,' Daddy said, 'it's some that can live their whole life out without asking about it and it's others has to know why it is, and this boy is one of the latters. He's going to be into everything!' " He put on his black hat and looked up suddenly and then away deep into the woods as if he were embarrassed again. "I'm sorry I don't have on a shirt before you ladies," he said, hunching his shoulders slightly, "We buried our clothes that we had on when we escaped and we're just making do until we can get better. We borrowed these from some folks we met," he explained.

"That's perfectly all right," the grandmother said. "Maybe Bailey has an extra shirt in his suitcase."

"I'll look and see terrectly," The Misfit said.

"Where are they taking him?" the children's mother screamed.

"Daddy was a card himself," The Misfit said. "You couldn't put anything over on him. He never got in trouble with the authorities though. Just had the knack of handling them."

"You could be honest too if you'd only try," said the grandmother. "Think how wonderful it would be to settle down and live a comfortable life and not have to think about somebody chasing you all the time."

The Misfit kept scratching in the ground with the butt of his gun as if he were thinking about it. "Yes'm, somebody is always after you," he murmured.

The grandmother noticed how thin his shoulder blades were just behind his hat because she was standing up looking down on him. "Do you ever pray?" she asked.

He shook his head. All she saw was the black hat wiggle between his shoulder blades. "Nome," he said.

There was a pistol shot from the woods, followed closely by another. Then silence. The old lady's head jerked around. She could hear the wind move through the tree tops like a long satisfied insuck of breath. "Bailey Boy!" she called.

"I was a gospel singer for a while," The Misfit said. "I been most everything. Been in the arm service, both land and sea, at home and abroad, been twict married, been an undertaker, been with the railroads, plowed Mother Earth, been in a tornado, see a man burnt alive oncet," and he looked up at the children's mother and the little girl who were sitting close together, their faces white and their eyes glassy; "I even seen a woman flogged," he said.

"Pray, pray," the grandmother began, "pray, pray. . . ."

"I never was a bad boy that I remember of," The Misfit said in an almost dreamy voice, "but somewheres along the line I done something wrong and got sent to the penitentiary. I was buried alive," and he looked up and held her attention to him by a steady stare.

"That's when you should have started to pray," she said. "What did you do to get sent to the penitentiary that first time?"

"Turn to the right, it was a wall," The Misfit said, looking up again at the cloudless sky. "Turn to the left, it was a wall. Look up it was a ceiling, look down it was a floor. I forget what I done, lady. I set there and set there, trying to remember what it was I done and I ain't recalled it to this day. Oncet in a while, I would think it was coming to me, but it never come."

"Maybe they put you in by mistake," the old lady said vaguely.

"Nome," he said. "It wasn't no mistake. They had the papers on me."

"You must have stolen something," she said.

The Misfit sneered slightly. "Nobody had nothing I wanted," he said. "It was a head-doctor at the penitentiary said what I had done was kill my daddy but I known that for a lie. My daddy died in nineteen ought nineteen of the epidemic flu and I never had a thing to do with it. He was buried in the Mount Hopewell Baptist churchyard and you can go there and see for yourself."

"If you would pray," the old lady said, "Jesus would help you."

"That's right," The Misfit said.

"Well then, why don't you pray?" she asked trembling with delight suddenly.

"I don't want no hep," he said. "I'm doing all right by myself."

Bobby Lee and Hiram came ambling back from the woods. Bobby Lee was dragging a yellow shirt with bright blue parrots in it.

"Throw me that shirt, Bobby Lee," The Misfit said. The shirt came flying at him and landed on his shoulder and he put it on. The grandmother couldn't name what the shirt reminded her of. "No, lady," The Misfit said while he was buttoning it up, "I found out the crime don't matter. You can do one thing or you can do another, kill a man or take a tire off his car, because sooner or later you're going to forget what it was you done and just be punished for it."

The children's mother had begun to make heaving noises as if she couldn't get her breath. "Lady," he asked, "would you and that little girl like to step off yonder with Bobby Lee and Hiram and join your husband?"

"Yes, thank you," the mother said faintly. Her left arm dangled helplessly and she was holding the baby, who had gone to sleep, in the other. "Hep that lady up, Hiram," The Misfit said as she struggled to climb out of the ditch, "and Bobby Lee, you hold onto that little girl's hand."

"I don't want to hold hands with him," June Star said. "He reminds me of a pig."

The fat boy blushed and laughed and caught her by the arm and pulled her off into the woods after Hiram and her mother.

Alone with The Misfit, the grandmother found that she had lost her voice. There was not a cloud in the sky nor any sun. There was nothing around her but woods. She wanted to tell him that he must pray. She opened and closed her mouth several times before anything came out. Finally she found herself saying, "Jesus, Jesus," meaning, Jesus will help you, but the way she was saying it, it sounded as if she might be cursing.

"Yes'm," The Misfit said as if he agreed. "Jesus thown everything off balance. It was the same case with Him as with me except He hadn't committed any crime and they could prove I had committed one because they had the papers on me. Of course," he said, "they never shown me my papers. That's why I sign myself now. I said long ago, you get you a signature and sign everything you do and keep a copy of it. Then you'll know what you done and you can hold up the crime to the punishment and see do they match and in the end you'll have something to prove you ain't been treated right. I call myself The Misfit," he said, "because I can't make what all I done wrong fit what all I gone through in punishment."

There was a piercing scream from the woods, followed closely by a pistol report. "Does it seem right to you, lady, that one is punished a heap and another ain't punished at all?"

"Jesus!" the old lady cried. "You've got good blood! I know you wouldn't shoot a lady! I know you come from nice people! Pray! Jesus, you ought not to shoot a lady. I'll give you all the money I've got!"

"Lady," The Misfit said, looking beyond her far into the woods, "there never was a body that give the undertaker a tip."

There were two more pistol reports and the grandmother raised her head like a parched old turkey hen crying for water and called, "Bailey Boy, Bailey Boy!" as if her heart would break.

"Jesus was the only One that ever raised the dead," The Misfit continued, "and He shouldn't have done it. He thown everything off balance. If He did what He said, then it's nothing for you to do but throw away everything and follow Him, and if He didn't, then it's nothing for you to do but enjoy the few minutes you got left the best way you can—by killing somebody or burning down his house or doing some other meanness to him. No pleasure but meanness," he said and his voice had become almost a snarl.

"Maybe He didn't raise the dead," the old lady mumbled, not knowing what she was saying and feeling so dizzy that she sank down in the ditch with her legs twisted under her.

"I wasn't there so I can't say He didn't," The Misfit said. "I wisht I had of been there," he said, hitting the ground with his fist. "It ain't right I wasn't there because if I had of been there I would of known. Listen lady," he said in a high voice, "if I had of been there I would of known and I wouldn't be like I am now." His voice seemed about to crack and the grandmother's head cleared for an instant. She saw the man's face twisted close to her own as if he were going to cry and she murmured, "Why you're one of my babies. You're one of my own children!" She reached out and touched him on the shoulder. The Misfit sprang back as if a snake had bitten him and shot her three times through the chest. Then he put his gun down on the ground and took off his glasses and began to clean them.

Hiram and Bobby Lee returned from the woods and stood over the ditch, looking down at the grandmother who half sat and half lay in a puddle of blood with her legs crossed under her like a child's and her face smiling up at the cloudless sky.

Without his glasses, The Misfit's eyes were red-rimmed and pale and defenseless-looking. "Take her off and thow her where you thown the others," he said, picking up the cat that was rubbing itself against his leg.

"She was a talker, wasn't she?" Bobby Lee said, sliding down the ditch with a yodel.

"She would of been a good woman," The Misfit said, "if it had been somebody there to shoot her every minute of her life."

"Some fun!" Bobby Lee said.

"Shut up, Bobby Lee," The Misfit said. "It's no real pleasure in life."

Thematic Tragedy

The analogy between narrative and thematic patterns is particularly close in tragedy. Because the narrative action ends in recognition, an act of understanding that replaces the spent emotions of the hero, we might expect to find many analogous themes in lyric poetry. And so it turns out: a central cluster of pastoral elegies surrounded by a galaxy of poems about death, time, love, fame, and immortality—the recurring subjects of much serious poetry. But it is misleading at the outset to identify "subject" with "theme," for subjects like love have elicited many themes throughout literary history that can more properly be described as romantic or comic or ironic. A tragic treatment of love in lyric poetry balances conflicting ideas and attitudes rather than a hero's acts and the consequences he must suffer. Action is implied rather than performed, and ideas that have been implicit as the meaning of action become the center of attention. Just as we have been speaking of the "shape" of an action in talking about narrative tragedy, we must now think of themes as "forces" in precarious equilibrium.

Recognition is the natural bridge between tragic narratives and tragic lyrics. As the hero's power to act decreases in narrative tragedy, his knowledge increases (or ours does). Thus recognition is the residue of lost physical power; the price of wisdom may be impotence. The transformation of suffering into understanding is one structuring principle of the classical elegy. The speaker must reconcile the fact of wasteful death with conceptions of human purpose and cosmic order. When Milton mourns for Edward King in "Lycidas" and Shelley for Keats in "Adonais," they assume the role of interpreters who "encroach" on the irrational, trying to contain it within the terms of human thought (just as Oedipus took on the far simpler task of solving the Sphinx's riddle). Their public stance, like that of the hero in narrative tragedy, is representative—the poet as spokesman for all mankind—and their tone is alternately one of protest and one of acceptance. Protest dominates in William Butler Yeats' "Easter 1916" and acceptance in Gerard Manley Hopkins' "Wreck of the

Loss and Reconciliation

Deutschland," but some opposition between the two attitudes is an impetus and a source of tension in both poems.

The event implied by most elegies is that of a remote death, off-stage, which must be accommodated to the more immediate scene within the imagination of the poet. Here painful experience can be distanced and transmuted through images of order, clarity, and proportion. In traditional elegies the harshness of grief is mollified by placing both the poet and his subject in an idyllic pastoral scene. Such elegies usually move rather quickly from concrete description of the dead person to myth. Thus for Milton the real Edward King becomes the impersonal Lycidas of pastoral convention, who is in turn associated with Christian and classical archetypes, Saint Peter and Orpheus, priest and poet. Similarly, for Shelley the real Keats, supposedly "killed" by harsh reviews of his work, becomes Adonais, a new embodiment of the mythical Adonis.

Other conventions of scene support the elegiac poet's movement toward reconciliation. The regular cycles of nature—sunset and sunrise, autumn and spring, salt sea and pure fountain—are an important source of meaning in both "Lycidas" and "Adonais." Images suggesting death and decay are enclosed within a context of recurrence and rejuvenation. The whole of Walt Whitman's "When Lilacs Last in the Dooryard Bloom'd" is dominated by three fully developed nature images—the blooming of lilacs, the setting of the evening star, and the song of the thrush—that surround the realistic vision of Abraham Lincoln's steadily moving funeral cortege. The listing of lives destroyed by the rebellion in Yeats' "Easter 1916" is punctuated by the refrain, "a terrible beauty is born," and the third stanza opposes the refrain by contrasting the stonelike "terrible beauty" with unceasing movement and transformation in nature.

The tendency to look to nature for comfort against death is characteristic of the elegy. The persona reconciles himself to the loss of a friend by placing that loss within some larger context of continuing life. In "Lycidas," the argument that accounts for King's premature death concludes with a double transfiguration: the young priest (associated with Saint Peter) mounts to heaven and the young poet (associated with Orpheus) becomes, metaphorically, the "genius of the shore," thus assuring the immortality of both his person and his fame. In "Adonais," a rhythm of alternating hope and despair culminates in a vision of Keats' influence throughout the world. And the tall nun in Hopkins' "Wreck of the Deutschland" is marked by the favor of God in the midst of the storm. In these elegies, the resolution reminds us of narrative tragedy. Just as a figure representing order arises in narrative tragedy to reconstitute society after the carnage, so the mourned dead in thematic tragedy are transformed into continuing presences or associated with undying gods. The conflict between an encroaching protagonist and the laws of his world reappears in thematic tragedy as the tension between individual mortality and cyclical regeneration in nature. Like the leader whose struggles represent our own in narrative tragedy, the persona of the traditional elegy speaks for us in trying to reconcile the meaning of existence with the fact of death.

As we move from the norm, represented by the elegy, toward the romantic phase, the persona's role and stance change significantly. The persona is speaking more for himself than for the world at large, and he is frequently addressing one person *in* the poem rather than all mankind. With this narrower audience there is a shift of interest: the poet is less concerned about justifying the course of destiny than about establishing the worth of a single personality, usually his own or that of his mistress. Signs of this interest also appear in the opening and closing stanzas of "Lycidas," where Milton speaks of the poem he is writing as a stage in his career. Normally, the persona seeks some form of immortality, actual or metaphorical, through public fame or private remembrance. Thus the final couplet in many of Shakespeare's sonnets argues that a mistress will not perish as long as the poem in which she is praised survives, and the speaker in Thomas Gray's "Elegy Written in a Country Churchyard" is wistfully preoccupied with inventing ways in which ordinary men should or might be remembered. A variation of the same interest appears in John Donne's "Valediction: Forbidding Mourning." By using a clever rhetorical stratagem, the persona first exaggerates the parting of lovers by treating it as a death within elegiac conventions, then, with this preparation behind him, further ennobles the commonplace through the claim that spiritual lovers endure "not yet / A breach, but an expansion, / Like gold to airy thinness beat."

Decay and indifference, the processes of time and of human forgetfulness, dominate poems of this phase. Like the innocent hero of James' "Pupil" or Lawrence's "Prussian Officer," the persona cannot adjust to reality. He has trouble accepting the death of a friend, the loss of a mistress, the aging of his own body, or most of all the fear that he may be forgotten when dead. Thomas Nashe bids farewell to "earth's bliss" only because he is quite sure of going to an even better place, and Shakespeare, after twelve lines of unallayed grief (in Sonnet 30), must find solace in the fragile "but if the while I think on thee . . . all losses are restored." The persona of W. H. Auden's "In Memory of W. B. Yeats" quite appropriately convinces himself that poets recede into their own words when their bodies are gone. Just as the hero of the romantic phase in narrative tragedy preserves his innocence or dignity by dying before he can be mutilated, so the persona assures himself that human personality matters.

No comparable hope redeems loss in the ironic phase of thematic tragedy. The persona has lost faith in fame and love as ways of surmounting death, so he is more likely to be preoccupied with the destruction of beauty or

The Search for Immortality

Submission to Impersonal Law

innocence per se. As compared to the persona of the tragic norm, his role and stance remain nearly constant—he is still trying to find a general justification for death—but his tone changes radically. The waste of human potentiality usually seems irremediable, although there are subtle differences among these poems. In mourning the death of his son, Ben Jonson overtly professes belief in Christian immortality, but he still manages to be plaintive in thinking his son better off for early deliverance from the evils of this world. Even less comforting are the visions of William Wordsworth's dead Lucy, "Rolled round in earth's diurnal course, / With rocks, and stones, and trees," and Dylan Thomas' anonymous child killed in a London air raid, now buried, "Robed in the long friends / The grains beyond age, the dark veins of her mother." Wordsworth's pantheism and Thomas' eloquent "refusal" to mourn cannot palliate the fact that these children have lost all semblance of human identity. In X. J. Kennedy's "Little Elegy," also about the death of a little girl, the tone becomes openly petulant—"and for her sake, trip up Death"—and the vision of the world—"the whirring edge of night"—is menacing. In such poems images of force and motion tend to dominate a tragic scene that overwhelms human personality, like the circumstances that prove too much for the trapped family in O'Connor's "A Good Man Is Hard to Find." Yet the poet finds a remnant of order, if only in the process of conceptualizing destruction. Impersonal forces and natural laws, by the regularity of their operation, provide a vision of a world not totally chaotic.

Tragic Transcendence: "In Memory of W. B. Yeats"

Some form of transcendence occurs in each of the thematic patterns. The comic poet transcends time momentarily by celebrating the simple but evanescent joys of life, and even the ironic poet gets beyond the state of being paralyzed in an inhospitable world when he is able to form a conception of it. The movements of transcendence in thematic romance and tragedy are more closely allied. In both, the persona leaps farther; there is greater distance between the concrete particulars of experience and the abstract ideas that he uses to make sense of them, and there seems to be a stronger impulse to generalize those ideas by associating them with divine beings or the course of history. The essential contrast with romance lies in the tragic poet's refusal to abandon the experience of this world for realms of higher and more satisfying order. He stops short of transfiguration because he balances the perfect world he can imagine against his sense of the real world as it is. His resting point is durable wisdom rather than vision or dream. Because thematic tragedy moves toward the reconciliation of desirable and undesirable worlds, it is likely to include strong romantic and ironic tendencies. W. H. Auden's "In Memory of W. B. Yeats" contains both.

W. H. AUDEN
b. 1907

In Memory of W. B. Yeats

(d. Jan. 1939)

1

He disappeared in the dead of winter:
The brooks were frozen, the airports almost
    deserted,
And snow disfigured the public statues;
The mercury sank in the mouth of the dying day.
O all the instruments agree   5
The day of his death was a dark cold day.

Far from his illness
The wolves ran on through the evergreen forests,
The peasant river was untempted by the fashionable
    quays;
By mourning tongues   10
The death of the poet was kept from his poems.

But for him it was his last afternoon as himself,
An afternoon of nurses and rumors;
The provinces of his body revolted,
The squares of his mind were empty,   15
Silence invaded the suburbs,
The current of his feeling failed: he became his
    admirers.

Now he is scattered among a hundred cities
And wholly given over to unfamiliar affections;
To find his happiness in another kind of wood   20
And be punished under a foreign code of con-
    science.
The words of a dead man
Are modified in the guts of the living.

But in the importance and noise of tomorrow
When the brokers are roaring like beasts on the
    floor of the Bourse,°   25
And the poor have the sufferings to which they are
    fairly accustomed,
And each in the cell of himself is almost convinced
    of his freedom;
A few thousand will think of this day

As one thinks of a day when one did something
    slightly unusual.
O all the instruments agree   30
The day of his death was a dark cold day.

2

You were silly like us: your gift survived it all;
The parish of rich women, physical decay,
Yourself; mad Ireland hurt you into poetry.
Now Ireland has her madness and her weather
    still,   35
For poetry makes nothing happen: it survives
In the valley of its saying where executives
Would never want to tamper; it flows south
From ranches of isolation and the busy griefs,
Raw towns that we believe and die in; it survives,
A way of happening, a mouth.   41

3

Earth, receive an honored guest;
William Yeats is laid to rest:
Let the Irish vessel lie
Emptied of its poetry.   45

Time that is intolerant
Of the brave and innocent,
And indifferent in a week
To a beautiful physique,

Worships language and forgives   50
Everyone by whom it lives;
Pardons cowardice, conceit,
Lays its honors at their feet.

Time that with this strange excuse
Pardoned Kipling and his views,°   55
And will pardon Paul Claudel,°
Pardons him for writing well.

In the nightmare of the dark
All the dogs of Europe bark,
And the living nations wait,   60
Each sequestered in its hate;

Intellectual disgrace
Stares from every human face,
And the seas of pity lie
Locked and frozen in each eye.   65

IN MEMORY OF W. B. YEATS. **25. Bourse:** French stock
exchange.

55. Kipling . . . views: allusion to Kipling's imperialism. **56.
Paul Claudel:** (1868–1955), French poet, politically far right.

Follow, poet, follow right
To the bottom of the night,
With your unconstraining voice
Still persuade us to rejoice;

With the farming of a verse   70
Make a vineyard of the curse,

Sing of human unsuccess
In a rapture of distress;

In the deserts of the heart
Let the healing fountain start,   75
In the prison of his days
Teach the free man how to praise.

The first section is largely ironic. The opening stanza sets the scene "in
the dead of winter" and piles up further images of sterility and inertness
in nature and society, ending with the speaker's obvious sarcasm as he
belittles the importance of human reason: "O all the instruments agree /
The day of his death was a dark cold day." The second stanza deepens the
irony by suggesting the insignificance of Yeats' death; the worlds of
nature and society go on much as before. This expansion of scene is
followed by a reduction to the hospital room, but the speaker does not
abandon the wider scene; death comes in the geographical metaphor of
"provinces," "squares," and "suburbs." The stanza ends with a suggestion
of poetic immortality—"he became his admirers"—but this conventional
notion that the poet lives on in his poems is not allowed to stand un-
qualified as it does in many of Shakespeare's sonnets. The whole of the
fourth stanza cuts it down as the images gradually become more ominous,
moving from "scattered" through "unfamiliar affections" to "punished
under a foreign code." This ironic movement recedes slightly as the closing
lines of the stanza reach equilibrium: "The words of a dead man" have
changed, but they are still *there*. Even this questionable form of immortality
is undercut by the sardonic tone of the last stanza in the section, with its
roaring beasts, its prison cell of self, and its talk of human life and death in
vapid terms like "something slightly unusual." The final stanza of the
section ends by repeating the impersonal closing lines of the first: "O all
the instruments agree / The day of his death was a dark cold day."

If the poem had ended at this point it would be clearly ironic, an attempt
at tragic resolution that failed. But the shorter second section moves
cautiously toward affirmation. The argument takes concessive form: even
though Ireland is mad, Yeats had many foibles, and poetry has no effect
on the world, "it survives." The "it" here is that part of the human spirit,
now generalized rather than specifically Yeats, that can be embodied in
poetry. The section closes with the reduction of poetry to "a mouth,"
reminding us of the first stanza where a mouth image was identified with
"the dying day." The speaker is groping toward transcendence of death,
but he has not yet arrived.

An abrupt shift of metrical form in the third section signals that arrival.
The long, colloquial lines of the first two sections are replaced by short
rhymed couplets in the ordered quatrains of an epitaph to Yeats. Images
of disorder still appear, especially in references to the chaos of the wider
scenes of the Spanish Civil War and the general disorder in Europe just

prior to the beginning of the Second World War. But the "barking dogs of Europe," the "intellectual disgrace," and the "frozen pity" are now contained and regulated by the form of the verse: "with the farming of a verse / Make a vineyard of the curse." The speaker now addresses the poet, whom he conceives as a teacher of mankind. Only the poet can fathom evil and "still persuade us to rejoice" through the magic of "an unconstraining voice." He has the magic of words, a power of creation that seemed to mean nothing at the beginning of the elegy. Thus the poet, although weak and mortal and perhaps mistaken like Kipling or Claudel, has a meaningful life because he can start the "healing fountain." He can teach men imprisoned in time and beset by evil "how to praise."

Auden's "unconstraining voice" of the poet "modified in the guts of the living" is emblematic of the tensions within tragedy. Like romance, tragedy seeks a vision at least partly compatible with human desires; like irony, it forms conceptions of human experience with all the intellectual rigor it can muster. These two impulses are locked together in the conflict of tragedy until they reach a state of equilibrium. In narrative tragedy, the hero begins with exorbitant desires and ends with a hard-earned understanding of his true place in the world. The persona of lyric poetry moves through the same cycle imaginatively, fusing hope and despair in the poise of a reconciliation. This rhythm repeats itself throughout literary history because it represents one of our most sustained efforts to connect thought and action in a world whose principles of order we never fully understand.

Loss and Reconciliation

JOHN MILTON
1608–1674

Lycidas

In this monody the author bewails a learned friend,° unfortunately drowned in his passage from Chester on the Irish Seas, 1637. And by occasion foretells the ruin of our corrupted clergy then in their height.

Yet once more, O ye laurels, and once more
Ye myrtles brown, with ivy° never sere,°
I come to pluck your berries harsh and crude,°
And with forced fingers rude,
Shatter your leaves before the mellowing year.°   5
Bitter constraint, and sad occasion dear,°
Compels me to disturb your season due:
For Lycidas is dead, dead ere his prime,
Young Lycidas, and hath not left his peer:
Who would not sing for Lycidas? he knew   10
Himself to sing, and build the lofty rhyme.
He must not float upon his watery bier
Unwept, and welter° to the parching wind,
Without the meed° of some melodious tear.
    Begin then, Sisters° of the sacred well,   15
That from beneath the seat of Jove doth spring,

Begin, and somewhat loudly sweep the string.°
Hence with denial vain, and coy excuse,
So may some gentle muse°
With lucky° words favor my destined urn,°   20
And as he passes turn,
And bid fair peace be to my sable shroud.
For° we were nursed upon the selfsame hill,
Fed the same flock, by fountain, shade, and rill.
    Together both, ere the high lawns appeared   25
Under the opening eyelids of the morn,
We drove afield, and both together heard
What time the gray-fly winds° her sultry horn,
Batt'ning° our flocks with the fresh dews of night,
Oft till the star that rose, at ev'ning, bright   30
Toward heav'n's descent° had sloped his westering
    wheel.
Meanwhile the rural ditties were not mute,
Tempered to th' oaten flute,
Rough satyrs danced, and fauns with clov'n heel
From the glad sound would not be absent long,   35
And old Damoetas° loved to hear our song.
    But O the heavy change, now thou art gone,
Now thou art gone, and never must return!
Thee shepherd, thee the woods, and desert caves,
With wild thyme and the gadding° vine o'ergrown,
And all their echoes mourn.   41
The willows, and the hazel copses green,
Shall now no more be seen,
Fanning their joyous leaves to thy soft lays.°
As killing as the canker to the rose,   45

LYCIDAS. **friend:** Edward King, a student with Milton at Christ's College, Cambridge, who was thought to have promise both as clergyman and poet. Lycidas is a traditional name used in pastoral poems. **1–2. laurels, myrtles, ivy:** evergreens sacred to Apollo, Venus, and Bacchus, respectively, which were traditionally used to crown poets. **2. sere:** dry, withered. **3. crude:** unripe. **5. before . . . year:** before the year has mellowed them. **6. dear:** costly. **13. welter:** toss. **14. meed:** reward. **15. Sisters:** Muses.

17. string: i.e., of a pastoral lyre. **19. muse:** poet. **20. lucky:** propitious. **urn:** burial urn. **23–36. For . . . song:** pastoral version of life at Cambridge. **28. winds:** blows. **29. Batt'n-ing:** feeding. **31. heav'n's descent:** i.e., the horizon. **36. Damoetas:** character in Virgil's third *Eclogue;* here probably an allusion to a tutor at Cambridge. **40. gadding:** straggling. **44. lays:** songs.

Or taint-worm to the weanling herds that graze,
Or frost to flowers, that their gay wardrobe wear,
When first the white-thorn blows;°
Such, Lycidas, thy loss to shepherd's ear.
    Where were ye nymphs° when the remorseless deep   50
Closed o'er the head of your loved Lycidas?
For° neither were ye playing on the steep,
Where your old bards, the famous Druids lie,
Nor on the shaggy top of Mona high,
Nor yet where Deva spreads her wizard° stream: 55
Ay me, I fondly° dream!
Had ye been there—for what could that have done?
What could the Muse herself that Orpheus bore,
The Muse herself, for her enchanting son
Whom universal nature did lament,   60
When by the rout that made the hideous roar,
His gory visage down the stream was sent,
Down the swift Hebrus to the Lesbian shore.°
    Alas! What boots° it with uncessant care
To tend the homely slighted shepherd's° trade, 65
And strictly meditate the thankless Muse,°
Were it not better done as others use,°
To sport with Amaryllis in the shade,
Or with the tangles of Neaera's° hair?°
Fame is the spur that the clear spirit doth raise 70
(That last infirmity of noble mind)
To scorn delights, and live laborious days;
But the fair guerdon° when we hope to find,
And think to burst out into sudden blaze,
Comes the blind Fury° with th' abhorrèd shears, 75
And slits the thin-spun life. But not the praise,
Phoebus° replied, and touched my trembling ears;
Fame is no plant that grows on mortal soil,
Nor in the glistering foil°
Set off to th' world, nor in broad rumor° lies, 80
But lives and spreads aloft by those pure eyes,
And perfect witness of all-judging Jove;

As he pronounces lastly on each deed,
Of so much fame in Heav'n expect thy meed.
    O Fountain Arethuse,° and thou honored flood,
Smooth-sliding Mincius,° crowned with vocal reeds,   86
That strain I heard was of a higher mood:
But now my oat° proceeds,
And listens to the herald of the sea°
That came in Neptune's plea.°   90
He asked the waves, and asked the felon winds,
What hard mishap hath doomed this gentle swain?
And questioned every gust of rugged wings
That blows from off each beakèd promontory;
They knew not of his story,   95
And sage Hippotades° their answer brings,
That not a blast was from his dungeon strayed,
The air was calm, and on the level brine,
Sleek Panope with all her sisters° played.
It was that fatal and perfidious bark   100
Built in th' eclipse, and rigged with curses dark,
That sunk so low that sacred head of thine.
    Next Camus,° reverend sire, went footing slow,
His mantle hairy, and his bonnet sedge,°
Inwrought with figures dim, and on the edge 105
Like to that sanguine flower inscribed with woe.°
"Ah! Who hath reft,"° quoth he, "my dearest pledge?"°
Last came, and last did go,
The pilot of the Galilean lake,
Two massy keys he bore of metals twain 110
(The golden opes, the iron shuts amain°).
He shook his mitered° locks, and stern bespake,
"How well could I have spared for thee young swain,
Enow of such as for their bellies' sake,
Creep and intrude, and climb into the fold! 115
Of other care they little reck'ning make,

---

48. blows: blooms. 50. nymphs: water deities. 52–55. For . . . stream: places on the Welsh coast of the Irish Sea, near the site of King's shipwreck. 55. wizard: prophetic (according to a legend about the Welsh river Dee). 56. fondly: foolishly. 58–63. the . . . shore: Calliope, Muse of epic poetry and mother of Orpheus, was unable to save her son from being torn to pieces by Thracian women celebrating the rites of Bacchus. 64. boots: benefits. 65. shepherd's: poet's. 66. And . . . Muse: study the art of poetry. 67. use: do. 68–69. Amaryllis, Neaera: pastoral shepherdesses. 73. guerdon: reward. 75. Fury: Atropos, the Fate who cut the threads of men's lives, after her two sisters had spun them. 77. Phoebus: Apollo, god of poetry. 79. glistering foil: setting for a gem. 80. rumor: reputation.

85–86. Arethuse, Mincius: fountain and river associated with the pastoral poets Theocritus and Virgil, respectively. 88. oat: pastoral pipe (i.e., song or poem). 89. herald of the sea: Triton. 90. plea: defense against the charge of drowning Lycidas. 96. Hippotades: Aeolus, god of the winds. 99. Panope . . . sisters: sea nymphs. 103. Camus: personification of the river Cam in Cambridge. 104. mantle . . . sedge: floating weeds and grass-lined banks. 106. sanguine . . . woe: the flower (not the one now called hyacinth) made by Apollo from the blood of Hyacinthus, whom he had killed accidentally; its petals were said to have markings resembling the Greek letters AI ("alas"). 107. reft: robbed. pledge: child. 109–11. pilot . . . amain: Saint Peter (formerly a fisherman), who holds the keys to heaven. 111. amain: powerfully. 112. mitered: with an ecclesiastical hat.

Than how to scramble at the shearers' feast,
And shove away the worthy bidden guest;
Blind mouths!° that scarce themselves know how to
    hold
A sheep-hook, or have learned aught else the
    least   120
That to the faithful herdsman's art belongs!
What recks it them?° What need they? They are
    sped;°
And when they list,° their lean and flashy songs°
Grate on their scrannel° pipes of wretched straw,
The hungry sheep look up, and are not fed,   125
But swoln with wind, and the rank mist° they draw,
Rot inwardly, and foul contagion spread:
Besides what the grim wolf with privy paw
Daily devours apace, and nothing said,
But that two-handed engine at the door,   130
Stands ready to smite once, and smite no more."°
    Return Alpheus,° the dread voice is past,
That shrunk thy streams; return Sicilian muse,°
And call the vales, and bid them hither cast
Their bells, and flowerets of a thousand hues.   135
Ye valleys low where the mild whispers use,°
Of shades and wanton winds, and gushing brooks,
On whose fresh lap the swart star° sparely looks,
Throw hither all your quaint enameled eyes,°
That on the green turf suck the honeyed showers,
And purple all the ground with vernal flowers.   141
Bring the rathe° primrose that forsaken dies,
The tufted crow-toe, and pale jessamine,
The white pink, and the pansy freaked° with jet,
The glowing violet,   145
The musk-rose, and the well-attired woodbine,
With cowslips wan that hang the pensive head,
And every flower that sad embroidery wears:
Bid amaranthus all his beauty shed,
And daffadillies fill their cups with tears,   150
To strew the laureate° hearse where Lycid lies.
For so to interpose a little ease,
Let our frail thoughts dally with false surmise.°

Ay me! Whilst thee the shores, and sounding seas
Wash far away, where'er thy bones are hurled,   155
Whether beyond the stormy Hebrides,
Where thou perhaps under the whelming tide
Visit'st the bottom of the monstrous world;°
Or whether thou to our moist° vows denied,
Sleep'st by the fable of Bellerus old,   160
Where the great vision of the guarded mount
Looks toward Namancos and Bayona's hold;°
Look homeward angel now, and melt with ruth,°
And, O ye dolphins, waft the hapless youth.°
    Weep no more, woeful shepherds weep no more,
For Lycidas your sorrow is not dead,   166
Sunk though he be beneath the watery floor,
So sinks the day-star° in the ocean bed,
And yet anon repairs his drooping head,   169
And tricks° his beams, and with new spangled ore,
Flames in the forehead of the morning sky:
So Lycidas sunk low, but mounted high,
Through the dear might of him that walked the
    waves,
Where other groves, and other streams along,
With nectar pure his oozy locks he laves,   175
And hears the unexpressive° nuptial song,
In the blest kingdom meek of joy and love.
There entertain him all the saints above,
In solemn troops, and sweet societies
That sing, and singing in their glory move,   180
And wipe the tears forever from his eyes.
Now Lycidas the shepherds weep no more;
Henceforth thou art the genius° of the shore,
In thy large recompense, and shalt be good
To all that wander in that perilous flood.   185
    Thus sang the uncouth° swain to th' oaks and rills,
While the still morn went out with sandals gray,
He touched the tender stops of various quills,°
With eager thought warbling his Doric° lay:
And now the sun had stretched out all the hills, 190
And now was dropped into the western bay;
At last he rose, and twitched° his mantle blue:
Tomorrow to fresh woods, and pastures new.°

---

119. **Blind mouths:** both gluttons and preachers lacking insight. 122. **What . . . them:** what do they care? **sped:** provided for. 123. **list:** wish. **songs:** sermons. 124. **scrannel:** thin, meager. 126. **wind . . . mist:** hollow and false preaching. 128–31. **wolf . . . more:** somewhat obscure allusions to seventeenth-century religious politics. 132. **Alpheus:** pastoral river. 133. **Sicilian muse:** Theocritus. 136. **use:** dwell. 138. **swart star:** black star, i.e., Sirius, associated with the scorching heat of late summer. 139. **enameled eyes:** decorated flowers. 142. **rathe:** early. 144. **freaked:** mottled, speckled. 151. **laureate:** crowned with laurel. 153. **false surmise:** false because King was "buried" at sea.

158. **monstrous world:** world of sea monsters. 159. **moist:** tearful. 160–62. **Sleep'st . . . hold:** The Archangel Michael was thought to sit at Land's End (Bellerus) looking toward Spain (Namancos and Bayona). 163. **ruth:** pity. 164. **dolphins . . . youth:** Dolphins saved the Greek poet Arion from drowning. 168. **day-star:** sun. 170. **tricks:** adorns. 176. **unexpressive:** indescribable, mystical. 183. **genius:** guardian spirit. 186. **uncouth:** unlearned; unknown. 188. **quills:** reed pipes. 189. **Doric:** Greek dialect associated with pastoral poetry. 192.**twitched:** threw on. 193.**Tomorrow . . . new:** to writing other kinds of poetry.

PERCY BYSSHE SHELLEY
1792–1822

Adonais

An Elegy on the Death of John Keats

1

I weep for Adonais°—he is dead!
O, weep for Adonais! though our tears
Thaw not the frost which binds so dear a head!
And thou, sad Hour, selected from all years
To mourn our loss, rouse thy obscure compeers,   5
And teach them thine own sorrow, say: "With me
Died Adonais; till the Future dares
Forget the Past, his fate and fame shall be
An echo and a light unto eternity!"

2

Where wert thou, mighty Mother,° when he lay,   10
When thy Son lay, pierced by the shaft which flies
In darkness? where was lorn Urania°
When Adonais died? With veilèd eyes,
'Mid listening Echoes, in her Paradise
She sate, while one,° with soft enamored breath,   15
Rekindled all the fading melodies,
With which, like flowers that mock the corse beneath,
He had adorned and hid the coming bulk of Death.

3

O, weep for Adonais—he is dead!
Wake, melancholy Mother, wake and weep! 20

ADONAIS. **1. Adonais:** Adonis, the handsome youth loved by Venus and killed by a boar. **10. Mother:** Venus in the role of earth mother, nature; the name is sometimes associated with Urania. **12. lorn Urania:** forlorn Muse of astronomy and of heavenly wisdom. **15. one:** the echo of Keats' poems.

Yet wherefore? Quench within their burning bed
Thy fiery tears, and let thy loud heart keep
Like his, a mute and uncomplaining sleep;
For he is gone, where all things wise and fair
Descend;—oh, dream not that the amorous Deep   25
Will yet restore him to the vital air;
Death feeds on his mute voice, and laughs at our despair.

4

Most musical of mourners, weep again!
Lament anew, Urania!—He° died,
Who was the Sire of an immortal strain,   30
Blind, old, and lonely, when his country's pride,
The priest, the slave, and the liberticide,
Trampled and mocked with many a loathèd rite
Of lust and blood; he went, unterrified,
Into the gulf of death; but his clear Sprite°   35
Yet reigns o'er earth; the third° among the sons of light.

5

Most musical of mourners, weep anew!
Not all to that bright station dared to climb;
And happier they their happiness who knew,
Whose tapers yet burn through that night of time   40
In which suns perished; others more sublime,
Struck by the envious wrath of man or god,
Have sunk, extinct in their refulgent prime;
And some yet live, treading the thorny road,
Which leads, through toil and hate, to Fame's serene abode.   45

6

But now, thy youngest, dearest one has perished—
The nursling of thy widowhood, who grew,
Like a pale flower by some sad maiden cherished,

29. He: Milton, who invoked Urania as the muse of *Paradise Lost*. **35. Sprite:** spirit. **36. third:** after Homer and Dante.

And fed with true-love tears, instead of dew;°
Most musical of mourners, weep anew!   50
Thy extreme hope, the loveliest and the last,
The bloom, whose petals, nipped before they
    blew,
Died on the promise of the fruit, is waste;
The broken lily lies—the storm is overpast.

7

To that high Capital,° where kingly Death 55
Keeps his pale court in beauty and decay,
He came; and bought, with price of purest
    breath,
A grave among the eternal.—Come away!
Haste, while the vault of blue Italian day
Is yet his fitting charnel-roof! while still   60
He lies, as if in dewy sleep he lay;
Awake him not! surely he takes his fill
Of deep and liquid rest, forgetful of all ill.

8

He will awake no more, oh, never more!—
Within the twilight chamber spreads apace 65
The shadow of white Death, and at the door
Invisible Corruption waits to trace
His extreme way to her dim dwelling-place;
The eternal Hunger sits, but pity and awe
Soothe her pale rage, nor dares she to deface 70
So fair a prey, till darkness, and the law
Of change, shall o'er his sleep the mortal curtain
    draw.

9

O, weep for Adonais!—The quick Dreams,°
The passion-wingèd Ministers of thought,
Who were his flocks, whom near the living
    streams   75
Of his young spirit he fed, and whom he
    taught
The love which was its music, wander not,—
Wander no more, from kindling brain to
    brain,
But droop there, whence they sprung; and
    mourn their lot

Round the cold heart, where, after their
    sweet pain,   80
They ne'er will gather strength, or find a home
    again.

10

And one with trembling hands clasps his cold
    head,
And fans him with her moonlight wings, and
    cries:
"Our love, our hope, our sorrow, is not dead;
See, on the silken fringe of his faint eyes,   85
Like dew upon a sleeping flower, there lies
A tear some Dream has loosened from his
    brain."
Lost Angel of a ruined Paradise!
She knew not 'twas her own; as with no stain
She faded, like a cloud which had outwept its
    rain.   90

11

One from a lucid urn of starry dew
Washed his light limbs as if embalming them;
Another clipped her profuse locks, and threw
The wreath upon him, like an anadem,°
Which frozen tears instead of pearls begem; 95
Another in her willful grief would break
Her bow and wingèd reeds, as if to stem
A greater loss with one which was more
    weak;
And dull the barbèd fire against his frozen cheek.

12

Another Splendor on his mouth alit,   100
That mouth, whence it was wont to draw the
    breath
Which gave it strength to pierce the guarded
    wit,°
And pass into the panting heart beneath
With lightning and with music: the damp
    death
Quenched its caress upon his icy lips;   105
And, as a dying meteor stains a wreath
Of moonlight vapor, which the cold night clips,
It flushed through his pale limbs, and passed to
    its eclipse.

49. And . . . dew: allusion to Keats' "Isabella." 55.
Capital: Rome. 73. Dreams: poetic inventions.

94. anadem: garland. 102. guarded wit: cautious intellect.

13

And others came . . . Desires and Adorations,
Wingèd Persuasions and veiled Destinies, 110
Splendors, and Glooms, and glimmering
    Incarnations
Of hopes and fears, and twilight fantasies;
And Sorrow, with her family of Sighs,
And Pleasure, blind with tears, led by the
    gleam
Of her own dying smile instead of eyes, 115
Came in slow pomp;—the moving pomp
    might seem
Like pageantry of mist on an autumnal stream.

14

All he had loved, and molded into thought,
From shape, and hue, and odor, and sweet
    sound,
Lamented Adonais. Morning sought   120
Her eastern watchtower, and her hair un-
    bound,
Wet with the tears which should adorn the
    ground,
Dimmed the aërial eyes that kindle day;
Afar the melancholy thunder moaned,
Pale Ocean in unquiet slumber lay,   125
And the wild winds flew round, sobbing in their
dismay.

15

Lost Echo sits amid the voiceless mountains,
And feeds her grief with his remembered lay,
And will no more reply to winds or fountains,
Or amorous birds perched on the young
    green spray,   130
Or herdsman's horn, or bell at closing day;
Since she can mimic not his lips, more dear
Than those for whose disdain she pined away
Into a shadow of all sounds°—a drear
Murmur, between their songs, is all the woodmen
hear.   135

16

Grief made the young Spring wild, and she
    threw down
Her kindling buds, as if she Autumn were,

133–34. those . . . sounds: The nymph Echo became a
voice because Narcissus did not return her love.

Or they dead leaves; since her delight is flown,
For whom should she have waked the sullen
    year?
To Phoebus was not Hyacinth° so dear   140
Nor to himself Narcissus, as to both
Thou, Adonais: wan they stand and sere°
Amid the faint companions of their youth,
With dew all turned to tears; odor, to sighing
ruth.°

17

Thy spirit's sister, the lorn nightingale,   145
Mourns not her mate with such melodious
    pain;
Not so the eagle, who like thee could scale
Heaven, and could nourish in the sun's
    domain
Her mighty youth with morning,° doth
    complain,   149
Soaring and screaming round her empty nest,
As Albion° wails for thee: the curse of Cain
Light on his° head who pierced thy innocent
    breast,
And scared the angel soul that was its earthly guest!

18

Ah, woe is me! Winter is come and gone,
But grief returns with the revolving year;   155
The airs and streams renew their joyous tone;
The ants, the bees, the swallows, reappear;
Fresh leaves and flowers deck the dead
    Seasons' bier;
The amorous birds now pair in every brake,°
And build their mossy homes in field and
    brere;°   160
And the green lizard, and the golden snake,
Like unimprisoned flames, out of their trance
awake.

140. Phoebus . . . Hyacinth: Phoebus Apollo accidentally
killed Hyacinthus, whom he loved. 142. sere: dry, withered.
144. ruth: pity. 148–49. could . . . morning: Cf. the legendary belief that eagles rejuvenated themselves by flying
toward the sun. 151. Albion: England. 152. his: the writer
(now known to be John Wilson Croker) of an anonymous
review damning Keats' "Endymion" in the Quarterly
Review, April, 1818; Shelley thought this attack partly
responsible for Keats' death. Keats was only twenty-five
when he died of tuberculosis. 159. brake: thicket. 160.
brere: briar.

19

Through wood and stream and field and hill
and Ocean
A quickening life from the Earth's heart has
burst
As it has ever done, with change and motion
From the great morning of the world when
first   166
God dawned on Chaos; in its stream im-
mersed,
The lamps of Heaven flash with a softer light;
All baser things pant with life's sacred thirst;
Diffuse themselves; and spend in love's
delight,   170
The beauty and the joy of their renewèd might.

20

The leprous corpse, touched by this spirit
tender,
Exhales itself in flowers of gentle breath;
Like incarnations of the stars, when splendor
Is changed to fragrance, they illumine death 175
And mock the merry worm that wakes
beneath;
Naught we know, dies. Shall that alone which
knows
Be as a sword consumed before the sheath°
By sightless lightning?—the intense atom
glows
A moment, then is quenched in a most cold re-
pose.   180

21

Alas! that all we loved of him should be,
But for our grief, as if it had not been,
And grief itself be mortal! Woe is me!
Whence are we, and why are we? of what
scene
The actors or spectators? Great and mean 185
Meet massed in death, who lends what life
must borrow.
As long as skies are blue, and fields are green,
Evening must usher night, night urge the
morrow,
Month follow month with woe, and year wake
year to sorrow.

178. **sword, sheath:** soul, body.

22

He will awake no more, oh, never more!   190
"Wake thou," cried Misery, "childless Mother,
rise
Out of thy sleep, and slake, in thy heart's core,
A wound more fierce than his with tears and
sighs."
And all the Dreams that watched Urania's
eyes,
And all the Echoes whom their sister's song 195
Had held in holy silence, cried: "Arise!"
Swift as a Thought by the snake Memory stung,
From her ambrosial rest the fading Splendor°
sprung.

23

She rose like an autumnal Night, that springs
Out of the East, and follows wild and drear 200
The golden Day, which, on eternal wings,
Even as a ghost abandoning a bier,
Had left the Earth a corpse. Sorrow and fear
So struck, so roused, so rapt° Urania;
So saddened round her like an atmosphere 205
Of stormy mist; so swept her on her way
Even to the mournful place where Adonais lay.

24

Out of her secret Paradise she sped,
Through camps and cities rough with stone
and steel,
And human hearts, which to her aëry tread 210
Yielding not, wounded the invisible
Palms of her tender feet where'er they fell:
And barbèd tongues, and thoughts more
sharp than they,
Rent the soft Form they never could repel,
Whose sacred blood, like the young tears of
May,   215
Paved with eternal flowers that undeserving way.

25

In the death-chamber for a moment Death,
Shamed by the presence of that living Might,
Blushed to annihilation, and the breath
Revisited those lips, and life's pale light   220

198. **Splendor:** Urania. 204. **rapt:** carried away.

Flashed through those limbs, so late her dear
delight.
"Leave me not wild and drear and comfortless,
As silent lightning leaves the starless night!
Leave me not!" cried Urania: her distress
Roused Death: Death rose and smiled, and met
her vain caress.   225

26

"Stay yet awhile! speak to me once again;
Kiss me, so long but as a kiss may live;
And in my heartless breast° and burning brain
That word, that kiss, shall all thoughts else
survive,
With food of saddest memory kept alive,   230
Now thou art dead, as if it were a part
Of thee, my Adonais! I would give
All that I am to be as thou now art!
But I am chained to Time, and cannot thence
depart!

27

"Oh gentle child, beautiful as thou wert,   235
Why didst thou leave the trodden paths of men
Too soon, and with weak hands though
mighty heart
Dare the unpastured dragon° in his den?
Defenseless as thou wert, oh, where was then
Wisdom the mirrored shield, or scorn the
spear?   240
Or hadst thou waited the full cycle, when
Thy spirit should have filled its crescent
sphere,
The monsters of life's waste had fled from thee like
deer.

28

"The herded wolves,° bold only to pursue;
The obscence ravens, clamorous o'er the
dead;   245
The vultures to the conqueror's banner true
Who feed where Desolation first has fed,
And whose wings rain contagion;—how they
fled,

When like Apollo, from his golden bow
The Pythian of the age° one arrow sped   250
And smiled!—The spoilers tempt no second
blow,
They fawn on the proud feet that spurn them
lying low.

29

"The sun comes forth, and many reptiles
spawn;
He sets, and each ephemeral insect then
Is gathered into death witnout a dawn,   255
And the immortal stars awake again;
So is it in the world of living men:
A godlike mind soars forth, in its delight
Making earth bare and veiling heaven,° and
when
It sinks, the swarms that dimmed or shared its
light   260
Leave to its kindred lamps the spirit's awful night."

30

Thus ceased she: and the mountain shepherds
came,
Their garlands sere, their magic mantles rent;
The Pilgrim of Eternity,° whose fame
Over his living head like Heaven is bent,   265
An early but enduring monument,
Came, veiling all the lightnings of his song
In sorrow; from her wilds Ierne° sent
The sweetest lyrist° of her saddest wrong,
And Love taught Grief to fall like music from his
tongue.   270

31

Midst others of less note, came one frail
Form,°
A phantom among men; companionless
As the last cloud of an expiring storm
Whose thunder is its knell; he, as I guess,

228. heartless breast: Dead Keats has her heart. 238. dragon:
literary reputation, here compared with dragon-killing
myths, such as those of Perseus and Medusa. 244. wolves:
critics.

250. Pythian . . . age: Byron, who demolished the
critics in *English Bards and Scotch Reviewers* (1809), is
being compared with Apollo, who slew the monster Python.
259. Making . . . heaven: revealing earth and blotting out
other stars. 264. Pilgrim of Eternity: epithet for Byron.
268. Ierne: Hibernia (Ireland). 269. lyrist: Thomas Moore
(1779–1852). 271. Form: Shelley.

Had gazed on Nature's naked loveliness, 275
Actaeon°-like, and now he fled astray
With feeble steps o'er the world's wilderness,
And his own thoughts, along that rugged way,
Pursued, like raging hounds, their father and their
prey.

32

A pardlike° Spirit beautiful and swift—   280
A Love in desolation masked;—a Power
Girt round with weakness;—it can scarce
    uplift
The weight of the superincumbent hour;
It is a dying lamp, a falling shower,
A breaking billow;—even whilst we speak 285
Is it not broken? On the withering flower
The killing sun smiles brightly: on a cheek
The life can burn in blood, even while the heart
may break.

33

His head was bound with pansies overblown,
And faded violets, white, and pied, and blue;
And a light spear topped with a cypress cone,
Round whose rude shaft dark ivy tresses
    grew°
Yet dripping with the forest's noonday dew,
Vibrated, as the ever-beating heart
Shook the weak hand that grasped it; of that
    crew   295
He came the last, neglected and apart;
A herd-abandoned deer struck by the hunter's dart.

34

All stood aloof, and at his partial° moan
Smiled through their tears; well knew that
    gentle band
Who in another's fate now wept his own,   300
As in the accents of an unknown land
He sung new sorrow; sad Urania scanned
The Stranger's mien, and murmured: "Who
art thou?"

He answered not, but with a sudden hand
Made bare his branded and ensanguined
    brow,   305
Which was like Cain's or Christ's—oh! that it
should be so!

35

What softer voice is hushed over the dead?
Athwart what brow is that dark mantle
    thrown?
What form leans sadly o'er the white deathbed,
In mockery° of monumental stone,   310
The heavy heart heaving without a moan?
If it be He,° who, gentlest of the wise,
Taught, soothed, loved, honored the departed
    one,
Let me not vex with inharmonious sighs,
The silence of that heart's accepted sacrifice.   315

36

Our Adonais has drunk poison—oh!
What deaf and viperous murderer could
    crown
Life's early cup with such a draft of woe?
The nameless worm° would now itself disown:
It felt, yet could escape, the magic tone   320
Whose prelude held° all envy, hate, and
    wrong,
But what was howling in one breast alone,
Silent with expectation of the song,
Whose master's hand is cold, whose silver lyre
unstrung.

37

Live thou, whose infamy is not thy fame!   325
Live! fear no heavier chastisement from me,
Thou noteless blot on a remembered name!
But be thyself, and know thyself to be!
And ever at thy season be thou free
To spill the venom when thy fangs o'erflow 330
Remorse and Self-contempt shall cling to thee;
Hot Shame shall burn upon thy secret brow,
And like a beaten hound tremble thou shalt—as
now.

---

276. Actaeon: Changed to a deer for gazing at Diana while she was bathing, Actaeon was torn to pieces by his own hounds. **280. pardlike:** leopardlike. **291–92. spear . . . grew:** like the staff carried by Dionysus, god of vegetation. **298. partial:** for himself.

310. mockery: imitation. **312. He:** Leigh Hunt (1784–1859), friend of Keats and Shelley. **319. nameless worm:** Croker's review was anonymous. **321. held:** checked.

38

Nor let us weep that our delight is fled
Far from these carrion kites that scream
　　below;　　　　　　　　　　　　　335
He wakes or sleeps with the enduring dead;
Thou canst not soar where he is sitting now.—
Dust to the dust! but the pure spirit shall
　flow
Back to the burning fountain whence it came,
A portion of the Eternal, which must glow 340
Through time and change, unquenchably the
　same,
Whilst thy° cold embers choke the sordid hearth of
shame.

39

Peace, peace! he is not dead, he doth not
　sleep—
He hath awakened from the dream of life—
'Tis we, who lost in stormy visions, keep　345
With phantoms an unprofitable strife,
And in mad trance, strike with our spirit's
　knife
Invulnerable nothings.—*We* decay
Like corpses in a charnel; fear and grief
Convulse us and consume us day by day,　350
And cold hopes swarm like worms within our
　living clay.

40

He has outsoared the shadow° of our night;
Envy and calumny and hate and pain,
And that unrest which men miscall delight,
Can touch him not and torture not again; 355
From the contagion of the world's slow stain
He is secure, and now can never mourn
A heart grown cold, a head grown gray in
　vain;
Nor, when the spirit's self has ceased to burn,
With sparkless ashes load an unlamented urn. 360

41

He lives, he wakes—'tis Death is dead, not he;
Mourn not for Adonais.—Thou young Dawn,

Turn all thy dew to splendor, for from thee
The spirit thou lamentest is not gone;
Ye caverns and ye forests, cease to moan! 365
Cease, ye faint flowers and fountains, and
　thou Air,
Which like a mourning veil thy scarf hadst
　thrown
O'er the abandoned Earth, now leave it bare
Even to the joyous stars which smile on its despair!

42

He is made one with Nature: there is heard 370
His voice in all her music, from the moan
Of thunder, to the song of night's sweet bird;
He is a presence to be felt and known
In darkness and in light, from herb and stone,
Spreading itself where'er that Power may
　move　　　　　　　　　　　　　375
Which has withdrawn his being to its own;
Which wields the world with never-wearied
　love,
Sustains it from beneath, and kindles it above.

43

He is a portion of the loveliness
Which once he made more lovely: he doth
　bear　　　　　　　　　　　　　380
His part, while the one Spirit's plastic° stress
Sweeps through the dull dense world, com-
　pelling there,
All new successions to the forms they wear;
Torturing th' unwilling dross that checks its
　flight
To its own likeness, as each mass may
　bear;°　　　　　　　　　　　　385
And bursting in its beauty and its might
From trees and beasts and men into the Heaven's
light.

44

The splendors of the firmament of time°
May be eclipsed, but are extinguished not;
Like stars to their appointed height they
　climb,　　　　　　　　　　　　390
And death is a low mist which cannot blot

---

342. thy: the reviewer's. 352. shadow: created by the earth's
obstructing the sun's rays.

381. plastic: forming. 385. as . . . bear: to the extent that
each substance can be formed (by spirit). 388. splendors
. . . time: great poets.

The brightness it may veil. When lofty
thought
Lifts a young heart above its mortal lair,
And love and life contend in it, for what
Shall be its earthly doom, the dead live there
And move like winds of light on dark and stormy
air.   396

45

The inheritors of unfulfilled renown°
Rose from their thrones, built beyond mortal
thought,
Far in the Unapparent.° Chatterton
Rose pale; his solemn agony had not   400
Yet faded from him; Sidney, as he fought
And as he fell and as he lived and loved,
Sublimely mild, a Spirit without spot,
Arose; and Lucan, by his death approved:°
Oblivion as they rose shrank like a thing re-
proved.   405

46

And many more, whose names on Earth are
dark,
But whose transmitted effluence cannot die
So long as fire outlives the parent spark,
Rose, robed in dazzling immortality.
"Thou art become as one of us," they cry, 410
"It was for thee yon kingless sphere has long
Swung blind in unascended majesty,
Silent alone amid an Heaven of Song.°
Assume thy wingèd throne, thou Vesper° of our
throng!"

47

Who mourns for Adonais? oh, come forth, 415
Fond° wretch! and know thyself and him
aright.
Clasp with thy panting soul the pendulous°
Earth;
As from a center, dart thy spirit's light
Beyond all worlds, until its spacious might

Satiate the void circumference: then shrink 420
Even to a point within our day and night;°
And keep thy heart light lest it make thee
sink
When hope has kindled hope, and lured thee to the
brink.

48

Or go to Rome,° which is the sepulcher,
Oh, not of him, but of our joy: 'tis nought 425
That ages, empires, and religions there
Lie buried in the ravage they have wrought;
For such as he can lend,—they borrow not
Glory from those who made the world their
prey;
And he is gathered to the kings of thought 430
Who waged contention with their time's
decay,
And of the past are all that cannot pass away.

49

Go thou to Rome,—at once the Paradise,
The grave, the city, and the wilderness;
And where its wrecks like shattered mountains
rise,   435
And flowering weeds, and fragrant copses
dress
The bones of Desolation's nakedness
Pass, till the Spirit of the spot shall lead
Thy footsteps to a slope of green access
Where, like an infant's smile, over the dead 440
A light of laughing flowers along the grass is
spread;

50

And gray walls molder round, on which dull
Time
Feeds, like slow fire upon a hoary brand;
And one keen pyramid with wedge sublime,°
Pavilioning the dust of him who planned 445
This refuge for his memory, doth stand
Like flame transformed to marble; and
beneath,

397. **inheritors . . . renown:** promising poets who died while
relatively young, three of whom are named in the stanza.
399. **Unapparent:** unrealized. 404. **approved:** proved
worthy. 413. **Heaven of Song:** music of the spheres. 414.
Vesper: the evening star. 416. **Fond:** foolish. 417. **pendulous:**
suspended.

421. **day and night:** also the cycle of life and death. 424.
Rome: Keats was buried in the Protestant Cemetery in
Rome. 444. **pyramid . . . sublime:** tomb of Gaius Cestius,
a Roman statesman.

A field is spread, on which a newer band
Have pitched in Heaven's smile their camp of
    death,
Welcoming him we lose with scarce extinguished
breath.   450

51

Here pause: these graves are all too young as
    yet
To have outgrown the sorrow which consigned
Its charge to each; and if the seal is set,
Here, on one fountain of a mourning mind,
Break it not thou! too surely shalt thou
    find   455
Thine own well full, if thou returnest home,
Of tears and gall. From the world's bitter
    wind
Seek shelter in the shadow of the tomb.
What Adonais is, why fear we to become?

52

The One remains, the many change and pass;
Heaven's light forever shines, Earth's shadows
    fly;   461
Life, like a dome of many-colored glass,
Stains the white radiance of Eternity,
Until Death tramples it to fragments.—Die,
If thou wouldst be with that which thou dost
    seek!   465
Follow where all is fled!—Rome's azure sky,
Flowers, ruins, statues, music, words, are weak
The glory they transfuse with fitting truth to speak.

53

Why linger, why turn back, why shrink, my
    Heart?
Thy hopes are gone before: from all things
    here   470
They have departed; thou shouldst now depart!
A light is passed from the revolving year,
And man, and woman; and what still is dear
Attracts to crush, repels to make thee wither.
The soft sky smiles,—the low wind whispers
    near: 475
'Tis Adonais calls! oh, hasten thither,
No more let Life divide what Death can join
together.

54

That Light whose smile kindles the Universe,
That Beauty in which all things work and
    move,
That Benediction which the eclipsing Curse 480
Of birth can quench not, that sustaining Love
Which through the web of being blindly wove
By man and beast and earth and air and sea,
Burns bright or dim, as each are mirrors of
The fire for which all thirst° now beams on
    me,   485
Consuming the last clouds of cold mortality.

55

The breath whose might I have invoked in
    song°
Descends on me; my spirit's bark is driven,
Far from the shore, far from the trembling
    throng   489
Whose sails were never to the tempest given;
The massy earth and spherèd skies are riven!
I am borne darkly, fearfully, afar;
Whilst, burning through the inmost veil of
    Heaven,
The soul of Adonais, like a star,
Beacons from the abode where the Eternal are. 495

WALT WHITMAN
1819–1892

When Lilacs Last
in the Dooryard Bloom'd

1

When lilacs° last in the dooryard bloom'd,
And the great star early droop'd in the western
    sky in the night,
I mourn'd, and yet shall mourn with ever-returning
    spring.

---

485. fire . . . thirst: desire of the human spirit to return
to its divine source. **487. breath . . . song:** Cf. Shelley's
"Ode to the West Wind," in which Shelley associates the
autumnal west wind with poetic inspiration.

Ever-returning spring, trinity sure to me you bring,
Lilac blooming perennial and drooping star in the
    west,   5
And thought of him I love.°

2

O powerful western fallen star!
O shades of night—O moody, tearful night!
O great star disappear'd—O the black murk that
    hides the star!
O cruel hands that hold me powerless—O helpless
    soul of me!   10
O harsh surrounding cloud that will not free my
    soul.

3

In the dooryard fronting an old farm-house near
    the white-wash'd palings,
Stands the lilac-bush tall-growing with heart-
    shaped leaves of rich green,
With many a pointed blossom rising delicate, with
    perfume strong I love,
With every leaf a miracle—and from this bush in
    the dooryard,   15
With delicate-color'd blossoms and heart-shaped
    leaves of rich green,
A sprig with its flower I break.

4

In the swamp in secluded recesses,
A shy and hidden bird is warbling a song.

Solitary the thrush,   20
The hermit withdrawn to himself, avoiding the
    settlements,
Sings by himself a song.

Song of the bleeding throat,
Death's outlet song of life, (for well dear brother
    I know,
If thou wast not granted to sing thou would'st
    surely die.)   25

5

Over the breast of the spring, the land, amid cities,
Amid lanes and through old woods, where lately
    the violets peep'd from the ground, spotting the
    gray debris,
Amid the grass in the fields each side of the lanes,
    passing the endless grass,
Passing the yellow-spear'd wheat, every grain from
    its shroud in the dark-brown fields uprisen,
Passing the apple-tree blows of white and pink in
    the orchards,   30
Carrying a corpse to where it shall rest in the grave,
Night and day journeys a coffin.°

6

Coffin that passes through lanes and streets,
Through day and night with the great cloud
    darkening the land,
With the pomp of the inloop'd flags with the cities
    draped in black,   35
With the show of the States themselves as of
    crape-veil'd women standing,
With processions long and winding and the
    flambeaus° of the night,
With the countless torches lit, with the silent sea of
    faces and the unbared heads,
With the waiting depot, the arriving coffin, and the
    somber faces,
With dirges through the night, with the thousand
    voices rising strong and solemn,   40
With all the mournful voices of the dirges pour'd
    around the coffin,
The dim-lit churches and the shuddering organs—
    where amid these you journey,
With the tolling tolling bells' perpetual clang,
Here, coffin that slowly passes,
I give you my sprig of lilac.   45

7

(Nor for you, for one alone,
Blossoms and branches green to coffins all I bring,
For fresh as the morning, thus would I chant a
    song for you O sane and sacred death.

All over bouquets of roses,

WHEN LILACS LAST IN THE DOORYARD BLOOM'D. **6. him I
love**: President Lincoln, who was assassinated in the spring
of 1865.

32. Night . . . coffin: Lincoln's funeral train made many
stops between Washington and Springfield, Illinois, where
he was buried. **37. flambeaus**: torches.

O death, I cover you over with roses and early
　lilies,　　　　　　　　　　　　　　　　50
But mostly and now the lilac that blooms the first,
Copious I break, I break the sprigs from the
　bushes,
With loaded arms I come, pouring for you,
For you and the coffins all of you O death.)

8

O western orb sailing the heaven,　　　　　55
Now I know what you must have meant as a
　month since I walk'd,
As I walk'd in silence the transparent shadowy
　night,
As I saw you had something to tell as you bent to
　me night after night,
As you droop'd from the sky low down as if to my
　side, (while the other stars all look'd on,)
As we wander'd together the solemn night, (for
　something I know not what kept me from
　sleep,)　　　　　　　　　　　　　　60
As the night advanced, and I saw on the rim of the
　west how full you were of woe,
As I stood on the rising ground in the breeze in the
　cool transparent night,
As I watch'd where you pass'd and was lost in the
　netherward black of the night,
As my soul in its trouble dissatisfied sank, as
　where you sad orb,
Concluded, dropt in the night, and was gone.　65

9

Sing on there in the swamp,
O singer bashful and tender, I hear your notes, I
　hear your call,
I hear, I come presently, I understand you,
But a moment I linger, for the lustrous star has
　detain'd me,
The star my departing comrade holds and detains
　me.　　　　　　　　　　　　　　　70

10

O how shall I warble myself for the dead one there
　I loved?
And how shall I deck my song for the large sweet
　soul that has gone?
And what shall my perfume be for the grave of
　him I love?

Sea-winds blown from east and west,
Blown from the Eastern sea and blown from the
　Western sea, till there on the prairies meeting, 75
These and with these and the breath of my chant,
I'll perfume the grave of him I love.

11

O what shall I hang on the chamber walls?
And what shall the pictures be that I hang on the
　walls,
To adorn the burial-house of him I love?　　80

Pictures of growing spring and farms and homes,
With the Fourth-month eve at sundown, and the
　gray smoke lucid and bright,
With floods of the yellow gold of the gorgeous,
　indolent, sinking sun, burning, expanding the
　air,
With the fresh sweet herbage under foot, and the
　pale green leaves of the trees prolific,
In the distance the flowing glaze, the breast of the
　river, with a wind-dapple here and there,　85
With ranging hills on the banks, with many a line
　against the sky, and shadows,
And the city at hand with dwellings so dense, and
　stacks of chimneys,
And all the scenes of life and the workshops, and
　the workmen homeward returning.

12

Lo, body and soul—this land,
My own Manhattan with spires, and the sparkling
　and hurrying tides, and the ships,　　　90
The varied and ample land, the South and the
　North in the light, Ohio's shores and flashing
　Missouri,
And ever the far-spreading prairies cover'd with
　grass and corn.

Lo, the most excellent sun so calm and haughty,
The violet and purple morn with just-felt breezes,
The gentle soft-born measureless light,　　95
The miracle spreading bathing all, the fulfill'd noon,
The coming eve delicious, the welcome night and
　the stars,
Over my cities shining all, enveloping man and
　land.

13

Sing on, sing on you gray-brown bird,
Sing from the swamps, the recesses, pour your
    chant from the bushes,   100
Limitless out of the dusk, out of the cedars and
    pines.

Sing on dearest brother, warble your reedy song,
Loud human song, with voice of uttermost woe.

O liquid and free and tender!
O wild and loose to my soul—O wondrous singer!
You only I hear—yet the star holds me, (but will
    soon depart,)   106
Yet the lilac with mastering odor holds me.

14

Now while I sat in the day and look'd forth,
In the close of the day with its light and the fields
    of spring, and the farmers preparing their crops,
In the large unconscious scenery of my land with
    its lakes and forests,   110
In the heavenly aerial beauty, (after the perturb'd
    winds and the storms,)
Under the arching heavens of the afternoon swift
    passing, and the voices of children and women,
The many-moving sea-tides, and I saw the ships
    how they sail'd,
And the summer approaching with richness, and
    the fields all busy with labor,
And the infinite separate houses, how they all
    went on, each with its meals and minutia of
    daily usages,   115
And the streets how their throbbings throbb'd, and
    the cities pent—lo, then and there,
Falling upon them all and among them all,
    enveloping me with the rest,
Appear'd the cloud, appear'd the long black trail,°
And I knew death, its thought, and the sacred
    knowledge of death.

Then with the knowledge of death as walking one
    side of me,   120
And the thought of death close-walking the other
    side of me,
And I in the middle as with companions, and as
    holding the hands of companions,

I fled forth to the hiding receiving night that talks
    not,
Down to the shores of the water, the path by the
    swamp in the dimness,
To the solemn shadowy cedars and ghostly pines
    so still.   125

And the singer so shy to the rest receiv'd me,
The gray-brown bird I know receiv'd us comrades
    three,
And he sang the carol of death, and a verse for
    him I love.

From deep secluded recesses,
From the fragrant cedars and the ghostly pines so
    still,   130
Came the carol of the bird.

And the charm of the carol rapt° me,
As I held as if by their hands my comrades in the
    night,
And the voice of my spirit tallied° the song of the
    bird.

Come lovely and soothing death,   135
Undulate round the world, serenely arriving,
    arriving,
In the day, in the night, to all, to each,
Sooner or later delicate death.

Prais'd be the fathomless universe,
For life and joy, and for objects and knowledge
    curious,   140
And for love, sweet love—but praise! praise!
    praise!
For the sure-enwinding arms of cool-enfolding death.

Dark mother always gliding near with soft feet,
Have none chanted for thee a chant of fullest
    welcome?
Then I chant it for thee, I glorify thee above all, 145
I bring thee a song that when thou must indeed
    come, come unfalteringly.

Approach strong deliveress,
When it is so, when thou hast taken them I joyously
    sing the dead,
Lost in the loving floating ocean of thee,
Laved in the flood of thy bliss O death.   150

---

118. long . . . trail: the funeral cortege.

132. rapt: carried away. **134. tallied:** corresponded to.

From me to thee glad serenades,
Dances for thee I propose saluting thee, adornments
*   and feastings for thee,*
And the sights of the open landscape and the high-
*   spread sky are fitting,*
And life and the fields, and the huge and thoughtful
*   night.*

The night in silence under many a star,   155
The ocean shore and the husky whispering wave
*   whose voice I know,*
And the soul turning to thee O vast and well-veil'd
*   death,*
And the body gratefully nestling close to thee.

Over the tree-tops I float thee a song,
Over the rising and sinking waves, over the myriad
*   fields and the prairies wide,*   160
Over the dense-pack'd cities all and the teeming
*   wharves and ways,*
I float this carol with joy, with joy to thee O death.

15

To the tally of my soul,
Loud and strong kept up the gray-brown bird,
With pure deliberate notes spreading filling the
    night.   165

Loud in the pines and cedars dim,
Clear in the freshness moist and the swamp-
    perfume,
And I with my comrades there in the night.

While my sight that was bound in my eyes un-
    closed,
As to long panoramas of visions.   170

And I saw askant the armies,
I saw as in noiseless dreams hundreds of battle-
    flags,
Borne through the smoke of the battles and
    pierc'd with missiles I saw them,
And carried hither and yon through the smoke,
    and torn and bloody,
And at last but a few shreds left on the staffs, (and
    all in silence,)   175
And the staffs all splinter'd and broken.

I saw battle-corpses, myriads of them,
And the white skeletons of young men, I saw them,
I saw the debris and debris of all the slain soldiers
    of the war,

But I saw they were not as was thought,   180
They themselves were fully at rest, they suffer'd
    not,
The living remain'd and suffer'd, the mother
    suffer'd,
And the wife and the child and the musing comrade
    suffer'd,
And the armies that remain'd suffer'd.

16

Passing the visions, passing the night,   185
Passing, unloosing the hold of my comrades'
    hands,
Passing the song of the hermit bird and the tallying
    song of my soul,
Victorious song, death's outlet song, yet varying
    ever-altering song,
As low and wailing, yet clear the notes, rising and
    falling, flooding the night,
Sadly sinking and fainting, as warning and warning,
    and yet again bursting with joy,   190
Covering the earth and filling the spread of the
    heaven,
As that powerful psalm in the night I heard from
    recesses,
Passing, I leave thee lilac with heart-shaped leaves,
I leave thee there in the door-yard, blooming,
    returning with spring.

I cease from my song for thee,   195
From my gaze on thee in the west, fronting the
    west, communing with thee,
O comrade lustrous with silver face in the night.

Yet each to keep and all, retrievements out of the
    night,
The song, the wondrous chant of the gray-brown
    bird,
And the tallying chant, the echo arous'd in my
    soul,   200
With the lustrous and drooping star with the
    countenance full of woe,
With the holders holding my hand nearing the
    call of the bird,
Comrades mine and I in the midst, and their
    memory ever to keep, for the dead I loved so
    well,
For the sweetest, wisest soul of all my days and
    lands—and this for his dear sake,

Lilac and star and bird twined with the chant of
my soul,   205
There in the fragrant pines and the cedars dusk
and dim.

GERARD MANLEY HOPKINS
1844–1889

The Wreck
of the Deutschland

*To the happy memory of five Franciscan Nuns,
exiles by the Falk Laws,° drowned between midnight and morning of Dec. 7th, 1875.*

PART THE FIRST

1

Thou mastering me
God! giver of breath and bread;
World's strand, sway of the sea;
Lord of living and dead;
Thou hast bound bones and veins in me, fastened
me flesh,   5
And after it almost unmade, what with dread,
Thy doing: and dost thou touch me
afresh?
Over again I feel thy finger and find thee.

2

I did say yes
O at lightning and lashed rod;   10
Thou heardst me truer than tongue confess
Thy terror, O Christ, O God;
Thou knowest the walls, altar and hour and
night:
The swoon of a heart that the sweep and the
hurl of thee trod
Hard down with a horror of height: 15
And the midriff astrain with leaning of, laced with
fire of stress.

THE WRECK OF THE DEUTSCHLAND. **Falk Laws:** repressive
penal measures against Roman Catholics enacted by
Prussian landowners in 1873 and administered by Adalbert
Falk, Prussian minister of cults, in 1874 and 1875.

3

The frown of his face
Before me, the hurtle of hell
Behind, where, where was a, where was a
place?
I whirled out wings that spell°   20
And fled with a fling of the heart to the heart
of the Host.
My heart, but you were dovewinged, I can tell,
Carrier-witted, I am bold to boast,
To flash from the flame to the flame then, tower
from the grace to the grace.

4

I am soft sift   25
In an hourglass—at the wall
Fast, but mined with a motion, a drift,
And it crowds and it combs° to the
fall;
I steady as a water in a well, to a poise, to a
pane,°
But roped with, always, all the way down
from the tall   30
Fells° or flanks of the voel,° a vein
Of the gospel proffer, a pressure, a principle,
Christ's gift.

5

I kiss my hand
To the stars, lovely-asunder
Starlight, wafting him out of it; and   35
Glow, glory in thunder;
Kiss my hand to the dappled-with-damson°
west:
Since, though he is under the world's splendor
and wonder,
His mystery must be instressed,° stressed;
For I greet him the days I meet him, and bless
when I understand.   40

6

Not out of his bliss
Springs the stress felt
Nor first from heaven (and few know this)
Swings the stroke dealt—

20. spell: time. **28. combs:** like a wave. **29. pane:** counterpane.
31. Fells: pasture. **voel:** bare hill. **37. damson:** dark purple
plum. **39. instressed:** inwardly felt; the illumination or act
of faith that for Hopkins leads to knowledge of ultimate
reality ("inscape").

Stroke and a stress that stars and storms
    deliver,   45
That guilt is hushed by, hearts are flushed by
    and melt—
    But it rides time like riding a river
(And here the faithful waver, the faithless fable
    and miss).

7

    It dates from day
    Of his going in Galilee;   50
Warm-laid grave of a womb-life gray;
    Manger, maiden's knee;
The dense and the driven Passion, and
    frightful sweat;
Thence the discharge of it, there its swelling
    to be,
    Though felt before, though in high flood
    yet—   55
What none would have known of it, only the heart,
    being hard at bay,

8

    Is out with it! Oh,
    We lash with the best or worst
Word last! How a lush-kept plush-
    capped sloe°
    Will, mouthed to flesh-burst,   60
Gush!—flush the man, the being with it,
    sour or sweet,
Brim, in a flash, full!—Hither then, last or
    first,
    To hero of Calvary, Christ's feet—
Never ask if meaning it, wanting it, warned of it—
    men go.

9

    Be adored among men,   65
    God, three-numberèd form;
Wring thy rebel, dogged in den,
    Man's malice, with wrecking and
    storm.
Beyond saying sweet, past telling of tongue,
Thou art lightning and love, I found it, a
    winter and warm;   70

59. **sloe:** blackthorn.

Father and fondler of heart thou hast
    wrung:
Hast thy dark descending and most art merciful
    then.

10

    With an anvil-ding
    And with fire in him forge thy will
    Or rather, rather then, stealing as
    Spring   75
    Through him, melt him but master
    him still:
Whether at once, as once at a crash Paul,
Or as Austin, a lingering-out swéet skíll,°
    Make mercy in all of us, out of us all
Mastery, but be adored, but be adored King.   80

PART THE SECOND

11

    "Some find me a sword; some
    The flange and the rail; flame,
Fang, or flood" goes Death on drum,
    And storms bugle his fame.
But wé dream we are rooted in earth—
    Dust!   85
Flesh falls within sight of us, we, though our
    flower the same,
    Wave with the meadow, forget that there
    must
The sour scythe cringe, and the blear share come.

12

    On Saturday sailed from Bremen,
    American-outward-bound,   90
Take settler and seamen, tell° men with
    women,
    Two hundred souls in the round—
O Father, not under thy feathers nor ever as
    guessing
The goal was a shoal, of a fourth the doom to
    be drowned;

77–78. crash . . . skill: Saint Paul was converted suddenly
on the road to Damascus; Saint Augustine was converted
over a long period of time. **91. tell:** count.

Yet did the dark side of the bay° of thy
blessing 95
Not vault them, the millions of rounds of thy
mercy not reeve° even them in?

13

Into the snows she sweeps,
Hurling the haven behind,
The Deutschland, on Sunday; and so
the sky keeps,
For the infinite air is unkind, 100
And the sea flint-flake, black-backed in the
regular blow,
Sitting Eastnortheast, in cursed quarter, the
wind;
Wiry and white-fiery and whirlwind-
swivelèd snow
Spins to the widow-making unchilding unfathering
deeps.

14

She drove in the dark to leeward, 105
She struck—not a reef or a rock
But the combs° of a smother of sand: night
drew her
Dead to the Kentish Knock;°
And she beat the bank down with her bows
and the ride of her keel:
The breakers rolled on her beam with ruinous
shock; 110
And canvas and compass, the whorl° and
the wheel
Idle forever to waft her or wind° her with, these
she endured.

15

Hope had grown gray hairs,
Hope had mourning on,
Trenched with tears, carved with cares, 115
Hope was twelve hours gone;
And frightful a nightfall folded rueful a day
Nor rescue, only rocket and lightship, shone,

And lives at last were washing away:
To the shrouds they took,—they shook in the
hurling and horrible airs. 120

16

One stirred from the rigging to save
The wild womankind below,
With a rope's end round the man, handy
and brave—
He was pitched to his death at a
blow,
For all his dreadnought breast and braids of
thew: 125
They could tell him for hours, dandled the to
and fro
Through the cobbled foam-fleece, what
could he do
With the burl° of the fountains of air, buck and
the flood of the wave?

17

They fought with God's cold—
And they could not and fell to the
deck 130
(Crushed them) or water (and drowned
them) or rolled
With the sea-romp over the wreck.
Night roared, with the heart-break hearing a
heart-broke rabble,
The woman's wailing, the crying of child
without check—
Till a lioness arose breasting the babble,
A prophetess towered in the tumult, a virginal
tongue told. 136

18

Ah, touched in your bower of bone
Are you! turned for an exquisite
smart,
Have you! make words break from me
here all alone,
Do you!—mother of being in me,
heart. 140
O unteachably after° evil, but uttering truth,

---

95. **bay**: body of water; in a building, space between
columns. 96. **reeve**: lead (as lines are led through blocks
or fairleads on sailing vessels). 107. **combs**: crests of
breaking seas. 108. **Kentish Knock**: sandbank in the
Thames estuary. 111. **whorl**: propeller. 112. **wind**: steer.

128. **burl**: knot in wood or lump in cloth, here suggesting
roughness. 141. **after**: desiring.

Why, tears! is it? tears; such a melting, a
    madrigal start!
    Never-eldering revel and river of youth,
What can it be, this glee? the good° you have there
    of your own?

19

    Sister, a sister calling   145
    A master, her master and mine!—
And the inboard seas run swirling and
    hawling;°
    The rash smart sloggering brine
Blinds her; but she that weather° sees one
    thing, one;
Has one fetch° in her: she rears herself to
    divine   150
    Ears, and the call of the tall nun
To the men in the tops and the tackle rode over
    the storm's brawling.

20

    She was first of a five and came
    Of a coifèd sisterhood.
    (O Deutschland, double a desperate
      name!   155
    O world wide of its good!
But Gertrude°, lily, and Luther, are two of a
    town,
    Christ's lily and beast of the waste wood:
    From life's dawn it is drawn down,
Abel is Cain's brother and breasts they have
    sucked the same.)   160

21

    Loathed for a love men knew in them,
    Banned by the land of their birth,
    Rhine refused them. Thames would ruin
      them;
    Surf, snow, river and earth
Gnashed: but thou art above, thou Orion° of
    light;   165

Thy unchanceling° poising palms were weigh-
    ing the worth,
    Thou martyr-master: in thy sight
Storm flakes were scroll-leaved flowers, lily
    showers—sweet heaven was astrew in them.

22

    Five! The finding and sake
    And cipher of suffering Christ.°   170
    Mark, the mark is of man's make
    And the word of it Sacrificed.
But he scores it in scarlet himself on his own
    bespoken,
    Before-time-taken, dearest prizèd and priced—
    Stigma,° signal, cinquefoil° token   175
For lettering of the lamb's fleece, ruddying of the
    rose-flake.°

23

    Joy fall to thee, father Francis,°
    Drawn to the Life that died;
    With the gnarls of the nails in thee, niche
      of the lance, his
    Lovescape° crucified   180
And seal of his seraph-arrival! and these thy
    daughters
    And five-livèd and leavèd favor and pride,
    Are sisterly sealed in wild waters,
To bathe in his fall-gold mercies, to breathe in his
    all-fire glances.

24

    Away in the lovable west,   185
    On a pastoral forehead° of Wales,
    I was under a roof here, I was at rest,
    And they the prey of the gales;
She to the black-about air, to the breaker, the
    thickly

144. **good:** courage. 147. **hawling:** hauling. 149. **that weather:** in that weather. 150. **fetch:** objective (as a sailing vessel is said to "fetch" a mark to windward). 154. **coifed:** hooded. 157. **Gertrude:** Catholic saint and mystic from Eisleben, Luther's birth-place. 165. **Orion:** God as hunter.

166. **unchanceling:** driving the nuns from sanctuary. 169–70. **Five . . . Christ:** reference to Christ's five wounds; in Hopkins' terminology, "finding" and "sake" are roughly equivalent to the process of coming to know and to the external symbol of the thing known. 175. **Stigma:** mark resembling Christ's wounds. **cinquefoil:** rose design with five petals. 176. **rose-flake:** symbolizes martyrdom. 177. **Francis:** Saint Francis of Assisi. 180. **Lovescape:** Christ's wounds were supposed to have appeared on the body of Saint Francis. 186. **forehead:** hill.

Falling flakes, to the throng that catches and
  quails   190
  Was calling "O Christ, Christ, come
  quickly":
The cross to her she calls Christ to her, christens
her wild-worst Best.

25

  The majesty! what did she mean?
  Breathe, arch and original Breath.
  Is it love in her of the being as her lover
  had been?   195
  Breathe, body of lovely Death.
They were else-minded then, altogether, the
  men
Woke thee with a *we are perishing* in the
  weather of Gennesareth.°
  Or is it that she cried for the crown then,
The keener to come at the comfort for feeling the
combating keen?   200

26

  For how to the heart's cheering
  The down-dugged ground-hugged
  grey
  Hovers off, the jay-blue heavens appearing
  Of pied° and peeled° May!
Blue-beating and hoary-glow height; or night,
  still higher,   205
With belled fire and the moth-soft Milky Way,
  What by your measure is the heaven of
  desire,
The treasurer never eyesight got, nor was ever
guessed what for the hearing?

27

  No, but it was not these.
  The jading and jar of the cart,   210
  Time's tasking, it is fathers° that asking
  for ease
    Of   the   sodden-with-its-sorrowing
    heart,
  Not danger, electrical horror; then further it
  finds

198. **Gennesareth:** Sea of Galilee, where Christ calmed
the storm (see Matthew 14). 204. **pied:** particolored.
peeled: polished. 211. **fathers:** produces, creates.

The appealing of the Passion is tenderer in
  prayer apart:
  Other, I gather, in measure her mind's 215
Burden, in wind's burly and beat of endragonèd
seas.

28

  But how shall I . . . make me room
  there:
  Reach me a . . . Fancy, come faster—
  Strike you the sight of it? look at it
  loom there,
    Thing that she . . . there then! the
    Master,   220
Ipse,° the only one, Christ, King, Head:
  He was to cure the extremity where he had
  cast her;
  Do, deal, lord it with living and dead;
Let him ride, her pride, in his triumph, despatch
and have done with his doom there.

29

  Ah! there was a heart right!   225
  There was single eye!°
  Read the unshapeable shock night
    And knew the who and the why;
  Wording it how but by him that present and
  past,
  Heaven and earth are word° of, worded
  by?—   230
  The Simon Peter° of a soul! to the blast
Tarpeian°-fast, but a blown beacon of light.

30

  Jesu, heart's light,
  Jesu, maid's son,
  What was the feast followed the night 235
    Thou hadst glory of this nun?—
Feast° of the one woman without stain.

221. **Ipse:** himself. 226. **single eye:** devoted to one purpose.
230. **word:** Cf. John 1:1: "In the beginning was the Word,
and the Word was with God, and the Word was God." 231.
Simon Peter: allusion relevant to both Peter's walking on
water to Christ (see Matthew 14:24–33) and his founding
of the Church of Rome. 232. **Tarpeian:** rock that is part of
the Capitoline, the highest of Rome's seven hills. 237.
Feast: December 8 is the Feast of the Immaculate Conception of the Blessed Virgin Mary.

For so conceivèd, so to conceive thee is done;
But here was heart-throe, birth of a brain,
Word, that heard and kept thee and uttered thee
outright.   240

31

Well, she has thee for the pain, for the
Patience; but pity of the rest of them!
Heart, go and bleed at a bitterer vein for
the
Comfortless unconfessed of them—
No not uncomforted: lovely-felicitous Pro-
vidence   245
Finger of a tender of, O of a feathery delicacy,
the breast of the
Maiden could obey so, be a bell to,
ring of it, and
Startle the poor sheep back! is the shipwrack then
a harvest, does tempest carry the grain for thee?

32

I admire thee, master of the tides,
Of the Yore-flood,° of the year's fall;
The recurb° and the recovery of the gulf's
sides,   251
The girth of it and the wharf° of it
and the wall;
Stanching, quenching ocean of a motionable
mind;
Ground of being, and granite of it: past all
Grasp God, throned behind   255
Death with a sovereignty that heeds but hides,
bodes but abides;

33

With a mercy that outrides
The all of water, an ark
For the listener; for the lingerer with a
love glides
Lower than death° and the dark; 260
A vein for the visiting of the past-prayer,
pent in prison,
The-last-breath penitent spirits—the utter-
most mark
Our passion-plungèd giant risen,
The Christ of the Father compassionate, fetched°
in the storm of his strides.

250. **Yore-flood:** Noah's flood. 251. **recurb:** reconfining.
252. **wharf:** shore. 260. **Lower . . . death:** in Purgatory.
262–64. **mark, fetched:** See note to l. 150.

34

Now burn, new born to the world,
Double-naturèd name,   266
The heaven-flung, heart-fleshed, maiden-
furled
Miracle-in-Mary-of-flame,
Mid-numbered He in three of the thunder-
throne!
Not a dooms-day dazzle in his coming nor
dark as he came;   270
Kind, but royally reclaiming his own;
A released shower, let flash to the shire, not a
lightning of fire hard-hurled.

35

Dame, at our door
Drowned, and among our shoals,
Remember us in the roads,° the heaven-
haven of the Reward: 275
Our King back, oh, upon English
souls!
Let him easter in us, be a dayspring to the
dimness of us, be a crimson-cresseted° east,
More brightening her, rare-dear Britain, as
his reign rolls,
Pride, rose, prince, hero of us, high-priest,
Our hearts' charity's hearth's fire, our thoughts'
chivalry's throng's Lord.   280

WILLIAM BUTLER YEATS
1865–1939

Easter 1916°

I have met them at close of day
Coming with vivid faces
From counter or desk among grey

275. **roads:** roadstead, harbor. 277. **crimson-cresseted:** as if
illuminated by cressets, or torches.
EASTER 1916. During the Easter Rising of 1916, Irish
Republicans temporarily seized parts of Dublin in defiance
of English rule; the leaders of the revolt were subsequently
executed. Many of them are specifically referred to in the
poem: Countess Markiewicz, an aristocrat; Patrick Pearse,
a schoolmaster; Thomas MacDonagh, James Connolly,
and Major John MacBride, other leaders of the revolution.

Eighteenth-century houses.
I have passed with a nod of the head   5
Or polite meaningless words,
Or have lingered awhile and said
Polite meaningless words,
And thought before I had done
Of a mocking tale or a gibe   10
To please a companion
Around the fire at the club,
Being certain that they and I
But lived where motley° is worn:
All changed, changed utterly: 15
A terrible beauty is born.

That woman's° days were spent
In ignorant good-will,
Her nights in argument
Until her voice grew shrill.   20
What voice more sweet than hers
When, young and beautiful,
She rode to harriers?°
This man° had kept a school
And rode our wingèd horse;°   25
This other° his helper and friend
Was coming into his force;
He might have won fame in the end,
So sensitive his nature seemed,
So daring and sweet his thought.   30
This other man° I had dreamed
A drunken, vainglorious lout.
He had done most bitter wrong
To some who are near my heart,
Yet I number him in the song;   35
He, too, has resigned his part
In the casual comedy;
He, too, has been changed in his turn,

14. **motley:** costume of variegated colors worn by court jesters; hence, appropriate to a land of comic humors rather than tragic actions. **17. That woman:** Countess Markiewicz. **23. harriers:** hounds. **24. This man:** Patrick Pearse. **25. winged horse:** Pegasus, horse of the Muses. **26. This other:** Thomas MacDonagh. **31. man:** Major John MacBride, who married Maud Gonne, a lifelong friend of Yeats'.

Transformed utterly:
A terrible beauty is born.   40

Hearts with one purpose alone
Through summer and winter seem
Enchanted to a stone
To trouble the living stream.
The horse that comes from the road,   45
The rider, the birds that range
From cloud to tumbling cloud,
Minute by minute they change;
A shadow of cloud on the stream
Changes minute by minute;   50
A horse-hoof slides on the brim,
And a horse plashes within it;
The long-legged moor-hens dive,
And hens to moor-cocks call;
Minute by minute they live: 55
The stone's in the midst of all.

Too long a sacrifice
Can make a stone of the heart.
O when may it suffice?
That is Heaven's part, our part   60
To murmur name upon name,
As a mother names her child
When sleep at last has come
On limbs that had run wild.
What is it but nightfall?   65
No, no, not night but death;
Was it needless death after all?
For England may keep faith
For all that is done and said.
We know their dream; enough   70
To know they dreamed and are dead;
And what if excess of love
Bewildered them till they died?
I write it out in a verse—
MacDonagh and MacBride   75
And Connolly and Pearse
Now and in time to be,
Wherever green is worn,
Are changed, changed utterly:
A terrible beauty is born.   80

The Search for Immortality

THOMAS NASHE
1567–1601

Adieu, Farewell,
Earth's Bliss

Adieu, farewell, earth's bliss.
This world uncertain is,
Fond° are life's lustful joys,
Death proves them all but toys;
None from his darts can fly;   5
I am sick, I must die:
  Lord, have mercy on us.

Rich men, trust not in wealth,
Gold cannot buy you health;
Physic° himself must fade.   10
All things to end are made,
The plague full swift goes by;
I am sick, I must die.
  Lord, have mercy on us.

Beauty is but a flower,   15
Which wrinkles will devour,
Brightness falls from the air,
Queens have died young and fair,
Dust hath closed Helen's eye.
I am sick, I must die: 20
  Lord, have mercy on us.

Strength stoops unto the grave,
Worms feed on Hector brave,

ADIEU, FAREWELL, EARTH'S BLISS. **3. Fond:** foolish. **10.
Physic:** the physician.

576

Swords may not fight with fate,
Earth still holds ope her gate.   25
Come, come, the bells do cry.
I am sick, I must die:
  Lord, have mercy on us.

Wit with his wantonness°
Tasteth death's bitterness: 30
Hell's executioner
Hath no ears for to hear
What vain art can reply.
I am sick, I must die:
  Lord, have mercy on us.   35

Haste therefore each degree,°
To welcome destiny:
Heaven is our heritage,
Earth but a player's stage,
Mount we unto the sky.   40
I am sick, I must die.
  Lord, have mercy on us!

WILLIAM SHAKESPEARE
1564–1616

Sonnet 30

When to the sessions° of sweet silent thought
I summon up remembrance of things past,
I sigh the lack of many a thing I sought,
And with old woes new wail my dear time's waste:

---

29. wantonness: extravagance. **36. degree:** rank in society.
SONNET 30. **1. sessions:** sittings of a law court.

Then can I drown an eye, unused to flow,   5
For precious friends hid in death's dateless night,
And weep afresh love's long since canceled woe,
And moan th' expense° of many a vanished sight.
Then can I grieve at grievances foregone,
And heavily from woe to woe tell° o'er   10
The sad account of fore-bemoanèd moan,
Which I new pay as if not paid before.
　　But if the while I think on thee, dear friend,
　　All losses are restored, and sorrows end.

Sonnet 55

Not marble, nor the gilded monuments
Of princes, shall outlive this powerful rhyme;
But you shall shine more bright in these contents
Than unswept stone, besmeared with sluttish time.
When wasteful war shall statues overturn,   5
And broils° root out the work of masonry,
Nor Mars his sword nor war's quick fire shall burn
The living record of your memory.
'Gainst death and all-oblivious enmity°
Shall you pace forth; your praise shall still find
　　room   10
Even in the eyes of all posterity
That wear this world out to the ending doom.°
　　So, till the judgment that° yourself arise,
　　You live in this, and dwell in lovers' eyes.

Sonnet 64

When I have seen by Time's fell hand defaced
The rich proud cost° of outworn buried age;
When sometime lofty towers I see down razed,
And brass° eternal slave to mortal rage;
When I have seen the hungry ocean gain   5
Advantage on the kingdom of the shore,
And the firm soil win of the watery main,
Increasing store with loss, and loss with store;
When I have seen such interchange of state,

8. **expense:** loss. 10. **tell:** count.

SONNET 55. 6. **broils:** conflicts. 9. **all-oblivious enmity:**
enmity of being forgotten. 12. **ending doom:** Judgment Day.
13. **that:** when.

SONNET 64. 2. **cost:** expensive memorials of an individual
or a civilization. 4. **brass:** artifacts made of brass.

Or state° itself confounded° to decay,   10
Ruin hath taught me thus to ruminate
That Time will come and take my love away.
　　This thought is as a death, which cannot choose
　　But weep to have that which it fears to lose.

Sonnet 73

That time of year thou mayst in me behold
When yellow leaves, or none, or few, do hang
Upon those boughs which shake against the cold,
Bare ruined choirs,° where late the sweet birds
　　sang.
In me thou seest the twilight of such day   5
As after sunset fadeth in the west,
Which by and by black night doth take away,
Death's second self that seals up all in rest.
In me thou seest the glowing of such fire
That on the ashes of his° youth doth lie,   10
As the deathbed whereon it must expire,
Consumed with that° which it was nourished by.
　　This thou perceiv'st, which makes thy love more
　　　strong,
　　To love that well which thou must leave ere long.

JOHN DONNE
1572–1631

A Valediction: Forbidding Mourning

As virtuous men pass mildly away,
　　And whisper to their souls to go,
Whilst some of their sad friends do say,
　　The breath goes now, and some say, no:

So let us melt, and make no noise,   5
　　No tear-floods, nor sigh-tempests move,

10. **state:** grandeur. **confounded:** deteriorated, wasted.

SONNET 73. 4. **choirs:** churches, where services were sung.
10. **his:** its. 12. **that:** the material that fed the fire, now
ashes.

'Twere profanation of our joys
  To tell the laity° our love.

Moving of the earth° brings harms and fears,
  Men reckon what it did and meant,   10
But trepidation of the spheres,°
  Though greater far, is innocent.

Dull sublunary° lovers' love
  (Whose soul is sense°) cannot admit
Absence, because it doth remove   15
  Those things which elemented° it.

But we by a love so much refined
  That our selves know not what it is,
Inter-assurèd of the mind,
  Care less, eyes, lips, and hands to miss.   20

Our two souls therefore, which are one,
  Though I must go, endure not yet
A breach, but an expansion,
  Like gold to airy thinness beat.

If they be two, they are two so   25
  As stiff twin compasses are two:
Thy soul, the fixed foot, makes no show
  To move, but doth if the other do.

And though it in the center sit,
  Yet when the other far doth roam,   30
It leans and hearkens after it,
  And grows erect as that comes home.

Such wilt thou be to me, who must,
  Like the other foot, obliquely run;
Thy firmness makes my circle just,°   35
  And makes me end where I begun.

A Nocturnal
Upon Saint Lucy's Day

'Tis the year's midnight, and it is the day's,
Lucy's,° who scarce seven hours herself unmasks.
  The sun is spent, and now his flasks°
  Send forth light squibs,° no constant rays;
    The world's whole sap is sunk;   5
The general balm° th' hydroptic° earth hath drunk,
Whither, as to the bed's-feet, life is shrunk,
Dead and interred; yet all these seem to laugh,
Compared with me, who am their epitaph.

Study me then, you who shall lovers be   10
At the next world, that is, at the next spring:
  For I am every dead thing,
    In whom love wrought new alchemy.
    For his art did express°
A quintessence even from nothingness,   15
From dull privations, and lean emptiness
He ruined me, and I am re-begot
Of° absence, darkness, death: things which are not.

All others from all things draw all that's good,
Life, soul, form, spirit, whence they being have; 20
  I, by love's limbec,° am the grave
    Of all that's nothing. Oft a flood
      Have we two wept, and so
Drowned the whole world, us two; oft did we grow
To be two chaoses, when we did show   25
Care to aught else; and often absences
Withdrew our souls, and made us carcases.

But I am by her death (which word wrongs her)
Of the first nothing the elixir° grown;
    Were I a man, that I were one   30
    I needs must know; I should prefer,
      If I were any beast,
Some ends, some means; yea plants, yea stones
    detest
And love; all, all some properties invest;°

A NOCTURNAL UPON SAINT LUCY'S DAY. **2. Lucy's:** Saint
Lucy's Day, December 13, was the shortest day of the year
according to the Julian calendar, which was used in England
until 1752. **3. flasks:** powder flasks. **4. squibs:** fireworks
that produce a series of minor explosions. **6. balm:** vital
sap. **hydroptic:** thirsty. **14. express:** press out (in alchemy).
18. Of: from. **21. limbec:** retort, a vessel used in distillation.
29. elixir: in alchemy, the substance that would transform
base metal to gold; hence the "quintessence" of the "first
nothing." **30–34. Were . . . invest:** allusion to the great
chain of being, a concept that ordered all existing things in a
hierarchy, specifying the nature and function of each.

A VALEDICTION: FORBIDDING MOURNING. **8. laity:** laymen,
i.e., outsiders in the mysteries of love. **9. Moving . . . earth:**
earthquakes. **11. trepidation . . . spheres:** wobbling of the
eighth sphere in the geocentric astronomy of Ptolemy,
which is one way of explaining the precession of the vernal
and autumnal equinoxes and thereby the change of seasons.
13. sublunary: under the moon, earthly. **14. sense:** physical
sensation. **16. elemented:** composed. **34. obliquely:** indirectly. **35. just:** perfect.

If I an ordinary nothing were,   35
As shadow, a light and body must be here.°

But I am none; nor will my sun° renew.
You lovers, for whose sake the lesser sun
  At this time to the Goat° is run
    To fetch new lust, and give it you,   40
    Enjoy your summer all;
Since she° enjoys her long night's festival,
Let me prepare towards her, and let me call
This hour her vigil, and her eve, since this
Both the year's and the day's deep midnight is. 45

THOMAS GRAY
1716–1771

Elegy
Written in a
Country Churchyard

The curfew tolls the knell of parting day,
The lowing herd wind slowly o'er the lea,°
The plowman homeward plods his weary way,
And leaves the world to darkness and to me.

Now fades the glimmering landscape on the sight,
And all the air a solemn stillness holds,   6
Save where the beetle wheels his droning flight,
And drowsy tinklings lull the distant folds;

Save that from yonder ivy-mantled tow'r
The moping owl does to the moon complain   10
Of such, as wand'ring near her secret bow'r,°
Molest her ancient solitary reign.

Beneath those rugged elms, that yew-tree's shade,
Where heaves the turf in many a mold'ring heap,
Each in his narrow cell forever laid,   15
The rude° forefathers of the hamlet sleep.

The breezy call of incense-breathing Morn,
The swallow twitt'ring from the straw-built shed,

The cock's shrill clarion, or the echoing horn,°
No more shall rouse them from their lowly bed. 20

For them no more the blazing hearth shall burn,
Or busy housewife ply her evening care:
No children run to lisp their sire's return,
Or climb his knees the envied kiss to share.

Oft did the harvest to their sickle yield,   25
Their furrow oft the stubborn glebe° has broke;
How jocund° did they drive their team afield!
How bowed the woods beneath their sturdy
  stroke!

Let not Ambition mock their useful toil,
Their homely joys, and destiny obscure;   30
Nor Grandeur hear with a disdainful smile
The short and simple annals of the poor.

The boast of heraldry,° the pomp of pow'r,
And all that beauty, all that wealth e'er gave,
Await alike th' inevitable hour.   35
The paths of glory lead but to the grave.

Nor you, ye proud, impute to these the fault,
If Mem'ry o'er their tomb no trophies° raise,
Where through the long-drawn aisle and fretted
  vault°
The pealing anthem swells the note of praise.   40

Can storied° urn or animated bust
Back to its mansion call the fleeting breath?
Can Honor's voice provoke° the silent dust,
Or Flatt'ry soothe the dull cold ear of Death?

Perhaps in this neglected spot is laid   45
Some heart once pregnant with celestial fire;
Hands, that rod of empire might have swayed,
Or waked to ecstasy the living lyre.

But Knowledge to their eyes her ample page
Rich with the spoils of time did ne'er unroll;   50
Chill Penury repressed their noble rage,
And froze the genial° current of the soul.

Full many a gem of purest ray serene,
The dark unfathomed caves of ocean bear:
Full many a flower is born to blush unseen,   55
And waste its sweetness on the desert air.

---

36. a . . . here: i.e., what is necessary to produce a
shadow. 37. sun: loved one. 39. Goat: Capricorn in the
zodiac; also associated with lust. 42. she: loved one.
ELEGY WRITTEN IN A COUNTRY CHURCHYARD. 2. lea:
pasture. 11. bow'r: dwelling. 16. rude: untaught.

19. horn: hunter's horn. 26. glebe: turf. 27. jocund: cheerfully. 33. heraldry: noble birth. 38. trophies: carvings that
represent the achievements of the dead man. 39. fretted vault:
ornamental arched ceiling. 41. storied: inscribed with an
epitaph. 43. provoke: call forth. 52. genial: animating.

Some village-Hampden,° that with dauntless breast
The little tyrant of his fields withstood;
Some mute inglorious Milton here may rest,
Some Cromwell guiltless of his country's blood. 60

Th' applause of list'ning senates to command,
The threats of pain and ruin to despise,
To scatter plenty o'er a smiling land,
And read their hist'ry in a nation's eyes,

Their lot forbade: nor circumscribed alone   65
Their growing virtues, but their crimes confined;
Forbade to wade through slaughter to a throne,
And shut the gates of mercy on mankind,

The struggling pangs of conscious truth to hide,
To quench the blushes of ingenuous shame,   70
Or heap the shrine of Luxury and Pride
With incense kindled at the Muse's flame.

Far from the madding crowd's ignoble strife,
Their sober wishes never learned to stray;
Along the cool sequestered vale of life   75
They kept the noiseless tenor of their way.

Yet ev'n these bones from insult to protect,
Some frail memorial still erected nigh,
With uncouth rhymes and shapeless sculpture
    decked,
Implores the passing tribute of a sigh.   80

Their name, their years, spelt by th' unlettered
    Muse,
The place of fame and elegy supply:
And many a holy text around she strews,
That teach the rustic moralist° to die.

For who to dumb Forgetfulness a prey,   85
This pleasing anxious being e'er resigned,
Left the warm precincts of the cheerful day,
Nor cast one longing ling'ring look behind?

On some fond breast the parting soul relies,
Some pious drops the closing eye requires;   90
Ev'n from the tomb the voice of Nature cries,
Ev'n in our ashes live their wonted° fires.

For thee,° who mindful of th' unhonored dead
Dost in these lines their artless tale relate;

If chance,° by lonely contemplation led,   95
Some kindred spirit shall inquire thy fate,

Haply° some hoary-headed swain° may say,
"Oft have we seen him at the peep of dawn
Brushing with hasty steps the dews away
To meet the sun upon the upland lawn.   100

"There at the foot of yonder nodding beech
That wreathes its old fantastic roots so high,
His listless length at noontide would he stretch,
And pore upon the brook that babbles by.

"Hard by yon wood, now smiling as in scorn,   105
Mutt'ring his wayward fancies he would rove,
Now drooping, woeful wan, like one forlorn,
Or crazed with care, or crossed in hopeless love.

"One morn I missed him on the customed hill,
Along the heath and near his fav'rite tree;   110
Another came; nor yet beside the rill,
Nor up the lawn, nor at the wood was he;

"The next with dirges due in sad array
Slow through the church-way path we saw him
    borne.   114
Approach and read (for thou canst read) the lay,
Graved on the stone beneath yon aged thorn."°

THE EPITAPH

Here rests his head upon the lap of Earth
A youth to Fortune and to Fame unknown.
Fair Science° frowned not on his humble birth,
And Melancholy marked him for her own.   120

Large was his bounty,° and his soul sincere,
Heav'n did a recompense as largely send:
He gave to Mis'ry all he had, a tear,
He gain'd from Heav'n ('twas all he wished) a friend.

No farther seek his merits to disclose,   125
Or draw his frailties from their dread abode
(There they alike in trembling hope repose),
The bosom of his Father and his God.

---

57. **Hampden:** John Hampden (1594–1643), hero of the Parliamentary forces in he English Civil War because he had defied the taxes of Charles I. 84. **moralist:** i.e., moral man. 92. **wonted:** customary. 93. **thee:** ambiguous reference to the stonecutter, the speaker of the poem, or perhaps to Gray himself.

95. **If chance:** if it should happen that. 97. **Haply:** perhaps. **swain:** rustic or shepherd, a traditional persona for the poet who mourns in the pastoral elegy. 116. **thorn:** hawthorn tree. 119. **Science:** learning or knowledge in general. 121. **bounty:** generosity.

Submission to Impersonal Law

BEN JONSON
1572–1637

On My First Son

Farewell, thou child of my right hand, and joy;
  My sin was too much hope of thee, loved boy.
Seven years thou wert lent to me, and I thee pay,
  Exacted by thy fate, on the just day.
Oh, could I lose all father° now. For why   5
  Will man lament the state he should envy?
To have so soon scaped world's and flesh's rage,
  And, if no other misery, yet age?
Rest in soft peace and, asked, say, "Here doth lie
  Ben Jonson his best piece of *poetry*."   10
For whose sake, henceforth, all his vows be such,
  As what he loves may never° like too much.

Epitaph on Elizabeth, L. H.

Wouldst thou hear what man can say
In a little? Reader, stay.
Underneath this stone doth lie
As much beauty as could die;
Which in life did harbor give   5
To more virtue than doth live.
If at all she had a fault,
Leave it buried in this vault.
One name was Elizabeth,

ON MY FIRST SON. **5. father:** fatherhood. **12. may never:**
may he never.

Th' other let it sleep with death;   10
Fitter, where it died to tell,
Than that it lived at all. Farewell.

ALEXANDER POPE
1688–1744

Elegy to the Memory
of an Unfortunate Lady

What beckoning ghost, along the moonlight shade
Invites my steps, and points to yonder glade?
'Tis she!—but why that bleeding bosom gored,
Why dimly gleams the visionary sword?°
O ever beauteous, ever friendly! tell,   5
Is it, in Heaven, a crime to love too well?
To bear too tender, or too firm a heart,
To act a lover's or a Roman's part?°
Is there no bright reversion in the sky,
For those who greatly think, or bravely die?   10
    Why bade ye else, ye Powers! her soul aspire
Above the vulgar flight of low desire?
Ambition first sprung from your blest abodes;
The glorious fault of angels and of gods:
Thence to their images on earth it flows,   15
And in the breasts of kings and heroes glows.
Most souls, 'tis true, but peep out once an age,
Dull sullen prisoners in the body's cage:

ELEGY TO THE MEMORY OF AN UNFORTUNATE LADY. **4.
sword:** used in committing suicide. **8. act . . . part:** commit
suicide because of unrequited love or military defeat.

581

Dim lights of life, that burn a length of years
Useless, unseen, as lamps in sepulchers;   20
Like Eastern kings a lazy state they keep,
And close confined to their own palace, sleep.

From these perhaps (ere Nature bade her die)
Fate snatched her early to the pitying sky.
As into air the purer spirits flow,   25
And separate from their kindred dregs below;°
So flew the soul to its congenial° place.
Nor left one virtue to redeem her race.°

But thou, false guardian of a charge too good,
Thou, mean deserter of thy brother's blood!   30
See on these ruby lips the trembling breath,
These cheeks, now fading at the blast of death;
Cold is that breast which warmed the world before,
And those love-darting eyes must roll no more.
Thus, if Eternal Justice rules the ball,°   35
Thus shall your wives, and thus your children fall:
On all the line a sudden vengeance waits,
And frequent hearses shall besiege your gates.
There passengers shall stand, and pointing say
(While the long funerals blacken all the way)   40
Lo, these were they, whose souls the Furies steeled,
And cursed with hearts unknowing how to yield.
Thus unlamented pass the proud away,
The gaze of fools, and pageant of a day!
So perish all, whose breast ne'er learned to glow 45
For others' good, or melt at others' woe.

What can atone (oh, ever-injured shade!)
Thy fate unpitied, and thy rites unpaid?
No friend's complaint,° no kind domestic tear
Pleased thy pale ghost, or graced thy mournful bier.
By foreign hands thy dying eyes were closed,   51
By foreign hands thy decent limbs composed,
By foreign hands thy humble grave adorned,
By strangers honored, and by strangers mourned!
What though no friends in sable weeds° appear, 55
Grieve for an hour, perhaps, then mourn a year,
And bear about the mockery of woe
To midnight dances, and the public show?
What though no weeping Loves thy ashes grace,
Nor polished marble emulate thy face?   60
What though no sacred earth allow thee room,°
Nor hallowed dirge be muttered o'er thy tomb?
Yet shall thy grave with rising flowers be dressed,
And the green turf lie lightly on thy breast:

There shall the morn her earliest tears bestow, 65
There the first roses of the year shall blow;°
While angels with their silver wings o'ershade
The ground, now sacred by thy reliques made.
So peaceful rests, without a stone, a name,
What once had beauty, titles, wealth, and fame. 70
How loved, how honored once, avails thee not,
To whom related, or by whom begot;
A heap of dust alone remains of thee,
'Tis all thou art, and all the proud° shall be!   74
Poets themselves must fall, like those they sung,
Deaf the praised ear, and mute the tuneful tongue.
Even he, whose soul now melts in mournful lays,
Shall shortly want the generous tear he pays;
Then from his closing eyes thy form shall part,
And the last pang shall tear thee from his heart, 80
Life's idle business at one gasp be o'er,
The Muse forgot, and thou beloved no more!

WILLIAM WORDSWORTH
1770–1850

She Dwelt
Among The Untrodden Ways

She dwelt among the untrodden ways
    Beside the springs of Dove,°
A maid whom there were none to praise
    And very few to love:

A violet by a mossy stone   5
    Half hidden from the eye!
—Fair as a star, when only one
    Is shining in the sky.

She lived unknown, and few could know
    When Lucy ceased to be;   10
But she is in her grave, and, oh,
    The difference to me!

25–26. As . . . below: as in chemical sublimation. 27.
congenial: kindred; natal. 28. race: family, lineage. 35.
ball: earth. 49. complaint: elegy. 55. sable weeds: black
clothes of mourning. 61. no . . . room: Suicides could not
be buried in consecrated ground.

66. blow: bloom. 74. the proud: the lady's unfeeling kin.
SHE DWELT AMONG THE UNTRODDEN WAYS. 2. Dove: small
river in central England.

A Slumber Did My Spirit Seal

A slumber did my spirit seal;
  I had no human fears:
She seemed a thing that could not feel
  The touch of earthly years.

No motion has she now, no force;   5
  She neither hears nor sees;
Rolled round in earth's diurnal course,
  With rocks, and stones, and trees.

WALTER SAVAGE LANDOR
1775–1864

Rose Aylmer

Ah what avails the sceptered race,°
  Ah what the form divine!
What every virtue, every grace!
  Rose Aylmer, all were thine.
Rose Aylmer, whom these wakeful eyes   5
  May weep, but never see,
A night of memories and of sighs
  I consecrate to thee.

On Seeing a Hair of Lucretia Borgia

Borgia,° thou once wert almost too august
And high for adoration—now thou'rt dust;
All that remains of thee these plaits infold,
Calm hair, meandering with pellucid gold!

DYLAN THOMAS
1914–1953

A Refusal to Mourn the Death, by Fire, of a Child in London

Never until the mankind° making
Bird beast and flower
Fathering and all humbling° darkness
Tells with silence the last light° breaking
And the still hour   5
Is come of the sea tumbling in harness

And I must enter again the round
Zion° of the water bead
And the synagogue of the ear of corn
Shall I let pray the shadow of a sound   10
Or sow my salt seed
In the least valley of sackcloth° to mourn

The majesty and burning of the child's death.
I shall not murder
The mankind of her going with a grave° truth   15
Nor blaspheme down the stations of the breath°
With any further
Elegy of innocence and youth.

Deep with the first dead lies London's daughter,
Robed in the long° friends,   20
The grains beyond age, the dark veins° of her
    mother,
Secret by the unmourning water
Of the riding Thames.
After the first death, there is no other.

ROSE AYLMER. **1. sceptered race:** Rose Aylmer was the daughter of a baron.

ON SEEING A HAIR OF LUCRETIA BORGIA. **1. Borgia:** Lucretia Borgia (1480–1519), duchess of Ferrara, whose many marriages played a part in the political intrigues of her father, Pope Alexander VI. As duchess of Ferrara, she was patroness of many scholars and artists, including Ariosto, Cardinal Bembo, and Titian.

A REFUSAL TO MOURN. **1–3. mankind . . . humbling:** modifiers of "darkness." **4. last light:** Day of Judgment. **8. Zion:** Jerusalem or Jewish religious culture as a whole. **10–12. shadow . . . sackcloth:** Cf. "valley of the shadow of death." **15. grave:** concerning death; also, trite and pompous. **16. stations . . . breath:** Cf. "stations of the cross." **20. long:** for a long time past and to come. **21. veins:** perhaps rivers; also, ore.

X. J. KENNEDY
b. 1929

Little Elegy

for a child who skipped rope

Here lies resting, out of breath,
Out of turns, Elizabeth

Whose quicksilver toes not quite
Cleared the whirring edge of night.

Earth whose circles round us skim   5
Till they catch the lightest limb,
Shelter now Elizabeth
And for her sake trip up Death.

COMEDY

Narrative Comedy

There is far less agreement about the nature of comedy than there is about her more dignified sister. Tragedy is easily associated with ideas about fate, cosmic order, and human pride, but comedy will not sit still for such an analysis. When we try to define comedy, we are likely to end up with a vacuous formula such as "criticism of life" or "thoughtful laughter." The diversity in what people mean when they use the word *comedy* should make the boldest generalizer wary. Comedy presumably includes farce, burlesque, travesty, parody, and some kinds of satire. Numbered among its techniques are wit, humor, sarcasm, exaggeration, understatement, and the like. Some of its effects are simple and immediately available, like the exhilaration of laughter and the benign reassurance of a happy ending, although its aims—the ridicule of human folly or the ritual purification of a sick society—may be intellectually complex and symbolic. Definitions of what is central to comedy tend to become narrow and exclusive as they gain in precision. Affectation, hypocrisy, rigidity, and excess in human conduct can explain much about the comic nature of such figures as the dandy, the machine politician, the "square" father, and the circus clown, but no one of them has the scope to do the whole job.

Part of the difficulty is semantic. Ways of limiting the established senses of the word *comedy* do not seem to reflect ordinary usage. A clumsy movement, a distorted face, the verbal play of puns and limericks, a conversation in which two people talk at cross purposes—all may strike us as being "comic," whereas we should be less likely to use the word *tragic* in comparable but sadder circumstances. One reason for this difference in usage is the constant availability of comic "material" in ordinary life; we derive our sense of comedy quite directly from experience. The comic is waiting for us every day wherever men and women congregate—in fragments of conversation that reveal poses, in rote actions, in quirks of temperament, in the ponderous workings of absurd bureaucracies. Stand as a detached observer for ten minutes in any room full of people and you will probably find a pompous fool, an intellectual snob, an egotist, an egregious flirt, a self-made man, a social climber, and any number of other "types," including yourself as a self-assured and realistic critic of the situation.

Such characters reveal themselves in almost any social context. We can recognize them immediately because their dominating traits are independent of any special circumstances in the past and will continue indefinitely in the future. Just the reverse seems to be true of tragic figures. We do know of men who sacrifice much of their lives for a cause or suffer to the limit of human endurance or set out to control nature and society, but we are not likely to meet Ahabs or Jobs or Fausts in the street. And even if we did, we would not be able to recognize tragic figures apart from their histories. They are embedded in time: their obsessions and illusions have special meaning only in the context that shapes and magnifies their lives, and this context is elaborated most fully in literary works. Historical figures—King Lear, Joan of Arc, Thomas à Becket—become tragic through literature or the legends closely associated with it, where their roles have a magnitude hard to sustain in less exalted contexts. If he were not king and his acts had no inevitable consequences, Lear's childish game with his daughters in the opening scene of the play might be comic, a version of tell-me-how-much-you-love-me. Although most comic types are also derived from literature, they have a different relation to it: particulars of time and place are accidental rather than essential. Shakespeare's Falstaff and Molière's Tartuffe are quintessentially the braggart soldier and the religious hypocrite; with different mannerisms, they can be found in Roman comedy and in nineteenth-century fiction, or outside of literature in veterans' conventions and church meetings. Evidently comic types are not dependent on literary contexts for their meaning in the same way that tragic heroes are. They exhibit principles that do not change much from setting to setting; they seem to be self-contained in such a way that their conduct is both transparent and predictable.

Our quick recognition of comic types, whether on or off stage, is the result of one rudimentary assumption about human temperament—its resistance to change. Characters whose eccentricity strikes us immediately and forcibly have been a staple of literature in the Renaissance comedy of humours, the eighteenth-century comedy of manners, and the twentieth-century comedy of the absurd. Although the types are constant in an abstract sense because the same feature of human nature is revealing itself again, their external trappings vary considerably from age to age. We no longer use a convention of "humours" to connect dominant traits with the balance of fluids in the human body, but we recognize a comic type in Shakespeare's Malvolio (*Twelfth Night*) and Jaques (*As You Like It*) whether or not we call them melancholics. There is, however, an important difference between the characters we see on stage and the distant relatives we meet at a family reunion. The conventions of literary comedy give us eccentricities and follies undiluted by normal behavior; the ingredients of the comic from everyday experience have been distilled and refined. Thus comedy is both natural and artificial, with sources in life and in literature, and it is clear that any attempt to reduce one source to the other can be a rather futile exercise in classification. We are more interested in the relationship between the constants of human nature and the literary conventions that draw our attention to them. Ultimately, comedy is ordinary experience given rhythm or shape, a pattern that simultaneously represents human behavior and implies attitudes toward it.

Many attempts to isolate the central principles of comedy have foundered in theories of laughter. The simplest rationale for identifying the comic with the laughable grows out of drama, where dialogue and action on stage evoke an immediate response in the audience. A number of difficulties make this way of defining comedy less useful than it seems. Laughter ranges from a half-formed smile to uncontrollable hysteria. When overtired or keyed up, anyone may fall into hilarity at the slightest excuse, and there are obvious differences of temperament among the habitually morose, the exuberant, and the phlegmatic that affect their tendency to laugh. Cultural traditions and political events also determine in more general ways what people find funny. The first production of John Millington Synge's *Playboy of the Western World* in Dublin produced a theater riot rather than laughter. Records parodying President Kennedy had to be withdrawn after his assassination. It is apparent that no simple correlation between laughter and literary comedy will stand much scrutiny.

The Motives in Comedy

Whatever laughter depends on must be much less specialized than the experience of literature because we laugh more often when we are not reading a novel or watching a play than when we are. Also, it seems impossible to limit the causes of laughter to the inherent qualities of what we are observing. Whether we laugh or not, apart from the individual variables of temperament and mood, depends on the rhetorical situation. The key relationship in stage comedy would seem to be distance: we do not leap up on the stage to straighten out a deluded character (violating this inhibition is the point of departure for "happenings" and "living theater"), yet we have no qualms about offering the same advice to a good friend. Because of our distance from the dramatic character, we laugh instead of act; identifying with the friend, however, we dare not laugh openly. Between these situations lies conversation at a formal dinner party, where a sense of decorum may reduce us to snickering when we want to laugh uproariously. Every rhetorical situation has its own conventions, and these conventions often restrict laughter. An incident that makes us laugh in one setting may not in another, although its structure and detail remain unchanged. Thus the causes of laughter are too complex and variable to be easily related to the literary form we call comedy.

Theorizing about literary comedy by discussing other effects it is supposed to produce is again a false start. A number of effects other than laughter have been proposed: the pleasure of simple joy, the vicarious release of aggressions, the extirpation of foolish attitudes, or the comfort of identifying with a group. Such effects may or may not take place in the audience; if they do, they are not totally governed by the literary work and thus are partly accidental. The essential nature of any work does not depend on what *happens* to any particular audience. Although their interpretations vary, literary works are relatively stable and permanent, and we value them because they provide representations of living that do not fade with time. Moreover, they give us human motives abstractly, as it were, without any demand for the interaction or direct response that we cannot totally avoid in "real" encounters. Thus we see human motives more clearly in literature than in life—they are uncluttered with the extraneous—and we understand them better because we have no worries about our own course of action. And the motives built into the represented "action" of literature are out in the open to be looked at, unlike the variable, semiprivate effects that the action may produce in a particular audience. The characters of fiction and drama are intelligible to us whether we identify with them, reject them, or remain indifferent. The surest ways of describing comedy will call attention to what we understand rather than what we feel, without denigrating the importance or value of the latter in the total experience of literature.

Preservation and Heightening of Vitality

Literary comedy uses at least three human motives. The first of these is the desire to preserve and heighten vitality, the impulse to grasp all the delights of living now. It is human energy asking for no limits, hindrances, postponements, or choices. It is based on the instinct of human beings to adapt themselves to changes in their environment, to be responsive and alert and flexible in conserving their own persons, to use what Susanne Langer calls "a brainy opportunism in face of an essentially dreadful universe." We value human energy because it must ultimately decay in sickness or senility and end in death. How we pass through time—how much joy and love and freshness we are able to pack into living—matters because we do not have enough of it. The vortex of action in comedy is often a character with boundless energy like Mosca in Ben Jonson's *Volpone*, Jim Dixon in Kingsley Amis' *Lucky Jim*, or Gulley Jimson in Joyce Cary's *Horse's Mouth*. Fast-paced, witty dialogue that contributes very little to plot or characterization (of the kind found in Richard Brinsley Sheridan's *School for Scandal*) displays such vitality for its own sake, and it is sometimes projected into roles like that of the fool in Elizabethan comedy.

The circus clown and the stock buffoon of slapstick go through antics that consume an exorbitant amount of human energy, as if there were no end to it. In such cases the impulses of vitality begin to parody themselves. Totally undirected energy becomes absurd, especially when stupid characters abuse their inheritance of vitality. The human being who cannot "case" his environment and adapt to it quickly is a caricature, a slave to his own routines and habits. Figures in slapstick comedy over-respond to their surroundings through rote movements suggesting the mechanical rather than the human—clumsiness, stiffness of limbs, rigid gestures, frozen facial expressions, inattention, and automatic repetition. The general principle is lack of balance, an incongruence between means and ends. Energy becomes dehumanized when there is no fit between what is being done and the manner of doing it, as if the actor were a misprogramed robot rather than a living being.

The desire for freedom from spurious constriction is a second motive in comedy. When television comedians imitate such stock types as filibustering senators, blustering tycoons, absent-minded professors, and milquetoast husbands, they expose the misuse of life possibilities. The targets of mimicry seem ridiculous because they confine themselves, huddling in corners when they could be moving freely through spacious rooms. The general principle here is reduction: men quixotically limit their own freedom of action by taking comfort in familiar faces and old ways of doing things, however senseless that may be in their present circumstances. The living, changing being is by his own will reduced to acting out those preformed, inflexible patterns of conduct we call habits; he becomes static, dull, and predictable, narrowly defining what he could be by what he has been. In literary comedy, such characters are more often old than young, and they usually represent the accumulated wealth and power of existing social classes. They cause malaise in society by imposing outworn sanctions on the young. The familiar types are usually anachronistic, behind the times from the standpoint of the young: filibustering senators use talk to avoid the real issues, self-made executives insist that others come up the hard way, absent-minded professors maintain a comfortable division between thought and action, bullied husbands accede to a truce less painful than fresh bickering. Hold the line, they all seem to say, where the young see infinite possibilities and unlimited freedom.

Freedom from Constriction

In comedy the illusions of the young are set against the delusions of the old. "There is no joke so true and deep in actual life," writes Emerson in his essay "The Comic,"

> as when some pure idealist goes up and down among the institutions of society, attended by a man who knows the world, and who, sympathizing with the philosopher's scrutiny, sympathizes also with the confusion and indignation of the detected, skulking institutions. His perception of disparity, his eye wandering perpetually from the rule to the crooked, lying, thieving fact, makes the eyes run over with laughter.

With laughter but not with rage. The gap between ideals and practice is not unbridgeable in comedy, as it is in irony. In comedy, defects in human conduct have the character of folly more than sin. Most vulnerable to ridicule are those who bluff or pretend, leading us to sense the disparity between inflated claims and minute accomplishment. In *Tom Jones* Henry Fielding presents a host of characters like Thwackum and Square, the parson who twists scripture to suit his own purposes and the philosopher of continence who is discovered in bed—and not alone. In the same novel

Squire Western showers friendship on Tom quite genuinely until he discovers that his daughter may want to marry the low-born fellow. Two centuries later the same affectations reappear in Saul Bellow's *Adventures of Augie March* or Joyce Cary's *Horse's Mouth*. Comedy claims folly as its special domain by assuming that human nature does not change much. Foolishness and hypocrisy are perennial, and the action of comedy exposes them in all their forms. Men can never be permanently cured of their absurd pretenses in comedy any more than they can avoid hubris in tragedy.

Ritual Purification of Society   With a slight change of tone, pretense and hypocrisy threaten human desires so strongly that comedy verges on irony. As comic action darkens, characters appear to be vicious rather than foolish, and the fabric of society is so rent that a good life seems impossible; vitality itself becomes more a menace than a boon. There is enough literature of this sort that is neither ironic nor tragic to suggest a third general motive in comedy: the ritual purification of society. Many comic dramas of the Renaissance and seventeenth century display this motive—Shakespeare's *Measure for Measure* and *Merchant of Venice*, Jonson's *Volpone*, and Molière's *Tartuffe*, to name just a few. In these plays the comic action frames aggressions that might produce catastrophe in a tragic context. At some point in each of them, the world is so much under the control of corrupt characters that reclaiming it seems impossible, yet comic action prevails and a shattered society is somehow put together again. The mechanism for accomplishing this nearly miraculous recovery is often an outside force, but the principle involved is a transfer of guilt. The festering sores of vice have spread so far throughout a society that it cannot redeem itself without ritual purification. Communal sins are loaded on a scapegoat who is then expelled, thus cleansing the other members of their past and renewing the possibility of normal life in society.

Within this general framework of ritual action, the relation of the scapegoat figure to the rest of society varies. At the darkest moment in Shakespeare's *Twelfth Night*, Malvolio is transformed from an object of ridicule into a scapegoat. He is vulnerable because he pompously refuses to condone festivity, but his imprisonment represents more than the liberation of the play's lower society of drunken revelers. When he is brought close to madness in the prison scene, the change of tone suggests that the heavy hand of Malvolio's priggishness has been replaced by total license, the unrestrained freedom of disorder. Molière's Tartuffe, the archetypal hypocrite in the play named for him, gains a specious and malignant power over society through his consummate skill in deceiving and manipulating others, just as Angelo does in Shakespeare's *Measure for Measure*; in both cases it takes the interference of a remote and more powerful ruler to save society from total corruption. A similar rite of expelling the scapegoat occurs at the end of Jonson's *Volpone*, but with a difference: in this case the vices of society are not concentrated in one man and his helper but uncovered by them, until there are few innocents left in the whole of Venice. Volpone and Mosca, as well as Corbaccio, Corvino, and Voltore, must be punished or exiled in a gesture of purification, a restorative closure to a play that could never end in celebration; the plague of vice and cruelty has been lifted, and the best that can be expected is a return to normalcy. The expulsion of a scapegoat and its reciprocal (the voluntary withdrawal of an individual from a society) are not limited to the darker forms of comedy. *Twelfth Night* is one of Shakespeare's most exuberant plays in spite of Malvolio; and when Alceste chooses to leave what he thinks is a corrupt society in Molière's *Misanthrope*, we are well aware of the values he rejects—tact, discretion, tolerance—for the sake of an inflexible candor. Similarly, there is loss as well as gain in the expulsion of Becky Sharp from the neat little domestic society cradled at the end of William Thackeray's *Vanity Fair*; the figure of wit and energy must give way to the dull Amelia and faithful Dobbin, who are the hero and heroine of the comic action. Even when more admirable heroes choose to exile themselves from constricting societies—Ozzie Freedman in Philip Roth's "Conversion of the Jews," Christy Mahon in Synge's *Playboy of the Western World*, Jim Dixon in Kingsley Amis' *Lucky Jim*—they have enough foibles to assure us that they are like the imperfect men and women we know.

Thus a ritual of purification never appears in deadly earnest, as it does in romance and tragedy, because comedy does not countenance such monolithic views of human nature. No single motive like the tragic protagonist's encroaching will or the romantic hero's desire for a quest dominates. Vanity, affectation, hypocrisy, and egoism are just a few of the obstacles in human character that comic action must overcome. Taken together, the three motives in comedy—the impulses of vitality, the desire for freedom from constriction, and the need for continual purification and renewal—explain much of comedy but not all. Without a clearer idea of the perspective that nourishes comic impulses, it is almost impossible to understand what saves *Volpone* from irony, what distinguishes *Twelfth Night* and "Rip Van Winkle" from romance, or even what one would have to do to convert *Romeo and Juliet* into comedy.

Comedy depends less on a fixed scene than on a way of seeing things. Like irony, it furnishes the audience with a double perspective on characters and events. For convenience, we can call these two perspectives *illusion* and *reality* if we mean by those terms two standards of judgment built into the narrative. Thus comic perspective works as a principle of relativity: we are asked to recognize as an illusion any conception of human society that reduces life possibilities to a rule, a formula, or a pattern. Although an illusion may not be pernicious in itself, it can become so as a part of any establishment. What many people now see as the confinement and dreary sameness of suburbia was once (just after the Second World

Comic Perspective

War) a dream of freedom and space in the country. The problem with any dream made real is that it stops changing: it becomes a "way of life" that the old hang on to grimly and the young rebel against. The basic illusion in comedy is the perception of existing categories—social classes based on wealth or heredity, laws decreed by a government or inherited from the past, traditional alliances or quarrels between groups of people—as if they were permanent fixtures of an unchanging world order. "Illusion is whatever is fixed or definable," comments Frye, "and reality is best understood as its negation: whatever reality is, it's not *that*." Establishments are not incarnations; they do not grow and adapt themselves to enhance the possibilities of life, but stiffen and die, leaving their imprint like fossils.

Comic perspective allows us to see illusions for what they are—attempts to make imperfect human conceptions permanent. Societies could not exist without illusions because no vision of a good life would be more than a dream if it did not take some shape in the real world. But as soon as that shape becomes established, an institution of society, it becomes static and potentially life defeating. So there is always a need for fresh illusions, for new attempts to transform human desire into social reality. In comedy, the existing social order is an outworn illusion, with an accretion of custom and power weighing it down. Those who would live fully must evade or defeat it. Thus the *structure* of events is not of crucial importance in comedy because we always anticipate some form of renewal, or at least relief from unwanted restrictions. Any reading of comic novels like Fielding's *Tom Jones*, Laurence Sterne's *Tristram Shandy*, Bellow's *Adventures of Augie March*, and Cary's *Horse's Mouth* should convince us that we have room to wander about within a spacious episodic structure—stopping to look more closely where it pleases us—without being preoccupied with that structure in itself. Even the more tightly ordered events of comic drama often have a fortuitous quality about them. The scenes of repartee in Sheridan's *School for Scandal*, where Lady Sneerwell, Snake, and Joseph Surface demonstrate their talents for slander, could be cut or expanded without altering the comic illusion they display. In the figure who talks well—Chauntecleer in Chaucer's "Nun's Priest's Tale," the wandering minstrel who is the persona of Ezra Pound's "Cino," Christy Mahon in *The Playboy of the Western World*, Dynamene in Christopher Fry's *Phoenix Too Frequent*—we see an emphasis on artifice for its own sake, the building of delightfully imagined worlds with words. In comedy, word play is a sign of exuberance, not a last hedge against despair as it sometimes is in irony. Even more important is its function in creating illusions—new ones that will replace the outworn ones in the moment of fresh hope toward which the action moves.

In this free-wheeling aspect of comedy, we notice a marked difference from the tight pattern of tragedy. The tragic hero bears the burden of recognition in a world that cannot be completely known; the comic world, by contrast, is complicated rather than mysterious, and when characters make discoveries they are often belated and trivial from our point of view.

What the hero and heroine learn is neither important nor arcane. Often it is a simple matter of discovering the hero's social or sexual identity: Tom Jones must be revealed as the nephew and heir of Squire Allworthy before he is allowed to marry Sophia Western, just as Oscar Wilde's *Importance of Being Earnest* parodies this ancient convention of mistaken identity by "losing" the hero as a baby in a London railway station. The alignment of two pairs of lovers in *Twelfth Night* depends on Viola's assuming her female role and being replaced by her brother Sebastian. In other cases what must be known is a fact perfectly obvious to the audience but nevertheless veiled from a few benevolent characters, usually those in control of society. *We* are not fooled by Joseph Surface's scheming in *The School for Scandal*, by the trick played on the cuckolded carpenter in "The Miller's Tale," by the manipulations of a father trying to unload his daughter in Malamud's "Magic Barrel," or by Mosca's net of intrigue in *Volpone*. Yet disguise and deception are endemic in comedy; the illusion created and perpetuated by ordinary human beings somehow hoodwinks a whole society. From the beginning of the action, we understand the principles that make the comic world work, and this rather minimal knowledge comes to us rather easily. What matters is the continued disparity between things as they seem and things as they are for the characters.

It is worth noting two other features of comic perspective. One of them is somewhat vaguely called "atmosphere." The double perspective of illusion and reality is common to both irony and comedy, but only in the latter does it seem to be tempered and "civilized." If the choice allowed human beings is a choice among socially perpetuated illusions, no one of which represents the nature of the universe, there should be more than enough room for tolerance, magnanimity, and courtesy. A central representative of comic urbanity might be the cultivated dilettante, a man so well aware of the variety of human experience that he is unwilling to restrict himself to one activity, one mode of living, or one criterion of judgment. Occasionally such a figure appears within comic structures as a master of ceremonies like Pisthetairos in Aristophanes' *Birds* or the host in Chaucer's *Canterbury Tales*. A nice sense of balance or proportion is usually implicit in the comic context. Exaggeration and excess of the kind that becomes increasingly dominant through the four books of *Gulliver's Travels* are alien to the comic spirit. When we get to the point in Book IV where Gulliver prefers horses to men, the tone is too full of savage venom to permit detachment. At least some freedom of attitude, some chance to find absurdity in institutions and in persons whom we also respect, or some note of grace in bureaucracies and fools, is an essential part of comedy.

The idea of proportion leads to a second feature of comic perspective that is more equivocal—its moral implications. A traditional defense of comedy against the perennial attacks of those who want to close theaters or ban books has been an affirmation of comedy's corrective function: cure vice and folly by exposing it to laughter. We have already shown how slippery any argument about the effects of literature is likely to be, and the history of obscenity legislation would suggest a similar conclusion, but it is still possible to think of comedy as a series of moral equations. Is the conflict of illusions a contest between good and evil? It is impossible to settle this question definitively, but we can reach a general principle: the darker the comedy, the larger the role of moral repugnance in controlling comic perspective. As characters become more vicious and their acts more destructive of social harmony, we move away from toleration toward judgment. But we can also recall our earlier example of Alceste in Molière's *Misanthrope*, whose blunt honesty is carried to such an extreme that it becomes a ridiculous virtue. Much comedy is sophisticated enough to refine any simplistic battle of vices and virtues out of existence. A prig, a plain dealer, or an earnest advocate of clean living may be morally right, but such characters are made out to be preposterous in comedy because they resist sociability. The typical action of comedy, which we shall look at next, moves toward a convergence and union of characters, a temporary resolution of differences in a society that is momentarily harmonious.

The Movement of Comedy

Three Patterns of Action

Since a structure of cause and effect is not our primary interest in comedy, it is not surprising to discover that plots are usually arbitrary, often trivial or silly, sometimes complicated to the point of absurdity, and seldom convincing as a representation of the way things happen in the world. Only in comedy do we expect young prodigals like Charles Surface in *The School for Scandal* to be rescued by the timely appearance of a rich uncle. The lack of variety in comic plots is more startling. In spite of superficial gimmicks, much comic action bears a strong family resemblance to a simple boy-girl triangle, with the third role filled by false lover, obstinate parent, or deceiving villain. This archetypal narrative pattern, which first appeared in later Greek comedy (often called New Comedy), is simple in outline. Two men struggle over a girl who is an object of sexual desire but not readily marriageable because she is tainted or because one of them is unworthy of her. The eventual loser is old but more powerful in society than his young competitor, who needs help from allies better able to manage the entrenched society. An impasse between the blocking elder and the usurper is broken only by some discovery of origin or status that makes the marriage of the girl and young man socially acceptable. The action ends in a celebration that includes the blocking figure and thus minimizes his loss. It is rather easy to see many of the comic narratives in this anthology as variations of the sexual triangle—"The Miller's Tale," *The School for Scandal*, "The Magic Barrel," *The Playboy of the Western World*, and *A Phoenix Too Frequent*.

But what of the others? In *Volpone*, "The Man that Corrupted Hadleyburg," "Ivy Day in the Committee Room," "The Conversion of the Jews," and "Holy Willie's Prayer" we see a second pattern derived from the older Greek comedy of Aristophanes (Old Comedy): a vulnerable society is subjected to the machinations of an outsider who preys upon its gullibility and quite mercilessly exposes hypocrisy and debasement; when the order sustaining the society is about to crumble, the outsider withdraws himself, or is expelled, and the society returns to a state of normalcy somewhat cleansed of its impurities. As we have already remarked, this "dark" comedy always threatens to spill over into irony because it is full of absurd acts and grotesque characters. There is also a sense in which the manipulator (Volpone, or the mysterious stranger in Mark Twain's "Man That Corrupted Hadleyburg") resembles the nemesis of tragedy. In Twain's story, the whole town is locked in the grip of a man who has no obvious power over citizens other than that which their hypocrisy and greed expose them to. Their vulnerability links them with the three revelers in Chaucer's "Pardoner's Tale" and the townspeople in Shirley Jackson's "Lottery"; if the mysterious stranger of Hadleyburg were sufficiently relentless, the story would take on a tragic or ironic shape. Nevertheless, it shares with New Comedy an impetus toward a better life. We might describe the contrast between New Comedy and Old Comedy as one of depth of movement: in the first case, the hero and heroine are simply restrained from bursting to the surface until the dénouement, whereas in the second, victims of manipulation almost touch bottom in human depravity before they are allowed to resume a normal life. Freedom is relative to the postulates of context: it can exist in a dark world as long as there is some chance of rescue. If the viciousness continues too long (as it does in Edward Albee's *Who's Afraid of Virginia Woolf* and Harold Pinter's *Homecoming*, where the characters all manipulate one another) human beings break and there is no return to normalcy.

A third comic pattern, the adventures of a wandering hero, is more often associated with fiction than drama. Though represented in "Rip Van Winkle," "A Story," "A Day on the Big Branch," and "Cino," it is characteristic of the more expansive forms of the novel—Fielding's *Joseph Andrews*, Daniel Defoe's *Moll Flanders*, and Tobias Smollett's *Humphrey Clinker* in the eighteenth century and more satiric counterparts like Bellow's *Adventures of Augie March*, John Barth's *Sot-Weed Factor*, and Cary's *Horse's Mouth* in the twentieth. The episodic narrative structure of these novels, inherited from the earlier picaresque novels of Spain, is one manifestation of the balance between continuity and change at the heart of comedy. Such structure appeals to a fundamental egoism in human nature: we want continued existence for ourselves without sameness in our surroundings. We want to meet challenges (successfully), grapple with opposing forces (as long as we win), be surprised by the unexpected (when we are prepared to handle it), and exercise all of our abilities in the great game of chance. This third form of comic action is essentially repetitive, with each episode containing its own *raison d'être*, its own justification in the simple joy of coping with life for the sake of doing it. Picaresque heroes represent the fulfillment of our desire to wander freely about the world armed only with a stock of wit, charm, and good luck. They carry the fragile moment of achieving one's heart's desire (normally achieved at the end of New Comedy) back into the real world again, where it gets buffeted about but survives.

From Bondage to Freedom

We are likely to think of the picaresque novel as a spacious form and of a comedy of manners like *The School for Scandal* as confined because the action of the latter is limited to drawing rooms and bedrooms, but whether episodic and loose or elaborately complicated, comic action seems to exemplify a movement from bondage to freedom. Within much comic action, either through the wanderings of a robust and somewhat roguish hero or through the deliverance of young lovers from the obstacles standing in the way of marriage, there is the spaciousness of unlimited possibilities. It is in this sense that comedy joins irony with romance; its principal characters break out of an initial confinement in which they have very little power of action—or keep doing so if they are wandering heroes—and gain that moment of total euphoria in which their desires and their situation coincide. They move from the helplessness of irony to the invulnerability of romance without shifting worlds because the ideal and the real merge. Often this occurs at the dénouement of comic action, suspended somewhat timelessly at the end so that it cannot be questioned in terms of quite realistic difficulties already overcome or of those that may be expected in an unromantic world. Real fathers do not always forgive sons and daughters who marry against the paternal will, and few people who are vain or foolish or hypocritical can in fact cast off the habit of years in a moment of conversion; but all these things happen quite regularly in comedy, and we do not question them.

Thus the action frequently closes in a carnival mood, a festival of communion and conversion, often a marriage feast celebrating new relationships that reverberate throughout the community as a whole. Like most festivals, the close of comedy has few restraints: anyone may kiss the bride, everyone drinks too much, no one worries about class distinctions, and tomorrow is forgotten completely. This culmination exhibits a second major principle: what happens to the group is more important than any individual fortune. The contrast with tragedy is marked here, for we are seldom concerned with a single hero in comedy. No one "represents" us by virtue of greater power or arrogance; the hero and heroine are sometimes rather pallid figures who need a great deal of help to win their freedom. In comedy the desire to conform and to belong is reinforced. The group temporarily congealed (or at least implied) by the action is one form of the ideal society in which we should all have perfect freedom.

Three stages of action precede this celebration, the final stage of comedy. In the first, some *obstacle* to desire appears in the form of a law, a belief, an obsession, a deception, or an unlucky turn of events. It may be a character's lust for power or revenge, as it is in *Volpone* and "The Man That Corrupted Hadleyburg," or it may be the residual inflexibility of social habit, as it is in *The School for Scandal* and "The Conversion of the Jews." Within the arbitrary plot sequences of comedy this obstacle is the "given" with which we start (comparable to the encroachment of tragedy), but it need be no more probable than Dynamene's voluntary incarceration with her dead husband in *A Phoenix Too Frequent* or more possible than Rip Van Winkle's long sleep. In the second stage of action a series of unforeseen *complications* takes place as a result of the initial obstacle. In New Comedy the power of the obstacle to thwart the hero's desires burgeons disproportionately, and in Old Comedy the outsider quickly snares victim after victim through the folly and vice of a vulnerable society. When the complications have been carried far enough to make the hero's marriage seem impossible or the recovery of equilibrium in society doubtful, there is usually a sudden reversal.

The typical occasion for this third stage is a *discovery*, but it is the kind of discovery that the mechanism of the plot requires rather than the philosophically loaded recognition of tragedy. Some disguise or deception is unveiled by conversations overheard (the stock device used in *Volpone* and *The School for Scandal*), by the arrival of a new character or the return of a powerful figure who had previously withdrawn (another stock device used in Jonson's *Alchemist* and Shakespeare's *Measure for Measure*), or by one of a number of other dramatic clichés. For example, in *The Playboy of the Western World* the boasts of young Christy are undercut by the arrival of his father, whom he has supposedly dispatched with a single blow. Discoveries in comedy tend to depend on sight or sound; when they occur they are unmistakable. Because the third stage is a complete solution to the problem that set the plot in motion, it melds quickly into the fourth and final stage of action, a *celebration* of deliverance from bondage and a consolidation of social unity. In addition to actual or ritual marriage, this stage often includes the expulsion of characters so vile that they cannot be accommodated to a new or restored society—Joseph Surface and Lady Sneerwell in *The School for Scandal*, almost the whole cast of characters in *Volpone*. It may culminate in a symbolic act that ritually kills the old society; Ozzie Freedman's jump from the rooftop of a synagogue in "The Conversion of the Jews" and the hanging of dead Virilius in *A Phoenix Too Frequent* remind us of the communal rites in which an effigy of the old year is beaten, burned, and thrown off a cliff. And this stage may conclude with the comic version of beatitude—some brief vision of a completely open society that needs no restrictions because it contains no evil.

Character Functions

Four character *functions* propel comic action through its stages. The distinction between "functions" and "types" is particularly important in comedy because types like the miser, the hypochondriac, the misanthrope, and the hypocrite—the central roles in four of Molière's plays—can perform different functions within comic action. The man of puffed-up expectations, for example, appears in the gulled victims of Volpone (Corbaccio, Corbino, and Voltore), in Malvolio, who is simultaneously the enemy of comic festivity and the occasion for it throughout much of *Twelfth Night*, and in immature heroes like Pip in Charles Dickens' *Great Expectations* and Christy in *The Playboy of the Western World*. Types are grounded in the stability of human nature; functions are necessary to make the action move in the three comic patterns we have described.

Blocking Figures   The most obvious of these functions is obstruction, performed by those characters who have a vested interest in the rigidity of society and who resist the movement toward freedom. They include such types as the humour characters of Jonson and Molière, the cuckolded husband in "The Miller's Tale," Rip Van Winkle's nagging wife who is a close relative of the wife in Dylan Thomas' "Story" and of Kate in Shakespeare's *Taming of the Shrew*, and Virilius, the meticulous and wooden husband in *A Phoenix Too Frequent*. Notice that any criterion of vice and virtue that might define this role breaks down sooner or later; in "The Miller's Tale" the cuckold John is ridiculous but not vicious in any sense, and certainly not comparable with Corvino, Corbaccio, and Voltore, yet all these characters perform the blocking function. Many of them are impostors or pretenders and most are self-deceived in some important way. In the comic love triangle, the irate or pompous father (sometimes called the "heavy" father) is a frequent type; in dark comedy the blocking figures are usually obsessed with lust, greed, or envy; in the picaresque novel, which puts a comic hero on the road, we often get the impression that the world is full of blocking figures, all trying to take advantage of the wandering hero's youth and innocence. Many compendious novels of the nineteenth century use all kinds of character types for blocking functions, as Dickens' world of caricatures reminds us, and some, like Thackeray's *Vanity Fair*, use social climbers as a "false" hero and heroine.

The New Society   Perhaps George Osborne and Becky Sharp are more interesting than Thackeray's true hero and heroine, Dobbin and Amelia, but the latter are models of the second function in comic action—those who are the nucleus of a new, freer society. Although some comic heroes like Jim Dixon in *Lucky Jim* vibrate with the energy of the action, others like Bonario and Celia in *Volpone* are strangely innocuous and peripheral. This makes sense when we remember that such heroes and heroines must be freed from the restrictions imposed on them by more powerful, and older, members of society. In addition to the hero and heroine, members of the new society include countless helpers and arrangers, usually social inferiors who have the necessary wit and dexterity to overcome blocking characters from behind the scenes. They often seem to dominate the action because they keep it moving; Mosca in *Volpone* and Knollwood in *The School for Scandal* are descendants of the tricky slaves who performed this function in Roman comedy. The same control is sometimes exercised by a withdrawing elder, an insider in the society who unostentatiously wields power even though he is absent during most of the action and who manages to reappear at the crucial moment. Sir Oliver Surface in *The School for Scandal* performs this function, especially when he returns in disguise to discover his nephews' true characters before rewarding one and punishing the other; Squire Allworthy has a comparable function through most of *Tom Jones*, serving as a background figure holding the ultimate power that benevolence has in comedy. Greek drama used the figure of a god descending from the heavens (*deus ex machina*) to resolve difficult situations, and we notice that the managers of the action who inherit this function tend to disappear and reappear somewhat mysteriously, as do the stranger in "The Man That Corrupted Hadleyburg" and the marriage broker in "The Magic Barrel." Because the hero's helpers and agents are usually unpretentious and self-deprecating, they are almost perfect foils for the blocking characters whom they outwit.

Buffoons

There is a similar polarity between the third and fourth functions, filled by subsidiary characters who create or deny the atmosphere of festivity or the process of exposure in dark comedy. The central figure of the supporting group is often a jester, fool, clown, or buffoon. Such figures are all dependents or parasites who must please their benefactors through some kind of dexterity—the verbal wit of Shakespeare's fools or the poetic skill of wandering minstrels like Pound's Cino. Sometimes the role of the buffoon is part of the hero's character, just as fools are identified with tragic protagonists at crucial points in *Hamlet* and *King Lear*. In *The Playboy of the Western World* Christy Mahon's power is almost entirely the power of words, and the hero's facial antics in *Lucky Jim* are a form of jubilant release from the strictures of academie.

The Establishment

Opposing such exuberance and vitality are characters performing the fourth function, the sour and pompous men who uphold the dignity of institutions and the solemnity of events. A host of Shakespeare's melancholics, such as Malvolio in *Twelfth Night* and Jaques in *As You Like It*, deny festivity, as does the legion of "professional" men—especially doctors, lawyers, clergymen, and professors—ridiculed for their self-importance and narrow-mindedness throughout the whole history of literary comedy. Even though he gets his revenge, Absalom in "The Miller's Tale" performs this function, and so does Chaunticleer in "The Nun's Priest's Tale" when he is parroting his learning. The only essential difference between these characters and the blocking figures whom they indirectly support is their peripheral position; when they are central, like Rabbi Binder in "The Conversion of the Jews," they assume the role of blocking figures. Another variant worth noting is the plain-spoken man who espouses the virtue of sincerity with all the priggishness at his command. If he were not hero, Molière's Alceste would be a good model for this type, which is likely to appear whenever a minor character has more pride than good sense. In comedy, tactlessness is the epitome of bad behavior because it fragments groups and creates dissension. When they are not blocking figures, the fearsome old matriarchs who run society perform this function, as do garrulous widows like Chaucer's Wife of Bath and the Widow Quin in *The Playboy of the Western World*.

The Phases of Comedy

It is quite apparent that character "types" can be used for different purposes in comic action. Understanding the general functions that characters have in a particular narrative will be helpful as long as we do not consider those functions rigid, exclusive categories. Given the diversity of comedy and its close imitation of the social milieu, the patterns and stages of action we have described are often modified, transformed, combined, and partially deleted. Moreover, comedy has no finite boundaries to separate it from romance and irony. Unlike tragedy, comedy is often said to be romantic or ironic solely on the basis of atmosphere, as is suggested by the modifying epithets commonly applied to specific plays and novels—"light," "heavy," "dark," and "serious." But it is also possible, and more useful, to trace structural affinities with romance and irony, since much of the sophistication we value in literature lies in the interweaving of narrative patterns.

The Comic Norm: Transformation of Ordinary Society

In the norm of comedy, members of the new society—the hero, the heroine, and their helpers—are subjected to restrictions that frustrate their aims, but they ultimately succeed in defeating, transforming, or at least neutralizing blocking forces in a movement toward greater freedom. Of the three patterns of action—the love triangle, the exposure of society's humors, and the wanderings of a roguish hero—the first is closest to the norm. Using familiar conventions of the medieval fable and beast epic, bawdy and refined versions of the battle between the sexes, Chaucer created "The Miller's Tale" and "The Nun's Priest's Tale"; the latter derives most of its comic effect from the juxtaposition of philosophical argument and the language of courtly love with barnyard drama. *The School for Scandal*, a pure example of the comedy of manners, is also on center. It exhibits a full repertoire of comic plot devices—the rich uncle, the January-May marriage (old husband and young wife), overheard interviews, sets of foils in character grouping (two brothers with opposing qualities, two heroines who display true and false judgment). All the machinery necessary to make this plot go complicates and expands the rather simple business of arranging marriages and liaisons, just as the scandalmongering theme is another way of embellishing the traditional battle of the sexes—the struggle for dominance between husbands and wives that Chaucer's Wife of Bath wins so handily. Such fullness of action gives us an image of human vitality as characters move rapidly through a maze of circumstances. In his simple "Story," Dylan Thomas creates the same effect by focusing on the final stage of comic action. After a bare suggestion of blocking action in the departure of the wife and hints of the "humors" embodied in various members of the "outing," the story is all celebration, a drunken revel purified by the innocence of its young narrator.

Other examples of the norm are more complex, carrying overtones of another phase. "The Magic Barrel" seems at first to be an almost perfect boy-gets-girl plot, with the young rabbi's inhibitions as an obstacle and the marriage broker as helping agent, until we find out that the girl is a whore being palmed off by that same helper, her father. The irony is obvious. Nevertheless the story remains an example of the norm because the young rabbi is freed from his inhibitions, and Pinye Salzman, a blocking figure as well as a helping agent, embraces the same restrictive code at the end of the story that the rabbi has just escaped from. There is a similar shift away from the norm toward the ironic in Robert Burns' "Holy Willie's Prayer," Robert Browning's "Soliloquy of the Spanish Cloister," and Pound's "Cino." These three dramatic monologues can best be considered fragments implying more complete comic actions. Pound's witty Cino finds his freedom in ridiculing the rigid caste system that suppresses him; Browning's subordinate monk inadvertently reveals his own pride and hypocrisy in railing at the hierarchy of the monastery; and Burns' Holy Willie is a radical example of the blocking figure, a hypocrite so perfect that his mere existence implies the action that must free men from such cant.

The Romantic Phase: Creation of a Free Society

The romantic and ironic phases of comedy have much in common. They are often combined in the same action, and they share a central feature: the "free" way of living cannot be realized *within* society. Just as romance includes a downward movement or "descent," irony implies an ideal world imagined as a contrast to the very unpleasant real one. And both perspectives are likely to appear when the comic norm of transforming society cannot be achieved.

The hero and his supporters in romantic comedy successfully abrogate or ignore the stifling conventions of ordinary society; unsuccessful in changing society, they escape by abandoning it. Thus Rip Van Winkle goes to the hills, Tegeus-Chromis in *A Phoenix Too Frequent* finds a tomb that is also a trysting place, and Ozzie Freedman in "The Conversion of the Jews" breaks out of his heritage by leaping from the roof of the synagogue. But the heroes of romantic comedy cannot *stay* outside a confining environment because visions of an ideal world usually last very little longer than the festival does in the comic norm. In romantic comedy the hero tunes in on both the real and the ideal more strongly because the disparity between the two cannot be reconciled.

The Ironic Phase: Exploitation of a Humorous Society

Volpone has often been called a tragicomedy but it is better described as an ironic comedy, a comedy of vulnerability. As in romantic comedy, the "free" way of living cannot be realized within society. The figures of energy, in this case Volpone and Mosca, are themselves impostors and deceivers who debase society by playing on latent vices, such as greed, lust, and envy, in effect restricting the freedom of other characters and forcing them to be more vicious than they would otherwise have been. Thus Corvino, Corbaccio, and Voltore are baited into conduct that they would ordinarily avoid through their fear of discovery—disinheriting one's son or cuckolding oneself would make them lose face in Venetian society. The impostors nearly succeed, and the vulnerable society remains essentially untransformed even though it is saved by a sudden reversal. The action starts, as in the comic norm, with a constricted society; however it then moves "downward" into the grotesquerie and absurdity of irony, and finally returns to the somewhat saner but still imperfect state of ordinary society. This description applies to "The Man That Corrupted Hadleyburg" as well, and to a host of plays, including *Measure for Measure*, *The Merchant of Venice*, *Tartuffe*, and *Who's Afraid of Virginia Woolf*.

Such structure is apt to seem both ironic and comic for several reasons. First, there are two perspectives built into the action, and each one has its own standard of judgment: within Venetian society, Volpone and Mosca are usurpers who must be expelled, blocking figures whose power has grown to terrifying and enormous proportions because they can elicit such exaggerated vices from ordinary people; on the other hand, for Volpone and Mosca Venetian society is a plaything to be fooled with, and their action is a continued movement toward greater freedom and power until it is suddenly thwarted by the belated efforts of "good" characters. Thus there are two contradictory ways of seeing and judging the action, one ironic and the other comic. Second, the comedy of vulnerability contains no vision of an untainted good, whether it is freedom, beauty, love, or an ideal society. Yet lesser and more equivocal goods can be developed with great subtlety, as they are in Joyce's "Ivy Day in the Committee Room" when Hines' lyric, though maudlin in itself, creates a momentary unity among a bunch of cynical ward-heelers. We get the same effect in Howard Nemerov's "Day on the Big Branch" when the impulse to reject the debauchery of modern city life and return to nature is suddenly undercut: the men willingly resume the habits that imprison them.

Both romantic and ironic comedy differ from the norm in one important respect: a central group of characters is excluded from society rather than incorporated into it. (Sometimes the hero alone leaves it, disdainfully.) Normally, some characters who cannot be converted because they are too vile (Lady Sneerwell and Joseph Surface in *The School for Scandal*) are left out, and a few, like the melancholics in Shakespeare's comedies, can refuse to join the festivities without disturbing the cohesion of the new and better society that has displaced the old. But whenever a comic hero willfully rejects society by pulling out of it completely, the action implies a disintegration of the human community that is hard to square with our sense of comedy. It is tempting to take an ethical view of comedy in order to solve the problem: if the society being abandoned is worse than the hero, we have romantic comedy; if it is better—although being exploited by a manipulating hero—we have ironic comedy. Unfortunately, black and white contrasts never carry us far enough. In *Volpone*, for example, Volpone's energy and imagination, his ability to *create* whole worlds for himself like the sickroom and the mountebank stand, make what he does less repugnant to us without diminishing the viciousness exposed in others. Molière's Alceste also elicits mixed responses, since the play shows us that it is possible to justify contradictory attitudes toward quite simple human acts: being tactless is both telling the truth and injuring someone else's self-respect; exposing a friend's stupidity is both good for the health of society and disloyal. Not either/or but both/and: such plays demand complex attitudes. The comedy that exposes anomalies in human motivation may not always be festive, but it is one of literature's most sophisticated responses to human experience.

A Comedy of Exclusion: *The Playboy of the Western World*

John Millington Synge's *Playboy of the Western World* is an interesting example of a comedy moving toward exclusion through both romantic and ironic structures. Yet when it was first produced in Dublin's famous Abbey Theatre in 1907, it was taken as a simple political tract by young nationalists in the audience, first on the pretext of their being scandalized by the word "shift" in Act III and by the slur upon the delicacy of Irish girls which that implied, but later more openly on the grounds that Synge had impugned the Irish character in general. One irate reviewer for the *Dublin Evening Mail* wrote: "If a man is stupid enough to suggest that the Irish people are cannibals or gorillas, my hand will not fumble for the sword-hilt." Groups of young patriots blew whistles throughout performances to drown out the lines, and before the week's run was over it took five hundred policemen to contain the riots the play occasioned. This melodramatic episode in theater history is a result of fundamental ambivalence in *The Playboy of the Western World*. Although the political climate of the time explains much of the exaggerated reaction, the play holds contradictory attitudes toward characters in such delicate balance that it is no wonder the simple-minded might mistake one possibility for all of them.

JOHN MILLINGTON SYNGE
1871–1909

The Playboy of the Western World

PERSONS IN THE PLAY

CHRISTOPHER MAHON

OLD MAHON, *his father, a squatter*

MICHAEL JAMES FLAHERTY (*called* MICHAEL JAMES), *a publican*

MARGARET FLAHERTY (*called* PEGEEN MIKE), *his daughter*

WIDOW QUIN, *a woman of about thirty*

SHAWN KEOGH, *her cousin, a young farmer*

PHILLY CULLEN and JIMMY FARRELL, *small farmers*

SARA TANSEY, SUSAN BRADY, HONOR BLAKE, and NELLY, *village girls*

A BELLMAN

SOME PEASANTS

The action takes place near a village, on a wild coast of Mayo. The first act passes on an evening of autumn, the other two acts on the following day.

ACT I

Country public-house or shebeen, very rough and untidy. There is a sort of counter on the right with shelves, holding many bottles and jugs, just seen above it. Empty barrels stand near the counter. At back, a little to left of counter, there is a door into the open air, then, more to the left, there is a settle with shelves above it, with more jugs, and a table beneath a window. At the left there is a large open fireplace, with turf fire, and a small door into inner room. PEGEEN, *a wild-looking but fine girl, of about twenty, is writing at table. She is dressed in the usual peasant dress.*

PEGEEN   [*Slowly as she writes*] Six yards of stuff for to make a yellow gown. A pair of lace boots with lengthy heels on them and brassy eyes. A hat is suited for a wedding-day. A fine-tooth comb. To be sent with three barrels of porter in Jimmy Farrell's creel cart on the evening of the coming fair to Mister Michael James Flaherty. With the best compliments of this season. Margaret Flaherty.

SHAWN KEOGH   [*A fat and fair young man comes in as she signs, looks round awkwardly, when he sees she is alone*] Where's himself?

PEGEEN   [*Without looking at him*] He's coming. [*She directs letter.*] To Mister Sheamus Mulroy, Wine and Spirit Dealer, Castlebar.

SHAWN   [*Uneasily*] I didn't see him on the road.

PEGEEN   How would you see him [*licks stamp and puts it on letter*] and it dark night this half-hour gone by?

SHAWN   [*Turning towards door again*] I stood a while outside wondering would I have a right to pass on or to walk in and see you, Pegeen Mike, [*comes to fire*] and I could hear the cows breathing and sighing in the stillness of the air, and not a step moving any place from this gate to the bridge.

PEGEEN   [*Putting letter in envelope*] It's above at the crossroads he is, meeting Philly Cullen and a couple more are going along with him to Kate Cassidy's wake.

SHAWN   [*Looking at her blankly*] And he's going that length in the dark night.

PEGEEN   [*Impatiently*] He is surely, and leaving me lonesome on the scruff of the hill. [*She gets up and puts envelope on dresser, then winds clock.*] Isn't it long the nights are now, Shawn Keogh, to be leaving a poor girl with her own self counting the hours to the dawn of day?

SHAWN   [*With awkward humor*] If it is, when we're wedded in a short while you'll have no call to complain, for I've little will to be walking off to wakes or weddings in the darkness of the night.

PEGEEN   [*With rather scornful good-humor*] You're making mighty certain, Shaneen, that I'll wed you now.

SHAWN   Aren't we after making a good bargain, the way we're only waiting these days on Father Reilly's dispensation[1] from the bishops, or the Court of Rome.

PEGEEN   [*Looking at him teasingly, washing up at dresser*] It's a wonder, Shaneen, the Holy Father'd be taking notice of the likes of you; for if I was him I wouldn't bother with this place where you'll meet none but Red Linahan, has a squint in his eye, and Patcheen is lame in his heel, or the mad Mulrannies were driven from California and they lost in their wits. We're a

THE PLAYBOY OF THE WESTERN WORLD.   **1. dispensation:** permitting the marriage of cousins.

queer lot these times to go troubling the Holy Father on his sacred seat.

SHAWN [*Scandalized*] If we are, we're as good this place as another, maybe, and as good these times as we were for ever.

PEGEEN [*With scorn*] As good, is it? Where now will you meet the like of Daneen Sullivan knocked the eye from a peeler;[2] or Marcus Quin, God rest him, got six months for maiming ewes, and he a great warrant to tell stories of holy Ireland till he'd have the old women shedding down tears about their feet. Where will you find the like of them, I'm saying?

SHAWN [*Timidly*] If you don't, it's a good job, maybe; for [*with peculiar emphasis on the words.*] Father Reilly has small conceit[3] to have that kind walking around and talking to the girls.

PEGEEN [*Impatiently throwing water from basin out of the door*] Stop tormenting me with Father Reilly [*imitating his voice*] when I'm asking only what way I'll pass these twelve hours of dark, and not take my death with the fear. [*Looking out of door.*]

SHAWN [*Timidly*] Would I fetch you the Widow Quin, maybe?

PEGEEN Is it the like of that murderer? You'll not, surely.

SHAWN [*Going to her, soothingly*] Then I'm thinking himself will stop along with you when he sees you taking on; for it'll be a long night-time with great darkness, and I'm after feeling[4] a kind of fellow above in the furzy ditch, groaning wicked like a maddening dog, the way it's good cause you have, maybe, to be fearing now.

PEGEEN [*Turning on him sharply*] What's that? Is it a man you seen?

SHAWN [*Retreating*] I couldn't see him at all; but I heard him groaning out, and breaking his heart. It should have been a young man from his words speaking.

PEGEEN [*Going after him*] And you never went near to see was he hurted or what ailed him at all?

SHAWN I did not, Pegeen Mike. It was a dark, lonesome place to be hearing the like of him.

PEGEEN Well, you're a daring fellow, and if they find his corpse stretched above in the dews of dawn, what'll you say then to the peelers, or the justice of the peace?

SHAWN [*Thunderstruck*] I wasn't thinking of that. For the love of God, Pegeen Mike, don't let on I was speaking of him. Don't tell your father and the men is coming above; for if they heard that story they'd have great blabbing this night at the wake.

PEGEEN I'll maybe tell them and I'll maybe not.

SHAWN They are coming at the door. Will you whisht, I'm saying?

PEGEEN Whisht yourself. [*She goes behind counter.* MICHAEL JAMES, *fat jovial publican, comes in followed by* PHILLY CULLEN, *who is thin and mistrusting, and* JIMMY FARRELL, *who is fat and amorous, about forty-five.*]

MEN [*Together*] God bless you! The blessing of God on this place!

PEGEEN God bless you kindly.

MICHAEL [*To men, who go to the counter*] Sit down now, and take your rest. [*Crosses to* SHAWN *at the fire.*] And how is it you are, Shawn Keogh? Are you coming over the sands to Kate Cassidy's wake?

SHAWN I am not, Michael James. I'm going home the short cut to my bed.

PEGEEN [*Speaking across the counter*] He's right, too, and have you no shame, Michael James, to be quitting off for the whole night, and leaving myself lonesome in the shop?

MICHAEL [*Good-humoredly*] Isn't it the same whether I go for the whole night or a part only? and I'm thinking it's a queer daughter you are if you'd have me crossing backward through the Stooks of the Dead Women, with a drop taken.

PEGEEN If I am a queer daughter, it's a queer father'd be leaving me lonesome these twelve hours of dark, and I piling the turf with the dogs barking, and the calves mooing, and my own teeth rattling with the fear.

JIMMY [*Flatteringly*] What is there to hurt you, and you a fine, hardy girl would knock the head of any two men in the place?

PEGEEN [*Working herself up*] Isn't there the harvest boys with their tongues red for drink, and the ten tinkers is camped in the east glen, and the thousand militia—bad cess[5] to them!—walking idle through the land. There's lots surely

---

2. peeler: English policeman. **3. conceit:** desire, pride. **4. feeling:** finding.

5. cess: luck.

to hurt me, and I won't stop alone in it, let himself do what he will.

MICHAEL If you're that afeard, let Shawn Keogh stop along with you. It's the will of God, I'm thinking, himself should be seeing to you now. [*They all turn on* SHAWN.]

SHAWN [*In horrified confusion*] I would and welcome, Michael James, but I'm afeard of Father Reilly; and what at all would the Holy Father and the cardinals of Rome be saying if they heard I did the like of that?

MICHAEL [*With contempt*] God help you! Can't you sit in by the hearth with the light lit and herself beyond in the room? You'll do that surely, for I've heard tell there's a queer fellow above, going mad or getting his death, maybe, in the gripe of the ditch, so she'd be safer this night with a person here.

SHAWN [*With plaintive despair*] I'm afeard of Father Reilly, I'm saying. Let you not be tempting me, and we near married itself.

PHILLY [*With cold contempt*] Lock him in the west room. He'll stay then and have no sin to be telling to the priest.

MICHAEL [*To* SHAWN, *getting between him and the door*] Go up now.

SHAWN [*At the top of his voice*] Don't stop me, Michael James. Let me out of the door, I'm saying, for the love of the Almighty God. Let me out. [*Trying to dodge past him.*] Let me out of it, and may God grant you his indulgence in the hour of need.

MICHAEL [*Loudly*] Stop your noising, and sit down by the hearth. [*Gives him a push and goes to counter laughing.*]

SHAWN [*Turning back, wringing his hands*] Oh, Father Reilly, and the saints of God, where will I hide myself today? Oh, Saint Joseph and Saint Patrick and Saint Brigid and Saint James, have mercy on me now! [SHAWN *turns round, sees door clear, and makes a rush for it.*]

MICHAEL [*Catching him by the coattail*] You'd be going, is it?

SHAWN [*Screaming*] Leave me go, Michael James, leave me go, you old Pagan, leave me go, or I'll get the curse of the priests on you, and of the scarlet-coated bishops of the Courts of Rome. [*With a sudden movement he pulls himself out of his coat, and disappears out of the door, leaving his coat in* MICHAEL's *hands.*]

MICHAEL [*Turning round, and holding up coat*] Well, there's the coat of a Christian man. Oh, there's sainted glory this day in the lonesome west; and by the will of God I've got you a decent man, Pegeen, you'll have no call to be spying after if you've a score of young girls, maybe, weeding in your fields.

PEGEEN [*Taking up the defense of her property*] What right have you to be making game of a poor fellow for minding the priest, when it's your own fault is, not paying a penny pot-boy to stand along with me and give me courage in the doing of my work? [*She snaps the coat away from him, and goes behind counter with it.*]

MICHAEL [*Taken aback*] Where would I get a potboy? Would you have me send the bellman screaming in the streets of Castlebar?

SHAWN [*Opening the door a chink and putting in his head, in a small voice*] Michael James!

MICHAEL [*Imitating him*] What ails you?

SHAWN The queer dying fellow's beyond looking over the ditch. He's come up, I'm thinking, stealing your hens. [*Looks over his shoulder.*] God help me, he's following me now [*he runs into room*], and if he's heard what I said, he'll be having my life, and I going home lonesome in the darkness of the night. [*For a perceptible moment they watch the door with curiosity. Someone coughs outside. Then* CHRISTY MAHON, *a slight young man, comes in very tired and frightened and dirty.*]

CHRISTY [*In a small voice*] God save all here!

MEN God save you kindly!

CHRISTY [*Going to the counter*] I'd trouble you for a glass of porter, woman of the house. [*He puts down coin.*]

PEGEEN [*Serving him*] You're one of the tinkers, young fellow, is beyond camped in the glen?

CHRISTY I am not; but I'm destroyed walking.

MICHAEL [*Patronizingly*] Let you come up then to the fire. You're looking famished with the cold.

CHRISTY God reward you. [*He takes up his glass and goes a little way across to the left, then stops and looks about him.*] Is it often the polis[6] do be coming into this place, master of the house?

MICHAEL If you'd come in better hours, you'd have seen "Licensed for the Sale of Beer and Spirits, to be Consumed on the Premises," written in white letters above the door, and what

6. **polis**: police.

would the polis want spying on me, and not a decent house within four miles, the way every living Christian is a bona fide,[7] saving one widow alone?

CHRISTY   [*With relief*] It's a safe house, so. [*He goes over to the fire, sighing and moaning. Then he sits down, putting his glass beside him, and begins gnawing a turnip, too miserable to feel the others staring at him with curiosity.*]

MICHAEL   [*Going after him*] Is it yourself is fearing the polis? You're wanting, maybe?

CHRISTY   There's many wanting.

MICHAEL   Many, surely, with the broken harvest and the ended wars. [*He picks up some stockings, etc., that are near the fire, and carries them away furtively.*] It should be larceny, I'm thinking?

CHRISTY   [*Dolefully*] I had it in my mind it was a different word and a bigger.

PEGEEN   There's a queer lad. Were you never slapped in school, young fellow, that you don't know the name of your deed?

CHRISTY   [*Bashfully*] I'm slow at learning, a middling scholar only.

MICHAEL   If you're a dunce itself, you'd have a right to know that larceny's robbing and stealing. Is it for the like of that you're wanting?

CHRISTY   [*With a flash of family pride*] And I the son of a strong farmer [*with a sudden qualm*], God rest his soul, could have bought up the whole of your old house a while since, from the butt of his tail-pocket, and not have missed the weight of it gone.

MICHAEL   [*Impressed*] If it's not stealing, it's maybe something big.

CHRISTY   [*Flattered*] Aye; it's maybe something big.

JIMMY   He's a wicked-looking young fellow. Maybe he followed after a young woman on a lonesome night.

CHRISTY   [*Shocked*] Oh, the saints forbid, mister; I was all times a decent lad.

PHILLY   [*Turning on JIMMY*] You're a silly man, Jimmy Farrell. He said his father was a farmer a while since, and there's himself now in a poor state. Maybe the land was grabbed from him, and he did what any decent man would do.

MICHAEL   [*To CHRISTY, mysteriously*] Was it bailiffs?

CHRISTY   The divil a one.

7. **bona fide**: respectable.

MICHAEL   Agents?

CHRISTY   The divil a one.

MICHAEL   Landlords?

CHRISTY   [*Peevishly*] Ah, not at all, I'm saying. You'd see the like of them stories on any little paper of a Munster town. But I'm not calling to mind any person, gentle, simple, judge or jury, did the like of me. [*They all draw nearer with delighted curiosity.*]

PHILLY   Well, that lad's a puzzle-the-world.

JIMMY   He'd beat Dan Davies' circus, or the holy missioners making sermons on the villainy of man. Try him again, Philly.

PHILLY   Did you strike golden guineas out of solder, young fellow, or shilling coins itself?

CHRISTY   I did not, mister, not sixpence nor a farthing coin.

JIMMY   Did you marry three wives maybe? I'm told there's a sprinkling have done that among the holy Luthers of the preaching north.

CHRISTY   [*Shyly*] I never married with one, let alone with a couple or three.

PHILLY   Maybe he went fighting for the Boers, the like of the man beyond, was judged to be hanged, quartered, and drawn. Were you off east, young fellow, fighting bloody wars for Kruger[8] and the freedom of the Boers?

CHRISTY   I never left my own parish till Tuesday was a week.

PEGEEN   [*Coming from counter*] He's done nothing, so. [*To CHRISTY.*] If you didn't commit murder or a bad, nasty thing; or false coining, or robbery, or butchery, or the like of them, there isn't anything that would be worth your troubling for to run from now. You did nothing at all.

CHRISTY   [*His feelings hurt*] That's an unkindly thing to be saying to a poor orphaned traveler, has a prison behind him, and hanging before, and hell's gap gaping below.

PEGEEN   [*With a sign to the men to be quiet*] You're only saying it. You did nothing at all. A soft lad the like of you wouldn't slit the windpipe of a screeching sow.

CHRISTY   [*Offended*] You're not speaking the truth.

PEGEEN   [*In mock rage*] Not speaking the truth, is it? Would you have me knock the head of you with the butt of the broom?

8. **Kruger**: Boer leader, opposed by England in the South African War, 1899–1902.

CHRISTY [*Twisting round on her with a sharp cry of horror*] Don't strike me. I killed my poor father, Tuesday was a week, for doing the like of that.

PEGEEN [*With blank amazement*] Is it killed your father?

CHRISTY [*Subsiding*] With the help of God I did, surely, and that the Holy Immaculate Mother may intercede for his soul.

PHILLY [*Retreating with* JIMMY] There's a daring fellow.

JIMMY Oh, glory be to God!

MICHAEL [*With great respect*] That was a hanging crime, mister honey. You should have good reason for doing the like of that.

CHRISTY [*In a very reasonable tone*] He was a dirty man, God forgive him, and he getting old and crusty, the way I couldn't put up with him at all.

PEGEEN And you shot him dead?

CHRISTY [*Shaking his head*] I never used weapons. I've no license, and I'm a law-fearing man.

MICHAEL It was with a hilted knife maybe? I'm told, in the big world, it's bloody knives they use.

CHRISTY [*Loudly, scandalized*] Do you take me for a slaughter-boy?

PEGEEN You never hanged him the way Jimmy Farrell hanged his dog from the license, and had it screeching and wriggling three hours at the butt of a string, and himself swearing it was a dead dog, and the peelers swearing it had life?

CHRISTY I did not, then. I just riz the loy[9] and let fall the edge of it on the ridge of his skull, and he went down at my feet like an empty sack, and never let a grunt or groan from him at all.

MICHAEL [*Making a sign to* PEGEEN *to fill* CHRISTY's *glass*] And what way weren't you hanged, mister? Did you bury him then?

CHRISTY [*Considering*] Aye. I buried him then. Wasn't I digging spuds in the field?

MICHAEL And the peelers never followed after you the eleven days that you're out?

CHRISTY [*Shaking his head*] Never a one of them, and I walking forward facing hog, dog, or divil on the highway of the road.

PHILLY [*Nodding wisely*] It's only with a common week-day kind of a murderer them lads would be trusting their carcass, and that man should be a great terror when his temper's roused.

MICHAEL He should then. [*To* CHRISTY.] And where was it, mister honey, that you did the deed?

CHRISTY [*Looking at him with suspicion*] Oh, a distant place, master of the house, a windy corner of high, distant hills.

PHILLY [*Nodding with approval*] He's a close man, and he's right, surely.

PEGEEN That'd be a lad with the sense of Solomon to have for a pot-boy, Michael James, if it's the truth you're seeking one at all.

PHILLY The peelers is fearing him, and if you'd that lad in the house there isn't one of them would come smelling around if the dogs itself were lapping poteen[10] from the dung-pit of the yard.

JIMMY Bravery's a treasure in a lonesome place, and a lad would kill his father, I'm thinking, would face a foxy divil with a pitchpike on the flags[11] of hell.

PEGEEN It's the truth they're saying, and if I'd that lad in the house, I wouldn't be fearing the loosèd kharki cutthroats, or the walking dead.

CHRISTY [*Swelling with surprise and triumph*] Well, glory be to God!

MICHAEL [*With deference*] Would you think well to stop here and be pot-boy, mister honey, if we gave you good wages, and didn't destroy you with the weight of work?

SHAWN [*Coming forward uneasily*] That'd be a queer kind to bring into a decent, quiet household with the like of Pegeen Mike.

PEGEEN [*Very sharply*] Will you whisht? Who's speaking to you?

SHAWN [*Retreating*] A bloody-handed murderer the like of . . .

PEGEEN [*Snapping at him*] Whisht, 1 am saying; we'll take no fooling from your like at all. [*To* CHRISTY *with a honeyed voice.*] And you, young fellow, you'd have a right to stop, I'm thinking, for we'd do our all and utmost to content your needs.

CHRISTY [*Overcome with wonder*] And I'd be safe this place from the searching law?

MICHAEL You would, surely. If they're not fearing you, itself, the peelers in this place is decent, drouthy[12] poor fellows, wouldn't touch a cur dog and not give warning in the dead of night.

PEGEEN [*Very kindly and persuasively*] Let you stop a short while anyhow. Aren't you destroyed

9. loy: spade.

10. poteen: home brew. 11. flags: flagstones. 12. drouthy: thirsty.

walking with your feet in bleeding blisters, and your whole skin needing washing like a Wicklow sheep?

CHRISTY [*Looking round with satisfaction*] It's a nice room, and if it's not humbugging me you are, I'm thinking that I'll surely stay.

JIMMY [*Jumps up*] Now, by the grace of God, herself will be safe this night, with a man killed his father holding danger from the door, and let you come on, Michael James, or they'll have the best stuff drunk at the wake.

MICHAEL [*Going to the door with men*] And begging your pardon, mister, what name will we call you, for we'd like to know?

CHRISTY   Christopher Mahon.

MICHAEL   Well, God bless you, Christy, and a good rest till we meet again when the sun'll be rising to the noon of day.

CHRISTY   God bless you all.

MEN   God bless you. [*They go out, except* SHAWN, *who lingers at the door.*]

SHAWN [*To* PEGEEN] Are you wanting me to stop along with you and keep you from harm?

PEGEEN [*Gruffly*] Didn't you say you were fearing Father Reilly?

SHAWN   There'd be no harm staying now, I'm thinking, and himself in it too.

PEGEEN   You wouldn't stay when there was need for you, and let you step off nimble this time when there's none.

SHAWN   Didn't I say it was Father Reilly . . .

PEGEEN   Go on, then, to Father Reilly [*in a jeering tone*], and let him put you in the holy brotherhoods, and leave that lad to me.

SHAWN   If I meet the Widow Quin . . .

PEGEEN   Go on, I'm saying, and don't be waking this place with your noise. [*She hustles him out and bolts door.*] That lad would wear the spirits from the saints of peace. [*Bustles about, then takes off her apron and pins it up in the window as a blind,* CHRISTY *watching her timidly. Then she comes to him and speaks with bland good-humor.*] Let you stretch out now by the fire, young fellow. You should be destroyed traveling.

CHRISTY [*Shyly again, drawing off his boots*] I'm tired surely, walking wild eleven days, and waking fearful in the night. [*He holds up one of his feet, feeling his blisters, and looking at them with compassion.*]

PEGEEN [*Standing beside him, watching him with delight*] You should have had great people in your family, I'm thinking, with the little, small feet you have, and you with a kind of quality name, the like of what you'd find on the great powers and potentates of France and Spain.

CHRISTY [*With pride*] We were great, surely, with wide and windy acres of rich Munster land.

PEGEEN   Wasn't I telling you, and you a fine handsome young fellow with a noble brow?

CHRISTY [*With a flash of delighted surprise*] Is it me?

PEGEEN   Aye. Did you never hear that from the young girls where you come from in the west or south?

CHRISTY [*With venom*] I did not, then. Oh, they're bloody liars in the naked parish where I grew a man.

PEGEEN   If they are itself, you've heard it these days, I'm thinking, and you walking the world telling out your story to young girls or old.

CHRISTY   I've told my story no place till this night, Pegeen Mike, and it's foolish I was here, maybe, to be talking free; but you're decent people, I'm thinking, and yourself a kindly woman, the way I wasn't fearing you at all.

PEGEEN [*Filling a sack with straw*] You've said the like of that, maybe, in every cot and cabin where you've met a young girl on your way.

CHRISTY [*Going over to her, gradually raising his voice*] I've said it nowhere till this night, I'm telling you; for I've seen none the like of you the eleven long days I am walking the world, looking over a low ditch or a high ditch on my north or south, into stony, scattered fields, or scribes[13] of bog, where you'd see young, limber girls, and fine, prancing women making laughter with the men.

PEGEEN   If you weren't destroyed traveling, you'd have as much talk and streeleen,[14] I'm thinking, as Owen Roe O'Sullivan or the poets of the Dingle Bay; and I've heard all times it's the poets are your like—fine, fiery fellows with great rages when their temper's roused.

CHRISTY [*Drawing a little nearer to her*] You've a power of rings, God bless you, and would there be any offense if I was asking are you single now?

PEGEEN   What would I want wedding so young?

CHRISTY [*With relief*] We're alike, so.

PEGEEN [*She puts sack on settle and beats it up*] I

13. **scribes:** enclosures (?)   14. **streeleen:** a line.

never killed my father. I'd be afeard to do that, except I was the like of yourself with blind rages tearing me within, for I'm thinking you should have had great tussling when the end was come.

CHRISTY [*Expanding with delight at the first confidential talk he has ever had with a woman*] We had not then. It was a hard woman was come over the hill; and if he was always a crusty kind when he'd a hard woman setting him on, not the divil himself or his four fathers could put up with him at all.

PEGEEN [*With curiosity*] And isn't it a great wonder that one wasn't fearing you?

CHRISTY [*Very confidentially*] Up to the day I killed my father, there wasn't a person in Ireland knew the kind I was, and I there drinking, waking, eating, sleeping, a quiet, simple poor fellow with no man giving me heed.

PEGEEN [*Getting a quilt out of cupboard and putting it on the sack*] It was the girls were giving you heed, maybe, and I'm thinking it's most conceit you'd have to be gaming with their like.

CHRISTY [*Shaking his head, with simplicity*] Not the girls itself, and I won't tell you a lie. There wasn't anyone heeding me in that place saving only the dumb beasts of the field. [*He sits down at fire.*]

PEGEEN [*With disappointment*] And I thinking you should have been living the like of a king of Norway or the eastern world. [*She comes and sits beside him after placing bread and mug of milk on the table.*]

CHRISTY [*Laughing piteously*] The like of a king, is it? And I after toiling, moiling, digging, dodging from the dawn till dusk; with never a sight of joy or sport saving only when I'd be abroad in the dark night poaching rabbits on hills, for I was a divil to poach, God forgive me, [*very naively*] and I near got six months for going with a dung fork and stabbing a fish.

PEGEEN   And it's that you'd call sport, is it, to be abroad in the darkness with yourself alone?

CHRISTY   I did, God help me, and there I'd be as happy as the sunshine of Saint Martin's Day, watching the light passing the north or the patches of fog, till I'd hear a rabbit starting to screech and I'd go running in the furze. Then, when I'd my full share, I'd come walking down where you'd see the ducks and geese stretched sleeping on the highway of the road, and before

I'd pass the dunghill, I'd hear himself snoring out, a loud, lonesome snore he'd be making all times, the while he was sleeping; and he a man'd be raging all times, the while he was waking, like a gaudy officer you'd hear cursing and damning and swearing oaths.

PEGEEN   Providence and Mercy, spare us all!

CHRISTY   It's that you'd say surely if you seen him and he after drinking for weeks, rising up in the red dawn, or before it maybe, and going out into the yard as naked as an ash-tree in the moon of May, and shying clods against the visage of the stars till he'd put the fear of death into the banbhs and the screeching sows.

PEGEEN   I'd be well-nigh afeard of that lad myself, I'm thinking. And there was no one in it but the two of you alone?

CHRISTY   The divil a one, though he'd sons and daughters walking all great states and territories of the world, and not a one of them, to this day, but would say their seven curses on him, and they rousing up to let a cough or sneeze, maybe, in the deadness of the night.

PEGEEN [*Nodding her head*] Well, you should have been a queer lot. I never cursed my father the like of that, though I'm twenty and more years of age.

CHRISTY   Then you'd have cursed mine, I'm telling you, and he a man never gave peace to any, saving when he'd get two months or three, or be locked in the asylums for battering peelers or assaulting men [*with depression*] the way it was a bitter life he led me till I did up a Tuesday and halve his skull.

PEGEEN [*Putting her hand on his shoulder*] Well, you'll have peace in this place, Christy Mahon, and none to trouble you, and it's near time a fine lad like you should have your good share of the earth.

CHRISTY   It's time surely, and I a seemly fellow with great strength in me and bravery of . . . [*Someone knocks.*]

CHRISTY [*Clinging to* PEGEEN] Oh, glory! it's late for knocking, and this last while I'm in terror of the peelers, and the walking dead. [*Knocking again.*]

PEGEEN   Who's there?

VOICE [*Outside*] Me.

PEGEEN   Who's me?

VOICE   The Widow Quin.

PEGEEN [*Jumping up and giving him the bread and milk*] Go on now with your supper, and let on to be sleepy, for if she found you were such a warrant to talk, she'd be stringing gabble till the dawn of day. [*He takes bread and sits shyly with his back to the door.*]

PEGEEN [*Opening door, with temper*] What ails you, or what is it you're wanting at this hour of the night?

WIDOW QUIN [*Coming in a step and peering at* CHRISTY] I'm after meeting Shawn Keogh and Father Reilly below, who told me of your curiosity man, and they fearing by this time he was maybe roaring, romping on your hands with drink.

PEGEEN [*Pointing to* CHRISTY] Look now is he roaring, and he stretched out drowsy with his supper and his mug of milk. Walk down and tell that to Father Reilly and to Shaneen Keogh.

WIDOW QUIN [*Coming forward*] I'll not see them again, for I've their word to lead that lad forward for to lodge with me.

PEGEEN [*In blank amazement*] This night is it?

WIDOW QUIN [*Going over*] This night. "It isn't fitting," says the priesteen, "to have his likeness lodging with an orphaned girl." [*To* CHRISTY.] God save you, mister!

CHRISTY [*Shyly*] God save you kindly!

WIDOW QUIN [*Looking at him with half-amazed curiosity*] Well, aren't you a little smiling fellow? It should have been great and bitter torments did rouse your spirits to a deed of blood.

CHRISTY [*Doubtfully*] It should, maybe.

WIDOW QUIN It's more than "maybe" I'm saying, and it'd soften my heart to see you sitting so simple with your cup and cake, and you fitter to be saying your catechism than slaying your da.

PEGEEN [*At counter, washing glasses*] There's talking when any'd see he's fit to be holding his head high with the wonders of the world. Walk on from this, for I'll not have him tormented, and he destroyed traveling since Tuesday was a week.

WIDOW QUIN [*Peaceably*] We'll be walking surely when his supper's done, and you'll find we're great company, young fellow, when it's of the like of you and me you'd hear the penny poets singing in an August Fair.

CHRISTY [*Innocently*] Did you kill your father?

PEGEEN [*Contemptuously*] She did not. She hit himself with a worn pick, and the rusted poison did corrode his blood the way he never overed it, and died after. That was a sneaky kind of murder did win small glory with the boys itself. [*She crosses to* CHRISTY'*s left.*]

WIDOW QUIN [*With good-humor*] If it didn't, maybe all knows a widow woman has buried her children and destroyed her man is a wiser comrade for a young lad than a girl, the like of you, who'd go helterskeltering after any man would let you a wink upon the road.

PEGEEN [*Breaking out into wild rage*] And you'll say that, Widow Quin, and you gasping with the rage you had racing the hill beyond to look on his face.

WIDOW QUIN [*Laughing derisively*] Me, is it? Well, Father Reilly has cuteness[15] to divide you now. [*She pulls* CHRISTY *up.*] There's great temptation in a man did slay his da, and we'd best be going, young fellow; so rise up and come with me.

PEGEEN [*Seizing his arm*] He'll not stir. He's pot-boy in this place, and I'll not have him stolen off and kidnapped while himself's abroad.

WIDOW QUIN It'd be a crazy pot-boy'd lodge him in the shebeen where he works by day, so you'd have a right to come on, young fellow, till you see my little houseen, a perch off on the rising hill.

PEGEEN Wait till morning, Christy Mahon. Wait till you lay eyes on her leaky thatch is growing more pasture for her buck goat than her square of fields, and she without a tramp itself to keep in order her place at all.

WIDOW QUIN When you see me contriving in my little gardens, Christy Mahon, you'll swear the Lord God formed me to be living lone, and that there isn't my match in Mayo for thatching, or mowing, or shearing a sheep.

PEGEEN [*With noisy scorn*] It's true the Lord God formed you to contrive indeed. Doesn't the world know you reared a black ram at your own breast, so that the Lord Bishop of Connaught felt the elements of a Christian, and he eating it after in a kidney stew? Doesn't the world know you've been seen shaving the foxy skipper from France for a threepenny-bit and a sop of grass tobacco would wring the liver from a mountain goat you'd meet leaping the hills?

---

15. cuteness: shrewdness.

WIDOW QUIN [*With amusement*] Do you hear her now, young fellow? Do you hear the way she'll be rating at your own self when a week is by?

PEGEEN [*To* CHRISTY] Don't heed her. Tell her to go on into her pigsty and not plague us here.

WIDOW QUIN I'm going; but he'll come with me.

PEGEEN [*Shaking him*] Are you dumb, young fellow?

CHRISTY [*Timidly to* WIDOW QUIN] God increase you; but I'm pot-boy in this place, and it's here I'd liefer stay.

PEGEEN [*Triumphantly*] Now you have heard him, and go on from this.

WIDOW QUIN [*Looking round the room*] It's lonesome this hour crossing the hill, and if he won't come along with me, I'd have a right maybe to stop this night with yourselves. Let me stretch out on the settle, Pegeen Mike; and himself can lie by the hearth.

PEGEEN [*Short and fiercely*] Faith, I won't. Quit off or I will send you now.

WIDOW QUIN [*Gathering her shawl up*] Well, it's a terror to be aged a score. [*To* CHRISTY.] God bless you now, young fellow, and let you be wary, or there's right torment will await you here if you go romancing with her like, and she waiting only, as they bade me say, on a sheepskin parchment to be wed with Shawn Keogh of Killakeen.

CHRISTY [*Going to* PEGEEN *as she bolts door*] What's that she's after saying?

PEGEEN Lies and blather, you've no call to mind. Well, isn't Shawn Keogh an impudent fellow to send up spying on me? Wait till I lay hands on him. Let him wait, I'm saying.

CHRISTY And you're not wedding him at all?

PEGEEN I wouldn't wed him if a bishop came walking for to join us here.

CHRISTY That God in glory may be thanked for that.

PEGEEN There's your bed now. I've put a quilt upon you I'm after quilting a while since with my own two hands, and you'd best stretch out now for your sleep, and may God give you a good rest till I call you in the morning when the cocks will crow.

CHRISTY [*As she goes to inner room*] May God and Mary and Saint Patrick bless you and reward you for your kindly talk. [*She shuts the door behind her. He settles his bed slowly, feeling the quilt with immense satisfaction.*] Well, it's a clean bed and soft with it, and it's great luck and company I've won me in the end of time—two fine women fighting for the likes of me—till I'm thinking this night wasn't I a foolish fellow not to kill my father in the years gone by.

ACT II

Scene as before. Brilliant morning light. CHRISTY, *looking bright and cheerful, is cleaning a girl's boots.*

CHRISTY [*To himself, counting jugs on dresser*] Half a hundred beyond. Ten there. A score that's above. Eighty jugs. Six cups and a broken one. Two plates. A power of glasses. Bottles, a schoolmaster'd be hard set to count, and enough in them, I'm thinking, to drunken all the wealth and wisdom of the county Clare. [*He puts down the boot carefully.*] There's her boots now, nice and decent for her evening use, and isn't it grand brushes she has? [*He puts them down and goes by degrees to the looking-glass.*] Well, this'd be a fine place to be my whole life talking out with swearing Christians, in place of my old dogs and cat; and I stalking around, smoking my pipe and drinking my fill, and never a day's work but drawing a cork an odd time, or wiping a glass or rinsing out a shiny tumbler for a decent man. [*He takes the looking-glass from the wall and puts it on the back of a chair; then sits down in front of it and begins washing his face.*] Didn't I know rightly, I was handsome, though it was the divil's own mirror we had beyond, would twist a squint across an angel's brow; and I'll be growing fine from this day, the way I'll have a soft lovely skin on me and won't be the like of the clumsy young fellows do be plowing all times in the earth and dung. [*He starts.*] Is she coming again? [*He looks out.*] Stranger girls. God help me, where'll I hide myself away and my long neck naked to the world? [*He looks out.*] I'd best go to the room maybe till I'm dressed again. [*He gathers up his coat and the looking-glass, and runs into the inner room. The door is pushed open, and* SUSAN BRADY *looks in, and knocks on door.*]

SUSAN There's nobody in it. [*Knocks again.*]

NELLY [*Pushing her in and following her, with* HONOR BLAKE *and* SARA TANSEY] It'd be early for them both to be out walking the hill.

SUSAN I'm thinking Shawn Keogh was making game of us, and there's no such man in it at all.

HONOR [*Pointing to straw and quilt*] Look at that. He's been sleeping there in the night. Well, it'll be a hard case if he's gone off now, the way we'll never set our eyes on a man killed his father, and we after rising early and destroying ourselves running fast on the hill.

NELLY Are you thinking them's his boots?

SARA [*Taking them up*] If they are, there should be his father's track on them. Did you never read in the papers the way murdered men do bleed and drip?

SUSAN Is that blood there, Sara Tansey?

SARA [*Smelling it*] That's bog water, I'm thinking; but it's his own they are, surely, for I never seen the like of them for whitey mud, and red mud, and turf on them and the fine sands of the sea. That man's been walking, I'm telling you. [*She goes down right, putting on one of his boots.*]

SUSAN [*Going to window*] Maybe he's stolen off to Belmullet with the boots of Michael James, and you'd have a right so to follow after him, Sara Tansye, and you the one yoked the ass cart and drove ten miles to set your eyes on the man bit the yellow lady's nostril on the northern shore. [*She looks out.*]

SARA [*Running to window, with one boot on*] Don't be talking, and we fooled today. [*Putting on the other boot.*] There's a pair do fit me well and I'll be keeping them for walking to the priest, when you'd be ashamed this place, going up winter and summer with nothing worthwhile to confess at all.

HONOR [*Who has been listening at door*] Whisht! there's someone inside the room. [*She pushes door a chink open.*] It's a man. [SARA *kicks off boots and puts them where they were. They all stand in a line looking through chink.*]

SARA I'll call him. Mister! Mister! [*He puts in his head.*] Is Pegeen within?

CHRISTY [*Coming in as meek as a mouse, with the looking-glass held behind his back*] She's above on the cnuceen, seeking the nanny goats, the way she'd have a sup of goats' milk for to color my tea.

SARA And asking your pardon, is it you's the man killed his father?

CHRISTY [*Sidling toward the nail where the glass was hanging*] I am, God help me!

SARA [*Taking eggs she had brought*] Then my thousand welcomes to you, and I've run up with a brace of duck's eggs for your food today. Pegeen's ducks is no use, but these are the real rich sort. Hold out your hand and you'll see it's no lie I'm telling you.

CHRISTY [*Coming forward shyly, and holding out his left hand*] They're a great and weighty size.

SUSAN And I run up with a pat of butter, for it'd be a poor thing to have you eating your spuds dry, and you after running a great way since you did destroy your da.

CHRISTY Thank you kindly.

HONOR And I brought you a little cut of a cake, for you should have a thin stomach on you, and you that length walking the world.

NELLY And I brought you a little laying pullet— boiled and all she is—was crushed at the fall of night by the curate's car. Feel the fat of that breast, mister.

CHRISTY It's bursting, surely. [*He feels it with the back of his hand, in which he holds the presents.*]

SARA Will you pinch it? Is your right hand too sacred for to use at all? [*She slips round behind him.*] It's a glass he has. Well, I never seen to this day a man with a looking-glass held to his back. Them that kills their fathers is a vain lot surely. [GIRLS *giggle.*]

CHRISTY [*Smiling innocently and piling presents on glass*] I'm very thankful to you all today. . . .

WIDOW QUIN [*Coming in quickly, at door*] Sara Tansey, Susan Brady, Honor Blake! What in glory has you here at this hour of day?

GIRLS [*Giggling*] That's the man killed his father.

WIDOW QUIN [*Coming to them*] I know well it's the man; and I'm after putting him down in the sports below for racing, leaping, pitching, and the Lord knows what.

SARA [*Exuberantly*] That's right, Widow Quin. I'll bet my dowry that he'll lick the world.

WIDOW QUIN If you will, you'd have a right to have him fresh and nourished in place of nursing a feast. [*Taking presents.*] Are you fasting or fed, young fellow?

CHRISTY Fasting, if you please.

WIDOW QUIN [*Loudly*] Well, you're the lot. Stir up now and give him his breakfast. [*To* CHRISTY.] Come here to me [*she puts him on bench beside her while the* GIRLS *make tea and get his breakfast*] and let you tell us your story before Pegeen will come, in place of grinning your ears off like the moon of May.

CHRISTY   [*Beginning to be pleased*] It's a long story; you'd be destroyed listening.

WIDOW QUIN   Don't be letting on to be shy, a fine, gamey, treacherous lad the like of you. Was it in your house beyond you cracked his skull?

CHRISTY   [*Shy but flattered*] It was not. We were digging spuds in his cold, sloping, stony, divil's patch of a field.

WIDOW QUIN   And you went asking money of him, or making talk of getting a wife would drive him from his farm?

CHRISTY   I did not, then; but there I was, digging and digging, and "You squinting idiot," says he, "let you walk down now and tell the priest you'll wed the Widow Casey in a score of days."

WIDOW QUIN   And what kind was she?

CHRISTY   [*With horror*] A walking terror from beyond the hills, and she twoscore and five years, and two hundred-weights and five pounds in the weighing scales, with a limping leg on her, and a blinded eye, and she a woman of noted misbehavior with the old and young.

GIRLS   [*Clustering round him, serving him*] Glory be.

WIDOW QUIN   And what did he want driving you to wed with her? [*She takes a bit of the chicken.*]

CHRISTY   [*Eating with growing satisfaction*] He was letting on I was wanting a protector from the harshness of the world, and he without a thought the whole while but how he'd have her hut to live in and her gold to drink.

WIDOW QUIN   There's maybe worse than a dry hearth and a widow woman and your glass at night. So you hit him then?

CHRISTY   [*Getting almost excited*] I did not. "I won't wed her," says I, "when all know she did suckle me for six weeks when I came into the world, and she a hag this day with a tongue on her has the crows and seabirds scattered, the way they wouldn't cast a shadow on her garden with the dread of her curse."

WIDOW QUIN   [*Teasingly*] That one should be right company.

SARA   [*Eagerly*] Don't mind her. Did you kill him then?

CHRISTY   "She's too good for the like of you," says he, "and go on now or I'll flatten you out like a crawling beast has passed under a dray."

"You will not if I can help it," says I. "Go on," says he, "or I'll have the divil making garters of your limbs tonight." "You will not if I can help it," says I. [*He sits up brandishing his mug.*]

SARA.   You were right surely.

CHRISTY   [*Impressively*] With that the sun came out between the cloud and the hill, and it shining green in my face. "God have mercy on your soul," says he, lifting a scythe. "Or on your own," says I, raising the loy.

SUSAN   That's a grand story.

HONOR   He tells it lovely.

CHRISTY   [*Flattered and confident, waving bone*] He gave a drive with the scythe, and I gave a lep to the east. Then I turned around with my back to the north, and I hit a blow on the ridge of his skull, laid him stretched out, and he split to the knob of his gullet. [*He raises the chicken bone to his Adam's apple.*]

GIRLS   [*Together*] Well, you're a marvel! Oh, God bless you! You're the lad, surely!

SUSAN   I'm thinking the Lord God sent him this road to make a second husband to the Widow Quin, and she with a great yearning to be wedded, though all dread her here. Lift him on her knee, Sara Tansey.

WIDOW QUIN   Don't tease him.

SARA   [*Going over to dresser and counter very quickly, and getting two glasses and porter*] You're heroes, surely, and let you drink a supeen with your arms linked like the outlandish lovers in the sailor's song. [*She links their arms and gives them the glasses.*] There now. Drink a health to the wonders of the western world, the pirates, preachers, poteen-makers, with the jobbing jockies; parching peelers, and the juries fill their stomachs selling judgments of the English law. [*Brandishing the bottle.*]

WIDOW QUIN   That's a right toast, Sara Tansey. Now, Christy. [*They drink with their arms linked, he drinking with his left hand, she with her right. As they are drinking, PEGEEN MIKE comes in with a milkcan and stands aghast. They all spring away from CHRISTY. He goes down left. WIDOW QUIN remains seated.*]

PEGEEN   [*Angrily, to SARA*] What is it you're wanting?

SARA   [*Twisting her apron*] An ounce of tobacco.

PEGEEN   Have you tuppence?

SARA   I've forgotten my purse.

PEGEEN   Then you'd best be getting it and not be fooling us here. [*To the* WIDOW QUIN, *with more elaborate scorn.*] And what is it you're wanting, Widow Quin?

WIDOW QUIN   [*Insolently*] A penn'orth of starch.

PEGEEN   [*Breaking out*] And you without a white shift or a shirt in your whole family since the dying of the flood. I've no starch for the like of you, and let you walk on now to Killamuck.

WIDOW QUIN   [*Turning to* CHRISTY, *as she goes out with the* GIRLS] Well, you're mighty huffy this day, Pegeen Mike, and you, young fellow, let you not forget the sports and racing when the noon is by. [*They go out.*]

PEGEEN   [*Imperiously*] Fling out that rubbish and put them cups away. [CHRISTY *tidies away in great haste.*] Shove in the bench by the wall. [*He does so.*] And hang that glass on the nail. What disturbed it at all?

CHRISTY   [*Very meekly*] I was making myself decent only, and this a fine country for young lovely girls.

PEGEEN   [*Sharply*] Whisht you talking of girls. [*Goes to counter on right.*]

CHRISTY   Wouldn't any wish to be decent in a place . . .

PEGEEN   Whisht, I'm saying.

CHRISTY   [*Looks at her face for a moment with great misgivings, then as a last effort takes up a loy, and goes towards her, with feigned assurance*] It was with a loy the like of that I killed my father.

PEGEEN   [*Still sharply*] You've told me that story six times since the dawn of day.

CHRISTY   [*Reproachfully*] It's a queer thing you wouldn't care to be hearing it and them girls after walking four miles to be listening to me now.

PEGEEN   [*Turning round astonished*] Four miles?

CHRISTY   [*Apologetically*] Didn't himself say there were only bona fides living in the place?

PEGEEN   It's bona fides by the road they are, but that lot came over the river lepping the stones. It's not three perches when you go like that, and I was down this morning looking on the papers the post-boy does have in his bag. [*With meaning and emphasis.*] For there was great news this day, Christopher Mahon. [*She goes into room on left.*]

CHRISTY   [*Suspiciously*] Is it news of my murder?

PEGEEN   [*Inside*] Murder, indeed.

CHRISTY   [*Loudly*] A murdered da?

PEGEEN   [*Coming in again and crossing right*] There was not, but a story filled half a page of the hanging of a man. Ah, that should be a fearful end, young fellow, and it worst of all for a man destroyed his da; for the like of him would get small mercies, and when it's dead he is they'd put him in a narrow grave, with cheap sacking wrapping him round, and pour down quicklime on his head, the way you'd see a woman pouring any frish-frash from a cup.

CHRISTY   [*Very miserably*] Oh, God help me. Are you thinking I'm safe? You were saying at the fall of night I was shut of jeopardy and I here with yourselves.

PEGEEN   [*Severely*] You'll be shut of jeopardy no place if you go talking with a pack of wild girls the like of them do be walking abroad with the peelers, talking whispers at the fall of night.

CHRISTY   [*With terror*] And you're thinking they'd tell?

PEGEEN   [*With mock sympathy*] Who knows, God help you?

CHRISTY   [*Loudly*] What joy would they have to bring hanging to the likes of me?

PEGEEN   It's queer joys they have, and who knows the thing they'd do, if it'd make the green stones cry itself to think of you swaying and swiggling at the butt of a rope, and you with a fine, stout neck, God bless you! the way you'd be a half an hour, in great anguish, getting your death.

CHRISTY   [*Getting his boots and putting them on*] If there's that terror of them, it'd be best, maybe, I went on wandering like Esau or Cain and Abel on the sides of Neifin or the Erris plain.

PEGEEN   [*Beginning to play with him*] It would, maybe, for I've heard the circuit judges this place is a heartless crew.

CHRISTY   [*Bitterly*] It's more than judges this place is a heartless crew. [*Looking up at her.*] And isn't it a poor thing to be starting again, and I a lonesome fellow will be looking out on women and girls the way the needy fallen spirits do be looking on the Lord?

PEGEEN   What call have you to be that lonesome when there's poor girls walking Mayo in their thousands now?

CHRISTY   [*Grimly*] It's well you know what call I have. It's well you know it's a lonesome thing to be passing small towns with the lights shining sideways when the night is down, or going in strange places with a dog noising before you and a dog noising behind, or drawn to the cities where you'd hear a voice kissing and talking deep love in every shadow of the ditch, and you passing on with an empty, hungry stomach failing from your heart.

PEGEEN I'm thinking you're an odd man, Christy Mahon. The oddest walking fellow I ever set my eyes on to this hour today.

CHRISTY What would any be but odd men and they living lonesome in the world?

PEGEEN I'm not odd, and I'm my whole life with my father only.

CHRISTY [*With infinite admiration*] How would a lovely, handsome woman the like of you be lonesome when all men should be thronging around to hear the sweetness of your voice, and the little infant children should be pestering your steps, I'm thinking, and you walking the roads.

PEGEEN I'm hard set to know what way a coaxing fellow the like of yourself should be lonesome either.

CHRISTY Coaxing?

PEGEEN Would you have me think a man never talked with the girls would have the words you've spoken today? It's only letting on you are to be lonesome, the way you'd get around me now.

CHRISTY I wish to God I was letting on; but I was lonesome all times, and born lonesome, I'm thinking, as the moon of dawn. [*Going to door.*]

PEGEEN [*Puzzled by his talk*] Well, it's a story I'm not understanding at all why you'd be worse than another, Christy Mahon, and you a fine lad with the great savagery to destroy your da.

CHRISTY It's little I'm understanding myself, saving only that my heart's scalded this day, and I going off stretching out the earth between us, the way I'll not be waking near you another dawn of the year till the two of us do arise to hope or judgment with the saints of God, and now I'd best be going with my wattle[16] in my hand, for hanging is a poor thing [*turning to go*], and it's little welcome only is left me in this house today.

PEGEEN [*Sharply*] Christy. [*He turns round.*] Come here to me. [*He goes towards her.*] Lay down that

switch and throw some sods on the fire. You're pot-boy in this place, and I'll not have you mitch[17] off from us now.

CHRISTY You were saying I'd be hanged if I stay.

PEGEEN [*Quite kindly at last*] I'm after going down and reading the fearful crimes of Ireland for two weeks or three, and there wasn't a word of your murder. [*Getting up and going over to the counter.*] They've likely not found the body. You're safe so with ourselves.

CHRISTY [*Astonished, slowly*] It's making game of me you were [*following her with fearful joy*], and I can stay so, working at your side, and I not lonesome from this mortal day.

PEGEEN What's to hinder you staying, except the widow woman or the young girls would inveigle you off?

CHRISTY [*With rapture*] And I'll have your words from this day filling my ears, and that look is come upon you meeting my two eyes, and I watching you loafing around in the warm sun, or rinsing your ankles when the night is come.

PEGEEN [*Kindly, but a little embarrassed*] I'm thinking you'll be a loyal young lad to have working around, and if you vexed me a while since with your leaguing with the girls, I wouldn't give a thraneen[18] for a lad hadn't a mighty spirit in him and a gamey heart. [SHAWN KEOGH *runs in carrying a cleeve*[19] *on his back, followed by the* WIDOW QUIN.]

SHAWN [*To* PEGEEN] I was passing below, and I seen your mountainy sheep eating cabbages in Jimmy's field. Run up or they'll be bursting, surely.

PEGEEN Oh, God mend them! [*She puts a shawl over her head and runs out.*]

CHRISTY [*Looking from one to the other. Still in high spirits*] I'd best go to her aid maybe. I'm handy with ewes.

WIDOW QUIN [*Closing the door*] She can do that much, and there is Shaneen has long speeches for to tell you now. [*She sits down with an amused smile.*]

SHAWN [*Taking something from his pocket and offering it to* CHRISTY] Do you see that, mister?

CHRISTY [*Looking at it*] The half of a ticket to the Western States!

---

16. wattle: stick or staff.

17. mitch: sneak. 18. thraneen: nickel. 19. cleeve: pack, hamper.

SHAWN [*Trembling with anxiety*] I'll give it to you and my new hat [*pulling it out of hamper*]; and my breeches with the double seat [*pulling it out*]; and my new coat is woven from the blackest shearings for three miles around [*giving him the coat*]; I'll give you the whole of them, and my blessing, and the blessing of Father Reilly itself, maybe, if you'll quit from this and leave us in the peace we had till last night at the fall of dark.

CHRISTY [*With a new arrogance*] And for what is it you're wanting to get shut of me?

SHAWN [*Looking to the* WIDOW *for help*] I'm a poor scholar with middling faculties to coin a lie, so I'll tell the truth, Christy Mahon. I'm wedding with Pegeen beyond, and I don't think well of having a clever, fearless man the like of you dwelling in her house.

CHRISTY [*Almost pugnaciously*] And you'd be using bribery for to banish me?

SHAWN [*In an imploring voice*] Let you not take it badly, mister honey; isn't beyond the best place for you, where you'll have golden chains and shiny coats and you riding upon hunters with the ladies of the land. [*He makes an eager sign to the* WIDOW QUIN *to come to help him.*]

WIDOW QUIN [*Coming over*] It's true for him, and you'd best quit off and not have that poor girl setting her mind on you, for there's Shaneen thinks she wouldn't suit you, though all is saying that she'll wed you now. [CHRISTY *beams with delight.*]

SHAWN [*In terrified earnest*] She wouldn't suit you, and she with the divil's own temper the way you'd be strangling one another in a score of days. [*He makes the movement of strangling with his hands.*] It's the like of me only that she's fit for; a quiet simple fellow wouldn't raise a hand upon her if she scratched itself.

WIDOW QUIN [*Putting* SHAWN'S *hat on* CHRISTY] Fit them clothes on you anyhow, young fellow, and he'd maybe loan them to you for the sports. [*Pushing him towards inner door.*] Fit them on and you can give your answer when you have them tried.

CHRISTY [*Beaming, delighted with the clothes*] I will then. I'd like herself to see me in them tweeds and hat. [*He goes into room and shuts the door.*]

SHAWN [*In great anxiety*] He'd like herself to see them. He'll not leave us, Widow Quin. He's a score of divils in him the way it's well-nigh certain he will wed Pegeen.

WIDOW QUIN [*Jeeringly*] It's true all girls are fond of courage and do hate the like of you.

SHAWN [*Walking about in desperation*] Oh, Widow Quin, what'll I be doing now? I'd inform again him but he'd burst from Kilmainham and he'd be sure and certain to destroy me. If I wasn't so God-fearing, I'd near have courage to come behind him and run a pike into his side. Oh, it's a hard case to be an orphan and not to have your father that you're used to, and you'd easy kill and make yourself a hero in the sight of all. [*Coming up to her.*] Oh, Widow Quin, will you find me some contrivance when I've promised you a ewe?

WIDOW QUIN A ewe's a small thing, but what would you give me if I did wed him and did save you so?

SHAWN [*With astonishment*] You?

WIDOW QUIN Aye. Would you give me the red cow you have and the mountainy ram, and the right of way across your rye path, and a load of dung at Michaelmas, and turbary[20] upon the western hill?

SHAWN [*Radiant with hope*] I would, surely, and I'd give you the wedding-ring I have, and the loan of a new suit, the way you'd have him decent on the wedding-day. I'd give you two kids for your dinner, and a gallon of poteen, and I'd call the piper on the long car to your wedding from Crossmolina or from Ballina. I'd give you . . .

WIDOW QUIN That'll do, so, and let you whisht, for he's coming now again. [CHRISTY *comes in very natty in the new clothes.* WIDOW QUIN *goes to him admiringly.*]

WIDOW QUIN If you seen yourself now, I'm thinking you'd be too proud to speak to at all, and it'd be a pity surely to have your like sailing from Mayo to the Western World.

CHRISTY [*As proud as a peacock*] I'm not going. If this is a poor place itself, I'll make myself contented to be lodging here. WIDOW QUIN *makes a sign to* SHAWN *to leave them.*]

SHAWN Well, I'm going measuring the racecourse while the tide is low, so I'll leave you the garments and my blessing for the sports today. God bless you! [*He wriggles out.*]

20. turbary: right to dig peat.

WIDOW QUIN [*Admiring* CHRISTY] Well, you're mighty spruce, young fellow. Sit down now while you're quiet till you talk with me.

CHRISTY [*Swaggering*] I'm going abroad on the hillside for to seek Pegeen.

WIDOW QUIN You'll have time and plenty for to seek Pegeen, and you heard me saying at the fall of night the two of us should be great company.

CHRISTY From this out I'll have no want of company when all sorts is bringing me their food and clothing [*he swaggers to the door, tightening his belt*], the way they'd set their eyes upon a gallant orphan cleft his father with one blow to the breeches belt. [*He opens door, then staggers back.*] Saints of glory! Holy angels from the throne of light!

WIDOW QUIN [*Going over*] What ails you?

CHRISTY It's the walking spirit of my murdered da?

WIDOW QUIN [*Looking out*] Is it that tramper?

CHRISTY [*Wildly*] Where'll I hide my poor body from that ghost of hell? [*The door is pushed open, and old* MAHON *appears on threshold.* CHRISTY *darts in behind door.*]

WIDOW QUIN [*In great amusement*] God save you, my poor man.

MAHON [*Gruffly*] Did you see a young lad passing this way in the early morning or the fall of night?

WIDOW QUIN You're a queer kind to walk in not saluting at all.

MAHON Did you see the young lad?

WIDOW QUIN [*Stiffly*] What kind was he?

MAHON An ugly young streeler with a murderous gob[21] on him, and a little switch in his hand. I met a tramper seen him coming this way at the fall of night.

WIDOW QUIN There's harvest hundreds do be passing these days for the Sligo boat. For what is it you're wanting him, my poor man?

MAHON I want to destroy him for breaking the head on me with the clout of a loy. [*He takes off a big hat, and shows his head in a mass of bandages and plaster, with some pride.*] It was he did that, and amn't I a great wonder to think I've traced him ten days with that rent in my crown?

WIDOW QUIN [*Taking his head in both hands and examining it with extreme delight*] That was a great blow. And who hit you? A robber maybe?

21. gob: lump.

MAHON It was my own son hit me, and he the divil a robber, or anything else, but a dirty, stuttering lout.

WIDOW QUIN [*Letting go his skull and wiping her hands in her apron*] You'd best be wary of a mortified scalp, I think they call it, lepping around with that wound in the splendor of the sun. It was a bad blow, surely, and you should have vexed him fearful to make him strike that gash in his da.

MAHON Is it me?

WIDOW QUIN [*Amusing herself*] Aye. And isn't it a great shame when the old and hardened do torment the young?

MAHON [*Raging*] Torment him is it? And I after holding out with the patience of a martyred saint till there's nothing but destruction on, and I'm driven out in my old age with none to aid me.

WIDOW QUIN [*Greatly amused*] It's a sacred wonder the way that wickedness will spoil a man.

MAHON My wickedness, is it? Amn't I after saying it is himself has me destroyed, and he a lier on walls, a talker of folly, a man you'd see stretched the half of the day in the brown ferns with his belly to the sun.

WIDOW QUIN Not working at all?

MAHON The divil a work, or if he did itself, you'd see him raising up a haystack like the stalk of a rush, or driving our last cow till he broke her leg at the hip, and when he wasn't at that he'd be fooling over little birds he had—finches and felts—or making mugs at his own self in the bit of a glass we had hung on the wall.

WIDOW QUIN [*Looking at* CHRISTY] What way was he so foolish? It was running wild after the girls maybe?

MAHON [*With a shout of derision*] Running wild, is it? If he seen a red petticoat coming swinging over the hill, he'd be off to hide in the sticks, and you'd see him shooting out his sheep's eyes between the little twigs and the leaves, and his two ears rising like a hare looking out through a gap. Girls, indeed!

WIDOW QUIN It was drink maybe?

MAHON And he a poor fellow would get drunk on the smell of a pint. He'd a queer rotten stomach, I'm telling you, and when I gave him three pulls from my pipe a while since, he was taken with contortions till I had to send him in the ass-cart to the females' nurse.

WIDOW QUIN [*Clasping her hands*] Well, I never, till this day, heard tell of a man the like of that!

MAHON I'd take a mighty oath you didn't, surely, and wasn't he the laughing joke of every female woman where four baronies meet, the way the girls would stop their weeding if they seen him coming the road to let a roar at him, and call him the looney of Mahon's.

WIDOW QUIN I'd give the world and all to see the like of him. What kind was he?

MAHON A small, low fellow.

WIDOW QUIN And dark?

MAHON Dark and dirty.

WIDOW QUIN [*Considering*] I'm thinking I seen him.

MAHON [*Eagerly*] An ugly young blackguard.

WIDOW QUIN A hideous, fearful villain, and the spit of you.

MAHON What way is he fled?

WIDOW QUIN Gone over the hills to catch a coasting steamer to the north or south.

MAHON Could I pull up on him now?

WIDOW QUIN If you'll cross the sands below where the tide is out, you'll be in it as soon as himself, for he had to go round ten miles by the top of the bay. [*She points to the door.*] Strike down by the head beyond and then follow on the roadway to the north and east. [MAHON *goes abruptly.*]

WIDOW QUIN [*Shouting after him*] Let you give him a good vengeance when you come up with him, but don't put yourself in the power of the law, for it'd be a poor thing to see a judge in his black cap reading out his sentence on a civil warrior the like of you. [*She swings the door to and looks at* CHRISTY, *who is cowering in terror, for a moment, then she bursts into a laugh.*] Well, you're the walking Playboy of the Western World, and that's the poor man you had divided to his breeches belt.

CHRISTY [*Looking out; then, to her*] What'll Pegeen say when she hears that story? What'll she be saying to me now?

WIDOW QUIN She'll knock the head of you, I'm thinking, and drive you from the door. God help her to be taking you for a wonder, and you a little schemer making up a story you destroyed your da.

CHRISTY [*Turning to the door, nearly speechless with rage, half to himself*] To be letting on he was dead, and coming back to his life, and following after me like an old weasel tracing a rat, and coming in here laying desolation between my own self and the fine women of Ireland, and he a kind of carcass that you'd fling upon the sea. . . .

WIDOW QUIN [*More soberly*] There's talking for a man's one only son.

CHRISTY [*Breaking out*] His one son, is it? May I meet him with one tooth and it aching, and one eye to be seeing seven and seventy divils in the twists of the road, and one old timber leg on him to limp into the scalding grave. [*Looking out.*] There he is now crossing the strands, and that the Lord God would send a high wave to wash him from the world.

WIDOW QUIN [*Scandalized*] Have you no shame? [*Putting her hand on his shoulder and turning him round.*] What ails you? Near crying, is it?

CHRISTY [*In despair and grief*] Amn't I after seeing the lovelight of the star of knowledge shining from her brow, and hearing words would put you thinking on the holy Brigid speaking to the infant saints, and now she'll be turning again, and speaking hard words to me, like an old woman with a spavindy[22] ass she'd have, urging on a hill.

WIDOW QUIN There's poetry talk for a girl you'd see itching and scratching, and she with a stale stink of poteen on her from selling in the shop.

CHRISTY [*Impatiently*] It's her like is fitted to be handling merchandise in the heavens above, and what'll I be doing now, I ask you, and I a kind of wonder was jilted by the heavens when a day was by. [*There is a distant noise of* GIRLS' *voices.* WIDOW QUIN *looks from window and comes to him, hurriedly.*]

WIDOW QUIN You'll be doing like myself, I'm thinking, when I did destroy my man, for I'm above many's the day, odd times in great spirits, abroad in the sunshine, darning a stocking or stitching a shift; and odd times again looking out on the schooners, hookers, trawlers is sailing the sea, and I thinking on the gallant hairy fellows are drifting beyond, and myself long years living alone.

CHRISTY [*Interested*] You're like me, so.

WIDOW QUIN I am your like, and it's for that I'm taking a fancy to you, and I with my little houseen above where there'd be myself to tend

22. **spavindy:** stiff-jointed.

you, and none to ask were you a murderer or what at all.

CHRISTY   And what would I be doing if I left Pegeen?

WIDOW QUIN   I've nice jobs you could be doing—gathering shells to make a whitewash for our hut within, building up a little goose-house, or stretching a new skin on an old curagh[23] I have, and if my hut is far from all sides, it's there you'll meet the wisest old men, I tell you, at the corner of my wheel, and it's there yourself and me will have great times whispering and hugging. . . .

VOICES   [Outside, calling far away] Christy! Christy Mahon! Christy!

CHRISTY   Is it Pegeen Mike?

WIDOW QUIN   It's the young girls, I'm thinking, coming to bring you to the sports below, and what is it you'll have me to tell them now?

CHRISTY   Aid me for to win Pegeen. It's herself only that I'm seeking now. [WIDOW QUIN gets up and goes to window.] Aid me for to win her, and I'll be asking God to stretch a hand to you in the hour of death, and lead you short cuts through the Meadows of Ease, and up the floor of Heaven to the Footstool of the Virgin's Son.

WIDOW QUIN   There's praying!

VOICES   [Nearer] Christy! Christy Mahon!

CHRISTY   [With agitation] They're coming. Will you swear to aid and save me, for the love of Christ?

WIDOW QUIN   [Looks at him for a moment] If I aid you, will you swear to give me a right of way I want, and a mountainy ram, and a load of dung at Michaelmas, the time that you'll be master here?

CHRISTY   I will, by the elements and stars of night.

WIDOW QUIN   Then we'll not say a word of the old fellow, the way Pegeen won't know your story till the end of time.

CHRISTY   And if he chances to return again?

WIDOW QUIN   We'll swear he's a maniac and not your da. I could take an oath I seen him raving on the sands today. [GIRLS run in.]

SUSAN   Come on to the sports below. Pegeen says you're to come.

SARA TANSEY   The lepping's beginning, and we've a jockey's suit to fit upon you for the mule race on the sands below.

HONOR   Come on, will you?

---

23. curagh: skin-covered boat.

CHRISTY   I will then if Pegeen's beyond.

SARA   She's in the boreen[24] making game of Shaneen Keogh.

CHRISTY   Then I'll be going to her now. [He runs out, followed by the GIRLS.]

WIDOW QUIN   Well, if the worst comes in the end of all, it'll be great game to see there's none to pity him but a widow woman, the like of me, has buried her children and destroyed her man. [She goes out.]

ACT III

Scene as before. Later in the day. JIMMY comes in, slightly drunk.

JIMMY   [Calls] Pegeen! [Crosses to inner door.] Pegeen Mike! [Comes back again into the room.] Pegeen! [PHILLY comes in in the same state—To PHILLY.] Did you see herself?

PHILLY   I did not; but I sent Shawn Keogh with the ass-cart for to bear him home. [Trying cupboards, which are locked.] Well, isn't he a nasty man to get into such staggers at a morning wake; and isn't herself the divil's daughter for locking, and she so fussy after that young gaffer, you might take your death with drouth and none to heed you?

JIMMY   It's little wonder she'd be fussy, and he after bringing bankrupt ruin on the roulette man, and the trick-o'-the-loop man, and breaking the nose of the cockshot-man, and winning all in the sports below, racing, lepping, dancing, and the Lord knows what! He's right luck, I'm telling you.

PHILLY   If he has, he'll be rightly hobbled yet, and he not able to say ten words without making a brag of the way he killed his father, and the great blow he hit with the loy.

JIMMY   A man can't hang by his own informing, and his father should be rotten by now. [OLD MAHON passes window slowly.]

PHILLY   Supposing a man's digging spuds in that field with a long spade, and supposing he flings up the two halves of that skull, what'll be said then in the papers and the courts of law?

JIMMY   They'd say it was an old Dane, maybe, was drowned in the flood. [OLD MAHON comes in and sits down near door listening.] Did you never hear

---

24. boreen: lane, narrow road.

tell of the skulls they have in the city of Dublin, ranged out like blue jugs in a cabin of Connaught?

PHILLY   And you believe that?

JIMMY   [*Pugnaciously*] Didn't a lad see them and he after coming from harvesting in the Liverpool boat? "They have them there," says he, "making a show of the great people there was one time walking the world. White skulls and black skulls and yellow skulls, and some with full teeth, and some haven't only but one."

PHILLY   It was no lie, maybe, for when I was a young lad there was a graveyard beyond the house with the remnants of a man who had thighs as long as your arm. He was a horrid man, I'm telling you, and there was many a fine Sunday I'd put him together for fun, and he with shiny bones, you wouldn't meet the like of these days in the cities of the world.

MAHON   [*Getting up*] You wouldn't, is it? Lay your eyes on that skull, and tell me where and when there was another the like of it, is splintered only from the blow of a loy.

PHILLY   Glory be to God! And who hit you at all?

MAHON   [*Triumphantly*] It was my own son hit me. Would you believe that?

JIMMY   Well, there's wonders hidden in the heart of man!

PHILLY   [*Suspiciously*] And what way was it done?

MAHON   [*Wandering about the room*] I'm after walking hundreds and long scores of miles, winning clean beds and the fill of my belly four times in the day, and I doing nothing but telling stories of that naked truth. [*He comes to them a little aggressively.*] Give me a supeen and I'll tell you now. [WIDOW QUIN *comes in and stands aghast behind him. He is facing* JIMMY *and* PHILLY, *who are on the left.*]

JIMMY   Ask herself beyond. She's the stuff hidden in her shawl.

WIDOW QUIN   [*Coming to* MAHON *quickly*] You here, is it? You didn't go far at all?

MAHON   I seen the coasting steamer passing, and I got a drouth upon me and a cramping leg, so I said, "The divil go along with him," and turned again. [*Looking under her shawl.*] And let you give me a supeen, for I'm destroyed traveling since Tuesday was a week.

WIDOW QUIN   [*Getting a glass, in a cajoling tone*] Sit down then by the fire and take your ease for a space. You've a right to be destroyed indeed, with your walking, and fighting, and facing the sun. [*Giving him poteen from a stone jar she has brought in.*] There now is a drink for you, and may it be to your happiness and length of life.

MAHON   [*Taking glass greedily, and sitting down by fire*] God increase you!

WIDOW QUIN   [*Taking men to the right stealthily*] Do you know what? That man's raving from his wound today, for I met him a while since telling a rambling tale of a tinker had him destroyed. Then he heard of Christy's deed, and he up and says it was his son had cracked his skull. Oh, isn't madness a fright, for he'll go killing someone yet, and he thinking it's the man has struck him so?

JIMMY   [*Entirely convinced*] It's a fright surely. I knew a party was kicked in the head by a red mare, and he went killing horses a great while, till he eat the insides of a clock and died after.

PHILLY   [*With suspicion*] Did he see Christy?

WIDOW QUIN   He didn't. [*With a warning gesture.*] Let you not be putting him in mind of him, or you'll be likely summoned if there's murder done. [*Looking round at* MAHON.] Whisht! He's listening. Wait now till you hear me taking him easy and unraveling all. [*She goes to* MAHON.] And what way are you feeling, mister? Are you in contentment now?

MAHON   [*Slightly emotional from his drink*] I'm poorly only, for it's a hard story the way I'm left today, when it was I did tend him from his hour of birth, and he a dunce never reached his second book, the way he'd come from school, many's the day, with his legs lamed under him, and he blackened with his beatings like a tinker's ass. It's a hard story, I'm saying, the way some do have their next and nighest raising up a hand of murder on them, and some is lonesome getting their death with lamentation in the dead of night.

WIDOW QUIN   [*Not knowing what to say*] To hear you talking so quiet, who'd know you were the same fellow we seen pass today?

MAHON   I'm the same surely. The wrack and ruin of threescore years; and it's a terror to live that length, I tell you, and to have your sons going to the dogs against you, and you wore out scolding them, and skelping[25] them, and God knows what.

25. **skelping:** spanking, slapping.

PHILLY [*To* JIMMY] He's not raving. [*To* WIDOW QUIN.] Will you ask him what kind was his son?

WIDOW QUIN [*To* MAHON, *with a peculiar look*] Was your son that hit you a lad of one year and a score maybe, a great hand at racing and lepping and licking the world?

MAHON [*Turning on her with a roar of rage*] Didn't you hear me say he was the fool of men, the way from this out he'll know the orphan's lot, with old and young making game of him, and they swearing, raging, kicking at him like a mangy cur. [*A great burst of cheering outside, some way off.*]

MAHON [*Putting his hands to his ears*] What in the name of God do they want roaring below?

WIDOW QUIN [*With the shade of a smile*] They're cheering a young lad, the champion Playboy of the Western World. [*More cheering.*]

MAHON [*Going to window*] It'd split my heart to hear them, and I with pulses in my brain-pan for a week gone by. Is it racing they are?

JIMMY [*Looking from door*] It is, then. They are mounting him for the mule race will be run upon the sands. That's the playboy on the winkered[26] mule.

MAHON [*Puzzled*] That lad, is it? If you said it was a fool he was, I'd have laid a mighty oath he was the likeness of my wandering son. [*Uneasily, putting his hand to his head.*] Faith, I'm thinking I'll go walking for to view the race.

WIDOW QUIN [*Stopping him, sharply*] You will not. You'd best take the road to Belmullet, and not be dilly-dallying in this place where there isn't a spot you could sleep.

PHILLY [*Coming forward*] Don't mind her. Mount there on the bench and you'll have a view of the whole. They're hurrying before the tide will rise, and it'd be near over if you went down the pathway through the crags below.

MAHON [*Mounts on bench,* WIDOW QUIN *beside him*] That's a right view again the edge of the sea. They're coming now from the point. He's leading. Who is he at all?

WIDOW QUIN He's the champion of the world, I tell you, and there isn't a hap'orth[27] isn't falling lucky to his hands today.

PHILLY [*Looking out, interested in the race*] Look at that. They're pressing him now.

26. winkered: with blinders. 27. hap'orth: a halfpenny's worth.

JIMMY He'll win it yet.

PHILLY Take your time, Jimmy Farrell. It's too soon to say.

WIDOW QUIN [*Shouting*] Watch him taking the gate. There's riding.

JIMMY [*Cheering*] More power to the young lad!

MAHON He's passing the third.

JIMMY He'll lick them yet.

WIDOW QUIN He'd lick them if he was running races with a score itself.

MAHON Look at the mule he has, kicking the stars.

WIDOW QUIN There was a lep! [*Catching hold of* MAHON *in her excitement.*] He's fallen? He's mounted again! Faith, he's passing them all!

JIMMY Look at him skelping her!

PHILLY And the mountain girls hooshing him on!

JIMMY It's the last turn! The post's cleared for them now!

MAHON Look at the narrow place. He'll be into the bogs! [*With a yell.*] Good rider! He's through it again!

JIMMY He neck and neck!

MAHON Good boy to him! Flames, but he's in! *Great cheering, in which all join.*]

MAHON [*With hesitation*] What's that? They're raising him up. They're coming this way. [*With a roar of rage and astonishment.*] It's Christy, by the stars of God! I'd know his way of spitting and he astride the moon. [*He jumps down and makes a run for the door, but* WIDOW QUIN *catches him and pulls him back.*]

WIDOW QUIN Stay quiet, will you? That's not your son. [*To* JIMMY.] Stop him, or you'll get a month for the abetting of manslaughter and be fined as well.

JIMMY I'll hold him.

MAHON [*Struggling*] Let me out! Let me out, the lot of you, till I have my vengeance on his head today.

WIDOW QUIN [*Shaking him, vehemently*] That's not your son. That's a man is going to make a marriage with the daughter of this house, a place with fine trade, with a license, and with poteen too.

MAHON [*Amazed*] That man marrying a decent and a moneyed girl! It is mad yous are? Is it in a crazy-house for females that I'm landed now?

WIDOW QUIN It's mad yourself is with the blow upon your head. That lad is the wonder of the Western World.

MAHON   I seen it's my son.

WIDOW QUIN   You seen that you're mad. [*Cheering outside.*] Do you hear them cheering him in the zigzags of the road? Aren't you after saying that your son's a fool, and how would they be cheering a true idiot born?

MAHON   [*Getting distressed*] It's maybe out of reason that that man's himself. [*Cheering again.*] There's none surely will go cheering him. Oh, I'm raving with a madness that would fright the world! [*He sits down with his hand to his head.*] There was one time I seen ten scarlet divils letting on they'd cork my spirit in a gallon can; and one time I seen rats as big as badgers sucking the lifeblood from the butt of my lug; but I never till this day confused that dribbling idiot with a likely man. I'm destroyed surely.

WIDOW QUIN   And who'd wonder when it's your brain-pan that is gaping now?

MAHON   Then the blight of the sacred drouth upon myself and him, for I never went mad to this day, and I not three weeks with the Limerick girls drinking myself silly and parlatic[28] from the dusk to dawn. [*To* WIDOW QUIN, *suddenly.*] Is my visage astray?

WIDOW QUIN   It is, then. You're a sniggering maniac, a child could see.

MAHON   [*Getting up more cheerfully*] Then I'd best be going to the union beyond, and there'll be a welcome before me, I tell you [*with great pride*], and I a terrible and fearful case, the way that there I was one time, screeching in a straightened waistcoat, with seven doctors writing out my sayings in a printed book. Would you believe that?

WIDOW QUIN   If you're a wonder itself, you'd best be hasty, for them lads caught a maniac one time and pelted the poor creature till he ran out, raving and foaming, and was drowned in the sea.

MAHON   [*With philosophy*] It's true mankind is the divil when your head's astray. Let me out now and I'll slip down the boreen, and not see them so.

WIDOW QUIN   [*Showing him out*] That's it. Run to the right, and not a one will see. [*He runs off.*]

PHILLY   [*Wisely*] You're at some gaming, Widow Quin; but I'll walk after him and give him his dinner and a time to rest, and I'll see then if he's raving or as sane as you.

WIDOW QUIN   [*Annoyed*] If you go near that lad,

28. **parlatic:** paralyzed.

let you be wary of your head, I'm saying. Didn't you hear him telling he was crazed at times?

PHILLY   I heard him telling a power; and I'm thinking we'll have right sport before night will fall. [*He goes out.*]

JIMMY   Well, Philly's a conceited and foolish man. How could that madman have his senses and his brain-pan slit? I'll go after them and see him turn on Philly now. [*He goes;* WIDOW QUIN *hides poteen behind counter. Then hubbub outside.*]

VOICES   There you are! Good jumper! Grand lepper! Darlint boy! He's the racer! Bear him on, will you! [CHRISTY *comes in, in jockey's dress, with* PEGEEN MIKE, SARA, *and other* GIRLS *and* MEN.]

PEGEEN   [*To crowd*] Go on now and don't destroy him and he drenching with sweat. Go along, I'm saying, and have your tug-of-warring till he's dried his skin.

CROWD   Here's his prizes! A bagpipes! A fiddle was played by a poet in the years gone by! A flat and three-thorned blackthorn[29] would lick the scholars out of Dublin town!

CHRISTY   [*Taking prizes from the* MEN] Thank you kindly, the lot of you. But you'd say it was little only I did this day if you'd seen me a while since striking my one single blow.

TOWN CRIER   [*Outside ringing a bell*] Take notice, last event of this day! Tug-of-warring on the green below! Come on, the lot of you! Great achievements for all Mayo men!

PEGEEN   Go on and leave him for to rest and dry. Go on, I tell you, for he'll do no more. [*She hustles crowd out;* WIDOW QUIN *following them.*]

MEN   [*Going*] Come on, then. Good luck for the while!

PEGEEN   [*Radiantly, wiping his face with her shawl*] Well, you're the lad, and you'll have great times from this out when you could win that wealth of prizes, and you sweating in the heat of noon!

CHRISTY   [*Looking at her with delight*] I'll have great times if I win the crowning prize I'm seeking now, and that's your promise that you'll wed me in a fortnight, when our banns is called.

PEGEEN   [*Backing away from him*] You've right daring to go ask me that, when all knows you'll be starting to some girl in your own townland, when your father's rotten in four months, or five.

CHRISTY   [*Indignantly*] Starting from you, is it?

29. **blackthorn:** cane.

[*He follows her.*] I will not, then, and when the airs is warming, in four months or five, it's then yourself and me should be pacing Neifin in the dews of night, the times sweet smells do be rising, and you'd see a little, shiny new moon, maybe, sinking on the hills.

PEGEEN   [*Looking at him playfully*] And it's that kind of a poacher's love you'd make, Christy Mahon, on the sides of Neifin, when the night is down?

CHRISTY   It's little you'll think if my love's a poacher's, or an earl's itself, when you'll feel my two hands stretched around you, and I squeezing kisses on your puckered lips, till I'd feel a kind of pity for the Lord God is all ages sitting lonesome in his golden chair.

PEGEEN   That'll be right fun, Christy Mahon, and any girl would walk her heart out before she'd meet a young man was your like for eloquence, or talk at all.

CHRISTY   [*Encouraged*] Let you wait, to hear me talking, till we're astray in Erris, when Good Friday's by, drinking a sup from a well, and making mighty kisses with our wetted mouths, or gaming in a gap of sunshine, with yourself stretched back unto your necklace, in the flowers of the earth.

PEGEEN   [*In a low voice, moved by his tone*] I'd be nice so, is it?

CHRISTY   [*With rapture*] If the mitered bishops seen you that time, they'd be the like of the holy prophets, I'm thinking, do be straining the bars of Paradise to lay eyes on the Lady Helen of Troy, and she abroad, pacing back and forward, with a nosegay in her golden shawl.

PEGEEN   [*With real tenderness*] And what is it I have, Christy Mahon, to make me fitting entertainment for the like of you, that has such poet's talking, and such bravery of heart.

CHRISTY   [*In a low voice*] Isn't there the light of seven heavens in your heart alone, the way you'll be an angel's lamp to me from this out, and I abroad in the darkness, spearing salmons in the Owen or the Carrowmore?

PEGEEN   If I was your wife I'd be along with you those nights, Christy Mahon, the way you'd see I was a great hand at coaxing bailiffs, or coining funny nicknames for the stars of night.

CHRISTY   You, is it? Taking your death in the hailstones, or in the fogs of dawn.

PEGEEN   Yourself and me would shelter easy in a narrow bush [*with a qualm of dread*], but we're only talking, maybe, for this would be a poor, thatched place to hold a fine lad is the like of you.

CHRISTY   [*Putting his arm round her*] If I wasn't a good Christian, it's on my naked knees I'd be saying my prayers and paters to every jackstraw you have roofing your head, and every stony pebble is paving the laneway to your door.

PEGEEN   [*Radiantly*] If that's the truth I'll be burning candles from this out to the miracles of God that have brought you from the south today, and I with my gowns bought ready, the way that I can wed you, and not wait at all.

CHRISTY   It's miracles, and that's the truth. Me there toiling a long while, and walking a long while, not knowing at all I was drawing all times nearer to this holy day.

PEGEEN   And myself, a girl, was tempted often to go sailing the seas till I'd marry a Jew-man, with ten kegs of gold, and I not knowing at all there was the like of you drawing nearer, like the stars of God.

CHRISTY   And to think I'm long years hearing women talking that talk, to all bloody fools, and this the first time I've heard the like of your voice talking sweetly for my own delight.

PEGEEN   And to think it's me is talking sweetly, Christy Mahon, and I the fright of seven townlands for my biting tongue. Well, the heart's a wonder; and, I'm thinking, there won't be our like in Mayo, for gallant lovers, from this hour today. [*Drunken singing is heard outside.*] There's my father coming from the wake, and when he's had his sleep we'll tell him, for he's peaceful then. [*They separate.*]

MICHAEL   [*Singing outside*]:
>   The jailer and the turnkey
>   They quickly ran us down,
>   And brought us back as prisoners
>   Once more to Cavan town.

[*He comes in supported by* SHAWN.]
>   There we lay bewailing
>   All in a prison bound. . . .

[*He sees* CHRISTY. *Goes and shakes him drunkenly by the hand, while* PEGEEN *and* SHAWN *talk on the left.*]

MICHAEL   [*To* CHRISTY] The blessing of God and the holy angels on your head, young fellow, I hear tell you're after winning all in the sports below; and wasn't it a shame I didn't bear you along with me to Kate Cassidy's wake, a fine, stout lad, the like of you, for you'd never see the match of it for flows of drink, the way when we sunk her bones at noonday in her narrow grave, there were five men, aye, and six men, stretched out retching speechless on the holy stones.

CHRISTY   [*Uneasily, watching* PEGEEN] Is that the truth?

MICHAEL   It is, then; and aren't you a louty schemer to go burying your poor father unbeknownst when you'd a right to throw him on the crupper of a Kerry mule and drive him westwards, like holy Joseph in the days gone by, the way we could have given him a decent burial, and not have him rotting beyond, and not a Christian drinking a smart drop to the glory of his soul?

CHRISTY   [*Gruffly*] It's well enough he's lying, for the likes of him.

MICHAEL   [*Slapping him on the back*] Well, aren't you a hardened slayer? It'll be a poor thing for the household man where you go sniffing for a female wife; and [*pointing to* SHAWN] look beyond at that shy and decent Christian I have chosen for my daughter's hand, and I after getting the gilded dispensation this day for to wed them now.

CHRISTY   And you'll be wedding them this day, is it?

MICHAEL   [*Drawing himself up*] Aye. Are you thinking, if I'm drunk itself, I'd leave my daughter living single with a little frisky rascal is the like of you?

PEGEEN   [*Breaking away from* SHAWN] Is it the truth the dispensation's come?

MICHAEL   [*Triumphantly*] Father Reilly's after reading it in gallous Latin, and "It's come in the nick of time," says he; "so I'll wed them in a hurry, dreading that young gaffer who'd capsize the stars."

PEGEEN   [*Fiercely*] He's missed his nick of time, for it's that lad, Christy Mahon, that I'm wedding now.

MICHAEL   [*Loudly, with horror*] You'd be making him a son to me, and he wet and crusted with his father's blood?

PEGEEN   Aye. Wouldn't it be a bitter thing for a girl to go marrying the like of Shaneen, and he a middling kind of a scarecrow, with no savagery or fine words in him at all?

MICHAEL   [*Gasping and sinking on a chair*] Oh, aren't you a heathen daughter to go shaking the fat of my heart, and I swamped and drownded with the weight of drink? Would you have them turning on me the way that I'd be roaring to the dawn of day with the wind upon my heart? Have you not a word to aid me, Shaneen? Are you not jealous at all?

SHAWN   [*In great misery*] I'd be afeared to be jealous of a man did slay his da!

PEGEEN   Well, it'd be a poor thing to go marrying your like. I'm seeing there's a world of peril for an orphan girl, and isn't it a great blessing I didn't wed you before himself came walking from the west or south?

SHAWN   It's a queer story you'd go picking a dirty tramp up from the highways of the world.

PEGEEN   [*Playfully*] And you think you're a likely beau to go straying along with the shiny Sundays of the opening year, when it's sooner on a bullock's liver you'd put a poor girl thinking than on the lily or the rose?

SHAWN   And have you no mind of my weight of passion, and the holy dispensation, and the drift of heifers I'm giving, and the golden ring?

PEGEEN   I'm thinking you're too fine for the like of me, Shawn Keogh of Killakeen, and let you go off till you'd find a radiant lady with droves of bullocks on the plains of Meath, and herself bedizened in the diamond jeweleries of Pharaoh's ma. That'd be your match, Shaneen. So God save you now! [*She retreats behind* CHRISTY.]

SHAWN   Won't you hear me telling you . . . ?

CHRISTY   [*With ferocity*] Take yourself from this, young fellow, or I'll maybe add a murder to my deeds today.

MICHAEL   [*Springing up with a shriek*] Murder is it? Is it mad yous are? Would you go making murder in this place, and it piled with poteen for our drink tonight? Go on to the foreshore if it's fighting you want, where the rising tide will wash all traces from the memory of man. [*Pushing* SHAWN *towards* CHRISTY.]

SHAWN   [*Shaking himself free, and getting behind* MICHAEL] I'll not fight him, Michael James. I'd liefer live a bachelor, simmering in passions to the end of time, than face a lepping savage the like of him has descended from the Lord knows where. Strike him yourself, Michael James, or you'll lose my drift of heifers and my blue bull from Sneem.

MICHAEL   Is it me fight him, when it's father-slaying he's bred to now? [*Pushing* SHAWN.] Go on, you fool, and fight him now.

SHAWN   [*Coming forward a little*] Will I strike him with my hand?

MICHAEL   Take the loy is on your western side.

SHAWN   I'd be afeard of the gallows if I struck with that.

CHRISTY   [*Taking up the loy*] Then I'll make you face the gallows or quit off from this. [SHAWN *flies out of the door.*]

CHRISTY   Well, fine weather be after him [*going to* MICHAEL, *coaxingly*], and I'm thinking you wouldn't wish to have that quaking blackguard in your house at all. Let you give us your blessing and hear her swear her faith to me, for I'm mounted on the spring-tide of the stars of luck, the way it'll be good for any to have me in the house.

PEGEEN   [*At the other side of* MICHAEL] Bless us now, for I swear to God I'll wed him, and I'll not renege.

MICHAEL   [*Standing up in the center, holding on to both of them*] It's the will of God, I'm thinking, that all should win an easy or a cruel end, and it's the will of God that all should rear up lengthy families for the nurture of the earth. What's a single man, I ask you, eating a bit in one house and drinking a sup in another, and he with no place of his own, like an old braying jackass strayed upon the rocks? [*To* CHRISTY.] It's many would be in dread to bring your life into their house for to end them, maybe, with a sudden end; but I'm a decent man of Ireland, and I'd liefer face the grave untimely and I seeing a score of grandsons growing up little gallant swearers by the name of God, than go peopling my bedside with puny weeds the like of what you'd breed, I'm thinking, out of Shaneen Keogh. [*He joins their hands.*] A daring fellow is the jewel of the world, and a man did split his father's middle with a single clout should have the bravery of ten, so may God and Mary and Saint Patrick bless you, and increase you from this mortal day.

CHRISTY AND PEGEEN   Amen, O Lord! [*Hubbub outside.* OLD MAHON *rushes in, followed by all the crowd, and* WIDOW QUIN. *He makes a rush at* CHRISTY, *knocks him down, and begins to beat him.*]

PEGEEN   [*Dragging back his arm*] Stop that, will you? Who are you at all?

MAHON   His father, God forgive me!

PEGEEN   [*Drawing back*] Is it rose from the dead?

MAHON   Do you think I look so easy quenched with the tap of a loy? [*Beats* CHRISTY *again.*]

PEGEEN   [*Glaring at* CHRISTY] And it's lies you told, letting on you had him slitted, and you nothing at all.

CHRISTY   [*Catching* MAHON'S *stick*] He's not my father. He's a raving maniac would scare the world. [*Pointing to* WIDOW QUIN.] Herself knows it is true.

CROWD   You're fooling Pegeen! The Widow Quin seen him this day, and you likely knew! You're a liar!

CHRISTY   [*Dumbfounded*] It's himself was a liar, lying stretched out with an open head on him, letting on he was dead.

MAHON   Weren't you off racing the hills before I got my breath with the start I had seeing you turn on me at all?

PEGEEN   And to think of the coaxing glory we had given him, and he after doing nothing but hitting a soft blow and chasing northward in a sweat of fear. Quit off from this.

CHRISTY   [*Piteously*] You've seen my doings this day, and let you save me from the old man; for why would you be in such a scorch of haste to spur me to destruction now?

PEGEEN   It's there your treachery is spurring me, till I'm hard set to think you're the one I'm after lacing in my heartstrings half an hour gone by. [*To* MAHON.] Take him on from this, for I think bad the world should see me raging for a Munster liar, and the fool of men.

MAHON   Rise up now to retribution, and come on with me.

CROWD   [*Jeeringly*] There's the playboy! There's the lad thought he'd rule the roost in Mayo! Slate him now, mister.

CHRISTY   [*Getting up in shy terror*] What is it drives you to torment me here, when I'd asked the thunders of the might of God to blast me if I ever did hurt to any saving only that one single blow.

MAHON   [*Loudly*] If you didn't, you're a poor

good-for-nothing, and isn't it by the like of you the sins of the whole world are committed?

CHRISTY [*Raising his hands*] In the name of the Almighty God . . .

MAHON Leave troubling the Lord God. Would you have him sending down droughts, and fevers, and the old hen and the cholera morbus?

CHRISTY [*To* WIDOW QUIN] Will you come between us and protect me now?

WIDOW QUIN I've tried a lot, God help me, and my share is done.

CHRISTY [*Looking round in desperation*] And I must go back into my torment is it, or run off like a vagabond straying through the unions with the dust of August making mudstains in the gullet of my throat; or the winds of March blowing on me till I'd take an oath I felt them making whistles of my ribs within?

SARA Ask Pegeen to aid you. Her like does often change.

CHRISTY I will not, then, for there's torment in the splendor of her like, and she a girl any moon of midnight would take pride to meet, facing southwards on the heaths of Keel. But what did I want crawling forward to scorch my understanding at her flaming brow?

PEGEEN [*To* MAHON, *vehemently, fearing she will break into tears*] Take him on from this or I'll set the young lads to destroy him here.

MAHON [*Going to him, shaking his stick*] Come on now if you wouldn't have the company to see you skelped.

PEGEEN [*Half-laughing, through her tears*] That's it, now the world will see him pandied, and he an ugly liar was playing off the hero, and the fright of men.

CHRISTY [*To* MAHON, *very sharply*] Leave me go!

CROWD That's it. Now, Christy. If them two set fighting, it will lick the world.

MAHON [*Making a grab at* CHRISTY] Come here to me.

CHRISTY [*More threateningly*] Leave me go, I'm saying.

MAHON I will, maybe, when your legs is limping, and your back is blue.

CROWD Keep it up, the two of you. I'll back the old one. Now the playboy.

CHRISTY [*In low and intense voice*] Shut your yelling, for if you're after making a mighty man of me this day by the power of a lie, you're

setting me now to think if it's a poor thing to be lonesome it's worse, maybe, go mixing with the fools of earth. [MAHON *makes a movement towards him.*]

CHRISTY [*Almost shouting*] Keep off . . . lest I do show a blow unto the lot of you would set the guardian angels winking in the clouds above. [*He swings round with a sudden rapid movement and picks up a loy.*]

CROWD [*Half-frightened, half-amused*] He's going mad! Mind yourselves! Run from the idiot!

CHRISTY If I am an idiot, I'm after hearing my voice this day saying words would raise the topknot on a poet in a merchant's town. I've won your racing, and your lepping, and . . .

MAHON Shut your gullet and come on with me.

CHRISTY I'm going, but I'll stretch you first. [*He runs at old* MAHON *with the loy, chases him out of the door, followed by crowd and* WIDOW QUIN. *There is a great noise outside, then a yell, and dead silence for a moment.* CHRISTY *comes in, half-dazed, and goes to fire.*]

WIDOW QUIN [*Coming in hurriedly, and going to him*] They're turning again you. Come on, or you'll be hanged, indeed.

CHRISTY I'm thinking, from this out, Pegeen'll be giving me praises, the same as in the hours gone by.

WIDOW QUIN [*Impatiently*] Come by the back-door. I'd think bad to have you stifled on the gallows tree.

CHRISTY [*Indignantly*] I will not, then. What good'd be my lifetime if I left Pegeen?

WIDOW QUIN Come on, and you'll be no worse than you were last night; and you with a double murder this time to be telling to the girls.

CHRISTY I'll not leave Pegeen Mike.

WIDOW QUIN [*Impatiently*] Isn't there the match of her in every parish public, from Binghamstown unto the plain of Meath? Come on, I tell you, and I'll find you finer sweethearts at each waning moon.

CHRISTY It's Pegeen I'm seeking only, and what'd I care if you brought me a drift of chosen females, standing in their shifts itself, maybe, from this place to the Eastern World?

SARA [*Runs in, pulling off one of her petticoats*] They're going to hang him. [*Holding out petticoat and shawl.*] Fit these upon him, and let him run off to the east.

WIDOW QUIN He's raving now; but we'll fit them on him, and I'll take him in the ferry to the Achill boat.

CHRISTY [*Struggling feebly*] Leave me go, will you? when I'm thinking of my luck today, for she will wed me surely, and I a proven hero in the end of all. [*They try to fasten petticoat round him.*]

WIDOW QUIN Take his left hand, and we'll pull him now. Come on, young fellow.

CHRISTY [*Suddenly starting up*] You'll be taking me from her? You're jealous, is it, of her wedding me? Go on from this. [*He snatches up a stool, and threatens them with it.*]

WIDOW QUIN [*Going*] It's in the madhouse they should put him, not in jail, at all. We'll go by the back-door to call the doctor, and we'll save him so. [*She goes out, with SARA, through inner room. MEN crowd in the doorway. CHRISTY sits down again by the fire.*]

MICHAEL [*In a terrified whisper*] Is the old lad killed surely?

PHILLY I'm after feeling the last gasps quitting his heart. [*They peer in at CHRISTY.*]

MICHAEL [*With a rope*] Look at the way he is. Twist a hangman's knot on it, and slip it over his head, while he's not minding at all.

PHILLY Let you take it, Shaneen. You're the soberest of all that's here.

SHAWN Is it me to go near him, and he the wickedest and worst with me? Let you take it, Pegeen Mike.

PEGEEN Come on, so. [*She goes forward with the others, and they drop the double hitch over his head.*]

CHRISTY What ails you?

SHAWN [*Triumphantly, as they pull the rope tight on his arms*] Come on to the peelers, till they stretch you now.

CHRISTY Me!

MICHAEL If we took pity on you the Lord God would, maybe, bring us ruin from the law today, so you'd best come easy, for hanging is an easy and a speedy end.

CHRISTY I'll not stir. [*To PEGEEN.*] And what is it you'll say to me, and I after doing it this time in the face of all?

PEGEEN I'll say, a strange man is a marvel, with his mighty talk; but what's a squabble in your back-yard, and the blow of a loy, have taught me

that there's a great gap between a gallous story and a dirty deed. [*To MEN.*] Take him on from this, or the lot of us will be likely put on trial for his deed today.

CHRISTY [*With horror in his voice*] And it's yourself will send me off, to have a horny-fingered hangman hitching his bloody slipknots at the butt of my ear.

MEN [*Pulling rope*] Come on, will you? [*He is pulled down on the floor.*]

CHRISTY [*Twisting his legs round the table*] Cut the rope, Pegeen, and I'll quit the lot of you, and live from this out, like the madmen of Keel, eating muck and green weeds on the faces of the cliffs.

PEGEEN And leave us to hang, is it, for a saucy liar, the like of you? [*To MEN.*] Take him on, out from this.

SHAWN Pull a twist on his neck, and squeeze him so.

PHILLY Twist yourself. Sure he cannot hurt you, if you keep your distance from his teeth alone.

SHAWN I'm afeard of him. [*To PEGEEN.*] Lift a lighted sod, will you, and scorch his leg.

PEGEEN [*Blowing the fire with a bellows*] Leave go now, young fellow, or I'll scorch your shins.

CHRISTY You're blowing for to torture me. [*His voice rising and growing stronger.*] That's your kind, is it? Then let the lot of you be wary, for, if I've to face the gallows, I'll have a gay march down, I tell you, and shed the blood of some of you before I die.

SHAWN [*In terror*] Keep a good hold, Philly. Be wary, for the love of God. For I'm thinking he would liefest wreak his pains on me.

CHRISTY [*Almost gaily*] If I do lay my hands on you, it's the way you'll be at the fall of night, hanging as a scarecrow for the fowls of hell. Ah, you'll have a gallous jaunt, I'm saying, coaching out through limbo with my father's ghost.

SHAWN [*To PEGEEN*] Make haste, will you? Oh, isn't he a holy terror, and isn't it true for Father Reilly, that all drink's a curse that has the lot of you so shaky and uncertain now?

CHRISTY If I can wring a neck among you, I'll have a royal judgment looking on the trembling jury in the courts of law. And won't there be crying out in Mayo the day I'm stretched upon the rope, with ladies in their silks and satins sniveling in their lacy kerchiefs, and they rhyming songs and ballads on the terror of my fate? [*He squirms round on the floor and bites* SHAWN's *leg*.]

SHAWN [*Shrieking*] My leg's bit on me. He's the like of a mad dog, I'm thinking, the way that I will surely die.

CHRISTY [*Delighted with himself*] You will, then, the way you can shake out hell's flags of welcome for my coming in two weeks or three, for I'm thinking Satan hasn't many have killed their da in Kerry, and in Mayo too. [OLD MAHON *comes in behind on all fours and looks on unnoticed*.]

MEN [*To* PEGEEN] Bring the sod, will you?

PEGEEN [*Coming over*] God help him so. [*Burns his leg*.]

CHRISTY [*Kicking and screaming*] Oh, glory be to God! [*He kicks loose from the table, and they all drag him towards the door*.]

JIMMY [*Seeing old* MAHON] Will you look what's come in? [*They all drop* CHRISTY *and run left*.]

CHRISTY [*Scrambling on his knees face to face with old* MAHON] Are you coming to be killed a third time, or what ails you now?

MAHON For what is it they have you tied?

CHRISTY They're taking me to the peelers to have me hanged for slaying you.

MICHAEL [*Apologetically*] It is the will of God that all should guard their little cabins from the treachery of law, and what would my daughter be doing if I was ruined or was hanged itself?

MAHON [*Grimly, loosening* CHRISTY] It's little I care if you put a bag on her back, and went picking cockles[30] till the hour of death; but my

30. cockles: weeds.

son and myself will be going our own way, and we'll have great times from this out telling stories of the villainy of Mayo, and the fools is here. [*To* CHRISTY, *who is freed*.] Come on now.

CHRISTY Go with you, is it? I will then, like a gallant captain with his heathen slave. Go on now and I'll see you from this day stewing my oatmeal and washing my spuds, for I'm master of all fights from now. [*Pushing* MAHON.] Go on, I'm saying.

MAHON Is it me?

CHRISTY Not a word out of you. Go on from this.

MAHON [*Walking out and looking back at* CHRISTY *over his shoulder*] Glory be to God! [*With a broad smile*.] I am crazy again. [*Goes*.]

CHRISTY The thousand blessings upon all that's here, for you've turned me a likely gaffer in the end of all, the way I'll go romancing through a romping lifetime from this hour to the dawning of the judgment day. [*He goes out*.]

MICHAEL By the will of God, we'll have peace now for our drinks. Will you draw the porter, Pegeen?

SHAWN [*Going up to her*] It's a miracle Father Reilly can wed us in the end of all, and we'll have none to trouble us when his vicious bite is healed.

PEGEEN [*Hitting him a box on the ear*] Quit my sight. [*Putting her shawl over her head and breaking out into wild lamentations*.] Oh my grief, I've lost him surely. I've lost the only Playboy of the Western World.

The absurd law or premise that gets comic action going is also the source of ambivalence in *The Playboy of the Western World*. Synge begins with a number of moral inversions. When Christy tells the lie that he murdered his "da" in a grand fit of passion (really only half a lie because he did hit his father with the "loy," unless we are to believe that old Mahon is faking it too) he is lionized for it, so we start with the uncomfortable equation of murderer with hero. And this is where we first encounter the basic problem in comic perspective: Are the people of Mayo monsters—as the reviewer for the *Dublin Evening Mail* saw them portrayed—or simply deluded fools, vicious or absurd? Synge's characters are truly naive, the primitive inhabitants of a wild and remote western coastline who are out of touch with the civilization of Dublin. For the people of Mayo amazement and wonder are naturally associated with any "marvel," any strange person or event; in their view English law made too little distinction between a deed of passion and calculated murder. Thus they see a great difference between Christy's murder of his father and the Widow Quin's murder of her husband. As we discover later, Christy is lying—although somewhat harmlessly—to make his way in the world. By the end of the first act, he has arrived: "Well, it's a clean bed and soft with it, and it's great luck and company I've won me in the end of time—two fine women fighting for the likes of me—till I'm thinking this night wasn't I a foolish fellow not to kill my father in the years gone by."

Christy's words make us uneasy because there is ambivalence in the glory of murdering one's "da," or even in making as much out of the tale as one can. In his lie Christy reenacts the Oedipus story with the added twist that he is supposed to have killed his father knowing who he was. And this fact makes Freudian interpretation of the act possible: perhaps the people of Mayo are responding not so much to Christy's "gallous" deed as to their own suppressed wishes for freedom from authority. Although the occasion for the blow did not involve Christy's mother, it did have sexual overtones because Christy's father was forcing him to marry a substitute mother, the old woman who had nursed him, and was constantly at him about his being "the laughing joke of every female woman where four baronies meet." Oedipus' murder allowed him to marry his mother, whereas Christy's "murder" freed him from marrying his nurse. Who would not want to be free of an old man (note that Mahon is pronounced "man") who refused to give an inch of ground to let the young one come into his own? In this sense Christy's lie is a sublimated release from the dreadful authority of a father who must be symbolically killed before the son can reach full potency, and the people of Mayo who stand in awe of the deed are identifying with Christy in a rite that renews them too. Life and death are intertwined in comedy, as Susanne Langer points out, since the value of one depends on the existence of the other.

The play's moral ambivalence is comic because Christy and the people of Mayo live in a world of words, not deeds. Christy's lie calls our attention to the gap between all words and the experience that they never fully represent. Words only *symbolize*, so Christy can even relish being hanged: "And won't there be crying out in Mayo the day I'm stretched upon the rope, with ladies in their silks and satins sniveling in their lacy kerchiefs, and they rhyming songs and ballads on the terror of my fate." The lie delights Christy because it *is* his power in the world, words doing the work of deeds, making things happen. As he retells the lie again and again, he embellishes it with the care of a poet. Ultimately he draws on the long tradition of epic boasting in literature; like Achilles and Beowulf, Christy discovers that gallant words do count. The comic type of the braggart soldier has been turned inside out. Christy becomes what he imagines himself to be, transformed from the defeated and frightened runt of Act I into the lover of Act II and the athlete of Act III. The constant refrain "Is it me?" underlines his amazement at the change in himself, just as

Old Mahon's use of the phrase at the end of the play reemphasizes that change when the roles of father and son have been reversed. Of course, the ultimate wielder of words is the poet, and Christy discovers that one can fashion whole worlds with words. He can turn Pegeen Mike, whom the Widow Quin enviously describes as "a girl you'd see itching and scratching, and she with a stale stink of poteen on her from selling in the shop" into an object of adoration: "If the mitred bishops seen you that time, they'd be the like of the holy prophets, I'm thinking, do be straining the bars of Paradise to lay eyes on the Lady Helen of Troy, and she abroad, pacing back and forward, with a nosegay in her golden shawl." And Pegeen Mike responds, as Christy has learned to do, by beginning to act out the role being created for her. The gap between words and deeds closes, and Christy and Pegeen seem headed toward marriage in a delightful world of their own imagining, a fit conclusion for a newly created hero and his rustic queen.

Yet this does not happen: the celebration we expect is replaced by judgments and separations. When the words of the characters lead to acts, those acts keep the characters from joining together in a new and better society. If we use the comic norm as a guide, everyone seems to be properly cast: Christy and Pegeen Mike are hero and heroine; Mahon, the Widow Quin, and Shawn Keogh are blockers; three subsidiary men (Michael James, Philly Cullen, and Jimmy Farrell) and three young women (Sara Tansey, Susan Brady, and Honor Blake) serve together, first as supporters and then as deniers of the comic drive toward celebration. Again, the stages of action seem relatively clear up to the third act. The obstacle to be overcome is old Mahon's repression, which makes Christy a self-depre-cating victim who has more latent power than he knows. The complications are also somewhat routine: two interlocked love triangles form one of them (Christy and Shawn after Pegeen, Pegeen and the Widow Quin after Christy), and the other is the return of old Mahon, which leads to the alliance of Christy and the Widow Quin, his manipulating agent. The discovery is quite naturally Mahon's identity—the first real evidence that something has gone wrong with the New Comedy plot. The dead man who has come alive (a withdrawing elder) brings oppression and belittlement to the hero rather than freeing him to marry the girl of his desires. Christy sees this quite clearly: "To be letting on he was dead, and coming back to his life, and following after me like an old weasel tracing a rat, and coming in here laying desolation between my own self and the fine women of Ireland, and he a kind of carcass that you'd fling upon the sea . . . ." Like the figure of the old year in a rite of spring, we might add. In spite of the petulant tone of this speech, we can sympathize with Christy's despair: the whole structure of the world of words is about to come crashing down around him, destroying the miracle of incarnation—words becoming deeds. Thus the discovery of old Mahon's identity effects an ironic rather than a comic reversal. The hero is returned to his initial position: deeds done on the strength of a lie are canceled out by the misdeed done only in words.

The final scene can be read in two ways. When the possibility of a festive celebration disappears in comedy, it is replaced by communal rites of a more menacing sort, often a trial. We welcome the return of legal justice in *Volpone* even if it is harsh and autocratic because that society can be made bearable in no other way. In *Playboy* the outcome is potentially horrifying—a lynching rather than a trial, complete with unnecessary, spiteful torture and the ultimate chaos of mob rule. Michael John, who had applauded his daughter's choice of the daring Christy over the puling Shawn Keogh a few scenes earlier, now plays the heavy father, and Pegeen repays Christy for her disillusionment: "I'll say, a strange man is a marvel, with his mighty talk; but what's a squabble in your backyard, and the blow of a loy, have taught me that there's a great gap between a gallous story and a dirty deed." Pegeen's wisdom is ironic, and if it were allowed to cancel out Christy's real achievement in Mayo the play would end with our sense of relief that we had not been fooled longer. But at this point the twice-struck father has been converted; on the spur of the moment Mahon *unbinds* Christy and indicts the society that has turned on him: "My son and myself will be going our own way, and we'll have great times from this out telling stories of the villainy of Mayo, and the fools is here." Father and son form a new group that is free of the entanglements of any society; they will go wandering about the world as they choose, "telling stories." Christy and his self-created world have the final word in the play: "Ten thousand blessings upon all that's here, for you've turned me a likely gaffer in the end of all, the way I'll go romancing through a romping lifetime from this hour to the dawning of the judgment day."

Thus the ambiguities of truth and lie, word and act, right and wrong produce a structure that combines all three patterns of action. The people of Mayo, like those of Venice in *Volpone*, are exposed as a humorous society that is not only gullible but also capable of viciousness. The new social group that might transform existing society is nearly formed when its absurd foundation in a lie makes it collapse, and the new group that does form is not hero and heroine but father and son. Marriages suggest the continued future of society, but this pairing off goes backward in generational time and puts the two out of society, yet with the freedom belonging to any set of picaresque rogues who may do what they will as long as they keep moving. A romantic hero has been built out of a tragic idea and immersed in a society that turns out to be ironic, yet this complex vision of human motives still ends in an exuberant celebration of the possibilities of life—elsewhere.

The Comic Norm:
Transformation of Ordinary Society

GEOFFREY CHAUCER
1340?–1400

The Miller's Tale

Whilom ther was dwellyng in Oxenford°
A riche gnof that gestes held to bord,°
And of his craft he was a carpenter.
With hym ther was dwellynge a poure scoler
Had lerned art,° but al his fantasie°   5
Was turned for to lerne astrologye,
And koude a certeyn of conclusions
To demen by interrogacions,°
If that men axed° hym in certein houres
Whan that men sholde have droghte or ellis°
    shoures,°   10
Or if men axed hym what sholde bifalle
Of everythyng—I may nat rekene hem° alle.
    This clerk was cleped hende° Nicholas.
Of derne° love he koude° and of solas,°
And therto he was sleigh° and ful pryvee°   15
And lyk a mayden meke for to see.
    A chambre hadde he in that hostelrye,
Allone withouten° any compaignye,

Ful fetisly dight° with herbes swoote,°
And he hymself as swete as is the roote   20
Of licorys° or any cetewale.°
    His *Almageste,*° and bokes grete and smale,
His astrelabye° longynge for° his art,
His augrym stones,° layen faire apart
On shelves couched at his beddes heed,°   25
His presse° y-covered with a faldyng reed.°
And al above ther lay a gay sautrye,°
On which he made anyghtes° melodye
So swetely that al the chambre rong,°
And *Angelus ad Virginem*° he song,   30
And after that he song the Kynges Note.°
Ful often blessed was his murye° throte.
And thus this swete clerk his tyme spente,
After his frendes fyndyng and his rente.°
    This carpenter had wedded newe° a wyf   35
Which that° he loved moore than his lyf.
Of eighteteene yeer she was of age.
Jalous he was and heeld hire narwe° in cage,
For she was wilde and yong, and he was old
And demed hymself been° lyk a cokewold.°   40
He knew nat Catoun,° for his wit was rude,

19. **fetisly dight:** daintily scented. **swoote:** sweet. 21. **licorys:** licorice. **cetewale:** zedoary. 22. **Almageste:** the second-century treatise by Ptolemy of Alexandria, which was still the standard textbook on astronomy. 23. **astrelabye:** astrolabe, an instrument once used for measuring the altitude of planets and stars. **longynge for:** belonging to. 24. **augrym stones:** algorism counters (for counting on an abacus). 25. **heed:** head. 26. **presse:** clothespress. **faldyng reed:** red cloth. 27. **sautrye:** psaltery (stringed instrument). 28. **anyghtes:** at night. 29. **rong:** rang. 30. **Angelus ad Virginem:** "The Angel to the Virgin," an Annunciation hymn. **song:** sang. 31. **Kynges Note:** a popular song. 32. **murye:** merry. 34. **After . . . rente:** with the support of his friends and his own income. 35. **newe:** newly. 36. **Which that:** whom. 38. **narwe:** strictly. 40. **been:** to be. **cokewold:** cuckold. 41. **Catoun:** Dionysius Cato, the reputed author of a collection of proverbs.

THE MILLER'S TALE. 1. **Oxenford:** Oxford. 2. **gnof . . . hord:** fellow who boarded guests. 5. **Had . . . art:** (who) had studied (the liberal) arts. **fantasie:** fancy. 7–8. **koude . . . interrogacions:** (he) knew a certain number of operations by which to determine (the future) through investigations (of the position of the planets). 9. **axed:** asked. 10. **ellis:** else. **shoures:** showers. 12. **may . . . hem:** cannot recount them. 13. **cleped hende:** called gentle. 14. **derne:** secret. **koude:** knew. **solas:** fun. 15. **sleigh:** sly. **pryvee:** secretive. 18. **withouten:** without.

That bad men° sholde wedde his similitude.°
Men sholde wedden after hir estaat,°
For youthe and elde° is often at debaat.
But, sith that° he was fallen in the snare,   45
He moste° endure as oother folk his care.
   Fair was this yonge wyf, and therwithal
As any wesele° hir body gent° and smal.°
A ceynt° she wered barred° al of silk,
A barmcloth° as whit as morne° mylk   50
Upon hir lendes,° ful of many a goore;°
Whit was hir smok,° and broyden° al bifore
And eek° bihynde on hir coler° aboute,
Of col-blak silk withinne and eek withoute;
The tapes of hir white voluper°   55
Were of the same sute of° hir coler,
Hir filet brood° of silk and set ful hye.
   And sikerly° she hadde a likerous° eye.
Ful smale y-pulled° were hir browes two,
And tho° were bent° and blake° as any slo.°   60
She was ful moore blisful on to see°
Than is the newe perjonette° tree,
And softer than the wolle° is of a wether,°
And by hir girdel heng a purs of lether,
Tasseled with silk and perled with latoun.°   65
In al this world to seken up and doun,
Ther nys° no man so wys that koude thenche°
So gay a popelote° or swich° a wenche.
Ful brighter was the shynyng of hir hewe°
Than in the Tour the noble y-forged newe.°   70
But of hir song, it was as loude and yerne°
As any swalwe° sittyng on a berne.°
Therto° she koude skippe and make game
As any kyde or calf folwynge his dame.°
Hir mouth was swete as bragot,° or the
   meeth,°   75

Or hoord of apples leyd° in hey or heeth.°
Wynsyng° she was as is a joly colt,
Long as a mast, and upright as a bolt.
A broche she bar° upon hir lowe coler
As brood as is the boos° of a bokeler.°   80
Hir shoes were laced on hir legges hye.
She was a prymerole,° a piggesnye,°
For any lord to leggen° in his bedde,
Or yet for any good yeman° to wedde.
   Now, sire, and eft,° sire, so bifel the cas°   85
That on a day this hende° Nicholas
Fil° with this yonge wyf to rage° and pleye,
Whil that hir housbonde was at Oseneye,°
As clerkes° been ful subtil and ful queynte,°
And pryvely° he caughte hire by the queynte   90
And seyde, "Ywis, but if ich° have my wille,
For derne love of thee, lemman,° I spille,"°
And heeld hire harde by the haunche bones
And seyde, "Lemman, love me al atones,°
Or I wol dyen, also° God me save!"   95
   And she sprong° as a colt doth in the trave,°
And with hir heed she wryed° faste awey.
She seyde, "I wol nat kisse thee, by my fey.°
Wy, lat be, quod ich.° Lat be, Nicholas,
Or I wol crye 'Out, harrow'° and 'Allas.'   100
Do wey° youre handes, for youre curteisye."
   This Nicholas gan° mercy for to crye,
And spak so faire and profred hym° so faste
That she hir love hym graunted atte° laste,
And swoor hir ooth by Seint Thomas° of Kent 105
That she wolde been at his comaundement
Whan that she may hir leyser° wel espie.
   "Myn housbonde is so ful of jalousie
That, but° ye wayte wel and be pryvee,
I woot° right wel I nam but deed,"° quod° she.   110
"Ye moste been ful derne as in this cas."°   111
   "Nay, thereof care thee noght," quod Nicholas.

---

42. **bad men**: ordered one that he. **similitude**: equal.
43. **after . . . estaat**: according to their status. 44. **elde**:
old age. 45. **sith that**: since. 46. **moste**: must. 48. **wesele**:
weasel. **gent**: graceful. **smal**: slim. 49. **ceynt**: belt. **wered
barred**: wore striped. 50. **barmcloth**: apron. **morne**:
morning. 51. **lendes**: loins. **goore**: fold. 52. **smok**: smock.
broyden: embroidered. 53. **eek**: also. **coler**: collar. 55. **vo-
luper**: cap. 56. **sute of**: kind as. 57. **filet brood**: headband
broad. 58. **sikerly**: certainly. **likerous**: lecherous. 59. **smale
y-pulled**: finely plucked. 60. **tho**: those. **bent**: arched.
blake: black. **slo**: sloe (the plumlike fruit of the blackthorn).
61. **on to see**: to look on. 62. **perjonette**: pear. 63. **wolle**:
wool. **wether**: bellwether. 65. **perled . . . latoun**: with buttons made of copper alloy. 67. **nys**: is. **thenche**: imagine.
68. **popelote**: doll. **swich**: such. 69. **hewe**: hue. 70. **in . . .
newe**: the noble (a gold coin) newly minted in the Tower (of
London). 71. **yerne**: lively. 72. **swalwe**: swallow. **berne**:
barn. 73. **Therto**: moreover. 74. **his dame**: its mother. 75.
bragot: honey ale. **meeth**: mead.

76. **leyd**: stored. **heeth**: heather. 77. **Wynsyng**: skittish. 79.
bar: wore. 80. **boos**: boss. **bokeler**: buckler (small shield).
82. **prymerole**: primrose. **piggesnye**: darling (lit., the pigsney
flower). 83. **leggen**: lay. 84. **yeman**: yeoman. 85. **eft**:
again. **cas**: case. 86. **hende**: gentle. 87. **Fil**: fell. **rage**: sport.
88. **Oseneye**: Osney, just west of Oxford. 89. **clerkes**:
scholars. **queynte**: ingenious. 90. **pryvely**: stealthily. **queynte**:
genitals. 91. **Ywis . . . ich**: indeed, unless I. 92. **lemman**:
sweetheart. **spille**: shall perish. 94. **al atones**: right now.
95. **also**: so. 96. **sprong**: sprang. **trave**: enclosure for handling a wild horse. 97. **wryed**: twisted. 98. **fey**: faith. 99.
quod ich: I said. 100. **harrow**: help. 101. **Do wey**: take
away. 102. **gan**: began. 103. **profred hym**: offered himself.
104. **atte**: at (the). 105. **Thomas**: Becket. 107. **leyser**: opportunity. 109. **but**: unless. 110. **woot**: know. **nam . . . deed**:
am no better than dead. **quod**: said. 111. **moste . . . cas**:
must be very stealthy in this matter.

"A clerk had litherly biset his while°
But if° he koude a carpenter bigyle."

And thus they been acorded° and y-sworn   115
To waite a tyme as I have told biforn.°

Whan Nicholas had doon thus everydel°
And thakked° hire aboute the lendes° wel,
He kiste hir swete, and taketh his sautrye°
And pleyeth faste and maketh melodye.   120

Thanne fil° it thus that to the parissh chirche,
Cristes owene werkes for to wirche,°
This goode wyf wente on an haliday.°
Hir forheed shoon as bright as any day,
So was it wasshen whan she leet° hir werk.   125

Now, was ther of that chirche a parissh clerk°
The which that was y-cleped° Absolon.
Crul° was his heer, and as the gold it shoon
And strouted° as a fanne large and brode;
Ful streight and evene lay his joly shode.°   130
His rode° was reed,° his eyen greye° as goos.

With Poules wyndow corven° on his shoos,
In hoses° rede he wente fetisly.°
Y-clad he was ful smal° and proprely
Al in a kirtel of a light waget;°   135
Ful faire and thikke been the poyntes set;°
And therupon he hadde a gay surplys
As whit as is the blosme° upon the rys.°

A mery child° he was, so God me save.
Wel koude he laten° blood, and clippe, and shave,
And maken a chartre of lond or aquitaunce.°   141
In twenty manere° koude he trippe and daunce,
After the scole of Oxenforde, tho,°
And with his legges casten° to and fro,
And pleyen songes on a smal rubible.°   145
Therto he song somtyme a loud quynyble,°

And as wel koude he pleye on a gyterne.°
In al the toun nas° brewhous ne taverne
That he ne visited with his solas,°
Ther° any gaylard tappestere° was.   150
But, sooth to seyn,° he was somdel squaymous°
Of fartyng, and of speche daungerous.°

This Absolon, that joly was and gay,
Goth° with a sencer° on the haliday,
Sensynge° the wyves of the parisshe faste,   155
And many a lovely look on hem° he caste,
And namely° on this carpenteres wyf.
To loke on hire hym thoughte° a mery lyf.
She was so propre° and swete and likerous,°
I dar wel seyn, if she had been a mous   160
And he a cat, he wolde hir hente anon.°
This parisshe clerk, this joly Absolon,
Hath in his herte swich a love-longynge
That of no wyf took he noon offrynge.
For° curteisye, he seyde, he wolde noon!°   165

The moone, whan it was nyght, ful brighte
    shoon,°
And Absolon his gyterne hath y-take.
For paramours° he thoghte for to wake.°
And forth he goth, jolyf and amorous,
Til he cam to the carpenteres hous   170
A litel after cokkes hadde y-crowe,
And dressed hym° up by a shot-wyndowe°
That was upon the carpenteres wal.
He syngeth in his voys gentil and smal,
"Now dere lady, if thy wille be,   175
I preye yow that ye wol rewe° on me,"
Ful wel acordant to° his giternynge.

This carpenter awook and herde hym synge,
And spak unto his wyf and seyde anon,
"What, Alison! Herestow noght° Absolon   180
That chaunteth thus under oure boures° wal?"

And she answered hir housbonde therwithal,
"Yis,° God wot,° John. I here it everydel."°

113. litherly . . . while: spent his time poorly. 114. But
if: unless. 115. been acorded: have agreed. 116. biforn:
before. 117. everydel: every bit. 118. thakked: stroked.
lendes: loins. 119. sautrye: psaltery. 121. fil: befell.
122. for to wirche: to perform. 123. haliday: holy day.
125. leet: left. 126. clerk: As parish clerk Absalom serves
at mass and collects the offering on holy days, but
on weekdays he does odd jobs such as barbering. 127.
The . . . y-cleped: who was called. 128. Crul: curly.
129. strouted: spread out. 130. shode: parting. 131. rode:
complexion. reed: red. greye: blue. 132. With . . .
corven: carved with a design like the tracery in the
windows of St. Paul's Cathedral. 133. hoses: leggings.
fetisly: daintily. 134. smal: trimly. 135. waget: blue. 136.
been . . . set: are the decorative tags set (on the kirtle).
138. blosme: blossom. rys: branch. 139. child: young man.
140. laten: let. 141. aquitaunce: written receipt. 142. manere:
manners, ways. 143. After . . . tho: according to the mode
of Oxford, though. 144. casten: leap. 145. rubible: a two-
stringed fiddle. 146. quynyble: falsetto.

147. gyterne: gittern, a kind of guitar. 148. nas: was no. 149.
solas: entertaining. 150. Ther: where. gaylard tappestere:
merry barmaid. 151. sooth to seyn: truth to tell. somdel
squaymous: somewhat censorious. 152. daungerous: fastidious. 154. Goth: goes. sencer: censer (incense burner). 155.
Sensynge: censing, swinging the censer (during the church
service) at. 156. hem: them. 157. namely: particularly. 158.
hym thoughte: seemed to him. 159. propre: trim. likerous:
lascivious. 161. wolde . . . anon: would at once have seized
her. 165. For: because of. noon: none. 166. shoon: shone. 168.
paramours: the cause of love. thoghte . . . wake: intended
to keep watch. 172. dressed hym: took his stance. shot-
wyndowe: hinged window. 176. rewe: take pity. 177. acordant to: harmonizing with. 180. Herestow noght: don't you
hear. 181. boures: bedroom's. 183. Yis: yes, indeed. wot:
knows. everydel: every bit.

This passeth forth. What wol ye bet° than wel?
Fro day to day this joly Absolon   185
So woweth° hire that hym° is wo bigon;
He waketh al the nyght and al the day.
He kembeth° his lokkes brode and made hym gay;
He woweth hire by menes° and brocage,°
And swoor he wolde been hir owene page;   190
He syngeth brokkyng° as a nyghtyngale,
He sente hir pyment,° meeth,° and spiced ale,
And wafres° pipyng hoot out of the glede;°
And, for° she was of towne, he profred mede,°
For som folk wol be wonnen° for richesse,°   195
And som for strokes, and som for gentilesse.°
Som tyme, to shewe his lightnesse° and maistrye,°
He pleyeth Herodes° upon a scaffold° hye.

　　But what availleth hym as in this cas?
She loveth so this hende Nicholas   200
That Absolon may blowe the bukkes horn.°
He ne had for his labour but° a scorn,
And thus she maketh Absolon hir ape,°
And al his ernest turneth til a jape.°
Ful sooth is this proverb, it is no lye;   205
Men seith right thus, "Alwey the nye slye
Maketh the ferre leeve to be looth."°
For, thogh that Absolon be wood° or wrooth,°
Bycause that he fer was from hir sighte,
This nye° Nicholas stood in his lighte.   210
　　Now bere thee° wel, thow hende Nicholas,
For Absolon may waille and synge "Allas."

　　And so bifel it on a Saterday,
This carpenter was goon til° Osenay,
And hende Nicholas and Alisoun   215
Acorded been° to this conclusioun
That Nicholas shal shapen hem a wyle°
This sely,° jalous housbonde to bigyle,

And if so be the game wente aright
She sholde slepen in his arm al nyght,   220
For this was hir desir and his also.
　　And right anoon, withouten wordes mo,°
This Nicholas no lenger wolde tarie
But doth ful softe unto his chambre carie
Bothe mete° and drynke for a day or tweye,°   225
And to hir housbonde bad° hir for to seye,
If that he axed after Nicholas,
She sholde seye she nyste° wher he was;
Of al that day she seigh° hym noght with eye;
She trowed° that he was in maladye,   230
For, for no cry, hir mayde koude hym calle;
He nolde° answere for nothyng that myghte falle.°
　　This passeth forth al thilke° Saterday
That Nicholas stille in his chambre lay,
And eet and sleep, or dide what hym leste,°   235
Til Sonday that° the sonne gooth to reste.
This sely carpenter hath greet mervaille°
Of Nicholas, or what thyng myghte hym aille,
And seyde, "I am adrad'° by seint Thomas,
It stondeth nat aright with Nicholas.   240
God shilde° that he deyde° sodeynly.
This world is now ful tikel,° sikerly.°
I saugh° today a corps y-born to chirche
That now on Monday last I saugh hym wirche.°
Go up" quod he, "unto his knave° anoon.   245
Clepe° at his dore, or knokke with a stoon.
Loke how it is, and tel me boldely."
　　This knave gooth hym° up ful sturdily,
And, at the chambre dore whil that he stood,
He cride and knokked as that° he were wood,°   250
"What! How! What do ye, maister Nicholay?
How may ye slepen al the longe day?"
　　But al for noght. He herde nat a word.
An hole he fond° ful lowe upon a bord
Ther-as° the cat was wont in for to crepe,   255
And at that hole he looked in ful depe,
And atte laste he hadde of hym a sighte.
This Nicholas sat evere capyng upright°
As° he had kiked° on the newe moone.

184. bet: better. 186. woweth: woos. hym: he. 188. kembeth: combs. 189. menes: go-betweens. brocage: agency. 191. brokkyng: quavering. 192. pyment: spiced wine. meeth: mead. 193. wafres: wafer cakes. glede: coal fire. 194. for: because. mede: money (which a townswoman might have accepted, though a courtly lady would not). 195. wonnen: won. for richesse: by riches. 196. gentilesse: courtliness. 197. lightnesse: dexterity. maistrye: skill. 198. Herodes: the violent role of Herod in the local production of a miracle play. scaffold: a pageant or platform used for the outdoor staging of a play. 201. blowe . . . horn: blow the buck's horn, that is, waste his efforts. 202. ne had but: had nothing but. 203. ape: fool. 204. til a jape: into a joke. 206–07. Alwey . . . looth: Always the sly one who is near makes the distant dear one loathsome. (That is, "out of sight, out of mind.") 208. wood: mad. wrooth: wrathful. 210. nye: near. 211. bere thee: conduct yourself. 214. goon til: gone to. 216. Acorded been: have agreed. 217. shapen . . . wyle: plan a scheme for them. 218. sely: simple.

222. mo: more. 225. mete: food. tweye: two. 226. bad: told. 228. nyste: didn't know. 229. seigh: saw. 230. trowed: supposed. 232. nolde: would (not). falle: befall. 233. thilke: that same. 235. hym leste: he wished. 236. that: when. 237. mervaille: marvel. 239. adrad: afraid. 241. shilde: forbid. deyde: should die. 242. tikel: unstable. sikerly: certainly. 243. saugh: saw. y-born: carried. 244. That . . . wirche: whom (that hym) . . . I saw working. 245. knave: boy servant. 246. Clepe: call. 248. gooth hym: goes. 250. that: if. wood: mad. 254. fond: found. 255. Ther-as: where. 258. capyng uprighte: gaping face-upwards. 259. As: as if. kiked: stared.

Adoun° he gooth and tolde his maister soone°
In what array he saugh this ilke° man.   261
    This carpenter to blessen hym° bigan
And seyde, "Help us, Seinte Frideswyde.°
A man woot° litel what hym shal bityde.
This man is falle° with his astromye°   265
In som woodnesse or in som agonye.
I thoghte ay° wel how that it sholde be!
Men sholde noght knowe of Goddes pryvetee.°
Ye,° blessed by alwey a lewed° man
That noght but oonly his bileve kan.°   270
So ferde° another clerk with astromye.
He walked in the feeldes for to prye
Upon the sterres what ther sholde bifalle,
Til he was in a marle° pit y-falle.
He saw nat that. But yet, by Seinte Thomas,   275
Me reweth sore of° hende Nicholas.
He shal be rated of° his studyyng,
If that I may,° by Jesus hevene° kyng!
Get me a staf that I man underspore,°
Whil that thow, Robyn, hevest up the dore.   280
He shal out of his studyyng, as I gesse."
    And to the chambre dore he gan hym dresse.°
His knave was a strong carl for the nones,°
And by the haspe he haf° it up atones.°
Into the floor the dore fil anoon.   285
    This Nicholas sat ay as stille as stoon
And evere caped upward into the eyr.
This carpenter wende° he were in despeyr,
And hente° hym by the shuldres myghtily,
And shook hym harde, and cride spitously,°   290
"What, Nicholay! What! How! Loke adoun.
Awake, and thenk on Cristes passioun.
I crouche° thee from elves and fro wightes."°
    Therwith the nyght-spel° seyde he anon rightes°
On foure halves° of the hous aboute   295

260. **Adoun**: down. **soone**: at once. 261. **ilke**: same. 262. **blessen hym**: cross himself. 263. **Frideswyde**: Frideswide, a local heroine enshrined in what later became the cathedral at Oxford. 264. **woot**: knows. 265. **is falle**: has fallen. **astromye**: the unlearned carpenter's mispronunciation of the word *astronomy*. 267. **thoghte ay**: always expected. 268. **pryvetee**: secrecy. 269. **Ye**: yes. **lewed**: ignorant. 270. **noght . . . kan**: knows nothing but his creed (alone). 271. **ferde**: fared. 274. **marle**: marl. 276. **Me . . . of**: I sorely pity. 277. **rated of**: scolded for. 278. **If . . . may**: if I can do anything about it. **hevene**: Heaven's. 279. **underspore**: pry underneath. 282. **gan . . . dresse**: betook himself. 283. **a . . . nones**: an exceptionally strong fellow. 284. **haf**: heaved. **atones**: at once. 288. **wende**: supposed. 289. **hente**: seized. 290. **spitously**: defiantly. 293. **crouche**: protect by marking with the sign of the cross. **wightes**: (other) creatures. 294. **nyght-spel**: charm against the dangers of the night, recorded here in an intentionally ludicrous form. **anon rightes**: right away. 295. **halves**: corners.

And on the threshfold on the dore withoute:
"Jesu Crist and Seint Benedight,°
Blesse this hous from every wikked wight.
For the nyghtes verye,° the white Pater-noster.°
Where wentestow,° Seint Petres soster?"°   300
And at the laste this hende Nicholas
Gan for to sike° soore and seyde, "Allas!
Shal al the world be lost eftsones° now?"
    This carpenter answerde, "What seistow?°
What! Thenk on God, as we doon, men that
    swynke."°   305
    This Nicholas answerde, "Fecche me drynke,
And after wol I speke in pryvetee
Of certein thyng that toucheth me and thee.
I wol telle it noon oother man, certayn."
    This carpenter gooth doun and comth agayn,
And broghte of myghty ale a large quart,   311
And whan that ech of hem had dronke his part,
This Nicholas his dore faste shette,°
And doun the carpenter by hym sette
And seyde, "John, myn hoost lief° and deere,   315
Thou shalt upon thy trouthe swere me heere
That to no wight thou shalt this counseil wreye,°
For it is Cristes counseil that I seye,
And, if thou telle it man, thou art forlore,°
For this vengeaunce thow shalt have therfore,   320
That, if thow wreye me, thow shalt be wood."°
    "Nay, Crist forbede it, for his holy blood,"
Quod tho° this sely man. "I nam no labbe,°
Ne, thogh I seye,° I nam nat lief to gabbe.°
Sey what thow wolt,° I shal it nevere telle   325
To child ne wyf, by hym that harwed° helle."
    "Now John," quod Nicholas, "I wol noght lye.
I have y-founde in myn astrologye,
As I have looked in the moone bright,
That now a° Monday next, at quarter-nyght,°   330
Shal falle a reyn, and that so wilde and wood,
That half so greet was nevere Noes° flood.

297. **Benedight**: Benedict. 299. **verye**: evil spirits. **white Pater-noster**: the name of a charm of this kind, presumably derived from some version of "Our Father" intended to effect white (legitimate) magic. 300. **wentestow**: did you go? **soster**: sister. 302. **sike**: sigh. 303. **eftsones**: very soon. 304. **seistow**: do you say? 305. **swynke**: work. 313. **shette**: shut. 315. **lief**: beloved. 317. **counseil wreye**: secret betray. 319. **forlore**: lost. 321. **be wood**: become insane (as a punishment). 323. **tho**: then. **labbe**: babbler. 324. **seye**: say (it myself). **nam . . . gabbe**: don't like to blab. 325. **wolt**: will. 326. **harwed**: harrowed (harassed). According to an apocryphal gospel, Christ after his crucifixion routed the evil spirits in hell and removed the souls of the patriarchs to heaven—a favorite episode in miracle plays. 330. **a**: on. **quarter-nyght**: the end of the first quarter of the night (9:00 P.M.). 332. **Noes**: Noah's.

This world," he seyde, "in lasse than in an hour
Shal al be dreynt,° so hidous is the shour.
Thus shal mankynde drenche° and lese hir° lif."
    This carpenter answerde, "Allas, my wyf!   336
And shal she drenche! Allas, myn Alisoun!"
    For sorwe of this he fil almoost adoun
And seyde, "Is ther no remedie in this cas?"
    "Why, yis, for Gode," quod hende Nicholas,
"If thow wolt werken after loore and reed.°   341
Thow mayst noght werken after thyn owene heed,°
For thus seith Salomon° that was ful trewe,
'Werk al by conseil, and thow shalt noght rewe.'°
And if thow werken wolt by good consayl,   345
I undertake, withouten mast or sayl,
Yit° shal I save hire and thee and me.
Hastow° nat herd how saved was Noe
Whan that Oure Lord had warned hym biforn°
That al the world with water sholde be lorn?"°
    "Yis," quod this carpenter, "ful yore° ago."   351
    "Hastow nat herd," quod Nicholas, "also
The sorwe of Noe with his felaweshipe°
Er that° he myghte gete his wyf to shipe.
Hym had levere,° I dar wel undertake,°   355
At thilke tyme than al hise wetheres blake°
That she hadde had a ship hirself allone!
And therfore wostow° what is best to done?°
This axeth° haste, and of an hastyf° thyng
Men may noght preche or maken tariyng.   360
Anon,° go gete us faste into this in°
A knedyng trogh, or ellis° a kemelyn°
For ech° of us, but looke that they be large
In which we mowen swymme° as in a barge,
And han therinne vitaille suffisaunt°   365
But for a day. Fy on the remenaunt.°
The water shal aslake° and goon away
Aboute pryme° upon the nexte day.
But Robyn may nat wite° of this, thy knave,°
Ne eek thy mayde Gille I may nat save.   370

Axe noght why, for thogh thou axe me,
I wol noght tellen Goddes pryvetee.°
Suffiseth thee, but if° thy wittes madde,°
To han as greet a grace as Noe hadde.
Thy wyf shal I wel saven, out of° doute!   375
Go now thy wey and speed thee heer-aboute.°
But whan thou hast, for hire and thee and me,
Y-geten° us thise kneydyng tubbes thre,
Thanne shaltow hange hem in the roof ful hye
That no man of oure purveiaunce espye;°   380
And whan thow thus hast doon as I have seyd,
And hast oure vitaille faire in hem y-leyd,°
And eek an ax to smyte the corde atwo,°
Whan that the water cometh, that we may go
And breke an hole an heigh° upon the gable   385
Unto the gardynward° over the stable
That we may frely passen° forth oure wey
Whan that the grete shour is goon awey.
Thanne shaltow swymme as murye, I undertake,
As doth the white doke° and his° drake.   390
Thanne wol I clepe,° 'How, Alison! How, John!
Be murye, for the flood wol passe anon.'
And thou wolt seyn, 'Hail, maister Nicholay!
Good morwe. I see thee wel, for it is day.'
    "And thanne shal we be lordes al oure lyf   395
Of al the world, as Noe and his wyf.
But of o° thyng I warne thee ful right.
Be wel avysed° on that ilke nyght
That we been° entred into shippes bord
That noon of us ne speke noght a word,   400
Ne clepe ne crye, but been in° his preyere,
For it is Goddes owene heste deere.°
Thy wyf and thow mote° hange fer atwynne°
For that bitwixe yow shal be no synne
Namoore in lookyng than ther shal in dede.   405
This ordinaunce is seyd. Go, God thee spede!
Tomorwe at nyght, when men been alle aslepe,
Into oure knedyng tubbes wol we crepe
And sitten ther, abidyng° Goddes grace.
Go now thy wey. I have no lenger space°   410

334. dreynt: drowned. **335. drenche:** drown. **lese hir:** lose their. **341. werken . . . reed:** act according to teaching and advice. **342. heed:** mind. **343. Salomon:** Solomon (the saying is actually from Ecclus. 32:19). **344. rewe:** rue. **347. Yit:** still. **348. Hastow:** have you. **349. biforn:** beforehand. **350. lorn:** lost. **351. yore:** long. **353. felaweshipe:** company. In the miracle plays Noah's wife provided comic relief by her obstreperousness. **354. Er that:** before. **355. Hym . . . levere:** he had sooner. **undertake:** assert. **356. wetheres blake:** black sheep. **358. wostow:** do you know. **done:** do. **359. axeth:** demands. **hastyf:** hasty. **361. Anon:** at once. **in:** house. **362. ellis:** else. **kemelyn:** tub. **363. ech:** each. **364. mowen swymme:** can float. **365. vitaille suffisaunt:** sufficient victuals. **366. Fy . . . remenaunt:** Never mind the remainder. **367. aslake:** slacken. **368. pryme:** prime (9:00 A.M.). **369. wite:** know. **knave:** servant boy.

372. pryvetee: secret. **373. but if:** unless. **madde:** become mad. **375. out of:** without. **376. speed . . . heer-aboute:** hurry about this business. **378. Y-geten:** gotten. **380. no . . . espye:** no one may discover our preparation. **382. y-leyd:** laid. **383. atwo:** in two. **385. an heigh:** on high. **386. Unto . . . gardynward:** on the gardenward side of the house. The same roof evidently runs over both house and stable. **387. frely passen:** freely pass. **390. doke:** duck. **his:** its. **391. clepe:** call out. **397. o:** one. **398. avysed:** advised. **399. That we been:** when we have. **401. in:** at. **402. heste deere:** commandment precious. **403. mote:** must. **fer atwynne:** far apart. **409. abidyng:** awaiting. **410. space:** time.

To make of this no lenger sermonyng.
Men seyn thus, 'Send the wise, and sey no thyng.'
Thow art so wys, it nedeth thee nat teche.°
Go save oure lyf, and that I thee b](seche.'"°
    This sely carpenter gooth forth his wey.   415
Ful ofte he seyde "Allas and weylawey."°
And to his wyf he tolde his pryvetee,
And she was war° and knew it bet° than he
What al this queynte cast was for to seye,°
But nathelees° she ferde as° she wolde deye   420
And seyde, "Allas! Go forth thy wey anon.
Help us to scape, or we been dede echon.°
I am thy trewe, verray° wedded wyf.
Go, deere spouse, and help to save oure lyf."
    Lo, which° a greet thyng is affeccioun!°   425
Men may dye of ymaginacioun,
So depe may impressioun be take.°
This sely carpenter bigynneth quake.
Hym thynketh verrailiche° that he may se
Noes flood come walwyng° as the see   430
To drenchen° Alison, his hony deere.
He wepeth, waileth, maketh sory cheere.
He siketh° with ful many a sory swogh,°
And gooth and geteth hym a knedyng trogh,
And after a tubbe and a kymelyn,°   435
And pryvely he sente hem to his in,°
And heeng hem in the roof in pryvetee.
His° owene hand he made laddres thre
To clymben by the ronges and the stalkes°
Unto the tubbes hangyng in the balkes°   440
And hem vitailled,° bothe trogh and tubbe,
With breed and chese and good ale in a jubbe,°
Suffisynge right ynogh as for a day.
    But er that he had maad al this array,
He sente his knave and eek his wenche also   445
Upon his nede° to Londoun for to go,
And on the Monday, whan it drogh° to nyght,
He shette his dore withouten candel lyght
And dressed° alle thyng as it sholde be,
And, shortly up they clomben alle thre.   450

They seten° stille wel a furlong-way.°
"Now Pater-noster, clum!"° seyde Nicholay.
And "Clum," quod John, and "Clum," seyde Alisoun.
    This carpenter seyde his devocioun,
And stille he sit° and biddeth° his prayere,   455
Awaitynge on the reyn if he it heere.
The dede sleep for wery bisynesse°
Fil on this carpenter right as I gesse
Aboute corfew° tyme or litel moore.
For travaille° of his goost° he groneth soore,   460
And eft° he routeth,° for his heed myslay.°
    Doun of the laddre stalketh Nicholay,
And Alisoun ful softe adoun she spedde.
Withouten wordes mo, they goon to bedde.
Theras° the carpenter is wont to lye,   465
Ther was the revel and the melodye!
And thus lyth° Alison and Nicholas
In bisynesse of myrthe and in solas°
Til that the belle of laudes° gan to rynge
And freres° in the chauncel gonne synge.   470
    This parissh clerk, this amorous Absolon,
That is for love alwey so wo-bigon,
Upon the Monday was at Oseneye
With compaignye hym to disporte and pleye,
And axed upon cas a cloisterer°   475
Ful pryvely after John the carpenter,
And he drogh hym apart out of the cherche°
And seyde, "I noot.° I saugh hym here noght werche°
Sith Saterday. I trowe° that he be went°
For tymber ther° oure abbot hath hym sent,   480
For he is wont for tymber for to go
And dwellen at the graunge° a day or two,
Or ellis he is at his hous certeyn.
Wher that he be, I kan noght soothly° seyn."
    This Absolon ful joly was and lyght   485
And thoughte, "Now is tyme to wake al nyght,
For sikerly° I saugh hym noght stirynge

---

413. nedeth . . . teche: it is not necessary to teach *you*. **414. biseche:** beseech. **416. weylawey:** woe. **418. war:** aware. **bet:** better. **419. queynte . . . seye:** ingenious plan meant. **420. nathelees:** nevertheless. **ferde as:** acted as if. **422. been . . . echon:** shall be dead each one. **423. trewe, verray:** faithful, true. **425. which:** what. **affeccioun:** a mental impression. **427. take:** received. **429. verrailiche:** truly. **430. walwyng:** welling. **431. drenchen:** drown. **433. siketh:** sighs. **swogh:** groan. **435. kymelyn:** tub. **436. in:** house. **438. His:** with his. **439. stalkes:** uprights. **440. in . . . balkes:** on the roof beams. **441. hem vitailled:** supplied them. **442. jubbe:** jug. **446. nede:** errand. **447. drogh:** drew. **449. dressed:** prepared.

451. seten: sat. **a furlong-way:** a few minutes (lit., as long as it takes to walk a furlong). **452. Pater-noster, clum:** (say) a paternoster, and then mum's the word! **455. sit:** sits. **biddeth:** prays. **457. wery bisynesse:** wearying activity. **459. corfew:** curfew (about 8:00 P.M.). **460. travaille:** disturbance. **goost:** spirit. **461. eft:** in turn. **routeth:** snores. **myslay:** lay in the wrong position. **465. Theras:** where. **467. lyth:** lie. **468. solas:** delight. **469. laudes:** the first service after midnight. **470. freres:** friars. **475. upon . . . cloisterer:** by chance a cloisterer (of Osney Abbey). **477. cherche:** church (of the abbey). **478. noot:** don't know. **saugh . . . werche:** haven't seen him work here. **479. trowe:** suppose. **be went:** has gone. **480. ther:** where. **482. graunge:** (abbey's) farmhouse. **484. soothly:** truly. **487. sikerly:** certainly.

Aboute his dore syn day bigan to sprynge.
So mote° I thryve, I shal at cokkes crowe°
Ful pryvely knokken at his wyndowe   490
That stant ful lowe upon his boures wal.
To Alison now wol I tellen al
My love longyng, for yit I shal nat mysse
That at the leeste wey° I shal hir kisse.
Som maner° confort shal I have, parfay!°   495
My mouth hath icched° al this longe day.
That is a signe of kissyng, atte leeste.
Al nyght me mette eek° I was at a feeste.
Therfore, I wol go slepe an houre or tweye,
And al the nyght than wol I wake and pleye!" 500
    Whan that the firste cok hath crowe, anon
Up rist° this joly lovere Absolon
And hym° arrayeth gay at poynt devys,°
But first he cheweth greyn° and likorys
To swellen swete, er° he hadde kembd° his heer.
Under his tonge a trewe-love° he beer,°   506
For therby wende° he to be gracious.
    He rometh to the carpenteres hous,
And stille he stant under the shot-wyndowe—
Unto his brest it raughte,° it was so lowe— 510
And softe he cougheth with a semysoun.°
"What do ye, honycomb, swete Alisoun,
My faire bryd,° my swete cynamome?
Awaketh, lemman° myn, and speketh to me.
Wel litel thynken ye upon my wo,   515
That for youre love I swete ther° I go.
No wonder is thogh that I swelte° and swete.
I moorne as dooth a lamb after the tete.°
Ywis,° lemman, I have swich love-longyng
That lyk a turtel° trewe is my moornyng.   520
I may nat ete namoore than a mayde."
    "Go fro the wyndow, Jakke fool,"° she seyde.
"As help me God, it wol nat be 'com pa° me.'
I love another—and ellis I were to blame°—
Wel bet than thee, by Jesu, Absolon.   525

Go forth thy wey, or I wol caste a stoon,
And lat me slepe, a twenty develwey."°
    "Allas," quod Absolon, "and weilawey
That trewe love was evere so yvel biset.°
Thanne kys me, syn it may be no bet,°   530
For Jesus love, and for the love of me."
    "Woltow thanne go thy wey therwith?" quod she.
    "Ye, certes, lemman," quod this Absolon.
    "Thanne make thee redy," quod she. "I come anon."
    And unto Nicholas she seyde stille,°   535
"Now hust,° and thou shalt laughen al thy fille."
    This Absolon doun sette hym on his knees
And seyde, "I am a lord at alle degrees,
For, after this, I hope ther cometh moore.
Lemman, thy grace, and, swete bryd, thyn oore."°
    The wyndow she undoth, and that in haste. 541
"Have do,"° quod she. "Com of, and speed thee faste
Lest that oure neighebores thee espye."
    This Absolon gan wipe his mouth ful drye.
Derk was the nyght as pych° or as the cole,° 545
And at the wyndow out she putte hir hole,
And Absolon hym fil° no bet ne wers°
But with his mouth he kiste hir naked ers°
Ful savourly° er he were war° of this.
    Abak he sterte° and thoghte it was amys,   550
For wel he wiste° a womman hath no berd.°
He felte a thyng al rogh and long y-herd,°
And seyde, "Fy, allas! What have I do?"
    "Tehee," quod she, and clapte the wyndow to,
And Absolon gooth forth a sory paas.°   555
    "A berd, a berd!" quod hende Nicholas.
"By Goddes corpus!° This gooth faire and wel!"
    This sely Absolon herde every del,°
And on his lippe he gan for anger byte,
And to hymself he seyde, "I shal thee quyte."° 560
Who rubbeth now, who froteth° now his lippes
With dust, with sond,° with straw, with clooth, with chippes
But Absolon, that seith ful ofte, "Allas!

---

489. mote: may. **crowe:** presumably at the *first* crow (as in l. 501), which was thought to occur at midnight. **494. at . . . wey:** at least. **495. maner:** sort of. **parfay:** in faith. **496. icched:** Itching was commonly interpreted as an omen. **498. me . . . eek:** I dreamed also. **502. rist:** rises. **503. hym:** himself. **gay . . . devys:** gaily to perfection. **504. greyn:** grain of paradise (an aromatic seed). **505. er:** before. **kembd:** combed. **506. trewe-love:** leaf of herb Paris, a medicinal herb growing in the shape of a truelove knot. **beer:** carried. **507. wende:** expected. **510. raughte:** reached. **511. semysoun:** half-sound. **513. bryd:** bird. **514. lemman:** sweetheart. **516. swete ther:** sweat where. **517. swelte:** faint. **518. tete:** teat. **519. Ywis:** indeed. **520. turtel:** turtledove. **522. Jakke fool:** jackass. **523. pa:** kiss. **524. were to blame:** would be blameworthy.

527. a . . . develwey: the Devil away with you, twenty times over. **529. yvel biset:** poorly bestowed. **530. bet:** better. **535. stille:** quietly. **536. hust:** hush. **540. oore:** mercy. **542. do:** done. **545. pych:** pitch. **the cole:** coal. **547. hym fil:** to him befell. **ne wers:** nor worse. **548. ers:** bottom. **549. savourly:** delightedly. **war:** aware. **550. sterte:** started. **551. wiste:** knew. **berd:** beard. **552. y-herd:** haired. **555. a . . . paas:** at a sorry pace. **557. corpus:** body. **558. del:** part. **560. quyte:** pay back. **561. froteth:** rub. **562. sond:** sand.

My soule bitake° I unto Sathanas,
But me were levere° than al this toun," quod he,
"Of this despit awreken for to be.°   566
Allas," quod he, "allas, I ne hadde y-bleynt!"°

His hote love was coold and al y-queynt,°
For, fro that tyme that he had kist hir ers,
Of paramours° he sette noght a kers,°   570
For he was heeled° of his maladye.
Ful ofte paramours he gan defye°
And weep° as dooth a child that is y-bete.

A softe paas° he wente over the strete
Until° a smyth men clepen daun° Gerveys,   575
That in his forge smythed plough harneys.
He sharpeth shaar° and cultour° bisily.

This Absolon knokketh al esily°
And seyde, "Undo, Gerveys, and that anon!"
    "What? Who artow?"° "It am I, Absolon."   580
    "What, Absolon! What, Cristes swete tree,°
Why rise ye so rathe,° ey, *benedicitee?*°
What eyleth yow? Som gay gerl, God it woot,
Hath broght yow thus upon the viritoot°—
By Seint Note, ye woot wel what I mene!"   585

This Absolon ne roghte nat a bene°
Of al his pley; no word agayn he yaf.°
He hadde moore tow° on his distaf
Then Gerveys knew and seyde, "Freend so deere,
That hoote cultour in the chymenee heere,   590
As lene° it me. I have therwith to doone.°
I wol brynge it thee agayn ful soone."

Gerveys answerde, "Certes, were it gold,
Or in a poke nobles al untold,°
Thow sholdest have, as I am trewe smyth.   595
Ey, Cristes foo!° What wol ye do therwith?"
    "Therof," quod Absolon, "be as be may.
I shal wel telle it thee tomorwe day,"
And caughte° the cultour by the colde stele.°

Ful softe out at the dore he gan to stele   600
And wente unto the carpenteres wal.

He cogheth first, and knokketh therwithal
Upon the wyndowe right as he dide er.°
    This Alison answerde, "Who is ther
That knokketh so? I warante it a theef!"   605
    "Why, nay," quod he. "God woot, my swete
        lief,°
I am thyn Absolon, thy derelyng.°
Of gold," quod he, "I have thee broght a ryng.
My moder yaf° it me, so God me save.
Ful fyn it is, and therto° wel y-grave.°   610
This wol I yeven° thee if thow me kisse."
    This Nicholas was risen for to pisse
And thoghte he wolde amenden° al the jape;°
He sholde kisse his ers er that he scape;°
And up the wyndow dide° he hastily,   615
And out his ers he putteth pryvely°
Over the buttok to the haunche bon.
    And therwith spak this clerk, this Absolon:
"Spek, swete brid,° I noot noght° wher thow art."
    This Nicholas anoon leet fle a fart   620
As greet as it hadde been a thonder dent,°
That with the strook he was almoost y-blent,°
And he was redy with his iren hoot,
And Nicholas in the ers he smoot.°
Of° gooth the skyn an hand brede° aboute;   625
The hoote cultour brende° so his toute°
That for the smert° he wende° for to dye.
As he were wood, for wo he gan to crye,
"Help! Water! Water! Help, for Goddes herte!"
    This carpenter out of his slomber sterte   630
And herde oon° cryen, "Water!" as he were wood
And thoghte, "Allas, now cometh Nowelys°
        flood."
He sette hym° up withoute wordes mo,
And with his ax he smoot the corde atwo,
And doun gooth al. He fond° neither to selle   635
Ne breed ne ale til he cam to the celle°
Upon the floor, and there aswowne° he lay.
    Up stirte hire° Alison and Nicholay
And criden, "Out!" and "Harrow!"° in the strete.

---

564. **bitake:** commit. 565. **me . . . levere:** I would sooner.
566. **despit . . . be:** insult be avenged. 567. **I . . . y-
bleynt:** that I didn't turn aside! 568. **y-queynt:** quenched.
570. **paramours:** lovers. **kers:** curse. 571. **heeled:** cured.
572. **gan defye:** renounced. 573. **weep:** wept. 574. **A . . .
paas:** quietly. 575. **Until:** to. **clepen daun:** called Master.
577. **shaar:** share. **cultour:** plow colter. 578. **esily:** gently.
580. **artow:** are you. 581. **swete tree:** precious cross. 582.
rathe: early. **benedicitee:** God bless you. 584. **upon . . .
viritoot:** on the move. 586. **ne . . . bene:** didn't care a bean.
587. **agayn he yaf:** he replied. 588. **tow:** tow (to spin). 591.
As lene: lend. **therwith to doone:** something to do with it.
594. **in . . . untold:** nobles (gold coins worth 6s. 8d.) all
uncounted in a bag. 596. **foo:** foot. 599. **caughte:** took.
stele: handle.

603. **er:** before. 606. **lief:** dear. 607. **derelyng:** darling. 609.
yaf: gave. 610. **therto:** besides. **y-grave:** carved. 611. **yeven:**
give. 613. **amenden:** improve upon. **jape:** joke. 614. **scape:**
escaped. 615. **dide:** put. 616. **pryvely:** stealthily. 619. **brid:**
bird. **noot noght:** don't know. 621. **dent:** dint. 622 **y-blent:**
blinded. 624. **smoot:** struck. 625. **Of:** off. **brede:** breadth.
626. **brende:** burned. **toute:** bottom. 627. **smert:** pain.
wende: expected. 631. **oon:** someone. 632. **Nowelys:** Noel's
(the Carpenter confuses the name of Noah with that of
Christmas). 633. **sette hym:** sat. 635. **fond:** found (the
opportunity). 636. **celle:** sill. 637. **aswowne:** aswoon. 638.
stirte hire: sprang. 639. **Harrow:** help.

The neighebores bothe smale and grete   640
In ronnen for to gauren° on this man
That aswowne lay bothe pale and wan,
For with the fal he brosten° hadde his arm.
But stonde he moste° unto his owene harm,
For whan he spak, he was anon bore doun°   645
With° hende Nicholas and Alisoun.
They tolden every man that he was wood;
He was agast° so of "Nowelys flood"
Thurgh fantasie that, of his vanytee,
He hadde y-boght hym knedyng tubbes thre   650
And hadde hem hanged in the roof above;
And that he preyed hem° for Goddes love
To sitten in the roof *par compaignye.*°
     The folk gan laughen at his fantasye.
Into the roof they kiken° and they cape°   655
And turned al his harm unto a jape,
For, what so that this carpenter answerde,
It was for noght; no man his reson° herde.
With othes° grete he was so sworn adoun
That he was holden° wood in al the toun,   660
For every clerk anon right heeld° with oother.
They seyde, "The man is wood, my leve brother."
And every wight gan laughen at this stryf.
     Thus swyved° was the carpenteres wyf
For al his kepyng° and his jalousye,   665
And Absolon hath kist hir nether eye,
And Nicholas is scalded in the toute.
This tale is doon, and God save al the route.°

The Nun's Priest's Tale

A poure widwe, somdel stape° in age,
Was whilom° dwellynge in a narwe° cotage
Biside a grove, stondyng in a dale.
This widwe of which I telle yow my tale,
Syn thilke° day that she was last a wyf,   5
In pacience ladde a ful symple lyf,
For litel was hire catel° and hire rente.°

By housbondrye of swich° as God hire sente
She foond° hireself and eek° hire doghtren° two.
Thre large sowes hadde she and namo,°   10
Thre kyn,° and eek a sheep that highte° Malle.
Ful sooty was hire bour° and eek hire halle,
In which she eet ful many a sklendre° meel.
Of poynaunt° sauce hir neded° never a deel.°
No deyntee morsel passed thurgh hir throte;   15
Hir diete was acordant to hir cote.°
Repleccioun ne made hire nevere syk;
Attempree° diete was al hir phisyk,
And excercise, and hertes suffisaunce.°
The goute lette° hire nothyng° for to daunce,   20
N' apoplexie shente nat hir heed.°
No wyn ne drank she, neither whit ne reed.
Hir bord° was served moost with whit and blak,
Milk and broun breed, in which she foond no lak,°
Seynd° bacoun, and some tyme an ey° or tweye,
For she was, as it were, a maner deye.°   26
     A yeerd she hadde, enclosed al aboute
With stikkes, and a drye dych° withoute,
In which she hadde a cok heet° Chauntecleer.
In al the land of crowyng nas° his peer.   30
His voys was murier° than the myrie orgon
On massedayes that in the chirche gon.°
Wel sikerer° was his crowyng in his logge°
Than is a clokke or any abbey orlogge.°
By° nature° he knew ech ascensioun   35
Of the equinoxial in thilke toun,
For whan degrees fiftene were ascended,
Thanne krew he that it myghte nat ben amended.°
His comb was redder than the fyn coral
And batailled as° it were a castel wal.   40
His byle° was blak, and as the jeet° it shoon.
Lyk asure° were hise legges and his toon,°
Hise nayles whitter than the lylye flour,

8. **swich:** such. 9. **foond:** supported. **eek:** also. **doghtren:** daughters. 10. **namo:** no more. 11. **kyn:** cows. **highte:** was called. 12. **bour:** bedroom. 13. **sklendre:** slender. 14. **poynaunt:** pungent. **hir neded:** she needed. **deel:** bit. 16: **cote:** means. 18. **Attempree:** temperate. 19. **suffisaunce:** sufficiency. 20. **lette:** hindered. **nothyng:** in no way. 21. **N' apoplexie. . .heed:** nor did apoplexy trouble her head. 23. **bord:** table. 24. **foond . . . lak:** found no fault. 25. **Seynd:** broiled. **ey:** egg. 26. **maner deye:** sort of dairywoman. 28. **dych:** ditch. 29. **heet:** named. 30. **nas:** (there) was not. 31. **murier:** merrier. 32. **gon:** plays. 33. **Wel sikerer:** much more accurate. **logge:** lodge. 34. **orlogge:** horologe (clock). 35–37. The sphere of the stars was thought of as rotating 360 degrees every twenty-four hours around the earth's equator. The equinoctial circle of the heaven thus turns or "ascends" 15 degrees every hour. 35. **nature:** instinct. 38. **that . . . amended:** so that it couldn't be bettered. 40. **batailled as:** battlemented as if. 41. **byle:** bill. **jeet:** jet. 42. **asure:** azure. **toon:** toes.

641. **gauren:** stare. 643. **brosten:** broken. 644. **stonde he moste:** he must attest. 645. **bore doun:** borne down. 646. **With:** by. 648. **agast:** afraid. 652. **hem:** them (Nicholas and Alisoun). 653. **par compaignye:** by way of company. 655. **kiken:** peer. **cape:** gape. 658. **reson:** argument. 659. **othes:** oaths. 660. **holden:** considered. 661. **heeld:** agreed. 664. **swyved:** lain with. 665. **kepyng:** watching. 668. **route:** company.

THE NUN'S PRIEST'S TALE. 1. **widwe . . . stape:** widow somewhat advanced. 2. **whilom:** once. **narwe:** small. 5. **Syn thilke:** since that same. 7. **catel:** property. **rente:** income.

And lyk the burned° gold was his colour.
This gentil cok hadde in his governaunce°   45
Sevene hennes for to doon al his plesaunce,°
Whiche were hise sustres° and his paramours,
And wonder° lyke to hym as of colours,
Of whiche the faireste hewed on hire throte
Was cleped° faire damoysele Pertelote.   50
Curteys she was, discreet, and debonaire,
And compaignable, and bar° hirself so faire
Syn thilke day that she was seven nyght oold
That, trewely, she hath the herte in hoold
Of Chauntecleer, loken° in every lith.°   55
He loved hire so that wel was hym ther-with.°
But swich a joye was it to here hem° synge,
Whan that the brighte sonne gan to sprynge,°
In swete acord "My leef is faren in londe."°
For thilke° tyme, as I have understonde,   60
Beestes and briddes° koude speke and synge.

   And so bifel that in a dawenynge,°
As Chauntecleer among hise wyves alle
Sat on his perche, that was in the halle,
And next hym sat this faire Pertelote,   65
This Chauntecleer gan gronen° in his throte
As man that in his dreem is drecched° soore.

   And whan that° Pertelote thus herde hym rore,
She was agast and seyde, "Herte deere,
What eyleth yow to grone in this manere?   70
Ye ben a verray° slepere. Fy, for shame!"

   And he answerde and seyde thus: "Madame,
I prey yow that ye take it nat agrief.°
By God, me mette° I was in swich meschief
Right now that yet myn herte is soore afright.   75
Now God," quod° he, "my swevene recche° aright,
And kepe my body out of foul prisoun.
Me mette how that I romed up and doun
Withinne oure yeerd, where-as I say° a beest,
Was lyk an hound and wolde han maad areest°   80
Upon my body and han° had me deed.
His colour was bitwixe yelow and reed,
And tipped was his tayl and bothe hise erys°

With blak unlik the remenaunt° of hise herys,°
His snowte smal, with glowyng eyen° tweye.   85
Yet of his look for fere almoost I deye.
This caused me my gronyng, doutelees."

   "Avoy!"° quod she. "Fy on yow, hertelees!°
Allas," quod she, "for, by that God above,
Now han ye lost myn herte and al my love.   90
I kan nat love a coward, by my feith!
For, certes,° what so° any womman seith,
We alle desiren, if it myghte be,
To han housbondes hardy, wise, and fre,°
And secree,° and no nygard, ne no fool,   95
Ne hym that is agast of every tool,°
Ne noon avauntour,° by that God above.
How dorste° ye seyn, for shame, unto youre love
That any thyng myghte make yow aferd?
Have ye no mannes herte and han a berd?   100

   "Allas, and konne ye ben agast° of swevenys!°
Nothyng, God woot,° but vanytee in swevene is.
Swevenes engendren of replexions,°
And ofte of fume° and of complexions,°
Whan humours ben to habundant in a wight.°   105
   "Certes, this dreem which ye han met to-nyght°
Comth of the grete superfluytee
Of youre rede colera,° pardee,°
Which causeth folk to dreden° in hir° dremes
Of arwes, and of fyr with rede lemes,°   110
Of rede bestes that they wol hem byte,
Of contek,° and of whelpes grete and lyte
Right° as the humour of malencolie
Causeth ful many a man in sleep to crie
For fere of blake beres,° or boles° blake,   115
Or elles blake develes, wol hem° take.
Of othere humours koude I telle also
That werken° many a man in sleep ful wo,°
But I wol passe as lightly as I kan.
Lo Catoun,° which that was so wys a man,   120

44. burned: burnished. **45. governaunce:** control. **46. plesaunce:** pleasure. **47. sustres:** sisters (sweethearts). **48. wonder:** wonderfully. **50. cleped:** called. **52. bar:** conducted. **55. loken:** locked. **lith:** limb. **56. wel . . . ther-with:** he was well contented. **57. hem:** them. **58. gan to sprynge:** began to rise. **59. leef . . . londe:** sweetheart has gone to the country. **60. thilke:** (at) that. **61. briddes:** birds. **62. in a dawenynge:** one dawn. **66. gan gronen:** began to groan. **67. drecched:** tormented. **68. whan that:** when. **71. verray:** sound. **73. agrief:** ill. **74. me mette:** I dreamed. **76. quod:** said. **my . . . recche:** may my dream work out. **79. where-as . . . say:** where I saw. **80. han . . . areest:** have seized. **81. han:** have. **83. erys:** ears.

84. remenaunt: rest. **herys:** hair. **85. eyen:** eyes. **88. Avoy:** shame. **hertelees:** faintheart. **92. certes:** certainly. **what so:** whatever. **94. fre:** generous. **95. secree:** discreet. **96. tool:** weapon. **97. avauntour:** boaster. **98. dorste:** dared. **101. agast:** afraid. **swevenys:** dreams. **102. woot:** knows. **103. engendren . . . replexions:** are engendered from repletion. **104. fume:** vapor. **complexions:** temperaments. **105. humours . . . wight:** humors are too abundant in a person. A super abundance of any one of the four humors affected the temperament. **106. han . . . to-nyght:** have dreamed this night. **108. rede colera:** red choler. **pardee:** certainly. **109. dreden:** be frightened. **hir:** their. **110. arwes:** arrows. **lemes:** flames. **112. contek:** strife. **113. Right:** just. **115. beres:** bears. **boles:** bulls. **116. wol hem:** (which) will them. **118. werken:** make. **wo:** woeful. **120. Catoun:** Dionysius Cato, to whom a well-known collection of Latin maxims was ascribed.

Seyde he nat thus: 'Ne do no fors of° dremes'?

   "Now sire," quod she, "whan we fle° fro the
      bemes,
For Goddes love, as taak° som laxatif.
Up° peril of my soule and of my lif,
I conseille yow the beste, I wol nat lye,   125
That bothe of colere and of malencolye
Ye purge yow. And, for° ye shal nat tarye,
Thogh in this toun is noon° apothecarye,
I shal myself to herbes techen° yow
That shul ben for youre heele° and for youre prow.°
And in oure yerd tho° herbes shal I fynde   131
The whiche han° of hire propretee by kynde°
To purge yow bynethe and eek° above.
Foryet nat this, for Goddes owene love:
Ye ben ful colerik of complexioun.   135
Ware° the sonne in his ascensioun,
Ne fynde yow nat replet of° humours hote,
And, if it do, I dar wel leye a grote°
That ye shul have a fevere terciane°
Or an agu that may be youre bane.°   140
A day or two ye shul have digestyves
Of wormes er° ye take youre laxatyves
Of lauriol,° centaure,° and fumetere,°
Or elles of ellebor° that groweth there,
Of katapuce,° or of gaitrys beryis,°   145
Of herbe yve° growyng in oure yerd, ther merye is.°
Pekke hem up right as they growe, and ete hem in.
Be myrie, housbonde, for youre fader kyn!°
Dredeth no dreem. I kan sey yow namoore."

   "Madame," quod he, "graunt mercy of youre
      loore.°   150
But nathelees, as touchyng daun Catoun,°
That hath of wisdom swich° a gret renoun,
Thogh that he bad no dremes for to drede,
By God, men may in olde bokes rede
Of many a man moore of auctoritee   155
Than evere Catoun was, so mote I thee,°

That al the revers° seyn of his sentence°
And han wel founden by experience
That dremes ben° significaciouns
As wel of joye as of tribulaciouns   160
That folk enduren in this lyf present.
Ther nedeth° make of this noon argument;
The verray preeve° sheweth it in dede.

   "Oon° of the gretteste auctor° that men rede
Seith thus, that whilom° two felawes° wente   165
On pilgrymage in a ful good entente,
And happed so they coomen in a toun
Where-as ther was swich congregacioun
Of peple and eek so streit of herbergage°
That they ne founde as muche as a cotage   170
In which they bothe myghte y-logged° be.
Wherfore they mosten° of necessitee,
As for° that nyght, departen° compaignye,
And ech of hem gooth to his hostelrye
And took his loggyng as it wolde falle.   175
That oon of hem was logged in a stalle
Fer in a yeerd° with oxen of the plow.
That oother man was logged wel ynow°
As was his aventure° or his fortune,
That us governeth alle as in commune.°   180

   "And so bifel that, longe er it were day,
This man mette° in his bed ther-as° he lay
How that his felawe gan upon hym calle
And seyde, 'Allas, for in an oxes stalle
This nyght I shal be mordred ther° I lye.   185
Now help me, deere brother, or I dye.
In alle haste com to me,' he sayde.

   "This man out of his sleep for feere abrayde,°
But whan that he was wakned of his sleep,
He turned hym and took of this no keep.°   190
Hym thoughte° his dreem nas but° a vanytee.
Thus twies° in his slepyng dremed he,
And atte thridde tyme yet his felawe
Cam, as hym thoughte, and seyde, 'I am now slawe.°
Bihoold my blody woundes, depe and wyde.   195
Arys up erly in the morwe tyde,°
And at the west gate of the toun,' quod he,

121. Ne . . . of: pay no attention to. 122. fle: fly down.
123. as taak: take. 124. Up: upon. 127. for: in order that.
128. noon: no. 129. techen: direct. 130. heele: healing. prow:
well-being. 131. tho: those. 132. The . . . han: which have.
kynde: nature. 133. eek: also. 136. Ware: beware that. 137.
replet of: overfilled with. 138. grote: groat (4*d*.). 139.
terciane: tertian (recurring every other day). 140. bane:
destruction. 142. er: before. 143. lauriol: spurge laurel.
centaure: centaury. fumetere: fumitory. 144. ellebor: helle-
bore. 145. katapuce: caper spurge. gaitrys beryis: gaitertree
berries (dogwood). 146. herbe yve: ground ivy. ther . . . is:
where it is pleasant. 148. fader kyn: father's kin. 150.
graunt . . . loore: much thanks for your instruction. 151.
daun Catoun: Master Cato. 152. swich: such. 156. mote I
thee: may I prosper.

157. revers: contrary. sentence: opinion. 159. ben: are.
162. Ther nedeth: there is (no) need to. 163. verray preeve:
very proof. 164. Oon: one. auctor: author(s). 165. whilom:
once. felawes: companions. 169. streit of herbergage: short
of lodgings. 171. y-logged: lodged. 172. mosten: must. 173.
As for: for. departen: part. 177. Fer . . . yeerd: far off in a
courtyard. 178. ynow: enough. 179. aventure: lot. 180. alle
. . . commune: all in common. 182. mette: dreamed. ther-
as: where. 185. ther: where. 188. abrayde: awoke. 190.
keep: heed. 191. Hym thoughte: it seemed to him. nas but:
was only. 192. twies: twice. 194. slawe: slain. 196. morwe
tyde: morning time.

'A carte ful of donge ther shaltow se,°
In which my body is hid ful pryvely.°
Do thilke° carte aresten° boldely.   200
My gold caused my mordre, sooth to seyn';°
And tolde hym every poynt how he was slayn
With a ful pitous face pale of hewe.
And truste wel his dreem he fond° ful trewe,
For on the morwe, as soone as it was day,   205
To his felawes in° he took the way,
And whan that he cam to this oxes stalle,
After° his felawe he bigan to calle.

   "The hostiler answerde hym anon°
And seyde, 'Sire, youre felawe is agon.   210
As soone as day he wente out of the toun.'
   "This man gan fallen in suspecioun,
Remembrynge on hise dremes that he mette,
And forth he gooth, no lenger wolde he lette,°
Unto the west gate of the toun and fond   215
A dong carte, wente° as it were to donge° lond,
That was arrayed in the same wise
As ye han herd the dede man devyse,°
And with an hardy herte he gan to crye
Vengeaunce and justice of this felonye.   220
'My felawe mordred is this same nyght,
And in this carte heere he lyth gapyng upright.°
I crye out on the mynystres,'° quod he,
'That sholden kepe and reulen this citee.
Harrow,° allas! Heere lyth my felawe slayn!'   225
What sholde I moore unto this tale sayn?
The peple out sterte° and caste the cart to grounde,
And in the myddel of the dong they founde
The dede man, that mordred was al newe.°

   "O blisful God, that art so just and trewe,   230
Lo how that thow biwreyest° mordre alway.
Mordre wol out, that se° we day by day.
Mordre is so wlatsom° and abhomynable
To God, that is so just and resonable,
That he ne wol nat suffre it heled° be,   235
Thogh it abyde° a yeer, or two, or thre.
Mordre wol out, this is my conclusioun.
And right anon ministres of that toun
Han hent° the cartere and so soore hym pyned°

And eek the hostiler so soore engyned°   240
That they biknewe° hir wikkednesse anon
And were an-hanged by the nekke bon.°
   "Heere may men seen that dremes ben to drede.°
And, certes, in the same book I rede,
Right in the nexte chapitre after this—   245
I gabbe° nat, so have I° joye or blys—
Two men that wolde han passed over see
For certeyn cause into a fer contree,
If that the wynd ne hadde ben contrarie,
That made hem in a citee for to tarie,   250
That stood ful myrie° upon an haven° syde.
But on a day, agayn the even tyde,°
The wynd gan chaunge and blew right as hem
     leste.°
Jolif° and glad they wente unto hir° reste
And casten hem° ful erly for to saille.   255
   "But herkneth! To that o° man fil° a greet
     mervaille,
That oon of hem, in slepyng as he lay,
Hym mette a wonder° dreem agayn° the day.
Hym thoughte a man stood by his beddes syde,
And hym comanded that he sholde abyde,   260
And seyde hym thus: 'If thow tomorwe wende,°
Thow shalt be dreynt.° My tale is at an ende.'
He wook, and tolde his felawe what he mette,
And preyde hym his viage° to lette.°
As for that day, he preyde hym to abyde.   265
His felawe, that lay by his beddes syde,
Gan for to laughe and scorned hym ful faste.
'No dreem,' quod he, 'may so myn herte agaste°
That I wol lette for to do my thynges.°
I sette nat a straw by thy dremynges,   270
For swevenes ben but vanytees and japes.°
Men dreme alday° of owles and of apes
And of many a maze° therwithal;
Men dreme of thyng that nevere was ne shal.°
But, sith I see that thow wolt here abyde,   275
And thus forslewthen wilfully° thy tyde,°
God woot,° it reweth me,° and have good day!'

240. engyned: racked. 241. biknewe: confessed. 242. bon:
bone. 243. ben to drede: are to be feared. 246. gabbe:
exaggerate. have I: may I have. 251. myrie: pleasant haven:
harbor. 252. agayn . . . tyde: towards evening time.
253. hem leste: they wished. 254. Jolif: jolly. hir: their. 255.
casten hem: decided. 256. o: one. fil: befell. 258. Hym . . .
wonder: dreamed a wonderful. agayn: before. 261. wende:
travel. 262. dreynt: drowned. 264. viage: voyage. lette:
delay. 268. agaste: frighten. 269. lette . . . thynges: stop
doing my business. 271. japes: follies. 272. alday: every day.
273. maze: wonder. 274. ne shal: nor shall (be). 276. forslewthen wilfully: squander willingly. tyde: time. 277. woot:
knows. it . . . me: I rue it.

198. shaltow se: you will see. 199. ful pryvely: very
secretly. 200. Do thilke: have that same. aresten: stopped.
201. sooth to seyn: truth to tell. 204. fond: found. 206.
felawes in: companion's lodging. 208. After: for. 209.
anon: at once. 214. lette: stay. 216. wente: (which) went.
donge: manure, fertilize. 218. devyse: describe. 222. upright:
face-upward. 223. mynystres: officers. 225. Harrow: help.
227. sterte: sprang. 229. al newe: just recently. 231. biwreyest:
dost reveal. 232. se: see. 233. wlatsom: foul. 235. heled concealed. 236. abyde: await. 239. hent: seized. pyned: tortured.

And thus he took his leve and wente his way,
But er that° he hadde half his cours y-seyled,
Noot I° nat why ne° what meschaunce it eyled,°
But casuelly° the shippes botme rente,°   281
And ship and man under the water wente
In sighte of othere shippes it bisyde°
That with hem seyled at the same tyde.
And therefore, faire Pertelote so deere,   285
By swiche ensamples° olde maystow leere°
That no man sholde been to recchelees°
Of dremes, for I sey thee, doutelees,
That many a dreem ful soore is for to dred.°
   "Lo, in the lyf of Seint Kenelm I rede,   290
That was Kenulphus sone,° the noble kyng
Of Mercenrike,° how Kenelm mette a thyng.
A lite er° he was mordred on a day,
His mordre in his avysioun° he say.°
His norice° hym expowned every del°   295
His swevene, and bad hym for to kepe hym° wel
For° traisoun, but he nas but° sevene yeer old,
And therfore litel tale° hath he told°
Of any dreem, so holy was his herte.
By God, I hadde levere° than my sherte   300
That ye hadde rad° his legende as have I.
Dame Pertelote, I sey yow trewely,
Macrobeus,° that writ° the avysioun
In Affrike of the worthy Cipioun,°
Affermeth dremes and seith that they ben   305
Warnynge of thynges that men after sen.°
And forther-moore, I pray yow, looketh wel
In the Olde Testament, of Daniel,°
If he heeld dremes any vanytee.
Rede eek of Joseph, and there shul ye see   310
Wher° dremes be somtyme, I sey nat alle,
Warnynge of thynges that shul after falle.

Looke of Egipte the kyng, daun Pharao,°
His bakere, and his butiller also,
Wher they ne felte noon effect in dremes.   315
Who-so° wol seke actes of sondry remes°
May rede of dremes many a wonder thyng.
Lo Cresus,° which that was of Lyde kyng,
Mette he nat° that he sat upon a tree,
Which signified he sholde an-hanged be?   320
Lo heere Andromacha,° Ectores° wyf,
That day that Ector sholde lese° his lyf,
She dremed on the same nyght biforn
How that the lyf of Ector sholde be lorn°
If thilke° day he wente in to bataille.   325
She warned hym, but it myghte nat availle;
He wente for to fighte, nathelees.°
But he was slayn anon of° Achilles.
But thilke tale is al to° long to telle,
And eek it is ny° day. I may nat dwelle.   330
   "Shortly I seye, as for conclusioun,
That I shal han of this avysioun
Adversitee, and I seye forther-moor
That I ne telle of laxatyves no stoor,°
For they ben venymes,° I woot it wel.   335
I hem deffye! I love hem never a del!°
   "Now lat us speke of myrthe and stynte° al this.
Madame Pertelote, so have I° blis,
Of o thyng God hath sent me large grace,
For whan I se the beautee of youre face,   340
Ye ben so scarlet reed aboute youre eyen,
It maketh al my drede for to dyen,
For, also siker as In principio,°
'Mulier est hominis confusio.'°
   "Madame, the sentence° of this Latyn is,   345
'Womman is mannes joye and al his blis.'
For whan I feele a-nyght youre softe syde,
Al be it that I may nat on yow ryde

279. er that: before. **280. Noot I:** I don't know, **ne:** nor. **eyled:** ailed. **281. casuelly:** by chance. **rente:** burst. **283. it bisyde:** beside it. **286. ensamples:** examples. **maystow leere:** you may learn. **287. to recchelees:** too heedless. **289. soore . . . dred:** sorely is to be feared. **291. Kenulphus sone:** Kenulphus' son. Kenelm dreamed that he had to fly to heaven; subsequently he was murdered by his aunt. **292. Mercenrike:** Mercia (central England). **293. lite er:** little before. **294. avysioun:** vision. **say:** saw. **295. norice:** nurse. **expowned . . . del:** expounded completely. **296. for . . . hym:** to guard himself. **297. For:** against. **nas but:** was only. **298. tale:** heed. **told:** paid. **300. levere:** rather. **301. rad:** read. **303. Macrobeus:** The commentary by Macrobius on Cicero's account of the dream of Scipio Africanus Minor was regarded as a standard authority on dream lore. **writ:** writes. **304. Cipioun:** Scipio. **306. after sen:** afterwards see. **308. Daniel:** The book of Daniel consists almost entirely of dreams and their interpretations. **311. Wher:** whether.

313. daun Pharao: Lord Pharaoh. Joseph correctly predicted the meaning of dreams both for him and for his butler and baker (Gen. 37, 40, and 41). **316. Who-so:** who-ever. **seke . . . remes:** search the history of various realms. **318. Cresus:** Croesus of Lydia, who according to legend was proud of his dream till his daughter told him that the tree signified the gallows. **319. nat:** not. **321. Andromacha:** Andromache. **Ectores:** Hector's. **322. lese:** lose. **324. lorn:** lost. **325. thilke:** that same. **327. nathelees:** nevertheless. **328. anon of:** immediately by. **329. to:** too. **330. ny:** near. **334. ne . . . stoor:** set no store on laxatives. **335. ben venymes:** are venomous. **336. hem . . . del:** them not at all. **337. stynte:** stop. **338. have I:** may I have. **343. also . . . principio:** as surely as "In the beginning (was the Word)," i.e., as surely as the gospel. **344. Mulier . . . confusio:** "Woman is man's ruin," a widely known Latin proverb carefully mistranslated by Chauntecleer in l. 346. **345. sentence:** meaning.

For that° oure perche is maad° so narwe,° allas,
I am so ful of joye and of solas° 350
That I deffye bothe swevene° and dreem."
　　And with that word he fley° doun fro the beem,
For it was day, and eke hise hennes alle.
And with a chuk he gan hem for to calle,
For he hadde founde a corn,° lay° in the yerd. 355
Real° he was; he was na moore aferd.°
He fethered Pertelote twenty tyme
And trad° as ofte er that it was pryme.°
He looketh as it were° a grym leoun,°
And on hise toos he rometh up and doun. 360
Hym deyned° nat to sette his foot to grounde.
He chukketh whan he hath a corn y-founde,
And to hym rennen thanne hise wyves alle.
Thus real as a prince is in his halle
Leve I this Chauntecleer in his pasture, 365
And after wol I telle his aventure.
　　Whan that the monthe in which the world bigan,
That highte° March, whan God first maked man,
Was complet, and passed were also,
Syn March bigan, thritty dayes and two, 370
Bifel° that Chauntecler in al his pryde,
Hise sevene wyves walkyng hym bisyde,
Caste up his eyen to the brighte sonne,
That in the signe of Taurus° hadde y-ronne 374
Twenty degrees and oon, and som-what moore,
And knew by kynde° and by noon oother loore
That it was pryme, and krew with blisful stevene.°
"The sonne," he seyde, "is clomben upon hevene
Fourty degrees and oon, and moore ywis.°
Madame Pertelote, my worldes blis, 380
Herkneth° thise blisful briddes, how they synge,
And se the fresshe floures how they sprynge.
Ful is myn herte of revel and solas."
But sodeynly hym fil° a sorweful cas,°
For evere the latter ende of joye is wo. 385
God woot that worldly joye is soone ago,°
And if a rethor° koude faire endite,°
He in a cronycle saufly myghte it write

As for a sovereyn notabilitee.°
Now every wys man, lat hym herkne° me; 390
This storie is also° trewe, I undertake,°
As is the book of *Launcelot de Lake,*°
That wommen holde in ful gret reverence.
Now wol I torne agayn to my sentence.°
　　A colfox° ful of sly iniquitee, 395
That in the grove hadde woned° yeres three,
By heigh ymaginacioun forncast,°
The same nyght thurgh-out the hegges brast°
Into the yerd ther Chauntecleer the faire
Was wont, and eek hise wyves, to repaire, 400
And in a bed of wortes° stille he lay
Til it was passed undren° of the day,
Waitynge his tyme on Chauntecleer to falle,
As gladly doon° thise homycides° alle
That in awayt liggen° to mordre men. 405
O false mordrour, lurkynge in thy den,
O newe Scariot,° newe Genyloun,°
False dissimilour,° O Greek Synoun,°
That broghtest Troye al outrely° to sorwe!
O Chauntecleer, acursed be that morwe° 410
That thow into the yerd flaugh° fro the bemes.
Thow were ful well y-warned by thy dremes
That thilke day was perilous to thee.
But what that God forwoot moot nedes° be
After° the opynyoun of certeyn clerkis.° 415
Witnesse on hym that any parfit clerk is,
That in scole is greet altercacioun
In this matere and greet disputisoun,°
And hath ben of an hundred thousand men.
But I ne kan nat bulte it to the bren° 420
As kan the holy doctour Augustyn,°

389. As . . . notabilitee: as a supreme observation. 390. herkne: hearken to. 391. also: as. undertake: vow. 392. Launcelot de Lake: an entirely fictitious romance concerning Lancelot, the lover of Guinevere, King Arthur's wife. 394. sentence: subject. 395. colfox: coal fox. 396. woned: lived. 397. heigh . . . forncast: divine knowledge foreordained. 398. hegges brast: hedges burst. 401. wortes: herbs. 402. undren: midmorning. 404. gladly doon: usually do. homycides: murderers. 405. in . . . liggen: lie in waiting. 407. Scariot: Judas Iscariot, who betrayed Christ. Genyloun: Ganelon, who betrayed Charlemagne's nephew Roland. 408. dissimilour: deceiver. Synoun: Sinon, who persuaded the Trojans to take the Greeks' wooden horse into Troy. 409. al outrely: utterly. 410. morwe: morning. 411. flaugh: flew. 414. forwoot . . . nedes: foreknows must needs. 415. After: according to. clerkis: scholars. 418. disputisoun: disputation. 420. I . . . bren: I can't sift it to the bran; i.e., I can't reach certainty in this much-disputed theological problem. (If God foreknows the future, to what extent has man free will?) 421. Augustyn: Saint Augustine of Hippo, who discussed the likelihood that man has "free choice" (l. 426) of action despite the infallibility of God's foreknowledge of future events.

349. For that: because. maad: made. narwe: narrow. 350. solas: pleasure. 351. swevene: vision. 352. fley: flew. 355. corn: grain of corn. lay: (which) lay. 356. Real: regal. na . . . aferd: no more afraid. 358. trad: trod (her). pryme: prime (9:00 A.M.). 359. looketh . . . were: looks like. leoun: lion. 361. Hym deyned: he deigned. 368. highte: is called. It was believed that the world was created in March. 371. Bifel: it befell. 374. Taurus: The date is May 3. (March, thirty days of April, and two days of May had passed.) 376. kynde: nature. 377. stevene: voice. 379. ywis: indeed. 381. Herkneth: listen to. 384. hym fil: befell him. cas: happening. 386. ago: gone. 387. rethor: rhetorician. endite: compose.

Or Boece,° or the bisshop Bradwardyn,°
Wheither that Goddes worthy forewityng°
Streyneth° me nedely° for to doon a thyng—
"Nedely" clepe° I symple necessitee—   425
Or ellis if fre choys be graunted me
To do that same thyng or do it noght,
Though God forwoot° it er that it was wroght;
Or if his wityng streyneth never a del°
But° by necessitee condicionel.   430
I wol nat han° to do of swich° matere.
My tale is of a cok, as ye may heere,
That took his conseil of his wyf with sorwe
To walken in the yerd upon that morwe
That he hadde met° the dreem that I yow tolde.
Wommens conseils ben ful ofte colde.°   436
Wommanes conseil broghte us first to wo
And made Adam fro Paradys to go,
Ther-as he was ful myrie and wel at ese.
But, for I noot° to whom it myghte displese   440
If I conseil of wommen wolde blame,
Passe over, for I seyde it in my game.°
Rede auctours° where they trete of swich matere,
And what they seyn° of wommen ye may heere.
Thise ben the cokkes wordes and nat myne;   445
I kan noon harm of no womman devyne.°

   Faire in the sond° to bathe hire myrily
Lith° Pertelote, and alle hir sustres by,
Agayn the sonne;° and Chauntecleer so free
Song myrier than the mermayde in the see,   450
For Phisiologus seithe sikerly°
How that they syngen wel and myrily.
   And so bifel that, as he caste his eye
Among the wortes° on a boterflye,
He was war° of this fox that lay ful lowe.   455

Nothyng ne liste hym thanne° for to crowe,
But cryde anon "Cok, cok," and up he sterte°
As man° that was affrayed° in his herte,
For naturelly° a beest desireth flee
Fro his contrarie,° if he may it see,   460
Though he nevere erst° hadde syn° it with his eye.
   This Chauntecleer, whan he gan hym espye,°
He wolde han fled but that the fox anon
Seyde, "Gentil sire, allas! Wher wol ye gon?
Be ye affrayed of me that am youre freend?   465
Now, certes, I were worse than a feend
If I to yow wolde° harm or vileynye.
I am nat come youre conseil for t' espye,°
But trewely the cause of my comynge
Was oonly for to herkne how that ye synge,   470
For trewely ye han as myrie a stevene°
As any aungel hath that is in hevene.
Ther-with ye han in musyk moore feelynge
Than hadde Boece° or any that kan synge.
My lord, youre fader—God his soule blesse!—
And eek youre moder, of hire gentillesse,°   476
Han in myn hous y-ben° to my greet ese.°
And, certes, sire, ful fayn° wolde I yow plese.
   "But, for° men speke of syngynge, I wol seye—
So mote I brouke° wel myne eyen tweye!—   480
Save yow I herde nevere man so synge
As dide youre fader in the morwenynge.
Certes, it was of herte,° al that he song.
And for to make his voys the moore strong,
He wolde so peyne hym° that with bothe hise eyen
He moste wynke,° so loude he wolde cryen,   486
And stonden on his tiptoon ther-with-al,
And strecche forth his nekke long and smal.
And eek he was of swich discrecioun
That ther nas no° man in no regioun   490
That hym in song or wisdom myghte passe.
I have wel rad° in Daun° Burnel the Asse,

422. Boece: Boethius, the author of the *Consolation of Philosophy,* who distinguished between the simple (l. 425) and the conditional (l. 430) necessity of man's actions. **Bradwardyn:** Archbishop Bradwardine of Canterbury (d. 1349), who lectured at Oxford on God's foreknowledge. **423. worthy forewityng:** excellent foreknowing. **424. Streyneth:** constrains. **nedely:** necessarily. **425. clepe:** call. **428. forwoot:** foreknows. **429. wityng . . . del:** knowing constrains not at all. **430. But:** except. **431. han:** have (anything). **of swich:** with such. **435. met:** dreamed. **436. colde:** fatal. **440. for I noot:** since I don't know. **442. in my game:** in jest. **443. auctours:** authors. **444. seyn:** say. **446. devyne:** imagine. **447. sond:** sand. **448. Lith:** lies. **449. Agayn . . . sonne:** in the sun. **451. Phisiologus . . . sikerly:** Physiologus says certainly. He was reputed to be the author of the first *Bestiary,* a compendium of lore about certain natural and supernatural creatures, including mermaids. The extreme popularity of its numerous adaptations arose less from the appended morals than from the fabulous marvels it recounted. **454. wortes:** plants. **455. war:** aware.

456. Nothyng . . . thanne: not at all did he wish then. **457. sterte:** sprang. **458. As man:** like someone. **affrayed:** frightened. **459. naturelly:** by nature. **460. contrarie:** opposite. Each thing and being was believed to have its contrary and to feel a natural antipathy to it. **461. erst:** before. **syn:** seen. **462. gan . . . espye:** noticed him. **467. wolde:** intended. **468. conseil . . . espye:** secret to discover. **471. stevene:** voice. **474. Boece:** Boethius also wrote a work entitled *On Music.* **476. gentillesse:** gentility. **477. y-ben:** been. **ese:** satisfaction. **478. fayn:** gladly. **479. for:** since. **480. mote I brouke:** may I use. **483. of herte:** hearty. **485. peyne hym:** strive. **486. moste wynke:** must shut (his eyes). **490. nas no:** was no. **492. rad:** read. **Daun:** *Master.* According to the twelfth-century poem, *Burnellus the Ass,* a young man threw a stone at a cock and broke its leg. Later, when he was to have been appointed to a benefice, the cock avenged itself by failing to crow in time to awaken him for the ordination.

Among his vers, how that ther was a cok,
For° a preestes sone yaf° hym a knok
Upon his leg, whil he was yong and nyce,°   495
He made hym for to lese° his benefice.
But, certeyn, ther nys no comparisoun
Bitwix the wisdom and discrecioun
Of youre fader and of his subtiltee.
Now syngeth, sire, for seinte° charitee!   500
Lat se, konne ye youre fader countrefete?"°
   This Chauntecleer hise wynges gan to bete
As man that koude his traysoun nat espie,°
So was he ravysshed with° his flaterie.
   Allas, ye lordes, many a fals flatour°   505
Is in youre court, and many a losengeour,°
That plesen° yow wel moore, by my feith,
Than he that soothfastnesse° unto yow seith.
Redeth Ecclesiaste of° flaterye.
Beth war,° ye lordes, of hir trecherye.   510
This Chauntecler stood hye upon his toos,
Strecchynge his nekke, and heeld hise eyen cloos,°
And gan to crowe loude for the nones.°
And daun Russell the fox stirte up atones,°
And by the gargat hente° Chauntecleer,   515
And on his bak toward the wode° hym beer,°
For yet ne was ther no man that hym sewed.°
   O destynee, that mayst nat ben eschewed!°
Allas that Chauntecler fleigh° fro the bemes!
Allas, his wif ne roghte nat° of dremes!   520
And on a Friday fil al this meschaunce.
   O Venus, that art goddesse of plesaunce,°
Syn that thy servant was this Chauntecleer,
And in thy servyce dide al his power
Moore for delit° than world to multiplie,   525
Why woldestow suffre° hym on thy day° to dye?
   O Gaufred,° deere maister soverayn,
That, whan thy worthy kyng Richard was slayn
With shot, compleynedest° his deth so soore,

Why ne hadde I now thy sentence° and thy loore°
The Friday for to chide, as diden ye?   531
For on a Friday, soothly,° slayn was he.
Thanne wolde I shewe yow how that I koude
   pleyne°
For Chauntecleres drede and for his peyne.
   Certes, swich cry ne lamentacioun   535
Was nevere of ladyes maad° whan Ylioun°
Was wonne, and Pirrus° with his streite swerd°
Whanne he hadde hent° kyng Priam by the berd
And slayn hym, as seith us *Eneydos,*°
As maden alle the hennes in the cloos°   540
Whan they hadde seyn° of Chauntecleer the sighte.
But sovereynly° dame Pertelote shrighte°
Ful louder than dide Hasdrubales° wyf
Whan that hire housbonde hadde lost his lyf
And that the Romayns hadden brend Cartage.°
She was so ful of torment and of rage   546
That wilfully° into the fyr she sterte°
And brende hirselven° with a stedefast herte.
   O woful hennes, right so cryden ye
As, whan that Nero brende the citee   550
Of Rome, cryden senatours wyves
For that° hir housbondes losten alle hire° lyves.
Withouten gilt this Nero hath hem slayn.
Now wol I turne to my tale agayn.
   The sely° widwe and eek hire doghtres two   555
Herden thise hennes crye and maken wo,
And out atte dores stirten they anon,
And syen° the fox toward the grove gon,
And bar° upon his bak the cok away,
And criden "Out! Harrow!" and "Weilaway!°   560
Ha, ha, the fox!" And after hym they ran,
And eek with staves° many another man.
Ran Colle oure dogge, and Talbot, and Gerland,
And Malkyn, with a distaf in hire hand.
Ran cow, and calf, and eek the verray hogges,   565
So fered° for the berkyng of the dogges
And showtynge° of the men and wommen eek.
They ronne so, hem thoughte hir herte breek.°

494. For: because. yaf: gave. 495. nyce: foolish. 496. lese: lose. 500. seinte: holy. 501. countrefete: imitate. 503. espie: perceive. 504. ravysshed with: overwhelmed by. 505. flatour: flatterer. 506. losengeour: deceiver. 507. plesen: please. 508. soothfastnesse: truth. 509. Ecclesiaste of: Ecclesiasticus on. 510. Beth war: beware. 512. cloos: closed. 513. nones: occasion. 514. stirte . . . atones: sprang up at once. 515. gargat hente: throat seized. 516. wode: wood. beer: bore. 517. sewed: pursued. 518. eschewed: avoided. 519. fleigh: flew. 520. ne . . . nat: took no heed. 522. plesaunce: pleasure. 525. delit: delight. 526. woldestow suffre: would you allow. thy day: Friday, the day of Venus. 527. Gaufred: Geoffrey de Vinsauf, who in his treatise on the composition of poetry offers as a sample of his highly rhetorical techniques an elegy for King Richard I, who was mortally wounded on a Friday. 529. compleynedest: lamented.

530. sentence: erudition. loore: learning. 532. soothly: truly. 533. pleyne: lament. 536. maad: made. Ylioun: Ilium (Troy). 537. Pirrus: Pyrrhus. streite swerd: drawn sword. 538. hent: seized. 539. seith . . . Eneydos: (the) *Aeneid* tells us. 540. cloos: enclosure. 541. seyn: seen. 542. sovereynly: especially. shrighte: shrieked. 543. Hasdrubales: Hasdrubal's. 545. brend Cartage: burned Carthage. 547. wilfully: voluntarily. sterte: leapt. 548. brende hirselven: burned herself. 552. For that: because. losten . . . hire: all lost their. 555. sely: poor. 558. syen: saw. 559. bar: carry (lit., carried). 560. Weilaway: alas. 562. staves: sticks. 566. fered: frightened. 567. showtynge: shouting. 568. hem . . . breek: they thought their heart would break.

They yelleden as fendes doon° in helle.
The dokes° cryden as men wolde hem quelle.°   570
The gees for feere flowen° over the trees.
Out of the hyve cam the swarm of bees.
So hydous° was the noyse, A, *benedicitee*,
Certes, he Jakke Straw and his meynee°
Ne made nevere shoutes half so shrille   575
Whan that they wolden any Flemyng kille
As thilke day was maad upon the fox.
Of bras they broghten bemes,° and of box,°
Of horn, of boon,° in whiche they blewe and
    powped,°
And ther-with-al they skryked,° and they howped.°
It semed as that° hevene sholde falle.   581
Now goode men, I prey yow, herkneth alle.
    Low, how Fortune turneth° sodeynly
The hope and pryde eek of hire enemy.
This cok that lay upon the foxes bak   585
In al his drede unto the fox he spak
And seyde, "Sire, if that I were as ye,
Yit sholde I seyn,° as wys God helpe me,
'Turneth agayn,° ye proude cherles° alle.
A verray pestilence upon yow falle.   590
Now I am come unto this wodes syde,
Maugree youre heed,° the cok shal here abyde.
I wol hym ete, in feith, and that anon.' "
    The fox answerde, "In feith, it shal be don."
And as he spak that word, al sodeynly   595
This cok brak° from his mouth delyverly,°
And hye upon a tree he fley anon.
And whan the fox say° that he was gon,
"Allas," quod he, "O Chauntecleer, allas!
I have to yow," quod he, "y-doon trespas°   600
In as muche as I maked yow aferd
Whan I you hente and broghte out the yerd.
But, sire, I dide it in no wikke° entente.
Com doun, and I shal telle yow what I mente.
I shal seye sooth to yow, God help me so."   605
    "Nay thanne," quod he, "I shrewe° us bothe
        two.

And first I shrewe myself, bothe blood and bones,
If thow bigile me any ofter° than ones.
Thow shalt namoore thurgh° thy flaterye
Do° me to synge and wynke with° myn eye,   610
For he that wynketh, whan he sholde see,
Al wilfully,° God lat hym nevere thee.'"°
    "Nay," quod the fox, "but God yeve° hym
        meschaunce°
That is so undiscreet of governaunce°
That jangleth° whan he sholde holde his pees."
    Lo, swich it is for to be recchelees,°   616
And necligent, and truste on flaterye.
    But ye that holden this tale a folye°
As of° a fox, or of a cok and hen,
Taketh the moralitee, goode men.   620
For Seint Poul° seith that al that writen is,
To oure doctryne° it is y-write,° ywis.°
Taketh the fruyt, and lat the chaf be stille.
Now goode God, if that it be thy wille,
As seith my lord, so make us alle goode men,   625
And brynge us to his heye blisse. Amen.

RICHARD BRINSLEY SHERIDAN
1751–1816

The School for Scandal

CHARACTERS

SIR PETER TEAZLE

SIR OLIVER SURFACE

JOSEPH SURFACE

CHARLES SURFACE

CRABTREE

SIR BENJAMIN BACKBITE

ROWLEY

MOSES

TRIP

SNAKE

CARELESS

SIR HARRY BUMPER

LADY TEAZLE

MARIA

LADY SNEERWELL

MRS. CANDOUR

GENTLEMEN, MAID, *and* SERVANTS

SCENE—*London.*

TIME—*Contemporary.*

PROLOGUE

WRITTEN BY MR. GARRICK°

A School for Scandal! tell me, I beseech you,
Needs there a school this modish art to teach you?
No need of lessons now, the knowing think;
We might as well be taught to eat and drink.   4
Caused by a dearth of scandal, should the vapors
Distress our fair ones—let them read the papers;
Their powerful mixtures such disorders hit;
Crave what you will—there's *quantum sufficit.*°
"Lord!" cries my Lady Wormwood (who loves
    tattle,
And puts much salt and pepper in her prattle), 10
Just ris'n at noon, all night at cards when threshing
Strong tea and scandal—"Bless me, how refreshing!

Give me the papers, Lisp—how bold and free!
    (*sips*)
Last night Lord L. (*sips*) *was caught with Lady D.*
For aching heads what charming sal volatile!°
    (*sips*)   15
If Mrs. B. will still continue flirting,
We hope she'll DRAW, *or we'll* UNDRAW *the curtain.*
Fine satire, poz—in public all abuse it,
But, by ourselves (*sips*), our praise we can't refuse
    it.
Now, Lisp, read you—there, at that dash and
    star."   20
"Yes, ma'am—*A certain lord had best beware,*
Who lives not twenty miles from Grosvenor Square;°
For should he Lady W. find willing,
Wormwood is bitter"—"Oh! that's me! the villain!
Throw it behind the fire, and never more   25
Let that vile paper come within my door."
Thus at our friends we laugh, who feel the dart;
To reach our feelings, we ourselves must smart.
Is our young bard so young, to think that he
Can stop the full spring-tide of calumny?   30
Knows he the world so little, and its trade?
Alas! the devil's sooner raised than laid.
So strong, so swift, the monster there's no gagging:
Cut Scandal's head off, still the tongue is wagging.
Proud of your smiles once lavishly bestowed,°   35
Again our young Don Quixote takes the road;
To show his gratitude he draws his pen,
And seeks this hydra, Scandal, in his den.
For your applause all perils he would through—
He'll fight—that's write—a cavalliero true,   40
Till every drop of blood—that's ink—is spilt for
    you.

ACT I

SCENE I. LADY SNEERWELL'*s house.*

[*Discovered,* LADY SNEERWELL *at her dressing-
table;* SNAKE *drinking chocolate.*]

LADY SNEERWELL The paragraphs, you say, Mr.
  Snake, were all inserted?

SNAKE They were, madam; and, as I copied them
  myself in a feigned hand, there can be no
  suspicion whence they came.

THE SCHOOL FOR SCANDAL: *Prologue.* **Garrick:** David
Garrick, famous eighteenth-century actor. **8. quantum
sufficit:** sufficient amount.

15. sal volatile: smelling salts. **22. Grosvenor Square:** the
fashionable residential quarter in the West End of London.
35. Proud . . . bestowed: i.e., for previous plays.

LADY SNEERWELL   Did you circulate the report of Lady Brittle's intrigue with Captain Boastall?

SNAKE   That's in as fine a train as your ladyship could wish. In the common course of things, I think it must reach Mrs. Clackitt's ears within four-and-twenty hours; and then, you know, the business is as good as done.

LADY SNEERWELL   Why, truly, Mrs. Clackitt has a very pretty talent, and a great deal of industry.

SNAKE   True, madam, and has been tolerably successful in her day. To my knowledge, she has been the cause of six matches being broken off and three sons disinherited, of four forced elopements and as many close confinements, nine separate maintenances and two divorces. Nay, I have more than once traced her causing a tête-à-tête in the *Town and Country Magazine*, when the parties, perhaps, had never seen each other's face before in the course of their lives.

LADY SNEERWELL   She certainly has talents, but her manner is gross.

SNAKE   'Tis very true. She generally designs well, has a free tongue and a bold invention; but her coloring is too dark and her outlines often extravagant. She wants that delicacy of tint and mellowness of sneer which distinguish your ladyship's scandal.

LADY SNEERWELL   You are partial, Snake.

SNAKE   Not in the least; everybody allows that Lady Sneerwell can do more with a word or look than many can with the most labored detail, even when they happen to have a little truth on their side to support it.

LADY SNEERWELL   Yes, my dear Snake; and I am no hypocrite to deny the satisfaction I reap from the success of my efforts. Wounded myself, in the early part of my life, by the envenomed tongue of slander, I confess I have since known no pleasure equal to the reducing others to the level of my own injured reputation.

SNAKE   Nothing can be more natural. But, Lady Sneerwell, there is one affair in which you have lately employed me, wherein, I confess, I am at a loss to guess your motives.

LADY SNEERWELL   I conceive you mean with respect to my neighbor, Sir Peter Teazle, and his family?

SNAKE   I do. Here are two young men to whom Sir Peter has acted as a kind of guardian since their father's death; the eldest possessing the most amiable character and universally well spoken of—the youngest, the most dissipated and extravagant young fellow in the kingdom, without friends or character: the former an avowed admirer of your ladyship, and apparently your favorite; the latter attached to Maria, Sir Peter's ward, and confessedly beloved by her. Now, on the face of these circumstances, it is utterly unaccountable to me why you, the widow of a city knight, with a good jointure,[1] should not close with the passion of a man of such character and expectations as Mr. Surface; and more so, why you should be so uncommonly earnest to destroy the mutual attachment subsisting between his brother Charles and Maria.

LADY SNEERWELL   Then, at once to unravel this mystery, I must inform you that love has no share whatever in the intercourse between Mr. Surface and me.

SNAKE   No!

LADY SNEERWELL   His real attachment is to Maria, or her fortune; but, finding in his brother a favored rival, he has been obliged to mask his pretensions and profit by my assistance.

SNAKE   Yet still I am more puzzled why you should interest yourself in his success.

LADY SNEERWELL   How dull you are! Cannot you surmise the weakness which I hitherto, through shame, have concealed even from you? Must I confess that Charles—that libertine, that extravagant, that bankrupt in fortune and reputation—that he it is for whom I'm thus anxious and malicious, and to gain whom I would sacrifice everything?

SNAKE   Now, indeed, your conduct appears consistent; but how came you and Mr. Surface so confidential?

LADY SNEERWELL   For our mutual interest. I have found him out a long time since. I know him to be artful, selfish, and malicious—in short, a sentimental knave; while with Sir Peter, and indeed with all his acquaintance, he passes for a youthful miracle of prudence, good sense, and benevolence.

SNAKE   Yes; yet Sir Peter vows he has not his equal in England, and, above all, he praises him as a man of sentiment.

LADY SNEERWELL   True; and with the assistance

Act I, scene i.   **1. jointure:** widow's inheritance from her husband.

of his sentiment and hypocrisy he has brought Sir Peter entirely into his interest with regard to Maria, while poor Charles has no friend in the house—though, I fear, he has a powerful one in Maria's heart, against whom we must direct our schemes.   [*Enter* SERVANT.]

SERVANT Mr. Surface.

LADY SNEERWELL Show him up. [*Exit* SERVANT.]
                              [*Enter* JOSEPH SURFACE.]

JOSEPH My dear Lady Sneerwell, how do you do today? Mr. Snake, your most obedient.

LADY SNEERWELL Snake has just been rallying me on our mutual attachment, but I have informed him of our real views. You know how useful he has been to us, and, believe me, the confidence is not ill placed.

JOSEPH Madam, it is impossible for me to suspect a man of Mr. Snake's sensibility and discernment.

LADY SNEERWELL Well, well, no compliments now; but tell me when you saw your mistress, Maria—or, what is more material to me, your brother.

JOSEPH I have not seen either since I left you, but I can inform you that they never meet. Some of your stories have taken a good effect on Maria.

LADY SNEERWELL Ah, my dear Snake! the merit of this belongs to you. But do your brother's distresses increase?

JOSEPH Every hour. I am told he has had another execution[2] in the house yesterday. In short, his dissipation and extravagance exceed anything I have ever heard of.

LADY SNEERWELL Poor Charles!

JOSEPH True, madam; notwithstanding his vices, one can't help feeling for him. Poor Charles! I'm sure I wish it were in my power to be of any essential service to him; for the man who does not share in the distresses of a brother, even though merited by his own misconduct, deserves—

LADY SNEERWELL O lud! you are going to be moral, and forget that you are among friends.

JOSEPH Egad, that's true! I'll keep that sentiment till I see Sir Peter. However, it is certainly a charity to rescue Maria from such a libertine, who, if he is to be reclaimed, can be so only by a person of your ladyship's superior accomplishments and understanding.

SNAKE I believe, Lady Sneerwell, here's company

2. **execution:** a repossession or lien on goods for debt.

coming. I'll go and copy the letter I mentioned to you. Mr. Surface, your most obedient.

JOSEPH Sir, your very devoted.   [*Exit* SNAKE.]
Lady Sneerwell, I am very sorry you have put any farther confidence in that fellow.

LADY SNEERWELL Why so?

JOSEPH I have lately detected him in frequent conference with old Rowley, who was formerly my father's steward, and has never, you know, been a friend of mine.

LADY SNEERWELL And do you think he would betray us?

JOSEPH Nothing more likely. Take my word for 't, Lady Sneerwell, that fellow hasn't virtue enough to be faithful even to his own villainy.—Ah, Maria!   [*Enter* MARIA.]

LADY SNEERWELL Maria, my dear, how do you do? What's the matter?

MARIA Oh! there's that disagreeable lover of mine, Sir Benjamin Backbite, has just called at my guardian's with his odious uncle, Crabtree; so I slipped out and ran hither to avoid them.

LADY SNEERWELL Is that all?

JOSEPH If my brother Charles had been of the party, madam, perhaps you would not have been so much alarmed.

LADY SNEERWELL Nay, now you are severe, for I dare swear the truth of the matter is, Maria heard *you* were here.—But, my dear, what has Sir Benjamin done, that you would avoid him so?

MARIA Oh, he has done nothing—but 'tis for what he has said: his conversation is a perpetual libel on all his acquaintance.

JOSEPH Aye, and the worst of it is, there is no advantage in not knowing him; for he'll abuse a stranger just as soon as his best friend, and his uncle's as bad.

LADY SNEERWELL Nay, but we should make allowance; Sir Benjamin is a wit and a poet.

MARIA For my part, I confess, madam, wit loses its respect with me when I see it in company with malice. What do you think, Mr. Surface?

JOSEPH Certainly, madam; to smile at the jest which plants a thorn in another's breast is to become a principal in the mischief.

LADY SNEERWELL Pshaw! there's no possibility of being witty without a little ill nature. The malice of a good thing is the barb that makes it stick. What's your opinion, Mr. Surface?

JOSEPH   To be sure, madam; that conversation where the spirit of raillery is suppressed, will ever appear tedious and insipid.

MARIA   Well, I'll not debate how far scandal may be allowable, but in a man, I am sure, it is always contemptible. We have pride, envy, rivalship, and a thousand motives to depreciate each other, but the male slanderer must have the cowardice of a woman before he can traduce one.

[*Enter* SERVANT.]

SERVANT   Madam, Mrs. Candour is below, and if your ladyship's at leisure, will leave her carriage.

LADY SNEERWELL   Beg her to walk in.

[*Exit* SERVANT.]

Now, Maria, here is a character to your taste, for though Mrs. Candour is a little talkative, everybody allows her to be the best-natured and best sort of woman.

MARIA   Yes, with a very gross affectation of good nature and benevolence, she does more mischief than the direct malice of old Crabtree.

JOSEPH   I' faith that's true, Lady Sneerwell; whenever I hear the current running against the characters of my friends, I never think them in such danger as when Candour undertakes their defence.

LADY SNEERWELL   Hush—here she is!

[*Enter* MRS. CANDOUR]

MRS. CANDOUR   My dear Lady Sneerwell, how have you been this century?—Mr. Surface, what news do you hear?—though indeed it is no matter, for I think one hears nothing else but scandal.

JOSEPH   Just so, indeed, ma'am.

MRS. CANDOUR   Oh, Maria! child—what, is the whole affair off between you and Charles? His extravagance, I presume—the town talks of nothing else.

MARIA   Indeed! I am very sorry, ma'am, the town is not better employed.

MRS. CANDOUR   True, true, child, but there's no stopping people's tongues. I own I was hurt to hear it, as I indeed was to learn from the same quarter that your guardian, Sir Peter, and Lady Teazle have not agreed lately as well as could be wished.

MARIA   'Tis strangely impertinent for people to busy themselves so.

MRS. CANDOUR   Very true, child, but what's to be done? People will talk—there's no preventing it.

Why, it was but yesterday I was told that Miss Gadabout had eloped with Sir Filigree Flirt. But, Lord! there's no minding what one hears—though, to be sure, I had this from very good authority.

MARIA   Such reports are highly scandalous.

MRS. CANDOUR   So they are, child—shameful, shameful! But the world is so censorious, no character escapes. Lord, now who would have suspected your friend, Miss Prim, of an indiscretion? Yet such is the ill-nature of people, that they say her uncle stopped her last week, just as she was stepping into the York diligence[3] with her dancing-master.

MARIA   I'll answer for 't there are no grounds for that report.

MRS. CANDOUR   Ah, no foundation in the world, I dare swear; no more, probably, than for the story circulated last month of Mrs. Festino's affair with Colonel Cassino—though, to be sure, that matter was never rightly cleared up.

JOSEPH   The license of invention some people take is monstrous, indeed.

MARIA   'Tis so; but in my opinion those who report such things are equally culpable.

MRS. CANDOUR   To be sure they are; tale-bearers are as bad as the tale-makers—'tis an old observation, and a very true one: but what's to be done, as I said before? How will you prevent people from talking? Today, Mrs. Clackitt assured me, Mr. and Mrs. Honeymoon were at last become mere man and wife, like the rest of their acquaintance. She likewise hinted that a certain widow, in the next street, had got rid of her dropsy and recovered her shape in a most surprising manner. And at the same time Miss Tattle, who was by, affirmed that Lord Buffalo had discovered his lady at a house of no extraordinary fame; and that Sir H. Bouquet and Tom Saunter were to measure swords on a similar provocation.—But Lord, do you think I would report these things! No, no! tale-bearers, as I said before, are just as bad as the tale-makers.

JOSEPH   Ah! Mrs. Candour, if everybody had your forbearance and good nature!

MRS. CANDOUR   I confess, Mr. Surface, I cannot bear to hear people attacked behind their backs; and when ugly circumstances come out against

3. **York diligence:** stagecoach.

our acquaintance, I own I always love to think the best. By-the-by, I hope 'tis not true that your brother is absolutely ruined?

JOSEPH   I am afraid his circumstances are very bad indeed, ma'am.

MRS. CANDOUR   Ah! I heard so—but you must tell him to keep up his spirits: everybody almost is in the same way—Lord Spindle, Sir Thomas Splint, Captain Quinze, and Mr. Nickitt—all up, I hear, within this week; so, if Charles is undone, he'll find half his acquaintance ruined too, and that, you know, is a consolation.

JOSEPH   Doubtless, ma'am—a very great one.

[*Enter* SERVANT.]

SERVANT   Mr. Crabtree and Sir Benjamin Backbite.   [*Exit* SERVANT.]

LADY SNEERWELL   So, Maria, you see your lover pursues you: positively, you shan't escape.

[*Enter* CRABTREE *and* SIR BENJAMIN BACKBITE.]

CRABTREE   Lady Sneerwell, I kiss your hand. Mrs. Candour, I don't believe you are acquainted with my nephew. Sir Benjamin Backbite? Egad, ma'am, he has a pretty wit, and is a pretty poet too; isn't he, Lady Sneerwell?

SIR BENJAMIN   Oh, fie, uncle!

CRABTREE   Nay, egad, it's true; I back him at a rebus[4] or a charade against the best rhymer in the kingdom. Has your ladyship heard the epigram he wrote last week on Lady Frizzle's feather catching fire?—Do, Benjamin, repeat it, or the charade you made last night extempore at Mrs. Drowzie's conversazione. Come now; your first is the name of a fish, your second a great naval commander, and—

SIR BENJAMIN   Uncle, now—prithee—

CRABTREE   I' faith, ma'am, 'twould surprise you to hear how ready he is at all these fine sort of things.

LADY SNEERWELL   I wonder, Sir Benjamin, you never publish anything.

SIR BENJAMIN   To say truth, ma'am, 'tis very vulgar to print; and as my little productions are mostly satires and lampoons on particular people, I find they circulate more by giving copies in confidence to the friends of the parties. However, I have some love elegies which, when favored with this lady's smiles, I mean to give the public.

[*Turning to* MARIA.]

CRABTREE   [*To* MARIA]   'Fore Heaven, ma'am,

4. rebus: game of making riddles.

they'll immortalize you!—you will be handed down to posterity, like Petrarch's Laura, or Waller's Sacharissa.[5]

SIR BENJAMIN   Yes, madam, I think you will like them when you shall see them on a beautiful quarto page where a neat rivulet of text shall meander through a meadow of margin. 'Fore Gad, they will be the most elegant things of their kind!

CRABTREE   But, ladies, that's true—have you heard the news?

MRS. CANDOUR   What, sir, do you mean the report of—

CRABTREE   No, ma'am, that's not it.—Miss Nicely is going to be married to her own footman.

MRS. CANDOUR   Impossible!

CRABTREE   Ask Sir Benjamin.

SIR BENJAMIN   'Tis very true, ma'am; everything is fixed, and the wedding liveries bespoke.

CRABTREE   Yes—and they do say there were pressing reasons for it.

LADY SNEERWELL   Why, I have heard something of this before.

MRS. CANDOUR   It can't be—and I wonder anyone should believe such a story of so prudent a lady as Miss Nicely.

SIR BENJAMIN   O lud! ma'am, that's the very reason 'twas believed at once. She has always been so cautious and so reserved that everybody was sure there was some reason for it at bottom.

MRS. CANDOUR   Why, to be sure, a tale of scandal is as fatal to the credit of a prudent lady of her stamp as a fever is generally to those of the strongest constitutions. But there is a sort of puny, sickly reputation that is always ailing, yet will outlive the robuster characters of a hundred prudes.

SIR BENJAMIN   True, madam, there are valetudinarians in reputation as well as constitution, who, being conscious of their weak part, avoid the least breath of air and supply their want of stamina by care and circumspection.

MRS. CANDOUR   Well, but this may be all a mistake. You know, Sir Benjamin, very trifling circumstances often give rise to the most injurious tales.

5. like . . . Sacharissa: absurd comparison of the ladies addressed in the sonnet sequences of Petrarch (1304–74) and Waller (1607–87), suggesting that the two poets are equivalent.

CRABTREE That they do, I'll be sworn, ma'am. Did you ever hear how Miss Piper came to lose her lover and her character last summer at Tunbridge?—Sir Benjamin, you remember it?

SIR BENJAMIN Oh, to be sure!—the most whimsical circumstance.

LADY SNEERWELL How was it, pray?

CRABTREE Why, one evening, at Mrs. Ponto's assembly, the conversation happened to turn on the breeding Nova Scotia sheep in this country. Says a young lady in company, "I have known instances of it; for, Miss Letitia Piper, a first cousin of mine, had a Nova Scotia sheep that produced her twins." "What!" cries the Lady Dowager Dundizzy (who you know is as deaf as a post), "has Miss Piper had twins?" This mistake, as you may imagine, threw the whole company into a fit of laughter. However, 'twas the next morning everywhere reported and in a few days believed by the whole town, that Miss Letitia Piper had actually been brought to bed of a fine boy and girl; and in less than a week there were some people who could name the father and the farmhouse where the babies were put to nurse.

LADY SNEERWELL Strange, indeed!

CRABTREE Matter of fact, I assure you. O lud; Mr. Surface, pray, is it true that your uncle, Sir Oliver, is coming home?

JOSEPH Not that I know of, indeed, sir.

CRABTREE He has been in the East Indies a long time. You can scarcely remember him, I believe. Sad comfort, whenever he returns, to hear how your brother has gone on!

JOSEPH Charles has been imprudent, sir, to be sure, but I hope no busy people have already prejudiced Sir Oliver against him. He may reform.

SIR BENJAMIN To be sure he may. For my part, I never believed him to be so utterly void of principle as people say, and, though he has lost all his friends, I am told nobody is better spoken of by the Jews.

CRABTREE That's true, egad, nephew. If the Old Jewry[6] was a ward, I believe Charles would be an alderman; no man more popular there, 'fore Gad! I hear he pays as many annuities as the

Irish tontine,[7] and that, whenever he is sick, they have prayers for the recovery of his health in all the synagogues.

SIR BENJAMIN Yet no man lives in greater splendor. They tell me, when he entertains his friends he will sit down to dinner with a dozen of his own securities, have a score of tradesmen waiting in the antechamber, and an officer[8] behind every guest's chair.

JOSEPH This may be entertainment to you, gentlemen, but you pay very little regard to the feelings of a brother.

MARIA [Aside] Their malice is intolerable!— [Aloud.] Lady Sneerwell, I must wish you a good morning; I'm not very well. [Exit MARIA.]

MRS. CANDOUR Oh, dear! she changes color very much.

LADY SNEERWELL Do, Mrs, Candour, follow her; she may want your assistance.

MRS. CANDOUR That I will, with all my soul, ma'am. Poor dear girl, who knows what her situation may be! [Exit MRS. CANDOUR.]

LADY SNEERWELL 'Twas nothing but that she could not bear to hear Charles reflected on, notwithstanding their difference.

SIR BENJAMIN The young lady's penchant is obvious.

CRABTREE But, Benjamin, you must not give up the pursuit for that; follow her and put her into good humor. Repeat her some of your own verses. Come, I'll assist you.

SIR BENJAMIN Mr. Surface, I did not mean to hurt you, but depend on 't your brother is utterly undone.

CRABTREE O lud, aye! undone as ever man was— can't raise a guinea.

SIR BENJAMIN And everything sold, I'm told, that was movable.

CRABTREE I have seen one that was at his house. Not a thing left but some empty bottles that were overlooked, and the family pictures, which I believe are framed in the wainscots.

SIR BENJAMIN [Going] And I'm very sorry also to hear some bad stories against him.

CRABTREE Oh, he has done many mean things, that's certain.

SIR BENJAMIN [Going] But, however, as he's your brother—

---

6. **Old Jewry:** section of London formerly inhabited by Jews.

7. **as many . . . tontine:** as much interest on his debts as the Irish pay to absentee English landlords. 8. **securities, officer:** servants.

CRABTREE We'll tell you all another opportunity.

[*Exeunt* CRABTREE *and* SIR BENJAMIN.]

LADY SNEERWELL Ha! ha! 'tis very hard for them to leave a subject they have not quite run down.

JOSEPH And I believe the abuse was no more acceptable to your ladyship than Maria.

LADY SNEERWELL I doubt[9] her affections are farther engaged than we imagine. But the family are to be here this evening, so you may as well dine where you are and we shall have an opportunity of observing farther; in the meantime, I'll go and plot mischief and you shall study sentiment.   [*Exeunt.*]

SCENE II. *A room in* SIR PETER TEAZLE'*s House.*

[*Enter* SIR PETER.]

SIR PETER When an old bachelor marries a young wife, what is he to expect? 'Tis now six months since Lady Teazle made me the happiest of men —and I have been the most miserable dog ever since. We tifted a little going to church, and fairly quarrelled before the bells had done ringing. I was more than once nearly choked with gall during the honeymoon, and had lost all comfort in life before my friends had done wishing me joy. Yet I chose with caution—a girl bred wholly in the country, who never knew luxury beyond one silk gown nor dissipation above the annual gala of a race ball. Yet she now plays her part in all the extravagant fopperies of the fashion and the town with as ready a grace as if she never had seen a bush or a grass-plot out of Grosvenor Square! I am sneered at by all my acquaintance and paragraphed in the newspapers. She dissipates my fortune and contradicts all my humors; yet the worst of it is, I doubt I love her, or I should never bear all this. However, I'll never be weak enough to own it.   [*Enter* ROWLEY.]

ROWLEY Oh! Sir Peter, your servant; how is it with you, sir?

SIR PETER Very bad, Master Rowley, very bad. I meet with nothing but crosses and vexations.

ROWLEY What can have happened to trouble you since yesterday?

SIR PETER A good question to a married man!

9. doubt: suspect.

ROWLEY Nay, I'm sure your lady, Sir Peter, can't be the cause of your uneasiness.

SIR PETER Why, has anybody told you she was dead?

ROWLEY Come, come, Sir Peter, you love her, notwithstanding your tempers don't exactly agree.

SIR PETER But the fault is entirely hers, Master Rowley. I am, myself, the sweetest-tempered man alive, and hate a teasing temper; and so I tell her a hundred times a day.

ROWLEY Indeed!

SIR PETER Aye; and what is very extraordinary, in all our disputes she is always in the wrong. But Lady Sneerwell and the set she meets at her house encourage the perverseness of her disposition. Then, to complete my vexation, Maria, my ward, whom I ought to have the power of a father over, is determined to turn rebel too, and absolutely refuses the man whom I have long resolved on for her husband—meaning, I suppose, to bestow herself on his profligate brother.

ROWLEY You know, Sir Peter, I have always taken the liberty to differ with you on the subject of these two young gentlemen. I only wish you may not be deceived in your opinion of the elder. For Charles, my life on 't! he will retrieve his errors yet. Their worthy father, once my honored master, was, at his years, nearly as wild a spark; yet when he died, he did not leave a more benevolent heart to lament his loss.

SIR PETER You are wrong, Master Rowley. On their father's death, you know, I acted as a kind of guardian to them both till their uncle Sir Oliver's liberality gave them an early independence; of course, no person could have more opportunities of judging of their hearts, and I was never mistaken in my life. Joseph is indeed a model for the young men of the age. He is a man of sentiment and acts up to the *sentiments* he professes; but for the other, take my word for 't, if he had any grain of virtue by descent, he has dissipated it with the rest of his inheritance. Ah! my old friend, Sir Oliver, will be deeply mortified when he finds how part of his bounty has been misapplied.

ROWLEY I am sorry to find you so violent against the young man, because this may be the most critical period of his fortune. I came hither with news that will surprise you.

SIR PETER   What! let me hear.

ROWLEY   Sir Oliver *is* arrived and at this moment in town.

SIR PETER   How! you astonish me! I thought you did not expect him this month.

ROWLEY   I did not, but his passage has been remarkably quick.

SIR PETER   Egad, I shall rejoice to see my old friend. 'Tis fifteen years since we met. We have had many a day together. But does he still enjoin us not to inform his nephews of his arrival?

ROWLEY   Most strictly. He means before it is known to make some trial of their dispositions.

SIR PETER   Ah! there needs no art to discover their merits—he shall have his way; but pray, does he know I am married?

ROWLEY   Yes, and will soon wish you joy.

SIR PETER   What, as we drink health to a friend in a consumption! Ah! Oliver will laugh at me. We used to rail at matrimony together, but he has been steady to his text. Well, he must be soon at my house, though—I'll instantly give orders for his reception. But, Master Rowley, don't drop a word that Lady Teazle and I ever disagree.

ROWLEY   By no means.

SIR PETER   For I should never be able to stand Noll's jokes; so I'd have him think, Lord forgive me! that we are a very happy couple.

ROWLEY   I understand you; but then you must be very careful not to differ while he is in the house with you.

SIR PETER   Egad, and so we must—and that's impossible. Ah! Master Rowley, when an old bachelor marries a young wife, he deserves—no —the crime carries its punishment along with it.

[*Exeunt.*]

ACT II

SCENE I.   *A room in* SIR PETER TEAZLE'*s house.*

[*Enter* SIR PETER *and* LADY TEAZLE.]

SIR PETER   Lady Teazle, Lady Teazle, I'll not bear it!

LADY TEAZLE   Sir Peter, Sir Peter, you may bear it or not, as you please; but I ought to have my own way in everything and what's more, I will too. What! though I was educated in the country, I know very well that women of fashion in

London are accountable to nobody after they are married.

SIR PETER   Very well, ma'am, very well; so a husband is to have no influence, no authority?

LADY TEAZLE   Authority! No, to be sure. If you wanted authority over me, you should have adopted me, and not married me: I am sure you were old enough.

SIR PETER   Old enough—aye, there it is. Well, well, Lady Teazle, though my life may be made unhappy by your temper, I'll not be ruined by your extravagance!

LADY TEAZLE   My extravagance! I'm sure I'm not more extravagant than a woman of fashion ought to be.

SIR PETER   No, no, madam, you shall throw away no more sums on such unmeaning luxury. 'Slife! to spend as much to furnish your dressing-room with flowers in winter as would suffice to turn the Pantheon[1] into a greenhouse, and give a *fête champêtre*[2] at Christmas.

LADY TEAZLE   And am I to blame, Sir Peter, because flowers are dear in cold weather? You should find fault with the climate, and not with me. For my part, I'm sure I wish it was spring all the year round and that roses grew under our feet.

SIR PETER   Oons! madam—if you had been born to this, I shouldn't wonder at your talking thus; but you forget what your situation was when I married you.

LADY TEAZLE   No, no, I don't; 'twas a very disagreeable one, or I should never have married you.

SIR PETER   Yes, yes, madam, you were then in somewhat a humbler style—the daughter of a plain country squire. Recollect, Lady Teazle, when I saw you first sitting at your tambour,[3] in a pretty figured linen gown, with a bunch of keys at your side, your hair combed smooth over a roll, and your apartment hung round with fruits in worsted of your own working.

LADY TEAZLE   Oh, yes! I remember it very well, and a curious life I led—my daily occupation to inspect the dairy, superintend the poultry, make extracts from the family receipt-book, and comb my aunt Deborah's lapdog.

Act II, scene i.   **1. Pantheon:** fashionable pleasure garden in London. **2. fete champetre:** garden party. **3. tambour:** embroidery frame.

SIR PETER   Yes, yes, ma'am, 'twas so indeed.

LADY TEAZLE   And then, you know, my evening amusements! to draw patterns for ruffles, which I had not materials to make up; to play Pope Joan[4] with the curate; to read a sermon to my aunt; or to be stuck down to an old spinet to strum my father to sleep after a fox-chase.

SIR PETER   I am glad you have so good a memory. Yes, madam, these were the recreations I took you from; but now you must have your coach—vis-à-vis[5]—and three powdered footmen before your chair; and, in the summer, a pair of white cats[6] to draw you to Kensington Gardens. No recollection, I suppose, when you were content to ride double, behind the butler, on a docked coach-horse.

LADY TEAZLE   No—I swear I never did that. I deny the butler and the coach-horse.

SIR PETER   This, madam, was your situation; and what have I done for you? I have made you a woman of fashion, of fortune, of rank—in short, I have made you my wife.

LADY TEAZLE   Well, then, and there is but one thing more you can make me to add to the obligation, and that is—

SIR PETER   My widow, I suppose?

LADY TEAZLE   Hem! hem!

SIR PETER   I thank you, madam—but don't flatter yourself; for, though your ill conduct may disturb my peace, it shall never break my heart, I promise you: however, I am equally obliged to you for the hint.

LADY TEAZLE   Then why will you endeavor to make yourself so disagreeable to me and thwart me in every little elegant expense?

SIR PETER   'Slife, madam, I say, had you any of these little elegant expenses when you married me?

LADY TEAZLE   Lud, Sir Peter! would you have me be out of the fashion?

SIR PETER   The fashion, indeed! what had you to do with the fashion before you married me?

LADY TEAZLE   For my part, I should think you would like to have your wife thought a woman of taste.

SIR PETER   Aye—there again—taste! Zounds! madam, you had no taste when you married me!

LADY TEAZLE   That's very true, indeed, Sir Peter; and, after having married you, I should never pretend to taste again, I allow. But now, Sir Peter, if we have finished our daily jangle, I presume I may go to my engagement at Lady Sneerwell's.

SIR PETER   Aye, there's another precious circumstance—a charming set of acquaintance you have made there!

LADY TEAZLE   Nay, Sir Peter, they are all people of rank and fortune, and remarkably tenacious of reputation.

SIR PETER   Yes, egad, they are tenacious of reputation with a vengeance, for they don't choose anybody should have a character but themselves! Such a crew! Ah! many a wretch has rid on a hurdle who has done less mischief than these utterers of forged tales, coiners of scandal, and clippers of reputation.

LADY TEAZLE   What, would you restrain the freedom of speech?

SIR PETER   Ah! they have made you just as bad as any one of the society.

LADY TEAZLE   Why, I believe I do bear a part with a tolerable grace. But I vow, I bear no malice against the people I abuse; when I say an ill-natured thing, 'tis out of pure good humor, and I take it for granted they deal exactly in the same manner with me. But Sir Peter, you know you promised to come to Lady Sneerwell's too.

SIR PETER   Well, well, I'll call in, just to look after my own character.

LADY TEAZLE   Then, indeed, you must make haste after me, or you'll be too late. So good-by to ye.

[*Exit* LADY TEAZLE.]

SIR PETER   So—I have gained much by my intended expostulation! Yet with what a charming air she contradicts everything I say, and how pleasingly she shows her contempt for my authority! Well, though I can't make her love me, there is great satisfaction in quarreling with her, and I think she never appears to such advantage as when she is doing everything in her power to plague me.

[*Exit.*]

SCENE II. *A room at* LADY SNEERWELL'S *house.*

[*Enter* LADY SNEERWELL, MRS. CANDOUR, CRABTREE, SIR BENJAMIN BACKBITE, *and* JOSEPH SURFACE.]

---

4. **Pope Joan:** card game. **5. vis-a-vis:** with seats facing each other for conversation. **6. white cats:** five horses.

LADY SNEERWELL   Nay, positively, we will hear it.

JOSEPH   Yes, yes, the epigram, by all means.

SIR BENJAMIN   Oh, plague on 't, uncle! 'tis mere nonsense.

CRABTREE   No, no; 'fore Gad, very clever for an extempore!

SIR BENJAMIN   But ladies, you should be acquainted with the circumstance. You must know that one day last week, as Lady Betty Curricle was taking the dust in Hyde Park, in a sort of duodecimo phaeton,[1] she desired me to write some verses on her ponies; upon which, I took out my pocketbook, and in one moment produced the following:

> Sure never were seen two such beautiful ponies;
> Other horses are clowns, but these macaronies:[2]
> To give them this title I'm sure can't be wrong,
> Their legs are so slim, and their tails are so long.

CRABTREE   There, ladies, done in the smack of a whip, and on horseback too.

JOSEPH   A very Phoebus,[3] mounted—indeed, Sir Benjamin!

SIR BENJAMIN   Oh! dear, sir! trifles—trifles.

[*Enter* LADY TEAZLE *and* MARIA.]

MRS. CANDOUR   I must have a copy.

LADY SNEERWELL   Lady Teazle, I hope we shall see Sir Peter?

LADY TEAZLE   I believe he'll wait on your ladyship presently.

LADY SNEERWELL   Maria, my love, you look grave. Come, you shall sit down to piquet with Mr. Surface.

MARIA   I take very little pleasure in cards—however, I'll do as you please.

LADY TEAZLE   [*Aside*] I am surprised Mr. Surface should sit down with her; I thought he would have embraced this opportunity of speaking to me before Sir Peter came.

MRS. CANDOUR   Now, I'll die, but you are so scandalous, I'll forswear your society.

LADY TEAZLE   What's the matter, Mrs. Candour?

MRS. CANDOUR   They'll not allow our friend Miss Vermilion to be handsome.

LADY SNEERWELL   Oh, surely she is a pretty woman.

CRABTREE   I am very glad you think so, ma'am.

MRS. CANDOUR   She has a charming fresh color.

LADY TEAZLE   Yes, when it is fresh put on.

Scene ii. **1. phaeton:** light carriage. **2. macaronies:** fops, dandies. **3. Phoebus:** Phoebus Apollo, the sun god.

MRS. CANDOUR   Oh, fie! I'll swear her color is natural; I have seen it come and go.

LADY TEAZLE   I dare swear you have, ma'am; it goes off at night and comes again in the morning.

SIR BENJAMIN   True, ma'am; it not only comes and goes, but what's more, egad, her maid can fetch and carry it!

MRS. CANDOUR   Ha! ha! ha! how I hate to hear you talk so! But surely, now, her sister *is*, or *was*, very handsome.

CRABTREE   Who? Mrs. Evergreen? O Lord! she's six-and-fifty if she's an hour!

MRS. CANDOUR   Now positively you wrong her; fifty-two or fifty-three is the utmost—and I don't think she looks more.

SIR BENJAMIN   Ah! there's no judging by her looks unless one could see her face.

LADY SNEERWELL   Well, well, if Mrs. Evergreen *does* take some pains to repair the ravages of time, you must allow she effects it with great ingenuity; and surely that's better than the careless manner in which the widow Ochre chalks her wrinkles.

SIR BENJAMIN   Nay now, Lady Sneerwell, you are severe upon the widow. Come, come, 'tis not that she paints so ill—but when she has finished her face, she joins it on so badly to her neck that she looks like a mended statue, in which the connoisseur may see at once that the head is modern, though the trunk's antique.

CRABTREE   Ha! ha! ha! Well said, nephew!

MRS. CANDOUR   Ha! ha! ha! Well, you make me laugh; but I vow I hate you for it. What do you think of Miss Simper?

SIR BENJAMIN   Why, she has very pretty teeth.

LADY TEAZLE   Yes, and on that account, when she is neither speaking nor laughing (which very seldom happens), she never absolutely shuts her mouth, but leaves it always on ajar, as it were—thus.   [*Shows her teeth.*]

MRS. CANDOUR   How can you be so ill-natured?

LADY TEAZLE   Nay, I allow even that's better than the pains Mrs. Prim takes to conceal her losses in front. She draws her mouth till it positively resembles the aperture of a poor's-box, and all her words appear to slide out edgewise as it were—thus: "How do you do, madam? Yes, madam."

LADY SNEERWELL   Very well, Lady Teazle; I see you can be a little severe.

LADY TEAZLE In defense of a friend, it is but justice. But here comes Sir Peter to spoil our pleasantry.   [*Enter* SIR PETER TEAZLE.]

SIR PETER Ladies, your most obedient—[*Aside*] Mercy on me, here is the whole set! a character dead at every word,[4] I suppose.

MRS. CANDOUR I am rejoiced you are come, Sir Peter. They have been so censorious—and Lady Teazle as bad as anyone.

SIR PETER That must be very distressing to *you*, Mrs. Candour, I dare swear.

MRS. CANDOUR Oh, they will allow good qualities to nobody—not even good nature to our friend Mrs. Pursy.

LADY TEAZLE What, the fat dowager who was at Mrs. Quadrille's last night?

MRS. CANDOUR Nay, her bulk is her misfortune; and, when she takes so much pains to get rid of it, you ought not to reflect on her.

LADY SNEERWELL That's very true, indeed.

LADY TEAZLE Yes, I know she almost lives on acids and small whey; laces herself by pulleys; and often, in the hottest noon in summer, you may see her on a little squat pony, with her hair plaited up behind like a drummer's and puffing round the Ring[5] on a full trot.

MRS. CANDOUR I thank you, Lady Teazle, for defending her.

SIR PETER Yes, a good defense, truly.

MRS. CANDOUR Truly, Lady Teazle is as censorious as Miss Sallow.

CRABTREE Yes, and she is a curious being to pretend to be censorious—an awkward gawky, without any one good point under heaven.

MRS. CANDOUR Positively you shall not be so very severe. Miss Sallow is a near relation of mine by marriage, and as for her person great allowance is to be made; for let me tell you, a woman labors under many disadvantages who tries to pass for a girl at six-and-thirty.

LADY SNEERWELL Though surely, she is handsome still!—and for the weakness in her eyes, considering how much she reads by candlelight, it is not to be wondered at.

MRS. CANDOUR True, and then as to her manner; upon my word, I think it is particularly graceful, considering she never had the least education;

for you know her mother was a Welsh milliner, and her father a sugar-baker at Bristol.

SIR BENJAMIN Ah! you are both of you too good-natured!

SIR PETER [*Aside*] Yes, damned good-natured! This their own relation! mercy on me!

MRS. CANDOUR For my part, I own I cannot bear to hear a friend ill spoken of.

SIR PETER No, to be sure!

SIR BENJAMIN Oh! you are of a moral turn. Mrs. Candour and I can sit for an hour and hear Lady Stucco talk sentiment.

LADY TEAZLE Nay, I vow Lady Stucco is very well with the dessert after dinner, for she's just like the French fruit[6] one cracks for mottoes—made up of paint and proverb.

MRS. CANDOUR Well, I will never join in ridiculing a friend, and so I constantly tell my cousin Ogle —and you all know what pretensions she has to be critical on beauty.

CRABTREE Oh, to be sure! she has herself the oddest countenance that ever was seen; 'tis a collection of features from all the different countries of the globe.

SIR BENJAMIN So she has, indeed—an Irish front—[7]

CRABTREE Caledonian locks—

SIR BENJAMIN Dutch nose—

CRABTREE Austrian lips—

SIR BENJAMIN Complexion of a Spaniard—

CRABTREE And teeth *à la chinoise*—

SIR BENJAMIN In short, her face resembles a *table d'hôte* at Spa,[8] where no two guests are of a nation—

CRABTREE Or a congress at the close of a general war—wherein all the members, even to her eyes, appear to have a different interest, and her nose and chin are the only parties likely to join issue.

MRS. CANDOUR Ha! ha! ha!

SIR PETER [*Aside*] Mercy on my life!—a person they dine with twice a week!

LADY SNEERWELL Go, go; you are a couple of provoking toads.

MRS. CANDOUR Nay, but I vow you shall not carry the laugh off so—for give me leave to say that Mrs. Ogle—

SIR PETER Madam, madam, I beg your pardon— there's no stopping these good gentlemen's

---

4. **a . . . word**: Cf. Pope, *Rape of the Lock*, iii.16: "At every word a reputation dies." 5. **Ring**: fashionable drive in Hyde Park.

6. **French fruit**: artificial fruit. 7. **front**: forehead. 8. **Spa**: fashionable watering place (resort) in Belgium.

tongues. But when I tell you, Mrs. Candour, that the lady they are abusing is a particular friend of mine, I hope you'll not take her part.

LADY SNEERWELL   Ha! ha! ha! well said, Sir Peter! but you are a cruel creature—too phlegmatic yourself for a jest and too peevish to allow wit in others.

SIR PETER   Ah, madam, true wit is more nearly allied to good nature than your ladyship is aware of.

LADY TEAZLE   True, Sir Peter: I believe they are so near akin that they can never be united.

SIR BENJAMIN   Or rather, madam, suppose them to be man and wife, because one seldom sees them together.

LADY TEAZLE   But Sir Peter is such an enemy to scandal, I believe he would have it put down by Parliament.

SIR PETER   'Fore Heaven, madam, if they were to consider the sporting with reputation of as much importance as poaching on manors, and pass an act for the preservation of fame as well as game, I believe many would thank them for the bill.

LADY SNEERWELL   O lud! Sir Peter; would you deprive us of our privileges?

SIR PETER   Aye, madam, and then no person should be permitted to kill characters and run down reputations but qualified old maids and disappointed widows.

LADY SNEERWELL   Go, you monster!

MRS. CANDOUR   But surely you would not be quite so severe on those who only report what they hear?

SIR PETER   Yes, madam, I would have law merchant[9] for them too; and in all cases of slander currency, whenever the drawer of the lie was not to be found, the injured parties should have a right to come on any of the endorsers.

CRABTREE   Well, for my part, I believe there never was a scandalous tale without some foundation.

SIR PETER   Oh, nine out of ten of the malicious inventions are founded on some ridiculous misrepresentation.

LADY SNEERWELL   Come, ladies, shall we sit down to cards in the next room?

    [Enter SERVANT, who whispers to SIR PETER.]

SIR PETER.   I'll be with them directly.

    [Exit SERVANT.]

[Aside] I'll get away unperceived.

9. **law merchant:** commercial law.

LADY SNEERWELL   Sir Peter, you are not going to leave us?

SIR PETER   Your ladyship must excuse me; I'm called away by particular business. But I leave my character behind me.   [Exit SIR PETER.]

SIR BENJAMIN   Well—certainly, Lady Teazle, that lord of yours is a strange being. I could tell you some stories of him would make you laugh heartily if he were not your husband.

LADY TEAZLE   Oh, pray don't mind that; come, do let's hear them. [Joins the rest of the company going into the next room.]

JOSEPH   Maria, I see you have no satisfaction in this society.

MARIA   How is it possible I should? If to raise malicious smiles at the infirmities or misfortunes of those who have never injured us be the province of wit or humor, Heaven grant me a double portion of dulness!

JOSEPH   Yet they appear more ill-natured than they are; they have no malice at heart.

MARIA   Then is their conduct still more contemptible, for in my opinion nothing could excuse the interference of their tongues but a natural and uncontrollable bitterness of mind.

JOSEPH   Undoubtedly, madam, and it has always been a sentiment of mine that to propagate a malicious truth wantonly is more despicable than to falsify from revenge. But can you, Maria, feel thus for others and be unkind to me alone? Is hope to be denied the tenderest passion?

MARIA   Why will you distress me by renewing this subject?

JOSEPH   Ah, Maria! you would not treat me thus and oppose your guardian Sir Peter's will but that I see that profligate Charles is still a favored rival.

MARIA   Ungenerously urged! But whatever my sentiments are for that unfortunate young man, be assured I shall not feel more bound to give him up because his distresses have lost him the regard even of a brother.

JOSEPH   Nay, but, Maria, do not leave me with a frown; by all that's honest, I swear—

    [Enter LADY TEAZLE behind.]

[Aside] Gad's life, here's Lady Teazle.

[Aloud to MARIA.] You must not—no, you shall not—for though I have the greatest regard for Lady Teazle—

MARIA   Lady Teazle!

JOSEPH Yet were Sir Peter to suspect—

[*Enter* LADY TEAZLE *and comes forward.*]

LADY TEAZLE What is this, pray? Do you take her for me?—Child, you are wanted in the next room.   [*Exit* MARIA.]
—What is all this, pray?

JOSEPH Oh, the most unlucky circumstance in nature! Maria has somehow suspected the tender concern I have for your happiness and threatened to acquaint Sir Peter with her suspicions, and I was just endeavoring to reason with her when you came in.

LADY TEAZLE Indeed! but you seemed to adopt a very tender mode of reasoning—do you usually argue on your knees?

JOSEPH Oh, she's a child, and I thought a little bombast—but, Lady Teazle, when are you to give me your judgment on my library, as you promised?

LADY TEAZLE No, no! I begin to think it would be imprudent, and you know I admit you as a lover no farther than fashion requires.

JOSEPH True—a mere Platonic cicisbeo[10]—what every wife is entitled to.

LADY TEAZLE Certainly, one must not be out of the fashion. However, I have so much of my country prejudices left that though Sir Peter's ill humor may vex me ever so, it never shall provoke me to—

JOSEPH The only revenge in your power. Well, I applaud your moderation.

LADY TEAZLE Go—you are an insinuating wretch! But we shall be missed—let us join the company.

JOSEPH But we had best not return together.

LADY TEAZLE Well, don't stay, for Maria shan't come to hear any more of your reasoning, I promise you.   [*Exit* LADY TEAZLE.]

JOSEPH A curious dilemma my politics have run me into! I wanted, at first, only to ingratiate myself with Lady Teazle, that she might not be my enemy with Maria; and I have, I don't know how, become her serious lover. Sincerely I begin to wish I had never made such a point of gaining so very good a character, for it has led me into so many cursed rogueries that I doubt I shall be exposed at last.   [*Exit.*]

10. cicisbeo: gallant; companion for a married woman.

SCENE III. *A room in* SIR PETER TEAZLE'*s house.*

[*Enter* ROWLEY *and* SIR OLIVER SURFACE.]

SIR OLIVER Ha! ha! ha! so my old friend is married, hey?—a young wife out of the country. Ha! ha! ha! that he should have stood bluff to old bachelor so long and sink into a husband at last!

ROWLEY But you must not rally him on the subject, Sir Oliver; 'tis a tender point, I assure you, though he has been married only seven months.

SIR OLIVER Then he has been just half a year on the stool of repentance!—Poor Peter! But you say he has entirely given up Charles—never sees him, hey?

ROWLEY His prejudice against him is astonishing, and I am sure greatly increased by a jealousy of him with Lady Teazle, which he has industriously been led into by a scandalous society in the neighborhood, who have contributed not a little to Charles's ill name. Whereas the trust is, I believe, if the lady is partial to either of them, his brother is the favorite.

SIR OLIVER Aye, I know there are a set of malicious, prating, prudent gossips, both male and female, who murder characters to kill time and will rob a young fellow of his good name before he has years to know the value of it. But I am not to be prejudiced against my nephew by such, I promise you! No, no; if Charles has done nothing false or mean, I shall compound for his extravagance.

ROWLEY Then, my life on 't, you will reclaim him. Ah, sir, it gives me new life to find that *your* heart is not turned against him, and that the son of my good old master has one friend, however, left.

SIR OLIVER What! shall I forget, Master Rowley, when I was at his years myself? Egad, my brother and I were neither of us very prudent youths, and yet, I believe, you have not seen many better men than your old master was.

ROWLEY Sir, 'tis this reflection gives me assurance that Charles may yet be a credit to his family. But here comes Sir Peter.

SIR OLIVER Egad, so he does! Mercy on me! he's greatly altered, and seems to have a settled married look! One may read "husband" in his face at this distance. [*Enter* SIR PETER TEAZLE.]

SIR PETER   Ha! Sir Oliver—my old friend! Welcome to England a thousand times!

SIR OLIVER   Thank you, thank you, Sir Peter and i' faith, I am glad to find you well, believe me!

SIR PETER   Oh! 'tis a long time since we met—fifteen years, I doubt, Sir Oliver, and many a cross accident in the time.

SIR OLIVER   Aye, I have had my share. But, what! I find you are married—hey? Well, well, it can't be helped, and so—I wish you joy with all my heart!

SIR PETER   Thank you, thank you, Sir Oliver.—Yes, I have entered into—the happy state; but we'll not talk of that now.

SIR OLIVER   True, true, Sir Peter; old friends should not begin on grievances at first meeting—no, no, no.

ROWLEY   [Aside to SIR OLIVER] Take care, pray, sir.

SIR OLIVER   Well, so one of my nephews is a wild fellow, hey?

SIR PETER   Wild! Ah! my old friend, I grieve for your disappointment there; he's a lost young man, indeed. However, his brother will make you amends; Joseph is, indeed, what a youth should be. Everybody in the world speaks well of him.

SIR OLIVER   I am sorry to hear it; he has too good a character to be an honest fellow. Everybody speaks well of him! Pshaw! then he has bowed as low to knaves and fools as to the honest dignity of genius and virtue.

SIR PETER   What, Sir Oliver! do you blame him for not making enemies?

SIR OLIVER   Yes, if he has merit enough to deserve them.

SIR PETER   Well, well—you'll be convinced when you know him. 'Tis edification to hear him converse; he professes the noblest sentiments.

SIR OLIVER   Oh, plague of his sentiments! If he salutes me with a scrap of morality in his mouth, I shall be sick directly. But, however, don't mistake me, Sir Peter; I don't mean to defend Charles's errors, but before I form my judgment of either of them, I intend to make a trial of their hearts, and my friend Rowley and I have planned something for the purpose.

ROWLEY   And Sir Peter shall own for once he has been mistaken.

SIR PETER   Oh, my life on Joseph's honor!

SIR OLIVER   Well—come, give us a bottle of good wine, and we'll drink the lads' health and tell you our scheme.

SIR PETER   Allons,[1] then!

SIR OLIVER   And don't, Sir Peter, be so severe against your old friend's son. Odds my life! I am not sorry that he has run out of the course a little. For my part, I hate to see prudence clinging to the green suckers of youth; 'tis like ivy round a sapling, and spoils the growth of the tree.   [Exeunt.]

ACT III

SCENE I. A room in SIR PETER TEAZLE's house.

[Enter SIR PETER TEAZLE, SIR OLIVER SURFACE, and ROWLEY.]

SIR PETER   Well then, we will see this fellow first and have our wine afterwards. But how is this, Master Rowley? I don't see the jest of your scheme.

ROWLEY   Why, sir, this Mr. Stanley, who I was speaking of, is nearly related to them by their mother. He was once a merchant in Dublin, but has been ruined by a series of undeserved misfortunes. He has applied, by letter, to Mr. Surface and Charles. From the former he has received nothing but evasive promises of future service, while Charles has done all that his extravagance has left him power to do; and he is, at this time, endeavoring to raise a sum of money, part of which, in the midst of his own distresses, I know he intends for the service of poor Stanley.

SIR OLIVER   Ah! he is my brother's son.

SIR PETER   Well, but how is Sir Oliver personally to—

ROWLEY   Why, sir, I will inform Charles and his brother that Stanley has obtained permission to apply personally to his friends; and as they have neither of them ever seen him, let Sir Oliver assume his character and he will have a fair opportunity of judging, at least of the benevolence of their dispositions. And believe me, sir, you will find in the youngest brother one who, in the midst of folly and dissipation, has still, as our immortal bard expresses it,

Scene iii.   1. Allons: let's go.

a heart to pity, and a hand
Open as day for melting charity.[1]

SIR PETER   Pshaw! What signifies his having an open hand or purse either when he has nothing left to give? Well, well—make the trial if you please. But where is the fellow whom you brought for Sir Oliver to examine relative to Charles's affairs?

ROWLEY   Below, waiting his commands, and no one can give him better intelligence. This, Sir Oliver, is a friendly Jew, who, to do him justice, has done everything in his power to bring your nephew to a proper sense of his extravagance.

SIR PETER   Pray, let us have him in.

ROWLEY   [*Apart to* SERVANT] Desire Mr. Moses to walk upstairs.

SIR PETER   But pray, why should you suppose he will speak the truth?

ROWLEY   Oh, I have convinced him that he has no chance of recovering certain sums advanced to Charles but through the bounty of Sir Oliver, who he knows is arrived; so that you may depend on his fidelity to his own interests. I have also another evidence in my power, one Snake, whom I have detected in a matter little short of forgery, and shall shortly produce him to remove some of your prejudices.

SIR PETER   I have heard too much on that subject.

ROWLEY   Here comes the honest Israelite.

[*Enter* MOSES.]

—This is Sir Oliver.

SIR OLIVER   Sir, I understand you have lately had great dealings with my nephew Charles.

MOSES   Yes, Sir Oliver, I have done all I could for him, but he was ruined before he came to me for assistance.

SIR OLIVER   That was unlucky, truly, for you have had no opportunity of showing your talents.

MOSES   None at all; I hadn't the pleasure of knowing his distresses till he was some thousands worse than nothing.

SIR OLIVER   Unfortunate, indeed! But I suppose you have done all in your power for him, honest Moses?

MOSES   Yes, he knows that. This very evening I was to have brought him a gentleman from the city, who does not know him and will, I believe, advance him some money.

SIR PETER   What, one Charles has never had money from before?

MOSES   Yes—Mr. Premium of Crutched Friars, formerly a broker.

SIR PETER   Egad, Sir Oliver, a thought strikes me! —Charles, you say, does not know Mr. Premium?

MOSES   Not at all.

SIR PETER   Now then, Sir Oliver, you may have a better opportunity of satisfying yourself than by an old romancing tale of a poor relation; go with my friend Moses and represent Premium, and then, I'll answer for it, you'll see your nephew in all his glory.

SIR OLIVER   Egad, I like this idea better than the other, and I may visit Joseph afterwards as old Stanley.

SIR PETER   True, so you may.

ROWLEY   Well, this is taking Charles rather at a disadvantage, to be sure. However, Moses, you understand Sir Peter and will be faithful?

MOSES   You may depend upon me.—This is near the time I was to have gone.

SIR OLIVER   I'll accompany you as soon as you please, Moses—But hold! I have forgot one thing; how the plague shall I be able to pass for a Jew?

MOSES   There's no need—the principal is Christian.

SIR OLIVER   Is he? I'm very sorry to hear it. But then again, an't I rather too smartly dressed to look like a moneylender?

SIR PETER   Not at all; 'twould not be out of character if you went in your own carriage— would it, Moses?

MOSES   Not in the least.

SIR OLIVER   Well, but how must I talk? there's certainly some cant of usury and mode of treating that I ought to know.

SIR PETER   Oh, there's not much to learn. The great point, as I take it, is to be exorbitant enough in your demands. Hey, Moses?

MOSES   Yes, that's a very great point.

SIR OLIVER   I'll answer for't I'll not be wanting in that. I'll ask him eight or ten percent on the loan, at least.

MOSES   If you ask him no more than that you'll be discovered immediately.

SIR OLIVER   Hey!—what the plague!—how much then?

Act III, scene i. **1.** Cf. *Henry IV, Part II,* IV.iv.31–32: "a tear for pity, and a hand / Open as day for melting charity."

MOSES   That depends upon the circumstances. If he appears not very anxious for the supply, you should require only forty or fifty percent; but if you find him in great distress and want the moneys very bad, you may ask double.

SIR PETER   A good honest trade you're learning, Sir Oliver.

SIR OLIVER   Truly, I think so—and not unprofitable.

MOSES   Then, you know, you haven't the moneys yourself, but are forced to borrow them for him of an old friend.

SIR OLIVER   Oh! I borrow it of a friend, do I?

MOSES   And your friend is an unconscionable dog: but you can't help that.

SIR OLIVER   My friend an unconscionable dog, is he?

MOSES   Yes, and he himself has not the moneys by him, but is forced to sell stock at a great loss.

SIR OLIVER   He is forced to sell stock at a great loss, is he? Well, that's very kind of him.

SIR PETER   I' faith, Sir Oliver—Mr. Premium, I mean—you'll soon be master of the trade. But, Moses! would not you have him run out a little against the Annuity Bill?[2] That would be in character, I should think.

MOSES   Very much.

ROWLEY   And lament that a young man now must be at years of discretion before he is suffered to ruin himself?

MOSES   Aye, great pity!

SIR PETER   And abuse the public for allowing merit to an act whose only object is to snatch misfortune and imprudence from the rapacious gripe of usury, and give the minor a chance of inheriting his estate without being undone by coming into possession.

SIR OLIVER   So, so—Moses shall give me farther instructions as we go together.

SIR PETER   You will not have much time, for your nephew lives hard by.

SIR OLIVER   Oh, never fear! my tutor appears so able that though Charles lived in the next street, it must be my own fault if I am not a complete rogue before I turn the corner.

[*Exit* SIR OLIVER SURFACE *and* MOSES.]

SIR PETER   So, now, I think Sir Oliver will be convinced. You are partial, Rowley, and would have prepared Charles for the other plot.

2. Annuity Bill: Act of Parliament controlling interest rates and prohibiting loans to minors.

ROWLEY   No, upon my word, Sir Peter.

SIR PETER   Well, go bring me this Snake, and I'll hear what he has to say presently. I see Maria, and want to speak with her. [*Exit* ROWLEY.] I should be glad to be convinced my suspicions of Lady Teazle and Charles were unjust. I have never yet opened my mind on this subject to my friend Joseph—I am determined I will do it—he will give me his opinion sincerely. [*Enter* MARIA.] So, child, has Mr. Surface returned with you?

MARIA   No, sir; he was engaged.

SIR PETER   Well, Maria, do you not reflect, the more you converse with that amiable young man, what return his partiality for you deserves?

MARIA   Indeed, Sir Peter, your frequent importunity on this subject distresses me extremely. You compel me to declare that I know no man who has ever paid me a particular attention whom I would not prefer to Mr. Surface.

SIR PETER   So—here's perverseness!—No, no, Maria, 'tis Charles only whom you would prefer. 'Tis evident his vices and follies have won your heart.

MARIA   This is unkind, sir. You know I have obeyed you in neither seeing nor corresponding with him: I have heard enough to convince me that he is unworthy my regard. Yet I cannot think it culpable if, while my understanding severely condemns his vices, my heart suggests some pity for his distresses.

SIR PETER   Well, well, pity him as much as you please, but give your heart and hand to a worthier object.

MARIA   Never to his brother!

SIR PETER   Go, perverse and obstinate! But take care, madam; you have never yet known what the authority of a guardian is; don't compel me to inform you of it.

MARIA   I can only say, you shall not have just reason. 'Tis true, by my father's will I am for a short period bound to regard you as his substitute; but must cease to think you so when you would compel me to be miserable. [*Exit* MARIA.]

SIR PETER   Was ever man so crossed as I am? everything conspiring to fret me! I had not been involved in matrimony a fortnight before her father, a hale and hearty man, died on purpose, I believe, for the pleasure of plaguing me with the care of his daughter. But here comes my helpmate! She appears in great good humor.

How happy I should be if I could tease her into loving me, though but a little!

[Enter LADY TEAZLE.]

LADY TEAZLE Lud! Sir Peter, I hope you haven't been quarrelling with Maria? It is not using me well to be ill-humored when I am not by.

SIR PETER Ah, Lady Teazle, you might have the power to make me good-humored at all times.

LADY TEAZLE I am sure I wish I had, for I want you to be in a charming sweet temper at this moment. Do be good-humored now and let me have two hundred pounds, will you?

SIR PETER Two hundred pounds! what, an't I to be in a good humor without paying for it? But speak to me thus and, i' faith, there's nothing I could refuse you. You shall have it, but seal me a bond for the repayment.

LADY TEAZLE *[Offering her hand]* Oh, no—there —my note of hand will do as well.

SIR PETER And you shall no longer reproach me with not giving you an independent settlement; I mean shortly to surprise you; but shall we always live thus, hey?

LADY TEAZLE If you please. I'm sure I don't care how soon we leave off quarrelling, provided you'll own you were tired first.

SIR PETER Well—then let our future contest be, who shall be most obliging.

LADY TEAZLE I assure you, Sir Peter, good nature becomes you. You look now as you did before we were married, when you used to walk with me under the elms and tell me stories of what a gallant you were in your youth; and chuck me under the chin, you would, and ask me if I thought I could love an old fellow who would deny me nothing—didn't you?

SIR PETER Yes, yes, and you were as kind and attentive—

LADY TEAZLE Aye, so I was, and would always take your part when my acquaintance used to abuse you and turn you into ridicule.

SIR PETER Indeed!

LADY TEAZLE Aye, and when my cousin Sophy has called you a stiff, peevish old bachelor, and laughed at me for thinking of marrying one who might be my father, I have always defended you and said I didn't think you so ugly by any means, and I dared say you'd make a very good sort of a husband.

SIR PETER And you prophesied right; and we shall now be the happiest couple—

LADY TEAZLE And never differ again?

SIR PETER No, never!—though at the same time, indeed, my dear Lady Teazle, you must watch your temper very seriously; for in all our little quarrels, my dear, if you recollect, my love, you always began first.

LADY TEAZLE I beg your pardon, my dear Sir Peter; indeed, you always gave the provocation.

SIR PETER Now see, my angel! take care—contradicting isn't the way to keep friends.

LADY TEAZLE Then don't you begin it, my love!

SIR PETER There now! you—you are going on. You don't perceive, my life, that you are just doing the very thing which you know always makes me angry.

LADY TEAZLE Nay, you know if you will be angry without any reason, my dear—

SIR PETER There! now you want to quarrel again.

LADY TEAZLE No, I'm sure I don't, but if you will be so peevish—

SIR PETER There now! who begins first?

LADY TEAZLE Why, you, to be sure. I said nothing —but there's no bearing your temper.

SIR PETER No, no, madam: the fault's in your own temper.

LADY TEAZLE Aye, you are just what my cousin Sophy said you would be.

SIR PETER Your cousin Sophy is a forward, impertinent gypsy.

LADY TEAZLE You are a great bear, I'm sure, to abuse my relations.

SIR PETER Now may all the plagues of marriage be doubled on me if ever I try to be friends with you any more!

LADY TEAZLE So much the better.

SIR PETER No, no, madam: 'tis evident you never cared a pin for me, and I was a madman to marry you—a pert, rural coquette that had refused half the honest 'squires in the neighborhood.

LADY TEAZLE And I am sure I was a fool to marry you—an old dangling bachelor who was single at fifty only because he never could meet with anyone who would have him.

SIR PETER Aye, aye, madam, but you were pleased enough to listen to me; you never had such an offer before.

LADY TEAZLE No! didn't I refuse Sir Tivy Terrier,

who everybody said would have been a better match? for his estate is just as good as yours, and he has broke his neck since we have been married.

SIR PETER   I have done with you, madam! You are an unfeeling, ungrateful—but there's an end of everything. I believe you capable of everything that is bad. Yes, madam, I now believe the reports relative to you and Charles, madam. Yes, madam, *you* and Charles are, not without grounds—

LADY TEAZLE   Take care, Sir Peter! you had better not insinuate any such thing! I'll not be suspected without cause, I promise you.

SIR PETER   Very well, madam! very well! A separate maintenance as soon as you please. Yes, madam, or a divorce! I'll make an example of myself for the benefit of all old bachelors. Let us separate, madam!

LADY TEAZLE   Agreed! agreed! And now, my dear Sir Peter, we are of a mind once more, we may be the happiest couple and never differ again, you know—ha! ha! ha! Well, you are going to be in a passion, I see, and I shall only interrupt you—so, bye! bye!   [*Exit.*]

SIR PETER   Plagues and tortures! can't I make her angry either! Oh, I am the most miserable fellow! But I'll not bear her presuming to keep her temper: no! she may break my heart, but she shan't keep her temper.   [*Exit.*]

SCENE II. *A room in* CHARLES SURFACE's *house.*

[*Enter* TRIP, MOSES, *and* SIR OLIVER SURFACE.]

TRIP   Here, Master Moses! if you'll stay a moment, I'll try whether—what's the gentleman's name?

SIR OLIVER   [*Aside*] Mr. Moses, what is my name?

MOSES   Mr. Premium.

TRIP   Premium—very well.
                    [*Exit* TRIP, *taking snuff.*]

SIR OLIVER   To judge by the servants, one wouldn't believe the master was ruined. But what!—sure, this was my brother's house?

MOSES   Yes, sir; Mr. Charles bought it of Mr. Joseph, with the furniture, pictures, etc., just as the old gentleman left it. Sir Peter thought it a piece of extravagance in him.

SIR OLIVER   In my mind, the other's economy in selling it to him was more reprehensible by half.
                    [*Enter* TRIP.]

TRIP   My master says you must wait, gentlemen: he has company and can't speak with you yet.

SIR OLIVER   If he knew who it was wanted to see him, perhaps he would not send such a message.

TRIP   Yes, yes, sir; he knows you are here—I did not forget little Premium: no, no, no!

SIR OLIVER   Very well; and I pray, sir, what may be your name?

TRIP   Trip, sir; my name is Trip, at your service.

SIR OLIVER   Well, then, Mr. Trip, you have a pleasant sort of place here, I guess?

TRIP   Why, yes—here are three or four of us pass our time agreeably enough; but then our wages are sometimes a little in arrear—and not very great either—but fifty pounds a year, and find our own bags[1] and bouquets.

SIR OLIVER   [*Aside*] Bags and bouquets? halters and bastinadoes!

TRIP   And á propos, Moses, have you been able to get me that little bill[2] discounted?

SIR OLIVER   [*Aside*] Wants to raise money too—mercy on me! Has his distresses too, I warrant, like a lord, and affects creditors and duns.

MOSES   'Twas not to be done, indeed, Mr. Trip.

TRIP   Good lack, you surprise me! My friend Brush has endorsed it, and I thought when he put his name at the back of a bill 'twas the same as cash.

MOSES   No, 'twouldn't do.

TRIP   A small sum—but twenty pounds. Hark'ee, Moses, do you think you couldn't get it me by way of annuity?[3]

SIR OLIVER   [*Aside*] An annuity! ha! ha! a footman raise money by way of annuity! Well done, luxury, egad!

MOSES   Well, but you must insure your place.

TRIP   Oh, with all my heart! I'll insure my place, and my life too, if you please.

SIR OLIVER   [*Aside*] It's more than I would your neck.

MOSES   But is there nothing you could deposit?

TRIP   Why, nothing capital of my master's

Scene ii. **1. find . . . bags:** provide our own wigs. **2. bill:** draft or check that could be cashed at a discount. **3. annuity:** loan; Moses asks for collateral in his next speech.

wardrobe has dropped lately, but I could give you a mortgage on some of his winter clothes, with equity of redemption before November—or you shall have the reversion of the French velvet, or a post-obit[4] on the blue and silver:—these, I should think, Moses, with a few pair of point ruffles as a collateral security—hey, my little fellow?

MOSES Well, well. [*Bell rings.*]

TRIP Egad, I heard the bell! I believe, gentlemen, I can now introduce you. Don't forget the annuity, little Moses! This way, gentlemen. I'll insure my place, you know.

SIR OLIVER [*Aside*] If the man be a shadow of the master, this is the temple of dissipation indeed!
[*Exeunt.*]

SCENE III. *Another room in the same.*

[CHARLES SURFACE *and his friends at a table with wine, etc.*]

CHARLES 'Fore Heaven, 'tis true!—there's the great degeneracy of the age. Many of our acquaintance have taste, spirit, and politeness, but, plague on 't, they won't drink.

CARELESS It is so indeed, Charles! they give in to all the substantial luxuries of the table, and abstain from nothing but wine and wit. Oh, certainly society suffers by it intolerably! for now, instead of the social spirit of raillery that used to mantle over a glass of bright Burgundy, their conversation is become just like the Spa water they drink, which has all the pertness and flatulence of champagne without the spirit or flavor.

FIRST GENTLEMAN But what are they to do who love play better than wine?

CARELESS True! there's Sir Harry diets himself for gaming, and is now under a hazard regimen.

CHARLES Then he'll have the worst of it. What! you wouldn't train a horse for the course by keeping him from corn? For my part, egad, I am never so successful as when I am a little merry; let me throw on a bottle of champagne, and I never lose—at least I never feel my losses, which is exactly the same thing.

SECOND GENTLEMAN Aye, that I believe.

CHARLES And then, what man can pretend to be a believer in love who is an abjurer of wine? 'Tis the test by which the lover knows his own heart. Fill a dozen bumpers to a dozen beauties, and she that floats atop is the maid that has bewitched you.

CARELESS Now then, Charles, be honest and give us your real favorite.

CHARLES Why, I have withheld her only in compassion to you. If I toast her, you must give a round of her peers, which is impossible—on earth.

CARELESS Oh! then we'll find some canonized vestals or heathen goddesses that will do, I warrant!

CHARLES Here then, bumpers, you rogues! bumpers! Maria! Maria!—

SIR HARRY Maria who?

CHARLES Oh, damn the surname—'tis too formal to be registered in Love's calendar; but now, Sir Harry, beware, we must have beauty superlative.

CARELESS Nay, never study, Sir Harry; we'll stand to the toast though your mistress should want an eye, and you know you have a song will excuse you.

SIR HARRY Egad, so I have! and I'll give him the song instead of the lady. [*Sings.*]

Here's to the maiden of bashful fifteen;
　　Here's to the widow of fifty;
Here's to the flaunting extravagant quean,[1]
　　And here's to the housewife that's thrifty.
CHORUS
　　　Let the toast pass—
　　　　Drink to the lass,
　　I'll warrant she'll prove an excuse for the glass.

Here's to the charmer whose dimples we prize;
　　Now to the maid who has none, sir;
Here's to the girl with a pair of blue eyes,
　　And here's to the nymph with but one, sir.
CHORUS
　　　Let the toast pass, etc.

Here's to the maid with a bosom of snow;
　　Now to her that's as brown as a berry;
Here's to the wife with a face full of woe,
　　And now to the damsel that's merry.
CHORUS
　　　Let the toast pass, etc.

4. **reverison, post-obit:** lien on or inheritance of the property being used as collateral.

Scene iii. **1. quean:** prostitute.

For let 'em be clumsy, or let 'em be slim,
    Young or ancient, I care not a feather;
So fill a pint bumper quite up to the brim,
    And let us e'en toast them together.
CHORUS
    Let the toast pass, etc.

ALL   Bravo! bravo!
    [*Enter* TRIP, *and whispers* CHARLES SURFACE.]
CHARLES   Gentlemen, you must excuse me a little.
Careless, take the chair, will you?
CARELESS   Nay, prithee, Charles, what now? This
is one of your peerless beauties, I suppose, has
dropped in by chance?
CHARLES   No, faith! To tell you the truth, 'tis a
Jew and a broker, who are come by appointment.
CARELESS   Oh, damn it! let's have the Jew in.
FIRST GENTLEMAN   Aye, and the broker too, by all
means.
SECOND GENTLEMAN   Yes, yes, the Jew and the
broker.
CHARLES   Egad, with all my heart! Trip, bid the
gentlemen walk in.   [*Exit* TRIP.]
—though there's one of them a stranger, I can
tell you.
CARELESS   Charles, let us give them some generous
Burgundy, and perhaps they'll grow conscien-
tious.
CHARLES   Oh, hang 'em, no! wine does but draw
forth a man's natural qualities, and to make
them drink would only be to whet their knavery.
    [*Enter* TRIP, *with* SIR OLIVER SURFACE *and* MOSES.]
CHARLES   So, honest Moses, walk in; walk in,
pray, Mr. Premium—that's the gentleman's
name, isn't it, Moses?
MOSES   Yes, sir.
CHARLES   Set chairs, Trip—Sit down, Mr. Premium
—Glasses, Trip.
    [TRIP *gives chairs and glasses, and exit.*]
—Sit down, Moses. Come, Mr. Premium, I'll
give you a sentiment; here's *Success to usury!*—
Moses, fill the gentlemen a bumper.
MOSES   Success to usury! [*Drinks.*]
CARELESS   Right, Moses—usury is prudence and
industry, and deserves to succeed.
SIR OLIVER   Then—here's all the success it de-
serves! [*Drinks.*]
CARELESS   No, no, that won't do! Mr. Premium,
you have demurred at the toast and must drink
it in a pint bumper.

FIRST GENTLEMAN   A pint bumper, at least.
MOSES   Oh, pray, sir, consider—Mr. Premium's a
gentleman.
CARELESS   And therefore loves good wine.
SECOND GENTLEMAN   Give Moses a quart glass—
this is mutiny, and a high contempt for the chair.
CARELESS   Here, now for 't! I'll see justice done,
to the last drop of my bottle.
SIR OLIVER   Nay, pray, gentlemen—I did not
expect this usage.
CHARLES   No, hang it, you shan't! Mr. Premium's
a stranger.
SIR OLIVER   [*Aside*] Odd! I wish I was well out of
their company.
CARELESS   Plague on 'em then! if they won't drink,
we'll not sit down with them. Come, Harry, the
dice are in the next room—Charles, you'll join
us when you have finished your business with the
gentlemen?
CHARLES   I will! I will!
    [*Exeunt* SIR HARRY BUMPER *and* GENTLEMEN,
            CARELESS *following.*]
—Careless!
CARELESS   [*Returning*] Well!
CHARLES   Perhaps I may want you.
CARELESS   Oh, you know I am always ready:
word, note, or bond, 'tis all the same to me.
    [*Exit.*]
MOSES   Sir, this is Mr. Premium, a gentleman of
the strictest honor and secrecy; and always performs what he undertakes. Mr. Premium, this is—
CHARLES   Pshaw! have done. Sir, my friend Moses
is a very honest fellow, but a little slow at
expression; he'll be an hour giving us our titles.
Mr. Premium, the plain state of the matter is
this: I am an extravagant young fellow who
wants to borrow money; you I take to be a
prudent old fellow who have got money to lend.
I am blockhead enough to give fifty percent
sooner than not have it; and you, I presume, are
rogue enough to take a hundred if you can get
it. Now, sir, you see we are acquainted at once,
and may proceed to business without farther
ceremony.
SIR OLIVER   Exceeding frank, upon my word. I see,
sir, you are not a man of many compliments.
CHARLES   Oh, no, sir! plain dealing in business I
always think best.
SIR OLIVER   Sir, I like you the better for it. However, you are mistaken in one thing; I have no

money to lend, but I believe I could procure some of a friend—but then, he's an unconscionable dog, isn't he, Moses?

MOSES But you can't help that.

SIR OLIVER And must sell stock to accommodate you—mustn't he, Moses?

MOSES Yes, indeed! You know I always speak the truth and scorn to tell a lie!

CHARLES Right. People that speak truth generally do. But these are trifles, Mr. Premium. What! I know money isn't to be bought without paying for 't.

SIR OLIVER Well, but what security could you give? You have no land, I suppose?

CHARLES Not a mole-hill nor a twig but what's in the bough-pots out of the window.

SIR OLIVER Nor any stock, I presume?

CHARLES Nothing but live stock—and that's only a few pointers and ponies. But pray, Mr. Premium, are you acquainted at all with any of my connections?

SIR OLIVER Why, to say truth, I am.

CHARLES Then you must know that I have a dev'lish rich uncle in the East Indies, Sir Oliver Surface, from whom I have the greatest expectations?

SIR OLIVER That you have a wealthy uncle, I have heard, but how your expectations will turn out is more, I believe, than you can tell.

CHARLES Oh, no!—there can be no doubt. They tell me I'm a prodigious favorite, and that he talks of leaving me everything.

SIR OLIVER Indeed! this is the first I've heard of it.

CHARLES Yes, yes, 'tis just so. Moses knows 'tis true; don't you, Moses?

MOSES Oh, yes! I'll swear to 't.

SIR OLIVER [Aside] Egad, they'll persuade me presently I'm at Bengal.

CHARLES Now I propose, Mr. Premium, if it's agreeable to you, a post-obit on Sir Oliver's life; though at the same time the old fellow has been so liberal to me that, I give you my word, I should be very sorry to hear that anything had happened to him.

SIR OLIVER Not more than I should, I assure you. But the bond you mention happens to be just the worst security you could offer me—for I might live to a hundred and never see the principal.

CHARLES Oh, yes, you would! the moment Sir Oliver dies, you know, you would come on me for the money.

SIR OLIVER Then I believe I should be the most unwelcome dun you ever had in your life.

CHARLES What! I suppose you're afraid that Sir Oliver is too good a life?

SIR OLIVER No, indeed I am not; though I have heard he is as hale and hearty as any man of his years in Christendom.

CHARLES There again, now, you are misinformed. No, no, the climate has hurt him considerably, poor Uncle Oliver. Yes, yes, he breaks apace, I'm told—and is so much altered lately that his nearest relations don't know him.

SIR OLIVER No! Ha! ha! ha! so much altered lately that his nearest relations would not know him! Ha! ha! ha! egad—ha! ha! ha!

CHARLES Ha! ha!—you're glad to hear that, little Premium?

SIR OLIVER No, no, I'm not.

CHARLES Yes, yes, you are—ha! ha! ha!—you know that mends your chance.

SIR OLIVER But I'm told Sir Oliver is coming over; nay, some say he is actually arrived.

CHARLES Pshaw! sure I must know better than you whether he's come or not. No, no, rely on 't he's at this moment at Calcutta—isn't he, Moses?

MOSES Oh, yes, certainly.

SIR OLIVER Very true, as you say, you must know better than I, though I have it from pretty good authority—haven't I, Moses?

MOSES Yes, most undoubted!

SIR OLIVER But, sir, as I understand you want a few hundreds immediately, is there nothing you could dispose of?

CHARLES How do you mean?

SIR OLIVER For instance, now, I have heard that your father left behind him a great quantity of massy old plate.

CHARLES O lud! that's gone long ago. Moses can tell you how better than I can.

SIR OLIVER [Aside] Good lack! all the family race-cups and corporation-bowls! [Aloud.] Then it was also supposed that his library was one of the most valuable and compact—

CHARLES Yes, yes, so it was—vastly too much so for a private gentleman. For my part, I was always of a communicative disposition; so I thought it a shame to keep so much knowledge to myself.

SIR OLIVER   [*Aside*] Mercy upon me! learning that had run in the family like an heirloom!—[*Aloud.*] Pray, what are become of the books?

CHARLES   You must inquire of the auctioneer, Master Premium, for I don't believe even Moses can direct you.

MOSES   I know nothing of books.

SIR OLIVER   So, so, nothing of the family property left, I suppose?

CHARLES   Not much, indeed, unless you have a mind to the family pictures. I have got a room full of ancestors above, and if you have a taste for old paintings, egad, you shall have 'em a bargain.

SIR OLIVER   Hey! what the devil! sure, you wouldn't sell your forefathers, would you?

CHARLES   Every man of them, to the best bidder.

SIR OLIVER   What! your great-uncles and aunts?

CHARLES   Aye, and my great-grandfathers and grandmothers too.

SIR OLIVER   [*Aside*] Now I give him up! [*Aloud.*] What the plague, have you no bowels for your own kindred? Odds life! do you take me for Shylock in the play[2] that you would raise money of me on your own flesh and blood?

CHARLES   Nay, my little broker, don't be angry; what need you care, if you have your money's worth?

SIR OLIVER   Well, I'll be the purchaser; I think I can dispose of the family canvas. [*Aside.*] Oh, I'll never forgive him this!—never!

[*Enter* CARELESS.]

CARELESS   Come, Charles, what keeps you?

CHARLES   I can't come yet i' faith, we are going to have a sale above stairs; here's little Premium will buy all my ancestors!

CARELESS   Oh, burn your ancestors!

CHARLES   No, he may do that afterwards if he pleases. Stay, Careless, we want you: egad, you shall be auctioneer—so come along with us.

CARELESS   Oh, have with you, if that's the case. [I can] handle a hammer as well as a dice-box!

SIR OLIVER   [*Aside*] Oh, the profligates!

CHARLES   Come, Moses, you shall be appraiser if we want one. Gad's life, little Premium, you don't seem to like the business?

SIR OLIVER   Oh, yes, I do, vastly! Ha! ha! ha! yes, yes, I think it a rare joke to sell one's family by auction—ha! ha!—[*Aside.*] Oh, the prodigal!

CHARLES   To be sure! when a man wants money, where the plague should he get assistance if he can't make free with his own relations?

[*Exeunt.*]

ACT IV

SCENE I. *Picture room at* CHARLES SURFACE'*s house.*

[*Enter* CHARLES SURFACE, SIR OLIVER SURFACE, MOSES, *and* CARELESS.]

CHARLES   Walk in, gentlemen, pray walk in; here they are, the family of the Surfaces up to the Conquest.

SIR OLIVER   And in my opinion a goodly collection.

CHARLES   Aye, aye, these are done in the true spirit of portrait-painting; no *volontaire grâce*[1] or expression. Not like the works of your modern Raphaels, who give you the strongest resemblance, yet contrive to make your portrait independent of you, so that you may sink the original and not hurt the picture. No, no; the merit of these is the inveterate likeness—all stiff and awkward as the originals, and like nothing in human nature besides.

SIR OLIVER   Ah! we shall never see such figures of men again.

CHARLES   I hope not. Well, you see, Master Premium, what a domestic character I am; here I sit of an evening surrounded by my family. But come, get to your pulpit, Mr. Auctioneer; here's an old gouty chair of my grandfather's will answer the purpose.

CARELESS   Aye, aye, this will do. But, Charles, I haven't a hammer; and what's an auctioneer without his hammer?

CHARLES   Egad, that's true. What parchment have we here? Oh, our genealogy in full. Here, Careless, you shall have no common bit of mahogany; here's the family tree for you, you rogue! This shall be your hammer, and now you may knock down my ancestors with their own pedigree.

SIR OLIVER   [*Aside*] What an unnatural rogue!—an *ex post facto* parricide!

2. the play: *The Merchant of Venice.*

Act IV, scene i.   1. volontaire grace: i.e., portraits done without much attempt to produce an exact likeness.

CARELESS Yes, yes, here's a list of your generation, indeed;—faith, Charles, this is the most convenient thing you could have found for the business, for 'twill not only serve as a hammer but a catalogue into the bargain. Come, begin—A-going, a-going, a-going!

CHARLES Bravo! Careless! Well, here's my great-uncle, Sir Richard Raveline, a marvelous good general in his day, I assure you. He served in all the duke of Marlborough's wars[2] and got that cut over his eye at the battle of Malplaquet. What say you, Mr. Premium? look at him—there's a hero! not cut out of his feathers, as your modern clipped captains are, but enveloped in wig and regimentals, as a general should be. What do you bid?

MOSES Mr. Premium would have *you* speak.

CHARLES Why, then, he shall have him for ten pounds, and I'm sure that's not dear for a staff officer.

SIR OLIVER [*Aside*] Heaven deliver me! his famous uncle Richard for ten pounds!—Very well, sir, I take him at that.

CHARLES Careless, knock down my uncle Richard. —Here, now, is a maiden sister of his, my great-aunt Deborah, done by Kneller, thought to be in his best manner and esteemed a very formidable likeness. There she is, you see, a shepherdess feeding her flock. You shall have her for five pounds ten—the sheep are worth the money.

SIR OLIVER [*Aside*] Ah! poor Deborah! a woman who set such a value on herself!—Five pounds ten—she's mine.

CHARLES Knock down my aunt Deborah! Here, now, are two that were a sort of cousins of theirs. You see, Moses, these pictures were done some time ago, when beaux wore wigs and the ladies their own hair.

SIR OLIVER Yes, truly, headdresses appear to have been a little lower in those days.

CHARLES Well, take that couple for the same.

MOSES 'Tis [a] good bargain.

CHARLES Careless!—this, now, is a grandfather of my mother's, a learned judge, well known on the western circuit.—What do you rate him at, Moses?

MOSES Four guineas.

CHARLES Four guineas! Gad's life, you don't bid me the price of his wig.—Mr. Premium, you have

2. **duke . . . wars:** Wars of the Spanish Succession (1701–14).

more respect for the woolsack; do let us knock his lordship down at fifteen.

SIR OLIVER By all means.

CARELESS Gone!

CHARLES And there are two brothers of his, William and Walter Blunt, Esquires, both members of Parliament and noted speakers; and, what's very extraordinary, I believe, this is the first time they were ever bought or sold.

SIR OLIVER That is very extraordinary, indeed! I'll take them at your own price, for the honour of Parliament.

CARELESS Well said, little Premium! I'll knock them down at forty.

CHARLES Here's a jolly fellow—I don't know what relation, but he was mayor of Manchester: take him at eight pounds.

SIR OLIVER No, no; six will do for the mayor.

CHARLES Come, make it guineas, and I'll throw you the two aldermen there into the bargain.

SIR OLIVER They're mine.

CHARLES Careless, knock down the mayor and aldermen. But, plague on 't! we shall be all day retailing in this manner; do let us deal wholesale. What say you, little Premium? Give me three hundred pounds for the rest of the family in the lump.

CARELESS Aye, aye, that will be the best way.

SIR OLIVER Well, well, anything to accommodate you; they are mine. But there is one portrait which you have always passed over.

CARELESS What, that ill-looking little fellow over the settee?

SIR OLIVER Yes, sir, I mean that, though I don't think him so ill-looking a little fellow, by any means.

CHARLES What, that?—Oh, that's my uncle Oliver; 'twas done before he went to India.

CARELESS Your uncle Oliver! Gad, then you'll never be friends, Charles. That, now, to me, is as stern a looking rogue as ever I saw—an unforgiving eye, and a damned disinheriting countenance!—an inveterate knave, depend on 't. Don't you think so, little Premium?

SIR OLIVER Upon my soul, sir, I do not; I think it is as honest a looking face as any in the room, dead or alive. But I suppose uncle Oliver goes with the rest of the lumber?

CHARLES No, hang it; I'll not part with poor Noll. The old fellow has been very good to me and, egad, I'll keep his picture while I've a room to put it in.

SIR OLIVER   [*Aside*] The rogue's my nephew after all!—But, sir, I have somehow taken a fancy to that picture.

CHARLES   I'm sorry for 't, for you certainly will not have it. Oons, haven't you got enough of them?

SIR OLIVER   [*Aside*] I forgive him everything!— But, sir, when I take a whim in my head, I don't value money. I'll give you as much for that as for all the rest.

CHARLES   Don't tease me, master broker; I tell you I'll not part with it, and there's an end of it.

SIR OLIVER   [*Aside*] How like his father the dog is! —Well, well, I have done.—[*Aside.*] I did not perceive it before, but I think I never saw such a striking resemblance.—Here is a draft for your sum.

CHARLES   Why, 'tis for eight hundred pounds!

SIR OLIVER   You will not let Sir Oliver go?

CHARLES   Zounds! no! I tell you once more.

SIR OLIVER   Then never mind the difference; we'll balance that another time. But give me your hand on the bargain. You are an honest fellow, Charles—I beg pardon, sir, for being so free.— Come, Moses.

CHARLES   Egad, this is a whimsical old fellow! But hark'ee, Premium, you'll prepare lodgings for these gentlemen.

SIR OLIVER   Yes, yes, I'll send for them in a day or two.

CHARLES   But hold; do now send a genteel conveyance for them, for I assure you, they were most of them used to ride in their own carriages.

SIR OLIVER   I will, I will—for all but Oliver.

CHARLES   Aye, all but the little nabob.

SIR OLIVER   You're fixed on that?

CHARLES   Peremptorily.

SIR OLIVER   [*Aside*] A dear extravagant rogue!— Good day!—Come, Moses.—[*Aside.*] Let me hear now who dares call him profligate!

[*Exeunt* SIR OLIVER SURFACE *and* MOSES.]

CARELESS   Why, this is the oddest genius of the sort I ever saw!

CHARLES   Egad, he's the prince of brokers, I think. I wonder how Moses got acquainted with so honest a fellow.—Hah, here's Rowley; do, Careless, say I'll join the company in a few moments.

CARELESS   I will—but don't let that old blockhead persuade you to squander any of that money on old musty debts, or any such nonsense; for tradesmen, Charles, are the most exorbitant fellows.

CHARLES   Very true, and paying them is only encouraging them.

CARELESS   Nothing else.

CHARLES   Aye, aye, never fear.   [*Exit* CARELESS.] —So! this was an odd old fellow, indeed. Let me see, two-thirds of this is mine by right—five hundred and thirty odd pounds. 'Fore Heaven! I find one's ancestors are more valuable relations than I took them for!—Ladies and gentlemen, your most obedient and very grateful servant. [*Bows.*]   [*Enter* ROWLEY.] Ha! old Rowley! egad, you are just come in time to take leave of your old acquaintance.

ROWLEY   Yes, I heard they were a-going. But I wonder you can have such spirits under so many distresses.

CHARLES   Why, there's the point! my distresses are so many that I can't afford to part with my spirits; but I shall be rich and splenetic, all in good time. However, I suppose you are surprised that I am not more sorrowful at parting with so many near relations. To be sure, 'tis very affecting; but you see they never move a muscle, so why should I?

ROWLEY   There's no making you serious a moment.

CHARLES   Yes, faith, I am so now. Here, my honest Rowley—here, get me this changed directly, and take a hundred pounds of it immediately to old Stanley.

ROWLEY   A hundred pounds! Consider only—

CHARLES   Gad's life, don't talk about it! poor Stanley's wants are pressing, and if you don't make haste we shall have someone call that has a better right to the money.

ROWLEY   Ah! there's the point! I never will cease dunning you with the old proverb—

CHARLES   "Be just before you're generous."— Why, so I would if I could, but Justice is an old lame, hobbling beldame, and I can't get her to keep pace with Generosity for the soul of me.

ROWLEY   Yes, Charles, believe me, one hour's reflection—

CHARLES   Aye, aye, it's all very true; but, hark'ee, Rowley, while I have, by Heaven, I'll give; so, damn your economy—and now for hazard.

[*Exeunt.*]

SCENE II. *The parlor.*

[*Enter* SIR OLIVER SURFACE *and* MOSES.]

MOSES   Well, sir, I think, as Sir Peter said, you have seen Mr. Charles in high glory; 'tis great pity he's so extravagant.

SIR OLIVER   True, but he would not sell my picture.

MOSES   And loves wine and women so much.

SIR OLIVER   But he would not sell my picture.

MOSES   And games so deep.

SIR OLIVER   But he would not sell my picture!— Oh, here's Rowley.   [*Enter* ROWLEY.]

ROWLEY   So, Sir Oliver, I find you have made a purchase—

SIR OLIVER   Yes, yes, our young rake has parted with his ancestors like old tapestry.

ROWLEY   And here has he commissioned me to re-deliver you part of the purchase money—I mean, though, in your necessitous character of old Stanley.

MOSES   Ah! there is the pity of all; he is so damned charitable.

ROWLEY   And I left a hosier and two tailors in the hall, who, I'm sure, won't be paid, and this hundred would satisfy them.

SIR OLIVER   Well, well, I'll pay his debts and his benevolence too. But now I am no more a broker, and you shall introduce me to the elder brother as old Stanley.

ROWLEY   Not yet awhile; Sir Peter, I know, means to call there about this time.   [*Enter* TRIP.]

TRIP   Oh, gentlemen, I beg pardon for not showing you out; this way—Moses, a word.

[*Exeunt* TRIP *and* MOSES.]

SIR OLIVER   There's a fellow for you! Would you believe it, that puppy intercepted the Jew on our coming and wanted to raise money before he got to his master!

ROWLEY   Indeed!

SIR OLIVER   Yes; they are now planning an annuity business. Ah, Master Rowley, in my days servants were content with the follies of their masters when they were worn a little threadbare; but now they have their vices, like their birthday clothes, with the gloss on.   [*Exeunt.*]

SCENE III. *A library in* JOSEPH SURFACE'S *house.*

[*Enter* JOSEPH SURFACE *and* SERVANT.]

JOSEPH   No letter from Lady Teazle?

SERVANT   No, sir.

JOSEPH   [*Aside*] I am surprised she has not sent if she is prevented from coming. Sir Peter certainly does not suspect me. Yet I wish I may not lose the heiress through the scrape I have drawn myself into with the wife; however, Charles's imprudence and bad character are great points in my favor.   [*Knocking without.*]

SERVANT   Sir, I believe that must be Lady Teazle.

JOSEPH   Hold! See whether it is or not before you go to the door. I have a particular message for you if it should be my brother.

SERVANT   'Tis her ladyship, sir; she always leaves her chair at the milliner's in the next street.

JOSEPH   Stay, stay; draw that screen before the window—that will do. My opposite neighbor is a maiden lady of so curious a temper.

[SERVANT *draws the screen, and exit.*]

I have a difficult hand to play in this affair. Lady Teazle has lately suspected my views on Maria, but she must by no means be let into that secret —at least till I have her more in my power.

[*Enter* LADY TEAZLE.]

LADY TEAZLE   What, sentiment in soliloquy now? Have you been very impatient? O lud! don't pretend to look grave. I vow I couldn't come before.

JOSEPH   O madam, punctuality is a species of constancy very unfashionable in a lady of quality.

LADY TEAZLE   Upon my word, you ought to pity me. Do you know Sir Peter is grown so ill-natured to me of late, and so jealous of Charles, too—that's the best of the story, isn't it?

JOSEPH   [*Aside*] I am glad my scandalous friends keep that up.

LADY TEAZLE   I am sure I wish he would let Maria marry him, and then perhaps he would be convinced; don't you, Mr. Surface?

JOSEPH   [*Aside*] Indeed I do not.—Oh, certainly I do! for then my dear Lady Teazle would also be convinced how wrong her suspicions were of my having any design on the silly girl.

LADY TEAZLE   Well, well, I'm inclined to believe you. But isn't it provoking to have the most ill-natured things said of one? And there's my friend Lady Sneerwell has circulated I don't know how many scandalous tales of me, and all without any foundation too; that's what vexes me.

JOSEPH   Aye, madam, to be sure, that is the provoking circumstance—without foundation; yes,

yes, there's the mortification, indeed, for when a scandalous story is believed against one, there certainly is no comfort like the consciousness of having deserved it.

LADY TEAZLE   No, to be sure, then I'd forgive their malice; but to attack me, who am really so innocent, and who never say an ill-natured thing of anybody—that is, of any friend; and then Sir Peter, too, to have him so peevish, and so suspicious, when I know the integrity of my own heart—indeed 'tis monstrous!

JOSEPH   But, my dear Lady Teazle, 'tis your own fault if you suffer it. When a husband entertains a groundless suspicion of his wife and withdraws his confidence from her, the original compact is broken and she owes it to the honor of her sex to outwit him.

LADY TEAZLE   Indeed! so that if he suspects me without cause, it follows that the best way of curing his jealousy is to give him reason for 't?

JOSEPH   Undoubtedly—for your husband should never be deceived in you, and in that case it becomes you to be frail in compliment to his discernment.

LADY TEAZLE   To be sure, what you say is very reasonable, and when the consciousness of my innocence—

JOSEPH   Ah, my dear madam, there is the great mistake! 'tis this very conscious innocence that is of the greatest prejudice to you. What is it makes you negligent of forms and careless of the world's opinion? why, the consciousness of your own innocence. What makes you thoughtless in your conduct and apt to run into a thousand little imprudences? why, the consciousness of your own innocence. What makes you impatient of Sir Peter's temper and outrageous at his suspicions? why, the consciousness of your innocence.

LADY TEAZLE   'Tis very true!

JOSEPH   Now, my dear Lady Teazle, if you would but once make a trifling *faux pas*, you can't conceive how cautious you would grow, and how ready to humor and agree with your husband.

LADY TEAZLE   Do you think so?

JOSEPH   Oh, I am sure on 't; and then you would find all scandal would cease at once, for—in short, your character at present is like a person in a plethora, absolutely dying from too much health.

LADY TEAZLE   So, so; then I perceive your prescription is that I must sin in my own defense and part with my virtue to preserve my reputation?

JOSEPH   Exactly so, upon my credit, ma'am.

LADY TEAZLE   Well, certainly this is the oddest doctrine and the newest receipt[1] for avoiding calumny!

JOSEPH   An infallible one, believe me. Prudence, like experience, must be paid for.

LADY TEAZLE   Why, if my understanding were once convinced—

JOSEPH   Oh, certainly, madam, your understanding should be convinced. Yes, yes—Heaven forbid I should persuade you to do anything you thought wrong. No, no, I have too much honor to desire it.

LADY TEAZLE   Don't you think we may as well leave *honor* out of the argument?

JOSEPH   Ah, the ill effects of your country education, I see, still remain with you.

LADY TEAZLE   I doubt they do, indeed; and I will fairly own to you that if I could be persuaded to do wrong, it would be by Sir Peter's ill usage sooner than your *honorable logic*, after all.

JOSEPH   [*Taking her hand*] Then, by this hand, which he is unworthy of—   [*Enter* SERVANT.] 'Sdeath, you blockhead—what do you want?

SERVANT   I beg your pardon, sir, but I thought you would not choose Sir Peter to come up without announcing him.

JOSEPH   Sir Peter!—Oons—the devil!

LADY TEAZLE   Sir Peter! O lud!—I'm ruined! I'm ruined!

SERVANT   Sir, 'twasn't I let him in.

LADY TEAZLE   Oh! I'm quite undone! What will become of me? Now, Mr. Logic—Oh! mercy, sir, he's on the stairs—I'll get behind here—and if ever I'm so imprudent again—
        [*Goes behind the screen.*]

JOSEPH   Give me that book.

[*Sits down.* SERVANT *pretends to adjust his chair.*]
        [*Enter* SIR PETER.]

SIR PETER   Aye, ever improving himself—Mr. Surface, Mr. Surface—

JOSEPH   Oh, my dear Sir Peter, I beg your pardon —[*Gaping, throws away the book.*] I have been dozing over a stupid book. Well, I am much obliged to you for this call. You haven't been

Scene iii. **1. receipt:** recipe.

here, I believe, since I fitted up this room. Books, you know, are the only things in which I am a coxcomb.

SIR PETER 'Tis very neat, indeed. Well, well, that's proper; and you can make even your screen a source of knowledge—hung, I perceive, with maps.

JOSEPH Oh, yes, I find great use in that screen.

SIR PETER I dare say you must, certainly, when you want to find anything in a hurry.

JOSEPH [Aside] Aye, or to hide anything in a hurry either.

SIR PETER Well, I have a little private business—

JOSEPH [To the SERVANT] You need not stay.

SERVANT No, sir.

JOSEPH Here's a chair, Sir Peter—I beg—

SIR PETER Well, now we are alone, there is a subject, my dear friend, on which I wish to unburden my mind to you—a point of the greatest moment to my peace; in short, my good friend, Lady Teazle's conduct of late has made me very unhappy.

JOSEPH Indeed! I am very sorry to hear it.

SIR PETER Yes, 'tis but too plain she has not the least regard for me; but what's worse I have pretty good authority to suppose she has formed an attachment to another.

JOSEPH Indeed! you astonish me!

SIR PETER Yes! and, between ourselves, I think I've discovered the person.

JOSEPH How! you alarm me exceedingly.

SIR PETER Aye, my dear friend, I knew you would sympathize with me!

JOSEPH Yes—believe me, Sir Peter, such a discovery would hurt me just as much as it would you.

SIR PETER I am convinced of it. Ah! it is a happiness to have a friend whom we can trust even with one's family secrets. But have you no guess who I mean?

JOSEPH I haven't the most distant idea. It can't be Sir Benjamin Backbite!

SIR PETER Oh, no! What say you to Charles?

JOSEPH My brother!—impossible!

SIR PETER Oh, my dear friend, the goodness of your own heart misleads you. You judge of others by yourself.

JOSEPH Certainly, Sir Peter, the heart that is conscious of its own integrity is ever slow to credit another's treachery.

SIR PETER True, but your brother has no sentiment —you never hear him talk so.

JOSEPH Yet I can't but think Lady Teazle herself has too much principle.

SIR PETER Aye, but what is principle against the flattery of a handsome, lively young fellow?

JOSEPH That's very true.

SIR PETER And there's, you know, the difference of our ages makes it very improbable that she should have any great affection for me; and if she were to be frail and I were to make it public, why the town would only laugh at me, the foolish old bachelor who had married a girl.

JOSEPH That's true, to be sure—they would laugh.

SIR PETER Laugh! aye, and make ballads, and paragraphs, and the devil knows what of me.

JOSEPH No, you must never make it public.

SIR PETER But then again—that the nephew of my old friend, Sir Oliver, should be the person to attempt such a wrong, hurts me more nearly.

JOSEPH Aye, there's the point. When ingratitude barbs the dart of injury, the wound has double danger in it.

SIR PETER Aye—I, that was, in a manner, left his guardian; in whose house he had been so often entertained; who never in my life denied him— my advice.

JOSEPH Oh, 'tis not to be credited! There may be a man capable of such baseness, to be sure; but for my part till you can give me positive proofs, I cannot but doubt it. However, if it should be proved on him, he is no longer a brother of mine—I disclaim kindred with him; for the man who can break the laws of hospitality and tempt the wife of his friend, deserves to be branded as the pest of society.

SIR PETER What a difference there is between you! What noble sentiments!

JOSEPH Yet I cannot suspect Lady Teazle's honor.

SIR PETER I am sure I wish to think well of her and to remove all ground of quarrel between us. She has lately reproached me more than once with having made no settlement on her, and in our last quarrel she almost hinted that she should not break her heart if I was dead. Now, as we seem to differ in our ideas of expense, I have resolved she shall have her own way and be her own mistress in that respect for the future; and if I were to die, she will find I have not been inattentive to her interest while living. Here, my friend, are the drafts of two deeds, which I wish to have your opinion on. By one she will enjoy eight hundred a year independent while I live, and by the other the bulk of my fortune at my death.

JOSEPH   This conduct, Sir Peter, is indeed truly generous. [*Aside*] I wish it may not corrupt my pupil.

SIR PETER   Yes, I am determined she shall have no cause to complain, though I would not have her acquainted with the latter instance of my affection yet awhile.

JOSEPH   [*Aside*] Nor I, if I could help it.

SIR PETER   And now, my dear friend, if you please, we will talk over the situation of your hopes with Maria.

JOSEPH   [*Softly*] Oh, no, Sir Peter; another time, if you please.

SIR PETER   I am sensibly chagrined at the little progress you seem to make in her affections.

JOSEPH   [*Softly*] I beg you will not mention it. What are my disappointments when your happiness is in debate! [*Aside.*] 'Sdeath, I shall be ruined every way!

SIR PETER   And though you are so averse to my acquainting Lady Teazle with your passion for Maria, I'm sure she's not your enemy in the affair.

JOSEPH   Pray, Sir Peter, now oblige me. I am really too much affected by the subject we have been speaking of, to bestow a thought on my own concerns.   The man who is entrusted with his friend's distresses can never— [*Enter* SERVANT.] Well, sir?

SERVANT   Your brother, sir, is speaking to a gentleman in the street, and says he knows you are within.

JOSEPH   'Sdeath, blockhead, I'm not within—I'm out for the day.

SIR PETER   Stay—hold—a thought has struck me: you shall be at home.

JOSEPH   Well, well, let him up.   [*Exit* SERVANT.] [*Aside.*] He'll interrupt Sir Peter, however.

SIR PETER   Now, my good friend, oblige me, I entreat you. Before Charles comes, let me conceal myself somewhere; then do you tax him on the point we have been talking, and his answer may satisfy me at once.

JOSEPH   Oh, fie, Sir Peter! would you have me join in so mean a trick—to trepan[2] my brother too?

SIR PETER   Nay, you tell me you are sure he is innocent; if so, you do him the greatest service by giving him an opportunity to clear himself, and you will set my heart at rest. Come, you shall not refuse me; here, behind the screen will be—Hey! what the devil! There seems to be one listener here already—I'll swear, I saw a petticoat!

JOSEPH   Ha! ha! ha! Well, this is ridiculous enough. I'll tell you, Sir Peter, though I hold a man of intrigue to be a most despicable character, yet, you know, it does not follow that one is to be an absolute Joseph either! Hark'ee, 'tis a little French milliner, a silly rogue that plagues me; and having some character to lose, on your coming, sir, she ran behind the screen.

SIR PETER   Ah, you rogue!—But, egad, she has overheard all I have been saying of my wife.

JOSEPH   Oh, 'twill never go any farther, you may depend upon it!

SIR PETER   No? then, faith, let her hear it out.— Here's a closet will do as well.

JOSEPH   Well, go in there.

SIR PETER   [*Going into the closet*] Sly rogue! sly rogue!

JOSEPH   A narrow escape, indeed! and a curious situation I'm in, to part man and wife in this manner.

LADY TEAZLE   [*Peeping*] Couldn't I steal off?

JOSEPH   Keep close, my angel!

SIR PETER   [*Peeping*] Joseph, tax him home.

JOSEPH   Back, my dear friend!

LADY TEAZLE   [*Peeping*] Couldn't you lock Sir Peter in?

JOSEPH   Be still, my life!

SIR PETER   [*Peeping*] You're sure the little milliner won't blab?

JOSEPH   In, in, my dear Sir Peter!—'Fore Gad, I wish I had a key to the door.

[*Enter* CHARLES SURFACE.]

CHARLES   Holla! brother, what has been the matter? Your fellow would not let me up at first. What! have you had a Jew or a wench with you?

JOSEPH   Neither, brother, I assure you.

CHARLES   But what has made Sir Peter steal off? I thought he had been with you.

2. trepan: ensnare.

JOSEPH He *was*, brother; but hearing you were coming, he did not choose to stay.

CHARLES What! was the old gentleman afraid I wanted to borrow money of him?

JOSEPH No, sir; but I am sorry to find, Charles, you have lately given that worthy man grounds for great uneasiness.

CHARLES Yes, they tell me I do that to a great many worthy men.—But how so, pray?

JOSEPH To be plain with you, brother, he thinks you are endeavoring to gain Lady Teazle's affection from him.

CHARLES Who, I? O lud! not I, upon my word. Ha! ha! ha! ha! So the old fellow has found out that he has got a young wife, has he?—or, what is worse, Lady Teazle has found out she has an old husband?

JOSEPH This is no subject to jest on, brother. He who can laugh—

CHARLES True, true, as you were going to say—then, seriously, I never had the least idea of what you charge me with, upon my honor.

JOSEPH [*Loudly*] Well, it will give Sir Peter great satisfaction to hear this.

CHARLES To be sure, I once thought the lady seemed to have taken a fancy to me, but upon my soul I never gave her the least encouragement. Besides, you know my attachment to Maria.

JOSEPH But sure, brother, even if Lady Teazle had betrayed the fondest partiality for you—

CHARLES Why, look'ee, Joseph, I hope I shall never deliberately do a dishonorable action, but if a pretty woman was purposely to throw herself in my way—and that pretty woman married to a man old enough to be her father—

JOSEPH Well—

CHARLES Why, I believe I should be obliged to borrow a little of your morality, that's all. But brother, do you know now that you surprise me exceedingly, by naming *me* with Lady Teazle; for i' faith, I always understood you were her favorite.

JOSEPH Oh, for shame, Charles! This retort is foolish.

CHARLES Nay, I swear I have seen you exchange such significant glances—

JOSEPH Nay, nay, sir, this is no jest.

CHARLES Egad, I'm serious! Don't you remember one day when I called here—

JOSEPH Nay, prithee, Charles—

CHARLES And found you together—

JOSEPH Zounds, sir, I insist—

CHARLES And another time when your servant—

JOSEPH Brother, brother, a word with you!—[*Aside.*] Gad, I must stop him.

CHARLES Informed, I say that—

JOSEPH Hush! I beg your pardon, but Sir Peter has overheard all we have been saying. I knew you would clear yourself, or I should not have consented.

CHARLES How, Sir Peter! Where is he?

JOSEPH [*Points to the closet*] Softly!—there!

CHARLES Oh, 'fore Heaven, I'll have him out—Sir Peter, come forth!

JOSEPH No, no—

CHARLES I say, Sir Peter, come into court.—[*Pulls in* SIR PETER.] What! my old guardian!—What! turn inquisitor and take evidence incog?

SIR PETER Give me your hand, Charles—I believe I have suspected you wrongfully; but you mustn't be angry with Joseph—'twas my plan!

CHARLES Indeed!

SIR PETER But I acquit you. I promise you I don't think near so ill of you as I did; what I have heard has given me great satisfaction.

CHARLES Egad, then, 'twas lucky you didn't hear any more, [*Apart to* JOSEPH] wasn't it, Joseph?

SIR PETER Ah! you would have retorted on him.

CHARLES Ah, aye, that was a joke.

SIR PETER Yes, yes, I know his honor too well.

CHARLES But you might as well have suspected *him* as *me* in this matter, for all that—[*Apart to* JOSEPH] mightn't he, Joseph?

SIR PETER Well, well, I believe you.

JOSEPH [*Aside*] Would they were both out of the room!

SIR PETER And in future, perhaps, we may not be such strangers.

[*Enter* SERVANT, *and whispers to* JOSEPH SURFACE.]

SERVANT Lady Sneerwell is below, and says she will come up.   [*Exit* SERVANT.]

JOSEPH Gentlemen, I beg pardon—I must wait on you downstairs; here is a person come on particular business.

CHARLES Well, you can see him in another room. Sir Peter and I have not met a long time, and I have something to say to him.

JOSEPH [*Aside*] They must not be left together.—I'll send this man away, and return directly.—

[*Apart to* SIR PETER.] Sir Peter, not a word of the French milliner.

SIR PETER   [*Apart to* JOSEPH] I! not for the world! [*Exit* JOSEPH SURFACE.]—Ah, Charles, if you associated more with your brother, one might indeed hope for your reformation. He is a man of sentiment. Well, there is nothing in the world so noble as a man of sentiment.

CHARLES   Pshaw! he is too moral by half; and so apprehensive of his "good name," as he calls it, that I suppose he would as soon let a priest into his house as a girl.

SIR PETER   No, no—come, come—you wrong him. No, no! Joseph is no rake, but he is no such saint either, in that respect.—[*Aside.*] I have a great mind to tell him—we should have a laugh at Joseph.

CHARLES   Oh, hang him! he's a very anchorite—a young hermit!

SIR PETER   Hark'ee—you must not abuse him; he may chance to hear of it again, I promise you.

CHARLES   Why, you won't tell him?

SIR PETER   No—but—this way. [*Aside.*] Egad, I'll tell him.—Hark'ee—have you a mind to have a good laugh at Joseph?

CHARLES   I should like it of all things.

SIR PETER   Then, i' faith, we will! I'll be quit with him for discovering me. He had a girl with him when I called.

CHARLES   What! Joseph? you jest.

SIR PETER   Hush!—a little French milliner—and the best of the jest is—she's in the room now.

CHARLES   The devil she is!

SIR PETER   Hush! I tell you. [*Points.*]

CHARLES   Behind the screen! 'Slife, let's unveil her!

SIR PETER   No, no, he's coming—you shan't, indeed!

CHARLES   Oh, egad, we'll have a peep at the little milliner!

SIR PETER   Not for the world!—Joseph will never forgive me.

CHARLES   I'll stand by you—

SIR PETER   Odds, here he is!

[JOSEPH SURFACE *enters just as* CHARLES SURFACE *throws down the screen.*]

CHARLES   Lady Teazle, by all that's wonderful!

SIR PETER   Lady Teazle, by all that's damnable!

CHARLES   Sir Peter, this is one of the smartest French milliners I ever saw. Egad, you seem all

to have been diverting yourselves here at hide and seek, and I don't see who is out of the secret. Shall I beg your ladyship to inform me? Not a word!—Brother, will you be pleased to explain this matter? What! is Morality dumb too?—Sir Peter, though I found you in the dark, perhaps you are not so now! All mute!—Well—though I can make nothing of the affair, I suppose you perfectly understand one another; so I'll leave you to yourselves.—[*Going.*] Brother, I'm sorry to find you have given that worthy man grounds for so much uneasiness.—Sir Peter! "there's nothing in the world so noble as a man of sentiment!"   [*Exit* CHARLES.]

[*They stand for some time looking at each other.*]

JOSEPH   Sir Peter—notwithstanding—I confess—that appearances are against me—if you will afford me your patience—I make no doubt—but I shall explain everything to your satisfaction.

SIR PETER   If you please, sir.

JOSEPH   The fact is, sir, that Lady Teazle, knowing my pretensions to your ward Maria—I say, sir, Lady Teazle, being apprehensive of the jealousy of your temper—and knowing my friendship to the family—she, sir, I say—called here—in order that—I might explain these pretensions—but on your coming—being apprehensive—as I said—of your jealousy—she withdrew—and this, you may depend on it, is the whole truth of the matter.

SIR PETER   A very clear account, upon my word, and I dare swear the lady will vouch for every article of it.

LADY TEAZLE   For not one word of it, Sir Peter.

SIR PETER   How! don't you think it worth while to agree in the lie!

LADY TEAZLE   There is not one syllable of truth in what that gentleman has told you.

SIR PETER   I believe you, upon my soul, ma'am!

JOSEPH   [*Aside*] 'Sdeath, madam, will you betray me?

LADY TEAZLE   Good Mr. Hypocrite, by your leave, I'll speak for myself.

SIR PETER   Aye, let her alone, sir; you'll find she'll make out a better story than you, without prompting.

LADY TEAZLE   Hear me, Sir Peter!—I came here on no matter relating to your ward, and even ignorant of this gentleman's pretensions to her. But I came, seduced by his insidious arguments, at least to listen to his pretended passion, if not to sacrifice your honor to his baseness.

SIR PETER Now, I believe, the truth is coming, indeed!

JOSEPH The woman's mad!

LADY TEAZLE No, sir; she has recovered her senses, and your own arts have furnished her with the means—Sir Peter, I do not expect you to credit me—but the tenderness you expressed for me when I am sure you could not think I was a witness to it, has so penetrated to my heart that had I left the place without the shame of this discovery, my future life should have spoken the sincerity of my gratitude. As for that smooth-tongued hypocrite, who would have seduced the wife of his too credulous friend while he affected honorable addresses to his ward—I behold him now in a light so truly despicable that I shall never again respect myself for having listened to him. [*Exit* LADY TEAZLE.]

JOSEPH Notwithstanding all this, Sir Peter, Heaven knows—

SIR PETER That you are a villain! and so I leave you to your conscience.

JOSEPH You are too rash, Sir Peter; you *shall* hear me. The man who shuts out conviction by refusing to—[*Exeunt* SIR PETER *and* JOSEPH SURFACE *talking*.]

ACT V

SCENE I. *The library in* JOSEPH SURFACE'*s house.*

[*Enter* JOSEPH SURFACE *and* SERVANT.]

JOSEPH Mr. Stanley! and why should you think I would see him? You must know he comes to ask something.

SERVANT Sir, I should not have let him in, but that Mr. Rowley came to the door with him.

JOSEPH Pshaw! blockhead! to suppose that I should now be in a temper to receive visits from poor relations!—Well, why don't you show the fellow up?

SERVANT I will, sir—Why, sir, it was not my fault that Sir Peter discovered my lady—

JOSEPH Go, fool! [*Exit* SERVANT.] Sure, Fortune never played a man of my policy such a trick before!—my character with Sir Peter, my hopes with Maria, destroyed in a moment! I'm in a rare humor to listen to other people's distresses! I shan't be able to bestow even a benevolent sentiment on Stanley.—So! here he comes, and Rowley with him. I must try to recover myself and put a little charity into my face, however.

[*Exit.*]

[*Enter* SIR OLIVER SURFACE *and* ROWLEY.]

SIR OLIVER What! does he avoid us? That was he, was it not?

ROWLEY It was, sir. But I doubt you are come a little too abruptly. His nerves are so weak that the sight of a poor relation may be too much for him. I should have gone first to break it to him.

SIR OLIVER Oh, plague of his nerves! Yet this is he whom Sir Peter extols as a man of the most benevolent way of thinking!

ROWLEY As to his way of thinking, I cannot pretend to decide; for to do him justice, he appears to have as much speculative benevolence as any private gentleman in the kingdom, though he is seldom so sensual as to indulge himself in the exercise of it.

SIR OLIVER Yet he has a string of charitable sentiments at his fingers' ends.

ROWLEY Or rather, at his tongue's end, Sir Oliver; for I believe there is no sentiment he has such faith in as that "charity begins at home."

SIR OLIVER And his, I presume, is of that domestic sort which never stirs abroad at all.

ROWLEY I doubt you'll find it so;—but he's coming. I mustn't seem to interrupt you; and you know, immediately as you leave him, I come in to announce your arrival in your real character.

SIR OLIVER True; and afterwards you'll meet me at Sir Peter's.

ROWLEY Without losing a moment. [*Exit.*]

SIR OLIVER I don't like the complaisance of his features. [*Enter* JOSEPH SURFACE.]

JOSEPH Sir, I beg you ten thousand pardons for keeping you a moment waiting.—Mr. Stanley, I presume.

SIR OLIVER At your service.

JOSEPH Sir, I beg you will do me the honor to sit down—I entreat you, sir.

SIR OLIVER Dear sir—there's no occasion.—[*Aside.*] Too civil by half!

JOSEPH I have not the pleasure of knowing you, Mr. Stanley, but I am extremely happy to see you look so well. You were nearly related to my mother, I think, Mr. Stanley?

SIR OLIVER I was sir—so nearly that my present poverty, I fear, may do discredit to her wealthy children, else I should not have presumed to trouble you.

JOSEPH Dear sir, there needs no apology; he that is in distress, though a stranger, has a right to claim kindred with the wealthy. I am sure I wish I was one of that class, and had it in my power to offer you even a small relief.

SIR OLIVER If your uncle, Sir Oliver, were here, I should have a friend.

JOSEPH I wish he was, sir, with all my heart; you should not want an advocate with him, believe me, sir.

SIR OLIVER I should not need one—my distresses would recommend me. But I imagined his bounty would enable you to become the agent of his charity.

JOSEPH My dear sir, you were strangely misinformed. Sir Oliver is a worthy man—a very worthy man; but avarice, Mr. Stanley, is the vice of age. I will tell you, my good sir, in confidence, what he has done for me has been a mere nothing—though people, I know, have thought otherwise, and for my part I never chose to contradict the report.

SIR OLIVER What! has he never transmitted you bullion—rupees—pagodas?[1]

JOSEPH Oh, dear sir, nothing of the kind! No, no; a few presents now and then—china, shawls, congou tea, avadavats,[2] and Indian crackers—little more, believe me.

SIR OLIVER [Aside] Here's gratitude for twelve thousand pounds!—avadavats and Indian crackers!

JOSEPH Then, my dear sir, you have heard, I doubt not, of the extravagance of my brother. There are very few would credit what I have done for that unfortunate young man.

SIR OLIVER [Aside] Not I, for one!

JOSEPH The sums I have lent him! Indeed I have been exceedingly to blame; it was an amiable weakness; however, I don't pretend to defend it—and now I feel it doubly culpable since it has deprived me of the pleasure of serving you, Mr. Stanley, as my heart dictates.

SIR OLIVER [Aside] Dissembler!—Then, sir, you can't assist me?

Act V, scene i. **1. pagodas:** Indian coins. **2. avadavats:** songbirds.

JOSEPH At present, it grieves me to say, I cannot; but whenever I have the ability, you may depend upon hearing from me.

SIR OLIVER I am extremely sorry—

JOSEPH Not more than I, believe me; to pity, without the power to relieve, is still more painful than to ask and be denied.

SIR OLIVER Kind sir, your modest obedient humble servant.

JOSEPH You leave me deeply affected, Mr. Stanley.—[Calls to SERVANT.] William, be ready to open the door.

SIR OLIVER Oh, dear sir, no ceremony.

JOSEPH Your very obedient.

SIR OLIVER Your most obsequious.

JOSEPH You may depend upon hearing from me whenever I can be of service.

SIR OLIVER Sweet sir, you are too good!

JOSEPH In the meantime I wish you health and spirits.

SIR OLIVER Your ever grateful and perpetual humble servant.

JOSEPH Sir, yours as sincerely.

SIR OLIVER [Aside] Charles, you are my heir!
[Exit.]

JOSEPH This is one bad effect of a good character; it invites application from the unfortunate, and there needs no small degree of address to gain the reputation of benevolence without incurring the expense. The silver ore of pure charity is an expensive article in the catalogue of a man's good qualities; whereas the sentimental French plate I use instead of it makes just as good a show and pays no tax.   [Enter ROWLEY.]

ROWLEY Mr. Surface, your servant. I was apprehensive of interrupting you, though my business demands immediate attention, as this note will inform you.

JOSEPH Always happy to see Mr. Rowley. [Reads the letter.] Sir Oliver Surface!—My uncle arrived!

ROWLEY He is, indeed; we have just parted—quite well, after a speedy voyage, and impatient to embrace his worthy nephew.

JOSEPH I am astonished!—William! stop Mr. Stanley if he's not gone.

ROWLEY Oh! he's out of reach, I believe.

JOSEPH Why did you not let me know this when you came in together?

ROWLEY I thought you had particular business. But I must be gone to inform your brother and appoint him here to meet your uncle. He will be with you in a quarter of an hour.

JOSEPH So he says. Well, I am strangely overjoyed at his coming.—[*Aside.*] Never, to be sure, was anything so damned unlucky!

ROWLEY You will be delighted to see how well he looks.

JOSEPH Oh! I'm overjoyed to hear it.—[*Aside.*] Just at this time!

ROWLEY I'll tell him how impatiently you expect him.

JOSEPH Do, do; pray, give my best duty and affection. Indeed, I cannot express the sensations I feel at the thought of seeing him.

[Exit ROWLEY.]

—Certainly his coming just at this time is the cruelest piece of ill-fortune.   [*Exit.*]

SCENE II. *A room in* SIR PETER TEAZLE'*s house.*

[Enter MRS. CANDOUR and MAID.]

MAID Indeed, ma'am, my lady will see nobody at present.

MRS. CANDOUR Did you tell her it was her friend Mrs. Candour?

MAID Yes, ma'am, but she begs you will excuse her.

MRS. CANDOUR Do go again; I shall be glad to see her, if it be only for a moment, for I am sure she must be in great distress.   [*Exit* MAID.]
Dear heart, how provoking! I'm not mistress of half the circumstances! We shall have the whole affair in the newspapers, with the names of the parties at length, before I have dropped the story at a dozen houses.

[Enter SIR BENJAMIN BACKBITE.]

—Oh, dear Sir Benjamin! you have heard, I suppose—

SIR BENJAMIN Of Lady Teazle and Mr. Surface—

MRS. CANDOUR And Sir Peter's discovery—

SIR BENJAMIN Oh, the strangest piece of business, to be sure!

MRS. CANDOUR Well, I never was so surprised in my life. I am so sorry for all parties, indeed.

SIR BENJAMIN Now, I don't pity Sir Peter at all; he was so extravagantly partial to Mr. Surface.

MRS. CANDOUR Mr. Surface! Why, 'twas with Charles Lady Teazle was detected.

SIR BENJAMIN No, no, I tell you—Mr. Surface is the gallant.

MRS. CANDOUR No such thing! Charles is the man. 'Twas Mr. Surface brought Sir Peter on purpose to discover them.

SIR BENJAMIN I tell you I had it from one—

MRS. CANDOUR And I have it from one—

SIR BENJAMIN Who had it from one who had it—

MRS. CANDOUR From one immediately—But here comes Lady Sneerwell; perhaps she knows the whole affair.   [*Enter* LADY SNEERWELL.]

LADY SNEERWELL So, my dear Mrs. Candour, here's a sad affair of our friend Lady Teazle!

MRS. CANDOUR Aye, my dear friend, who would have thought—

LADY SNEERWELL Well, there is no trusting appearances—though, indeed, she was always too lively for me.

MRS. CANDOUR To be sure her manners were a little too free; but then, she was so young!

LADY SNEERWELL And had, indeed, some good qualities.

MRS. CANDOUR So she had, indeed. But have you heard the particulars?

LADY SNEERWELL No, but everybody says that Mr. Surface—

SIR BENJAMIN Aye, there! I told you Mr. Surface was the man.

MRS. CANDOUR No, no! indeed, the assignation was with Charles.

LADY SNEERWELL With Charles! You alarm me, Mrs. Candour!

MRS. CANDOUR Yes, yes; he was the lover. Mr. Surface, to do him justice, was only the informer.

SIR BENJAMIN Well, I'll not dispute with you, Mrs. Candour, but be it which it may, I hope that Sir Peter's wound will not—

MRS. CANDOUR Sir Peter's wound! Oh, mercy! I didn't hear a word of their fighting.

LADY SNEERWELL Nor I, a syllable.

SIR BENJAMIN No! what, no mention of the duel?

MRS. CANDOUR Not a word.

SIR BENJAMIN Oh, yes! they fought before they left the room.

LADY SNEERWELL Pray, let us hear!

MRS. CANDOUR Aye, do oblige us with the duel!

SIR BENJAMIN "Sir," says Sir Peter, immediately after the discovery, "you are a most ungrateful fellow."

MRS. CANDOUR Aye to Charles—

SIR BENJAMIN   No, no—to Mr. Surface—"a most ungrateful fellow; and old as I am, sir," says he, "I insist on immediate satisfaction."

MRS. CANDOUR   Aye, that must have been to Charles, for 'tis very unlikely Mr. Surface should fight in his own house.

SIR BENJAMIN   Gad's life, ma'am, not at all—"giving me immediate satisfaction." On this, ma'am, Lady Teazle, seeing Sir Peter in such danger, ran out of the room in strong hysterics, and Charles after her, calling out for hartshorn[1] and water; then, madam, they began to fight with swords—   [Enter CRABTREE.]

CRABTREE   With pistols, nephew—pistols! I have it from undoubted authority.

MRS. CANDOUR   Oh, Mr. Crabtree, then it is all true!

CRABTREE   Too true, indeed, madam and Sir Peter is dangerously wounded—

SIR BENJAMIN   By a thrust in second quite through his left side—

CRABTREE   By a bullet lodged in the thorax.

MRS. CANDOUR   Mercy on me! Poor Sir Peter!

CRABTREE   Yes, madam—though Charles would have avoided the matter if he could.

MRS. CANDOUR   I knew Charles was the person.

SIR BENJAMIN   My uncle, I see, knows nothing of the matter.

CRABTREE   But Sir Peter taxed him with the basest ingratitude—

SIR BENJAMIN   That I told you, you know—

CRABTREE   Do, nephew, let me speak!—and insisted on immediate—

SIR BENJAMIN   Just as I said—

CRABTREE   Odds life, nephew, allow others to know something too! A pair of pistols lay on the bureau (for Mr. Surface, it seems, had come home the night before late from Salthill, where he had been to see the Montem[2] with a friend who has a son at Eton), so, unluckily, the pistols were left charged.

SIR BENJAMIN   I heard nothing of this.

CRABTREE   Sir Peter forced Charles to take one, and they fired, it seems, pretty nearly together. Charles's shot took effect, as I tell you, and Sir Peter's missed; but what is very extraordinary, the ball struck against a little bronze Shakespeare that stood over the fireplece, grazed out of the

window at a right angle, and wounded the postman, who was just coming to the door with a double letter from Northamptonshire.

SIR BENJAMIN   My uncle's account is more circumstantial, I confess; but I believe mine is the true one, for all that.

LADY SNEERWELL   [Aside] I am more interested in this affair than they imagine, and must have better information.   [Exit LADY SNEERWELL.]

SIR BENJAMIN   Ah! Lady Sneerwell's alarm is very easily accounted for.

CRABTREE   Yes, yes, they certainly do say—but that's neither here nor there.

MRS. CANDOUR   But pray, where is Sir Peter at present?

CRABTREE   Oh! they brought him home, and he is now in the house, though the servants are ordered to deny him.

MRS. CANDOUR   I believe so; and Lady Teazle, I suppose, attending him.

CRABTREE   Yes, yes; and I saw one of the faculty[3] enter just before me.

SIR BENJAMIN   Hey! who comes here?

CRABTREE   Oh, this is he—the physician, depend on 't.

MRS. CANDOUR   Oh, certainly! it must be the physician; and now we shall know.

[Enter SIR OLIVER SURFACE.]

CRABTREE   Well, doctor, what hopes?

MRS. CANDOUR   Aye, doctor, how's your patient?

SIR BENJAMIN   Now, doctor, isn't it a wound with a small-sword?

CRABTREE   A bullet lodged in the thorax, for a hundred!

SIR OLIVER   Doctor!—a wound with a small-sword! and a bullet in the thorax!—Oons! are you mad, good people?

SIR BENJAMIN   Perhaps, sir, you are not a doctor?

SIR OLIVER   Truly, I am to thank you for my degree if I am.

CRABTREE   Only a friend of Sir Peter's then, I presume. But, sir, you must have heard of his accident?

SIR OLIVER   Not a word!

CRABTREE   Not of his being dangerously wounded?

SIR OLIVER   The devil he is!

SIR BENJAMIN   Run through the body—

CRABTREE   Shot in the breast—

SIR BENJAMIN   By one Mr. Surface—

Scene ii.   1. **hartshorn**: smelling salts.   2. **Montem**: festival at Eton.

3. **faculty**: i.e., a doctor.

CRABTREE   Aye, the younger.

SIR OLIVER   Hey! what the plague! you seem to differ strangely in your accounts; however, you agree that Sir Peter is dangerously wounded.

SIR BENJAMIN   Oh, yes, we agree in that.

CRABTREE   Yes, yes, I believe there can be no doubt of that.

SIR OLIVER   Then, upon my word, for a person in that situation, he is the most imprudent man alive; for here he comes, walking as if nothing at all was the matter. [*Enter* SIR PETER TEAZLE.] Odds heart, Sir Peter, you are come in good time, I promise you, for we had just given you over!

SIR BENJAMIN   [*Aside to* CRABTREE] Egad, uncle, this is the most sudden recovery!

SIR OLIVER   Why, man! what do you out of bed with a small-sword through your body and a bullet lodged in your thorax?

SIR PETER   A small-sword and a bullet!

SIR OLIVER   Aye; these gentlemen would have killed you without law or physic, and wanted to dub me a doctor to make me an accomplice.

SIR PETER   Why, what is all this?

SIR BENJAMIN   We rejoice, Sir Peter, that the story of the duel is not true, and are sincerely sorry for your other misfortune.

SIR PETER   [*Aside*] So, so—all over the town already!

CRABTREE   Though, Sir Peter, you were certainly vastly to blame to marry at your years.

SIR PETER   Sir, what business is that of yours?

MRS. CANDOUR   Though, indeed, as Sir Peter made so good a husband, he's very much to be pitied.

SIR PETER   Plague on your pity, ma'am! I desire none of it.

SIR BENJAMIN   However, Sir Peter, you must not mind the laughing and jests you will meet with on the occasion.

SIR PETER   Sir, sir! I desire to be master in my own house.

CRABTREE   'Tis no uncommon case, that's one comfort.

SIR PETER   I insist on being left to myself—without ceremony, I insist on your leaving my house directly!

MRS. CANDOUR   Well, well, we are going; and depend on 't, we'll make the best report of it we can.   [*Exit.*]

SIR PETER   Leave my house!

CRABTREE   —And tell how hardly you've been treated.   [*Exit.*]

SIR PETER   Leave my house!

SIR BENJAMIN   —And how patiently you bear it.   [*Exit.*]

SIR PETER   Fiends! vipers! furies! Oh! that their own venom would choke them!

SIR OLIVER   They are very provoking indeed, Sir Peter.   [*Enter* ROWLEY.]

ROWLEY   I heard high words; what has ruffled you, sir?

SIR PETER   Pshaw! what signifies asking? Do I ever pass a day without my vexations?

ROWLEY   Well, I'm not inquisitive.

SIR OLIVER   Well, Sir Peter, I have seen both my nephews in the manner we proposed.

SIR PETER   A precious couple they are!

ROWLEY   Yes, and Sir Oliver is convinced that your judgment was right, Sir Peter.

SIR OLIVER   Yes, I find Joseph is indeed the man, after all.

ROWLEY   Aye, as Sir Peter says, he is a man of sentiment.

SIR OLIVER   And acts up to the sentiments he professes.

ROWLEY   It certainly is edification to hear him talk.

SIR OLIVER   Oh, he's a model for the young men of the age!—But how's this, Sir Peter? you don't join us in your friend Joseph's praise as I expected.

SIR PETER   Sir Oliver, we live in a damned wicked world, and the fewer we praise the better.

ROWLEY   What! do you say so, Sir Peter, who were never mistaken in your life?

SIR PETER   Pshaw! plague on you both! I see by your sneering you have heard the whole affair. I shall go mad among you!

ROWLEY   Then, to fret you no longer, Sir Peter, we are indeed acquainted with it all. I met Lady Teazle coming from Mr. Surface's so humbled that she deigned to request me to be her advocate with you.

SIR PETER   And does Sir Oliver know all this?

SIR OLIVER   Every circumstance.

SIR PETER   What—of the closet and the screen, hey?

SIR OLIVER   Yes, yes, and the little French milliner. Oh, I have been vastly diverted with the story! ha! ha! ha!

SIR PETER 'Twas very pleasant.

SIR OLIVER I never laughed more in my life, I assure you—ha! ha! ha!

SIR PETER Oh, vastly diverting—ha! ha! ha!

ROWLEY To be sure, Joseph with his sentiments! ha! ha! ha!

SIR PETER Yes, yes, his sentiments! ha! ha! ha!—Hypocritical villain!

SIR OLIVER Aye, and that rogue Charles to pull Sir Peter out of the closet: ha! ha! ha!

SIR PETER Ha! ha! 'twas devilish entertaining, to be sure!

SIR OLIVER Ha! ha! ha! Egad, Sir Peter, I should like to have seen your face when the screen was thrown down: ha! ha!

SIR PETER Yes, yes, my face when the screen was thrown down: ha! ha! ha! Oh, I must never show my head again!

SIR OLIVER But come, come, it isn't fair to laugh at you neither, my old friend; though, upon my soul, I can't help it.

SIR PETER Oh, pray, don't restrain your mirth on my account; it does not hurt me at all. I laugh at the whole affair myself. Yes, yes, I think being a standing jest for all one's acquaintance a very happy situation. Oh, yes, and then of a morning to read the paragraphs about Mr. S——, Lady T——, and Sir P——, will be so entertaining!

ROWLEY Without affectation, Sir Peter, you may despise the ridicule of fools. But I see Lady Teazle going towards the next room; I am sure you must desire a reconciliation as earnestly as she does.

SIR OLIVER Perhaps my being here prevents her coming to you. Well, I'll leave honest Rowley to mediate between you; but he must bring you all presently to Mr. Surface's, where I am now returning, if not to reclaim a libertine at least to expose hypocrisy.

SIR PETER Ah, I'll be present at your discovering yourself there with all my heart; though 'tis a vile unlucky place for discoveries.

ROWLEY We'll follow. [*Exit* SIR OLIVER SURFACE.]

SIR PETER She is not coming here, you see, Rowley.

ROWLEY No, but she has left the door of that room open, you perceive. See, she is in tears.

SIR PETER Certainly a little mortification appears very becoming in a wife. Don't you think it will do her good to let her pine a little?

ROWLEY Oh, this is ungenerous in you!

SIR PETER Well, I know not what to think. You remember the letter I found of hers evidently intended for Charles?

ROWLEY A mere forgery, Sir Peter, laid in your way on purpose. This is one of the points which I intend Snake shall give you conviction of.

SIR PETER I wish I were once satisfied of that. She looks this way. What a remarkably elegant turn of the head she has! Rowley, I'll go to her.

ROWLEY Certainly.

SIR PETER Though when it is known that we are reconciled, people will laugh at me ten times more.

ROWLEY Let them laugh, and retort their malice only by showing them you are happy in spite of it.

SIR PETER I' faith, so I will! and, if I'm not mistaken, we may yet be the happiest couple in the country.

ROWLEY Nay, Sir Peter, he who once lays aside suspicion—

SIR PETER Hold, Master Rowley! if you have any regard for me, never let me hear you utter anything like a sentiment; I have had enough of them to serve me the rest of my life. [*Exeunt.*]

SCENE III. *The library in* JOSEPH SURFACE'*s house.*

[*Enter* JOSEPH SURFACE *and* LADY SNEERWELL.]

LADY SNEERWELL Impossible! Will not Sir Peter immediately be reconciled to Charles, and of course no longer oppose his union with Maria? The thought is distraction to me.

JOSEPH Can passion furnish a remedy?

LADY SNEERWELL No, nor cunning neither. Oh, I was a fool, an idiot, to league with such a blunderer!

JOSEPH Sure, Lady Sneerwell, I am the greatest sufferer; yet you see, I bear the accident with calmness.

LADY SNEERWELL Because the disappointment doesn't reach your heart; your interest only attached you to Maria. Had you felt for her what I have for that ungrateful libertine, neither your temper nor hypocrisy could prevent your showing the sharpness of your vexation.

JOSEPH But why should your reproaches fall on me for this disappointment?

LADY SNEERWELL Are you not the cause of it? Had you not a sufficient field for your roguery in imposing upon Sir Peter and supplanting your brother, but you must endeavor to seduce his wife? I hate such an avarice of crimes; 'tis an unfair monopoly, and never prospers.

JOSEPH Well, I admit I have been to blame. I confess I deviated from the direct road of wrong, but I don't think we're so totally defeated neither.

LADY SNEERWELL No!

JOSEPH You tell me you have made a trial of Snake since we met, and that you still believe him faithful to us?

LADY SNEERWELL I do believe so.

JOSEPH And that he has undertaken, should it be necessary, to swear and prove that Charles is at this time contracted by vows and honor to your ladyship, which some of his former letters to you will serve to support.

LADY SNEERWELL This, indeed, might have assisted.

JOSEPH Come, come; it is not too late yet. [Knocking at the door.] But hark! this is probably my uncle, Sir Oliver. Retire to that room; we'll consult farther when he is gone.

LADY SNEERWELL Well, but if he should find you out too?

JOSEPH Oh, I have no fear of that. Sir Peter will hold his tongue for his own credit's sake—and you may depend on it, I shall soon discover Sir Oliver's weak side!

LADY SNEERWELL I have no diffidence of your abilities! Only be constant to one roguery at a time. [Exit LADY SNEERWELL.]

JOSEPH I will, I will! So! 'tis confounded hard, after such bad fortune, to be baited by one's confederate in evil. Well, at all events my character is so much better than Charles's that I certainly—hey—what—this is not Sir Oliver, but old Stanley again. Plague on 't that he should return to tease me just now! I shall have Sir Oliver come and find him here—and— [Enter SIR OLIVER SURFACE.] Gad's life, Mr. Stanley, why have you come back to plague me at this time? You must not stay now, upon my word.

SIR OLIVER Sir, I hear your uncle Oliver is expected here, and though he has been so penurious to you. I'll try what he'll do for me.

JOSEPH Sir, 'tis impossible for you to stay now; so I must beg—Come any other time, and I promise you, you shall be assisted.

SIR OLIVER No; Sir Oliver and I must be acquainted.

JOSEPH Zounds, sir! then I insist on your quitting the room directly.

SIR OLIVER Nay, sir—

JOSEPH Sir, I insist on 't—Here, William! show this gentleman out. Since you compel me, sir, not one moment—this is such insolence!
[Going to push him out.]
[Enter CHARLES SURFACE.]

CHARLES Heyday! what's the matter now? What the devil, have you got hold of my little broker here? Zounds, brother, don't hurt little Premium. What's the matter, my little fellow?

JOSEPH So! he has been with you, too, has he?

CHARLES To be sure, he has. Why, he's as honest a little—But sure, Joseph, you have not been borrowing money too, have you?

JOSEPH Borrowing! no! But brother, you know we expect Sir Oliver here every—

CHARLES O Gad, that's true! Noll mustn't find the little broker here, to be sure.

JOSEPH Yet, Mr. Stanley insists—

CHARLES Stanley! why, his name's Premium.

JOSEPH No, sir, Stanley.

CHARLES No, no, Premium.

JOSEPH Well, no matter which—but—

CHARLES Aye, aye, Stanley or Premium, 'tis the same thing, as you say; for I suppose he goes by half a hundred names, besides "A.B." at the coffeehouse. [Knocking.]

JOSEPH 'Sdeath! here's Sir Oliver at the door. Now, I beg, Mr. Stanley—

CHARLES Aye, aye, and I beg, Mr. Premium—

SIR OLIVER Gentlemen—

JOSEPH Sir, by Heaven, you shall go!

CHARLES Aye, out with him, certainly!

SIR OLIVER This violence—

JOSEPH Sir, 'tis your own fault.

CHARLES Out with him, to be sure!
[Both forcing SIR OLIVER out.]
[Enter SIR PETER and LADY TEAZLE, MARIA, and ROWLEY.]

SIR PETER My old friend, Sir Oliver—hey! what in the name of wonder—here are dutiful nephews—assault their uncle at a first visit!

LADY TEAZLE Indeed, Sir Oliver, 'twas well we came to rescue you.

ROWLEY Truly it was; for I perceive, Sir Oliver, the character of old Stanley was no protection to you.

SIR OLIVER Nor of Premium either: the necessities of the former could not extort a shilling from that benevolent gentleman, and now, egad, with the other I stood a chance of faring worse than my ancestors, and being knocked down without being bid for.

JOSEPH Charles!

CHARLES Joseph!

JOSEPH 'Tis now complete!

CHARLES Very!

SIR OLIVER Sir Peter, my friend, and Rowley too —look on that elder nephew of mine. You know what he has already received from my bounty, and you also know how gladly I would have regarded half my fortune as held in trust for him: judge, then, my disappointment in discovering him to be destitute of faith, charity, and gratitude!

SIR PETER Sir Oliver, I should be more surprised at this declaration if I had not myself found him to be mean, treacherous, and hypocritical.

LADY TEAZLE And if the gentleman pleads not guilty to these, pray let him call *me* to his character.

SIR PETER Then I believe we need add no more. If he knows himself, he will consider it as the most perfect punishment, that he is known to the world.

CHARLES [*Aside*] If they talk this way to Honesty, what will they say to me by and by?

SIR OLIVER As for that prodigal, his brother, there—

CHARLES [*Aside*] Aye, now comes my turn: the damned family pictures will ruin me!

JOSEPH Sir Oliver—uncle, will you honor me with a hearing?

CHARLES [*Aside*] Now if Joseph would make one of his long speeches, I might recollect myself a little.

SIR OLIVER [*To* JOSEPH] I suppose you would undertake to justify yourself entirely.

JOSEPH I trust I could.

SIR OLIVER [*To* CHARLES] Well, sir!—and you could justify yourself too, I suppose?

CHARLES Not that I know of, Sir Oliver.

SIR OLIVER What!—Little Premium has been let too much into the secret, I suppose?

CHARLES True, sir; but they were *family* secrets, and should not be mentioned again, you know.

ROWLEY Come, Sir Oliver, I know you cannot speak of Charles's follies with anger.

SIR OLIVER Odds heart, no more I can; nor with gravity either. Sir Peter, do you know the rogue bargained with me for all his ancestors—sold me judges and generals by the foot, and maiden aunts as cheap as broken china.

CHARLES To be sure, Sir Oliver, I did make a little free with the family canvas, that's the truth on 't. My ancestors may rise in judgment against me, there's no denying it; but believe me sincere when I tell you—and upon my soul I would not say so if I was not—that if I do not appear mortified at the exposure of my follies, it is because I feel at this moment the warmest satisfaction in seeing you, my liberal benefactor.

SIR OLIVER Charles, I believe you; give me your hand again. The ill-looking little fellow over the settee has made your peace.

CHARLES Then, sir, my gratitude to the original is still increased.

LADY TEAZLE Yet, I believe, Sir Oliver, here is one whom Charles is still more anxious to be reconciled to.

SIR OLIVER Oh, I have heard of his attachment there; and, with the young lady's pardon, if I construe right—that blush—

SIR PETER Well, child, speak your sentiments!

MARIA Sir, I have little to say, but that I shall rejoice to hear that he is happy; for me, whatever claim I had to his attention, I willingly resign to one who has a better title.

CHARLES How, Maria!

SIR PETER Heyday! what's the mystery now? While he appeared an incorrigible rake, you would give your hand to no one else; and now that he is likely to reform, I'll warrant you won't have him!

MARIA His own heart and Lady Sneerwell know the cause.

CHARLES Lady Sneerwell!

JOSEPH Brother, it is with great concern I am obliged to speak on this point, but my regard to justice compels me, and Lady Sneerwell's injuries can no longer be concealed.

[*Opens the door.*]

[*Enter* LADY SNEERWELL.]

SIR PETER So! another French milliner! Egad, he has one in every room in the house, I suppose!

LADY SNEERWELL Ungrateful Charles! Well may you be surprised, and feel for the indelicate situation your perfidy has forced me into.

CHARLES Pray, uncle, is this another plot of yours? For, as I have life, I don't understand it.

JOSEPH I believe, sir, there is but the evidence of one person more necessary to make it extremely clear.

SIR PETER And that person, I imagine, is Mr. Snake.—Rowley, you were perfectly right to bring him with us, and pray let him appear.

ROWLEY Walk in, Mr. Snake. [*Enter* SNAKE.] I thought his testimony might be wanted; however, it happens unluckily that he comes to confront Lady Sneerwell, not to support her.

LADY SNEERWELL A villain! Treacherous to me at last! Speak, fellow; have you too conspired against me?

SNAKE I beg your ladyship ten thousand pardons: you paid me extremely liberally for the lie in question; but I unfortunately have been offered double to speak the truth.

SIR PETER Plot and counterplot, egad!

LADY SNEERWELL [*Going*] The torments of shame and disappointment on you all!

LADY TEAZLE Hold, Lady Sneerwell—before you go, let me thank you for the trouble you and that gentleman have taken, in writing letters from me to Charles and answering them yourself; and let me also request you to make my respects to the scandalous college of which you are president, and inform them that Lady Teazle, licentiate, begs leave to return the diploma they granted her, as she leaves off practice and kills characters no longer.

LADY SNEERWELL You, too, madam!—provoking—insolent! May your husband live these fifty years! [*Exit.*]

SIR PETER Oons! what a fury!

LADY TEAZLE A malicious creature, indeed!

SIR PETER Hey!—not for her last wish!

LADY TEAZLE Oh, no!

SIR OLIVER Well, sir, and what have you to say now?

JOSEPH Sir, I am so confounded to find that Lady Sneerwell could be guilty of suborning Mr. Snake in this manner to impose on us all, that I know

not what to say; however, lest her revengeful spirit should prompt her to injure my brother, I had certainly better follow her directly. [*Exit.*]

SIR PETER Moral to the last drop!

SIR OLIVER Aye, and marry her, Joseph, if you can. Oil and vinegar, egad! you'll do very well together.

ROWLEY I believe we have no more occasion for Mr. Snake at present?

SNAKE Before I go, I beg pardon once for all for whatever uneasiness I have been the humble instrument of causing to the parties present.

SIR PETER Well, well, you have made atonement by a good deed at last.

SNAKE But I must request of the company that it shall never be known.

SIR PETER Hey! what the plague! are you ashamed of having done a right thing once in your life?

SNAKE Ah, sir, consider—I live by the badness of my character; I have nothing but my infamy to depend on, and if it were once known that I had been betrayed into an honest action, I should lose every friend I have in the world.

SIR OLIVER Well, well, we'll not traduce you by saying anything in your praise; never fear. [*Exit* SNAKE.]

SIR PETER There's a precious rogue!

LADY TEAZLE See, Sir Oliver, there needs no persuasion now to reconcile your nephew and Maria.

SIR OLIVER Aye, aye, that's as it should be, and, egad, we'll have the wedding tomorrow morning.

CHARLES Thank you, dear uncle.

SIR PETER What, you rogue! don't you ask the girl's consent first?

CHARLES Oh, I have done that a long time—a minute ago—and she has looked *yes*.

MARIA For shame, Charles!—I protest, Sir Peter, there has not been a word.

SIR OLIVER Well, then, the fewer the better; may your love for each other never know abatement!

SIR PETER And may you live as happily together as Lady Teazle and I intend to do!

CHARLES Rowley, my old friend, I am sure you congratulate me; and I suspect that I owe you much.

SIR OLIVER You do, indeed, Charles.

ROWLEY If my efforts to serve you had not succeeded, you would have been in my debt for the attempt; but deserve to be happy, and you overpay me.

SIR PETER   Aye, honest Rowley always said you would reform.

CHARLES   Why, as to reforming, Sir Peter, I'll make no promises, and that I take to be a proof that I intend to set about it. But here shall be my monitor—my gentle guide—ah! can I leave the virtuous path those eyes illumine?

Though thou, dear maid, shouldst waive thy beauty's sway,
Thou still must rule, because I will obey:
An humble fugitive from Folly, view,
No sanctuary near but Love and you.
                              [*To the audience.*]
You can, indeed, each anxious fear remove,
For even Scandal dies if you approve.
                              [*Exeunt omnes.*]

EPILOGUE

BY MR. COLMAN°
SPOKEN BY LADY TEAZLE

I, who was late so volatile and gay,
Like a tradewind must now blow all one way,
Bend all my cares, my studies, and my vows,
To one dull rusty weathercock—my spouse!
So wills our virtuous bard—the motley Bayes   5
Of crying epilogues and laughing plays!
Old bachelors who marry smart young wives,
Learn from our play to regulate their lives:
Each bring his dear to town, all faults upon her—
London will prove the very source of honor.   10
Plunged fairly in, like a cold bath it serves,
When principles relax, to brace the nerves.
Such is my case; and yet I must deplore
That the gay dream of dissipation's o'er.
And say, ye fair! was ever lively wife,   15
Born with a genius for the highest life,
Like me untimely blasted in her bloom,
Like me condemned to such a dismal doom?
Save money—when I just knew how to waste it!
Leave London—just as I began to taste it!   20
Must I then watch the early crowing cock,
The melancholy ticking of a clock,
In a lone rustic hall forever pounded,

With dogs, cats, rats, and squalling brats surrounded?
With humble curate can I now retire   25
(While good Sir Peter boozes with the squire),
And at backgammon mortify my soul,
That pants for loo,° or flutters at a vole?°
"Seven's the main!" Dear sound that must expire,
Lost at hot cockles° round a Christmas fire!   30
The transient hour of fashion too soon spent,
Farewell the tranquil mind, farewell content!
Farewell the plumèd head, the cushioned tête,
That takes the cushion from its proper seat!
That spirit-stirring drum!—card drums° I mean,
Spadille—odd trick—pam—basto—king and queen!°   36
And you, ye knockers, that, with brazen throat,
The welcome visitors' approach denote;
Farewell all quality of high renown,
Pride, pomp, and circumstance of glorious town!
Farewell! your revels I partake no more,   41
And Lady Teazle's occupation's o'er!
All this I told our bard; he smiled, and said 'twas clear
I ought to play deep tragedy next year.
Meanwhile he drew wise morals from his play,   45
And in these solemn periods stalked away:
"Bless'd were the fair like you; her faults who stopped
And closed her follies when the curtain dropped!
No more in vice or error to engage,
Or play the fool at large on life's great stage."   50

DYLAN THOMAS
1914–1953

A Story

If you can call it a story. There's no real beginning or end and there's very little in the middle. It is all about a day's outing, by charabanc,[1] to Porthcawl,[2]

---

28. loo, vole: maneuvers in card games. 30. hot cockles: rustic game somewhat like blindman's bluff. 35. card drums: large card parties. 36. Spadille . . . queen: more technical terms of cardplaying.

A STORY. 1. charabanc: sightseeing bus. 2. Porthcawl: Welsh seacoast town on the Bristol Channel.

Epilogue. **Colman:** George Colman (1732–94), a contemporary playwright.

which, of course, the charabanc never reached, and it happened when I was so high and much nicer.

I was staying at the time with my uncle and his wife. Although she was my aunt, I never thought of her as anything but the wife of my uncle, partly because he was so big and trumpeting and red-hairy and used to fill every inch of the hot little house like an old buffalo squeezed into an airing cupboard, and partly because she was so small and silk and quick and made no noise at all as she whisked about on padded paws, dusting the china dogs, feeding the buffalo, setting the mousetraps that never caught her; and once she sleaked out of the room, to squeak in a nook or nibble in the hayloft, you forgot she had ever been there.

But there he was, always, a steaming hulk of an uncle, his braces[3] straining like hawsers, crammed behind the counter of the tiny shop at the front of the house, and breathing like a brass band; or guzzling and blustery in the kitchen over his gutsy supper, too big for everything except the great black boats of his boots. As he ate, the house grew smaller; he billowed out over the furniture, the loud check meadow of his waistcoat littered, as though after a picnic, with cigarette ends, peelings, cabbage stalks, birds' bones, gravy; and the forest fire of his hair crackled among the hooked hams from the ceiling. She was so small she could hit him only if she stood on a chair; and every Saturday night at half-past ten he would lift her up, under his arm, onto a chair, in the kitchen so that she could hit him on the head with whatever was handy, which was always a china dog. On Sundays, and when pickled, he sang high tenor, and had won many cups.

The first I heard of the annual outing was when I was sitting one evening on a bag of rice behind the counter, under one of my uncle's stomachs, reading an advertisement for sheep-dip, which was all there was to read. The shop was full of my uncle, and when Mr. Benjamin Franklyn, Mr. Weazley, Noah Bowen, and Will Sentry came in, I thought it would burst. It was like all being together in a drawer that smelled of cheese and turps, and twist tobacco and sweet biscuits and snuff and waistcoat. Mr. Benjamin Franklyn said that he had collected enough money for the charabanc and twenty cases of pale ale and a

pound apiece over that he would distribute among the members of the outing when they first stopped for refreshment, and he was about sick and tired, he said, of being followed by Will Sentry.

"All day long, wherever I go," he said, "he's after me like a collie with one eye. I got a shadow of my own *and* a dog. I don't need no Tom, Dick or Harry pursuing me with his dirty muffler on."

Will Sentry blushed, and said, "It's only oily. I got a bicycle."

"A man has no privacy at all," Mr. Franklyn went on. "I tell you he sticks so close I'm afraid to go out the back in case I sit in his lap. It's a wonder to me," he said, "he don't follow me into bed at night."

"Wife won't let," Will Sentry said.

And that started Mr. Franklyn off again, and they tried to soothe him down by saying, "Don't you mind Will Sentry." "No harm in old Will." "He's only keeping an eye on the money, Benjie."

"Aren't I honest?" asked Mr. Franklyn in surprise. There was no answer for some time; then Noah Bowen said, "You know what the committee is. Ever since Bob the Fiddle they don't feel safe with a new treasurer."

"Do you think *I'm* going to drink the outing funds, like Bob the Fiddle did?" said Mr. Franklyn.

"You *might*," said my uncle, slowly.

"I resign," said Mr. Franklyn.

"Not with our money you won't," Will Sentry said.

"Who put the dynamite in the salmon pool?" said Mr. Weazley, but nobody took any notice of him. And, after a time, they all began to play cards in the thickening dusk of the hot, cheesy shop, and my uncle blew and bugled whenever he won, and Mr. Weazley grumbled like a dredger, and I fell to sleep on the gravy-scented mountain meadow of uncle's waistcoat.

On Sunday morning, after Bethesda,[4] Mr. Franklyn walked into the kitchen where my uncle and I were eating sardines from the tin with spoons because it was Sunday and his wife would not let us play draughts.[5] She was somewhere in the kitchen, too. Perhaps she was inside the grand-mother clock, hanging from the weights and breathing. Then, a second later, the door opened again and Will Sentry edged into the room,

---

3. **braces:** suspenders.

4. **Bethesda:** chapel. 5. **draughts:** checkers.

twiddling his hard, round hat. He and Mr. Franklyn sat down on the settee, stiff and mothballed and black in their chapel and funeral suits.

"I brought the list," said Mr. Franklyn. "Every member full paid. You ask Will Sentry."

My uncle put on his spectacles, wiped his whiskery mouth with a handkerchief big as a Union Jack, laid down his spoon of sardines, took Mr. Franklyn's list of names, removed the spectacles so that he could read, and then ticked the names off one by one.

"Enoch Davies. Aye. He's good with his fists. You never know. Little Gerwain. Very melodious bass. Mr. Cadwalladwr. That's right. He can tell opening time better than my watch. Mr. Weazley. Of course. He's been to Paris. Pity he suffers so much in the charabanc. Stopped us nine times last year between the Beehive and the Red Dragon. Noah Bowen. Ah, very peaceable. He's got a tongue like a turtledove. Never a argument with Noah Bowen. Jenkins Loughor. Keep him off economics. It cost us a plateglass window. And ten pints for the Sergeant. Mr. Jervis. Very tidy."

"He tried to put a pig in the charra,"[6] Will Sentry said.

"Live and let live," said my uncle.

Will Sentry blushed.

"Sinbad the Sailor's Arms. Got to keep in with him. Old O. Jones."

"Why old O. Jones?" said Will Sentry.

"Old O. Jones always goes," said my uncle.

I looked down at the kitchen table. The tin of sardines was gone. By Gee, I said to myself, Uncle's wife is quick as a flash.

"Cuthbert Johnny Fortnight. Now there's a card," said my uncle.

"He whistles after women," Will Sentry said.

"So do you," said Mr. Benjamin Franklyn, "in your mind."

My uncle at last approved the whole list, pausing only to say, when he came across one name, "If we weren't a Christian community, we'd chuck that Bob the Fiddle in the sea."

"We can do that in Porthcawl," said Mr. Franklyn, and soon after that he went, Will Sentry no more than an inch behind him, their Sunday-bright boots squeaking on the kitchen cobbles.

And then, suddenly, there was my uncle's wife standing in front of the dresser, with a china dog

6. **charra:** charabanc.

in one hand. By Gee, I said to myself again, did you ever see such a woman, if that's what she is. The lamps were not lit yet in the kitchen and she stood in a wood of shadows, with the plates on the dresser behind her shining—like pink and white eyes.

"If you go on that outing on Saturday, Mr. Thomas," she said to my uncle in her small, silk voice, "I'm going home to my mother's."

Holy Mo, I thought, she's got a mother. Now that's one old bald mouse of a hundred and five I won't be wanting to meet in a dark lane.

"It's me or the outing, Mr. Thomas."

I would have made my choice at once, but it was almost half a minute before my uncle said, "Well, then, Sarah, it's the outing, my love." He lifted her up, under his arm, onto a chair in the kitchen, and she hit him on the head with the china dog. Then he lifted her down again, and then I said good night.

For the rest of the week my uncle's wife whisked quiet and quick round the house with her darting duster, my uncle blew and bugled and swole, and I kept myself busy all the time being up to no good. And then at breakfast time on Saturday morning, the morning of the outing, I found a note on the kitchen table. It said, "There's some eggs in the pantry. Take your boots off before you go to bed." My uncle's wife had gone, as quick as a flash.

When my uncle saw the note, he tugged out the flag of his handkerchief and blew such a hubbub of trumpets that the plates on the dresser shook. "It's the same every year," he said. And then he looked at me. "But this year it's different. *You'll* have to come on the outing too, and what the members will say I dare not think."

The charabanc drew up outside, and when the members of the outing saw my uncle and me squeeze out of the shop together, both of us catlicked and brushed in our Sunday best, they snarled like a zoo.

"Are you bringing a *boy?*" asked Mr. Benjamin Franklyn as we climbed into the charabanc. He looked at me with horror.

"Boys is nasty," said Mr. Weazley.

"He hasn't paid his contributions," Will Sentry said.

"No room for boys. Boys get sick in charabancs."

"So do you, Enoch Davies," said my uncle.

"Might as well bring *women*."

The way they said it, women were worse than boys.

"Better than bringing grandfathers."

"Grandfathers is nasty, too," said Mr. Weazley.

"What can we do with him when we stop for refreshments?"

"I'm a grandfather," said Mr. Weazley.

"Twenty-six minutes to opening time," shouted an old man in a panama hat, not looking at a watch. They forgot me at once.

"Good old Mr. Cadwalladwr," they cried, and the charabanc started off down the village street.

A few cold women stood at their doorways, grimly watching us go. A very small boy waved good-by, and his mother boxed his ears. It was a beautiful August morning.

We were out of the village, and over the bridge, and up the hill toward Steeplehat Wood, when Mr. Franklyn, with his list of names in his hand, called out loud, "Where's old O. Jones?"

"Where's old O.?"

"We've left old O. behind."

"Can't go without old O."

And though Mr. Weazley hissed all the way, we turned and drove back to the village, where, outside the Prince of Wales, old O. Jones was waiting patiently and alone with a canvas bag.

"I didn't want to come at all," old O. Jones said as they hoisted him into the charabanc and clapped him on the back and pushed him on a seat and stuck a bottle in his hand, "but I always go." And over the bridge and up the hill and under the deep green wood and along the dusty road we wove, slow cows and ducks flying by, until "Stop the bus!" Mr. Weazley cried, "I left my teeth on the mantelpiece."

"Never you mind," they said, "you're not going to bite nobody," and they gave him a bottle with a straw.

"I might want to smile," he said.

"Not you," they said.

"What's the time, Mr. Cadwalladwr?"

"Twelve minutes to go," shouted back the old man in the panama, and they all began to curse him.

The charabanc pulled up outside the Mountain Sheep, a small, unhappy public house with a thatched roof like a wig with ringworm. From a flagpole by the Gents fluttered the flag of Siam. I knew it was the flag of Siam because of cigarette cards. The landlord stood at the door to welcome us, simpering like a wolf. He was a long, lean, black-fanged man with a greased love-curl and pouncing eyes. "What a beautiful August day!" he said, and touched his love-curl with a claw. That was the way he must have welcomed the Mountain Sheep before he ate it, I said to myself. The members rushed out, bleating, and into the bar.

"You keep an eye on the charra," my uncle said, "see nobody steals it now."

"There's nobody to steal it," I said, "except some cows," but my uncle was gustily blowing his bugle in the bar. I looked at the cows opposite, and they looked at me. There was nothing else for us to do. Forty-five minutes passed, like a very slow cloud. The sun shone down on the lonely road, the lost, unwanted boy, and the lake-eyed cows. In the dark bar they were so happy they were breaking glasses. A Shoni-Onion Breton man, with a beret and a necklace of onions, bicycled down the road and stopped at the door.

"*Quelle un grand matin, monsieur,*"[7] I said.

"There's French, boy bach!" he said.

I followed him down the passage, and peered into the bar. I could hardly recognize the members of the outing. They had all changed color. Beetroot, rhubarb and puce, they hollered and rollicked in that dark, damp hole like enormous ancient bad boys, and my uncle surged in the middle, all red whiskers and bellies. On the floor was broken glass and Mr. Weazley.

"Drinks all round," cried Bob the Fiddle, a small, absconding man with bright blue eyes and a plump smile.

"Who's been robbing the orphans?"

"Who sold his little babby to the gyppoes?"

"Trust old Bob, he'll let you down."

"You will have your little joke," said Bob the Fiddle, smiling like a razor, "but I forgive you, boys."

Out of the fug and babel I heard: "Where's old O. Jones?" "Where are you, old O.?" "He's in the kitchen cooking his dinner." "He never forgets his dinner time." "Good old O. Jones." "Come out and fight." "No, not now, later." "No, now when I'm in a temper." "Look at Will Sentry, he's proper snobbled." "Look at his willful feet." "Look at Mr. Weazley lording it on the floor."

Mr. Weazley got up, hissing like a gander. "That boy pushed me down deliberate," he said,

7. Quelle . . . monsieur: "What a fine morning, sir."

pointing to me at the door, and I slunk away down the passage and out to the mild, good cows.

Time clouded over, the cows wondered, I threw a stone at them and they wandered, wondering, away. Then out blew my uncle, ballooning, and one by one the members lumbered after him in a grizzle. They had drunk the Mountain Sheep dry. Mr. Weazley had won a string of onions that the Shoni-Onion man had raffled in the bar.

"What's the good of onions if you left your teeth on the mantelpiece?" he said. And when I looked through the back window of the thundering charabanc, I saw the pub grow smaller in the distance. And the flag of Siam, from the flagpole by the Gents, fluttered now at half mast.

The Blue Bull, the Dragon, the Star of Wales, the Twll in the Wall, the Sour Grapes, the Shepherd's Arms, the Bells of Aberdovey: I had nothing to do in the whole wild August world but remember the names where the outing stopped and keep an eye on the charabanc. And whenever it passed a public house, Mr. Weazley would cough like a billy goat and cry, "Stop the bus, I'm dying of breath." And back we would all have to go.

Closing time meant nothing to the members of that outing. Behind locked doors, they hymned and rumpused all the beautiful afternoon. And, when a policeman entered the Druid's Tap by the back door, and found them all choral with beer, "Sssh!" said Noah Bowen, "the pub is shut."

"Where do you come from?" he said in his buttoned, blue voice.

They told him.

"I got a auntie there," the policeman said. And very soon he was singing "Asleep in the Deep."

Off we drove again at last, the charabanc bouncing with tenors and flagons, and came to a river that rushed along among willows.

"Water!" they shouted.

"Porthcawl!" sang my uncle.

"Where's the donkeys?" said Mr. Weazley.

And out they lurched, to paddle and whoop in the cool, white, winding water. Mr. Franklyn, trying to polka on the slippery stones, fell in twice. "Nothing is simple," he said with dignity as he oozed up the bank.

"It's cold!" they cried.

"It's lovely!"

"It's smooth as a moth's nose!"

"It's *better* than Porthcawl!"

And dusk came down warm and gentle on thirty wild, wet, pickled, splashing men without a care in the world at the end of the world in the west of Wales. And "Who goes there?" called Will Sentry to a wild duck flying.

They stopped at the Hermit's Nest for a rum to keep out the cold. "I played for Aberavon in 1898," said a stranger to Enoch Davies.

"Liar," said Enoch Davies.

"I can show the photos," said the stranger.

"Forged," said Enoch Davies.

"And I'll show you my cap at home."

"Stolen."

"I got friends to prove it," the stranger said in a fury.

"Bribed," said Enoch Davies.

On the way home, through the simmering moon-splashed dark, old O. Jones began to cook his supper on a primus stove in the middle of the charabanc. Mr. Weazley coughed himself blue in the smoke. "Stop the bus!" he cried, "I'm dying of breath." We all climbed down into the moonlight. There was not a public house in sight. So they carried out the remaining cases, and the primus stove, and old O. Jones himself, and took them into a field, and sat down in a circle in the field and drank and sang while old O. Jones cooked sausage and mash and the moon flew above us. And there I drifted to sleep against my uncle's mountainous waistcoat, and, as I slept, "Who goes there?" called out Will Sentry to the flying moon.

BERNARD MALAMUD
b. 1914

The Magic Barrel

Not long ago there lived in uptown New York, in a small, almost meager room, though crowded with books, Leo Finkle, a rabbinical student in the Yeshivah University. Finkle, after six years of study, was to be ordained in June and had been advised by an acquaintance that he might find it easier to win himself a congregation if he were married. Since he had no present prospects of marriage, after two tormented days of turning it over in his mind, he called in Pinye Salzman, a marriage broker whose two-line advertisement he had read in the *Forward*.

The matchmaker appeared one night out of the dark fourth-floor hallway of the graystone rooming house where Finkle lived, grasping a black, strapped portfolio that had been worn thin with use. Salzman, who had been long in the business, was of slight but dignified build, wearing an old hat, and an overcoat too short and tight for him. He smelled frankly of fish, which he loved to eat, and although he was missing a few teeth, his presence was not displeasing, because of an amiable manner curiously contrasted with mournful eyes. His voice, his lips, his wisp of beard, his bony fingers were animated, but give him a moment of repose and his mild blue eyes revealed a depth of sadness, a characteristic that put Leo a little at ease although the situation, for him, was inherently tense.

He at once informed Salzman why he had asked him to come, explaining that his home was in Cleveland, and that but for his parents, who had married comparatively late in life, he was alone in the world. He had for six years devoted himself almost entirely to his studies, as a result of which, understandably, he had found himself without time for a social life and the company of young women. Therefore he thought it the better part of trial and error—of embarrassing fumbling—to call in an experienced person to advise him on these matters. He remarked in passing that the function of the marriage broker was ancient and honorable, highly approved in the Jewish community, because it made practical the necessary without hindering joy. Moreover, his own parents had been brought together by a matchmaker. They had made, if not a financially profitable marriage—since neither had possessed any worldly goods to speak of—at least a successful one in the sense of their everlasting devotion to each other. Salzman listened in embarrassed surprise, sensing a sort of apology. Later, however, he experienced a glow of pride in his work, an emotion that had left him years ago, and he heartily approved of Finkle.

The two went to their business. Leo had led Salzman to the only clear place in the room, a table near a window that overlooked the lamp-lit city. He seated himself at the matchmaker's side but facing him, attempting by an act of will to suppress the unpleasant tickle in his throat. Salzman eagerly unstrapped his portfolio and removed a loose rubber band from a thin packet of much-handled cards. As he flipped through them, a gesture and sound that physically hurt Leo, the student pretended not to see and gazed steadfastly out of the window. Although it was still February, winter was on its last legs, signs of which he had for the first time in years begun to notice. He now observed the round white moon, moving high in the sky through a cloud menagerie, and watched with half-open mouth as it penetrated a huge hen, and dropped out of her like an egg laying itself. Salzman, though pretending through eyeglasses he had just slipped on, to be engaged in scanning the writing on the cards, stole occasional glances at the young man's distinguished face, noting with pleasure the long, severe scholar's nose, brown eyes heavy with learning, sensitive yet ascetic lips, and a certain, almost hollow quality of the dark cheeks. He gazed around at shelves upon shelves of books and let out a soft, contented sigh.

When Leo's eyes fell upon the cards, he counted six spread out in Salzman's hand.

"So few?" he asked in disappointment.

"You wouldn't believe me how much cards I got in my office," Salzman replied. "The drawers are already filled to the top, so I keep them now in a barrel, but is every girl good for a new rabbi?"

Leo blushed at this, regretting all he had revealed of himself in a curriculum vitae he had sent to Salzman. He had thought it best to acquaint him with his strict standards and specifications, but in having done so, felt he had told the marriage broker more than was absolutely necessary.

He hesitantly inquired, "Do you keep photographs of your clients on file?"

"First comes family, amount of dowry, also what kind promises," Salzman replied, unbuttoning his tight coat and settling himself in the chair. "After comes pictures, rabbi."

"Call me Mr. Finkle. I'm not yet a rabbi."

Salzman said he would, but instead called him doctor, which he changed to rabbi when Leo was not listening too attentively.

Salzman adjusted his horn-rimmed spectacles, gently cleared his throat and read in an eager voice the contents of the top card:

"Sophie P. Twenty-four years. Widow one year. No children. Educated high school and two years college. Father promises eight thousand dollars. Has wonderful wholesale business. Also real estate. On the mother's side comes teachers, also one actor. Well known on Second Avenue."

Leo gazed up in surprise. "Did you say a widow?"

"A widow don't mean spoiled, rabbi. She lived with her husband maybe four months. He was a sick boy she made a mistake to marry him."

"Marrying a widow has never entered my mind."

"This is because you have no experience. A widow, especially if she is young and healthy like this girl, is a wonderful person to marry. She will be thankful to you the rest of her life. Believe me, if I was looking now for a bride, I would marry a widow."

Leo reflected, then shook his head.

Salzman hunched his shoulders in an almost imperceptible gesture of disappointment. He placed the card down on the wooden table and began to read another:

"Lily H. High school teacher. Regular. Not a substitute. Has savings and new Dodge car. Lived in Paris one year. Father is successful dentist thirty-five years. Interested in professional man. Well Americanized family. Wonderful opportunity."

"I knew her personally," said Salzman. "I wish you could see this girl. She is a doll. Also very intelligent. All day you could talk to her about books and theyater and what not. She also knows current events."

"I don't believe you mentioned her age?"

"Her age?" Salzman said, raising his brows. "Her age is thirty-two years."

Leo said after a while, "I'm afraid that seems a little too old."

Salzman let out a laugh. "So how old are you, rabbi?"

"Twenty-seven."

"So what is the difference, tell me, between twenty-seven and thirty-two? My own wife is seven years older than me. So what did I suffer?— Nothing. If Rothschild's a daughter wants to marry you, would you say on account her age, no?"

"Yes," Leo said dryly.

Salzman shook off the no in the yes. "Five years don't mean a thing. I give you my word that when you will live with her for one week you will forget her age. What does it mean five years—that she

lived more and knows more than somebody who is younger? On this girl, God bless her, years are not wasted. Each one that it comes makes better the bargain."

"What subject does she teach in high school?"

"Languages. If you heard the way she speaks French, you will think it is music. I am in the business twenty-five years, and I recommend her with my whole heart. Believe me, I know what I'm talking, rabbi."

"What's on the next card?" Leo said abruptly.

Salzman reluctantly turned up the third card:

"Ruth K. Nineteen years. Honor student. Father offers thirteen thousand cash to the right bridegroom. He is a medical doctor. Stomach specialist with marvelous practice. Brother-in-law owns own garment business. Particular people."

Salzman looked as if he had read his trump card.

"Did you say nineteen?" Leo asked with interest.

"On the dot."

"Is she attractive?" He blushed. "Pretty?"

Salzman kissed his finger tips. "A little doll. On this I give you my word. Let me call the father tonight and you will see what means pretty."

But Leo was troubled. "You're sure she's that young?"

"This I am positive. The father will show you the birth certificate."

"Are you positive there isn't something wrong with her?" Leo insisted.

"Who says there is wrong?"

"I don't understand why an American girl her age should go to a marriage broker."

A smile spread over Salzman's face.

"So for the same reason you went, she comes."

Leo flushed. "I am pressed for time."

Salzman, realizing he had been tactless, quickly explained. "The father came, not her. He wants she should have the best, so he looks around himself. When we will locate the right boy he will introduce him and encourage. This makes a better marriage than if a young girl without experience takes for herself. I don't have to tell you this."

"But don't you think this young girl believes in love?" Leo spoke uneasily.

Salzman was about to guffaw but caught himself and said soberly, "Love comes with the right person, not before."

Leo parted dry lips but did not speak. Noticing

that Salzman had snatched a glance at the next card, he cleverly asked, "How is her health?"

"Perfect," Salzman said, breathing with difficulty. "Of course, she is a little lame on her right foot from an auto accident that it happened to her when she was twelve years, but nobody notices on account she is so brilliant and also beautiful."

Leo got up heavily and went to the window. He felt curiously bitter and upbraided himself for having called in the marriage broker. Finally, he shook his head.

"Why not?" Salzman persisted, the pitch of his voice rising.

"Because I detest stomach specialists."

"So what do you care what is his business? After you marry her do you need him? Who says he must come every Friday night in your house?"

Ashamed of the way the talk was going, Leo dismissed Salzman, who went home with heavy, melancholy eyes.

Though he had felt only relief at the marriage broker's departure, Leo was in low spirits the next day. He explained it as arising from Salzman's failure to produce a suitable bride for him. He did not care for his type of clientele. But when Leo found himself hesitating whether to seek out another matchmaker, one more polished than Pinye, he wondered if it could be—his protestations to the contrary, and although he honored his father and mother—that he did not, in essence, care for the matchmaking institution? This thought he quickly put out of mind yet found himself still upset. All day he ran around in the woods—missed an important appointment, forgot to give out his laundry, walked out of a Broadway cafeteria without paying and had to run back with the ticket in his hand; had even not recognized his landlady in the street when she passed with a friend and courteously called out, "A good evening to you, Doctor Finkle." By nightfall, however, he had regained sufficient calm to sink his nose into a book and there found peace from his thoughts.

Almost at once there came a knock on the door. Before Leo could say enter, Salzman, commercial cupid, was standing in the room. His face was gray and meager, his expression hungry, and he looked as if he would expire on his feet. Yet the marriage broker managed, by some trick of the muscles, to display a broad smile.

"So good evening. I am invited?"

Leo nodded, disturbed to see him again, yet unwilling to ask the man to leave.

Beaming still, Salzman laid his portfolio on the table. "Rabbi, I got for you tonight good news."

"I've asked you not to call me rabbi. I'm still a student."

"Your worries are finished. I have for you a first-class bride."

"Leave me in peace concerning this subject." Leo pretended lack of interest.

"The world will dance at your wedding."

"Please, Mr. Salzman, no more."

"But first must come back my strength," Salzman said weakly. He fumbled with the portfolio straps and took out of the leather case an oily paper bag, from which he extracted a hard, seeded roll and a small, smoked white fish. With a quick motion of his hand he stripped the fish out of its skin and began ravenously to chew. "All day in a rush," he muttered.

Leo watched him eat.

"A sliced tomato you have maybe?" Salzman hesitantly inquired.

"No."

The marriage broker shut his eyes and ate. When he had finished he carefully cleaned up the crumbs and rolled up the remains of the fish, in the paper bag. His spectacled eyes roamed the room until he discovered, amid some piles of books, a one-burner gas stove. Lifting his hat he humbly asked, "A glass tea you got, rabbi?"

Conscience-stricken, Leo rose and brewed the tea. He served it with a chunk of lemon and two cubes of lump sugar, delighting Salzman.

After he had drunk his tea, Salzman's strength and good spirits were restored.

"So tell me, rabbi," he said amiably, "you considered some more the three clients I mentioned yesterday?"

"There was no need to consider."

"Why not?"

"None of them suits me."

"What then suits you?"

Leo let it pass because he could give only a confused answer.

Without waiting for a reply, Salzman asked, "You remember this girl I talked to you—the high school teacher?"

"Age thirty-two?"

But, surprisingly, Salzman's face lit in a smile. "Age twenty-nine."

Leo shot him a look. "Reduced from thirty-two?"

"A mistake," Salzman avowed. "I talked today with the dentist. He took me to his safety deposit box and showed me the birth certificate. She was twenty-nine years last August. They made her a party in the mountains where she went for her vacation. When her father spoke to me the first time I forgot to write the age and I told you thirty-two, but now I remember this was a different client, a widow."

"The same one you told me about? I thought she was twenty-four?"

"A different. Am I responsible that the world is filled with widows?"

"No, but I'm not interested in them, nor for that matter, in school teachers."

Salzman pulled his clasped hands to his breast. Looking at the ceiling he devoutly exclaimed, "Yiddishe kinder, what can I say to somebody that he is not interested in high school teachers? So what then you are interested?"

Leo flushed but controlled himself.

"In what else will you be interested," Salzman went on, "if you not interested in this fine girl that she speaks four languages and has personally in the bank ten thousand dollars? Also her father guarantees further twelve thousand. Also she has a new car, wonderful clothes, talks on all subjects, and she will give you a first-class home and children. How near do we come in our life to paradise?"

"If she's so wonderful, why wasn't she married ten years ago?"

"Why?" said Salzman with a heavy laugh. "—Why? Because she is *partikiler*. This is why. She wants the *best*."

Leo was silent, amused at how he had entangled himself. But Salzman had aroused his interest in Lily H., and he began seriously to consider calling on her. When the marriage broker observed how intently Leo's mind was at work on the facts he had supplied, he felt certain they would soon come to an agreement.

Late Saturday afternoon, conscious of Salzman, Leo Finkle walked with Lily Hirschorn along Riverside Drive. He walked briskly and erectly, wearing with distinction the black fedora he had that morning taken with trepidation out of the dusty hat box on his closet shelf, and the heavy black Saturday coat he had thoroughly whisked clean. Leo also owned a walking stick, a present from a distant relative, but quickly put temptation aside and did not use it. Lily, petite and not unpretty, had on something signifying the approach of spring. She was au courant, animatedly, with all sorts of subjects, and he weighed her words and found her surprisingly sound—score another for Salzman, whom he uneasily sensed to be somewhere around, hiding perhaps high in a tree along the street, flashing the lady signals with a pocket mirror; or perhaps a cloven-hoofed Pan, piping nuptial ditties as he danced his invisible way before them, strewing wild buds on the walk and purple grapes in their path, symbolizing fruit of a union, though there was of course still none.

Lily startled Leo by remarking, "I was thinking of Mr. Salzman, a curious figure, wouldn't you say?"

Not certain what to answer, he nodded.

She bravely went on, blushing, "I for one am grateful for his introducing us. Aren't you?"

He courteously replied, "I am."

"I mean," she said with a little laugh—and it was all in good taste, or at least gave the effect of being not in bad—"do you mind that we came together so?"

He was not displeased with her honesty, recognizing that she meant to set the relationship aright, and understanding that it took a certain amount of experience in life, and courage, to want to do it quite that way. One had to have some sort of past to make that kind of beginning.

He said that he did not mind. Salzman's function was traditional and honorable—valuable for what it might achieve, which, he pointed out, was frequently nothing.

Lily agreed with a sigh. They walked on for a while and she said after a long silence, again with a nervous laugh, "Would you mind if I asked you something a little bit personal? Frankly, I find the subject fascinating." Although Leo shrugged, she went on half embarrassedly, "How was it that you came to your calling? I mean was it a sudden passionate inspiration?"

Leo, after a time, slowly replied, "I was always interested in the Law."

"You saw revealed in it the presence of the Highest?"

He nodded and changed the subject. "I understand that you spent a little time in Paris, Miss Hirschorn?"

"Oh, did Mr. Salzman tell you, Rabbi Finkle?" Leo winced but she went on, "It was ages ago and almost forgotten. I remember I had to return for my sister's wedding."

And Lily would not be put off. "When," she asked in a trembly voice, "did you become enamored of God?"

He stared at her. Then it came to him that she was talking not about Leo Finkle, but of a total stranger, some mystical figure, perhaps even passionate prophet that Salzman had dreamed up for her—no relation to the living or dead. Leo trembled with rage and weakness. The trickster had obviously sold her a bill of goods, just as he had him, who'd expected to become acquainted with a young lady of twenty-nine, only to behold, the moment he laid eyes upon her strained and anxious face, a woman past thirty-five and aging rapidly. Only his self-control had kept him this long in her presence.

"I am not," he said gravely, "a talented religious person," and in seeking words to go on, found himself possessed by shame and fear. "I think," he said in a strained manner, "that I came to God not because I loved Him, but because I did not."

This confession he spoke harshly because its unexpectedness shook him.

Lily wilted. Leo saw a profusion of loaves of bread go flying like ducks high over his head, not unlike the winged loaves by which he had counted himself to sleep last night. Mercifully, then, it snowed, which he would not put past Salzman's machinations.

He was infuriated with the marriage broker and swore he would throw him out of the room the minute he reappeared. But Salzman did not come that night, and when Leo's anger had subsided, an unaccountable despair grew in its place. At first he thought this was caused by his disappointment in Lily, but before long it became evident that he had involved himself with Salzman without a true knowledge of his own intent. He gradually realized —with an emptiness that seized him with six hands —that he had called in the broker to find him a bride because he was incapable of doing it himself. This terrifying insight he had derived as a result of his meeting and conversation with Lily Hirschorn.

Her probing questions had somehow irritated him into revealing—to himself more than her—the true nature of his relationship to God, and from that it had come upon him, with shocking force, that apart from his parents, he had never loved anyone. Or perhaps it went the other way, that he did not love God so well as he might, because he had not loved man. It seemed to Leo that his whole life stood starkly revealed and he saw himself for the first time as he truly was—unloved and loveless. This bitter but somehow not fully unexpected revelation brought him to a point of panic, controlled only by extraordinary effort. He covered his face with his hands and cried.

The week that followed was the worst of his life. He did not eat and lost weight. His beard darkened and grew ragged. He stopped attending seminars and almost never opened a book. He seriously considered leaving the Yeshivah, although he was deeply troubled at the thought of the loss of all his years of study—saw them like pages torn from a book, strewn over the city—and at the devastating effect of this decision upon his parents. But he had lived without knowledge of himself, and never in the Five Books and all the Commentaries[1]—mea culpa—had the truth been revealed to him. He did not know where to turn, and in all this desolating loneliness there was no *to whom*, although he often thought of Lily but not once could bring himself to go downstairs and make the call. He became touchy and irritable, especially with his landlady, who asked him all manner of personal questions; on the other hand, sensing his own disagreeableness, he waylaid her on the stairs and apologized abjectly, until mortified, she ran from him. Out of this, however, he drew the consolation that he was a Jew and that a Jew suffered. But gradually, as the long and terrible week drew to a close, he regained his composure and some idea of purpose in life: to go on as planned. Although he was imperfect, the ideal was not. As for his quest of a bride, the thought of continuing afflicted him with anxiety and heartburn, yet perhaps with this new knowledge of himself he would be more successful than in the past. Perhaps love would now come to him and a bride to that love. And for this sanctified seeking who needed a Salzman?

THE MAGIC BARREL. 1. Five . . . Commentaries: the Pentateuch and the corpus of Jewish Law derived from them.

The marriage broker, a skeleton with haunted eyes, returned that very night. He looked, withal, the picture of frustrated expectancy—as if he had steadfastly waited the week at Miss Lily Hirschorn's side for a telephone call that never came.

Casually coughing, Salzman came immediately to the point: "So how did you like her?"

Leo's anger rose and he could not refrain from chiding the matchmaker: "Why did you lie to me, Salzman?"

Salzman's pale face went dead white, the world had snowed on him.

"Did you not state that she was twenty-nine?" Leo insisted.

"I give you my word—"

"She was thirty-five, if a day. *At least* thirty-five."

"Of this don't be too sure. Her father told me—"

"Never mind. The worst of it was that you lied to her."

"How did I lie to her, tell me?"

"You told her things about me that weren't true. You made me out to be more, consequently less than I am. She had in mind a totally different person, a sort of semimystical Wonder Rabbi."

"All I said, you was a religious man."

"I can imagine."

Salzman sighed. "This is my weakness that I have," he confessed. "My wife says to me I shouldn't be a salesman, but when I have two fine people that they would be wonderful to be married, I am so happy that I talk too much." He smiled wanly. "This is why Salzman is a poor man."

Leo's anger left him. "Well, Salzman, I'm afraid that's all."

The marriage broker fastened hungry eyes on him.

"You don't want any more a bride?"

"I do," said Leo, "but I have decided to seek her in a different way. I am no longer interested in an arranged marriage. To be frank, I now admit the necessity of premarital love. That is, I want to be in love with the one I marry."

"Love?" said Salzman, astounded. After a moment he remarked, "For us, our love is our life, not for the ladies. In the ghetto they—"

"I know, I know," said Leo. "I've thought of it often. Love, I have said to myself, should be a by-product of living and worship rather than its own

end. Yet for myself I find it necessary to establish the level of my need and fulfill it."

Salzman shrugged but answered, "Listen, rabbi, if you want love, this I can find for you also. I have such beautiful clients that you will love them the minute your eyes will see them."

Leo smiled unhappily. "I'm afraid you don't understand."

But Salzman hastily unstrapped his portfolio and withdrew a manila packet from it.

"Pictures," he said, quickly laying the envelope on the table.

Leo called after him to take the pictures away, but as if on the wings of the wind, Salzman had disappeared.

March came. Leo had returned to his regular routine. Although he felt not quite himself yet—lacked energy—he was making plans for a more active social life. Of course it would cost something, but he was an expert in cutting corners; and when there were no corners left he would make circles rounder. All the while Salzman's pictures had lain on the table, gathering dust. Occasionally as Leo sat studying, or enjoying a cup of tea, his eyes fell on the manila envelope, but he never opened it.

The days went by and no social life to speak of developed with a member of the opposite sex—it was difficult, given the circumstances of his situation. One morning Leo toiled up the stairs to his room and stared out the window at the city. Although the day was bright his view of it was dark. For some time he watched the people in the street below hurrying along and then turned with a heavy heart to his little room. On the table was the packet. With a sudden relentless gesture he tore it open. For a half-hour he stood by the table in a state of excitement, examining the photographs of the ladies Salzman had included. Finally, with a deep sigh he put them down. There were six, of varying degrees of attractiveness, but look at them long enough and they all became Lily Hirschorn: all past their prime, all starved behind bright smiles, not a true personality in the lot. Life, despite their frantic yoohooings, had passed them by; they were pictures in a briefcase that stank of fish. After a while, however, as Leo attempted to return the photographs into the envelope, he found in it another, a snapshot of the type taken by a machine for a quarter. He gazed at it a moment and let out a cry.

Her face deeply moved him. Why, he could at first not say. It gave him the impression of youth —spring flowers, yet age—a sense of having been used to the bone, wasted; this came from the eyes, which were hauntingly familiar, yet absolutely strange. He had a vivid impression that he had met her before, but try as he might he could not place her although he could almost recall her name, as if he had read it in her own handwriting. No, this couldn't be; he would have remembered her. It was not, he affirmed, that she had an extraordinary beauty—no, though her face was attractive enough; it was that *something* about her moved him. Feature for feature, even some of the ladies of the photographs could do better; but she leaped forth to his heart—had *lived*, or wanted to—more than just wanted, perhaps regretted how she had lived— had somehow deeply suffered: it could be seen in the depth of those reluctant eyes, and from the way the light enclosed and shone from her, and within her, opening realms of possibility: this was her own. Her he desired. His head ached and eyes narrowed with the intensity of his gazing, then as if an obscure fog had blown up in the mind, he experienced fear of her and was aware that he had received an impression, somehow, of evil. He shuddered, saying softly, it is thus with us all. Leo brewed some tea in a small pot and sat sipping it without sugar, to calm himself. But before he had finished drinking, again with excitement he examined the face and found it good: good for Leo Finkle. Only such a one could understand him and help him seek whatever he was seeking. She might, perhaps, love him. How she had happened to be among the discards in Salzman's barrel he could never guess, but he knew he must urgently go find her.

Leo rushed downstairs, grapped up the Bronx telephone book, and searched for Salzman's home address. He was not listed, nor was his office. Neither was he in the Manhattan book. But Leo remembered having written down the address on a slip of paper after he had read Salzman's advertisement in the "personals" column of the *Forward*. He ran up to his room and tore through his papers, without luck. It was exasperating. Just when he needed the matchmaker he was nowhere to be found. Fortunately Leo remembered to look in his wallet. There on a card he found his name written and a Bronx address. No phone number was listed, the reason—Leo now recalled—he had originally communicated with Salzman by letter. He got on his coat, put a hat on over his skull cap and hurried to the subway station. All the way to the far end of the Bronx he sat on the edge of his seat. He was more than once tempted to take out the picture and see if the girl's face was as he remembered it, but he refrained, allowing the snapshot to remain in his inside coat pocket, content to have her so close. When the train pulled into the station he was waiting at the door and bolted out. He quickly located the street Salzman had advertised.

The building he sought was less than a block from the subway, but it was not an office building, nor even a loft, nor a store in which one could rent office space. It was a very old tenement house. Leo found Salzman's name in pencil on a soiled tag under the bell and climbed three dark flights to his apartment. When he knocked, the door was opened by a thin, asthmatic, gray-haired woman, in felt slippers.

"Yes?" she said, expecting nothing. She listened without listening. He could have sworn he had seen her, too, before but knew it was an illusion.

"Salzman—does he live here? Pinye Salzman," he said, "the matchmaker?"

She stared at him a long minute. "Of course."

He felt embarrassed. "Is he in?"

"No." Her mouth, though left open, offered nothing more.

"The matter is urgent. Can you tell me where his office is?"

"In the air." She pointed upward.

"You mean he has no office?" Leo asked.

"In his socks."

He peered into the apartment. It was sunless and dingy, one large room divided by a half-open curtain, beyond which he could see a sagging metal bed. The near side of a room was crowded with rickety chairs, old bureaus, a three-legged table, racks of cooking utensils, and all the apparatus of a kitchen. But there was no sign of Salzman or his magic barrel, probably also a figment of the imagination. An odor of frying fish made Leo weak to the knees.

"Where is he?" he insisted. "I've got to see your husband."

At length she answered, "So who knows where he is? Every time he thinks a new thought he runs to a different place. Go home, he will find you."

"Tell him Leo Finkle."

She gave no sign she had heard.

He walked downstairs, depressed.

But Salzman, breathless, stood waiting at his door.

Leo was astounded and overjoyed. "How did you get here before me?"

"I rushed."

"Come inside."

They entered. Leo fixed tea, and a sardine sandwich for Salzman. As they were drinking he reached behind him for the packet of pictures and handed them to the marriage broker.

Salzman put down his glass and said expectantly, "You found somebody you like?"

"Not among these."

The marriage broker turned away.

"Here is the one I want." Leo held forth the snapshot.

Salzman slipped on his glasses and took the picture into his trembling hand. He turned ghastly and let out a groan.

"What's the matter?" cried Leo.

"Excuse me. Was an accident this picture. She isn't for you."

Salzman frantically shoved the manila packet into his portfolio. He thrust the snapshot into his pocket and fled down the stairs.

Leo, after momentary paralysis, gave chase and cornered the marriage broker in the vestibule. The landlady made hysterical outcries but neither of them listened.

"Give me back the picture, Salzman."

"No." The pain in his eyes was terrible.

"Tell me who she is then."

"This I can't tell you. Excuse me."

He made to depart, but Leo, forgetting himself, seized the matchmaker by his tight coat and shook him frenziedly.

"Please," sighed Salzman. "*Please.*"

Leo ashamedly let him go. "Tell me who she is," he begged. "It's very important for me to know."

"She is not for you. She is a wild one—wild, without shame. This is not a bride for a rabbi."

"What do you mean wild?"

"Like an animal. Like a dog. For her to be poor was a sin. This is why to me she is dead now."

"In God's name, what do you mean?"

"Her I can't introduce to you," Salzman cried.

"Why are you so excited?"

"Why, he asks," Salzman said, bursting into tears. "This is my baby, my Stella, she should burn in hell."

Leo hurried up to bed and hid under the covers. Under the covers he thought his life through. Although he soon fell asleep he could not sleep her out of his mind. He woke, beating his breast. Though he prayed to be rid of her, his prayers went unanswered. Through days of torment he endlessly struggled not to love her; fearing success, he escaped it. He then concluded to convert her to goodness, himself to God. The idea alternately nauseated and exalted him.

He perhaps did not know that he had come to a final decision until he encountered Salzman in a Broadway cafeteria. He was sitting alone at a rear table, sucking the bony remains of a fish. The marriage broker appeared haggard, and transparent to the point of vanishing.

Salzman looked up at first without recognizing him. Leo had grown a pointed beard and his eyes were weighted with wisdom.

"Salzman," he said, "love has at last come to my heart."

"Who can love from a picture?" mocked the marriage broker.

"It is not impossible."

"If you can love her, then you can love anybody. Let me show you some new clients that they just sent me their photographs. One is a little doll."

"Just her I want," Leo murmured.

"Don't be a fool, doctor. Don't bother with her."

"Put me in touch with her, Salzman," Leo said humbly. "Perhaps I can be of service."

Salzman had stopped eating and Leo understood with emotion that it was now arranged.

Leaving the cafeteria, he was, however, afflicted by a tormenting suspicion that Salzman had planned it all to happen this way.

Leo was informed by letter that she would meet him on a certain corner, and she was there one spring night, waiting under a street lamp. He appeared, carrying a small bouquet of violets and rosebuds. Stella stood by the lamp post, smoking. She wore white with red shoes, which fitted his expectations, although in a troubled moment he had imagined the dress red, and only the shoes white. She waited uneasily and shyly. From afar he saw that her eyes —clearly her father's—were filled with desperate innocence. He pictured, in her, his own redemption. Violins and lit candles revolved in the sky. Leo ran forward with flowers outthrust.

Around the corner, Salzman, leaning against a wall, chanted prayers for the dead.

ROBERT BURNS
1759–1796

Holy Willie's Prayer°

O thou, wha in the Heavens dost dwell,
Wha, as it pleases best thysel',
Sends ane to heaven and ten to hell,
    A' for thy glory,
And no for ony guid or ill   5
    They've done afore thee!°

I bless and praise thy matchless might,
Whan thousands thou hast left in night,
That I am here afore thy sight,
    For gifts an' grace   10
A burnin' an' a shinin' light,
    To a' this place.°

What was I, or my generation,°
That I should get sic° exaltation?
I, wha deserve most just damnation,   15
    For broken laws,
Sax° thousand years 'fore my creation,
    Through Adam's cause.

When frae my mither's womb I fell,
Thou might hae plungéd me in hell,   20
To gnash my gums, to weep and wail,
    In burnin' lakes,
Where damnéd devils roar and yell,
    Chained to their stakes;

Yet I am here a chosen sample,   25
To show thy grace is great and ample;
I'm here a pillar in thy temple,
    Strong as a rock,
A guide, a buckler, an example
    To a' thy flock.   30

O Lord, thou kens° what zeal I bear,
When drinkers drink, and swearers swear,
And singin' there and dancin' here,
    Wi' great an' sma':
For I am keepit by thy fear   35
    Free frae them a'.

But yet, O Lord! confess I must
At times I'm fashed° wi' fleshly lust;
An' sometimes too, in warldly trust,
    Vile self gets in;   40
But thou remembers we are dust,
    Defiled in sin.

O Lord! yestreen,° thou kens, wi' Meg—
Thy pardon I sincerely beg;
O' may't ne'er be a livin' plague   45
    To my dishonor,
An' I'll ne'er lift a lawless leg
    Again upon her.

Besides I farther maun° allow,
Wi' Lizzie's lass, three times I trow—   50
But, Lord, that Friday I was fou,°
    When I cam near her,
Or else thou kens thy servant true
    Wad never steer° her.

May be thou lets this fleshly thorn   55
Beset thy servant e'en and morn
Lest he owre high and proud should turn,
    That he's sae gifted;
If sae, thy hand maun e'en be borne,
    Until thou lift it.   60

Lord, bless thy chosen in this place,
For here thou hast a chosen race;
But God confound their stubborn face,
    And blast their name,
Wha bring thy elders to disgrace   65
    An' public shame.

Lord, mind Gawn Hamilton's° deserts,
He drinks, an' swears, an' plays at cartes,°
Yet has sae mony takin' arts
    Wi' grit° an' sma',   70
Frae God's ain priest the people's hearts
    He steals awa'.

HOLY WILLIE'S PRAYER. The speaker is an elder of the Scottish kirk who assumes that he is one of the "elect" predestined to God's grace. 5-6. And . . . thee: In Calvinist dogma, election did not depend on moral conduct. 12. this place: the parish. 13. generation: begetting. 14. sic: such. 17. Sax: six.

31. kens: knowest. 38. fashed: irked, troubled. 43. yestreen: last night. 49. maun: must. 51. fou: drunk. 54. steer: molest. 67. Gawn Hamilton: a friend of Burns' who was brought before the Presbytery of Ayr by the model for Holy Willie, William Fisher of Mauchline. 68. cartes: cards. 70. grit: great.

An' when we chastened him therefor,
Thou kens how he bred sic a splore°
As set the warld in a roar   75
    O' laughin' at us;
Curse thou his basket and his store,
    Kail° and potatoes.

Lord, hear my earnest cry an' pray'r,
Against that presbyt'ry o' Ayr;   80
Thy strong right hand, Lord, make it bare
    Upo' their heads;
Lord, weigh it down, and dinna spare,
    For their misdeeds.

O Lord my God, that glib-tongued Aiken,°   85
My very heart and soul are quakin',
To think how we stood sweatin', shakin',
    An' pissed wi' dread,
While he, wi' hingin' lips and snakin',°
    Held up his head.   90

Lord, in the day of vengeance try him;
Lord, visit° them wha did employ him.
And pass not in thy mercy by them,
    No hear their pray'r:
But, for thy people's sake, destroy them,   95
    And dinna spare.

But, Lord, remember me and mine
Wi' mercies temp'ral and divine,
That I for gear° and grace may shine
    Excelled by name,   100
And a' the glory shall be thine,
    Amen, Amen!

ROBERT BROWNING
1812–1889

Soliloquy of the Spanish Cloister

Gr-r-r—there go, my heart's abhorrence!
    Water your damned flowerpots, do!
If hate killed men, Brother Lawrence,

74. splore: row. 78. Kail: broth. 85. Aiken: counsel for
Hamilton (see l. 67). 89. hingin' . . . snakin': hanging and
sneering lips. 92. visit: in the biblical sense of wreaking
vengeance. 99. gear: wealth.

    God's blood,° would not mine kill you!
What? your myrtle-bush wants trimming?   5
    Oh, that rose has prior claims—
Needs its leaden vase filled brimming?
    Hell dry you up with its flames!

At the meal we sit together;
    Salve tibi!° I must hear   10
Wise talk of the kind of weather,
    Sort of season, time of year:
Not a plenteous cork-crop: scarcely
    Dare we hope oak-galls,° I doubt:
What's the Latin name for "parsley"?   15
    What's the Greek name for Swine's Snout?

Whew! We'll have our platter burnished,
    Laid with care on our own shelf!
With a fire-new spoon we're furnished,
    And a goblet for ourself,   20
Rinsed like something sacrificial
    Ere 'tis fit to touch our chaps°—
Marked with L. for our initial!
    (He-he! There his lily snaps!)

Saint, forsooth! While brown Dolores   25
    Squats outside the Convent bank
With Sanchicha, telling stories,
    Steeping tresses in the tank,
Blue-black, lustrous, thick like horsehairs,
    —Can't I see his dead eye glow,   30
Bright as 'twere a Barbary corsair's?
    (That is, if he'd let it show!)

When he finishes refection,
    Knife and fork he never lays
Crosswise, to my recollection,   35
    As do I, in Jesu's praise.
I the Trinity illustrate,
    Drinking watered orange-pulp—
In three sips the Arian° frustrate;
    While he drains his at one gulp!   40

Oh, those melons! If he's able
    We're to have a feast! so nice!
One goes to the Abbot's table,
    All of us get each a slice.

SOLILOQUY OF THE SPANISH CLOISTER. 4. God's blood:
strong oath generally regarded as shocking in British
culture. 10. Salve tibi: Hail to thee. 14. oak-galls: used for
making ink. 22. chaps: jaws. 39. Arian: follower of Arius,
a third-century Greek theologian who denied the doctrine
of the Trinity.

How go on your flowers? None double?° 45
  Not one fruit-sort can you spy?
Strange!—And I, too, at such trouble
  Keep them close-nipped on the sly!

There's a great text in Galatians,
  Once you trip on it, entails 50
Twenty-nine distinct damnations,
  One sure, if another fails:
If I trip him just a-dying,
  Sure of Heaven as sure can be,
Spin him round and send him flying 55
  Off to Hell, a Manichee?°

Or, my scrofulous French novel°
  On gray paper with blunt type!
Simply glance at it, you grovel
  Hand and foot in Belial's gripe: 60
If I double° down its pages
  At the woeful sixteenth print,
When he gathers his greengages,°
  Ope a sieve° and slip it in 't?

Or, there's Satan!—one might venture 65
  Pledge one's soul to him, yet leave
Such a flaw in the indenture
  As he'd miss, till, past retrieve,
Blasted lay that rose-acacia°
  We're so proud of! *Hy, Zy, Hine°* . . . 70
'St, there's Vespers! *Plena gratiâ*
  Ave, Virgo!° Gr-r-r—you swine!

45. **double:** multiply. 56. **Manichee:** follower of Manes, a third-century Persian prophet who believed the world to be controlled by two separate forces of good and evil. 57. **French novel:** pornographic trash. 61. **double:** turn. 63. **greengages:** plums. 64. **sieve:** basket. 69. **rose-acacia:** i.e., Brother Lawrence. 70. **Hy, Zy, Hine:** perhaps an imitation of bells calling the monks to vespers. 71–72. **Plena . . . Virgo:** Hail, Virgin, full of grace.

EZRA POUND
b. 1885

Cino°

Italian Campagna 1309, the open road

Bah! I have sung women in three cities,
But it is all the same;
And I will sing of the sun.

Lips, words, and you snare them,
Dreams, words, and they are as jewels, 5
Strange spells of old deity,
Ravens, nights, allurement:
And they are not;
Having become the souls of song.

Eyes, dreams, lips, and the night goes. 10
Being upon the road once more,
They are not.
Forgetful in their towers of our tuneing
Once for Wind-runeing°
They dream us-toward and 15
Sighing, say, "Would Cino,
Passionate Cino, of the wrinkling eyes,
Gay Cino, of quick laughter,
Cino, of the dare, the jibe,
Frail Cino, strongest of his tribe° 20
That tramp old ways beneath the sunlight,
Would Cino of the Luth° were here!"

Once, twice, a year—
Vaguely thus word they:
  "Cino?" "Oh, eh, Cino Polnesi 25
  The singer is 't you mean?"
  "Ah yes, passed once our way,
  A saucy fellow, but . . .
  (Oh they are all one these vagabonds),
  Peste! 'tis his own songs? 30
  Or some other's that he sings?
  But *you*, My Lord, how with your city?"
But you "My Lord," God's pity!
And° all I knew were out, My Lord, you
Were Lack-land Cino, e'en as I am, 35
O Sinistro.°

I have sung women in three cities.
But it is all one.
I will sing of the sun.
. . . eh? . . . they mostly had gray eyes,   40
But it is all one, I will sing of the sun.

    " 'Pollo Phoibee,° old tin pan, you
    Glory to Zeus' aegis-day,°
    Shield o' steel-blue, th' heaven o'er us
    Hath for boss thy luster gay!   45

    'Pollo Phoibee, to our way-fare°
    Make thy laugh our wander-lied;°

42. 'Pollo Phoibee: Phoebus Apollo, the god of the sun.
The following lines are a parody of the kind of epithet-laden
song used by minstrels to flatter princes. 43. aegis-day: day
of remembrance. 46. way-fare: perhaps a combination of
"welfare" and "wayfaring." 47. wander-lied: song of
wandering.

Bid thy 'fulgence° bear away care.
Cloud and rain-tears pass they fleet°!

Seeking e'er the new-laid rast-way°   50
To the gardens of the sun . . .

  .   .   .   .   .

I have sung women in three cities
But it is all one.

I will sing of the white birds
In the blue waters of heaven,   55
The clouds that are spray to its sea.

48. 'fulgence: effulgence. 49. fleet: quickly. 50. rast-way:
perhaps a pun on *rest*.

The Romantic Phase:
Creation of a Free Society

WASHINGTON IRVING
1783–1859

Rip Van Winkle

A Posthumous Writing of Diedrich Knickerbocker

By Woden,[1] God of Saxons,
From whence comes Wensday, that is Wodensday.
Truth is a thing that ever I will keep
Unto thylke day in which I creep into
My sepulcher—

CARTWRIGHT[2]

[The following tale was found among the papers of the late Diedrich Knickerbocker,[3] an old gentleman of New York, who was very curious in the Dutch history of the province, and the manners of the descendants from its primitive settlers. His historical researches, however, did not lie so much among books as among men; for the former are lamentably scanty on his favorite topics; whereas he found the old burghers, and still more their wives, rich in that legendary lore so invaluable to true history. Whenever, therefore, he happened upon a genuine Dutch family, snugly shut up in its low-roofed farmhouse, under a spreading sycamore, he looked upon it as a little clasped volume of black-letter, and studied it with the zeal of a bookworm.

The result of all these researches was a history of the province during the reign of the Dutch governors, which he published some years since. There have been various opinions as to the literary character of his work, and, to tell the truth, it is not a whit better than it should be. Its chief merit is its scrupulous accuracy, which indeed was a little questioned on its first appearance, but has since been completely established; and it is now admitted into all historical collections as a book of unquestionable authority.

The old gentleman died shortly after the publication of his work; and now that he is dead and gone, it cannot do much harm to his memory to say that his time might have been much better employed in weightier labors. He, however, was apt to ride his hobby his own way; and though it did now and then kick up the dust a little in the eyes of his neighbors, and grieve the spirit of some friends, for whom he felt the truest deference and affection, yet his errors and follies are remembered "more in sorrow than in anger,"[4] and it begins to be suspected that he never intended to injure or offend. But however his memory may be appreciated by critics, it is still held dear by many folk whose good opinion is well worth having; particularly by certain biscuit-bakers, who have gone so far as to imprint his likeness on their New-Year cakes; and have thus given him a chance of immortality, almost equal to the being stamped on a Waterloo Medal, or a Queen Anne's Farthing.][5]

RIP VAN WINKLE. **1. Woden:** in Teutonic mythology, the god of wisdom, war, and storms. **2. Cartwright:** The lines quoted are spoken by a pedant in William Cartwright's play *The Ordinary* (1651), III.i.1050–54. **3. Knickerbocker:** the fictitious Dutch historian from Irving's earlier work *A History of New York* (1809).

4. more . . . anger: *Hamlet* I.ii.231–32. **5. Waterloo . . . Farthing:** silver medals given to those who fought in the Battle of Waterloo and bronze farthings stamped with the image of Queen Anne, respectively.

Whoever has made a voyage up the Hudson must remember the Kaatskill mountains. They are a dismembered branch of the great Appalachian family, and are seen away to the west of the river, swelling up to a noble height, and lording it over the surrounding country. Every change of season, every change of weather, indeed, every hour of the day, produces some change in the magical hues and shapes of these mountains, and they are regarded by all the good wives, far and near, as perfect barometers. When the weather is fair and settled, they are clothed in blue and purple, and print their bold outlines on the clear evening sky; but sometimes, when the rest of the landscape is cloudless, they will gather a hood of gray vapors about their summits, which, in the last rays of the setting sun, will glow and light up like a crown of glory.

At the foot of these fairy mountains, the voyager may have descried the light smoke curling up from a village, whose shingle-roofs gleam among the trees, just where the blue tints of the upland melt away into the fresh green of the nearer landscape. It is a little village, of great antiquity, having been founded by some of the Dutch colonists in the early times of the province, just about the beginning of the government of the good Peter Stuyvesant[6] (may he rest in peace!), and there were some of the houses of the original settlers standing within a few years, built of small yellow bricks brought from Holland, having latticed windows and gable fronts, surmounted with weathercocks.

In that same village, and in one of these very houses (which, to tell the precise truth, was sadly time-worn and weather-beaten), there lived, many years since, while the country was yet a province of Great Britain, a simple, good-natured fellow, of the name of Rip Van Winkle. He was a descendant of the Van Winkles who figured so gallantly in the chivalrous days of Peter Stuyvesant, and accompanied him to the siege of Fort Christina.[7] He inherited, however, but little of the martial character of his ancestors. I have observed that he was a simple, good-natured man; he was, moreover, a kind neighbor, and an obedient, hen-pecked husband. Indeed, to the latter circumstance might be owing that meekness of spirit which

gained him such universal popularity; for those men are most apt to be obsequious and conciliating abroad, who are under the discipline of shrews at home. Their tempers, doubtless, are rendered pliant and malleable in the fiery furnace of domestic tribulation; and a curtain-lecture is worth all the sermons in the world for teaching the virtues of patience and long-suffering. A termagant wife may, therefore, in some respects be considered a tolerable blessing; and if so, Rip Van Winkle was thrice blessed.

Certain it is, that he was a great favorite among all the good wives of the village, who, as usual with the amiable sex, took his part in all family squabbles; and never failed, whenever they talked those matters over in their evening gossipings, to lay all the blame on Dame Van Winkle. The children of the village, too, would shout with joy whenever he approached. He assisted at their sports, made their playthings, taught them to fly kites and shoot marbles, and told them long stories of ghosts, witches and Indians. Whenever he went dodging about the village, he was surrounded by a troop of them, hanging on his skirts, clambering on his back, and playing a thousand tricks on him with impunity; and not a dog would bark at him throughout the neighborhood.

The great error in Rip's composition was an insuperable aversion to all kinds of profitable labor. It could not be from the want of assiduity or perseverance; for he would sit on a wet rock, with a rod as long and heavy as a Tartar's lance, and fish all day without a murmur, even though he should not be encouraged by a single nibble. He would carry a fowling-piece on his shoulder for hours together, trudging through woods and swamps, and up hill and down dale, to shoot a few squirrels or wild pigeons. He would never refuse to assist a neighbor even in the roughest toil, and was a foremost man at all country frolics for husking Indian corn, or building stone fences; the women of the village, too, used to employ him to run their errands, and to do such little odd jobs as their less obliging husbands would not do for them. In a word, Rip was ready to attend to anybody's business but his own; but as to doing family duty, and keeping his farm in order, he found it impossible.

In fact, he declared it was of no use to work on his farm; it was the most pestilent little piece of

6. **Peter Stuyvesant:** early governor of the Dutch colony of New Amsterdam. 7. **Fort Christina:** a Swedish fort on the Delaware captured by Stuyvesant's forces in 1655.

ground in the whole country; everything about it went wrong, and would go wrong, in spite of him. His fences were continually falling to pieces; his cow would either go astray, or get among the cabbages; weeds were sure to grow quicker in his fields than anywhere else; the rain always made a point of setting in just as he had some outdoor work to do; so that though his patrimonial estate had dwindled away under his management, acre by acre, until there was little more left than a mere patch of Indian corn and potatoes, yet it was the worst conditioned farm in the neighborhood.

His children, too, were as ragged and wild as if they belonged to nobody. His son Rip, an urchin begotten in his own likeness, promised to inherit the habits, with the old clothes, of his father. He was generally seen trooping like a colt at his mother's heels, equipped in a pair of his father's cast-off galligaskins,[8] which he had much ado to hold up with one hand, as a fine lady does her train in bad weather.

Rip Van Winkle, however, was one of those happy mortals, of foolish, well-oiled dispositions, who take the world easy, eat white bread or brown, whichever can be got with least thought or trouble, and would rather starve on a penny than work for a pound. If left to himself, he would have whistled life away in perfect contentment; but his wife kept continually dinning in his ears about his idleness, his carelessness, and the ruin he was bringing on his family. Morning, noon, and night, her tongue was incessantly going, and everything he said or did was sure to produce a torrent of household eloquence. Rip had but one way of replying to all lectures of this kind, and that, by frequent use, had grown into a habit. He shrugged his shoulders, shook his head, cast up his eyes, but said nothing. This, however, always provoked a fresh volley from his wife; so that he was fain to draw off his forces, and take to the outside of the house—the only side which, in truth, belongs to a hen-pecked husband.

Rip's sole domestic adherent was his dog Wolf, who was as much hen-pecked as his master; for Dame Van Winkle regarded them as companions in idleness, and even looked upon Wolf with an evil eye, as the cause of his master's going so often astray. True it is, in all points of spirit befitting an honorable dog, he was as courageous an

8. **galligaskins:** knee breeches.

animal as ever scoured the woods; but what courage can withstand the ever-during and all-besetting terrors of a woman's tongue? The moment Wolf entered the house his crest fell, his tail drooped to the ground, or curled between his legs, he sneaked about with a gallows air, casting many a sidelong glance at Dame Van Winkle, and at the least flourish of a broomstick or ladle he would fly to the door with yelping precipitation.

Times grew worse and worse with Rip Van Winkle as years of matrimony rolled on; a tart temper never mellows with age, and a sharp tongue is the only edged tool that grows keener with constant use. For a long while he used to console himself, when driven from home, by frequenting a kind of perpetual club of the sages, philosophers, and other idle personages of the village, which held its sessions on a bench before a small inn, designated by a rubicund portrait of his Majesty George the Third. Here they used to sit in the shade through a long, lazy summer's day, talking listlessly over village gossip, or telling endless sleepy stories about nothing. But it would have been worth any statesman's money to have heard the profound discussions that sometimes took place, when by chance an old newspaper fell into their hands from some passing traveler. How solemnly they would listen to the contents, as drawled out by Derrick Van Bummel, the schoolmaster, a dapper learned little man, who was not to be daunted by the most gigantic word in the dictionary; and how sagely they would deliberate upon public events some months after they had taken place.

The opinions of this junto were completely controlled by Nicholas Vedder, a patriarch of the village, and landlord of the inn, at the door of which he took his seat from morning till night, just moving sufficiently to avoid the sun and keep in the shade of a large tree; so that the neighbors could tell the hour by his movements as accurately as by a sun-dial. It is true he was rarely heard to speak, but smoked his pipe incessantly. His adherents, however (for every great man has his adherents), perfectly understood him, and knew how to gather his opinions. When anything that was read or related displeased him, he was observed to smoke his pipe vehemently, and to send forth short, frequent, and angry puffs; but when pleased, he would inhale the smoke slowly and tranquilly, and emit it in light and placid clouds; and sometimes, taking the pipe from his mouth, and letting the fragrant vapor curl about his nose, would gravely nod his head in token of perfect approbation.

From even this stronghold the unlucky Rip was at length routed by his termagant wife, who would suddenly break in upon the tranquility of the assemblage and call the members all to naught; nor was that august personage, Nicholas Vedder himself, sacred from the daring tongue of this terrible virago,[9] who charged him outright with encouraging her husband in habits of idleness.

Poor Rip was at last reduced almost to despair; and his only alternative, to escape from the labor of the farm and clamor of his wife, was to take gun in hand and stroll away into the woods. Here he would sometimes seat himself at the foot of a tree, and share the contents of his wallet with Wolf, with whom he sympathized as a fellow-sufferer in persecution. "Poor Wolf," he would say, "thy mistress leads thee a dog's life of it; but never mind, my lad, whilst I live thou shalt never want a friend to stand by thee!" Wolf would wag his tail, look wistfully in his master's face; and if dogs can feel pity, I verily believe he reciprocated the sentiment with all his heart.

In a long ramble of the kind on a fine autumnal day, Rip had unconsciously scrambled to one of the highest parts of the Kaatskill mountains. He was after his favorite sport of squirrel-shooting, and the still solitudes had echoed and reechoed with the reports of his gun. Panting and fatigued, he threw himself, late in the afternoon, on a green knoll, covered with mountain herbage, that crowned the brow of a precipice. From an opening between the trees he could overlook all the lower country for many a mile of rich woodland. He saw at a distance the lordly Hudson, far, far below him, moving on its silent but majestic course, with the reflection of a purple cloud, or the sail of a lagging bark, here and there sleeping on its glassy bosom, and at last losing itself in the blue highlands.

On the other side he looked down into a deep mountain glen, wild, lonely, and shagged, the bottom filled with fragments from the impending cliffs, and scarcely lighted by the reflected rays of the setting sun. For some time Rip lay musing on this scene; evening was gradually advancing; the mountains began to throw their long blue shadows

9. virago: sharp-tongued, nagging woman.

over the valleys; he saw that it would be dark long before he could reach the village, and he heaved a heavy sigh when he thought of encountering the terrors of Dame Van Winkle.

As he was about to descend, he heard a voice from a distance, hallooing, "Rip Van Winkle, Rip Van Winkle!" He looked round, but could see nothing but a crow winging its solitary flight across the mountain. He thought his fancy must have deceived him, and turned again to descend, when he heard the same cry ring through the still evening air: "Rip Van Winkle! Rip Van Winkle!" —at the same time Wolf bristled up his back, and giving a low growl, skulked to his master's side, looking fearfully down into the glen. Rip now felt a vague apprehension stealing over him; he looked anxiously in the same direction, and perceived a strange figure slowly toiling up the rocks, and bending under the weight of something he carried on his back. He was surprised to see any human being in this lonely and unfrequented place; but supposing it to be some one of the neighborhood in need of his assistance, he hastened down to yield it.

On nearer approach he was still more surprised at the singularity of the stranger's appearance. He was a short, square-built old fellow, with thick bushy hair, and a grizzled beard. His dress was of the antique Dutch fashion—a cloth jerkin strapped round his waist—several pair of breeches, the outer one of ample volume, decorated with rows of buttons down the sides, and bunches at the knees. He bore on his shoulder a stout keg, that seemed full of liquor, and made signs for Rip to approach and assist him with the load. Though rather shy and distrustful of this new acquaintance, Rip complied with his usual alacrity; and mutually relieving one another, they clambered up a narrow gully, apparently the dry bed of a mountain torrent. As they ascended, Rip every now and then heard long, rolling peals, like distant thunder, that seemed to issue out of a deep ravine, or rather cleft, between lofty rocks, toward which their rugged path conducted. He paused for an instant, but supposing it to be the muttering of one of those transient thundershowers which often take place in mountain heights, he proceeded. Passing through the ravine, they came to a hollow, like a small amphitheater, surrounded by perpendicular precipices, over the brinks of which impending trees shot their branches, so that you only caught glimpses of the azure sky and the bright evening cloud. During the whole time Rip and his companion had labored on in silence; for though the former marveled greatly what could be the object of carrying a keg of liquor up this wild mountain, yet there was something strange and incomprehensible about the unknown, that inspired awe and checked familiarity.

On entering the amphitheater, new objects of wonder presented themselves. On a level spot in the center was a company of odd-looking personages playing at ninepins.[10] They were dressed in a quaint, outlandish fashion; some wore short doublets, others jerkins, with long knives in their belts, and most of them had enormous breeches, of similar style with that of the guide's. Their visages, too, were peculiar: one had a large beard, broad face, and small piggish eyes; the face of another seemed to consist entirely of nose, and was surmounted by a white sugar-loaf hat, set off with a little red cock's tail. They all had beards, of various shapes and colors. There was one who seemed to be the commander. He was a stout old gentleman, with a weather-beaten countenance; he wore a laced doublet, broad belt and hanger,[11] high crowned hat and feather, red stockings, and high-heeled shoes, with roses[12] in them. The whole group reminded Rip of the figures in an old Flemish painting, in the parlor of Dominie Van Shaick, the village parson, and which had been brought over from Holland at the time of the settlement.

What seemed particularly odd to Rip was, that, though these folks were evidently amusing themselves, yet they maintained the gravest faces, the most mysterious silence, and were, withal, the most melancholy party of pleasure he had ever witnessed. Nothing interrupted the stillness of the scene but the noise of the balls, which, whenever they were rolled, echoed along the mountains like rumbling peals of thunder.

As Rip and his companion approached them, they suddenly desisted from their play, and stared at him with such fixed, statuelike gaze, and such strange, uncouth, lackluster countenances, that his heart turned within him, and his knees smote together. His companion now emptied the contents of the keg into large flagons, and made signs to him to wait upon the company. He obeyed with

fear and trembling; they quaffed the liquor in profound silence, and then returned to their game.

By degrees Rip's awe and apprehension subsided. He even ventured, when no eye was fixed upon him, to taste the beverage, which he found had much of the flavor of excellent Hollands.[13] He was naturally a thirsty soul, and was soon tempted to repeat the draft. One taste provoked another; and he reiterated his visits to the flagon so often that at length his senses were overpowered, his eyes swam in his head, his head gradually declined, and he fell into a deep sleep.

On waking, he found himself on the green knoll whence he had first seen the old man of the glen. He rubbed his eyes—it was a bright sunny morning. The birds were hopping and twittering among the bushes, and the eagle was wheeling aloft, and breasting the pure mountain breeze. "Surely," thought Rip, "I have not slept here all night." He recalled the occurrences before he fell asleep. The strange man with a keg of liquor—the mountain ravine—the wild retreat among the rocks—the woe-begone party at ninepins—the flagon—"Oh! that flagon! that wicked flagon!" thought Rip,— "what excuse shall I make to Dame Van Winkle?"

He looked round for his gun, but in place of the clean, well-oiled fowling-piece, he found an old firelock lying by him, the barrel incrusted with rust, the lock falling off, and the stock worm-eaten. He now suspected that the grave roisters of the mountain had put a trick upon him, and, having dosed him with liquor, had robbed him of his gun. Wolf, too, had disappeared, but he might have strayed away after a squirrel or partridge. He whistled after him, and shouted his name, but all in vain; the echoes repeated his whistle and shout, but no dog was to be seen.

He determined to revisit the scene of the last evening's gambol, and if he met with any of the party, to demand his dog and gun. As he rose to walk, he found himself stiff in the joints, and wanting in his usual activity. "These mountain beds do not agree with me," thought Rip, "and if this frolic should lay me up with a fit of the rheumatism, I shall have a blessed time with Dame Van Winkle." With some difficulty he got down into the glen: he found the gully up which he and his companion had ascended the preceding evening; but to his astonishment a mountain stream was now foaming

10. **ninepins:** bowling. **11. hanger:** sword. **12. roses:** rosettes.

13. **Hollands:** Dutch gin.

down it, leaping from rock to rock, and filling the glen with babbling murmurs. He, however, made shift to scramble up its sides, working his toilsome way through thickets of birch, sassafras, and witchhazel, and sometimes tripped up or entangled by the wild grapevines that twisted their coils or tendrils from tree to tree, and spread a kind of network in his path.

At length he reached to where the ravine had opened through the cliffs to the amphitheater; but no traces of such opening remained. The rocks presented a high, impenetrable wall, over which the torrent came tumbling in a sheet of feathery foam, and fell into a broad deep basin, black from the shadows of the surrounding forest. Here, then, poor Rip was brought to a stand. He again called and whistled after his dog; he was only answered by the cawing of a flock of idle crows, sporting high in air about a dry tree that overhung a sunny precipice; and who, secure in their elevation, seemed to look down and scoff at the poor man's perplexities. What was to be done? the morning was passing away, and Rip felt famished for want of his breakfast. He grieved to give up his dog and gun; he dreaded to meet his wife; but it would not do to starve among the mountains. He shook his head, shouldered the rusty firelock, and, with a heart full of trouble and anxiety, turned his steps homeward.

As he approached the village he met a number of people, but none whom he knew, which somewhat surprised him, for he had thought himself acquainted with everyone in the country round. Their dress, too, was of a different fashion from that to which he was accustomed. They all stared at him with equal marks of surprise, and whenever they cast their eyes upon him, invariably stroked their chins. The constant recurrence of this gesture induced Rip, involuntarily, to do the same, when, to his astonishment, he found his beard had grown a foot long!

He had now entered the skirts of the village. A troop of strange children ran at his heels, hooting after him, and pointing at his gray beard. The dogs, too, not one of which he recognized for an old acquaintance, barked at him as he passed. The very village was altered; it was larger and more populous. There were rows of houses which he had never seen before, and those which had been his familiar haunts had disappeared. Strange names were over the doors—strange faces at the windows—everything was strange. His mind now misgave him; he began to doubt whether both he and the world around him were not bewitched. Surely this was his native village, which he had left but the day before. There stood the Kaatskill mountains—there ran the silver Hudson at a distance—there was every hill and dale precisely as it had always been. Rip was sorely perplexed. "That flagon last night," thought he, "has addled my poor head sadly!"

It was with some difficulty that he found the way to his own house, which he approached with silent awe, expecting every moment to hear the shrill voice of Dame Van Winkle. He found the house gone to decay—the roof fallen in, the windows shattered, and the doors off the hinges. A half-starved dog that looked like Wolf was skulking about it. Rip called him by name, but the cur snarled, showed his teeth, and passed on. This was an unkind cut indeed. "My very dog," sighed poor Rip, "has forgotten me!"

He entered the house, which, to tell the truth, Dame Van Winkle had always kept in neat order. It was empty, forlorn, and apparently abandoned. This desolateness overcame all his connubial fears —he called loudly for his wife and children—the lonely chambers rang for a moment with his voice, and then all again was silence.

He now hurried forth, and hastened to his old resort, the village inn—but it too was gone. A large rickety wooden building stood in its place, with great gaping windows, some of them broken and mended with old hats and petticoats, and over the door was painted, "The Union Hotel, by Jonathan Doolittle." Instead of the great tree that used to shelter the quiet little Dutch inn of yore, there now was reared a tall naked pole, with something on the top that looked like a red nightcap,[14] and from it was fluttering a flag, on which was a singular assemblage of stars and stripes;—all this was strange and incomprehensible. He recognized on the sign, however, the ruby face of King George under which he had smoked so many a peaceful pipe; but even this was singularly metamorphosed. The red coat was changed for one of blue and buff, a sword was held in the hand instead of a scepter,

14. **pole . . . nightcap:** The "liberty" pole and cap of the French Revolution were used also to commemorate the American Revolution.

the head was decorated with a cocked hat, and underneath was painted in large characters, GENERAL WASHINGTON.

There was, as usual, a crowd of folk about the door, but none that Rip recollected. The very character of the people seemed changed. There was a busy, bustling, disputatious tone about it, instead of the accustomed phlegm and drowsy tranquility. He looked in vain for the sage Nicholas Vedder, with his broad face, double chin, and fair long pipe, uttering clouds of tobacco-smoke instead of idle speeches; or Van Bummel, the schoolmaster, doling forth the contents of an ancient newspaper. In place of these, a lean, bilious-looking fellow, with his pockets full of handbills, was haranguing vehemently about rights of citizens—elections—members of congress—liberty—Bunker's Hill—heroes of seventy-six—and other words, which were a perfect Babylonish[15] jargon to the bewildered Van Winkle.

The appearance of Rip, with his long, grizzled beard, his rusty fowling-piece, his uncouth dress, and an army of women and children at his heels, soon attracted the attention of the tavern-politicians. They crowded round him, eying him from head to foot with great curiosity. The orator bustled up to him, and, drawing him partly aside, inquired "On which side he voted?" Rip stared in vacant stupidity. Another short but busy little fellow pulled him by the arm, and, rising on tiptoe, inquired in his ear, "Whether he was Federal or Democrat?"[16] Rip was equally at a loss to comprehend the question; when a knowing, self-important old gentleman, in a sharp cocked hat, made his way through the crowd, putting them to the right and left with his elbows as he passed, and planting himself before Van Winkle, with one arm akimbo, the other resting on his cane, his keen eyes and sharp hat penetrating, as it were, into his very soul, demanded, in an austere tone, "What brought him to the election with a gun on his shoulder, and a mob at his heels; and whether he meant to breed a riot in the village?"—"Alas! gentlemen," cried Rip, somewhat dismayed, "I am a poor quiet man, a native of the place, and a loyal subject of the king, God bless him!"

Here a general shout burst from the bystanders

—"A tory! a tory! a spy! a refugee! hustle him! away with him!" It was with great difficulty that the self-important man in the cocked hat restored order; and, having assumed a tenfold austerity of brow, demanded again of the unknown culprit, what he came there for, and whom he was seeking? The poor man humbly assured him that he meant no harm, but merely came there in search of some of his neighbors, who used to keep about the tavern.

"Well—who are they?—name them."

Rip bethought himself a moment, and inquired, "Where's Nicholas Vedder?"

There was a silence for a little while, when an old man replied, in a thin piping voice, "Nicholas Vedder! why, he is dead and gone these eighteen years! There was a wooden tombstone in the churchyard that used to tell all about him, but that's rotten and gone too."

"Where's Brom Dutcher?"

"Oh, he went off to the army in the beginning of the war; some say he was killed at the storming of Stony Point—others say he was drowned in a squall at the foot of Antony's Nose.[17] I don't know—he never came back again."

"Where's Van Bummel, the schoolmaster?"

"He went off to the wars too, was a great militia general, and is now in congress."

Rip's heart died away at hearing of these sad changes in his home and friends, and finding himself thus alone in the world. Every answer puzzled him too, by treating of such enormous lapses of time, and of matters which he could not understand: war—congress—Stony Point;—he had no courage to ask after any more friends, but cried out in despair, "Does nobody here know Rip Van Winkle?"

"Oh, Rip Van Winkle!" exclaimed two or three, "oh, to be sure! that's Rip Van Winkle yonder, leaning against the tree."

Rip looked, and beheld a precise counterpart of himself, as he went up the mountain; apparently as lazy, certainly as ragged. The poor fellow was now completely confounded. He doubted his own identity, and whether he was himself or another man. In the midst of his bewilderment, the man in the cocked hat demanded who he was, and what was his name.

"God knows," exclaimed he, at his wit's end;

15. **Babylonish:** like the Tower of Babel. 16. **Federal or Democrat:** advocate of the political ideals of Hamilton or Jefferson.

17. **Stony . . . Nose:** battles of the American Revolution.

"I'm not myself—I'm somebody else—that's me yonder—no—that's somebody else got into my shoes—I was myself last night, but I fell asleep on the mountain, and they've changed my gun, and everything's changed, and I'm changed, and I can't tell what's my name, or who I am!"

The bystanders began now to look at each other, nod, wink significantly, and tap their fingers against their foreheads. There was a whisper, also, about securing the gun, and keeping the old fellow from doing mischief, at the very suggestion of which the self-important man in the cocked hat retired with some precipitation. At this critical moment a fresh, comely woman pressed through the throng to get a peep at the gray-bearded man. She had a chubby child in her arms, which, frightened at his looks, began to cry. "Hush, Rip," cried she, "hush, you little fool; the old man won't hurt you." The name of the child, the air of the mother, the tone of her voice, all awakened a train of recollections in his mind. "What is your name, my good woman?" asked he.

"Judith Gardenier."

"And your father's name?"

"Ah, poor man, Rip Van Winkle was his name, but it's twenty years since he went away from home with his gun, and never has been heard of since,—his dog came home without him; but whether he shot himself, or was carried away by the Indians, nobody can tell. I was then but a little girl."

Rip had but one question more to ask; but he put it with a faltering voice:

"Where's your mother?"

"Oh, she too had died but a short time since; she broke a bloodvessel in a fit of passion at a New-England peddler."

There was a drop of comfort, at least, in this intelligence. The honest man could contain himself no longer. He caught his daughter and her child in his arms. "I am your father!" cried he—"Young Rip Van Winkle once—old Rip Van Winkle now!—Does nobody know poor Rip Van Winkle?"

All stood amazed, until an old woman, tottering out from among the crowd, put her hand to her brow, and peering under it in his face for a moment, exclaimed, "Sure enough! it is Rip Van Winkle—it is himself! Welcome home again, old neighbor. Why, where have you been these twenty long years?"

Rip's story was soon told, for the whole twenty years had been to him but as one night. The neighbors stared when they heard it; some were seen to wink at each other, and put their tongues in their cheeks: and the self-important man in the cocked hat, who, when the alarm was over, had returned to the field, screwed down the corners of his mouth, and shook his head—upon which there was a general shaking of the head throughout the assemblage.

It was determined, however, to take the opinion of old Peter Vanderdonk, who was seen slowly advancing up the road. He was a descendant of the historian of that name, who wrote one of the earliest accounts of the province. Peter was the most ancient inhabitant of the village, and well versed in all the wonderful events and traditions of the neighborhood. He recollected Rip at once, and corroborated his story in the most satisfactory manner. He assured the company that it was a fact, handed down from his ancestor the historian, that the Kaatskill mountains had always been haunted by strange beings. That it was affirmed that the great Hendrick Hudson, the first discoverer of the river and country, kept a kind of vigil there every twenty years, with his crew of the Half-moon; being permitted in this way to revisit the scenes of his enterprise, and keep a guardian eye upon the river and the great city called by his name. That his father had once seen them in their old Dutch dresses playing at ninepins in a hollow of the mountain; and that he himself had heard, one summer afternoon, the sound of their balls, like distant peals of thunder.

To make a long story short, the company broke up and returned to the more important concerns of the election. Rip's daughter took him home to live with her; she had a snug, well-furnished house, and a stout, cheery farmer for a husband, whom Rip recollected for one of the urchins that used to climb upon his back. As to Rip's son and heir, who was the ditto of himself, seen leaning against the tree, he was employed to work on the farm; but evinced an hereditary disposition to attend to anything else but his business.

Rip now resumed his old walks and habits; he soon found many of his former cronies, though all rather the worse for the wear and tear of time; and preferred making friends among the rising generation, with whom he soon grew into great favor.

Having nothing to do at home, and being arrived at that happy age when a man can be idle with impunity, he took his place once more on the bench at the inn-door, and was reverenced as one of the patriarchs of the village, and a chronicle of the old times "before the war." It was some time before he could get into the regular track of gossip, or could be made to comprehend the strange events that had taken place during his torpor. How that there had been a revolutionary war,—that the country had thrown off the yoke of old England,— and that, instead of being a subject of his Majesty George the Third, he was now a free citizen of the United States. Rip, in fact, was no politician; the changes of states and empires made but little impression on him; but there was one species of despotism under which he had long groaned, and that was—petticoat government. Happily that was at an end; he had got his neck out of the yoke of matrimony, and could go in and out whenever he pleased, without dreading the tyranny of Dame Van Winkle. Whenever her name was mentioned, however, he shook his head, shrugged his shoulders, and cast up his eyes; which might pass either for an expression of resignation to his fate, or joy at his deliverance.

He used to tell his story to every stranger that arrived at Mr. Doolittle's hotel. He was observed, at first, to vary on some points every time he told it, which was, doubtless, owing to his having so recently awaked. It at last settled down precisely to the tale I have related, and not a man, woman, or child in the neighborhood but knew it by heart. Some always pretended to doubt the reality of it, and insisted that Rip had been out of his head, and that this was one point on which he always remained flighty. The old Dutch inhabitants, however, almost universally gave it full credit. Even to this day they never hear a thunderstorm of a summer afternoon about the Kaatskill, but they say Hendrick Hudson and his crew are at their game of ninepins; and it is a common wish of all henpecked husbands in the neighborhood, when life hangs heavy on their hands, that they might have a quieting draft out of Rip Van Winkle's flagon.

CHRISTOPHER FRY
b. 1907

A Phoenix Too Frequent

CHARACTERS

DYNAMENE
DOTO
TEGEUS-CHROMIS

SCENE—*The tomb of Virilius, near Ephesus; night.*
NOTE—*The story was got from Jeremy Taylor who had it from Petronius.°*

"To whom conferred a peacock's undecent,
A squirrel's harsh, a phoenix too frequent."
Robert Burton quoting Martial

[*An underground tomb, in darkness except for the very low light of an oil-lamp. Above ground the starlight shows a line of trees on which hang the bodies of several men. It also penetrates a gate and falls on to the first of the steps which descend into the darkness of the tomb.* DOTO *talks to herself in the dark.*]

DOTO Nothing but the harmless day gone into
    black
  Is all the dark is. And so what's my trouble?
  Demons is so much wind. Are so much wind.
  I've plenty to fill my thoughts. All that I ask
  Is don't keep turning men over in my mind,   5
  Venerable Aphrodite. I've had my last one
  And thank you. I thank thee. He smelt of sour
    grass
  And was likable. He collected ebony quoits.
    [*An owl hoots near at hand.*]
  O Zeus! O some god or other, where is the oil?
  Fire's from Prometheus. I thank thee. If I   10
  Mean to die I'd better see what I'm doing.
[*She fills the lamp with oil. The flame burns up brightly and shows* DYNAMENE, *beautiful and young, leaning asleep beside a bier.*]

A PHOENIX TOO FREQUENT. **from Petronius:** The story of the "Widow of Ephesus" comes from *The Satyricon* of Petronius, Roman author of the first century A.D., and is retold by Jeremy Taylor, a seventeenth-century English clergyman, in *Holy Living and Holy Dying* (1650–51), where it is used as an exemplum to illustrate the excesses of grief.

Honestly, I would rather have to sleep
With a bald beekeeper who was wearing his
  boots
Than spend more days fasting and thirsting and
  crying
In a tomb. I shouldn't have said it. Pretend   15
I didn't hear myself. But life and death
Is cat and dog in this double-bed of a world.
My master, my poor master, was a man
Whose nose was as straight as a little buttress,
And now he has taken it into Elysium   20
Where it won't be noticed among all the other
  straightness.
[*The owl cries again and wakens* DYNAMENE.]
Oh, them owls. Those owls. It's woken her.

DYNAMENE   Ah! I'm breathless. I caught up with
  the ship
But it spread its wings, creaking a cry of *Dew,
Dew!* and flew figurehead foremost into the sun.

DOTO   How crazy, madam.   26

DYNAMENE   Doto, draw back the curtains.
I'll take my barley-water.

DOTO   We're not at home
Now, madam. It's the master's tomb.

DYNAMENE   Of course!
Oh, I'm wretched. Already I have disfigured
My vigil. My cynical eyelids have soon dropped
  me   30
In a dream.

DOTO   But then it's possible, madam, you might
Find yourself in bed with him again
In a dream, madam. Was he on the ship?

DYNAMENE   He was the ship.

DOTO   Oh. That makes it different.

DYNAMENE   He was the ship. He had such a deck,
  Doto,   35
Such a white, scrubbed deck. Such a stern prow,
Such a proud stern, so slim from port to star-
  board.
If ever you meet a man with such fine masts
Give your life to him, Doto. The figurehead
Bore his own features, so serene in the brow   40
And hung with a little seaweed. O Virilius,
My husband, you have left a wake in my soul.
You cut the glassy water with a diamond keel.
I must cry again.

DOTO   What, when you mean to join him?
Don't you believe he will be glad to see you,
  madam?   45
Thankful to see you, I should imagine, among

Them shapes and shades; all shapes of shapes
  and all
Shades of shades, from what I've heard. I know
I shall feel odd at first with Cerberus,
Sop or no sop. Still, I know how you feel,
  madam.   50
You think he may find a temptation in Hades.
I shouldn't worry. It would help him to settle
  down.
[DYNAMENE *weeps*.]
It would only be *fun*, madam. He couldn't go far
With a shade.

DYNAMENE   He was one of the coming men.
He was certain to have become the most well-
  organized provost   55
The town has known, once they had made him
  provost.
He was so punctual, you could regulate
The sun by him. He made the world succumb
To his daily revolution of habit. But who,
In the world he has gone to, will appreciate that?
O poor Virilius! To be a coming man   61
Already gone—it must be distraction.
Why did you leave me walking about our
  ambitions
Like a cat in the ruins of a house? Promising
  husband,
Why did you insult me by dying? Virilius,   65
Now I keep no flower, except in the vase
Of the tomb.

DOTO   O poor madam! O poor master!
I presume so far as to cry somewhat for myself
As well. I know you won't mind, madam. It's two
Days not eating makes me think of my uncle's
Shop in the country, where he has a hardware
  business,   71
Basins, pots, ewers, and alabaster birds.
He makes you die of laughing. O madam,
Isn't it sad?
[*They both weep*.]

DYNAMENE   How could I have allowed you
To come and die of my grief? Doto, it puts   75
A terrible responsibility on me. Have you
No grief of your own you could die of?

DOTO   Not really, madam.

DYNAMENE   Nothing?

DOTO   Not really. They was all one to me.
Well, all but two was all one to me. And they,
Strange enough, was two who kept recurring.   80
I could never be sure if they had gone for good

Or not; and so that kept things cheerful, madam.
One always gave a wink before he deserted me,
The other slapped me as it were behind, madam;
Then they would be away for some months.
DYNAMENE   Oh Doto, 85
What an unhappy life you were having to lead.
DOTO Yes, I'm sure. But never mind, madam,
It seemed quite lively then. And now I know
It's what you say; life is more big than a bed
And full of miracles and mysteries like   90
One man made for one woman, etcetera,
  etcetera.
Lovely. I feel sung, madam, by a baritone
In mixed company with everyone pleased.
And so I had to come with you here, madam,
For the last sad chorus of me. It's all   95
Fresh to me. Death's a new interest in life,
If it doesn't disturb you, madam, to have me
  crying.
It's because of us not having breakfast again.
And the master, of course. And the beautiful
  world.
And you crying too, madam. Oh—Oh!   100
DYNAMENE I can't forbid your crying; but you
  must cry
On the other side of the tomb. I'm becoming
  confused.
This is my personal grief and my sacrifice
Of self, solus. Right over there, darling girl.
DOTO What here?
DYNAMENE Now, if you wish, you may cry, Doto.
But our tears are very different. For me   106
The world is all with Charon, all, all,
Even the metal and plume of the rose garden,
And the forest where the sea fumes overhead
In vegetable tides, and particularly   110
The entrance to the warm baths in Arcite Street
Where we first met;—all!—the sun itself
Trails an evening hand in the sultry river
Far away down by Acheron. I am lonely,
Virilius. Where is the punctual eye   115
And where is the cautious voice which made
Balance-sheets sound like Homer and Homer
  sound
Like balance-sheets? The precision of limbs, the
  amiable
Laugh, the exact festivity? Gone from the world.
You were the peroration of nature, Virilius. 120
You explained everything to me, even the
  extremely

Complicated gods. You wrote them down
In seventy columns. Dear curling calligraphy!
Gone from the world, once and for all. And I
  taught you
In your perceptive moments to appreciate me.
You said I was harmonious, Virilius,   126
Molded and harmonious, little matronal
Ox-eye, your package. And then I would walk
Up and down largely, as it were making my own
Sunlight. What a mad blacksmith creation is
Who blows his furnaces until the stars fly
  upward   131
And iron time is hot and politicians glow
And bulbs and roots sizzle into hyacinth
And orchis, and the sand puts out the lion,
Roaring yellow, and oceans bud with porpoises,
Blenny, tunny and the almost unexisting   136
Blindfish; throats are cut, the masterpiece
Looms out of labor; nations and rebellions
Are spat out to hang on the wind—and all is
  gone
In one Virilius, wearing his office tunic,   140
Checking the pence column as he went.
Where's animation now? What is there that
  stays
To dance? The eye of the one-eyed world is out.
                [*She weeps.*]
DOTO I shall try to grieve a little, too.
It would take lessons, I imagine, to do it out
  loud   145
For long. If I could only remember
Any one of those fellows without wanting to
  laugh.
Hopeless, I am. Now those good pair of shoes
I gave away without thinking, that's a different—
Well, I've cried enough about *them*, I suppose.
Poor madam, poor master.   151
[TEGEUS-CHROMIS *comes through the gate to the top*
                of the steps.]
TEGEUS-CHROMIS   What's your trouble?
DOTO   Oh!
Oh! Oh, a man. I thought for a moment it was
  something
With harm in it. Trust a man to be where it's
  dark.
What is it? Can't you sleep?
TEGEUS-CHROMIS   Now, listen—
DOTO   Hush!
Remember you're in the grave. You must go
  away.   155

Madam is occupied.

TEGEUS-CHROMIS   What, here?

DOTO   Becoming
Dead. We both are.

TEGEUS-CHROMIS   What's going on here?

DOTO   Grief.
Are you satisfied now?

TEGEUS-CHROMIS   Less and less. Do you know
What the time is?

DOTO   I'm not interested.
We've done with all that. Go away. Be a gentle-
man.   160
If we can't be free of men in a grave
Death's a dead loss.

TEGEUS-CHROMIS   It's two in the morning. All
I ask is what are women doing down here
At two in the morning?

DOTO   Can't you see she's crying?
Or is she sleeping again? Either way   165
She's making arrangements to join her husband.

TEGEUS-CHROMIS   Where?

DOTO   Good god, in the underworld, dear man.
Haven't you learnt
About life and death?

TEGEUS-CHROMIS   In a manner, yes; in a manner;
The rudiments. So the lady means to die?   170

DOTO   For love; beautiful, curious madam.

TEGEUS-CHROMIS   Not curious;
I've had thoughts like it. Death is a kind of love.
Not anything I can explain.

DOTO   You'd better come in
And sit down.

TEGEUS-CHROMIS   I'd be grateful.

DOTO   Do. It will be my last
Chance to have company, in the flesh.

TEGEUS-CHROMIS   Do you mean   175
You're going too?

DOTO   Oh, certainly I am.
Not anything I can explain.
It all started with madam saying a man
Was two men really, and I'd only noticed one,
One each, I mean. It seems he has a soul   180
As well as his other troubles. And I like to know
What I'm getting with a man. I'm inquisitive,
I suppose you'd call me.

TEGEUS-CHROMIS   It takes some courage.

DOTO   Well, yes
And no. I'm fond of change.

TEGEUS-CHROMIS   Would you object
To have me eating my supper here?

DOTO   Be careful   185
Of the crumbs. We don't want a lot of squeaking
mice
Just when we're dying.

TEGEUS-CHROMIS   What a sigh she gave then.
Down the air like a slow comet.
And now she's all dark again. Mother of me.
How long has this been going on?

DOTO   Two days   190
It should have been three by now, but at first
Madam had difficulty with the Town Council.
They said
They couldn't have a tomb used as a private
residence.
But madam told them she wouldn't be eating
here,
Only suffering, and they thought that would be
all right.   195

TEGEUS-CHROMIS   Two of you. Marvelous. Who
would have said
I should ever have stumbled on anything like
this?
Do you have to cry? Yes, I suppose so. It's all
Quite reasonable.

DOTO   Your supper and your knees.
That's what's making me cry. I can't bear
sympathy   200
And they're sympathetic.

TEGEUS-CHROMIS   Please eat a bit of something.
I've no appetite left.

DOTO   And see her go ahead of me?
Wrap it up; put it away. You sex of wicked
beards!
It's no wonder you have to shave off your black
souls
Every day as they push through your chins. 205
I'll turn my back on you. It means utter
Contempt. Eat? Utter contempt. Oh, little new
rolls!

TEGEUS-CHROMIS   Forget it, forget it; please forget
it. Remember
I've had no experience of this kind of thing
before.
Indeed I'm as sorry as I know how to be. Ssh,
We'll disturb her. She sighed again. O Zeus, 211
It's terrible! Asleep, and still sighing.
Mourning has made a warren in her spirit,
All that way below. Ponos!° the heart

214. Ponos: slangy, familiar reference to a god, perhaps one
whose name ends in *ponos.*

Is the devil of a medicine.

DOTO   And I don't intend   215
To turn round.

TEGEUS-CHROMIS I understand how you must feel.
Would it be—have you any objection
To my having a drink? I have a little wine here.
And, you probably see how it is: grief's in order,
And death's in order, and women—I can
  usually   220
Manage that too; but not all three together
At this hour of the morning. So you'll excuse
  me.
How about you? It would make me more
  comfortable
If you'd take a smell of it.

DOTO   One for the road?

TEGEUS-CHROMIS One for the road.

DOTO   It's the dust in my throat.   225
The tomb
Is so dusty. Thanks, I will. There's no point in
  dying
Of everything, simultaneously.

TEGEUS-CHROMIS   It's lucky
I brought two bowls. I was expecting to keep
A drain for my relief when he comes in the
  morning.   230

DOTO   Are you on duty?

TEGEUS-CHROMIS   Yes.

DOTO   It looks like it.

TEGEUS-CHROMIS   Well,
Here's your good health.

DOTO   What good is that going to do me?
Here's to an easy crossing and not too much
  waiting
About on the bank. Do you have to tremble like
  that?

TEGEUS-CHROMIS The idea—I can't get used to it.

DOTO   For a member   235
Of the forces, you're peculiarly queasy. I wish
Those owls were in Hades—oh no; let them stay
  where they are.
Have you never had nothing to do with corpses
  before?

TEGEUS-CHROMIS I've got six of them outside.

DOTO   Morpheus, that's plenty.
What are they doing there?   240

TEGEUS-CHROMIS Hanging.°

---

241. Hanging: In *The Satyricon* they were crucified.
Crucifixion was a customary form of capital punishment in
the ancient world.

DOTO   Hanging?

TEGEUS-CHROMIS   On trees.
Five plane trees and a holly. The holly-berries
Are just reddening. Another drink?

DOTO   Why not?

TEGEUS-CHROMIS It's from Samos. Here's—

DOTO   All right. Let's just drink it.
—How did you get in that predicament?   245

TEGEUS-CHROMIS The sandy-haired fellow said we
  should collaborate
With everybody; the little man said he wouldn't
Collaborate with anybody; the old one
Said that the Pleiades weren't sisters but cousins
And anyway were manufactured in Lacedaemon.
The fourth said that we hanged men for nothing.
The other two said nothing. Now they hang   252
About at the corner of the night, they're present
And absent, horribly obsequious to every
Move in the air, and yet they keep me standing
For five hours at a stretch.   256

DOTO   The wine has gone
Down to my knees.

TEGEUS-CHROMIS   And up to your cheeks.
  You're looking
Fresher. If only—

DOTO   Madam? She never would.
Shall I ask her?

TEGEUS-CHROMIS No; no, don't dare, don't
  breathe it.
This is privilege, to come so near   260
To what is undeceiving and uncorrupt
And undivided; this is the clear fashion
For all souls, a ribbon to bind the unruly
Curls of living, a faith, a hope, Zeus
Yes, a fine thing. I am human, and this   265
Is human fidelity, and we can be proud
And unphilosophical.

DOTO   I need to dance
But I haven't the use of my legs.

TEGEUS-CHROMIS   No, no, don't dance,
Or, at least, only inwards; don't dance; cry
Again. We'll put a moat of tears   270
Round her bastion of love, and save
The world. It's something, it's more than some-
  thing,
It's regeneration, to see how a human cheek
Can become as pale as a pool.

DOTO   Do you love me, handsome?

TEGEUS-CHROMIS To have found life, after all,
  unambiguous!   275

DOTO   Did you say Yes?

TEGEUS-CHROMIS   Certainly; just as now I love all
men.

DOTO   So do I.

TEGEUS-CHROMIS   And the world is a good creature
again.
I'd begun to see it as mildew, verdigris,
Rust, woodrot, or as though the sky had uttered
An oval twirling blasphemy with occasional
vistas   280
In country districts. I was within an ace
Of volunteering for overseas service. Despair
Abroad can always nurse pleasant thoughts of
home.
Integrity, by god!

DOTO   I love all the world   284
And the movement of the apple in your throat.
So shall you kiss me? It would be better, I should
think,
To go moistly to Hades.

TEGEUS-CHROMIS   Her's is the way,
Luminous with sorrow.

DOTO   Then I'll take
Another little swiggy. I love all men,
Everybody, even you, and I'll pick you   290
Some outrageous honeysuckle for your helmet,
If only it lived here. Pardon.

DYNAMENE   Doto. Who is it?

DOTO   Honeysuckle, madam. Because of the bees.
Go back to sleep, madam.

DYNAMENE   What person is it?

DOTO   Yes, I see what you mean, madam. It's a
kind of   295
Corporal talking to his soul, on a five-hour shift,
Madam, with six bodies. He's been having his
supper.

TEGEUS-CHROMIS   I'm going. It's terrible that we
should have disturbed her.

DOTO   He was delighted to see you so sad, madam.
It has stopped him going abroad.

DYNAMENE   One with six bodies? 300
A messenger, a guide to where we go.
It is possible he has come to show us the way
Out of these squalid suburbs of life, a shade,
A gorgon, who has come swimming up, against
The falls of my tears (for which in truth he would
need   305
Many limbs) to guide me to Virilius.
I shall go quietly.

TEGEUS-CHROMIS   I do assure you—

Such clumsiness, such a vile and unforgivable
Intrusion. I shall obliterate myself
Immediately.

DOTO   Oblit—oh, what a pity   310
To oblit. Pardon. Don't let him, the nice fellow.

DYNAMENE   Sir: your other five bodies: where are
they?

TEGEUS-CHROMIS   Madam—
Outside; I have them outside. On trees.

DYNAMENE   Quack!

TEGEUS-CHROMIS   What do I reply?

DYNAMENE   Quack, charlatan!
You've never known the gods. You came to
mock me.   315
Doto, this never was a gorgon, never.
Nor a gentleman either. He's completely
spurious.
Admit it, you creature. Have you even a feather
Of the supernatural in your system? Have you?

TEGEUS-CHROMIS   Some of my relations—

DYNAMENE   Well?

TEGEUS-CHROMIS   Are dead, I think; 320
This is to say I have connections—

DYNAMENE   Connections
With pickpockets. It'a shameless imposition.
Does the army provide you with no amusements?
If I were still of the world, and not cloistered
In a colorless landscape of winter thought   325
Where the approaching spring is desired oblivion,
I should write sharply to your commanding
officer.
It should be done, it should be done. If my fingers
Weren't so cold I would do it now. But they are,
Horribly cold. And why should insolence
matter   330
When my color of life is unreal, a blush on death,
A partial mere diaphane? I don't know
Why it should matter. Oafish, noncommissioned
Young man! The boots of your conscience will
pinch forever
If life's dignity has any self-protection.   335
Oh, I have to sit down. The tomb's going round.

DOTO   Oh, madam, don't give over. I can't
remember
When things were so lively. He looks marvelously
Marvelously uncomfortable. Go on, madam.
Can't you, madam? Oh, madam, don't you feel
up to it?   340
There, do you see her, you acorn-chewing
infantryman?

You've made her cry, you square-bashing
  barbarian.

TEGEUS-CHROMIS O history, my private history,
  why
Was I led here? What stigmatism has got
Into my stars? Why wasn't it my brother? 345
He has a tacit misunderstanding with everybody
And washes in it. Why wasn't it my mother?
She makes a collection of other people's tears
And dries them all. Let them forget I came;
And lie in the terrible black crystal of grief 350
Which held them, before I broke it. Outside,
  Tegeus.

DOTO Hey, I don't think so, I shouldn't say so.
  Come
Down again, uniform. Do you think you're
  going
To half kill an unprotected lady and then
Back out upwards? Do you think you can leave
  her like this? 355

TEGEUS-CHROMIS Yes, yes, I'll leave her. O direc-
  torate of gods,
How can I? Beauty's bit is between my teeth.
She has added another torture to me. Bottom
Of Hades' bottom.

DOTO   Madam. Madam, the corporal
Has some wine here. It will revive you, madam.
And then you can go at him again, madam. 361

TEGEUS-CHROMIS It's the opposite of everything
  you've said,
I swear. I swear by Horkos and the Styx,
I swear by the nine acres of Tityos, 364
I swear the Hypnotic oath, by all the Titans—
By Koeos, Krios, Iapetos, Kronos, and so on—
By the three Hekatoncheires, by the insomnia
Of Tisiphone, by Jove, by jove, and the dew
On the feet of my boyhood, I am innocent
Of mocking you. Am I a Salmoneus 370
That, seeing such a flame of sorrow—°

DYNAMENE   You needn't
Labor to prove your secondary education.
Perhaps I jumped to a wrong conclusion, perhaps
I was hasty.

DOTO   How easy to swear if you're properly
  educated.
Wasn't it pretty, madam? Pardon.

363–71. by Horkos . . . sorrow: The clumsy oaths of
Tegeus-Chromis are derived from figures in Aeneas' visit
to Hades, proving only that Tegeus had read Virgil's
Aeneid and making Dynamene's response in line 373 quite
appropriate.

DYNAMENE   If I misjudged you 375
I apologize, I apologize. Will you please leave us?
You were wrong to come here. In a place of
  mourning
Light itself is a trespasser; nothing can have
The right of entrance except those natural symbols
Of mortality, the jabbing, funeral, sleek- 380
With-omen raven, the deathwatch beetle which
  mocks
Time: particularly, I'm afraid, the spider
Weaving his home with swift self-generated
Threads of slaughter; and, of course, the worm.
I wish it could be otherwise. Oh dear, 385
They aren't easy to live with.

DOTO   Not even a *little* wine, madam?

DYNAMENE Here, Doto?

DOTO   Well, on the steps perhaps,
Except it's so drafty.

DYNAMENE   Doto! Here?

DOTO   No, madam;
I quite see.

DYNAMENE I might be wise to strengthen myself
In order to fast again; it would make me abler
For grief. I will breathe a little of it, Doto. 391

DOTO Thank god. Where's the bottle?

DYNAMENE   What an exquisite bowl.

TEGEUS-CHROMIS Now that it's peacetime we have
  pottery classes.

DYNAMENE You made it yourself?

TEGEUS-CHROMIS   Yes. Do you see the design?
The corded god, tied also by the rays 395
Of the sun, and the astonished ship erupting
Into vines and vine-leaves, inverted pyramids
Of grapes, the uplifted hands of the men (the
  raiders),
And here the headlong sea, itself almost
Venturing into leaves and tendrils, and Proteus
With his beard braiding the wind, and this 401
Held by other hands is a drowned sailor—

DYNAMENE Always, always.

DOTO   Hold the bowl steady, madam.
Pardon.

DYNAMENE Doto, have you been drinking?

DOTO   Here, madam?
I coaxed some a little way towards my mouth,
  madam, 405
But I scarcely swallowed except because I had
  to. The hiccup
Is from no breakfast, madam, and not meant to
  be funny.

DYNAMENE   You may drink this too. Oh, how the
 inveterate body,
Even when cut from the heart, insists on leaf,
Puts out, with a separate meaningless will,   410
Fronds to intercept the thankless sun.
How it does, oh, how it does. And how it confuses
The nature of the mind.
TEGEUS-CHROMIS   Yes, yes, the confusion;
 That's something I understand better than any-
 thing.
DYNAMENE   When the thoughts would die, the
 instincts will set sail   415
For life. And when the thoughts are alert for life
The instincts will rage to be destroyed on the
 rocks.
To Virilius it was not so; his brain was an
 ironing-board
For all crumpled indecision: and I follow him,
The hawser of my world. You don't belong here,
You see; you don't belong here at all.   421
TEGEUS-CHROMIS   If only
 I did. If only you knew the effort it costs me
To mount those steps again into an untrust-
 worthy,
Unpredictable, unenlightened night,
And turn my back on—on a state of affairs, 425
I can only call it a vision, a hope, a promise,
A—By that I mean loyalty, enduring passion,
Unrecking bravery and beauty all in one.
DOTO   He means you, or you and me; or me,
 madam.
TEGEUS-CHROMIS   It only remains for me to thank
 you, and to say   430
That whatever awaits me and for however long
I may be played by this poor musician, existence,
Your person and sacrifice will leave their trace
As clear upon me as the shape of the hills
Around my birthplace. Now I must leave you to
 your husband.   435
DOTO   Oh! You, madam.
DYNAMENE   I'll tell you what I will do.
 I will drink with you to the memory of my
 husband,
Because I have been curt, because you are kind,
And because I'm extremely thirsty. And then
 we will say
Good-by and part to go to our opposite corrup-
 tions,   440
The world and the grave.
TEGEUS-CHROMIS   The climax to the vision.

DYNAMENE   [*Drinking*] My husband, and all he
 stood for.
TEGEUS-CHROMIS   Stands for.
DYNAMENE   Stands for.
TEGEUS-CHROMIS   Your husband.
DOTO   The master.
DYNAMENE   How good it is,
 How it sings to the throat, purling with summer.
TEGEUS-CHROMIS   It has a twin nature, winter and
 warmth in one,   446
Moon and meadow. Do you agree?
DYNAMENE   Perfectly;
 A cold bell sounding in a golden month.
TEGEUS-CHROMIS   Crystal in harvest.
DYNAMENE   Perhaps a nightingale
 Sobbing among the pears.
TEGEUS-CHROMIS In an old autumnal midnight.
DOTO   Grapes—Pardon. There's some more here.
TEGEUS-CHROMIS   Plenty.
 I drink to the memory of your husband.   452
DYNAMENE   My husband.
DOTO   The master.
DYNAMENE   He was careless in his choice of wines.
TEGEUS-CHROMIS   And yet
 Rendering to living its rightful poise is not
Unimportant.
DYNAMENE A mystery's in the world   455
 Where a little liquid, with flavor, quality, and
 fume
Can be as no other, can hint and flute our senses
As though a music played in harvest hollows
And a movement was in the swathes of our
 memory.
Why should scent, why should flavor come 460
With such wings upon us? Parsley, for instance.
TEGEUS-CHROMIS   Seaweed.
DYNAMENE   Lime trees.
DOTO   Horses.
TEGEUS-CHROMIS   Fruit in the fire.
DYNAMENE   Do I know your name?
TEGEUS-CHROMIS   Tegeus.
DYNAMENE   That's very thin for you,
 It hardly covers your bones. Something quite
 different,
Altogether other. I shall think of it presently.
TEGEUS-CHROMIS   Darker vowels, perhaps.   466
DYNAMENE   Yes, certainly darker vowels.
 And your consonants should have a slight angle,
And a certain temperature. Do you know what I
 mean?

It will come to me.

TEGEUS-CHROMIS   Now *your* name—

DYNAMENE   It is nothing
To any purpose. I'll be to you the She   470
In the tomb. You have the air of a natural-
historian
As though you were accustomed to handling
birds' eggs,
Or tadpoles, or putting labels on moths. You see?
The genius of dumb things, that they are
nameless.
Have I found the seat of the weevil in human
brains?   475
Our names. They make us broody; we sit and sit
To hatch them into reputation and dignity.
And then they set upon us and become despair,
Guilt and remorse. We go where they lead. We
dance
Attendance on something wished upon us by the
wife   480
Of our mother's physician. But insects meet and
part
And put the woods about them, fill the dusk
And freckle the light and go and come without
A name among them, without the wish of a
name
And very pleasant too. Did I interrupt you? 485

TEGEUS-CHROMIS   I forget. We'll have no names
then.

DYNAMENE   I should like
You to have a name, I don't know why; a small
one
To fill out the conversation.

TEGEUS-CHROMIS   I should like
You to have a name too, if only for something
To remember. Have you still some wine in your
bowl?   490

DYNAMENE   Not altogether.

TEGEUS-CHROMIS   We haven't come to the end
By several inches. Did I splash you?

DYNAMENE   It doesn't matter.
Well, here's to my husband's name.

TEGEUS-CHROMIS   Your husband's name.

DOTO   The master.

DYNAMENE   It was kind of you to come.

TEGEUS-CHROMIS   It was more than coming. I
followed my future here,   495
As we all do if we're sufficiently inattentive
And don't vex ourselves with questions; or do I
mean

Attentive? If so, attentive to what? Do I sound
Incoherent?

DYNAMENE   You're wrong. There isn't a future
here,
Not here, not for you.   500

TEGEUS-CHROMIS   Your name's Dynamene.

DYNAMENE   Who—Have I been utterly irreverent?
Are you—
Who made you say that? Forgive me the
question,
But are you dark or light? I mean which shade
Of the supernatural? Or if neither, what
prompted you?

TEGEUS-CHROMIS   Dynamene——

DYNAMENE   No, but I'm sure
you're the friend of nature,   505
It must be so, I think I see little Phoebuses°
Rising and setting in your eyes.

DOTO   They're not little Phoebuses,
They're hoodwinks, madam. Your name is on
your brooch.
No little Phoebuses tonight.

DYNAMENE   That's twice
You've played me a trick. Oh, I know practical
jokes   510
Are common on Olympus, but haven't we at all
Developed since the gods were born? Are gods
And men both to remain immortal adolescents?
How tiresome it all is.

TEGEUS-CHROMIS   It was you, each time,
Who said I was supernatural. When did I say
so?   515
You're making me into whatever you imagine
And then you blame me because I can't live up
to it.

DYNAMENE   I shall call you Chromis. It has a
breadlike sound.
I think of you as a crisp loaf.

TEGEUS-CHROMIS   And now
You'll insult me because I'm not sliceable.   520

DYNAMENE   I think drinking is harmful to our
tempers.

TEGEUS-CHROMIS   If I seem to be frowning, that is
only because
I'm looking directly into your light: I must look
Angrily, or shut my eyes.

DYNAMENE   Shut them.—Oh,
You have eyelashes! A new perspective of you.

---

506. Phoebuses: reference to Phoebus Apollo, the Greek
sun god.

Is that how you look when you sleep?   526

TEGEUS-CHROMIS   My jaw drops down.

DYNAMENE   Show me how.

TEGEUS-CHROMIS   Like this.

DYNAMENE   It makes an irresistible
Moron of you. Will you waken now?
It's morning; I see a thin dust of daylight
Blowing on to the steps.

TEGEUS-CHROMIS   Already? Dynamene,   530
You're tricked again. This time by the moon.

DYNAMENE   Oh, well,
Moon's daylight, then. Doto is asleep.

TEGEUS-CHROMIS   Doto
Is asleep . . .

DYNAMENE   Chromis, what made you walk about
In the night? What, I wonder, made you not
stay   534
Sleeping wherever you slept? Was it the friction
Of the world on your mind? Those two are
difficult
To make agree. Chromis—now try to learn
To answer your name. I won't say Tegeus.

TEGEUS-CHROMIS   And I
Won't say Dynamene.

DYNAMENE   Not?

TEGEUS-CHROMIS   It makes you real.
Forgive me, a terrible thing has happened. Shall I
Say it and perhaps destroy myself for you?   541
Forgive me first, or, more than that, forgive
Nature who winds her furtive stream all through
Our reason. Do you forgive me?

DYNAMENE   I'll forgive
Anything, if it's the only way I can know   545
What you have to tell me.

TEGEUS-CHROMIS   I felt us to be alone;
Here in a grave, separate from any life,
I and the only one of beauty, the only
Persuasive key to all my senses,
In spite of my having lain day after day   550
And pored upon the sepals, corolla, stamen, and
bracts
Of the yellow bog-iris. Then my body ventured
A step towards interrupting your perfection of
purpose
And my own renewed faith in human nature.
Would you have believed that possible?

DYNAMENE   I have never   555
Been greatly moved by the yellow bog-iris. Alas,
It's as I said. This place is for none but the spider,
Raven and worms, not for a living man.

TEGEUS-CHROMIS   It has been a place of blessing to
me. It will always
Play in me, a fountain of confidence   560
When the world is arid. But I know it is true
I have to leave it, and though it withers my soul
I must let you make your journey.

DYNAMENE   No.

TEGEUS-CHROMIS   Not true?

DYNAMENE   We can talk of something quite
different.

TEGEUS-CHROMIS   Yes, we can!
Oh yes, we will! Is it your opinion   565
That no one believes who hasn't learned to
doubt?
Or, another thing, if we persuade ourselves
To one particular persuasion, become Sophist,
Stoic, Platonist, anything whatever,   569
Would you say that there must be areas of
soul
Lying unproductive therefore, or dishonored
Or blind?

DYNAMENE   No, I don't know.

TEGEUS-CHROMIS   No. It's impossible
To tell. Dynamene, if only I had
Two cakes of pearl-barley and hydromel
I could see you to Hades, leave you with your
husband   575
And come back to the world.

DYNAMENE   Ambition, I suppose,
Is an appetite particular to man.
What is your definition?

TEGEUS-CHROMIS   The desire to find
A reason for living.

DYNAMENE   But then, suppose it leads,
As often, one way or another, it does, to death.

TEGEUS-CHROMIS   Then that may be life's reason.
Oh, but how   581
Could I bear to return, Dynamene? The earth's
Daylight would be my grave if I had left you
In that unearthly night.

DYNAMENE   O Chromis——

TEGEUS-CHROMIS   Tell me,
What is your opinion of progress? Does it, for
example,   585
Exist? Is there ever progression without retro-
gression?
Therefore is it not true that mankind
Can more justly be said increasingly to gress?
As the material improves, the craftsmanship
deteriorates

And honor and virtue remain the same. I love
you, 590
Dynamene.

DYNAMENE   Would you consider we go round and
round?

TEGEUS-CHROMIS   We concertina, I think; taking
each time
A larger breath, so that the farther we go out
The farther we have to go in.

DYNAMENE   There'll come a time
When it will be unbearable to continue. 595

TEGEUS-CHROMIS   Unbearable.

DYNAMENE   Perhaps we had better have something
To eat. The wine has made your eyes so quick
I am breathless beside them. It *is*
Your eyes, I think; or your intelligence
Holding my intelligence up above you 600
Between its hands. Or the cut of your uniform.

TEGEUS-CHROMIS   Here's a new roll with honey. In
the gods' names
Let's sober ourselves.

DYNAMENE   As soon as possible.

TEGEUS-CHROMIS   Have you
Any notion of algebra?

DYNAMENE   We'll discuss you, Chromis.
We will discuss you, till you're nothing but
words. 605

TEGEUS-CHROMIS   I? There is nothing, of course, I
would rather discuss,
Except—if it would be no intrusion—you,
Dynamene.

DYNAMENE   No, you couldn't want to. But your
birthplace, Chromis,
With the hills that placed themselves in you
forever
As you say, where was it?

TEGEUS-CHROMIS   My father's farm at Pyxa. 610

DYNAMENE   There? Could it be there?

TEGEUS-CHROMIS   I was born in the hills
Between showers, a quarter of an hour before
milking time.
Do you know Pyxa? It stretches to the crossing
of two
Troublesome roads, and buries its back in
beechwood,
From which come the white owls of our nights
And the mulling and cradling of doves in the
day. 616
I attribute my character to those shadows
And heavy roots; and my interest in music

To the sudden melodious escape of the young
river
Where it breaks from nosing through the cresses
and kingcups. 620
That's honestly so.

DYNAMENE   You used to climb about
Among the windfallen tower of Phrasidemus
Looking for bees' nests.

TEGEUS-CHROMIS   What? When have I
Said so?

DYNAMENE   Why, all the children did.

TEGEUS-CHROMIS   Yes: but, in the name of light,
how do you *know* that? 625

DYNAMENE   I played there once, on holiday.

TEGEUS-CHROMIS   O Klotho,
Lachesis and Atropos!°

DYNAMENE   It's the strangest chance:
I may have seen, for a moment, your boyhood.

TEGEUS-CHROMIS   I may
Have seen something like an early flower
Something like a girl. If I only could remember
how I must 630
Have seen you. Were you after the short white
violets?
Maybe I blundered past you, taking your look,
And scarcely acknowledged how a star
Ran through me, to live in the brooks of my
blood forever.
Or I saw you playing at hiding in the cave 635
Where the ferns are and the water drips.

DYNAMENE   I was quite plain and fat and I was
usually
Hitting someone. I wish I could remember you.
I'm envious of the days and children who saw
you
Then. It is curiously a little painful 640
Not to share your past.

TEGEUS-CHROMIS   How did it come
Our stars could mingle for an afternoon
So long ago, and then forget us or tease us
Or helplessly look on the dark high seas
Of our separation, while time drank 645
The golden hours? What hesitant fate is that?

DYNAMENE   Time? Time? Why—how old are we?

TEGEUS-CHROMIS   Young,
Thank both our mothers, but still we're older
than tonight
And so older than we should be. Wasn't I born

626–27. Klotho . . . Atropos: the three Fates.

In love with what, only now, I have grown to
  meet?   650
I'll tell you something else. I was born entirely
For this reason. I was born to fill a gap
In the world's experience, which had never
  known
Chromis loving Dynamene.

DYNAMENE   You are so   654
  Excited, poor Chromis. What is it? Here you sit
  With a woman who has wept away all claims
  To appearance, unbecoming in her oldest clothes,
  With not a trace of liveliness, a drab
  Of melancholy, entirely shadow without
  A smear of sun. Forgive me if I tell you   660
  That you fall easily into superlatives.

TEGEUS-CHROMIS   Very well. I'll say nothing, then.
  I'll fume
  With feeling.

DYNAMENE   Now you go to the extreme. Certainly
  You must speak. You may have more to say.
    Besides   664
  You might let your silence run away with you
  And not say something that you should. And
    how
  Should I answer you then? Chromis, you boy,
  I can't look away from you. You use
  The lamplight and the moon so skillfully,
  So arrestingly, in and around your furrows. 670
  A humorous plowman goes whistling to a team
  Of sad sorrow, to and fro in your brow
  And over your arable cheek. Laugh for me.
    Have you
  Cried for women, ever?

TEGEUS-CHROMIS   In looking about for you.
  But I have recognized them for what they were.

DYNAMENE   What were they?   676

TEGEUS-CHROMIS   Never you: never, although
  They could walk with bright distinction into all
    men's
  Longest memories, never you, by a hint
  Or a faint quality, or at least not more
  Than reflectively, stars lost and uncertain 680
  In the sea, compared with the shining salt, the
    shiners,
  The galaxies, the clusters, the bright grain
    whirling
  Over the black threshing-floor of space.
  Will you make some effort to believe that?

DYNAMENE   No, no effort.
  It lifts me and carries me. It may be wild 685

But it comes to me with a charm, like trust indeed,
And eats out of my heart, dear Chromis,
Absurd, disconcerting Chromis. You make me
Feel I wish I could look my best for you.
I wish, at least, that I could believe myself 690
To be showing some beauty for you, to put in
  the scales
Between us. But they dip to you, they sink
With masculine victory.

TEGEUS-CHROMIS   Eros, no! No!
  If this is less than your best, then never, in my
    presence
  Be more than your less: never! If you should
    bring   695
  More to your mouth or to your eyes, a moisture
  Or a flake of light, anything, anything fatally
  More, perfection would fetch her unsparing rod
  Out of pickle to flay me, and what would have
    been love
  Will be the end of me. O Dynamene,   700
  Let me unload something of my lips' longing
  On to yours receiving. Oh, when I cross
  Like this the hurt of the little space between us
  I come a journey from the wrenching ice
  To walk in the sun. That is the feeling.

DYNAMENE   Chromis, 705
  Where am I going? No, don't answer. It's death
  I desire, not you.

TEGEUS-CHROMIS   Where is the difference? Call me
  Death instead of Chromis. I'll answer to any-
    thing.
  It's desire all the same, of death in me, or me
  In death, but Chromis either way. Is it so? 710
  Do you not love me, Dynamene?

DYNAMENE   How could it happen?
  I'm going to my husband. I'm too far on the way
  To admit myself to life again. Love's in Hades.

TEGEUS-CHROMIS   Also here. And here are we, not
    there
  In Hades. Is your husband expecting you?   715

DYNAMENE   Surely, surely?

TEGEUS-CHROMIS   Not necessarily. I,
  If I had been your husband, would never dream
  Of expecting you. I should remember your body
  Descending stairs in the floating light, but not
  Descending in Hades. I should say "I have left
  My wealth warm on the earth, and, hell, earth
    needs it."   721
  "Was all I taught her of love," I should say, "so
    poor

That she will leave her flesh and become
  shadow?"
"Wasn't our love for each other" (I should
  continue)
"Infused with life, and life infused with our
  love?   725
Very well; repeat me in love, repeat me in life,
And let me sing in your blood forever."

DYNAMENE   Stop, stop, I shall be dragged apart!
Why should the fates do everything to keep me
From dying honorably? They must have got
Tired of honor in Elysium. Chromis, it's terrible
To be susceptible to two conflicting norths.   732
I have the constitution of a whirlpool.
Am I actually twirling, or is it just sensation?

TEGEUS-CHROMIS   You're still; still as the darkness.

DYNAMENE   What appears   735
Is so unlike what is. And what is madness
To those who only observe, is often wisdom
To those to whom it happens.

TEGEUS-CHROMIS   Are we compelled
To go into all this?

DYNAMENE   Why, how could I return
To my friends? Am I to be an entertainment?

TEGEUS-CHROMIS   That's for tomorrow. Tonight I
  need to kiss you,   741
Dynamene. Let's see what the whirlpool does
Between my arms; let it whirl on my breast. O
  love,
Come in.

DYNAMENE   I am there before I reach you; my
  body
Only follows to join my longing which   745
Is holding you already.—Now I am
All one again.

TEGEUS-CHROMIS   I feel as the gods feel:
This is their sensation of life, not a man's:
Their suspension of immortality, to enrich
Themselves with time. O life, O death, O body,
O spirit, O Dynamene.

DYNAMENE   O all   751
In myself; it so covets all in you,
My care, my Chromis. Then I shall be
Creation.

TEGEUS-CHROMIS   You have the skies already;
Out of them you are buffeting me with your
  gales   755
Of beauty. Can we be made of dust, as they tell
  us?
What! dust with dust releasing such a light

And such an apparition of the world
Within one body? A thread of your hair has
  stung me.
Why do you push me away?

DYNAMENE   There's so much metal   760
About you. Do I have to be imprisoned
In an armory?

TEGEUS-CHROMIS   Give your hand to the buckles
  and then
To me.

DYNAMENE   Don't help; I'll do them all myself.

TEGEUS-CHROMIS   O time and patience! I want you
  back again.

DYNAMENE   We have a lifetime. O Chromis, think,
  think   765
Of that. And even unfastening a buckle
Is loving. And not easy. Very well,
You can help me. Chromis, what zone of
  miracle
Did you step into to direct you in the dark
To where I waited, not knowing I waited?

TEGEUS-CHROMIS   I saw   770
The lamplight. That was only the appearance
Of some great gesture in the bed of fortune.
I saw the lamplight.

DYNAMENE   But here? So far from life?
What brought you near enough to see lamplight?

TEGEUS-CHROMIS   Zeus,
That reminds me.

DYNAMENE   What is it, Chromis?

TEGEUS-CHROMIS   I'm on duty.   775

DYNAMENE   Is it warm enough to do without your
  greaves?

TEGEUS-CHROMIS   Darling loom of magic, I must
  go back
To take a look at those boys. The whole business
Of guard had gone out of my mind.

DYNAMENE   What boys, my heart?

TEGEUS-CHROMIS   My six bodies.

DYNAMENE   Chromis, not that joke   780
Again.

TEGEUS-CHROMIS   No joke, sweet. Today our city
Held a sextuple hanging. I'm minding the bodies
Until five o'clock. Already I've been away
For half an hour.

DYNAMENE   What can they do, poor bodies,
In half an hour, or half a century?   785
You don't really mean to go?

TEGEUS-CHROMIS   Only to make
My conscience easy. Then, Dynamene,

No cloud can rise on love, no hovering thought
Fidget, and the night will be only to *us*.

DYNAMENE   But if every half-hour——

TEGEUS-CHROMIS   Hush, smile of my soul,   790
My sprig, my sovereign: this is to hold your eyes,
I sign my lips on them both: this is to keep
Your forehead—do you feel the claim of my kiss
Falling into your thought? And now your throat
Is a white branch and my lips two singing
    birds—   795
They are coming to rest. Throat, remember me
Until I come back in five minutes. Over all
Here is my parole: I give it to your mouth
To give me again before it's dry. I promise:
Before it's dry, or not long after.

DYNAMENE   Run,   800
Run all the way. You needn't be afraid of
    stumbling.
There's plenty of moon. The fields are blue. Oh,
    wait,
Wait! My darling. No, not now: it will keep
Until I see you; I'll have it here at my lips.
Hurry.

TEGEUS-CHROMIS   So long, my haven.

DYNAMENE   Hurry, hurry!   805

[*Exit* TEGEUS-CHROMIS.]

DOTO   Yes, madam, hurry; of course. Are we
    there
Already? How nice. Death doesn't take
Any doing at all. We were gulped into Hades
As easy as an oyster.

DYNAMENE   Doto!

DOTO   Hurry, hurry,
Yes, madam.—But they've taken out all my
    bones.   810
I haven't a bone left. I'm a shadow: wonderfully
    shady
In the legs. We shall have to sit out eternity,
    madam,
If they've done the same to you.

DYNAMENE   You'd better wake up.
If you can't go to sleep again, you'd better wake
    up.
Oh dear!—We're still alive, Doto, do you hear
    me?   815

DOTO   You must speak for yourself, madam. I'm
    quite dead.
I'll tell you how I know. I feel
Invisible. I'm a wraith, madam; I'm only
Waiting to be wafted.

DYNAMENE   If only you *would* be.   819
Do you see where you are? Look. Do you see?

DOTO   Yes. You're right, madam. We're still alive.
Isn't it enough to make you swear?
Here we are, dying to be dead,
And where does it get us?

DYNAMENE   Perhaps you should try to die
In some other place. Yes! Perhaps the air here
Suits you too well. You were sleeping very
    heavily.   826

DOTO   And all the time you alone and dying.
I shouldn't have. Has the corporal been long
    gone,
Madam?

DYNAMENE   He came and went, came and went,
You know the way.   830

DOTO   Very well I do. And went
He should have, come he should never. Oh dear,
    he must
Have disturbed you, madam.

DYNAMENE   He could be said
To've disturbed me. Listen; I have something to
    say to you.

DOTO   I expect so, madam. Maybe I *could* have
    kept him out
But men are in before I wish they wasn't.   835
I think quickly enough, but I get behindhand
With what I ought to be saying. It's a kind of
    stammer
In my way of life, madam.

DYNAMENE   I have been unkind,
I have sinfully wronged you, Doto.

DOTO   Never, madam.

DYNAMENE   Oh yes. I was letting you die with me,
    Doto, without   840
Any fair reason. I was drowning you
In grief that wasn't yours. That was wrong,
    Doto.

DOTO   But I haven't got anything against dying,
    madam.
I may *like* the situation, as far as I like
Any situation, madam. Now if you'd said
    mangling,   845
A lot of mangling, I might have thought twice
    about staying.
We all have our dislikes, madam.

DYNAMENE   I'm asking you
To leave me, Doto, at once, as quickly as
    possible,
Now, before—now, Doto, and let me forget

My bad mind which confidently expected you
To companion me to Hades. Now good-by,   851
Good-by.

DOTO   No, it's not good-by at all.
I shouldn't know another night of sleep, wonder-
ing
How you got on, or what I was missing, come
to that.
I should be anxious about you, too. When you
belong   855
To an upper class, the netherworld might come
strange.
Now I was born nether, madam, though not
As nether as some. No, it's not good-by, madam.

DYNAMENE   Oh Doto, go; you must, you must!
And if I seem
Without gratitude, forgive me. It isn't so,   860
It is far, far from so. But I can only
Regain my peace of mind if I know you're
gone.

DOTO   Besides, look at the time, madam. Where
should I go
At three in the morning? Even if I was to think
Of going; and think of it I never shall.   865

DYNAMENE   Think of the unmatchable world,
Doto.

DOTO   I do
Think of it, madam. And when I think of it, what
Have I thought? Well, it depends, madam.

DYNAMENE   I insist,
Obey me! At once! Doto!

DOTO   Here I sit.

DYNAMENE   What shall I do with you?

DOTO   Ignore me, madam.   870
I know my place. I shall die quite unobtrusive.
Oh look, the corporal's forgotten to take his
equipment.

DYNAMENE   Could he be so careless?

DOTO   I shouldn't hardly have thought so.
Poor fellow. They'll go and deduct it off his
credits.
I suppose, madam, I suppose he couldn't be
thinking   875
Of coming back?

DYNAMENE   He'll think of these. He will notice
He isn't wearing them. He'll come; he is sure to
come.

DOTO   Oh.

DYNAMENE   I know he will.

DOTO   Oh, oh.

Is that all for tonight, madam? May I go now,
madam?

DYNAMENE   Doto! Will you?

DOTO   Just you try to stop me, madam.   880
Sometimes going is a kind of instinct with me.
I'll leave death to some other occasion.

DYNAMENE   Do,
Doto. Any other time. Now you must hurry.
I won't delay you from life another moment.
Oh, Doto, good-by.

DOTO   Good-by. Life is unusual,   885
Isn't it, madam? Remember me to Cerberus.
[Reenter TEGEUS-CHROMIS. DOTO passes him on
the steps.]

DOTO   [As she goes] You left something behind.
Ye gods, what a moon!

DYNAMENE   Chromis, it's true; my lips are hardly
dry.
Time runs again; the void is space again;
Space has life again; Dynamene has Chromis.

TEGEUS-CHROMIS   It's over.   891

DYNAMENE   Chromis, you're sick. As white
as wool.
Come, you covered the distance too quickly.
Rest in my arms; get your breath again.

TEGEUS-CHROMIS   I've breathed one night too
many. Why did I see you,
Why in the name of life did I see you?

DYNAMENE   Why?   895
Weren't we gifted with each other? O heart,
What do you mean?

TEGEUS-CHROMIS   I mean that joy is nothing
But the parent of doom. Why should I have
found
Your constancy such balm to the world and yet
Find, by the same vision, its destruction   900
A necessity? We're set upon by love
To make us incompetent to steer ourselves,
To make us docile to fate. I should have known:
Indulgences, not fulfillment, is what the world
Permits us.

DYNAMENE   Chromis, is this intelligible?   905
Help me to follow you. What did you meet in
the fields
To bring about all this talk? Do you still love me?

TEGEUS-CHROMIS   What good will it do us? I've
lost a body.

DYNAMENE   A body?
One of the six? Well, it isn't with them you
propose   909

To love me; and you couldn't keep it forever.
Are we going to allow a body that isn't there
To come between us?

TEGEUS-CHROMIS   But I'm responsible for it.
I have to account for it in the morning. Surely
You see, Dynamene, the horror we're faced with?
The relatives have had time to cut him down
And take him away for burial. It means   916
A court martial. No doubt about the sentence.
I shall take the place of the missing man.
To be hanged, Dynamene! Hanged, Dynamene!

DYNAMENE   No; it's monstrous! Your life is yours,
Chromis.   920

TEGEUS-CHROMIS   Anything but. That's why I have
to take it.
At the best we live our lives on loan,
At the worst in chains. And I was never born
To have life. Then for what? To be had by it,
And so are we all. But I'll make it what it is,
By making it nothing.   926

DYNAMENE   Chromis, you're frightening me.
What are you meaning to do?

TEGEUS-CHROMIS   I have to die,
Dance of my heart, I have to die, to die,
To part us, to go to my sword and let it part us.
I'll have my free will even if I'm compelled to it.
I'll kill myself.

DYNAMENE   Oh, no! No, Chromis!   931
It's all unreasonable—no such horror
Can come of a pure accident. Have you hanged?
How can they hang you for simply not being
somewhere?   934
How can they hang you for losing a dead man?
They must have wanted to lose him, or they
wouldn't
Have hanged him. No, you're scaring yourself
for nothing
And making me frantic.

TEGEUS-CHROMIS   It's section six, paragraph
Three in the regulations. That's my doom.
I've read it for myself. And, by my doom,   940
Since I have to die, let me die here, in love,
Promoted by your kiss to tower, in dying,
High above my birth. For god's sake let me die
On a wave of life, Dynamene, with an action
I can take pride in. How could I settle to
death   945
Knowing that you last saw me stripped and
strangled
On a holly tree? Demoted first and then hanged!

DYNAMENE   Am I supposed to love the corporal
Or you? It's you I love, from head to foot
And out to the ends of your spirit. What shall I
do   950
If you die? How could I follow you? I should
find you
Discussing me with my husband, comparing your
feelings,
Exchanging   reactions.   Where   should   I   put
myself?
Or am I to live on alone, or find in life
Another source of love, in memory   955
Of Virilius and of you?

TEGEUS-CHROMIS   Dynamene,
Not that! Since everything in the lives of men
Is brief to indifference, let our love at least
Echo and perpetuate itself uniquely
As long as time allows you. Though you go   960
To the limit of age, it won't be far to contain me.

DYNAMENE   It will seem like eternity ground into
days and days.

TEGEUS-CHROMIS   Can I be certain of you, forever?

DYNAMENE   But, Chromis,
Surely you said——

TEGEUS-CHROMIS   Surely we have sensed
Our passion to be greater than mortal? Must I
Die believing it is dying with me?

DYNAMENE   Chromis,   966
You must never die, never! It would be
An offense against truth.

TEGEUS-CHROMIS   I cannot live to be hanged.
It would be an offense against life. Give me my
sword,
Dynamene. O Hades, when you look pale   970
You take the heart out of me. I could die
Without a sword by seeing you suffer. Quickly!
Give me my heart back again with your lips
And I'll live the rest of my ambitions
In a last kiss.

DYNAMENE   Oh, no, no, no!   975
Give my blessing to your desertion of me?
Never, Chromis, never. Kiss you and then
Let you go? Love you, for death to have you?
Am I to be made the fool of courts martial?
Who are they who think they can discipline
souls   980
Right off the earth? What discipline is that?
Chromis, love is the only discipline
And we're the disciples of love. I hold you to
that:

Hold you, hold you.

TEGEUS-CHROMIS   We have no chance. It's
   determined
In section six, paragraph three, of the regulations.
That has more power than love. It can snuff the
   great   986
Candles of creation. It makes me able
To do the impossible, to leave you, to go from
   the light
That keeps you.

DYNAMENE   No!

TEGEUS-CHROMIS   O dark, it does. Good-by,
My memory of earth, my dear most dear   990
Beyond every expectation. I was wrong
To want you to keep our vows existent
In the vacuum that's coming. It would make you
A heaviness to the world, when you should be,
As you are, a form of light. Dynamene, turn
Your head away. I'm going to let my sword
Solve all the riddles.   997

DYNAMENE   Chromis, I have it! I know!
Virilius will help you.

TEGEUS-CHROMIS   Virilius?

DYNAMENE My husband. He can be the other
   body.

TEGEUS-CHROMIS Your husband can?   1000

DYNAMENE   He has no further use
For what he left of himself to lie with us here.
Is there any reason why he shouldn't hang
On your holly tree?° Better, far better, he,
Than you who are still alive, and surely better
Than *idling* into corruption?   1005

TEGEUS-CHROMIS   Hang your husband?
Dynamene, it's terrible, horrible.

DYNAMENE How little you can understand. I loved
His life not his death. And now we can give his
   death
The power of life. Not horrible: wonderful!
Isn't it so? That I should be able to feel   1010
He moves again in the world, accomplishing
Our welfare? It's more than my grief could do.

TEGEUS-CHROMIS What can I say?

DYNAMENE   That you love me; as I love him
And you. Let's celebrate your safety then.
Where's the bottle? There's some wine unfinished
   in this bowl.   1015
I'll share it with you. Now forget the fear

1003. **holly tree:** often symbolic of life and vitality because
it remains green throughout winter; cf. the rejuvenation of
the phoenix.

We were in; look at me, Chromis. Come away
From the pit you nearly dropped us in. **My**
   darling,
I give you Virilius.

TEGEUS-CHROMIS   Virilius.
And all that follows.

DOTO [*On the steps, with the bottle*]
        The master. Both the masters.   1020

PHILIP ROTH
b. 1933

The Conversion of the Jews

You're a real one for opening your mouth in the
first place," Itzie said. "What do you open your
mouth all the time for?"

"I didn't bring it up, Itz, I didn't," Ozzie said.

"What do you care about Jesus Christ for anyway?"

"I didn't bring up Jesus Christ. He did. I didn't
even know what he was talking about. Jesus is
historical, he kept saying. Jesus is historical."
Ozzie mimicked the monumental voice of Rabbi
Binder.

"Jesus was a person that lived like you and me,"
Ozzie continued. "That's what Binder said—"

"Yeah? . . . So what! What do I give two cents
whether he lived or not. And what do you gotta
open your mouth!" Itzie Lieberman favored closed-
mouthedness, especially when it came to Ozzie
Freedman's questions. Mrs. Freedman had to see
Rabbi Binder twice before about Ozzie's questions
and this Wednesday at four-thirty would be the
third time. Itzie preferred to keep *his* mother in the
kitchen; he settled for behind-the-back subtleties
such as gestures, faces, snarls and other less delicate
barnyard noises.

"He was a real person, Jesus, but he wasn't like
God, and we don't believe he is God." Slowly,
Ozzie was explaining Rabbi Binder's position to
Itzie, who had been absent from Hebrew School
the previous afternoon.

"The Catholics," Itzie said helpfully, "they
believe in Jesus Christ, that he's God." Itzie

Lieberman used "the Catholics" in its broadest sense—to include the Protestants.

Ozzie received Itzie's remark with a tiny head bob, as though it were a footnote, and went on. "His mother was Mary, and his father probably was Joseph," Ozzie said. "But the New Testament says his real father was God."

"His *real* father?"

"Yeah," Ozzie said, "that's the big thing, his father's supposed to be God."

"Bull."

"That's what Rabbi Binder says, that it's impossible—"

"Sure it's impossible. That stuff's all bull. To have a baby you gotta get laid," Itzie theologized. "Mary hadda get laid."

"That's what Binder says: 'The only way a woman can have a baby is to have intercourse with a man.'"

"He said *that*, Ozz?" For a moment it appeared that Itzie had put the theological question aside. "He said that, intercourse?" A little curled smile shaped itself in the lower half of Itzie's face like a pink mustache. "What you guys do, Ozz, you laugh or something?"

"I raised my hand."

"Yeah? Whatja say?"

"That's when I asked the question."

Itzie's face lit up. "Whatja ask about—intercourse?"

"No, I asked the question about God, how if he could create the heaven and earth in six days, and make all the animals and the fish and the light in six days—the light especially, that's what always gets me, that he could make the light. Making fish and animals, that's pretty good—"

"That's damn good." Itzie's appreciation was honest but unimaginative: it was as though God had just pitched a one-hitter.

"But making light . . . I mean when you think about it, it's really something," Ozzie said. "Anyway, I asked Binder if he could make all that in six days, and he could *pick* the six days he wanted right out of nowhere, why couldn't he let a woman have a baby without having intercourse."

"You said intercourse, Ozz, to Binder?"

"Yeah."

"Right in class?"

"Yeah."

Itzie smacked the side of his head.

"I mean, no kidding around," Ozzie said, "that'd really be nothing. After all that other stuff, that'd practically be nothing."

Itzie considered a moment. "What'd Binder say?"

"He started all over again explaining how Jesus was historical and how he lived like you and me but he wasn't God. So I said I under*stood* that. What I wanted to know was different."

What Ozzie wanted to know was always different. The first time he had wanted to know how Rabbi Binder could call the Jews "The Chosen People" if the Declaration of Independence claimed all men to be created equal. Rabbi Binder tried to distinguish for him between political equality and spiritual legitimacy, but what Ozzie wanted to know, he insisted vehemently, was different. That was the first time his mother had to come.

Then there was the plane crash. Fifty-eight people had been killed in a plane crash at La Guardia. In studying a casualty list in the newspaper his mother had discovered among the list of those dead eight Jewish names (his grandmother had nine but she counted Miller as a Jewish name); because of the eight she said the plane crash was "a tragedy." During free-discussion time on Wednesday Ozzie had brought to Rabbi Binder's attention this matter of "some of his relations" always picking out the Jewish names. Rabbi Binder had begun to explain cultural unity and some other things when Ozzie stood up at his seat and said that what he wanted to know was different. Rabbi Binder insisted that he sit down and it was then that Ozzie shouted that he wished all fifty-eight were Jews. That was the second time his mother came.

"And he kept explaining about Jesus being historical, and so I kept asking him. No kidding, Itz, he was trying to make me look stupid."

"So what he finally do?"

"Finally he starts screaming that I was deliberately simple-minded and a wise guy, and that my mother had to come, and this was the last time. And that I'd never get bar-mitzvahed[1] if he could help it. Then, Itz, then he starts talking in that voice like a statue, real slow and deep, and he says that I better think over what I said about the Lord. He told me to go to his office and think it over."

THE CONVERSION OF THE JEWS. 1. **bar-mitzvahed**: barmitzvah is the ceremony of religious initiation for Jewish boys.

Ozzie leaned his body towards Itzie. "Itz, I thought it over for a solid hour, and now I'm convinced God could do it."

Ozzie had planned to confess his latest transgression to his mother as soon as she came home from work. But it was a Friday night in November and already dark, and when Mrs. Freedman came through the door she tossed off her coat, kissed Ozzie quickly on the face, and went to the kitchen table to light the three yellow candles, two for the Sabbath and one for Ozzie's father.

When his mother lit the candles she would move her two arms slowly towards her, dragging them through the air, as though persuading people whose minds were half made up. And her eyes would get glassy with tears. Even when his father was alive Ozzie remembered that her eyes had gotten glassy, so it didn't have anything to do with his dying. It had something to do with lighting the candles.

As she touched the flaming match to the unlit wick of a Sabbath candle, the phone rang, and Ozzie, standing only a foot from it, plucked it off the receiver and held it muffled to his chest. When his mother lit candles Ozzie felt there should be no noise; even breathing, if you could manage it, should be softened. Ozzie pressed the phone to his breast and watched his mother dragging whatever she was dragging, and he felt his own eyes get glassy. His mother was a round, tired, gray-haired penguin of a woman whose gray skin had begun to feel the tug of gravity and the weight of her own history. Even when she was dressed up she didn't look like a chosen person. But when she lit candles she looked like something better; like a woman who knew momentarily that God could do anything.

After a few mysterious minutes she was finished. Ozzie hung up the phone and walked to the kitchen table where she was beginning to lay the two places for the four-course Sabbath meal. He told her that she would have to see Rabbi Binder next Wednesday at four-thirty, and then he told her why. For the first time in their life together she hit Ozzie across the face with her hand.

All through the chopped liver and chicken soup part of the dinner Ozzie cried; he didn't have any appetite for the rest.

On Wednesday, in the largest of the three basement classrooms of the synagogue, Rabbi Marvin Binder, a tall, handsome, broad-shouldered man of thirty with thick strong-fibered black hair, removed his watch from his pocket and saw that it was four o'clock. At the rear of the room Yakov Blotnik, the seventy-one-year-old custodian, slowly polished the large window, mumbling to himself, unaware that it was four o'clock or six o'clock, Monday or Wednesday. To most of the students Yakov Blotnik's mumbling, along with his brown curly beard, scythe nose, and two heel-trailing black cats, made of him an object of wonder, a foreigner, a relic, towards whom they were alternately fearful and disrespectful. To Ozzie the mumbling had always seemed a monotonous, curious prayer; what made it curious was that old Blotnik had been mumbling so steadily for so many years, Ozzie suspected he had memorized the prayers and forgotten all about God.

"It is now free-discussion time," Rabbi Binder said. "Feel free to talk about any Jewish matter at all—religion, family, politics, sports—"

There was silence. It was a gusty, clouded November afternoon and it did not seem as though there ever was or could be a thing called baseball. So nobody this week said a word about that hero from the past, Hank Greenberg—which limited free discussion considerably.

And the soul-battering Ozzie Freedman had just received from Rabbi Binder had imposed its limitation. When it was Ozzie's turn to read aloud from the Hebrew book the rabbi had asked him petulantly why he didn't read more rapidly. He was showing no progress. Ozzie said he could read faster but that if he did he was sure not to understand what he was reading. Nevertheless, at the rabbi's repeated suggestion Ozzie tried, and showed a great talent, but in the midst of a long passage he stopped short and said he didn't understand a word he was reading, and started in again at a drag-footed pace. Then came the soul-battering.

Consequently when free-discussion time rolled around none of the students felt too free. The rabbi's invitation was answered only by the mumbling of feeble old Blotnik.

"Isn't there anything at all you would like to discuss?" Rabbi Binder asked again, looking at his watch. "No questions or comments?"

There was a small grumble from the third row. The rabbi requested that Ozzie rise and give the rest of the class the advantage of his thought.

Ozzie rose. "I forget it now," he said, and sat down in his place.

Rabbi Binder advanced a seat towards Ozzie and poised himself on the edge of the desk. It was Itzie's desk and the rabbi's frame only a dagger's-length away from his face snapped him to sitting attention.

"Stand up again, Oscar," Rabbi Binder said calmly, "and try to assemble your thoughts."

Ozzie stood up. All his classmates turned in their seats and watched as he gave an unconvincing scratch to his forehead.

"I can't assemble any," he announced, and plunked himself down.

"Stand up!" Rabbi Binder advanced from Itzie's desk to the one directly in front of Ozzie; when the rabbinical back was turned Itzie gave it five-fingers off the tip of his nose, causing a small titter in the room. Rabbi Binder was too absorbed in squelching Ozzie's nonsense once and for all to bother with titters. "Stand up, Oscar. What's your question about?"

Ozzie pulled a word out of the air. It was the handiest word. "Religion."

"Oh, now you remember?"

"Yes."

"What is it?"

Trapped, Ozzie blurted the first thing that came to him. "Why can't he make anything he wants to make!"

As Rabbi Binder prepared an answer, a final answer, Itzie, ten feet behind him, raised one finger on his left hand, gestured it meaningfully towards the rabbi's back, and brought the house down.

Binder twisted quickly to see what had happened and in the midst of the commotion Ozzie shouted into the rabbi's back what he couldn't have shouted to his face. It was a loud, toneless sound that had the timbre of something stored inside for about six days.

"You don't know! You don't know anything about God!"

The rabbi spun back towards Ozzie. "What?"

"You don't know—you don't—"

"Apologize, Oscar, apologize!" It was a threat.

"You don't—"

Rabbi Binder's hand flicked out at Ozzie's cheek. Perhaps it had only been meant to clamp the boy's mouth shut, but Ozzie ducked and the palm caught him squarely on the nose.

The blood came in a short, red spurt on to Ozzie's shirt front.

The next moment was all confusion. Ozzie screamed, "You bastard, you bastard!" and broke for the classroom door. Rabbi Binder lurched a step backwards, as though his own blood had started flowing violently in the opposite direction, then gave a clumsy lurch forward and bolted out the door after Ozzie. The class followed after the rabbi's huge blue-suited back, and before old Blotnik could turn from his window, the room was empty and everyone was headed full speed up the three flights leading to the roof.

If one should compare the light of day to the life of man: sunrise to birth; sunset—the dropping down over the edge—to death; then as Ozzie Freedman wiggled through the trapdoor of the synagogue roof, his feet kicking backwards bronco-style at Rabbi Binder's outstretched arms—at that moment the day was fifty years old. As a rule, fifty or fifty-five reflects accurately the age of late afternoons in November, for it is in that month, during those hours, that one's awareness of light seems no longer a matter of seeing, but of hearing: light begins clicking away. In fact, as Ozzie locked shut the trapdoor in the rabbi's face, the sharp click of the bolt into the lock might momentarily have been mistaken for the sound of the heavier gray that had just throbbed through the sky.

With all his weight Ozzie kneeled on the locked door; any instant he was certain that Rabbi Binder's shoulder would fling it open, splintering the wood into shrapnel and catapulting his body into the sky. But the door did not move and below him he heard only the rumble of feet, first loud then dim, like thunder rolling away.

A question shot through his brain. "Can this be *me*?" For a thirteen-year-old who had just labeled his religious leader a bastard, twice, it was not an improper question. Louder and louder the question came to him—"Is it me? It is me?"—until he discovered himself no longer kneeling, but racing crazily towards the edge of the roof, his eyes crying, his throat screaming, and his arms flying every-whichway as though not his own.

"Is it me? Is it me Me ME ME ME! It has to be me—but is it!"

It is the question a thief must ask himself the night he jimmies open his first window, and it is said to be the question with which bridegrooms quiz themselves before the altar.

In the few wild seconds it took Ozzie's body to propel him to the edge of the roof, his self-examination began to grow fuzzy. Gazing down at the street, he became confused as to the problem beneath the question: was it, is-it-me-who-called-Binder-a-bastard? or, is-it-me-prancing-around-on-the-roof? However, the scene below settled all, for there is an instant in any action when whether it is you or somebody else is academic. The thief crams the money in his pockets and scoots out the window. The bridegroom signs the hotel register for two. And the boy on the roof finds a streetful of people gaping at him, necks stretched backwards, faces up, as though he were the ceiling of the Hayden Planetarium. Suddenly you know it's you.

"Oscar! Oscar Freedman!" A voice rose from the center of the crowd, a voice that, could it have been seen, would have looked like the writing on scroll. "Oscar Freedman, get down from there. Immediately!" Rabbi Binder was pointing one arm stiffly up at him; and at the end of that arm, one finger aimed menacingly. It was the attitude of a dictator, but one—the eyes confessed all—whose personal valet had spit neatly in his face.

Ozzie didn't answer. Only for a blink's length did he look towards Rabbi Binder. Instead his eyes began to fit together the world beneath him, to sort out people from places, friends from enemies, participants from spectators. In little jagged star-like clusters his friends stood around Rabbi Binder, who was still pointing. The topmost point on a star compounded not of angels but of five adolescent boys was Itzie. What a world it was, with those stars below, Rabbi Binder below . . . Ozzie, who a moment earlier hadn't been able to control his own body, started to feel the meaning of the word control: he felt Peace and he felt Power.

"Oscar Freedman, I'll give you three to come down."

Few dictators give their subjects three to do anything; but, as always, Rabbi Binder only looked dictatorial.

"Are you ready, Oscar?"

Ozzie nodded his head yes, although he had no intention in the world—the lower one or the celestial one he'd just entered—of coming down even if Rabbi Binder should give him a million.

"All right then," said Rabbi Binder. He ran a hand through his black Samson hair[2] as though it were the gesture prescribed for uttering the first digit. Then, with his other hand cutting a circle out of the small piece of sky around him, he spoke. "One!"

There was no thunder. On the contrary, at that moment, as though "one" was the cue for which he had been waiting, the world's least thunderous person appeared on the synagogue steps. He did not so much come out the synagogue door as lean out, onto the darkening air. He clutched at the doorknob with one hand and looked up at the roof.

"Oy!"

Yakov Blotnik's old mind hobbled slowly, as if on crutches, and though he couldn't decide precisely what the boy was doing on the roof, he knew it wasn't good—that is, it wasn't-good-for-the-Jews. For Yakov Blotnik life had fractioned itself simply: things were either good-for-the-Jews or no-good-for-the-Jews.

He smacked his free hand to his in-sucked cheek, gently. "Oy, Gut!" And then quickly as he was able, he jacked down his head and surveyed the street. There was Rabbi Binder (like a man at an auction with only three dollars in his pocket, he had just delivered a shaky "Two!"); there were the students, and that was all. So far it-wasn't-so-bad-for-the-Jews. But the boy had to come down immediately, before anybody saw. The problem: how to get the boy off the roof?

Anybody who has ever had a cat on the roof knows how to get him down. You call the fire department. Or first you call the operator and you ask her for the fire department. And the next thing there is great jamming of brakes and clanging of bells and shouting of instructions. And then the cat is off the roof. You do the same thing to get a boy off the roof.

That is, you do the same thing if you are Yakov Blotnik and you once had a cat on the roof.

When the engines, all four of them, arrived, Rabbi Binder had four times given Ozzie the count of three. The big hook-and-ladder swung around the corner and one of the firemen leaped from it, plunging headlong towards the yellow fire hydrant in front of the synagogue. With a huge wrench he began to unscrew the top nozzle. Rabbi Binder raced over to him and pulled at his shoulder.

2. **Samson hair:** Samson's hair was the source of his strength.

"There's no fire . . ."

The fireman mumbled back over his shoulder and, heatedly, continued working at the nozzle.

"But there's no fire, there's no fire . . ." Binder shouted. When the fireman mumbled again, the rabbi grasped his face with both his hands and pointed it up at the roof.

To Ozzie it looked as though Rabbi Binder was trying to tug the fireman's head out of his body, like a cork from a bottle. He had to giggle at the picture they made: it was a family portrait—rabbi in black skullcap, fireman in red fire hat, and the little yellow hydrant squatting beside like a kid brother, bareheaded. From the edge of the roof Ozzie waved at the portrait, a one-handed, flapping, mocking wave; in doing it his right foot slipped from under him. Rabbi Binder covered his eyes with his hands.

Firemen work fast. Before Ozzie had even regained his balance, a big, round, yellowed net was being held on the synagogue lawn. The firemen who held it looked up at Ozzie with stern, feelingless faces.

One of the firemen turned his head towards Rabbi Binder. "What, is the kid nuts or something?"

Rabbi Binder unpeeled his hands from his eyes, slowly, painfully, as if they were tape. Then he checked: nothing on the sidewalk, no dents in the net.

"Is he gonna jump, or what?" the fireman shouted.

In a voice not at all like a statue, Rabbi Binder finally answered. "Yes, Yes, I think so . . . He's been threatening to . . ."

Threatening to? Why, the reason he was on the roof, Ozzie remembered, was to get away; he hadn't even thought about jumping. He had just run to get away, and the truth was that he hadn't really headed for the roof as much as he'd been chased there.

"What's his name, the kid?"

"Freedman," Rabbi Binder answered. "Oscar Freedman."

The fireman looked up at Ozzie. "What is it with you, Oscar? You gonna jump, or what?"

Ozzie did not answer. Frankly, the question had just arisen.

"Look, Oscar, if you're gonna jump, jump—and if you're not gonna jump, don't jump. But don't waste our time, willya?"

Ozzie looked at the fireman and then at Rabbi Binder. He wanted to see Rabbi Binder cover his eyes one more time.

"I'm going to jump."

And then he scampered around the edge of the roof to the corner, where there was no net below, and he flapped his arms at his sides, swishing the air and smacking his palms to his trousers on the downbeat. He began screaming like some kind of engine, "Wheeeee . . . wheeeeee," and leaning way out over the edge with the upper half of his body. The firemen whipped around to cover the ground with the net. Rabbi Binder mumbled a few words to Somebody and covered his eyes. Everything happened quickly, jerkily, as in a silent movie. The crowd, which had arrived with the fire engines, gave out a long, Fourth-of-July fireworks ooohaahhh. In the excitement no one had paid the crowd much heed, except, of course, Yakov Blotnik, who swung from the doorknob counting heads. "Fier und tsvantsik . . . finf und tsvantsik[3] . . . Oy, Gut!" It wasn't like this with the cat.

Rabbi Binder peeked through his fingers, checked the sidewalk and net. Empty. But there was Ozzie racing to the other corner. The firemen raced with him but were unable to keep up. Whenever Ozzie wanted to he might jump and splatter himself upon the sidewalk, and by the time the firemen scooted to the spot all they could do with their net would be to cover the mess.

"Wheeeee . . . wheeeee . . ."

"Hey, Oscar," the winded fireman yelled, "What the hell is this, a game or something?"

"Wheeeee . . . wheeeee . . ."

"Hey, Oscar—"

But he was off now to the other corner, flapping his wings fiercely. Rabbi Binder couldn't take it any longer—the fire engines from nowhere, the screaming suicidal boy, the net. He fell to his knees, exhausted, and with his hands curled together in front of his chest like a little dome, he pleaded, "Oscar, stop it, Oscar. Don't jump, Oscar. Please come down . . . Please don't jump."

And further back in the crowd a single voice, a single young voice, shouted a lone word to the boy on the roof.

"Jump!"

It was Itzie. Ozzie momentarily stopped flapping.

"Go ahead, Ozz—jump!" Itzie broke off his

3. **Fier . . . tsvantsik:** twenty-four . . . twenty-five.

point of the star and courageously, with the inspiration not of a wise-guy but of a disciple, stood alone. "Jump, Ozz, jump!"

Still on his knees, his hands still curled, Rabbi Binder twisted his body back. He looked at Itzie, then, agonizingly, back to Ozzie.

"Oscar, don't jump! Please, don't jump . . . please please . . ."

"Jump!" This time it wasn't Itzie but another point of the star. By the time Mrs. Freedman arrived to keep her four-thirty appointment with Rabbi Binder, the whole little upside down heaven was shouting and pleading for Ozzie to jump, and Rabbi Binder no longer was pleading with him not to jump, but was crying into the dome of his hands.

Understandably Mrs. Freedman couldn't figure out what her son was doing on the roof. So she asked.

"Ozzie, my Ozzie, what are you doing? My Ozzie, what is it?"

Ozzie stopped wheeeeeing and slowed his arms down to a cruising flap, the kind birds use in soft winds, but he did not answer. He stood against the low, clouded, darkening sky—light clicked down swiftly now, as on a small gear—flapping softly and gazing down at the small bundle of a woman who was his mother.

"What are you doing, Ozzie?" She turned towards the kneeling Rabbi Binder and rushed so close that only a paper-thickness of dusk lay between her stomach and his shoulders.

"What is my baby doing?"

Rabbi Binder gaped up at her but he too was mute. All that moved was the dome of his hands; it shook back and forth like a weak pulse.

"Rabbi, get him down! He'll kill himself. Get him down, my only baby . . ."

"I can't," Rabbi Binder said, "I can't . . ." and he turned his handsome head towards the crowd of boys behind him. "It's them. Listen to them."

And for the first time Mrs. Freedman saw the crowd of boys, and she heard what they were yelling.

"He's doing it for them. He won't listen to me. It's them." Rabbi Binder spoke like one in a trance.

"For them?"

"Yes."

"Why for them?"

"They want him to . . ."

Mrs. Freedman raised her two arms upward as though she were conducting the sky. "For them he's doing it!" And then in a gesture older than pyramids, older than prophets and floods, her arms came slapping down to her sides. "A martyr I have. Look!" She tilted her head to the roof. Ozzie was still flapping softly. "My martyr."

"Oscar, come down, please," Rabbi Binder groaned.

In a startlingly even voice Mrs. Freedman called to the boy on the roof. "Ozzie, come down, Ozzie. Don't be a martyr, my baby."

As though it were a litany, Rabbi Binder repeated her words. "Don't be a martyr, my baby. Don't be a martyr."

"Gawhead, Ozz—be a Martin!" It was Itzie. "Be a Martin, be a Martin," and all the voices joined in singing for Martindom, whatever it was. "Be a Martin, be a Martin . . ."

Somehow when you're on a roof the darker it gets the less you can hear. All Ozzie knew was that two groups wanted two new things: his friends were spirited and musical about what they wanted; his mother and the rabbi were even-toned, chanting, about what they didn't want. The rabbi's voice was without tears now and so was his mother's.

The big net stared up at Ozzie like a sightless eye. The big, clouded sky pushed down. From beneath it looked like a gray corrugated board. Suddenly, looking up into that unsympathetic sky, Ozzie realized all the strangeness of what these people, his friends, were asking: they wanted him to jump, to kill himself; they were singing about it now—it made them that happy. And there was an even greater strangeness: Rabbi Binder was on his knees, trembling. If there was a question to be asked now it was not "Is it me?" but rather "Is it us? . . . Is it us?"

Being on the roof, it turned out, was a serious thing. If he jumped would the singing become dancing? Would it? What would jumping stop? Yearningly, Ozzie wished he could rip open the sky, plunge his hands through, and pull out the sun; and on the sun, like a coin, would be stamped JUMP or DON'T JUMP.

Ozzie's knees rocked and sagged a little under him as though they were setting him for a dive. His arms tightened, stiffened, froze, from shoulders to fingernails. He felt as if each part of his body were going to vote as to whether he should kill himself or not—and each part as though it were independent of *him*.

The light took an unexpected click down and the new darkness, like a gag, hushed the friends singing for this and the mother and rabbi chanting for that.

Ozzie stopped counting votes, and in a curiously high voice, like one who wasn't prepared for speech, he spoke.

"Mamma?"

"Yes, Oscar."

"Mamma, get down on your knees, like Rabbi Binder."

"Oscar—"

"Get down on your knees," he said, "or I'll jump."

Ozzie heard a whimper, then a quick rustling, and when he looked down where his mother had stood he saw the top of a head and beneath that a circle of dress. She was kneeling beside Rabbi Binder.

He spoke again. "Everybody kneel." There was the sound of everybody kneeling.

Ozzie looked around. With one hand he pointed towards the synagogue entrance. "Make *him* kneel."

There was a noise, not of kneeling, but of body-and-cloth stretching. Ozzie could hear Rabbi Binder saying in a gruff whisper, ". . . or he'll *kill* himself," and when next he looked there was Yakov Blotnik off the doorknob and for the first time in his life upon his knees in the Gentile posture of prayer.

As for the firemen—it is not as difficult as one might imagine to hold a net taut while you are kneeling.

Ozzie looked around again; and then he called to Rabbi Binder.

"Rabbi?"

"Yes, Oscar."

"Rabbi Binder, do you believe in God."

"Yes."

"Do you believe God can do Anything?" Ozzie leaned his head out into the darkness. "Anything?"

"Oscar, I think—"

"Tell me you believe God can do Anything."

There was a second's hesitation. Then: "God can do Anything."

"Tell me you believe God can make a child without intercourse."

"He can."

"Tell me!"

"God," Rabbi Binder admitted, "can make a child without intercourse."

"Mamma, you tell me."

"God can make a child without intercourse," his mother said.

"Make *him* tell me." There was no doubt who *him* was.

In a few moments Ozzie heard an old comical voice say something to the increasing darkness about God.

Next, Ozzie made everybody say it. And then he made them all say they believed in Jesus Christ—first one at a time, then all together.

When the catechizing was through it was the beginning of evening. From the street it sounded as if the boy on the roof might have sighed.

"Ozzie?" A woman's voice dared to speak. "You'll come down now?"

There was no answer, but the woman waited, and when a voice finally did speak it was thin and crying, and exhausted as that of an old man who has just finished pulling the bells.

"Mamma, don't you see—you shouldn't hit me. He shouldn't hit me. You shouldn't hit me about God, Mamma. You should never hit anybody about God—"

"Ozzie, please come down now."

"Promise me, promise me you'll never hit anybody about God."

He had asked only his mother, but for some reason everyone kneeling in the street promised he would never hit anybody about God.

Once again there was silence.

"I can come down now, Mamma," the boy on the roof finally said. He turned his head both ways as though checking the traffic lights. "Now I can come down . . ."

And he did, right into the center of the yellow net that glowed in the evening's edge like an overgrown halo.

The Ironic Phase:
Exploitation of a Humorous Society

BEN JONSON
1572–1637

Volpone, or The Fox

THE PERSONS OF THE PLAY[1]

VOLPONE, *a magnifico*[2]
MOSCA, *his parasite*[3]
VOLTORE, *an advocate*[4]
CORBACCIO, *an old gentleman*
CORVINO, *a merchant*
AVOCATORI, *four magistrates*
NOTARIO, *the register*[5]
NANO, *a dwarf*
CASTRONE, *an eunuch*
SIR POLITIC WOULDBE, *a knight*
PEREGRINE, *a gentleman-traveler*
BONARIO, *a young gentleman* (*son of Corbaccio*)
FINE MADAME WOULDBE, *the knight's wife*
CELIA, *the merchant's wife*
COMMENDATORI, *officers*
MERCATORI, *three merchants*
ANDROGYNO, *a hermaphrodite*
SERVITORE, *a servant*
GREGE
WOMEN

VOLPONE. **1. The . . . Play:** The play is based on a conventional fable, the beast epic, in which human traits are associated with specific animals. Mosca, fly; Voltore, vulture; Corbaccio, raven; Corvino, crow; Sir Pol(itic), parrot; Peregrine, hunting hawk. **2. magnifico:** rich and distinguished man. **3. parasite:** flattering dependent, hanger-on. **4. advocate:** lawyer. **5. register:** clerk of the court.

SCENE—*Venice.*

THE ARGUMENT

V olpone, childless, rich, feigns sick, despairs,
O ffers his state° to hopes of several heirs,
L ies languishing; his Parasite receives
P resents of all, assures, deludes; then weaves
O ther cross plots, which ope themselves, are
    told.°   5
N ew tricks for safety are sought; they thrive;
    when, bold,
E ach tempts th' other again, and all are sold.°

PROLOGUE

Now, luck yet send us, and a little wit
    Will serve to make our play hit;
According to the palates of the season,
    Here is rhyme not empty of reason.
This we were bid to credit° from our poet,   5
    Whose true scope,° if you would know it,
In all his poems still hath been this measure:
    To mix profit with your pleasure;
And not as some, whose throats their envy failing,
    Cry hoarsely, "All he writes is railing,"   10
And when his plays come forth, think they can
    flout them,
    With saying, "He was a year about them."
To these there needs no lie but this his creature,
    Which was two months since no feature;
And though he dares give them five lives to mend
    it,   15

The Argument. **2. state:** property. **5. told:** exposed. **7. sold:** defrauded.
Prologue. **5. credit:** believe. **6. scope:** aim.

'Tis known, five weeks fully penned it,
From his own hand, without a coadjutor,
　　Novice, journeyman, or tutor.
Yet thus much I can give you as a token
　　Of his play's worth: no eggs are broken,   20
Nor quaking custards with fierce teeth affrighted,°
　　Wherewith your rout are so delighted;
Nor hales° he in a gull° old ends° reciting,
　　To stop gaps in his loose writing,
With such a deal of monstrous and forced action,
　　As might make Bedlam a faction;°   26
Nor made he 'his play for jests stol'n from each
　　table,
　　But makes jests to fit his fable.
And so presents quick comedy refined,
　　As best critics have designed;   30
The laws of time, place, persons° he observeth,
　　From no needful rule he swerveth.
All gall and copperas° from his ink he draineth,
　　Only a little salt remaineth,
Wherewith he'll rub your cheeks, till red with
　　laughter,   35
　　They shall look fresh a week after.

ACT I

SCENE I. VOLPONE's _house._

VOLPONE   Good morning to the day; and next,
　　my gold!
Open the shrine that I may see my saint.
[MOSCA _opens a curtain disclosing piles of gold._]
Hail the world's soul, and mine! More glad than
　　is
The teeming earth to see the longed-for sun
Peep through the horns of the celestial Ram,°   5
Am I, to view thy splendor darkening his;
That lying here, amongst my other hoards,
Showst like a flame by night, or like the day
Struck out of chaos,° when all darkness fled
Unto the center.° O thou son of Sol,°   10

20–21. no . . . affrighted: somwhat obscure allusion to
the tomfoolery prevalent in contemporary stage burlesques.
23. hales: hauls. gull: fool. old ends: scraps of poetry.
26. make . . . faction: make Bedlam (a London insane
asylum) more disorderly. 31. laws . . . persons: the dramatic
unities. 33. copperas: vitriol (used in making green ink).
Act I, scene i. 5. Peep . . . Ram: In late March, the
sun enters the sign of the Ram in the zodiac. 8–9. day . . .
chaos: first day of creation. 10. center: of the earth. son of
Sol: In alchemy, gold was thought to be ripened by the sun,
and it is therefore, metaphorically, a kind of offspring.

But brighter than thy father, let me kiss,
With adoration, thee, and every relic
Of sacred treasure in this blessed room.
Well did wise poets by thy glorious name
Title that age° which they would have the best,
Thou being the best of things, and far tran-
　　scending   16
All style of joy in children, parents, friends,
Or any other waking dream on earth.
Thy looks when they to Venus did ascribe,
They should have giv'n her twenty thousand
　　cupids,   20
Such are thy beauties and our loves! Dear saint,
Riches, the dumb god° that givst all men tongues,
That canst do nought, and yet mak'st men do
　　all things;
The price of souls; even hell, with thee to boot,
Is made worth heaven! Thou art virtue, fame,
Honor, and all things else. Who can get thee, 26
He shall be noble, valiant, honest, wise—
MOSCA   And what he will, sir. Riches are in
　　fortune
A greater good than wisdom is in nature.
VOLPONE   True, my belovèd Mosca. Yet, I glory
More in the cunning purchase° of my wealth 31
Than in the glad possession, since I gain
No common way: I use no trade, no venture;°
I wound no earth with ploughshares; fat no
　　beasts
To feed the shambles;° have no mills for iron,
Oil, corn, or men, to grind 'em into powder; 36
I blow no subtle° glass; expose no ships
To threat'nings of the furrow-facèd sea;
I turn no monies in the public bank,
Nor usure° private—
MOSCA   　　　　No, sir, nor devour   40
Soft prodigals.° You shall ha' some will swallow
A melting heir as glibly as your Dutch
Will pills of butter, and ne'er purge° for 't;
Tear forth the fathers of poor families
Out of their beds, and coffin them, alive,   45
In some kind, clasping prison, where their bones
May be forthcoming, when the flesh is rotten.
But, your sweet nature doth abhor these courses;

---

15. that age: the Golden Age, that period of time envisioned
by classical poets when life was simple and perfect. 22.
dumb god: "Silence is golden." 31. purchase: acquisition.
33. venture: risk of capital. 35. shambles: slaughterhouse.
37. subtle: delicate (Venetian). 40. usure: usury, i.e., loans
at exorbitant interest rates. 41. prodigals: spendthrifts. 43.
purge: take a laxative.

You loathe the widow's or the orphan's tears
Should wash your pavements, or their piteous cries   50
Ring in your roofs, and beat the air for vengeance—

VOLPONE   Right, Mosca, I do loathe it.

MOSCA   And, besides, sir,
You are not like the thresher that doth stand
With a huge flail, watching a heap of corn,   54
And, hungry, dares not taste the smallest grain,
But feeds on mallows° and such bitter herbs;
Nor like the merchant, who hath filled his vaults
With Romagnia° and rich Candian° wines,
Yet drinks the lees of Lombard's vinegar.
You will not lie in straw, whilst moths and worms   60
Feed on your sumptuous hangings and soft beds.
You know the use of riches, and dare give, now,
From that bright heap, to me, your poor observer,°
Or to your dwarf, or your hermaphrodite,
Your eunuch, or what other household trifle   65
Your pleasure allows maintenance—

VOLPONE   Hold thee, Mosca,
        [Gives him money.]
Take, of my hand; thou strik'st on truth in all,
And they are envious term thee parasite.
Call forth my dwarf, my eunuch, and my fool,
And let 'em make me sport. What should I do
                            [Exit MOSCA.]   70
But cocker up my genius° and live free
To all delights my fortune calls me to?
I have no wife, no parent, child, ally,
To give my substance to; but whom I make°
Must be my heir, and this makes men observe me.   75
This draws new clients, daily, to my house,
Women and men of every sex and age,
That bring me presents, send me plate, coin, jewels,
With hope that when I die (which they expect
Each greedy minute) it shall then return   80
Tenfold upon them; whilst some, covetous
Above the rest, seek to engross° me, whole,
And counterwork the one unto° the other,
Contend in gifts, as they would seem in love.

All which I suffer, playing with their hopes,   85
And am content to coin 'em into profit,
And look upon their kindness, and take more,
And look on that; still bearing them in hand,°
Letting the cherry knock against their lips,
And draw it by their mouths, and back again.
How now!   91

SCENE II

[MOSCA enters with NANO, ANDROGYNO, and CASTRONE prepared to put on an entertainment.]

NANO   Now, room for fresh gamesters, who do will you to know,
They do bring you neither play nor university show;°
And therefore do entreat you that whatsoever they rehearse,
May not fare a whit the worse, for the false pace of the verse.
If you wonder at this, you will wonder more ere we pass,   5
For know, here° is enclosed the soul of Pythagoras,°
        [Pointing to ANDROGYNO.]
That juggler divine, as hereafter shall follow;
Which soul, fast and loose, sir, came first from Apollo,
And was breathed into Aethalides,° Mercurius his son,
Where it had the gift to remember all that ever was done.   10
From thence it fled forth, and made quick transmigration
To goldy-locked Euphorbus,° who was killed in good fashion,
At the siege of old Troy, by the cuckold of Sparta.°
Hermotimus° was next (I find it in my charta)
To whom it did pass, where no sooner it was missing,   15

88. bearing . . . hand: leading them on.
        Scene ii. 2. university show: student production of classical drama. 6. here: in Androgyno. soul of Pythagoras: by transmigration, one of the doctrines of Pythagoras. 9. Aethalides: Mercury's son, herald of the Argonauts. 12. Euphorbus: the Trojan who first wounded Patroclus (the Iliad, XVI). 13. cuckold of Sparta: Menelaus, husband of Helen of Troy, who was abducted by Paris. 14. Hermotimus: Greek philosopher.

56. mallows: coarse plants. 58. Romagnia: Greek wine. Candian: Cretan. 63. observer: servant. 71. cocker . . . genius: cultivate my talents. 74. make: choose. 82. engross: absorb. 83. unto: against.

But with one Pyrrhus of Delos° it learned to go
    afishing;
And thence did it enter the sophist of Greece.°
From Pythagore, she went into a beautiful piece,
Hight° Aspasia,° the meretrix;° and the next toss
    of her
Was again of a whore, she became a philosopher,
Crates the Cynic, as itself doth relate it.   21
Since, kings, knights, and beggars, knaves, lords,
    and fools gat it,
Besides ox and ass, camel, mule, goat, and
    brock,°
In all which it hath spoke, as in the Cobbler's
    cock.°
But I come not here to discourse of that matter,
Or his one, two, or three, or his great oath, "By
    Quater!"°   26
His musics, his trigon,° his golden thigh,°
Or his telling how elements shift; but I
Would ask, how of late thou hast suffered
    translation,°
And shifted thy coat in these days of reforma-
    tion?°   30
ANDROGYNO   Like one of the reformèd,° a fool, as
    you see,
Counting all old doctrine heresy.
NANO   But not on thine own forbid meats° hast
    thou ventured?
ANDROGYNO   On fish, when first a Carthusian° I
    entered.
NANO   Why, then thy dogmatical° silence hath left
    thee?   35
ANDROGYNO   Of that an obstreperous° lawyer
    bereft me.
NANO   O wonderful change! When Sir Lawyer
    forsook thee,
For Pythagore's sake, what body then took thee?
ANDROGYNO   A good, dull moyle.
NANO   And how! by that means

Thou wert brought to allow of the eating of
    beans?   40
ANDROGYNO   Yes.
NANO   But from the moyle into whom
    didst thou pass?
ANDROGYNO   Into a very strange beast, by some
    writers called an ass;
By others, a precise,° pure, illuminate° brother,
Of those devour flesh, and sometimes one
    another,
And will drop you forth a libel, or a sanctified
    lie,   45
Betwixt every spoonful of a nativity pie.°
NANO   Now quit thee, for heaven, of that profane
    nation,
And gently report thy next transmigration.
ANDROGYNO   To the same that I am.
NANO   A creature of delight,
And what is more than a fool, an hermaphrodite?
Now, 'pray thee, sweet soul, in all thy variation,
Which body wouldst thou choose to take up thy
    station?   52
ANDROGYNO   Troth, this I am in, even here would
    I tarry.
NANO   'Cause here the delight of each sex thou
    canst vary?
ANDROGYNO   Alas, those pleasures be stale and
    forsaken;   55
No, 'tis your fool wherewith I am so taken,
The only one creature that I can call blessèd,
For all other forms I have proved most distressèd.
NANO   Spoke true, as thou wert in Pythagoras still.
This learned opinion we celebrate will,   60
Fellow eunuch, as behooves us, with all our wit
    and art,
To dignify that whereof ourselves are so great
    and special a part.
VOLPONE   Now, very, very pretty! Mosca, this
Was thy invention?
MOSCA   If it please my patron,
    Not else.
VOLPONE   It doth, good Mosca.
MOSCA   Then it was, sir.   65
                            Song
Fools, they are the only nation
Worth men's envy or admiration;
Free from care or sorrow-taking,
Selves and others merry making,

16. Pyrrhus of Delos: another Greek philosopher (not
clearly identifiable). 17. sophist of Greece: Pythagoras. 19.
Hight: named. Aspasia: the mistress of Pericles. meretrix:
courtesan. 23. brock: badger. 24. Cobbler's cock: who
speaks in the dialogue about the transmigration of souls
written by Lucian, Greek satirist of the second century.
26. "By Quater": by four; the mystical numerology of
the Pythagorean sect. 27. trigon: triangle. golden thigh:
Pythagoras was believed to have one. 29. translation: transmigration. 30. reformation: the Protestant Reformation.
31. reformed: a Puritan. 33. forbid meats: Pythagoreans did
not eat fish. 34. Carthusian: austere Catholic religious order.
35. dogmatical silence: Pythagoreans took a vow to hold
silence for five years. 36. obstreperous: noisy.

43. precise: puritanical. illuminate: with "inner light." 46.
nativity pie: Christmas pie.

All they speak or do is sterling. 70
Your fool, he is your great man's dearling,
And your ladies' sport and pleasure;
Tongue and bable° are his treasure.
E'en his face begetteth laughter,
And he speaks truth free from slaughter.° 75
He's the grace of every feast,
And, sometimes, the chiefest guest:
Hath his trencher° and his stool,
When wit waits upon the fool.
    Oh, who would not be 80
    Hee, hee, hee?   *[One knocks without.]*

VOLPONE   Who's that? Away! Look, Mosca.
MOSCA   Fool, begone!
      [Exeunt NANO, CASTRONE, ANDROGYNO.]
'Tis Signior Voltore, the advocate;
I know him by his knock.
VOLPONE   Fetch me my gown,
My furs,° and night-caps; say my couch is
   changing, 85
And let him entertain himself awhile
Without i' th' gallery. *[Exit* MOSCA.] Now, now,
   my clients
Begin their visitation! Vulture, kite,
Raven, and gorcrow,° all my birds of prey, 89
That think me turning carcass, now they come.
I am not for 'em yet. *[Enter* MOSCA.] How now?
   the news?
MOSCA   A piece of plate,° sir.
VOLPONE   Of what bigness?
MOSCA   Huge,
Massy, and antique, with your name inscribed,
And arms engraven.
VOLPONE   Good! and not a fox 94
Stretched on the earth, with fine delusive sleights
Mocking a gaping crow?° ha, Mosca!
MOSCA   Sharp, sir.
VOLPONE   Give me my furs. Why dost thou laugh
   so, man?
MOSCA   I cannot choose, sir, when I apprehend
What thoughts he has, without, now, as he
   walks: 99
That this might be the last gift he should give;
That this would fetch you; if you died today,
And gave him all, what he should be tomorrow;

---

73. **bable:** mock scepter carried by professional jesters.
75. **free . . . slaughter:** with impunity. 78. **trencher:** platter.
85. **furs:** robes. 89. **gorcrow:** carrion crow. 92. **piece of
plate:** gold dish. 96. **gaping crow:** in Aesop's fable the crow
that dropped the cheese when inveigled into singing by the
fox.

What large return would come of all his ventures;
How he should worshipped be, and reverenced;
Ride with his furs, and foot-cloths; waited on
By herds of fools and clients; have clear way 106
Made for his moyle, as lettered° as himself;
Be called the great and learnèd advocate:
And then concludes, there's nought impossible.
VOLPONE   Yes, to be learnèd, Mosca. 110
MOSCA   Oh, no; rich
Implies it. Hood an ass with reverend purple,
So you can hide his two ambitious ears,
And he shall pass for a cathedral doctor.
VOLPONE   My caps, my caps, good Mosca. Fetch
   him in.
MOSCA   Stay, sir; your ointment for your eyes. 115
VOLPONE   That's true;
Dispatch, dispatch. I long to have possession
Of my new present.
MOSCA   That, and thousands more,
I hope to see you lord of.
VOLPONE   Thanks, kind Mosca.
MOSCA   And that, when I am lost in blended
   dust,
And hundreds such as I am,° in succession—120
VOLPONE   Nay, that were too much, Mosca.
MOSCA   You shall live
Still to delude these harpies.
VOLPONE   Loving Mosca!
      [Looking into a mirror.]
'Tis well. My pillow now, and let him enter.
                   [Exit MOSCA.]
Now, my feigned cough, my phthisic,° and my
   gout,
My apoplexy, palsy, and catarrhs, 125
Help, with your forcèd functions, this my
   posture,°
Wherein, this three year, I have milked their
   hopes.
He comes, I hear him—uh! uh! uh! uh! Oh—

SCENE III

[Enter MOSCA *with* VOLTORE. VOLPONE *in bed.]*
MOSCA   You still are what you were, sir. Only you,
Of all the rest, are he° commands his love,
And you do wisely to preserve it thus,

---

107. **lettered:** learned. 120. **such . . . am:** servants. 124.
phthisic: consumption. 126. **posture:** deception.
Scene iii. 2. **he:** the one who.

With early visitation, and kind notes
Of your good meaning to him, which, I know, 5
Cannot but come most grateful. Patron, sir.
Here's Signior Voltore is come—

VOLPONE [*Faintly*]   What say you?

MOSCA Sir, Signior Voltore is come this morning
To visit you.

VOLPONE   I thank him.

MOSCA   And hath brought
A piece of antique plate, bought of Saint Mark,°
With which he here presents you.   11

VOLPONE   He is welcome.
Pray him to come more often.

MOSCA   Yes.

VOLTORE   What says he?

MOSCA He thanks you and desires you see him
often.

VOLPONE Mosca.

MOSCA   My patron?

VOLPONE   Bring him near, where is he?
I long to feel his hand.

MOSCA [*Directing* VOLPONE'*s groping hands*] The
plate is here, sir.   15

VOLTORE How fare you, sir?

VOLPONE   I thank you, Signior Voltore.
Where is the plate? mine eyes are bad.

VOLTORE [*Putting it into his hands*]   I'm sorry
To see you still thus weak.

MOSCA [*Aside*]   That he is not weaker.

VOLPONE You are too munificent.

VOLTORE   No, sir; would to heaven
I could as well give health to you as that plate!

VOLPONE You give, sir, what you can. I thank
you. Your love   21
Hath taste in this, and shall not be unanswered.
I pray you see me often.

VOLTORE   Yes, I shall, sir.

VOLPONE Be not far from me.

MOSCA [*To* VOLTORE] Do you observe that, sir?

VOLPONE Hearken unto me still; it will concern
you.   25

MOSCA You are a happy man, sir; know your
good.

VOLPONE I cannot now last long—

MOSCA   You are his heir, sir.

VOLTORE Am I?

VOLPONE   I feel me going, uh! uh! uh! uh!
I am sailing to my port, uh! uh! uh! uh!
And I am glad I am so near my haven.   30

10. **Saint Mark:** goldsmith in the Piazza del San Marco.

MOSCA Alas, kind gentleman. Well, we must all
go—

VOLTORE But, Mosca—

MOSCA   Age will conquer.

VOLTORE   Pray thee, hear me.
Am I inscribed his heir for certain?

MOSCA   Are you?
I do beseech you, sir, you will vouchsafe
To write me i' your family.° All my hopes   35
Depend upon your worship. I am lost
Except the rising sun do shine on me.

VOLTORE It shall both shine and warm thee,
Mosca.

MOSCA   Sir,
I am a man that have not done your love
All the worst offices. Here I wear your keys,   40
See all your coffers and your caskets locked,
Keep the poor inventory of your jewels,
Your plate, and monies; am your steward, sir,
Husband your goods here.

VOLTORE   But am I sole heir?

MOSCA Without a partner, sir, confirmed this
morning;   45
The wax is warm yet, and the ink scarce dry
Upon the parchment.

VOLTORE   Happy, happy me!
By what good chance, sweet Mosca?

MOSCA   Your desert, sir;
I know no second cause.

VOLTORE   Thy modesty
Is loth to know it; well, we shall requite it.   50

MOSCA He ever liked your course,° sir; that first
took him.
I oft have heard him say how the admired
Men of your large° profession, could speak
To every cause, and things mere contraries,°
Till they were hoarse again, yet all be law;   55
That, with most quick agility, could turn
And re-turn; make knots, and undo them;
Give forkèd° counsel; take provoking gold°
On either hand, and put it up.° These men,
He knew, would thrive with their humility.   60
And, for his part, he thought he should be bless'd
To have his heir of such a sufferint° spirit,
So wise, so grave, of so perplexed° a tongue,

35. **write . . . family:** make me a servant in your household.
51. **course:** behavior. 53. **large:** liberal. 54. **To . . . con-**
traries: convincingly on both sides of any case at law. 58.
forked: split, going two ways at once. **provoking gold:**
payment for initiating a legal action. 59. **put it up:** pocket
it. 63. **perplexed:** intricate, double-dealing.

And loud withal, that would not wag, nor scarce
Lie still, without a fee; when every word   65
Your worship but lets fall, is a chequin!°
                              [*Another knocks.*]
Who's that? One knocks. I would not have you
      seen, sir.
And yet—pretend you came and went in haste;
I'll fashion an excuse. And, gentle sir,
When you do come to swim in golden lard,   70
Up to the arms in honey, that your chin
Is borne up stiff with fatness of the flood,
Think on your vassal; but remember me:
I ha' not been your worst of clients.
VOLTORE   Mosca—
MOSCA When will you have your inventory
      brought, sir?   75
Or see a copy of the will? [*Calling out to the one
      knocking.*] Anon.
I'll bring 'em to you, sir. Away, be gone,
Put business i' your face.   [*Exit* VOLTORE.]
VOLPONE   Excellent, Mosca!
Come hither, let me kiss thee.
MOSCA   Keep you still, sir.
Here is Corbaccio.
VOLPONE   Set the plate away.   80
The vulture's gone, and the old raven's come.

SCENE IV

MOSCA Betake you to your silence, and your sleep.
                    [*Sets the plate aside.*]
Stand there and multiply. Now shall we see
A wretch who is indeed more impotent
Than this° can feign to be, yet hopes to hop
Over his grave. [*Enter* CORBACCIO.] Signior
      Corbaccio!   5
You're very welcome, sir.
CORBACCIO   How does your patron?
MOSCA Troth, as he did, sir; no amends.
CORBACCIO [*Cupping his ear*] What? mends he?°
MOSCA [*Shouting*] No, sir. He is rather worse.
CORBACCIO   That's well. Where is he?
MOSCA Upon his couch, sir, newly fall'n asleep.
CORBACCIO Does he sleep well?
MOSCA   No wink, sir, all this night,   10
Nor yesterday, but slumbers.°
CORBACCIO   Good! he should take

---

66. chequin: sequin, a Venetian gold coin.
 Scene iv. 4. this: Volpone. 7. What . . . he: Corbaccio
is deaf. 11. slumbers: dozes.

Some counsel of physicians. I have brought him
An opiate here, from mine own doctor—
MOSCA He will not hear of drugs.
CORBACCIO   Why? I myself
Stood by while 't was made, saw all th'ingredi-
      ents,   15
And know it cannot but most gently work.
My life for his, 'tis but to make him sleep.
VOLPONE [*Aside*] Aye, his last sleep, if he would
      take it.
MOSCA Sir,
He has no faith in physic.
CORBACCIO   Say you, say you?
MOSCA He has no faith in physic: he does think
Most of your doctors are the greater danger,   21
And worse disease t'escape. I often have
Heard him protest that your° physician
Should never be his heir.
CORBACCIO   Not I his heir?
MOSCA Not your physician, sir.
CORBACCIO   Oh, no, no, no,   25
I do not mean it.
MOSCA   No, sir, nor their fees
He cannot brook; he says they flay a man
Before they kill him.
CORBACCIO   Right, I do conceive you.
MOSCA And then, they do it by experiment,
For which the law not only doth absolve 'em,
But gives them great reward; and he is loth   31
To hire his death so.
CORBACCIO   It is true, they kill
With as much license as a judge.
MOSCA   Nay, more;
For he but kills, sir, where the law condemns,
And these can kill him too.
CORBACCIO   Aye, or me,   35
Or any man. How does his apoplex?
Is that strong on him still?
MOSCA   Most violent.
His speech is broken, and his eyes are set,
His face drawn longer than 't was wont—
CORBACCIO   How! how!
Stronger than he was wont?
MOSCA   No, sir; his face   40
Drawn longer than 't was wont.
CORBACCIO   Oh, good.
MOSCA   His mouth
Is ever gaping, and his eyelids hang.
CORBACCIO   Good.

---

23. your: any.

MOSCA   A freezing numbness stiffens all his joints,
And makes the color of his flesh like lead.
CORBACCIO   'Tis good.
MOSCA   His pulse beats slow and dull.
CORBACCIO   Good symptoms still.   45
MOSCA   And from his brain—
CORBACCIO   Ha! How? not from his brain?
MOSCA   Yes, sir, and from his brain—
CORBACCIO   I conceive you; good.
MOSCA   Flows a cold sweat, with a continual
      rheum,
Forth the resolvèd° corners of his eyes.
CORBACCIO   Is 't possible? Yet I am better, ha! 50
How does he with the swimming of his head?
MOSCA   Oh, sir, 'tis past the scotomy;° he now
Hath lost his feeling, and hath left to snort;°
You hardly can perceive him that he breathes.
CORBACCIO   Excellent, excellent; sure I shall
      outlast him!   55
This makes me young again, a score of years.
MOSCA   I was a-coming for you, sir.
CORBACCIO   Has he made his will?
What has he given me?
MOSCA   No, sir.
CORBACCIO   Nothing? ha!
MOSCA   He has not made his will, sir.
CORBACCIO   Oh, oh, oh.
What then did Voltore, the lawyer, here?   60
MOSCA   He smelled a carcass, sir, when he but
      heard
My master was about his testament;
As I did urge him to it for your good—
CORBACCIO   He came unto him, did he? I thought
so.   64
MOSCA   Yes, and presented him this piece of plate.
CORBACCIO   To be his heir?
MOSCA   I do not know, sir.
CORBACCIO   True,
I know it too.
MOSCA   [Aside] By your own scale,° sir.
CORBACCIO   Well,
I shall prevent° him yet. See, Mosca, look,
Here I have brought a bag of bright chequins,
Will quite weigh down his plate.
MOSCA   [Taking the bag]   Yea, marry, sir.   70
This is true physic, this your sacred medicine;
No talk of opiates to this great elixir.

CORBACCIO   'Tis aurum palpabile,° if not potabile.°
MOSCA   It shall be ministered to him, in his bowl?
CORBACCIO   Aye, do, do, do.
MOSCA   Most blessed cordial!°   75
This will recover him.
CORBACCIO   Yes, do, do, do.
MOSCA   I think it were not best, sir.
CORBACCIO   What?
MOSCA   To recover him.
CORBACCIO   Oh, no, no, no; by no means.
MOSCA   Why, sir, this
Will work some strange effect if he but feel it.
CORBACCIO   'Tis true, therefore forbear; I'll take
      my venture;   80
Give me 't again.
MOSCA   At no hand. Pardon me.
You shall not do yourself that wrong, sir. I
Will advise you, you shall have it all.
CORBACCIO   How?
MOSCA   All, sir; 'tis your right, your own; no man
Can claim a part; 'tis yours without a rival,   85
Decreed by destiny.
CORBACCIO   How, how, good Mosca?
MOSCA   I'll tell you, sir. This fit he shall recover—
CORBACCIO   I do conceive you.
MOSCA   And on first advantage
Of his gained senses, will I re-importune him
Unto the making of his testament,   90
And show him this. [Points to the bag of gold.]
CORBACCIO   Good, good.
MOSCA   'Tis better yet,
If you will hear, sir.
CORBACCIO   Yes, with all my heart.
MOSCA   Now would I counsel you, make home
      with speed;
There, frame a will whereto you shall inscribe
My master your sole heir.
CORBACCIO   And disinherit   95
My son?
MOSCA   Oh, sir, the better; for that color°
Shall make it much more taking.
CORBACCIO   Oh, but color?
MOSCA   This will, sir, you shall send it unto me.
Now, when I come to enforce,° as I will do,
Your cares, your watchings, and your many
      prayers,   100

---

49. **resolved:** rotting. 52. **scotomy:** dimness of sight and
dizziness. 53. **left to snort:** stopped snoring. 67. **scale:**
standard. 68. **prevent:** get ahead of.

73. **palpabile:** touchable. **potabile:** drinkable (elixer of gold
was supposed to be a sovereign remedy for illness). 75.
cordial: heart stimulant. 96. **color:** pretense. 99. **enforce:**
urge.

Your more than many gifts, your this day's
    present,
And, last, produce your will; where, without
    thought
Or least regard unto your proper issue,°
A son so brave and highly meriting,
The stream of your diverted love hath thrown
    you   105
Upon my master, and made him your heir:
He cannot be so stupid, or stone dead,
But out of conscience and mere gratitude—

CORBACCIO He must pronounce me his?

MOSCA   'Tis true.

CORBACCIO   This plot
Did I think on before.

MOSCA   I do believe it.   110

CORBACCIO Do you not believe it?

MOSCA   Yes, sir.

CORBACCIO   Mine own project.

MOSCA Which, when he hath done, sir—

CORBACCIO   Published me his heir?

MOSCA And you so certain to survive him—

CORBACCIO   Ay.

MOSCA Being so lusty a man—

CORBACCIO   'Tis true.

MOSCA   Yes, sir—

CORBACCIO I thought on that too. See, how he
    should be   115
The very organ to express my thoughts!

MOSCA You have not only done yourself a good—

CORBACCIO But multiplied it on my son?

MOSCA   'Tis right, sir.

CORBACCIO Still my invention.

MOSCA   'Las, sir, heaven knows
It hath been all my study, all my care,   120
(I e'en grow grey withal) how to work things—

CORBACCIO I do conceive, sweet Mosca.

MOSCA   You are he
For whom I labor here.

CORBACCIO   Aye, do, do, do.
I'll straight about it. [Going.]

[MOSCA now begins to bow and smile while speaking
    too softly for CORBACCIO to hear.]

MOSCA   Rook go with you,° raven!

CORBACCIO I know thee honest.

MOSCA   You do lie, sir.

CORBACCIO   And—   125

MOSCA Your knowledge is no better than your
    ears, sir.

CORBACCIO I do not doubt to be a father to thee.

MOSCA Nor I to gull° my brother° of his blessing.

CORBACCIO I may ha' my youth restored to me,
    why not?

MOSCA Your worship is a precious ass—   130

CORBACCIO   What sayst thou?

MOSCA I do desire your worship to make haste,
    sir.

CORBACCIO 'Tis done, 'tis done, I go.   [Exit.]

VOLPONE [Leaping up]   Oh, I shall burst!
Let out my sides, let out my sides.

MOSCA   Contain
Your flux° of laughter, sir. You know this hope
Is such a bait it covers any hook.   135

VOLPONE Oh, but thy working, and thy placing it!
I cannot hold; good rascal, let me kiss thee.
I never knew thee in so rare a humor.

MOSCA Alas, sir, I but do as I am taught;
Follow your grave° instructions; give 'em
    words;   140
Pour oil into their ears,° and send them hence.

VOLPONE 'Tis true, 'tis true. What a rare punish-
    ment
Is avarice to itself!

MOSCA   Aye, with our help, sir.

VOLPONE So many cares, so many maladies,
So many fears attending on old age.   145
Yea, death so often called on as no wish
Can be more frequent with 'em. Their limbs
    faint,
Their senses dull, their seeing, hearing, going,°
All dead before them; yea, their very teeth,
Their instruments of eating, failing them.   150
Yet this is reckoned life! Nay, here was one,
Is now gone home, that wishes to live longer!
Feels not his gout, nor palsy; feigns himself
Younger by scores of years, flatters his age
With confident belying it; hopes he may   155
With charms, like Aeson° have his youth
    restored;
And with these thoughts so battens,° as if fate
Would be as easily cheated on as he,

                [Another knocks.]

128. gull: cheat, fleece. **my brother:** Corbaccio's son (taking off from "father" of l. 127). **134. flux:** flood. **140. grave:** wise (also a pun on *grave*). **141. Pour . . . ears:** flatter them. **148. going:** motion. **156. Aeson:** Jason's father, who was rejuvenated by Medea's magic. **157. battens:** grows fat.

103. proper issue: own child. **124. Rook . . . you:** May you be cheated (a pun on the two meanings of *rook:* "crow" and "cheat").

And all turns air! Who's that, there, now? a
   third?

MOSCA Close to your couch again; I hear his
   voice.   160

It is Corvino, our spruce merchant.

VOLPONE [Lies down]   Dead.

MOSCA Another bout, sir, with your eyes. Who's
   there?

SCENE V

[Enter CORVINO.]

MOSCA Signior Corvino! come most wished for!
   Oh,

How happy were you, if you knew it, now!

CORVINO Why? what? wherein?

MOSCA   The tardy hour is come, sir.

CORVINO He is not dead?

MOSCA   Not dead, sir, but as good;
   He knows no man.

CORVINO   How shall I do then?

MOSCA   Why, sir?   5

CORVINO I have brought him here a pearl.

MOSCA   Perhaps he has
So much remembrance left as to know you, sir.
He still calls on you, nothing but your name
Is in his mouth. Is your pearl orient,° sir?

CORVINO Venice was never owner of the like. 10

VOLPONE [Faintly] Signior Corvino.

MOSCA   Hark.

VOLPONE   Signior Corvino.

MOSCA He calls you; step and give it him. He is
   here, sir.

And he has brought you a rich pearl.

CORVINO   How do you, sir?
Tell him it doubles the twelfth caract.°

MOSCA   Sir,
He cannot understand, his hearing's gone, 15
And yet it comforts him to see you—

CORVINO   Say
I have a diamond for him, too.

MOSCA   Best show 't, sir,
Put it into his hand; 'tis only there
He apprehends, he has his feeling yet.

       [VOLPONE seizes the pearl.]
See how he grasps it!

CORVINO   'Las, good gentleman. 20
How pitiful the sight is!

MOSCA   Tut, forget, sir.
The weeping of an heir should still be laughter
Under a visor.°

CORVINO   Why, am I his heir?

MOSCA Sir, I am sworn, I may not show the will
Till he be dead. But here has been Corbaccio, 25
Here has been Voltore, here were others too,
I cannot number 'em, they were so many;
All gaping here for legacies; but I,
Taking the vantage of his naming you,
"Signior Corvino, Signior Corvino," took 30
Paper, and pen, and ink, and there I asked him
Whom he would have his heir? "Corvino." Who
Should be executor? "Corvino." And
To any question he was silent to,
I still interpreted the nods he made, 35
Through weakness, for consent; and sent home
   th' others,
Nothing bequeathed them but to cry and curse.

          [They embrace.]

CORVINO Oh, my dear Mosca. Does he not
   perceive us?

MOSCA No more than a blind harper.° He knows
   no man,
No face of friend, nor name of any servant, 40
Who 't was that fed him last, or gave him drink;
Not those he hath begotten, or brought up,
Can he remember.

CORVINO   Has he children?

MOSCA   Bastards,
Some dozen, or more, that he begot on beggars,
Gypsies, and Jews, and black-moors when he
   was drunk. 45
Knew you not that, sir? 'Tis the common fable,°
The dwarf, the fool, the eunuch are all his;
He's the true father of his family,
In all save me, but he has given 'em nothing.

CORVINO That's well, that's well. Art sure he does
   not hear us? 50

MOSCA Sure, sir? why, look you, credit your own
   sense.

       [Shouts in VOLPONE's ear.]
The pox° approach and add to your diseases,
If it would send you hence the sooner, sir,
For, your incontinence, it hath deserved it
Throughly and throughly, and the plague to
   boot. 55

Scene v. **9. orient:** precious. **14. doubles . . . caract:** is
equal to pure (24-karat) gold.

23. visor: mask. **39. harper:** any man in a crowd. **46.
fable:** gossip. **52. pox:** syphilis.

You may come near, sir—Would you would
    once close
Those filthy eyes of yours that flow with slime
Like two frog-pits,° and those same hanging
    cheeks,
Covered with hide instead of skin—Nay, help,°
    sir—
That look like frozen dish-clouts° set on end. 60
CORVINO Or, like an old smoked wall, on which
    the rain
Ran down in streaks.
MOSCA   Excellent, sir, speak out.
    You may be louder yet; a culverin°
Dischargèd in his ear would hardly bore it.
CORVINO His nose is like a common sewer, still
    running.   65
MOSCA 'Tis good! And what his mouth?
CORVINO   A very draft.°
MOSCA Oh, stop it up— [Starting to smother him.]
CORVINO   By no means.
MOSCA   Pray you, let me.
    Faith I could stifle him rarely° with a pillow,
    As well as any woman that should keep him.
CORVINO Do as you will, but I'll be gone.
MOSCA   Be so.
    It is your presence makes him last so long.   71
CORVINO I pray you, use no violence.
MOSCA   No, sir? why?
    Why should you be thus scrupulous, pray you, sir?
CORVINO Nay, at your discretion.
MOSCA   Well, good sir, be gone.
CORVINO I will not trouble him now to take my
    pearl?   75
MOSCA Puh! nor your diamond. What a needless
    care

            [taking the jewels]

    Is this afflicts you! is not all here yours?
    Am not I here, whom you have made? Your
        creature?
    That owe my being to you?
CORVINO   Grateful Mosca!
    Thou art my friend, my fellow, my companion,
    My partner, and shalt share in all my fortunes.
MOSCA Excepting one.   82
CORVINO   What's that?
MOSCA   Your gallant wife, sir.
            [Exit CORVINO hurriedly.]

Now is he gone; we had no other means
To shoot him hence but this.
VOLPONE   My divine Mosca!
    Thou hast today outgone thyself. [Another
        knocks.] Who's there?   85
    I will be troubled with no more. Prepare
    Me music, dances, banquets, all delights;
    The Turk is not more sensual in his pleasures
    Than will Volpone. [Exit MOSCA.] Let me see: a
        pearl!
    A diamond! plate! chequins! good morning's
        purchase.°   90
    Why, this is better than rob churches, yet,
    Or fat,° by eating once a month a man.
                        [Enter MOSCA.]
    Who is't?
MOSCA   The beauteous Lady Wouldbe, sir,
    Wife to the English knight, Sir Politic Wouldbe—
    This is the style,° sir, is directed me—   95
    Hath sent to know how you have slept tonight,
    And if you would be visited?
VOLPONE   Not now.
    Some three hours hence.
MOSCA   I told the squire° so much.
VOLPONE When I am high with mirth and wine,
        then, then.
    'Fore heaven, I wonder at the desperate valor
    Of the bold English, that they dare let loose 101
    Their wives to all encounters!
MOSCA   Sir, this knight
    Had not his name for nothing; he is politic,
    And knows, howe'er his wife affect strange
        airs,
    She hath not yet the face to be dishonest.° 105
    But had she Signior Corvino's wife's face—
VOLPONE Has she so rare a face?
MOSCA   Oh, sir, the wonder,
    The blazing star of Italy, a wench
    O' the first year!° a beauty ripe as harvest!
    Whose skin is whiter than a swan, all over! 110
    Than silver, snow, or lilies! a soft lip,
    Would tempt you to eternity of kissing!
    And flesh that melteth in the touch to blood!°
    Bright as your gold! and lovely as your gold!
VOLPONE Why had not I known this before?
MOSCA   Alas, sir, 115
    Myself but yesterday discovered it.

---

58. frog-pits: frog's eggs. 59. help: join in the abuse. 60.
dish-clouts: rags. 63. culverin: cannon. 66. draft: cesspool.
68. rarely: perfectly.

90. purchase: loot. 92. fat: grow fat. 95. style: grand
manner. 98. squire: servant. 105. face . . . dishonest:
enough beauty to be unfaithful. 109. O' . . . year: Of the
first order. 113. to blood: blushes and (perhaps) passion.

VOLPONE   How might I see her?

MOSCA   Oh, not possible;
  She's kept as warily as is your gold,
  Never does come abroad, never takes air
  But at a window. All her looks are sweet   120
  As the first grapes or cherries, and are watched
  As near as they are.

VOLPONE   I must see her—

MOSCA   Sir,
  There is a guard, of ten spies thick, upon her;
  All his whole household; each of which is set
  Upon his fellow, and have all their charge,°   125
  When he° goes out, when he comes in, examined.

VOLPONE   I will go see her, though but at her
  window.

MOSCA   In some disguise then.

VOLPONE   That is true. I must
  Maintain mine own shape still the same: we'll
  think.   [Exeunt.]

ACT II

SCENE I. *The public square, before* CORVINO's
house.

[*Enter* POLITIC WOULDBE, PEREGRINE.]

SIR POLITIC   Sir, to a wise man, all the world's his
  soil.
  It is not Italy, nor France, nor Europe,
  That must bound me, if my fates call me forth.
  Yet, I protest, it is no salt° desire
  Of seeing countries, shifting a religion   5
  Nor any disaffection to the state
  Where I was bred, and unto which I owe
  My dearest plots,° hath brought me out; much
  less
  That idle, antique, stale, gray-headed project
  Of knowing men's minds, and manners, with
  Ulysses;   10
  But a peculiar humor of my wife's,
  Laid for this height° of Venice, to observe,
  To quote,° to learn the language, and so forth.
  I hope you travel, sir, with license?°

PEREGRINE   Yes.

SIR POLITIC   I dare the safelier converse. How long,
  sir,   15

Since you left England?

PEREGRINE   Seven weeks.

SIR POLITIC   So lately!
  You ha' not been with my lord ambassador?

PEREGRINE   Not yet, sir.

SIR POLITIC   'Pray you, what news, sir, vents our
  climate?°
  I heard, last night, a most strange thing reported
  By some of my lord's followers, and I long   20
  To hear how 'twill be seconded.°

PEREGRINE   What was 't, sir?

SIR POLITIC   Marry, sir, of a raven,° that should
  build
  In a ship royal of the king's.

PEREGRINE   [*Aside*]   —This fellow,
  Does he gull me, trow?° or is gulled?—Your
  name, sir?

SIR POLITIC   My name is Politic Wouldbe.   25

PEREGRINE   [*Aside*]   —Oh, that speaks him—
  A knight, sir?

SIR POLITIC   A poor knight, sir.

PEREGRINE   Your lady
  Lies° here, in Venice, for intelligence°
  Of tires,° and fashions, and behavior
  Among the courtesans?° The fine Lady Wouldbe?

SIR POLITIC   Yes, sir, the spider and the bee
  ofttimes   30
  Suck from one flower.

PEREGRINE   Good Sir Politic!
  I cry you mercy;° I have heard much of you.
  'Tis true, sir, of your raven.

SIR POLITIC   On your knowledge?

PEREGRINE   Yes, and your lion's whelping in the
  Tower.°

SIR POLITIC   Another whelp!

PEREGRINE   Another, sir.

SIR POLITIC   Now heaven!   35
  What prodigies be these? The fires° at Berwick!
  And the new star! These things concurring,
  strange!
  And full of omen! Saw you those meteors?

PEREGRINE   I did, sir.

SIR POLITIC   Fearful! Pray you, sir, confirm me,

---

125. **charge:** responsibility. 126. **he:** Corvino.
  Act II, scene i. 4. **salt:** keen. 8. **dearest plots:** desires
and plans. 12. **height:** latitude (peculiarly inappropriate to
Venice). 13. **quote:** note down. 14. **license:** passport.

18. **vents our climate:** comes from England. 21. **seconded:**
confirmed. 22. **raven:** the bird of ill omen, perhaps a
foolishly oblique reference to a traitor. 24. **trow:** I wonder.
27. **Lies:** stays. **intelligence:** knowledge. 28. **tires:** clothes.
29. **courtesans:** fashionable prostitutes. 32. **cry you mercy:**
ask your pardon. 34. **lion's . . . Tower:** Lions were kept in
the Tower of London. 36. **fires:** meteors, taken as omens of
coming political disorder.

Were there three porpoises seen above the
   bridge,°   40
As they give out?°
PEREGRINE   Six, and a sturgeon, sir.
SIR POLITIC   I am astonished!
PEREGRINE   Nay, sir, be not so;
I'll tell you a greater prodigy than these—
SIR POLITIC   What should these things portend?
PEREGRINE   The very day
   (Let me be sure) that I put forth from London,
There was a whale discovered in the river,   46
As high as Woolwich, that had waited there,
Few know how many months, for the subversion°
Of the Stode fleet.°
SIR POLITIC   Is't possible? Believe it,
'Twas either sent from Spain, or the archduke's!°
Spinola's° whale, upon my life, my credit!   51
Will they not leave these projects? Worthy sir,
Some other news.
PEREGRINE   Faith, Stone° the fool is dead,
And they do lack a tavern fool extremely.
SIR POLITIC   Is Mas' Stone dead?
PEREGRINE   He's dead, sir; why, I hope   55
   You thought him not immortal? [*Aside*.]—Oh,
   this knight,
Were he well known, would be a precious thing
To fit our English stage. He that should write
But such a fellow, should be thought to feign
Extremely, if not maliciously.—
SIR POLITIC   Stone dead!   60
PEREGRINE   Dead. Lord, how deeply, sir, you
   apprehend° it!
He was no kinsman to you?
SIR POLITIC   That° I know of.
Well, that same fellow was an unknown° fool.
PEREGRINE   And yet you know him, it seems?
SIR POLITIC   I did so. Sir,
I knew him one of the most dangerous heads°
Living within the state, and so I held him.   66
PEREGRINE   Indeed, sir?
SIR POLITIC   While he lived, in action.
He has received weekly intelligence,
Upon my knowledge, out of the Low Countries,

For all parts of the world, in cabbages;   70
And those dispensed, again, t'ambassadors,
In oranges, musk-melons, apricots,
Lemons, pome-citrons, and suchlike; sometimes
In Colchester oysters, and your Selsey cockles.
PEREGRINE   You make me wonder.
SIR POLITIC   Sir, upon my knowledge.   75
Nay, I have observed him at your public ordinary°
Take his advertisement° from a traveler,
A concealed° statesman, in a trencher of meat;
And, instantly, before the meal was done,
Convey an answer in a toothpick.
PEREGRINE   Strange!   80
How could this be, sir?
SIR POLITIC   Why, the meat was cut
So like his character,° and so laid as he
Must easily read the cipher.
PEREGRINE   I have heard
He could not read, sir.
SIR POLITIC   So 'twas given out,
In policy,° by those that did employ him;   85
But he could read, and had your languages,
And to 't,° as sound a noddle—
PEREGRINE   I have heard, sir,
That your baboons were spies, and that they
   were
A kind of subtle nation near to China.
SIR POLITIC   Aye, aye, your Mamaluchi.° Faith,
   they had   90
Their hand in a French plot, or two; but they
Were so extremely given to women as°
They made discovery of all; yet I
Had my advices° here, on Wednesday last,
From one of their own coat,° they were returned,
Made their relations,° as the fashion is,   96
And now stand fair° for fresh employment.
PEREGRINE   [*Aside*]   —'Heart!°
This Sir Pol will be ignorant of nothing—
It seems, sir, you know all.
SIR POLITIC   Not all, sir. But
I have some general notions; I do love   100
To note and to observe: though I live out,
Free from the active torrent, yet I'd mark

---

40. **the bridge:** London Bridge. **41. give out:** report. **48.
subversion:** destruction. **49. Stode fleet:** from Stode, near
Hamburg. **50. archduke:** ruler of the Spanish Netherlands.
51. Spinola: Spanish general at this time who used ingenious
weapons. **53. Stone:** court fool to James I. **61. apprehend:**
feel, take. **62. That:** not that. **63. unknown:** pretended, i.e.,
not known for what he really was. **65. dangerous heads:**
subversive persons.

76. **ordinary:** tavern. **77. advertisement:** information.
78. concealed statesman: secret agent. **82. character:** handwriting. **85. In policy:** craftily. **87. And to 't:** in addition.
90. Mamaluchi: Mamelukes, former Christian slaves of
the Turks; they held power in Egypt in the thirteenth
century. **92. as:** that. **94. advices:** dispatches. **95. coat:** party.
96. relations: reports. **97. stand fair:** are ready. **'Heart:**
God's heart! (a curse).

The currents and the passages of things
For mine own private use; and know the ebbs
And flows of state.

PEREGRINE   Believe it, sir, I hold   105
Myself in no small tie° unto my fortunes
For casting me thus luckily upon you,
Whose knowledge, if your bounty° equal it,
May do me great assistance in instruction
For my behavior, and my bearing, which   110
Is yet so rude and raw.

SIR POLITIC   Why? came you forth
Empty of rules for travel?

PEREGRINE   Faith, I had
Some common ones, from out that vulgar°
grammar,
Which he that cried° Italian to me, taught me.

SIR POLITIC   Why, this it is that spoils all our brave
bloods,   115
Trusting our hopeful gentry unto pedants,
Fellows of outside,° and mere bark. You seem
To be a gentleman, of ingenuous race—°
I not profess it,° but my fate hath been
To be where I have been consulted with   120
In this high kind,° touching some great men's
sons,
Persons of blood and honor—

PEREGRINE   Who be these, sir?

SCENE II

[Enter MOSCA and NANO, disguised as mountebank's
attendants, with materials to erect a scaffold stage.
A crowd follows them.]

MOSCA   Under that window, there't must be. The
same.

SIR POLITIC   Fellows to mount a bank!° Did your
instructor
In the dear° tongues, never discourse to you
Of the Italian mountebanks?

PEREGRINE   Yes, sir.

SIR POLITIC   Why,
Here shall you see one.

PEREGRINE   They are quacksalvers, 5
Fellows that live by venting° oils and drugs.

SIR POLITIC   Was that the character he gave you
of them?

PEREGRINE   As I remember.

SIR POLITIC   Pity his ignorance.
They are the only knowing men of Europe!
Great general scholars, excellent physicians,   10
Most admired statesmen, professed favorites
And cabinet counselors to the greatest princes!
The only languaged men of all the world!

PEREGRINE   And I have heard they are most lewd°
impostors,
Made all of terms and shreds;° no less beliers
Of° great men's favors than their own vile
medicines;   16
Which they will utter° upon monstrous oaths,°
Selling that drug for twopence, ere they part,
Which they have valued at twelve crowns before.

SIR POLITIC   Sir, calumnies are answered best with
silence.   20
Yourself shall judge. Who is it mounts, my
friends?

MOSCA   Scoto of Mantua,° sir.

SIR POLITIC   Is't he? Nay, then
I'll proudly promise, sir, you shall behold
Another man than has been fantasied° to you.
I wonder, yet, that he should mount his bank 25
Here, in this nook, that has been wont t'appear
In face of the Piazza! Here he comes.
[Enter VOLPONE, disguised as a mountebank.]

VOLPONE   [To NANO] Mount, zany.

GREGE   Follow, follow, follow, follow, follow.
[VOLPONE mounts the stage.]

SIR POLITIC   See how the people follow him! He's
a man   30
May write ten thousand crowns in bank here.
Note,
Mark but his gesture. I do use to observe
The state° he keeps in getting up!

PEREGRINE   'Tis worth it, sir.

VOLPONE   Most noble gentlemen, and my worthy
patrons, it may seem strange that I, your Scoto
Mantuano, who was ever wont to fix my bank
in face of the public Piazza, near the shelter of the
Portico to the Procuratia,° should now, after

---

106. tie: obligation. 108. bounty: generosity. 113. vulgar:
commonplace. 114. cried: taught. 117. outside: pretense.
118. ingenuous race: good birth. 119. I . . . it: I do not
teach young gentlemen. 121. high kind: important matter.
   Scene ii. 2. bank: platform (pun on mountebank). 3.
dear: esteemed. 6. venting: selling.

14. lewd: ignorant. 15. terms and shreds: jargon and unrelated scraps of learning. 15–16. beliers of: pretenders
to. 17. utter: sell. oaths: testimonials. 22. Scoto of Mantua:
juggler known in London. 24. fantasied: misrepresented.
33. state: formal bearing. 38. Procuratia: residences of
civic officials along the north side of the Piazza del San
Marco.

eight months' absence from this illustrious city of Venice, humbly retire myself into an obscure nook of the Piazza.   41

SIR POLITIC   Did not I now object° the same?

PEREGRINE   Peace, sir.

VOLPONE   Let me tell you: I am not, as your Lombard proverb saith, cold on my feet, or content to part with my commodities at a cheaper rate than I accustomed. Look not for it. Nor that the calumnious reports of that impudent detractor, and shame to our profession, Alessandro Buttone° I mean, who gave out, in public, I was condemned a sforzato° to the galleys, for poisoning the Cardinal Bembo's°—cook, hath at all attached,° much less dejected me. No, no, worthy gentlemen; to tell you true, I cannot endure to see the rabble of these ground ciarlitani° that spread their cloaks on the pavement as if they meant to do feats of activity,° and then come in lamely with their moldy tales out of Boccaccio, like stale Tabarin,° the fabulist:° some of them discoursing their travels, and of their tedious captivity in the Turk's galleys, when, indeed, were the truth known, they were the Christian's galleys, where very temperately they eat bread, and drunk water, as a wholesome penance enjoined them° by their confessors, for base pilferies.   65

SIR POLITIC   Note but his bearing and contempt of these.

VOLPONE   These turdy-facy-nasty-paty-lousy-fartical rogues, with one poor groatsworth of unprepared antimony, finely wrapped up in several scartoccios,° are able, very well, to kill their twenty a week, and play; yet these meager, starved spirits, who have half stopped the organs of their minds with earthy oppilations,° want not their favorers among your shriveled salad-eating artisans,° who are overjoyed that they may have their half-pe'rth° of physic; though it purge 'em into another world, 't makes no matter.   78

SIR POLITIC   Excellent! ha' you heard better language, sir?   80

VOLPONE   Well, let 'em go. And, gentlemen, honorable gentlemen, know that for this time our bank, being thus removed from the clamors of the canaglia,° shall be the scene of pleasure and delight; for I have nothing to sell, little or nothing to sell.   86

SIR POLITIC   I told you, sir, his end.

PEREGRINE   You did so, sir.

VOLPONE   I protest, I and my six servants are not able to make of this precious liquor so fast as it is fetched away from my lodging by gentlemen of your city, strangers of the Terra Firma,° worshipful merchants, aye, and senators too, who, ever since my arrival, have detained me to their uses by their splendidous liberalities. And worthily. For what avails your rich men to have his magazines° stuft with moscadelli,° or of the purest grape, when his physicians prescribe him, on pain of death, to drink nothing but water cocted° with aniseeds? O health! health! the blessing of the rich! the riches of the poor! who can buy thee at too dear a rate, since there is no enjoying this world without thee? Be not then so sparing of your purses, honorable gentlemen, as to abridge the natural course of life—   105

PEREGRINE   You see his end?

SIR POLITIC   Aye, is't not good?

VOLPONE   For, when a humid flux°, or catarrh, by the mutability of air falls from your head into an arm or shoulder, or any other part, take you a ducat, or your chequin of gold, and apply to the place affected: see, what good effect it can work. No, no, 'tis this blessed unguento,° this rare extraction, that hath only power to disperse all malignant humours° that proceed either of hot, cold, moist, or windy causes—   115

PEREGRINE   I would he had put in dry too.

SIR POLITIC   'Pray you, observe.

VOLPONE   To fortify the most indigest and crude°

42. object: surmise. 48–49. Alessandro Buttone: rival mountebank. 50. a sforzato: at forced labor. 51. Cardinal Bembo: secretary to Pope Leo X. (The dash suggests that Volpone was about to say "mistress" instead of "cook.") 52. attached: bothered. 55. ciarlitani: quacks, charlatans. 56. feats of activity: trembling. 58. Tabarin: stock comedian in traveling companies of players. fabulist: storyteller. 64. enjoined them: imposed upon them. 70–71. several scartoccios: separate papers. 74. oppilations: obstructions to the functioning of internal organs. 75–76. salad-eating artisans: poor workers. 77. half-pe'rth: half-penny's worth.

84. canaglia: canaille, rabble. 92. Terra Firma: "land" possessions of Venice on the mainland. 97. magazines: warehouses. moscadelli: muscatel wines. 100. cocted: boiled. 107. flux: discharge. 112. unguento: salve. 114. humours: in Renaissance medical theory, the four fluids of the body (blood, phlegm, choler, black bile), which corresponded to the four elements of nature (air, water, fire, earth) and to four kinds of temperament (sanguine, phlegmatic, choleric, melancholic). Perfect health depended on a balance of the humours, but in most men one was thought to dominate, thus forming the essential personality. 117. crude: sour.

stomach, ay, were it of one that through extreme weakness vomited blood, applying only a warm napkin to the place, after the unction and fricace;° for the vertigine° in the head, putting but a drop into your nostrils, likewise behind the ears; a most sovereign and approved remedy: the *mal caduco*,° cramps, convulsions, paralyses, epilepsies, *tremor cordia*,° retired° nerves, ill vapors of the spleen, stoppings of the liver, the stone, the strangury,° *hernia ventosa*,° *iliaca passio*;° stops a *dysenteria* immediately; easeth the torsion° of the small guts; and cures *melancholia hypocondriaca*,° being taken and applied according to my printed receipt. [*Pointing to his bill and his glass.*] For, this is the physician, this the medicine; this counsels, this cures; this gives the direction, this works the effect; and, in sum, both together may be termed an abstract of the theoric and practic in the Aesculapian art.° 'Twill cost you eight crowns. And, Zan Fritada,° pray thee sing a verse, extempore, in honor of it.   139

SIR POLITIC   How do you like him, sir?
PEREGRINE   Most strangely, I!
SIR POLITIC   Is not his language rare?
PEREGRINE   But° alchemy
I never heard the like, or Broughton's° books.

Song
Had old Hippocrates° or Galen,°
That to their books put med'cines all in,
But known this secret, they had never,   145
Of which they will be guilty ever,
Been murderers of so much paper,
Or wasted many a hurtless° taper.
No Indian drug had e'er been famèd,
Tobacco, sassafras not namèd;   150
Ne° yet of guacum° one small stick, sir,
Nor Raymond Lully's great elixir.°

Ne had been known the Danish Gonswart,°
Or Paracelsus,° with his long sword.   154
PEREGRINE   All this, yet, will not do; eight crowns is high.
VOLPONE   No more. Gentlemen, if I had but time to discourse to you the miraculous effects of this my oil, surnamed *Oglio del Scoto*, with the countless catalogue of those I have cured of th'aforesaid, and many more diseases; the patents and privileges of all the princes and commonwealths of Christendom; or but the depositions of those that appeared on my part, before the signiory of the *Sanita*° and most learned college of physicians; where I was authorized, upon notice taken of the admirable virtues of my medicaments, and mine own excellency in matter of rare and unknown secrets, not only to disperse them publicly in this famous city, but in all the territories that happily joy under the government of the most pious and magnificent states of Italy. But may some other gallant fellow say, "Oh, there be divers that make profession to have as good and as experimented receipts° as yours." Indeed, very many have assayed, like apes, in imitation of that, which is really and essentially in me, to make of this oil; bestowed great cost in furnaces, stills, alembics, continual fires,° and preparation of the ingredients (as indeed there goes to it six hundred several simples,° besides some quantity of human fat, for the conglutination, which we buy of the anatomists), but, when these practitioners come to the last decoction, blow, blow, puff, puff, and all flies in fumo.° Ha, ha, ha! Poor wretches! I rather pity their folly and indiscretion than their loss of time and money; for those may be recovered by industry; but to be a fool born is a disease incurable. For myself, I always from my youth have endeavored to get the rarest secrets, and book° them, either in exchange or for money; I spared nor cost nor labor where anything was worthy to be learned. And gentlemen, honorable gentlemen, I will undertake, by virtue of chemical art, out of the honorable hat that covers your head to extract the four elements, that is to say, the fire, air,

121. fricace: massage. vertigine: dizziness. 124. mal caduco: epilepsy. 125. tremor cordia: heart tremors. retired: atrophied. 127. strangury: strangulated urination. hernia ventosa: gaseous hernia. 127–28. iliaca passio: colic. 129. torsion: griping. 129–30. melancholia hypochondriaca: acute depression. 136. Aesculapian art: medicine. 137. Zan Fritada: famous Italian comedian (probably addressed to Nano). 141. But: except for. 142. Broughton: eccentric Puritan theologian. 143. Hippocrates, Galen: Greek founders of the art of medicine. 148. hurtless: harmless. 151. Ne: nor. guacum: drug used to treat gout. 152. Raymund . . . elixir: drug capable of prolonging life and health, supposedly discovered by Lully, a medieval alchemist.

153. Gonswart: another alchemist. 154. Paracelsus: sixteenth-century alchemist, reputed to have carried alchemical essences in his sword. 165. signiory . . . Sanita: medical licensing board of Venice. 175. experimented receipts: tested prescriptions. 179. furnaces . . . fires: alchemical equipment. 181. simples: herbs. 184. fumo: smoke. 191. book: note.

water, and earth, and return you your felt without burn or stain. For, whilst others have been at the balloo,° I have been at my book, and am now past the craggy paths of study, and come to the flowery plains of honor and reputation. 202

SIR POLITIC   I do assure you, sir, that is his aim.

VOLPONE   But to our price—

PEREGRINE   And that withal,° Sir Pol.

VOLPONE   You all know, honorable gentlemen, I never valued this *ampulla*, or vial, at less than eight crowns, but for this time I am content to be deprived of it for six; six crowns is the price, and less in courtesy I know you cannot offer me; take it or leave it, howsoever, both it and I am at your service. I ask you not as the value of the thing,° for then I should demand of you a thousand crowns; so the cardinals Montalto, Farnese, the great duke of Tuscany, my gossip,° with divers other princes have given me; but I despise money. Only to show my affection to you, honorable gentlemen, and your illustrious state here, I have neglected the messages of these princes, mine own offices, framed my journey hither, only to present you with the fruits of my travels. [*To* NANO *and* MOSCA.] Tune your voices once more to the touch of your instruments, and give the honorable assembly some delightful recreation.   224

PEREGRINE   What monstrous and most painful circumstance
Is here, to get some three or four *gazets!*°
Some threepence i' th' whole, for that 'twill come to

Song

You that would last long, list to my song,
Make no more coil,° but buy of this oil.
Would you be ever fair? and young?   230
Stout of teeth? and strong of tongue?
Tart of palate? quick of ear?
Sharp of sight? of nostril clear?
Moist of hand? and light of foot?
Or I will come nearer to 't,   235
Would you live free from all diseases?
Do the act your mistress pleases,
Yet fright all aches from your bones?
Here's a med'cine for the nones.°   239

VOLPONE   Well, I am in a humor, at this time, to make a present of the small quantity my coffer contains to the rich, in courtesy, and to the poor, for God's sake. Wherefore, now mark: I asked you six crowns, and six crowns at other times you have paid me; you shall not give me six crowns, nor five, nor four, nor three, nor two, nor one; nor half a ducat; no, not a *moccenigo*.° Six-pence it will cost you, or six hundred pound —expect no lower price, for by the banner of my front, I will not bate° a bagatine;° that I will have, only, a pledge of your loves, to carry something from amongst you to show I am not contemned by you. Therefore, now, toss your handkerchiefs, cheerfully, cheerfully; and be advertised° that the first heroic spirit that deigns to grace me with a handkerchief, I will give it a little remembrance of something beside, shall please it better than if I had presented it with a double pistolet.°   259

PEREGRINE   Will you be that heroic spark, Sir Pol?
[CELIA *at the window throws down her handkerchief.*]
O see! the window has prevented° you.   261

VOLPONE   Lady, I kiss your bounty, and for this timely grace you have done your poor Scoto of Mantua, I will return you, over and above my oil, a secret of that high and inestimable nature shall make you forever enamored on that minute wherein your eye first descended on so mean, yet not altogether to be despised, an object. Here is a poulder concealed in this paper of which, if I should speak to the worth, nine thousand volumes were but as one page, that page as a line, that line as a word: so short is this pilgrimage of man, which some call life, to the expressing of it. Would I reflect on the price? Why, the whole world were but as an empire, that empire as a province, that province as a bank, that bank as a private purse to the purchase of it. I will, only, tell you: it is the poulder that made Venus a goddess (given her by Apollo), that kept her perpetually young, cleared her wrinkles, firmed her gums, filled her skin, colored her hair. From her derived to Helen, and at the sack of Troy unfortunately lost; till now, in this our age, it

---

200. balloo: Venetian ball game. 204. withal: as well.
211–12. as . . . thing: what it is worth. 214. gossip: god-father. 226. gazets: small Venetian coins. 229. coil: fuss.
239. nones: purpose.

247. moccenigo: small coin. 250. bate: come down. bagatine:
very small coin. 254–55. be advertised: understand. 259.
double pistolet: gold coin of some worth. 261. prevented:
anticipated.

was as happily recovered by a studious antiquary
out of some ruins of Asia, who sent a moiety°
of it to the court of France (but much sophisticated), wherewith the ladies there now color their
hair. The rest, at this present, remains with me;
extracted to a quintessence, so that wherever it
but touches in youth it perpetually preserves, in
age restores the complexion; seats your teeth,
did they dance like virginal jacks,° firm as a wall;
makes them white as ivory, that were black
as—   294

SCENE III

[*Enter* CORVINO.]

CORVINO Spite o' the devil, and my shame!
[*To* VOLPONE.]   Come down here;
Come down! No house but mine to make your
scene?
       [*He beats away the mountebank, &c.*]
Signior Flaminio,° will you down, sir? down?
What, is my wife your Franciscina°, sir?
No windows on the whole Piazza, here,   5
To make your properties, but mine? but mine?
Heart! ere tomorrow I shall be new christened,
And called the Pantalone° di Besogniosi
About the town.   [*Exit.*]
PEREGRINE   What should this mean, Sir Pol?
SIR POLITIC Some trick of state, believe it. I will
home.   10
PEREGRINE It may be some design on you.
SIR POLITIC   I know not.
I'll stand upon my guard.
PEREGRINE   It is your best, sir.
SIR POLITIC This three weeks all my advices, all
my letters,
They have been intercepted.
PEREGRINE   Indeed, sir?
Best have a care.
SIR POLITIC   Nay, so I will.
PEREGRINE   This knight,   15
I may not lose him for my mirth, till night.
                                       [*Exit.*]

---

285. **moiety:** part. 292. **virginal jacks:** keys of a small
spinet.
Scene iii. **3. Flaminio:** noted actor in the *commedia
dell' arte*, improvised plays performed by wandering
troupes during the sixteenth and seventeenth centuries in
Italy. **4. Franciscina:** clever, amorous servant, one of the
stock characters of *commedia dell' arte*. **8. Pantalone:**
another stock character, the old merchant who is cuckolded.

SCENE IV. VOLPONE's *house.*

[VOLPONE *and* MOSCA.]

VOLPONE Oh, I am wounded!
MOSCA   Where, sir?
VOLPONE   Not without;
Those blows were nothing, I could bear them
ever.
But angry Cupid, bolting from her eyes,
Hath shot himself into me like a flame;
Where, now, he flings about his burning heat, 5
As in a furnace an ambitious° fire
Whose vent is stopped. The fight is all within me.
I cannot live except thou help me, Mosca;
My liver melts, and I, without the hope
Of some soft air from her refreshing breath,   10
Am but a heap of cinders.
MOSCA   'Las, good sir!
Would you had never seen her!
VOLPONE   Nay, would thou
Hadst never told me of her.
MOSCA   Sir, 'tis true;
I do confess I was unfortunate,
And you unhappy; but I'm bound in conscience,
No less than duty, to effect my best   16
To your release of torment, and I will, sir.
VOLPONE Dear Mosca, shall I hope?
MOSCA   Sir, more than dear,
I will not bid you to despair of aught
Within a human compass.°
VOLPONE   Oh, there spoke   20
My better angel. Mosca, take my keys,
Gold, plate, and jewels, all's at thy devotion;
Employ them how thou wilt; nay, coin me too,
So thou in this but crown my longings—Mosca?
MOSCA Use but your patience.
VOLPONE   So I have.
MOSCA   I doubt not   25
To bring success to your desires.
VOLPONE   Nay, then,
I not° repent me of my late disguise.
MOSCA If you can horn° him, sir, you need not.
VOLPONE   True.
Besides, I never meant him for my heir.
Is not the color° o' my beard and eyebrows   30
To make me known?
MOSCA   No jot.
VOLPONE   I did it well.

Scene iv. **6. ambitious:** swelling. **20. compass:** possibility.
27. not: do not. **28. horn:** cuckold. **30. color:** distinctive red.

MOSCA   So well, would I could follow you in mine,
   With half the happiness; and yet, I would
   Escape your epilogue.°
VOLPONE   But were they gulled
   With a belief that I was Scoto?
MOSCA   Sir,   35
   Scoto himself could hardly have distinguished!
   I have not time to flatter you now; we'll part,
   And as I prosper, so applaud my art. [*Exeunt.*]

SCENE V. CORVINO'*s house.*

[*Enter* CORVINO, CELIA.]

CORVINO   Death of mine honor, with the city's
   fool?
   A juggling, tooth-drawing, prating mountebank?
   And at a public window? where, whilst he,
   With his strained action,° and his dole of faces,°
   To his drug-lecture draws your itching ears,   5
   A crew of old, unmarried, noted lechers
   Stood leering up like satyrs: and you smile
   Most graciously, and fan your favors forth,
   To give your hot spectators satisfaction!
   What, was your mountebank their call? their
   whistle?   10
   Or were y'enamored on his copper rings?
   His saffron jewel, with the toad stone° in't?
   Or his embroider'd suit, with the cope-stitch,
   Made of a hearse cloth?° or his old tilt-feather?°
   Or his starched beard! Well, you shall have him,
   yes.   15
   He shall come home and minister unto you
   The fricace° for the mother. Or, let me see,
   I think you'd rather mount? would you not
   mount?
   Why, if you'll mount, you may; yes truly, you
   may,
   And so you may be seen, down to th' foot.   20
   Get you a cittern,° Lady Vanity,°
   And be a dealer° with the virtuous man;°

Make one. I'll but protest myself a cuckold,
   And save your dowry. I am a Dutchman,° I!
   For if you thought me an Italian,   25
   You would be damned ere you did this, you
   whore!
   Thou'dst tremble to imagine that the murder
   Of father, mother, brother, all thy race,
   Should follow as the subject of my justice.
CELIA   Good sir, have patience!
CORVINO   What couldst thou propose°   30
   Less to thyself than in this heat of wrath,
   And stung with my dishonor, I should strike
      [*waves his sword*]
   This steel into thee, with as many stabs
   As thou wert gazed upon with goatish eyes?
CELIA   Alas, sir, be appeased! I could not think 35
   My being at the window should more now
   Move your impatience than at other times.
CORVINO   No? not to seek and entertain a parley
   With a known knave? before a multitude?
   You were an actor with your handkerchief,   40
   Which he, most sweetly, kissed in the receipt.
   And might, no doubt, return it with a letter,
   And point the place where you might meet: your
   sister's,
   Your mother's, or your aunt's might serve the
   turn.
CELIA   Why, dear sir, when do I make these
   excuses?   45
   Or ever stir abroad but to the church?
   And that so seldom—
CORVINO   Well, it shall be less;
   And thy restraint before was liberty
   To what I now decree, and therefore mark me.
   First, I will have this bawdy light° dammed up;
   And till't be done, some two, or three yards off
   I'll chalk a line, o'er which if thou but chance 52
   To set thy desp'rate foot, more hell, more horror,
   More wild, remorseless rage shall seize on thee
   Than on a conjurer that had heedless left   55
   His circle's safety ere his devil was laid.°
   Then, here's a lock° which I will hang upon thee,
   And, now I think on't, I will keep thee back-
   wards;
   Thy lodging shall be backwards, thy walks
   backwards,

---

34. **epilogue:** the blows, and perhaps the end that Mosca plans for Volpone.
  Scene v.   **4. strained action:** overdone gestures. **dole of faces:** repertory of theatrical expressions. **12. toad-stone:** stonelike substance supposedly formed in the head of a toad according to popular belief, and valued as a charm against illness. **14. hearse cloth:** rich hanging over a tomb. **tilt-feather:** large feather worn on a helmet. **17. fricace . . . mother:** massage for hysteria. The line also suggests that Volpone will seduce Celia. **21. cittern:** zither. **Lady Vanity:** stock character in English morality plays. **22. dealer:** whore. **virtuous man:** pun on *virtuoso.*

24. **Dutchman:** thrifty. **30. propose:** expect. **50. light:** window. **55–56. heedless . . . laid:** stepped out of the safe magic circle before disposing of the devil he had called up. **57. lock:** chastity belt.

Thy prospect—all be backwards, and no pleasure,
That thou shalt know but backwards. Nay, since
   you force   61
My honest nature, know it is your own
Being too open makes me use you thus.
Since you will not contain your subtle nostrils
In a sweet room, but they must snuff the air 65
Of rank and sweaty passengers°—
      [*Knock within.*]
               One knocks.
Away, and be not seen, pain of thy life;
Not look toward the window; if thou dost—
      [CELIA *starts to leave.*]
Nay, stay, hear this, let me not prosper, whore,
But I will make thee an anatomy,°   70
Dissect thee mine own self, and read a lecture
Upon thee to the city, and in public.
Away! [*Exit* CELIA.] Who's there?
             [*Enter* SERVANT.]
SERVANT   'Tis Signior Mosca, sir.

SCENE VI

CORVINO Let him come in, his master's dead.
  There's yet
Some good to help the bad. [*Enter* MOSCA.] My
  Mosca, welcome!
I guess your news.
MOSCA   I fear you cannot, sir.
CORVINO Is't not his death?
MOSCA   Rather the contrary.
CORVINO Not his recovery?
MOSCA   Yes, sir.
CORVINO   I am cursed, 5
I am bewitched, my crosses meet to vex me.
How? how? how? how?
MOSCA   Why, sir, with Scoto's oil!
Corbaccio and Voltore brought of it,
Whilst I was busy in an inner room—
CORVINO Death! that damned mountebank! but
  for the law,   10
Now, I could kill the rascal; 't cannot be
His oil should have that virtue. Ha' not I
Known him a common rogue, come fiddling in
To th'*osterìa*,° with a tumbling whore,°
And, when he has done all his forced tricks, been
  glad   15

Of a poor spoonful of dead wine, with flies in't?
It cannot be. All his ingredients
Are a sheep's gall, a roasted bitch's marrow,
Some few sod earwigs,° pounded caterpillars,
A little capon's grease, and fasting° spittle; 20
I know 'em to a dram.
MOSCA   I know not, sir;
But some on 't,° there, they poured into his ears,
Some in his nostrils, and recovered him,
Applying but the fricace.
CORVINO   Pox o' that fricace.
MOSCA And since, to seem the more officious 25
And flatt'ring of his health, there they have had,
At extreme fees, the college of physicians
Consulting on him how they might restore him;
Where one would have a cataplasm° of spices,
Another a flayed ape clapped to his breast, 30
A third would ha' it a dog, a fourth an oil
With wild cats' skins. At last, they all resolved
That to preserve him was no other means
But some young woman must be straight sought
  out,
Lusty, and full of juice, to sleep by him; 35
And to this service, most unhappily
And most unwillingly, am I now employed,
Which here I thought to pre-acquaint you with,
For your advice, since it concerns you most,
Because I would not do that thing might cross
Your ends, on whom I have my whole depen-
  dence, sir.   41
Yet, if I do it not they may delate°
My slackness to my patron, work me out
Of his opinion; and there all your hopes,
Ventures, or whatsoever, are all frustrate. 45
I do but tell you, sir. Besides, they are all
Now striving who shall first present° him.
  Therefore,
I could entreat you, briefly, conclude somewhat.°
Prevent 'em if you can.
CORVINO   Death to my hopes!
This is my villainous fortune! Best to hire 50
Some common courtesan?
MOSCA   Aye, I thought on that, sir.
But they are all so subtle, full of art,
And age° again doting and flexible,

---

66. **passengers:** passers-by. 70. **anatomy:** cadaver.
  Scene vi. 14. **osteria:** inn. **tumbling whore:** female
acrobat.

19. **sod earwigs:** boiled insects. 20. **fasting:** of a starving
man. 22. **on 't:** of it. 29. **cataplasm:** poultice. 42. **delate:**
report. 47. **present:** i.e., with the young woman. 48. **conclude somewhat:** decide on something. 53. **age:** "old"
Volpone.

So as—I cannot tell—we may perchance
Light on a quean may cheat us all.
CORVINO   'Tis true.   55
MOSCA   No, no; it must be one that has no tricks,
   sir,
   Some simple thing, a creature made unto° it;
   Some wench you may command. Ha' you no
      kinswoman?
   God's so—Think, think, think, think, think,
      think, think, sir.
   One o' the doctors offered there his daughter.   60
CORVINO   How!
MOSCA   Yes, Signior Lupo, the physician.
CORVINO   His daughter!
MOSCA   And a virgin, sir. Why, alas,
   He knows the state of's body, what it is;
   That nought can warm his blood, sir, but a
      fever;
   Nor any incantation raise his spirit;   65
   A long forgetfulness hath seized that part.
   Besides, sir, who shall know it? Some one or
      two—
CORVINO   I pray thee give me leave.
   [*Walks up and down and talks to himself.*]
                                    If any man
   But I had had this luck—The thing in'tself,
   I know, is nothing—Wherefore should not I   70
   As well command my blood and my affections
   As this dull doctor? In the point of honor
   The cases are all one of wife and daughter.
MOSCA   [*Aside*] I hear him coming.°
CORVINO   She shall do 't. 'Tis done.
   'Slight, if this doctor, who is not engaged,°   75
   Unless't be for his counsel, which is nothing,
   Offer his daughter, what should I that am
   So deeply in? I will prevent him. Wretch!
   Covetous wretch! Mosca, I have determined.
MOSCA   How, sir?
CORVINO   We'll make all sure. The party
      you wot° of   80
   Shall be mine own wife, Mosca.
MOSCA   Sir, the thing
   But that I would not seem to counsel you,
   I should have motioned° to you at the first.
   And make your count,° you have cut all their
      throats.
   Why, 'tis directly taking a possession!   85

And in his next fit, we may let him go.
'Tis but to pull the pillow from his head,
And he is throttled; 't had been done before
But for your scrupulous doubts.   89
CORVINO   Aye, a plague on 't,
   My conscience fools my wit! Well, I'll be brief,
   And so be thou, lest they should be before us.
   Go home, prepare him, tell him with what zeal
   And willingness I do it; swear it was
   On the first hearing, as thou mayst do, truly,
   Mine own free motion.
MOSCA   Sir, I warrant you,   95
   I'll so possess him with it that the rest
   Of his starved clients shall be banished all;
   And only you received. But come not, sir,
   Until I send, for I have something else
   To ripen for your good, you must not know 't.
CORVINO   But do not you forget to send now. 101
MOSCA   Fear not.
                                    [*Exit* MOSCA.]

SCENE VII

CORVINO   Where are you, wife? My Celia? wife?
                    [*Enter* CELIA *crying.*]
                                    What, blubbering?
   Come, dry those tears. I think thou thoughtst me
      in earnest?
   Ha? by this light I talked so but to try thee.
   Methinks the lightness° of the occasion
   Should ha' confirmed° thee. Come, I am not
      jealous.   5
CELIA   No?
CORVINO   Faith I am not, I, nor never was;
   It is a poor unprofitable humor.
   Do not I know if women have a will°
   They'll do 'gainst all the watches o' the world?
   And that the fiercest spies are tamed with gold?
   Tut, I am confident in thee, thou shalt see 't;   11
   And see I'll give thee cause too, to believe it.
   Come, kiss me. Go, and make thee ready straight
   In all thy best attire, thy choicest jewels,
   Put 'em all on, and, with 'em, thy best looks. 15
   We are invited to a solemn feast
   At old Volpone's, where it shall appear
   How far I am free from jealousy or fear.
                                    [*Exeunt.*]

---

57. **made unto:** coached for. **74. coming:** coming round.
75. engaged: involved. **80. wot:** know. **83. motioned:**
suggested. **84. count:** of Volpone's goods.

Scene vii.   **4. lightness:** triviality. **5. confirmed:** reassured.
8. will: sexual desire.

ACT III

SCENE I. *A street.*

[MOSCA *alone.*]

MOSCA   I fear I shall begin to grow in love
With my dear self and my most prosp'rous
    parts,°
They do so spring and burgeon; I can feel
A whimsy i' my blood. I know not how,
Success hath made me wanton. I could skip   5
Out of my skin, now, like a subtle snake,
I am so limber. O! your parasite
Is a most precious thing, dropped from above,
Not bred 'mongst clods and clodpolls,° here on
    earth.
I muse the mystery° was not made a science, 10
It is so liberally professed!° Almost
All the wise world is little else in nature
But parasites or sub-parasites. And yet,
I mean not those that have your bare town-art,
To know who's fit to feed 'em; have no house,
No family, no care, and therefore mold   16
Tales for men's ears, to bait° that sense; or get
Kitchen-invention, and some stale receipts°
To please the belly, and the groin; nor those,
With their court-dog-tricks, that can fawn and
    fleer,°   20
Make their revènue out of legs° and faces,
Echo my lord, and lick away a moth.°
But your fine, elegant rascal, that can rise
And stoop, almost together, like an arrow;
Shoot through the air as nimbly as a star;   25
Turn short as doth a swallow; and be here,
And there, and here, and yonder, all at once;
Present to any humor, all occasion;
And change a visor° swifter than a thought,
This is the creature had the art born with him;
Toils not to learn it, but doth practice it   31
Out of most excellent nature: and such sparks
Are the true parasites, others but their zanies.°

Act III, scene i.   **2. parts:** talents. **9. clodpolls:** dolts.
10. mystery: profession. **11. liberally professed:** widely
practiced. **17. bait:** feed. **18. receipts:** recipes. **20. fleer:**
smile obsequiously. **21. legs:** bows. **22. lick . . . mote:** pick
small objects from a lord's coat, an extreme form of
servility. **29. visor:** mask, expression. **33. zanies:** assistants,
clowns, like Nano.

SCENE II

[*Enter* BONARIO.]

MOSCA   Who's this? Bonario? Old Corbaccio's
    son?
The person I was bound to seek. Fair sir,
You are happ'ly met.
BONARIO   That cannot be by thee.
MOSCA   Why, sir?
BONARIO   Nay, 'pray thee know thy way and leave
    me:
I would be loth to interchange discourse   5
With such a mate as thou art.
MOSCA   Courteous sir,
Scorn not my poverty.
BONARIO   Not I, by heaven;
But thou shalt give me leave to hate thy baseness.
MOSCA   Baseness?
BONARIO   Aye, answer me, is not thy sloth
Sufficient argument? thy flattery?   10
Thy means of feeding?
MOSCA   Heaven be good to me!
These imputations are too common, sir,
And eas'ly stuck on virtue when she's poor.
You are unequal° to me, and howe'er
Your sentence may be righteous, yet you are
    not,   15
That ere you know me, thus proceed in censure.
Saint Mark bear witness 'gainst you, 'tis inhuman.
[*He cries.*]
BONARIO   [*Aside*] What? does he weep? the sign
    is soft and good.
I do repent me that I was so harsh.
MOSCA   'Tis true that swayed by strong necessity,
I am enforced to eat my carefull° bread   21
With too much obsequy;° 'tis true, beside,
That I am fain to spin mine own poor raiment
Out of my mere observance,° being not born
To a free fortune; but that I have done   25
Base offices, in rending friends asunder,
Dividing families, betraying counsels,
Whispering false lies, or mining° men with
    praises,
Trained their credulity with perjuries,
Corrupted chastity, or am in love   30
With mine own tender ease, but would not
    rather

Scene ii.   **14. unequal:** unjust. **21. carefull:** won with care,
toil. **22. obsequy:** humility. **24. observance:** service. **28.
mining:** undermining.

Prove° the most rugged and laborious course,
That might redeem my present estimation,
Let me here perish, in all hope of goodness.

BONARIO [*Aside*]—This cannot be a personated°
    passion—   35
    I was to blame, so to mistake thy nature;
    Pray thee forgive me and speak out thy business.

MOSCA Sir, it concerns you, and though I may seem
    At first to make a main offence in manners,
    And in my gratitude unto my master,   40
    Yet, for the pure love which I bear all right,
    And hatred of the wrong, I must reveal it.
    This very hour your father is in purpose
    To disinherit you—

BONARIO   How!

MOSCA   And thrust you forth
    As a mere stranger to his blood; 'tis true, sir. 45
    The work no way engageth me, but as
    I claim an interest in the general state
    Of goodness and true virtue, which I hear
    T'abound in you, and for which mere respect,
    Without a second aim, sir, I have done it.   50

BONARIO This tale hath lost thee much of the late
    trust
    Thou hadst with me; it is impossible.
    I know not how to lend it any thought
    My father should be so unnatural.

MOSCA It is a confidence that well becomes   55
    Your piety, and formed, no doubt, it is
    From your own simple innocence, which makes
    Your wrong more monstrous and abhorred. But,
    sir,
    I now tell you more. This very minute
    It is, or will be doing; and if you   60
    Shall be but pleased to go with me, I'll bring
    you,
    I dare not say where you shall see, but where
    Your ear shall be a witness of the deed;
    Hear yourself written bastard and professed
    The common issue° of the earth.

BONARIO   I'm mazed! 65

MOSCA Sir, if I do it not, draw your just sword
    And score your vengeance on my front and face;
    Mark me your villain. You have too much wrong,
    And I do suffer for you, sir. My heart
    Weeps blood in anguish—

BONARIO   Lead, I follow thee. 70
                        [*Exeunt.*]

---

32. **Prove**: endure. 35. **personated**: pretended. 65. **common
issue**: without family or position.

SCENE III. VOLPONE's *house.*

VOLPONE Mosca stays long, methinks. Bring forth
    your sports
    And help to make the wretched time more sweet.
    [*Enter* NANO, CASTRONE, ANDROGYNO.]

NANO Dwarf, fool, and eunuch, well met here we
    be.
    A question it were now, whether° of us three,
    Being, all, the known delicates° of a rich man, 5
    In pleasing him, claim the precedency can?

CASTRONE I claim for myself.

ANDROGYNO   And so doth the fool.

NANO 'Tis foolish indeed, let me set you both to
    school.
    First for your dwarf, he's little and witty,
    And everything, as it is little, is pretty;   10
    Else, why do men say to a creature of my shape,
    So soon as they see him, "It's a pretty little
    ape"?
    And, why a pretty ape? but for pleasing imitation
    Of greater men's action, in a ridiculous fashion.
    Beside, this feat° body of mine doth not crave
    Half the meat, drink, and cloth one of your bulks
    will have.   16
    Admit your fool's face be the mother of laughter,
    Yet, for his brain, it must always come after;
    And though that do feed him, it's a pitiful case
    His body is beholding to such a bad face.   20
                [*One knocks.*]

VOLPONE Who's there? My couch, away, look,
    Nano, see;
    Give me my caps first—go, inquire.
           [*Exeunt* CASTRONE, ANDROGYNO.]
    [VOLPONE *lies down in his bed.*]
                      Now Cupid
    Send it be Mosca, and with fair return.

NANO It is the beauteous madam—

VOLPONE   Wouldbe—is it?

NANO The same.   25

VOLPONE   Now, torment on me; squire her in,
    For she will enter, or dwell here forever.
    Nay, quickly, that my fit were past. I fear
                    [*Exit* NANO.]
    A second hell too: that my loathing this
    Will quite expel my appetite to the other.   29
    Would she were taking, now, her tedious leave.
    Lord, how it threats me, what I am to suffer!

Scene iii. 4. **whether**: which. 5. **known delicates**:
acknowledged favorites. 15. **feat**: dainty.

SCENE IV

[*Enter* NANO *with* LADY WOULDBE.]

LADY WOULDBE [*To* NANO] I thank you, good sir.
   Pray you signify
Unto your patron I am here—This band
Shows not my neck enough.—I trouble you, sir;
Let me request you bid one of my women
Come hither to me. In good faith, I am dressed
Most favorably today! It is no matter;   6
'Tis well enough. [*Enter* FIRST WOMAN.] Look, see
   these petulant things!
How they have done this!

VOLPONE [*Aside*]   —I do feel the fever
Ent'ring in at mine ears. O for a charm
To fright it hence—

LADY WOULDBE   Come nearer. Is this curl 10
In his right place? or this? Why is this higher
Than all the rest? You ha' not washed your eyes
   yet?
Or do they not stand even i' your head?
Where's your fellow? Call her.
                [*Exit* FIRST WOMAN.]

NANO [*Aside*]   Now, Saint Mark
Deliver us! Anon she'll beat her women 15
Because her nose is red.
   [*Reenter* FIRST WOMAN *with* SECOND WOMAN.]

LADY WOULDBE   I pray you, view
This tire,° forsooth; are all things apt, or no?

FIRST WOMAN One hair a little, here, sticks out,
   forsooth.

LADY WOULDBE Dost so, forsooth? And where
   was your dear sight
When it did so, forsooth? What now! Bird-
   eyed?°   20
And you too? Pray you both approach and
   mend it.
Now, by that light, I muse you're not ashamed!
I, that have preached these things, so oft, unto
   you,
Read you the principles, argued all the grounds,
Disputed every fitness, every grace,   25
Called you to counsel of so frequent dressings—

NANO [*Aside*] More carefully than of your fame
   or honor.

LADY WOULDBE Made you acquainted what an
   ample dowry
The knowledge of these things would be unto you,
Able, alone, to get you noble husbands 30

Scene iv. **17. tire:** headdress. **20. Bird-eyed:** startled.

At your return; and you, thus, to neglect it!
Besides, you seeing what a curious° nation
Th' Italians are, what will they say of me?
"The English lady cannot dress herself."
Here's a fine imputation to our country!   35
Well, go your ways, and stay i' the next room.
This fucus° was too coarse, too; it's no matter.
Good sir, you'll give 'em entertainment?
             [*Exit* NANO *with* WOMEN.]

VOLPONE The storm comes toward me.

LADY WOULDBE   How does my Volp?

VOLPONE Troubled with noise, I cannot sleep;
   I dreamt   40
That a strange fury entered, now, my house,
And, with the dreadful tempest of her breath,
Did cleave my roof asunder.

LADY WOULDBE   Believe me, and I
Had the most *fearful* dream, could I remember
   't—

VOLPONE [*Aside*] Out on my fate! I ha' giv'n her
   the occasion   45
How to torment me. She will tell me hers.

LADY WOULDBE Methought the golden mediocrity,°
   Polite and delicate—

VOLPONE   Oh, if you do love me,
No more; I sweat, and suffer, at the mention
Of *any* dream; feel how I tremble yet.   50
      [*Placing her hand on his heart.*]

LADY WOULDBE Alas, good soul! the passion of
   the heart,°
Seed-pearl were good now, boiled with syrup of
   apples,
Tincture of gold, and coral, citron-pills,
Your elecampane root, myrobalanes—

VOLPONE [*Aside*] Aye me, I have ta'en a grass-
   hopper° by the wing!   55

LADY WOULDBE Burnt silk and amber. You have
   muscadel
Good in the house—

VOLPONE   You will not drink and part?

LADY WOULDBE No, fear not that. I doubt we shall
   not get
Some English saffron, half a dram would serve,
Your sixteen cloves, a little musk, dried mints,
Bugloss, and barley-meal°—

VOLPONE [*Aside*]   She's in again.   61

32. curious: fastidious. **37. fucus:** pancake make-up. **47.
golden mediocrity:** Aristotle's "golden mean," somehow
personified. **51. passion . . . heart:** heartburn. **52–61. Seed-
pearl . . . meal:** popular remedies for melancholy. **55.
grasshopper:** i.e., noisy thing.

Before I feigned diseases, now I have one.

LADY WOULDBE   And these applied with a right°
  scarlet cloth.

VOLPONE   [*Aside*] Another flood of words! a very
  torrent!

LADY WOULDBE   Shall I, sir, make you a poultice?

VOLPONE   No, no, no.   65
  I'm very well, you need prescribe no more.

LADY WOULDBE   I have, a little, studied physic;
  but now
  I'm all for music, save, i' the forenoons
  An hour or two for painting. I would have
  A lady, indeed, to have all letters and arts,   70
  Be able to discourse, to write, to paint,
  But principal, as Plato holds, your music,
  And so does wise Pythagoras, I take it,
  Is your true rapture, when there is concent°
  In face, in voice, and clothes, and is, indeed,   75
  Our sex's chiefest ornament.

VOLPONE   The poet°
  As old in time as Plato, and as knowing,
  Says that your highest female grace is silence.

LADY WOULDBE   Which o' your poets? Petrarch?
  or Tasso? or Dante?
  Guarini? Ariosto? Aretine?   80
  Cieco di Hadria? I have read them all.

VOLPONE   [*Aside*] Is everything a cause to my
  destruction?

LADY WOULDBE   I think I ha' two or three of 'em
  about me.

VOLPONE   [*Aside*] The sun, the sea, will sooner
  both stand still
  Than her eternal tongue! Nothing can scape it.

LADY WOULDBE   Here's *Pastor Fido*°—   86
     [*Producing a book.*]

VOLPONE   [*Aside*]   Profess obstinate silence;
  That's now my safest.

LADY WOULDBE   All our English writers,
  I mean such as are happy in th' Italian,
  Will deign to steal out of this author, mainly;
  Almost as much as from Montagniè.   90
  He has so modern and facile a vein,
  Fitting the time, and catching the court-ear.
  Your Petrarch is more passionate, yet he,
  In days of sonneting, trusted° 'em with much.
  Dante is hard, and few can understand him.   95
  But for a desperate wit, there's Aretine!

Only, his pictures are a little obscene—
You mark me not.

VOLPONE   Alas, my mind's perturbed.

LADY WOULDBE   Why, in such cases, we must cure
  ourselves,
  Make use of our philosophy—

VOLPONE   O'y me!   100

LADY WOULDBE   And as we find our passions do
  rebel,
  Encounter 'em with reason, or divert 'em
  By giving scope unto some other humor
  Of lesser danger: as, in politic bodies°
  There's nothing more doth overwhelm the
   judgment,   105
  And clouds the understanding, than too much
  Settling and fixing, and, as 'twere, subsiding
  Upon one object. For the incorporating
  Of these same outward things into that part
  Which we call mental, leaves some certain feces
  That stop the organs, and, as Plato says,   111
  Assassinates our knowledge.

VOLPONE   [*Aside*]   Now, the spirit
  Of patience help me!

LADY WOULDBE   Come, in faith, I must
  Visit you more adays and make you well;
  Laugh and be lusty.

VOLPONE   [*Aside*]   My good angel save me!

LADY WOULDBE   There was but one sole man in all
  the world   116
  With whom I e'er could sympathize; and he
  Would lie you often, three, four hours together
  To hear me speak, and be sometime so rapt,
  As he would answer me quite from the purpose,
  Like you, and you are like him, just. I'll dis-
   course,   121
  An't be but only, sir, to bring you asleep,
  How we did spend our time and loves together,
  For some six years.

VOLPONE   Oh, oh, oh, oh, oh, oh.

LADY WOULDBE   For we were *coaetanei,*° and
  brought up—   125

VOLPONE   Some power, some fate, some fortune
  rescue me!

---

63. **right**: genuine. 74. **concent**: harmony. 76. **poet**:
Sophocles (*Ajax*, 293). 86. **Pastor Fido**: *The Faithful
Shepherd* (1590), a play by Guarini. 94. **trusted**: provided.

104. **politic bodies**: kingdoms. 125. **coaetanei**: of the same
age.

SCENE V

[*Enter* MOSCA.]

MOSCA   God save you, madam!

LADY WOULDBE   Good sir.

VOLPONE   Mosca, welcome!
Welcome to my redemption.

MOSCA   Why, sir?

VOLPONE   Oh,
Rid me of this my torture quickly, there,
My madam with the everlasting voice;
The bells in time of pestilence ne'er made   5
Like noise, or were in that perpetual motion!
The cock-pit° comes not near it. All my house,
But now, steamed like a bath with her thick
   breath.
A lawyer could not have been heard; nor scarce
Another woman, such a hail of words   10
She has let fall. For hell's sake, rid her hence.

MOSCA   Has she presented?°

VOLPONE   Oh, I do not care;
I'll take her absence upon any price,
With any loss.

MOSCA   Madam—

LADY WOULDBE   I ha' brought your patron
A toy, a cap here, of mine own work.   15

MOSCA   'Tis well.
I had forgot to tell you I saw your knight
Where you'd little think it.

LADY WOULDBE   Where?

MOSCA   Marry,
Where yet, if you make haste, you may apprehend
   him,
Rowing upon the water in a gondole,
With the most cunning courtesan of Venice.   20

LADY WOULDBE   Is't true?

MOSCA   Pursue 'em, and believe your eyes.
Leave me to make your gift. [*Exit* LADY
   WOULDBE.] I knew 'twould take.
For lightly,° they that use themselves most
   license,
Are still most jealous.

VOLPONE   Mosca, hearty thanks
For thy quick fiction and delivery of me.   25
Now to my hopes, what sayst thou?

                              [*Reenter* LADY WOULDBE.]

LADY WOULDBE   But do you hear, sir?

VOLPONE   Again! I fear a paroxysm.

Scene v.   **7. cock-pit:** where cockfights were held. **12.
presented:** given a present. **23. lightly:** commonly.

LADY WOULDBE   Which way
Rowed they together?

MOSCA   Toward the Rialto.

LADY WOULDBE   I pray you lend me your dwarf.

MOSCA   I pray you, take him.
                              [*Exit* LADY WOULDBE.]
Your hopes, sir, are like happy blossoms: fair,
And promise timely fruit, if you will stay   31
But the maturing; keep you at your couch.
Corbaccio will arrive straight with the will;
When he is gone, I'll tell you more.

                              [*Exit* MOSCA.]

VOLPONE   My blood,
My spirits are returned; I am alive;   35
And, like your wanton gamester at primero,°
Whose thought had whispered to him, not go°
   less,
Methinks I lie, and draw°—for an encounter.°
   [*He draws the curtains across his bed.*]

SCENE VI

[MOSCA *leads* BONARIO *on stage and hides him.*]

MOSCA   Sir, here concealed you may hear all. But
   pray you   [*One knocks.*]
Have patience, sir; the same's your father
   knocks.
I am compelled to leave you.

BONARIO   Do so. Yet
Cannot my thought imagine this a truth.

SCENE VII

[MOSCA *opens door and admits* CORVINO *and*
CELIA.]

MOSCA   Death on me! you are come too soon,
   what meant you?
Did not I say I would send?

CORVINO   Yes, but I feared
You might forget it, and then they prevent us.

MOSCA   Prevent! [*Aside.*]—Did e'er man haste so
   for his horns?
A courtier would not ply it so for a place.°—   5
Well, now there's no helping it, stay here;
I'll presently return. [*He moves to one side.*]

CORVINO   Where are you, Celia?

36. primero: card game. **37. go:** bet. **38. draw, encounter:**
terms used in primero.
   Scene vii.   **5. place:** office at court.

You know not wherefore I have brought you hither?

CELIA Not well, except° you told me.

CORVINO   Now I will:
Hark hither. [*He leads her aside and whispers to her.*]

MOSCA [*To* BONARIO] Sir, your father hath sent word,   10
It will be half an hour ere he come;
And therefore, if you please to walk the while
Into that gallery—at the upper end
There are some books to entertain the time.
And I'll take care no man shall come unto you, sir.   15

BONARIO Yes, I will stay there. [*Aside.*] I do doubt this fellow.   [*Exit.*]

MOSCA There, he is far enough; he can hear nothing.
And for his father, I can keep him off.
[*Returns to* VOLPONE's *couch, opens the curtains, whispers to him.*]

CORVINO Nay, now, there is no starting back, and therefore
Resolve upon it: I have so decreed.   20
It must be done. Nor would I move° 't afore,
Because I would avoid all shifts and tricks,
That might deny me.

CELIA   Sir, let me beseech you,
Affect not these strange trials; if you doubt
My chastity, why, lock me up forever;   25
Make me the heir of darkness. Let me live
Where I may please your fears, if not your trust.

CORVINO Believe it, I have no such humor, I.
All that I speak I mean; yet I am not mad;
Not horn-mad,° see you? Go to, show yourself
Obedient, and a wife.   31

CELIA   O heaven!

CORVINO   I say it,
Do so.

CELIA Was this the train?°

CORVINO   I've told you reasons:
What the physicians have set down; how much
It may concern me; what my engagements° are; 35
My means, and the necessity of those means
For my recovery; wherefore, if you be
Loyal and mine, be won, respect my venture.

CELIA Before your honor?

CORVINO   Honor! tut, a breath.
There's no such thing in nature; a mere term
Invented to awe fools. What, is my gold   40
The worse for touching? clothes for being looked on?
Why, this 's no more. An old, decrepit wretch,
That has no sense,° no sinew; takes his meat
With others' fingers; only knows to gape
When you do scald his gums; a voice, a shadow;
And what can this man hurt you?   46

CELIA   Lord, what spirit
Is this hath entered him?

CORVINO   And for your fame,
That's such a jig;° as if I would go tell it,
Cry it, on the Piazza! Who shall know it
But he that cannot speak it, and this fellow, 50
Whose lips are i' my pocket, save yourself.
—If you'll proclaim 't, you may—I know no other
Should come to know it.

CELIA   Are heaven and saints then nothing?
Will they be blind, or stupid?

CORVINO   How?

CELIA   Good sir,
Be jealous still, emulate them, and think   55
What hate they burn with toward every sin.

CORVINO I grant you. If I thought it were a sin
I would not urge you. Should I offer this
To some young Frenchman, or hot Tuscan blood
That had read Aretine, conned all his prints, 60
Knew every quirk within lust's labyrinth,
And were professed critic in lechery;
And I would look upon him, and applaud him,
This were a sin; but here, 'tis contrary
A pious work, mere charity, for physic   65
And honest policy to assure mine own.

CELIA O heaven! canst thou suffer such a change?

VOLPONE Thou art mine honor, Mosca, and my pride,
My joy, my tickling, my delight! Go, bring 'em.

MOSCA Please you draw near, sir.

CORVINO   Come on, what—   70
[*She hangs back.*]
You will not be rebellious? By that light—
[*He drags her to the bed.*]

MOSCA [*To* VOLPONE] Sir, Signior Corvino, here, is come to see you.

VOLPONE Oh!

---

9. except: unless. 21. move: suggest. 30. horn-mad: fearing cuckoldry. 32. train: trap. 34. engagements: financial commitments.

43. sense: sensation. 48. jig: farce, joke.

MOSCA   And hearing of the consultation had,
So lately, for your health, is come to offer,
Or rather, sir, to prostitute—   75
CORVINO   Thanks, sweet Mosca.
MOSCA   Freely, unasked, or unentreated—
CORVINO   Well.
MOSCA   As the true, fervent instance of his love,
His own most fair and proper wife, the beauty
Only of price° in Venice—
CORVINO   'Tis well urged.
MOSCA   To be your comfortress, and to preserve
you.   80
VOLPONE   Alas, I'm past already! Pray you, thank
him
For his good care and promptness; but for that,
'Tis a vain labor e'en to fight 'gainst heaven;
Applying fire to a stone, uh, uh, uh, uh!
Making a dead leaf grow again. I take   85
His wishes gently, though; and you may tell him
What I've done for him. Marry, my state is
hopeless!
Will him to pray for me, and t' use his fortune
With reverence when he comes to 't.
MOSCA   Do you hear, sir?
Go to him with your wife.   90
CORVINO   [To CELIA]   Heart of my father!
Wilt thou persist thus? Come, I pray thee,
come.
Thou seest 'tis nothing, Celia. By this hand
                [Raising his hand.]
I shall grow violent. Come, do 't, I say.
CELIA   Sir, kill me rather. I will take down poison,
Eat burning coals, do anything—
CORVINO   Be damned! 95
Heart! I will drag thee hence home by the
hair,
Cry thee a strumpet through the streets, rip up
Thy mouth unto thine ears, and slit thy nose,
Like a raw rotchet!°—Do not tempt me, come.
Yield, I am loth—Death! I will buy some
slave   100
Whom I will kill, and bind thee to him, alive;
And at my window hang you forth, devising
Some monstrous crime, which I, in capital
letters,
Will eat into thy flesh with aquafortis,°   104
And burning cor'sives,° on this stubborn breast.
Now, by the blood thou hast incensed, I'll do 't!

CELIA   Sir, what you please, you may; I am your
martyr.
CORVINO   Be not thus obstinate, I ha' not deserved
it.
Think who it is entreats you. Pray thee, sweet;
Good faith, thou shalt have jewels, gowns,
attires,   110
What thou wilt, think and ask. Do, but go kiss
him.
Or touch him, but. For my sake. At my suit.
This once. [She refuses.] No? Not? I shall
remember this.
Will you disgrace me thus? D' you thirst my
undoing?
MOSCA   Nay, gentle lady, be advised.
CORVINO   No, no.   115
She has watched her time. God's precious, this
is scurvy,
'Tis very scurvy; and you are—
MOSCA   Nay, good sir.
CORVINO   An errant° locust, by heaven, a locust!
Whore,
Crocodile, that hast thy tears prepared,
Expecting how thou'lt bid 'em flow.   120
MOSCA   Nay, pray you, sir!
She will consider.
CELIA   Would my life would serve
To satisfy.
CORVINO   'Sdeath! if she would but speak to him,
And save my reputation, 'twere somewhat;
But spitefully to effect utter ruin!
MOSCA   Aye, now you've put your fortune in her
hands.   125
Why i' faith, it is her modesty, I must quit° her.
If you were absent, she would be more coming;°
I know it, and dare undertake° for her.
What woman can before her husband? Pray you,
Let us depart and leave her here.   130
CORVINO   Sweet Celia,
Thou mayst redeem all yet; I'll say no more.
If not, esteem yourself as lost. [She begins to
leave with him.] Nay, stay there.
                [Exit MOSCA and CORVINO.]
CELIA   O God, and his good angels! whither,
whither,
Is shame fled human breasts? that with such ease
Men dare put off your honors, and their own?

---

79. Only of price: most precious. **99. rotchet:** fish. **104. aquafortis:** nitric caid. **105. cor'sives:** corrosives.

118. errant: out-and-out. **126. quit:** excuse, defend. **127. coming:** agreeable. **128. undertake:** vouch.

Is that, which ever was a cause of life,° 136
Now placed beneath the basest circumstance,
And modesty an exile made, for money?

VOLPONE Aye, in Corvino, and such earth-fed minds,

[*He leaps off from the couch.*]

That never tasted the true heaven of love. 140
Assure thee, Celia, he that would sell thee,
Only for hope of gain, and that uncertain,
He would have sold his part of Paradise
For ready money, had he met a cope-man.°
Why art thou mazed to see me thus revived?
Rather applaud thy beauty's miracle; 146
'Tis thy great work, that hath, not now alone,
But sundry times raised me in several shapes,
And, but this morning, like a mountebank,
To see thee at thy window. Aye, before 150
I would have left my practice° for thy love,
In varying figures I would have contended
With the blue Proteus, or the hornèd flood.°
Now, art thou welcome.

CELIA   Sir!

VOLPONE   Nay, fly me not.
Nor let thy false imagination 155
That I was bed-rid, make thee think I am so:
Thou shalt not find it. I am, now, as fresh,
As hot, as high, and in as jovial plight
As when in that so celebrated scene
At recitation of our comedy, 160
For entertainment of the great Valois,°
I acted young Antinous,° and attracted
The eyes and ears of all the ladies present,
T' admire each graceful gesture, note, and footing.

Song

Come, my Celia, let us prove,° 165
While we can, the sports of love;
Time will not be ours forever,
He, at length, our good will sever;
Spend not then his gifts in vain.
Suns that set may rise again; 170
But if once we lose this light,
'Tis with us perpetual night.
Why should we defer our joys?

Fame and rumor are but toys.
Cannot we delude the eyes 175
Of a few poor household spies?
Or his easier ears beguile,
Thus removèd by our wile?
'Tis no sin love's fruits to steal,
But the sweet thefts to reveal: 180
To be taken, to be seen,
These have crimes accounted been.

CELIA Some serene° blast me, or dire lightning strike
This my offending face.

VOLPONE   Why droops my Celia?
Thou hast in place of a base husband found 185
A worthy lover; use thy fortune well,
With secrecy and pleasure. See, behold,

[*Pointing to his treasure.*]

What thou art queen of; not in expectation,
As I feed others, but possessed and crowned.
See, here, a rope of pearl, and each more orient 190
Than that the brave Egyptian queen caroused;°
Dissolve and drink 'em. See, a carbuncle°
May put out both the eyes of° our Saint Mark;
A diamond would have bought Lollia Paulina°
When she came in like star-light, hid with jewels 195
That were the spoils of provinces; take these,
And wear, and lose 'em; yet remains an earring
To purchase them again, and this whole state.
A gem but worth a private patrimony°
Is nothing; we will eat such at a meal. 200
The heads of parrots, tongues of nightingales,
The brains of peacocks, and of estriches
Shall be our food, and, could we get the phoenix,
Though nature lost her kind,° she were our dish.

CELIA Good sir, these things might move a mind affected 205
With such delights; but I, whose innocence
Is all I can think wealthy, or worth th' enjoying,
And which, once lost, I have nought to lose beyond it,
Cannot be taken with these sensual baits.
If you have conscience— 210

---

136. **cause of life:** i.e., honor of marriage. **144. cope-man:** merchant. **151. practice:** plotting. **153. horned flood:** Achelous, the river god who changes his shape just as the sea god Proteus does. **161. Valois:** Henry III of France, who visited Venice in 1574. **162. Antinous:** handsome youth favored by the Roman emperor Hadrian. **165. prove:** try.

183. **serene:** poisonous fog. **191. brave . . . caroused:** Cleopatra is supposed to have dissolved pearls in vinegar at a banquet. **192. carbuncle:** ruby. **193. May . . . of:** outshining. **194. Lollia Paulina:** wife of the Roman emperor Caligula. **199. private patrimony:** single inheritance. **204. kind:** species.

VOLPONE   'Tis the beggar's virtue;
If thou hast wisdom, hear me, Celia.
Thy baths shall be the juice of July-flowers,°
Spirit of roses, and of violets,
The milk of unicorns, and panthers' breath   214
Gathered in bags and mixed with Cretan wines.
Our drink shall be preparèd gold and amber,
Which we will take until my roof whirl round
With the vertigo; and my dwarf shall dance,
My eunuch sing, my fool make up the antic.
Whilst we, in changèd shapes, act Ovid's tales,°
Thou like Europa now, and I like Jove,   221
Then I like Mars, and thou like Erycine;°
So of the rest, till we have quite run through,
And wearied all the fables of the gods.   224
Then will I have thee in more modern forms,
Attirèd like some sprightly dame of France,
Brave Tuscan lady, or proud Spanish beauty;
Sometimes unto the Persian Sophy's° wife,
Or the Grand Signior's° mistress; and, for
    change,
To one of our most artful courtesans,   230
Or some quick Negro, or cold Russian;
And I will meet thee in as many shapes;
Where we may, so, transfuse our wand'ring souls
                         [Kissing her.]
Out at our lips and score up sums of pleasures,
    That the curious shall not know   235
    How to tell° them as they flow;
    And the envious, when they find
    What their number is, be pined.
CELIA If you have ears that will be pierced, or
    eyes   239
That can be opened, a heart may be touched,
Or any part that yet sounds man° about you;
If you have touch of holy saints, or heaven,
Do me the grace to let me 'scape. If not,
Be bountiful and kill me. You do know
I am a creature hither ill betrayed   245
By one whose shame I would forget it were.
If you will deign me neither of these graces,
Yet feed your wrath, sir, rather than your lust,
It is a vice comes nearer manliness,
And punish that unhappy crime of nature,   250
Which you miscall my beauty: flay my face,
Or poison it with ointments for seducing

212. **July-flowers:** gillyflowers, of the mustard or the pink
family. **220. Ovid's tales:** *The Metamorphoses.* **222. Erycine:**
Venus. **228. Sophy:** Shah. **229. Grand Signior:** Sultan of
Turkey. **236. tell:** count. **241. sounds man:** i.e., more than
a beast.

Your blood to this rebellion. Rub these hands
With what may cause an eating leprosy,
E'en to my bones and marrow; anything   255
That may disfavor me, save in my honor,
And I will kneel to you, pray for you, pay down
A thousand hourly vows, sir, for your health;
Report, and think you virtuous—
VOLPONE   Think me cold,
Frozen, and impotent, and so report me?   260
That I had Nestor's hernia° thou wouldst think.
I do degenerate and abuse my nation
To play with opportunity thus long;
I should have done the act, and then have
    parleyed.
Yield, or I'll force thee. [*He seizes her.*]   265
CELIA   O! just God!
VOLPONE   In vain—
BONARIO Forbear, foul ravisher! libidinous swine!
[*He leaps out from where* MOSCA *had placed him.*]
Free the forced lady, or thou diest, impostor.
But that I am loth to snatch thy punishment
Out of the hand of justice, thou shouldst yet
Be made the timely sacrifice of vengeance,   270
Before this altar, and this dross, thy idol.
                    [*Points to the gold.*]
Lady, let's quit the place, it is the den
Of villainy; fear nought, you have a guard;
And he ere long shall meet his just reward.   274
                    [*Exeunt* BONARIO *and* CELIA.]
VOLPONE Fall on me, roof, and bury me in ruin!
Become my grave, that wert my shelter! O!
I am unmasked, unspirited, undone,
Betrayed to beggary, to infamy—

                    SCENE VIII

            [*Enter* MOSCA, *bleeding.*]
MOSCA Where shall I run, most wretched shame
    of men,
To beat out my unlucky brains?
VOLPONE   Here, here.
What! dost thou bleed?
MOSCA   Oh, that his well-driven sword
Had been so courteous to have cleft me down
Unto the navel, ere I lived to see   5
My life, my hopes, my spirits, my patron, all
Thus desperately engagèd by my error.
VOLPONE Woe on thy fortune!
MOSCA   And my follies, sir.

261. Nestor's hernia: an old man's impotence.

VOLPONE   Th' hast made me miserable.

MOSCA   And myself, sir.
Who would have thought he would have
hearkened so?   10

VOLPONE   What shall we do?

MOSCA   I know not; if my heart
Could expiate the mischance, I'd pluck it out.
Will you be pleased to hang me, or cut my
throat?
And I'll requite you, sir. Let's die like Romans,°
Since we have lived like Grecians.°   15
              [*They knock without.*]

VOLPONE   Hark! who's there?
I hear some footing;° officers, the *saffi,*°
Come to apprehend us! I do feel the brand
Hissing already at my forehead; now,
Mine ears are boring.°

MOSCA   To your couch, sir; you
Make that place good, however.° Guilty men   20
              [VOLPONE *lies down.*]
Suspect what they deserve still.° [MOSCA *opens
door.*] Signior Corbaccio!

                    SCENE IX

              [*Enter* CORBACCIO.]

CORBACCIO   Why, how now, Mosca?

MOSCA   Oh, undone, amazed, sir.
Your son, I know not by what accident,
Acquainted with your purpose to my patron,
Touching your will, and making him your heir,
Entered our house with violence, his sword
drawn,   5
Sought for you, called you wretch, unnatural,
Vowed he would kill you.

CORBACCIO   Me?

MOSCA   Yes, and my patron.

CORBACCIO   This act shall disinherit him indeed.
Here is the will.

MOSCA   'Tis well, sir.

CORBACCIO   Right and well.
Be you as careful now for me.
              [*Enter* VOLTORE *behind.*]

MOSCA   My life, sir,   10
Is not more tendered;° I am only yours.

CORBACCIO   How does he? Will he die shortly,
thinkst thou?

MOSCA   I fear
He'll outlast May.

CORBACCIO   Today?

MOSCA   [*Shouting*]   No, last out May, sir.

CORBACCIO   Couldst thou not gi' him a dram?

MOSCA   Oh, by no means, sir.

CORBACCIO   Nay, I'll not bid you.   15

VOLTORE   [*Stepping forward*] This is a knave, I see.

MOSCA   [*Aside*] How! Signior Voltore! Did he
hear me?

VOLTORE   Parasite!

MOSCA   Who's that? Oh, sir, most timely welcome.

VOLTORE   Scarce
To° the discovery of your tricks, I fear.
You are his, only? And mine, also, are you not?
[CORBACCIO *wanders to the side of the stage, and
              stands there.*]

MOSCA   Who? I, sir?   20

VOLTORE   You, sir. What device is this
About a will?

MOSCA   A plot for you, sir.

VOLTORE   Come,
Put not your foists° upon me; I shall scent 'em.

MOSCA   Did you not hear it?

VOLTORE   Yes, I hear Corbaccio
Hath made your patron, there, his heir.

MOSCA   'Tis true,
By my device, drawn to it by my plot,   25
With hope—

VOLTORE   Your patron should reciprocate?
And you have promised?

MOSCA   For your good I did, sir.
Nay, more, I told his son, brought, hid him here,
Where he might hear his father pass the deed;
Being persuaded to it by this thought, sir: 30
That the unnaturalness, first, of the act,
And then his father's oft disclaiming in him,
Which I did mean t' help on, would sure enrage
him
To do some violence upon his parent.
On which the law should take sufficient hold, 35
And you be stated° in a double hope.°
Truth be my comfort, and my conscience,
My only aim was to dig you a fortune
Out of these two old, rotten sepulchres—

Scene viii. **14. like Romans:** by suicide. **15. like Grecians:** luxuriously. **16. footing:** footsteps. **saffi:** police. **19.
boring:** being cut out, a common punishment for criminals.
20. however: whatever happens. **21. still:** always.
Scene ix. **11. tendered:** watched over.

18. To: because of. **22. foists:** tricks (also farts). **36. stated:**
set up. **double hope:** two fortunes.

VOLTORE I cry thee mercy, Mosca. 40
MOSCA   Worth your patience,
  And your great merit, sir. And see the change!
VOLTORE Why, what success?
MOSCA   Most hapless! you must help, sir.
  Whilst we expected th' old raven, in comes
  Corvino's wife, sent hither by her husband—
VOLTORE What, with a present? 45
MOSCA   No, sir, on visitation;
  I'll tell you how anon—and staying long,
  The youth he grows impatient, rushes forth,
  Seizeth the lady, wounds me, makes her swear—
  Or he would murder her, that was his vow—
  T' affirm my patron to have done her rape, 50
  Which how unlike it is, you see! and hence,
  With that pretext he's gone t' accuse his father,
  Defame my patron, defeat you—
VOLTORE   Where's her husband?
  Let him be sent for straight.
MOSCA   Sir, I'll go fetch him.
VOLTORE Bring him to the *Scrutineo*.° 55
MOSCA   Sir, I will.
VOLTORE This must be stopped.
MOSCA   Oh, you do nobly, sir.
  Alas, 'twas labored all, sir, for your good;
  Nor was there want of counsel in the plot.
  For Fortune can, at any time, o'erthrow
  The projects of a hundred learned clerks,° sir.
CORBACCIO What's that? 61
[*Suddenly becoming aware that others are present.*]
VOLTORE [*To* CORBACCIO]
                Will 't please you, sir, to go along?
                [*Exeunt* CORBACCIO *and* VOLTORE.]
MOSCA [*To* VOLPONE] Patron, go in and pray for
  our success.
VOLPONE Need makes devotion; heaven your
  labor bless!

ACT IV

SCENE I. *A street in Venice.*

[*Enter* SIR POLITIC *and* PEREGRINE.]
SIR POLITIC I told you, sir, it was a plot; you see
  What observation is! You mentioned° me
  For some instructions; I will tell you, sir,
  Since we are met here in this height of Venice,

Some few particulars I have set down 5
  Only for this meridian, fit to be known
  Of your crude° traveler; and they are these.
  I will not touch, sir, at your phrase,° or clothes,
  For they are old.
PEREGRINE   Sir, I have better.
SIR POLITIC   Pardon,
  I meant as they are themes.
PEREGRINE   Oh, sir, proceed. 10
  I'll slander you no more of wit, good sir.
SIR POLITIC First, for your garb,° it must be grave
    and serious,
  Very reserved and locked; not tell a secret
  On any terms, not to your father; scarce
  A fable but with caution; make sure choice 15
  Both of your company and discourse; beware
  You never speak a truth—
PEREGRINE   How!
SIR POLITIC   Not to strangers,
  For those be they you must converse with most;
  Others I would not know, sir, but at distance,
  So as I still might be a saver in 'em.° 20
  You shall have tricks, else, passed upon you
    hourly.
  And then, for your religion, profess none,
  But wonder at the diversity of all;
  And, for your part, protest were there no other
  But simply the laws o' th' land, you could
    content you. 25
  Nick Machiavel° and Monsieur Bodin° both
  Were of this mind. Then must you learn the use
  And handling of your silver fork at meals,
  The metal° of your glass (these are main matters
  With your Italian), and to know the hour 30
  When you must eat your melons and your figs.
PEREGRINE Is that a point of state too?
SIR POLITIC   Here it is.
  For your Venetian, if he see a man
  Preposterous° in the least, he has him straight;°
  He has, he strips him. I'll acquaint you, sir. 35
  I now have lived here 'tis some fourteen months;
  Within the first week of my landing here,
  All took me for a citizen of Venice,
  I knew the forms so well—
PEREGRINE [*Aside*]   And nothing else.

7. crude: naive. **8. phrase:** manner of speaking. **12. garb:** conduct, bearing. **20. So . . . 'em:** to play it safe. **26. Nick Machiavel:** Niccolò Machiavelli (1467–1527), author of *The Prince.* **Bodin:** French political philosopher who advocated religious toleration. **29. metal:** material. **34. Preposterous:** incorrect (in observing customs). **straight:** at once.

55. Scrutineo: Senate House. **60. clerks:** scholars.
Act IV, scene i. **2. mentioned:** called on.

SIR POLITIC   I had read Contarini,° took me a
house,   40
Dealt with my Jews to furnish it with movables—
Well, if I could but find one man, one man
To mine own heart, whom I durst trust, I
would—

PEREGRINE   What, what, sir?

SIR POLITIC   Make him rich, make him a fortune:
He should not think again. I would command it.

PEREGRINE   As how?   46

SIR POLITIC   With certain projects that I have,
Which I may not discover.°

PEREGRINE   [Aside]   If I had
But one to wager with, I would lay odds, now,
He tells me instantly.

SIR POLITIC   One is, and that   49
I care not greatly who knows, to serve the state
Of Venice with red herrings for three years,
And at a certain rate, from Rotterdam,
Where I have correspondence. There's a letter
    [Showing a greasy sheet of paper.]
Sent me from one o' th' States,° and to that
purpose;
He cannot write his name, but that's his mark.

PEREGRINE   He is a chandler?°   56

SIR POLITIC   No, a cheesemonger.
There are some other too with whom I treat
About the same negotiation;
And I will undertake it: for 'tis thus
I'll do 't with ease, I've cast° it all. Your hoy° 60
Carries but three men in her, and a boy;
And she shall make me three returns a year.
So, if there come but one of three, I save;
If two, I can defalk.° But this is now
If my main project fail.   65

PEREGRINE   Then you have others?

SIR POLITIC   I should be loath to draw the subtle
air
Of such a place without my thousand aims.
I'll not dissemble, sir; where'er I come
I love to be considerative, and 'tis true
I have at my free hours thought upon   70
Some certain goods unto the state of Venice,
Which I do call my cautions;° and, sir, which
I mean, in hope of pension, to propound

To the Great Council, then unto the Forty,
So to the Ten.° My means are made already—

PEREGRINE   By whom?   76

SIR POLITIC   Sir, one that though his
place be obscure,
Yet he can sway, and they will hear him. He's
A commendatore.

PEREGRINE   What, a common sergeant?

SIR POLITIC   Sir, such as they are put it in their
mouths
What they should say, sometimes, as well as
greater.°   80
I think I have my notes to show you—
    [Searching his pockets.]

PEREGRINE   Good sir.

SIR POLITIC   But you shall swear unto me, on your
gentry,
Not to anticipate—

PEREGRINE   I, sir?

SIR POLITIC   Nor reveal
A circumstance—My paper is not with me.

PEREGRINE   Oh, but you can remember, sir.

SIR POLITIC   My first is 85
Concerning tinderboxes. You must know
No family is here without its box.
Now, sir, it being so portable a thing,
Put case° that you or I were ill affected
Unto the state; sir, with it in our pockets   90
Might not I go into the Arsenal?
Or you? Come out again? And none the wiser?

PEREGRINE   Except yourself, sir.

SIR POLITIC   Go to, then. I therefore
Advertise to the state how fit it were
That none but such as were known patriots,   95
Sound lovers of their country, should be suffered
T'enjoy them in their houses; and even those
Sealed at some office, and at such a bigness
As might not lurk in pockets.

PEREGRINE   Admirable!

SIR POLITIC   My next is, how t'inquire, and be
resolved   100
By present demonstration,° whether a ship
Newly arrivèd from Syria, or from
Any suspected part of all the Levant,
Be guilty of the plague. And where they use
To lie out forty, fifty days, sometimes,   105

---

40. Contarini: Cardinal Contarini, who wrote a book on
Venice that was translated into English in 1599. **47. discover:**
disclose. **54. States:** Low Countries. **56. chandler:** candle
seller (because the letter is so greasy). **60. cast:** calculated.
hoy: Dutch coastal vessel. **64. defalk:** make reductions. **72.
cautions:** precautions.

74–75. Great . . . Ten: governing bodies of Venice, in order
of importance. **79–80. such . . . greater:** to influence important people, it is sometimes necessary to use their
subordinates. **89. Put case:** assume. **101. present demonstration:** immediate inspection.

About the *Lazaretto*° for their trial,
I'll save that charge and loss unto the merchant,
And in an hour clear the doubt.

PEREGRINE   Indeed, sir!

SIR POLITIC   Or—I will lose my labor.

PEREGRINE   My faith, that's much.

SIR POLITIC   Nay, sir, conceive me. 'Twill cost me,
   in onions,   110
Some thirty livres—

PEREGRINE   Which is one pound sterling.

SIR POLITIC   Beside my waterworks. For this I do,
   sir:
First, I bring in your ship 'twixt two brick walls—
But those the state shall venture. On the one
I strain me a fair tarpaulin, and in that   115
I stick my onions, cut in halves; the other
Is full of loopholes, out at which I thrust
The noses of my bellows; and those bellows
I keep, with waterworks, in perpetual motion,
Which is the easiest matter of a hundred.   120
Now, sir, your onion, which doth naturally
Attract th' infection, and your bellows blowing
The air upon him, will show instantly
By his changed color if there be contagion,
Or else remain as fair as at the first.   125
Now 'tis known, 'tis nothing.

PEREGRINE   You are right, sir.

SIR POLITIC   I would I had my note.
                 [*Searching his pockets.*]

PEREGRINE   Faith, so would I.
But you ha' done well for once, sir.

SIR POLITIC   Were I false,°
Or would be made so, I could show you reasons
How I could sell this state, now, to the Turk—
Spite of their galleys, or their—   131
     [*Still frantically searching his pocket.*]

PEREGRINE   Pray you, Sir Pol.

SIR POLITIC   I have 'em not about me.

PEREGRINE   That I feared.
They're there, sir?
     [*Pulling a book from* SIR POL's *pocket.*]

SIR POLITIC   No, this is my diary,
Wherein I note my actions of the day.

PEREGRINE   Pray you let's see, sir. What is here?
—"*Notandum,*   135
A rat had gnawn my spur leathers; notwith-
   standing,
I put on new and did go forth; but first
I threw three beans over the threshold. Item,

106. **Lazaretto:** a quarantine hospital. **128. false:** traitorous.

I went and bought two toothpicks, whereof one
I burst, immediately, in a discourse   140
With a Dutch merchant 'bout *ragion del stato.*°
From him I went and paid a *moccenigo*
For piecing my silk stockings; by the way
I cheapened° sprats, and at Saint Mark's I
   urined."
Faith, these are politic notes!

SIR POLITIC   Sir, I do slip   145
No action of my life, thus but I quote it.

PEREGRINE   Believe me it is wise!

SIR POLITIC   Nay, sir, read forth.

SCENE II

[*Enter* LADY WOULDBE, NANO, *and two* WOMEN.]

LADY WOULDBE   Where should this loose° knight
   be, trow? Sure, he's housed.

NANO   Why, then he's fast.°

LADY WOULDBE   Aye, he plays both° with me.
I pray you stay. This heat will do more harm
To my complexion than his heart is worth.
I do not care to hinder, but to take him.   5
How it comes off! [*Rubbing her make-up.*]

FIRST WOMAN   My master's yonder. [*Pointing.*]

LADY WOULDBE   Where?

SECOND WOMAN   With a young gentleman.

LADY WOULDBE   That same's the party!
In man's apparel! Pray you, sir, jog my knight.
I will be tender to his reputation,
However he demerit.°

SIR POLITIC   My lady!

PEREGRINE   Where?   10

SIR POLITIC   'Tis she indeed; sir, you shall know
   her. She is,
Were she not mine, a lady of that merit
For fashion, and behavior, and for beauty
I durst compare—

PEREGRINE   It seems you are not jealous,
That dare commend her.   15

SIR POLITIC   Nay, and for discourse—

PEREGRINE   Being your wife, she cannot miss that.
              [*The parties join.*]

SIR POLITIC   Madam,
Here is a gentleman; pray you, use him fairly;
He seems a youth, but he is—

141. **ragion del stato:** politics. **144. cheapened:** bargained
for.
   Scene ii. **1. loose:** lascivious. **2. fast:** safe. **both:** i.e.,
fast and loose. **10. demerit:** does not deserve it.

LADY WOULDBE None?

SIR POLITIC Yes, one
Has put his face as soon into the world—

LADY WOULDBE You mean, as early? But today?

SIR POLITIC How's this? 20

LADY WOULDBE Why, in this habit,° sir; you
apprehend me!
Well, Master Wouldbe, this doth not become
you.
I had thought the odor, sir, of your good name
Had been more precious to you; that you would
not
Have done this dire massàcre on your honor, 25
One of your gravity, and rank besides!
But knights, I see, care little for the oath
They make to ladies, chiefly their own ladies.

SIR POLITIC Now, by my spurs, the symbol of my
knighthood—

PEREGRINE [Aside] Lord, how his brain is
humbled° for an oath! 30

SIR POLITIC I reach° you not.

LADY WOULDBE Right sir, your policy
May bear it through thus. [To PEREGRINE.] Sir, a
word with you,
I would be loath to contest publicly
With any gentlewoman, or to seem
Froward,° or violent, as The Courtier° says. 35
It comes too near rusticity in a lady,
Which I would shun by all means. And, however
I may deserve from Master Wouldbe, yet
T' have one fair gentlewoman, thus, be made
Th'unkind instrument to wrong another, 40
And one she knows not, ay, and to persèver,
In my poor judgment, is not warranted
From being a solecism° in our sex,
If not in manners.

PEREGRINE How is this!

SIR POLITIC Sweet madam,
Come nearer to your aim. 45

LADY WOULDBE Marry, and will, sir.
Since you provoke me with your impudence
And laughter of your light° land-siren here,
Your Sporus,° your hermaphrodite—

PEREGRINE What's here?
Poetic fury and historic storms!

SIR POLITIC The gentleman, believe it, is of worth,
And of our nation. 51

LADY WOULDBE Aye, your Whitefriars° nation!
Come, I blush for you, Master Wouldbe, aye;
And am ashamed you should ha' no more
forehead°
Than thus to be the patron, or Saint George,
To a lewd harlot, a base fricatrice,° 55
A female devil in a male outside.

SIR POLITIC Nay,
And° you be such a one, I must bid adieu
To your delights. The case appears too liquid.°
[Exit.]

LADY WOULDBE Aye, you may carry't clear, with
your state-face!°
But for your carnival concupiscence, 60
Who here is fled for liberty of conscience,
From furious persecution of the marshal,°
Her will I disc'ple.°

PEREGRINE This is fine, i'faith!
And do you use this often? Is this part
Of your wit's exercise, 'gainst you have
occasion?° 65
Madam—

LADY WOULDBE Go to sir.

PEREGRINE Do you hear me, lady?
Why, if your knight have set you to beg shirts,
Or to invite me home, you might have done it
A nearer° way by far.

LADY WOULDBE This cannot work you
Out of my snare.

PEREGRINE Why, am I in it, then? 70
Indeed, your husband told me you were fair,
And so you are; only your nose inclines—
That side that's next the sun—to the queen-
apple.°

LADY WOULDBE This cannot be endured by any
patience.

SCENE III

[Enter MOSCA.]

MOSCA What's the matter, madam?

LADY WOULDBE If the Senate

---

21. habit: i.e., dressed as a man. **30. humbled:** brought low. **31. reach:** understand. **35. Froward:** perverse. **the courtier:** Castiglione's *The Courtier* (1528), a guide to proper behavior at court (translated into English in 1561). **43. solecism:** impropriety. **47. light:** immoral. **48. Sporus:** Nero's eunuch.

51. Whitefriars: i.e., criminal (referring to a bad section of London). **53. forehead:** shame. **55. fricatrice:** prostitute. **57. And:** if. **58. liquid:** clear. **59. state-face:** solemn manner. **60–62. But . . . marshal:** applies to both husband and supposed prostitute in the confused manner of Lady Wouldbe. **63. disc'ple:** discipline. **65. 'gainst . . . occasion:** i.e., to keep in practice. **69. nearer:** more direct. **73. queen-apple:** bright red.

Right not my quest° in this, I will protest 'em
To all the world no aristocracy.
MOSCA   What is the injury, lady?
LADY WOULDBE   Why, the callet°
You told me of, I have ta'en disguised.   5
MOSCA   Who? This! What means your ladyship?
The creature
I mentioned to you is apprehended, now
Before the Senate. You shall see her—
LADY WOULDBE   Where?
MOSCA   I'll bring you to her. This young gentle-
man,
I saw him land this morning at the port.   10
LADY WOULDBE   Is 't possible? How has my
judgment wandered!
Sir, I must, blushing, say to you, I have erred;
And plead your pardon.
PEREGRINE   What, more changes yet?
LADY WOULDBE   I hope y' ha' not the malice to
remember
A gentlewoman's passion. If you stay   15
In Venice, here, please you to use° me, sir—
MOSCA   Will you go, madam?
LADY WOULDBE   Pray you, sir, use me. In faith,
The more you see me, the more I shall conceive
You have forgot our quarrel.   [Exeunt
        LADY WOULDBE, MOSCA, NANO, and WOMEN.]
PEREGRINE   This is rare!
Sir Politic Wouldbe? No, Sir Politic Bawd,   20
To bring me, thus, acquainted with his wife!
Well, wise Sir Pol, since you have practiced thus
Upon my freshmanship, I'll try your salt-head,°
What proof it is against a counterplot.   [Exit.]

SCENE IV. *The Scrutineo, the Venetian court of
law.*

[*Enter* VOLTORE, CORBACCIO, CORVINO, *and* MOSCA.]
VOLTORE   Well, now you know the carriage° of the
business,
Your constancy is all that is required,
Unto the safety of it.
MOSCA   Is the lie
Safely conveyed amongst us? Is that sure?
Knows every man his burden?
CORVINO   Yes.   5

MOSCA   Then shrink not.
CORVINO   [*Aside to* MOSCA] But knows the advocate
the truth?
MOSCA   O sir,
By no means. I devised a formal tale°
That salved° your reputation. But be valiant, sir.
CORVINO   I fear no one but him, that this his
pleading
Should make him stand for a co-heir—   10
MOSCA   Co-halter!
Hang him, we will but use his tongue, his noise,
As we do Croaker's° here.
            [*Pointing to* CORBACCIO.]
CORVINO   Aye, what shall he do?
MOSCA   When we ha' done, you mean?
CORVINO   Yes.
MOSCA   Why, we'll think:
Sell him for mummia,° he's half dust already.
[*Turns away from* CORVINO *and speaks to* VOLTORE.]
Do not you smile to see this buffalo,°   15
How he doth sport it with his head?—I should,
If all were well and past. [*To* CORBACCIO.] Sir,
only you
Are he that shall enjoy the crop of all,
And these not know for whom they toil.
CORBACCIO   Aye, peace.
MOSCA   [*To* CORVINO] But you shall eat it.—
Much!—
            [*To* VOLTORE.] Worshipful sir,   20
Mercury° sit upon your thund'ring tongue,
Or the French Hercules,° and make your
language
As conquering as his club, to beat along,
As with a tempest, flat, our adversaries;
But much more yours, sir.   25
VOLTORE   Here they come, ha' done.
MOSCA   I have another witness if you need, sir,
I can produce.
VOLTORE   Who is it!
MOSCA   Sir, I have her.°

Scene iii.   **2. quest:** request, petition. **protest:** publish.
4. callet: prostitute. **16. use:** call on, make use of. **23. salt-
head:** experience.
Scene iv.   **1. carriage:** management.

7. formal tale: believable story. **8. salved:** saved. **12.
Croaker's:** Corbaccio's **14. mummia:** drug made from the
liquid that oozes from embalmed human bodies. **15.
buffalo:** i.e., with horns (cuckold). **21. Mercury:** in his
role as god of eloquence. **22. French Hercules:** also symbolic of eloquence. **27. her:** Lady Wouldbe.

SCENE V

[*Enter four* AVOCATORI, BONARIO, CELIA,
NOTARIO, COMMENDATORI, *and* OTHERS.]

FIRST AVOCATORE   The like of this the Senate never
heard of.

SECOND AVOCATORE   'Twill come most strange to
them when we report it.

FOURTH AVOCATORE   The gentlewoman has been
ever held
Of unreprovèd name.

THIRD AVOCATORE   So the young man.

FOURTH AVOCATORE   The more unnatural part,
that of his father.   5

SECOND AVOCATORE   More of the husband.

FIRST AVOCATORE   I not know to give
His act a name, it is so monstrous!

FOURTH AVOCATORE   But the impostor, he is a
thing created
T'exceed example.

FIRST AVOCATORE   And all after-times!

SECOND AVOCATORE   I never heard a true voluptu-
ary   10
Described but him.

THIRD AVOCATORE   Appear yet those were cited?°

NOTARIO   All but the old magnifico, Volpone.

FIRST AVOCATORE   Why is not he here?

MOSCA   Please your fatherhoods,°
Here is his advocate. Himself's so weak,
So feeble—

FOURTH AVOCATORE   What are you?   15

BONARIO   His parasite,
His knave, his pander! I beseech the court
He may be forced to come, that your grave eyes
May bear strong witness of his strange impos-
tures.

VOLTORE   Upon my faith and credit with your
virtues,
He is not able to endure the air.   20

SECOND AVOCATORE   Bring him, however.

THIRD AVOCATORE   We will see him.

FOURTH AVOCATORE   Fetch him.

VOLTORE   Your fatherhoods' fit pleasures be
obeyed,
But sure the sight will rather move your pities
Than indignation. May it please the court,
In the meantime he may be heard in me!   25
I know this place most void of prejudice,

And therefore crave it, since we have no reason
To fear our truth should hurt our cause.

THIRD AVOCATORE   Speak free.

VOLTORE   Then know, most honored fathers, I
must now
Discover to your strangely abusèd ears   30
The most prodigious and most frontless° piece
Of solid impudence, and treachery,
That ever vicious nature yet brought forth
To shame the state of Venice. This lewd woman,
[*pointing to* CELIA]
That wants° no artificial looks or tears   35
To help the visor she has now put on,
Hath long been known a close° adulteress
To that lascivious youth, there; [*pointing to*
BONARIO] not suspected,
I say, but known, and taken, in the act,
With him; and by this man, the easy husband,
[*pointing to* CORVINO]
Pardoned; whose timeless bounty° makes him
now   41
Stand here, the most unhappy, innocent person
That ever man's own goodness made accused.
For these, not knowing how to owe° a gift
Of that dear° grace but with their shame, being
placed   45
So above all powers of their gratitude,
Began to hate the benefit, and in place
Of thanks, devise t'extirp° the memory
Of such an act. Wherein, I pray your fatherhoods
To observe the malice, yea, the rage of creatures
Discovered in their evils; and what heart   51
Such take, even from their crimes. But that anon
Will more appear. This gentleman, the father,
[*pointing to* CORBACCIO]
Hearing of this foul fact,° with many others,
Which daily struck at his too tender ears,   55
And grieved in nothing more than that he could
not
Preserve himself a parent (his son's ills°
Growing to that strange flood) at last decreed
To disinherit him.

FIRST AVOCATORE   These be strange turns!°

SECOND AVOCATORE   The young man's fame was
ever fair and honest.   60

VOLTORE   So much more full of danger is his vice,

Scene v. **11. cited:** summoned. **13. fatherhoods:** conventional form of address to important civic officials.

31. frontless: shameless. **35. wants:** lacks. **37. close:** secret.
41. timeless bounty: untimely mercy. **44. owe:** value. **45.
dear:** rich, costly. **48. extirp:** eradicate. **54. fact:** crime.
57. ills: wrongdoings. **59. turns:** events.

That can beguile so under shade of virtue.
But as I said, my honored sires, his father
Having this settled purpose—by what means
To him betrayed, we know not—and this day 65
Appointed for the deed, that parricide,
I cannot style him better, by confederacy
Preparing this his paramour to be there,
Entered Volpone's house—who was the man,
Your fatherhoods must understand, designed 70
For the inheritance—there sought his father.
But with what purpose sought he him, my lords?
I tremble to pronounce it, that a son
Unto a father, and to such a father,
Should have so foul, felonious intent: 75
It was, to murder him! When, being prevented
By his more happy absence, what then did he?
Not check his wicked thoughts? No, now new
   deeds—
Mischief doth ever end where it begins—
An act of horror, fathers! He dragged forth 80
The agèd gentleman, that had there lain bed-rid
Three years, and more, out off his innocent
   couch,
Naked, upon the floor, there left him; wounded
His servant in the face; and, with this strumpet,
The stale to his forged practice,° who was glad
To be so active—I shall here desire   86
Your fatherhoods to note but my collections°
As most remarkable—thought at once to stop
His father's ends, discredit his free choice
In the old gentleman, redeem themselves   90
By laying infamy upon this man,
To whom, with blushing, they should owe their
   lives.
FIRST AVOCATORE   What proofs have you of this?
BONARIO   Most honored fathers,
   I humbly crave there be no credit given
   To this man's mercenary tongue.
SECOND AVOCATORE   Forbear.   95
BONARIO   His soul moves in his fee.
THIRD AVOCATORE   Oh, sir!
BONARIO   This fellow,
   For six sols° more would plead against his
     Maker.
FIRST AVOCATORE   You do forget yourself.
VOLTORE   Nay, nay, grave fathers,
   Let him have scope. Can any man imagine
   That he will spare's accuser, that would not 100

85. stale . . . practice: cover for his deception. 87. collections: evidence. 97. sols: coins of small value.

Have spared his parent?
FIRST AVOCATORE   Well, produce your proofs.
CELIA   I would I could forget I were a creature!°
VOLTORE   Signior Corbaccio!
FOURTH AVOCATORE   What is he?
VOLTORE   The father.
SECOND AVOCATORE   Has he had an oath?
NOTARIO   Yes.
CORBACCIO   What must I do now?
NOTARIO   Your testimony's craved.
CORBACCIO   [Cupping his ear] Speak to the knave?
   I'll ha' my mouth first stopped with earth. My
    heart   106
   Abhors his knowledge.° I disclaim in° him.
FIRST AVOCATORE   But for what cause?
CORBACCIO   The mere portent° of nature.
   He is an utter stranger to my loins.
BONARIO   Have they made° you to this?   110
CORBACCIO   I will not hear thee,
   Monster of men, swine, goat, wolf, parricide!
   Speak not, thou viper.
BONARIO   Sir, I will sit down,
   And rather wish my innocence should suffer,
   Than I resist the authority of a father.
VOLTORE   Signior Corvino!
SECOND AVOCATORE   This is strange.   115
FIRST AVOCATORE   Who's this?
NOTARIO   The husband.
FOURTH AVOCATORE   Is he sworn?
NOTARIO   He is.
THIRD AVOCATORE   Speak, then.
CORVINO   This woman, please your fatherhoods, is
   a whore
   Of most hot exercise, more than a partridge,°
   Upon record°—
FIRST AVOCATORE   No more.
CORVINO   Neighs like a jennet.
NOTARIO   Preserve the honor of the court.   120
CORVINO   I shall,
   And modesty of your most reverend ears.
   And, yet, I hope that I may say these eyes
   Have seen her glued unto that piece of cedar,
   That fine, well-timbered gallant, and that here°
    [tapping his forehead]
   The letters may be read, thorough the horn,° 125

102. a creature: alive. 107. his knowledge: knowing him. disclaim in: disown. 108. portent: monster. 110. made: deluded.
118. partridge: supposedly a lecherous bid. 119. Upon
record: generally known. 124. here: on his head (making a
V with his fingers). 125. horn: of the cuckold and the primer
(hornbook).

That make the story perfect.

MOSCA   Excellent, sir.

[MOSCA *and* CORVINO *whisper.*]

CORVINO   There is no shame in this now, is there?

MOSCA   None.

CORVINO   Or if I said I hoped that she were
    onward

To her damnation, if there be a hell

Greater than whore and woman;° a good
    Catholic   130

May make the doubt.°

THIRD AVOCATORE   His grief hath made him
    frantic.

FIRST AVOCATORE   Remove him hence.

[*She* (CELIA) *swoons.*]

SECOND AVOCATORE   Look to the woman.

CORVINO   Rare!

Prettily feigned! Again!

FOURTH AVOCATORE   Stand from about her.

FIRST AVOCATORE   Give her the air.

THIRD AVOCATORE   [*To* MOSCA] What can you say?

MOSCA   My wound,

May 't please your wisdoms, speaks for me,
    received   135

In aid of my good patron, when he missed

His sought-for father, when that well-taught
    dame

Had her cue given her to cry out a rape.

BONARIO   O most laid° impudence! Fathers—

THIRD AVOCATORE   Sir, be silent,

You had your hearing free, so must they theirs.

SECOND AVOCATORE   I do begin to doubt th'impos-
    ture here.   141

FOURTH AVOCATORE   This woman has too many
    moods.

VOLTORE   Grave fathers,

She is a creature of a most professed°

And prostituted lewdness.

CORVINO   Most impetuous,

Unsatisfied, grave fathers!

VOLTORE   May her feignings

Not take your wisdoms; but° this day she
    baited°   146

A stranger, a grave knight, with her loose eyes

And more lascivious kisses. This man saw 'em

Together on the water in a gondola.

MOSCA   Here is the lady herself that saw 'em too,

Without; who, then, had in the open streets 151

Pursued them, but for saving her knight's honor.

FIRST AVOCATORE   Produce that lady.

[MOSCA *beckons to the wings.*]

SECOND AVOCATORE   Let her come.

FOURTH AVOCATORE   These things.

They strike with wonder!

THIRD AVOCATORE   I am turned a stone!

SCENE VI

[*Enter* LADY WOULDBE.]

MOSCA   Be resolute, madam.

LADY WOULDBE   [*Pointing to* CELIA] Aye, this same
    is she.

Out, thou chameleon harlot! Now thine eyes

Vie tears with the hyena. Darst thou look

Upon my wrongèd face? I cry your pardons.

[*To the Court.*]

I fear I have forgettingly transgressed   5

Against the dignity of the court—

SECOND AVOCATORE   No, madam.

LADY WOULDBE   And been exorbitant°—

FOURTH AVOCATORE   You have not, lady.

These proofs are strong.

LADY WOULDBE   Surely, I had no purpose

To scandalize your honors, or my sex's.

THIRD AVOCATORE   We do believe it.   10

LADY WOULDBE   Surely, you may believe it.

SECOND AVOCATORE   Madam, we do.

LADY WOULDBE   Indeed, you may; my breeding

Is not so coarse—

FOURTH AVOCATORE   We know it.

LADY WOULDBE   To offend

With pertinacy°—

THIRD AVOCATORE   Lady—

LADY WOULDBE   Such a presence.

No, surely.

FIRST AVOCATORE   We well think it.

LADY WOULDBE   You may think it.

FIRST AVOCATORE   Let her o'ercome.° [*To* BONARIO.]

What witness have you   15

To make good your report?

BONARIO   Our consciences.

CELIA   And heaven, that never fails the innocent.

FOURTH AVOCATORE   These are no testimonies.

BONARIO   Not in your courts,

Where multitude and clamor overcomes.

---

130. **whore and woman**: i.e., a woman being a whore. **131.
make the doubt**: question. **139. laid**: calculated. **143. professed**: open. **146. but**: only. **baited**: enticed.

Scene vi. **7. exorbitant**: disorderly. **13. pertinacy**:
pertinacity. **15. o'ercome**: win the battle of compliments.

FIRST AVOCATORE   Nay, then you do wax insolent.
[VOLPONE *is brought in, as impotent.*]
VOLPONE   Here, here,   20
The testimony comes that will convince,
And put to utter dumbness their bold tongues.
See here, grave fathers, here's the ravisher,
The rider on men's wives, the great impostor,
The grand voluptuary! Do you not think   25
These limbs should affect venery?° Or these
   eyes
Covet a concubine? Pray you, mark these
   hands.
Are they not fit to stroke a lady's breasts?
Perhaps he doth dissemble!
BONARIO   So he does.
VOLTORE   Would you ha' him tortured?   30
BONARIO   I would have him proved.°
VOLTORE   Best try him, then, with goads, or
   burning irons;
Put him to the strappado.° I have heard
The rack hath cured the gout. Faith, give it
   him
And help him of° a malady; be courteous.
I'll undertake, before these honored fathers,   35
He shall have yet as many left diseases
As she has known adulterers, or thou strumpets.
O my most equal° hearers, if these deeds,
Acts of this bold and most exorbitant strain
May pass with sufferance, what one citizen   40
But owes the forfeit of his life, yea, fame,
To him that dares traduce him? Which of you
Are safe, my honored fathers? I would ask,
With leave of your grave fatherhoods, if their
   plot
Have any face or color like to truth?   45
Or if, unto the dullest nostril here,
It smell not rank and most abhorrèd slander?
I crave your care of this good gentleman,
Whose life is much endangered by their fable;
And as for them, I will conclude with this: 50
That vicious persons when they are hot and
   fleshed
In impious acts, their constancy° abounds:
Damned deeds are done with greatest confidence.
FIRST AVOCATORE   Take 'em to custody, and sever°
   them.   [CELIA *and* BONARIO *are taken out.*]

26. venery: lust. 30. proved: tested. 32. strappado: torture in
which a man with his arms tied behind him is hoisted by his
arms in order to dislocate his shoulders. 34. of: get rid of.
38. equal: just, judicious. 52. constancy: determination. 54.
sever: put them in separate cells.

SECOND AVOCATORE   'Tis pity two such prodigies
   should live.   55
FIRST AVOCATORE   Let the old gentleman be
   returned with care.
I'm sorry our credulity wronged him.
               [*Exeunt* OFFICERS *with* VOLPONE.]
FOURTH AVOCATORE   These are two creatures!
THIRD AVOCATORE   I have an earthquake in me!
SECOND AVOCATORE   Their shame, even in their
   cradles, fled their faces.
FOURTH AVOCATORE   [*To* VOLTORE] You've done a
   worthy service to the state, sir,   60
In their discovery.
FIRST AVOCATORE   You shall hear ere night
What punishment the court decrees upon 'em.
VOLTORE   We thank your fatherhoods.—
               [*Exeunt* COURT OFFICIALS.]
                              How like you it?
MOSCA   Rare.
I'd ha' your tongue, sir, tipped with gold for
   this;
I'd ha' you be the heir to the whole city;   65
The earth I'd have want men, ere you want
   living.
They're bound to erect your statue in Saint
   Mark's.
               [VOLTORE *moves to one side.*]
Signior Corvino, I would have you go
And show yourself, that you have conquered.
CORVINO   Yes.
MOSCA   It was much better that you should
   profess   70
Yourself a cuckold, thus, than that the other
Should have been proved.
CORVINO   Nay, I considered that.
Now, it is her fault.
MOSCA   Then, it had been yours.
CORVINO   True. I do doubt this advocate still.
MOSCA   I'faith,
You need not; I dare ease you of that care.   75
CORVINO   I trust thee, Mosca.
MOSCA   As your own soul, sir.
                              [*Exit* CORVINO.]
CORBACCIO   Mosca!
MOSCA   Now for your business, sir.
CORBACCIO   How! Ha' you business?
MOSCA   Yes, yours, sir.
CORBACCIO   Oh, none else?
MOSCA   None else, not I.
CORBACCIO   Be careful then.

MOSCA   Rest you with both your eyes,° sir.
CORBACCIO   Dispatch it.
MOSCA   Instantly.   80
CORBACCIO   And look that all
   Whatever be put in: jewels, plate, moneys,
   Household stuff, bedding, curtains.
MOSCA   Curtain-rings, sir;
   Only the advocate's fee must be deducted.
CORBACCIO   I'll pay him now; you'll be too
   prodigal.
MOSCA   Sir, I must tender it.   85
CORBACCIO   Two chequins is well?
MOSCA   No, six, sir.
CORBACCIO   'Tis too much.
MOSCA   He talked a great while,
   You must consider that, sir.
CORBACCIO   Well, there's three—
MOSCA   I'll give it him.
CORBACCIO   Do so, and there's for thee.
          [Gives MOSCA money and exits.]
MOSCA   Bountiful bones! What horrid, strange
   offense
   Did he commit 'gainst nature in his youth,   90
   Worthy this age? [To VOLTORE.] You see, sir,
   how I work
   Unto your ends; take you no notice.
VOLTORE   No,
   I'll leave you.
MOSCA   All is yours, [exit VOLTORE] —the
   devil and all,
   Good advocate!— [To LADY WOULDBE.] Madam,
   I'll bring you home.
LADY WOULDBE   No, I'll go see your patron.   95
MOSCA   That you shall not.
   I'll tell you why: my purpose is to urge
   My patron to reform his will, and for
   The zeal you've shown today, whereas before
   You were but third or fourth, you shall be now
   Put in the first; which would appear as begged
   If you were present. Therefore—   101
LADY WOULDBE   You shall sway me.
          [Exeunt.]

---

79. Rest . . . eyes: Leave it to me.

ACT V

SCENE I. VOLPONE's house.

[Enter VOLPONE.]

VOLPONE   Well, I am here, and all this brunt° is
   past.
   I ne'er was in dislike with my disguise
   Till this fled moment. Here, 'twas good, in
   private,
   But in your public—Cave,° whilst I breathe.   4
   'Fore God, my left leg 'gan to have the cramp,
   And I apprehended, straight, some power had
   struck me
   With a dead palsy. Well, I must be merry
   And shake it off. A many of these fears
   Would put me into some villainous disease
   Should they come thick upon me. I'll prevent
   'em.   10
   Give me a bowl of lusty wine to fright
   This humor from my heart. Hum, hum, hum!
          [He drinks.]
   'Tis almost gone already; I shall conquer.
   Any device, now, of rare, ingenious knavery
   That would possess me with a violent laughter,
   Would make me up° again. So, so, so, so.   16
          [Drinks again.]
   This heat is life; 'tis blood by this time! Mosca!

SCENE II

[Enter MOSCA.]

MOSCA   How now, sir? Does the day look clear
   again?
   Are we recovered? and wrought out of error
   Into our way, to see our path before us?
   Is our trade free once more?
VOLPONE   Exquisite Mosca!
MOSCA   Was it not carried learnedly?
VOLPONE   And stoutly.   5
   Good wits are greatest in extremities.
MOSCA   It were a folly beyond thought to trust
   Any grand act unto a cowardly spirit.
   You are not taken with it enough, methinks?
VOLPONE   Oh, more than if I had enjoyed the
   wench.   10
   The pleasure of all womankind's not like it.

Act V, scene i. 1. brunt: confusion, danger. 4. Cave:
beware. 16. make me up: restore me.

MOSCA Why, now you speak, sir! We must here be fixed;

Here we must rest. This is our masterpiece;
We cannot think to go beyond this.

VOLPONE   True,
Th'ast played thy prize, my precious Mosca. 15

MOSCA   Nay, sir,
To gull the court—

VOLPONE   And quite divert the torrent
Upon the innocent.

MOSCA   Yes, and to make
So rare a music out of discords—

VOLPONE   Right.
That yet to me 's the strangest; how th'ast borne° it!

That these, being so divided 'mongst themselves,
Should not scent somewhat, or in me or° thee,
Or doubt their own side.   22

MOSCA   True, they will not see 't.
Too much light° blinds 'em, I think. Each of 'em
Is so possessed and stuffed with his own hopes
That anything unto the contrary,   25
Never so true, or never so apparent,
Never so palpable, they will resist it—

VOLPONE   Like a temptation of the devil.

MOSCA   Right, sir.
Merchants may talk of trade, and your great signiors

Of land that yields well; but if Italy   30
Have any glebe° more fruitful than these fellows,
I am deceived. Did not your advocate rare?°

VOLPONE   O—"My most honored fathers, my grave fathers,

Under correction of your fatherhoods,
What face of truth is here? If these strange deeds   35

May pass, most honored fathers"—I had much ado
To forbear laughing.

MOSCA   'T seemed to me you sweat, sir.

VOLPONE   In troth, I did a little.

MOSCA   But confess, sir;
Were you not daunted?

VOLPONE   In good faith, I was
A little in a mist, but not dejected;   40
Never but still myself.

MOSCA   I think it, sir.
Now, so truth help me, I must needs say this, sir,

And out of conscience for your advocate:
He's taken pains, in faith, sir, and deserved,
In my poor judgment, I speak it under favor, 45
Not to contrary you, sir, very richly—
Well—to be cozened.°

VOLPONE   Troth, and I think so too,
By that I heard him in the latter end.°

MOSCA Oh, but before, sir, had you heard him first

Draw it to certain heads,° then aggravate,°   50
Then use his vehement figures°—I looked still°
When he would shift° a shirt; and doing this
Out of pure love, no hope of gain—

VOLPONE   'Tis right.
I cannot answer° him, Mosca, as I would,
Not yet; but for thy sake, at any entreaty,   55
I will begin e'en now to vex 'em all,
This very instant.

MOSCA   Good, sir.

VOLPONE   Call the dwarf
And eunuch forth.

MOSCA   Castrone! Nano!

[Enter CASTRONE and NANO.]

NANO   Here.

VOLPONE   Shall we have a jig now?

MOSCA   What you please, sir.

VOLPONE   Go,
Straight give out about the streets, you two, 60
That I am dead; do it with constancy,
Sadly,° do you hear? Impute it to the grief
Of this late slander.

[Exeunt CASTRONE and NANO.]

MOSCA   What do you mean, sir?

VOLPONE   Oh,
I shall have instantly my vulture, crow,
Raven, come flying hither on the news   65
To peck for carrion, my she-wolf and all,
Greedy and full of expectation—

MOSCA And then to have it ravished from their mouths?

VOLPONE   'Tis true. I will ha' thee put on a gown,
And take upon thee as thou wert mine heir; 70
Show 'em a will. Open that chest and reach
Forth one of those that has the blanks. I'll straight
Put in thy name.

Scene ii. **19. borne:** managed. **21. or . . . or:** either . . . or. **23. light:** greed. **31. glebe:** soil. **32. rare:** rarely.

47. cozened: tricked. **48. By . . . end:** Judging by the tail end of his speech, which I heard. **50. heads:** topics. **aggravate:** emphasize. **51. figures:** figures of speech. **still:** constantly. **52. shift:** change. **54. answer:** repay. **62. Sadly:** gravely, seriously.

MOSCA   It will be rare, sir.

VOLPONE   Aye,
When they e'en gape, and find themselves
    deluded—

MOSCA Yes.   75

VOLPONE   And thou use them scurvily! Dispatch,
Get on thy gown.

MOSCA   But what, sir, if they ask
After the body?

VOLPONE   Say it was corrupted.

MOSCA I'll say it stunk, sir; and was fain t' have it
Coffined up instantly and sent away.

VOLPONE Anything, what thou wilt. Hold, here's
    my will.   80
Get thee a cap, a count-book, pen and ink,
Papers afore thee; sit as thou wert taking
An inventory of parcels. I'll get up
Behind the curtain, on a stool, and hearken;
Sometime peep over, see how they do look,   85
With what degrees their blood doth leave their
    faces.
Oh, 'twill afford me a rare meal of laughter!

MOSCA Your advocate will turn stark dull upon it.

VOLPONE   It will take off his oratory's edge.

MOSCA But your *clarissimo*,° old round-back,° he
Will crump you° like a hog-louse with the
    touch.   91

VOLPONE   And what Corvino?

MOSCA   O sir, look for him
Tomorrow morning with a rope and dagger
To visit all the streets; he must run mad.
My lady too, that came into the court   95
To bear false witness for your worship—

VOLPONE   Yes,
And kissed me 'fore the fathers, when my face
Flowed all with oils—

MOSCA   And sweat, sir. Why, your gold
Is such another med'cine, it dries up
All those offensive savors! It transforms   100
The most deformèd, and restores 'em lovely
As 'twere the strange poetical girdle.° Jove
                            [*Cestus.*]
Could not invent t' himself a shroud more subtle
To pass Acrisius'° guards. It is the thing
Makes° all the world her grace, her youth, her
    beauty.   105

VOLPONE I think she loves me.

MOSCA   Who? The lady, sir?
She's jealous of you.

VOLPONE   Dost thou say so?
                [*Knocking without.*]

MOSCA   Hark,
There's some already.

VOLPONE   Look!

MOSCA [*Peering out*]   It is the vulture;
He has the quickest scent.

VOLPONE   I'll to my place,
Thou to thy posture.

MOSCA   I am set.

VOLPONE   But Mosca,   110
Play the artificer now, torture 'em rarely.

SCENE III

[*Enter* VOLTORE.]

VOLTORE How now, my Mosca?

MOSCA [*Writing*]   Turkey carpets, nine—

VOLTORE Taking an inventory? That is well.

MOSCA Two suits of bedding, tissue—

VOLTORE   Where's the will?
Let me read that the while.
[*Enter bearers carrying* CORBACCIO *in a chair.*]

CORBACCIO   So, set me down,
And get you home.   [*Exeunt bearers.*]

VOLTORE   Is he come now, to trouble us?   5

MOSCA Of cloth of gold, two more—

CORBACCIO   Is it done, Mosca?

MOSCA Of several vellets, eight—

VOLTORE   I like his care.

CORBACCIO Dost thou not hear? [*Enter* CORVINO.]

CORVINO   Ha! Is the hour come, Mosca?

VOLPONE [*Aside*] Aye, now they muster.
        [*Peeps from behind a traverse.*]

CORVINO   What does the advocate here,
Or this Corbaccio?

CORBACCIO   What do these here?   10
                [*Enter* LADY WOULDBE.]

LADY WOULDBE   Mosca!
Is his thread spun?

MOSCA   Eight chests of linen—

VOLPONE [*Aside*]   Oh,
My fine Dame Wouldbe, too!

CORVINO   Mosca, the will,
That I may show it these and rid 'em hence.

---

90. clarissimo: Venetian of high rank. **round-back:** Corbaccio, a stooping old man. **91. crump you:** curl up. **102. girdle:** of Venus. **104. Acrisius:** the father of Danaë, whom Jove visited as a shower of gold. **105. Makes:** gives to.

MOSCA   Six chests of diaper,° four of damask—
  There.
[*Gives them the will and continues to write.*]
CORBACCIO   Is that the will?
MOSCA   Down-beds, and bolsters—
VOLPONE   [*Aside*]   Rare!   15
  Be busy still. Now they begin to flutter;
  They never think of me. Look, see, see, see!
  How their swift eyes run over the long deed
  Unto the name, and to the legacies,
  What is bequeathed them there.   20
MOSCA   Ten suits of hangings—
VOLPONE   [*Aside*] Aye, i' their garters,° Mosca.
  Now their hopes
  Are at the gasp.
VOLTORE   Mosca the heir!
CORBACCIO   What's that?
VOLPONE   [*Aside*] My advocate is dumb; look to
  my merchant.
  He has heard of some strange storm, a ship is lost,
  He faints; my lady will swoon. Old glazen-eyes
  He hath not reached his despair, yet.   26
CORBACCIO   All these
  Are out of hope; I'm sure the man.
CORVINO   But, Mosca—
MOSCA   Two cabinets—
CORVINO   Is this in earnest?
MOSCA   One
  Of ebony—
CORVINO   Or do you but delude me?
MOSCA   The other, mother of pearl—I am very
  busy.   30
  Good faith, it is a fortune thrown upon me—
  Item, one salt° of agate—not my seeking.
LADY WOULDBE   Do you hear, sir?
MOSCA   A perfumed box—Pray you forbear,
  You see I'm troubled—made of an onyx—
LADY WOULDBE   How?
MOSCA   Tomorrow, or next day, I shall be at
  leisure   35
  To talk with you all.
CORVINO   Is this my large hope's issue?
LADY WOULDBE   Sir, I must have a fairer answer.
MOSCA   Madam!
  Marry, and shall: pray you, fairly quit my house.
  Nay, raise no tempest with your looks; but hark
  you,
  Remember what your ladyship offered me   40

Scene iii.   **14. diaper:** kind of damask. **21. i' . . .
garters:** i.e., a ridiculous form of suicide. **32. salt:** saltcellar.

To put you in an heir; go to, think on 't.
And what you said e'en your best madams did
For maintenance, and why not you? Enough.
Go home and use the poor Sir Pol, your knight,
  well,
For fear I tell some riddles. Go, be melancholic.
                        [*Exit* LADY WOULDBE.]
VOLPONE   [*Aside*] O my fine devil!   46
CORVINO   Mosca, pray you a word.
MOSCA   Lord! Will not you take your dispatch°
  hence yet?
  Methinks of all you should have been th'example.
  Why should you stay here? With what thought?
  What promise?
  Hear you: do not you know I know you an
  ass,   50
  And that you would most fain have been a wittol°
  If fortune would have let you? That you are
  A declared cuckold, on good terms? This pearl,
                        [*Holding up jewels.*]
  You'll say, was yours? Right. This diamond?
  I'll not deny 't, but thank you. Much here
  else?   55
  It may be so. Why, think that these good works
  May help to hide your bad. I'll not betray you,
  Although you be but extraordinary,
  And have it only in title,° it sufficeth.
  Go home, be melancholic too, or mad.   60
                        [*Exit* CORVINO.]
VOLPONE   [*Aside*] Rare, Mosca! How his villainy
  becomes him!
VOLTORE   Certain he doth delude all these for me.
CORBACCIO   Mosca the heir?
                [*Still straining to read the will.*]
VOLPONE   [*Aside*] Oh, his four eyes° have found it!
CORBACCIO   I'm cozened, cheated, by a parasite
  slave!
  Harlot,° th'ast gulled me.   65
MOSCA   Yes, sir. Stop your mouth,
  Or I shall draw the only tooth is left.
  Are not you he, that filthy, covetous wretch
  With the three legs,° that here, in hope of prey,
  Have, any time this three year, snuffed about
  With your most grov'ling nose, and would have
  hired   70
  Me to the pois'ning of my patron, sir?

---

47. dispatch: dismissal. **51. wittol:** willing cuckold. **59.
have . . . title:** only nominal cuckoldry. **63. four eyes:** He
wears glasses. **65. Harlot:** vicious fellow (used of both
sexes). **68. three legs:** He uses a cane.

Are not you he that have, today, in court,
Professed the disinheriting of your son?
Perjured yourself? Go home, and die, and stink.
If you but croak a syllable, all comes out.   75
Away, and call your porters! Go, go, stink.

                    [*Exit* CORBACCIO.]

VOLPONE   [*Aside*] Excellent varlet!
VOLTORE   Now, my faithful Mosca,
I find thy constancy.
MOSCA   Sir?
VOLTORE   Sincere.
MOSCA   A table
Of porphyry—I mar'l° you'll be thus trouble-
  some.
VOLTORE   Nay, leave off now, they are gone.
MOSCA   Why, who are you?   80
What! Who did send for you? Oh, cry you
  mercy,
Reverend sir! Good faith, I am grieved for you,
That any chance of mine should thus defeat
Your—I must needs say—most deserving
  travails.
But I protest, sir, it was cast upon me,   85
And I could, almost, wish to be without it,
But that the will o' th' dead must be observed.
Marry, my joy is that you need it not;
You have a gift, sir—thank your education—
Will never let you want while there are men   90
And malice to breed causes.° Would I had
But half the like, for all my fortune, sir.
If I have any suits—as I do hope,
Things being so easy and direct, I shall not—
I will make bold with your obstreperous° aid;
Conceive° me, for your fee, sir. In meantime, 96
You that have so much law, I know ha' the
  conscience
Not to be covetous of what is mine.
Good sir, I thank you for my plate: 'twill help
To set up a young man. Good faith, you look
As you were costive;° best go home and purge,
  sir.   101

                    [*Exit* VOLTORE.]

VOLPONE   Bid him eat lettuce well! My witty
  mischief,

       [*Coming from behind curtain.*]

Let me embrace thee. O that I could now
Transform thee to a Venus—Mosca, go,

Straight take my habit of *clarissimo,*°   105
And walk the streets; be seen, torment 'em more.
We must pursue as well as plot. Who would
Have lost this feast?
MOSCA   I doubt it will lose them.
VOLPONE   O, my recovery shall recover all.
That I could now but think on some disguise
To meet 'em in, and ask 'em questions.   111
How I would vex 'em still at every turn!
MOSCA   Sir, I can fit you.
VOLPONE   Canst thou?
MOSCA   Yes, I know
One o' th' *commendatori,* sir, so like you;
Him will I straight make drunk, and bring you
  his habit.   115
VOLPONE   A rare disguise, and answering° thy
  brain!
Oh, I will be a sharp disease unto 'em.
MOSCA   Sir, you must look for curses—
VOLPONE   Till they burst;
The fox fares ever best when he is cursed.

                       [*Exeunt.*]

SCENE IV. SIR POLITIC'*s house.*

[*Enter* PEREGRINE *disguised, and three* MERCHANTS.]

PEREGRINE   Am I enough disguised?
FIRST MERCHANT   I warrant you.
PEREGRINE   All my ambition is to fright him only.
SECOND MERCHANT   If you could ship him away,
  'twere excellent.
THIRD MERCHANT   To Zant,° or to Aleppo?°
PEREGRINE   Yes, and ha' his
Adventures put i' th' Book of Voyages,°   5
And his gulled story registered for truth?
Well, gentlemen, when I am in a while,
And that you think us warm in our discourse,
Know your approaches.°
FIRST MERCHANT   Trust it to our care.

              [*Exeunt* MERCHANTS.]
            [*Enter* WOMAN.]

PEREGRINE   Save you, fair lady. Is Sir Pol within?
WOMAN   I do not know, sir.   11
PEREGRINE   Pray you say unto him,

---

79. mar'l: marvel. 91. causes: lawsuits. 95. obstreperous:
clamorous. 96. Conceive: understand. 101. costive: con-
stipated.

105. habit of clarissimo: robe befitting a nobleman. 116.
answering: resembling.
  Scene iv.   4. Zant: Greek island. Aleppo: city in Syria.
5. Book of Voyages: by Hakluyt, one of the popular collections of voyages at this time. 9. Know . . . approaches:
Know when to come in.

Here is a merchant, upon earnest business,
Desires to speak with him.

WOMAN   I will see, sir.

PEREGRINE   Pray you.

[*Exit* WOMAN.]

I see the family is all female here.

[*Reenter* WOMAN.]

WOMAN   He says, sir, he has weighty affairs of
state   15
That now require him whole;° some other time
You may possess him.

PEREGRINE   Pray you, say again,
If those require him whole, these will exact° him,
Whereof I bring him tidings. [*Exit* WOMAN.]
    What might be
His grave affair of state now? How to make   20
Bolognian sausages here in Venice, sparing
One o' th'ingredients? [*Reenter* WOMAN.]

WOMAN   Sir, he says he knows
By your word "tidings" that you are no states-
man,
And therefore wills you stay.

PEREGRINE   Sweet, pray you return him:
I have not read so many proclamations   25
And studied them for words, as he has done,
But—Here he deigns to come.

[*Enter* SIR POLITIC.]

SIR POLITIC   Sir, I must crave
Your courteous pardon. There hath chanced
today
Unkind disaster 'twixt my lady and me,
And I was penning my apology   30
To give her satisfaction, as you came now.

PEREGRINE   Sir, I am grieved I bring you worse
disaster:
The gentleman you met at th' port today,
That told you he was newly arrived—

SIR POLITIC   Aye, was
A fugitive punk?°

PEREGRINE   No, sir, a spy set on you,   35
And he has made relation to the Senate
That you professed to him to have a plot
To sell the state of Venice to the Turk.

SIR POLITIC   Oh me!

PEREGRINE   For which warrants are signed by this
time
To apprehend you and to search your study   40
For papers—

SIR POLITIC   Alas, sir, I have none but notes

16. **whole:** wholly. 18. **exact:** force. 35. **punk:** whore.

Drawn out of play-books°—

PEREGRINE   All the better, sir.

SIR POLITIC   And some essays. What shall I do?

PEREGRINE   Sir, best
Convey yourself into a sugar-chest,
Or, if you could lie round, a frail° were rare,   45
And I could send you abroad.

SIR POLITIC   Sir, I but talked so
For discourse' sake merely.

[*They knock without.*]

PEREGRINE   Hark, they are there.

SIR POLITIC   I am a wretch, a wretch!

PEREGRINE   What will you do, sir?
Ha' you ne'er a currant-butt° to leap into?
They'll put you to the rack, you must be
sudden.   50

SIR POLITIC   Sir, I have an engine°—

THIRD MERCHANT   [*Calling from off-stage*] Sir
Politic Wouldbe!

SECOND MERCHANT   Where is he?

SIR POLITIC   That I have thought upon beforetime.

PEREGRINE   What is it?

SIR POLITIC   I shall ne'er endure the torture!
Marry, it is, sir, of a tortoise-shell,
Fitted for these extremities. Pray you, sir, help
me.   55

[*He gets into a large tortoise shell.*]

Here I've a place, sir, to put back my legs;
Please you to lay it on, sir. With this cap
And my black gloves, I'll lie, sir, like a tortoise,
Till they are gone.

PEREGRINE   And call you this an engine?

SIR POLITIC   Mine own device—Good sir, bid my
wife's women   60
To burn my papers.

[*They (the three* MERCHANTS) *rush in.*]

FIRST MERCHANT   Where's he hid?

THIRD MERCHANT   We must,
And will, sure, find him.

SECOND MERCHANT   Which is his study?

FIRST MERCHANT   What
Are you, sir?

PEREGRINE   I'm a merchant that came here
To look upon this tortoise.

THIRD MERCHANT   How!

FIRST MERCHANT   Saint Mark!
What beast is this?

42. **play-books:** printed plays. 45. **frail:** rush basket. 49. **currant-butt:** cask for currants. 51. **engine:** device, con-traption.

PEREGRINE   It is a fish.

SECOND MERCHANT   [*Striking the tortoise*] Come
  out here!   65

PEREGRINE   Nay, you may strike him, sir, and
  tread upon him.
  He'll bear a cart.

FIRST MERCHANT   What, to run over him?

PEREGRINE   Yes.

THIRD MERCHANT   Let's jump upon him.

SECOND MERCHANT   Can he not go?

PEREGRINE   He creeps, sir.

FIRST MERCHANT   Let's see him creep. [*Prodding
  him.*]

PEREGRINE   No, good sir, you will hurt him.

SECOND MERCHANT   Heart, I'll see him creep, or
  prick his guts.   70

THIRD MERCHANT   Come out here!

PEREGRINE   [*Aside to* SIR POLITIC] Pray you, sir,
  creep a little.

FIRST MERCHANT   Forth!

SECOND MERCHANT   Yet further.

PEREGRINE   [*Aside to* SIR POLITIC] Good sir, creep.

SECOND MERCHANT   We'll see his legs.
  [*They pull off the shell and discover him.*]

THIRD MERCHANT   Godso, he has garters!

FIRST MERCHANT   Aye, and gloves!

SECOND MERCHANT   Is this
  Your fearful tortoise?

PEREGRINE   Now, Sir Pol, we are even;
  [*Throwing off his disguise.*]
  For your next project I shall be prepared.   75
  I am sorry for the funeral of your notes, sir.

FIRST MERCHANT   'Twere a rare motion° to be seen
  in Fleet Street.

SECOND MERCHANT   Aye, i' the term.°

FIRST MERCHANT   Or Smithfield, in the fair.

THIRD MERCHANT   Methinks 'tis but a melancholic
  sight.

PEREGRINE   Farewell, most politic tortoise!   80
  [*Exeunt* PEREGRINE *and* MERCHANTS.]

SIR POLITIC   Where's my lady?
  Knows she of this?

WOMAN   I know not, sir.

SIR POLITIC   Inquire. [*Exit* WOMAN.]
  Oh, I shall be the fable of all feasts,
  The freight° of the *gazetti*,° ship-boys' tale,
  And, which is worst, even talk for ordinaries.°
  [*Reenter* WOMAN.]

WOMAN   My lady's come most melancholic home,
  And says, sir, she will straight to sea, for
  physic.   86

SIR POLITIC   And I, to shun this place and clime
  forever,
  Creeping with house on back, and think it well
  To shrink my poor head in my politic shell.
  [*Exeunt.*]

SCENE V. VOLPONE'*s house.*

[*Enter* VOLPONE *in the habit of a commendatore,*
  MOSCA *of a clarissimo.*]

VOLPONE   Am I then like him?

MOSCA   O sir, you are he;
  No man can sever° you.

VOLPONE   Good.

MOSCA   But what am I?

VOLPONE   'Fore heav'n, a brave *clarissimo*, thou
  becomst it!
  Pity thou wert not born one.

MOSCA   If I hold
  My made one, 'twill be well.

VOLPONE   I'll go and see   5
  What news, first, at the court.

MOSCA   Do so. My fox
  Is out on° his hole, and ere he shall re-enter,
  I'll make him languish in his borrowed case,°
  Except to come to composition° with me.
  Androgyno, Castrone, Nano!
  [*Enter* ANDROGYNO, CASTRONE, *and* NANO.]

ALL   Here.   10

MOSCA   Go recreate° yourselves abroad, go sport.
  [*Exeunt the three.*]
  So, now I have the keys and am possessed.
  Since he will needs be dead afore his time,
  I'll bury him, or gain by him. I'm his heir,
  And so will keep me,° till he share at least.   15
  To cozen him of all were but a cheat
  Well placed; no man would construe it a sin.
  Let his sport pay for 't. This is called the fox-
  trap.   [*Exit.*]

Scene v. **2. sever:** tell you apart. **7. on:** of. **8. case:**
disguise. **9. composition:** terms. **11. recreate:** enjoy. **15.
keep me:** remain.

77. motion: sight. **78. term:** the court season. **83. freight:**
topic. **gazetti:** newspapers. **84. ordinaries:** taverns.

SCENE VI. *A Venetian street.*

[*Enter* CORBACCIO *and* CORVINO.]

CORBACCIO   They say the court is set.

CORVINO   We must maintain
Our first tale good, for both our reputations.

CORBACCIO   Why, mine's no tale! My son would,
there, have killed me.

CORVINO   That's true, I had forgot. Mine is, I am
sure.
But for your will, sir.

CORBACCIO   Aye, I'll come upon him
For that hereafter, now his patron's dead.   6
[*Enter* VOLPONE *in disguise.*]

VOLPONE   Signior Corvino! And Corbaccio! Sir,
Much joy unto you.

CORVINO   Of what?

VOLPONE   The sudden good
Dropped down upon you—

CORBACCIO   Where?

VOLPONE   And none knows how,
From old Volpone, sir.

CORBACCIO   Out, arrant knave!   10

VOLPONE   Let not your too much wealth, sir, make
you furious.

CORBACCIO   Away, thou varlet.

VOLPONE   Why, sir?

CORBACCIO   Dost thou mock me?

VOLPONE   You mock the world, sir; did you not
change wills?

CORBACCIO   Out, harlot!

VOLPONE   O! Belike you are the man,
Signior Corvino? Faith, you carry it well;   15
You grow not mad withal. I love your spirit.
You are not over-leavened° with your fortune.
You should ha' some would swell now like a
wine-fat°
With such an autumn—Did he gi' you all, sir?

CORVINO   Avoid,° you rascal.

VOLPONE   Troth, your wife has shown   20
Herself a very° woman! But you are well,
You need not care, you have a good estate
To bear it out, sir, better by this chance.
Except Corbaccio have a share?

CORBACCIO   Hence, varlet.

VOLPONE   You will not be a'known,° sir? Why, 'tis
wise.   25

Thus do all gamesters, at all games, dissemble.
No man will seem to win.
[*Exeunt* CORVINO *and* CORBACCIO.]
Here comes my vulture,
Heaving his beak up i' the air, and snuffing.

SCENE VII

[*Enter* VOLTORE *to* VOLPONE.]

VOLTORE   Outstripped thus, by a parasite! A slave,
Would run on errands, and make legs° for
crumbs?
Well, what I'll do—

VOLPONE   The court stays for your worship.
I e'en rejoice, sir, at your worship's happiness,
And that it fell into so learned hands,   5
That understand the fingering—

VOLTORE   What do you mean?

VOLPONE   I mean to be a suitor to your worship
For the small tenement, out of reparations,°
That at the end of your long row of houses,
By the *Pescheria;*° it was, in Volpone's time,   10
Your predecessor, ere he grew diseased,
A handsome, pretty, customed° bawdy-house
As any was in Venice—none dispraised°—
But fell with him. His body and that house
Decayed together.   15

VOLTORE   Come, sir, leave your prating.

VOLPONE   Why, if your worship give me but your
hand,
That I may ha' the refusal,° I have done.
'Tis a mere toy to you, sir, candle-rents.°
As your learned worship knows—

VOLTORE   What do I know?

VOLPONE   Marry, no end of your wealth, sir, God
decrease it.   20

VOLTORE   Mistaking knave! What, mock'st thou
my misfortune?

VOLPONE   His blessing on your heart, sir; would
'twere more!   [*Exit* VOLTORE.]
Now, to my first again, at the next corner.

Scene vi. **17. over-leavened:** puffed up. **18. wine-fat:**
wine vat. **20. Avoid:** get out! **21. very:** true, faithful. **25. be
a' known:** admit it.

Scene vii. **2. legs:** bows. **8. reparations:** repair. **10.
Pescheria:** fish market. **12. customed:** well patronized. **13.
none dispraised:** not to run down the others. **17. refusal:**
option. **18. candle-rents:** slum rent.

SCENE VIII

[VOLPONE *remains on stage to one side.* CORBACCIO
and CORVINO *enter.* MOSCA *passes slowly across
stage.*]

CORBACCIO See, in our habit!° See the impudent
  varlet!

CORVINO That I could shoot mine eyes at him,
  like gunstones!°   [*Exit* MOSCA.]

VOLPONE But is this true, sir, of the parasite?

CORBACCIO Again t'afflict us? Monster!

VOLPONE   In good faith, sir,
  I'm heartily grieved a beard of your grave
    length   5
  Should be so over-reached.° I never brooked°
  That parasite's hair; methought his nose should
    cozen.
  There still was somewhat in his look did promise
  The bane of a *clarissimo.*

CORBACCIO   Knave—

VOLPONE   Methinks
  Yet you, that are so traded° i' the world,   10
  A witty merchant, the fine bird Corvino,
  That have such moral emblems° on your name,
  Should not have sung your shame, and dropped
    your cheese,
  To let the fox laugh at your emptiness.

CORVINO Sirrah, you think the privilege of the
  place,   15
  And your red, saucy cap, that seems to me
  Nailed to your jolt-head° with those two
    chequins,°
  Can warrant your abuses. Come you hither:
  You shall perceive, sir, I dare beat you.
    Approach.

VOLPONE No haste, sir. I do know your valor
  well,   20
  Since you durst publish what you are, sir.

CORVINO   Tarry,
  I'd speak with you.

VOLPONE   Sir, sir, another time—
    [*Backing away.*]

CORVINO Nay, now.

VOLPONE   O God, sir! I were a wise man

Would° stand the fury of a distracted cuckold.
    [MOSCA *walks by 'em.*]

CORBACCIO What, come again!

VOLPONE [*Aside*]   Upon 'em, Mosca; save me.

CORBACCIO The air's infected where he breathes.

CORVINO   Let's fly him.   26
    [*Exeunt* CORVINO *and* CORBACCIO.]

VOLPONE Excellent basilisk!° Turn upon the
  vulture.

SCENE IX

[*Enter* VOLTORE.]

VOLTORE Well, flesh-fly,° it is summer with you
  now;
  Your winter will come on.

MOSCA   Good advocate,
  Pray thee not rail, nor threaten out of place thus;
  Thou'lt make a solecism, as madam° says.
  Get you a biggen more,° your brain breaks
    loose.   [*Exit.*]

VOLTORE Well, sir.   6

VOLPONE   Would you ha' me beat the insolent
  slave?
  Throw dirt upon his first good clothes?

VOLTORE   This same
  Is doubtless some familiar!°

VOLPONE   Sir, the court,
  In troth, stays for you. I am mad;° a mule
  That never read Justinian,° should get up   10
  And ride an advocate! Had you no quirk°
  To avoid gullage,° sir, by such a creature?
  I hope you do but jest; he has not done 't;
  This's but confederacy to blind the rest.
  You are the heir?

VOLTORE   A strange, officious,   15
  Troublesome knave! Thou dost torment me.

VOLPONE [*Aside*]   —I know—
  It cannot be, sir, that you should be cozened;
  'Tis not within the wit of man to do it.
  You are so wise, so prudent, and 'tis fit   19
  That wealth and wisdom still should go
    together.   [*Exeunt.*]

    Scene viii. **1. habit:** dress. **2. gunstones:** cannonballs.
6. over-reached: outsmarted. **brooked:** could endure. **10.
traded:** experienced. **12. moral emblems:** another reference
to the fable of the fox and the crow (see I.ii.96 and note).
16–17. red . . . chequins: reference to the hat worn by
commendatori (Volpone's disguise). **17. jolt-head:** blockhead.

24. Would: if I would. **27. basilisk:** mythical serpent that
could kill with a look.
    Scene ix. **1. flesh-fly:** carrion fly (Mosca). **4. Madam:**
Lady Wouldbe. **5. biggen more:** large lawyer's cap. **8.
familiar:** attending demon. **9. I am mad:** it is madness that.
10. Justinian: Roman emperor Justinian ordered the
compilation of the Roman legal code. **11. quirk:** device.
12. gullage: being tricked.

SCENE X. *The Scrutineo.*

[*Enter four* AVOCATORI, NOTARIO, COMMENDATORI,
    BONARIO, CELIA, CORBACCIO, CORVINO.]
FIRST AVOCATORE   Are all the parties here?
NOTARIO   All but the advocate.
SECOND AVOCATORE   And here he comes.
      [*Enter* VOLTORE, VOLPONE *following him.*]
AVOCATORI   Then bring 'em forth to sentence.
VOLTORE   O my most honored fathers, let your
    mercy
    Once win upon your justice, to forgive—
    I am distracted—
VOLPONE   [*Aside*]   What will he do now?
VOLTORE   Oh,   5
    I know not what t'address myself to first,
    Whether your fatherhoods, or these innocents—
CORVINO   [*Aside*] Will he betray himself?
VOLTORE   Whom equally
    I have abused, out of most covetous ends—
CORVINO   The man is mad!
CORBACCIO   What's that?   10
CORVINO   He is possessed.°
VOLTORE   For which, now struck in conscience,
    here I prostrate
    Myself at your offended feet, for pardon.
                              [*He kneels.*]
FIRST, SECOND AVOCATORI   Arise.
CELIA   O heav'n, how just thou art!
VOLPONE   [*Aside*]   I'm caught
    I' mine own noose.
CORVINO   [*Aside to* CORBACCIO] Be constant,° sir,
    nought now
    Can help but impudence.
FIRST AVOCATORE   Speak forward.   15
COMMENDATORE   [*To the courtroom*]   Silence!
VOLTORE   It is not passion in me, reverend fathers,
    But only conscience, conscience, my good sires,
    That makes me now tell truth. That parasite,
    That knave, hath been the instrument of all.
AVOCATORI   Where is that knave? Fetch him.
VOLPONE   I go. [*Exit.*]
CORVINO   Grave fathers,
    This man's distracted, he confessed it now,   21
    For, hoping to be old Volpone's heir,
    Who now is dead—
THIRD AVOCATORE   How!
SECOND AVOCATORE   Is Volpone dead?

CORVINO   Dead since,° grave fathers—
BONARIO   O sure vengeance!
FIRST AVOCATORE   Stay.
    Then he was no deceiver.
VOLTORE   Oh, no, none;   25
    The parasite, grave fathers.
CORVINO   He does speak
    Out of mere envy, 'cause the servant's made
    The thing he gaped for. Please your fatherhoods,
    This is the truth; though I'll not justify
    The other, but he may be some-deal° faulty.   30
VOLTORE   Aye, to your hopes, as well as mine,
    Corvino.
    But I'll use modesty.° Pleaseth your wisdoms
    To view these certain notes, and but confer° them;
                    [*Gives them notes.*]
    As I hope favor, they shall speak clear truth.
CORVINO   The devil has entered him!   35
BONARIO   Or bides in you.
FOURTH AVOCATORE   We have done ill, by a public
    officer
    To send for him, if he be heir.
SECOND AVOCATORE   For whom?
FOURTH AVOCATORE   Him that they call the parasite.
THIRD AVOCATORE   'Tis true,
    He is a man of great estate now left.
FOURTH AVOCATORE   Go you, and learn his name,
    and say the court   40
    Entreats his presence here, but to° the clearing
    Of some few doubts.   [*Exit* NOTARIO.]
SECOND AVOCATORE   This same's a labyrinth!
FIRST AVOCATORE   Stand you unto your first report?
CORVINO   My state,
    My life, my fame—
BONARIO   Where is't?
CORVINO   Are at the stake.
FIRST AVOCATORE   Is yours so too?   45
CORBACCIO   The advocate's a knave,
    And has a forkèd tongue—
SECOND AVOCATORE   Speak to the point.
CORBACCIO   So is the parasite too.
FIRST AVOCATORE   This is confusion.
VOLTORE   I do beseech your fatherhoods, read but
    those.
CORVINO   And credit nothing the false spirit hath
    writ.   49
    It cannot be but he is possessed, grave fathers.

Scene x. **10. possessed:** i.e., by the devil, mad. **14. Be
constant:** stick to the old line.

24. since: since the trial. **30. some-deal:** somewhat.
32. modesty: moderation, restraint. **33. confer:** compare.
41. but to: only for.

SCENE XI. *A street.*

[VOLPONE *alone.*]

VOLPONE   To make a snare for mine own neck!
      and run
   My head into it willfully, with laughter!
   When I had newly 'scaped, was free and clear!
   Out of mere wantonness! Oh, the dull devil
   Was in this brain of mine when I devised it,   5
   And Mosca gave it second; he must now
   Help to sear up this vein, or we bleed dead.

      [*Enter* NANO, ANDROGYNO, *and* CASTRONE.]

   How now! Who let you loose? Whither go you
      now?
   What, to buy gingerbread, or to drown kitlings?°
NANO   Sir, Master Mosca called us out of doors,
   And bid us all go play, and took the keys.   11
ANDROGYNO   Yes.
VOLPONE   Did Master Mosca take the keys? Why,
      so!
   I am farther in. These are my fine conceits!°
   I must be merry, with a mischief to me!
   What a vile wretch was I, that could not bear   15
   My fortune soberly; I must ha' my crotchets°
   And my conundrums! Well, go you and seek
      him.
   His meaning may be truer than my fear.
   Bid him, he straight come to me to the court;
   Thither will I, and if 't be possible,   20
   Unscrew my advocate,° upon new hopes.
   When I provoked him, then I lost myself.
                              [*Exeunt.*]

SCENE XII. *The Scrutineo.*

[*Four* AVOCATORI, NOTARIO, VOLTORE, BONARIO,
      CELIA, CORBACCIO, CORVINO.]

FIRST AVOCATORE   [*Looking over* VOLTORE's *notes*]
   These things can ne'er be reconciled. He here
   Professeth that the gentleman was wronged,
   And that the gentlewoman was brought thither,
   Forced by her husband, and there left.
VOLTORE   Most true.
CELIA   How ready is heav'n to those that pray!   5
FIRST AVOCATORE   But that
   Volpone would have ravished her, he holds
   Utterly false, knowing his impotence.

Scene xi. **9. kitlings:** kittens. **13. conceits:** plans,
schemes. **16. crotchets:** whims. **21. Unscrew my advocate:**
Make him reverse himself again.

CORVINO   Grave fathers, he is possessed; again, I
      say,
   Possessed. Nay, if there be possession
   And obsession,° he has both.   10
THIRD AVOCATORE   Here comes our officer.
                  [*Enter* VOLPONE, *still disguised.*]
VOLPONE   The parasite will straight be here, grave
      fathers.
FOURTH AVOCATORE   You might invent some other
      name, sir varlet.
THIRD AVOCATORE   Did not the notary meet him?
VOLPONE   Not that I know.
FOURTH AVOCATORE   His coming will clear all.
SECOND AVOCATORE   Yet, it is misty.
VOLTORE   May 't please your fatherhoods—   15
VOLPONE   Sir, the parasite
            [VOLPONE *whispers (to) the* ADVOCATE.]
   Willed me to tell you that his master lives;
   That you are still the man; your hopes the same;
   And this was only a jest—
VOLTORE   How?
VOLPONE   Sir, to try
   If you were firm, and how you stood affected.°
VOLTORE   Art sure he lives?
VOLPONE   Do I live, sir?   20
VOLTORE   O me!
   I was too violent.
VOLPONE   Sir, you may redeem it:
   They said you were possessed: fall down, and
      seem so.
   I'll help to make it good. God bless the man!
                        [VOLTORE *falls.*]
   [*Aside to* VOLTORE.] —Stop your wind hard,° and
      swell—See, see, see, see!
   He vomits crooked pins! His eyes are set   25
   Like a dead hare's hung in a poulter's shop!
   His mouth's running away! Do you see, signior?
   Now, 'tis in his belly.°
CORVINO   Aye, the devil!
VOLPONE   Now, in his throat.
CORVINO   Aye, I perceive it plain.
VOLPONE   'Twill out, 'twill out! Stand clear. See
      where it flies!   30
   In shape of a blue toad, with a bat's wings!
                  [*Pointing.*]
   Do you not see it, sir?

Scene xii. **9–10. possession and obsession:** both external
and internal madness. **19. stood affected:** truly felt. **24.
Stop . . . hard:** hold your breath. **25–28. He . . . belly:**
symptoms of being (literally) possessed by a devil.

CORBACCIO   What? I think I do.

CORVINO   'Tis too manifest.

VOLPONE   Look! He comes t' himself.

VOLTORE   Where am I?

VOLPONE   Take good heart, the worst is past, sir.
You are dispossessed.

FIRST AVOCATORE   What accident is this?   35

SECOND AVOCATORE   Sudden, and full of wonder!

THIRD AVOCATORE   If he were
Possessed, as it appears, all this is nothing.
                    [*Waving notes.*]

CORVINO   He has been often subject to these fits.

FIRST AVOCATORE   Show him that writing.—Do
you know it, sir?

VOLPONE   [*Aside*] Deny it sir, forswear it, know it
not.   40

VOLTORE   Yes, I do know it well, it is my hand;
But all that it contains is false.

BONARIO   O practice!°

SECOND AVOCATORE   What maze is this!

FIRST AVOCATORE   Is he not guilty then,
Whom you, there, name the parasite?

VOLTORE   Grave fathers,
No more than his good patron, old Volpone.   45

FOURTH AVOCATORE   Why, he is dead.

VOLTORE   Oh, no, my honored fathers.
He lives—

FIRST AVOCATORE   How! Lives?

VOLTORE   Lives.

SECOND AVOCATORE   This is subtler yet!

THIRD AVOCATORE   You said he was dead.

VOLTORE   Never.

THIRD AVOCATORE   You said so!

CORVINO   I heard so.

FOURTH AVOCATORE   Here comes the gentleman,
make him way.   [*Enter* MOSCA.]

THIRD AVOCATORE   A stool!

FOURTH AVOCATORE   A proper° man and, were
Volpone dead,   50
A fit match for my daughter.

THIRD AVOCATORE   Give him way.

VOLPONE   [*Aside to* MOSCA] Mosca, I was almost
lost; the advocate
Had betrayed all; but now it is recovered.
All's o' the hinge again. Say I am living.

MOSCA   What busy knave is this? Most reverend
fathers,   55
I sooner had attended your grave pleasures,
But that my order for the funeral

42. **practice:** intrigue. 50. **proper:** handsome.

Of my dear patron did require me—

VOLPONE   [*Aside*]   Mosca!

MOSCA   Whom I intend to bury like a gentleman.

VOLPONE   [*Aside*] Aye, quick,° and cozen me of all.

SECOND AVOCATORE   Still stranger!
More intricate!   61

FIRST AVOCATORE   And come about again!

FOURTH AVOCATORE   [*Aside*] It is a match, my
daughter is bestowed.

MOSCA   [*Aside to* VOLPONE] Will you gi' me half?

VOLPONE   [*Half aloud*]   First I'll be hanged.

MOSCA   [*Aside*]   I know
Your voice is good, cry not so loud.

FIRST AVOCATORE   Demand
The advocate. Sir, did not you affirm   65
Volpone was alive?

VOLPONE   Yes, and he is;
This gent'man told me so. [*Aside to* MOSCA.]
Thou shalt have half.

MOSCA   Whose drunkard is this same? Speak,
some that know him.
I never saw his face. [*Aside to* VOLPONE.] I cannot
now
Afford it you so cheap.

VOLPONE   [*Aside*]   No?

FIRST AVOCATORE   [*To* VOLTORE]
                    What say you?   70

VOLTORE   The officer told me.

VOLPONE   I did, grave fathers,
And will maintain he lives with mine own life,
And that this creature told me. [*Aside.*] I was born
With all good stars my enemies!

MOSCA   Most grave fathers,
If such an insolence as this must pass   75
Upon me, I am silent; 'twas not this
For which you sent, I hope.

SECOND AVOCATORE   Take him away.

VOLPONE   [*Aside*] Mosca!

THIRD AVOCATORE   Let him be whipped.

VOLPONE   [*Aside*]   Wilt thou betray me?
Cozen me?

THIRD AVOCATORE   And taught to bear himself
Toward a person of his rank.
            [*The* OFFICERS *seize* VOLPONE.]

FOURTH AVOCATORE   Away.   80

MOSCA   I humbly thank your fatherhoods.

VOLPONE   [*Aside*]   Soft, soft. Whipped?
And lose all that I have? If I confess,
It cannot be much more.

60. **quick:** alive.

FOURTH AVOCATORE [*To* MOSCA] Sir, are you married?

VOLPONE [*Aside*] They'll be allied anon; I must be resolute:
The fox shall here uncase.
              [*He puts off his disguise.*]

MOSCA   Patron!

VOLPONE   Nay, now   85
My ruins shall not come alone; your match
I'll hinder sure. My substance° shall not glue you,
Nor screw you, into a family.

MOSCA   Why, patron!

VOLPONE I am Volpone, and this is my knave;
This, his own knave; this, avarice's fool;   90
This, a chimera° of wittol, fool, and knave.
And, reverend fathers, since we all can hope
Nought but a sentence, let's not now despair it.
You hear me brief.

CORVINO   May it please your fatherhoods—

COMMENDATORE   Silence.

FIRST AVOCATORE The knot is now undone by miracle!   95

SECOND AVOCATORE Nothing can be more clear.

THIRD AVOCATORE   Or can more prove
These innocent.

FIRST AVOCATORE Give 'em their liberty.

BONARIO Heaven could not long let such gross crimes be hid.

SECOND AVOCATORE If this be held the highway to get riches,
May I be poor!

THIRD AVOCATORE This's not the gain, but torment.   100

FIRST AVOCATORE These possess wealth as sick men possess fevers,
Which trulier may be said to possess them.

SECOND AVOCATORE Disrobe that parasite.

CORVINO, MOSCA   Most honored fathers—

FIRST AVOCATORE Can you plead aught to stay the course of justice?
If you can, speak.

CORVINO, VOLTORE We beg favor.

CELIA   And mercy.   105

FIRST AVOCATORE You hurt your innocence, suing for the guilty.
Stand forth; and first the parasite. You appear
T'have been the chiefest minister, if not plotter,

In all these lewd impostures; and now, lastly,
Have with your impudence abused the court,
And habit of a gentleman of Venice,   111
Being a fellow of no birth or blood.
For which our sentence is, first thou be whipped;
Then live perpetual prisoner in our galleys.

VOLPONE I thank you for him.   115

MOSCA   Bane to° thy wolfish nature.

FIRST AVOCATORE Deliver him to the *saffi.* [MOSCA *is taken out.*] Thou Volpone,
By blood and rank a gentleman, canst not fall
Under like censure; but our judgment on thee
Is that thy substance all be straight confiscate
To the hospital of the *Incurabili.*°   120
And since the most was gotten by imposture,
By feigning lame, gout, palsy, and such diseases,
Thou art to lie in prison, cramped with irons,
Till thou be'st sick and lame indeed. Remove him.

VOLPONE This is called mortifying° of a fox.   125

FIRST AVOCATORE Thou, Voltore, to take away the scandal
Thou hast giv'n all worthy men of thy profession,
Art banished from their fellowship, and our state.
Corbaccio, bring him near! We here possess
Thy son of all thy state, and confine thee   130
To the monastery of *San' Spirito;*
Where, since thou knewst not how to live well here,
Thou shalt be learned° to die well.

CORBACCIO [*Cupping his ear*] Ha! What said he?

COMMENDATORE You shall know anon, sir.

FIRST AVOCATORE   Thou, Corvino, shalt
Be straight embarked from thine own house, and rowed   135
Round about Venice, through the Grand Canal,
Wearing a cap with fair long ass's ears
Instead of horns; and so to mount, a paper
Pinned on thy breast, to the *Berlina*°—

CORVINO   Yes,
And have mine eyes beat out with stinking fish,
Bruised fruit, and rotten eggs—'Tis well, I'm glad   141
I shall not see my shame yet.

FIRST AVOCATORE   And to expiate
Thy wrongs done to thy wife, thou art to send her

---

87. **substance:** wealth. 91. **chimera:** the mythical combination of lion, goat, and serpent.

115. **Bane to:** a curse on. 120. **Incurabili:** incurables.
125. **mortifying:** slowly killing. 133. **learned:** taught. 139.
Berlina: pillory.

Home to her father, with her dowry trebled.
And these are all your judgments.   145
ALL   Honored fathers!
FIRST AVOCATORE Which may not be revoked.
  Now you begin,
  When crimes are done and past, and to be
     punished,
  To think what your crimes are. Away with them!
  Let all that see these vices thus rewarded,
  Take heart, and love to study 'em. Mischiefs
     feed   150
  Like beasts, till they be fat, and then they bleed.
                              [*Exeunt.*]
              [VOLPONE *comes forward.*]
VOLPONE The seasoning of a play is the applause.
  Now, though the fox be punished by the laws,
  He yet doth hope there is no suff'ring due
  For any fact° which he hath done 'gainst you.
  If there be, censure him; here he doubtful
     stands.   156
  If not, fare jovially, and clap your hands.

MARK TWAIN
1835–1910

The Man That Corrupted
Hadleyburg

1

It was many years ago. Hadleyburg was the most
honest and upright town in all the region round
about. It had kept that reputation unsmirched
during three generations, and was prouder of it
than of any other of its possessions. It was so proud
of it, and so anxious to insure its perpetuation, that
it began to teach the principles of honest dealing to
its babies in the cradle, and made the like teachings
the staple of their culture thenceforward through
all the years devoted to their education. Also,
throughout the formative years temptations were
kept out of the way of the young people, so that
their honesty could have every chance to harden
and solidify, and become a part of their very bone.

155. fact: crime, offense.

The neighboring towns were jealous of this honorable supremacy, and affected to sneer at Hadleyburg's pride in it and call it vanity; but all the same
they were obliged to acknowledge that Hadleyburg
was in reality an incorruptible town; and if pressed
they would also acknowledge that the mere fact
that a young man hailed from Hadleyburg was
all the recommendation he needed when he went
forth from his natal town to seek for responsible
employment.

But at last, in the drift of time, Hadleyburg had
the ill luck to offend a passing stranger—possibly
without knowing it, certainly without caring, for
Hadleyburg was sufficient unto itself, and cared not
a rap for strangers or their opinions. Still, it would
have been well to make an exception in this one's
case, for he was a bitter man and revengeful. All
through his wanderings during a whole year he
kept his injury in mind, and gave all his leisure
moments to trying to invent a compensating satisfaction for it. He contrived many plans, and all of
them were good, but none of them was quite
sweeping enough; the poorest of them would hurt
a great many individuals, but what he wanted was
a plan which would comprehend the entire town,
and not let so much as one person escape unhurt.
At last he had a fortunate idea, and when it fell
into his brain it lit up his whole head with an evil
joy. He began to form a plan at once, saying to
himself, "That is the thing to do—I will corrupt the
town."

Six months later he went to Hadleyburg, and
arrived in a buggy at the house of the old cashier
of the bank about ten at night. He got a sack out
of the buggy, shouldered it, and staggered with it
through the cottage yard, and knocked at the door.
A woman's voice said "Come in," and he entered,
and set his sack behind the stove in the parlor,
saying politely to the old lady who sat reading the
Missionary Herald by the lamp:

"Pray keep your seat, madam, I will not disturb
you. There—now it is pretty well concealed; one
would hardly know it was there. Can I see your
husband a moment, madam?"

No, he was gone to Brixton, and might not
return before morning.

"Very well, madam, it is no matter. I merely
wanted to leave that sack in his care, to be delivered
to the rightful owner when he shall be found. I am
a stranger; he does not know me; I am merely

passing through the town tonight to discharge a matter which has been long in my mind. My errand is now completed, and I go pleased and a little proud, and you will never see me again. There is a paper attached to the sack which will explain everything. Good-night, madam.''

The old lady was afraid of the mysterious big stranger, and was glad to see him go. But her curiosity was roused, and she went straight to the sack and brought away the paper. It began as follows:

TO BE PUBLISHED; or, the right man sought out by private inquiry—either will answer. This sack contains gold coin weighing a hundred and sixty pounds four ounces—

"Mercy on us, and the door not locked!"

Mrs. Richards flew to it all in a tremble and locked it, then pulled down the window-shades and stood frightened, worried, and wondering if there was anything else she could do toward making herself and the money more safe. She listened awhile for burglars, then surrendered to curiosity and went back to the lamp and finished reading the paper:

I am a foreigner, and am presently going back to my own country, to remain there permanently. I am grateful to America for what I have received at her hands during my stay under her flag; and to one of her citizens—a citizen of Hadleyburg—I am especially grateful for a great kindness done me a year or two ago. Two great kindnesses; in fact. I will explain. I was a gambler. I say I WAS. I was a ruined gambler. I arrived in this village at night, hungry and without a penny. I asked for help —in the dark; I was ashamed to beg in the light. I begged of the right man. He gave me twenty dollars— that is to say, he gave me life, as I considered it. He also gave me fortune; for out of that money I have made myself rich at the gaming-table. And finally, a remark which he made to me has remained with me to this day, and has at last conquered me; and in conquering has saved the remnant of my morals; I shall gamble no more. Now I have no idea who that man was, but I want him found, and I want him to have this money, to give away, throw away or keep, as he pleases. It is merely my way of testifying my gratitude to him. If I could stay, I would find him myself; but no matter, he will be found. This is an honest town, an incorruptible town, and I know I can trust it without fear. This man can be identified by the remark which he made to me; I feel persuaded that he will remember it.

And now my plan is this: If you prefer to conduct the inquiry privately, do so. Tell the contents of this present writing to anyone who is likely to be the right man. If he shall answer, "I am the man; the remark I made was so-and-so," apply the test—to wit: open the sack, and

in it you will find a sealed envelope containing that remark. If the remark mentioned by the candidate tallies with it, give him the money, and ask no further questions, for he is certainly the right man.

But if you shall prefer a public inquiry, then publish this present writing in the local paper—with these instructions added, to wit: Thirty days from now, let the candidate appear at the town-hall at eight in the evening (Friday), and hand his remark, in a sealed envelope, to the Rev. Mr. Burgess (if he will be kind enough to act); and let Mr. Burgess there and then destroy the seals on the sack, open it, and see if the remark is correct; if correct, let the money be delivered, with my sincere gratitude, to my benefactor thus identified.

Mrs. Richards sat down, gently, quivering with excitement, and was soon lost in thinking—after this pattern: "What a strange thing it is! . . . And what a fortune for that kind man who set his bread afloat upon the waters! . . . If he had only been my husband that did it!—for we are so poor, so old and poor! . . ." Then, with a sigh—"But it was not my Edward; no, it was not he that gave the stranger twenty dollars. It is a pity too; I see it now. . . ." Then, with a shudder—"But it is *gambler's* money! the wages of sin: we couldn't take it; we couldn't touch it. I don't like to be near it; it seems a defilement." She moved to a farther chair. . . . "I wish Edward would come, and take it to the bank; a burglar might come at any moment; it is dreadful to be here all alone with it."

At eleven Mr. Richards arrived, and while his wife was saying, "I am *so* glad you've come!" he was saying, "I'm so tired—tired clear out; it is dreadful to be poor, and have to make these dismal journeys at my time of life. Always at the grind, grind, grind, on a salary—another man's slave, and he sitting at home in his slippers, rich and comfortable."

"I am so sorry for you, Edward, you know that; but be comforted; we have our livelihood; we have our good name—"

"Yes, Mary, and that is everything. Don't mind my talk—it's just a moment's irritation and doesn't mean anything. Kiss me—there, it's all gone now, and I am not complaining any more. What have you been getting? What's in the sack?"

Then his wife told him the great secret. It dazed him for a moment; then he said:

"It weighs a hundred and sixty pounds? Why, Mary, it's for-ty thou-sand dollars—think of it—a whole fortune! Not ten men in this village are worth that much. Give me the paper."

He skimmed through it and said:

"Isn't it an adventure! Why, it's a romance; it's like the impossible things one reads about in books, and never sees in life." He was well stirred up now; cheerful, even gleeful. He tapped his old wife on the cheek, and said, humorously, "Why, we're rich, Mary, rich; all we've got to do is to bury the money and burn the papers. If the gambler ever comes to inquire, we'll merely look coldly upon him and say: 'What is this nonsense you are talking? We have never heard of you and your sack of gold before'; and then he would look foolish, and—"

"And in the meantime, while you are running on with your jokes, the money is still here, and it is fast getting along toward burglar-time."

"True. Very well, what shall we do—make the inquiry private? No, not that: it would spoil the romance. The public method is better. Think what a noise it will make! And it will make all the other towns jealous; for no stranger would trust such a thing to any town but Hadleyburg, and they know it. It's a great card for us. I must get to the printing-office now, or I shall be too late."

"But stop—stop—don't leave me here alone with it, Edward!"

But he was gone. For only a little while, however. Not far from his own house he met the editor-proprietor of the paper, and gave him the document, and said, "Here is a good thing for you, Cox—put it in."

"It may be too late, Mr. Richards, but I'll see."

At home again he and his wife sat down to talk the charming mystery over; they were in no condition for sleep. The first question was, Who could the citizen have been who gave the stranger the twenty dollars? It seemed a simple one; both answered it in the same breath—

"Barclay Goodson."

"Yes," said Richards, "he could have done it, and it would have been like him, but there's not another in the town."

"Everybody will grant that, Edward—grant it privately, anyway. For six months, now, the village has been its own proper self once more—honest, narrow, self-righteous, and stingy."

"It is what he always called it, to the day of his death—said it right out publicly, too."

"Yes, and he was hated for it."

"Oh, of course; but he didn't care. I reckon he was the best-hated man among us, except the Reverend Burgess."

"Well, Burgess deserves it—he will never get another congregation here. Mean as the town is, it knows how to estimate *him*. Edward, doesn't it seem odd that the stranger should appoint Burgess to deliver the money?"

"Well, yes—it does. That is—that is—"

"Why so much that-*is*-ing? Would *you* select him?"

"Mary, maybe the stranger knows him better than this village does."

"Much *that* would help Burgess!"

The husband seemed perplexed for an answer; the wife kept a steady eye upon him, and waited. Finally Richards said, with the hesitancy of one who is making a statement which is likely to encounter doubt:

"Mary, Burgess is not a bad man."

His wife was certainly surprised.

"Nonsense!" she exclaimed.

"He is not a bad man. I know. The whole of his unpopularity had its foundation in that one thing—the thing that made so much noise."

"That 'one thing,' indeed! As if that 'one thing' wasn't enough, all by itself."

"Plenty. Plenty. Only he wasn't guilty of it."

"How you talk! Not guilty of it! Everybody knows he *was* guilty."

"Mary, I give you my word—he was innocent."

"I can't believe it, and I don't. How do you know?"

"It is a confession. I am ashamed, but I will make it. I was the only man who knew he was innocent. I could have saved him, and—and—well, you know how the town was wrought up—I hadn't the pluck to do it. It would have turned everybody against me. I felt mean, ever so mean; but I didn't dare; I hadn't the manliness to face that."

Mary looked troubled, and for a while was silent. Then she said, stammeringly:

"I—I don't think it would have done for you to —to—One mustn't—er—public opinion—one has to be so careful—so—" It was a difficult road, and she got mired; but after a little she got started again. "It was a great pity, but—Why, we couldn't afford it, Edward—we couldn't indeed. Oh, I wouldn't have had you do it for anything!"

"It would have lost us the good-will of so many people, Mary; and then—and then—"

"What troubles me now is, what *he* thinks of us, Edward."

"He? *He* doesn't suspect that I could have saved him."

"Oh," exclaimed the wife, in a tone of relief, "I'm glad of that. As long as he doesn't know that you could have saved him, he—he—well, that makes it a great deal better. Why, I might have known he didn't know, because he is always trying to be friendly with us, as little encouragement as we give him. More than once people have twitted me with it. There's the Wilsons, and the Wilcoxes, and the Harknesses, they take a mean pleasure in saying, '*Your friend* Burgess,' because they know it pesters me. I wish he wouldn't persist in liking us so; I can't think why he keeps it up."

"I can explain it. It's another confession. When the thing was new and hot, and the town made a plan to ride him on a rail, my conscience hurt me so that I couldn't stand it, and I went privately and gave him notice, and he got out of the town and stayed out till it was safe to come back."

"Edward! If the town had found it out—"

"*Don't!* It scares me yet, to think of it. I repented of it the minute it was done; and I was even afraid to tell you, lest your face might betray it to somebody. I didn't sleep any that night, for worrying. But after a few days I saw that no one was going to suspect me, and after that I got to feeling glad I did it. And I feel glad yet, Mary—glad through and through."

"So do I, now, for it would have been a dreadful way to treat him. Yes, I'm glad; for really you did owe him that, you know. But, Edward, suppose it should come out yet, some day!"

"It won't."

"Why!"

"Because everybody thinks it was Goodson."

"Of course they would!"

"Certainly. And of course *he* didn't care. They persuaded poor old Sawlsberry to go and charge it on him, and he went blustering over there and did it. Goodson looked him over, like as if he was hunting for a place on him that he could despise the most, then he says, 'So you are the Committee of Inquiry, are you?' Sawlsberry said that was about what he was. 'Hm. Do they require particulars, or do you reckon a kind of a *general* answer will do?' 'If they require particulars, I will come back, Mr. Goodson; I will take the general answer

first.' 'Very well, then, tell them to go to hell—I reckon that's general enough. And I'll give you some advice, Sawlsberry; when you come back for the particulars, fetch a basket to carry the relics of yourself home in.' "

"Just like Goodson; it's got all the marks. He had only vanity; he thought he could give advice better than any other person."

"It settled the business, and saved us, Mary. The subject was dropped."

"Bless you, I'm not doubting *that*."

Then they took up the gold-sack mystery again, with strong interest. Soon the conversation began to suffer breaks—interruptions caused by absorbed thinkings. The breaks grew more and more frequent. At last Richards lost himself wholly in thought. He sat long, gazing vacantly at the floor, and by-and-by he began to punctuate his thoughts with little nervous movements of his hands that seemed to indicate vexation. Meantime his wife too had relapsed into a thoughtful silence, and her movements were beginning to show a troubled discomfort. Finally Richards got up and strode aimlessly about the room, plowing his hands through his hair, much as a somnambulist might do who was having a bad dream. Then he seemed to arrive at a definite purpose; and without a word he put on his hat and passed quickly out of the house. His wife sat brooding, with a drawn face, and did not seem to be aware that she was alone. Now and then she murmured, "Lead us not into t . . . but —but—we are so poor, so poor! . . . Lead us not into . . . Ah, who would be hurt by it?—and no one would ever know. . . . Lead us . . ." The voice died out in mumblings. After a little she glanced up and muttered in a half-frightened, half-glad way—

"He is gone! But, oh dear, he may be too late —too late. . . . Maybe not—maybe there is still time." She rose and stood thinking, nervously clasping and unclasping her hands. A slight shudder shook her frame, and she said, out of a dry throat, "God forgive me—it's awful to think such things —but . . . Lord, how we are made—how strangely we are made!"

She turned the light low, and slipped stealthily over and kneeled down by the sack and felt of its ridgy sides with her hands, and fondled them lovingly; and there was a gloating light in her poor old eyes. She fell into fits of absence; and came half out of them at times to mutter, "If we had only waited!—oh, if we had only waited a little, and not been in such a hurry!"

Meantime Cox had gone home from his office and told his wife all about the strange thing that had happened, and they had talked it over eagerly, and guessed that the late Goodson was the only man in the town who could have helped a suffering stranger with so noble a sum as twenty dollars. Then there was a pause, and the two became thoughtful and silent. And by-and-by nervous and fidgety. At last the wife said, as if to herself:

"Nobody knows this secret but the Richardses . . . and us . . . nobody."

The husband came out of his thinkings with a slight start, and gazed wistfully at his wife, whose face was become very pale; then he hesitatingly rose, and glanced furtively at his hat, then at his wife—a sort of mute inquiry. Mrs. Cox swallowed once or twice, with her hand at her throat, then in place of speech she nodded her head. In a moment she was alone, and mumbling to herself.

And now Richards and Cox were hurrying through the deserted streets, from opposite directions. They met, panting, at the foot of the printing-office stairs; by the night-light there they read each other's face. Cox whispered:

"Nobody knows about this but us?"

The whispered answer was,

"Not a soul—on honor, not a soul!"

"If it isn't too late to—"

The men were starting upstairs; at this moment they were overtaken by a boy, and Cox asked:

"Is that you, Johnny?"

"Yes, sir."

"You needn't ship the early mail—nor *any* mail; wait till I tell you."

"It's already gone, sir."

"*Gone?*" It had the sound of an unspeakable disappointment in it.

"Yes, sir. Timetable for Brixton and all the towns beyond changed today, sir—had to get the papers in twenty minutes earlier than common. I had to rush; if I had been two minutes later—"

The men turned and walked slowly away, not waiting to hear the rest. Neither of them spoke during ten minutes; then Cox said, in a vexed tone:

"What possessed you to be in such a hurry, *I* can't make out."

The answer was humble enough:

"I see it now, but somehow I never thought, you know, until it was too late. But the next time—"

"Next time be hanged! It won't come in a thousand years."

Then the friends separated without a good-night, and dragged themselves home with the gait of mortally stricken men. At their homes their wives sprang up with an eager "Well?"—then saw the answer with their eyes and sank down sorrowing, without waiting for it to come in words. In both houses a discussion followed of a heated sort—a new thing; there had been discussions before, but not heated ones, not ungentle ones. The discussions tonight were a sort of seeming plagiarisms of each other. Mrs. Richards said,

"If you had only waited, Edward—if you had only stopped to think; but no, you must run straight to the printing-office and spread it all over the world."

"It *said* publish it."

"That is nothing; it also said do it privately, if you liked. There, now—is that true, or not?"

"Why, yes—yes, it is true; but when I thought what a stir it would make, and what a compliment it was to Hadleyburg that a stranger should trust it so—"

"Oh, certainly, I know all that; but if you had only stopped to think, you would have seen that you *couldn't* find the right man, because he is in his grave, and hasn't left chick nor child nor relation behind him; and as long as the money went to somebody that awfully needed it, and nobody would be hurt by it, and—and—"

She broke down, crying. Her husband tried to think of some comforting thing to say, and presently came out with this:

"But after all, Mary, it must be for the best—it *must* be; we know that. And we must remember that it was so ordered—"

"Ordered! Oh, everything's *ordered*, when a person has to find some way out when he has been stupid. Just the same, it was *ordered* that the money should come to us in this special way, and it was you that must take it on yourself to go meddling with the designs of Providence—and who gave you the right? It was wicked, that is what it was—just blasphemous presumption, and no more becoming to a meek and humble professor of—"

"But, Mary, you know how we have been trained all our lives long, like the whole village, till it is absolutely second nature to us to stop not a single moment to think when there's an honest thing to be done—"

Oh, I know it, I know it—it's been one everlasting training and training and training in honesty—honesty shielded, from the very cradle, against every possible temptation, and so it's *artificial* honesty, and weak as water when temptation comes, as we have seen this night. God knows I never had shade nor shadow of a doubt of my petrified and indestructible honesty until now—and now, under the very first big and real temptation, I—Edward, it is my belief that this town's honesty is as rotten as mine; as rotten as yours is. It is a mean town, a hard, stingy town, and hasn't a virtue in the world but this honesty it is so celebrated for and so conceited about; and so help me, I do believe that if ever the day comes that its honesty falls under great temptation, its grand reputation will go to ruin like a house of cards. There, now, I've made confession, and I feel better; I am a humbug, and I've been one all my life, without knowing it. Let no man call me honest again—I will not have it."

"I—Well, Mary, I feel a good deal as you do; I certainly do. It seems strange, too, so strange. I never could have believed it—never."

A long silence followed; both were sunk in thought. At last the wife looked up and said:

"I know what you are thinking, Edward."

Richards had the embarrassed look of a person who is caught.

"I am ashamed to confess it, Mary, but—"

"It's no matter, Edward, I was thinking the same question myself."

"I hope so. State it."

"You were thinking, if a body could only guess out *what the remark was* that Goodson made to the stranger."

"It's perfectly true. I feel guilty and ashamed. And you?"

"I'm past it. Let us make a pallet[1] here; we've got to stand watch till the bank vault opens in the morning and admits the sack. . . . Oh, dear, oh, dear—if we hadn't made the mistake!"

The pallet was made, and Mary said:

"The open sesame—what could it have been? I do wonder what that remark could have been? But come; we will get to bed now."

THE MAN THAT CORRUPTED HADLEYBURG.   **1. pallet:** bed.

"And sleep?"

"No; think."

"Yes, think."

By this time the Coxes too had completed their spat and their reconciliation, and were turning in—to think, to think, and toss, and fret, and worry over what the remark could possibly have been which Goodson made to the stranded derelict: that golden remark; that remark worth forty thousand dollars, cash.

The reason that the village telegraph-office was open later than usual that night was this: The foreman of Cox's paper was the local representative of the Associated Press. One might say its honorary representative, for it wasn't four times a year that he could furnish thirty words that would be accepted. But this time it was different. His despatch stating what he had caught got an instant answer:

Send the whole thing—all the details—twelve hundred words.

A colossal order! The foreman filled the bill; and he was the proudest man in the State. By breakfast-time the next morning the name of Hadleyburg the Incorruptible was on every lip in America, from Montreal to the Gulf, from the glaciers of Alaska to the orange-groves of Florida; and millions and millions of people were discussing the stranger and his money-sack, and wondering if the right man would be found, and hoping some more news about the matter would come soon—right away.

2

Hadleyburg village woke up world-celebrated—astonished—happy—vain. Vain beyond imagination. Its nineteen principal citizens and their wives went about shaking hands with each other, and beaming, and smiling, and congratulating, and saying *this* thing adds a new word to the dictionary—*Hadleyburg*, synonym for *incorruptible*—destined to live in dictionaries forever! And the minor and unimportant citizens and their wives went around acting in much the same way. Everybody ran to the bank to see the gold-sack; and before noon grieved and envious crowds began to flock in from Brixton and all the neighboring towns; and that afternoon and next day reporters began to arrive from everywhere to verify the sack and its history and write the whole thing up anew, and make dashing freehand pictures of the sack and of Richards's house, and the bank, and the Presbyterian church, and the Baptist church, and the public square, and the town-hall where the test would be applied and the money delivered; and damnable portraits of the Richardses and Pinkerton the banker, and Cox, and the foreman, and Reverend Burgess, and the postmaster—and even of Jack Halliday, who was the loafing, good-natured, no-account, irreverent fisherman, hunter, boys' friend, stray-dog's friend, typical "Sam Lawson"[2] of the town. The little mean, smirking, oily Pinkerton showed the sack to all comers, and rubbed his sleek palms together pleasantly, and enlarged upon the town's fine old reputation for honesty and upon this wonderful endorsement of it, and hoped and believed that the example would now spread far and wide over the American world, and be epoch-making in the matter of moral regeneration. And so on, and so on.

By the end of a week things had quieted down again; the wild intoxication of pride and joy had sobered to a soft, sweet, silent delight—a sort of deep, nameless, unutterable content. All faces bore a look of peaceful, holy happiness.

Then a change came. It was a gradual change: so gradual that its beginnings were hardly noticed; maybe were not noticed at all, except by Jack Halliday, who always noticed everything; and always made fun of it, too, no matter what it was. He began to throw out chaffing remarks about people not looking quite so happy as they did a day or two ago; and next he claimed that the new aspect was deepening to positive sadness; next, that it was taking on a sick look; and finally he said that everybody was becoming so moody, thoughtful, and absent-minded that he could rob the meanest man in town of a cent out of the bottom of his breeches pocket and not disturb his revery.

At this stage—or at about this stage—a saying like this was dropped at bed-time—with a sigh, usually—by the head of each of the nineteen principal households: "Ah, what *could* have been the remark that Goodson made!"

And straightway—with a shudder—came this, from the man's wife:

2. **Sam Lawson:** a lazy homespun philosopher created by Harriet Beecher Stowe who appears in *Oldtown Folks* (1869) and narrates *Sam Lawson's Oldtown Fireside Stories* (1872).

"Oh, *don't!* What horrible thing are you mulling in your mind? Put it away from you, for God's sake!"

But that question was wrung from those men again the next night—and got the same retort. But weaker.

And the third night the men uttered the question yet again—with anguish, and absently. This time—and the following night—the wives fidgeted feebly, and tried to say something. But didn't.

And the night after that they found their tongues and responded—longingly,

"Oh, if we *could* only guess!"

Halliday's comments grew daily more and more sparklingly disagreeable and disparaging. He went diligently about, laughing at the town, individually and in mass. But his laugh was the only one left in the village: it fell upon a hollow and mournful vacancy and emptiness. Not even a smile was findable anywhere. Halliday carried a cigar-box around on a tripod, playing that it was a camera, and halted all passers and aimed the thing and said, "Ready!—now look pleasant, please," but not even this capital joke could surprise the dreary faces into any softening.

So three weeks passed—one week was left. It was Saturday evening—after supper. Instead of the aforetime Saturday-evening flutter and bustle and shopping and larking, the streets were empty and desolate. Richards and his old wife sat apart in their little parlor—miserable and thinking. This was become their evening habit now: the lifelong habit which had preceded it, of reading, knitting, and contented chat, or receiving or paying neighborly calls, was dead and gone and forgotten, ages ago—two or three weeks ago; nobody talked now, nobody read, nobody visited—the whole village sat at home, sighing, worrying, silent. Trying to guess out that remark.

The postman left a letter. Richards glanced listlessly at the superscription and the postmark—unfamiliar, both—and tossed the letter on the table and resumed his might-have-beens and his hopeless dull miseries where he had left them off. Two or three hours later his wife got wearily up and was going away to bed without a good-night—custom now—but she stopped near the letter and eyed it awhile with a dead interest, then broke it open, and began to skim it over. Richards, sitting there with his chair tilted back against the wall and his chin between his knees, heard something fall. It was his wife. He sprang to her side, but she cried out:

"Leave me alone, I am too happy. Read the letter—read it!"

He did. He devoured it, his brain reeling. The letter was from a distant state, and it said:

I am a stranger to you, but no matter: I have something to tell. I have just arrived home from Mexico, and learned about that episode. Of course you do not know who made that remark, but I know, and I am the only person living who does know. It was GOODSON. I knew him well, many years ago. I passed through your village that very night, and was his guest till the midnight train came along. I overheard him make that remark to the stranger in the dark—it was in Hale Alley. He and I talked of it the rest of the way home, and while smoking in his house. He mentioned many of your villagers in the course of his talk—most of them in a very uncomplimentary way, but two or three favorably: among these latter yourself. I say "favorably"—nothing stronger. I remember his saying he did not actually LIKE any person in the town—not one; but that you—I THINK he said you—am almost sure, had done him a very great service once, possibly without knowing the full value of it, and he wished he had a fortune, he would leave it to you when he died, and a curse apiece for the rest of the citizens. Now, then, if it was you that did him that service, you are his legitimate heir, and entitled to the sack of gold. I know that I can trust to your honor and honesty, for in a citizen of Hadleyburg these virtues are an unfailing inheritance, and so I am going to reveal to you the remark, well satisfied that if you are not the right man you will seek and find the right one and see that poor Goodson's debt of gratitude for the service referred to is paid. This is the remark: "YOU ARE FAR FROM BEING A BAD MAN: GO, AND REFORM."

HOWARD L. STEPHENSON

"Oh, Edward, the money is ours, and I am so grateful, *oh*, so grateful—kiss me, dear, it's forever since we kissed—and we needed it so—the money —and now you are free of Pinkerton and his bank, and nobody's slave any more; it seems to me I could fly for joy."

It was a happy half-hour that the couple spent there on the settee caressing each other; it was the old days come again—days that had begun with their courtship and lasted without a break till the stranger brought the deadly money. By-and-by the wife said:

"Oh, Edward, how lucky it was you did him that grand service, poor Goodson! I never liked him, but I love him now. And it was fine and beautiful of you never to mention it or brag about it." Then, with a touch of reproach, "But you ought to have told *me*, Edward, you ought to have told your wife, you know."

"Well, I—er—well, Mary, you see——"

"Now stop hemming and hawing, and tell me about it, Edward. I always loved you, and now I'm proud of you. Everybody believes there was only one good generous soul in this village, and now it turns out that you—Edward, why don't you tell me?"

"Well—er—er— Why, Mary, I can't!"

"You *can't? Why* can't you?"

"You see, he—well, he—he made me promise I wouldn't."

The wife looked him over, and said, very slowly,

"Made—you—promise? Edward, what do you tell me that for?"

"Mary, do you think I would lie?"

She was troubled and silent for a moment, then she laid her hand within his and said:

"No . . . no. We have wandered far enough from our bearings—God spare us that! In all your life you have never uttered a lie. But now—now that the foundations of things seem to be crumbling from under us, we—we—" She lost her voice for a moment, then said, brokenly, "Lead us not into temptation. . . . I think you made the promise, Edward. Let it rest so. Let us keep away from that ground. Now—that is all gone by; let us be happy again; it is no time for clouds."

Edward found it something of an effort to comply, for his mind kept wandering—trying to remember what the service was that he had done Goodson.

The couple lay awake the most of the night, Mary happy and busy, Edward busy, but not so happy. Mary was planning what she would do with the money. Edward was trying to recall that service. At first his conscience was sore on account of the lie he had told Mary—if it was a lie. After much reflection—suppose it *was* a lie? What then? Was it such a great matter? Aren't we always *acting* lies? Then why not *tell* them? Look at Mary—look what she had done. While he was hurrying off on his honest errand, what was she doing? Lamenting because the papers hadn't been destroyed and the money kept! Is theft better than lying?

That point lost its sting—the lie dropped into the background and left comfort behind it. The next point came to the front: *had* he rendered that service? Well, here was Goodson's own evidence as reported in Stephenson's letter; there could be no better evidence than that—it was even *proof* that he had rendered it. Of course. So that point was settled. . . . No, not quite. He recalled with a wince that this unknown Mr. Stephenson was just a trifle unsure as to whether the performer of it was Richards or some other—and, oh dear, he had to put Richards on his honor! He must himself decide whither that money must go—and Mr. Stephenson was not doubting that if he was the wrong man he would go honorably and find the right one. Oh, it was odious to put a man in such a situation—ah, why couldn't Stephenson have left out that doubt! What did he want to intrude that for?

Further reflection. How did it happen that *Richards's* name remained in Stephenson's mind as indicating the right man, and not some other man's name? That looked good. Yes, that looked very good. In fact, it went on looking better and better, straight along—until by-and-by it grew into positive *proof*. And then Richards put the matter at once out of his mind, for he had a private instinct that a proof once established is better left so.

He was feeling reasonably comfortable now, but there was still one other detail that kept pushing itself on his notice: of course he had done that service—that was settled; but what *was* that service? He must recall it—he would not go to sleep till he had recalled it; it would make his peace of mind perfect. And so he thought and thought. He thought of a dozen things—possible services, even probable services—but none of them seemed adequate, none of them seemed large enough, none of them seemed worth the money—worth the fortune Goodson had wished he could leave in his will. And besides, he couldn't remember having done them, anyway. Now, then—now, then—what *kind* of a service would it be that would make a man so inordinately grateful? Ah—the saving of his soul! That must be it. Yes, he could remember, now, how he once set himself the task of converting Goodson, and labored at it as much as—he was going to say three months; but upon closer examination it shrunk to a month, then to a week, then to a day, then to nothing. Yes, he remembered now, and with unwelcome vividness, that Goodson had told him to go to thunder and mind his own business—*he* wasn't hankering to follow Hadleyburg to heaven!

So that solution was a failure—he hadn't saved

Goodson's soul. Richards was discouraged. Then after a little came another idea: had he saved Goodson's property? No, that wouldn't do—he hadn't any. His life? This is it! Of course. Why, he might have thought of it before. This time he was on the right track, sure. His imagination was hard at work in a minute, now.

Thereafter during a stretch of two exhausting hours he was busy saving Goodson's life. He saved it in all kinds of difficult and perilous ways. In every case he got it saved satisfactorily up to a certain point; then, just as he was beginning to get well persuaded that it had really happened, a troublesome detail would turn up which made the whole thing impossible. As in the matter of drowning, for instance. In that case he had swum out and tugged Goodson ashore in an unconscious state with a great crowd looking on and applauding, but when he had got it all thought out and was just beginning to remember all about it a whole swarm of disqualifying details arrived on the ground: the town would have known of it, it would glare like a limelight in his own memory instead of being an inconspicuous service which he had possibly rendered "without knowing its full value." And at this point he remembered that he couldn't swim, anyway.

Ah—*there* was a point which he had been overlooking from the start: it had to be a service which he had rendered "possibly without knowing the full value of it." Why, really, that ought to be an easy hunt—much easier than those others. And sure enough, by-and-by he found it. Goodson, years and years ago, came near marrying a very sweet and pretty girl, named Nancy Hewitt, but in some way or other the match had been broken off; the girl died, Goodson remained a bachelor, and by-and-by became a soured one and a frank despairer of the human species. Soon after the girl's death the village found out, or thought it had found out, that she carried a spoonful of Negro blood in her veins. Richards worked at these details a good while, and in the end he thought he remembered things concerning them which must have gotten mislaid in his memory through long neglect. He seemed to dimly remember that it was *he* that found out about the Negro blood; that it was he that told the village; that the village told Goodson where they got it; that he thus saved Goodson from marrying the tainted girl; that he had done him this great service "without knowing the full value of it," in fact without knowing that he *was* doing it; but that Goodson knew the value of it, and what a narrow escape he had had, and so went to his grave grateful to his benefactor and wishing he had a fortune to leave him. It was all clear and simple now, and the more he went over it the more luminous and certain it grew; and at last, when he nestled to sleep satisfied and happy, he remembered the whole thing just as if it had been yesterday. In fact, he dimly remembered Goodson's *telling* him his gratitude once. Meantime Mary had spent six thousand dollars on a new house for herself and a pair of slippers for her pastor, and then had fallen peacefully to rest.

That same Saturday evening the postman had delivered a letter to each of the other principal citizens—nineteen letters in all. No two of the envelopes were alike, and no two of the super-scriptions were in the same hand, but the letters inside were just like each other in every detail but one. They were exact copies of the letter received by Richards—handwriting and all—and were all signed by Stephenson, but in place of Richards's name each receiver's own name appeared.

All night long eighteen principal citizens did what their caste-brother Richards was doing at the same time—they put in their energies trying to remember what notable service it was that they had unconsciously done Barclay Goodson. In no case was it a holiday job; still they succeeded.

And while they were at this work, which was difficult, their wives put in the night spending the money, which was easy. During that one night the nineteen wives spent an average of seven thousand dollars each out of the forty thousand in the sack —a hundred and thirty-three thousand altogether.

Next day there was a surprise for Jack Halliday. He noticed that the faces of the nineteen chief citizens and their wives bore that expression of peaceful and holy happiness again. He could not understand it, neither was he able to invent any remarks about it that could damage it or disturb it. And so it was his turn to be dissatisfied with life. His private guesses at the reasons for the happiness failed in all instances, upon examination. When he met Mrs. Wilcox and noticed the placid ecstasy in her face, he said to himself, "Her cat has had kittens"—and went and asked the cook; it was not so; the cook had detected the happiness, but did

not know the cause. When Halliday found the duplicate ecstasy in the face of "Shadbelly" Billson (village nickname), he was sure some neighbor of Billson's had broken his leg, but inquiry showed that this had not happened. The subdued ecstasy in Gregory Yates's face could mean but one thing— he was a mother-in-law short; it was another mistake. "And Pinkerton—Pinkerton—he has col-lected ten cents that he thought he was going to lose." And so on, and so on. In some cases the guesses had to remain in doubt, in the others they proved distinct errors. In the end Halliday said to himself, "Anyway, it foots up that there's nineteen Hadleyburg families temporarily in heaven: I don't know how it happened; I only know Providence is off duty today."

An architect and builder from the next state had lately ventured to set up a small business in this unpromising village, and his sign had now been hanging out a week. Not a customer yet; he was a discouraged man, and sorry he had come. But his weather changed suddenly now. First one and then another chief citizen's wife said to him privately:

"Come to my house Monday week—but say nothing about it for the present. We think of building."

He got eleven invitations that day. That night he wrote his daughter and broke off her match with her student. He said she could marry a mile higher than that.

Pinkerton the banker and two or three other well-to-do men planned country-seats—but waited. That kind don't count their chickens until they are hatched.

The Wilsons devised a grand new thing—a fancy-dress ball. They made no actual promises, but told all their acquaintanceship in confidence that they were thinking the matter over and thought they should give it—"And if we do, you will be invited, of course." People were surprised, and said, one to another, "Why, they are crazy, those poor Wilsons, they can't afford it." Several among the nineteen said privately to their husbands, "It is a good idea, we will keep still till their cheap thing is over, then *we* will give one that will make it sick."

The days drifted along, and the bill of future squanderings rose higher and higher, wilder and wilder, more and more foolish and reckless. It began to look as if every member of the nineteen would not only spend his whole forty thousand dollars before receiving-day, but be actually in debt by the time he got the money. In some cases light-headed people did not stop with planning to spend, they really spent—on credit. They bought land, mortgages, farms, speculative stocks, fine clothes, horses, and various other things, paid down the bonus,[3] and made themselves liable for the rest—at ten days. Presently the sober second thought came, and Halliday noticed that a ghastly anxiety was beginning to show up in a good many faces. Again he was puzzled, and didn't know what to make of it. "The Wilcox kittens aren't dead, for they weren't born; nobody's broken a leg; there's no shrinkage in mother-in-laws; *nothing* has happened—it is an insolvable mystery."

There was another puzzled man, too—the Rev. Mr. Burgess. For days, wherever he went, people seemed to follow him or to be watching out for him; and if he ever found himself in a retired spot, a member of the nineteen would be sure to appear, thrust an envelope privately into his hand, whisper "To be opened at the town-hall Friday evening," then vanish away like a guilty thing. He was expecting that there might be one claimant for the sack—doubtful, however, Goodson being dead—but it never occurred to him that all this crowd might be claimants. When the great Friday came at last, he found that he had nineteen envelopes.

3

The town-hall had never looked finer. The platform at the end of it was backed by a showy draping of flags; at intervals along the walls were festoons of flags; the gallery fronts were clothed in flags; the supporting columns were swathed in flags; all this was to impress the stranger, for he would be there in considerable force, and in a large degree he would be connected with the press. The house was full. The 412 fixed seats were occupied; also the 68 extra chairs which had been packed into the aisles; the steps of the platform were occupied; some distinguished strangers were given seats on the platform; at the horseshoe of tables which fenced the front and sides of the platform sat a strong force of special correspondents who had come from everywhere. It was the best-dressed house the town had ever produced. There were some tolerably expensive toilets there, and in several cases the

3. **bonus:** deposit.

ladies who wore them had the look of being unfamiliar with that kind of clothes. At least the town thought they had that look, but the notion could have arisen from the town's knowledge of the fact that these ladies had never inhabited such clothes before.

The gold-sack stood on a little table at the front of the platform where all the house could see it. The bulk of the house gazed at it with a burning interest, a mouth-watering interest, a wistful and pathetic interest; a minority of nineteen couples gazed at it tenderly, lovingly, proprietarily, and the male half of this minority kept saying over to themselves the moving little impromptu speeches of thankfulness for the audience's applause and congratulations which they were presently going to get up and deliver. Every now and then one of these got a piece of paper out of his vest pocket and privately glanced at it to refresh his memory.

Of course there was a buzz of conversation going on—there always is; but at last when the Rev. Mr. Burgess rose and laid his hand on the sack he could hear his microbes gnaw, the place was so still. He related the curious history of the sack, then went on to speak in warm terms of Hadleyburg's old and well-earned reputation for spotless honesty, and of the town's just pride in this reputation. He said that this reputation was a treasure of priceless value; that under Providence its value had now become inestimably enhanced, for the recent episode had spread this fame far and wide, and thus had focused the eyes of the American world upon this village, and made its name for all time, as he hoped and believed, a synonym for commercial incorruptibility. [*Applause.*] "And who is to be the guardian of this noble treasure—the community as a whole? No! The responsibility is individual, not communal. From this day forth each and every one of you is in his own person its special guardian and individually responsible that no harm shall come to it. Do you—does each of you—accept this great trust? [*Tumultuous assent.*] Then all is well. Transmit it to your children and to your children's children. Today your purity is beyond reproach—see to it that it shall remain so. Today there is not a person in your community who could be beguiled to touch a penny not his own—see to it that you abide in this grace. ["*We will! we will!*"] This is not the place to make comparisons between ourselves and other communities—some of them ungracious toward us; they have their ways, we have ours; let us be content. [*Applause.*] I am done. Under my hand, my friends, rests a stranger's eloquent recognition of what we are: through him the world will always henceforth know what we are. We do not know who he is, but in your name I utter your gratitude, and ask you to raise your voices in endorsement."

The house rose in a body and made the walls quake with the thunders of its thankfulness for the space of a long minute. Then it sat down, and Mr. Burgess took an envelope out of his pocket. The house held its breath while he slit the envelope open and took from it a slip of paper. He read its contents—slowly and impressively—the audience listening with tranced attention to this magic document, each of whose words stood for an ingot of gold:

"*The remark which I made to the distressed stranger was this: "You are very far from being a bad man; go, and reform."*'" Then he continued: "We shall know in a moment now whether the remark here quoted corresponds with the one concealed in the sack; and if that shall prove to be so —and it undoubtedly will—this sack of gold belongs to a fellow-citizen who will henceforth stand before the nation as the symbol of the special virtue which has made our town famous throughout the land—Mr. Billson!"

The house had gotten itself all ready to burst into a proper tornado of applause; but instead of doing it, it seemed stricken with a paralysis; there was a deep hush for a moment or two, then a wave of whispered murmurs swept the place—of about this tenor: "*Billson!* oh, come, this is *too* thin! Twenty dollars to a stranger—or *anybody*— *Billson!* Tell it to the marines!" And now at this point the house caught its breath all of a sudden in a new access of astonishment, for it discovered that whereas in one part of the hall Deacon Billson was standing up with his head meekly bowed, in another part of it Lawyer Wilson was doing the same. There was a wondering silence now for a while. Everybody was puzzled, and nineteen couples were surprised and indignant.

Billson and Wilson turned and stared at each other. Billson asked, bitingly,

"Why do *you* rise, Mr. Wilson?"

"Because I have a right to. Perhaps you will be good enough to explain to the house why *you* rise?"

"With great pleasure. Because I wrote that paper."

"It is an impudent falsity! I wrote it myself."

It was Burgess's turn to be paralyzed. He stood looking vacantly at first one of the men and then the other, and did not seem to know what to do. The house was stupefied. Lawyer Wilson spoke up, now, and said,

"I ask the Chair to read the name signed to that paper."

That brought the Chair to itself, and it read out the name,

"'John Wharton *Billson*.'"

"There!" shouted Billson, "what have you got to say for yourself, now? And what kind of apology are you going to make to me and to this insulted house for the imposture which you have attempted to play here?"

"No apologies are due, sir; and as for the rest of it, I public charge you with pilfering my note from Mr. Burgess and substituting a copy of it signed with your own name. There is no other way by which you could have gotten hold of the test-remark; I alone, of living men, possessed the secret of its wording."

There was likely to be a scandalous state of things if this went on; everybody noticed with distress that the shorthand scribes were scribbling like mad; many people were crying "Chair, Chair! Order! order!" Burgess rapped with his gavel, and said:

"Let us not forget the proprieties due. There has evidently been a mistake somewhere, but surely that is all. If Mr. Wilson gave me an envelope— and I remembered now that he did—I still have it."

He took one out of his pocket, opened it, glanced at it, looked surprised and worried, and stood silent a few moments. Then he waved his hand in a wandering and mechanical way, and made an effort or two to say something, then gave it up, despondently. Several voices cried out:

"Read it! read it! What is it?"

So he began in a dazed and sleepwalker fashion:

"*The remark which I made to the unhappy stranger was this: "You are far from being a bad man. [The house gazed at him, marveling.] Go, and reform."*' [MURMURS "Amazing! what can this mean?"] This one," said the Chair, "is signed Thurlow G. Wilson."

"There!" cried Wilson, "I reckon that settles it! I knew perfectly well my note was purloined."

"Purloined!" retorted Billson. "I'll let you know that neither you nor any man of your kidney must venture to—"

THE CHAIR "Order, gentlemen, order! Take your seats, both of you, please."

They obeyed, shaking their heads and grumbling angrily. The house was profoundly puzzled; it did not know what to do with this curious emergency. Presently Thompson got up. Thompson was the hatter. He would have liked to be a Nineteener; but such was not for him; his stock of hats was not considerable enough for the position. He said:

"Mr. Chairman, if I may be permitted to make a suggestion, can both of these gentlemen be right? I put it to you, sir, can both have happened to say the very same words to the stranger? It seems to me—"

The tanner got up and interrupted him. The tanner was a disgruntled man; he believed himself entitled to be a Nineteener, but he couldn't get recognition. It made him a little unpleasant in his ways and speech. Said he:

"Sho, *that's* not the point! *That* could happen— twice in a hundred years—but not the other thing. *Neither* of them gave the twenty dollars!" [*A ripple of applause.*]

BILLSON "I did!"

WILSON "I did!"

Then each accused the other of pilfering.

THE CHAIR "Order! Sit down, if you please— both of you. Neither of the notes has been out of my possession at any moment."

A VOICE "Good—that settles *that!*"

THE TANNER "Mr. Chairman, one thing is now plain: one of these men has been eavesdropping under the other one's bed, and filching family secrets. If it is not unparliamentary to suggest it, I will remark that both are equal to it. [THE CHAIR "Order! order!"] I withdraw the remark, sir, and will confine myself to suggesting that *if* one of them has overheard the other reveal the test-remark to his wife, we shall catch him now."

A VOICE "How?"

THE TANNER "Easily. The two have not quoted the remark in exactly the same words. You would have noticed that, if there hadn't been a considerable stretch of time and an exciting quarrel inserted between the two readings."

A VOICE "Name the difference."

THE TANNER "The word *very* is in Billson's note, and not in the other."

MANY VOICES "That's so—he's right."

THE TANNER "And so, if the Chair will examine the test-remark in the sack, we shall know which of these two frauds— [THE CHAIR "Order!"]— which of these two adventurers—[THE CHAIR "Order! order!"]—which of these two gentlemen —[*laughter and applause*]—is entitled to wear the belt as being the first dishonest blatherskite ever bred in this town—which he has dishonored, and which will be a sultry place for him from now on!" [*Vigorous applause.*]

MANY VOICES "Open it!—open the sack!"

Mr. Burgess made a slit in the sack, slid his hand in and brought out an envelope. In it were a couple of folded notes. He said:

"One of these is marked, 'Not to be examined until all written communications which have been addressed to the Chair—if any—shall have been read.' The other is marked '*The Test*.' Allow me. It is worded—to wit:

"I do not require that the first half of the remark which was made to me by my benefactor shall be quoted with exactness, for it was not striking, and could be forgotten; but its closing fifteen words are quite striking, and I think easily rememberable; unless *these* shall be accurately reproduced, let the applicant be regarded as an impostor. My benefactor began by saying he seldom gave advice to any one, but that it always bore the hallmark of high value when he did give it. Then he said this— and it has never faded from my memory: " *You are far from being a bad man*— ' "

FIFTY VOICES "That settles it—the money's Wilson's! Wilson! Wilson! Speech! Speech!"

People jumped up and crowded around Wilson, wringing his hand and congratulating fervently— meantime the Chair was hammering with the gavel and shouting:

"Order, gentlemen! Order! Order! Let me finish reading, please." When quiet was restored, the reading was resumed—as follows:

" ' "*Go, and reform—or, mark my words—some day, for your sins, you will die and go to hell or Hadleyburg*—TRY AND MAKE IT THE FORMER.' " "

A ghastly silence followed. First an angry cloud began to settle darkly upon the faces of the citizenship; after a pause the cloud began to rise, and a tickled expression tried to take its place; tried so hard that it was only kept under with great and painful difficulty; the reporters, the Brixtonites, and other strangers bent their heads down and shielded their faces with their hands, and managed to hold in by main strength and heroic courtesy. At this most inopportune time burst upon the stillness the roar of a solitary voice—Jack Halliday's:

"*That's* got the hallmark on it!"

Then the house let go, strangers and all. Even Mr. Burgess's gravity broke down presently, then the audience considered itself officially absolved from all restraint, and it made the most of its privilege. It was a good long laugh, and a tempestuously wholehearted one, but it ceased at last—long enough for Mr. Burgess to try to resume, and for the people to get their eyes partially wiped; then it broke out again; and afterward yet again; then at last Burgess was able to get out these serious words:

"It is useless to try to disguise the fact—we find ourselves in the presence of a matter of grave import. It involves the honor of your town, it strikes at the town's good name. The difference of a single word between the test-remarks offered by Mr. Wilson and Mr. Billson was itself a serious thing, since it indicated that one or the other of these gentlemen had committed a theft—"

The two men were sitting limp, nerveless, crushed; but at these words both were electrified into movement, and started to get up—

"Sit down!" said the Chair, sharply, and they obeyed. "That, as I have said, was a serious thing. And it was—but for only one of them. But the matter has become graver; for the honor of *both* is now in formidable peril. Shall I go even further, and say in inextricable peril? *Both* left out the crucial fifteen words." He paused. During several moments he allowed the pervading stillness to gather and deepen its impressive effects, then added: "There would seem to be but one way whereby this could happen. I ask these gentlemen —Was there *collusion?—agreement?*"

A low murmur sifted through the house; its import was, "He's got them both."

Billson was not used to emergencies; he sat in a helpless collapse. But Wilson was a lawyer. He struggled to his feet, pale and worried, and said:

"I ask the indulgence of the house while I explain this most painful matter. I am sorry to say what I am about to say, since it must inflict irreparable injury upon Mr. Billson, whom I have always esteemed and respected until now, and in whose invulnerability to temptation I entirely believed— as did you all. But for the preservation of my own honor I must speak—and with frankness. I confess with shame—and I now beseech your pardon for it—that I said to the ruined stranger all of the words contained in the test-remark, including the disparaging fifteen. [*Sensation.*] When the late publication was made I recalled them, and I resolved to claim the sack of coin, for by every right I was entitled to it. Now I will ask you to consider this point, and weigh it well: that stranger's gratitude to me that night knew no bounds; he said himself that he could find no words for it that were adequate, and that if he should ever be able he would repay me a thousandfold. Now, then, I ask you this: could I expect—could I believe—could I even remotely imagine—that, feeling as he did, he would do so ungrateful a thing as to add those quite unnecessary fifteen words to his test?—set a trap for me?—expose me as a slanderer of my own town before my own people assembled in a public hall? It was preposterous; it was impossible. His test would contain only the kindly opening clause of my remark. Of that I had no shadow of doubt. You would have thought as I did. You would not have expected a base betrayal from one whom you had befriended and against whom you had committed no offence. And so, with perfect confidence, perfect trust, I wrote on a piece of paper the opening words—ending with 'Go, and reform,'— and signed it. When I was about to put it in an envelope I was called into my back office, and without thinking I left the paper lying open on my desk." He stopped, turned his head slowly toward Billson, waited a moment, then added: "I ask you to note this: when I returned, a little later, Mr. Billson was retiring by my street door." [*Sensation.*]

In a moment Billson was on his feet and shouting:

"It's a lie! It's an infamous lie!"

THE CHAIR "Be seated, sir! Mr. Wilson has the floor."

Billson's friends pulled him into his seat and quieted him, and Wilson went on:

"Those are the simple facts. My note was now lying in a different place on the table from where I had left it. I noticed that, but attached no importance to it, thinking a draft had blown it there. That

Mr. Billson would read a private paper was a thing which could not occur to me; he was an honorable man, and he would be above that. If you will allow me to say it, I think his extra word '*very*' stands explained; it is attributable to a defect of memory. I was the only man in the world who could furnish here any detail of the test-mark—by *honorable* means. I have finished."

There is nothing in the world like a persuasive speech to fuddle the mental apparatus and upset the convictions and debauch the emotions of an audience not practiced in the tricks and delusions of oratory. Wilson sat down victorious. The house submerged him in tides of approving applause; friends swarmed to him and shook him by the hand and congratulated him, and Billson was shouted down and not allowed to say a word. The Chair hammered and hammered with its gavel, and kept shouting:

"But let us proceed, gentlemen, let us proceed!"

At last there was a measurable degree of quiet, and the hatter said:

"But what is there to proceed with, sir, but to deliver the money?"

VOICES   "That's it! That's it! Come forward, Wilson!"

THE HATTER   "I move three cheers for Mr. Wilson, symbol of the special virtue which—"

The cheers burst forth before he could finish; and in the midst of them—and in the midst of the clamor of the gavel also—some enthusiasts mounted Wilson on a big friend's shoulder and were going to fetch him in triumph to the platform. The Chair's voice now rose above the noise—

"Order! To your places! You forget that there is still a document to be read." When quiet had been restored he took up the document, and was going to read it, but laid it down again, saying, "I forgot; this is not to be read until all written communications received by me have first been read." He took an envelope out of his pocket, removed its enclosure, glanced at it—seemed astonished—held it out and gazed at it—stared at it.

Twenty or thirty voices cried out:

"What is it? Read it! read it!"

And he did—slowly, and wondering:

" 'The remark which I made to the stranger— [VOICES   "Hello! how's this?"]—was this: "You are far from being a bad man. [VOICES   "Great Scott!"] Go, and reform." ' [VOICE   "Oh, saw my leg off!"] Signed by Mr. Pinkerton the banker."

The pandemonium of delight which turned itself loose now was of a sort to make the judicious weep. Those whose withers were unwrung[4] laughed till the tears ran down; the reporters, in throes of laughter, set down disordered pothooks[5] which would never in the world be decipherable; and a sleeping dog jumped up, scared out of its wits, and barked itself crazy at the turmoil. All manner of cries were scattered through the din: "We're getting rich—*two* Symbols of Incorruptibility!—without counting Billson!" "*Three !*—count Shadbelly in— we can't have too many!" "All right—Billson's elected!" "Alas, poor Wilson—victim of *two* thieves!"

A POWERFUL VOICE   "Silence! The Chair's fished up something more out of its pocket."

VOICES   "Hurrah! Is it something fresh? Read it! read! read!"

THE CHAIR   [*Reading*]   " 'The remark which I made,' etc. 'You are far from being a bad man. Go,' etc. Signed, 'Gregory Yates.' "

TORNADO OF VOICES   "Four Symbols!" " 'Rah for Yates!" "Fish again!"

The house was in a roaring humor now, and ready to get all the fun out of the occasion that might be in it. Several Nineteeners, looking pale and distressed, got up and began to work their way toward the aisles, but a score of shouts went up:

"The doors, the doors—close the doors; no Incorruptible shall leave this place! Sit down, everybody!"

The mandate was obeyed.

"Fish again! Read! read!"

The Chair fished again, and once more the familiar words began to fall from its lips—" 'You are far from being a bad man—' "

"Name! name! What's his name?"

" 'L. Ingoldsby Sargent.' "

"Five elected! Pile up the Symbols! Go on, go on!"

" 'You are far from being a bad—' "

"Name! name!"

" 'Nicholas Whitworth.' "

"Hooray! hooray! it's a symbolical day!"

Somebody wailed in, and began to sing this rhyme (leaving out "it's") to the lovely "Mikado"

---

4. withers . . . unwrung: mock "poetic" cliché for unstrung feelings. **5. pothooks:** scrawls.

tune of "When a man's afraid, a beautiful maid[6]—"; the audience joined in, with joy; then, just in time, somebody contributed another line—

And don't you this forget——

The house roared it out. A third line was at once furnished—

Corruptibles far from Hadleyburg are——

The house roared that one too. As the last note died, Jack Halliday's voice rose high and clear, freighted with a final line—

But the Symbols are here, you bet!

That was sung, with booming enthusiasm. Then the happy house started in at the beginning and sang the four lines through twice, with immense swing and dash, and finished up with a crashing three-times-three and a tiger for "Hadleyburg the Incorruptible and all Symbols of it which we shall find worthy to receive the hallmark to-night."

Then the shoutings at the Chair began again, all over the place:

"Go on! go on! Read! read some more! Read all you've got!"

"That's it—go on! We are winning eternal celebrity!"

A dozen men got up now and began to protest. They said that this farce was the work of some abandoned joker, and was an insult to the whole community. Without a doubt these signatures were all forgeries—

"Sit down! sit down! Shut up! You are confessing. We'll find *your* names in the lot."

"Mr. Chairman, how many of those envelopes have you got?"

The Chair counted.

"Together with those that have been already examined, there are nineteen."

A storm of derisive applause broke out.

"Perhaps they all contain the secret. I move that you open them all and read every signature that is attached to a note of that sort—and read also the first eight words of the note."

"Second the motion!"

It was put and carried—uproariously. Then poor old Richards got up, and his wife rose and stood at his side. Her head was bent down, so that none

might see that she was crying. Her husband gave her his arm, and so supporting her, he began to speak in a quavering voice:

"My friends, you have known us two—Mary and me—all our lives, and I think you have liked us and respected us—"

The Chair interrupted him:

"Allow me. It is quite true—that which you are saying, Mr. Richards; this town *does* know you two; it *does* like you; it *does* respect you; more— it honors you and *loves* you—"

Halliday's voice rang out:

"That's the hallmarked truth, too! If the Chair is right, let the house speak up and say it. Rise! Now, then—hip! hip! hip!—all together!"

The house rose in mass, faced toward the old couple eagerly, filled the air with a snowstorm of waving handkerchiefs, and delivered the cheers with all its affectionate heart.

The Chair then continued:

"What I was going to say is this: We know your good heart, Mr. Richards, but this is not a time for the exercise of charity toward offenders. [*Shouts of "Right! right!"*] I see your generous purpose in your face, but I cannot allow you to plead for these men—"

"But I was going to—"

"Please take your seat, Mr. Richards. We must examine the rest of these notes—simple fairness to the men who have already been exposed requires this. As soon as that has been done—I give you my word for this—you shall be heard."

MANY VOICES "Right!—the Chair is right—no interruption can be permitted at this stage! Go on! —the names! the names!—according to the terms of the motion!"

The old couple sat reluctantly down, and the husband whispered to the wife, "It is pitifully hard to have to wait; the shame will be greater than ever when they find we were only going to plead for *ourselves*."

Straightway the jollity broke loose again with the reading of the names.

" 'You are far from being a bad man—' Signature, 'Robert J. Titmarsh.' "

" 'You are far from being a bad man—' Signature, 'Eliphalet Weeks.' "

" 'You are far from being a bad man—' Signature, 'Oscar B. Wilder.' "

At this point the house lit upon the idea of

6. When . . . maid: "when a man's afraid, / a beautiful maid / Is a cheering sight to see." (*Mikado*, Act III).

taking the eight words out of the Chairman's hands. He was not unthankful for that. Thenceforward he held up each note in its turn, and waited. The house droned out the eight words in a massed and measured and musical deep volume of sound (with a daringly close resemblance to a well-known church chant)—" 'You are f-a-r from being a b-a-a-a-d man.' " Then the Chair said, "Signature, 'Archibald Wilcox.' " And so on, and so on, name after name, and everybody had an increasingly and gloriously good time except the wretched Nineteen. Now and then, when a particularly shining name was called, the house made the Chair wait while it chanted the whole of the test-remark from the beginning to the closing words, "And go to hell or Hadleyburg—try and make it the for-or-m-e-r!" and in these special cases they added a grand and agonized and imposing "A-a-a-a-*men!*"

The list dwindled, dwindled, dwindled, poor old Richards keeping tally of the count, wincing when a name resembling his own was pronounced, and waiting in miserable suspense for the time to come when it would be his humiliating privilege to rise with Mary and finish his plea, which he was intending to word thus: ". . . for until now we have never done any wrong thing, but have gone our humble way unreproached. We are very poor, we are old, and have no chick nor child to help us; we were sorely tempted, and we fell. It was my purpose when I got up before to make confession and beg that my name might not be read out in this public place, for it seemed to us that we could not bear it; but I was prevented. It was just; it was our place to suffer with the rest. It has been hard for us. It is the first time we have ever heard our name fall from any one's lips—sullied. Be merciful—for the sake of the better days; make our shame as light to bear as in your charity you can." At this point in his reverie Mary nudged him, perceiving that his mind was absent. The house was chanting. "You are f-a-r," etc.

"Be ready," Mary whispered. "Your name comes now; he has read eighteen."

The chant ended.

"Next! next! next!" came volleying from all over the house.

Burgess put his hand into his pocket. The old couple, trembling, began to rise, Burgess fumbled a moment, then said,

"I find I have read them all."

Faint with joy and surprise, the couple sank into their seats, and Mary whispered:

"Oh, bless God, we are saved!—he has lost ours —I wouldn't give this for a hundred of those sacks!"

The house burst out with its "Mikado" travesty, and sang it three times with ever-increasing enthusiasm, rising to its feet when it reached for the third time the closing line—

But the Symbols are here, you bet!

and finished up with cheers and a tiger for "Hadleyburg purity and our eighteen immortal representatives of it."

Then Wingate, the saddler, got up and proposed cheers "for the cleanest man in town, the one solitary important citizen in it who didn't try to steal that money—Edward Richards."

They were given with great and moving heartiness; then somebody proposed that Richards be elected sole Guardian and Symbol of the now Sacred Hadleyburg Tradition, with power and right to stand up and look the whole sarcastic world in the face.

Passed, by acclamation; then they sang the "Mikado" again, and ended it with,

And there's *one* Symbol left, you bet!

There was a pause; then—

A VOICE   "Now, then, who's to get the sack?"

THE TANNER   [*With bitter sarcasm*] "That's easy. The money has to be divided among the eighteen Incorruptibles. They gave the suffering stranger twenty dollars apiece—and that remark—each in his turn—it took twenty-two minutes for the procession to move past. Staked the stranger—total contribution, $360. All they want is just the loan back—and interest—forty thousand dollars altogether."

MANY VOICES   [*Derisively*]   "That's it! Divvy! divvy! Be kind to the poor—don't keep them waiting!"

THE CHAIR   "Order! I now offer the stranger's remaining document. It says: 'If no claimant shall appear [*grand chorus of groans*], I desire that you open the sack and count out the money to the principal citizens of your town, they to take it in trust [*Cries of* "Oh! Oh! Oh!"], and use it in such ways as to them shall seem best for the propagation and preservation of your community's noble reputation for incorruptible honesty [*more cries*]—a reputation to which their names and their efforts will add a new and far-reaching lustre.' [*Enthusiastic outburst of sarcastic applause.*] That seems to be all. No—here is a postscript:

" 'P. S.—CITIZENS OF HADLEYBURG: There *is* no test-remark—nobody made one. [*Great sensation.*] There wasn't any pauper stranger, nor any twenty-dollar contribution, nor any accompanying benediction and compliment—these are all inventions. [*General buzz and hum of astonishment and delight.*] Allow me to tell my story—it will take but a word or two. I passed through your town at a certain time, and received a deep offense which I had not earned. Any other man would have been content to kill one or two of you and call it square, but to me that would have been a trivial revenge, and inadequate; for the dead do not *suffer*. Besides, I could not kill you all—and, anyway, made as I am, even that would not have satisfied me. I wanted to damage every man in the place, and every woman —and not in their bodies or in their estate, but in their vanity—the place where feeble and foolish people are most vulnerable. So I disguised myself and came back and studied you. You were easy game. You had an old and lofty reputation for honesty, and naturally you were proud of it—it was your treasure of treasures, the very apple of your eye. As soon as I found out that you carefully and vigilantly kept yourselves and your children *out of temptation*, I knew how to proceed. Why, you simple creatures, the weakest of all weak things is a virtue which has not been tested in the fire. I laid a plan, and gathered a list of names. My project was to corrupt Hadleyburg the incorruptible. My idea was to make liars and thieves of nearly half a hundred smirchless men and women who had never in their lives uttered a lie or stolen a penny. I was afraid of Goodson. He was neither born nor reared in Hadleyburg. I was afraid that if I started to operate my scheme by getting my letter laid before you, you would say to yourselves, "Goodson is the only man among us who would give away twenty dollars to a poor devil"—and then you might not bite at my bait. But Heaven took Goodson; then I knew I was safe, and I set my trap and baited it. It may be that I shall not catch all the men to whom I mailed the pretended test secret, but I shall catch the most of them, if I know Hadleyburg nature. [VOICES "Right—he got every last one of

them."] I believe they will even steal ostensible *gamble*-money, rather than miss, poor, tempted, and mistrained fellows. I am hoping to eternally and everlastingly squelch your vanity and give Hadleyburg a new renown—one that will *stick*— and spread far. If I have succeeded, open the sack and summon the Committee on Propagation and Preservation of the Hadleyburg Reputation.' "

A CYCLONE OF VOICES "Open it! Open it! The Eighteen to the front! Committee on Propagation of the Tradition! Forward—the Incorruptibles!"

The Chair ripped the sack wide, and gathered up a handful of bright, broad, yellow coins, shook them together, then examined them—

"Friends, they are only gilded disks of lead!"

There was a crashing outbreak of delight over this news, and when the noise had subsided, the tanner called out:

"By right of apparent seniority in this business, Mr. Wilson is Chairman of the Committee on Propagation of the Tradition. I suggest that he step forward on behalf of his pals, and receive in trust the money."

A HUNDRED VOICES "Wilson! Wilson! Wilson! Speech! Speech!"

WILSON [*in a voice trembling with anger*] "You will allow me to say, without apologies for my language, *damn* the money!"

A VOICE "Oh, and him a Baptist!"

A VOICE "Seventeen Symbols left! Step up, gentlemen, and assume your trust!"

There was a pause—no response.

THE SADDLER "Mr. Chairman, we've got *one* clean man left, anyway, out of the late aristocracy; and he needs money, and deserves it. I move that you appoint Jack Halliday to get up there and auction off that sack of gilt twenty-dollar pieces, and give the result to the right man—the man whom Hadleyburg delights to honor—Edward Richards."

This was received with great enthusiasm, the dog taking a hand again; the saddler started the bids at a dollar, the Brixton folk and Barnum's representative fought hard for it, the people cheered every jump that the bids made, the excitement climbed moment by moment higher and higher, the bidders got on their mettle and grew steadily more and more daring, more and more determined, the jumps went from a dollar up to five, then to ten, then to twenty, then fifty, then to a hundred, then—

At the beginning of the auction Richards whispered in distress to his wife: "Oh, Mary, can we allow it? It—it—you see, it is an honor-reward, a testimonial to purity of character, and—and—can we allow it? Hadn't I better get up and—Oh, Mary, what ought we to do?—what do you think we—" [HALLIDAY's *voice* "*Fifteen I'm bid!—fifteen for the sack!—twenty!—ah, thanks!—thirty thanks again! Thirty, thirty, thirty!—do—I hear forty?—forty it is! Keep the ball rolling, gentlemen, keep it rolling!—fifty!—thanks, noble Roman!—going at fifty, fifty, fifty!—seventy!—ninety!—splendid!—a hundred!—pile it up, pile it up!—hundred and twenty—forty!—just in time!—hundred and fifty!—*TWO *hundred!—superb! Do I hear two h—thanks! two hundred and fifty!*——"]

"It is another temptation, Edward—I'm all in a tremble—but, oh, we've escaped *one* temptation, and that ought to warn us, to—[*"Six did I hear?—thanks!—six fifty, six f—*SEVEN *hundred!"*] And yet, Edward, when you think—nobody susp—[*"Eight hundred dollars!—hurrah!—make it nine!—Mr. Parsons, did I hear you say—thanks!—nine!—this noble sack of virgin lead going at only nine hundred dollars, gilding and all—come! do I hear—a thousand!—gratefully yours!—did some one say eleven?—a sack which is going to be the most celebrated in the whole Uni——"*] Oh, Edward" [*beginning to sob*], "we are *so* poor!—but—but—do as you think best—do as you think best."

Edward fell—that is, he sat still; sat with a conscience which was not satisfied, but which was overpowered by circumstances.

Meanwhile a stranger, who looked like an amateur detective gotten up as an impossible English earl, had been watching the evening's proceedings with manifest interest, and with a contented expression in his face; and he had been privately commenting to himself. He was now soliloquizing somewhat like this: "None of the Eighteen are bidding; that is not satisfactory; I must change that—the dramatic unities require it; they must buy the sack they tried to steal; they must pay a heavy price, too—some of them are rich. And another thing, when I make a mistake in Hadleyburg nature the man that puts that error upon me is entitled to a high honorarium, and someone must pay it. This poor old Richards has brought my judgment to shame; he is an honest man;—I don't understand it, but I acknowledge it.

Yes, he saw my deuces—*and* with a straight flush, and by rights the pot is his. And it shall be a jackpot, too, if I can manage it. He disappointed me, but let that pass."

He was watching the bidding. At a thousand, the market broke; the prices tumbled swiftly. He waited—and still watched. One competitor dropped out; then another, and another. He put in a bid or two, now. When the bids had sunk to ten dollars, he added a five; some one raised him a three; he waited a moment, then flung in a fifty-dollar jump, and the sack was his—at $1,282. The house broke out in cheers—then stopped; for he was on his feet and had lifted his hand. He began to speak.

"I desire to say a word, and ask a favor. I am a speculator in rarities, and I have dealings with persons interested in numismatics all over the world. I can make a profit on this purchase, just as it stands; but there is a way, if I can get your approval, whereby I can make every one of these leaden twenty-dollar pieces worth its face in gold, and perhaps more. Grant me that approval, and I will give part of my gains to your Mr. Richards, whose invulnerable probity you have so justly and so cordially recognized tonight; his share shall be ten thousand dollars, and I will hand him the money tomorrow. [*Great applause from the house.* But the "invulnerable probity" made the Richardses blush prettily; however, it went for modesty, and did no harm.] If you will pass my proposition by a good majority—I would like a two-thirds vote—I will regard that as the town's consent, and that is all I ask. Rarities are always helped by any device which will rouse curiosity and compel remark. Now if I may have your permission to stamp upon the faces of each of these ostensible coins the names of the eighteen gentlemen who—"

Nine-tenths of the audience were on their feet in a moment—dog and all—and the proposition was carried with a whirlwind of approving applause and laughter.

They sat down, and all the Symbols except "Dr." Clay Harkness got up, violently protesting against the proposed outrage, and threatening to—

"I beg you not to threaten me," said the stranger, calmly. "I know my legal rights, and am not accustomed to being frightened at bluster." [*Applause.*] He sat down. "Dr." Harkness saw an opportunity here. He was one of the two very rich men of the place, and Pinkerton was the other.

Harkness was proprietor of a mint; that is to say, a popular patent medicine. He was running for the legislature on one ticket, and Pinkerton on the other. It was a close race and a hot one, and getting hotter every day. Both had strong appetites for money; each had bought a great tract of land, with a purpose; there was going to be a new railway, and each wanted to be in the legislature and help locate the route to his own advantage; a single vote might make the decision, and with it two or three fortunes. The stake was large, and Harkness was a daring speculator. He was sitting close to the stranger. He leaned over while one or another of the other Symbols was entertaining the house with protests and appeals, and asked, in a whisper,

"What is your price for the sack?"

"Forty thousand dollars."

"I'll give you twenty."

"No."

"Twenty-five."

"No."

"Say thirty."

"The price is forty thousand dollars; not a penny less."

"All right, I'll give it. I will come to the hotel at ten in the morning. I don't want it known; will see you privately."

"Very good." Then the stranger got up and said to the house:

"I find it late. The speeches of these gentlemen are not without merit, not without interest, not without grace; yet if I may be excused I will take my leave. I thank you for the great favor which you have shown me in granting my petition. I ask the Chair to keep the sack for me until tomorrow, and to hand these three five-hundred-dollar notes to Mr. Richards." They were passed up to the Chair. "At nine I will call for the sack, and at eleven will deliver the rest of the ten thousand to Mr. Richards in person, at his home. Good-night."

Then he slipped out, and left the audience making a vast noise, which was composed of a mixture of cheers, the "Mikado" song, dog-disapproval, and the chant, "you are f-a-r from being a b-a-a-d man—a-a-a-a-men!"

4

At home the Richardses had to endure congratulations and compliments until midnight. Then they were left to themselves. They looked a little sad, and they sat silent and thinking. Finally Mary sighed and said,

"Do you think we are to blame, Edward—*much* to blame?" and her eyes wandered to the accusing triplet of big banknotes lying on the table, where the congratulators had been gloating over them and reverently fingering them. Edward did not answer at once; then he brought out a sigh and said, hesitatingly:

"We—we couldn't help it, Mary. It—well, it was ordered. *All* things are."

Mary glanced up and looked at him steadily, but he didn't return the look. Presently she said:

"I thought congratulations and praises always tasted good. But—it seems to me, now—Edward?"

"Well?"

"Are you going to stay in the bank?"

"N-no."

"Resign?"

"In the morning—by note."

"It does seem best."

Richards bowed his head in his hands and muttered:

"Before, I was not afraid to let oceans of people's money pour through my hands, but—Mary, I am so tired, so tired—"

"We will go to bed."

At nine in the morning the stranger called for the sack and took it to the hotel in a cab. At ten Harkness had a talk with him privately. The stranger asked for and got five checks on a metropolitan bank—drawn to "Bearer,"—four for $1,500 each, and one for $34,000. He put one of the former in his pocketbook, and the remainder, representing $38,500, he put in an envelope, and with these he added a note, which he wrote after Harkness was gone. At eleven he called at the Richards house and knocked. Mrs. Richards peeped through the shutters, then went and received the envelope, and the stranger disappeared without a word. She came back flushed and a little unsteady on her legs, and gasped out:

"I am sure I recognized him! Last night it seemed to me that maybe I had seen him somewhere before."

"He is the man that brought the sack here?"

"I am almost sure of it."

"Then he is the ostensible Stephenson too, and sold every important citizen in this town with his bogus secret. Now if he has sent checks instead of money, we are sold too, after we thought we had escaped. I was beginning to feel fairly comfortable once more, after my night's rest, but the look of that envelope makes me sick. It isn't fat enough; $8,500 in even the largest banknotes makes more bulk than that."

"Edward, why do you object to checks?"

"Checks signed by Stephenson! I am resigned to take the $8,500 if it could come in banknotes—for it does seem that it was so ordered, Mary—but I have never had much courage, and I have not the pluck to try to market a check signed with that disastrous name. It would be a trap. That man tried to catch me; we escaped somehow or other; and now he is trying a new way. If it is checks——"

"Oh, Edward, it is *too* bad!" and she held up the checks and began to cry.

"Put them in the fire! quick! we mustn't be tempted. It is a trick to make the world laugh at *us*, along with the rest, and—Give them to *me*, since you can't do it!" He snatched them and tried to hold his grip till he could get to the stove; but he was human, he was a cashier, and he stopped a moment to make sure of the signature. Then he came near to fainting.

"Fan me, Mary, fan me! They are the same as gold!"

"Oh, how lovely, Edward! Why?"

"Signed by Harkness. What can the mystery of that be, Mary?"

"Edward, do you think——"

"Look here—look at this! Fifteen—fifteen—fifteen—thirty-four. Thirty-eight thousand five hundred! Mary, the sack isn't worth twelve dollars, and Harkness—apparently—has paid about par for it."

"And does it all come to us, do you think—instead of the ten thousand?"

"Why, it looks like it. And the checks are made to 'Bearer,' too."

"Is that good, Edward? What is it for?"

"A hint to collect them at some distant bank, I reckon. Perhaps Harkness doesn't want the matter known. What is that—a note?"

"Yes. It was with the checks."

It was in the "Stephenson" handwriting, but there was no signature. It said:

I am a disappointed man. Your honesty is beyond the reach of temptation. I had a different idea about it, but

I wronged you in that, and I beg pardon, and do it sincerely. I honor you—and that is sincere, too. This town is not worthy to kiss the hem of your garment. Dear sir, I made a square bet with myself that there were nineteen debauchable men in your self-righteous community. I have lost Take the whole pot, you are entitled to it.

Richards drew a deep sigh, and said:

"It seems written with fire—it burns so. Mary—I am miserable again."

"I, too. Ah, dear, I wish——"

"To think, Mary—he *believes* in me."

"Oh, don't, Edward—I can't bear it."

"If those beautiful words were deserved, Mary—and God knows I believed I deserved them once—I think I could give the forty thousand dollars for them. And I would put that paper away, as representing more than gold and jewels, and keep it always. But now—We could not live in the shadow of its accusing presence, Mary."

He put it in the fire.

A messenger arrived and delivered an envelope. Richards took from it a note and read it; it was from Burgess.

You saved me, in a difficult time. I saved you last night. It was at cost of a lie, but I made the sacrifice freely, and out of grateful heart. None in this village knows so well as I know how brave and good and noble you are. At bottom you cannot respect me, knowing as you do of that matter of which I am accused, and by the general voice condemned; but I beg that you will at least believe that I am a grateful man; it will help me to bear my burden.

[*Signed*] BURGESS.

"Saved, once more. And on such terms!" He put the note in the fire. "I—I wish I were dead, Mary, I wish I were out of it all."

"Oh, these are bitter, bitter days, Edward. The stabs, through their very generosity, are so deep—and they come so fast!"

Three days before the election each of two thousand voters suddenly found himself in possession of a prized memento—one of the renowned bogus double-eagles. Around one of its faces was stamped these words: "THE REMARK I MADE TO THE POOR STRANGER WAS—" Around the other face was stamped these: "GO, AND REFORM. [SIGNED] PINKERTON." Thus the entire remaining refuse of the renowned joke was emptied upon a single head, and with calamitous effect. It revived the recent vast laugh and concentrated it upon Pinkerton; and Harkness's election was a walk-over.

Within twenty-four hours after the Richardses had received their checks their consciences were quieting down, discouraged; the old couple were learning to reconcile themselves to the sin which they had committed. But they were to learn, now, that a sin takes on new and real terrors when there seems a chance that it is going to be found out. This gives it a fresh and most substantial and important aspect. At church the morning sermon was of the usual pattern; it was the same old things said in the same old way; they had heard them a thousand times and found them innocuous, next to meaningless, and easy to sleep under; but now it was different: the sermon seemed to bristle with accusations; it seemed aimed straight and specially at people who were concealing deadly sins. After church they got away from the mob of congratulators as soon as they could, and hurried homeward, chilled to the bone at they did not know what—vague, shadowy, indefinite fears. And by chance they caught a glimpse of Mr. Burgess as he turned a corner. He paid no attention to their nod of recognition! He hadn't seen it; but they did not know that. What could his conduct mean? It might mean—it might mean—oh, a dozen dreadful things. Was it possible that he knew that Richards could have cleared him of guilt in that bygone time, and had been silently waiting for a chance to even up accounts? At home, in their distress they got to imagining that their servant might have been in the next room listening when Richards revealed the secret to his wife that he knew of Burgess's innocence; next, Richards began to imagine that he had heard the swish of a gown in there at that time; next, he was sure he *had* heard it. They would call Sarah in, on a pretext, and watch her face: if she had been betraying them to Mr. Burgess, it would show in her manner. They asked her some questions—questions which were so random and incoherent and seemingly purposeless that the girl felt sure that the old people's mind had been affected by their sudden good fortune; the sharp and watchful gaze which they bent upon her frightened her, and that completed the business. She blushed, she became nervous and confused, and to the old people these were plain signs of guilt—guilt of some fearful sort or other—without doubt she was a spy and a traitor. When they were alone again they began to piece many unrelated things together and get horrible results out of the combi-

nation. When things had got about to the worst, Richards was delivered of a sudden gasp, and his wife asked:

"Oh, what is it?—what is it?"

"The note—Burgess's note! Its language was sarcastic, I see it now." He quoted: "At bottom you cannot respect me, *knowing*, as you do, of *that matter* of which I am accused'—oh, it is perfectly plain, now, God help me! He knows that I know! You see the ingenuity of the phrasing. It was a trap—and like a fool, I walked into it. And Mary —?"

"Oh, it is dreadful—I know what you are going to say—he didn't return your transcript of the pretended test-remark."

"No—kept it to destroy us with. Mary, he has exposed us to some already. I know it—I know it well. I saw it in a dozen faces after church. Ah, he wouldn't answer our nod of recognition—*he* knew what he had been doing!"

In the night the doctor was called. The news went around in the morning that the old couple were rather seriously ill—prostrated by the exhausting excitement growing out of their great windfall, the congratulations, and the late hours, the doctor said. The town was sincerely distressed; for these old people were about all it had left to be proud of, now.

Two days later the news was worse. The old couple were delirious, and were doing strange things. By witness of the nurses, Richards had exhibited checks—for $8,500? No—for an amazing sum—$38,500! What could be the explanation of this gigantic piece of luck?

The following day the nurses had more news—and wonderful. They had concluded to hide the checks, lest harm come to them; but when they searched they were gone from under the patient's pillow—vanished away. The patient said:

"Let the pillow alone; what do you want?"

"We thought it best that the checks——"

"You will never see them again—they are destroyed. They came from Satan. I saw the hell-brand on them, and I knew they were sent to betray me to sin." Then he fell to gabbling strange and dreadful things which were not clearly understandable, and which the doctor admonished them to keep to themselves.

Richards was right; the checks were never seen again.

A nurse must have talked in her sleep, for within two days the forbidden gabblings were the property of the town; and they were of a surprising sort. They seemed to indicate that Richards had been a claimant for the sack himself, and that Burgess had concealed that fact and then maliciously betrayed it.

Burgess was taxed with this and stoutly denied it. And he said it was not fair to attach weight to the chatter of a sick old man who was out of his mind. Still, suspicion was in the air, and there was much talk.

After a day or two it was reported that Mrs. Richards's delirious deliveries were getting to be duplicates of her husband's. Suspicion flamed up into conviction, now, and the town's pride in the purity of its one undiscredited important citizen began to dim down and flicker toward extinction.

Six days passed, then came more news. The old couple were dying. Richards's mind cleared in his latest hour, and he sent for Burgess. Burgess said:

"Let the room be cleared. I think he wishes to say something in privacy."

"No!" said Richards; "I want witnesses. I want you all to hear my confession, so that I may die a man, and not a dog. I was clean—artificially—like the rest; and like the rest I fell when temptation came. I signed a lie, and claimed the miserable sack. Mr. Burgess remembered that I had done him a service, and in gratitude (and ignorance) he suppressed my claim and saved me. You know the thing that was charged against Burgess years ago. My testimony, and mine alone, could have cleared him, and I was a coward, and left him to suffer disgrace—"

"No—no—Mr. Richards, you—"

"My servant betrayed my secret to him—"

"No one has betrayed anything to me—"

—"and then he did a natural and justifiable thing, he repented of the saving kindness which he had done me, and he *exposed* me—as I deserved—"

"Never!—I make oath—"

"Out of my heart I forgive him."

Burgess's impassioned protestations fell upon deaf ears; the dying man passed away without knowing that once more he had done poor Burgess a wrong. The old wife died that night.

The last of the sacred Nineteen had fallen a prey to the fiendish sack; the town was stripped of the last rag of its ancient glory. Its mourning was not showy, but it was deep.

By act of the legislature—upon prayer and petition—Hadleyburg was allowed to change its name to (never mind what—I will not give it away), and leave one word out of the motto that for many generations had graced the town's official seal.

It is an honest town once more, and the man will have to rise early that catches it napping again.

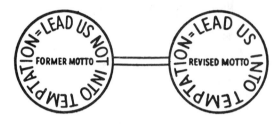

JAMES JOYCE
1882–1941

Ivy Day° in the Committee Room

Old Jack raked the cinders together with a piece of cardboard and spread them judiciously over the whitening dome of coals. When the dome was thinly covered his face lapsed into darkness but, as he set himself to fan the fire again, his crouching shadow ascended the opposite wall and his face slowly reemerged into light. It was an old man's face, very bony and hairy. The moist blue eyes blinked at the fire and the moist mouth fell open at times, munching once or twice mechanically when it closed. When the cinders had caught he laid the piece of cardboard against the wall, sighed and said:

"That's better now, Mr. O'Connor."

IVY DAY IN THE COMMITTEE ROOM. **Ivy Day:** Ivy Day, celebrated October 6, commemorates the death of one of Ireland's greatest political leaders, Charles Stewart Parnell (1846–91), the almost legendary "chief" of the story. Although he survived the repression of the English after the Phoenix Park murder of Lord Cavendish in 1882 and brought Ireland close to home rule in 1886, his involvement as corespondent in the O'Shea divorce proceedings led ultimately to the loss of all his political power in 1890.

Mr. O'Connor, a gray-haired young man, whose face was disfigured by many blotches and pimples, had just brought the tobacco for a cigarette into a shapely cylinder but when spoken to he undid his handiwork meditatively. Then he began to roll the tobacco again meditatively and after a moment's thought decided to lick the paper.

"Did Mr. Tierney say when he'd be back?" he asked in a husky falsetto.

"He didn't say."

Mr. O'Connor put his cigarette into his mouth and began to search his pockets. He took out a pack of thin pasteboard cards.

"I'll get you a match," said the old man.

"Never mind, this'll do," said Mr. O'Connor.

He selected one of the cards and read what was printed on it:

MUNICIPAL ELECTIONS

ROYAL EXCHANGE WARD

Mr. Richard J. Tierney, P.L.G., respectfully solicits the favor of your vote and influence at the coming election in the Royal Exchange Ward.

Mr. O'Connor had been engaged by Tierney's agent to canvass one part of the ward but, as the weather was inclement and his boots let in the wet, he spent a great part of the day sitting by the fire in the Committee Room in Wicklow Street with Jack, the old caretaker. They had been sitting thus since the short day had grown dark. It was the sixth of October, dismal and cold out of doors.

Mr. O'Connor tore a strip off the card and, lighting it, lit his cigarette. As he did so the flame lit up a leaf of dark glossy ivy[1] in the lapel of his coat. The old man watched him attentively and then, taking up the piece of cardboard again, began to fan the fire slowly while his companion smoked.

"Ah, yes," he said, continuing, "it's hard to know what way to bring up children. Now who'd think he'd turn out like that! I sent him to the Christian Brothers[2] and I done what I could for him, and there he goes boozing about. I tried to make him someway decent."

He replaced the cardboard wearily.

"Only I'm an old man now I'd change his tune for him I'd take the stick to his back and beat him while I could stand over him—as I done many a time before. The mother, you know, she cocks him up with this and that. . . ."

"That's what ruins children," said Mr. O'Connor.

"To be sure it is," said the old man. "And little thanks you get for it, only impudence. He takes th' upper hand of me whenever he sees I've a sup taken. What's the world coming to when sons speaks that way to their fathers?"

"What age is he?" said Mr. O'Connor.

"Nineteen," said the old man.

"Why don't you put him to something?"

"Sure, amn't I never done at the drunken bowsy every since he left school? 'I won't keep you,' I says. 'You must get a job for yourself.' But, sure, it's worse whenever he gets a job; he drinks it all."

Mr. O'Connor shook his head in sympathy, and the old man fell silent, gazing into the fire. Someone opened the door of the room and called out:

"Hello! Is this a Freemason's meeting?"[3]

"Who's that?" said the old man.

"What are you doing in the dark?" asked a voice.

"Is that you, Hynes?" asked Mr. O'Connor.

"Yes. What are you doing in the dark?" said Mr. Hynes, advancing into the light of the fire.

He was a tall, slender young man with a light brown mustache. Imminent little drops of rain hung at the brim of his hat and the collar of his jacket-coat was turned up.

"Well, Mat," he said to Mr. O'Connor, "how goes it?"

Mr. O'Connor shook his head. The old man left the hearth, and after stumbling about the room returned with two candlesticks which he thrust one after the other into the fire and carried to the table. A denuded room came into view and the fire lost all its cheerful color. The walls of the room were bare except for a copy of an election address. In the middle of the room was a small table on which papers were heaped.

Mr. Hynes leaned against the mantelpiece and asked:

"Has he paid you yet?"

"Not yet," said Mr. O'Connor. "I hope to God he'll not leave us in the lurch tonight."

Mr. Hynes laughed.

---

1. **ivy:** symbol of remembrance for Parnell that also suggests rejuvenation. 2. **Christian Brothers:** a parochial school.

3. **Freemason's meeting:** i.e., because of the dim light.

"Oh, he'll pay you. Never fear," he said.

"I hope he'll look smart about it if he means business," said Mr. O'Connor.

"What do you think, Jack?" said Mr. Hynes satirically to the old man.

The old man returned to his seat by the fire, saying:

"It isn't but he has it, anyway. Not like the other tinker."

"What other tinker?" said Mr. Hynes.

"Colgan," said the old man scornfully.

"It is because Colgan's a workingman you say that? What's the difference between a good honest bricklayer and a publican—eh? Hasn't the working-man as good a right to be in the Corporation[4] as anyone else—ay, and a better right than those shoneens that are always hat in hand before any fellow with a handle to his name? Isn't that so, Mat?" said Mr. Hynes, addressing Mr. O'Connor.

"I think you're right," said Mr. O'Connor.

"One man is a plain honest man with no hunker-sliding about him. He goes in to represent the labor classes. This fellow you're working for only wants to get some job or other."

"Of course, the working-classes should be represented," said the old man.

"The workingman," said Mr. Hynes, "gets all kicks and no halfpence. But it's labor produces everything. The workingman is not looking for fat jobs for his sons and nephews and cousins. The workingman is not going to drag the honor of Dublin in the mud to please a German monarch."[5]

"How's that?" said the old man.

"Don't you know they want to present an address of welcome to Edward Rex if he comes here next year? What do we want kowtowing to a foreign king?"

"Our man won't vote for the address," said Mr. O'Connor. "He goes in on the Nationalist ticket."

"Won't he?" said Mr. Hynes. "Wait till you see whether he will or not. I know him. Is it Tricky Dicky Tierney?"

"By God! perhaps you're right, Joe," said Mr. O'Connor. "Anyway, I wish he'd turn up with the spondulics."

The three men fell silent. The old man began to rake more cinders together. Mr. Hynes took off his

hat, shook it and then turned down the collar of his coat, displaying, as he did so, an ivy leaf in the lapel.

"If this man was alive," he said, pointing to the leaf, "we'd have no talk of an address of welcome."

"That's true," said Mr. O'Connor.

"Musha, God be with them times!" said the old man. "There was some life in it then."

The room was silent again. Then a bustling little man with a snuffling nose and very cold ears pushed in the door. He walked over quickly to the fire, rubbing his hands as if he intended to produce a spark from them.

"No money, boys," he said.

"Sit down here, Mr. Henchy," said the old man, offering him his chair.

"Oh, don't stir, Jack, don't stir," said Mr. Henchy.

He nodded curtly to Mr. Hynes and sat down on the chair which the old man vacated.

"Did you serve Aungier Street?" he asked Mr. O'Connor.

"Yes," said Mr. O'Connor, beginning to search his pockets for memoranda.

"Did you call on Grimes?"

"I did."

"Well? How does he stand?"

"He wouldn't promise. He said: 'I won't tell anyone what way I'm going to vote.' But I think he'll be all right."

"Why so?"

"He asked me who the nominators were; and I told him. I mentioned Father Burke's name. I think it'll be all right."

Mr. Henchy began to snuffle and to rub his hands over the fire at a terrific speed. Then he said:

"For the love of God, Jack, bring us a bit of coal. There must be some left."

The old man went out of the room.

"It's no go," said Mr. Henchy, shaking his head. "I asked the little shoeboy, but he said: 'Oh, now, Mr. Henchy, when I see the work going on properly I won't forget you, you may be sure'. Mean little tinker! 'Usha, how could he be anything else?"

"What did I tell you, Mat?" said Mr. Hynes. "Tricky Dicky Tierney."

"Oh, he's as tricky as they make 'em," said Mr. Henchy. "He hasn't got those little pigs' eyes for nothing. Blast his soul! Couldn't he pay up like a

---

4. **Corporation:** city government.   5. **German monarch:** Edward VIII, king of England from 1901–1910, came partly of German ancestry.

man instead of: "Oh, now, Mr. Henchy, I must speak to Mr. Fanning. . . . I've spent a lot of money'? Mean little schoolboy of hell! I suppose he forgets the time his little old father kept the hand-me-down shop in Mary's Lane."

"But is that a fact?" asked Mr. O'Connor.

"God, yes," said Mr. Henchy. "Did you never hear that? And the men used to go in on Sunday morning before the houses were open to buy a waistcoat or a trousers—moya! But Tricky Dicky's little old father always had a tricky little black bottle up in a corner. Do you mind now? That's that. That's where he first saw the light."

The old man returned with a few lumps of coal which he placed here and there on the fire.

"That's a nice how-do-you-do," said Mr. O'Connor. "How does he expect us to work for him if he won't stump up?"

"I can't help it," said Mr. Henchy. "I expect to find the bailiffs in the hall when I go home."

Mr. Hynes laughed and, shoving himself away from the mantelpiece with the aid of his shoulders, made ready to leave.

"It'll be all right when King Eddie comes," he said. "Well, boys, I'm off for the present. See you later. 'Bye, 'bye."

He went out of the room slowly. Neither Mr. Henchy nor the old man said anything, but, just as the door was closing, Mr. O'Connor, who had been staring moodily into the fire, called out suddenly:

"'Bye, Joe."

Mr. Henchy waited a few moments and then nodded in the direction of the door.

"Tell me," he said across the fire, "what brings our friend in here? What does he want?"

"'Usha, poor Joe!" said Mr. O'Connor, throwing the end of his cigarette into the fire, "he's hard up, like the rest of us."

Mr. Henchy snuffled vigorously and spat so copiously that he nearly put out the fire, which uttered a hissing protest.

"To tell you my private and candid opinion," he said, "I think he's a man from the other camp. He's a spy of Colgan's, if you ask me. Just go round and try and find out how they're getting on. They won't suspect you. Do you twig?"[6]

"Ah, poor Joe is a decent skin," said Mr. O'Connor.

6. **twig**: understand.

"His father was a decent, respectable man," Mr. Henchy admitted. "Poor old Larry Hynes! Many a good turn he did in his day! But I'm greatly afraid our friend is not nineteen carat. Damn it, I can understand a fellow being hard up, but what I can't understand is a fellow sponging. Couldn't he have some spark of manhood about him?"

"He doesn't get a warm welcome from me when he comes," said the old man. "Let him work for his own side and not come spying around here."

"I don't know," said Mr. O'Connor dubiously, as he took out cigarette-papers and tobacco. "I think Joe Hynes is a straight man. He's a clever chap, too, with the pen. Do you remember that thing he wrote . . . ?"

"Some of these hillsiders and fenians[7] are a bit too clever if you ask me," said Mr. Henchy. "Do you know what my private and candid opinion is about some of those little jokers? I believe half of them are in the pay of the Castle."[8]

"There's no knowing," said the old man.

"Oh, but I know it for a fact," said Mr. Henchy. "They're Castle hacks. . . . I don't say Hynes. . . . No, damn it, I think he's a stroke above that. . . . But there's a certain little nobleman with a cock-eye—you know the patriot I'm alluding too?"

Mr. O'Connor nodded.

"There's a lineal descendant of Major Sirr[9] for you if you like! Oh, the heart's blood of a patriot! That's a fellow now that'd sell his country for fourpence—aye—and go down on his bended knees and thank the Almighty Christ he had a country to sell."

There was a knock at the door.

"Come in!" said Mr. Henchy.

A person resembling a poor clergyman or a poor actor appeared in the doorway. His black clothes were tightly buttoned on his short body and it was impossible to say whether he wore a clergyman's collar or a layman's, because the collar of his shabby frock-coat, the uncovered buttons of which reflected the candlelight, was turned up about his neck. He wore a round hat of hard black felt. His face, shining with raindrops, had the appearance of damp yellow cheese save where two rosy spots indicated the cheekbones. He opened his very long mouth suddenly to express disappointment

7. **fenians**: Irish nationalists. 8. **Castle**: i.e., the English who governed Ireland. 9. **Major Sirr**: a traitor.

and at the same time opened wide his very bright blue eyes to express pleasure and surprise.

"O Father Keon!"[10] said Mr. Henchy, jumping up from his chair. "Is that you? Come in!"

"Oh, no, no, no!" said Father Keon quickly, pursing his lips as if he were addressing a child.

"Won't you come in and sit down?"

"No, no, no!" said Father Keon, speaking in a discreet, indulgent, velvety voice. "Don't let me disturb you now! I'm just looking for Mr. Fanning. . . ."

"He's round at the *Black Eagle*," said Mr. Henchy. "But won't you come in and sit down a minute?"

"No, no, thank you. It was just a little business matter," said Father Keon. "Thank you, indeed."

He retreated from the doorway and Mr. Henchy, seizing one of the candlesticks, went to the door to light him downstairs.

"Oh, don't trouble, I beg!"

"No, but the stairs is so dark."

"No, no, I can see. . . . Thank you, indeed."

"Are you right now?"

"All right, thanks. . . . Thanks."

Mr. Henchy returned with the candlestick and put it on the table. He sat down again at the fire. There was silence for a few moments.

"Tell me, John," said Mr. O'Connor, lighting his cigarette with another pasteboard card.

"Hm?"

"What he is exactly?"

"Ask me an easier one," said Mr. Henchy.

"Fanning and himself seem to me very thick. They're often in Kavanagh's together. Is he a priest at all?"

"Mmmyes, I believe so. . . . I think he's what you call a black sheep. We haven't many of them, thank God! but we have a few. . . . He's an unfortunate man of some kind. . . ."

"And how does he knock it out?" asked Mr. O'Connor.

"That's another mystery."

"Is he attached to any chapel or church or institution or——"

"No," said Mr. Henchy, "I think he's traveling on his own account. . . . God forgive me," he added, "I thought he was the dozen of stout."

"Is there any chance of a drink itself?" asked Mr. O'Connor.

"I'm dry too," said the old man.

"I asked that little shoeboy three times," said Mr. Henchy, "would he send up a dozen of stout. I asked him again now, but he was leaning on the counter in his shirtsleeves having a deep goster[11] with Alderman Cowley."

"Why didn't you remind him?" said Mr. O'Connor.

"Well, I couldn't go over while he was talking to Alderman Cowley. Just waited till I caught his eye, and said: 'About that little matter I was speaking to you about. . . .' 'That'll be all right, Mr. H.,' he said. Yerra, sure the little hop-o'-my-thumb has forgotten all about it."

"There's some deal on in that quarter," said Mr. O'Connor thoughtfully. "I saw the three of them hard at it yesterday at Suffolk Street corner."

"I think I know the little game they're at," said Mr. Henchy. "You must owe the city fathers money nowadays if you want to be made lord mayor. Then they'll make you lord mayor. By God! I'm thinking seriously of becoming a city father myself. What do you think? Would I do for the job?"

Mr. O'Connor laughed.

"So far as owing money goes. . . ."

"Driving out of the Mansion House," said Mr. Henchy, "in all my vermin,[12] with Jack here standing up behind me in a powdered wig—eh?"

"And make me your private secretary, John."

"Yes. And I'll make Father Keon my private chaplain. We'll have a family party."

"Faith, Mr. Henchy," said the old man, "you'd keep up better style than some of them. I was talking one day to old Keegan, the porter. 'And how do you like your new master, Pat?' says I to him. 'You haven't much entertaining now,' says I. 'Entertaining!' says he. 'He'd live on the smell of an oil-rag.' And do you know what he told me? Now, I declare to God, I didn't believe him."

"What?" said Mr. Henchy and Mr. O'Connor.

"He told me: 'What do you think of a lord mayor of Dublin sending out for a pound of chops for his dinner? How's that for high living?' says he. 'Wisha! wisha,' says I. 'A pound of chops,' says he, 'coming into the Mansion House.'

---

10. **Father Keon:** the Catholic Church played an important part in discrediting Parnell.

11. **goster:** conversation. 12. **vermin:** furs.

'Wisha!' says I, 'what kind of people is going at all now?''

At this point there was a knock at the door, and a boy put in his head.

"What is it?" said the old man.

"From the *Black Eagle*," said the boy, walking in sideways and depositing a basket on the floor with a noise of shaken bottles.

The old man helped the boy to transfer the bottles from the basket to the table and counted the full tally. After the transfer the boy put his basket on his arm and asked:

"Any bottles?"

"What bottles?" said the old man.

"Won't you let us drink them first?" said Mr. Henchy.

"I was told to ask for the bottles."

"Come back tomorrow," said the old man.

"Here, boy!" said Mr. Henchy, "will you run over to O'Farrell's and ask him to lend us a corkscrew—for Mr. Henchy, say. Tell him we won't keep it a minute. Leave the basket there."

The boy went out and Mr. Henchy began to rub his hands cheerfully, saying:

"Ah, well, he's not so bad after all. He's as good as his word, anyhow."

"There's no tumblers," said the old man.

"Oh, don't let that trouble you, Jack," said Mr. Henchy, "Many's the good man before now drank out of the bottle."

"Anyway, it's better than nothing," said Mr. O'Connor.

"He's not a bad sort," said Mr. Henchy, "only Fanning has such a loan of him. He means well, you know, in his own tinpot way."

The boy came back with the corkscrew. The old man opened three bottles and was handing back the corkscrew when Mr. Henchy said to the boy:

"Would you like a drink, boy?"

"If you please, sir," said the boy.

The old man opened another bottle grudgingly, and handed it to the boy.

"What age are you?" he asked.

"Seventeen," said the boy.

As the old man said nothing further, the boy took the bottle, said: "Here's my best respects, sir, to Mr. Henchy," drank the contents, put the bottle back on the table and wiped his mouth with his sleeve. Then he took up the corkscrew and

went out of the door sideways, muttering some form of salutation.

"That's the way it begins," said the old man.

"The thin edge of the wedge," said Mr. Henchy.

The old man distributed the three bottles which he had opened and the men drank from them simultaneously. After having drunk each placed his bottle on the mantelpiece within hand's reach and drew in a long breath of satisfaction.

"Well, I did a good day's work today," said Mr. Henchy, after a pause.

"That so, John?"

"Yes. I got him one or two sure things in Dawson Street, Crofton and myself. Between ourselves, you know, Crofton (he's a decent chap, of course), but he's not worth a damn as a canvasser. He hasn't a word to throw to a dog. He stands and looks at the people while I do the talking."

Here two men entered the room. One of them was a very fat man, whose blue serge clothes seemed to be in danger of falling from his sloping figure. He had a big face which resembled a young ox's face in expression, staring blue eyes and a grizzled mustache. The other man, who was much younger and frailer, had a thin, clean-shaven face. He wore a very high double collar and a wide-brimmed bowler hat.

"Hello, Crofton!" said Mr. Henchy to the fat man. "Talk of the devil . . ."

"Where did the booze come from?" asked the young man. "Did the cow calve?"

"Oh, of course, Lyons spots the drink first thing!" said Mr. O'Connor, laughing.

"Is that the way you chaps canvass," said Mr. Lyons, "and Crofton and I out in the cold and rain looking for votes?"

"Why, blast your soul," said Mr. Henchy, "I'd get more votes in five minutes than you two'd get in a week."

"Open two bottles of stout, Jack," said Mr. O'Connor.

"How can I?" said the old man, "when there's no corkscrew?"

"Wait now, wait now!" said Mr. Henchy, getting up quickly. "Did you ever see this little trick?"

He took two bottles from the table and, carrying them to the fire, put them on the hob. Then he sat down again by the fire and took another drink from his bottle. Mr. Lyons sat on the edge of the table, pushed his hat towards the nape of his neck and began to swing his legs.

"Which is my bottle?" he asked.

"This, lad," said Mr. Henchy.

Mr. Crofton sat down on a box and looked fixedly at the other bottle on the hob. He was silent for two reasons. The first reason, sufficient in itself, was that he had nothing to say; the second reason was that he considered his companions beneath him. He had been a canvasser for Wilkins, the Conservative, but when the Conservatives had withdrawn their man and, choosing the lesser of two evils, given their support to the Nationalist candidate, he had been engaged to work for Mr. Tierney.

In a few minutes an apologetic "Pok!" was heard as the cork flew out of Mr. Lyons' bottle. Mr. Lyons jumped off the table, went to the fire, took his bottle and carried it back to the table.

"I was just telling them, Crofton," said Mr. Henchy, "that we got a good few votes today."

"Who did you get?" asked Mr. Lyons.

"Well, I got Parkes for one, and I got Atkinson for two, and I got Ward of Dawson Street. Fine old chap he is, too—regular old toff,[13] old Conservative! 'But isn't your candidate a Nationalist?' said he. 'He's a respectable man,' said I. 'He's in favor of whatever will benefit this country. He's a big ratepayer,' I said. 'He has extensive house property in the city and three places of business and isn't it to his own advantage to keep down the rates? He's a prominent and respected citizen,' said I, "and a Poor Law Guardian, and he doesn't belong to any party, good, bad, or indifferent.' That's the way to talk to 'em."

"And what about the address to the king?" said Mr. Lyons, after drinking and smacking his lips.

"Listen to me," said Mr. Henchy. "What we want in this country, as I said to old Ward, is capital. The king's coming here will mean an influx of money into this country. The citizens of Dublin will benefit by it. Look at all the factories down by the quays there, idle! Look at all the money there is in the country if we only worked the old industries, the mills, the shipbuilding yards and factories. It's capital we want."

"But look here, John," said Mr. O'Connor. "Why should we welcome the king of England? Didn't Parnell himself . . ."

13. toff: gentleman.

"Parnell," said Mr. Henchy, "is dead. Now, here's the way I look at it. Here's this chap come to the throne after his old mother keeping him out of it till the man was gray. He's a man of the world, and he means well by us. He's a jolly fine decent fellow, if you ask me, and no damn nonsense about him. He just says to himself: 'The old one never went to see these wild Irish. By Christ, I'll go myself and see what they're like.' And are we going to insult the man when he comes over here on a friendly visit? Eh? Isn't that right, Crofton?"

Mr. Crofton nodded his head.

"But after all now," said Mr. Lyons argumentatively, "King Edward's life, you know, is not the very . . ."

"Let bygones be bygones," said Mr. Henchy. "I admire the man personally. He's just an ordinary knockabout like you and me. He's fond of his glass of grog and he's a bit of a rake, perhaps, and he's a good sportsman. Damn it, can't we Irish play fair?"

"That's all very fine," said Mr. Lyons. "But look at the case of Parnell now."

"In the name of God," said Mr. Henchy, "where's the analogy between the two cases?"

"What I mean," said Mr. Lyons, "is we have our ideals. Why, now, would we welcome a man like that? Do you think now after what he did Parnell was a fit man to lead us? And why, then, would we do it for Edward the Seventh?"

"This is Parnell's anniversary," said Mr. O'Connor, "and don't let us stir up any bad blood. We all respect him now that he's dead and gone—even the Conservatives," he added, turning to Mr. Crofton.

Pok! The tardy cork flew out of Mr. Crofton's bottle. Mr. Crofton got up from his box and went to the fire. As he returned with his capture he said in a deep voice:

"Our side of the house respects him, because he was a gentleman."

"Right you are, Crofton!" said Mr. Henchy fiercely. "He was the only man that could keep that bag of cats in order. 'Down, ye dogs! Lie down, ye curs!' That's the way he treated them. Come in, Joe! Come in!" he called out, catching sight of Mr. Hynes in the doorway.

Mr. Hynes came in slowly.

"Open another bottle of stout, Jack," said Mr.

Henchy. "Oh, I forgot there's no corkscrew! Here, show me one here and I'll put it at the fire."

The old man handed him another bottle and he placed it on the hob.

"Sit down, Joe," said Mr. O'Connor, "we're just talking about the Chief."——— *PARNELL*

"Aye, aye!" said Mr. Henchy.

Mr. Hynes sat on the side of the table near Mr. Lyons but said nothing.

"There's one of them, anyhow," said Mr. Henchy, "that didn't renege him. By God, I'll say for you, Joe! No, by God, you stuck to him like a man!"

"Oh, Joe," said Mr. O'Connor suddenly. "Give us that thing you wrote—do you remember? Have you got it on you?"

"Oh, aye!" said Mr. Henchy. "Give us that. Did you ever hear that. Crofton? Listen to this now: splendid thing."

"Go on," said Mr. O'Connor. "Fire away, Joe."

Mr. Hynes did not seem to remember at once the piece to which they were alluding, but, after reflecting a while, he said:

"Oh, that thing is it. . . . Sure, that's old now."

"Out with it, man!" said Mr. O'Connor.

"'Sh, 'sh," said Mr. Henchy. "Now, Joe!"

Mr. Hynes hesitated a little longer. Then amid the silence he took off his hat, laid it on the table and stood up. He seemed to be rehearsing the piece in his mind. After a rather long pause he announced:

THE DEATH OF PARNELL

6th October, 1891

He cleared his throat once or twice and then began to recite:

He is dead. Our Uncrowned King is dead.
  O, Erin, mourn with grief and woe
For he lies dead whom the fell gang
  Of modern hypocrites laid low.

He lies slain by the coward hounds
  He raised to glory from the mire;
And Erin's hopes and Erin's dreams
  Perish upon her monarch's pyre.

In palace, cabin or in cot
  The Irish heart where'er it be
Is bowed with woe—for he is gone
  Who would have wrought her destiny.

He would have had his Erin famed,
  The green flag gloriously unfurled,
Her statesmen, bards and warriors raised
  Before the nations of the World.

He dreamed (alas, 'twas but a dream!)
  Of Liberty: but as he strove
To clutch that idol, treachery
  Sundered him from the thing he loved.

Shame on the coward, caitiff hands
  That smote their Lord or with a kiss
Betrayed him to the rabble-rout
  Of fawning priests—no friends of his.

May everlasting shame consume
  The memory of those who tried
To befoul and smear the exalted name
  Of one who spurned them in his pride.

He fell as fall the mighty ones,
  Nobly undaunted to the last,
And death has now united him
  With Erin's heroes of the past.

No sound of strife disturb his sleep!
  Calmly he rests: no human pain
Or high ambition spurs him now
  The peaks of glory to attain.

They had their way: they laid him low.
  But Erin, list, his spirit may
Rise, like the Phoenix[14] from the flames,
  When breaks the dawning of the day,

The day that brings us Freedom's reign.
  And on that day may Erin well
Pledge in the cup she lifts to Joy
  One grief—the memory of Parnell.

Mr. Hynes sat down again on the table. When he had finished his recitation there was a silence and then a burst of clapping: even Mr. Lyons clapped. The applause continued for a little time. When it had ceased all the auditors drank from their bottles in silence.

14. **Phoenix:** probably a double allusion, both to the legendary bird that rises from its own ashes and to the assassination of Lord Cavendish in Phoenix Park.

Pok! The cork flew out of Mr. Hynes' bottle, but Mr. Hynes remained sitting flushed and bareheaded on the table. He did not seem to have heard the invitation.

"Good man, Joe!" said Mr. O'Connor, taking out his cigarette papers and pouch the better to hide his emotion.

"What do you think of that, Crofton?" cried Mr. Henchy. "Isn't that fine? What?"

Mr. Crofton said that it was a very fine piece of writing.

HOWARD NEMEROV
b. 1920

A Day on the Big Branch

Still half drunk, after a night at cards,
with the gray dawn taking us unaware
among our guilty kings and queens, we drove
far north in the morning, winners, losers,
to a stream in the high hills, to climb up to a place 5
one of us knew, with some vague view
of cutting losses or consolidating gains
by the old standard appeal to the wilderness,
the desert, the empty places of our exile,
bringing only the biblical bread and cheese   10
and cigarettes got from a grocer's on the way,
expecting to drink only the clear cold water
among the stones, and remember, or forget.
Though no one said anything about atonement,
there was still some purgatorial idea   15
in all those aching heads and aging hearts
as we climbed the giant stair of the stream,
reaching the place around noon.

It was as promised, a wonder, with granite walls
enclosing ledges, long and flat, of limestone,   20
or, rolling, of lava; within the ledges
the water, fast and still, pouring its yellow light
and green, over the tilted slabs of the floor,
blackened at shady corners, falling in a foam
of crystal to a calm where the waterlight   25
dappled the ledges as they leaned
against the sun; big blue dragonflies hovered
and darted and dipped a wing, hovered again

against the low wind moving over the stream,
and shook the flakes of light from their clear
    wings.   30
This surely was it, was what we had come for,
was nature, though it looked like art with its
gray fortress walls and laminated benches
as in the waiting room of some petrified station,
But we believed; and what it was we believed   35
made of the place a paradise
for ruined poker players, win or lose,
who stripped naked and bathed and dried out on
    the rocks
like gasping trout (the water they drank
making them drunk again), lit cigarettes and lay
    back   40
waiting for nature to say the last word
—as though the stones were Memnon° stones,
which, caught in a certain light, would sing.

The silence (and even the noise of the waters
was silence) grew pregnant; that is the phrase,   45
grew pregnant; but nothing else did.
The mountain brought forth not a mouse, and the
    rocks,
unlike the ones you would expect to find
on the slopes of purgatory or near Helicon,°
mollified by muses and with a little give to 'em,   50
were modern American rocks, and hard as rocks.
Our easy bones groaned, our flesh baked
on one side and shuddered on the other; and each
    man
thought bitterly about primitive simplicity
and decadence, and how he had been ruined   55
by civilization and forced by circumstances
to drink and smoke and sit up all night
inspecting those perfectly arbitrary cards
until he was broken-winded as a trout on a rock
and had no use for the doctrines° of Jean Jacques 60
Rousseau, and could no longer afford
a savagery whether noble or not; some
would never batter that battered copy of Walden
again.

    But all the same,   65
the water, the sunlight, and the wind
did something; even the dragonflies
did something to the minds full of telephone

A DAY ON THE BIG BRANCH.   **42. Memnon:** statue at Thebes that is supposed to sing at dawn. **49. Helicon:** mountain home of the Muses. **60. doctrines:** of the harmony between man and nature.

numbers and flushes, to the flesh
sweating bourbon on one side and freezing on the
    other. 70
And the rocks, the old and tumbling boulders
which formed the giant stair of the stream,
induced (again) some purgatorial ideas
concerning humility, concerning patience
and enduring what had to be endured, 75
winning and losing and breaking even;
ideas of weathering in whatever weather,
being eroded, or broken, or ground down into
    pebbles
by the stream's necessitous and grave currents.
But to these ideas did any purgatory 80
respond? Only this one: that in a world
where even the Memnon stones were carved in soap
one might at any rate wash with the soap.

After a time we talked about the War,°
about what we had done in the War, and how
    near 85
some of us had been to being drowned, and burned,
and shot, and how many people we knew
who had been drowned, or burned, or shot;
and would it have been better to have died

84. **War:** the Second World War.

in the War, the peaceful old War, where we were
    young? 90
But the mineral peace, or paralysis, of those
great stones, the moving stillness of the waters,
entered our speech; the ribs and blood
of the earth, from which all fables grow,
established poetry and truth in us, 95
so that at last one said, "I shall play cards
until the day I die," and another said,
"in bourbon whisky are all the vitamins
and minerals needed to sustain man's life,"
and still another, "I shall live on smoke 100
until my spirit has been cured of flesh."

Climbing downstream again, on the way home
to the lives we had left empty for a day,
we noticed, as not before, how of three bridges
not one had held the stream, which in its floods 105
had twisted the girders, splintered the boards,
    hurled
boulder on boulder, and had broken into rubble,
smashed practically back to nature,
the massive masonry of span after span
with its indifferent rage; this was a sight 110
that sobered us considerably, and kept us quiet
both during the long drive home and after,
till it was time to deal the cards.

Thematic Comedy

Thematic analogues to narrative comedy are as plentiful and diverse as the human acts worth celebrating. There is a sense in which singing and the lyric are clearly identified, as the name of the latter suggests. Throughout the long history of dramatic comedy, the culminating scene on stage has often been a festival celebrated in song and dance, and this finale has become the whole substance of musical comedy. Many songs from plays, like those in Shakespeare's and Jonson's comedies, can stand on their own as lyrics. There is, however, a more fundamental connection between comic narrative and many poems. Using the analogies developed in the General Introduction, we can describe some of the principles in this relationship. The comic poet, like the singer, assumes the role of finding and celebrating harmony in *this* world. He is neither prophet or seer like the romantic poet because he has a strong sense of the limitations of his knowledge and a respect for the tangible beauties of human life and nature. Thus the celebrative tone and the frequent recurrence of such subjects as youth, flowers, spring, love, and growth are appropriate, since they represent the joys of life potentially available to all of us. In the midst of commonly shared—if transitory—experience, he usually speaks for the individual man, anyone and everyone. Parallel to the movement toward freedom in comic narrative, there is often a movement from one attitude or mood to another until the poet is able to connect his own wishes with the outer world, to *find* them reflected there. In the perspective of the comic poet, nature is benign rather than menacing; unlike the tragic poet, he does not need to be reconciled to it. Through the generating power of his imagination, which works by intuition and flashes of insight, he is able to envision this world as a fit home for man, satisfying his desires and fulfilling his needs if he will only get in tune with it. Just as incorporation into a social group is the normal outcome for narrative comedy, perception of man harmonious with nature is a typical achievement of the comic poet. The imagery, dominated by things that grow and develop, is organic rather than mechanical.

This set of features is characteristic of Elizabethan songs and early nineteenth-century odes, but it appears in many other forms of poetry as well. Comic poetry has no conventions as marked as those of the heroic poem of romance, the tragic elegy, or the demonic apocalypse of irony. A few specific themes, such as Horace's *carpe diem* (literally "seize the day," reminding the young to make use of time while they can), have a long history, but because of the comic stress on individuality and imagination are not easily associated with particular literary conventions. What we can sense, with some accuracy, is a number of broad processes analogous to the action of the narrative phases. Three of these are the discovery and affirmation of the power implicit in human imagination, the celebration of temporal experience, and the invention of partial order as a substitute for the more inclusive vision of romance or tragedy.

The Poetic Process: Discovery and Affirmation A number of lyrics concern the poetic process itself. The imaginative faculty is the source of delight, and its operations are somewhat analogous to what happens in the norm of narrative comedy: a man of genius and sensitivity, usually a poet, transforms and synthesizes ordinary experience in his imagination and discovers an intricate, sustaining order in nature and man. He comes to feel at home in the world he finds. In John Dryden's "A Song for Saint Cecilia's Day," music is the symbol of a harmony in both heaven and mankind that will last until the Day of Judgment, when "music shall untune the sky." The discovery and affirmation of order is an active process: it requires some creation on the part of man. That creation may be as simple as the conscious memory of the speaker in William Wordsworth's "Lines Composed a Few Miles above Tintern Abbey," who is still

> A lover of the meadows and the woods,
> And mountains; and of all that we behold
> From this green earth; of all the mighty world
> Of eye, and ear,—both what they half create,
> And what perceive; . . ."

The closing couplet of Ralph Waldo Emerson's "Each and All" implies a similar linkage between perception of the natural world and creation of ideas about it within a single process: "Beauty through my senses stole; / I yielded myself to the perfect whole." And the "secret working mind" is equated with the "profane perfection of mankind" in Yeats' "Under Ben Bulben." In all these poems the act of imagination is central because it helps to constitute the world that is perceived and thereby to form and shape that world into a fit habitation for human beings—the processes of imagining a friendly universe and seeing it merge. In contrast to the romantic poet, the comic poet helps to make what he sees; in contrast to the tragic poet, he likes what he sees.

The simplest process in comic poetry is parallel to entering the "green" world of romantic comedy: the persona celebrates some delightful temporal experience for its own sake without trying to connect it with anything else in life. In medieval lyrics about spring and in many poems by A. C. Swinburne and Lawrence, the coming of spring can be enjoyed directly and immediately. Sound, whether in the simple form of exuberant repetition, as in the refrain ("Sing cuccu!") of "Sumer Is Icumen In," or in the elaborate alliteration of Swinburne's "When the Hounds of Spring," is likely to play a large part in the act of celebrating. Often the poet attempts a transformation of what he sees into what we can hear, as Herrick does in two miniature lyrics on women's dress: the "glittering" of Julia's clothes becomes a "brave vibration," a "liquefaction" that "sweetly flows." Synaesthesia, the transfer of perceptions from one sense to another, is a way of making the sounds of poetry do for sights—standing in, as it were, for the immediate sensations that the celebrative poet would have us enjoy with him. It is tempting to associate such unworried enjoyment of living with subjects like love and spring, but Keats gives autumn the same lush treatment in the ode "To Autumn," calling it the "season of mists and mellow fruitfulness" that can "fill all fruit with ripeness to the core."

Generally, such lyrics create the illusion of a scene in the immediate present. In Lawrence's "Spring Morning," for example, the past ("We are not our old selves any more") and the future ("And we're going to be summer-happy") are contained in the present moment: "See, how gorgeous the world is / Outside the door!" Comic poems that use the rhetorical form of poetic argument, such as Herrick's "Corinna's Going a-Maying," may enclose it within real or imagined present movements, in this case those of the speaker and his love walking through the village and out into the fields to join in the festival of spring. The *carpe diem* theme gets full statement in the last stanza of this poem:

> Come, let us go while we are in our prime;
> And take the harmless folly of the time.
> > We shall grow old apace, and die
> > Before we know our liberty.
> > Our life is short; and our days run
> > As fast away as does the sun:
> And, as a vapor, or a drop of rain,
> Once lost, can ne'er be found again:
> > So when or you or I are made
> > A fable, song, or fleeting shade,
> > All love, all liking, all delight
> > Lies drowned with us in endless night.
> Then while time serves, and we are but decaying,
> Come, my Corinna, come, let's go a-Maying.

The *carpe diem* theme has tragic implications, but Herrick's speaker uses an awareness of the transitory nature of human joy only as an argument to seduce the beloved. The opening and closing lines, which frame the stanza, are imperatives, a call to action in the present that supersedes any philosophic reflection the argument itself might invite. In this way rhetorical form is an essential feature in poems of celebration.

Invention of Partial Order

When comprehensive visions of harmony between man and nature or mind and sense break down, we get the psychological process closest to irony: the whole world is no longer orderly, but the poet finds something to hang on to in a sea of confusion, and he is grateful for it. Thus we get poems affirming partial order or celebrating fragments of beauty. In Donne's "Sun Rising" the whole world contracts to a lover's bed, but that is enough. Both Archibald MacLeish and Stephen Spender find beauty in unexpected places—MacLeish in the bleak great plains of the midwest, which he conceives in images of "dust" and "smoke" and in dark colors ("Landscape as a Nude") and Spender in the concrete pylons trailing "black wire," which he sees as precursors of beautiful cities "where clouds shall lean their swan-white neck" ("The Pylons"). W. H. Auden and Philip Larkin look for a sense of order and continuity in human institutions that are inadequate or decaying. In "Law Like Love" the speaker asserts his analogy between law and love "timidly," and the persona of "Church Going" gives us the sense that there *was* something there as he visits old churches.

In the final stanza of Wallace Stevens' poem "Sunday Morning," the closing image of the undulating bird disappearing into darkness barely gives us a vision of order rather than chaos:

> in the isolation of the sky,
> At evening, casual flocks of pigeons make
> Ambiguous undulations as they sink,
> Downward to darkness, on extended wings.

And in e. e. cummings' poem, "anyone" and "noone" were the only fully human beings in a pretty dead town, but they nevertheless affirmed the modicum of life that everyone else forgot.

Affirmation and *vitality* have been key words throughout our discussion of narrative and thematic comedy because they epitomize the processes at work. Comic action moves toward an attainable freedom, a freedom within our grasp although we cannot hold on to it for long; comic themes give us the image of a world that is harmonious and sustaining. "There is a comic as well as a tragic control of life," claims Wylie Sypher in "The Meanings of Comedy," "and the comic control may be more usable, more relevant to the human condition in all its normalcy and confusion, its many unreconciled directions." Confusion and control, change and continuity, experience and desire—all these come together in comedy as they do nowhere else, assuring us that it is still possible to live well in a sometimes preposterous world.

Perception and Imagination in "The Idea of Order at Key West"

The relationship between poetic creation and reality is the central subject of Wallace Stevens' "Idea of Order at Key West," in which the persona explores the intricacies of human imagination to the vanishing point, the "ghostlier demarcations" and "keener sounds" of the final line. In one sense this poem is as abstruse as its goal is elusive, yet it contains a perfectly clear scene: the speaker and his companion were walking along the beach at Key West at dusk (as far out into the ocean as one can get in the United States) with their backs to the town. As the speaker recalls listening to the sound of the surf, he starts a series of speculations about what his own perceptions might mean. The first word of the poem is the initial creative act from which all else follows; the speaker constructs and personifies an unidentified "she" as the hypothetical form of human imagination, the way in which mind and world meet to become something more than either one alone. From the outset the marriage of poetic process and theme is almost perfect: the pursuit of knowledge about the imagination is itself an exercise of that imagination "since what she sang was uttered word by word."

WALLACE STEVENS
1879–1955

The Idea of Order at Key West

She sang beyond the genius of the sea.
The water never formed to mind or voice,
Like a body wholly body, fluttering
Its empty sleeves; and yet its mimic motion
Made constant cry, caused constantly a cry,   5
That was not ours although we understood,
Inhuman, of the veritable ocean.

These a was not a mask. No more was she.
The song and water were not medleyed sound
Even if what she sang was what she heard,   10
Since what she sang was uttered word by word.
It may be that in all her phrases stirred

The grinding water and the gasping wind;
But it was she and not the sea we heard.

For she was the maker of the song she sang.   15
The ever-hooded, tragic-gestured sea
Was merely a place by which she walked to sing.
Whose spirit is this? we said, because we knew
It was the spirit that we sought and knew
That we should ask this often as she sang.   20

If it was only the dark voice of the sea
That rose, or even colored by many waves;
If it was only the outer voice of sky
And cloud, of the sunken coral water-walled,
However clear, it would have been deep air,   25
The heaving speech of air, a summer sound
Repeated in a summer without end
And sound alone. But it was more than that,
More even than her voice, and ours, among
The meaningless plungings of water and the wind,

Theatrical distances, bronze shadows heaped   30
On high horizons, mountainous atmospheres
Of sky and sea.
           It was her voice that made
The sky acutest at its vanishing.
She measured to the hour its solitude.   35
She was the single artificer of the world
In which she sang. And when she sang, the sea,
Whatever self it had, became the self
That was her song, for she was the maker. Then we,
As we beheld her striding there alone,   40
Knew that there never was a world for her
Except the one she sang and, singing, made.

Ramon Fernandez,° tell me, if you know,
Why, when the singing ended and we turned
Toward the town, tell why the glassy lights,   45
The lights in the fishing boats at anchor there,
As the night descended, tilting in the air,
Mastered the night and portioned out the sea,
Fixing emblazoned zones and fiery poles,
Arranging, deepening, enchanting night.   50

Oh! Blessed rage for order, pale Ramon,
The maker's rage to order words of the sea,
Words of the fragrant portals, dimly-starred,
And of ourselves and of our origins,
In ghostlier demarcations, keener sounds.   55

THE IDEA OF ORDER AT KEY WEST. **43. Ramon Fernandez:** twentieth-century French literary critic interested in the creative process, poetry as a way of ordering experience.

What the persona is trying to grasp is not easily won; much of the poem is a series of attempts—negations, if-then deductions, hypotheses, and images. "She" is not mere sound, the "inhuman" ocean, nor is she a "mask" for some metaphysical reality behind nature. Then a syntactical change introduced by a question ("Whose spirit is this?") transforms two parts of the relationship between listener and sound into four: the spirit becomes "it" which is "more than" sound (1), "more even than her voice" (2), "and ours" (3)—therefore something (4) that transcends inanimate nature itself, as well as human consciousness. At this point the persona has carried philosophical analysis as far as it will go, to an ultimate paradox that involves contradiction. Jumping intuitively, he discovers a self-creating whole that articulates all these possible relationships without explaining them:

> She was the single artificer of the world
> In which she sang. And when she sang, the sea,
> Whatever self it had, became the self
> That was her song, for she was the maker. Then we
> As we beheld her striding there alone,
> Knew that there never was a world for her
> Except the one she sang and, singing, made.

The poet has reached an idea of order that is essentially an aesthetic vision rather than a philosophical assertion; the perception of harmony validates itself. The final section recalls turning back toward town, where the speaker and his companion see the riding lights of fishing boats rolling in the roadstead not as discrete objects but as movements of the whole, "Fixing emblazoned zones and fiery poles, / Arranging, deepening, enchanting night." Thus the speaker ends by celebrating what the imagination's "rage for order" can do in creating perceptions of man and nature, in leading us to those "fragrant portals" where sensation and thought, maker and thing made, are one.

The Poetic Process:
Discovery and Affirmation

JOHN DRYDEN
1631–1700

A Song
for Saint Cecilia's Day°

1

From harmony, from heav'nly harmony°
  This universal frame began.
  When Nature underneath a heap
    Of jarring atoms lay,
  And could not heave her head,   5
The tuneful voice was heard from high,
  "Arise, ye more than dead."
Then cold and hot and moist and dry°
In order to their stations leap,
  And Music's pow'r obey.   10
From harmony, from heav'nly harmony
  This universal frame began:
  From harmony to harmony
Through all the compass of the notes it ran,
The diapason closing full in Man.   15

2

What passion cannot Music raise and quell!
  When Jubal° struck the corded shell
  His list'ning brethren stood around
  And, wond'ring, on their faces fell
  To worship that celestial sound.   20
Less than a god they thought there could not dwell
  Within the hollow of that shell
  That spoke so sweetly and so well.
What passion cannot Music raise and quell!

3

  The Trumpet's loud clangor   25
    Excites us to arms,
  With shrill notes of anger,
    And mortal alarms.
  The double double double beat
    Of the thundering Drum   30
Cries, "Hark the foes come;
Charge, charge, 'tis too late to retreat."

4

  The soft complaining Flute
  In dying notes discovers
  The woes of hopeless lovers,   35
Whose dirge is whispered by the warbling Lute.

5

Sharp Violins proclaim
Their jealous pangs, and desperation,
Fury, frantic indignation,
Depth of pains, and height of passion,   40
  For the fair, disdainful dame.

A SONG FOR SAINT CECILIA'S DAY. This ode was composed in 1687 for a concert given annually on November 22; it was set to music by Giovanni Baptista Draghi. Saint Cecilia is the patron saint of music. **1. heav'nly harmony:** harmony produced by the perfect alignment of the orbits of the planets, a Platonic conception of the order of the universe. The analogy between music and the creation of the world continues throughout the first stanza. **8. cold . . . dry:** the four elements: earth, fire, water and air.

17. Jubal: inventor of musical instruments (see Genesis 4:21).

6

But oh! what art can teach,
What human voice can reach
The sacred Organ's praise?
    Notes inspiring holy love,   45
Notes that wing their heav'nly ways
    To mend° the choirs above.

7

Orpheus could lead the savage race;
And trees unrooted left their place;
    Sequacious of° the lyre;   50
But bright Cecilia raised the wonder high'r;
When to her Organ, vocal breath was giv'n
An angel° heard, and straight appeared
    Mistaking earth for heaven.

GRAND CHORUS

As from the pow'r of sacred lays   55
    The spheres began to move,
And sung the great Creator's praise
    To all the blest above;
So when the last and dreadful hour°
This crumbling pageant shall devour,   60
The Trumpet shall be heard on high,
The dead shall live, the living die,
And Music shall untune the sky.

WILLIAM WORDSWORTH
1770–1850

Lines

*Composed a Few Miles Above Tintern Abbey,° on
Revisiting the Banks of the Wye During a Tour.
July 13, 1798.*

Five years have past; five summers, with the length
Of five long winters! and again I hear

---

47. **mend:** excel. 50. **Sequacious of:** following unreasoningly.
53. **angel:** Saint Cecilia's guardian angel, here attracted
to earth by harmony. 59. **dreadful hour:** Day of Judgment,
which complements the creation of the first stanza.

LINES COMPOSED A FEW MILES ABOVE TINTERN ABBEY. **Tintern Abbey:** a ruin in Western England.

These waters, rolling from their mountain-springs
With a soft inland° murmur—Once again
Do I behold these steep and lofty cliffs,   5
That on a wild secluded scene impress
Thoughts of more deep seclusion; and connect
The landscape with the quiet of the sky.
The day is come when I again repose
Here, under this dark sycamore, and view   10
These plots of cottage-ground, these orchard-tufts,
Which at this season, with their unripe fruits,
Are clad in one green hue, and lose themselves
'Mid groves and copses.° Once again I see
These hedgerows, hardly hedgerows, little lines 15
Of sportive wood run wild: these pastoral farms,
Green to the very door; and wreaths of smoke
Sent up, in silence, from among the trees!
With some uncertain notice, as might seem
Of vagrant dwellers in the houseless woods,   20
Or of some Hermit's cave, where by his fire
The Hermit sits alone.

                  These beauteous forms,
Through a long absence, have not been to me
As is a landscape to a blind man's eye:
But oft, in lonely rooms, and 'mid the din   25
Of towns and cities, I have owed to them
In hours of weariness, sensations sweet,
Felt in the blood, and felt along the heart;
And passing even into my purer mind,
With tranquil restoration:—feelings too   30
Of unremembered pleasure: such, perhaps,
As have no slight or trivial influence
On that best portion of a good man's life,
His little, nameless, unremembered, acts
Of kindness and of love. Nor less, I trust,   35
To them I may have owed another gift,
Of aspect more sublime; that blessed mood
In which the burthen of the mystery,
In which the heavy and the weary weight
Of all this unintelligible world,   40
Is lightened:—that serene and blessed mood,
In which the affections° gently lead us on,—
Until, the breath of this corporeal frame
And even the motion of our human blood
Almost suspended, we are laid asleep   45
In body, and become a living soul:
While with an eye made quiet by the power
Of harmony, and the deep power of joy,
We see into the life of things.

---

4. **inland:** i.e., above the tidal region of the river. 14.
copses: thickets. 42. **affections:** feelings, emotions.

                    If this
Be but a vain belief, yet, oh! how oft—   50
In darkness and amid the many shapes
Of joyless daylight; when the fretful stir
Unprofitable, and the fever of the world,
Have hung upon the beatings of my heart—
How oft, in spirit, have I turned to thee   55
O sylvan Wye! thou wanderer through the woods,
How often has my spirit turned to thee!

And now, with gleams of half-extinguished thought,
With many recognitions dim and faint,
And somewhat of a sad perplexity,   60
The picture of the mind revives again:
While here I stand, not only with the sense
Of present pleasure, but with pleasing thoughts
That in this moment there is life and food
For future years. And so I dare to hope,   65
Though changed, no doubt, from what I was when
    first
I came among these hills; when like a roe
I bounded o'er the mountains, by the sides
Of the deep rivers, and the lonely streams,
Wherever nature led: more like a man   70
Flying from something that he dreads than one
Who sought the thing he loved. For nature then
(The coarser pleasures of my boyish days,
And their glad animal movements all gone by)
To me was all in all.—I cannot paint   75
What then I was. The sounding cataract
Haunted me like a passion: the tall rock,
The mountain, and the deep and gloomy wood,
Their colors and their forms, were then to me
An appetite; a feeling and a love,   80
That had no need of a remoter charm,
By thought supplied, nor any interest
Unborrowed from the eye.—That time is past,
And all its aching joys are now no more,
And all its dizzy raptures. Not for this   85
Faint I, nor mourn nor murmur; other gifts
Have followed; for such loss, I would believe,
Abundant recompense. For I have learned
To look on nature, not as in the hour
Of thoughtless youth; but hearing oftentimes   90
The still, sad music of humanity,
Nor harsh nor grating, though of ample power
To chasten and subdue. And I have felt
A presence that disturbs me with the joy
Of elevated thoughts; a sense sublime   95
Of something far more deeply interfused,

Whose dwelling is the light of setting suns,
And the round ocean and the living air,
And the blue sky, and in the mind of man:
A motion and a spirit, that impels   100
All thinking things, all objects of all thought,
And rolls through all things. Therefore am I still
A lover of the meadows and the woods,
And mountains; and of all that we behold
From this green earth; of all the mighty world   105
Of eye, and ear,—both what they half create,
And what perceive; well pleased to recognize
In nature and the language of the sense°
The anchor of my purest thoughts, the nurse,
The guide, the guardian of my heart, and soul 110
Of all my moral being.

                    Nor perchance,
If I were not thus taught, should I the more
Suffer my genial° spirits to decay:
For thou art with me here upon the banks
Of this fair river; thou my dearest Friend,°   115
My dear, dear Friend; and in thy voice I catch
The language of my former heart, and read
My former pleasures in the shooting lights
Of thy wild eyes. Oh! yet a little while
May I behold in thee what I was once,   120
My dear, dear Sister! and this prayer I make,
Knowing that Nature never did betray
The heart that loved her; 'tis her privilege,
Through all the years of this our life, to lead
From joy to joy: for she can so inform   125
The mind that is within us, so impress
With quietness and beauty, and so feed
With lofty thoughts, that neither evil tongues,
Rash judgments, nor the sneers of selfish men,
Nor greetings where no kindness is, nor all   130
The dreary intercourse of daily life,
Shall e'er prevail against us, or disturb
Our cheerful faith, that all which we behold
Is full of blessings. Therefore let the moon
Shine on thee in thy solitary walk;   135
And let the misty mountain-winds be free
To blow against thee: and, in after years,
When these wild ecstasies shall be matured
Into a sober pleasure: when thy mind
Shall be a mansion for all lovely forms,   140
Thy memory be as a dwelling place
For all sweet sounds and harmonies; oh! then,

108. sense: senses. **113. genial:** vital. **115. Friend:** Wordsworth's sister Dorothy.

If solitude, or fear, or pain, or grief,
Should be thy portion, with what healing thoughts
Of tender joy wilt thou remember me,   145
And these my exhortations! Nor, perchance—
If I should be where I no more can hear
Thy voice, nor catch from thy wild eyes these
  gleams
Of past existence—wilt thou then forget
That on the banks of this delightful stream   150
We stood together; and that I, so long
A worshiper of Nature, hither came
Unwearied in that service: rather say
With warmer love—oh! with far deeper zeal
Of holier love. Nor wilt thou then forget,   155
That after many wanderings, many years
Of absence, these steep woods and lofty cliffs,
And this green pastoral landscape, were to me
More dear, both for themselves and for thy sake!

RALPH WALDO EMERSON
1803–1882

Each and All

Little thinks, in the field, yon red-cloaked clown
Of thee from the hilltop looking down;
The heifer that lows in the upland farm,
Far-heard, lows not thine ear to charm;
The sexton, tolling his bell at noon,   5
Deems not that great Napoleon
Stops his horse, and lists with delight,
Whilst his files sweep round yon Alpine height;
Nor knowest thou what argument
Thy life to thy neighbor's creed has lent.   10
All are needed by each one;
Nothing is fair or good alone.
I thought the sparrow's note from heaven,
Singing at dawn on the alder bough;
I brought him home, in his nest, at even;   15
He sings the song, but it cheers not now,
For I did not bring home the river and sky;—
He sang to my ear—they sang to my eye.
The delicate shells lay on the shore;
The bubbles of the latest wave   20
Fresh pearls to their enamel gave,
And the bellowing of the savage sea

Greeted their safe escape to me.
I wiped away the weeds and foam,
I fetched my sea-born treasures home;   25
But the poor, unsightly, noisome things
Had left their beauty on the shore
With the sun and the sand and the wild uproar.
The lover watched his graceful maid,
As 'mid the virgin train she strayed,   30
Nor knew her beauty's best attire
Was woven still by the snow-white choir.
At last she came to his hermitage,
Like the bird from the woodlands to the cage;—
The gay enchantment was undone,   35
A gentle wife, but fairy none.
Then I said, "I covet truth;
Beauty is unripe childhood's cheat;
I leave it behind with the games of youth":—
As I spoke, beneath my feet   40
The ground-pine curled its pretty wreath,
Running over the club-moss burrs;
I inhaled the violet's breath;
Around me stood the oaks and firs;
Pine-cones and acorns lay on the ground;   45
Over me soared the eternal sky,
Full of light and of deity;
Again I saw, again I heard,
The rolling river, the morning bird;—
Beauty through my senses stole;   50
I yielded myself to the perfect whole.

The Snowstorm

Announced by all the trumpets of the sky,
Arrives the snow, and, driving o'er the fields,
Seems nowhere to alight: the whited air
Hides hills and woods, the river, and the heaven,
And veils the farmhouse at the garden's end.   5
The sled and traveler stopped, the courier's feet
Delayed, all friends shut out, the housemates sit
Around the radiant fireplace, enclosed
In a tumultuous privacy of storm.

Come see the north wind's masonry.   10
Out of an unseen quarry evermore
Furnished with tile, the fierce artificer
Curves his white bastions with projected roof
Round every windward stake, or tree, or door.
Speeding, the myriad-handed, his wild work   15
So fanciful, so savage, nought cares he

For number or proportion. Mockingly,
On coop or kennel he hangs Parian° wreaths;
A swanlike form invests the hidden thorn;
Fills up the farmer's lane from wall to wall,   20
Maugre° the farmer's sighs; and at the gate
A tapering turret overtops the work.
And when his hours are numbered, and the world
Is all his own, retiring, as he were not,
Leaves, when the sun appears, astonished Art   25
To mimic in slow structures, stone by stone,
Built in an age, the mad wind's night-work,
The frolic architecture of the snow.

WALLACE STEVENS
1879–1955

Sunday Morning

1

Complacencies of the peignoir,° and late
Coffee and oranges in a sunny chair,
And the green freedom of a cockatoo
Upon a rug mingle to dissipate
The holy hush of ancient sacrifice.°   5
She dreams a little, and she feels the dark
Encroachment of that old catastrophe,
As a calm darkens among water-lights.
The pungent oranges and bright, green wings
Seem things in some procession of the dead,   10
Winding across wide water, without sound.
The day is like wide water, without sound,
Stilled for the passing of her dreaming feet
Over the seas, to silent Palestine,
Dominion of the blood and sepulcher.   15

2

Why should she give her bounty to the dead?
What is divinity if it can come
Only in silent shadows and in dreams?
Shall she not find in comforts of the sun,
In pungent fruit and bright, green wings, or else   20
In any balm or beauty of the earth,

THE SNOWSTORM.   **18. Parian:** white marble. **21. Maugre:**
In spite of.

SUNDAY MORNING.   **1. peignoir:** dressing-gown. **5. ancient
sacrifice:** the Crucifixion.

Things to be cherished like the thought of heaven?
Divinity must live within herself:
Passions of rain, or moods in falling snow;
Grievings in loneliness, or unsubdued   25
Elations when the forest blooms; gusty
Emotions on wet roads on autumn nights;
All pleasures and all pains, remembering
The bough of summer and the winter branch.
These are the measures destined for her soul.   30

3

Jove in the clouds had his inhuman birth.
No mother suckled him, no sweet land gave
Large-mannered motions to his mythy mind.
He moved among us, as a muttering king,
Magnificent, would move among his hinds,°   35
Until our blood, commingling, virginal,
With heaven, brought such requital° to desire
The very hinds discerned it, in a star.
Shall our blood fail? Or shall it come to be
The blood of paradise? And shall the earth   40
Seem all of paradise that we shall know?
The sky will be much friendlier then than now,
A part of labor and a part of pain,
And next in glory to enduring love,
Not this dividing and indifferent blue.   45

4

She says, "I am content when wakened birds,
Before they fly, test the reality
Of misty fields, by their sweet questionings;
But when the birds are gone, and their warm fields
Return no more, where, then, is paradise?"   50
There is not any haunt of prophecy,
Nor any old chimera° of the grave,
Neither the golden underground, nor isle
Melodious, where spirits gat° them home,
Nor visionary south, nor cloudy palm   55
Remote on heaven's hill, that has endured
As April's green endures; or will endure
Like her remembrance of awakened birds,
Or her desire for June and evening, tipped
By the consummation of the swallow's wings.   60

5

She says, "But in contentment I still feel
The need of some imperishable bliss."

35. hinds: servants. **37. requital:** repayment. **52. chimera:**
grotesque monster with a lion's head, a goat's body, and a
serpent's tail. **54. gat:** got.

Death is the mother of beauty; hence from her,
Alone, shall come fulfillment to our dreams
And our desires. Although she strews the leaves 65
Of sure obliteration on our paths,
The path sick sorrow took, the many paths
Where triumph rang its brassy phrase, or love
Whispered a little out of tenderness,
She makes the willow shiver in the sun   70
For maidens who were wont to sit and gaze
Upon the grass, relinquished to their feet.
She causes boys to pile new plums and pears
On disregarded plate. The maidens taste
And stray impassioned in the littering leaves.   75

6

Is there no change of death in paradise?
Does ripe fruit never fall? Or do the boughs
Hang always heavy in that perfect sky,
Unchanging, yet so like our perishing earth,
With rivers like our own that seek for seas   80
They never find, the same receding shores
That never touch with inarticulate pang?
Why set the pear upon those river-banks
Or spice the shores with odors of the plum?
Alas, that they should wear our colors there,   85
The silken weavings of our afternoons,
And pick the strings of our insipid lutes!
Death is the mother of beauty, mystical,
Within whose burning bosom we devise
Our earthly mothers waiting, sleeplessly.   90

7

Supple and turbulent, a ring of men
Shall chant in orgy on a summer morn
Their boisterous devotion to the sun,
Not as a god, but as a god might be,
Naked among them, like a savage source.   95
Their chant shall be a chant of paradise,
Out of their blood, returning to the sky;
And in their chant shall enter, voice by voice,
The windy lake wherein their lord delights,
The trees, like serafin, and echoing hills,   100
That choir among themselves long afterward.
They shall know well the heavenly fellowship
Of men that perish and of summer morn.
And whence they came and whither they shall go
The dew upon their feet shall manifest.   105

8

She hears, upon that water without sound,
A voice that cries, "The tomb in Palestine
Is not the porch of spirits lingering.
It is the grave of Jesus, where he lay."
We live in an old chaos of the sun,   110
Or old dependency of day and night,
Or island solitude, unsponsored, free,
Of that wide water, inescapable.
Deer walk upon our mountains, and the quail
Whistle about us their spontaneous cries;   115
Sweet berries ripen in the wilderness;
And, in the isolation of the sky,
At evening, casual flocks of pigeons make
Ambiguous undulations as they sink,
Downward to darkness, on extended wings.   120

WILLIAM BUTLER YEATS
1865–1939

Under Ben Bulben

1

Swear by what the sages spoke
Round the Mareotic Lake°
That the Witch of Atlas knew,
Spoke and set the cocks a-crow.

Swear by those horsemen,° by those women   5
Complexion and form prove superhuman,
That pale, long-visaged company
That air in immortality
Completeness of their passions won;
Now they ride the wintry dawn   10
Where Ben Bulben° sets the scene.

Here's the gist of what they mean.

2

Many times man lives and dies
Between his two eternities,
That of race and that of soul,   15
And ancient Ireland knew it all.

UNDER BEN BULBEN. **2. Mareotic Lake:** in Egypt. **5. those horsemen:** superhuman horsemen of Irish folklore. **11. Ben Bulben:** mountain in Ireland.

Whether man die in his bed
Or the rifle knocks him dead,
A brief parting from those dear
Is the worst man has to fear.　　　　20
Though grave-diggers' toil is long,
Sharp their spades, their muscles strong,
They but thrust their buried men
Back in the human mind again.

3

You that Mitchel's° prayer have heard,　　25
"Send war in our time, O Lord!"
Know that when all words are said
And a man is fighting mad,
Something drops from eyes long blind,
He completes his partial mind,　　　　30
For an instant stands at ease,
Laughs aloud, his heart at peace.
Even the wisest man grows tense
With some sort of violence
Before he can accomplish fate,　　　　35
Know his work or choose his mate.

4

Poet and sculptor, do the work,
Nor let the modish painter shirk
What his great forefathers did,
Bring the soul of man to God,　　　　40
Make him fill the cradles right.

Measurement began our might:
Forms a stark Egyptian thought,
Forms that gentler Phidias° wrought.
Michael Angelo left a proof　　　　45
On the Sistine Chapel roof,
Where but half-awakened Adam
Can disturb globe-trotting Madam
Till her bowels are in heat,
Proof that there's a purpose set　　　50
Before the secret working mind:
Profane perfection of mankind.

Quattrocento° put in paint
On backgrounds for a God or Saint
Gardens where a soul's at ease;　　　55
Where everything that meets the eye,
Flowers and grass and cloudless sky,
Resemble forms that are or seem

When sleepers wake and yet still dream,
And when it's vanished still declare,　　60
With only bed and bedstead there,
That heavens had opened.
　　　　　　　Gyres° run on;
When that greater dream had gone
Calvert and Wilson, Blake and Claude,°
Prepared a rest for the people of God,　　65
Palmer's° phrase, but after that
Confusion fell upon our thought.

5

Irish poets, learn your trade,
Sing whatever is well made,
Scorn the sort now growing up　　　70
All out of shape from toe to top,
Their unremembering hearts and heads
Base-born products of base beds.
Sing the peasantry, and then
Hard-riding country gentlemen,　　　75
The holiness of monks, and after
Porter-drinkers' randy laughter;
Sing the lords and ladies gay
That were beaten into the clay
Through seven heroic centuries;°　　80
Cast your mind on other days
That we in coming days may be
Still the indomitable Irishry.

6

Under bare Ben Bulben's head
In Drumcliff churchyard° Yeats is laid.　　85
An ancestor was rector there
Long years ago, a church stands near,
By the road an ancient cross.
No marble, no conventional phrase;
On limestone quarried near the spot　　90
By his command these words are cut:
　　　　Cast a cold eye
　　　　On life, on death.
　　　　Horseman, pass by!

62. Gyres: part of Yeats' private mythology, here representing the antithesis of historical eras. **64. Calvert . . . Claude:** Denis Calvert (1540–1619), Flemish painter; Richard Wilson (1714–82), English landscape painter; William Blake (1757–1827), English poet, mystic, and painter; Claude Lorrain (1600–82), French landscape painter. **66. Palmer:** Samuel Palmer (1805–81), English etcher who illustrated an edition of Milton's poems. **80. seven . . . centuries:** of Irish history. **85. Drumcliff churchyard:** in County Sligo, where Yeats' great-grandfather was rector.

25. Mitchel: John Mitchell (1815–75?), an Irish patriot. **44. Phidias:** ancient Greek sculptor. **53. Quattrocento:** the fifteenth century, a great age of Italian art.

The Celebration
of Temporal Experience

Sumer is Icumen In

ca. 1225

Sumer° is icumen in,
  Loude sing cuccu!
Groweth sed° and bloweth med°
  And springth the wude° nu.°
    Sing cuccu!   5
Awe° bleteth after lomb,
  Loweth after calve cu;°
Bulluc sterteth,° bucke verteth;°
  Murie sing cuccu!
    Cuccu, cuccu,   10
Wel singes thu, cuccu:
Ne swik° thu naver nu.
Sing cuccu nu! Sing cuccu!
Sing cuccu! Sing cuccu nu!

Bitweene Merch and Averil

ca. 1320

Bitweene° Merch and Averil,
When spray biginneth to springe,
The litel fowl hath hire° wil°
On hire leod° to singe.
Ich° libbe° in love-longinge   5
For semlokest° of alle thinge.
Heo° may me blisse bringe:

SUMER IS ICUMEN IN. **1. Sumer:** spring. **3. sed:** seed. **bloweth med:** the meadow blossoms. **4. wude:** woods. **nu:** now. **6. Awe:** ewe. **7. cu:** cow. **8. sterteth:** leaps. **verteth:** breaks wind. **12. swik:** cease, stop.

BITWEENE MERCH AND AVERIL. **1. Bitweene:** during. **3. hire:** her. **wil:** pleasure. **4. leod:** language. **5. Ich:** I. **libbe:** live. **6. semlokest:** seemliest, fairest. **7. Heo:** she.

Ich am in hire baundoun.°
  An hendy hap ich habbe yhent,°
  Ichoot° from hevene it is me sent: 10
  From alle° wommen my love is lent,°
  And light° on Alisoun.

On hew° hire heer° is fair ynough,
Hire browe browne, hire yë° blake,
With lossum cheere° heo on me lough,°   15
With middel smal and wel ymake.
But° heo me wolle to hire take
For to been hire owen make,°
Longe to liven ichulle° forsake,
And feye° fallen adown.   20
  An hendy hap, etc.

Nightes when I wende° and wake,
Forthy° mine wonges° waxeth wan:
Levedy,° al for thine sake
Longinge is ylent me on.°   25
In world nis noon so witer° man
That al hire bountee° telle can:
Hire swire° is whittere° than the swan,
And fairest may° in town.
  An hendy, etc.   30

Ich am for wowing° al forwake,°
Wery as water in wore.°

8. baundoun: power, control. **9. An . . . yhent:** I have received a gracious fortune. **10. Ichoot:** I know. **11. alle:** all other. **lent:** taken away. **12. light:** alights. **13. On hew:** in hue. **heer:** hair. **14. ye:** eye. **15. lossum cheere:** lovely face. **lough:** smiled. **17. But:** unless. **18. make:** mate. **19. ichulle:** I will. **20. feye:** doomed. **22. wende:** turn, toss. **23. Forthy:** therefore. **wonges:** cheeks. **24. Levedy:** lady. **25. is . . . on:** has come upon me. **26. witer:** wise, clever. **27. bountee:** excellence. **28. swire:** neck. **whittere:** whiter. **29. fairest may:** [she is the] fairest maid. **31. wowing:** wooing. **forwake:** worn out from lying awake. **32. wore:** pool (meaning unclear).

Lest any reve me° my make
Ich habbe y-yerned yore.°
Bettere is tholien° while° sore   35
Than mournen evermore.
Geinest under gore,°
Herkne to my roun:°
  An hendy, etc.

SIR JOHN SUCKLING
1609–1642

The Siege

'Tis now, since I sat down before
  That foolish fort, a heart,
(Time strangely spent) a year and more,
  And still I did my part,

Made my approaches, from her hand   5
  Unto her lip did rise,
And did already understand
  The language of her eyes;

Proceeded on with no less art—
  My tongue was engineer: 10
I thought to undermine the heart
  By whispering in the ear.

When this did nothing, I brought down
  Great cannon-oaths, and shot
A thousand thousand to the town;   15
  And still it yielded not.

I then resolved to starve the place
  By cutting off all kisses,
Praising and gazing on her face,
  And all such little blisses.   20

To draw her out, and from her strength,
  I drew all batteries in;
And brought myself to lie at length,
  As if no siege had been.

When I had done what man could do   25
  And thought the place mine own,
The enemy lay quiet too,
  And smiled at all was done.

I sent to know from whence, and where,
  These hopes, and this relief?   30
A spy informed, Honor was there,
  And did command in chief.

"March, march", quoth I; "the word straight give.
  Let's lose no time, but leave her:
That giant upon air will live,   35
  And hold it out forever.

"To such a place our camp remove
  As will no siege abide:
I hate a fool that starves her love,
  Only to feed her pride."   40

Oh! For Some Honest
Lover's Ghost

Oh! for some honest lover's ghost,
  Some kind unbodied post
  Sent from the shades below!
  I strangely long to know
Whether the nobler chaplets° wear,   5
Those that their mistress' scorn did bear,
  Or those that were used kindly.

For whatsoe'er they tell us here
  To make those sufferings dear,
  'Twill there, I fear, be found   10
  That to the being crowned
T' have loved alone will not suffice,
Unless we also have been wise,
  And have our loves enjoyed.

What posture can we think him in,   15
  That here unloved again
  Departs, and 's thither gone
  Where each sits by his own?
Or how can that Elysium be,
Where I my mistress still must see   20
  Circled in others' arms?

---

33. **reve me**: deprive me. 34. **y-yerned yore**: been worrying for a long time. 35. **tholien**: to endure. **while**: for a while. 37. **Geinest . . . gore**: fairest beneath gown. 38. **roun**: speech, song.

OH! FOR SOME HONEST LOVER'S GHOST. **5. chaplets**: garlands.

For there the judges all are just,
  And Sophonisba° must
  Be his whom she held dear,
  Not his who loved her here: 25
The sweet Philoclea, since she died,
Lies by her Pirocles his side,
  Not by Amphialus.°

Some bays, perchance, or myrtle bough,
  For difference crowns the brow   30
  Of those kind souls that were
  The noble martyrs here;
And if that be the only odds,
(As who can tell?) ye kinder gods,
  Give me the woman here.   35

Constancy

Out upon it! I have loved
  Three whole days together;
And am like to love three more,
  If it prove fair weather.

Time shall molt away his wings,   5
  Ere he shall discover
In the whole wide world again
  Such a constant lover.

But the spite on't is, no praise
  Is due at all to me: 10
Love with me had made no stays,
  Had it any been but she.

Had it any been but she,
  And that very face,
There had been at least ere this   15
  A dozen dozen in her place.

ROBERT HERRICK
1591–1674

Upon Julia's Clothes

Whenas in silks my Julia goes,
Then, then (methinks) how sweetly flows
That liquefaction of her clothes.

Next, when I cast mine eyes, and see
That brave vibration each way free;   5
Oh, how that glittering taketh me!

Delight in Disorder

A sweet disorder in the dress
Kindles in clothes a wantonness:
A lawn° about the shoulders thrown
Into a fine distraction:
An erring lace, which here and there   5
Enthralls the crimson stomacher:°
A cuff neglectful, and thereby
Ribbands to flow confusedly:
A winning wave (deserving note)
In the tempestuous petticoat: 10
A careless shoestring, in whose tie
I see a wild civility;
Do more bewitch me, than when art
Is too precise in every part.

To the Virgins,
to Make Much of Time

Gather ye rosebuds while ye may,
  Old time is still a-flying:
And this same flower that smiles today,
  Tomorrow will be dying.

The glorious lamp of heaven, the sun,   5
  The higher he's a-getting:
The sooner will his race be run,
  And nearer he's to setting.

23. **Sophonisba:** conventional name for the lady addressed in love poetry. **26–28. Philoclea, Pirocles, Amphialus:** characters in Sir Philip Sidney's *Arcadia* (1590); Pirocles, rather than Amphialus, is the object of Philoclea's love.

DELIGHT IN DISORDER. **3. lawn:** shawl. **6. stomacher:** article of clothing worn by women over the breast and stomach.

That age is best, which is the first,
    When youth and blood are warmer;   10
But being spent, the worse, and worst
    Times, still succeed the former.

Then be not coy, but use your time,
    And while ye may, go marry:
For having lost but once your prime,   15
    You may forever tarry.

Corinna's Going A-Maying

Get up, get up for shame, the blooming morn
Upon her wings presents the god unshorn.
    See how Aurora throws her fair
    Fresh-quilted colors through the air.
    Get up, sweet slug-a-bed, and see   5
    The dew bespangling herb and tree.
Each flower has wept, and bowed toward the east
Above an hour since, yet you not dressed,
    Nay! not so much as out of bed?
    When all the birds have matins said,   10
    And sung their thankful hymns, 'tis sin,
    Nay, profanation to keep in,
Whenas a thousand virgins on this day,
Spring, sooner than the lark, to fetch in May.°

Rise; and put on your foliage, and be seen   15
To come forth, like the springtime, fresh and
    green;
    And sweet as Flora. Take no care
    For jewels for your gown or hair:
    Fear not; the leaves will strew
    Gems in abundance upon you: 20
Besides, the childhood of the day has kept,
Against° you come, some orient° pearls unwept:
    Come and receive them while the light
    Hangs on the dew-locks of the night:
    And Titan° on the eastern hill   25
    Retires himself, or else stands still
Till you come forth. Wash, dress, be brief in
    praying:
Few beads are best, when once we go a-Maying.

Come, my Corinna, come; and, coming, mark
How each field turns a street, each street a park 30
    Made green and trimmed with trees, see how
    Devotion gives each house a bough
    Or branch: each porch, each door, ere this,
    An ark, a tabernacle is
Made up of whitethorn neatly interwove;   35
As if here were those cooler shades of love.
    Can such delights be in the street
    And open fields, and we not see 't?
    Come, we'll abroad; and let's obey
    The proclamation made for May: 40
And sin no more, as we have done, by staying;
But, my Corinna, come, let's go a-Maying.

There's not a budding boy or girl this day,
But is got up and gone to bring in May.
    A deal of youth, ere this, is come   45
    Back, and with whitethorn laden home.
    Some have dispatched their cakes and cream,
    Before that we have left to dream:
And some have wept, and wooed, and plighted
    troth,
And chose their priest, ere we can cast off sloth: 50
    Many a green-gown has been given,
    Many a kiss, both odd and even:
    Many a glance too has been sent
    From out the eye, love's firmament,
Many a jest told of the keys° betraying   55
This night, and locks° picked, yet we're not
    a-Maying.

Come, let us go while we are in our prime;
And take the harmless folly of the time.
    We shall grow old apace, and die
    Before we know our liberty.   60
    Our life is short; and our days run
    As fast away as does the sun:
And, as a vapor, or a drop of rain,
Once lost, can ne'er be found again:
    So when or you or I are made   65
    A fable, song, or fleeting shade,
    All love, all liking, all delight
    Lies drowned with us in endless night.
Then while time serves, and we are but decaying,
Come, my Corinna, come, let's go a-Maying.   70

CORINNA'S GOING A-MAYING. **14. fetch in May:** gather
flowers. **22. Against:** until. **orient:** precious. **25. Titan:** the
sun.

55–56. keys, locks: of chastity belts.

JOHN KEATS
1795–1821

To Autumn

Season of mists and mellow fruitfulness,
    Close bosom-friend of the maturing sun:
Conspiring with him how to load and bless
    With fruit the vines that round the thatch-eves
        run;
To bend with apples the mossed cottage-trees,   5
    And fill all fruit with ripeness to the core;
        To swell the gourd, and plump the hazel
        shells
With a sweet kernel; to set budding more,
    And still more, later flowers for the bees,
Until they think warm days will never cease,   10
    For Summer has o'er-brimmed their clammy
        cells.

Who hath not seen thee° oft amid thy store?
    Sometimes whoever seeks abroad may find
Thee sitting careless on a granary floor,
    Thy hair soft-lifted by the winnowing wind;   15
Or on a half-reaped furrow sound asleep,
    Drowsed with the fume of poppies, while thy
        hook°
    Spares the next swath and all its twinèd
        flowers:
And sometimes like a gleaner thou dost keep
    Steady thy laden head across a brook;   20
    Or by a cider-press, with patient look,
        Thou watchest the last oozings hours by hours.

Where are the songs of Spring? Aye, where are
    they?
    Think not of them, thou hast thy music too,—
While barrèd clouds bloom the soft-dying day,   25
    And touch the stubble-plains with rosy hue;
Then in a wailful choir the small gnats mourn
    Among the river sallows,° borne aloft
    Or sinking as the light wind lives or dies;
And full-grown lambs loud bleat from hilly
    bourn;°   30
    Hedge-crickets sing; and now with treble soft
    The red-breast whistles from a garden-croft;°
    And gathering swallows twitter in the skies.

TO AUTUMN. **12. thee:** female personification of autumn.
17. hook: sickle. **28. sallows:** willow trees. **30. bourn:**
region. **32. croft:** area.

Ode to Psyche

O Goddess!° hear these tuneless numbers,°
    wrung
By sweet enforcement and remembrance dear,
And pardon that thy secrets should be sung
    Even into thine own soft-conchèd ear:
Surely I dreamt today, or did I see   5
    The wingèd Psyche with awakened eyes?
I wandered in a forest thoughtlessly,
    And, on the sudden, fainting with surprise,
Saw two fair creatures, couchèd side by side
    In deepest grass, beneath the whisp'ring roof   10
    Of leaves and trembled blossoms, where there
        ran
        A brooklet, scarce espied:

Mid hushed, cool-rooted flowers, fragrant-eyed,
    Blue, silver-white, and budded Tyrian,°
They lay calm-breathing on the bedded grass;   15
    Their arms embracèd, and their pinions° too;
    Their lips touched not, but had not bade adieu,
As if disjoinèd by soft-handed slumber,
    And ready still past kisses to outnumber
    At tender eye-dawn of aurorean love: 20
        The wingèd boy I knew:
But who wast thou, O happy, happy dove?
        His Psyche true!

O latest born° and loveliest vision far
    Of all Olympus' faded hierarchy!   25
Fairer than Phoebe's sapphire-regioned star,°
    Or Vesper,° amorous glowworm of the sky;
Fairer than these, though temple thou hast none,
    Nor altar heaped with flowers;
Nor virgin-choir to make delicious moan   30
    Upon the midnight hours;
No voice, no lute, no pipe, no incense sweet
    From chain-swung censer teeming;
No shrine, no grove, no oracle, no heat
    Of pale-mouthed prophet dreaming.   35

ODE TO PSYCHE. **1. Goddess:** Psyche (Greek "soul"), a
beautiful maiden whom Cupid loved but was forced to
abandon because of her curiosity to see him; eventually she
was restored to him when Jupiter made her immortal.
numbers: metrical lines. **14. Tyrian:** purple. **16. pinions:**
wings. **24. latest born:** The myth of Cupid and Psyche first
appeared in the second century A.D. in *The Golden Ass* of
Apuleius. **26. Phoebe's . . . star:** the moon, of which
Phoebe, or Diana, was goddess. **27. Vesper:** the evening
star (Venus).

O brightest! though too late for antique vows,°
  Too, too late for the fond believing lyre,
When holy were the haunted forest boughs,
  Holy the air, the water, and the fire;
Yet even in these days so far retired   40
  From happy pieties, thy lucent fans,°
  Fluttering among the faint Olympians,
I see, and sing, by my own eyes inspired.
So let me be thy choir, and make a moan
    Upon the midnight hours;   45
Thy voice, thy lute, thy pipe, thy incense sweet
  From swingèd censer teeming;
Thy shrine, thy grove, thy oracle, thy heat
  Of pale-mouthed prophet dreaming.

Yes, I will be thy priest, and build a fane°   50
  In some untrodden region of my mind,
Where branchèd thoughts, new grown with
    pleasant pain,
  Instead of pines shall murmur in the wind:
Far, far around shall those dark-clustered trees
  Fledge° the wild-ridged mountains steep by
    steep;   55
And there by zephyrs, streams, and birds, and bees,
  The moss-lain Dryads° shall be lulled to sleep;
And in the midst of this wide quietness
  A rosy sanctuary will I dress
With the wreathed trellis of a working brain,   60
  With buds, and bells, and stars without a name,
With all the gardener Fancy e'er could feign,
  Who breeding flowers, will never breed the
    same:
And there shall be for thee all soft delight
  That shadowy thought can win,   65
A bright torch, and a casement ope at night,
  To let the warm Love in!

ALGERNON CHARLES
SWINBURNE
1837–1909

When the Hounds of Spring°

When the hounds of spring are on winter's traces,
  The mother of months° in meadow or plain
Fills the shadows and windy places
  With lisp of leaves and ripple of rain;
And the brown bright nightingale° amorous   5
Is half assuaged for Itylus,°
For the Thracian ships and the foreign faces,
  The tongueless vigil° and all the pain.

Come with bows bent and with emptying of
    quivers,
  Maiden most perfect, lady of light,   10
With a noise of winds and many rivers,
  With a clamor of waters, and with might;
Bind on thy sandals, O thou most fleet,
Over the splendor and speed of thy feet;
For the faint east quickens, the wan west shivers,   15
  Round the feet of the day and the feet of the
    night.

Where shall we find her, how shall we sing to her,
  Fold our hands round her knees, and cling?
O that man's heart were as fire and could spring to
    her,
  Fire, or the strength of the streams that spring!   20
For the stars and the winds are unto her
  As raiment, as songs of the harp player;
For the risen stars and the fallen cling to her,
  And the southwest-wind and the west-wind sing.

For winter's rains and ruins are over,   25
  And all the season of snows and sins;
The days dividing lover and lover,
  The light that loses, the night that wins;

WHEN THE HOUNDS OF SPRING. The poem is the opening
chorus of Swinburne's tragedy *Atalanta in Calydon*,
addressed to Diana (Artemis), goddess of the moon and
the hunt, protector of virgins. **2. mother of months:** because
of the relation of the moon to changing seasons. **5. nightingale:** Philomela, raped by her brother-in-law, Tereus, a
Thracian king, and changed into a nightingale. **6. Itylus:**
son of Procne, Philomela's sister, and Tereus. Procne
killed him and fed him to Tereus to avenge her sister.
8. tongueless vigil: Tereus had Philomela's tongue cut out
to keep her from telling of the rape.

---

36. **antique vows:** worship in Greece. Psyche was not regarded as a goddess until Roman times. **41. lucent fans:**
bright wings. **50. fane:** temple. **55. Fledge:** cover with
feathers. **57. Dryads:** tree nymphs.

And time remembered is grief forgotten,
And frosts are slain and flowers begotten,   30
And in green underwood and cover
  Blossom by blossom the spring begins.

The full streams feed on flower of rushes,
  Ripe grasses trammel a traveling foot,
The faint fresh flame of the young year flushes 35
  From leaf to flower and flower to fruit;
And fruit and leaf are as gold and fire,
And the oat° is heard above the lyre,
And the hoofèd heel of a satyr crushes
  The chestnut-husk at the chestnut-root.   40

And Pan by noon and Bacchus by night,
  Fleeter of foot than the fleet-foot kid,
Follows with dancing and fills with delight
  The Maenad and the Bassarid;°
And soft as lips that laugh and hide,   45
The laughing leaves of the trees divide,
And screen from seeing and leave in sight
  The god pursuing, the maiden hid.

The ivy falls with the Bacchanal's° hair
  Over her eyebrows hiding her eyes;   50
The wild vine slipping down leaves bare
  Her bright breast shortening into sighs;
The wild vine slips with the weight of its leaves,
But the berried ivy catches and cleaves
To the limbs that glitter, the feet that scare   55
  The wolf that follows, the fawn that flies.

An Interlude

In the greenest growth of the Maytime,
  I rode where the woods were wet,
Between the dawn and the daytime;
  The spring was glad that we met.

There was something the season wanted,   5
  Though the ways and the woods smelt sweet;
The breath at your lips that panted,
  The pulse of the grass at your feet.

You came, and the sun came after,
  And the green grew golden above;   10

And the flag-flowers lightened with laughter,
  And the meadow-sweet shook with love.

Your feet in the full-grown grasses
  Moved soft as a weak wind blows;
You passed me as April passes,   15
  With face made out of a rose.

By the stream where the stems were slender,
  Your bright foot paused at the sedge;
It might be to watch the tender
  Light leaves in the springtime hedge,   20

On boughs that the sweet month blanches
  With flowery frost of May:
It might be a bird in the branches,
  It might be a thorn in the way.

I waited to watch you linger   25
  With foot drawn back from the dew,
Till a sunbeam straight like a finger
  Struck sharp through the leaves at you.

And a bird overhead sang *Follow*,
  And a bird to the right sang *Here;*   30
And the arch of the leaves was hollow,
  And the meaning of May was clear.

I saw where the sun's hand pointed,
  I knew what the bird's note said;
By the dawn and the dewfall anointed,   35
  You were queen by the gold on your head.

As the glimpse of a burnt-out ember
  Recalls a regret of the sun,
I remember, forget, and remember
  What Love saw done and undone.   40

I remember the way we parted,
  The day and the way we met;
You hoped we were both broken-hearted,
  And knew we should both forget.

And May with her world in flower   45
  Seemed still to murmur and smile
As you murmured and smiled for an hour;
  I saw you turn at the stile.

A hand like a white wood-blossom
  You lifted, and waved, and passed   50
With head hung down to the bosom,
  And pale, as it seemed, at last.

---

38. oat: musical pipe made of straw, that symbolizes the poet's song in the conventions of pastoral poetry. **44. Maenad . . . Bassarid:** attendants of Bacchus in his revels. **49. Bacchanal:** female follower of Bacchus.

And the best and the worst of this is
   That neither is most to blame
If you've forgotten my kisses   55
   And I've forgotten your name.

D. H. LAWRENCE
1885–1930

Gloire de Dijon

When she rises in the morning
I linger to watch her;
She spreads the bath-cloth underneath the window
And the sunbeams catch her
Glistening white on the shoulders,   5
While down her sides the mellow
Golden shadow glows as
She stoops to the sponge, and the swung breasts
Sway like full-blown yellow
Gloire de Dijon roses.   10

She drips herself with water, and her shoulders
Glisten as silver, they crumple up
Like wet and falling roses, and I listen
For the sluicing of their rain-disheveled petals.
In the window full of sunlight   15
Concentrates her golden shadow
Fold on fold, until it glows as
Mellow as the glory roses.

Spring Morning

Ah, through the open door
Is there an almond-tree
Aflame with blossom!
   —Let us fight no more.

Among the pink and blue   5
Of the sky and the almond flowers
A sparrow flutters.
   —We have come through,

It is really spring!—See,
When he thinks himself alone   10
How he bullies the flowers.
   —Ah, you and me

How happy we'll be!—See him?
He clouts the tufts of flowers
In his impudence.   15
   —But, did you dream

It would be so bitter? Never mind
It is finished, the spring is here.
And we're going to be summer-happy
   And summer-kind.   20

We have died, we have slain and been slain,
We are not our old selves any more.
I feel new and eager
   To start again.

It is gorgeous to live and forget.   25
And to feel quite new.
See the bird in the flowers?—he's making
   A rare to-do!

He thinks the whole blue sky
Is much less than the bit of blue egg   30
He's got in his nest—we'll be happy,
   You and I, I and you.

With nothing to fight any more—
In each other, at least.
See, how gorgeous the world is   35
   Outside the door!

My Way Is Not Thy Way°

My way is not thy way, and thine is not mine.
But come, before we part
Let us separately go to the Morning Star,°
And meet there.

I do not point you to my road, nor yet   5
Call: "Oh come!"
But the Star is the same for both of us,
Winsome.

The good ghost of me goes down the distance
To the Holy Ghost.°   10

MY WAY IS NOT THY WAY. This poem was originally published as a Quetzalcoatl hymn (psalmlike song of praise in Lawrence's version of a revived Aztec religion) in the final chapter of Lawrence's novel *The Plumed Serpent*. **3. Morning Star:** In the symbolism of the Quetzalcoatl religion of the novel, the morning and evening stars are associated with spirit and body, respectively. **10. Holy Ghost:** In the novel Jesus returns to heaven, regarding Christianity as a cycle of belief that will be replaced by the religion of Quetzalcoatl; here the Holy Ghost is applied to the new religion.

Oh you, in the tent of the cloven flame
Meet me, you I like most.

Each man his own way forever, but towards
The hoverer between;
Who opens his flame like a tent-flap,   15
As we slip in unseen.

A man cannot tread like a woman,
Nor a woman step out like a man.
The ghost of each through the leaves of shadow
Moves as it can.   20

But the Morning Star and the Evening Star
Pitch tents of flame
Where we foregather like gypsies, none knowing
How the other came.

I ask for nothing except to slip   25
In the tent of the Holy Ghost
And be there in the house of the cloven flame,
Guest of the Host.

Be with me there, my woman,
Be bodily there.   30
Then let the flame wrap round us
Like a snare.

Be there along with me, oh men!
Reach across the hearth,
And laugh with me, while the woman rests,   35
For all we are worth.

The Invention
of Partial Order

JOHN DONNE
1572–1631

The Sun Rising

Busy old fool, unruly sun,
    Why dost thou thus,
Through windows, and through curtains, call on us?
Must to thy motions lovers' seasons run?
      Saucy pedantic wretch, go chide   5
      Late schoolboys and sour prentices,
  Go tell court-huntsmen that the king will ride,
  Call country ants to harvest offices;
Love, all alike, no season knows, nor clime,
Nor hours, days, months, which are the rags of
    time.   10

      Thy beams, so reverend and strong
      Why shouldst thou think?
I could eclipse and cloud them with a wink,
But that I would not lose her sight so long:
      If her eyes have not blinded thine,   15
      Look, and tomorrow late, tell me,
  Whether both th' Indias of spice and mine°
  Be where thou leftst them, or lie here with me.
Ask for those kings whom thou saw'st yesterday,
And thou shalt hear, All here in one bed lay.   20

      She is all states, and all princes I,
      Nothing else is.
Princes do but play us; compared to this,
All honor's mimic, all wealth alchemy.°

Thou, sun, art half as happy as we,   25
In that the world's contracted thus;
Thine age asks° ease, and since thy duties be
To warm the world, that's done in warming us.
Shine here to us, and thou art everywhere;
This bed thy center is, these walls, thy sphere.   30

Love's Diet

To what a cumbersome unwieldiness
And burdensome corpulence my love had grown,
    But that I did, to make it less,
    And keep it in proportion,
Give it a diet, made it feed upon   5
That which love worst endures, *discretion.*

Above one sigh a day I allowed him not,
Of which my fortune and my faults had part;°
    And if sometimes by stealth he got
    A she-sigh from my mistress' heart,   10
And thought to feast on that, I let him see
'Twas neither very sound, nor meant to me.

If he wrung from me a tear, I brined° it so
With scorn or shame, that him it nourished not;
    If he sucked hers, I let him know   15
    'Twas not a tear which he had got,
His drink was counterfeit, as was his meat;°
For eyes which roll towards all, weep not, but
    sweat.

Whatever he would dictate, I writ that,
But burnt my letters; when she writ to me,   20

THE SUN RISING. **17. both . . . mine:** the East Indies (spice)
and West Indies (gold and silver). **24. alchemy:** here seen to
be fraudulent.

LOVE'S DIET. **8. Of . . . part:** i.e., part of which had
nothing to do with love. **13. brined:** salted. **17. meat:** sighs.

27. **asks:** requires, needs.

And that that favor made him fat,°
I said, if any title be
Conveyed by this, ah, what doth it avail
To be the fortieth name in an entail?°

Thus I reclaimed° my buzzard love, to fly   25
At what, and when, and how, and where I choose;
  Now negligent of sport I lie,
  And now, as other falconers use,
I spring° a mistress, swear, write, sigh and weep:
And the game killed, or lost, go talk, and sleep. 30

ARCHIBALD MACLEISH
b. 1892

Not Marble
Nor the Gilded Monuments°

The praisers of women in their proud and beautiful
  poems
Naming the grave mouth and the hair and the eyes,
Boasted those they loved should be forever
  remembered:
These were lies.

The words sound but the face in the Istrian° sun is
  forgotten.   5
The poet speaks but to her dead ears no more.
The sleek throat is gone—and the breast that was
  troubled to listen:
Shadow from door.

Therefore I will not praise your knees nor your
  fine walking
Telling you men shall remember your name as
  long   10
As lips move or breath is spent or the iron of
  English
Rings from a tongue.

<hr>

21. And . . . fat: i.e., when she replied that his writing made
love grow. 24. fortieth . . . entail: the fortieth person in
line to inherit an estate. 25. reclaimed: tamed. 29. spring:
start, flush (an animal).

NOT MARBLE NOR THE GILDED MONUMENTS. The first line
of Shakespeare's Sonnet 55. 5. Istrian: peninsula along the
Yugoslavian coast of the Adriatic.

I shall say you were young, and your arms straight,
  and your mouth scarlet:
I shall say you will die and none will remember you:
Your arms change, and none remember the swish
  of your garments: 15
Nor the click of your shoe:

Not with my hand's strength, not with difficult
  labor
Springing the obstinate words to the bones of your
  breast
And the stubborn line to your young stride and
  the breath to your breathing
And the beat to your haste   20
Shall I prevail on the hearts of unborn men to
  remember.

(What is a dead girl but a shadowy ghost
Or a dead man's voice but a distant and vain
  affirmation
Like dream words most)

Therefore I will not speak of the undying glory of
  women.   25
I will say you were young and straight and your
  skin fair
And you stood in the door and the sun was a
  shadow of leaves on your shoulders
And a leaf on your hair—

I will not speak of the famous beauty of dead
  women:
I will say the shape of a leaf lay once on your
  hair.   30
Till the world ends and the eyes are out and the
  mouths broken
Look! It is there!

Landscape as a Nude

She lies on her left side her flank golden:
Her hair is burned black with the strong sun.
The scent of her hair is of rain in the dust on her
  shoulders:
She has brown breasts and the mouth of no other
  country.

Ah she is beautiful here in the sun where she
  lies: 5
She is not like the soft girls naked in vineyards

Nor the soft naked girls of the English islands
Where the rain comes in with the surf on an east
   wind:

Hers is the west wind and the sunlight: the west
Wind is the long clean wind of the continents— 10
The wind turning with earth, the wind descending
Steadily out of the evening and following on.

The wind here where she lies is west: the trees
Oak ironwood cottonwood hickory: standing in
Great groves they roll on the wind as the sea
   would.   15
The grasses of Iowa Illinois Indiana

Run with the plunge of the wind as a wave tumbling.

Under her knees there is no green lawn of the
   Florentines:
Under her dusty knees is the corn stubble:
Her belly is flecked with the flickering light of the
   corn.   20

She lies on her left side her flank golden:
Her hair is burned black with the strong sun.
The scent of her hair is of dust and of smoke on
   her shoulders:
She has brown breasts and the mouth of no other
   country.

STEPHEN SPENDER
b. 1909

The Express

After the first powerful plain manifesto
The black statement of pistons, without more fuss
But gliding like a queen, she leaves the station.
Without bowing and with restrained unconcern
She passes the houses which humbly crowd
   outside,   5
The gasworks, and at last the heavy page
Of death, printed by gravestones in the cemetery.
Beyond the town, there lies the open country
Where, gathering speed, she acquires mystery,
The luminous self-possession of ships on ocean. 10

It is now she begins to sing—at first quite low
Then loud, and at last with a jazzy madness—
The song of her whistle screaming at curves,
Of deafening tunnels, brakes, innumerable bolts.
And always light, aerial, underneath,   15
Retreats the elate meter of her wheels.
Steaming through metal landscape on her lines,
She plunges new eras of white happiness,
Where speed throws up strange shapes, broad
   curves
And parallels clean like trajectories from guns. 20
At last, further than Edinburgh or Rome,
Beyond the crest of the world, she reaches night
Where only a low stream-line brightness
Of phosphorus on the tossing hills is light.
Ah, like a comet through flame, she moves en-
   tranced,   25
Wrapped in her music no bird song, no, nor bough
Breaking with honey buds, shall ever equal.

The Pylons

The secret of these hills was stone, and cottages
Of that stone made,
And crumbling roads
That turned on sudden hidden villages.

Now over these small hills, they have built the
   concrete   5
That trails black wire;
Pylons, those pillars
Bare like nude giant girls that have no secret.

The valley with its gilt and evening look
And the green chestnut   10
Of customary root
Are mocked dry like the parched bed of a brook.

But far above and far as sight endures
Like whips of anger
With lightning's danger   15
There runs the quick perspective of the future.

This dwarfs our emerald country by its trek
So tall with prophecy:
Dreaming of cities
Where often clouds shall lean their swan-white
   neck.   20

W. H. AUDEN
b. 1907

Law Like Love

Law, say the gardeners, is the sun,
Law is the one
All gardeners obey
Tomorrow, yesterday, today.

Law is the wisdom of the old   5
The impotent grandfathers shrilly scold;
The grandchildren put out a treble tongue,
Law is the senses of the young.

Law, says the priest with a priestly look,
Expounding to an unpriestly people,   10
Law is the words in my priestly book,
Law is my pulpit and my steeple.

Law, says the judge as he looks down his nose,
Speaking clearly and most severely,
Law is as I've told you before,   15
Law is as you know I suppose,
Law is but let me explain it once more,
Law is The Law.

Yet law-abiding scholars write;
Law is neither wrong nor right,   20
Law is only crimes
Punished by places and by times,
Law is the clothes men wear
Anytime, anywhere,
Law is Good-morning and Good-night.   25

Others say, Law is our Fate;
Others say, Law is our State;
Others say, others say
Law is no more
Law is gone away.   30

And always the loud angry crowd
Very angry and very loud
Law is We,
And always the soft idiot softly Me.

If we, dear, know we know no more   35
Than they about the law,
If I no more than you
Know what we should and should not do
Except that all agree
Gladly or miserably   40

That the law is
And that all know this,
If therefore thinking it absurd
To identify Law with some other word,
Unlike so many men   45
I cannot say Law is again,
No more than they can we suppress
The universal wish to guess
Or slip out of our own position
Into an unconcerned condition.   50
Although I can at least confine
Your vanity and mine
To stating timidly
A timid similarity,
We shall boast anyway: 55
Like love I say.

Like love we don't know where or why
Like love we can't compel or fly
Like love we often weep
Like love we seldom keep.   60

E. E. CUMMINGS
1894–1962

anyone lived in a pretty how town

anyone lived in a pretty how town
(with up so floating many bells down)
spring summer autumn winter
he sang his didn't he danced his did.

Women and men(both little and small)   5
cared for anyone not at all
they sowed their isn't they reaped their same
sun moon stars rain

children guessed(but only a few
and down they forgot as up they grew   10
autumn winter spring summer)
that noone loved him more by more

when by now and tree by leaf
she laughed his joy she cried his grief
bird by snow and stir by still   15
anyone's any was all to her

someones married their everyones
laughed their cryings and did their dance

(sleep wake hope and then)they
said their nevers they slept their dream   20

stars rain sun moon
(and only the snow can begin to explain
how children are apt to forget to remember
with up so floating many bells down)

one day anyone died i guess   25
(and noone stooped to kiss his face)
busy folk buried them side by side
little by little and was by was

all by all and deep by deep
and more by more they dream their sleep   30
noone and anyone earth by april
wish by spirit and if by yes.

Women and men(both dong and ding)
summer autumn winter spring
reaped their sowing and went their came   35
sun moon stars rain

PHILIP LARKIN
b. 1922

Church Going

Once I am sure there's nothing going on
I step inside, letting the door thud shut.
Another church: matting, seats, and stone,
And little books; sprawlings of flowers, cut
For Sunday, brownish now; some brass and stuff 5
Up at the holy end; the small neat organ;
And a tense, musty, unignorable silence,
Brewed God knows how long. Hatless, I take off
My cycle-clips in awkward reverence,

Move forward, run my hand around the font.   10
From where I stand, the roof looks almost new—
Cleaned or restored? Someone would know: I
     don't.
Mounting the lectern, I peruse a few
Hectoring large-scale verses and pronounce
"Here endeth" much more loudly than I'd meant.
The echoes snigger briefly. Back at the door   16
I sign the book, donate an Irish sixpence,
Reflect the place was not worth stopping for.

Yet stop I did: in fact I often do,
And always end much at a loss like this,   20
Wondering what to look for; wondering, too,
When churches fall completely out of use
What we shall turn them into, if we shall keep
A few cathedrals chronically on show,
Their parchment, plate and pyx° in locked cases, 25
And let the rest rent-free to rain and sheep.
Shall we avoid them as unlucky places?

Or, after dark, will dubious women come
To make their children touch a particular stone;
Pick simples° for a cancer; or in some   30
Advised night see walking a dead one?
Power of some sort or other will go on
In games, in riddles, seemingly at random;
But superstition, like belief, must die,
And what remains when disbelief has gone?   35
Grass, weedy pavement, brambles, buttress, sky,

A shape less recognizable each week,
A purpose more obscure. I wonder who
Will be the last, the very last, to seek
This place for what it was: one of the crew   40
That tap and jot and know what rood-lofts were?
Some ruin-bibber, randy° for antique,
Or Christmas-addict, counting on a whiff
Of gown-and-bands and organ-pipes and myrrh?
Or will he be my representative,   45

Bored, uninformed, knowing the ghostly silt
Dispersed, yet tending to this cross of ground
Through suburb scrub because it held unspilt
So long and equably what since is found
Only in separation—marriage, and birth,   50
And death, and thoughts of these—for whom was
     built
This special shell? For, though I've no idea
What this accoutered frowsty° barn is worth,
It pleases me to stand in silence here;

A serious house on serious earth it is,   55
In whose blent air all our compulsions meet,
Are recognized, and robed as destinies.
And that much never can be obsolete,
Since someone will forever be surprising
A hunger in himself to be more serious,   60
And gravitating with it to this ground,
Which, he once heard, was proper to grow wise in,
If only that so many dead lie round.

CHURCH GOING. **25. pyx:** box for keeping the reserved
Eucharist. **30. simples:** herbs. **42. randy:** overzealous. **53.
frowsty:** musty.

IRONY

Narrative Irony

Narrative irony has never received the critical attention given to tragedy, comedy, and even romance. So little has been written on it that we might question whether irony in fact has the status of the other narrative patterns. There may be a good reason for this in the nature of irony itself. More than the other forms, it demands an unusual sensitivity to the author's "real" position or role. To read it correctly we must refuse to take the ironist's words at face value; we must remember to anticipate his ironic feint. It is possible that we are so conditioned to looking warily ahead to the ironic meaning of the story that we tend to think little about the narrative structure we have just read through. Most of the descriptions of irony, therefore, refer to thematic rather than narrative elements.

Satire, a form often associated with irony, encourages this habit. By definition satire ridicules and criticizes human follies and vices; and however general an author's attack may be, we naturally look for historical or biographical details that will reveal his specific animosities. The dispute between the Big-Endians and the Little-Endians in *Gulliver's Travels* is an example of literary burlesque, but we read it almost immediately as evidence of Jonathan Swift's view of theological controversy in eighteenth-century England. Both the equivocal and the satiric elements of irony, then, divert our attention from the work and to the author, prompting us to ask what *he* meant and what, in his own experience, provoked *his* scorn. This is not to deny the interest in these questions, but rather to suggest one reason for the scarcity of critical works on the narrative pattern of irony.

The fact that we use phrases like "the narrative pattern of irony" or "ironic narratives" is indicative: the vocabulary of criticism relegates the term *irony* to the position of the modifier. While the language provides the other modes with familiar nouns for their narrative patterns—*romance*, *tragedy*, *comedy*—to speak of a work as an irony, although it may pass grammatically, gives no assurance that the reference is to the plot or narrative. The term *irony* by itself is not usually associated with narrative pattern. Other terms, like *antiromance*, seem awkward and too dependent on another mode, or like *satire*, give an unwarranted importance to one feature of irony—one, incidentally, that is not exclusive to it, for tragedy and, more particularly, comedy are as often satiric. Lacking any better term, then, we will take irony as a noun for the narrative pattern and hope that usage will justify it later, for we suspect that its lack of currency may simply reflect the fact that the mode has come to dominate literary history only in our own time and even now its protean nature awaits the critic who can pin it down.

From Verbal to Narrative Irony

Let us assume that what is true for the ironic sentence holds for the ironic narrative and begin with what we understand as ironic in its most common or colloquial forms. For a conversational remark—"A fine day, isn't it?" —to have ironic force, there must be some context, a grim sky or pouring rain, or some gesture or inflection that establishes a contrast between statement and implication. To understand the irony we must choose the remark's negative implication rather than its apparent meaning. There is a possible model for irony here: it begins with a simple and apparent affirmative; it then negates that affirmative by implying its opposite; and finally that implication is underscored with a degree of emphasis greater than it could have had as an unequivocal statement. Irony begins with a guileful assent to commonplace assumptions—people mean what they say —works with inversions and negations, and somehow manages to create out of two opposed meanings a third with a force greater than the sum of its parts. It is perhaps instructive that when things go right, when the weather changes, the ironist is often at a loss for words. This is to say more than that irony thrives on bad luck; it may suggest something like a set of "rules" governing ironic expression and intimately connected with the conventional assumptions implicit in the ironic view of experience.

The vocabulary of criticism adds to our understanding of verbal irony. Both dramatic and Socratic irony depend on a contrast between sophistication and naiveté, or understanding and ignorance. In the first, the contrast is between the understanding of the audience and the ignorance of a character, and the classic example is Oedipus' curse on the murderer of the former king, whom the audience knows to be Oedipus himself. The conventional philosophic role of Socrates combines these extremes of knowledge: the wisest of philosophers proclaimed himself the most ignorant of men. Thus irony, probably more than any other mode, clearly requires a very sharp sense of the subtleties of rhetoric. This rigorous demand for attention to ambiguities of language may explain why we conceive of irony as more in the texture than in the structure of a work.

If there are similarities between an ironic sentence and an ironic narrative, they should center about some major contrast or paradox. The common characteristic of the examples of verbal irony is their dependence on the effect of a contrast between the stated and the implied, between conventional expectations and their opposites, or between the assumed and real roles of a character. Two sets of expectations must work together, and the reader must share these with the author, even if only tentatively, for irony to have its effect. At first we assume that the ironist means what he says, then we catch his implication, and finally we sense that he means something more emphatic than the simple negative implication. This is an obvious attenuation of an instantaneous response, but it provides a model for understanding the narrative pattern of irony. The pattern of events in an ironic story tentatively establishes one set of positive assumptions, undercuts it with a second, and produces a third. Irony usually demands a "second reading" of the preliminaries to which we initially assigned a positive value. In the total context of irony these seem more foreboding than promising, if only because we have discovered that in the ironist's world hope is the prelude to disaster.

Consider the structure of one of Alexander Pope's couplets as an example of the model for irony. (He inscribed these lines on a collar for a dog he gave to his friend the Prince of Wales in 1736.)

> I am his Highness' dog at Kew;
> Pray tell me sir, whose dog are you?

The first line strikes us as a guileless and simple statement of fact, recognizing not only that there are dogs and masters in this world, but also that there may be men without masters, perhaps like the individual who reads the lines. But the second line infuses the term of address with a canine sneer and demolishes the implications of the first. Finally, we reconsider the couplet and see that it does more than simply say that all men, like dogs, serve some master, for in a world where everyone is someone else's dog, the dog who knows it and can ask the question is somehow more of a man.

The "tension" in the couplet between statement and implication may in longer forms appear to exist between earlier and later elements of the narrative. However we think of it, the contrast rests on the discrepancy between conventions or sets of assumptions shared by the author and his audience. To take a popular example: in a satiric cartoon a beautiful princess encounters a frog in the forest; touching it with her wand, she transforms it into a handsome prince; they marry and retire for the night, when the prince, seeing a fly on the ceiling, flicks out a long and glutinous tongue and devours the fly. The humor, such as it is, in this "ironic" narrative, assumes a familiarity with the convention of the fairy tale it mocks, the legend of the Beauty and the Beast. That much is obvious, but it is less apparent that its form, the comic-strip panels and the rather distorted figures, prepares us for that mocking finale.

Another "principle" of irony, then, may rest in the requirement that we simultaneously assent to some external convention of narrative and yet doubt that it will turn out as that convention would lead us to expect. Just as verbal irony demands that we recognize both statement and implication, so narrative irony requires us to see events as part of two narrative patterns. One of these patterns must be familiar enough to allow the ironist to elicit our expectations in order to deny them. Yet, in the double vision of irony, that denial is also part of what we expect and is undoubtedly a more sophisticated aspect of this complex convention. Put another way, irony presents us with a balanced set of opposed narrative expectations, both of which, if we would read irony rightly, should be held in suspension at the outset, and one of which—usually the darker of the two—should more accurately predict the conclusion.

Narratives like Nathaniel Hawthorne's "My Kinsman, Major Molineux" support this notion: in the early scenes the story establishes a delicate equilibrium between Robin's enthusiastic hopes and the more threatening forecasts of his failure. Both views are part of a set of tacit assumptions about the shape and consequence of human action. Both are essential to the later comprehension of the old gentleman's prophecies and of the reason for the universal and diabolic laughter, to which the boy adds his own new-found voice. It is likely, however, that the *primary* impetus for our sense of pattern in the narrative derives from a view of things analogous to Robin's: a young man in search of a respected kinsman comes to the city and, whatever obstacles he meets, he usually wins his inheritance—a series of events familiar to us from romance. Moreover, it is likely that only a *secondary* impetus for our sense of narrative pattern derives from a view similar to that of the threatening and ambiguous commentators on Robin's progress. It is a secondary impulse in that it depends on some prior expectation that it negates. Irony does not say, expect nothing; it says, rather, do not expect something.

The idea that irony operates on some such denial of a formal or structural expectation underlies Northrop Frye's original concept of the narrative pattern: "As structure," he suggests, "the central principle of ironic myth is best approached as a parody of romance: the application of romantic mythical forms to a more realistic content which fits them in unexpected ways." The important term is parody. Although we usually think of parody as the humorous use of the writer's style to treat a subject strikingly uncharacteristic of his work, there is a familiar tradition in literature of "structural" parodies. Whether stylistic or structural—and admittedly the line is hard to draw—the effect of parody depends on some violation of a convention that requires an equivalence between manner and matter, form and content. Literary burlesque, for example, commonly treats an ordinary subject in an inappropriately lofty manner, as Pope invests a card game with the proportions of an epic battle in "The Rape of the Lock," or it reduces the lofty to the ordinary, as Byron does the divine courts in "The Vision of Judgment." In each case, style is parodied, yet each mocks the structure of a conventional narrative pattern: in Pope, the romantic quest, in Byron, the apotheosis of the romantic hero. The common element in most parody and burlesque is the author's expectation, in fact his dependence on, his reader's awareness and momentary acceptance of the style, the narrative conventions, and the implicit conceptual system of a structural pattern other than the one he is in the midst of creating.

As verbal irony says one thing and means another, so narrative irony often alludes to one structure and creates another. It is this allusive design that leads critics to speak of irony in terms of the other three major narrative patterns: a work may seem ironic because it is "structurally close to" but not quite comedy, or because it "isolates" one and only one element from tragedy, or because it "adopts" a feature from romance and then transmutes it into its opposite. All these insights strike us as valid, if only because to define irony by what it is not is to affirm the negative principle that is the hallmark of the mode.

Beyond the Conventions of Irony

If conventional irony is founded on a covenant between writer and reader in which the reader, as straight-man, agrees to be tricked according to more or less prescribed rules, then there is some question as to what can be made of those emerging contemporary works that seem to violate even the minimal rules of the most radical irony. There is in the work of contemporary ironists a variety of compounded duplicity, in the face of which the innocent general reader has little assurance that there is a meaning system on which he and the author would agree or at least consistently disagree. When John Cheever tells us that one of his characters' "work in Washington was so secret that it cannot be discussed here," he is toying with the very first assumption we thought we shared with him on the question of what is fiction and what is reality. Other contemporary writers go even further. The plays within plays within plays of Peter Weiss' *Marat/Sade* and Tom Stoppard's *Rosencrantz and Guildenstern Are Dead*, the infinitely receding reflections between the opposed mirrors of poem and commentary in Vladimir Nabokov's *Pale Fire*, and the most recent fiction of John Barth—in one instance merging a narrative with authorial comments derived from a manual on the writing of narrative—all these imply a restiveness with the limits of irony and an urge to break through them into another mode.

One example of irony that goes beyond conventional limits is the "put-on," the facetious and bizarre event or discourse that for all its apparent structure and intention we cannot interpret as either serious or conventionally satiric. In a *New Yorker* magazine article on the put-on in 1967, Jacob Brackman provided a variety of examples from a press conference in which the Beatles responded to every question with "Woof, woof" to a contemporary play in which the chorale from Beethoven's Ninth Symphony is sung by a chorus of apes. And there are others in this era so conscious of the new media and so indifferent to the old messages. At a well-publicized university lecture on "The Literature of Silence" the speaker walked on the stage, pinned a blank sheet of paper to the lectern, and walked off. The point of such nonevents is that they have no point: the most that one can do with them is to identify some general target toward which they are directed and which often turns out to be, as in these instances, the mode of expression itself. Thus, the put-on is an extension of one of the primary features of irony, the tendency to turn in upon itself and against the resources of language, to question and ultimately demolish the medium that gives it life. But unlike conventional irony the put-on defies analysis. As Brackman notes, "Irony is unsuccessful when misunderstood. But the put-on, inherently, *cannot* be understood." As the examples demonstrate, it is satiric in that an object is criticized—the press conference, the play, the professional lecture—but the put-on "has only the *form* of satire, without the content, without the rules. It attacks, but from no real position of its own. Not holding any real position, it is itself invulnerable to attack."

It may be that we are witnessing in the put-on the appearance of one of the cultural forms of a postironic era. A generation once burned by believing that there were positions on which one could take a stand, that the language of politics and the rituals of society could be taken straight, might well react by adopting a new mode that denies or disguises *any* position and manipulates expressive forms to negate expression itself. Whatever historical or cultural significance we may find in this phenomenon, it is interesting to us for the way in which it points up contrasting features in irony: irony works by indirection and its confusions are finally resolved; the put-on works by misdirection and its confusions are unresolved. The put-on artist takes no position, follows no rules; the ironist depends on a complex set of conventions to establish his and his audience's position. The rules of his game are intricate and sophisticated—perhaps enough in itself to turn off some artists whose reaction to an age of irony will be to put us on.

The Pattern of Irony   Part of our difficulty in characterizing the conceptions that order and shape irony lies in the fact that we get little assistance from the ironic author. He is rarely didactic, his meanings issue in indirection and implication, and we catch his intention, if at all, out of the corner of our eye. The "rules" of irony seem to exclude the explicit judgment or the tidy moral. The ironist recognizes few ethical norms and those only after an exhausting and literally demoralizing quest that ends in a no more than temporary certitude. When he takes his stand he does so with the sense not that he has won a victory but that he has found a position where he can best go down to defeat. The tone of his statements is governed by the negative, ranging in intensity from Herman Melville's "No, in thunder" to Robert Frost's more reticent denials.

The ironist's typical introspective vision demands self-deprecation. At the end of Joseph Conrad's *Heart of Darkness,* for example, the narrator Marlow visits Kurtz's betrothed to tell her of his death.

> "I heard his very last words. . . ." I stopped in a fright.
> "Repeat them," she murmured in a heartbroken tone. "I want
> —I want—something—something—to—to live with."

I was on the point of crying at her, "Don't you hear them?"
The dusk was repeating them in a persistent whisper all around
us, in a whisper that seemed to swell menacingly like the first
whisper of a rising wind. "The horror! The horror!"

"His last word—to live with," she insisted. "Don't you understand I loved him—I loved him—I loved him!"

I pulled myself together and spoke slowly.

"The last word he pronounced was—your name."

The scene demonstrates the stance the ironist takes toward the general
uncomprehending public. His narrative has revealed the truth to those
elite listeners on the yacht at anchor in the Thames; but for the rest, like
Kurtz's betrothed, there is only the lie made necessary by their incompre-
hension, a lie that in itself is of little significance. For a moment Marlow
felt that the heavens would fall upon him, "but nothing happened. The
heavens do not fall for such a trifle." There is little point in explaining to
the uninitiated, and for the initiated there is no need, because in either
instance the consequences are trivial. This is not to say, however, that the
burden of Kurtz's vision and Marlow's experience are trifling, but that
this work, like most ironic narratives, lets its case rest in the implications
of the narrative or the intensity of the narrator's unspoken commitment
to his experience. There is an instructive difference between the final
summary scenes that seem a requirement in Shakespeare's tragedies and
comedies and the bitter irresolution and self-pity of Pandarus' epilogue in
Troilus and Cressida.

Our first impressions of the narrative pattern of irony are of an action
that is arbitrary, a sequence of events governed—if that is the term—
more by chance than by causality. Men's actions have an ambiguity not
found in the other narrative patterns: when the knight sets out on his
quest in romance, when the tragic hero disturbs the equilibrium of things,
when the gouty old man of comedy leers at the young heroine, we know
where we are and what to expect. Not so in irony. And our intuition is
correct; it is our terminology that begs the question: in what sense is the
action of irony arbitrary, a matter of chance, or lacking causality? There
is, after all, nothing any less arbitrary or more causal in the set of events
that seems somehow naturally to follow from a knight's finding a beleaguered maiden in the power of a dragon than in those that occur in
Cheever's "Swimmer" or Shirley Jackson's "Lottery." The most that can
be said is that a different sort of causality is at work in each of the major
narrative patterns, and that in the light of one any other may be made to
seem arbitrary. If, however, it seems that irony is somehow unique in its
capricious structures, then that sense of it must arise out of some reversal
of those tacit expectations formed in our experience of other literary
conventions. Irony, then, is essentially derivative, and the sophistication
it demands from its readers is uniquely literary.

One motive in irony is to question or deny the assumptions that govern the other narrative patterns. The quest pattern, so ordered and determined in the romance, takes a meandering route through the ironic world and finally affirms little more than the pointlessness of such ventures and of the conventional assumptions that ordinarily invest them with meaning. The ironic hero sacrifices himself for a kind of moral life insurance only to find that the tragic policy has lapsed. And as comedy picks up the strains of irony, the trickster who ordinarily gets away with his comic manipulations is as often caught and punished for his wiles. The most generally understood sign for the presence of an ironic narrative, then, is a complex denial of expectations derived from our experience with other narrative forms— a denial that we finally realize was inevitable. It is this realization that accounts for the effect of irony: the sense that events have worked out in the only possible way and that we should have known better than to count on our first expectations. The sense of unrealized expectations accounts for the incongruous in irony; the sense that we should have known better than to entertain those expectations accounts for the inevitable in irony. These two features, the incongruous and the inevitable, exist as polarities. The ironist neither combines nor resolves them as the writer of tragedy does, because to do so would be to invoke the explanatory powers of some extrahuman order and consequently attribute too large a measure of dignity to the victim, an unacceptable gesture.

It follows that the audience witnessing the ironic narrative forms a community different from the visionary company of romance, the celebrants of the new comic society, and the purged and enlightened chorus of tragedy. The tragic chorus, like that in *Samson Agonistes*, is "with peace and consolation . . . dismist / And . . . all passion spent." They are united by a common perception of moral law. This affirmative or at least reconciling perception of order is seldom experienced in irony. The tension between the incongruous and the inevitable is unrelaxed; whatever passion is spent, little or no peace or consolation is acquired. Without the several varieties of the tragic or comic visions there is little that the ironic audience can rally about but the aesthetic experience of irony itself. Thus the ironic community, if it exists at all, is often an elite group drawn to the ironist and sharing a perception that is *primarily* literary in a sense that the final perceptions of romance, tragedy, and comedy are not.

Whatever judgment is implied—and every speech-act implies a judgment —the primary significance of the ironic narrative lies in its cold-blooded articulation of experience. For all Marlow's protestations to the contrary, Kurtz's speaking "The horror! The horror!" is finally less important as a judgment—who, after all, is Kurtz to judge?—than as a statement. Then, at "the last opportunity for pronouncement," the remarkable thing about Kurtz is that "he had something to say. He said it." In a way this is the most that the ironic writer aspires to: to say it, to be known as one who at some final moment looked into the dark heart of things and spoke.

Our perception of literary form takes on an importance in irony that might well be distracting in the other narrative forms. Frye identifies the mode through a hero who is "inferior in power or intelligence to ourselves, so that we have the sense of looking down on a scene of bondage, frustration or absurdity," but he adds that this "is still true when the reader feels that he is or might be in the same situation, as the situation is being judged by the norms of a greater freedom." This is one of the distinctive features of irony. Those norms of freedom we enjoy are greater than any fictional character's simply because we are readers, free participants in an aesthetic event. And they figure importantly in irony *in lieu of* other norms in other fictions that depend less on our consciousness of our status as readers.

Pervaded by incongruity, irony resists our terms and categories, and we are reduced, more often than is critically comfortable, to negative definitions and to working through antonyms from the other narrative forms *toward* irony. Our sense of the divine that gives order to the narratives of romance leads us to recognize the principle of disorder that confuses the ironic narrative. When the supernatural appears in irony it is most often diabolic, as in Keats' "Lamia," or is part of the mechanism of satire and parody, as in ironic poems by Dryden, Pope, and Byron. If there is a design it is Frost's "design of darkness to appall," a fortuitous semblance of order that brings a terror just within the reach of expression and just beyond that of explanation. Whereas romance is organized by some supernal order and tragedy and comedy by conceptions of fate and fortune, the pattern of irony is, in a sense, deformed by their absence.

The controlling metaphor in the ironic mode is the disappearance or dismemberment of the hero. As if in obedience to the metaphor its narrative structures are most often fragmentary and episodic, the picaresque story with its discontinuous plot and the brief lyric with its momentary vision. There may be vestiges of other narrative forms— "My Kinsman, Major Molineux" momentarily suggests a romance and "The Killers" a tragedy—but their function is primarily parodic, serving, once again, to raise and to chasten our presumption in believing that those forms and their conceptual systems would be possible in this world. From romance irony borrows the ordered elements of the quest and dislocates them in the haphazard events and loose ends of the picaresque form. From tragedy it takes the sense of an arbitrary fate but refuses to lessen its nagging incongruities with a redeeming moral order. From comedy it draws out the conflict between the new and old societies but turns it to more corrosive satiric purposes.

Fragmentary, incongruous, indirect—terms like these point to the eclectic nature of irony and the paradoxical fact that the ironist, assuming the most independent of roles, is in fact the most dependent on the conventions of literature. Indeed, irony seems somehow parasitical, living on the other narrative patterns and drawing its sustenance from another value system, for there is nothing in its abstract and negative vision that can, in itself, generate anything like a conventional pattern of action.

**The
Characters
of Irony**

The ironic glance stuns the world it looks upon, investing its literature with images of humankind frozen, dismembered, incarcerated, waiting with its face to the wall. The recurrent characters of irony, like the narrative pattern, suggest inversions or perversions of the types and their functions in other patterns.

The pure, invincible hero of romance, with his singleness of purpose, has an ironic counterpart in the antihero, the term Ihab Hassan uses in *Radical Innocence* for "a ragged assembly of victims: the fool, the clown, the hipster, the criminal, the poor sod, the freak, the outsider, the scapegoat, the scrubby opportunist, the rebel without a cause, the 'hero' in the ashcan, the 'hero' on the leash." Although Shakespeare's Pandarus and Thersites would be at home in this desperate company drawn largely from contemporary fiction, one would have to add others of a somewhat nobler stature though no less defeated, like Troilus, and to accommodate the satiric intent, still others with more cultivated pretensions and vanities, like Dryden's Shadwell, Pope's belles and fops, and Byron's George III. What we notice about these characters is that except where satire is the intent, there are few who have the clarity and definition of romantic or tragic figures. It is as if the distinctions among their personalities and motives have been lost as irony obscures the significance of their actions. Where some definition does occur it seems to derive not so much from what characters do as from what is done to them, and not so much from what they strive for as from what they struggle against. Hassan's critical portrait of the rebel-victim of contemporary fiction attributes something of the heroic to the ironic antihero: as rebel he "denies without saying No to life" and as victim he "succumbs without saying Yes to oppression." This composite role suggests the ironic hero's line of descent from both tragedy and comedy: insofar as he rebels he partakes of the revolutionary spirit of comedy but has lost all save the last remnant of its affirmative nature, and insofar as he is victimized he participates in something like a tragic action but without the sense of reconciliation tragedy usually conveys. This is the very best that one can say of the central figure in irony; indeed the description is a little too heroic to apply to Edgar Allan Poe's Montresor, Ernest Hemingway's Nick Adams or Ole Andreson, much less the characters created by George Orwell, Franz Kafka, and Samuel Beckett.

The characters that surround the antihero and in part define him are in turn inversions of characters in other narratives. The ironic villains have none of the clear black definition of those in romance and are invulnerable to the moral weaponry of romance. The ironically ministering Beast in Robert Graves' "Saint" will not stay buried but rolls in the city gutter, "praising the Knight for all his valorous deeds," until the hero is shamed to death. The humorous and mechanical figures of comedy become the gigantic automata and soulless machines irrevocably programed to withstand the hero's diminished powers. Social systems and natural laws become antagonists denying any dignity in man's struggle, or, worse yet, they simply turn away from his challenge with a terrifying indifference. Like the reporter in Stephen Crane's "Open Boat," the antihero, realizing "that nature does not regard him as important," would "throw bricks at the temple" but for "the fact that there are no bricks and no temples." Rituals no longer have meaning; retaining enough force to torture their human participants, they become, like the lottery in Shirley Jackson's story, antagonistic powers in themselves. "Although the villagers had forgotten the ritual and lost the original black box, they still remembered to use stones." So confronted, the best the ironic victim can do is to cry at the last moment, "It isn't fair, it isn't right."

The women of irony are a pitiful and unattractive lot. The roles they assume, when they become more than types of female vanity, are often inversions of those in romance. The sibylline older woman, the wise mother who sets the romantic quest and awaits the hero's return, has a hideous counterpart in Ambrose Bierce's "Chickamauga." There the child, imitating the warring conventions of the older generation and nurtured by romantic stories of military ventures, wanders into a field of battle and a company of mutilated men, and then returns home to find his mother brained by a shell. The fair maiden who waited passively as the reward for the hero's romantic quest becomes a prostitute, a nagging wife, or a hard, sexless woman, masculine in dress and manner, whose intent is to emasculate the hero, the role played by the Circe-figures who are sisters to Brett Ashley in Hemingway's *The Sun Also Rises*. No longer instruments of love, they have learned karate. Antihero and antiheroine get what they deserve, responding to each other like W. H. Auden's Victor and Anna:

> They were married early in August,
>   She said; "Kiss me, you funny boy":
> Victor took her in his arms and said;
>   "O my Helen of Troy."

Later he does her in with a carving knife for her infidelity.

The World of Irony

The only appropriate world for characters such as these is a hostile one, with an antagonism unmitigated by the promise of comedy and tragedy that suffering is either finite or educative. With the exception of those satiric works in which the setting is used for humor, the ironic environment is a harsh, inhospitable place—the indifferent wasteland, the entangling and malevolent jungle, and the corrupt city. It is curious that we tend to speak of irony as a vision of the "real" world, the world of experience, in contrast to the "ideal" world of romance, the world of innocence. There is nothing any more or less real about Conrad's Congo than Shakespeare's noble courts or John Millington Synge's Irish public house. Perhaps the better strategy is to characterize the world of irony in the negative, to speak of it as "unidealized existence," without laying claim to a greater realism, a claim dictated more by our contemporary tastes than by critical understanding. The world of irony is unidealized in a rather particular way in that it recognizes the implicit idealizations in the patterns of the other narrative forms and resolutely questions and ridicules their assumptions, beginning of course, with their premises about the hero's power of action. Yet as we approach irony through the less affirmative versions of tragedy and comedy, we sense, as Frye has it, that just as art has an upper limit in the visionary experience of an eternal world, so it has a "lower limit in actual life. This is the condition of savagery, the world in which comedy consists of inflicting pain on a helpless victim, and tragedy in enduring it." The savage condition is that brutish state where pain is inflicted or endured without the articulating and partially redeeming conceptions of an eternal order, a justifying fate, or temporary bad luck. It is life without art, without form or coherence, and thus without meaning. Now, as irony mocks other literary conventions and seems to rebel against expression itself, it approaches the boundary between the virtual and the real, by suggesting, if only momentarily, that we imagine a world stripped of the imaginative orders of art. Irony never crosses that line and, as an art, never can; but by disavowing the ideal, it raises the possibility of a silent and formless condition, unmediated by the structures of perception and therefore closer to the real, in one sense, but useless for the human imagination.

Whatever definition of reality we find in irony, the world it displays is marked by fragmentation and incoherence. If any order obtains it is in the oppressive and faceless systems where men become mechanisms like Hemingway's killers, and machines assume an inhuman life of their own as in science fiction. Cities are dark and labyrinthine, lit only by the ominous carnival lights that flicker through Hawthorne's "Major Molineux" and Poe's "Cask of Amontillado"; men exist as parts of this impersonal environment until, like Herman Melville's Bartleby, they can only stare at blank walls and mutter their defiance in ambiguous terms. The only communal experience is the Sunday hangover of Cheever's suburban dwellers, terrifying rituals like the lottery, and the inhuman expulsion of the scapegoat as in "Major Molineux."

The natural world offers no solace for this life. The central metaphor for the images of thematic irony is the waste land, an inimical environment like T. S. Eliot's where

> the dead tree gives no shelter, the cricket no relief,
> And the dry stone no sound of water.

Nature, so supremely ordered in romance and so regenerating in comedy is, in irony, sterile at best and at worst poisonous. The people of irony live through days that "are dragon-ridden" and move through landscapes torn by war or paved into the "charter'd" streets of William Blake's "London" or dying under the regularities of modern developments. Even the primitive luxuriance of an unspoiled land mocks them with indifference and overwhelms the mind as its timeless and boundless expanses lead them back toward crippling visions of their own hearts of darkness. The magic pools, royal fountains, or soft rain—images of water we find in other modes—give way in irony to the East River, the mirage, and Matthew Arnold's "unplumbed, salt, estranging sea." Reading through the ironic lyrics of Blake, Frost, Eliot, and Lowell, we see that all living things mock or threaten man. The invisible worm at the rose, the fly that interposes a final vision before death, the dimpled spider, the ponderous nightmare-bred draft horse, the bats with baby faces, all by opposition remind us of other worlds where living things consort with man's dream or witness the dignity of his struggle.

The ironic conceptions of time and space reflect the powerlessness of the hero and the dismembered world in which he exists. These infinite and unbounded abstractions overpower him; his journey is "through a pitch-dark limitless grove," and time displays that sterile prospect that Andrew Marvell saw in "deserts of vast eternity." With no sense of spatial limits the ironic hero can neither control nor understand his experience. Time is neither consistent nor absolute. The clock in the lunchroom in Hemingway's "Killers" is always incorrect, twenty minutes fast; Cheever's Neddy Merrill swims through a series of pools to his home only to find that he has swum forward through time to a season of desolation and despair. Both time and space shift ambiguously in the uncertain vision of the ironic hero. Robin Molineux watches the pillars of a city building become the trees of home in an experience that taunts him with his ineptitude. Like the young heroes of romance, the boy in "Chickamauga" progresses on a circular journey, but he returns to his burned home without bringing order to the desolate countryside.

The disintegration of temporal and spatial laws is repeated in the fragmentation of literary forms; conventional types and styles are broken down, traditional notions of sequence and description give way to abrupt shifts of time and place. Finally, sentences and words themselves disintegrate and, like the other fragments of the ironist's artistic material, are shored against his final ruined vision.

The Phases of Irony: Three Definitions

Narrative irony resists formal explanations and does not immediately reveal the features that allow us to describe the phases of tragedy, comedy, and romance. Our experience argues, however, that irony ought to conform to the other patterns. There are some apparently regular differences among works that we agree are ironic; for example, it is more natural to associate "Major Molineux" with "The Killers" than with "The Cask of Amontillado" and "The Cask of Amontillado" with "The Lottery" than with "Chickamauga." And since we think of irony as deriving partly from comedy and tragedy, it might well reflect the formal properties of their narrative patterns, just as its "opposition" to romance might have structural consequences. Reasonable as that expectation is, there is little beyond it but speculation on the phases of irony. Our best strategy, then, is to examine the most inclusive of the current descriptions of the phases, particularly at those points where, having approached irony from different directions, they overlap and reinforce one another.

The Influence of Comedy and Tragedy

Frye's survey of irony assumes the influence of comedy and tragedy. His definition of what we will call first-phase irony includes the conventional kinds of satire, or "militant irony," that are "structurally close to the comic." The emphasis on fantasy, the grotesque, the inclusion of at least dark humor, and the characteristic opposition of two societies or two standards of morality or behavior—the conventional and the unconventional—all imply some connection with comedy. That connection is obscured as satire shifts its aim from the unconventional to the conventional, drops any pretension to a positive standard for judgment or ridicule, and turns contemptuously away from society rather than trying to reform it. In the ironic norm the familiar narrative is the picaresque tale, the random and unconnected adventures of the unprincipled rogue. Out of this convention may come our sense of the antiquest, for the adventures seem to be more a series of departures, movements from something, than movements toward some goal as in the romantic quest. When satire turns against the conventional and begins to question even the norms of common sense and sensory experience, when the grotesque becomes obscene, then irony moves beyond the influence of comedy to that of tragedy. In last-phase irony we have versions of tragedy that are human rather than heroic. Random victimization with no sign of an alleviating sense of order and a fatalistic vision of events single out and magnify the "sense of arbitrariness" from the tragic situation. At this extreme, we witness scenes dominated by images of bondage and torture and governed by the implacable revolutions of the wheel of fortune. The antihero assumes the role of the ironic scapegoat, the character who is "neither innocent or guilty" but simply suffers. Like Mrs. Hutchinson in her apron, hurrying from her dishwashing to her doom, the victim is an emblem of "human nature under sentence of death."

The Influence of Character Types

In *Radical Innocence* Ihab Hassan simplifies and extends Frye's description of the forms of irony in order to survey contemporary American fiction. He retains the initial assumption that irony derives variety from the influence of comedy and tragedy, but he establishes a three-part structure, each part of which takes its form from a controlling character. In the first phase, the ironic hero "appears primarily in the guise of the rebel, the rogue, or self-inflating *alazon* [impostor]. He enjoys considerable freedom, and gives the illusion of escaping from necessity." The form that results is open to "real change in the life of the hero [and to] self-renewal." This "clownish or marginal figure" does not escape the ironic world, he is simply and unceremoniously sent on his way. The central form of irony finds its antihero in the *eiron*, the self-deprecating figure, and under his influence adopts from romance "the quest myth, turning it into a study of self-deception, and the dream of wishfulfillment, transforming it into nightmare." Under conditions of limited freedom, the central character enjoys an "uneasy truce with necessity," and the form gives the impression of being "suspended" or equivocal on the question of the possibilities for change or renewal. Finally, in its last phase, the figure of the *pharmakos* or scapegoat dominates the form, reflecting the "sense of isolation" and unrelieved suffering in a pattern of action that allows no freedom and is as closed to the opportunities for change as the prisons and torture chambers the victim inhabits.

A third pattern for the phases of irony develops Frye's comment that "the central principle of ironic myth is best approached as a parody of romance: the application of romantic mythical forms to a more realistic content." That application, as Frye notes, occurs "in unexpected ways. No one in a romance, Don Quixote protests, ever asks who pays for the hero's accommodation." Irony insists on presenting the bill, and in a manner that catches us unawares in our quixotic attachment to the details of romance. With this as our first premise and with our earlier concept of the specific forms of romance as our second, we would expect the phases of irony to parody those recurrent events we found in the romantic pattern. *The Influence of Romance*

The first phase mocks the initiation and the advent of the hero. The early trials and preliminary adventures that prepare the romantic hero for his career destroy the ironic hero or at the least make him incapable of further action. The ironic hero in this phase may well have some of the features of the comic impostor: usually young, he is filled with pretensions to the heroic—witness the swaggering behavior of Hawthorne's Robin Molineux and Hemingway's Nick Adams. The world he enters, like that of comedy as well as that of first-phase romance, presents two opposed worlds, that of the young and that of the old, with the difference that the conflict is most often resolved against the hero. In the ironic version of the comic initiation, as Hassan says, "the process of encounter and discovery . . . denies its own purpose."

The ironic norm inverts the quest; the antihero embarks on a series of uncertain adventures that lead, if anywhere, to a struggle that is either indecisive or anticlimactic compared to those in romance. He wanders through an ambiguous and shattered world, as does Troilus through a world that echoes the cynicism of Thersites' invective, where pandering and diplomacy are equated and women are as false as Cressida. The weak, the cynical, the tortured, all seem less in pursuit of a goal than in flight from some terror, and in the struggle to escape they return to the original source of horror. The civilized Thames stretches toward the heart of darkness as much as does the savage Congo; all the mocking figures Robin Molineux leaves behind finally gather for the last diabolic laugh.

The last phase of irony, like that of romance, has a compelling quality about it that seems to derive from its involvement in the occult. Drawing partly on the mystery we associate with tragedy, with its central figure of the tragic scapegoat, and partly on the contrasting phase of romance, it presents a world of frozen agony, where the characters display a fixed grimace that parodies tragedy's suffering and romance's apotheosis. Rituals are demonized: the romantic pattern of descent and recognition is travestied as the ironic heroes enter some physical or spiritual underworld never to return and never to achieve any other wisdom than the sense of their own human frailty. In its inversions of religious events or divine rituals, this phase of irony draws our attention to those black versions of the archetypes of romance: the entombment in "The Cask of Amontillado," the paradisal vision in James Joyce's "Grace," and the rite of the scapegoat in "The Lottery." Much of the fascination of irony rests in these specific forms in which, if anywhere, we can test the provocative notion that "irony returns to myth."

Three Definitions Combined   The correspondences among these three concepts of the ironic pattern offer a framework for a general theory of narrative irony. Each suggests as a central event the antiquest, with its physical or spiritual journey from place to place rather than toward some haven that redeems the quest. If there is a withdrawal and return, the withdrawal does not revitalize or educate and the return denies the point of the adventure. All the roles of romance are reversed or confused: the fair maiden becomes mannish, cuts her hair, and natters. In Graves' poem "Saint," a version of the Blatant Beast follows the hero, becomes "his seneschal," and finally kills him with solicitude. And the hero, like the dismembered Captain Carpenter in John Crowe Ransom's poem, exhibits "an anatomy with little to lose."

In romance the successful quest was bounded by two similar initiatory rituals, the advent of the hero and his apotheosis into the divine realm. A demonic analogue of that pattern exists in irony. At either end of the antiquest are two ritualistic events. The ironic parody of the romantic initiation involves elements of the comic antagonism between the old and the new societies, but in nearly every instance the older society wins or works a hard lesson on the younger. Except in a satire like Dryden's "Mac Flecknoe" or a luxuriant poem like Keats' "Lamia," the initiates are young men striking poses of rebellion like so many adolescent braggart soldiers. They are taught a cruel lesson, the benefits of which are less than likely to do them any good. The whole event is presided over by older figures, like George in "The Killers," who are mock versions of the wise elders of romance. At the other extreme, irony draws on elements of tragedy, isolates the victim and subjects him to pointless rituals and parodic versions of divine illumination. In romance, the final "initiation" takes the form of a descent into hell that marks the hero with wisdom and power and culminates in a transcendent death. In irony, the initiation is destructive, driving men mad like Fortunato, to the Tombs like Bartleby, or to some delusion like the mercantile grace that descends on Joyce's sanctimonious Dubliners.

In its resolute denial of the meaning or efficacy of tragic fate and comic fortune, and in its insistence on negations and inversions of romantic forms, irony, often under the pretense of denying the premises of literary form, forces us to reexamine the original principles of literature. But the very force of its opposition, its negative imperative, becomes a structuring energy. In its antipathy to the assumptions of other modes irony is shaped by the structures it opposes, until the denial of convention becomes a convention in itself.

Demonic Parody in "The Cask of Amontillado"

Most critical commentaries on Edgar Allan Poe's "Cask of Amontillado" agree that it is a well-made story of an obscurely motivated yet intricately achieved revenge in which the avenger, for all his insight and subtlety, is finally a victim of his own scheme. Whatever the deciding insult was, we realize in the last moments of the story that Montresor has not been able to "punish with impunity." His screams, surpassing Fortunato's, and his heart-sickness suggest that the epitaph, *In pace requiescat*, is intended for both his unquiet victim and himself.

EDGAR ALLAN POE
1809–1849

The Cask of Amontillado

The thousand injuries of Fortunato I had borne as best I could; but when he ventured upon insult, I vowed revenge. You, who so well know the nature of my soul, will not suppose, however, that I gave utterance to a threat. *At length* I would be avenged; this was a point definitively settled—but the very definitiveness with which it was resolved precluded the idea of risk. I must not only punish, but punish with impunity. A wrong is unredressed when retribution overtakes its redresser. It is equally unredressed when the avenger fails to make himself felt as such to him who has done the wrong.

It must be understood that neither by word nor deed had I given Fortunato cause to doubt my goodwill. I continued, as was my wont, to smile in his face, and he did not perceive that my smile *now* was at the thought of his immolation.

He had a weak point—this Fortunato—although in other regards he was a man to be respected and even feared. He prided himself on his connoisseurship, in wine. Few Italians have the true virtuoso spirit. For the most part their enthusiasm is adopted to suit the time and opportunity—to practice imposture upon the British and Austrian millionaires. In painting and gemmary, Fortunato, like his countrymen, was a quack—but in the matter of old wines he was sincere. In this respect I did not differ from him materially: I was skillful in the Italian vintages myself, and bought largely whenever I could.

It was about dusk, one evening during the supreme madness of the carnival season, that I encountered my friend. He accosted me with excessive warmth, for he had been drinking much. The man wore motley. He had on a tight-fitting parti-striped dress, and his head was surmounted by the conical cap and bells. I was so pleased to see him that I thought I should never have done wringing his hand.

I said to him, "My dear Fortunato, you are luckily met. How remarkably well you are looking today! But I have received a pipe[1] of what passes for amontillado, and I have my doubts."

THE CASK OF AMONTILLADO. **1. pipe:** large cask.

"How?" said he. "Amontillado? A pipe? Impossible! And in the middle of the carnival!"

"I have my doubts," I replied; "and I was silly enough to pay the full amontillado price without consulting you in the matter. You were not to be found, and I was fearful of losing a bargain."

"Amontillado!"

"I have my doubts."

"Amontillado!"

"And I must satisfy them."

"Amontillado!"

"As you are engaged, I am on my way to Luchesi. If anyone has a critical turn, it is he. He will tell me——"

"Luchesi cannot tell amontillado from sherry."

"And yet some fools will have it that his taste is a match for your own."

"Come, let us go."

"Whither?"

"To your vaults."

"My friend, no; I will not impose upon your good-nature. I perceive you have an engagement. Luchesi——"

"I have no engagement;—come."

"My friend, no. It is not the engagement, but the severe cold with which I perceive you are afflicted. The vaults are insufferably damp. They are encrusted with niter."

"Let us go, nevertheless. The cold is merely nothing. Amontillado! You have been imposed upon. And as for Luchesi, he cannot distinguish sherry from amontillado."

Thus speaking, Fortunato possessed himself of my arm. Putting on a mask of black silk, and drawing a roquelaire[2] closely about my person, I suffered him to hurry me to my palazzo.

There were no attendants at home; they had absconded to make merry in honor of the time. I had told them that I should not return until the morning, and had given them explicit orders not to stir from the house. These orders were sufficient, I well knew, to insure their immediate disappearance, one and all, as soon as my back was turned.

I took from their sconces two flambeaus, and giving one to Fortunato, bowed him through several suites of rooms to the archway that led into the vaults. I passed down a long and winding staircase, requesting him to be cautious as he followed. We came at length to the foot of the descent, and

stood together on the damp ground of the catacombs of the Montresors.

The gait of my friend was unsteady, and the bells upon his cap jingled as he strode.

"The pipe," said he.

"It is farther on," said I; "but observe the white web-work which gleams from these cavern walls."

He turned towards me, and looked into my eyes with two filmy orbs that distilled the rheum of intoxication.

"Niter?" he asked, at length.

"Niter," I replied. "How long have you had that cough?"

"Ugh! ugh! ugh!—ugh! ugh! ugh—ugh! ugh! ugh!—ugh! ugh! ugh!—ugh! ugh! ugh!"

My poor friend found it impossible to reply for many minutes.

"It is nothing," he said, at last.

"Come," I said, with decision, "we will go back; your health is precious. You are rich, respected, admired, beloved; you are happy, as once I was. You are a man to be missed. For me it is no matter. We will go back; you will be ill, and I cannot be responsible. Besides, there is Luchesi——"

"Enough," he said; "the cough is a mere nothing; it will not kill me. I shall not die of a cough."

"True—true," I replied; "and, indeed, I had no intention of alarming you unnecessarily—but you should use all proper caution. A draft of this Médoc will defend us from the damps."

Here I knocked off the neck of a bottle which I drew from a long row of its fellows that lay upon the mold.

"Drink," I said, presenting him the wine.

He raised it to his lips with a leer. He paused and nodded to me familiarly, while his bells jingled.

"I drink," he said, "to the buried that repose around us."

"And I to your long life."

He again took my arm, and we proceeded.

"These vaults," he said, "are extensive."

"The Montresors," I replied, "were a great and numerous family."

"I forget your arms."

"A huge human foot d'or, in a field azure; the foot crushes a serpent rampant whose fangs are imbedded in the heel."

"And the motto?"

"*Nemo me impune lacessit.*"[3]

2. **roquelaire:** roquelaure, a knee-length cloak.

3. **Nemo . . . lacessit:** No one attacks me with impunity.

"Good!" he said.

The wine sparkled in his eyes and the bells jingled. My own fancy grew warm with the Médoc. We had passed through walls of piled bones, with casks and puncheons intermingling, into the inmost recesses of the catacombs. I paused again, and this time I made bold to seize Fortunato by an arm above the elbow.

"The niter!" I said: "see, it increases. It hangs like moss upon the vaults. We are below the river's bed. The drops of moisture trickle among the bones. Come, we will go back ere it is too late. Your cough——"

"It is nothing," he said; "let us go on. But first, another draft of the Médoc."

I broke and reached him a flagon of De Grâve. He emptied it at a breath. His eyes flashed with a fierce light. He laughed and threw the bottle upwards with a gesticulation I did not understand.

I looked at him in surprise. He repeated the movement—a grotesque one.

"You do not comprehend?" he said.

"Not I," I replied.

"Then you are not of the brotherhood."

"How?"

"You are not of the masons."

"Yes, yes," I said, "yes, yes."

"You? Impossible! A mason?"

"A mason," I replied.

"A sign," he said.

"It is this," I answered, producing a trowel from beneath the folds of my roquelaire.

"You jest," he exclaimed, recoiling a few paces. "But let us proceed to the amontillado."

"Be it so," I said, replacing the tool beneath the cloak, and again offering him my arm. He leaned upon it heavily. We continued our route in search of the amontillado. We passed through a range of low arches, descended, passed on, and, descending again, arrived at a deep crypt, in which the foulness of the air caused our flambeaus rather to glow than flame.

At the most remote end of the crypt there appeared another less spacious. Its walls had been lined with human remains, piled to the vault overhead, in the fashion of the great catacombs of Paris. Three sides of this interior crypt were still ornamented in this manner. From the fourth the bones had been thrown down, and lay promiscuously upon the earth, forming at one point a mound of some size. Within the wall thus exposed by the displacing of the bones, we perceived a still interior recess, in depth about four feet, in width three, in height six or seven. It seemed to have been constructed for no especial use within itself, but formed merely the interval between two of the colossal supports of the roof of the catacombs, and was backed by one of their circumscribing walls of solid granite.

It was in vain that Fortunato, uplifting his dull torch, endeavored to pry into the depth of the recess. Its termination the feeble light did not enable us to see.

"Proceed," I said; "herein is the amontillado. As for Luchesi——"

"He is an ignoramus," interrupted my friend, as he stepped unsteadily forward, while I followed immediately at his heels. In an instant he had reached the extremity of the niche, and finding his progress arrested by the rock, stood stupidly bewildered. A moment more and I had fettered him to the granite. In its surface were two iron staples, distant from each other about two feet, horizontally. From one of these depended a short chain, from the other a padlock. Throwing the links about his waist, it was but the work of a few seconds to secure it. He was too much astounded to resist. Withdrawing the key, I stepped back from the recess.

"Pass your hand," I said, "over the wall; you cannot help feeling the niter. Indeed it is *very* damp. Once more let me *implore* you to return. No? Then I must positively leave you. But I must first render you all the little attentions in my power."

"The amontillado!" ejaculated my friend, not yet recovered from his astonishment.

"True," I replied; "the amontillado."

As I said these words I busied myself among the pile of bones of which I have before spoken. Throwing them aside, I soon uncovered a quantity of building stone and mortar. With these materials and with the aid of my trowel, I began vigorously to wall up the entrance of the niche.

I had scarcely laid the first tier of the masonry when I discovered that the intoxication of Fortunato had in a great measure worn off. The earliest indication I had of this was a low moaning cry from the depth of the recess. It was *not* the cry of a drunken man. There was then a long and obstinate silence. I laid the second tier, and the third, and the fourth; and then I heard the furious vibrations of the chain. The noise lasted for several minutes, during which, that I might harken to it with the more satisfaction, I ceased my labors and sat down upon the bones. When at last the clanking subsided, I resumed the trowel, and finished without interruption the fifth, the sixth, and the seventh tier. The wall was now nearly upon a level with my breast. I again paused, and holding the flambeaus over the mason-work, threw a few feeble rays upon the figure within.

A succession of loud and shrill screams, bursting suddenly from the throat of the chained form, seemed to thrust me violently back. For a brief moment I hesitated—I trembled. Unsheathing my rapier, I began to grope with it about the recess; but the thought of an instant reassured me. I placed my hand upon the solid fabric of the catacombs, and felt satisfied. I reapproached the wall, I replied to the yells of him who clamored. I re-echoed—I aided—I surpassed them in volume and in strength. I did this, and the clamorer grew still.

It was now midnight, and my task was drawing to a close. I had completed the eighth, the ninth, and the tenth tier. I had finished a portion of the last and the eleventh; there remained but a single stone to be fitted and plastered in. I struggled with its weight; I placed it partially in its destined position. But now there came from out the niche a low laugh that erected the hairs upon my head. It was succeeded by a sad voice, which I had difficulty in recognizing as that of the noble Fortunato. The voice said—

"Ha! ha! ha!—he! he! he!—a very good joke indeed—an excellent jest. We will have many a rich laugh about it at the palazzo—he! he! he!—over our wine—he! he! he!"

"The amontillado!" I said.

"He! he! he!—he! he! he!—yes, the amontillado. But is it not getting late? Will not they be awaiting us at the palazzo,—the Lady Fortunato and the rest? Let us be gone."

"Yes," I said, "let us be gone."

"*For the love of God, Montresor!*"

"Yes," I said, "for the love of God!"

But to these words I harkened in vain for a reply. I grew impatient. I called aloud—

"Fortunato!"

No answer. I called again—

"Fortunato!"

No answer still. I thrust a torch through the remaining aperture and let it fall within. There came forth in return only a jingling of the bells. My heart grew sick—on account of the dampness of the catacombs. I hastened to make an end of my labor. I forced the last stone into its position; I plastered it up. Against the new masonry I reerected the old rampart of bones. For the half of a century no mortal has disturbed them. *In pace requiescat.*[4]

4. **In . . . requiescat:** May he rest in peace.

The ambiguity of that ending and its reversal of our expectations identifies the story as an ironic narrative. Nearly every passage of dialogue, gesture, and symbol contributes to a remarkably sustained ironic texture. Montresor's remarks that Fortunato is "luckily met" and "a man to be missed"; his sinister assent to his victim's comment that "he will not die of a cough"; the name Fortunato, which means both a fortunate man and a man ruled by fate; the ambiguous epitaph—all these features share the equivocal meaning of one of the major images of the story, Montresor's family arms and motto. The image of a human foot crushing a serpent whose fangs are imbedded in the heel, and the words *Nemo me impune lacessit* (No one attacks me with impunity) support the ambiguity of the conclusion, for by implication both attacker and attacked are destroyed in the symbolic act. The arms represent not only the revenge of Montresor but the more universal antagonism between man and the archetypal image of evil. In Genesis, God condemns the serpent, saying "I will put enmity between thee and the woman, and between thy seed and her seed; it shall bruise thy head, and thou shalt bruise his heel."

This much is more or less obvious, but there has been little comment on the relationships between the pervasively ironic texture, the thematic concerns that seem to coalesce in the ambiguity of the Montresor arms and motto, and the motivation, indeterminate as it may be, in both the narrative and the narration—what moved Montresor to murder Fortunato and later compelled him to reveal the crime.

Whatever the insult added to the "thousand injuries" Montresor had received from Fortunato, the narrative leads us to suspect that it grew out of an antagonism between Montresor's proud, aristocratic, and ancient but declining family, one that looked back on its traditions and lived by its arms and mottoes, and Fortunato's, probably a more recent line, as proud as the older group but with a pride born out of their more recent ascendence, with enthusiasms "adopted to suit the time and opportunity," in short the *nouveaux riches* who make a point of remarking that "the Montresors . . . *were* a great and numerous family." The difference between the family that looks to the past and one that looks to the future is indicated in the toasts that each man gives to the other on their journey into the catacombs: Fortunato drinks "to the buried that repose around us" and Montresor, with more conscious irony, to Fortunato's "long life." During one of the interludes in their descent, Fortunato admits that he has forgotten the Montresor arms and motto, implying a lack of concern bordering on contempt for the old family now without respect, admiration, or heirs. And in another interlude, Fortunato tosses a bottle from him with an odd gesture:

> "You do not comprehend?" he said.
> "Not I," I replied.
> "Then you are not of the brotherhood."
> "How?"
> "You are not of the masons."
> "Yes, yes," I said, "yes, yes."
> "You? Impossible! A mason?"

To prove the point, Montresor produces a trowel.

Now for a writer who once wrote that "in the whole composition there should be no word written, of which the tendency . . . is not to the one preestablished design," such an egregious visual pun so laboriously engineered should be justifiable in the design of the work. Whatever else Poe may have intended, the identification of Fortunato as a Mason suggests another range of the antagonism between him and Montresor. Fortunato's initial shock at hearing that Montresor is a Mason stems from the fact that he knows his companion is a Catholic and would have been specifically prohibited from joining that fraternal order, particularly at the time in which the story is set, presumably no later than the late eighteenth century. Montresor's Catholicism is established by the fact, among others, that he is telling the story some fifty years after the event, probably on his deathbed, to his confessor—"You, who so well know the nature of my soul . . . ." Roman Catholic disapproval of Masonry dates from the early eighteenth century and was articulated in several papal bulls; in Italy the antagonism between the two orders at times broke into open warfare. The origin of the conflict is obscure but the issues are clearly those between the older, more hierarchical, autocratic, and orthodox religion and the newer, more democratic, ecumenical, secret, and fraternal order. Whether this clarifies or simply extends the range of the conflict between the two men, it does force another reading of Montresor's last words to Fortunato and the conclusion of the story. After his mad cries have failed, Fortunato makes one last appeal:

> "Will not they be awaiting us at the palazzo,—the Lady
> Fortunato and the rest? Let us be gone."
> "Yes," I said, "let us be gone."
> *"For the love of God, Montresor!"*
> "Yes," I said, "for the love of God!"

Montresor, in answer to his victim's appeal to the divinity for salvation, echoes the words as an ironic *explanation* of his motive. He then proceeds to finish the incarceration.

> I forced the last stone into its position; I plastered it up. Against
> the new masonry I reerected the old rampart of bones.

The old ramparts of orthodoxy, benightedly moved to vengeance for the love of God, are reestablished over the new order.

In a consistently ironic work about an act of revenge, motivated at least in part by militant religious feelings, then confessed at a time near death, and concluded with an *"In pace requiescat"* for both victim and avenger, we should expect a narrative pattern at once parodic and dependent for its parody on our recognition of an archetypal religious event or ritual. Once the antagonism, Montresor's rules for revenge, and Fortunato's fatal connoisseurship are established, the narrative displays a pattern associated with the last phase of irony, the descent into an underworld from which there is no return, literally for the victim and metaphorically for the avenger. There is nothing to indicate that in his confession Montresor has been able to erase the memory of his crime and return in spirit from the catacombs; one last irony of his deathbed confession is that he will soon join Fortunato in a similar entombment in his family vaults.

The specific details of the descent point to the religious event it parodies. During the carnival season, just before Lent, which commemorates Christ's fasting in the wilderness, Montresor meets Fortunato dressed in the garb of a fool and deceives him into visiting his catacombs to try a cask of rare amontillado. They walk through the darkened streets to the avenger's palace. There they begin a long descent into the catacombs, during which they pause three times: once when they drink a mutual toast, a second time when they discuss the Montresor arms and motto, and a third when each reveals himself as a Mason of sorts. Finally the victim is led to a crypt, where he is pinned to the wall and entombed.

Paraphrased and abstracted, the narrative assumes the nature of a black version, or inversion, of the Crucifixion. These events provide an ironic parallel to the events surrounding Christ's death: betrayed, dressed in purple robes and a crown of thorns, mocked and led through the streets, he began an ascent, during which, according to tradition, he fell three times, and then was nailed to the cross at Golgotha, which literally means the place of the skull. The two narratives, Poe's and the New Testament's, reverse dimensions like mirror images. One is at carnival time, when men bid farewell to flesh (*carne vale*) in the last orgy before fasting; the other is at Easter, when Christ sacrificed his body that men might live free from sin. In one a rare wine, offered in deception and sought in drunkenness, leads to death; in the other redeeming blood, symbolized in the sacramental wine, is shed for eternal life. One is a pointless sacrifice of a witless fool for no more than the injured pride of a lonely aristocrat; the other is Christ's sacrifice for no less than the eternal life of all men. One gives us the fool's motley and cap and bells, the other the purple robe and crown of thorns; one the wine vaults and cavernous catacombs, the other the Holy Grail and the sacred hill.

Analogies such as these clarify our understanding of this least known and most recalcitrant of literary patterns by confirming the hypothesis that irony, particularly in its last or tragic phase, "returns to myth" through structural parodies or inversions of the religious or mystic rituals and events associated with the last phase of romance. The interest here, however, lies in the way our experience of the story is enlarged or enhanced by the concept of narrative irony. In this context the story is more than an ironic tour de force describing an intricate revenge for a nameless insult. The narrative structure, read as a demonic analogue to the Passion of Christ, illuminates the underlying unity of all its complex elements. The ironic verbal texture of narration and dialogue reveals a deeper irony in the relationship between motive, act, and narration. At its deepest level the narrative pattern suggests an ultimately ironic link between motive and confession. However various the differences between avenger and victim, the tale suggests that the seed of controversy was a religious antagonism. Otherwise the reference to Masonry is only a gratuitous pun, and Montresor's reply, "Yes, for the love of God," is an empty remark rather than a very literal and immediate "confession" of his motive as well as a fulfillment of that criterion he had already established, that it should be accomplished with a "definitiveness." It is appropriate to the ironic narrative that a resolution of a partially religious antagonism should take on the form of a black crucifixion. And there is a similarly ironic connection between the implications of the narrative sequence and the final confession. The last irony of the story may rest in the fact that Montresor is seeking from Christ remission for a sin in which he reenacted his final agony. If Christ suffered and died that all men might achieve eternal life free from sin, then in the murder of any one man, and most especially in one done "for the love of God," his passion and death are mocked not only in the act itself but in its form. Such a recognition might well have begun for Montresor when he echoed and surpassed the terrified screams of his victim. For Montresor's confession is revealed most profoundly in its ironic form.

First-Phase Irony: Demonic Advent and Initiation

JOHN DRYDEN
1631–1700

Mac Flecknoe

A Satire upon the True-blue-Protestant Poet, T. S.°

All human things are subject to decay,
And when Fate summons, monarchs must obey.
This Flecknoe found, who, like Augustus, young
Was called to empire, and had governed long:
In prose and verse, was owned, without dispute, 5
Through all the realms of Nonsense, absolute.
This aged prince, now flourishing in peace,
And blest with issue of a large increase,
Worn out with business, did at length debate
To settle the succession of the state; 10
And, pond'ring which of all his sons was fit
To reign, and wage immortal war with wit,
Cried: " 'Tis resolved; for Nature pleads, that he
Should only rule, who most resembles me.
Sh—— alone my perfect image bears, 15
Mature in dullness from his tender years:
Sh—— alone of all my sons is he
Who stands confirmed in full stupidity.
The rest to some faint meaning make pretense,
But Sh—— never deviates into sense. 20

Some beams of wit on other souls may fall,
Strike through, and make a lucid interval;
But Sh——'s genuine night admits no ray,
His rising fogs prevail upon the day.
Besides, his goodly fabric fills the eye, 25
And seems designed for thoughtless majesty:
Thoughtless as monarch oaks that shade the plain,
And, spread in solemn state, supinely reign.
Heywood and Shirley were but types° of thee,
Thou last great prophet of tautology. 30
Even I, a dunce of more renown than they,
Was sent before but to prepare thy way:
And coarsely clad in Norwich drugget° came
To teach the nations in thy greater name.
My warbling lute, the lute I whilom strung, 35
When to King John of Portugal I sung,
Was but the prelude to that glorious day,
When thou on silver Thames didst cut thy way,
With well-timed oars before the royal barge,
Swelled with the pride of thy celestial charge; 40
And big with hymn, commander of a host,
The like was ne'er in Epsom blankets° tossed.
Methinks I see the new Arion° sail,
The lute still trembling underneath thy nail.
At thy well-sharpened thumb from shore to shore
The treble squeaks for fear, the basses roar; 46
Echoes from Pissing Alley Sh—— call,
And Sh—— they resound from Aston Hall.
About thy boat the little fishes throng,

MAC FLECKNOE. Dryden's victim in this satire is the Whig (and thus "True-blue Protestant") playwright Thomas Shadwell (1640–92), with whom he quarreled over political and literary matters. Dryden presents him as the son of ("Mac") Richard Flecknoe (d. 1678), a less than minor Irish poet, whose qualities Shadwell "inherited."

29. Heywood . . . types: Thomas Heywood and James Shirley, popular in the first half of the century but out of fashion by 1682, thus prototypes of Shadwell. 33. Norwich drugget: woolen cloth. 42. Epsom blankets: allusion to Shadwell's play *Epsom Wells* and to another farce in which a character is tossed in a blanket. 43. Arion: legendary Greek poet who saved himself from drowning by charming a dolphin with his music.

As at the morning toast that floats along.   50
Sometimes, as prince of thy harmonious band,
Thou wield'st thy papers in thy threshing hand.
St. André's° feet ne'er kept more equal time,
Not ev'n the feet of thy own *Psyche*'s rhyme:
Though they in number as in sense excel,   55
So just, so like tautology, they fell,
That, pale with envy, Singleton° forswore
The lute and sword, which he in triumph bore,
And vowed he ne'er would act Villerius° more."
Here stopped the good old sire, and wept for joy
In silent raptures of the hopeful boy.   61
All arguments, but most his plays, persuade,
That for anointed dullness he was made.

   Close to the walls which fair Augusta° bind,
(The fair Augusta much to fears inclined)   65
An ancient fabric raised t' inform the sight,
There stood of yore, and Barbican it hight:°
A watchtower once; but now, so fate ordains,
Of all the pile an empty name remains.
From its old ruins brothel-houses rise,   70
Scenes of lewd loves, and of polluted joys,
Where their vast courts the mother-strumpets keep,
And, undisturbed by watch, in silence sleep.
Near these a Nursery° erects its head,
Where queens are formed, and future heroes bred;
Where unfledged actors learn to laugh and cry,   76
Where infant punks their tender voices try,
And little Maximins° the gods defy.
Great Fletcher never treads in buskins here,
Nor greater Jonson dares in socks appear;°   80
But gentle Simkin° just reception finds
Amidst this monument of vanished minds:
Pure clinches° the suburbian Muse affords,
And Panton° waging harmless war with words.
Here Flecknoe, as a place to fame well known,   85
Ambitiously designed his Sh——'s throne;
For ancient Dekker° prophesied long since,
That in this pile should reign a mighty prince,
Born for a scourge of wit, and flail of sense,

To whom true dullness should some *Psyches* owe,
But worlds of *Misers* from his pen should flow;   91
Humorists and *Hypocrites*° it should produce,
Whole Raymond families, and tribes of Bruce.°
   Now Empress Fame had published the renown
Of Sh——'s coronation through the town.   95
Roused by report of Fame, the nations meet,
From near Bunhill, and distant Watling Street.°
No Persian carpets spread th' imperial way,
But scattered limbs of mangled poets lay;
From dusty shops neglected authors come,   100
Martyrs of pies, and relics of the bum.°
Much Heywood, Shirley, Ogleby° there lay,
But loads of Sh—— almost choked the way.
Bilked stationers for yeomen stood prepared
And Herringman° was captain of the guard.   105
The hoary prince in majesty appeared,
High on a throne of his own labors reared.
At his right hand our young Ascanius° sat,
Rome's other hope, and pillar of the state.
His brows thick fogs, instead of glories, grace,   110
And lambent dullness played around his face.
As Hannibal° did to the altars come,
Sworn by his sire a mortal foe to Rome;
So Sh—— swore, nor should his vow be vain,
That he till death true dullness would maintain;   115
And, in his father's right, and realm's defense,
Ne'er to have peace with wit, nor truce with sense.
The king himself the sacred unction made,
As king by office, and as priest by trade.
In his sinister° hand, instead of ball,   120
He placed a mighty mug of potent ale;
Love's Kingdom° to his right he did convey.
At once his scepter, and his rule of sway;
Whose righteous lore the prince had practiced young
And from whose loins recorded *Psyche* sprung.   125
His temples, last, with poppies were o'erspread,
That nodding seemed to consecrate his head:
Just at that point of time, if fame not lie,

---

53. St. Andre: choreographer of Shadwell's opera *Psyche*. **57. Singleton:** John Singleton, a court musician. **59. Villerius:** character in William Davenant's opera *Siege of Rhodes*. **64. Augusta:** London. **67. hight:** called. **74. Nursery:** school for young actors. **78. Maximin:** cruel and bombastic emperor in Dryden's *Tyrannic Love*. **79–80. Fletcher . . . appear:** John Fletcher, with Francis Beaumont, a writer of tragedies, of which the buskin was a symbol; Ben Jonson, writer of comedies, of which the sock was a symbol. **81. Simkin:** farce character. **83. clinches:** puns. **84. Panton:** punster. **87. Dekker:** Thomas Dekker, a playwright.

91–92. Misers . . . Hypocrites: three Shadwell plays. **93. Raymond . . . Bruce:** Raymond and Bruce are characters in his plays. **97. Bunhill . . . Street:** two London streets nearby and in a middle-class district, implying the range and character of Shadwell's plays. **101. Martyrs . . . bum:** Unsold books were variously used in bakeries and privies. **102. Ogleby:** John Ogleby, a translator of the classics. **105. Herringman:** John Herringman, one-time publisher of both Dryden and Shadwell. **108. Ascanius:** son of Aeneas, "Rome's other hope." **112. Hannibal:** Hannibal took an oath at an early age and nearly conquered Rome. **120. sinister:** left. **122. Love's Kingdom:** another dull Shadwell play.

On his left hand twelve reverend owls did fly.
So Romulus, 'tis sung, by Tiber's brook,   130
Presage of sway from twice six vultures° took.
Th' admiring throng loud acclamations make,
And omens of his future empire take.
The sire then shook the honors of his head,
And from his brows damps of oblivion shed   135
Full on the filial dullness: long he stood,
Repelling from his breast the raging god;
At length burst out in this prophetic mood:
    "Heavens bless my son, from Ireland let him
      reign
To far Barbadoes on the western main;   140
Of his dominion may no end be known,
And greater than his father's be his throne;
Beyond *Love's Kingdom* let him stretch his pen!"
He paused, and all the people cried, "Amen."
Then thus continued he: "My son, advance   145
Still in new impudence, new ignorance.
Success let others reach, learn thou from me
Pangs without birth, and fruitless industry.
Let *Virtuosos*° in five years be writ;
Yet not one thought accuse thy toil of wit.   150
Let gentle George° in triumph tread the stage,
Make Dorimant betray, and Loveit rage;
Let Cully, Cockwood, Fopling,° charm the pit,
And in their folly shew the writer's wit.
Yet still thy fools shall stand in thy defense   155
And justify their author's want of sense.
Let 'em be all by thy own model made
Of dullness, and desire no foreign aid,
That they to future ages may be known,
Not copies drawn, but issue of thy own.   160
Nay, let thy men of wit too be the same,
All full of thee, and differing but in name.
But let no alien S—dl—y° interpose,
To lard with wit thy hungry *Epsom* prose.
And when false flowers of rhetoric thou wouldst
      cull,   165
Trust nature, do not labor to be dull;
But write thy best, and top; and, in each line,
Sir Formal's° oratory will be thine:
Sir Formal, though unsought, attends thy quill,

And does thy northern dedications° fill.   170
Nor let false friends seduce thy mind to fame,
By arrogating Jonson's hostile name.
Let father Flecknoe fire thy mind with praise,
And uncle Ogleby thy envy raise.
Thou art my blood, where Jonson has no part: 175
What share have we in nature, or in art?
Where did his wit on learning fix a brand,
And rail at arts he did not understand?
Where made he love in Prince Nicander's vein,°
Or swept the dust in *Psyche*'s humble strain?   180
Where sold he bargains, 'whipstitch,° kiss my arse,'
Promised a play and dwindled to a farce?
When did his Muse from Fletcher scenes purloin,
As thou whole Eth'rege dost transfuse to thine?
But so transfused, as oil on water's flow,   185
His always floats above, thine sinks below.
This is thy province, this thy wondrous way,
New humors to invent for each new play:
This is that boasted bias of thy mind,
By which one way, to dullness, 'tis inclined,   190
Which makes thy writings lean on one side still,
And, in all changes, that way bends thy will.
Nor let thy mountain-belly make pretense
Of likeness; thine's a tympany° of sense.
A tun of man in thy large bulk is writ,   195
But sure thou'rt but a kilderkin of wit.
Like mine, thy gentle numbers feebly creep;
Thy tragic Muse gives smiles, thy comic sleep.
With whate'er gall thou sett'st thyself to write,
Thy inoffensive satires never bite.   200
In thy felonious heart though venom lies,
It does but touch thy Irish pen, and dies.
Thy genius calls thee not to purchase fame
In keen iambics, but mild anagram.
Leave writing plays, and choose for thy command
Some peaceful province in acrostic land.   206
There thou may'st wings display, and altars raise,°
And torture one poor word ten thousand ways;
Or, if thou wouldst thy diff'rent talents suit,
Set thy own songs, and sing them to thy lute."   210
    He said: but his last words were scarcely heard,

129–31. owls . . . vultures: Dryden substitutes owls, presumably asleep, for the vultures whose flight marked the site on which Romulus founded Rome. **149. Virtuosos:** another Shadwell play. **151. George:** George Etherege, brilliant author of satiric comedies. **152–53. Dorimant . . . Fopling:** some of Etherege's famous characters. **163. S—dl—y:** Charles Sedley, author of the prologue and, by implication, the wittier lines in Shadwell's play. **168. Sir Formal:** pompous orator in *The Virtuoso*.

170. northern dedications: Shadwell often dedicated his works to the duke of Newcastle and his family in northern England. **179. Prince Nicander's vein:** in *Psyche*. **181. sold . . . 'whipstitch':** To sell a bargain is to give a coarse answer to an innocent question; *whipstitch* is a nonsense word used by a character in *The Virtuoso*. **194. tympany:** swelling in the body. **207. wings . . . raise:** as in George Herbert's poetry, which was originally printed in the shape of angels' wings and church altars.

For Bruce and Longvil° had a trap prepared,
And down they sent the yet declaiming bard.
Sinking he left his drugget robe behind,
Borne upwards by a subterranean wind.   215
The mantle fell to the young prophet's part,
With double portion of his father's art.

JOHN KEATS
1795–1821

Lamia

PART I

Upon a time, before the faery broods
Drove nymph and satyr from the prosperous
     woods,
Before King Oberon's° bright diadem,
Scepter, and mantle, clasped with dewy gem,
Frighted away the dryads and the fauns   5
From rushes green, and brakes, and cowslipped
     lawns,
The ever-smitten Hermes° empty left
His golden throne, bend warm on amorous theft:°
From high Olympus had he stolen light,
On this side of Jove's clouds, to escape the sight   10
Of his great summoner, and made retreat
Into a forest on the shores of Crete.
For somewhere in that sacred island dwelt
A nymph, to whom all hoofèd satyrs knelt;
At whose white feet the languid Tritons poured   15
Pearls, while on land they withered and adored.
Fast by the springs where she to bathe was wont,
And in those meads where sometimes she might
     haunt,
Were strewn rich gifts, unknown to any Muse,
Though Fancy's casket were unlocked to choose.
Ah, what a world of love was at her feet!   21
So Hermes thought, and a celestial heat
Burnt from his wingèd heels to either ear,
That from a whiteness, as the lily clear,
Blushed into roses 'mid his golden hair,   25

Fallen in jealous curls about his shoulders bare.
From vale to vale, from wood to wood, he flew,
Breathing upon the flowers his passion new,
And wound with many a river to its head,
To find where this sweet nymph prepared her secret
     bed: 30
In vain; the sweet nymph might nowhere be found,
And so he rested, on the lonely ground,
Pensive, and full of painful jealousies
Of the wood-gods, and even the very trees.
There as he stood, he heard a mournful voice,   35
Such as once heard, in gentle heart, destroys
All pain but pity: thus the lone voice spake:
"When from this wreathèd tomb shall I awake!
When move in a sweet body fit for life,
And love, and pleasure, and the ruddy strife   40
Of hearts and lips! Ah, miserable me!"
The god, dove-footed, glided silently
Round bush and tree, soft-brushing, in his speed,
The taller grasses and full-flowering weed,
Until he found a palpitating snake,   45
Bright, and cirque-couchant° in a dusky brake.

She was a gordian shape of dazzling hue,
Vermilion-spotted, golden, green, and blue;
Striped like a zebra, freckled like a pard,°
Eyed like a peacock, and all crimson barred;   50
And full of silver moons, that, as she breathed,
Dissolved, or brighter shone, or interwreathed
Their lusters with the gloomier tapestries—
So rainbow-sided, touched with miseries,
She seemed, at once, some penanced lady elf,   55
Some demon's mistress, or the demon's self.
Upon her crest she wore a wannish° fire
Sprinkled with stars, like Ariadne's tiar:°
Her head was serpent, but ah, bittersweet!
She had a woman's mouth with all its pearls
     complete: 60
And for her eyes: what could such eyes do there
But weep, and weep, that they were born so fair?
As Proserpine still weeps for her Sicilian air.°
Her throat was serpent, but the words she spake
Came, as through bubbling honey, for Love's sake,
And thus; while Hermes on his pinions lay,   66
Like a stooped falcon° ere he takes his prey.

---

212. Bruce and Longvil: In *The Virtuoso* they so dispose of
Sir Formal.

LAMIA: *Part I.* **3. Oberon:** king of the fairies, who replaced
minor classical deities, nymphs, satyrs, dryads, and fauns.
7. Hermes: the often amorous messenger of the gods.

46. cirque-couchant: coiled. **49. pard:** leopard. **57. wannish:**
darkish. **58. Ariadne's tiar:** in Greek myth a woman transformed into a constellation in which her tiara became a
group of stars. **63. Proserpine . . . air:** Pluto carried
Proserpine to Hades from her home in Sicily. **67. stooped
falcon:** In falconry to stoop is to plunge.

"Fair Hermes, crowned with feathers, fluttering
    light,
I had a splendid dream of thee last night:
I saw thee sitting, on a throne of gold,   70
Among the Gods, upon Olympus old,
The only sad one; for thou didst not hear
The soft, lute-fingered Muses chaunting clear,
Nor even Apollo when he sang alone,
Deaf to his throbbing throat's long, long melodious
    moan.   75
I dreamt I saw thee, robed in purple flakes,
Break amorous through the clouds, as morning
    breaks,
And, swiftly as bright Phoebean dart,°
Strike for the Cretan isle; and here thou art!
Too gentle Hermes, hast thou found the maid?"
Whereat the star of Lethe° not delayed   81
His rosy eloquence and thus inquired:
"Thou smooth-lipped serpent, surely high inspired!
Thou beauteous wreath, with melancholy eyes,
Possess whatever bliss thou canst devise,   85
Telling me only where my nymph is fled—
Where she doth breathe!" "Bright planet, thou
    hast said,"
Returned the snake, "but seal with oaths, fair god!"
"I swear," said Hermes, "by my serpent rod,
And by thine eyes, and by thy starry crown!"   90
Light flew his earnest words, among the blossoms
    blown.
Then thus again the brilliance feminine:
"Too frail of heart! for this lost nymph of thine,
Free as the air, invisibly, she strays
About these thornless wilds; her pleasant days   95
She tastes unseen; unseen her nimble feet
Leave traces in the grass and flowers sweet;
From weary tendrils, and bowed branches green,
She plucks the fruit unseen, she bathes unseen:
And by my power is her beauty veiled   100
To keep it unaffronted, unassailed
By the love-glances of unlovely eyes,
Of satyrs, fauns, and bleared Silenus'° sighs.
Pale grew her immortality, for woe
Of all these lovers, and she grievèd so   105
I took compassion on her, bade her steep
Her hair in weïrd° syrups, that would keep
Her loveliness invisible, yet free

To wander as she loves, in liberty.
Thou shalt behold her, Hermes, thou alone,   110
If thou wilt, as thou swearest, grant my boon!"
Then, once again, the charmèd god began
An oath, and through the serpent's ears it ran
Warm, tremulous, devout, psalterian.
Ravished, she lifted her Circean° head,   115
Blushed a live damask, and swift-lisping said,
"I was a woman, let me have once more
A woman's shape, and charming as before.
I love a youth of Corinth—O the bliss!
Give me my woman's form, and place me where
    he is.   120
Stoop, Hermes, let me breathe upon thy brow,
And thou shalt see thy sweet nymph even now."
The god on half-shut feathers sank serene,
She breathed upon his eyes, and swift was seen
Of both the guarded nymph near-smiling on the
    green.   125
It was no dream; or say a dream it was,
Real are the dreams of gods, and smoothly pass
Their pleasures in a long immortal dream.
One warm, flushed moment, hovering, it might
    seem
Dashed by the wood-nymph's beauty, so he
    burned;   130
Then, lighting on the printless verdure, turned
To the swooned serpent, and with languid arm,
Delicate, put to proof the lithe caducean° charm.
So done, upon the nymph his eyes he bent
Full of adoring tears and blandishment,   135
And towards her stepped: she, like a moon in wane,
Faded before him, cowered, nor could restrain
Her fearful sobs, self-folding like a flower
That faints into itself at evening hour:
But the god fostering her chillèd hand,   140
She felt the warmth, her eyelids opened bland,
And, like new flowers at morning song of bees,
Bloomed, and gave up her honey to the lees.
Into the green-recessèd woods they flew;
Nor grew they pale, as mortal lovers do.   145

Left to herself, the serpent now began
To change; her elfin blood in madness ran,
Her mouth foamed, and the grass, therewith
    besprent,°
Withered at dew so sweet and virulent;
Her eyes in torture fixed, and anguish drear,   150

---

78. Phoebean dart: ray from the sun god, Phoebus Apollo.
81. star of Lethe: Hermes appeared as a star when guiding
the souls of the dead to Lethe in Hades. **103. Silenus:** a
drunken satyr. **107. weird:** occult.

115. Circean: Circe was an enchantress in the *Odyssey*.
133. caducean: The caduceus was Hermes' snake-entwined
staff. **148. besprent:** sprinkled.

Hot, glazed, and wide, with lid-lashes all sear,
Flashed phosphor and sharp sparks, without one
    cooling tear.
The colors all inflamed throughout her train,
She writhed about, convulsed with scarlet pain:
A deep volcanian yellow took the place   155
Of all her milder-moonèd body's grace;
And, as the lava ravishes the mead,
Spoilt all her silver mail, and golden brede;°
Made gloom of all her frecklings, streaks and bars,
Eclipsed her crescents, and licked up her stars: 160
So that, in moments few, she was undressed
Of all her sapphires, greens, and amethyst,
And rubious-argent:° of all these bereft,
Nothing but pain and ugliness were left.
Still shone her crown; that vanished, also she   165
Melted and disappeared as suddenly;
And in the air, her new voice luting soft,
Cried, "Lycius! gentle Lycius!"—Borne aloft
With the bright mists about the mountains hoar
These words dissolved: Crete's forests heard no
    more.   170

Whither fled Lamia, now a lady bright,
A full-born beauty new and exquisite?
She fled into that valley they pass o'er
Who go to Corinth from Cenchreas'° shore;
And rested at the foot of those wild hills,   175
The rugged founts of the Peraean rills,
And of that other ridge whose barren back
Stretches, with all its mist and cloudy rack,
Southwestward to Cleone. There she stood
About a young bird's flutter from a wood,   180
Fair, on a sloping green of mossy tread,
By a clear pool, wherein she passionèd°
To see herself escaped from so sore ills,
While her robes flaunted with the daffodils.

Ah, happy Lycius!—for she was a maid   185
More beautiful than ever twisted braid,
Or sighed, or blushed, or on spring-flowered lea
Spread a green kirtle to the minstrelsy:
A virgin purest lipped, yet in the lore
Of love deep learnèd to the red heart's core: 190
Not one hour old, yet of sciential brain
To unperplex bliss from its neighbor pain;
Define their pettish limits, and estrange°

158. **brede:** embroidery. 163. **rubious-argent:** silvery red.
174. **Cenchreas:** Cenchrea, a port of Corinth. 182. **passioned:**
responded passionately. 191–93. **of . . . estrange:** of
knowledgeable brain to distinguish bliss from pain, determine their disputed limits, and separate.

Their points of contact, and swift counterchange;
Intrigue with the specious chaos, and dispart   195
Its most ambiguous atoms with sure art;
As though in Cupid's college she had spent
Sweet days a lovely graduate, still unshent,°
And kept his rosy terms in idle languishment.

Why this fair creature chose so faerily   200
By the wayside to linger, we shall see;
But first 'tis fit to tell how she could muse
And dream, when in the serpent prison-house,
Of all she list° strange or magnificent:
How, ever, where she willed, her spirit went;   205
Whether to faint Elysium, or where
Down through tress-lifting waves the Nereids fair
Wind into Thetis' bower by many a pearly stair;
Or where god Baachus drains his cups divine,
Stretched out, at ease, beneath a glutinous pine; 210
Or where in Pluto's gardens palatine
Mulciber's° columns gleam in far piazzian line.
And sometimes into cities she would send
Her dream, with feast and rioting to blend;
And once, while among mortals dreaming thus,
She saw the young Corinthian Lycius   216
Charioting foremost in the envious race,
Like a young Jove with calm uneager face,
And fell into a swooning love of him.
Now on the moth-time of that evening dim   220
He would return that way, as well she knew,
To Corinth from the shore; for freshly blew
The eastern soft wind, and his galley now
Grated the quaystones with her brazen prow
In port Cenchreas, from Egina isle   225
Fresh anchored; whither he had been awhile
To sacrifice to Jove, whose temple there
Waits with high marble doors for blood and incense
    rare.
Jove heard his vows, and bettered his desire;
For by some freakful chance he made retire   230
From his companions, and set forth to walk,
Perhaps grown wearied of their Corinth talk:
Over the solitary hills he fared,
Thoughtless at first, but ere eve's star appeared
His fantasy was lost, where reason fades,   235
In the calmed twilight of Platonic shades.°
Lamia beheld him coming, near, more near—
Close to her passing, in indifference drear,
His silent sandals swept the mossy green;

198. **unshent:** unspoiled. 204. **list:** wished. 212. **Mulciber:**
Vulcan. 236. **Platonic shades:** i.e., obscure aspects of
Plato's philosophy.

So neighbored to him, and yet so unseen   240
She stood: he passed, shut up in mysteries,
His mind wrapped like his mantle, while her eyes
Followed his steps, and her neck regal white
Turned—syllabling thus, "Ah, Lycius bright,
And will you leave me on the hills alone?   245
Lycius, look back! and be some pity shown."
He did; not with cold wonder fearingly,
But Orpheus-like at an Eurydice;°
For so delicious were the words she sung,
It seemed he had loved them a whole summer
    long: 250
And soon his eyes had drunk her beauty up,
Leaving no drop in the bewildering cup,
And still the cup was full—while he, afraid
Lest she should vanish ere his lip had paid
Due adoration, thus began to adore;   255
Her soft look growing coy, she saw his chain so
    sure:
"Leave thee alone! Look back! Ah, goddess, see
Whether my eyes can ever turn from thee!
For pity do not this sad heart belie—
Even as thou vanishest so shall I die.   260
Stay! though a naiad of the rivers, stay!
To thy far wishes will thy streams obey:
Stay! though the greenest woods be thy domain,
Alone they can drink up the morning rain:
Though a descended Pleiad, will not one   265
Of thine harmonious sisters keep in tune
Thy spheres, and as thy silver proxy shine?
So sweetly to these ravished ears of mine
Came thy sweet greeting, that if thou shouldst fade
Thy memory will waste me to a shade—   270
For pity do not melt!"—"If I should stay "
Said Lamia, "here, upon this floor of clay,
And pain my steps upon these flowers too rough,
What canst thou say or do of charm enough
To dull the nice° remembrance of my home?   275
Thou canst not ask me with thee here to roam
Over these hills and vales, where no joy is—
Empty of immortality and bliss!
Thou art a scholar, Lycius, and must know
That finer spirits cannot breathe below   280
In human climes, and live: Alas! poor youth,
What taste of purer air hast thou to soothe
My essence? What serener palaces,
Where I may all my many senses please,

And by mysterious sleights a hundred thirsts
    appease?   285
It cannot be—Adieu!" So said, she rose
Tiptoe with white arms spread. He, sick to lose
The amorous promise of her lone complain,
Swooned, murmuring of love, and pale with pain.
The cruel lady, without any show   290
Of sorrow for her tender favorite's woe,
But rather, if her eyes could brighter be,
With brighter eyes and slow amenity,
Put her new lips to his, and gave afresh
The life she had so tangled in her mesh: 295
And as he from one trance was wakening
Into another, she began to sing,
Happy in beauty, life, and love, and everything,
A song of love, too sweet for earthly lyres,
While, like held breath, the stars drew in their
    panting fires.   300
And then she whispered in such trembling tone,
As those who, safe together met alone
For the first time through many anguished days,
Use other speech than looks; bidding him raise
His drooping head, and clear his soul of doubt,   305
For that she was a woman, and without
Any more subtle fluid in her veins
Than throbbing blood, and that the selfsame pains
Inhabited her frail-strung heart as his.
And next she wondered how his eyes could miss
Her face so long in Corinth, where, she said,   311
She dwelt but half retired, and there had led
Days happy as the gold coin could invent
Without the aid of love; yet in content
Till she saw him, as once she passed him by,   315
Where 'gainst a column he leant thoughtfully
At Venus' temple porch, 'mid baskets heaped
Of amorous herbs and flowers, newly reaped
Late on that eve, as 'twas the night before
The Adonian feast;° whereof she saw no more,   320
But wept alone those days, for why should she
    adore?
Lycius from death awoke into amaze,
To see her still, and singing so sweet lays;
Then from amaze into delight he fell
To hear her whisper woman's lore so well;   325
And every word she spake enticed him on
To unperplexed delight and pleasure known.
Let the mad poets say whate'er they please
Of the sweets of faeries, peris,° goddesses,

248. **Orpheus-like . . . Eurydice:** as Orpheus, prohibited
from looking back at his wife, did when he led her from
Hades and lost her once more. 275. **nice:** fine, detailed.

320. **Adonian feast:** feast of Adonis. 329. **peris:** fairies in
Persian myth.

There is not such a treat among them all,   330
Haunters of cavern, lake, and waterfall,
As a real woman, lineal indeed
From Pyrrha's pebbles° or old Adam's seed.
Thus gentle Lamia judged, and judged aright,
That Lycius could not love in half a fright,   335
So threw the goddess off, and won his heart
More pleasantly by playing woman's part,
With no more awe than what her beauty gave,
That, while it smote, still guaranteed to save.
Lycius to all made eloquent reply,   340
Marrying to every word a twinborn sigh;
And last, pointing to Corinth, asked her sweet,
If 'twas too far that night for her soft feet.
The way was short, for Lamia's eagerness
Made, by a spell, the triple league decrease   345
To a few paces; not at all surmised
By blinded Lycius, so in her comprised.
They passed the city gates, he knew not how,
So noiseless, and he never thought to know.

As men talk in a dream, so Corinth all,   350
Throughout her palaces imperial,
And all her populous streets and temples lewd,
Muttered, like tempest in the distance brewed,
To the wide-spreaded night above her towers.
Men, women, rich and poor, in the cool hours,   355
Shuffled their sandals o'er the pavement white,
Companioned or alone; while many a light
Flared, here and there, from wealthy festivals,
And threw their moving shadows on the walls,
Or found them clustered in the corniced shade   360
Of some arched temple door, or dusky colonnade.

Muffling his face, of greeting friends in fear,
Her fingers he pressed hard, as one came near
With curled gray beard, sharp eyes, and smooth
    bald crown,
Slow-stepped, and robed in philosophic gown: 365
Lycius shrank closer, as they met and passed,
Into his mantle, adding wings to haste,
While hurried Lamia trembled: "Ah," said he,
"Why do you shudder, love, so ruefully?
Why does your tender palm dissolve in dew?"—
"I'm wearied," said fair Lamia: "tell me who   371
Is that old man? I cannot bring to mind
His features—Lycius! wherefore did you blind
Yourself from his quick eyes?" Lycius replied,
" 'Tis Apollonius sage, my trusty guide   375

333. **Pyrrha's pebbles:** In Greek myth, Pyrrha and Deucalion
created a new race of men out of pebbles after the flood.

And good instructor; but tonight he seems
The ghost of folly haunting my sweet dreams."

While yet he spake they had arrived before
A pillared porch, with lofty portal door,
Where hung a silver lamp, whose phosphor glow
Reflected in the slabbèd steps below,   381
Mild as a star in water; for so new,
And so unsullied was the marble hue,
So through the crystal polish, liquid fine,
Ran the dark veins, that none but feet divine   385
Could e'er have touched there. Sounds Aeolian
Breathed from the hinges, as the ample span
Of the wide doors disclosed a place unknown
Some time to any, but those two alone,
And a few Persian mutes, who that same year   390
Were seen about the markets: none knew where
They could inhabit; the most curious
Were foiled, who watched to trace them to their
    house:
And but the flitter-wingèd verse must tell,
For truth's sake, what woe afterwards befell,   395
'Twould humor many a heart to leave them thus,
Shut from the busy world of more incredulous.

PART II

Love in a hut, with water and a crust,
Is—Love, forgive us!—cinders, ashes, dust;
Love in a palace is perhaps at last
More grievous torment than a hermit's fast:
That is a doubtful tale from faery land,   5
Hard for the non-elect to understand.
Had Lycius lived to hand his story down,
He might have given the moral a fresh frown,
Or clenched it quite: but too short was their bliss
To breed distrust and hate, that make the soft voice
    hiss.   10
Beside, there, nightly, with terrific glare,
Love, jealous grown of so complete a pair,
Hovered and buzzed his wings, with fearful roar,
Above the lintel of their chamber door,
And down the passage cast a glow upon the floor.

For all this came a ruin: side by side   16
They were enthronèd, in the eventide,
Upon a couch, near to a curtaining
Whose airy texture, from a golden string,
Floated into the room, and let appear   20
Unveiled the summer heaven, blue and clear,
Betwixt two marble shafts; there they reposed,

Where use had made it sweet, with eyelids closed,
Saving a tithe which love still open kept,
That they might see each other while they almost
    slept;   25
When from the slope side of a suburb hill,
Deafening the swallow's twitter, came a thrill
Of trumpets—Lycius started—the sounds fled,
But left a thought, a buzzing in his head.
For the first time, since first he harbored in   30
That purple-linèd palace of sweet sin,
His spirit passed beyond its golden bourn
Into the noisy world almost forsworn.
The lady, ever watchful, penetrant,
Saw this with pain, so arguing a want   35
Of something more, more than her empery
Of joys; and she began to moan and sigh
Because he mused beyond her, knowing well
That but a moment's thought is passion's passing
    bell.
"Why do you sigh, fair creature?" whispered he:
"Why do you think?" returned she tenderly: 41
"You have deserted me—where am I now?
Not in your heart while care weighs on your brow:
No, no, you have dismissed me; and I go
From your breast houseless; aye, it must be so."
He answered, bending to her open eyes,   46
Where he was mirrored small in paradise,
"My silver planet, both of eve and morn!°
Why will you plead yourelf so sad forlorn,
While I am striving how to fill my heart   50
With deeper crimson, and a double smart?
How to entangle, trammel up, and snare
Your soul in mine, and labyrinth you there
Like the hid scent in an unbudded rose?
Aye, a sweet kiss—you see your mighty woes.   55
My thoughts! shall I unveil them? Listen then!
What mortal hath a prize, that other men
May be confounded and abashed withal,
But lets it sometimes pace abroad majestical,
And triumph, as in thee I should rejoice   60
Amid the hoarse alarm of Corinth's voice.
Let my foes choke, and my friends shout afar,
While through the throngèd streets your bridal car
Wheels round its dazzling spokes."—The lady's
    cheek
Trembled; she nothing said, but, pale and meek,
Arose and knelt before him, wept a rain   66
Of sorrows at his words; at last with pain
Beseeching him, the while his hand she wrung,

Part II. **48. silver . . . morn:** planet Venus.

To change his purpose. He thereat was stung,
Perverse, with stronger fancy to reclaim   70
Her wild and timid nature to his aim:
Besides, for all his love, in self-despite,
Against his better self, he took delight
Luxurious in her sorrows, soft and new.
His passion, cruel grown, took on a hue   75
Fierce and sanguineous as 'twas possible
In one whose brow had no dark veins to swell.
Fine was the mitigated fury, like
Apollo's presence when in act to strike
The serpent—Ha, the serpent! certes, she   80
Was none. She burnt, she loved the tyranny,
And, all subdued, consented to the hour
When to the bridal he should lead his paramour.
Whispering in midnight silence, said the youth,
"Sure some sweet name thou hast, though, by my
    truth,   85
I have not asked it, ever thinking thee
Not mortal, but of heavenly progeny,
As still I do. Hast any mortal name,
Fit appellation for this dazzling frame?
Or friends or kinsfolk on the cited earth,   90
To share our marriage feast and nuptial mirth?"
"I have no friends," said Lamia, "no, not one;
My presence in wide Corinth hardly known:
My parents' bones are in their dusty urns
Sepulchered, where no kindled incense burns,   95
Seeing all their luckless race are dead, save me,
And I neglect the holy rite for thee.
Even as you list invite your many guests;
But if, as now it seems, your vision rests
With any pleasure on me, do not bid   100
Old Apollonius—from him keep me hid."
Lycius, perplexed at words so blind and blank,
Made close inquiry; from whose touch she shrank,
Feigning a sleep; and he to the dull shade
Of deep sleep in a moment was betrayed.   105

It was the custom then to bring away
The bride from home at blushing shut of day,
Veiled, in a chariot, heralded along
By strewn flowers, torches, and a marriage song,
With other pageants: but this fair unknown   110
Had not a friend. So being left alone
(Lycius was gone to summon all his kin),
And knowing surely she could never win
His foolish heart from its mad pompousness,
She set herself, high-thoughted, how to dress   115
The misery in fit magnificence.

She did so, but 'tis doubtful how and whence
Came, and who were her subtle servitors.
About the halls, and to and from the doors,
There was a noise of wings, till in short space 120
The glowing banquet room shone with wide-
    archèd grace.
A haunting music, sole perhaps and lone
Supportress of the faery roof, made moan
Throughout, as fearful the whole charm might fade.
Fresh carvèd cedar, mimicking a glade 125
Of palm and plantain, met from either side,
High in the midst, in honor of the bride:
Two palms and then two plaintains, and so on,
From either side their stems branched one to one
All down the aislèd place; and beneath all 130
There ran a stream of lamps straight on from wall
    to wall.
So canopied, lay an untasted feast
Teeming with odors. Lamia, regal dressed,
Silently paced about, and as she went,
In pale contented sort of discontent, 135
Missioned her viewless servants to enrich
The fretted splendor of each nook and niche.
Between the tree stems, marbled plain at first,
Came jasper panels; then, anon, there burst
Forth creeping imagery of slighter trees, 140
And with the larger wove in small intricacies.
Approving all, she faded at self-will,
And shut the chamber up, close, hushed and still,
Complete and ready for the revels rude,
When dreadful guests would come to spoil her
    solitude. 145

The day appeared, and all the gossip rout.
O senseless Lycius! Madman! wherefore flout
The silent-blessing fate, warm cloistered hours,
And show to common eyes these secret bowers?
The herd approached; each guest, with busy brain,
Arriving at the portal, gazed amain,° 151
And entered marveling: for they knew the street,
Remembered it from childhood all complete
Without a gap, yet ne'er before had seen
That royal porch, that high-built fair demesne; 155
So in they hurried all, 'mazed, curious and keen:
Save one, who looked thereon with eye severe,
And with calm-planted steps walked in austere;
'Twas Apollonius: something too he laughed,
As though some knotty problem, that had daft 160

His patient thought, had now begun to thaw,
And solve and melt—'twas just as he foresaw.

He met within the murmurous vestibule
His young disciple. " 'Tis no common rule,
Lycius," said he, "for uninvited guest 165
To force himself upon you, and infest
With an unbidden presence the bright throng
Of younger friends; yet must I do this wrong,
And you forgive me." Lycius blushed, and led
The old man through the inner doors broad-
    spread; 170
With reconciling words and courteous mien
Turning into sweet milk the sophist's spleen.

Of wealthy luster was the banquet room,
Filled with pervading brilliance and perfume:
Before each lucid panel fuming stood 175
A censer fed with myrrh and spicèd wood,
Each by a sacred tripod held aloft,
Whose slender feet wide-swerved upon the soft
Wool-woofèd carpets: fifty wreaths of smoke
From fifty censers their light voyage took 180
To the high roof, still mimicked as they rose
Along the mirrored walls by twin-clouds odorous.
Twelve spherèd tables, by silk seats ensphered,
High as the level of a man's breast reared
On libbard's° paws, upheld the heavy gold 185
Of cups and goblets, and the store thrice told
Of Ceres' horn° and, in huge vessels, wine
Come from the gloomy tun with merry shine.
Thus loaded with a feast the tables stood,
Each shrining in the midst the image of a god. 190

When in an antechamber every guest
Had felt the cold full sponge to pleasure pressed,
By minist'ring slaves, upon his hands and feet,
And fragrant oils with ceremony meet
Poured on his hair, they all moved to the feast 195
In white robes, and themselves in order placed
Around the silken couches, wondering
When all this mighty cost and blaze of wealth could
    spring.

Soft went the music the soft air along,
While fluent Greek a voweled undersong 200
Kept up among the guests, discoursing low
At first, for scarcely was the wine at flow;
But when the happy vintage touched their brains,
Louder they talk, and louder come the strains

151. **amain:** intently.

185. **libbard:** leopard. 187. **Ceres' horn:** horn of plenty.

Of powerful instruments—the gorgeous dyes, 205
The space, the splendor of the draperies,
The roof of awful richness, nectarous cheer,
Beautiful slaves, and Lamia's self, appear,
Now, when the wine has done its rosy deed,
And every soul from human trammels freed, 210
No more so strange; for merry wine, sweet wine,
Will make Elysian shades not too fair, too divine.
Soon was god Bacchus at meridian height;
Flushed were their cheeks, and bright eyes double
    bright.
Garlands of every green, and every scent 215
From vales deflowered, or forest trees branch-rent,
In baskets of bright osiered° gold were brought
High as the handles heaped, to suit the thought
Of every guest; that each, as he did please,
Might fancy-fit his brows, silk-pillowed at his
    ease. 220

What wreath for Lamia? What for Lycius?
What for the sage, old Apollonius?
Upon her aching forehead be there hung
The leaves of willow and of adder's tongue;
And for the youth, quick, let us strip for him 225
The thyrsus,° that his watching eyes may swim
Into forgetfulness; and, for the sage,
Let spear-grass and the spiteful thistle wage
War on his temples. Do not all charms fly
At the mere touch of cold philosophy? 230
There was an awful° rainbow once in heaven:
We know her woof, her texture, she is given
In the dull catalogue of common things.
Philosophy will clip an angel's wings,
Conquer all mysteries by rule and line, 235
Empty the haunted air, and gnomèd mine°—
Unweave a rainbow, as it erewhile made
The tender-personed Lamia melt into a shade.

By her glad Lycius sitting, in chief place,
Scarce saw in all the room another face, 240
Till, checking his love trance, a cup he took
Full brimmed, and opposite sent forth a look
'Cross the broad table, to beseech a glance
From his old teacher's wrinkled countenance,
And pledge him. The bald-head philosopher 245
Had fixed his eye, without a twinkle or stir
Full on the alarmèd beauty of the bride,

217. osiered: woven like osiers, or willow branches. 226.
thyrsus: Bacchus' vine-covered staff. 231. awful: awe-
inspiring. 236. gnomèd mine: Traditionally, gnomes guarded
mines.

Brow-beating her fair form, and troubling her
    sweet pride.
Lycius then pressed her hand, with devout touch,
As pale it lay upon the rosy couch: 250
'Twas icy, and the cold ran through his veins;
Then sudden it grew hot, and all the pains
Of an unnatural heat shot to his heart.
"Lamia, what means this? Wherefore dost thou
    start?
Know'st thou that man?" Poor Lamia answered
    not. 255
He gazed into her eyes, and not a jot
Owned they the lovelorn piteous appeal:
More, more he gazed: his human senses reel:
Some hungry spell that loveliness absorbs;
There was no recognition in those orbs. 260
"Lamia!" he cried—and no soft-toned reply.
The many heard, and the loud revelry
Grew hush; the stately music no more breathes;
The myrtle sickened in a thousand wreaths.
By faint degrees, voice, lute, and pleasure ceased;
A deadly silence step by step increased, 266
Until it seemed a horrid presence there,
And not a man but felt the terror in his hair.
"Lamia!" he shrieked; and nothing but the shriek
With its sad echo did the silence break. 270
"Begone, foul dream!" he cried, gazing again
In the bride's face, where now no azure vein
Wandered on fair-spaced temples; no soft bloom
Misted the cheek; no passion to illume
The deep-recessèd vision—all was blight; 275
Lamia, no longer fair, there sat a deadly white.
"Shut, shut those juggling eyes, thou ruthless man!
Turn them aside, wretch! or the righteous ban
Of all the gods, whose dreadful images
Here represent their shadowy presences, 280
May pierce them on the sudden with the thorn
Of painful blindness; leaving thee forlorn,
In trembling dotage to the feeblest fright
Of conscience, for their long offended might,
For all thine impious proud-heart sophistries, 285
Unlawful magic, and enticing lies.
Corinthians! look upon that gray-beard wretch!
Mark how, possessed, his lashless eyelids stretch
Around his demon eyes! Corinthians, see!
My sweet bride withers at their potency." 290
"Fool!" said the sophist, in an undertone
Gruff with contempt; which a death-nighing moan
From Lycius answered, as heart-struck and lost,
He sank supine beside the aching ghost.

"Fool! Fool!" repeated he, while his eyes still   295
Relented not, nor moved; "from every ill
Of life have I preserved thee to this day,
And shall I see thee made a serpent's prey?"
Then Lamia breathed death breath; the sophist's
    eye,
Like a sharp spear, went through her utterly,   300
Keen, cruel, perceant,° stinging: she, as well
As her weak hand could any meaning tell,
Motioned him to be silent; vainly so,
He looked and looked again a level—No!
"A serpent!" echoed he; no sooner said,   305
Than with a frightful scream she vanishèd:
And Lycius' arms were empty of delight,
As were his limbs of life, from that same night.
On the high couch he lay!—his friends came
    round—   309
Supported him—no pulse, or breath they found,
And, in its marriage robe, the heavy body wound.

301. perceant: piercing.

NATHANIEL HAWTHORNE
1804–1864

My Kinsman, Major Molineux

After the kings of Great Britain had assumed the right of appointing the colonial governors, the measures of the latter seldom met with the ready and generous approbation which had been paid to those of their predecessors, under the original charters. The people looked with most jealous scrutiny to the exercise of power which did not emanate from themselves, and they usually rewarded their rulers with slender gratitude for the compliances by which, in softening their instructions from beyond the sea, they had incurred the reprehension of those who gave them. The annals of Massachusetts Bay will inform us, that of six governors in the space of about forty years from the surrender of the old charter, under James II, two were imprisoned by a popular insurrection; a third, as Hutchinson inclines to believe, was driven from the province by the whizzing of a musket-ball; a fourth, in the opinion of the same historian, was hastened to his grave by continual bickerings with the House of Representatives; and the remaining two, as well as their successors, till the Revolution, were favored with few and brief intervals of peaceful sway.[1] The inferior members of the court party, in times of high political excitement, led scarcely a more desirable life. These remarks may serve as a preface to the following adventures, which chanced upon a summer night, not far from a hundred years ago. The reader, in order to avoid a long and dry detail of colonial affairs, is requested to dispense with an account of the train of circumstances that had caused much temporary inflammation of the popular mind.

It was near nine o'clock of a moonlight evening, when a boat crossed the ferry with a single passenger, who had obtained his conveyance at that unusual hour by the promise of an extra fare. While he stood on the landing place, searching in either pocket for the means of fulfilling his agreement, the ferryman lifted a lantern, by the aid of which, and the newly-risen moon, he took a very accurate survey of the stranger's figure. He was a youth of barely eighteen years, evidently country-bred, and now, as it should seem, upon his first visit to town. He was clad in a coarse gray coat, well worn, but in excellent repair; his under garments were durably constructed of leather, and fitted tight to a pair of serviceable and well-shaped limbs; his stockings of blue yarn were the incontrovertible work of a mother or a sister; and on his head was a three-cornered hat, which in its better days had perhaps sheltered the graver brow of the lad's father. Under his left arm was a heavy cudgel, formed of an oak sapling, and retaining a part of the hardened root; and his equipment was completed by a wallet, not so abundantly stocked as to incommode the vigorous shoulders on which it hung. Brown, curly hair, well-shaped features, and bright, cheerful eyes, were nature's gifts, and worth all that art could have done for his adornment.

The youth, one of whose names was Robin, finally drew from his pocket the half of a little

MY KINSMAN, MAJOR MOLINEUX.   **1. The annals . . . sway:** To gain control over the colonial governors, the people of Massachusetts appealed to England to annul its charter. The six governors were Simon Bradstreet, Sir Edmund Andros, Sir William Phips, Richard Coote, Earl of Bellomont, Joseph Dudley, and Samuel Shute. The charter was annulled in 1684. Hawthorne refers to Thomas Hutchinson's *History of the Colony of Massachusetts Bay (1764–1828).*

province bill of five shillings, which, in the depreciation of that sort of currency, did but satisfy the ferryman's demand, with the surplus of a sexangular piece of parchment, valued at three pence. He then walked forward into the town, with as light a step as if his day's journey had not already exceeded thirty miles, and with as eager an eye as if he were entering London city, instead of the little metropolis of a New England colony. Before Robin had proceeded afar, however, it occurred to him that he knew not whither to direct his steps; so he paused, and looked up and down the narrow street, scrutinizing the small and mean wooden buildings that were scattered on either side.

"This low hovel cannot be my kinsman's dwelling," thought he, "nor yonder old house, where the moonlight enters at the broken casement; and truly I see none hereabouts that might be worthy of him. It would have been wise to inquire my way of the ferryman, and doubtless he would have gone with me, and earned a shilling from the Major for his pains. But the next man I meet will do as well."

He resumed his walk, and was glad to perceive that the street now became wider, and the houses more respectable in their appearance. He soon discerned a figure moving on moderately in advance, and hastened his steps to overtake it. As Robin drew nigh, he saw that the passenger was a man in years, with a full periwig of gray hair, a wide-skirted coat of dark cloth, and silk stockings rolled above his knees. He carried a long and polished cane, which he struck down perpendicularly before him at every step; and at regular intervals he uttered two successive hems, of a peculiarly solemn and sepulchral intonation. Having made these observations, Robin laid hold of the skirt of the old man's coat, just when the light from the open door and windows of a barber's shop fell upon both their figures.

"Good evening to you, honored sir," said he, making a low bow, and still retaining his hold of the skirt. "I pray you tell me whereabouts is the dwelling of my kinsman, Major Molineux."

The youth's question was uttered very loudly; and one of the barbers, whose razor was descending on a well-soaped chin, and another who was dressing a Ramillies wig,[2] left their occupations,

2. **Ramillies wig:** braided wig with bows from Ramillies, Belgium.

and came to the door. The citizen, in the meantime, turned a long-favored countenance upon Robin, and answered him in a tone of excessive anger and annoyance. His two sepulchral hems, however, broke into the very center of his rebuke, with most singular effect, like a thought of the cold grave obtruding among wrathful passions.

"Let go my garment, fellow! I tell you, I know not the man you speak of. What! I have authority, I have—hem, hem—authority; and if this be the respect you show for your betters, your feet shall be brought acquainted with the stocks by daylight, tomorrow morning!"

Robin released the old man's skirt, and hastened away, pursued by an ill-mannered roar of laughter from the barber's shop. He was at first considerably surprised by the result of his question, but, being a shrewd youth, soon thought himself able to account for the mystery.

"This is some country representative," was his conclusion, "who has never seen the inside of my kinsman's door, and lacks the breeding to answer a stranger civilly. The man is old, or verily—I might be tempted to turn back and smite him on the nose. Ah, Robin, Robin! even the barber's boys laugh at you for choosing such a guide! You will be wiser in time, friend Robin."

He now became entangled in a succession of crooked and narrow streets, which crossed each other, and meandered at no great distance from the water-side. The smell of tar was obvious to his nostrils, the masts of vessels pierced the moonlight above the tops of the buildings, and the numerous signs, which Robin paused to read, informed him that he was near the center of business. But the streets were empty, the shops were closed, and lights were visible only in the second stories of a few dwelling-houses. At length, on the corner of a narrow lane, through which he was passing, he beheld the broad countenance of a British hero swinging before the door of an inn, whence proceeded the voices of many guests. The casement of one of the lower windows was thrown back, and a very thin curtain permitted Robin to distinguish a party at supper, round a well-furnished table. The fragrance of the good cheer steamed forth into the outer air, and the youth could not fail to recollect that the last remnant of his traveling stock of provision had yielded to his morning appetite, and that noon had found, and left him, dinnerless.

"Oh, that a parchment three-penny might give me a right to sit down at yonder table!" said Robin, with a sigh. "But the Major will make me welcome to the best of his victuals; so I will even step boldly in, and inquire my way to his dwelling."

He entered the tavern, and was guided by the murmur of voices, and the fumes of tobacco, to the public room. It was a long and low apartment, with oaken walls, grown dark in the continual smoke, and a floor, which was thickly sanded, but of no immaculate purity. A number of persons— the larger part of whom appeared to be mariners, or in some way connected with the sea—occupied the wooden benches, or leather-bottomed chairs, conversing on various matters, and occasionally lending their attention to some topic of general interest. Three or four little groups were draining as many bowls of punch, which the West India trade had long since made a familiar drink in the colony. Others, who had the appearance of men who lived by regular and laborious handicraft, preferred the insulated bliss of an unshared pota- tion, and became more taciturn under its influence. Nearly all, in short, evinced a predilection for the Good Creature in some of its various shapes, for this is a vice to which, as Fast Day sermons[3] of a hundred years ago will testify, we have a long hereditary claim. The only guests to whom Robin's sympathies inclined him were two or three sheepish countrymen, who were using the inn somewhat after the fashion of a Turkish cara- vansary; they had gotten themselves into the dark- est corner of the room, and heedless of the Nicotian atmosphere,[4] were supping on the bread of their own ovens, and the bacon cured in their own chimney-smoke. But though Robin felt a sort of brotherhood with these strangers, his eyes were attracted from them to a person who stood near the door, holding whispered conversation with a group of ill-dressed associates. His features were separately striking almost to grotesqueness, and the whole face left a deep impression on the mem- ory. The forehead bulged out into a double promi- nence, with a vale between; the nose came boldly forth in a an irregular curve, and its bridge was of more than a finger's breadth; the eyebrows were

deep and shaggy, and the eyes glowed beneath them like fire in a cave.

While Robin deliberated of whom to inquire re- specting his kinsman's dwelling, he was accosted by the innkeeper, a little man in a stained white apron, who had come to pay his professional wel- come to the stranger. Being in the second genera- tion from a French Protestant,[5] he seemed to have inherited the courtesy of his parent nation; but no variety of circumstances was ever known to change his voice from the one shrill note in which he now addressed Robin.

"From the country, I presume, sir?" said he, with a profound bow. "Beg leave to congratulate you on your arrival, and trust you intend a long stay with us. Fine town here, sir, beautiful buildings, and much that may interest a stranger. May I hope for the honor of your commands in respect to supper?"

"The man sees a family likeness! the rogue has guessed that I am related to the Major!" thought Robin, who had hitherto experienced little super- fluous civility.

All eyes were now turned on the country lad, standing at the door, in his worn three-cornered hat, gray coat, leather breeches, and blue yarn stockings, leaning on an oaken cudgel, and bearing a wallet on his back.

Robin replied to the courteous innkeeper, with such an assumption of confidence as befitted the Major's relative. "My honest friend," he said, "I shall make it a point to patronize your house on some occasion, when"—here he could not help lowering his voice—"when I may have more than a parchment three-pence in my pocket. My present business," continued he, speaking with lofty confidence, "is merely to inquire my way to the dwelling of my kinsman, Major Molineux."

There was a sudden and general movement in the room, which Robin interpreted as expressing the eagerness of each individual to become his guide. But the innkeeper turned his eyes to a written paper on the wall, which he read, or seemed to read, with occasional recurrences to the young man's figure.

"What have we here?" said he, breaking his speech into little dry fragments. "Left the house of the subscriber, bounden servant,[6] Hezekiah

---

3. **Fast Day sermons:** delivered on days of public penance.
4. **Nicotian atmosphere:** air filled with tobacco smoke.

5. **French Protestant:** Huguenot refugee from France. 6. **bounden servant:** servant indentured to a master for seven years.

Mudge,—had on, when he went away, gray coat, leather breeches, master's third-best hat. One pound currency reward to whosoever shall lodge him in any jail of the province. Better trudge, boy; better trudge!''

Robin had begun to draw his hand towards the lighter end of the oak cudgel, but a strange hostility in every countenance induced him to relinquish his purpose of breaking the courteous innkeeper's head. As he turned to leave the room, he encountered a sneering glance from the bold-featured personage whom he had before noticed; and no sooner was he beyond the door, than he heard a general laugh, in which the innkeeper's voice might be distinguished, like the dropping of small stones in a kettle.

"Now, is it not strange," thought Robin, with his usual shrewdness,—"is it not strange that the confession of an empty pocket should outweigh the name of my kinsman, Major Molineux? Oh, if I had one of those grinning rascals in the woods, where I and my oak sapling grew up together, I would teach him that my arm is heavy though my purse be light!"

On turning the corner of the narrow lane, Robin found himself in a spacious street, with an unbroken line of lofty houses on each side, and a steepled building at the upper end, whence the ringing of a bell announced the hour of nine. The light of the moon, and the lamps from the numerous shop-windows, discovered people promenading on the pavement, and amongst them Robin had hoped to recognize his hitherto inscrutable relative. The result of his former inquiries made him unwilling to hazard another, in a scene of such publicity, and he determined to walk slowly and silently up the street, thrusting his face close to that of every elderly gentleman, in search of the Major's lineaments. In his progress, Robin encountered many gay and gallant figures. Embroidered garments of showy colors, enormous periwigs, gold-laced hats, and silver-hilted swords glided past him and dazzled his optics. Traveled youths, imitators of the European fine gentlemen of the period, trod jauntily along, half dancing to the fashionable tunes which they hummed, and making poor Robin ashamed of his quiet and natural gait. At length, after many pauses to examine the gorgeous display of goods in the shop-windows, and after suffering some rebukes for the impertinence of his

scrutiny into people's faces, the Major's kinsman found himself near the steepled building, still unsuccessful in his search. As yet, however, he had seen only one side of the thronged street; so Robin crossed, and continued the same sort of inquisition down the opposite pavement, with stronger hopes than the philosopher seeking an honest man, but with no better fortune. He had arrived about midway towards the lower end, from which his course began, when he overheard the approach of some one, who struck down a cane on the flag-stones at every step, uttering, at regular intervals, two sepulchral hems.

"Mercy on us!" quoth Robin, recognizing the sound.

Turning a corner, which chanced to be close at his right hand, he hastened to pursue his researches in some other part of the town. His patience now was wearing low, and he seemed to feel more fatigue from his rambles since he crossed the ferry, than from his journey of several days on the other side. Hunger also pleaded loudly within him, and Robin began to balance the propriety of demanding, violently, and with lifted cudgel, the necessary guidance from the first solitary passenger whom he should meet. While a resolution to this effect was gaining strength, he entered a street of mean appearance, on either side of which a row of ill-built houses was straggling towards the harbor. The moonlight fell upon no passenger along the whole extent, but in the third domicile which Robin passed there was a half-opened door, and his keen glance detected a woman's garment within.

"My luck may be better here," said he to himself.

Accordingly, he approached the door, and beheld it shut closer as he did so; yet an open space remained, sufficing for the fair occupant to observe the stranger, without a corresponding display on her part. All that Robin could discern was a strip of scarlet petticoat, and the occasional sparkle of an eye, as if the moonbeams were trembling on some bright thing.

"Pretty mistress," for I may call her so with a good conscience, thought the shrewd youth, since I know nothing to the contrary,—"my sweet pretty mistress, will you be kind enough to tell me whereabouts I must seek the dwelling of my kinsman, Major Molineux?"

Robin's face was plaintive and winning, and the

female, seeing nothing to be shunned in the handsome country youth, thrust open the door, and came forth into the moonlight. She was a dainty little figure, with a white neck, round arms, and a slender waist, at the extremity of which her scarlet petticoat jutted out over a hoop, as if she were standing in a balloon. Moreover, her face was oval and pretty, her hair dark beneath the little cap, and her bright eyes possessed a sly freedom, which triumphed over those of Robin.

"Major Molineux dwells here," said this fair woman.

Now, her voice was the sweetest Robin had heard that night, yet he could not help doubting whether that sweet voice spoke Gospel truth. He looked up and down the mean street, and then surveyed the house before which they stood. It was a small, dark edifice of two stories, the second of which projected over the lower floor, and the front apartment had the aspect of a shop for petty commodities.

"Now, truly, I am in luck," replied Robin, cunningly, "and so indeed is my kinsman, the Major, in having so pretty a housekeeper. But I prithee trouble him to step to the door; I will deliver him a message from his friends in the country, and then go back to my lodgings at the inn."

"Nay, the Major has been abed this hour or more," said the lady of the scarlet petticoat; "and it would be to little purpose to disturb him tonight, seeing his evening draft was of the strongest. But he is a kind-hearted man, and it would be as much as my life's worth to let a kinsman of his turn away from the door. You are the good old gentleman's very picture, and I could swear that was his rainy-weather hat. Also he has garments very much resembling those leather small-clothes. But come in, I pray, for I bid you hearty welcome in his name."

So saying, the fair and hospitable dame took our hero by the hand; and the touch was light, and the force was gentleness, and though Robin read in her eyes what he did not hear in her words, yet the slender-waisted woman in the scarlet petticoat proved stronger than the athletic country youth. She had drawn his half-willing footsteps nearly to the threshold, when the opening of a door in the neighborhood startled the Major's housekeeper, and, leaving the Major's kinsman, she vanished speedily into her own domicile. A heavy yawn

preceded the appearance of a man, who, like the Moonshine of Pyramus and Thisbe,[7] carried a lantern, needlessly aiding his sister luminary in the heavens. As he walked sleepily up the street, he turned his broad, dull face on Robin, and displayed a long staff, spiked at the end.

"Home, vagabond, home!" said the watchman in accents that seemed to fall asleep as soon as they were uttered. "Home, or we'll set you in the stocks, by peep of day!"

"This is the second hint of the kind," thought Robin. "I wish they would end my difficulties, by setting me there tonight."

Nevertheless, the youth felt an instinctive antipathy towards the guardian of midnight order, which at first prevented him from asking his usual question. But just when the man was about to vanish behind the corner, Robin resolved not to lose the opportunity, and shouted lustily after him,—

"I say, friend! will you guide me to the house of my kinsman, Major Molineux?"

The watchman made no reply, but turned the corner and was gone; yet Robin seemed to hear the sound of drowsy laughter stealing along the solitary street. At that moment, also, a pleasant titter saluted him from the open window above his head; he looked up, and caught the sparkle of a saucy eye; a round arm beckoned to him, and next he heard light footsteps descending the staircase within. But Robin, being of the household of a New England clergyman, was a good youth, as well as a shrewd one; so he resisted temptation, and fled away.

He now roamed desperately, and at random, through the town, almost ready to believe that a spell was on him, like that by which a wizard of his country had once kept three pursuers wandering, a whole winter night, within twenty paces of the cottage which they sought. The streets lay before him, strange and desolate, and the lights were extinguished in almost every house. Twice, however, little parties of men, among whom Robin distinguished individuals in outlandish attire, came hurrying along; but, though on both occasions, they paused to address him, such intercourse did not at all enlighten his perplexity. They did but utter a few words in some language of which Robin

7. **Moonshine . . . Thisbe:** see Shakespeare, *A Midsummer Night's Dream,* V.i.130ff.

knew nothing, and perceiving his inability to answer, bestowed a curse upon him in plain English and hastened away. Finally, the lad determined to knock at the door of every mansion that might appear worthy to be occupied by his kinsman, trusting that perseverance would overcome the fatality that had hitherto thwarted him. Firm in this resolve, he was passing beneath the walls of a church, which formed the corner of two streets, when, as he turned into the shade of its steeple, he encountered a bulky stranger, muffled in a cloak. The man was proceeding with the speed of earnest business, but Robin planted himself full before him, holding the oak cudgel with both hands across his body as a bar to further passage.

"Halt, honest man, and answer me a question," said he, very resolutely. "Tell me, this instant, whereabouts is the dwelling of my kinsman, Major Molineux!"

"Keep your tongue between your teeth, fool, and let me pass!" said a deep, gruff voice, which Robin partly remembered. "Let me pass, or I'll strike you to the earth!"

"No, no, neighbor!" cried Robin, flourishing his cudgel, and then thrusting its larger end close to the man's muffled face. "No, no, I'm not the fool you take me for, nor do you pass till I have an answer to my question. Whereabouts is the dwelling of my kinsman, Major Molineux?"

The stranger, instead of attempting to force his passage, stepped back into the moonlight, unmuffled his face, and stared full into that of Robin.

"Watch here an hour, and Major Molineux will pass by," said he.

Robin gazed with dismay and astonishment on the unprecedented physiognomy of the speaker. The forehead with its double prominence, the broad hooked nose, the shaggy eyebrows, and fiery eyes, were those which he had noticed at the inn, but the man's complexion had undergone a singular, or, more properly, a twofold change. One side of the face blazed an intense red, while the other was black as midnight, the division line being in the broad bridge of the nose; and a mouth which seemed to extend from ear to ear was black or red, in contrast to the color of the cheek. The effect was as if two individual devils, a fiend of fire and a fiend of darkness, had united themselves to form this infernal visage. The stranger grinned in

Robin's face, muffled his parti-colored features, and was out of sight in a moment.

"Strange things we travelers see!" ejaculated Robin.

He seated himself, however, upon the steps of the church-door, resolving to wait the appointed time for his kinsman. A few moments were consumed in philosophical speculations upon the species of man who had just left him; but having settled this point shrewdly, rationally, and satisfactorily, he was compelled to look elsewhere for his amusement. And first he threw his eyes along the street. It was of more respectable appearance than most of those into which he had wandered, and the moon, creating, like the imaginative power, a beautiful strangeness in familiar objects, gave something of romance to a scene that might not have possessed it in the light of day. The irregular and often quaint architecture of the houses, some of whose roofs were broken into numerous little peaks, while others ascended, steep and narrow, into a single point, and others again were square; the pure snow-white of some of their complexions, the aged darkness of others, and the thousand sparklings, reflected from bright substances in the walls of many; these matters engaged Robin's attention for a while, and then began to grow wearisome. Next he endeavored to define the forms of distant objects, starting away, with almost ghostly indistinctness, just as his eye appeared to grasp them; and finally he took a minute survey of an edifice which stood on the opposite side of the street, directly in front of the church-door, where he was stationed. It was a large, square mansion, distinguished from its neighbors by a balcony, which rested on tall pillars, and by an elaborate Gothic window, communicating therewith.

"Perhaps this is the very house I have been seeking," thought Robin.

Then he strove to speed away the time, by listening to a murmur which swept continually along the street, yet was scarcely audible, except to an unaccustomed ear like his; it was a low, dull, dreamy sound, compounded of many noises, each of which was at too great a distance to be separately heard. Robin marveled at this snore of a sleeping town, and marveled more whenever its continuity was broken by now and then a distant shout, apparently loud where it originated. But altogether it was a sleep-inspiring sound, and, to shake off its drowsy influence, Robin arose, and climbed a window-frame, that he might view the interior of the church. There the moonbeams came trembling in, and fell down upon the deserted pews, and extended along the quiet aisles. A fainter yet more awful radiance was hovering around the pulpit, and one solitary ray had dared to rest upon the open page of the great Bible. Had nature, in that deep hour, become a worshiper in the house which man had builded? Or was that heavenly light the visible sanctity of the place,— visible because no earthly and impure feet were within the walls? The scene made Robin's heart shiver with a sensation of loneliness stronger than he had ever felt in the remotest depths of his native woods; so he turned away and sat down again before the door. There were graves around the church, and now an uneasy thought obtruded into Robin's breast. What if the object of his search, which had been so often and so strangely thwarted, were all the time mouldering in his shroud? What if his kinsman should glide through yonder gate, and nod and smile to him in dimly passing by?

"Oh that any breathing thing were here with me!" said Robin.

Recalling his thoughts from this uncomfortable track, he sent them over forest, hill, and stream, and attempted to imagine how that evening of ambiguity and weariness had been spent by his father's household. He pictured them assembled at the door, beneath the tree, the great old tree, which had been spared for its huge twisted trunk, and venerable shade, when a thousand leafy brethren fell. There, at the going down of the summer sun, it was his father's custom to perform domestic worship, that the neighbors might come and join with him like brothers of the family, and that the wayfaring man might pause to drink at that fountain, and keep his heart pure by freshening the memory of home. Robin distinguished the seat of every individual of the little audience; he saw the good man in the midst, holding the Scriptures in the golden light that fell from the western clouds; he beheld him close the book and all rise up to pray. He heard the old thanksgivings for daily mercies, the old supplications for their continuance, to which he had so often listened in weariness, but which were now among his dear remembrances. He perceived the slight inequality of his father's

voice when he came to speak of the absent one; he noted how his mother turned her face to the broad and knotted trunk; how his elder brother scorned, because the beard was rough upon his upper lip, to permit his features to be moved; how the younger sister drew down a low hanging branch before her eyes; and how the little one of all, whose sports had hitherto broken the decorum of the scene, understood the prayer for her playmate, and burst into clamorous grief. Then he saw them go in at the door; and when Robin would have entered also, the latch tinkled into its place, and he was excluded from his home.

"Am I here, or there?" cried Robin, starting; for all at once, when his thoughts had become visible and audible in a dream, the long, wide, solitary street shone out before him.

He aroused himself, and endeavored to fix his attention steadily upon the large edifice which he had surveyed before. But still his mind kept vibrating between fancy and reality; by turns, the pillars of the balcony lengthened into the tall, bare stems of pines, dwindled down to human figures, and settled again into their true shape and size, and then commenced a new succession of changes. For a single moment, when he deemed himself awake, he could have sworn that a visage—one which he seemed to remember, yet could not absolutely name as his kinsman's—was looking towards him from the Gothic window. A deeper sleep wrestled with and nearly overcame him, but fled at the sound of footsteps along the opposite pavement. Robin rubbed his eyes, discerned a man passing at the foot of the balcony, and addressed him in a loud, peevish, and lamentable cry.

"Hallo, friend! must I wait here all night for my kinsman, Major Molineux?"

The sleeping echoes awoke, and answered the voice; and the passenger, barely able to discern a figure sitting in the oblique shade of the steeple, traversed the street to obtain a nearer view. He was himself a gentleman in his prime, of open, intelligent, cheerful, and altogether prepossessing countenance. Perceiving a country youth, apparently homeless and without friends, he accosted him in a tone of real kindness, which had become strange to Robin's ears.

"Well, my good lad, why are you sitting here?" inquired he. "Can I be of service to you in any way?"

"I am afraid not, sir," replied Robin, despondingly; "yet I shall take it kindly, if you'll answer me a single question. I've been searching, half the night, for one Major Molineux; now, sir, is there really such a person in these parts, or am I dreaming?"

"Major Molineux! The name is not altogether strange to me," said the gentleman, smiling. "Have you any objection to telling me the nature of your business with him?"

Then Robin briefly related that his father was a clergyman, settled on a small salary, at a long distance back in the country, and that he and Major Molineux were brothers' children. The Major, having inherited riches, and acquired civil and military rank, had visited his cousin, in great pomp, a year or two before; had manifested much interest in Robin and an elder brother, and, being childless himself, had thrown out hints respecting the future establishment of one of them in life. The elder brother was destined to succeed to the farm which his father cultivated in the interval of sacred duties; it was therefore determined that Robin should profit by his kinsman's generous intentions, especially as he seemed to be rather the favorite, and was thought to possess other necessary endowments.

"For I have the name of being a shrewd youth," observed Robin, in this part of his story.

"I doubt not you deserve it," replied his new friend, good-naturedly; "but pray proceed."

"Well, sir, being nearly eighteen years old, and well-grown, as you see," continued Robin, drawing himself up to his full height, "I thought it high time to begin the world. So my mother and sister put me in handsome trim, and my father gave me half the remnant of his last year's salary, and five days ago I started for this place, to pay the Major a visit. But, would you believe it, sir! I crossed the ferry a little after dark, and have yet found nobody that would show me the way to his dwelling;—only, an hour or two since, I was told to wait here, and Major Molineux would pass by."

"Can you describe the man who told you this?" inquired the gentleman.

"Oh, he was a very ill-favored fellow, sir," replied Robin, "with two great bumps on his forehead, a hook nose, fiery eyes,—and, what struck me as the strangest, his face was of two different colors. Do you happen to know such a man, sir?"

"Not intimately," answered the stranger, "but I chanced to meet him a little time previous to your stopping me. I believe you may trust his word, and that the Major will very shortly pass through this street. In the meantime, as I have a singular curiosity to witness your meeting, I will sit down here upon the steps, and bear you company."

He seated himself accordingly, and soon engaged his companion in animated discourse. It was but of brief continuance, however, for a noise of shouting, which had long been remotely audible, drew so much nearer that Robin inquired its cause.

"What may be the meaning of this uproar?" asked he. "Truly, if your town be always as noisy, I shall find little sleep, while I am an inhabitant."

"Why, indeed, friend Robin, there do appear to be three or four riotous fellows abroad tonight," replied the gentleman. "You must not expect all the stillness of your native woods, here in our streets. But the watch will shortly be at the heels of these lads, and—"

"Aye, and set them in the stocks by peep of day," interrupted Robin, recollecting his own encounter with the drowsy lantern-bearer. "But, dear sir, if I may trust my ears, an army of watchmen would never make head against such a multitude of rioters. There were at least a thousand voices went up to make that one shout."

"May not a man have several voices, Robin, as well as two complexions?" said his friend.

"Perhaps a man may; but Heaven forbid that a woman should!" responded the shrewd youth, thinking of the seductive tones of the Major's housekeeper.

The sounds of a trumpet in some neighboring street now became so evident and continual, that Robin's curiosity was strongly excited. In addition to the shouts, he heard frequent bursts from many instruments of discord, and a wild and confused laughter filled up the intervals. Robin rose from the steps, and looked wistfully towards a point whither people seemed to be hastening.

"Surely some prodigious merry-making is going on," exclaimed he. "I have laughed very little since I left home, sir, and should be sorry to lose an opportunity. Shall we step round the corner by the darkish house, and take our share of the fun?"

"Sit down again, sit down, good Robin," replied the gentleman, laying his hand on the skirt of the gray coat. "You forget that we must wait here for your kinsman; and there is reason to believe that he will pass by, in the course of a very few moments."

The near approach of the uproar had now disturbed the neighborhood; windows flew open on all sides; and many heads, in the attire of the pillow, and confused by sleep suddenly broken, were protruded to the gaze of whoever had leisure to observe them. Eager voices hailed each other from house to house, all demanding the explanation, which not a soul could give. Half-dressed men hurried towards the unknown commotion, stumbling as they went over the stone steps that thrust themselves into the narrow foot-walk. The shouts, the laughter, and the tuneless bray, the antipodes of music, came onwards with increasing din, till scattered individuals, and then denser bodies, began to appear round a corner at the distance of a hundred yards.

"Will you recognize your kinsman, if he passes in this crowd?" inquired the gentleman.

"Indeed, I can't warrant it, sir; but I'll take my stand here, and keep a bright lookout," answered Robin, descending to the outer edge of the pavement.

A mighty stream of people now emptied into the street, and came rolling slowly towards the church. A single horseman wheeled the corner in the midst of them and close behind him came a band of fearful wind-instruments, sending forth a fresher discord, now that no intervening buildings kept it from the ear. Then a redder light disturbed the moonbeams, and a dense multitude of torches shone along the street, concealing, by their glare, whatever object they illuminated. The single horseman, clad in a military dress, and bearing a drawn sword, rode onward as the leader, and, by his fierce and variegated countenance, appeared like war personified: the red of one cheek was an emblem of fire and sword; the blackness of the other betokened the mourning that attends them. In his train were wild figures in the Indian dress, and many fantastic shapes without a model, giving the whole march a visionary air, as if a dream had broken forth from some feverish brain, and were sweeping visibly through the midnight streets. A mass of people, inactive, except as applauding spectators, hemmed the procession in; and several women ran along the sidewalk, piercing the confusion of heavier sounds with their shrill voices of mirth or terror.

"The double-faced fellow has his eye upon me," muttered Robin, with an indefinite but an uncomfortable idea that he was himself to bear a part in the pageantry.

The leader turned himself in the saddle, and fixed his glance full upon the country youth, as the steed went slowly by. When Robin had freed his eyes from those fiery ones, the musicians were passing before him, and the torches were close at hand; but the unsteady brightness of the latter formed a veil which he could not penetrate. The rattling of wheels over the stones sometimes found its way to his ear, and confused traces of a human form appeared at intervals, and then melted into the vivid light. A moment more, and the leader thundered a command to halt: the trumpets vomited a horrid breath, and then held their peace; the shouts and laughter of the people died away, and there remained only a universal hum, allied to silence. Right before Robin's eyes was an uncovered cart. There the torches blazed the brightest, there the moon shone out like day, and there, in tar-and-feathery dignity, sat his kinsman, Major Molineux!

He was an elderly man, of large and majestic person, and strong, square features, betokening a steady soul; but steady as it was, his enemies had found means to shake it. His face was pale as death, and far more ghastly; the broad forehead was contracted in his agony, so that his eyebrows formed one grizzled line; his eyes were red and wild, and the foam hung white upon his quivering lip. His whole frame was agitated by a quick and continual tremor, which his pride strove to quell, even in those circumstances of overwhelming humiliation. But perhaps the bitterest pang of all was when his eyes met those of Robin; for he evidently knew him on the instant, as the youth stood witnessing the foul disgrace of a head grown gray in honor. They stared at each other in silence, and Robin's knees shook, and his hair bristled, with a mixture of pity and terror. Soon, however, a bewildering excitement began to seize upon his mind; the preceding adventures of the night, the unexpected appearance of the crowd, the torches, the confused din and the hush that followed, the specter of his kinsman reviled by that great multitude,—all this, and, more than all, a perception of tremendous ridicule in the whole scene, affected him with a sort of mental inebriety. At that moment a voice of sluggish merriment saluted Robin's ears; he turned instinctively, and just behind the corner of the church stood the lantern-bearer, rubbing his eyes, and drowsily enjoying the lad's amazement. Then he heard a peal of laughter like the ringing of silvery bells; a woman twitched his arm, a saucy eye met his, and he saw the lady of the scarlet petticoat. A sharp, dry cachinnation appealed to his memory, and, standing on tiptoe in the crowd, with his white apron over his head, he beheld the courteous little innkeeper. And lastly, there sailed over the heads of the multitude a great, broad laugh, broken in the midst by two sepulchral hems; thus, "Haw, haw, haw,—hem, hem,—haw, haw, haw, haw!"

The sound proceeded from the balcony of the opposite edifice, and thither Robin turned his eyes. In front of the Gothic window stood the old citizen, wrapped in a wide gown, his gray periwig exchanged for a nightcap, which was thrust back from his forehead, and his silk stockings hanging about his legs. He supported himself on his polished cane in a fit of convulsive merriment, which manifested itself on his solemn old features like a funny inscription on a tombstone. Then Robin seemed to hear the voices of the barbers, of the guests of the inn, and of all who had made sport of him that night. The contagion was spreading among the multitude, when, all at once, it seized upon Robin, and he sent forth a shout of laughter that echoed through the street;—every man shook his sides, every man emptied his lungs, but Robin's shout was the loudest there. The cloud-spirits peeped from their silvery islands, as the congregated mirth went roaring up the sky! The Man in the Moon heard the far bellow. "Oho," quoth he, "the old earth is frolicsome tonight!"

When there was a momentary calm in that tempestuous sea of sound, the leader gave the sign, the procession resumed its march. On they went, like fiends that throng in mockery around some dead potentate, mighty no more, but majestic still in his agony. On they went, in counterfeited pomp, in senseless uproar, in frenzied merriment, trampling all on an old man's heart. On swept the tumult, and left a silent street behind.

"Well, Robin, are you dreaming?" inquired the gentleman, laying his hand on the youth's shoulder.

Robin started, and withdrew his arm from the stone post to which he had instinctively clung, as the living stream rolled by him. His cheek was somewhat pale, and his eye not quite as lively as in the earlier part of the evening.

"Will you be kind enough to show me the way to the ferry?" said he, after a moment's pause.

"You have, then, adopted a new subject of inquiry?" observed his companion, with a smile.

"Why, yes, sir," replied Robin, rather dryly. "Thanks to you, and to my other friends, I have at last met my kinsman, and he will scarce desire to see my face again. I begin to grow weary of a town life, sir. Will you show me the way to the ferry?"

"No, my good friend Robin,—not tonight, at least," said the gentleman. "Some few days hence, if you wish it, I will speed you on your journey. Or, if you prefer to remain with us, perhaps, as you are a shrewd youth, you may rise in the world without the help of your kinsman, Major Molineux."

AMBROSE BIERCE
1842–1914?

Chickamauga°

One sunny autumn afternoon a child strayed away from its rude home in a small field and entered a forest unobserved. It was happy in a new sense of freedom from control, happy in the opportunity of exploration and adventure; for this child's spirit, in bodies of its ancestors, had for thousands of years been trained to memorable feats of discovery and conquest—victories in battles whose critical moments were centuries, whose victors' camps were cities of hewn stone. From the cradle of its race it had conquered its way through two continents and passing a great sea had penetrated a third, there to be born to war and dominion as a heritage.

The child was a boy aged about six years, the son of a poor planter. In his younger manhood the father had been a soldier, had fought against naked

CHICKAMAUGA. The Chickamauga is a creek in northwestern Georgia, the site of a major Civil War battle on September 20, 1863, in which the Union forces were defeated.

savages and followed the flag of his country into the capital of a civilized race to the far South. In the peaceful life of a planter the warrior-fire survived; once kindled, it is never extinguished. The man loved military books and pictures and the boy had understood enough to make himself a wooden sword, though even the eye of his father would hardly have known it for what it was. This weapon he now bore bravely, as became the son of an heroic race, and pausing now and again in the sunny space of the forest assumed, with some exaggeration, the postures of aggression and defense that he had been taught by the engraver's art. Made reckless by the ease with which he overcame invisible foes attempting to stay his advance, he committed the common enough military error of pushing the pursuit to a dangerous extreme, until he found himself upon the margin of a wide but shallow brook, whose rapid waters barred his direct advance against the flying foe that had crossed with illogical ease. But the intrepid victor was not to be baffled; the spirit of the race which had passed the great sea burned unconquerable in that small breast and would not be denied. Finding a place where some boulders in the bed of the stream lay but a step or a leap apart, he made his way across and fell again upon the rear-guard of his imaginary foe, putting all to the sword.

Now that the battle had been won, prudence required that he withdraw to his base of operations. Alas; like many a mightier conqueror, and like one, the mightiest, he could not

curb the lust for war,
Nor learn that tempted Fate will leave the loftiest star.

Advancing from the bank of the creek he suddenly found himself confronted with a new and more formidable enemy: in the path that he was following, sat, bolt upright, with ears erect and paws suspended before it, a rabbit! With a startled cry the child turned and fled, he knew not in what direction, calling with inarticulate cries for his mother, weeping, stumbling, his tender skin cruelly torn by brambles, his little heart beating hard with terror—breathless, blind with tears—lost in the forest! Then, for more than an hour, he wandered with erring feet through the tangled undergrowth, till at last, overcome by fatigue, he lay down in a narrow space between two rocks, within a few yards of the stream and still grasping his toy sword, no longer a weapon but a companion,

sobbed himself to sleep. The wood birds sang merrily above his head; the squirrels, whisking their bravery of tail, ran barking from tree to tree, unconscious of the pity of it, and somewhere far away was a strange, muffled thunder, as if the partridges were drumming in celebration of nature's victory over the son of her immemorial enslavers. And back at the little plantation, where white men and black were hastily searching the fields and hedges in alarm, a mother's heart was breaking for her missing child.

Hours passed, and then the little sleeper rose to his feet. The chill of the evening was in his limbs, the fear of the gloom in his heart. But he had rested, and he no longer wept. With some blind instinct which impelled to action he struggled through the undergrowth about him and came to a more open ground—on his right the brook, to the left a gentle acclivity studded with infrequent trees; over all, the gathering gloom of twilight. A thin, ghostly mist rose along the water. It frightened and repelled him; instead of recrossing, in the direction whence he had come, he turned his back upon it, and went forward toward the dark inclosing wood. Suddenly he saw before him a strange moving object which he took to be some large animal—a dog, a pig—he could not name it; perhaps it was a bear. He had seen pictures of bears, but knew of nothing to their discredit and had vaguely wished to meet one. But something in form or movement of this object—something in the awkwardness of its approach—told him that it was not a bear, and curiosity was stayed by fear. He stood still and as it came slowly on gained courage every moment, for he saw that at least it had not the long menacing ears of the rabbit. Possibly his impressionable mind was half conscious of something familiar in its shambling, awkward gait. Before it had approached near enough to resolve his doubts he saw that it was followed by another and another. To right and to left were many more; the whole open space about him were alive with them—all moving toward the brook.

They were men. They crept upon their hands and knees. They used their hands only, dragging their legs. They used their knees only, their arms hanging idle at their sides. They strove to rise to their feet, but fell prone in the attempt. They did nothing naturally, and nothing alike, save only to advance foot by foot in the same direction. Singly,

in pairs and in little groups, they came on through
the gloom, some halting now and again while
others crept slowly past them, then resuming their
movement. They came by dozens and by hundreds;
as far on either hand as one could see in the deepening gloom they extended and the black wood
behind them appeared to be inexhaustible. The
very ground seemed in motion toward the creek.
Occasionally one who had paused did not again
go on, but lay motionless. He was dead. Some,
pausing, made strange gestures with their hands,
erected their arms and lowered them again, clasped
their heads; spread their palms upward, as men are
sometimes seen to do in public prayer.

Not all of this did the child note; it is what would
have been noted by an elder observer; he saw little
but that these were men, yet crept like babes. Being
men, they were not terrible, though unfamiliarly
clad. He moved among them freely, going from one
to another and peering into their faces with childish
curiosity. All their faces were singularly white and
many were streaked and gouted with red. Something in this—something too, perhaps, in their
grotesque attitudes and movements—reminded him
of the painted clown whom he had seen last summer
in the circus, and he laughed as he watched them.
But on and ever on they crept, these maimed and
bleeding men, as heedless as he of the dramatic
contrast between his laughter and their own ghastly
gravity. To him it was a merry spectacle. He had
seen his father's Negroes creep upon their hands
and knees for his amusement—had ridden them so,
"making believe" they were his horses. He now
approached one of these crawling figures from behind and with an agile movement mounted it
astride. The man sank upon his breast, recovered,
flung the small boy fiercely to the ground as an
unbroken colt might have done, then turned upon
him a face that lacked a lower jaw—from the upper
teeth to the throat was a great red gap fringed with
hanging shreds of flesh and splinters of bone. The
unnatural prominence of nose, the absence of chin,
the fierce eyes, gave this man the appearance of a
great bird of prey crimsoned in throat and breast
by the blood of its quarry. The man rose to his
knees, the child to his feet. The man shook his fist
at the child; the child, terrified at last, ran to a tree
near by, got upon the farther side of it and took a
more serious view of the situation. And so the
clumsy multitude dragged itself slowly and painfully

along in hideous pantomime—moved forward
down the slope like a swarm of great black beetles,
with never a sound of going—in silence profound,
absolute.

Instead of darkening, the haunted landscape
began to brighten. Through the belt of trees beyond
the brook shone a strange red light, the trunks and
branches of the trees making a black lacework
against it. It struck the creeping figures and gave
them monstrous shadows, which caricatured their
movements on the lit grass. It fell upon their faces,
touching their whiteness with a ruddy tinge, accentu-
ating the stains with which so many of them were
freaked and maculated. It sparkled on buttons and
bits of metal in their clothing. Instinctively the child
turned toward the growing splendor and moved
down the slope with his horrible companions; in a
few moments had passed the foremost of the throng
—not much of a feat, considering his advantages.
He placed himself in the lead, his wooden sword still
in hand, and solemnly directed the march, con-
forming his pace to theirs and occasionally turning
as if to see that his forces did not straggle. Surely
such a leader never before had such a following.

Scattered about upon the ground now slowly
narrowing by the encroachment of this awful march
to water, were certain articles to which, in the
leader's mind, were coupled no significant associations: an occasional blanket tightly rolled length-
wise, doubled and the ends bound together with a
string; a heavy knapsack here, and there a broken
rifle—such things, in short, as are found in the rear
of retreating troops, the "spoor"[1] of men flying
from their hunters. Everywhere near the creek,
which here had a margin of lowland, the earth was
trodden into mud by the feet of men and horses.
An observer of better experience in the use of his
eyes would have noticed that these footprints
pointed in both directions; the ground had been
twice passed over—in advance and in retreat. A
few hours before, these desperate, stricken men,
with their more fortunate and now distant comrades, had penetrated the forest in thousands. Their
successive battalions, breaking into swarms and
reforming in lines, had passed the child on every
side—had almost trodden on him as he slept. The
rustle and murmur of their march had not awakened
him. Almost within a stone's throw of where he lay
they had fought a battle; but all unheard by him

1. **spoor:** track or trail of an animal.

were the roar of the musketry, the shock of the cannon, "the thunder of the captains and the shouting." He had slept through it all, grasping his little wooden sword with perhaps a tighter clutch in unconscious sympathy with his martial environment, but as heedless of the grandeur of the struggle as the dead who had died to make the glory.

The fire beyond the belt of woods on the farther side of the creek, reflected to earth from the canopy of its own smoke, was now suffusing the whole landscape. It transformed the sinuous line of mist to the vapor of gold. The water gleamed with dashes of red, and red, too, were many of the stones protruding above the surface. But that was blood; the less desperately wounded had stained them in crossing. On them, too, the child now crossed with eager steps; he was going to the fire. As he stood upon the farther bank he turned about to look at the companions of his march. The advance was arriving at the creek. The stronger had already drawn themselves to the brink and plunged their faces into the flood. Three or four who lay without motion appeared to have no heads. At this the child's eyes expanded with wonder; even his hospitable understanding could not accept a phenomenon implying such vitality as that. After slaking their thirst these men had not had the strength to back away from the water, nor to keep their heads above it. They were drowned. In rear of these, the open spaces of the forest showed the leader as many formless figures of his grim command as at first; but not nearly so many were in motion. He waved his cap for their encouragement and smilingly pointed with his weapon in the direction of the guiding light—a pillar of fire to this strange exodus.

Confident of the fidelity of his forces, he now entered the belt of woods, passed through it easily in the red illumination, climbed a fence, ran across a field, turning now and again to coquet with his responsive shadow, and so approached the blazing ruin of a dwelling. Desolation everywhere! In all the wide glare not a living thing was visible. He cared nothing for that; the spectacle pleased, and he danced with glee in imitation of the wavering flames. He ran about, collecting fuel, but every object that he found was too heavy for him to cast in from the distance to which the heat limited his approach. In despair he flung in his sword—a

surrender to the superior forces of nature. His military career was at an end.

Shifting his position, his eyes fell upon some outbuildings which had an oddly familiar appearance, as if he had dreamed of them. He stood considering them with wonder, when suddenly the entire plantation, with its inclosing forest, seemed to turn as if upon a pivot. His little world swung half around; the points of the compass were reversed. He recognized the blazing building as his own home!

For a moment he stood stupefied by the power of the revelation, then ran with stumbling feet, making a half-circuit of the ruin. There, conspicuous in the light of the conflagration, lay the dead body of a woman—the white face turned upward, the hands thrown out and clutched full of grass, the clothing deranged, the long dark hair in tangles and full of clotted blood. The greater part of the forehead was torn away, and from the jagged hole the brain protruded, overflowing the temple, a frothy mass of gray, crowned with clusters of crimson bubbles—the work of a shell.

The child moved his little hands, making wild, uncertain gestures. He uttered a series of inarticulate and indescribable cries—something between the chattering of an ape and the gobbling of a turkey—a startling, soulless, unholy sound, the language of a devil. The child was a deaf mute.

Then he stood motionless, with quivering lips, looking down upon the wreck.

ERNEST HEMINGWAY
1899–1961

The Killers

The door of Henry's lunchroom opened and two men came in. They sat down at the counter.

"What's yours?" George asked them.

"I don't know," one of the men said. "What do you want to eat, Al?"

"I don't know," said Al. "I don't know what I want to eat."

Outside it was getting dark. The street-light came

on outside the window. The two men at the counter read the menu. From the other end of the counter Nick Adams watched them. He had been talking to George when they came in.

"I'll have a roast pork tenderloin with apple sauce and mashed potatoes," the first man said.

"It isn't ready yet."

"What the hell do you put it on the card for?"

"That's the dinner," George explained. "You can get that at six o'clock."

George looked at the clock on the wall behind the counter.

"It's five o'clock."

"The clock says twenty minutes past five," the second man said.

"It's twenty minutes fast."

"Oh, to hell with the clock," the first man said. "What have you got to eat?"

"I can give you any kind of sandwiches," George said. "You can have ham and eggs, bacon and eggs, liver and bacon, or a steak."

"Give me chicken croquettes with green peas and cream sauce and mashed potatoes."

"That's the dinner."

"Everything we want's the dinner, eh? That's the way you work it."

"I can give you ham and eggs, bacon and eggs, liver—"

"I'll take ham and eggs," the man called Al said. He wore a derby hat and a black overcoat buttoned across the chest. His face was small and white and he had tight lips. He wore a silk muffler and gloves.

"Give me bacon and eggs," said the other man. He was about the same size as Al. Their faces were different, but they were dressed like twins. Both wore overcoats too tight for them. They sat leaning forward, their elbows on the counter.

"Got anything to drink?" Al asked.

"Silver beer, bevo, ginger-ale," George said.

"I mean you got anything to *drink*?"

"Just those I said."

"This is a hot town," said the other. "What do they call it?"

"Summit."

"Ever hear of it?" Al asked his friend.

"No," said the friend.

"What do you do here nights?" Al asked.

"They eat the dinner," his friend said. "They all come here and eat the big dinner."

"That's right," George said.

"So you think that's right?" Al asked George.

"Sure," said George.

"You're a pretty bright boy, aren't you?"

"Sure," said George.

"Well, you're not," said the other little man. "Is he, Al?"

"He's dumb," said Al. He turned to Nick. "What's your name?"

"Adams."

"Another bright boy," Al said. "Ain't he a bright boy, Max?"

"The town's full of bright boys," Max said.

George put the two platters, one of ham and eggs, the other of bacon and eggs, on the counter. He set down two side-dishes of fried potatoes and closed the wicket into the kitchen.

"Which is yours?" he asked Al.

"Don't you remember?"

"Ham and eggs."

"Just a bright boy," Max said. He leaned forward and took the ham and eggs. Both men ate with their gloves on. George watched them eat.

"What are *you* looking at?" Max looked at George.

"Nothing."

"The hell you were. You were looking at me."

"Maybe the boy meant it for a joke, Max," Al said.

George laughed.

"*You* don't have to laugh," Max said to him. "*You* don't have to laugh at all, see?"

"All right," said George.

"So he thinks it's all right." Max turned to Al. "He thinks it's all right. That's a good one."

"Oh, he's a thinker," Al said. They went on eating.

"What's the bright boy's name down the counter?" Al asked Max.

"Hey, bright boy," Max said to Nick. "You go around on the other side of the counter with your boy friend."

"What's the idea?" Nick asked.

"There isn't any idea."

"You better go around, bright boy," Al said. Nick went around behind the counter.

"What's the idea?" George asked.

"None of your damn business," Al said. "Who's out in the kitchen?"

"The nigger."

"What do you mean the nigger?"

"The nigger that cooks."

"Tell him to come in."

"What's the idea?"

"Tell him to come in."

"Where do you think you are?"

"We know damn well where we are," the man called Max said. "Do we look silly?"

"You talk silly," Al said to him. "What the hell do you argue with this kid for? Listen," he said to George, "tell the nigger to come out here."

"What are you going to do to him?"

"Nothing. Use your head, bright boy. What would we do to a nigger?"

George opened the slit that opened back into the kitchen. "Sam," he called. "Come in here a minute."

The door to the kitchen opened and the nigger came in. "What was it?" he asked. The two men at the counter took a look at him.

"All right, nigger. You stand right there," Al said.

Sam, the nigger, standing in his apron, looked at the two men sitting at the counter. "Yes, sir," he said. Al got down from his stool.

"I'm going back to the kitchen with the nigger and bright boy," he said. "Go on back to the kitchen, nigger. You go with him, bright boy." The little man walked after Nick and Sam, the cook, back into the kitchen. The door shut after them. The man called Max sat at the counter opposite George. He didn't look at George but looked in the mirror that ran along back of the counter. Henry's had been made over from a saloon into a lunch-counter.

"Well, bright boy," Max said, looking into the mirror, "why don't you say something?"

"What's it all about?"

"Hey, Al," Max called, "bright boy wants to know what it's all about."

"Why don't you tell him?" Al's voice came from the kitchen.

"What do you think it's all about?"

"I don't know."

"What do you think?"

Max looked into the mirror all the time he was talking.

"I wouldn't say."

"Hey, Al, bright boy says he wouldn't say what he thinks it's all about."

"I can hear you, all right," Al said from the kitchen. He had propped open the slit that dishes passed through into the kitchen with a catsup bottle. "Listen, bright boy," he said from the kitchen to George. "Stand a little further along the bar. You move a little to the left, Max." He was like a photographer arranging for a group picture.

"Talk to me, bright boy," Max said. "What do you think's going to happen?"

George did not say anything.

"I'll tell you," Max said. "We're going to kill a Swede. Do you know a big Swede named Ole Andreson?"

"Yes."

"He comes here to eat every night, don't he?"

"Sometimes he comes here."

"He comes here at six o'clock, don't he?"

"If he comes."

"We know all that, bright boy," Max said. "Talk about something else. Ever go to the movies?"

"Once in a while."

"You ought to go to the movies more. The movies are fine for a bright boy like you."

"What are you going to kill Ole Andreson for? What did he ever do to you?"

"He never had a chance to do anything to us. He never even seen us."

"And he's only going to see us once," Al said from the kitchen.

"What are you going to kill him for, then?" George asked.

"We're killing him for a friend. Just to oblige a friend, bright boy."

"Shut up," said Al from the kitchen. "You talk too goddam much."

"Well, I got to keep bright boy amused. Don't I, bright boy?"

"You talk too damn much," Al said. "The nigger and my bright boy are amused by themselves. I got them tied up like a couple of girl friends in the convent."

"I suppose you were in a convent."

"You never know."

"You were in a kosher convent. That's where you were."

George looked up at the clock.

"If anybody comes in you tell them the cook is off, and if they keep after it, you tell them you'll go back and cook yourself. Do you get that, bright boy?"

"All right," George said. "What you going to do with us afterward?"

"That'll depend," Max said. "That's one of those things you never know at the time."

George looked up at the clock. It was a quarter past six. The door from the street opened. A streetcar motorman came in.

"Hello, George," he said. "Can I get supper?"

"Sam's gone out," George said. "He'll be back in about half an hour."

"I'd better go up the street," the motorman said. George looked at the clock. It was twenty minutes past six.

"That was nice, bright boy," Max said. "You're a regular little gentleman."

"He knew I'd blow his head off," Al said from the kitchen.

"No," said Max. "It ain't that. Bright boy is nice. He's a nice boy. I like him."

At six-fifty-five George said: "He's not coming."

Two other people had been in the lunchroom. Once George had gone out to the kitchen and made a ham-and-egg sandwich "to go" that a man wanted to take with him. Inside the kitchen he saw Al, his derby hat tipped back, sitting on a stool beside the wicket with the muzzle of a sawed-off shotgun resting on the ledge. Nick and the cook were back to back in the corner, a towel tied in each of their mouths. George had cooked the sandwich, wrapped it up in oiled paper, put it in a bag, brought it in, and the man had paid for it and gone out.

"Bright boy can do everything," Max said. "He can cook and everything. You'd make some girl a nice wife, bright boy."

"Yes?" George said. "Your friend, Ole Andreson, isn't going to come."

"We'll give him ten minutes," Max said.

Max watched the mirror and the clock. The hands of the clock marked seven o'clock, and then five minutes past seven.

"Come on, Al," said Max. "We'd better go. He's not coming."

"Better give him five minutes," Al said from the kitchen.

In the five minutes a man came in, and George explained that the cook was sick.

"Why the hell don't you get another cook?" the man asked. "Aren't you running a lunch-counter?" He went out.

"Come on, Al," Max said.

"What about the two bright boys and the nigger?"

"They're all right."

"You think so?"

"Sure. We're through with it."

"I don't like it," said Al. "It's sloppy. You talk too much."

"Oh, what the hell," said Max. "We got to keep amused, haven't we?"

"You talk too much, all the same," Al said. He came out from the kitchen. The cut-off barrels of the shotgun made a slight bulge under the waist of his too tight-fitting overcoat. He straightened his coat with his gloved hands.

"So long, bright boy," he said to George. "You got a lot of luck."

"That's the truth," Max said. "You ought to play the races, bright boy."

The two of them went out the door. George watched them, through the window, pass under the arc-light and cross the street. In their tight overcoats and derby hats they looked like a vaudeville team. George went back through the swinging-door into the kitchen and untied Nick and the cook.

"I don't want any more of that," said Sam, the cook. "I don't want any more of that,"

Nick stood up. He had never had a towel in his mouth before.

"Say," he said. "What the hell?" He was trying to swagger it off.

"They were going to kill Ole Andreson," George said. "They were going to shoot him when he came in to eat."

"Ole Andreson?"

"Sure."

The cook felt the corners of his mouth with his thumbs.

"They all gone?" he asked.

"Yeah," said George. "They're gone now."

"I don't like it," said the cook. "I don't like any of it at all."

"Listen," George said to Nick. "You better go see Ole Andreson."

"All right."

"You better not have anything to do with it at all," Sam, the cook, said. "You better stay way out of it."

"Don't go if you don't want to," George said.

"Mixing up in this ain't going to get you anywhere," the cook said. "You stay out of it."

"I'll go see him," Nick said to George. "Where does he live?"

The cook turned away.

"Little boys always know what they want to do," he said.

"He lives up at Hirsch's rooming-house," George said to Nick.

"I'll go up there."

Outside the arc-light shone through the bare branches of a tree. Nick walked up the street beside the car-tracks and turned at the next arc-light down a side-street. Three houses up the street was Hirsch's rooming-house. Nick walked up the two steps and pushed the bell. A woman came to the door.

"Is Ole Andreson here?"

"Do you want to see him?"

"Yes, if he's in."

Nick followed the woman up a flight of stairs and back to the end of a corridor. She knocked on the door.

"Who is it?"

"It's somebody to see you, Mr. Andreson," the woman said.

"It's Nick Adams."

"Come in."

Nick opened the door and went into the room. Ole Andreson was lying on the bed with all his clothes on. He had been a heavyweight prizefighter and he was too long for the bed. He lay with his head on two pillows. He did not look at Nick.

"What was it?" he asked.

"I was up at Henry's," Nick said, "and two fellows came in and tied up me and the cook, and they said they were going to kill you."

It sounded silly when he said it. Ole Andreson said nothing.

"They put us out in the kitchen," Nick went on. "They were going to shoot you when you came in to supper."

Ole Andreson looked at the wall and did not say anything.

"George thought I better come and tell you about it."

"There isn't anything I can do about it," Ole Andreson said.

"I'll tell you what they were like."

"I don't want to know what they were like," Ole

Andreson said. He looked at the wall. "Thanks for coming to tell me about it."

"That's all right."

Nick looked at the big man lying on the bed.

"Don't you want me to go and see the police?"

"No," Ole Andreson said. "That wouldn't do any good."

"Isn't there something I could do?"

"No. There ain't anything to do."

"Maybe it was just a bluff."

"No. It ain't just a bluff."

Ole Andreson rolled over toward the wall.

"The only thing is," he said, talking toward the wall, "I just can't make up my mind to go out. I been in here all day."

"Couldn't you get out of town?"

"No," Ole Andreson said. "I'm through with all that running around."

He looked at the wall.

"There ain't anything to do now."

"Couldn't you fix it up some way?"

"No. I got in wrong." He talked in the same flat voice. "There ain't anything to do. After a while I'll make up my mind to go out."

"I better go back and see George," Nick said.

"So long," said Ole Andreson. He did not look toward Nick. "Thanks for coming around."

Nick went out. As he shut the door he saw Ole Andreson with all his clothes on, lying on the bed looking at the wall.

"He's been in his room all day," the landlady said downstairs. "I guess he don't feel well. I said to him: 'Mr. Andreson, you ought to go out and take a walk on a nice fall day like this,' but he didn't feel like it."

"He doesn't want to go out."

"I'm sorry he don't feel well," the woman said. "He's an awfully nice man. He was in the ring, you know."

"I know it."

"You'd never know it except from the way his face is," the woman said. They stood talking just inside the street door. "He's just as gentle."

"Well, good-night, Mrs. Hirsch," Nick said.

"I'm not Mrs. Hirsch," the woman said. "She owns the place. I just look after it for her. I'm Mrs. Bell."

"Well, good-night, Mrs. Bell," Nick said.

"Good-night," the woman said.

Nick walked up the dark street to the corner

under the arc-light, and then along the car-tracks to Henry's eating-house. George was inside, back of the counter.

"Did you see Ole?"

"Yes," said Nick. "He's in his room and he won't go out."

The cook opened the door from the kitchen when he heard Nick's voice.

"I don't even listen to it," he said and shut the door.

"Did you tell him about it?" George asked.

"Sure. I told him but he knows what it's all about."

"What's he going to do?"

"Nothing."

"They'll kill him."

"I guess they will."

"He must have got mixed up in something in Chicago."

"I guess so," said Nick.

"It's a hell of a thing."

"It's an awful thing," Nick said.

They did not say anything. George reached down for a towel and wiped the counter.

"I wonder what he did?" Nick said.

"Double-crossed somebody. That's what they kill them for."

"I'm going to get out of this town," Nick said.

"Yes," said George. "That's a good thing to do."

"I can't stand to think about him waiting in the room and knowing he's going to get it. It's too damned awful."

"Well," said George. "you better not think about it."

The Ironic Norm:
Inversion of the Quest

WILLIAM SHAKESPEARE
1564–1616

Troilus and Cressida

DRAMATIS PERSONAE

PRIAM, *king of Troy*
HECTOR ⎫
TROILUS ⎪
PARIS ⎬ *his sons*
DEIPHOBUS ⎪
HELENUS ⎭
MARGARELON, *a bastard son of Priam*
AENEAS ⎫
ANTENOR ⎬ *Trojan commanders*
CALCHAS, *a Trojan priest, taking part with the Greeks*
PANDARUS, *uncle to Cressida*
AGAMEMNON, *the Grecian general*
MENELAUS, *his brother*
ACHILLES ⎫
AJAX ⎪
ULYSSES ⎪
NESTOR ⎬ *Grecian commanders*
DIOMEDES ⎪
PATROCLUS ⎭
THERSITES, *a deformed and scurrilous Grecian*
ALEXANDER, *servant to Cressida*
SERVANT *to Troilus*
SERVANT *to Paris*
SERVANT *to Diomedes*

HELEN, *wife to Menelaus*

ANDROMACHE, *wife to Hector*
CASSANDRA, *daughter to Priam; a prophetess*
CRESSIDA, *daughter to Calchas*

TROJAN *and* GREEK SOLDIERS, *and* ATTENDANTS

SCENE—*Troy, and the Grecian camp.*

PROLOGUE

In Troy there lies the scene. From isles of Greece
The princes orgulous,° their high blood chafed,°
Have to the port of Athens sent their ships,
Fraught° with the ministers and instruments
Of cruel war. Sixty and nine that wore   5
Their crownets° regal from the Athenian bay
Put forth toward Phrygia,° and their vow is made
To ransack Troy, within whose strong immures°
The ravished Helen, Menelaus' queen,
With wanton Paris sleeps, and that's the quarrel.
To Tenedos° they come,   11
And the deep-drawing barks do there disgorge
Their warlike fraughtage. Now on Dardan° plains
The fresh and yet unbruisèd Greeks do pitch
Their brave pavilions. Priam's six-gated city,   15
Dardan, and Timbria, Helias, Chetas, Troien,
And Antenorides,° with massy° staples,
And corresponsive and fulfilling bolts,
Sperr° up the sons of Troy.
Now expectation, tickling skittish spirits,   20
On one and other side, Trojan and Greek,

TROILUS AND CRESSIDA. *Prologue.* **2. orgulous:** proud. **chafed:** enraged. **4. Fraught:** laden. **6. crownets:** coronets, worn by petty kings. **7. Phrygia:** Asia Minor. **8. immures:** walls. **11. Tenedos:** a Greek island in the Aegean Sea. **13. Dardan:** Trojan. **16–17. Dardan . . . Antenorides:** the names of the gates of Troy. **17. massy:** massive. **19. Sperr:** shut.

Sets all on hazard. And hither am I come
A Prologue armed, but not in confidence
Of author's pen or actor's voice, but suited
In like conditions as our argument,°   25
To tell you, fair beholders, that our play
Leaps o'er the vaunt and firstlings° of those broils,
Beginning in the middle, starting thence away
To what may be digested in a play.
Like, or find fault, do as your pleasures are.   30
Now good or bad, 'tis but the chance of war.

ACT I

SCENE I. *Troy. Before* PRIAM's *palace.*

[*Enter* PANDARUS *and* TROILUS.]

TROILUS   Call here my varlet,° I'll unarm again.
Why should I war without° the walls of Troy,
That find such cruel battle here within?
Each Trojan that is master of his heart,
Let him to field. Troilus, alas, hath none!   5
PANDARUS   Will this gear° ne'er be mended?
TROILUS   The Greeks are strong and skillful to
their strength,
Fierce to their skill and to their fierceness valiant.
But I am weaker than a woman's tear,
Tamer than sleep, fonder° than ignorance,   10
Less valiant than the virgin in the night,
And skill-less as unpracticed infancy.
PANDARUS   Well, I have told you enough of this.
For my part, I'll not meddle nor make no
farther. He that will have a cake out of the wheat
must needs tarry the grinding.   16
TROILUS   Have I not tarried?
PANDARUS   Aye, the grinding. But you must tarry
the bolting.°
TROILUS   Have I not tarried?
PANDARUS   Aye, the bolting. But you must tarry
the leavening.   20
TROILUS   Still have I tarried.
PANDARUS   Aye, to the leavening. But here's yet
in the word *hereafter* the kneading, the making
of the cake, the heating of the oven, and the
baking. Nay, you must stay the cooling too, or
you may chance to burn your lips.   26

TROILUS   Patience herself, what goddess e'er she be,
Doth lesser blench° at sufferance° than I do.
At Priam's royal table do I sit,
And when fair Cressid comes into my thoughts—
So, traitor!—"When she comes!"—When is she
thence?   31
PANDARUS   Well, she looked yesternight fairer
than ever I saw her look, or any woman else.
TROILUS   I was about to tell thee—when my heart,
As wedgèd with a sigh, would rive° in twain   35
Lest Hector or my father should perceive me,
I have, as when the sun doth light a storm,
Buried this sigh in wrinkle of a smile.
But sorrow that is couched in seeming gladness
Is like that mirth fate turns to sudden sadness.   40
PANDARUS   An° her hair were not somewhat
darker than Helen's—well, go to—there were no
more comparison between the women. But for
my part, she is my kinswoman. I would not, as
they term it, praise her. But I would somebody
had heard her talk yesterday, as I did. I will not
dispraise your sister Cassandra's wit, but—   47
TROILUS   O Pandarus! I tell thee, Pandarus—
When I do tell thee, there my hopes lie drowned,
Reply not in how many fathoms deep   50
They lie indrenched.° I tell thee I am mad
In Cressid's love. Thou answer'st "she is fair,"
Pour'st in the open ulcer of my heart
Her eyes, her hair, her cheek, her gait, her voice,
Handlest in thy discourse, oh, that her hand,   55
In whose comparison all whites are ink
Writing their own reproach, to whose soft seizure
The cygnet's down is harsh, and spirit of sense
Hard as the palm of plowman.° This thou tell'st
me,
As true thou tell'st me, when I say I love her.   60
But, saying thus, instead of oil and balm,
Thou lay'st in every gash that love hath given me
The knife that made it.
PANDARUS   I speak no more than truth.
TROILUS   Thou dost not speak so much.   65
PANDARUS   Faith, I'll not meddle in 't. Let her be
as she is. If she be fair, 'tis the better for her. An
she be not, she has the mends in her own
hands.°

---

25. **argument:** plot, theme. 27. **vaunt . . . firstlings:** van and
beginning.
    Act I, scene i. 1. **varlet:** servant, valet. 2. **without:**
outside. 6. **gear:** business. 10. **fonder:** more foolish. 18.
bolting: sifting of the flour.

28. **blench:** shy (like a horse). **sufferance:** pain. 35. **rive:**
split. 41. **An:** if. 51. **indrenched:** soaked. 57–59. **to . . .
plowman:** Compared with Cressida's gentle grasp, swan's-
down is hard, and the most sensitive of feeling as rough as a
plowman's hand. 68–69. **has . . . hands:** i.e., can make herself up.

TROILUS   Good Pandarus, how now, Pandarus! 70

PANDARUS   I have had my labor for my travail, ill-thought-on of her and ill-thought-on of you— gone between and between, but small thanks for my labor.

TROILUS   What, art thou angry, Pandarus? What, with me? 75

PANDARUS   Because she's kin to me, therefore she's not so fair as Helen. An she were not kin to me, she would be as fair on Friday as Helen is on Sunday.° But what care I? I care not an she were a blackamoor, 'tis all one to me. 80

TROILUS   Say I she is not fair?

PANDARUS   I do not care whether you do or no. She's a fool to stay behind her father.° Let her to the Greeks, and so I'll tell her the next time I see her. For my part, I'll meddle nor make no more i' the matter. 86

TROILUS   Pandarus——

PANDARUS   Not I.

TROILUS   Sweet Pandarus——

PANDARUS   Pray you, speak no more to me. I will leave all as I found it, and there an end. 91
     [Exit. An alarum.]

TROILUS   Peace, you ungracious clamors! Peace, rude sounds!
Fools on both sides! Helen must needs be fair
When with your blood you daily paint her thus.
I cannot fight upon this argument, 95
It is too starved a subject for my sword.
But Pandarus——O gods, how do you plague me!
I cannot come to Cressid but by Pandar,
And he's as tetchy° to be wooed to woo
As she is stubborn-chaste against all suit. 100
Tell me, Apollo, for thy Daphne's° love,
What Cressid is, what Pandar, and what we.
Her bed is India,° there she lies, a pearl.
Between our Ilium and where she resides,
Let it be called the wild and wandering flood, 105
Ourself the merchant, and this sailing Pandar
Our doubtful hope, our convoy and our bark.°
     [Alarum. Enter AENEAS.]

AENEAS   How now, Prince Troilus! Wherefore not afield?

TROILUS   Because not there. This woman's answer sorts,°
For womanish it is to be from thence. 110
What news, Aeneas, from the field today?

AENEAS   That Paris is returned home, and hurt.

TROILUS   By whom, Aeneas?

AENEAS   Troilus, by Menelaus.

TROILUS   Let Paris bleed. 'Tis but a scar to scorn.
Paris is gored with Menelaus' horn.° [Alarum.]

AENEAS   Hark, what good sport is out of town today! 116

TROILUS   Better at home if "would I might" were "may."
But to the sport abroad. Are you bound thither?

AENEAS   In all swift haste.

TROILUS   Come, go we then together. [Exeunt.]

SCENE II. *The same. A street.*

[*Enter* CRESSIDA *and* ALEXANDER *her man.*]

CRESSIDA   Who were those went by?

ALEXANDER   Queen Hecuba and Helen.

CRESSIDA   And whither go they?

ALEXANDER   Up to the eastern tower,
Whose height commands as subject all the vale,
To see the battle. Hector, whose patience
Is as a virtue fixed, today was moved. 5
He chid Andromache and struck his armorer,
And, like as there were husbandry° in war,
Before the sun rose he was harnessed° light,
And to the field goes he, where every flower
Did, as a prophet, weep what it foresaw 10
In Hector's wrath.

CRESSIDA   What was his cause of anger?

ALEXANDER   The noise goes, this: There is among the Greeks
A lord of Trojan blood, nephew to Hector.
They call him Ajax.

CRESSIDA   Good, and what of him?

ALEXANDER   They say he is a very man per se,°
And stands alone. 16

CRESSIDA   So do all men, unless they are drunk, sick, or have no legs.

ALEXANDER   This man, lady, hath robbed many beasts of their particular additions.° He is as valiant as the lion, churlish as the bear, slow

---

78–79. **on Sunday:** i.e., in her Sunday best. **83. She's . . . father:** Cressida's father, Calchas, deserted to the Greeks. **99. tetchy:** touchy. **101. Daphne:** one of Apollo's unsuccessful loves. To avoid his approaches she was changed into a laurel. **103. India:** symbol of distant, wealthy, and romantic lands. **107. bark:** ship.

109. sorts: fits. **115. horn:** i.e., because Menelaus is a cuckold.
Scene ii. **7. husbandry:** economy; i.e., he got up early to make the most of daylight. **8. harnessed:** armored. **14. per se:** by himself, unique. **20. additions:** distinctive attributes.

as the elephant—a man into whom Nature hath so crowded humors° that his valor is crushed into folly, his folly sauced with discretion. There is no man hath a virtue that he hath not a glimpse of, nor any man an attaint° but he carries some stain of it. He is melancholy without cause and merry against the hair.° He hath the joints of everything, but everything so out of joint that he is a gouty Briareus,° many hands and no use, or purblind Argus,° all eyes and no sight.   31

CRESSIDA   But how should this man, that makes me smile, make Hector angry?

ALEXANDER   They say he yesterday coped° Hector in the battle and struck him down, the disdain and shame whereof hath ever since kept Hector fasting and waking.   37

[*Enter* PANDARUS.]

CRESSIDA   Who comes here?

ALEXANDER   Madam, your uncle Pandarus.

CRESSIDA   Hector's a gallant man.   40

ALEXANDER   As may be in the world, lady.

PANDARUS   What's that? What's that?

CRESSIDA   Good morrow, Uncle Pandarus.

PANDARUS   Good morrow, Cousin° Cressid. What do you talk of? Good morrow, Alexander. How do you, cousin? When were you at Ilium?°   46

CRESSIDA   This morning, uncle.

PANDARUS   What were you talking of when I came? Was Hector armed and gone ere you came to Ilium? Helen was not up, was she?   50

CRESSIDA   Hector was gone, but Helen was not up.

PANDARUS   E'en so. Hector was stirring early.

CRESSIDA   That were we talking of, and of his anger.

PANDARUS   Was he angry?

CRESSIDA   So he says here.

PANDARUS   True, he was so. I know the cause too. He'll lay about him today, I can tell them that. And there's Troilus will not come far behind him. Let them take heed of Troilus, I can tell them that too.

CRESSIDA   What, is he angry too?

PANDARUS   Who, Troilus? Troilus is the better man of the two.

CRESSIDA   Oh Jupiter! There's no comparison.   65

PANDARUS   What, not between Troilus and Hector? Do you know a man if you see him?

CRESSIDA   Aye, if I ever saw him before and knew him.

PANDARUS   Well, I say Troilus is Troilus.   70

CRESSIDA   Then you say as I say, for I am sure he is not Hector.

PANDARUS   No, nor Hector is not Troilus in some degrees.°   74

CRESSIDA   'Tis just to each of them, he is himself.

PANDARUS   Himself! Alas, poor Troilus! I would he were.

CRESSIDA   So he is.

PANDARUS   Condition, I had gone° barefoot to India.   80

CRESSIDA   He is not Hector.

PANDARUS   Himself! No, he's not himself. Would a'° were himself! Well, the gods are above, time must friend or end. Well, Troilus, well, I would my heart were in her body! No, Hector is not a better man than Troilus.   86

CRESSIDA   Excuse me.

PANDARUS   He is elder.

CRESSIDA   Pardon me, pardon me.

PANDARUS   Th' other's not come to't. You shall tell me another tale when th' other's come to 't. Hector shall not have his wit this year.   92

CRESSIDA   He shall not need it if he have his own.

PANDARUS   Nor his qualities.

CRESSIDA   No matter.   95

PANDARUS   Nor his beauty.

CRESSIDA   'Twould not become him, his own's better.

PANDARUS   You have no judgment, niece. Helen herself swore th' other day that Troilus, for a brown favor°—for so 'tis, I must confess—not brown neither——   102

CRESSIDA   No, but brown.

PANDARUS   Faith, to say truth, brown and not brown.   105

CRESSIDA   To say the truth, true and not true.

PANDARUS   She praised his complexion above Paris.

CRESSIDA   Why, Paris hath color enough.

PANDARUS   So he has.

CRESSIDA   Then Troilus should have too much. If she praised him above, his complexion is

---

23. humors: whims. **26. attaint:** disgrace. **28. against . . . hair:** i.e., the natural lie of the hair; "against the grain." **30. Briareus:** a monster with a hundred hands. **31. Argus:** a monster with a hundred eyes. **34. coped:** encountered. **44. Cousin:** used for any near relation. **46. Ilium:** the citadel of Troy, the royal palace.

73–74. in . . . degrees: by some distance. **79. Condition . . . gone:** i.e., I wish Troilus was himself even if I had to go. **83. a':** he. **101. brown favor:** dark complexion.

higher than his. He having color enough, and the other higher, is too flaming a praise for a good complexion. I had as lief Helen's golden tongue had commended Troilus for a copper° nose. 116

PANDARUS I swear to you I think Helen loves him better than Paris.

CRESSIDA Then she's a merry Greek° indeed.

PANDARUS Nay, I am sure she does. She came to him th' other day into the compassed° window —and you know he has not past three or four hairs on his chin—— 123

CRESSIDA Indeed, a tapster's arithmetic° may soon bring his particulars therein to a total. 125

PANDARUS Why, he is very young. And yet will he, within three pound, lift as much as his brother Hector.

CRESSIDA Is he so young a man and so old a lifter?°

PANDARUS But to prove to you that Helen loves him—she came and puts me her white hand to his cloven chin—— 132

CRESSIDA Juno have mercy! How came it cloven?

PANDARUS Why you know 'tis dimpled. I think his smiling becomes him better than any man in all Phrygia. 136

CRESSIDA Oh, he smiles valiantly.

PANDARUS Does he not?

CRESSIDA Oh yes, an 'twere a cloud in autumn.

PANDARUS Why, go to, then. But to prove to you that Helen loves Troilus—— 141

CRESSIDA Troilus will stand to the proof, if you'll prove it so.

PANDARUS Troilus! Why, he esteems her no more than I esteem an addle° egg. 145

CRESSIDA If you love an addle egg as well as you love an idle head, you would eat chickens i' the shell.

PANDARUS I cannot choose but laugh to think how she tickled his chin. Indeed she has a marvelous white hand, I must needs confess—— 151

CRESSIDA Without the rack.°

PANDARUS And she takes upon her to spy a white hair on his chin.

CRESSIDA Alas, poor chin! Many a wart is richer. 156

PANDARUS But there was such laughing! Queen Hecuba laughed, that her eyes ran o'er.

CRESSIDA With millstones.°

PANDARUS And Cassandra laughed. 160

CRESSIDA But there was more temperate fire under the pot° of her eyes. Did her eyes run o'er too?

PANDARUS And Hector laughed.

CRESSIDA At what was all this laughing? 165

PANDARUS Marry,° at the white hair that Helen spied on Troilus' chin.

CRESSIDA An 't had been a green hair, I should have laughed too.

PANDARUS They laughed not so much at the hair as at his pretty answer. 171

CRESSIDA What was his answer?

PANDARUS Quoth she, "Here's but two and fifty hairs on your chin, and one of them is white."

CRESSIDA This is her question. 175

PANDARUS That's true, make no question of that. "Two and fifty hairs," quoth he, "and one white. That white hair is my father, and all the rest are his sons."° "Jupiter!" quoth she. "Which of these hairs is Paris my husband?" "The forked one,"° quoth he. "Pluck 't out, and give it him." But there was such laughing! And Helen so blushed, and Paris so chafed, and all the rest so laughed, that it passed. 184

CRESSIDA So let it° now, for it has been a great while going by.

PANDARUS Well, cousin, I told you a thing yesterday. Think on 't.

CRESSIDA So I do.

PANDARUS I'll be sworn 'tis true. He will weep you an 'twere° a man born in April.° 191

CRESSIDA And I'll spring up in his tears as 'twere a nettle against May.   [A retreat sounded.]

PANDARUS Hark! They are coming from the field. Shall we stand up here and see them as they pass toward Ilium? Good niece, do, sweet Niece Cressida. 197

CRESSIDA At your pleasure.

PANDARUS Here, here, here's an excellent place, here we may see most bravely. I'll tell you them all by their names as they pass by, but mark Troilus above the rest. 202

116. copper: red. 119. merry Greek: The Greeks were considered gay folk, so *merry Greek* came to be a proverbial phrase for a lighthearted, frivolous person. 121. compassed: round. 124. tapster's arithmetic: such slight ability to add as a bartender (*tapster*) needs. 129. lifter: thief. 145. addle: addled, bad. 152. Without . . . rack: i.e., without being put to torture.

159. With millstones: "by the pailful." 162. pot: socket. 166. Marry: Mary, by the Virgin. 176. his sons: Priam had fifty sons. 180–81. forked one: i.e., the cuckold. 185. it: i.e., this interminable tale. 191. an 'twere: as if he was. born in April: the rainy month of Aquarius.

[AENEAS *passes*.]

CRESSIDA   Speak not so loud.

PANDARUS   That's Aeneas. Is not that a brave
man? He's one of the flowers of Troy, I can tell
you. But mark Troilus, you shall see anon.   206

CRESSIDA   Who's that?

[ANTENOR *passes*.]

PANDARUS   That's Antenor. He has a shrewd wit,
I can tell you, and he's a man good enough. He's
one o' the soundest judgments in Troy, whosoever, and a proper man of person.° When comes
Troilus? I'll show you Troilus anon. If he see
me, you shall see him nod at me.   213

CRESSIDA   Will he give you the nod?°

PANDARUS   You shall see.   215

CRESSIDA   If he do, the rich shall have more.°

[HECTOR *passes*.]

PANDARUS   That's Hector, that, that, look you,
that. There's a fellow! Go thy way, Hector!
There's a brave man, niece. O, brave Hector!
Look how he looks! There's a countenance! Is 't
not a brave man?   221

CRESSIDA   Oh, a brave man!

PANDARUS   Is a' not? It does a man's heart good.
Look you what hacks are on his helmet! Look
you yonder, do you see? Look you there—there's
no jesting, there's laying on, take 't off who will,
as they say. There be hacks!   227

CRESSIDA   Be those with swords?

PANDARUS   Swords! Anything, he cares not. An
the Devil come to him, it's all one. By God's lid,°
it does one's heart good. Yonder comes Paris,
yonder comes Paris. [PARIS *passes*.] Look ye
yonder, niece. Is 't not a gallant man too, is
't not? Why, this is brave now. Who said he came
hurt home today? He's not hurt. Why, this will
do Helen's heart good now, ha! Would I could
see Troilus now! You shall see Troilus anon.   237

CRESSIDA   Who's that?

[HELENUS *passes*.]

PANDARUS   That's Helenus. I marvel where Troilus
is. That's Helenus. I think he went not forth
today. That's Helenus.   241

CRESSIDA   Can Helenus fight, uncle?

PANDARUS   Helenus! No, yes, he'll fight indiffer-
ent° well. I marvel where Troilus is. Hark! Do

you not hear the people cry "Troilus"? Helenus
is a priest.   246

CRESSIDA   What sneaking fellow comes yonder?

[TROILUS *passes*.]

PANDARUS   Where? Yonder? That's Deiphobus.
'Tis Troilus! There's a man, niece! Hem! Brave
Troilus! The prince of chivalry!   250

CRESSIDA   Peace, for shame, peace!

PANDARUS   Mark him, note him. Oh, brave
Troilus! Look well upon him, niece. Look you
how his sword is bloodied, and his helm more
hacked than Hector's, and how he looks, and
how he goes! Oh, admirable youth! He never
saw° three-and-twenty. Go thy way, Troilus,
go thy way! Had I a sister were a grace, or a
daughter a goddess, he should take his choice.
Oh, admirable man! Paris? Paris is dirt to him,
and I warrant Helen, to change, would give an
eye to boot.°   262

[COMMON SOLDIERS *pass*.]

CRESSIDA   Here come more.

PANDARUS   Asses, fools, dolts! Chaff and bran,
chaff and bran! Porridge after meat! I could live
and die i' the eyes of° Troilus. Ne'er look, ne'er
look, the eagles are gone—crows and daws,°
crows and daws! I had rather be such a man as
Troilus than Agamemnon and all Greece.   269

CRESSIDA   There is among the Greeks Achilles, a
better man than Troilus.

PANDARUS   Achilles! A drayman,° a porter, a very
camel.

CRESSIDA   Well, well.   274

PANDARUS   Well, well! Why, have you any discretion? Have you any eyes? Do you know what
a man is? Is not birth, beauty, good shape,
discourse, manhood. learning, gentleness, virtue,
youth, liberality, and suchlike the spice and salt
that season a man?   280

CRESSIDA   Aye, a minced° man. And then to be
baked with no date in the pie, for then the man's
date is out.°

PANDARUS   You are such a woman! One knows
not at what ward° you lie.   285

CRESSIDA   Upon my back, to defend my belly;
upon my wit, to defend my wiles; upon my

---

211. proper . . . person: a fine handsome man. **214. give
. . . nod:** i.e., recognize you. **216. rich . . . more:** i.e., if he
nods to you, you will be a greater noddy (simpleton) than
ever. **230. lid:** eyelid. **243–44. indifferent:** fairly.

256–57. never saw: i.e., is not yet. **262. to boot:** in addition;
i.e., to get Troilus, Helen would give Paris and one of her
eyes. **266. i' . . . of:** gazing at. **267. daws:** jackdaws. **272.
drayman:** man who drives a heavy cart. **281. minced:** with
a pun on mincing, affected. **283. date is out:** time is up.
285. ward: position of defense.

secrecy, to defend mine honesty;° my mask,° to defend my beauty; and you, to defend all these. And at all these wards I lie, at a thousand watches.   291

PANDARUS Say one of your watches.

CRESSIDA Nay, I'll watch you for that, and that's one of the chiefest of them too. If I cannot ward what I would not have hit, I can watch you for telling how I took the blow—unless it swell past hiding, and then it's past watching.°   297

PANDARUS You are such another!

[*Enter* TROILUS' BOY.]

BOY Sir, my lord would instantly speak with you.   300

PANDARUS Where?

BOY At your own house. There he unarms him.

PANDARUS Good boy, tell him I come. [*Exit* BOY.] I doubt° he be hurt. Fare ye well, good niece.

CRESSIDA Adieu, uncle.   305

PANDARUS I will be with you, niece, by and by.

CRESSIDA To bring, uncle?

PANDARUS Aye, a token from Troilus.

CRESSIDA By the same token, you are a bawd.°

[*Exit* PANDARUS.]

Words, vows, gifts, tears, and love's full sacrifice, He offers in another's enterprise.   311

But more in Troilus thousandfold I see Than in the glass° of Pandar's praise may be.

Yet hold I off. Women are angels, wooing.°

Things won are done, joy's soul lies in the doing.   315

That she beloved° knows naught that knows not this—

Men prize the thing ungained more than it is.

That she was never yet that ever knew°

Love got so sweet as when desire did sue.

Therefore this maxim out of love I teach: 320

Achievement is command; ungained, beseech.°

Then though my heart's content firm love doth bear,

Nothing of that shall from mine eyes appear.

[*Exeunt.*]

SCENE III. *The Grecian camp. Before* AGAMEMNON'*s tent.*

[*Sennet.° Enter* AGAMEMNON, NESTOR, ULYSSES, MENELAUS, *with others.*]

AGAMEMNON Princes,

What grief hath set the jaundice on your cheeks? The ample proposition that hope makes In all designs begun on earth below Fails in the promised largeness.° Checks and disasters   5

Grow in the veins of actions highest reared,°

As knots, by the conflux of meeting sap, Infect the sound pine and divert his grain Tortive° and errant from his course of growth.

Nor, princes, is it matter new to us   10

That we come short of our suppose° so far That after seven years' siege yet Troy walls stand; Sith° every action that hath gone before, Whereof we have recórd, trial did draw Bias° and thwart,° not answering the aim   15

And that unbodied° figure of the thought That gave 't surmised shape. Why then, you princes,

Do you with cheeks abashed behold our works, And call them shames? Which are indeed naught else

But the protractive° trials of great Jove   20

To find persistive constancy° in men.

The fineness of which metal is not found In Fortune's love,° for then the bold and coward, The wise and fool, the artist° and unread, The hard and soft, seem all affined° and kin. 25

But in the wind and tempest of her frown, Distinction with a broad and powerful fan, Puffing at all, winnows the light away, And what hath mass or matter, by itself Lies rich in virtue and unmingled.°   30

NESTOR With due observance of thy godlike seat,° Great Agamemnon, Nestor shall apply Thy latest words. In the reproof of chance° Lies the true proof of men. The sea being smooth, How many shallow bauble° boats dare sail   35

---

288. honesty: chastity. mask: Ladies wore masks to prevent sun tan. 297. watching: caring for. 304. doubt: am afraid. 309. bawd: one who introduces the customer to a prostitute. 313. glass: reflection. 314. wooing: while still being wooed. 316. That . . . beloved: i.e., any woman who has a lover. 318. That . . . knew: there was never a woman who did not know. 321. Achievement . . . beseech: When a woman is won, she is at her man's command; but before he has won her, he will beg.

Scene iii. s.d., Sennet: trumpet call. 5. promised largeness: expected good results. 6. highest reared: undertaken on a large scale. 9. Tortive: twisting. 11. suppose: estimate. 13. Sith: since. 15. Bias: out of the direct course. thwart: awry. 16. unbodied: i.e., existing in the mind. 20. protractive: long-drawn-out. 21. persistive constancy: firmness to persist. 23. Fortune's love: i.e., when all goes well. 24. artist: scholar. 25. affined: related. 30. unmingled: i.e., with baser qualities. 31. seat: authority. 33. reproof of chance: defiance of fortune. 35. bauble: trifling.

Upon her patient breast, making their way
With those of nobler bulk!
But let the ruffian Boreas° once enrage
The gentle Thetis,° and anon behold
The stronged-ribbed bark through liquid moun-
   tains cut,   40
Bounding between the two moist elements°
Like Perseus' horse.° Where's then the saucy
   boat,
Whose weak untimbered sides but even now
Corivaled° greatness? Either to harbor fled,
Or made a toast for Neptune. Even so   45
Doth valor's show° and valor's worth divide
In storms of Fortune. For in her ray and
   brightness
The herd hath more annoyance by the breese°
Than by the tiger. But when the splitting wind
Makes flexible the knees of knotted oaks,   50
And flies fled under shade, why then the thing of
   courage
As roused with rage with rage doth sympathize,
And with an accent tuned in selfsame key
Retorts to chiding Fortune.
ULYSSES   Agamemnon,
Thou great commander, nerve° and bone of
   Greece,   55
Heart of our numbers, soul and only spirit
In whom the tempers and the minds of all
Should be shut up,° hear what Ulysses speaks.
Besides the applause and approbation
The which, [To AGAMEMNON] most mighty for thy
   place and sway,   60
[To NESTOR] And thou most reverend for thy
   stretched-out life,
I give to both your speeches, which were such
As Agamemnon and the hand of Greece
Should hold up high in brass,° and such again
As venerable Nestor, hatched in silver,°   65
Should with a bond of air, strong as the axletree
On which heaven rides, knit all the Greekish ears
To his experienced tongue, yet let it please both,
Thou great, and wise, to hear Ulysses speak.

AGAMEMNON   Speak, prince of Ithaca, and be 't of
   less expect   70
That matter needless, of importless burden,
Divide thy lips than we are confident
When rank Thersites opes his mastic° jaws
We shall hear music, wit, and oracle.°   74
ULYSSES   Troy, yet upon his basis, had been down,
And the great Hector's sword had lacked a
   master,
But for these instances.°
The specialty of rule° hath been neglected.
And look how many Grecian tents do stand
Hollow upon this plain, so many hollow
   factions.   80
When that the general is not like the hive
To whom the foragers shall all repair,
What honey is expected? Degree° being
   vizarded,°
The unworthiest shows as fairly in the mask.°
The heavens themselves, the planets and this
   center,°   85
Observe degree, priority, and place,
Insisture,° course, proportion, season, form,
Office, and custom, in all line of order.
And therefore is the glorious planet Sol
In noble eminence enthroned and sphered   90
Amidst the other,° whose medicinable eye
Corrects the ill aspécts of planets evil,
And posts° like the commandment of a king,
Sans° check to good and bad. But when the
   planets
In evil mixture to disorder wander,   95
What plagues and what portents, what mutiny,
What raging of the sea, shaking of earth,
Commotion in the winds, frights, changes,
   horrors,
Divert and crack, rend and deracinate,°
The unity and married calm of states   100
Quite from their fixure!° Oh, when degree is
   shaked,

70–74. Speak . . . oracle: This obscure speech may be
paraphrased: "Speak, prince of Ithaca, for we know that
we shall hear nothing worthless from you, as we know that
when Thersites opens his bitter mouth we shall hear neither
harmony nor sense." mastic: lit., scourging, satirical; a
word coined by Shakespeare from *mastix* (a scourge). 77.
instances: reasons. 78. specialty of rule: special authority
of the commander; i.e., discipline. 83. Degree: rank. being
vizarded: wearing a mask, obscured. 84. mask: entertainment at which all the partakers are masked. 85. center:
earth. 87. Insisture: regularity. 91. other: others. 93. posts:
rides fast. 94. Sans: without. 99. deracinate: root out. 101.
fixure: fixed place.

<hr/>

38. Boreas: the north wind. 39. Thetis: a sea nymph,
so the sea. 41. moist elements: i.e., air and water. 42.
Perseus' horse: The Greek hero Perseus killed the sorceress
Medea, and from her head came Pegasus, a winged horse,
which Perseus rode. 44. Corivaled: competed with. 46.
show: i.e., outward show. 48. breese: gadfly. 55. nerve:
sinew. 58. shut up: confined. 64. hold . . . brass: set up aloft
inscribed in brass for all to read. 65. hatched in silver: lit.,
inlaid with silver, streaked with white.

Which is the ladder to all high designs,
The enterprise is sick! How could communities,
Degrees in schools° and brotherhoods in cities,
Peaceful commerce from dividable° shores,   105
The primogenitive° and due of birth,
Prerogative° of age, crowns, scepters, laurels,
But by degree, stand in authentic place?
Take but degree away, untune that string,
And hark, what discord follows! Each thing
    meets   110
In mere oppugnancy.° The bounded° waters
Should lift their bosoms higher than the shores,
And make a sop of all this solid globe.
Strength should be lord of imbecility,°
And the rude son should strike his father dead.
Force should be right, or rather, right and
    wrong,   116
Between whose endless jar° justice resides,
Should lose their names, and so should justice
    too.
Then everything includes itself in power,
Power into will, will into appetite,   120
And appetite, a universal wolf,
So doubly seconded with° will and power,
Must make perforce a universal prey,
And last eat up himself. Great Agamemnon,
This chaos, when degree is suffocate,   125
Follows the choking.
And this neglection of degree it is
That by a pace goes backward, with a purpose
It hath to climb.° The general's disdained
By him one step below, he by the next,   130
That next by him beneath. So every step,
Exampled by the first pace that is sick
Of his superior, grows to an envious fever
Of pale and bloodless emulation.°
And 'tis this fever that keeps Troy on foot,   135
Not her own sinews. To end a tale of length,
Troy in our weakness stands, not in her strength.
NESTOR   Most wisely hath Ulysses here discovered°
The fever whereof all our power is sick.

AGAMEMNON   The nature of the sickness found,
    Ulysses,   140
What is the remedy?
ULYSSES   The great Achilles, whom opinion
    crowns
The sinew and the forehand of our host,
Having his ear full of his airy fame,
Grows dainty of his worth, and in his tent   145
Lies mocking our designs. With him, Patroclus,
Upon a lazy bed, the livelong day
Breaks scurril° jests,
And with ridiculous and awkward action,
Which, slanderer, he imitation calls,   150
He pageants° us. Sometime, great Agamemnon,
Thy topless deputation° he puts on,
And like a strutting player whose conceit°
Lies in his hamstring,° and doth think it rich
To hear the wooden dialogue and sound   155
'Twixt his stretched footing° and the scaffold-
    age,°
Such to-be-pitied and o'erwrested° seeming
He acts thy greatness in. And when he speaks,
'Tis like a chime a-mending,° with terms un-
    squared,°
Which, from the tongue of roaring Typhon°
    dropped,   160
Would seem hyperboles. At this fusty stuff,
The large Achilles, on his pressed bed lolling,
From his deep chest laughs out a loud applause,
Cries "Excellent! 'Tis Agamemnon just.°   164
Now play me Nestor, hem, and stroke thy beard,
As he being dressed° to some oration."
That's done, as near as the extremest ends
Of parallels, as like as Vulcan and his wife.°
Yet god Achilles still cries "Excellent!
'Tis Nestor right. Now play him me, Patroclus,
Arming to answer in a night alarm."   171
And then, forsooth, the faint defects of age
Must be the scene of mirth, to cough and spit
And, with a palsy fumbling on his gorget,°
Shake in and out the rivet. And at this sport   175

---

104. **Degrees in schools:** i.e., the three degrees in universities: Bachelor, Master, Doctor. 105. **dividable:** divided. 106. **primogenitive:** right of the firstborn. 107. **Prerogative:** privilege. 111. **mere oppugnancy:** utter conflict. **bounded:** confined. 114. **Strength . . . imbecility:** i.e., the strong young man should control his feeble father. 117. **jar:** conflict. 122. **seconded with:** supported by. 127–29. **And . . . climb:** This neglect of degree makes us go back when we seek to climb. 133–34. **grows . . . emulation:** becomes a feverish jealousy which makes our bravery (*emulation*) pale and bloodless. 138. **discovered:** revealed.

148. **scurril:** scurrilous. 151. **pageants:** mimics. 152. **topless deputation:** supreme authority. 153. **conceit:** intelligence. 154. **hamstring:** ridiculous posing; lit., the tendon behind the knee. 156. **stretched footing:** exaggerated stalking. **scaffoldage:** stage. 157. **o'erwrested:** overstrained. 159. **chime a-mending:** peal of bells out of tune. **unsquared:** inappropriate. 160. **Typhon:** a roaring monster buried beneath Mount Etna. 164. **just:** exactly. 166. **dressed:** about to begin. 168. **Vulcan . . . wife:** Vulcan was the blacksmith of the gods, unsuitably married to Venus. 174. **gorget:** armor for the throat.

Sir Valor dies, cries "Oh, enough, Patroclus,
Or give me ribs of steel! I shall split all
In pleasure of my spleen."° And in this fashion
All our abilities, gifts, natures, shapes,
Severals° and generals of grace exact, 180
Achievements, plots, orders, preventions,
Excitements to the field or speech for truce,
Success or loss, what is or is not, serves
As stuff for these two to make paradoxes.°

NESTOR And in the imitation of these twain, 185
Who, as Ulysses says, opinion crowns
With an imperial voice,° many are infect.
Ajax is grown self-willed, and bears his head
In such a rein, in full as proud a place
As broad Achilles; keeps his tent like him; 190
Makes factious feasts; rails on our state of war
Bold as an oracle; and sets Thersites,
A slave whose gall coins slanders like a mint,
To match us in comparisons with dirt,
To weaken and discredit our exposure, 195
How rank soever rounded in with danger.°

ULYSSES They tax° our policy and call it cowardice,
Count wisdom as no member of the war,
Forestall prescience,° and esteem no act
But that of hand. The still and mental parts 200
That do contrive how many hands shall strike
When fitness calls them on, and know by measure
Of their observant toil the enemies' weight—
Why, this hath not a finger's dignity. 204
They call this bed work,° mappery,° closet war.
So that the ram° that batters down the wall,
For the great swing and rudeness of his poise,
They place before his hand that made the engine,
Or those that with the fineness of their souls
By reason guide his execution. 210

NESTOR Let this be granted, and Achilles' horse
Makes many Thetis' sons.° [Tucket.°]

AGAMEMNON What trumpet? Look, Menelaus.

MENELAUS From Troy.

[Enter AENEAS.]

AGAMEMNON What would you 'fore our tent? 215

AENEAS Is this great Agamemnon's tent, I pray
you?

AGAMEMNON Even this.

AENEAS May one that is a herald and a prince
Do a fair message to his kingly ears?

AGAMEMNON With surety stronger than Achilles'
arm 220
'Fore all the Greekish heads, which with one
voice
Call Agamemnon head and general.

AENEAS Fair leave and large security. How may
A stranger to those most imperial looks
Know them from eyes of other mortals? 225

AGAMEMNON How!

AENEAS Aye.
I ask that I might waken reverence,
And bid the cheek be ready with a blush
Modest as morning when she coldly eyes
The youthful Phoebus.° 230
Which is that god in office, guiding men?
Which is the high and mighty Agamemnon?

AGAMEMNON This Trojan scorns us, or the men of
Troy
Are ceremonious courtiers. 234

AENEAS Courtiers as free, as debonair, unarmed,
As bending° angels, that's their fame in peace.
But when they would seem soldiers, they have
galls,°
Good arms, strong joints, true swords, and,
Jove's accord,°
Nothing so full of heart. But peace, Aeneas,
Peace, Trojan, lay thy finger on thy lips! 240
The worthiness of praise distains° his worth
If that the praised himself bring the praise forth.
But what the repining enemy commends,
That breath fame blows, that praise, sole pure,
transcends.

AGAMEMNON Sir, you of Troy, call you yourself
Aeneas? 245

AENEAS Aye, Greek, that is my name.

AGAMEMNON What's your affair, I pray you?

AENEAS Sir, pardon, 'tis for Agamemnon's ears.

AGAMEMNON He hears naught privately that comes
from Troy.

AENEAS Nor I from Troy come not to whisper
him. 250
I bring a trumpet to awake his ear,

---

178. spleen: excessive laughter. 180. Severals: particular qualities. 184. paradoxes: absurdities. 186–87. opinion . . . voice: general opinion would wish to have commander. 195–96. exposure . . . danger: our exposure to danger however excessive. 197. tax: criticize. 199. Forestall prescience: condemn forethought. 205. bed work: armchair strategy. mappery: mere making of maps. 206. ram: battering-ram. 211–12. Achilles' . . . sons: Achilles' horse is worth many an Achilles (who was the son of Thetis). 212. s.d., Tucket: trumpet call.

230. Phoebus: the sun. 236. bending: adoring. 237. galls: bitterness. 238. Jove's accord: Jove is with them. 241. distains: sullies.

To set his sense on the attentive bent,°
And then to speak.

AGAMEMNON　　　　Speak frankly as the wind.
It is not Agamemnon's sleeping hour.
That thou shalt know, Trojan, he is awake,　　255
He tells thee so himself.

AENEAS　　　　　　Trumpet, blow loud,
Send thy brass voice through all these lazy tents,
And every Greek of mettle, let him know
What Troy means fairly shall be spoke aloud.
　　　　　　　　　　　　[*Trumpet sounds.*]
We have, great Agamemnon, here in Troy　　260
A prince called Hector—Priam is his father—
Who in this dull and long-continued truce
Is rusty grown. He bade me take a trumpet,
And to this purpose speak; Kings, princes, lords!
If there be one among the fair'st of Greece　　265
That holds his honor higher than his ease,
That seeks his praise more than he fears his peril,
That knows his valor and knows not his fear,
That loves his mistress more than in confession
With truant° vows to her own lips he loves,　　270
And dare avow° her beauty and her worth
In other arms than hers—to him this challenge.
Hector, in view of Trojans and of Greeks,
Shall make it good, or do his best to do it,
He hath a lady, wiser, fairer, truer,　　275
Than ever Greek did compass in his arms,
And will tomorrow with his trumpet call
Midway between your tents and walls of Troy,
To rouse a Grecian that is true in love.
If any come, Hector shall honor him.　　280
If none, he'll say in Troy, when he retires,
The Grecian dames are sunburnt° and not worth
The splinter of a lance. Even so much.

AGAMEMNON　　This shall be told our lovers, Lord
　　Aeneas.
If none of them have soul in such a kind,　　285
We left them all at home. But we are soldiers,
And may that soldier a mere recreant° prove
That means not, hath not, or is not in love!
If then one is, or hath, or means to be,　　289
That one meets Hector. If none else, I am he.

NESTOR　　Tell him of Nestor, one that was a man
When Hector's grandsire sucked. He is old now,
But if there be not in our Grecian host

One noble man that hath one spark of fire,
To answer for his love, tell him from me　　295
I'll hide my silver beard in a gold beaver,°
And in my vantbrace° put this withered brawn,
And meeting him will tell him that my lady
Was fairer than his grandam, and as chaste
As may be in the world. His youth in flood,°　　300
I'll prove this truth with my three drops of blood.

AENEAS　　Now heavens forbid such scarcity of
　　youth!

ULYSSES　　Amen.

AGAMEMNON　　Fair Lord Aeneas, let me touch your
　　hand.
To our pavilion shall I lead you, sir.　　305
Achilles shall have word of this intent,
So shall each lord of Greece, from tent to tent.
Yourself shall feast with us before you go,
And find the welcome of a noble foe.
　　　　　　[*Exeunt all but* ULYSSES *and* NESTOR.]

ULYSSES　　Nestor!　　310

NESTOR　　What says Ulysses?

ULYSSES　　I have a young conception° in my brain.
Be you my time to bring it to some shape.

NESTOR　　What is 't?

ULYSSES　　This 'tis:　　315
Blunt wedges rive hard knots. The seeded pride
That hath to this maturity blown up
In rank° Achilles must or° now be cropped,
Or, shedding,° breed a nursery of like evil,
To overbulk° us all.

NESTOR　　　　　　Well, and how?　　320

ULYSSES　　This challenge that the gallant Hector
　　sends,
However it is spread in general name,
Relates in purpose only to Achilles.

NESTOR　　The purpose is perspicuous even as sub-
　　stance,
Whose grossness little characters sum up.°　　325
And, in the publication, make no strain,
But that Achilles, were his brain as barren
As banks of Libya°—though Apollo knows,
'Tis dry enough—will, with great speed of judg-
　　ment—

---

252. **attentive bent:** lit., stretched taut to hear. 270. **truant:** runaway. 271. **avow:** declare. 282. **sunburnt:** i.e., mere country wenches. 287. **recreant:** traitor.

296. **beaver:** face piece of the helmet. 297. **vantbrace:** armor for the forearm. 300. **His . . . flood:** though his manhood be in its prime. 312. **young conception:** fresh idea. 318. **rank:** lit., overfull of blood, proud. **or:** either. 319. **shedding:** i.e., its seeds. 320. **overbulk:** overwhelm. 325. **grossness: . . . up:** size is made up of little figures. 328. **Libya:** the African desert.

Aye, with celerity—find Hector's purpose 330
Pointing to him.
ULYSSES   And wake him to the answer, think you?
NESTOR   Yes, 'tis most meet. Who may you else
oppose
That can from Hector bring his honor off,°
If not Achilles? Though 't be a sportful combat,
Yet in this trial much opinion° dwells,   336
For here the Trojans taste our dear'st repute
With their finest palate. And trust to me,
Ulysses,
Our imputation° shall be oddly poised°
In this wild action. For the success,   340
Although particular, shall give a scantling°
Of good or bad unto the general,°
And in such indexes, although small pricks°
To their subsequent volumes, there is seen
The baby figure of the giant mass   345
Of things to come at large. It is supposed
He that meets Hector issues from our choice.
And choice, being mutual act of all our souls,
Makes merit her election,° and doth boil
As 'twere from forth us all, a man distilled   350
Out of our virtues. Who miscarrying,
What heart from hence receives the conquering
part,
To steel a strong opinion to themselves?°
Which entertained, limbs are his instruments,
In no less working than are swords and bows 355
Directive by the limbs.
ULYSSES   Give pardon to my speech.
Therefore 'tis meet Achilles meet not Hector.
Let us, like merchants, show our foulest wares,
And think perchance they'll sell. If not,   360
The luster of the better yet to show
Shall show the better. Do not consent
That ever Hector and Achilles meet,
For both our honor and our shame in this
Are dogged with two strange followers.   365
NESTOR   I see them not with my old eyes. What are
they?
ULYSSES   What glory our Achilles shares from
Hector,
Were he not proud, we all should share with him.

But he already is too insolent,
And we were better parch in Afric sun   370
Than in the pride and salt° scorn of his eyes,
Should he 'scape Hector fair. If he were foiled,°
Why then we did our main opinion crush
In taint of our best man.° No, make a lottery,
And by device° let blockish° Ajax draw   375
The sort° to fight with Hector. Among ourselves
Give him allowance for the better man;
For that will physic° the great Myrmidon°
Who broils in loud applause, and make him fall°
His crest that prouder than blue Iris° bends. 380
If the dull brainless Ajax comes safe off,
We'll dress him up in voices.° If he fail,
Yet go we under our opinion still
That we have better men. But, hit or miss,
Our project's life this shape of sense assumes, 385
Ajax employed plucks down Achilles' plumes.
NESTOR   Ulysses,
Now I begin to relish thy advice,
And I will give a taste of it forthwith
To Agamemnon. Go we to him straight.   390
Two curs shall tame each other. Pride alone
Must tarre° the mastiffs on, as 'twere their bone.
[Exeunt.]

ACT II

SCENE I. *The Grecian camp.*

[*Enter* AJAX *and* THERSITES.]
AJAX   Thersites!
THERSITES   Agamemnon—how if he had boils—
full, all over, generally?
AJAX   Thersites!   4
THERSITES   And those boils did run?—Say so—did
not the general run then? Were not that a botchy
core?°
AJAX   Dog!
THERSITES   Then would come some matter from
him. I see none now.   10

---

334. bring . . . off: win honor. 336. opinion: reputation.
339. imputation: good fame. oddly poised: unevenly
balanced. 341. scantling: sample. 342. general: army as a
whole. 343. small pricks: mere dots. 349. Makes . . . election: chooses the best man. 351–53. Who . . . themselves:
if he fails, what an encouragement the winning side will
gain to strengthen (steel) their self-confidence (opinion).

371. salt: bitter. 372. foiled: defeated. 373–74. did . . . man:
lost our reputation (opinion) in the failure of our best man.
375. device: a trick. blockish: blockheaded. 376. sort: lot.
378. physic: give a dose to. Myrmidon: i.e., Achilles, who
was commander of the Myrmidons. 379. fall: lower. 380.
Iris: the rainbow. 382. dress . . . voices: congratulate him
loudly. 392. tarre: urge on to fight.
Act II, scene i. 6–7. botchy core: boil full of matter.

AJAX   Thou bitch wolf's son, canst thou not hear? Feel, then.   [*Strikes him.*]

THERSITES   The plague of Greece upon thee, thou mongrel beef-witted° lord!   14

AJAX   Speak then, thou vinewed'st° leaven, speak. I will beat thee into handsomeness.

THERSITES   I shall sooner rail thee into wit and holiness. But I think thy horse will sooner con° an oration than thou learn a prayer without book. Thou canst strike, canst thou? A red murrain° o' thy jade's° tricks!   21

AJAX   Toadstool, learn° me the proclamation.

THERSITES   Dost thou think I have no sense,° thou strikest me thus?

AJAX   The proclamation!   25

THERSITES   Thou art proclaimed a fool, I think.

AJAX   Do not, porpentine,° do not. My fingers itch.   28

THERSITES   I would thou didst itch from head to foot, and I had the scratching of thee. I would make thee the loathsomest scab in Greece. When thou art forth in the incursions,° thou strikest as slow as another.   33

AJAX   I say, the proclamation!

THERSITES   Thou grumblest and railest every hour on Achilles, and thou art as full of envy at his greatness as Cerberus° is at Proserpina's° beauty —aye, that thou barkest at him.

AJAX   Mistress Thersites!

THERSITES   Thou shouldst strike him.   40

AJAX   Cobloaf!°

THERSITES   He would pun° thee into shivers with his fist, as a sailor breaks a biscuit.

AJAX   [*Beating him*] You whoreson° cur!

THERSITES   Do, do.   45

AJAX   Thou stool° for a witch!

THERSITES   Aye, do, do, thou sodden-witted lord! Thou hast no more brain than I have in mine elbows, an assinego° may tutor thee. Thou scurvy-valiant ass! Thou art here but to thrash Trojans, and thou art bought and sold among those of any wit, like a barbarian slave. If thou use to beat me, I will begin at thy heel and

14. **beef-witted:** too much meat was believed to be bad for the wits. 15. **vinewed'st:** moldy. 18. **con:** learn by heart. 20. **murrain:** plague. 21. **jade:** bad-tempered horse. 22. **learn:** tell. 23. **sense:** feeling. 27. **porpentine:** porcupine. 32. **incursions:** raids. 37. **Cerberus:** the three-headed dog guarding the mouth of Hades. **Proserpina.** queen of the underworld. 41. **Cobloaf:** little loaf with a round head. 42. **pun:** pound. 44. **whoreson:** bastard. 46. **stool:** closestool, privy. 49. **assinego:** little ass.

tell what thou art by inches, thou thing of no bowels° thou!   55

AJAX   You dog!

THERSITES   You scurvy lord!

AJAX   [*Beating him*] You cur!

THERSITES   Mars his idiot!° Do, rudeness, do, camel, do, do.   60

[*Enter* ACHILLES *and* PATROCLUS.]

ACHILLES   Why, how now, Ajax! Wherefore do ye thus? How now, Thersites! What's the matter, man?

THERSITES   You see him there, do you?

ACHILLES   Aye. What's the matter?   65

THERSITES   Nay, look upon him.

ACHILLES   So I do. What's the matter?

THERSITES   Nay, but regard him well.

ACHILLES   Well! Why, so I do.

THERSITES   But yet you look not well upon him, for whosoever you take him to be, he is Ajax.   71

ACHILLES   I know that, fool.

THERESITES   Aye, but that fool knows not himself.

AJAX   Therefore I beat thee.   74

THERSITES   Lo, lo, lo, lo, what modicums of wit he utters! His evasions have ears thus long.° I have bobbed° his brain more than he has beat my bones. I will buy nine sparrows for a penny, and his pia mater° is not worth the ninth part of a sparrow. This lord, Achilles—Ajax, who wears his wit in his belly and his guts in his head—I'll tell you what I say of him.   82

ACHILLES   What?

THERSITES   I say, this Ajax——

[AJAX *offers to strike him.*]

ACHILLES   Nay, good Ajax.   85

THERSITES   Has not so much wit——

ACHILLES   Nay, I must hold you.

THERSITES   As will stop the eye of Helen's needle, for whom he comes to fight.

ACHILLES   Peace, fool!   90

THERSITES   I would have peace and quietness, but the fool will not. He there, that he. Look you there!

AJAX   O thou damned cur! I shall——

ACHILLES   Will you set your wit to a fool's?   95

THERSITES   No, I warrant you, for a fool's will shame it.

PATROCLUS   Good words, Thersites.

55. **bowels:** mercy. 59. **Mars . . . idiot:** the fool of the god of war. 76. **evasions . . . long:** i.e., his utterances are as long as an ass's ears. 77. **bobbed:** struck. 79. **pia mater:** brain.

ACHILLES   What's the quarrel?   99

AJAX   I bade the vile owl go learn me the tenor of the proclamation, and he rails upon me.

THERSITES   I serve thee not.

AJAX   Well, go to, go to.

THERSITES   I serve here voluntary.°   104

ACHILLES   Your last service was sufferance, 'twas not voluntary, no man is beaten voluntary. Ajax was here the voluntary, and you as under an impress.°   108

THERSITES   E'en so, a great deal of your wit too lies in your sinews, or else there be liars. Hector shall have a great catch if he knock out either of your brains. A' were as good crack a fusty nut with no kernel.

ACHILLES   What, with me too, Thersites?   114

THERSITES   There's Ulysses and old Nestor, whose wit was moldy ere your grandsires had nails on their toes, yoke you° like draft oxen, and make you plow up the wars.

ACHILLES   What? What?

THERSITES   Yes, good sooth. To, Achilles! To, Ajax! To!   121

AJAX   I shall cut out your tongue.

THERSITES   'Tis no matter, I shall speak as much as thou afterward.

PATROCLUS   No more words, Thersites, peace!

THERSITES   I will hold my peace when Achilles' brooch° bids me, shall I?   127

ACHILLES   There's for you, Patroclus.

THERSITES   I will see you hanged, like clotpoles,° ere I come any more to your tents. I will keep where there is wit stirring, and leave the faction of fools.   [*Exit.*]

PATROCLUS   A good riddance.

ACHILLES   Marry, this, sir, is proclaimed through all our host:
That Hector, by the fifth hour of the sun,   135
Will with a trumpet 'twixt our tents and Troy
Tomorrow morning call some knight to arms
That hath a stomach,° and such a one that dare
Maintain—I know not what. 'Tis trash. Farewell.

AJAX   Farewell. Who shall answer him?   140

ACHILLES   I know not. 'Tis put to lottery, otherwise

He knew his man.

AJAX   Oh, meaning you. I will go learn more of it.
[*Exeunt.*]

SCENE II. *Troy. A room in* PRIAM'*s palace.*

[*Enter* PRIAM, HECTOR, TROILUS, PARIS,
and HELENUS.]

PRIAM   After so many hours, lives, speeches spent,
Thus once again says Nestor from the Greeks:
"Deliver Helen, and all damage else,
As honor, loss of time, travail, expense,
Wounds, friends, and what else dear that is consumed   5
In hot digestion of this cormorant° war,
Shall be struck off." Hector, what say you to 't?

HECTOR   Though no man lesser fears the Greeks than I
As far as toucheth my particular,
Yet, dread Priam,   10
There is no lady of more softer bowels,
More spongy to suck in the sense of fear,
More ready to cry out "Who knows what follows?"
Than Hector is. The wound of peace is surety,
Surety secure. But modest doubt is called   15
The beacon of the wise, the tent° that searches
To the bottom of the worst.° Let Helen go.
Since the first sword was drawn about this question
Every tithe soul, 'mongst many thousand dismes,°
Hath been as dear as Helen—I mean, of ours.
If we have lost so many tenths of ours   21
To guard a thing not ours, nor worth to us,
Had it our name, the value of one ten,
What merit's in that reason which denies
The yielding of her up?

TROILUS   Fie, fie, my brother!   25
Weigh you the worth and honor of a king
So great as our dread father in a scale
Of common ounces? Will you with counters° sum°

Scene ii. **6. cormorant:** devouring. The cormorant is a rapacious sea bird. **14–17. wound . . . worst:** peace is wounded by self-confidence (*surety*), careless (*secure*) self-confidence; but a modest doubt of success is like a guiding light (*beacon*) to the wise, or a probe (*tent*) which cleans the wound to the bottom. **16. tent:** lit., a piece of lint used to probe and clean out a wound. **19. tithe . . . dismes:** both mean tenth; i.e., since Helen came one man in ten of many ten thousands. **28. counters:** used in calculating large sums. **sum:** reckon.

---

104. voluntary: as a volunteer. **107–08. as . . . impress:** forced to serve. **117. yoke you:** i.e., treat you two like beasts of burden. **127. brooch:** an ornament that he hangs about him; i.e., Patroclus. **129. clotpoles:** blockheads. **138. stomach:** i.e., for a fight.

The past proportion of his infinite?
And buckle in a waist most fathomless   30
With spans° and inches so diminutive
As fears and reasons? Fie, for godly shame!
HELENUS No marvel, though you bite so sharp at
   reasons,
   You are so empty of them. Should not our father
   Bear the great sway of his affairs with reasons,
   Because your speech hath none that tells him
   so?   36
TROILUS You are for dreams and slumbers,
   brother priest.
   You fur your gloves with reason.° Here are your
   reasons:
   You know an enemy intends you harm,
   You know a sword employed is perilous,   40
   And reason flies the object of all harm.
   Who marvels, then, when Helenus beholds
   A Grecian and his sword, if he do set
   The very wings of reason to his heels,
   And fly like chidden Mercury from Jove,   45
   Or like a star disorbed?° Nay, if we talk of
   reason,
   Let's shut our gates, and sleep. Manhood and
   honor
   Should have hare hearts, would they but fat their
   thoughts
   With this crammed reason. Reason and respect°
   Make livers° pale and lustihood deject.   50
HECTOR Brother, she is not worth what she doth
   cost
   The holding.
TROILUS   What's aught but as 'tis valued?
HECTOR But value dwells not in particular will.°
   It holds his estimate and dignity
   As well wherein 'tis precious of itself   55
   As in the prizer. 'Tis mad idolatry
   To make the service greater than the god.
   And the will dotes that is attributive
   To what infectiously itself affects,
   Without some image of the affected merit.°   60
TROILUS I take° today a wife, and my election°

Is led on in the conduct of my will,°
My will enkindled by mine eyes and ears,
Two traded° pilots 'twixt the dangerous shores
Of will and judgment. How may I avoid,   65
Although my will distaste what it elected,
The wife I chose? There can be no evasion
To blench° from this, and to stand firm by honor.
We turn not back the silks upon the merchant
When we have soiled them, nor the remainder
   viands   70
We do not throw in unrespective sieve°
Because we now are full. It was thought meet
Paris should do some vengeance on the Greeks.
Your breath of full consent bellied° his sails.
The seas and winds, old wranglers, took a
   truce,
And did him service. He touched the ports de-
   sired,   76
And for an old aunt whom the Greeks held
   captive
He brought a Grecian queen, whose youth and
   freshness
Wrinkles Apollo's° and makes stale the morning.
Why keep we her? The Grecians keep our aunt.
Is she worth keeping? Why, she is a pearl,   81
Whose price hath launched above a thousand
   ships,°
And turned crowned kings to merchants.
If you'll avouch 'twas wisdom Paris went—   84
As you must needs, for you all cried "Go, go"—
If you'll confess he brought home noble prize—
As you must needs, for you all clapped your
   hands
And cried "Inestimable!"—why do you now
The issue° of your proper° wisdoms rate,°
And do a deed that Fortune never did,°   90
Beggar the estimation° which you prized
Richer than sea and land? Oh, theft most base,
That we have stol'n what we do fear to keep!
But thieves unworthy of a thing so stol'n,
That in their country did them that disgrace,   95

---

31. spans: little calculations; lit., the distance between thumb and little finger in the outstretched hand; i.e., 9 inches. 38. fur . . . reason: line your gloves with reasons; i.e., cowardly arguments. 46. disorbed: shot out of its course. 49. respect: counting the consequences. 50. livers: The liver was regarded as the seat of courage. 53. particular will: individual desire. 58–60. And . . . merit: Desire is mad when it inclines to what will cause it harm without even the show of any advantage. 61. I take: suppose that I choose. election: choice.

62. will: desire, lust. 64. traded: experienced. 68. blench: start aside, refuse. 71. unrespective sieve: senseless garbage can. 74. bellied: blew out. 79. Wrinkles Apollo's: i.e., makes the god Apollo look wrinkled. 82. Whose . . . ships: a deliberate echo of Faustus' famous address to Helen in Marlowe's Dr. Faustus: "Was this the face that launched a thousand ships?" 89. issue: result. proper: own. rate: estimate the value of. 90. And . . . did: i.e., show yourselves more fickle even than Fortune. 91. Beggar . . . estimation: make worthless the thing of value.

We fear to warrant in our native place!°
CASSANDRA [*Within*] Cry, Trojans, cry!
PRIAM   What noise? What shriek is this?
TROILUS 'Tis our mad sister, I do know her voice.
CASSANDRA [*Within*] Cry, Trojans!   100
HECTOR It is Cassandra.
[*Enter* CASSANDRA, *raving, with her hair about her
ears.*]
CASSANDRA Cry, Trojans, cry! Lend me ten
    thousand eyes,
And I will fill them with prophetic tears.
HECTOR Peace, sister, peace!
CASSANDRA Virgins and boys, mid-age and
    wrinkled eld,°   105
Soft infancy, that nothing canst but cry,
Add to my clamors! Let us pay betimes
A moiety° of that mass of moan to come.
Cry, Trojans, cry! Practice your eyes with tears!
Troy must not be, nor goodly Ilion° stand,   110
Our firebrand brother, Paris, burns us all.
Cry, Trojans, cry! A Helen and a woe.
Cry, cry! Troy burns, or else let Helen go. [*Exit.*]
HECTOR Now, youthful Troilus, do not these high
    strains
Of divination in our sister work   115
Some touches of remorse?° Or is your blood
So madly hot that no discourse of reason,
Nor fear of bad success in a bad cause,
Can qualify° the same?
TROILUS   Why, Brother Hector,
We may not think the justness of each act   120
Such and no other than event° doth form it,
Nor once deject the courage of our minds,
Because Cassandra's mad. Her brainsick raptures
Cannot distaste° the goodness of a quarrel
Which hath our several honors all engaged   125
To make it gracious. For my private part,
I am no more touched than all Priam's sons.
And Jove forbid there should be done amongst us
Such things as might offend the weakest spleen°
To fight for and maintain!   130
PARIS Else might the world convince° of levity

As well my undertakings as your counsels.
But I attest° the gods your full consent
Gave wings to my propension,° and cut off
All fears attending on so dire a project.   135
For what, alas, can these my single arms?
What propugnation° is in one man's valor,
To stand the push and enmity of those
This quarrel would excite? Yet I protest
Were I alone to pass the difficulties,   140
And had as ample power as I have will,
Paris should ne'er retract what he hath done,
Nor faint in the pursuit.
PRIAM   Paris, you speak
Like one besotted on your sweet delights.
You have the honey still, but these the gall, 145
So to be valiant is no praise at all.
PARIS Sir, I propose not merely to myself
The pleasures such a beauty brings with it,
But I would have the soil of her fair rape
Wiped off in honorable keeping her.   150
What treason were it to the ransacked queen,
Disgrace to your great worths, and shame to me,
Now to deliver her possession up
On terms of base compulsion! Can it be
That so degenerate a strain as this   155
Should once set footing in your generous°
    bosoms?
There's not the meanest spirit on our party
Without a heart to dare, or sword to draw,
When Helen is defended, nor none so noble
Whose life were ill bestowed, or death unfamed,
Where Helen is the subject. Then, I say,   161
Well may we fight for her, whom, we know well,
The world's large spaces cannot parallel.
HECTOR Paris and Troilus, you have both said
    well,
And on the cause and question now in hand 165
Have glozed,° but superficially, not much
Unlike young men, whom Aristotle° thought
Unfit to hear moral philosophy.
The reasons you allege do more conduce
To the hot passion of distempered° blood   170
Than to make up a free determination
'Twixt right and wrong; for pleasure and
    revenge

92–96. Oh . . . place: We are like thieves who have stolen
something too good for us, which disgraces us in our own
country; we are afraid to admit the worth of (*fear to
warrant*) Helen in Troy; i.e., you were all enthusiastic when
Paris brought Helen back to Troy, but now you basely
pretend that she is not worth keeping. 105. eld: old age.
108. moiety: part. 110. Ilion: Ilium, the citadel of Troy.
116. remorse: pity. 119. qualify: moderate. 121. event:
consequences. 124. distaste: give a bad taste to. 129. spleen:
temper. 131. convince: convict.

133. attest: call to witness. 134. propension: inclination.
137. propugnation: defense. 156. generous: noble. 166.
glozed: commented. 167. Aristotle: the Greek philosopher
who died in 322 B.C.—about ten centuries after the siege of
Troy. 170. distempered: drunken.

Have ears more deaf than adders to the voice
Of any true decision. Nature craves
All dues be rendered to their owners. Now, 175
What nearer debt in all humanity
Than wife is to the husband? If this law
Of nature be corrupted through affection,°
And that great minds, of partial indulgence
To their benumbèd wills, resist the same, 180
There is a law in each well-ordered nation
To curb those raging appetites that are
Most disobedient and refractory.
If Helen then be wife to Sparta's king,
As it is known she is, these moral laws 185
Of nature and of nations speak aloud
To have her back returned. Thus to persist
In doing wrong extenuates not wrong,
But makes it much more heavy. Hector's opinion
Is this in way of truth. Yet ne'ertheless, 190
My spritely brethren, I propend° to you
In resolution to keep Helen still,
For 'tis a cause that hath no mean dependence
Upon° our joint and several dignities.
TROILUS Why, there you touched the life of our
  design. 195
Were it not glory that we more affected
Than the performance of our heaving spleens,
I would not wish a drop of Trojan blood
Spent more in her defense. But, worthy Hector,
She is a theme of honor and renown, 200
A spur to valiant and magnanimous deeds
Whose present courage may beat down our foes,
And fame in time to come canónize° us.
For I presume brave Hector would not lose
So rich advantage of a promised glory 205
As smiles upon the forehead of this action
For the wide world's revenue.
HECTOR   I am yours,
You valiant offspring of great Priamus.
I have a roisting° challenge sent amongst
The dull and factious nobles of the Greeks 210
Will strike amazement to their drowsy spirits.
I was advértised° their great general slept
Whilst emulation° in the army crept.
This, I presume, will wake him.   [Exeunt.]

SCENE III. *The Grecian camp. Before the tent of*
ACHILLES.

[*Enter* THERSITES, *solus.*]

THERSITES How now, Thersites! What, lost in the
labyrinth of thy fury! Shall the elephant Ajax
carry it thus? He beats me, and I rail at him, oh,
worthy satisfaction! Would it were otherwise—
that I could beat him whilst he railed at me.
'Sfoot,° I'll learn to conjure and raise devils, but
I'll see some issue of my spiteful execrations.
Then there's Achilles, a rare enginer.° If Troy be
not taken till these two undermine it, the walls
will stand till they fall of themselves. O thou
great thunder-darter of Olympus, forget that
thou art Jove, the king of gods, and, Mercury,
lose all the serpentine craft of thy caduceus°
if ye take not that little little less than little
wit from them that they have! Which short-armed
ignorance itself knows is so abundant scarce it
will not in circumvention° deliver a fly from a
spider without drawing their massy irons and
cutting the web. After this, the vengeance on the
whole camp! Or rather the Neapolitan boneache,°
for that methinks is the curse dependent on those
that war for a placket.° I have said my prayers,
and devil Envy say amen. What ho! My Lord
Achilles!   24

[*Enter* PATROCLUS.]

PATROCLUS Who's there? Thersites! Good Thersites, come in and rail.   26

THERSITES If I could ha' remembered a gilt
counterfeit,° thou wouldst not have slipped out
of my contemplation. But it is no matter, thyself
upon thyself! The common curse of mankind,
folly and ignorance, be thine in great revenue!
Heaven bless thee° from a tutor, and discipline
come not near thee! Let thy blood be thy
direction° till thy death! Then if she that lays
thee out says thou art a fair corse, I'll be sworn
and sworn upon 't she never shrouded any but
lazars.° Amen. Where's Achilles?   37

PATROCLUS What, art thou devout? Wast thou in
prayer?

---

178. affection: lust. 191. propend: incline. 193–94. hath . . .
Upon: does not lightly concern. 203. canonize: set us in the
calendar of the heroes. 209. roisting: blustering. 212.
advertised: informed. 213. emulation: jealous rivalry.

Scene iii. 6. 'Sfoot: by God's foot. 8. enginer: engineer.
13. caduceus: Mercury's snake-entwined wand. 17. circum-
vention: cunning. 20. Neapolitan boneache: venereal
disease. 22. placket: opening in a petticoat; i.e., wench.
27–28. gilt counterfeit: false money, counter; called also a
slip. 31–32. bless thee: preserve you. 33–34. blood . . .
direction: desires lead you. 37. lazars: lepers.

THERSITES Aye, the heavens hear me!   40

PATROCLUS Amen.

    [*Enter* ACHILLES.]

ACHILLES Who's there?

PATROCLUS Thersites, my lord.

ACHILLES Where, where? Art thou come? Why, my cheese, my digestion, why hast thou not served thyself in to my table so many meals? Come, what's Agamemnon?   47

THERSITES Thy commander, Achilles. Then tell me, Patroclus, what's Achilles?

PATROCLUS Thy lord, Thersites. Then tell me, I pray thee, what's thyself?   51

THERSITES Thy knower, Patroclus. Then tell me, Patroclus, what art thou?

PATROCLUS Thou mayst tell that knowest.

ACHILLES Oh, tell, tell.   55

THERSITES I'll decline° the whole question. Agamemnon commands Achilles, Achilles is my lord, I am Patroclus' knower, and Patroclus is a fool.

PATROCLUS You rascal!

THERSITES Peace, fool! I have not done.   60

ACHILLES He is a privileged man. Proceed, Thersites.

THERSITES Agamemnon is a fool, Achilles is a fool, Thersites is a fool, and, as aforesaid, Patroclus is a fool.   65

ACHILLES Derive this, come.

THERSITES Agamemnon is a fool to offer to command Achilles, Achilles is a fool to be commanded of Agamemnon, Thersites is a fool to serve such a fool, and Patroclus is a fool positive.   71

PATROCLUS Why am I a fool?

THERSITES Make that demand of the prover. It suffices me thou art. Look you, who comes here?

ACHILLES Patroclus, I'll speak with nobody. Come in with me, Thersites.   [*Exit.*]

THERSITES Here is such patchery,° such juggling, and such knavery! All the argument is a cuckold and a whore, a good quarrel to draw emulous° factions and bleed to death upon. Now, the dry serpigo° on the subject!° And war and lechery confound all!   [*Exit*].

[*Enter* AGAMEMNON, ULYSSES, NESTOR, DIOMEDES, *and* AJAX.]

AGAMEMNON Where is Achilles?   83

PATROCLUS Within his tent, but ill-disposed, my lord.

AGAMEMNON Let it be known to him that we are here.   85

He shent° our messengers, and we lay by
Our appertainments,° visiting of him.
Let him be told so, lest perchance he think
We dare not move° the question of our place,°
Or know not what we are.   90

PATROCLUS   I shall say so to him. [*Exit.*]

ULYSSES We saw him at the opening of his tent.
He is not sick.

AJAX Yes, lion sick, sick of proud heart. You may call it melancholy, if you will favor the man, but, by my head, 'tis pride. But why, why? Let him show us the cause. A word, my lord.   96

    [*Takes* AGAMEMNON *aside.*]

NESTOR What moves Ajax thus to bay° at him?

ULYSSES Achilles hath inveigled his fool from him.

NESTOR Who, Thersites?

ULYSSES He.   100

NESTOR Then will Ajax lack matter, if he have lost his argument.°

ULYSSES No, you see he is his argument that has his argument, Achilles.   104

NESTOR All the better. Their fraction° is more our wish than their faction. But it was a strong composure° a fool could disunite.

ULYSSES The amity that wisdom knits not, folly may easily untie. [*Reenter* PATROCLUS.] Here comes Patroclus.   110

NESTOR No Achilles with him.

ULYSSES The elephant hath joints, but none for courtesy. His legs are legs for necessity, not for flexure.°   114

PATROCLUS Achilles bids me say he is much sorry
If anything more than your sport and pleasure
Did move your greatness and this noble state
To call upon him. He hopes it is no other
But for your health and your digestion sake,
An after-dinner's breath.°   120

AGAMEMNON   Hear you, Patroclus.
We are too well acquainted with these answers.
But his evasion, winged thus swift with scorn,

---

56. decline: go through. 77. patchery: pretense. 79. emulous: jealous. 80–81. dry serpigo: eruptions on the skin. 81. the subject: everyone.

86. shent: rebuked. 87. appertainments: privileges of rank. 89. We . . . move: we are afraid of asserting. place: i.e., as commander. 97. bay: bark. 102. argument: topic of conversation; i.e., Thersites. 105. fraction: division, quarrel. 106–07. composure: unity. 114. flexure: bending. It was once believed that the elephant had no leg joints. 120. breath: exercise.

Cannot outfly our apprehensions.°
Much attribute° he hath, and much the reason
Why we ascribe it to him. Yet all his virtues,   125
Not virtuously on his own part beheld,
Do in our eyes begin to lose their gloss—
Yea, like fair fruit in an unwholesome dish,
Are like to rot untasted. Go and tell him
We come to speak with him, and you shall not
    sin   130
If you do say we think him overproud
And underhonest; in self-assumption greater
Than in the note of judgment; and worthier than
    himself
Here tend° the savage strangeness he puts on,   134
Disguise the holy strength of their command,
And underwrite in an observing kind
His humorous predominance°—yea, watch
His pettish lunes,° his ebbs, his flows, as if
The passage and whole carriage of this action
Rode on his tide. Go tell him this, and add   140
That if he overhold his price so much,
We'll none of him, but let him, like an engine°
Not portable,° lie under this report:
"Bring action hither, this cannot go to war.
A stirring dwarf we do allowance give   145
Before a sleeping giant." Tell him so.
PATROCLUS   I shall, and bring his answer pre-
    sently.°   [*Exit.*]
AGAMEMNON   In second voice we'll not be satisfied,
We come to speak with him. Ulysses, enter
    you.   [*Exit* ULYSSES.]
AJAX   What is he more than another?   150
AGAMEMNON   No more than what he thinks he is.
AJAX   Is he so much? Do you not think he thinks
himself a better man than I am?
AGAMEMNON   No question.   154
AJAX   Will you subscribe° his thought and say he
is?
AGAMEMNON   No, noble Ajax. You are as strong,
as valiant, as wise, no less noble, much more
gentle, and altogether more tractable.   159
AJAX   Why should a man be proud? How doth
pride grow? I know not what pride is.
AGAMEMNON   Your mind is the clearer, Ajax, and

your virtues the fairer. He that is proud eats up
himself. Pride is his own glass, his own trumpet,
his own chronicle, and whatever praises itself
but in the deed devours the deed in the praise.
AJAX   I do hate a proud man as I hate the engen-
dering of toads.
NESTOR   [*Aside*] Yet he loves himself. Is 't not
strange?   170
              [*Reenter* ULYSSES.]
ULYSSES   Achilles will not to the field tomorrow.
AGAMEMNON   What's his excuse?
ULYSSES   He doth rely on none,
But carries on the stream of his dispose
Without observance or respect of any,
In will peculiar and in self-admission.°   175
AGAMEMNON   Why will he not, upon our fair
    request,
Untent his person, and share the air with us?
ULYSSES   Things small as nothing, for request's
    sake only°
He makes important. Possessed he is with
    greatness,
And speaks not to himself but with a pride   180
That quarrels at self-breath. Imagined worth
Holds in his blood such swoln and hot discourse
That 'twixt his mental and his active parts
Kingdomed° Achilles in commotion rages   184
And batters down himself. What should I say?
He is so plaguy proud that the death tokens° of it
Cry "No recovery."
AGAMEMNON   Let Ajax go to him.
Dear lord, go you and greet him in his tent.
'Tis said he holds you well, and will be led
At your request a little from himself.   190
ULYSSES   O Agamemnon, let it not be so!
We'll consecrate the steps that Ajax makes
When they go from Achilles. Shall the proud
    lord
That bastes his arrogance with his own seam,°
And never suffers matter of the world   195
Enter his thoughts, save such as do revolve
And ruminate himself, shall he be worshiped
Of that we hold an idol more than he?°
No, this thrice worthy and right valiant lord

---

123. outfly . . . apprehensions: outdistance our understanding. 124. attribute: honor. 134. tend: wait upon. 136–37.
underwrite . . . predominance: submit to but observe his
moody superiority. 138. lunes: freaks. 142. engine: military
machine, battering-ram. 143. Not portable: too heavy to be
moved. 147. presently: immediately. 155. subscribe: agree
with.

175. self-admission: admitting only his own judgment. 178.
for . . . only: only because they are asked for. 184. King-
domed: like a kingdom. 186. death tokens: plague spots
indicating that the disease has taken a fatal turn. 194. seam:
grease. 198. Of . . . he: a man whom we regard as more
worshipful than he.

Must not so stale his palm,° noble acquired, 200
Nor, by my will, assubjugate° his merit,
As amply titled as Achilles is,
By going to Achilles.
That were to enlard his fat-already pride, 204
And add more coals to Cancer when he burns
With entertaining great Hyperion.°
This lord go to him! Jupiter forbid,
And say in thunder "Achilles go to him."

NESTOR   [Aside] Oh, this is well. He rubs the vein
of him.°

DIOMEDES   [Aside] And how his silence drinks up
this applause!   210

AJAX   If I go to him, with my armèd fist
I'll pash° him o'er the face.

AGAMEMNON   Oh, no, you shall not go.

AJAX   An a' be proud with me, I'll pheeze° his
pride.
Let me go to him.   215

ULYSSES   Not for the worth that hangs upon our
quarrel.

AJAX   A paltry, insolent fellow!

NESTOR   [Aside] How he describes himself!

AJAX   Can he not be sociable?

ULYSSES   [Aside] The raven chides blackness. 220

AJAX   I'll let his humors blood.°

AGAMEMNON   [Aside] He will be the physician that
should be the patient.

AJAX   An all men were o' my mind——

ULYSSES   [Aside] Wit would be out of fashion. 225

AJAX   A'° should not bear it so, a' should eat
swords first. Shall pride carry it?

NESTOR   [Aside] An 'twould, you 'd carry half.

ULYSSES   [Aside] A' would have ten shares.

AJAX   I will knead him, I'll make him supple. 230

NESTOR   [Aside] He's not yet through° warm.
Force° him with praises. Pour in, pour in, his
ambition is dry.

ULYSSES   [To AGAMEMNON] My lord, you feed too
much on this dislike.

NESTOR   Our noble general, do not do so.   235

DIOMEDES   You must prepare to fight without
Achilles.

ULYSSES   Why, 'tis this naming of him does him
harm.
Here is a man—but 'tis before his face,
I will be silent.

NESTOR   Wherefore should you so?
He is not emulous,° as Achilles is.   240

ULYSSES   Know the whole world, he is as valiant.

AJAX   A whoreson dog, that shall palter thus with
us!
Would he were a Trojan!

NESTOR   What a vice were it in Ajax now——

ULYSSES   If he were proud——   245

DIOMEDES   Or covetous of praise——

ULYSSES   Aye, or surly borne——

DIOMEDES   Or strange,° or self-affected!°

ULYSSES   Thank the heavens, lord, thou art of
sweet composure.   249
Praise him that got° thee, she that gave thee suck.
Famed be thy tutor, and thy parts of nature
Thrice-famed beyond, beyond all erudition.°
But he that disciplined thine arms to fight,
Let Mars divide eternity in twain
And give him half. And for thy vigor,   255
Bull-bearing Milo° his addition yield°
To sinewy Ajax. I will not praise thy wisdom,
Which, like a bourn,° a pale,° a shore, confines
Tny spacious and dilated° parts. Here's Nestor,
Instructed by the antiquary times,   260
He must, he is, he cannot but be wise.
But pardon, Father Nestor, were your days
As green° as Ajax', and your brain so tempered,
You should not have the eminence of him,
But be as Ajax.

AJAX   Shall I call you father?   265

NESTOR   Aye, my good son.

DIOMEDES   Be ruled by him, Lord Ajax.

ULYSSES   There is no tarrying here. The hart
Achilles
Keeps thicket. Please it our great general
To call together all his state of war.°
Fresh kings are come to Troy. Tomorrow   270
We must with all our main of° power stand fast.
And here's a lord, come knights from east to
west,

---

200. stale . . . palm: make his glory cheap. 201. assubjugate: lower. 205–06. add . . . Hyperion: make summer hotter: The sun (Hyperion) enters the sign of Cancer in June. 209. rubs . . . him: flatters his disposition. 213. pash: smash. 214. pheeze: do for. 221. I'll . . . blood: I'll bleed his moodiness. Bleeding was a recognized remedy for many complaints. 226. A': he. 231. through: thoroughly. 232. Force: stuff.

240. emulous: envious. 248. strange: standoffish, haughty. self-affected: conceited. 250. got: begot. 252. erudition: learning. 256. Milo: a prodigiously strong Greek athlete. addition yield: give up his claims to fame. 258. bourn: boundary. pale: fence. 259. dilated: spread far and wide. 263. green: young. 269. state of war: chief commanders. 271. main of: full.

And cull their flower,° Ajax shall cope the best.

AGAMEMNON Go we to council. Let Achilles sleep.
Light boats sail swift, though greater hulks draw deep.   [*Exeunt.*]

ACT III

SCENE I. *Troy. A room in* PRIAM's *palace.*

[*Enter* PANDARUS *and a* SERVANT.]

PANDARUS Friend you, pray you, a word. Do you not follow° the young Lord Paris?

SERVANT Aye, sir, when he goes before me.

PANDARUS You depend upon him, I mean?

SERVANT Sir, I do depend upon the Lord.   5

PANDARUS You depend upon a noble gentleman. I must needs praise him.

SERVANT The Lord be praised!

PANDARUS You know me, do you not?

SERVANT Faith, sir, superficially.   10

PANDARUS Friend, know me better. I am the Lord Pandarus.

SERVANT I hope I shall know your honor better.

PANDARUS I do desire it.

SERVANT You are in the state of grace.°   15

PANDARUS Grace! Not so, friend. Honor and lordship are my titles.° [*Music within.*] What music is this?

SERVANT I do but partly know, sir. It is music in parts.°   20

PANDARUS Know you the musicians?

SERVANT Wholly, sir.

PANDARUS Who play they to?

SERVANT To the hearers, sir.

PANDARUS At whose pleasure, friend?   25

SERVANT At mine, sir, and theirs that love music.

PANDARUS Command, I mean, friend.

SERVANT Who shall I command, sir?

PANDARUS Friend, we understand not one another. I am too courtly, and thou art too cunning.° At whose request do these men play?   31

SERVANT That's to 't, indeed, sir. Marry, sir, at the

request of Paris my lord, who is there in person; with him, the mortal Venus, the heartblood of beauty, love's invisible soul.   35

PANDARUS Who, my cousin Cressida?

SERVANT No, sir, Helen. Could not you find out that by her attributes?

PANDARUS It should seem, fellow, that thou hast not seen the Lady Cressida. I come to speak with Paris from the Prince Troilus. I will make a complimental assault° upon him, for my business seethes.°   43

SERVANT Sodden business! There's a stewed phrase indeed!   45

[*Enter* PARIS *and* HELEN, *attended.*]

PANDARUS Fair be to you, my lord, and to all this fair company! Fair desires, in all fair measure, fairly guide them! Especially to you, fair queen! Fair thoughts be your fair pillow!

HELEN Dear lord, you are full of fair words.   50

PANDARUS You speak your fair pleasure, sweet queen. Fair prince, here is good broken music.°

PARIS You have broke it, cousin. And, by my life, you shall make it whole again, you shall piece it out° with a piece of your performance. Nell, he is full of harmony.   56

PANDARUS Truly, lady, no.

HELEN O sir——

PANDARUS Rude,° in sooth, in good sooth,° very rude.   60

PARIS Well said, my lord! Well, you say so in fits.°

PANDARUS I have business to my lord, dear queen. My lord, will you vouchsafe me a word?

HELEN Nay, this shall not hedge us out. We'll hear you sing, certainly.   65

PANDARUS Well, sweet queen, you are pleasant with me. But, marry, thus, my lord. My dear lord, and most esteemed friend, your brother Troilus——   69

HELEN My Lord Pandarus, honey-sweet lord——

PANDARUS Go to, sweet queen, go to—commends himself most affectionately to you——

HELEN You shall not bob° us out of our melody. If you do, our melancholy upon your head!

PANDARUS Sweet queen, sweet queen, that's a sweet queen, i' faith.   76

---

273. cull . . . flower: i.e., take the pick of them. *Act III, scene i.* 2. follow: serve. 15. state of grace: highly favored. 16–17. Grace . . . titles: Pandarus, who is not used to the literal-mindedness of the servant, replies that *grace* (the courtesy title of a duke) is not appropriate—he is merely entitled to be called "your honor" or "your lordship." 19–20. music in parts: i.e., with several instruments. 30–31. cunning: clever.

41–42. make . . . assault: attack him with compliments. 43. seethes: is urgent; lit., boils. 52. broken music: music performed by different kinds of instruments. 54–50. piece it out: fill it up. 59. Rude: i.e., my voice is rough. sooth: truth. 61. in fits: in starts, with a pun on *fit* meaning the division of a song or tune. 73. bob: cheat.

HELEN And to make a sweet lady sad is a sour offense.

PANDARUS Nay, that shall not serve your turn, that shall it not, in truth, la. Nay, I care not for such words, no, no. And my lord, he desires you that if the king call for him at supper, you will make his excuse.   83

HELEN My Lord Pandarus——

PANDARUS What says my sweet queen, my very very sweet queen?   86

PARIS What exploit 's in hand? Where sups he tonight?

HELEN Nay, but, my lord——

PANDARUS What says my sweet queen? My cousin will fall out with you. You must not know where he sups.   92

PARIS I'll lay my life, with my disposer° Cressida.

PANDARUS No, no, no such matter, you are wide. Come, your disposer is sick.   95

PARIS Well, I'll make excuse.

PANDARUS Aye, good my lord. Why should you say Cressida? No, your poor disposer's sick.

PARIS I spy.

PANDARUS You spy! What do you spy? Come, give me an instrument. Now, sweet queen.   101

HELEN Why, this is kindly done.

PANDARUS My niece is horribly in love with a thing you have, sweet queen.

HELEN She shall have it, my lord, if it be not my lord Paris.   106

PANDARUS He! No, she'll none of him, they two are twain.°

HELEN Falling in, after falling out, may make them three.   110

PANDARUS Come, come, I'll hear no more of this. I'll sing you a song now.

HELEN Aye, aye, prithee now. By my troth, sweet lord, thou hast a fine forehead.

PANDARUS Aye, you may,° you may.   115

HELEN Let thy song be love. This love will undo us all. O Cupid, Cupid, Cupid!

PANDARUS Love! Aye, that it shall, i' faith.

PARIS Aye, good now, love, love, nothing but love.

PANDARUS In good troth, it begins so. [*Sings.*] 120
"Love, love, nothing but love, still more!
    For, oh, love's bow
    Shoots buck and doe.

The shafts confounds,
    Not that it wounds,   125
But tickles still the sore.°
These lovers cry 'Oh! oh!' they die.
    Yet that which seems the wound to kill,
    Doth turn oh! oh! to ha! ha! he!
    So dying love lives still.   130
Oh! oh! a while, but ha! ha! ha!
Oh! oh! groans out for ha! ha! ha!"
Heigh-ho!

HELEN In love, i' faith, to the very tip of the nose.

PARIS He eats nothing but doves, love, and that breeds hot blood, and hot blood begets hot thoughts, and hot thoughts beget hot deeds, and hot deeds is love.   138

PANDARUS Is this the generation° of love? Hot blood, hot thoughts, and hot deeds? Why, they are vipers. Is love a generation of vipers? Sweet lord, who's afield today?   142

PARIS Hector, Deiphobus, Helenus, Antenor, and all the gallantry of Troy. I would fain have armed today, but my Nell would not have it so. How chance my brother Troilus went not? 146

HELEN He hangs the lip at° something. You know all, Lord Pandarus.

PANDARUS Not I, honey-sweet queen. I long to hear how they sped today. You'll remember your brother's excuse?   151

PARIS To a hair.

PANDARUS Farewell, sweet queen.

HELEN Commend me to your niece.

PANDARUS I will, sweet queen.   [*Exit.*]
                                   [*A retreat sounded.*]

PARIS They're come from field. Let us to Priam's hall   156
To greet the warriors. Sweet Helen, I must woo you
To help unarm our Hector. His stubborn buckles,
With these your white enchanting fingers touched,
Shall more obey than to the edge of steel   160
Or force of Greekish sinews. You shall do more
Than all the island kings°—disarm great Hector.

HELEN 'Twill make us proud to be his servant, Paris.

---

93. disposer: either one disposed to merriment, gay friend, or controller. **108. twain:** separated. **115. you may:** i.e., jest at my expense. **126. sore:** lit., a buck in its fourth year, with a pun on *sore*, meaning hurt. **139. generation:** descent, breeding. **147. hangs . . . at:** is troubled by. **162. island kings:** kings of the Greek isles.

Yea, what he shall receive of us in duty
Gives us more palm° in beauty than we have—
Yea, overshines ourself.   166
PARIS   Sweet, above thought I love thee. [*Exeunt.*]

SCENE II. *An orchard to* PANDARUS' *house.*

[*Enter* PANDARUS *and* TROILUS' BOY, *meeting.*]
PANDARUS   How now! Where's thy master? At my
cousin Cressida's?
BOY   No, sir, he stays for you to conduct him
thither.
PANDARUS   Oh, here he comes. [*Enter* TROILUS.]
How now, how now!   6
TROILUS   Sirrah,° walk off.   [*Exit* BOY.]
PANDARUS   Have you seen my cousin?
TROILUS   No, Pandarus. I stalk about her door
Like a strange soul upon the Stygian° banks 10
Staying for waftage.° Oh, be thou my Charon,
And give me swift transportation to those fields
Where I may wallow in the lily beds
Proposed for the deserver! O gentle Pandarus,
From Cupid's shoulder pluck his painted wings,
And fly with me to Cressid!   16
PANDARUS   Walk here i' the orchard, I'll bring her
straight.   [*Exit.*]
TROILUS   I am giddy, expectation whirls me round.
The imaginary relish is so sweet   20
That it enchants my sense. What will it be
When that the watery palates taste indeed
Love's thrice repurèd° nectar? Death, I fear me,
Swounding° destruction, or some joy too fine,
Too subtle-potent, tuned too sharp in sweetness,
For the capacity of my ruder powers.   26
I fear it much, and I do fear besides
That I shall lose distinction in my joys,
As doth a battle when they charge on heaps
The enemy flying.   30
                [*Reenter* PANDARUS.]
PANDARUS   She's making her ready, she'll come
straight. You must be witty now. She does so
blush, and fetches her wind so short, as if she
were frayed with a sprite:° I'll fetch her. It is the
prettiest villain. She fetches her breath as short
as a new-ta'en sparrow.   [*Exit.*]

TROILUS   Even such a passion doth embrace my
bosom.   37
My heart beats thicker than a feverous pulse,
And all my powers do their bestowing lose,
Like vassalage° at unawares encountering   40
The eye of majesty.
            [*Reenter* PANDARUS *with* CRESSIDA.]
PANDARUS   Come, come, what need you blush?
Shame's a baby. Here she is now. Swear the
oaths now to her that you have sworn to me.
What, are you gone again? You must be watched
ere you be made tame, must you? Come your
ways, come your ways. An you draw backward,
we'll put you i' the fills.° Why do you not speak
to her? Come, draw this curtain° and let's see your
picture. Alas the day, how loath you are to
offend daylight! An 'twere dark, you'd close
sooner. So, so, rub on, and kiss the mistress.°
How now! A kiss in fee farm!° Build there,
carpenter, the air is sweet. Nay, you shall fight
your hearts out ere I part you. The falcon as the
tercel,° for all the ducks i' the river. Go to, go
to.   57
TROILUS   You have bereft me of all words, lady.
PANDARUS   Words pay no debts, give her deeds.
But she'll bereave you o' the deeds too if she call
your activity in question. What, billing again?
Here's "In witness whereof the parties interchangeably"°——Come in, come in. I'll go get
a fire.   [*Exit.*]
CRESSIDA   Will you walk in, my lord?   65
TROILUS   O Cressida, how often have I wished me
thus!
CRESSIDA   Wished, my lord?—The gods grant——
O my lord!   69
TROILUS   What should they grant? What makes
this pretty abruption?° What too curious dreg
espies my sweet lady in the fountain of our love?
CRESSIDA   More dregs than water, if my fears have
eyes.   74
TROILUS   Fears make devils of cherubins, they
never see truly.
CRESSIDA   Blind fear that seeing reason leads finds

---

165. palm: reward.
  Scene ii. 7. Sirrah: term of address used to an inferior.
10. Stygian: the river Styx, which surrounded the underworld and across which souls were transported by Charon
the ferryman. 11. waftage: passage. 23. repured: refined. 24.
Swounding: swooning. 34. frayed . . . sprite: frightened
by a ghost.

40. vassalage: servant. 48. fills: shafts (of a cart). 49.
curtain: veil. 52. rub . . . mistress: a metaphor from bowls.
rub on: roll on. *mistress*: the "jack." 53. fee farm: perpetual
possession. 56. tercel: male of a small species of hawk.
62–63. In . . . interchangeably: a legal phrase in agreements,
which continues "set to their hands and seals." 71. abruption: breaking off.

safer footing than blind reason stumbling without fear. To fear the worst oft cures the worse. 79

TROILUS Oh, let my lady apprehend no fear. In all Cupid's pageant there is presented no monster.

CRESSIDA Nor nothing monstrous neither? 82

TROILUS Nothing but our undertakings—when we vow to weep seas, live in fire, eat rocks, tame tigers, thinking it harder for our mistress to devise imposition enough than for us to undergo any difficulty imposed. This is the monstruosity in love, lady, that the will is infinite and the execution confined, that the desire is boundless and the act a slave to limit.° 90

CRESSIDA They say all lovers swear more performance than they are able, and yet reserve an ability that they never perform, vowing more than the perfection of ten, and discharging less than the tenth part of one. They that have the voice of lions and the act of hares, are they not monsters? 97

TROILUS Are there such? Such are not we. Praise us as we are tasted, allow us as we prove, our head shall go bare till merit crown it. No perfection in reversion° shall have a praise in present. We will not name desert° before his birth, and being born, his addition° shall be humble. Few words to fair faith. Troilus shall be such to Cressid as what envy can say worst shall be a mock for his truth, and what truth can speak truest, not truer than Troilus.° 107

CRESSIDA Will you walk in, my lord?

[*Reenter* PANDARUS.]

PANDARUS What, blushing still? Have you not done talking yet? 110

CRESSIDA Well, uncle, what folly I commit, I dedicate to you.

PANDARUS I thank you for that. If my lord get a boy of you, you'll give him me. Be true to my lord. If he flinch, chide me for it. 115

TROILUS You know now your hostages—your uncle's word and my firm faith.

PANDARUS Nay, I'll give my word for her too. Our kindred, though they be long ere they are wooed, they are constant being won. They are

90. slave to limit: only able to be performed to a limited degree. 101. in reversion: a legal phrase meaning property which will pass on the death of some other person; so "in the future." 102. desert: merit. 103. addition: title. 103–07. Few . . . Troilus: good faith needs few words. Troilus will be so true to Cressida that the worst that Envy can utter will be a mockery of the truth, and when Truth is speaking its truest, it will not be truer than Troilus.

burrs, I can tell you, they'll stick where they are thrown. 122

CRESSIDA Boldness comes to me now, and brings me heart.
 Prince Troilus, I have loved you night and day
 For many weary months. 125

TROILUS Why was my Cressid then so hard to win?

CRESSIDA Hard to seem won. But I was won, my lord,
 With the first glance that ever—pardon me,
 If I confess much, you will play the tyrant.
 I love you now, but not, till now, so much 130
 But I might master it. In faith, I lie.
 My thoughts were like unbridled° children, grown
 Too headstrong for their mother. See, we fools!
 Why have I blabbed? Who shall be true to us
 When we are so unsecret to ourselves? 135
 But though I loved you well, I wooed you not.
 And yet, good faith, I wished myself a man,
 Or that we women had men's privilege
 Of speaking first. Sweet, bid me hold my tongue,
 For in this rapture° I shall surely speak 140
 The thing I shall repent. See, see, your silence,
 Cunning in dumbness, from my weakness draws
 My very soul of counsel!° Stop my mouth.

TROILUS And shall, albeit sweet music issues thence.

PANDARUS Pretty, i' faith. 145

CRESSIDA My lord, I do beseech you pardon me,
 'Twas not my purpose thus to beg a kiss.
 I am ashamed. Oh heavens, what have I done?
 For this time will I take my leave, my lord.

TROILUS Your leave, sweet Cressid? 150

PANDARUS Leave! An you take leave till tomorrow morning——

CRESSIDA Pray you content you.

TROILUS What offends you, lady?

CRESSIDA Sir, mine own company. 155

TROILUS You cannot shun yourself.

CRESSIDA Let me go and try.
 I have a kind of self resides with you,
 But an unkind self that itself will leave
 To be another's fool. I would be gone. 160
 Where is my wit? I know not what I speak.

TROILUS Well know they what they speak that speak so wisely.

132. unbridled: uncontrolled. 140. rapture: ecstasy. 143. soul of counsel: secret of my heart.

CRESSIDA   Perchance, my lord, I show more craft
than love,
And fell so roundly° to a large° confession   164
To angle for your thoughts. But you are wise,
Or else you love not, for to be wise and love
Exceeds man's might, that dwells with gods
above.

TROILUS   Oh, that I thought it could be in a
woman—
As, if it can, I will presume in you—
To feed for aye her lamp and flames of love, 170
To keep her constancy in plight° and youth,
Outliving beauty's outward, with a mind
That doth renew swifter than blood decays!
Or that persuasion could but thus convince me
That my integrity and truth to you   175
Might be affronted with the match and weight°
Of such a winnowed purity in love.
How were I then uplifted! But alas!
I am as true as truth's simplicity,
And simpler than the infancy of truth.   180

CRESSIDA   In that I'll war with you.

TROILUS   Oh, virtuous fight
When right with right wars who shall be most
right!
True swains° in love shall in the world to come
Approve° their truths by Troilus. When their
rhymes,
Full of protest, of oath and big compare,   185
Want similes, truth tired with iteration°—
"As true as steel, as plantage to the moon,°
As sun to day, as turtle° to her mate,
As iron to adamant,° as earth to the center"—
Yet, after all comparisons of truth,   190
As truth's authentic author to be cited,
"As true as Troilus" shall crown up the verse
And sanctify the numbers.°

CRESSIDA   Prophet may you be!
If I be false, or swerve a hair from truth,
When time is old and hath forgot itself,   195
When waterdrops have worn the stones of Troy,
And blind oblivion swallowed cities up,
And mighty states characterless are grated°

To dusty nothing, yet let memory,
From false to false, among false maids in love,
Upbraid my falsehood! When they've said "as
false   201
As air, as water, wind, or sandy earth,
As fox to lamb, or wolf to heifer's calf,
Pard° to the hind, or stepdame to her son,"
"Yea," let them say, to stick the heart of false-
hood,   205
"As false as Cressid."

PANDARUS   Go to, a bargain made. Seal it, seal it,
I'll be the witness. Here I hold your hand, here
my cousin's. If ever you prove false one to another, since I have taken such pains to bring you
together, let all pitiful goers-between be called
to the world's end after my name—call them all
Pandars, let all constant men be Troiluses, all
false women Cressids, and all brokers-between
Pandars! Say "Amen."   215

TROILUS   Amen.

CRESSIDA   Amen.

PANDARUS   Amen. Whereupon I will show you a
chamber with a bed, which bed, because it shall
not speak of your pretty encounters, press it to
death. Away!   [Exeunt TROILUS and CRESSIDA.]
And Cupid grant all tongue-tied maidens here
Bed, chamber, Pandar to provide this gear!   223
[Exit.]

SCENE III. *The Grecian camp.*

[*Flourish. Enter* AGAMEMNON, ULYSSES, DIOMEDES,
NESTOR, AJAX, MENELAUS, *and* CALCHAS.]

CALCHAS   Now, princes, for the service I have done
you,
The advantage of the time prompts me aloud
To call for recompense. Appear it to your mind
That, through the sight I bear in things to love,
I have abandoned Troy, left my possession,   5
Incurred a traitor's name, exposed myself,
From certain and possessed conveniences,
To doubtful fortunes, sequestering° from me all
That time, acquaintance, custom, and condition
Made tame and most familiar to my nature,   10
And here, to do you service, am become
As new into the world, strange, unacquainted.
I do beseech you, as in way of taste,°
To give me now a little benefit

---

164. **roundly:** directly. **large:** full. **171. plight:** promise. **176.
affronted . . . weight:** met by equal truth. **183. swains:**
lovers. **184. Approve:** confirm. **186. iteration:** simile. **187.
plantage . . . moon:** as plants are true to the moon. It is still
a very general belief that the growth of plants is controlled
by the moon. **188. turtle:** dove. **189. adamant:** the hardest
steel. **193. numbers:** verses. **198. characterless . . . grated:**
are ground so small that not a letter remains.

204. **Pard:** panther.
Scene iii. **8. sequestering:** separating. **13. taste:** foretaste.

Out of those many registered in promise,   15
Which you say live to come in my behalf.

AGAMEMNON   What wouldst thou of us, Trojan?
Make demand.

CALCHAS   You have a Trojan prisoner called
Antenor,
Yesterday took. Troy holds him very dear.
Oft have you—often have you thanks there-
fore—   20
Desired my Cressid in right great exchange,
Whom Troy hath still° denied. But this Antenor
I know is such a wrest° in their affairs
That their negotiations all must slack
Wanting his manage, and they will almost   25
Give us a prince of blood, a son of Priam,
In change of him. Let him be sent, great princes,
And he shall buy my daughter, and her presence
Shall quite strike off° all service I have done
In most accepted pain.°   30

AGAMEMNON   Let Diomedes bear him,
And bring us Cressid hither. Calchas shall have
What he requests of us. Good Diomed,
Furnish you° fairly for this interchange.
Withal, bring word if Hector will tomorrow
Be answered in his challenge. Ajax is ready.   35

DIOMEDES   This shall I undertake, and 'tis a burden
Which I am proud to bear.

                    [*Exeunt* DIOMEDES *and* CALCHAS.]
[*Enter* ACHILLES *and* PATROCLUS, *before their tent.*]

ULYSSES   Achilles stands i' the entrance of his tent.
Please it° our general pass strangely by him,
As if he were forgot, and, princes all,   40
Lay negligent and loose regard° upon him.
I will come last. 'Tis like he'll question me
Why such unplausive° eyes are bent on him.
If so, I have derision medicinable
To use between your strangeness and his pride,
Which his own will shall have desire to drink.   46
It may do good. Pride hath no other glass
To show itself but pride, for supple knees
Feed arrogance and are the proud man's fees.

AGAMEMNON   We'll execute your purpose and put
on   50
A form of strangeness as we pass along.
So do each lord, and either greet him not

Or else disdainfully, which shall shake him more
Than if not looked on. I will lead the way.

ACHILLES   What, comes the general to speak with
me?   55
You know my mind, I'll fight no more 'gainst
Troy.

AGAMEMNON   What says Achilles? Would he aught
with us?

NESTOR   Would you, my lord, aught with the
general?

ACHILLES   No.

NESTOR   Nothing, my lord.   60

AGAMEMNON   The better.
                    [*Exeunt* AGAMEMNON *and* NESTOR.]

ACHILLES   Good day, good day.

MENELAUS   How do you? How do you?   [*Exit.*]

ACHILLES   What, does the cuckold scorn me?

AJAX   How now, Patroclus!   65

ACHILLES   Good morrow, Ajax.

AJAX   Ha?

ACHILLES   Good morrow.

AJAX   Aye, and good next day too.   [*Exit.*]

ACHILLES   What mean these fellows? Know they
not Achilles?   70

PATROCLUS   They pass by strangely. They were
used to bend,
To send their smiles before them to Achilles,
To come as humbly as they used to creep
To holy altars.

ACHILLES   What, am I poor of late?
'Tis certain greatness, once fall'n out with
fortune,   75
Must fall out with men too. What the declined is,
He shall as soon read in the eyes of others
As feel in his own fall. For men, like butterflies,
Show not their mealy° wings but to the summer,
And not a man, for being simply man,   80
Hath any honor but honor for those honors
That are without him, as place, riches, and favor,
Prizes of accident as oft as merit.
Which when they fall, as being slippery standers,
The love that leaned on them as slippery too,   85
Do one pluck down another and together
Die in the fall. But 'tis not so with me.
Fortune and I are friends. I do enjoy
At ample point° all that I did possess,
Save these men's looks, who do methinks find
out   90
Something not worth in me such rich beholding

---

22. **still:** always. 23. **wrest:** controlling instrument; lit., the key which tightens the pegs in a musical instrument. 29. **strike off:** pay for. 30. **accepted pain:** agreeable labor. 33. **Furnish you:** equip yourself. 39. **Please it:** let it please . . . to. 41. **regard:** look. 43. **unplausive:** disapproving.

79. **mealy:** powdery. 89. **At . . . point:** fully.

As they have often given. Here is Ulysses.
I'll interrupt his reading.
How now, Ulysses!

ULYSSES   Now, great Thetis' son!

ACHILLES   What are you reading?   95

ULYSSES   A strange fellow here
Writes me: "That man, how dearly ever parted,°
How much in having, or without or in,
Cannot make boast to have that which he hath,
Nor feels not what he owes,° but by reflection,
As when his virtues shining upon others   100
Heat them, and they retort that heat again
To the first giver."

ACHILLES   This is not strange, Ulysses.
The beauty that is borne here in the face
The bearer knows not, but commends itself
To others' eyes. Nor doth the eye itself,   105
That most pure spirit of sense, behold itself,
Not going from itself, but eye to eye opposed
Salutes each other with each other's form.
For speculation° turns not to itself
Till it hath traveled and is mirrored there   110
Where it may see itself. This is not strange at all.

ULYSSES   I do not strain at the position—°
It is familiar—but at the author's drift,
Who in his circumstance expressly proves
That no man is the lord of anything,   115
Though in and of him there be much consisting,
Till he communicate his parts to others.
Nor doth he of himself know them for aught
Till he behold them formed in the applause
Where they're extended,° who, like an arch,
    reverberates   120
The voice again, or like a gate of steel
Fronting the sun, receives and renders back
His figure and his heat. I was much rapt in° this,
And apprehended here immediately
The unknown Ajax.   125
Heavens, what a man is there! A very horse,
That has he knows not what. Nature, what things
    there are,
Most abject in regard and dear in use!°
What things again most dear in the esteem

And poor in worth! Now shall we see tomor-
    row—   130
An act that very chance doth throw upon him—
Ajax renowned. O heavens, what some men do
While some men leave to do!
How some men creep in skittish fortune's hall
Whiles others play the idiots in her eyes!   135
How one man eats into another's pride
While pride is fasting in his wantonness!
To see these Grecian lords! Why, even already
They clap the lubber° Ajax on the shoulder
As if his foot were on brave Hector's breast   140
And great Troy shrieking.

ACHILLES   I do believe it, for they passed by me
As misers do by beggars, neither gave to me
Good word nor look. What, are my deeds
    forgot?

ULYSSES   Time hath, my lord, a wallet at his back
Wherein he puts alms for oblivion,   146
A great-sized monster of ingratitudes.
Those scraps are good deeds past, which are
    devoured
As fast as they are made, forgot as soon
As done. Perseverance, dear my lord,   150
Keeps honor bright. To have done is to hang
Quite out of fashion, like a rusty mail
In monumental mockery.° Take the instant way,
For honor travels in a strait° so narrow,
Where one but goes abreast. Keep then the path,
For emulation° hath a thousand sons   156
That one by one pursue. If you give way,
Or hedge aside from the direct forthright,°
Like to an entered tide they all rush by
And leave you hindmost.   160
Or like a gallant horse fall'n in first rank,
Lie there for pavement to the abject rear,
O'errun and trampled on. Then what they do in
    present,
Though less than yours in past, must o'ertop
    yours.
For time is like a fashionable host   165
That slightly shakes his parting guest by the hand,
And with his arms outstretched, as he would fly,
Grasps in the comer. Welcome ever smiles,
And farewell goes out sighing. Oh, let not virtue
    seek

---

96. how . . . parted: however richly endowed. **99. owes:** owns. **109. speculation:** power of sight. It was thought that the eye shot out a beam (like a searchlight) which caused the object to be visible to the beholder. So in this image *speculation* cannot see itself until the beam has passed out and been reflected back. **112. position:** assertion. **120. extended:** bestowed. **123. rapt in:** taken by. **128. abject . . . use:** despised but invaluable.

139. lubber: lout. **152–53. rusty . . . mockery:** neglected suit of armor, which is a mocking memorial of the knight who once wore it. **154. strait:** path. **156. emulation:** jealousy. **158. forthright:** straightforward path.

Remuneration for the thing it was;   170
For beauty, wit,
High birth, vigor of bone, desert in service,
Love, friendship, charity, are subjects all
To envious and calumniating time.   174
One touch of nature makes the whole world kin,°
That all with one consent praise newborn gawds,°
Though they are made and molded of things past,
And give to dust that is a little gilt
More laud than gilt o'erdusted.
The present eye praises the present object.   180
Then marvel not, thou great and complete man,
That all the Greeks begin to worship Ajax,
Since things in motion sooner catch the eye
Than what not stirs. The cry went once on thee,
And still it might, and yet it may again,   185
If thou wouldst not entomb thyself alive
And case thy reputation in thy tent,
Whose glorious deeds, but in these fields of late,
Made emulous missions 'mongst the gods themselves,
And drave great Mars to faction.°   190

ACHILLES   Of this my privacy
I have strong reasons.

ULYSSES   But 'gainst your privacy
The reasons are more potent and heroical.
'Tis known, Achilles, that you are in love
With one of Priam's daughters.°

ACHILLES   Ha! Known?

ULYSSES   Is that a wonder?   195
The providence that's in a watchful state
Knows almost every grain of Plutus'° gold,
Finds bottom in the uncomprehensive° deeps,
Keeps place with thought, and almost like the gods
Does thoughts unveil in their dumb cradles.   200
There is a mystery, with whom relation
Durst never meddle,° in the soul of state,
Which hath an operation more divine
Than breath or pen can give expressure to.
All the commerce that you have had with Troy
As perfectly is ours as yours, my lord,   206
And better would it fit Achilles much

To throw down Hector than Polyxena.
But it must grieve young Pyrrhus° now at home
When fame shall in our islands sound her trump,   210
And all the Greekish girls shall tripping sing
"Great Hector's sister did Achilles win,
But our great Ajax bravely beat down him."
Farewell, my lord. I as your lover speak.
The fool slides o'er the ice that you should break.
                              [*Exit.*]

PATROCLUS   To this effect, Achilles, have I moved you.   216
A woman impudent and mannish grown
Is not more loathed than an effeminate man
In time of action. I stand condemned for this,
They think my little stomach° to the war   220
And your great love to me restrains you thus.
Sweet, rouse yourself, and the weak wanton Cupid
Shall from your neck unloose his amorous fold
And, like a dewdrop from the lion's mane,
Be shook to air.   225

ACHILLES   Shall Ajax fight with Hector?

PATROCLUS   Aye, and perhaps receive much honor by him.

ACHILLES   I see my reputation is at stake,
My fame is shrewdly gored.°

PATROCLUS   Oh, then beware.
Those wounds heal ill that men do give themselves.
Omission to do what is necessary   230
Seals a commission to a blank of danger,°
And danger, like an ague, subtly taints
Even then when we sit idly in the sun.

ACHILLES   Go call Thersites hither, sweet Patroclus.
I'll send the fool to Ajax, and desire him   235
To invite the Trojan lords after the combat
To see us here unarmed. I have a woman's longing,°
An appetite that I am sick withal,
To see great Hector in his weeds° of peace,
To talk with him, and to behold his visage,   240
Even to my full of view.
                    [*Enter* THERSITES.]
                    —A labor saved!

---

175. **One . . . kin:** One natural inclination (*touch*) unites everyone. 176. **gawds:** trifles. 189–90. **Made . . . faction:** caused the gods to grow jealous and take sides (*to faction*). In the *Iliad* each of the heroes was the favorite of one of the gods or goddesses, who were constantly squabbling. 194. **one . . . daughters:** i.e., Polyxena. 197. **Plutus:** god of wealth. 198. **uncomprehensive:** unplumbed. 201–02. **relation . . . meddle:** that which must never be pried into.

209. **Pyrrhus:** Achilles' son. 220. **stomach:** appetite. 228. **shrewdly gored:** grievously wounded. 231. **Seals . . . danger:** gives danger a blank check. 237. **woman's longing:** the unsatiable longing of a pregnant woman. 239. **weeds:** garments.

THERSITES   A wonder!

ACHILLES   What?

THERSITES   Ajax goes up and down the field asking for himself.   245

ACHILLES   How so?

THERSITES   He must fight singly tomorrow with Hector, and is so prophetically proud of a heroical cudgeling that he raves in saying nothing.

ACHILLES   How can that be?   250

THERSITES   Why, a' stalks up and down like a peacock—a stride and a stand. Ruminates like a hostess° that hath no arithmetic but her brain to set down her reckoning. Bites his lip with a politic regard,° as who should say "There were wit in this head, an 'twould out." And so there is, but it lies as coldly in him as fire in a flint, which will not show without knocking. The man's undone forever, for if Hector break not his neck i' the combat, he'll break 't himself in vainglory. He knows not me. I said, "Good morrow, Ajax," and he replies "Thanks, Agamemnon." What think you of this man, that takes me for the general? He's grown a very land fish,° languageless, a monster. A plague of opinion!° A man may wear it on both sides, like a leather jerkin.

ACHILLES   Thou must be my ambassador to him, Thersites.   268

THERSITES   Who, I? Why, he'll answer nobody, he professes not answering. Speaking is for beggars, he wears his tongue in 's arms. I will put on his presence.° Let Patroclus make demands to me, you shall see the pageant° of Ajax.   273

ACHILLES   To him Patroclus. Tell him I humbly desire the valiant Ajax to invite the most valorous Hector to come unarmed to my tent, and to procure safe-conduct for his person of the magnanimous and most illustrious six-or-seven-times-honored Captain General of the Grecian army, Agamemnon, et cetera. Do this.   280

PATROCLUS   Jove bless great Ajax!

THERSITES   Hum!

PATROCLUS   I come from the worthy Achilles——

THERSITES   Ha!

PATROCLUS   Who most humbly desires you to invite Hector to his tent——   286

THERSITES   Hum!

PATROCLUS   And to procure safe-conduct from Agamemnon.

THERSITES   Agamemnon?   290

PATROCLUS   Aye, my lord.

THERSITES   Ha!

PATROCLUS   What say you to 't?

THERSITES   God be wi' you, with all my heart.

PATROCLUS   Your answer, sir.   295

THERSITES   If tomorrow be a fair day, by eleven of the clock it will go one way or other. Howsoever, he shall pay for me ere he has me.

PATROCLUS   Your answer, sir.

THERSITES   Fare you well, with all my heart.   300

ACHILLES   Why, but he is not in this tune, is he?

THERSITES   No, but he's out o' tune thus. What music will be in him when Hector has knocked out his brains I know not, but I am sure none unless the fiddler Apollo get his sinews to make catlings° on.   306

ACHILLES   Come, thou shalt bear a letter to him straight.

THERSITES   Let me bear another to his horse, for that's the more capable° creature.   310

ACHILLES   My mind is troubled like a fountain stirred,
And I myself see not the bottom of it.
                    [Exeunt ACHILLES and PATROCLUS.]

THERSITES   Would the fountain of your mind were clear again, that I might water an ass at it! I had rather be a tick in a sheep than such a valiant ignorance.   [Exit.]

ACT IV

SCENE I. *Troy. A street.*

[*Enter, at one side,* AENEAS, *and* SERVANT *with a torch; at the other,* PARIS, DEIPHOBUS, ANTENOR, DIOMEDES, *and others, with torches.*]

PARIS   See, ho! Who is that there?

DEIPHOBUS   It is the lord Aeneas.

AENEAS   Is the prince there in person?
Had I so good occasion to lie long
As you, Prince Paris, nothing but heavenly business   5
Should rob my bedmate of my company.

DIOMEDES   That's my mind too. Good morrow, Lord Aeneas.

---

253. **hostess:** tavernkeeper. 254–55. **politic regard:** look of a politician. 264. **land fish:** freak of nature. 265. **opinion:** conceit. 271–72. **put . . . presence:** imitate his manner. 273. **pageant:** play.

306. **catlings:** catgut fiddle strings. 310. **capable:** intelligent.

PARIS A valiant Greek, Aeneas—take his hand—
Witness the process° of your speech, wherein
You told how Diomed a whole week by days 10
Did haunt you in the field.

AENEAS Health to you, valiant sir,
During all question° of the gentle truce.
But when I meet you armed, as black defiance
As heart can think or courage execute. 15

DIOMEDES The one and other Diomed embraces.
Our bloods are now in calm, and, so long, health.
But when contention and occasion° meet,
By Jove, I'll play the hunter for thy life
With all my force, pursuit, and policy.° 20

AENEAS And thou shalt hunt a lion that will fly
With his face backward. In humane gentleness,
Welcome to Troy! Now, by Anchises'° life,
Welcome indeed! By Venus' hand I swear
No man alive can love in such a sort 25
The thing he means to kill more excellently.

DIOMEDES We sympathize.° Jove, let Aeneas live,
If to my sword his fate be not the glory,
A thousand complete courses of the sun!
But in mine emulous honor, let him die, 30
With every joint a wound, and that tomorrow.

AENEAS We know each other well.

DIOMEDES We do, and long to know each other
worse.

PARIS This is the most despiteful° gentle greeting,
The noblest hateful love, that e'er I heard of. 35
What business, lord, so early?

AENEAS I was sent for to the king, but why I know
not.

PARIS His purpose meets you. 'Twas to bring this
Greek
To Calchas' house, and there to render° him,
For the enfreed Antenor, the fair Cressid. 40
Let's have your company, or, if you please,
Haste there before us. I constantly do think,
Or rather, call my thought a certain knowledge,
My brother Troilus lodges there tonight.
Rouse him and give him note of our approach,
With the whole quality° wherefore. I fear 46
We shall be much unwelcome.

AENEAS That I assure you.
Troilus had rather Troy were borne to Greece

Than Cressid borne from Troy.

PARIS There is no help,
The bitter disposition of the time 50
Will have it so. Oh, lord, we'll follow you.

AENEAS Good morrow, all. [Exit, with SERVANT.]

PARIS And tell me, noble Diomed, faith, tell me
true,
Even in the soul of sound good-fellowship,
Who, in your thoughts, deserves fair Helen best,
Myself or Menelaus?

DIOMEDES Both alike. 56
He merits well to have her that doth seek her
Not making any scruple of her soilure,°
With such a hell of pain and world of charge.°
And you as well to keep her that defend her 60
Not palating° the taste of her dishonor
With such a costly loss of wealth and friends.
He, like a puling cuckold, would drink up
The lees and dregs of a flat tamed piece.°
You, like a lecher, out of whorish loins 65
Are pleased to breed out your inheritors.°
Both merits poised, each weighs nor less nor
more,
But he as he, the heavier for a whore.°

PARIS You are too bitter to your countrywoman.

DIOMEDES She's bitter to her country. Hear me,
Paris. 70
For every false drop in her bawdy veins
A Grecian's life hath sunk; for every scruple°
Of her contaminated carrion weight
A Trojan hath been slain. Since she could speak,
She hath not given so many good words breath
As for her Greeks and Trojans suffered death. 76

PARIS Fair Diomed, you do as chapmen° do,
Dispraise the thing that you desire to buy.
But we in silence hold this virtue well,
We'll not commend what we intend to sell. 80
Here lies our way. [Exeunt.]

SCENE II. *Court of* PANDARUS' *house.*

[*Enter* TROILUS *and* CRESSIDA.]

TROILUS Dear, trouble not yourself. The morn is
cold.

Act IV, scene i. **9. process:** gist. **13. question:** converse.
18. occasion: opportunity. **20. policy:** cunning. **23. Anchises:**
father of Aeneas, whose mother was Venus. **27. sympathize:**
have the same feeling. **34. despiteful:** hateful. **39. render:**
restore. **46. quality:** nature of the business.

58. Not . . . soilure: regardless of her dishonor. **59. charge:**
expense. **61. palating:** relishing. **64. flat . . . piece:** woman
whose best has been enjoyed by others. **66. inheritors:**
children. **67–68. each . . . whore:** both weigh alike, but you
who have her are heavier for having a whore as wife. **72.
scruple:** smallest part. **77. chapmen:** haggling traders.

CRESSIDA   Then, sweet my lord, I'll call mine uncle down.

He shall unbolt the gates.

TROILUS   Trouble him not.

To bed, to bed. Sleep kill° those pretty eyes,
And give as soft attachment° to thy senses   5
As infants' empty of all thought!

CRESSIDA   Good morrow, then.

TROILUS   I prithee now, to bed.

CRESSIDA   Are you aweary of me?

TROILUS   O Cressida! But that the busy day,
Waked by the lark, hath roused the ribald crows,
And dreaming night will hide our joys no
longer,   10
I would not from thee.

CRESSIDA   Night hath been too brief.

TROILUS   Beshrew° the witch! With venomous
wights° she stays

As tediously as hell, but flies the grasps of love
With wings more momentary-swift than thought.
You will catch cold, and curse me.   15

CRESSIDA   Prithee tarry.

You men will never tarry.

O foolish Cressid! I might have still held off,
And then you would have tarried. Hark! There's
one up.

PANDARUS   [Within] What, 's all the doors open
here?

TROILUS   It is your uncle.   20

CRESSIDA   A pestilence on him! Now will he be
mocking.

I shall have such a life!

[Enter PANDARUS.]

PANDARUS   How now, how now! How go° maiden-
heads? Here, you maid! Where's my cousin
Cressid?   25

CRESSIDA   Go hang yourself, you naughty mocking
uncle!

You bring me to do—and then you flout me too.

PANDARUS   To do what? To do what? Let her say
what.

What have I brought you to do?

CRESSIDA   Come, come, beshrew your heart!
You'll ne'er be good,   30
Nor suffer others.

PANDARUS   Ha, ha! Alas, poor wretch! A poor
capocchia!° Hast not slept tonight? Would he

not, a naughty man, let it sleep? A bugbear take
him!   35

CRESSIDA   Did not I tell you? Would he were
knocked i' the head!   [One knocks.]

Who's that at door? Good uncle, go and see.

My lord, come you again into my chamber.

You smile and mock me, as if I meant naughtily.

TROILUS   Ha, ha!   40

CRESSIDA   Come, you are deceived, I think of no
such thing.   [Knocking.]

How earnestly they knock! Pray you come in.

I could not for half Troy have you seen here.

[Exeunt TROILUS and CRESSIDA.]

PANDARUS   Who's there? What's the matter? Will
you beat down the door? How now! What's the
matter?   46

[Enter AENEAS.]

AENEAS   Good morrow, lord, good morrow.

PANDARUS   Who's there? My Lord Aeneas! By my
troth, I knew you not. What news with you so
early?   50

AENEAS   Is not Prince Troilus here?

PANDARUS   Here! What should he do here?

AENEAS   Come, he is here, my lord, do not deny
him.

It doth import him much° to speak with me.

PANDARUS   Is he here, say you? 'Tis more than I
know, I'll be sworn. For my own part, I came in
late. What should he do here?   57

AENEAS   Who! Nay then, come, come, you'll do
him wrong ere you are ware. You'll be so true to
him to be false to him. Do not you know of him,
but yet go fetch him hither, go.   61

[Reenter TROILUS.]

TROILUS   How now! What's the matter?

AENEAS   My lord, I scarce have leisure to salute you,
My matter is so rash.° There is at hand
Paris your brother and Deiphobus,   65
The Grecian Diomed, and our Antenor
Delivered to us, and for him forthwith,
Ere the first sacrifice, within this hour,
We must give up to Diomedes' hand
The Lady Cressida.

TROILUS   Is it so concluded?   70

AENEAS   By Priam and the general state° of Troy.
They are at hand and ready to effect it.

TROILUS   How my achievements° mock me!

Scene ii.   **4. kill:** overcome. **5. attachment:** seizure. **12.
Beshrew:** curse. **wights:** men. **23. How go:** what's the price
of. **33. capocchia:** lit., knob of stick (used obscenely).

54. It . . . much: it is of great importance for him. **64.
rash:** urgent. **71. state:** assembly. **73. achievements:**
winnings, luck.

I will go meet them. And, my Lord Aeneas,
We met by chance, you did not find me here. 75
AENEAS Good, good, my lord. The secrets of
nature
Have not more gift in taciturnity.

[*Exeunt* TROILUS *and* AENEAS.]

PANDARUS Is 't possible? No sooner got but lost?
The devil take Antenor! The young prince will go
mad. A plague upon Antenor! I would they had
broke 's neck!   81

[*Reenter* CRESSIDA.]

CRESSIDA How now! What's the matter? Who was
here?
PANDARUS Ah, ah!
CRESSIDA Why sigh you so profoundly? Where's
my lord? Gone! Tell me, sweet uncle, what's the
matter?   87
PANDARUS Would I were as deep under the earth
as I am above!
CRESSIDA Oh, the gods! What's the matter?   90
PANDARUS Prithee get thee in. Would thou hadst
ne'er been born! I knew thou wouldst be his
death. Oh, poor gentleman! A plague upon
Antenor!
CRESSIDA Good uncle, I beseech you, on my knees
I beseech you, what's the matter?   96
PANDARUS Thou must be gone, wench, thou must
be gone, thou art changed° for Antenor. Thou
must to thy father, and be gone from Troilus.
'Twill be his death, 'twill be his bane,° he cannot
bear it.   101
CRESSIDA O you immortal gods! I will not go.
PANDARUS Thou must.
CRESSIDA I will not, uncle. I have forgot my
father,
I know no touch of consanguinity,°   105
No kin, no love, no blood, no soul, so near me
As the sweet Troilus. O you gods divine!
Make Cressid's name the very crown of falsehood
If ever she leave Troilus! Time, force, and death
Do to this body what extremes you can,   110
But the strong base and building of my love
Is as the very center of the earth,
Drawing all things to it. I'll go in and weep——
PANDARUS Do, do.
CRESSIDA Tear my bright hair and scratch my
praisèd cheeks,   115

Crack my clear voice with sobs, and break my
heart
With sounding Troilus. I will not go from Troy.

[*Exeunt.*]

SCENE III. *Before* PANDARUS' *house.*

[*Enter* PARIS, TROILUS, AENEAS, DEIPHOBUS,
ANTENOR, *and* DIOMEDES.]

PARIS It is great morning,° and the hour prefixed
For her delivery to this valiant Greek
Comes fast upon. Good my brother Troilus,
Tell you the lady what she is to do,
And haste her to the purpose.   5
TROILUS   Walk into her house,
I'll bring her to the Grecian presently.
And to his hand when I deliver her,
Think it an altar, and thy brother Troilus
A priest, there offering to it his own heart.

[*Exit.*]

PARIS I know what 'tis to love,   10
And would, as I shall pity, I could help!
Please you walk in, my lords.   [*Exeunt.*]

SCENE IV. *A room in* PANDARUS' *house.*

[*Enter* PANDARUS *and* CRESSIDA.]

PANDARUS Be moderate, be moderate.
CRESSIDA Why tell you me of moderation?
The grief is fine, full, perfect, that I taste,
And violenteth° in a sense as strong
As that which causeth it. How can I moderate it?
If I could temporize° with my affection,   6
Or brew it to a weak and colder palate,
The like allayment could I give my grief.
My love admits no qualifying dross,°
No more my grief, in such a precious loss.   10
PANDARUS Here, here, here he comes. [*Enter*
TROILUS.] Ah, sweet ducks!
CRESSIDA O Troilus! Troilus!   [*Embracing him.*]
PANDARUS What a pair of spectacles is here! Let
me embrace too. "O heart," as the goodly
saying is,   16
    "O heart, heavy heart,

---

98. **changed:** exchanged. 100. **bane:** destruction. 105. **con-**
sanguinity: blood relationship.

Scene iii. **1. great morning:** broad daylight.
Scene iv. **4. violenteth:** is violent. **6. temporize:** compromise. **9. qualifying dross:** alloy to make it less than pure
gold.

Why sigh'st thou without breaking?''
where he answers again,
  "Because thou canst not ease thy smart   20
    By friendship nor by speaking.''
There was never a truer rhyme. Let us cast away
nothing, for we may live to have need of such a
verse. We see it, we see it. How now, lambs!

TROILUS   Cressid, I love thee in so strained° a
    purity   25
  That the blest gods, as angry with my fancy,°
  More bright in zeal than the devotion which
  Cold lips blow to their deities, take thee from me.

CRESSIDA   Have the gods envy?   29

PANDARUS   Aye, aye, aye, aye, 'tis too plain a case.

CRESSIDA   And is it true that I must go from Troy?

TROILUS   A hateful truth.

CRESSIDA   What, and from Troilus too?

TROILUS   From Troy and Troilus.

CRESSIDA   Is it possible?

TROILUS   And suddenly, where injury of chance°
  Puts back leave-taking, justles roughly by   35
  All time of pause, rudely beguiles our lips
  Of all rejoindure,° forcibly prevents
  Our locked embrasures,° strangles our dear vows
  Even in the birth of our own laboring breath.
  We two, that with so many thousand sighs   40
  Did buy each other, must poorly sell ourselves
  With the rude brevity and discharge of one.
  Injurious time now with a robber's haste
  Crams his rich thievery° up, he knows not how.
  As many farewells as be stars in heaven,   45
  With distinct breath and consigned kisses to
    them,°
  He fumbles up into a loose adieu,
  And scants us with a single famished kiss
  Distasted° with the salt of broken tears.

AENEAS   [Within] My lord, is the lady ready?   50

TROILUS   Hark! You are called. Some say the
    Genius° so
  Cries "Come!" to him that instantly must die.
  Bid them have patience, she shall come anon.

PANDARUS   Where are my tears? Rain, to lay this
  wind, or my heart will be blown up by the root.
                                        [Exit.]

CRESSIDA   I must then to the Grecians?   56

TROILUS   No remedy.

CRESSIDA   A woeful Cressid 'mongst the merry
    Greeks!°
  When shall we see again?

TROILUS   Hear me, my love. Be thou but true of
    heart.

CRESSIDA   I true! How now! What wicked deem°
    is this?   60

TROILUS   Nay, we must use expostulation° kindly,
  For it is parting from us.°
  I speak not "Be thou true" as fearing thee,
  For I will throw my glove to° Death himself
  That there's no maculation° in thy heart.   65
  But "Be thou true" say I to fashion in
  My sequent protestation.° Be thou true,
  And I will see thee.

CRESSIDA   Oh, you shall be exposed, my lord, to
    dangers
  As infinite as imminent. But I'll be true.   70

TROILUS   And I'll grow friend with danger. Wear
    this sleeve.°

CRESSIDA   And you this glove. When shall I see
    you?

TROILUS   I will corrupt the Grecian sentinels,
  To give thee nightly visitation.
  But yet, be true.   75

CRESSIDA   Oh heavens! "Be true" again!

TROILUS   Hear why I speak it, love.
  The Grecian youths are full of quality,°
  They're loving, well composed with gifts of
    nature,
  And flowing o'er with arts and exercise.°
  How novelties may move and parts with person,°
  Alas, a kind of godly jealousy—   81
  Which, I beseech you, call a virtuous sin—
  Makes me afeard.

CRESSIDA   Oh heavens! You love me not.

TROILUS   Die I a villain, then!
  In this I do not call your faith in question,   85
  So mainly as my merit. I cannot sing,
  Nor heel the high lavolt,° nor sweeten talk,
  Nor play at subtle games—fair virtues all,

---

25. **strained:** i.e., of all impurities. **26. fancy:** love. **34. injury of chance:** the ill done us by Fortune. **37. rejoindure:** reunion. **38. embrasures:** embraces. **44. thievery:** plunder. **46. With . . . them:** each farewell with its own sigh and added kiss. **49. Distasted:** distasteful. **51. Genius:** guardian angel.

57. **merry Greeks:** See I.ii.119,n. **60. deem:** thought. **61. expostulation:** talk. **62. For . . . us:** for it is our last chance of talking. **64. throw . . . to:** challenge to combat. **65. maculation:** stain. **66–67. to . . . protestation:** to prepare for my vow which follows. **71. sleeve:** often richly embroidered and worn separately from the main garment. **77. quality:** natural gifts. **79. exercise:** skill. **80. parts . . . person:** accomplishments added to personal charm. **87. lavolt:** lavolta, a high stepping dance.

To which the Grecians are most prompt and
    pregnant,°
But I can tell that in each grace of these   90
There lurks a still and dumb-discoursive° devil
That tempts most cunningly. But be not tempted.

CRESSIDA   Do you think I will?

TROILUS   No.
But something may be done that we will not. 95
And sometimes we are devils to ourselves,
When we will tempt the frailty of our powers,
Presuming on their changeful potency.°

AENEAS   [Within] Nay, good my lord!

TROILUS   Come, kiss, and let us part.

PARIS   [Within] Brother Troilus!   100

TROILUS   Good brother, come you hither,
And bring Aeneas and the Grecian with you.

CRESSIDA   My lord, will you be true?

TROILUS   Who, I? Alas, it is my vice, my fault.
Whiles others fish with craft for great opinion,°
I with great truth catch mere simplicity.   105
Whilst some with cunning gild their copper
    crowns,°
With truth and plainness I do wear mine bare.
Fear not my truth. The moral of my wit
Is "plain and true," there's all the reach of it.
    [Enter AENEAS, PARIS, ANTENOR, DEIPHOBUS,
          and DIOMEDES.]
Welcome, Sir Diomed! Here is the lady   110
Which for Antenor we deliver you.
At the port,° lord, I'll give her to thy hand,
And by the way possess° thee what she is.
Entreat her fair, and by my soul, fair Greek,
If e'er thou stand at mercy of my sword,   115
Name Cressid and thy life shall be as safe
As Priam is in Ilion.

DIOMEDES   Fair Lady Cressid,
So please you, save the thanks this prince
    expects.
The luster in your eye, heaven in your cheek,
Pleads your fair usage, and to Diomed   120
You shall be mistress, and command him wholly.

TROILUS   Grecian, thou dost not use me court-
    eously,
To shame the zeal of my petition to thee
In praising her. I tell thee, lord of Greece,
She is as far high-soaring o'er thy praises   125

As thou unworthy to be called her servant.
I charge thee use her well, even for my charge,
For, by the dreadful Pluto,° if thou dost not,
Though the great bulk Achilles be thy guard,
I'll cut thy throat.   130

DIOMEDES   Oh, be not moved, Prince Troilus.
Let me be privileged by my place and message
To be a speaker free. When I am hence,
I'll answer to my lust.° And know you, lord,
I'll nothing do on charge.° To her own worth
She shall be prized, but that° you say "Be 't so,"
I'll speak it in my spirit and honor "No!"   136

TROILUS   Come, to the port. I'll tell thee, Diomed,
This brave° shall oft make thee to hide thy head.
Lady, give my your hand, and as we walk
To our own selves bend we our needful talk. 140
    [Exeunt TROILUS, CRESSIDA, and DIOMEDES.]
               [A trumpet sounds.]

PARIS   Hark! Hector's trumpet.

AENEAS   How have we spent this morning!
The prince must think me tardy and remiss,
That swore to ride before him to the field.

PARIS   'Tis Troilus' fault. Come, come, to field
    with him.

DEIPHOBUS   Let us make ready straight.   145

AENEAS   Yea, with a bridegroom's fresh alacrity,
Let us address° to tend on Hector's heels.
The glory of our Troy doth this day lie
On his fair worth and single chivalry.° [Exeunt.]

SCENE V. *The Grecian camp. Lists set out.°*

    [Enter AJAX, armed; AGAMEMNON, ACHILLES,
PATROCLUS, MENELAUS, ULYSSES, NESTOR, and others.]

AGAMEMNON   Here art thou in appointment° fresh
    and fair,
Anticipating time with starting courage.
Give with thy trumpet a loud note to Troy,
Thou dreadful Ajax, that the appallèd air
May pierce the head of the great combatant   5
And hale° him hither.

89. **pregnant:** apt. 91. **dumb-discoursive:** silently eloquent.
98. **changeful potency:** fickle power. 104. **opinion:** reputation. 106. **gild . . . crowns:** Copper gilt was the poorest
kind of imitation gold. 112. **port:** gate. 113. **possess:** tell.

128. **Pluto:** king of the underworld. 133. **to my lust:** as I
please. 134. **on charge:** because I am bidden. 135. **that:** if.
138. **brave:** boast. 147. **address:** make ready. 149. **chivalry:**
knightly combat.
    Scene v. **Lists . . . out:** place of combat prepared.
Shakespeare and his contemporaries, as well as earlier
writers, imagined the worthies of the Trojan war as medieval
knights, fighting in full armor, according to the rules of
chivalry. 1. **appointment:** equipment. 6. **hale:** draw, haul.
trumpet: trumpeter.

AJAX   Thou, trumpet,° there's my purse.
Now crack thy lungs, and split thy brazen pipe.
Blow, villain, till thy spherèd bias cheek°
Outswell the colic of puffed Aquilon.°
Come, stretch thy chest, and let thy eyes spout
blood.   10
Thou blow'st for Hector.   [*Trumpet sounds.*]
ULYSSES   No trumpet answers.
ACHILLES   'Tis but early days.
AGAMEMNON   Is not yond Diomed, with Calchas'
daughter?
ULYSSES   'Tis he, I ken° the manner of his gait,
He rises on the toe. That spirit of his   15
In aspiration lifts him from the earth.
[*Enter* DIOMEDES, *with* CRESSIDA.]
AGAMEMNON   Is this the lady Cressid?
DIOMEDES   Even she.
AGAMEMNON   Most dearly welcome to the Greeks,
sweet lady.
NESTOR   Our general doth salute you with a kiss.
ULYSSES   Yet is the kindness but particular,   20
'Twere better she were kissed in general.
NESTOR   And very courtly counsel. I'll begin.
So much for Nestor.
ACHILLES   I'll take that winter° from your lips, fair
lady.
Achilles bids you welcome.   25
MENELAUS   I had good argument for kissing once.
PATROCLUS   But that's no argument for kissing now,
For thus popped Paris in his hardiment,°
And parted thus you and your argument.
ULYSSES   O deadly gall, and theme of all our
scorns!   30
For which we lose our heads to gild his horns.°
PATROCLUS   The first was Menelaus' kiss, this,
mine.
Patroclus kisses you.
MENELAUS   Oh, this is trim!
PATROCLUS   Paris and I kiss evermore for him.
MENELAUS   I'll have my kiss, sir. Lady, by your
leave.   35
CRESSIDA   In kissing, do you render or receive?
PATROCLUS   Both take and give.
CRESSIDA   I'll make my match to live,
The kiss you take is better than you give,
Therefore no kiss.

MENELAUS   I'll give you boot,° I'll give you three
for one.   40
CRESSIDA   You're an odd man. Give even, or give
none.
MENELAUS   An odd man, lady! Every man is odd.
CRESSIDA   No, Paris is not, for you know 'tis true
That you are odd, and he is even with you.
MENELAUS   You fillip° me o' the head.   45
CRESSIDA   No, I'll be sworn.
ULYSSES   It were no match, your nail against his
horn.
May I, sweet lady, beg a kiss of you?
CRESSIDA   You may.
ULYSSES   I do desire it.
CRESSIDA   Why, beg, then.
ULYSSES   Why then, for Venus' sake, give me a kiss
When Helen is a maid again, and his.°   50
CRESSIDA   I am your debtor, claim it when 'tis due.
ULYSSES   Never's my day, and then a kiss of you.
DIOMEDES   Lady, a word. I'll bring you to your
father.   [*Exit with* CRESSIDA.]
NESTOR   A woman of quick sense.°   54
ULYSSES   Fie, fie upon her!
There's language in her eye, her cheek, her lip—
Nay, her foot speaks, her wanton spirits look out
At every joint and motive° of her body.
Oh, these encounterers, so glib of tongue,
That give accosting welcome ere it comes,
And wide unclasp° the tables° of their thoughts
To every ticklish° reader! Set them down   61
For sluttish spoils of opportunity,°
And daughters of the game.   [*Trumpet within.*]
ALL   The Trojans' trumpet.
AGAMEMNON   Yonder comes the troop.
[*Flourish. Enter* HECTOR, *armed;* AENEAS, TROILUS,
and other TROJANS, *with* ATTENDANTS.]
AENEAS   Hail, all the state of Greece! What shall
be done   65
To him that victory commands? Or do you
purpose
A victor shall be known?° Will you the knights
Shall to the edge of all extremity°
Pursue each other, or shall they be divided
By any voice or order of the field?   70
Hector bade ask.

---

8. sphered . . . cheek: cheek blown out like a bowl. 9.
Aquilon: northwest wind. 14. ken: know. 24. winter: i.e.,
old Nestor's cold kiss. 28. hardiment: boldness. 31. gild . . .
horns: i.e., to do honor to our cuckold Menelaus.

40. boot: advantage, extra payment. 45. fillip: flip. 50.
his: i.e., restored to Menelaus. 54. sense: feeling. 57.
motive: limb. 60. unclasp: open. tables: notebook. 61.
ticklish: lecherous. 62. sluttish . . . opportunity: sluts to be
picked up as desired. 67. A . . . known: i.e., a combat to a
decisive end. 68. edge . . . extremity: to the death.

AGAMEMNON   Which way would Hector have it?

AENEAS He cares not. He'll obey conditions.

ACHILLES 'Tis done like Hector, but securely°
done,
A little proudly, and great deal misprizing°
The knight opposed.

AENEAS   If not Achilles, sir,   75
What is your name?

ACHILLES   If not Achilles, nothing.

AENEAS Therefore Achilles. But whate'er, know
this.
In the extremity of great and little,
Valor and pride excel themselves in Hector,
The one almost as infinite as all,   80
The other blank as nothing. Weigh him well,
And that which looks like pride is courtesy.
This Ajax is half made of Hector's blood.°
In love whereof, half Hector stays at home;   84
Half heart, half hand, half Hector comes to seek
This blended knight, half Trojan and half Greek.

ACHILLES A maiden° battle, then? Oh, I perceive
you.

[Reenter DIOMEDES.]

AGAMEMNON Here is Sir Diomed. Go, gentle
knight,
Stand by our Ajax. As you and Lord Aeneas
Consent upon the order of their fight,   90
So be it, either to the uttermost
Or else a breath. The combatants being kin
Half stints their strife before their strokes begin.

[AJAX and HECTOR enter the lists.]

ULYSSES They are opposed already.

AGAMEMNON What Trojan is that same that looks
so heavy?   95

ULYSSES The youngest son of Priam, a true knight,
Not yet mature, yet matchless, firm of word,
Speaking in deeds and deedless in his tongue,
Not soon provoked nor being provoked soon
calmed;
His heart and hand both open and both free;   100
For what he has he gives, what thinks he shows,
Yet gives he not till judgment guide his bounty,
Nor dignifies an impair° thought with breath;
Manly as Hector, but more dangerous,
For Hector in his blaze of wrath subscribes   105
To tender objects,° but he in heat of action

Is more vindicative° than jealous love.
They call him Troilus, and on him erect
A second hope, as fairly built as Hector.
Thus says Aeneas, one that knows the youth   110
Even to his inches, and with private soul°
Did in great Ilion thus translate° him to me.

[Alarum. HECTOR and AJAX fight.]

AGAMEMNON They are in action.

NESTOR Now, Ajax, hold thine own!

TROILUS   Hector, thou sleep'st.
Awake thee!   115

AGAMEMNON His blows are well disposed. There,
Ajax!

DIOMEDES You must no more. [Trumpets cease.]

AENEAS   Princes, enough, so please you.

AJAX I am not warm yet, let us fight again.

DIOMEDES As Hector pleases.

HECTOR   Why, then will I no more.
Thou art, great lord, my father's sister son,   120
A cousin-german° to great Priam's seed.
The obligation of our blood forbids
A gory emulation 'twixt us twain.
Were thy commixtion° Greek and Trojan so
That thou couldst say, "This hand is Grecian all,
And this is Trojan, the sinews of this leg   126
All Greek and this all Troy, my mother's blood
Runs on the dexter° cheek and this sinister°
Bounds in my father's," by Jove multipotent,
Thou shouldst not bear from me a Greekish
member°   130
Wherein my sword had not impressure made
Of our rank feud. But the just gods gainsay°
That any drop thou borrow'dst from thy mother,
My sacred aunt, should by my mortal sword
Be drained! Let me embrace thee, Ajax.   135
By him that thunders, thou hast lusty arms.
Hector would have them fall upon him thus.
Cousin, all honor to thee!

AJAX   I thank thee, Hector.
Thou art too gentle and too free° a man.
I came to kill thee, cousin, and bear hence   140
A great addition° earnèd in thy death.

HECTOR Not Neoptolemus° so mirable,°
On whose bright crest Fame with her loud'st Oyes°

---

73. **securely:** foolhardily. 74. **misprizing:** disdaining. 83. **half . . . blood:** explained later at ll. 120–35. 87. **maiden:** bloodless. 103. **impair:** unfit. 105–06. **subscribes . . . objects:** i.e., shows mercy.

107. **vindicative:** vindictive. 111. **with . . . soul:** confidentially. 112. **translate:** interpret. 121. **cousin-german:** kinsman. 124. **commixtion:** mixture. 128. **dexter:** right. **sinister:** left. 130. **member:** limb. 132. **gainsay:** forbid. 139. **free:** generous. 141. **addition:** honor. 142. **Neoptolemus:** son of Achilles, but presumably Achilles is meant. **mirable:** marvelous. 143. **Oyes:** Oyez (hear ye), the herald's warning to his hearers.

Cries, "This is he," could promise to himself
A thought of added honor torn from Hector. 145

AENEAS There is expectance here from both the sides,
What further you will do.

HECTOR   We'll answer it,
The issue° is embracement. Ajax, farewell.

AJAX If I might in entreaties find success—
As seld I have the chance—I would desire   150
My famous cousin to our Grecian tents.

DIOMEDES 'Tis Agamemnon's wish, and great Achilles
Doth long to see unarmed the valiant Hector.

HECTOR Aeneas, call my brother Troilus to me.
And signify this loving interview   155
To the expecters° of our Trojan part,
Desire them home. Give me thy hand, my cousin.
I will go eat with thee, and see your knights.

AJAX Great Agamemnon comes to meet us here.

HECTOR The worthiest of them tell me name by name,   160
But for Achilles, my own searching eyes
Shall find him by his large and portly size.

AGAMEMNON Worthy of arms! As welcome as to one
That would be rid of such an enemy,
But that's no welcome. Understand more clear
What's past and what's to come is strewed with husks   166
And formless ruin of oblivion.°
But in this extant° moment, faith and troth,
Strained purely from all hollow bias-drawing,°
Bids thee, with most divine integrity,   170
From heart of very heart, great Hector, welcome.

HECTOR I thank thee, most imperious Agamemnon.

AGAMEMNON [To TROILUS] My well-famed lord of Troy, no less to you.

MENELAUS Let me confirm my princely brother's greeting.
You brace of warlike brothers, welcome hither.

HECTOR Who must we answer?   176

AENEAS   The noble Menelaus.

HECTOR Oh, you, my lord! By Mars his gauntlet, thanks!
Mock not that I affect the untraded° oath,

Your quondam° wife swears still by Venus' glove.
She's well, but bade me not commend her to you.

MENELAUS Name her not now, sir, she's a deadly theme.   181

HECTOR Oh, pardon, I offend.

NESTOR I have, thou gallant Trojan, seen thee oft,
Laboring for destiny,° make cruel way
Through ranks of Greekish youth. And I have seen thee,   185
As hot as Perseus,° spur thy Phrygian steed,
Despising many forfeits and subduements,°
When thou hast hung° thy advancèd sword i' the air,
Not letting it decline on the declined,
That I have said to some my standers-by   190
"Lo, Jupiter is yonder, dealing life!"
And I have seen thee pause and take thy breath
When that a ring of Greeks have hemmed thee in,
Like an Olympian° wrestling. This have I seen.
But this thy countenance, still locked in steel,°
I never saw till now. I knew thy grandsire,   196
And once fought with him. He was a soldier good,
But, by great Mars the captain of us all,
Never like thee. Let an old man embrace thee,
And, worthy warrior, welcome to our tents. 200

AENEAS 'Tis the old Nestor.

HECTOR Let me embrace thee, good old chronicle,°
That hast so long walked hand in hand with time.
Most reverend Nestor, I am glad to clasp thee.

NESTOR I would my arms could match thee in contention,   205
As they contend with thee in courtesy.

HECTOR I would they could.

NESTOR Ha!
By this white beard, I'd fight with thee tomorrow.
Well, welcome, welcome!—I have seen the time.   210

ULYSSES I wonder now how yonder city stands,
When we have here her base and pillar by us.

HECTOR I know your favor, Lord Ulysses, well.
Ah, sir, there's many a Greek and Trojan dead

---

148. **issue:** end. 156. **expecters:** supporters; lit., those who wait for news. 166–67. **husks . . . oblivion:** In time to come nothing will be left but shapeless ruins. 168. **extant:** present. 169. **bias-drawing:** crooked dealing. 178. **untraded:** unusual.

179. **quondam:** former. 184. **Laboring . . . destiny:** working for Fate. 186. **Perseus:** See I.iii. 42,n. 187. **forfeits . . . subduements:** men vanquished who have forfeited their lives. 188. **hung:** i.e., refrained from striking. 194. **Olympian:** god. 195. **still . . . steel:** always enclosed in armor. 202. **chronicle:** i.e., record of the past.

Since first I saw yourself and Diomed 215
In Ilion, on your Greekish embassy.

ULYSSES Sir, I foretold you then what would ensue.
My prophecy is but half his journey yet,
For yonder walls that pertly front° your town,
Yond towers whose wanton tops do buss° the clouds, 220
Must kiss their own feet.

HECTOR I must not believe you.
There they stand yet, and modestly I think
The fall of every Phrygian stone will cost
A drop of Grecian blood. The end crowns all,
And that old common arbitrator, Time, 225
Will one day end it.

ULYSSES So to him we leave it.
Most gentle and most valiant Hector, welcome.
After the general, I beseech you next
To feast with me and see me at my tent.

ACHILLES I shall forestall thee, Lord Ulysses, thou! 230
Now, Hector, I have fed mine eyes on thee,
I have with exact view perused thee, Hector,
And quoted° joint by joint.

HECTOR Is this Achilles?

ACHILLES I am Achilles.

HECTOR Stand fair, I pray thee. Let me look on thee. 235

ACHILLES Behold thy fill.

HECTOR Nay, I have done already.

ACHILLES Thou art too brief. I will the second time,
As I would buy thee, view thee limb by limb.

HECTOR Oh, like a book of sport thou'lt read me o'er,
But there's more in me than thou understand'st.
Why dost thou so oppress me with thine eye? 241

ACHILLES Tell me, you heavens, in which part of his body
Shall I destroy him? Whether there, or there, or there?
That I may give the local wound a name,
And make distinct the very breach whereout 245
Hector's great spirit flew. Answer me, Heavens!

HECTOR It would discredit the blest gods, proud man,
To answer such a question. Stand again.
Think'st thou to catch my life so pleasantly
As to prenominate° in nice conjecture 250

Where thou wilt hit me dead?

ACHILLES I tell thee yea.

HECTOR Wert thou an oracle to tell me so,
I'd not believe thee. Henceforth guard thee well,
For I'll not kill thee there, nor there, nor there,
But, by the forge that stithied° Mars his helm, 255
I'll kill thee everywhere—yea, o'er and o'er.
You wisest Grecians, pardon me this brag.
His insolence draws folly from my lips,
But I'll endeavor deeds to match these words,
Or may I never—— 260

AJAX Do not chafe thee, cousin.
And you, Achilles, let these threats alone
Till accident or purpose bring you to 't.
You may have every day enough of Hector,
If you have stomach. The general state, I fear,
Can scarce entreat you to be odd with him.° 265

HECTOR I pray you let us see you in the field.
We have had pelting° wars since you refused
The Grecians' cause.

ACHILLES Dost thou entreat me, Hector?
Tomorrow do I meet thee, fell° as death,
Tonight all friends. 270

HECTOR Thy hand upon that match.

AGAMEMNON First, all you peers of Greece, go to my tent,
There in the full convive we.° Afterward,
As Hector's leisure and your bounties shall
Concur together, severally° entreat him. 274
Beat loud the tabourines,° let the trumpets blow,
That this great soldier may his welcome know.

[*Exeunt all but* TROILUS *and* ULYSSES.]

TROILUS My Lord Ulysses, tell me, I beseech you,
In what place of the field doth Calchas keep?°

ULYSSES At Menelaus' tent, most princely Troilus.
There Diomed doth feast with him tonight, 280
Who neither looks upon the heaven nor earth,
But gives all gaze and bent of amorous view
On the fair Cressid.

TROILUS Shall I, sweet lord, be bound to you so much,
After we part from Agamemnon's tent, 285
To bring me thither?

ULYSSES You shall command me, sir.
As gentle tell me, of what honor was

---

219. **front:** stand in front of. 220. **buss:** kiss. 233. **quoted:** noted. 250. **prenominate:** foretell.

255. **stithied:** forged. 263–65. **You . . . him:** i.e., you can fight Hector any day you choose, but our army (*general state*) can hardly persuade you to come out. 267. **pelting:** paltry. 269. **fell:** fearful. 272. **convive we:** let us feast. 274. **severally:** individually. 275. **tabourines:** drums. 278. **keep:** lodge.

This Cressida in Troy? Had she no lover there
That wails her absence?
TROILUS   Oh, sir, to such as boasting show their
   scars   290
A mock is due. Will you walk on, my lord?
She was beloved, she loved; she is, and doth.
But still sweet love is food for fortune's tooth.
                                          [*Exeunt.*]

ACT V

SCENE I. *The Grecian camp. Before* ACHILLES'
                         tent.

[*Enter* ACHILLES *and* PATROCLUS.]
ACHILLES   I'll heat his blood with Greekish wine
   tonight,
Which with my scimitar I'll cool tomorrow.
Patroclus, let us feast him to the height.
PATROCLUS   Here comes Thersites.
                    [*Enter* THERSITES.]
ACHILLES   How now, thou core° of envy!
Thou crusty batch° of nature, what's the news? 5
THERSITES   Why, thou picture of what thou seem-
est, and idol of idiot-worshipers, here's a letter
for thee.
ACHILLES   From whence, fragment?
THERSITES   Why, thou full dish of fool, from Troy.
PATROCLUS   Who keeps the tent now?°   11
THERSITES   The surgeon's box, or the patient's
wound.°
PATROCLUS   Well said, adversity! And what needs
these tricks?   15
THERSITES   Prithee be silent, boy, I profit not by
thy talk. Thou art thought to be Achilles' male
varlet.   18
PATROCLUS   Male varlet, you rogue! What's that?
THERSITES   Why, his masculine whore. Now the
rotten diseases of the south,° the guts-griping,
ruptures, catarrhs, loads o' gravel i' the back,
lethargies, cold palsies, raw eyes, dirt-rotten
livers, wheezing lungs, bladders full of imposthume,° sciaticas, limekilns i' the palm,° incurable

---

Act V, scene i. **4. core:** center of a boil. **5. crusty batch:**
overbaked loaf; i.e., black, hard, and bitter. **11. Who . . .
now:** i.e., the news that Thersites has a letter from Troy
quickly brings Achilles out of his tent. **12–13. The . . .
wound:** Thersites deliberately misunderstands tent as lint. See
II.ii.16,n. **21. south:** regarded as an unhealthy quarter. **24–25.
imposthume:** abscess. **25. limekilns . . . palm:** arthritis.

boneache, and the riveled fee simple of the tetter,°
take and take again such preposterous dis-
coveries!°   28
PATROCLUS   Why, thou damnable box of envy
thou, what mean'st thou to curse thus?   30
THERSITES   Do I curse thee?
PATROCLUS   Why, no, you ruinous butt,° you
whoreson indistinguishable° cur, no.   33
THERSITES   No! Why art thou then exasperate,
thou idle immaterial skein of sleave silk,° thou
green sarcenet° flap for a sore eye, thou tassel of a
prodigal's purse thou?° Ah, how the poor world
is pestered with such water flies,° diminutives of
nature!   39
PATROCLUS   Out, gall!   40
THERSITES   Finch-egg!°
ACHILLES   My sweet Patroclus, I am thwarted quite
From my great purpose in tomorrow's battle.
Here is a letter from Queen Hecuba,
A token from her daughter, my fair love,   45
Both taxing° me and gaging° me to keep
An oath that I have sworn. I will not break it.
Fall Greeks, fail fame, honor or go or stay,
My major vow lies here, this I'll obey.
Come, come, Thersites, help to trim my tent. 50
This night in banqueting must all be spent.
Away, Patroclus!
                [*Exeunt* ACHILLES *and* PATROCLUS.]
THERSITES   With too much blood and too little
brain, these two may run mad, but if with too
much brain and too little blood they do, I'll be a
curer of madmen. Here's Agamemnon, an honest
fellow enough and one that loves quails,° but he
has not so much brain as earwax. And the goodly
transformation of Jupiter there, his brother, the
bull, the primitive statue and oblique° memorial
of cuckolds, a thrifty shoeing horn in a chain
hanging at his brother's leg—to what form but
that he is should wit larded° with malice and
malice forced° with wit turn him to? To an ass

---

26. riveled . . . tetter: permanent ownership (*fee simple*) of
eruptions (*tetter*) that pucker (*rivel*) the skin. **27–28. discoveries:** revelations. **32. ruinous butt:** broken-down barrel.
33. indistinguishable: shapeless. **34–37. thou . . . thou:**
Thersites now turns to curse Patroclus' appearance.
Patroclus is played as a dapper effeminate youth, prettily
dressed in green silk. **sleave silk:** skein of raw silk. **sarcenet:**
fine soft silk. **38. water flies:** useless little creatures that flit
about. **41. Finch-egg:** i.e., little smooth thing. **46. taxing:**
blaming. **gaging:** pledging. **57. quails:** courtesans. **60.
oblique:** indirect, symbolic. **63. larded:** basted. **64. forced:**
stuffed.

were nothing, he is both ass and ox. To an ox were nothing, he is both ox and ass. To be a dog, a mule, a cat, a fitchew,° a toad, a lizard, an owl, a puttock,° or a herring without a rope, I would not care. But to be Menelaus! I would conspire against destiny. Ask me not what I would be if I were not Thersites, for I care not to be the louse of a lazar,° so I were not Menelaus. Hoy-day!° Spirits and fires!   73

[*Enter* HECTOR, TROILUS, AJAX, AGAMEMNON,
ULYSSES, NESTOR, MENELAUS, *and* DIOMEDES,
with lights.]

AGAMEMNON   We go wrong, we go wrong.
AJAX   No, yonder 'tis,
There, where we see the lights.
HECTOR   I trouble you. 75
AJAX   No, not a whit.

[*Reenter* ACHILLES.]

ULYSSES   Here comes himself to guide you.
ACHILLES   Welcome, brave Hector, welcome, princes all.
AGAMEMNON   So now, fair prince of Troy, I bid good night.
Ajax commands the guard to tend on you.
HECTOR   Thanks and good night to the Greeks' general.   80
MENELAUS   Good night, my lord.
HECTOR   Good night, sweet Lord Menelaus.
THERSITES   Sweet draught.° Sweet, quoth a'! Sweet sink, sweet sewer.
ACHILLES   Good night and welcome, both at once, to those
That go or tarry.   85
AGAMEMNON   Good night.

[*Exeunt* AGAMEMNON *and* MENELAUS.]

ACHILLES   Old Nestor tarries, and you too, Diomed,
Keep Hector company an hour or two.
DIOMEDES   I cannot, lord, I have important business
The tide° whereof is now. Good night, great Hector.   90
HECTOR   Give me your hand.
ULYSSES   [*Aside to* TROILUS] Follow his torch, he goes to Calchas' tent.
I'll keep you company.
TROILUS   Sweet sir, you honor me.

HECTOR   And so good night.

[*Exit* DIOMEDES; ULYSSES *and* TROILUS *following.*]

ACHILLES   Come, come, enter my tent.   95

[*Exeunt* ACHILLES, HECTOR, AJAX, *and* NESTOR.]

THERSITES   That same Diomed's a false-hearted rogue, a most unjust knave. I will no more trust him when he leers than I will a serpent when he hisses. He will spend his mouth° and promise, like Brabbler the hound, but when he performs, astronomers foretell it.° It is prodigious,° there will come some change,° the sun borrows of the moon when Diomed keeps his word. I will rather leave to see° Hector than not to dog him. They say he keeps a Trojan drab and uses the traitor Calchas' tent. I'll after. Nothing but lechery! All incontinent varlets!   [*Exit.*]

SCENE II. *The same. Before* CALCHAS' *tent.*

[*Enter* DIOMEDES.]

DIOMEDES   What, are you up here, ho? Speak.
CALCHAS   [*Within*] Who calls?
DIOMEDES   Diomed. Calchas, I think. Where's your daughter?
CALCHAS   [*Within*] She comes to you.   5

[*Enter* TROILUS *and* ULYSSES, *at a distance; after them,* THERSITES.]

ULYSSES   Stand where the torch may not discover us.

[*Enter* CRESSIDA.]

TROILUS   Cressid comes forth to him.
DIOMEDES   How now, my charge!
CRESSIDA   Now, my sweet guardian! Hark, a word with you.   [*Whispers.*]
TROILUS   Yea, so familiar!
ULYSSES   She will sing any man at first sight.   10
THERSITES   And any man may sing her, if he can take her cliff.° She's noted.°
DIOMEDES   Will you remember?
CRESSIDA   Remember! Yes.
DIOMEDES   Nay, but do, then,   15
And let your mind be coupled with your words.
TROILUS   What should she remember?
ULYSSES   List.
CRESSIDA   Sweet honey Greek, tempt me no more to folly.

---

67. fitchew: polecat. 68. puttock: kite. 72. lazar: leper. Hoy-day: an exclamation of surprise, as he sees lights approaching. 82. draught: privy. 90. tide: decisive moment.

99. spend . . . mouth: bark. 101. astronomers . . . it: astrologers prophesy it. prodigious: an omen. 102. change: revolution. 104. leave to see: lose seeing.
Scene ii. 12. cliff: clef, a key in music. noted: observed, with a pun on musical notes.

THERSITES   Roguery!   20
DIOMEDES   Nay, then——
CRESSIDA   I'll tell you what——
DIOMEDES   Foh, foh! Come, tell a pin.° You are forsworn.
CRESSIDA   In faith, I cannot. What would you have me do?   26
THERSITES   A juggling trick—to be secretly open.
DIOMEDES   What did you swear you would bestow on me?
CRESSIDA   I prithee do not hold me to mine oath. Bid me do anything but that, sweet Greek.   30
DIOMEDES   Good night.
TROILUS   Hold, patience!
ULYSSES   How now, Trojan!
CRESSIDA   Diomed——   34
DIOMEDES   No, no, good night. I'll be your fool no more.
TROILUS   Thy better° must.
CRESSIDA   Hark, one word in your ear.
TROILUS   Oh, plague and madness!
ULYSSES   You are moved, prince. Let us depart, I pray you,   40
Lest your displeasure should enlarge itself
To wrathful terms. This place is dangerous,
The time right deadly. I beseech you, go.
TROILUS   Behold, I pray you!
ULYSSES   Nay, good my lord, go off.
You flow to great distraction.° Come, my lord.
TROILUS   I pray thee stay.   46
ULYSSES   You have not patience, come.
TROILUS   I pray you stay. By hell and all hell's torments,
I will not speak a word.
DIOMEDES   And so good night.
CRESSIDA   Nay, but you part in anger.
TROILUS   Doth that grieve thee?
Oh, withered truth!
ULYSSES   Why, how now, lord!   50
TROILUS   By Jove,
I will be patient.
CRESSIDA   Guardian—Why, Greek!
DIOMEDES   Foh, foh! Adieu, you palter.
CRESSIDA   In faith, I do not. Come hither once again.
ULYSSES   You shake, my lord, at something. Will you go?
You will break out.

TROILUS   She strokes his cheek!   55
ULYSSES   Come, come.
TROILUS   Nay, stay, by Jove. I will not speak a word.
There is between my will and all offenses
A guard of patience. Stay a little while.
THERSITES   How the devil luxury,° with his fat rump and potato finger,° tickles these together! Fry, lechery, fry!   61
DIOMEDES   But will you, then?
CRESSIDA   In faith, I will, la. Never trust me else.
DIOMEDES   Give me some token for the surety of it.
CRESSIDA   I'll fetch you one.   [Exit.]
ULYSSES   You have sworn patience.   66
TROILUS   Fear me not, sweet lord.
I will not be myself, nor have cognition
Of what I feel. I am all patience.
[Reenter CRESSIDA.] Now the pledge, now, now, now!
CRESSIDA   Here, Diomed, keep this sleeve.   70
TROILUS   O beauty! Where is thy faith?
ULYSSES   My lord——
TROILUS   I will be patient, outwardly I will.
CRESSIDA   You look upon that sleeve, behold it well.
He loved me.—O false wench!—Give 't me again.
DIOMEDES   Whose was 't?   75
CRESSIDA   It is no matter, now I have 't again.
I will not meet with you tomorrow night.
I prithee, Diomed, visit me no more.
THERSITES   Now she sharpens. Well said, whetstone!   80
DIOMEDES   I shall have it.
CRESSIDA   What, this?
DIOMEDES   Aye, that.
CRESSIDA   Oh, all you gods! O pretty, pretty pledge!
Thy master now lies thinking in his bed
Of thee and me, and sighs, and takes my glove,
And gives memorial dainty kisses to it,   85
As I kiss thee. Nay, do not snatch it from me.
He that takes that doth take my heart withal.
DIOMEDES   I had your heart before, this follows it.
TROILUS   I did swear patience.
CRESSIDA   You shall not have it, Diomed, faith, you shall not.   90
I'll give you something else.

DIOMEDES   I will have this. Whose was it?

CRESSIDA   It is no matter.

DIOMEDES   Come, tell me whose it was.

CRESSIDA   'Twas one's that loved me better than
you will.
But now you have it, take it.

DIOMEDES   Whose was it?   95

CRESSIDA   By all Diana's waiting women° yond,
And by herself, I will not tell you whose.

DIOMEDES   Tomorrow will I wear it on my helm,
And grieve his spirit that dares not challenge it.

TROILUS   Wert thou the devil, and worest it on thy
horn,   100
It should be challenged.

CRESSIDA   Well, well, 'tis done, 'tis past. And yet it
is not.
I will not keep my word.

DIOMEDES   Why then, farewell.
Thou never shalt mock Diomed again.

CRESSIDA   You shall not go. One cannot speak a
word   105
But it straight starts you.

DIOMEDES   I do not like this fooling.

THERSITES   Nor I, by Pluto. But that
that likes° not you
Pleases me best.

DIOMEDES   What, shall I come? The hour?

CRESSIDA   Aye, come. O Jove!   110
Do come. I shall be plagued.

DIOMEDES   Farewell till then.

CRESSIDA   Good night, I prithee come.
[*Exit* DIOMEDES.]
Troilus, farewell! One eye yet looks on thee,
But with my heart the other eye doth see.
Ah, poor our sex! This fault in us I find,   115
The error of our eye directs our mind.
What error leads must err. Oh, then conclude
Minds swayed by eyes are full of turpitude. [*Exit.*]

THERSITES   A proof of strength she could not
publish more
Unless she said "My mind is now turned whore."

ULYSSES   All's done, my lord.

TROILUS   It is.   121

ULYSSES   Why stay we, then?

TROILUS   To make a recordation to° my soul
Of every syllable that here was spoke.
But if I tell how these two did coact,
Shall I not lie in publishing a truth?   125

Sith° yet there is a credence in my heart,
An esperance° so obstinately strong
That doth invert the attest° of eyes and ears,
As if those organs had deceptious functions,
Created only to calumniate.   130
Was Cressid here?

ULYSSES   I cannot conjure,° Trojan.

TROILUS   She was not, sure.

ULYSSES   Most sure she was.

TROILUS   Why, my negation hath no taste of madness.°

ULYSSES   Nor mine, my lord. Cressid was here but
now.   134

TROILUS   Let it not be believed for womanhood!
Think, we had mothers. Do not give advantage
To stubborn critics, apt without a theme
For depravation, to square° the general sex
By Cressid's rule.° Rather think this not Cressid.

ULYSSES   What hath she done, prince, that can soil
our mothers?   140

TROILUS   Nothing at all, unless that this were she.

THERSITES   Will a' swagger himself out on 's own
eyes?

TROILUS   This she? No, this is Diomed's Cressida.
If beauty have a soul, this is not she.
If souls guide vows, if vows be sanctimonies, 145
If sanctimony be the gods' delight,
If there be rule in unity itself,
This is not she. Oh, madness of discourse
That cause sets up with and against itself!
Bifold authority! Where reason can revolt   150
Without perdition, and loss assume all reason
Without revolt.° This is, and is not, Cressid!
Within my soul there doth conduce a fight
Of this strange nature, that a thing inseparate°
Divides more wider than the sky and earth,   155
And yet the spacious breadth of this division
Admits no orifex° for a point as subtle
As Ariachne's broken woof° to enter.

96. **waiting women**: i.e., the stars, Diana being the moon.
108. **likes**: pleases. 122. **recordation to**: remembrance in.

126. **Sith**: since. 127. **esperance**: hope. 128. **invert . . . at-test**: refuse to believe the evidence. 131. **I . . . conjure**: i.e., these were not spirits. 133. **negation . . . madness**: my denial has no taint of madness; i.e., I am not mad to deny it. 138. **square**: measure. 139. **rule**: carpenter's rule. 148–52. **Oh . . . revolt**: a mad argument that is at the same time for and against itself. Divided authority where reason can turn against itself without becoming madness, and destruction (*loss*) become reasonable; i.e., it is both reason-able and insane to believe or to disbelieve what I have seen. 154. **inseparate**: inseparable. 157. **orifex**: point of entry. 158. **Ariachne's . . . woof**: the thread of a spider's web. Ariachne for Arachne, who was turned into a spider.

Instance,° oh instance, strong as Pluto's gates,
Cressid is mine, tied with the bonds of heaven.
Instance, oh instance, strong as heaven itself,
The bonds of heaven are slipped, dissolved, and
    loosed,   162
And with another knot, five-finger-tied,
The fractions of her faith, orts° of her love,
The fragments, scraps, the bits and greasy relics
Of her o'ereaten° faith, are bound to Diomed.

ULYSSES May worthy Troilus be half attached 167
With° that which here his passion doth express?

TROILUS Aye, Greek, and that shall be divulgèd
    well
In characters as red as Mars his heart   170
Inflamed with Venus. Never did young man
    fancy
With so eternal and so fixed a soul.
Hark, Greek. As much as I do Cressid love,
So much by weight hate I her Diomed.   174
That sleeve is mine that he'll bear on his helm.
Were it a casque° composed by Vulcan's skill,
My sword should bite it. Not the dreadful spout°
Which shipmen do the hurricano call,
Constringed in mass° by the almighty sun,
Shall dizzy with more clamor Neptune's ear 180
In his descent than shall my prompted sword
Falling on Diomed.

THERSITES He'll tickle it for his concupy.°

TROILUS O Cressid! O false Cressid! False, false,
    false!
Let all untruths stand by thy stainèd name, 185
And they'll seem glorious.

ULYSSES   Oh, contain yourself.
Your passion draws ears hither.

                  [Enter AENEAS.]

AENEAS I have been seeking you this hour, my
    lord.
Hector by this is arming him in Troy,
Ajax your guard stays to conduct you home. 190

TROILUS Have with you, prince. My courteous
    lord, adieu.
Farewell, revolted fair! And, Diomed,
Stand fast, and wear a castle on thy head!°

ULYSSES I'll bring you to the gates.

TROILUS Accept distracted thanks.   195

---

159. Instance: proof. 164. orts: scraps. 166. o'ereaten: over-
eaten, gorged. 167–68. attached With: affected by. 176.
casque: helmet. 177. spout: waterspout. 179. Constringed
in mass: drawn together. 183. He'll . . . concupy: He'll
be tickled for his lust. 193. wear . . . head: i.e., nothing
less than a castle will protect you.

[Exeunt TROILUS, AENEAS, and ULYSSES.]

THERSITES Would I could meet that rogue
    Diomed! I would croak like a raven, I would
    bode,° I would bode. Patroclus will give me any-
    thing for the intelligence of this whore. The
    parrot will not do more for an almond° than he
    for a commodious° drab. Lechery, lechery! Still
    wars and lechery! Nothing else holds fashion. A
    burning devil take them!   [Exit.]

SCENE III. Troy. Before PRIAM's palace.

[Enter HECTOR and ANDROMACHE.]

ANDROMACHE When was my lord so much un-
    gently tempered
To stop his ears against admonishment?
Unarm, unarm, and do not fight today.

HECTOR You train° me to offend you, get you in.
By all the everlasting gods, I'll go!   5

ANDROMACHE My dreams will sure prove ominous
    to the day.

HECTOR No more, I say.

                  [Enter CASSANDRA.]

CASSANDRA   Where is my brother Hector?

ANDROMACHE Here, sister, armed, and bloody in
    intent.
Consort with me in loud and dear petition,
Pursue we him on knees, for I have dreamed   10
Of bloody turbulence, and this whole night
Hath nothing been but shapes and forms of
    slaughter.

CASSANDRA Oh, 'tis true.

HECTOR   Ho! Bid my trumpet sound!

CASSANDRA No notes of sally, for the heavens,
    sweet brother.

HECTOR Be gone, I say. The gods have heard me
    swear.   15

CASSANDRA The gods are deaf to hot and peevish°
    vows,
They are polluted offerings, more abhorred
Than spotted livers in the sacrifice.

ANDROMACHE Oh, be persuaded! Do not count it
    holy
To hurt by being just. It is as lawful,   20
For we would give much, to use violent thefts
And rob in the behalf of charity.

---

198. bode: prophesy disaster. 200. parrot . . . almond: The
love of parrots for almonds is proverbial. 201. commodious:
accommodating.
  Scene iii. 4. train: encourage. 16. peevish: obstinate.

CASSANDRA It is the purpose that makes strong
the vow,
But vows to every purpose must not hold.
Unarm, sweet Hector.
HECTOR   Hold you still, I say.   25
Mine honor keeps the weather of° my fate.
Life every man holds dear, but the dear man
Holds honor far more precious-dear than life.
[*Enter* TROILUS.] How now, young man! Mean'st
thou to fight today?
ANDROMACHE Cassandra, call my father to per-
suade.   [*Exit* CASSANDRA.]
HECTOR No, faith, young Troilus. Doff thy
harness, youth.   31
I am today i' the vein of chivalry.°
Let grow thy sinews till their knots be strong,
And tempt not yet the brushes of the war.
Unarm thee, go, and doubt thou not, brave boy,
I'll stand today for thee and me and Troy.   36
TROILUS Brother, you have a vice of mercy in you
Which better fits a lion than a man.
HECTOR What vice is that, good Troilus? Chide
me for it.
TROILUS When many times the captive Grecian
falls,   40
Even in the fan and wind of your fair sword,
You bid them rise and live.
HECTOR Oh, 'tis fair play.
TROILUS   Fool's play, by heaven, Hector.
HECTOR How now! How now!
TROILUS   For the love of all the gods,
Let's leave the hermit pity with our mother,   45
And when we have our armors buckled on,
The venomed vengeance ride upon our swords,
Spur them to ruthful work,° rein them from ruth!
HECTOR Fie, savage, fie!
TROILUS   Hector, then 'tis wars.
HECTOR Troilus, I would not have you fight today.
TROILUS Who should withhold me?   51
Not fate, obedience, nor the hand of Mars
Beckoning with fiery truncheon my retire—
Not Priamus and Hecuba on knees,
Their eyes o'ergallèd° with recourse° of tears; 55
Nor you, my brother, with your true sword
drawn—
Opposed to hinder me should stop my way

---

26. keeps . . . of: has the advantage of. 32. i' . . . chivalry:
i.e., fighting for honor. 48. ruthful work: work that will rouse
pity; i.e., be ruthless. 55. o'ergalled: inflamed. recourse:
flowing.

But by my ruin.
[*Reenter* CASSANDRA, *with* PRIAM.]
CASSANDRA Lay hold upon him, Priam, hold him
fast.
He is thy crutch. Now if thou lose thy stay,   60
Thou on him leaning and all Troy on thee,
Fall all together.
PRIAM   Come, Hector, come, go back.
Thy wife hath dreamed, thy mother hath had
visions,
Cassandra doth foresee, and I myself
Am like a prophet suddenly enrapt,°   65
To tell thee that this day is ominous,
Therefore, come back,
HECTOR   Aeneas is afield,
And I do stand engaged° to many Greeks,
Even in the faith of valor, to appear
This morning to them.   70
PRIAM   Aye, but thou shalt not go.
HECTOR I must not break my faith.
You know me dutiful, therefore, dear sir,
Let me not shame respect, but give me leave
To take that course by your consent and voice
Which you do here forbid me, royal Priam.   75
CASSANDRA O Priam, yield not to him!
ANDROMACHE   Do not, dear father.
HECTOR Andromache, I am offended with you.
Upon the love you bear me, get you in.
[*Exit* ANDROMACHE.]
TROILUS This foolish, dreaming, superstitious girl
Makes all these bodements.°   80
CASSANDRA   Oh, farewell, dear Hector!
Look how thou diest! Look how thy eye turns
pale!
Look how thy wounds do bleed at many vents!°
Hark how Troy roars, how Hecuba cries out!
How poor Andromache shrills her dolors forth!
Behold, distraction, frenzy, and amazement,   85
Like witless antics,° one another meet,
And all cry "Hector! Hector's dead! Oh,
Hector!"
TROILUS Away! Away!
CASSANDRA Farewell. Yet, soft! Hector, I take my
leave.
Thou dost thyself and all our Troy deceive.   90
[*Exit.*]
HECTOR You are amazed, my liege, at her
exclaim.

---

65. enrapt: inspired. 68. engaged: pledged. 80. bodements:
gloomy prophecies. 82. vents: openings. 86. antics: buffoons.

Go in and cheer the town. We'll forth and fight,
Do deeds worth praise and tell you them at night.
PRIAM Farewell. The gods with safety stand
about thee!

> [*Exeunt severally*° PRIAM *and* HECTOR.
> *Alarum.*]

TROILUS They are at it, hark! Proud Diomed,
believe,   95
I come to lose my arm or win my sleeve.

> [*Enter* PANDARUS.]

PANDARUS Do you hear, my lord? Do you hear?
TROILUS What now?
PANDARUS Here's a letter come from yond poor
girl.
TROILUS Let me read.   100
PANDARUS A whoreson tisick,° a whoreson rascally tisick so troubles me, and the foolish
fortune of this girl; and what one thing, what
another, that I shall leave you one o' these days.
And I have a rheum in mine eyes too, and such
an ache in my bones that, unless a man were
cursed, I cannot tell what to think on 't. What
says she there?   108
TROILUS Words, words, mere words, no matter
from the heart.
The effect doth operate another way.   110

> [*Tearing the letter.*]

Go, wind, to wind, there turn and change
together.
My love with words and errors still she feeds,
But edifies another with her deeds.

> [*Exeunt severally.*]

SCENE IV. *The field between Troy and the
Grecian camp.*

[*Alarums. Excursions. Enter* THERSITES.]

THERSITES Now they are clapper-clawing° one another. I'll go look on. That dissembling abominable varlet Diomed has got that same scurvy
doting foolish young knave's sleeve of Troy
there in his helm. I would fain see them meet,
that that same young Trojan ass, that loves the
whore there, might send that Greekish whore-
masterly villain with the sleeve back to the
dissembling luxurious drab, of a sleeveless°
errand. O' the t'other side, the policy of those

crafty swearing rascals, that stale old mouse-eaten
dry cheese Nestor, and that same dog fox
Ulysses, is not proved worth a blackberry. They
set me up in policy° that mongrel cur Ajax
against that dog of as bad a kind, Achilles. And
now is the cur Ajax prouder than the cur Achilles,
and will not arm today, whereupon the Grecians
begin to proclaim barbarism,° and policy grows
into an ill opinion.° Soft! Here comes sleeve, and
t'other.   20

> [*Enter* DIOMEDES *and* TROILUS.]

TROILUS Fly not, for shouldst thou take the river
Styx,
I would swim after.
DIOMEDES   Thou dost miscall retire.
I do not fly, but advantageous care
Withdrew me from the odds of multitude.
Have at thee!   25
THERSITES Hold thy whore, Grecian! Now for thy
whore, Trojan! Now the sleeve, now the sleeve!

> [*Exeunt* TROILUS *and* DIOMEDES, *fighting.*]
> [*Enter* HECTOR.]

HECTOR What art thou, Greek? Art thou for
Hector's match?
Art thou of blood and honor?
THERSITES No, no, I am a rascal,° a scurvy railing
knave, a very filthy rogue.   31
HECTOR I do believe thee. Live.   [*Exit.*]
THERSITES God-a-mercy° that thou wilt believe
me, but a plague break thy neck for frighting me!
What's become of the wenching rogues? I think
they have swallowed one another. I would laugh
at that miracle—yet in a sort lechery eats itself.
I'll seek them.   [*Exit.*]

SCENE V. *Another part of the field.*

[*Enter* DIOMEDES *and* SERVANT.]

DIOMEDES Go, go, my servant, take thou Troilus'
horse,
Present the fair steed to my Lady Cressid.
Fellow, commend my service to her beauty.
Tell her I have chastised the amorous Trojan,
And am her knight by proof.   5
SERVANT   I go, my lord. [*Exit.*]

> [*Enter* AGAMEMNON.]

---

94. severally: by different exits. **101. tisick:** cough.
Scene iv. **1. clapper-clawing:** scratching and clawing. **9.
sleeveless:** futile.

14. set . . . policy: thought it a clever plan to support.
18. proclaim barbarism: declare that ignorance is prefer-
able. **18–19. policy . . . opinion:** cleverness gets a bad name.
30. rascal: lit., a deer in poor condition. **33. God-a-mercy:**
thank God.

AGAMEMNON   Renew, renew! The fierce Polydamas
Hath beat down Menon. Bastard Margarelon
Hath Doreus prisoner,
And stands colossus-wise, waving his beam,°
Upon the pashèd corses° of the kings   10
Epistrophus and Cedius. Polyxenes is slain,
Amphimachus and Thoas deadly hurt,
Patroclus ta'en or slain, and Palamedes
Sore hurt and bruised. The dreadful sagittary°
Appals our numbers. Haste we, Diomed,   15
To reinforcement, or we perish all.

[*Enter* NESTOR.]

NESTOR   Go, bear Patroclus' body to Achilles,
And bid the snail-paced Ajax arm for shame.
There is a thousand Hectors in the field.
Now here he fights on Galathe his horse,   20
And there lacks work. Anon he's there afoot,
And there they fly or die, like scalèd sculls°
Before the belching whale. Then is he yonder,
And there the strawy° Greeks, ripe for his edge,
Fall down before him like the mower's swath.   25
Here, there, and everywhere he leaves and takes,
Dexterity so obeying appetite
That what he will he does, and does so much
That proof is called impossibility.

[*Enter* ULYSSES.]

ULYSSES   Oh, courage, courage, princes! Great
   Achilles   30
Is arming, weeping, cursing, vowing vengeance.
Patroclus' wounds have roused his drowsy blood,
Together with his mangled Myrmidons,°
That noseless, handless, hacked and chipped,
   come to him,
Crying on Hector. Ajax hath lost a friend,   35
And foams at mouth, and he is armed, and at it,
Roaring for Troilus, who hath done today
Mad and fantastic execution,
Engaging and redeeming of himself
With such a careless force and forceless care   40
As if that luck, in very spite of cunning,
Bade him win all.

[*Enter* AJAX.]

AJAX   Troilus! Thou coward Troilus!   [*Exit.*]
DIOMEDES   Aye, there, there.
NESTOR   So, so, we draw together.

[*Enter* ACHILLES.]

Scene *v.* **9. beam:** huge spear. **10. pashed corses:**
mangled corpses. **14. sagittary:** centaur, half man, half
horse, who helped the Trojans. **22. scaled sculls:** shoals of
scaly fish. **24. strawy:** weak as straw. **33. Myrmidons:**
Achilles' followers.

ACHILLES   Where is this Hector?
Come, come, thou boy-queller,° show thy face,
Know what it is to meet Achilles angry.   46
Hector! Where's Hector? I will none but Hector.

[*Exeunt.*]

SCENE VI. *Another part of the field.*

[*Enter* AJAX.]

AJAX   Troilus, thou coward Troilus, show thy
   head!

[*Enter* DIOMEDES.]

DIOMEDES   Troilus, I say! Where's Troilus?
AJAX   What wouldst thou?
DIOMEDES   I would correct him.
AJAX   Were I the general, thou shouldst have my
   office
Ere that correction.° Troilus, I say! What,
   Troilus!   5

[*Enter* TROILUS.]

TROILUS   O traitor Diomed! Turn thy false face,
   thou traitor,
And pay thy life thou owest me for my horse.
DIOMEDES   Ha, art thou there?
AJAX   I'll fight with him alone. Stand, Diomed.
DIOMEDES   He is my prize, I will not look upon. 10
TROILUS   Come both, you cogging° Greeks, have
   at you both!   [*Exeunt, fighting.*]

[*Enter* HECTOR.]

HECTOR   Yea, Troilus? Oh, well fought, my youngest brother!

[*Enter* ACHILLES.]

ACHILLES   Now do I see thee, ha! Have at thee,
   Hector!
HECTOR   Pause, if thou wilt.
ACHILLES   I do disdain thy courtesy, proud Trojan.
Be happy that my arms are out of use.   16
My rest and negligence befriends thee now,
But thou anon shalt hear of me again.
Till when, go seek thy fortune.   [*Exit.*]
HECTOR   Fare thee well.
I would have been much more a fresher man   20
Had I expected thee.
[*Reenter* TROILUS.]   How now, my brother!
TROILUS   Ajax hath ta'en Aeneas. Shall it be?
No, by the flame of yonder glorious heaven,

---

45. boy-queller: boy-killer, because he has killed Patroclus.
Scene *vi.* **5. Ere . . . correction:** before you should take
from me the privilege of correcting him. **11. cogging:**
cheating.

He shall not carry him. I'll be ta'en too,
Or bring him off.° Fate, hear me what I say!   25
I reck not though I end my life today.   [*Exit.*]
[*Enter one in sumptuous armor.*]

HECTOR Stand, stand, thou Greek, thou art a
  goodly mark.
No? Wilt thou not? I like thy armor well.
I'll frush° it, and unlock the rivets all,
But I'll be master of it. Wilt thou not, beast,
  abide?   30
Why then, fly on, I'll hunt thee for thy hide.
                              [*Exeunt.*]

SCENE VII. *Another part of the field.*

[*Enter* ACHILLES, *with* MYRMIDONS.]

ACHILLES Come here about me, you my Myr-
  midons,
Mark what I say. Attend me where I wheel.
Strike not a stroke, but keep yourselves in breath.
And when I have the bloody Hector found,
Empale° him with your weapons round about,   5
In fellest manner execute your aims.
Follow me, sirs, and my proceedings eye.
It is decreed Hector the great must die.
                              [*Exeunt.*]
[*Enter* MENELAUS *and* PARIS, *fighting: then*
                    THERSITES.]

THERSITES The cuckold and the cuckold-maker are
at it. Now, bull! Now, dog! 'Loo,° Paris, 'loo!
Now, my double-henned sparrow! 'Loo, Paris,
'loo! The bull has the game. Ware horns, ho!   12
                    [*Exeunt* PARIS *and* MENELAUS.]
[*Enter* MARGARELON.]

MARGARELON Turn, slave, and fight.

THERSITES What art thou?

MARGARELON A bastard son of Priam's.   15

THERSITES I am a bastard too, I love bastards. I
am a bastard begot, bastard instructed, bastard
in mind, bastard in valor, in everything illegitimate. One bear will not bite another, and wherefore should one bastard? Take heed, the quarrel's
most ominous to us. If the son of a whore fight
for a whore, he tempts judgment. Farewell,
bastard.   [*Exit.*]

MARGARELON The Devil take thee, coward!   24
                              [*Exit.*]

25. bring . . . off: rescue him. 29. frush: bruise.
Scene vii. 5. Empale: hedge in. 10. Now . . . 'Loo:
Thersites shouts encouragement as if a spectator in the
bullring.

SCENE VIII. *Another part of the field.*

[*Enter* HECTOR.]

HECTOR Most putrefied core, so fair without,
Thy goodly armor thus hath cost thy life.
Now is my day's work done. I'll take good breath.
Rest, sword, thou hast thy fill of blood and death.
        [*Puts off his helmet and hangs
                    his shield behind him.*]
[*Enter* ACHILLES *and* MYRMIDONS.]

ACHILLES Look, Hector, how the sun begins to
  set,   5
How ugly night comes breathing at his heels.
Even with the vail° and darking of the sun
To close the day up, Hector's life is done.

HECTOR I am unarmed, forgo this vantage, Greek.

ACHILLES Strike, fellows, strike, this is the man I
  seek.   [HECTOR *falls.*]
So, Ilion, fall thou next! Now, Troy, sink down!
Here lies thy heart, thy sinews, and thy bone.   12
On, Myrmidons, and cry you all amain,
"Achilles hath the mighty Hector slain."
                              [*A retreat sounded.*]
Hark! A retire upon our Grecian part.   15

MYRMIDONS The Trojan trumpets sound the like,
  my lord.

ACHILLES The dragon wing of night o'erspreads
  the earth,
And stickler-like° the armies separates.
My half-supped sword that frankly would have
  fed,
Pleased with this dainty bait, thus goes to bed.   20
                              [*Sheathes his sword.*]
Come, tie his body to my horse's tail.
Along the field I will the Trojan trail.
                    [*Exeunt. A retreat sounded.*]

SCENE IX. *Another part of the field.*

[*Enter* AGAMEMNON, AJAX, MENELAUS, NESTOR,
DIOMEDES, *and the rest, marching. Shouts within.*]

AGAMEMNON Hark! Hark! What shout is that?

NESTOR Peace, drums!

[*Within*] "Achilles! Achilles! Hector's slain!
  Achilles!"

DIOMEDES The bruit° is Hector's slain, and by
  Achilles.

Scene viii. 7. vail: lowering. 18. stickler-like: The
stickler was the umpire who intervened in a friendly combat.
Scene ix. 4. bruit: rumor.

AJAX   If it be so, yet bragless let it be,   5
Great Hector was a man as good as he.
AGAMEMNON   March patiently along. Let one be
sent
To pray Achilles see us at our tent.
If in his death the gods have us befriended,
Great Troy is ours, and our sharp wars are
ended.   [*Exeunt, marching.*]

SCENE X. *Another part of the field.*

[*Enter* AENEAS, PARIS, ANTENOR, *and* DEIPHOBUS.]
AENEAS   Stand, ho! Yet are we masters of the field.
Never go home, here starve we out the night.
                       [*Enter* TROILUS.]
TROILUS   Hector is slain.
ALL   Hector! The gods forbid!
TROILUS   He's dead, and at the murderer's horse's
tail
In beastly sort dragged through the shameful
field.   5
Frown on, you heavens, effect your rage with
speed!
Sit, gods, upon your thrones, and smile at Troy!
I say, at once let your brief plagues be mercy,
And linger not our sure destructions on!
AENEAS   My lord, you do discomfort all the host. 10
TROILUS   You understand me not that tell me so.
I do not speak of flight, of fear, of death,
But dare all imminence° that gods and men
Address° their dangers in. Hector is gone.
Who shall tell Priam so, or Hecuba?   15
Let him that will a screech owl aye° be called
Go in to Troy, and say there "Hector's dead."
There is a word will Priam turn to stone,
Make wells and Niobes° of the maids and wives,
Cold statues of the youth, and, in a word,   20
Scare Troy out of itself. But march away.
Hector is dead, there is no more to say.
Stay yet. You vile abominable tents,
Thus proudly pight° upon our Phrygian plains,
Let Titan° rise as early as he dare,   25

Scene x. **13. imminence:** impending evil. **14. Address:**
make ready. **16. aye:** always. **19. Niobe:** She wept so grievously for her dead children that she was turned into a stone
fountain. **24. pight:** pitched. **25. Titan:** the sun.

I'll through and through you! And, thou great-
sized coward,
No space of earth shall sunder our two hates.
I'll haunt thee like a wicked conscience still,°
That moldeth goblins swift as frenzy's thoughts.
Strike a free march to Troy! With comfort go. 30
Hope of revenge shall hide our inward woe.
                       [*Exeunt* AENEAS *and* TROJANS.]
[*As* TROILUS *is going out, enter, from the other side,*
PANDARUS.]
PANDARUS   But hear you, hear you!
TROILUS   Hence, broker lackey! Ignomy and
shame
Pursue thy life, and live aye with thy name!   34
                                        [*Exit.*]
PANDARUS   A goodly medicine for my aching
bones! O world, world, world! Thus is the poor
agent despised! O traitors and bawds, how earn-
estly are you set a-work, and how ill requited!
Why should our endeavor be so loved and the
performance so loathed? What verse for it?
What instance for it? Let me see: 41
   "Full merrily the humblebee doth sing
   Till he hath lost his honey and his sting,
   And being once subdued in armèd tail,
   Sweet honey and sweet notes together fail." 45
Good traders in the flesh, set this in your painted
cloths:°
   "As many as be here of Pandar's hall,
   Your eyes, half out, weep out at Pandar's fall.
   Or if you cannot weep, yet give some groans, 50
   Though not for me, yet for your aching bones.
   Brethren and sisters of the hold-door trade,
   Some two months hence my will shall here
        be made.
   It should be now, but that my fear is this—
   Some gallèd° goose of Winchester° would hiss.
   Till then I'll sweat and seek about for eases, 56
   And at that time bequeath you my diseases."
                                        [*Exit.*]

28. still: always. **46–47. painted cloths:** imitation tapestry,
painted with Scriptural or allegorical scenes. **55. galled:**
sore. **goose of Winchester:** prostitute. Prostitutes were called
"Winchester geese" because they inhabited property in
Southwark owned by the bishop of Winchester.

ALEXANDER POPE
1688–1744

The Rape of the Lock

An Heroi-comical Poem

Nolueram, Belinda, tuos violare capillos;
sed juvat hoc precibus me tribuisse tuis.[1]
                              MARTIAL

TO MRS. ARABELLA FERMOR[2]

Madam,

It will be in vain to deny that I have some regard for this piece, since I dedicate it to you. Yet you may bear me witness, it was intended only to divert a few young ladies, who have good sense and good humor enough to laugh not only at their sex's little unguarded follies, but at their own. But it was communicated with the air of a secret, it soon found its way into the world. An imperfect copy having been offered to a bookseller, you had the good nature for my sake to consent to the publication of one more correct; this I was forced to, before I had executed half my design, for the machinery was entirely wanting to complete it.

The machinery, madam, is a term invented by the critics, to signify that part which the deities, angels, or demons are made to act in a poem; for the ancient poets are in one respect like many modern ladies: let an action be never so trivial in itself, they always make it appear of the utmost importance. These machines I determined to raise on a very new and odd foundation, the Rosicrucian doctrine of spirits.

I know how disagreeable it is to make use of hard words before a lady; but 'tis so much the concern of a poet to have his works understood, and particularly by your sex, that you must give me leave to explain two or three difficult terms.

The Rosicrucians are a people I must bring you acquainted with. The best account I know of them is in a French book called *Le Comte de Gabalis*,[3] which both in its title and size is so like a novel, that many of the fair sex have read it for one by mistake. According to these gentlemen, the four elements are inhabited by spirits, which they call Sylphs, Gnomes, Nymphs, and Salamanders. The Gnomes, or Demons of earth, delight in mischief; but the Sylphs, whose habitation is in the air, are the best-conditioned creatures imaginable. For they say, any mortals may enjoy the most intimate familiarities with these gentle spirits, upon a condition very easy to all true adepts, an inviolate preservation of chastity.

As to the following cantos, all the passages of them are as fabulous as the vision at the beginning, or the transformation at the end; (except the loss of your hair, which I always mention with reverence). The human persons are as fictitious as the airy ones; and the character of Belinda, as it is now managed, resembles you in nothing but in beauty.

If this poem had as many graces as there are in your person, or in your mind, yet I could never hope it should pass through the world half so uncensured as you have done. But let its fortune be what it will, mine is happy enough, to have given me this occasion of assuring you that I am, with the truest esteem,

Madam,
Your most obedient, humble servant,
                              A. POPE

CANTO I

What dire offense from amorous causes springs,
What mighty contests rise from trivial things,
I sing—This verse to Caryll, Muse! is due:
This, even Belinda may vouchsafe to view:
Slight is the subject, but not so the praise,   5
If she inspire, and he approve my lays.
    Say what strange motive, goddess! could compel
A well-bred lord to assault a gentle belle?
Oh, say what stranger cause, yet unexplored,
Could make a gentle belle reject a lord?   10
In tasks so bold can little men engage,
And in soft bosoms dwells such mighty rage?
    Sol through white curtains shot a timorous ray,

THE RAPE OF THE LOCK.   **1. Nolueram . . . tuis:** "I was unwilling, Belinda, to ravish your locks; but I rejoice to have conceded this to your prayers." Martial, *Epigrams*, XII. lxxxiv.1–2, with the substitution of Belinda for Polytimus in the original. **2. Mrs. Arabella Fermor:** The occasion for the poem was Lord Petre's cutting a lock of Mrs. Fermor's hair and the ensuing quarrel between the two families; Pope's friend and benefactor John Caryll (l. 3) suggested the subject for a poem that might settle the controversy.

3. Le . . . Gabalis: by the Abbé de Montfaucon, published in 1670.

And oped those eyes that must eclipse the day.
Now lapdogs give themselves the rousing shake,   15
And sleepless lovers just at twelve awake:
Thrice rung the bell, the slipper knocked the
    ground,
And the pressed watch° returned a silver sound.
Belinda still her downy pillow pressed,
Her guardian Sylph prolonged the balmy rest: 20
'Twas he had summoned to her silent bed
The morning dream that hovered o'er her head.
A youth more glittering than a birthnight beau°
(That even in slumber caused her cheek to glow)
Seemed to her ear his winning lips to lay,   25
And thus in whispers said, or seemed to say:
    "Fairest of mortals, thou distinguished care
Of thousand bright inhabitants of air!
If e'er one vision touched thy infant thought,
Of all the nurse and all the priest have taught,   30
Of airy elves by moonlight shadows seen,
The silver token, and the circled green,°
Or virgins visited by angel powers,
With golden crowns and wreaths of heavenly
    flowers,
Hear and believe! thy own importance know,   35
Nor bound thy narrow views to things below.
Some secret truths, from learned pride concealed,
To maids alone and children are revealed:
What though no credit doubting wits may give?
The fair and innocent shall still believe.   40
Know, then, unnumbered spirits round thee fly,
The light militia of the lower sky:
These, though unseen, are ever on the wing,
Hang o'er the box,° and hover round the Ring.°
Think what an equipage thou hast in air,   45
And view with scorn two pages and a chair.°
As now your own, our beings were of old,
And once enclosed in woman's beauteous mold;
Thence, by a soft transition, we repair
From earthly vehicles to these of air.   50
Think not, when woman's transient breath is fled,
That all her vanities at once are dead:
Succeeding vanities she still regards,
And though she plays no more, o'erlooks the cards.
Her joy in gilded chariots, when alive,   55

Canto I. **18. pressed watch:** one that chimes the hour and the quarter-hour when its stem is pressed. **23. birthnight beau:** courtier finely dressed for his sovereign's birthday. **32. silver . . . green:** In folklore, fairies skim cream from milk and leave a coin in payment, and rings of bright green grass indicate where they have danced. **44. box:** theater box. **Ring:** circular drive in Hyde Park. **46. chair:** sedan chair.

And love of ombre,° after death survive.
For when the Fair in all their pride expire,
To their first elements° their souls retire:
The sprites of fiery termagants in flame
Mount up, and take a Salamander's name.   60
Soft yielding minds to water glide away,
And sip, with Nymphs, their elemental tea.
The graver prude sinks downward to a Gnome,
In search of mischief still on earth to roam.
The light coquettes in Sylphs aloft repair,   65
And sport and flutter in the fields of air.
    "Know further yet; whoever fair and chaste
Rejects mankind, is by some Sylph embraced:
For spirits, freed from mortal laws, with ease
Assume what sexes and what shapes they please.   70
What guards the purity of melting maids,
In courtly balls, and midnight masquerades,
Safe from the treacherous friend, the daring spark,
The glance by day, the whisper in the dark,
When kind occasion prompts their warm desires,   75
When music softens, and when dancing fires?
'Tis but their Sylph, the wise Celestials know,
Though honor is the word with men below.
    "Some nymphs there are, too conscious of their
    face,
For life predestined to the Gnomes' embrace.   80
These swell their prospects and exalt their pride,
When offers are disdained, and love denied:
Then gay ideas° crown the vacant brain,
While peers, and dukes, and all their sweeping
    train,
And garters, stars, and coronets appear,   85
And in soft sounds, 'your grace' salutes their ear.
'Tis these that early taint the female soul,
Instruct the eyes of young coquettes to roll,
Teach infant cheeks a bidden blush to know,
And little hearts to flutter at a beau.   90
    "Oft, when the world imagine women stray,
The Sylphs through mystic mazes guide their way,
Through all the giddy circle they pursue,
And old impertinence expel by new.
What tender maid but must a victim fall   95
To one man's treat, but for another's ball?
When Florio speaks what virgin could withstand,
If gentle Damon did not squeeze her hand?
With varying vanities, from every part,

56. ombre: card game. **58. first elements:** fire, air, earth, and water from which all things are made; as one of the "humors" each may dominate a person's character. **83. ideas:** images.

They shift the moving toyshop of their heart;   100
Where wigs with wigs, with sword-knots sword-
     knots strive,
Beaux banish beaux, and coaches coaches drive.
This erring mortals levity may call;
Oh, blind to truth! the Sylphs contrive it all.
     "Of these am I, who thy protection claim,   105
A watchful sprite, and Ariel is my name.
Late, as I ranged the crystal wilds of air,
In the clear mirror of thy ruling star
I saw, alas! some dread event impend,
Ere to the main this morning sun descend,   110
But Heaven reveals not what, or how, or where:
Warned by the Sylph, O pious maid, beware!
This to disclose is all thy guardian can:
Beware of all, but most beware of man!"
     He said; when Shock,° who thought she slept
     too long,   115
Leaped up, and waked his mistress with his tongue.
'Twas then, Belinda, if report say true,
Thy eyes first opened on a billet-doux;
Wounds, charms, and ardors were no sooner read,
But all the vision vanished from thy head.   120
     And now, unveiled, the toilet stands displayed,
Each silver vase in mystic order laid.
First, roved in white, the nymph intent adores,
With head uncovered, the cosmetic powers.
A heavenly image in the glass appears;   125
To that she bends, to that her eyes she rears.
The inferior priestess, at her altar's side,
Trembling begins the sacred rites of pride.
Unnumbered treasures ope at once, and here
The various offerings of the world appear;   130
From each she nicely culls with curious toil,
And decks the goddess with the glittering spoil.
This casket India's glowing gems unlocks,
And all Arabia breathes from yonder box.
The tortoise here and elephant unite,   135
Transformed to combs, the speckled and the white.
Here files of pins extend their shining rows,
Puffs, powders, patches,° Bibles, billet-doux.
Now awful Beauty puts on all its arms;
The fair each moment rises in her charms,   140
Repairs her smiles, awakens every grace,
And calls forth all the wonders of her face;
Sees by degrees a purer blush arise,
And keener lightnings quicken in her eyes.
The busy Sylphs surround their darling care,   145

These set the head, and those divide the hair,
Some fold the sleeve, whilst others plait the gown;
And Betty's° praised for labors not her own.

CANTO II

Not with more glories, in the ethereal plain,
The sun first rises o'er the purpled main,
Than, issuing forth, the rival of his beams
Launched on the bosom of the silver Thames.
Fair nymphs and well-dressed youths around her
     shone,   5
But every eye was fixed on her alone.
On her white breast a sparkling cross she wore,
Which Jews might kiss, and infidels adore.
Her lively looks a sprightly mind disclose,
Quick as her eyes, and as unfixed as those: 10
Favors to none, to all she smiles extends;
Oft she rejects, but never once offends.
Bright as the sun, her eyes the gazers strike,
And, like the sun, they shine on all alike.
Yet graceful ease, and sweetness void of pride,   15
Might hide her faults, if belles had faults to hide:
If to her share some female errors fall,
Look on her face, and you'll forget 'em all.
     This nymph, to the destruction of mankind,
Nourished two locks which graceful hung behind 20
In equal curls, and well conspired to deck
With shining ringlets the smooth ivory neck.
Love in these labyrinths his slaves detains,
And mighty hearts are held in slender chains.
With hairy springes° we the birds betray,   25
Slight lines of hair surprise the finny prey,
Fair tresses man's imperial race ensnare,
And beauty draws us with a single hair.
     The adventurous baron the bright locks admired,
He saw, he wished, and to the prize aspired.   30
Resolved to win, he meditates the way,
By force to ravish, or by fraud betray;
For when success a lover's toil attends,
Few ask if fraud or force attained his ends.
     For this, ere Phoebus rose, he had implored   35
Propitious Heaven, and every power adored,
But chiefly Love—to Love an altar built,
Of twelve vast French romances, neatly gilt.
There lay three garters, half a pair of gloves,
And all the trophies of his former loves.   40
With tender billet-doux he lights the pyre,

---

115. Shock: Belinda's lapdog. **138. patches:** beauty spots
applied to the face.

148. Betty: Belinda's maid.
     Canto II.   **25. springes:** traps, snares

And breathes three amorous sighs to raise the fire.
Then prostrate falls, and begs with ardent eyes
Soon to obtain, and long possess the prize:
The powers gave ear, and granted half his prayer, 45
The rest the winds dispersed in empty air.

But now secure the painted vessel glides,
The sunbeams trembling on the floating tides,
While melting music steals upon the sky,
And softened sounds along the waters die.　　50
Smooth flow the waves, the zephyrs gently play,
Belinda smiled, and all the world was gay.
All but the Sylph—with careful thoughts oppressed,
The impending woe sat heavy on his breast.
He summons straight his denizens of air;　　55
The lucid squadrons round the sails repair:
Soft o'er the shrouds aërial whispers breathe
That seemed but zephyrs to the train beneath.
Some to the sun their insect-wings unfold,
Waft on the breeze, or sink in clouds of gold.　60
Transparent forms too fine for mortal sight,
Their fluid bodies half dissolved in light,
Loose to the wind their airy garments flew,
Thin glittering textures of the filmy dew,
Dipped in the richest tincture of the skies,　　65
Where light disports in ever-mingling dyes,
While every beam new transient colors flings,
Colors that change whene'er they wave their wings.
Amid the circle, on the gilded mast,
Superior by the head was Ariel placed;　　70
His purple pinions opening to the sun,
He raised his azure wand, and thus begun:

"Ye Sylphs and Sylphids, to your chief give ear!
Fays, Fairies, Genii, Elves, and Daemons, hear!
Ye know the spheres and various tasks assigned 75
By laws eternal to the aërial kind.
Some in the fields of purest ether play,
And bask and whiten in the blaze of day.
Some guide the course of wandering orbs on high,
Or roll the planets through the boundless sky.　80
Some less refined, beneath the moon's pale light
Pursue the stars that shoot athwart the night,
Or suck the mists in grosser air below,
Or dip their pinions in the painted bow,
Or brew fierce tempests on the wintry main,　85
Or o'er the glebe° distill the kindly rain.
Others on earth o'er human race preside,
Watch all their ways, and all their actions guide:
Of these the chief the care of nations own,
And guard with arms divine the British throne.　90

86. glebe: cultivated field.

"Our humbler province is to tend the Fair,
Not a less pleasing, though less glorious care:
To save the powder from too rude a gale,
Nor let the imprisoned essences exhale;
To draw fresh colors from the vernal flowers;　95
To steal from rainbows e'er they drop in showers
A brighter wash;° to curl their waving hairs,
Assist their blushes, and inspire their airs;
Nay oft, in dreams invention we bestow,
To change a flounce, or add a furbelow.　　100

"This day black omens threat the brightest fair,
That e'er deserved a watchful spirit's care;
Some dire disaster, or by force or slight,
But what, or where, the Fates have wrapped in night:
Whether the nymph shall break Diana's law,° 105
Or some frail china jar receive a flaw,
Or stain her honor or her new brocade,
Forget her prayers, or miss a masquerade,
Or lose her heart, or necklace, at a ball;
Or whether Heaven has doomed that Shock must fall.　　110
Haste, then, ye spirits! to your charge repair:
The fluttering fan be Zephyretta's care;
The drops° to thee, Brillante, we consign;
And, Momentilla, let the watch be thine;
Do thou, Crispissa, tend her favorite Lock;　115
Ariel himself shall be the guard of Shock.

"To fifty chosen Sylphs, of special note,
We trust the important charge, the petticoat;
Oft have we known that sevenfold fence to fail,
Though stiff with hoops, and armed with ribs of whale.　　120
Form a strong line about the silver bound,
And guard the wide circumference around.

"Whatever spirit, careless of his charge,
His post neglects, or leaves the fair at large,
Shall feel sharp vengeance soon o'ertake his sins,
Be stopped in vials, or transfixed with pins,　126
Or plunged in lakes of bitter washes lie,
Or wedged whole ages in a bodkin's eye;°
Gums and pomatums shall his flight restrain,
While clogged he beats his silken wings in vain, 130
Or alum styptics with contracting power
Shrink his thin essence like a riveled° flower:
Or, as Ixion fixed, the wretch shall feel
The giddy motion of the whirling mill,

97. wash: face lotion. 105. Diana's law: chastity. 113.
drops: diamond earrings. 128. bodkin's eye: the large eye
of a blunt needle. 132. riveled: wrinkled.

In fumes of burning chocolate shall glow,   135
And tremble at the sea that froths below!"
    He spoke; the spirits from the sails descend;
Some, orb in orb, around the nymph extend;
Some thread the mazy ringlets of her hair;
Some hang upon the pendants of her ear: 140
With beating hearts the dire event they wait,
Anxious, and trembling for the birth of Fate.

CANTO III

Close by those meads, forever crowned with flowers,
Where Thames with pride surveys his rising towers,
There stands a structure of majestic frame,
Which from the neighboring Hampton takes its
    name.°
Here Britain's statesmen oft the fall foredoom   5
Of foreign tyrants and of nymphs at home;
Here thou, great Anna! whom three realms obey,
Dost sometimes counsel take—and sometimes tea.
    Hither the heroes and the nymphs resort,
To taste awhile the pleasures of a court;   10
In various talk the instructive hours they passed,
Who gave the ball, or paid the visit last;
One speaks the glory of the British queen,
And one describes a charming Indian screen;
A third interprets motions, looks, and eyes;   15
At every word a reputation dies.
Snuff, or the fan, supply each pause of chat,
With singing, laughing, ogling, and all that.
    Meanwhile, declining from the noon of day,
The sun obliquely shoots his burning ray;   20
The hungry judges soon the sentence sign,
And wretches hang that jurymen may dine;
The merchant from the Exchange returns in peace,
And the long labors of the toilet cease.
Belinda now, whom thirst of fame invites,   25
Burns to encounter two adventurous knights,
At ombre° singly to decide their doom,
And swells her breast with conquests yet to come.
Straight the three bands prepare in arms to join,
Each band the number of the sacred nine.   30

Canto III. **4. name:** Hampton Court. **27. ombre:** In this
complicated card game, arranged here so that Belinda
defeats the baron and another player, each person has nine
cards (l. 30). The three cards of highest value are called
the Matadors (l. 33); when spades are trump, they are
Spadillio, the ace of spades (l. 49), Manillio, the deuce of
spades (l. 51), and Basto, the ace of clubs (l. 53), all in
Belinda's hand.

Soon as she spreads her hand, the aërial guard
Descend, and sit on each important card:
First Ariel perched upon a Matador,
Then each according to the rank they bore;
For Sylphs, yet mindful of their ancient race,   35
Are, as when women, wondrous fond of place.
    Behold, four Kings in majesty revered,
With hoary whiskers and a forky beard;
And four fair Queens whose hands sustain a flower,
The expressive emblem of their softer power;   40
Four Knaves in garbs succinct,° a trusty band,
Caps on their heads, and halberts in their hand;
And particolored troops, a shining train,
Draw forth to combat on the velvet plain.
    The skillful nymph reviews her force with care;
"Let Spades be trumps!" she said, and trumps they
    were.   46
    Now move to war her sable Matadors,
In show like leaders of the swarthy Moors.
Spadillio first, unconquerable lord!
Led off two captive trumps, and swept the board.   50
As many more Manillio forced to yield,
And marched a victor from the verdant field.
Him Basto followed, but his fate more hard
Gained but one trump and one plebeian card.
With his broad saber next, a chief in years,   55
The hoary Majesty of Spades appears,
Puts forth one manly leg, to sight revealed,
The rest his many-colored robe concealed.
The rebel Knave, who dares his prince engage,
Proves the just victim of his royal rage.   60
Even mighty Pam, that kings and queens o'erthrew
And mowed down armies in the fights of loo,°
Sad chance of war! now destitute of aid,
Falls undistinguished by the victor Spade.
    Thus far both armies to Belinda yield;   65
Now to the baron fate inclines the field.
His warlike amazon her host invades,
The imperial consort of the crown of Spades.
The Club's black tyrant first her victim died,
Spite of his haughty mien and barbarous pride.   70
What boots the regal circle on his head,
His giant limbs, in state unwieldy spread?
That long behind he trails his pompous robe,
And of all monarchs only grasps the globe?
    The baron now his Diamonds pours apace;   75
The embroidered King who shows but half his face,
And his refulgent Queen, with powers combined

---

41. succinct: bound up. **61–62. Pam . . . loo:** knave of
clubs, highest card in the game of loo.

Of broken troops an easy conquest find.
Clubs, Diamonds, Hearts, in wild disorder seen,
With throngs promiscuous strew the level green.   80
Thus when dispersed a routed army runs,
Of Asia's troops, and Afric's sable sons,
With like confusion different nations fly,
Of various habit, and of various dye,
The pierced battalions disunited fall   85
In heaps on heaps; one fate o'erwhelms them all.
  The Knave of Diamonds tries his wily arts,
And wins (oh, shameful chance!) the Queen of
    Hearts.
At this, the blood the virgin's cheek forsook,
A vivid paleness spreads o'er all her look;
She sees, and trembles at the approaching ill,
Just in the jaws of ruin, and Codille,°
And now (as oft in some distempered state)
On one nice trick depends the general fate.
An Ace of Hearts steps forth: the King unseen   95
Lurked in her hand, and mourned his captive
    Queen.
He springs to vengeance with an eager pace,
And falls like thunder on the prostrate Ace.
The nymph exulting fills with shouts the sky,
The walls, the woods, and long canals reply.   100
  O thoughtless mortals! ever blind to fate,
Too soon dejected, and too soon elate:
Sudden these honors shall be snatched away,
And cursed forever this victorious day.
  For lo! the board with cups and spoons is
    crowned,   105
The berries crackle, and the mill turns round;°
On shining altars of Japan° they raise
The silver lamp; the fiery spirits blaze:
From silver spouts the grateful liquors glide,
While China's earth receives the smoking tide. 110
At once they gratify their scent and taste,
And frequent cups prolong the rich repast.
Straight hover round the fair her airy band;
Some, as she sipped, the fuming liquor fanned,
Some o'er her lap their careful plumes displayed,
Trembling, and conscious of the rich brocade.   116
Coffee (which makes the politician wise,
And see through all things with his half-shut eyes)
Sent up in vapors to the baron's brain
New stratagems, the radiant Lock to gain.   120
Ah, cease, rash youth! desist ere 'tis too late,

Fear the just gods, and think of Scylla's fate!
Changed to a bird, and sent to flit in air,
She dearly pays for Nisus' injured hair!°
  But when to mischief mortals bend their will, 125
How soon they find fit instruments of ill!
Just then, Clarissa drew with tempting grace
A two-edged weapon from her shining case:
So ladies in romance assist their knight,
Present the spear, and arm him for the fight.   130
He takes the gift with reverence, and extends
The little engine on his fingers' ends;
This just behind Belinda's neck he spread,
As o'er the fragrant steams she bends her head.
Swift to the Lock a thousand sprites repair,   135
A thousand wings, by turns, blow back the hair,
And thrice they twitched the diamond in her ear,
Thrice she looked back, and thrice the foe drew
    near.
Just in that instant, anxious Ariel sought
The close recesses of the virgin's thought;   140
As on the nosegay in her breast reclined,
He watched the ideas rising in her mind,
Sudden he viewed, in spite of all her art,
An earthly lover lurking at her heart.
Amazed, confused, he found his power expired,   145
Resigned to fate, and with a sigh retired.
  The peer now spreads the glittering forfex° wide,
To enclose the Lock; now joins it, to divide.
Even then, before the fatal engine closed,
A wretched Sylph too fondly interposed;   150
Fate urged the shears, and cut the Sylph in twain
(But airy substance soon unites again):
The meeting points the sacred hair dissever
From the fair head, forever, and forever!
  Then flashed the living lightning from her eyes,
And screams of horror rend the affrighted skies. 156
Not louder shrieks to pitying heaven are cast,
When husbands, or when lapdogs breathe their last;
Or when rich china vessels fallen from high,
In glittering dust and painted fragments lie!   160
"Let wreaths of triumph now my temples twine,"
The victor cried, "the glorious prize is mine!
While fish in streams, or birds delight in air,
Or in a coach and six the British Fair,
As long as *Atalantis*° shall be read,   165
Or the small pillow grace a lady's bed,

92. **Codille:** means losing the game. **106. berries . . . round:** coffee being roasted and ground. **107. altars of Japan:** small lacquered tables.

122–24. **Scylla's . . . hair:** To aid her lover, Minos, who was besieging her father's city, Scylla cut off the lock of her father's hair on which his safety depended. **147. forfex:** scissors. **165. Atalantis:** contemporary novel popular for its allusions to court and party scandals.

While visits shall be paid on solemn days,
When numerous wax-lights in bright order blaze,
While nymphs take treats, or assignations give,
So long my honor, name, and praise shall live!   170
What Time would spare, from Steel receives its
date,
And monuments, like men, submit to fate!
Steel could the labor of the gods destroy,
And strike to dust the imperial towers of Troy;
Steel could the works of mortal pride confound, 175
And hew triumphal arches to the ground.
What wonder then, fair nymph! thy hairs should
feel,
The conquering force of unresisted Steel?"

CANTO IV

But anxious cares the pensive nymph oppressed,
And secret passions labored in her breast.
Not youthful kings in battle seized alive,
Not scornful virgins who their charms survive,
Not ardent lovers robbed of all their bliss,   5
Not ancient ladies when refused a kiss,
Not tyrants fierce that unrepenting die,
Not Cynthia when her manteau's° pinned awry,
E'er felt such rage, resentment, and despair,
As thou, sad virgin! for thy ravished hair.   10
  For, that sad moment, when the Sylphs withdrew
And Ariel weeping from Belinda flew,
Umbriel, a dusky, melancholy sprite
As ever sullied the fair face of light,
Down to the central earth, his proper scene,   15
Repaired to search the gloomy Cave of Spleen.
  Swift on his sooty pinions flits the Gnome,
And in a vapor reached the dismal dome.
No cheerful breeze this sullen region knows,
The dreaded east is all the wind that blows.   20
Here in a grotto, sheltered close from air,
And screened in shades from day's detested glare,
She sighs forever on her pensive bed,
Pain at her side, and Megrim° at her head.
  Two handmaids wait the throne: alike in place,
But differing far in figure and in face.   26
Here stood Ill-Nature like an ancient maid,
Her wrinkled form in black and white arrayed;
With store of prayers for mornings, nights, and
noons,
Her hand is filled; her bosom with lampoons.   30

Canto IV. 8. manteau: loose robe. 24. Megrim: head-
ache.

There Affectation, with a sickly mien,
Shows in her cheek the roses of eighteen,
Practiced to lisp, and hang the head aside,
Faints into airs, and languishes with pride,
On the rich quilt sinks with becoming woe,   35
Wrapped in a gown, for sickness and for show.
The fair ones feel such maladies as these,
When each new nightdress gives a new disease.
  A constant vapor° o'er the palace flies,
Strange phantoms rising as the mists arise;   40
Dreadful as hermit's dreams in haunted shades,
Or bright as visions of expiring maids.
Now glaring fiends, and snakes on rolling spires,°
Pale specters, gaping tombs, and purple fires;
Now lakes of liquid gold, Elysian scenes,   45
And crystal domes, and angels in machines.°
  Unnumbered throngs on every side are seen
Of bodies changed to various forms by Spleen.
Here living teapots stand, one arm held out,
One bent; the handle this, and that the spout: 50
A pipkin there, like Homer's tripod, walks;°
Here sighs a jar, and there a goose pie talks;
Men prove with child, as powerful fancy works,
And maids, turned bottles, call aloud for corks.
  Safe passed the Gnome through this fantastic
band,   55
A branch of healing spleenwort° in his hand.
Then thus addressed the power: "Hail, wayward
queen!
Who rule the sex to fifty from fifteen:
Parent of vapors and of female wit,
Who give the hysteric or poetic fit,   60
On various tempers act by various ways,
Make some take physic, others scribble plays;
Who cause the proud their visits to delay,
And send the godly in a pet to pray.
A nymph there is that all your power disdains, 65
And thousands more in equal mirth maintains.
But oh! if e'er thy Gnome could spoil a grace,
Or raise a pimple on a beauteous face,
Like citron-waters° matrons' cheeks inflame,
Or change complexions at a losing game;   70
If e'er with airy horns° I planted heads,

39. **vapor:** representative of the "vapors, hypochon-
dria, melancholy, peevishness, considered fashionable
among society ladies. **43. spires:** coils. **46. machines:**
theatrical devices for spectacular effects. **51. pipkin . . .
walks:** earthen pot like the three-legged stools Vulcan gives
the gods in the *Iliad*, XVIII.373–77. **56. spleenwort:** herb
for ailments of the spleen. **69. citron-waters:** orange- or
lemon-flavored brandy. **71. horns:** of the cuckold.

Or rumpled petticoats, or tumbled beds,
Or caused suspicion when no soul was rude,
Or discomposed the headdress of a prude,
O e'er to costive lapdog gave disease,   75
Which not the tears of brightest eyes could ease,
Hear me, and touch Belinda with chagrin.
That single act gives half the world the spleen."
  The goddess with a discontented air
Seems to reject him though she grants his prayer. 80
A wondrous bag with both her hands she binds,
Like that where once Ulysses held the winds;°
There she collects the force of female lungs,
Sighs, sobs, and passions, and the war of tongues.
A vial next she fills with fainting fears,   85
Soft sorrows, melting griefs, and flowing tears.
The Gnome rejoicing bears her gifts away,
Spreads his black wings, and slowly mounts to day.
  Sunk in Thalestris'° arms the nymph he found,
Her eyes dejected and her hair unbound.   90
Full o'er their heads the swelling bag he rent,
And all the Furies issued at the vent.
Belinda burns with more than mortal ire,
And fierce Thalestris fans the rising fire.
"O wretched maid!" she spread her hands, and
      cried   95
(While Hampton's echoes, "Wretched maid!"
      replied),
"Was it for this you took such constant care
The bodkin, comb, and essence to prepare?
For this your locks in paper durance bound,
For this with torturing irons wreathed around?   100
For this with fillets strained your tender head,
And bravely bore the double loads of lead?°
Gods! shall the ravisher display your hair,
While the fops envy, and the ladies stare!
Honor forbid! at whose unrivaled shrine   105
Ease, pleasure, virtue, all, our sex resign.
Methinks already I your tears survey,
Already hear the horrid things they say,
Already see you a degraded toast,
And all your honor in a whisper lost!   110
How shall I, then, your helpless fame defend?
'Twill then be infamy to seem your friend!
And shall this prize, the inestimable prize,
Exposed through crystal to the gazing eyes,
And heightened by the diamond's circling rays,   115

On that rapacious hand forever blaze?
Sooner shall grass in Hyde Park Circus grow,
And wits take lodgings in the sound of Bow;°
Sooner let earth, air, sea, to chaos fall,
Men, monkeys, lapdogs, parrots, perish all!"   120
  She said; then raging to Sir Plume repairs,
And bids her beau demand the precious hairs
(Sir Plume of amber snuffbox justly vain,
And the nice conduct of a clouded cane).
With earnest eyes, and round unthinking face,   125
He first the snuffbox opened, then the case,
And thus broke out—"My Lord, why, what the
      devil!
Z——ds! damn the lock! 'fore Gad, you must be
      civil!
Plague on 't! 'tis past a jest—nay prithee, pox!
Give her the hair"—he spoke, and rapped his box.
  "It grieves me much," replied the peer again, 131
"Who speaks so well should ever speak in vain.
But by this Lock, this sacred Lock I swear
(Which never more shall join its parted hair;
Which never more its honors shall renew,   135
Clipped from the lovely head where late it grew),
That while my nostrils draw the vital air,
This hand, which won it, shall forever wear."
He spoke, and speaking, in proud triumph spread
The long-contended honors of her head.   140
  But Umbriel, hateful Gnome, forbears not so;
He breaks the vial whence the sorrows flow.
Then see! the nymph in beauteous grief appears,
Her eyes half languishing, half drowned in tears;
On her heaved bosom hung her drooping head,   145
Which with a sigh she raised, and thus she said:
  "Forever cursed be this detested day,
Which snatched my best, my favorite curl away!
Happy! ah, ten times happy had I been,
If Hampton Court these eyes had never seen!   150
Yet am not I the first mistaken maid,
By love of courts to numerous ills betrayed.
Oh, had I rather unadmired remained
In some lone isle, or distant northern land;
Where the gilt chariot never marks the way,   155
Where none learn ombre, none e'er taste bohea!°
There kept my charms concealed from mortal eye,
Like roses that in deserts bloom and die.
What moved my mind with youthful lords to roam?
Oh, had I stayed, and said my prayers at home!   160

---

82. **Ulysses . . . winds:** Aeolus gave Ulysses a bag of adverse
winds in the *Odyssey*, X.19ff. 89. **Thalestris:** fierce and
warlike queen of the Amazons. 102. **lead:** frames for
elaborate coiffures.

118. **Bow:** church of Saint Mary-le-Bow; anyone born
within the sound of its bells was considered a cockney. 156.
bohea: black tea.

'Twas this the morning omens seemed to tell,
Thrice from my trembling hand the patch box° fell;
The tottering china shook without a wind,
Nay, Poll sat mute, and Shock was most unkind!
A Sylph too warned me of the threats of fate,   165
In mystic visions, now believed too late!
See the poor remnants of these slighted hairs!
My hands shall rend what e'en thy rapine spares.
These in two sable ringlets taught to break,
Once gave new beauties to the snowy neck;   170
The sister lock now sits uncouth, alone,
And in its fellow's fate foresees its own;
Uncurled it hangs, the fatal shears demands,
And tempts once more thy sacrilegious hands.
Oh, hadst thou, cruel! been content to seize   175
Hairs less in sight, or any hairs but these!"

CANTO V

She said: the pitying audience melt in tears,
But Fate and Jove had stopped the baron's ears.
In vain Thalestris with reproach assails,
For who can move when fair Belinda fails?
Not half so fixed the Trojan° could remain,   5
While Anna begged and Dido raged in vain.
Then grave Clarissa graceful waved her fan;
Silence ensued, and thus the nymph began:
   "Say why are beauties praised and honored most,
The wise man's passion, and the vain man's toast?
Why decked with all that land and sea afford,   11
Why angels called, and angel-like adored?
Why round our coaches crowd the white-gloved
      beaux,
Why bows the side box from its inmost rows?
How vain are all these glories, all our pains,   15
Unless good sense preserve what beauty gains;
That men may say when we the front box grace,
'Behold the first in virtue as in face!'
Oh! if to dance all night, and dress all day,
Charmed the smallpox, or chased old age away,   20
Who would not scorn what housewife's cares
      produce,
Or who would learn one earthly thing of use?
To patch, nay ogle, might become a saint,
Nor could it sure be such a sin to paint.
But since, alas! frail beauty must decay,   25
Curled or uncurled, since locks will turn to gray;
Since painted, or not painted, all shall fade,

Canto V. **5. Trojan**: Aeneas forsook Dido in spite of her rage and her sister's pleading.

And she who scorns a man must die a maid;
What then remains but well our power to use,
And keep good humor still whate'er we lose?   30
And trust me, dear, good humor can prevail
When airs, and flights, and screams, and scolding
      fail.
Beauties in vain their pretty eyes may roll;
Charms strike the sight, but merit wins the soul."
   So spoke the dame, but no applause ensued;   35
Belinda frowned, Thalestris called her prude.
"To arms, to arms!" the fierce virago cries,
And swift as lightning to the combat flies.
All side in parties, and begin the attack;
Fans clap, silks rustle, and tough whalebones
      crack;   40
Heroes' and heroines' shouts confusedly rise,
And bass and treble voices strike the skies.
No common weapons in their hands are found,
Like gods they fight, nor dread a mortal wound.
   So when bold Homer makes the gods engage,   45
And heavenly breasts with human passions rage;
'Gainst Pallas, Mars; Latona, Hermes arms;
And all Olympus rings with loud alarms:
Jove's thunder roars, heaven trembles all around,
Blue Neptune storms, the bellowing deeps resound:
Earth shakes her nodding towers, the ground gives
      way,   51
And the pale ghosts start at the flash of day!
   Triumphant Umbriel on a sconce's height
Clapped his glad wings, and sat to view the fight:
Propped on the bodkin spears, the sprites survey   55
The growing combat, or assist the fray.
   While through the press enraged Thalestris flies,
And scatters death around from both her eyes,
A beau and witling perished in the throng,
One died in metaphor, and one in song.   60
"O cruel nymph! a living death I bear,"
Cried Dapperwit, and sunk beside his chair.
A mournful glance Sir Fopling upwards cast,
"Those eyes are made so killing"—was his last.
Thus on Maeander's flowery margin lies   65
The expiring swan, and as he sings he dies.
   When bold Sir Plume had drawn Clarissa down,
Chloe stepped in, and killed him with a frown;
She smiled to see the doughty hero slain,
But, at her smile, the beau revived again.   70
   Now Jove suspends his golden scales in air,
Weighs the men's wits against the lady's hair;
The doubtful beam long nods from side to side;
At length the wits mount up, the hairs subside.

See, fierce Belinda on the baron flies, 75
With more than usual lightning in her eyes;
Nor feared the chief the unequal fight to try,
Who sought no more than on his foe to die.

But this bold lord with manly strength endued,
She with one finger and a thumb subdued: 80
Just where the breath of life his nostrils drew,
A charge of snuff the wily virgin threw;
The Gnomes direct, to every atom just,
The pungent grains of titillating dust.
Sudden, with starting tears each eye o'erflows, 85
And the high dome re-echoes to his nose.

"Now meet thy fate," incensed Belinda cried,
And drew a deadly bodkin from her side.
(The same, his ancient personage to deck,
Her great-great-grandsire wore about his neck, 90
In three seal rings; which after, melted down,
Formed a vast buckle for his widow's gown:
Her infant grandame's whistle next it grew,
The bells she jingled, and the whistle blew;
Then in a bodkin graced her mother's hairs, 95
Which long she wore, and now Belinda wears.)

"Blast not my fall," he cried, "insulting foe!
Thou by some other shalt be laid as low.
Nor think to die dejects my lofty mind:
All that I dread is leaving you behind! 100
Rather than so, ah, let me still survive,
And burn in Cupid's flames—but burn alive."

"Restore the Lock!" she cries; and all around
"Restore the Lock!" the vaulted roofs rebound.
Not fierce Othello in so loud a strain 105
Roared for the handkerchief that caused his pain.°
But see how oft ambitious aims are crossed,
And chiefs content till all the prize is lost!
The lock, obtained with guilt, and kept with pain,
In every place is sought, but sought in vain: 110
With such a prize no mortal must be blessed,
So Heaven decrees! with Heaven who can contest?

Some thought it mounted to the lunar sphere,
Since all things lost on earth are treasured there.
There heroes' wits are kept in ponderous vases, 115
And beaux' in snuffboxes and tweezer cases.
There broken vows and deathbed alms are found,
And lovers' hearts with ends of riband bound,
The courtier's promises, and sick man's prayers,
The smiles of harlots, and the tears of heirs, 120
Cages for gnats, and chains to yoke a flea,

Dried butterflies, and tomes of casuistry.
But trust the Muse—she saw it upward rise,
Though marked by none but quick, poetic eyes
(So Rome's great founder to the heavens with-
    drew,° 125
To Proculus alone confessed in view);
A sudden star, it shot through liquid air,
And drew behind a radiant trail of hair.
Not Berenice's locks first rose so bright,°
The heavens bespangling with disheveled light. 130
The Sylphs behold it kindling as it flies,
And pleased pursue its progress through the skies.
This the beau monde shall from the Mall°
    survey,
And hail with music its propitious ray.
This the blest lover shall for Venus take, 135
And send up vows from Rosamonda's Lake.°
This Partridge° soon shall view in cloudless skies,
When next he looks through Galileo's eyes;
And hence the egregious wizard shall foredoom
The fate of Louis, and the fall of Rome. 140
Then cease, bright nymph! to mourn thy ravished
    hair,
Which adds new glory to the shining sphere!
Not all the tresses that fair head can boast,
Shall draw such envy as the Lock you lost.
For, after all the murders of your eye, 145
When, after millions slain, yourself shall die:
When those fair suns shall set, as set they must,
And all those tresses shall be laid in dust,
This Lock the Muse shall consecrate to fame,
And 'midst the stars inscribe Belinda's name. 150

105–06. Othello . . . pain: in Shakespeare's *Othello*, IV.i, the Moor takes Iago's possession of Desdemona's handkerchief as proof of her infidelity.

125. Rome's . . . withdrew: Romulus, first king of Rome, was taken up into heaven in a storm cloud. 129. Berenice's . . . bright: Berenice dedicated a lock of her hair to the gods to insure the return of her husband Ptolemy III from the war; the lock became a constellation. 133. Mall: a walk in Saint James's Park. 136. Rosamonda's Lake: a pond in Saint James's Park associated with disappointed lovers. 137. Partridge: John Partridge, a contemporary astrologer.

JOSEPH CONRAD
1857–1924

Heart of Darkness

1

The *Nellie*, a cruising yawl, swung to her anchor without a flutter of the sails, and was at rest. The flood had made, the wind was nearly calm, and being bound down the river, the only thing for it was to come to and wait for the turn of the tide.

The sea-reach of the Thames stretched before us like the beginning of an interminable waterway. In the offing the sea and the sky were welded together without a joint, and in the luminous space the tanned sails of the barges drifting up with the tide seemed to stand still in red clusters of canvas sharply peaked, with gleams of varnished sprits. A haze rested on the low shores that ran out to sea in vanishing flatness. The air was dark above Gravesend,[1] and farther back still seemed condensed into a mournful gloom, brooding motionless over the biggest, and the greatest, town on earth.

The Director of Companies was our captain and our host. We four affectionately watched his back as he stood in the bows looking to seaward. On the whole river there was nothing that looked half so nautical. He resembled a pilot, which to a seaman is trustworthiness personified. It was difficult to realize his work was not out there in the luminous estuary, but behind him, within the brooding gloom.

Between us there was, as I have already said somewhere, the bond of the sea. Besides holding our hearts together through long periods of separation, it had the effect of making us tolerant of each other's yarns—and even convictions. The Lawyer—the best of old fellows—had, because of his many years and many virtues, the only cushion on deck, and was lying on the only rug. The Accountant had brought out already a box of dominoes, and was toying architecturally with the bones. Marlow sat cross-legged right aft, leaning against the mizzenmast. He had sunken cheeks, a yellow complexion, a straight back, an ascetic aspect, and, with his

arms dropped, the palms of hands outwards, resembled an idol. The Director, satisfied the anchor had good hold, made his way aft and sat down amongst us. We exchanged a few words lazily. Afterwards there was silence on board the yacht. For some reason or other we did not begin that game of dominoes. We felt meditative, and fit for nothing but placid staring. The day was ending in a serenity of still and exquisite brilliance. The water shone pacifically; the sky, without a speck, was a benign immensity of unstained light; the very mist on the Essex marshes was like a gauzy and radiant fabric, hung from the wooded rises inland, and draping the low shores in diaphanous folds. Only the gloom to the west, brooding over the upper reaches, became more somber every minute, as if angered by the approach of the sun.

And at last, in its curved and imperceptible fall, the sun sank low, and from glowing white changed to a dull red without rays and without heat, as if about to go out suddenly, stricken to death by the touch of that gloom brooding over a crowd of men.

Forthwith a change came over the waters, and the serenity became less brilliant but more profound. The old river in its broad reach rested unruffled at the decline of day, after ages of good service done to the race that peopled its banks, spread out in the tranquil dignity of a waterway leading to the uttermost ends of the earth. We looked at the venerable stream not in the vivid flush of a short day that comes and departs for ever, but in the august light of abiding memories. And indeed nothing is easier for a man who has, as the phrase goes, "followed the sea" with reverence and affection, than to evoke the great spirit of the past upon the lower reaches of the Thames. The tidal current runs to and fro in its unceasing service, crowded with memories of men and ships it has borne to the rest of home or to the battles of the sea. It had known and served all the men of whom the nation is proud, from Sir Francis Drake to Sir John Franklin,[2] knights all, titled and untitled—the great knights-errant of the sea. It had borne all the ships whose names are like jewels flashing in the night of time, from the *Golden Hind* returning with her round flanks full of treasure, to be visited

---

HEART OF DARKNESS.   **1. Gravesend:** town at the mouth of the Thames.

2. Drake . . . Franklin: Drake sailed the *Golden Hind* in the service of Queen Elizabeth; Franklin explored the Northwest Passage in the *Erebus* and the *Terror* in the 1840's.

by the Queen's Highness and thus pass out of the gigantic tale, to the *Erebus* and *Terror*, bound on other conquests—and that never returned. It had known the ships and the men. They had sailed from Deptford, from Greenwich, from Erith—the adventurers and the settlers; kings' ships and the ships of men on 'Change; captains, admirals, the dark "interlopers" of the Eastern trade, and the commissioned "generals" of East India fleets.[3] Hunters for gold or pursuers of fame, they all had gone out on that stream, bearing the sword, and often the torch, messengers of the might within the land, bearers of a spark from the sacred fire. What greatness had not floated on the ebb of that river into the mystery of an unknown earth! . . . The dreams of men, the seed of commonwealths, the germs of empires.

The sun set; the dusk fell on the stream, and lights began to appear along the shore. The Chapman lighthouse, a three-legged thing erect on a mud-flat, shone strongly. Lights of ships moved in the fairway—a great stir of lights going up and going down. And farther west on the upper reaches the place of the monstrous town was still marked ominously on the sky, a brooding gloom in sunshine, a lurid glare under the stars.

"And this also," said Marlow suddenly, "has been one of the dark places of the earth."

He was the only man of us who still "followed the sea." The worst that could be said of him was that he did not represent his class. He was a seaman, but he was a wanderer too, while most seamen lead, if one may so express it, a sedentary life. Their minds are of the stay-at-home order, and their home is always with them—the ship; and so is their country—the sea. One ship is very much like another, and the sea is always the same. In the immutability of their surroundings the foreign shores, the foreign faces, the changing immensity of life, glide past, veiled not by a sense of mystery but by a slightly disdainful ignorance; for there is nothing mysterious to a seaman unless it be the sea itself, which is the mistress of his existence and as inscrutable as Destiny. For the rest, after his hours of work, a casual stroll or a casual spree on shore suffices to unfold for him the secret of a whole continent, and generally he finds the secret not worth knowing. The yarns of seamen have a direct simplicity, the whole meaning of which lies within the shell of a cracked nut. But Marlow was not typical (if his propensity to spin yarns be excepted), and to him the meaning of an episode was not inside like a kernel but outside, enveloping the tale which brought it out only as a glow brings out a haze, in the likeness of one of these misty halos that sometimes are made visible by the spectral illumination of moonshine.

His remark did not seem at all surprising. It was just like Marlow. It was accepted in silence. No one took the trouble to grunt even; and presently he said, very slow:

"I was thinking of very old times, when the Romans first came here, nineteen hundred years ago—the other day. . . . Light came out of this river since—you say knights? Yes; but it is like a running blaze on a plain, like a flash of lightning in the clouds. We live in the flicker—may it last as long as the old earth keeps rolling! But darkness was here yesterday. Imagine the feelings of a commander of a fine—what d'ye call 'em?—trireme[4] in the Mediterranean, ordered suddenly to the north; run overland across the Gauls in a hurry; put in charge of one of these craft the legionaries—a wonderful lot of handy men they must have been too—used to build, apparently by the hundred, in a month or two, if we may believe what we read. Imagine him here—the very end of the world, a sea the color of lead, a sky the color of smoke, a kind of ship about as rigid as a concertina—and going up this river with stores, or orders, or what you like. Sandbanks, marches, forests, savages—precious little to eat fit for a civilized man, nothing but Thames water to drink. No Falernian wine here, no going ashore. Here and there a military camp lost in a wilderness, like a needle in a bundle of hay—cold, fog, tempests, disease, exile, and death—death skulking in the air, in the water, in the bush. They must have been dying like flies here. Oh yes—he did it. Did it very well, too, no doubt, and without thinking much about it either, except afterwards to brag of what he had gone through in his time, perhaps. They were men enough to face the darkness. And perhaps he was cheered by keeping his eye on a chance of promotion to the fleet at Ravenna by and by, if he had good friends

3. **Deptford . . . fleets:** From these three ports on the Thames a variety of ships sailed, some financed by men on the Exchange, the financial center in London, some by men in the East India Company.

4. **trireme:** galley with three banks of oars.

in Rome and survived the awful climate. Or think of a decent young citizen in a toga—perhaps too much dice, you know—coming out here in the train of some prefect, or tax-gatherer, or trader, even, to mend his fortunes. Land in a swamp, march through the woods, and in some inland post feel the savagery, the utter savagery, had closed round him —all that mysterious life of the wilderness that stirs in the forest, in the jungles, in the hearts of wild men. There's no initiation either into such mysteries. He has to live in the midst of the incomprehensible, which is also detestable. And it has a fascination, too, that goes to work upon him. The fascination of the abomination—you know. Imagine the growing regrets, the longing to escape, the powerless disgust, the surrender, the hate."

He paused.

"Mind," he began again, lifting one arm from the elbow, the palm of the hand outwards, so that, with his legs folded before him, he had the pose of a Buddha preaching in European clothes and without a lotus-flower—"Mind, none of us would feel exactly like this. What saves us is efficiency—the devotion to efficiency. But these chaps were not much account, really. They were no colonists; their administration was merely a squeeze, and nothing more, I suspect. They were conquerors, and for that you want only brute force—nothing to boast of, when you have it, since your strength is just an accident arising from the weakness of others. They grabbed what they could get for the sake of what was to be got. It was just robbery with violence, aggravated murder on a great scale, and men going at it blind—as is very proper for those who tackle a darkness. The conquest of the earth, which mostly means the taking it away from those who have a different complexion or slightly flatter noses than ourselves, is not a pretty thing when you look into it too much. What redeems it is the idea only. An idea at the back of it; not a sentimental pretense but an idea; and an unselfish belief in the idea— something you can set up, and bow down before, and offer a sacrifice to. . . ."

He broke off. Flames glided in the river, small green flames, red flames, white flames, pursuing, overtaking, joining, crossing each other—then separating slowly or hastily. The traffic of the great city went on in the deepening night upon the sleepless river. We looked on, waiting patiently— there was nothing else to do till the end of the flood;

but it was only after a long silence, when he said, in a hesitating voice, "I suppose you fellows remember I did once turn fresh-water sailor for a bit," that we knew we were fated, before the ebb began to run, to hear about one of Marlow's inconclusive experiences.

"I don't want to bother you much with what happened to me personally," he began, showing in this remark the weakness of many tellers of tales who seem so often unaware of what their audience would best like to hear; "yet to understand the effect of it on me you ought to know how I got out there, what I saw, how I went up that river to the place where I first met the poor chap. It was the farthest point of navigation and the culminating point of my experience. It seemed somehow to throw a kind of light on everything about me—and into my thoughts. It was somber enough too—and pitiful—not extraordinary in any way—not very clear either. No, not very clear. And yet it seemed to throw a kind of light.

"I had then, as you remember, just returned to London after a lot of Indian Ocean, Pacific, China Seas—a regular dose of the East—six years or so, and I was loafing about, hindering you fellows in your work and invading your homes, just as though I had got a heavenly mission to civilize you. It was very fine for a time, but after a bit I did get tired of resting. Then I began to look for a ship—I should think the hardest work on earth. But the ships wouldn't even look at me. And I got tired of that game too.

"Now when I was a little chap I had a passion for maps. I would look for hours at South America, or Africa, or Australia, and lose myself in all the glories of exploration. At that time there were many blank spaces on the earth, and when I saw one that looked particularly inviting on a map (but they all look that) I would put my finger on it and say, When I grow up I will go there. The North Pole was one of these places, I remember. Well, I haven't been there yet, and shall not try now. The glamor's off. Other places were scattered about the Equator, and in every sort of latitude all over the two hemispheres. I have been in some of them, and . . . well, we won't talk about that. But there was one yet—the biggest, the most blank, so to speak—that I had a hankering after.

"True, by this time it was not a blank space any more. It had got filled since my boyhood with rivers and lakes and names. It had ceased to be a blank space of delightful mystery—a white patch for a boy to dream gloriously over. It had become a place of darkness. But there was in it one river especially, a mighty big river, that you could see on the map, resembling an immense snake uncoiled, with its head in the sea, its body at rest curving afar over a vast country, and its tail lost in the depths of the land. And as I looked at the map of it in a shop-window, it fascinated me as a snake would a bird—a silly little bird. Then I remembered there was a big concern, a Company for trade on that river. Dash it all! I thought to myself, they can't trade without using some kind of craft on that lot of fresh water—steamboats! Why shouldn't I try to get charge of one? I went on along Fleet Street,[5] but could not shake off the idea. The snake had charmed me.

"You understand it was a Continental concern, that Trading Society; but I have a lot of relations living on the Continent, because it's cheap and not so nasty as it looks, they say.

"I am sorry to own I began to worry them. This was already a fresh departure for me. I was not used to get things that way, you know. I always went my own road and on my own legs where I had a mind to go. I wouldn't have believed it of myself; but, then—you see—I felt somehow I must get there by hook or by crook. So I worried them. The men said, 'My dear fellow,' and did nothing. Then —would you believe it?—I tried the women. I, Charlie Marlow, set the women to work—to get a job. Heavens! Well, you see, the notion drove me. I had an aunt, a dear enthusiastic soul. She wrote: 'It will be delightful. I am ready to do anything, anything for you. It is a glorious idea. I know the wife of a very high personage in the Administration, and also a man who has lots of influence with,' etc. etc. She was determined to make no end of fuss to get me appointed skipper of a river steamboat, if such was my fancy.

"I got my appointment—of course; and I got it very quick. It appears the Company had received news that one of their captains had been killed in a scuffle with the natives. This was my chance, and it made me the more anxious to go. It was only months and months afterwards, when I made the attempt to recover what was left of the body, that

I heard the original quarrel arose from a misunder-standing about some hens. Yes, two black hens. Fresleven—that was the fellow's name, a Dane—thought himself wronged somehow in the bargain, so he went ashore and started to hammer the chief of the village with a stick. Oh, it didn't surprise me in the least to hear this, and at the same time to be told that Fresleven was the gentlest, quietest creature that ever walked on two legs. No doubt he was; but he had been a couple of years already out there engaged in the noble cause, you know, and he probably felt the need at last of asserting his self-respect in some way. Therefore he whacked the old nigger mercilessly, while a big crowd of his people watched him, thunderstruck, till some man —I was told the chief's son—in desperation at hearing the old chap yell, made a tentative jab with a spear at the white man—and of course it went quite easy between the shoulder-blades. Then the whole population cleared into the forest, expecting all kinds of calamities to happen, while, on the other hand, the steamer Fresleven commanded left also in a bad panic, in charge of the engineer, I believe. Afterwards nobody seemed to trouble much about Fresleven's remains, till I got out and stepped into his shoes. I couldn't let it rest, though; but when an opportunity offered at last to meet my predecessor, the grass growing through his ribs was tall enough to hide his bones. They were all there. The supernatural being had not been touched after he fell. And the village was deserted, the huts gaped black, rotting, all askew within the fallen enclosures. A calamity had come to it, sure enough. The people had vanished. Mad terror had scattered them, men, women, and children, through the bush, and they had never returned. What became of the hens I don't know either. I should think the cause of progress got them, anyhow. However, through this glorious affair I got my appointment, before I had fairly begun to hope for it.

"I flew around like mad to get ready, and before forty-eight hours I was crossing the Channel to show myself to my employers, and sign the contract. In a very few hours I arrived in a city that always makes me think of a whited sepulchre. Prejudice no doubt. I had no difficulty in finding the Company's offices. It was the biggest thing in the town, and everybody I met was full of it. They were going to run an oversea empire, and make no end of coin by trade.

5. **Fleet Street:** major London business street.

"A narrow and deserted street in deep shadow, high houses, innumerable windows with venetian blinds, a dead silence, grass sprouting between the stones, imposing carriage archways right and left, immense double doors standing ponderously ajar. I slipped through one of these cracks, went up a swept and ungarnished staircase, as arid as a desert, and opened the first door I came to. Two women, one fat and the other slim, sat on straw-bottomed chairs, knitting black wool. The slim one got up and walked straight at me—still knitting with downcast eyes—and only just as I began to think of getting out of her way, as you would for a somnambulist, stood still, and looked up. Her dress was as plain as an umbrella-cover, and she turned round without a word and preceded me into a waiting-room. I gave my name, and looked about. Deal table in the middle, plain chairs all round the walls, on one end a large shining map, marked with all the colors of a rainbow. There was a vast amount of red—good to see at any time, because one knows that some real work is done in there, a deuce of a lot of blue, a little green, smears of orange, and, on the East Coast, a purple patch, to show where the jolly pioneers of progress drink the jolly lager-beer. However, I wasn't going into any of these. I was going into the yellow. Dead in the center. And the river was there—fascinating—deadly—like a snake. Ough! A door opened, a white-haired secretarial head, but wearing a compassionate expression, appeared, and a skinny forefinger beckoned me into the sanctuary. Its light was dim, and a heavy writing-desk squatted in the middle. From behind that structure came out an impression of pale plumpness in a frock-coat. The great man himself. He was five feet six, I should judge, and had his grip on the handle-end of ever so many millions. He shook hands, I fancy, murmured vaguely, was satisfied with my French. *Bon voyage*.

"In about forty-five seconds I found myself again in the waiting-room with the compassionate secretary, who, full of desolation and sympathy, made me sign some document. I believe I undertook amongst other things not to disclose any trade secrets. Well, I am not going to.

"I began to feel slightly uneasy. You know I am not used to such ceremonies, and there was something ominous in the atmosphere. It was just as though I had been let into some conspiracy—I don't know—something not quite right; and I was glad to get out. In the outer room the two women knitted black wool feverishly. People were arriving, and the younger one was walking back and forth introducing them. The old one sat on her chair. Her flat cloth slippers were propped up on a foot-warmer, and a cat reposed on her lap. She wore a starched white affair on her head, had a wart on one cheek, and silver-rimmed spectacles hung on the tip of her nose. She glanced at me above the glasses. The swift and indifferent placidity of that look troubled me. Two youths with foolish and cheery countenances were being piloted over, and she threw at them the same quick glance of unconcerned wisdom. She seemed to know all about them and about me too. An eerie feeling came over me. She seemed uncanny and fateful. Often far away there I thought of these two, guarding the door of Darkness, knitting black wool as for a warm pall, one introducing, introducing continuously to the unknown, the other scrutinising the cheery and foolish faces with unconcerned old eyes. *Ave!* Old knitter of black wool. *Morituri te salutant*.[6] Not many of those she looked at ever saw her again—not half, by a long way.

"There was yet a visit to the doctor. 'A simple formality,' assured me the secretary, with an air of taking an immense part in all my sorrows. Accordingly a young chap wearing his hat over the left eyebrow, some clerk I suppose—there must have been clerks in the business, though the house was as still as a house in a city of the dead—came from somewhere upstairs, and led me forth. He was shabby and careless, with ink-stains on the sleeves of his jacket, and his cravat was large and billowy, under a chin shaped like the toe of an old boot. It was a little too early for the doctor, so I proposed a drink, and thereupon he developed a vein of joviality. As we sat over our vermouths he glorified the Company's business, and by and by I expressed casually my surprise at him not going out there. He became very cool and collected all at once. 'I am not such a fool as I look, quoth Plato to his disciples,' he said sententiously, emptied his glass with great resolution, and we rose.

"The old doctor felt my pulse, evidently thinking of something else the while. 'Good, good for there,' he mumbled, and then with a certain eagerness

6. **Morituri te salutant:** "Those who are about to die salute you," traditional gladiator's salute to the Roman emperor.

asked me whether I would let him measure my head. Rather surprised, I said yes, when he produced a thing like callipers and got the dimensions back and front and every way, taking notes carefully. He was an unshaven little man in a threadbare coat like a gaberdine, with his feet in slippers, and I thought him a harmless fool. 'I always ask leave, in the interests of science, to measure the crania of those going out there,' he said. 'And when they come back too?' I asked. 'Oh, I never see them,' he remarked; 'and, moreover, the changes take place inside, you know.' He smiled, as if at some quiet joke. 'So you are going out there. Famous. Interesting too.' He gave me a searching glance, and made another note. 'Ever any madness in your family?' he asked, in a matter-of-fact tone. I felt very annoyed. 'Is that question in the interests of science too?' 'It would be,' he said, without taking notice of my irritation, 'interesting for science to watch the mental changes of individuals, on the spot, but . . .' 'Are you an alienist?'[7] I interrupted. 'Every doctor should be—a little,' answered that original imperturbably. 'I have a little theory which you messieurs who go out there must help me to prove. This is my share in the advantages my country shall reap from the possession of such a magnificent dependency. The mere wealth I leave to others. Pardon my questions, but you are the first Englishman coming under my observation . . .' I hastened to assure him I was not in the least typical. 'If I were,' said I, 'I wouldn't be talking like this with you.' 'What you say is rather profound, and probably erroneous,' he said, with a laugh. 'Avoid irritation more than exposure to the sun. Adieu. How do you English say, eh? Good-bye. Ah! Good-bye. Adieu. In the tropics one must before everything keep calm.' . . . He lifted a warning forefinger. . . . '*Du calme, du calme. Adieu.*'

"One thing more remained to do—say good-bye to my excellent aunt. I found her triumphant. I had a cup of tea—the last decent cup of tea for many days—and in a room that most soothingly looked just as you would expect a lady's drawing-room to look, we had a long quiet chat by the fireside. In the course of these confidences it became quite plain to me I had been represented to the wife of the high dignitary, and goodness knows to how many more people besides, as an exceptional and gifted

7. **alienist:** early term for a psychiatrist.

creature—a piece of good fortune for the Company —a man you don't get hold of every day. Good Heavens! and I was going to take charge of a two-penny-half-penny river-steamboat with a penny whistle attached! It appeared, however, I was also one of the Workers, with a capital—you know. Something like an emissary of light, something like a lower sort of apostle. There had been a lot of such rot let loose in print and talk just about that time, and the excellent woman, living right in the rush of all that humbug, got carried off her feet. She talked about 'weaning those ignorant millions from their horrid ways,' till, upon my word, she made me quite uncomfortable. I ventured to hint that the Company was run for profit.

" 'You forget, dear Charlie, that the laborer is worthy of his hire,' she said brightly. It's queer how out of touch with truth women are. They live in a world of their own, and there had never been anything like it, and never can be. It is too beautiful altogether, and if they were to set it up it would go to pieces before the first sunset. Some confounded fact we men have been living contentedly with ever since the day of creation would start up and knock the whole thing over.

"After this I got embraced, told to wear flannel, be sure to write often, and so on—and I left. In the street—I don't know why—a queer feeling came to me that I was an impostor. Odd thing that I, who used to clear out for any part of the world at twenty-four hours' notice, with less thought than most men give to the crossing of a street, had a moment—I won't say of hesitation, but of startled pause, before this commonplace affair. The best way I can explain it to you is by saying that, for a second or two, I felt as though, instead of going to the center of a continent, I were about to set off for the center of the earth.

"I left in a French steamer, and she called in every blamed port they have out there, for, as far as I could see, the sole purpose of landing soldiers and custom-house officers. I watched the coast. Watching a coast as it slips by the ship is like thinking about an enigma. There it is before you— smiling, frowning, inviting, grand, mean, insipid, or savage, and always mute with an air of whispering, Come and find out. This one was almost featureless, as if still in the making, with an aspect of monotonous grimness. The edge of a colossal jungle, so dark green as to be almost black, fringed with white surf, ran straight, like a ruled line, far, far away along a blue sea whose glitter was blurred by a creeping mist. The sun was fierce, the land seemed to glisten and drip with steam. Here and there grayish-whitish specks showed up clustered inside the white surf, with a flag flying above them perhaps—settlements some centuries old, and still no bigger than pinheads on the untouched expanse of their background. We pounded along, stopped, landed soldiers; went on, landed custom-house clerks to levy toll in what looked like a God-forsaken wilderness, with a tin shed and a flagpole lost in it; landed more soldiers—to take care of the custom-house clerks presumably. Some, I heard, got drowned in the surf; but whether they did or not, nobody seemed particularly to care. They were just flung out there, and on we went. Every day the coast looked the same, as though we had not moved; but we passed various places—trading places—with names like Gran' Bassam, Little Popo; names that seemed to belong to some sordid farce acted in front of a sinister back-cloth. The idleness of a passenger, my isolation amongst all these men with whom I had no point of contact, the oily and languid sea, the uniform somberness of the coast, seemed to keep me away from the truth of things, within the toil of a mournful and senseless delusion. The voice of the surf heard now and then was a positive pleasure, like the speech of a brother. It was something natural, that had its reason, that had a meaning. Now and then a boat from the shore gave one a momentary contact with reality. It was paddled by black fellows. You could see from afar the white of their eyeballs glistening. They shouted, sang; their bodies streamed with perspiration; they had faces like grotesque masks—these chaps; but they had bone, muscle, a wild vitality, an intense energy of movement, that was as natural and true as the surf along their coast. They wanted no excuse for being there. They were a great comfort to look at. For a time I would feel I belonged still to a world of straight-forward facts; but the feeling would not last long. Something would turn up to scare it away. Once, I remember, we came upon a man-of-war anchored off the coast. There wasn't even a shed there, and she was shelling the bush. It appears the French had one of their wars going on thereabouts. Her ensign dropped limp like a rag; the muzzles of the long six-inch guns stuck out all over the low hull; the greasy, slimy swell swung her up lazily and let her down, swaying her thin masts. In the empty immensity of earth, sky, and water, there she was, incomprehensible, firing into a continent. Pop, would go one of the six-inch guns; a small flame would dart and vanish, a little white smoke would disappear, a tiny projectile would give a feeble screech—and nothing happened. Nothing could happen. There was a touch of insanity in the proceeding, a sense of lugubrious drollery in the sight; and it was not dissipated by somebody on board assuring me earnestly there was a camp of natives—he called them enemies!—hidden out of sight somewhere.

"We gave her her letters (I heard the men in that lonely ship were dying of fever at the rate of three a day) and went on. We called at some more places with farcical names, where the merry dance of death and trade goes on in a still and earthy atmosphere as of an overheated catacomb; all along the formless coast bordered by dangerous surf, as if Nature herself had tried to ward off intruders; in and out of rivers, streams of death in life, whose banks were rotting into mud, whose waters, thickened into slime, invaded the contorted mangroves, that seemed to writhe at us in the extremity of an impotent despair. Nowhere did we stop long enough to get a particularized impression, but the general sense of vague and oppressive wonder grew upon me. It was like a weary pilgrimage amongst hints for nightmares.

"It was upward of thirty days before I saw the mouth of the big river. We anchored off the seat of the government. But my work would not begin till some two hundred miles farther on. So as soon as I could I made a start for a place thirty miles higher up.

"I had my passage on a little sea-going steamer. Her captain was a Swede, and knowing me for a seaman, invited me on the bridge. He was a young man, lean, fair, and morose, with lanky hair and a shuffling gait. As we left the miserable little wharf, he tossed his head contemptuously at the shore. 'Been living there?' he asked. I said, 'Yes.' 'Fine lot these government chaps—are they not?' he went on, speaking English with great precision and considerable bitterness. 'It is funny what some people will do for a few francs a month. I wonder what becomes of that kind when it goes up country?' I said to him I expected to see that soon.

'So-o-o!' he exclaimed. He shuffled athwart, keeping one eye ahead vigilantly. 'Don't be too sure,' he continued. 'The other day I took up a man who hanged himself on the road. He was a Swede, too.' 'Hanged himself! Why, in God's name?' I cried. He kept on looking out watchfully. 'Who knows? The sun too much for him, or the country perhaps.'

"At last we opened a reach. A rocky cliff appeared, mounds of turned-up earth by the shore, houses on a hill, others with iron roofs, amongst a waste of excavations, or hanging to the declivity. A continuous noise of the rapids above hovered over this scene of inhabited devastation. A lot of people, mostly black and naked, moved about like ants. A jetty projected into the river. A blinding sunlight drowned all this at times in a sudden recrudescence of glare. 'There's your Company's station,' said the Swede, pointing to three wooden barracklike structures on the rocky slope. 'I will send your things up. Four boxes did you say? So. Farewell.'

"I came upon a boiler wallowing in the grass, then found a path leading up the hill. It turned aside for the boulders, and also for an undersized railway truck lying there on its back with its wheels in the air. One was off. The thing looked as dead as the carcass of some animal. I came upon more pieces of decaying machinery, a stack of rusty rails. To the left a clump of trees made a shady spot, where dark things seemed to stir feebly. I blinked, the path was steep. A horn tooted to the right, and I saw the black people run. A heavy and dull detonation shook the ground, a puff of smoke came out of the cliff, and that was all. No change appeared on the face of the rock. They were building a railway. The cliff was not in the way or anything; but this objectless blasting was all the work going on.

"A slight clinking behind me made me turn my head. Six black men advanced in a file, toiling up the path. They walked erect and slow, balancing small baskets full of earth on their heads, and the clink kept time with their footsteps. Black rags were wound round their loins, and the short ends behind waggled to and fro like tails. I could see every rib, the joints of their limbs were like knots in a rope; each had an iron collar on his neck, and all were connected together with a chain whose bights swung between them, rhythmically clinking. Another report from the cliff made me think suddenly of that ship of war I had seen firing into a continent. It was the same kind of ominous voice; but these men could by no stretch of imagination be called enemies. They were called criminals, and the outraged law, like the bursting shells, had come to them, an insoluble mystery from the sea. All their meager breasts panted together, the violently dilated nostrils quivered, the eyes stared stonily uphill. They passed me within six inches, without a glance, with that complete, deathlike indifference of unhappy savages. Behind this raw matter one of the reclaimed, the product of the new forces at work, strolled despondently, carrying a rifle by its middle. He had a uniform jacket with one button off, and seeing a white man on the path, hoisted his weapon to his shoulder with alacrity. This was simple prudence, white men being so much alike at a distance that he could not tell who I might be. He was speedily reassured, and with a large, white, rascally grin, and a glance at his charge, seemed to take me into partnership in his exalted trust. After all, I also was a part of the great cause of these high and just proceedings.

"Instead of going up, I turned and descended to the left. My idea was to let that chain-gang get out of sight before I climbed the hill. You know I am not particularly tender; I've had to strike and to fend off. I've had to resist and to attack sometimes —that's only one way of resisting—without counting the exact cost, according to the demands of such sort of life as I had blundered into. I've seen the devil of violence, and the devil of greed, and the devil of hot desire; but, by all the stars! these were strong, lusty, red-eyed devils, that swayed and drove men—men, I tell you. But as I stood on this hillside, I foresaw that in the blinding sunshine of that land I would become acquainted with a flabby, pretending, weak-eyed devil of a rapacious and pitiless folly. How insidious he could be, too, I was only to find out several months later and a thousand miles farther. For a moment I stood appalled, as though by a warning. Finally I descended the hill, obliquely, towards the trees I had seen.

"I avoided a vast artificial hole somebody had been digging on the slope, the purpose of which I found it impossible to divine. It wasn't a quarry or a sandpit, anyhow. It was just a hole. It might have been connected with the philanthropic desire of giving the criminals something to do. I don't know.

Then I nearly fell into a very narrow ravine, almost no more than a scar in the hillside. I discovered that a lot of imported drainage-pipes for the settlement had been tumbled in there. There wasn't one that was not broken. It was a wanton smash-up. At last I got under the trees. My purpose was to stroll into the shade for a moment; but no sooner within than it seemed to me I had stepped into the gloomy circle of some inferno. The rapids were near, and an uninterrupted, uniform, headlong, rushing noise filled the mournful stillness of the grove, where not a breath stirred, not a leaf moved, with a mysterious sound—as though the tearing pace of the launched earth had suddenly become audible.

"Black shapes crouched, lay, sat between the trees, leaning against the trunks, clinging to the earth, half coming out, half effaced within the dim light, in all the attitudes of pain, abandonment, and despair. Another mine on the cliff went off, followed by a slight shudder of the soil under my feet. The work was going on. The work! And this was the place where some of the helpers had withdrawn to die.

"They were dying slowly—it was very clear. They were not enemies, they were not criminals, they were nothing earthly now—nothing but black shadows of disease and starvation, lying confusedly in the greenish gloom. Brought from all the recesses of the coast in all the legality of time contracts, lost in uncongenial surroundings, fed on unfamiliar food, they sickened, became inefficient, and were then allowed to crawl away and rest. These moribund shapes were free as air—and nearly as thin. I began to distinguish the gleam of the eyes under the trees. Then, glancing down, I saw a face near my hand. The black bones reclined at full length with one shoulder against the tree, and slowly the eyelids rose and the sunken eyes looked up at me, enormous and vacant, a kind of blind, white flicker in the depths of the orbs, which died out slowly. The man seemed young—almost a boy —but you know with them it's hard to tell. I found nothing else to do but to offer him one of my good Swede's ship's biscuits I had in my pocket. The fingers closed slowly on it and held—there was no other movement and no other glance. He had tied a bit of white worsted round his neck—Why? Where did he get it? Was it a badge—an ornament —a charm—a propitiatory act? Was there any idea at all connected with it? It looked startling

round his black neck, this bit of white thread from beyond the seas.

"Near the same tree two more bundles of acute angles sat with their legs drawn up. One, with his chin propped on his knees, stared at nothing, in an intolerable and appalling manner: his brother phantom rested its forehead, as if overcome with a great weariness; and all about others were scattered in every pose of contorted collapse, as in some picture of a massacre or a pestilence. While I stood horror-struck, one of these creatures rose to his hands and knees, and went off on all-fours towards the river to drink. He lapped out of his hand, then sat up in the sunlight, crossing his shins in front of him, and after a time let his woolly head fall on his breastbone.

"I didn't want any more loitering in the shade, and I made haste towards the station. When near the buildings I met a white man, in such an unexpected elegance of get-up that in the first moment I took him for a sort of vision. I saw a high starched collar, white cuffs, a light alpaca jacket, snowy trousers, a clean necktie, and varnished boots. No hat. Hair parted, brushed, oiled, under a green-lined parasol held in a big white hand. He was amazing, and had a pen-holder behind his ear.

"I shook hands with this miracle, and I learned he was the Company's chief accountant, and that all the bookkeeping was done at this station. He had come out for a moment, he said, 'to get a breath of fresh air.' The expression sounded wonderfully odd, with its suggestion of sedentary desk-life. I wouldn't have mentioned the fellow to you at all, only it was from his lips that I first heard the name of the man who is so indissolubly connected with the memories of that time. Moreover, I respected the fellow. Yes; I respected his collars, his vast cuffs, his brushed hair. His appearance was certainly that of a hairdresser's dummy; but in the great demoralization of the land he kept up his appearance. That's backbone. His starched collars and got-up shirt-fronts were achievements of character. He had been out nearly three years; and, later, I could not help asking him how he managed to sport such linen. He had just the faintest blush, and said modestly, 'I've been teaching one of the native women about the station. It was difficult. She had a distaste for the work.' Thus this man had verily accomplished something.

And he was devoted to his books, which were in apple-pie order.

"Everything else in the station was in a muddle, —heads, things, buildings. Strings of dusty niggers with splay feet arrived and departed; a stream of manufactured goods, rubbishy cottons, beads, and brass-wire set into the depths of darkness, and in return came a precious trickle of ivory.

"I had to wait in the station for ten days—an eternity. I lived in a hut in the yard, but to be out of the chaos I would sometimes get into the accountant's office. It was built of horizontal planks, and so badly put together that, as he bent over his high desk, he was barred from neck to heels with narrow strips of sunlight. There was no need to open the big shutter to see. It was hot there too; big flies buzzed fiendishly, and did not sting, but stabbed. I sat generally on the floor, while, of faultless appearance (and even slightly scented), perching on a high stool, he wrote, he wrote. Sometimes he stood up for exercise. When a truckle-bed with a sick man (some invalided agent from up-country) was put in there, he exhibited a gentle annoyance. 'The groans of this sick person,' he said, 'distract my attention. And without that it is extremely difficult to guard against clerical errors in this climate.'

"One day he remarked, without lifting his head, 'In the interior you will no doubt meet Mr. Kurtz.' On my asking who Mr. Kurtz was, he said he was a first-class agent; and seeing my disappointment at this information, he added slowly, laying down his pen, 'He is a very remarkable person.' Further questions elicited from him that Mr. Kurtz was at present in charge of a trading-post, a very important one, in the true ivory-country, at 'the very bottom of there. Sends in as much ivory as all the others put together . . .' He began to write again. The sick man was too ill to groan. The flies buzzed in a great peace.

"Suddenly there was a growing murmur of voices and a great tramping of feet. A caravan had come in. A violent babble of uncouth sounds burst out on the other side of the planks. All the carriers were speaking together, and in the midst of the uproar the lamentable voice of the chief agent was heard 'giving it up' tearfully for the twentieth time that day. . . . He rose slowly. 'What a frightful row,' he said. He crossed the room gently to look at the sick man, and returning, said to me, 'He does not hear.' 'What! Dead?' I asked, startled. 'No, not yet,' he answered, with great composure. Then, alluding with a toss of the head to the tumult in the station-yard, 'When one has got to make correct entries, one comes to hate those savages— hate them to the death.' He remained thoughtful for a moment. 'When you see Mr. Kurtz,' he went on, 'tell him from me that everything here'—he glanced at the desk—'is very satisfactory. I don't like to write to him—with those messengers of ours you never know who may get hold of your letter—at that Central Station.' He stared at me for a moment with his mild, bulging eyes. 'Oh, he will go far, very far,' he began again. 'He will be a somebody in the Administration before long. They, above—the Council in Europe, you know— mean him to be.'

"He turned to his work. The noise outside had ceased, and presently in going out I stopped at the door. In the steady buzz of flies the homeward-bound agent was lying flushed and insensible; the other, bent over his books, was making correct entries of perfectly correct transactions; and fifty feet below the doorstep I could see the still treetops of the grove of death.

"Next day I left that station at last, with a caravan of sixty men, for a two-hundred-mile tramp.

"No use telling you much about that. Paths, paths, everywhere; a stamped-in network of paths spreading over the empty land, through long grass, through burnt grass, through thickets, down and up chilly ravines, up and down stony hills ablaze with heat; and a solitude, a solitude, nobody, not a hut. The population had cleared out a long time ago. Well, if a lot of mysterious niggers armed with all kinds of fearful weapons suddenly took to traveling on the road between Deal and Gravesend, catching the yokels right and left to carry heavy loads for them, I fancy every farm and cottage thereabouts would get empty very soon. Only here the dwellings were gone too. Still, I passed through several abandoned villages. There's something pathetically childish in the ruins of grass walls. Day after day, with the stamp and shuffle of sixty pair of bare feet behind me, each pair under a sixty-pound load. Camp, cook, sleep; strike camp, march. Now and then a carrier dead in harness, at rest in the long grass near the path, with an empty water-gourd and his long staff lying by his side. A great silence around and above.

Perhaps on some quiet night the tremor of far-off drums, sinking, swelling, a tremor vast, faint; a sound weird, appealing, suggestive, and wild— and perhaps with as profound a meaning as the sound of bells in a Christian country. Once a white man in an unbuttoned uniform, camping on the path with an armed escort of lank Zanzibaris,[8] very hospitable and festive—not to say drunk. Was looking after the upkeep of the road, he declared. Can't say I saw any road or any upkeep, unless the body of a middle-aged Negro, with a bullet-hole in the forehead, upon which I absolutely stumbled three miles farther on, may be considered as a permanent improvement. I had a white companion too, not a bad chap, but rather too fleshy and with the exasperating habit of fainting on the hot hillsides, miles away from the least bit of shade and water. Annoying, you know, to hold your own coat like a parasol over a man's head while he is coming to. I couldn't help asking him once what he meant by coming there at all. 'To make money, of course. What do you think?' he said scornfully. Then he got fever, and had to be carried in a hammock slung under a pole. As he weighed sixteen stone I had no end of rows with the carriers. They jibbed, ran away, sneaked off with their loads in the night—quite a mutiny. So, one evening, I made a speech in English with gestures, not one of which was lost to the sixty pairs of eyes before me, and the next morning I started the hammock off in front all right. An hour afterwards I came upon the whole concern wrecked in a bush—man, hammock, groans, blankets, horrors. The heavy pole had skinned his poor nose. He was very anxious for me to kill somebody, but there wasn't the shadow of a carrier near. I remembered the old doctor—'It would be interesting for science to watch the mental changes of individuals, on the spot.' I felt I was becoming scientifically interesting. However, all that is to no purpose. On the fifteenth day I came in sight of the big river again, and hobbled into the Central Station. It was on a backwater surrounded by scrub and forest, with a pretty border of smelly mud on one side, and on the three others enclosed by a crazy fence of rushes. A neglected gap was all the gate it had, and the first glance at the place was enough to let you see the flabby devil was running that show. White men

8. **Zanzibaris:** Natives of Zanzibar were often employed as mercenaries.

with long staves in their hands appeared languidly from amongst the buildings, strolling up to take a look at me, and then retired out of sight somewhere. One of them, a stout, excitable chap with black mustaches, informed me with great volubility and many digressions, as soon as I told him who I was, that my steamer was at the bottom of the river. I was thunderstruck. What, how, why? Oh, it was 'all right.' The 'manager himself' was there. All quite correct. 'Everybody had behaved splendidly! splendidly!'—'You must,' he said in agitation, 'go and see the general manager at once. He is waiting.'

"I did not see the real significance of that wreck at once. I fancy I see it now, but I am not sure— not at all. Certainly the affair was too stupid— when I think of it—to be altogether natural. Still . . . But at the moment it presented itself simply as a confounded nuisance. The steamer was sunk. They had started two days before in a sudden hurry up the river with the manager on board, in charge of some volunteer skipper, and before they had been out three hours they tore the bottom out of her on stones, and she sank near the south bank. I asked myself what I was to do there, now my boat was lost. As a matter of fact, I had plenty to do in fishing my command out of the river. I had to set about it the very next day. That, and the repairs when I brought the pieces to the station, took some months.

"My first interview with the manager was curious. He did not ask me to sit down after my twenty-mile walk that morning. He was commonplace in complexion, in feature, in manners, and in voice. He was of middle size and of ordinary build. His eyes, of the usual blue, were perhaps remarkably cold, and he certainly could make his glance fall on one as trenchant and heavy as an ax. But even at these times the rest of his person seemed to disclaim the intention. Otherwise there was only an indefinable, faint expression of his lips, something stealthy—a smile—not a smile—I remember it, but I can't explain. It was unconscious, this smile was, though just after he had said something it got intensified for an instant. It came at the end of his speeches like a seal applied on the words to make the meaning of the commonest phrase appear absolutely inscrutable. He was a common trader, from his youth up employed in these parts— nothing more. He was obeyed, yet he inspired neither love nor fear, nor even respect. He inspired uneasiness. That was it! Uneasiness. Not a definite mistrust—just uneasiness—nothing more. You have no idea how effective such a . . . a . . . faculty can be. He had no genius for organizing, for initiative, or for order even. That was evident in such things as the deplorable state of the station. He had no learning, and no intelligence. His position had come to him—why? Perhaps because he was never ill . . . He had served three terms of three years out there . . . Because triumphant health in the general rout of constitutions is a kind of power in itself. When he went home on leave he rioted on a large scale—pompously. Jack ashore—with a difference—in externals only. This one could gather from his casual talk. He originated nothing, he could keep the routine going—that's all. But he was great. He was great by this little thing that it was impossible to tell what could control such a man. He never gave that secret away. Perhaps there was nothing within him. Such a suspicion made one pause—for out there there were no external checks. Once when various tropical diseases had laid low almost every 'agent' in the station, he was heard to say, 'Men who come out here should have no entrails.' He sealed the utterance with that smile of his, as though it had been a door opening into a darkness he had in his keeping. You fancied you had seen things—but the seal was on. When annoyed at meal-times by the constant quarrels of the white men about precedence, he ordered an immense round table to be made, for which a special house had to be built. This was the station's mess-room. Where he sat was the first place—the rest were nowhere. One felt this to be his unalterable conviction. He was neither civil or uncivil. He was quiet. He allowed his 'boy'—an overfed young Negro from the coast —to treat the white men, under his very eyes, with provoking insolence.

"He began to speak as soon as he saw me. I had been very long on the road. He could not wait. Had to start without me. The up-river stations had to be relieved. There had been so many delays already that he did not know who was dead and who was alive, and how they got on—and so on, and so on. He paid no attention to my explanations, and, playing with a stick of sealing-wax, repeated several times that the situation was 'very grave, very grave.' There were rumors that a very important station was in jeopardy, and its chief, Mr. Kurtz, was ill. Hoped it was not true. Mr. Kurtz was . . . I felt weary and irritable. Hang Kurtz, I thought. I interrupted him by saying I had heard of Mr. Kurtz on the coast. 'Ah! So they talk of him down there,' he murmured to himself. Then he began again, assuring me Mr. Kurtz was the best agent he had, an exceptional man, of the greatest importance to the Company: therefore I could understand his anxiety. He was, he said, 'very, very uneasy.' Certainly he fidgeted on his chair a good deal, exclaimed, 'Ah, Mr. Kurtz!' broke the stick of sealing-wax and seemed dumbfounded by the accident. Next thing he wanted to know 'how long it would take to'. . . I interrupted him again. Being hungry, you know, and kept on my feet too, I was getting savage. 'How can I tell?' I said. 'I haven't even seen the wreck yet—some months, no doubt.' All this talk seemed to me so futile. 'Some months,' he said. 'Well, let us say three months before we can make a start. Yes. That ought to do the affair.' I flung out of his hut (he lived all alone in a clay hut with a sort of veranda) muttering to myself my opinion of him. He was a chattering idiot. Afterwards I took it back when it was borne in upon me startlingly with what extreme nicety he had estimated the time requisite for the 'affair.'

"I went to work the next day, turning, so to speak, my back on that station. In that way only it seemed to me I could keep my hold on the redeeming facts of life. Still, one must look about sometimes; and then I saw this station, these men strolling aimlessly about in the sunshine of the yard. I asked myself sometimes what it all meant. They wandered here and there with their absurd long staves in their hands, like a lot of faithless pilgrims bewitched inside a rotten fence. The word *ivory* rang in the air, was whispered, was sighed. You would think they were praying to it. A taint of imbecile rapacity blew through it all, like a whiff from some corpse. By Jove! I've never seen anything so unreal in my life. And outside, the silent wilderness surrounding this cleared speck on the earth struck me as something great and invincible, like evil or truth, waiting patiently for the passing away of this fantastic invasion.

"Oh, those months! Well, never mind. Various things happened. One evening a grass shed full of calico, cotton prints, beads, and I don't know what else, burst into a blaze so suddenly that you would have thought the earth had opened to let an avenging fire consume all that trash. I was smoking my pipe quietly by my dismantled steamer, and saw them all cutting capers in the light, with their arms lifted high, when the stout man with mustaches came tearing down to the river, a tin pail in his hand, assured me that everybody was 'behaving splendidly, splendidly,' dipped about a quart of water and tore back again. I noticed there was a hole in the bottom of his pail.

"I strolled up. There was no hurry. You see the thing had gone off like a box of matches. It had been hopeless from the very first. The flame had leaped high, driven everybody back, lighted up everything—and collapsed. The shed was already a heap of embers glowing fiercely. A nigger was being beaten near by. They said he had caused the fire in some way; be that as it may, he was screeching most horribly. I saw him, later, for several days, sitting in a bit of shade looking very sick and trying to recover himself: afterwards he arose and went out—and the wilderness without a sound took him into its bosom again. As I approached the glow from the dark I found myself at the back of two men, talking. I heard the name of Kurtz pronounced, then the words, 'take advantage of this unfortunate accident.' One of the men was the manager. I wished him a good evening. 'Did you ever see anything like it—eh? it is incredible,' he said, and walked off. The other man remained. He was a first-class agent, young, gentlemanly, a bit reserved, with a forked little beard and a hooked nose. He was standoffish with the other agents, and they on their side said he was the manager's spy upon them. As to me, I had hardly ever spoken to him before. We got into talk, and by and by we strolled away from the hissing ruins. Then he asked me to his room, which was in the main building of the station. He struck a match, and I perceived that this young aristocrat had not only a silver-mounted dressing-case but also a whole candle all to himself. Just at that time the manager was the only man supposed to have any right to candles. Native mats covered the clay walls; a collection of spears, assegais,[9] shields, knives, was hung up in trophies. The business entrusted to this fellow was the making of bricks —so I had been informed; but there wasn't a

9. **assegais:** light South African throwing spears.

fragment of a brick anywhere in the station, and he had been there more than a year—waiting. It seems he could not make bricks without something, I don't know what—straw maybe. Anyway, it could not be found there, and as it was not likely to be sent from Europe, it did not appear clear to me what he was waiting for. An act of special creation perhaps. However, they were all waiting— all the sixteen or twenty pilgrims of them—for something; and upon my word it did not seem an uncongenial occupation, from the way they took it, though the only thing that ever came to them was disease—as far as I could see. They beguiled the time by backbiting and intriguing against each other in a foolish kind of way. There was an air of plotting about that station, but nothing came of it, of course. It was as unreal as everything else—as the philanthropic pretense of the whole concern, as their talk, as their government, as their show of work. The only real feeling was a desire to get appointed to a trading-post where ivory was to be had, so that they could earn percentages. They intrigued and slandered and hated each other only on that account—but as to effectually lifting a little finger—oh no. By heavens! there is something after all in the world allowing one man to steal a horse while another must not look at a halter. Steal a horse straight out. Very well. He has done it. Perhaps he can ride. But there is a way of looking at a halter that would provoke the most charitable of saints into a kick.

"I had no idea why he wanted to be sociable, but as we chatted in there it suddenly occurred to me the fellow was trying to get at something—in fact, pumping me. He alluded constantly to Europe, to the people I was supposed to know there—putting leading questions as to my acquaintances in the sepulchral city, and so on. His little eyes glittered like mica disks—with curiosity—though he tried to keep up a bit of superciliousness. At first I was astonished, but very soon I became awfully curious to see what he would find out from me. I couldn't possibly imagine what I had in me to make it worth his while. It was very pretty to see how he baffled himself, for in truth my body was full only of chills, and my head had nothing in it but that wretched steamboat business. It was evident he took me for a perfectly shameless prevaricator. At last he got angry, and, to conceal a movement of furious annoyance, he yawned, I rose. Then I noticed a small sketch in oils, on a panel, representing a woman, draped and blindfolded, carrying a lighted torch. The background was somber—almost black. The movement of the woman was stately, and the effect of the torchlight on the face was sinister.

"It arrested me, and he stood by civilly, holding an empty half-pint champagne bottle (medical comforts) with the candle stuck in it. To my question he said Mr. Kurtz had painted this—in this very station more than a year ago—while waiting for means to go to his trading-post. 'Tell me, pray,' said I, 'who is this Mr. Kurtz?'

" 'The chief of the Inner Station,' he answered in a short tone, looking away. 'Much obliged,' I said, laughing. 'And you are the brickmaker of the Central Station. Everyone knows that.' He was silent for a while. 'He is a prodigy,' he said at last. 'He is an emissary of pity, and science, and progress, and devil knows what else. We want,' he began to declaim suddenly, 'for the guidance of the cause entrusted to us by Europe, so to speak, higher intelligence, wide sympathies, a singleness of purpose.' 'Who says that?' I asked. 'Lots of them,' he replied. 'Some even write that; and so *he* comes here, a special being, as you ought to know.' 'Why ought I to know?' I interrupted, really surprised. He paid no attention. 'Yes. Today he is chief of the best station, next year he will be assistant-manager, two years more and . . . but I daresay you know what he will be in two years' time. You are of the new gang—the gang of virtue. The same people who sent him specially also recommended you. Oh, don't say no. I've my own eyes to trust.' Light dawned upon me. My dear aunt's influential acquaintances were producing an unexpected effect upon that young man. I nearly burst into a laugh. 'Do you read the Company's confidential correspondence?' I asked. He hadn't a word to say. It was great fun. 'When Mr. Kurtz,' I continued severely, 'is General Manager, you won't have the opportunity.'

"He blew the candle out suddenly, and we went outside. The moon had risen. Black figures strolled about listlessly, pouring water on the glow, whence proceeded a sound of hissing; steam ascended in the moonlight; the beaten nigger groaned somewhere. 'What a row the brute makes!' said the indefatigable man with the mustaches, appearing near us. 'Serve him right. Transgression—punishment —bang! Pitiless, pitiless. That's the only way. This will prevent all conflagrations for the future. I was just telling the manager . . .' He noticed my companion, and became crestfallen all at once. 'Not in bed yet,' he said, with a kind of servile heartiness; 'it's so natural. Ha! Danger—agitation.' He vanished. I went on to the riverside, and the other followed me. I heard a scathing murmur at my ear, 'Heaps of muffs—go to.' The pilgrims could be seen in knots gesticulating, discussing. Several had still their staves in their hands. I verily believe they took these sticks to bed with them. Beyond the fence the forest stood up spectrally in the moonlight, and through the dim stir, through the faint sounds of that lamentable courtyard, the silence of the land went home to one's very heart —its mystery, its greatness, the amazing reality of its concealed life. The hurt nigger moaned feebly somewhere near by, and then fetched a deep sigh that made me mend my pace away from there. I felt a hand introducing itself under my arm. 'My dear sir,' said the fellow, 'I don't want to be misunderstood, and especially by you, who will see Mr. Kurtz long before I can have that pleasure. I wouldn't like him to get a false idea of my disposition. . . .'

"I let him run on, this papier-mâché Mephistopheles, and it seemed to me that if I tried I could poke my forefinger through him, and would find nothing inside but a little loose dirt, maybe. He, don't you see, had been planning to be assistant-manager by and by under the present man, and I could see that the coming of that Kurtz had upset them both not a little. He talked precipitately, and I did not try to stop him. I had my shoulders against the wreck of my steamer, hauled up on the slope like a carcass of some big river animal. The smell of mud, of primeval mud, by Jove! was in my nostrils, the high stillness of primeval forest was before my eyes; there were shiny patches on the black creek. The moon had spread over everything a thin layer of silver—over the rank grass, over the mud, upon the wall of matted vegetation standing higher than the wall of a temple, over the great river I could see through a somber gap glittering, glittering, as it flowed broadly by without a murmur. All this was great, expectant, mute, while the man jabbered about himself. I wondered whether the stillness on the face of the immensity looking at us two were meant as an appeal or as a menace. What were we who had strayed in here? Could we handle that dumb thing, or would it handle us? I felt how big, how confoundedly big, was that thing that couldn't talk and perhaps was deaf as well. What was in there? I could see a little ivory coming out from there, and I had heard Mr. Kurtz was in there. I had heard enough about it too—God knows! Yet somehow it didn't bring any image with it—no more than if I had been told an angel or a fiend was in there. I believed it in the same way one of you might believe there are inhabitants in the planet Mars. I knew once a Scotch sailmaker who was certain, dead sure, there were people in Mars. If you asked him for some idea how they looked and behaved, he would get shy and mutter something about 'walking on all-fours.' If you as much as smiled, he would—though a man of sixty—offer to fight you. I would not have gone so far as to fight for Kurtz, but I went for him near enough to a lie. You know I hate, detest, and can't bear a lie, not because I am straighter than the rest of us, but simply because it appals me. There is a taint of death, a flavor of mortality in lies—which is exactly what I hate and detest in the world—what I want to forget. It makes me miserable and sick, like biting something rotten would do. Temperament, I suppose. Well, I went near enough to it by letting the young fool there believe anything he liked to imagine as to my influence in Europe. I became in an instant as much of a pretense as the rest of the bewitched pilgrims. This simply because I had a notion it somehow would be of help to that Kurtz whom at the time I did not see—you understand. He was just a word for me. I did not see the man in the name any more than you do. Do you see him? Do you see the story? Do you see anything? It seems to me I am trying to tell you a dream—making a vain attempt, because no relation of a dream can convey the dream-sensation, that commingling of absurdity, surprise, and bewilderment in a tremor of struggling revolt, that notion of being captured by the incredible which is of the very essence of dreams. . . ."

He was silent for a while.

". . . No, it is impossible; it is impossible to convey the life-sensation of any given epoch of one's existence—that which makes its truth, its meaning—its subtle and penetrating essence. It is impossible. We live, as we dream—alone. . . ."

He paused again as if reflecting, then added:

"Of course in this you fellows see more than I could then. You see me, whom you know. . . ."

It had become so pitch dark that we listeners could hardly see one another. For a long time already he, sitting apart, had been no more to us than a voice. There was not a word from anybody. The others might have been asleep, but I was awake. I listened, I listened on the watch for the sentence, for the word, that would give me the clue to the faint uneasiness inspired by this narrative that seemed to shape itself without human lips in the heavy night-air of the river.

". . . Yes—I let him run on," Marlow began again, "and think what he pleased about the powers that were behind me. I did! And there was nothing behind me! There was nothing but that wretched, old, mangled steamboat I was leaning against, while he talked fluently about 'the necessity for every man to get on.' 'And when one comes out here, you conceive, it is not to gaze at the moon.' Mr. Kurtz was a 'universal genius,' but even a genius would find it easier to work with 'adequate tools—intelligent men.' He did not make bricks—why, there was a physical impossibility in the way—as I was well aware; and if he did secretarial work for the manager, it was because 'no sensible man rejects wantonly the confidence of his superiors.' Did I see it? I saw it. What more did I want? What I really wanted was rivets, by heaven! Rivets. To get on with the work—to stop the hole. Rivets I wanted. There were cases of them down at the coast—cases—piled up—burst—split! You kicked a loose rivet at every second step in that station yard on the hillside. Rivets had rolled into the grove of death. You could fill your pockets with rivets for the trouble of stooping down—and there wasn't one rivet to be found where it was wanted. We had plates that would do, but nothing to fasten them with. And every week the messenger, a lone Negro, letter-bag on shoulder and staff in hand, left our station for the coast. And several times a week a coast caravan came in with trade goods—ghastly glazed calico that made you shudder only to look at it, glass beads value about a penny a quart, confounded spotted cotton handkerchiefs. And no rivets. Three carriers could have brought all that was wanted to set that steamboat afloat.

"He was becoming confidential now, but I fancy my unresponsive attitude must have exasperated him at last, for he judged it necessary to inform me he feared neither God nor devil, let alone any mere man. I said I could see that very well, but what I wanted was a certain quantity of rivets—and rivets were what really Mr. Kurtz wanted, if he had only known it. Now letters went to the coast every week. . . . 'My dear sir,' he cried, 'I write from dictation.' I demanded rivets. There was a way—for an intelligent man. He changed his manner; became very cold, and suddenly began to talk about a hippopotamus; wondered whether sleeping on board the steamer (I stuck to my salvage night and day) I wasn't disturbed. There was an old hippo that had the bad habit of getting out on the bank and roaming at night over the station grounds. The pilgrims used to turn out in a body and empty every rifle they could lay hands on at him. Some even had sat up o' nights for him. All this energy was wasted, though. 'That animal has a charmed life,' he said; 'but you can say this only of brutes in this country. No man—you apprehend me?—no man here bears a charmed life.' He stood there for a moment in the moonlight with his delicate hooked nose set a little askew, and his mica eyes glittering without a wink, then, with a curt Good-night, he strode off. I could see he was disturbed and considerably puzzled, which made me feel more hopeful than I had been for days. It was a great comfort to turn from that chap to my influential friend, the battered, twisted, ruined, tin-pot steamboat. I clambered on board. She rang under my feet like an empty Huntley & Palmer biscuit-tin kicked along a gutter; she was nothing so solid in make, and rather less pretty in shape, but I had expended enough hard work on her to make me love her. No influential friend would have served me better. She had given me a chance to come out a bit—to find out what I could do. No, I don't like work. I had rather laze about and think of all the fine things that can be done. I don't like work—no man does—but I like what is in the work —the chance to find yourself. Your own reality— for yourself, not for others—what no other man can ever know. They can only see the mere show, and never can tell what it really means.

"I was not surprised to see somebody sitting aft, on the deck, with his legs dangling over the mud. You see I rather chummed with the few mechanics there were in that station, whom the other pilgrims naturally despised—on account of their imperfect

manners, I suppose. This was the foreman—a boiler-maker by trade—a good worker. He was a lank, bony, yellow-faced man, with big intense eyes. His aspect was worried, and his head was as bald as the palm of my hand; but his hair in falling seemed to have stuck to his chin, and had prospered in the new locality, for his beard hung down to his waist. He was a widower with six young children (he had left them in charge of a sister of his to come out there), and the passion of his life was pigeon-flying. He was an enthusiast and a connoisseur. He would rave about pigeons. After work hours he used sometimes to come over from his hut for a talk about his children and his pigeons; at work, when he had to crawl in the mud under the bottom of the steamboat, he would tie up that beard of his in a kind of white serviette he brought for the purpose. It had loops to go over his ears. In the evening he could be seen squatted on the bank rinsing that wrapper in the creek with great care, then spreading it solemnly on a bush to dry.

"I slapped him on the back and shouted 'We shall have rivets!' He scrambled to his feet exclaiming 'No! Rivets!' as though he couldn't believe his ears. Then in a low voice, 'You . . . eh?' I don't know why we behaved like lunatics. I put my finger to the side of my nose and nodded mysteriously. 'Good for you!' he cried, snapped his fingers above his head, lifting one foot. I tried a jig. We capered on the iron deck. A frightful clatter came out of that hulk, and the virgin forest on the other bank of the creek sent it back in a thundering roll upon the sleeping station. It must have made some of the pilgrims sit up in their hovels. A dark figure obscured the lighted doorway of the manager's hut, vanished, then, a second or so after, the doorway itself vanished too. We stopped, and the silence driven away by the stamping of our feet flowed back again from the recesses of the land. The great wall of vegetation, an exuberant and entangled mass of trunks, branches, leaves, boughs, festoons, motionless in the moonlight, was like a rioting invasion of soundless life, a rolling wave of plants, piled up, crested, ready to topple over the creek, to sweep every little man of us out of his little existence. And it moved not. A deadened burst of mighty splashes and snorts reached us from afar, as though an ichthyosaurus had been taking a bath of glitter in the great river. 'After all,' said the boiler-maker in a reasonable tone, 'why shouldn't we get the rivets?' Why not, indeed! I did not know of any reason why we shouldn't. 'They'll come in three weeks,' I said confidently.

"But they didn't. Instead of rivets there came an invasion, an infliction, a visitation. It came in sections during the next three weeks, each section headed by a donkey carrying a white man in new clothes and tan shoes, bowing from that elevation right and left to the impressed pilgrims. A quarrelsome band of footsore sulky niggers trod on the heels of the donkey; a lot of tents, campstools, tin boxes, white cases, brown bales would be shot down in the courtyard, and the air of mystery would deepen a little over the muddle of the station. Five such installments came, with their absurd air of disorderly flight with the loot of innumerable outfit shops and provision stores, that, one would think, they were lugging, after a raid, into the wilderness for equitable division. It was an inextricable mess of things decent in themselves but that human folly made look like the spoils of thieving.

"This devoted band called itself the Eldorado Exploring Expedition, and I believe they were sworn to secrecy. Their talk, however, was the talk of sordid buccaneers: it was reckless without hardihood, greedy without audacity, and cruel without courage, there was not an atom of foresight or of serious intention in the whole batch of them, and they did not seem aware these things are wanted for the work of the world. To tear treasure out of the bowels of the land was their desire, with no more moral purpose at the back of it than there is in burglars breaking into a safe. Who paid the expenses of the noble enterprise I don't know; but the uncle of our manager was leader of that lot.

"In exterior he resembled a butcher in a poor neighborhood, and his eyes had a look of sleepy cunning. He carried his fat paunch with ostentation on his short legs, and during the time his gang infested the station spoke to no one but his nephew. You could see these two roaming about all day long with their heads close together in an everlasting confab.

"I had given up worrying myself about the rivets. One's capacity for that kind of folly is more limited than you would suppose. I said Hang!— and let things slide. I had plenty of time for meditation, and now and then I would give some thought to Kurtz. I wasn't very interested in him. No. Still, I was curious to see whether this man, who had come out equipped with moral ideas of some sort, would climb to the top after all, and how he would set about his work when there."

2

"One evening as I was lying flat on the deck of my steamboat, I heard voices approaching—and there were the nephew and the uncle strolling along the bank. I laid my head on my arm again, and had nearly lost myself in a doze, when somebody said in my ear, as it were: 'I am as harmless as a little child, but I don't like to be dictated to. Am I the manager—or am I not? I was ordered to send him there. It's incredible.' . . . I became aware that the two were standing on the shore alongside the forepart of the steamboat, just below my head. I did not move; it did not occur to me to move: I was sleepy. 'It *is* unpleasant,' grunted the uncle. 'He has asked the Administration to be sent there,' said the other, 'with the idea of showing what he could do; and I was instructed accordingly. Look at the influence that man must have. Is it not frightful?' They both agreed it was frightful, then made several bizarre remarks: "Make rain and fine weather—one man—the Council—by the nose'—bits of absurd sentences that got the better of my drowsiness, so that I had pretty near the whole of my wits about me when the uncle said, 'The climate may do away with this difficulty for you. Is he alone there?' 'Yes,' answered the manager; 'he sent his assistant down the river with a note to me in these terms: "Clear this poor devil out of the country, and don't bother sending more of that sort. I had rather be alone than have the kind of men you can dispose of with me." It was more than a year ago. Can you imagine such impudence?' 'Anything since then?' asked the other hoarsely. 'Ivory,' jerked the nephew; 'lots of it— prime sort—lots—most annoying, from him.' 'And with that?' questioned the heavy rumble. 'Invoice,' was the reply fired out, so to speak. Then silence. They had been talking about Kurtz.

"I was broad awake by this time, but, lying perfectly at ease, remained still, having no inducement to change my position. 'How did that ivory come all this way?' growled the elder man, who seemed very vexed. The other explained that it had come with a fleet of canoes in charge of an English half-caste clerk Kurtz had with him; that Kurtz had apparently intended to return himself, the station being by that time bare of goods and stores, but after coming three hundred miles, had suddenly decided to go back, which he started to do alone in a small dugout with four paddlers, leaving the half-caste to continue down the river with the ivory. The two fellows there seemed astounded at anybody attempting such a thing. They were at a loss for an adequate motive. As for me, I seemed to see Kurtz for the first time. It was a distinct glimpse: the dugout, four paddling savages, and the lone white man turning his back suddenly on the headquarters, on relief, on thoughts of home— perhaps, setting his face towards the depths of the wilderness, towards his empty and desolate station. I did not know the motive. Perhaps he was just simply a fine fellow who stuck to his work for its own sake. His name, you understand, had not been pronounced once. He was 'that man.' The half-caste, who, as far as I could see, had conducted a difficult trip with great prudence and pluck, was invariably alluded to as 'that scoundrel.' The 'scoundrel' had reported that the 'man' had been very ill—had recovered imperfectly. . . . The two below me moved away then a few paces, and strolled back and forth at some little distance. I heard: 'Military post—doctor—two hundred miles— quite alone now—unavoidable delays—nine months—no news—strange rumors.' They approached again, just as the manager was saying, 'No one, as far as I know, unless a species of wandering trader—a pestilential fellow, snapping ivory from the natives.' Who was it they were talking about now? I gathered in snatches that this was some man supposed to be in Kurtz's district, and of whom the manager did not approve. 'We will not be free from unfair competition till one of these fellows is hanged for an example,' he said. 'Certainly,' grunted the other; 'get him hanged! Why not? Anything—anything can be done in this country. That's what I say; nobody here, you understand, *here*, can endanger your position. And why? You stand the climate—you outlast them all. The danger is in Europe; but there before I left I took care to——' They moved off and whispered, then their voices rose again. 'The extraordinary series of delays is not my fault. I did my possible.' The fat man sighed, 'Very sad.' 'And the pestiferous

absurdity of his talk,' continued the other; 'he bothered me enough when he was here. "Each station should be like a beacon on the road towards better things, a center for trade of course, but also for humanizing, improving, instructing." Conceive you—that ass! And he wants to be manager! No, it's——' Here he got choked by excessive indignation, and I lifted my head the least bit. I was surprised to see how near they were—right under me. I could have spat upon their hats. They were looking on the ground, absorbed in thought. The manager was switching his leg with a slender twig: his sagacious relative lifted his head. 'You have been well since you came out this time?' he asked. The other gave a start. 'Who? I? Oh! Like a charm —like a charm. But the rest—oh, my goodness! All sick. They die so quick, too, that I haven't the time to send them out of the country—it's incredible!' 'H'm. Just so,' grunted the uncle. 'Ah! my boy, trust to this—I say, trust to this.' I saw him extend his short flipper of an arm for a gesture that took in the forest, the creek, the mud, the river—seemed to beckon with a dishonoring flourish before the sunlit face of the land a treacherous appeal to the lurking death, to the hidden evil, to the profound darkness of its heart. It was so startling that I leaped to my feet and looked back at the edge of the forest, as though I had expected an answer of some sort to that black display of confidence. You know the foolish notions that come to one sometimes. The high stillness confronted these two figures with its ominous patience, waiting for the passing away of a fantastic invasion.

"They swore aloud together—out of sheer fright, I believe—then, pretending not to know anything of my existence, turned back to the station. The sun was low; and leaning forward side by side, they seemed to be tugging painfully uphill their two ridiculous shadows of unequal length, that trailed behind them slowly over the tall grass without bending a single blade.

"In a few days the Eldorado Expedition went into the patient wilderness, that closed upon it as the sea closes over a diver. Long afterwards the news came that all the donkeys were dead. I know nothing as to the fate of the less valuable animals. They, no doubt, like the rest of us, found what they deserved. I did not inquire. I was then rather excited at the prospect of meeting Kurtz very soon. When I say very soon I mean it comparatively. It was just two months from the day we left the creek when we came to the bank below Kurtz's station.

"Going up that river was like traveling back to the earliest beginnings of the world, when vegetation rioted on the earth and the big trees were kings. An empty stream, a great silence, an impenetrable forest. The air was warm, thick, heavy, sluggish. There was no joy in the brilliance of sunshine. The long stretches of the waterway ran on, deserted, into the gloom of overshadowed distances. On silvery sandbanks hippos and alligators sunned themselves side by side. The broadening waters flowed through a mob of wooded islands; you lost your way on that river as you would in a desert, and butted all day long against shoals, trying to find the channel, till you thought yourself bewitched and cut off forever from everything you had known once—somewhere—far away—in another existence perhaps. There were moments when one's past came back to one, as it will sometimes when you have not a moment to spare to yourself; but it came in the shape of an unrestful and noisy dream, remembered with wonder amongst the overwhelming realities of this strange world of plants, and water, and silence. And this stillness of life did not in the least resemble a peace. It was the stillness of an implacable force brooding over an inscrutable intention. It looked at you with a vengeful aspect. I got used to it afterwards; I did not see it any more; I had no time. I had to keep guessing at the channel; I had to discern, mostly by inspiration, the signs of hidden banks; I watched for sunken stones; I was learning to clap my teeth smartly before my heart flew out, when I shaved by a fluke some infernal sly old snag that would have ripped the life out of the tin-pot steamboat and drowned all the pilgrims; I had to keep a lookout for the signs of dead wood we could cut up in the night for next day's steaming. When you have to attend to things of that sort, to the mere incidents of the surface, the reality—the reality, I tell you—fades. The inner truth is hidden—luckily, luckily. But I felt it all the same; I felt often its mysterious stillness watching me at my monkey tricks, just as it watches you fellows performing on your respective tightropes for—what is it? half a crown a tumble——"

"Try to be civil, Marlow," growled a voice, and I knew there was at least one listener awake besides myself.

"I beg your pardon. I forgot the heartache which makes up the rest of the price. And indeed what does the price matter, if the trick be well done? You do your tricks very well. And I didn't do badly either, since I managed not to sink that steamboat on my first trip. It's a wonder to me yet. Imagine a blindfolded man set to drive a van over a bad road. I sweated and shivered over that business considerably, I can tell you. After all, for a seaman, to scrape the bottom of the thing that's supposed to float all the time under his care is the unpardonable sin. No one may know of it, but you never forget the thump—eh? A blow on the very heart. You remember it, you dream of it, you wake up at night and think of it—years after—and go hot and cold all over. I don't pretend to say that steamboat floated all the time. More than once she had to wade for a bit, with twenty cannibals splashing around and pushing. We had enlisted some of these chaps on the way for a crew. Fine fellows—cannibals—in their place. They were men one could work with, and I am grateful to them. And, after all, they did not eat each other before my face: they had brought along a provision of hippo-meat which went rotten, and made the mystery of the wilderness stink in my nostrils. Phoo! I can sniff it now. I had the manager on board and three or four pilgrims with their staves—all complete. Sometimes we came upon a station close by the bank, clinging to the skirts of the unknown, and the white men rushing out of a tumble-down hovel, with great gestures of joy and surprise and welcome, seemed very strange—had the appearance of being held there captive by a spell. The word *ivory* would ring in the air for a while—and on we went again into the silence, along empty reaches, round the still bends, between the high walls of our winding way, reverberating in hollow claps the ponderous beat of the stern-wheel. Trees, trees, millions of trees, massive, immense, running up high; and at their foot, hugging the bank against the stream, crept the little begrimed steamboat, like a sluggish beetle crawling on the floor of a lofty portico. It made you feel very small, very lost, and yet it was not altogether depressing, that feeling. After all, if you were small, the grimy beetle crawled on—which was just what you wanted it to do. Where the pilgrims imagined it crawled to I don't know. To some place where they expected to get something, I bet! For me it crawled towards Kurtz—

exclusively; but when the steam-pipes started leaking we crawled very slow. The reaches opened before us and closed behind, as if the forest had stepped leisurely across the water to bar the way for our return. We penetrated deeper and deeper into the heart of darkness. It was very quiet there. At night sometimes the roll of drums behind the curtain of trees would run up the river and remain sustained faintly, as if hovering in the air high over our heads, till the first break of day. Whether it meant war, peace, or prayer we could not tell. The dawns were heralded by the descent of a chill stillness; the woodcutters slept, their fires burned low; the snapping of a twig would make you start. We were wanderers on a prehistoric earth, on an earth that wore the aspect of an unknown planet. We could have fancied ourselves the first of men taking possession of an accursed inheritance, to be subdued at the cost of profound anguish and of excessive toil. But suddenly, as we struggled round a bend, there would be a glimpse of rush walls, of peaked grass-roofs, a burst of yells, a whirl of black limbs, a mass of hands clapping, of feet stamping, of bodies swaying, of eyes rolling, under the droop of heavy and motionless foliage. The steamer toiled along slowly on the edge of a black and incomprehensible frenzy. The prehistoric man was cursing us, praying to us, welcoming us—who could tell? We were cut off from the comprehension of our surroundings; we glided past like phantoms, wondering and secretly appalled, as sane men would be before an enthusiastic outbreak in a madhouse. We could not understand because we were too far and could not remember, because we were traveling in the night of first ages, of those ages that are gone, leaving hardly a sign—and no memories.

"The earth seemed unearthly. We are accustomed to look upon the shackled form of a conquered monster, but there—there you could look at a thing monstrous and free. It was unearthly, and the men were—— No, they were not inhuman. Well, you know, that was the worst of it—this suspicion of their not being inhuman. It would come slowly to one. They howled and leaped, and spun, and made horrid faces; but what thrilled you was just the thought of their humanity—like yours—the thought of your remote kinship with this wild and passionate uproar. Ugly. Yes, it was ugly enough; but if you were man enough you would admit to yourself that there was in you just the faintest trace of a response to the terrible frankness of that noise, a dim suspicion of there being a meaning in it which you—you so remote from the night of first ages—could comprehend. And why not? The mind of man is capable of anything—because everything is in it, all the past as well as all the future. What was there after all? Joy, fear, sorrow, devotion, valor, rage—who can tell?—but truth—truth stripped of its cloak of time. Let the fool gape and shudder—the man knows, and can look on without a wink. But he must at least be as much of a man as these on the shore. He must meet that truth with his own true stuff—with his own inborn strength. Principles? Principles won't do. Acquisitions, clothes, pretty rags—rags that would fly off at the first good shake. No; you want a deliberate belief. An appeal to me in this fiendish row—is there? Very well; I hear; I admit, but I have a voice too, and for good or evil mine is the speech that cannot be silenced. Of course, a fool, what with sheer fright and fine sentiments, is always safe. Who's that grunting? You wonder I didn't go ashore for a howl and a dance? Well, no —I didn't. Fine sentiments, you say? Fine sentiments be hanged! I had no time. I had to mess about with white-lead and strips of woollen blanket helping to put bandages on those leaky steam-pipes—I tell you. I had to watch the steering, and circumvent those snags, and get the tin-pot along by hook or by crook. There was surface-truth enough in these things to save a wiser man. And between whiles I had to look after the savage who was fireman. He was an improved specimen; he could fire up a vertical boiler. He was there below me, and, upon my word, to look at him was as edifying as seeing a dog in a parody of breeches and a feather hat, walking on his hind legs. A few months of training had done for that really fine chap. He squinted at the steam-gauge and at the water-gauge with an evident effort of intrepidity— and he had filed teeth too, the poor devil, and the wool of his pate shaved into queer patterns, and three ornamental scars on each of his cheeks. He ought to have been clapping his hands and stamping his feet on the bank, instead of which he was hard at work, a thrall to strange witchcraft, full of improving knowledge. He was useful because he had been instructed; and what he knew was this— that should the water in that transparent thing disappear, the evil spirit inside the boiler would get angry through the greatness of his thirst, and take a terrible vengeance. So he sweated and fired up and watched the glass fearfully (with an impromptu charm, made of rags, tied to his arm, and a piece of polished bone, as big as a watch, stuck flatways through his lower lip), while the wooded banks slipped past us slowly, the short noise was left behind, the interminable miles of silence—and we crept on, towards Kurtz. But the snags were thick, the water was treacherous and shallow, the boiler seemed indeed to have a sulky devil in it, and thus neither that fireman nor I had any time to peer into our creepy thoughts.

"Some fifty miles below the Inner Station we came upon a hut of reeds, an inclined and melancholy pole, with the unrecognizable tatters of what had been a flag of some sort flying from it, and a neatly stacked woodpile. This was unexpected. We came to the bank, and on the stack of firewood found a flat piece of board with some faded pencil-writing on it. When deciphered it said: 'Wood for you. Hurry up. Approach cautiously.' There was a signature, but it was illegible—not Kurtz—a much longer word. 'Hurry up.' Where? Up the river? 'Approach cautiously.' We had not done so. But the warning could not have been meant for the place where it could be only found after approach. Something was wrong above. But what—and how much? That was the question. We commented adversely upon the imbecility of that telegraphic style. The bush around said nothing, and would not let us look very far, either. A torn curtain of red twill hung in the doorway of the hut, and flapped sadly in our faces. The dwelling was dismantled; but we could see a white man had lived there not very long ago. There remained a rude table—a plank on two posts; a heap of rubbish reposed in a dark corner, and by the door I picked up a book. It had lost its covers, and the pages had been thumbed into a state of extremely dirty softness; but the back had been lovingly stitched afresh with white cotton thread, which looked clean yet. It was an extraordinary find. Its title was, *An Inquiry into some Points of Seamanship*, by a man Towser, Towson—some such name—Master in His Majesty's Navy. The matter looked dreary reading enough, with illustrative diagrams and repulsive tables of figures, and the copy was sixty years old. I handled this amazing antiquity with the greatest possible tenderness, lest it should dissolve in my hands. Within, Towson or Towser was inquiring earnestly into the breaking strain of ships' chains and tackle, and other such matters. Not a very enthralling book; but at the first glance you could see there a singleness of intention, an honest concern for the right way of going to work, which made these humble pages, thought out so many years ago, luminous with another than a professional light. The simple old sailor, with his talk of chains and purchases, made me forget the jungle and the pilgrims in a delicious sensation of having come upon something unmistakably real. Such a book being there was wonderful enough; but still more astounding were the notes penciled in the margin, and plainly referring to the text. I couldn't believe my eyes! They were in cipher! Yes, it looked like cipher. Fancy a man lugging with him a book of that description into this nowhere and studying it—and making notes—in cipher at that! It was an extravagant mystery.

"I had been dimly aware for some time of a worrying noise, and when I lifted my eyes I saw the woodpile was gone, and the manager, aided by all the pilgrims, was shouting at me from the riverside. I slipped the book into my pocket. I assure you to leave off reading was like tearing myself away from the shelter of an old and solid friendship.

"I started the lame engine ahead. 'It must be this miserable trader—this intruder,' exclaimed the manager, looking back malevolently at the place we had left. 'He must be English,' I said. 'It will not save him from getting into trouble if he is not careful,' muttered the manager darkly. I observed with assumed innocence that no man was safe from trouble in this world.

"The current was more rapid now, the steamer seemed at her last gasp, the stern-wheel flopped languidly, and I caught myself listening on tiptoe for the next beat of the float,[10] for in sober truth I expected the wretched thing to give up every moment. It was like watching the last flickers of a life. But still we crawled. Sometimes I would pick out a tree a little way ahead to measure our progress towards Kurtz by, but I lost it invariably before we got abreast. To keep the eyes so long on one thing was too much for human patience. The manager displayed a beautiful resignation. I fretted and fumed and took to arguing with myself whether

10. **float:** regulator for water level.

or no I would talk openly with Kurtz; but before I could come to any conclusion it occurred to me that my speech or my silence, indeed any action of mine, would be a mere futility. What did it matter what any one knew or ignored? What did it matter who was manager? One gets sometimes such a flash of insight. The essentials of this affair lay deep under the surface, beyond my reach, and beyond my power of meddling.

"Towards the evening of the second day we judged ourselves about eight miles from Kurtz's station. I wanted to push on; but the manager looked grave, and told me the navigation up there was so dangerous that it would be advisable, the sun being very low already, to wait where we were till next morning. Moreover, he pointed out that if the warning to approach cautiously were to be followed, we must approach in daylight—not at dusk, or in the dark. This was sensible enough. Eight miles meant nearly three hours' steaming for us, and I could also see suspicious ripples at the upper end of the reach. Nevertheless, I was annoyed beyond expression at the delay, and most unreasonably too, since one night more could not matter much after so many months. As we had plenty of wood, and caution was the word, I brought up in the middle of the stream. The reach was narrow, straight, with high sides like a railway cutting. The dusk came gliding into it long before the sun had set. The current ran smooth and swift, but a dumb immobility sat on the banks. The living trees, lashed together by the creepers and every living bush of the undergrowth, might have been changed into stone, even to the slenderest twig, to the lightest leaf. It was not sleep—it seemed unnatural, like a state of trance. Not the faintest sound of any kind could be heard. You looked on amazed, and began to suspect yourself of being deaf—then the night came suddenly, and struck you blind as well. About three in the morning some large fish leaped, and the loud splash made me jump as though a gun had been fired. When the sun rose there was a white fog, very warm and clammy, and more blinding than the night. It did not shift or drive; it was just there, standing all round you like something solid. At eight or nine, perhaps, it lifted as a shutter lifts. We had a glimpse of the towering multitude of trees, of the immense matted jungle, with the blazing little ball of the sun hanging over it—all

perfectly still—and then the white shutter came down again, smoothly, as if sliding in greased grooves. I ordered the chain, which we had begun to heave in, to be paid out again. Before it stopped running with a muffled rattle, a cry, a very loud cry, as of infinite desolation, soared slowly in the opaque air. It ceased. A complaining clamor, modulated in savage discords, filled our ears. The sheer unexpectedness of it made my hair stir under my cap. I don't know how it struck the others: to me it seemed as though the mist itself had screamed, so suddenly, and apparently from all sides at once, did this tumultuous and mournful uproar arise. It culminated in a hurried outbreak of almost intolerably excessive shrieking, which stopped short, leaving us stiffened in a variety of silly attitudes, and obstinately listening to the nearly as appalling and excessive silence. 'Good God! What is the meaning——?' stammered at my elbow one of the pilgrims—a little fat man, with sandy hair and red whiskers, who wore side-spring boots, and pink pajamas tucked into his socks. Two others remained open-mouthed a whole minute, then dashed into the little cabin, to rush out incontinently and stand darting scared glances, with Winchesters at 'ready' in their hands. What we could see was just the steamer we were on, her outlines blurred as though she had been on the point of dissolving, and a misty strip of water, perhaps two feet broad, around her—and that was all. The rest of the world was nowhere, as far as our eyes and ears were concerned. Just nowhere. Gone, disappeared; swept off without leaving a whisper or a shadow behind.

"I went forward, and ordered the chain to be hauled in short, so as to be ready to trip the anchor and move the steamboat at once if necessary. 'Will they attack?' whispered an awed voice. 'We will all be butchered in this fog,' murmured another. The faces twitched with the strain, the hands trembled slightly, the eyes forgot to wink. It was very curious to see the contrast of expressions of the white men and of the black fellows of our crew, who were as much strangers to that part of the river as we, though their homes were only eight hundred miles away. The whites, of course greatly discomposed, had besides a curious look of being painfully shocked by such an outrageous row. The others had an alert, naturally interested expression; but their faces were essentially quiet, even those of the one or two who grinned as they hauled at the chain. Several exchanged short, grunting phrases, which seemed to settle the matter to their satisfaction. Their head-man, a young, broad-chested black, severely draped in dark-blue fringed cloths, with fierce nostrils and his hair all done up artfully in oily ringlets, stood near me. 'Aha!' I said, just for good fellowship's sake. 'Catch 'im,' he snapped, with a bloodshot widening of his eyes and a flash of sharp teeth—'catch 'im. Give 'im to us.' 'To you, eh?' I asked; 'what would you do with them?' 'Eat 'im!' he said curtly, and, leaning his elbow on the rail, looked out into the fog in a dignified and profoundly pensive attitude. I would no doubt have been properly horrified, had it not occurred to me that he and his chaps must be very hungry: that they must have been growing increasingly hungry for at least this month past. They had been engaged for six months (I don't think a single one of them had any clear idea of time, as we at the end of countless ages have. They still belonged to the beginnings of time—had no inherited experience to teach them, as it were), and of course, as long as there was a piece of paper written over in accordance with some farcical law or other made down the river, it didn't enter anybody's head to trouble how they would live. Certainly they had brought with them some rotten hippo-meat, which couldn't have lasted very long, anyway, even if the pilgrims hadn't, in the midst of a shocking hullabaloo, thrown a considerable quantity of it overboard. It looked like a high-handed proceeding; but it was really a case of legitimate self-defense. You can't breathe dead hippo waking, sleeping, and eating, and at the same time keep your precarious grip on existence. Besides that, they had given them every week three pieces of brass wire, each about nine inches long; and the theory was they were to buy their provisions with that currency in riverside villages. You can see how *that* worked. There were either no villages, or the people were hostile, or the director, who like the rest of us fed out of tins, with an occasional old he-goat thrown in, didn't want to stop the steamer for some more or less recondite reason. So, unless they swallowed the wire itself, or made loops of it to snare the fishes with, I don't see what good their extravagant salary could be to them. I must say it was paid with a regularity worthy of a large and honorable

trading company. For the rest, the only thing to eat—though it didn't look eatable in the least—I saw in their possession was a few lumps of some stuff like half-cooked dough, of a dirty lavender color, they kept wrapped in leaves, and now and then swallowed a piece of, but so small that it seemed done more for the look of the thing than for any serious purpose of sustenance. Why in the name of all the gnawing devils of hunger they didn't go for us—they were thirty to five—and have a good tuck-in for once, amazes me now when I think of it. They were big powerful men, with not much capacity to weigh the consequences, with courage, with strength, even yet, though their skins were no longer glossy and their muscles no longer hard. And I saw that something restraining, one of those human secrets that baffle probability, had come into play there. I looked at them with a swift quickening of interest—not because it occurred to me I might be eaten by them before very long, though I own to you that just then I perceived—in a new light, as it were—how unwholesome the pilgrims looked, and I hoped, yes, I positively hoped, that my aspect was not so—what shall I say?—so—unappetizing: a touch of fantastic vanity which fitted well with the dream-sensation that pervaded all my days at that time. Perhaps I had a little fever too. One can't live with one's finger everlastingly on one's pulse. I had often 'a little fever,' or a little touch of other things—the playful paw-strokes of the wilderness, the preliminary trifling before the more serious onslaught which came in due course. Yes; I looked at them as you would on any human being, with a curiosity of their impulses, motives, capacities, weaknesses, when brought to the test of an inexorable physical necessity. Restraint! What possible restraint? Was it superstition, disgust, patience, fear—or some kind of primitive honor? No fear can stand up to hunger, no patience can wear it out, disgust simply does not exist where hunger is; and as to superstition, beliefs, and what you may call principles, they are less than chaff in a breeze. Don't you know the devilry of lingering starvation, its exasperating torment, its black thoughts, its somber and brooding ferocity? Well, I do. It takes a man all his inborn strength to fight hunger properly. It's really easier to face bereavement, dishonor, and the perdition of one's soul—than this kind of prolonged hunger. Sad, but true. And these chaps too had no earthly reason for any kind of scruple. Restraint! I would just as soon have expected restraint from a hyena prowling amongst the corpses of a battlefield. But there was the fact facing me—the fact dazzling, to be seen, like the foam on the depths of the sea, like a ripple on an unfathomable enigma, a mystery greater—when I thought of it—than the curious, inexplicable note of desperate grief in this savage clamor that had swept by us on the riverbank, behind the blind whiteness of the fog.

"Two pilgrims were quarreling in hurried whispers as to which bank. 'Left.' 'No, no; how can you? Right, right, of course.' 'It is very serious,' said the manager's voice behind me; 'I would be desolated if anything should happen to Mr. Kurtz before we came up.' I looked at him, and had not the slightest doubt he was sincere. He was just the kind of man who would wish to preserve appearances. That was his restraint. But when he muttered something about going on at once, I did not even take the trouble to answer him. I knew, and he knew, that it was impossible. Were we to let go our hold of the bottom, we would be absolutely in the air—in space. We wouldn't be able to tell where we were going to—whether up or down stream, or across—till we fetched against one bank or the other—and then we wouldn't know at first which it was. Of course I made no move. I had no mind for a smash-up. You couldn't imagine a more deadly place for a shipwreck. Whether drowned at once or not, we were sure to perish speedily in one way or another. 'I authorize you to take all the risks,' he said, after a short silence. 'I refuse to take any,' I said shortly; which was just the answer he expected, though its tone might have surprised him. 'Well, I must defer to your judgment. You are captain,' he said, with marked civility. I turned my shoulder to him in sign of my appreciation, and looked into the fog. How long would it last? It was the most hopeless lookout. The approach to this Kurtz grubbing for ivory in the wretched bush was beset by as many dangers as though he had been an enchanted princess sleeping in a fabulous castle. 'Will they attack, do you think?' asked the manager, in a confidential tone.

"I did not think they would attack, for several obvious reasons. The thick fog was one. If they left the bank in their canoes they would get lost in it, as we would be if we attempted to move. Still, I had also judged the jungle of both banks quite impenetrable—and yet eyes were in it, eyes that had seen us. The riverside bushes were certainly very thick; but the undergrowth behind was evidently penetrable. However, during the short lift I had seen no canoes anywhere in the reach—certainly not abreast of the steamer. But what made the idea of attack inconceivable to me was the nature of the noise—of the cries we had heard. They had not the fierce character boding of immediate hostile intention. Unexpected, wild, and violent as they had been, they had given me an irresistible impression of sorrow. The glimpse of the steamboat had for some reason filled those savages with unrestrained grief. The danger, if any, I expounded, was from our proximity to a great human passion let loose. Even extreme grief may ultimately vent itself in violence—but more generally takes the form of apathy. . . .

"You should have seen the pilgrims stare! They had no heart to grin, or even to revile me; but I believe they thought me gone mad—with fright, maybe. I delivered a regular lecture. My dear boys, it was no good bothering. Keep a lookout? Well, you may guess I watched the fog for the signs of lifting as a cat watches a mouse; but for anything else our eyes were of no more use to us than if we had been buried miles deep in a heap of cotton-wool. It felt like it too—choking, warm, stifling. Besides, all I said, though it sounded extravagant, was absolutely true to fact. What we afterwards alluded to as an attack was really an attempt at repulse. The action was very far from being aggressive—it was not even defensive, in the usual sense: it was undertaken under the stress of desperation, and in its essence was purely protective.

"It developed itself, I should say, two hours after the fog lifted, and its commencement was at a spot, roughly speaking, about a mile and a half below Kurtz's station. We had just floundered and flopped round a bend, when I saw an islet, a mere grassy hummock of bright green, in the middle of the stream. It was the only thing of the kind; but as we opened the reach more, I perceived it was the head of a long sandbank, or rather a chain of shallow patches stretching down the middle of the river. They were discolored, just awash, and the whole lot was seen just under the water, exactly as a man's backbone is seen running down the middle of his back under the skin. Now, as far as I did see, I could go to the right or to the left of this. I didn't know either channel, of course. The banks looked pretty well alike, the depth appeared the same; but as I had been informed the station was on the west side, I naturally headed for the western passage.

"No sooner had we fairly entered it than I became aware it was much narrower than I had supposed. To the left of us there was the long uninterrupted shoal, and to the right a high steep bank heavily overgrown with bushes. Above the bush the trees stood in serried ranks. The twigs overhung the current thickly, and from distance to distance a large limb of some tree projected rigidly over the stream. It was then well on in the afternoon, the face of the forest was gloomy, and a broad strip of shadow had already fallen on the water. In this shadow we steamed up—very slowly, as you may imagine. I sheered her well inshore—the water being deepest near the bank, as the sounding-pole informed me.

"One of my hungry and forbearing friends was sounding in the bows just below me. This steamboat was exactly like a decked scow. On the deck there were two little teakwood houses, with doors and windows. The boiler was in the fore-end, and the machinery right astern. Over the whole there was a light roof, supported on stanchions. The funnel projected through that roof, and in front of the funnel a small cabin built of light planks served for a pilothouse. It contained a couch, two campstools, a loaded Martini-Henry[11] leaning in one corner, a tiny table, and the steering-wheel. It had a wide door in front and a broad shutter at each side. All these were always thrown open, of course. I spent my days perched up there on the extreme fore-end of that roof, before the door. At night I slept, or tried to, on the couch. An athletic black belonging to some coast tribe, and educated by my poor predecessor, was the helmsman. He sported a pair of brass earrings, wore a blue cloth wrapper from the waist to the ankles, and thought all the world of himself. He was the most unstable kind of fool I had ever seen. He steered with no end of a swagger while you were by; but if he lost sight of you, he became instantly the prey of an

11. **Martini-Henry:** breech-action rifle.

abject funk, and would let that cripple of a steamboat get the upper hand of him in a minute.

"I was looking down at the sounding-pole, and feeling much annoyed to see at each try a little more of it stick out of that river, when I saw my poleman give up the business suddenly, and stretch himself flat on the deck, without even taking the trouble to haul his pole in. He kept hold on it though, and it trailed in the water. At the same time the fireman, whom I could also see below me, sat down abruptly before his furnace and ducked his head. I was amazed. Then I had to look at the river mighty quick, because there was a snag in the fairway. Sticks, little sticks, were flying about—thick: they were whizzing before my nose, dropping below me, striking behind me against my pilothouse. All this time the river, the shore, the woods, were very quiet—perfectly quiet. I could only hear the heavy splashing thump of the stern-wheel and the patter of these things. We cleared the snag clumsily. Arrows, by Jove! We were being shot at! I stepped in quickly to close the shutter on the land-side. That fool-helmsman, his hands on the spokes, was lifting his knees high, stamping his feet, champing his mouth, like a reined-in horse. Confound him! And we were staggering within ten feet of the bank. I had to lean right out to swing the heavy shutter, and I saw a face amongst the leaves on the level with my own, looking at me very fierce and steady; and then suddenly, as though a veil had been removed from my eyes, I made out, deep in the tangled gloom, naked breasts, arms, legs, glaring eyes—the bush was swarming with human limbs in movement, glistening, of bronze color. The twigs shook, swayed, and rustled, the arrows flew out of them, and then the shutter came to. 'Steer her straight,' I said to the helmsman. He held his head rigid, face forward; but his eyes rolled, he kept on lifting and setting down his feet gently, his mouth foamed a little. 'Keep quiet'! I said in a fury. I might just as well have ordered a tree not to sway in the wind. I darted out. Below me there was a great scuffle of feet on the iron deck; confused exclamations; a voice screamed, 'Can you turn back?' I caught sight of a V-shaped ripple on the water ahead. What? Another snag! A fusillade burst out under my feet. The pilgrims had opened with their Winchesters, and were simply squirting lead into that bush. A deuce of a lot of smoke came up and drove slowly forward. I swore at it.

Now I couldn't see the ripple or the snag either. I stood in the doorway, peering, and the arrows came in swarms. They might have been poisoned, but they looked as though they wouldn't kill a cat. The bush began to howl. Our woodcutters raised a warlike whoop; the report of a rifle just at my back deafened me. I glanced over my shoulder, and the pilothouse was yet full of noise and smoke when I made a dash at the wheel. The fool-nigger had dropped everything, to throw the shutter open and let off that Martini-Henry. He stood before the wide opening, glaring, and I yelled at him to come back, while I straightened the sudden twist out of that steamboat. There was no room to turn even if I had wanted to, the snag was somewhere very near ahead in that confounded smoke, there was no time to lose, so I just crowded her into the bank —right into the bank, where I knew the water was deep.

"We tore slowly along the overhanging bushes in a whirl of broken twigs and flying leaves. The fusillade below stopped short, as I had foreseen it would when the squirts got empty. I threw my head back to a glinting whiz that traversed the pilot-house, in at one shutter-hole and out at the other. Looking past that mad helmsman, who was shaking the empty rifle and yelling at the shore, I saw vague forms of men running bent double, leaping, gliding, distinct, incomplete, evanescent. Something big appeared in the air before the shutter, the rifle went overboard, and the man stepped back swiftly, looked at me over his shoulder in an extraordinary, profound, familiar manner, and fell upon my feet. The side of his head hit the wheel twice, and the end of what appeared a long cane clattered round and knocked over a little campstool. It looked as though after wrenching that thing from somebody ashore he had lost his balance in the effort. The thin smoke had blown away, we were clear of the snag, and looking ahead I could see that in another hundred yards or so I would be free to sheer off, away from the bank; but my feet felt so very warm and wet that I had to look down. The man had rolled on his back and stared straight up at me; both his hands clutched that cane. It was the shaft of a spear that, either thrown or lunged through the opening, had caught him in the side just below the ribs; the blade had gone in out of sight, after making a frightful gash; my shoes were full; a pool of blood lay very still,

gleaming dark-red under the wheel; his eyes shone with an amazing luster. The fusillade burst out again. He looked at me anxiously, gripping the spear like something precious, with an air of being afraid I would try to take it away from him. I had to make an effort to free my eyes from his gaze and attend to the steering. With one hand I felt above my head for the line of the steam whistle, and jerked out screech after screech hurriedly. The tumult of angry and warlike yells was checked instantly, and then from the depths of the woods went out such a tremulous and prolonged wail of mournful fear and utter despair as may be imagined to follow the flight of the last hope from the earth. There was a great commotion in the bush; the shower of arrows stopped, a few dropping shots rang out sharply—then silence, in which the languid beat of the stern-wheel came plainly to my ears. I put the helm hard a-starboard at the moment when the pilgrim in pink pajamas, very hot and agitated, appeared in the doorway. 'The manager sends me ——' he began in an official tone, and stopped short. 'Good God!' he said, glaring at the wounded man.

"We two whites stood over him, and his lustrous and inquiring glance enveloped us both. I declare it looked as though he would presently put to us some question in an understandable language; but he died without uttering a sound, without moving a limb, without twitching a muscle. Only in the very last moment, as though in response to some sign we could not see, to some whisper we could not hear, he frowned heavily, and that frown gave to his black death-mask an inconceivably somber, brooding, and menacing expression. The luster of inquiring glance faded swiftly into vacant glassiness. 'Can you steer?' I asked the agent eagerly. He looked very dubious; but I made a grab at his arm, and he understood at once I meant him to steer whether or no. To tell you the truth, I was morbidly anxious to change my shoes and socks. 'He is dead,' murmured the fellow, immensely impressed. 'No doubt about it,' said I, tugging like mad at the shoelaces. 'And by the way, I suppose Mr. Kurtz is dead as well by this time.'

"For the moment that was the dominant thought. There was a sense of extreme disappointment, as though I had found out I had been striving after something altogether without a substance. I couldn't have been more disgusted if I had traveled all this way for the sole purpose of talking with Mr. Kurtz. Talking with . . . I flung one shoe overboard, and became aware that that was exactly what I had been looking forward to—a talk with Kurtz. I made the strange discovery that I had never imagined him as doing, you know, but as discoursing. I didn't say to myself, 'Now I will never see him,' or 'Now I will never shake him by the hand,' but, 'Now I will never hear him.' The man presented himself as a voice. Not of course that I did not connect him with some sort of action. Hadn't I been told in all the tones of jealousy and admiration that he had collected, bartered, swindled, or stolen more ivory than all the other agents together? That was not the point. The point was in his being a gifted creature, and that of all his gifts the one that stood out preeminently, that carried with it a sense of real presence, was his ability to talk, his words—the gift of expression, the bewildering, the illuminating, the most exalted and the most contemptible, the pulsating stream of light, or the deceitful flow from the heart of an impenetrable darkness.

"The other shoe went flying unto the devil-god of that river. I thought, By Jove! it's all over. We are too late; he has vanished—the gift has vanished, by means of some spear, arrow, or club. I will never hear that chap speak after all—and my sorrow had a startling extravagance of emotion, even such as I had noticed in the howling sorrow of these savages in the bush. I couldn't have felt more of lonely desolation somehow, had I been robbed of a belief or had missed my destiny in life. . . . Why do you sigh in this beastly way, somebody? Absurd? Well, absurd. Good Lord! mustn't a man ever—— Here, give me some tobacco." . . .

There was a pause of profound stillness, then a match flared, and Marlow's lean face appeared, worn, hollow, with downward folds and dropped eyelids, with an aspect of concentrated attention; and as he took vigorous draws at his pipe, it seemed to retreat and advance out of the night in the regular flicker of the tiny flame. The match went out.

"Absurd!" he cried. "This is the worst of trying to tell . . . Here you all are, each moored with two good addresses, like a hulk with two anchors, a butcher round one corner, a policeman round another, excellent appetites, and temperature normal—you hear—normal from year's end to year's end. And you say, Absurd! Absurd be—exploded! Absurd! My dear boys, what can you expect from a man who out of sheer nervousness had just flung overboard a pair of new shoes? Now I think of it, it is amazing I did not shed tears. I am, upon the whole, proud of my fortitude. I was cut to the quick at the idea of having lost the inestimable privilege of listening to the gifted Kurtz. Of course I was wrong. The privilege was waiting for me. Oh yes, I heard more than enough. And I was right, too. A voice. He was very little more than a voice. And I heard—him—it—this voice—other voices—all of them were so little more than voices—and the memory of that time itself lingers around me, impalpable, like a dying vibration of one immense jabber, silly, atrocious, sordid, savage, or simply mean, without any kind of sense. Voices, voices—even the girl herself—now—"

He was silent for a long time.

"I laid the ghost of his gifts at last with a lie," he began suddenly. "Girl! What? Did I mention a girl? Oh, she is out of it—completely. They—the women I mean—are out of it—should be out of it. We must help them to stay in that beautiful world of their own, lest ours gets worse. Oh, she had to be out of it. You should have heard the disinterred body of Mr. Kurtz saying, 'My Intended.' You would have perceived directly then how completely she was out of it. And the lofty frontal bone of Mr. Kurtz! They say the hair goes on growing sometimes, but this—ah—specimen was impressively bald. The wilderness had patted him on the head, and, behold, it was like a ball—an ivory ball; it had caressed him, and—lo!—he had withered; it had taken him, loved him, embraced him, got into his veins, consumed his flesh, and sealed his soul to its own by the inconceivable ceremonies of some devilish initiation. He was its spoiled and pampered favorite. Ivory? I should think so. Heaps of it, stacks of it. The old mud shanty was bursting with it. You would think there was not a single tusk left either above or below the ground in the whole country. 'Mostly fossil,' the manager had remarked disparagingly. It was no more fossil than I am; but they call it fossil when it is dug up. It appears these niggers do bury the tusks sometimes—but evidently they couldn't bury this parcel deep enough to save the gifted Mr. Kurtz from his fate. We filled the steamboat with it, and had to pile a lot on the deck. Thus he could see and enjoy as long as he could see, because the appreciation of this favor had remained with him to the last. You should have heard him say, 'My ivory.' Oh yes, I heard him. 'My Intended, my ivory, my station, my river, my——' everything belonged to him. It made me hold my breath in expectation of hearing the wilderness burst into a prodigious peal of laughter that would shake the fixed stars in their places. Everything belonged to him—but that was a trifle. The thing was to know what he belonged to, how many powers of darkness claimed him for their own. That was the reflection that made you creepy all over. It was impossible—it was not good for one either—trying to imagine. He had taken a high seat amongst the devils of the land— I mean literally. You can't understand. How could you?—with solid pavement under your feet, surrounded by kind neighbors ready to cheer you or to fall on you, stepping delicately between the butcher and the policeman, in the holy terror of scandal and gallows and lunatic asylums—how can you imagine what particular region of the first ages a man's untrammeled feet may take him into by the way of solitude—utter solitude without a police-man—by the way of silence—utter silence, where no warning voice of a kind neighbor can be heard whispering of public opinion? These little things make all the great difference. When they are gone you must fall back upon your own innate strength, upon your own capacity for faithfulness. Of course you may be too much of a fool to go wrong—too dull even to know you are being assaulted by the powers of darkness. I take it, no fool ever made a bargain for his soul with the devil: the fool is too much of a fool, or the devil too much of a devil—I don't know which. Or you may be such a thunder-ingly exalted creature as to be altogether deaf and blind to anything but heavenly sights and sounds. Then the earth for you is only a standing place— and whether to be like this is your loss or your gain I won't pretend to say. But most of us are neither one nor the other. The earth for us is a place to live in, where we must put up with sights, with sounds, with smells, too, by Jove!—breathe dead hippo, so to speak, and not be contaminated. And there, don't you see? your strength comes in, the faith in your ability for the digging of unostentatious holes to bury the stuff in—your power of devotion, not to yourself, but to an obscure, backbreaking business. And that's difficult enough. Mind, I am not trying to excuse or even explain—I am trying to account to myself for—for—Mr. Kurtz—for the shade of Mr. Kurtz. This initiated wraith from the back of Nowhere honored me with its amazing confidence before it vanished altogether. This was because it could speak English to me. The original Kurtz had been educated partly in England, and—as he was good enough to say himself—his sympathies were in the right place. His mother was half-English, his father was half-French. All Europe contributed to the making of Kurtz; and by and by I learned that, most appro-priately, the International Society for the Sup-pression of Savage Customs had entrusted him with the making of a report, for its future guidance. And he had written it too, I've seen it. I've read it. It was eloquent, vibrating with eloquence, but too high-strung, I think. Seventeen pages of close writing he had found time for! But this must have been before his—let us say—nerves went wrong, and caused him to preside at certain midnight dances ending with unspeakable rites, which—as far as I reluctantly gathered from what I heard at various times—were offered up to him—do you understand?—to Mr. Kurtz himself. But it was a beautiful piece of writing. The opening paragraph, however, in the light of later information, strikes me now as ominous. He began with the argument that we whites, from the point of development we had arrived at, 'must necessarily appear to them [savages] in the nature of supernatural beings—we approach them with the might as of a deity,' and so on, and so on. 'By the simple exercise of our will we can exert a power for good practically unbounded,' etc. etc. From that point he soared and took me with him. The peroration was mag-nificent, though difficult to remember, you know. It gave me the notion of an exotic Immensity ruled by an august Benevolence. It made me tingle with enthusiasm. This was the unbounded power of eloquence—of words—of burning noble words. There were no practical hints to interrupt the magic current of phrases, unless a kind of note at the foot of the last page, scrawled evidently much later, in an unsteady hand, may be regarded as the exposi-tion of a method. It was very simple, and at the end of that moving appeal to every altruistic sentiment it blazed at you, luminous and terrifying, like a flash of lightning in a serene sky: 'Exterminate all the brutes!' The curious part was that he had apparently forgotten all about that valuable postscriptum, because, later on, when he in a sense came to himself, he repeatedly entreated me to take good care of 'my pamphlet' (he called it), as it was sure to have in the future a good influence upon his career. I had full information about all these things, and, besides, as it turned out, I was to have the care of his memory. I've done enough for it to give me the indisputable right to lay it, if I choose, for an everlasting rest in the dustbin of progress amongst all the sweepings and, figuratively speaking, all the dead cats of civilization. But then, you see, I can't choose. He won't be forgotten. Whatever he was, he was not common. He had the power to charm or frighten rudimentary souls into an aggravated witch-dance in his honor; he could also fill the small souls of the pilgrims with bitter misgivings: he had one devoted friend at least, and he had conquered one soul in the world that was neither rudimentary nor tainted with self-seeking. No; I can't forget him, though I am not prepared to affirm the fellow was exactly worth the life we lost in getting to him. I missed my late helmsman awfully—I missed him even while his body was still lying in the pilothouse. Perhaps you will think it passing strange this regret for a savage who was no more account than a grain of sand in a black Sahara. Well, don't you see, he had done something, he had steered; for months I had him at my back—a help—an instrument. It was a kind of partnership. He steered for me—I had to look after him, I worried about his deficiencies, and thus a subtle bond had been created, of which I only became aware when it was suddenly broken. And the intimate profundity of that look he gave me when he received his hurt remains to this day in my memory—like a claim of distant kinship affirmed in a supreme moment.

"Poor fool! If he had only left that shutter alone. He had no restraint, no restraint—just like Kurtz —a tree swayed by the wind. As soon as I had put on a dry pair of slippers, I dragged him out, after first jerking the spear out of his side, which operation I confess I performed with my eyes shut tight. His heels leaped together over the little doorstep; his shoulders were pressed to my breast; I hugged him from behind desperately. Oh! he was heavy, heavy; heavier than any man on earth, I should imagine. Then without more ado I tipped him overboard. The current snatched him as though he had

been a wisp of grass, and I saw the body roll over twice before I lost sight of it forever. All the pilgrims and the manager were then congregated on the awning-deck about the pilothouse, chattering at each other like a flock of excited magpies, and there was a scandalized murmur at my heartless promptitude. What they wanted to keep that body hanging about for I can't guess. Embalm it, maybe. But I had also heard another, and a very ominous, murmur on the deck below. My friends the woodcutters were likewise scandalized, and with a better show of reason—though I admit that the reason itself was quite inadmissible. Oh, quite! I had made up my mind that if my late helmsman was to be eaten, the fishes alone should have him. He had been a very second-rate helmsman while alive, but now he was dead he might have become a first-class temptation, and possibly cause some startling trouble. Besides, I was anxious to take the wheel, the man in pink pajamas showing himself a hopeless duffer at the business.

"This I did directly the simple funeral was over. We were going half-speed, keeping right in the middle of the stream, and I listened to the talk about me. They had given up Kurtz, they had given up the station; Kurtz was dead, and the station had been burnt—and so on, and so on. The red-haired pilgrim was beside himself with the thought that at least this poor Kurtz had been properly revenged. 'Say! We must have made a glorious slaughter of them in the bush. Eh? What do you think? Say?' He positively danced, the blood-thirsty little gingery beggar.[12] And he had nearly fainted when he saw the wounded man! I could not help saying, 'You made a glorious lot of smoke, anyhow.' I had seen, from the way the tops of the bushes rustled and flew, that almost all the shots had gone too high. You can't hit anything unless you take aim and fire from the shoulder; but these chaps fired from the hip with their eyes shut. The retreat, I maintained—and I was right—was caused by the screeching of the steam-whistle. Upon this they forgot Kurtz, and began to howl at me with indignant protests.

"The manager stood by the wheel murmuring confidentially about the necessity of getting well away down the river before dark at all events, when I saw in the distance a clearing on the riverside and the outlines of some sort of building. 'What's

12. **gingery beggar:** (slang) red-headed rascal.

this?' I asked. He clapped his hands in wonder. 'The station!' he cried. I edged in at once, still going half-speed.

"Through my glasses I saw the slope of a hill interspersed with rare trees and perfectly free from undergrowth. A long decaying building on the summit was half buried in the high grass; the large holes in the peaked roof gaped black from afar; the jungle and the woods made a background. There was no enclosure or fence of any kind; but there had been one apparently, for near the house half a dozen slim posts remained in a row, roughly trimmed, and with their upper ends ornamented with round carved balls. The rails, or whatever there had been between, had disappeared. Of course the forest surrounded all that. The riverbank was clear, and on the water side I saw a white man under a hat like a cart-wheel beckoning persistently with his whole arm. Examining the edge of the forest above and below, I was almost certain I could see movements—human forms gliding here and there. I steamed past prudently, then stopped the engines and let her drift down. The man on the shore began to shout, urging us to land. 'We have been attacked,' screamed the manager. 'I know— I know. It's all right,' yelled back the other, as cheerful as you please. 'Come along. It's all right. I am glad.'

"His aspect reminded me of something I had seen—something funny I had seen somewhere. As I maneuvred to get alongside, I was asking myself, 'What does this fellow look like?' Suddenly I got it. He looked like a harlequin. His clothes had been made of some stuff that was brown holland[13] probably, but it was covered with patches all over, with bright patches, blue, red, and yellow—patches on the back, patches on the front, patches on elbows, on knees; colored binding round his jacket, scarlet edging at the bottom of his trousers; and the sunshine made him look extremely gay and wonderfully neat withal, because you could see how beautifully all this patching had been done. A beardless, boyish face, very fair, no features to speak of, nose peeling, little blue eyes, smiles and frowns chasing each other over that open countenance like sunshine and shadow on a wind-swept plain. 'Look out, captain!' he cried; 'there's a snag lodged in here last night.' What! Another snag? I confess I swore shamefully. I had nearly holed my

13. **holland:** linen or cotton cloth.

cripple, to finish off that charming trip. The harlequin on the bank turned his little pug-nose up to me. 'You English?' he asked, all smiles. 'Are you?' I shouted from the wheel. The smiles vanished, and he shook his head as if sorry for my disappointment. Then he brightened up. 'Never mind!' he cried encouragingly. 'Are we in time?' I asked. 'He is up there,' he replied, with a toss of the head up the hill, and becoming gloomy all of a sudden. His face was like the autumn sky, overcast one moment and bright the next.

"When the manager, escorted by the pilgrims, all of them armed to the teeth, had gone to the house, this chap came on board. 'I say, I don't like this. These natives are in the bush,' I said. He assured me earnestly it was all right. 'They are simple people,' he added; 'well, I am glad you came. It took me all my time to keep them off.' 'But you said it was all right,' I cried. 'Oh, they meant no harm,' he said; and as I stared he corrected himself, 'Not exactly.' Then vivaciously, 'My faith, your pilothouse wants a clean-up!' In the next breath he advised me to keep enough steam on the boiler to blow the whistle in case of any trouble. 'One good screech will do more for you than all your rifles. They are simple people,' he repeated. He rattled away at such a rate he quite overwhelmed me. He seemed to be trying to make up for lots of silence, and actually hinted, laughing, that such was the case. 'Don't you talk with Mr. Kurtz?' I said. 'You don't talk with that man—you listen to him,' he exclaimed with severe exaltation. 'But now——' He waved his arm, and in the twinkling of an eye was in the uttermost depths of despondency. In a moment he came up again with a jump, possessed himself of both my hands, shook them continuously, while he gabbled: 'Brother sailor . . . honor . . . pleasure . . . delight . . . introduce myself . . . Russian . . . son of an arch-priest . . . Government of Tambov . . . What? Tobacco! English tobacco; the excellent English tobacco! Now, that's brotherly. Smoke? Where's a sailor that does not smoke?'

"The pipe soothed him, and gradually I made out he had run away from school, had gone to sea in a Russian ship; ran away again; served some time in English ships; was now reconciled with the arch-priest. He made a point of that. 'But when one is young one must see things, gather experience, ideas; enlarge the mind.' 'Here!' I interrupted.

'You can never tell! Here I met Mr. Kurtz,' he said, youthfully solemn and reproachful. I held my tongue after that. It appears he had persuaded a Dutch trading-house on the coast to fit him out with stores and goods, and had started for the interior with a light heart, and no more idea of what would happen to him than a baby. He had been wandering about that river for nearly two years alone, cut off from everybody and everything. 'I am not so young as I look. I am twenty-five,' he said. 'At first old Van Shuyten would tell me to go to the devil,' he narrated with keen enjoyment; 'but I stuck to him, and talked and talked, till at last he got afraid I would talk the hind-leg off his favorite dog, so he gave me some cheap things and a few guns, and told me he hoped he would never see my face again. Good old Dutchman, Van Shuyten. I sent him one small lot of ivory a year ago, so that he can't call me a little thief when I get back. I hope he got it. And for the rest, I don't care. I had some wood stacked for you. That was my old house. Did you see?'

"I gave him Towson's book. He made as though he would kiss me, but restrained himself. 'The only book I had left, and I thought I had lost it,' he said, looking at it ecstatically. 'So many accidents happen to a man going about alone, you know. Canoes get upset sometimes—and sometimes you've got to clear out so quick when the people get angry.' He thumbed the pages. 'You made notes in Russian?' I asked. He nodded. 'I thought they were written in cipher,' I said. He laughed, then became serious. 'I had lots of trouble to keep these people off,' he said. 'Did they want to kill you?' I asked. 'Oh no!' he cried, and checked himself. 'Why did they attack us?' I pursued. He hesitated, then said shamefacedly, 'They don't want him to go.' 'Don't they?' I said curiously. He nodded a nod full of mystery and wisdom. 'I tell you,' he cried, 'this man has enlarged my mind.' He opened his arms wide, staring at me with his little blue eyes that were perfectly round."

3

"I looked at him, lost in astonishment. There he was before me, in motley, as though he had absconded from a troupe of mimes, enthusiastic, fabulous. His very existence was improbable, inexplicable, and altogether bewildering. He was an insoluble problem. It was inconceivable how he had existed, how he had succeeded in getting so far, how he had managed to remain—why he did not instantly disappear. 'I went a little farther,' he said, 'then still a little farther—till I had gone so far that I don't know how I'll ever get back. Never mind. Plenty time. I can manage. You take Kurtz away quick—quick—I tell you.' The glamor of youth enveloped his particolored rags, his destitution, his loneliness, the essential desolation of his futile wanderings. For months—for years—his life hadn't been worth a day's purchase; and there he was gallantly, thoughtlessly alive, to all appearance indestructible solely by the virtue of his few years and of his unreflecting audacity. I was seduced into something like admiration—like envy. Glamor urged him on, glamor kept him unscathed. He surely wanted nothing from the wilderness but space to breathe in and to push on through. His need was to exist, and to move onwards at the greatest possible risk, and with a maximum of privation. If the absolutely pure, uncalculating, unpractical spirit of adventure had ever ruled a human being, it ruled this be-patched youth. I almost envied him the possession of this modest and clear flame. It seemed to have consumed all thought of self so completely, that, even while he was talking to you, you forgot that it was he—the man before your eyes—who had gone through these things. I did not envy him his devotion to Kurtz, though. He had not meditated over it. It came to him, and he accepted it with a sort of eager fatalism. I must say that to me it appeared about the most dangerous thing in every way he had come upon so far.

"They had come together unavoidably, like two ships becalmed near each other, and lay rubbing sides at last. I suppose Kurtz wanted an audience, because on a certain occasion, when encamped in the forest, they had talked all night, or more probably Kurtz had talked. 'We talked of everything,' he said, quite transported at the recollection. 'I forgot there was such a thing as sleep. The night did not seem to last an hour. Everything! Everything! . . . Of love too.' 'Ah, he talked to you of love!' I said, much amused. 'It isn't what you think,' he cried, almost passionately. 'It was in general. He made me see things—things.'

"He threw his arms up. We were on deck at the time, and the head-man of my woodcutters, lounging near by, turned upon him his heavy and glittering eyes. I looked around, and I don't know why, but I assure you that never, never before, did this land, this river, this jungle, the very arch of this blazing sky, appear to me so hopeless and so dark, so impenetrable to human thought, so pitiless to human weakness. 'And, ever since, you have been with him, of course?' I said.

"On the contrary. It appears their intercourse had been very much broken by various causes. He had, as he informed me proudly, managed to nurse Kurtz through two illnesses (he alluded to it as you would to some risky feat), but as a rule Kurtz wandered alone, far in the depths of the forest. 'Very often coming to this station, I had to wait days and days before he would turn up,' he said. 'Ah, it was worth waiting for!—sometimes.' 'What was he doing? exploring or what?' I asked. 'Oh yes, of course'; he had discovered lots of villages, a lake too—he did not know exactly in what direction; it was dangerous to inquire too much—but mostly his expeditions had been for ivory. 'But he had no goods to trade with by that time,' I objected. 'There's a good lot of cartridges left even yet,' he answered, looking away. 'To speak plainly, he raided the country,' I said. He nodded. 'Not alone, surely!' He muttered something about the villages round that lake. 'Kurtz got the tribe to follow him, did he?' I suggested. He fidgeted a little. 'They adored him,' he said. The tone of these words was so extraordinary that I looked at him searchingly. It was curious to see his mingled eagerness and reluctance to speak of Kurtz. The man filled his life, occupied his thoughts, swayed his emotions. 'What can you expect?' he burst out; 'he came to them with thunder and lightning, you know—and they had never seen anything like it—and very terrible. He could be very terrible. You can't judge Mr. Kurtz as you would an ordinary man. No, no, no! Now—just to give you an idea—I don't mind telling you, he wanted to shoot me too one day—but I don't judge him.' 'Shoot you!' I cried. 'What for?' 'Well, I had a small lot of ivory the chief of that village near my house gave me. You see I used to shoot game for them. Well, he wanted it, and wouldn't hear reason. He declared he would shoot me unless I gave him the ivory and then cleared out of the country, because he could do so, and had a fancy for it, and there was nothing on earth to prevent him killing

whom he jolly well pleased. And it was true too. I gave him the ivory. What did I care! But I didn't clear out. No, no. I couldn't leave him. I had to be careful, of course, till we got friendly again for a time. He had his second illness then. Afterwards I had to keep out of the way; but I didn't mind. He was living for the most part in those villages on the lake. When he came down to the river, sometimes he would take to me, and sometimes it was better for me to be careful. This man suffered too much. He hated all this, and somehow he couldn't get away. When I had a chance I begged him to try and leave while there was time; I offered to go back with him. And he would say yes, and then he would remain; go off on another ivory hunt; disappear for weeks; forget himself amongst these people—forget himself—you know.' 'Why! he's mad,' I said. He protested indignantly. Mr. Kurtz couldn't be mad. If I had heard him talk, only two days ago, I wouldn't dare hint at such a thing. . . . I had taken up my binoculars while we talked, and was looking at the shore, sweeping the limit of the forest at each side and at the back of the house. The consciousness of there being people in that bush, so silent, so quiet—as silent and quiet as the ruined house on the hill—made me uneasy. There was no sign on the face of nature of this amazing tale that was not so much told as suggested to me in desolate exclamations, completed by shrugs, in interrupted phrases, in hints ending in deep sighs. The woods were unmoved, like a mask—heavy, like the closed door of a prison—they looked with their air of hidden knowledge, of patient expectation, of unapproachable silence. The Russian was explaining to me that it was only lately that Mr. Kurtz had come down to the river, bringing along with him all the fighting men of that lake tribe. He had been absent for several months—getting himself adored, I suppose—and had come down unexpectedly, with the intention to all appearance of making a raid either across the river or down stream. Evidently the appetite for more ivory had got the better of the—what shall I say?—less material aspirations, However, he had got much worse suddenly. 'I heard he was lying helpless, and so I came up—took my chance,' said the Russian. 'Oh, he is bad, very bad.' I directed my glass to the house. There were no signs of life, but there were the ruined roof, the long mud wall peeping above the grass, with three little square window-holes, no two of the same size; all this brought within reach of my hand, as it were. And then I made a brusque movement, and one of the remaining posts of that vanished fence leaped up in the field of my glass. You remember I told you I had been struck at the distance by certain attempts at ornamentation, rather remarkable in the ruinous aspect of the place. Now I had suddenly a nearer view, and its first result was to make me throw my head back as if before a blow. Then I went carefully from post to post with my glass, and I saw my mistake. These round knobs were not ornamental but symbolic; they were expressive and puzzling, striking and disturbing—food for thought and also for vultures if there had been any looking down from the sky; but at all events for such ants as were industrious enough to ascend the pole. They would have been even more impressive, those heads on the stakes, if their faces had not been turned to the house. Only one, the first I had made out, was facing my way. I was not so shocked as you may think. The start back I had given was really nothing but a movement of surprise. I had expected to see a knob of wood there, you know. I returned deliberately to the first I had seen—and there it was, black, dried, sunken, with closed eyelids—a head that seemed to sleep at the top of that pole, and, with the shrunken dry lips showing a narrow white line of the teeth, was smiling too, smiling continuously at some endless and jocose dream of that eternal slumber.

"I am not disclosing any trade secrets. In fact the manager said afterwards that Mr. Kurtz's methods had ruined the district. I have no opinion on that point, but I want you clearly to understand that there was nothing exactly profitable in these heads being there. They only showed that Mr. Kurtz lacked restraint in the gratification of his various lusts, that there was something wanting in him—some small matter which, when the pressing need arose, could not be found under his magnificent eloquence. Whether he knew of this deficiency himself I can't say. I think the knowledge came to him at last—only at the very last. But the wilderness had found him out early, and had taken on him a terrible vengeance for the fantastic invasion. I think it had whispered to him things about himself which he did not know, things of which he had no conception till he took counsel with this great solitude—and the whisper had proved irresistibly

fascinating. It echoed loudly within him because he was hollow at the core. . . . I put down the glass, and the head that had appeared near enough to be spoken to seemed at once to have leaped away from me into inaccessible distance.

"The admirer of Mr. Kurtz was a bit crestfallen. In a hurried, indistinct voice he began to assure me he had not dared to take these—say, symbols —down. He was not afraid of the natives; they would not stir till Mr. Kurtz gave the word. His ascendancy was extraordinary. The camps of these people surrounded the place, and the chiefs came every day to see him. They would crawl . . . 'I don't want to know anything of the ceremonies used when approaching Mr. Kurtz,' I shouted. Curious, this feeling that came over me that such details would be more intolerable than those heads drying on the stakes under Mr. Kurtz's windows. After all, that was only a savage sight, while I seemed at one bound to have been transported into some lightless region of subtle horrors, where pure, uncomplicated savagery was a positive relief, being something that had a right to exist— obviously—in the sunshine. The young man looked at me with surprise. I suppose it did not occur to him that Mr. Kurtz was no idol of mine. He forgot I hadn't heard any of these splendid monologues on, what was it? on love, justice, conduct of life— or what not. If it had come to crawling before Mr. Kurtz, he crawled as much as the veriest savage of them all. I had no idea of the conditions, he said: these heads were the heads of rebels. I shocked him excessively by laughing. Rebels! What would be the next definition I was to hear? There had been enemies, criminals, workers—and these were rebels. Those rebellious heads looked very subdued to me on their sticks. 'You don't know how such a life tries a man like Kurtz,' cried Kurtz's last disciple. 'Well, and you?' I said. 'I! I! I am a simple man. I have no great thoughts. I want nothing from anybody. How can you compare me to . . . ?' His feelings were too much for speech, and suddenly he broke down. 'I don't understand,' he groaned. 'I've been doing my best to keep him alive, and that's enough. I had no hand in all this. I have no abilities. There hasn't been a drop of medicine or a mouthful of invalid food for months here. He was shamefully abandoned. A man like this, with such ideas. Shamefully! Shamefully! I— I—haven't slept for the last ten nights. . . .'

"His voice lost itself in the calm of the evening. The long shadows of the forest had slipped downhill while we talked, had gone far beyond the ruined hovel, beyond the symbolic row of stakes. All this was in the gloom, while we down there were yet in the sunshine, and the stretch of the river abreast of the clearing glittered in a still and dazzling splendor, with a murky and overshadowed bend above and below. Not a living soul was seen on the shore. The bushes did not rustle.

"Suddenly round the corner of the house a group of men appeared, as though they had come up from the ground. They waded waist-deep in the grass, in a compact body, bearing an improvised stretcher in their midst. Instantly, in the emptiness of the landscape, a cry arose whose shrillness pierced the still air like a sharp arrow flying straight to the very heart of the land; and, as if by enchantment, streams of human beings—of naked human beings—with spears in their hands, with bows, with shields, with wild glances and savage movements, were poured into the clearing by the dark-faced and pensive forest. The bushes shook, the grass swayed for a time, and then everything stood still in attentive immobility.

" 'Now, if he does not say the right thing to them we are all done for,' said the Russian at my elbow. The knot of men with the stretcher had stopped too, halfway to the steamer, as if petrified. I saw the man on the stretcher sit up, lank and with an uplifted arm, above the shoulders of the bearers. 'Let us hope that the man who can talk so well of love in general will find some particular reason to spare us this time,' I said. I resented bitterly the absurd danger of our situation, as if to be at the mercy of that atrocious phantom had been a dishonoring necessity. I could not hear a sound, but through my glasses I saw the thin arm extended commandingly, the lower jaw moving, the eyes of that apparition shining darkly far in its bony head that nodded with grotesque jerks. Kurtz—Kurtz —that means 'short' in German—don't it? Well, the name was as true as everything else in his life— and death. He looked at least seven feet long. His covering had fallen off, and his body emerged from it pitiful and appalling as from a winding-sheet. I could see the cage of his ribs all astir, the bones of his arm waving. It was as though an animated image of death carved out of old ivory had been shaking its hand with menaces at a motionless crowd of men made of dark and glittering bronze. I saw him open his mouth wide—it gave him a weirdly voracious aspect, as though he had wanted to swallow all the air, all the earth, all the men before him. A deep voice reached me faintly. He must have been shouting. He fell back suddenly. The stretcher shook as the bearers staggered forward again, and almost at the same time I noticed that the crowd of savages was vanishing without any perceptible movement of retreat, as if the forest that had ejected these beings so suddenly had drawn them in again as the breath is drawn in a long aspiration.

"Some of the pilgrims behind the stretcher carried his arms—two shotguns, a heavy rifle, and a light revolver-carbine—the thunderbolts of that pitiful Jupiter. The manager bent over him murmuring as he walked beside his head. They laid him down in one of the little cabins—just a room for a bed-place and a campstool or two, you know. We had brought his belated correspondence, and a lot of torn envelopes and open letters littered his bed. His hand roamed feebly amongst these papers. I was struck by the fire of his eyes and the composed languor of his expression. It was not so much the exhaustion of disease. He did not seem in pain. This shadow looked satiated and calm, as though for the moment it had had its fill of all the emotions.

"He rustled one of the letters, and looking straight in my face said, 'I am glad.' Somebody had been writing to him about me. These special recommendations were turning up again. The volume of tone he emitted without effort, almost without the trouble of moving his lips, amazed me. A voice! a voice! It was grave, profound, vibrating, while the man did not seem capable of a whisper. However, he had enough strength in him—factitious no doubt—to very nearly make an end of us, as you shall hear directly.

"The manager appeared silently in the doorway; I stepped out at once and he drew the curtain after me. The Russian, eyed curiously by the pilgrims, was staring at the shore. I followed the direction of his glance.

"Dark human shapes could be made out in the distance, flitting indistinctly against the gloomy border of the forest, and near the river two bronze figures, leaning on tall spears, stood in the sunlight under fantastic headdresses of spotted skins, warlike and still in statuesque repose. And from right to left along the lighted shore moved a wild and gorgeous apparition of a woman.

"She walked with measured steps, draped in striped and fringed cloths, treading the earth proudly, with a slight jingle and flash of barbarous ornaments. She carried her head high; her hair was done in the shape of a helmet; she had brass leggings to the knees, brass wire gauntlets to the elbow, a crimson spot on her tawny cheek, innumerable necklaces of glass beads on her neck; bizarre things, charms, gifts of witch-men, that hung about her, glittered and trembled at every step. She must have had the value of several elephant tusks upon her. She was savage and superb, wild-eyed and magnificent; there was something ominous and stately in her deliberate progress. And in the hush that had fallen suddenly upon the whole sorrowful land, the immense wilderness, the colossal body of the fecund and mysterious life seemed to look at her, pensive, as though it had been looking at the image of its own tenebrous and passionate soul.

"She came abreast of the steamer, stood still, and faced us. Her long shadow fell to the water's edge. Her face had a tragic and fierce aspect of wild sorrow and of dumb pain mingled with the fear of some struggling, half-shaped resolve. She stood looking at us without a stir, and like the wilderness itself, with an air of brooding over an inscrutable purpose. A whole minute passed, and then she made a step forward. There was a low jingle, a glint of yellow metal, a sway of fringed draperies, and she stopped as if her heart had failed her. The young fellow by my side growled. The pilgrims murmured at my back. She looked at us all as if her life had depended upon the unswerving steadiness of her glance. Suddenly she opened her bared arms and threw them up rigid above her head, as though in an uncontrollable desire to touch the sky, and at the same time the swift shadows darted out on the earth, swept around on the river, gathering the steamer in a shadowy embrace. A formidable silence hung over the scene.

"She turned away slowly, walked on, following the bank, and passed into the bushes to the left. Once only her eyes gleamed back at us in the dusk of the thickets before she disappeared.

" 'If she had offered to come aboard I really think I would have tried to shoot her,' said the man of patches nervously. 'I had been risking my life every day for the last fortnight to keep her out of the house. She got in one day and kicked up a row about those miserable rags I picked up in the storeroom to mend my clothes with. I wasn't decent. At least it must have been that, for she talked like a fury to Kurtz for an hour, pointing at me now and then. I don't understand the dialect of this tribe. Luckily for me, I fancy Kurtz felt too ill that day to care, or there would have been mischief. I don't understand. . . . No—it's too much for me. Ah, well, it's all over now.'

"At this moment I heard Kurtz's deep voice behind the curtain: 'Save me!—save the ivory, you mean. Don't tell me. Save *me*! Why, I've had to save you. You are interrupting my plans now. Sick! Sick! Not so sick as you would like to believe. Never mind. I'll carry my ideas out yet—I will return. I'll show you what can be done. You with your little peddling notions—you are interfering with me. I will return. I . . .'

"The manager came out. He did me the honor to take me under the arm and lead me aside. 'He is very low, very low,' he said. He considered it necessary to sigh, but neglected to be consistently sorrowful. 'We have done all we could for him— haven't we? But there is no disguising the fact, Mr. Kurtz has done more harm than good to the Company. He did not see the time was not ripe for vigorous action. Cautiously, cautiously—that's my principle. We must be cautious yet. The district is closed to us for a time. Deplorable! Upon the whole, the trade will suffer. I don't deny there is a remarkable quantity of ivory—mostly fossil. We must save it, at all events—but look how precarious the position is—and why? Because the method is unsound.' 'Do you,' said I, looking at the shore, 'call it "unsound method"?' 'Without doubt,' he exclaimed hotly. 'Don't you?' . . . 'No method at all,' I murmured after a while. 'Exactly,' he exulted. 'I anticipated this. Shows a complete want of judgment. It is my duty to point it out in the proper quarter.' 'Oh,' said I, 'that fellow—what's his name? —the brickmaker, will make a readable report for you.' He appeared confounded for a moment. It seemed to me I had never breathed an atmosphere so vile, and I turned mentally to Kurtz for relief— positively for relief. 'Nevertheless, I think Mr. Kurtz is a remarkable man,' I said with emphasis.

He started, dropped on me a cold heavy glance, said very quietly, 'He *was*,' and turned his back on me. My hour of favor was over; I found myself lumped along with Kurtz as a partisan of methods for which the time was not ripe: I was unsound! Ah! but it was something to have at least a choice of nightmares.

"I had turned to the wilderness really, not to Mr. Kurtz, who, I was ready to admit, was as good as buried. And for a moment it seemed to me as if I also were buried in a vast grave full of unspeakable secrets. I felt an intolerable weight oppressing my breast, the smell of the damp earth, the unseen presence of victorious corruption, the darkness of an impenetrable night. . . . The Russian tapped me on the shoulder. I heard him mumbling and stammering something about 'brother seaman— couldn't conceal—knowledge of matters that would affect Mr. Kurtz's reputation.' I waited. For him evidently Mr. Kurtz was not in his grave; I suspect that for him Mr. Kurtz was one of the immortals. 'Well!' said I at last, 'speak out. As it happens, I am Mr. Kurtz's friend—in a way.'

"He stated with a good deal of formality that had we not been 'of the same profession,' he would have kept the matter to himself without regard to consequences. He suspected 'there was an active ill-will towards him on the part of these white men that——' 'You are right,' I said, remembering a certain conversation I had overheard. 'The manager thinks you ought to be hanged.' He showed a concern at this intelligence which amused me at first. 'I had better get out of the way quietly,' he said earnestly. 'I can do no more for Kurtz now, and they would soon find some excuse. What's to stop them? There's a military post three hundred miles from here.' 'Well, upon my word,' said I, 'perhaps you had better go if you have any friends amongst the savages near by.' 'Plenty,' he said. 'They are simple people—and I want nothing, you know.' He stood biting his lip, then: 'I don't want any harm to happen to these whites here, but of course I was thinking of Mr. Kurtz's reputation— but you are a brother seaman and——' 'All right,' said I, after a time. 'Mr. Kurtz's reputation is safe with me.' I did not know how truly I spoke.

"He informed me, lowering his voice, that it was Kurtz who had ordered the attack to be made on the steamer. 'He hated sometimes the idea of being taken away—and then again . . . But I don't understand these matters. I am a simple man. He thought it would scare you away—that you would give it up, thinking him dead. I could not stop him. Oh, I had an awful time of it this last month.' 'Very well,' I said. 'He is all right now.' 'Ye-e-es,' he muttered, not very convinced apparently. 'Thanks,' said I; 'I shall keep my eyes open.' 'But quiet—eh?' he urged anxiously. 'It would be awful for his reputation if anybody here——' I promised a complete discretion with great gravity. 'I have a canoe and three black fellows waiting not very far. I am off. Could you give me a few Martini-Henry cartridges?' I could, and did, with proper secrecy. He helped himself, with a wink at me, to a handful of my tobacco. 'Between sailors—you know— good English tobacco.' At the door of the pilot-house he turned round—'I say, haven't you a pair of shoes you could spare?' He raised one leg. 'Look.' The soles were tied with knotted strings sandal-wise under his bare feet. I rooted out an old pair, at which he looked with admiration before tucking it under his left arm. One of his pockets (bright red) was bulging with cartridges, from the other (dark blue) peeped *Towson's Inquiry*, etc. etc. He seemed to think himself excellently well equipped for a renewed encounter with the wilderness. 'Ah! I'll never, never meet such a man again. You ought to have heard him recite poetry—his own too it was, he told me. Poetry!' He rolled his eyes at the recollection of these delights. 'Oh, he enlarged my mind!' 'Good-bye,' said I. He shook hands and vanished in the night. Sometimes I ask myself whether I had ever really seen him—whether it was possible to meet such a phenomenon! . . .

"When I woke up shortly after midnight his warning came to my mind with its hint of danger that seemed, in the starred darkness, real enough to make me get up for the purpose of having a look round. On the hill a big fire burned, illuminating fitfully a crooked corner of the station-house. One of the agents with a picket of a few of our blacks, armed for the purpose, was keeping guard over the ivory; but deep within the forest, red gleams that wavered, that seemed to sink and rise from the ground amongst confused columnar shapes of intense blackness, showed the exact position of the camp where Mr. Kurtz's adorers were keeping their uneasy vigil. The monotonous beating of a big drum filled the air with muffled shocks and a lingering vibration. A steady droning sound of many men chanting each to himself some weird incantation came out from the black, flat wall of the woods as the humming of bees comes out of a hive, and had a strange narcotic effect upon my half-awake senses. I believe I dozed off leaning over the rail, till an abrupt burst of yells, an overwhelming outbreak of a pent-up and mysterious frenzy, woke me up in a bewildered wonder. It was cut short all at once, and the low droning went on with an effect of audible and soothing silence. I glanced casually into the little cabin. A light was burning within, but Mr. Kurtz was not there.

"I think I would have raised an outcry if I had believed my eyes. But I didn't believe them at first —the thing seemed so impossible. The fact is, I was completely unnerved by a sheer blank fright, pure abstract terror, unconnected with any distinct shape of physical danger. What made this emotion so overpowering was—how shall I define it?—the moral shock I received, as if something altogether monstrous, intolerable to thought and odious to the soul, had been thrust upon me unexpectedly. This lasted of course the merest fraction of a second, and then the usual sense of commonplace, deadly danger, the possibility of a sudden onslaught and massacre, or something of the kind, which I saw impending, was positively welcome and composing. It pacified me, in fact, so much, that I did not raise an alarm.

"There was an agent buttoned up inside an ulster and sleeping on a chair on deck within three feet of me. The yells had not awakened him; he snored very slightly; I left him to his slumbers and leaped ashore. I did not betray Mr. Kurtz—it was ordered I should never betray him—it was written I should be loyal to the nightmare of my choice. I was anxious to deal with this shadow by myself alone—and to this day I don't know why I was so jealous of sharing with anyone the peculiar blackness of that experience.

"As soon as I got on the bank I saw a trail—a broad trail through the grass. I remember the exultation with which I said to myself, 'He can't walk—he is crawling on all-fours—I've got him.' The grass was wet with dew. I strode rapidly with clenched fists. I fancy I had some vague notion of falling upon him and giving him a drubbing. I don't know. I had some imbecile thoughts. The knitting old woman with the cat obtruded herself upon my memory as a most improper person to be

sitting at the other end of such an affair. I saw a row of pilgrims squirting lead in the air out of Winchesters held to the hip. I thought I would never get back to the steamer, and imagined myself living alone and unarmed in the woods to an advanced age. Such silly things—you know. And I remember I confounded the beat of the drum with the beating of my heart, and was pleased at its calm regularity.

"I kept to the track though—then stopped to listen. The night was very clear; a dark blue space, sparkling with dew and starlight, in which black things stood very still. I thought I could see a kind of motion ahead of me. I was strangely cocksure of everything that night. I actually left the track and ran in a wide semicircle (I verily believe chuckling to myself) so as to get in front of that stir, of that motion I had seen—if indeed I had seen anything. I was circumventing Kurtz as though it had been a boyish game.

"I came upon him, and, if he had not heard me coming, I would have fallen over him too, but he got up in time. He rose, unsteady, long, pale, indistinct, like a vapor exhaled by the earth, and swayed slightly, misty and silent before me; while at my back the fires loomed between the trees, and the murmur of many voices issued from the forest. I had cut him off cleverly; but when actually confronting him I seemed to come to my senses, I saw the danger in its right proportion. It was by no means over yet. Suppose he began to shout? Though he could hardly stand, there was still plenty of vigour in his voice. 'Go away—hide yourself,' he said, in that profound tone. It was very awful. I glanced back. We were within thirty yards from the nearest fire. A black figure stood up, strode on long black legs, waving long black arms, across the glow. It had horns—antelope horns, I think—on its head. Some sorcerer, some witchman, no doubt: it looked fiendlike enough. 'Do you know what you are doing?' I whispered. 'Perfectly,' he answered, raising his voice for that single word: it sounded to me far off and yet loud, like a hail through a speaking-trumpet. If he makes a row we are lost, I thought to myself. This clearly was not a case for fisticuffs, even apart from the very natural aversion I had to beat that Shadow —this wandering and tormented thing. 'You will be lost,' I said—'utterly lost.' One gets sometimes such a flash of inspiration, you know. I did say the right thing, though indeed he could not have been more irretrievably lost than he was at this very moment, when the foundations of our intimacy were being laid—to endure—to endure—even to the end—even beyond.

" 'I had immense plans,' he muttered irresolutely. 'Yes,' said I; 'but if you try to shout I'll smash your head with——' There was not a stick or a stone near. 'I will throttle you for good,' I corrected myself. 'I was on the threshold of great things,' he pleaded, in a voice of longing, with a wistfulness of tone that made my blood run cold. 'And now for this stupid scoundrel——' 'Your success in Europe is assured in any case,' I affirmed steadily. I did not want to have the throttling of him, you understand—and indeed it would have been very little use for any practical purpose. I tried to break the spell—the heavy, mute spell of the wilderness—that seemed to draw him to its pitiless breast by the awakening of forgotten and brutal instincts, by the memory of gratified and monstrous passions. This alone, I was convinced, had driven him out to the edge of the forest, to the bush, towards the gleam of fires, the throb of drums, the drone of weird incantations; this alone had beguiled his unlawful soul beyond the bounds of permitted aspirations. And, don't you see, the terror of the position was not in being knocked on the head—though I had a very lively sense of that danger too—but in this, that I had to deal with a being to whom I could not appeal in the name of anything high or low. I had, even like the niggers, to invoke him—himself—his own exalted and incredible degradation. There was nothing either above or below him, and I knew it. He had kicked himself loose of the earth. Confound the man! he had kicked the very earth to pieces. He was alone, and I before him did not know whether I stood on the ground or floated in the air. I've been telling you what we said—repeating the phrases we pronounced—but what's the good? They were common everyday words—the familiar, vague sounds exchanged on every waking day of life. But what of that? They had behind them, to my mind, the terrific suggestiveness of words heard in dreams, of phrases spoken in nightmares. Soul! If anybody had ever struggled with a soul, I am the man. And I wasn't arguing with a lunatic either. Believe me or not, his intelligence was perfectly clear—concentrated, it is true, upon himself with horrible intensity, yet clear; and therein was my only chance—barring, of course,

the killing him there and then, which wasn't so good, on account of unavoidable noise. But his soul was mad. Being alone in the wilderness, it had looked within itself, and, by heavens! I tell you, it had gone mad. I had—for my sins, I suppose, to go through the ordeal of looking into it myself. No eloquence could have been so withering to one's belief in mankind as his final burst of sincerity. He struggled with himself too. I saw it—I heard it. I saw the inconceivable mystery of a soul that knew no restraint, no faith, and no fear, yet struggling blindly with itself. I kept my head pretty well; but when I had him at last stretched on the couch, I wiped my forehead, while my legs shook under me as though I had carried half a ton on my back down that hill. And yet I had only supported him, his bony arm clasped round my neck—and he was not much heavier than a child.

"When next day we left at noon, the crowd, of whose presence behind the curtain of trees I had been acutely conscious all the time, flowed out of the woods again, filled the clearing, covered the slope with a mass of naked, breathing, quivering, bronze bodies. I steamed up a bit, then swung downstream, and two thousand eyes followed the evolutions of the splashing, thumping, fierce river-demon beating the water with its terrible tail and breathing black smoke into the air. In front of the first rank, along the river, three men, plastered with bright red earth from head to foot, strutted to and fro restlessly. When we came abreast again, they faced the river, stamped their feet, nodded their horned heads, swayed their scarlet bodies; they shook towards the fierce river-demon a bunch of black feathers, a mangy skin with a pendent tail —something that looked like a dried gourd; they shouted periodically together strings of amazing words that resembled no sounds of human language; and the deep murmurs of the crowd, interrupted suddenly, were like the responses of some satanic litany.

"We had carried Kurtz into the pilothouse: there was more air there. Lying on the couch, he stared through the open shutter. There was an eddy in the mass of human bodies, and the woman with helmeted head and tawny cheeks rushed out to the very brink of the stream. She put out her hands, shouted something, and all that wild mob took up the shout in a roaring chorus of articulated, rapid, breathless utterance.

" 'Do you understand this?' I asked.

"He kept on looking out past me with fiery, longing eyes, with a mingled expression of wistfulness and hate. He made no answer, but I saw a smile, a smile of indefinable meaning, appear on his colorless lips that a moment after twitched convulsively. 'Do I not?' he said slowly, gasping, as if the words had been torn out of him by a supernatural power.

"I pulled the string of the whistle, and I did this because I saw the pilgrims on deck getting out their rifles with an air of anticipating a jolly lark. At the sudden screech there was a movement of abject terror through that wedged mass of bodies. 'Don't! don't you frighten them away,' cried someone on deck disconsolately. I pulled the string time after time. They broke and ran, they leaped, they crouched, they swerved, they dodged the flying terror of the sound. The three red chaps had fallen flat, face down on the shore, as though they had been shot dead. Only the barbarous and superb woman did not so much as flinch, and stretched tragically her bare arms after us over the somber and glittering river.

"And then that imbecile crowd down on the deck started their little fun, and I could see nothing more for smoke.

"The brown current ran swiftly out of the heart of darkness, bearing us down towards the sea with twice the speed of our upward progress; and Kurtz's life was running swiftly too, ebbing, ebbing out of his heart into the sea of inexorable time. The manager was very placid, he had no vital anxieties now, he took us both in with a comprehensive and satisfied glance: the 'affair' had come off as well as could be wished. I saw the time approaching when I would be left alone of the party of 'unsound method.' The pilgrims looked upon me with disfavor. I was, so to speak, numbered with the dead. It is strange how I accepted this unforeseen partnership, this choice of nightmares forced upon me in the tenebrous land invaded by these mean and greedy phantoms.

"Kurtz discoursed. A voice! a voice! It rang deep to the very last. It survived his strength to hide in the magnificent folds of eloquence the barren darkness of his heart. Oh, he struggled! he struggled! The wastes of his weary brain were haunted by shadowy images now—images of wealth and fame revolving obsequiously round his unextinguishable gift of noble and lofty expression. My Intended, my station, my career, my ideas—these were the subjects for the occasional utterances of elevated sentiments. The shade of the original Kurtz frequented the bedside of the hollow sham, whose fate it was to be buried presently in the mould of primeval earth. But both the diabolic love and the unearthly hate of the mysteries it had penetrated fought for the possession of that soul satiated with primitive emotions, avid of lying fame, of sham distinction, of all the appearances of success and power.

"Sometimes he was contemptibly childish. He desired to have kings meet him at railway stations on his return from some ghastly Nowhere, where he intended to accomplish great things. 'You show them you have in you something that is really profitable, and then there will be no limits to the recognition of your ability,' he would say. 'Of course you must take care of the motives—right motives—always.' The long reaches that were like one and the same reach, monotonous bends that were exactly alike, slipped past the steamer with their multitude of secular[14] trees looking patiently after this grimy fragment of another world, the forerunner of change, of conquest, of trade, of massacres, of blessings. I looked ahead—piloting. 'Close the shutter,' said Kurtz suddenly one day; 'I can't bear to look at this.' I did so. There was a silence. 'Oh, but I will wring your heart yet!' he cried at the invisible wilderness.

"We broke down—as I had expected—and had to lie up for repairs at the head of an island. This delay was the first thing that shook Kurtz's confidence. One morning he gave me a packet of papers and a photograph—the lot tied together with a shoestring. 'Keep this for me,' he said. 'This noxious fool' (meaning the manager) 'is capable of prying into my boxes when I am not looking.' In the afternoon I saw him. He was lying on his back with closed eyes, and I withdrew quietly, but I heard him mutter, 'Live rightly, die, die . . .' I listened. There was nothing more. Was he rehearsing some speech in his sleep, or was it a fragment of a phrase from some newspaper article? He had been writing for the papers and meant to do so again, 'for the furthering of my ideas. It's a duty.'

14. **secular:** aged, ancient.

"His was an impenetrable darkness. I looked at him as you peer down at a man who is lying at the bottom of a precipice where the sun never shines. But I had not much time to give him, because I was helping the engine-driver to take to pieces the leaky cylinders, to straighten a bent connecting-rod, and in other such matters. I lived in an infernal mess of rust, filings, nuts, bolts, spanners, hammers, ratchet-drills—things I abominate, because I don't get on with them. I tended the little forge we fortunately had aboard; I toiled wearily in a wretched scrap-heap—unless I had the shakes too bad to stand.

"One evening coming in with a candle I was startled to hear him say a little tremulously, 'I am lying here in the dark waiting for death.' The light was within a foot of his eyes. I forced myself to murmur, 'Oh, nonsense!' and stood over him as if transfixed.

"Anything approaching the change that came over his features I have never seen before, and hope never to see again. Oh, I wasn't touched. I was fascinated. It was as though a veil had been rent. I saw on that ivory face the expression of somber pride, of ruthless power, of craven terror—of an intense and hopeless despair. Did he live his life again in every detail of desire, temptation, and surrender during that supreme moment of complete knowledge? He cried in a whisper at some image, at some vision—he cried out twice, a cry that was no more than a breath:

" 'The horror! The horror!'

"I blew the candle out and left the cabin. The pilgrims were dining in the mess-room, and I took my place opposite the manager, who lifted his eyes to give me a questioning glance, which I successfully ignored. He leaned back, serene, with that peculiar smile of his sealing the unexpressed depths of his meanness. A continuous shower of small flies streamed upon the lamp, upon the cloth, upon our hands and faces. Suddenly the manager's boy put his insolent black head in the doorway, and said in a tone of scathing contempt:

" 'Mistah Kurtz—he dead.'

"All the pilgrims rushed out to see. I remained, and went on with my dinner. I believe I was considered brutally callous. However, I did not eat much. There was a lamp in there—light, don't you know—and outside it was so beastly, beastly dark. I went no more near the remarkable man who had pronounced a judgment upon the adventures of his soul on this earth. The voice was gone. What else had been there? But I am of course aware that next day the pilgrims buried something in a muddy hole.

"And then they very nearly buried me.

"However, as you see, I did not go to join Kurtz there and then. I did not. I remained to dream the nightmare out to the end, and to show my loyalty to Kurtz once more. Destiny. My destiny! Droll thing life is—that mysterious arrangement of merciless logic for a futile purpose. The most you can hope from it is some knowledge of yourself—that comes too late—a crop of unextinguishable regrets. I have wrestled with death. It is the most unexciting contest you can imagine. It takes place in an impalpable grayness, with nothing underfoot, with nothing around, without spectators, without clamor, without glory, without the great desire of victory, without the great fear of defeat, in a sickly atmosphere of tepid scepticism, without much belief in your own right, and still less in that of your adversary. If such is the form of ultimate wisdom, then life is a greater riddle than some of us think it to be. I was within a hair's-breadth of the last opportunity for pronouncement, and I found with humiliation that probably I would have nothing to say. This is the reason why I affirm that Kurtz was a remarkable man. He had something to say. He said it. Since I had peeped over the edge myself, I understand better the meaning of his stare, that could not see the flame of the candle, but was wide enough to embrace the whole universe, piercing enough to penetrate all the hearts that beat in the darkness. He had summed up—he had judged. 'The horror!' He was a remarkable man. After all, this was the expression of some sort of belief; it had candor, it had conviction, it had a vibrating note of revolt in its whisper, it had the appalling face of a glimpsed truth—the strange commingling of desire and hate. And it is not my own extremity I remember best—a vision of grayness without form filled with physical pain, and a careless contempt for the evanescence of all things—even of this pain itself. No! It is his extremity that I seem to have lived through. True, he had made that last stride, he had stepped over the edge, while I had been permitted to draw back by hesitating foot. And perhaps in this is the whole difference; perhaps all the wisdom, and all truth, and all sincerity, are just compressed into that inappreciable moment of time in which we step over the threshold of the invisible. Perhaps! I like to think my summing-up would not have been a word of careless contempt. Better his cry—much better. It was an affirmation, a moral victory paid for by innumerable defeats, by abominable terrors, by abominable satisfactions. But it was a victory! That is why I have remained loyal to Kurtz to the last, and even beyond, when a long time after I heard once more, not his own voice, but the echo of his magnificent eloquence thrown to me from a soul as translucently pure as a cliff of crystal.

"No, they did not bury me, though there is a period of time which I remember mistily, with a shuddering wonder, like a passage through some inconceivable world that had no hope in it and no desire. I found myself back in the sepulchral city resenting the sight of people hurrying through the streets to filch a little money from each other, to devour their infamous cookery, to gulp their unwholesome beer, to dream their insignificant and silly dreams. They trespassed upon my thoughts. They were intruders whose knowledge of life was to me an irritating pretense, because I felt so sure they could not possibly know the things I knew. Their bearing, which was simply the bearing of commonplace individuals going about their business in the assurance of perfect safety, was offensive to me like the outrageous flauntings of folly in the face of a danger it is unable to comprehend. I had no particular desire to enlighten them, but I had some difficulty in restraining myself from laughing in their faces, so full of stupid importance. I daresay I was not very well at that time. I tottered about the streets—there were various affairs to settle—grinning bitterly at perfectly respectable persons. I admit my behavior was inexcusable, but then my temperature was seldom normal in these days. My dear aunt's endeavors to 'nurse up my strength' seemed altogether beside the mark. It was not my strength that wanted nursing, it was my imagination that wanted soothing. I kept the bundle of papers given me by Kurtz, not knowing exactly what to do with it. His mother had died lately, watched over, as I was told, by his Intended. A clean-shaved man, with an official manner and wearing gold-rimmed spectacles, called on me one day and made inquiries, at first circuitous, afterwards suavely pressing, about what he was pleased to denominate certain 'documents.' I was not surprised, because I had had two rows with the manager on the subject out there. I had refused to give up the smallest scrap out of that package, and I took the same attitude with the spectacled man. He became darkly menacing at last, and with much heat argued that the Company had the right to every bit of information about its 'territories.' And, said he, 'Mr. Kurtz's knowledge of unexplored regions must have been necessarily extensive and peculiar—owing to his great abilities and to the deplorable circumstances in which he had been placed: therefore——' I assured him Mr. Kurtz's knowledge, however extensive, did not bear upon the problems of commerce or administration. He invoked then the name of science. 'It would be an incalculable loss if,' etc. etc. I offered him the report on the 'Suppression of Savage Customs,' with the postscriptum torn off. He took it up eagerly, but ended by sniffing at it with an air of contempt. 'This is not what we had a right to expect,' he remarked. 'Expect nothing else,' I said. 'There are only private letters.' He withdrew upon some threat of legal proceedings, and I saw him no more; but another fellow, calling himself Kurtz's cousin, appeared two days later, and was anxious to hear all the details about his dear relative's last moments. Incidentally he gave me to understand that Kurtz had been essentially a great musician. 'There was the making of an immense success,' said the man, who was an organist, I believe, with lank gray hair flowing over a greasy coat-collar. I had no reason to doubt his statement; and to this day I am unable to say what was Kurtz's profession, whether he ever had any—which was the greatest of his talents. I had taken him for a painter who wrote for the papers, or else for a journalist who could paint—but even the cousin (who took snuff during the interview) could not tell me what he had been—exactly. He was a universal genius—on that point I agreed with the old chap, who thereupon blew his nose noisily into a large cotton handkerchief and withdrew in senile agitation, bearing off some family letters and memoranda without importance. Ultimately a journalist anxious to know something of the fate of his 'dear colleague' turned up. This visitor informed me Kurtz's proper sphere ought to have been politics 'on the popular side.' He had furry straight eyebrows, bristly hair cropped short, an eyeglass on a broad ribbon, and, becoming expansive, confessed his opinion that Kurtz really couldn't write a bit—but heavens! how that man could talk! He electrified large meetings. He had faith—don't you see?—he had the faith. He could get himself to believe anything—anything. He would have been a splendid leader of an extreme party.' 'What party?' I asked. 'Any party,' answered the other. 'He was an—an—extremist.' Did I not think so? I assented. Did I know, he asked, with a sudden flash of curiosity, 'what it was that had induced him to go out there?' 'Yes,' said I, and forthwith handed him the famous report for publication, if he thought fit. He glanced through it hurriedly, mumbling all the time, judged 'it would do,' and took himself off with this plunder.

"Thus I was left at last with a slim packet of letters and the girl's portrait. She struck me as beautiful—I mean she had a beautiful expression. I know that the sunlight can be made to lie too, yet one felt that no manipulation of light and pose could have conveyed the delicate shade of truthfulness upon those features. She seemed ready to listen without mental reservation, without suspicion, without a thought for herself. I concluded I would go and give her back her portrait and those letters myself. Curiosity? Yes; and also some other feeling perhaps. All that had been Kurtz's had passed out of my hands: his soul, his body, his station, his plans, his ivory, his career. There remained only his memory and his Intended—and I wanted to give that up too to the past, in a way—to surrender personally all that remained of him with me to that oblivion which is the last word of our common fate. I don't defend myself. I had no clear perception of what it was I really wanted. Perhaps it was an impulse of unconscious loyalty, or the fulfillment of one of those ironic necessities that lurk in the facts of human existence. I don't know. I can't tell. But I went.

"I thought his memory was like the other memories of the dead that accumulate in every man's life—a vague impress on the brain of shadows that had fallen on it in their swift and final passage; but before the high and ponderous door, between the tall houses of a street as still and decorous as a well-kept alley in a cemetery, I had a vision of him on the stretcher, opening his mouth voraciously, as if to devour all the earth with all its mankind. He lived then before me; he lived as much as he had ever lived—a shadow insatiable of splendid appearances, of frightful realities; a shadow darker than the shadow of the night, and draped nobly in the folds of a gorgeous eloquence. The vision seemed to enter the house with me—the stretcher, the phantom-bearers, the wild crowd of obedient worshipers, the gloom of the forests, the glitter of the reach between the murky bends, the beat of the drum, regular and muffled like the beating of a heart—the heart of a conquering darkness. It was a moment of triumph for the wilderness, an invading and vengeful rush which, it seemed to me, I would have to keep back alone for the salvation of another soul. And the memory of what I had heard him say afar there, with the horned shapes stirring at my back, in the glow of fires, within the patient woods, those broken phrases came back to me, were heard again in their ominous and terrifying simplicity. I remembered his abject pleading, his abject threats, the colossal scale of his vile desires, the meanness, the torment, the tempestuous anguish of his soul. And later on I seemed to see his collected languid manner, when he said one day, 'This lot of ivory now is really mine. The Company did not pay for it. I collected it myself at a very great personal risk. I am afraid they will try to claim it as theirs though. H'm. It is a difficult case. What do you think I ought to do—resist? Eh? I want no more than justice.' . . . He wanted no more than justice—no more than justice. I rang the bell before a mahogany door on the first floor, and while I waited he seemed to stare at me out of the glassy panel—stare with that wide and immense stare embracing, condemning, loathing all the universe. I seemed to hear the whispered cry, 'The horror! The horror!'

"The dusk was falling. I had to wait in a lofty drawing-room with three long windows from floor to ceiling that were like three luminous and bedraped columns. The bent gilt legs and backs of the furniture shone in indistinct curves. The tall marble fireplace had a cold and monumental whiteness. A grand piano stood massively in a corner; with dark gleams on the flat surfaces like a somber and polished sarcophagus. A high door opened—closed. I rose.

"She came forward, all in black, with a pale head, floating towards me in the dusk. She was in mourning. It was more than a year since his death, more than a year since the news came; she seemed as though she would remember and mourn forever. She took both my hands in hers and murmured, 'I had heard you were coming.' I noticed she was not very young—I mean not girlish. She had a mature capacity for fidelity, for belief, for suffering. The room seemed to have grown darker, as if all the sad light of the cloudy evening had taken refuge on her forehead. This fair hair, this pale visage, this pure brow, seemed surrounded by an ashy halo from which the dark eyes looked out at me. Their glance was guileless, profound, confident, and trustful. She carried her sorrowful head as though she were proud of that sorrow, as though she would say, I—I alone know how to mourn for him as he deserves. But while we were still shaking hands, such a look of awful desolation came upon her face that I perceived she was one of those creatures that are not the playthings of Time. For her he had died only yesterday. And, by Jove! the impression was so powerful that for me too he seemed to have died only yesterday—nay, this very minute. I saw her and him in the same instant of time—his death and her sorrow—I saw her sorrow in the very moment of his death. Do you understand? I saw them together—I heard them together. She had said, with a deep catch of the breath, 'I have survived'; while my strained ears seemed to hear distinctly, mingled with her tone of despairing regret, the summing-up whisper of his eternal condemnation. I asked myself what I was doing there, with a sensation of panic in my heart as though I had blundered into a place of cruel and absurd mysteries not fit for a human being to behold. She motioned me to a chair. We sat down. I laid the packet gently on the little table, and she put her hand over it. . . . 'You knew him well,' she murmured, after a moment of mourning silence.

" 'Intimacy grows quickly out there,' I said. 'I knew him as well as it is possible for one man to know another.'

" 'And you admired him,' she said. 'It was impossible to know him and not to admire him. Was it?'

" 'He was a remarkable man,' I said unsteadily. Then before the appealing fixity of her gaze, that seemed to watch for more words on my lips, I went on, 'It was impossible not to——'

" 'Love him,' she finished eagerly, silencing me into an appalled dumbness. 'How true! how true!

But when you think that no one knew him so well as I! I had all his noble confidence. I knew him best.'

" 'You knew him best,' I repeated. And perhaps she did. But with every word spoken the room was growing darker, and only her forehead, smooth and white, remained illumined by the unextinguishable light of belief and love.

" 'You were his friend,' she went on. 'His friend,' she repeated, a little louder. 'You must have been, if he had given you this, and sent you to me. I feel I can speak to you—and oh! I must speak. I want you—you who have heard his last words—to know I have been worthy of him. . . . It is not pride. . . . Yes! I am proud to know I understood him better than anyone on earth—he told me so himself. And since his mother died I have had no one—no one—to—to——'

"I listened. The darkness deepened. I was not even sure whether he had given me the right bundle. I rather suspect he wanted me to take care of another batch of his papers which, after his death, I saw the manager examining under the lamp. And the girl talked, easing her pain in the certitude of my sympathy; she talked as thirsty men drink. I had heard that her engagement with Kurtz had been disapproved by her people. He wasn't rich enough or something. And indeed I don't know whether he had not been a pauper all his life. He had given me some reason to infer that it was his impatience of comparative poverty that drove him out there.

" '. . . Who was not his friend who had heard him speak once?' she was saying. 'He drew men towards him by what was best in them.' She looked at me with intensity. 'It is the gift of the great,' she went on, and the sound of her low voice seemed to have the accompaniment of all the other sounds, full of mystery, desolation, and sorrow, I had ever heard—the ripple of the river, the soughing of the trees swayed by the wind, the murmurs of the crowds, the faint ring of incomprehensible words cried from afar, the whisper of a voice speaking from beyond the threshold of an eternal darkness. But you have heard him! You know!' she cried.

" 'Yes, I know,' I said with something like despair in my heart, but bowing my head before the faith that was in her, before that great and saving illusion that shone with an unearthly glow in the darkness, in the triumphant darkness from which I could not have defended her—from which I could not even defend myself.

" 'What a loss to me—to us!'—she corrected herself with beautiful generosity; then added in a murmur, 'To the world.' By the last gleams of twilight I could see the glitter of her eyes, full of tears—of tears that would not fall.

" 'I have been very happy—very fortunate—very proud,' she went on. 'Too fortunate. Too happy for a little while. And now I am unhappy for—for life.'

"She stood up; her fair hair seemed to catch all the remaining light in a glimmer of gold. I rose too.

" 'And of all this,' she went on mournfully, 'of all his promise, and of all his greatness, of his generous mind, of his noble heart, nothing remains—nothing but a memory. You and I——'

" 'We shall always remember him,' I said hastily.

" 'No!' she cried. 'It is impossible that all this should be lost—that such a life should be sacrificed to leave nothing—but sorrow. You know what vast plans he had. I knew of them too—I could not perhaps understand—but others knew of them. Something must remain. His words, at least, have not died.'

" 'His words will remain,' I said.

" 'And his example,' she whispered to herself. 'Men looked up to him—his goodness shone in every act. His example——'

" 'True,' I said; 'his example too. Yes, his example. I forgot that.'

" 'But I do not. I cannot—I cannot believe—not yet. I cannot believe that I shall never see him again, that nobody will see him again, never, never, never.'

"She put out her arms as if after a retreating figure, stretching them back and with clasped pale hands across the fading and narrow sheen of the window. Never see him! I saw him clearly enough then. I shall see this eloquent phantom as long as I live, and I shall see her too, a tragic and familiar shade, resembling in this gesture another one, tragic also, and bedecked with powerless charms, stretching bare brown arms over the glitter of the infernal stream, the stream of darkness. She said suddenly very low, 'He died as he lived.'

" 'His end,' said I, with dull anger stirring in me, 'was in every way worthy of his life.'

" 'And I was not with him,' she murmured. My anger subsided before a feeling of infinite pity.

" 'Everything that could be done——' I mumbled.

" 'Ah, but I believed in him more than anyone on earth—more than his own mother, more than —himself. He needed me! Me! I would have treasured every sigh, every word, every sign, every glance.'

"I felt like a chill grip on my chest. 'Don't,' I said, in a muffled voice.

" 'Forgive me. I—I—have mourned so long in silence—in silence. . . . You were with him—to the last? I think of his loneliness. Nobody near to understand him as I would have understood. Perhaps no one to hear . . .'

" 'To the very end,' I said shakily. 'I heard his very last words. . . .' I stopped in a fright.

" 'Repeat them,' she murmured in a heartbroken tone. 'I want—I want—something—something—to—to live with.'

"I was on the point of crying at her, 'Don't you hear them?' The dusk was repeating them in a persistent whisper all around us, in a whisper that seemed to swell menacingly like the first whisper of a rising wind. 'The horror! The horror!'

" 'His last word—to live with,' she insisted. 'Don't you understand I loved him—I loved him —I loved him!'

"I pulled myself together and spoke slowly.

" 'The last word he pronounced was—your name.'

"I heard a light sigh and then my heart stood still, stopped dead short by an exulting and terrible cry, by the cry of inconceivable triumph and of unspeakable pain. 'I knew it—I was sure!' . . . She knew. She was sure. I heard her weeping; she had hidden her face in her hands. It seemed to me that the house would collapse before I could escape, that the heavens would fall upon my head. But nothing happened. The heavens do not fall for such a trifle. Would they have fallen, I wonder, if I had rendered Kurtz that justice which was his due? Hadn't he said he wanted only justice? But I couldn't. I could not tell her. It would have been too dark—to dark altogether. . . ."

Marlow ceased, and sat apart, indistinct and silent, in the pose of a meditating Buddha. Nobody moved for a time. "We have lost the first of the ebb," said the Director suddenly. I raised my head. The offing was barred by a black bank of clouds, and the tranquil waterway leading to the uttermost ends of the earth flowed somber under an overcast sky—seemed to lead into the heart of an immense darkness.

JOHN CHEEVER
b. 1912

The Swimmer

It was one of those midsummer Sundays when everyone sits around saying: "I *drank* too much last night." You might have heard it whispered by the parishioners leaving church, heard it from the lips of the priest himself, struggling with his cassock in the *vestiarium*, heard it from the golf links and the tennis courts, heard it from the wild-life preserve where the leader of the Audubon group was suffering from a terrible hangover. "I *drank* too much," said Donald Westerhazy. "We all *drank* too much," said Lucinda Merrill. "It must have been the wine," said Helen Westerhazy. "I *drank* too much of that claret."

This was at the edge of the Westerhazys' pool. The pool, fed by an artesian well with a high iron content, was a pale shade of green. It was a fine day. In the west there was a massive stand of cumulus cloud so like a city seen from a distance —from the bow of an approaching ship—that it might have had a name. Lisbon. Hackensack. The sun was hot. Neddy Merrill sat by the green water, one hand in it, one around a glass of gin. He was a slender man—he seemed to have the especial slenderness of youth—and while he was far from young he had slid down his banister that morning and given the bronze backside of Aphrodite on the hall table a smack, as he jogged toward the smell of coffee in his dining room. He might have been compared to a summer's day, particularly the last hours of one, and while he lacked a tennis racket or a sail bag the impression was definitely one of youth, sport, and clement weather. He had been swimming and now he was breathing deeply, stertorously as if he could gulp into his lungs the components of that moment, the heat of the sun, the intenseness of his pleasure. It all seemed to flow into his chest. His own house stood in Bullet

Park, eight miles to the south, where his four beautiful daughters would have had their lunch and might be playing tennis. Then it occurred to him that by taking a dogleg to the southwest he could reach his home by water.

His life was not confining and the delight he took in this observation could not be explained by its suggestion of escape. He seemed to see, with a cartographer's eye, that string of swimming pools, that quasi-subterranean stream that curved across the county. He had made a discovery, a contribution to modern geography; he would name the stream Lucinda after his wife. He was not a practical joker nor was he a fool but he was determinedly original and had a vague and modest idea of himself as a legendary figure. The day was beautiful and it seemed to him that a long swim might enlarge and celebrate its beauty.

He took off a sweater that was hung over his shoulders and dove in. He had an inexplicable contempt for men who did not hurl themselves into pools. He swam a choppy crawl, breathing either with every stroke or every fourth stroke and counting somewhere well in the back of his mind the one-two one-two of a flutter kick. It was not a serviceable stroke for long distances but the domestication of swimming had saddled the sport with some customs and in his part of the world a crawl was customary. To be embraced and sustained by the light green water was less a pleasure, it seemed, than the resumption of a natural condition, and he would have liked to swim without trunks, but this was not possible, considering his project. He hoisted himself up on the far curb—he never used the ladder—and started across the lawn. When Lucinda asked where he was going he said he was going to swim home.

The only maps and charts he had to go by were remembered or imaginary but these were clear enough. First there were the Grahams, the Hammers, the Lears, the Howlands, and the Crosscups. He would cross Ditmar Street to the Bunkers and come, after a short portage, to the Levys, the Welchers, and the public pool in Lancaster. Then there were the Hallorans, the Sachses, the Biswangers, Shirley Adams, the Gilmartins, and the Clydes. The day was lovely, and that he lived in a world so generously supplied with water seemed like a clemency, a beneficence. His heart was high and he ran across the grass. Making his way home by an uncommon route gave him the feeling that he was a pilgrim, an explorer, a man with a destiny, and he knew that he would find friends all along the way; friends would line the banks of the Lucinda River.

He went through a hedge that separated the Westerhazys' land from the Grahams', walked under some flowering apple trees, passed the shed that housed their pump and filter, and came out at the Grahams' pool. "Why, Neddy," Mrs. Graham said, "what a marvelous surprise. I've been trying to get you on the phone all morning. Here, let me get you a drink." He saw then, like any explorer, that the hospitable customs and traditions of the natives would have to be handled with diplomacy if he was ever going to reach his destination. He did not want to mystify or seem rude to the Grahams nor did he have the time to linger there. He swam the length of their pool and joined them in the sun and was rescued, a few minutes later, by the arrival of two carloads of friends from Connecticut. During the uproarious reunions he was able to slip away. He went down by the front of the Grahams' house, stepped over a thorny hedge, and crossed a vacant lot to the Hammers'. Mrs. Hammer, looking up from her roses, saw him swim by although she wasn't quite sure who it was. The Lears heard him splashing past the open windows of their living room. The Howlands and the Crosscups were away. After leaving the Howlands' he crossed Ditmar Street and started for the Bunkers', where he could hear, even at that distance, the noise of a party.

The water refracted the sound of voices and laughter and seemed to suspend it in midair. The Bunkers' pool was on a rise and he climbed some stairs to a terrace where twenty-five or thirty men and women were drinking. The only person in the water was Rusty Towers, who floated there on a rubber raft. Oh how bonny and lush were the banks of the Lucinda River! Prosperous men and women gathered by the sapphire-colored waters while caterer's men in white coats passed them cold gin. Overhead a red de Haviland trainer was circling around and around and around in the sky with something like the glee of a child in a swing. Ned felt a passing affection for the scene, a tenderness for the gathering, as if it was something he might touch. In the distance he heard thunder. As soon as Enid Bunker saw him she began to scream: "Oh

look who's here! What a marvelous surprise! When Lucinda said that you couldn't come I thought I'd *die*." She made her way to him through the crowd, and when they had finished kissing she led him to the bar, a progress that was slowed by the fact that he stopped to kiss eight or ten other women and shake the hands of as many men. A smiling bartender he had seen at a hundred parties gave him a gin and tonic and he stood by the bar for a moment, anxious not to get stuck in any conversation that would delay his voyage. When he seemed about to be surrounded he dove in and swam close to the side to avoid colliding with Rusty's raft. At the far end of the pool he bypassed the Tomlinsons with a broad smile and jogged up the garden path. The gravel cut his feet but this was the only unpleasantness. The party was confined to the pool, and as he went toward the house he heard the brilliant, watery sound of voices fade, heard the noise of a radio from the Bunkers' kitchen, where someone was listening to a ballgame. Sunday afternoon. He made his way through the parked cars and down the grassy border of their driveway to Alewives' Lane. He did not want to be seen on the road in his bathing trunks but there was no traffic and he made the short distance to the Levys' driveway, marked with a private property sign and a green tube for the *New York Times*. All the doors and windows of the big house were open but there were no signs of life; not even a dog barked. He went around the side of the house to the pool and saw that the Levys had only recently left. Glasses and bottles and dishes of nuts were on a table at the deep end, where there was a bathhouse or gazebo, hung with Japanese lanterns. After swimming the pool he got himself a glass and poured a drink. It was his fourth or fifth drink and he had swum nearly half the length of the Lucinda River. He felt tired, clean, and pleased at that moment to be alone; pleased with everything.

It would storm. The stand of cumulus cloud—that city—had risen and darkened, and while he sat there he heard the percussiveness of thunder again. The de Haviland trainer was still circling overhead and it seemed to Ned that he could almost hear the pilot laugh with pleasure in the afternoon; but when there was another peal of thunder he took off for home. A train whistle blew and he wondered what time it had gotten to be.

Four? Five? He thought of the provincial station at that hour, where a waiter, his tuxedo concealed by a raincoat, a dwarf with some flowers wrapped in newspaper, and a woman who had been crying would be waiting for the local. It was suddenly growing dark; it was that moment when the pin-headed birds seem to organize their song into some acute and knowledgeable recognition of the storm's approach. Then there was a fine noise of rushing water from the crown of an oak at his back, as if a spigot there had been turned. Then the noise of fountains came from the crowns of all the tall trees. Why did he love storms, what was the meaning of his excitement when the door sprang open and the rain wind fled rudely up the stairs, why had the simple task of shutting the windows of an old house seemed fitting and urgent, why did the first watery notes of a storm wind have for him the unmistakable sound of good news, cheer, glad tidings? Then there was an explosion, a smell of cordite, and rain lashed the Japanese lanterns that Mrs. Levy had bought in Kyoto the year before last, or was it the year before that?

He stayed in the Levys' gazebo until the storm had passed. The rain had cooled the air and he shivered. The force of the wind had stripped a maple of its red and yellow leaves and scattered them over the grass and the water. Since it was mid-summer the tree must be blighted, and yet he felt a peculiar sadness at this sign of autumn. He braced his shoulders, emptied his glass, and started for the Welchers' pool. This meant crossing the Lindleys' riding ring and he was surprised to find it overgrown with grass and all the jumps dismantled. He wondered if the Lindleys had sold their horses or gone away for the summer and put them out to board. He seemed to remember having heard something about the Lindleys and their horses but the memory was unclear. On he went, barefoot through the wet grass, to the Welchers', where he found their pool was dry.

This breach in his chain of water disappointed him absurdly, and he felt like some explorer who seeks a torrential headwater and finds a dead stream. He was disappointed and mystified. It was common enough to go away for the summer but no one ever drained his pool. The Welchers had definitely gone away. The pool furniture was folded, stacked, and covered with a tarpaulin. The bathhouse was locked. All the windows of the

house were shut, and when he went around to the driveway in front he saw a for-sale sign nailed to a tree. When had he last heard from the Welchers—when, that is, had he and Lucinda last regretted an invitation to dine with them. It seemed only a week or so ago. Was his memory failing or had he so disciplined it in the repression of unpleasant facts that he had damaged his sense of the truth? Then in the distance he heard the sound of a tennis game. This cheered him, cleared away all his apprehensions and let him regard the overcast sky and the cold air with indifference. This was the day that Neddy Merrill swam across the county. That was the day! He started off then for his most difficult portage.

Had you gone for a Sunday afternoon ride that day you might have seen him, close to naked, standing on the shoulders of Route 424, waiting for a chance to cross. You might have wondered if he was the victim of foul play, had his car broken down, or was he merely a fool. Standing barefoot in the deposits of the highway—beer cans, rags, and blowout patches—exposed to all kinds of ridicule, he seemed pitiful. He had known when he started that this was a part of his journey—it had been on his maps—but confronted with the lines of traffic, worming through the summery light, he found himself unprepared. He was laughed at, jeered at, a beer can was thrown at him, and he had no dignity or humor to bring to the situation. He could have gone back, back to the Westerhazys', where Lucinda would still be sitting in the sun. He had signed nothing, vowed nothing, pledged nothing not even to himself. Why, believing as he did, that all human obduracy was susceptible to common sense, was he unable to turn back? Why was he determined to complete his journey even if it meant putting his life in danger? At what point had this prank, this joke, this piece of horseplay become serious? He could not go back, he could not even recall with any clearness the green water at the Westerhazys', the sense of inhaling the day's components, the friendly and relaxed voices saying that they had *drunk* too much. In the space of an hour, more or less, he had covered a distance that made his return impossible.

An old man, tooling down the highway at fifteen miles an hour, let him get to the middle of the road, where there was a grass divider. Here he was exposed to the ridicule of the northbound traffic, but after ten or fifteen minutes he was able to cross. From here he had only a short walk to the Recreation Center at the edge of the Village of Lancaster, where there were some handball courts and a public pool.

The effect of the water on voices, the illusion of brilliance and suspense, was the same here as it had been at the Bunkers' but the sounds here were louder, harsher, and more shrill, and as soon as he entered the crowded enclosure he was confronted with regimentation. "ALL SWIMMERS MUST TAKE A SHOWER BEFORE USING THE POOL. ALL SWIMMERS MUST USE THE FOOTBATH. ALL SWIMMERS MUST WEAR THEIR IDENTIFICATION DISKS." He took a shower, washed his feet in a cloudy and bitter solution and made his way to the edge of the water. It stank of chlorine and looked to him like a sink. A pair of lifeguards in a pair of towers blew police whistles at what seemed to be regular intervals and abused the swimmers through a public address system. Neddy remembered the sapphire water at the Bunkers' with longing and thought that he might contaminate himself—damage his own prosperousness and charm—by swimming in this murk, but he reminded himself that he was an explorer, a pilgrim, and that this was merely a stagnant bend in the Lucinda River. He dove, scowling with distaste, into the chlorine and had to swim with his head above water to avoid collisions, but even so he was bumped into, splashed and jostled. When he got to the shallow end both lifeguards were shouting at him: "Hey, you, you without the identification disk, get outa the water." He did, but they had no way of pursuing him and he went through the reek of suntan oil and chlorine out through the hurricane fence and passed the handball courts. By crossing the road he entered the wooded part of the Halloran estate. The woods were not cleared and the footing was treacherous and difficult until he reached the lawn and the clipped beech hedge that encircled their pool.

The Hallorans were friends, an elderly couple of enormous wealth who seemed to bask in the suspicion that they might be Communists. They were zealous reformers but they were not Communists, and yet when they were accused, as they sometimes were, of subversion, it seemed to gratify and excite them. Their beech hedge was yellow and he guessed this had been blighted like the Levys'

maple. He called hullo, hullo, to warn the Hallorans of his approach, to palliate his invasion of their privacy. The Hallorans, for reasons that had never been explained to him, did not wear bathing suits. No explanations were in order, really. Their nakedness was a detail in their uncompromising zeal for reform and he stepped politely out of his trunks before he went through the opening in the hedge.

Mrs. Halloran, a stout woman with white hair and a serene face, was reading the *Times*. Mr. Halloran was taking beech leaves out of the water with a scoop. They seemed not surprised or displeased to see him. Their pool was perhaps the oldest in the county, a fieldstone rectangle, fed by a brook. It had no filter or pump and its waters were the opaque gold of the stream.

"I'm swimming across the county," Ned said.

"Why, I didn't know one could," exclaimed Mrs. Halloran.

"Well, I've made it from the Westerhazys'," Ned said. "That must be about four miles."

He left his trunks at the deep end, walked to the shallow end, and swam this stretch. As he was pulling himself out of the water he heard Mrs. Halloran say: "We've been *terribly* sorry to hear about all your misfortunes, Neddy."

"My misfortunes?" Ned asked. "I don't know what you mean."

"Why, we heard that you'd sold the house and that your poor children . . ."

"I don't recall having sold the house," Ned said, "and the girls are at home."

"Yes," Mrs. Halloran sighed. "Yes . . ." Her voice filled the air with an unseasonable melancholy and Ned spoke briskly. "Thank you for the swim."

"Well, have a nice trip," said Mrs. Halloran.

Beyond the hedge he pulled on his trunks and fastened them. They were loose and he wondered if, during the space of an afternoon, he could have lost some weight. He was cold and he was tired and the naked Hallorans and their dark water had depressed him. The swim was too much for his strength but how could he have guessed this, sliding down the banister that morning and sitting in the Westerhazys' sun? His arms were lame. His legs felt rubbery and ached at the joints. The worst of it was the cold in his bones and the feeling that he might never be warm again. Leaves were falling down around him and he smelled wood-smoke on the wind. Who would be burning wood at this time of year?

He needed a drink. Whisky would warm him, pick him up, carry him through the last of his journey, refresh his feeling that it was original and valorous to swim across the county. Channel swimmers took brandy. He needed a stimulant. He crossed the lawn in front of the Hallorans' house and went down a little path to where they had built a house for their only daughter Helen and her husband Eric Sachs. The Sachses' pool was small and he found Helen and her husband there.

"Oh, *Neddy*," Helen said. "Did you lunch at mother's?"

"Not *really*," Ned said. "I *did* stop to see your parents." This seemed to be explanation enough. "I'm terribly sorry to break in on you like this but I've taken a chill and I wonder if you'd give me a drink."

"Why, I'd *love* to," Helen said, "but there hasn't been anything in this house to drink since Eric's operation. That was three years ago."

Was he losing his memory, had his gift for concealing painful facts let him forget that he had sold his house, that his children were in trouble, and that his friend had been ill? His eyes slipped from Eric's face to his abdomen, where he saw three pale, sutured scars, two of them at least a foot long. Gone was his navel, and what, Neddy thought, would the roving hand, bed-checking one's gifts at 3 A.M. make of a belly with no navel, no link to birth, this breach in the succession?

"I'm sure you can get a drink at the Biswangers'," Helen said. "They're having an enormous do. You can hear it from here. Listen!"

She raised her head and from across the road, the lawns, the gardens, the woods, the fields, he heard again the brilliant noise of voices over water. "Well, I'll get wet," he said, still feeling that he had no freedom of choice about his means of travel. He dove into the Sachses' cold water and, gasping, close to drowning, made his way from one end of the pool to the other. "Lucinda and I want *terribly* to see you," he said over his shoulder, his face set towards the Biswangers'. "We're sorry it's been so long and we'll call you *very* soon."

He crossed some fields to the Biswangers' and the sounds of revelry there. They would be honored to give him a drink, they would be happy to give him a drink, they would in fact be lucky to give him a drink. The Biswangers invited him and Lucinda for dinner four times a year, six weeks in advance. They were always rebuffed and yet they continued to send out their invitations, unwilling to comprehend the rigid and undemocratic realities of their society. They were the sort of people who discussed the price of things at cocktails, exchanged market tips during dinner, and after dinner told dirty stories to mixed company. They did not belong to Neddy's set—they were not even on Lucinda's Christmas card list. He went toward their pool with feelings of indifference, charity, and some unease, since it seemed to be getting dark and these were the longest days of the year. The party when he joined it was noisy and large. Grace Biswanger was the kind of hostess who asked the optometrist, the veterinarian, the real-estate dealer and the dentist. No one was swimming and the twilight, reflected on the water of the pool, had a wintry gleam. There was a bar and he started for this. When Grace Biswanger saw him she came toward him, not affectionately as he had every right to expect, but bellicosely.

"Why, this party has everything," she said loudly, "including a gate crasher."

She could not deal him a social blow—there was no question about this and he did not flinch. "As a gate crasher," he asked politely, "do I rate a drink?"

"Suit yourself," she said. "You don't seem to pay much attention to invitations."

She turned her back on him and joined some guests, and he went to the bar and ordered a whisky. The bartender served him but he served him rudely. His was a world in which the caterer's men kept the social score, and to be rebuffed by a part-time barkeep meant that he had suffered some loss of social esteem. Or perhaps the man was new and uninformed. Then he heard Grace at his back say: "They went for broke overnight—nothing but income—and he showed up drunk one Sunday and asked us to loan him five thousand dollars. . . ." She was always talking about money. It was worse than eating your peas off a knife. He dove into the pool, swam its length and went away.

The next pool on his list, the last but two, belonged to his old mistress, Shirley Adams. If he had suffered any injuries at the Biswangers' they would be cured here. Love—sexual roughhouse in fact—was the supreme elixir, the painkiller, the brightly colored pill that would put the spring back into his step, the joy of life in his heart. They had had an affair last week, last month, last year. He couldn't remember. It was he who had broken it off, his was the upper hand, and he stepped through the gate of the wall that surrounded her pool with nothing so considered as self-confidence. It seemed in a way to be his pool as the lover, particularly the illicit lover, enjoys the possessions of his mistress with an authority unknown to holy matrimony. She was there, her hair the color of brass, but her figure, at the edge of the lighted, cerulean water, excited in him no profound memories. It had been, he thought, a lighthearted affair, although she had wept when he broke it off. She seemed confused to see him and he wondered if she was still wounded. Would she, God forbid, weep again?

"What do you want?" she asked.

"I'm swimming across the county."

"Good Christ. Will you ever grow up?"

"What's the matter?"

"If you've come here for money," she said, "I won't give you another cent."

"You could give me a drink."

"I could but I won't. I'm not alone."

"Well, I'm on my way."

He dove in and swam the pool, but when he tried to haul himself up onto the curb he found that the strength in his arms and his shoulders had gone, and he paddled to the ladder and climbed out. Looking over his shoulder he saw, in the lighted bathhouse, a young man. Going out onto the dark lawn he smelled chrysanthemums or marigolds—some stubborn autumnal fragrance—on the night air, strong as gas. Looking overhead he saw that the stars had come out, but why should he seem to see Andromeda, Cepheus, and Cassiopeia? What had become of the constellations of mid-summer? He began to cry.

It was probably the first time in his adult life that he had ever cried, certainly the first time in his life that he had ever felt so miserable, cold, tired, and bewildered. He could not understand the rudeness of the caterer's barkeep or the rudeness of a mistress who had come to him on her knees and showered his trousers with tears. He had swum too long, he had been immersed too long, and his nose and his throat were sore from the water. What he needed then was a drink, some company, and some clean dry clothes, and while he could have cut directly across the road to his home he went on to the Gilmartins' pool. Here, for the first time in his life, he did not dive but went down the steps into the icy water and swam a hobbled side stroke that he might have learned as a youth. He staggered with fatigue on his way to the Clydes' and paddled the length of their pool, stopping again and again with his hand on the curb to rest. He climbed up the ladder and wondered if he had the strength to get home. He had done what he wanted, he had swum the county, but he was so stupefied with exhaustion that his triumph seemed vague. Stooped, holding onto the gateposts for support, he turned up the driveway of his own house.

The place was dark. Was it so late that they had all gone to bed? Had Lucinda stayed at the Westerhazys' for supper? Had the girls joined her there or gone someplace else? Hadn't they agreed, as they usually did on Sunday, to regret all their invitations and stay at home? He tried the garage doors to see what cars were in but the doors were locked and rust came off the handles onto his hands. Going toward the house, he saw that the force of the thunderstorm had knocked one of the rain gutters loose. It hung down over the front door like an umbrella rib, but it could be fixed in the morning. The house was locked, and he thought that the stupid cook or the stupid maid must have locked the place up until he remembered that it had been some time since they had employed a maid or a cook. He shouted, pounded on the door, tried to force it with his shoulder, and then, looking in at the windows, saw that the place was empty.

JOHN CROWE RANSOM
b. 1888

Captain Carpenter

Captain Carpenter rose up in his prime
Put on his pistols and went riding out
But had got well nigh nowhere at that time
Till he fell in with ladies in a rout.

It was a pretty lady and all her train   5
That played with him so sweetly but before
An hour she'd taken a sword with all her main
And twined him of his nose for evermore.

Captain Carpenter mounted up one day
And rode straight way into a stranger rogue   10
That looked unchristian but be that as it may
The Captain did not wait upon prologue.

But drew upon him out of his great heart
The other swung against him with a club
And cracked his two legs at the shinny part   15
And let him roll and stick like any tub.

Captain Carpenter rode many a time
From male and female took he sundry harms
He met the wife of Satan crying "I'm
The she-wolf bids you shall bear no more arms."   20

Their strokes and counters whistled in the wind
I wish he had delivered half his blows
But where she should have made off like a hind
The bitch bit off his arms at the elbows.

And Captain Carpenter parted with his ears   25
To a black devil that used him in this wise
O Jesus ere his threescore and ten years
Another had plucked out his sweet blue eyes.

Captain Carpenter got up on his roan
And sallied from the gate in hell's despite   30
I heard him asking in the grimmest tone
If any enemy yet there was to fight?

"To any adversary it is fame
If he risk to be wounded by my tongue
Or burnt in two beneath my red heart's flame   35
Such are the perils he is cast among.

"But if he can he has a pretty choice
From an anatomy with little to lose
Whether he cut my tongue and take my voice
Or whether it be my round red heart he choose."   40

It was the neatest knave that ever was seen
Stepping in perfume from his lady's bower
Who at this word put in his merry mien
And fell on Captain Carpenter like a tower.

I would not knock old fellows in the dust   45
But there lay Captain Carpenter on his back
His weapons were the old heart in his bust
And a blade shook between rotten teeth alack.

The rogue in scarlet and gray soon knew his mind
He wished to get his trophy and depart;   50
With gentle apology and touch refined
He pierced him and produced the Captain's heart.

God's mercy rest on Captain Carpenter now
I thought him Sirs an honest gentleman
Citizen husband soldier and scholar enow   55
Let jangling kites eat of him if they can.

But God's deep curses follow after those
That shore him of his goodly nose and ears
His legs and strong arms at the two elbows
And eyes that had not watered seventy years.   60

The curse of hell upon the sleek upstart
Who got the Captain finally on his back
And took the red red vitals of his heart
And made the kites to whet their beaks clack clack.

ROBERT GRAVES
b. 1895

Saint

This Blatant Beast° was finally overcome
And in no secret tourney: wit and fashion
Flocked out and for compassion
Wept as the Red Cross Knight° pushed the blade
    home.

The people danced and sang the paeans due,   5
Roasting whole oxen on the public spit;
Twelve mountain peaks were lit
With bonfires; yet their hearts were doubt and rue.

Therefore no grave was deep enough to hold
The Beast, who after days came thrusting out,   10
Wormy from rump to snout,
His yellow cerecloth patched with the grave's mold.

Nor could sea hold him: anchored with huge rocks,
He swelled and buoyed them up, paddling ashore
As evident as before   15
With deep-sea ooze and salty creaking bones.

SAINT. **1. Blatant Beast:** embodiment of scandal in *The Faerie Queene*, Book VI. **4. Red . . . Knight:** champion of Truth in *The Faerie Queene*, Book I.

Lime could not burn him nor the sulfur fire:
So often as the good Knight bound him there,
With stink of singeing hair
And scorching flesh the corpse rolled from the
    pyre. 20

In the city-gutter would the Beast lie
Praising the Knight for all his valorous deeds:
"Aye, on those water-meads
He slew even me. These death-wounds testify."

The Knight governed that city, a man shamed 25
And shrunken: for the Beast was over-dead,
With wounds no longer red
But gangrenous and loathsome and inflamed.

Not all the righteous judgments he could utter,
Nor mild laws frame, nor public works repair, 30
Nor wars wage, in despair,
Could bury that same Beast, crouched in the gutter.

A fresh remembrance-banquet to forestall,
The Knight turned hermit, went without farewell
To a far mountain-cell; 35
But the Beast followed as his seneschal,

And there drew water for him and hewed wood
With vacant howling laughter; else all day
Noisome with long decay
Sunning himself at the cave's entry stood. 40

Would bawl to pilgrims for a dole of bread
To feed the sick saint who once vanquished him
With spear so stark and grim;
Would set a pillow of grass beneath his head,
Would fetch him feverwort from the pool's brim—
And crept into his grave when he was dead. 46

W. H. AUDEN
b. 1907

Victor Was a Little Baby

(*Tune: Frankie & Johnny*)

Victor was a little baby,
    Into this world he came;
His father took him on his knee and said:
    "Don't dishonor the family name."

Victor looked up at his father 5
    Looked up with big round eyes:
His father said; "Victor, my only son,
    Don't you ever ever tell lies."

Victor and his father went riding
    Out in a little dog-cart; 10
His father took a Bible from his pocket and read;
    "Blessed are the pure in heart."

It was a frosty December,
    It wasn't the season for fruits;
His father fell dead of heart disease 15
    While lacing up his boots.

It was a frosty December
    When into his grave he sank;
His uncle found Victor a post as cashier
    In the Midland Counties Bank. 20

It was a frosty December
    Victor was only eighteen,
But his figures were neat and his margins straight
    And his cuffs were always clean.

He took a room at the Peveril, 25
    A respectable boarding-house;
And Time watched Victor day after day
    As a cat will watch a mouse.

The clerks slapped Victor on the shoulder;
    "Have you ever had a woman?" they said,
"Come down town with us on Saturday night," 31
    Victor smiled and shook his head.

The manager sat in his office,
    Smoked a Corona cigar:
Said; "Victor's a decent fellow but 35
    He's too mousey to go far."

Victor went up to his bedroom,
    Set the alarum bell;
Climbed into bed, took his Bible and read
    Of what happened to Jezebel. 40

It was the First of April,
    Anna to the Peveril came;
Her eyes, her lips, her breasts, her hips
    And her smile set men aflame.

She looked as pure as a schoolgirl 45
    On her First Communion day,
But her kisses were like the best champagne
    When she gave herself away.

It was the Second of April,
    She was wearing a coat of fur;   50
Victor met her upon the stairs
    And he fell in love with her.

The first time he made his proposal,
    She laughed, said; "I'll never wed";
The second time there was a pause;   55
    Then she smiled and shook her head.

Anna looked into her mirror,
    Pouted and gave a frown:
Said; "Victor's as dull as a wet afternoon
    But I've got to settle down."   60

The third time he made his proposal,
    As they walked by the Reservoir:
She gave him a kiss like a blow on the head,
    Said; "You are my heart's desire."

They were married early in August,   65
    She said; "Kiss me, you funny boy":
Victor took her in his arms and said;
    "O my Helen of Troy."

It was the middle of September,
    Victor came to the office one day;   70
He was wearing a flower in his buttonhole,
    He was late but he was gay.

The clerks were talking of Anna,
    The door was just ajar:
One said; "Poor old Victor, but where ignorance
    Is bliss, etcetera."   76

Victor stood still as a statue,
    The door was just ajar:
One said; "God, what fun I had with her
    In that Baby Austin car."   80

Victor walked out into the High Street,
    He walked to the edge of the town;
He came to the allotments and the rubbish heaps
    And his tears came tumbling down.

Victor looked up at the sunset   85
    As he stood there all alone;
Cried: "Are you in Heaven, Father?"
    But the sky said "Address not known."

Victor looked up at the mountains,
    The mountains all covered with snow: 90
Cried; "Are you pleased with me, Father?"
    And the answer came back, "No."

Victor came to the forest,
    Cried: "Father, will she ever be true?"
And the oaks and the beeches shook their heads   95
    And they answered: "Not to you."

Victor came to the meadow
    Where the wind went sweeping by:
Cried; "O Father, I love her so,"
    But the wind said, "She must die."   100

Victor came to the river
    Running so deep and so still:
Crying; "O Father, what shall I do?"
    And the river answered, "Kill."

Anna was sitting at table,   105
    Drawing cards from a pack;
Anna was sitting at table
    Waiting for her husband to come back.

It wasn't the Jack of Diamonds
    Nor the Joker she drew at first;   110
It wasn't the King or the Queen of Hearts
    But the Ace of Spades reversed.

Victor stood in the doorway,
    He didn't utter a word:
She said; "What's the matter, darling?"   115
    He behaved as if he hadn't heard.

There was a voice in his left ear,
    There was a voice in his right,
There was a voice at the base of his skull
    Saying, "She must die tonight."   120

Victor picked up a carving-knife,
    His features were set and drawn,
Said; "Anna, it would have been better for you
    If you had not been born."

Anna jumped up from the table,   125
    Anna started to scream,
But Victor came slowly after her
    Like a horror in a dream.

She dodged behind the sofa,
    She tore down a curtain rod,   130
But Victor came slowly after her:
    Said; "Prepare to meet thy God."

She managed to wrench the door open,
    She ran and she didn't stop.
But Victor followed her up the stairs   135
    And he caught her at the top.

He stood there above the body,
  He stood there holding the knife;
And the blood ran down the stairs and sang,
  "I'm the Resurrection and the Life."   140

They tapped Victor on the shoulder,
  They took him away in a van;
He sat as quiet as a lump of moss
  Saying, "I am the Son of Man."

Victor sat in a corner   145
  Making a woman of clay:
Saying; "I am Alpha and Omega,° I shall come
  To judge the earth one day."

VICTOR WAS A LITTLE BABY. **147. Alpha and Omega:** first
and last letters of the Greek alphabet, thus the Beginning
and the End (see Revelation 22:13).

Last-Phase Irony:
Demonic Ritual and Expulsion

GEORGE GORDON, LORD BYRON
1788–1824

The Vision of Judgment°

By Quevedo Redivivus

Suggested by the Composition so Entitled by the
Author of *Wat Tyler*

"A Daniel come to judgment! yea, a Daniel!
I thank thee, Jew, for teaching me that word."

1

Saint Peter sat by the celestial gate:
   His keys were rusty, and the lock was dull,
So little trouble had been given of late;
   Not that the place by any means was full,
But since the Gallic era "eighty-eight"°   5
   The devils had ta'en a longer, stronger pull,
And "a pull altogether," as they say
At sea—which drew most souls another way.

2

The angels all were singing out of tune,
   And hoarse with having little else to do,   10
Excepting to wind up the sun and moon,
   Or curb a runaway young star or two,
Or wild colt of a comet, which too soon
   Broke out of bounds o'er th' ethereal blue,
Splitting some planet with its playful tail,   15
As boats are sometimes by a wanton whale.

3

The guardian seraphs had retired on high,
   Finding their charges past all care below;
Terrestrial business filled nought in the sky
   Save the recording angel's black bureau;   20
Who found, indeed, the facts to multiply
   With such rapidity of vice and woe,
That he had stripped off both his wings in quills,
And yet was in arrear of human ills.

4

His business so augmented of late years,   25
   That he was forced, against his will no doubt
(Just like those cherubs, earthly ministers),
   For some resource to turn himself about,
And claim the help of his celestial peers,
   To aid him ere he should be quite worn out   30
By the increased demand for his remarks;
Six angels and twelve saints were named his clerks.

5

This was a handsome board—at least for heaven;
   And yet they had even then enough to do,

THE VISION OF JUDGMENT. The poem is a satiric parody of
Robert Southey's poem of the same name, in which
Southey has a vision of George III's entrance into heaven.
Southey had earlier written and suppressed a radical play,
Wat Tyler; he then turned Tory and became laureate, and
to his embarrassment the play was pirated and published.
He and Byron openly attacked each other on political and
literary issues. Quevedo is the name of a seventeenth-
century Spanish author of satirical visions. *Redivivus* means
"revived." The epigraph is a misquotation of *The Merchant
of Venice*, IV.i.340–41. **5. eighty-eight:** 1788, the last year
of the old regime before the French Revolution.

So many conquerors' cars were daily driven, 35
   So many kingdoms fitted up anew;
Each day too slew its thousands six or seven,
   Till at the crowning carnage, Waterloo,
They threw their pens down in divine disgust—
The page was so besmeared with blood and dust. 40

6

This by the way; 'tis not mine to record
   What angels shrink from: even the very devil
On this occasion his own work abhorred,
   So surfeited with the infernal revel:
Though he himself had sharpened every sword, 45
   It almost quenched his innate thirst of evil.
(Here Satan's sole good work deserves insertion—
'Tis, that he has both generals in reversion.°)

7

Let's skip a few short years of hollow peace,
   Which peopled earth no better, hell as wont, 50
And heaven none—they form the tyrant's lease,
   With nothing but new names subscribed upon 't;
'Twill one day finish: meantime they increase,
   "With seven heads and ten horns," and all in front,
Like Saint John's foretold beast;° but ours are born 55
Less formidable in the head than horn.

8

In the first year of freedom's second dawn°
   Died George the Third; although no tyrant, one
Who shielded tyrants, till each sense withdrawn
   Left him nor mental nor external sun: 60
A better farmer ne'er brushed dew from lawn,
   A worse king never left a realm undone!
He died—but left his subjects still behind,
One half as mad—and t'other no less blind.

9

He died! his death made no great stir on earth; 65
   His burial made some pomp; there was profusion

Of velvet, gilding, brass, and no great dearth
   Of aught but tears—save those shed by collusion.
For these things may be bought at their true worth;
   Of elegy there was the due infusion— 70
Bought also; and the torches, cloaks, and banners,
Heralds, and relics of old Gothic manners,

10

Formed a sepulchral melodrame. Of all
   The fools who flocked to swell or see the show,
Who cared about the corpse? The funeral 75
   Made the attraction, and the black the woe.
There throbbed not there a thought which pierced the pall;
   And when the gorgeous coffin was laid low,
It seemed the mockery of hell to fold
The rottenness of eighty years in gold. 80

11

So mix his body with the dust! It might
   Return to what it *must* far sooner, were
The natural compound left alone to fight
   Its way back into earth, and fire, and air;
But the unnatural balsams° merely blight 85
   What nature made him at his birth, as bare
As the mere million's base unmummied clay—
Yet all his spices but prolong decay.

12

He's dead—and upper earth with him has done;
   He's buried; save the undertaker's bill, 90
Or lapidary scrawl, the world is gone
   For him, unless he left a German will;
But where's the proctor who will ask his son?°
   In whom his qualities are reigning still,
Except that household virtue, most uncommon, 95
Of constancy to a bad, ugly woman.

13

"God save the king!" It is a large economy
   In God to save the like; but if he will
Be saving, all the better; for not one am I
   Of those who think damnation better still: 100

---

48. both . . . reversion: Both generals at Waterloo, Napoleon and Wellington, are legally Satan's in the future. **55. beast:** See Revelation 13:1. **57. second dawn:** 1820, a year of new revolutions in southern Europe.

85. balsams: embalming fluids. **93. proctor . . . son:** the official who intervenes when a will is suspect; an allusion to such an instance in the will of George I.

I hardly know too if not quite alone am I
  In this small hope of bettering future ill
By circumscribing, with some slight restriction,
  The eternity of hell's hot jurisdiction.

14

I know this is unpopular; I know   105
  'Tis blasphemous; I know one may be damned
For hoping no one else may e'er be so;
  I know my catechism; I know we're crammed
With the best doctrines till we quite o'erflow;
  I know that all save England's church have
      shammed,   110
And that the other twice two hundred churches
And synagogues have made a *damned* bad purchase.

15

God help us all! God help me too! I am,
  God knows, as helpless as the devil can wish,
And not a whit more difficult to damn,   115
  Than is to bring to land a late-hooked fish,
Or to the butcher to purvey the lamb;
  Not that I'm fit for such a noble dish,
As one day will be that immortal fry
Of almost everybody born to die.   120

16

Saint Peter sat by the celestial gate,
  And nodded o'er his keys; when, lo! there came
A wondrous noise he had not heard of late—
  A rushing sound of wind, and stream, and flame;
In short, a roar of things extremely great,   125
  Which would have made aught save a saint
      exclaim;
But he, with first a start and then a wink,
Said, "There's another star gone out, I think!"

17

But ere he could return to his repose,
  A cherub flapped his right wing o'er his eyes—
At which Saint Peter yawned, and rubbed his nose;
  "Saint porter," said the angel, "prithee rise!" 132
Waving a goodly wing, which glowed, as glows
  An earthly peacock's tail, with heavenly dyes:

To which the saint replied, "Well, what's the
  matter?   135
"Is Lucifer come back with all this clatter?"

18

"No," quoth the cherub; "George the Third is
  dead."
  "And who *is* George the Third?" replied the
    apostle:
"*What George? what Third?*" "The king of
  England," said
The angel. "Well! he won't find kings to jostle
Him on his way; but does he wear his head;   141
  Because the last we saw here had a tustle,
And ne'er would have got into heaven's good
    graces,
Had he not flung his head in all our faces.°

19

"He was, if I remember, king of France;   145
  That head of his, which could not keep a crown
On earth, yet ventured in my face to advance
  A claim to those of martyrs—like my own:
If I had had my sword, as I had once
  When I cut ears off, I had cut him down;°   150
But having but my *keys*, and not my brand,
I only knocked his head from out his hand.

20

"And then he set up such a headless howl,
  That all the saints came out and took him in;
And there he sits by Saint Paul, cheek by jowl;
  That fellow Paul—the parvenu! The skin   156
Of Saint Bartholomew,° which makes his cowl
  In heaven, and upon earth redeemed his sin
So as to make a martyr, never sped
Better than did this weak and wooden head.   160

21

"But had it come up here upon its shoulders,
  There would have been a different tale to tell:

144. flung . . . faces: Louis XVI, guillotined in 1793. **150.
cut . . . down:** Simon Peter cut off the ear of one of the
men sent to arrest Jesus at Gethsemane (see John 18:10).
157. Saint Bartholomew: martyr who was flayed before
death.

The fellow-feeling in the saint's beholders
  Seems to have acted on them like a spell;
And so this very foolish head heaven solders   165
  Back on its trunk: it may be very well,
And seems the custom here to overthrow
Whatever has been wisely done below."

22

The angel answered, "Peter! do not pout:
  The king who comes has head and all entire,   170
And never knew much what it was about—
  He did as doth the puppet—by its wire,
And will be judged like all the rest, no doubt:
  My business and your own is not to inquire
Into such matters, but to mind our cue—   175
Which is to act as we are bid to do."

23

While thus they spake, the angelic caravan,
  Arriving like a rush of mighty wind,
Cleaving the fields of space, as doth the swan
  Some silver stream (say Ganges, Nile, or Inde,
Or Thames, or Tweed), and 'midst them an old
    man   181
  With an old soul, and both extremely blind,
Halted before the gate, and in his shroud
Seated their fellow traveler on a cloud.

24

But bringing up the rear of this bright host   185
  A spirit of a different aspect waved
His wings, like thunder clouds above some coast
  Whose barren beach with frequent wrecks is
    paved:
His brow was like the deep when tempest-tossed;
  Fierce and unfathomable thoughts engraved   190
Eternal wrath on his immortal face,
And *where* he gazed a gloom pervaded space.

25

As he drew near, he gazed upon the gate
  Ne'er to be entered more by him or Sin,
With such a glance of supernatural hate,   195
  As made Saint Peter wish himself within;
He pattered with his keys at a great rate,

And sweated through his apostolic skin:
Of course his perspiration was but ichor,
Or some such other spiritual liquor.   200

26

The very cherubs huddled all together,
  Like birds when soars the falcon; and they felt
A tingling to the tip of every feather,
  And formed a circle like Orion's belt
Around their poor old charge; who scarce knew
    whither   205
  His guards had led him, though they gently dealt
With royal manes° (for by many stories,
And true, we learn the angels all are Tories).

27

As things were in this posture, the gate flew
  Asunder, and the flashing of its hinges   210
Flung over space an universal hue
  Of many-colored flames, until its tinges
Reached even our speck of earth, and made a new
  Aurora borealis spread its fringes
O'er the North Pole; the same seen, when ice-
    bound,   215
By Captain Parry's° crew, in "Melville's Sound."

28

And from the gate thrown open issued beaming
  A beautiful and mighty thing of light,
Radiant with glory, like a banner streaming
  Victorious from some world-o'erthrowing fight:
My poor comparisons must needs be teeming   221
  With earthly likenesses, for here the night
Of clay obscures our best conceptions, saving
Johanna Southcote,° or Bob Southey raving.

29

'Twas the archangel Michael: all men know   225
  The make of angels and archangels, since
There's scarce a scribbler has not one to show,

207. manes: spirits of the dead. **216. Captain Parry:**
explorer of the Northwest Passage in 1819–20. **224.**
Johanna Southcote: religious mystic and founder of a cult
who proclaimed in 1813 that she would give birth to the
world's redeemer; her "pregnancy," however, was caused
by a tumor from which she died.

From the fiends' leader to the angels' prince.
There also are some altarpieces, though
    I really can't say that they much evince   230
One's inner notions of immortal spirits;
But let the connoisseurs explain *their* merits.

30

Michael flew forth in glory and in good;
    A goodly work of him from whom all glory
And good arise; the portal past—he stood;   235
    Before him the young cherubs and saints hoary—
(I say *young*, begging to be understood
    By looks, not years; and should be very sorry
To state, they were not older than Saint Peter.
But merely that they seemed a little sweeter).   240

31

The cherubs and the saints bowed down before
    That arch-angelic hierarch, the first
Of essences angelical, who wore
    The aspect of a god; but this ne'er nursed
Pride in his heavenly bosom, in whose core   245
    No thought, save for his Master's service, durst
Intrude, however glorified and high;
He knew him but the viceroy of the sky.

32

He and the somber silent spirit met—
    They knew each other both for good and ill;   250
Such was their power, that neither could forget
    His former friend and future foe; but still
There was a high, immortal, proud regret
    In either's eye, as if 'twere less their will
Than destiny to make the eternal years   255
Their date of war, and their "champ clos"° the
    spheres.

33

But here they were in neutral space: we know
    From Job, that Satan hath the power to pay
A heavenly visit thrice a year or so;
    And that the "sons of God," like those of clay,
Must keep him company;° and we might show   261

256. champ clos: enclosed fields for tournaments. 258-61.
Satan . . . company: See Job 1:6.

From the same book, in how polite a way
The dialogue is held between the powers
Of good and evil—but 'twould take up hours.

34

And this is not a theologic tract,   265
    To prove with Hebrew and with Arabic
If Job be allegory or a fact,
    But a true narrative; and thus I pick
From out the whole but such and such an act
    As sets aside the slightest thought of trick.   270
'Tis every tittle true, beyond suspicion,
And accurate as any other vision.

35

The spirits were in neutral space, before
    The gate of heaven; like eastern thresholds is
The place where Death's grand cause is argued
    o'er,°   275
    And souls despatched to that world or to this;
And therefore Michael and the other wore
    A civil aspect: though they did not kiss,
Yet still between his darkness and his brightness
There passed a mutual glance of great politeness.

36

The archangel bowed, not like a modern beau, 281
    But with a graceful oriental bend,
Pressing one radiant arm just where below
    The heart in good men is supposed to tend.
He turned as to an equal, not too low,   285
    But kindly; Satan met his ancient friend
With more hauteur, as might an old Castilian
Poor noble meet a mushroom rich civilian.

37

He merely bent his diabolic brow
    An instant; and then raising it, he stood   290
In act to assert his right or wrong, and show
    Cause why King George by no means could or
    should
Make out a case to be exempt from woe
    Eternal, more than other kings, endued

274-75. eastern . . . o'er: The gateways of Middle Eastern
cities were often used as places for debate and admin-
istering justice.

With better sense and hearts, whom history mentions,   295
Who long have "paved hell with their good intentions."

38

Michael began: "What wouldst thou with this man,
    Now dead, and brought before the Lord? What
        ill
Hath he wrought since his mortal race began,
    That thou canst claim him? Speak! and do thy
        will,   300
If it be just: if in this earthly span
    He hath been greatly failing to fulfill
His duties as a king and mortal, say,
And he is thine; if not, let him have way."

39

"Michael!" replied the Prince of Air, "even here,
    Before the gate of him thou servest, must   306
I claim my subject: and will make appear
    That as he was my worshiper in dust,
So shall he be in spirit, although dear
    To thee and thine, because nor wine nor lust 310
Were of his weaknesses; yet on the throne
He reigned o'er millions to serve me alone.

40

"Look to our earth, or rather mine; it was,
    Once, more thy master's: but I triumph not
In this poor planet's conquest; nor, alas!   315
    Need he thou servest envy me my lot:
With all the myriads of bright worlds which pass
    In worship round him, he may have forgot
Yon weak creation of such paltry things:
I think few worth damnation save their kings— 320

41

"And these but as a kind of quitrent, to
    Assert my right as lord: and even had
I such an inclination, 'twere (as you
    Well know) superfluous; they are grown so bad,
That hell has nothing better left to do   325
    Than leave them to themselves: so much more
        mad

And evil by their own internal curse,
Heaven cannot make them better, nor I worse.

42

"Look to the earth, I said, and say again:
    When this old, blind, mad, helpless, weak, poor
        worm   330
Began in youth's first bloom and flush to reign,
    The world and he both wore a different form,
And much of earth and all the watery plain
    Of ocean called him king: through many a storm
His isles had floated on the abyss of time;   335
For the rough virtues chose them for their clime.

43

"He came to his scepter young; he leaves it old:
    Look to the state in which he found his realm,
And left it; and his annals too behold,
    How to a minion° first he gave the helm,   340
How grew upon his heart a thirst for gold,
    The beggar's vice, which can but overwhelm
The meanest hearts; and for the rest, but glance
Thine eye along America and France.

44

" 'Tis true, he was a tool from first to last   345
    (I have the workmen safe); but as a tool
So let him be consumed. From out the past
    Of ages, since mankind have known the rule
Of monarchs—from the bloody rolls amassed
    Of sin and slaughter—from the Caesar's school,
Take the worst pupil; and produce a reign   351
More drenched with gore, more cumbered with the
        slain.

45

"He ever warred with freedom and the free:
    Nations as men, home subjects, foreign foes,
So that they uttered the word 'Liberty!'   355
    Found George the Third their first opponent.
        Whose
History was ever stained as his will be
    With national and individual woes?
I grant his household abstinence; I grant
His neutral virtues, which most monarchs want; 360

340. minion: the earl of Bute, who became prime minister
in 1761.

46

"I know he was a constant consort; own
    He was a decent sire, and middling lord.
All this is much, and most upon a throne;
    As temperance, if at Apicius' board,°
Is more than at an anchorite's supper shown.   365
    I grant him all the kindest can accord;
And this was well for him, but not for those
Millions who found him what oppression chose.

47

"The New World shook him off; the Old yet groans
    Beneath what he and his prepared, if not   370
Completed: he leaves heirs on many thrones
    To all his vices, without what begot
Compassion for him—his tame virtues; drones
    Who sleep, or despots who have now forgot
A lesson which shall be retaught them, wake   375
Upon the thrones of earth; but let them quake!

48

"Five millions of the primitive,° who hold
    The faith which makes ye great on earth, implored
A *part* of that vast *all* they held of old—
    Freedom to worship—not alone your Lord,   380
Michael, but you, and you, Saint Peter! Cold
    Must be your souls, if you have not abhorred
The foe to Catholic participation
In all the license of a Christian nation.

49

"True! he allowed them to pray God; but as   385
    A consequence of prayer, refused the law
Which would have placed them upon the same base
    With those who did not hold the saints in awe."
But here Saint Peter started from his place,
    And cried, "You may the prisoner withdraw: 390
Ere heaven shall ope her portals to this Guelph,°
While I am guard, may I be damned myself!

364. Apicius' board: Apicius was a famous Roman epicure.
377. Five . . . primitive: Irish Catholics, who were
denied the right to hold public office by George III's
opposition to the Catholic Emancipation Bill in 1795
(ll. 385–88). **391. Guelph:** The Hanovers were descended
from the German Guelphs.

50

"Sooner will I with Cerberus exchange
    My office (and *his* is no sinecure)
Than see this royal Bedlam bigot range   395
    The azure fields of heaven, of that be sure!"
"Saint!" replied Satan, "you do well to avenge
    The wrongs he made your satellites endure;
And if to this exchange you should be given,
I'll try to coax *our* Cerberus up to heaven."   400

51

Here Michael interposed: "Good saint! and devil!
    Pray, not so fast; you both outrun discretion.
Saint Peter! you were wont to be more civil!
    Satan! excuse this warmth of his expression,
And condescension to the vulgar's level: 405
    Even saints sometimes forget themselves in session.
Have you got more to say?"—"No."—"If you please,
I'll trouble you to call your witnesses."

52

Then Satan turned and waved his swarthy hand,
    Which stirred with its electric qualities   410
Clouds farther off than we can understand,
    Although we find him sometimes in our skies;
Infernal thunder shook both sea and land
    In all the planets, and hell's batteries
Let off the artillery, which Milton mentions   415
As one of Satan's most sublime inventions.

53

This was a signal unto such damned souls
    As have the privilege of their damnation
Extended far beyond the mere controls
    Of worlds past, present, or to come; no station
Is theirs particularly in the rolls   421
    Of hell assigned; but where their inclination
Or business carries them in search of game,
They may range freely—being damned the same.

54

They're proud of this—as very well they may,   425
    It being a sort of knighthood, or gilt key

Stuck in their loins,° or like an "entré"
  Up the back stairs, or such freemasonry.
I borrow my comparisons from clay,
  Being clay myself. Let not those spirits be   430
Offended with such base low likenesses;
We know their posts are nobler far than these.

55

When the great signal ran from heaven to hell—
  About ten million times the distance reckoned
From our sun to its earth, as we can tell   435
  How much time it takes up, even to a second,
For every ray that travels to dispel
  The fogs of London, through which, dimly
    beaconed,
The weathercocks are gilt some thrice a year,
If that the *summer* is not too severe—   440

56

I say that I can tell—'twas half a minute;
  I know the solar beams take up more time
Ere, packed up for their journey, they begin it;
  But then their telegraph is less sublime,
And if they ran a race, they would not win it   445
  'Gainst Satan's couriers bound for their own
    clime.
The sun takes up some years for every ray
To reach its goal—the Devil not half a day.

57

Upon the verge of space, about the size
  Of half-a-crown, a little speck appeared   450
(I've seen a something like it in the skies
  In the Aegean, ere a squall); it neared,
And, growing bigger, took another guise;
  Like an aërial ship it tacked, and steered,
Or *was* steered (I am doubtful of the grammar   455
Of the last phrase, which makes the stanza
    stammer—

58

But take your choice); and then it grew a cloud;
  And so it was—a cloud of witnesses.
But such a cloud! No land e'er saw a crowd

426–27: gilt . . . loins: gold key hung from the belt as a symbol of the lord chamberlain's office.

Of locusts numerous as the heavens saw these;
  They shadowed with their myriads space; their
    loud   461
And varied cries were like those of wild geese
(If nations may be likened to a goose),
And realized the phrase of "hell broke loose."

59

Here crashed a sturdy oath of stout John Bull,   465
  Who damned away his eyes as heretofore:
There Paddy brogued "By Jasus!"—"What's your
    wull?"
  The temperate Scot exclaimed: the French ghost
    swore
In certain terms I shan't translate in full,
  As the first coachman will; and 'midst the war,
The voice of Jonathan° was heard to express,   471
"*Our* president is going to war, I guess."

60

Besides there were the Spaniard, Dutch, and Dane;
  In short, an universal shoal of shades,
From Otaheite's isle° to Salisbury Plain,   475
  Of all climes and professions, years and trades,
Ready to swear against the good king's reign,
  Bitter as clubs in cards are against spades;
All summoned by this grand "subpoena," to
Try if kings mayn't be damned like me or you.   480

61

When Michael saw this host, he first grew pale,
  As angels can; next, like Italian twilight,
He turned all colors—as a peacock's tail,
  Or sunset streaming through a Gothic skylight
In some old abbey, or a trout not stale,   485
  Or distant lightning on the horizon *by* night,
Or a fresh rainbow, or a grand review
Of thirty regiments in red, green, and blue.

62

Then he addressed himself to Satan: "Why—
  My good old friend, for such I deem you,
    though   490

471. Jonathan: name for Americans and America. 475. Otaheite's isle: Tahiti.

Our different parties make us fight so shy,
    I ne'er mistake you for a *personal* foe;
Our difference is *political*, and I
    Trust that, whatever may occur below,
You know my great respect for you: and this   495
Makes me regret whate'er you do amiss—

63

"Why, my dear Lucifer, would you abuse
    My call for witnesses? I did not mean
That you should half of earth and hell produce;
    'Tis even superfluous, since two honest, clean,   500
True testimonies are enough: we lose
    Our time, nay, our eternity, between
The accusation and defense: if we
Hear both, 'twill stretch our immortality."

64

Satan replied, "To me the matter is   505
    Indifferent, in a personal point of view:
I can have fifty better souls than this
    With far less trouble than we have gone through
Already; and I merely argued his
    Late majesty of Britain's case with you   510
Upon a point of form: you may dispose
Of him; I've kings enough below, God knows!"

65

Thus spoke the demon (late called "multifaced"
    By multo-scribbling Southey). "Then we'll call
One or two persons of the myriads placed   515
    Around our congress, and dispense with all
The rest," quoth Michael: "Who may be so graced
    As to speak first? there's choice enough—who
      shall
It be?" Then Satan answered, "There are many;
But you may choose Jack Wilkes° as well as any."

66

A merry, cock-eyed, curious-looking sprite   521
    Upon the instant started from the throng,

520. Jack Wilkes: John Wilkes, an eighteenth-century wit
and radical politician who attacked the monarchy and was
exiled; he later returned to Parliament and had his record
cleared (ll. 557–58), and in his last years he rose in society
(l. 570).

Dressed in a fashion now forgotten quite;
    For all the fashions of the flesh stick long
By people in the next world; where unite   525
    All the costumes since Adam's, right or wrong,
From Eve's fig leaf down to the petticoat,
Almost as scanty, of days less remote.

67

The spirit looked around upon the crowds
    Assembled, and exclaimed, "My friends of all   530
The spheres, we shall catch cold amongst these
      clouds;
    So let's to business: why this general call?
If those are freeholders I see in shrouds,
    And 'tis for an election that they bawl,
Behold a candidate with unturned coat!   535
Saint Peter, may I count upon your vote?"

68

"Sir," replied Michael, "you mistake; these things
    Are of a former life, and what we do
Above is more august; to judge of kings
    Is the tribunal met: so now you know."   540
"Then I presume those gentlemen with wings,"
    Said Wilkes, "are cherubs; and that soul below
Looks much like George the Third, but to my mind
A good deal older—Bless me! is he blind?"

69

"He is what you behold him, and his doom   545
    Depends upon his deeds," the angel said.
"If you have aught to arraign in him, the tomb
    Gives license to the humblest beggar's head
To lift itself against the loftiest."—"Some,"
    Said Wilkes, "don't wait to see them laid in lead,
For such a liberty—and I, for one,   551
Have told them what I thought beneath the sun."

70

"*Above* the sun repeat, then, what thou hast
    To urge against him," said the archangel.
      "Why,"
Replied the spirit, "since old scores are past,   555
    Must I turn evidence? In faith, not I.
Besides, I beat him hollow at the last,

With all his Lords and Commons: in the sky
I don't like ripping up old stories, since
His conduct was but natural in a prince.   560

71

"Foolish, no doubt, and wicked, to oppress
   A poor unlucky devil without a shilling;
But then I blame the man himself much less
   Than Bute and Grafton,° and shall be unwilling
To see him punished here for their excess,   565
   Since they were both damned long ago, and still
   in
Their place below: for me, I have forgiven,
And vote his 'habeas corpus' into heaven."

72

"Wilkes," said the Devil, "I understand all this;
   You turned to half a courtier ere you died,   570
And seem to think it would not be amiss
   To grow a whole one on the other side
Of Charon's ferry; you forget that *his*
   Reign is concluded; whatsoe'er betide,
He won't be sovereign more: you've lost your
   labor   575
For at the best he will but be your neighbor.

73

"However, I knew what to think of it,
   When I beheld you in your jesting way
Flitting and whispering round about the spit
   Where Belial, upon duty for the day,   580
With Fox's lard was basting William Pitt,°
   His pupil; I knew what to think, I say:
That fellow even in hell breeds farther ills;
I'll have him *gagged*—'twas one of his own bills.°

74

"Call Junius!"° From the crowd a shadow stalked,
   And at the name there was a general squeeze,   586
So that the very ghosts no longer walked

564. **Grafton:** the duke of Grafton, one of the king's
servile ministers. 581. **Fox's . . . Pitt:** Charles James Fox,
a fat prime minister who attacked William Pitt. 584. **bills:**
Alien and Sedition Bills of 1795. 585. **Junius:** pseudonym
for a satirist who wrote against the monarchy; his works
were variously attributed to Edmund Burke, John Horne
Tooke, and Sir Philip Francis (ll. 631–32).

In comfort, at their own aërial ease,
But were all rammed, and jammed (but to be
   balked,
   As we shall see), and jostled hands and knees,   590
Like wind compressed and pent within a bladder,
Or like a human colic, which is sadder.

75

The shadow came—a tall, thin, gray-haired figure,
   That looked as it had been a shade on earth;
Quick in its motions, with an air of vigor,   595
   But nought to mark its breeding or its birth:
Now it waxed little, then again grew bigger,
   With now an air of gloom, or savage mirth;
But as you gazed upon its features, they
Changed every instant—to *what*, none could say.

76

The more intently the ghosts gazed, the less   601
   Could they distinguish whose the features were;
The Devil himself seemed puzzled even to guess;
   They varied like a dream—now here, now there;
And several people swore from out the press,   605
   They knew him perfectly; and one could swear
He was his father: upon which another
Was sure he was his mother's cousin's brother:

77

Another, that he was a duke, or knight,
   An orator, a lawyer, or a priest,   610
A nabob, a man-midwife; but the wight
   Mysterious changed his countenance at least
As oft as they their minds: though in full sight
   He stood, the puzzle only was increased;
The man was a phantasmagoria in   615
Himself—he was so volatile and thin.

78

The moment that you had pronounced him *one*,
   Presto! his face changed, and he was another;
And when that change was hardly well put on,
   It varied, till I don't think his own mother   620
(If that he had a mother) would her son
   Have known, he shifted so from one to t'other;

Till guessing from a pleasure grew a task,
At this epistolary "Iron Mask."°

79

For sometimes he like Cerberus would seem— 625
    "Three gentlemen at once" (as sagely says
Good Mrs. Malaprop°); then you might deem
    That he was not even *one*; now many rays
Were flashing round him; and now a thick steam
    Hid him from sight—like fogs on London days:
Now Burke, now Tooke, he grew to people's
    fancies,   631
And certes often like Sir Philip Francis.

80

I've an hypothesis—'tis quite my own;
    I never let it out till now, for fear
Of doing people harm about the throne,   635
    And injuring some minister or peer,
On whom the stigma might perhaps be blown;
    It is—my gentle public, lend thine ear!
'Tis, that what Junius we are wont to call
Was *really*, *truly*, nobody at all.   640

81

I don't see wherefore letters should not be
    Written without hands, since we daily view
Them written without heads; and books, we see,
    Are filled as well without the latter too:
And really till we fix on somebody   645
    For certain sure to claim them as his due,
Their author, like the Niger's mouth,° will bother
The world to say if *there* be mouth or author.

82

"And who and what art thou?" the archangel said.
    "For *that* you may consult my title page," 650
Replied this mighty shadow of a shade:
    "If I have kept my secret half an age,
I scarce shall tell it now."—"Canst thou upbraid,"

624. **Iron Mask:** The "Man in the Iron Mask" was a state
prisoner during Louis XIV's reign whose identity has never
been established. 627. **Mrs. Malaprop:** character in R. B.
Sheridan's *The Rivals* noted for her misuse of words. 647.
Niger's mouth: Several expeditions to this river had failed
recently.

Continued Michael, "George Rex, or allege
Aught further?" Junius answered, "You had
    better   655
First ask him for *his* answer to my letter:

83

"My charges upon record will outlast
    The brass of both his epitaph and tomb."
"Repent'st thou not," said Michael, "of some past
    Exaggeration? something which may doom   660
Thyself if false, as him if true? Thou wast
    Too bitter—is it not so?—in thy gloom
Of passion?"—"Passion!" cried the phantom dim,
"I loved my country, and I hated him.

84

"What I have written, I have written:° let   665
    The rest be on his head or mine!" So spoke
Old "*Nominis Umbra*";° and while speaking yet,
    Away he melted in celestial smoke.
Then Satan said to Michael, "Don't forget
    To call George Washington, and John Horne
    Tooke,°   670
And Franklin"—but at this time there was heard
A cry for room, though not a phantom stirred.

85

At length with jostling, elbowing, and the aid
    Of cherubim appointed to that post,
The devil Asmodeus° to the circle made   675
    His way, and looked as if his journey cost
Some trouble. When his burden down he laid,
    "What's this?" cried Michael; "why, 'tis not a
    ghost?"
"I know it," quoth the incubus; "but he
Shall be one, if you leave the affair to me.   680

86

"Confound the renegado! I have sprained
    My left wing, he's so heavy; one would think
Some of his works about his neck were chained.

665. **What . . . written:** the words of Pontius Pilate (see
John 19:22). 667. **Nominis Umbra:** the shadow of a name.
670. **Tooke:** He opposed the war against the colonies. 675.
Asmodeus: a devil in Alain René Le Sage's *The Lame Devil*
who transports a character to a mountain-top.

But to the point; while hovering o'er the brink
Of Skiddaw° (where as usual it still rained),   685
    I saw a taper, far below me, wink,
And stooping, caught this fellow at a libel—
No less on history than the Holy Bible.

87

"The former is the Devil's scripture, and
    The latter yours, good Michael: so the affair   690
Belongs to all of us, you understand.
    I snatched him up just as you see him there,
And brought him off for sentence out of hand:
    I've scarcely been ten minutes in the air—
At least a quarter it can hardly be: 695
    I dare say that his wife is still at tea."

88

Here Satan said, "I know this man of old,
    And have expected him for some time here;
A sillier fellow you will scarce behold,
    Or more conceited in his petty sphere: 700
But surely it was not worth while to fold
    Such trash below your wing, Asmodeus dear:
We had the poor wretch safe (without being bored
With carriage) coming of his own accord.

89

"But since he's here, let's see what he has done."
    "Done!" cried Asmodeus, "he anticipates   706
The very business you are now upon,
    And scribbles as if head clerk to the Fates.
Who knows to what his ribaldry may run,
    When such an ass as this, like Balaam's,°
        prates?"   710
"Let's hear," quoth Michael, "what he has to say:
You know we're bound to that in every way."

90

Now the bard, glad to get an audience, which
    By no means often was his case below,
Began to cough, and hawk, and hem, and pitch   715
    His voice into that awful note of woe
To all unhappy hearers within reach

Of poets when the tide of rhyme's in flow;
    But stuck fast with his first hexameter,
Not one of all whose gouty feet would stir.   720

91

But ere the spavined dactyls could be spurred
    Into recitative, in great dismay
Both cherubim and seraphim were heard
    To murmur loudly through their long array;
And Michael rose ere he could get a word   725
    Of all his foundered verses under way,
And cried, "For God's sake stop, my friend!
        'twere best—
Non Di, non homines°—you know the rest."

92

A general bustle spread throughout the throng,
    Which seemed to hold all verse in detestation;
The angels had of course enough of song   731
    When upon service; and the generation
Of ghosts had heard too much in life, not long
    Before, to profit by a new occasion:
The monarch, mute till then, exclaimed, "What!
        what!   735
Pye° come again? No more—no more of that!"

93

The tumult grew; an universal cough
    Convulsed the skies, as during a debate,
When Castlereagh° has been up long enough
    (Before he was first minister of state,   740
I mean—the *slaves hear now*); some cried "Off,
        off!"
    As at a farce; till, grown quite desperate,
The bard Saint Peter prayed to interpose
(Himself an author) only for his prose.

94

The varlet was not an ill-favored knave;   745
    A good deal like a vulture in the face,

---

728. Non Di, non homines: "Mediocrity in poets has never
been tolerated by *either men, or gods*, or booksellers"
(Horace, "Art of Poetry," ll. 372–73). **736. Pye:** Henry
James Pye, a bad poet, often ridiculed, who was laureate
before Southey. **739. Castlereagh:** Viscount Castlereagh,
foreign secretary whom the House of Commons will hear as
slaves (l. 741).

685. Skiddaw: mountain near Southey's home. **710. Balaam:**
See Numbers 22:1–35.

With a hook nose and a hawk's eye, which gave
　　A smart and sharper-looking sort of grace
To his whole aspect, which, though rather grave,
　　Was by no means so ugly as his case;　　750
But that, indeed, was hopeless as can be,
Quite a poetic felony "*de se.*"°

95

Then Michael blew his trump, and stilled the noise
　　With one still greater, as is yet the mode
On earth besides; except some grumbling voice, 755
　　Which now and then will make a slight inroad
Upon decorous silence, few will twice
　　Lift up their lungs when fairly overcrowed;
And now the bard could plead his own bad cause,
With all the attitudes of self-applause.　　760

96

He said—(I only give the heads)—he said,
　　He meant no harm in scribbling; 'twas his way
Upon all topics; 'twas, besides, his bread,
　　Of which he buttered both sides; 'twould delay
Too long the assembly (he was pleased to dread),
　　And take up rather more time than a day,　766
To name his works—he would but cite a few—
"Wat Tyler"—"Rhymes on Blenheim"—"Water-
　　loo."

97

He had written praises of a regicide;°
　　He had written praises of all kings whatever; 770
He had written for republics far and wide,
　　And then against them bitterer than ever:
For pantisocracy° he once had cried
　　Aloud, a scheme less moral than 'twas clever;
Then grew a hearty anti-jacobin—　　775
Had turned his coat—and would have turned his
　　skin.

98

He had sung against all battles, and again
　　In their high praise and glory; he had called
Reviewing "the ungentle craft," and then
　　Become as base a critic as e'er crawled—　780
Fed, paid, and pampered by the very men
　　By whom his muse and morals had been mauled:
He had written much blank verse, and blanker
　　prose,
And more of both than anybody knows.

99

He had written Wesley's life—here turning round
　　To Satan, "Sir, I'm ready to write yours,　786
In two octavo volumes, nicely bound,
　　With notes and preface, all that most allures
The pious purchaser; and there's no ground
　　For fear, for I can choose my own reviewers:
So let me have the proper documents,　　791
That I may add you to my other saints."

100

Satan bowed, and was silent. "Well, if you,
　　With amiable modesty, decline
My offer, what says Michael? There are few　795
　　Whose memoirs could be rendered more divine.
Mine is a pen of all work; not so new
　　As it was once, but I would make you shine
Like your own trumpet. By the way, my own
Has more of brass in it, and is as well blown. 800

101

"But talking about trumpets, here's my vision!
　　Now you shall judge, all people; yes, you shall
Judge with my judgment, and by my decision
　　Be guided who shall enter heaven or fall.
I settle all these things by intuition,　　805
　　Times present, past, to come, heaven, hell, and
　　all,
Like King Alfonso.° When I thus see double,
I save the Deity some worlds of trouble."

---

752. **felony de se:** (felony against himself) suicide. **769.**
praises of a regicide: Southey wrote a poem to Henry Martin,
one of the judges who condemned Charles I. **773. panti-**
socracy: utopian community planned by Southey and
Coleridge.

807. **King Alfonso:** [Byron's note] King Alfonso [a thirteenth-century Spaniard], speaking of the Ptolomean system,
said that "had he been consulted at the creation of the
world, he would have spared the Maker some absurdities."

102

He ceased, and drew forth an MS.; and no
   Persuasion on the part of devils, saints,   810
Or angels, now could stop the torrent; so
   He read the first three lines of the contents;
But at the fourth, the whole spiritual show
   Had vanished, with variety of scents,
Ambrosial and sulfureous, as they sprang,   815
Like lightning, off from his "melodious twang."

103

Those grand heroics acted as a spell:
   The angels stopped their ears and plied their
      pinions;
   The devils ran howling, deafened, down to hell;
   The ghosts fled, gibbering, for their own do-
      minions—   820
(For 'tis not yet decided where they dwell,
   And I leave every man to his opinions);
Michael took refuge in his trump—but, lo!
His teeth were set on edge, he could not blow!

104

Saint Peter, who has hitherto been known   825
   For an impetuous saint, upraised his keys,
And at the fifth line knocked the poet down;
   Who fell like Phaeton, but more at ease,
Into his lake, for there he did not drown;
   A different web being by the Destinies   830
Woven for the laureate's final wreath, whene'er
Reform shall happen either here or there.

105

He first sank to the bottom—like his works,
   But soon rose to the surface—like himself;
For all corrupted things are buoyed like corks,
   By their own rottenness, light as an elf,   836
Or wisp that flits o'er a morass: he lurks,
   It may be, still, like dull books on a shelf,
In his own den, to scrawl some "Life" or "Vision,"
As Welborn says—"the devil turned precisian."°

---

840. **Welborn . . . precisian:** A character in Philip Mas-
singer's play *A New Way to Pay Old Debts* speaks these
lines; a precisian is a Puritan.

106

As for the rest, to come to the conclusion   841
   Of this true dream, the telescope is gone
Which kept my optics free from all delusion,
   And showed me what I in my turn have shown;
All I saw farther, in the last confusion,   845
   Was, that King George slipped into heaven for
      one;
And when the tumult dwindled to a calm,
I left him practicing the hundredth psalm.

HERMAN MELVILLE
1819–1891

Bartleby, The Scrivener: A Story of Wall Street

I am a rather elderly man. The nature of my avocations, for the last thirty years, has brought me into more than ordinary contact with what would seem an interesting and somewhat singular set of men, of whom, as yet, nothing, that I know of, has ever been written—I mean, the law-copyists, or scriveners. I have known very many of them, professionally and privately, and, if I pleased, could relate divers histories, at which good-natured gentlemen might smile, and sentimental souls might weep. But I waive the biographies of all other scriveners, for a few passages in the life of Bartleby, who was a scrivener, the strangest I ever saw, or heard of. While, of other law-copyists, I might write the complete life, of Bartleby nothing of that sort can be done. I believe that no materials exist for a full and satisfactory biography of this man. It is an irreparable loss to literature. Bartleby was one of those beings of whom nothing is ascertainable, except from the original sources, and, in his case, those are very small. What my own astonished eyes saw of Bartleby, *that* is all I know of him, except, indeed, one vague report, which will appear in the sequel.

Ere introducing the scrivener, as he first appeared to me, it is fit I make some mention of myself, my *employés*, my business, my chambers, and general surroundings; because some such description is indispensable to an adequate understanding of the chief character about to be presented. Imprimis: I am a man who, from his youth upwards, has been filled with a profound conviction that the easiest way of life is the best. Hence, though I belong to a profession proverbially energetic and nervous, even to turbulence, at times, yet nothing of that sort have I ever suffered to invade my peace. I am one of those unambitious lawyers who never addresses a jury, or in any way draws down public applause; but, in the cool tranquility of a snug retreat, do a snug business among rich men's bonds, and mortgages, and title-deeds. All who know me, consider me an eminently *safe* man. The late John Jacob Astor,[1] a personage little given to poetic enthusiasm, had no hesitation in pronouncing my first grand point to be prudence; my next, method. I do not speak it in vanity, but simply record the fact, that I was not unemployed in my profession by the late John Jacob Astor; a name which, I admit, I love to repeat; for it hath a rounded and orbicular sound to it, and rings like unto bullion. I will freely add, that I was not insensible to the late John Jacob Astor's good opinion.

Some time prior to the period at which this little history begins, my avocations had been largely increased. The good old office, now extinct in the State of New York, of a Master in Chancery, had been conferred upon me. It was not a very arduous office, but very pleasantly remunerative. I seldom lose my temper; much more seldom indulge in dangerous indignation at wrongs and outrages; but, I must be permitted to be rash here, and declare, that I consider the sudden and violent abrogation of the office of Master in Chancery, by the new constitution, as a ———— premature act; inasmuch as I had counted upon a life-lease of the profits, whereas I only received those of a few short years. But this is by the way.

My chambers were up stairs, at No. —— Wall Street. At one end, they looked upon the white wall of the interior of a spacious skylight shaft, penetrating the building from top to bottom.

This view might have been considered rather tame than otherwise, deficient in what landscape painters call "life." But, if so, the view from the other end of my chambers offered, at least, a contrast, if nothing more. In that direction, my windows commanded an unobstructed view of a lofty brick wall, black by age and everlasting shade; which wall required no spyglass to bring out its lurking beauties, but, for the benefit of all nearsighted spectators, was pushed up to within ten feet of my window panes. Owing to the great height of the surrounding buildings, and my chambers being on the second floor, the interval between this wall and mine not a little resembled a huge square cistern.

At the period just preceding the advent of Bartleby, I had two persons as copyists in my employment, and a promising lad as an office-boy. First, Turkey; second, Nippers; third, Ginger Nut. These may seem names, the like of which are not usually found in the directory. In truth, they were nicknames, mutually conferred upon each other by my three clerks, and were deemed expressive of their respective persons or characters. Turkey was a short, pursy Englishman, of about my own age —that is, somewhere not far from sixty. In the morning, one might say, his face was of a fine florid hue, but after twelve o'clock, meridian—his dinner hour—it blazed like a grate full of Christmas coals; and continued blazing—but, as it were, with a gradual wane—till six o'clock P.M., or thereabouts; after which, I saw no more of the proprietor of the face, which, gaining its meridian with the sun, seemed to set with it, to rise, culminate, and decline the following day, with the like regularity and undiminished glory. There are many singular coincidences I have known in the course of my life, not the least among which was the fact, that, exactly when Turkey displayed his fullest beams from his red and radiant countenance, just then, too, at that critical moment, began the daily period when I considered his business capacities as seriously disturbed for the remainder of the twenty-four hours. Not that he was absolutely idle, or averse to business, then; far from it. The difficulty was, he was apt to be altogether too energetic. There was a strange, inflamed, flurried, flighty recklessness of activity about him. He would be incautious in dipping his pen into his inkstand. All his blots upon my documents were dropped there after twelve o'clock meridian. Indeed, not only would he be reckless, and sadly given to making blots in the afternoon, but, some days, he went

BARTLEBY, THE SCRIVENER. **1. Astor:** John Jacob Astor (1763–1848), a penniless immigrant who became rich in the western fur trade.

further, and was rather noisy. At such times, too, his face flamed with augmented blazonry, as if cannel coal had been heaped on anthracite. He made an unpleasant racket with his chair; spilled his sand-box; in mending his pens, impatiently split them all to pieces, and threw them on the floor in a sudden passion; stood up, and leaned over his table, boxing his papers about in a most indecorous manner, very sad to behold in an elderly man like him. Nevertheless, as he was in many ways a most valuable person to me, and all the time before twelve o'clock meridian, was the quickest, steadiest creature, too, accomplishing a great deal of work in a style not easily to be matched—for these reasons, I was willing to overlook his eccentricities, though, indeed, occasionally, I remonstrated with him. I did this very gently, however, because, though the civilest, nay, the blandest and most reverential of men in the morning, yet, in the afternoon, he was disposed, upon provocation, to be slightly rash with his tongue—in fact, insolent. Now, valuing his morning services as I did, and resolved not to lose them—yet, at the same time, made uncomfortable by his inflamed ways after twelve o'clock—and being a man of peace, unwilling by my admonitions to call forth unseemly retorts from him, I took upon me, one Saturday noon (he was always worse on Saturdays) to hint to him, very kindly, that, perhaps, now that he was growing old, it might be well to abridge his labors; in short, he need not come to my chambers after twelve o'clock, but, dinner over, had best go home to his lodgings, and rest himself till teatime. But no; he insisted upon his afternoon devotions. His countenance became intolerably fervid, as he oratorically assured me—gesticulating with a long ruler at the other end of the room—that if his services in the morning were useful, how indispensable, then, in the afternoon?

"With submission, sir," said Turkey, on this occasion, "I consider myself your right-hand man. In the morning I but marshal and deploy my columns; but in the afternoon I put myself at their head and gallantly charge the foe, thus"—and he made a violent thrust with the ruler.

"But the blots, Turkey," intimated I.

"True; but, with submission, sir, behold these hairs! I am getting old. Surely, sir, a blot or two of a warm afternoon is not to be severely urged against gray hairs. Old age—even if it blot the page—is honorable. With submission, sir, we *both* are getting old."

This appeal to my fellow-feeling was hardly to be resisted. At all events, I saw that go he would not. So, I made up my mind to let him stay, resolving, nevertheless, to see to it that, during the afternoon, he had to do with my less important papers.

Nippers, the second on my list, was a whiskered, sallow, and, upon the whole, rather piratical-looking young man, of about five and twenty. I always deemed him the victim of two evil powers—ambition and indigestion. The ambition was evinced by a certain impatience of the duties of a mere copyist, an unwarrantable usurpation of strictly professional affairs, such as the original drawing up of legal documents. The indigestion seemed betokened in an occasional nervous testiness and grinning irritability, causing the teeth to audibly grind together over mistakes committed in copying; unnecessary maledictions, hissed, rather than spoken, in the heat of business; and especially by a continual discontent with the height of the table where he worked. Though of a very ingenious, mechanical turn, Nippers could never get this table to suit him. He put chips under it, blocks of various sorts, bits of pasteboard, and at last went so far as to attempt an exquisite adjustment, by final pieces of folded blotting-paper. But no invention would answer. If, for the sake of easing his back, he brought the table lid at a sharp angle well up towards his chin, and wrote there like a man using the steep roof of a Dutch house for his desk, then he declared that it stopped the circulation in his arms. If now he lowered the table to his waistbands, and stooped over it in writing, then there was a sore aching in his back. In short, the truth of the matter was, Nippers knew not what he wanted. Or, if he wanted anything, it was to be rid of a scrivener's table altogether. Among the manifestations of his diseased ambition was a fondness he had for receiving visits from certain ambiguous-looking fellows in seedy coats, whom he called his clients. Indeed, I was aware that not only was he, at times, considerable of a ward-politician, but he occasionally did a little business at the Justices' courts, and was not unknown on the steps of the Tombs. I have good reason to believe, however, that one individual who called upon him at my chambers, and who, with a grand air, he insisted was his client, was no other than a dun, and the alleged title-deed, a bill. But, with all his failings, and the annoyances he caused me, Nippers, like his compatriot Turkey, was a very useful man to me; wrote a neat, swift hand; and, when he chose, was not deficient in a gentlemanly sort of deportment. Added to this, he always dressed in a gentlemanly sort of way; and so, incidentally, reflected credit upon my chambers. Whereas, with respect to Turkey, I had much ado to keep him from being a reproach to me. His clothes were apt to look oily, and smell of eating-houses. He wore his pantaloons very loose and baggy in summer. His coats were execrable; his hat not to be handled. But while the hat was a thing of indifference to me, inasmuch as his natural civility and deference, as a dependent Englishman, always led him to doff it the moment he entered the room, yet his coat was another matter. Concerning his coats, I reasoned with him; but with no effect. The truth was, I suppose, that a man with so small an income could not afford to sport such a lustrous face and a lustrous coat at one and the same time. As Nippers once observed, Turkey's money went chiefly for red ink. One winter day, I presented Turkey with a highly respectable-looking coat of my own—a padded gray coat, of a most comfortable warmth, and which buttoned straight up from the knee to the neck. I thought Turkey would appreciate the favor, and abate his rashness and obstreperousness of afternoons. But no; I verily believe that buttoning himself up in so downy and blanketlike a coat had a pernicious effect upon him—upon the same principle that too much oats are bad for horses. In fact, precisely as a rash, restive horse is said to feel his oats, so Turkey felt his coat. It made him insolent. He was a man whom prosperity harmed.

Though, concerning the self-indulgent habits of Turkey, I had my own private surmises, yet, touching Nippers, I was well persuaded that, whatever might be his faults in other respects, he was, at least, a temperate young man. But, indeed, nature herself seemed to have been his vintner, and, at his birth, charged him so thoroughly with an irritable, brandylike disposition, that all subsequent potations were needless. When I consider how, amid the stillness of my chambers, Nippers would sometimes impatiently rise from his seat, and stooping over his table, spread his arms wide apart, seize the whole desk, and move it, and jerk

it, with a grim, grinding motion on the floor, as if the table were a perverse voluntary agent and vexing him, I plainly perceive that, for Nippers, brandy-and-water were altogether superfluous.

It was fortunate for me that, owing to its peculiar cause—indigestion—the irritability and consequent nervousness of Nippers were mainly observable in the morning, while in the afternoon he was comparatively mild. So that, Turkey's paroxysms only coming on about twelve o'clock, I never had to do with their eccentricities at one time. Their fits relieved each other, like guards. When Nippers's was on, Turkey's was off; and vice versa. This was a good natural arrangement, under the circumstances.

Ginger Nut, the third on my list, was a lad, some twelve years old. His father was a carman, ambitious of seeing his son on the bench instead of a cart, before he died. So he sent him to my office, as student at law, errand-boy, cleaner and sweeper, at the rate of one dollar a week. He had a little desk to himself; but he did not use it much. Upon inspection, the drawer exhibited a great array of the shells of various sorts of nuts. Indeed, to this quick-witted youth, the whole noble science of the law was contained in a nutshell. Not the least among the employments of Ginger Nut, as well as one which he discharged with the most alacrity, was his duty as cake and apple purveyor for Turkey and Nippers. Copying law-papers being proverbially a dry, husky sort of business, my two scriveners were fain to moisten their mouths very often with Spitzenbergs,[2] to be had at the numerous stalls nigh the custom house and post office. Also, they sent Ginger Nut very frequently for that peculiar cake—small, flat, round, and very spicy—after which he had been named by them. Of a cold morning, when business was but dull, Turkey would gobble up scores of these cakes, as if they were mere wafers—indeed, they sell them at the rate of six or eight for a penny—the scrape of his pen blending with the crunching of the crisp particles in his mouth. Rashest of all the fiery afternoon blunders and flurried rashnesses of Turkey, was his once moistening a ginger-cake between his lips, and clapping it on to a mortgage, for a seal. I came within an ace of dismissing him then. But he mollified me by making an oriental bow, and saying—

2. **Spitzenbergs:** fine variety of apple.

"With submission, sir, it was generous of me to find you in stationery on my own account."

Now my original business—that of a conveyancer and title hunter, and drawer-up of recondite documents of all sorts—was considerably increased by receiving the master's office. There was now great work for scriveners. Not only must I push the clerks already with me, but I must have additional help.

In answer to my advertisement, a motionless young man one morning stood upon my office threshold, the door being open, for it was summer. I can see that figure now—pallidly neat, pitiably respectable, incurably forlorn! It was Bartleby.

After a few words touching his qualifications, I engaged him, glad to have among my corps of copyists a man of so singularly sedate an aspect, which I thought might operate beneficially upon the flighty temper of Turkey, and the fiery one of Nippers.

I should have stated before that ground glass folding-doors divided my premises into two parts, one of which was occupied by my scriveners, the other by myself. According to my humor, I threw open these doors, or closed them. I resolved to assign Bartleby a corner by the folding-doors, but on my side of them, so as to have this quiet man within easy call, in case any trifling thing was to be done. I placed his desk close up to a small side-window in that part of the room, a window which originally had afforded a lateral view of certain grimy backyards and bricks, but which, owing to subsequent erections, commanded at present no view at all, though it gave some light. Within three feet of the panes was a wall, and the light came down from far above, between two lofty buildings, as from a very small opening in a dome. Still further to a satisfactory arrangement, I procured a high green folding screen, which might entirely isolate Bartleby from my sight, though not remove him from my voice. And thus, in a manner, privacy and society were conjoined.

At first, Bartleby did an extraordinary quantity of writing. As if long famishing for something to copy, he seemed to gorge himself on my documents. There was no pause for digestion. He ran a day and night line, copying by sunlight and by candle-light. I should have been quite delighted with his application, had he been cheerfully industrious. But he wrote on silently, palely, mechanically.

It is, of course, an indispensable part of a scrivener's business to verify the accuracy of his copy, word by word. Where there are two or more scriveners in an office, they assist each other in this examination, one reading from the copy, the other holding the original. It is a very dull, wearisome, and lethargic affair. I can readily imagine that, to some sanguine temperaments, it would be altogether intolerable. For example, I cannot credit that the mettlesome poet, Byron, would have contentedly sat down with Bartleby to examine a law document of, say five hundred pages, closely written in a crimpy hand.

Now and then, in the haste of business, it had been my habit to assist in comparing some brief document myself, calling Turkey or Nippers for this purpose. One object I had, in placing Bartleby so handy to me behind the screen, was to avail myself of his services on such trivial occasions. It was on the third day, I think, of his being with me, and before any necessity had arisen for having his own writing examined, that, being much hurried to complete a small affair I had in hand, I abruptly called to Bartleby. In my haste and natural expectancy of instant compliance, I sat with my head bent over the original on my desk, and my right hand sideways, and somewhat nervously extended with the copy, so that, immediately upon emerging from his retreat, Bartleby might snatch it and proceed to business without the least delay.

In this very attitude did I sit when I called to him, rapidly stating what it was I wanted him to do—namely, to examine a small paper with me. Imagine my surprise, nay, my consternation, when, without moving from his privacy, Bartleby, in a singularly mild, firm voice, replied, "I would prefer not to."

I sat awhile in perfect silence, rallying my stunned faculties. Immediately it occurred to me that my ears had deceived me, or Bartleby had entirely misunderstood my meaning. I repeated my request in the clearest tone I could assume; but in quite as clear a one came the previous reply, "I would prefer not to."

"Prefer not to," echoed I, rising in high excitement, and crossing the room with a stride. "What do you mean? Are you moonstruck? I want you to help me compare this sheet here—take it," and I thrust it towards him.

"I would prefer not to," said he.

I looked at him steadfastly. His face was leanly composed; his gray eye dimly calm. Not a wrinkle of agitation rippled him. Had there been the least uneasiness, anger, impatience, or impertinence in his manner; in other words, had there been any thing ordinarily human about him, doubtless I should have violently dismissed him from the premises. But as it was, I should have as soon thought of turning my pale plaster-of-paris bust of Cicero out of doors. I stood gazing at him awhile, as he went on with his own writing, and then reseated myself at my desk. This is very strange, thought I. What had one best do? But my business hurried me. I concluded to forget the matter for the present, reserving it for my future leisure. So calling Nippers from the other room, the paper was speedily examined.

A few days after this, Bartleby concluded four lengthy documents, being quadruplicates of a week's testimony taken before me in my High Court of Chancery. It became necessary to examine them. It was an important suit, and great accuracy was imperative. Having all things arranged, I called Turkey, Nippers, and Ginger Nut from the next room, meaning to place the four copies in the hands of my four clerks, while I should read from the original. Accordingly, Turkey, Nippers, and Ginger Nut had taken their seats in a row, each with his document in his hand, when I called to Bartleby to join this interesting group.

"Bartleby! quick, I am waiting."

I heard a slow scrape of his chair legs on the uncarpeted floor, and soon he appeared standing at the entrance of his hermitage.

"What is wanted?" said he, mildly.

"The copies, the copies," said I, hurriedly. "We are going to examine them. There—" and I held towards him the fourth quadruplicate.

"I would prefer not to," he said, and gently disappeared behind the screen.

For a few moments I was turned into a pillar of salt, standing at the head of my seated column of clerks. Recovering myself, I advanced towards the screen, and demanded the reason for such extraordinary conduct.

"*Why* do you refuse?"

"I would prefer not to."

With any other man I should have flown outright into a dreadful passion, scorned all further words, and thrust him ignominiously from my presence. But there was something about Bartleby that not only strangely disarmed me, but in a wonderful manner, touched and disconcerted me. I began to reason with him.

"These are your own copies we are about to examine. It is labor saving to you, because one examination will answer for your four papers. It is common usage. Every copyist is bound to help examine his copy. Is it not so? Will you not speak? Answer!"

"I prefer not to," he replied in a flutelike tone. It seemed to me that, while I had been addressing him, he carefully revolved every statement that I made; fully comprehended the meaning; could not gainsay the irresistible conclusion; but, at the same time, some paramount consideration prevailed with him to reply as he did.

"You are decided, then, not to comply with my request—a request made according to common usage and common sense?"

He briefly gave me to understand, that on that point my judgment was sound. Yes: his decision was irreversible.

It is not seldom the case that, when a man is browbeaten in some unprecedented and violently unreasonable way, he begins to stagger in his own plainest faith. He begins, as it were, vaguely to surmise that, wonderful as it may be, all the justice and all the reason is on the other side. Accordingly, if any disinterested persons are present, he turns to them for some reinforcement of his own faltering mind.

"Turkey," said I, "what do you think of this? Am I not right?"

"With submission, sir," said Turkey, in his blandest tone, "I think that you are."

"Nippers," said I, "what do *you* think of it?"

"I think I should kick him out of the office."

(The reader, of nice[3] perceptions, will here perceive that, it being morning, Turkey's answer is couched in polite and tranquil terms, but Nippers replies in ill-tempered ones. Or, to repeat a previous sentence, Nippers's ugly mood was on duty, and Turkey's off.)

"Ginger Nut," said I, willing to enlist the smallest suffrage in my behalf, "what do *you* think of it?"

---

3. **nice:** fine, discriminating.

"I think, sir, he's a little *luny*," replied Ginger Nut, with a grin.

"You hear what they say," said I, turning towards the screen, "come forth and do your duty."

But he vouchsafed no reply. I pondered a moment in sore perplexity. But once more business hurried me. I determined again to postpone the consideration of this dilemma to my future leisure. With a little trouble we made out to examine the papers without Bartleby, though at every page or two Turkey deferentially dropped his opinion, that this proceeding was quite out of the common; while Nippers, twitching in his chair with a dyspeptic nervousness, ground out, between his set teeth, occasional hissing maledictions against the stubborn oaf behind the screen. And for his (Nippers's) part, this was the first and the last time he would do another man's business without pay.

Meanwhile Bartleby sat in his hermitage, oblivious to everything but his own peculiar business there.

Some days passed, the scrivener being employed upon another lengthy work. His late remarkable conduct led me to regard his ways narrowly. I observed that he never went to dinner; indeed, that he never went anywhere. As yet I had never, of my personal knowledge, known him to be outside of my office. He was a perpetual sentry in the corner. At about eleven o'clock though, in the morning, I noticed that Ginger Nut would advance toward the opening in Bartleby's screen, as if silently beckoned thither by a gesture invisible to me where I sat. The boy would then leave the office, jingling a few pence, and reappear with a handful of ginger-nuts, which he delivered in the hermitage, receiving two of the cakes for his trouble.

He lives, then, on ginger-nuts, thought I; never eats a dinner, properly speaking; he must be a vegetarian, then; but no; he never eats even vegetables; he eats nothing but ginger-nuts. My mind then ran on in reveries concerning the probable effects upon the human constitution of living entirely on ginger-nuts. Ginger-nuts are so called, because they contain ginger as one of their peculiar constituents, and the final flavoring one. Now, what was ginger? A hot, spicy thing. Was Bartleby hot and spicy? Not at all. Ginger, then, had no effect upon Bartleby. Probably he preferred it should have none.

Nothing so aggravates an earnest person as a passive resistance. If the individual so resisted be of a not inhumane temper, and the resisting one perfectly harmless in his passivity, then, in the better moods of the former, he will endeavor charitably to construe to his imagination what proves impossible to be solved by his judgment. Even so, for the most part, I regarded Bartleby and his ways. Poor fellow! thought I, he means no mischief; it is plain he intends no insolence; his aspect sufficiently evinces that his eccentricities are involuntary. He is useful to me. I can get along with him. If I turn him away, the chances are he will fall in with some less-indulgent employer, and then he will be rudely treated, and perhaps driven forth miserably to starve. Yes. Here I can cheaply purchase a delicious self-approval. To befriend Bartleby; to humor him in his strange willfulness, will cost me little or nothing, while I lay up in my soul what will eventually prove a sweet morsel for my conscience. But this mood was not invariable with me. The passiveness of Bartleby sometimes irritated me. I felt strangely goaded on to encounter him in new opposition—to elicit some angry spark from him answerable to my own. But, indeed, I might as well have essayed to strike fire with my knuckles against a bit of Windsor soap. But one afternoon the evil impulse in me mastered me, and the following little scene ensued:

"Bartleby," said I, "when those papers are all copied, I will compare them with you."

"I would prefer not to."

"How? Surely you do not mean to persist in that mulish vagary?"

No answer.

I threw open the folding-doors near by, and, turning upon Turkey and Nippers, exclaimed:

"Bartleby a second time says, he won't examine his papers. What do you think of it, Turkey?"

It was afternoon, be it remembered. Turkey sat glowing like a brass boiler; his bald head steaming; his hands reeling among his blotted papers.

"Think of it?" roared Turkey; "I think I'll just step behind his screen, and black his eyes for him!"

So saying, Turkey rose to his feet and threw his arms into a pugilistic position. He was hurrying away to make good his promise, when I detained him, alarmed at the effect of incautiously rousing Turkey's combativeness after dinner.

"Sit down, Turkey," said I, "and hear what

Nippers has to say. What do you think of it, Nippers? Would I not be justified in immediately dismissing Bartleby?"

"Excuse me, that is for you to decide, sir. I think his conduct quite unusual, and, indeed, unjust, as regards Turkey and myself. But it may only be a passing whim."

"Ah," exclaimed I, "you have strangely changed your mind, then—you speak very gently of him now."

"All beer," cried Turkey; "gentleness is effects of beer—Nippers and I dined together today. You see how gentle *I* am, sir. Shall I go and black his eyes?"

"You refer to Bartleby, I suppose. No, not today, Turkey," I replied; "pray, put up your fists."

I closed the doors, and again advanced towards Bartleby. I felt additional incentives tempting me to my fate. I burned to be rebelled against again. I remembered that Bartleby never left the office.

"Bartleby," said I, "Ginger Nut is away; just step around to the post office, won't you? (it was but a three minutes' walk), and see if there is anything for me."

"I would prefer not to."

"You *will* not?"

"I *prefer* not."

I staggered to my desk, and sat there in a deep study. My blind inveteracy returned. Was there any other thing in which I could procure myself to be ignominiously repulsed by this lean, penniless wight?—my hired clerk? What added thing is there, perfectly reasonable, that he will be sure to refuse to do?

"Bartleby!"

No answer.

"Bartleby," in a louder tone.

No answer.

"Bartleby," I roared.

Like a very ghost, agreeably to the laws of magical invocation, at the third summons, he appeared at the entrance of his hermitage.

"Go to the next room, and tell Nippers to come to me."

"I prefer not to," he respectfully and slowly said, and mildly disappeared.

"Very good, Bartleby," said I, in a quiet sort of serenely-severe, self-possessed tone, intimating the unalterable purpose of some terrible retribution very close at hand. At the moment I half intended something of the kind. But upon the whole, as it was drawing towards my dinner-hour, I thought it best to put on my hat and walk home for the day, suffering much from perplexity and distress of mind.

Shall I acknowledge it? The conclusion of this whole business was, that it soon became a fixed fact of my chambers, that a pale young scrivener, by the name of Bartleby, had a desk there; that he copied for me at the usual rate of four cents a folio (one hundred words); but he was permanently exempt from examining the work done by him, that duty being transferred to Turkey and Nippers, out of compliment, doubtless, to their superior acuteness; moreover, said Bartleby was never, on any account, to be dispatched on the most trivial errand of any sort; and that even if entreated to take upon him such a matter, it was generally understood that he would "prefer not to"—in other words, that he would refuse pointblank.

As days passed on, I became considerably reconciled to Bartleby. His steadiness, his freedom from all dissipation, his incessant industry (except when he chose to throw himself into a standing reverie behind his screen), his great stillness, his unalterableness of demeanor under all circumstances, made him a valuable acquisition. One prime thing was this—*he was always there*—first in the morning, continually through the day, and the last at night. I had a singular confidence in his honesty. I felt my most precious papers perfectly safe in his hands. Sometimes, to be sure, I could not, for the very soul of me, avoid falling into sudden spasmodic passions with him. For it was exceeding difficult to bear in mind all the time those strange peculiarities, privileges, and unheard of exemptions, forming the tacit stipulations on Bartleby's part under which he remained in my office. Now and then, in the eagerness of dispatching pressing business, I would inadvertently summon Bartleby, in a short, rapid tone, to put his finger, say, on the incipient tie of a bit of red tape with which I was about compressing some papers. Of course, from behind the screen the usual answer, "I prefer not to," was sure to come; and then, how could a human creature, with the common infirmities of our nature, refrain from bitterly exclaiming upon such perverseness—such unreasonableness. However, every added repulse of this sort which I received only tended to lessen the probability of my repeating the inadvertence.

Here it must be said, that according to the custom of most legal gentlemen occupying chambers in densely-populated law buildings, there were several keys to my door. One was kept by a woman residing in the attic, which person weekly scrubbed and daily swept and dusted my apartments. Another was kept by Turkey for convenience sake. The third I sometimes carried in my own pocket. The fourth I knew not who had.

Now, one Sunday morning I happened to go to Trinity Church, to hear a celebrated preacher, and finding myself rather early on the ground I thought I would walk around to my chambers for a while. Luckily I had my key with me; but upon applying it to the lock, I found it resisted by something inserted from the inside. Quite surprised, I called out; when to my consternation a key was turned from within; and thrusting his lean visage at me, and holding the door ajar, the apparition of Bartleby appeared, in his shirt sleeves, and otherwise in a strangely tattered *déshabille*, saying quietly that he was sorry, but he was deeply engaged just then, and—preferred not admitting me at present. In a brief word or two, he moreover added, that perhaps I had better walk around the block two or three times, and by that time he would probably have concluded his affairs.

Now, the utterly unsurmised appearance of Bartleby, tenanting my law-chambers of a Sunday morning, with his cadaverously gentlemanly *nonchalance*, yet withal firm and self-possessed, had such a strange effect upon me, that incontinently I slunk away from my own door, and did as desired. But not without sundry twinges of impotent rebellion against the mild effrontery of this unaccountable scrivener. Indeed, it was his wonderful mildness chiefly, which not only disarmed me, but unmanned me as it were. For I consider that one, for the time, is somehow unmanned when he tranquilly permits his hired clerk to dictate to him, and order him away from his own premises. Furthermore, I was full of uneasiness as to what Bartleby could possibly be doing in my office in his shirt sleeves, and in an otherwise dismantled condition of a Sunday morning. Was anything amiss going on? Nay, that was out of the question. It was not to be thought of for a moment that Bartleby was an immoral person. But what could he be doing there?—copying? Nay again, whatever might be his eccentricities, Bartleby was an eminently

decorous person. He would be the last man to sit down to his desk in any state approaching to nudity. Besides, it was Sunday; and there was something about Bartleby that forbade the supposition that he would by any secular occupation violate the proprieties of the day.

Nevertheless, my mind was not pacified; and full of a restless curiosity, at last I returned to the door. Without hindrance I inserted my key, opened it, and entered. Bartleby was not to be seen. I looked round anxiously, peeped behind his screen; but it was very plain that he was gone. Upon more closely examining the place, I surmised that for an indefinite period Bartleby must have eaten, dressed, and slept in my office, and that, too, without plate, mirror, or bed. The cushioned seat of a rickety old sofa in one corner bore the faint impress of a lean, reclining form. Rolled away under his desk, I found a blanket; under the empty grate, a blacking box and brush; on a chair, a tin basin, with soap and a ragged towel; in a newspaper a few crumbs of ginger-nuts and a morsel of cheese. Yes, thought I, it is evident enough that Bartleby has been making his home here, keeping bachelor's hall all by himself. Immediately then the thought came sweeping across me, what miserable friendlessness and loneliness are here revealed! His poverty is great; but his solitude, how horrible! Think of it. Of a Sunday, Wall Street is deserted as Petra;[4] and every night of every day it is an emptiness. This building, too, which of weekdays hums with industry and life, at nightfall echoes with sheer vacancy, and all through Sunday is forlorn. And here Bartleby makes his home; sole spectator of a solitude which he has seen all populous—a sort of innocent and transformed Marius[5] brooding among the ruins of Carthage!

For the first time in my life a feeling of overpowering stinging melancholy seized me. Before, I had never experienced aught but a not unpleasing sadness. The bond of a common humanity now drew me irresistibly to gloom. A fraternal melancholy! For both I and Bartleby were sons of Adam. I remembered the bright silks and sparkling faces I had seen that day, in gala trim, swanlike sailing down the Mississippi of Broadway;

---

4. **Petra:** ruined ancient Palestinian city rediscovered in 1812. 5. **Marius:** Gaius Marius, a plebeian general of Rome in the second century B.C., noted for his victories in Africa and later betrayed by the patricians and exiled.

and I contrasted them with the pallid copyist, and thought to myself, Ah, happiness courts the light, so we deem the world is gay; but misery hides aloof, so we deem that misery there is none. These sad fancyings—chimeras, doubtless, of a sick and silly brain—led on to other and more special thoughts, concerning the eccentricities of Bartleby. Presentiments of strange discoveries hovered round me. The scrivener's pale form appeared to me laid out, among uncaring strangers, in its shivering winding sheet.

Suddenly I was attracted by Bartleby's closed desk, the key in open sight left in the lock.

I mean no mischief, seek the gratification of no heartless curiosity, thought I; besides, the desk is mine, and its contents, too, so I will make bold to look within. Everything was methodically arranged, the papers smoothly placed. The pigeon holes were deep, and removing the files of documents, I groped into their recesses. Presently I felt something there, and dragged it out. It was an old bandanna handkerchief, heavy and knotted. I opened it, and saw it was a savings bank.

I now recalled all the quiet mysteries which I had noted in the man. I remembered that he never spoke but to answer; that, though at intervals he had considerable time to himself, yet I had never seen him reading—no, not even a newspaper; that for long periods he would stand looking out, at his pale window behind the screen, upon the dead brick wall; I was quite sure he never visited any refectory or eating house; while his pale face clearly indicated that he never drank beer like Turkey, or tea and coffee even, like other men; that he never went anywhere in particular that I could learn; never went out for a walk, unless, indeed, that was the case at present; that he had declined telling who he was, or whence he came, or whether he had any relatives in the world; that though so thin and pale, he never complained of ill health. And more than all, I remembered a certain unconscious air of pallid—how shall I call it?—of pallid haughtiness, say, or rather an austere reserve about him, which had positively awed me into my tame compliance with his eccentricities, when I had feared to ask him to do the slightest incidental thing for me, even though I might know, from his long-continued motionlessness, that behind his screen he must be standing in one of those dead-wall reveries of his.

Revolving all these things, and coupling them with the recently discovered fact, that he made my office his constant abiding place and home, and not forgetful of his morbid moodiness; revolving all these things, a prudential feeling began to steal over me. My first emotions had been those of pure melancholy and sincerest pity; but just in proportion as the forlornness of Bartleby grew and grew to my imagination, did that same melancholy merge into fear, that pity into repulsion. So true it is, and so terrible, too, that up to a certain point the thought or sight of misery enlists our best affections; but, in certain special cases, beyond that point it does not. They err who would assert that invariably this is owing to the inherent selfishness of the human heart. It rather proceeds from a certain hopelessness of remedying excessive and organic ill. To a sensitive being, pity is not seldom pain. And when at last it is perceived that such pity cannot lead to effectual succor, common sense bids the soul be rid of it. What I saw that morning persuaded me that the scrivener was the victim of innate and incurable disorder. I might give alms to his body; but his body did not pain him; it was his soul that suffered, and his soul I could not reach.

I did not accomplish the purpose of going to Trinity Church that morning. Somehow, the things I had seen disqualified me for the time from church-going. I walked homeward, thinking what I would do with Bartleby. Finally, I resolved upon this—I would put certain calm questions to him the next morning, touching his history, etc., and if he declined to answer them openly and unreservedly (and I supposed he would prefer not), then to give him a twenty dollar bill over and above whatever I might owe him, and tell him his services were no longer required; but that if in any other way I could assist him, I would be happy to do so, especially if he desired to return to his native place, wherever that might be, I would willingly help to defray the expenses. Moreover, if, after reaching home, he found himself at any time in want of aid, a letter from him would be sure of a reply.

The next morning came.

"Bartleby," said I, gently calling to him behind his screen.

No reply.

"Bartleby," said I, in a still gentler tone, "come here; I am not going to ask you to do anything you would prefer not to do—I simply wish to speak to you."

Upon this he noiselessly slid into view.

"Will you tell me, Bartleby, where you were born?"

"I would prefer not to."

"Will you tell me *anything* about yourself?"

"I would prefer not to."

"But what reasonable objection can you have to speak to me? I feel friendly towards you."

He did not look at me while I spoke, but kept his glance fixed upon my bust of Cicero, which, as I then sat, was directly behind me, some six inches above my head.

"What is your answer, Bartleby," said I, after waiting a considerable time for a reply, during which his countenance remained immovable, only there was the faintest conceivable tremor of the white attenuated mouth.

"At present I prefer to give no answer," he said, and retired into his hermitage.

It was rather weak in me I confess, but his manner, on this occasion, nettled me. Not only did there seem to lurk in it a certain calm disdain, but his perverseness seemed ungrateful, considering the undeniable good usage and indulgence he had received from me.

Again I sat ruminating what I should do. Mortified as I was at his behavior, and resolved as I had been to dismiss him when I entered my office, nevertheless I strangely felt something superstitious knocking at my heart, and forbidding me to carry out my purpose, and denouncing me for a villain if I dared to breathe one bitter word against this forlornest of mankind. At last, familiarly drawing my chair behind his screen, I sat down and said: "Bartleby, never mind, then, about revealing your history; but let me entreat you, as a friend, to comply as far as may be with the usages of this office. Say now, you will help to examine papers tomorrow or next day: in short, say now, that in a day or two you will begin to be a little reasonable: —say so, Bartleby."

"At present I would prefer not to be a little reasonable," was his mildly cadaverous reply.

Just then the folding-doors opened, and Nippers approached. He seemed suffering from an unusually bad night's rest, induced by severer indigestion than common. He overheard those final words of Bartleby.

"*Prefer not*, eh?" gritted Nippers—"I'd *prefer* him, if I were you, sir," addressing me—"I'd *prefer* him; I'd give him preferences, the stubborn mule! What is it, sir, pray, that he *prefers* not to do now?"

Bartleby moved not a limb.

"Mr. Nippers," said I, "I'd prefer that you would withdraw for the present."

Somehow, of late, I had got into the way of involuntarily using this word *prefer* upon all sorts of not exactly suitable occasions. And I trembled to think that my contact with the scrivener had already and seriously affected me in a mental way. And what further and deeper aberration might it not yet produce? This apprehension had not been without efficacy in determining me to summary measures.

As Nippers, looking very sour and sulky, was departing, Turkey blandly and deferentially approached.

"With submission, sir," said he, "yesterday I was thinking about Bartleby here, and I think that if he would but prefer to take a quart of good ale every day, it would do much towards mending him, and enabling him to assist in examining his papers."

"So you have got the word, too," said I, slightly excited.

"With submission, what word, sir," asked Turkey, respectfully crowding himself into the contracted space behind the screen, and by so doing, making me jostle the scrivener. "What word, sir?"

"I would prefer to be left alone here," said Bartleby, as if offended at being mobbed in his privacy.

"*That's* the word, Turkey," said I—"*that's* it."

"Oh, *prefer?* oh yes—queer word. I never use it myself. But sir, as I was saying, if he would but prefer—"

"Turkey," interrupted I, "you will please withdraw."

"Oh certainly, sir, if you prefer that I should."

As he opened the folding-door to retire, Nippers at his desk caught a glimpse of me, and asked whether I would prefer to have a certain paper copied on blue paper or white. He did not in the least roguishly accent the word *prefer*. It was plain that it involuntarily rolled from his tongue. I thought to myself, surely I must get rid of a demented man, who already has in some degree turned the tongues, if not the heads of myself and clerks. But I thought it prudent not to break the dismission at once.

The next day I noticed that Bartleby did nothing but stand at his window in his dead-wall reverie. Upon asking him why he did not write, he said that he had decided upon doing no more writing.

"Why, how now? what next?" exclaimed I, "do no more writing?"

"No more."

"And what is the reason?"

"Do you not see the reason for yourself," he indifferently replied.

I looked steadfastly at him, and perceived that his eyes looked dull and glazed. Instantly it occurred to me, that his unexampled diligence in copying by his dim window for the first few weeks of his stay with me might have temporarily impaired his vision.

I was touched. I said something in condolence with him. I hinted that of course he did wisely in abstaining from writing for a while; and urged him to embrace that opportunity of taking wholesome exercise in the open air. This, however, he did not do. A few days after this, my other clerks being absent, and being in a great hurry to dispatch certain letters by the mail, I thought that, having nothing else earthly to do, Bartleby would surely be less inflexible than usual, and carry these letters to the post office. But he blankly declined. So, much to my inconvenience, I went myself.

Still added days went by. Whether Bartleby's eyes improved or not, I could not say. To all appearance I thought they did. But when I asked him if they did, he vouchsafed no answer. At all events, he would do no copying. At last, in reply to my urgings, he informed me that he had permanently given up copying.

"What!" exclaimed I; "suppose your eyes should get entirely well—better than ever before—would you not copy then?"

"I have given up copying," he answered, and slid aside.

He remained as ever, a fixture in my chamber. Nay—if that were possible—he became still more of a fixture than before. What was to be done? He would do nothing in the office; why should he stay there? In plain fact, he had now become a millstone to me, not only useless as a necklace, but afflictive to bear. Yet I was sorry for him. I speak less than truth when I say that, on his own account, he occasioned me uneasiness. If he would but have named a single relative or friend, I would instantly have written, and urged their taking the poor fellow away to some convenient retreat. But he seemed alone, absolutely alone in the universe. A bit of wreck in the mid Atlantic. At length, necessities connected with my business tyrannized over all other considerations. Decently as I could, I told Bartleby that in six days time he must unconditionally leave the office. I warned him to take measures, in the interval, for procuring some other abode. I offered to assist him in his endeavor, if he himself would but take the first step towards a removal. "And when you finally quit me, Bartleby," added I, "I shall see that you go not away entirely unprovided. Six days from this hour, remember."

At the expiration of that period, I peeped behind the screen, and lo! Bartleby was there.

I buttoned up my coat, balanced myself; advanced slowly towards him, touched his shoulder, and said, "The time has come; you must quit this place; I am sorry for you; here is money; but you must go."

"I would prefer not," he replied, with his back still towards me.

"You *must*."

He remained silent.

Now I had an unbounded confidence in this man's common honesty. He had frequently restored to me sixpences and shillings carelessly dropped upon the floor, for I am apt to be very reckless in such shirt-button affairs. The proceeding, then, which followed will not be deemed extraordinary.

"Bartleby," said I, "I owe you twelve dollars on account; here are thirty-two; the odd twenty are yours—Will you take it?" and I handed the bills towards him.

But he made no motion.

"I will leave them here, then," putting them under a weight on the table. Then taking my hat and cane and going to the door, I tranquilly turned and added—"After you have removed your things from these offices, Bartleby, you will of course lock the door—since everyone is now gone for the day but you—and if you please, slip your key underneath the mat, so that I may have it in the morning. I shall not see you again; so good-by to you. If, hereafter, in your new place of abode, I can be of any service to you, do not fail to advise me by letter. Good-by, Bartleby, and fare you well.

But he answered not a word; like the last column of some ruined temple, he remained standing mute and solitary in the middle of the otherwise deserted room.

As I walked home in a pensive mood, my vanity got the better of my pity. I could not but highly plume myself on my masterly management in getting rid of Bartleby. Masterly I call it, and such it must appear to any dispassionate thinker. The beauty of my procedure seemed to consist in its perfect quietness. There was no vulgar bullying, no bravado of any sort, no choleric hectoring, and striding to and fro across the apartment, jerking out vehement commands for Bartleby to bundle himself off with his beggarly traps. Nothing of the kind. Without loudly bidding Bartleby depart—as an inferior genius might have done—I *assumed* the ground that depart he must; and upon that assumption built all I had to say. The more I thought over my procedure, the more I was charmed with it. Nevertheless, next morning, upon awakening, I had my doubts—I had somehow slept off the fumes of vanity. One of the coolest and wisest hours a man has, is just after he awakes in the morning. My procedure seemed as sagacious as ever—but only in theory. How it would prove in practice—there was the rub. It was truly a beautiful thought to have assumed Bartleby's departure; but, after all, that assumption was simply my own, and none of Bartleby's. The great point was, not whether I had assumed that he would quit me, but whether he would prefer so to do. He was more a man of preferences than assumptions.

After breakfast, I walked down town, arguing the probabilities pro and con. One moment I thought it would prove a miserable failure, and Bartleby would be found all alive at my office as usual; the next moment it seemed certain that I should find his chair empty. And so I kept veering about. At the corner of Broadway and Canal Street, I saw quite an excited group of people standing in earnest conversation.

"I'll take odds he doesn't," said a voice as I passed.

"Doesn't go?—done!" said I; "put up your money."

I was instinctively putting my hand in my pocket to produce my own, when I remembered that this was an election day. The words I had overheard bore no reference to Bartleby, but to the success or nonsuccess of some candidate for the mayoralty. In my intent frame of mind, I had, as it were, imagined that all Broadway shared in my excitement, and were debating the same question with me. I passed on, very thankful that the uproar of the street screened my momentary absent-mindedness.

As I had intended, I was earlier than usual at my office door. I stood listening for a moment. All was still. He must be gone. I tried the knob. The door was locked. Yes, my procedure had worked to a charm; he indeed must be vanished. Yet a certain melancholy mixed with this: I was almost sorry for my brilliant success. I was fumbling under the door mat for the key, which Bartleby was to have left there for me, when accidentally my knee knocked against a panel, producing a summoning sound, and in response a voice came to me from within—"Not yet; I am occupied."

It was Bartleby.

I was thunderstruck. For an instant I stood like the man who, pipe in mouth, was killed one cloudless afternoon long ago in Virginia, by summer lightning; at his own warm open window he was killed, and remained leaning out there upon the dreamy afternoon, till some one touched him, when he fell.

"Not gone!" I murmured at last. But again obeying that wondrous ascendancy which the inscrutable scrivener had over me, and from which ascendancy, for all my chafing, I could not completely escape, I slowly went down stairs and out into the street, and while walking round the block, wondered what I should next do in this unheard-of perplexity. Turn the man out by an actual thrusting I could not; to drive him away by calling him hard names would not do; calling in the police was an unpleasant idea; and yet, permit him to enjoy his cadaverous triumph over me—this, too, I could not think of. What was to be done? or, if nothing could be done, was there anything further that I could *assume* in the matter? Yes, as before I had prospectively assumed that Bartleby would depart, so now I might retrospectively assume that departed he was. In the legitimate carrying out of this assumption, I might enter my office in a great hurry, and pretending not to see Bartleby at all, walk straight against him as if he were air. Such a proceeding would in a singular degree have the appearance of a home-thrust. It was hardly possible that Bartleby could withstand such an application of the doctrine of assumptions. But upon second thoughts the success of the plan seemed rather dubious. I resolved to argue the matter over with him again.

"Bartleby," said I, entering the office, with a quietly severe expression, "I am seriously displeased. I am pained, Bartleby. I had thought better of you. I had imagined you of such a gentlemanly organization, that in any delicate dilemma a slight hint would suffice—in short, an assumption. But it appears I am deceived. Why," I added, unaffectedly starting, "you have not even touched that money yet," pointing to it, just where I had left it the evening previous.

He answered nothing.

"Will you, or will you not, quit me?" I now demanded in a sudden passion, advancing close to him.

"I would prefer *not* to quit you," he replied, gently emphasizing the *not*.

"What earthly right have you to stay here? Do you pay any rent? Do you pay my taxes? Or is this property yours?"

He answered nothing.

"Are you ready to go on and write now? Are your eyes recovered? Could you copy a small paper for me this morning? or help examine a few lines? or step round to the post office? In a word, will you do anything at all, to give a coloring to your refusal to depart the premises?"

He silently retired into his hermitage.

I was now in such a state of nervous resentment that I thought it but prudent to check myself at present from further demonstrations. Bartleby and I were alone. I remembered the tragedy of the unfortunate Adams and the still more unfortunate Colt in the solitary office of the latter; and how poor Colt, being dreadfully incensed by Adams, and imprudently permitting himself to get wildly excited, was at unawares hurried into his fatal act—an act which certainly no man could possibly deplore more than the actor himself.[6] Often it

6. **himself:** In a famous murder case of 1841, John C. Colt killed Samuel Adams, a printer, with an unpremeditated blow during an argument.

had occurred to me in my ponderings upon the subject, that had that altercation taken place in the public street, or at a private residence, it would not have terminated as it did. It was the circumstance of being alone in a solitary office, up stairs, of a building entirely unhallowed by humanizing domestic associations—an uncarpeted office, doubtless, of a dusty, haggard sort of appearance—this it must have been, which greatly helped to enhance the irritable desperation of the hapless Colt.

But when this old Adam of resentment rose in me and tempted me concerning Bartleby, I grappled him and threw him. How? Why, simply by recalling the divine injunction: "A new commandment give I unto you, that ye love one another." Yes, this it was that saved me. Aside from higher considerations, charity often operates as a vastly wise and prudent principle—a great safeguard to its possessor. Men have committed murder for jealousy's sake, and anger's sake, and hatred's sake, and selfishness' sake, and spiritual pride's sake; but no man, that ever I heard of, ever committed a diabolical murder for sweet charity's sake. Mere self-interest, then, if no better motive can be enlisted, should, especially with high-tempered men, prompt all beings to charity and philanthropy. At any rate, upon the occasion in question, I strove to drown my exasperated feelings towards the scrivener by benevolently construing his conduct. Poor fellow, poor fellow! thought I, he don't mean anything; and besides, he has seen hard times, and ought to be indulged.

I endeavored, also, immediately to occupy myself, and at the same time to comfort my despondency. I tried to fancy, that in the course of the morning, at such time as might prove agreeable to him, Bartleby, of his own free accord, would emerge from his hermitage and take up some decided line of march in the direction of the door. But no. Half-past twelve o'clock came; Turkey began to glow in the face, overturn his inkstand, and become generally obstreperous; Nippers abated down into quietude and courtesy; Ginger Nut munched his noon apple; and Bartleby remained standing at his window in one of his profoundest dead-wall reveries. Will it be credited? Ought I to acknowledge it? That afternoon I left the office without saying one further word to him.

Some days now passed, during which, at leisure

intervals I looked a little into "Edwards[7] on the Will," and "Priestley[8] on Necessity." Under the circumstances, those books induced a salutary feeling. Gradually I slid into the persuasion that these troubles of mine, touching the scrivener, had been all predestinated from eternity, and Bartleby was billeted upon me for some mysterious purpose of an allwise Providence, which it was not for a mere mortal like me to fathom. Yes, Bartleby, stay there behind your screen, thought I; I shall persecute you no more; you are harmless and noiseless as any of these old chairs; in short, I never feel so private as when I know you are here. At last I see it, I feel it; I penetrate to the predestinated purpose of my life. I am content. Others may have loftier parts to enact; but my mission in this world, Bartleby, is to furnish you with office-room for such period as you may see fit to remain.

I believe that this wise and blessed frame of mind would have continued with me, had it not been for the unsolicited and uncharitable remarks obtruded upon me by my professional friends who visited the rooms. But thus it often is, that the constant friction of illiberal minds wears out at last the best resolves of the more generous. Though to be sure, when I reflected upon it, it was not strange that people entering my office should be struck by the peculiar aspect of the unaccountable Bartleby, and so be tempted to throw out some sinister observations concerning him. Sometimes an attorney, having business with me, and calling at my office, and finding no one but the scrivener there, would undertake to obtain some sort of precise information from him touching my whereabouts; but without heeding his idle talk, Bartleby would remain standing immovable in the middle of the room. So after contemplating him in that position for a time, the attorney would depart, no wiser than he came.

Also, when a reference was going on, and the room full of lawyers and witnesses, and business driving fast, some deeply-occupied legal gentleman present, seeing Bartleby wholly unemployed, would request him to run round to his (the legal gentleman's) office and fetch some papers for him. Thereupon, Bartleby would tranquilly decline, and yet remain idle as before. Then the lawyer would give a great stare, and turn to me. And what could I say? At last I was made aware that all through the circle of my professional acquaintance, a whisper of wonder was running round, having reference to the strange creature I kept at my office. This worried me very much. And as the idea came upon me of his possibly turning out a long-lived man, and keep occupying my chambers, and denying my authority; and perplexing my visitors; and scandalizing my professional reputation; and casting a general gloom over the premises; keeping soul and body together to the last upon his savings (for doubtless he spent but half a dime a day), and in the end perhaps outlive me, and claim possession of my office by right of his perpetual occupancy: as all these dark anticipations crowded upon me more and more, and my friends continually intruded their relentless remarks upon the apparition in my room; a great change was wrought in me. I resolved to gather all my faculties together, and forever rid me of this intolerable incubus.

Ere revolving any complicated project, however, adapted to this end, I first simply suggested to Bartleby the propriety of his permanent departure. In a calm and serious tone, I commended the idea to his careful and mature consideration. But, having taken three days to meditate upon it, he apprised me, that his original determination remained the same; in short, that he still preferred to abide with me.

What shall I do? I now said to myself, buttoning up my coat to the last button. What shall I do? what ought I to do? what does conscience say I *should* do with this man, or, rather, ghost. Rid myself of him, I must; go, he shall. But how? You will not thrust him, the poor, pale, passive mortal —you will not thrust such a helpless creature out of your door? you will not dishonor yourself by such cruelty? No, I will not, I cannot do that. Rather would I let him live and die here, and then mason up his remains in the wall. What, then, will you do? For all your coaxing, he will not budge. Bribes he leaves under your own paperweight on your table; in short, it is quite plain that he prefers to cling to you.

7. Edwards: Jonathan Edwards, a New England minister and famed theologian, wrote *The Freedom of the Will* (1754) in which he defended the Calvinist position that the will is not free. **8. Priestley:** Joseph Priestley, eighteenth-century English scientist and nonconformist Unitarian who also denied the concept of the freedom of the will but on grounds of natural determinism rather than Calvinist arguments.

Then something severe, something unusual must be done. What! surely you will not have him collared by a constable, and commit his innocent pallor to the common jail? And upon what ground could you procure such a thing to be done?—a vagrant, is he? What! he a vagrant, a wanderer, who refuses to budge? It is because he will *not* be a vagrant, then, that you seek to count him *as* a vagrant. That is too absurd. No visible means of support: there I have him. Wrong again: for indubitably he *does* support himself, and that is the only unanswerable proof that any man can show of his possessing the means so to do. No more, then. Since he will not quit me, I must quit him. I will change my offices; I will move elsewhere, and give him fair notice, that if I find him on my new premises I will then proceed against him as a common trespasser.

Acting accordingly, next day I thus addressed him: "I find these chambers too far from the city hall; the air is unwholesome. In a word, I propose to remove my offices next week, and shall no longer require your services. I tell you this now, in order that you may seek another place."

He made no reply; and nothing more was said.

On the appointed day I engaged carts and men, proceeded to my chambers, and, having but little furniture, everything was removed in a few hours. Throughout, the scrivener remained standing behind the screen, which I directed to be removed the last thing. It was withdrawn; and, being folded up like a huge folio, left him the motionless occupant of a naked room. I stood in the entry watching him a moment, while something from within me upbraided me.

I reentered, with my hand in my pocket—and—and my heart in my mouth.

"Good-by, Bartleby; I am going—good-by, and God some way bless you; and take that," slipping something in his hand. But it dropped upon the floor, and then—strange to say—I tore myself from him whom I had so longed to be rid of.

Established in my new quarters, for a day or two I kept the door locked, and started at every footfall in the passages. When I returned to my rooms, after any little absence, I would pause at the threshold for an instant, and attentively listen, ere applying my key. But these fears were needless. Bartleby never came nigh me.

I thought all was going well, when a perturbed-looking stranger visited me, inquiring whether I was the person who had recently occupied rooms at No. — Wall Street.

Full of forebodings, I replied that I was.

"Then, sir," said the stranger, who proved a lawyer, "you are responsible for the man you left there. He refuses to do any copying; he refuses to do anything; he says he prefers not to; and he refuses to quit the premises."

"I am very sorry, sir," said I, with assumed tranquility, but an inward tremor, "but, really, the man you allude to is nothing to me—he is no relation or apprentice of mine, that you should hold me responsible for him."

"In mercy's name, who is he?"

"I certainly cannot inform you. I know nothing about him. Formerly I employed him as a copyist; but he has done nothing for me now for some time past."

"I shall settle him, then—good morning, sir."

Several days passed, and I heard nothing more; and, though I often felt a charitable prompting to call at the place and see poor Bartleby, yet a certain squeamishness, of I know not what, withheld me.

All is over with him, by this time, thought I, at last, when, through another week, no further intelligence reached me. But, coming to my room the day after, I found several persons waiting at my door in a high state of nervous excitement.

"That's the man—here he comes," cried the foremost one, whom I recognized as the lawyer who had previously called upon me alone.

"You must take him away, sir, at once," cried a portly person among them, advancing upon me, and whom I knew to be the landlord of No. — Wall Street. "These gentlemen, my tenants, cannot stand it any longer; Mr. B——," pointing to the lawyer, "has turned him out of his room, and he now persists in haunting the building generally, sitting upon the banisters of the stairs by day, and sleeping in the entry by night. Everybody is concerned; clients are leaving the offices; some fears are entertained of a mob; something you must do, and that without delay."

Aghast at this torrent, I fell back before it, and would fain have locked myself in my new quarters. In vain I persisted that Bartleby was nothing to me—no more than to any one else. In vain—I was the last person known to have anything to do with him, and they held me to the terrible account.

Fearful, then, of being exposed to the papers (as one person present obscurely threatened), I considered the matter, and, at length, said, that if the lawyer would give me a confidential interview with the scrivener, in his (the lawyer's) own room, I would, that afternoon, strive my best to rid them of the nuisance they complained of.

Going up stairs to my old haunt, there was Bartleby silently sitting upon the banister at the landing.

"What are you doing here, Bartleby?" said I.

"Sitting upon the banister," he mildly replied.

I motioned him into the lawyer's room, who then left us.

"Bartleby," said I, "are you aware that you are the cause of great tribulation to me, by persisting in occupying the entry after being dismissed from the office?"

No answer.

"Now one of two things must take place. Either you must do something, or something must be done to you. Now what sort of business would you like to engage in? Would you like to reengage in copying for someone?"

"No; I would prefer not to make any change."

"Would you like a clerkship in a dry-goods store?"

"There is too much confinement about that. No, I would not like a clerkship; but I am not particular."

"Too much confinement," I cried, "why you keep yourself confined all the time!"

"I would prefer not to take a clerkship," he rejoined, as if to settle that little item at once.

"How would a bartender's business suit you? There is no trying of the eyesight in that."

"I would not like it at all; though, as I said before, I am not particular."

His unwonted wordiness inspirited me. I returned to the charge.

"Well, then, would you like to travel through the country collecting bills for the merchants? That would improve your health."

"No, I would prefer to be doing something else."

"How, then, would going as a companion to Europe, to entertain some young gentleman with your conversation—how would that suit you?"

"Not at all. It does not strike me that there is anything definite about that. I like to be stationary. But I am not particular."

"Stationary you shall be, then," I cried, now losing all patience, and, for the first time in all my exasperating connection with him, fairly flying into a passion. "If you do not go away from these premises before night, I shall feel bound—indeed, I *am* bound—to—to—to quit the premises myself!" I rather absurdly concluded, knowing not with what possible threat to try to frighten his immobility into compliance. Despairing of all further efforts, I was precipitately leaving him, when a final thought occurred to me—one which had not been wholly unindulged before.

"Bartleby," said I, in the kindest tone I could assume under such exciting circumstances, "will you go home with me now—not to my office, but my dwelling—and remain there till we can conclude upon some convenient arrangement for you at our leisure? Come, let us start now, right away."

"No: at present I would prefer not to make any change at all."

I answered nothing; but, effectually dodging everyone by the suddenness and rapidity of my flight, rushed from the building, ran up Wall Street towards Broadway, and, jumping into the first omnibus, was soon removed from pursuit. As soon as tranquility returned, I distinctly perceived that I had now done all that I possibly could, both in respect of the demands of the landlord and his tenants, and with regard to my own desire and sense of duty, to benefit Bartleby, and shield him from rude persecution. I now strove to be entirely carefree and quiescent; and my conscience justified me in the attempt; though, indeed, it was not so successful as I could have wished. So fearful was I of being again hunted out by the incensed landlord and his exasperated tenants, that, surrendering my business to Nippers, for a few days, I drove about the upper part of the town and through the suburbs, in my rockaway; crossed over to Jersey City and Hoboken, and paid fugitive visits to Manhattanville and Astoria. In fact, I almost lived in my rockaway for the time.

When again I entered my office, lo, a note from the landlord lay upon the desk. I opened it with trembling hands. It informed me that the writer had sent to the police, and had Bartleby removed to the Tombs as a vagrant. Moreover, since I knew more about him than anyone else, he wished me to appear at that place, and make a suitable statement of the facts. These tidings had a conflicting effect upon me. At first I was indignant; but, at last, almost approved. The landlord's energetic, summary disposition, had led him to adopt a procedure which I do not think I would have decided upon myself; and yet, as a last resort, under such peculiar circumstances, it seemed the only plan.

As I afterwards learned, the poor scrivener, when told that he must be conducted to the Tombs, offered not the slightest obstacle, but, in his pale, unmoving way, silently acquiesced.

Some of the compassionate and curious bystanders joined the party; and headed by one of the constables arm in arm with Bartleby, the silent procession filed its way through all the noise, and heat, and joy of the roaring thoroughfares at noon.

The same day I received the note, I went to the Tombs, or, to speak more properly, the Halls of Justice. Seeking the right officer, I stated the purpose of my call, and was informed that the individual I described was, indeed, within. I then assured the functionary that Bartleby was a perfectly honest man, and greatly to be compassionated, however unaccountably eccentric. I narrated all I knew, and closed by suggesting the idea of letting him remain in as indulgent confinement as possible, till something less harsh might be done—though, indeed, I hardly knew what. At all events, if nothing else could be decided upon, the almshouse must receive him. I then begged to have an interview.

Being under no disgraceful charge, and quite serene and harmless in all his ways, they had permitted him freely to wander about the prison, and, especially, in the inclosed grass-platted yards thereof. And so I found him there, standing all alone in the quietest of the yards, his face towards a high wall, while all around, from the narrow slits of the jail windows, I thought I saw peering out upon him the eyes of murderers and thieves.

"Bartleby!"

"I know you," he said, without looking round—"and I want nothing to say to you."

"It was not I that brought you here, Bartleby," said I, keenly pained at his implied suspicion. "And to you, this should not be so vile a place. Nothing reproachful attaches to you by being here. And see, it is not so sad a place as one might think. Look, there is the sky, and here is the grass."

"I know where I am," he replied, but would say nothing more, and so I left him.

As I entered the corridor again, a broad meat-like man, in an apron, accosted me, and jerking his thumb over his shoulder, said—"Is that your friend?"

"Yes."

"Does he want to starve? If he does, let him live on the prison fare, that's all."

"Who are you?" asked I, not knowing what to make of such an unofficially speaking person in such a place.

"I am the grub-man. Such gentlemen as have friends here, hire me to provide them with something good to eat."

"Is this so?" said I, turning to the turnkey.

He said it was.

"Well, then," said I, slipping some silver into the grub-man's hands (for so they called him), "I want you to give particular attention to my friend there; let him have the best dinner you can get. And you must be as polite to him as possible."

"Introduce me, will you?" said the grub-man, looking at me with an expression which seemed to say he was all impatience for an opportunity to give a specimen of his breeding.

Thinking it would prove of benefit to the scrivener, I acquiesced; and, asking the grub-man his name, went up with him to Bartleby.

"Bartleby, this is a friend; you will find him very useful to you."

"Your sarvant, sir, your sarvant," said the grubman, making a low salutation behind his apron. "Hope you find it pleasant here, sir; nice grounds—cool apartments—hope you'll stay with us sometime—try to make it agreeable. What will you have for dinner today?"

"I prefer not to dine today," said Bartleby, turning away. "It would disagree with me; I am unused to dinners." So saying, he slowly moved to the other side of the enclosure, and took up a position fronting the dead-wall.

"How's this?" said the grub-man, addressing me with a stare of astonishment. "He's odd, ain't he?"

"I think he is a little deranged," said I, sadly.

"Deranged? deranged is it? Well, now, upon my word, I thought that friend of yourn was a gentleman forger; they are always pale and genteellike, them forgers. I can't help pity 'em—can't help it, sir. Did you know Monroe Edwards?" he added, touchingly, and paused. Then, laying his hand piteously on my shoulder, sighed, "he died of consumption at Sing Sing. So you weren't acquainted with Monroe?"

"No, I was never socially acquainted with any forgers. But I cannot stop longer. Look to my friend yonder. You will not lose by it. I will see you again."

Some few days after this, I again obtained admission to the Tombs, and went through the corridors in quest of Bartleby; but without finding him.

"I saw him coming from his cell not long ago," said a turnkey, "may be he's gone to loiter in the yards."

So I went in that direction.

"Are you looking for the silent man?" said another turnkey, passing me. "Yonder he lies— sleeping in the yard there. 'Tis not twenty minutes since I saw him lie down."

The yard was entirely quiet. It was not accessible to the common prisoners. The surrounding walls, of amazing thickness, kept off all sounds behind them. The Egyptian character of the masonry weighed upon me with its gloom. But a soft imprisoned turf grew under foot. The heart of the eternal pyramids, it seemed, wherein, by some strange magic, through the clefts, grass-seed, dropped by birds, had sprung.

Strangely huddled at the base of the wall, his knees drawn up, and lying on his side, his head touching the cold stones, I saw the wasted Bartleby. But nothing stirred. I paused; then went close up to him; stooped over, and saw that his dim eyes were open; otherwise he seemed profoundly sleeping. Something prompted me to touch him. I felt his hand, when a tingling shiver ran up my arm and down my spine to my feet.

The round face of the grub-man peered upon me now. "His dinner is ready. Won't he dine today, either? Or does he live without dining?"

"Lives without dining," said I, and closed the eyes.

"Eh!—He's asleep, ain't he?"

"With kings and counselors,"[9] murmured I.

There would seem little need for proceeding further in this history. Imagination will readily supply the meager recital of poor Bartleby's interment. But, ere parting with the reader, let me say,

9. With . . . counselors: See Job 3:13–14.

that if this little narrative has sufficiently interested him, to awaken curiosity as to who Bartleby was, and what manner of life he had prior to the present narrator's making his acquaintance, I can only reply, that in such curiosity I fully share, but am wholly unable to gratify it. Yet here I hardly know whether I should divulge one little item of rumor, which came to my ear a few months after the scrivener's decease. Upon what basis it rested, I could never ascertain; and hence, how true it is I cannot now tell. But, inasmuch as this vague report has not been without a certain suggestive interest to me, however said, it may prove the same with some others; and so I will briefly mention it. The report was this: that Bartleby had been a subordinate clerk in the Dead Letter Office at Washington, from which he had been suddenly removed by a change in the administration. When I think over this rumor, hardly can I express the emotions which seize me. Dead letters! does it not sound like dead men? Conceive a man by nature and misfortune prone to a pallid hopelessness, can any business seem more fitted to heighten it than that of continually handling these dead letters, and assorting them for the flames? For by the cartload they are annually burned. Sometimes from out the folded paper the pale clerk takes a ring—the finger it was meant for, perhaps, molders in the grave; a bank-note sent in swiftest charity—he whom it would relieve, nor eats nor hungers any more; pardon for those who died despairing; hope for those who died unhoping; good tidings for those who died stifled by unrelieved calamities. On errands of life, these letters speed to death.

Ah, Bartleby! Ah, humanity!

JAMES JOYCE
1882–1941

Grace

Two gentlemen who were in the lavatory at the time tried to lift him up: but he was quite helpless. He lay curled up at the foot of the stairs down which he had fallen. They succeeded in turning him over. His hat had rolled a few yards away and his clothes were smeared with the filth and ooze of the floor on which he had lain, face downwards. His eyes were closed and he breathed with a grunting noise. A thin stream of blood trickled from the corner of his mouth.

These two gentlemen and one of the curates[1] carried him up the stairs and laid him down again on the floor of the bar. In two minutes he was surrounded by a ring of men. The manager of the bar asked everyone who he was and who was with him. No one knew who he was but one of the curates said he had served the gentleman with a small rum.

"Was he by himself?" asked the manager.

"No, sir. There was two gentlemen with him."

"And where are they?"

No one knew; a voice said:

"Give him air. He's fainted."

The ring of onlookers distended and closed again elastically. A dark medal of blood had formed itself near the man's head on the tessellated floor. The manager, alarmed by the gray pallor of the man's face, sent for a policeman.

His collar was unfastened and his necktie undone. He opened his eyes for an instant, sighed and closed them again. One of the gentlemen who had carried him upstairs held a dinged[2] silk hat in his hand. The manager asked repeatedly did no one know who the injured man was or where had his friends gone. The door of the bar opened and an immense constable entered. A crowd which had followed him down the laneway collected outside the door, struggling to look in through the glass panels.

The manager at once began to narrate what he knew. The constable, a young man with thick immobile features, listened. He moved his head slowly to right and left and from the manager to the person on the floor, as if he feared to be the victim of some delusion. Then he drew off his glove, produced a small book from his waist, licked the lead of his pencil and made ready to indite. He asked in a suspicious provincial accent:

"Who is the man? What's his name and address?"

A young man in a cycling-suit cleared his way through the ring of bystanders. He knelt down promptly beside the injured man and called for water. The constable knelt down also to help. The

GRACE.   1. curates: bartenders.   2. dinged: dented.

young man washed the blood from the injured man's mouth and then called for some brandy. The constable repeated the order in an authoritative voice until a curate came running with the glass. The brandy was forced down the man's throat. In a few seconds he opened his eyes and looked about him. He looked at the circle of faces and then, understanding, strove to rise to his feet.

"You're all right now?" asked the young man in the cycling-suit.

"Sha, 's nothing," said the injured man, trying to stand up.

He was helped to his feet. The manager said something about a hospital and some of the bystanders gave advice. The battered silk hat was placed on the man's head. The constable asked:

"Where do you live?"

The man, without answering, began to twirl the ends of his mustache. He made light of his accident. It was nothing, he said: only a little accident. He spoke very thickly.

"Where do you live?" repeated the constable.

The man said they were to get a cab for him. While the point was being debated a tall agile gentleman of fair complexion, wearing a long yellow ulster, came from the far end of the bar. Seeing the spectacle, he called out:

"Hallo, Tom, old man! What's the trouble?"

"Sha, 's nothing," said the man.

The newcomer surveyed the deplorable figure before him and then turned to the constable, saying:

"It's all right, constable. I'll see him home."

The constable touched his helmet and answered:

"All right, Mr. Power!"

"Come now, Tom," said Mr. Power, taking his friend by the arm. "No bones broken. What? Can you walk?"

The young man in the cycling-suit took the man by the other arm and the crowd divided.

"How did you get yourself into this mess?" asked Mr. Power.

"The gentleman fell down the stairs," said the young man.

"I 'ery 'uch o'liged to you, sir," said the injured man.

"Not at all."

" 'ant we have a little . . . ?"

"Not now. Not now."

The three men left the bar and the crowd sifted

through the doors in to the laneway. The manager brought the constable to the stairs to inspect the scene of the accident. They agreed that the gentleman must have missed his footing. The customers returned to the counter and a curate set about removing the traces of blood from the floor.

When they came out into Grafton Street, Mr. Power whistled for an outsider.[3] The injured man said again as well as he could:

"I 'ery 'uch o'liged to you, sir. I hope we'll 'eet again. 'y na'e is Kernan."

The shock and the incipient pain had partly sobered him.

"Don't mention it," said the young man.

They shook hands. Mr. Kernan was hoisted on to the car and, while Mr. Power was giving directions to the carman, he expressed his gratitude to the young man and regretted that they could not have a little drink together.

"Another time," said the young man.

The car drove off towards Westmoreland Street. As it passed the Ballast Office the clock showed half-past nine. A keen east wind hit them, blowing from the mouth of the river. Mr. Kernan was huddled together with cold. His friend asked him to tell how the accident had happened.

"I 'an't 'an," he answered, " 'y 'ongue is hurt."

"Show."

The other leaned over the well of the car and peered into Mr. Kernan's mouth but he could not see. He struck a match and, sheltering it in the shell of his hands, peered again into the mouth which Mr. Kernan opened obediently. The swaying movement of the car brought the match to and from the opened mouth. The lower teeth and gums were covered with clotted blood and a minute piece of the tongue seemed to have been bitten off. The match was blown out.

"That's ugly," said Mr. Power.

"Sha, 's nothing," said Mr. Kernan, closing his mouth and pulling the collar of his filthy coat across his neck.

Mr. Kernan was a commercial traveler of the old school which believed in the dignity of its calling. He had never been seen in the city without a silk hat of some decency and a pair of gaiters. By grace of these two articles of clothing, he said, a man could always pass muster. He carried on the tradition of his Napoleon, the great Blackwhite,

3. **outsider:** cab.

whose memory he evoked at times by legend and mimicry. Modern business methods had spared him only so far as to allow him a little office in Crowe Street, on the window blind of which was written the name of his firm with the address—London, E. C. On the mantelpiece of this little office a little leaden battalion of canisters was drawn up and on the table before the window stood four or five china bowls which were usually half full of a black liquid. From these bowls Mr. Kernan tasted tea. He took a mouthful, drew it up, saturated his palate with it and then spat it forth into the grate. Then he paused to judge.

Mr. Power, a much younger man, was employed in the Royal Irish Constabulary Office in Dublin Castle. The arc of his social rise intersected the arc of his friend's decline, but Mr. Kernan's decline was mitigated by the fact that certain of those friends who had known him at his highest point of success still esteemed him as a character. Mr. Power was one of these friends. His inexplicable debts were a byword in his circle; he was a debonair young man.

The car halted before a small house on the Glasnevin road and Mr. Kernan was helped into the house. His wife put him to bed, while Mr. Power sat downstairs in the kitchen asking the children where they went to school and what book they were in. The children—two girls and a boy, conscious of their father's helplessness and of their mother's absence, began some horseplay with him. He was surprised at their manners and at their accents, and his brow grew thoughtful. After a while Mrs. Kernan entered the kitchen, exclaiming:

"Such a sight! Oh, he'll do for himself one day and that's the holy alls of it. He's been drinking since Friday."

Mr. Power was careful to explain to her that he was not responsible, that he had come on the scene by the merest accident. Mrs. Kernan, remembering Mr. Power's good offices during domestic quarrels, as well as many small, but opportune loans, said:

"Oh, you needn't tell me that, Mr. Power. I know you're a friend of his, not like some of the others he does be with. They're all right so long as he has money in his pocket to keep him out from his wife and family. Nice friends! Who was he with tonight, I'd like to know?"

Mr. Power shook his head but said nothing.

"I'm so sorry," she continued, "that I've nothing

in the house to offer you. But if you wait a minute I'll send round to Fogarty's, at the corner."

Mr. Power stood up.

"We were waiting for him to come home with the money. He never seems to think he has a home at all."

"Oh, now, Mrs. Kernan," said Mr. Power, "we'll make him turn over a new leaf. I'll talk to Martin. He's the man. We'll come here one of these nights and talk it over."

She saw him to the door. The carman was stamping up and down the footpath, and swinging his arms to warm himself.

"It's very kind of you to bring him home," she said.

"Not at all," said Mr. Power.

He got up on the car. As it drove off he raised his hat to her gaily.

"We'll make a new man of him," he said. "Good-night, Mrs. Kernan."

Mrs. Kernan's puzzled eyes watched the car till it was out of sight. Then she withdrew them, went into the house and emptied her husband's pockets.

She was an active, practical woman of middle age. Not long before she had celebrated her silver wedding and renewed her intimacy with her husband by waltzing with him to Mr. Power's accompaniment. In her days of courtship, Mr. Kernan had seemed to her a not ungallant figure: and she still hurried to the chapel door whenever a wedding was reported and, seeing the bridal pair, recalled with vivid pleasure how she had passed out of the Star of the Sea Church in Sandymount, leaning on the arm of a jovial well-fed man, who was dressed smartly in a frock-coat and lavender trousers and carried a silk hat gracefully balanced upon his other arm. After three weeks she had found a wife's life irksome and, later on, when she was beginning to find it unbearable, she had become a mother. The part of mother presented to her no insuperable difficulties and for twenty-five years she had kept house shrewdly for her husband. Her two eldest sons were launched. One was in a draper's shop in Glasgow and the other was clerk to a tea-merchant in Belfast. They were good sons, wrote regularly and sometimes sent home money. The other children were still at school.

Mr. Kernan sent a letter to his office next day and remained in bed. She made beef-tea for him and scolded him roundly. She accepted his frequent intemperance as part of the climate, healed him dutifully whenever he was sick and always tried to make him eat a breakfast. There were worse husbands. He had never been violent since the boys had grown up, and she knew that he would walk to the end of Thomas Street and back again to book even a small order.

Two nights after, his friends came to see him. She brought them up to his bedroom, the air of which was impregnated with a personal odor, and gave them chairs at the fire. Mr. Kernan's tongue, the occasional stinging pain of which had made him somewhat irritable during the day, became more polite. He sat propped up in the bed by pillows and the little color in his puffy cheeks made them resemble warm cinders. He apologized to his guests for the disorder of the room, but at the same time looked at them a little proudly, with a veteran's pride.

He was quite unconscious that he was the victim of a plot which his friends, Mr. Cunningham, Mr. M'Coy and Mr. Power had disclosed to Mrs. Kernan in the parlor. The idea had been Mr. Power's, but its development was entrusted to Mr. Cunningham. Mr. Kernan came of Protestant stock and, though he had been converted to the Catholic faith at the time of his marriage, he had not been in the pale of the Church for twenty years. He was fond, moreover, of giving side-thrusts at Catholicism.

Mr. Cunningham was the very man for such a case. He was an elder colleague of Mr. Power. His own domestic life was not very happy. People had great sympathy with him, for it was known that he had married an unpresentable woman who was an incurable drunkard. He had set up house for her six times; and each time she had pawned the furniture on him.

Everyone had respect for poor Martin Cunningham. He was a thoroughly sensible man, influential and intelligent. His blade of human knowledge, natural astuteness particularized by long association with cases in the police courts, had been tempered by brief immersions in the waters of general philosophy. He was well informed. His friends bowed to his opinions and considered that his face was like Shakespeare's.

When the plot had been disclosed to her, Mrs. Kernan had said:

"I leave it all in your hands, Mr. Cunningham."

After a quarter of a century of married life, she had very few illusions left. Religion for her was a habit, and she suspected that a man of her husband's age would not change greatly before death. She was tempted to see a curious appropriateness in his accident and, but that she did not wish to seem bloody-minded, she would have told the gentlemen that Mr. Kernan's tongue would not suffer by being shortened. However, Mr. Cunningham was a capable man; and religion was religion. The scheme might do good and, at least, it could do no harm. Her beliefs were not extravagant. She believed steadily in the Sacred Heart as the most generally useful of all Catholic devotions and approved of the sacraments. Her faith was bounded by her kitchen, but, if she was put to it, she could believe also in the banshee and in the Holy Ghost.

The gentlemen began to talk of the accident. Mr. Cunningham said that he had once known a similar case. A man of seventy had bitten off a piece of his tongue during an epileptic fit and the tongue had filled in again, so that no one could see a trace of the bite.

"Well, I'm not seventy," said the invalid.

"God forbid," said Mr. Cunningham.

"It doesn't pain you now?" asked Mr. M'Coy.

Mr. M'Coy had been at one time a tenor of some reputation. His wife, who had been a soprano, still taught young children to play the piano at low terms. His line of life had not been the shortest distance between two points and for short periods he had been driven to live by his wits. He had been a clerk in the Midland Railway, a canvasser for advertisements for *The Irish Times* and for *The Freeman's Journal*, a town traveler for a coal firm on commission, a private inquiry agent, a clerk in the office of the sub-sheriff, and he had recently become secretary to the city coroner. His new office made him professionally interested in Mr. Kernan's case.

"Pain? Not much," answered Mr. Kernan. "But it's so sickening. I feel as if I wanted to retch off."

"That's the booze," said Mr. Cunningham firmly.

"No," said Mr. Kernan. "I think I caught cold on the car. There's something keeps coming into my throat, phlegm or——"

"Mucus," said Mr. M'Coy.

"It keeps coming like from down in my throat; sickening thing."

"Yes, yes," said Mr. M'Coy, "that's the thorax."

He looked at Mr. Cunningham and Mr. Power at the same time with an air of challenge. Mr. Cunningham nodded his head rapidly and Mr. Power said:

"Ah, well, all's well that ends well."

"I'm very much obliged to you, old man," said the invalid.

Mr. Power waved his hand.

"Those other two fellows I was with——"

"Who were you with?" asked Mr. Cunningham.

"A chap. I don't know his name. Damn it now, what's his name? Little chap with sandy hair. . . ."

"And who else?"

"Harford."

"Hm," said Mr. Cunningham.

When Mr. Cunningham made that remark, people were silent. It was known that the speaker had secret sources of information. In this case the monosyllable had a moral intention. Mr. Harford sometimes formed one of a little detachment which left the city shortly after noon on Sunday with the purpose of arriving as soon as possible at some public-house on the outskirts of the city where its members duly qualified themselves as bona fide travelers.[4] But his fellow-travelers had never consented to overlook his origin. He had begun life as an obscure financier by lending small sums of money to workmen at usurious interest. Later on he had become the partner of a very fat, short gentleman, Mr. Goldberg, in the Liffey Loan Bank. Though he had never embraced more than the Jewish ethical code, his fellow-Catholics, whenever they had smarted in person or by proxy under his exactions, spoke of him bitterly as an Irish Jew and an illiterate, and saw divine disapproval of usury made manifest through the person of his idiot son. At other times they remembered his good points.

"I wonder where did he go to," said Mr. Kernan.

He wished the details of the incident to remain vague. He wished his friends to think there had been some mistake, that Mr. Harford and he had missed each other. His friends, who knew quite well Mr.

4. **bona fide travelers:** travelers who may drink at pubs officially closed to local customers.

Harford's manners in drinking, were silent. Mr. Power said again:

"All's well that ends well."

Mr. Kernan changed the subject at once.

"That was a decent young chap, that medical fellow," he said. "Only for him——"

"Oh, only for him," said Mr. Power, "it might have been a case of seven days, without the option of a fine."

"Yes, yes," said Mr. Kernan, trying to remember. "I remember now there was a policeman. Decent young fellow, he seemed. How did it happen at all?"

"It happened that you were peloothered,[5] Tom," said Mr. Cunningham gravely.

"True bill," said Mr. Kernan, equally gravely.

"I suppose you squared the constable, Jack," said Mr. M'Coy.

Mr. Power did not relish the use of his Christian name. He was not strait-laced, but he could not forget that Mr. M'Coy had recently made a crusade in search of valises and portmanteaus to enable Mrs. M'Coy to fulfill imaginary engagements in the country. More than he resented the fact that he had been victimized he resented such low playing of the game. He answered the question, therefore, as if Mr. Kernan had asked it.

The narrative made Mr. Kernan indignant. He was keenly conscious of his citizenship, wished to live with his city on terms mutually honourable and resented any affront put upon him by those whom he called country bumpkins.

"Is this what we pay rates for?" he asked. "To feed and clothe these ignorant bostooms[6] . . . and they're nothing else."

Mr. Cunningham laughed. He was a Castle official only during office hours.

"How could they be anything else, Tom?" he said.

He assumed a thick, provincial accent and said in a tone of command:

"65,[7] catch your cabbage!"

Everyone laughed. Mr. M'Coy, who wanted to enter the conversation by any door, pretended that he had never heard the story. Mr. Cunningham said:

"It is supposed—they say, you know—to take

place in the depot where they get these thundering big country fellows, omadhauns, you know, to drill. The sergeant makes them stand in a row against the wall and hold up their plates."

He illustrated the story by grotesque gestures.

"At dinner, you know. Then he has a bloody big bowl of cabbage before him on the table and a bloody big spoon like a shovel. He takes up a wad of cabbage on the spoon and pegs it across the room and the poor devils have to try and catch it on their plates: *65, catch your cabbage.*"

Everyone laughed again: but Mr. Kernan was somewhat indignant still. He talked of writing a letter to the papers.

"These yahoos coming up here," he said, "think they can boss the people. I needn't tell you, Martin, what kind of men they are."

Mr. Cunningham gave a qualified assent.

"It's like everything else in this world," he said. "You get some bad ones and you get some good ones."

"Oh yes, you get some good ones, I admit," said Mr. Kernan, satisfied.

"It's better to have nothing to say to them," said Mr. M'Coy. "That's my opinion!"

Mrs. Kernan entered the room and, placing a tray on the table, said:

"Help yourselves, gentlemen."

Mr. Power stood up to officiate, offering her his chair. She declined it, saying she was ironing downstairs, and, after having exchanged a nod with Mr. Cunningham behind Mr. Power's back, prepared to leave the room. Her husband called out to her:

"And have you nothing for me, duckie?"

"Oh, you! The back of my hand to you!" said Mrs. Kernan tartly.

Her husband called after her:

"Nothing for poor little hubby!"

He assumed such a comical face and voice that the distribution of the bottles of stout took place amid general merriment.

The gentlemen drank from their glasses, set the glasses again on the table and paused. Then Mr. Cunningham turned towards Mr. Power and said casually:

"On Thursday night, you said, Jack?"

"Thursday, yes," said Mr. Power.

"Righto!" said Mr. Cunningham promptly.

"We can meet in M'Auley's," said Mr. M'Coy. "That'll be the most convenient place."

---

5. **peloothered:** presumably, drunk. 6. **bostooms:** derogatory term applied here to the constabulary. 7. **65:** constable number 65.

"But we mustn't be late," said Mr. Power earnestly, "because it is sure to be crammed to the doors."

"We can meet at half-seven," said Mr. M'Coy.

"Righto!" said Mr. Cunningham.

"Half-seven at M'Auley's be it!"

There was a short silence. Mr. Kernan waited to see whether he would be taken into his friends' confidence. Then he asked:

"What's in the wind?"

"Oh, it's nothing," said Mr. Cunningham. "It's only a little matter that we're arranging about for Thursday."

"The opera, is it?" said Mr. Kernan.

"No, no," said Mr. Cunningham in an evasive tone, "it's just a little . . . spiritual matter."

"Oh," said Mr. Kernan.

There was silence again. Then Mr. Power said, pointblank:

"To tell you the truth, Tom, we're going to make a retreat."

"Yes, that's it," said Mr. Cunningham, "Jack and I and M'Coy here—we're all going to wash the pot."

He uttered the metaphor with a certain homely energy and, encouraged by his own voice, proceeded:

"You see, we may as well all admit we're a nice collection of scoundrels, one and all. I say, one and all," he added with gruff charity and turning to Mr. Power. "Own up now!"

"I own up," said Mr. Power.

"And I own up," said Mr. M'Coy.

"So we're going to wash the pot together," said Mr. Cunningham.

A thought seemed to strike him. He turned suddenly to the invalid and said:

"D'ye know what, Tom, has just occurred to me? You might join in and we'd have a four-handed reel."

"Good idea," said Mr. Power. "The four of us together."

Mr. Kernan was silent. The proposal conveyed very little meaning to his mind, but, understanding that some spiritual agencies were about to concern themselves on his behalf, he thought he owed it to his dignity to show a stiff neck. He took no part in the conversation for a long while, but listened, with an air of calm enmity, while his friends discussed the Jesuits.

"I haven't such a bad opinion of the Jesuits," he said, intervening at length. "They're an educated order. I believe they mean well, too."

"They're the grandest order in the Church, Tom," said Mr. Cunningham, with enthusiasm. "The general of the Jesuits stands next to the pope."

"There's no mistake about it," said Mr. M'Coy, "if you want a thing well done and no flies about, you go to a Jesuit. They're the boyos have influence. I'll tell you a case in point. . . ."

"The Jesuits are a fine body of men," said Mr. Power.

"It's a curious thing," said Mr. Cunningham, "about the Jesuit Order. Every other order of the Church had to be reformed at some time or other but the Jesuit Order was never once reformed. It never fell away."

"Is that so?" asked Mr. M'Coy.

"That's a fact," said Mr. Cunningham. "That's history."

"Look at their church, too," said Mr. Power. "Look at the congregation they have."

"The Jesuits cater for the upper classes," said Mr. M'Coy.

"Of course," said Mr. Power.

"Yes," said Mr. Kernan. "That's why I have a feeling for them. It's some of those secular priests, ignorant, bumptious——"

"They're all good men," said Mr. Cunningham, "each in his own way. The Irish priesthood is honored all the world over."

"Oh yes," said Mr. Power.

"Not like some of the other priesthoods on the Continent," said Mr. M'Coy, "unworthy of the name."

"Perhaps you're right," said Mr. Kernan, relenting.

"Of course I'm right," said Mr. Cunningham. "I haven't been in the world all this time and seen most sides of it without being a judge of character."

The gentlemen drank again, one following another's example. Mr. Kernan seemed to be weighing something in his mind. He was impressed. He had a high opinion of Mr. Cunningham as a judge of character and as a reader of faces. He asked for particulars.

"Oh, it's just a retreat, you know," said Mr. Cunningham. "Father Purdon is giving it. It's for businessmen, you know."

"He won't be too hard on us, Tom," said Mr. Power persuasively.

"Father Purdon? Father Purdon?" said the invalid.

"Oh, you must know him, Tom," said Mr. Cunningham stoutly. "Fine, jolly fellow! He's a man of the world like ourselves."

"Ah, . . . yes. I think I know him. Rather red face; tall."

"That's the man."

"And tell me, Martin. . . . Is he a good preacher?"

"Munno. . . . It's not exactly a sermon, you know. It's just a kind of a friendly talk, you know, in a common-sense way."

Mr. Kernan deliberated. Mr. M'Coy said:

"Father Tom Burke, that was the boy!"

"Oh, Father Tom Burke," said Mr. Cunningham, "that was a born orator. Did you ever hear him, Tom?"

"Did I ever hear him!" said the invalid, nettled. "Rather! I heard him. . . ."

"And yet they say he wasn't much of a theologian," said Mr. Cunningham.

"Is that so?" said Mr. M'Coy.

"Oh, of course, nothing wrong, you know. Only sometimes, they say, he didn't preach what was quite orthodox."

"Ah! . . . he was a splendid man," said Mr. M'Coy.

"I heard him once," Mr. Kernan continued. "I forget the subject of his discourse now. Crofton and I were in the back of the . . . pit, you know . . . the——"

"The body," said Mr. Cunningham.

"Yes, in the back near the door. I forget now what. . . . Oh, yes, it was on the pope, the late pope.[8] I remember it well. Upon my word it was magnificent, the style of the oratory. And his voice! God! hadn't he a voice! *The Prisoner of the Vatican*, he called him. I remember Crofton saying to me when we came out——"

"But he's an Orangeman, Crofton, isn't he?" said Mr. Power.

" 'Course he is," said Mr. Kernan, "and a damned decent Orangeman, too. We went into Butler's in Moore Street—faith, I was genuinely

moved, tell you the God's truth—and I remember well his very words. *Kernan*, he said, *we worship at different altars*, he said, *but our belief is the same*. Struck me as very well put."

"There's a good deal in that," said Mr. Power. "There used always be crowds of Protestants in the chapel where Father Tom was preaching."

"There's not much difference between us," said Mr. M'Coy. "We both believe in——"

He hesitated for a moment.

". . . in the Redeemer. Only they don't believe in the pope and in the mother of God."

"But, of course," said Mr. Cunningham quietly and effectively, "our religion is *the* religion, the old, original faith."

"Not a doubt of it," said Mr. Kernan warmly.

Mrs. Kernan came to the door of the bedroom and announced:

"Here's a visitor for you!"

"Who is it?"

"Mr. Fogarty."

"Oh, come in! come in!"

A pale, oval face came forward into the light. The arch of its fair trailing mustache was repeated in the fair eyebrows looped above pleasantly astonished eyes. Mr. Fogarty was a modest grocer. He had failed in business in a licensed house in the city because his financial condition had constrained him to tie himself to second-class distillers and brewers. He had opened a small shop on Glasnevin Road where, he flattered himself, his manners would ingratiate him with the housewives of the district. He bore himself with a certain grace, complimented little children and spoke with a neat enunciation. He was not without culture.

Mr. Fogarty brought a gift with him, a half-pint of special whisky. He inquired politely for Mr. Kernan, placed his gift on the table and sat down with the company on equal terms. Mr. Kernan appreciated the gift all the more since he was aware that there was a small account for groceries unsettled between him and Mr. Fogarty. He said:

"I wouldn't doubt you, old man. Open that, Jack, will you?"

Mr. Power again officiated. Glasses were rinsed and five small measures of whisky were poured out. This new influence enlivened the conversation. Mr. Fogarty, sitting on a small area of the chair, was specially interested.

"Pope Leo XIII," said Mr. Cunningham, "was

---

8. the late pope: Leo XIII, a scholar and poet, who was notably pro-Irish. Pope from 1878 until his death in 1903, he considered himself a prisoner of the Vatican.

one of the lights of the age. His great idea, you know, was the union of the Latin and Greek churches. That was the aim of his life."

"I often heard he was one of the most intellectual men in Europe," said Mr. Power. "I mean, apart from his being pope."

"So he was," said Mr. Cunningham, "if not *the* most so. His motto, you know, as pope, was *Lux upon Lux—Light upon Light*."

"No, no," said Mr. Fogarty eagerly. "I think you're wrong there. It was *Lux in Tenebris*,[9] I think—*Light in Darkness*."

"Oh yes," said Mr. M'Coy, "*Tenebrae*."

"Allow me," said Mr. Cunningham positively, "it was *Lux upon Lux*. And Pius IX his predecessor's motto was *Crux upon Crux*—that is, *Cross upon Cross*—to show the difference between their two pontificates."

The inference was allowed. Mr. Cunningham continued.

"Pope Leo, you know, was a great scholar and a poet."

"He had a strong face," said Mr. Kernan.

"Yes," said Mr. Cunningham. "He wrote Latin poetry."

"Is that so?" said Mr. Fogarty.

Mr. M'Coy tasted his whisky contentedly and shook his head with a double intention, saying:

"That's no joke, I can tell you."

"We didn't learn that, Tom," said Mr. Power, following Mr. M'Coy's example, "when we went to the penny-a-week school."

"There was many a good man went to the penny-a-week school with a sod of turf under his oxter," said Mr. Kernan sententiously. "The old system was the best: plain honest education. None of your modern trumpery. . . ."

"Quite right," said Mr. Power.

"No superfluities," said Mr. Fogarty.

He enunciated the word and then drank gravely.

"I remember reading," said Mr. Cunningham, "that one of Pope Leo's poems was on the invention of the photograph—in Latin, of course."

"On the photograph!" exclaimed Mr. Kernan.

"Yes," said Mr. Cunningham.

He also drank from his glass.

"Well, you know," said Mr. M'Coy, "isn't the photograph wonderful when you come to think of it?"

"Oh, of course," said Mr. Power, "great minds can see things."

"As the poet says: *Great minds are very near to madness*," said Mr. Fogarty.

Mr. Kernan seemed to be troubled in mind. He made an effort to recall the Protestant theology on some thorny points and in the end addressed Mr. Cunningham.

"Tell me, Martin," he said. "Weren't some of the popes—of course, not our present man, or his predecessor, but some of the old popes—not exactly . . . you know . . . up to the knocker?"

There was a silence. Mr. Cunningham said:

"Oh, of course, there were some bad lots. . . . But the astonishing thing is this. Not one of them, not the biggest drunkard, not the most . . . out-and-out ruffian, not one of them ever preached *ex cathedra* a word of false doctrine. Now isn't that an astonishing thing?"

"That is," said Mr. Kernan.

"Yes, because when the pope speaks *ex cathedra*," Mr. Fogarty explained, "he is infallible."

"Yes," said Mr. Cunningham.

"Oh, I know about the infallibility of the pope. I remember I was younger then. . . . Or was it that——?"

Mr. Fogarty interrupted. He took up the bottle and helped the others to a little more. Mr. M'Coy, seeing that there was not enough to go round, pleaded that he had not finished his first measure. The others accepted under protest. The light music of whisky falling into glasses made an agreeable interlude.

"What's that you were saying, Tom?" asked Mr. M'Coy.

"Papal infallibility," said Mr. Cunningham, "that was the greatest scene in the whole history of the Church."

"How was that, Martin?" asked Mr. Power.

Mr. Cunningham held up two thick fingers.

"In the sacred college, you know, of cardinals and archbishops and bishops there were two men who held out against it while the others were all for it. The whole conclave except these two was unanimous. No! They wouldn't have it!"

"Ha!" said Mr. M'Coy.

"And they were a German cardinal by the name of Dolling[10] . . . or Dowling . . . or——"

---

9. Lux in Tenebris: the correct motto of Leo XIII.

10. Dolling: Professor Dollinger of Munich, who left the Church in 1871.

"Dowling was no German, and that's a sure five," said Mr. Power, laughing.

"Well, this great German cardinal, whatever his name was, was one; and the other was John MacHale."[11]

"What?" cried Mr. Kernan. "Is it John of Tuam?"

"Are you sure of that now?" asked Mr. Fogarty dubiously. "I thought it was some Italian or American."

"John of Tuam," repeated Mr. Cunningham, "was the man."

He drank and the other gentlemen followed his lead. Then he resumed:

"There they were at it, all the cardinals and bishops and archbishops from all the ends of the earth and these two fighting dog and devil until at last the pope himself stood up and declared infallibility a dogma of the Church *ex cathedra*. On the very moment John MacHale, who had been arguing and arguing against it, stood up and shouted out with the voice of a lion: '*Credo!*'"

"*I believe!*" said Mr. Fogarty.

"*Credo!*" said Mr. Cunningham. "That showed the faith he had. He submitted the moment the pope spoke."

"And what about Dowling?" asked Mr. M'Coy.

"The German cardinal wouldn't submit. He left the Church."

Mr. Cunningham's words had built up the vast image of the Church in the minds of his hearers. His deep, raucous voice had thrilled them as it uttered the word of belief and submission. When Mrs. Kernan came into the room, drying her hands, she came into a solemn company. She did not disturb the silence, but leaned over the rail at the foot of the bed.

"I once saw John MacHale," said Mr. Kernan, "and I'll never forget it as long as I live."

He turned towards his wife to be confirmed.

"I often told you that?"

Mrs. Kernan nodded.

"It was at the unveiling of Sir John Gray's statue. Edmund Dwyer Gray[12] was speaking, blathering away, and here was this old fellow,

crabbed-looking old chap, looking at him from under his bushy eyebrows."

Mr. Kernan knitted his brows and, lowering his head like an angry bull, glared at his wife.

"God!" he exclaimed, resuming his natural face, "I never saw such an eye in a man's head. It was as much as to say: *I have you properly taped, my lad.* He had an eye like a hawk."

"None of the Grays was any good," said Mr. Power.

There was a pause again. Mr. Power turned to Mrs. Kernan and said with abrupt joviality:

"Well, Mrs. Kernan, we're going to make your man here a good holy pious and God-fearing Roman Catholic."

He swept his arm round the company inclusively.

"We're all going to make a retreat together and confess our sins—and God knows we want it badly."

"I don't mind," said Mr. Kernan, smiling a little nervously.

Mrs. Kernan thought it would be wiser to conceal her satisfaction. So she said:

"I pity the poor priest that has to listen to your tale."

Mr. Kernan's expression changed.

"If he doesn't like it," he said bluntly, "he can . . . do the other thing. I'll just tell him my little tale of woe. I'm not such a bad fellow——"

Mr. Cunningham intervened promptly.

"We'll all renounce the devil," he said, "together, not forgetting his works and pomps."

"Get behind me, Satan!" said Mr. Fogarty, laughing and looking at the others.

Mr. Power said nothing. He felt completely outgeneraled. But a pleased expression flickered across his face.

"All we have to do," said Mr. Cunningham, "is to stand up with lighted candles in our hands and renew our baptismal vows."

"Oh, don't forget the candle, Tom," said Mr. M'Coy, "whatever you do."

"What?" said Mr. Kernan. "Must I have a candle?"

"Oh yes," said Mr. Cunningham.

"No, damn it all," said Mr. Kernan sensibly, "I draw the line there. I'll do the job right enough. I'll do the retreat business and confession, and . . . all that business. But . . . no candles! No, damn it all, I bar the candles!"

---

11. **John MacHale:** an Irish archbishop of Tuam, noted for his activities in aiding Ireland's poor. 12. **Edmund Dwyer Gray:** son of Sir John Gray, proprietor of *The Freeman's Journal*, a patriotic Irish newspaper to which John MacHale contributed articles for the reform of England's Irish policy.

He shook his head with farcical gravity.

"Listen to that!" said his wife.

"I bar the candles," said Mr. Kernan, conscious of having created an effect on his audience and continuing to shake his head to and fro. "I bar the magic-lantern business."

Everyone laughed heartily.

"There's a nice Catholic for you!" said his wife.

"No candles!" repeated Mr. Kernan obdurately. "That's off!"

The transept of the Jesuit Church in Gardiner Street was almost full; and still at every moment gentlemen entered from the side door and, directed by the lay-brother, walked on tip-toe along the aisles until they found seating accommodation. The gentlemen were all well dressed and orderly. The light of the lamps of the church fell upon an assembly of black clothes and white collars, relieved here and there by tweeds, on dark mottled pillars of green marble and on lugubrious canvases. The gentlemen sat in the benches, having hitched their trousers slightly above their knees and laid their hats in security. They sat well back and gazed formally at the distant speck of red light which was suspended before the high altar.

In one of the benches near the pulpit sat Mr. Cunningham and Mr. Kernan. In the bench behind sat Mr. M'Coy alone: and in the bench behind him sat Mr. Power and Mr. Fogarty. Mr. M'Coy had tried unsuccessfully to find a place in the bench with the others, and, when the party had settled down in the form of a quincunx,[13] he had tried unsuccessfully to make comic remarks. As these had not been well received, he had desisted. Even he was sensible of the decorous atmosphere and even he began to respond to the religious stimulus. In a whisper, Mr. Cunningham drew Mr. Kernan's attention to Mr. Harford, the moneylender, who sat some distance off, and to Mr. Fanning, the registration agent and mayor maker of the city, who was sitting immediately under the pulpit beside one of the newly elected councilors of the ward. To the right sat old Michael Grimes, the owner of three pawnbroker's shops, and Dan Hogan's nephew, who was up for the job in the town clerk's office. Farther in front sat Mr. Hendrick, the chief reporter of *The Freeman's*

Journal, and poor O'Carroll, an old friend of Mr. Kernan's, who had been at one time a considerable commercial figure. Gradually, as he recognized familiar faces, Mr. Kernan began to feel more at home. His hat, which had been rehabilitated by his wife, rested upon his knees. Once or twice he pulled down his cuffs with one hand while he held the brim of his hat lightly, but firmly, with the other hand.

A powerful-looking figure, the upper part of which was draped with a white surplice, was observed to be struggling up into the pulpit. Simultaneously the congregation unsettled, produced handkerchiefs and knelt upon them with care. Mr. Kernan followed the general example. The priest's figure now stood upright in the pulpit, two-thirds of its bulk, crowned by a massive red face, appearing above the balustrade.

Father Purdon knelt down, turned towards the red speck of light and, covering his face with his hands, prayed. After an interval, he uncovered his face and rose. The congregation rose also and settled again on its benches. Mr. Kernan restored his hat to its original position on his knee and presented an attentive face to the preacher. The preacher turned back each wide sleeve of his surplice with an elaborate large gesture and slowly surveyed the array of faces. Then he said:

"For the children of this world are wiser in their generation than the children of light. Wherefore make unto yourselves friends out of the mammon of iniquity so that when you die they may receive you into everlasting dwellings."[14]

Father Purdon developed the text with resonant assurance. It was one of the most difficult texts in all the Scriptures, he said, to interpret properly. It was a text which might seem to the casual observer at variance with the lofty morality elsewhere preached by Jesus Christ. But, he told his hearers, the text had seemed to him specially adapted for the guidance of those whose lot it was to lead the life of the world and who yet wished to lead that life not in the manner of worldlings. It was a text for businessmen and professional men. Jesus Christ, with his divine understanding of every cranny of our human nature, understood that all men were not called to the religious life, that by far the vast

13. **quincunx:** arrangement of five points in a square, one at each corner and one in the center, often a symbol of Christ's five wounds.

14. **For . . . dwellings:** a paraphrase of Luke 16:8–9; but see 16:13, "Ye cannot serve God and mammon."

majority were forced to live in the world, and, to a certain extent, for the world: and in this sentence he designed to give them a word of counsel, setting before them as exemplars in the religious life those very worshipers of Mammon who were of all men the least solicitous in matters religious.

He told his hearers that he was there that evening for no terrifying, no extravagant purpose; but as a man of the world speaking to his fellow-men. He came to speak to businessmen and he would speak to them in a businesslike way. If he might use the metaphor, he said, he was their spiritual account- ant; and he wished each and every one of his hearers to open his books, the books of his spiritual life, and see if they tallied accurately with con- science.

Jesus Christ was not a hard taskmaster. He understood our little failings, understood the weakness of our poor fallen nature, understood the temptations of this life. We might have had, we all had from time to time, our temptations: we might have, we all had, our failings. But one thing only, he said, he would ask of his hearers. And that was: to be straight and manly with God. If their accounts tallied in every point to say:

"Well, I have verified my accounts. I find all well."

But if, as might happen, there were some dis- crepancies, to admit the truth, to be frank and say like a man:

"Well, I have looked into my accounts. I find this wrong and this wrong. But, with God's grace, I will rectify this and this. I will set right my accounts."

SHIRLEY JACKSON
1919–1965

The Lottery

The morning of June 27th was clear and sunny, with the fresh warmth of a full-summer day; the flowers were blossoming profusely and the grass was richly green. The people of the village began to gather in the square, between the post office and the bank, around ten o'clock; in some towns there were so many people that the lottery took two days and had to be started on June 26th, but in this village, where there were only about three hundred people, the whole lottery took only about two hours, so it could begin at ten o'clock in the morn- ing and still be through in time to allow the villagers to get home for noon dinner.

The children assembled first, of course. School was recently over for the summer, and the feeling of liberty sat uneasily on most of them; they tended to gather together quietly for a while before they broke into boisterous play, and their talk was still of the classroom and the teacher, of books and reprimands. Bobby Martin had already stuffed his pockets full of stones, and the other boys soon followed his example, selecting the smoothest and roundest stones; Bobby and Harry Jones and Dickie Delacroix—the villagers pronounced this name "Dellacroy"—eventually made a great pile of stones in one corner of the square and guarded it against the raids of the other boys. The girls stood aside, talking among themselves, looking over their shoulders at the boys, and the very small children rolled in the dust or clung to the hands of their older brothers or sisters.

Soon the men began to gather, surveying their own children, speaking of planting and rain, tractors and taxes. They stood together, away from the pile of stones in the corner, and their jokes were quiet and they smiled rather than laughed. The women, wearing faded house dresses and sweaters, came shortly after their menfolk. They greeted one another and exchanged bits of gossip as they went to join their husbands. Soon the women, standing by their husbands, began to call to their children, and the children came reluctantly, having to be called four or five times. Bobby Martin ducked under his mother's grasping hand and ran, laughing, back to the pile of stones. His father spoke up sharply, and Bobby came quickly and took his place between his father and his oldest brother.

The lottery was conducted—as were the square dances, the teen-age club, the Halloween program —by Mr. Summers, who had time and energy to devote to civic activities. He was a round-faced, jovial man and he ran the coal business, and people were sorry for him, because he had no children and his wife was a scold. When he arrived in the square, carrying the black wooden box, there was a mur- mur of conversation among the villagers, and he waved and called, "Little late today, folks." The postmaster, Mr. Graves, followed him, carrying a three-legged stool, and the stool was put in the center of the square and Mr. Summers set the black box down on it. The villagers kept their distance, leaving a space between themselves and the stool, and when Mr. Summers said, "Some of you fellows want to give me a hand?" there was a hesitation before two men, Mr. Martin and his oldest son, Baxter, came forward to hold the box steady on the stool while Mr. Summers stirred up the papers inside it.

The original paraphernalia for the lottery had been lost long ago, and the black box now resting on the stool had been put into use even before Old Man Warner, the oldest man in town, was born. Mr. Summers spoke frequently to the villagers about making a new box, but no one liked to upset even as much tradition as was represented by the black box. There was a story that the present box had been made with some pieces of the box that had preceded it, the one that had been constructed when the first people settled down to make a village here. Every year, after the lottery, Mr. Summers began talking again about a new box, but every year the subject was allowed to fade off without anything's being done. The black box grew shabbier each year; by now it was no longer completely black but splintered badly along one side to show the original wood color, and in some places faded or stained.

Mr. Martin and his oldest son, Baxter, held the black box securely on the stool until Mr. Summers had stirred the papers thoroughly with his hand. Because so much of the ritual had been forgotten or discarded, Mr. Summers had been successful in having slips of paper substituted for the chips of wood that had been used for generations. Chips of wood, Mr. Summers had argued, had been all very well when the village was tiny, but now that the population was more than three hundred and likely to keep on growing, it was necessary to use something that would fit more easily into the black box. The night before the lottery, Mr. Summers and Mr. Graves made up the slips of paper and put them into the box, and it was then taken to the safe of Mr. Summers' coal company and locked up until Mr. Summers was ready to take it to the square next morning. The rest of the year, the box was put away, sometimes one place, sometimes

another; it had spent one year in Mr. Graves' barn and another year underfoot in the post office, and sometimes it was set on a shelf in the Martin grocery and left there.

There was a great deal of fussing to be done before Mr. Summers declared the lottery open. There were the lists to make up—of heads of families, heads of households in each family, members of each household in each family. There was the proper swearing-in of Mr. Summers by the postmaster, as the official of the lottery; at one time, some people remembered, there had been a recital of some sort, performed by the official of the lottery, a perfunctory, tuneless chant that had been rattled off duly each year; some people believed that the official of the lottery used to stand just so when he said or sang it, others believed that he was supposed to walk among the people, but years and years ago this part of the ritual had been allowed to lapse. There had been, also, a ritual salute, which the official of the lottery had had to use in addressing each person who came up to draw from the box, but this also had changed with time, until now it was felt necessary only for the official to speak to each person approaching. Mr. Summers was very good at all this; in his clean white shirt and blue jeans, with one hand resting carelessly on the black box, he seemed very proper and important as he talked interminably to Mr. Graves and the Martins.

Just as Mr. Summers finally left off talking and turned to the assembled villagers, Mrs. Hutchinson came hurriedly along the path to the square, her sweater thrown over her shoulders, and slid into place in the back of the crowd. "Clean forgot what day it was," she said to Mrs. Delacroix, who stood next to her, and they both laughed softly. "Thought my old man was out back stacking wood," Mrs. Hutchinson went on, "and then I looked out the window and the kids was gone, and then I remembered it was the twenty-seventh and came a-running." She dried her hands on her apron, and Mrs. Delacroix said, "You're in time, though. They're still talking away up there."

Mrs. Hutchinson craned her neck to see through the crowd and found her husband and children standing near the front. She tapped Mrs. Delacroix on the arm as a farewell and began to make her way through the crowd. The people separated good-humoredly to let her through; two or three people said, in voices just loud enough to be heard across the crowd, "Here comes your Mrs., Hutchinson," and "Bill, she made it after all." Mrs. Hutchinson reached her husband, and Mr. Summers, who had been waiting, said cheerfully, "Thought we were going to have to get on without you, Tessie." Mrs. Hutchinson said, grinning, "Wouldn't have me leave m'dishes in the sink, now, would you, Joe?" and soft laughter ran through the crowd as the people stirred back into position after Mr. Hutchinson's arrival.

"Well, now," Mr. Summers said soberly, "guess we better get started, get this over with, so's we can go back to work. Anybody ain't here?"

"Dunbar," several people said. "Dunbar, Dunbar."

Mr. Summers consulted his list. "Clyde Dunbar," he said. "That's right. He's broke his leg, hasn't he? Who's drawing for him?"

"Me, I guess," a woman said, and Mr. Summers turned to look at her. "Wife draws for her husband," Mr. Summers said. "Don't you have a grown boy to do it for you, Janey?" Although Mr. Summers and everyone else in the village knew the answer perfectly well, it was the business of the official of the lottery to ask such questions formally. Mr. Summers waited with an expression of polite interest while Mrs. Dunbar answered.

"Horace's not but sixteen yet," Mrs. Dunbar said regretfully. "Guess I gotta fill in for the old man this year."

"Right," Mr. Summers said. He made a note on the list he was holding. Then he asked, "Watson boy drawing this year?"

A tall boy in the crowd raised his hand. "Here," he said. "I'm drawing for m'mother and me." He blinked his eyes nervously and ducked his head as several voices in the crowd said things like "Good fellow, Jack," and "Glad to see your mother's got a man to do it."

"Well," Mr. Summers said, "guess that's everyone. Old Man Warner make it?"

"Here," a voice said, and Mr. Summers nodded.

A sudden hush fell on the crowd as Mr. Summers cleared his throat and looked at the list. "All ready?" he called. "Now, I'll read the names—heads of families first—and the men come up and take a paper out of the box. Keep the paper folded in your hand without looking at it until everyone has had a turn. Everything clear?"

The people had done it so many times that they only half listened to the directions; most of them were quiet, wetting their lips, not looking around. Then Mr. Summers raised one hand high and said, "Adams." A man disengaged himself from the crowd and came forward. "Hi, Steve," Mr. Summers said, and Mr. Adams said, "Hi, Joe." They grinned at one another humorlessly and nervously. Then Mr. Adams reached into the black box and took out a folded paper. He held it firmly by one corner as he turned and went hastily back to his place in the crowd, where he stood a little apart from his family, not looking down at his hand.

"Allen," Mr. Summers said. "Anderson. . . . Bentham."

"Seems like there's no time at all between lotteries any more," Mrs. Delacroix said to Mrs. Graves in the back row. "Seems like we got through with the last one only last week."

"Time sure goes fast," Mrs. Graves said.

"Clark. . . . Delacroix."

"There goes my old man," Mrs. Delacroix said. She held her breath while her husband went forward.

"Dunbar," Mr. Summers said, and Mrs. Dunbar went steadily to the box while one of the women said, "Go on, Janey," and another said, "There she goes."

"We're next," Mrs. Graves said. She watched while Mr. Graves came around from the side of the box, greeted Mr. Summers gravely, and selected a slip of paper from the box. By now, all through the crowd there were men holding the small folded papers in their large hands, turning them over and over nervously. Mrs. Dunbar and her two sons stood together, Mrs. Dunbar holding the slip of paper.

"Harburt. . . . Hutchinson."

"Get up there, Bill," Mrs. Hutchinson said, and the people near her laughed.

"Jones."

"They do say," Mr. Adams said to Old Man Warner, who stood next to him, "that over in the north village they're talking of giving up the lottery."

Old Man Warner snorted. "Pack of crazy fools," he said. "Listening to the young folks, nothing's good enough for *them*. Next thing you know, they'll be wanting to go back to living in caves, nobody work any more, live *that* way for a while. Used to be a saying about 'Lottery in June, corn be heavy soon.' First thing you know, we'd all be eating stewed chickenweed and acorns. There's *always* been a lottery," he added petulantly. "Bad enough to see young Joe Summers up there joking with everybody."

"Some places have already quit lotteries," Mrs. Adams said.

"Nothing but trouble in *that*," Old Man Warner said stoutly. "Pack of young fools."

"Martin." And Bobby Martin watched his father go forward. "Overdyke. . . . Percy."

"I wish they'd hurry," Mrs. Dunbar said to her older son. "I wish they'd hurry."

"They're almost through," her son said.

"You get ready to run tell Dad," Mrs. Dunbar said.

Mr. Summers called his own name and then stepped forward precisely and selected a slip from the box. Then he called, "Warner."

"Seventy-seventh year I been in the lottery," Old Man Warner said as he went through the crowd. "Seventy-seventh time."

"Watson." The tall boy came awkwardly through the crowd. Someone said, "Don't be nervous, Jack," and Mr. Summers said, "Take your time, son."

"Zanini."

After that, there was a long pause, a breathless pause, until Mr. Summers, holding his slip of paper in the air, said, "All right, fellows." For a minute, no one moved, and then all the slips of paper were opened. Suddenly, all the women began to speak at once, saying, "Who is it?" "Who's got it?" "Is it the Dunbars?" "Is it the Watsons?" Then the voices began to say, "It's Hutchinson. It's Bill," "Bill Hutchinson's got it."

"Go tell your father," Mrs. Dunbar said to her older son.

People began to look around to see the Hutchinsons. Bill Hutchinson was standing quiet, staring down at the paper in his hand. Suddenly, Tessie Hutchinson shouted to Mr. Summers, "You didn't give him time enough to take any paper he wanted. I saw you. It wasn't fair!"

"Be a good sport, Tessie," Mrs. Delacroix called, and Mrs. Graves said, "All of us took the same chance."

"Shut up, Tessie," Bill Hutchinson said.

"Well, everyone," Mr. Summers said, "that was done pretty fast, and now we've got to be hurrying a little more to get done in time." He consulted his next list. "Bill," he said, "you draw for the Hutchinson family. You got any other households in the Hutchinsons?"

"There's Don and Eva," Mrs. Hutchinson yelled. "Make *them* take their chance!"

"Daughters draw with their husbands' families, Tessie," Mr. Summers said gently. "You know that as well as anyone else."

"It wasn't *fair*," Tessie said.

"I guess not, Joe," Bill Hutchinson said regretfully. "My daughter draws with her husband's family, that's only fair. And I've got no other family except the kids."

"Then, as far as drawing for families is concerned, it's you," Mr. Summers said in explanation, "and as far as drawing for households is concerned, that's you, too. Right?"

"Right," Bill Hutchinson said.

"How many kids, Bill?" Mr. Summers asked formally.

"Three," Bill Hutchinson said. "There's Bill, Jr., and Nancy, and little Dave. And Tessie and me."

"All right, then," Mr. Summers said. "Harry, you got their tickets back?"

Mr. Graves nodded and held up the slips of paper. "Put them in the box, then," Mr. Summers directed. "Take Bill's and put it in."

"I think we ought to start over," Mrs. Hutchinson said, as quietly as she could. "I tell you it wasn't *fair*. You didn't give him time enough to choose. *Every*body saw that."

Mr. Graves had selected the five slips and put them in the box, and he dropped all the papers but those onto the ground, where the breeze caught them and lifted them off.

"Listen, everybody," Mrs. Hutchinson was saying to the people around her.

"Ready, Bill?" Mr. Summers asked, and Bill Hutchinson, with one quick glance around at his wife and children, nodded.

"Remember," Mr. Summers said, "take the slips and keep them folded until each person has taken one. Harry, you help little Dave." Mr. Graves took the hand of the little boy, who came willingly with him up to the box. "Take a paper out of the box, Davy," Mr. Summers said. Davy put his hand into the box and laughed. "Take just *one* paper," Mr. Summers said. "Harry, you hold it for him." Mr. Graves took the child's hand and removed the folded paper from the tight fist and held it while little Dave stood next to him and looked up at him wonderingly.

"Nancy next," Mr. Summers said. Nancy was twelve, and her school friends breathed heavily as she went forward, switching her skirt, and took a slip daintily from the box. "Bill, Jr.," Mr. Summers said, and Billy, his face red and his feet overlarge, nearly knocked the box over as he got a paper out. "Tessie," Mr. Summers said. She hesitated for a minute, looking around defiantly, and then set her lips and went up to the box. She snatched a paper out and held it behind her.

"Bill," Mr. Summers said, and Bill Hutchinson reached into the box and felt around, bringing his hand out at last with the slip of paper in it.

The crowd was quiet. A girl whispered, "I hope it's not Nancy," and the sound of the whisper reached the edges of the crowd.

"It's not the way it used to be," Old Man Warner said clearly. "People ain't the way they used to be."

"All right," Mr. Summers said. "Open the papers. Harry, you open little Dave's."

Mr. Graves opened the slip of paper and there was a general sigh through the crowd as he held it up and everyone could see that it was blank. Nancy and Bill, Jr., opened theirs at the same time, and both beamed and laughed, turning around to the crowd and holding their slips of paper above their heads.

"Tessie," Mr. Summers said. There was a pause, and then Mr. Summers looked at Bill Hutchinson, and Bill unfolded his paper and showed it. It was blank.

"It's Tessie," Mr. Summers said, and his voice was hushed. "Show us her paper, Bill."

Bill Hutchinson went over to his wife and forced the slip of paper out of her hand. It had a black spot on it, the black spot Mr. Summers had made the night before with the heavy pencil in the coal-company office. Bill Hutchinson held it up, and there was a stir in the crowd.

"All right, folks," Mr. Summers said. "Let's finish quickly."

Although the villagers had forgotten the ritual and lost the original black box, they still remembered to use stones. The pile of stones the boys had made earlier was ready; there were stones on the ground with the blowing scraps of paper that had come out of the box. Mrs. Delacroix selected a stone so large she had to pick it up with both hands and turned to Mrs. Dunbar. "Come on," she said. "Hurry up."

Mrs. Dunbar had small stones in both hands, and she said, gasping for breath, "I can't run at all. You'll have to go ahead and I'll catch up with you."

The children had stones already, and someone gave little Davy Hutchinson a few pebbles.

Tessie Hutchinson was in the center of a cleared space by now, and she held her hands out desperately as the villagers moved in on her. "It isn't fair," she said. A stone hit her on the side of the head.

Old Man Warner was saying, "Come on, come on, everyone." Steve Adams was in the front of the crowd of villagers, with Mrs. Graves beside him.

"It isn't fair, it isn't right," Mrs. Hutchinson screamed, and then they were upon her.

Thematic Irony

The lyric has a special attraction for the ironic poet. Of all the major genres, it offers the shortest and most intensive forms, and while they are no less difficult than others, they relieve the ironist of the demands of structure and causality in the more extensive structures of fiction and drama. The introspective stance and the intensity of engagement in the subject that we associate with the lyric correspond with certain ironic attitudes. The lyric's emphasis on the associative rather than the logical pattern and its reliance on the implication of image and metaphor rather than the more direct and "rational" forms of discourse appeal to the ironist's taste for the laconic and his suspicion of rhetoric. As a consequence, there is a large selection of lyrics to draw on to test the analogy between the narrative and thematic forms of irony.

The Vision of the Demonic

When the romantic poet experiences his supernatural vision, although it isolates him from his audience through an ecstasy in a literally absorbing act, the effect is to give form and meaning to experience. The ironic poet's vision originates with the demonic rather than the divine, and the effect is more often shattering than unifying. The substantial world for Arnold is "Swept with confused alarms" and for Lowell is a "black classic, breaking up / like killer kings on an Etruscan cup." The ironic lyricist does not usually provide a summary moral unless his motive is primarily satiric, as was that of many eighteenth-century poets. If he does he speaks in the insistent negatives of Arnold, certain only of uncertainty, in a world that "Hath really neither joy nor love, nor light, / Nor certitude, nor peace, nor help for pain." When the poet does find a grandeur in the world, as Emily Dickinson does in the northern lights in "Of Bronze— and Blaze," it "Infects . . . / With Taints of Majesty" and contrasts with man's arrogance and pretension to anything more than a "menagerie" of human splendors that end in the "dishonored Grass." The event of death, conventionally a moment of insight and final clarification of mystery, no longer affords that resolution: in "I heard a Fly buzz—when I died" Dickinson contemplates that instant of the "last Onset—when the

King / Be witnessed" (her use of the subjunctive and dashes leaves the verb ambiguous) but then a fly interposes, shutting off the light, until she "could not see to see." In all these visionary poems, clarity and definition are transitory: the ironic illumination flickers over a dark background into which it fades like an afterimage. And however sharp the vision, the subject simply exists in its terrifying actuality, or displaying the fortuitousness of Frost's spider, moth, and flower, it takes on the character of a hallucination.

At best, the experience is unsettling enough to cast doubt on the validity of any extended comment by the poet. Blake may rage against the "mind-forged manacles" that bind mankind, Arnold may find some resolution in identifying the God that severed man from man and "enisled" him in the sea of life, and Frost may avoid the ultimate despair of no design by attributing his experience to a "design of darkness" that at least considers him worthy enough to appall. But measured against the substance of the vision, the ironic poet's response is unusually laconic. The poem utters more than the poet, for he avoids the role of the teacher, a role with which he is manifestly ill at ease. The ironist customarily places his subject against a backdrop of chaos and darkness and affords it only the fitful illumination of a momentary vision. The light of that vision may extend outward to reveal the anarchy of the human condition, but more often it reveals the dimensions of a more personal demonic experience. Such a moment may have the initiating effect that we find in the first phase of narrative irony, incorporating in thematic forms the withering illuminations of contemporary fiction. Or, once again, if the intent is to satirize, these visionary moments may contrast the bewildering confusion of an anomalous world with the bleak but ordered moral sense of the satirist's anger, but there is usually little occasion for moralizing. The vision seems to have a life and purpose of its own. Like the skunk in Lowell's poem, it "will not scare," or like Poe's "City in the Sea," its hallucinatory grandeur will not allow the comfort of a generalization.

The Dismembered World of Experience

The longer poems in the ironic mode bear witness to a dismembered world and the necessarily fragmented vision of the poet who attempts to survey it. In our own times, the more panoramic poems—Eliot's "Waste Land," Ezra Pound's "Cantos," and William Carlos Williams' "Paterson" —seem more like the random gatherings of the remains of a broken culture than any consistent articulation of an ordered world. They assume the form of an anthology of lyrics that represent less a structure than, as for Eliot, makeshift fragments shored against a ruin. This, of course, is not to deny these poems any structure at all but simply to note that whatever aesthetic form they have is meant in at least one way to reflect the disorder in the world they envision.

The longer poems of earlier periods, particularly those of the seventeenth and eighteenth centuries, imply a more unified vision, perhaps because they drew on the formal conventions of the classical verse satire and epistle. But if the traditions of satire provided poets like Rochester, Pope, and Swift with an unwavering moral point of view and a consistent though bitter vision of things, the world they presented was still anatomized, dissected with an analytic wit, and held up to scorn on the point of an epigrammatic couplet. Rochester sees mankind strayed from "right reason" and no better than the beast, if as good. Pope, with his vision of the good man who walks "innoxious through his age," takes on a whole society of patronizing lords and ladies, scribbling hacks, pretentious literati, poetasters, and critical quibblers in an age when "The Dog Star rages! nay 'tis past a doubt / All Bedlam; or Parnassus, is let out." In his long epitaph Swift ironically imagines his meager fame dwindling fast upon his death, a fame that might have lasted longer had he been less honest with others and himself. Only a few friends are faithful to his memory; the rest damn themselves with their specious estimations of his value, while he pays off his age and nation with an appropriate legacy:

> He gave the little wealth he had
> To build a house for fools and mad;
> And showed by one satiric touch,
> No nation wanted it so much.

Whatever sure moral sense and integrity of vision these poems have, they all present us with a world ethically deformed and a society whose most fitting metaphor is the madhouse. Honesty is rare; men are deluded; taste, good sense, reason are all perverted. The best strategy for the poet is to retreat: "Shut, shut the door, good John! (fatigued, I said), / Tie up the knocker, say I'm sick, I'm dead." These poets withdrew, alone or with a select company of like-minded ironists, like Pope into a quiet room or like Swift to his imagined grave, in order to establish a detached moral or intellectual position. This withdrawn stance, designed to dissociate the poet from a world of turmoil and allow him a vantage point for the panoramic vision, was a harbinger of the further retreat of the poet in our own time. In contemporary poetry the satiric voice is still heard, and still with the accents of a prophet castigating a generation of vipers, but now the poet speaks more often through a persona or mask. In place of the authoritative tones of Pope or Swift we hear only the querulous voices of Eliot's characters or the convoluted dialogues among the various masks of Yeats. In "The Waste Land" Eliot notes that Tiresias is, "although a mere spectator, . . . the most important personage in the poem, uniting all the rest." There is a contemporary significance in Eliot's blind seer who represents all the personages of the poet's world, witnesses the tawdry events of our time, and hopelessly records them. The anarchy earlier poets saw in the world they satirized seems to have infected the poetic vision itself; chaos is now so obvious that any moral commentary on it is redundant.

Yeats' "Nineteen Hundred and Nineteen" seems to mark a moment in history when irony turns against itself. He calls on his generation to mock the great, the wise, and the good, and then destroys even the bitter solace of that extreme pessimism:

> Mock mockers after that
> That would not lift a hand maybe
> To help good, wise or great
> To bar that foul storm out, for we
> Traffic in mockery.

This is not the final version of despair—Yeats still entertains the possibility of greatness, wisdom, and goodness—but in that admission he comes close to a point that seriously challenges the conventional position of the ironist. When the ironist begins to question the conceptual system of his own poem, as Yeats seems to in this one, the effect, particularly on the formal features of his work, is profound. To indict satire with trafficking in mockery is to question the validity of a number of ironic roles, and such withering self-scrutiny may account for the contemporary ironist's predilection for the persona or the mask, a long-standing convention but one neither as often nor as insistently adopted by earlier poets. Moreover, something of that modern doubt may account for the striking difference between the almost discursive form of the earlier verse satire and epistle and the allusive and more lyric form of the longer contemporary poems. The poems in both groups survey an expansive realm of the human situation; in both the poet assumes some variation of the detached position and views the human scene and history as lacking form and relation. The classical satirist draws on this anatomized condition for the force of his epigrams with their unexpected connections, as in Pope's "All Bedlam; or Parnassus, is let out." The contemporary poet, reviving the mock-heroic convention, uses allusion and parody to juxtapose fragments of a broken culture, at one time implying the timelessness of man's corruption and at another the decadence of our age in the scales of history. Eliot, for example, sets the modern Thames, a place for assignations among the nymphs and "the loitering heirs of city directors," against the lyric appeal to that river in Edmund Spenser's epithalamion, "Sweet Thames, run softly till I end my song."

Yeats' vision of man's bestiality in war may reiterate Rochester's and Swift's, and Eliot's final position in *The Waste Land* is close to Pope's in the "Epistle to Dr. Arbuthnot." There are, after all, a limited number of attitudes one can take toward man in the moral abstract. But these similarities finally serve to point up differences among these works, and the most striking of these are structural or stylistic. Rochester, Pope, and Swift share a style that, whether colloquial or formal, seems close to the discursive and draws on firm rational or logical orders. Metaphor and imagery, if not subservient to the pattern of discourse, is at least not primary. The modern poets, however, avoid the discursive, the plain statement, and depend more often for their meaning on the allusive and presentational force of the metaphor and symbol. Pope speaks of humility, Eliot conveys the idea in the arcane syllables of the voice of the thunder; Pope castigates his enemies with an aphoristic syntax, Eliot more often lets them damn themselves with their own words. The poets of the eighteenth century give us the arguments for their anger and despair; the poets of today give us images and scenes. As the moral position for satire becomes more difficult to assume, the poet becomes more like Stephen Dedalus' ideal artist, "within or behind or beyond or above his handiwork, invisible, refined out of existence, indifferent, paring his fingernails." The poem is left to speak for itself through the unmediated symbol. In *The Waste Land,* images, scenes, fragments of conversation, the vestiges of a broken and sterile civilization gather to present us with a vast and chaotic panorama of history, in which we glimpse here and there the brief and silent images of terrifying import. All discourse and commentary are silenced by that vision. Yeats in "Nineteen Hundred and Nineteen" may lament the loss of political innocence and denounce all mankind as "but weasels fighting in a hole," but a curious stillness falls on the poem as a horrifying image stalks forth with a meaning almost beyond language:

> There lurches past, his great eyes without thought
> Under the shadow of stupid straw-pale locks,
> That insolent fiend Robert Artisson
> To whom the lovelorn Lady Kyteler brought
> Bronzed peacock feathers, red combs of her cocks.

The Denial of the Poetic

In Yeats' vision of the bloody and anarchic era that 1919 ushered in, there is an image that counters the demonic meeting of the fiend Robert Artisson and the lascivious Lady Kyteler. The art of Loie Fuller's Chinese dancers, prophetic though it is of a barbarous time, seems to create out of floating ribbons "a dragon of air," born in the aesthetic act and bearing with it some promise of order and meaning if not hope. Now that the monstrous has become the usual thing, all that is left for the poet after the holocaust is his art, chastened by experience and stripped of any pretensions to being anything other than itself. So Dylan Thomas writes of his "craft or sullen art," Marianne Moore looks "beyond all this fiddle" for something more genuine than a poetry "so derivative as to become unintelligible," and William Carlos Williams finds the artist, Mr. T., "in a soiled undershirt," performing a perfectly achieved *entrechat* in a poem that, like the figure, is unexpected, momentary, perfect, existing in and of itself, but now complete, finished.

The ironic poet's role is implicit in this conception of the "true" nature of the poem. The poem is seen as the product of a craft, something anti-poetic or at least anticonventional, a perfectly executed but utterly unpredictable gesture that, as in Williams' poem, leaves us speechless. If this is so, then the poet's role has become significantly diminished and, para-doxically, significantly enlarged. The ironic poet is not a visionary of the divine, like the thematic poet of romance, or a spokesman for society, like the thematic poet of tragedy, or a celebrator of creative imagination, like the thematic poet of comedy; he is simply the reticent craftsman, the artist in his undershirt, whose audiences, by his own admission, "pay no praise or wages / Nor heed my craft or art." But in another way he has achieved a nearly total freedom. Since he is not a seer, he need not serve the divine order and, in fact, can play the role of the god himself. He need not obey the constraints and conventions of his society or the traditions of "the towering dead / With their nightingales and psalms." He need not assume even that most liberal of roles, the inspired poet of the creative and revolutionary imagination that Shelley wrote of: to play the "unacknow-ledged legislator of the world" is unattractive and limiting to the poet, upon whom the only apparent restraints are those embodied in the rules of his art. He may even challenge those rules and defy outworn conven-tion to discover, almost in spite of himself, convention in its radical form.

In turning away from the public, the ironic poet loses the esteem granted the poet in earlier ages but wins a new freedom from the social constraints implicit in their roles. He denies the earlier conventions of the poet's relationship to his audience and in so doing creates another audi-ence, those elite who agree to his terms and conditions for audienceship and are initiated into the group through the simple witnessing of the poetic act. Like the lovers in Thomas' poem, they may be as indifferent to him as he is to others, yet they are united in their perception of "the griefs of the ages." The ironic audience joins the poet in his contempt for con-ventional forms and for conventional poets. He demands the genuine—poets who are, in Marianne Moore's words, "'literalists of the imagination'" and who present "for inspection, 'imaginary gardens with real toads in them'"—a poetic version of our initial concept of irony, romantic form with realistic content. The audience's initiation is a sudden perception of the artistic act that takes one by surprise, as it does the poet's mother in "The Artist"; for the rest, like the artist's wife, who comes in from the kitchen, the show is over.

This impulse toward the literal in the ironic mode is another manifesta-tion of the poet's attempt to break through convention and to reveal that dimension of meaning in the thing itself. Although the poet is necessarily and at times unhappily restricted to words, his poem is commonly pre-sented as a replica of the significant object or gesture that, if it speaks at all, speaks for itself, and is independent of the timeworn and suspect traditions of rhetoric and commentary. Trapped by words, the ironic poet, like Archibald MacLeish, strives for the poem that is "wordless." As one surveys the work of the major poets in our time, it seems more than coinci-dental that these poets conceptualize the ideal artist not as a poet, but as a painter, sculptor, dancer, or musician. They do so in part because, like all poets, they find words incapable of capturing the poetic vision, but more because they consider a poem a tangible thing, a silent abstract object, a symbolic line or shape or color, or a momentary figure or gesture transcending language. In his classic statement of this position MacLeish envisions poetry as mute, dumb, silent, and motionless in time. Pure images, like those in a still life, are meant to be symbolically equivalent to the common emotions and experiences of man's life rather than true. Poetry exists as an object, mysteriously emblematic; it "should not mean / But be." Williams demonstrates that mystery in "The Dish of Fruit" with an analogy between a table and a poem. He suggests that no analysis of the poem's form, the four lines "by which it becomes a poem," can ever characterize its content or reveal its true purpose, which is to lift to our view the poetic object, the dish of fruit.

The exaltation of the object and the nonverbal aesthetic act is a result of the ironic poet's renunciation not so much of language, for speak he must, but of the discredited rhetorical conventions and formulas of morality that, given the world as he sees it, are at best irrelevant and at worst obscene. In his cheerless vision of things there is no place for the accents of the orator or the onetime moving and persuasive tropes of the didact. Guilty through such associations, words themselves have become suspect and must testify to the innocence of their purpose by their references to the silent things of the world. It is as if to mean something is to be dishonest or to suggest an ulterior motive.

Believing that the oracular, if it exists at all, is in the objects of the world rather than the men who live in it, the poet can only advise the prophet—whose imminent arrival the terror of modern life makes inevitable—to be unprophetic. The traditional proclamations of doom and the usual jeremiads will not move an ironic generation to belief or even self-pity. The ironic prophet, if he is to succeed at all, must force our contemplation of a world without its last and lasting things,

> In which we have said the rose of our love and the clean
> Horse of our courage, in which beheld
> The singing locust of the soul unshelled,
> And all we mean or wish to mean.

For the seer of romance the ultimate vision rests in the divine Word; for the prophet of irony his scant and flickering vision rests in the existential Object. Irony finally drives the poet to the limits of language, to the unmarked boundary between the realm where words stand for things and that where things take the place of words. He can imagine a condition beyond language and even desire it, but he can never cross the line into silence. Such a prospect—like the statement in Williams' *Paterson*, "Say it, no ideas but in things"—ultimately contradicts language. For the idea *of* ideas existing only in things does not itself exist in a thing but in words. It depends on the structures of language for its existence, and the imperative, "Say it," is an admission of the transcendent and necessary structures of the verbal art, one of which is the ironic convention of the poem that denies the poetic.

Demonic Ritual in "The Draft Horse"

Many of Robert Frost's most characteristic poems—"Stopping By Woods on a Snowy Evening," "Desert Places," and "Design"—reveal a pattern or structure similar to the one underlying "The Draft Horse." In each, a narrator or character unexpectedly witnesses some compelling and seemingly chance event in a deserted natural scene. He subjects it to colloquial scrutiny, shifting between the whimsical and the deadly serious, and concludes with lines that seem offhand but imply an aphoristic summary of the event's meaning. The irony in these poems usually centers on the disparity between the expectation, which is the prologue to the event, and the implied commentary, which is its epilogue. "The Draft Horse" embodies one of the darker versions of this pattern.

ROBERT FROST
1880–1963

The Draft Horse

With a lantern that wouldn't burn
In too frail a buggy we drove
Behind too heavy a horse
Through a pitch-dark limitless grove.

And a man came out of the trees   5
And took our horse by the head
And reaching back to his ribs
Deliberately stabbed him dead.

The ponderous beast went down
With a crack of a broken shaft.   10
And the night drew through the trees
In one long invidious draft.

The most unquestioning pair
That ever accepted fate
And the least disposed to ascribe   15
Any more than we had to to hate.

We assumed that the man himself
Or someone he had to obey
Wanted us to get down
And walk the rest of the way.   20

The event in this poem has the enormity of a nightmare, and the distance between it and the explanatory comment is vast. The world of the poem offers a nearly complete paradigm of the archetypal images of a demonic cosmos. The couple drives through a sinister, "pitch-dark," and "limitless" wood, denied the least light from "a lantern that wouldn't burn," in a scene reminiscent of Kafka's fiction and Ingmar Bergman's films. The horse is monstrous, a "ponderous beast," and "too heavy" for the frail buggy that seems an instrument of torture in its inappropriateness for this journey. Within this scene mysterious events occur: a man appears, moving like an automaton, and carefully kills the horse; the night, embodied in the wind, draws through the trees; and the unwitting couple speculate on the motive for this apparently senseless act. The scene is more than an appropriate setting for the act; it is the only one in which the act is possible, and in this way it is not so much a setting for the act as it is a part of the act. To prove this assertion we need only try to imagine the event within the edenic groves of romance, the formal gardens of tragedy, or the productive hayfields of comedy.

The inadequacy of the couple's response and their assumptions about the man's motive force us to reexamine the act. The simple-mindedness of their statement, so manifestly off the mark, compels us to interpret the event differently. It most obviously does not enjoin them or us literally to walk through the woods or figuratively to take the hard way through "life." By their own admission these two unfortunates are a "most unquestioning pair," accustomed to settling the unknown with an easy abstraction like fate or a simple personal motive like hate. The closest they come to any real sense of what they have witnessed is to suspect that there was "someone "the man had to obey, some force or power beyond their comfortable explanation.

Reconsidering the act of the poem, then, we find two features that are not comprehended by the couple's final comment. The first is the conscious and almost predetermined manner in which the man "took our horse by the head / And reaching back to his ribs / Deliberately stabbed him dead." This mysterious figure, appearing "out of the trees," acts in what seems a preordained way, as if following the dictates of some ancient ritual. Moreover, the immediate effect of this act, as integral to it as the deliberation with which it was performed, is not the accidental breaking of the shaft, but a draft of wind: "the night drew through the trees / In one long invidious draft." It is as if the ominous night, now figured in the draft of wind, draws through the trees, invidiously, with hatred, ill-will, and envy. The causal link between the killing of the horse and the withdrawal of the wind lies in the pun on draft. The horse, a draft animal used for drawing heavy loads, is transformed, as his last breath is drawn, into the draft of wind that draws through the trees like some mysterious power, whose odium and envy have now been placated with the death of the animal victim. This much suggests that the enigmatic event was, in some inexplicable way, a ritual sacrifice, that the real victims of the night's dark enmity were the witless couple themselves, and that the innocent horse is killed as a scapegoat, burdened with their sins for their salvation. Though none of this is explicit in the act and though all of it is lost on the uncomprehending couple, the events seem to allude through parody or inversion to some ritualistic killing of an animal, in whose death one's sins are vicariously assumed and atoned. So it is not surprising to find that the deliberation with which the man performs the ritual and the gesture of the hand on the horse's head are in fact analogues to the directions for the rites of atonement through the sacrifice of beasts described in the first eight chapters of Leviticus.

Whatever final meaning we get from this ritualistic poem comes, as it so often does in irony, not from what the incurious and benighted say but from what they do not say. Meaning in irony is never found in the explicit and discursive "morals" with which we may be accustomed to comprehend such poems and with which the couple here tries to understand their experience; rather it arises out of the recognition of the somehow allusive and yet predictable ironic patterns that inform so much of our literary experience.

This poem gives us some grasp on the concept that in the hidden and yet evocative patterns of irony we may find those forms that return by the way of parody to the original structures of literature in ritual and myth. We, like the poor couple in Frost's poem, may well be unexpectedly challenged by the seeming terror and discord of the ironic world, but perhaps only then can we perceive those informing orders of act and thought that irony imposes on the most profound and ambiguous of man's experiences.

The Vision of the Demonic

WILLIAM BLAKE
1757–1827

The Sick Rose

O Rose, thou art sick!
The invisible worm,
That flies in the night,
In the howling storm,

Has found out thy bed   5
Of crimson joy,
And his dark secret love
Does thy life destroy.

London

I wander thro' each charter'd° street,
Near where the charter'd Thames does flow,
And mark in every face I meet
Marks of weakness, marks of woe.

In every cry of every Man,   5
In every Infant's cry of fear,
In every voice, in every ban,
The mind-forg'd manacles I hear.

How the Chimney-sweeper's cry
Every blackning Church appalls;   10
And the hapless Soldier's sigh
Runs in blood down Palace walls.

LONDON. **1. charter'd:** suggests both liberated and restricted.

But most thro' midnight streets I hear
How the youthful Harlot's curse
Blasts the new born Infant's tear,°   15
And blights with plagues the Marriage hearse.

EDGAR ALLAN POE
1809–1849

The City in the Sea

Lo! Death has reared himself a throne
In a strange city lying alone
Far down within the dim West,
Where the good and the bad and the worst and the best
Have gone to their eternal rest.   5
There shrines and palaces and towers
(Time-eaten towers that tremble not!)
Resemble nothing that is ours.
Around, by lifting winds forgot,
Resignedly beneath the sky   10
The melancholy waters lie.

No rays from the holy heaven come down
On the long night-time of that town;
But light from out the lurid sea
Streams up the turrets silently—   15
Gleams up the pinnacles far and free—
Up domes—up spires—up kingly halls—
Up fanes—up Babylon-like walls—

14–15. Harlot's . . . tear: suggests venereal disease resulting in the infant's blindness.

Up shadowy long-forgotten bowers
Of sculptured ivy and stone flowers—   20
Up many and many a marvelous shrine
Whose wreathèd friezes intertwine
The viol, the violet, and the vine.

Resignedly beneath the sky
The melancholy waters lie.   25
So blend the turrets and shadows there
That all seem pendulous in air,
While from a proud tower in the town
Death looks gigantically down.

There open fanes and gaping graves   30
Yawn level with the luminous waves;
But not the riches there that lie
In each idol's diamond eye—
Not the gaily-jeweled dead
Tempt the waters from their bed;   35
For no ripples curl, alas!
Along that wilderness of glass—
No swellings tell that winds may be
Upon some far-off happier sea—
No heavings hint that winds have been   40
On seas less hideously serene.

But lo, a stir is in the air!
The wave—there is a movement there!
As if the towers had thrust aside,
In slightly sinking, the dull tide—   45
As if their tops had feebly given
A void within the filmy heaven.

The waves have now a redder glow—
The hours are breathing faint and low—
And when, amid no earthly moans,   50
Down, down that town shall settle hence,
Hell, rising from a thousand thrones,
Shall do it reverence.

So preconcerted with itself
So distant—to alarms—   5
An Unconcern so sovreign
To Universe, or me—
Infects my simple spirit
With Taints of Majesty—
Till I take vaster attitudes—   10
And strut upon my stem—
Disdaining Men, and Oxygen,
For Arrogance of them—

My Splendors, are Menagerie—
But their Competeless Show   15
Will entertain the Centuries
When I, am long ago,
An Island in dishonored Grass—
Whom none but Daisies, know.

465

I heard a Fly buzz—when I died—
The Stillness in the Room
Was like the Stillness in the Air—
Between the Heaves of Storm—

The Eyes around—had wrung them dry—   5
And Breaths were gathering firm
For that last Onset—when the King
Be witnessed—in the Room—

I willed my Keepsakes—Signed away
What portion of me be   10
Assignable—and then it was
There interposed a Fly—

With Blue—uncertain stumbling Buzz—
Between the light—and me—
And then the Windows failed—and then   15
I could not see to see—

EMILY DICKINSON
1830–1886

290

Of Bronze—and Blaze—
The North—Tonight—
So adequate—it forms—

MATTHEW ARNOLD
1822–1888

To Marguerite—Continued

Yes! in the sea of life enisled,
With echoing straits between us thrown,
Dotting the shoreless watery wild,

We mortal millions live *alone*.
The islands feel the enclasping flow,   5
And then their endless bounds they know.

But when the moon their hollows lights,
And they are swept by balms of spring,
And in their glens, on starry nights,
The nightingales divinely sing;   10
And lovely notes, from shore to shore,
Across the sounds and channels pour—

Oh! then a longing like despair
Is to their farthest caverns sent;
For surely once, they feel, we were   15
Parts of a single continent!
Now round us spreads the watery plain—
Oh might our marges meet again!

Who ordered that their longing's fire
Should be, as soon as kindled, cooled?   20
Who renders vain their deep desire?—
A God, a God their severance ruled!
And bade between their shores to be
The unplumbed, salt, estranging sea.

Dover Beach

The sea is calm tonight.
The tide is full, the moon lies fair
Upon the straits;—on the French coast the light
Gleams and is gone; the cliffs of England stand,
Glimmering and vast, out in the tranquil bay.   5
Come to the window, sweet is the night-air!
Only, from the long line of spray
Where the sea meets the moon-blanched land,
Listen! you hear the grating roar
Of pebbles which the waves draw back, and
    fling,   10
At their return, up the high strand,
Begin, and cease, and then again begin,
With tremulous cadence slow, and bring
The eternal note of sadness in.

Sophocles long ago   15
Heard it on the Aegean, and it brought
Into his mind the turbid ebb and flow
Of human misery; we
Find also in the sound a thought,
Hearing it by this distant northern sea.   20

The Sea of Faith
Was once, too, at the full, and round earth's shore
Lay like the folds of a bright girdle furled.
But now I only hear
Its melancholy, long, withdrawing roar,   25
Retreating, to the breath
Of the night-wind, down the vast edges drear
And naked shingles of the world.

Ah, love, let us be true
To one another! for the world, which seems   30
To lie before us like a land of dreams
So various, so beautiful, so new,
Hath really neither joy, nor love, nor light,
Nor certitude, nor peace, nor help for pain;
And we are here as on a darkling plain   35
Swept with confused alarms of struggle and flight,
Where ignorant armies clash by night.

ROBERT FROST
1874–1963

Design

I found a dimpled spider, fat and white,
On a white heal-all,° holding up a moth
Like a white piece of rigid satin cloth—
Assorted characters of death and blight
Mixed ready to begin the morning right,   5
Like the ingredients of a witches' broth—
A snow-drop spider, a flower like a froth,
And dead wings carried like a paper kite.

What had that flower to do with being white,
The wayside blue and innocent heal-all?   10
What brought the kindred spider to that height,
Then steered the white moth thither in the night?
What but design of darkness to appall?—
If design govern in a thing so small.

DESIGN. **2. heal-all:** popular name for a variety of plants
used as universal remedies, sometimes called the self-heal,
usually blue-flowered (l. 10).

ROBERT LOWELL
b. 1917

Beyond the Alps

(On the train from Rome to Paris. 1950, the year Pius XII defined the dogma of Mary's bodily assumption.)

Reading how even the Swiss had thrown the sponge
in once again and Everest was still
unscaled, I watched our Paris pullman lunge
mooning across the fallow Alpine snow.
O bella Roma!° I saw our stewards go   5
forward on tiptoe banging on their gongs.°
Life changed to landscape. Much against my will
I left the City of God° where it belongs.
There the skirt-mad Mussolini unfurled
the eagle° of Caesar. He was one of us   10
only, pure prose. I envy the conspicuous
waste of our grandparents on their grand tours—
long-haired Victorian sages accepted the universe,
while breezing on their trust funds through the world.

When the Vatican made Mary's Assumption
    dogma,   15
the crowds at San Pietro screamed *Papa.°*
The Holy Father dropped his shaving glass,
and listened. His electric razor purred,
his pet canary chirped on his left hand.
The lights of science couldn't hold a candle   20
to Mary risen—at one miraculous stroke,
angel-winged, gorgeous as a jungle bird!
But who believed this? Who could understand?
Pilgrims still kissed Saint Peter's brazen sandal.
The Duce's° lynched, bare, booted skull still
    spoke.   25
God herded his people to the *coup de grâce*—
the costumed Switzers° sloped their pikes to push,
O Pius, through the monstrous human crush. . . .

Our mountain-climbing train had come to earth.
Tired of the querulous hush-hush of the wheels, 30
the blear-eyed ego kicking in my berth
lay still, and saw Apollo plant his heels
on terra firma through the morning's thigh . . .
each backward, wasted Alp, a Parthenon,
fire-branded socket of the Cyclops' eye.   35
There were no tickets for that altitude
once held by Hellas, when the goddess stood,
prince, pope, philosopher and golden bough,
pure mind and murder at the scything prow—
Minerva, the miscarriage of the brain.°   40

Now Paris, our black classic, breaking up
like killer kings on an Etruscan cup.

Skunk Hour

(For Elizabeth Bishop)

Nautilus Island's hermit
heiress still lives through winter in her Spartan
    cottage;
her sheep still graze above the sea.
Her son's a bishop. Her farmer
is first selectman in our village;   5
she's in her dotage.

Thirsting for
the hierarchic privacy
of Queen Victoria's century,
she buys up all   10
the eyesores facing her shore,
and lets them fall.

The season's ill—
we've lost our summer millionaire,
who seemed to leap from an L. L. Bean   15
catalogue.° His nine-knot yawl°
was auctioned off to lobstermen.
A red fox stain covers Blue Hill.

BEYOND THE ALPS. **5. O bella Roma:** O beautiful Rome. **6. gongs:** sounded to announce a meal. **8. City of God:** Rome, also suggesting Augustine's *City of God.* **10. eagle:** symbol of Roman legions. **16. crowds . . . Papa:** crowds at Saint Peter's in Rome cheered the pope (*Papa*). **25. Duce:** (Italian) leader. Benito Mussolini (1883–1945), Fascist prime minister of Italy. Executed by Italian partisans, he and his mistress were hung by the heels in a square in Milan. **27. costumed Switzers:** The pope's Swiss guard dressed in medieval costumes and carried pikes.

37–40. goddess . . . brain: Athena, Greek goddess of wisdom, skills, and warfare, also associated here with myth; see J. G. Frazer's *The Golden Bough.* Athena sprang full-grown from the head of Zeus. Minerva is her Roman counterpart.

SKUNK HOUR. **15–16. L. L. Bean catalogue:** catalogue for the sporting goods mail order house. **16. nine-knot yawl:** yawl capable of nine nautical miles per hour.

And now our fairy
decorator brightens his shop for fall;   20
his fishnet's filled with orange cork,
orange, his cobbler's bench and awl;
there is no money in his work,
he'd rather marry.

One dark night,   25
my Tudor Ford climbed the hill's skull;
I watched for love-cars. Lights turned down,
they lay together, hull to hull,
where the graveyard shelves on the town. . . .
My mind's not right.   30

A car radio bleats,
"Love, O careless Love. . . ." I hear
my ill-spirit sob in each blood cell,
as if my hand were at its throat. . . .

I myself am hell;°   35
nobody's here—

only skunks, that search
in the moonlight for a bite to eat.
They march on their soles up Main Street:
white stripes, moonstruck eyes' red fire   40
under the chalk-dry and spar spire
of the Trinitarian Church.

I stand on top
of our back steps and breathe the rich air—
a mother skunk with her column of kittens swills
       the garbage pail.   45
She jabs her wedge-head in a cup
of sour cream, drops her ostrich tail,
and will not scare.

35. myself am hell: spoken by Satan in *Paradise Lost*, IV.75,
when he admits his guilt but refuses to repent. Later Satan
enviously watches the innocent Adam and Eve in each
other's arms.

The Dismembered World of Experience

JOHN WILMOT, EARL OF
ROCHESTER
1647–1680

A Satire Against Mankind

Were I, who to my cost already am,
One of those strange, prodigious creatures, man,
A spirit free, to choose for my own share,
What case of flesh and blood I pleased to wear,
I'd be a dog, a monkey, or a bear,   5
Or anything but that vain animal,
Who is so proud of being rational.
The senses are too gross, and he'll contrive
A sixth, to contradict the other five:
And before certain instinct will prefer   10
Reason, which fifty times for one does err.
Reason, an *ignis fatuus*° of the mind,
Which leaves the light of nature, sense, behind.
Pathless and dangerous, wandering ways it takes,
Through error's fenny bogs, and thorny brakes: 15
Whilst the misguided follower climbs with pain,
Mountains of whimsies heaped in his own brain:
Stumbling from thought to thought, falls headlong
    down
Into doubt's boundless sea, where like to drown
Books bear him up awhile, and make him try   20
To swim with bladders° of philosophy:
In hopes still to o'ertake the skipping light,
The vapor dances in his dazzled sight,
Till spent, it leaves him to eternal night.

Then old age, and experience, hand in hand,   25
Lead him to death, and make him understand,
After a search so painful, and so long,
That all his life he has been in the wrong;
Huddled in dirt, the reasoning engine lies,
Who was so proud, so witty, and so wise.   30
Pride drew him in, as cheats their bubbles° catch,
And made him venture to be made a wretch:
His wisdom did his happiness destroy,
Aiming to know the world he should enjoy.
And wit was his vain frivolous pretense,   35
Of pleasing others at his own expense.
For wits are treated just like common whores;
First they're enjoyed, and then kicked out of doors.
The pleasure past, a threatening doubt remains,
That frights the enjoyer with succeeding pains.   40
Women, and men of wit, are dangerous tools,
And ever fatal to admiring fools.
Pleasure allures, and when the fops escape,
'Tis not that they're beloved, but fortunate;
And therefore what they fear, at heart they hate.   45
    But now, methinks, some formal Band and
        Beard°
Takes me to task. Come on, sir, I'm prepared:
"Then, by your favor, anything that's writ
Against this gibing, jingling knack, called wit,
Likes° me abundantly; but you'll take care   50
Upon this point, not to be too severe.
Perhaps my Muse were fitter for this part,
For, I profess, I can be very smart
On wit, which I abhor with all my heart.
I long to lash it, in some sharp essáy,   55
But your grand indiscretion bids me stay,

A SATIRE AGAINST MANKIND.   **12. ignis fatuus:** will-o'-the-wisp. **21. bladders:** inflated bladders used as life-preservers.

31. bubbles: dupes. **46. Band . . . Beard:** older clergyman (bearded) wearing a Geneva band or neckcloth. **50. Likes:** pleases.

And turns my tide of ink another way.
What rage ferments in your degenerate mind,
To make you rail at reason and mankind?
Blest glorious man! to whom alone kind heaven   60
An everlasting soul has freely given;
Whom his great Maker took such care to make,
That from himself he did the image take,
And this fair frame in shining reason dressed,
To dignify his nature above beast.   65
Reason, by whose aspiring influence,
We take a flight beyond material sense,
Dive into mysteries, then soaring pierce
The flaming limits of the universe,
Search heaven and hell, find out what's acted
    there,   70
And give the world true grounds of hope and fear."
  Hold, mighty man, I cry; all this we know,
From the pathetic pen of Ingelo,
From Patrick's *Pilgrim*, Sibbe's *Soliloquies*,°
And 'tis this very reason I despise,   75
This supernatural gift, that makes a mite
Think he's the image of the Infinite;
Comparing his short life, void of all rest,
To the eternal and the ever blest;
This busy, puzzling stirrer up of doubt,   80
That frames deep mysteries, then finds 'em out,
Filling with frantic crowds of thinking fools,
Those reverend Bedlams, colleges and schools,
Borne on whose wings, each heavy sot can pierce
The limits of the boundless universe: 85
So charming ointments make an old witch fly,
And bear a crippled carcass through the sky.
'Tis this exalted power, whose business lies
In nonsense and impossibilities:
This made a whimsical philosopher,   90
Before the spacious world his tub° prefer,
And we have modern cloistered coxcombs, who
Retire to think, 'cause they have nought to do.
But thoughts were given for action's government;
Where action ceases, thought's impertinent.   95
Our sphere of action is life's happiness,
And he who thinks beyond, thinks like an ass.
Thus whilst against false reasoning I inveigh,
I own right reason, which I would obey:
That reason, that distinguishes by sense,   100

And gives us rules of good and ill from thence;
That bounds desires with a reforming will,
To keep them more in vigor, not to kill.
Your reason hinders, mine helps to enjoy;
Renewing appetites, yours would destroy.   105
My reason is my friend, yours is a cheat:
Hunger calls out, my reason bids me eat;
Perversely yours, your appetite does mock;
This asks for food, that answers, "What's o'clock?"
This plain distinction, sir, your doubt secures;   110
'Tis not true reason I despise, but yours.
Thus, I think reason righted: but for man,
I'll ne'er recant, defend him if you can.
For all his pride, and his philosophy,
'Tis evident beasts are, in their degree,   115
As wise at least, and better far than he.
Those creatures are the wisest, who attain,
By surest means, the ends at which they aim.
If therefore Jowler finds, and kills his hares,
Better than Meres° supplies committee chairs;   120
Though one's a statesman, the other but a hound,
Jowler in justice will be wiser found.
You see how far Man's wisdom here extends:
Look next if human nature makes amends;
Whose principles most generous are and just,   125
And to those whose morals you would sooner trust.
Be judge yourself, I'll bring it to the test,
Which is the basest creature, man or beast?
Birds feed on birds, beasts on each other prey,
But savage man alone does man betray.   130
Pressed by necessity, *they* kill for food,
Man undoes man to do himself no good.
With teeth and claws by nature armed, *they* hunt
Nature's allowance, to supply their want:
But man, with smiles, embraces, friendships,
    praise,   135
Unhumanly, his fellow's life betrays:
With voluntary pains works his distress;
Not through necessity, but wantonness.
For hunger, or for love, *they* bite or tear,
Whilst wretched man is still in arms for fear: 140
For fear he arms, and is of arms afraid;
From fear to fear successively betrayed.
Base fear, the source whence his best passions came,
His boasted honor, and his dear-bought fame,
That lust of power, to which he's such a slave,   145
And for the which alone he dares be brave:
To which his various projects are designed,

73–74. Ingelo . . . Soliloquies: Nathaniel Ingelo's romance *Bentivoli and Urania*, Simon Patrick's *Parable of the Pilgrim* and Richard Sibbe's discourses were contemporary allegorical works intended for moral instruction. **90–91. philosopher . . . tub:** Diogenes the Cynic is supposed to have lived in a tub.

120. Meres: Sir Thomas Meres, a Whig member of Parliament.

Which makes him generous, affable, and kind,
For which he takes such pains to be thought wise,
And screws° his actions, in a forced disguise: 150
Leading a tedious life, in misery,
Under laborious, mean hypocrisy.
Look to the bottom of his vast design,
Wherein man's wisdom, power, and glory join;
The good he acts, the ill he does endure,   155
'Tis all from fear, to make himself secure.
Merely for safety, after fame we thirst,
For all men would be cowards if they durst:
And honesty's against all common sense:
Men must be knaves; 'tis in their own defense.   160
Mankind's dishonest; if you think it fair,
Amongst known cheats, to play upon the square,
You'll be undone——
Nor can weak truth your reputation save;
The knaves will all agree to call you knave.   165
Wronged shall he live, insulted o'er, oppressed,
Who dares be less a villain than the rest.
Thus, sir, you see what human nature craves,
Most men are cowards, all men should be knaves.
The difference lies, as far as I can see,   170
Not in the thing itself, but the degree;
And all the subject matter of debate,
Is only who's a knave of the first rate.

ALEXANDER POPE
1688–1744

An Epistle to Dr. Arbuthnot°

P. Shut, shut the door, good John!° (fatigued, I
   said),
Tie up the knocker, say I'm sick, I'm dead.
The Dog Star rages! nay 'tis past a doubt
All Bedlam; or Parnassus, is let out:
Fire in each eye, and papers in each hand,   5
They rave, recite, and madden round the land.
   What walls can guard me, or what shades can
      hide?
They pierce my thickets, through my grot° they
   glide,

150. **screws:** distorts.

EPISTLE TO DR. ARBUTHNOT. In his last illness, Pope's friend Dr. John Arbuthnot urged Pope to continue his satiric writing. **1. John:** John Serle, Pope's servant. **8. grot:** decorated grotto on Pope's estate at Twickenham (l. 21).

By land, by water, they renew the charge,
They stop the chariot, and they board the barge.   10
No place is sacred, not the church is free;
Even Sunday shines no Sabbath day to me:
Then from the Mint° walks forth the man of rhyme,
Happy to catch me just at dinner time.
   Is there a parson, much bemused in beer,   15
A maudlin poetess, a rhyming peer,
A clerk foredoomed his father's soul to cross,
Who pens a stanza when he should engross?°
Is there who, locked from ink and paper, scrawls
With desperate charcoal round his darkened walls?
All fly to Twit'nam, and in humble strain   21
Apply to me to keep them mad or vain.
Arthur, whose giddy son neglects the laws,°
Imputes to me and my damned works the cause:
Poor Cornus° sees his frantic wife elope,   25
And curses wit, and poetry, and Pope.
   Friend to my life (which did not you prolong,
The world had wanted many an idle song)
What drop or nostrum can this plague remove?
Or which must end me, a fool's wrath or love?   30
A dire dilemma! either way I'm sped,
If foes, they write, if friends, they read me dead.
Seized and tied down to judge, how wretched I!
Who can't be silent, and who will not lie.
To laugh were want of goodness and of grace,   35
And to be grave exceeds all power of face.
I sit with sad civility, I read
With honest anguish and an aching head,
And drop at last, but in unwilling ears,
This saving counsel, "Keep your piece nine years."°
   "Nine years!" cries he, who high in Drury Lane,
Lulled by soft zephyrs through the broken pane,   42
Rhymes ere he wakes, and prints before term ends,
Obliged by hunger and request of friends:
"The piece, you think, is incorrect? why, take it,   45
I'm all submission, what you'd have it, make it."
   Three things another's modest wishes bound,
My friendship, and a prologue, and ten pound.
   Pitholeon° sends to me: "You know his grace,
I want a patron; ask him for a place."   50

12–13. Sunday . . . Mint: The Mint was a place where debtors were safe from arrest, as they were anywhere on Sunday. **18. engross:** write legal documents. **23. Arthur . . . laws:** Arthur Moore's son, James Moore-Smythe, cribbed lines from Pope in a play. **25. Cornus:** (Latin) horn, thus cuckold. **40. Keep . . . years:** Horace's advice in "Ars Poetica." **49. Pitholeon:** [Pope's note] The name taken from a foolish poet at Rhodes, who pretended much to Greek. [The reference is to Leonard Welsted, a translator who attacked Pope (l. 375).]

Pitholeon libeled me—"but here's a letter
Informs you, sir, 'twas when he knew no better.
Dare you refuse him? Curll° invites to dine,
He'll write a *Journal*, or he'll turn divine."
Bless me! a packet.—" 'Tis a stranger sues,   55
A virgin tragedy, an orphan Muse."
If I dislike it, "Furies, death, and rage!"
If I approve, "Commend it to the stage."
There (thank my stars) my whole commission ends,
The players and I are, luckily, no friends.   60
Fired that the house reject him, " 'Sdeath, I'll
     print it,
And shame the fools—Your interest, sir, with
     Lintot!"°
Lintot, dull rogue, will think your price too much.
"Not, sir, if you revise it, and retouch."
All my demurs but double his attacks;   65
At last he whispers, "Do; and we go snacks."°
Glad of a quarrel, straight I clap the door,
"Sir, let me see your works and you no more."
'Tis sung, when Midas' ears began to spring
(Midas, a sacred person and a king),   70
His very minister who spied them first,
(Some say his queen) was forced to speak, or burst.
And is not mine, my friend, a sorer case,
When every coxcomb perks them in my face?
     A. Good friend, forbear! you deal in dangerous
          things.   75
I'd never name queens, ministers, or kings;
Keep close to ears, and those let asses prick;
'Tis nothing—— P. Nothing? if they bite and kick?
Out with it, *Dunciad!*° let the secret pass,
That secret to each fool, that he's an ass: 80
The truth once told (and wherefore should we lie?)
The queen of Midas slept, and so may I.
     You think this cruel? take it for a rule,
No creature smarts so little as a fool.
Let peals of laughter, Codrus!° round thee break,
Thou unconcerned canst hear the mighty crack,   86
Pit, box, and gallery in convulsions hurled,
Thou stand'st unshook amidst a bursting world.
Who shames a scribbler? break one cobweb
     through,
He spins the slight, self-pleasing thread anew: 90
Destroy his fib or sophistry, in vain;
The creature's at his dirty work again,

Throned in the center of his thin designs,
Proud of a vast extent of flimsy lines.
Whom have I hurt? has poet yet or peer   95
Lost the arched eyebrow or Parnassian sneer?
And has not Colley° still his lord and whore?
His butchers Henley? his freemasons Moore?
Does not one table Bavius° still admit?
Still to one bishop Philips seem a wit?   100
Still Sappho—— A. Hold! for God's sake—you'll
     offend.
No names—be calm—learn prudence of a friend.
I too could write, and I am twice as tall;
But foes like these!—— P. One flatterer's worse
     than all.
Of all mad creatures, if the learn'd are right,   105
It is the slaver kills, and not the bite.
A fool quite angry is quite innocent:
Alas! 'tis ten times worse when they repent.
     One dedicates in high heroic prose,
And ridicules beyond a hundred foes;   110
One from all Grub Street will my fame defend,
And, more abusive, calls himself my friend.
This prints my letters, that expects a bribe,
And others roar aloud, "Subscribe, subscribe!"
     There are, who to my person pay their court: 115
I cough like Horace, and, though lean, am short;
Ammon's great son° one shoulder had too high,
Such Ovid's nose, and "Sir! you have an eye—"
Go on, obliging creatures, make me see
All that disgraced my betters met in me.   120
Say for my comfort, languishing in bed,
"Just so immortal Maro° held his head":
And when I die, be sure you let me know
Great Homer died three thousand years ago.
     Why did I write? what sin to me unknown   125
Dipped me in ink, my parents', or my own?
As yet a child, nor yet a fool to fame,
I lisped in numbers, for the numbers came.
I left no calling for this idle trade,
No duty broke, no father disobeyed.   130
The Muse but served to ease some friend, not wife,
To help me through this long disease, my life,
To second, Arbuthnot! thy art and care,

97–101. Colley . . . Sappho: some of Pope's frequent targets: Colley Cibber, laureate; John Henley, an eloquent preacher among the lower classes; James Moore; Ambrose Philips, a sentimental poet much admired by the Bishop of Armagh; and Lady Mary Wortley Montagu, whom Pope referred to as Sappho. **99. Bavius:** a bad poet mentioned by Virgil in his third eclogue. **117. son:** Alexander the Great. **122. Maro:** Virgil.

---

53. Curll: Edmund Curll, a disreputable bookseller who published some of Pope's letters without permission. **62. Lintot:** Bernard Lintot, an early publisher of Pope. **66. go snacks:** go shares. **79. Dunciad:** Pope's mock-heroic poem. **85. Codrus:** poet ridiculed by Virgil and Juvenal.

And teach the being you preserved, to bear.
 A. But why then publish? P. Granville the
  polite,   135
And knowing Walsh, would tell me I could write;
Well-natured Garth inflamed with early praise,
And Congreve loved, and Swift endured my lays;
The courtly Talbot, Somers, Sheffield, read;
Even mitered Rochester would nod the head, 140
And Saint John's self (great Dryden's friends
 before)
With open arms received one poet more.
Happy my studies, when by these approved!
Happier their author, when by these beloved!
From these the world will judge of men and
 books,   145
Not from the Burnets, Oldmixons, and Cookes.°

Soft were my numbers; who could take offense
While pure description held the place of sense?
Like gentle Fanny's was my flowery theme,
A painted mistress, or a purling stream. 150
Yet then did Gildon draw his venal quill;
I wished the man a dinner, and sat still.
Yet then did Dennis° rave in furious fret;
I never answered, I was not in debt.
If want provoked, or madness made them print, 155
I waged no war with Bedlam or the Mint.

 Did some more sober critic come abroad?
If wrong, I smiled; if right, I kissed the rod.
Pains, reading, study are their just pretense,
And all they want is spirit, taste, and sense. 160
Commas and points they set exactly right,
And 'twere a sin to rob them of their mite.
Yet ne'er one sprig of laurel graced these ribalds,
From slashing Bentley down to piddling Tibbalds.°
Each wight who reads not, and but scans and
 spells,   165
Each word-catcher that lives on syllables,
Even such small critics some regard may claim,

Preserved in Milton's or in Shakespeare's name.
Pretty! in amber to observe the forms
Of hairs, or straws, or dirt, or grubs, or worms!
The things, we know, are neither rich nor rare, 171
But wonder how the devil they got there.

 Were others angry? I excused them too;
Well might they rage; I gave them but their due.
A man's true merit 'tis not hard to find; 175
But each man's secret standard in his mind,
That casting weight° pride adds to emptiness,
This, who can gratify? for who can guess?
The bard whom pilfered pastorals renown,
Who turns a Persian tale for half a crown,° 180
Just writes to make his barrenness appear,
And strains from hard-bound brains eight lines a
 year:
He, who still wanting, though he lives on theft,
Steals much, spends little, yet has nothing left;
And he who now to sense, now nonsense leaning,
Means not, but blunders round about a meaning:
And he whose fustian's so sublimely bad, 187
It is not poetry, but prose run mad:
All these, my modest satire bade translate,
And owned that nine such poets made a Tate.° 190
How did they fume, and stamp, and roar, and chafe!
And swear, not Addison° himself was safe.

 Peace to all such! but were there one whose fires
True Genius kindles, and fair Fame inspires;
Blessed with each talent and each art to please, 195
And born to write, converse, and live with ease:
Should such a man, too fond to rule alone,
Bear, like the Turk, no brother near the throne;
View him with scornful, yet with jealous eyes,
And hate for arts that caused himself to rise; 200
Damn with faint praise, assent with civil leer,
And without sneering, teach the rest to sneer;
Willing to wound, and yet afraid to strike,
Just hint a fault, and hesitate dislike;
Alike reserved to blame or to commend, 205
A timorous foe, and a suspicious friend;
Dreading even fools; by flatterers besieged,
And so obliging that he ne'er obliged;
Like Cato, give his little senate laws,

135–46. **Granville . . . Cookes:** friends and supporters who link Pope with Dryden: George Granville, Lord Lansdowne; William Walsh; Sir Samuel Garth; William Congreve; Charles Talbot, duke of Shrewsbury; Lord Sommers; John Sheffield, duke of Buckinghamshire; and Francis Atterbury, bishop of Rochester. Their opinion outweighs that of Thomas Burnet, John Oldmixon, and Thomas Cooke, whom Pope identifies in a note as "authors of . . . scandalous history." 149–53. **Fanny . . . Dennis:** John, Lord Hervey (ll. 305–33); Charles Gildon and John Dennis, both unfriendly critics of Pope. 164. **Bentley . . . Tibbalds:** Richard Bentley, an editor who set in square brackets (slashed) those parts of Milton he felt were bad and thus not by Milton; Lewis Theobald, an editor who pointed out defects in Pope's editing of Shakespeare.

177. **casting weight:** deciding weight in a balance. 179–80. **bard . . . crown:** Ambrose Philips, pastoral poet and translator of Persian tales. 190. **Tate:** Nahum Tate, laureate and editor who "revised" *King Lear* with a happy ending. 192. **Addison:** Joseph Addison, author of the successful play *Cato* (l. 209), for which Pope wrote the Prologue; Addison is referred to as Atticus (109–32 B.C.) a wise man of letters and friend of Cicero.

And sit attentive to his own applause;   210
While wits and Templars every sentence raise,
And wonder with a foolish face of praise—
Who but must laugh, if such a man there be?
Who would not weep, if Atticus° were he?

    What though my name stood rubric on the
      walls   215
Or plastered posts, with claps,° in capitals?
Or smoking forth, a hundred hawkers' load,
On wings of winds came flying all abroad?
I sought no homage from the race that write;
I kept, like Asian monarchs, from their sight: 220
Poems I heeded (now berhymed so long)
No more than thou, great George! a birthday song.
I ne'er with wits or witlings passed my days
To spread about the itch of verse and praise;
Nor like a puppy daggled through the town   225
To fetch and carry sing-song up and down;
Nor at rehearsals sweat, and mouthed, and cried,
With handkerchief and orange at my side;
But sick of fops, and poetry, and prate,
To Bufo left the whole Castalian state.°   230

    Proud as Apollo on his forkéd hill,
Sat full-blown Bufo, puffed by every quill;
Fed with soft dedication all day long,
Horace and he went hand in hand in song.
His library (where busts of poets dead   235
And a true Pindar stood without a head)
Received of wits an undistinguished race,
Who first his judgment asked, and then a place:
Much they extolled his pictures, much his seat,
And flattered every day, and some days eat: 240
Till grown more frugal in his riper days,
He paid some bards with port, and some with
    praise;
To some a dry rehearsal was assigned,
And others (harder still) he paid in kind.
Dryden alone (what wonder?) came not nigh;   245
Dryden alone escaped this judging eye:
But still the great have kindness in reserve;
He helped to bury whom he helped to starve.

    May some choice patron bless each gray goose
    quill!
May every Bavius have his Bufo still!   250
So when a statesman wants a day's defense,
Or Envy holds a whole week's war with Sense,

Or simple Pride for flattery makes demands,
May dunce by dunce be whistled off my hands!
Blessed be the great! for those they take away, 255
And those they left me—for they left me Gay,
Left me to see neglected genius bloom,
Neglected die, and tell it on his tomb;
Of all thy blameless life the sole return
My verse, and Queensberry° weeping o'er thy urn!
Oh, let me live my own, and die so too!   261
("To live and die is all I have to do")
Maintain a poet's dignity and ease,
And see what friends, and read what books I please;
Above a patron, though I condescend   265
Sometimes to call a minister my friend.
I was not born for courts or great affairs;
I pay my debts, believe, and say my prayers,
Can sleep without a poem in my head,
Nor know if Dennis be alive or dead.   270

    Why am I asked what next shall see the light?
Heavens! was I born for nothing but to write?
Has life no joys for me? or (to be grave)
Have I no friend to serve, no soul to save?
"I found him close with Swift"—"Indeed? no
    doubt"   275
Cries prating Balbus, "something will come out."
'Tis all in vain, deny it as I will.
"No, such a genius never can lie still,"
And then for mine obligingly mistakes
The first lampoon Sir Will or Bubo° makes.   280
Poor guiltless I! and can I choose but smile,
When every coxcomb knows me by my style?

    Cursed be the verse, how well soe'er it flow,
That tends to make one worthy man my foe,
Give Virtue scandal, Innocence a fear,   285
Or from the soft-eyed virgin steal a tear!
But he who hurts a harmless neighbor's peace,
Insults fallen worth, or Beauty in distress,
Who loves a lie, lame Slander helps about.
Who writes a libel, or who copies out: 290
That fop whose pride affects a patron's name,
Yet absent, wounds an author's honest fame;
Who can your merit selfishly approve,
And show the sense of it without the love;
Who has the vanity to call you friend,   295
Yet wants the honor, injured, to defend;
Who tells whate'er you think, whate'er you say,

---

216. **claps:** posters. 230. **Bufo . . . Castalian state:** Bufo, a
tasteless patron of the arts. The Castalian spring on twin-
peaked Mount Parnassus (l. 231) was sacred to Apollo
and the Muses.

256–60. **Gay . . . Queensberry:** John Gay, author of *The
Beggar's Opera,* who failed to gain patronage from the court
and was befriended later by the duke of Queensberry.
280. **Sir . . . Bubo:** Sir William Yonge, politician and minor
poet; George Bubb Dodington, patron of letters.

And, if he lie not, must at least betray:
Who to the dean and silver bell can swear,
And sees at Cannons what was never there:°   300
Who reads but with a lust to misapply,
Make satire a lampoon, and fiction, lie:
A lash like mine no honest man shall dread,
But all such babbling blockheads in his stead.
    Let Sporus° tremble—— A. What? that thing of
    silk,   305
Sporus, that mere white curd of ass's milk?°
Satire or sense, alas! can Sporus feel?
Who breaks a butterfly upon a wheel?
    P. Yet let me flap this bug with gilded wings,
This painted child of dirt, that stinks and stings; 310
Whose buzz the witty and the fair annoys,
Yet wit ne'er tastes, and beauty ne'er enjoys;
So well-bred spaniels civilly delight
In mumbling of the game they dare not bite.
Eternal smiles his emptiness betray,   315
As shallow streams run dimpling all the way.
Whether in florid impotence he speaks,
And, as the prompter breathes, the puppet squeaks;
Or at the ear of Eve,° familiar toad,
Half froth, half venom, spits himself abroad,   320
In puns, or politics, or tales, or lies,
Or spite, or smut, or rhymes, or blasphemies.
His wit all seesaw between *that* and *this*,
Now high, now low, now master up, now miss,
And he himself one vile antithesis.   325
Amphibious thing! that acting either part,
The trifling head or the corrupted heart,
Fop at the toilet, flatterer at the board,
Now trips a lady, and now struts a lord.
Eve's tempter thus the rabbins have expressed, 330
A cherub's face, a reptile all the rest;
Beauty that shocks you, parts that none will trust,
Wit that can creep, and pride that licks the dust.
    Not Fortune's worshiper, nor Fashion's fool,
Not Lucre's madman, nor Ambition's tool,   335
Not proud, nor servile, be one poet's praise,
That if he pleased, he pleased by manly ways:
That flattery, even to kings, he held a shame,
And thought a lie in verse or prose the same:

That not in fancy's maze he wandered long,   340
But stooped to truth, and moralized his song:
That not for fame, but Virtue's better end,
He stood the furious foe, the timid friend,
The damning critic, half approving wit,
The coxcomb hit, or fearing to be hit;   345
Laughed at the loss of friends he never had,
The dull, the proud, the wicked, and the mad;
The distant threats of vengeance on his head,
The blow unfelt, the tear he never shed;
The tale revived, the lie so oft o'erthrown,   350
The imputed trash, and dullness not his own;
The morals blackened when the writings 'scape,
The libeled person, and the pictured shape;
Abuse on all he loved, or loved him, spread,
A friend in exile, or a father dead;   355
The whisper, that to greatness still too near,
Perhaps yet vibrates on his Sovereign's ear—
Welcome for thee, fair Virtue! all the past!
For thee, fair Virtue! welcome even the last!
    A. But why insult the poor, affront the great? 360
P. A knave's a knave to me in every state:
Alike my scorn, if he succeed or fail,
Sporus at court, or Japhet° in a jail,
A hireling scribbler, or a hireling peer,
Knight of the post° corrupt, or of the shire,   365
If on a pillory, or near a throne,
He gain his prince's ear, or lose his own.
    Yet soft by nature, more a dupe than wit,
Sappho can tell you how this man was bit:
This dreaded satirist Dennis will confess   370
Foe to his pride, but friend to his distress:°
So humble, he has knocked at Tibbald's door,
Has drunk with Cibber, nay, has rhymed for
    Moore.
Full ten years slandered, did he once reply?
Three thousand suns went down on Welsted's lie.
To please a mistress one aspersed his life;   376
He lashed him not, but let her be his wife.
Let Budgell charge low Grub Street on his quill,
And write whate'er he pleased, except his will;°
Let the two Curlls of town and court,° abuse   380
His father, mother, body, soul, and muse.

299–300. dean . . . there: Pope was accused of satirizing
Cannons, the duke of Chandos' estate, in the "Epistle to
Burlington," a point he disproves by noting that the
description in his poem does not fit the dean and bell
at Cannons. 305. Sporus: a boy whom the Roman emperor
Nero publicly married. Pope is referring to Lord Hervey,
an effeminate courtier to Queen Caroline. 306. ass's milk:
drunk by invalids. 319. Eve: See *Paradise Lost* IV.799–809.
Pope is referring to Queen Caroline.

363. Japhet: Japhet Crook, a famous forger. 365. Knight
. . . post: seller of false evidence. 371. friend . . . distress:
Pope wrote a prologue for a benefit performance of a
play for the critic shortly before he died. 378–79. Budgell
. . . will: Eustace Budgell attacked the *Grub Street Journal*
for printing the charge, attributed to Pope, that he had
forged a will. 380. two . . . court: the publisher and Lord
Hervey.

Yet why? that father held it for a rule,
It was a sin to call our neighbor fool;
That harmless mother thought no wife a whore:
Hear this, and spare his family, James Moore! 385
Unspotted names, and memorable long,
If there be force in virtue, or in song.
    Of gentle blood (part shed in honor's cause,
While yet in Britain honor had applause)
Each parent sprung—— A. What fortune, pray?
    —— P. Their own,   390
And better got than Bestia's° from the throne.
Born to no pride, inheriting no strife,
Nor marrying discord in a noble wife,
Stranger to civil and religious rage,
The good man walked innoxious through his age.
No courts he saw, no suits would ever try,   396
Nor dared an oath,° nor hazarded a lie.
Unlearn'd, he knew no schoolman's subtle art,
No language but the language of the heart.
By nature honest, by experience wise,   400
Healthy by temperance, and by exercise;
His life, though long, to sickness passed unknown,
His death was instant, and without a groan.
Oh, grant me thus to live, and thus to die!
Who sprung from kings shall know less joy than I.
    O friend! may each domestic bliss be thine! 406
Be no unpleasing melancholy mine:
Me, let the tender office long engage,
To rock the cradle of reposing Age,
With lenient arts extend a mother's breath,°   410
Make Languor smile, and smooth the bed of Death,
Explore the thought, explain the asking eye,
And keep a while one parent from the sky!
On cares like these if length of days attend,
May Heaven, to bless those days, preserve my
        friend,   415
Preserve him social, cheerful, and serene,
And just as rich as when he served a queen!
A. Whether that blessing be denied or given,
Thus far was right—the rest belong to Heaven.

---

391. Bestia: a corrupt Roman consul. Pope is probably referring to the duke of Marlborough, who acquired his fortune through royal favoritism. **397. dared an oath:** Pope's father, a Catholic, refused to take the oath against the pope and therefore suffered under anti-Catholic laws. **410. mother's breath:** in 1731 Pope nursed his mother through a serious illness.

JONATHAN SWIFT
1667–1745

Verses on the Death
of Dr. Swift

OCCASIONED BY READING A MAXIM IN
ROCHEFOUCAULD

*Dans l'adversité de nos meilleurs amis nous trouvons
toujours quelque chose, qui ne nous déplaît pas.*°

As Rochefoucauld his maxims drew
From nature, I believe 'em true;
They argue no corrupted mind
In him; the fault is in mankind.
    This maxim more than all the rest   5
Is thought too base for human breast:
"In all distresses of our friends
We first consult our private ends,
While Nature, kindly bent to ease us,
Points out some circumstance to please us." 10
    If this perhaps your patience move,
Let reason and experience prove.
    We all behold with envious eyes
Our equal raised above our size.
Who would not at a crowded show   15
Stand high himself, keep others low?
I love my friend as well as you,
But why should he obstruct my view?
Then let me have the higher post;
Suppose it but an inch at most.   20
    If in a battle you should find
One, whom you love of all mankind,
Had some heroic action done,
A champion killed, or trophy won;
Rather than thus be overtopped,   25
Would you not wish his laurels cropped?
    Dear honest Ned is in the gout,
Lies racked with pain, and you without:
How patiently you hear him groan!
How glad the case is not your own!   30
    What poet would not grieve to see
His brethren write as well as he?
But rather than they should excel,

VERSES ON THE DEATH OF DR. SWIFT. **Dans . . . pas:** "In the misfortune of our best friends, we always find something that does not displease us." François de La Rochefoucauld.

He'd wish his rivals all in hell.
    Her end when Emulation misses,   35
She turns to envy, stings, and hisses:
The strongest friendship yields to pride,
Unless the odds be on our side.
    Vain humankind! fantastic race!
Thy various follies who can trace?   40
Self-love, ambition, envy, pride,
Their empire in our hearts divide.
Give others riches, power, and station;
'Tis all on me an usurpation;
I have no title to aspire,   45
Yet, when you sink, I seem the higher.
In Pope I cannot read a line,
But with a sigh I wish it mine:
When he can in one couplet fix
More sense than I can do in six,   50
It gives me such a jealous fit,
I cry, "Pox take him and his wit!"
    I grieve to be outdone by Gay°
In my own humorous biting way.
Arbuthnot° is no more my friend,   55
Who dares to irony pretend,
Which I was born to introduce,
Refined it first, and showed its use.
St. John, as well as Pulteney,° knows
That I had some repute for prose;   60
And, till they drove me out of date,
Could maul a minister of state.
If they have mortified my pride,
And made me throw my pen aside;
If with such talents Heaven hath blessed 'em,   65
Have I not reason to detest 'em?
    To all my foes, dear Fortune, send
Thy gifts, but never to my friend:
I tamely can endure the first,
But this with envy makes me burst.   70
    Thus much may serve by way of proem;
Proceed we therefore to our poem.
    The time is not remote, when I
Must by the course of nature die;
When, I foresee, my special friends   75
Will try to find their private ends:
Though it is hardly understood

53. Gay: John Gay, author of *The Beggar's Opera* and friend of Pope's and Swift's. **55. Arbuthnot:** John Arbuthnot, physician, wit, and friend of Pope's and Swift's. **59. St. John . . . Pulteney:** Henry St. John, Lord Bolingbroke, and William Pulteney (l. 194), two of those in opposition to Sir Robert Walpole's government who published the journal the *Craftsman* and thus rivaled Swift as political pamphleteers.

Which way my death can do them good;
Yet thus, methinks, I hear 'em speak:
"See how the Dean° begins to break!   80
Poor gentleman! he droops apace!
You plainly find it in his face.
That old vertigo in his head
Will never leave him till he's dead.
Besides, his memory decays;   85
He recollects not what he says;
He cannot call his friends to mind;
Forgets the place where last he dined;
Plies you with stories o'er and o'er,
He told them fifty times before.   90
How does he fancy we can sit
To hear his out-of-fashion wit?
But he takes up with younger folks,
Who for his wine will bear his jokes.
Faith, he must make his stories shorter.   95
Or change his comrades once a quarter;
In half the time he talks them round,
There must another set be found.
    "For poetry, he's past his prime;
He takes an hour to find a rhyme;   100
His fire is out, his wit decayed,
His fancy sunk, his Muse a jade.
I'd have him throw away his pen—
But there's no talking to some men."
    And then their tenderness appears   105
By adding largely to my years:
"He's older than he would be reckoned,
And well remembers Charles the Second.
He hardly drinks a pint of wine;
And that, I doubt, is no good sign.   110
His stomach, too, begins to fail;
Last year we thought him strong and hale;
But now he's quite another thing;
I wish he may hold out till spring."
They hug themselves, and reason thus: 115
"It is not yet so bad with us."
    In such a case they talk in tropes,
And by their fears express their hopes.
Some great misfortune to portend
No enemy can match a friend.   120
With all the kindness they profess,
The merit of a lucky guess
(When daily how-d'ye's come of course,
And servants answer, "Worse and worse"!)
Would please 'em better, than to tell   125

80. Dean: Swift was dean of Saint Patrick's Cathedral in Dublin.

That God be praised! The Dean is well.
Then he who prophesied the best,
Approves his foresight to the rest:
"You know I always feared the worst,
And often told you so at first." 130
He'd rather choose that I should die,
Than his prediction prove a lie.
Not one foretells I shall recover,
But all agree to give me over.

    Yet, should some neighbor feel a pain 135
Just in the parts where I complain,
How many a message would he send!
What hearty prayers that I should mend!
Inquire what regimen I kept;
What gave me ease, and how I slept, 140
And more lament, when I was dead,
Than all the snivelers round my bed.

    My good companions, never fear;
For though you may mistake a year,
Though your prognostics run too fast, 145
They must be verified at last.

    Behold the fatal day arrive!
"How is the Dean?"—"He's just alive."
Now the departing prayer is read.
"He hardly breathes"—"The Dean is dead." 150
Before the passing bell begun,
The news through half the town has run.
"Oh! may we all for death prepare!
What has he left? and who's his heir?"
"I know no more than what the news is; 155
'Tis all bequeathed to public uses."
"To public use! a perfect whim!
What had the public done for him?
Mere envy, avarice, and pride:
He gave it all—but first he died. 160
And had the Dean in all the nation
No worthy friend, no poor relation?
So ready to do strangers good,
Forgetting his own flesh and blood?"
Now Grub Street° wits are all employed; 165
With elegies the town is cloyed;
Some paragraph in every paper
To curse the Dean, or bless the Drapier.°

    The doctors, tender of their fame,
Wisely on me lay all the blame. 170
"We must confess his case was nice;°

But he would never take advice.
Had he been ruled, for aught appears,
He might have lived these twenty years:
For, when we opened him, we found, 175
That all his vital parts were sound."

    From Dublin soon to London spread,
'Tis told at court, "The Dean is dead."
Kind Lady Suffolk,° in the spleen,
Runs laughing up to tell the queen. 180
The queen, so gracious, mild and good,
Cries, "Is he gone? 'tis time he should.
He's dead, you say; why, let him rot:
I'm glad the medals° were forgot.
I promised him, I own; but when? 185
I only was the princess then;
But now, as consort of the king.
You know, 'tis quite a different thing."

    Now Chartres, at Sir Robert's° levee,°
Tells with a sneer the tidings heavy: 190
"Why, is he dead without his shoes?"
Cries Bob, "I'm sorry for the news:
Oh, were the wretch but living still,
And in his place my good friend Will!
Or had a miter on his head, 195
Provided Bolingbroke were dead!"

    Now Curll° his shop from rubbish drains:
Three genuine tomes of Swift's remains!
And then, to make them pass the glibber,
Revised by Tibbalds, Moore, and Cibber.° 200
He'll treat me as he does my betters,
Publish my will, my life, my letters;
Revive the libels born to die,
Which Pope must bear, as well as I.

    Here shift the scene, to represent 205
How those I love my death lament.
Poor Pope will grieve a month, and Gay
A week, and Arbuthnot a day.

    St. John himself will scarce forbear
To bite his pen, and drop a tear. 210
The rest will give a shrug, and cry,
"I'm sorry—but we all must die!"

    Indifference clad in wisdom's guise
All fortitude of mind supplies:

179. Lady Suffolk: George II's mistress. **184. medals:** honorary medals promised by Caroline when she was Princess of Wales. **189. Chartres . . . Robert:** Colonel Francis Chartres, a famous debauchee; Sir Robert Walpole. **levee:** morning reception. **197. Curll:** Edmund Curll, a disreputable bookseller and publisher. **200. Tibbalds . . . Cibber:** Lewis Theobald, editor; James Moore, minor poet; and Colley Cibber, untalented laureate, satirized by Pope and Swift.

165. Grub Street: frequented by and thus known for its hack writers. **168. Drapier:** Swift assumed the persona of a Dublin draper in some of his political writings. **171. nice:** delicate.

For how can stony bowels melt   215
In those who never pity felt?
When *we* are lashed, *they* kiss the rod,
Resigning to the will of God.

The fools, my juniors by a year,
Are tortured with suspense and fear;   220
Who wisely thought my age a screen,
When death approached, to stand between:
The screen removed, their hearts are trembling;
They mourn for me without dissembling.

My female friends, whose tender hearts   225
Have better learned to act their parts,
Receive the news in doleful dumps:
"The Dean is dead (and what is trumps?)
Then, Lord have mercy on his soul!
(Ladies, I'll venture for the vole.°)   230
Six deans, they say, must bear the pall.
(I wish I knew what king to call.)
Madam, your husband will attend
The funeral of so good a friend?"
"No, madam, 'tis a shocking sight;   235
And he's engaged tomorrow night:
My Lady Club would take it ill,
If he should fail her at quadrille.
He loved the Dean—(I lead a heart)
But dearest friends, they say, must part.   240
His time was come; he ran his race;
We hope he's in a better place."

Why do we grieve that friends should die?
No loss more easy to supply.
One year is past; a different scene!   245
No further mention of the Dean,
Who now, alas! no more is missed,
Than if he never did exist.
Where's now this favorite of Apollo?
Departed—and his works must follow,   250
Must undergo the common fate;
His kind of wit is out of date.

Some country squire to Lintot° goes,
Inquires for Swift in verse and prose.
Says Lintot, "I have heard the name;   255
He died a year ago."—"The same."
He searches all the shop in vain.
"Sir, you may find them in Duck Lane:°
I sent them, with a load of books,
Last Monday to the pastry-cook's.°   260

To fancy they could live a year!
I find you're but a stranger here.
The Dean was famous in his time,
And had a kind of knack at rhyme.
His way of writing now is past: 265
The town has got a better taste.
I keep no antiquated stuff;
But spick and span I have enough.
Pray do but give me leave to show 'em:
Here's Colley Cibber's birthday poem.   270
This ode you never yet have seen
By Stephen Duck° upon the queen.
Then here's a letter finely penned
Against the *Craftsman* and his friend;
It clearly shows that all reflection   275
On ministers is disaffection.
Next, here's Sir Robert's vindication,
    And Mr. Henley's last oration.°
The hawkers have not got them yet:
Your honor please to buy a set?   280
    "Here's Woolston's tracts,° the twelfth edition;
'Tis read by every politician:
The country members, when in town,
To all their boroughs send them down;
You never met a thing so smart;   285
The courtiers have them all by heart;
Those maids of honor (who can read)
Are taught to use them for their creed.
The reverend author's good intention
Has been rewarded with a pension.   290
He does an honor to his gown,
By bravely running priestcraft down;
He shows, as sure as God's in Gloucester,
That Jesus was a grand impostor;
That all his miracles were cheats,   295
Performed as jugglers do their feats:
The Church had never such a writer;
A shame he has not got a miter!"
    Suppose me dead; and then suppose
A club assembled at the Rose;   300
Where, from discourse of this and that,
I grow the subject of their chat.
And while they toss my name about,
With favor some, and some without,
One, quite indifferent in the cause,   305

230. venture . . . vole: large bid in the game of quadrille.
253. Lintot: Bernard Lintot, early publisher of Pope. 258.
Duck Lane: street with second-hand bookstores. 260.
pastry-cook's: to be used for wrapping parcels.

272. Stephen Duck: the "thresher poet," a farmer with little
talent who was patronized by the court. 278. Henley's . . .
oration: John Henley was an eloquent preacher who appealed to the lower classes. 281. Woolston's tracts: Thomas
Woolston wrote radical tracts on the divine miracles of
Jesus.

My character impartial draws:
"The Dean, if we believe report,
Was never ill received at court.
As for his works in verse and prose,
I own myself no judge of those; 310
Nor can I tell what critics thought 'em:
But this I know, all people bought 'em,
As with a moral view designed
To cure the vices of mankind.
"His vein, ironically grave, 315
Exposed the fool and lashed the knave,
To steal a hint was never known,
But what he writ was all his own.
"He never thought an honor done him,
Because a duke was proud to own him, 320
Would rather slip aside and choose
To talk with wits in dirty shoes;
Despised the fools with stars and garters,
So often seen caressing Chartres.
He never courted men in station, 325
Nor persons held in admiration;
Of no man's greatness was afraid,
Because he sought for no man's aid.
Though trusted long in great affairs,
He gave himself no haughty airs; 330
Without regarding private ends,
Spent all his credit for his friends;
And only chose the wise and good;
No flatterers, no allies in blood;
But succored virtue in distress, 335
And seldom failed of good success;
As numbers in their hearts must own,
Who, but for him, had been unknown.
"With princes kept a due decorum,
But never stood in awe before 'em. 340
He followed David's lesson° just;
In princes never put thy trust:
And would you make him truly sour,
Provoke him with a slave in power.
The Irish senate if you named, 345
With what impatience he declaimed!
Fair Liberty was all his cry,
For her he stood prepared to die;
For her he boldly stood alone;
For her he oft exposed his own. 350
Two kingdoms, just as faction led,
Had set a price upon his head,
But not a traitor could be found,

To sell him for six hundred pound.°
"Had he but spared his tongue and pen, 355
He might have rose like other men;
But power was never in his thought,
And wealth he valued not a groat:
Ingratitude he often found,
And pitied those who meant the wound; 360
But kept the tenor of his mind,
To merit well of human kind:
Nor made a sacrifice of those
Who still were true, to please his foes.
He labored many a fruitless hour, 365
To reconcile his friends in power;
Saw mischief by a faction brewing,
While they pursued each other's ruin.
But finding vain was all his care,
He left the court in mere despair.° 370
"And, oh! how short are human schemes!
Here ended all our golden dreams.
What St. John's skill in state affairs,
What Ormonde's° valor, Oxford's cares,
To save their sinking country lent, 375
Was all destroyed by one event.°
Too soon that precious life was ended,
On which alone our weal depended.
When up a dangerous faction° starts,
With wrath and vengeance in their hearts; 380
By solemn league and covenant bound,
To ruin, slaughter, and confound;
To turn religion to a fable,
And make the government a Babel;
Pervert the laws, disgrace the gown, 385
Corrupt the senate, rob the crown;
To sacrifice old England's glory,
And make her infamous in story:
When such a tempest shook the land,
How could unguarded Virtue stand? 390
With horror, grief, despair, the Dean
Beheld the dire destructive scene:
His friends in exile, or the Tower,
Himself within the frown of power,
Pursued by base envenomed pens, 395

341. David's lesson: See Psalm 147.

354. sell . . . pound: The British government in 1714 and
the Irish in 1724 offered rewards of £300 for the name
of the author of certain of Swift's anonymous political
writings. 365–70. He . . . despair: Two of Swift's friends,
Robert Harley, earl of Oxford, and Bolingbroke, quarreled
and jeopardized the Tory ministry; Swift tried to reconcile
them but failed and retired to Ireland. 374. Ormonde:
James Butler, duke of Ormonde, was commander of the
English armies on the Continent. 376. event: death of
Queen Anne in 1714. 379. faction: Whig party.

Far to the land of slaves and fens;°
A servile race in folly nursed,
Who truckle most, when treated worst.
    "By innocence and resolution,
He bore continual persecution;   400
While numbers to preferment rose,
Whose merits were to be his foes;
When even his own familiar friends,
Intent upon their private ends,
Like renegadoes now he feels,   405
Against him lifting up their heels.
    "The Dean did, by his pen, defeat
An infamous destructive cheat;°
Taught fools their interest how to know,
And gave them arms to ward the blow.   410
Envy has owned it was his doing,
To save that hapless land from ruin;
While they who at the steerage stood,
And reaped the profit, sought his blood.
    "To save them from their evil fate,   415
In him was held a crime of state.
A wicked monster on the bench,°
Whose fury blood could never quench;
As vile and profligate a villain,
As modern Scroggs, or old Tresilian;°   420
Who long all justice had discarded,
Nor feared he God, nor man regarded;
Vowed on the Dean his rage to vent,
And make him of his zeal repent:
But Heaven his innocence defends,   425
The grateful people stand his friends;
Not strains of law, nor judge's frown,
Nor topics brought to please the crown,
Nor witness hired, nor jury picked,
Prevail to bring him in convict.   430
    "In exile, with a steady heart,
He spent his life's declining part;
Where folly, pride, and faction sway
Remote from St. John, Pope, and Gay.
    "His friendships there, to few confined,   435
Were always of the middling kind;
No fools of rank, a mongrel breed,
Who fain would pass for lords indeed:

Where titles give no right or power,
And peerage is a withered flower;   440
He would have held it a disgrace,
If such a wretch had known his face.
On rural squires, that kingdom's bane,
He vented oft his wrath in vain;
Biennial squires° to market brought: 445
Who sell their souls, and votes for naught;
The nation stripped, go joyful back,
To rob the church, their tenants rack,
Go snacks with rogues and rapparees;°
And keep the peace to pick up fees;   450
In every job to have a share,
A jail or barrack to repair;
And turn the tax for public roads,
Commodious to their own abodes.
    "Perhaps I may allow the Dean   455
Had too much satire in his vein;
And seemed determined not to starve it,
Because no age could more deserve it.
Yet malice never was his aim;
He lashed the vice, but spared the name; 460
No individual could resent,
Where thousands equally were meant;
His satire points at no defect,
But what all mortals may correct;
For he abhorred that senseless tribe   465
Who call it humor when they gibe:
He spared a hump, or crooked nose,
Whose owners set not up for beaux.
True genuine dullness moved his pity,
Unless it offered to be witty.   470
Those who their ignorance confessed,
He ne'er offended with a jest;
But laughed to hear an idiot quote
A verse from Horace learned by rote.
    "He knew an hundred pleasant stories, 475
With all the turns of Whigs and Tories:
Was cheerful to his dying day;
And friends would let him have his way.
    "He gave the little wealth he had
To build a house for fools and mad; 480
And showed by one satiric touch,
No nation wanted it so much.
That kingdom he hath left his debtor,
I wish it soon may have a better."

396. **land . . . fens:** Ireland. **407–08. The . . . cheat:** Swift's *Drapier's Letters* helped to stop a scheme to introduce a copper halfpenny into Ireland. **417. monster . . . bench:** William Whitshed, Lord Chief Justice, who tried unsuccessfully to force a jury to convict Swift for sedition. **420. Scroggs . . . Tresilian:** Sir William Scroggs in 1678 and Robert Tresilian in the Peasants' Revolt in 1381, examples of vindictive justices.

445. **Biennial squires:** members of the Irish Parliament. 449. **Go . . . rapparees:** go shares with rogues and highwaymen.

WILLIAM BUTLER YEATS
1865–1939

Nineteen Hundred and Nineteen

1

Many ingenious lovely things are gone
That seemed sheer miracle to the multitude,
Protected from the circle of the moon
That pitches common things about. There stood
Amid the ornamental bronze and stone   5
An ancient image made of olive wood—
And gone are Phidias' famous ivories°
And all the golden grasshoppers and bees.

We too had many pretty toys when young:
A law indifferent to blame or praise,   10
To bribe or threat; habits that made old wrong
Melt down, as it were wax in the sun's rays;
Public opinion ripening for so long
We thought it would outlive all future days.
O what fine thought we had because we thought   15
That the worst rogues and rascals had died out.

All teeth were drawn, all ancient tricks unlearned,
And a great army but a showy thing;
What matter that no cannon had been turned
Into a plowshare? Parliament and king   20
Thought that unless a little powder burned
The trumpeters might burst with trumpeting
And yet it lack all glory; and perchance
The guardsmen's drowsy chargers would not
     prance.

Now days° are dragon-ridden, the nightmare   25
Rides upon sleep: a drunken soldiery
Can leave the mother, murdered at her door,
To crawl in her own blood, and go scot-free;
The night can sweat with terror as before
We pieced our thoughts into philosophy,   30
And planned to bring the world under a rule,
Who are but weasels fighting in a hole.

He who can read the signs nor sink unmanned
Into the half-deceit of some intoxicant
From shallow wits; who knows no work can
     stand,   35
Whether health, wealth or peace of mind were
     spent
On master-work of intellect or hand,
No honor leave its mighty monument,
Has but one comfort left: all triumph would
But break upon his ghostly solitude.   40

But is there any comfort to be found?
Man is in love and loves what vanishes,
What more is there to say? That country round
None dared admit, if such a thought were his,
Incendiary or bigot could be found   45
To burn that stump on the Acropolis,
Or break in bits the famous ivories
Or traffic in the grasshoppers or bees.

2

When Loie Fuller's° Chinese dancers enwound
A shining web, a floating ribbon of cloth,   50
It seemed that a dragon of air
Had fallen among dancers, had whirled them round
Or hurried them off on its own furious path;
So the Platonic Year
Whirls out new right and wrong,   55
Whirls in the old instead;
All men are dancers and their tread
Goes to the barbarous clangor of a gong.

3

Some moralist or mythological poet°
Compares the solitary soul to a swan;   60
I am satisfied with that,
Satisfied if a troubled mirror show it,
Before that brief gleam of its life be gone,
An image of its state;
The wings half spread for flight,   65
The breast thrust out in pride
Whether to play, or to ride
Those winds that clamor of approaching night.

A man in his own secret meditation
Is lost amid the labyrinth that he has made   70

NINETEEN HUNDRED AND NINETEEN. **7. ivories:** gold and
ivory statues of Zeus and Athena destroyed in war.
25. days: reference to the terrorist activities of the British
Black and Tan Auxiliaries against the Irish Republican
Army.

49. Loie Fuller: American dancer who lived in Paris,
famed for dances in which she swirled draperies under
colored lights. **59. poet:** Socrates in Plato's *Phaedo.*

In art or politics;
Some Platonist affirms that in the station
Where we should cast off body and trade
The ancient habit sticks,
And that if our works could   75
But vanish with our breath
That were a lucky death,
For triumph can but mar our solitude.

The swan has leaped into the desolate heaven:
That image can bring wildness, bring a rage   80
To end all things, to end
What my laborious life imagined, even
The half-imagined, the half-written page;
O but we dreamed to mend
Whatever mischief seemed   85
To afflict mankind, but now
That winds of winter blow
Learn that we were crack-pated when we dreamed.

4

We, who seven years ago
Talked of honor and of truth,   90
Shriek with pleasure if we show
The weasel's twist, the weasel's tooth.

5

Come let us mock at the great
That had such burdens on the mind
And toiled so hard and late   95
To leave some monument behind,
Nor thought of the leveling wind.

Come let us mock at the wise;
With all those calendars whereon
They fixed old aching eyes,   100
They never saw how seasons run,
And now but gape at the sun.

Come let us mock at the good
That fancied goodness might be gay,
And sick of solitude   105
Might proclaim a holiday:
Wind shrieked—and where are they?

Mock mockers after that
That would not lift a hand maybe
To help good, wise or great   110
To bar that foul storm out, for we
Traffic in mockery.

6

Violence upon the roads: violence of horses;
Some few have handsome riders, are garlanded
On delicate sensitive ear or tossing mane,   115
But wearied running round and round in their
    courses
All break and vanish, and evil gathers head:
Herodias' daughters° have returned again,
A sudden blast of dusty wind and after
Thunder of feet, tumult of images,   120
Their purpose in the labyrinth of the wind;
And should some crazy hand dare touch a daughter
All turn with amorous cries, or angry cries,
According to the wind, for all are blind.
But now wind drops, dust settles; thereupon   125
There lurches past, his great eyes without thought
Under the shadow of stupid straw-pale locks,
That insolent fiend Robert Artisson
To whom the lovelorn Lady Kyteler° brought
Bronzed peacock feathers, red combs of her
    cocks.   130

T. S. ELIOT
1888–1965

The Waste Land

"Nam Sibyllam quidem Cumis ego ipse oculis
meis vidi in ampulla pendere, et cum illi pueri
dicerent: Σίβυλλα τί θέλεις; respondebat illa:
ἀποθανεῖν θέλω."°

FOR EZRA POUND
il miglior fabbro.°

118. **Herodias' daughters:** the Sidhe, often sinister supernatural beings who ride the wind. **128–29. Robert . . .
Kyteler:** Artisson was the incubus of Dame Alice Kyteler,
a fourteenth-century witch and dealer in magic charms.

THE WASTE LAND.   The following notes translate foreign
quotations and make the identifications necessary for a
first reading of the poem. Most of the allusions, some of
which are cited in Eliot's notes, are too complex and
extensive for these notes. For further study of the poem
consult the extensive commentary in Kimon Friar and John
Malcolm Brinnin, eds., *Modern Poetry.* **Nam . . . θέλω:**
"For once I saw with my own eyes the Sibyl at Cumae,
hanging in a cage, and when the boys said, 'What do you
wish, O Sibyl?' she replied, 'I wish to die' " (Petronius,
Satyricon XLVIII). **il miglior fabbro:** "the better craftsman"
(Dante, *Purgatory* XXVI.117).

I. THE BURIAL OF THE DEAD

April is the cruellest month, breeding
Lilacs out of the dead land, mixing
Memory and desire, stirring
Dull roots with spring rain.
Winter kept us warm, covering   5
Earth in forgetful snow, feeding
A little life with dried tubers.
Summer surprised us, coming over the Starnber-
    gersee°
With a shower of rain; we stopped in the colon-
    nade,
And went on in sunlight, into the Hofgarten,°   10
And drank coffee, and talked for an hour.
Bin gar keine Russin, stamm' aus Litauen, echt
    deutsch.°
And when we were children, staying at the arch-
    duke's,
My cousin's, he took me out on a sled,
And I was frightened. He said, Marie,   15
Marie, hold on tight. And down we went.
In the mountains, there you feel free.
I read, much of the night, and go south in the
    winter.

What are the roots that clutch, what branches grow
Out of this stony rubbish? Son of man,   20
You cannot say, or guess, for you know only
A heap of broken images, where the sun beats,
And the dead tree gives no shelter, the cricket no
    relief,
And the dry stone no sound of water. Only
There is shadow under this red rock,   25
(Come in under the shadow of this red rock),
And I will show you something different from
    either
Your shadow at morning striding behind you
Or your shadow at evening rising to meet you;
I will show you fear in a handful of dust.   30
        Frisch weht der Wind
        Der Heimat zu
        Mein Irisch Kind,
        Wo weilest du?°
"You gave me hyacinths first a year ago;   35
"They called me the hyacinth girl."

—Yet when we came back, late, from the Hyacinth
    garden,
Your arms full, and your hair wet, I could not
Speak, and my eyes failed. I was neither
Living nor dead, and I knew nothing,   40
Looking into the heart of light, the silence.
Oed' und leer das Meer.°

Madame Sosostris, famous clairvoyante,
Had a bad cold, nevertheless
Is known to be the wisest woman in Europe,   45
With a wicked pack of cards. Here, said she,
Is your card, the drowned Phoenician Sailor,
(Those are pearls that were his eyes. Look!)
Here is Belladonna, the Lady of the Rocks,
The lady of situations.   50
Here is the man with three staves, and here the
    Wheel,
And here is the one-eyed merchant, and this card,
Which is blank, is something he carries on his back,
Which I am forbidden to see. I do not find
The Hanged Man. Fear death by water.   55
I see crowds of people, walking round in a ring.
Thank you. If you see dear Mrs. Equitone,
Tell her I bring the horoscope myself:
One must be so careful these days.

Unreal City,   60
Under the brown fog of a winter dawn,
A crowd flowed over London Bridge, so many,
I had not thought death had undone so many.
Sighs, short and infrequent, were exhaled,
And each man fixed his eyes before his feet.   65
Flowed up the hill and down King William Street,
To where Saint Mary Woolnoth° kept the hours
With a dead sound on the final stroke of nine.
There I saw one I knew, and stopped him, crying:
    "Stetson!
"You who were with me in the ships at Mylae!°   70
"That corpse you planted last year in your garden,
"Has it begun to sprout? Will it bloom this year?
"Or has the sudden frost disturbed its bed?
"Oh keep the Dog far hence, that's friend to men,
"Or with his nails he'll dig it up again!   75
"You! hypocrite lecteur!—mon semblable,—mon
    frère!"°

---

8. Starnbergersee: resort lake near Munich. **10. Hofgarten:** Munich park with cafes. **12. Bin . . . deutsch:** "I am not a Russian, I come from Lithuania, a true German." **31–34. Frisch . . . du:** "The wind blows fresh toward home; my Irish child, where are you waiting?"

42. Oed' . . . Meer: "Wide and empty is the sea." **67. Saint Mary Woolnoth:** small church in the business district of London. **70. Mylae:** site of the Roman defeat of the Carthaginian fleet in the First Punic War. **76. hypocrite . . . frere:** "hypocrite reader, my likeness, my brother."

II. A GAME OF CHESS

The Chair she sat in, like a burnished throne,
Glowed on the marble, where the glass
Held up by standards wrought with fruited vines
From which a golden Cupidon peeped out   80
(Another hid his eyes behind his wing)
Doubled the flames of sevenbranched candelabra
Reflecting light upon the table as
The glitter of her jewels rose to meet it,
From satin cases poured in rich profusion;   85
In vials of ivory and coloured glass
Unstoppered, lurked her strange synthetic per-
    fumes,
Unguent, powdered, or liquid—troubled, confused
And drowned the sense in odours; stirred by the
    air
That freshened from the window, these ascended 90
In fattening the prolonged candle-flames,
Flung their smoke into the laquearia,
Stirring the pattern on the coffered ceiling.
Huge sea-wood fed with copper
Burned green and orange, framed by the coloured
    stone,   95
In which sad light a carvèd dolphin swam.
Above the antique mantel was displayed
As though a window gave upon the sylvan scene
The change of Philomel, by the barbarous king°
So rudely forced; yet there the nightingale   100
Filled all the desert with inviolable voice
And still she cried, and still the world pursues,
"Jug Jug"° to dirty ears.
And other withered stumps of time
Were told upon the walls; staring forms   105
Leaned out, leaning, hushing the room enclosed.
Footsteps shuffled on the stair.
Under the firelight, under the brush, her hair
Spread out in fiery points
Glowed into words, then would be   savagely
    still.   110

"My nerves are bad to-night. Yes, bad. Stay with
    me.
"Speak to me. Why do you never speak. Speak.
"What are you thinking of? What thinking?
    What?

"I never know what you are thinking. Think."

I think we are in rats' alley   115
Where the dead men lost their bones.

"What is that noise?"
                                    The wind under the door.
"What is that noise now? What is the wind doing?"
                                    Nothing again nothing.   120
                                                              "Do
"You know nothing? Do you see nothing? Do you
    remember
"Nothing?"

I remember
Those are pearls that were his eyes.   125
"Are you alive, or not? Is there nothing in your
    head?"
                                                        But
O O O O that Shakespeherian Rag—
It's so elegant
So intelligent   130
"What shall I do now? What shall I do?"
"I shall rush out as I am, and walk the street
"With my hair down, so. What shall we do to-
    morrow?
"What shall we ever do?"
                                    The hot water at ten. 135
And if it rains, a closed car at four.
And we shall play a game of chess,
Pressing lidless eyes and waiting for a knock upon
    the door.

When Lil's husband got demobbed, I said—
I didn't mince my words, I said to her myself, 140
HURRY UP PLEASE ITS TIME°
Now Albert's coming back, make yourself a bit
    smart.
He'll want to know what you done with that money
    he gave you
To get yourself some teeth. He did, I was there.
You have them all out, Lil, and get a nice set, 145
He said, I swear, I can't bear to look at you.
And no more can't I, I said, and think of poor
    Albert,
He's been in the army four years, he wants a good
    time,
And if you don't give it him, there's others will, I
    said.
Oh is there, she said. Something o' that, I said.   150

99. **Philomel . . . king:** In Greek myth, Philomela was raped by her brother-in-law, Tereus (l. 206); aided by her sister, she murdered his son in revenge, fled, and was changed into a nightingale. 103. **Jug Jug:** in Elizabethan lyrics a conventional representation of the nightingale's song.

141. **Hurry . . . time:** pubkeeper's call at closing time.

Then I'll know who to thank, she said, and give me
    a straight look.
HURRY UP PLEASE ITS TIME
If you don't like it you can get on with it, I said.
Others can pick and choose if you can't.
But if Albert makes off, it won't be for lack of
    telling.   155
You ought to be ashamed, I said, to look so
    antique.
(And her only thirty-one.)
I can't help it, she said, pulling a long face,
It's them pills I took, to bring it off, she said.
(She's had five already, and nearly died of young
    George.)   160
The chemist said it would be all right, but I've
    never been the same.
You are a proper fool, I said.
Well, if Albert won't leave you alone, there it is, I
    said,
What you get married for if you don't want
    children?
HURRY UP PLEASE ITS TIME   165
Well, that Sunday Albert was home, they had a hot
    gammon,
And they asked me in to dinner, to get the beauty
    of it hot—
HURRY UP PLEASE ITS TIME
HURRY UP PLEASE ITS TIME
Goonight Bill. Goonight Lou. Goonight May.
    Goonight.   170
Ta ta. Goonight. Goonight.
Good night, ladies, good night, sweet ladies, good
    night, good night.

III. THE FIRE SERMON

The river's tent is broken: the last fingers of leaf
Clutch and sink into the wet bank. The wind
Crosses the brown land, unheard. The nymphs are
    departed.   175
Sweet Thames, run softly, till I end my song.
The river bears no empty bottles, sandwich papers,
Silk handkerchiefs, cardboard boxes, cigarette
    ends
Or other testimony of summer nights. The nymphs
    are departed.
And their friends, the loitering heirs of city
    directors;   180
Departed, have left no addresses.
By the waters of Leman I sat down and wept . . .

Sweet Thames, run softly till I end my song,
Sweet Thames, run softly, for I speak not loud or
    long.
But at my back in a cold blast I hear   185
The rattle of the bones, and chuckle spread from
    ear to ear.
A rat crept softly through the vegetation
Dragging its slimy belly on the bank
While I was fishing in the dull canal
On a winter evening round behind the gashouse. 190
Musing upon the king my brother's wreck
And on the king my father's death before him.
White bodies naked on the low damp ground
And bones cast in a little low dry garret,
Rattled by the rat's foot only, year to year.   195
But at my back from time to time I hear
The sound of horns and motors, which shall bring
Sweeney to Mrs. Porter in the spring.
O the moon shone bright on Mrs. Porter
And on her daughter   200
They wash their feet in soda water
Et O ces voix d'enfants, chantant dans la coupole!°

Twit twit twit
Jug jug jug jug jug jug
So rudely forc'd.   205
Tereu

Unreal City
Under the brown fog of a winter noon
Mr. Eugenides, the Smyrna merchant
Unshaven, with a pocket full of currants   210
C.i.f. London: documents at sight,
Asked me in demotic French
To luncheon at the Cannon Street Hotel
Followed by a weekend at the Metropole.

At the violet hour, when the eyes and back   215
Turn upward from the desk, when the human
    engine waits
Like a taxi throbbing waiting,
I Tiresias, though blind, throbbing between two
    lives,
Old man with wrinkled female breasts, can see
At the violet hour, the evening hour that strives 220
Homeward, and brings the sailor home from sea,
The typist home at teatime, clears her breakfast,
    lights
Her stove, and lays out food in tins.

202. Et . . . coupole: "And, O those children's voices,
chanting in the dome."

Out of the window perilously spread
Her drying combinations touched by the sun's last
          rays,   225
On the divan are piled (at night her bed)
Stockings, slippers, camisoles, and stays.
I Tiresias, old man with wrinkled dugs
Perceived the scene, and foretold the rest—
I too awaited the expected guest.   230
He, the young man carbuncular, arrives,
A small house agent's clerk, with one bold stare,
One of the low on whom assurance sits
As a silk hat on a Bradford° millionaire.
The time is now propitious, as he guesses,   235
The meal is ended, she is bored and tired,
Endeavours to engage her in caresses
Which still are unreproved, if undesired.
Flushed and decided, he assaults at once;
Exploring hands encounter no defence;   240
His vanity requires no response,
And makes a welcome of indifference.
(And I Tiresias have foresuffered all
Enacted on this same divan or bed;
I who have sat by Thebes below the wall   245
And walked among the lowest of the dead.)
Bestows one final patronising kiss,
And gropes his way, finding the stairs unlit . . .

She turns and looks a moment in the glass,
Hardly aware of her departed lover: 250
Her brain allows one half-formed thought to pass:
"Well now that's done: and I'm glad it's over."
When lovely woman stoops to folly and
Paces about her room again, alone,
She smoothes her hair with automatic hand,   255
And puts a record on the gramophone.

"This music crept by me upon the waters"
And along the Strand, up Queen Victoria Street.
O City city, I can sometimes hear
Beside a public bar in Lower Thames Street,   260
The pleasant whining of a mandoline
And a clatter and a chatter from within
Where fishmen lounge at noon: where the walls
Of Magnus Martyr hold
Inexplicable splendour of Ionian white and gold.

          The river sweats   266
          Oil and tar
          The barges drift
          With the turning tide

234. **Bradford**: British manufacturing town.

          Red sails   270
          Wide
          To leeward, swing on the
               heavy spar.
          The barges wash
          Drifting logs
          Down Greenwich reach   275
          Past the Isle of Dogs.°
               Weialala leia
               Wallala leialala

          Elizabeth and Leicester
          Beating oars   280
          The stern was formed
          A gilded shell
          Red and gold
          The brisk swell
          Rippled both shores   285
          Southwest wind
          Carried down stream
          The peal of bells
          White towers
               Weialala leia   290
               Wallala leialala

"Trams and dusty trees.
Highbury bore me. Richmond and Kew°
Undid me. By Richmond I raised my knees
Supine on the floor of a narrow canoe."   295

"My feet are at Moorgate,° and my heart
Under my feet. After the event
He wept. He promised 'a new start.'
I made no comment. What should I resent?"

"On Margate Sands.°   300
I can connect
Nothing with nothing.
The broken fingernails of dirty hands.
My people humble people who expect
Nothing."   305
          la la

To Carthage then I came

Burning burning burning burning
O Lord Thou pluckest me out
O Lord Thou pluckest   310

burning

275–76. **Greenwich . . . Dogs**: London district south of
the Thames and a peninsula opposite it. 293. **Highbury
. . . Kew**: three residential London suburbs on the Thames.
296. **Moorgate**: London slum area. 300. **Margate Sands**:
seaside resort on the Thames estuary.

IV. DEATH BY WATER

Phlebas the Phoenician, a fortnight dead,
Forgot the cry of gulls, and the deep sea swell
And the profit and loss.
           A current under sea   315
Picked his bones in whispers. As he rose and fell
He passed the stages of his age and youth
Entering the whirlpool.
              Gentile or Jew
O you who turn the wheel and look to windward,
Consider Phlebas, who was once handsome and
    tall as you.   321

V. WHAT THE THUNDER SAID

After the torchlight red on sweaty faces
After the frosty silence in the gardens
After the agony in stony places
The shouting and the crying   325
Prison and palace and reverberation
Of thunder of spring over distant mountains
He who was living is now dead
We who were living are now dying
With a little patience   330

Here is no water but only rock
Rock and no water and the sandy road
The road winding above among the mountains
Which are mountains of rock without water
If there were water we should stop and drink 335
Amongst the rock one cannot stop or think
Sweat is dry and feet are in the sand
If there were only water amongst the rock
Dead mountain mouth of carious teeth that cannot
    spit
Here one can neither stand nor lie nor sit   340
There is not even silence in the mountains
But dry sterile thunder without rain
There is not even solitude in the mountains
But red sullen faces sneer and snarl
From doors of mudcracked houses   345
                If there were water
  And no rock
  If there were rock
  And also water
  And water   350
  A spring
  A pool among the rock
  If there were the sound of water only
  Not the cicada
  And dry grass singing   355

But sound of water over a rock
Where the hermit-thrush sings in the pine trees
Drip drop drip drop drop drop drop
But there is no water

Who is the third who walks always beside you? 360
When I count, there are only you and I together
But when I look ahead up the white road
There is always another one walking beside you
Gliding wrapt in a brown mantle, hooded
I do not know whether a man or a woman   365
—But who is that on the other side of you?

What is that sound high in the air
Murmur of maternal lamentation
Who are those hooded hordes swarming
Over endless plains, stumbling in cracked earth 370
Ringed by the flat horizon only
What is the city over the mountains
Cracks and reforms and bursts in the violet air
Falling towers
Jerusalem Athens Alexandria   375
Vienna London
Unreal

A woman drew her long black hair out tight
And fiddled whisper music on those strings
And bats with baby faces in the violet light 380
Whistled, and beat their wings
And crawled head downward down a blackened
    wall
And upside down in air were towers
Tolling reminiscent bells, that kept the hours
And voices singing out of empty cisterns and
    exhausted wells.   385

In this decayed hole among the mountains
In the faint moonlight, the grass is singing
Over the tumbled graves, about the chapel
There is the empty chapel, only the wind's home.
It has no windows, and the door swings,   390
Dry bones can harm no one.
Only a cock stood on the rooftree
Co co rico co co rico
In a flash of lightning. Then a damp gust
Bringing rain   395

Ganga was sunken, and the limp leaves
Waited for rain, while the black clouds
Gathered far distant, over Himavant.°

396–98. Ganga . . . Himavant: perhaps the Ganges; in Indian myth, Himavant is a personification of the Himalayan Mountains.

The jungle crouched, humped in silence.
Then spoke the thunder   400
DA
Datta: what have we given?
My friend, blood shaking my heart
The awful daring of a moment's surrender
Which an age of prudence can never retract   405
By this, and this only, we have existed
Which is not to be found in our obituaries
Or in memories draped by the beneficent spider
Or under seals broken by the lean solicitor
In our empty rooms   410
DA
Dayadhvam: I have heard the key
Turn in the door once and turn once only
We think of the key, each in his prison
Thinking of the key, each confirms a prison   415
Only at nightfall, aethereal rumours
Revive for a moment a broken Coriolanus
DA
Damyata: The boat responded
Gaily, to the hand expert with sail and oar   420
The sea was calm, your heart would have responded
Gaily, when invited, beating obedient
To controlling hands

        I sat upon the shore
Fishing, with the arid plain behind me   425
Shall I at least set my lands in order?
London Bridge is falling down falling down falling
    down
Poi s'ascose nel foco che gli affina°
Quando fiam uti chelidon°—O swallow swallow
Le Prince d'Aquitaine à la tour abolie°   430
These fragments I have shored against my ruins
Why then Ile fit you. Hieronymo's mad againe.
Datta. Dayadhvam. Damyata.
      Shantih   shantih   shantih

NOTES ON "THE WASTE LAND"

Not only the title, but the plan and a good deal of the incidental symbolism of the poem were suggested by Miss Jessie L. Weston's book on the Grail legend: *From Ritual to Romance* (Cambridge). Indeed, so deeply am I indebted, Miss Weston's book will elucidate the difficulties of the poem much better than my

428. Poi . . . affina: "Then he hid himself in the fire which refines them." **429. Quando . . . chelidon:** "When shall I be as the swallow." **430. Le . . . abolie:** "The prince of Aquitaine in the ruined tower."

notes can do; and I recommend it (apart from the great interest of the book itself) to any who think such elucidation of the poem worth the trouble. To another work of anthropology I am indebted in general, one which has influenced our generation profoundly; I mean *The Golden Bough;* I have used especially the two volumes *Adonis, Attis, Osiris.* Anyone who is acquainted with these works will immediately recognise in the poem certain references to vegetation ceremonies.

I. THE BURIAL OF THE DEAD

Line 20. Cf. Ezekiel II, i.
   23. Cf. Ecclesiastes XII, v.
   31. V. Tristan und Isolde, I, verses 5–8.
   42. Id. III, verse 24.
   46. I am not familiar with the exact constitution of the Tarot pack of cards, from which I have obviously departed to suit my own convenience. The Hanged Man, a member of the traditional pack, fits my purpose in two ways: because he is associated in my mind with the Hanged God of Frazer, and because I associate him with the hooded figure in the passage of the disciples to Emmaus in Part V. The Phoenician Sailor and the Merchant appear later; also the "crowds of people," and Death by Water is executed in Part IV. The Man with Three Staves (an authentic member of the Tarot pack) I associate, quite arbitrarily, with the Fisher King himself.
   60. Cf. Baudelaire:
     "Fourmillante cité, cité pleine de rêves,
     "Où le spectre en plein jour raccroche le passant."[1]
   63. Cf. Inferno III, 55–57:
           "si lunga tratta
    di gente, ch'io non avrei mai creduto
    che morte tanta n'avesse disfatta."[2]
   64. Cf. Inferno IV, 25–27:
     "Quivi, secondo che per ascoltare,
     "non avea pianto, ma' che di sospiri,
     "che l'aura eterna facevan tremare."[3]
   68. A phenomenon which I have often noticed.
   74. Cf. the Dirge in Webster's *White Devil.*
   76. V. Baudelaire, Preface to *Fleurs du Mal.*

II. A GAME OF CHESS

   77. Cf. *Antony and Cleopatra*, II, ii, l. 190.
   92. Laquearia. V. *Aeneid*, I, 726:
     dependent lychni laquearibus aureis incensi, et
noctem flammis funalia vincunt.[4]

NOTES ON *The Waste Land.* **1. Fourmillante . . . passant:** "Swarming city, city full of dreams, / Where the specter in broad daylight accosts the passerby" (*Les Sept Vieillards*). **2. si . . . disfatta:** "So long a train of people, / that I should never have believed / that death had undone so many." **3. Quivi . . . tremare:** "Here, so far as I could tell by listening, / there was no lamentation except sighs, / which caused the eternal air to tremble." **4. dependent . . . vincunt:** "Blazing torches hang from the gold-paneled ceiling, and torches conquer the night with flames."

98. Sylvan scene. V. Milton. *Paradise Lost*, IV, 140.
99. V. Ovid, *Metamorphoses*, VI, Philomela.
100. Cf. Part III, l. 204.
115. Cf. Part III, l. 195.
118. Cf. Webster: "Is the wind in that door still?"
126. Cf. Part I, l. 37, 48.
138. Cf. the game of chess in Middleton's *Women beware Women*.

III. THE FIRE SERMON

176. V. Spenser, *Prothalamion*.
192. Cf. *The Tempest*, I, ii.
196. Cf. Marvell, *To His Coy Mistress*.
197. Cf. Day, *Parliament of Bees*:
"When of the sudden, listening, you shall hear,
"A noise of horns and hunting, which shall bring
"Actaeon to Diana in the spring,
"Where all shall see her naked skin . . ."
199. I do not know the origin of the ballad from which these lines are taken: it was reported to me from Sydney, Australia.
202. V. Verlaine, *Parsifal*.
210. The currants were quoted at a price "carriage and insurance free to London"; and the Bill of Lading etc. were to be handed to the buyer upon payment of the sight draft.
218. Tiresias, although a mere spectator and not indeed a "character," is yet the most important personage in the poem, uniting all the rest. Just as the one-eyed merchant, seller of currants, melts into the Phoenician Sailor, and the latter is not wholly distinct from Ferdinand Prince of Naples, so all the women are one woman, and the two sexes meet in Tiresias. What Tiresias *sees*, in fact, is the substance of the poem. The whole passage from Ovid is of great anthropological interest:

'. . . Cum Iunone iocos et maior vestra profecto est
Quam, quae contingit maribus,' dixisse, 'voluptas.'
Illa negat; placuit quae sit sententia docti
Quaerere Tiresiae: venus huic erat utraque nota.
Nam duo magnorum viridi coeuntia silva
Corpora serpentum baculi violaverat ictu
Deque viro factus, mirabile, femina septem
Egerat autumnos; octavo rursus eosdem
Vidit et 'est vestrae si tanta potentia plagae,'
Dixit 'ut auctoris sortem in contraria mutet,
Nunc quoque vos feriam!' percussis anguibus isdem
Forma prior rediit genetivaque venit imago.
Arbiter hic igitur sumptus de lite iocosa
Dicta Iovis firmat; gravius Saturnia iusto
Nec pro materia fertur doluisse suique
Iudicis aeterna damnavit lumina nocte,
At pater omnipotens (neque enim licet inrita cuiquam

Facta dei fecisse deo) pro lumine adempto
Scire futura dedit peonamque levavit honore.[5]
221. This may not appear as exact as Sappho's lines, but I had in mind the "longshore" or "dory" fisherman, who returns at nightfall.
253. V. Goldsmith, the song in *The Vicar of Wakefield*.
257. V. *The Tempest*, as above.
264. The interior of St. Magnus Martyr is to my mind one of the finest among Wren's interiors. See *The Proposed Demolition of Nineteen City Churches*: (P. S. King & Son, Ltd.).
266. The Song of the (three) Thames-daughters begins here. From line 292 to 306 inclusive they speak in turn. V. *Götterdämmerung*, III, i: the Rhine-daughters.
279. V. Froude, *Elizabeth*, Vol. I, ch. iv, letter of De Quadra to Philip of Spain:
"In the afternoon we were in a barge, watching the games on the river. (The queen) was along with Lord Robert and myself on the poop, when they began to talk nonsense, and went so far that Lord Robert at last said, as I was on the spot there was no reason why they should not be married if the queen pleased."
293. Cf. *Purgatorio*, V. 133:
"Ricorditi di me, che son la Pia;
"Siena mi fe', disfecemi Maremma."[6]
307. V. St. Augustine's *Confessions*: "to Carthage then I came, where a cauldron of unholy loves sang all about mine ears."
308. The complete text of the Buddha's Fire Sermon (which corresponds in importance to the Sermon on the Mount) from which these words are taken, will be found translated in the late Henry Clarke Warren's *Buddhism in Translation* (Harvard Oriental Series). Mr. Warren was one of the great pioneers of Buddhist studies in the Occident.
309. From St. Augustine's *Confessions* again. The collocation of these two representatives of eastern and western asceticism, as the culmination of this part of the poem, is not an accident.

5. Cum . . . honore: "[Jove, having drunk a great deal,] jested with Juno. He said, 'Your pleasure in love is really greater than that enjoyed by men.' She denied it; so they decided to seek the opinion of the wise Tiresias, for he knew both aspects of love. For once, with a blow of his staff, he had committed violence on two huge snakes as they copulated in the green forest; and—wonderful to tell —was turned from a man into a woman and thus spent seven years. In the eighth year he saw the same snakes again and said, 'If a blow struck at you is so powerful that it changes the sex of the giver, I will now strike at you again.' With these words he struck the snakes, and his former shape was restored to him and he became as he had been born. So he was appointed arbitrator in the playful quarrel and supported Jove's statement. It is said that Saturnia [i.e., Juno] was quite disproportionately upset and condemned the arbitrator to perpetual blindness. But the almighty father (for no god may undo what has been done by another god), in return for the sight that was taken away, gave him the power to know the future and so lightened the penalty paid by the honor." **6. Ricorditi . . . Maremma:** "Remember me, who am La Pia. / Siena made me, Maremma undid me."

V. WHAT THE THUNDER SAID

In the first part of Part V three themes are employed: the journey to Emmaus, the approach to the Chapel Perilous (see Miss Weston's book) and the present decay of eastern Europe.

357. This is *Turdus aonalaschkae pallasii*, the hermit-thrush which I have heard in Quebec Province. Chapman says (*Handbook of Birds of Eastern North America*) "it is most at home in secluded woodland and thickety retreats. . . Its notes are not remarkable for variety or volume, but in purity and sweetness of tone and exquisite modulation they are unequalled." Its "water-dripping song" is justly celebrated.

360. The following lines were stimulated by the account of one of the Antarctic expeditions (I forget which, but I think one of Shackleton's): it was related that the party of explorers, at the extremity of their strength, had the constant delusion that there was *one more member* than could actually be counted.

367–77. Cf. Hermann Hesse, *Blick ins Chaos*: "Schon ist halb Europa, schon ist zumindest der halbe Osten Europas auf dem Wege zum Chaos, fährt betrunken im heiligem Wahn am Abgrund entlang und singt dazu, singt betrunken und hymnisch wie Dmitri Karamasoff sang. Ueber diese Lieder lacht der Bürger beleidigt, der Heilige und Seher hört sie mit Tränen."[7]

402. "Datta, dayadhvam, damyata" (Give, sympathise, control). The fable of the meaning of the Thunder is found in the *Brihadaranyaka—Upanishad*, 5, 1. A translation is found in Deussen's *Sechzig Upanishads des Veda*, p. 489.

7. **Schon . . . Tranen:** "Already half of Europe, already at least half of Eastern Europe, on the way to Chaos, drives drunk in sacred infatuation along the edge of the precipice, sings drunkenly, as Dmitri Karamazov sang. The offended bourgeois laughs at these songs; the saint and seer hears them with tears."

408. Cf. Webster, *The White Devil*, V, vi:
". . . they'll remarry
Ere the worm pierce your winding-sheet, ere the spider
Make a thin curtain for your epitaphs."

412. Cf. *Inferno*, XXXIII, 46:
"ed io sentii chiavar l'uscio di sotto
all'orribile torre."[8]

Also F. H. Bradley, *Appearance and Reality*, p. 346. "My external sensations are no less private to myself than are my thoughts or my feelings. In either case my experience falls within my own circle, a circle closed on the outside; and, with all its elements alike, every sphere is opaque to the others which surround it. . . . In brief, regarded as an existence which appears in a soul, the whole world for each is peculiar and private to that soul."

425. V. Weston: *From Ritual to Romance*; chapter on the Fisher King.

428. V. *Purgatorio*, XXVI, 148.
" 'Ara vos prec per aquella valor
'que vos guida al som de l'escalina,
'sovegna vos a temps de ma dolor.'
Poi s'ascose nel foco che gli affina."[9]

429. V. *Pervigilium Veneris*. Cf. Philomela in Parts II and III.

430. V. Gerard de Nerval, Sonnet *El Desdichado*.

432. V. Kyd's *Spanish Tragedy*.

434. Shantih. Repeated as here, a formal ending to an Upanishad. "The Peace which passeth understanding" is our equivalent to this word.

8. **ed . . . torre:** "And I heard below the door of the horrible tower being locked up." 9. **Ara . . . affina:** " 'Now I pray you, by that virtue / which guides you to the summit of the stairway, / be mindful in due time of my pain.' / Then he hid himself in the fire which refines them."

The Denial of the Poetic

MARIANNE MOORE
1887–1972

Poetry

I, too, dislike it: there are things that are important
    beyond all this fiddle.
  Reading it, however, with a perfect contempt for
    it, one discovers in
  it after all, a place for the genuine.
    Hands that can grasp, eyes
    that can dilate, hair that can rise   5
      if it must, these things are important not
    because a

high-sounding interpretation can be put upon them
    but because they are
  useful. When they become so derivative as to
    become unintelligible,
  the same thing may be said for all of us, that we
    do not admire what   10
  we cannot understand: the bat
    holding on upside down or in quest of
    something to

eat, elephants pushing, a wild horse taking a roll,
    a tireless wolf under
  a tree, the immovable critic twitching his skin
    like a horse that feels a flea, the base-
  ball fan, the statistician—   15
    nor is it valid
      to discriminate against "business documents
    and

school-books"; all these phenomena are important.
    One must make a distinction

however: when dragged into prominence by half
    poets, the result is not poetry,
nor till the poets among us can be   20
  "literalists of
    the imagination"—above
    insolence and triviality and can present

for inspection, "imaginary gardens with real toads
    in them" shall we have
  it. In the meantime, if you demand on the one
    hand,   25
  the raw material of poetry in
    all its rawness and
    that which is on the other hand
      genuine, you are interested in poetry.

ARCHIBALD MACLEISH
b. 1892

Ars Poetica°

A poem should be palpable and mute
As a globed fruit,

Dumb
As old medallions to the thumb,

Silent as the sleeve-worn stone   5
Of casement ledges where the moss has grown—

A poem should be wordless
As the flight of birds.

ARS POETICA.   The Art of Poetry.

A poem should be motionless in time
As the moon climbs,   10

Leaving, as the moon releases
Twig by twig the night-entangled trees,

Leaving, as the moon behind the winter leaves,
Memory by memory the mind—

A poem should be motionless in time   15
As the moon climbs.

A poem should be equal to:
Not true.

For all the history of grief
An empty doorway and a maple leaf.   20

For love
The leaning grasses and two lights above the sea—

A poem should not mean
But be.

DYLAN THOMAS
1914–1953

In My Craft or Sullen Art

In my craft or sullen art
Exercised in the still night
When only the moon rages
And the lovers lie abed
With all their griefs in their arms,   5
I labor by singing light
Not for ambition or bread
Or the strut and trade of charms
On the ivory stages
But for the common wages   10
Of their most secret heart.

Not for the proud man apart
From the raging moon I write
On these spindrift pages
Not for the towering dead   15
With their nightingales and psalms
But for the lovers, their arms
Round the griefs of the ages,
Who pay no praise or wages
Nor heed my craft or art.   20

WILLIAM CARLOS WILLIAMS
1883–1963

The Dish of Fruit

The table describes
nothing: four legs, by which
it becomes a table. Four lines
by which it becomes a quatrain,

the poem that lifts the dish
of fruit, if we say it is like
a table—how will it describe
the contents of the poem?

The Artist

Mr. T.
          bareheaded
                    in a soiled undershirt
his hair standing out
          on all sides   5
                    stood on his toes
heels together
          arms gracefully
                    for the moment
curled above his head.   10
          Then he whirled about
                    bounded
into the air
          and with an *entrechat*
                    perfectly achieved   15
completed the figure.
          My mother
                    taken by surprise
where she sat
          in her invalid's chair   20
                    was left speechless.
Bravo! she cried at last
          and clapped her hands.
                    The man's wife
came from the kitchen: 25
          What goes on here? she said.
                    But the show was over.

RICHARD WILBUR
b. 1921

Advice to a Prophet

When you come, as you soon must, to the streets
    of our city,
Mad-eyed from stating the obvious,
Not proclaiming our fall but begging us
In God's name to have self-pity,

Spare us all word of the weapons, their force and
    range,   5
The long numbers that rocket the mind;
Our slow, unreckoning hearts will be left behind,
Unable to fear what is too strange.

Nor shall you scare us with talk of the death of
    the race.
How should we dream of this place without us?—
The sun mere fire, the leaves untroubled about us,
A stone look on the stone's face?   12

Speak of the world's own change. Though we can-
    not conceive
Of an undreamt thing, we know to our cost
How the dreamt cloud crumbles, the vines are
    blackened by frost,   15
How the view alters. We could believe,

If you told us so, that the white-tailed deer will slip
Into perfect shade, grown perfectly shy,
The lark avoid the reaches of our eye,
The jack-pine lose its knuckled grip   20

On the cold ledge, and every torrent burn
As Xanthus° once, its gliding trout
Stunned in a twinkling. What should we be without
The dolphin's arc, the dove's return,

These things in which we have seen ourselves and
    spoken?   25
Ask us, prophet, how we shall call
Our natures forth when that live tongue is all
Dispelled, that glass obscured or broken

In which we have said the rose of our love and the
    clean
Horse of our courage, in which beheld   30
The singing locust of the soul unshelled,
And all we mean or wish to mean.

Ask us, ask us whether with the worldless rose
Our hearts shall fail us; come demanding
Whether there shall be lofty or long standing   35
When the bronze annals of the oak-tree close.

ADVICE TO A PROPHET. **22. Xanthus:** in Greek myth, a
river scalded by Hephaestus, god of fire.

Generic
Table of
Contents

Generic
Table of
Contents

The following table of contents arranges the selections in this anthology according to the conventional genres: drama, fiction, narrative poetry, and lyric poetry. Within each genre the selections are listed chronologically by the author's date of birth or, in the case of anonymous poems, by the probable date of composition. When there is more than one selection by an author, they follow the order in which they appear in this text.

As we indicate in the General Introduction, the distinction between narrative and thematic works is not an absolute one; there are narrative and thematic elements in every work of literature. In some instances we have ignored the distinction in order to illustrate a theme and have considered a poem like Tennyson's "Ulysses" as a lyric, even though it is as much a dramatic poem as Burns' "Holy Willie's Prayer," and Thomas' "A Winter's Tale" as a narrative poem, even though it is a more thematic work than "The Phoenix."

The prose versions of *Havelok the Dane* and *Sir Orfeo* are listed under narrative poetry, the genre in which they were originally written.

DRAMA

FICTION

NARRATIVE POETRY

Index

Index

Numbers in *italics* indicate pages on which selections appear.

B 3
C 4
D 5
E 6
F 7
G 8
H 9
I 0
J 1